College Edition

HARPER COLLINS
FRENCH
DICTIONARY

College Edition

HARPER COLLINS
FRENCH
DICTIONARY

FRENCH·ENGLISH   ENGLISH·FRENCH

HarperCollinsPublishers

by/par
Pierre-Henri Cousin, Lorna Sinclair,
Jean-François Allain, Catherine E. Love

contributors/avec la collaboration de
Claude Nimmo, Vivian Marr

American language consultant/anglais américain
Dr. Donald Windham

editorial staff/secrétariat de rédaction
Elspeth Anderson, Angela Campbell,
Barbara Christie

ISBN 0-06-275508-0
ISBN 0-06-276506-X (pbk)

TABLE DES MATIÈRES

CONTENTS

Les marques déposées

Note on trademarks

Pour comprendre l'anglais

Ce dictionnaire nouveau, résolument tourné vers le monde moderne, rend compte de l'usage actuel de la langue anglaise, y compris dans les domaines du commerce et de la micro-informatique, et contient un choix étendu d'abréviations, sigles et noms géographiques fréquemment rencontrés dans la presse. Pour faciliter les recherches, les formes irrégulières des verbes et substantifs anglais font l'objet d'une entrée séparée qui renvoie à la forme de base suivie de sa traduction.

Pour vous exprimer en anglais

Pour vous aider à vous exprimer dans un anglais correct et idiomatique, de nombreuses indications précisant le sens ou le domaine d'emploi sont là pour vous guider et vous orienter vers la traduction la mieux adaptée à votre contexte. Tous les termes courants sont traités en détail et illustrés d'exemples.

Un compagnon de travail

Par le soin apporté à sa confection, ce nouveau dictionnaire Collins constitue un outil fiable et facile d'emploi qui saura répondre à vos besoins linguistiques et se montrer un fidèle compagnon de route dans vos études ou votre travail.

Understanding French

This new and thoroughly up-to-date dictionary provides the user with wide-ranging, practical coverage of current usage, including terminology relevant to business and office automation, and a comprehensive selection of abbreviations, acronyms and geographical names commonly found in the press. You will also find, for ease of consultation, irregular forms of French verbs and nouns with a cross-reference to the basic form where a translation is given.

Self-expression in French

To help you express yourself correctly and idiomatically in French, numerous indications – think of them as signposts – guide you to the most appropriate translation for your context. All the most commonly used words are given detailed treatment, with many examples of typical usage.

A working companion

Much care has been taken to make this new Collins dictionary thoroughly reliable, easy to use and relevant to your work and study. We hope it will become a long-serving companion for all your foreign language needs.

ABRÉVIATIONS

ABBREVIATIONS

adjectif, locution adjective	**a**	adjective, adjectival phrase
abréviation	**ab(b)r**	abbreviation
adverbe, locution adverbiale	**ad**	adverb, adverbial phrase
administration	**ADMIN**	administration
agriculture	**AGR**	agriculture
anatomie	**ANAT**	anatomy
architecture	**ARCHIT**	architecture
l'automobile	**AUT(O)**	automobiles
aviation, voyages aériens	**AVIAT**	flying, air travel
biologie	**BIO(L)**	biology
botanique	**BOT**	botany
anglais de Grande-Bretagne	**Brit**	British English
conjonction	**cj**	conjunction
langue familière (! emploi vulgaire)	**col (!)**	colloquial usage (! particularly offensive)
commerce, finance, banque	**COMM**	commerce, finance, banking
informatique	**COMPUT**	computing
construction	**CONSTR**	building
nom utilisé comme adjectif, ne peut s'employer ni comme attribut, ni après le nom qualifié	**cpd**	compound element: noun used as an adjective and which cannot follow the noun it qualifies
cuisine, art culinaire	**CULIN**	cookery
déterminant: article, adjectif démonstratif ou indéfini etc	**dét, det**	determiner: article, demonstrative etc
économie	**ECON**	economics
électricité, électronique	**ELEC**	electricity, electronics
exclamation, interjection	**excl**	exclamation, interjection
féminin	**f**	feminine
langue familière (! emploi vulgaire)	**fam (!)**	colloquial usage (! particularly offensive)
emploi figuré	**fig**	figurative use
(verbe anglais) dont la particule est inséparable du verbe	**fus**	(phrasal verb) where the particle cannot be separated from main verb
dans la plupart des sens; généralement	**gén, gen**	in most or all senses; generally
géographie, géologie	**GEO**	geography, geology
géométrie	**GEOM**	geometry
histoire	**HIST**	history
informatique	**INFORM**	computing
invariable	**inv**	invariable
irrégulier	**irg**	irregular
domaine juridique	**JUR**	law
grammaire, linguistique	**LING**	grammar, linguistics
masculin	**m**	masculine
mathématiques, algèbre	**MATH**	mathematics, calculus
médecine	**MED**	medical term, medicine
masculin ou féminin, suivant le sexe	**m/f**	either masculine or feminine depending on sex
domaine militaire, armée	**MIL**	military matters
musique	**MUS**	music
nom	**n**	noun

ABRÉVIATIONS

ABBREVIATIONS

navigation, nautisme	**NAVIG, NAUT**	sailing, navigation
adjectif ou nom numérique	**num**	numeral adjective or noun
	o.s.	oneself
péjoratif	**péj, pej**	derogatory, pejorative
photographie	**PHOT(O)**	photography
physiologie	**PHYSIOL**	physiology
pluriel	**pl**	plural
politique	**POL**	politics
participe passé	**pp**	past participle
préposition	**prép, prep**	preposition
psychologie, psychiatrie	**PSYCH**	psychology, psychiatry
temps du passé	**pt**	past tense
nom non comptable: ne peut s'utiliser au pluriel	**q**	collective (uncountable) noun: is not used in the plural
quelque chose	**qch**	
quelqu'un	**qn**	
religions, domaine ecclésiastique	**REL**	religions, church service
	sb	somebody
enseignement, système scolaire et universitaire	**SCOL**	education, schools and universities
singulier	**sg**	singular
	sth	something
subjonctif	**sub**	subjunctive
sujet (grammatical)	**su(b)j**	(grammatical) subject
techniques, technologie	**TECH**	technical term, technology
télécommunications	**TEL**	telecommunications
télévision	**TV**	television
typographie	**TYP(O)**	typography, printing
anglais des USA	**US**	American English
verbe	**vb**	verb
verbe ou groupe verbal à fonction intransitive	**vi**	verb or phrasal verb used intransitively
verbe ou groupe verbal à fonction transitive	**vt**	verb or phrasal verb used transitively
zoologie	**ZOOL**	zoology
marque déposée	®	registered trademark
indique une équivalence culturelle	≈	introduces a cultural equivalent

TRANSCRIPTION PHONÉTIQUE

CONSONNES — CONSONANTS

NB. **p, b, t, d, k, g** sont suivis d'une aspiration en anglais.

NB. **p, b, t, d, k, g** are not aspirated in French.

Français		Anglais
pou*p*ée	p	*p*u*pp*y
*b*om*b*e	b	*b*a*b*y
*t*en*te t*hermal	t	*t*en*t*
*d*in*d*e	d	*d*og ro*d*
*c*o*q* qui *k*épi	k	*c*ork *k*iss *ch*ord
*g*ag ba*g*ue	g	*g*ag *g*uess
*s*ale *ce* na*t*ion	s	*s*o ri*ce* ki*ss*
*z*éro ro*s*e	z	cou*s*in bu*zz*
ta*ch*e *ch*at	sh	*sh*eep *s*ugar
*g*ilet *j*uge	zh	plea*s*ure vi*s*ion
	ch	*ch*ur*ch*
	j	*j*ud*g*e *g*eneral
*f*er *ph*are	f	*f*arm hal*f*
val*v*e	v	*v*ery e*v*e
	th	*th*in bo*th*
	th	*th*at o*th*er
*l*ent sa*ll*e	l	*l*ittle ba*ll*
*r*are *r*ent*r*er	r	*r*at *r*a*r*e
*m*aman fe*mm*e	m	*m*ove co*mb*
*n*on *n*o*nn*e	n	*n*o ra*n*
ag*n*eau vi*gn*e	ny	
campi*ng*	ng	si*ng*ing ba*n*k
	h	*h*at re*h*earse
*y*eux pa*ill*e p*i*ed	y	*y*et
no*u*er o*u*i	w	*w*all a*w*ay

DIVERS — MISCELLANEOUS

pour l'anglais: suit la syllabe accentuée

'

in French transcription: no liaison

indique que les deux consonnes se prononcent séparément

.

shows where two consonants should be pronounced separately

PHONETIC TRANSCRIPTION

VOYELLES

VOWELS

NB. La mise en équivalence de certains sons n'indique qu'une ressemblance approximative.

NB. The pairing of some vowel sounds only indicates approximate equivalence.

	a	add map laugh
plat amour	å	
bas pâte	â	palm father odd
jouer été	ā	ace rate gauge
	är	care air
lait jouet merci	e	set tent
ici vie lyre	ē	heel bead
le premier	ə	darken above
	i	hit pity
	ī	ice dime aisle
or homme	o	
	ô	law dog order
mot eau gauche	ō	open so
genou roue	o͞o	pool food
	o͝o	took full
	yo͞o	use few
beurre peur	oe	
peu deux	o͞e	
	u	fun done up
urne huile rue	ü	
	ûr	urn term

DIPHTONGUES

DIPHTHONGS

	oi	oil boy
	ou	out now

NASALES

NASAL VOWELS

matin plein	aṅ	
brun	œṅ	
sang an dans	âṅ	
non pont	ôṅ	

FRENCH VERB FORMS

1 Participe présent *2* Participe passé *3* Présent *4* Imparfait *5* Futur *6* Conditionnel *7* Subjonctif présent

acquérir *1* acquérant *2* acquis *3* acquiers, acquérons, acquièrent *4* acquérais *5* acquerrai *7* acquière

ALLER *1* allant *2* allé *3* vais, vas, va, allons, allez, vont *4* allais *5* irai *6* irais *7* aille

asseoir *1* asseyant *2* assis *3* assieds, asseyons, asseyez, asseyent *4* asseyais *5* assiérai *7* asseye

atteindre *1* atteignant *2* atteint *3* atteins, atteignons *4* atteignais *7* atteigne

AVOIR *1* ayant *2* eu *3* ai, as, a, avons, avez, ont *4* avais *5* aurai *6* aurais *7* aie, aies, ait, ayons, ayez, aient

battre *1* battant *2* battu *3* bats, bat, battons *4* battais *7* batte

boire *1* buvant *2* bu *3* bois, buvons, boivent *4* buvais *7* boive

bouillir *1* bouillant *2* bouilli *3* bous, bouillons *4* bouillais *7* bouille

conclure *1* concluant *2* conclu *3* conclus, concluons *4* concluais *7* conclue

conduire *1* conduisant *2* conduit *3* conduis, conduisons *4* conduisais *7* conduise

connaître *1* connaissant *2* connu *3* connais, connaît, connaissons *4* connaissais *7* connaisse

coudre *1* cousant *2* cousu *3* couds, cousons, cousez, cousent *4* cousais *7* couse

courir *1* courant *2* couru *3* cours, courons *4* courais *5* courrai *7* coure

couvrir *1* couvrant *2* couvert *3* couvre, couvrons *4* couvrais *7* couvre

craindre *1* craignant *2* craint *3* crains, craignons *4* craignais *7* craigne

croire *1* croyant *2* cru *3* crois, croyons, croient *4* croyais *7* croie

croître *1* croissant *2* crû, crue, crus, crues *3* croîs, croissons *4* croissais *7* croisse

cueillir *1* cueillant *2* cueilli *3* cueille, cueillons *4* cueillais *5* cueillerai *7* cueille

devoir *1* devant *2* dû, due, dus, dues *3* dois, devons, doivent *4* devais *5* devrai *7* doive

dire *1* disant *2* dit *3* dis, disons, dites, disent *4* disais *7* dise

dormir *1* dormant *2* dormi *3* dors, dormons *4* dormais *7* dorme

écrire *1* écrivant *2* écrit *3* écris, écrivons *4* écrivais *7* écrive

ÊTRE *1* étant *2* été *3* suis, es, est, sommes, êtes, sont *4* étais *5* serai *6* serais *7* sois, sois, soit, soyons, soyez, soient

FAIRE *1* faisant *2* fait *3* fais, fais, fait, faisons, faites, font *4* faisais *5* ferai *6* ferais *7* fasse

falloir *2* fallu *3* faut *4* fallait *5* faudra *7* faille

FINIR *1* finissant *2* fini *3* finis, finis, finit, finissons, finissez, finissent *4* finissais *5* finirai *6* finirais *7* finisse

fuir *1* fuyant *2* fui *3* fuis, fuyons, fuient *4* fuyais *7* fuie

joindre *1* joignant *2* joint *3* joins, joignons *4* joignais *7* joigne

lire *1* lisant *2* lu *3* lis, lisons *4* lisais *7* lise

luire *1* luisant *2* lui *3* luis, luisons *4* luisais *7* luise

maudire *1* maudissant *2* maudit *3* maudis, maudissons *4* maudissait *7* maudisse

mentir *1* mentant *2* menti *3* mens, mentons *4* mentais *7* mente

mettre *1* mettant *2* mis *3* mets, mettons *4* mettais *7* mette

mourir *1* mourant *2* mort *3* meurs, mourons, meurent *4* mourais *5* mourrai *7* meure

naître *1* naissant *2* né *3* nais, naît, naissons *4* naissais *7* naisse

offrir *1* offrant *2* offert *3* offre, offrons *4* offrais *7* offre

PARLER *1* parlant *2* parlé *3* parle, parles, parle, parlons, parlez, parlent *4* parlais, parlais, parlait, parlions, parliez, parlaient *5* parlerai, parleras, parlera, parlerons, parlerez, parleront *6* parlerais, parlerais, parlerait, parlerions, parleriez, parleraient *7* parle, parles, parle, parlons, parliez, parlent *impératif* parle! parlez!

partir *1* partant *2* parti *3* pars, partons *4* partais *7* parte

plaire *1* plaisant *2* plu *3* plais, plaît, plaisons *4* plaisais *7* plaise

pleuvoir *1* pleuvant *2* plu *3* pleut, pleuvent *4* pleuvait *5* pleuvra *7* pleuve

pourvoir *1* pourvoyant *2* pourvu *3* pourvois, pourvoyons, pourvoient *4* pourvoyais *7* pourvoie

pouvoir *1* pouvant *2* pu *3* peux, peut, pouvons, peuvent *4* pouvais *5* pourrai *7* puisse

prendre *1* prenant *2* pris *3* prends, prenons, prennent *4* prenais *7* prenne

prévoir *like* voir *5* prévoirai

RECEVOIR *1* recevant *2* reçu *3* reçois, reçois, reçoit, recevons, recevez, reçoivent *4* recevais *5* recevrai *6* recevrais *7* reçoive

RENDRE *1* rendant *2* rendu *3* rends, rends, rend, rendons, rendez, rendent *4* rendais *5* rendrai *6* rendrais *7* rende

résoudre *1* résolvant *2* résolu *3* résous, résout, résolvons *4* résolvais *7* résolve

rire *1* riant *2* ri *3* ris, rions *4* riais *7* rie

savoir *1* sachant *2* su *3* sais, savons, savent *4* savais *5* saurai *7* sache *impératif* sache, sachons, sachez

servir *1* servant *2* servi *3* sers, servons *4* servais *7* serve

sortir *1* sortant *2* sorti *3* sors, sortons *4* sortais *7* sorte

souffrir *1* souffrant *2* souffert *3* souffre, souffrons *4* souffrais *7* souffre

suffire *1* suffisant *2* suffi *3* suffis, suffisons *4* suffisais *7* suffise

suivre *1* suivant *2* suivi *3* suis, suivons *4* suivais *7* suive

taire *1* taisant *2* tu *3* tais, taisons *4* taisais *7* taise

tenir *1* tenant *2* tenu *3* tiens, tenons, tiennent *4* tenais *5* tiendrai *7* tienne

vaincre *1* vainquant *2* vaincu *3* vaincs, vainc, vainquons *4* vainquais *7* vainque

valoir *1* valant *2* valu *3* vaux, vaut, valons *4* valais *5* vaudrai *7* vaille

venir *1* venant *2* venu *3* viens, venons, viennent *4* venais *5* viendrai *7* vienne

vivre *1* vivant *2* vécu *3* vis, vivons *4* vivais *7* vive

voir *1* voyant *2* vu *3* vois, voyons, voient *4* voyais *5* verrai *7* voie

vouloir *1* voulant *2* voulu *3* veux, veut, voulons, veulent *4* voulais *5* voudrai *7* veuille *impératif* veuillez

LE VERBE ANGLAIS

present	pt	pp	present	pt	pp
arise (arising)	arose	arisen	eat	ate	eaten
awake (awaking)	awoke	awaked	fall	fell	fallen
			feed	fed	fed
be (am, is, are, being)	was, were	been	feel	felt	felt
			fight	fought	fought
bear	bore	born(e)	find	found	found
beat	beat	beaten	flee	fled	fled
become (becoming)	became	become	fling	flung	flung
befall	befell	befallen	fly (flies)	flew	flown
begin (beginning)	began	begun	forbid (forbidding)	forbade	forbidden
behold	beheld	beheld	forecast	forecast	forecast
bend	bent	bent	forego	forewent	foregone
beseech	besought	besought	foresee	foresaw	foreseen
beset (besetting)	beset	beset	foretell	foretold	foretold
bet (betting)	bet (also betted)	bet (also betted)	forget (forgetting)	forgot	forgotten
bid (bidding)	bid (also bade)	bid (also bidden)	forgive (forgiving)	forgave	forgiven
bind	bound	bound	forsake (forsaking)	forsook	forsaken
bite (biting)	bit	bitten	freeze (freezing)	froze	frozen
bleed	bled	bled	get (getting)	got	got, (US) gotten
blow	blew	blown	give (giving)	gave	given
break	broke	broken	go (goes)	went	gone
breed	bred	bred	grind	ground	ground
bring	brought	brought	grow	grew	grown
build	built	built	hang	hung (also hanged)	hung (also hanged)
burn	burned (also burnt)	burned (also burnt)	have (has; having)	had	had
burst	burst	burst	hear	heard	heard
buy	bought	bought	hide (hiding)	hid	hidden
can	could	(been able)	hit (hitting)	hit	hit
cast	cast	cast	hold	held	held
catch	caught	caught	hurt	hurt	hurt
choose (choosing)	chose	chosen	keep	kept	kept
cling	clung	clung	kneel	knelt (also kneeled)	knelt (also kneeled)
come (coming)	came	come	know	knew	known
cost	cost	cost	lay	laid	laid
creep	crept	crept	lead	led	led
cut (cutting)	cut	cut	lean	leaned (also leant)	leaned (also leant)
deal	dealt	dealt	leap	leaped (also leapt)	leaped (also leapt)
dig (digging)	dug	dug	learn	learned (also learnt)	learned (also learnt)
do (3rd person: he/she/it/does)	did	done	leave (leaving)	left	left
draw	drew	drawn	lend	lent	lent
dream	dreamed (also dreamt)	dreamed also dreamt)	let (letting)	let	let
drink	drank	drunk	lie (lying)	lay	lain
drive (driving)	drove	driven	light	lighted (also lit)	lighted (also lit)
dwell	dwelt	dwelt	lose (losing)	lost	lost

present	pt	pp	present	pt	pp
make (making)	made	made	spell	spelled (*also* spelt)	spelled (*also* spelt)
may	might	—	spend	spent	spent
mean	meant	meant	spill	spilled (*also* spilt)	spilled (*also* spilt)
meet	met	met	spin (spinning)	spun	spun
mistake (mistaking)	mistook	mistaken	spit (spitting)	spat	spat
mow	mowed	mowed (*also* mown)	split (splitting)	split	split
must	(had to)	(had to)	spoil	spoiled (*also* spoilt)	spoiled (*also* spoilt)
pay	paid	paid	spread	spread	spread
put (putting)	put	put	spring	sprang	sprung
quit (quitting)	quit (*also* quitted)	quit (*also* quitted)	stand	stood	stood
read	read	read	steal	stole	stolen
rend	rent	rent	stick	stuck	stuck
rid (ridding)	rid	rid	sting	stung	stung
ride (riding)	rode	ridden	stink	stank	stunk
ring	rang	rung	stride (striding)	strode	stridden
rise (rising)	rose	risen	strike (striking)	struck	struck (*also* stricken)
run (running)	ran	run	strive (striving)	strove	striven
saw	sawed	sawn	swear	swore	sworn
say	said	said	sweep	swept	swept
see	saw	seen	swell	swelled	swelled (*also* swollen)
seek	sought	sought			
sell	sold	sold	swim (swimming)	swam	swum
send	sent	sent			
set (setting)	set	set	swing	swung	swung
shake (shaking)	shook	shaken	take (taking)	took	taken
shall	should	—	teach	taught	taught
shear	sheared	sheared (*also* shorn)	tear	tore	torn
			tell	told	told
shed (shedding)	shed	shed	think	thought	thought
shine (shining)	shone	shone	throw	threw	thrown
shoot	shot	shot	thrust	thrust	thrust
show	showed	shown	tread	trod	trodden
shrink	shrank	shrunk	wake (waking)	woke (*also* waked)	waked (*also* woken)
shut (shutting)	shut	shut	waylay	waylaid	waylaid
sing	sang	sung	wear	wore	worn
sink	sank	sunk	weave (weaving)	wove (*also* weaved)	woven (*also* weaved)
sit (sitting)	sat	sat			
slay	slew	slain	wed (wedding)	wedded	wedded (*also* wed)
sleep	slept	slept			
slide (sliding)	slid	slid	weep	wept	wept
sling	slung	slung	win (winning)	won	won
slit (slitting)	slit	slit	wind	wound	wound
smell	smelled (*Brit* smelt)	smelled (*Brit* smelt)	withdraw	withdrew	withdrawn
			withhold	withheld	withheld
sow	sowed	sown (*also* sowed)	withstand	withstood	withstood
			wring	wrung	wrung
speak	spoke	spoken	write (writing)	wrote	written
speed	sped (*also* speeded)	sped (*also* speeded)			

LES NOMBRES

NUMBERS

un(une)	1	one
deux	2	two
trois	3	three
quatre	4	four
cinq	5	five
six	6	six
sept	7	seven
huit	8	eight
neuf	9	nine
dix	10	ten
onze	11	eleven
douze	12	twelve
treize	13	thirteen
quatorze	14	fourteen
quinze	15	fifteen
seize	16	sixteen
dix-sept	17	seventeen
dix-huit	18	eighteen
dix-neuf	19	nineteen
vingt	20	twenty
vingt et un(une)	21	twenty-one
vingt-deux	22	twenty-two
trente	30	thirty
quarante	40	forty
cinquante	50	fifty
soixante	60	sixty
soixante-dix	70	seventy
soixante et onze	71	seventy-one
soixante-douze	72	seventy-two
quatre-vingts	80	eighty
quatre-vingt-un(-une)	81	eighty-one
quatre-vingt-dix	90	ninety
quatre-vingt-onze	91	ninety-one
cent	100	a hundred
cent un(une)	101	a hundred and one
trois cents	300	three hundred
trois cent un(une)	301	three hundred and one
mille	1 000	a thousand
un million	1 000 000	a million

premier(première), 1er	first, 1st
deuxième, 2e or 2ème	second, 2nd
troisième, 3e or 3ème	third, 3rd
quatrième	fourth, 4th
dixième	tenth
onzième	eleventh
douzième	twelfth
treizième	thirteenth
dix-septième	seventeenth
dix-huitième	eighteenth
dix-neuvième	nineteenth
vingtième	twentieth
vingt-et-unième	twenty-first
vingt-deuxième	twenty-second
trentième	thirtieth
centième	hundredth
cent-unième	hundred-and-first
millième	thousandth

FRANÇAIS-ANGLAIS
FRENCH-ENGLISH

A

A, a [á] *nm inv* A, a ♦ *abr* = **anticyclone, are;** (= *ampère*) amp; (= *autoroute*) ≈ I (*US*), ≈ M (*Brit*); **A comme Anatole** A for Able; **de a à z** from a to z; **prouver qch par a + b** to prove sth conclusively.

a [á] *vb voir* **avoir.**

à [á] (*à* + *le* = **au,** *à* + *les* = **aux**) [á, ō] *prép* (*situation*) at, in; (*direction, attribution*) to; (*provenance*) from; (*moyen*) with, by; **donner qch à qn** to give sb sth, give sth to sb; **prendre de l'eau à la fontaine** to take some water from the fountain; **payé au mois** paid by the month; **100 km/unités à l'heure** 100 km/units per hour; **à 3 heures/minuit** at 3 o'clock/midnight; **il habite à 5 minutes de la gare** he lives 5 minutes (away) from the station; **ils vivent à deux heures de Paris, par la route** they live two hours' drive (away) from Paris; **au mois de juin** in the month of June; **au départ** at the start, at the outset; **se chauffer au gaz/à l'électricité** to heat one's house with gas/electricity, to have gas/electric heating; **à la main/machine** by hand/machine; **à bicyclette** by bicycle *ou* on a bicycle; **à pied** by *ou* on foot; **être/aller à la campagne** to be in/go to the country; **l'homme aux yeux bleus/à la veste rouge** the man with the blue eyes/with *ou* in the red jacket; **un ami à moi** a friend of mine; **cinq à six heures** five to six hours; **à demain/la semaine prochaine!** see you tomorrow/next week!; **à la russe** the Russian way, in the Russian fashion; **à bien réfléchir** if you think about it; **maison à vendre** house for sale; **à sa grande surprise** to his great surprise; **à ce qu'il prétend** according to him, from what he says; **tasse à café** coffee cup.

Å *abr* (= *Angstrom*) A ou Å.

A2 *abr* (= *Antenne 2*) *French TV channel.*

abaissement [ábesmáñ] *nm* lowering; pulling down.

abaisser [ábāsā] *vt* to lower, bring down; (*manette*) to pull down; (*fig*) to debase; to humiliate; **s'~** *vi* to go down; (*fig*) to demean o.s.; **s'~ à faire/à qch** to stoop *ou* descend to doing/to sth.

abandon [ábáñdóñ] *nm* abandoning; deserting; giving up; withdrawal; surrender, relinquishing; (*fig*) lack of constraint; relaxed pose *ou* mood; **être à l'~** to be in a state of neglect; **laisser à l'~** to abandon.

abandonné, e [ábáñdónā] *a* (*solitaire*) deserted; (*route, usine*) disused; (*jardin*) abandoned.

abandonner [ábáñdónā] *vt* to leave, abandon, desert; (*projet, activité*) to abandon, give up; (*SPORT*) to retire *ou* withdraw from; (*céder*) to surrender, relinquish; **s'~** *vi* to let o.s. go;

s'~ à (*paresse, plaisirs*) to give o.s. up to; **~ qch à qn** to give sth up to sb.

abasourdir [ábázōōrdēr] *vt* to stun, stagger.

abat [ábá] *etc vb voir* **abattre.**

abat-jour [ábázhōōr] *nm inv* lampshade.

abats [ábá] *vb voir* **abattre** ♦ *nmpl* (*de bœuf, porc*) entrails (*US*), offal *sg* (*Brit*); (*de volaille*) giblets.

abattage [ábátázh] *nm* cutting down, felling.

abattant [ábátáñ] *vb voir* **abattre** ♦ *nm* leaf, flap.

abattement [ábátmáñ] *nm* (*physique*) enfeeblement; (*moral*) dejection, despondency; (*déduction*) reduction; **~ fiscal** ≈ tax allowance.

abattis [ábátē] *vb voir* **abattre** ♦ *nmpl* giblets.

abattoir [ábátwàr] *nm* abattoir (*Brit*), slaughterhouse.

abattre [ábátr(ə)] *vt* (*arbre*) to cut down, fell; (*mur, maison*) to pull down; (*avion, personne*) to shoot down; (*animal*) to shoot, kill; (*fig: physiquement*) to wear out, tire out; (: *moralement*) to demoralize; **s'~** *vi* to crash down; **s'~ sur** (*suj: pluie*) to beat down on; (: *coups, injures*) to rain down on; **~ ses cartes** (*aussi fig*) to lay one's cards on the table; **~ du travail** *ou* **de la besogne** to get through a lot of work.

abattu, e [ábátü] *pp de* **abattre** ♦ *a* (*déprimé*) downcast.

abbaye [ábāē] *nf* abbey.

abbé [ábā] *nm* priest; (*d'une abbaye*) abbot; **M l'~** Father.

abbesse [ábes] *nf* abbess.

abc, ABC [ábāsā] *nm* alphabet primer; (*fig*) rudiments *pl*.

abcès [ápse] *nm* abscess.

abdication [ábdēkásyóñ] *nf* abdication.

abdiquer [ábdēkā] *vi* to abdicate ♦ *vt* to renounce, give up.

abdomen [ábdomen] *nm* abdomen.

abdominal, e, aux [ábdomēnál, -ō] *a* abdominal ♦ *nmpl*: **faire des abdominaux** to do exercises for the stomach muscles.

abécédaire [ábāsāder] *nm* alphabet primer.

abeille [ábey] *nf* bee.

aberrant, e [áberáñ, -áñt] *a* absurd.

aberration [áberásyóñ] *nf* aberration.

abêtir [ábātēr] *vt* to make morons (*ou* a moron) of.

abhorrer [áborā] *vt* to abhor, loathe.

abîme [ábēm] *nm* abyss, gulf.

abîmer [ábēmā] *vt* to spoil, damage; **s'~** *vi* to get spoilt *ou* damaged; (*fruits*) to spoil; (*tomber*) to sink, founder; **s'~ les yeux** to ruin one's eyes *ou* eyesight.

abject, e [ábzhckt] *a* abject, despicable.

abjurer [ábzhürā] *vt* to abjure, renounce.

ablation [ȧblȧsyôǹ] *nf* removal.
ablutions [ȧblüsyôǹ] *nfpl*: **faire ses** ~ to perform one's ablutions.
abnégation [ȧbnāgȧsyôǹ] *nf* (self-)abnegation.
aboie [ȧbwȧ] *etc vb voir* **aboyer**.
aboiement [ȧbwȧmȧ́ǹ] *nm* bark, barking *q*.
aboierai [ȧbwȧyərȧ] *etc vb voir* **aboyer**.
abois [ȧbwȧ] *nmpl*: **aux** ~ at bay.
abolir [ȧbolēr] *vt* to abolish.
abolition [ȧbolēsyôǹ] *nf* abolition.
abolitionniste [ȧbolēsyonēst(ə)] *a*, *nm/f* abolitionist.
abominable [ȧbomēnȧbl(ə)] *a* abominable.
abomination [ȧbomēnȧsyôǹ] *nf* abomination.
abondamment [ȧbôǹdȧmȧ́ǹ] *ad* abundantly.
abondance [ȧbôǹdȧ́ǹs] *nf* abundance; *(richesse)* affluence; **en** ~ in abundance.
abondant, e [ȧbôǹdȧ́ǹ, -ȧ́ǹt] *a* plentiful, abundant, copious.
abonder [ȧbôǹdā] *vi* to abound, be plentiful; ~ **en** to be full of, abound in; ~ **dans le sens de qn** to concur with sb.
abonné, e [ȧbonā] *nm/f* subscriber; season ticket holder ♦ *a*: **être** ~ **à un journal** to subscribe to *ou* have a subscription to a periodical; **être** ~ **au téléphone** to have a (tele)phone.
abonnement [ȧbonmȧ́ǹ] *nm* subscription; *(pour transports en commun, concerts)* season ticket.
abonner [ȧbonā] *vt*: **s'**~ **à** to subscribe to, take out a subscription to.
abord [ȧbor] *nm*: **être d'un** ~ **facile** to be approachable; **être d'un** ~ **difficile** *(personne)* to be unapproachable; *(lieu)* to be hard to reach *ou* difficult to get to; **de prime** ~, **au premier** ~ at first sight; **d'**~ *ad* first; **tout d'**~ first of all.
abordable [ȧbordȧbl(ə)] *a* *(personne)* approachable; *(marchandise)* reasonably priced; *(prix)* affordable, reasonable.
abordage [ȧbordȧzh] *nm* boarding.
aborder [ȧbordā] *vi* to land ♦ *vt* *(sujet, difficulté)* to tackle; *(personne)* to approach; *(rivage etc)* to reach; *(NAVIG: attaquer)* to board; *(: heurter)* to collide with.
abords [ȧbor] *nmpl* surroundings.
aborigène [ȧborēzhen] *nm* aborigine, native.
Abou Dhabî, Abu Dhabi [ȧbo͞odȧbē] *nm* Abu Dhabi.
aboulique [ȧbo͞olēk] *a* totally lacking in will-power.
aboutir [ȧbo͞otēr] *vi* *(négociations etc)* to succeed; *(abcès)* to come to a head; ~ **à/dans/sur** to end up at/in/on.
aboutissants [ȧbo͞otēsȧ́ǹ] *nmpl voir* **tenants**.
aboutissement [ȧbo͞otēsmȧ́ǹ] *nm* success; *(de concept, projet)* successful realization; *(d'années de travail)* successful conclusion.
aboyer [ȧbwȧyā] *vi* to bark.
abracadabrant, e [ȧbrȧkȧdȧbrȧ́ǹ, -ȧ́ǹt] *a* incredible, preposterous.
abrasif, ive [ȧbrȧzēf, -ēv] *a*, *nm* abrasive.
abrégé [ȧbrāzhā] *nm* summary; **en** ~ in a shortened *ou* abbreviated form.
abréger [ȧbrāzhā] *vt* *(texte)* to shorten, abridge; *(mot)* to shorten, abbreviate; *(réunion, voyage)* to cut short, shorten.
abreuver [ȧbrœvā] *vt* to water; *(fig)*: ~ **qn de**

to shower *ou* swamp sb with; *(injures etc)* to shower sb with; **s'**~ *vi* to drink.
abreuvoir [ȧbrœvwȧr] *nm* watering place.
abréviation [ȧbrāvyȧsyôǹ] *nf* abbreviation.
abri [ȧbrē] *nm* shelter; **à l'**~ under cover; **être/se mettre à l'**~ to be/get under cover *ou* shelter; **à l'**~ **de** sheltered from; *(fig)* safe from.
abricot [ȧbrēkō] *nm* apricot.
abricotier [ȧbrēkotyā] *nm* apricot tree.
abrité, e [ȧbrētā] *a* sheltered.
abriter [ȧbrētā] *vt* to shelter; *(loger)* to accommodate; **s'**~ to shelter, take cover.
abrogation [ȧbrogȧsyôǹ] *nf* *(JUR)* repeal, abrogation.
abroger [ȧbrozhā] *vt* to repeal, abrogate.
abrupt, e [ȧbrüpt] *a* sheer, steep; *(ton)* abrupt.
abruti, e [ȧbrütē] *nm/f* *(fam)* idiot, moron.
abrutir [ȧbrütēr] *vt* to daze; *(fatiguer)* to exhaust; *(abêtir)* to stupefy.
abrutissant, e [ȧbrütēsȧ́ǹ, -ȧ́ǹt] *a* *(bruit, travail)* stupefying.
abscisse [ȧpsēs] *nf* X axis, abscissa.
absence [ȧpsȧ́ǹs] *nf* absence; *(MÉD)* blackout; *(distraction)* mental blank; **en l'**~ **de** in the absence of.
absent, e [ȧpsȧ́ǹ, -ȧ́ǹt] *a* absent; *(chose)* missing, lacking; *(distrait: air)* vacant, faraway ♦ *nm/f* absentee.
absentéisme [ȧpsȧ́ǹtācsm(ə)] *nm* absenteeism.
absenter [ȧpsȧ́ǹtā]: **s'**~ *vi* to take time off work; *(sortir)* to leave, go out.
abside [ȧpsēd] *nf* *(ARCHIT)* apse.
absinthe [ȧpsȧ́ǹt] *nf* *(boisson)* absinth(e); *(BOT)* wormwood, absinth(e).
absolu, e [ȧpsolü] *a* absolute; *(caractère)* rigid, uncompromising ♦ *nm* *(PHILOSOPHIE)*: **l'**~ the Absolute; **dans l'**~ in the absolute, in a vacuum.
absolument [ȧpsolümȧ́ǹ] *ad* absolutely.
absolution [ȧpsolüsyôǹ] *nf* absolution; *(JUR)* dismissal *(of case)*.
absolutisme [ȧpsolütēsm(ə)] *nm* absolutism.
absolvais [ȧpsolve] *etc vb voir* **absoudre**.
absorbant, e [ȧpsorbȧ́ǹ, -ȧ́ǹt] *a* absorbent; *(tâche)* absorbing, engrossing.
absorbé, e [ȧpsorbā] *a* absorbed, engrossed.
absorber [ȧpsorbā] *vt* to absorb; *(gén MÉD: manger, boire)* to take; *(ÉCON: firme)* to take over, absorb.
absorption [ȧpsorpsyôǹ] *nf* absorption.
absoudre [ȧpso͞odr(ə)] *vt* to absolve; *(JUR)* to dismiss.
absous, oute [ȧpso͞o, -o͞ot] *pp de* **absoudre**.
abstenir [ȧpstənēr]: **s'**~ *vi* *(POL)* to abstain; **s'**~ **de qch/de faire** to refrain from sth/from doing.
abstention [ȧpstȧ́ǹsyôǹ] *nf* abstention.
abstentionniste [ȧpstȧ́ǹsyonēst(ə)] *nm* abstentionist.
abstenu, e [ȧpstənü] *pp de* **abstenir**.
abstiendrai [ȧpstyȧ́ǹdrȧ], **abstiens** [ȧpstyȧǹ] *etc voir* **abstenir**.
abstinence [ȧpstēnȧ́ǹs] *nf* abstinence; **faire** ~ to abstain *(from meat on Fridays)*.
abstint [ȧpstȧǹ] *etc vb voir* **abstenir**.
abstraction [ȧpstrȧksyôǹ] *nf* abstraction; **faire** ~ **de** to set *ou* leave aside; ~ **faite de** ...

leaving aside ....

abstraire [ápstrer] *vt* to abstract; **s'~** *vi*: **s'~ (de)** (*s'isoler*) to cut o.s. off (from).

abstrait, e [ápstre, -et] *pp de* **abstraire** ♦ *a* abstract ♦ *nm*: **dans l'~** in the abstract.

abstraitement [ápstretmáṅ] *ad* abstractly.

abstrayais [ápstreye] *etc vb voir* **abstraire**.

absurde [ápsürd(ə)] *a* absurd ♦ *nm* absurdity; (*PHILOSOPHIE*): **l'~** absurd; **par l'~** *ad* absurdum.

absurdité [ápsürdētá] *nf* absurdity.

abus [ábü] *nm* (*excès*) abuse, misuse; (*injustice*) abuse; **~ de confiance** breach of trust; (*détournement de fonds*) embezzlement; **~ de pouvoir** abuse of power.

abuser [ábüzá] *vi* to go too far, overstep the mark ♦ *vt* to deceive, mislead; **s'~** *vi* (*se méprendre*) to be mistaken; **~ de** *vt* (*force, droit*) to misuse; (*alcool*) to take to excess; (*violer, duper*) to take advantage of.

abusif, ive [ábüzēf, -ēv] *a* exorbitant; (*punition*) excessive; (*pratique*) improper.

abusivement [ábüzēvmáṅ] *ad* exorbitantly; excessively; improperly.

AC *sigle f* (= *appellation contrôlée*) *guarantee of quality of wine*.

acabit [ákábē] *nm*: **du même ~** of the same type.

acacia [ákásyá] *nm* (*BOT*) acacia.

académicien, ne [ákádāmēsyaṅ, -en] *nm/f* academician.

académie [ákádāmē] *nf* (*société*) learned society; (*école: d'art, de danse*) academy; (*ART: nu*) nude; (*SCOL: circonscription*) ≈ regional education authority; **l'A~ (française)** the French Academy.

académique [ákádāmēk] *a* academic.

Acadie [ákádē] *nf*: **l'~** the Maritime Provinces.

acadien, ne [ákádyaṅ, -en] *a* Acadian, of *ou* from the Maritime Provinces.

acajou [ákázhōō] *nm* mahogany.

acariâtre [ákáryátr(ə)] *a* cantankerous.

accablant, e [ákábláṅ, -áṅt] *a* (*témoignage, preuve*) overwhelming.

accablement [ákábləmáṅ] *nm* deep despondency.

accabler [ákáblá] *vt* to overwhelm, overcome; (*suj: témoignage*) to condemn, damn; **~ qn d'injures** to heap *ou* shower abuse on sb; **~ qn de travail** to overburden sb with work; **accablé de dettes/soucis** weighed down with debts/cares.

accalmie [ákálmē] *nf* lull.

accaparant, e [ákápáráṅ, -áṅt] *a* that takes up all one's time *ou* attention.

accaparer [ákápárá] *vt* to monopolize; (*suj: travail etc*) to take up (all) the time *ou* attention of.

accéder [áksādá]: **~ à** *vt* (*lieu*) to reach; (*fig: pouvoir*) to accede to; (*: poste*) to attain; (*accorder: requête*) to grant, accede to.

accélérateur [áksālárátœr] *nm* accelerator.

accélération [áksālárásyóṅ] *nf* speeding up; acceleration.

accéléré [áksālārá] *nm*: **en ~** (*CINÉMA*) speeded up.

accélérer [áksālārá] *vt* (*mouvement, travaux*) to speed up ♦ *vi* (*AUTO*) to accelerate.

accent [áksáṅ] *nm* accent; (*inflexions expressives*) tone (of voice); (*PHONÉTIQUE, fig*) stress; **aux ~s de** (*musique*) to the strains of; **mettre l'~ sur** (*fig*) to stress; **~ aigu/grave/circonflexe** acute/grave/circumflex accent.

accentuation [áksáṅtüásyóṅ] *nf* accenting; stressing.

accentué, e [áksáṅtüā] *a* marked, pronounced.

accentuer [áksáṅtüā] *vt* (*LING: orthographe*) to accent; (*: phonétique*) to stress, accent; (*fig*) to accentuate, emphasize; (*: effort, pression*) to increase; **s'~** *vi* to become more marked *ou* pronounced.

acceptable [ákseptábl(ə)] *a* satisfactory, acceptable.

acceptation [ákseptásyóṅ] *nf* acceptance.

accepter [ákseptá] *vt* to accept; (*tolérer*): **~ que qn fasse** to agree to sb doing; **~ de faire** to agree to do.

acception [áksepsyóṅ] *nf* meaning, sense; **dans toute l'~ du terme** in the full sense *ou* meaning of the word.

accès [ákse] *nm* (*à un lieu, INFORM*) access; (*MÉD*) attack; (*: de toux*) fit, bout ♦ *nmpl* (*routes etc*) means of access, approaches; **d'~ facile/malaisé** easily/not easily accessible; **donner ~ à** (*lieu*) to give access to; (*carrière*) to open the door to; **avoir ~ auprès de qn** to have access to sb; **l'~ aux quais est interdit aux personnes non munies d'un billet** ticket-holders only on platforms, no access to platforms without a ticket; **~ de colère** fit of anger; **~ de joie** burst of joy.

accessible [áksāsēbl(ə)] *a* accessible; (*personne*) approachable; (*livre, sujet*): **~ à qn** within the reach of sb; (*sensible*): **~ à la pitié/l'amour** open to pity/love.

accession [áksesyóṅ] *nf*: **~ à** accession to; (*à un poste*) attainment of; **~ à la propriété** home-ownership.

accessit [áksāsēt] *nm* (*SCOL*) ≈ certificate of merit.

accessoire [áksāswár] *a* secondary, of secondary importance; (*frais*) incidental ♦ *nm* accessory; (*THÉÂTRE*) prop.

accessoirement [áksāswármáṅ] *ad* secondarily; incidentally.

accessoiriste [áksāswárēst(ə)] *nm/f* (*TV, CINÉMA*) property man/woman.

accident [áksēdáṅ] *nm* accident; **par ~** by chance; **~ de parcours** mishap; **~ de la route** road accident; **~ du travail** accident at work; industrial injury *ou* accident; **~s de terrain** unevenness of the ground.

accidenté, e [áksēdáṅtá] *a* damaged *ou* injured (in an accident); (*relief, terrain*) uneven; hilly.

accidentel, le [áksēdáṅtel] *a* accidental.

accidentellement [áksēdáṅtelmáṅ] *ad* (*par hasard*) accidentally; (*mourir*) in an accident.

accidenter [áksēdáṅtá] *vt* (*personne*) to injure; (*véhicule*) to damage.

accise [áksēz] *nf*: **droit d'~(s)** excise duty.

acclamation [áklámásyóṅ] *nf*: **par ~** (*vote*) by acclamation; **~s** *nfpl* cheers, cheering *sg*.

acclamer [áklámá] *vt* to cheer, acclaim.

acclimatation [åklēmátâsyôṅ] *nf* acclimatization.

acclimater [åklēmátā] *vt* to acclimatize; **s'~** *vi* to become acclimatized.

accointances [åkwaṅtâṅs] *nfpl*: **avoir des ~ avec** to have contacts with.

accolade [åkolád] *nf* (*amicale*) embrace; (*signe*) brace; **donner l'~ à qn** to embrace sb.

accoler [åkolā] *vt* to place side by side.

accommodant, e [åkomodâṅ, -âṅt] *a* accommodating, easy-going.

accommodement [åkomodmâṅ] *nm* compromise.

accommoder [åkomodā] *vt* (CULIN) to prepare; (*points de vue*) to reconcile; **~ qch à** (*adapter*) to adapt sth to; **s'~ de** to put up with; (*se contenter de*) to make do with; **s'~ à** (*s'adapter*) to adapt to.

accompagnateur, trice [åkôṅpáṅyátœr, -trēs] *nm/f* (MUS) accompanist; (*de voyage*) guide; (: *de voyage organisé*) courier; (*d'enfants*) accompanying adult.

accompagnement [åkôṅpáṅymâṅ] *nm* (MUS) accompaniment; (MIL) support.

accompagner [åkôṅpáṅyā] *vt* to accompany, be *ou* go *ou* come with; (MUS) to accompany; **s'~ de** to bring, be accompanied by.

accompli, e [åkôṅplē] *a* accomplished.

accomplir [åkôṅplēr] *vt* (*tâche, projet*) to carry out; (*souhait*) to fulfill (US), fulfil (Brit); **s'~** *vi* to be fulfilled.

accomplissement [åkôṅplēsmâṅ] *nm* carrying out; fulfillment (US), fulfilment (Brit).

accord [åkor] *nm* (*entente, convention,* LING) agreement; (*entre des styles, tons etc*) harmony; (*consentement*) agreement, consent; (MUS) chord; **donner son ~** to give one's agreement; **mettre 2 personnes d'~** to make 2 people come to an agreement, reconcile 2 people; **se mettre d'~** to come to an agreement (with each other); **être d'~** to agree; **être d'~ avec qn** to agree with sb; **d'~!** OK!, right!; **d'un commun ~** of one accord; **~ parfait** (MUS) tonic chord.

accord-cadre, *pl* **accords-cadres** [åkorkâdr(ə)] *nm* framework *ou* outline agreement.

accordéon [åkordâôṅ] *nm* (MUS) accordion.

accordéoniste [åkordâonēst(ə)] *nm/f* accordionist.

accorder [åkordā] *vt* (*faveur, délai*) to grant; (*attribuer*): **~ de l'importance/de la valeur à qch** to attach importance/value to sth; (*harmoniser*) to match; (MUS) to tune; **s'~** to get on together; (*être d'accord*) to agree; (*couleurs, caractères*) to go together, match; (LING) to agree; **je vous accorde que ... I** grant you that ....

accordeur [åkordœr] *nm* (MUS) tuner.

accoster [åkostā] *vt* (NAVIG) to draw alongside; (*personne*) to accost ♦ *vi* (NAVIG) to berth.

accotement [åkotmâṅ] *nm* (*de route*) shoulder; **~ stabilisé/non stabilisé** hard shoulder/soft shoulder.

accoter [åkotā] *vt*: **~ qch contre/à** to lean *ou* rest sth against/on; **s'~ contre/à** to lean against/on.

accouchement [åkōōshmâṅ] *nm* delivery,

(child) birth; (*travail*) labor (US), labour (Brit); **~ à terme** delivery at (full) term; **~ sans douleur** natural childbirth.

accoucher [åkōōshā] *vi* to give birth, have a baby; (*être en travail*) to be in labor (US) *ou* labour (Brit) ♦ *vt* to deliver; **~ d'un garçon** to give birth to a boy.

accoucheur [åkōōshœr] *nm*: **(médecin) ~** obstetrician.

accoucheuse [åkōōshēz] *nf* midwife.

accouder [åkōōdā]: **s'~** *vi*: **s'~ à/contre/sur** to rest one's elbows on/against/on; **accoudé à la fenêtre** leaning on the windowsill.

accoudoir [åkōōdwár] *nm* armrest.

accouplement [åkōōpləmâṅ] *nm* coupling; mating.

accoupler [åkōōplā] *vt* to couple; (*pour la reproduction*) to mate; **s'~** to mate.

accourir [åkōōrēr] *vi* to rush *ou* run up.

accoutrement [åkōōtrəmâṅ] *nm* (*péj*) outfit.

accoutrer [åkōōtrā] (*péj*) *vt* to do *ou* get up; **s'~** to do *ou* get o.s. up.

accoutumance [åkōōtümâṅs] *nf* (*gén*) adaptation; (MÉD) addiction.

accoutumé, e [åkōōtümā] *a* (*habituel*) customary, usual; **comme à l'~e** as is customary *ou* usual.

accoutumer [åkōōtümā] *vt*: **~ qn à qch/faire** to accustom sb to sth/to doing; **s'~ à** to get accustomed *ou* used to.

accréditer [åkrādētā] *vt* (*nouvelle*) to substantiate; **~ qn (auprès de)** to accredit sb (to).

accro [åkrō] *nm/f* (*fam*: = *accroché(e)*) addict.

accroc [åkrō] *nm* (*déchirure*) tear; (*fig*) hitch, snag; **sans ~** without a hitch; **faire un ~ à** (*vêtement*) to make a tear in; tear; (*fig: règle etc*) to infringe.

accrochage [åkrosházh] *nm* hanging (up); hitching (up); (AUTO) (minor) collision; (MIL) encounter, engagement; (*dispute*) clash, brush.

accroche-cœur [åkroshkœr] *nm* spit curl (US), kiss-curl (Brit).

accrocher [åkroshā] *vt* (*suspendre*): **~ qch à** to hang sth (up) on; (*attacher: remorque*): **~ qch à** to hitch sth (up) to; (*heurter*) to catch; to hit; (*déchirer*): **~ qch (à)** to catch sth (on); (MIL) to engage; (*fig*) to catch, attract ♦ *vi* to stick, get stuck; (*fig: pourparlers etc*) to hit a snag; (*plaire: disque etc*) to catch on; **s'~** (*se disputer*) to have a clash *ou* brush; (*ne pas céder*) to hold one's own, hang on in (*fam*); **s'~ à** (*rester pris à*) to catch on; (*agripper, fig*) to hang on *ou* cling to.

accrocheur, euse [åkroshœr, -ēz] *a* (*vendeur, concurrent*) tenacious; (*publicité*) eye-catching; (*titre*) catchy, eye-catching.

accroire [åkrwár] *vt*: **faire** *ou* **laisser ~ à qn qch/que** to give sb to believe sth/that.

accroîs [åkrwâ], **accroissais** [åkrwâsc] *etc vb voir* **accroître**.

accroissement [åkrwâsmâṅ] *nm* increase.

accroître [åkrwâtr(ə)] *vt*, **s'~** *vi* to increase.

accroupi, e [åkrōōpē] *a* squatting, crouching (down).

accroupir [åkrōōpēr]: **s'~** *vi* to squat, crouch

(down).

accru, e |àkrü| *pp de* **accroître.**

accu |àkü| *nm (fam: = accumulateur)* battery.

accueil |àkœy| *nm* welcome; *(endroit)* reception (desk); *(: dans une gare)* information kiosk; **comité/centre d'~** reception committee/center.

accueillant, e |àkœyàn̄, -àn̄t| *a* welcoming, friendly.

accueillir |àkœyēr| *vt* to welcome; *(loger)* to accommodate.

acculer |àkülä| *vt:* ~ **qn à** *ou* **contre** to drive sb back against; ~ **qn dans** to corner sb in; ~ **qn à** *(faillite)* to drive sb to the brink of.

accumulateur |àkümülàtœr| *nm* battery.

accumulation |àkümülâsyôn̄| *nf* accumulation; **chauffage/radiateur à** ~ (night-)storage heating/heater.

accumuler |àkümülä| *vt* to accumulate, amass; **s'~** *vi* to accumulate; to pile up.

accusateur, trice |àküzàtœr, -trēs| *nm/f* accuser ♦ *a* accusing; *(document, preuve)* incriminating.

accusatif |àküzàtēf| *nm (LING)* accusative.

accusation |àküzâsyôn̄| *nf (gén)* accusation; *(JUR)* charge; *(partie):* **l'~** the prosecution; **mettre en** ~ to indict; **acte d'~** bill of indictment.

accusé, e |àküzä| *nm/f* accused; *(prévenu(e))* defendant ♦ *nm:* ~ **de réception** acknowledgement of receipt.

accuser |àküzä| *vt* to accuse; *(fig)* to emphasize, bring out; *(: montrer)* to show; **s'~** *vi* *(s'accentuer)* to become more marked; ~ **qn de** to accuse sb of; *(JUR)* to charge sb with; ~ **qn/qch de qch** *(rendre responsable)* to blame sb/sth for sth; **s'~ de qch/d'avoir fait qch** to admit sth/having done sth; to blame o.s. for sth/for having done sth; ~ **réception de** to acknowledge receipt of; ~ **le coup** *(aussi fig)* to be visibly affected.

acerbe |àserb(ə)| *a* caustic, acid.

acéré, e |àsàrä| *a* sharp.

acétate |àsàtàt| *nm* acetate.

acétique |àsàtēk| *a:* **acide** ~ acetic acid.

acétone |àsàton| *nf* acetone.

acétylène |àsàtēlen| *nm* acetylene.

ACF *sigle m (= Automobile Club de France)* ≈ AAA *(US),* ≈ AA *(Brit).*

ach. *abr* = **achète.**

achalandé, e |àshàlàn̄dä| *a:* **bien/mal** ~ well-/poorly stocked.

acharné, e |àshàrnä| *a (lutte, adversaire)* fierce, bitter; *(travail)* relentless, unremitting.

acharnement |àshàrnəmàn̄| *nm* fierceness; relentlessness.

acharner |àshàrnä| **s'~** *vi:* **s'~ sur** to go at fiercely, hound; **s'~ contre** to set o.s. against; to dog, pursue; *(suj: malchance)* to hound; **s'~ à faire** to try doggedly to do; to persist in doing.

achat |àshà| *nm* buying *q; (article acheté)* purchase; **faire l'~ de** to buy, purchase; **faire des ~s** to do some shopping, buy a few things.

acheminement |àshmēnmàn̄| *nm* conveyance.

acheminer |àshmēnä| *vt (courrier)* to forward, dispatch; *(troupes)* to convey, transport;

(train) to route; **s'~ vers** to head for.

acheter |àshtä| *vt* to buy, purchase; *(soudoyer)* to buy, bribe; ~ **qch à** *(marchand)* to buy *ou* purchase sth from; *(ami etc: offrir)* to buy sth for; ~ **à crédit** to buy on credit.

acheteur, euse |àshtœr, -œz| *nm/f* buyer; shopper; *(COMM)* buyer; *(JUR)* vendee, purchaser.

achevé, e |àshvä| *a:* **d'un ridicule** ~ thoroughly *ou* absolutely ridiculous; **d'un comique** ~ absolutely hilarious.

achèvement |àshevmàn̄| *nm* completion, finishing.

achever |àshvä| *vt* to complete, finish; *(blessé)* to finish off; **s'~** *vi* to end.

achoppement |àshopmàn̄| *nm:* **pierre d'~** stumbling block.

acide |àsēd| *a* sour, sharp; *(ton)* acid, biting; *(CHIMIE)* acid(ic) ♦ *nm* acid.

acidifier |àsēdēfyä| *vt* to acidify.

acidité |àsēdētä| *nf* sharpness; acidity.

acidulé, e |àsēdülä| *a* slightly acid; **bonbons ~s** ≈ lemon drops *(US),* acid drops *(Brit).*

acier |àsyä| *nm* steel; ~ **inoxydable** stainless steel.

aciérie |àsyàrē| *nf* steelworks *sg.*

acné |àknä| *nf* acne.

acolyte |àkolēt| *nm (péj)* associate.

acompte |àkôn̄t| *nm* deposit; *(versement régulier)* installment *(US),* instalment *(Brit);* *(sur somme due)* payment on account; *(sur salaire)* advance; **un ~ de 100 F** 100 F on account.

acoquiner |àkokēnä| **s'~ avec** *vt (péj)* to team up with.

Açores |àsor| *nfpl:* **les** ~ the Azores.

à-côté |àkōtä| *nm* side-issue; *(argent)* extra.

à-coup |àkōō| *nm (du moteur)* (hic)cough; *(fig)* jolt; **sans ~s** smoothly; **par ~s** by fits and starts.

acoustique |àkōōstēk| *nf (d'une salle)* acoustics *pl; (science)* acoustics *sg* ♦ *a* acoustic.

acquéreur |àkàrœr| *nm* buyer, purchaser; **se porter/se rendre ~ de qch** to announce one's intention to purchase/to purchase sth.

acquérir |àkàrēr| *vt* to acquire; *(par achat)* to purchase, acquire; *(valeur)* to gain; *(résultats)* to achieve; **ce que ses efforts lui ont acquis** what his efforts have won *ou* gained (for) him.

acquiers |àkyer| *etc vb voir* **acquérir.**

acquiescement |àkyesmàn̄| *nm* acquiescence, agreement.

acquiescer |àkyäsä| *vi (opiner)* to agree; *(consentir):* ~ **(à qch)** to acquiesce *ou* assent (to sth).

acquis, e |àkē, -ēz| *pp de* **acquérir** ♦ *nm* (accumulated) experience; *(avantage)* gain ♦ *a (voir acquérir)* acquired; gained; achieved; **être ~ à** *(plan, idée)* to be in full agreement with; **son aide nous est ~e** we can count on *ou* be sure of his help; **tenir qch pour ~** to take sth for granted.

acquisition |àkēzēsyôn̄| *nf* acquisition; *(achat)* purchase; **faire l'~ de** to acquire; to purchase.

acquit |àkē| *vb voir* **acquérir** ♦ *nm (quittance)* receipt; **pour** ~ received; **par ~ de**

conscience to set one's mind at rest.
acquittement [àkētmáṅ] *nm* acquittal; payment, settlement.
acquitter [àkētá] *vt* (*JUR*) to acquit; (*facture*) to pay, settle; **s'~ de** to discharge; (*promesse, tâche*) to fulfill (*US*), fulfil (*Brit*), carry out.
âcre [àkr(ə)] *a* acrid, pungent.
âcreté [àkrətá] *nf* acridness, pungency.
acrobate [àkrobát] *nm/f* acrobat.
acrobatie [àkrobàsē] *nf* (*art*) acrobatics *sg*; (*exercice*) acrobatic feat; **~ aérienne** aerobatics *sg*.
acrobatique [àkrobátēk] *a* acrobatic.
acronyme [àkronēm] *nm* acronym.
Acropole [àkropol] *nf*: **l'~** the Acropolis.
acrylique [àkrēlēk] *a, nm* acrylic.
acte [àktœr] *nm* act, action; (*THÉÂTRE*) act; **~s** *nmpl* (*compte-rendu*) proceedings; **prendre ~ de** to note, take note of; **faire ~ de présence** to put in an appearance; **faire ~ de candidature** to submit an application; **~ d'accusation** bill of indictment; **~ de baptême** baptismal certificate; **~ de mariage/naissance** marriage/birth certificate; **~ de vente** bill of sale.
acteur [àktœr] *nm* actor.
actif, ive [àktēf, -ēv] *a* active ♦ *nm* (*COMM*) assets *pl*; (*LING*) active (voice); (*fig*): **avoir à son ~** to have to one's credit; **~s** *nmpl* people in employment; **mettre à son ~** to add to one's list of achievements; **l'~ et le passif** assets and liabilities; **prendre une part active à qch** to take an active part in sth; **population active** working population.
action [àksyóṅ] *nf* (*gén*) action; (*COMM*) share; **une bonne/mauvaise ~** a good/an unkind deed; **mettre en ~** to put into action; **passer à l'~** to take action; **sous l'~ de** under the effect of; **l'~ syndicale** (the) union action; **un film d'~** an action film *ou* movie; **~ en diffamation** libel suit; **~ de grâce(s)** (*REL*) thanksgiving.
actionnaire [àksyoner] *nm/f* shareholder.
actionner [àksyoná] *vt* to work; to activate; to operate.
active [àktēv] *af voir* **actif**.
activement [àktēvmáṅ] *ad* actively.
activer [àktēvá] *vt* to speed up; (*CHIMIE*) to activate; **s'~** *vi* (*s'affairer*) to bustle about; (*se hâter*) to hurry up.
activisme [àktēvēsm(ə)] *nm* activism.
activiste [àktēvēst(ə)] *nm/f* activist.
activité [àktēvētá] *nf* activity; **en ~** (*volcan*) active; (*fonctionnaire*) in active life; (*militaire*) on active service.
actrice [àktrēs] *nf* actress.
actualiser [àktüálēzá] *vt* to actualize; (*mettre à jour*) to bring up to date.
actualité [àktüálētá] *nf* (*d'un problème*) topicality; (*événements*): **l'~** current events; **les ~s** (*CINÉMA, TV*) the news; **l'~ politique/sportive** the political/sports news; **les ~s télévisées** the television news; **d'~** topical.
actuel, le [àktüel] *a* (*présent*) present; (*d'actualité*) topical; (*non virtuel*) actual; **à l'heure ~le** at this moment in time, at the moment.

actuellement [àktüelmáṅ] *ad* at present, at the present time.
acuité [àküētá] *nf* acuteness.
acuponcteur, acupuncteur [àküpóṅktœr] *nm* acupuncturist.
acuponcture, acupuncture [àküpóṅktür] *nf* acupuncture.
adage [àdázh] *nm* adage.
adaptable [àdáptábl(ə)] *a* adaptable.
adaptateur, trice [àdáptátœr, -trēs] *nm/f* adapter.
adaptation [àdáptásyóṅ] *nf* adaptation.
adapter [àdáptá] *vt* to adapt; **s'~ (à)** (*suj: personne*) to adapt (to); (*: objet, prise etc*) to apply (to); **~ qch à** (*approprier*) to adapt sth to (fit); **~ qch sur/dans/à** (*fixer*) to fit sth on/into/to.
addenda [àdándá] *nm inv* addenda.
Addis-Ababa [àdēsábábá], **Addis-Abeba** [àdēsábəbá] *n* Addis Ababa.
additif [àdētēf] *nm* additional clause; (*substance*) additive; **~ alimentaire** food additive.
addition [àdēsyóṅ] *nf* addition; (*au café*) bill.
additionnel, le [àdēsyonel] *a* additional.
additionner [àdēsyoná] *vt* to add (up); **s'~** *vi* to add up; **~ un produit d'eau** to add water to a product.
adduction [àdüksyóṅ] *nf* (*de gaz, d'eau*) conveyance.
ADEP *sigle f* (= *Agence nationale pour le développement de l'éducation permanente*) national body which promotes adult education.
adepte [àdept(ə)] *nm/f* follower.
adéquat, e [àdákwá, -át] *a* appropriate, suitable.
adéquation [àdákwásyóṅ] *nf* appropriateness; (*LING*) adequacy.
adhérence [àdáráns] *nf* adhesion.
adhérent, e [àdáráṅ, -áṅt] *nm/f* (*de club*) member.
adhérer [àdárá] *vi* (*coller*) to adhere, stick; **~ à** (*coller*) to adhere *ou* stick to; (*se rallier à: parti, club*) to join; to be a member of; (*: opinion, mouvement*) to support.
adhésif, ive [àdázēf, -ēv] *a* adhesive, sticky ♦ *nm* adhesive.
adhésion [àdázyóṅ] *nf* (*à un club*) joining; membership; (*à un opinion*) support.
ad hoc [àdok] *a* ad hoc.
adieu, x [àdyœ] *excl* goodbye ♦ *nm* farewell; **dire ~ à qn** to say goodbye *ou* farewell to sb; **dire ~ à qch** (*renoncer*) to say *ou* wave goodbye to sth.
adipeux, euse [àdēpœ, -œz] *a* bloated, fat; (*ANAT*) adipose.
adjacent, e [àdzhásáṅ, -áṅt] *a*: **~ (à)** adjacent (to).
adjectif [àdzhektēf] *nm* adjective; **~ attribut** adjectival complement; **~ épithète** attributive adjective.
adjoignais [àdzhwánye] *etc vb voir* **adjoindre**.
adjoindre [àdzhwaṅdr(ə)] *vt*: **~ qch à** to attach sth to; (*ajouter*) to add sth to; **~ qn à** (*personne*) to appoint sb as an assistant to; (*comité*) to appoint sb to, attach sb to; **s'~** *vt* (*collaborateur etc*) to take on, appoint.
adjoint, e [àdzhwaṅ, -waṅt] *pp de* **adjoindre** ♦

nm/f assistant; **directeur** ~ assistant manager.

adjonction [àdzhóṅksyóṅ] *nf* (*voir adjoindre*) attaching; addition; appointment.

adjudant [àdzhüdáṅ] *nm* (*MIL*) warrant officer; ~**-chef** ≈ chief warrant officer (*US*), ≈ warrant officer 1st class (*Brit*).

adjudicataire [àdzhüdēkáter] *nm/f* successful bidder, purchaser; (*pour travaux*) successful bidder.

adjudicateur, trice [àdzhüdēkátœr, -trēs] *nm/f* (*aux enchères*) seller.

adjudication [àdzhüdēkàsyóṅ] *nf* sale by auction; (*pour travaux*) invitation to bid.

adjuger [àdzhüzhā] *vt* (*prix, récompense*) to award; (*lors d'une vente*) to auction (off); **s'**~ *vt* to take for o.s; **adjugé!** (*vendu*) gone!, sold!

adjurer [àdzhürā] *vt*: ~ **qn de faire** to implore *ou* beg sb to do.

adjuvant [àdzhüvàṅ] *nm* (*médicament*) adjuvant; (*additif*) additive; (*stimulant*) stimulant.

admettre [àdmetr(ə)] *vt* (*visiteur, nouveau-venu*) to admit, let in; (*candidat*: *SCOL*) to pass; (*TECH*: *gaz, eau, air*) to admit; (*tolérer*) to allow, accept; (*reconnaître*) to admit, acknowledge; (*supposer*) to suppose; **j'admets que** ... I admit that ...; **je n'admets pas que tu fasses cela** I won't allow you to do that; **admettons que** ... let's suppose that ...; **admettons** let's suppose so.

administrateur, trice [àdmēnēstrátœr, -trēs] *nm/f* (*COMM*) director; (*ADMIN*) administrator; ~ **délégué** managing director; ~ **judiciaire** receiver.

administratif, ive [àdmēnēstrátēf, -ēv] *a* administrative ♦ *nm* person in administration.

administration [àdmēnēstràsyóṅ] *nf* administration; **l'A**~ ≈ the Civil Service.

administré, e [àdmēnēstrā] *nm/f* ≈ citizen.

administrer [àdmēnēstrā] *vt* (*firme*) to manage, run; (*biens, remède, sacrement etc*) to administer.

admirable [àdmēràbl(ə)] *a* admirable, wonderful.

admirablement [àdmēràbləmàṅ] *ad* admirably.

admirateur, trice [àdmēràtœr, -trēs] *nm/f* admirer.

admiratif, ive [àdmēràtēf, -ēv] *a* admiring.

admiration [àdmēràsyóṅ] *nf* admiration; **être en** ~ **devant** to be lost in admiration before.

admirativement [àdmēràtēvmàṅ] *ad* admiringly.

admirer [àdmērā] *vt* to admire.

admis, e [àdmē, -ēz] *pp de* **admettre**.

admissibilité [àdmēsēbēlētā] *nf* eligibility; admissibility, acceptability.

admissible [àdmēsēbl(ə)] *a* (*candidat*) eligible; (*comportement*) admissible, acceptable; (*JUR*) receivable.

admission [àdmēsyóṅ] *nf* admission; **tuyau d'**~ intake pipe; **demande d'**~ application for membership; **service des** ~**s** admissions.

admonester [àdmonestā] *vt* to admonish.

ADN *sigle m* (= *acide désoxyribonucléique*) DNA.

ado [àdō] *nm/f* (*fam*: = *adolescent(e)*) adolescent, teenager.

adolescence [àdolāsàṅs] *nf* adolescence.

adolescent, e [àdolāsàṅ, -àṅt] *nm/f* adolescent, teenager.

adonner [àdonā]: **s'**~ **à** *vt* (*sport*) to devote o.s. to; (*boisson*) to give o.s. over to.

adopter [àdoptā] *vt* to adopt; (*projet de loi etc*) to pass.

adoptif, ive [àdoptēf, -ēv] *a* (*parents*) adoptive; (*fils, patrie*) adopted.

adoption [àdopsyóṅ] *nf* adoption; **son pays/sa ville d'**~ his adopted country/town.

adorable [àdoràbl(ə)] *a* adorable.

adoration [àdoràsyóṅ] *nf* adoration; (*REL*) worship; **être en** ~ **devant** to be lost in adoration before.

adorer [àdorā] *vt* to adore; (*REL*) to worship.

adosser [àdōsā] *vt*: ~ **qch à** *ou* **contre** to stand sth against; **s'**~ **à** *ou* **contre** to lean with one's back against; **être adossé à** *ou* **contre** to be leaning with one's back against.

adoucir [àdōōsēr] *vt* (*goût, température*) to make milder; (*avec du sucre*) to sweeten; (*peau, voix, eau*) to soften; (*caractère, personne*) to mellow; (*peine*) to soothe, allay; **s'**~ *vi* to become milder; to soften; to mellow.

adoucissement [àdōōsēsmàṅ] *nm* becoming milder; sweetening; softening; mellowing; soothing.

adoucisseur [àdōōsēsœr] *nm*: ~ (**d'eau**) water softener.

adr. *abr* = **adresse, adresser**.

adrénaline [àdrānálēn] *nf* adrenaline.

adresse [àdres] *nf* (*voir adroit*) skill, dexterity; (*domicile, INFORM*) address; **à l'**~ **de** (*pour*) for the benefit of.

adresser [àdrāsā] *vt* (*lettre*: *expédier*) to send; (*: écrire l'adresse sur*) to address; (*injure, compliments*) to address; ~ **qn à un docteur/bureau** to refer *ou* send sb to a doctor/an office; ~ **la parole à qn** to speak to *ou* address sb; **s'**~ **à** (*parler à*) to speak to, address; (*s'informer auprès de*) to go and see, go and speak to; (*: bureau*) to enquire at; (*suj: livre, conseil*) to be aimed at.

Adriatique [àdrēyàtēk] *nf*: **l'**~ the Adriatic.

adroit, e [àdrwà, -wàt] *a* (*joueur, mécanicien*) skillful (*US*), skilful (*Brit*), dext(e)rous; (*politicien etc*) shrewd, skilled.

adroitement [àdrwàtmàṅ] *ad* skillfully (*US*), skilfully (*Brit*), dext(e)rously; shrewdly.

AdS *sigle f* = **Académie des Sciences**.

aduler [àdülā] *vt* to adulate.

adulte [àdült(ə)] *nm/f* adult, grown-up ♦ *a* (*personne, attitude*) adult, grown-up; (*chien, arbre*) fully-grown, mature; **l'âge** ~ adulthood; **formation/film pour** ~**s** adult training/film.

adultère [àdülter] *a* adulterous ♦ *nm/f* adulterer/adulteress ♦ *nm* (*acte*) adultery.

adultérin, e [àdültáràṅ, -ēn] *a* born of adultery.

advenir [àdvənēr] *vi* to happen; **qu'est-il advenu de?** what has become of?; **quoi qu'il advienne** whatever befalls *ou* happens.

adventiste [àdvàṅtēst(ə)] *nm/f* (*REL*) Adventist.

adverbe [àdverb(ə)] *nm* adverb; **~ de manière** adverb of manner.

adverbial, e, aux [àdverbyàl, -ō] *a* adverbial.

adversaire [àdverser] *nm/f* (*SPORT*, *gén*) opponent, adversary; (*MIL*) adversary, enemy.

adverse [àdvers(ə)] *a* opposing.

adversité [àdversētà] *nf* adversity.

AE *sigle m* (= *adjoint d'enseignement*) noncertificated teacher.

AELE *sigle f* (= *Association européenne de libre échange*) EFTA (= *European Free Trade Association*).

AEN *sigle f* (= *Agence pour l'énergie nucléaire*) ≈ AEC (= *Atomic Energy Commission*).

aérateur [àārātœr] *nm* ventilator.

aération [àārāsyōn] *nf* airing; (*circulation de l'air*) ventilation; **conduit d'~** ventilation shaft; **bouche d'~** air vent.

aéré, e [àārā] *a* (*pièce*, *local*) airy, well-ventilated; (*tissu*) loose-woven; **centre ~** outdoor (recreation) center.

aérer [àārā] *vt* to air; (*fig*) to lighten; **s'~** *vi* to get some (fresh) air.

aérien, ne [àāryan, -en] *a* (*AVIAT*) air *cpd*, aerial; (*câble*, *métro*) overhead; (*fig*) light; **compagnie ~ne** airline (company); **ligne ~ne** airline.

aérobic [àārobēk] *nm* aerobics *sg*.

aérobie [àārobē] *a* aerobic.

aéro-club [àāroklœb] *nm* flying club.

aérodrome [àārodrom] *nm* airfield, airdrome (*US*), aerodrome (*Brit*).

aérodynamique [àārodēnàmēk] *a* aerodynamic, streamlined ♦ *nf* aerodynamics *sg*.

aérogare [àārogár] *nf* airport (buildings); (*en ville*) air terminal.

aéroglisseur [àāroglēsœr] *nm* hovercraft.

aérogramme [àārográm] *nm* air letter, aerogram(me).

aéromodélisme [àāromodālēsm(ə)] *nm* model aircraft making.

aéronaute [àāronōt] *nm/f* aeronaut.

aéronautique [àāronōtēk] *a* aeronautical ♦ *nf* aeronautics *sg*.

aéronaval, e [àāronávàl] *a* air and sea *cpd* ♦ *nf*: **l'A~e** ≈ the Naval Air Force (*US*), ≈ the Fleet Air Arm (*Brit*).

aéronef [àāronef] *nm* aircraft.

aérophagie [àārofàzhē] *nf* aerophagy.

aéroport [àāropor] *nm* airport; **~ d'embarquement** departure airport.

aéroporté, e [àāroportā] *a* airborne, airlifted.

aéroportuaire [àāroportüer] *a* of an *ou* the airport, airport *cpd*.

aéropostal, e, aux [àāropostàl, -ō] *a* airmail *cpd*.

aérosol [àārosol] *nm* aerosol.

aérospatial, e, aux [àārospásyàl, -ō] *a* aerospace ♦ *nf* the aerospace industry.

aérostat [àārostá] *nm* aerostat.

aérotrain [àārotran] *nm* hovertrain.

AF *sigle fpl* = **allocations familiales** ♦ *sigle f* (*Suisse*) = *Assemblée fédérale*.

AFAT [àfát] *sigle m* (= *Auxiliaire féminin de l'armée de terre*) member of the women's army.

affable [àfàbl(ə)] *a* affable.

affabulateur, trice [àfàbülàtœr, -trēs] *nm/f* storyteller.

affabuler [àfàbülā] *vi* to make up stories.

affacturage [àfàktüràzh] *nm* factoring.

affadir [àfàdēr] *vt* to make insipid *ou* tasteless.

affaiblir [àfàblēr] *vt* to weaken; **s'~** *vi* to weaken, grow weaker; (*vue*) to grow dim.

affaiblissement [àfàblēsmán] *nm* weakening.

affaire [àfer] *nf* (*problème*, *question*) matter; (*criminelle*, *judiciaire*) case; (*scandaleuse etc*) affair; (*entreprise*) business; (*marché*, *transaction*) (business) deal, (piece of) business *q*; (*occasion intéressante*) good deal, bargain; **~s** *nfpl* affairs; (*activité commerciale*) business *sg*; (*effets personnels*) things, belongings; **tirer qn/se tirer d'~** to get sb/o.s. out of trouble; **ceci fera l'~** this will do (nicely); **avoir ~ à** (*comme adversaire*) to be faced with; (*en contact*) to be dealing with; **tu auras ~ à moi!** (*menace*) you'll have me to contend with!; **c'est une ~ de goût/d'argent** it's a question *ou* matter of taste/money; **c'est l'~ d'une minute/heure** it'll only take a minute/an hour; **ce sont mes ~s** (*cela me concerne*) that's my business; **toutes ~s cessantes** forthwith; **les ~s étrangères** (*POL*) foreign affairs.

affairé, e [àfārā] *a* busy.

affairer [àfārā]: **s'~** *vi* to busy o.s., bustle about.

affairisme [àfārēsm(ə)] *nm* (political) racketeering.

affaissement [àfesmán] *nm* subsidence; collapse.

affaisser [àfāsā]: **s'~** *vi* (*terrain*, *immeuble*) to subside, sink; (*personne*) to collapse.

affaler [àfàlā]: **s'~** *vi*: **s'~ dans/sur** to collapse *ou* slump into/onto.

affamé, e [àfàmā] *a* starving, famished.

affamer [àfàmā] *vt* to starve.

affectation [àfektàsyōn] *nf* (*voir affecter*) allotment; appointment; posting; (*voir affecté*) affectedness.

affecté, e [àfektā] *a* affected.

affecter [àfektā] *vt* (*émouvoir*) to affect, move; (*feindre*) to affect, feign; (*telle ou telle forme etc*) to take on, assume; **~ qch à** to allocate *ou* allot sth to; **~ qn à** to appoint sb to; (*diplomate*) to post sb to; **~ qch de** (*de coefficient*) to modify sth by.

affectif, ive [àfektēf, -ēv] *a* emotional, affective.

affection [àfeksyōn] *nf* affection; (*mal*) ailment; **avoir de l'~ pour** to feel affection for; **prendre en ~** to become fond of.

affectionner [àfeksyonā] *vt* to be fond of.

affectueusement [àfektüēzmán] *ad* affectionately.

affectueux, euse [àfektüē, -ēz] *a* affectionate.

afférent, e [àfārán, -ánt] *a*: **~ à** pertaining *ou* relating to.

affermir [àfermēr] *vt* to consolidate, strengthen.

affichage [àfēshàzh] *nm* billposting, billsticking; (*électronique*) display; **"~ interdit"** "post no bills"; **~ à cristaux liquides** liquid crystal display, LCD; **~ numérique** *ou* **digital** digital display.

affiche [áfēsh] *nf* poster; *(officielle)* (public) notice; *(THÉÂTRE)* bill; **être à l'~** *(THÉÂTRE)* to be on; **tenir l'~** to run.

afficher [áfēshā] *vt (affiche)* to put up, post up; *(réunion)* to put up a notice about; *(électroniquement)* to display; *(fig)* to exhibit, display; **s'~** *(péj)* to flaunt o.s.; **"défense d'~"** "post no bills".

affichette [áfēshet] *nf* small poster *ou* notice.

affilé, e [áfēlā] *a* sharp.

affilée [áfēlā]: **d'~** *ad* at a stretch.

affiler [áfēlā] *vt* to sharpen.

affiliation [áfēlyâsyôṅ] *nf* affiliation.

affilié, e [áfēlyā] *a*: **être ~ à** to be affiliated with ♦ *nm/f* affiliated party *ou* member.

affilier [áfēlyā] *vt*: **s'~ à** to become affiliated with.

affiner [áfēnā] *vt* to refine; **s'~** *vi* to become (more) refined.

affinité [áfēnētā] *nf* affinity.

affirmatif, ive [áfērmátēf, -ēv] *a* affirmative ♦ *nf*: **répondre par l'affirmative** to reply in the affirmative; **dans l'affirmative** *(si oui)* if (the answer is) yes, if he does *(ou* you do *etc)*.

affirmation [áfērmásyôṅ] *nf* assertion.

affirmativement [áfērmátēvmáṅ] *ad* affirmatively, in the affirmative.

affirmer [áfērmā] *vt (prétendre)* to maintain, assert; *(autorité etc)* to assert; **s'~** to assert o.s.; to assert itself.

affleurer [áflœrā] *vi* to show on the surface.

affliction [áflēksyôṅ] *nf* affliction.

affligé, e [áflēzhā] *a* distressed, grieved; **~ de** *(maladie, tare)* afflicted with.

affligeant, e [áflēzhâṅ, -âṅt] *a* distressing.

affliger [áflēzhā] *vt (peiner)* to distress, grieve.

affluence [áflüáṅs] *nf* crowds *pl*; **heures d'~** rush hour *sg*; **jours d'~** busiest days.

affluent [áflüâṅ] *nm* tributary.

affluer [áflüā] *vi (secours, biens)* to flood in, pour in; *(sang)* to rush, flow.

afflux [áflü] *nm* flood, influx; rush.

affolant, e [áfolâṅ, -âṅt] *a* terrifying.

affolé, e [áfolā] *a* a panic-stricken, panicky.

affolement [áfolmáṅ] *nm* panic.

affoler [áfolā] *vt* to throw into a panic; **s'~** *vi* to panic.

affranchir [áfráṅshēr] *vt* to put a stamp *ou* stamps on; *(à la machine)* to meter *(US)*, frank *(Brit)*; *(esclave)* to enfranchise, emancipate; *(fig)* to free, liberate; **s'~ de** to free o.s. from; **machine à ~** franking machine, postage meter.

affranchissement [áfráṅshēsmáṅ] *nm* metering *(US)*, franking *(Brit)*; freeing; *(POSTES: prix payé)* postage; **tarifs d'~** postage rates.

affres [áfr(ə)] *nfpl*: **dans les ~ de** in the throes of.

affréter [áfrātā] *vt* to charter.

affreusement [áfrœzmáṅ] *ad* dreadfully, awfully.

affreux, euse [áfrœ̄, -œ̄z] *a* dreadful, awful.

affriolant, e [áfrēyolâṅ, -âṅt] *a* tempting, enticing.

affront [áfrôṅ] *nm* affront.

affrontement [áfrôṅtmáṅ] *nm (MIL, POL)* clash, confrontation.

affronter [áfrôṅtā] *vt* to confront, face; **s'~** to confront each other.

affubler [áfüblā] *vt (péj)*: **~ qn de** to rig out *ou* deck sb out in; *(surnom)* to attach to sb.

affût [áfü] *nm (de canon)* gun carriage; **à l'~ (de)** *(gibier)* lying in wait (for); *(fig)* on the look-out (for).

affûter [áfütā] *vt* to sharpen, grind.

afghan, e [áfgáṅ, -áṅ] *a* Afghan.

Afghanistan [áfgánēstáṅ] *nm*: **l'~** Afghanistan.

afin [áfaṅ]: **~ que** *cj* so that, in order that; **~ de faire** in order to do, so as to do.

AFNOR [áfnor] *sigle f (= Association française de normalisation)* industrial standards authority.

a fortiori [áforsyorē] *ad* all the more, a fortiori.

AFP *sigle f = Agence France-Presse.*

AFPA *sigle f = Association pour la formation professionnelle des adultes.*

africain, e [áfrēkaṅ, -en] *a* African ♦ *nm/f*: **A~, e** African.

afrikaans [áfrēkáṅ] *nm, a inv* Afrikaans.

Afrikaner [áfrēkáncr], **Afrikander** [áfrēkáṅdcr] *nm/f* Afrikaner.

Afrique [áfrēk] *nf*: **l'~** Africa; **l'~ australe/du Nord/du Sud** southern/North/South Africa.

afro [áfrō] *a inv*: **coupe ~** Afro hairstyle ♦ *nm/f*: **A~** Afro.

afro-américain, e [áfrōámārēkaṅ, -en] *a* Afro-American.

afro-asiatique [áfroázyátēk] *a* Afro-Asian.

AG *sigle f = assemblée générale.*

ag. *abr = agence.*

agaçant, e [ágásâṅ, -âṅt] *a* irritating, aggravating.

agacement [ágásmáṅ] *nm* irritation, aggravation.

agacer [ágásā] *vt* to pester, tease; *(involontairement)* to irritate, aggravate; *(aguicher)* to excite, lead on.

agapes [ágáp] *nfpl (humoristique: festin)* feast.

agate [ágát] *nf* agate.

AGE *sigle f = assemblée générale extraordinaire.*

âge [ázh] *nm* age; **quel ~ as-tu?** how old are you?; **une femme d'un certain ~** a middle-aged woman, a woman who is getting on (in years); **bien porter son ~** to wear well; **prendre de l'~** to be getting on (in years), grow older; **limite d'~** age limit; **dispense d'~** special exemption from age limit; **troisième ~** *(période)* retirement; *(personnes âgées)* senior citizens; **l'~ ingrat** the awkward *ou* difficult age; **~ légal** legal age; **~ mental** mental age; **l'~ mûr** maturity, middle age; **~ de raison** age of reason.

âgé, e [ázhā] *a* old, elderly; **~ de 10 ans** 10 years old.

agence [ázhâṅs] *nf* agency, office; *(succursale)* branch; **~ immobilière** real estate agency *(US)*, estate agent's (office) *(Brit)*; **~ matrimoniale** marriage bureau; **~ de placement** employment agency; **~ de publicité** advertising agency; **~ de voyages** travel agency.

agencé, e [ázhâṅsā] *a*: **bien/mal ~** well/badly put together; well/badly laid out *ou* arranged.

agencement [ázhâṅsmáṅ] *nm* putting

together; arrangement, laying out.

agencer |àzhâṅsā| *vt* to put together; (*local*) to arrange, lay out.

agenda |àzhaṅdà| *nm* appointment book, diary (*Brit*).

agenouiller |àzhnōōyā|: **s'~** *vi* to kneel (down).

agent |àzhâṅ| *nm* (*aussi*: ~ **de police**) policeman; (*ADMIN*) official, officer; (*fig: élément, facteur*) agent; ~ **d'assurances** insurance agent (*US*) *ou* broker (*Brit*); ~ **de change** stockbroker; ~ **commercial** sales representative; ~ **immobilier** realtor (*US*), estate agent (*Brit*); ~ **(secret)** (secret) agent.

agglomérat |àglomàrā| *nm* (*GÉO*) agglomerate.

agglomération |àglomārâsyóṅ| *nf* town; (*AUTO*) built-up area; **l'~ parisienne** the urban area of Paris.

aggloméré |àglomārā| *nm* (*bois*) particleboard (*US*), chipboard (*Brit*); (*pierre*) conglomerate.

agglomérer |àglomàrā| *vt* to pile up; (*TECH: bois, pierre*) to compress; **s'~** *vi* to pile up.

agglutiner |àglütēnā| *vt* to stick together; **s'~** *vi* to congregate.

aggravant, e |àgràvàṅ, -àṅt| *a*: **circonstances ~es** aggravating circumstances.

aggravation |àgràvàsyóṅ| *nf* worsening, aggravation; increase.

aggraver |àgràvā| *vt* to worsen, aggravate; (*JUR: peine*) to increase; **s'~** *vi* to worsen; ~ **son cas** to make one's case worse.

agile |àzhēl| *a* agile, nimble.

agilité |àzhēlētā| *nf* agility, nimbleness.

agio |àzhyō| *nm* (bank) charges *pl*.

agir |àzhēr| *vi* (*se comporter*) to behave, act; (*faire quelque chose*) to act, take action; (*avoir de l'effet*) to act; **il s'agit de** it's a matter *ou* question of; it is about; (*il importe que*): **il s'agit de faire** we (*ou* you *etc*) must do; **de quoi s'agit-il?** what is it about?

agissements |àzhēsmàṅ| *nmpl* (*gén péj*) schemes, intrigues.

agitateur, trice |àzhētàtœr, -trēs| *nm/f* agitator.

agitation |àzhētàsyóṅ| *nf* (hustle and) bustle; (*trouble*) agitation, excitement; (*politique*) unrest, agitation.

agité, e |àzhētā| *a* (*remuant*) fidgety, restless; (*troublé*) agitated, perturbed; (*journée*) hectic; (*mer*) rough; (*sommeil*) disturbed, broken.

agiter |àzhētā| *vt* (*bouteille, chiffon*) to shake; (*bras, mains*) to wave; (*préoccuper, exciter*) to trouble, perturb; **s'~** *vi* to bustle about; (*dormeur*) to toss and turn; (*enfant*) to fidget; (*POL*) to grow restless; **"~ avant l'emploi"** "shake before use".

agneau, x |àṅyō| *nm* lamb; (*toison*) lambswool.

agnelet |àṅyle| *nm* little lamb.

agnostique |àgnostēk| *a, nm/f* agnostic.

agonie |àgonē| *nf* mortal agony, death pangs *pl*; (*fig*) death throes *pl*.

agonir |àgonēr| *vt*: ~ **qn d'injures** to hurl abuse at sb.

agoniser |àgonēzā| *vi* to be dying; (*fig*) to be in its death throes.

agrafe |àgràf| *nf* (*de vêtement*) hook, fastener; (*de bureau*) staple; (*MÉD*) clip.

agrafer |àgràfā| *vt* to fasten; to staple.

agrafeuse |àgràfœz| *nf* stapler.

agraire |àgrer| *a* agrarian; (*mesure, surface*) land *cpd*.

agrandir |àgràṅdēr| *vt* (*magasin, domaine*) to extend, enlarge; (*trou*) to enlarge, make bigger; (*PHOTO*) to enlarge, blow up; **s'~** *vi* to be extended; to be enlarged.

agrandissement |àgràṅdēsmàṅ| *nm* extension; enlargement; (*photographie*) enlargement.

agrandisseur |àgràṅdēsœr| *nm* (*PHOTO*) enlarger.

agréable |àgrāàbl(ə)| *a* pleasant, nice.

agréablement |àgrāàbləmàṅ| *ad* pleasantly.

agréé, e |àgrāā| *a*: **concessionnaire ~** registered dealer; **magasin ~** registered dealer('s).

agréer |àgrāā| *vt* (*requéte*) to accept; ~ **à** *vt* to please, suit; **veuillez ~ ...** (*formule épistolaire*) sincerely yours (*US*), yours faithfully (*Brit*).

agrég |àgreg| *nf* (*fam*) = **agrégation**.

agrégat |àgrāgà| *nm* aggregate.

agrégation |àgrāgàsyóṅ| *nf* highest teaching diploma in France (*competitive examination*).

agrégé, e |àgràzhā| *nm/f* holder of the *agrégation*.

agréger |àgrāzhā|: **s'~** *vi* to aggregate.

agrément |àgrāmàṅ| *nm* (*accord*) consent, approval; (*attraits*) charm, attractiveness; (*plaisir*) pleasure; **voyage/jardin d'~** pleasure trip/garden.

agrémenter |àgrāmàṅtā| *vt*: ~ **(de)** to embellish (with), adorn (with).

agrès |àgre| *nmpl* (gymnastics) apparatus *sg*.

agresser |àgràsā| *vt* to attack.

agresseur |àgrescœr| *nm* aggressor.

agressif, ive |àgresēf, -ēv| *a* aggressive.

agression |àgresyóṅ| *nf* attack; (*POL, MIL, PSYCH*) aggression.

agressivement |àgresēvmàṅ| *ad* aggressively.

agressivité |àgresēvētā| *nf* aggressiveness.

agreste |àgrest(ə)| *a* rustic.

agricole |àgrēkol| *a* agricultural, farm *cpd*.

agriculteur, trice |àgrēkültœr, -trēs| *nm/f* farmer.

agriculture |àgrēkültür| *nf* agriculture; farming.

agripper |àgrēpā| *vt* to grab, clutch; (*pour arracher*) to snatch, grab; **s'~ à** to cling (on) to, clutch, grip.

agro-alimentaire |àgroàlēmàṅter| *a* farming *cpd* ♦ *nm*: **l'~** agribusiness.

agronomique |àgronomēk| *a* agronomic(al).

agrumes |àgrüm| *nmpl* citrus fruit(s).

aguerrir |àgàrēr| *vt* to harden; **s'~ (contre)** to become hardened (to).

aguets |àge|: **aux ~** *ad*: **être aux ~** to be on the look-out.

aguichant, e |àgēshàṅ, -àṅt| *a* enticing.

aguicher |àgēshā| *vt* to entice.

aguicheur, euse |àgēshœr, -œz| *a* enticing.

ah |à| *excl* ah!; ~ **bon?** really?, is that so?; ~ **mais ...** yes, but ...; ~ **non!** oh no!

ahuri, e |àürē| *a* (*stupéfait*) flabbergasted;

(*idiot*) dim-witted.

ahurir [äürēr] *vt* to stupefy, stagger.

ahurissant, e [äürēsåǹ, -åǹt] *a* stupefying, staggering.

ai [ä] *vb voir* **avoir**.

aide [ed] *nm/f* assistant ♦ *nf* assistance, help; (*secours financier*) aid; **à l'~ de** with the help *ou* aid of; **aller à l'~ de qn** to go to sb's aid, go to help sb; **venir en ~ à qn** to help sb, come to sb's assistance; **appeler (qn) à l'~** to call for help (from sb); **à l'~!** help!; ~ **de camp** *nm* aide-de-camp; ~ **comptable** *nm* accountant's assistant; ~ **électricien** *nm* electrician's helper (*US*) *ou* mate (*Brit*); ~ **familiale** *nf* mother's helper (*US*) *ou* help (*Brit*), ≈ home help; ~ **judiciaire** *nf* legal aid; ~ **de laboratoire** *nm/f* laboratory assistant; ~ **ménagère** *nf* ≈ home help; ~ **sociale** *nf* (*assistance*) welfare (*US*), social security (*Brit*); ~ **soignant, e** *nm/f* nurse's aide (*US*), auxiliary nurse (*Brit*); ~ **technique** *nf* ≈ Peace Corps (*US*), ≈ VSO (*Brit*).

aide-mémoire [edmāmwàr] *nm inv* (key facts) handbook.

aider [ādā] *vt* to help; ~ **à qch** to help (towards) sth; ~ **qn à faire qch** to help sb to do sth; **s'~ de** (*se servir de*) to use, make use of.

aie [e] *etc vb voir* **avoir**.

aïe [äy] *excl* ouch!

AIEA *sigle f* (= *Agence internationale de l'énergie nucléaire*) IAEA (= *International Atomic Energy Agency*).

aïeul, e [äyœl] *nm/f* grandparent, grandfather/grandmother; (*ancêtre*) forebear.

aïeux [äyœ̄] *nmpl* grandparents; forebears, forefathers.

aigle [egl(ə)] *nm* eagle.

aiglefin [egləfåǹ] *nm* = **églefin**.

aigre [egr(ə)] *a* sour, sharp; (*fig*) sharp, cutting; **tourner à l'~** to turn sour.

aigre-doux, -douce [egrədōō, -dōōs] *a* (*fruit*) bitter-sweet; (*sauce*) sweet and sour.

aigrefin [egrəfåǹ] *nm* swindler.

aigrelet, te [egrəlɛ, -et] *a* (*taste*) sourish; (*voix, son*) sharpish.

aigrette [egret] *nf* (*plume*) feather.

aigreur [egrœr] *nf* sourness; sharpness; ~**s d'estomac** heartburn *sg*.

aigri, e [āgrē] *a* embittered.

aigrir [āgrēr] *vt* (*personne*) to embitter; (*caractère*) to sour; **s'~** *vi* to become embittered; to sour; (*lait etc*) to turn sour.

aigu, ë [āgü] *a* (*objet, arête*) sharp, pointed; (*son, voix*) high-pitched, shrill; (*note*) high(-pitched); (*douleur, intelligence*) acute, sharp.

aigue-marine, *pl* **aigues-marines** [egmárēn] *nf* aquamarine.

aiguillage [āgüēyázh] *nm* (*RAIL*) switch (*US*), points *pl* (*Brit*).

aiguille [āgüēy] *nf* needle; (*de montre*) hand; ~ **à tricoter** knitting needle.

aiguiller [āgüēyā] *vt* (*orienter*) to direct; (*RAIL*) to switch (*US*), shunt (*Brit*).

aiguillette [āgüēyet] *nf* (*CULIN*) aiguillette.

aiguilleur [āgüēyœr] *nm* (*RAIL*) switchman (*US*), pointsman (*Brit*); ~ **du ciel** air traffic controller.

aiguillon [āgüēyóǹ] *nm* (*d'abeille*) sting; (*fig*) spur, stimulus.

aiguillonner [āgüēyonā] *vt* to spur *ou* goad on.

aiguiser [āgēzā] *vt* to sharpen, grind; (*fig*) to stimulate; (: *esprit*) to sharpen; (: *sens*) to excite.

aïkido [áykēdō] *nm* aikido.

ail [áy] *nm* garlic.

aile [el] *nf* wing; (*de voiture*) fender (*US*), wing (*Brit*); **battre de l'~** (*fig*) to be in a sorry state; **voler de ses propres ~s** to stand on one's own two feet; ~ **libre** hang-glider.

ailé, e [ālā] *a* winged.

aileron [elróǹ] *nm* (*de requin*) fin; (*d'avion*) aileron.

ailette [elet] *nf* (*TECH*) fin; (: *de turbine*) blade.

ailier [ālyā] *nm* (*SPORT*) wing (*US*), winger (*Brit*).

aille [áy] *etc vb voir* **aller**.

ailleurs [áyœr] *ad* elsewhere, somewhere else; **partout/nulle part** ~ everywhere/nowhere else; **d'~** *ad* (*du reste*) moreover, besides; **par** ~ *ad* (*d'autre part*) moreover, furthermore.

ailloli [áyolē] *nm* garlic mayonnaise.

aimable [emábl(ə)] *a* kind, nice; **vous êtes bien** ~ that's very nice *ou* kind of you, how kind (of you)!

aimablement [emábləmåǹ] *ad* kindly.

aimant [emåǹ] *nm* magnet.

aimant, e [emåǹ, -åǹt] *a* loving, affectionate.

aimanté, e [emåǹtā] *a* magnetic.

aimanter [emåǹtā] *vt* to magnetize.

aimer [āmā] *vt* to love; (*d'amitié, affection, par goût*) to like; (*souhait*): **j'aimerais ...** I would like ...; **s'~** to love each other; to like each other; **je n'aime pas beaucoup Paul** I don't like Paul much, I don't care much for Paul; ~ **faire qch** to like doing sth, like to do sth; **aimeriez-vous que je vous accompagne?** would you like me to come with you?; **j'aimerais (bien) m'en aller** I should (really) like to go; **bien** ~ **qn/qch** to like sb/sth; **j'aime mieux Paul (que Pierre)** I prefer Paul (to Pierre); **j'aime mieux** *ou* **autant vous dire que** I may as well tell you that; **j'aimerais autant** *ou* **mieux y aller maintenant** I'd sooner *ou* rather go now; **j'aime assez aller au cinéma** I quite like going to the cinema.

aine [en] *nf* groin.

aîné, e [ānā] *a* elder, older; (*le plus âgé*) eldest, oldest ♦ *nm/f* oldest child *ou* one, oldest boy *ou* son/girl *ou* daughter; ~**s** *nmpl* (*fig: anciens*) elders; **il est mon** ~ **(de 2 ans)** he's (2 years) older than me, he's 2 years my senior.

aînesse [enes] *nf*: **droit d'~** birthright.

ainsi [åǹsē] *ad* (*de cette façon*) like this, in this way, thus; (*ce faisant*) thus ♦ *cj* thus, so; ~ **que** (*comme*) (just) as; (*et aussi*) as well as; **pour** ~ **dire** so to speak, as it were; ~ **donc** and so; ~ **soit-il** (*REL*) so be it; **et** ~ **de suite** and so on (and so forth).

aïoli [áyolē] *nm* = **ailloli**.

air [er] *nm* air; (*mélodie*) tune; (*expression*) look, air; (*atmosphère, ambiance*): **dans l'~**

in the air *(fig)*; **prendre de grands ~s (avec qn)** to give o.s. airs (with sb); **en l'~** (up) into the air; **tirer en l'~** to fire shots in the air; **paroles/menaces en l'~** idle words/ threats; **prendre l'~** to get some (fresh) air; *(avion)* to take off; **avoir l'~ triste** to look *ou* seem sad; **avoir l'~ de qch** to look like sth; **avoir l'~ de faire** to look as though one is doing, appear to be doing; **courant d'~** draft *(US)*, draught *(Brit)*; **le grand ~** the open air; **mal de l'~** air-sickness; **tête en l'~** scatterbrain; **~ comprimé** compressed air; **~ conditionné** air-conditioning.

aire |er| *nf (zone, fig, MATH)* area; *(nid)* eyrie, aerie *(US)*; **~ d'atterrissage** landing strip; landing patch; **~ de jeu** play area; **~ de lancement** launching site; **~ de stationnement** parking area.

airelle |erel| *nf* bilberry.

aisance |ezãs| *nf* ease; *(COUTURE)* easing, freedom of movement; *(richesse)* affluence; **être dans l'~** to be well-off *ou* affluent.

aise |ez| *nf* comfort ♦ *a*: **être bien ~ de/que** to be delighted to/that; **~s** *nfpl*: **aimer ses ~s** to like one's (creature) comforts; **prendre ses ~s** to make o.s. comfortable; **frémir d'~** to shudder with pleasure; **être à l'~** *ou* à son ~ to be comfortable; *(pas embarrassé)* to be at ease; *(financièrement)* to be comfortably off; **se mettre à l'~** to make o.s. comfortable; **être mal à l'~** *ou* à son ~ to be uncomfortable; *(gêné)* to be ill at ease; **mettre qn à l'~** to put sb at his *(ou* her) ease; **mettre qn mal à l'~** to make sb feel ill at ease; **à votre ~** please yourself, just as you like; **en faire à son ~** to do as one likes; **en prendre à son ~ avec qch** to be free and easy with sth, do as one likes with sth.

aisé, e |ãzã| *a* easy; *(assez riche)* well-to-do, well-off.

aisément |ãzãmã| *ad* easily.

aisselle |esel| *nf* armpit.

ait |e| *vb voir* **avoir**.

ajonc |ãzhõ| *nm* gorse *q.*

ajouré, e |ãzhōōrã| *a* openwork *cpd.*

ajournement |ãzhōōrnãmã| *nm* adjournment; deferment, postponement.

ajourner |ãzhōōrnã| *vt (réunion)* to adjourn; *(décision)* to defer, postpone; *(candidat)* to fail; *(conscrit)* to defer.

ajout |ãzhōō| *nm* addition.

ajouter |ãzhōōtã| *vt* to add; *(INFORM)* to append; **~ à** *vt (accroître)* to add to; **s'~ à** to add to; **~ que** to add that; **~ foi à** to lend *ou* give credence to.

ajustage |ãzhüstãzh| *nm* fitting.

ajusté, e |ãzhüstã| *a*: **bien ~** *(robe etc)* close-fitting.

ajustement |ãzhüstãmã| *nm* adjustment.

ajuster |ãzhüstã| *vt (régler)* to adjust; *(vêtement)* to alter; *(arranger)*: **~ sa cravate** to adjust one's tie; *(coup de fusil)* to aim; *(cible)* to aim at; *(adapter)*: **~ qch à** to fit sth to.

ajusteur |ãzhüstœr| *nm* metal worker.

al *abr* = **année-lumière**.

alaise |ãlez| *nf* = **alèse**.

alambic |ãlãbēk| *nm* still.

alambiqué, e |ãlãbēkã| *a* convoluted, over-

complicated.

alangui, e |ãlãgē| *a* languid.

alanguir |ãlãgēr|: **s'~** *vi* to grow languid.

alarme |ãlãrm(ə)| *nf* alarm; **donner l'~** to give *ou* raise the alarm; **jeter l'~** to cause alarm.

alarmer |ãlãrmã| *vt* to alarm; **s'~** *vi* to become alarmed.

alarmiste |ãlãrmēst(ə)| *a* alarmist.

Alaska |ãlãskã| *nm*: **l'~** Alaska.

albanais, e |ãlbãne, -ez| *a* Albanian ♦ *nm (LING)* Albanian ♦ *nm/f*: **A~, e** Albanian.

Albanie |ãlbãnē| *nf*: **l'~** Albania.

albâtre |ãlbãtr(ə)| *nm* alabaster.

albatros |ãlbãtrõs| *nm* albatross.

albigeois, e |ãlbēzhwã, -wãz| *a* of *ou* from Albi.

albinos |ãlbēnõs| *nm/f* albino.

album |ãlbom| *nm* album; **~ à colorier** coloring book; **~ de timbres** stamp album.

albumen |ãlbümen| *nm* albumen.

albumine |ãlbümēn| *nf* albumin; **avoir** *ou* **faire de l'~** to suffer from albuminuria.

alcalin, e |ãlkãlã, -ēn| *a* alkaline.

alchimiste |ãlshēmēst(ə)| *nm* alchemist.

alcool |ãlkol| *nm*: **l'~** alcohol; **un ~** a spirit, a brandy; **~ à brûler** wood alcohol *(US)*, methylated spirit(s) *(Brit)*; **~ à 90°** rubbing alcohol *(US)*, surgical spirit *(Brit)*; **~ camphré** camphorated alcohol; **~ de prune** *etc* plum *etc* brandy.

alcoolémie |ãlkolãmē| *nf* blood alcohol level.

alcoolique |ãlkolēk| *a*, *nm/f* alcoholic.

alcoolisé, e |ãlkolēzã| *a* alcoholic.

alcoolisme |ãlkolēsm(ə)| *nm* alcoholism.

alco(o)test |ãlkotest| *nm* ® *(objet)* Breathalyzer ®; *(test)* breath-test; **faire subir l'~ à qn** to Breathalyze ® sb.

alcôve |ãlkõv| *nf* alcove, recess.

aléas |ãlãã| *nmpl* hazards.

aléatoire |ãlããtwãr| *a* uncertain; *(INFORM, STATISTIQUE)* random.

alentour |ãlãtōōr| *ad* around (about); **~s** *nmpl* surroundings; **aux ~s de** in the vicinity *ou* neighborhood of, around about; *(temps)* around about.

Aléoutiennes |ãlãōōsyen| *nfpl*: **les (îles) ~** the Aleutian Islands.

alerte |ãlert(ə)| *a* agile, nimble; *(style)* brisk, lively ♦ *nf* alert; warning; **donner l'~** to give the alert; **à la première ~** at the first sign of trouble *ou* danger.

alerter |ãlertã| *vt* to alert.

alèse |ãlez| *nf (drap)* undersheet, drawsheet.

aléser |ãlãzã| *vt* to ream.

alevin |ãlvã| *nm* alevin, young fish.

alevinage |ãlvēnãzh| *nm* fish farming.

Alexandrie |ãleksãdrē| *n* Alexandria.

alexandrin |ãleksãdrã| *nm* alexandrine.

alezan, e |ãlzã, -ãn| *a* chestnut.

algarade |ãlgãrãd| *nf* row, dispute.

algèbre |ãlzhebr(ə)| *nf* algebra.

Alger |ãlzhã| *n* Algiers.

Algérie |ãlzhãrē| *nf*: **l'~** Algeria.

algérien, ne |ãlzhãryã, -en| *a* Algerian ♦ *nm/f*: **A~, ne** Algerian.

algérois, e |ãlzhãrwã, -wãz| *a* of *ou* from Algiers ♦ *nm*: **l'A~** *(région)* the Algiers region.

algorithme |ãlgorētm(ə)| *nm* algorithm.

algue [álg(ə)] *nf* (*gén*) seaweed *q*; (*BOT*) alga (*pl* -ae).

alias [áljás] *ad* alias.

alibi [álébē] *nm* alibi.

aliénation [áljānâsyóň] *nf* alienation.

aliéné, e [áljānā] *nm/f* insane person, lunatic (*péj*).

aliéner [áljānā] *vt* to alienate; (*bien, liberté*) to give up; **s'~** *vt* to alienate.

alignement [álēnymâň] *nm* alignment, lining up; **à l'~** in line.

aligner [álēnyā] *vt* to align, line up; (*idées, chiffres*) to string together; (*adapter*): **~ qch sur** to bring sth into alignment with; **s'~** (*soldats etc*) to line up; **s'~ sur** (*POL*) to align o.s. with.

aliment [álēmâň] *nm* food; **~ complet** natural (*US*) *ou* whole (*Brit*) food.

alimentaire [álēmâńter] *a* food *cpd*; (*péj: besogne*) done merely to earn a living; **produits ~s** foodstuffs, foods.

alimentation [álēmâńtâsyóň] *nf* feeding; supplying, supply; (*commerce*) food trade; (*produits*) groceries *pl*; (*régime*) diet; (*IN-FORM*) feed; **~ (générale)** (general) grocer's; **~ de base** staple diet; **~ en feuilles/en continu/en papier** form/continuous/sheet feed.

alimenter [álēmâńtā] *vt* to feed; (*TECH*): **~ (en)** to supply (with), feed (with); (*fig*) to sustain, keep going.

alinéa [álēnáá] *nm* paragraph; **"nouvel ~"** "new paragraph".

aliter [álētā]: **s'~** *vi* to take to one's bed; **infirme alité** bedridden person *ou* invalid.

alizé [álēzā] *a, nm*: **(vent)** ~ trade wind.

allaitement [álětmâň] *nm* feeding; **~ maternel/au biberon** breast-/bottle-feeding; **~ mixte** mixed feeding.

allaiter [álātā] *vt* (*suj: femme*) to (breast-) feed, nurse; (*suj: animal*) to suckle; **~ au biberon** to bottle-feed.

allant [álâň] *nm* drive, go.

alléchant, e [álāshâň, -âňt] *a* tempting, enticing.

allécher [álāshā] *vt*: **~ qn** to make sb's mouth water; to tempt sb, entice sb.

allée [álā] *nf* (*de jardin*) path; (*en ville*) avenue, drive; **~s et venues** comings and goings.

allégation [álāgâsyóň] *nf* allegation.

alléger [álāzhā] *vt* (*voiture*) to make lighter; (*chargement*) to lighten; (*souffrance*) to alleviate, soothe.

allégorie [álāgorē] *nf* allegory.

allégorique [álāgorēk] *a* allegorical.

allègre [álegr(ə)] *a* lively, jaunty (*Brit*); (*personne*) cheerful.

allégresse [álāgres] *nf* elation, gaiety.

alléguer [álāgā] *vt* to offer (as proof *ou* an excuse).

Allemagne [álmány] *nf*: **l'~** Germany; **l'~ de l'Est/Ouest** East/West Germany; **l'~ fédérale (RFA)** the Federal Republic of Germany (FRG).

allemand, e [álmâň, -âňd] *a* German ♦ *nm* (*LING*) German ♦ *nm/f*: **A~, e** German; **A~ de l'Est/l'Ouest** East/West German.

aller [álā] *nm* (*trajet*) outward journey;

(*billet*): **~ (simple)** one-way ticket *ou* single (*Brit*); **~ (et) retour (AR)** (*trajet*) round trip (*US*), return trip *ou* journey (*Brit*); (*billet*) round-trip (*US*) *ou* return (*Brit*) ticket ♦ *vi* (*gén*) to go; **~ à** (*convenir*) to suit; (*suj: forme, pointure etc*) to fit; **cela me va** (*couleur*) that suits me; (*vêtement*) that suits me; that fits me; (*projet, disposition*) that suits me, that's fine *ou* OK by me; **~ à la chasse/pêche** to go hunting/fishing; **~ avec** (*couleurs, style etc*) to go (well) with; **je vais le faire/me fâcher** I'm going to do it/to get angry; **~ voir/chercher qn** to go and see/look for sb; **comment allez-vous?** how are you?; **comment ça va?** how are you?; (*affaires etc*) how are things?; **ça va? — oui (ça va)!** how are things? — fine!; **ça va (comme ça)** that's fine (as it is); **il va bien/mal** he's well/not well, he's fine/ill; **ça va bien/mal** (*affaires etc*) it's going well/not going well; **tout va bien** everything's fine; **ça ne va pas!** (*mauvaise humeur etc*) that won't do!; hey, come on!; **ça ne va pas sans difficultés** it's not without difficulties; **~ mieux** to be better; **il y va de leur vie** their lives are at stake; **se laisser** ~ to let o.s. go; **s'en** ~ *vi* (*partir*) to be off, go, leave; (*disparaître*) to go away; **~ jusqu'à** to go as far as; **ça va de soi, ça va sans dire** that goes without saying; **tu y vas un peu fort** you're going a bit (too) far; **allez!** go on!; come on!; **allons-y!** let's go!; **allez, au revoir** right *ou* OK then, bye-bye!

allergie [álerzhē] *nf* allergy.

allergique [álerzhēk] *a* allergic; **~ à** allergic to.

allez [álā] *vb voir* **aller.**

alliage [ályázh] *nm* alloy.

alliance [ályâńs] *nf* (*MIL, POL*) alliance; (*mariage*) marriage; (*bague*) wedding ring; **neveu par** ~ nephew by marriage.

allié, e [ályā] *nm/f* ally; **parents et ~s** relatives and relatives by marriage.

allier [ályā] *vt* (*métaux*) to alloy; (*POL, gén*) to ally; (*fig*) to combine; **s'~** to become allies; (*éléments, caractéristiques*) to combine; **s'~ à** to become allied to *ou* with.

alligator [álēgátor] *nm* alligator.

allitération [álētārâsyóň] *nf* alliteration.

allô [álō] *excl* hello, hallo.

allocataire [álokáter] *nm/f* beneficiary.

allocation [álokâsyóň] *nf* allowance; **~ (de) chômage** unemployment benefit; **~ (de) logement** rent allowance; **~s familiales** ≈ family allowance *ou* subsidy; **~s de maternité** maternity allowance.

allocution [áloküsyóň] *nf* short speech.

allongé, e [álóňzhā] *a* (*étendu*): **être** ~ to be stretched out *ou* lying down; (*long*) long; (*étiré*) elongated; (*oblong*) oblong; **rester** ~ to be lying down; **mine ~e** long face.

allonger [álóňzhā] *vt* to lengthen, make longer; (*étendre: bras, jambe*) to stretch (out); (*sauce*) to spin out, make go further; **s'~** *vi* to get longer; (*se coucher*) to lie down, stretch out; **~ le pas** to hasten one's step(s).

allouer [álwā] *vt*: **~ qch à** to allocate sth to, allot sth to.

allumage [álümázh] *nm* (*AUTO*) ignition.

allume-cigare [álümsēgár] *nm inv* cigar lighter.

allume-gaz [àlümgáz] *nm inv* gas lighter.

allumer [àlümā] *vt* (*lampe, phare, radio*) to turn *ou* switch on; (*pièce*) to turn *ou* switch the light(s) on in; (*feu, bougie, cigare, pipe, gaz*) to light; (*chauffage*) to turn on; **s'~** *vi* (*lumière, lampe*) to come *ou* go on; **~ (la lumière** *ou* **l'électricité)** to turn on the light.

allumette [àlümet] *nf* match; (*morceau de bois*) matchstick; (*CULIN*): **~ au fromage** cheese straw; **~ de sûreté** safety match.

allumeuse [àlümœ̄z] *nf* (*péj*) tease (*woman*).

allure [àlür] *nf* (*vitesse*) speed; (: *à pied*) pace; (*démarche*) walk; (*maintien*) bearing; (*aspect, air*) look; **avoir de l'~** to have style *ou* a certain elegance; **à toute ~** at top *ou* full speed.

allusion [àlüzyôñ] *nf* allusion; (*sous-entendu*) hint; **faire ~ à** to allude *ou* refer to; to hint at.

alluvions [àlüvyôñ] *nfpl* alluvial deposits, alluvium *sg*.

almanach [àlmáná] *nm* almanac.

aloès [àloes] *nm* (*BOT*) aloe.

aloi [àlwà] *nm*: **de bon/mauvais ~** of genuine/ doubtful worth *ou* quality.

alors [àlor] *ad* then, at that time ♦ *cj* then, so; **~, Paul?** well, Paul?; **~? quoi de neuf?** well *ou* so? what's new?; **et ~?** and then (what)?; (*indifférence*) so?; **jusqu'~** up till *ou* until then; **ça ~!** well really!; **~ que** *cj* (*au moment où*) when, as; (*pendant que*) while, when; (*opposition*) whereas, while.

alouette [àlwet] *nf* (sky)lark.

alourdir [àlōōrdēr] *vt* to weigh down, make heavy; **s'~** *vi* to grow heavy *ou* heavier.

aloyau [àlwàyō] *nm* sirloin.

alpaga [àlpágá] *nm* (*tissu*) alpaca.

alpage [àlpàzh] *nm* high mountain pasture.

Alpes [àlp(ə)] *nfpl*: **les ~** the Alps.

alpestre [àlpestr(ə)] *a* alpine.

alphabet [àlfábe] *nm* alphabet; (*livre*) ABC (book), primer.

alphabétique [àlfábātēk] *a* alphabetic(al); **par ordre ~** in alphabetical order.

alphabétisation [àlfábātēzásyôñ] *nf* literacy teaching.

alphabétiser [àlfábātēzā] *vt* to teach to read and write; (*pays*) to eliminate illiteracy in.

alphanumérique [àlfánümārēk] *a* alphanumeric.

alpin, e [àlpañ, -ēn] *a* (*plante etc*) alpine; (*club*) climbing.

alpinisme [àlpēnēsm(ə)] *nm* mountaineering, climbing.

alpiniste [àlpēnēst(ə)] *nm/f* mountaineer, climber.

Alsace [àlzás] *nf*: **l'~** Alsace.

alsacien, ne [àlzásyañ, -en] *a* Alsatian.

altercation [àlterkásyôñ] *nf* altercation.

alter ego [àlterāgō] *nm* alter ego.

altérer [àltārā] *vt* (*faits, vérité*) to falsify, distort; (*qualité*) to debase, impair; (*données*) to corrupt; (*donner soif à*) to make thirsty; **s'~** *vi* to deteriorate; to spoil.

alternance [àlternáñs] *nf* alternation; **en ~** alternately; **formation en ~** work-study program (*US*), sandwich course (*Brit*).

alternateur [àlternátœr] *nm* alternator.

alternatif, ive [àlternátēf, -ēv] *a* alternating ♦ *nf* alternative.

alternativement [àlternàtēvmâñ] *ad* alternately.

alterner [àlternā] *vt* to alternate ♦ *vi*: **~ (avec)** to alternate (with); (**faire**) **~ qch avec qch** to alternate sth with sth.

Altesse [àltes] *nf* Highness.

altier, ière [àltyā, -yer] *a* haughty.

altimètre [àltēmetr(ə)] *nm* altimeter.

altiport [àltēpor] *nm* mountain airfield.

altiste [àltēst(ə)] *nm/f* viola player, violist.

altitude [àltētüd] *nf* altitude, height; **à 1000 m d'~** at a height *ou* an altitude of 1000 m; **en ~** at high altitudes; **perdre/prendre de l'~** to lose/gain height; **voler à haute/basse ~** to fly at a high/low altitude.

alto [àltō] *nm* (*instrument*) viola ♦ *nf* (contr)alto.

altruisme [àltrüēsm(ə)] *nm* altruism.

altruiste [àltrüēst(ə)] *a* altruistic.

aluminium [àlümēnyom] *nm* aluminum (*US*), aluminium (*Brit*).

alun [àlœñ] *nm* alum.

alunir [àlünēr] *vi* to land on the moon.

alvéole [àlváol] *nf* (*de ruche*) alveolus; **alvéolé, e** [àlváolā] *a* honeycombed.

AM *sigle f* = **assurance maladie**.

amabilité [àmábēlētā] *nf* kindness; **il a eu l'~ de** he was kind *ou* good enough to.

amadou [àmádōō] *nm* touchwood, amadou.

amadouer [àmádwā] *vt* to coax, cajole; (*adoucir*) to mollify, soothe.

amaigrir [àmāgrēr] *vt* to make thin *ou* thinner.

amaigrissant, e [àmāgrēsáñ, -áñt] *a*: **régime ~** weight-reduction (*US*) *ou* slimming (*Brit*) diet.

amalgame [àmálgám] *nm* amalgam; (*fig: de gens, d'idées*) hotch-potch, mixture.

amalgamer [àmálgámā] *vt* to amalgamate.

amande [àmáñd] *nf* (*de l'amandier*) almond; (*de noyau de fruit*) kernel; **en ~** (*yeux*) almond *cpd*, almond-shaped.

amandier [àmáñdyā] *nm* almond (tree).

amant [àmáñ] *nm* lover.

amarre [àmár] *nf* (*NAVIG*) (mooring) rope *ou* line; **~s** *nfpl* moorings.

amarrer [àmárā] *vt* (*NAVIG*) to moor; (*gén*) to make fast.

amaryllis [àmárēlēs] *nf* amaryllis.

amas [àmá] *nm* heap, pile.

amasser [àmásā] *vt* to amass; **s'~** *vi* to pile up, accumulate; (*foule*) to gather.

amateur [àmátœr] *nm* amateur; **en ~** (*péj*) amateurishly; **musicien/sportif ~** amateur musician/sportsman; **~ de musique/sport** *etc* music/sports *etc* lover.

amateurisme [àmátœrēsm(ə)] *nm* amateurism; (*péj*) amateurishness.

Amazone [àmázon] *nf*: **l'~** the Amazon; **en a~** sidesaddle.

Amazonie [àmázonē] *nf*: **l'~** Amazonia.

ambages [àñbázh]: **sans ~** *ad* without beating about the bush, plainly.

ambassade [àñbásád] *nf* embassy; (*mission*): **en ~** on a mission.

ambassadeur, drice [àñbásádœr, -drēs] *nm/f* ambassador/ambassadress.

ambiance [àñbyáñs] *nf* atmosphere; **il y a de**

l'~ everyone's having a good time.
ambiant, e [ãbyã, -ãt] a (air, milieu) surrounding; (température) ambient.
ambidextre [ãbēdɛkstr(ə)] a ambidextrous.
ambigu, ë [ãbēgü] a ambiguous.
ambiguïté [ãbēgüētã] nf ambiguousness q, ambiguity.
ambitieux, euse [ãbēsyœ, -œz] a ambitious.
ambition [ãbēsyõ] nf ambition.
ambitionner [ãbēsyonã] vt to have as one's aim ou ambition.
ambivalent, e [ãbēvãlã, -ãt] a ambivalent.
amble [ãbl(ə)] nm: **aller l'~** to amble.
ambre [ãbr(ə)] nm: **~ (jaune)** amber; **~ gris** ambergris.
ambré, e [ãbrã] a (couleur) amber; (parfum) ambergris-scented.
ambulance [ãbülãs] nf ambulance.
ambulancier, ière [ãbülãsyã, -ycr] paramedic (US), ambulanceman/woman (Brit).
ambulant, e [ãbülã, -ãt] a traveling (US), travelling (Brit), itinerant.
âme [ãm] nf soul; **rendre l'~** to give up the ghost; **bonne ~** (aussi ironique) kind soul; **un joueur/tricheur dans l'~** a gambler/cheat through and through; **~ sœur** kindred spirit.
amélioration [ãmãlyorãsyõ] nf improvement.
améliorer [ãmãlyorã] vt to improve; **s'~** vi to improve, get better.
aménagement [ãmãnãzhmã] nm fitting out; laying out; development; **~s** nmpl developments; **l'~ du territoire** ≈ town and country planning; **~s fiscaux** tax adjustments.
aménager [ãmãnãzhã] vt (agencer: espace, local) to fit out; (: terrain) to lay out; (: quartier, territoire) to develop; (installer) to fix up, put in; **ferme aménagée** converted farmhouse.
amende [ãmãd] nf fine; **mettre à l'~** to penalize; **faire ~ honorable** to make amends.
amendement [ãmãdmã] nm (JUR) amendment.
amender [ãmãdã] vt (loi) to amend; (terre) to enrich; **s'~** vi to mend one's ways.
amène [ãmɛn] a affable; **peu ~** unkind.
amener [ãmnã] vt to bring; (causer) to bring about; (baisser: drapeau, voiles) to strike; **s'~** vi (fam) to show up, turn up; **~ qn à qch/à faire** to lead sb to sth/to do.
amenuiser [ãmɔnüēzã]: **s'~** vi to dwindle; (chances) to grow slimmer, lessen.
amer, amère [ãmɛr] a bitter.
amèrement [ãmɛrmã] ad bitterly.
américain, e [ãmãrēkã, -ɛn] a American ♦ nm (LING) American (English) ♦ nm/f: **A~, e** American; **en vedette ~e** as a special guest (star).
américaniser [ãmãrēkãnēzã] vt to Americanize.
américanisme [ãmãrēkãnēsm(ə)] nm Americanism.
amérindien, ne [ãmãrãdyã, -ɛn] a Amerindian, American Indian.
Amérique [ãmãrēk] nf America; **l'~ centrale** Central America; **l'~ latine** Latin America; **l'~ du Nord** North America; **l'~ du Sud** South America.
amerloque [ãmɛrlok] n (péj) Yank, Yankee.
amerrir [ãmãrēr] vi to land (on the sea);

(capsule spatiale) to splash down.
amerrissage [ãmãrēsãzh] nm landing (on the sea); splash-down.
amertume [ãmɛrtüm] nf bitterness.
améthyste [ãmãtɛst(ə)] nf amethyst.
ameublement [ãmœblǝmã] nm furnishing; (meubles) furniture; **articles d'~** furnishings; **tissus d'~** home furnishings, upholstery fabrics.
ameuter [ãmœtã] vt (badauds) to draw a crowd of; (peuple) to rouse, stir up.
ami, e [ãmē] nm/f friend; (amant/maîtresse) boyfriend/girlfriend ♦ a: **pays/groupe ~** friendly country/group; **être (très) ~ avec qn** to be (very) friendly with sb; **être ~ de l'ordre** to be a lover of order; **un ~ des arts** a patron of the arts; **un ~ des chiens** a dog lover; **petit ~/petite ~e** (fam) boyfriend/girlfriend.
amiable [ãmyãbl(ə)]: **à l'~** ad (JUR) out of court; (gén) amicably.
amiante [ãmyãt] nm asbestos.
amibe [ãmēb] nf amoeba (pl -ae).
amical, e, aux [ãmēkãl, -ō] a friendly ♦ nf (club) association.
amicalement [ãmēkãlmã] ad in a friendly way; (formule épistolaire) regards.
amidon [ãmēdõ] nm starch.
amidonner [ãmēdonã] vt to starch.
amincir [ãmãsēr] vt (objet) to thin (down); **s'~** vi to get thinner ou slimmer; **~ qn** to make sb thinner ou slimmer.
aminé, e [ãmēnã] a: **acide ~** amino acid.
amiral, aux [ãmērãl, -ō] nm admiral.
amirauté [ãmērōtã] nf admiralty.
amitié [ãmētyã] nf friendship; **prendre en ~** to take a liking to; **faire** ou **présenter ses ~s à qn** to send sb one's best wishes; **~s** (formule épistolaire) (with) best wishes.
ammoniac [ãmonyãk] nm: **(gaz) ~** ammonia.
ammoniaque [ãmonyãk] nf ammonia (water).
amnésie [ãmnãzē] nf amnesia.
amniocentèse [ãmnyōsãtez] nf amniocentesis.
amnistie [ãmnēstē] nf amnesty.
amnistier [ãmnēstyã] vt to amnesty.
amoindrir [ãmwãdrēr] vt to reduce.
amollir [ãmolēr] vt to soften.
amonceler [ãmõslã] vt, **s'~** vi to pile ou heap up; (fig) to accumulate.
amoncellement [ãmõsɛlmã] nm piling ou heaping up; accumulation; (tas) pile, heap; accumulation.
amont [ãmõ]: **en ~** ad upstream; (sur une pente) uphill; **en ~ de** prép upstream from; uphill from, above.
amoral, e, aux [ãmorãl, -ō] a amoral.
amorce [ãmors(ə)] nf (sur un hameçon) bait; (explosif) cap; (tube) primer; (: contenu) priming; (fig: début) beginning(s), start.
amorcer [ãmorsã] vt to bait; to prime; (commencer) to begin, start.
amorphe [ãmorf(ə)] a passive, lifeless.
amortir [ãmortēr] vt (atténuer: choc) to absorb, cushion; (bruit, douleur) to deaden; (COMM: dette) to pay off, amortize; (: mise de fonds, matériel) to write off; **~ un abonnement** to make a season ticket pay (for itself).

amortissable [ámortēsábl(ə)]. *a* (*COMM*) that can be paid off.

amortissement [ámortēsmáṅ] *nm* (*de matériel*) writing off; (*d'une dette*) paying off.

amortisseur [ámortēsœr] *nm* shock absorber.

amour [ámōōr] *nm* love; (*liaison*) love affair, love; (*statuette etc*) cupid; **un ~ de** a lovely little; **faire l'~** to make love.

amouracher [ámōōráshā]: **s'~ de** *vt* (*péj*) to become infatuated with.

amourette [ámōōret] *nf* passing fancy.

amoureusement [ámōōrœzmáṅ] *ad* lovingly.

amoureux, euse [ámōōrœ̄, -œ̄z] *a* (*regard, tempérament*) amorous; (*vie, problèmes*) love *cpd*; (*personne*): **~ (de qn)** in love (with sb) ♦ *nm/f* lover ♦ *nmpl* courting couple(s); **tomber ~ de qn** to fall in love with sb; **être ~ de qch** to be passionately fond of sth; **un ~ de la nature** a nature lover.

amour-propre,   *pl*   **amours-propres** [ámōōrpropr(ə)] *nm* self-esteem.

amovible [ámovēbl(ə)] *a* removable, detachable.

ampère [áṅper] *nm* amp(ere).

ampèremètre [áṅpermetr(ə)] *nm* ammeter.

amphétamine [áṅfātámēn] *nf* amphetamine.

amphi [áṅfē] *nm* (*SCOL fam*: = *amphithéâtre*) lecture hall *ou* theater.

amphibie [áṅfēbē] *a* amphibious.

amphibien [áṅfēbyaṅ] *nm* (*ZOOL*) amphibian.

amphithéâtre [áṅfētāātr(ə)] *nm* amphitheater (*US*), amphitheatre (*Brit*); (*d'université*) lecture hall, auditorium.

amphore [áṅfor] *nf* amphora.

ample [áṅpl(ə)] *a* (*vêtement*) roomy, ample; (*gestes, mouvement*) broad; (*ressources*) ample; **jusqu'à plus ~ informé** (*ADMIN*) until further details are available.

amplement [áṅpləmáṅ] *ad* amply; **~ suffisant** ample, more than enough.

ampleur [áṅplœr] *nf* scale, size; extent, magnitude.

ampli [áṅplē] *nm* (*fam*: = *amplificateur*) amplifier, amp.

amplificateur [áṅplēfēkátœr] *nm* amplifier.

amplification [áṅplēfēkásyóṅ] *nf* amplification; expansion, increase.

amplifier [áṅplēfyā] *vt* (*son, oscillation*) to amplify; (*fig*) to expand, increase.

amplitude [áṅplētüd] *nf* amplitude; (*des températures*) range.

ampoule [áṅpōōl] *nf* (*électrique*) bulb; (*de médicament*) phial; (*aux mains, pieds*) blister.

ampoulé, e [áṅpōōlā] *a* (*péj*) pompous, bombastic.

amputation [áṅpütásyóṅ] *nf* amputation.

amputer [áṅpütā] *vt* (*MÉD*) to amputate; (*fig*) to cut *ou* reduce drastically; **~ qn d'un bras/pied** to amputate sb's arm/foot.

Amsterdam [ámsterdàm] *n* Amsterdam.

amulette [ámület] *nf* amulet.

amusant, e [ámüzáṅ, -áṅt] *a* (*divertissant, spirituel*) entertaining, amusing; (*comique*) funny, amusing.

amusé, e [ámüzā] *a* amused.

amuse-gueule [ámüzgœl] *nm inv* appetizer, snack.

amusement [ámüzmáṅ] *nm* (*voir amusé*) amusement; (*voir amuser*) entertaining, amusing; (*jeu etc*) pastime, diversion.

amuser [ámüzā] *vt* (*divertir*) to entertain, amuse; (*égayer, faire rire*) to amuse; (*détourner l'attention de*) to distract; **s'~** *vi* (*jouer*) to amuse o.s., play; (*se divertir*) to enjoy o.s., have fun; (*fig*) to mess around; **s'~ de qch** (*trouver comique*) to find sth amusing; **s'~ avec** *ou* **de qn** (*duper*) to make a fool of sb.

amusette [ámüzet] *nf* idle pleasure, trivial pastime.

amuseur [ámüzœr] *nm* entertainer; (*péj*) clown.

amygdale [ámēdál] *nf* tonsil; **opérer qn des ~s** to take sb's tonsils out.

amygdalite [ámēdálēt] *nf* tonsillitis.

AN *sigle f* = **Assemblée nationale**.

an [áṅ] *nm* year; **être âgé de** *ou* **avoir 3 ~s** to be 3 (years old); **en l'~ 1980** in the year 1980; **le jour de l'~, le premier de l'~, le nouvel ~** New Year's Day.

anabolisant [ánábolēzáṅ] *nm* anabolic steroid.

anachronique [ánákronĕk] *a* anachronistic.

anachronisme [ánákronēsm(ə)] *nm* anachronism.

anaconda [ánákóṅdà] *nm* (*ZOOL*) anaconda.

anagramme [ánágrám] *nf* anagram.

ANAH *sigle f* = *Agence nationale pour l'amélioration de l'habitat*.

anal, e, aux [ánál, -ō] *a* anal.

analgésique [ánálzhāzĕk] *nm* analgesic.

anallergique [ánálerzhĕk] *a* hypoallergenic.

analogie [ánálozhē] *nf* analogy.

analogique [ánálozhĕk] *a* (*LOGIQUE*: *raisonnement*) analogical; (*calculateur, montre etc*) analog (*US*), analogue (*Brit*); (*INFORM*) analog.

analogue [ánálog] *a*: **~ (à)** analogous (to), similar (to).

analphabète [ánálfábet] *nm/f* illiterate.

analphabétisme [ánálfábātēsm(ə)] *nm* illiteracy.

analyse [ánálēz] *nf* analysis; (*MÉD*) test; **faire l'~ de** to analyze (*US*), analyse (*Brit*); **une ~ approfondie** an in-depth analysis; **en dernière ~** in the last analysis; **avoir l'esprit d'~** to have an analytical turn of mind; **~ grammaticale** grammatical analysis, parsing (*SCOL*).

analyser [ánálēzā] *vt* to analyze (*US*), analyse (*Brit*); (*MÉD*) to test.

analyste [ánálēst(ə)] *nm/f* analyst; (*psychanalyste*) (psycho)analyst.

analyste-programmeur, euse, *pl* **analystes-programmeurs, euses** [ánálēstprográmœr, -œ̄z] *nm/f* systems analyst.

analytique [ánálētĕk] *a* analytical.

analytiquement [ánálētēkmáṅ] *ad* analytically.

ananas [ánáná] *nm* pineapple.

anarchie [ánárshē] *nf* anarchy.

anarchique [ánárshĕk] *a* anarchic.

anarchisme [ánárshēsm(ə)] *nm* anarchism.

anarchiste [ánárshēst(ə)] *a* anarchistic ♦ *nm/f* anarchist.

anathème [ánátem] *nm*: **jeter l'~ sur, lancer l'~ contre** to anathematize, curse.

anatomie [ánátomē] *nf* anatomy.

anatomique [ànátomēk] *a* anatomical.
ancestral, e, aux [ànsestrál, -ō] *a* ancestral.
ancêtre [ànsetr(ə)] *nm/f* ancestor; (*fig*): **l'~ de** the forerunner of.
anche [ànsh] *nf* reed.
anchois [ànshwá] *nm* anchovy.
ancien, ne [ànsyań, -en] *a* old; (*de jadis, de l'antiquité*) ancient; (*précédent, ex-*) former, old ♦ *nm* (*mobilier ancien*): **l'~** antiques *pl* ♦ *nm/f* (*dans une tribu etc*) elder; **un ~ minis-tre** a former minister; **mon ~ne voiture** my previous car; **être plus ~ que qn dans une maison** to have been in a firm longer than sb; (*dans l'hiérarchie*) to be senior to sb in a firm; **~ combattant** ex-serviceman; **~ (élève)** (*SCOL*) alumnus (*US*), ex-pupil (*Brit*).
anciennement [ànsyenmáń] *ad* formerly.
ancienneté [ànsyentā] *nf* oldness; antiquity; (*ADMIN*) (length of) service; seniority.
ancrage [ànkràzh] *nm* anchoring; (*NAVIG*) anchorage; (*CONSTR*) anchor.
ancre [ànkr(ə)] *nf* anchor; **jeter/lever l'~** to cast/weigh anchor; **à l'~** at anchor.
ancrer [ànkrā] *vt* (*CONSTR*) to anchor; (*fig*) to fix firmly; **s'~** *vi* (*NAVIG*) to (cast) anchor.
andalou, ouse [àndálōō, -ōōz] *a* Andalusian.
Andalousie [àndálōōzē] *nf*: **l'~** Andalusia.
andante [àndáńt] *ad, nm* andante.
Andes [ànd] *nfpl*: **les ~** the Andes.
Andorre [àndor] *n* Andorra.
andouille [àndōōy] *nf* (*CULIN*) sausage made of chitterlings; (*fam*) dope, knucklehead (*US*).
andouillette [àndōōyet] *nf* small andouille.
âne [àn] *nm* donkey, ass; (*péj*) dunce, fool.
anéantir [ànāáńtēr] *vt* to annihilate, wipe out; (*fig*) to obliterate, destroy; (*déprimer*) to overwhelm.
anecdote [ànekdot] *nf* anecdote.
anecdotique [ànekdotēk] *a* anecdotal.
anémie [ànāmē] *nf* anemia (*US*), anaemia (*Brit*).
anémié, e [ànāmyā] *a* anemic (*US*), anaemic (*Brit*); (*fig*) enfeebled.
anémique [ànāmēk] *a* anemic (*US*), anaemic (*Brit*).
anémone [ànāmon] *nf* anemone; **~ de mer** sea anemone.
ânerie [ànrē] *nf* stupidity; (*parole etc*) stupid *ou* idiotic comment *etc*.
anéroïde [ànāroēd] *a voir* **baromètre**.
ânesse [ànes] *nf* she-ass.
anesthésie [ànestāzē] *nf* anesthesia (*US*), anaesthesia (*Brit*); **sous ~** under anesthetic; **~ générale/locale** general/local anesthetic; **faire une ~ locale à qn** to give sb a local anesthetic.
anesthésier [ànestāzyā] *vt* to anesthetize (*US*), anaesthetize (*Brit*).
anesthésique [ànestāzēk] *a* anesthetic (*US*), anaesthetic (*Brit*).
anesthésiste [ànestāzēst(ə)] *nm/f* anesthesiolo-gist (*US*), anaesthetist (*Brit*).
anfractuosité [ànfráktūōzētā] *nf* crevice.
ange [ànzh] *nm* angel; **être aux ~s** to be in seventh heaven; **~ gardien** guardian angel.
angélique [ànzhālēk] *a* angelic(al) ♦ *nf* angelica.
angelot [ànzhlō] *nm* cherub.

angélus [ànzhālüs] *nm* angelus; (*cloches*) eve-ning bells *pl*.
angevin, e [ànzhvań, -ēn] *a* of *ou* from Anjou; of *ou* from Angers.
angine [ànzhēn] *nf* sore throat, throat infec-tion; **~ de poitrine** angina (pectoris).
angiome [ànzhyōm] *nm* angioma.
anglais, e [àngle, -ez] *a* English ♦ *nm* (*LING*) English ♦ *nm/f*: **A~,** e Englishman/woman; **les A~** the English; **filer à l'~e** to take French leave; **à l'~e** (*CULIN*) boiled.
anglaises [ànglez] *nfpl* (*cheveux*) ringlets.
angle [àngl(ə)] *nm* angle; (*coin*) corner; **~ droit/obtus/aigu/mort** right/obtuse/acute/ dead angle.
Angleterre [àngləter] *nf*: **l'~** England.
anglican, e [ànglēkáń, -àn] *a, nm/f* Anglican.
anglicisme [ànglēsēsm(ə)] *nm* anglicism.
angliciste [ànglēsēst(ə)] *nm/f* English scholar; (*étudiant*) student of English.
anglo... [ànglo] (*préfixe*) Anglo-, anglo(-).
anglo-américain, e [àngloámārēkań, -en] *a* Anglo-American ♦ *nm* (*LING*) American English.
anglo-arabe [àngloáráb] *a* Anglo-Arab.
anglo-canadien, ne [ànglokánádyań, -en] *a* Anglo-Canadian ♦ *nm* (*LING*) Canadian English.
anglo-normand, e [ànglonormáń, -áńd] *a* Anglo-Norman; **les îles ~es** the Channel Islands.
anglophile [ànglofēl] *a* anglophilic.
anglophobe [ànglofob] *a* anglophobic.
anglophone [ànglofon] *a* English-speaking.
anglo-saxon, ne [ànglosáksóń, -on] *a* Anglo-Saxon.
angoissant, e [àngwásáń, -áńt] *a* harrowing.
angoisse [àngwás] *nf*: **l'~** anguish *q*.
angoissé, e [àngwásā] *a* anguished; (*personne*) full of anxieties *ou* hang-ups (*fam*).
angoisser [àngwásā] *vt* to harrow, cause anguish to ♦ *vi* to worry, fret.
Angola [àngolá] *nm*: **l'~** Angola.
angolais, e [àngole, -ez] *a* Angolan.
angora [àngorá] *a, nm* angora.
anguille [àngēy] *nf* eel; **~ sous roche** (*fig*) there's some-thing going on, there's something beneath all this.
angulaire [àngüler] *a* angular.
anguleux, euse [àngülœ, -œz] *a* angular.
anicroche [ànēkrosh] *nf* hitch, snag.
animal, e, aux [ànēmál, -ō] *a, nm* animal; **~ domestique/sauvage** domestic/wild animal.
animalier [ànēmályā] *a*: **peintre ~** animal painter.
animateur, trice [ànēmátœr, -trēs] *nm/f* (*de télévision*) host; (*de music-hall*) MC, emcee (*US*), compère (*Brit*); (*de groupe*) leader, organizer; (*CINÉMA: technicien*) animator.
animation [ànēmásyóń] *nf* (*voir animé*) busy-ness; liveliness; (*CINÉMA: technique*) anima-tion; (*activité*): **~s** activities; **centre d'~** ≈ community center.
animé, e [ànēmā] *a* (*rue, lieu*) busy, lively; (*conversation, réunion*) lively, animated; (*opposé à inanimé, aussi LING*) animate.
animer [ànēmā] *vt* (*ville, soirée*) to liven up,

enliven; (*mettre en mouvement*) to drive; (*stimuler*) to drive, impel; **s'~** *vi* to liven up, come to life.

animosité [ánēmōzētā] *nf* animosity.

anis [ánē] *nm* (*CULIN*) aniseed; (*BOT*) anise.

anisette [ánēzet] *nf* anisette.

Ankara [áṅkárá] *n* Ankara.

ankyloser [áṅkēlōzā]: **s'~** *vi* to get stiff, ankylose.

annales [ánál] *nfpl* annals.

anneau, x [ánō] *nm* ring; (*de chaîne*) link; (*SPORT*): **exercices aux ~x** ring exercises.

année [ánā] *nf* year; **souhaiter la bonne ~ à qn** to wish sb a Happy New Year; **tout au long de l'~** all year long; **d'une ~ à l'autre** from one year to the next; **d'~ en ~** from year to year; **l'~ scolaire/fiscale** the school/tax year.

année-lumière,   *pl*   **années-lumières** [ánālümyer] *nf* light year.

annexe [áneks(ə)] *a* (*problème*) related; (*document*) appended; (*salle*) adjoining ♦ *nf* (*bâtiment*) annex(e); (*de document, ouvrage*) annex, appendix; (*jointe à une lettre, un dossier*) enclosure.

annexer [áneksā] *vt* to annex; **s'~** (*pays*) to annex; **~ qch à** (*joindre*) to append sth to.

annexion [áneksyóń] *nf* annexation.

annihiler [áñēēlā] *vt* to annihilate.

anniversaire [áñēverser] *nm* birthday; (*d'un événement, bâtiment*) anniversary ♦ *a*: **jour ~** anniversary.

annonce [ánóńs] *nf* announcement; (*signe, indice*) sign; (*aussi:* **~ publicitaire**) advertisement; (*CARTES*) declaration; **~ personnelle** personal message; **les petites ~s** the want (*US*) *ou* classified ads.

annoncer [ánóńsā] *vt* to announce; (*être le signe de*) to herald; (*CARTES*) to declare; **je vous annonce que ...** I wish to tell you that ...; **s'~ bien/difficile** to look promising/difficult; **~ la couleur** (*fig*) to lay one's cards on the table.

annonceur, euse [ánóńsœr, -ēz] *nm/f* (*TV, RADIO: speaker*) announcer; (*publicitaire*) advertiser.

annonciateur, trice [ánóńsyátœr, -trēs] *a*: **~ d'un événement** presaging an event.

Annonciation [ánóńsyâsyóń] *nf*: **l'~** (*REL*) the Annunciation; (*jour*) Annunciation Day.

annotation [ánotâsyóń] *nf* annotation.

annoter [ánotā] *vt* to annotate.

annuaire [ánüer] *nm* yearbook, annual; **~ téléphonique** (telephone) directory, phone book.

annuel, le [ánüel] *a* annual, yearly.

annuellement [ánüelmáń] *ad* annually, yearly.

annuité [ánüētā] *nf* annual installment.

annulaire [ánüler] *nm* ring finger, fourth (*US*) *ou* third (*Brit*) finger.

annulation [ánülâsyóń] *nf* cancellation; annulment; repeal (*US*), quashing (*Brit*).

annuler [ánülā] *vt* (*rendez-vous, voyage*) to cancel, call off; (*mariage*) to annul; (*jugement*) to repeal (*US*), quash (*Brit*); (*résultats*) to declare void; (*MATH, PHYSIQUE*) to cancel out; **s'~** to cancel each other out.

anoblir [ánoblēr] *vt* to ennoble.

anode [ánod] *nf* anode.

anodin, e [ánodań, -ēn] *a* harmless; (*sans importance*) insignificant, trivial.

anomalie [ánomálē] *nf* anomaly.

ânon [ánóń] *nm* baby donkey; (*petit âne*) little donkey.

ânonner [ánonā] *vi, vt* to read in a drone; (*hésiter*) to read in a fumbling manner.

anonymat [ánonēmá] *nm* anonymity; **garder l'~** to remain anonymous.

anonyme [ánonēm] *a* anonymous; (*fig*) impersonal.

anonymement [ánonēmmáń] *ad* anonymously.

anorak [ánorák] *nm* anorak.

anorexie [ánoreksē] *nf* anorexia.

anormal, e, aux [ánormál, -ō] *a* abnormal; (*insolite*) unusual, abnormal.

anormalement [ánormálmáń] *ad* abnormally; unusually.

ANPE *sigle f* (= *Agence nationale pour l'emploi*) *national employment agency* (functions include job creation).

anse [áńs] *nf* handle; (*GÉO*) cove.

antagonisme [áńtágonēsm(ə)] *nm* antagonism.

antagoniste [áńtágonēst(ə)] *a* antagonistic ♦ *nm* antagonist.

antan [áńtáń]: **d'~** *a* of yesteryear, of long ago.

antarctique [áńtárktēk] *a* Antarctic ♦ *nm*: **l'A~** the Antarctic; **le cercle A~** the Antarctic Circle; **l'océan A~** the Antarctic Ocean.

antécédent [áńtāsādáń] *nm* (*LING*) antecedent; **~s** *nmpl* (*MÉD etc*) past history *sg*; **~s professionnels** record, career to date.

antédiluvien, ne [áńtādēlüvyań, -en] *a* (*fig*) ancient, antediluvian.

antenne [áńten] *nf* (*de radio, télévision*) aerial; (*d'insecte*) antenna (*pl* -ae), feeler; (*poste avancé*) outpost; (*petite succursale*) sub-branch; **sur l'~** on the air; **passer à/avoir l'~** to go/be on the air; **2 heures d'~** 2 hours' broadcasting time; **hors ~** off the air; **~ chirurgicale** (*MIL*) advance surgical unit.

antépénultième [áńtāpānültyem] *a* antepenultimate.

antérieur, e [áńtāryœr] *a* (*d'avant*) previous, earlier; (*de devant*) front; **~ à** prior *ou* previous to; **passé/futur ~** (*LING*) past/future anterior.

antérieurement [áńtāryœrmáń] *ad* earlier; (*précédemment*) previously; **~ à** prior *ou* previous to.

antériorité [áńtāryorētā] *nf* precedence (*in time*).

anthologie [áńtolozhē] *nf* anthology.

anthracite [áńtrásēt] *nm* anthracite ♦ *a*: **(gris) ~** charcoal (gray).

anthropologie [áńtropolozhē] *nf* anthropology.

anthropologue [áńtropolog] *nm/f* anthropologist.

anthropomorphisme [áńtropomorfēsm(ə)] *nm* anthropomorphism.

anthropophagie [áńtropofázhē] *nf* cannibalism, anthropophagy.

anti... [áńtē] *préfixe* anti....

antiaérien, ne [áńtēáāryań, -en] *a* anti-aircraft; **abri ~** air-raid shelter.

antialcoolique [ǻṅtēálkolēk] *a* anti-alcohol; **ligue** ~ temperance league.
antiatomique [ǻṅtēátomēk] *a*: **abri** ~ fallout shelter.
antibiotique [ǻṅtēbyotēk] *nm* antibiotic.
antibrouillard [ǻṅtēbrōōyár] *a*: **phare** ~ fog light.
antibruit [ǻṅtēbrüē] *a inv*: **mur** ~ (*sur auto-route*) sound-muffling wall.
antibuée [ǻṅtēbüä] *a inv*: **dispositif** ~ defogger (*US*), demister (*Brit*); **bombe** ~ antifog (*US*) *ou* demister (*Brit*) spray.
anticancéreux, euse [ǻṅtēkáṅsārœ̄, -œ̄z] *a* cancer *cpd*.
anticasseur(s) [ǻṅtēkâsœr] *a*: **loi/mesure** ~ law/measure against damage done by demonstrators.
antichambre [ǻṅtēsháṅbr(ə)] *nf* antechamber, anteroom; **faire** ~ to wait (for an audience).
antichar [ǻṅtēshár] *a* anti-tank.
antichoc [ǻṅtēshok] *a* shockproof.
anticipation [ǻṅtēsēpásyóṅ] *nf* anticipation; (*COMM*) payment in advance; **par** ~ in anticipation, in advance; **livre/film d'**~ science fiction book/film.
anticipé, e [ǻṅtēsēpä] *a* (*règlement, paiement*) early, in advance; (*joie etc*) anticipated, early; **avec mes remerciements** ~**s** thanking you in advance *ou* anticipation.
anticiper [ǻṅtēsēpä] *vt* to anticipate, foresee; (*paiement*) to pay *ou* make in advance ♦ *vi* to look *ou* think ahead; (*en racontant*) to jump ahead; (*prévoir*) to anticipate; ~ **sur** to anticipate.
anticlérical, e, aux [ǻṅtēklārēkàl, -ō] *a* anticlerical.
anticoagulant, e [ǻṅtēkoágüláṅ, -áṅt] *a, nm* anticoagulant.
anticonceptionnel, le [ǻṅtēkóṅsepsyonel] *a* contraceptive.
anticonformisme [ǻṅtēkóṅformēsm(ə)] *nm* nonconformism.
anticonstitutionnel, le [ǻṅtēkóṅstētüsyonel] *a* unconstitutional.
anticorps [ǻṅtēkor] *nm* antibody.
anticyclone [ǻṅtēsēklōn] *nm* anticyclone.
antidater [ǻṅtēdátä] *vt* to backdate, predate.
antidémocratique [ǻṅtēdámokrátēk] *a* antidemocratic; (*peu démocratique*) undemocratic.
antidérapant, e [ǻṅtēdārápáṅ, -áṅt] *a* non-skid.
antidopage [ǻṅtēdopázh], **antidoping** [ǻṅtēdopēng] *a* (*lutte*) against drugs; (*contrôle*) drug *cpd*.
antidote [ǻṅtēdot] *nm* antidote.
antienne [áṅtyen] *nf* (*fig*) chant, refrain.
antigang [ǻṅtēgáṅg] *a inv*: **brigade** ~ commando unit.
antigel [ǻṅtēzhel] *nm* antifreeze.
antigène [ǻṅtēzhen] *nm* antigen.
antigouvernemental, e, aux [ǻṅtēgōōvernə-máṅtál, -ō] *a* anti-government.
Antigua et Barbude [ǻṅtēgáábárbüd] *nf* Antigua and Barbuda.
antihistaminique [ǻṅtēēstámēnēk] *nm* antihistamine.
anti-inflammatoire [ǻṅtēáṅflámátwár] *a* anti-inflammatory.

anti-inflationniste [ǻṅtēáṅflâsyonēst(ə)] *a* anti-inflationary.
antillais, e [áṅtēye, -ez] *a* West Indian.
Antilles [áṅtēy] *nfpl*: **les** ~ the West Indies; **les Grandes/Petites** ~ the Greater/Lesser Antilles.
antilope [áṅtēlop] *nf* antelope.
antimilitariste [áṅtēmēlētárēst(ə)] *a* antimilitarist.
antimissile [áṅtēmēsēl] *a* antimissile.
antimite(s) [áṅtēmēt] *a, nm*: (**produit**) ~ mothproofer, moth repellent.
antinucléaire [áṅtēnüklāer] *a* antinuclear.
antioxydant [áṅtēoksēdáṅ] *nm* antioxidant.
antiparasite [áṅtēpárázēt] *a* (*RADIO, TV*) anti-interference; **dispositif** ~ suppressor.
antipathie [áṅtēpátē] *nf* antipathy.
antipathique [áṅtēpátēk] *a* unpleasant, disagreeable.
antipelliculaire [áṅtēpālēküler] *a* anti-dandruff.
antiphrase [áṅtēfráz] *nf*: **par** ~ ironically.
antipodes [áṅtēpod] *nmpl* (*GÉO*): **les** ~ the antipodes; (*fig*): **être aux** ~ **de** to be the opposite extreme of.
antipoison [áṅtēpwázóṅ] *a inv*: **centre** ~ poison control center.
antipoliomyélitique [áṅtēpolyomyālētēk] *a* polio *cpd*.
antiprotectionniste [áṅtēproteksyonēst(ə)] *a* free-trade.
antiquaire [áṅtēker] *nm/f* antique dealer.
antique [áṅtēk] *a* antique; (*très vieux*) ancient, antiquated.
antiquité [áṅtēkētä] *nf* (*objet*) antique; **l'A**~ Antiquity; **magasin/marchand d'**~**s** antique shop/dealer.
antirabique [áṅtērábēk] *a* rabies *cpd*.
antiraciste [áṅtērásēst(ə)] *a* antiracist, anti-racialist.
antirépublicain, e [áṅtērāpüblēkáṅ, -en] *a* antirepublican.
antirides [áṅtērēd] *a* (*crème*) anti-wrinkle.
antirouille [áṅtērōōy] *a inv*: **peinture** ~ anti-rust paint; **traitement** ~ rustproofing.
antisémite [áṅtēsámēt] *a* anti-semitic.
antisémitisme [áṅtēsámētēsm(ə)] *nm* anti-semitism.
antiseptique [áṅtēseptēk] *a, nm* antiseptic.
antisocial, e, aux [áṅtēsosyál, -ō] *a* antisocial.
antisportif, ive [áṅtēsportēf, -ēv] *a* unsporting; (*hostile au sport*) against sport, anti-sport.
antitétanique [áṅtētātánēk] *a* tetanus *cpd*.
antithèse [áṅtētez] *nf* antithesis.
antitrust [áṅtētrœst] *a inv* (*loi, mesures*) anti-trust (*US*), anti-monopoly (*Brit*).
antituberculeux, euse [áṅtētüberkülœ̄, -œ̄z] *a* tuberculosis *cpd*.
antitussif, ive [áṅtētüsēf, -ēv] *a* antitussive, cough *cpd*.
antivariolique [áṅtēváryolēk] *a* smallpox *cpd*.
antivol [áṅtēvol] *a, nm*: (**dispositif**) ~ anti-theft device; (*pour vélo*) padlock.
antonyme [áṅtonēm] *nm* antonym.
antre [áṅtr(ə)] *nm* den, lair.
anus [ánüs] *nm* anus.
Anvers [áṅver] *n* Antwerp.
anxiété [áṅksyätä] *nf* anxiety.
anxieusement [áṅksyœ̄zmáṅ] *ad* anxiously.

anxieux, euse [ãksyœ̃, -œ̃z] *a* anxious, worried; **être ~ de faire** to be anxious to do.

AOC *sigle f* (= *Appellation d'origine contrôlée*) guarantee of quality of wine.

aorte [àort(ə)] *nf* aortạ.

août [ōō] *nm* August; *voir aussi* **juillet**.

aoûtien, ne [àōōsyań, -en] *nm/f* August vacationer (*US*) *ou* holiday-maker (*Brit*).

AP *sigle f* = **Assistance publique**.

apaisement [àpezmãń] *nm* calming; soothing; (*aussi POL*) appeasement; **~s** *nmpl* soothing reassurances; (*pour calmer*) pacifying words.

apaiser [àpāzā] *vt* (*colère*) to calm, quell, soothe; (*faim*) to appease, assuage; (*douleur*) to soothe; (*personne*) to calm (down), pacify; **s'~** *vi* (*tempête, bruit*) to die down, subside.

apanage [àpánázh] *nm*: **être l'~ de** to be the privilege *ou* prerogative of.

aparté [àpártā] *nm* (*THÉÂTRE*) aside; (*entretien*) private conversation; **en ~** *ad* in an aside; (*entretien*) in private.

apartheid [àpárted] *nm* apartheid.

apathie [àpátē] *nf* apathy.

apathique [àpátēk] *a* apathetic.

apatride [àpátrēd] *nm/f* stateless person.

Apennins [àpenań] *nmpl*: **les ~** the Apennines.

apercevoir [àpersəvwàr] *vt* to see; **s'~ de** *vt* to notice; **s'~ que** to notice that; **sans s'en ~** without realizing *ou* noticing.

aperçu, e [àpersü] *pp de* **apercevoir** ♦ *nm* (*vue d'ensemble*) general survey; (*intuition*) insight.

apéritif, ive [àpārētēf, -ēv] *a* which stimulates the appetite ♦ *nm* (*boisson*) aperitif; (*réunion*) (pre-lunch *ou* -dinner) drinks *pl*; **prendre l'~** to have drinks (before lunch *ou* dinner) *ou* an aperitif.

apesanteur [àpəzãñtœr] *nf* weightlessness.

à-peu-près [àpœ̃pre] *nm inv* (*péj*) vague approximation.

apeuré, e [àpœrā] *a* frightened, scared.

aphone [àfon] *a* voiceless.

aphorisme [àforēsm(ə)] *nm* aphorism.

aphrodisiaque [àfrodēzyák] *a, nm* aphrodisiac.

aphte [àft(ə)] *nm* mouth ulcer.

aphteuse [àftœ̃z] *af*: **fièvre ~** foot-and-mouth disease.

apicole [àpēkol] *a* beekeeping *cpd*.

apiculture [àpēkültür] *nf* beekeeping, apiculture.

apitoiement [àpētwámáń] *nm* pity, compassion.

apitoyer [àpētwàyā] *vt* to move to pity; **~ qn sur qn/qch** to move sb to pity for sb/over sth; **s'~ (sur qn/qch)** to feel pity *ou* compassion (for sb/over sth).

ap. J.-C. *abr* (= *après Jésus-Christ*) AD.

APL *sigle f* (= *aide personnalisée au logement*) type of loan for house purchase.

aplanir [àplánēr] *vt* to level; (*fig*) to smooth away, iron out.

aplati, e [àplátē] *a* flat, flattened.

aplatir [àplátēr] *vt* to flatten; **s'~** *vi* to become flatter; (*écrasé*) to be flattened; (*fig*) to lie flat on the ground; (*: fam*) to fall flat on one's face; (*: péj*) to grovel.

aplomb [àplóń] *nm* (*équilibre*) balance, equilibrium; (*fig*) self-assurance; (*: péj*) nerve; **d'~** *ad* steady; (*CONSTR*) plumb.

apocalypse [àpokálēps(ə)] *nf* apocalypse.

apocalyptique [àpokálēptēk] *a* (*fig*) apocalyptic.

apocryphe [àpokrēf] *a* apocryphal.

apogée [àpozhā] *nm* (*fig*) peak, apogee.

apolitique [àpolētēk] *a* (*indifférent*) apolitical; (*indépendant*) unpolitical, non-political.

apologie [àpolozhē] *nf* praise; (*JUR*) vindication.

apoplexie [àpopleksē] *nf* apoplexy.

a posteriori [àpostāryorē] *ad* after the event, with hindsight, a posteriori.

apostolat [àpostolá] *nm* (*REL*) apostolate, discipleship; (*gén*) evangelism.

apostolique [àpostolēk] *a* apostolic.

apostrophe [àpostrof] *nf* (*signe*) apostrophe; (*appel*) interpellation.

apostropher [àpostrofā] *vt* (*interpeller*) to shout at, address sharply.

apothéose [àpotāōz] *nf* pinnacle (of achievement); (*MUS etc*) grand finale.

apothicaire [àpotēker] *nm* apothecary.

apôtre [àpōtr(ə)] *nm* apostle, disciple.

Appalaches [àpálásh] *nmpl*: **les ~** the Appalachian Mountains.

appalachien, ne [àpáláshyań, -en] *a* Appalachian.

apparaître [àpáretr(ə)] *vi* to appear ♦ *vb avec attribut* to appear, seem.

apparat [àpárá] *nm*: **tenue/dîner d'~** ceremonial dress/dinner.

appareil [àpárey] *nm* (*outil, machine*) piece of apparatus, device; (*électrique etc*) appliance; (*politique, syndical*) machinery; (*avion*) (air)plane (*US*), (aero)plane (*Brit*), aircraft *inv*; (*téléphonique*) telephone; (*dentier*) braces (*US*), brace (*Brit*); **~ digestif/ reproducteur** digestive/reproductive system *ou* apparatus; **l'~ productif** the means of production; **qui est à l'~?** who's speaking?; **dans le plus simple ~** in one's birthday suit; **~ (photographique)** camera; **~ 24 x 36** *ou* **petit format** 35 mm camera.

appareillage [àpáreyázh] *nm* (*appareils*) equipment; (*NAVIG*) casting off, getting under way.

appareiller [àpárāyā] *vi* (*NAVIG*) to cast off, get under way ♦ *vt* (*assortir*) to match up.

appareil-photo, *pl* **appareils-photos** [àpáreyfoto] *nm* camera.

apparemment [àpárámáń] *ad* apparently.

apparence [àpáráńs] *nf* appearance; **malgré les ~s** despite appearances; **en ~** apparently, seemingly.

apparent, e [àpáráń, -áńt] *a* visible; (*évident*) obvious; (*superficiel*) apparent; **coutures ~es** topstitched seams; **poutres ~es** exposed beams.

apparenté, e [àpáráńtā] *a*: **~ à** related to; (*fig*) similar to.

apparenter [àpáráńtā]: **s'~ à** *vt* to be similar to.

apparier [àpáryā] *vt* (*gants*) to pair, match.

appariteur [àpárētœr] *nm* attendant, porter (*in French universities*), ≈ campus policeman (*US*).

apparition [ápárēsyôǹ] *nf* appearance; (*surnaturelle*) apparition; **faire son** ~ to appear.

appartement [ápártəmâǹ] *nm* apartment (*US*), flat (*Brit*).

appartenance [ápártənáǹs] *nf*: ~ **à** belonging to, membership in (*US*) *ou* of (*Brit*).

appartenir [ápártənēr]: ~ **à** *vt* to belong to; (*faire partie de*) to belong to, be a member of; **il lui appartient de** it is up to him to.

appartiendrai [ápártyaǹdrā], **appartiens** [ápártyaǹ] *etc voir* **appartenir**.

apparu, e [ápárü] *pp de* **apparaître**.

appas [ápâ] *nmpl* (*d'une femme*) charms.

appât [ápâ] *nm* (*PÊCHE*) bait; (*fig*) lure, bait.

appâter [ápâtā] *vt* (*hameçon*) to bait; (*poisson, fig*) to lure, entice.

appauvrir [ápōvrēr] *vt* to impoverish; **s'**~ *vi* to grow poorer, become impoverished.

appauvrissement [ápōvrēsmâǹ] *nm* impoverishment.

appel [ápel] *nm* call; (*nominal*) roll call; (*SCOL*) roll, register (*Brit*); (*MIL: recrutement*) call-up; (*JUR*) appeal; **faire** ~ **à** (*invoquer*) to appeal to; (*avoir recours à*) to call on; (*nécessiter*) to call for, require; **faire ou interjeter** ~ (*JUR*) to appeal, file (*US*) *ou* lodge (*Brit*) an appeal; **faire l'**~ to call the roll; to call the register; **indicatif d'**~ call sign; **numéro d'**~ (*TÉL*) number; **produit d'**~ (*COMM*) loss leader; **sans** ~ (*fig*) final, irrevocable; ~ **d'air** in-draft (*US*), in-draught (*Brit*); ~ **d'offres** (*COMM*) invitation to bid; **faire un** ~ **de phares** to flash one's headlights; ~ **(téléphonique)** (tele)phone call.

appelé [áplā] *nm* (*MIL*) draftee.

appeler [áplā] *vt* to call; (*TÉL*) to call, ring; (*faire venir: médecin etc*) to call, send for; (*fig: nécessiter*) to call for, demand; ~ **au secours** to call for help; ~ **qn à l'aide** *ou* **au secours** to call to sb to help; ~ **qn à un poste/des fonctions** to appoint sb to a post/ assign duties to sb; **être appelé à** (*fig*) to be destined to; ~ **qn à comparaître** (*JUR*) to summon sb to appear; **en** ~ **à** to appeal to; **s'**~: **elle s'appelle Gabrielle** her name is Gabrielle, she's called Gabrielle; **comment ça s'appelle?** what is it *ou* that called?

appellation [áplásyôǹ] *nf* designation, appellation; **vin d'**~ **contrôlée** 'appellation contrôlée' wine, *wine guaranteed of a certain quality*.

appelle [ápel] *etc vb voir* **appeler**.

appendice [ápaǹdēs] *nm* appendix.

appendicite [ápaǹdēsēt] *nf* appendicitis.

appentis [ápâǹtē] *nm* lean-to.

appert [áper] *vb*: **il** ~ **que** it appears that, it is evident that.

appesantir [ápzâǹtēr]: **s'**~ *vi* to grow heavier; **s'**~ **sur** (*fig*) to dwell at length on.

appétissant, e [ápātēsâǹ, -âǹt] *a* appetizing, mouth-watering.

appétit [ápātē] *nm* appetite; **couper l'**~ **à qn** to take away sb's appetite; **bon** ~! enjoy your meal!

applaudimètre [áplōdēmetr(ə)] *nm* applause meter.

applaudir [áplōdēr] *vt* to applaud ♦ *vi* to applaud, clap; ~ **à** *vt* (*décision*) to applaud, commend.

applaudissements [áplōdēsmâǹ] *nmpl* applause *sg*, clapping *sg*.

applicable [áplēkábl(ə)] *a* applicable.

applicateur [áplēkátœr] *nm* applicator.

application [áplēkâsyôǹ] *nf* application; (*d'une loi*) enforcement; **mettre en** ~ to implement.

applique [áplēk] *nf* wall lamp.

appliqué, e [áplēkā] *a* (*élève etc*) industrious, assiduous; (*science*) applied.

appliquer [áplēkā] *vt* to apply; (*loi*) to enforce; (*donner: gifle, châtiment*) to give; **s'**~ *vi* (*élève etc*) to apply o.s.; **s'**~ **à** (*loi, remarque*) to apply to; **s'**~ **à faire qch** to apply o.s. to doing sth, take pains to do sth; **s'**~ **sur** (*coïncider avec*) to fit over.

appoint [ápwaǹ] *nm* (*extra*) contribution *ou* help; **avoir/faire l'**~ (*en payant*) to have/give the exact change; **chauffage d'**~ extra heating.

appointements [ápwaǹtmâǹ] *nmpl* salary *sg*, stipend (*surtout REL*).

appointer [ápwaǹtā] *vt*: **être appointé à l'année/au mois** to be paid yearly/monthly.

appontement [ápôǹtmâǹ] *nm* landing stage, wharf.

apponter [ápôǹtā] *vi* (*avion, hélicoptère*) to land.

apport [ápor] *nm* supply; (*argent, biens etc*) contribution.

apporter [áportā] *vt* to bring; (*preuve*) to give, provide; (*modification*) to make; (*suj: remarque*) to contribute, add.

apposer [ápōzā] *vt* to append; (*sceau etc*) to affix.

apposition [ápōzēsyôǹ] *nf* appending; affixing; (*LING*): **en** ~ in apposition.

appréciable [áprāsyábl(ə)] *a* (*important*) appreciable, significant.

appréciation [áprāsyâsyôǹ] *nf* appreciation; estimation, assessment; ~**s** *nfpl* (*avis*) assessment *sg*, appraisal *sg*.

apprécier [áprāsyā] *vt* to appreciate; (*évaluer*) to estimate, assess; **j'apprécierais que tu ... I** should appreciate (it) if you ....

appréhender [áprāâǹdā] *vt* (*craindre*) to dread; (*arrêter*) to apprehend; ~ **que** to fear that; ~ **de faire** to dread doing.

appréhensif, ive [áprāâǹsēf, -ēv] *a* apprehensive.

appréhension [áprāâǹsyôǹ] *nf* apprehension.

apprendre [ápráǹdr(ə)] *vt* to learn; (*événement, résultats*) to learn of, hear of; ~ **qch à qn** (*informer*) to tell sb (of) sth; (*enseigner*) to teach sb sth; **tu me l'apprends!** that's news to me!; ~ **à faire qch** to learn to do sth; ~ **à qn à faire qch** to teach sb to do sth.

apprenti, e [ápráǹtē] *nm/f* apprentice; (*fig*) novice, beginner.

apprentissage [ápráǹtēsázh] *nm* learning; (*COMM, SCOL: période*) apprenticeship; **école ou centre d'**~ training school *ou* center; **faire l'**~ **de qch** (*fig*) to be initiated into sth.

apprêt [ápre] *nm* (*sur un cuir, une étoffe*) dressing; (*sur un mur*) size; (*sur un papier*) finish; **sans** ~ (*fig*) without artifice, unaffectedly.

apprêté, e [áprātā] *a* (*fig*) affected.

apprêter [áprātā] *vt* to dress, finish; **s'~** *vi*: **s'~ à qch/à faire qch** to prepare for sth/for doing sth.

appris, e [áprē, -ēz] *pp de* **apprendre**.

apprivoisé, e [áprēvwázā] *a* tame, tamed.

apprivoiser [áprēvwázā] *vt* to tame.

approbateur, trice [áprobátœr, -trēs] *a* approving.

approbatif, ive [áprobátēf, -ēv] *a* approving.

approbation [áprobásyôn] *nf* approval; **digne d'~** (*conduite, travail*) praiseworthy, commendable.

approchant, e [áproshân, -ânt] *a* similar, close; **quelque chose d'~** something similar.

approche [áprosh] *nf* approaching; (*arrivée, attitude*) approach; **~s** *nfpl* (*abords*) surroundings; **à l'~ du bateau/de l'ennemi** as the ship/enemy approached *ou* drew near; **l'~ d'un problème** the approach to a problem; **travaux d'~** (*fig*) maneuvers.

approché, e [áproshā] *a* approximate.

approcher [áproshā] *vi* to approach, come near ♦ *vt* (*vedette, artiste*) to come close to, approach; (*rapprocher*): **~ qch (de qch)** to bring *ou* put *ou* move sth near (to sth); **~ de** *vt* to draw near to; (*quantité, moment*) to approach; **s'~ de** *vt* to approach, go *ou* come *ou* move near to; **approchez-vous** come *ou* go nearer.

approfondi, e [áprofôndē] *a* thorough, detailed.

approfondir [áprofôndēr] *vt* to deepen; (*question*) to go further into; **sans ~** without going too deeply into it.

appropriation [áproprēyásyôn] *nf* appropriation.

approprié, e [áproprēyā] *a*: **~ (à)** appropriate (to), suited to.

approprier [áproprēyā] *vt* (*adapter*) adapter; **s'~** *vt* to appropriate, take over.

approuver [áprōōvā] *vt* to agree with; (*autoriser: loi, projet*) to approve, pass; (*trouver louable*) to approve of; **je vous approuve entièrement/ne vous approuve pas** I agree with you entirely/don't agree with you; **lu et approuvé** (read and) approved.

approvisionnement [áprovēzyonmân] *nm* supplying; (*provisions*) supply, stock.

approvisionner [áprovēzyonā] *vt* to supply; (*compte bancaire*) to pay funds into; **~ qn en** to supply sb with; **s'~** *vi*: **s'~ dans un certain magasin/au marché** to shop in a certain shop/at the market; **s'~ en** to stock up with.

approximatif, ive [áproksēmátēf, -ēv] *a* approximate, rough; (*imprécis*) vague.

approximation [áproksēmásyôn] *nf* approximation.

approximativement [áproksēmátēvmân] *ad* approximately, roughly; vaguely.

appt *abr* = **appartement**.

appui [ápüē] *nm* support; **prendre ~ sur** to lean on; (*objet*) to rest on; **point d'~** fulcrum; (*fig*) something to lean on; **à l'~ de** (*pour prouver*) in support of; **à l'~** *ad* to support one's argument; **l'~ de la fenêtre** the windowsill, the window ledge.

appuie [ápüē] *etc vb voir* **appuyer**.

appui-tête, appuie-tête [ápüētet] *nm inv* head-rest.

appuyé, e [ápüēyā] *a* (*regard*) meaningful; (: *insistant*) intent, insistent; (*excessif: politesse, compliment*) exaggerated, over-done.

appuyer [ápüēyā] *vt* (*poser*): **~ qch sur/contre/à** to lean *ou* rest sth on/against/on; (*soutenir: personne, demande*) to support, back (up) ♦ *vi*: **~ sur** (*bouton, frein*) to press, push; (*mot, détail*) to stress, emphasize; (*suj: chose: peser sur*) to rest (heavily) on, press against; **s'~ sur** *vt* to lean on; (*compter sur*) to rely on; **s'~ sur qn** to lean on sb; **~ contre** (*toucher: mur, porte*) to lean *ou* rest against; **~ à droite** *ou* **sur sa droite** to bear (to the) right; **~ sur le champignon** to put one's foot down.

apr. *abr* = **après**.

âpre [ápr(ə)] *a* acrid, pungent; (*fig*) harsh; (*lutte*) bitter; **~ au gain** grasping, greedy.

après [ápre] *prép* after ♦ *ad* afterwards; **2 heures ~** 2 hours later; **~ qu'il est** *ou* **soit parti/avoir fait** after he left/having done; **courir ~ qn** to run after sb; **crier ~ qn** to shout at sb; **être toujours ~ qn** (*critiquer etc*) to be always nagging (at) sb; **~ quoi** after which; **d'~** *prép* (*selon*) according to; **d'~ lui** according to him; **d'~ moi** in my opinion; **~ coup** *ad* after the event, afterwards; **~ tout** *ad* (*au fond*) after all; **et (puis) ~?** so what?

après-demain [ápredmân] *ad* the day after tomorrow.

après-guerre [ápreger] *nm* post-war years *pl*; **d'~** *a* post-war.

après-midi [ápremēdē] *nm ou nf inv* after-noon.

après-rasage [áprerázazh] *nm inv*: **(lotion) ~** after-shave (lotion).

après-ski [ápreskē] *nm inv* (*chaussure*) snow boot; (*moment*) après-ski.

après-vente [áprevânt] *a inv* after-sales *cpd*.

âpreté [ápratā] *nf* (*voir âpre*) pungency; harshness; bitterness.

à-propos [ápropō] *nm* (*d'une remarque*) apt-ness; **faire preuve d'~** to show presence of mind, do the right thing; **avec ~** suitably, aptly.

apte [ápt(ə)] *a*: **~ à qch/faire qch** capable of sth/doing sth; **~ (au service)** (*MIL*) fit (for service).

aptitude [áptētüd] *nf* ability, aptitude.

apurer [ápürā] *vt* to balance.

aquaplanage [ákwáplánázh] *nm* (*AUTO*) aqua-planing.

aquaplane [ákwáplán] *nm* (*planche*) aqua-plane; (*sport*) aquaplaning.

aquarelle [ákwárel] *nf* (*tableau*) watercolor (*US*), watercolour (*Brit*); (*genre*) water-colo(u)rs *pl*, aquarelle.

aquarium [ákwáryom] *nm* aquarium.

aquatique [ákwátēk] *a* aquatic, water *cpd*.

aqueduc [ákdük] *nm* aqueduct.

aqueux, euse [ákœ, -œz] *a* aqueous.

aquilin [ákēlan] *am*: **nez ~** aquiline nose.

AR *sigle m* (= *accusé de réception*): **lettre/paquet avec ~** ≈ certified letter/parcel (*US*), ≈ recorded delivery letter/parcel (*Brit*); (*AVIAT, RAIL etc*) = **aller (et) retour** ♦ *abr*

(*AUTO*) = **arrière**.

arabe [àráb] *a* Arabic; (*désert, cheval*) Arabian; (*nation, peuple*) Arab ♦ *nm* (*LING*) Arabic ♦ *nm/f*: **A~** Arab.

arabesque [àràbesk(ə)] *nf* arabesque.

Arabie [àràbē] *nf*: **l'~** Arabia; **l'~ Saoudite** *ou* **Séoudite** Saudi Arabia.

arable [àrábl(ə)] *a* arable.

arachide [àráshēd] *nf* groundnut (plant); (*graine*) peanut, groundnut.

araignée [àrànyá] *nf* spider; **~ de mer** spider crab.

araser [àrázā] *vt* to level; (*en rabotant*) to plane (down).

aratoire [àràtwàr] *a*: **instrument ~** plowing (*US*) *ou* ploughing (*Brit*) implement.

arbalète [àrbálet] *nf* crossbow.

arbitrage [àrbētrázh] *nm* refereeing; umpiring; arbitration.

arbitraire [àrbētrer] *a* arbitrary.

arbitrairement [àrbētrermáñ] *ad* arbitrarily.

arbitre [àrbētr(ə)] *nm* (*SPORT*) referee; (*TENNIS, CRICKET*) umpire; (*fig*) arbiter, judge; (*JUR*) arbitrator.

arbitrer [àrbētrā] *vt* to referee; to umpire; to arbitrate.

arborer [àrborā] *vt* to bear, display; (*avec ostentation*) to sport.

arborescence [àrborāsáñs] *nf* tree structure.

arboriculture [àrborēkültür] *nf* arboriculture; **~ fruitière** fruit (tree) growing.

arbre [àrbr(ə)] *nm* tree; (*TECH*) shaft; **~ à cames** (*AUTO*) camshaft; **~ fruitier** fruit tree; **~ généalogique** family tree; **~ de Noël** Christmas tree; **~ de transmission** (*AUTO*) driveshaft.

arbrisseau, x [àrbrēsō] *nm* shrub.

arbuste [àrbüst(ə)] *nm* small shrub, bush.

arc [àrk] *nm* (*arme*) bow; (*GÉOM*) arc; (*ARCHIT*) arch; **~ de cercle** arc of a circle; **en ~ de cercle** *a* semi-circular.

arcade [àrkád] *nf* arch(way); **~s** *nfpl* arcade *sg*, arches; **~ sourcilière** arch of the eyebrows.

arcanes [àrkán] *nmpl* mysteries.

arc-boutant, pl arcs-boutants [àrkbōōtáñ] *nm* flying buttress.

arc-bouter [àrkbōōtā]: **s'~** *vi*: **s'~ contre** to lean *ou* press against.

arceau, x [àrsō] *nm* (*métallique etc*) hoop.

arc-en-ciel, pl arcs-en-ciel [àrkáñsyel] *nm* rainbow.

archaïque [àrkáēk] *a* archaic.

archaïsme [àrkáēsm(ə)] *nm* archaism.

archange [àrkánzh] *nm* archangel.

arche [àrsh(ə)] *nf* arch; **~ de Noé** Noah's Ark.

archéologie [àrkāolozhē] *nf* arch(a)eology.

archéologique [àrkāolozhēk] *a* arch(a)eological.

archéologue [àrkāolog] *nm/f* arch(a)eologist.

archer [àrshā] *nm* archer.

archet [àrshe] *nm* bow.

archétype [àrkātēp] *nm* archetype.

archevêché [àrshəvāshā] *nm* archbishopric; (*palais*) archbishop's palace.

archevêque [àrshəvek] *nm* archbishop.

archi... [àrshē] *préfixe* (*très*) dead, extra.

archibondé, e [àrshēbóñdā] *a* chock-a-block (*Brit*), packed solid.

archiduc [àrshēdük] *nm* archduke.

archiduchesse [àrshēdüshes] *nf* archduchess.

archipel [àrshēpel] *nm* archipelago.

archisimple [àrshēsañpl(ə)] *a* dead easy *ou* simple.

architecte [àrshētekt(ə)] *nm* architect.

architectural, e, aux [àrshētektürál, -ō] *a* architectural.

architecture [àrshētektür] *nf* architecture.

archive [àrshēv] *nf* file; **~s** *nfpl* archives.

archiver [àrshēvā] *vt* to file.

archiviste [àrshēvēst(ə)] *nm/f* archivist.

arçon [àrsóñ] *nm voir* **cheval**.

arctique [àrktēk] *a* Arctic ♦ *nm*: **l'A~** the Arctic; **le cercle A~** the Arctic Circle; **l'océan A~** the Arctic Ocean.

ardemment [àrdámáñ] *ad* ardently, fervently.

ardent, e [àrdáñ, -áñt] *a* (*soleil*) blazing; (*fièvre*) raging; (*amour*) ardent, passionate; (*prière*) fervent.

ardeur [àrdœr] *nf* blazing heat; (*fig*) fervor (*US*), fervour (*Brit*), ardor (*US*), ardour (*Brit*).

ardoise [àrdwáz] *nf* slate.

ardu, e [àrdü] *a* arduous, difficult; (*pente*) steep, abrupt.

are [àr] *nm* are, 100 square meters.

arène [àren] *nf* arena; (*fig*): **l'~ politique/littéraire** the political/literary arena; **~s** *nfpl* bull-ring *sg*.

arête [àret] *nf* (*de poisson*) bone; (*d'une montagne*) ridge; (*GÉOM etc*) edge (*where two faces meet*).

arg. *abr* = **argus**.

argent [àrzháñ] *nm* (*métal*) silver; (*monnaie*) money; (*couleur*) silver; **en avoir pour son ~** to get one's money's worth; **gagner beaucoup d'~** to earn a lot of money; **~ comptant** (hard) cash; **~ liquide** ready money, (ready) cash; **~ de poche** pocket money.

argenté, e [àrzháñtā] *a* silver(y); (*métal*) silver-plated.

argenter [àrzháñtā] *vt* to silver(-plate).

argenterie [àrzháñtrē] *nf* silverware; (*en métal argenté*) silver plate.

argentin, e [àrzháñtañ, -ēn] *a* (*son*) silvery; (*d'Argentine*) Argentinian, Argentine ♦ *nm/f*: **A~, e** Argentinian, Argentine.

Argentine [àrzháñtēn] *nf*: **l'~** Argentina, the Argentine.

argile [àrzhēl] *nf* clay.

argileux, euse [àrzhēlœ, -œz] *a* clayey.

argot [àrgō] *nm* slang.

argotique [àrgotēk] *a* slang *cpd*; (*très familier*) slangy.

arguer [àrgüā]: **~ de** *vt* to put forward as a pretext *ou* reason; **~ que** to argue that.

argument [àrgümáñ] *nm* argument.

argumentaire [àrgümáñter] *nm* list of selling points; (*brochure*) sales brochure.

argumenter [àrgümáñtā] *vi* to argue.

argus [àrgüs] *nm* guide to second-hand car etc prices.

arguties [àrgüsē] *nfpl* quibbles.

aride [àrēd] *a* arid.

aridité [àrēdētā] *nf* aridity.

arien, ne [àryañ, -en] *a* Arian.

aristocrate [àrēstokrát] *nm/f* aristocrat.

aristocratie [årēstokråsē] *nf* aristocracy.
aristocratique [årēstokråtēk] *a* aristocratic.
arithmétique [årētmåtēk] *a* arithmetic(al) ♦ *nf* arithmetic.
armagnac [årmånyåk] *nm* armagnac.
armateur [årmåtœr] *nm* shipowner.
armature [årmåtür] *nf* framework; (*de tente etc*) frame; (*de corset*) bone; (*de soutien-gorge*) underwiring.
arme [årm(ə)] *nf* weapon; (*section de l'armée*) arm; **~s** *nfpl* weapons, arms; (*blason*) (coat of) arms; **les ~s** (*profession*) soldiering *sg*; **à ~s égales** on equal terms; **en ~s** up in arms; **passer par les ~s** to execute (by firing squad); **prendre/présenter les ~s** to take up/present arms; **se battre à l'~ blanche** to fight with blades; **~ à feu** firearm.
armé, e [årmå] *a* armed; **~ de** armed with.
armée [årmå] *nf* army; **~ de l'air** Air Force; **l'~ du Salut** the Salvation Army; **~ de terre** Army.
armement [årməmån] *nm* (*matériel*) arms *pl*, weapons *pl*; (*: d'un pays*) arms *pl*, armament; (*action d'équiper: d'un navire*) fitting out; **~s nucléaires** nuclear armaments; **course aux ~s** arms race.
Arménie [årmånē] *nf:* **l'~** Armenia.
arménien, ne [årmånyań, -en] *a* Armenian ♦ *nm* (*LING*) Armenian ♦ *nm/f:* **A~, ne** Armenian.
armer [årmå] *vt* to arm; (*arme à feu*) to cock; (*appareil-photo*) to wind on; **~ qch de** to fit sth with; (*renforcer*) to reinforce sth with; **~ qn de** to arm *ou* equip sb with; **s'~ de** to arm o.s. with.
armistice [årmēstēs] *nm* armistice; **l'A~** ≈ Veterans (*US*) *ou* Remembrance (*Brit*) Day.
armoire [årmwår] *nf* (tall) cupboard; (*penderie*) closet, wardrobe (*Brit*); **~ à pharmacie** medicine chest.
armoiries [årmwårē] *nfpl* coat of arms *sg*.
armure [årmür] *nf* armor *q* (*US*), armour *q* (*Brit*), suit of armor.
armurerie [årmürrē] *nf* arms factory; (*magasin*) gunsmith's (shop).
armurier [årmüryå] *nm* gunsmith; (*MIL, d'armes blanches*) armorer (*US*), armourer (*Brit*).
ARN *sigle m* (= *acide ribonucléique*) RNA.
arnaque [årnåk] *nf:* **de l'~** highway (*US*) *ou* daylight (*Brit*) robbery.
arnaquer [årnåkå] *vt* to do (*fam*), swindle; **se faire ~** to be had (*fam*) *ou* done.
arnaqueur [årnåkœr] *nm* swindler.
arnica [årnēkå] *nm:* (**teinture d'**)**~** arnica.
aromates [åromåt] *nmpl* seasoning *sg*, herbs (and spices).
aromatique [åromåtēk] *a* aromatic.
aromatiser [åromåtēzå] *vt* to flavor (*US*) *ou* flavour (*Brit*).
arôme [årōm] *nm* aroma; (*d'une fleur etc*) fragrance.
arpège [årpezh] *nm* arpeggio.
arpentage [årpåntåzh] *nm* (land) surveying.
arpenter [årpåntå] *vt* to pace up and down.
arpenteur [årpåntœr] *nm* land surveyor.
arqué, e [årkå] *a* arched; (*jambes*) bow *cpd*, bandy.
arr. *abr* = **arrondissement**.

arrachage [åråshåzh] *nm:* **~ des mauvaises herbes** weeding.
arraché [åråshå] *nm* (*SPORT*) snatch; **obtenir à l'~** (*fig*) to snatch.
arrache-pied [åråshpyå]: **d'~** *ad* relentlessly.
arracher [åråshå] *vt* to pull out; (*page etc*) to tear off, tear out; (*déplanter: légume*) to lift; (*: herbe, souche*) to pull up; (*bras etc: par explosion*) to blow off; (*: par accident*) to tear off; **s'~** *vt* (*article très recherché*) to fight over; **~ qch à qn** to snatch sth from sb; (*fig*) to wring sth out of sb, wrest sth from sb; **~ qn à** (*solitude, rêverie*) to drag sb out of; (*famille etc*) to tear *ou* wrench sb away from; **se faire ~ une dent** to have a tooth out *ou* pulled (*US*); **s'~ de** (*lieu*) to tear o.s. away from; (*habitude*) to force o.s. out of.
arraisonner [årezonå] *vt* to board and search.
arrangeant, e [årånzhån, -ånt] *a* accommodating, obliging.
arrangement [årånzhmån] *nm* arrangement.
arranger [årånzhå] *vt* to arrange; (*réparer*) to fix, put right; (*régler*) to settle, sort out; (*convenir à*) to suit, be convenient for; **s'~** (*se mettre d'accord*) to come to an agreement *ou* arrangement; (*s'améliorer: querelle, situation*) to be sorted out; (*se débrouiller*): **s'~ pour que ...** to arrange things so that ...; **je vais m'~** I'll manage; **ça va s'~** it'll sort itself out; **s'~ pour faire** to make sure that *ou* see to it that one can do.
arrangeur [årånzhœr] *nm* (*MUS*) arranger.
arrestation [åreståsyôn] *nf* arrest.
arrêt [åre] *nm* stopping; (*de bus etc*) stop; (*JUR*) judgment, decision; (*FOOTBALL*) save; **~s** *nmpl* (*MIL*) arrest *sg*; **être à l'~** to be stopped, have come to a halt; **rester** *ou* **tomber en ~ devant** to stop short in front of; **sans ~** without stopping, non-stop; (*fréquemment*) continually; **~ d'autobus** bus stop; **~ facultatif** request stop; **~ de mort** death sentence; **~ de travail** stoppage (of work).
arrêté, e [åråtå] *a* (*idées*) firm, fixed ♦ *nm* order, decree; **~ municipal** ≈ bylaw, byelaw.
arrêter [åråtå] *vt* to stop; (*chauffage etc*) to turn off, switch off; (*COMM: compte*) to settle; (*COUTURE: point*) to fasten off; (*fixer: date etc*) to appoint, decide on; (*criminel, suspect*) to arrest; **s'~** *vi* to stop; (*s'interrompre*) to stop o.s.; **~ de faire** to stop doing; **arrête de te plaindre** stop complaining; **ne pas ~ de faire** to keep on doing; **s'~ de faire** to stop doing; **s'~ sur** (*suj: choix, regard*) to fall on.
arrhes [år] *nfpl* deposit *sg*.
arrière [åryer] *nm* back; (*SPORT*) fullback ♦ *a inv:* **siège/roue ~** back *ou* rear seat/wheel; **~s** *nmpl* (*fig*): **protéger ses ~s** to protect the rear; **à l'~** *ad* behind, at the back; **en ~** *ad* behind; (*regarder*) back, behind; (*tomber, aller*) backwards; **en ~ de** *prép* behind.
arriéré, e [åryårå] *a* (*péj*) backward ♦ *nm* (*d'argent*) arrears *pl*.
arrière-boutique [åryerbootēk] *nf* back shop.
arrière-cour [åryerkoor] *nf* backyard.
arrière-cuisine [åryerküēzēn] *nf* scullery.
arrière-garde [åryergård(ə)] *nf* rearguard.
arrière-goût [åryergoo] *nm* aftertaste.

arrière-grand-mère, _pl_ **arrière-grand-mères** [áryergráⁿmer] _nf_ great-grandmother.

arrière-grand-père, _pl_ **arrière-grands-pères** [áryergráⁿper] _nm_ great-grandfather.

arrière-grands-parents [áryergráⁿpáráⁿ] _nmpl_ great-grandparents.

arrière-pays [áryerpáē] _nm inv_ hinterland.

arrière-pensée [áryerpáⁿsã] _nf_ ulterior motive; _(doute)_ mental reservation.

arrière-petite-fille, _pl_ **arrière-petites-filles** [áryerpətētfēy] _nf_ great-granddaughter.

arrière-petit-fils, _pl_ **arrière-petits-fils** [áryerpətēfēs] _nm_ great-grandson.

arrière-petits-enfants [áryerpətēzáⁿfáⁿ] _nmpl_ great-grandchildren.

arrière-plan [áryerpláⁿ] _nm_ background; **d'~** _a (INFORM)_ background _cpd._

arriérer [áryārã]: **s'~** _vi (COMM)_ to fall into arrears.

arrière-saison [áryersezôⁿ] _nf_ late fall _(US)_ or autumn.

arrière-salle [áryersál] _nf_ back room.

arrière-train [áryertraⁿ] _nm_ hindquarters _pl._

arrimer [árēmã] _vt_ to stow; _(fixer)_ to secure, fasten securely.

arrivage [árēvázh] _nm_ arrival.

arrivant, e [árēváⁿ, -áⁿt] _nm/f_ newcomer.

arrivée [árēvã] _nf_ arrival; _(ligne d'arrivée)_ finish; **~ d'air/de gaz** air/gas inlet; **courrier à l'~** incoming mail; **à mon ~** when I arrived.

arriver [árēvã] _vi_ to arrive; _(survenir)_ to happen, occur; **j'arrive!** (I'm) just coming!; **il arrive à Paris à 8h** he gets to _ou_ arrives in Paris at 8; **~ à destination** to arrive at one's destination; **~ à** _(atteindre)_ to reach; **~ à (faire) qch** _(réussir)_ to manage (to do) sth; **~ à échéance** to fall due; **en ~ à faire** to end up doing, get to the point of doing; **il arrive que** it happens that; **il lui arrive de faire** he sometimes does.

arrivisme [árēvēsm(ə)] _nm_ ambition, ambitiousness.

arriviste [árēvēst(ə)] _nm/f_ go-getter.

arrogance [árogáⁿs] _nf_ arrogance.

arrogant, e [árogáⁿ, -áⁿt] _a_ arrogant.

arroger [ározhã]: **s'~** _vt_ to assume (without right); **s'~ le droit de ...** to assume the right to ....

arrondi, e [árôⁿdē] _a_ round ♦ _nm_ roundness.

arrondir [árôⁿdēr] _vt (forme, objet)_ to round; _(somme)_ to round off; **s'~** _vi_ to become round(ed); **~ ses fins de mois** to supplement one's pay.

arrondissement [árôⁿdēsmáⁿ] _nm (ADMIN)_ ≈ district.

arrosage [árōzázh] _nm_ watering; **tuyau d'~** hose(pipe).

arroser [árōzã] _vt_ to water; _(victoire etc)_ to celebrate (over a drink); _(CULIN)_ to baste.

arroseur [árōzœr] _nm (tourniquet)_ sprinkler.

arroseuse [árōzœz] _nf_ street cleaning truck.

arrosoir [árōzwár] _nm_ watering can.

arrt _abr =_ **arrondissement**.

arsenal, aux [ársənál, -ō] _nm (NAVIG)_ naval dockyard; _(MIL)_ arsenal; _(fig)_ gear, paraphernalia.

arsenic [ársənēk] _nm_ arsenic.

art [ár] _nm_ art; **avoir l'~ de faire** _(fig:_ personne)_ to have a talent for doing; **les ~s** the arts; **livre/critique d'~** art book/critic; **objet d'~** objet d'art; **~ dramatique** dramatic art; **~s et métiers** industrial _(US) ou_ applied _(Brit)_ arts and crafts; **~s ménagers** home economics _sg;_ **~s plastiques** plastic arts.

art. _abr =_ **article**.

artère [árter] _nf (ANAT)_ artery; _(rue)_ main road.

artériel, le [ártāryel] _a_ arterial.

artériosclérose [ártāryosklārōz] _nf_ arteriosclerosis.

arthrite [ártrēt] _nf_ arthritis.

arthrose [ártrōz] _nf_ (degenerative) osteoarthritis.

artichaut [ártēshō] _nm_ artichoke.

article [ártēkl(ə)] _nm_ article; _(COMM)_ item, article; _(INFORM)_ record, item; **faire l'~** _(COMM)_ to give one's sales pitch; **faire l'~ de** _(fig)_ to sing the praises of; **à l'~ de la mort** at the point of death; **~ défini/indéfini** definite/indefinite article; **~ de fond** _(PRESSE)_ feature article; **~s de bureau** office equipment; **~s de voyage** travel goods _ou_ items.

articulaire [ártēküler] _a_ of the joints, articular.

articulation [ártēkülásyôⁿ] _nf_ articulation; _(ANAT)_ joint.

articulé, e [ártēkülã] _a (membre)_ jointed; _(poupée)_ with moving joints.

articuler [ártēkülã] _vt_ to articulate; **s'~ (sur)** _(ANAT, TECH)_ to articulate (with); **s'~ autour de** _(fig)_ to center around _ou_ on, turn on.

artifice [ártēfēs] _nm_ device, trick.

artificiel, le [ártēfēsyel] _a_ artificial.

artificiellement [ártēfēsyelmáⁿ] _ad_ artificially.

artificier [ártēfēsyã] _nm_ pyrotechnist.

artificieux, euse [ártēfēsyœ̄, -œ̄z] _a_ guileful, deceitful.

artillerie [ártēyrē] _nf_ artillery, ordnance.

artilleur [ártēyœr] _nm_ artilleryman, gunner.

artisan [ártēzáⁿ] _nm_ artisan, (self-employed) craftsman; **l'~ de la victoire/du malheur** the architect of victory/of the disaster.

artisanal, e, aux [ártēzánál, -ō] _a_ of _ou_ made by craftsmen; _(péj)_ cottage industry _cpd_, unsophisticated.

artisanat [ártēzáná] _nm_ arts and crafts _pl._

artiste [ártēst(ə)] _nm/f_ artist; _(THÉÂTRE, MUS)_ artist, performer; _(: de variétés)_ entertainer.

artistique [ártēstēk] _a_ artistic.

artistiquement [ártēstēkmáⁿ] _ad_ artistically.

aryen, ne [áryaⁿ, -en] _a_ Aryan.

AS _sigle fpl (ADMIN) =_ **assurances sociales** ♦ _sigle f (SPORT) = Association sportive._

as _vb_ [á] _voir_ **avoir** ♦ _nm_ [ás] ace.

a/s _abr (= aux soins de)_ c/o.

ASBL _sigle f (= association sans but lucratif)_ non-profit-making organization.

asc. _abr =_ **ascenseur**.

ascendance [ásáⁿdáⁿs] _nf (origine)_ ancestry; _(ASTROLOGIE)_ ascendant.

ascendant, e [ásáⁿdáⁿ, -áⁿt] _a_ upward ♦ _nm_ influence; **~s** _nmpl_ ascendants.

ascenseur [ásáⁿsœr] _nm_ elevator _(US)_, lift _(Brit)._

ascension [ásáⁿsyôⁿ] _nf_ ascent; climb; **l'A~** _(REL)_ the Ascension; **(île de) l'A~** Ascension

Island.

ascète [áset] *nm/f* ascetic.

ascétisme [ásātēsm(ə)] *nm* asceticism.

ascorbique [áskorbēk] *a*: **acide ~** ascorbic acid.

ASE *sigle f* (= *Agence spatiale européenne*) ESA (= *European Space Agency*).

asepsie [ásepsē] *nf* asepsis.

aseptique [áseptēk] *a* aseptic.

aseptiser [áseptēzā] *vt* to sterilize; (*plaie*) to disinfect.

Asiate [ázyát] *nm/f* Asian.

asiatique [ázyátēk] *a* Asian, Asiatic ♦ *nm/f*: **A~** Asian.

Asie [ázē] *nf*: **l'~** Asia.

asile [ázēl] *nm* (*refuge*) refuge, sanctuary; (*POL*): **droit d'~** (political) asylum; (*pour malades, vieillards etc*) home; **accorder l'~ politique à qn** to grant *ou* give sb political asylum; **chercher/trouver ~ quelque part** to seek/find refuge somewhere.

asocial, e, aux [ásosyál, -ō] *a* antisocial.

aspect [áspe] *nm* appearance, look; (*fig*) aspect, side; (*LING*) aspect; **à l'~ de** at the sight of.

asperge [ásperzh(ə)] *nf* asparagus *q*.

asperger [ásperzhā] *vt* to spray, sprinkle.

aspérité [áspārētā] *nf* excrescence, protruding bit (of rock *etc*).

aspersion [áspersyôň] *nf* spraying, sprinkling.

asphalte [ásfált(ə)] *nm* asphalt.

asphyxie [ásfēksē] *nf* suffocation, asphyxia, asphyxiation.

asphyxier [ásfēksyā] *vt* to suffocate, asphyxiate; (*fig*) to stifle; **mourir asphyxié** to die of suffocation *ou* asphyxiation.

aspic [áspēk] *nm* (*ZOOL*) asp; (*CULIN*) aspic.

aspirant, e [áspēráň, -áňt] *a*: **pompe ~e** suction pump ♦ *nm* (*NAVIG*) midshipman.

aspirateur [áspērátœr] *nm* vacuum cleaner.

aspiration [áspērásyôň] *nf* inhalation; sucking (up); drawing up; **~s** *nfpl* (*ambitions*) aspirations.

aspirer [áspērā] *vt* (*air*) to inhale; (*liquide*) to suck (up); (*suj: appareil*) to suck *ou* draw up; **~ à** *vt* to aspire to.

aspirine [áspērēn] *nf* aspirin.

assagir [ásázhēr] *vt*, **s'~** *vi* to quieten down, sober down.

assaillant, e [ásàyáň, -àňt] *nm/f* assailant, attacker.

assaillir [ásàyēr] *vt* to assail, attack; **~ qn de** (*questions*) to assail *ou* bombard sb with.

assainir [ásānēr] *vt* to clean up; (*eau, air*) to purify.

assainissement [ásānēsmáň] *nm* cleaning up; purifying.

assaisonnement [ásezonmáň] *nm* seasoning.

assaisonner [ásezonā] *vt* to season; **bien assaisonné** highly seasoned.

assassin [ásásaň] *nm* murderer; assassin.

assassinat [ásásēnā] *nm* murder; assassination.

assassiner [ásásēnā] *vt* to murder; (*surtout POL*) to assassinate.

assaut [ásō] *nm* assault, attack; **prendre d'~** to (take by) storm, assault; **donner l'~ (à)** to attack; **faire ~ de** (*rivaliser*) to vie with *ou* rival each other in.

assèchement [áseshmáň] *nm* draining, drainage.

assécher [ásāshā] *vt* to drain.

ASSEDIC [ásādēk] *sigle f* (= *Association pour l'emploi dans l'industrie et le commerce*) unemployment insurance plan.

assemblage [ásáňblázh] *nm* assembling; (*MENUISERIE*) joint; **un ~ de** (*fig*) a collection of; **langage d'~** (*INFORM*) assembly language.

assemblée [ásáňblā] *nf* (*réunion*) meeting; (*public, assistance*) gathering; assembled people; (*POL*) assembly; (*REL*): **l'~ des fidèles** the congregation; **l'A~ nationale (AN)** the (French) National Assembly.

assembler [ásáňblā] *vt* (*joindre, monter*) to assemble, put together; (*amasser*) to gather (together), collect (together); **s'~** *vi* to gather, collect.

assembleur [ásáňblœr] *nm* assembler, fitter; (*INFORM*) assembler.

assener, asséner [ásánā] *vt*: **~ un coup à qn** to deal sb a blow.

assentiment [ásáňtēmáň] *nm* assent, consent; (*approbation*) approval.

asseoir [áswár] *vt* (*malade, bébé*) to sit up; (*personne debout*) to sit down; (*autorité, réputation*) to establish; **s'~** *vi* to sit (o.s.) up; to sit (o.s.) down; **faire ~ qn** to ask sb to sit down; **~ qch sur** to build sth on; (*appuyer*) to base sth on.

assermenté, e [ásermáňtā] *a* sworn, on oath.

assertion [ásersyôň] *nf* assertion.

asservir [áservēr] *vt* to subjugate, enslave.

assesseur [ásásœr] *nm* (*JUR*) assessor.

asseyais [áseye] *etc vb voir* **asseoir**.

assez [ásā] *ad* (*suffisamment*) enough, sufficiently; (*passablement*) rather, quite, fairly; **~!** enough!, that'll do!; **~/pas ~ cuit** well enough done/underdone; **est-il ~ fort/rapide?** is he strong/fast enough *ou* sufficiently strong/fast?; **il est passé ~ vite** he went past rather *ou* quite *ou* fairly fast; **~ de pain/livres** enough *ou* sufficient bread/books; **vous en avez ~?** have you got enough?; **en avoir ~ de qch** (*en être fatigué*) to have had enough of sth; **travailler ~** to work sufficiently (hard), work (hard) enough.

assidu, e [ásēdü] *a* assiduous, painstaking; (*régulier*) regular; **~ auprès de qn** attentive towards sb.

assiduité [ásēdüētā] *nf* assiduousness, painstaking; regularity; attentiveness; **~s** *nfpl* assiduous attentions.

assidûment [ásēdümáň] *ad* assiduously, painstakingly; attentively.

assied [ásyā] *etc vb voir* **asseoir**.

assiéger [ásyāzhā] *vt* to besiege, lay siege to; (*suj: foule, touristes*) to mob, besiege.

assiérai [ásyārā] *etc vb voir* **asseoir**.

assiette [ásyet] *nf* plate; (*contenu*) plate(ful); (*équilibre*) seat; (*de colonne*) seating; (*de navire*) trim; **~ anglaise** assorted cold meats; **~ creuse** (soup) dish, soup plate; **~ à dessert** dessert *ou* side plate; **~ de l'impôt** basis of (tax) assessment; **~ plate** (dinner) plate.

assiettée [ásyātā] *nf* plateful.

assignation [ásēňyásyôň] *nf* assignation; (*JUR*)

summons; (: *de témoin*) subpoena.
assigner [àsĕnyā] *vt*: ~ **qch à** to assign *ou*
allot sth to; (*valeur, importance*) to attach
sth to; (*somme*) to allocate sth to; (*limites*)
to set *ou* fix sth to; (*cause, effet*) to ascribe
ou attribute sth to; ~ **qn à** (*affecter*) to
assign sb to; ~ **qn à résidence** (*JUR*) to
place sb under house arrest.
assimilable [àsĕmēlàbl(ə)] *a* easily assimilated
ou absorbed.
assimilation [àsĕmēlàsyôñ] *nf* assimilation,
absorption.
assimiler [àsĕmēlā] *vt* to assimilate, absorb;
(*comparer*): ~ **qch/qn à** to liken *ou* compare
sth/sb to; ~ **vi** (*s'intégrer*) to be
assimilated *ou* absorbed; **ils sont assimilés
aux infirmières** (*ADMIN*) they are classed as
nurses.
assis, e [àsĕ, -ēz] *pp de* **asseoir** ♦ *a* sitting
(down), seated ♦ *nf* (*CONSTR*) course; (*GÉO*)
stratum (*pl* -a); (*fig*) basis (*pl* bases),
foundation; ~ **en tailleur** sitting cross-legged.
assises [àsēz] *nfpl* (*JUR*) assizes; (*congrès*)
(annual) conference.
assistanat [àsĕstáná] *nm* assistantship; (*à
l'université*) instructorship (*US*), lectureship
(*Brit*).
assistance [àsĕstâñs] *nf* (*public*) audience;
(*aide*) assistance; **porter** *ou* **prêter** ~ **à qn** to
give sb assistance; **A~ publique (AP)** *public
health service*; **enfant de l'A~ (publique)**
ward of the state; ~ **technique** technical aid.
assistant, e [àsĕstáñ, -âñt] *nm/f* assistant;
(*d'université*) instructor (*US*), lecturer
(*Brit*); **les** ~**s** *nmpl* (*auditeurs etc*) those
present; ~**e sociale** social worker.
assisté, e [àsĕstā] *a* (*AUTO*) power assisted ♦
nm/f person receiving aid from the State.
assister [àsĕstā] *vt* to assist; ~ **à** *vt* (*scène,
événement*) to witness; (*conférence, sémi-
naire*) to attend, be (present) at; (*spectacle,
match*) to be at, see.
association [àsosyâsyôñ] *nf* association;
(*COMM*) partnership; ~ **d'idées/images**
association of ideas/images.
associé, e [àsosyā] *nm/f* associate; (*COMM*)
partner.
associer [àsosyā] *vt* to associate; ~ **qn à**
(*profits*) to give sb a share of; (*affaire*) to
make sb a partner in; (*joie, triomphe*) to include sb in; ~ **qch à** (*joindre, allier*) to
combine sth with; **s'**~ *vi* to join together;
(*COMM*) to form a partnership ♦ *vt* (*collaborateur*) to take on (as a partner); **s'**~ **à** to be
combined with; (*opinions, joie de qn*) to
share in; **s'**~ **à** *ou* **avec qn pour faire** to join
(forces) *ou* join together with sb to do.
assoie [àswá] *etc vb voir* **asseoir**.
assoiffé, e [àswáfā] *a* thirsty; (*fig*): ~ **de**
(*sang*) thirsting for; (*gloire*) thirsting after.
assoirai [àswàrá], **assois** [àswá] *etc vb voir*
asseoir.
assolement [àsolmâñ] *nm* (systematic) rotation of crops.
assombrir [àsôñbrēr] *vt* to darken; (*fig*) to fill
with gloom; **s'**~ *vi* to darken; (*devenir
nuageux, fig: visage*) to cloud over; (*fig*) to
become gloomy.
assommer [àsomā] *vt* (*étourdir, abrutir*) to

knock out, stun; (*fam: ennuyer*) to bore stiff.
Assomption [àsôñpsyôñ] *nf*: **l'**~ the Assumption.
assorti, e [àsortē] *a* matched, matching;
fromages/légumes ~**s** assorted cheeses/
vegetables; ~ **à** matching; ~ **de**
accompanied with; (*conditions, conseils*)
coupled with; **bien/mal** ~ well/ill-matched.
assortiment [àsortēmáñ] *nm* (*choix*) assortment, selection; (*harmonie de couleurs, formes*) arrangement; (*COMM: lot, stock*) selection.
assortir [àsortēr] *vt* to match; **s'**~ to go well
together, match; ~ **qch à** to match sth with;
~ **qch de** to accompany sth with; **s'**~ **de** to
be accompanied by.
assoupi, e [àsōōpē] *a* dozing, sleeping; (*fig*)
(be)numbed; (*sens*) dulled.
assoupir [àsōōpēr]: **s'**~ *vi* (*personne*) to doze
off; (*sens*) to go numb.
assoupissement [àsōōpēsmáñ] *nm* (*sommeil*)
dozing; (*fig: somnolence*) drowsiness.
assouplir [àsōōplēr] *vt* to make supple, soften;
(*membres, corps*) to limber up, make supple;
(*fig*) to relax; (: *caractère*) to soften, make
more flexible; **s'**~ *vi* to soften; to limber up;
to relax; to become more flexible.
assouplissement [àsōōplēsmáñ] *nm* softening; limbering up; relaxation; **exercices d'**~
limbering up exercises.
assourdir [àsōōrdēr] *vt* (*bruit*) to deaden,
muffle; (*suj: bruit*) to deafen.
assourdissant, e [àsōōrdēsáñ, -âñt] *a* (*bruit*)
deafening.
assouvir [àsōōvēr] *vt* to satisfy, appease.
assoyais [àswáye] *etc vb voir* **asseoir**.
ASSU [àsü] *sigle f* = *Association du sport
scolaire et universitaire*.
assujetti, e [àsüzhātē] *a*: ~ **(à)** subject (to);
(*ADMIN*): ~ **à l'impôt** subject to tax(ation).
assujettir [àsüzhātēr] *vt* to subject, subjugate;
(*fixer: planches, tableau*) to secure, fix
securely; ~ **qn à** (*règle, impôt*) to subject sb
to.
assujettissement [àsüzhātēsmáñ] *nm* subjection, subjugation.
assumer [àsümā] *vt* (*fonction, emploi*) to
assume, take on; (*accepter: conséquence,
situation*) to accept.
assurance [àsürâñs] *nf* (*certitude*) assurance;
(*confiance en soi*) (self-)confidence; (*contrat*)
insurance (policy); (*secteur commercial*) insurance; **prendre une** ~ **contre** to take out
insurance *ou* an insurance policy against; ~
contre l'incendie fire insurance; ~ **contre le
vol** insurance against theft; **société d'**~,
compagnie d'~**s** insurance company; ~
maladie (AM) health insurance; ~ **au tiers**
third party insurance; ~ **tous risques**
(*AUTO*) comprehensive insurance; ~**s
sociales (AS)** ≈ Social Security (*US*), ≈
National Insurance (*Brit*).
assurance-vie, *pl* **assurances-vie** [àsürâñsvē]
nf life insurance *ou* assurance (*Brit*).
assurance-vol, *pl* **assurances-vol** [àsürâñsvol]
nf insurance against theft.
assuré, e [àsürā] *a* (*victoire etc*) certain, sure;
(*démarche, voix*) assured, (self-)confident;
(*certain*): ~ **de** confident of; (*ASSURANCES*)

insured ♦ *nm/f* insured (person); ~ **social** ≈ member of the Social Security plan (*US*) *ou* National Insurance scheme (*Brit*).
assurément [àsürámáɲ] *ad* assuredly, most certainly.
assurer [àsürá] *vt* (*COMM*) to insure; (*stabiliser*) to steady, stabilize; (*victoire etc*) to ensure, make certain; (*frontières, pouvoir*) to make secure; (*service, garde*) to provide, operate; ~ **qch à qn** (*garantir*) to secure *ou* guarantee sth for sb; (*certifier*) to assure sb of sth; ~ **à qn que** to assure sb that; **je vous assure que non/si** I assure you that that is not the case/is the case; ~ **qn de** to assure sb of; ~ **ses arrières** (*fig*) to be sure one has something to fall back on; **s'~ (contre)** (*COMM*) to insure o.s. (against); **s'~ de/que** (*vérifier*) to make sure of/that: **s'~ (de)** (*aide de qn*) to secure; **s'~ sur la vie** to take out a life insurance; **s'~ le concours/la collaboration de qn** to secure sb's aid/collaboration.
assureur [àsürœr] *nm* insurance agent; (*société*) insurers *pl*.
Assyrie [àsērē] *nf*: **l'~** Assyria.
assyrien, ne [àsēryàn, -en] *a* Assyrian.
astérisque [àstārēsk(ə)] *nm* asterisk.
asthmatique [àsmátēk] *a* asthmatic.
asthme [àsm(ə)] *nm* asthma.
asticot [àstēkō] *nm* maggot.
astigmate [àstēgmát] *a* (*MÉD*: *personne*) astigmatic, having an astigmatism.
astiquer [àstēká] *vt* to polish, shine.
astrakan [àstrákáɲ] *nm* astrakhan.
astral, e, aux [àstrál, -ō] *a* astral.
astre [àstr(ə)] *nm* star.
astreignant, e [àstrenyàɲ, -áɲt] *a* demanding.
astreindre [àstràɲdr(ə)] *vt*: ~ **qn à qch** to force sth upon sb; ~ **qn à faire** to compel *ou* force sb to do; **s'~ à** to compel *ou* force o.s. to.
astringent, e [àstrànžáɲ, -áɲt] *a* astringent.
astrologie [àstrolozhē] *nf* astrology.
astrologique [àstrolozhēk] *a* astrological.
astrologue [àstrolog] *nm/f* astrologer.
astronaute [àstronōt] *nm/f* astronaut.
astronome [àstronom] *nm/f* astronomer.
astronomie [àstronomē] *nf* astronomy.
astronomique [àstronomēk] *a* astronomic(al).
astrophysicien, ne [àstrofēzēsyàɲ, -en] *nm/f* astrophysicist.
astuce [àstüs] *nf* shrewdness, astuteness; (*truc*) trick, clever way; (*plaisanterie*) wisecrack.
astucieusement [àstüsyēzmáɲ] *ad* shrewdly, cleverly, astutely.
astucieux, euse [àstüsyœ̄. -ēz] *a* shrewd, clever, astute.
asymétrique [àsēmātrēk] *a* asymmetric(al).
AT *sigle m* (= *Ancien Testament*) OT.
atavisme [àtávēsm(ə)] *nm* atavism, heredity.
atelier [àtəlyá] *nm* workshop; (*de peintre*) studio.
atermoiements [àtermwámáɲ] *nmpl* procrastination *sg*.
atermoyer [àtermwàyá] *vi* to temporize, procrastinate.
athée [àtá] *a* atheistic ♦ *nm/f* atheist.
athéisme [àtáēsm(ə)] *nm* atheism.

Athènes [áten] *n* Athens.
athénien, ne [àtānyàɲ. -en] *a* Athenian.
athlète [átlet] *nm/f* (*SPORT*) athlete; (*costaud*) muscleman.
athlétique [átlātēk] *a* athletic.
athlétisme [àtlātēsm(ə)] *nm* athletics *sg*; **faire de l'~** to do athletics; **tournoi d'~** athletics meet (*US*) *ou* meeting (*Brit*).
Atlantide [átláɲtēd] *nf*: **l'~** Atlantis.
atlantique [àtláɲtēk] *a* Atlantic ♦ *nm*: **l'(océan) A~** the Atlantic (Ocean).
atlantiste [àtláɲtēst(ə)] *a*, *nm/f* Atlanticist.
Atlas [átlâs] *nm*: **l'~** the Atlas Mountains.
atlas [átlâs] *nm* atlas.
atmosphère [átmosfer] *nf* atmosphere.
atmosphérique [àtmosfārēk] *a* atmospheric.
atoll [àtol] *nm* atoll.
atome [àtōm] *nm* atom.
atomique [àtomēk] *a* atomic, nuclear; (*usine*) nuclear; (*nombre, masse*) atomic.
atomiseur [àtomēzœr] *nm* atomizer.
atomiste [àtomēst(ə)] *nm/f* (*aussi*: **savant, ingénieur** *etc* ~) atomic scientist.
atone [àton] *a* lifeless; (*LING*) unstressed, unaccented.
atours [àtōōr] *nmpl* attire *sg*, finery *sg*.
atout [àtōō] *nm* trump; (*fig*) asset; (: *plus fort*) trump card; **"~ pique/trèfle"** "spades/clubs are trumps".
ATP *sigle f* (= *Association des tennismen professionnels*) ATP (= *Association of Tennis Professionals*) ♦ *sigle mpl* (= *arts et traditions populaires*): **musée des ~** ≈ folk museum.
âtre [âtr(ə)] *nm* hearth.
atroce [àtros] *a* atrocious, horrible.
atrocement [àtrosmáɲ] *ad* atrociously, horribly.
atrocité [àtrosētá] *nf* atrocity.
atrophie [átrofē] *nf* atrophy.
atrophier [átrofyá]: **s'~** *vi* to atrophy.
atropine [àtropēn] *nf* (*CHIMIE*) atropine.
attabler [átáblá]: **s'~** *vi* to sit down at (the) table; **s'~ à la terrasse** to sit down (at a table) on the terrace.
attachant, e [átásháɲ. -áɲt] *a* engaging, likeable.
attache [àtásh] *nf* clip, fastener; (*fig*) tie; ~**s** *nfpl* (*relations*) connections; **à l'~** (*chien*) tied up.
attaché, e [átáshá] *a*: **être ~ à** (*aimer*) to be attached to ♦ *nm* (*ADMIN*) attaché; ~ **de presse/d'ambassade** press/embassy attaché; ~ **commercial** commercial attaché.
attaché-case [àtáshākez] *nm inv* attaché case, briefcase.
attachement [àtáshmáɲ] *nm* attachment.
attacher [átáshá] *vt* to tie up; (*étiquette*) to attach, tie on; (*souliers*) to tie ♦ *vi* (*poêle, riz*) to stick; **s'~** (*robe etc*) to button up; **s'~ à** (*par affection*) to become attached to; **s'~ à faire qch** to endeavor to do sth; ~ **qch à** to tie *ou* fasten *ou* attach sth to; ~ **qn à** (*fig*: *lier*) to attach sb to; ~ **du prix/de l'importance à** to attach great value/attach importance to.
attaquant [átákáɲ] *nm* (*MIL*) attacker; (*SPORT*) striker, forward.
attaque [àták] *nf* attack; (*cérébrale*) stroke;

(*d'épilepsie*) fit; **être/se sentir d'~** to be/feel in top form; **~ à main armée** armed attack.

attaquer [àtàkā] *vt* to attack; (*en justice*) to bring an action against, sue; (*travail*) to tackle, set about ♦ *vi* to attack; **s'~ à** to attack; (*épidémie, misère*) to tackle, attack.

attardé, e [àtárdā] *a* (*passants*) late; (*enfant*) backward; (*conceptions*) old-fashioned.

attarder [àtárdā]: **s'~** *vi* (*sur qch, en chemin*) to linger; (*chez qn*) to stay on.

atteignais [àtānyc] *etc vb voir* **atteindre**.

atteindre [àtaɴdr(ə)] *vt* to reach; (*blesser*) to hit; (*contacter*) to reach, contact, get in touch with; (*émouvoir*) to affect.

atteint, e [àtaɴ, -aɴt] *pp de* **atteindre** ♦ *a* (*MÉD*): **être ~ de** to be suffering from ♦ *nf* attack; **hors d'~e** out of reach; **porter ~e à** to strike a blow at, undermine.

attelage [àtlàzh] *nm* (*de remorque etc*) (trailer) hitch (*US*), coupling (*Brit*); (*animaux*) team; (*harnachement*) harness; (: *de bœufs*) yoke.

atteler [àtlā] *vt* (*cheval, bœufs*) to hitch up; (*wagons*) to couple; **s'~ à** (*travail*) to buckle down to.

attelle [àtɛl] *nf* splint.

attenant, e [àtnáɴ, -àɴt] *a*: **~ (à)** adjoining.

attendant [àtáɴdáɴ]: **en ~** *ad* (*dans l'intervalle*) meanwhile, in the meantime.

attendre [àtáɴdr(ə)] *vt* to wait for; (*être destiné ou réservé à*) to await, be in store for ♦ *vi* to wait; **je n'attends plus rien (de la vie)** I expect nothing more (from life); **attendez que je réfléchisse** wait while I think; **s'~ à (ce que)** (*escompter*) to expect (that); **je ne m'y attendais pas** I didn't expect that; **ce n'est pas ce à quoi je m'attendais** that's not what I expected; **~ un enfant** to be expecting a baby; **~ de pied ferme** to wait determinedly; **~ de faire/d'être** to wait until one does/is; **~ que** to wait until; **~ qch de** to expect sth of; **faire ~ qn** to keep sb waiting; **se faire ~** to keep people (*ou us etc*) waiting; **en attendant** *ad voir* **attendant**.

attendri, e [àtáɴdrē] *a* tender.

attendrir [àtáɴdrēr] *vt* to move (to pity); (*viande*) to tenderize; **s'~ (sur)** to be moved *ou* touched (by).

attendrissant, e [àtáɴdrēsáɴ, -àɴt] *a* moving, touching.

attendrissement [àtáɴdrēsmáɴ] *nm* (*tendre*) emotion; (*apitoyé*) pity.

attendrisseur [àtáɴdrēsœr] *nm* tenderizer.

attendu, e [àtáɴdü] *pp de* **attendre** ♦ *a* long-awaited; (*prévu*) expected ♦ *nm*: **~s** *reasons adduced for a judgment*; **~ que** *cj* considering that, since.

attentat [àtáɴtá] *nm* (*contre une personne*) assassination attempt; (*contre un bâtiment*) attack; **~ à la bombe** bomb attack; **~ à la pudeur** (*exhibitionnisme*) indecent exposure *q*; (*agression*) indecent assault *q*.

attente [àtáɴt] *nf* wait; (*espérance*) expectation; **contre toute ~** contrary to (all) expectations.

attenter [àtáɴtā]: **~ à** *vt* (*liberté*) to violate; **~ à la vie de qn** to make an attempt on sb's life; **~ à ses jours** to make an attempt on one's life.

attentif, ive [àtáɴtēf, -ēv] *a* (*auditeur*) attentive; (*soin*) scrupulous; (*travail*) careful; **~ à** paying attention to; (*devoir*) mindful of; **~ à faire** careful to do.

attention [àtáɴsyôɴ] *nf* attention; (*prévenance*) attention, thoughtfulness *q*; **mériter ~** to be worthy of attention; **à l'~ de** for the attention of; **porter qch à l'~ de qn** to bring sth to sb's attention; **attirer l'~ de qn sur qch** to draw sb's attention to sth; **faire ~ (à)** to be careful (of); **faire ~ (à ce) que** to be *ou* make sure that; **~!** careful!, watch!, watch out!; **~, si vous ouvrez cette lettre** (*sanction*) just watch out, if you open that letter; **~, respectez les consignes de sécurité** be sure to observe the safety instructions.

attentionné, e [àtáɴsyonā] *a* thoughtful, considerate.

attentisme [àtáɴtēsm(ə)] *nm* wait-and-see policy.

attentiste [àtáɴtēst(ə)] *a* (*politique*) wait-and-see ♦ *nm/f* believer in a wait-and-see policy.

attentivement [àtáɴtēvmáɴ] *ad* attentively.

atténuant, e [àtānüáɴ, -áɴt] *a*: **circonstances ~es** extenuating circumstances.

atténuer [àtānüā] *vt* to alleviate, ease; (*diminuer*) to lessen; (*amoindrir*) to mitigate the effects of; **s'~** *vi* to ease; (*violence etc*) to abate.

atterrer [àtārā] *vt* to dismay, appal(l).

atterrir [àtārēr] *vi* to land.

atterrissage [àtārēsàzh] *nm* landing; **~ sur le ventre/sans visibilité/forcé** belly/blind/forced landing.

attestation [àtestàsyôɴ] *nf* certificate, testimonial; **~ médicale** doctor's certificate.

attester [àtestā] *vt* to testify to, vouch for; (*démontrer*) to attest, testify to; **~ que** to testify that.

attiédir [àtyādēr]: **s'~** *vi* to become lukewarm; (*fig*) to cool down.

attifé, e [àtēfā] *a* (*fam*) decked out.

attifer [àtēfā] *vt* to deck out.

attique [àtēk] *nm*: **appartement en ~** penthouse (apartment (*US*) *ou* flat (*Brit*)).

attirail [àtēráy] *nm* gear; (*péj*) paraphernalia.

attirance [àtēráɴs] *nf* attraction; (*séduction*) lure.

attirant, e [àtēráɴ, -áɴt] *a* attractive, appealing.

attirer [àtērā] *vt* to attract; (*appâter*) to lure, entice; **~ qn dans un coin/vers soi** to draw sb into a corner/towards one; **~ l'attention de qn** to attract sb's attention; **~ l'attention de qn sur qch** to draw sb's attention to sth; **~ des ennuis à qn** to make trouble for sb; **s'~ des ennuis** to bring trouble upon o.s., get into trouble.

attiser [àtēzā] *vt* (*feu*) to poke (up), stir up; (*fig*) to fan the flame of, stir up.

attitré, e [àtētrā] *a* qualified; (*agréé*) accredited, appointed.

attitude [àtētüd] *nf* attitude; (*position du corps*) bearing.

attouchements [àtōōshmáɴ] *nmpl* touching *sg*; (*sexuels*) fondling *sg*, stroking *sg*.

attraction [àtràksyôɴ] *nf* attraction; (*de cabaret, cirque*) number.

attrait [àtrɛ] *nm* appeal, attraction; (*plus fort*)

lure; **~s** *nmpl* attractions; **éprouver de l'~ pour** to be attracted to.

attrape [átráp] *nf voir* **farce**.

attrape-nigaud [átrápnēgō] *nm* con.

attraper [átrápā] *vt* to catch; (*habitude, amende*) to get, pick up; (*fam: duper*) to con.

attrayant, e [átreyáń, -áńt] *a* attractive.

attribuer [átrēbüā] *vt* (*prix*) to award; (*rôle, tâche*) to allocate, assign; (*imputer*): **~ qch à** to attribute sth to, ascribe sth to, put sth down to; **s'~** *vt* (*s'approprier*) to claim for o.s.

attribut [átrēbü] *nm* attribute; (*LING*) complement.

attribution [átrēbüsyóń] *nf* (*voir* **attribuer**) awarding; allocation, assignment; attribution; **~s** *nfpl* (*compétence*) attributions; **complément d'~** (*LING*) indirect object.

attrister [átrēstā] *vt* to sadden; **s'~ de qch** to be saddened by sth.

attroupement [átrōōpmáń] *nm* crowd, mob.

attrouper [átrōōpā]: **s'~** *vi* to gather.

au [ō] *prép* + *dét voir* **à**.

aubade [ōbád] *nf* dawn serenade.

aubaine [ōben] *nf* godsend; (*financière*) windfall; (*COMM*) bonanza.

aube [ōb] *nf* dawn, daybreak; (*REL*) alb; **à l'~** at dawn *ou* daybreak; **à l'~ de** (*fig*) at the dawn of.

aubépine [ōbāpēn] *nf* hawthorn.

auberge [ōberzh(ə)] *nf* inn; **~ de jeunesse** youth hostel.

aubergine [ōbärzhēn] *nf* eggplant, aubergine.

aubergiste [ōberzhēst(ə)] *nm/f* inn-keeper, hotel-keeper.

auburn [ōbœrn] *a inv* auburn.

aucun, e [ōkœn, -ün] *dét* no, *tournure négative* + any; (*positif*) any ♦ *pronom* none, *tournure négative* + any; (*positif*) any(one); **il n'y a ~ livre** there isn't any book, there is no book; **je n'en vois ~ qui** I can't see any which, I (can) see none which; **~ homme** no man; **sans ~ doute** without any doubt; **sans ~e hésitation** without hesitation; **plus qu'~ autre** more than any other; **plus qu'~ de ceux qui** ... more than any of those who ...; **en ~e façon** in no way at all; **~ des deux** neither of the two; **~ d'entre eux** none of them; **d'~s** (*certains*) some.

aucunement [ōkünmáń] *ad* in no way, not in the least.

audace [ōdás] *nf* daring, boldness; (*péj*) audacity; **il a eu l'~ de** ... he had the audacity to ...; **vous ne manquez pas d'~!** you're not lacking in nerve *ou* cheek!

audacieux, euse [ōdásyœ, -œz] *a* daring, bold.

au-dedans [ōdədáń] *ad, prép* inside.

au-dehors [ōdəor] *ad, prép* outside.

au-delà [ōdlà] *ad* beyond ♦ *nm*: **l'~** the hereafter; **~ de** *prép* beyond.

au-dessous [ōdsōō] *ad* underneath; below; **~ de** *prép* under(neath), below; (*limite, somme etc*) below, under; (*dignité, condition*) below.

au-dessus [ōdsü] *ad* above; **~ de** *prép* above.

au-devant [ōdváń]: **~ de** *prép*: **aller ~ de** to go (out) and meet; (*souhaits de qn*) to anticipate.

audible [ōdēbl(ə)] *a* audible.

audience [ōdyáńs] *nf* audience; (*JUR: séance*) hearing; **trouver ~ auprès de** to arouse much interest among, get the (interested) attention of.

audiogramme [ōdyográm] *nm* audiogram (*US*), audiogramme (*Brit*).

audio-visuel, le [ōdyovēzüel] *a* audio-visual ♦ *nm* (*équipement*) audio-visual aids *pl*; (*méthodes*) audio-visual methods *pl*; **l'~** radio and television.

auditeur, trice [ōdētœr, -trēs] *nm/f* (*à la radio*) listener; (*à une conférence*) member of the audience, listener; **~ libre** auditor (*US*), unregistered student (*attending lectures*).

auditif, ive [ōdētēf, -ēv] (*mémoire*) auditory; **appareil ~** hearing aid.

audition [ōdēsyóń] *nf* (*ouïe, écoute*) hearing; (*JUR: de témoins*) examination; (*MUS, THÉÂTRE: épreuve*) audition.

auditionner [ōdēsyonā] *vt, vi* to audition.

auditoire [ōdētwár] *nm* audience.

auditorium [ōdētoryom] *nm* (*public*) studio.

auge [ōzh] *nf* trough.

augmentation [ogmáńtâsyóń] *nf* (*action*) increasing; raising; (*résultat*) increase; **~ (de salaire)** (pay) raise (*US*), rise (in salary) (*Brit*).

augmenter [ogmáńtā] *vt* to increase; (*salaire, prix*) to increase, raise, put up; (*employé*) to increase the salary of, give a (pay) raise (*US*) *ou* (salary) rise (*Brit*) to ♦ *vi* to increase; **~ de poids/volume** to gain (in) weight/volume.

augure [ogür] *nm* soothsayer, oracle; **de bon/mauvais ~** of good/ill omen.

augurer [ogürā] *vt*: **~ qch de** to foresee sth (coming) from *ou* out of; **~ bien de** to augur well for.

auguste [ogüst(ə)] *a* august, noble, majestic.

aujourd'hui [ōzhōōrdüē] *ad* today; **~ en huit/quinze** a week/two weeks from now *ou* from today; **à dater** *ou* **partir d'~** from today('s date).

aumône [omōn] *nf* alms *sg* (*pl inv*); **faire l'~ (à qn)** to give alms (to sb); **faire l'~ de qch à qn** (*fig*) to favor sb with sth.

aumônerie [omōnrē] *nf* chaplaincy.

aumônier [omōnyā] *nm* chaplain.

auparavant [ōpáráváń] *ad* before(hand).

auprès [ōpre]: **~ de** *prép* next to, close to; (*recourir, s'adresser*) to; (*en comparaison de*) compared with, next to; (*dans l'opinion de*) in the opinion of.

auquel [ōkel] *prép* + *pronom voir* **lequel**.

aurai [orā] *etc vb voir* **avoir**.

auréole [orāol] *nf* halo; (*tache*) ring.

auréolé, e [orāolā] *a* (*fig*): **~ de gloire** crowned with *ou* in glory.

auriculaire [orēküler] *nm* little finger.

aurore [oror] *nf* dawn, daybreak; **~ boréale** northern lights *pl*.

ausculter [oskültā] *vt* to sound.

auspices [ospēs] *nmpl*: **sous les ~ de** under the patronage *ou* auspices of; **sous de bons/mauvais ~** under favorable/unfavorable auspices.

aussi [ōsē] *ad* (*également*) also, too; (*de comparaison*) as ♦ *cj* therefore, consequently; **~ fort que** as strong as; **lui ~** (*sujet*) he too;

(objet) him too; ~ **bien que** *(de même que)* as well as.

aussitôt [ōsētō] *ad* straight away, immediately; ~ **que** as soon as; ~ **envoyé** as soon as it is *(ou* was) sent; ~ **fait** no sooner done.

austère [oster] *a* austere; *(sévère)* stern.

austérité [ostārētā] *nf* austerity; **plan/budget d'~** austerity plan/budget.

austral, e [ostrál] *a* southern; **l'océan A~** the Antarctic Ocean; **les Terres A~es** Antarctica.

Australie [ostrálē] *nf:* **l'~** Australia.

australien, ne [ostrályań, -en] *a* Australian ♦ *nm/f:* **A~, ne** Australian.

autant [ōtáń] *ad* so much; *(comparatif):* ~ **(que)** as much (as); *(nombre)* as many (as); ~ **(de)** so much *(ou* many); as much *(ou* many); **n'importe qui aurait pu en faire** ~ anyone could have done the same *ou* as much; ~ **partir** we *(ou* you *etc)* may as well leave; ~ **ne rien dire** best not say anything; ~ **dire que** ... one might as well say that ...; **fort** ~ **que courageux** as strong as he is brave; **il n'est pas découragé pour** ~ he isn't discouraged for all that; **pour** ~ **que** *cj* assuming, as long as; **d'~** accordingly, in proportion; **d'~ plus/mieux (que)** all the more/the better (since).

autarcie [ōtársē] *nf* autarky, self-sufficiency.

autel [otel] *nm* altar.

auteur [ōtœr] *nm* author; **l'~ de cette remarque** the person who said that; **droit d'~** copyright.

authenticité [otáńtēsētā] *nf* authenticity.

authentifier [otáńtēfyā] *vt* to authenticate.

authentique [otáńtēk] *a* authentic, genuine.

auto [otō] *nf* car; ~**s tamponneuses** bumper cars, dodgems.

auto... [otō] *préfixe* auto..., self-.

autobiographie [otobyográfē] *nf* autobiography.

autobiographique [otobyográfēk] *a* autobiographical.

autobus [otobüs] *nm* bus.

autocar [otokár] *nm* bus, coach *(Brit)*.

autochtone [otokton] *nm/f* native.

autocollant, e [otokoláń, -áńt] *a* self-adhesive; *(enveloppe)* self-seal ♦ *nm* sticker.

auto-couchettes [otokōōshet] *a inv:* **train** ~ car sleeper train, motorail ® train *(Brit)*.

autocratique [otokrátēk] *a* autocratic.

autocritique [otokrētēk] *nf* self-criticism.

autocuiseur [otokwēzœr] *nm (CULIN)* pressure cooker.

autodéfense [otodáfáńs] *nf* self-defence; **groupe d'~** vigilante committee.

autodétermination [otodātermēnâsyóń] *nf* self-determination.

autodidacte [otodēdákt(ə)] *nm/f* self-taught person.

autodiscipline [otodēsēplēn] *nf* self-discipline.

autodrome [otodrōm] *nm* motor-racing stadium.

auto-école [otoákol] *nf* driving school.

autofinancement [otofēnáńsmáń] *nm* self-financing.

autogéré, e [otozhārā] *a* self-managed, managed internally.

autographe [otográf] *nm* autograph.

autoguidé, e [otogēdā] *a* self-guided.

automate [otomát] *nm (robot)* automaton; *(machine)* (automatic) machine.

automatique [otomátēk] *a, nm* automatic; **l'~** *(TÉL)* ≈ direct dialling.

automatiquement [otomátēkmáń] *ad* automatically.

automatiser [otomátēzā] *vt* to automate.

automatisme [otomátēsm(ə)] *nm* automatism.

automédication [otomādēkásyóń] *nf* self-medication.

automitrailleuse [otomētráyœz] *nf* armored *(US)* ou armoured *(Brit)* car.

automnal, e, aux [otonál, -ō] *a* autumnal.

automne [oton] *nm* fall *(US)*, autumn.

automobile [otomobēl] *a* motor *cpd* ♦ *nf* (motor) car; **l'~** motoring; *(industrie)* the car *ou* automobile *(US)* industry.

automobiliste [otomobēlēst(ə)] *nm/f* motorist.

autonettoyant, e [otonetwáyáń, -áńt] *a:* **four** ~ self-cleaning oven.

autonome [otonom] *a* autonomous; *(INFORM)* stand-alone; **(en mode)** ~ off line.

autonomie [otonomē] *nf* autonomy; *(POL)* self-government, autonomy; ~ **de vol** range.

autoportrait [otoportre] *nm* self-portrait.

autopsie [otopsē] *nf* post-mortem (examination), autopsy.

autopsier [otopsyā] *vt* to carry out a post-mortem *ou* an autopsy on.

autoradio [otorádyō] *nf* car radio.

autorail [otoráy] *nm* railcar.

autorisation [otorēzásyóń] *nf* permission, authorization; *(papiers)* permit; **donner à qn l'~ de** to give sb permission to, authorize sb to; **avoir l'~ de faire** to be allowed *ou* have permission to do, be authorized to do.

autorisé, e [otorēzā] *a (opinion, sources)* authoritative; *(permis):* ~ **à faire** authorized *ou* permitted to do; **dans les milieux ~s** in official circles.

autoriser [otorēzā] *vt* to give permission for, authorize; *(fig)* to allow (of), sanction; ~ **qn à faire** to give permission to sb to do, authorize sb to do.

autoritaire [otorēter] *a* authoritarian.

autoritarisme [otorētárēsm(ə)] *nm* authoritarianism.

autorité [otorētā] *nf* authority; **faire** ~ to be authoritative; **~s constituées** constitutional authorities.

autoroute [otorōōt] *nf* expressway *(US)*, motorway *(Brit)*.

autoroutier, ière [otorōōtyā, -yer] *a* expressway *cpd (US)*, motorway *cpd (Brit)*.

autosatisfaction [otosátēsfáksyóń] *nf* self-satisfaction.

auto-stop [otostop] *nm:* **l'~** hitch-hiking; **faire de l'~** to hitch-hike; **prendre qn en** ~ to give sb a lift.

auto-stoppeur, euse [otostopœr, -œz] *nm/f* hitch-hiker.

autosuffisant, e [otosüfēzáń, -áńt] *a* self-sufficient.

autosuggestion [otosügzhestyóń] *nf* auto-suggestion.

autour [ōtōōr] *ad* around; ~ **de** *prép* around; *(environ)* around, about; **tout** ~ *ad* all around.

autre [ōtr(ə)] *a* other; **un ~ verre** (*supplémentaire*) one more glass, another glass; (*différent*) another glass, a different glass; **un ~** another (one); **l'~** the other (one); **les ~s** (*autrui*) others; **l'un et l'~** both (of them); **se détester** *etc* **l'un l'~/les uns les ~s** to hate *etc* each other/one another; **ni l'un ni l'~** neither (one) of them; **d'une semaine à l'~** from one week to the next; (*incessamment*) any week now; **de temps à ~** from time to time; **d'~s** others; **d'~s verres** other glasses; **j'en ai vu d'~s** I've seen worse; **à d'~s!** tell that to the marines!; **se sentir ~** to feel different; **la difficulté est ~** the difficulty is not there, that's not the difficulty; **~ chose** something else; **~ part** *ad* somewhere else; **d'~ part** *ad* on the other hand; **entre ~s** (*gens*) among others; (*choses*) among other things; **nous/vous ~s** us/you.

autrefois [ōtrəfwà] *ad* in the past.

autrement [ōtrəmåṅ] *ad* differently; (*d'une manière différente*) in another way; (*sinon*) otherwise; **je n'ai pas pu faire ~** I couldn't do anything else, I couldn't do otherwise; **~ dit** in other words; (*c'est-à-dire*) that is to say.

Autriche [ōtrēsh] *nf*: **l'~** Austria.

autrichien, ne [ōtrēshyaṅ, -en] *a* Austrian ♦ *nm/f*: **A~, ne** Austrian.

autruche [ōtrüsh] *nf* ostrich; **faire l'~** (*fig*) to bury one's head in the sand.

autrui [ōtrüē] *pronom* others.

auvent [ōvåṅ] *nm* canopy.

auvergnat, e [overnyà, -àt] *a* of *ou* from the Auvergne.

Auvergne [overny(ə)] *nf*: **l'~** the Auvergne.

aux [ō] *prép* + *dét voir* **à.**

auxiliaire [oksēlyer] *a*, *nm/f* auxiliary.

auxquels, auxquelles [ōkel] *prép* + *pronom voir* **lequel.**

AV *sigle m* (*BANQUE*: = *avis de virement*) advice of bank transfer ♦ *abr* (*AUTO*) = **avant.**

av. *abr* (= *avenue*) Av(e).

avachi, e [àvàshē] *a* limp, flabby; (*chaussure, vêtement*) out-of-shape; (*personne*): **~ sur qch** slumped on *ou* across sth.

avais [àve] *etc vb voir* **avoir.**

aval [àvàl] *nm* (*accord*) endorsement, backing; (*GÉO*): **en ~** downstream, downriver; (*sur une pente*) downhill; **en ~ de** downstream *ou* downriver from; downhill from.

avalanche [àvàlåṅsh] *nf* avalanche; **~ poudreuse** powder snow avalanche.

avaler [àvàlā] *vt* to swallow.

avaliser [àvàlēzā] *vt* (*plan, entreprise*) to back, support; (*COMM, JUR*) to guarantee.

avance [àvåṅs] *nf* (*de troupes etc*) advance; (*progrès*) progress; (*d'argent*) advance; (*opposé à retard*) lead; being ahead of schedule; **~s** *nfpl* overtures; (*amoureuses*) advances; **une ~ de 300 m/4 h** (*SPORT*) a 300 m/4 hour lead; (**être**) **en ~** (to be) early; (*sur un programme*) (to be) ahead of schedule; **on n'est pas en ~!** we're kind of late!; **être en ~ sur qn** to be ahead of sb; **d'~, à l'~, par ~** in advance; **~ (du) papier**

(*INFORM*) paper advance.

avancé, e [àvåṅsā] *a* advanced; (*travail etc*) well on, well under way; (*fruit, fromage*) overripe ♦ *nf* projection; overhang; **il est ~ pour son âge** he is advanced for his age.

avancement [àvåṅsmåṅ] *nm* (*professionnel*) promotion; (*de travaux*) progress.

avancer [àvåṅsā] *vi* to move forward, advance; (*projet, travail*) to make progress; (*être en saillie*) to overhang; to project; (*montre, réveil*) to be fast; (*: d'habitude*) to gain ♦ *vt* to move forward, advance; (*argent*) to advance; (*montre, pendule*) to put forward; (*faire progresser: travail etc*) to advance, move on; **s'~** *vi* to move forward, advance; (*fig*) to commit o.s.; (*faire saillie*) to overhang; to project; **j'avance** (**d'une heure**) I'm (an hour) fast.

avanies [àvànē] *nfpl* insults.

avant [àvåṅ] *prép* before ♦ *ad*: **trop/plus ~** too far/further forward ♦ *a inv*: **siège/roue ~** front seat/wheel ♦ *nm* front; (*SPORT*: *joueur*) forward; **~ qu'il parte/de partir** before he leaves/leaving; **~ qu'il (ne) pleuve** before it rains (*ou* rained); **~ tout** (*surtout*) above all; **à l'~** (*dans un véhicule*) in (the) front; **en ~** *ad* forward(s); **en ~ de** *prép* in front of; **aller de l'~** to steam ahead (*fig*), make good progress.

avantage [àvåṅtàzh] *nm* advantage; (*TENNIS*): **~ service/dehors** advantage *ou* ad (*US*) *ou* van (*Brit*) in/out; **tirer ~ de** to take advantage of; **vous auriez ~ à faire** you would be well-advised to do, it would be to your advantage to do; **à l'~ de qn** to sb's advantage; **être à son ~** to be at one's best; **~s en nature** benefits in kind; **~s sociaux** fringe benefits.

avantager [àvåṅtàzhā] *vt* (*favoriser*) to favor (*US*) *ou* favour (*Brit*); (*embellir*) to flatter.

avantageux, euse [àvåṅtàzhœ̄, -œ̄z] *a* attractive; (*intéressant*) attractively priced; (*portrait, coiffure*) flattering; **conditions avantageuses** favorable terms.

avant-bras [àvåṅbrà] *nm inv* forearm.

avant-centre [àvåṅsåṅtr(ə)] *nm* center forward (*US*), centre-forward (*Brit*).

avant-coureur [àvåṅkōōrœr] *a inv* (*bruit etc*) precursory; **signe ~** advance indication *ou* sign.

avant-dernier, ière [àvåṅdernyà, -yer] *a*, *nm/f* next to last, last but one.

avant-garde [àvåṅgàrd(ə)] *nf* (*MIL*) vanguard; (*fig*) avant-garde; **d'~** avant-garde.

avant-goût [àvåṅgōō] *nm* foretaste.

avant-hier [àvåṅtyer] *ad* the day before yesterday.

avant-poste [àvåṅpost(ə)] *nm* outpost.

avant-première [àvåṅprəmyer] *nf* (*de film*) preview; **en ~** as a preview, in a preview showing.

avant-projet [àvåṅprozhe] *nm* preliminary draft.

avant-propos [àvåṅpropō] *nm* foreword.

avant-veille [àvåṅvey] *nf*: **l'~** two days before.

avare [àvàr] *a* miserly, avaricious ♦ *nm/f* miser; **~ de compliments** stingy *ou* sparing with one's compliments.

avarice [àvàrēs] *nf* avarice, miserliness.

avaricieux, euse [àvàrēsyœ̄, -œ̄z] *a* miserly, niggardly.

avarié, e [àvàryā] *a* (*viande, fruits*) rotting; (*NAVIG*: *navire*) damaged.

avaries [àvàrē] *nfpl* (*NAVIG*) damage *sg.*

avatar [àvàtàr] *nm* misadventure; (*transformation*) metamorphosis (*pl* -phoses).

avec [àvek] *prép* with; (*à l'égard de*) to(wards), with ♦ *ad* (*fam*) with it (*ou* him *etc*); ~ **habileté/lenteur** skilfully/slowly; ~ **eux/ces maladies** with them/these diseases; ~ **ça** (*malgré ça*) for all that; **et** ~ **ça?** (*dans un magasin*) anything *ou* something else?

avenant, e [àvnâǹ, -âǹt] *a* pleasant ♦ *nm* (*ASSURANCES*) additional clause; **à l'**~ *ad* in keeping.

avènement [àvenmáǹ] *nm* (*d'un roi*) accession, succession; (*d'un changement*) advent; (*d'une politique, idée*) coming.

avenir [àvnēr] *nm*: **l'**~ the future; **à l'**~ in future; **sans** ~ with no future, without a future; **carrière/politicien d'**~ career/politician with prospects *ou* a future.

Avent [àvâǹ] *nm*: **l'**~ Advent.

aventure [àvâǹtür] *nf*: **l'**~ adventure; **une** ~ an adventure; (*amoureuse*) an affair; **partir à l'**~ to go off in search of adventure; (*au hasard*) to go where one's fancy takes one; **roman/film d'**~ adventure story/film.

aventurer [àvâǹtürā] *vt* (*somme, réputation, vie*) to stake; (*remarque, opinion*) to venture; **s'**~ *vi* to venture; **s'**~ **à faire qch** to venture into sth.

aventureux, euse [àvâǹtürœ̄, -œ̄z] *a* adventurous, venturesome; (*projet*) risky, chancy.

aventurier, ière [àvâǹtüryā, -yer] *nm/f* adventurer ♦ *nf* (*péj*) adventuress.

avenu, e [àvnü] *a*: **nul et non** ~ null and void.

avenue [àvnü] *nf* avenue.

avéré, e [àvārā] *a* recognized, acknowledged.

avérer [àvārā]: **s'**~ *vb avec attribut*: **s'**~ **faux/coûteux** to prove (to be) wrong/expensive.

averse [àvers(ə)] *nf* shower.

aversion [àversyóǹ] *nf* aversion, loathing.

averti, e [àvertē] *a* (well-)informed.

avertir [àvertēr] *vt*: ~ **qn** (**de qch/que**) to warn sb (of sth/that); (*renseigner*) to inform sb (of sth/that); ~ **qn de ne pas faire qch** to warn sb not to do sth.

avertissement [àvertēsmáǹ] *nm* warning.

avertisseur [àvertēscœr] *nm* horn, siren; ~ (**d'incendie**) (fire) alarm.

aveu, x [àvœ̄] *nm* confession; **passer aux** ~**x** to make a confession; **de l'**~ **de** according to.

aveuglant, e [àvœglâǹ, -âǹt] *a* blinding.

aveugle [àvœgl(ə)] *a* blind ♦ *n* blind person; **les** ~**s** the blind; **test en** (**double**) ~ (double) blind test.

aveuglement [àvœgləmáǹ] *nm* blindness.

aveuglément [àvœglāmáǹ] *ad* blindly.

aveugler [àvœglā] *vt* to blind.

aveuglette [àvœglet]: **à l'**~ groping one's way along; (*fig*) in the dark, blindly.

avez [àvā] *vb voir* **avoir**.

aviateur, trice [àvyàtœr, -trēs] *nm/f* aviator, pilot.

aviation [àvyâsyóǹ] *nf* (*secteur commercial*) aviation; (*sport, métier de pilote*) flying; (*MIL*) air force; **terrain d'**~ airfield; ~ **de chasse** fighter force.

aviculteur, trice [àvēkültœr, -trēs] *nm/f* poultry farmer; bird breeder.

avide [àvēd] *a* eager; (*péj*) greedy, grasping; ~ **de** (*sang etc*) thirsting for; ~ **d'honneurs/d'argent** greedy for honors/money; ~ **de connaître/d'apprendre** eager to know/learn.

avidité [àvēdētā] *nf* eagerness; greed.

avilir [àvēlēr] *vt* to debase.

avilissant, e [àvēlēsâǹ, -âǹt] *a* degrading.

aviné, e [àvēnā] *a* drunken.

avion [àvyóǹ] *nm* (air)plane (*US*), (aero)plane (*Brit*); **aller** (**quelque part**) **en** ~ to go (somewhere) by plane, fly (somewhere); **par** ~ by airmail; ~ **de chasse** fighter; ~ **de ligne** airliner; ~ **à réaction** jet (plane).

avion-cargo [àvyóǹkàrgō] *nm* air freighter.

avion-citerne [àvyóǹsētern(ə)] *nm* air tanker.

aviron [àvēróǹ] *nm* oar; (*sport*): **l'**~ rowing.

avis [àvē] *nm* opinion; (*notification*) notice; (*COMM*): ~ **de crédit/débit** credit/debit advice; **à mon** ~ in my opinion; **je suis de votre** ~ I share your opinion, I am of your opinion; **être d'**~ **que** to be of the opinion that; **changer d'**~ to change one's mind; **sauf** ~ **contraire** unless you hear to the contrary; **sans** ~ **préalable** without notice; **jusqu'à nouvel** ~ until further notice; ~ **de décès** death announcement.

avisé, e [àvēzā] *a* sensible, wise; **être bien/mal** ~ **de faire** to be well-/ill-advised to do.

aviser [àvēzā] *vt* (*voir*) to notice, catch sight of; (*informer*): ~ **qn de/que** to advise *ou* inform *ou* notify sb of/that ♦ *vi* to think about things, assess the situation; **s'**~ **de qch/que** to become suddenly aware of sth/that; **s'**~ **de faire** to take it into one's head to do.

aviver [àvēvā] *vt* (*douleur, chagrin*) to intensify; (*intérêt, désir*) to sharpen; (*colère, querelle*) to stir up; (*couleur*) to brighten up.

av. J.-C. *abr* (= *avant Jésus-Christ*) BC.

avocat, e [àvokà, -àt] *nm/f* (*JUR*) lawyer, ≈ barrister (*Brit*); (*fig*) advocate, champion ♦ *nm* (*CULIN*) avocado (pear); **se faire l'**~ **du diable** to be the devil's advocate; **l'**~ **de la défense/partie civile** the counsel for the defense/plaintiff; ~ **d'affaires** business lawyer; ~ **général** prosecuting attorney (*US*), assistant public prosecutor (*Brit*).

avocat-conseil, *pl* **avocats-conseils** [àvokàkóǹsey] *nm* ≈ attorney (*US*), ≈ barrister (*Brit*).

avoine [àvwàn] *nf* oats *pl.*

avoir [àvwàr] *nm* assets *pl*, resources *pl*; (*COMM*): ~ (**fiscal**) (tax) credit ♦ *vt* (*gén*) to have; (*fam*: *duper*) to do, have ♦ *vb auxiliaire* to have; **vous avez du sel?** do you have any salt?, have you got any salt?; ~ **à faire qch** to have to do sth; **tu n'as pas à me poser de questions** it's not for you to ask me questions; **il a 3 ans** he is 3 (years old); *voir* **faim, peur** *etc*; ~ **3 mètres de haut** to be 3 metres high; ~ **les cheveux blancs/un chapeau rouge** to have white hair/a red hat; ~ **mangé/dormi** to have eaten/slept; **il y a** there is + *sg*, there are + *pl*; (*temporel*): **il y**

a 10 ans 10 years ago; **il y a 10 ans/ longtemps que je le sais** I've known (it) for 10 years/a long time; **il y a 10 ans qu'il est arrivé** it's 10 years since he arrived; **qu'y-a-t-il?, qu'est-ce qu'il y a?** what is it?, what's the matter?; **il doit y ~** there must be; **il ne peut y en ~ qu'un** there can only be one; **il n'y a qu'à ...** we (ou you etc) will just have to ...; **en ~ à** ou **contre qn** to have a grudge against sb; **en ~ assez** to be fed up; **j'en ai pour une demi-heure** it'll take me half an hour; **n'~ que faire de qch** to have no use for sth.

avoisinant, e [ávwázēnáṅ, -áṅt] a neighboring (US), neighbouring (Brit).

avoisiner [ávwázēnā] vt to be near ou close to; (fig) to border ou verge on.

avons [ávóṅ] vb voir **avoir**.

avortement [ávortəmáṅ] nm abortion.

avorter [ávortā] vi (MÉD) to have an abortion; (fig) to fail; **faire ~** to abort; **se faire ~** to have an abortion.

avorton [ávortóṅ] nm (péj) little runt.

avoué, e [ávwā] a avowed ♦ nm (JUR) lawyer.

avouer [ávwā] vt (crime, défaut) to confess (to) ♦ vi (se confesser) to confess; (admettre) to admit; **~ avoir fait/que** to admit ou confess to having done/that; **~ que oui/non** to admit that that is so/not so; **s'~ vaincu** to admit defeat.

avril [ávrēl] nm April; voir aussi **juillet**.

avt abr = **avant**.

axe [áks(ə)] nm axis (pl axes); (de roue etc) axle; (prolongement): **dans l'~ de** directly in line with; (fig) main line; **~ routier** main road.

axer [áksā] vt: **~ qch sur** to center sth on.

axial, e, aux [áksyál, -ō] a axial.

axiome [áksyōm] nm axiom.

ayant [eyáṅ] vb voir **avoir** ♦ nm: **~ droit** assignee; **~ droit à** (pension etc) person eligible for ou entitled to.

ayons [eyóṅ] etc vb voir **avoir**.

azalée [ázálā] nf azalea.

azimut [ázēmüt] nm azimuth; **tous ~s** a (fig) omnidirectional.

azote [ázot] nm nitrogen.

azoté, e [ázotā] a nitrogenous.

aztèque [áztèk] a Aztec.

azur [ázür] nm (couleur) azure, sky blue; (ciel) sky, skies pl.

azyme [ázēm] a: **pain ~** unleavened bread.

B

B, b [bā] nm inv B, b ♦ abr (= bien) g (= good); **B comme Bertha** B for Baker.

BA sigle f (= bonne action) good deed.

baba [bábá] a inv: **en être ~** (fam) to be flabbergasted ♦ nm: **~ au rhum** rum baba.

babil [bábē] nm prattle.

babillage [bábēyázh] nm chatter.

babiller [bábēyā] vi to prattle, chatter; (bébé) to babble.

babines [bábēn] nfpl chops.

babiole [bábyol] nf (bibelot) trinket; (vétille) trifle.

bâbord [bábor] nm: **à** ou **par ~** to port, on the port side.

babouin [bábwaṅ] nm baboon.

baby-foot [bábēfōōt] nm inv table football.

Babylone [bábēlon] n Babylon.

babylonien, ne [bábēlonyaṅ, -en] a Babylonian.

baby-sitter [bábēsētœr] nm/f baby-sitter.

baby-sitting [bábēsētēng] nm baby-sitting.

bac [bák] nm (SCOL) = **baccalauréat**; (bateau) ferry; (récipient) tub; (: PHOTO etc) tray; (: INDUSTRIE) tank; **~ à glace** ice-tray; **~ à légumes** vegetable compartment ou rack.

baccalauréat [bákálorāä] nm ≈ high school diploma (US), ≈ GCE A-levels pl (Brit).

bâche [básh] nf tarpaulin, canvas sheet.

bachelier, ière [báshəlyā, -yer] nm/f holder of the baccalauréat.

bâcher [báshā] vt to cover (with a canvas sheet ou a tarpaulin).

bachot [báshō] nm = **baccalauréat**.

bachotage [báshotázh] nm (SCOL) cramming.

bachoter [báshotā] vi (SCOL) to cram (for an exam).

bacille [básēl] nm bacillus (pl -i).

bâcler [báklā] vt to botch (up).

bactéricide [báktārēsēd] nm (MÉD) bactericide.

bactérie [báktārē] nf bacterium (pl -ia).

bactériologie [báktāryolozhē] nf bacteriology.

bactériologique [báktāryolozhēk] a bacteriological.

bactériologiste [báktāryolozhēst(ə)] nm/f bacteriologist.

badaud, e [bádō, -ōd] nm/f idle onlooker, stroller.

baderne [bádern(ə)] nf (péj): **(vieille) ~** old fossil.

badge [bádzh(ə)] nm badge.

badigeon [bádēzhóṅ] nm distemper; whitewash.

badigeonner [bádēzhonā] vt to distemper; to whitewash; (péj: barbouiller) to daub; (MÉD) to paint.

badin, e [bádaṅ, -ēn] a light-hearted, playful.

badinage [bádēnázh] nm banter.

badine [bádēn] nf switch (stick).

badiner [bádēnā] vi: **~ avec qch** to treat sth lightly; **ne pas ~ avec qch** not to trifle with sth.

badminton [bádmēnton] nm badminton.

BAFA [báfá] sigle m (= Brevet d'aptitude aux fonctions d'animation) diploma for youth leaders and workers.

baffe [báf] nf (fam) slap, clout.

Baffin [báfēn] nf: **terre de ~** Baffin Island.

baffle [báfl(ə)] nm baffle (board).

bafouer [báfwā] vt to deride, ridicule.

bafouillage [báfōōyázh] nm (fam: propos incohérents) jumble of words.

bafouiller [báfōōyā] vi, vt to stammer.

bâfrer [báfrā] vi, vt (fam) to guzzle, gobble.

bagage [bágázh] nm: **~s** luggage sg, baggage sg; **~ littéraire** (stock of) literary knowledge;

~s à main hand-luggage.

bagarre [bágár] *nf* fight, brawl; **il aime la** ~ he loves a fight, he likes fighting.

bagarrer [bágárã]: **se** ~ *vi* to (have a) fight.

bagarreur, euse [bágárœr, -œz] *a* pugnacious ♦ *nm/f*: **il est** ~ he loves a fight.

bagatelle [bágátel] *nf* trifle, trifling sum (*ou* matter).

Bagdad, Baghdâd [bágdâd] *n* Baghdad.

bagnard [bányár] *nm* convict.

bagne [bány] *nm* penal colony; **c'est le** ~ (*fig*) it's forced labor.

bagnole [bányol] *nf* (*fam*) car, wheels *pl*.

bagout [bágōō] *nm* glibness; **avoir du** ~ to have the gift of the gab.

bague [bág] *nf* ring; ~ **de fiançailles** engagement ring; ~ **de serrage** clip.

baguenauder [bágnōdã]: **se** ~ *vi* to trail around, loaf around.

baguer [bágã] *vt* to ring.

baguette [báget] *nf* stick; (*cuisine chinoise*) chopstick; (*de chef d'orchestre*) baton; (*pain*) stick of (French) bread; (*CONSTR*: *moulure*) beading; **mener qn à la** ~ to rule sb with a rod of iron; ~ **magique** magic wand; ~ **de sourcier** divining rod; ~ **de tambour** drumstick.

Bahamas [bàámàs] *nfpl*: **les (îles)** ~ the Bahamas.

Bahrein [báren] *nm* Bahrain *ou* Bahrein.

bahut [báü] *nm* chest.

bai, e [be] *a* (*cheval*) bay.

baie [be] *nf* (*GÉO*) bay; (*fruit*) berry; ~ **(vitrée)** picture window.

baignade [benyád] *nf* (*action*) bathing; (*bain*) bathe; (*endroit*) bathing place.

baigné, e [bányã] *a*: ~ **de** bathed in; (*trempé*) soaked with; (*inondé*) flooded with.

baigner [bányã] *vt* (*bébé*) to bath ♦ *vi*: ~ **dans son sang** to lie in a pool of blood; ~ **dans la brume** to be shrouded in mist; **se** ~ *vi* to go swimming *ou* bathing; (*dans une baignoire*) to have a bath; **ça baigne!** (*fam*) everything's great!

baigneur, euse [benyœr, -œz] *nm/f* bather ♦ *nm* (*poupée*) baby doll.

baignoire [benywár] *nf* bath(tub); (*THÉÂTRE*) ground-floor box.

bail, baux [báy, bō] *nm* lease; **donner** *ou* **prendre qch à** ~ to lease sth.

bâillement [báymân] *nm* yawn.

bâiller [báyã] *vi* to yawn; (*être ouvert*) to gape.

bailleur [báyœr] *nm*: ~ **de fonds** sponsor, backer; (*COMM*) silent *ou* sleeping (*Brit*) partner.

bâillon [báyôn] *nm* gag.

bâillonner [báyonã] *vt* to gag.

bain [bán] *nm* (*dans une baignoire, PHOTO, TECH*) bath; (*dans la mer, une piscine*) swim; **costume de** ~ bathing suit, swimsuit; **prendre un** ~ to have a bath; **se mettre dans le** ~ (*fig*) to get into the swing of it *ou* things; ~ **de bouche** mouthwash; ~ **de foule** walkabout; ~ **de pieds** footbath; (*au bord de la mer*) wade; ~ **de siège** hip bath; ~ **de soleil** sunbathing *q*; **prendre un** ~ **de soleil** to sunbathe; ~**s de mer** sea bathing *sg*; ~**s(-douches) municipaux** public baths.

bain-marie, *pl* **bains-marie** [bânmárē] *nm* double boiler; **faire chauffer au** ~ (*boîte etc*) to immerse in boiling water.

baïonnette [báyonet] *nf* bayonet; (*ÉLEC*): **douille à** ~ snap-up (*US*) *ou* bayonet (*Brit*) socket; **ampoule à** ~ bulb with a bayonet fitting.

baisemain [bezmań] *nm* kissing a lady's hand.

baiser [bāzā] *nm* kiss ♦ *vt* (*main, front*) to kiss; (*fam!*) to screw (!).

baisse [bes] *nf* fall, drop; (*COMM*): "~ **sur la viande**" "meat prices down"; **en** ~ (*cours, action*) falling; **à la** ~ downwards.

baisser [bāsā] *vt* to lower; (*radio, chauffage*) to turn down; (*AUTO: phares*) to dim (*US*), lower (*US*), dip (*Brit*) ♦ *vi* to fall, drop, go down; **se** ~ *vi* to bend down.

bajoues [bàzhōō] *nfpl* chaps, chops.

bal [bál] *nm* dance; (*grande soirée*) ball; ~ **costumé/masqué** fancy-dress/masked ball; ~ **musette** dance (*with accordion accompaniment*).

balade [bálád] *nf* walk, stroll; (*en voiture*) drive; **faire une** ~ to go for a walk *ou* stroll; to go for a drive.

balader [báládã] *vt* (*traîner*) to carry around; **se** ~ *vi* to go for a walk *ou* stroll; to go for a drive.

baladeur [báládœr] *nm* personal stereo.

baladeuse [báládœz] *nf* trouble light (*US*), inspection lamp (*Brit*).

baladin [báládań] *nm* wandering entertainer.

balafre [báláfr(ə)] *nf* gash, slash; (*cicatrice*) scar.

balafrer [báláfrã] *vt* to gash, slash.

balai [bále] *nm* broom, brush; (*AUTO: d'essuie-glace*) blade; (*MUS: de batterie etc*) brush; **donner un coup de** ~ to give the floor a sweep; ~ **mécanique** carpet sweeper.

balai-brosse, *pl* **balais-brosses** [bálebros] *nm* (long-handled) scrubbing brush.

balance [báláns] *nf* (*à plateaux*) scales *pl*; (*de précision*) balance; (*COMM, POL*): ~ **des comptes** *ou* **paiements** balance of payments; (*signe*): **la B~** Libra, the Scales; **être de la B~** to be Libra; ~ **commerciale** balance of trade; ~ **des forces** balance of power; ~ **romaine** steelyard.

balancelle [bálánsel] *nf* glider (*US*), garden hammock-seat (*Brit*).

balancer [bálánsã] *vt* to swing; (*lancer*) to fling, chuck; (*renvoyer, jeter*) to chuck out ♦ *vi* to swing; **se** ~ *vi* to swing; (*bateau*) to rock; (*branche*) to sway; **se** ~ **de qch** (*fam*) not to give a darn about sth.

balancier [bálánsyã] *nm* (*de pendule*) pendulum; (*de montre*) balance wheel; (*perche*) (balancing) pole.

balançoire [bálánswár] *nf* swing; (*sur pivot*) seesaw.

balayage [báleyàzh] *nm* sweeping; scanning.

balayer [báleyã] *vt* (*feuilles etc*) to sweep up, brush up; (*pièce, cour*) to sweep; (*chasser*) to sweep away *ou* aside; (*suj: radar*) to scan; (*: phares*) to sweep across.

balayette [báleyet] *nf* small brush.

balayeur, euse [báleyœr, -œz] *nm/f* streetsweeper ♦ *nf* (*engin*) streetsweeper.

balayures [báleyür] *nfpl* sweepings.

balbutiement [bálbüsēmáṅ] *nm* (*paroles*) stammering *q*; ~**s** *nmpl* (*fig: débuts*) first faltering steps.

balbutier [bálbüsyā] *vi*, *vt* to stammer.

balcon [bálkóṅ] *nm* balcony; (*THÉÂTRE*) dress circle.

baldaquin [báldákaṅ] *nm* canopy.

Bâle [bál] *n* Basle *ou* Basel.

Baléares [bálāár] *nfpl*: **les** ~ the Balearic Islands.

baleine [bálen] *nf* whale; (*de parapluie*) rib; (*de corset*) bone.

baleinier [bálānyā] *nm* (*NAVIG*) whaler.

baleinière [bálenyer] *nf* whaleboat.

balisage [bálēzázh] *nm* (*signaux*) beacons *pl*; buoys *pl*; runway lights *pl*; signs *pl*, markers *pl*.

balise [bálēz] *nf* (*NAVIG*) beacon, (marker) buoy; (*AVIAT*) runway light, beacon; (*AUTO*, *SKI*) sign, marker.

baliser [bálēzā] *vt* to mark out (with beacons *ou* lights *etc*).

balistique [bálēstēk] *a* (*engin*) ballistic ♦ *nf* ballistics.

balivernes [bálēvern(ə)] *nfpl* twaddle *sg*, nonsense *sg*.

balkanique [bálkánēk] *a* Balkan.

Balkans [bálkáṅ] *nmpl*: **les** ~ the Balkans.

ballade [bálád] *nf* ballad.

ballant, e [báláṅ, -áṅt] *a* dangling.

ballast [bálást] *nm* ballast.

balle [bál] *nf* (*de fusil*) bullet; (*de sport*) ball; (*du blé*) chaff; (*paquet*) bale; (*fam: franc*) franc; ~ **perdue** stray bullet.

ballerine [bálrēn] *nf* ballet dancer; (*chaussure*) pump, ballerina.

ballet [bále] *nm* ballet; (*fig*): ~ **diplomatique** diplomatic to-ings and fro-ings.

ballon [bálóṅ] *nm* (*de sport*) ball; (*jouet*, *AVIAT*, *de bande dessinée*) balloon; (*de vin*) glass; ~ **d'essai** (*météorologique*) trial (*US*) *ou* pilot balloon; (*fig*) feeler(s); ~ **de football** football; ~ **d'oxygène** oxygen bottle.

ballonner [bálonā] *vt*: **j'ai le ventre ballonné** I feel bloated.

ballon-sonde, *pl* **ballons-sondes** [bálóṅsôṅd] *nm* sounding balloon.

ballot [bálō] *nm* bundle; (*péj*) nitwit.

ballottage [bálotázh] *nm* (*POL*) second ballot.

ballotter [bálotā] *vi* to roll around; (*bateau etc*) to toss ♦ *vt* to shake *ou* throw about; to toss; **être ballotté entre** (*fig*) to be shunted between; (*: indécis*) to be torn between.

ballottine [báloten] *nf* (*CULIN*): ~ **de volaille** meat loaf made with poultry.

ball-trap [báltráp] *nm* (*appareil*) trap; (*tir*) clay pigeon shooting.

balluchon [bálüshóṅ] *nm* bundle (of clothes).

balnéaire [bálnāer] *a* seaside *cpd*.

balnéothérapie [bálnāotárápē] *nf* spa bath therapy.

BALO *sigle m* (= *Bulletin des annonces légales obligatoires*) ≈ Legal (*US*) *ou* Public (*Brit*) Notices (*in newspapers etc*).

balourd, e [bálōōr, -ōōrd(ə)] *a* clumsy ♦ *nm/f* clodhopper.

balourdise [bálōōrdēz] *nf* clumsiness; (*gaffe*) blunder.

balte [bált] *a* Baltic ♦ *nm/f*: **B**~ native of the Baltic States.

baltique [báltēk] *a* Baltic ♦ *nf*: **la (mer) B**~ the Baltic (Sea).

baluchon [bálüshóṅ] *nm* = **balluchon**.

balustrade [bálüstrád] *nf* railings *pl*, handrail.

bambin [báṅbaṅ] *nm* little child.

bambou [báṅbōō] *nm* bamboo.

ban [báṅ] *nm* round of applause, cheer; **être/mettre au** ~ **de** to be outlawed/to outlaw from; **le** ~ **et l'arrière-**~ **de sa famille** every last one of his relatives; ~**s (de mariage)** banns, bans.

banal, e [bánál] *a* banal, commonplace; (*péj*) trite; **four/moulin** ~ village oven/mill.

banalisé, e [bánálēzá] *a* (*voiture de police*) unmarked.

banalité [bánálētá] *nf* banality; (*remarque*) truism, trite remark.

banane [bánán] *nf* banana.

bananeraie [bánánre] *nf* banana plantation.

bananier [bánányā] *nm* banana tree; (*bateau*) banana boat.

banc [báṅ] *nm* seat, bench; (*de poissons*) school (*US*), shoal (*Brit*); ~ **des accusés** dock; ~ **d'essai** (*fig*) testing ground; ~ **de sable** sandbank; ~ **des témoins** witness stand.

bancaire [bánker] *a* banking, bank *cpd*.

bancal, e [báṅkál] *a* wobbly; (*personne*) bow-legged; (*fig: projet*) shaky.

bandage [báṅdázh] *nm* bandaging; (*pansement*) bandage; ~ **herniaire** truss.

bande [báṅd] *nf* (*de tissu etc*) strip; (*MÉD*) bandage; (*motif*, *dessin*) stripe; (*CINÉMA*) film; (*INFORM*) tape; (*RADIO*, *groupe*) band; (*péj*): **une** ~ **de** a bunch *ou* crowd of; **par la** ~ in a roundabout way; **donner de la** ~ to list; **faire** ~ **à part** to keep to o.s.; ~ **dessinée (BD)** comic strip, strip cartoon (*Brit*); ~ **magnétique** magnetic tape; ~ **perforée** punched tape; ~ **de roulement** (*de pneu*) tread; ~ **sonore** sound track; ~ **de terre** strip of land; ~ **Velpeau** ® (*MÉD*) Ace ® (*US*) *ou* crêpe (*Brit*) bandage.

bandé, e [báṅdá] *a* bandaged; **les yeux** ~**s** blindfold.

bande-annonce, *pl* **bandes-annonces** [báṅdánóṅs] *nf* (*CINÉMA*) trailer.

bandeau, x [báṅdō] *nm* headband; (*sur les yeux*) blindfold; (*MÉD*) head bandage.

bandelette [báṅdlet] *nf* strip of cloth, bandage.

bander [báṅdā] *vt* to bandage; (*muscle*) to tense; (*arc*) to bend ♦ *vi* (*fam!*) to have a hard on (*!*); ~ **les yeux à qn** to blindfold sb.

banderole [báṅdrol] *nf* banderole; (*dans un défilé etc*) streamer.

bande-son, *pl* **bandes-son** [báṅdsóṅ] *nf* (*CINÉMA*) soundtrack.

bande-vidéo, *pl* **bandes-vidéo** [báṅdvēdāō] *nf* video tape.

bandit [báṅdē] *nm* bandit.

banditisme [báṅdētēsm(ə)] *nm* violent crime, armed robberies *pl*.

bandoulière [báṅdōōlyer] *nf*: **en** ~ (slung *ou* worn) across the shoulder.

Bangkok [báṅgkok] *n* Bangkok.

Bangla Desh [báṅgládesh] *nm*: **le** ~ Bangladesh.

banjo [bãn(d)zhõ] *nm* banjo.
banlieue [bãnlyœ̃] *nf* suburbs *pl*; **lignes/ quartiers de** ~ suburban lines/areas; **trains de** ~ commuter trains.
banlieusard, e [bãnlyœ̃zár, -árd(ə)] *nm/f* suburbanite.
bannière [bányer] *nf* banner.
bannir [bánēr] *vt* to banish.
banque [bãnk] *nf* bank; (*activités*) banking; ~ **des yeux/du sang** eye/blood bank; ~ **d'affaires** commercial (*US*) *ou* merchant (*Brit*) bank; ~ **de dépôt** deposit bank; ~ **de données** (*INFORM*) data bank; ~ **d'émission** bank of issue.
banqueroute [bánkrōōt] *nf* bankruptcy.
banquet [bánke] *nm* (*de club*) dinner; (*de noces*) reception; (*d'apparat*) banquet.
banquette [bánket] *nf* seat.
banquier [bánkyā] *nm* banker.
banquise [bánkēz] *nf* ice field.
bantou, e [bántōō] *a* Bantu.
baptême [bàtem] *nm* (*sacrement*) baptism; (*cérémonie*) christening, baptism; (*d'un navire*) launching; (*d'une cloche*) consecration, dedication; ~ **de l'air** first flight.
baptiser [bàtēzā] *vt* to christen; to baptize; to launch; to consecrate, dedicate.
baptismal, e, aux [bàtēsmál, -ō] *a*: **eau** ~**e** baptismal water.
baptiste [bàtēst(ə)] *a*, *nm/f* Baptist.
baquet [bàke] *nm* tub, bucket.
bar [bár] *nm* bar; (*poisson*) bass.
baragouin [bàrágwán] *nm* gibberish.
baragouiner [bàrágwēnā] *vi* to gibber, jabber.
baraque [bàrák] *nf* shed; (*fam*) house; ~ **foraine** fairground stand.
baraqué, e [bàrákā] *a* well-built, hefty.
baraquements [bàrákmã́n] *nmpl* huts (*for refugees, workers etc*).
baratin [bàrátán] *nm* (*fam*) smooth talk, patter.
baratiner [bàrátēnā] *vt* to sweet-talk.
baratte [bàrát] *nf* churn.
Barbade [bàrbád] *nf*: **la** ~ Barbados.
barbant, e [bàrbán, -áńt] *a* (*fam*) deadly (boring).
barbare [bàrbár] *a* barbaric ♦ *nm/f* barbarian.
Barbarie [bàrbárē] *nf*: **la** ~ the Barbary Coast.
barbarie [bàrbárē] *nf* barbarism; (*cruauté*) barbarity.
barbarisme [bàrbárēsm(ə)] *nm* (*LING*) barbarism.
barbe [bàrb(ə)] *nf* beard; (**au nez et) à la** ~ **de qn** (*fig*) under sb's very nose; **quelle** ~! (*fam*) what a drag *ou* bore!; ~ **à papa** cotton candy (*US*), candy-floss (*Brit*).
barbecue [bàrbəkyōō] *nm* barbecue.
barbelé [bàrbəlā] *nm* barbed wire *q*.
barber [bàrbā] *vt* (*fam*) to bore stiff.
barbiche [bàrbēsh] *nf* goatee.
barbichette [bàrbēshet] *nf* small goatee.
barbiturique [bàrbētürēk] *nm* barbiturate.
barboter [bàrbotā] *vi* to paddle, dabble ♦ *vt* (*fam*) to filch.
barboteuse [bàrbotœ̃z] *nf* rompers *pl*.
barbouiller [bàrbōōyā] *vt* to daub; (*péj*: *écrire, dessiner*) to scribble; **avoir l'estomac barbouillé** to feel queasy *ou* sick.
barbu, e [bàrbü] *a* bearded.

barbue [bàrbü] *nf* (*poisson*) brill.
Barcelone [bàrsəlon] *n* Barcelona.
barda [bàrdá] *nm* (*fam*) kit, gear.
barde [bàrd(ə)] *nf* (*CULIN*) piece of fat bacon ♦ *nm* (*poète*) bard.
bardé, e [bàrdā] *a*: ~ **de médailles** *etc* bedecked with medals *etc*.
bardeaux [bàrdō] *nmpl* shingle *q*.
barder [bàrdā] *vt* (*CULIN*: *rôti, volaille*) to bard ♦ *vi* (*fam*): **ça va** ~ sparks will fly, things are going to get hot.
barème [bàrem] *nm* scale; (*liste*) table; ~ **des salaires** salary scale.
barguigner [bàrgēnyā] *vi*: **sans** ~ without (any) hemming and hawing *ou* shilly-shallying.
baril [bàrēl] *nm* (*tonneau*) barrel; (*de poudre*) keg.
barillet [bàrēye] *nm* (*de revolver*) cylinder.
bariolé, e [bàryolā] *a* many-colored, rainbow-colored.
barman [bàrmán] *nm* bartender (*US*), barman.
baromètre [bàrometr(ə)] *nm* barometer; ~ **anéroïde** aneroid barometer.
baron [bàróń] *nm* baron.
baronne [bàron] *nf* baroness.
baroque [bàrok] *a* (*ART*) baroque; (*fig*) weird.
baroud [bàrōōd] *nm*: ~ **d'honneur** gallant last stand.
baroudeur [bàrōōdœr] *nm* (*fam*) fighter.
barque [bàrk(ə)] *nf* small boat.
barquette [bàrket] *nf* small boat-shaped tart; (*récipient*: *en aluminium*) tub; (: *en bois*) basket.
barracuda [bàráküdá] *nm* barracuda.
barrage [bàrázh] *nm* dam; (*sur route*) roadblock, barricade; ~ **de police** police roadblock.
barre [bár] *nf* (*de fer etc*) rod, bar; (*NAVIG*) helm; (*écrite*) line, stroke; (*DANSE*) barre; (*JUR*): **comparaître à la** ~ to appear as a witness; **être à** *ou* **tenir la** ~ (*NAVIG*) to be at the helm; **coup de** ~ (*fig*): **c'est le coup de** ~! it's highway (*US*) *ou* daylight (*Brit*) robbery!; **j'ai le coup de** ~! I'm exhausted!; ~ **fixe** (*GYM*) horizontal bar; ~ **de mesure** (*MUS*) bar line; ~ **à mine** crowbar; ~**s parallèles/asymétriques** (*GYM*) parallel/asymmetric bars.
barreau, x [bàrō] *nm* bar; (*JUR*): **le** ~ the Bar.
barrer [bàrā] *vt* (*route etc*) to block; (*mot*) to cross out; (*chèque*) to mark "for deposit only" (*US*), cross (*Brit*); (*NAVIG*) to steer; **se** ~ *vi* (*fam*) to clear out.
barrette [bàret] *nf* (*pour cheveux*) (hair) clip (*US*) *ou* slide (*Brit*); (*REL*: *bonnet*) biretta; (*broche*) brooch.
barreur [bàrœr] *nm* helmsman; (*aviron*) coxswain.
barricade [bàrēkàd] *nf* barricade.
barricader [bàrēkádā] *vt* to barricade; **se** ~ **chez soi** (*fig*) to lock o.s. in.
barrière [bàryer] *nf* fence; (*obstacle*) barrier; (*porte*) gate; **la Grande B**~ the Great Barrier Reef; ~ **de dégel** (*ADMIN*: *on roadsigns*) no heavy vehicles - road liable to subsidence due to thaw; ~**s douanières** trade barriers.

barrique [bàrēk] *nf* barrel, cask.

barrir [bàrēr] *vi* to trumpet.

baryton [bàrētóñ] *nm* baritone.

BAS *sigle m* (= *bureau d'aide sociale*) ≈ Welfare office (*US*), ≈ social security office (*Brit*).

bas, basse [bâ, bâs] *a* low; (*action*) low, ignoble ♦ *nm* (*vêtement*) stocking; (*partie inférieure*): **le ~ de** the lower part *ou* foot *ou* bottom of ♦ *nf* (*MUS*) bass ♦ *ad* low; (*parler*) softly; **plus ~** lower down; more softly; (*dans un texte*) further on, below; **la tête basse** with lowered head; (*fig*) with head hung low; **avoir la vue basse** to be short-sighted; **au ~ mot** at the lowest estimate; **enfant en ~ âge** infant, young child; **en ~** down below; at (*ou* to) the bottom; (*dans une maison*) downstairs; **en ~ de** at the bottom of; **de ~ en haut** upwards; from the bottom to the top; **des hauts et des ~** ups and downs; **un ~ de laine** (*fam*: *économies*) money under the mattress (*fig*); **mettre ~** *vi* to give birth; **à ~ la dictature!** down with dictatorship!; **~ morceaux** (*viande*) cheap cuts.

basalte [bàzàlt(ə)] *nm* basalt.

basané, e [bàzànā] *a* tanned, bronzed; (*immigré etc*) swarthy.

bas-côté [bàkōtā] *nm* (*de route*) shoulder; (*d'église*) (side) aisle.

bascule [bàskül] *nf*: **(jeu de) ~** seesaw; **(balance à) ~** scales *pl*; **fauteuil à ~** rocking chair; **système à ~** tip-over device; rocker device.

basculer [bàskülā] *vi* to fall over, topple (over); (*benne*) to tip up ♦ *vt* (*aussi*: **faire ~**) to topple over; to tip out, tip up.

base [bàz] *nf* base; (*POL*): **la ~** the rank and file, the grass roots; (*fondement, principe*) basis (*pl* bases); **jeter les ~s de** to lay the foundations of; **à la ~ de** (*fig*) at the root of; **sur la ~ de** (*fig*) on the basis of; **de ~** basic; **à ~ de café** *etc* coffee *etc* -based; **~ de données** (*INFORM*) database; **~ de lancement** launching site.

base-ball [bezbōl] *nm* baseball.

baser [bàzā] *vt*: **~ qch sur** to base sth on; **se ~ sur** (*données, preuves*) to base one's argument on; **être basé à/dans** (*MIL*) to be based at/in.

bas-fond [bàfóñ] *nm* (*NAVIG*) shallow; **~s** *nmpl* (*fig*) dregs.

BASIC [bàzēk] *nm* BASIC.

basilic [bàzēlēk] *nm* (*CULIN*) basil.

basilique [bàzēlēk] *nf* basilica.

basket(-ball) [bàsket(bōl)] *nm* basketball.

baskets [bàsket] *nmpl* (*chaussures*) sneakers (*US*), trainers (*Brit*).

basketteur, euse [bàsketœr, -ēz] *nm/f* basketball player.

basquaise [bàskez] *af* Basque ♦ *nf*: **B~** Basque.

basque [bàsk(ə)] *a, nm* (*LING*) Basque ♦ *nm/f*: **B~** Basque; **le Pays ~** the Basque country.

basques [bàsk(ə)] *nfpl* skirts; **pendu aux ~ de qn** constantly pestering sb; (*mère etc*) hanging on sb's apron strings.

bas-relief [bàrəlyef] *nm* bas-relief.

basse [bàs] *af, nf voir* **bas**.

basse-cour, *pl* **basses-cours** [bàskōōr] *nf* farmyard; (*animaux*) farmyard animals.

bassement [bàsmáñ] *ad* basely.

bassesse [bàses] *nf* baseness; (*acte*) base act.

basset [bàse] *nm* (*ZOOL*) basset (hound).

bassin [bàsañ] *nm* (*cuvette*) bowl; (*pièce d'eau*) pond, pool; (*de fontaine*, *GÉO*) basin; (*ANAT*) pelvis; (*portuaire*) dock; **~ houiller** coalfield.

bassine [bàsēn] *nf* basin; (*contenu*) bowl, bowlful.

bassiner [bàsēnā] *vt* (*plaie*) to bathe; (*lit*) to warm with a warming pan; (*fam*: *ennuyer*) to bore; (*: importuner*) to bug, pester.

bassiste [bàsēst(ə)] *nm/f* (double) bass player.

basson [bàsóñ] *nm* bassoon.

bastide [bàstēd] *nf* (*maison*) country house (*in Provence*); (*ville*) walled town (*in SW France*).

bastingage [bàstañgàzh] *nm* (ship's) rail.

bastion [bàstyóñ] *nm* (*aussi fig*, *POL*) bastion.

bas-ventre [bàvàñtr(ə)] *nm* (lower part of the) stomach.

bât [bâ] *nm* packsaddle.

bataille [bàtáy] *nf* battle; **en ~** (*en travers*) at an angle; (*en désordre*) awry; **~ rangée** pitched battle.

bataillon [bàtáyóñ] *nm* battalion.

bâtard, e [bâtàr, -àrd(ə)] *a* (*enfant*) illegitimate; (*fig*) hybrid ♦ *nm/f* illegitimate child, bastard (*péj*) ♦ *nm* (*BOULANGERIE*) ≈ Vienna loaf; **chien ~** mongrel.

batavia [bàtàvyà] *nf* ≈ Webb lettuce.

bateau, x [bàtō] *nm* boat; (*grand*) ship ♦ *a inv* (*banal, rebattu*) hackneyed; **~ de pêche/à moteur** fishing/motor boat.

bateau-citerne [bàtōsētern(ə)] *nm* tanker.

bateau-mouche [bàtōmōōsh] *nm* (passenger) pleasure boat (*on the Seine*).

bateau-pilote [bàtōpēlot] *nm* pilot ship.

bateleur, euse [bàtlœr, -ēz] *nm/f* street performer.

batelier, ière [bàtəlyā, -yer] *nm/f* ferryman/woman.

bat-flanc [bàflâñ] *nm inv* raised boards for sleeping, in cells, army huts etc.

bâti, e [bâtē] *a* (*terrain*) developed ♦ *nm* (*armature*) frame; (*COUTURE*) tacking; **bien ~** (*personne*) well-built.

batifoler [bàtēfolā] *vi* to frolic *ou* lark about.

batik [bàtēk] *nm* batik.

bâtiment [bâtēmáñ] *nm* building; (*NAVIG*) ship, vessel; (*industrie*): **le ~** the building trade.

bâtir [bàtēr] *vt* to build; (*COUTURE*: *jupe, ourlet*) to tack; **fil à ~** (*COUTURE*) tacking thread.

bâtisse [bâtēs] *nf* building.

bâtisseur, euse [bâtēsœr, -ēz] *nm/f* builder.

batiste [bàtēst(ə)] *nf* (*COUTURE*) batiste, cambric.

bâton [bâtóñ] *nm* stick; **mettre des ~s dans les roues à qn** to throw a monkey wrench (*US*) *ou* a spanner (*Brit*) into the works for sb; **à ~s rompus** informally; **~ de rouge (à lèvres)** lipstick; **~ de ski** ski pole.

bâtonnet [bàtone] *nm* short stick *ou* rod.

bâtonnier [bàtonyā] *nm* (*JUR*) ≈ President of the Bar.

batraciens [bátràsyań] *nmpl* amphibians.

battage [bátázh] *nm* (*publicité*) (hard) plugging.

battant, e [bátáń, -áńt] *vb voir* **battre** ♦ *a:* **pluie** ~**e** pelting rain ♦ *nm* (*de cloche*) clapper; (*de volets*) shutter, flap; (*de porte*) side; (*fig: personne*) fighter; **porte à double** ~ double door; **tambour** ~ briskly.

batte [bát] *nf* (*SPORT*) bat.

battement [bátmáń] *nm* (*de cœur*) beat; (*intervalle*) interval (*between classes, trains etc*); ~ **de paupières** blinking *q* (of eyelids); **un** ~ **de 10 minutes, 10 minutes de** ~ 10 minutes to spare.

batterie [bátrē] *nf* (*MIL, ÉLEC*) battery; (*MUS*) drums *pl*, drum set (*US*) ou kit (*Brit*); ~ **de cuisine** kitchen utensils *pl*; (*casseroles etc*) pots and pans *pl*; **une** ~ **de tests** a string of tests.

batteur [bátœr] *nm* (*MUS*) drummer; (*appareil*) whisk.

batteuse [bátœz] *nf* (*AGR*) threshing machine.

battoir [bátwár] *nm* (*à linge*) beetle (*for laundry*); (*à tapis*) (carpet) beater.

battre [bátr(ə)] *vt* to beat; (*suj: pluie, vagues*) to beat ou lash against; (*œufs etc*) to beat up, whisk; (*blé*) to thresh; (*cartes*) to shuffle; (*passer au peigne fin*) to scour ♦ *vi* (*cœur*) to beat; (*volets etc*) to bang, rattle; **se** ~ *vi* to fight; ~ **la mesure** to beat time; ~ **en brèche** (*MIL: mur*) to batter; (*fig: théorie*) to demolish; (*: institution etc*) to attack; ~ **son plein** to be at its height, be going full swing; ~ **pavillon britannique** to fly the British flag; ~ **des mains** to clap one's hands; ~ **des ailes** to flap its wings; ~ **de l'aile** (*fig*) to be in a bad way ou in bad shape; ~ **la semelle** to stamp one's feet; ~ **en retraite** to beat a retreat.

battu, e [bátü] *pp de* **battre** ♦ *nf* (*chasse*) beat; (*policière etc*) search, hunt.

baud [bō(d)] *nm* baud.

baudruche [bōdrüsh] *nf:* **ballon en** ~ (toy) balloon; (*fig*) windbag.

baume [bōm] *nm* balm.

bauxite [bōksēt] *nf* bauxite.

bavard, e [bávár, -árd(ə)] *a* (very) talkative; gossipy.

bavardage [bávárdàzh] *nm* chatter *q*; gossip *q*.

bavarder [bávárdā] *vi* to chatter; (*indiscrètement*) to gossip; (*: révéler un secret*) to blab.

bavarois, e [bávárwá, -wáz] *a* Bavarian ♦ *nm ou nf* (*CULIN*) Bavarian cream (*US*), bavarois (*Brit*).

bave [báv] *nf* dribble; (*de chien etc*) slobber, drool (*US*), slaver (*Brit*); (*d'escargot*) slime.

baver [bává] *vi* to dribble; to slobber, drool (*US*), slaver (*Brit*); (*encre, couleur*) to run; **en** ~ (*fam*) to have a hard time (of it).

bavette [bávet] *nf* bib.

baveux, euse [bávœ̄, -œ̄z] *a* dribbling; (*omelette*) runny.

Bavière [bávyer] *nf:* **la** ~ Bavaria.

bavoir [bávwár] *nm* (*de bébé*) bib.

bavure [bávür] *nf* smudge; (*fig*) hitch; blunder.

bayer [báyā] *vi:* ~ **aux corneilles** to stand gaping.

bazar [bázár] *nm* general store; (*fam*) jumble.

bazarder [bázárdā] *vt* (*fam*) to chuck out.

BCBG *sigle a* (= *bon chic bon genre*) ≈ preppy.

BCG *sigle m* (= *bacille Calmette-Guérin*) BCG.

bcp *abr* = **beaucoup**.

BD *sigle f* = **bande dessinée**; (= *base de données*) DB.

bd *abr* = **boulevard**.

b.d.c. *abr* (*TYPO:* = *bas de casse*) l.c.

béant, e [bááń, -áńt] *a* gaping.

béarnais, e [báárne, -ez] *a* of ou from the Béarn.

béat, e [báá, -át] *a* showing open-eyed wonder; (*sourire etc*) blissful.

béatitude [báátētüd] *nf* bliss.

beau (bel), belle, beaux [bō, bel] *a* beautiful, lovely; (*homme*) handsome ♦ *nf* (*SPORT*) deciding game ♦ *ad:* **il fait** ~ the weather's fine ♦ *nm:* **avoir le sens du** ~ to have an aesthetic sense; **le temps est au** ~ the weather is set fair; **un** ~ **geste** (*fig*) a fine gesture; **un** ~ **salaire** a good salary; **un** ~ **gâchis/rhume** a fine mess/nasty cold; **en faire/dire de belles** to do/say (some) stupid things; **le** ~ **monde** high society; ~ **parleur** smooth talker; **un** ~ **jour** one (fine) day; **de plus belle** more than ever, even more; **bel et bien** well and truly; (*vraiment*) really (and truly); **le plus** ~ **c'est que** ... the best of it is that ...; **c'est du** ~! that's great, that is!; **on a** ~ **essayer** however hard ou no matter how hard we try; **il a** ~ **jeu de protester** *etc* it's easy for him to protest *etc*; **faire le** ~ (*chien*) to sit up and beg.

beauceron, ne [bōsróń, -on] *a* of ou from the Beauce.

beaucoup [bōkōō] *ad* a lot; much (*gén en tournure négative*); **il ne boit pas** ~ he doesn't drink much ou a lot; ~ **de** (*nombre*) many, a lot of; (*quantité*) a lot of, much; **pas** ~ **de** not much ou not a lot of; ~ **plus/trop** far ou much more/too much; **de** ~ *ad* by far.

beau-fils, *pl* **beaux-fils** [bōfēs] *nm* son-in-law; (*remariage*) stepson.

beau-frère, *pl* **beaux-frères** [bōfrer] *nm* brother-in-law.

beau-père, *pl* **beaux-pères** [bōper] *nm* father-in-law; (*remariage*) stepfather.

beauté [bōtá] *nf* beauty; **de toute** ~ beautiful; **en** ~ *ad* with a flourish, brilliantly.

beaux-arts [bōzár] *nmpl* fine arts.

beaux-parents [bōpáráń] *nmpl* wife's/husband's family *sg ou pl*, in-laws.

bébé [bábá] *nm* baby.

bébé-éprouvette, *pl* **bébés-éprouvette** [bábááprōōvet] *nm* test-tube baby.

bec [bek] *nm* beak, bill; (*de plume*) nib; (*de cafetière etc*) spout; (*de casserole etc*) lip; (*d'une clarinette etc*) mouthpiece; (*fam*) mouth; **clouer le** ~ **à qn** (*fam*) to shut sb up; **ouvrir le** ~ (*fam*) to open one's mouth; ~ **de gaz** (street) gaslamp; ~ **verseur** pouring lip.

bécane [bákàn] *nf* (*fam*) bike.

bécarre [bákár] *nm* (*MUS*) natural.

bécasse [bákás] *nf* (*ZOOL*) woodcock; (*fam*)

silly goose.

bec-de-cane, pl **becs-de-cane** |bɛkdəkán| nm (poignée) door handle.

bec-de-lièvre, pl **becs-de-lièvre** |bɛkdə-lyɛvr(ə)| nm harelip.

béchamel |bāshámɛl| nf: **(sauce)** ~ white sauce, bechamel sauce.

bêche |bɛsh| nf spade.

bêcher |bɛshā| vt (terre) to dig; (personne: critiquer) to criticize severely; (: snober) to look down on.

bêcheur, euse |bɛshœr, -œz| a (fam) stuck-up ♦ nm/f fault-finder; (snob) stuck-up person.

bécoter |bākotā|: **se** ~ vi to smooch.

becquée |bākā| nf: **donner la** ~ **à** to feed.

becqueter |bɛktā| vt (fam) to eat.

bedaine |bədɛn| nf paunch.

bédé |bādā| nf (fam: = bande dessinée) comic strip.

bedeau, x |bədō| nm beadle.

bedonnant, e |bədonáṅ, -áṅt| a paunchy, potbellied.

bée |bā| a: **bouche** ~ gaping.

beffroi |bāfrwà| nm belfry.

bégaiement |bāgɛmáṅ| nm stammering.

bégayer |bāgāyā| vt, vi to stammer.

bégonia |bāgonyá| nm (BOT) begonia.

bègue |bɛg| nm/f: **être** ~ to have a stammer.

bégueule |bāgœl| a prudish.

béguin |bāgaṅ| nm: **avoir le** ~ **de** ou **pour** to have a crush on.

beige |bɛzh| a beige.

beignet |bɛnyɛ| nm fritter.

bel |bɛl| am voir **beau.**

bêler |bālā| vi to bleat.

belette |bəlɛt| nf weasel.

belge |bɛlzh(ə)| a Belgian ♦ nm/f: **B~** Belgian.

Belgique |bɛlzhēk| nf: **la** ~ Belgium.

Belgrade |bɛlgrád| n Belgrade.

bélier |bālyā| nm ram; (engin) (battering) ram; (signe): **le B~** Aries, the Ram; **être du B~** to be Aries.

Bélize |bālēz| nm: **le** ~ Belize.

bellâtre |bɛlâtr(ə)| nm dandy.

belle |bɛl| af, nf voir **beau.**

belle-famille, pl **belles-familles** |bɛlfámēy| nf (fam) in-laws pl.

belle-fille, pl **belles-filles** |bɛlfēy| nf daughter-in-law; (remariage) stepdaughter.

belle-mère, pl **belles-mères** |bɛlmɛr| nf mother-in-law; (remariage) stepmother.

belle-sœur, pl **belles-sœurs** |bɛlsœr| nf sister-in-law.

belliciste |bālēsēst(ə)| a warmongering.

belligérance |bālēzhāráṅs| nf belligerence.

belligérant, e |bālēzhāráṅ, -áṅt| a belligerent.

belliqueux, euse |bālēkœ, -œz| a aggressive, warlike.

belote |bəlot| nf belote (card game).

belvédère |bɛlvāder| nm panoramic viewpoint (or small building there).

bémol |bāmol| nm (MUS) flat.

ben |baṅ| excl (fam) well.

bénédiction |bānādēksyóṅ| nf blessing.

bénéfice |bānāfēs| nm (COMM) profit; (avantage) benefit; **au** ~ **de** in aid of.

bénéficiaire |bānāfēsyer| nm/f beneficiary.

bénéficier |bānāfēsyā| vi: ~ **de** to enjoy; (profiter) to benefit by ou from; (obtenir) to get, be given.

bénéfique |bānāfēk| a beneficial.

Bénélux |bānālüks| nm: **le** ~ Benelux, the Benelux countries.

benêt |bənɛ| nm simpleton.

bénévolat |bānāvolá| nm voluntary service ou work.

bénévole |bānāvol| a voluntary, unpaid.

bénévolement |bānāvolmáṅ| ad voluntarily.

Bengale |bàṅgál| nm: **le** ~ .Bengal; **le golfe du** ~ the Bay of Bengal.

bengali |bàṅgálē| a Bengali, Bengalese ♦ nm (LING) Bengali.

Bénin |bānaṅ| nm: **le** ~ Benin.

bénin, igne |bānaṅ, -ēny| a minor, mild; (tumeur) benign.

bénir |bānēr| vt to bless.

bénit, e |bānē, -ēt| a consecrated; **eau** ~**e** holy water.

bénitier |bānētyā| nm stoup, font (for holy water).

benjamin, e |bàṅzhámaṅ, -ēn| nm/f youngest child; (SPORT) under-13.

benne |bɛn| nf tub (US), skip (Brit); (de téléphérique) (cable) car; ~ **basculante** dump ou dumper truck.

benzine |bàṅzēn| nf benzine.

béotien, ne |bāosyaṅ, -ɛn| nm/f philistine.

BEP sigle m (= Brevet d'études professionnelles) school-leaving diploma, taken at approx. 18 years.

BEPA |bāpá| sigle m (= Brevet d'études professionnelles agricoles) school-leaving diploma in agriculture, taken at approx. 18 years.

BEPC sigle m (= Brevet d'études du premier cycle) former school certificate (taken at approx. 16 years).

béquille |bākēy| nf crutch; (de bicyclette) stand.

berbère |berber| a Berber ♦ nm (LING) Berber ♦ nm/f: **B~** Berber.

bercail |berkáy| nm fold.

berceau, x |bersō| nm cradle, crib.

bercer |bersā| vt to rock, cradle; (suj: musique etc) to lull; ~ **qn de** (promesses etc) to delude sb with.

berceur, euse |bersœr, -œz| a soothing ♦ nf (chanson) lullaby.

béret (basque) |bāre(básk(ə))| nm beret.

bergamote |bergàmot| nf (BOT) bergamot.

berge |berzh(ə)| nf bank.

berger, ère |berzhā, -er| nm/f shepherd/shepherdess; ~ **allemand** (chien) German shepherd (dog) (US), alsatian (dog) (Brit).

bergerie |berzhərē| nf sheep pen.

béribéri |bārēbārē| nm beriberi.

Berlin |berlaṅ| n Berlin; ~**-Est/-Ouest** East/West Berlin.

berline |berlēn| nf (AUTO) sedan (US), saloon (car) (Brit).

berlingot |berlàṅgō| nm (emballage) carton (pyramid shaped); (bonbon) lozenge.

berlinois, e |berlēnwà, -wáz| a of ou from Berlin ♦ nm/f: **B~, e** Berliner.

berlue |bārlü| nf: **j'ai la** ~ I must be seeing things.

bermuda |bermüdá| nm (short) Bermuda shorts.

Bermudes [bermüd] *nfpl*: **les (îles)** ~ Bermuda.
Berne [bern(ə)] *n* Bern.
berne [bern(ə)] *nf*: **en** ~ at half-mast; **mettre en** ~ to fly at half-mast.
berner [bernā] *vt* to fool.
bernois, e [bernwá, -wáz] *a* Bernese.
berrichon, ne [berēshóṅ, -on] *a* of *ou* from the Berry.
besace [bəzás] *nf* beggar's bag.
besogne [bəzony] *nf* work *q*, job.
besogneux, euse [bəzonyœ̄, -œ̄z] *a* hardworking.
besoin [bəzwaṅ] *nm* need; (*pauvreté*): **le** ~ need, want; **le** ~ **d'argent/de gloire** the need for money/glory; ~**s (naturels)** nature's needs; **faire ses** ~**s** to relieve o.s.; **avoir** ~ **de qch/faire qch** to need sth/to do sth; **il n'y a pas** ~ **de (faire)** there is no need to (do); **au** ~, **si** ~ **est** if need be; **pour les** ~**s de la cause** for the purpose in hand.
bestial, e, aux [bestyál, -ō] *a* bestial, brutish ♦ *nmpl* cattle.
bestiole [bestyol] *nf* (tiny) creature.
bétail [bātáy] *nm* livestock, cattle *pl*.
bétaillère [bātáyer] *nf* livestock truck.
bête [bet] *nf* animal; (*bestiole*) insect, creature ♦ *a* stupid, silly; **les** ~**s (the)** animals; **chercher la petite** ~ to nit-pick; ~ **noire** pet peeve (*US*) *ou* hate (*Brit*); ~ **sauvage** wild beast; ~ **de somme** beast of burden.
bêtement [betmáṅ] *ad* stupidly; **tout** ~ quite simply.
Bethléem [betlāem] *n* Bethlehem.
bêtifier [bātēfyā] *vi* to talk nonsense.
bêtise [bātēz] *nf* stupidity; (*action, remarque*) stupid thing (to say *ou* do); (*bonbon*) *type of mint candy* (*US*) *ou sweet* (*Brit*); **faire/dire une** ~ to do/say something stupid.
béton [bātóṅ] *nm* concrete; **(en)** ~ (*fig: alibi, argument*) cast iron; ~ **armé** reinforced concrete; ~ **précontraint** prestressed concrete.
bétonner [bātonā] *vt* to concrete (over).
bétonnière [bātonyer] *nf* cement mixer.
bette [bet] *nf* (*BOT*) Chinese cabbage.
betterave [betráv] *nf* (*rouge*) beet (*US*), beetroot (*Brit*); ~ **fourragère** mangel-wurzel; ~ **sucrière** sugar beet.
beugler [bœ̄glā] *vi* to low; (*péj: radio etc*) to blare ♦ *vt* (*péj: chanson etc*) to belt out.
Beur [bœr] *a, nm/f second-generation Arab immigrant.*
beurre [bœr] *nm* butter; **mettre du** ~ **dans les épinards** (*fig*) to add a little to the kitty; ~ **de cacao** cocoa butter; ~ **noir** brown butter (sauce).
beurrer [bœrā] *vt* to butter.
beurrier [bœryā] *nm* butter dish.
beuverie [bœvrē] *nf* drinking session.
bévue [bāvü] *nf* blunder.
Beyrouth [bārōōt] *n* Beirut.
Bhoutan [bōōtáṅ] *nm*: **le** ~ Bhutan.
bi... [bē] *préfixe* bi..., two-.
biais [bye] *nm* (*moyen*) device, expedient; (*aspect*) angle; (*bande de tissu*) piece of cloth cut on the bias; **en** ~, **de** ~ (*obliquement*) at an angle; (*fig*) indirectly.
biaiser [byāzā] *vi* (*fig*) to sidestep the issue.

bibelot [bēblō] *nm* trinket, curio.
biberon [bēbróṅ] *nm* (feeding) bottle; **nourrir au** ~ to bottle-feed.
bible [bēbl(ə)] *nf* bible.
bibliobus [bēblēyobüs] *nm* bookmobile (*US*), mobile library van (*Brit*).
bibliographie [bēblēyográfē] *nf* bibliography.
bibliophile [bēblēyofēl] *nm/f* book-lover.
bibliothécaire [bēblēyotāker] *nm/f* librarian.
bibliothèque [bēblēyotek] *nf* library; (*meuble*) bookcase; ~ **municipale** public library.
biblique [bēblēk] *a* biblical.
bicarbonate [bēkárbonát] *nm*: ~ **(de soude)** bicarbonate of soda.
bicentenaire [bēsáṅtner] *nm* bicentenary.
biceps [bēseps] *nm* biceps.
biche [bēsh] *nf* doe.
bichonner [bēshonā] *vt* to groom.
bicolore [bēkolor] *a* two-colored (*US*), two-coloured (*Brit*).
bicoque [bēkok] *nf* (*péj*) shack, dump.
bicorne [bēkorn(ə)] *nm* cocked hat.
bicyclette [bēsēklet] *nf* bicycle.
bide [bēd] *nm* (*fam: ventre*) belly; (*THÉÂTRE*) flop.
bidet [bēde] *nm* bidet.
bidirectionnel, le [bēdēreksyonel] *a* bidirectional.
bidon [bēdóṅ] *nm* can ♦ *a inv* (*fam*) phoney.
bidonville [bēdóṅvēl] *nm* shanty town.
bidule [bēdül] *nm* (*fam*) thingamajig.
bielle [byel] *nf* connecting rod; (*AUTO*) tie (*US*) *ou* track (*Brit*) rod.
bien [byaṅ] *nm* good; (*patrimoine*) property *q*; **le** ~ **public** the public good; **faire du** ~ **à qn** to do sb good; **dire/penser du** ~ **de** to speak/think well of; **changer en** ~ to turn to the good; ~**s de consommation/ d'équipement** consumer/capital goods; ~**s durables** durables ♦ *ad* (*travailler*) well; (*approximativement*): **il y a** ~ **2 ans** at least 2 years ago; (*intensif*): ~ **jeune** rather young; ~ **assez** quite enough; ~ **mieux** very much better; ~ **du temps/des gens** quite a time/a number of people; **j'espère** ~ **y aller** I do hope to go; **il semble** ~ **que** it really seems that; **je veux** ~ **le faire** I'm (quite) willing *ou* happy to do it; **il faut** ~ **le faire** it has to be done; **tu as eu** ~ **raison de faire ça** you were quite right to do that; ~ **sûr**, ~ **entendu** certainly, of course; **c'est** ~ **fait** (*mérité*) it serves him (*ou* her *etc*) right; **croyant** ~ **faire** thinking he *etc* was doing the right thing; **faire** ~ **de ...** to be right to ...; **peut-être** ~ it could well be; **aimer** ~ to like; **aller** ~ to be well; **eh** ~! well!; **si** ~ **que** with the result that ♦ *excl* right!, OK!, fine! ♦ *a inv* good; (*joli*) good-looking; (*à l'aise*): **être** ~ to be fine; **ce n'est pas** ~ **de** it's not right to; **c'est (très)** ~ **(comme ça)** it's fine (like that); **ce n'est pas si** ~ **que ça** it's not as good *ou* great as all that; **c'est** ~? is that all right?; **des gens** ~ respectable people; **être** ~ **avec qn** to be on good terms with sb.
bien-aimé, e [byaṅnāmā] *a, nm/f* beloved.
bien-être [byaṅnetr(ə)] *nm* well-being.
bienfaisance [byaṅfəzáṅs] *nf* charity.

bienfaisant, e [byañfəzáñ, -áñt] *a* (*chose*) beneficial.

bienfait [byañfe] *nm* act of generosity, benefaction; (*de la science etc*) benefit.

bienfaiteur, trice [byañfetœr, -trēs] *nm/f* benefactor/benefactress.

bien-fondé [byañfóñdā] *nm* soundness.

bien-fonds [byañfóñ] *nm* property.

bienheureux, euse [byañnœrœ̄, -œ̄z] *a* happy; (*REL*) blessed, blest.

biennal, e, aux [byānál, -ō] *a* biennial.

bien-pensant, e [byañpáñsáñ, -áñt] *a* right-thinking ♦ *nm/f*: **les ~s** right-minded people.

bien que [byañk(ə)] *cj* although.

bienséance [byañsááñs] *nf* propriety, decorum *q*; **les ~s** (*convenances*) the proprieties.

bienséant, e [byañsááñ, -áñt] *a* proper, seemly.

bientôt [byañtō] *ad* soon; **à ~** see you soon.

bienveillance [byañveyáñs] *nf* kindness.

bienveillant, e [byañveyáñ, -áñt] *a* kindly.

bienvenu, e [byañvnü] *a* welcome ♦ *nm/f*: **être le ~/la ~e** to be welcome ♦ *nf*: **souhaiter la ~e à** to welcome; **~e à** welcome to.

bière [byer] *nf* (*boisson*) beer; (*cercueil*) bier; **~ blonde** light beer, lager (*Brit*); **~ brune** dark beer, brown ale (*Brit*); **~ (à la) pression** draft (*US*) *ou* draught (*Brit*) beer.

biffer [bēfā] *vt* to cross out.

bifteck [bēftek] *nm* steak.

bifurcation [bēfürkásyóñ] *nf* fork (*in road*); (*fig*) new direction.

bifurquer [bēfürkā] *vi* (*route*) to fork; (*véhicule*) to turn off.

bigame [bēgám] *a* bigamous.

bigamie [bēgámē] *nf* bigamy.

bigarré, e [bēgárā] *a* multicolored (*US*), multicoloured (*Brit*); (*disparate*) motley.

bigarreau, x [bēgárō] *nm* type of cherry.

bigorneau, x [bēgornō] *nm* winkle.

bigot, e [bēgō, -ot] (*péj*) *a* bigoted ♦ *nm/f* bigot.

bigoterie [bēgotrē] *nf* bigotry.

bigoudi [bēgōōdē] *nm* curler.

bigrement [bēgrəmáñ] *ad* (*fam*) fantastically.

bijou, x [bēzhōō] *nm* jewel.

bijouterie [bēzhōōtrē] *nf* (*magasin*) jewelry store (*US*), jeweller's (shop) (*Brit*); (*bijoux*) jewelry (*US*), jewellery (*Brit*).

bijoutier, ière [bēzhōōtyā, -yer] *nm/f* jeweler (*US*), jeweller (*Brit*).

bikini [bēkēnē] *nm* bikini.

bilan [bēláñ] *nm* (*COMM*) balance sheet(s); (*annuel*) end of year statement; (*fig*) (net) outcome; (*: de victimes*) toll; **faire le ~ de** to assess; to review; **déposer son ~** to file a bankruptcy statement; **~ de santé** (*MÉD*) check-up; **~ social** statement of a firm's policies towards its employees.

bilatéral, e, aux [bēlátárál, -ō] *a* bilateral.

bilboquet [bēlboke] *nm* (*jouet*) cup-and-ball game.

bile [bēl] *nf* bile; **se faire de la ~** (*fam*) to worry o.s. sick.

biliaire [bēlyer] *a* biliary.

bilieux, euse [bēlyœ̄, -œ̄z] *a* bilious; (*fig: colérique*) testy.

bilingue [bēlañg] *a* bilingual.

bilinguisme [bēlañgüēsm(ə)] *nm* bilingualism.

billard [bēyár] *nm* billiards *sg*; (*table*) billiard table; **c'est du ~** (*fam*) it's a cinch; **passer sur le ~** (*fam*) to have an (*ou* one's) operation; **~ électrique** pinball.

bille [bēy] *nf* ball; (*du jeu de billes*) marble; (*de bois*) log; **jouer aux ~s** to play marbles.

billet [bēye] *nm* (*aussi*: **~ de banque**) (bank)note; (*de cinéma, de bus etc*) ticket; (*courte lettre*) note; **~ à ordre** *ou* **de commerce** (*COMM*) promissory note, IOU; **~ d'avion/de train** plane/train ticket; **~ circulaire** round-trip ticket; **~ doux** love letter; **~ de faveur** complimentary ticket; **~ de loterie** lottery ticket; **~ de quai** platform ticket.

billetterie [bēyetrē] *nf* ticket office; (*distributeur*) ticket dispenser; (*BANQUE*) cash dispenser.

billion [bēlyóñ] *nm* trillion (*US*), billion (*Brit*).

billot [bēyō] *nm* block.

BIMA *sigle m* = *Bulletin d'information du ministère de l'agriculture*.

bimbeloterie [bañblotrē] *nf* (*objets*) knick-knacks *pl*.

bimensuel, le [bēmáñsüel] *a* bimonthly, twice-monthly.

bimestriel, le [bēmestrēyel] *a* bimonthly, two-monthly.

bimoteur [bēmotœr] *a* twin-engined.

binaire [bēner] *a* binary.

biner [bēnā] *vt* to hoe.

binette [bēnet] *nf* (*outil*) hoe.

binoclard, e [bēnoklár, -árd(ə)] (*fam*) *nm/f* four-eyes.

binocle [bēnokl(ə)] *nm* pince-nez.

binoculaire [bēnokülœr] *a* binocular.

binôme [bēnōm] *nm* binomial.

bio... [byo] *préfixe* bio....

biochimie [byoshēmē] *nf* biochemistry.

biochimique [byoshēmēk] *a* biochemical.

biochimiste [byoshēmēst(ə)] *nm/f* biochemist.

biodégradable [byodāgrádábl(ə)] *a* biodegradable.

biographe [byográf] *nm/f* biographer.

biographie [byográfē] *nf* biography.

biographique [byográfēk] *a* biographical.

biologie [byolōzhē] *nf* biology.

biologique [byolōzhēk] *a* biological.

biologiste [byolozhēst(ə)] *nm/f* biologist.

biopsie [byopsē] *nf* (*MÉD*) biopsy.

biosphère [byosfer] *nf* biosphere.

bipartisme [bēpártēsm(ə)] *nm* bipartisanship.

bipède [bēped] *nm* biped, two-footed creature.

biphasé, e [bēfázā] *a* (*ÉLEC*) two-phase.

biplace [bēplás] *a, nm* (*avion*) two-seater.

biplan [bēpláñ] *nm* biplane.

bique [bēk] *nf* nanny goat; (*péj*) old hag.

biquet, te [bēke, -et] *nm/f*: **mon ~** (*fam*) my lamb.

biréacteur [bērāáktœr] *nm* twin-engined jet.

birman, e [bērmáñ, -án] *a* Burmese.

Birmanie [bērmánē] *nf*: **la ~** Burma.

bis, e [bē, bēz] *a* (*couleur*) grayish (*US*) *ou* greyish (*Brit*) brown ♦ *ad* [bēs]: **12 ~** 12a *ou* A ♦ *excl, nm* [bēs] encore ♦ *nf* (*baiser*) kiss; (*vent*) North wind.

bisaïeul, e [bēsáyœl] *nm/f* great-grandfather/great-grandmother.

bisannuel, le [bēzánüel] *a* biennial.

bisbille [bēsbēy] *nf*: **être en ~ avec qn** to be at loggerheads with sb.

Biscaye [bēskā] *nf*: **le golfe de ~** the Bay of Biscay.

biscornu, e [bēskornü] *a* crooked; (*bizarre*) weird(-looking).

biscotte [bēskot] *nf* ≈ melba toast.

biscuit [bēskūē] *nm* cookie (*US*), biscuit (*Brit*); (*gateau*) sponge cake; **~ à la cuiller** ladyfinger (*US*), sponge finger (*Brit*).

biscuiterie [bēskūētrē] *nf* cookie (*US*) *ou* biscuit (*Brit*) manufacturing.

bise [bēz] *af, nf voir* **bis**.

biseau, x [bēzō] *nm* bevelled edge; **en ~** bevelled.

biseauter [bēzōtā] *vt* to bevel.

bisexué, e [bēseksüā] *a* bisexual.

bismuth [bēsmüt] *nm* bismuth.

bison [bēzôṅ] *nm* bison.

bisou [bēzōō] *nm* (*fam*) kiss.

bisque [bēsk(ə)] *nf*: **~ d'écrevisses** shrimp bisque.

bissectrice [bēsektrēs] *nf* bisector.

bisser [bēsā] *vt* (*faire rejouer: artiste, chanson*) to encore; (*rejouer: morceau*) to give an encore of.

bissextile [bēsekstēl] *a*: **année ~** leap year.

bistouri [bēstōōrē] *nm* lancet.

bistre [bēstr(ə)] *a* (*couleur*) bistre; (*peau, teint*) tanned.

bistro(t) [bēstrō] *nm* bistro, café.

BIT *sigle m* (= *Bureau international du travail*) ILO.

bit [bēt] *nm* (*INFORM*) bit.

biterrois, e [bēterwà, -wàz] *a* of *ou* from Béziers.

bitte [bēt] *nf*: **~ d'amarrage** bollard (*NAUT*).

bitume [bētüm] *nm* asphalt.

bitumer [bētümā] *vt* to asphalt.

bivalent, e [bēválåṅ, -åṅt] *a* bivalent.

bivouac [bēvwàk] *nm* bivouac.

bivouaquer [bēvwàkā] *vi* to bivouac.

bizarre [bēzár] *a* strange, odd.

bizarrement [bēzàrmåṅ] *ad* strangely, oddly.

bizarrerie [bēzàrrē] *nf* strangeness, oddness.

blackbouler [blákbōōlā] *vt* (*à une élection*) to blackball.

blafard, e [blàfàr, -àrd(ə)] *a* wan.

blague [blàg] *nf* (*propos*) joke; (*farce*) trick; **sans ~!** no kidding!; **~ à tabac** tobacco pouch.

blaguer [blàgā] *vi* to joke ♦ *vt* to tease.

blagueur, euse [blàgœr, -œz] *a* teasing ♦ *nm/f* joker.

blair [bler] *nm* (*fam*) beak.

blaireau, x [blerō] *nm* (*ZOOL*) badger; (*brosse*) shaving brush.

blairer [blārā] *vt*: **je ne peux pas le ~** I can't bear *ou* stand him.

blâmable [blàmábl(ə)] *a* blameworthy.

blâme [blàm] *nm* blame; (*sanction*) reprimand.

blâmer [blàmā] *vt* (*réprouver*) to blame; (*réprimander*) to reprimand.

blanc, blanche [blåṅ, blåṅsh] *a* white; (*non imprimé*) blank; (*innocent*) pure ♦ *nm/f* white, white man/woman ♦ *nm* (*couleur*) white; (*linge*): **le ~** whites *pl*; (*espace non écrit*) blank; (*aussi*: **~ d'œuf**) (egg-)white;

(*aussi*: **~ de poulet**) breast, white meat; (*aussi*: **vin ~**) white wine ♦ *nf* (*MUS*) half note (*US*), minim (*Brit*); **d'une voix blanche** in a toneless voice; **aux cheveux ~s** white-haired; **le ~ de l'œil** the white of the eye; **laisser en ~** to leave blank; **chèque en ~** blank check; **à ~** *ad* (*chauffer*) white-hot; (*tirer, charger*) with blanks; **saigner à ~** to bleed white; **~ cassé** off-white.

blanc-bec, pl blancs-becs [blåṅbek] *nm* greenhorn.

blanchâtre [blåṅshâtr(ə)] *a* (*teint, lumière*) whitish.

blancheur [blåṅshœr] *nf* whiteness.

blanchir [blåṅshēr] *vt* (*gén*) to whiten; (*linge, fig: argent*) to launder; (*CULIN*) to blanch; (*fig: disculper*) to clear ♦ *vi* to grow white; (*cheveux*) to go white; **blanchi à la chaux** whitewashed.

blanchissage [blåṅshēsázh] *nm* (*du linge*) laundering.

blanchisserie [blåṅshēsrē] *nf* laundry.

blanchisseur, euse [blåṅshēsœr, -œz] *nm/f* launderer.

blanc-seing, pl blancs-seings [blåṅsaṅ] *nm* signed blank paper.

blanquette [blåṅket] *nf* (*CULIN*): **~ de veau** veal in a white sauce, blanquette de veau.

blasé, e [blàzā] *a* blasé.

blaser [blàzā] *vt* to make blasé.

blason [blàzôṅ] *nm* coat of arms.

blasphémateur, trice [blásfāmátœr, -trēs] *nm/f* blasphemer.

blasphématoire [blásfāmátwár] *a* blasphemous.

blasphème [blàsfem] *nm* blasphemy.

blasphémer [blásfāmā] *vi* to blaspheme ♦ *vt* to blaspheme against.

blatte [blát] *nf* cockroach.

blazer [blàzer] *nm* blazer.

blé [blā] *nm* wheat; **~ en herbe** wheat on the ear; **~ noir** buckwheat.

bled [bled] *nm* (*péj*) hole; (*en Afrique du Nord*): **le ~** the interior.

blême [blem] *a* pale.

blêmir [blāmēr] *vi* (*personne*) to (turn) pale; (*lueur*) to grow pale.

blennorragie [blānorázhē] *nf* gonorrhoea.

blessant, e [blesåṅ, -åṅt] *a* hurtful.

blessé, e [blāsā] *a* injured ♦ *nm/f* injured person, casualty; **un ~ grave, un grand ~** a seriously injured *ou* wounded person.

blesser [blāsā] *vt* to injure; (*délibérément: MIL etc*) to wound; (*suj: souliers etc, offenser*) to hurt; **se ~** to injure o.s.; **se ~ au pied** *etc* to injure one's foot *etc*.

blessure [blāsür] *nf* injury; wound.

blet, te [ble, blet] *a* overripe.

blette [blet] *nf* = **bette**.

bleu, e [blœ] *a* blue; (*bifteck*) very rare ♦ *nm* (*couleur*) blue; (*novice*) greenhorn; (*contusion*) bruise; (*vêtement: aussi*: **~s**) coveralls *pl* (*US*), overalls *pl* (*Brit*); **avoir une peur ~e** to be scared stiff; **zone ~e** ≈ restricted parking area; **fromage ~** blue cheese; **au ~** (*CULIN*) au bleu; **~ (de lessive)** ≈ bluing (*US*), ≈ blue bag (*Brit*); **~ de méthylène** (*MÉD*) methylene blue; **~ marine/nuit/roi** navy/midnight/royal blue.

bleuâtre [blœ̃âtr(ə)] *a* (*fumée etc*) bluish, blueish.

bleuet [blœ̃e] *nm* cornflower.

bleuir [blœ̃ēr] *vt, vi* to turn blue.

bleuté, e [blœ̃tã] *a* blue-shaded.

blindage [blaṅdâzh] *nm* armor-plating (*US*), armour-plating (*Brit*).

blindé, e [blaṅdã] *a* armored (*US*), armoured (*Brit*); (*fig*) hardened ♦ *nm* armored *ou* armoured car; (*char*) tank.

blinder [blaṅdã] *vt* to armor (*US*), armour (*Brit*); (*fig*) to harden.

blizzard [blēzãr] *nm* blizzard.

bloc [blok] *nm* (*de pierre etc*, *INFORM*) block; (*de papier à lettres*) pad; (*ensemble*) group, block; **serré à ~** tightened right down; **en ~** as a whole; wholesale; **faire ~** to unite; **~ opératoire** operating rooms (*US*), theatre block (*Brit*); **~ sanitaire** toilet block; **~ sténo** shorthand notebook.

blocage [blokâzh] *nm* (*voir bloquer*) blocking; jamming; freezing; (*PSYCH*) hang-up.

bloc-cuisine, *pl* **blocs-cuisines** [blokkü̃ēzēn] *nm* kitchen unit.

bloc-cylindres, *pl* **blocs-cylindres** [bloksēlaṅdr(ə)] *nm* cylinder block.

bloc-évier, *pl* **blocs-éviers** [blokãvyã] *nm* sink unit.

bloc-moteur, *pl* **blocs-moteurs** [blokmotœr] *nm* engine block.

bloc-notes, *pl* **blocs-notes** [bloknot] *nm* note pad.

blocus [blokü̃s] *nm* blockade.

blond, e [blóṅ, -óṅd] *a* fair; (*plus clair*) blond; (*sable, blés*) golden ♦ *nm/f* fair-haired *ou* blond man/woman; **~ cendré** ash blond.

blondeur [blóṅdœr] *nf* fairness; blondness.

blondin, e [blóṅdaṅ, -ēn] *nm/f* fair-haired *ou* blond child *ou* young person.

blondinet, te [blóṅdēne, -et] *nm/f* blondy.

blondir [blóṅdēr] *vi* (*personne, cheveux*) to go fair *ou* blond.

bloquer [blokã] *vt* (*passage*) to block; (*pièce mobile*) to jam; (*crédits, compte*) to freeze; (*personne, négociations etc*) to hold up; (*regrouper*) to group; **~ les freins** to jam on the brakes.

blottir [blotēr]: **se ~** *vi* to huddle up.

blousant, e [blõõzaṅ, âṅt] *a* blousing out.

blouse [blõõz] *nf* smock.

blouser [blõõzã] *vi* to blouse out.

blouson [blõõzóṅ] *nm* blouson (jacket); **~ noir** (*fig*) ≈ hell's angel.

blue-jean(s) [blõõdzhēn(s)] *nm* jeans.

blues [blõõz] *nm* blues *pl*.

bluet [blü̃e] *nm* = **bleuet**.

bluff [blœf] *nm* bluff.

bluffer [blœfã] *vi, vt* to bluff.

BN *sigle f* = *Bibliothèque nationale*.

BNP *sigle f* = *Banque nationale de Paris*.

boa [boá] *nm* (*ZOOL*): **~ (constricteur)** boa (constrictor); (*tour de cou*) (feather *ou* fur) boa.

bobard [bobár] *nm* (*fam*) tall story.

bobèche [bobesh] *nf* bobeche (*US*), candlering (*Brit*).

bobine [bobēn] *nf* (*de fil*) reel; (*de machine à coudre*) spool; (*de machine à écrire*) ribbon; (*ÉLEC*) coil; **~ (d'allumage)** (*AUTO*) coil; **~**

de pellicule (*PHOTO*) roll of film.

bobo [bõbõ] *nm* (*aussi fig*) sore spot.

bob(sleigh) [bob(sleg)] *nm* bobsled (*US*), bob(sleigh) (*Brit*).

bocage [bokâzh] *nm* (*GÉO*) bocage, *farmland criss-crossed by hedges and trees*; (*bois*) grove, copse.

bocal, aux [bokál, -õ] *nm* jar.

bock [bok] *nm* (*beer*) glass; (*contenu*) glass of beer.

bœuf [bœf, *pl* bœ̃] *nm* ox (*pl* oxen), steer; (*CULIN*) beef.

bof [bof] *excl* (*fam*: *indifférence*) don't care!; (: *pas terrible*) nothing special.

Bogotá [bogotá] *n* Bogotá.

Bohême [boem] *nf*: **la ~** Bohemia.

bohème [boem] *a* happy-go-lucky, unconventional.

bohémien, ne [boãmyaṅ, -en] *a* Bohemian ♦ *nm/f* gipsy.

boire [bwár] *vt* to drink; (*s'imprégner de*) to soak up; **~ un coup** to have a drink.

bois [bwá] *vb voir* **boire** ♦ *nm* wood; (*ZOOL*) antler; (*MUS*): **les ~** the woodwinds (*US*), the woodwind (*Brit*); **de ~, en ~** wooden; **~ vert** green wood; **~ mort** deadwood; **~ de lit** bedstead.

boisé, e [bwázã] *a* woody, wooded.

boiser [bwázã] *vt* (*galerie de mine*) to timber; (*chambre*) to panel; (*terrain*) to plant with trees.

boiseries [bwázrē] *nfpl* panelling *sg*.

boisson [bwásóṅ] *nf* drink; **pris de ~** drunk, intoxicated; **~s alcoolisées** alcoholic beverages *ou* drinks; **~s non alcoolisées** soft drinks.

boit [bwá] *vb voir* **boire**.

boîte [bwát] *nf* box; (*fam*: *entreprise*) firm, company; **aliments en ~** canned *ou* tinned (*Brit*) foods; **~ de sardines/petits pois** can *ou* tin (*Brit*) of sardines/peas; **mettre qn en ~** (*fam*) to have a laugh at sb's expense; **~ d'allumettes** box of matches; (*vide*) matchbox; **~ de conserves** can *ou* tin (*Brit*) (of food); **~ crânienne** cranium; **~ à gants** glove compartment; **~ aux lettres** letter box, mailbox (*US*); (*INFORM*) mailbox; **~ à musique** music box; **~ noire** (*AVIAT*) black box; **~ de nuit** night club; **~ à ordures** trash can (*US*), dustbin (*Brit*); **~ postale (BP)** PO box; **~ de vitesses** transmission (*US*), gear box (*Brit*).

boiter [bwátã] *vi* to limp; (*fig*) to wobble; (*raisonnement*) to be shaky.

boiteux, euse [bwátœ̃, -œ̃z] *a* lame; wobbly; shaky.

boîtier [bwátyã] *nm* case; (*d'appareil-photo*) body; **~ de montre** watch case.

boitiller [bwátēyã] *vi* to limp slightly, have a slight limp.

boive [bwáv] *etc vb voir* **boire**.

bol [bol] *nm* bowl; (*contenu*): **un ~ de café** *etc* a bowl of coffee *etc*; **un ~ d'air** a breath of fresh air; **en avoir ras le ~** (*fam*) to have had a bellyful.

bolée [bolã] *nf* bowlful.

bolet [bole] *nm* boletus (mushroom).

bolide [bolēd] *nm* racing car; **comme un ~** like a rocket.

Bolivie [bolēvē] *nf*: **la** ~ Bolivia.
bolivien, ne [bolēvyań, -en] *a* Bolivian ♦ *nm/f*: **B~, ne** Bolivian.
bolognais, e [bolonyc, -cz] *a* Bolognese.
Bologne [bolony] *n* Bologna.
bombance [bôńbáńs] *nf*: **faire** ~ to have a feast, revel.
bombardement [bôńbàrdəmáń] *nm* bombing.
bombarder [bôńbàrdā] *vt* to bomb; ~ **qn de** *(cailloux, lettres)* to bombard sb with; ~ **qn directeur** to thrust sb into the director's seat.
bombardier [bôńbàrdyā] *nm (avion)* bomber; *(aviateur)* bombardier.
bombe [bôńb] *nf* bomb; *(atomiseur)* (aerosol) spray; *(ÉQUITATION)* riding cap; **faire la** ~ *(fam)* to go on a binge; ~ **atomique** atomic bomb; ~ **à retardement** time bomb.
bombé, e [bôńbā] *a* rounded; *(mur)* bulging; *(front)* domed; *(route)* steeply cambered.
bomber [bôńbā] *vi* to bulge; *(route)* to camber ♦ *vt*: ~ **le torse** to swell out one's chest.
bon, bonne [bôń, bon] *a* good; *(charitable)*: ~ **(envers)** good (to), kind (to); *(juste)*: **le** ~ **numéro/moment** the right number/moment; *(intensif)*: **un** ~ **nombre** a good number; *(approprié)*: ~ **à/pour** fit to/for ♦ *nm (billet)* voucher; *(aussi)*: ~ **cadeau)** gift certificate *(US)*, gift voucher *(Brit)* ♦ *nf (domestique)* maid ♦ *ad*: **il fait** ~ it's *ou* the weather's fine ♦ *excl* right!, good!; **vous êtes trop** ~ you are too kind; **avoir** ~ **goût** to taste nice *ou* good; *(fig)* to have good taste; **avoir** ~ **dos** to be always willing to shoulder responsibility; *(chose)* to be a good excuse; **bonne heure** early; **sentir** ~ to smell good; **tenir** ~ to stand firm, hold out; **pour de** ~ for good; **à quoi** ~ **(...)?** what's the good *ou* use (of ...)?; **juger** ~ **de faire ...** to think fit to do ...; **ah** ~? (oh) really?; **il y a du** ~ **dans cela** there are some advantages in it; **il y a du** ~ **dans ce qu'il dit** there is some sense in what he says; ~ **anniversaire!** happy birthday!; ~ **voyage!** have a good journey!, enjoy your trip!; **bonne chance!** good luck!; **bonne année!** happy New Year!; **bonne nuit!** good night!; ~ **de caisse** cash voucher; ~ **enfant** *a inv* accommodating, easy-going; ~ **d'essence** *(US) ou* petrol *(Brit)* coupon; ~ **marché** *a inv, ad* cheap; ~ **mot** witticism; ~ **sens** common sense; ~ **à tirer** ready *(US) ou* pass *(Brit)* for press; ~ **du Trésor** Treasury bond; ~ **vivant** jovial chap; **bonne d'enfant** nanny; **bonne femme** *(péj)* woman; female *(péj)*; **bonne sœur** nun; **bonne à tout faire** general help; **bonnes œuvres** charitable works; charities.
bonasse [bonás] *a* soft, meek.
bonbon [bôńbôń] *nm* (boiled) candy *(US) ou* sweet *(Brit)*.
bonbonne [bôńbon] *nf* demijohn; carboy.
bonbonnière [bôńbonycr] *nf* candy *(US) ou* sweet *(Brit)* box.
bond [bôń] *nm* leap; *(d'une balle)* rebound, ricochet; **faire un** ~ to leap in the air; **d'un seul** ~ in one bound, with one leap; ~ **en avant** *(fig: progrès)* leap forward.
bonde [bôńd] *nf (d'évier etc)* plug; *(: trou)* plughole; *(de tonneau)* bung; bunghole.

bondé, e [bôńdā] *a* packed (full).
bondieuserie [bôńdyœzrē] *nf (péj: objet)* religious knick-knack.
bondir [bôńdēr] *vi* to leap; ~ **de joie** *(fig)* to jump for joy; ~ **de colère** *(fig)* to be hopping mad.
bonheur [bonœr] *nm* happiness; **avoir le** ~ **de** to have the good fortune to; **porter** ~ **(à qn)** to bring (sb) luck; **au petit** ~ haphazardly; **par** ~ fortunately.
bonhomie [bonomē] *nf* goodnaturedness.
bonhomme [bonom], *pl* **bonshommes** [bôńzom] *nm* fellow ♦ *a* good-natured; **un vieux** ~ an old chap; **aller son** ~ **de chemin** to carry on in one's own sweet way; ~ **de neige** snowman.
boni [bonē] *nm* profit.
bonification [bonēfēkâsyôń] *nf* bonus.
bonifier [bonēfyā] *vt*, **se** ~ *vi* to improve.
boniment [bonēmáń] *nm* patter *q*.
bonjour [bôńzhōōr] *excl, nm* hello; *(selon l'heure)* good morning *(ou* afternoon*)*; **donner** *ou* **souhaiter le** ~ **à qn** to bid sb good morning *ou* afternoon.
Bonn [bon] *n* Bonn.
bonne [bon] *af, nf voir* **bon**.
bonne-maman, *pl* **bonnes-mamans** [bonmámáń] granny, grandma, gran.
bonnement [bonmáń] *ad*: **tout** ~ quite simply.
bonnet [bonc] *nm* bonnet, hat; *(de soutien-gorge)* cup; ~ **d'âne** dunce's cap; ~ **de bain** bathing cap; ~ **de nuit** nightcap.
bonneterie [bonetrē] *nf* hosiery.
bon-papa, *pl* **bons-papas** [bôńpápá] *nm* grandpa, grandad.
bonsoir [bôńswàr] *excl* good evening.
bonté [bôńtā] *nf* kindness *q*; **avoir la** ~ **de** to be kind *ou* good enough to.
bonus [bonüs] *nm (assurances)* no-claims discount *(US) ou* bonus *(Brit)*.
bonze [bôńz] *nm (REL)* bonze.
boomerang [bōōmráṅg] *nm* boomerang.
borborygme [borborēgm(ə)] *nm* rumbling noise.
bord [bor] *nm (de table, verre, falaise)* edge; *(de rivière, lac)* bank; *(de route)* side; *(de vêtement)* edge, border; *(de chapeau)* brim; *(monter)* **à** ~ (to go) on board; **jeter par-dessus** ~ to throw overboard; **le commandant/les hommes du** ~ the ship's captain/crew; **du même** ~ *(fig)* of the same opinion; **au** ~ **de la mer/route** at the seaside/roadside; **être au** ~ **des larmes** to be on the verge of tears; **virer de** ~ *(NAVIG)* to tack; **sur les** ~s *(fig)* slightly; **de tous** ~s on all sides; ~ **du trottoir** curb *(US)*, kerb *(Brit)*.
bordage [bordàzh] *nm (NAVIG)* planking *q*; plating *q*.
bordeaux [bordō] *nm* Bordeaux ♦ *a inv* maroon.
bordée [bordā] *nf* broadside; **une** ~ **d'injures** a volley of abuse; **tirer une** ~ to go on the town.
bordel [bordcl] *nm* brothel; *(fam!)* goddamn *(US) ou* bloody *(Brit)* mess *(!)* ♦ *excl* hell!
bordelais, e [bordəlc, -cz] *a* of *ou* from Bordeaux.

border [bordā] *vt* (*être le long de*) to border, line; (*garnir*): ~ **qch de** to line sth with; to trim sth with; (*qn dans son lit*) to tuck in.

bordereau, x [bordərō] *nm* docket, slip.

bordure [bordür] *nf* border; (*sur un vêtement*) trim(ming), border; **en** ~ **de** on the edge of.

boréal, e, aux [borāāl, -ō] *a* boreal, northern.

borgne [borny(ə)] *a* one-eyed; **hôtel** ~ shady hotel; **fenêtre** ~ obstructed window.

bornage [bornazh] *nm* (*d'un terrain*) demarcation.

borne [born(ə)] *nf* boundary stone; (*aussi*: ~ **kilométrique**) kilometer-marker, ≈ milestone; ~s *nfpl* (*fig*) limits; **dépasser les** ~s to go too far; **sans** ~(s) boundless.

borné, e [bornā] *a* narrow; (*obtus*) narrowminded.

Bornéo [bornāō] *nm*: **le** ~ Borneo.

borner [bornā] *vt* (*délimiter*) to limit; (*limiter*) to confine; **se** ~ **à faire** to content o.s. with doing; to limit o.s. to doing.

bosniaque [boznyák] *a* Bosnian.

bosnien, ne [boznyań, -en] *a* Bosnian.

Bosphore [bosfor] *nm*: **le** ~ the Bosphorus.

bosquet [boske] *nm* copse, grove.

bosse [bos] *nf* (*de terrain etc*) bump; (*enflure*) lump; (*du bossu, du chameau*) hump; **avoir la** ~ **de l'anglais** *etc* to have a gift for English *etc*; **il a roulé sa** ~ he's been around.

bosseler [boslā] *vt* (*ouvrer*) to emboss; (*abîmer*) to dent.

bosser [bosā] *vi* (*fam*) to work; (*: dur*) to slave (away).

bosseur, euse [bosœr, -œz] *nm/f* (hard) worker.

bossu, e [bosü] *nm/f* hunchback.

bot [bō] *am*: **pied** ~ club foot.

botanique [botánēk] *nf* botany ♦ *a* botanic(al).

botaniste [botánēst(ə)] *nm/f* botanist.

Botswana [botswáná] *nm*: **le** ~ Botswana.

botte [bot] *nf* (*soulier*) (high) boot; (*ESCRIME*) thrust; (*gerbe*): ~ **de paille** bundle of straw; ~ **de radis/d'asperges** bunch of radishes/asparagus; ~s **de caoutchouc** wellington boots.

botter [botā] *vt* to put boots on; (*donner un coup de pied à*) to kick; (*fam*): **ça me botte** I like that.

bottier [botyā] *nm* bootmaker.

bottillon [boteȳoń] *nm* bootee.

bottin [botań] *nm* ® directory.

bottine [botēn] *nf* ankle boot.

botulisme [botülēsm(ə)] *nm* botulism.

bouc [boōk] *nm* goat; (*barbe*) goatee; ~ **émissaire** scapegoat.

boucan [boōkáń] *nm* din, racket.

bouche [boōsh] *nf* mouth; **une** ~ **à nourrir** a mouth to feed; **les** ~s **inutiles** the nonproductive members of the population; **faire le** ~ **à** ~ **à qn** to give sb mouth-to-mouth resuscitation; **de** ~ **à oreille** confidentially; **pour la bonne** ~ (*pour la fin*) till last; **faire venir l'eau à la** ~ to make one's mouth water; ~ **cousue!** mum's the word!; ~ **d'aération** air vent; ~ **de chaleur** hot air vent; ~ **d'égout** manhole; ~ **d'incendie** fire hydrant; ~ **de métro** métro entrance.

bouché, e [boōshā] *a* (*flacon etc*) stoppered; (*temps, ciel*) overcast; (*carrière*) blocked; (*péj: personne*) thick; (*trompette*) muted; **avoir le nez** ~ to have a stuffy (*US*) *ou* blocked(-up) (*Brit*) nose.

bouchée [boōshā] *nf* mouthful; **ne faire qu'une** ~ **de** (*fig*) to make short work of; **pour une** ~ **de pain** (*fig*) for next to nothing; ~s **à la reine** chicken vol-au-vents.

boucher [boōshā] *nm* butcher ♦ *vt* (*pour colmater*) to stop up; to fill up; (*obstruer*) to block (up); **se** ~ (*tuyau etc*) to block up, get blocked up; **se** ~ **le nez** to hold one's nose.

bouchère [boōsher] *nf* butcher; (*femme du boucher*) butcher's wife.

boucherie [boōshrē] *nf* butcher's (shop); (*métier*) butchery; (*fig*) slaughter, butchery.

bouche-trou [boōshtroō] *nm* (*fig*) stop-gap.

bouchon [boōshoń] *nm* (*en liège*) cork; (*autre matière*) stopper; (*fig: embouteillage*) hold-up; (*PÊCHE*) float; ~ **doseur** measuring cap.

bouchonner [boōshonā] *vt* to rub down ♦ *vi* to form a traffic jam.

bouchot [boōshō] *nm* mussel bed.

bouclage [boōklázh] *nm* sealing off.

boucle [boōkl(ə)] *nf* (*forme, figure, aussi IN-FORM*) loop; (*objet*) buckle; ~ **(de cheveux)** curl; ~ **d'oreilles** earring.

bouclé, e [boōklā] *a* curly; (*tapis*) uncut.

boucler [boōklā] *vt* (*fermer: ceinture etc*) to fasten; (*: magasin*) to shut; (*terminer*) to finish off; (*: circuit*) to complete; (*budget*) to balance; (*enfermer*) to shut away; (*: condamné*) to lock up; (*: quartier*) to seal off ♦ *vi* to curl; **faire** ~ (*cheveux*) to curl; ~ **la boucle** (*AVIAT*) to loop the loop.

bouclette [boōklet] *nf* small curl.

bouclier [boōklēyā] *nm* shield.

bouddha [boōdà] *nm* Buddha.

bouddhisme [boōdēsm(ə)] *nm* Buddhism.

bouddhiste [boōdēst(ə)] *nm/f* Buddhist.

bouder [boōdā] *vi* to sulk ♦ *vt* (*chose*) to turn one's nose up at; (*personne*) to refuse to have anything to do with.

bouderie [boōdrē] *nf* sulking *q*.

boudeur, euse [boōdœr, -œz] *a* sullen, sulky.

boudin [boōdań] *nm* (*CULIN*) blood sausage (*US*), black pudding (*Brit*); (*TECH*) roll; ~ **blanc** sausage (*US*), white pudding (*Brit*).

boudiné, e [boōdēnā] *a* (*doigt*) podgy; (*serré*): ~ **dans** (*vêtement*) bulging out of.

boudoir [boōdwár] *nm* boudoir; (*biscuit*) ladyfinger (*US*), sponge finger (*Brit*).

boue [boō] *nf* mud.

bouée [bwā] *nf* buoy; (*de baigneur*) rubber ring; ~ **(de sauvetage)** lifebuoy; (*fig*) lifeline.

boueux, euse [bwœ, -œz] *a* muddy ♦ *nm* garbage (*US*) *ou* refuse (*Brit*) collector.

bouffant, e [boōfàń, -àńt] *a* puffed out.

bouffe [boōf] *nf* (*fam*) grub, food.

bouffée [boōfā] *nf* puff; ~ **de chaleur** blast of hot air; ~ **de fièvre/de honte** flush of fever/shame; ~ **d'orgueil** fit of pride.

bouffer [boōfā] *vi* (*fam*) to eat; (*COUTURE*) to puff out ♦ *vt* (*fam*) to eat.

bouffi, e [boōfē] *a* swollen.

bouffon, ne [boōfoń, -on] *a* farcical, comical ♦ *nm* jester.

bouge [boozh] *nm* (*bar louche*) (low) dive; (*taudis*) hovel.

bougeoir [boozhwár] *nm* candlestick.

bougeotte [boozhot] *nf*: **avoir la ~** to have the fidgets.

bouger [boozhā] *vi* to move; (*dent etc*) to be loose; (*changer*) to alter; (*agir*) to stir ♦ *vt* to move; **se ~** (*fam*) to move (o.s.).

bougie [boozhē] *nf* candle; (*AUTO*) spark plug.

bougon, ne [boogóń, -on] *a* grumpy.

bougonner [boogonā] *vi, vt* to grumble.

bougre [boogr(ə)] *nm* chap; (*fam*): **ce ~ de** ... that confounded ....

bouillabaisse [booyábes] *nf type of fish soup*.

bouillant, e [booyáń, -áńt] *a* (*qui bout*) boiling; (*très chaud*) boiling (hot); (*fig: ardent*) hot-headed; **~ de colère** *etc* seething with anger *etc*.

bouilleur [booyœr] *nm*: **~ de cru** (home) distiller.

bouillie [booyē] *nf* gruel; (*de bébé*) cereal; **en ~** (*fig*) crushed.

bouillir [booyēr] *vi* to boil ♦ *vt* (*aussi*: **faire ~**: *CULIN*) to boil; **~ de colère** *etc* to seethe with anger *etc*.

bouilloire [booywár] *nf* kettle.

bouillon [booyóń] *nm* (*CULIN*) stock *q*; (*bulles, écume*) bubble; **~ de culture** culture medium.

bouillonnement [booyonmáń] *nm* (*d'un liquide*) bubbling; (*des idées*) ferment.

bouillonner [booyonā] *vi* to bubble; (*fig*) to bubble up; (*torrent*) to foam.

bouillotte [booyot] *nf* hot-water bottle.

boulanger, ère [boolánzhā, -er] *nm/f* baker ♦ *nf* (*femme du boulanger*) baker's wife.

boulangerie [boolánzhrē] *nf* bakery, baker's (shop); (*commerce*) bakery; **~ industrielle** bakery.

boulangerie-pâtisserie, *pl* **boulangeries-pâtisseries** [boolánzhrēpátēsrē] *nf* baker's and confectioner's (shop).

boule [bool] *nf* (*gén*) ball; (*pour jouer*) bowl; (*de machine à écrire*) typing element (*US*), golf ball (*Brit*); **roulé en ~** curled up in a ball; **se mettre en ~** (*fig*) to fly off the handle, blow one's top; **perdre la ~** (*fig: fam*) to go off one's rocker; **~ de gomme** (*bonbon*) gum(drop), pastille; **~ de neige** snowball; **faire ~ de neige** (*fig*) to snowball.

bouleau, x [boolō] *nm* (silver) birch.

bouledogue [booldog] *nm* bulldog.

boulet [boole] *nm* (*aussi*: **~ de canon**) cannonball; (*de bagnard*) ball and chain; (*charbon*) briquette.

boulette [boolet] *nf* ball.

boulevard [boolvár] *nm* boulevard.

bouleversant, e [boolversáń, -áńt] *a* (*récit*) deeply distressing; (*nouvelle*) shattering.

bouleversé, e [boolversā] *a* (*ému*) deeply distressed; shattered.

bouleversement [boolversəmáń] *nm* (*politique, social*) upheaval.

bouleverser [boolversā] *vt* (*émouvoir*) to overwhelm; (*causer du chagrin à*) to distress; (*pays, vie*) to disrupt; (*papiers, objets*) to turn upside down, upset.

boulier [boolyā] *nm* abacus; (*de jeu*) scoring board.

boulimie [boolēmē] *nf* compulsive eating.

boulingrin [boolańgrań] *nm* lawn.

bouliste [boolēst(ə)] *nm/f* bowler.

boulocher [booloshā] *vi* (*laine etc*) to develop little snarls.

boulodrome [boolodrom] *nm* bowling ground.

boulon [boolóń] *nm* bolt.

boulonner [boolonā] *vt* to bolt.

boulot [boolō] *nm* (*fam: travail*) work.

boulot, te [boolō, -ot] *a* plump, tubby.

boum [boom] *nm* bang ♦ *nf* party.

bouquet [booke] *nm* (*de fleurs*) bunch (of flowers), bouquet; (*de persil etc*) bunch; (*parfum*) bouquet; (*fig*) crowning piece; **c'est le ~!** that's the last straw!; **~ garni** (*CULIN*) bouquet garni.

bouquetin [booktań] *nm* ibex.

bouquin [bookań] *nm* (*fam*) book.

bouquiner [bookēnā] *vi* (*fam*) to read.

bouquiniste [bookēnēst(ə)] *nm/f* bookseller.

bourbeux, euse [boorbœ̄, -œ̄z] *a* muddy.

bourbier [boorbyā] *nm* (*quag*)mire.

bourde [boord(ə)] *nf* (*erreur*) howler; (*gaffe*) blunder.

bourdon [boordóń] *nm* bumblebee.

bourdonnement [boordonmáń] *nm* buzzing *q*, buzz; **avoir des ~s d'oreilles** to have a buzzing (noise) in one's ears.

bourdonner [boordonā] *vi* to buzz; (*moteur*) to hum.

bourg [boor] *nm* small market town (*ou* village).

bourgade [boorgád] *nf* township.

bourgeois, e [boorzhwá, -wáz] *a* (*péj*) ≈ (upper) middle class; bourgeois; (*maison etc*) very comfortable ♦ *nm/f* (*autrefois*) burgher.

bourgeoisie [boorzhwázē] *nf* ≈ upper middle classes *pl*; bourgeoisie; **petite ~** middle classes.

bourgeon [boorzhóń] *nm* bud.

bourgeonner [boorzhonā] *vi* to bud.

Bourgogne [boorgony] *nf*: **la ~** Burgundy ♦ *nm*: **b~** burgundy (wine).

bourguignon, ne [boorgēnyóń, -on] *a* of *ou* from Burgundy, Burgundian; **bœuf ~** bœuf bourguignon.

Bourkina [boorkēnā] *nm*: **le ~** Burkina Faso.

bourlinguer [boorlańgā] *vi* to knock about a lot, get around a lot.

bourrade [boorád] *nf* shove, thump.

bourrage [boorázh] *nm* (*papier*) jamming; **~ de crâne** brainwashing; (*SCOL*) cramming.

bourrasque [boorásk(ə)] *nf* squall.

bourratif, ive [booratēf, -ēv] *a* filling, stodgy.

bourre [boor] *nf* (*de coussin, matelas etc*) stuffing.

bourré, e [boorā] *a* (*rempli*): **~ de** crammed full of; (*fam: ivre*) pickled, plastered.

bourreau, x [boorō] *nm* executioner; (*fig*) torturer; **~ de travail** workaholic, glutton for work.

bourrelé, e [boorlā] *a*: **être ~ de remords** to be racked by remorse.

bourrelet [boorle] *nm* weather strip(ping); (*de peau*) fold *ou* roll (of flesh).

bourrer [boorā] *vt* (*pipe*) to fill; (*poêle*) to pack; (*valise*) to cram (full); **~ de** to cram (full) with, stuff with; ~ **de coups** to hammer blows on, pummel; ~ **le crâne à qn** to pull the wool over sb's eyes; (*endocriner*) to brainwash sb.

bourricot [bŏŏrēkŏ] *nm* small donkey.

bourrique [bŏŏrēk] *nf* (*âne*) ass.

bourru, e [bŏŏrü] *a* surly, gruff.

bourse [bŏŏrs(ə)] *nf* (*subvention*) scholarship; (*porte-monnaie*) purse; **sans** ~ **délier** without spending a penny; **la B**~ the Stock Exchange; ~ **du travail** ≈ labor (*US*) *ou* trades (*Brit*) union council (regional headquarters).

boursicoter [bŏŏrsēkotā] *vi* (*COMM*) to dabble on the Stock Exchange.

boursier, ière [bŏŏrsyā, -yer] *a* (*COMM*) Stock Market *cpd* ♦ *nm/f* (*SCOL*) scholarship holder.

boursouflé, e [bŏŏrsŏŏflā] *a* swollen, puffy; (*fig*) bombastic, turgid.

boursoufler [bŏŏrsŏŏflā] *vt* to puff up, bloat; **se** ~ *vi* (*visage*) to swell *ou* puff up; (*peinture*) to blister.

boursouflure [bŏŏrsŏŏflür] *nf* (*du visage*) swelling, puffiness; (*de la peinture*) blister; (*fig: du style*) pomposity.

bous [bŏŏ] *vb voir* **bouillir**.

bousculade [bŏŏskülád] *nf* (*hâte*) rush; (*poussée*) crush.

bousculer [bŏŏskülā] *vt* to knock over; to knock into; (*fig*) to push, rush.

bouse [bŏŏz] *nf*: ~ **(de vache)** (cow) dung *q*, manure *q*.

bousiller [bŏŏzēyā] *vt* (*fam*) to wreck.

boussole [bŏŏsol] *nf* compass.

bout [bŏŏ] *vb voir* **bouillir** ♦ *nm* bit; (*extrémité: d'un bâton etc*) tip; (: *d'une ficelle, table, rue, période*) end; **au** ~ **de** at the end of, after; **au** ~ **du compte** at the end of the day; **pousser qn à** ~ to push sb to the limit (of his patience); **venir à** ~ **de** to manage to finish (off) *ou* overcome; ~ **à** ~ end to end; **à tout** ~ **de champ** at every turn; **d'un** ~ **à l'autre, de** ~ **en** ~ from one end to the other; **à** ~ **portant** at point-blank range; **un** ~ **de chou** (*enfant*) a little tot; ~ **d'essai** (*CINÉMA etc*) screen test; ~ **filtre** filter tip.

boutade [bŏŏtád] *nf* quip, sally.

boute-en-train [bŏŏtántrań] *nm inv* live wire (*fig*).

bouteille [bŏŏtey] *nf* bottle; (*de gaz butane*) cylinder.

boutiquaire [bŏŏtēker] *a*: **niveau** ~ shopping level.

boutique [bŏŏtēk] *nf* store (*US*), shop; (*de grand couturier, de mode*) boutique.

boutiquier, ière [bŏŏtēkyā, -yer] *nm/f* storekeeper (*US*), shopkeeper.

boutoir [bŏŏtwár] *nm*: **coup de** ~ (*choc*) thrust; (*fig: propos*) barb.

bouton [bŏŏtóń] *nm* (*de vêtement, électrique etc*) button; (*BOT*) bud; (*sur la peau*) spot; (*de porte*) knob; ~ **de manchette** cuff-link; ~ **d'or** buttercup.

boutonner [bŏŏtonā] *vt* to button up; **se** ~ to button one's clothes up.

boutonneux, euse [bŏŏtonœ̈, -œz] *a* pimply.

boutonnière [bŏŏtonyer] *nf* buttonhole.

bouton-poussoir, *pl* **boutons-poussoirs** [bŏŏtóńpŏŏswár] *nm* push button.

bouton-pression, *pl* **boutons-pression** [bŏŏtóńprāsyóń] *nm* snap fastener.

bouture [bŏŏtür] *nf* cutting; **faire des** ~s to take cuttings.

bouvreuil [bŏŏvrœy] *nm* bullfinch.

bovidé [bovēdā] *nm* bovine.

bovin, e [bovań, -ēn] *a* bovine ♦ *nm*: ~s cattle.

bowling [bolēng] *nm* (tenpin) bowling; (*salle*) bowling alley.

box [boks] *nm* lock-up stall (*US*), lock-up (garage) (*Brit*); (*de salle, dortoir*) cubicle; (*d'écurie*) box stall (*US*), loose-box (*Brit*); **le** ~ **des accusés** the dock.

box(-calf) [boks(kálf)] *nm inv* box calf.

boxe [boks(ə)] *nf* boxing.

boxer [boksā] *vi* to box ♦ *nm* [bokser] (*chien*) boxer.

boxeur [boksœr] *nm* boxer.

boyau, x [bwáyŏ] *nm* (*corde de raquette etc*) (cat) gut; (*galerie*) passage(way); (narrow) gallery; (*pneu de bicyclette*) tubeless tire (*US*) *ou* tyre (*Brit*) ♦ *nmpl* (*viscères*) entrails, guts.

boycottage [boēkotázh] *nm* (*d'un produit*) boycotting.

boycotter [boykotā] *vt* to boycott.

BP *sigle f* = **boîte postale**.

BPAL *sigle f* (= *base de plein air et de loisir*) open-air leisure center.

BPF *sigle* (= *bon pour francs*) *printed on checks before space for amount to be inserted.*

brabançon, ne [brábáńsóń, -on] *a* of *ou* from Brabant.

Brabant [brábáń] *nm*: **le** ~ Brabant.

bracelet [brásle] *nm* bracelet.

bracelet-montre [bráslemóńtr(ə)] *nm* wristwatch.

braconnage [brákonázh] *nm* poaching.

braconner [brákonā] *vi* to poach.

braconnier [brákonyā] *nm* poacher.

brader [brádā] *vt* to sell off, sell cheaply.

braderie [brádrē] *nf* clearance sale; (*par des particuliers*) ≈ garage sale (*US*), ≈ car boot sale (*Brit*); (*magasin*) discount store; (*sur marché*) cut-rate (*US*) *ou* cut-price (*Brit*) stall.

braguette [bráget] *nf* zipper (*US*), fly, flies *pl* (*Brit*).

braille [bráy] *nm* Braille.

braillement [bráymáń] *nm* (*cri*) bawling *q*, yelling *q*.

brailler [bráyā] *vi* to bawl, yell ♦ *vt* to bawl out, yell out.

braire [brer] *vi* to bray.

braise [brez] *nf* embers *pl*.

braiser [brāzā] *vt* to braise; **bœuf braisé** braised steak.

bramer [brámā] *vi* to bell; (*fig*) to wail.

brancard [bráńkár] *nm* (*civière*) stretcher; (*bras, perche*) shaft.

brancardier [bráńkárdyā] *nm* stretcher-bearer.

branchages [bráńsházh] *nmpl* branches, boughs.

branche [bráńsh] *nf* branch; (*de lunettes*) side(-piece).

branché, e [bráńshā] *a* (*fam*) switched-on, trendy ♦ *nm/f* (*fam*) trendy.

branchement [brȧńshmȧ́ń] *nm* connection.

brancher [brȧńshā] *vt* to connect (up); (*en mettant la prise*) to plug in; ~ **qn/qch sur** (*fig*) to get sb/sth launched onto.

branchies [brȧńshē] *nfpl* gills.

brandade [brȧńdȧd] *nf* brandade (*cod dish*).

brandebourgeois, e [brȧńdbōōrzhwȧ, -wȧz] *a* of *ou* from Brandenburg.

brandir [brȧńdēr] *vt* (*arme*) to brandish, wield; (*document*) to flourish, wave.

brandon [brȧńdȯń] *nm* firebrand.

branlant, e [brȧńlȧ́ń, -ȧ́ńt] *a* (*mur, meuble*) shaky.

branle [brȧńl] *nm*: **mettre en** ~ to set swinging; **donner le** ~ **à** to set in motion.

branle-bas [brȧńlbȧ́] *nm inv* commotion.

branler [brȧńlā] *vi* to be shaky, be loose ♦ *vt*: ~ **la tête** to shake one's head.

braquage [brȧkȧzh] *nm* (*fam*) stick-up, hold-up; (*AUTO*): **rayon de** ~ turning radius (*US*) *ou* circle (*Brit*).

braque [brȧk] *nm* (*ZOOL*) pointer.

braquer [brȧkā] *vi* (*AUTO*) to turn (the wheel) ♦ *vt* (*revolver etc*): ~ **qch sur** to aim sth at, point sth at; (*mettre en colère*): ~ **qn** to antagonize sb, put sb's back up; ~ **son regard sur** to fix one's gaze on; **se** ~ *vi*: **se** ~ **(contre)** to take a stand (against).

bras [brȧ] *nm* arm; (*de fleuve*) branch ♦ *nmpl* (*fig: travailleurs*) labor *sg* (*US*), labour *sg* (*Brit*), hands; ~ **dessus** ~ **dessous** arm in arm; **à** ~ **raccourcis** with fists flying; **à tour de** ~ with all one's might; **baisser les** ~ to give up; ~ **droit** (*fig*) right hand man; ~ **de fer** arm-wrestling; **une partie de** ~ **de fer** (*fig*) a trial of strength; ~ **de levier** lever arm; ~ **de mer** arm of the sea, sound.

brasero [brȧzȧrō] *nm* brazier.

brasier [brȧzyā] *nm* blaze, (blazing) inferno; (*fig*) inferno.

Brasilia [brȧzēlyȧ] *n* Brasilia.

bras-le-corps [brȧlkor]: **à** ~ *ad* (a)round the waist.

brassage [brȧsȧzh] *nm* (*de la bière*) brewing; (*fig*) mixing.

brassard [brȧsȧr] *nm* armband.

brasse [brȧs] *nf* (*nage*) breast-stroke; (*mesure*) fathom; ~ **papillon** butterfly(-stroke).

brassée [brȧsā] *nf* armful; **une** ~ **de** (*fig*) a number of.

brasser [brȧsā] *vt* (*bière*) to brew; (*remuer: salade*) to toss; (*: cartes*) to shuffle; (*fig*) to mix; ~ **l'argent/les affaires** to handle a lot of money/business.

brasserie [brȧsrē] *nf* (*restaurant*) bar (*selling food*), brasserie; (*usine*) brewery.

brasseur [brȧsœr] *nm* (*de bière*) brewer; ~ **d'affaires** big businessman.

brassière [brȧsyer] *nf* (baby's) undershirt (*US*) *ou* vest (*Brit*); (*de sauvetage*) life jacket.

bravache [brȧvȧsh] *nm* blusterer, braggart.

bravade [brȧvȧd] *nf*: **par** ~ out of bravado.

brave [brȧv] *a* (*courageux*) brave; (*bon, gentil*) good, kind.

bravement [brȧvmȧ́ń] *ad* bravely; (*résolument*) boldly.

braver [brȧvā] *vt* to defy.

bravo [brȧvō] *excl* bravo! ♦ *nm* cheer.

bravoure [brȧvōōr] *nf* bravery.

BRB *sigle f* (*POLICE*: = *Brigade de répression du banditisme*) ≈ serious crime squad.

break [brɛk] *nm* (*AUTO*) station wagon (*US*), estate car (*Brit*).

brebis [brəbē] *nf* ewe; ~ **galeuse** black sheep.

brèche [bresh] *nf* breach, gap; **être sur la** ~ (*fig*) to be on the go.

bredouille [brədōōy] *a* empty-handed.

bredouiller [brədōōyā] *vi, vt* to mumble, stammer.

bref, brève [brɛf, brɛv] *a* short, brief ♦ *ad* in short ♦ *nf* (*voyelle*) short vowel; (*information*) brief news item; **d'un ton** ~ sharply, curtly; **en** ~ in short, in brief; **à** ~ **délai** shortly.

brelan [brəlȧ́ń] *nm*: **un** ~ three of a kind; **un** ~ **d'as** three aces.

breloque [brəlok] *nf* charm.

brème [brem] *nf* bream.

Brésil [brāzēl] *nm*: **le** ~ Brazil.

brésilien, ne [brāzēlyȧ́ń, -en] *a* Brazilian ♦ *nm/f*: **B~, ne** Brazilian.

bressan, e [bresȧ́ń, -ȧ́ń] *a* of *ou* from Bresse.

Bretagne [brətȧny] *nf*: **la** ~ Brittany.

bretelle [brətɛl] *nf* (*de fusil etc*) sling; (*de vêtement*) strap; (*d'autoroute*) on *ou* off ramp (*US*), slip road (*Brit*); ~**s** *nfpl* (*pour pantalon*) suspenders (*US*), braces (*Brit*); ~ **de contournement** (*AUTO*) bypass; ~ **de raccordement** (*AUTO*) access road.

breton, ne [brətȯ́ń, -on] *a* Breton ♦ *nm* (*LING*) Breton ♦ *nm/f*: **B~, ne** Breton.

breuvage [brœvȧzh] *nm* beverage, drink.

brève [brɛv] *af, nf voir* bref.

brevet [brəvɛ] *nm* diploma, certificate; ~ **(d'invention)** patent; ~ **d'apprentissage** certificate of apprenticeship; ~ **(des collèges)** *school certificate, taken at approx. 16 years.*

breveté, e [brəvtā] *a* patented; (*diplômé*) qualified.

breveter [brəvtā] *vt* to patent.

bréviaire [brāvyer] *nm* breviary.

BRGM *sigle m* = *Bureau de recherches géologiques et minières.*

briard, e [brēyȧr, -ȧrd(ə)] *a* of *ou* from Brie ♦ *nm* (*chien*) briard.

bribes [brēb] *nfpl* bits, scraps; (*d'une conversation*) snatches; **par** ~ piecemeal.

bric [brɛk]: **de** ~ **et de broc** *ad* with any old thing.

bric-à-brac [brɛkȧbrȧk] *nm inv* bric-a-brac, jumble.

bricolage [brēkolȧzh] *nm*: **le** ~ do-it-yourself (jobs); (*péj*) patched-up job.

bricole [brēkol] *nf* (*babiole, chose insignifiante*) trifle; (*petit travail*) small job.

bricoler [brēkolā] *vi* to do odd jobs; (*en amateur*) to do do-it-yourself jobs; (*passe-temps*) to putter around (*US*), potter about (*Brit*) ♦ *vt* (*réparer*) to fix up; (*mal réparer*) to tinker with; (*trafiquer: voiture etc*) to doctor, fix.

bricoleur, euse [brēkolœr, -œz] *nm/f* handyman/woman, do-it-yourselfer.

bride [brēd] *nf* bridle; (*d'un bonnet*) string, tie; **à** ~ **abattue** flat out, hell for leather;

tenir en ~ to keep in check; **lâcher la** ~ **à, laisser la** ~ **sur le cou à** to give free rein to.

bridé, e [brēdä] *a*: **yeux** ~s slit eyes.

brider [brēdä] *vt* (*réprimer*) to keep in check; (*cheval*) to bridle; (*CULIN*: *volaille*) to truss.

bridge [brēdzh(ə)] *nm* bridge.

brie [brē] *nm* Brie (*cheese*).

brièvement [brēyɛvmäň] *ad* briefly.

brièveté [brēyɛvtä] *nf* brevity.

brigade [brēgàd] *nf* squad; (*MIL*.) brigade.

brigadier [brēgàdyä] *nm* (*POLICE*) ≈ sergeant; (*MIL*.) bombardier; corporal.

brigadier-chef, *pl* **brigadiers-chefs** [brēgàdyäshef] *nm* corporal acting temporarily as a sergeant.

brigand [brēgàň] *nm* brigand.

brigandage [brēgàňdäzh] *nm* robbery.

briguer [brēgä] *vt* to aspire to; (*suffrages*) to canvass.

brillamment [brēyàmàň] *ad* brilliantly.

brillant, e [brēyàň, -àňt] *a* brilliant; bright; (*luisant*) shiny, shining ♦ *nm* (*diamant*) brilliant.

briller [brēyä] *vi* to shine.

brimade [brēmàd] *nf* vexation, harassment *q*; bullying *q*.

brimbaler [braňbälä] *vb* = **bringuebaler**.

brimer [brēmä] *vt* to harass; to bully.

brin [braň] *nm* (*de laine, ficelle etc*) strand; (*fig*) **un** ~ **de** a bit of; **un** ~ **mystérieux** *etc* (*fam*) a weeny bit mysterious *etc*; ~ **d'herbe** blade of grass; ~ **de muguet** sprig of lily of the valley; ~ **de paille** wisp of straw.

brindille [braňdēy] *nf* twig.

bringue [braňg] *nf* (*fam*): **faire la** ~ to go on a binge.

bringuebaler [braňgbälä] *vi* to shake (about) ♦ *vt* to cart about.

brio [brēyō] *nm* brilliance; (*MUS*) brio; **avec** ~ brilliantly, with panache.

brioche [brēyosh] *nf* brioche (bun); (*fam*: *ventre*) paunch.

brioché, e [brēyoshä] *a* brioche-style.

brique [brēk] *nf* brick; (*fam*) 10,000 francs ♦ *a inv* brick red.

briquer [brēkä] *vt* (*fam*) to polish up.

briquet [brēkɛ] *nm* (*cigarette*) lighter.

briqueterie [brēktrē] *nf* brickyard.

bris [brē] *nm*: ~ **de clôture** (*JUR*) breaking in; ~ **de glaces** (*AUTO*) breaking of windows.

brisant [brēzàň] *nm* reef; (*vague*) breaker.

brise [brēz] *nf* breeze.

brisé, e [brēzä] *a* broken; ~ (**de fatigue**) exhausted; **d'une voix** ~e in a voice broken with emotion; **pâte** ~e pie crust (*US*) *ou* shortcrust (*Brit*) pastry.

brisées [brēzä] *nfpl*: **aller** *ou* **marcher sur les** ~ **de qn** to compete with sb in his own province.

brise-glace [brēzglàs] *nm inv* icebreaker.

brise-jet [brēzzhe] *nm inv* spray filter.

brise-lames [brēzläm] *nm inv* breakwater.

briser [brēzä] *vt* to break; **se** ~ *vi* to break.

brise-tout [brēztōō] *nm inv* wrecker.

briseur, euse [brēzœr, -ēz] *nm/f*: ~ **de grève** strike-breaker.

brise-vent [brēzvàň] *nm inv* windbreak.

bristol [brēstol] *nm* (*carte de visite*) visiting card.

britannique [brētànĕk] *a* British ♦ *nm/f*: **B**~ Briton, British person; **les B**~**s** the British.

broc [brō] *nm* pitcher.

brocante [brokàňt] *nf* (*objets*) secondhand goods *pl*, junk; (*commerce*) secondhand trade; junk dealing.

brocanteur, euse [brokàňtœr, -ēz] *nm/f* junk-shop owner; junk dealer.

brocart [brokár] *nm* brocade.

broche [brosh] *nf* brooch; (*CULIN*) spit; (*fiche*) spike, peg; (*MÉD*) pin; **à la** ~ spit-roasted, roasted on a spit.

broché, e [broshä] *a* (*livre*) paper-backed; (*tissu*) brocaded.

brochet [broshe] *nm* pike *inv*.

brochette [broshet] *nf* skewer; ~ **de décorations** row of medals.

brochure [broshür] *nf* pamphlet, brochure, booklet.

brocoli [brokolē] *nm* broccoli.

brodequins [brodkaň] *nmpl* (*de marche*) (lace-up) boots.

broder [brodä] *vt* to embroider ♦ *vi*: ~ (**sur des faits** *ou* **une histoire**) to embroider the facts.

broderie [brodrē] *nf* embroidery.

bromure [bromür] *nm* bromide.

broncher [brōňshä] *vi*: **sans** ~ without flinching, without turning a hair.

bronches [brōňsh] *nfpl* bronchial tubes.

bronchite [brōňshĕt] *nf* bronchitis.

broncho-pneumonie [brōňkopnēĕmonē] *nf* broncho-pneumonia *q*.

bronzage [brōňzäzh] *nm* (*hâle*) (sun)tan.

bronze [brōňz] *nm* bronze.

bronzé, e [brōňzä] *a* tanned.

bronzer [brōňzä] *vt* to tan ♦ *vi* to get a tan; **se** ~ to sunbathe.

brosse [bros] *nf* brush; **donner un coup de** ~ **à qch** to give sth a brush; **coiffé en** ~ with a crewcut; ~ **à cheveux** hairbrush; ~ **à dents** toothbrush; ~ **à habits** clothesbrush.

brosser [brosä] *vt* (*nettoyer*) to brush; (*fig*: *tableau etc*) to paint; to draw; **se** ~ to brush one's clothes; **se** ~ **les dents** to brush one's teeth; **tu peux te** ~! (*fam*) you can whistle for it!

brou [brōō] *nm*: ~ **de noix** (*pour bois*) walnut stain; (*liqueur*) walnut liqueur.

brouette [brōōet] *nf* wheelbarrow.

brouhaha [brōōàä] *nm* hubbub.

brouillage [brōōyäzh] *nm* (*d'une émission*) jamming.

brouillard [brōōyàr] *nm* fog; **être dans le** ~ (*fig*) to be all at sea.

brouille [brōōy] *nf* quarrel.

brouillé, e [brōōyä] *a* (*fâché*): **il est** ~ **avec ses parents** he has fallen out with his parents; (*teint*) muddy.

brouiller [brōōyä] *vt* to mix up; to confuse; (*RADIO*) to cause interference to; (: *délibérément*) to jam; (*rendre trouble*) to cloud; (*désunir*: *amis*) to set at odds; **se** ~ *vi* (*ciel, vue*) to cloud over; (*détails*) to become confused; **se** ~ (**avec**) to fall out (with); ~ **les pistes** to cover one's tracks; (*fig*) to confuse the issue.

brouillon, ne [brōōyoň, -on] *a* disorganized, unmethodical ♦ *nm* (first) draft; **cahier de** ~

notebook for rough drafts.
broussailles [broosây] *nfpl* undergrowth *sg*.
broussailleux, euse [broosâyœ̃. -œ̃z] *a* bushy.
brousse [broos] *nf*: **la** ~ the bush.
brouter [brootā] *vt* to graze on ◊ *vi* to graze; (*AUTO*) to chatter (*US*), judder (*Brit*).
broutille [brootēy] *nf* trifle.
broyer [brwâyā] *vt* to crush; ~ **du noir** to be down in the dumps.
bru [brü] *nf* daughter-in-law.
brucelles [brüsel] *nfpl*: **(pinces)** ~ tweezers.
brugnon [brünyôn] *nm* nectarine.
bruine [brüēn] *nf* drizzle.
bruiner [brüēnā] *vb impersonnel*: **il bruine** it's drizzling, there's a drizzle.
bruire [brüēr] *vi* (*eau*) to murmur; (*feuilles, étoffe*) to rustle.
bruissement [brüēsmân] *nm* murmuring; rustling.
bruit [brüē] *nm*: **un** ~ a noise, a sound; (*fig: rumeur*) a rumor (*US*), a rumour (*Brit*); **le** ~ noise; **pas/trop de** ~ no/too much noise; **sans** ~ without a sound, noiselessly; **faire du** ~ to make a noise; ~ **de fond** background noise.
bruitage [brüētazh] *nm* sound effects *pl*.
bruiteur, euse [brüētœr, -œ̃z] *nm/f* sound-effects engineer.
brûlant, e [brülân, -ânt] *a* burning (hot); (*liquide*) boiling (hot); (*regard*) fiery; (*sujet*) red-hot.
brûlé, e [brülā] *a* (*fig: démasqué*) blown; (: *homme politique etc*) discredited ◊ *nm*: **odeur de** ~ smell of burning.
brûle-pourpoint [brülpoorpwań]: **à** ~ *ad* point-blank.
brûler [brülā] *vt* to burn; (*suj: eau bouillante*) to scald; (*consommer: électricité, essence*) to use; (*feu rouge, signal*) to run ◊ *vi* to burn; (*jeu*): **tu brûles** you're getting warm *ou* hot; **se** ~ to burn o.s.; to scald o.s.; **se** ~ **la cervelle** to blow one's brains out; ~ **les étapes** to make rapid progress; (*aller trop vite*) to cut corners; ~ **(d'impatience) de faire qch** to burn with impatience to do sth, be dying to do sth.
brûleur [brülœr] *nm* burner.
brûlot [brülō] *nm* (*CULIN*) flaming brandy; **un** ~ **de contestation** (*fig*) a hotbed of dissent.
brûlure [brülür] *nf* (*lésion*) burn; (*sensation*) burning *q*, burning sensation; **~s d'estomac** heartburn *sg*.
brume [brüm] *nf* mist.
brumeux, euse [brümœ̃. -œ̃z] *a* misty; (*fig*) hazy.
brun, e [brœn. -ün] *a* brown; (*cheveux, personne*) dark ◊ *nm* (*couleur*) brown.
brunâtre [brünâtr(ə)] *a* brownish.
Brunei [brünāē] *nm*: **le** ~ Brunei.
brunir [brünēr] *vi* (*aussi*: **se** ~) to get a tan ◊ *vt* to tan.
brushing [brœshēng] *nm* blow-dry.
brusque [brüsk(ə)] *a* (*soudain*) abrupt, sudden; (*rude*) abrupt, brusque.
brusquement [brüskəmân] *ad* (*soudainement*) abruptly, suddenly.
brusquer [brüskā] *vt* to rush.
brusquerie [brüskərē] *nf* abruptness, brusqueness.

brut, e [brüt] *a* raw, crude, rough; (*diamant*) uncut; (*soie, minéral, INFORM*: *données*) raw; (*COMM*) gross ◊ *nf* brute; **(champagne)** ~ brut champagne; **(pétrole)** ~ crude (oil).
brutal, e, aux [brütál, -ō] *a* brutal.
brutalement [brütálmân] *ad* brutally.
brutaliser [brütálēzā] *vt* to handle roughly, manhandle.
brutalité [brütálētā] *nf* brutality *q*.
brute [brüt] *af, nf voir* **brut**.
Bruxelles [brüsel] *n* Brussels.
bruxellois, e [brüselwâ, -wâz] *a* of *ou* from Brussels ◊ *nm/f*: **B~, e** inhabitant *ou* native of Brussels.
bruyamment [brüēyàmân] *ad* noisily.
bruyant, e [brüēyân, -ânt] *a* noisy.
bruyère [brüyer] *nf* heather.
BT *sigle m* (= *Brevet de technicien*) *vocational training certificate, taken at approx. 18 years*.
BTA *sigle m* (= *Brevet de technicien agricole*) *agricultural training certificate, taken at approx. 18 years*.
BTP *sigle mpl* (= *Bâtiments et travaux publics*) *public buildings and works sector*.
BTS *sigle m* (= *Brevet de technicien supérieur*) *vocational training certificate taken at end of 2-year higher education course*.
BU *sigle f* = *Bibliothèque universitaire*.
bu, e [bü] *pp de* **boire**.
buanderie [büândrē] *nf* laundry.
Bucarest [bükárest] *n* Bucharest.
buccal, e, aux [bükál, -ō] *a*: **par voie** ~**e** orally.
bûche [büsh] *nf* log; **prendre une** ~ (*fig*) to fall flat on one's face; ~ **de Noël** Yule log.
bûcher [büshā] *nm* pyre; bonfire ◊ *vi* (*fam*: *étudier*) to grind (*US*), swot (*Brit*) ◊ *vt* to cram.
bûcheron [büshrôn] *nm* woodcutter.
bûchette [büshet] *nf* (*de bois*) stick, twig; (*pour compter*) rod.
bûcheur, euse [büshœr, -œ̃z] *nm/f* (*fam*: *étudiant*) grind (*US*), swot (*Brit*).
bucolique [bükolēk] *a* bucolic, pastoral.
Budapest [büdápest] *n* Budapest.
budget [büdzhe] *nm* budget.
budgétaire [büdzhāter] *a* a budgetary, budget *cpd*.
budgétiser [büdzhātēzā] *vt* to budget (for).
buée [büā] *nf* (*sur une vitre*) mist; (*de l'haleine*) steam.
Buenos Aires [bwãnozer] *n* Buenos Aires.
buffet [büfe] *nm* (*meuble*) sideboard; (*de réception*) buffet; ~ **(de gare)** (station) buffet, snack bar.
buffle [büfl(ə)] *nm* buffalo.
buis [büē] *nm* box tree; (*bois*) box(wood).
buisson [büēsôn] *nm* bush.
buissonnière [büēsonyer] *af*: **faire l'école** ~ to play hooky, skip school.
bulbe [bülb(ə)] *nm* (*BOT, ANAT*) bulb; (*coupole*) onion-shaped dome.
bulgare [bülgár] *a* a Bulgarian ◊ *nm* (*LING*) Bulgarian ◊ *nm/f*: **B~** Bulgarian, Bulgar.
Bulgarie [bülgárē] *nf*: **la** ~ Bulgaria.
bulldozer [booldōzœr] *nm* bulldozer.
bulle [bül] *a, nm*: **(papier)** ~ manil(l)a paper ◊ *nf* bubble; (*de bande dessinée*) balloon; (*papale*) bull; ~ **de savon** soap bubble.

bulletin [bültañ] *nm* (*communiqué, journal*) bulletin; (*papier*) form; (: *de bagages*) baggage check (*US*) *ou* ticket (*Brit*); (*SCOL*) report card (*US*), report (*Brit*); ~ **d'informations** news bulletin; ~ **météorologique** weather report; ~ **de naissance** birth certificate; ~ **de salaire** check stub (*US*), pay slip (*Brit*); ~ **de santé** medical bulletin; ~ (**de vote**) ballot paper.

buraliste [bürálést(ə)] *nm/f* (*de bureau de tabac*) tobacconist; (*de poste*) clerk.

bure [bür] *nf* homespun; (*de moine*) frock.

bureau, x [bürō] *nm* (*meuble*) desk; (*pièce, service*) office; ~ **de change** (foreign) exchange office *ou* bureau; ~ **d'embauche** employment office; ~ **d'études** research department; ~ **de location** box office; ~ **de placement** employment agency; ~ **de poste** post office; ~ **de tabac** cigar store (*US*), tobacco shop (*US*), tobacconist's (shop) (*Brit*); ~ **de vote** polling station.

bureaucrate [bürōkrát] *nm* bureaucrat.
bureaucratie [bürōkrásē] *nf* bureaucracy.
bureaucratique [bürōkrátēk] *a* bureaucratic.
bureautique [bürōtēk] *nf* office automation.
burette [büret] *nf* (*de mécanicien*) oilcan; (*de chimiste*) burette.

burin [bürañ] *nm* cold chisel; (*ART*) burin.
buriné, e [bürēnā] *a* (*fig: visage*) craggy, seamed.

burlesque [bürlesk(ə)] *a* ridiculous; (*LITTÉRATURE*) burlesque.

burnous [bürnōō(s)] *nm* burnous.
Burundi [bōōrōōndē] *nm*: **le** ~ Burundi.
BUS *sigle m* = *Bureau universitaire de statistiques.*

bus *vb* [bü] *voir* **boire** ♦ *nm* [büs] (*véhicule, aussi INFORM*) bus.

busard [büzár] *nm* harrier.
buse [büz] *nf* buzzard.
busqué, e [büskā] *a*: **nez** ~ hook(ed) nose.
buste [büst(ə)] *nm* (*ANAT*) chest; (: *de femme*) bust; (*sculpture*) bust.

bustier [büstyā] *nm* (*soutien-gorge*) long-line bra.

but [bü] *vb voir* **boire** ♦ *nm* (*cible*) target; (*fig*) goal, aim; (*FOOTBALL etc*) goal; **de** ~ **en blanc** point-blank; **avoir pour** ~ **de faire** to aim to do; **dans le** ~ **de** with the intention of.

butane [bütan] *nm* butane; (*domestique*) butane, calor gas ® (*Brit*).

buté, e [bütā] *a* stubborn, obstinate, ♦ *nf* (*TECH*) stop; (*ARCHIT*) abutment.

buter [bütā] *vi*: ~ **contre** *ou* **sur** to bump into; (*trébucher*) to stumble against ♦ *vt* to antagonize; **se** ~ *vi* to get obstinate, dig in one's heels.

buteur [bütœr] *nm* goal-scorer.
butin [bütañ] *nm* booty, spoils *pl*; (*d'un vol*) loot.

butiner [bütēnā] *vi* to gather nectar.
butor [bütor] *nm* (*fig*) lout.
butte [büt] *nf* mound, hillock; **être en** ~ **à** to be exposed to.

buvable [büvábl(ə)] *a* (*eau, vin*) drinkable; (*MÉD: ampoule etc*) to be taken orally; (*fig: roman etc*) reasonable.

buvais [büve] *etc vb voir* **boire**.

buvard [büvár] *nm* blotter.
buvette [büvet] *nf* refreshment stand; (*comptoir*) bar.

buveur, euse [büvœr, -œz] *nm/f* drinker.
buvons [büvôñ] *etc vb voir* **boire**.
BVP *sigle m* (= *Bureau de vérification de la publicité*) *advertising standards authority.*

Byzance [bēzáñs] *n* Byzantium.
byzantin, e [bēzáñtañ, -ēn] *a* Byzantine.
BZH *abr* (= *Breizh*) Brittany.

C

C, c [sā] *nm inv* C, c ♦ *abr* (= *centime*) c; (= *Celsius*) C; **C comme Célestin** C for Charlie.

c' [s] *dét voir* **ce**.

CA *sigle m* = **chiffre d'affaires, conseil d'administration, corps d'armée** ♦ *sigle f* = **chambre d'agriculture.**

ca *abr* (= *centiare*) 1 m².

ça [sá] *pronom* (*pour désigner*) this; (: *plus loin*) that; (*comme sujet indéfini*) it; ~ **m'étonne que** it surprises me that; ~ **va?** how are you?; how are things?; (*d'accord?*) OK?, all right?; ~ **alors!** (*désapprobation*) well!, really!; (*étonnement*) heavens!; **c'est** ~ that's right.

çà [sá] *ad*: ~ **et là** here and there.
cabale [kábál] *nf* (*THÉÂTRE, POL*) cabal, clique.

caban [kábáñ] *nm* reefer jacket.
cabane [kában] *nf* hut, cabin.
cabanon [kábánôñ] *nm* chalet; (*country*) cottage.

cabaret [kábáre] *nm* night club.
cabas [kábá] *nm* shopping bag.
cabestan [kábestáñ] *nm* capstan.
cabillaud [kábēyō] *nm* cod *inv*.
cabine [kábēn] *nf* (*de bateau*) cabin; (*de plage*) (beach) hut; (*de piscine etc*) cubicle; (*de camion, train*) cab; (*d'avion*) cockpit; ~ (**d'ascenseur**) elevator car (*US*), lift cage (*Brit*); ~ **d'essayage** fitting room; ~ **de projection** projection room; ~ **spatiale** space capsule; ~ (**téléphonique**) (tele)phone booth, call *ou* (tele)phone box (*Brit*).

cabinet [kábēne] *nm* (*petite pièce*) closet; (*de médecin*) office (*US*), surgery (*Brit*); (*de notaire etc*) office; (: *clientèle*) practice; (*POL*) cabinet; (*d'un ministre*) advisers *pl*; ~**s** *nmpl* (*w.-c.*) toilet *sg*; ~ **d'affaires** business consultants' (bureau), business partnership; ~ **de toilette** washroom; ~ **de travail** study.

câble [kábl(ə)] *nm* cable.
câblé, e [káblā] *a* (*fam*) switched on; (*TECH*) linked to cable television.
câbler [káblā] *vt* to cable.
câblogramme [káblográm] *nm* cablegram.
cabosser [kábosā] *vt* to dent.
cabot [kábō] *nm* (*péj: chien*) mutt.
cabotage [kábotázh] *nm* coastal navigation.

caboteur [kábotœr] *nm* coaster.

cabotin, e [kábotañ, -ēn] *nm/f* (*péj: personne maniérée*) poseur; (*: acteur*) ham ♦ *a* dramatic, theatrical.

cabotinage [kábotēnázh] *nm* playacting; third-rate acting, ham acting.

cabrer [kábrā]: **se ~** *vi* (*cheval*) to rear up; (*avion*) to nose up; (*fig*) to revolt, rebel; to jib.

cabri [kábrē] *nm* kid.

cabriole [kábrēyol] *nf* caper; (*gymnastique etc*) somersault.

cabriolet [kábrēyole] *nm* convertible.

CAC [kák] *sigle f* (= *Compagnie des agents de change*): **indice ~** ≈ Dow Jones average (*US*); ≈ FT index (*Brit*).

caca [káká] *nm* (*langage enfantin*) pooh; (*couleur*): **~ d'oie** greenish-yellow; **faire ~** (*fam*) to go pooh-pooh (*US*), do a pooh (*Brit*).

cacahuète [kákáüet] *nf* peanut.

cacao [kákáō] *nm* cocoa (powder); (*boisson*) cocoa.

cachalot [káshálō] *nm* sperm whale.

cache [kásh] *nm* mask, card (*for masking*) ♦ *nf* hiding place.

cache-cache [káshkásh] *nm*: **jouer à ~** to play hide-and-seek.

cache-col [káshkol] *nm* scarf (*pl* scarves).

cachemire [káshmēr] *nm* cashmere ♦ *a*: **dessin ~** paisley pattern; **le C~** Kashmir.

cache-nez [káshnā] *nm inv* scarf (*pl* scarves), muffler.

cache-pot [káshpō] *nm inv* flower-pot holder.

cache-prise [káshprēz] *nm inv* socket cover.

cacher [káshā] *vt* to hide, conceal; **~ qch à qn** to hide *ou* conceal sth from sb; **se ~** to hide; to be hidden *ou* concealed; **il ne s'en cache pas** he makes no secret of it.

cache-sexe [káshseks] *nm inv* G-string.

cachet [káshe] *nm* (*comprimé*) tablet; (*sceau: du roi*) seal; (*: de la poste*) postmark; (*rétribution*) fee; (*fig*) style, character.

cacheter [káshtā] *vt* to seal; **vin cacheté** vintage wine.

cachette [káshet] *nf* hiding place; **en ~** on the sly, secretly.

cachot [káshō] *nm* dungeon.

cachotterie [káshotrē] *nf* mystery; **faire des ~s** to be secretive.

cachottier, ière [káshotyā, -yer] *a* secretive.

cachou [káshōō] *nm*: **(pastille de) ~** cachou (*candy*).

cacophonie [kákofonē] *nf* cacophony, din.

cactus [káktüs] *nm* cactus.

c-à-d *abr* (= *c'est-à-dire*) i.e.

cadastre [kádástr(ə)] *nm* land register.

cadavéreux, euse [kádávārœ, -œz] *a* (*teint, visage*) deathly pale.

cadavérique [kádávārēk] *a* deathly (pale), deadly pale.

cadavre [kádávr(ə)] *nm* corpse, (dead) body.

caddie [kádē] *nm* shopping cart (*US*), (supermarket) trolley (*Brit*).

cadeau, x [kádō] *nm* present, gift; **faire un ~ à qn** to give sb a present *ou* gift; **faire ~ de qch à qn** to make a present of sth to sb, give sb sth as a present.

cadenas [kádná] *nm* padlock.

cadenasser [kádnásā] *vt* to padlock.

cadence [kádâñs] *nf* (*MUS*) cadence; (*: rythme*) rhythm; (*de travail etc*) rate; **~s** *nfpl* (*en usine*) production rate *sg*; **en ~** rhythmically; in time.

cadencé, e [kádâñsā] *a* rhythmic(al); **au pas ~** (*MIL*) in quick time.

cadet, te [káde, -et] *a* younger; (*le plus jeune*) youngest ♦ *nm/f* youngest child *ou* one, youngest boy *ou* son/girl *ou* daughter; **il est mon ~ de deux ans** he's 2 years younger than me, he's 2 years my junior; **les ~s** (*SPORT*) the juniors (*15 - 17 years*); **le ~ de mes soucis** the least of my worries.

cadran [kádrâñ] *nm* dial; **~ solaire** sundial.

cadre [kádr(ə)] *nm* frame; (*environnement*) surroundings *pl*; (*limites*) scope ♦ *nm/f* (*ADMIN*) managerial employee, executive ♦ *a*: **loi ~** outline *ou* blueprint law; **~ moyen/ supérieur** (*ADMIN*) middle/senior management employee, junior/senior executive; **rayer qn des ~s** to discharge sb; to dismiss sb; **dans le ~ de** (*fig*) within the framework *ou* context of.

cadrer [kádrā] *vi*: **~ avec** to tally *ou* correspond with ♦ *vt* (*CINÉMA*) to center (*US*) *ou* centre (*Brit*).

cadreur, euse [kádrœr, -œz] *nm/f* (*CINÉMA*) cameraman/woman.

caduc, uque [kádük] *a* obsolete; (*BOT*) deciduous.

CAF *sigle f* (= *Caisse d'allocations familiales*) *family allowance office.*

caf *abr* (= *coût, assurance, fret*) cif.

cafard [káfár] *nm* cockroach; **avoir le ~** to be down in the dumps, be feeling low.

cafardeux, euse [káfárdœ, -œz] *a* (*personne, ambiance*) depressing, melancholy.

café [káfā] *nm* coffee; (*bistro*) café ♦ *a inv* coffee *cpd*; **~ crème** coffee with cream; **~ au lait** coffee with milk (*US*), white coffee (*Brit*); **~ noir** black coffee; **~ en grains** coffee beans; **~ en poudre** instant coffee; **~ tabac** tobacconist's *or* newsagent's *also* serving coffee and spirits; **~ liégeois** coffee ice cream with whipped cream.

café-concert, *pl* **cafés-concerts** [káfākôñser] *nm* (*aussi*: **caf'conc'**) *café with a cabaret.*

caféine [káfāēn] *nf* caffeine.

cafétéria [káfātāryá] *nf* cafeteria.

café-théâtre, *pl* **cafés-théâtres** [káfātáâtr(ə)] *nm* *café used as a venue by* (*experimental*) *theatre groups.*

cafetier, ière [káftyā, -yer] *nm/f* café-owner ♦ *nf* (*pot*) coffee-pot.

cafouillage [káfōōyázh] *nm* shambles *sg*.

cafouiller [káfōōyā] *vi* to get in a shambles; (*machine etc*) to work in fits and starts.

cage [kázh] *nf* cage; **~ (des buts)** goal; **en ~** in a cage, caged up *ou* in; **~ d'ascenseur** elevator (*US*) *ou* lift shaft (*Brit*); **~ d'escalier** (stair)well; **~ thoracique** rib cage.

cageot [kázhō] *nm* crate.

cagibi [kázhēbē] *nm* shed.

cagneux, euse [kányœ, -œz] *a* knock-kneed.

cagnotte [kányot] *nf* kitty.

cagoule [kágōōl] *nf* cowl; hood.

cahier [káyā] *nm* notebook; (*TYPO*) signature; (*revue*): **~s** journal; **~ de revendications/ doléances** list of claims/grievances; **~ de**

brouillon notebook for rough drafts; ~ **des charges** specifications *pl* (*US*), specification (*Brit*); ~ **d'exercices** workbook.

cahin-caha [káàńkáá] *ad*: **aller** ~ to jog along; (*fig*) to be so-so.

cahot [káō] *nm* jolt, bump.

cahoter [káotā] *vi* to bump along, jog along.

cahoteux, euse [káotœ̄, -œ̄z] *a* bumpy.

cahute [káüt] *nf* shack, hut.

caïd [káēd] *nm* big chief, boss.

caillasse [káyàs] *nf* (*pierraille*) loose stones *pl*.

caille [kây] *nf* quail.

caillé, e [kâyā] *a*: **lait** ~ curdled milk, curds *pl*.

caillebotis [kâybotē] *nm* duckboard.

cailler [kâyā] *vi* (*lait*) to curdle; (*sang*) to clot; (*fam*) to be cold.

caillot [kâyō] *nm* (blood) clot.

caillou, x [kâyōō] *nm* (little) stone.

caillouter [kâyōōtā] *vt* (*chemin*) to metal.

caillouteux, euse [kâyōōtœ̄, -œ̄z] *a* stony, pebbly.

cailloutis [kâyōōtē] *nm* (*petits graviers*) gravel.

caïman [káēmáń] *nm* cayman.

Caïmans [káēmáń] *nfpl*: **les** ~ the Cayman Islands.

Caire [ker] *nm*: **le** ~ Cairo.

caisse [kes] *nf* box; (*où l'on met la recette*) cashbox; (: *machine*) till; (*où l'on paye*) checkout counter; (: *au supermarché*) checkout; (*de banque*) cashier's desk; (*TECH*) case, casing; **faire sa** ~ (*COMM*) to count the takings; ~ **claire** (*MUS*) side *ou* snare drum; ~ **éclair** express checkout; ~ **enregistreuse** cash register; ~ **d'épargne (CE)** savings bank; ~ **noire** slush fund; ~ **de retraite** pension fund; ~ **de sortie** checkout; *voir* **grosse.**

caissier, ière [kàsyā, -yer] *nm/f* cashier.

caisson [kesóń] *nm* box, case.

cajoler [kàzholā] *vt* to wheedle, coax; to surround with love and care, make a fuss of.

cajoleries [kàzholrē] *nfpl* coaxing *sg*, flattery *sg*.

cajou [kàzhōō] *nm* cashew nut.

cake [kek] *nm* fruit cake.

CAL *sigle m* (= *Comité d'action lycéen*) *pupils' action group seeking to reform school system.*

cal [kàl] *nm* callus.

cal. *abr* = **calorie.**

calamar [kàlàmár] *nm* = **calmar.**

calaminé, e [kàlámēnā] *a* (*AUTO*) caked with soot.

calamité [kàlàmētā] *nf* calamity, disaster.

calandre [kàlâńdr(ə)] *nf* radiator grill; (*machine*) calender, mangle.

calanque [kàlâńk] *nf* rocky inlet.

calcaire [kàlker] *nm* limestone ♦ *a* (*eau*) hard; (*GÉO*) limestone *cpd*.

calciné, e [kàlsēnā] *a* burnt to ashes.

calcium [kàlsyom] *nm* calcium.

calcul [kàlkül] *nm* calculation; **le** ~ (*SCOL*) arithmetic; ~ **différentiel/intégral** differential/integral calculus; ~ **mental** mental arithmetic; ~ **(biliaire)** (gall)stone; ~ **(rénal)** (kidney) stone; **d'après mes** ~**s** by my reckoning.

calculateur [kàlkülàtœr] *nm*, **calculatrice** [kàlkülàtrēs] *nf* calculator.

calculé, e [kàlkülā] *a*: **risque** ~ calculated risk.

calculer [kàlkülā] *vt* to calculate, work out, reckon; (*combiner*) to calculate; ~ **qch de tête** to work sth out in one's head.

calculette [kàlkület] *nf* (pocket) calculator.

cale [kàl] *nf* (*de bateau*) hold; (*en bois*) wedge, chock; ~ **sèche** *ou* **de radoub** dry dock.

calé, e [kàlā] *a* (*fam*) clever, bright.

calebasse [kàlbás] *nf* calabash, gourd.

calèche [kàlesh] *nf* horse-drawn carriage.

caleçon [kàlsóń] *nm* pair of underpants, trunks *pl*; ~ **de bain** bathing trunks *pl*.

calembour [kàlâńbōōr] *nm* pun.

calendes [kàlâńd] *nfpl*: **renvoyer aux** ~ **grecques** to postpone indefinitely.

calendrier [kàlâńdrēyā] *nm* calendar; (*fig*) timetable.

cale-pied [kàlpyā] *nm inv* toe clip.

calepin [kàlpàń] *nm* notebook.

caler [kàlā] *vt* to wedge, chock up; ~ **(son moteur/véhicule)** to stall (one's engine/vehicle); **se** ~ **dans un fauteuil** to make o.s. comfortable in an armchair.

calfater [kàlfátā] *vt* to caulk.

calfeutrer [kàlfœtrā] *vt* to (make) draftproof (*US*) *ou* draughtproof (*Brit*); **se** ~ to make o.s. snug and comfortable.

calibre [kàlēbr(ə)] *nm* (*d'un fruit*) grade; (*d'une arme*) bore, caliber (*US*), calibre (*Brit*); (*fig*) caliber, calibre.

calibrer [kàlēbrā] *vt* to grade.

calice [kàlēs] *nm* (*REL*) chalice; (*BOT*) calyx.

calicot [kàlēkō] *nm* (*tissu*) calico.

Californie [kàlēfornē] *nf*: **la** ~ California.

californien, ne [kàlēfornyàń, -en] *a* Californian.

califourchon [kàlēfōōrshóń]: **à** ~ *ad* astride; **à** ~ **sur** astride, straddling.

câlin, e [kâlàń, -ēn] *a* cuddly, cuddlesome; tender.

câliner [kâlēnā] *vt* to fondle, cuddle.

câlineries [kâlēnrē] *nfpl* cuddles.

calisson [kàlēsóń] *nm diamond-shaped candy made with ground almonds.*

calleux, euse [kàlœ̄, -œ̄z] *a* horny, callous.

calligraphie [kàlēgráfē] *nf* calligraphy.

callosité [kàlōzētā] *nf* callus.

calmant [kàlmáń] *nm* tranquillizer, sedative; (*contre la douleur*) painkiller.

calmar [kàlmár] *nm* squid.

calme [kàlm(ə)] *a* calm, quiet ♦ *nm* calm(ness), quietness; **sans perdre son** ~ without losing one's cool *ou* calmness; ~ **plat** (*NAVIG*) dead calm.

calmer [kàlmā] *vt* to calm (down); (*douleur, inquiétude*) to ease, soothe; **se** ~ to calm down.

calomniateur, trice [kàlomnyátœr, -trēs] *nm/f* slanderer; libeller.

calomnie [kàlomnē] *nf* slander; (*écrite*) libel.

calomnier [kàlomnyā] *vt* to slander; to libel.

calomnieux, euse [kàlomnyœ̄, -œ̄z] *a* slanderous; libel(l)ous.

calorie [kàlorē] *nf* calorie.

calorifère [kàlorēfer] *nm* stove.

calorifique [kàlorēfēk] *a* calorific.

calorifuge [kàlorēfüzh] *a* (heat-)insulating, heat-retaining.

calot [kálō] *nm* overseas *ou* garrison cap (*US*), forage cap (*Brit*).

calotte [kálot] *nf* (*coiffure*) skullcap; (*gifle*) slap; **la ~** (*péj: clergé*) the cloth, the clergy; **~ glaciaire** icecap.

calque [kálk(ə)] *nm* (*aussi*: **papier ~**) tracing paper; (*dessin*) tracing; (*fig*) carbon copy.

calquer [kálkā] *vt* to trace; (*fig*) to copy exactly.

calvados [kálvádōs] *nm* Calvados (*apple brandy*).

calvaire [kálver] *nm* (*croix*) wayside cross, calvary; (*souffrances*) suffering, martyrdom.

calvitie [kálvēsē] *nf* baldness.

camaïeu [kámáyœ̄] *nm*: **(motif en) ~** monochrome motif.

camarade [kámárád] *nm/f* friend, pal; (*POL*) comrade.

camaraderie [kámárádrē] *nf* friendship.

camarguais, e [kámárge, -ez] *a* of *ou* from the Camargue.

Camargue [kámárg] *nf*: **la ~** the Camargue.

cambiste [kánbēst(ə)] *nm* (*COMM*) foreign exchange dealer, exchange agent.

Cambodge [kánbodzh] *nm*: **le ~** Cambodia.

cambodgien, ne [kánbodzhyañ, -en] *a* Cambodian ♦ *nm/f*: **C~, ne** Cambodian.

cambouis [kánbwē] *nm* dirty oil *ou* grease.

cambré, e [kánbrā] *a*: **avoir les reins ~s** to have an arched back; **avoir le pied très ~** to have very high arches *ou* insteps.

cambrer [kánbrā] *vt* to arch; **se ~** to arch one's back; **~ la taille** *ou* **les reins** to arch one's back.

cambriolage [kánbrēyolázh] *nm* burglary.

cambrioler [kánbrēyolā] *vt* to burglarize (*US*), burgle (*Brit*).

cambrioleur, euse [kánbrēyolœr, -ēz] *nm/f* burglar.

cambrure [kánbrür] *nf* (*du pied*) arch; (*de la route*) camber; **~ des reins** small of the back.

cambuse [kánbüz] *nf* storeroom.

came [kám] *nf*: **arbre à ~s** camshaft; **arbre à ~s en tête** overhead camshaft.

camée [kámā] *nm* cameo.

caméléon [kámālāōñ] *nm* chameleon.

camélia [kámālyá] *nm* camellia.

camelot [kámlō] *nm* street pedlar.

camelote [kámlot] *nf* rubbish, trash, junk.

camembert [kámánber] *nm* Camembert (*cheese*).

caméra [kámárá] *nf* (*CINÉMA, TV*) camera; (*d'amateur*) cine-camera.

Cameroun [kámrōōn] *nm*: **le ~** Cameroon.

camerounais, e [kámrōōne, -ez] *a* Cameroonian.

camescope [kámskop] *nm* camcorder.

camion [kámyôñ] *nm* truck; (*plus petit, fermé*): (*charge*): **~ de sable/cailloux** truck-load of sand/stones; **~ de dépannage** tow (*US*) *ou* breakdown (*Brit*) truck.

camion-citerne, *pl* **camions-citernes** [kámyôñsētern(ə)] *nm* tanker.

camionnage [kámyonázh] *nm* trucking (*US*), haulage (*Brit*); **frais/entreprise de ~** haulage costs/business.

camionnette [kámyonet] *nf* (small) truck.

camionneur [kámyonœr] *nm* (*entrepreneur*) trucker (*US*), haulage contractor (*Brit*); (*chauffeur*) truck driver; van driver.

camisole [kámēzol] *nf*: **~ (de force)** straitjacket.

camomille [kámomēy] *nf* camomile; (*boisson*) camomile tea.

camouflage [kámōōflázh] *nm* camouflage.

camoufler [kámōōflā] *vt* to camouflage; (*fig*) to conceal, cover up.

camouflet [kámōōfle] *nm* (*fam*) snub.

camp [káñ] *nm* camp; (*fig*) side; **~ de nudistes/vacances** nudist/vacation (*US*) *ou* holiday (*Brit*) camp; **~ de concentration** concentration camp.

campagnard, e [kánpányár, -árd(ə)] *a* country *cpd* ♦ *nm/f* countryman/woman.

campagne [kánpány] *nf* country, countryside; (*MIL, POL, COMM*) campaign; **en ~** (*MIL*) in the field; **à la ~** in/to the country; **faire ~ pour** to campaign for; **~ électorale** election campaign; **~ de publicité** advertising campaign.

campé, e [kánpā] *a*: **bien ~** (*personnage, tableau*) well-drawn.

campement [kánpmáñ] *nm* camp, encampment.

camper [kánpā] *vi* to camp ♦ *vt* (*chapeau etc*) to pull *ou* put on firmly; (*dessin*) to sketch; **se ~ devant** to plant o.s. in front of.

campeur, euse [kánpœr, -ēz] *nm/f* camper.

camphre [kánfr(ə)] *nm* camphor.

camphré, e [kánfrā] *a* camphorated.

camping [kánpēng] *nm* camping; (*terrain de*) **~** campsite, camping site; **faire du ~** to go camping; **faire du ~ sauvage** to camp in the wild.

camping-car [kánpēngkár] *nm* camper.

campus [kánpüs] *nm* campus.

camus, e [kámü, -üz] *a*: **nez ~** pug nose.

Canada [kánádá] *nm*: **le ~** Canada.

canadair [kánáder] *nm* ® fire-fighting plane.

canadien, ne [kánádyañ, -en] *a* Canadian ♦ *nm/f*: **C~, ne** Canadian ♦ *nf* (*veste*) fur-lined jacket.

canaille [kánáy] *nf* (*péj*) scoundrel; (*populace*) riff-raff ♦ *a* raffish, rakish.

canal, aux [kánál, -ō] *nm* canal; (*naturel*) channel; (*ADMIN*): **par le ~ de** through (the medium of), via; **~ de distribution/télévision** distribution/television channel; **~ de Panama/Suez** Panama/Suez Canal.

canalisation [kánálēzásyôñ] *nf* (*tuyau*) pipe.

canaliser [kánálēzā] *vt* to canalize; (*fig*) to channel.

canapé [kánápā] *nm* settee, sofa; (*CULIN*) canapé, open sandwich.

canapé-lit, *pl* **canapés-lits** [kánápálē] *nm* sofa bed.

canaque [kánák] *a* of *ou* from New Caledonia ♦ *nm/f*: **C~** native of New Caledonia.

canard [kánár] *nm* duck.

canari [kánárē] *nm* canary.

Canaries [kánárē] *nfpl*: **les (îles) ~** the Canary Islands, the Canaries.

cancaner [kánkánā] *vi* to gossip (maliciously); (*canard*) to quack.

cancanier, ière [kánkányâ, -yer] *a* gossiping.

cancans [kánkáñ] *nmpl* (malicious) gossip *sg*.

cancer [kánser] *nm* cancer; (*signe*): **le C~**

Cancer, the Crab; **être du C~** to be Cancer; **il a un ~** he has cancer.

cancéreux, euse [kãsārœ̃, -œ̃z] *a* cancerous; *(personne)* suffering from cancer.

cancérigène [kãsārēzhen] *a* carcinogenic.

cancérologue [kãsārolog] *nm/f* cancer specialist.

cancre [kãkr(ə)] *nm* dunce.

cancrelat [kãkrəlá] *nm* cockroach.

candélabre [kãdālábr(ə)] *nm* candelabrum; *(lampadaire)* street lamp, lamppost.

candeur [kãdœr] *nf* ingenuousness, guilelessness.

candi [kãdē] *a inv:* **sucre ~** (sugar-)candy.

candidat, e [kãdēdá, -át] *nm/f* candidate; *(à un poste)* applicant, candidate.

candidature [kãdēdátür] *nf* candidacy; application; **poser sa ~** to submit an application, apply.

candide [kãdēd] *a* ingenuous, guileless, naïve.

cane [kán] *nf* (female) duck.

caneton [kãtõ] *nm* duckling.

canette [kãnet] *nf (de bière)* (flip-top) bottle; *(de machine à coudre)* spool.

canevas [kãvá] *nm (COUTURE)* canvas (for tapestry work); *(fig)* framework, structure.

caniche [kãnēsh] *nm* poodle.

caniculaire [kãnēküler] *a (chaleur, jour)* scorching.

canicule [kãnēkül] *nf* scorching heat; midsummer heat, dog days *pl*.

canif [kãnēf] *nm* penknife, pocket knife.

canin, e [kãnañ, -ēn] *a* canine ♦ *nf* canine (tooth), eye tooth; **exposition ~e** dog show.

caniveau, x [kãnēvō] *nm* gutter.

cannabis [kãnábēs] *nm* cannabis.

canne [kán] *nf* (walking) stick; **~ à pêche** fishing rod; **~ à sucre** sugar cane; **les ~s blanches** *(les aveugles)* the blind.

canné, e [kãná] *a (chaise)* cane *cpd*.

cannelé, e [kãnlā] *a* fluted.

cannelle [kãnel] *nf* cinnamon.

cannelure [kãnlür] *nf* fluting *q*.

canner [kãnā] *vt (chaise)* to make *ou* repair with cane.

cannibale [kãnēbál] *nm/f* cannibal.

canoë [kãnoā] *nm* canoe; *(sport)* canoeing; **~ (kayak)** kayak.

canon [kãnõ] *nm (arme)* gun; *(HIST)* cannon; *(d'une arme: tube)* barrel; *(fig)* model; *(MUS)* canon ♦ *a:* **droit ~** canon law; **~ rayé** rifled barrel.

cañon [kãnyõ] *nm* canyon.

canonique [kãnonēk] *a:* **âge ~** respectable age.

canoniser [kãnonēzā] *vt* to canonize.

canonnade [kãnonád] *nf* cannonade.

canonnier [kãnonyā] *nm* gunner.

canonnière [kãnonyer] *nf* gunboat.

canot [kãnō] *nm* boat, ding(h)y; **~ pneumatique** rubber *ou* inflatable ding(h)y; **~ de sauvetage** lifeboat.

canotage [kãnotázh] *nm* rowing.

canoter [kãnotā] *vi* to go rowing.

canoteur, euse [kãnotœr, -œ̃z] *nm/f* rower.

canotier [kãnotyā] *nm* boater.

Cantal [kãtál] *nm:* **le ~** Cantal.

cantate [kãtát] *nf* cantata.

cantatrice [kãtátrēs] *nf* (opera) singer.

cantilène [kãtēlen] *nf (MUS)* cantilena.

cantine [kãtēn] *nf* canteen; *(réfectoire d'école)* dining hall.

cantique [kãtēk] *nm* hymn.

canton [kãtõ] *nm* district *consisting of several communes*; *(en Suisse)* canton.

cantonade [kãtonád]: **à la ~** *ad* to everyone in general; *(crier)* from the rooftops.

cantonais, e [kãtone, -ez] *a* Cantonese ♦ *nm (LING)* Cantonese.

cantonner [kãtonā] *vt (MIL)* to billet, quarter; to station; **se ~ dans** to confine o.s. to.

cantonnier [kãtonyā] *nm* roadmender.

canular [kãnülár] *nm* hoax.

CAO *sigle f* (= *conception assistée par ordinateur*) CAD.

caoutchouc [kã-ootshoo] *nm* rubber; **~ mousse** foam rubber; **en ~** rubber *cpd*.

caoutchouté, e [kã-ootshootā] *a* rubberized.

caoutchouteux, euse [kã-ootshootœ̃, -œ̃z] *a* rubbery.

CAP *sigle m* (= *Certificat d'aptitude professionnelle*) vocational training certificate taken at high school.

cap [káp] *nm (GÉO)* cape; headland; *(fig)* hurdle; watershed; *(NAVIG)*: **changer de ~** to change course; **mettre le ~ sur** to head *ou* steer for; **doubler** *ou* **passer le ~** *(fig)* to get over the worst; **Le C~** Cape Town; **le ~ de Bonne Espérance** the Cape of Good Hope; **le ~ Horn** Cape Horn; **les îles du C~ Vert** *(aussi:* **le C~-Vert**) the Cape Verde Islands.

capable [kápábl(ə)] *a* able, capable; **~ de qch/faire** capable of sth/doing; **il est ~ d'oublier** he could easily forget; **spectacle/livre ~ d'intéresser** show/book liable *ou* likely to be of interest.

capacité [kápásētā] *nf (compétence)* ability; *(JUR, INFORM, d'un récipient)* capacity; **~ (en droit)** basic legal qualification.

caparaçonner [kápárásonā] *vt (fig)* to clad.

cape [káp] *nf* cape, cloak; **rire sous ~** to laugh up one's sleeve.

capeline [káplēn] *nf* wide-brimmed hat.

CAPES [kápes] *sigle m* (= *Certificat d'aptitude au professorat de l'enseignement du second degré*) secondary teaching diploma.

capésien, ne [kápāsyañ, -en] *nm/f person who holds the CAPES*.

CAPET [kápet] *sigle m* (= *Certificat d'aptitude au professorat de l'enseignement technique*) technical teaching diploma.

capharnaüm [káfárnáom] *nm* shambles *sg*.

capillaire [kápēler] *a (soins, lotion)* hair *cpd*; *(vaisseau etc)* capillary; **artiste ~** hair artist *ou* designer.

capillarité [kápēlárētā] *nf* capillary action.

capilliculteur [kápēlēkültœr] *nm* hair-care specialist.

capilotade [kápēlotád]: **en ~** *ad* crushed to a pulp; smashed to pieces.

capitaine [kápēten] *nm* captain; **~ des pompiers** fire marshal *(US)*, fire chief *(Brit)*; **~ au long cours** master mariner.

capitainerie [kápētenrē] *nf (du port)* harbor *(US) ou* harbour *(Brit)* master's (office).

capital, e, aux [kápētál, -ō] *a* major; of paramount importance; fundamental; *(JUR)* capital ♦ *nm* capital; (*fig*) stock; asset ♦ *nf* (*ville*) capital; (*lettre*) capital (letter); ♦ *nmpl* (*fonds*) capital *sg*, money *sg*; **les sept péchés capitaux** the seven deadly sins; **peine ~e** capital punishment; **~ (social)** capital stock (*US*), authorized capital (*Brit*); **~ d'exploitation** working capital.

capitaliser [kápětálēzá] *vt* to amass, build up; (*COMM*) to capitalize ♦ *vi* to save.

capitalisme [kápětálēsm(ə)] *nm* capitalism.

capitaliste [kápětálēst(ə)] *a, nm/f* capitalist.

capiteux, euse [kápětœ, -œz] *a* (*vin, parfum*) heady; (*sensuel*) sensuous, alluring.

capitonné, e [kápětoná] *a* padded.

capitulation [kápětülásyóň] *nf* capitulation.

capituler [kápětülá] *vi* to capitulate.

caporal, aux [káporál, -ō] *nm* ≈ corporal (*US*), ≈ lance corporal (*Brit*).

caporal-chef, *pl* **caporaux-chefs** [káporálshef, káporō-] *nm* corporal.

capot [kápō] *nm* (*AUTO*) hood (*US*), bonnet (*Brit*) ♦ *a inv* (*CARTES*): **être ~** to lose without taking a single trick.

capote [kápot] *nf* (*de voiture*) top (*US*), hood (*Brit*); (*de soldat*) greatcoat; **~ (anglaise)** (*fam*) rubber, condom.

capoter [kápotá] *vi* to overturn; (*négociations*) to founder.

câpre [kápr(ə)] *nf* caper.

caprice [káprēs] *nm* whim, caprice; passing fancy; **~s** *nmpl* (*de la mode etc*) vagaries; **faire un ~** to throw a tantrum; **faire des ~s** to be temperamental.

capricieux, euse [káprēsyœ, -œz] *a* capricious; whimsical; temperamental.

Capricorne [káprēkorn] *nm*: **le ~** Capricorn, the Goat; **être du ~** to be Capricorn.

capsule [kápsül] *nf* (*de bouteille*) cap; (*amorce*) primer; cap; (*BOT etc, spatiale*) capsule.

capter [káptá] *vt* (*ondes radio*) to pick up; (*eau*) to harness; (*fig*) to win, capture.

capteur [káptœr] *nm*: **~ solaire** solar collector.

captieux, euse [kápsyœ, -œz] *a* specious.

captif, ive [káptēf, -ēv] *a, nm/f* captive.

captiver [káptēvá] *vt* to captivate.

captivité [káptēvētá] *nf* captivity; **en ~** in captivity.

capture [káptür] *nf* capture, catching *q*; catch.

capturer [káptürá] *vt* to capture, catch.

capuche [kápüsh] *nf* hood.

capuchon [kápüshóň] *nm* hood; (*de stylo*) cap, top.

capucin [kápüsáň] *nm* Capuchin monk.

capucine [kápüsēn] *nf* (*BOT*) nasturtium.

caquelon [káklóň] *nm* (*ustensile de cuisson*) fondue pot.

caquet [káke] *nm*: **rabattre le ~ à qn** to bring sb down a peg or two.

caqueter [káktá] *vi* (*poule*) to cackle; (*fig*) to prattle.

car [kár] *nm* bus, coach (*Brit*) ♦ *cj* because, for; **~ de police** police van; **~ de reportage** broadcasting *ou* radio van.

carabine [kárábēn] *nf* carbine, rifle; **~ à air comprimé** airgun.

carabiné, e [kárábēná] *a* violent; (*cocktail, amende*) stiff.

Caracas [kárákás] *n* Caracas.

caracoler [kárákolá] *vi* to caracole, prance.

caractère [kárákter] *nm* (*gén*) character; **en ~s gras** in bold type; **en petits ~s** in small print; **en ~s d'imprimerie** in block letters; **avoir du ~** to have character; **avoir bon/mauvais ~** to be good-/ill-natured *ou* tempered; **~ de remplacement** wild card (*INFORM*); **~s/seconde (cps)** characters per second (cps).

caractériel, le [káráktáryel] *a* (*enfant*) (emotionally) disturbed ♦ *nm/f* problem child; **troubles ~s** emotional problems.

caractérisé, e [káráktárēzá] *a*: **c'est une grippe/de l'insubordination ~e** it is a clear(-cut) case of flu/insubordination.

caractériser [káráktárēzá] *vt* to characterize; **se ~ par** to be characterized *ou* distinguished by.

caractéristique [káráktárēstěk] *a, nf* characteristic.

carafe [káráf] *nf* decanter; carafe.

carafon [káráfóň] *nm* small carafe.

caraïbe [káráēb] *a* Caribbean; **les C~s** *nfpl* the Caribbean (Islands); **la mer des C~s** the Caribbean Sea.

carambolage [káráňbolázh] *nm* multiple crash, pileup.

caramel [kárámel] *nm* (*bonbon*) caramel, toffee; (*substance*) caramel.

caraméliser [kárámálēzá] *vt* to caramelize.

carapace [kárápás] *nf* shell.

carapater [kárápátá]: **se ~** *vi* to take to one's heels, scram.

carat [kárá] *nm* carat; **or à 18 ~s** 18-carat gold.

caravane [káráván] *nf* (*véhicule*) trailer (*US*), caravan (*Brit*).

caravanier [káráványá] *nm* camper (*using a trailer/caravan* (*Brit*)).

caravaning [kárávánēng] *nm* camping with a trailer (*US*), caravanning (*Brit*); (*emplacement*) campground (*US*), caravan site (*Brit*).

caravelle [kárável] *nf* caravel.

carbonate [kárbonát] *nm* (*CHIMIE*): **~ de soude** sodium carbonate.

carbone [kárbon] *nm* carbon; (*feuille*) carbon, sheet of carbon paper; (*double*) carbon (copy).

carbonique [kárbonēk] *a*: **gaz ~** carbon dioxide; **neige ~** dry ice.

carbonisé, e [kárbonēzá] *a* charred; **mourir ~** to be burned to death.

carboniser [kárbonēzá] *vt* to carbonize; (*brûler complètement*) to burn down, reduce to ashes.

carburant [kárbüráň] *nm* (motor) fuel.

carburateur [kárbürátœr] *nm* carburetor (*US*), carburettor (*Brit*).

carburation [kárbürásyóň] *nf* carburetion (*US*), carburation (*Brit*).

carburer [kárbürá] *vi* (*moteur*): **bien/mal ~** to be well/badly tuned.

carcan [kárkáň] *nm* (*fig*) yoke, shackles *pl*.

carcasse [kárkás] *nf* carcass; (*de véhicule etc*) frame.

carcéral, e, aux [kársárál, -ō] *a* prison *cpd*.

carcinogène [kársēnozhen] *a* carcinogenic.

cardan [kárdáň] *nm* universal joint.

carder [kárdā] *vt* to card.

cardiaque [kárdyák] *a* cardiac, heart *cpd* ♦ *nm/f* heart patient; **être** ~ to have a heart condition.

cardigan [kárdēgáṅ] *nm* cardigan.

cardinal, e, aux [kárdēnál, -ō] *a* cardinal ♦ *nm* (*REL*) cardinal.

cardiologie [kárdyolozhē] *nf* cardiology.

cardiologue [kárdyolog] *nm/f* cardiologist, heart specialist.

cardio-vasculaire [kárdyováskülœr] *a* cardio-vascular.

cardon [kárdôṅ] *nm* cardoon.

carême [kárɛm] *nm*: **le C**~ Lent.

carence [káráṅs] *nf* incompetence, inadequacy; (*manque*) deficiency; ~ **vitaminique** vitamin deficiency.

carène [kárɛn] *nf* hull.

caréner [kárānā] *vt* (*NAVIG*) to careen; (*carrosserie*) to streamline.

caressant, e [kárɛsáṅ, -áṅt] *a* affectionate; caressing, tender.

caresse [kárɛs] *nf* caress.

caresser [kárāsā] *vt* to caress, stroke, fondle; (*fig: projet, espoir*) to toy with.

cargaison [kárgezôṅ] *nf* cargo, freight.

cargo [kárgō] *nm* cargo boat, freighter; ~ **mixte** cargo and passenger ship.

cari [kárē] *nm* = **curry**.

caricatural, e, aux [kárēkátürál, -ō] *a* caricatural, caricature-like.

caricature [kárēkátür] *nf* caricature; (*politique etc*) (satirical) cartoon.

caricaturer [kárēkátürā] *vt* (*personne*) to caricature; (*politique etc*) to satirize.

caricaturiste [kárēkátürēst(ə)] *nm/f* caricaturist; (satirical) cartoonist.

carie [kárē] *nf*: **la** ~ **(dentaire)** tooth decay; **une** ~ a bad tooth.

carié, e [káryā] *a*: **dent** ~**e** bad *ou* decayed tooth.

carillon [kárēyôṅ] *nm* (*d'église*) bells *pl*; (*de pendule*) chimes *pl*; (*de porte*): ~ **(électrique)** (electric) door chime *ou* bell.

carillonner [kárēyonā] *vi* to ring, chime, peal.

carlingue [kárlaṅg] *nf* cabin.

carmin [kármaṅ] *a inv* crimson.

carnage [kárnázh] *nm* carnage, slaughter.

carnassier, ière [kárnásyā, -yer] *a* carnivorous ♦ *nm* carnivore.

carnation [kárnásyôṅ] *nf* complexion; ~**s** *nfpl* (*PEINTURE*) flesh tones.

carnaval [kárnávál] *nm* carnival.

carné, e [kárnā] *a* meat *cpd*, meat-based.

carnet [kárnɛ] *nm* (*calepin*) notebook; (*de tickets, timbres etc*) book; (*d'école*) report card (*US*), school report (*Brit*); (*journal intime*) diary; ~ **d'adresses** address book; ~ **de chèques** check (*US*) *ou* cheque (*Brit*) book; ~ **de commandes** order book; ~ **de notes** (*SCOL*) report card (*US*), (school) report (*Brit*); ~ **à souches** stub (*US*) *ou* counterfoil (*Brit*) book.

carnier [kárnyā] *nm* gamebag.

carnivore [kárnēvor] *a* carnivorous ♦ *nm* carnivore.

Carolines [károlēn] *nfpl*: **les** ~ the Caroline Islands.

carotide [károtēd] *nf* carotid (artery).

carotte [károt] *nf* (*aussi fig*) carrot.

Carpates [kárpát] *nfpl*: **les** ~ the Carpathians, the Carpathian Mountains.

carpe [kárp(ə)] *nf* carp.

carpette [kárpɛt] *nf* rug.

carquois [kárkwá] *nm* quiver.

carre [kár] *nf* (*de ski*) edge.

carré, e [kárā] *a* square; (*fig: franc*) straightforward ♦ *nm* (*de terrain, jardin*) patch, plot; (*NAVIG: salle*) wardroom; (*MATH*) square; (*CARTES*): ~ **d'as/de rois** four aces/kings; **élever un nombre au** ~ to square a number; **mètre/kilomètre** ~ square meter/kilometer; ~ **de soie** silk headscarf; ~ **d'agneau** loin of lamb.

carreau, x [kárō] *nm* (*en faïence etc*) (floor) tile; (wall) tile; (*de fenêtre*) (window) pane; (*motif*) check, square; (*CARTES: couleur*) diamonds *pl*; (: *carte*) diamond; **tissu à** ~**x** checked fabric; **papier à** ~**x** squared paper.

carrefour [kárfōōr] *nm* crossroads *sg*.

carrelage [kárlázh] *nm* tiling; (tiled) floor.

carreler [kárlā] *vt* to tile.

carrelet [kárlɛ] *nm* (*poisson*) plaice.

carreleur [kárlœr] *nm* (floor) tiler.

carrément [kárāmáṅ] *ad* (*franchement*) straight out, bluntly; (*sans détours, sans hésiter*) straight; (*nettement*) definitely; **il l'a** ~ **mis à la porte** he threw him straight out.

carrer [kárā]: **se** ~ *vi*: **se** ~ **dans un fauteuil** to settle o.s. comfortably *ou* ensconce o.s. in an armchair.

carrier [káryā] *nm*: **(ouvrier)** ~ quarryman, quarrier.

carrière [káryɛr] *nf* (*de roches*) quarry; (*métier*) career; **militaire de** ~ professional soldier; **faire** ~ **dans** to make one's career in.

carriole [káryol] *nf* (*péj*) old cart.

carrossable [károsábl(ə)] *a* suitable for (motor) vehicles.

carrosse [káros] *nm* (horse-drawn) coach.

carrosserie [károsrē] *nf* body; (*activité, commerce*) (car) body manufacturing; **atelier de** ~ (*pour réparations*) body shop.

carrossier [károsyā] *nm* (car) body repairer; (*dessinateur*) car designer.

carrousel [károozɛl] *nm* (*ÉQUITATION*) carousel; (*fig*) merry-go-round.

carrure [kárür] *nf* build; (*fig*) stature.

cartable [kártábl(ə)] *nm* (*d'écolier*) satchel, (school) bag.

carte [kárt(ə)] *nf* (*de géographie*) map; (*marine, du ciel*) chart; (*de fichier, d'abonnement etc, à jouer*) card; (*au restaurant*) menu; (*aussi*: ~ **postale**) (post)card; (*aussi*: ~ **de visite**) (visiting) card; **avoir/donner** ~ **blanche** to have/give carte blanche *ou* a free hand; **tirer les** ~**s à qn** to read sb's cards; **jouer aux** ~**s** to play cards; **jouer** ~**s sur table** (*fig*) to put one's cards on the table; **à la** ~ (*au restaurant*) à la carte; ~ **bancaire** banking (*US*) *ou* cash (*Brit*) card; ~ **à circuit imprimé** printed circuit; ~ **de crédit** credit card; ~ **d'état-major** ≈ Geological (*US*) *ou* Ordnance (*Brit*) Survey map; **la** ~ **grise** (*AUTO*) ≈ the (car) registration document; ~ **d'identité** identity card; ~ **perforée** punch(ed) card; ~ **de séjour**

residence permit; ~ **routière** road map; ~
verte (AUTO) international insurance
certificate; **la ~ des vins** the wine list.

cartel [kártel] nm cartel.

carte-lettre, pl cartes-lettres [kártəletr(ə)] nf
letter-card.

carte-mère, pl cartes-mères [kártəmer] nf (IN-
FORM) mother board.

carter [kárter] nm (AUTO: d'huile) oil pan
(US), sump (Brit); (: de la boîte de vitesses)
housing (US), casing (Brit); (de bicyclette)
chain guard.

carte-réponse, pl **cartes-réponses**
[kárt(ə)rāpôns] nf reply card.

Carthage [kártázh] n Carthage.

carthaginois, e [kártázhēnwà, -wáz] a
Carthaginian.

cartilage [kártēlázh] nm (ANAT) cartilage.

cartilagineux, euse [kártēlázhēnœ̄, -œ̄z] a
(viande) gristly.

cartographe [kártográf] nm/f cartographer.

cartographie [kártográfē] nf cartography,
map-making.

cartomancie [kártomânsē] nf fortune-telling,
card-reading.

cartomancien, ne [kártomânsyan, -en] nm/f
fortune-teller (with cards).

carton [kártôn] nm (matériau) cardboard;
(boîte) (cardboard) box; (d'invitation) invitation card; (ART) sketch; cartoon; **en ~** cardboard cpd; **faire un ~** (au tir) to have a go
at the rifle range; to score a hit; **~ (à dessin)**
portfolio.

cartonnage [kártonázh] nm cardboard (packing).

cartonné, e [kártonā] a (livre) hardback,
cased.

carton-pâte [kártônpát] nm pasteboard; **de ~**
(fig) cardboard cpd.

cartouche [kártōōsh] nf cartridge; (de cigarettes) carton.

cartouchière [kártōōshyer] nf cartridge belt.

cas [kâ] nm case; **faire peu de ~/grand ~ de**
to attach little/great importance to; **le ~**
échéant if need be; **en aucun ~** on no
account, under no circumstances (whatsoever); **au ~ où** in case; **dans ce ~** in that
case; **en ~ de** in case of, in the event of; **en**
~ de besoin if need be; **en ~ d'urgence** in
an emergency; **en ce ~** in that case; **en tout**
~ in any case, at any rate; **~ de conscience**
matter of conscience; **~ de force majeure**
case of absolute necessity; (ASSURANCES) act
of God; **~ limite** borderline case; **~ social**
social problem.

Casablanca [kázáblánkà] n Casablanca.

casanier, ière [kázànyā, -yer] a stay-at-home.

casaque [kázák] nf (de jockey) blouse.

cascade [káskád] nf waterfall, cascade; (fig)
stream, torrent.

cascadeur, euse [káskádœr, -œ̄z] nm/f
stuntman/girl.

case [kâz] nf (hutte) hut; (compartiment)
compartment; (pour le courrier) pigeonhole;
(de mots croisés, d'échiquier) square; (sur
un formulaire) box.

casemate [kázmát] nf blockhouse.

caser [kázā] vt (mettre) to put; (loger) to put
up; (péj) to find a job for; to marry off; **se**

~ (personne) to settle down.

caserne [kázern(ə)] nf barracks.

casernement [kázernəmân] nm barrack buildings pl.

cash [kàsh] ad: **payer ~** to pay cash.

casier [kázyā] nm (à journaux etc) rack; (de
bureau) filing cabinet; (: à cases) set of
pigeonholes; (case) compartment; pigeonhole; (: à clef) locker; (PÊCHE) lobster pot;
~ à bouteilles bottle rack; **~ judiciaire**
police record.

casino [kázēnō] nm casino.

casque [kásk(ə)] nm helmet; (chez le coiffeur)
(hair-)drier; (pour audition) (head-)phones
pl, headset; **les C~s bleus** the UN peace-
keeping force.

casquer [káskā] vi (fam) to cough up.

casquette [kásket] nf cap.

cassable [kásábl(ə)] a (fragile) breakable.

cassant, e [kásán, -ánt] a brittle; (fig)
brusque, abrupt.

cassate [kását] nf: (glace) ~ cassata.

cassation [kásásyôn] nf: **se pourvoir en ~** to
lodge an appeal; **recours en ~** appeal to the
Supreme Court.

casse [kás] nf (pour voitures): **mettre à la ~**
to scrap; (dégâts): **il y a eu de la ~** there
were a lot of breakages; (TYPO): **haut/bas**
de ~ upper/lower case.

cassé, e [kásā] a (voix) cracked; (vieillard)
bent.

casse-cou [káskōō] a inv daredevil, reckless;
crier ~ à qn to warn sb (against a risky
undertaking).

casse-croûte [káskrōōt] nm inv snack.

casse-noisette(s) [kásnwázet], **casse-noix**
[kásnwá] nm inv nutcracker (US), nutcrack-
ers pl (Brit).

casse-pieds [káspyā] a, nm/f inv (fam): **il est**
~, c'est un ~ he's a pain (in the neck).

casser [kásā] vt to break; (ADMIN: gradé) to
demote; (JUR) to quash; (COMM): **~ les prix**
to slash prices; **se ~** vi to break; (fam) to
go, leave ♦ vt: **se ~ la jambe/une jambe** to
break one's leg/a leg; **à tout ~** fantastic,
brilliant; **se ~ net** to break clean off.

casserole [kásrol] nf saucepan; **à la ~**
(CULIN) braised.

casse-tête [kástet] nm inv (fig) brain teaser;
(difficultés) headache (fig).

cassette [káset] nf (bande magnétique) cassette; (coffret) casket.

casseur [kásœr] nm hooligan; rioter.

cassis [kásēs] nm blackcurrant; (de la route)
dip, bump.

cassonade [kásonád] nf brown sugar.

cassoulet [kásōōle] nm sausage and bean hotpot.

cassure [kásür] nf break, crack.

castagnettes [kástányet] nfpl castanets.

caste [kást(ə)] nf caste.

castillan, e [kástēyán, -án] a Castilian ♦ nm
(LING) Castilian.

Castille [kástēy] nf: **la ~** Castile.

castor [kástor] nm beaver.

castrer [kástrā] vt (mâle) to castrate;
(femelle) to spay; (cheval) to geld; (chat,
chien) to fix (US), doctor (Brit).

cataclysme [kátáklēsm(ə)] nm cataclysm.

catacombes [kátákôṅb] *nfpl* catacombs.
catadioptre [kàtádyoptr(ə)] *nm* = **cataphote**.
catafalque [kàtáfálk(ə)] *nm* catafalque.
catalan, e [kátálàṅ, -áṅ] *a* Catalan, Catalonian ♦ *nm* (*LING*) Catalan.
Catalogne [kátálony] *nf*: **la** ~ Catalonia.
catalogue [kátálog] *nm* catalogue.
cataloguer [kátálogá] *vt* to catalogue, list; (*péj*) to put a label on.
catalyse [kátálēz] *nf* catalysis.
catalyseur [kátálēzœr] *nm* catalyst.
catamaran [kàtàmáráṅ] *nm* (*voilier*) catamaran.
cataphote [kátáfot] *nm* reflector.
cataplasme [kàtàplásm(ə)] *nm* poultice.
catapulte [kátápült(ə)] *nf* catapult.
catapulter [kátápültá] *vt* to catapult.
cataracte [kátárákt(ə)] *nf* cataract; **opérer qn de la** ~ to operate on sb for a cataract.
catarrhe [kátár] *nm* catarrh.
catarrheux, euse [kátàrœ̄, -œ̄z] *a* catarrhal.
catastrophe [kátástrof] *nf* catastrophe, disaster; **atterrir en** ~ to make an emergency landing; **partir en** ~ to rush away.
catastropher [kátástrofá] *vt* (*personne*) to shatter.
catastrophique [kátástrofēk] *a* catastrophic, disastrous.
catch [kátsh] *nm* freestyle (*US*) *ou* all-in (*Brit*) wrestling.
catcheur, euse [kátshœr, -œ̄z] *nm/f* freestyle (*US*) *ou* (all-in) (*Brit*) wrestler.
catéchiser [kátáshēzá] *vt* to indoctrinate; to lecture.
catéchisme [kátáshēsm(ə)] *nm* catechism.
catéchumène [kátákümen] *nm/f* catechumen, *person attending religious instruction prior to baptism.*
catégorie [kátágorē] *nf* category; (*BOUCHERIE*): **morceaux de première/deuxième** ~ prime/second cuts.
catégorique [kátágorēk] *a* categorical.
catégoriquement [kátágorēkmáṅ] *ad* categorically.
catégoriser [kátágorēzá] *vt* to categorize.
caténaire [kátánɛr] *nf* (*RAIL*) overhead line.
cathédrale [kátádrál] *nf* cathedral.
cathéter [kátátɛr] *nm* (*MÉD*) catheter.
cathode [kátod] *nf* cathode.
cathodique [kátodēk] *a*: **rayons** ~**s** cathode rays; **tube/écran** ~ cathode-ray tube/screen.
catholicisme [kátolēsēsm(ə)] *nm* (Roman) Catholicism.
catholique [kátolēk] *a*, *nm/f* (Roman) Catholic; **pas très** ~ a bit shady *ou* fishy.
catimini [kátēmēnē]: **en** ~ *ad* on the sly, on the quiet.
catogan [kátogáṅ] *nm* bow (*tying hair on neck*).
Caucase [kokáz] *nm*: **le** ~ the Caucasus (Mountains).
caucasien, ne [kokázyaṅ, -en] *a* Caucasian.
cauchemar [koshmár] *nm* nightmare.
cauchemardesque [koshmárdesk(ə)] *a* nightmarish.
caudal, e, aux [kōdál, -ō] *a* caudal, tail *cpd*.
causal, e [kōzál] *a* causal.
causalité [kōzálētá] *nf* causality.
cause [kōz] *nf* cause; (*JUR*) lawsuit, case;

brief; **faire** ~ **commune avec qn** to take sides with sb; **être** ~ **de** to be the cause of; **à** ~ **de** because of, owing to; **pour** ~ **de** on account of; owing to; (**et**) **pour** ~ and for (a very) good reason; **être en** ~ (*intérêts*) to be at stake; (*personne*) to be involved; (*qualité*) to be in question; **mettre en** ~ to implicate; to call into question; **remettre en** ~ to challenge, call into question; **c'est hors de** ~ it's out of the question; **en tout état de** ~ in any case.
causer [kōzá] *vt* to cause ♦ *vi* to chat, talk.
causerie [kōzrē] *nf* talk.
causette [kōzet] *nf*: **faire la** *ou* **un brin de** ~ to have a chat.
caustique [kōstēk] *a* caustic.
cauteleux, euse [kōtlœ̄, -œ̄z] *a* wily.
cautériser [kotárēzá] *vt* to cauterize.
caution [kōsyóṅ] *nf* guarantee, security; deposit; (*JUR*) bail (bond); (*fig*) backing, support; **payer la** ~ **de qn** to go (*US*) *ou* stand (*Brit*) bail for sb; **se porter** ~ **pour qn** to stand surety for sb; **libéré sous** ~ released on bail; **sujet à** ~ unconfirmed.
cautionnement [kōsyonmáṅ] *nm* (*somme*) guarantee, surety.
cautionner [kōsyoná] *vt* to guarantee; (*soutenir*) to support.
cavalcade [káválkád] *nf* (*fig*) stampede.
cavale [kávál] *nf*: **en** ~ on the run.
cavalerie [káválrē] *nf* cavalry.
cavalier, ière [kávályá, -yer] *a* (*désinvolte*) offhand ♦ *nm/f* rider; (*au bal*) partner ♦ *nm* (*ÉCHECS*) knight; **faire** ~ **seul** to go it alone; **allée** *ou* **piste cavalière** riding path.
cave [káv] *nf* cellar; (*cabaret*) (cellar) nightclub ♦ *a*: **yeux** ~**s** sunken eyes; **joues** ~**s** hollow cheeks.
caveau, x [kávō] *nm* vault.
caverne [kávern(ə)] *nf* cave.
caverneux, euse [kávernœ̄, -œ̄z] *a* cavernous.
caviar [kávyár] *nm* caviar(e).
cavité [kávētá] *nf* cavity.
Cayenne [káyen] *n* Cayenne.
CB [sēbē] *sigle f* (= *citizens' band, canaux banalisés*) CB.
CC *sigle m* = **corps consulaire, compte courant.**
CCI *sigle f* = **Chambre de commerce et d'industrie.**
CCP *sigle m* = **compte chèque postal.**
CD *sigle m* (= *chemin départemental*) secondary road; (= *compact disc*) CD; (= *comité directeur*) steering committee; (*POL*) = **corps diplomatique.**
CDF, CdF *sigle mpl* (= *Charbonnages de France*) national coal board.
CDI *sigle m* (= *Centre de documentation et d'information*) school library.
CDS *sigle m* (= *Centre des démocrates sociaux*) political party.
CE *sigle f* (= *Communauté européenne*) EEC, EC (*Brit*); (*COMM*) = **caisse d'épargne** ♦ *sigle m* (*INDUSTRIE*) = **comité d'entreprise**; (*SCOL*) = **cours élémentaire.**
ce (c'), cet, cette, ces [sə, set, sā] *dét* (*gén*) this; these *pl*; (*non-proximité*) that; those *pl*; **cette nuit** (*qui vient*) tonight; (*passée*) last night ♦ *pronom*: ~ **qui**, ~ **que** what; (*chose*

qui ...): **il est bête, ~ qui me chagrine** he's stupid, which saddens me; **tout ~ qui bouge** everything that *ou* which moves; **tout ~ que je sais** all I know; **~ dont j'ai parlé** what I talked about; **~ que c'est grand!** how big it is!, what a size it is!; **c'est: c'est petit/ grand/un livre** it's *ou* it is small/big/a book; **c'est un peintre** he's *ou* he is a painter; **~ sont des livres/ peintres** they're *ou* they are books/painters; **c'est le facteur** *etc* (*à la porte*) it's the mailman *etc*; **qui est-~?** who is it?; (*en désignant*) who is he/she?; **qu'est-~?** what is it?; **c'est ça** (*correct*) that's it, that's right; **c'est qu'il n'a pas faim** the fact is he's not hungry; **ce n'est pas à moi de faire** it's not up to me to do; *voir aussi* **-ci, est-ce que, n'est-ce pas, c'est- à-dire.**

CEA *sigle m* (= *Commissariat à l'énergie atomique*) ≈ AEC (= *Atomic Energy Commission*) (*US*), ≈ AEA (= *Atomic Energy Authority*) (*Brit*).

CECA [sākā] *sigle f* (= *Communauté européenne du charbon et de l'acier*) ECSC (= *European Coal and Steel Community*).

ceci [səsē] *pronom* this.

cécité [sāsētā] *nf* blindness.

céder [sādā] *vt* to give up ♦ *vi* (*pont, barrage*) to give way; (*personne*) to give in; **~ à** to yield to, give in to.

CEDEX [sādeks] *sigle m* (= *courrier d'entreprise à distribution exceptionnelle*) *accelerated postal service for bulk users.*

cédille [sādēy] *nf* cedilla.

cèdre [sedr(ə)] *nm* cedar.

CEE *sigle f* (= *Communauté économique européenne*) EEC.

CEG *sigle m* (= *Collège d'enseignement général*) ≈ junior high school.

ceindre [sãdr(ə)] *vt* (*mettre*) to put on, don; (*entourer*): **~ qch de qch** to put sth around sth.

ceinture [sãtür] *nf* belt; (*taille*) waist; (*fig*) ring; belt; circle; **~ de sauvetage** lifebelt; **~ de sécurité** safety *ou* seat belt; **~ (de sécurité) à enrouleur** inertia reel seat belt; **~ verte** green belt.

ceinturer [sãtürā] *vt* (*saisir*) to grasp (around the waist); (*entourer*) to surround.

ceinturon [sãtüróñ] *nm* belt.

cela [səlá] *pronom* that; (*comme sujet indéfini*) it; **~ m'étonne que** it surprises me that; **quand/où ~?** when/where (was that)?

célébrant [sālābrãñ] *nm* (*REL*) celebrant.

célébration [sālābrãsyóñ] *nf* celebration.

célèbre [sālebr(ə)] *a* famous.

célébrer [sālābrā] *vt* to celebrate; (*louer*) to extol.

célébrité [sālābrētā] *nf* fame; (*star*) celebrity.

céleri [sālrē] *nm*: **~(-rave)** celeriac; **~ (en branche)** celery.

célérité [sālārētā] *nf* speed, swiftness.

céleste [sālest(ə)] *a* celestial; heavenly.

célibat [sālēbá] *nm* celibacy; bachelor/ spinsterhood.

célibataire [sālēbáter] *a* single, unmarried ♦ *nm/f* bachelor/unmarried *ou* single woman; **mère ~** single *ou* unmarried mother.

celle, celles [sel] *pronom voir* **celui.**

cellier [sālyā] *nm* storeroom.

cellophane [sālofán] *nf* ® cellophane.

cellulaire [sālüler] *a* (*BIO*) cell *cpd*, cellular; **voiture** *ou* **fourgon ~** prison *ou* police van; **régime ~** confinement.

cellule [sālül] *nf* (*gén*) cell; **~ (photo- élec- trique)** electronic eye.

cellulite [sālülēt] *nf* cellulite.

celluloïd [sālüloēd] *nm* ® Celluloid.

cellulose [sālülōz] *nf* cellulose.

celte [selt(ə)], **celtique** [seltēk] *a* Celt, Celtic.

celui, celle, ceux, celles [səlüē, sel, sœ̄] *pronom* the one; **~ qui bouge** the one which *ou* that moves; (*personne*) the one who moves; **~ que je vois** the one (which *ou* that) I see; the one (whom) I see; **~ dont je parle** the one I'm talking about; **~ qui veut** (*valeur indéfinie*) whoever wants, the one *ou* person who wants; **~ du salon/du dessous** the one in (*ou* from) the lounge/below; **~ de mon frère** my brother's; **celui-ci/-là, celle-ci/-là** this/that one; the latter/former; **ceux- ci, celles-ci** these ones; the latter; **ceux-là, celles-là** those (ones); the former.

cénacle [sānákl(ə)] *nm* (*literary*) coterie *ou* set.

cendre [sãdr(ə)] *nf* ash; **~s** (*d'un foyer*) ash(es), cinders; (*volcaniques*) ash *sg*; (*d'un défunt*) ashes; **sous la ~** (*CULIN*) in (the) embers.

cendré, e [sãdrā] *a* (*couleur*) ashen; (*piste*) **~e** cinder track.

cendreux, euse [sãdrœ̄, -œ̄z] *a* (*terrain, substance*) cindery; (*teint*) ashen.

cendrier [sãdrēyā] *nm* ashtray.

cène [sen] *nf*: **la ~** (Holy) Communion; (*ART*) the Last Supper.

censé, e [sãsā] *a*: **être ~ faire** to be supposed to do.

censément [sãsāmãñ] *ad* supposedly.

censeur [sãser] *nm* (*SCOL*) assistant- *ou* vice-principal; (*CINÉMA, POL*) censor.

censure [sãsür] *nf* censorship.

censurer [sãsürā] *vt* (*CINÉMA, PRESSE*) to censor; (*POL*) to censure.

cent [sãñ] *num* a hundred, one hundred; **pour ~ (%)** per cent (%); **faire les ~ pas** to pace up and down.

centaine [sãten] *nf*: **une ~ (de)** about a hundred, a hundred or so; (*COMM*) a hundred; **plusieurs ~s (de)** several hundred; **des ~s (de)** hundreds (of).

centenaire [sãtner] *a* hundred-year-old ♦ *nm/f* centenarian ♦ *nm* (*anniversaire*) centenary.

centième [sãtyem] *num* hundredth.

centigrade [sãtēgrád] *nm* centigrade.

centigramme [sãtēgram] *nm* centigramme.

centilitre [sãtēlētr(ə)] *nm* centiliter (*US*), centilitre (*Brit*).

centime [sãtēm] *nm* centime.

centimètre [sãtēmetr(ə)] *nm* centimeter (*US*), centimetre (*Brit*); (*ruban*) tape measure, measuring tape.

centrafricain, e [sãtráfrēkañ, -en] *a* of *ou* from the Central African Republic.

central, e, aux [sãtrál, -ō] *a* central ♦ *nm*: **~ (téléphonique)** (telephone) exchange ♦ *nf*: **~e d'achat** (*COMM*) central buying service; **~e électrique/nucléaire** electric/nuclear power station; **~e syndicale** group of affiliated trade unions.

centralisation [såntrålēzåsyôṅ] *nf* centralization.

centraliser [såntrålēzā] *vt* to centralize.

centraméricain, e [såntråmårēkaṅ, -en] *a* Central American.

centre [såntr(ə)] *nm* center (*US*), centre (*Brit*); ~ **commercial/sportif/culturel** shopping/sports/arts center; ~ **aéré** outdoor (recreation) center; ~ **d'apprentissage** training college; ~ **d'attraction** center of attraction; ~ **de gravité** center of gravity; ~ **hospitalier** hospital complex; ~ **de tri** (*POSTES*) sorting office; ~**s nerveux** (*ANAT*) nerve centers.

centrer [såntrā] *vt* to center (*US*), centre (*Brit*) ♦ *vi* (*FOOTBALL*) to center (*US*) *ou* centre (*Brit*) the ball.

centre-ville, *pl* **centres-villes** [såntrəvēl] *nm* town center (*US*) *ou* centre (*Brit*), downtown (area) (*US*).

centrifuge [såntrēfüzh] *a*: **force** ~ centrifugal force.

centrifuger [såntrēfüzhā] *vt* to centrifuge.

centrifugeuse [såntrēfüzhœz] *nf* (*pour fruits*) juice extractor.

centripète [såntrēpet] *a*: **force** ~ centripetal force.

centriste [såntrēst(ə)] *a, nm/f* centrist.

centuple [såntüpl(ə)] *nm*: **le** ~ **de qch** a hundred times sth; **au** ~ a hundredfold.

centupler [såntüplā] *vi, vt* to increase a hundredfold.

CEP *sigle m* = **Certificat d'études (primaires)**.

cep [sep] *nm* (vine) stock.

cépage [sāpàzh] *nm* (type of) vine.

cèpe [sep] *nm* (edible) boletus.

cependant [səpåndåṅ] *ad* however, nevertheless.

céramique [sårámēk] *a* ceramic ♦ *nf* ceramic; (*art*) ceramics *sg*.

céramiste [sårámēst(ə)] *nm/f* ceramist.

cerbère [serber] *nm* (*fig: péj*) bad-tempered doorkeeper.

cerceau, x [sersō] *nm* (*d'enfant, de tonnelle*) hoop.

cercle [serkl(ə)] *nm* circle; (*objet*) band, hoop; **décrire un** ~ (*avion*) to circle; (*projectile*) to describe a circle; ~ **d'amis** circle of friends; ~ **de famille** family circle; ~ **vicieux** vicious circle.

cercler [serklā] *vt*: **lunettes cerclées d'or** gold-rimmed glasses.

cercueil [serkœy] *nm* coffin.

céréale [sårāál] *nf* cereal.

céréalier, ière [sårāályā, -yer] *a* (*production, cultures*) cereal *cpd*.

cérébral, e, aux [sårābrál, -ō] *a* (*ANAT*) cerebral, brain *cpd*; (*fig*) mental, cerebral.

cérémonial [sårāmonyál] *nm* ceremonial.

cérémonie [sårāmonē] *nf* ceremony; ~**s** *nfpl* (*péj*) fuss *sg*, to-do *sg*.

cérémonieux, euse [sårāmonyœ, -œz] *a* ceremonious, formal.

CERES [sāres] *sigle m* (= *Centre d'études, de recherches et d'éducation socialiste*) (*formerly*) intellectual section of the French Socialist party.

cerf [ser] *nm* stag.

cerfeuil [serfœy] *nm* chervil.

cerf-volant [servolåṅ] *nm* kite; **jouer au** ~ to fly a kite.

cerisaie [sərēze] *nf* cherry orchard.

cerise [sərēz] *nf* cherry.

cerisier [sərēzyā] *nm* cherry (tree).

CERN [sern] *sigle m* (= *Conseil européen pour la recherche nucléaire*) CERN.

cerné, e [sernā] *a*: **les yeux** ~**s** with dark rings *ou* shadows under the eyes.

cerner [sernā] *vt* (*MIL etc*) to surround; (*fig: problème*) to delimit, define.

cernes [sern(ə)] *nfpl* (dark) rings, shadows (under the eyes).

certain, e [sertaṅ, -en] *a* certain; (*sûr*): ~ (**de/que**) certain *ou* sure (of/ that) ♦ *dét* certain; **d'un** ~ **âge** past one's prime, not so young; **un** ~ **temps** (quite) some time; **sûr et** ~ absolutely certain; ~**s** *pronom* some.

certainement [sertenmåṅ] *ad* (*probablement*) most probably *ou* likely; (*bien sûr*) certainly, of course.

certes [sert(ə)] *ad* admittedly; of course; indeed (yes).

certificat [sertēfēkà] *nm* certificate; **C~ d'études (primaires) (CEP)** *former school leaving certificate* (*taken at the end of primary education*); **C~ de fin d'études secondaires (CFES)** school leaving certificate.

certifié, e [sertēfyā] *a*: **professeur** ~ qualified teacher; (*ADMIN*): **copie** ~**e conforme (à l'original)** certified copy (of the original).

certifier [sertēfyā] *vt* to certify, guarantee; ~ **à qn que** to assure sb that, guarantee to sb that; ~ **qch à qn** to guarantee sth to sb.

certitude [sertētüd] *nf* certainty.

cérumen [sārümen] *nm* (ear)wax.

cerveau, x [servō] *nm* brain; ~ **électronique** electronic brain.

cervelas [servəlà] *nm* saveloy.

cervelle [servel] *nf* (*ANAT*) brain; (*CULIN*) brain(s); **se creuser la** ~ to rack one's brains.

cervical, e, aux [servēkàl, -ō] *a* cervical.

cervidés [servēdā] *nmpl* cervidae.

CES *sigle m* (= *Collège d'enseignement secondaire*) junior high school.

ces [sā] *dét voir* **ce**.

césarienne [sāzåryen] *nf* caesarean (section).

cessantes [sesåṅt] *afpl*: **toutes affaires** ~ forthwith.

cessation [sesàsyôṅ] *nf*: ~ **des hostilités** suspension of hostilities; ~ **de paiements/ commerce** suspension of payments/trading.

cesse [ses]: **sans** ~ *ad* continually, constantly; continuously; **il n'avait de** ~ **que** he would not rest until.

cesser [sesā] *vt* to stop ♦ *vi* to stop, cease; ~ **de faire** to stop doing; **faire** ~ (*bruit, scandale*) to put a stop to.

cessez-le-feu [sesālfœ] *nm inv* ceasefire.

cession [sesyôṅ] *nf* transfer.

c'est [se] *pronom + vb voir* **ce**.

c'est-à-dire [setàder] *ad* that is (to say); (*demander de préciser*): ~**?** what does that mean?; ~ **que** ... (*en conséquence*) which means that ...; (*manière d'excuse*) well, in fact ....

CET *sigle m* (= *Collège d'enseignement*

technique) formerly technical school.

cet [set] *dét voir* **ce.**

cétacé [sātāsā] *nm* cetacean.

cette [set] *dét voir* **ce.**

ceux [sœ̃] *pronom voir* **celui.**

cévenol, e [sãvnol] *a of ou* from the Cévennes region.

cf. *abr* (= *confer*) cf, cp.

CFAO *sigle f* (= *conception de fabrication assistée par ordinateur*) CAM.

CFDT *sigle f* (= *Confédération française et démocratique du travail*) trade union.

CFES *sigle m* = **Certificat de fin d'études secondaires.**

CFF *sigle m* (= *Chemin de fer fédéral*) Swiss railroad.

CFL *sigle m* (= *Chemin de fer luxembourgeois*) Luxembourg railroad.

CFP *sigle m* = *Centre de formation professionnelle* ♦ *sigle f* = *Compagnie française des pétroles.*

CFTC *sigle f* (= *Confédération française des travailleurs chrétiens*) trade union.

CGC *sigle f* (= *Confédération générale des cadres*) management union.

CGPME *sigle f* = *Confédération générale des petites et moyennes entreprises.*

CGT *sigle f* (= *Confédération générale du travail*) trade union.

CH *abr* (= *Confédération helvétique*) CH.

ch. *abr* = **charges, chauffage, cherche.**

chacal [shākāl] *nm* jackal.

chacun, e [shākœ̃, -ün] *pronom* each; (*indéfini*) everyone, everybody.

chagrin, e [shāgrañ, -ēn] *a* morose ♦ *nm* grief, sorrow; **avoir du** ~ to be grieved *ou* sorrowful.

chagriner [shāgrēnā] *vt* to grieve, distress; (*contrarier*) to bother, worry.

chahut [shāü] *nm* uproar.

chahuter [shāütā] *vt* to rag, bait ♦ *vi* to make an uproar.

chahuteur, euse [shāütœr, -œz] *nm/f* rowdy.

chai [she] *nm* wine and spirit store(house).

chaîne [shen] *nf* chain; (*RADIO, TV*) channel; (*INFORM*) string; ~**s** *nfpl* (*liens, asservissement*) fetters, bonds; **travail à la** ~ production line work; **réactions en** ~ chain reactions; **faire la** ~ to form a (human) chain; ~ **d'entraide** mutual aid association; ~ **(haute-fidélité** *ou* **hi-fi)** hi-fi system; ~ **(de montage** *ou* **de fabrication)** production *ou* assembly line; ~ **(de montagnes)** (mountain) range; ~ **de solidarité** solidarity network; ~ **(stéréo** *ou* **audio)** stereo (system).

chaînette [shenet] *nf* (small) chain.

chaînon [shenóñ] *nm* link.

chair [sher] *nf* flesh ♦ *a*: **(couleur)** ~ flesh-colored; **avoir la** ~ **de poule** to have goosepimples *ou* gooseflesh; **bien en** ~ plump, well-padded; **en** ~ **et en os** in the flesh; ~ **à saucisses** sausage meat.

chaire [sher] *nf* (*d'église*) pulpit; (*d'université*) chair.

chaise [shez] *nf* chair; ~ **de bébé** high chair; ~ **électrique** electric chair; ~ **longue** deck-chair.

chaland [shālāñ] *nm* (*bateau*) barge.

châle [shāl] *nm* shawl.

chalet [shāle] *nm* chalet.

chaleur [shālœr] *nf* heat; (*fig*) warmth; fire, fervor (*US*), fervour (*Brit*); heat; **en** ~ (*ZOOL*) on heat.

chaleureusement [shālœrœzmāñ] *ad* warmly.

chaleureux, euse [shālœrœ̃, -œz] *a* warm.

challenge [shālāñzh] *nm* contest, tournament.

challenger [shālāñzher] *nm* (*SPORT*) challenger.

chaloupe [shālōōp] *nf* launch; (*de sauvetage*) lifeboat.

chalumeau, x [shālümō] *nm* blowtorch.

chalut [shālü] *nm* trawl (net); **pêcher au** ~ to trawl.

chalutier [shālütyā] *nm* trawler; (*pêcheur*) trawlerman.

chamade [shāmād] *nf*: **battre la** ~ to beat wildly.

chamailler [shāmāyā]: **se** ~ *vi* to squabble, bicker.

chamarré, e [shāmārā] *a* richly brocaded.

chambard [shāñbār] *nm* rumpus.

chambardement [shāñbārdəmāñ] *nm*: **c'est le grand** ~ everything has been (*ou* is being) turned upside down.

chambarder [shāñbārdā] *vt* to turn upside down.

chamboulement [shāñbōōlmāñ] *nm* disruption.

chambouler [shāñbōōlā] *vt* to disrupt, turn upside down.

chambranle [shāñbrāñl] *nm* (door) frame.

chambre [shāñbr(ə)] *nf* bedroom; (*TECH*) chamber; (*POL*) chamber, house; (*JUR*) court; (*COMM*) chamber; federation; **faire** ~ **à part** to sleep in separate rooms; **stratège/alpiniste en** ~ armchair strategist/mountaineer; ~ **à un lit/deux lits** single/twin-bedded room; ~ **pour une/deux personne(s)** single/double room; ~ **d'accusation** court of criminal appeal; ~ **d'agriculture** body responsible for the agricultural interests of a *département*; ~ **à air** (*de pneu*) (inner) tube; ~ **d'amis** spare *ou* guest room; ~ **de combustion** combustion chamber; ~ **de commerce et d'industrie (CCI)** chamber of commerce and industry; ~ **à coucher** bedroom; **la C~ des députés** the Chamber of Deputies, ≈ the House of Representatives (*US*), ≈ the House (of Commons) (*Brit*); ~ **forte** strongroom; ~ **froide** *ou* **frigorifique** cold room; ~ **à gaz** gas chamber; ~ **d'hôte** ≈ bed and breakfast (*in private home*); ~ **des machines** engine-room; ~ **des métiers (CM)** *chamber of commerce for trades*; ~ **meublée** furnished room; ~ **noire** (*PHOTO*) dark room.

chambrée [shāñbrā] *nf* room.

chambrer [shāñbrā] *vt* (*vin*) to bring to room temperature.

chameau, x [shāmō] *nm* camel.

chamois [shāmwā] *nm* chamois ♦ *a*: **(couleur)** ~ fawn, buff.

champ [shāñ] *nm* (*aussi INFORM*) field; (*PHOTO*): **dans le** ~ in the picture; **prendre du** ~ to draw back; **laisser le** ~ **libre à qn** to leave sb a clear field; ~ **d'action** sphere of operation(s); ~ **de bataille** battlefield; ~ **de courses** racecourse; ~ **d'honneur** field of honor; ~ **de manœuvre** (*MIL*) parade ground; ~ **de mines** minefield; ~ **de tir** shooting *ou* rifle range; ~ **visuel** field of vision.

Champagne [shâṅpány] *nf*: **la** ~ Champagne, the Champagne region.

champagne [shâṅpány] *nm* champagne.

champenois, e [shâṅpənwá, -wáz] *a* of *ou* from Champagne; (*vin*): **méthode** ~**e** champagne-type.

champêtre [shâṅpetr(ə)] *a* country *cpd*, rural.

champignon [shâṅpēṅyóṅ] *nm* mushroom; (*terme générique*) fungus (*pl* -i); (*fam*: *accélérateur*) accelerator, gas pedal (*US*); ~ **de couche** *ou* **de Paris** button mushroom; ~ **vénéneux** toadstool, poisonous mushroom.

champion, ne [shâṅpyóṅ, -on] *a*, *nm/f* champion.

championnat [shâṅpyoná] *nm* championship.

chance [shâṅs] *nf*: **la** ~ luck; **une** ~ a stroke *ou* piece of luck *ou* good fortune; (*occasion*) a lucky break; ~**s** *nfpl* (*probabilités*) chances; **avoir de la** ~ to be lucky; **il a des** ~**s de ga-gner** he has a chance of winning; **il y a de fortes** ~**s pour que Paul soit malade** it's highly probable that Paul is ill; **bonne** ~**!** good luck!; **encore une** ~ **que tu viennes!** it's lucky you're coming; **je n'ai pas de** ~ I'm out of luck; (*toujours*) I never have any luck; **donner sa** ~ **à qn** to give sb a chance.

chancelant, e [shâṅslâṅ, -âṅt] *a* (*personne*) tottering; (*santé*) failing.

chanceler [shâṅslá] *vi* to totter.

chancelier [shâṅsəlyá] *nm* (*allemand*) chancellor; (*d'ambassade*) secretary.

chancellerie [shâṅselrē] *nf* (*en France*) min-istry of justice; (*en Allemagne*) chancellery; (*d'ambassade*) chancery.

chanceux, euse [shâṅsœ̄, -œ̄z] *a* lucky, for-tunate.

chancre [shâṅkr(ə)] *nm* canker.

chandail [shâṅdáy] *nm* (thick) sweater.

Chandeleur [shâṅdlœr] *nf*: **la** ~ Candlemas.

chandelier [shâṅdəlyá] *nm* candlestick; (*à plusieurs branches*) candelabra.

chandelle [shâṅdel] *nf* (tallow) candle; (*TENNIS*): **faire une** ~ to lob; (*AVIAT*): **monter en** ~ to climb vertically; **tenir la** ~ to be the odd one out in a threesome, play gooseberry (*Brit*); **dîner aux** ~**s** candlelight dinner.

change [shâṅzh] *nm* (*COMM*) exchange; **opérations de** ~ (foreign) exchange transac-tions; **contrôle des** ~**s** exchange control; **gagner/perdre au** ~ to be better/worse off (for it); **donner le** ~ **à qn** (*fig*) to lead sb down (*US*) *ou* up (*Brit*) the garden path.

changeant, e [shâṅzhâṅ, -âṅt] *a* changeable, fickle.

changement [shâṅzhmâṅ] *nm* change; ~ **de vitesse** (*dispositif*) gears *pl*; (*action*) gear change.

changer [shâṅzhá] *vt* (*modifier*) to change, alter; (*remplacer*, *COMM*, *rhabiller*) to change ♦ *vi* to change, alter; **se** ~ to change (o.s.); ~ **de** (*remplacer*: *adresse*, *nom etc*) to change one's; (*échanger*, *alterner*: *côté*, *place*, *train etc*) to change + *npl*; ~ **d'air** to have a change of scenery *ou* air (*Brit*); ~ **de couleur/direction** to change color/direction;

~ **d'idée** to change one's mind; ~ **de place avec qn** to change places with sb; ~ **de vitesse** (*AUTO*) to change gear; ~ **qn/qch de place** to move sb/sth to another place; ~ (**de train** *etc*) to change (trains *etc*); ~ **qch en** to change sth into.

changeur [shâṅzhœr] *nm* (*personne*) money-changer; ~ **automatique** change machine; ~ **de disques** record changer.

chanoine [shánwán] *nm* canon.

chanson [shâṅsóṅ] *nf* song.

chansonnette [shâṅsonet] *nf* ditty.

chansonnier [shâṅsonyá] *nm* cabaret artist (*specializing in political satire*); (*recueil*) song book.

chant [shâṅ] *nm* song; (*art vocal*) singing; (*d'église*) hymn; (*de poème*) canto; (*TECH*): **posé de** *ou* **sur** ~ placed edgeways; ~ **de Noël** Christmas carol.

chantage [shâṅtázh] *nm* blackmail; **faire du** ~ to use blackmail; **soumettre qn à un** ~ to blackmail sb.

chantant, e [shâṅtâṅ, -âṅt] *a* (*accent*, *voix*) sing-song.

chanter [shâṅtá] *vt*, *vi* to sing; ~ **juste/faux** to sing in tune/out of tune; **si cela lui chante** (*fam*) if he feels like it *ou* fancies it (*Brit*).

chanterelle [shâṅtrel] *nf* chanterelle (*edible mushroom*).

chanteur, euse [shâṅtœr, -œ̄z] *nm/f* singer; ~ **de charme** crooner.

chantier [shâṅtyá] *nm* (building) site; (*sur une route*) (road) construction (*US*), roadworks *pl* (*Brit*); **mettre en** ~ to start work on; ~ **naval** shipyard.

chantilly [shâṅtēyē] *nf voir* **crème**.

chantonner [shâṅtoná] *vi*, *vt* to sing to one-self, hum.

chantre [shâṅtr(ə)] *nm* (*fig*) eulogist.

chanvre [shâṅvr(ə)] *nm* hemp.

chaos [káō] *nm* chaos.

chaotique [káotēk] *a* chaotic.

chap. *abr* (= *chapitre*) ch.

chapardage [shápárdázh] *nm* pilfering.

chaparder [shápárdá] *vt* to swipe.

chapeau, x [shápō] *nm* hat; (*PRESSE*) introductory paragraph; ~**!** well done!; ~ **melon** derby (*US*) *ou* bowler (*Brit*) hat; ~ **mou** fedora (*US*), trilby (*Brit*); ~**x de roues** hub caps.

chapeauter [shápōtá] *vt* (*ADMIN*) to head, oversee.

chapelain [sháplaṅ] *nm* (*REL*) chaplain.

chapelet [sháple] *nm* (*REL*) rosary; (*fig*): **un** ~ **de** a string of; **dire son** ~ to tell one's beads.

chapelier, ière [shápəlyá, -yer] *nm/f* hatter; milliner.

chapelle [shápel] *nf* chapel; ~ **ardente** mor-tuary chapel.

chapelure [sháplür] *nf* (dried) bread-crumbs *pl*.

chaperon [shápróṅ] *nm* chaperon.

chaperonner [sháproná] *vt* to chaperon.

chapiteau, x [shápētō] *nm* (*ARCHIT*) capital; (*de cirque*) big top.

chapitre [shápetr(ə)] *nm* chapter; (*fig*) sub-ject, matter; **avoir voix au** ~ to have a say in the matter.

chapitrer [shàpētrā] *vt* to lecture, reprimand.

chapon [shàpôñ] *nm* capon.

chaque [shàk] *dét* each, every; (*indéfini*) every.

char [shàr] *nm* (*à foin etc*) cart, wagon; (*de carnaval*) float; ~ **(d'assaut)** tank.

charabia [shàràbyà] *nm* (*péj*) gibberish, gobbledygook.

charade [shàràd] *nf* riddle; (*mimée*) charade.

charbon [shàrbôñ] *nm* coal; ~ **de bois** charcoal.

charbonnage [shàrbonàzh] *nm*: les ~s de France the (French) Coal Board *sg*.

charbonnier [shàrbonyā] *nm* coalman.

charcuterie [shàrkütrē] *nf* (*magasin*) pork butcher's shop and delicatessen; (*produits*) cooked pork meats *pl*.

charcutier, ière [shàrkütyā, -yer] *nm/f* pork butcher.

chardon [shàrdôñ] *nm* thistle.

chardonneret [shàrdonre] *nm* goldfinch.

charentais, e [shàrâñte, -ez] *a* of *ou* from Charente ♦ *nf* (*pantoufle*) slipper.

charge [shàrzh(ə)] *nf* (*fardeau*) load; (*explosif, ÉLEC, MIL, JUR*) charge; (*rôle, mission*) responsibility; ~s *nfpl* (*du loyer*) service charges; **à la ~ de** (*dépendant de*) dependent upon, supported by; (*aux frais de*) chargeable to, payable by; **j'accepte, à ~ de revanche** I accept, provided I can do the same for you (in return) one day; **prendre en ~** to take charge of; (*suj: véhicule*) to take on; (*dépenses*) to take care of; ~ **utile** (*AUTO*) live load; (*COMM*) payload; ~s **sociales** social security contributions.

chargé [shàrzhā] *a* (*voiture, animal, personne*) laden; (*fusil, caméra*) loaded; (*batterie*) charged; (*occupé: emploi du temps, journée*) busy, full; (*estomac*) heavy, full; (*langue*) coated (*US*), furred (*Brit*); (*décoration, style*) heavy, ornate ♦ *nm*: ~ **d'affaires** chargé d'affaires; ~ **de cours** ≈ assistant professor (*US*), ≈ lecturer (*Brit*); ~ **de** (*responsable de*) responsible for.

chargement [shàrzhəmâñ] *nm* (*action*) loading; charging; (*objets*) load.

charger [shàrzhā] *vt* (*voiture, fusil, caméra, INFORM*) to load; (*batterie*) to charge ♦ *vi* (*MIL etc*) to charge; **se ~ de** *vt* to see to, take care of; ~ **qn de qch/faire qch** to give sb the responsibility for sth/of doing sth; to put sb in charge of sth/doing sth; **se ~ de faire qch** to take it upon o.s. to do sth.

chargeur [shàrzhœr] *nm* (*dispositif: d'arme à feu*) magazine; (*: PHOTO*) cartridge; ~ **de batterie** (*ÉLEC*) battery charger.

chariot [shàryō] *nm* cart (*US*), trolley (*Brit*); (*charrette*) wagon; (*de machine à écrire*) carriage; ~ **élévateur** fork-lift truck.

charisme [kàrēsm(ə)] *nm* charisma.

charitable [shàrētàbl(ə)] *a* charitable; kind.

charité [shàrētā] *nf* charity; **faire la ~** to give to charity; to do charitable works; **faire la ~ à** to give (something) to; **fête/vente de ~** fête/sale in aid of charity.

charivari [shàrēvàrē] *nm* hullabaloo.

charlatan [shàrlàtâñ] *nm* charlatan.

charmant, e [shàrmâñ, -âñt] *a* charming.

charme [shàrm(ə)] *nm* charm; ~s *nmpl* (*appas*) charms; **c'est ce qui en fait le ~** that is its attraction; **faire du ~** to be charming, turn on the charm; **aller** *ou* **se porter comme un ~** to be in the pink.

charmer [shàrmā] *vt* to charm; **je suis charmé de** I'm delighted to.

charmeur, euse [shàrmœr, -ēz] *nm/f* charmer; ~ **de serpents** snake charmer.

charnel, le [shàrnel] *a* carnal.

charnier [shàrnyā] *nm* mass grave.

charnière [shàrnyer] *nf* hinge; (*fig*) turning-point.

charnu, e [shàrnü] *a* fleshy.

charogne [shàrony] *nf* carrion *q*; (*fam!*) bastard (*!*).

charolais, e [shàrole, -ez] *a* of *ou* from the Charolais.

charpente [shàrpâñt] *nf* frame(work); (*fig*) structure, framework; (*carrure*) build, frame.

charpenté, e [shàrpâñtā] *a*: **bien** *ou* **solidement ~** (*personne*) well-built; (*texte*) well-constructed.

charpenterie [shàrpâñtrē] *nf* carpentry.

charpentier [shàrpâñtyā] *nm* carpenter.

charpie [shàrpē] *nf*: **en ~** (*fig*) in shreds *ou* ribbons.

charretier [shàrtyā] *nm* carter; **de ~** (*péj: langage, manières*) uncouth.

charrette [shàret] *nf* cart.

charrier [shàryā] *vt* to carry (along); to cart, carry ♦ *vi* (*fam*) to exaggerate.

charrue [shàrü] *nf* plow (*US*), plough (*Brit*).

charte [shàrt(ə)] *nf* charter.

charter [tshàrtœr] *nm* (*vol*) charter flight; (*avion*) charter plane.

chasse [shàs] *nf* hunting; (*au fusil*) shooting; (*poursuite*) chase; (*aussi:* ~ **d'eau**) flush; **la ~ est ouverte** the hunting season is open; **la ~ est fermée** it is the closed (*US*) *ou* close (*Brit*) season; **aller à la ~** to go hunting; **prendre en ~, donner la ~ à** to give chase to; **tirer la ~ (d'eau)** to flush the toilet; ~ **aérienne** aerial pursuit; ~ **à courre** hunting; ~ **à l'homme** manhunt; ~ **gardée** private hunting grounds *pl*; ~ **sous-marine** underwater fishing.

châsse [shàs] *nf* reliquary, shrine.

chassé-croisé [shàsākrwàzā] *pl* **chassés-croisés** *nm* (*DANSE*) chassé-croisé; (*fig*) mix-up (*where people miss each other in turn*).

chasse-neige [shàsnezh] *nm inv* snowplow (*US*), snowplough (*Brit*).

chasser [shàsā] *vt* to hunt; (*expulser*) to chase away *ou* out, drive away *ou* out; (*dissiper*) to chase *ou* sweep away; to dispel, drive away.

chasseur, euse [shàsœr, -ēz] *nm/f* hunter ♦ *nm* (*avion*) fighter; (*domestique*) messenger (boy); ~ **d'images** roving photographer; ~ **de têtes** (*fig*) headhunter; ~s **alpins** mountain infantry.

chassieux, euse [shàsyœ, -ēz] *a* sticky, gummy.

châssis [shàsē] *nm* (*AUTO*) chassis; (*cadre*) frame; (*de jardin*) cold frame.

chaste [shàst(ə)] *a* chaste.

chasteté [shàstətā] *nf* chastity.

chasuble [shàzübl(ə)] *nf* chasuble; **robe ~**

jumper (*US*), pinafore dress (*Brit*).
chat [shá] *nm* cat; ~ **sauvage** wildcat.
châtaigne [sháteny] *nf* chestnut.
châtaignier [shátányá] *nm* chestnut (tree).
châtain [shátáñ] *a inv* chestnut (brown); (*personne*) chestnut-haired.
château, x [shátō] *nm* castle; ~ **d'eau** water tower; ~ **fort** stronghold, fortified castle; ~ **de sable** sandcastle.
châtelain, e [shátlañ, -cn] *nm/f* lord/lady of the manor ♦ *nf* (*ceinture*) chatelaine.
châtier [shátyá] *vt* to punish, castigate; (*fig: style*) to polish, refine.
chatière [shátyer] *nf* (*porte*) cat door (*US*) *ou* flap (*Brit*).
châtiment [shátēmáñ] *nm* punishment, castigation; ~ **corporel** corporal punishment.
chatoiement [shátwámáñ] *nm* shimmer(ing).
chaton [shátôñ] *nm* (*ZOOL*) kitten; (*BOT*) catkin; (*de bague*) bezel; stone.
chatouiller [shátōōyá] *vt* to tickle; (*l'odorat, le palais*) to titillate.
chatouilleux, euse [shátōōyœ̄, -œ̄z] *a* ticklish; (*fig*) touchy, over-sensitive.
chatoyant, e [shátwáyáñ, -áñt] *a* (*reflet, étoffe*) shimmering; (*couleurs*) sparkling.
chatoyer [shátwáyá] *vi* to shimmer.
châtrer [shátrá] *vt* (*mâle*) to castrate; (*femelle*) to spay; (*cheval*) to geld; (*chat, chien*) to fix (*US*), doctor (*Brit*); (*fig*) to mutilate.
chatte [shát] *nf* (she-)cat.
chatterton [shátertoñ] *nm* (*ruban isolant: ÉLEC*) (adhesive) insulating tape.
chaud, e [shō, -ōd] *a* (*gén*) warm; (*très chaud*) hot; (*fig: félicitations*) hearty; (*discussion*) heated; **il fait** ~ it's warm; it's hot; **manger** ~ to have something hot to eat; **avoir** ~ to be warm; to be hot; **tenir** ~ to keep hot; **ça me tient** ~ it keeps me warm; **tenir au** ~ to keep in a warm place; **rester au** ~ to stay where it's warm.
chaudement [shōdmáñ] *ad* warmly; (*fig*) hotly.
chaudière [shōdyer] *nf* boiler.
chaudron [shōdrôñ] *nm* cauldron.
chaudronnerie [shōdronrē] *nf* (*usine*) boiler-works; (*activité*) boilermaking; (*boutique*) coppersmith's workshop.
chauffage [shōfázh] *nm* heating; ~ **au gaz/à l'électricité** gas/electric heating; ~ **au charbon** heating with coal (*US*), solid fuel heating (*Brit*); ~ **central** central heating; ~ **par le sol** underfloor heating.
chauffagiste [shōfázhēst(ə)] *nm* (*installateur*) heating specialist (*US*) *ou* engineer (*Brit*).
chauffant, e [shōfáñ, -áñt]: **couverture** ~**e** electric blanket; **plaque** ~**e** hotplate.
chauffard [shōfár] *nm* (*péj*) reckless driver; roadhog; (*après un accident*) hit-and-run driver.
chauffe-bain [shōfbáñ] *nm* = **chauffe-eau**.
chauffe-biberon [shōfbēbróñ] *nm* (baby's) bottle warmer.
chauffe-eau [shōfō] *nm inv* water heater.
chauffe-plats [shōfplá] *nm inv* dish warmer.
chauffer [shōfá] *vt* to heat ♦ *vi* to heat up, warm up; (*trop chauffer: moteur*) to overheat; **se** ~ (*se mettre en train*) to warm up;

(*au soleil*) to warm o.s.
chaufferie [shōfrē] *nf* boiler room.
chauffeur [shōfœr] *nm* driver; (*privé*) chauffeur; **voiture avec/sans** ~ chauffeur-driven/self-drive car.
chauffeuse [shōfœ̄z] *nf* fireside chair.
chauler [shōlá] *vt* (*mur*) to whitewash.
chaume [shōm] *nm* (*du toit*) thatch; (*tiges*) stubble.
chaumière [shōmyer] *nf* (thatched) cottage.
chaussée [shōsá] *nf* road(way); (*digue*) causeway.
chausse-pied [shōspyá] *nm* shoe-horn.
chausser [shōsá] *vt* (*bottes, skis*) to put on; (*enfant*) to put shoes on; (*suj: soulier*) to fit; ~ **du 38/42** to take size 38/42; ~ **grand** to be too big; ~ **bien** to fit well; **se** ~ to put one's shoes on.
chausse-trappe [shōstráp] *nf* trap.
chaussette [shōset] *nf* sock.
chausseur [shōsœr] *nm* (*marchand*) footwear specialist, shoemaker.
chausson [shōsôñ] *nm* slipper; (*de bébé*) bootee; ~ (**aux pommes**) (apple) turnover.
chaussure [shōsür] *nf* shoe; (*commerce*): **la** ~ the shoe industry *ou* trade; ~**s basses** flat shoes; ~**s montantes** ankle boots; ~**s de ski** ski boots.
chaut [shō] *vb*: **peu me** ~ it matters little to me.
chauve [shōv] *a* bald.
chauve-souris, pl chauves-souris [shōvsōōrē] *nf* bat.
chauvin, e [shōvañ, -ēn] *a* chauvinistic; jingoistic.
chauvinisme [shōvēnēsm(ə)] *nm* chauvinism; jingoism.
chaux [shō] *nf* lime; **blanchi à la** ~ whitewashed.
chavirer [shávērá] *vi* to capsize, overturn.
chef [shef] *nm* head, leader; (*patron*) boss; (*de cuisine*) chef; **au premier** ~ extremely, to the nth degree; **de son propre** ~ on his *ou* her own initiative; **général en** ~ general (*US*), general-in-chief (*Brit*); **commandant en** ~ commander-in-chief; ~ **d'accusation** (*JUR*) charge, count (of indictment); ~ **d'atelier** (shop) foreman; ~ **de bureau** head of department; ~ **d'entreprise** company manager (*US*) *ou* head (*Brit*); ~ **d'équipe** team leader; ~ **d'état** head of state; ~ **de famille** head of the family; ~ **de file** (*de parti etc*) leader; ~ **de gare** station master; ~ **d'orchestre** conductor; ~ **de rayon** department(al) supervisor; ~ **de service** departmental head.
chef-d'œuvre, pl chefs-d'œuvre [shedœvr(ə)] *nm* masterpiece.
chef-lieu, pl chefs-lieux [sheflyœ̄] *nm* county seat.
cheftaine [sheften] *nf* girl scout troop leader (*US*), (guide) captain (*Brit*).
cheik [shek] *nm* sheik.
chemin [shəmañ] *nm* path; (*itinéraire, direction, trajet*) way; **en** ~, ~ **faisant** on the way; ~ **de fer** railroad (*US*), railway (*Brit*); **par** ~ **de fer** by rail; **les** ~**s de fer** the railroad (*US*), the railways (*Brit*); ~ **de terre** dirt road.

cheminée [shəmēnā] *nf* chimney; (*à l'intérieur*) chimney piece, fireplace; (*de bateau*) funnel.
cheminement [shəmēnmân] *nm* progress; course.
cheminer [shəmēnā] *vi* to walk (along).
cheminot [shəmēnō] *nm* railroad worker (*US*), railwayman (*Brit*).
chemise [shəmēz] *nf* shirt; (*dossier*) folder; ~ **de nuit** nightgown (*US*), nightdress (*Brit*).
chemiserie [shəmēzrē] *nf* men's shop, (gentlemen's) outfitters' (*Brit*).
chemisette [shəmēzet] *nf* short-sleeved shirt.
chemisier [shəmēzyā] *nm* blouse.
chenal, aux [shənàl, -ō] *nm* channel.
chenapan [shənàpân] *nm* (*garnement*) rascal; (*péj: vaurien*) rogue.
chêne [shen] *nm* oak (tree); (*bois*) oak.
chenet [shəne] *nm* fire-dog, andiron.
chenil [shənēl] *nm* kennels *pl*.
chenille [shənēy] *nf* (*ZOOL*) caterpillar; (*AUTO*) caterpillar track; **véhicule à ~s** caterpillar (*vehicle*).
chenillette [shənēyet] *nf* caterpillar (*vehicle*).
cheptel [sheptel] *nm* livestock.
chèque [shek] *nm* check (*US*), cheque (*Brit*); **faire/toucher un** ~ to write/cash a check; **par** ~ by check; ~ **barré** check marked "for deposit only" (*US*), crossed cheque (*Brit*); ~ **sans provision** bad check; ~ **en blanc** blank check; ~ **au porteur** bearer check; ~ **postal** post office check; ~ **de voyage** traveler's check.
chèque-cadeau, *pl* **chèques-cadeaux** [shekkàdō] *nm* gift certificate (*US*) *ou* token (*Brit*).
chèque-repas, *pl* **chèques-repas** [shekrəpâ], **chèque-restaurant,** *pl* **chèques-restaurant** [shekrestorân] *nm* ≈ luncheon voucher.
chéquier [shākyā] *nm* check book (*US*), cheque book (*Brit*).
cher, ère [sher] *a* (*aimé*) dear; (*coûteux*) expensive, dear ♦ *ad*: **coûter/payer** ~ to cost/pay a lot; **cela coûte** ~ it's expensive, it costs a lot of money ♦ *nf*: **la bonne chère** good food; **mon** ~, **ma chère** my dear.
chercher [shershā] *vt* to look for; (*gloire etc*) to seek; (*INFORM*) to search; ~ **des ennuis/la bagarre** to be looking for trouble/a fight; **aller** ~ to go for, go and get; ~ **à faire** to try to do.
chercheur, euse [shershœr, -œz] *nm/f* researcher, research worker; ~ **de** seeker of; hunter of; ~ **d'or** gold digger.
chère [sher] *af*, *nf voir* **cher**.
chèrement [shermân] *ad* dearly.
chéri, e [shārē] *a* beloved, dear; (**mon**) ~ darling.
chérir [shārēr] *vt* to cherish.
cherté [shertā] *nf*: **la** ~ **de la vie** the high cost of living.
chérubin [shārübàn] *nm* cherub.
chétif, ive [shātēf, -ēv] *a* puny, stunted.
cheval, aux [shəvàl, -ō] *nm* horse; (*AUTO*): ~ **(vapeur) (CV)** horsepower *q*; **50 chevaux (au frein)** 50 brake horsepower, 50 b.h.p.; **10 chevaux (fiscaux)** 10 horsepower (*for tax purposes*); **faire du** ~ to go (horseback) riding; **à** ~ on horseback; **à** ~ **sur** astride,

straddling; (*fig*) overlapping; ~ **d'arçons** pommel (*US*) *ou* vaulting (*Brit*) horse; ~ **à bascule** rocking horse; ~ **de bataille** charger; (*fig*) hobby-horse; ~ **de course** race horse; **chevaux de bois** (*des manèges*) wooden (fairground) horses; (*manège*) merry-go-round.
chevaleresque [shəvàlresk(ə)] *a* chivalrous.
chevalerie [shəvàlrē] *nf* chivalry; knighthood.
chevalet [shəvàle] *nm* easel.
chevalier [shəvàlyā] *nm* knight; ~ **servant** escort.
chevalière [shəvàlyer] *nf* signet ring.
chevalin, e [shəvàlàn, -ēn] *a* of horses, equine; (*péj*) horsy; **boucherie** ~**e** horse-meat butcher's.
cheval-vapeur, *pl* **chevaux-vapeur** [shəvàlvàpœr, shəvō-] *nm voir* **cheval.**
chevauchée [shəvōshā] *nf* ride; cavalcade.
chevauchement [shəvōshmân] *nm* overlap.
chevaucher [shəvōshā] *vi* (*aussi:* **se** ~) to overlap (each other) ♦ *vt* to be astride, straddle.
chevaux [shəvō] *nmpl voir* **cheval.**
chevelu, e [shəvlü] *a* with a good head of hair, hairy (*péj*).
chevelure [shəvlür] *nf* hair *q*.
chevet [shəve] *nm*: **au** ~ **de qn** at sb's bedside; **lampe de** ~ bedside lamp.
cheveu, x [shəvœ] *nm* hair ♦ *nmpl* (*chevelure*) hair *sg*; **avoir les** ~**x courts/en brosse** to have short hair/a crew cut; **se faire couper les** ~**x** to get *ou* have one's hair cut; **tiré par les** ~**x** (*histoire*) far-fetched.
cheville [shəvēy] *nf* (*ANAT*) ankle; (*de bois*) peg; (*pour enfoncer une vis*) plug; **être en** ~ **avec qn** to be in cahoots with sb; ~ **ouvrière** (*fig*) kingpin.
chèvre [shevr(ə)] *nf* (she-)goat; **ménager la** ~ **et le chou** to try to please everyone.
chevreau, x [shəvrō] *nm* kid.
chèvrefeuille [shevrəfœy] *nm* honeysuckle.
chevreuil [shəvrœy] *nm* roe deer *inv*; (*CULIN*) venison.
chevron [shəvrôn] *nm* (*poutre*) rafter; (*motif*) chevron, v(-shape); **à** ~**s** chevron-patterned; (*petits*) herringbone.
chevronné, e [shəvronā] *a* seasoned, experienced.
chevrotant, e [shəvrotân, -ânt] *a* quavering.
chevroter [shəvrotā] *vi* (*personne, voix*) to quaver.
chevrotine [shəvrotēn] *nf* buckshot *q*.
chewing-gum [shwēnggom] *nm* chewing gum.
chez [shā] *prép* (*à la demeure de*): ~ **qn** at (*ou* to) sb's house *ou* place; (*parmi*) among; ~ **moi** at home; (*avec direction*) home; ~ **le boulanger** (*à la boulangerie*) at the baker's; ~ **les Français** (*dans leur caractère*) among the French; ~ **ce musicien/poète** (*dans ses œuvres*) in this musician/poet.
chez-soi [shāswà] *nm inv* home.
Chf. cent. *abr* (= *chauffage central*) c.h.
chic [shēk] *a inv* chic, smart; (*généreux*) nice, decent ♦ *nm* stylishness; **avoir le** ~ **de** *ou* **pour** to have the knack of *ou* for; **de** ~ *ad* off the cuff; ~**!** great!, terrific!
chicane [shēkàn] *nf* (*obstacle*) zigzag; (*querelle*) squabble.

chicaner [shēkånā] *vi* (*ergoter*): ~ **sur** to quibble about.

chiche [shēsh] *a* (*mesquin*) niggardly, mean; (*pauvre*) meager (*US*), meagre (*Brit*) ♦ *excl* (*en réponse à un défi*) you're on!; **tu n'es pas** ~ **de lui parler!** you wouldn't (dare) speak to her!

chichement [shēshmån] *ad* (*pauvrement*) meagerly (*US*), meagrely (*Brit*); (*mesquinement*) meanly.

chichi [shēshē] *nm* (*fam*) fuss; **faire des** ~s to make a fuss.

chicorée [shēkorā] *nf* (*café*) chicory; (*salade*) endive; ~ **frisée** curly endive.

chicot [shēkō] *nm* stump.

chien [shyań] *nm* dog; (*de pistolet*) hammer; **temps de** ~ rotten weather; **vie de** ~ dog's life; **couché en** ~ **de fusil** curled up; ~ **d'aveugle** guide dog; ~ **de chasse** gun dog; ~ **de garde** guard dog; ~ **policier** police dog; ~ **de race** pedigree dog; ~ **de traineau** husky.

chiendent [shyańdåń] *nm* couch grass.

chien-loup, *pl* **chiens-loups** [shyańlōō] *nm* wolfhound.

chienne [shyen] *nf* (she-)dog, bitch.

chier [shyā] *vi* (*fam!*) to crap (*!*), shit (*!*); **faire** ~ **qn** (*importuner*) to bug sb; (*causer des ennuis à*) to piss sb off (*US!*) *ou* around (*Brit!*); **se faire** ~ (*s'ennuyer*) to be bored stiff.

chiffe [shēf] *nf*: **il est mou comme une** ~, **c'est une** ~ **molle** he's spineless.

chiffon [shēfóń] *nm* (piece of) rag.

chiffonné, **e** [shēfonā] *a* (*fatigué: visage*) worn-looking.

chiffonner [shēfonā] *vt* to crumple, crease; (*tracasser*) to concern.

chiffonnier [shēfonyā] *nm* ragman; (*meuble*) chiffonier.

chiffrable [shēfråbl(ə)] *a* numerable.

chiffre [shēfr(ə)] *nm* (*représentant un nombre*) figure; numeral; (*montant, total*) total, sum; (*d'un code*) code, cipher; ~**s romains/arabes** roman/arabic numerals; **en** ~**s ronds** in round figures; **écrire un nombre en** ~**s** to write a number in figures; ~ **d'affaires (CA)** turnover; ~ **de ventes** sales figures.

chiffrer [shēfrā] *vt* (*dépense*) to put a figure to, assess; (*message*) to (en)code, cipher ♦ *vi*: ~ **à, se** ~ **à** to add up to.

chignole [shēnyol] *nf* drill.

chignon [shēnyóń] *nm* chignon, bun.

Chili [shēlē] *nm*: **le** ~ Chile.

chilien, **ne** [shēlyań, -en] *a* Chilean ♦ *nm/f*: **C**~, **ne** Chilean.

chimère [shēmer] *nf* (wild) dream; pipe dream, idle fancy.

chimérique [shēmårēk] *a* (*utopique*) fanciful.

chimie [shēmē] *nf* chemistry.

chimio [shēmyo], **chimiothérapie** [shēmyotårāpē] *nf* chemotherapy.

chimique [shēmēk] *a* chemical; **produits** ~**s** chemicals.

chimiste [shēmēst(ə)] *nm/f* chemist.

chinchilla [shańshēlā] *nm* chinchilla.

Chine [shēn] *nf*: **la** ~ China; **la** ~ **libre**, **la république de** ~ the Republic of China, Nationalist China (*Taiwan*).

chine [shēn] *nm* rice paper; (*porcelaine*) china (vase).

chiné, **e** [shēnā] *a* flecked.

chinois, **e** [shēnwå, -wåz] *a* Chinese; (*fig: péj*) persnickety, fussy ♦ *nm* (*LING*) Chinese ♦ *nm/f*: **C**~, **e** Chinese.

chinoiserie(s) [shēnwåzrē] *nf(pl)* (*péj*) red tape, fuss.

chiot [shyō] *nm* pup(py).

chiper [shēpā] *vt* (*fam*) to swipe.

chipie [shēpē] *nf* shrew.

chipolata [shēpolåtå] *nf* chipolata.

chipoter [shēpotā] *vi* (*manger*) to nibble; (*ergoter*) to quibble, haggle.

chips [shēps] *nfpl* (*aussi*: **pommes** ~) (potato) chips (*US*), crisps (*Brit*).

chique [shēk] *nf* quid, chew.

chiquenaude [shēknōd] *nf* flick, flip.

chiquer [shēkā] *vi* to chew tobacco.

chiromancie [kēromåńsē] *nf* palmistry.

chiromancien, **ne** [kēromåńsyań, -en] *nm/f* palmist.

chiropracteur [kēropråktœr] *nm*, **chiropracticien**, **ne** [kēropråktēsyań, -en] *nm/f* chiropractor.

chirurgical, **e**, **aux** [shērürzhēkål, -ō] *a* surgical.

chirurgie [shērürzhē] *nf* surgery; ~ **esthétique** cosmetic *ou* plastic surgery.

chirurgien [shērürzhyań] *nm* surgeon; ~ **dentiste** dental surgeon.

chiure [shyür] *nf*: ~**s de mouche** fly specks.

ch.-l. *abr* = **chef-lieu.**

chlore [klor] *nm* chlorine.

chloroforme [kloroform(ə)] *nm* chloroform.

chlorophylle [klorofēl] *nf* chlorophyll.

chlorure [klorür] *nm* chloride.

choc [shok] *nm* impact; shock; crash; (*moral*) shock; (*affrontement*) clash ♦ *a*: **prix** ~ amazing *ou* incredible price/prices; **de** ~ (*troupe, traitement*) shock *cpd*; (*patron etc*) high-powered; ~ **opératoire/nerveux** post-operative/nervous shock; ~ **en retour** return shock; (*fig*) backlash.

chocolat [shokolå] *nm* chocolate; (*boisson*) (hot) chocolate; ~ **à cuire** cooking chocolate; ~ **au lait** milk chocolate; ~ **en poudre** drrrinking chocolate.

chocolaté, **e** [shokolåtā] *a* chocolate *cpd*, chocolate-flavoured.

chocolaterie [shokolåtrē] *nf* (*fabrique*) chocolate factory.

chocolatier, **ière** [shokolåtyå, -yer] *nm/f* chocolate maker.

chœur [kœr] *nm* (*chorale*) choir; (*OPÉRA, THÉÂTRE*) chorus; (*ARCHIT*) choir, chancel; **en** ~ in chorus.

choir [shwår] *vi* to fall.

choisi, **e** [shwåzē] *a* (*de premier choix*) carefully chosen; select; **textes** ~**s** selected writings.

choisir [shwåzēr] *vt* to choose; (*entre plusieurs*) to choose, select; ~ **de faire qch** to choose *ou* opt to do sth.

choix [shwå] *nm* choice; selection; **avoir le** ~ to have the choice; **je n'avais pas le** ~ I had no choice; **de premier** ~ (*COMM*) class *ou* grade one; **de** ~ choice *cpd*, selected; **au** ~ as you wish *ou* prefer; **de mon/son** ~ of my/his ou her choosing.

choléra |kolárá| *nm* cholera.

cholestérol |kolestárol| *nm* cholesterol.

chômage |shōmázh| *nm* unemployment; **mettre au ~** to make redundant, put out of work; **être au ~** to be unemployed *ou* out of work; **~ partiel** short-time working; **~ structurel** structural unemployment; **~ technique** lay-offs *pl.*

chômer |shōmā| *vi* to be unemployed, be idle; **jour chômé** public holiday.

chômeur, euse |shōmœr, -œz| *nm/f* unemployed person, person out of work.

chope |shop| *nf* tankard.

choquant, e |shokáṅ, -áṅt| *a* shocking.

choquer |shokā| *vt* (*offenser*) to shock; (*commotionner*) to shake (up).

choral, e |korál| *a* choral ♦ *nf* choral society, choir.

chorégraphe |korāgráf| *nm/f* choreographer.

chorégraphie |korāgráfē| *nf* choreography.

choriste |korēst(ə)| *nm/f* choir member; (*OPÉRA*) chorus member.

chorus |korüs| *nm*: **faire ~ (avec)** to voice one's agreement (with).

chose |shōz| *nf* thing ♦ *nm* (*fam: machin*) thingamajig ♦ *a inv*: **être/se sentir tout ~** (*bizarre*) to be/feel a bit odd; (*malade*) to be/feel out of sorts; **dire bien des ~s à qn** to give sb's regards to sb; **parler de ~(s) et d'autre(s)** to talk about one thing and another; **c'est peu de ~** it's nothing much.

chou, x |shōō| *nm* cabbage ♦ *a inv* cute; **mon petit ~** (my) sweetheart; **faire ~ blanc** to draw a blank; **feuille de ~** (*fig: journal*) rag; **~ à la crème** cream puff (*made of choux pastry*); **~ de Bruxelles** Brussels sprout.

choucas |shōōká| *nm* jackdaw.

chouchou, te |shōōshōō, -ōōt| *nm/f* (*SCOL*) teacher's pet.

chouchouter |shōōshōōtā| *vt* to pet.

choucroute |shōōkrōōt| *nf* sauerkraut; **~ garnie** sauerkraut with cooked meats and potatoes.

chouette |shwet| *nf* owl ♦ *a* (*fam*) great, neat (*US*).

chou-fleur, *pl* **choux-fleurs** |shōōflœr| *nm* cauliflower.

chou-rave, *pl* **choux-raves** |shōōráv| *nm* kohlrabi.

choyer |shwáyā| *vt* to cherish; to pamper.

CHR *sigle m* = *Centre hospitalier régional.*

chrétien, ne |krātyaṅ, -en| *a, nm/f* Christian.

chrétiennement |krātyenmáṅ| *ad* in a Christian way *ou* spirit.

chrétienté |krātyaṅtā| *nf* Christendom.

Christ |krēst| *nm*: **le ~** Christ; **c~** (*crucifix etc*) figure of Christ; **Jésus ~** Jesus Christ.

christianiser |krēstyáṅēzā| *vt* to convert to Christianity.

christianisme |krēstyáṅēsm(ə)| *nm* Christianity.

Christmas |krēstmás| *nf*: **(l'île) ~** Christmas Island.

chromatique |kromátēk| *a* chromatic.

chrome |krōm| *nm* chromium; (*revêtement*) chrome, chromium.

chromé, e |krōmā| *a* chrome-plated,

chromium-plated.

chromosome |kromōzōm| *nm* chromosome.

chronique |kronēk| *a* chronic ♦ *nf* (*de journal*) column, page; (*historique*) chronicle; (*RADIO, TV*): **la ~ sportive/théâtrale** the sports/theater review; **la ~ locale** local news and gossip.

chroniqueur |kronēkœr| *nm* columnist; chronicler.

chronologie |kronolozhē| *nf* chronology.

chronologique |kronolozhēk| *a* chronological.

chronomètre |kronometr(ə)| *nm* stopwatch.

chronométrer |kronomātrā| *vt* to time.

chronométreur |kronomātrœr| *nm* timekeeper.

chrysalide |krēzálēd| *nf* chrysalis.

chrysanthème |krēzáṅtem| *nm* chrysanthemum.

CHU *sigle m* (= *Centre hospitalo-universitaire*) ≈ (teaching) hospital.

chu, e |shü| *pp de* **choir.**

chuchotement |shüshotmáṅ| *nm* whisper.

chuchoter |shüshotā| *vt, vi* to whisper.

chuintement |shüaṅtmáṅ| *nm* hiss.

chuinter |shüaṅtā| *vi* to hiss.

chut *excl* |shüt| sh! ♦ *vb* |shü| *voir* **choir.**

chute |shüt| *nf* fall; (*de bois, papier: déchet*) scrap; **la ~ des cheveux** hair loss; **faire une ~ (de 10 m)** to fall (10 m); **~s de pluie/neige** rain/snowfalls; **~ (d'eau)** waterfall; **~ du jour** nightfall; **~ libre** free fall; **~ des reins** small of the back.

Chypre |shēpr| *nm*: **le ~** Cyprus.

chypriote |shēprēot| *a, nm/f* = **cypriote.**

CIA *sigle f* CIA.

cial *abr* = **commercial.**

ciao |tsháō| *excl* (*fam*) (bye-)bye.

ci-après |sēáprè| *ad* hereafter.

cibiste |sēbēst(ə)| *nm* CB enthusiast.

cible |sēbl(ə)| *nf* target.

cibler |sēblā| *vt* to target.

ciboire |sēbwár| *nm* ciborium (*vessel*).

ciboule |sēbōōl| *nf* (large) chive.

ciboulette |sēbōōlet| *nf* (small) chive.

cicatrice |sēkátrēs| *nf* scar.

cicatriser |sēkátrēzā| *vt* to heal; **se ~** to heal (up), form a scar.

ci-contre |sēkôṅtr(ə)| *ad* opposite.

ci-dessous |sēdəsōō| *ad* below.

ci-dessus |sēdəsü| *ad* above.

ci-devant |sēdəváṅ| *nm/f inv* aristocrat who lost his/her title in the French Revolution.

CIDEX *sigle m* (= *Courrier individuel à distribution exceptionnelle*) *system which groups mailboxes in country areas, rather than each house having its mailbox at its front door.*

CIDJ *sigle m* (= *Centre d'information et de documentation de la jeunesse*) *careers advisory service.*

cidre |sēdr(ə)| *nm* cider.

CIDUNATI |sēdünátē| *sigle m* (= *Comité interprofessionnel de défense de l'union nationale des artisans et travailleurs indépendants*) *union of self-employed craftsmen.*

Cie *abr* (= *compagnie*) Co.

ciel |syel| *nm* sky; (*REL*) heaven; **~s** *nmpl* (*PEINTURE etc*) skies; **cieux** *nmpl* sky *sg,* skies; (*REL*) heaven *sg*; **à ~ ouvert** open-air;

(*mine*) opencut (*US*), opencast (*Brit*);
tomber du ~ (*arriver à l'improviste*) to appear out of the blue; (*être stupéfait*) to be unable to believe one's eyes; **C~!** good heavens!; **~ de lit** canopy.

cierge |syerzh(ə)| *nm* candle; **~ pascal** Easter candle.

cieux |syœ̃| *nmpl voir* **ciel**.

cigale |sĕgál| *nf* cicada.

cigare |sĕgár| *nm* cigar.

cigarette |sĕgáret| *nf* cigarette; **~ (à) bout filtre** filter cigarette.

ci-gît |sĕzhĕ| *ad* here lies.

cigogne |sĕgony| *nf* stork.

ciguë |sĕgü| *nf* hemlock.

ci-inclus, e |sĕaṅklü, -üz| *a, ad* enclosed.

ci-joint, e |sĕzhwaṅ, -aṅt| *a, ad* enclosed; **veuillez trouver ~** please find enclosed.

cil |sĕl| *nm* (eye)lash.

ciller |sĕyā| *vi* to blink.

cimaise |sĕmez| *nf* picture rail.

cime |sĕm| *nf* top; (*montagne*) peak.

ciment |sĕmaṅ| *nm* cement; **~ armé** reinforced concrete.

cimenter |sĕmaṅtā| *vt* to cement.

cimenterie |sĕmaṅtrē| *nf* cement works *sg*.

cimetière |sĕmtyer| *nm* cemetery; (*d'église*) churchyard; **~ de voitures** junkyard.

cinéaste |sĕnāāst(ə)| *nm/f* film-maker.

ciné-club |sĕnāklœb| *nm* film club; film society.

cinéma |sĕnāmá| *nm* cinema; **aller au ~** to go to the cinema *ou* movies; **~ d'animation** cartoon (film).

cinémascope |sĕnāmáskop| *nm* ® Cinemascope ®.

cinémathèque |sĕnāmátek| *nf* film archives *pl ou* library.

cinématographie |sĕnāmátográfē| *nf* cinematography.

cinématographique |sĕnāmátográfēk| *a* film *cpd*, cinema *cpd*.

cinéphile |sĕnāfēl| *nm/f* film buff.

cinérama |sĕnārámá| *nm* ®: **en ~** in Cinerama ®.

cinétique |sĕnātēk| *a* kinetic.

cing(h)alais, e |saṅgále, -ez| *a* Sin(g)halese.

cinglant, e |saṅglaṅ, -aṅt| *a* (*propos, ironie*) scathing, biting; (*échec*) crushing.

cinglé, e |saṅglā| *a* (*fam*) crazy.

cingler |saṅglā| *vt* to lash; (*fig*) to sting ♦ *vi* (*NAVIG*): **~ vers** to make *ou* head for.

cinq |saṅk| *num* five.

cinquantaine |saṅkáṅten| *nf*: **une ~ (de)** about fifty; **avoir la ~** (*âge*) to be around fifty.

cinquante |saṅkáṅt| *num* fifty.

cinquantenaire |saṅkáṅtner| *a, nm/f* fifty-year-old.

cinquantième |saṅkáṅtyem| *num* fiftieth.

cinquième |saṅkyem| *num* fifth.

cinquièmement |saṅkyemmáṅ| *ad* fifthly.

cintre |saṅtr(ə)| *nm* coat-hanger; (*ARCHIT*) arch; **plein ~** semicircular arch.

cintré, e |saṅtrā| *a* curved; (*chemise*) fitted, slim-fitting.

CIO *sigle m* (= *Comité international olympique*) IOC (= *International Olympic Committee*).

cirage |sĕrázh| *nm* (shoe) polish.

circoncis, e |sĕrkóṅsĕ, -ēz| *a* circumcised.

circoncision |sĕrkóṅsĕzyóṅ| *nf* circumcision.

circonférence |sĕrkóṅfāráṅs| *nf* circumference.

circonflexe |sĕrkóṅfleks(ə)| *a*: **accent ~** circumflex accent.

circonscription |sĕrkóṅskrēpsyóṅ| *nf* district; **~ électorale** (*d'un député*) constituency; **~ militaire** military area.

circonscrire |sĕrkóṅskrēr| *vt* to define, delimit; (*incendie*) to contain; (*propriété*) to mark out; (*sujet*) to define.

circonspect, e |sĕrkóṅspekt| *a* circumspect, cautious.

circonspection |sĕrkóṅspeksyóṅ| *nf* circumspection, caution.

circonstance |sĕrkóṅstáṅs| *nf* circumstance; (*occasion*) occasion; **œuvre de ~** occasional work; **air de ~** fitting air; **tête de ~** appropriate demeanor (*US*) *ou* demeanour (*Brit*); **~s atténuantes** mitigating circumstances.

circonstancié, e |sĕrkóṅstáṅsyā| *a* detailed.

circonstanciel, le |sĕrkóṅstáṅsyel| *a*: **complément/proposition ~(le)** adverbial phrase/clause.

circonvenir |sĕrkóṅvnēr| *vt* to circumvent.

circonvolutions |sĕrkóṅvolüsyóṅ| *nfpl* twists, convolutions.

circuit |sĕrküē| *nm* (*trajet*) tour, (round) trip; (*ÉLEC, TECH*) circuit; **~ automobile** motor circuit; **~ de distribution** distribution network; **~ fermé** closed circuit; **~ intégré** integrated circuit.

circulaire |sĕrküler| *a, nf* circular.

circulation |sĕrkülásyóṅ| *nf* circulation; (*AUTO*): **la ~** (the) traffic; **bonne/mauvaise ~** good/bad circulation; **mettre en ~** to put into circulation.

circulatoire |sĕrkülátwár| *a*: **avoir des troubles ~s** to have problems with one's circulation.

circuler |sĕrkülā| *vi* to drive (along); to walk along; (*train etc*) to run; (*sang, devises*) to circulate; **faire ~** (*nouvelle*) to spread (around), circulate; (*badauds*) to move on.

cire |sĕr| *nf* wax; **~ à cacheter** sealing wax.

ciré |sĕrā| *nm* oilskin.

cirer |sĕrā| *vt* to wax, polish.

cireur |sĕrœr| *nm* shoeshine-boy.

cireuse |sĕrœz| *nf* floor polisher.

cireux, euse |sĕrœ̃, -œ̃z| *a* (*fig: teint*) sallow, waxen.

cirque |sĕrk(ə)| *nm* circus; (*arène*) amphitheater (*US*), amphitheatre (*Brit*); (*GÉO*) cirque; (*fig: désordre*) chaos, bedlam; (*: chichis*) fuss.

cirrhose |sĕrōz| *nf*: **~ du foie** cirrhosis of the liver.

cisailler |sĕzāyā| *vt* to clip.

cisaille(s) |sĕzáy| *nf(pl)* (gardening) shears *pl*.

ciseau, x |sĕzō| *nm*: **~ (à bois)** chisel ♦ *nmpl* (pair of) scissors; **sauter en ~x** to do a scissors jump; **~ à froid** cold chisel.

ciseler |sĕzlā| *vt* to chisel, carve.

ciselure |sĕzlür| *nf* engraving; (*bois*) carving.

Cisjordanie |sĕszhordánē| *nf*: **la ~** the West Bank (of Jordan).

citadelle [sētádel] *nf* citadel.
citadin, e [sētádań, -ēn] *nm/f* city dweller ♦ *a* town *cpd*, city *cpd*, urban.
citation [sētásyóń] *nf* (*d'auteur*) quotation; (*JUR*) summons *sg*; (*MIL*: *récompense*) citation (*US*), mention (*Brit*).
cité [sētā] *nf* town; (*plus grande*) city; **~ ouvrière** (workers') housing development; **~ universitaire** students' residences *pl*.
cité-dortoir, *pl* **cités-dortoirs** [sētādortwár] *nf* bedroom community (*US*), dormitory town (*Brit*).
cité-jardin, *pl* **cités-jardins** [sētāzhárdań] *nf* garden city.
citer [sētā] *vt* (*un auteur*) to quote (from); (*nommer*) to name; (*JUR*) to summon; **~ (en exemple)** (*personne*) to hold up (as an example); **je ne veux ~ personne** I don't want to name names.
citerne [sētern(ə)] *nf* tank.
cithare [sētár] *nf* zither.
citoyen, ne [sētwáyań, -en] *nm/f* citizen.
citoyenneté [sētwáyentā] *nf* citizenship.
citrique [sētrēk] *a*: **acide ~** citric acid.
citron [sētróń] *nm* lemon; **~ pressé** (fresh) lemon juice; **~ vert** lime.
citronnade [sētronád] *nf* lemonade.
citronné, e [sētronā] *a* (*boisson*) lemonflavored (*US*) *ou* -flavoured (*Brit*); (*eau de toilette*) lemon-scented.
citronnier [sētronyā] *nm* lemon tree.
citrouille [sētrōōy] *nf* pumpkin.
cive(s) [sēv] *nf(pl)* (*BOT*) chive(s); (*CULIN*) chives.
civet [sēve] *nm* stew; **~ de lièvre** ≈ rabbit stew, jugged hare (*Brit*).
civette [sēvet] *nf* (*BOT*) chives *pl*; (*ZOOL*) civet (cat).
civière [sēvyer] *nf* stretcher.
civil, e [sēvēl] *a* (*JUR, ADMIN, poli*) civil; (*non militaire*) civilian ♦ *nm* civilian; **en ~** in civilian clothes; **dans le ~** in civilian life.
civilement [sēvēlmáń] *ad* (*poliment*) civilly; **se marier ~** to have a civil wedding.
civilisation [sēvēlēzásyóń] *nf* civilization.
civilisé, e [sēvēlēzā] *a* civilized.
civiliser [sēvēlēzā] *vt* to civilize.
civilité [sēvēlētā] *nf* civility; **présenter ses ~s** to present one's compliments.
civique [sēvēk] *a* civic; **instruction ~** (*SCOL*) civics *sg*.
civisme [sēvēsm(ə)] *nm* public-spiritedness.
cl. *abr* (= *centilitre*) cl.
clafoutis [kláfōōtē] *nm* batter pudding (*containing fruit*).
claie [kle] *nf* grid, riddle.
clair, e [kler] *a* light; (*chambre*) light, bright; (*eau, son, fig*) clear ♦ *ad*: **voir ~** to see clearly ♦ *nm*: **mettre au ~** (*notes etc*) to tidy up; **tirer qch au ~** to clear sth up, clarify sth; **bleu ~** light blue; **pour être ~** so as to make it plain; **y voir ~** (*comprendre*) to understand, see; **le plus ~ de son temps/ argent** the better part of his time/money; **~ de lune** moonlight.
claire [kler] *nf*: **(huître de) ~** fattened oyster.
clairement [klermáń] *ad* clearly.
claire-voie [klervwá]: **à ~** *a* letting the light through; openwork *cpd*.

clairière [kleryer] *nf* clearing.
clair-obscur, *pl* **clairs-obscurs** [kleropskür] *nm* half-light; (*fig*) uncertainty.
clairon [kleróń] *nm* bugle.
claironner [kleronā] *vt* (*fig*) to trumpet, shout from the rooftops.
clairsemé, e [klersəmā] *a* sparse.
clairvoyant, e [klervwáyań, -áńt] *a* perceptive, clear-sighted.
clam [klám] *nm* (*ZOOL*) clam.
clamer [klámā] *vt* to proclaim.
clameur [klámœr] *nf* clamor (*US*), clamour (*Brit*).
clandestin, e [kláńdestań, -ēn] *a* clandestine, covert; (*POL*) underground, clandestine; **passager ~** stowaway.
clandestinité [kláńdestēnētā] *nf*: **dans la ~** (*en secret*) under cover; (*en se cachant: vivre*) underground; **entrer dans la ~** to go underground.
clapet [klápe] *nm* (*TECH*) valve.
clapier [klápyā] *nm* (rabbit) hutch.
clapotement [klápotmáń] *nm* lap(ping).
clapoter [klápotā] *vi* to lap.
clapotis [klápotē] *nm* lap(ping).
claquage [klákázh] *nm* pulled *ou* strained muscle.
claque [klák] *nf* (*gifle*) slap; (*THÉÂTRE*) claque ♦ *nm* (*chapeau*) opera hat.
claquement [klákmáń] *nm* (*de porte: bruit répété*) banging; (*: bruit isolé*) slam.
claquemurer [klákmürā]: **se ~** *vi* to shut o.s. away, closet o.s.
claquer [klákā] *vi* (*drapeau*) to flap; (*porte*) to bang, slam; (*coup de feu*) to ring out ♦ *vt* (*porte*) to slam, bang; (*doigts*) to snap; **elle claquait des dents** her teeth were chattering; **se ~ un muscle** to pull *ou* strain a muscle.
claquettes [kláket] *nfpl* tap-dancing *sg*.
clarification [klárēfēkásyóń] *nf* (*fig*) clarification.
clarifier [klárēfyā] *vt* (*fig*) to clarify.
clarinette [klárēnet] *nf* clarinet.
clarinettiste [klárēnātēst(ə)] *nm/f* clarinettist.
clarté [klártā] *nf* lightness; brightness; (*d'un son, de l'eau*) clearness; (*d'une explication*) clarity.
classe [klás] *nf* class; (*SCOL*: *local*) class(room); (*: leçon*) class; (*: élèves*) class, grade (*US*), form (*Brit*); **1ère/2ème ~** 1st/ 2nd class; **un (soldat de) deuxième ~** (*MIL*: *armée de terre*) ≈ private (soldier); (*: armée de l'air*) ≈ airman basic (*US*), ≈ aircraftman (*Brit*); **de ~** luxury *cpd*; **faire ses ~s** (*MIL*) to go through basic training; **faire la ~** (*SCOL*) to be a *ou* the teacher; to teach; **aller en ~** to go to school; **aller en ~ verte/ de neige/de mer** to go to the countryside/ skiing/to the seaside with the school; **~ ouvrière** working class; **~ sociale** social class; **~ touriste** economy class.
classement [klásmáń] *nm* classifying; filing; grading; closing; (*rang: SCOL*) rank (*US*), place (*Brit*); (*: SPORT*) ranking (*US*), placing (*Brit*); (*liste: SCOL*) class list (in order of merit); (*: SPORT*) rankings *pl* (*US*), placings *pl* (*Brit*); **premier au ~ général** (*SPORT*) first overall.
classer [klásā] *vt* (*idées, livres*) to classify;

(*papiers*) to file; (*candidat, concurrent*) to grade; (*personne: juger: péj*) to rate; (*JUR: affaire*) to close; **se ~ premier/dernier** to come first/last; (*SPORT*) to finish first/last.

classeur [klâsœr] *nm* (*cahier*) file; (*meuble*) filing cabinet; **~ à feuillets mobiles** ring binder.

classification [klàsēfēkâsyôń] *nf* classification.

classifier [klâsēfyā] *vt* to classify.

classique [klásēk] *a* classical; (*sobre: coupe etc*) classic(al); (*habituel*) standard, classic ♦ *nm* classic; classical author; **études ~s** classical studies, classics.

claudication [klōdēkâsyôń] *nf* limp.

clause [klōz] *nf* clause.

claustrer [klōstrā] *vt* to confine.

claustrophobie [klōstrofobē] *nf* claustrophobia.

clavecin [klàvsań] *nm* harpsichord.

claveciniste [klávsēnēst(ə)] *nm/f* harpsichordist.

clavicule [klàvēkül] *nf* clavicle, collarbone.

clavier [klàvyā] *nm* keyboard.

clé *ou* **clef** [klā] *nf* key; (*MUS*) clef; (*de mécanicien*) wrench (*US*), spanner (*Brit*) ♦ *a*: **problème/position ~** key problem/position; **mettre sous ~** to place under lock and key; **prendre la ~ des champs** to run away, make off; **prix ~s en main** (*d'une voiture*) sticker (*US*) *ou* on-the-road (*Brit*) price; (*d'un appartement*) ready-for-occupancy price (*US*), price with immediate entry (*Brit*); **~ de sol/de fa/d'ut** treble/bass/alto clef; **livre/film** etc **à ~** book/film etc in which real people are depicted under fictitious names; **à la ~** (*à la fin*) at the end of it all; **~ anglaise = ~ à molette**; **~ de contact** ignition key; **~ à molette** adjustable wrench, monkey wrench; **~ de voûte** keystone.

clématite [klāmátēt] *nf* clematis.

clémence [klāmáńs] *nf* mildness; leniency.

clément, e [klāmâń, -âńt] *a* (*temps*) mild; (*indulgent*) lenient.

clémentine [klāmâńtēn] *nf* (*BOT*) tangerine (*US*), clementine (*Brit*).

clenche [klâńsh] *nf* latch.

cleptomane [kleptomán] *nm/f* = **kleptomane**.

clerc [kler] *nm*: **~ de notaire** *ou* **d'avoué** lawyer's clerk.

clergé [klerzhā] *nm* clergy.

clérical, e, aux [klārēkál, -ō] *a* clerical.

cliché [klēshā] *nm* (*PHOTO*) negative; print; (*TYPO*) (printing) plate; (*LING*) cliché.

client, e [klēyáń, -áńt] *nm/f* (*acheteur*) customer, client; (*d'hôtel*) guest, patron; (*du docteur*) patient; (*de l'avocat*) client.

clientèle [klēyáńtel] *nf* (*du magasin*) customers *pl*, clientèle; (*du docteur, de l'avocat*) practice; **accorder sa ~** à to give one's business to; **retirer sa ~** à to take one's business away from.

cligner [klēnyā] *vi*: **~ des yeux** to blink (one's eyes); **~ de l'œil** to wink.

clignotant [klēnyotáń] *nm* (*AUTO*) turn signal (*US*), indicator (*Brit*).

clignoter [klēnyotā] *vi* (*étoiles etc*) to twinkle; (*lumière: à intervalles réguliers*) to flash; (*: vaciller*) to flicker; (*yeux*) to blink.

climat [klēmá] *nm* climate.

climatique [klēmátēk] *a* climatic.

climatisation [klēmátēzásyôń] *nf* air conditioning.

climatisé, e [klēmátēzā] *a* air-conditioned.

climatiseur [klēmátēzœr] *nm* air conditioner.

clin d'œil [klańdœy] *nm* wink; **en un ~** in a flash.

clinique [klēnēk] *a* clinical ♦ *nf* nursing home, (*private*) clinic.

clinquant, e [klańkâń, -âńt] *a* flashy.

clip [klēp] *nm* (*pince*) clip; (*vidéo*) pop (*ou* promotional) video.

clique [klēk] *nf* (*péj: bande*) clique, set; **prendre ses ~s et ses claques** to pack one's bags.

cliqueter [klēktā] *vi* to clash; (*ferraille, clefs, monnaie*) to jangle, jingle; (*verres*) to clink.

cliquetis [klēktē] *nm* jangle, jingle; clink.

clitoris [klētorēs] *nm* clitoris.

clivage [klēvàzh] *nm* cleavage; (*fig*) rift, split.

cloaque [kloák] *nm* (*fig*) cesspool.

clochard, e [kloshár, -árd(ə)] *nm/f* tramp.

cloche [klosh] *nf* (*d'église*) bell; (*fam*) idiot, dope; (*chapeau*) cloche (hat); **~ à fromage** cheese-cover.

cloche-pied [kloshpyā]: **à ~** *ad* on one leg, hopping (along).

clocher [kloshā] *nm* church tower; (*en pointe*) steeple ♦ *vi* (*fam*) to be *ou* go wrong; **de ~** (*péj*) parochial.

clocheton [kloshtôń] *nm* pinnacle.

clochette [kloshet] *nf* bell.

clodo [klodō] *nm* (*fam*: = *clochard*) tramp.

cloison [klwàzôń] *nf* partition (wall); **~ étanche** (*fig*) impenetrable barrier, brick wall (*fig*).

cloisonner [klwàzonā] *vt* to partition (off); to divide up; (*fig*) to compartmentalize.

cloître [klwátr(ə)] *nm* cloister.

cloîtrer [klwátrā] *vt*: **se ~** to shut o.s. up *ou* away; (*REL*) to enter a convent *ou* monastery.

clone [klon] *nm* clone.

clope [klop] *nm* (*fam*) cigarette.

clopin-clopant [klopańklopáń] *ad* hobbling along; (*fig*) so-so.

clopiner [klopēnā] *vi* to hobble along.

cloporte [kloport(ə)] *nm* pill *ou* sow bug (*US*), woodlouse (*pl* -lice) (*Brit*).

cloque [klok] *nf* blister.

cloqué, e [klokā] *a*: **étoffe ~e** seersucker.

cloquer [klokā] *vi* (*peau, peinture*) to blister.

clore [klor] *vt* to close; **~ une session** (*INFORM*) to log out.

clos, e [klō, -ōz] *pp de* **clore** ♦ *a voir* **maison, huis, vase** ♦ *nm* (enclosed) field.

clôt [klō] *vb voir* **clore**.

clôture [klōtür] *nf* closure, closing; (*barrière*) enclosure, fence.

clôturer [klōtürā] *vt* (*terrain*) to enclose, close off; (*festival, débats*) to close.

clou [klōō] *nm* nail; (*MÉD*) boil; **~s** *nmpl* = **passage clouté**; **pneus à ~s** studded tires; **le ~ du spectacle** the highlight of the show; **~ de girofle** clove.

clouer [klōōā] *vt* to nail down (*ou* up); (*fig*): **~ sur/contre** to pin to/against.

clouté, e [klōōtā] *a* studded.

clown [klo͞on] *nm* clown; **faire le** ~ (*fig*) to clown (around), play the fool.

CLT *sigle f* = *Compagnie Luxembourgeoise de Télévision*.

club [klœb] *nm* club.

CM *sigle f* = **chambre des métiers** ♦ *sigle m* = **conseil municipal**; (*SCOL*) = **cours moyen.**

cm. *abr* (= *centimètre*) cm.

CNAT *sigle f* (= *Commission nationale d'aménagement du territoire*) *national development agency.*

CNC *sigle m* (= *Conseil national de la consommation*) *national consumers' council.*

CNCL *sigle f* (= *Commission nationale de la communication et des libertés*) *independent broadcasting authority.*

CNDP *sigle m* = *Centre national de documentation pédagogique.*

CNE *sigle f* (= *Caisse nationale d'épargne*) *national savings bank.*

CNEC *sigle m* = *Centre national de l'enseignement par correspondance.*

CNIL *sigle f* (= *Commission nationale de l'informatique et des libertés*) *board which enforces law on data protection.*

CNIT *sigle m* (= *Centre national des industries et des techniques*) *exhibition center in Paris.*

CNJA *sigle m* (= *Centre national des jeunes agriculteurs*) *farmers' union.*

CNL *sigle f* (= *Confédération nationale du logement*) *consumer group for housing.*

CNP *sigle f* (= *Caisse nationale de prévoyance*) *savings bank.*

CNPF *sigle m* (= *Conseil national du patronat français*) *national council of French employers.*

CNRS *sigle m* = *Centre national de la recherche scientifique.*

c/o *abr* (= *care of*) c/o.

coagulant [koágüláñ] *nm* (*MÉD*) coagulant.

coaguler [koágülä] *vi, vt,* **se** ~ *vi* to coagulate.

coaliser [koálēzä]: **se** ~ *vi* to unite, join forces.

coalition [koálēsyóñ] *nf* coalition.

coasser [koásä] *vi* to croak.

coauteur [ko͞otœr] *nm* co-author.

cobalt [kobált] *nm* cobalt.

cobaye [kobáy] *nm* guinea-pig.

COBOL *ou* **Cobol** [kobol] *nm* COBOL.

cobra [kobrá] *nm* cobra.

coca [koká] *nm* ® Coke ®.

cocagne [kokány] *nf*: **pays de** ~ land of plenty; **mât de** ~ greasy pole (*fig*).

cocaïne [kokáēn] *nf* cocaine.

cocarde [kokárd(ə)] *nf* rosette.

cocardier, ière [kokárdyä, -yer] *a* jingoistic, chauvinistic; militaristic.

cocasse [kokás] *a* comical, funny.

coccinelle [koksēnel] *nf* ladybug (*US*), ladybird (*Brit*).

coccyx [koksēs] *nm* coccyx.

cocher [koshä] *nm* coachman ♦ *vt* to check off; (*entailler*) to notch.

cochère [kosher] *af*: **porte** ~ carriage entrance.

cochon, ne [koshóñ, -on] *nm* pig ♦ *nm/f* (*péj*: *sale*) (filthy) pig; (*: méchant*) swine ♦ *a*

(*fam*) dirty, smutty; ~ **d'Inde** guinea-pig; ~ **de lait** (*CULIN*) suckling (*US*) *ou* sucking (*Brit*) pig.

cochonnaille [koshonáy] *nf* (*péj*: *charcuterie*) (cold) pork.

cochonnerie [koshonrē] *nf* (*fam*: *saleté*) filth; (*: marchandises*) rubbish, trash.

cochonnet [koshone] *nm* (*BOULES*) jack.

cocker [koker] *nm* cocker spaniel.

cocktail [koktel] *nm* cocktail; (*réception*) cocktail party.

coco [kokō] *nm voir* **noix**; (*fam*) dude (*US*), bloke (*Brit*).

cocon [kokóñ] *nm* cocoon.

cocorico [kokorēkō] *excl, nm* cock-a-doodle-do.

cocotier [kokotyä] *nm* coconut palm.

cocotte [kokot] *nf* (*en fonte*) casserole; **ma** ~ (*fam*) sweetie (pie); ~ **(minute)** ® pressure cooker; ~ **en papier** paper shape.

cocu [kokü] *nm* cuckold.

code [kod] *nm* code; **se mettre en** ~**(s)** to dim (*US*) *ou* dip (*Brit*) one's (head)lights; ~ **à barres** bar code; ~ **de caractère** (*INFORM*) character code; ~ **civil** Civil Code (*US*), Common Law (*Brit*); ~ **machine** machine code; ~ **pénal** penal code; ~ **postal** (*numéro*) zip code (*US*), postcode (*Brit*); ~ **de la route** rules of the road; ~ **secret** secret code, cipher (*Brit*).

codéine [kodáēn] *nf* codeine.

coder [kodä] *vt* to (en)code.

codétenu, e [kodetnü] *nm/f* fellow prisoner *ou* inmate.

codicille [kodēsēl] *nm* codicil.

codifier [kodēfyä] *vt* to codify.

codirecteur, trice [kodērektœr, -trēs] *nm/f* co-director.

coéditeur, trice [koādētœr, -trēs] *nm/f* co-publisher; (*rédacteur*) co-editor.

coefficient [koáfēsyáñ] *nm* coefficient; ~ **d'erreur** margin of error.

coéquipier, ière [koākēpyä, -yer] *nm/f* team-mate, partner.

coercition [koersēsyóñ] *nf* coercion.

cœur [kœr] *nm* heart; (*CARTES*: *couleur*) hearts *pl*; (*: carte*) heart; (*CULIN*): ~ **de laitue/d'artichaut** lettuce/artichoke heart; (*fig*): ~ **du débat** heart of the debate; ~ **de l'été** height of summer; ~ **de la forêt** depths *pl* of the forest; **affaire de** ~ love affair; **avoir bon** ~ to be kind-hearted; **avoir mal au** ~ to feel sick to one's stomach; **contre** *ou* **sur son** ~ to one's breast; **opérer qn à** ~ **ouvert** to perform open-heart surgery on sb; **recevoir qn à** ~ **ouvert** to welcome sb with open arms; **parler à** ~ **ouvert** to open one's heart; **de tout son** ~ with all one's heart; **avoir le** ~ **gros** *ou* **serré** to have a heavy heart; **en avoir le** ~ **net** to be clear in one's own mind (about it); **par** ~ by heart; **de bon** ~ willingly; **avoir à** ~ **de faire** to be very eager to do; **cela lui tient à** ~ that's (very) close to his heart; **prendre les choses à** ~ to take things to heart; **à** ~ **joie** to one's heart's content; **être de tout** ~ **avec qn** to be (completely) in accord with sb.

coexistence [koegzēstáñs] *nf* coexistence.

coexister [koágzēstä] *vi* to coexist.

coffrage [kofrázh] *nm* (*CONSTR*: *dispositif*)

form.

coffre [kofr(ə)] *nm* (*meuble*) chest; (*coffre-fort*) safe; (*d'auto*) trunk (*US*), boot (*Brit*); **avoir du ~** (*fam*) to have a lot of breath.

coffre-fort, *pl* **coffres-fortes** [kofrəfor] *nm* safe.

coffrer [kofrā] *vt* (*fam*) to put inside, lock up.

coffret [kofre] *nm* casket; **~ à bijoux** jewel box.

cogérant, e [kozhāráń, -áńt] *nm/f* joint manager/manageress.

cogestion [kozhāstyóń] *nf* joint management.

cogiter [kozhētā] *vi* to cogitate.

cognac [konyák] *nm* brandy, cognac.

cognement [konymáń] *nm* knocking.

cogner [konyā] *vi* to knock, bang; **se ~** to bump o.s.

cohabitation [koábētásyóń] *nf* living together; (*POL, JUR*) cohabitation.

cohabiter [koábētā] *vi* to live together.

cohérence [koārâns] *nf* coherence.

cohérent, e [koārâń, -áńt] *a* coherent.

cohésion [koāzyóń] *nf* cohesion.

cohorte [koort(ə)] *nf* troop.

cohue [koü] *nf* crowd.

coi, coite [kwá, kwát] *a:* **rester ~** to remain silent.

coiffe [kwáf] *nf* headdress.

coiffé, e [kwáfā] *a:* **bien/mal ~** with tidy/untidy hair; **~ d'un béret** wearing a beret; **~ en arrière** with one's hair brushed ou combed back; **~ en brosse** with a crew cut.

coiffer [kwáfā] *vt* (*fig*) to cover, top; **~ qn** to do sb's hair; **~ qn d'un béret** to put a beret on sb; **se ~** to do one's hair; **to put on a** *ou* one's hat.

coiffeur, euse [kwáfœr, -œz] *nm/f* hairdresser ♦ *nf* (*table*) dressing table.

coiffure [kwáfür] *nf* (*cheveux*) hairstyle, hairdo; (*chapeau*) hat, headgear *q*; (*art*): **la ~** hairdressing.

coin [kwań] *nm* corner; (*pour graver*) die; (*pour coincer*) wedge; (*poinçon*) hallmark; **l'épicerie du ~** the local grocer; **dans le ~** (*aux alentours*) in the area, around about; locally; **au ~ du feu** by the fireside; **du ~ de l'œil** out of the corner of one's eye; **regard en ~** side(ways) glance; **sourire en ~** half-smile.

coincé, e [kwáńsā] *a* stuck, jammed; (*fig: inhibé*) inhibited, with hang-ups.

coincer [kwáńsā] *vt* to jam; (*fam*) to catch; to nab; **se ~** to get stuck *ou* jammed.

coïncidence [koáńsēdáńs] *nf* coincidence.

coïncider [koáńsēdā] *vi:* **~ (avec)** to coincide (with); (*correspondre: témoignage etc*) to correspond *ou* tally (with).

coin-coin [kwáńkwań] *nm inv* quack.

coing [kwań] *nm* quince.

coït [koēt] *nm* coitus.

coite [kwát] *af voir* **coi.**

coke [kok] *nm* coke.

col [kol] *nm* (*de chemise*) collar; (*encolure, cou*) neck; (*de montagne*) pass; **~ du fémur** neck of the thighbone; **~ roulé** polo-neck; **~ de l'utérus** cervix.

coléoptère [kolāopter] *nm* beetle.

colère [koler] *nf* anger; **une ~** a fit of anger; **être en ~ (contre qn)** to be angry (with sb);

mettre qn en ~ to make sb angry; **se mettre en ~** to get angry.

coléreux, euse [kolārœ, -œz] *a,* **colérique** [kolārēk] *a* quick-tempered, irascible.

colibacillose [kolēbásēlōz] *nf* colibacillosis.

colifichet [kolēfēshe] *nm* trinket.

colimaçon [kolēmàsóń] *nm:* **escalier en ~** spiral staircase.

colin [kolań] *nm* hake.

colin-maillard [kolańmáyár] *nm* (*jeu*) blind man's buff.

colique [kolēk] *nf* diarrhea (*US*), diarrhoea (*Brit*); (*douleurs*) colic (pains *pl*); (*fam: personne ou chose ennuyeuse*) pain.

colis [kolē] *nm* parcel; **par ~ postal** by parcel post.

colistier, ière [kolēstyā, -yer] *nm/f* fellow candidate.

colite [kolēt] *nf* colitis.

coll. *abr* = **collection**; (= *collaborateurs*): **et ~ et al.**

collaborateur, trice [koláborátœr, -trēs] *nm/f* (*aussi POL*) collaborator; (*d'une revue*) contributor.

collaboration [koláborásyóń] *nf* collaboration.

collaborer [koláborā] *vi* to collaborate; **~ à** to collaborate on; (*revue*) to contribute to.

collage [kolázh] *nm* (*ART*) collage.

collant, e [koláń, -áńt] *a* sticky; (*robe etc*) clinging, skintight; (*péj*) clinging ♦ *nm* (*bas*) pantyhose *pl* (*US*), tights *pl* (*Brit*).

collatéral, e, aux [kolátárál, -ō] *nm/f* collateral.

collation [kolásyóń] *nf* light meal.

colle [kol] *nf* glue; (*à papiers peints*) (wallpaper) paste; (*devinette*) teaser, riddle; (*SCOL fam*) detention; **~ forte** superglue ®.

collecte [kolekt(ə)] *nf* collection; **faire une ~** to take up a collection.

collecter [kolektā] *vt* to collect.

collecteur [kolektœr] *nm* (*égout*) main sewer.

collectif, ive [kolektēf, -ēv] *a* collective; (*visite, billet etc*) group *cpd* ♦ *nm*: **~ budgétaire** mid-term budget; **immeuble ~** apartment building (*US*), block of flats (*Brit*).

collection [koleksyóń] *nf* collection; (*ÉDITION*) series; **pièce de ~** collector's item; **faire (la) ~ de** to collect; **(toute) une ~ de ...** (*fig*) a (complete) set of ....

collectionner [koleksyonā] *vt* (*tableaux, timbres*) to collect.

collectionneur, euse [koleksyonœr, -œz] *nm/f* collector.

collectivement [kolektēvmáń] *ad* collectively.

collectiviste [kolektēvēst(ə)] *a* collectivist.

collectivité [kolektēvētā] *nf* group; **la ~** the community, the collectivity; **les ~s locales** local governments.

collège [kolezh] *nm* (*école*) (high) school; (*assemblée*) body; **~ électoral** electoral college; **~ d'enseignement secondaire (CES)** ≈ junior high school.

collégial, e, aux [kolāzhyàl, -ō] *a* collegiate.

collégien, ne [kolāzhyáń, -en] *nm/f* high school student (*US*), secondary school pupil (*Brit*).

collègue [koleg] *nm/f* colleague.

coller [kolā] *vt* (*papier, timbre*) to stick (on); (*affiche*) to stick up; (*appuyer, placer contre*): **~ son front à la vitre** to press one's face to the window; (*enveloppe*) to seal; (*morceaux*) to stick *ou* glue together; (*fam*: *mettre, fourrer*) to stick, shove; (*SCOL fam*) to keep in, give detention to ♦ *vi* (*être collant*) to be sticky; (*adhérer*) to stick; ~ **qch sur** to stick (*ou* paste *ou* glue) sth on(to); ~ **à** to stick to; (*fig*) to cling to.

collerette [kolret] *nf* ruff; (*TECH*) flange.

collet [kole] *nm* (*piège*) snare, noose; (*cou*): **prendre qn au** ~ to grab sb by the throat; ~ **monté** *a inv* straight-laced.

colleter [kolta] *vt* (*adversaire*) to collar, grab by the throat; **se** ~ **avec** to wrestle with.

colleur [kolœr] *nm*: ~ **d'affiches** bill-poster.

collier [kolya] *nm* (*bijou*) necklace; (*de chien, TECH*) collar; ~ **(de barbe), barbe en** ~ narrow beard along the line of the jaw; ~ **de serrage** choke collar.

collimateur [kolēmátœr] *nm*: **être dans le** ~ (*fig*) to be in the firing line; **avoir qn/qch dans le** ~ (*fig*) to have sb/sth in one's sights.

colline [kolēn] *nf* hill.

collision [kolēzyóń] *nf* collision, crash; **entrer en** ~ **(avec)** to collide (with).

colloque [kolok] *nm* colloquium, symposium.

collusion [kolüzyóń] *nf* collusion.

collutoire [kolütwàr] *nm* (*MÉD*) oral medication; (*en bombe*) throat spray.

collyre [kolēr] *nm* (*MÉD*) eye lotion.

colmater [kolmátā] *vt* (*fuite*) to seal off; (*brèche*) to plug, fill in.

Cologne [kolony] *n* Cologne.

colombe [kolôńb] *nf* dove.

Colombie [kolôńbē] *nf*: **la** ~ Colombia.

colombien, ne [kolôńbyań, -en] *a* Colombian ♦ *nm/f*: **C~, ne** Colombian.

colon [kolóń] *nm* settler; (*enfant*) boarder (*in children's summer camp*).

côlon [kōlóń] *nm* colon (*MÉD*).

colonel [kolonel] *nm* colonel; (*armée de l'air*) colonel (*US*), group captain (*Brit*).

colonial, e, aux [kolonyàl, -ō] *a* colonial.

colonialisme [kolonyálēsm(ə)] *nm* colonialism.

colonie [kolonē] *nf* colony; ~ **(de vacances)** summer camp (*for children*).

colonisation [kolonēzàsyóń] *nf* colonization.

coloniser [kolonēzā] *vt* to colonize.

colonnade [kolonád] *nf* colonnade.

colonne [kolon] *nf* column; **se mettre en** ~ **par deux/quatre** to line up two/four abreast; **en** ~ **par deux** in double file; ~ **de secours** rescue party; ~ **(vertébrale)** spine, spinal column.

colonnette [kolonet] *nf* small column.

colophane [kolofán] *nf* rosin.

colorant [koloráń] *nm* coloring (*US*), colouring (*Brit*).

coloration [kolorásyóń] *nf* color(ing) (*US*), colour(ing) (*Brit*); **se faire faire une** ~ (*chez le coiffeur*) to have one's hair dyed.

coloré, e [kolorā] *a* (*fig*) colorful (*US*), colourful (*Brit*).

colorer [kolorā] *vt* to color (*US*), colour (*Brit*); **se** ~ *vi* to turn red; to blush.

coloriage [koloryázh] *nm* coloring (*US*), colouring (*Brit*).

colorier [koloryā] *vt* to color (*US*) *ou* colour (*Brit*) (in); **album à** ~ coloring book.

coloris [kolorē] *nm* color (*US*), colour (*Brit*),

shade.

coloriste [kolorēst(ə)] *nm/f* colorist (*US*), colourist (*Brit*).

colossal, e, aux [kolosàl, -ō] *a* colossal, huge.

colosse [kolos] *nm* giant.

colostrum [kolostrom] *nm* colostrum.

colporter [kolportā] *vt* to hawk, peddle.

colporteur, euse [kolportœr, -ēz] *nm/f* hawker, pedlar.

colt [kolt] *nm* revolver, Colt ®.

coltiner [koltēnā] *vt* to lug around.

colza [kolzà] *nm* rape(seed).

coma [komá] *nm* coma; **être dans le** ~ to be in a coma.

comateux, euse [komátœ, -ēz] *a* comatose.

combat [kôńbá] *vb voir* **combattre** ♦ *nm* fight; fighting *q*; ~ **de boxe** boxing match; ~ **de rues** street fighting *q*; ~ **singulier** single combat.

combatif, ive [kôńbátēf, -ēv] *a* with a lot of fight.

combativité [kôńbátēvētā] *nf* fighting spirit.

combattant [kôńbátáń] *vb voir* **combattre** ♦ *nm* combatant; (*d'une rixe*) brawler; **ancien** ~ war veteran.

combattre [kôńbátr(ə)] *vi* to fight ♦ *vt* to fight; (*épidémie, ignorance*) to combat, fight (against).

combien [kôńbyań] *ad* (*quantité*) how much; (*nombre*) how many; (*exclamatif*) how; ~ **de** how much; how many; ~ **de temps** how long, how much time; ~ **coûte/pèse ceci?** how much does this cost/weigh?; **vous mesurez** ~? what size are you?; **ça fait** ~ **en largeur?** how wide is that?

combinaison [kôńbēnezóń] *nf* combination; (*astuce*) device, scheme; (*de femme*) slip; (*d'aviateur*) jump suit; (*d'homme-grenouille*) wetsuit; (*bleu de travail*) coveralls *pl* (*US*); boilersuit (*Brit*).

combine [kôńbēn] *nf* trick; (*péj*) scheme.

combiné [kôńbēnā] *nm* (*aussi*: ~ **téléphonique**) receiver; (*SKI*) combination (event); (*vêtement de femme*) corselet.

combiner [kôńbēnā] *vt* to combine; (*plan, horaire*) to work out, devise.

comble [kôńbl(ə)] *a* (*salle*) packed (full) ♦ *nm* (*du bonheur, plaisir*) height; ~**s** *nmpl* (*CONSTR*) attic *sg*, loft *sg*; **de fond en** ~ from top to bottom; **pour** ~ **de malchance** to cap it all; **c'est le** ~! that beats everything!; **sous les** ~**s** in the attic.

combler [kôńblā] *vt* (*trou*) to fill in; (*besoin, lacune*) to fill; (*déficit*) to make good; (*satisfaire*) to gratify, fulfill (*US*), fulfil (*Brit*); ~ **qn de joie** to fill sb with joy; ~ **qn d'honneurs** to shower sb with honors.

combustible [kôńbüstēbl(ə)] *a* combustible ♦ *nm* fuel.

combustion [kôńbüstyóń] *nf* combustion.

COMECON [komákon] *sigle m* Comecon.

comédie [komādē] *nf* comedy; (*fig*) playacting *q*; **jouer la** ~ (*fig*) to put on an act; ~ **musicale** musical.

comédien, ne [komādyań, -en] *nm/f* actor/actress; (*comique*) comedy actor/actress, comedian/comedienne; (*fig*) sham.

COMES [komes] *sigle m* = *Commissariat à l'énergie solaire*.

comestible [komestēbl(ə)] *a* edible; ~s *nmpl* foods.

comète [komet] *nf* comet.

comice [komēs] *nm*: ~ **agricole** agricultural show.

comique [komēk] *a* (*drôle*) comical; (*THÉÂTRE*) comic ♦ *nm* (*artiste*) comic, comedian; **le** ~ **de qch** the funny *ou* comical side of sth.

comité [komētā] *nm* committee; **petit** ~ select group; ~ **directeur** executive (*US*) *ou* management (*Brit*) committee; ~ **d'entreprise (CE)** work council; ~ **des fêtes** festival committee.

commandant [komāndān] *nm* (*gén*) commander, commandant; (*MIL*: *grade*) major; (: *armée de l'air*) major (*US*), squadron leader (*Brit*); (*NAVIG*) captain; ~ **(de bord)** (*AVIAT*) captain.

commande [komānd] *nf* (*COMM*) order; (*INFORM*) command; ~s *nfpl* (*AVIAT etc*) controls; **passer une** ~ **(de)** to put in an order (for); **sur** ~ to order; ~ **à distance** remote control; **véhicule à double** ~ vehicle with dual controls.

commandement [komāndmān] *nm* command; (*ordre*) command, order; (*REL*) commandment.

commander [komāndā] *vt* (*COMM*) to order; (*diriger, ordonner*) to command; ~ **à** (*MIL*) to command; (*contrôler, maîtriser*) to have control over; ~ **à qn de faire** to command *ou* order sb to do.

commanditaire [komāndēter] *nm* silent (*US*) *ou* sleeping (*Brit*) partner.

commandite [komāndēt] *nf*: **(société en)** ~ limited partnership.

commanditer [komāndētā] *vt* (*COMM*) to finance, back; to commission.

commando [komāndō] *nm* commando (squad).

comme [kom] *prép* like; (*en tant que*) as ♦ *cj* as; (*parce que, puisque*) as, since ♦ *ad*: ~ **il est fort/c'est bon!** how strong he is/good it is!; **donner** ~ **prix/heure** to give the price/ time as; ~ **si** as if, as though; ~ **quoi** (*disant que*) with the result that; (*d'où il s'ensuit que*) which shows that; **faites-le** ~ **cela** *ou* **ça** do it like this *ou* this way; ~ **ça** *ou* **cela on n'aura pas d'ennuis** that way we won't have any problems; **comment ça va?** — ~ **ça** how are things? — OK; ~ **ci** ~ **ça** so-so, middling; **joli** ~ **tout** ever so pretty; ~ **on dit** as they say; ~ **de juste** needless to say; ~ **il faut** properly.

commémoration [komāmorāsyōn] *nf* commemoration.

commémorer [komāmorā] *vt* to comemorate.

commencement [komānsmān] *nm* beginning, start, commencement; ~s *nmpl* (*débuts*) beginnings.

commencer [komānsā] *vt* to begin, start, commence; (*être placé au début de*) to begin ♦ *vi* to begin, start, commence; ~ **à** *ou* **de faire** to begin *ou* start doing; ~ **par qch** to begin with sth; ~ **par faire qch** to begin by doing sth.

commensal, e, aux [komānsál, -ō] *nm/f* table companion.

comment [komān] *ad* how; ~? (*que dites-vous*) (I beg your) pardon?; ~! what! ♦ *nm*: **le** ~ **et le pourquoi** the whys and wherefores; **et** ~! and how!; ~ **donc!** of course!; ~ **faire?** how will we do it?; ~ **se fait-il que?** how is it that?

commentaire [komānter] *nm* comment; remark; ~ **(de texte)** (*SCOL*) commentary; ~ **sur image** voice-over.

commentateur, trice [komāntātœr, -trēs] *nm/f* commentator.

commenter [komāntā] *vt* (*jugement, événement*) to comment (up)on; (*RADIO, TV*: *match, manifestation*) to cover, give a commentary on.

commérages [komārázh] *nmpl* gossip *sg*.

commerçant, e [komersān, -ānt] *a* commercial; trading; (*rue*) shopping; (*personne*) commercially shrewd ♦ *nm/f* shopkeeper, trader.

commerce [komers(ə)] *nm* (*activité*) trade, commerce; (*boutique*) business; **le petit** ~ small business owners *pl*; **faire** ~ **de** to trade in; (*fig*: *péj*) to trade on; **chambre de** ~ Chamber of Commerce; **livres de** ~ (account) books; **vendu dans le** ~ sold in the stores; **vendu hors**-~ sold directly to the public; ~ **en** *ou* **de gros/détail** wholesale/ retail trade; ~ **intérieur/extérieur** domestic/ foreign market.

commercer [komersā] *vi*: ~ **avec** to trade with.

commercial, e, aux [komersyál, -ō] *a* commercial, trading; (*péj*) commercial ♦ *nm*: **les commerciaux** the commercial people.

commercialisation [komersyálēzásyōn] *nf* marketing.

commercialiser [komersyálēzā] *vt* to market.

commère [komer] *nf* gossip.

commettant [komātān] *vb voir* **commettre** ♦ *nm* (*JUR*) principal.

commettre [kometr(ə)] *vt* to commit; **se** ~ to compromise one's good name.

commis [komē] *vb voir* **commettre** ♦ *nm* (*de magasin*) sales clerk (*US*), (shop) assistant (*Brit*); (*de banque*) clerk; ~ **voyageur** traveling salesman.

commis, e [komē, -ēz] *pp de* **commettre**.

commisération [komēzārāsyōn] *nf* commiseration.

commissaire [komēser] *nm* (*de police*) ≈ (police) captain (*US*), (police) superintendent (*Brit*); (*de rencontre sportive etc*) steward; ~ **du bord** (*NAVIG*) purser; ~ **aux comptes** (*ADMIN*) auditor.

commissaire-priseur, *pl* **commissaires-priseurs** [komēserprēzœr] *nm* (official) auctioneer.

commissariat [komēsáryà] *nm* police station; (*ADMIN*) commissionership.

commission [komēsyōn] *nf* (*comité, pourcentage*) commission; (*message*) message; (*course*) errand; ~s *nfpl* (*achats*) shopping *sg*; ~ **d'examen** examining board.

commissionnaire [komēsyoner] *nm* delivery boy (*ou* man); messenger; (*TRANSPORTS*) (forwarding) agent.

commissure [komɛsür] *nf*: **les** ~**s des lèvres** the corners of the mouth.

commode [komod] *a* (*pratique*) convenient, handy; (*facile*) easy; (*air, personne*) easygoing; (*personne*): **pas** ~ awkward (to deal with) ♦ *nf* chest of drawers.

commodité [komodētā] *nf* convenience.

commotion [komōsyōn] *nf*: ~ (**cérébrale**) concussion.

commotionné, e [komōsyonā] *a* shocked, shaken.

commuer [komüā] *vt* to commute.

commun, e [komœn, -ün] *a* common; (*pièce*) communal, shared; (*réunion, effort*) joint ♦ *nf* (*ADMIN*) commune, ≈ district; (: *urbaine*) ≈ borough; ~**s** *nmpl* (*bâtiments*) outbuildings; **cela sort du** ~ it's out of the ordinary; **le** ~ **des mortels** the common run of people; **sans** ~**e mesure** incomparable; **être** ~ **à** (*suj: chose*) to be shared by; **en** ~ (*faire*) jointly; **mettre en** ~ to pool, share; **peu** ~ unusual; **d'un** ~ **accord** of one accord; with one accord.

communal, e, aux [komünál, -ō] *a* (*ADMIN*) of the commune, ≈ (district *ou* borough) council *cpd*.

communautaire [komünōter] *a* community *cpd*.

communauté [komünōtā] *nf* community; (*JUR*): **régime de la** ~ joint estate settlement.

commune [komün] *af, nf voir* **commun.**

Communes [komün] *nfpl* (*Brit: parlement*) Commons.

communiant, e [komünyân, -ânt] *nm/f* communicant; **premier** ~ child taking his first communion.

communicant, e [komünēkân, -ânt] *a* communicating.

communicatif, ive [komünēkátēf, -ēv] *a* (*personne*) communicative; (*rire*) infectious.

communication [komünēkâsyōn] *nf* communication; ~ (**téléphonique**) (telephone) call; **avoir la** ~ (**avec**) to get through (to); **vous avez la** ~ your party is on the line (*US*), you're through (*Brit*); **donnez-moi la** ~ **avec** put me through to; **mettre qn en** ~ **avec qn** (*en contact*) to put sb in touch with sb; (*au téléphone*) to connect sb with sb; ~ **interurbaine** long-distance call; ~ **en PCV** collect (*US*) *ou* reverse charge (*Brit*) call; ~ **avec préavis** person-to-person call.

communier [komünyā] *vi* (*REL*) to receive communion; (*fig*) to be united.

communion [komünyōn] *nf* communion.

communiqué [komünēkā] *nm* communiqué; ~ **de presse** press release.

communiquer [komünēkā] *vt* (*nouvelle, dossier*) to pass on, convey; (*maladie*) to pass on; (*peur etc*) to communicate; (*chaleur, mouvement*) to transmit ♦ *vi* to communicate; ~ **avec** (*suj: salle*) to communicate with; **se** ~ **à** (*se propager*) to spread to.

communisant, e [komünēzân, -ânt] *a* communistic ♦ *nm/f* communist sympathizer.

communisme [komünēsm(ə)] *nm* communism.

communiste [komünēst(ə)] *a, nm/f* communist.

commutateur [komütâtœr] *nm* (*ÉLEC*) (change-over) switch, commutator.

commutation [komütâsyōn] *nf* (*INFORM*): ~ **de messages** message switching; ~ **de paquets** packet switching.

Comores [komor] *nfpl*: **les** (**îles**) ~ the Comoros (Islands).

comorien, ne [komoryan, -en] *a* of *ou* from the Comoros.

compact, e [kōnpákt] *a* dense; compact.

compagne [kōnpány] *nf* companion.

compagnie [kōnpányē] *nf* (*firme, MIL*) company; (*groupe*) gathering; (*présence*): **la** ~ **de qn** sb's company; **homme/femme de** ~ escort; **tenir** ~ **à qn** to keep sb company; **fausser** ~ **à qn** to give sb the slip, slip *ou* sneak away from sb; **en** ~ **de** in the company of; **Dupont et** ~, **Dupont et Cie** Dupont and Company, Dupont and Co; ~ **aérienne** airline (company).

compagnon [kōnpányōn] *nm* companion; (*autrefois: ouvrier*) craftsman; journeyman.

comparable [kōnpárábl(ə)] *a*: ~ (**à**) comparable (to).

comparais [kōnpáre] *etc vb voir* **comparaître.**

comparaison [kōnpárezōn] *nf* comparison; (*métaphore*) simile; **en** ~ (**de**) in comparison (with); **par** ~ (**à**) by comparison (with).

comparaître [kōnpáretr(ə)] *vi*: ~ (**devant**) to appear (before).

comparatif, ive [kōnpárátēf, -ēv] *a, nm* comparative.

comparativement [kōnpárátēvmân] *ad* comparatively; ~ **à** by comparison with.

comparé, e [kōnpárā] *a*: **littérature** *etc* ~**e** comparative literature *etc*.

comparer [kōnpárā] *vt* to compare; ~ **qch/qn à** *ou* **et** (*pour choisir*) to compare sth/sb with *ou* and; (*pour établir une similitude*) to compare sth/sb to *ou* and.

comparse [kōnpárs(ə)] *nm/f* (*péj*) associate, stooge.

compartiment [kōnpártmân] *nm* compartment.

compartimenté, e [kōnpártēmântā] *a* partitioned; (*fig*) compartmentalized.

comparu, e [kōnpárü] *pp de* **comparaître.**

comparution [kōnpárüsyōn] *nf* appearance.

compas [kōnpá] *nm* (*GÉOM*) (pair of) compasses *pl*; (*NAVIG*) compass.

compassé, e [kōnpásā] *a* starchy, formal.

compassion [kōnpásyōn] *nf* compassion.

compatibilité [kōnpátēbēlētā] *nf* compatibility.

compatible [kōnpátēbl(ə)] *a*: ~ (**avec**) compatible (with).

compatir [kōnpátēr] *vi*: ~ (**à**) to sympathize (with).

compatissant, e [kōnpátēsân, -ânt] *a* sympathetic.

compatriote [kōnpátrēyot] *nm/f* compatriot, fellow countryman/woman.

compensateur, trice [kōnpânsátœr, -trēs] *a* compensatory.

compensation [kōnpânsâsyōn] *nf* compensation; (*BANQUE*) clearing; **en** ~ in *ou* as compensation.

compensé, e [kōnpânsā] *a*: **semelle** ~**e** platform sole.

compenser [kôṅpâṅsā] *vt* to compensate for, make up for.

compère [kôṅper] *nm* accomplice; fellow musician *ou* comedian *etc*.

compétence [kôṅpátâṅs] *nf* competence.

compétent, e [kôṅpātâṅ, -âṅt] *a* (*apte*) competent, capable; (*JUR*) competent.

compétitif, ive [kôṅpātētēf, -ēv] *a* competitive.

compétition [kôṅpātēsyôṅ] *nf* (*gén*) competition; (*SPORT*: *épreuve*) event; **la** ~ competitive sport; **être en** ~ **avec** to be competing with; **la** ~ **automobile** car racing.

compétitivité [kôṅpātētēvētā] *nf* competitiveness.

compilateur [kôṅpēlátœr] *nm* (*INFORM*) compiler.

compiler [kôṅpēlā] *vt* to compile.

complainte [kôṅplaṅt] *nf* lament.

complaire [kôṅpler]: **se** ~ *vi*: **se** ~ **dans/ parmi** to take pleasure in/in being among.

complaisais [kôṅpleze] *etc vb voir* **complaire**.

complaisamment [kôṅplezámâṅ] *ad* kindly; complacently.

complaisance [kôṅplezâṅs] *nf* kindness; (*péj*) indulgence; (: *fatuité*) complacency; **attestation de** ~ *certificate produced to oblige a patient etc*; **pavillon de** ~ flag of convenience.

complaisant, e [kôṅplezâṅ, -âṅt] *vb voir* **complaire** ♦ *a* (*aimable*) kind; obliging; (*péj*) accommodating; (: *fat*) complacent.

complaît [kôṅple] *vb voir* **complaire**.

complément [kôṅplāmâṅ] *nm* complement; (*reste*) remainder; (*LING*) complement; ~ **d'information** (*ADMIN*) supplementary *ou* further information; ~ **d'agent** agent; ~ (**d'objet**) **direct/indirect** direct/indirect object; ~ (**circonstanciel**) **de lieu/temps** adverbial phrase of place/time; ~ **de nom** possessive phrase.

complémentaire [kôṅplāmâṅter] *a* complementary; (*additionnel*) supplementary.

complet, ète [kôṅple, -et] *a* complete; (*plein*: *hôtel etc*) full ♦ *nm* (*aussi*: ~**-veston**) suit; **au** (**grand**) ~ all together.

complètement [kôṅpletmâṅ] *ad* (*en entier*) completely; (*absolument*: *fou, faux etc*) absolutely; (*à fond*: *étudier etc*) fully, in depth.

compléter [kôṅplātā] *vt* (*porter à la quantité voulue*) to complete; (*augmenter*) to complement, supplement; to add to; **se** ~ (*personnes*) to complement one another; (*collection etc*) to become complete.

complexe [kôṅpleks(ə)] *a* complex ♦ *nm* (*PSYCH*) complex, hang-up; (*bâtiments*): ~ **hospitalier/industriel** hospital/industrial complex.

complexé, e [kôṅpleksā] *a* mixed-up, hung-up.

complexité [kôṅpleksētā] *nf* complexity.

complication [kôṅplēkâsyôṅ] *nf* complexity, intricacy; (*difficulté, ennui*) complication; ~**s** *nfpl* (*MÉD*) complications.

complice [kôṅples] *nm* accomplice.

complicité [kôṅplēsētā] *nf* complicity.

compliment [kôṅplēmâṅ] *nm* (*louange*) compliment; ~**s** *nmpl* (*félicitations*) congratulations.

complimenter [kôṅplēmâṅtā] *vt*: ~ **qn** (**sur** *ou* **de**) to congratulate *ou* compliment sb (on).

compliqué, e [kôṅplēkā] *a* complicated, complex, intricate; (*personne*) complicated.

compliquer [kôṅplēkā] *vt* to complicate; **se** ~ *vi* (*situation*) to become complicated; **se** ~ **la vie** to make life difficult *ou* complicated for o.s.

complot [kôṅplō] *nm* plot.

comploter [kôṅplotā] *vi, vt* to plot.

complu, e [kôṅplü] *pp de* **complaire**.

comportement [kôṅportəmâṅ] *nm* behavior (*US*), behaviour (*Brit*); (*TECH*: *d'une pièce, d'un véhicule*) behavior (*US*), behaviour (*Brit*), performance.

comporter [kôṅportā] *vt* to be composed of, consist of, comprise; (*être équipé de*) to have; (*impliquer*) to entail, involve; **se** ~ *vi* to behave; (*TECH*) to behave, perform.

composant [kôṅpōzâṅ] *nm* component, constituent.

composante [kôṅpōzâṅt] *nf* component.

composé, e [kôṅpōzā] *a* (*visage, air*) studied; (*BIO, CHIMIE, LING*) compound ♦ *nm* (*CHIMIE, LING*) compound; ~ **de** made up of.

composer [kôṅpōzā] *vt* (*musique, texte*) to compose; (*mélange, équipe*) to make up; (*faire partie de*) to make up, form; (*TYPO*) (*type*)set ♦ *vi* (*SCOL*) to take a test; (*transiger*) to come to terms; **se** ~ **de** to be composed of, be made up of; ~ **un numéro** (*au téléphone*) to dial a number.

composite [kôṅpōzēt] *a* heterogeneous.

compositeur, trice [kôṅpōzētœr, -trēs] *nm/f* (*MUS*) composer; (*TYPO*) compositor, typesetter.

composition [kôṅpōzēsyôṅ] *nf* composition; (*SCOL*) test; (*TYPO*) (type)setting, composition; **de bonne** ~ (*accommodant*) easy to deal with; **amener qn à** ~ to get sb to come to terms; ~ **française** (*SCOL*) French essay.

compost [kôṅpost] *nm* compost.

composter [kôṅpostā] *vt* to date-stamp; to punch.

composteur [kôṅpostœr] *nm* date stamp; punch; (*TYPO*) composing stick.

compote [kôṅpot] *nf* stewed fruit *q*; ~ **de pommes** stewed apples.

compotier [kôṅpotyā] *nm* fruit dish *ou* bowl.

compréhensible [kôṅprāâṅsēbl(ə)] *a* comprehensible; (*attitude*) understandable.

compréhensif, ive [kôṅprāâṅsēf, -ēv] *a* understanding.

compréhension [kôṅprāâṅsyôṅ] *nf* understanding; comprehension.

comprendre [kôṅprâṅdr(ə)] *vt* to understand; (*se composer de*) to comprise, consist of; (*inclure*) to include; **se faire** ~ to make o.s. understood; to get one's ideas across; **mal** ~ to misunderstand.

compresse [kôṅpres] *nf* compress.

compresser [kôṅprāsā] *vt* to squash in, crush together.

compresseur [kôṅprescœr] *am voir* **rouleau**.

compressible [kôṅprāsēbl(ə)] *a* (*PHYSIQUE*) compressible; (*dépenses*) reducible.

compression [kôṅpresyôṅ] *nf* compression; (*d'un crédit etc*) reduction.

comprimé, e [kôṅprēmā] *a*: **air** ~ compressed

air ♦ *nm* tablet.

comprimer [kôṅprēmā] *vt* to compress; *(fig: crédit etc)* to reduce, cut down.

compris, e [kôṅprē̱, -ēz] *pp de* **comprendre** ♦ *a (inclus)* included; **~?** understood?, is that clear?; **~ entre** *(situé)* contained between; **la maison ~e/non ~e, y/non ~ la maison** including/excluding the house; **service ~** service (charge) included; **100 F tout ~** 100 F all-inclusive.

compromettre [kôṅprometr(ə)] *vt* to compromise.

compromis [kôṅpromē] *vb voir* **compromettre** ♦ *nm* compromise.

compromission [kôṅpromēsyôṅ] *nf* compromise, deal.

comptabiliser [kôṅtábēlēzā] *vt (valeur)* to post; *(fig)* to evaluate.

comptabilité [kôṅtábēlētā] *nf (activité, technique)* accounting, accountancy; *(d'une société: comptes)* accounts *pl*, books *pl*; *(: service)* accounts office *ou* department; **~ à partie double** double-entry book-keeping.

comptable [kôṅtábl(ə)] *nm/f* accountant ♦ *a* accounts *cpd*, accounting.

comptant [kôṅtáṅ] *ad*: **payer ~** to pay cash; **acheter ~** to buy for cash.

compte [kôṅt] *nm* count, counting; *(total, montant)* count, (right) number; *(bancaire, facture)* account; **~s** *nmpl* accounts, books; *(fig)* explanation *sg*; **ouvrir un ~** to open an account; **rendre des ~s à qn** *(fig)* to be answerable to sb; **faire le ~ de** to count up, make a count of; **tout ~ fait** on the whole; **à ce ~-là** *(dans ce cas)* in that case; *(à ce train-là)* at that rate; **en fin de ~** *(fig)* all things considered, weighing it all up; **au bout du ~** in the final analysis; **à bon ~** at a favorable price; *(fig)* lightly; **avoir son ~** *(fig: fam)* to have had it; **pour le ~ de** on behalf of; **pour son propre ~** for one's own benefit; **sur le ~ de qn** *(à son sujet)* about sb; **travailler à son ~** to work for oneself; **mettre qch sur le ~ de qn** *(le rendre responsable)* to attribute sth to sb; **prendre qch à son ~** to take responsibility for sth; **trouver son ~ à qch** to profit by sth; **régler un ~** *(s'acquitter de qch)* to settle an account; *(se venger)* to settle a score; **rendre ~ (à qn) de qch** to give (sb) an account of sth; **tenir ~ de qch** to take sth into account; **~ tenu de** taking into account; **~ chèque(s)** checking *(US) ou* current *(Brit)* account; **~ chèque postal (CCP)** Post Office account; **~ client** *(sur bilan)* accounts receivable; **~ courant (CC)** checking *(US) ou* current *(Brit)* account; **~ de dépôt** deposit account; **~ d'exploitation** operating account; **~ fournisseur** *(sur bilan)* accounts payable; **~ à rebours** countdown; **~ rendu** account, report; *(de film, livre)* review; *voir aussi* **rendre**.

compte-gouttes [kôṅtgo͞ot] *nm inv* dropper.

compter [kôṅtā] *vt* to count; *(facturer)* to charge for; *(avoir à son actif, comporter)* to have; *(prévoir)* to allow, reckon; *(tenir compte de, inclure)* to include; *(penser, espérer)*: **~ réussir/revenir** to expect to succeed/return ♦ *vi* to count; *(être économe)*

to economize; *(être non négligeable)* to count, matter; *(valoir)*: **~ pour** to count for; *(figurer)*: **~ parmi** to be *ou* rank among; **~ sur** to count (up)on; **~ avec qch/qn** to reckon with *ou* take account of sth/sb; **~ sans qch/qn** to reckon without sth/sb; **sans ~ que** besides which; **à ~ du 10 janvier** *(COMM)* (as) from 10th January.

compte-tours [kôṅtto͞or] *nm inv* rev(olution) counter.

compteur [kôṅtœr] *nm* meter; **~ de vitesse** speedometer.

comptine [kôṅtēn] *nf* nursery rhyme.

comptoir [kôṅtwár] *nm (de magasin)* counter; *(de café)* counter, bar; *(colonial)* trading post.

compulser [kôṅpülsā] *vt* to consult.

comte, comtesse [kôṅt, kôṅtes] *nm/f* count/countess.

con, ne [kôṅ, kon] *a (fam!)* damned *ou* bloody *(Brit)* stupid *(!)*.

concasser [kôṅkásā] *vt (pierre, sucre)* to crush; *(poivre)* to grind.

concave [kôṅkáv] *a* concave.

concéder [kôṅsādā] *vt* to grant; *(défaite, point)* to concede; **~ que** to concede that.

concentration [kôṅsáṅtrâsyôṅ] *nf* concentration.

concentrationnaire [kôṅsáṅtrâsyoner] *a* of *ou* in concentration camps.

concentré [kôṅsáṅtrā] *nm* concentrate; **~ de tomates** tomato purée.

concentrer [kôṅsáṅtrā] *vt* to concentrate; **se ~** to concentrate.

concentrique [kôṅsáṅtrēk] *a* concentric.

concept [kôṅsept] *nm* concept.

concepteur, trice [kôṅseptœr, -trēs] *nm/f* designer.

conception [kôṅsepsyôṅ] *nf* conception; *(d'une machine etc)* design.

concernant [kôṅsernáṅ] *prép (se rapportant à)* concerning; *(en ce qui concerne)* as regards.

concerner [kôṅsernā] *vt* to concern; **en ce qui me concerne** as far as I am concerned; **en ce qui concerne ceci** as far as this is concerned, with regard to this.

concert [kôṅser] *nm* concert; **de ~** *ad* in unison; together.

concertation [kôṅsertásyôṅ] *nf (échange de vues)* dialogue; *(rencontre)* meeting.

concerter [kôṅsertā] *vt* to devise; **se ~** *vi (collaborateurs etc)* to put our *(ou* their *etc)* heads together, consult (each other).

concertiste [kôṅsertēst(ə)] *nm/f* concert artist.

concerto [kôṅsertō] *nm* concerto.

concession [kôṅsāsyôṅ] *nf* concession.

concessionnaire [kôṅsāsyoner] *nm/f* agent, dealer.

concevable [kôṅsvábl(ə)] *a* conceivable.

concevoir [kôṅsvwár] *vt (idée, projet)* to conceive (of); *(méthode, plan d'appartement, décoration etc)* to plan, design; *(enfant)* to conceive; **maison bien/mal conçue** well-/badly-designed *ou* -planned house.

concierge [kôṅsyerzh(ə)] *nm/f* caretaker; *(d'hôtel)* head porter.

conciergerie [kôṅsyerzhərē] *nf* caretaker's lodge.

concile [kôṅsēl] *nm* council, synod.

conciliable [kôṅsēlyábl(ə)] *a* (*opinions etc*) reconcilable.

conciliabules [kôṅsēlyábül] *nmpl* (private) discussions.

conciliant, e [kôṅsēlyáṅ, -áṅt] *a* conciliatory.

conciliateur, trice [kôṅsēlyátœr, -trēs] *nm/f* mediator, go-between.

conciliation [kôṅsēlyásyôṅ] *nf* conciliation.

concilier [kôṅsēlyā] *vt* to reconcile; **se ~ qn/ l'appui de qn** to win sb over/sb's support.

concis, e [kôṅsē, -ēz] *a* concise.

concision [kôṅsēzyôṅ] *nf* concision, conciseness.

concitoyen, ne [kôṅsētwáyaṅ, -en] *nm/f* fellow citizen.

conclave [kôṅkláv] *nm* conclave.

concluant, e [kôṅklüáṅ, -áṅt] *vb voir* **conclure** ♦ *a* conclusive.

conclure [kôṅklür] *vt* to conclude; (*signer: accord, pacte*) to enter into; (*déduire*): **~ qch de qch** to deduce sth from sth; **~ à l'acquittement** to decide in favor of an acquittal; **~ au suicide** to come to the conclusion (*ou* (*JUR*) to pronounce) that it is a case of suicide; **~ un marché** to clinch a deal; **j'en conclus que** from that I conclude that.

conclusion [kôṅklüzyôṅ] *nf* conclusion; **~s** *nfpl* (*JUR*) submissions; findings; **en ~** in conclusion.

concocter [kôṅkoktā] *vt* to concoct.

conçois [kôṅswá], **conçoive** [kôṅswáv] *etc vb voir* **concevoir**.

concombre [kôṅkôṅbr(ə)] *nm* cucumber.

concomitant, e [kôṅkomētáṅ, -áṅt] *a* concomitant.

concordance [kôṅkordáṅs] *nf* concordance; **la ~ des temps** (*LING*) the sequence of tenses.

concordant, e [kôṅkordáṅ, -áṅt] *a* (*témoignages, versions*) corroborating.

concorde [kôṅkord(ə)] *nf* concord.

concorder [kôṅkordā] *vi* to tally, agree.

concourir [kôṅkōōrēr] *vi* (*SPORT*) to compete; **~ à** *vt* (*effet etc*) to work towards.

concours [kôṅkōōr] *vb voir* **concourir** ♦ *nm* competition; (*SCOL*) competitive examination; (*assistance*) aid, help; **recrutement par voie de ~** recruitment by (competitive) examination; **apporter son ~ à** to give one's support to; **~ de circonstances** combination of circumstances; **~ hippique** horse show; *voir* **hors**.

concret, ète [kôṅkre, -et] *a* concrete.

concrètement [kôṅkretmáṅ] *ad* in concrete terms.

concrétiser [kôṅkrātēzā] *vt* to realize; **se ~** *vi* to materialize.

conçu, e [kôṅsü] *pp de* **concevoir**.

concubin, e [kôṅkübaṅ, -ēn] *nm/f* (*JUR*) cohabitant.

concubinage [kôṅkübēnázh] *nm* (*JUR*) cohabitation.

concupiscence [kôṅküpēsáṅs] *nf* concupiscence.

concurremment [kôṅkürámáṅ] *ad* concurrently; jointly.

concurrence [kôṅküráṅs] *nf* competition; **jusqu'à ~ de** up to; **~ déloyale** unfair competition.

concurrent, e [kôṅküráṅ, -áṅt] *a* competing ♦ *nm/f* (*SPORT, ÉCON etc*) competitor; (*SCOL*) competitor (*US*), candidate (*Brit*).

conçus [kôṅsü] *vb voir* **concevoir**.

condamnable [kôṅdánábl(ə)] *a* (*action, opinion*) reprehensible.

condamnation [kôṅdánásyôṅ] *nf* (*action*) condemnation; sentencing; (*peine*) sentence; conviction; **~ à mort** death sentence.

condamné, e [kôṅdánā] *nm/f* (*JUR*) convict.

condamner [kôṅdánā] *vt* (*blâmer*) to condemn; (*JUR*) to sentence; (*porte, ouverture*) to fill in, block up; (*malade*) to give up (hope for); (*obliger*): **~ qn à qch/faire** to condemn sb to sth/to do; **~ qn à 2 ans de prison** to sentence sb to 2 years' imprisonment; **~ qn à une amende** to impose a fine on sb.

condensateur [kôṅdáṅsátœr] *nm* condenser.

condensation [kôṅdáṅsásyôṅ] *nf* condensation.

condensé [kôṅdáṅsā] *nm* digest.

condenser [kôṅdáṅsā] *vt*, **se ~** *vi* to condense.

condescendant, e [kôṅdāsáṅdáṅ, -áṅt] *a* (*personne, attitude*) condescending.

condescendre [kôṅdāsáṅdr(ə)] *vi*: **~ à** to condescend to.

condiment [kôṅdēmáṅ] *nm* condiment.

condisciple [kôṅdēsēpl(ə)] *nm/f* school fellow, fellow student.

condition [kôṅdēsyôṅ] *nf* condition; **~s** *nfpl* (*tarif, prix*) terms; (*circonstances*) conditions; **sans ~** *a* unconditional ♦ *ad* unconditionally; **sous ~ que** on condition that; **à ~ de** *ou* **que** provided that; **en bonne ~** in good condition; **mettre en ~** (*SPORT etc*) to get fit; (*PSYCH*) to condition (mentally); **~s de vie** living conditions.

conditionnel, le [kôṅdēsyonel] *a* conditional ♦ *nm* conditional (tense).

conditionnement [kôṅdēsyonmáṅ] *nm* (*emballage*) packaging; (*fig*) conditioning.

conditionner [kôṅdēsyonā] *vt* (*déterminer*) to determine; (*COMM: produit*) to package; (*fig: personne*) to condition; **air conditionné** air conditioning; **réflexe conditionné** conditioned reflex.

condoléances [kôṅdolāáṅs] *nfpl* condolences.

conducteur, trice [kôṅdüktœr, -trēs] *a* (*ÉLEC*) conducting ♦ *nm/f* (*AUTO etc*) driver; (*machine*) operator ♦ *nm* (*ÉLEC etc*) conductor.

conduire [kôṅdüēr] *vt* (*véhicule, passager*) to drive; (*délégation, troupeau*) to lead; **se ~** *vi* to behave; **~ vers/à** to lead towards/to; **~ qn quelque part** to take sb somewhere; to drive sb somewhere.

conduit, e [kôṅdüē, -ēt] *pp de* **conduire** ♦ *nm* (*TECH*) conduit, pipe; (*ANAT*) duct, canal.

conduite [kôṅdüēt] *nf* (*en auto*) driving; (*comportement*) behavior (*US*), behaviour (*Brit*); (*d'eau, de gaz*) pipe; **sous la ~ de** led by; **~ forcée** penstock (*US*), pressure pipe (*Brit*); **~ à gauche** left-hand drive; **~ intérieure** sedan (*US*), saloon (car) (*Brit*).

cône [kōn] *nm* cone; **en forme de ~** cone-shaped.

conf. *abr* (= *confort*): **tt ~** all modern conveniences.

confection [kôṅfeksyôṅ] *nf* (*fabrication*) making; (*COUTURE*): **la** ~ the clothing industry, the rag trade (*fam*); **vêtement de** ~ ready-to-wear garment, off-the-rack (*US*) *ou* off-the-peg (*Brit*) garment.

confectionner [kôɲfeksyonā] *vt* to make.

confédération [kôɲfādārâsyôɲ] *nf* confederation.

conférence [kôɲfārâɲs] *nf* (*exposé*) lecture; (*pourparlers*) conference; ~ **de presse** press conference; ~ **au sommet** summit (conference).

conférencier, ière [kôɲfārâɲsyā, -ycr] *nm/f* lecturer.

conférer [kôɲfārā] *vt*: ~ **à qn** (*titre, grade*) to confer on sb; ~ **à qch/qn** (*aspect etc*) to endow sth/sb with, give (to) sth/sb.

confesser [kôɲfāsā] *vt* to confess; **se** ~ *vi* (*REL*) to go to confession.

confesseur [kôɲfāscœr] *nm* confessor.

confession [kôɲfesyôɲ] *nf* confession; (*culte: catholique etc*) denomination.

confessionnal, aux [kôɲfāsyonál, -ō] *nm* confessional.

confessionnel, le [kôɲfāsyonel] *a* denominational.

confetti [kôɲfātē] *nm* confetti *q*.

confiance [kôɲfyâɲs] *nf* confidence, trust; faith; **avoir** ~ **en** to have confidence *ou* faith in, trust; **faire** ~ **à** to trust; **en toute** ~ with complete confidence; **de** ~ trustworthy, reliable; **mettre qn en** ~ to win sb's trust; **vote de** ~ (*POL*) vote of confidence; **inspirer** ~ **à** to inspire confidence in; ~ **en soi** self-confidence; *voir* **question.**

confiant, e [kôɲfyâɲ, -âɲt] *a* confident; trusting.

confidence [kôɲfēdâɲs] *nf* confidence.

confident, e [kôɲfēdâɲ, -âɲt] *nm/f* confidant/confidante.

confidentiel, le [kôɲfēdâɲsyel] *a* confidential.

confier [kôɲfyā] *vt*: ~ **à qn** (*objet en dépôt, travail etc*) to entrust to sb; (*secret, pensée*) to confide to sb; **se** ~ **à qn** to confide in sb.

configuration [kôɲfēgürâsyôɲ] *nf* configuration, layout; (*INFORM*) configuration.

confiné, e [kôɲfēnā] *a* enclosed; (*air*) stale.

confiner [kôɲfēnā] *vt*: ~ **à** to confine to; (*toucher*) to border on; **se** ~ **dans** *ou* **à** to confine o.s. to.

confins [kôɲfaɲ] *nmpl*: **aux** ~ **de** on the borders of.

confirmation [kôɲfērmâsyôɲ] *nf* confirmation.

confirmer [kôɲfērmā] *vt* to confirm; ~ **qn dans une croyance/ses fonctions** to strengthen sb in a belief/his duties.

confiscation [kôɲfēskâsyôɲ] *nf* confiscation.

confiserie [kôɲfēzrē] *nf* (*magasin*) confectioner's *ou* candy store (*US*), sweet shop (*Brit*); ~**s** *nfpl* (*bonbons*) confectionery *sg*, candy *q*, sweets (*Brit*).

confiseur, euse [kôɲfēzœr, -œz] *nm/f* confectioner.

confisquer [kôɲfēskā] *vt* to confiscate.

confit, e [kôɲfē, -ēt] *a*: **fruits** ~**s** candied fruits ♦ *nm*: ~ **d'oie** potted goose.

confiture [kôɲfētür] *nf* jam; ~ **d'oranges** (orange) marmalade.

conflagration [kôɲflâgrâsyôɲ] *nf* cataclysm.

conflictuel, le [kôɲflēktücl] *a* full of clashes *ou*

conflicts.

conflit [kôɲflē] *nm* conflict.

confluent [kôɲflüâɲ] *nm* confluence.

confondre [kôɲfôɲdr(ə)] *vt* (*jumeaux, faits*) to confuse, mix up; (*témoin, menteur*) to confound; **se** ~ *vi* to merge; **se** ~ **en excuses** to offer profuse apologies, apologize profusely; ~ **qch/qn avec qch/qn d'autre** to mistake sth/sb for sth/sb else.

confondu, e [kôɲfôɲdü] *pp de* **confondre** ♦ *a* (*stupéfait*) speechless, overcome; **toutes catégories** ~**es** taking all categories together.

conformation [kôɲformâsyôɲ] *nf* conformation.

conforme [kôɲform(ə)] *a*: ~ **à** (*en accord avec*) in accordance with, in keeping with; (*identique à*) true to; **copie certifiée** ~ (*ADMIN*) certified copy; ~ **à la commande** as per order.

conformé, e [kôɲformā] *a*: **bien** ~ well-formed.

conformément [kôɲformâmâɲ] *ad*: ~ **à** in accordance with.

conformer [kôɲformā] *vt*: ~ **qch à** to model sth on; **se** ~ **à** to conform to.

conformisme [kôɲformēsm(ə)] *nm* conformity.

conformiste [kôɲformēst(ə)] *a, nm/f* conformist.

conformité [kôɲformētā] *nf* conformity; agreement; **en** ~ **avec** in accordance with.

confort [kôɲfor] *nm* comfort; **tout** ~ (*COMM*) with all modern conveniences.

confortable [kôɲfortábl(ə)] *a* comfortable.

confortablement [kôɲfortábləmâɲ] *ad* comfortably.

conforter [kôɲfortā] *vt* to reinforce, strengthen.

confrère [kôɲfrcr] *nm* colleague; fellow member.

confrérie [kôɲfrārē] *nf* brotherhood.

confrontation [kôɲfrôɲtâsyôɲ] *nf* confrontation. ·

confronté, e [kôɲfrôɲtā] *a*: ~ **à** confronted by, facing.

confronter [kôɲfrôɲtā] *vt* to confront; (*textes*) to compare, collate.

confus, e [kôɲfü, -üz] *a* (*vague*) confused; (*embarrassé*) embarrassed.

confusément [kôɲfüzâmâɲ] *ad* (*distinguer, ressentir*) vaguely; (*parler*) confusedly.

confusion [kôɲfüzyôɲ] *nf* (*voir confus*) confusion; embarrassment; (*voir confondre*) confusion; mixing up; (*erreur*) confusion; ~ **des peines** (*JUR*) concurrency of sentences.

congé [kôɲzhā] *nm* (*vacances*) vacation (*US*), holiday (*Brit*); (*arrêt de travail*) time off *q*; leave *q*; (*MIL*) leave *q*; (*avis de départ*) notice; **en** ~ on vacation (*US*) *ou* holiday (*Brit*); off (work); on leave; **semaine/jour de** ~ week/day off; **prendre** ~ **de qn** to take one's leave of sb; **donner son** ~ **à** to hand *ou* give one's notice to; ~ **de maladie** sick leave; ~ **de maternité** maternity leave; ~**s payés** paid vacation *ou* leave.

congédier [kôɲzhādyā] *vt* to dismiss.

congélateur [kôɲzhālátœr] *nm* freezer, deep freeze.

congeler [kôṅzhlā] *vt*, **se** ~ *vi* to freeze.

congénère [kôṅzhāner] *nm/f* 'fellow (bear *ou* lion *etc*), fellow creature.

congénital, e, aux [kôṅzhānētàl, -ō] *a* congenital.

congère [kôṅzher] *nf* snowdrift.

congestion [kôṅzhestyôṅ] *nf* congestion; ~ **cérébrale** stroke; ~ **pulmonaire** congestion of the lungs.

congestionner [kôṅzhestyonā] *vt* to congest; (*MÉD*) to flush.

conglomérat [kôṅglomàrá] *nm* conglomerate.

Congo [kôṅgō] *nm*: **le** ~ (*pays, fleuve*) the Congo.

congolais, e [kôṅgole, -ez] *a* Congolese ♦ *nm/f*: **C~, e** Congolese.

congratuler [kôṅgrátülā] *vt* to congratulate.

congre [kôṅgr(ə)] *nm* conger (eel).

congrégation [kôṅgrāgásyôṅ] *nf* (*REL*) congregation; (*gén*) assembly; gathering.

congrès [kôṅgre] *nm* congress.

congressiste [kôṅgrāsēst(ə)] *nm/f* delegate, participant (at a congress).

congru, e [kôṅgrü] *a*: **la portion** ~e the smallest *ou* meanest share.

conifère [konēfer] *nm* conifer.

conique [konēk] *a* conical.

conjecture [kôṅzhektür] *nf* conjecture, speculation *q*.

conjecturer [kôṅzhektürā] *vt, vi* to conjecture.

conjoint, e [kôṅzhwaṅ, -waṅt] *a* joint ♦ *nm/f* spouse.

conjointement [kôṅzhwaṅtmáṅ] *ad* jointly.

conjonctif, ive [kôṅzhôṅktēf, -ēv] *a*: **tissu** ~ connective tissue.

conjonction [kôṅzhôṅksyôṅ] *nf* (*LING*) conjunction.

conjonctivite [kôṅzhôṅktēvēt] *nf* conjunctivitis.

conjoncture [kôṅzhôṅktür] *nf* circumstances *pl*; **la** ~ **(économique)** the economic climate *ou* situation.

conjugaison [kôṅzhügezôṅ] *nf* (*LING*) conjugation.

conjugal, e, aux [kôṅzhügàl, -ō] *a* conjugal; married.

conjuguer [kôṅzhügā] *vt* (*LING*) to conjugate; (*efforts etc*) to combine.

conjuration [kôṅzhürásyôṅ] *nf* conspiracy.

conjuré, e [kôṅzhürā] *nm/f* conspirator.

conjurer [kôṅzhürā] *vt* (*sort, maladie*) to avert; (*implorer*): ~ **qn de faire qch** to beseech *ou* entreat sb to do sth.

connais [kone], **connaissais** [konesc] *etc vb voir* **connaître**.

connaissance [konesáṅs] *nf* (*savoir*) knowledge *q*; (*personne connue*) acquaintance; (*conscience, perception*) consciousness; ~**s** *nfpl* knowledge *q*; **être sans** ~ to be unconscious; **perdre/reprendre** ~ to lose/regain consciousness; **à ma/sa** ~ to (the best of) my/his knowledge; **faire** ~ **avec qn** *ou* **la** ~ **de qn** (*rencontrer*) to meet sb; (*apprendre à connaître*) to get to know sb; **avoir** ~ **de** to be aware of; **prendre** ~ **de** (*document etc*) to peruse; **en** ~ **de cause** with full knowledge of the facts; **de** ~ (*personne, visage*) familiar.

connaissant [konesáṅ] *etc vb voir* **connaître**.

connaissement [konesmáṅ] *nm* bill of lading.

connaisseur, euse [konescœr, -œz] *nm/f* connoisseur ♦ *a* expert.

connaître [konetr(ə)] *vt* to know; (*éprouver*) to experience; (*avoir*) to have; to enjoy; ~ **de nom/vue** to know by name/sight; **se** ~ to know each other; (*soi-même*) to know o.s.; **ils se sont connus à Genève** they (first) met in Geneva; **s'y** ~ **en qch** to know about sth.

connecté, e [konektā] *a* (*INFORM*) on line.

connecter [konektā] *vt* to connect.

connerie [konrē] *nf* (*fam*) damn-fool (*US*) *ou* (bloody) stupid (*Brit*) thing to do *ou* say.

connexe [koneks(ə)] *a* closely related.

connexion [koneksyôṅ] *nf* connection.

connivence [konēvàṅs] *nf* connivance.

connu, e [konü] *pp de* **connaître** ♦ *a* (*célèbre*) well-known.

conquérant, e [kôṅkāràṅ, -àṅt] *nm/f* conqueror.

conquérir [kôṅkārēr] *vt* to conquer, win.

conquerrai [kôṅkerrā] *etc vb voir* **conquérir**.

conquête [kôṅket] *nf* conquest.

conquière, conquiers [kôṅkyer] *etc vb voir* **conquérir**.

conquis, e [kôṅkē, -ēz] *pp de* **conquérir**.

consacrer [kôṅsákrā] *vt* (*REL*): ~ **qch (à)** to consecrate sth (to); (*fig: usage etc*) to sanction, establish; (*employer*): ~ **qch à** to devote *ou* dedicate sth to; **se** ~ **à qch/faire** to dedicate *ou* devote o.s. to sth/to doing.

consanguin, e [kôṅsáṅgaṅ, -ēn] *a* between blood relations; **frère** ~ half-brother (*on father's side*); **mariage** ~ intermarriage.

consciemment [kôṅsyámáṅ] *ad* consciously.

conscience [kôṅsyáṅs] *nf* conscience; (*perception*) consciousness; **avoir/prendre** ~ **de** to be/become aware of; **perdre/reprendre** ~ to lose/regain consciousness; **avoir bonne/ mauvaise** ~ to have a clear/guilty conscience; **en (toute)** ~ in all conscience; ~ **professionnelle** professional conscience.

consciencieux, euse [kôṅsyáṅsyœ̄, -œz] *a* conscientious.

conscient, e [kôṅsyáṅ, -áṅt] *a* conscious; ~ **de** aware *ou* conscious of.

conscription [kôṅskrēpsyôṅ] *nf* draft.

conscrit [kôṅskrē] *nm* draftee.

consécration [kôṅsākrásyôṅ] *nf* consecration.

consécutif, ive [kôṅsākütēf, -ēv] *a* consecutive; ~ **à** following upon.

consécutivement [kôṅsākütēvmáṅ] *ad* consecutively; ~ **à** following on.

conseil [kôṅsey] *nm* (*avis*) piece of advice, advice *q*; (*assemblée*) council; (*expert*): ~ **en recrutement** recruitment consultant ♦ *a*: **ingénieur-**~ consulting engineer, engineering consultant; **tenir** ~ to hold a meeting; to deliberate; **donner un** ~ *ou* **des** ~**s à qn** to give sb (a piece of) advice; **demander** ~ **à qn** to ask sb's advice; **prendre** ~ **(auprès de qn)** to seek advice (from sb); ~ **d'administration (CA)** board (of directors); ~ **de classe** (*SCOL*) meeting of teachers, parents and class representatives to discuss pupils' progress; ~ **de discipline** disciplinary committee; ~ **général** regional council; ~ **de guerre** court-martial; **le** ~ **des ministres** ≈ the Cabinet; ~ **municipal (CM)** town council;

~ **régional** *regional board of elected representatives*; ~ **de révision** recruitment *ou* draft (*US*) board.

conseiller [kɔ̃sɛyā] *vt* (*personne*) to advise; (*méthode, action*) to recommend, advise; ~ **qch à qn** to recommend sth to sb; ~ **à qn de faire qch** to advise sb to do sth.

conseiller, ère [kɔ̃sɛyā, -er] *nm/f* adviser; ~ **matrimonial** marriage guidance counsellor; ~ **municipal** town *ou* city councilman (*US*), town councillor (*Brit*).

consentement [kɔ̃sɑ̃tmɑ̃] *nm* consent.

consentir [kɔ̃sɑ̃tēr] *vt*: ~ (**à qch/faire**) to agree *ou* consent (to sth/to doing); ~ **qch à qn** to grant sb sth.

conséquence [kɔ̃sākɑ̃s] *nf* consequence, outcome; ~**s** *nfpl* consequences, repercussions; **en** ~ (*donc*) consequently; (*de façon appropriée*) accordingly; **ne pas tirer à** ~ to be unlikely to have any repercussions; **sans** ~ unimportant; **de** ~ important.

conséquent, e [kɔ̃sākɑ̃, -ɑ̃t] *a* logical, rational; (*fam: important*) substantial; **par** ~ consequently.

conservateur, trice [kɔ̃sɛrvátœr, -trēs] *a* conservative ♦ *nm/f* (*POL*) conservative; (*de musée*) curator.

conservation [kɔ̃sɛrvâsyɔ̃] *nf* retention; keeping; preserving; preservation.

conservatoire [kɔ̃sɛrvátwár] *nm* academy; (*ÉCOLOGIE*) conservation area.

conserve [kɔ̃sɛrv(ə)] *nf* (*gén pl*) canned food; ~**s de poisson** canned fish; **en** ~ canned; **de** ~ (*ensemble*) in concert; (*naviguer*) in convoy.

conservé, e [kɔ̃sɛrvā] *a*: **bien** ~ (*personne*) well-preserved.

conserver [kɔ̃sɛrvā] *vt* (*faculté*) to retain, keep; (*habitude*) to keep up; (*amis, livres*) to keep; (*préserver, aussi CULIN*) to preserve; **se** ~ *vi* (*aliments*) to keep; "~ **au frais**" "store in a cool place".

conserverie [kɔ̃sɛrvərē] *nf* canning factory.

considérable [kɔ̃sēdārábl(ə)] *a* considerable, significant, extensive.

considération [kɔ̃sēdārásyɔ̃] *nf* consideration; (*estime*) esteem, respect; ~**s** *nfpl* (*remarques*) reflections; **prendre en** ~ to take into consideration *ou* account; **ceci mérite** ~ this is worth considering; **en** ~ **de** given, because of.

considéré, e [kɔ̃sēdārā] *a* respected; **tout bien** ~ all things considered.

considérer [kɔ̃sēdārā] *vt* to consider; (*regarder*) to consider, study; ~ **qch comme** to regard sth as.

consigne [kɔ̃sēɲ] *nf* (*COMM*) deposit; (*de gare*) checkroom (*US*), left luggage (office) (*Brit*); (*punition: SCOL*) detention; (: *MIL*) confinement to barracks; (*ordre, instruction*) instructions *pl*; ~ **automatique** luggage locker; ~**s de sécurité** safety instructions.

consigné, e [kɔ̃sēɲā] *a* (*COMM: bouteille, emballage*) returnable; **non** ~ non-returnable.

consigner [kɔ̃sēɲā] *vt* (*note, pensée*) to record; (*marchandises*) to deposit; (*punir: MIL*) to confine to barracks; (: *élève*) to keep in; (*COMM*) to put a deposit on.

consistance [kɔ̃sēstɑ̃s] *nf* consistency.

consistant, e [kɔ̃sēstɑ̃, -ɑ̃t] *a* thick; solid.

consister [kɔ̃sēstā] *vi*: ~ **en/dans/à faire** to consist of/in/in doing.

consœur [kɔ̃sœr] *nf* (*lady*) colleague; fellow member.

consolation [kɔ̃sɔlásyɔ̃] *nf* consolation *q*, comfort *q*.

console [kɔ̃sɔl] *nf* console; ~ **graphique** *ou* **de visualisation** (*INFORM*) visual display unit, VDU.

consoler [kɔ̃sɔlā] *vt* to console; **se** ~ (**de qch**) to console o.s. (for sth).

consolider [kɔ̃sɔlēdā] *vt* to strengthen, reinforce; (*fig*) to consolidate; **bilan consolidé** consolidated balance sheet.

consommateur, trice [kɔ̃sɔmátœr, -trēs] *nm/f* (*ÉCON*) consumer; (*dans un café*) customer.

consommation [kɔ̃sɔmásyɔ̃] *nf* consumption; (*JUR*) consummation; (*boisson*) drink; ~ **aux 100 km** (*AUTO*) (fuel) consumption per 100 km, ≈ miles per gallon (mpg), ≈ gas mileage (*US*); **de** ~ (*biens, société*) consumer *cpd*.

consommé, e [kɔ̃sɔmā] *a* consummate ♦ *nm* consommé.

consommer [kɔ̃sɔmā] *vt* (*suj: personne*) to eat *ou* drink, consume; (*suj: voiture, usine, poêle*) to use, consume; (*JUR*) to consummate ♦ *vi* (*dans un café*) to (have a) drink.

consonance [kɔ̃sɔnɑ̃s] *nf* consonance; **nom à** ~ **étrangère** foreign-sounding name.

consonne [kɔ̃sɔn] *nf* consonant.

consorts [kɔ̃sɔr] *nmpl*: **et** ~ (*péj*) and company, and his bunch *ou* like.

conspirateur, trice [kɔ̃spērátœr, -trēs] *nm/f* conspirator, plotter.

conspiration [kɔ̃spērásyɔ̃] *nf* conspiracy.

conspirer [kɔ̃spērā] *vi* to conspire, plot; ~ **à** (*tendre à*) to conspire to.

conspuer [kɔ̃spüā] *vt* to boo, shout down.

constamment [kɔ̃stámɑ̃] *ad* constantly.

constant, e [kɔ̃stɑ̃, -ɑ̃t] *a* constant; (*personne*) steadfast ♦ *nf* constant.

Constantinople [kɔ̃stɑ̃tēnopl(ə)] *n* Constantinople.

constat [kɔ̃stá] *nm* (*d'huissier*) certified report (*by bailiff*); (*de police*) report; (*observation*) (observed) fact, observation; (*affirmation*) statement; ~ (**à l'amiable**) (*jointly agreed*) statement for insurance purposes.

constatation [kɔ̃státásyɔ̃] *nf* noticing; certifying; (*remarque*) observation.

constater [kɔ̃státā] *vt* (*remarquer*) to note, notice; (*ADMIN, JUR: attester*) to certify; (*dégâts*) to note; ~ **que** (*dire*) to state that.

constellation [kɔ̃stālásyɔ̃] *nf* constellation.

constellé, e [kɔ̃stālā] *a*: ~ **de** (*étoiles*) studded *ou* spangled with; (*taches*) spotted with.

consternation [kɔ̃stɛrnásyɔ̃] *nf* consternation, dismay.

consterner [kɔ̃stɛrnā] *vt* to dismay.

constipation [kɔ̃stēpásyɔ̃] *nf* constipation.

constipé, e [kɔ̃stēpā] *a* constipated; (*fig*) stiff.

constituant, e [kɔ̃stētüɑ̃, -ɑ̃t] *a* (*élément*)

constituent; **assemblée** ~**e** (POL) constituent assembly.

constitué, e [kôṅstētüä] a: ~ **de** made up ou composed of; **bien** ~ of sound constitution; well-formed.

constituer [kôṅstētüä] vt (comité, équipe) to set up, form; (dossier, collection) to put together, build up; (suj: éléments, parties: composer) to make up, constitute; (re-présenter, être) to constitute; **se** '~ **prisonnier** to give o.s. up; **se** ~ **partie civile** to bring an independent action for damages.

constitution [kôṅstētüsyôṅ] nf setting up; building up; (composition) composition, make-up; (santé, POL) constitution.

constitutionnel, le [kôṅstētüsyonel] a constitutional.

constructeur [kôṅstrüktœr] nm manufacturer, builder.

constructif, ive [kôṅstrüktēf, -ēv] a (positif) constructive.

construction [kôṅstrüksyôṅ] nf construction, building.

construire [kôṅstrüēr] vt to build, construct; **se** ~: **l'immeuble s'est construit très vite** the building went up ou was built very quickly.

consul [kôṅsül] nm consul.

consulaire [kôṅsüler] a consular.

consulat [kôṅsülä] nm consulate.

consultatif, ive [kôṅsültätēf, -ēv] a advisory.

consultation [kôṅsültäsyôṅ] nf consultation; ~**s** nfpl (POL) talks; **être en** ~ (délibération) to be in consultation; (médecin) to be consulting; **aller à la** ~ (MÉD) to go to the doctor's office (US) ou surgery (Brit); **heures de** ~ (MÉD) office (US) ou surgery (Brit) hours.

consulter [kôṅsültä] vt to consult ♦ vi (médecin) to be in (the office) (US), hold surgery (Brit); **se** ~ to confer.

consumer [kôṅsümä] vt to consume; **se** ~ vi to burn; **se** ~ **de chagrin/douleur** to be consumed with sorrow/grief.

consumérisme [kôṅsümärēsm(ə)] nm consumerism.

contact [kôṅtäkt] nm contact; **au** ~ **de** (air, peau) on contact with; (gens) through contact with; **mettre/couper le** ~ (AUTO) to switch on/off the ignition; **entrer en** ~ (fils, objets) to come into contact, make contact; **se mettre en** ~ **avec** (RADIO) to make contact with; **prendre** ~ **avec** (relation d'affaires, connaissance) to get in touch ou contact with.

contacter [kôṅtäktä] vt to contact, get in touch with.

contagieux, euse [kôṅtäzhyœ, -œz] a contagious; infectious.

contagion [kôṅtäzhyôṅ] nf contagion.

container [kôṅtener] nm container.

contaminer [kôṅtämēnä] vt to contaminate.

conte [kôṅt] nm tale; ~ **de fées** fairy tale.

contemplation [kôṅtäṅpläsyôṅ] nf contemplation; (REL, PHILOSOPHIE) meditation.

contempler [kôṅtäṅplä] vt to contemplate, gaze at.

contemporain, e [kôṅtäṅporaṅ, -en] a, nm/f contemporary.

contenance [kôṅtnâṅs] nf (d'un récipient) capacity; (attitude) bearing, attitude; **perdre** ~ to lose one's composure; **se donner une** ~ to give the impression of composure; **faire bonne** ~ **(devant)** to put on a bold front (in the face of).

conteneur [kôṅtnœr] nm container.

conteneurisation [kôṅtnœrēzâsyôṅ] nf containerization.

contenir [kôṅtnēr] vt to contain; (avoir une capacité de) to hold; **se** ~ (se retenir) to control o.s. ou one's emotions, contain o.s.

content, e [kôṅtâṅ, -âṅt] a pleased, glad; ~ **de** pleased with; **je serais** ~ **que tu** ... I would be pleased if you ....

contentement [kôṅtâṅtmâṅ] nm contentment, satisfaction.

contenter [kôṅtâṅtä] vt to satisfy, please; (envie) to satisfy; **se** ~ **de** to content o.s. with.

contentieux [kôṅtâṅsyœ] nm (COMM) litigation; (: service) litigation department; (POL etc) contentious issues pl.

contenu, e [kôṅtnü] pp de **contenir** ♦ nm (d'un bol) contents pl; (d'un texte) content.

conter [kôṅtä] vt to recount, relate; **en** ~ **de belles à qn** to tell tall stories to sb.

contestable [kôṅtestâbl(ə)] a questionable.

contestataire [kôṅtestáter] a (journal, étudiant) anti-establishment ♦ nm/f (anti-establishment) protester.

contestation [kôṅtestâsyôṅ] nf questioning, contesting; (POL): **la** ~ anti-establishment activity, protest.

conteste [kôṅtest(ə)]: **sans** ~ ad unquestionably, indisputably.

contesté, e [kôṅtestä] a (roman, écrivain) controversial.

contester [kôṅtestä] vt to question, contest ♦ vi (POL, gén) to protest, rebel (against established authority).

conteur, euse [kôṅtœr, -œz] nm/f story-teller.

contexte [kôṅtekst(ə)] nm context.

contiendrai [kôṅtyäṅdrä], **contiens** [kôṅtyaṅ] etc vb voir **contenir**.

contigu, ë [kôṅtēgü] a: ~ **(à)** adjacent (to).

continent [kôṅtēnâṅ] nm continent.

continental, e, aux [kôṅtēnâṅtál, -ō] a continental.

contingences [kôṅtäṅzhâṅs] nfpl contingencies.

contingent [kôṅtäṅzhâṅ] nm (MIL) contingent; (COMM) quota.

contingenter [kôṅtäṅzhâṅtä] vt (COMM) to fix a quota on.

contins [kôṅtaṅ] etc vb voir **contenir**.

continu, e [kôṅtēnü] a continuous; **(courant)** ~ direct current, DC.

continuation [kôṅtēnüäsyôṅ] nf continuation.

continuel, le [kôṅtēnüel] a (qui se répète) constant, continual; (continu) continuous.

continuellement [kôṅtēnüelmâṅ] ad continually; continuously.

continuer [kôṅtēnüä] vt (travail, voyage etc) to continue (with), carry on (with), go on (with); (prolonger: alignement, rue) to continue ♦ vi (pluie, vie, bruit) to continue, go on; (voyageur) to go on; **se** ~ vi to carry on; ~ **à** ou **de faire** to go on ou continue doing.

continuité [kôṅtēnüētä] nf continuity; continuation.

contondant, e [kôǹtôǹdâǹ, -âǹt] *a*: **arme ~e** blunt instrument.

contorsion [kôǹtorsyôǹ] *nf* contortion.

contorsionner [kôǹtorsyonâ]: **se ~** *vi* to contort o.s., writhe about.

contour [kôǹtōōr] *nm* outline, contour; **~s** *nmpl* (*d'une rivière etc*) windings.

contourner [kôǹtōōrnâ] *vt* to bypass, walk (*ou* drive) around.

contraceptif, ive [kôǹtrâseptēf, -ēv] *a, nm* contraceptive.

contraception [kôǹtrâsepsyôǹ] *nf* contraception.

contracté, e [kôǹtrâktâ] *a* (*muscle*) tense, contracted; (*personne: tendu*) tense, tensed up; **article ~** (*LING*) contracted article.

contracter [kôǹtrâktâ] *vt* (*muscle etc*) to tense, contract; (*maladie, dette, obligation*) to contract; (*assurance*) to take out; **se ~** *vi* (*métal, muscles*) to contract.

contraction [kôǹtrâksyôǹ] *nf* contraction.

contractuel, le [kôǹtrâktücl] *a* contractual ♦ *nm/f* (*agent*) traffic policeman (*US*)/meter maid (*US*), traffic warden (*Brit*); (*employé*) contract employee.

contradiction [kôǹtrâdēksyôǹ] *nf* contradiction.

contradictoire [kôǹtrâdēktwâr] *a* contradictory, conflicting; **débat ~** (open) debate.

contraignant, e [kôǹtrenyâǹ, -âǹt] *vb voir* **contraindre** ♦ *a* restricting.

contraindre [kôǹtraǹdr(ǝ)] *vt*: **~ qn à faire** to force *ou* compel sb to do.

contraint, e [kôǹtraǹ, -aǹt] *pp de* **contraindre** ♦ *a* (*mine, air*) constrained, forced ♦ *nf* constraint; **sans ~e** unrestrainedly, unconstrainedly.

contraire [kôǹtrɛr] *a, nm* opposite; **~ à** contrary to; **au ~** *ad* on the contrary.

contrairement [kôǹtrɛrmâǹ] *ad*: **~ à** contrary to, unlike.

contralto [kôǹtrâltō] *nm* contralto.

contrariant, e [kôǹtrâryâǹ, -âǹt] *a* (*personne*) contrary, perverse; (*incident*) annoying.

contrarier [kôǹtrâryâ] *vt* (*personne*) to annoy, bother; (*fig*) to impede; to thwart, frustrate.

contrariété [kôǹtrâryâtâ] *nf* annoyance.

contraste [kôǹtrâst(ǝ)] *nm* contrast.

contraster [kôǹtrâstâ] *vt, vi* to contrast.

contrat [kôǹtrâ] *nm* contract; (*fig: accord, pacte*) agreement; **~ de travail** employment contract.

contravention [kôǹtrâvâǹsyôǹ] *nf* (*infraction*): **~ à** infraction (*US*) *ou* contravention (*Brit*) of; (*amende*) fine; (*PV pour stationnement interdit*) parking ticket; **dresser ~ à** (*automobiliste*) to write out a parking ticket for.

contre [kôǹtr(ǝ)] *prép* against; (*en échange*) (in exchange) for; **par ~** on the other hand.

contre-amiral, aux [kôǹtrâmērâl, -ō] *nm* rear admiral.

contre-attaque [kôǹtrâtâk] *nf* counter-attack.

contre-attaquer [kôǹtrâtâkâ] *vi* to counter-attack.

contre-balancer [kôǹtrǝbâlâǹsâ] *vt* to counter-balance; (*fig*) to offset.

contrebande [kôǹtrǝbâǹd] *nf* (*trafic*) contraband, smuggling; (*marchandise*) contraband, smuggled goods *pl*; **faire la ~ de** to smuggle.

contrebandier, ière [kôǹtrǝbâǹdyâ, -yɛr] *nm/f* smuggler.

contrebas [kôǹtrǝbâ]: **en ~** *ad* (down) below.

contrebasse [kôǹtrǝbâs] *nf* (double) bass.

contrebassiste [kôǹtrǝbâsēst(ǝ)] *nm/f* (double) bass player.

contre-braquer [kôǹtrǝbrâkâ] *vi* to steer into a skid.

contrecarrer [kôǹtrǝkârâ] *vt* to thwart.

contrechamp [kôǹtrǝshâǹ] *nm* (*CINÉMA*) reverse shot.

contrecœur [kôǹtrǝkœr]: **à ~** *ad* (be)grudgingly, reluctantly.

contrecoup [kôǹtrǝkōō] *nm* repercussions *pl*; **par ~** as an indirect consequence.

contre-courant [kôǹtrǝkōōrâǹ]: **à ~** *ad* against the current.

contredire [kôǹtrǝdēr] *vt* (*personne*) to contradict; (*témoignage, assertion, faits*) to refute; **se ~** to contradict o.s.

contredit, e [kôǹtrǝdē, -ēt] *pp de* **contredire** ♦ *nm*: **sans ~** without question.

contrée [kôǹtrâ] *nf* region; land.

contre-écrou [kôǹtrâkrōō] *nm* lock nut.

contre-espionnage [kôǹtrespyonâzh] *nm* counter-espionage.

contre-expertise [kôǹtrekspertēz] *nf* second (expert) assessment.

contrefaçon [kôǹtrǝfâsôǹ] *nf* forgery; **~ de brevet** patent infringement.

contrefaire [kôǹtrǝfɛr] *vt* (*document, signature*) to forge, counterfeit; (*personne, démarche*) to mimic; (*dénaturer: sa voix etc*) to disguise.

contrefait, e [kôǹtrǝfɛ, -ɛt] *pp de* **contrefaire** ♦ *a* misshapen, deformed.

contrefasse [kôǹtrǝfâs], **contreferai** [kôǹtrǝfrâ] *etc vb voir* **contrefaire**.

contre-filet [kôǹtrǝfēlɛ] *nm* (*CULIN*) sirloin.

contreforts [kôǹtrǝfor] *nmpl* foothills.

contre-haut [kôǹtrǝō]: **en ~** *ad* (up) above.

contre-indication [kôǹtraǹdēkâsyôǹ] *nf* contra-indication.

contre-interrogatoire [kôǹtraǹtârogâtwâr] *nm*: **faire subir un ~ à qn** to cross-examine sb.

contre-jour [kôǹtrǝzhōōr]: **à ~** *ad* against the light.

contremaître [kôǹtrǝmɛtr(ǝ)] *nm* foreman.

contre-manifestation [kôǹtrǝmâǹēfestâsyôǹ] *nf* counter-demonstration.

contremarque [kôǹtrǝmârk(ǝ)] *nf* (*ticket*) pass-out check (*US*) *ou* ticket (*Brit*).

contre-offensive [kôǹtrofâǹsēv] *nf* counter-offensive.

contre-ordre [kôǹtrordr(ǝ)] *nm* = **contrordre**.

contrepartie [kôǹtrǝpârtē] *nf* compensation; **en ~** in compensation; in return.

contre-performance [kôǹtrǝperformâǹs] *nf* below-average performance.

contrepèterie [kôǹtrǝpɛtrē] *nf* spoonerism.

contre-pied [kôǹtrǝpyâ] *nm* (*inverse, opposé*): **le ~ de ...** the exact opposite of ...; **prendre le ~ de** to take the opposing view of; to take the opposite course to; **prendre qn à ~** (*SPORT*) to throw sb off balance.

contre-plaqué [kôṅtrəplákā] *nm* plywood.
contre-plongée [kôṅtrəplóṅzhā] *nf* low-angle shot.
contrepoids [kôṅtrəpwá] *nm* counterweight, counterbalance; **faire** ~ to act as a counterbalance.
contrepoil [kôṅtrəpwál]: **à** ~ *ad* the wrong way.
contrepoint [kôṅtrəpwaṅ] *nm* counterpoint.
contrepoison [kôṅtrəpwázôṅ] *nm* antidote.
contrer [kôṅtrā] *vt* to counter.
contre-révolution [kôṅtrərāvolüsyóṅ] *nf* counter-revolution.
contresens [kôṅtrəsáṅs] *nm* misinterpretation; (*mauvaise traduction*) mistranslation; (*absurdité*) nonsense *q*; **à** ~ *ad* the wrong way.
contresigner [kôṅtrəsēnyā] *vt* to countersign.
contretemps [kôṅtrətáṅ] *nm* hitch, contretemps; **à** ~ *ad* (*MUS*) out of time; (*fig*) at an inopportune moment.
contre-terrorisme [kôṅtrəterorēsm(ə)] *nm* counter-terrorism.
contre-torpilleur [kôṅtrətorpēyœr] *nm* destroyer.
contrevenant, e [kôṅtrəvnáṅ, -áṅt] *vb voir* **contrevenir ♦** *nm/f* offender.
contrevenir [kôṅtrəvnēr]: ~ **à** *vt* to contravene.
contrevoie [kôṅtrəvwá]: **à** ~ *ad* (*en sens inverse*) on the wrong track; (*du mauvais côté*) on the wrong side.
contribuable [kôṅtrēbüábl(ə)] *nm/f* taxpayer.
contribuer [kôṅtrēbüā]: ~ **à** *vt* to contribute towards.
contribution [kôṅtrēbüsyóṅ] *nf* contribution; **les** ~**s** (*bureaux*) the tax office; **mettre à** ~ to call upon; ~**s directes/indirectes** direct/indirect taxation.
contrit, e [kôṅtrē, -ēt] *a* contrite.
contrôle [kôṅtrōl] *nm* checking *q*, check; supervision; monitoring; (*test*) test, examination; **perdre le** ~ **de son véhicule** to lose control of one's vehicle; ~ **des changes** (*COMM*) exchange controls; ~ **continu** (*SCOL*) continuous assessment; ~ **d'identité** identity check; ~ **des naissances** birth control; ~ **des prix** price control.
contrôler [kôṅtrōlā] *vt* (*vérifier*) to check; (*surveiller*) to supervise; to monitor, control; (*maîtriser*, *COMM*: *firme*) to control; **se** ~ to control o.s.
contrôleur, euse [kôṅtrōlœr, -œz] *nm/f* (*de train*) (ticket) inspector; (*de bus*) (bus) conductor/tress; ~ **de la navigation aérienne** air traffic controller; ~ **financier** financial controller.
contrordre [kôṅtrordr(ə)] *nm* counter-order, countermand; **sauf** ~ unless otherwise directed.
controverse [kôṅtrovers(ə)] *nf* controversy.
controversé, e [kôṅtroversā] *a* (*personnage, question*) controversial.
contumace [kôṅtümás]: **par** ~ *ad* in absentia.
contusion [kôṅtüzyóṅ] *nf* bruise, contusion.
contusionné, e [kôṅtüzyonā] *a* bruised.
conurbation [konürbásyóṅ] *nf* conurbation.
convaincant, e [kôṅvaṅkáṅ, -áṅt] *vb voir* **convaincre ♦** *a* convincing.

convaincre [kôṅvaṅkr(ə)] *vt*: ~ **qn (de qch)** to convince sb (of sth); ~ **qn (de faire)** to persuade sb (to do); ~ **qn de** (*JUR*: *délit*) to convict sb of.
convaincu, e [kôṅvaṅkü] *pp de* **convaincre ♦** *a*: **d'un ton** ~ with conviction.
convainquais [kôṅvaṅkc] *etc vb voir* **convaincre**.
convalescence [kôṅválāsáṅs] *nf* convalescence; **maison de** ~ convalescent home.
convalescent, e [kôṅválāsáṅ, -áṅt] *a*, *nm/f* convalescent.
convenable [kôṅvnábl(ə)] *a* suitable; (*décent*) acceptable, proper; (*assez bon*) decent, acceptable; adequate, passable.
convenablement [kôṅvnábləmáṅ] *ad* (*placé, choisi*) suitably; (*s'habiller, s'exprimer*) properly; (*payé, logé*) decently.
convenance [kôṅvnáṅs] *nf*: **à ma/votre** ~ to my/your liking; ~**s** *nfpl* proprieties.
convenir [kôṅvnēr] *vt* to be suitable; ~ **à** to suit; **il convient de** it is advisable to; (*bienséant*) it is right *ou* proper to; ~ **de** (*bien-fondé de qch*) to admit (to), acknowledge; (*date, somme etc*) to agree upon; ~ **que** (*admettre*) to admit that, acknowledge the fact that; ~ **de faire qch** to agree to do sth; **il a été convenu que** it has been agreed that; **comme convenu** as agreed.
convention [kôṅváṅsyóṅ] *nf* convention; ~**s** *nfpl* (*convenances*) convention *sg*, social conventions; **de** ~ conventional; ~ **collective** (*ÉCON*) collective agreement.
conventionné, e [kôṅváṅsyonā] *a* (*ADMIN*) applying charges laid down by the state.
conventionnel, le [kôṅváṅsyoncl] *a* conventional.
conventuel, le [kôṅváṅtücl] *a* monastic; monastery *cpd*; conventual, convent *cpd*.
convenu, e [kôṅvnōō] *pp de* **convenir ♦** *a* agreed.
convergent, e [kôṅverzháṅ, -áṅt] *a* convergent.
converger [kôṅverzhā] *vi* to converge; ~ **vers** *ou* **sur** to converge on.
conversation [kôṅversásyóṅ] *nf* conversation; **avoir de la** ~ to be a good conversationalist.
converser [kôṅversā] *vi* to converse.
conversion [kôṅversyóṅ] *nf* conversion; (*SKI*) kick turn.
convertible [kôṅvertēbl(ə)] *a* (*ÉCON*) convertible; (**canapé**) ~ sofa bed.
convertir [kôṅvertēr] *vt*: ~ **qn (à)** to convert sb (to); ~ **qch en** to convert sth into; **se** ~ **(à)** to be converted (to).
convertisseur [kôṅvertēsœr] *nm* (*ÉLEC*) converter.
convexe [kôṅveks(ə)] *a* convex.
conviction [kôṅvēksyóṅ] *nf* conviction.
conviendrai [kôṅvyaṅdrā], **conviens** [kôṅvyaṅ] *etc vb voir* **convenir**.
convier [kôṅvyā] *vt*: ~ **qn à** (*dîner etc*) to (cordially) invite sb to; ~ **qn à faire** to urge sb to do.
convint [kôṅvaṅ] *etc vb voir* **convenir**.
convive [kôṅvēv] *nm/f* guest (*at table*).
convivial, e [kôṅvēvyál] *a* (*INFORM*) user-friendly.

convocation [kôṅvokâsyôṅ] *nf* (*voir convoquer*) convening, convoking; summoning; invitation; (*document*) notification to attend; summons *sg*.

convoi [kôṅvwȧ] *nm* (*de voitures, prisonniers*) convoy; (*train*) train; ~ **(funèbre)** funeral procession.

convoiter [kôṅvwȧtȧ] *vt* to covet.

convoitise [kôṅvwȧtēz] *nf* covetousness; (*sexuelle*) lust, desire.

convoler [kôṅvolȧ] *vi*: ~ **(en justes noces)** to be wed.

convoquer [kôṅvokȧ] *vt* (*assemblée*) to convene, convoke; (*subordonné, témoin*) to summon; (*candidat*) to ask to attend; ~ **qn (à)** (*réunion*) to invite sb (to attend).

convoyer [kôṅvwȧyȧ] *vt* to escort.

convoyeur [kôṅvwȧyœr] *nm* (*NAVIG*) escort ship; ~ **de fonds** security guard.

convulsé, e [kôṅvülsȧ] *a* (*visage*) distorted.

convulsions [kôṅvülsyôṅ] *nfpl* convulsions.

coopérant [koopārȧṅ] *nm* ≈ member of the Peace Corps (*US*), ≈ person doing Voluntary Service Overseas (*Brit*).

coopératif, ive [koopārȧtēf, -ēv] *a*, *nf* co-operative.

coopération [koopārȧsyôṅ] *nf* co-operation; (*ADMIN*): **la C~** ≈ the Peace Corps (*US*), *done as alternative to military service*, ≈ Voluntary Service Overseas (*Brit*).

coopérer [koopārȧ] *vi*: ~ **(à)** to co-operate (in).

coordination [koordēnȧsyôṅ] *nf* coordination.

coordonné, e [koordonȧ] *a* coordinated ♦ *nf* (*LING*) coordinate clause; ~**s** *nmpl* (*vêtements*) coordinates; ~**es** *nfpl* (*MATH*) co-ordinates; (*détails personnels*) address, phone number, schedule *etc*; whereabouts.

coordonner [koordonȧ] *vt* to coordinate.

copain, copine [kopȧṅ, kopēn] *nm/f* pal, chum ♦ *a*: **être** ~ **avec** to be chummy with.

copeau, x [kopō] *nm* shaving; (*de métal*) turning.

Copenhague [kopǝnȧg] *n* Copenhagen.

copie [kopē] *nf* copy; (*SCOL*) paper; exercise; ~ **certifiée conforme** certified copy; ~ **papier** (*INFORM*) hard copy.

copier [kopyȧ] *vt, vi* to copy; ~ **sur** to copy from.

copieur [kopyœr] *nm* (photo)copier.

copieusement [kopyœzmȧṅ] *ad* copiously.

copieux, euse [kopyœ̄, -œz] *a* copious, hearty.

copilote [kopēlot] *nm* (*AVIAT*) co-pilot; (*AUTO*) co-driver, navigator.

copine [kopēn] *nf voir* **copain**.

copiste [kopēst(ǝ)] *nm/f* copyist, transcriber.

coproduction [koprodüksyôṅ] *nf* coproduction, joint production.

copropriété [koproprēyȧtȧ] *nf* co-ownership, joint ownership; **acheter en** ~ to buy on a co-ownership basis.

copulation [kopülȧsyôṅ] *nf* copulation.

coq [kok] *nm* cock, rooster ♦ *a inv* (*BOXE*): **poids** ~ bantamweight; ~ **de bruyère** grouse; ~ **du village** (*fig*: *péj*) ladykiller.

coq-à-l'âne [kokȧlȧn] *nm inv* abrupt change of subject.

coque [kok] *nf* (*de noix, mollusque*) shell; (*de bateau*) hull; **à la** ~ (*CULIN*) (soft-)boiled.

coquelet [koklȅ] *nm* (*CULIN*) cockerel.

coquelicot [koklȅkō] *nm* poppy.

coqueluche [koklüsh] *nf* whooping-cough; (*fig*): **être la** ~ **de qn** to be sb's flavor of the month.

coquet, te [kokȅ, -et] *a* appearance-conscious; (*joli*) pretty.

coquetier [koktyȧ] *nm* egg-cup.

coquettement [kokȅtmȧṅ] *ad* (*s'habiller*) attractively; (*meubler*) prettily.

coquetterie [kokȅtrȅ] *nf* appearance-conciousness.

coquillage [kokȅyȧzh] *nm* (*mollusque*) shellfish *inv*; (*coquille*) shell.

coquille [kokȅy] *nf* shell; (*TYPO*) misprint; ~ **de beurre** shell of butter; ~ **d'œuf** *a* (*couleur*) eggshell; ~ **de noix** nutshell; ~ **St Jacques** scallop.

coquillettes [kokȅyet] *nfpl* pasta shells.

coquin, e [kokȧṅ, -ēn] *a* mischievous, roguish; (*polisson*) naughty ♦ *nm/f* (*péj*) rascal.

cor [kor] *nm* (*MUS*) horn; (*MÉD*): ~ **(au pied)** corn; **réclamer à** ~ **et à cri** to clamor for; ~ **anglais** English horn, cor anglais; ~ **de chasse** hunting horn.

corail, aux [korȧy, -ō] *nm* coral *q*.

Coran [korȧṅ] *nm*: **le** ~ the Koran.

coraux [korō] *pl de* **corail**.

corbeau, x [korbō] *nm* crow.

corbeille [korbȅy] *nf* basket; (*BOURSE*): **la** ~ ≈ the floor of the Stock Exchange); ~ **de mariage** (*fig*) wedding presents *pl*; ~ **à ouvrage** work-basket; ~ **à pain** bread-basket; ~ **à papier** waste paper basket *ou* bin.

corbillard [korbȅyȧr] *nm* hearse.

cordage [kordȧzh] *nm* rope; ~**s** *nmpl* (*de voilure*) rigging *sg*.

corde [kord(ǝ)] *nf* rope; (*de violon, raquette, d'arc*) string; (*trame*): **la** ~ the thread; (*ATHLÉTISME, AUTO*): **la** ~ the rails *pl*; **les** ~**s** (*BOXE*) the ropes; **les (instruments à)** ~**s** (*MUS*) the strings, the stringed instruments; **semelles de** ~ rope soles; **tenir la** ~ (*ATHLÉTISME, AUTO*) to be in the inside lane; **tomber des** ~**s** to rain cats and dogs; **tirer sur la** ~ to go too far; **la** ~ **sensible** the right chord; **usé jusqu'à la** ~ threadbare; ~ **à linge** clothes line; ~ **lisse** (climbing) rope; ~ **à nœuds** knotted climbing rope; ~ **raide** tight-rope; ~ **à sauter** jump (*US*) *ou* skipping (*Brit*) rope; ~**s vocales** vocal cords.

cordeau, x [kordō] *nm* string, line; **tracé au** ~ as straight as an arrow.

cordée [kordȧ] *nf* (*d'alpinistes*) rope, roped party.

cordelière [kordǝlyȅr] *nf* cord (belt).

cordial, e, aux [kordyȧl, -ō] *a* warm, cordial ♦ *nm* cordial, pick-me-up.

cordialement [kordyȧlmȧṅ] *ad* cordially, heartily; (*formule épistolaire*) (kind) regards.

cordialité [kordyȧlȅtȧ] *nf* warmth, cordiality.

cordillère [kordȅyer] *nf*: **la** ~ **des Andes** the Andes cordillera *ou* range.

cordon [kordôṅ] *nm* cord, string; ~ **sanitaire/de police** sanitary/police cordon; ~ **littoral** sandbank, sandbar; ~ **ombilical** umbilical cord.

cordon-bleu [kordôṅblœ̄] *a*, *nm/f* cordon bleu.

cordonnerie [kordonrē] *nf* shoe repairer's *ou* mender's (shop).

cordonnier [kordonyā] *nm* shoe repairer *ou* mender, cobbler.

cordouan, e [kordōōáṅ, -áṅ] *a* Cordovan.

Cordoue [kordōō] *n* Cordoba.

Corée [korā] *nf*: **la ~** Korea; **la ~ du Sud/du Nord** South/North Korea; **la République (démocratique populaire) de ~** the (Democratic People's) Republic of Korea.

coréen, ne [korāaṅ, -en] *a* Korean ♦ *nm* (*LING*) Korean ♦ *nm/f*: **C~, ne** Korean.

coreligionnaire [korəlēzhyoner] *nm/f* fellow Christian/Muslim/Jew *etc*.

Corfou [korfōō] *n* Corfu.

coriace [koryás] *a* tough.

Corinthe [koraṅt] *n* Corinth.

cormoran [kormoráṅ] *nm* cormorant.

cornac [kornák] *nm* elephant driver.

corne [korn(ə)] *nf* horn; (*de cerf*) antler; (*de la peau*) callus; **~ d'abondance** horn of plenty; **~ de brume** (*NAVIG*) foghorn.

cornée [kornā] *nf* cornea.

corneille [korney] *nf* crow.

cornélien, ne [kornālyaṅ, -en] *a* (*débat etc*) where love and duty conflict.

cornemuse [kornəmüz] *nf* bagpipes *pl*; **joueur de ~** piper.

corner *nm* [korner] (*FOOTBALL*) corner (kick) ♦ *vb* [kornā] *vt* (*pages*) to make dog-eared ♦ *vi* (*klaxonner*) to blare out.

cornet [korne] *nm* (paper) cone; (*de glace*) cornet, cone; **~ à piston** cornet.

cornette [kornet] *nf* cornet (*headgear*).

corniaud [kornyō] *nm* (*chien*) mongrel; (*péj*) dope, idiot.

corniche [kornēsh] *nf* (*de meuble, neigeuse*) cornice; (*route*) coast road.

cornichon [kornēshóṅ] *nm* gherkin.

Cornouailles [kornwáy] *nf(pl)* Cornwall.

cornue [kornü] *nf* retort.

corollaire [koroler] *nm* corollary.

corolle [korol] *nf* corolla.

coron [koróṅ] *nm* mining cottage; mining village.

coronaire [koroner] *a* coronary.

corporation [korporásyóṅ] *nf* corporate body; (*au moyen-âge*) guild.

corporel, le [korporel] *a* bodily; (*punition*) corporal; **soins ~s** care *sg* of the body.

corps [kor] *nm* (*gén*) body; (*cadavre*) (dead) body; **à son ~ défendant** against one's will; **à ~ perdu** headlong; **perdu ~ et biens** lost with all hands; **prendre ~** to take shape; **faire ~ avec** to be joined to; to form one body with; **~ d'armée (CA)** army corps; **~ de ballet** corps de ballet; **~ constitués** (*POL*) constitutional bodies; **le ~ consulaire (CC)** the consular corps; **~ à ~** *ad* hand-to-hand; **~ du délit** (*JUR*) corpus delicti; **le ~ diplomatique (CD)** the diplomatic corps; **le ~ électoral** the electorate; **le ~ enseignant** the teaching profession; **~ étranger** (*MÉD*) foreign body; **~ expéditionnaire** task force; **~ de garde** guardroom; **~ législatif** legislative body; **le ~ médical** the medical profession.

corpulence [korpülâṅs] *nf* build; (*embonpoint*) stoutness, corpulence; **de forte ~** of large build.

corpulent, e [korpülâṅ, -áṅt] *a* stout, corpulent.

correct, e [korekt] *a* (*exact*) accurate, correct; (*bienséant, honnête*) correct; (*passable*) adequate.

correctement [korektəmâṅ] *ad* accurately; correctly; adequately.

correcteur, trice [korektœr, -trēs] *nm/f* (*SCOL*) examiner, grader (*US*), marker (*Brit*); (*TYPO*) proofreader.

correctif, ive [korektēf, -ēv] *a* corrective ♦ *nm* (*mise au point*) rider, qualification.

correction [koreksyóṅ] *nf* (*voir corriger*) correction; grading (*US*), marking (*Brit*); (*voir correct*) correctness; (*rature, surcharge*) correction, emendation; (*coups*) thrashing; **~ sur écran** (*INFORM*) screen editing; **~ (des épreuves)** proofreading.

correctionnel, le [koreksyonel] *a* (*JUR*): **tribunal ~** ≈ criminal court.

corrélation [korālâsyóṅ] *nf* correlation.

correspondance [korespóṅdâṅs] *nf* correspondence; (*de train, d'avion*) connection; **ce train assure la ~ avec l'avion de 10 heures** this train connects with the 10 o'clock plane; **cours par ~** correspondence course; **vente par ~** mail-order business.

correspondancier, ière [korespóṅdâṅsyā, -yer] *nm/f* correspondence clerk.

correspondant, e [korespóṅdâṅ, -âṅt] *nm/f* correspondent; (*TÉL*) person phoning (*ou* being phoned).

correspondre [korespóṅdr(ə)] *vi* (*données, témoignages*) to correspond, tally; (*chambres*) to communicate; **~ à** to correspond to; **~ avec qn** to correspond with sb.

corrida [korēdá] *nf* bullfight.

corridor [korēdor] *nm* corridor, passage.

corrigé [korēzhā] *nm* (*SCOL*) correct version; fair copy.

corriger [korēzhā] *vt* (*devoir*) to correct, grade (*US*), mark (*Brit*); (*texte*) to correct, emend; (*erreur, défaut*) to correct, put right; (*punir*) to thrash; **~ qn de** (*défaut*) to cure sb of; **se ~ de** to cure o.s. of.

corroborer [koroborā] *vt* to corroborate.

corroder [korodā] *vt* to corrode.

corrompre [koróṅpr(ə)] *vt* (*dépraver*) to corrupt; (*acheter: témoin etc*) to bribe.

corrompu, e [koróṅpü] *a* corrupt.

corrosif, ive [korōzēf, -ēv] *a* corrosive.

corrosion [korōzyóṅ] *nf* corrosion.

corruption [korüpsyóṅ] *nf* corruption; bribery.

corsage [korsázh] *nm* (*d'une robe*) bodice; (*chemisier*) blouse.

corsaire [korser] *nm* pirate, corsair; privateer.

corse [kors(ə)] *a* Corsican ♦ *nm/f*: **C~** Corsican ♦ *nf*: **la C~** Corsica.

corsé, e [korsā] *a* vigorous; (*café etc*) full-flavored (*US*) *ou* -flavoured (*Brit*); (*goût*) full; (*fig*) spicy; tricky.

corselet [korsəle] *nm* corselet.

corser [korsā] *vt* (*difficulté*) to aggravate; (*intrigue*) to liven up; (*sauce*) to add spice to.

corset [korse] *nm* corset; (*d'une robe*) bodice; **~ orthopédique** surgical corset.

corso [korsō] *nm*: **~ fleuri** procession of floral

floats.

cortège [kortezh] *nm* procession.
cortisone [kortēzon] *nf* (*MÉD*) cortisone.
corvée [korvā] *nf* chore, drudgery *q*; (*MIL*)
fatigue (duty).
cosignataire [kosēnyáter] *a*, *nm/f* co-signatory.
cosinus [kosēnüs] *nm* (*MATH*) cosine.
cosmétique [kosmātēk] *nm* (*pour les cheveux*) hair-oil; (*produit de beauté*) beauty care product.
cosmique [kosmēk] *a* cosmic.
cosmonaute [kosmonōt] *nm/f* cosmonaut, astronaut.
cosmopolite [kosmopolēt] *a* cosmopolitan.
cosmos [kosmos] *nm* outer space; cosmos.
cosse [kos] *nf* (*BOT*) pod, hull.
cossu, e [kosü] *a* opulent-looking, well-to-do.
Costa Rica [kostárēká] *nm*: **le ~** Costa Rica.
costaricien, ne [kostárēsyan, -en] *a* Costa Rican ♦ *nm/f*: **C~, ne** Costa Rican.
costaud, e [kostō, -ōd] *a* strong, sturdy.
costume [kostüm] *nm* (*d'homme*) suit; (*de théâtre*) costume.
costumé, e [kostümā] *a* dressed up.
costumier, ière [kostümyā, -yer] *nm/f* (*fabricant, loueur*) costumier; (*THÉÂTRE*) wardrobe master/mistress.
cotangente [kotáñzháñt] *nf* (*MATH*) cotangent.
cotation [kotâsyóñ] *nf* quoted value.
cote [kot] *nf* (*en Bourse etc*) quotation; quoted value; (*d'un cheval*): **la ~ de** the odds *pl* on; (*d'un candidat etc*) rating; (*mesure: sur une carte*) elevation point (*US*), spot height (*Brit*); (*: sur un croquis*) dimension; (*de classement*) reference number; **avoir la ~** to be very popular; **inscrit à la ~** listed on the Stock Exchange; **~ d'alerte** danger *ou* flood level; **~ mal taillée** (*fig*) compromise; **~ de popularité** popularity rating.
coté, e [kotā] *a*: **être ~** to be listed *ou* quoted; **être ~ en Bourse** to be listed on the Stock Exchange; **être bien/mal ~** to be highly/poorly rated.
côte [kōt] *nf* (*rivage*) coast(line); (*pente*) slope; (*: sur une route*) hill; (*ANAT*) rib; (*d'un tricot, tissu*) rib, ribbing *q*; **~ à ~** *ad* side by side; **la C~** (**d'Azur**) the (French) Riviera; **la C~ d'Ivoire** the Ivory Coast.
côté [kotā] *nm* (*gén*) side; (*direction*) way, direction; **de chaque ~ (de)** on each side of; **de tous les ~s** from all directions; **de quel ~ est-il parti?** which way *ou* in which direction did he go?; **de ce/de l'autre ~** this/the other way; **d'un ~ ... de l'autre ~** (*alternative*) on (the) one hand ... on the other (hand); **du ~ de** (*provenance*) from; (*direction*) towards; **du ~ de Lyon** (*proximité*) near Lyons; **du ~ gauche** on the left-hand side; **de ~** *ad* sideways; on one side; to one side; aside; **laisser de ~** to leave aside; **mettre de ~** to put aside; **de mon ~** (*quant à moi*) for my part; **à ~** *ad* (right) nearby; beside; next door; (*d'autre part*) besides; **à ~ de** beside; next to; (*fig*) in comparison to; **à ~ (de la cible)** off target, wide (of the mark); **être aux ~s de** to be by the side of.
coteau, x [kotō] *nm* hill.
côtelé, e [kōtlā] *a* ribbed; **pantalon en velours**

~ corduroy pants *pl*.
côtelette [kōtlet] *nf* chop.
coter [kotā] *vt* (*BOURSE*) to quote.
coterie [kotrē] *nf* set.
côtier, ière [kōtyā, -yer] *a* coastal.
cotisation [kotēzâsyóñ] *nf* subscription, dues *pl*; (*pour une pension*) contributions *pl*.
cotiser [kotēzā] *vi*: **~ (à)** to pay contributions (to); (*à une association*) to subscribe (to); **se ~** to club together.
coton [kotóñ] *nm* cotton; **~ hydrophile** absorbent cotton (*US*), cotton wool (*Brit*).
cotonnade [kotonàd] *nf* cotton (fabric).
coton-tige [kotóñtēzh] *nm* ® Q-tip ® (*US*), cotton bud ® (*Brit*).
côtoyer [kōtwáyā] *vt* to be close to; (*rencontrer*) to rub shoulders with; (*longer*) to run alongside; (*fig: friser*) to be bordering *ou* verging on.
cotte [kot] *nf*: **~ de mailles** coat of mail.
cou [kōō] *nm* neck.
couac [kwàk] *nm* (*fam*) squawk.
couard, e [kwàr, -àrd(ə)] *a* cowardly.
couchage [kōōsházh] *nm voir* **sac.**
couchant [kōōshàñ] *a*: **soleil ~** setting sun.
couche [kōōsh] *nf* (*strate: gén*, *GÉO*) layer, stratum (*pl* -a); (*de peinture, vernis*) coat; (*de poussière, crème*) layer; (*de bébé*) diaper (*US*), nappy (*Brit*); **~s** *nfpl* (*MÉD*) childbirth; **~s sociales** social levels *ou* strata.
couché, e [kōōshā] *a* (*étendu*) lying down; (*au lit*) in bed.
couche-culotte, *pl* **couches-culottes** [kōōshkülot] *nf* (plastic-coated) disposable diaper (*US*) *ou* nappy (*Brit*).
coucher [kōōshā] *nm* (*du soleil*) setting ♦ *vt* (*personne*) to put to bed; (*: loger*) to put up; (*objet*) to lay on its side; (*écrire*) to inscribe, couch ♦ *vi* (*dormir*) to sleep, spend the night; **~ avec qn** to sleep with sb, go to bed with sb; **se ~** *vi* (*pour dormir*) to go to bed; (*pour se reposer*) to lie down; (*soleil*) to set, go down; **à prendre avant le ~** (*MÉD*) take at night *ou* before going to bed; **~ de soleil** sunset.
couchette [kōōshet] *nf* berth, couchette; (*de marin*) bunk.
coucheur [kōōshœr] *nm*: **mauvais ~** tough customer.
couci-couça [kōōsēkōōsá] *ad* (*fam*) so-so.
coucou [kōōkōō] *nm* cuckoo ♦ *excl* peek-a-boo.
coude [kōōd] *nm* (*ANAT*) elbow; (*de tuyau, de la route*) bend; **~ à ~** *ad* shoulder to shoulder, side by side.
coudée [kōōdā] *nf*: **avoir ses ~s franches** (*fig*) to have a free rein.
cou-de-pied, *pl* **cous-de-pied** [kōōdpyā] *nm* instep.
coudoyer [kōōdwáyā] *vt* to brush past *ou* against; (*fig*) to rub shoulders with.
coudre [kōōdr(ə)] *vt* (*bouton*) to sew on; (*robe*) to sew (up) ♦ *vi* to sew.
couenne [kwán] *nf* (*de lard*) rind.
couette [kwet] *nf* duvet, (continental) quilt; **~s** *nfpl* (*cheveux*) bunches.
couffin [kōōfañ] *nm* wicker cradle.
couilles [kōōy] *nfpl* (*fam!*) balls (!).
couiner [kwēnā] *vi* to squeal.
coulage [kōōlázh] *nm* (*COMM*) loss of stock

(due to theft or negligence).

coulant, e [koolã́n, -ã́nt] a (indulgent) easy-going; (fromage etc) runny.

coulée [koolā́] nf (de lave, métal en fusion) flow; ~ **de neige** snowslide.

couler [koolā́] vi to flow, run; (fuir: stylo, récipient) to leak; (sombrer: bateau) to sink ♦ vt (cloche, sculpture) to cast; (bateau) to sink; (fig) to ruin, bring down; (: passer): ~ **une vie heureuse** to enjoy a happy life; **se ~ dans** (interstice etc) to slip into; **faire ~** (eau) to run; **faire ~ un bain** to run a bath; **il a coulé une bielle** (AUTO) his crankshaft broke; ~ **de source** to follow on naturally; ~ **à pic** to sink ou go straight to the bottom.

couleur [koolœr] nf color (US), colour (Brit); (CARTES) suit; ~**s** nfpl (du teint) color sg; **les** ~**s** (MIL) the colors; **en** ~**s** (film) in color; **télévision en** ~**s** color television; **de** ~ (homme, femme) colored; **sous** ~ **de** on the pretext of.

couleuvre [koolœvr(ə)] nf grass snake.

coulisse [koolēs] nf (TECH) runner; ~**s** nfpl (THÉÂTRE) wings; (fig): **dans les** ~**s** behind the scenes; **porte à** ~ sliding door.

coulisser [koolēsā] vi to slide, run.

couloir [koolwàr] nm corridor, passage; (de bus) aisle; (: sur la route) bus lane; (SPORT: de piste) lane; (GÉO) gully; ~ **aérien** air corridor ou lane; ~ **de navigation** shipping lane.

coulpe [koolp(ə)] nf: **battre sa** ~ to repent openly.

coup [koo] nm (heurt, choc) knock; (affectif) blow, shock; (agressif) blow; (avec arme à feu) shot; (de l'horloge) chime; stroke; (SPORT) stroke; shot; blow; (fam: fois) time; (ÉCHECS) move; ~ **de coude/genou** nudge (with the elbow)/with the knee; **à** ~**s de hache/marteau** (hitting) with an axe/a hammer; ~ **de tonnerre** clap of thunder; ~ **de sonnette** ring of the bell; ~ **de crayon/pinceau** stroke of the pencil/brush; **donner un** ~ **de balai** to sweep up, give the floor a sweep; **donner un** ~ **de chiffon** to dust; **avoir le** ~ (fig) to have the knack; **être dans le/hors du** ~ to be/not to be in on it; **boire un** ~ to have a drink; **d'un seul** ~ (subitement) suddenly; (à la fois) at one try; in one blow; **du** ~ so (you see); **du premier** ~ first time, at the first attempt; **du même** ~ at the same time; **à** ~ **sûr** definitely, without fail; **après** ~ afterwards; ~ **sur** ~ in quick succession; **être sur un** ~ to be on to something; **sur le** ~ outright; **sous le** ~ **de** (surprise etc) under the influence of; **tomber sous le** ~ **de la loi** to constitute a statutory offense; **à tous les** ~**s** every time; **il a raté son** ~ he didn't pull it off; **pour le** ~ for once; ~ **bas** (fig): **donner un** ~ **bas à qn** to hit sb below the belt; ~ **de chance** stroke of luck; ~ **de chapeau** (fig) pat on the back; ~ **de couteau** stab (of a knife); ~ **dur** hard blow; ~ **d'éclat** (great) feat; ~ **d'envoi** kick-off; ~ **d'essai** first attempt; ~ **d'état** coup d'état; ~ **de feu** shot; ~ **de filet** (POLICE) haul; ~ **de foudre** (fig) love at first sight; ~ **fourré** stab in the back; ~ **franc** free kick; ~ **de frein** (sharp) braking q; ~

de fusil rifle shot; ~ **de grâce** coup de grâce; ~ **du lapin** (AUTO) whiplash; ~ **de main**: **donner un** ~ **de main à qn** to give sb a (helping) hand; ~ **de maître** master stroke; ~ **d'œil** glance; ~ **de pied** kick; ~ **de poing** punch; ~ **de soleil** sunburn q; ~ **de téléphone** phone call; ~ **de tête** (fig) (sudden) impulse; ~ **de théâtre** (fig) dramatic turn of events; ~ **de vent** gust of wind; **en** ~ **de vent** (rapidement) in a great hurry.

coupable [koopábl(ə)] a guilty; (pensée) guilty, culpable ♦ nm/f (gén) culprit; (JUR) guilty party; ~ **de** guilty of.

coupant, e [koopã́n, -ã́nt] a (lame) sharp; (fig: voix, ton) cutting.

coupe [koop] nf (verre) goblet; (à fruits) dish; (SPORT) cup; (de cheveux, de vêtement) cut; (graphique, plan) (cross) section; **être sous la** ~ **de** to be under the control of; **faire des** ~**s sombres dans** to make drastic cuts in.

coupé, e [koopā́] a (communications, route) cut, blocked; (vêtement): **bien/mal** ~ well/badly cut ♦ nm (AUTO) coupé.

coupe-circuit [koopsērküē] nm inv cutout, circuit breaker.

coupée [koopā́] nf (NAVIG) gangway.

coupe-feu [koopfœ́] nm inv firebreak.

coupe-gorge [koopgorzh(ə)] nm inv cut-throats' den.

coupe-ongles [koopóngl(ə)] nm inv (pince) nail clippers; (ciseaux) nail scissors.

coupe-papier [kooppápyā́] nm inv paper knife.

couper [koopā́] vt to cut; (retrancher) to cut (out), take out; (route, courant) to cut off; (appétit) to take away; (fièvre) to take down, reduce; (vin, cidre) to blend; (: à table) to dilute (with water) ♦ vi to cut; (prendre un raccourci) to take a short-cut; (CARTES: diviser le paquet) to cut; (: avec l'atout) to trump; **se** ~ (se blesser) to cut o.s.; (en témoignant etc) to give o.s. away; ~ **l'appétit à qn** to spoil sb's appetite; ~ **la parole à qn** to cut sb short; ~ **les vivres à qn** to cut off sb's vital supplies; ~ **le contact** ou **l'allumage** (AUTO) to turn off the ignition; ~ **les ponts avec qn** to break with sb; **se faire** ~ **les cheveux** to have ou get one's hair cut.

couperet [kooprε] nm cleaver, chopper.

couperosé, e [kooprōzā́] a blotchy.

couple [koopl(ə)] nm couple; ~ **de torsion** torque.

coupler [kooplā́] vt to couple (together).

couplet [kooplε] nm verse.

coupleur [kooplœr] nm: ~ **acoustique** acoustic coupler.

coupole [koopol] nf dome; cupola.

coupon [koopóń] nm (ticket) coupon; (de tissu) remnant; roll.

coupon-réponse, pl **coupons-réponses** [koopóńrāpóńs] nm reply coupon.

coupure [koopür] nf cut; (billet de banque) note; (de journal) cutting; ~ **de courant** power cut.

cour [koor] nf (de ferme, jardin) (court)yard; (d'immeuble) back yard; (JUR, royale) court; **faire la** ~ **à qn** to court sb; ~ **d'appel**

appellate court (US), appeal court (Brit); ~ **d'assises** court of assizes; ~ **de cassation** final court of appeal; ~ **des comptes** (ADMIN) ≈ General Accounting Office (US), revenue court (Brit); ~ **martiale** court-martial; ~ **de récréation** (SCOL) schoolyard, playground.

courage [kŏŏrázh] nm courage, bravery.

courageux, euse [kŏŏrázhœ̄, -œ̄z] a brave, courageous.

couramment [kŏŏrámáń] ad commonly; (parler) fluently.

courant, e [kŏŏráń, -áńt] a (fréquent) common; (COMM, gén: normal) standard; (en cours) current ♦ nm current; (fig) movement; trend; **être au** ~ **(de)** (fait, nouvelle) to know (about); **mettre qn au** ~ **(de)** (fait, nouvelle) to tell sb (about); (nouveau travail etc) to teach sb the basics (of), brief sb (about); **se tenir au** ~ **(de)** (techniques etc) to keep o.s. up-to-date (on); **dans le** ~ **de** (pendant) in the course of; ~ **octobre** etc in the course of October etc; **le 10** ~ (COMM) the 10th of this month; ~ **d'air** draft (US), draught (Brit); ~ **électrique** (electric) current, power.

courbature [kŏŏrbátür] nf ache.

courbaturé, e [kŏŏrbátürá] a aching.

courbe [kŏŏrb(ə)] a curved ♦ nf curve; ~ **de niveau** contour line.

courber [kŏŏrbā] vt to bend; ~ **la tête** to bow one's head; **se** ~ vi (branche etc) to bend, curve; (personne) to bend (down).

courbette [kŏŏrbet] nf low bow.

coure [kŏŏr] etc vb voir **courir**.

coureur, euse [kŏŏrœr, -œ̄z] nm/f (SPORT) runner (ou driver); (péj) womanizer/ manhunter; ~ **cycliste/automobile** racing cyclist/driver.

courge [kŏŏrzh(ə)] nf (BOT) gourd; (CULIN) marrow.

courgette [kŏŏrzhet] nf zucchini (US), cour-gette (Brit).

courir [kŏŏrēr] vi (gén) to run; (se dépêcher) to rush; (fig: rumeurs) to go around; (COMM: intérêt) to accrue ♦ vt (SPORT: épreuve) to compete in; (risque) to run; (danger) to face; ~ **les cafés/bals** to make the rounds of the cafés/dances; **le bruit court que** ... the rumor is going around that ..., rumor has it that ...; **par les temps qui courent** at the present time; ~ **après qn** to run after sb, chase (after) sb; **laisser** ~ to let things alone; **faire** ~ **qn** to make sb run around (all over the place); **tu peux (toujours)** ~! you can always try!

couronne [kŏŏron] nf crown; (de fleurs) wreath, circlet; ~ **(funéraire** ou **mortuaire)** (funeral) wreath.

couronnement [kŏŏronmáń] nm coronation, crowning; (fig) crowning achievement.

couronner [kŏŏronā] vt to crown.

courons [kŏŏróń], **courrai** [kŏŏrā] etc vb voir **courir**.

courre [kŏŏr] vb voir **chasse**.

courrier [kŏŏryā] nm mail, post; (lettres à écrire) letters pl; (rubrique) column; quality ~ letter quality; **long/moyen** ~ a (AVIAT) long-/medium-haul; ~ **du cœur** advice

column; ~ **électronique** electronic mail.

courroie [kŏŏrwâ] nf strap; (TECH) belt; ~ **de transmission/de ventilateur** driving/fan belt.

courrons [kŏŏróń] etc vb voir **courir**.

courroucé, e [kŏŏrōōsā] a wrathful.

cours [kŏŏr] vb voir **courir** ♦ nm (leçon) lesson; class; (série de leçons) course; (cheminement) course; (écoulement) flow; (avenue) walk; (COMM) rate; price; (BOURSE) quotation; **donner libre** ~ **à** to give free expression to; **avoir** ~ (monnaie) to be legal tender; (fig) to be current; (SCOL) to have a class ou lecture; **en** ~ (année) current; (travaux) in progress; **en** ~ **de route** on the way; **au** ~ **de** in the course of, during; **le** ~ **du change** the exchange rate; ~ **d'eau** waterway; ~ **élémentaire (CE)** 2nd and 3rd years of grade school; ~ **moyen (CM)** 4th and 5th years of grade school; ~ **préparatoire** ≈ 1st grade (US), ≈ infants' class (Brit); ~ **du soir** night school.

course [kŏŏrs(ə)] nf running; (SPORT: épreuve) race; (trajet: du soleil) course; (: d'un projectile) flight; (: d'une pièce mécanique) travel; (excursion) outing; climb; (d'un taxi, autocar) journey, trip; (petite mission) errand; ~**s** nfpl (achats) shopping sg; (HIPPISME) races; **faire les** ou **ses** ~**s** to go shopping; **jouer aux** ~**s** to bet on the races; **à bout de** ~ (épuisé) exhausted; ~ **automobile** motor race; ~ **de côte** (AUTO) hill climb; ~ **par étapes** ou **d'étapes** race in stages; ~ **d'obstacles** obstacle race; ~ **à pied** walking race; ~ **de vitesse** sprint; ~**s de chevaux** horse racing.

court, e [kŏŏr, kŏŏrt(ə)] a short ♦ ad short ♦ nm: ~ **(de tennis)** (tennis) court; **tourner** ~ to come to a sudden end; **couper** ~ **à** to cut short; **à** ~ **de** short of; **prendre qn de** ~ to catch sb unawares; **pour faire** ~ briefly, to cut a long story short; **ça fait** ~ that's not very long; **tirer à la** ~**e paille** to draw lots; **faire la** ~**e échelle à qn** to give sb a boost (US) ou leg up (Brit); ~ **métrage** (CINÉMA) short (film).

court-bouillon, pl **courts-bouillons** [kŏŏrbōōyóń] nm court-bouillon.

court-circuit, pl **courts-circuits** [kŏŏrsērküē] nm short circuit.

court-circuiter [kŏŏrsērküētā] vt (fig) to by-pass.

courtier, ière [kŏŏrtēā, -yer] nm/f broker.

courtisan [kŏŏrtēzáń] nm courtier.

courtisane [kŏŏrtēzán] nf courtesan.

courtiser [kŏŏrtēzā] vt to court, woo.

courtois, e [kŏŏrtwâ, -wâz] a courteous.

courtoisie [kŏŏrtwâzē] nf courtesy.

couru, e [kŏŏrü] pp de **courir** ♦ a (spectacle etc) popular; **c'est** ~ **(d'avance)**! (fam) it's a safe bet!

cousais [kŏŏzc] etc vb voir **coudre**.

couscous [kŏŏskōōs] nm couscous.

cousin, e [kŏŏzáń, -čn] nm/f cousin ♦ nm (ZOOL) mosquito; ~ **germain** first cousin.

cousons [kŏŏzóń] etc vb voir **coudre**.

coussin [kŏŏsáń] nm cushion; ~ **d'air** (TECH) air cushion.

cousu, e [kŏŏzü] pp de **coudre** ♦ a: ~ **d'or** rolling in riches.

coût [kōō] *nm* cost; **le ~ de la vie** the cost of living.

coûtant [kōōtáñ] *am*: **au prix ~** at cost price.

couteau, x [kōōtō] *nm* knife; **~ à cran d'arrêt** switchblade (knife); **~ de cuisine** kitchen knife; **~ à pain** bread knife; **~ de poche** pocket knife.

couteau-scie, *pl* **couteaux-scies** [kōōtōsē] *nm* serrated(-edged) knife.

coutellerie [kōōtelrē] *nf* cutlery shop; cutlery.

coûter [kōōtā] *vt* to cost ♦ *vi*: **~ à qn** to cost sb a lot; **~ cher** to be expensive; **~ cher à qn** (*fig*) to cost sb dear *ou* dearly; **combien ça coûte?** how much is it?, what does it cost?; **coûte que coûte** at all costs.

coûteux, euse [kōōtœ, -œz] *a* costly, expensive.

coutume [kōōtüm] *nf* custom; **de ~** usual, customary.

coutumier, ière [kōōtümyā, -ycr] *a* customary: **elle est coutumière du fait** that's her usual trick.

couture [kōōtür] *nf* sewing; dress-making; (*points*) seam.

couturier [kōōtüryā] *nm* fashion designer, couturier.

couturière [kōōtürycr] *nf* dressmaker.

couvée [kōōvā] *nf* brood, clutch.

couvent [kōōváñ] *nm* (*de sœurs*) convent; (*de frères*) monastery; (*établissement scolaire*) convent (school).

couver [kōōvā] *vt* to hatch; (*maladie*) to be coming down with ♦ *vi* (*feu*) to smolder (*US*), smoulder (*Brit*); (*révolte*) to be brewing; **~ qn/qch des yeux** to look lovingly at sb/sth; (*convoiter*) to look longingly at sb/sth.

couvercle [kōōverkl(ə)] *nm* lid; (*de bombe aérosol etc, qui se visse*) cap, top.

couvert, e [kōōver, -ert(ə)] *pp de* **couvrir** ♦ *a* (*ciel*) overcast; (*coiffé d'un chapeau*) wearing a hat ♦ *nm* place setting; (*place à table*) place; (*au restaurant*) cover charge; **~s** *nmpl* place settings; cutlery *sg*; **~ de** covered with *ou* in; **bien ~** (*habillé*) well wrapped up; **mettre le ~** to set the table; **à ~ under cover; sous le ~ de** under the shelter of; (*fig*) under cover of.

couverture [kōōvertür] *nf* (*de lit*) blanket; (*de bâtiment*) roofing; (*de livre, fig: d'un espion etc*) cover; (*ASSURANCES*) coverage (*US*), cover (*Brit*); (*PRESSE*) coverage; **de ~** (*lettre etc*) covering; **~ chauffante** electric blanket.

couveuse [kōōvœz] *nf* (*à poules*) sitter, brooder; (*de maternité*) incubator.

couvre [kōōvr(ə)] *etc vb voir* **couvrir.**

couvre-chef [kōōvrəshef] *nm* hat.

couvre-feu, x [kōōvrəfœ] *nm* curfew.

couvre-lit [kōōvrəlē] *nm* bedspread.

couvre-pieds [kōōvrəpyā] *nm inv* quilt.

couvreur [kōōvrœr] *nm* roofer.

couvrir [kōōvrēr] *vt* to cover; (*dominer, étouffer: voix, pas*) to drown out; (*erreur*) to cover up; (*ZOOL: s'accoupler à*) to cover; **se ~** (*ciel*) to cloud over; (*s'habiller*) to cover up, wrap up; (*se coiffer*) to put on one's hat; (*par une assurance*) to cover o.s.; **se ~ de** (*fleurs, boutons*) to become covered in.

coyote [koyot] *nm* coyote.

CP *sigle m* = **cours préparatoire.**

CPAM *sigle f* (= *Caisse primaire d'assurances maladie*) health insurance office.

cps *abr* (= *caractères par seconde*) cps.

cpt *abr* = **comptant.**

CQFD *abr* (= *ce qu'il fallait démontrer*) QED (= *quod erat demonstrandum*).

CR *sigle m* = **compte rendu.**

crabe [kráb] *nm* crab.

crachat [kráshá] *nm* spittle *q*, spit *q*.

craché, e [kráshā] *a*: **son père tout ~** the spitting image of his (*ou* her) father.

cracher [kráshā] *vi* to spit ♦ *vt* to spit out; (*fig: lave etc*) to belch (out); **~ du sang** to spit blood.

crachin [kráshañ] *nm* drizzle.

crachiner [kráshēnā] *vi* to drizzle.

crachoir [kráshwár] *nm* spittoon; (*de dentiste*) basin.

crachoter [kráshotā] *vi* (*haut-parleur, radio*) to crackle.

crack [krák] *nm* (*intellectuel*) whizzkid; (*sportif*) ace; (*poulain*) hot favorite (*US*) *ou* favourite (*Brit*).

Cracovie [krákovē] *n* Kraków (*US*), Cracow (*Brit*).

cradingue [krádañg] *a* (*fam*) disgustingly dirty, filthy-dirty.

craie [kre] *nf* chalk.

craignais [krenye] *etc vb voir* **craindre.**

craindre [krañdr(ə)] *vt* to fear, be afraid of; (*être sensible à: chaleur, froid*) to be easily damaged by; **~ de/que** to be afraid of/that; **je crains qu'il (ne) vienne** I am afraid he may come.

crainte [krañt] *nf* fear; **de ~ de/que** for fear of/that.

craintif, ive [krañtēf, -ēv] *a* timid.

cramoisi, e [krámwázē] *a* crimson.

crampe [kráñp] *nf* cramp; **~ d'estomac** stomach cramp.

crampon [kráñpóñ] *nm* (*de semelle*) cleat (*US*), stud (*Brit*); (*ALPINISME*) crampon.

cramponner [kráñponā]: **se ~** *vi*: **se ~ (à)** to hang *ou* cling on (to).

cran [kráñ] *nm* (*entaille*) notch; (*de courroie*) hole; (*courage*) guts *pl*; **~ d'arrêt** safety catch; **~ de mire** bead; **~ de sûreté** safety catch.

crâne [krán] *nm* skull.

crâner [kránā] *vi* (*fam*) to swank, show off.

crânien, ne [krányañ, -en] *a* cranial, skull *cpd*, brain *cpd*.

crapaud [krápo] *nm* toad.

crapule [krápül] *nf* villain.

crapuleux, euse [krápülœ, -œz] *a*: **crime ~** villainous crime.

craquelure [kráklür] *nf* crack; crackle *q*.

craquement [krákmáñ] *nm* crack, snap; (*du plancher*) creak, creaking *q*.

craquer [krákā] *vi* (*bois, plancher*) to creak; (*fil, branche*) to snap; (*couture*) to come apart, burst; (*fig*) to break down, fall apart; (: *être enthousiasmé*) to go wild ♦ *vt*: **~ une allumette** to strike a match.

crasse [krás] *nf* grime, filth ♦ *a* (*fig: ignorance*) crass.

crassier [krásyā] *nm* slag heap.

cratère [kráter] *nm* crater.

cravache [kráválsh] *nf* (riding) crop.

cravacher [kráváshã] *vt* to use the crop on.

cravate [krávát] *nf* tie.

cravater [krávátã] *vt* to put a tie on; (*fig*) to grab around the neck.

crawl [krōl] *nm* crawl.

crawlé, e [krōlã] *a*: **dos ~** backstroke.

crayeux, euse [kreyœ̃, -œ̃z] *a* chalky.

crayon [kreyóñ] *nm* pencil; (*de rouge à lèvres etc*) stick, pencil; **écrire au ~** to write in pencil; **~ à bille** ball-point pen; **~ de couleur** crayon; **~ optique** light pen.

crayon-feutre,   *pl*   **crayons-feutres** [kreyóñfœ̃tr(ə)] *nm* felt(-tip) pen.

crayonner [kreyonã] *vt* to scribble, sketch.

CRDP *sigle m* (= *Centre régional de documentation pédagogique*) *teachers' resource center.*

créance [krãáñs] *nf* (*COMM*) (financial) claim, (recoverable) debt; **donner ~ à qch** to lend credence to sth.

créancier, ière [krãáñsyã, -yer] *nm/f* creditor.

créateur, trice [krãátœr, -trẽs] *a* creative ♦ *nm/f* creator; **le C~** (*REL*) the Creator.

créatif, ive [krãátẽf, -ẽv] *a* creative.

création [krããsyóñ] *nf* creation.

créativité [krãátẽvẽtã] *nf* creativity.

créature [krãátür] *nf* creature.

crécelle [krãsel] *nf* rattle.

crèche [kresh] *nf* (*de Noël*) manger; (*garderie*) day-care center (*US*), day nursery (*Brit*).

crédence [krãdãñs] *nf* (small) sideboard.

crédibilité [krãdẽbẽlẽtã] *nf* credibility.

crédible [krãdẽbl(ə)] *a* credible.

CREDIF [krãdẽf] *sigle m* (= *Centre de recherche et d'étude pour la diffusion du français*) *official body promoting use of the French language.*

crédit [krãdẽ] *nm* (*gén*) credit; **~s** *nmpl* funds; **payer/acheter à ~** to pay/buy on credit *ou* on easy terms; **faire ~ à qn** to give sb credit; **~ municipal** pawnshop; **~ relais** bridge (*US*) *ou* bridging (*Brit*) loan.

crédit-bail, *pl* **crédits-bails** [krãdẽbáy] *nm* (*ÉCON*) leasing.

créditer [krãdẽtã] *vt*: **~ un compte (de)** to credit an account (with).

créditeur, trice [krãdẽtœr, -trẽs] *a* in credit, credit *cpd* ♦ *nm/f* customer in credit.

credo [krãdō] *nm* credo, creed.

crédule [krãdül] *a* credulous, gullible.

crédulité [krãdülẽtã] *nf* credulity, gullibility.

créer [krãã] *vt* to create; (*THÉÂTRE*: *pièce*) to produce (for the first time); (*: rôle*) to create.

crémaillère [krãmáyer] *nf* (*RAIL*) rack; (*tige crantée*) trammel; **direction à ~** (*AUTO*) rack and pinion steering; **pendre la ~** to have a house-warming party.

crémation [krãmãsyóñ] *nf* cremation.

crématoire [krãmátwár] *a*: **four ~** crematorium.

crème [krem] *nf* cream; (*entremets*) cream dessert ♦ *a inv* cream; **un (café) ~** ≈ coffee with cream (*US*), ≈ a white coffee (*Brit*); **~ chantilly** whipped cream, crème Chantilly; **~ fouettée** whipped cream; **~ glacée** ice cream; **~ à raser** shaving cream.

crémerie [kremrẽ] *nf* dairy; (*restaurant*) tearoom.

crémeux, euse [krãmœ̃, -œ̃z] *a* creamy.

crémier, ière [krãmyã, -yer] *nm/f* dairyman/woman.

créneau, x [krãnō] *nm* (*de fortification*) crenel(le); (*fig, aussi COMM*) gap, slot; (*AUTO*): **faire un ~** to reverse into a parking space (*between cars alongside the curb*).

créole [krãol] *a, nm/f* Creole.

créosote [krãōzot] *nf* creosote.

crêpe [krep] *nf* (*galette*) pancake ♦ *nm* (*tissu*) crêpe; (*de deuil*) black mourning crêpe; (*ruban*) black armband (*ou* hatband *ou* ribbon); **semelle (de) ~** crêpe sole; **~ de Chine** crêpe de Chine.

crêpé, e [krãpã] *a* (*cheveux*) backcombed.

crêperie [kreprẽ] *nf* pancake shop *ou* restaurant.

crépi [krãpẽ] *nm* roughcast.

crépir [krãpẽr] *vt* to roughcast.

crépiter [krãpẽtã] *vi* to sputter, splutter, crackle.

crépon [krãpóñ] *nm* seersucker.

CREPS [kreps] *sigle m* (= *Centre régional d'éducation physique et sportive*) ≈ sports *ou* recreation center (*US*) *ou* centre (*Brit*).

crépu, e [krãpü] *a* frizzy, fuzzy.

crépuscule [krãpüskül] *nm* twilight, dusk.

crescendo [krãshendō] *nm, ad* (*MUS*) crescendo; **aller ~** (*fig*) to rise higher and higher, grow ever greater.

cresson [krãsóñ] *nm* watercress.

Crète [kret] *nf*: **la ~** Crete.

crête [kret] *nf* (*de coq*) comb; (*de vague, montagne*) crest.

crétin, e [krãtañ, -ẽn] *nm/f* cretin.

crétois, e [krãtwà, -wàz] *a* Cretan.

cretonne [krãton] *nf* cretonne.

creuser [krœ̃zã] *vt* (*trou, tunnel*) to dig; (*sol*) to dig a hole in; (*bois*) to hollow out; (*fig*) to go (deeply) into; **ça creuse** that gives you a real appetite; **se ~ (la cervelle)** to rack one's brains.

creuset [krœ̃ze] *nm* crucible; (*fig*) melting pot; (*severe*) test.

creux, euse [krœ̃, -œ̃z] *a* hollow ♦ *nm* hollow; (*fig*: *sur graphique etc*) trough; **heures creuses** slack periods; off-peak periods; **le ~ de l'estomac** the pit of the stomach.

crevaison [krəvezóñ] *nf* puncture, flat.

crevasse [krəvàs] *nf* (*dans le sol*) crack, fissure; (*de glacier*) crevasse; (*de la peau*) crack.

crevé, e [krəvã] *a* (*fam: fatigué*) worn out, dead beat.

crève-cœur [krevkœr] *nm inv* heartbreak.

crever [krəvã] *vt* (*papier*) to tear, break; (*tambour, ballon*) to burst ♦ *vi* (*pneu*) to burst; (*automobiliste*) to have a flat (tire) (*US*) *ou* a puncture (*Brit*); (*abcès, outre, nuage*) to burst (open); (*fam*) to die; **cela lui a crevé un œil** it blinded him in one eye; **~ l'écran** to have real screen presence.

crevette [krəvet] *nf*: **~ (rose)** prawn; **~ grise** shrimp.

cri [krẽ] *nm* cry, shout; (*d'animal: spécifique*) cry, call; **à grands ~s** at the top of one's voice; **c'est le dernier ~** (*fig*) it's the latest fashion.

criant, e [krēyáṅ, -áṅt] *a* (*injustice*) glaring.

criard, e [krēyár, -árd(ə)] *a* (*couleur*) garish, loud; (*voix*) yelling.

crible [krēbl(ə)] *nm* riddle; (*mécanique*) screen, jig; **passer qch au ~** to put sth through a riddle; (*fig*) to go over sth with a fine-tooth comb.

criblé, e [krēblā] *a*: **~ de** riddled with.

cric [krēk] *nm* (*AUTO*) jack.

cricket [krēket] *nm* cricket.

criée [krēyā] *nf*: **(vente à la) ~** (sale by) auction.

crier [krēyā] *vi* (*pour appeler*) to shout, cry (out); (*de peur, de douleur etc*) to scream, yell; (*fig: grincer*) to squeal, screech ♦ *vt* (*ordre, injure*) to shout (out), yell (out); **sans ~ gare** without warning; **~ grâce** to cry for mercy; **~ au secours** to shout for help.

crieur, euse [krēyœr, -ǣz] *nm/f*: **~ de journaux** newspaper seller.

crime [krēm] *nm* crime; (*meurtre*) murder.

Crimée [krēmā] *nf*: **la ~** the Crimea.

criminaliste [krēmēnálēst(ə)] *nm/f* specialist in criminal law.

criminalité [krēmēnálētā] *nf* criminality, crime.

criminel, le [krēmēnel] *a* criminal ♦ *nm/f* criminal; murderer; **~ de guerre** war criminal.

criminologiste [krēmēnolozhēst(ə)] *nm/f* criminologist.

crin [kraṅ] *nm* hair *q*; (*fibre*) horsehair; **à tous ~s, à tout ~** diehard, out-and-out.

crinière [krēnyer] *nf* mane.

crique [krēk] *nf* creek, inlet.

criquet [krēke] *nm* grasshopper.

crise [krēz] *nf* crisis (*pl* crises); (*MÉD*) attack; fit; **~ cardiaque** heart attack; **~ de foi** crisis of belief; **~ de foie** bilious attack; **~ de nerfs** attack of nerves.

crispant, e [krēspáṅ, -áṅt] *a* annoying, irritating.

crispation [krēspásyôṅ] *nf* (*spasme*) twitch; (*contraction*) contraction; tenseness.

crispé, e [krēspā] *a* tense, nervous.

crisper [krēspā] *vt* to tense; (*poings*) to clench; **se ~** to tense; to clench; (*personne*) to get tense.

crissement [krēsmáṅ] *nm* crunch; rustle; screech.

crisser [krēsā] *vi* (*neige*) to crunch; (*tissu*) to rustle; (*pneu*) to screech.

cristal, aux [krēstál, -ō] *nm* crystal ♦ *nmpl* (*objets*) crystal(ware) *sg*; **~ de plomb** (lead) crystal; **~ de roche** rock-crystal; **cristaux de soude** washing soda *sg*.

cristallin, e [krēstálaṅ, -ēn] *a* crystal-clear ♦ *nm* (*ANAT*) crystalline lens.

cristalliser [krēstálēzā] *vi*, *vt*, **se ~** *vi* to crystallize.

critère [krēter] *nm* criterion (*pl* -ia).

critiquable [krētēkábl(ə)] *a* open to criticism.

critique [krētēk] *a* critical ♦ *nm/f* (*de théâtre, musique*) critic ♦ *nf* criticism; (*THÉÂTRE etc*: *article*) review; **la ~** (*activité*) criticism; (*personnes*) the critics *pl*.

critiquer [krētēkā] *vt* (*dénigrer*) to criticize;

(*évaluer, juger*) to assess, examine (critically).

croasser [kroásā] *vi* to caw.

croate [kroát] *a* Croatian ♦ *nm* (*LING*) Croat, Croatian.

Croatie [kroásē] *nf*: **la ~** Croatia.

croc [krō] *nm* (*dent*) fang; (*de boucher*) hook.

croc-en-jambe, *pl* **crocs-en-jambe** [krokáṅyáṅb] *nm*: **faire un ~ à qn** to trip sb up.

croche [krosh] *nf* (*MUS*) eighth note (*US*), quaver (*Brit*); **double ~** sixteenth note (*US*), semiquaver (*Brit*).

croche-pied [kroshpyā] *nm* = **croc-en-jambe**.

crochet [kroshe] *nm* hook; (*clef*) picklock; (*détour*) detour; (*BOXE*): **~ du gauche** left hook; (*TRICOT*: *aiguille*) crochet hook; (*: technique*) crochet; **~s** *nmpl* (*TYPO*) square brackets; **vivre aux ~s de qn** to live *ou* sponge off sb.

crocheter [kroshtā] *vt* (*serrure*) to pick.

crochu, e [kroshü] *a* hooked; claw-like.

crocodile [krokodēl] *nm* crocodile.

crocus [kroküs] *nm* crocus.

croire [krwár] *vt* to believe; **~ qn honnête** to believe sb (to be) honest; **se ~ fort** to think one is strong; **~ que** to believe *ou* think that; **vous croyez?** do you think so?; **~ être/faire** to think one is/does; **~ à, ~ en** to believe in.

crois [krwá] *etc vb voir* **croître**.

croisade [krwázád] *nf* crusade.

croisé, e [krwázā] *a* (*veston*) double-breasted ♦ *nm* (*guerrier*) crusader ♦ *nf* (*fenêtre*) window, casement; **~e d'ogives** intersecting ribs; **à la ~e des chemins** at the crossroads.

croisement [krwázmáṅ] *nm* (*carrefour*) crossroads *sg*; (*BIO*) crossing; crossbreed.

croiser [krwázā] *vt* (*personne, voiture*) to pass; (*route*) to cross, cut across; (*BIO*) to cross ♦ *vi* (*NAVIG*) to cruise; **~ les jambes/bras** to cross one's legs/fold one's arms; **se ~** (*personnes, véhicules*) to pass each other; (*routes*) to cross, intersect; (*lettres*) to cross (in the mail); (*regards*) to meet; **se ~ les bras** (*fig*) to twiddle one's thumbs.

croiseur [krwázœr] *nm* cruiser (*warship*).

croisière [krwázyer] *nf* cruise; **vitesse de ~** (*AUTO etc*) cruising speed.

croisillon [krwázēyôṅ] *nm*: **motif/fenêtre à ~s** lattice pattern/window.

croissais [krwásc] *etc vb voir* **croître**.

croissance [krwásáṅs] *nf* growing, growth; **troubles de la ~** growing pains; **maladie de ~** growth disease; **~ économique** economic growth.

croissant, e [krwásáṅ, -áṅt] *vb voir* **croître** ♦ *a* growing; rising ♦ *nm* (*à manger*) croissant; (*motif*) crescent; **~ de lune** crescent moon.

croître [krwátr(ə)] *vi* to grow; (*lune*) to wax.

croix [krwá] *nf* cross; **en ~** *a*, *ad* in the form of a cross; **la C~ Rouge** the Red Cross.

croquant, e [krokáṅ, -áṅt] *a* crisp, crunchy ♦ *nm/f* (*péj*) yokel, (country) bumpkin.

croque-madame [krokmádám] *nm inv* toasted cheese sandwich with a fried egg on top.

croque-mitaine [krokmēten] *nm* bog(e)y-man (*pl* -men).

croque-monsieur [krokməsyǣ] *nm inv*

toasted ham and cheese sandwich.

croque-mort [krokmor] *nm* (*péj*) pallbearer.

croquer [krokā] *vt* (*manger*) to crunch; to munch; (*dessiner*) to sketch ♦ *vi* to be crisp *ou* crunchy; **chocolat à ~** plain dessert chocolate.

croquet [kroke] *nm* croquet.

croquette [kroket] *nf* croquette.

croquis [krokē] *nm* sketch.

cross(-country), *pl* **cross(-countries)** [kros(kōōntrē)] *nm* cross-country race *ou* run; cross-country racing *ou* running.

crosse [kros] *nf* (*de fusil*) butt; (*de revolver*) grip; (*d'évêque*) crook, crosier; (*de hockey*) hockey stick.

crotale [krotál] *nm* rattlesnake.

crotte [krot] *nf* droppings *pl*; **~!** (*fam*) damn!

crotté, e [krotā] *a* muddy, mucky.

crottin [krotań] *nm:* **~ (de cheval)** (horse) dung *ou* manure.

croulant, e [krōōláń, -áńt] *nm/f* (*fam*) old fogey.

crouler [krōōlā] *vi* (*s'effondrer*) to collapse; (*être délabré*) to be crumbling.

croupe [krōōp] *nf* croup, rump; **en ~** pillion.

croupier [krōōpyā] *nm* croupier.

croupir [krōōpēr] *vi* to stagnate.

CROUS [krōōs] *sigle m* (= *Centre régional des œuvres universitaires et scolaires*) *students' representative body.*

croustillant, e [krōōstēyáń, -áńt] *a* crisp; (*fig*) spicy.

croustiller [krōōstēyā] *vi* to be crisp *ou* crusty.

croûte [krōōt] *nf* crust; (*du fromage*) rind; (*de vol-au-vent*) shell; (*MÉD*) scab; **en ~** (*CULIN*) in pastry, in a pie; **~ aux champignons** mushrooms on toast; **~ au fromage** cheese on toast *q*; **~ de pain** (*morceau*) crust (of bread); **~ terrestre** earth's crust.

croûton [krōōtóń] *nm* (*CULIN*) crouton (*bout du pain*) crust, heel.

croyable [krwáyábl(ə)] *a* believable, credible.

croyais [krwáye] *etc vb voir* **croire.**

croyance [krwáyáńs] *nf* belief.

croyant, e [krwáyáń, -áńt] *vb voir* **croire** ♦ *a:* **être/ne pas être ~** to be/not to be a believer ♦ *nm/f* believer.

Crozet [krōzε] *n:* **les îles ~** the Crozet Islands.

CRS *sigle fpl* (= *Compagnies républicaines de sécurité*) *state security police force* ♦ *sigle m* member of the CRS.

cru, e [krü] *pp de* **croire** ♦ *a* (*non cuit*) raw; (*lumière, couleur*) harsh; (*description*) crude; (*paroles, langage: franc*) blunt; (*: grossier*) crude ♦ *nm* (*vignoble*) vineyard; (*vin*) wine ♦ *nf* (*d'un cours d'eau*) swelling, rising; **de son (propre) ~** (*fig*) of his own devising; **monter à ~** to ride bareback; **du ~** local; **en ~e** in spate.

crû [krü] *pp de* **croître.**

cruauté [krüötā] *nf* cruelty.

cruche [krüsh] *nf* pitcher, (earthenware) jug.

crucial, e, aux [krüsyál, -ō] *a* crucial.

crucifier [krüsēfyā] *vt* to crucify.

crucifix [krüsēfē] *nm* crucifix.

crucifixion [krüsēfēksyóń] *nf* crucifixion.

cruciforme [krüsēform(ə)] *a* cruciform, cross-shaped.

cruciverbiste [krüsēverbēst(ə)] *nm/f* crossword puzzle enthusiast.

crudité [krüdētā] *nf* crudeness *q*; harshness *q*; **~s** *nfpl* (*CULIN*) mixed salads (*as hors-d'œuvre*).

crue [krü] *nf voir* **cru.**

cruel, le [krüel] *a* cruel.

cruellement [krüelmáń] *ad* cruelly.

crûment [krümáń] *ad* (*voir cru*) harshly; bluntly; crudely.

crus, crûs [krü] *etc vb voir* **croire, croître.**

crustacés [krüstásā] *nmpl* shellfish.

crypte [krēpt(ə)] *nf* crypt.

cse *abr* = **cause.**

CSEN *sigle f* (= *Confédération des syndicats de l'éducation nationale*) *group of teachers' unions.*

Cte *abr* = **Comtesse.**

CU *sigle f* = *communauté urbaine.*

Cuba [kübá] *nf:* **la ~** Cuba.

cubage [kübázh] *nm* cubage, cubic content.

cubain, e [kübań, -en] *a* Cuban ♦ *nm/f:* **C~, e** Cuban.

cube [küb] *nm* cube; (*jouet*) brick, building block; **gros ~** powerful motorbike; **mètre ~** cubic meter; **2 au ~ = 8** 2 cubed is 8; **élever au ~** to cube.

cubique [kübēk] *a* cubic.

cubisme [kübēsm(ə)] *nm* cubism.

cubitus [kübētüs] *nm* ulna.

cueillette [kœyet] *nf* picking, gathering; harvest *ou* crop (of fruit).

cueillir [kœyēr] *vt* (*fruits, fleurs*) to pick, gather; (*fig*) to catch.

cuiller *ou* **cuillère** [küēyer] *nf* spoon; **~ à café** coffee spoon; (*CULIN*) ≈ teaspoonful; **~ à soupe** soup spoon; (*CULIN*) ≈ tablespoonful.

cuillerée [küēyrā] *nf* spoonful; (*CULIN*): **~ à soupe/café** tablespoonful/teaspoonful.

cuir [küēr] *nm* leather; (*avant tannage*) hide; **~ chevelu** scalp.

cuirasse [küērás] *nf* breastplate.

cuirassé [küērásā] *nm* (*NAVIG*) battleship.

cuire [küēr] *vt* (*aliments*) to cook; (*au four*) to bake; (*poterie*) to fire ♦ *vi* to cook; (*picoter*) to smart, sting, burn; **bien cuit** (*viande*) well done; **trop cuit** overdone; **pas assez cuit** underdone; **cuit à point** medium done; done to a turn.

cuisant, e [küēzáń, -áńt] *vb voir* **cuire** ♦ *a* (*douleur*) smarting, burning; (*fig: souvenir, échec*) bitter.

cuisine [küēzēn] *nf* (*pièce*) kitchen; (*art culinaire*) cookery, cooking; (*nourriture*) cooking, food; **faire la ~** to cook.

cuisiné, e [küēzēnā] *a:* **plat ~** ready-made meal *ou* dish.

cuisiner [küēzēnā] *vt* to cook; (*fam*) to grill ♦ *vi* to cook.

cuisinette [küēzēnet] *nf* kitchenette.

cuisinier, ière [küēzēnyā, -yer] *nm/f* cook ♦ *nf* (*poêle*) cooker.

cuisis [küēzē] *etc vb voir* **cuire.**

cuissardes [küēsárd] *nfpl* (*de pêcheur*) waders; (*de femme*) thigh boots.

cuisse [küēs] *nf* (*ANAT*) thigh; (*CULIN*) leg.

cuisson [küēsóń] *nf* cooking; (*de poterie*) firing.

cuissot [küēsō] *nm* haunch.

cuistre [küēstr(ə)] *nm* prig.

cuit, e [küē, -ēt] *pp de* **cuire**.

cuivre [küēvr(ə)] *nm* copper; **les ~s** (*MUS*) the brass; **~ rouge** copper; **~ jaune** brass.

cuivré, e [küēvrā] *a* coppery; (*peau*) bronzed.

cul [kü] *nm* (*fam!*) ass (*US !*), arse (*Brit !*); **~ de bouteille** bottom of a bottle.

culasse [küläs] *nf* (*AUTO*) cylinder-head; (*de fusil*) breech.

culbute [külbüt] *nf* somersault; (*accidentelle*) tumble, fall.

culbuter [külbütā] *vi* to (take a) tumble, fall (head over heels).

culbuteur [külbütœr] *nm* (*AUTO*) rocker arm.

cul-de-jatte, *pl* **culs-de-jatte** [küdzhát] *nm/f* legless cripple.

cul-de-sac, *pl* **culs-de-sac** [küdsák] *nm* cul-de-sac.

culinaire [külēner] *a* culinary.

culminant, e [külmēnáṅ, -áṅt] *a*: **point ~** highest point; (*fig*) height, climax.

culminer [külmēnā] *vi* to reach its highest point; to tower.

culot [külō] *nm* (*d'ampoule*) base (*US*), cap (*Brit*); (*effronterie*) nerve.

culotte [külot] *nf* (*de femme*) panties *pl*; (*d'homme*) underpants *pl*; (*pantalon*) trousers *pl*, pants *pl* (*US*); **~ de cheval** riding breeches *pl*.

culotté, e [külotā] *a* (*pipe*) seasoned; (*cuir*) mellowed; (*effronté*) sassy (*US*), cheeky (*Brit*).

culpabiliser [külpábēlēzā] *vt*: **~ qn** to make sb feel guilty.

culpabilité [külpábēlētā] *nf* guilt.

culte [kült(ə)] *nm* (*religion*) religion; (*hommage, vénération*) worship; (*protestant*) service.

cultivateur, trice [kültēvátœr, -trēs] *nm/f* farmer.

cultivé, e [kültēvā] *a* (*personne*) cultured, cultivated.

cultiver [kültēvā] *vt* to cultivate; (*légumes*) to grow, cultivate.

culture [kültür] *nf* cultivation; growing; (*connaissances etc*) culture; **(champs de) ~s** land(s) under cultivation.

culturel, le [kültürel] *a* cultural.

culturisme [kültürēsm(ə)] *nm* body-building.

culturiste [kültürēst(ə)] *nm/f* body-builder.

cumin [kümaṅ] *nm* (*CULIN*) caraway seeds *pl*; cumin.

cumul [kümül] *nm* (*voir cumuler*) holding (*ou* drawing) concurrently; **~ de peines** sentences to run consecutively.

cumuler [kümülā] *vt* (*emplois, honneurs*) to hold concurrently; (*salaires*) to draw concurrently; (*JUR: droits*) to accumulate.

cupide [küpēd] *a* greedy, grasping.

curable [kürábl(ə)] *a* curable.

Curaçao [kürásō] *n* Curaçao ♦ *nm*: **c~** curaçao.

curatif, ive [kürátēf, -ēv] *a* curative.

cure [kür] *nf* (*MÉD*) course of treatment; (*REL*) cure; presbytery; ≈ vicarage; **faire une ~ de fruits** to go on a fruit cure *ou* diet; **faire une ~ thermale** to visit a spa; **n'avoir ~ de** to pay no attention to; **~ d'amaigrissement** reducing *ou* weight-loss treatment (*US*), slimming course (*Brit*); **~ de repos**

rest cure; **~ de sommeil** sleep therapy *q*.

curé [kürā] *nm* parish priest; **M le ~** ≈ Vicar.

cure-dent [kürdáṅ] *nm* toothpick.

curée [kürā] *nf* (*fig*) scramble for the pickings.

cure-ongles [küróṅgl(ə)] *nm inv* nail cleaner.

cure-pipe [kürpēp] *nm* pipe cleaner.

curer [kürā] *vt* to clean out; **se ~ les dents** to pick one's teeth.

curieusement [küryœzmáṅ] *ad* oddly.

curieux, euse [küryœ, -œz] *a* (*étrange*) strange, curious; (*indiscret*) curious, inquisitive; (*intéressé*) inquiring, curious ♦ *nmpl* (*badauds*) onlookers, bystanders.

curiosité [küryōzētā] *nf* curiosity, inquisitiveness; (*objet*) curio(sity); (*site*) unusual feature *ou* sight.

curiste [kürēst(ə)] *nm/f spa guest.*

curriculum vitae (CV) [kürēkülomvētā] *nm inv* curriculum vitae (CV).

curry [kürē] *nm* curry; **poulet au ~** curried chicken, chicken curry.

curseur [kürsœr] *nm* (*INFORM*) cursor; (*de règle*) slide; (*de fermeture-éclair*) slider.

cursif, ive [kürsēf, -ēv] *a*: **écriture cursive** cursive script.

cursus [kürsüs] *nm* degree course.

cutané, e [kütánā] *a* cutaneous, skin *cpd*.

cuti-réaction [kütēráāksyóṅ] *nf* (*MÉD*) skintest.

cuve [küv] *nf* vat; (*à mazout etc*) tank.

cuvée [küvā] *nf* vintage.

cuvette [küvet] *nf* (*récipient*) bowl, basin; (*du lavabo*) (wash)basin; (*des w.-c.*) bowl; (*GÉO*) basin.

CV *sigle m* (*AUTO*) = **cheval vapeur**; (*ADMIN*) = **curriculum vitae.**

CVS *sigle a* (= *corrigées des variations saisonnières*) seasonally adjusted.

cx *abr* (= *coefficient de pénétration dans l'air*) drag coefficient.

cyanure [syánür] *nm* cyanide.

cybernétique [sēbernātēk] *nf* cybernetics *sg*.

cyclable [sēklábl(ə)] *a*: **piste ~** bike path *ou* lane.

cyclamen [sēklámen] *nm* cyclamen.

cycle [sēkl(ə)] *nm* cycle; (*SCOL*): **premier/second ~** ≈ junior/senior high school (*US*), ≈ middle/upper school (*Brit*).

cyclique [sēklēk] *a* cyclic(al).

cyclisme [sēklēsm(ə)] *nm* cycling.

cycliste [sēklēst(ə)] *nm/f* cyclist ♦ *a* cycle *cpd*; **coureur ~** racing cyclist.

cyclo-crosse [sēklokros] *nm* (*SPORT*) cyclocross; (*épreuve*) cyclo-cross race.

cyclomoteur [sēklomotœr] *nm* moped.

cyclomotoriste [sēklomotorēst(ə)] *nm/f* moped rider.

cyclone [sēklōn] *nm* cyclone, hurricane.

cyclotourisme [sēklotōōrēsm(ə)] *nm* (bi)cycle touring.

cygne [sēny] *nm* swan.

cylindre [sēláṅdr(ə)] *nm* cylinder; **moteur à 4 ~s en ligne** straight-4 engine.

cylindrée [sēláṅdrā] *nf* (*AUTO*) (cubic) capacity; **une (voiture de) grosse ~** a big-engined car.

cylindrique [sēláṅdrēk] *a* cylindrical.

cymbale [saṅbál] *nf* cymbal.

cynique [sēnēk] *a* cynical.

cynisme [sēnēsm(ə)] *nm* cynicism.
cyprès [sēprε] *nm* cypress.
cypriote [sēprēyot] *a* Cypriot ♦ *nm/f*: **C~** Cypriot.
cyrillique [sērēlēk] *a* Cyrillic.
cystite [sēstēt] *nf* cystitis.
cytise [sētēz] *nm* laburnum.
cytologie [sētolozhē] *nf* cytology.

D

D, d [dā] *nm inv* D, d ♦ *abr*: **D** (*MÉTÉO*: = *dépression*) low, depression; **D comme Désiré** D for Dog; *voir* **système.**
d' *prép, dét voir* **de.**
Dacca [dàkà] *n* Dacca.
dactylo [dàktēlō] *nf* (*aussi*: **~graphe**) typist; (*aussi*: **~graphie**) typing, typewriting.
dactylographier [dàktēlográfyā] *vt* to type (out).
dada [dàdà] *nm* hobby-horse.
dadais [dàde] *nm* ninny, lump.
dague [dàg] *nf* dagger.
dahlia [dàlyà] *nm* dahlia.
dahoméen, ne [dàomàań, -en] *a* Dahomean.
Dahomey [dàomā] *nm*: **le ~** Dahomey.
daigner [dānyā] *vt* to deign.
daim [dań] *nm* (fallow) deer *inv*; (*peau*) buckskin; (*imitation*) suede.
dais [de] *nm* (*tenture*) canopy.
Dakar [dàkàr] *n* Dakar.
dal. *abr* (= *décalitre*) dal.
dallage [dàlàzh] *nm* paving.
dalle [dàl] *nf* slab; (*au sol*) paving stone, flag(stone); **que ~** nothing at all, zilch.
daller [dàlā] *vt* to pave.
dalmate [dàlmát] *a* Dalmatian.
Dalmatie [dàlmàsē] *nf*: **la ~** Dalmatia.
dalmatien, ne [dàlmàsyań, -en] *nm/f* (*chien*) Dalmatian.
daltonien, ne [dàltonyań, -en] *a* color-blind (*US*), colour-blind (*Brit*).
daltonisme [dàltonēsm(ə)] *nm* color (*US*) *ou* colour (*Brit*) blindness.
dam [dàń] *nm*: **au grand ~ de** much to the detriment (*ou* annoyance) of.
Damas [dàmà] *n* Damascus.
damas [dàmà] *nm* (*étoffe*) damask.
damassé, e [dàmàsā] *a* damask *cpd*.
dame [dàm]' *nf* lady; (*CARTES*, *ÉCHECS*) queen; **~s** *nfpl* (*jeu*) checkers *sg* (*US*), draughts *sg* (*Brit*); **les (toilettes des) ~s** the ladies' (toilets); **~ de charité** benefactress; **~ de compagnie** lady's companion.
dame-jeanne, pl dames-jeannes [dàmzhân] *nf* demijohn.
damer [dàmā] *vt* to ram *ou* pack down; **~ le pion à** (*fig*) to get the better of.
damier [dàmyā] *nm* checkerboard (*US*), draughtboard (*Brit*); (*dessin*) check (pattern); **en ~** check.
damner [dànā] *vt* to damn.

dancing [dânsēng] *nm* dance hall.
dandiner [dândēnā]: **se ~** *vi* to sway about; (*en marchant*) to waddle along.
Danemark [dànmárk] *nm*: **le ~** Denmark.
danger [dânzhā] *nm* danger; **mettre en ~** to endanger, put in danger; **être en ~ de mort** to be in peril of one's life; **être hors de ~** to be out of danger.
dangereusement [dânzhrœzmâń] *ad* dangerously.
dangereux, euse [dânzhrœ, -œz] *a* dangerous.
danois, e [dànwà, -wàz] *a* Danish ♦ *nm* (*LING*) Danish ♦ *nm/f*: **D~, e** Dane.
dans [dâń] *prép* in; (*direction*) into, to; (*à l'intérieur de*) in, inside; **je l'ai pris ~ le tiroir/la chambre** I took it out of *ou* from the drawer/the bedroom; **boire ~ un verre** to drink out of *ou* from a glass; **~ 2 mois** in 2 months, in 2 months' time, 2 months from now; **~ quelques instants** in a few minutes; **~ quelques jours** in a few days' time; **il part ~ quinze jours** he's leaving in two weeks' (time); **~ les 20 F** about 20 F.
dansant, e [dânsâń, -âńt] *a*: **soirée ~e** evening of dancing; (*bal*) dinner dance.
danse [dâńs] *nf*: **la ~** dancing; (*classique*) (ballet) dancing; **une ~** a dance; **~ du ventre** belly dancing.
danser [dâńsā] *vi, vt* to dance.
danseur, euse [dâńsœr, -œz] *nm/f* ballet dancer; (*au bal etc*) dancer; (: **cavalier**) partner; **~ de claquettes** tap-dancer; **en danseuse** (*à vélo*) standing on the pedals.
Danube [dànüb] *nm*: **le ~** the Danube.
DAO *sigle m* (= *dessin assisté par ordinateur*) CAD.
dard [dàr] *nm* sting (*organ*).
Dardanelles [dàrdànel] *nfpl*: **les ~** the Dardanelles.
darder [dàrdā] *vt* to shoot, send forth.
dare-dare [dàrdàr] *ad* in double-quick time.
Dar es Salaam, Dar-es-Salam [dàresàlám] *n* Dar es Salaam.
darse [dàrs(ə)] *nf* sheltered dock (*in a Mediterranean port*).
datation [dàtàsyôń] *nf* dating.
date [dàt] *nf* date; **faire ~** to mark a milestone; **de longue ~** a longstanding; **~ de naissance** date of birth; **~ limite** deadline; (*d'un aliment*: *aussi*: **~ limite de vente**) sell-by date.
dater [dàtā] *vt, vi* to date; **~ de** to date from, go back to; **à ~ de** (as) from.
dateur [dàtœr] *nm* (*de montre*) date indicator; **timbre ~** date stamp.
datif [dàtēf] *nm* dative.
datte [dàt] *nf* date.
dattier [dàtyā] *nm* date palm.
daube [dōb] *nf*: **bœuf en ~** beef casserole.
dauphin [dōfań] *nm* (*ZOOL*) dolphin; (*du roi*) dauphin; (*fig*) heir apparent.
Dauphiné [dōfēnā] *nm*: **le ~** the Dauphiné.
dauphinois, e [dōfēnwà, -wàz] *a* of *ou* from the Dauphiné.
daurade [dorád] *nf* sea bream.
davantage [dàvâńtázh] *ad* more; (*plus longtemps*) longer; **~ de** more; **~ que** more than.
DB *sigle f* (*MIL*) = *division blindée*.

DCT *sigle m* (= *diphtérie coqueluche tétanos*) DPT.

DDASS [dås] *sigle f* (= *Direction départementale d'action sanitaire et sociale*) ≈ SSA (= *Social Security Administration*) (*US*), ≈ DHSS (= *Department of Health and Social Security*) (*Brit*).

DDT *sigle m* (= *dichloro-diphénol-trichloréthane*) DDT.

de (*de* + *le* = **du**, *de* + *les* = **des**) [də, dü, dā] *prép* of; (*provenance*) from; (*moyen*) with; **la voiture d'Élisabeth/de mes parents** Elizabeth's/my parents' car; **un mur de brique/bureau d'acajou** a brick wall/ mahogany desk; **augmenter** *etc* **de 10 F** to increase *etc* by 10 F; **une pièce de 2 m de large** *ou* **large de 2 m** a room 2 m wide *ou* in width, a 2 m wide room; **un bébé de 10 mois** a 10-month-old baby; **un séjour de 2 ans** a 2-year stay; **12 mois de crédit/travail** 12 months' credit/work; **de 14 à 18h** from 2pm till 6pm ♦ *dét*: **du vin, de l'eau, des pommes** (some) wine, (some) water, (some) apples; **des enfants sont venus** some children came; **a-t-il du vin?** has he got any wine?; **il ne veut pas de pommes** he doesn't want any apples; **il n'a pas d'enfants** he has no children, he hasn't (got) any children; **pendant des mois** for months.

dé [dā] *nm* (*à jouer*) die *ou* dice (*pl* dice); (*aussi*: ~ **à coudre**) thimble; ~**s** *nmpl* (*jeu*) (game of) dice; **un coup de** ~**s** a throw of the dice; **couper en** ~**s** (*CULIN*) to dice.

DEA *sigle m* (= *Diplôme d'études approfondies*) post-graduate diploma.

déambuler [dāáñbülā] *vi* to stroll about.

déb. *abr* = **débutant**; (*COMM*) = *à débattre*.

débâcle [dābákl(ə)] *nf* rout.

déballer [dābálā] *vt* to unpack.

débandade [dābáñdád] *nf* scattering; (*déroute*) rout.

débander [dābáñdā] *vt* to unbandage.

débaptiser [dābátēzā] *vt* (*rue*) to rename.

débarbouiller [dābárbōōyā] *vt* to wash; **se** ~ to wash (one's face).

débarcadère [dābárkáder] *nm* wharf, pier.

débardeur [dābárdœr] *nm* docker, stevedore; (*maillot*) slipover, tank top.

débarquement [dābárkəmáñ] *nm* unloading, landing; disembarcation; (*MIL*) landing; **le D**~ the Normandy landings.

débarquer [dābárkā] *vt* to unload, land ♦ *vi* to disembark; (*fig*) to turn up.

débarras [dābárá] *nm* junk room; (*placard*) junk closet (*US*) *ou* cupboard (*Brit*); (*remise*) outbuilding, shed; **bon** ~! good riddance!

débarrasser [dābárásā] *vt* to clear ♦ *vi* (*enlever le couvert*) to clear; ~ **qn de** (*vêtements, paquets*) to relieve sb of; (*habitude, ennemi*) to rid sb of; ~ **qch de** (*fouillis etc*) to clear sth of; **se** ~ **de** *vt* to get rid of; to rid o.s. of.

débat [dābá] *vb voir* **débattre** ♦ *nm* discussion, debate; ~**s** *nmpl* (*POL*) proceedings, debates.

débattre [dābátr(ə)] *vt* to discuss, debate; **se** ~ *vi* to struggle.

débauche [dābōsh] *nf* debauchery; **une** ~ **de** (*fig*) a profusion of; (: *de couleurs*) a riot of.

débauché, e [dābōshā] *a* debauched ♦ *nm/f*
profligate.

débaucher [dābōshā] *vt* (*licencier*) to lay off, dismiss; (*entraîner*) to lead astray, debauch; (*inciter à la grève*) to incite.

débile [dābēl] *a* weak, feeble; (*fam: idiot*) dim-witted ♦ *nm/f*: ~ **mental, e** mental defective.

débilitant, e [dābēlētáñ, -áñt] *a* debilitating.

débilité [dābēlētā] *nf* debility; (*fam: idiotie*) stupidity; ~ **mentale** mental debility.

débiner [dābēnā]: **se** ~ *vi* to clear out, do a bunk (*Brit*).

débit [dābē] *nm* (*d'un liquide, fleuve*) (rate of) flow; (*d'un magasin*) turnover (of goods); (*élocution*) delivery; (*bancaire*) debit; **avoir un** ~ **de 10 F** to be 10 F in debit; ~ **de boissons** drinking establishment; ~ **de tabac** tobacco shop (*US*), tobacconist's (shop) (*Brit*).

débiter [dābētā] *vt* (*compte*) to debit; (*liquide, gaz*) to yield, produce, give out; (*couper: bois, viande*) to cut up; (*vendre*) to retail; (*péj: paroles etc*) to come out with, churn out.

débiteur, trice [dābētœr, -trēs] *nm/f* debtor ♦ *a* in debit; (*compte*) debit *cpd*.

déblai [dāble] *nm* earth (*moved*).

déblaiement [dāblemáñ] *nm* clearing; **travaux de** ~ earth moving *sg*.

déblatérer [dāblátārā] *vi*: ~ **contre** to go on about.

déblayer [dāblāyā] *vt* to clear; ~ **le terrain** (*fig*) to clear the ground.

débloquer [dāblokā] *vt* (*frein, fonds*) to release; (*prix*) to free ♦ *vi* (*fam*) to talk nonsense.

débobiner [dābobēnā] *vt* to unwind.

déboires [dābwár] *nmpl* setbacks.

déboisement [dābwázmáñ] *nm* deforestation.

déboiser [dābwázā] *vt* to clear of trees; (*région*) to deforest; **se** ~ *vi* (*colline, montagne*) to become bare of trees.

déboîter [dābwátā] *vt* (*AUTO*) to pull out; **se** ~ **le genou** *etc* to dislocate one's knee *etc*.

débonnaire [dāboner] *a* easy-going, good-natured.

débordant, e [dābordáñ, -áñt] *a* (*joie*) unbounded; (*activité*) exuberant.

débordé, e [dābordā] *a*: **être** ~ **de** (*travail, demandes*) to be snowed under with.

débordement [dābordəmáñ] *nm* overflowing.

déborder [dābordā] *vi* to overflow; (*lait etc*) to boil over ♦ *vt* (*MIL, SPORT*) to outflank; ~ (**de**) **qch** (*dépasser*) to extend beyond sth; ~ **de** (*joie, zèle*) to be brimming over with *ou* bursting with.

débouché [dābōōshā] *nm* (*pour vendre*) outlet; (*perspective d'emploi*) opening; (*sortie*): **au** ~ **de la vallée** where the valley opens out (onto the plain).

déboucher [dābōōshā] *vt* (*évier, tuyau etc*) to unblock; (*bouteille*) to uncork, open ♦ *vi*: ~ **de** to emerge from, come out of; ~ **sur** to come out onto; to open out onto; (*fig*) to arrive at, lead up to.

débouler [dābōōlā] *vi* to go (*ou* come) tumbling down; (*sans tomber*) to come careering down ♦ *vt*: ~ **l'escalier** to belt down the stairs.

déboulonner [dāboolonā] *vt* to dismantle; *(fig: renvoyer)* to dismiss; *(: détruire le prestige de)* to discredit.

débours [dāboor] *nmpl* outlay.

débourser [dāboorsā] *vt* to pay out, lay out.

déboussoler [dāboosolā] *vt* to disorientate, disorient.

debout [dāboo] *ad*: **être** ~ *(personne)* to be standing, stand; *(: levé, éveillé)* to be up (and about); *(chose)* to be upright; **être encore** ~ *(fig: en état)* to be still going; to be still standing; to be still up; **mettre qn** ~ to get sb to his feet; **mettre qch** ~ to stand sth up; **se mettre** ~ to get up (on one's feet); **se tenir** ~ to stand; ~! get up!; **cette histoire ne tient pas** ~ this story doesn't hold water.

débouter [dābootā] *vt* (*JUR*) to dismiss; ~ **qn de sa demande** to dismiss sb's petition.

déboutonner [dābootonā] *vt* to undo, unbutton; **se** ~ *vi* to come undone *ou* unbuttoned.

débraillé, e [dābrāyā] *a* slovenly, untidy.

débrancher [dābrānshā] *vt* (*appareil électrique*) to unplug; (*téléphone, courant électrique*) to disconnect, cut off.

débrayage [dābreyázh] *nm* (*AUTO*) clutch; *(: action)* disengaging the clutch; (*grève*) stoppage; **faire un double** ~ to ,uble-clutch (*US*) *ou* double-declutch (*Brit*).

débrayer [dābrāyā] *vi* (*AUTO*) to declutch, disengage the clutch; (*cesser le travail*) to stop work.

débridé, e [dābrēdā] *a* unbridled, unrestrained.

débrider [dābrēdā] *vt* (*cheval*) to unbridle; (*CULIN: volaille*) to untruss.

débris [dābrē] *nm* (*fragment*) fragment ♦ *nmpl* (*déchets*) pieces, debris *sg*; garbage *sg* (*US*); rubbish *sg* (*Brit*).

débrouillard, e [dābrooyár, -árd(ə)] *a* smart, resourceful.

débrouillardise [dābrooyárdēz] *nf* smartness, resourcefulness.

débrouiller [dābrooyā] *vt* to disentangle, untangle; (*fig*) to sort out, unravel; **se** ~ *vi* to manage.

débroussailler [dābroosáyā] *vt* to clear (of brushwood).

débusquer [dābüskā] *vt* to drive out (from cover).

début [dābü] *nm* beginning, start; ~**s** *nmpl* beginnings; (*de carrière*) début *sg*; **faire ses** ~**s** to start out; **au** ~ in *ou* at the beginning, at first; **au** ~ **de** at the beginning *ou* start of; **dès le** ~ from the start.

débutant, e [dābütán, -ánt] *nm/f* beginner, novice.

débuter [dābütā] *vi* to begin, start; (*faire ses débuts*) to start out.

deçà [dəsá]: **en** ~ **de** *prép* this side of; **en** ~ *ad* on this side.

décacheter [dākáshtā] *vt* to unseal, open.

décade [dākád] *nf* (*10 jours*) (period of) ten days; (*10 ans*) decade.

décadence [dākádáńs] *nf* decadence; decline.

décadent, e [dākádáń, -áńt] *a* decadent.

décaféiné, e [dākáfáēnā] *a* decaffeinated, caffeine-free.

décalage [dākálázh] *nm* move forward *ou* back; shift forward *ou* back; (*écart*) gap; (*désaccord*) discrepancy; ~ **horaire** time difference (between time zones), time-lag.

décalaminer [dākálámēnā] *vt* to decarbonize (*US*), decoke (*Brit*).

décalcomanie [dākálkománē] *nf* decal (*US*), transfer.

décaler [dākálā] *vt* (*dans le temps: avancer*) to move forward; (*: retarder*) to put back; (*changer de position*) to shift forward *ou* back; ~ **de 10 cm** to move forward *ou* back by 10 cm; ~ **de 2 h** to bring *ou* move forward 2 hours; to put back 2 hours.

décalitre [dākálētr(ə)] *nm* decaliter (*US*), decalitre (*Brit*).

décalquer [dākálkā] *vt* to trace; (*par pression*) to transfer.

décamètre [dākámetr(ə)] *nm* decameter (*US*), decametre (*Brit*).

décamper [dākáńpā] *vi* to clear out *ou* off.

décan [dākáń] *nm* (*ASTROLOGIE*) decan.

décanter [dākáńtā] *vt* to (allow to) settle (and decant); **se** ~ *vi* to settle.

décapage [dākápázh] *nm* stripping; scouring; sanding.

décapant [dākápáń] *nm* acid solution; scouring agent; paint stripper.

décaper [dākápā] *vt* to strip; (*avec abrasif*) to scour; (*avec papier de verre*) to sand.

décapiter [dākápētā] *vt* to behead; (*par accident*) to decapitate; (*fig*) to cut the top off; (*: organisation*) to remove the top people from.

décapotable [dākápotábl(ə)] *a* convertible.

décapoter [dākápotā] *vt* to put down the top of.

décapsuler [dākápsülā] *vt* to take the cap *ou* top off.

décapsuleur [dākápsülœr] *nm* bottle-opener.

décathlon [dākátlóń] *nm* decathlon.

décati, e [dākátē] *a* faded, aged.

décédé, e [dāsādā] *a* deceased.

décéder [dāsādā] *vi* to die.

déceler [dāslā] *vt* to discover, detect; (*révéler*) to indicate, reveal.

décélération [dāsālārásyóń] *nf* deceleration.

décélérer [dāsālārā] *vi* to decelerate, slow down.

décembre [dāsáńbr(ə)] *nm* December; *voir aussi* **juillet**.

décemment [dāsámáń] *ad* decently.

décence [dāsáńs] *nf* decency.

décennal, e, aux [dāsánál, -ō] *a* (*qui dure dix ans*) having a term of ten years, ten-year; (*qui revient tous les dix ans*) ten-yearly.

décennie [dāsánē] *nf* decade.

décent, e [dāsáń, -áńt] *a* decent.

décentralisation [dāsáńtrálēzásyóń] *nf* decentralization.

décentraliser [dāsáńtrálēzā] *vt* to decentralize.

décentrer [dāsáńtrā] *vt* to decenter (*US*) *ou* decentre (*Brit*); **se** ~ to move off-center (*US*) *ou* off-centre (*Brit*).

déception [dāsepsyóń] *nf* disappointment.

décerner [dāsernā] *vt* to award.

décès [dāse] *nm* death, decease; **acte de** ~ death certificate.

décevant, e [dəsváń, -áńt] *a* disappointing.

décevoir [desvwár] *vt* to disappoint.

déchaîné, e |dāshānā| *a* unbridled, raging.

déchaîner |dāshānā| *vt* (*passions, colère*) to unleash; (*rires etc*) to give rise to, arouse; **se ~** *vi* to be unleashed; (*rires*) to burst out; (*se mettre en colère*) to fly into a rage; **se ~ contre qn** to unleash one's fury on sb.

déchanter |dāshântā| *vi* to become disillusioned.

décharge |dāshàrzh(ə)| *nf* (*dépôt d'ordures*) garbage dump (*US*), rubbish tip *ou* dump (*Brit*); (*électrique*) electrical discharge; (*salve*) volley of shots; **à la ~ de** in defense of.

déchargement |dāshárzhəmáň| *nm* unloading.

décharger |dāshàrzhā| *vt* (*marchandise, véhicule*) to unload; (*ÉLEC*) to discharge; (*arme: neutraliser*) to unload; (*: faire feu*) to discharge, fire; **~ qn de** (*responsabilité*) to relieve sb of, release sb from; **~ sa colère (sur)** to vent one's anger (on); **~ sa conscience** to unburden one's conscience; **se ~ dans** (*se déverser*) to flow into; **se ~ d'une affaire sur qn** to hand a matter over to sb.

décharné, e |dāshárnā| *a* bony, emaciated, fleshless.

déchaussé, e |dāshōsā| *a* (*dent*) loose.

déchausser |dāshōsā| *vt* (*personne*) to take the shoes off; (*skis*) to take off; **se ~** to take off one's shoes; (*dent*) to come ou work loose.

dèche |dēsh| *nf* (*fam*): **être dans la ~** to be flat broke.

déchéance |dāshāáňs| *nf* (*déclin*) degeneration, decay, decline; (*chute*) fall.

déchet |dāshē| *nm* (*de bois, tissu etc*) scrap; (*perte: gén* COMM) wastage, waste; **~s** *nmpl* (*ordures*) refuse *sg*, garbage *sg* (*US*), rubbish *sg* (*Brit*); **~s radioactifs** radioactive waste.

déchiffrage |dāshēfrázh| *nm* sight-reading.

déchiffrer |dāshēfrā| *vt* to decipher.

déchiqueté, e |dāshēktā| *a* jagged(-edged), ragged.

déchiqueter |dāshēktā| *vt* to tear *ou* pull to pieces.

déchirant, e |dāshēràň, -áňt| *a* heart-breaking, heart-rending.

déchiré, e |dāshērā| *a* torn; (*fig*) heart-broken.

déchirement |dāshērmáň| *nm* (*chagrin*) wrench, heartbreak; (*gén pl: conflit*) rift, split.

déchirer |dāshērā| *vt* to tear, rip; (*mettre en morceaux*) to tear up; (*pour ouvrir*) to tear off; (*arracher*) to tear out; (*fig*) to tear apart; **se ~** *vi* to tear, rip; **se ~ un muscle/tendon** to tear a muscle/tendon.

déchirure |dāshērür| *nf* (*accroc*) tear, rip; **~ musculaire** torn muscle.

déchoir |dāshwàr| *vi* (*personne*) to lower o.s., demean o.s; **~ de** to fall from.

déchu, e |dāshü| *pp de* **déchoir ♦** *a* fallen; (*roi*) deposed.

décibel |dāsēbel| *nm* decibel.

décidé, e |dāsēdā| *a* (*personne, air*) determined; **c'est ~** it's decided; **être ~ à faire** to be determined to do.

décidément |dāsēdāmáň| *ad* undoubtedly; really.

décider |dāsēdā| *vt*: **~ qch** to decide on sth; **~ de faire/que** to decide to do/that; **~ qn (à**

faire qch) to persuade *ou* induce sb (to do sth); **~ de qch** to decide upon sth; (*suj: chose*) to determine sth; **se ~** *vi* (*personne*) to decide, make up one's mind; (*problème, affaire*) to be resolved; **se ~ à qch** to decide on sth; **se ~ à faire** to decide *ou* make up one's mind to do; **se ~ pour qch** to decide on *ou* in favor of sth.

décilitre |dāsēlētr(ə)| *nm* deciliter (*US*), decilitre (*Brit*).

décimal, e, aux |dāsēmál, -ō| *a, nf* decimal.

décimalisation |dāsēmálēzàsyóň| *nf* decimalization.

décimaliser |dāsēmálēzā| *vt* to decimalize.

décimer |dāsēmā| *vt* to decimate.

décimètre |dāsēmetr(ə)| *nm* decimeter (*US*), decimetre (*Brit*); **double ~** (20 cm) ruler.

décisif, ive |dāsēzēf, -ēv| *a* decisive; (*qui l'emporte*): **le facteur/l'argument ~** the deciding factor/argument.

décision |dāsēzyóň| *nf* decision; (*fermeté*) decisiveness, decision; **prendre une ~** to make a decision; **prendre la ~ de faire** to make the decision to do; **emporter** *ou* **faire la ~** to be decisive.

déclamation |dāklámásyóň| *nf* declamation; (*péj*) ranting, spouting.

déclamatoire |dāklámátwàr| *a* declamatory.

déclamer |dāklámā| *vt* to declaim; (*péj*) to spout ♦ *vi*: **~ contre** to rail against.

déclarable |dāklárábl(ə)| *a* (*marchandise*) dutiable; (*revenus*) declarable.

déclaration |dāklárásyóň| *nf* declaration; registration; (*discours:* POL *etc*) statement; (*compte rendu*) report; **fausse ~** misrepresentation; **~ (d'amour)** declaration; **~ de décès** registration of death; **~ de guerre** declaration of war; **~ (d'impôts)** statement of income, tax declaration, ≈ tax return; **~ (de sinistre)** (*insurance*) claim; **~ de revenus** statement of income.

déclaré, e |dāklárā| *a* (*juré*) avowed.

déclarer |dāklárā| *vt* to declare, announce; (*revenus, employés, marchandises*) to declare; (*décès, naissance*) to register; (*vol etc: à la police*) to report; **se ~** *vi* (*feu, maladie*) to break out; **~ la guerre** to declare war.

déclassé, e |dāklásā| *a* relegated, downgraded; (*matériel*) (to be) sold off.

déclassement |dāklásmáň| *nm* relegation, downgrading; (RAIL *etc*) change of class.

déclasser |dāklásā| *vt* to relegate, downgrade; (*déranger: fiches, livres*) to get out of order.

déclenchement |dākláňshmáň| *nm* release; setting off.

déclencher |dāklāňshā| *vt* (*mécanisme etc*) to release; (*sonnerie*) to set off, activate; (*attaque, grève*) to launch; (*provoquer*) to trigger off; **se ~** *vi* to release itself; to go off.

déclencheur |dāklāňshœr| *nm* release mechanism.

déclic |dāklēk| *nm* trigger mechanism; (*bruit*) click.

déclin |dāklaň| *nm* decline.

déclinaison |dāklēnєzóň| *nf* declension.

décliner |dāklēnā| *vi* to decline ♦ *vt* (*invitation*) to decline, refuse; (*responsabilité*) to re-

fuse to accept; (*nom, adresse*) to state; (*LING*) to decline; **se** ~ (*LING*) to decline.
déclivité [dāklēvētā] *nf* slope, incline; **en** ~ sloping, on the incline.
décloisonner [dāklwåzonā] *vt* to decompartmentalize.
déclouer [dāklōōā] *vt* to unnail.
décocher [dākoshā] *vt* to hurl; (*flèche, regard*) to shoot.
décoction [dākoksyôṅ] *nf* decoction.
décodage [dākodázh] *nm* deciphering, decoding.
décoder [dākodā] *vt* to decipher, decode.
décodeur [dākodœr] *nm* decoder.
décoiffé, e [dākwáfā] *a*: **elle est toute** ~**e** her hair is in a mess.
décoiffer [dākwáfā] *vt*: ~ **qn** to disarrange *ou* mess up sb's hair; to take sb's hat off; **se** ~ to take off one's hat.
décoincer [dākwaṅsā] *vt* to unjam, loosen.
déçois [dāswà] *etc*, **déçoive** [dāswàv] *etc vb voir* **décevoir**.
décolérer [dākolārā] *vi*: **il ne décolère pas** he's still angry, he hasn't calmed down.
décollage [dākolázh] *nm* (*AVIAT, ÉCON*) takeoff.
décollé, e [dākolā] *a*: **oreilles** ~**es** sticking-out ears.
décollement [dākolmáṅ] *nm* (*MÉD*): ~ **de la rétine** retinal detachment.
décoller [dākolā] *vt* to unstick ♦ *vi* to take off; (*projet, entreprise*) to take off, get off the ground; **se** ~ *vi* to come unstuck.
décolleté, e [dākoltā] *a* low-necked, low-cut; (*femme*) wearing a low-cut dress ♦ *nm* low neck(line); (*épaules*) (bare) neck and shoulders; (*plongeant*) cleavage.
décolleter [dākoltā] *vt* (*vêtement*) to give a low neckline to; (*TECH*) to cut.
décoloniser [dākolonēzā] *vt* to decolonize.
décolorant [dākoloráṅ] *nm* decolorant, bleaching agent.
décoloration [dākolorâsyôṅ] *nf*: **se faire faire une** ~ (*chez le coiffeur*) to have one's hair bleached *ou* lightened.
décoloré, e [dākolorā] *a* (*vêtement*) faded; (*cheveux*) bleached.
décolorer [dākolorā] *vt* (*tissu*) to fade; (*cheveux*) to bleach, lighten; **se** ~ *vi* to fade.
décombres [dākôṅbr(ə)] *nmpl* rubble *sg*, debris *sg*.
décommander [dākomâṅdā] *vt* to cancel; (*invités*) to put off; **se** ~ to cancel, cry off.
décomposé, e [dākôṅpōzā] *a* (*pourri*) decomposed; (*visage*) haggard, distorted.
décomposer [dākôṅpōzā] *vt* to break up; (*CHIMIE*) to decompose; (*MATH*) to factor (*US*), factorize (*Brit*); **se** ~ *vi* to decompose.
décomposition [dākôṅpōzēsyôṅ] *nf* breaking up; decomposition; factorization; **en** ~ (*organisme*) in a state of decay, decomposing.
décompresseur [dākôṅprăscœr] *nm* decompressor.
décompression [dākôṅprăsyôṅ] *nf* decompression.
décomprimer [dākôṅprēmā] *vt* to decompress.
décompte [dākôṅt] *nm* deduction; (*facture*) breakdown (of an account), detailed account.
décompter [dākôṅtā] *vt* to deduct.

déconcentration [dākôṅsâṅtrásyôṅ] *nf* (*des industries etc*) dispersal; ~ **des pouvoirs** devolution.
déconcentré, e [dākôṅsâṅtrā] *a* (*sportif etc*) who has lost (his/her) concentration.
déconcentrer [dākôṅsâṅtrā] *vt* (*ADMIN*) to disperse; **se** ~ *vi* to lose (one's) concentration.
déconcertant, e [dākôṅsertâṅ, -âṅt] *a* disconcerting.
déconcerter [dākôṅsertā] *vt* to disconcert, confound.
déconfit, e [dākôṅfē, -ēt] *a* crestfallen, downcast.
déconfiture [dākôṅfētür] *nf* collapse, ruin; (*morale*) defeat.
décongélation [dākôṅzhālâsyôṅ] *nf* defrosting, thawing.
décongeler [dākôṅzhlā] *vt* to thaw (out).
décongestionner [dākôṅzhestyonā] *vt* (*MÉD*) to decongest; (*rues*) to relieve congestion in.
déconnecter [dākonektā] *vt* to disconnect.
déconner [dākonā] *vi* (*fam!*: *en parlant*) to talk (a load of) garbage (*US*) *ou* rubbish (*Brit*); (: *faire des bêtises*) to mess around; **sans** ~ no kidding.
déconseiller [dākôṅsāyā] *vt*: ~ **qch (à qn)** to advise (sb) against sth; ~ **à qn de faire** to advise sb against doing; **c'est déconseillé** it's not advised *ou* advisable.
déconsidérer [dākôṅsēdārā] *vt* to discredit.
décontaminer [dākôṅtámēnā] *vt* to decontaminate.
décontenancer [dākôṅtnâṅsā] *vt* to disconcert, discountenance.
décontracté, e [dākôṅtráktā] *a* relaxed.
décontracter [dākôṅtráktā] *vt*, **se** ~ *vi* to relax.
décontraction [dākôṅtráksyôṅ] *nf* relaxation.
déconvenue [dākôṅvnü] *nf* disappointment.
décor [dākor] *nm* décor; (*paysage*) scenery; ~**s** *nmpl* (*THÉÂTRE*) scenery *sg*, decor *sg*; (*CINÉMA*) set *sg*; **changement de** ~ (*fig*) change of scene; **entrer dans le** ~ (*fig*) to run off the road; **en** ~ **naturel** (*CINÉMA*) on location.
décorateur, trice [dākoråtœr, -trēs] *nm/f* (interior) decorator; (*CINÉMA*) set designer.
décoratif, ive [dākorátēf, -ēv] *a* decorative.
décoration [dākorâsyôṅ] *nf* decoration.
décorer [dākorā] *vt* to decorate.
décortiqué, e [dākortēkā] *a* shelled; hulled.
décortiquer [dākortēkā] *vt* to shell; (*riz*) to hull; (*fig*) to dissect.
décorum [dākorom] *nm* decorum; etiquette.
décote [dākot] *nf* tax relief.
découcher [dākōōshā] *vi* to spend the night away.
découdre [dākōōdr(ə)] *vt* (*vêtement, couture*) to unpick, take the stitching out of; (*bouton*) to take off; **se** ~ *vi* to come unstitched; (*bouton*) to come off; **en** ~ (*fig*) to fight, do battle.
découler [dākōōlā] *vi*: ~ **de** to ensue *ou* follow from.
découpage [dākōōpázh] *nm* cutting up; carving; (*image*) cut-out (figure); ~ **électoral** division into constituencies.
découper [dākōōpā] *vt* (*papier, tissu etc*) to cut up; (*volaille, viande*) to carve; (*déta-*

cher: manche, article) to cut out; **se ~ sur** (*ciel, fond*) to stand out against.

découplé, e [dākōōplā] *a*: **bien ~** well-built, well-proportioned.

découpure [dākōōpür] *nf*: **~s** (*morceaux*) cut-out bits; (*d'une côte, arête*) indentations, jagged outline *sg*.

découragement [dākōōrāzhmáṅ] *nm* discouragement, despondency.

décourager [dākōōrázhā] *vt* to discourage, dishearten; (*dissuader*) to discourage, put off; **se ~** *vi* to lose heart, become discouraged; **~ qn de faire/de qch** to discourage sb from doing/from sth, put sb off doing/sth.

décousu, e [dākōōzü] *pp de* **découdre** ♦ *a* unstitched; (*fig*) disjointed, disconnected.

découvert, e [dākōōver, -ert(ə)] *pp de* **découvrir** ♦ *a* (*tête*) bare, uncovered; (*lieu*) open, exposed ♦ *nm* (*bancaire*) overdraft ♦ *nf* discovery; **à ~** *ad* (*MIL*) exposed, without cover; (*fig*) openly ♦ *a* (*COMM*) overdrawn; **à visage ~** openly; **aller à la ~e de** to go in search of.

découvrir [dākōōvrēr] *vt* to discover; (*apercevoir*) to see; (*enlever ce qui couvre ou protège*) to uncover; (*montrer, dévoiler*) to reveal; **se ~** to take off one's hat; (*se déshabiller*) to take something off; (*au lit*) to uncover o.s.; (*ciel*) to clear; **se ~ des talents** to find hidden talents in o.s.

décrasser [dākrásā] *vt* to clean.

décrêper [dākrāpā] *vt* (*cheveux*) to straighten.

décrépi, e [dākrāpē] *a* peeling; with roughcast rendering removed.

décrépit, e [dākrāpē, -ēt] *a* decrepit.

décrépitude [dākrāpētüd] *nf* decrepitude, decay.

decrescendo [dākrāshendō] *nm* (*MUS*) decrescendo; **aller ~** (*fig*) to decline, be on the wane.

décret [dākre] *nm* decree.

décréter [dākrātā] *vt* to decree; (*ordonner*) to order.

décret-loi [dākrelwá] *nm* statutory order.

décrié, e [dākrēyā] *a* disparaged.

décrire [dākrēr] *vt* to describe; (*courbe, cercle*) to follow, describe.

décrisper [dākrēspā] *vt* to defuse.

décrit, e [dākrē, -ēt] *pp de* **décrire**.

décrivais [dākrēve] *etc vb voir* **décrire**.

décrochement [dākroshmáṅ] *nm* (*d'un mur etc*) recess.

décrocher [dākroshā] *vt* (*dépendre*) to take down; (*téléphone*) to take off the hook; (: *pour répondre*): **~** (**le téléphone**) to pick up *ou* lift the receiver; (*fig: contrat etc*) to get, land ♦ *vi* to drop out; to switch off; **se ~** *vi* (*tableau, rideau*) to fall down.

décrois [dākrwá] *etc vb voir* **décroître**.

décroiser [dākrwázā] *vt* (*bras*) to unfold; (*jambes*) to uncross.

décroissant, e [dākrwásáṅ, -áṅt] *vb voir* **décroître** ♦ *a* decreasing, declining, diminishing; **par ordre ~** in descending order.

décroître [dākrwátr(ə)] *vi* to decrease, decline, diminish.

décrotter [dākrotā] *vt* (*chaussures*) to clean the mud from; **se ~ le nez** to pick one's nose.

décru, e [dākrü] *pp de* **décroître**.

décrue [dākrü] *nf* drop in level (of the waters).

décrypter [dākrēptā] *vt* to decipher.

déçu, e [dāsü] *pp de* **décevoir** ♦ *a* disappointed.

déculotter [dākülotā] *vt*: **~ qn** to take off sb's pants (*US*) *ou* trousers (*Brit*); **se ~** to take off one's pants *ou* trousers.

déculpabiliser [dākülpábēlēzā] *vt* (*personne*) to relieve of guilt; (*chose*) to decriminalize.

décuple [dāküpl(ə)] *nm*: **le ~ de** ten times; **au ~** tenfold.

décupler [dāküplā] *vt, vi* to increase tenfold.

déçut [dāsü] *etc vb voir* **décevoir**.

dédaignable [dādenyábl(ə)] *a*: **pas ~** not to be despised.

dédaigner [dādānyā] *vt* to despise, scorn; (*négliger*) to disregard, spurn; **~ de faire** to consider it beneath one to do, not deign to do.

dédaigneusement [dādenyœzmáṅ] *ad* scornfully, disdainfully.

dédaigneux, euse [dādenyœ, -œz] *a* scornful, disdainful.

dédain [dādáṅ] *nm* scorn, disdain.

dédale [dādál] *nm* maze.

dedans [dədáṅ] *ad* inside; (*pas en plein air*) indoors, inside ♦ *nm* inside; **au ~** on the inside; inside; **en ~** (*vers l'intérieur*) inwards; *voir aussi* **là**.

dédicace [dādēkás] *nf* (*imprimée*) dedication; (*manuscrite, sur une photo etc*) inscription.

dédicacer [dādēkásā] *vt*: **~ (à qn)** to sign (for sb), autograph (for sb), inscribe (to sb).

dédié, e [dādyā] *a*: **ordinateur ~** dedicated computer.

dédier [dādyā] *vt* to dedicate.

dédire [dādēr]: **se ~** *vi* to go back on one's word; (*se rétracter*) to retract, recant.

dédit, e [dādē, -ēt] *pp de* **dédire** ♦ *nm* (*COMM*) forfeit, penalty.

dédommagement [dādomázhmáṅ] *nm* compensation.

dédommager [dādomázhā] *vt*: **~ qn (de)** to compensate sb (for); (*fig*) to repay sb (for).

dédouaner [dādwánā] *vt* to clear through customs.

dédoublement [dādōōbləmáṅ] *nm* splitting; (*PSYCH*): **~ de la personnalité** split *ou* dual personality.

dédoubler [dādōōblā] *vt* (*classe, effectifs*) to split (into two); (*couverture etc*) to unfold; (*manteau*) to remove the lining of; **~ un train/les trains** to run a relief train/additional trains; **se ~** *vi* (*PSYCH*) to have a split personality.

dédramatiser [dādrámátēzā] *vt* (*situation*) to defuse; (*événement*) to play down.

déductible [dādüktēbl(ə)] *a* deductible.

déduction [dādüksyôṅ] *nf* (*d'argent*) deduction; (*raisonnement*) deduction, inference.

déduire [dādüēr] *vt*: **~ qch (de)** (*ôter*) to deduct sth (from); (*conclure*) to deduce *ou* infer sth (from).

déesse [dāes] *nf* goddess.

DEFA *sigle m* (= *Diplôme d'État relatif aux fonctions d'animation*) *diploma for senior youth leaders*.

défaillance [dāfáyáṅs] *nf* (*syncope*) blackout; (*fatigue*) (sudden) weakness *q*; (*technique*) fault, failure; (*morale etc*) weakness; **~**

cardiaque heart failure.
défaillant, e [dăfáyáǹ, -ȧ̇ńt] a defective; (JUR: témoin) defaulting.
défaillir [dăfáyēr] vi to faint; to feel faint; (mémoire etc) to fail.
défaire [dăfer] vt (installation, échafaudage) to take down, dismantle; (paquet etc, nœud, vêtement) to undo; (bagages) to unpack; (ouvrage) to undo, unpick; (cheveux) to undo, let down; **se ~** vi to come undone; **~ de** vt (se débarrasser de) to get rid of; (se séparer de) to part with; **~ le lit** (pour changer les draps) to strip the bed; (pour se coucher) to turn back the bedclothes.
défait, e [dăfe, -et] pp de **défaire** ♦ a (visage) haggard, ravaged ♦ nf defeat.
défaites [dăfet] vb voir **défaire**.
défaitisme [dăfātēsm(ə)] nm defeatism.
défaitiste [dăfātēst(ə)] a, nm/f defeatist.
défalcation [dăfálkásyóǹ] nf deduction.
défalquer [dăfálkā] vt to deduct.
défasse [dăfás] etc vb voir **défaire**.
défausser [dăfōsá] vt to get rid of; **se ~** vi (CARTES) to discard.
défaut [dăfō] nm (moral) fault, failing, defect; (d'étoffe, métal) fault, flaw, defect; (manque, carence): **~ de** lack of; shortage of; (IN-FORM) bug; **~ de la cuirasse** (fig) chink in the armor; **en ~** at fault; in the wrong; **faire ~** (manquer) to be lacking; **à ~** ad failing that; **à ~ de** for lack ou want of; **par ~** (JUR) in his (ou her etc) absence.
défaveur [dăfávœr] nf disfavor (US), disfavour (Brit).
défavorable [dăfávorábl(ə)] a unfavorable (US), unfavourable (Brit).
défavoriser [dăfávorēzā] vt to put at a disadvantage.
défectif, ive [dăfektēf, -ēv] a: **verbe ~** defective verb.
défection [dăfeksyóǹ] nf defection, failure to give support ou assistance; failure to appear; **faire ~** (d'un parti etc) to withdraw one's support, leave.
défectueux, euse [dăfektüœ̈, -œ̈z] a faulty, defective.
défectuosité [dăfeküōzētā] nf defectiveness q; (défaut) defect, fault.
défendable [dăfȧ̇ńdábl(ə)] a defensible.
défendeur, eresse [dăfȧ̇ńdœr, -dres] nm/f (JUR) defendant.
défendre [dăfȧ̇ńdr(ə)] vt to defend; (interdire) to forbid; **~ à qn qch/de faire** to forbid sb sth/to do; **il est défendu de cracher** spitting (is) prohibited ou is not allowed; **c'est défendu** it is forbidden; **se ~** to defend o.s.; **il se défend** (fig) he can hold his own; **ça se défend** (fig) it holds together; **se ~ de/contre** (se protéger) to protect o.s. from/against; **se ~ de** (se garder de) to refrain from; (nier): **se ~ de vouloir** to deny wanting.
défenestrer [dăfȧ̇ńestrā] vt to throw out of the window.
défense [dăfȧ̇ńs] nf defense (US), defence (Brit); (d'éléphant etc) tusk; **ministre de la ~** Secretary of Defense (US), Minister of Defence (Brit); **la ~ nationale** defense; **la ~ contre avions** anti-aircraft defense; **"~ de fumer/cracher"** "no smoking/spitting", "smoking/spitting prohibited"; **prendre la ~ de qn** to stand up for sb; **~ des consommateurs** consumerism.
défenseur [dăfȧ̇ńsœr] nm defender; (JUR) counsel for the defense (US) ou defence (Brit).
défensif, ive [dăfȧ̇ńsēf, -ēv] a, nf defensive; **être sur la défensive** to be on the defensive.
déferai [dăfrā] etc vb voir **défaire**.
déférence [dăfārȧ̇ńs] nf deference.
déférent, e [dăfārȧ̇ń, -ȧ̇ńt] a (poli) deferential, deferent.
déférer [dăfārā] vt (JUR) to refer; **~ à** vt (requête, décision) to defer to; **~ qn à la justice** to hand sb over to justice.
déferlant, e [dăferlȧ̇ń, -ȧ̇ńt] a: **vague ~e** breaker.
déferlement [dăferləmȧ̇ń] nm breaking; surge.
déferler [dăferlā] vi (vagues) to break; (fig) to surge.
défi [dăfē] nm (provocation) challenge; (bravade) defiance; **mettre qn au ~ de faire qch** to challenge sb to do sth; **relever un ~** to take up ou accept a challenge.
défiance [dăfyȧ̇ńs] nf mistrust, distrust.
déficeler [dăfēslā] vt (paquet) to undo, untie.
déficience [dăfēsyȧ̇ńs] nf deficiency.
déficient, e [dăfēsyȧ̇ń, -ȧ̇ńt] a deficient.
déficit [dăfēsēt] nm (COMM) deficit; (PSYCH etc: manque) defect; **~ budgétaire** budget deficit; **être en ~** to be in deficit.
déficitaire [dăfēsēter] a (année, récolte) bad; **entreprise/budget ~** business/budget in deficit.
défier [dăfyā] vt (provoquer) to challenge; (fig) to defy, brave; **se ~ de** (se méfier de) to distrust, mistrust; **~ qn de faire** to challenge ou defy sb to do; **~ qn à** to challenge sb to; **~ toute comparaison/concurrence** to be incomparable/unbeatable.
défigurer [dăfēgürā] vt to disfigure; (suj: boutons etc) to mar ou spoil (the looks of); (fig: œuvre) to mutilate, deface.
défilé [dăfēlā] nm (GÉO) (narrow) gorge ou pass; (soldats) parade; (manifestants) procession, march; **un ~ de** (voitures, visiteurs etc) a stream of.
défiler [dăfēlā] vi (troupes) to march past; (sportifs) to parade; (manifestants) to march; (visiteurs) to pour, stream; **se ~** vi (se dérober) to slip away, sneak off; **faire ~** (bande, film) to put on; (INFORM) to scroll.
défini, e [dăfēnē] a definite.
définir [dăfēnēr] vt to define.
définissable [dăfēnēsábl(ə)] a definable.
définitif, ive [dăfēnētēf, -ēv] a (final) final, definitive; (pour longtemps) permanent, definitive; (sans appel) final, definite ♦ nf: **en définitive** eventually; (somme toute) when all is said and done.
définition [dăfēnēsyóǹ] nf definition; (de mots croisés) clue; (TV) (picture) resolution.
définitivement [dăfēnētēvmáǹ] ad definitively; permanently; definitely.
défit [dăfē] etc vb voir **défaire**.
déflagration [dăflágrásyóǹ] nf explosion.
déflation [dăflásyóǹ] nf deflation.

déflationniste [dāflásyonēst(ə)] *a* deflationist, deflationary.

déflecteur [dāflɛktœr] *nm* (*AUTO*) deflector (*US*), quarterlight (*Brit*).

déflorer [dāflōrā] *vt* (*jeune fille*) to deflower; (*fig*) to spoil the charm of.

défoncé, e [dāfôǹsā] *a* smashed in; broken down; (*route*) full of potholes ♦ *nm/f* addict.

défoncer [dāfôǹsā] *vt* (*caisse*) to stave in; (*porte*) to smash in *ou* down; (*lit, fauteuil*) to burst (the springs of); (*terrain, route*) to rip up, plow (*US*) *ou* plough (*Brit*) up; **se ~** *vi* (*se donner à fond*) to give it all one's got.

défont [dāfôǹ] *vb voir* **défaire**.

déformant, e [dāfôrmàǹ, -àǹt] *a*: **glace** *ou* **miroir ~(e)** distorting mirror.

déformation [dāformàsyôǹ] *nf* loss of shape; deformation; distortion; **~ professionnelle** conditioning by one's job.

déformer [dāformā] *vt* to put out of shape; (*corps*) to deform; (*pensée, fait*) to distort; **se ~** *vi* to lose its shape.

défoulement [dāfōōlmàǹ] *nm* release of tension; unwinding.

défouler [dāfōōlā]: **se ~** *vi* (*PSYCH*) to work off one's tensions, release one's pent-up feelings; (*gén*) to unwind, let off steam.

défraîchi, e [dāfrāshē] *a* faded; (*article à vendre*) shopworn (*US*), shop-soiled (*Brit*).

défraîchir [dāfrāshēr]: **se ~** *vi* to fade; to become shopworn (*US*) *ou* shop-soiled (*Brit*).

défrayer [dāfrāyā] *vt*: **~ qn** to pay sb's expenses; **~ la chronique** to be in the news; **~ la conversation** to be the main topic of conversation.

défrichement [dāfrēshmàǹ] *nm* clearance.

défricher [dāfrēshā] *vt* to clear (for cultivation).

défriser [dāfrēzā] *vt* (*cheveux*) to straighten; (*fig*) to annoy.

défroisser [dāfrwàsā] *vt* to smooth out.

défroque [dāfrok] *nf* castoff.

défroqué [dāfrokā] *nm* former monk (*ou* priest).

défroquer [dāfrokā] *vi* (*aussi*: **se ~**) to give up the cloth, renounce one's vows.

défunt, e [dāfœǹ, -œǹt] *a*: **son ~ père** his late father ♦ *nm/f* deceased.

dégagé, e [dāgázhā] *a* clear; (*ton, air*) casual, jaunty.

dégagement [dāgázhmàǹ] *nm* emission; freeing; clearing; (*espace libre*) clearing; passage; clearance; (*FOOTBALL*) clearance; **voie de ~** on *ou* off ramp (*US*), slip road (*Brit*); **itinéraire de ~** alternative route (*to relieve traffic congestion*).

dégager [dāgázhā] *vt* (*exhaler*) to give off, emit; (*délivrer*) to free, extricate; (*MIL*: *troupes*) to relieve; (*désencombrer*) to clear; (*isoler, mettre en valeur*) to bring out; (*crédits*) to release; **se ~** *vi* (*odeur*) to emanate, be given off; (*passage, ciel*) to clear; **~ qn de** (*engagement, parole etc*) to release *ou* free sb from; **se ~ de** (*fig*: *engagement etc*) to get out of; (*: promesse*) to go back on.

dégaine [dāgen] *nf* awkward way of walking.

dégainer [dāgānā] *vt* to draw.

dégarni, e [dāgárnē] *a* bald.

dégarnir [dāgárnēr] *vt* (*vider*) to empty, clear; **se ~** *vi* to empty; to be cleaned out *ou* cleared; (*tempes, crâne*) to go bald.

dégâts [dāgá] *nmpl* damage *sg*; **faire des ~** to damage.

dégazer [dāgázā] *vi* (*pétrolier*) to clean its tanks.

dégel [dāzhel] *nm* thaw; (*fig: des prix etc*) unfreezing.

dégeler [dāzhlā] *vt* to thaw (out); (*fig*) to unfreeze ♦ *vi* to thaw (out); **se ~** *vi* (*fig*) to thaw out.

dégénéré, e [dāzhānārā] *a*, *nm/f* degenerate.

dégénérer [dāzhānārā] *vi* to degenerate; (*empirer*) to go from bad to worse; (*devenir*): **~ en** to degenerate into.

dégénérescence [dāzhānārāsáǹs] *nf* degeneration.

dégingandé, e [dāzhàǹgàǹdā] *a* gangling, lanky.

dégivrage [dāzhēvrázh] *nm* defrosting; de-icing.

dégivrer [dāzhēvrā] *vt* (*frigo*) to defrost; (*vitres*) to de-ice.

dégivreur [dāzhēvrœr] *nm* defroster; de-icer.

déglinguer [dāglàǹgā] *vt* to bust.

déglutir [dāglütēr] *vt*, *vi* to swallow.

déglutition [dāglütēsyóǹ] *nf* swallowing.

dégonflé, e [dāgóǹflā] *a* (*pneu*) flat; (*fam*) chicken ♦ *nm/f* (*fam*) chicken.

dégonfler [dāgóǹflā] *vt* (*pneu, ou ballon*) to let down, deflate ♦ *vi* (*désenfler*) to go down; **se ~** *vi* (*fam*) to chicken out.

dégorger [dāgorzhā] *vi* (*CULIN*): **faire ~** to (leave to) sweat; (*aussi*: **se ~**: *rivière*): **~ dans** to flow into ♦ *vt* to disgorge.

dégoter [dāgotā] *vt* (*fam*) to dig up, find.

dégouliner [dāgōōlēnā] *vi* to trickle, drip; **~ de** to be dripping with.

dégoupiller [dāgōōpēyā] *vt* (*grenade*) to take the pin out of.

dégourdi, e [dāgōōrdē] *a* smart, resourceful.

dégourdir [dāgōōrdēr] *vt* to warm (up); **se ~ (les jambes)** to stretch one's legs.

dégoût [dāgōō] *nm* disgust, distaste.

dégoûtant, e [dāgōōtàǹ, -àǹt] *a* disgusting.

dégoûté, e [dāgōōtā] *a* disgusted; **~ de** sick of.

dégoûter [dāgōōtā] *vt* to disgust; **cela me dégoûte** I find this disgusting *ou* revolting; **~ qn de qch** to put sb off sth; **se ~ de** to get *ou* become sick of.

dégoutter [dāgōōtā] *vi* to drip; **~ de** to be dripping with.

dégradant, e [dāgrádàǹ, -àǹt] *a* degrading.

dégradation [dāgrádásyôǹ] *nf* reduction in rank; defacement; degradation, debasement; deterioration; (*aussi*: **~s**: *dégâts*) damage *q*.

dégradé, e [dāgrádā] *a* (*couleur*) shaded off; (*teintes*) faded; (*cheveux*) layered ♦ *nm* (*PEINTURE*) gradation.

dégrader [dāgrádā] *vt* (*MIL*: *officier*) to degrade; (*abîmer*) to damage, deface; (*avilir*) to degrade, debase; **se ~** *vi* (*relations, situation*) to deteriorate.

dégrafer [dāgráfā] *vt* to unclip, unhook, unfasten.

dégraissage [dāgrɛsázh] *nm* (*ÉCON*) cutbacks *pl*; **~ et nettoyage à sec** dry cleaning.

dégraissant [dāgresáṅ] *nm* spot remover.

dégraisser [dāgrāsā] *vt* (*soupe*) to skim; (*vêtement*) to take the grease marks out of; (*ÉCON*) to cut back; (*: entreprise*) to slim down.

degré [dəgrā] *nm* degree; (*d'escalier*) step; **brûlure au 1er/2ème** ~ 1st/2nd degree burn; **équation du 1er/2ème** ~ linear/quadratic equation; **le premier** ~ (*SCOL*) elementary (*US*) ou primary (*Brit*) level; **alcool à 90** ~**s** rubbing alcohol (*US*), surgical spirit (*Brit*); **vin de 10** ~**s** 10° wine (*on Gay-Lussac scale*); **par** ~(**s**) *ad* by degrees, gradually.

dégressif, ive [dāgrāsēf, -ēv] *a* on a decreasing scale, degressive; **tarif** ~ decreasing rate of charge.

dégrèvement [dāgrevmáṅ] *nm* tax relief.

dégrever [dāgrəvā] *vt* to grant tax relief to; to reduce the tax burden on.

dégriffé, e [dāgrēfā] *a* (*vêtement*) sold without the designer's label.

dégringolade [dāgraṅgolád] *nf* tumble; (*fig*) collapse.

dégringoler [dāgraṅgolā] *vi* to tumble (down); (*fig: prix, monnaie etc*) to collapse.

dégriser [dāgrēzā] *vt* to sober up.

dégrossir [dāgrōsēr] *vt* (*bois*) to trim; (*fig*) to rough out; (*: personne*) to knock the rough edges off.

déguenillé, e [degnēyā] *a* ragged, tattered.

déguerpir [dāgerpēr] *vi* to clear out.

dégueulasse [dāgœlás] *a* (*fam*) disgusting.

dégueuler [dāgœlā] *vi* (*fam*) to puke, throw up.

déguisé, e [dāgēzā] *a* disguised; dressed up; ~ **en** disguised (*ou* dressed up) as.

déguisement [dāgēzmáṅ] *nm* disguise; (*habits: pour s'amuser*) dressing-up clothes; (*: pour tromper*) disguise.

déguiser [dāgēzā] *vt* to disguise; **se** ~ (**en**) (*se costumer*) to dress up (as); (*pour tromper*) to disguise o.s. (as).

dégustation [dāgüstásyóṅ] *nf* tasting; sampling; savoring (*US*), savouring (*Brit*); (*séance*): ~ **de vin(s)** wine-tasting.

déguster [dāgüstā] *vt* (*vins*) to taste; (*fromages etc*) to sample; (*savourer*) to enjoy, savor (*US*), savour (*Brit*).

déhancher [dāáṅshā]: **se** ~ *vi* to sway one's hips; to lean (one's weight) on one hip.

dehors [dəor] *ad* outside; (*en plein air*) outdoors, outside ♦ *nm* outside ♦ *nmpl* (*apparences*) appearances, exterior *sg*; **mettre** *ou* **jeter** ~ to throw out; **au** ~ outside; (*en apparence*) outwardly; **au** ~ **de** outside; **de** ~ from outside; **en** ~ outside; outwards; **en** ~ **de** apart from.

déifier [dāēfyā] *vt* to deify.

déjà [dāzhá] *ad* already; (*auparavant*) before, already; **as-tu** ~ **été en France?** have you been to France before?; **c'est** ~ **pas mal** that's not too bad (at all); **c'est** ~ **quelque chose** (at least) it's better than nothing; **quel nom,** ~? what was the name again?

déjanter [dāzháṅtā]: **se** ~ *vi* (*pneu*) to come off the rim.

déjà-vu [dāzhávü] *nm*: **c'est du** ~ there's nothing new in that.

déjeté, e [dezhtā] *a* lop-sided, crooked.

déjeuner [dāzhœnā] *vi* to (have) lunch; (*le matin*) to have breakfast ♦ *nm* lunch; (*petit déjeuner*) breakfast; ~ **d'affaires** business lunch.

déjouer [dāzhwā] *vt* to elude; to foil, thwart.

déjuger [dāzhüzhā]: **se** ~ *vi* to reverse one's opinion.

delà [dəlá] *ad*: **par** ~, **en** ~ (**de**), **au** ~ (**de**) beyond.

délabré, e [dālâbrā] *a* dilapidated, broken-down.

délabrement [dālâbrəmáṅ] *nm* decay, dilapidation.

délabrer [dālâbrā]: **se** ~ *vi* to fall into decay, become dilapidated.

délacer [dālásā] *vt* to unlace, untie.

délai [dāle] *nm* (*attente*) waiting period; (*sursis*) extension (of time); (*temps accordé: aussi*: ~**s**) time limit; **sans** ~ without delay; **à bref** ~ shortly, very soon; at short notice; **dans les** ~**s** within the time limit; **un** ~ **de 30 jours** a period of 30 days; **comptez un** ~ **de livraison de 10 jours** allow 10 days for delivery.

délaissé, e [dālāsā] *a* abandoned, deserted; neglected.

délaisser [dālāsā] *vt* (*abandonner*) to abandon, desert; (*négliger*) to neglect.

délassant, e [dālásáṅ, -áṅt] *a* relaxing.

délassement [dālásmáṅ] *nm* relaxation.

délasser [dālásā] *vt* (*reposer*) to relax; (*divertir*) to divert, entertain; **se** ~ *vi* to relax.

délateur, trice [dālátœr, -trēs] *nm/f* informer.

délation [dālásyóṅ] *nf* denouncement, informing.

délavé, e [dālávā] *a* faded.

délayage [dāleyázh] *nm* mixing; thinning down.

délayer [dālāyā] *vt* (*CULIN*) to mix (with water etc); (*peinture*) to thin down; (*fig*) to pad out, spin out.

delco [delkō] *nm* ® (*AUTO*) distributor; **tête de** ~ distributor cap.

délectation [dālektásyóṅ] *nf* delight.

délecter [dālektā]: **se** ~ *vi*: **se** ~ **de** to revel *ou* delight in.

délégation [dālāgásyóṅ] *nf* delegation; ~ **de pouvoir** delegation of power.

délégué, e [dālāgā] *a* delegated ♦ *nm/f* delegate; representative; **ministre** ~ **à** minister with special responsibility for.

déléguer [dālāgā] *vt* to delegate.

délestage [dālestázh] *nm*: **itinéraire de** ~ alternative route (*to relieve traffic congestion*).

délester [dālestā] *vt* (*navire*) to unballast; ~ **une route** to relieve traffic congestion on a road by diverting traffic.

Delhi [delē] *n* Delhi.

délibérant, e [dālēbāráṅ, -áṅt] *a*: **assemblée** ~**e** deliberative assembly.

délibératif, ive [dālēbārátēf, -ēv] *a*: **avoir voix délibérative** to have voting rights.

délibération [dālēbārásyóṅ] *nf* deliberation.

délibéré, e [dālēbārā] *a* (*conscient*) deliberate; (*déterminé*) determined, resolute; **de propos** ~ (*à dessein, exprès*) intentionally.

délibérément [dālēbārāmáṅ] *ad* deliberately;

(*résolument*) resolutely.
délibérer [dālēbārā] *vi* to deliberate.
délicat, e [dālēkà, -àt] *a* delicate; (*plein de tact*) tactful; (*attentionné*) thoughtful; (*exigeant*) fussy, particular; **procédés peu ~s** unscrupulous methods.
délicatement [dālēkátmáṅ] *ad* delicately; (*avec douceur*) gently.
délicatesse [dālēkàtes] *nf* delicacy; tactfulness; thoughtfulness; **~s** *nfpl* attentions, consideration *sg*.
délice [dālēs] *nm* delight.
délicieusement [dālēsyōēzmáṅ] *ad* deliciously; delightfully.
délicieux, euse [dālēsyōē, -ēz] *a* (*au goût*) delicious; (*sensation, impression*) delightful.
délictueux, euse [dālēktüēē, -ēz] *a* criminal.
délié, e [dālyā] *a* nimble, agile; (*mince*) slender, fine ♦ *nm*: **les ~s** the upstrokes (*in handwriting*).
délier [dālyā] *vt* to untie; **~ qn de** (*serment etc*) to free *ou* release sb from.
délimitation [dālēmētàsyóṅ] *nf* delimitation.
délimiter [dālēmētā] *vt* to delimit.
délinquance [dālaṅkáṅs] *nf* criminality; **~ juvénile** juvenile delinquency.
délinquant, e [dālaṅkáṅ, -áṅt] *a*, *nm/f* delinquent.
déliquescence [dālēkāsáṅs] *nf*: **en ~** in a state of decay.
déliquescent, e [dālēkāsáṅ, -áṅt] *a* decaying.
délirant, e [dālēráṅ, -áṅt] *a* (*MÉD*: *fièvre*) delirious; (*imagination*) frenzied; (*fam*: *déraisonnable*) crazy.
délire [dālēr] *nm* (*fièvre*) delirium; (*fig*) frenzy; (: *folie*) lunacy.
délirer [dālērā] *vi* to be delirious; (*fig*) to be raving.
délit [dālē] *nm* (criminal) offense (*US*) *ou* offence (*Brit*); **~ de droit commun** violation of common law; **~ de fuite** failure to stop after an accident; **~ de presse** violation of the press laws.
délivrance [dālēvráṅs] *nf* freeing, release; (*sentiment*) relief.
délivrer [dālēvrā] *vt* (*prisonnier*) to (set) free, release; (*passeport, certificat*) to issue; **~ qn de** (*ennemis*) to set sb free from, deliver *ou* free sb from; (*fig*) to rid sb of.
déloger [dālozhā] *vt* (*locataire*) to evict; (*objet coincé, ennemi*) to dislodge.
déloyal, e, aux [dālwàyál, -ō] *a* (*personne, conduite*) disloyal; (*procédé*) unfair.
Delphes [delf] *n* Delphi.
delta [deltá] *nm* (*GÉO*) delta.
deltaplane [deltáplán] *nm* ® hang glider.
déluge [dālüzh] *nm* (*biblique*) Flood, Deluge; (*grosse pluie*) downpour, deluge; (*grand nombre*): **~ de** flood of.
déluré, e [dālürā] *a* smart, resourceful; (*péj*) forward, pert.
démagogie [dāmágozhē] *nf* demagogy.
démagogique [dāmágozhēk] *a* demagogic, popularity-seeking; (*POL*) vote-catching.
démagogue [dāmágog] *a* demagogic ♦ *nm* demagogue.
démaillé, e [dāmáyā] *a* (*bas*) with a run (*ou* runs), laddered (*Brit*).
demain [dəmaṅ] *ad* tomorrow; **~ matin/soir**

tomorrow morning/evening; **~ midi** tomorrow at midday; **à ~!** see you tomorrow!
demande [dəmáṅd] *nf* (*requête*) request; (*revendication*) demand; (*ADMIN, formulaire*) application; (*ÉCON*): **la ~** demand; **"~s d'emploi"** "jobs *ou* work wanted" (*US*), "situations wanted" (*Brit*); **à la ~ générale** by popular request; **~ en mariage** (marriage) proposal; **faire sa ~ (en mariage)** to propose (marriage); **~ de naturalisation** application for naturalization; **~ de poste** job application.
demandé, e [dəmáṅdā] *a* (*article etc*): **très ~** (very) much in demand.
demander [dəmáṅdā] *vt* to ask for; (*question: date, heure, chemin*) to ask; (*requérir, nécessiter*) to require, demand; **~ qch à qn** to ask sb for sth, ask sb sth; **ils demandent 2 secrétaires et un ingénieur** they're looking for 2 secretaries and an engineer; **~ la main de qn** to ask for sb's hand (in marriage); **~ pardon à qn** to apologize to sb; **~ à ou de voir/faire** to ask to see/ask if one can do; **~ à qn de faire** to ask sb to do; **~ que/pourquoi** to ask that/why; **se ~ si/pourquoi** *etc* to wonder if/why *etc*; (*sens purement réfléchi*) to ask o.s. if/why *etc*; **on vous demande au téléphone** you're wanted on the phone, there's someone for you on the phone; **il ne demande que ça** that's all he wants; **je ne demande pas mieux** I'm asking nothing more; **il ne demande qu'à faire** all he wants is to do.
demandeur, euse [dəmáṅdœr, -ēz] *nm/f*: **~ d'emploi** job-seeker.
démangeaison [dāmáṅzhezóṅ] *nf* itching.
démanger [dāmáṅzhā] *vi* to itch; **la main me démange** my hand is itching; **l'envie** *ou* **ça me démange de faire** I'm itching to do.
démanteler [dāmáṅtlā] *vt* to break up; to demolish.
démaquillant [dāmákēyáṅ] *nm* make-up remover.
démaquiller [dāmákēyā] *vt*: **se ~** to remove one's make-up.
démarcage [dāmárkázh] *nm* = démarquage.
démarcation [dāmárkásyóṅ] *nf* demarcation.
démarchage [dāmársházh] *nm* (*COMM*) door-to-door selling.
démarche [dāmársh(ə)] *nf* (*allure*) gait, walk; (*intervention*) step; approach; (*fig: intellectuelle*) thought processes *pl*; approach; **faire** *ou* **entreprendre des ~s** to take action; **faire des ~s auprès de qn** to approach sb.
démarcheur, euse [dāmárshœr, -ēz] *nm/f* (*COMM*) door-to-door salesman/woman; (*POL etc*) canvasser.
démarquage [dāmárkázh] *nm* marking down.
démarque [dāmárk(ə)] *nf* (*COMM*: *d'un article*) markdown.
démarqué, e [dāmárkā] *a* (*FOOTBALL*) unmarked; (*COMM*) reduced; **prix ~s** marked-down prices.
démarquer [dāmárkā] *vt* (*prix*) to mark down; (*joueur*) to stop marking; **se ~** *vi* (*SPORT*) to shake off one's marker.
démarrage [dāmárázh] *nm* starting *q*, start; **~ en côte** hill start.
démarrer [dāmárā] *vt* to start up ♦ *vi* (*con-*

ducteur) to start (up); (*véhicule*) to move off; (*travaux, affaire*) to get moving; (*coureur: accélérer*) to pull away.

démarreur [dāmárœr] *nm* (*AUTO*) starter.

démasquer [dāmáskā] *vt* to unmask; **se ~** to unmask; (*fig*) to drop one's mask.

démâter [dāmâtā] *vt* to dismast ♦ *vi* to be dismasted.

démêlant, e [dāmālâṅ, -âṅt] *a*: **baume ~, crème ~e** (hair) conditioner.

démêler [dāmālā] *vt* to untangle, disentangle.

démêlés [dāmālā] *nmpl* problems.

démembrer [dāmáṅbrā] *vt* to slice up, tear apart.

déménagement [dāmānázhmáṅ] *nm* (*du point de vue du locataire etc*) moving; (*: du déménageur*) moving (*US*), removal (*Brit*); **entreprise/camion de ~** moving (*US*) *ou* removal (*Brit*) firm/van.

déménager [dāmānázhā] *vt* (*meubles*) to (re)move ♦ *vi* to move.

déménageur [dāmānázhœr] *nm* (furniture) mover (*US*), removal man (*Brit*); (*entrepreneur*) furniture mover (*US*) *ou* remover (*Brit*).

démence [dāmâṅs] *nf* madness, insanity; (*MÉD*) dementia.

démener [dāmnā]: **se ~** *vi* to thrash about; (*fig*) to exert o.s.

dément, e [dāmâṅ, -âṅt] *vb voir* **démentir** ♦ *a* (*fou*) crazy; (*fam*) brilliant, fantastic.

démentiel, le [dāmáṅsyel] *a* insane.

démentir [dāmáṅtēr] *vt* (*nouvelle, témoin*) to refute; (*suj: faits etc*) to belie, refute; **~ que** to deny that; **ne pas se ~** not to fail, keep up.

démerder [dāmœrdā]: **se ~** *vi* (*fam!*) to look after o.s., look out for o.s.

démériter [dāmārētā] *vi*: **~ auprès de qn** to come down in sb's esteem.

démesure [dāmзzür] *nf* immoderation, immoderateness.

démesuré, e [dāmзzürā] *a* immoderate, disproportionate.

démesurément [dāmзzürāmáṅ] *ad* disproportionately.

démettre [dāmetr(з)] *vt*: **~ qn de** (*fonction, poste*) to dismiss sb from; **se ~ (de ses fonctions)** to resign (from) one's duties; **se ~ l'épaule** *etc* to dislocate one's shoulder *etc*.

demeurant [dзmœráṅ]: **au ~** *ad* for all that.

demeure [dзmœr] *nf* residence; (*fig*) last resting place; **mettre qn en ~ de faire** to enjoin *ou* order sb to do; **à ~** *ad* permanently.

demeuré, e [dзmœrā] *a* backward ♦ *nm/f* backward person.

demeurer [dзmœrā] *vi* (*habiter*) to live; (*séjourner*) to stay; (*rester*) to remain; **en ~ là** (*suj: personne*) to leave it at that; (*: choses*) to be left at that.

demi, e [dзmē] *a*: **et ~: trois heures/ bouteilles et ~es** three and a half hours/ bottles, three hours/bottles and a half ♦ *nm* (*bière*) ≈ half-pint (*.25 litre*); (*FOOTBALL*) halfback; **il est 2 heures/midi et ~e** it's half past 2/12; **~ de mêlée/d'ouverture** (*RUGBY*) scrum/stand-off half; **à ~** *ad* half-; **ouvrir à ~** to half-open; **faire les choses à ~** to do

things by halves; **à la ~e** (*heure*) on the half-hour.

demi... [dзmē] *préfixe* half-, semi..., demi-.

demi-bas [dзmēbá] *nm inv* (*chaussette*) kneesock.

demi-bouteille [dзmēbōōtey] *nf* half-bottle.

demi-cercle [dзmēserkl(з)] *nm* semicircle; **en ~** *a* semicircular ♦ *ad* in a semicircle.

demi-douzaine [dзmēdōōzen] *nf* half-dozen, half a dozen.

demi-finale [dзmēfēnál] *nf* semifinal.

demi-finaliste [dзmēfēnálēst(з)] *nm/f* semifinalist.

demi-fond [dзmēfôṅ] *nm* (*SPORT*) mediumdistance running.

demi-frère [dзmēfrer] *nm* half-brother.

demi-gros [dзmēgrō] *nm inv* wholesale trade.

demi-heure [dзmēœr] *nf*: **une ~** a half-hour, half an hour.

demi-jour [dзmēzhōōr] *nm* half-light.

demi-journée [dзmēzhōōrnā] *nf* half-day, half a day.

démilitariser [dāmēlētárēzā] *vt* to demilitarize.

demi-litre [dзmēlētr(з)] *nm* half-liter (*US*), half-litre (*Brit*), half a liter *ou* litre.

demi-livre [dзmēlēvr(з)] *nf* half-pound, half a pound.

demi-longueur [dзmēlôṅgœr] *nf* (*SPORT*) half-length, half a length.

demi-lune [dзmēlün]: **en ~** *a inv* semicircular.

demi-mal [dзmēmál] *nm*: **il n'y a que ~** there's not much harm done.

demi-mesure [dзmēmзür] *nf* half-measure.

demi-mot [dзmēmō]: **à ~** *ad* without having to spell things out.

déminer [dāmēnā] *vt* to clear of mines.

démineur [dāmēnœr] *nm* bomb disposal expert.

demi-pension [dзmēpáṅsyôṅ] *nf* half-board; **être en ~** (*SCOL*) to buy lunch at school.

demi-pensionnaire [dзmēpáṅsyoner] *nm/f* (*SCOL*) day student (*US*) *ou* pupil (*Brit*).

demi-place [dзmēplás] *nf* half-price; (*TRANSPORTS*) half-fare.

démis, e [dāmē, -ēz] *pp de* **démettre** ♦ *a* (*épaule etc*) dislocated.

demi-saison [dзmēsezôṅ] *nf*: **vêtements de ~** spring *ou* fall (*US*) *ou* autumn (*Brit*) clothing.

demi-sel [dзmēsel] *a inv* slightly salted.

demi-sœur [dзmēsœr] *nf* half-sister.

demi-sommeil [dзmēsomey] *nm* doze.

demi-soupir [dзmēsōōpēr] *nm* (*MUS*) eighth (*US*) *ou* quaver (*Brit*) rest.

démission [dāmēsyôṅ] *nf* resignation; **donner sa ~** to give *ou* hand in one's notice, hand in one's resignation.

démissionnaire [dāmēsyoner] *a* outgoing ♦ *nm/f* person resigning.

démissionner [dāmēsyonā] *vi* (*de son poste*) to resign, give *ou* hand in one's notice.

demi-tarif [dзmētárēf] *nm* half-price; (*TRANSPORTS*) half-fare.

demi-ton [dзmētôṅ] *nm* (*MUS*) half step (*US*), semitone.

demi-tour [dзmētōōr] *nm* about-face (*US*), about-turn (*Brit*); **faire un ~** (*MIL etc*) to make an about-face (*US*) *ou* about-turn (*Brit*); **faire ~** to turn (and go) back;

(*AUTO*) to make a U-turn.

démobilisation [dāmobēlēzâsyóń] *nf* demobilization; (*fig*) demotivation, demoralization.

démobiliser [dāmobēlēzā] *vt* to demobilize; (*fig*) to demotivate, demoralize.

démocrate [dāmokrát] *a* democratic ♦ *nm/f* democrat.

démocrate-chrétien, ne [dāmokrátkrātyań, -en] *nm/f* Christian Democrat.

démocratie [dāmokrásē] *nf* democracy; ~ **populaire/libérale** people's/liberal democracy.

démocratique [dāmokrátēk] *a* democratic.

démocratiquement [dāmokrátēkmáń] *ad* democratically.

démocratiser [dāmokrátēzā] *vt* to democratize.

démodé, e [dāmodā] *a* old-fashioned.

démoder [dāmodā]: **se** ~ *vi* to go out of fashion.

démographie [dāmográfē] *nf* demography.

démographique [dāmográfēk] *a* demographic; **poussée** ~ increase in population.

demoiselle [dəmwázel] *nf* (*jeune fille*) young lady; (*célibataire*) single lady, maiden lady; ~ **d'honneur** bridesmaid.

démolir [dāmolēr] *vt* to demolish; (*fig: personne*) to do in.

démolisseur [dāmolēsœr] *nm* demolition worker.

démolition [dāmolēsyóń] *nf* demolition.

démon [dāmóń] *nm* demon, fiend; evil spirit; (*enfant turbulent*) devil, demon; **le** ~ **du jeu/des femmes** a mania for gambling/women; **le D**~ the Devil.

démonétiser [dāmonātēzā] *vt* to demonetize.

démoniaque [dāmonyák] *a* fiendish.

démonstrateur, trice [dāmóństrátœr, -trēs] *nm/f* demonstrator.

démonstratif, ive [dāmóństrátēf, -ēv] *a, nm* (*aussi LING*) demonstrative.

démonstration [dāmóństrâsyóń] *nf* demonstration; (*aérienne, navale*) display.

démontable [dāmóńtábl(ə)] *a* folding.

démontage [dāmóńtázh] *nm* dismantling.

démonté, e [dāmóńtā] *a* (*fig*) raging, wild.

démonte-pneu [dāmóńtəpnœ̄] *nm* tire iron (*US*), tyre lever (*Brit*).

démonter [dāmóńtā] *vt* (*machine etc*) to take down, dismantle; (*pneu, porte*) to take off; (*cavalier*) to throw, unseat; (*fig: personne*) to disconcert; **se** ~ *vi* (*personne*) to lose countenance.

démontrable [dāmóńtrábl(ə)] *a* demonstrable.

démontrer [dāmóńtrā] *vt* to demonstrate, show.

démoralisant, e [dāmorálēzáń, -áńt] *a* demoralizing.

démoralisateur, trice [dāmorálēzátœr, -trēs] *a* demoralizing.

démoraliser [dāmorálēzā] *vt* to demoralize.

démordre [dāmordr(ə)] *vi*: **ne pas** ~ **de** to refuse to give up, stick to.

démouler [dāmōōlā] *vt* (*gâteau*) to unmold (*US*), turn out (*Brit*).

démoustiquer [dāmōōstēkā] *vt* to clear of mosquitoes.

démultiplication [dāmültēplēkâsyóń] *nf* reduction; reduction ratio.

démuni, e [dāmünē] *a* (*sans argent*) impoverished; ~ **de** without, lacking in.

démunir [dāmünēr] *vt*: ~ **qn de** to deprive sb of; **se** ~ **de** to part with, give up.

démuseler [dāmüzlā] *vt* to unmuzzle.

démystifier [dāmēstēfyā] *vt* to demystify.

démythifier [dāmētēfyā] *vt* to demythologize.

dénatalité [dānátálētā] *nf* fall in the birth rate.

dénationalisation [dānásyonálēzâsyóń] *nf* denationalization.

dénationaliser [dānásyonálēzā] *vt* to denationalize.

dénaturé, e [dānátürā] *a* (*alcool*) denatured (*US*), denaturized (*Brit*); (*goûts*) unnatural.

dénaturer [dānátürā] *vt* (*goût*) to alter (completely); (*pensée, fait*) to distort, misrepresent.

dénégations [dānāgâsyóń] *nfpl* denials.

déneigement [dānezhmáń] *nm* snow removal.

déneiger [dānāzhā] *vt* to remove *ou* shovel snow from.

déni [dānē] *nm*: ~ **(de justice)** denial of justice.

déniaiser [dānyāzā] *vt*: ~ **qn** to teach sb about life.

dénicher [dānēshā] *vt* to unearth.

dénicotinisé, e [dānēkotēnēzā] *a* nicotine-free.

denier [dənyā] *nm* (*monnaie*) formerly, a coin of small value; (*de bas*) denier; ~ **du culte** contribution to parish upkeep; ~**s publics** public money; **de ses (propres)** ~**s** out of one's own pocket.

dénier [dānyā] *vt* to deny; ~ **qch à qn** to deny sb sth.

dénigrer [dānēgrā] *vt* to denigrate, run down.

dénivelé, e [dānēvlā] *a* (*chaussée*) on a lower level ♦ *nm* difference in height.

déniveler [dānēvlā] *vt* to make uneven; to put on a lower level.

dénivellation [dānēvelâsyóń] *nf*, **dénivellement** [dānēvelmáń] *nm* difference in level; (*pente*) ramp; (*creux*) dip.

dénombrer [dānóńbrā] *vt* (*compter*) to count; (*énumérer*) to enumerate, list.

dénominateur [dānomēnátœr] *nm* denominator; ~ **commun** common denominator.

dénomination [dānomēnásyóń] *nf* designation, appellation.

dénommé, e [dānomā] *a*: **le** ~ **Dupont** the man by the name of Dupont.

dénommer [dānomā] *vt* to name.

dénoncer [dānóńsā] *vt* to denounce; **se** ~ to give o.s. up, come forward.

dénonciation [dānóńsyâsyóń] *nf* denunciation.

dénoter [dānotā] *vt* to denote.

dénouement [dānōōmáń] *nm* outcome, conclusion; (*THÉÂTRE*) dénouement.

dénouer [dānwā] *vt* to unknot, undo.

dénoyauter [dānwáyōtā] *vt* to pit (*US*), stone (*Brit*); **appareil à** ~ pitter (*US*), stoner (*Brit*).

dénoyauteur [dānwáyōtœr] *nm* pitter (*US*), stoner (*Brit*).

denrée [dáńrā] *nf* commodity; (*aussi*: ~ **alimentaire**) food(stuff).

dense [dáńs] *a* dense.

densité [dáńsētā] *nf* denseness; (*PHYSIQUE*) density.

dent [dáń] *nf* tooth (*pl* teeth); **avoir/garder**

une ~ **contre qn** to have/hold a grudge against sb; **se mettre qch sous la** ~ to eat sth; **être sur les** ~**s** to be on one's last legs; **faire ses** ~**s** to teethe, cut (one's) teeth; **en** ~**s de scie** serrated; (*irrégulier*) jagged; **avoir les** ~**s longues** (*fig*) to be ruthlessly ambitious; ~ **de lait/sagesse** milk/wisdom tooth.

dentaire [dȧṅter] *a* dental; **cabinet** ~ dentist's office (*US*), dental surgery (*Brit*); **école** ~ dental school.

denté, e [dȧṅtā] *a*: **roue** ~**e** cog wheel.

dentelé, e [dȧṅtlā] *a* jagged, indented.

dentelle [dȧṅtel] *nf* lace *q*.

dentelure [dȧṅtlür] *nf* (*aussi:* ~**s**) jagged outline.

dentier [dȧṅtyā] *nm* denture.

dentifrice [dȧṅtēfrēs] *a, nm*: (**pâte**) ~ toothpaste; **eau** ~ mouthwash.

dentiste [dȧṅtēst(ə)] *nm/f* dentist.

dentition [dȧṅtēsyóṅ] *nf* teeth *pl*, dentition.

dénucléariser [dānüklāárēzā] *vt* to make nuclear-free.

dénudé, e [dānüdā] *a* bare.

dénuder [dānüdā] *vt* to bare; **se** ~ (*personne*) to strip.

dénué, e [dānüā] *a*: ~ **de** lacking in; (*intérêt*) devoid of.

dénuement [dānümáṅ] *nm* destitution.

dénutrition [dānütrēsyóṅ] *nf* undernourishment.

déodorant [dāodoráṅ] *nm* deodorant.

déodoriser [dāodorēzā] *vt* to deodorize.

déontologie [dāóṅtolozhē] *nf* code of ethics; (*professionnelle*) (professional) code of practice.

dép. *abr* (*ADMIN*: = *département*) dept; (= *départ*) dep.

dépannage [dāpánázh] *nm*: **service/camion de** ~ (*AUTO*) breakdown service/truck.

dépanner [dāpánā] *vt* (*voiture, télévision*) to fix, repair; (*fig*) to bail out, help out.

dépanneur [dāpáncer] *nm* (*AUTO*) breakdown mechanic; (*TV*) television repairman.

dépanneuse [dāpáncēz] *nf* tow truck (*US*), breakdown lorry (*Brit*).

dépareillé, e [dāpárāyā] *a* (*collection, service*) incomplete; (*gant, volume, objet*) odd.

déparer [dāpárā] *vt* to spoil, mar.

départ [dāpár] *nm* leaving *q*, departure; (*SPORT*) start; (*sur un horaire*) departure; **à son** ~ when he left; **au** ~ (*au début*) initially, at the start; **courrier au** ~ outgoing mail.

départager [dāpártázhā] *vt* to decide between.

département [dāpártəmáṅ] *nm* department.

départemental, e, aux [dāpártəmáṅtál, -ō] *a* departmental.

départementaliser [dāpártəmáṅtálēzā] *vt* to devolve authority to.

départir [dāpártēr]: **se** ~ **de** *vt* to abandon, depart from.

dépassé, e [dāpásā] *a* superseded, outmoded; (*fig*) out of one's depth.

dépassement [dāpásmáṅ] *nm* (*AUTO*) passing.

dépasser [dāpásā] *vt* (*véhicule, concurrent*) to pass; (*endroit*) to pass, go past; (*somme, limite*) to exceed; (*fig: en beauté etc*) to

surpass, outshine; (*être en saillie sur*) to jut out above (*ou* in front of); (*dérouter*): **cela me dépasse** it's beyond me ♦ *vi* (*AUTO*) to pass; (*jupon*) to show; **se** ~ to outdo o.s.

dépassionner [dāpásyonā] *vt* (*débat etc*) to take the heat out of.

dépaver [dāpávā] *vt* to remove the cobblestones from.

dépaysé, e [dāpāēzā] *a* disorientated.

dépaysement [dāpāēzmáṅ] *nm* disorientation; change of scenery.

dépayser [dāpāēzā] *vt* (*désorienter*) to disorientate; (*changer agréablement*) to provide with a change of scenery.

dépecer [dāpəsā] *vt* (*suj: boucher*) to joint, cut up; (*suj: animal*) to dismember.

dépêche [dāpcsh] *nf* dispatch; ~ (**télégraphique**) telegram, wire.

dépêcher [dāpāshā] *vt* to dispatch; **se** ~ *vi* to hurry; **se** ~ **de faire qch** to hasten to do sth, to hurry (in order) to do sth.

dépeindre [dāpáṅdr(ə)] *vt* to depict.

dépendance [dāpáṅdáṅs] *nf* (*interdépendance*) dependence *q*, dependency; (*bâtiment*) outbuilding.

dépendant, e [dāpáṅdáṅ, -áṅt] *vb voir* **dépendre** ♦ *a* (*financièrement*) dependent.

dépendre [dāpáṅdr(ə)] *vt* (*tableau*) to take down; ~ **de** *vt* to depend on; (*financièrement etc*) to be dependent on; (*appartenir*) to belong to.

dépens [dāpáṅ] *nmpl*: **aux** ~ **de** at the expense of.

dépense [dāpáṅs] *nf* spending *q*, expense, expenditure *q*; (*fig*) consumption; (*: de temps, de forces*) expenditure; **pousser qn à la** ~ to make sb incur an expense; ~ **physique** (physical) exertion; ~ **de temps** investment of time; ~**s de fonctionnement** revenue expenditure; ~**s d'investissement** capital expenditure; ~**s publiques** government spending.

dépenser [dāpáṅsā] *vt* to spend; (*gaz, eau*) to use; (*fig*) to expend, use up; **se** ~ (*se fatiguer*) to exert o.s.

dépensier, ière [dāpáṅsyā, -ycr] *a*: **il est** ~ he's a spendthrift.

déperdition [dāperdēsyóṅ] *nf* loss.

dépérir [dāpārēr] *vi* (*personne*) to waste away; (*plante*) to wither.

dépersonnaliser [dāpersonálēzā] *vt* to depersonalize.

dépêtrer [dāpātrā] *vt*: **se** ~ **de** (*situation*) to extricate o.s. from.

dépeuplé, e [dāpœplā] *a* depopulated.

dépeupler [dāpœplā] *vt* to depopulate; **se** ~ to be depopulated.

déphasage [dāfázázh] *nm* (*fig*) being out of touch.

déphasé, e [dāfázā] *a* (*ÉLEC*) out of phase; (*fig*) out of touch.

déphaser [dāfázā] *vt* (*fig*) to put out of touch.

dépilation [dāpēlásyóṅ] *nf* hair loss; hair removal.

dépilatoire [dāpēlátwár] *a* depilatory, hairremoving.

dépiler [dāpēlā] *vt* (*épiler*) to depilate, remove hair from.

dépistage [dāpēstázh] *nm* (*MÉD*) screening.

dépister |dāpēstā| *vt* to detect; (*MÉD*) to screen; (*voleur*) to track down; (*poursuivants*) to throw off the scent.

dépit |dāpē| *nm* vexation, frustration; **en ~ de** *prép* in spite of; **en ~ du bon sens** contrary to all good sense.

dépité, e |dāpētā| *a* vexed, frustrated.

dépiter |dāpētā| *vt* to vex, frustrate.

déplacé, e |dāplásā| *a* (*propos*) out of place, uncalled-for; **personne ~e** displaced person.

déplacement |dāplásmáń| *nm* moving; shifting; transfer; (*voyage*) trip, traveling *q* (*US*), travelling *q* (*Brit*); **en ~** away (on a trip); **~ d'air** displacement of air; **~ de vertèbre** slipped disc.

déplacer |dāplásā| *vt* (*table, voiture*) to move, shift; (*employé*) to transfer, move; **se ~** *vi* (*objet*) to move; (*organe*) to become displaced; (*personne: bouger*) to move, walk; (: *voyager*) to travel ♦ *vt* (*vertèbre etc*) to displace.

déplaire |dāplɛr| *vi*: **ceci me déplaît** I don't like this, I dislike this; **il cherche à nous ~** he's trying to displease us *ou* be disagreeable to us; **se ~ quelque part** to dislike it *ou* be unhappy somewhere.

déplaisant, e |dāplɛzáń, -áńt| *vb voir* **déplaire** ♦ *a* disagreeable, unpleasant.

déplaisir |dāplāzēr| *nm* displeasure, annoyance.

déplaît |dāplɛ| *vb voir* **déplaire.**

dépliant |dāplēyáń| *nm* leaflet.

déplier |dāplēyā| *vt* to unfold; **se ~** (*parachute*) to open.

déplisser |dāplēsā| *vt* to smooth out.

déploiement |dāplwámáń| *nm* (*voir* **déployer**) deployment; display.

déplomber |dāplóńbā| *vt* (*caisse, compteur*) to break (open) the seal of.

déplorable |dāplorábl(ə)| *a* deplorable, lamentable.

déplorer |dāplorā| *vt* (*regretter*) to deplore; (*pleurer sur*) to lament.

déployer |dāplwáyā| *vt* to open out, spread; (*MIL*) to deploy; (*montrer*) to display, exhibit.

déplu |dāplü| *pp de* **déplaire.**

dépointer |dāpwáńtā| *vi* to punch (*US*) *ou* clock (*Brit*) out.

dépoli, e |dāpolē| *a*: **verre ~** frosted glass.

dépolitiser |dāpolētēzā| *vt* to depoliticize.

déportation |dāportásyóń| *nf* deportation.

déporté, e |dāportā| *nm/f* deportee; (*1939-45*) concentration camp prisoner.

déporter |dāportā| *vt* (*POL*) to deport; (*dévier*) to carry off course; **se ~** *vi* (*voiture*) to swerve.

déposant, e |dāpōzáń, -áńt| *nm/f* (*épargnant*) depositor.

dépose |dāpōz| *nf* taking out; taking down.

déposé, e |dāpōzā| *a* registered; *voir aussi* **marque.**

déposer |dāpōzā| *vt* (*gén: mettre, poser*) to lay down, put down, set down; (*à la banque, à la consigne*) to deposit; (*caution*) to put down; (*passager*) to drop (off); (*démonter: serrure, moteur*) to take out; (: *rideau*) to take down; (*roi*) to depose; (*ADMIN: faire enregistrer*) to file; to register ♦ *vi* to form a

sediment *ou* deposit; (*JUR*): **~ (contre)** to testify *ou* give evidence (against); **se ~** *vi* to settle; **~ son bilan** (*COMM*) to go into (voluntary) liquidation.

dépositaire |dāpozētɛr| *nm/f* (*JUR*) depository; (*COMM*) agent; **~ agréé** authorized agent.

déposition |dāpōzēsyóń| *nf* (*JUR*) deposition.

déposséder |dāposādā| *vt* to dispossess.

dépôt |dāpō| *nm* (*à la banque, sédiment*) deposit; (*entrepôt, réserve*) warehouse, store; (*gare*) depot; (*prison*) cells *pl*; **~ d'ordures** garbage (*US*) *ou* rubbish (*Brit*) dump; **~ de bilan** (voluntary) liquidation; **~ légal** registration of copyright.

dépoter |dāpotā| *vt* (*plante*) to take from the pot, transplant.

dépotoir |dāpotwár| *nm* dumping ground, garbage (*US*) *ou* rubbish (*Brit*) dump; **~ nucléaire** nuclear (waste) dump.

dépouille |dāpōōy| *nf* (*d'animal*) skin, hide; (*humaine*): **~ (mortelle)** mortal remains *pl*.

dépouillé, e |dāpōōyā| *a* (*fig*) bare, bald; **~ de** stripped of; lacking in.

dépouillement |dāpōōymáń| *nm* (*de scrutin*) count, counting *q*.

dépouiller |dāpōōyā| *vt* (*animal*) to skin; (*spolier*) to deprive of one's possessions; (*documents*) to go through, peruse; **~ qn/qch de** to strip sb/sth of; **~ le scrutin** to count the votes.

dépourvu, e |dāpōōrvü| *a*: **~ de** lacking in, without; **au ~** *ad*: **prendre qn au ~** to catch sb unawares.

dépoussiérer |dāpōōsyārā| *vt* to remove dust from.

dépravation |dāprávásyóń| *nf* depravity.

dépravé, e |dāprávā| *a* depraved.

dépraver |dāprávā| *vt* to deprave.

dépréciation |dāprāsyásyóń| *nf* depreciation.

déprécier |dāprāsyā| *vt, se ~* *vi* to depreciate.

déprédations |dāprādásyóń| *nfpl* damage *sg*.

dépressif, ive |dāprāsēf, -ēv| *a* depressive.

dépression |dāpresyóń| *nf* depression; **~ (nerveuse)** (nervous) breakdown.

déprimant, e |dāprēmáń, -áńt| *a* depressing.

déprime |dāprēm| *nf* (*fam*): **la ~** depression.

déprimé, e |dāprēmā| *a* (*découragé*) depressed.

déprimer |dāprēmā| *vt* to depress.

déprogrammer |dāprográmā| *vt* (*supprimer*) to cancel.

DEPS *sigle* (= *dernier entré premier sorti*) LIFO (= *last in first out*).

dépt *abr* (= *département*) dept.

dépuceler |dāpüslā| *vt* (*fam*) to take the virginity of.

depuis |dəpüē| *prép* (*temps: date*) since; (: *période*) for; (*lieu*) since, from; (*quantité, rang*) from ♦ *ad* (ever) since; **~ que** (*temps*) (ever) since; **je le connais ~ 3 ans** I've known him for 3 years; **il est parti ~ mardi** he has been gone since Tuesday; **~ quand le connaissez-vous?** how long have you known him?; **elle a téléphoné ~ Valence** she phoned from Valence; **~ lors** since then.

dépuratif, ive |dāpürátēf, -ēv| *a* depurative, purgative.

députation |dāpütásyóń| *nf* deputation; (*fonction*) position of deputy, ≈ seat in Congress

(US), ≈ parliamentary seat (Brit).

député, e [dāpütā] nm/f (POL) deputy, ≈ Congressman/woman (US), ≈ Member of Parliament (Brit).

députer [dāpütā] vt to delegate; ~ qn auprès de to send sb (as a representative) to.

déraciner [dārásēnā] vt to uproot.

déraillement [dārâymâŋ] nm derailment.

dérailler [dārâyā] vi (train) to be derailed, go off ou jump the rails; (fam) to be completely off the track; **faire** ~ to derail.

dérailleur [dārâycer] nm (de vélo) derailleur (US), dérailleur gears pl (Brit).

déraison [dārezóŋ] nf unreasonableness.

déraisonnable [dārezonábl(ə)] a unreasonable.

déraisonner [dārezonā] vi to talk nonsense, rave.

dérangement [dārâŋzhmâŋ] nm (gêne, déplacement) trouble; (gastrique etc) disorder; (mécanique) breakdown; **en** ~ (téléphone) out of order.

déranger [dārâŋzhā] vt (personne) to trouble, bother, disturb; (projets) to disrupt, upset; (objets, vêtements) to disarrange; **se** ~ to put o.s. out; (se déplacer) to (take the trouble to) come (ou go) out; **est-ce que cela vous dérange si ...?** do you mind if ...?; **ça te dérangerait de faire ...?** would you mind doing ...?; **ne vous dérangez pas** don't go to any trouble; don't disturb yourself.

dérapage [dārápázh] nm skid, skidding q; going out of control.

déraper [dārápā] vi (voiture) to skid; (personne, semelles, couteau) to slip; (fig: économie etc) to go out of control.

dératé, e [dārátā] nm/f: **courir comme un** ~ to run like the wind.

dératiser [dārátēzā] vt to rid of rats.

déréglé, e [dārāglā] a (mœurs) dissolute.

dérèglement [dāregləmâŋ] nm upsetting q, upset.

dérégler [dārāglā] vt (mécanisme) to put out of order, cause to break down; (estomac) to upset; **se** ~ vi to break down, go wrong.

dérider [dārēdā] vt, **se** ~ vi to brighten ou cheer up.

dérision [dārēzyóŋ] nf derision; **tourner en** ~ to deride; **par** ~ in mockery.

dérisoire [dārēzwár] a derisory.

dérivatif [dārēvátēf] nm distraction.

dérivation [dārēvásyóŋ] nf derivation; diversion.

dérive [dārēv] nf (de dériveur) centerboard (US), centreboard (Brit); **aller à la** ~ (NAVIG, fig) to drift; ~ **des continents** (GÉO) continental drift.

dérivé, e [dārēvā] a derived ♦ nm (LING) derivative; (TECH) by-product ♦ nf (MATH) derivative.

dériver [dārēvā] vt (MATH) to derive; (cours d'eau etc) to divert ♦ vi (bateau) to drift; ~ de to derive from.

dériveur [dārēvœr] nm sailing dinghy.

dermatite [dermâtēt] nf dermatitis.

dermato [dermâtō] nm/f (fam: = dermatologue) dermatologist.

dermatologie [dermâtolozhē] nf dermatology.

dermatologue [dermâtolog] nm/f dermatologist.

dermite [dermēt] nf = **dermatite**.

dernier, ière [dernyā, -yer] a (dans le temps, l'espace) last; (le plus récent: gén avant n) latest, last; (final, ultime: effort) final; (échelon, grade) top, highest ♦ nm (étage) top floor; **lundi/le mois** ~ last Monday/month; **du** ~ **chic** extremely smart; **le** ~ **cri** the last word (in fashion); **les** ~**s honneurs** the last tribute; **le** ~ **soupir: rendre le** ~ **soupir** to breathe one's last; **en** ~ ad last; **ce** ~, **cette dernière** the latter.

dernièrement [dernyermâŋ] ad recently.

dernier-né, dernière-née [dernyānā, dernyernā] nm/f (enfant) last-born.

dérobade [dārobád] nf side-stepping q.

dérobé, e [dārobā] a (porte) secret, hidden; **à la** ~**e** surreptitiously.

dérober [dārobā] vt to steal; (cacher): ~ **qch à (la vue de) qn** to conceal ou hide sth from sb('s view); **se** ~ vi (s'esquiver) to slip away; (fig) to shy away; **se** ~ **sous** (s'effondrer) to give way beneath; **se** ~ **à** (justice, regards) to hide from; (obligation) to shirk.

dérogation [dārogâsyóŋ] nf (special) dispensation.

déroger [dārozhā]: ~ **à** vt to go against, depart from.

dérouiller [dārōōyā] vt: **se** ~ **les jambes** to stretch one's legs.

déroulement [dārōōlmâŋ] nm (d'une opération etc) progress.

dérouler [dārōōlā] vt (ficelle) to unwind; (papier) to unroll; **se** ~ vi to unwind; to unroll, come unrolled; (avoir lieu) to take place; (se passer) to go.

déroutant, e [dārōōtâŋ, -âŋt] a disconcerting.

déroute [dārōōt] nf (MIL) rout; (fig) total collapse; **mettre en** ~ to rout; **en** ~ routed.

dérouter [dārōōtā] vt (avion, train) to reroute, divert; (étonner) to disconcert, throw (off).

derrière [deryer] ad, prép behind ♦ nm (d'une maison) back; (postérieur) behind, bottom; **les pattes de** ~ the back legs, the hind legs; **par** ~ from behind; (fig) in an underhanded (US) ou underhand way, behind one's back.

des [dā] dét, prép + dét voir **de**.

dès [de] prép from; ~ **que** cj as soon as; ~ **à présent** here and now; ~ **son retour** as soon as he was (ou is) back; ~ **réception** upon receipt; ~ **lors** ad from then on; ~ **lors que** cj from the moment (that).

désabusé, e [dāzábüzā] a disillusioned.

désaccord [dāzákor] nm disagreement.

désaccordé, e [dāzàkordā] a (MUS) out of tune.

désacraliser [dāsákrálēzā] vt to deconsecrate; (fig: profession, institution) to take the mystique out of.

désaffecté, e [dāzáfektā] a disused.

désaffection [dāzáfeksyóŋ] nf: ~ **pour** estrangement from.

désagréable [dāzágráábl(ə)] a unpleasant, disagreeable.

désagréablement [dāzàgráábləmâŋ] ad disagreeably, unpleasantly.

désagrégation [dāzàgrāgásyóŋ] nf disintegration.

désagréger [dāzágrāzhā]: **se ~** *vi* to disintegrate, break up.

désagrément [dāzágrāmáṅ] *nm* annoyance, trouble *q*.

désaltérant, e [dāzáltāráṅ, -áṅt] *a* thirst-quenching.

désaltérer [dāzáltārā] *vt*: **se ~** to quench one's thirst; **ça désaltère** it's thirst-quenching, it quenches your thirst.

désamorcer [dāzámorsā] *vt* to remove the primer from; *(fig)* to defuse; *(: prévenir)* to forestall.

désappointé, e [dāzápwáṅtā] *a* disappointed.

désapprobateur, trice [dāzáprobátœr, -trēs] *a* disapproving.

désapprobation [dāzáprobāsyóṅ] *nf* disapproval.

désapprouver [dāzáprōōvā] *vt* to disapprove of.

désarçonner [dāzársonā] *vt* to unseat, throw; *(fig)* to throw, nonplus, disconcert.

désargenté, e [dāzárzháṅtā] *a* impoverished.

désarmant, e [dāzármáṅ, -áṅt] *a* disarming.

désarmé, e [dāzármā] *a (fig)* disarmed.

désarmement [dāzármɔmáṅ] *nm* disarmament.

désarmer [dāzármā] *vt (MIL, aussi fig)* to disarm; *(NAVIG)* to lay up; *(fusil)* to unload; *(: mettre le cran de sûreté)* to put the safety catch on ♦ *vi (pays)* to disarm; *(haine)* to wane; *(personne)* to give up.

désarrimer [dāzárēmā] *vt* to shift.

désarroi [dāzárwá] *nm* helplessness, disarray.

désarticulé, e [dāzártēkülā] *a (pantin, corps)* dislocated.

désarticuler [dāzártēkülā] *vt*: **se ~** to contort (o.s.).

désassorti, e [dāzásortē] *a* unmatching, unmatched; *(magasin, marchand)* sold out.

désastre [dāzástr(ɔ)] *nm* disaster.

désastreux, euse [dāzástrœ̄, -œ̄z] *a* disastrous.

désavantage [dāzáváṅtázh] *nm* disadvantage; *(inconvénient)* drawback, disadvantage.

désavantager [dāzáváṅtázhā] *vt* to put at a disadvantage.

désavantageux, euse [dāzáváṅtázhœ̄, -œ̄z] *a* unfavorable *(US)*, unfavourable *(Brit)*, disadvantageous.

désaveu [dāzávœ̄] *nm* repudiation; *(déni)* disclaimer.

désavouer [dāzávwā] *vt* to disown, repudiate, disclaim.

désaxé, e [dāzáksā] *a (fig)* unbalanced.

désaxer [dāzáksā] *vt (roue)* to put out of true; *(personne)* to throw off balance.

desceller [dāsálā] *vt (pierre)* to pull free.

descendance [dāsáṅdáṅs] *nf (famille)* descendants *pl*, issue; *(origine)* descent.

descendant, e [dāsáṅdáṅ, -áṅt] *vb voir* **descendre** ♦ *nm/f* descendant.

descendeur, euse [dāsáṅdœr, -œ̄z] *nm/f (SPORT)* downhiller.

descendre [dāsáṅdr(ɔ)] *vt (escalier, montagne)* to go *(ou* come) down; *(valise, paquet)* to take *ou* get down; *(étagère etc)* to lower; *(fam: abattre)* to shoot down; *(: boire)* to knock back ♦ *vi* to go *(ou* come) down; *(passager: s'arrêter)* to get out, alight; *(niveau, température)* to go *ou* come

down, fall, drop; *(marée)* to go out; **~ à pied/en voiture** to walk/drive down, go down on foot/by car; **~ de** *(famille)* to be descended from; **~ du train** to get out of *ou* off the train; **~ d'un arbre** to climb down from a tree; **~ de cheval** to dismount, get off one's horse; **~ à l'hôtel** to stay at a hotel; **~ dans la rue** *(manifester)* to take to the streets; **~ en ville** to go into town, go down town.

descente [dāsáṅt] *nf* descent, going down; *(chemin)* way down; *(SKI)* downhill (race); **au milieu de la ~** halfway down; **freinez dans les ~s** use the brakes going downhill; **~ de lit** bedside rug; **~ (de police)** (police) raid.

descriptif, ive [dɛskrēptēf, -ēv] *a* descriptive ♦ *nm* explanatory leaflet.

description [dɛskrēpsyóṅ] *nf* description.

désembourber [dāzáṅbōōrbā] *vt* to pull out of the mud.

désembourgeoiser [dāzáṅbōōrzhwázā] *vt*: **~ qn** to get sb out of his *(ou* her) middle-class attitudes.

désembuer [dāzáṅbüā] *vt* to defog *(US)*, demist *(Brit)*.

désemparé, e [dāzáṅpárā] *a* bewildered, distraught; *(bateau, avion)* crippled.

désemparer [dāzáṅpárā] *vi*: **sans ~** without stopping.

désemplir [dāzáṅplēr] *vi*: **ne pas ~** to be always full.

désenchanté, e [dāzáṅsháṅtā] *a* disenchanted, disillusioned.

désenchantement [dāzáṅsháṅtmáṅ] *nm* disenchantment, disillusion.

désenclaver [dāzáṅklávā] *vt* to open up.

désencombrer [dāzáṅkóṅbrā] *vt* to clear.

désenfler [dāzáṅflā] *vi* to become less swollen.

désengagement [dāzáṅgázhmáṅ] *nm (POL)* disengagement.

désensabler [dāzáṅsáblā] *vt* to pull out of the sand.

désensibiliser [dāsáṅsēbēlēzā] *vt (MÉD)* to desensitize.

désenvenimer [dāzáṅvnēmā] *vt (plaie)* to remove the poison from; *(fig)* to take the sting out of.

désépaissir [dāzápāsēr] *vt* to thin (out).

déséquilibre [dāzākēlēbr(ɔ)] *nm (position)*: **être en ~** to be unsteady; *(fig: des forces, du budget)* imbalance; *(PSYCH)* unbalance.

déséquilibré, e [dāzākēlēbrā] *nm/f (PSYCH)* unbalanced person.

déséquilibrer [dāzākēlēbrā] *vt* to throw off balance.

désert, e [dāzɛr, -ɛrt(ɔ)] *a* deserted ♦ *nm* desert.

déserter [dāzɛrtā] *vi, vt* to desert.

déserteur [dāzɛrtœr] *nm* deserter.

désertion [dāzɛrsyóṅ] *nf* desertion.

désertique [dāzɛrtēk] *a* desert *cpd*; *(inculte)* barren, empty.

désescalade [dāzeskálád] *nf (MIL)* de-escalation.

désespérant, e [dāzespāráṅ, -áṅt] *a* hopeless, despairing.

désespéré, e [dāzespārā] *a* desperate; *(regard)* despairing; **état ~** *(MÉD)* hopeless condition.

désespérément [dāzespārāmáɲ] *ad* desperately.

désespérer [dāzespārā] *vt* to drive to despair ♦ *vi*, **se** ~ *vi* to despair; ~ **de** to despair of.

désespoir [dāzespwár] *nm* despair; **être** *ou* **faire le** ~ **de qn** to be the despair of sb; **en** ~ **de cause** in desperation.

déshabillé, e [dāzábēyā] *a* undressed ♦ *nm* negligee.

déshabiller [dāzábēyā] *vt* to undress; **se** ~ to undress (o.s.).

déshabituer [dāzábētüā] *vt*: **se** ~ **de** to get out of the habit of.

désherbant [dāzerbáɲ] *nm* weed-killer.

désherber [dāzerbā] *vt* to weed.

déshérité, e [dāzārētā] *a* disinherited ♦ *nm/f*: **les** ~**s** (*pauvres*) the underprivileged, the deprived.

déshériter [dāzārētā] *vt* to disinherit.

déshonneur [dāzonœr] *nm* dishonor (*US*), dishonour (*Brit*), disgrace.

déshonorer [dāzonorā] *vt* to dishonor (*US*), dishonour (*Brit*), bring disgrace upon; **se** ~ to bring dishono(u)r on o.s.

déshumaniser   [dāzümánēzā]   *vt*   to dehumanize.

déshydratation [dāzēdrátásyóɲ] *nf* dehydration.

déshydraté, e [dāzēdrátā] *a* dehydrated.

déshydrater [dāzēdrátā] *vt* to dehydrate.

desiderata [dāzēdārátā] *nmpl* requirements.

design [dēzáyn] *a* (*mobilier*) designer *cpd* ♦ *nm* (industrial) design.

désignation [dāzēnyásyóɲ] *nf* naming, appointment; (*signe, mot*) name, designation.

designer [dēzáyner] *nm* designer.

désigner [dāzēnyā] *vt* (*montrer*) to point out, indicate; (*dénommer*) to denote, refer to; (*nommer: candidat etc*) to name, appoint.

désillusion [dāzēlüzyóɲ] *nf* disillusion(ment).

désillusionner [dāzēlüzyonā] *vt* to disillusion.

désincarné, e [dāzáɲkárnā] *a* disembodied.

désinence [dāzēnáɲs] *nf* ending, inflection.

désinfectant, e [dāzáɲfektáɲ, -áɲt] *a*, *nm* disinfectant.

désinfecter [dāzáɲfektā] *vt* to disinfect.

désinformation [dāzáɲformásyóɲ] *nf* disinformation.

désintégrer [dāzáɲtāgrā] *vt*, **se** ~ *vi* to disintegrate.

désintéressé, e [dāzáɲtārāsā] *a* (*généreux, bénévole*) disinterested, unselfish.

désintéressement [dāzáɲtáresmáɲ] *nm* (*générosité*) disinterestedness.

désintéresser [dāzáɲtārāsā] *vt*: **se** ~ **(de)** to lose interest (in).

désintérêt [dāzáɲtāre] *nm* (*indifférence*) disinterest.

désintoxication [dāzáɲtoksēkásyóɲ] *nf* treatment for alcoholism (*ou* drug addiction); **faire une cure de** ~ to have *ou* undergo treatment for alcoholism (*ou* drug addiction).

désintoxiquer [dāzáɲtoksēkā] *vt* to treat for alcoholism (*ou* drug addiction).

désinvolte [dāzáɲvolt(ə)] *a* casual, off-hand.

désinvolture [dāzáɲvoltür] *nf* casualness.

désir [dāzēr] *nm* wish; (*fort, sensuel*) desire.

désirer [dāzērā] *vt* to want, wish for; (*sexuelle-*

ment) to desire; **je désire** ... (*formule de politesse*) I would like ...; **il désire que tu l'aides** he would like *ou* he wants you to help him; ~ **faire** to want *ou* wish to do; **ça laisse à** ~ it leaves something to be desired.

désireux, euse [dāzērœ̄, -œ̄z] *a*: ~ **de faire** anxious to do.

désistement [dāzēstəmáɲ] *nm* withdrawal.

désister [dāzēstā]: **se** ~ *vi* to withdraw.

désobéir [dāzobāēr] *vi*: ~ **(à qn/qch)** to disobey (sb/sth).

désobéissance [dāzobāēsáɲs] *nf* disobedience.

désobéissant, e [dāzobāēsáɲ, -áɲt] *a* disobedient.

désobligeant, e [dāzoblēzháɲ, -áɲt] *a* disagreeable, unpleasant.

désobliger [dāzoblēzhā] *vt* to offend.

désodorisant [dāzodorēzáɲ] *nm* air freshener, deodorizer.

désodoriser [dāzodorēzā] *vt* to deodorize.

désœuvré, e [dāzœvrā] *a* idle.

désœuvrement [dāzœvrəmáɲ] *nm* idleness.

désolant, e [dāzoláɲ, -áɲt] *a* distressing.

désolation [dāzolásyóɲ] *nf* (*affliction*) distress, grief; (*d'un paysage etc*) desolation, devastation.

désolé, e [dāzolā] *a* (*paysage*) desolate; **je suis** ~ I'm sorry.

désoler [dāzolā] *vt* to distress, grieve; **se** ~ to be upset.

désolidariser [dāsolēdárēzā] *vt*: **se** ~ **de** *ou* **d'avec** to dissociate o.s. from.

désopilant, e [dāzopēláɲ, -áɲt] *a* screamingly funny, hilarious.

désordonné, e [dāzordonā] *a* untidy, disorderly.

désordre [dāzordr(ə)] *nm* disorder(liness), untidiness; (*anarchie*) disorder; ~**s** *nmpl* (*POL*) disturbances, disorder *sg*; **en** ~ in a mess, untidy.

désorganiser [dāzorgánēzā] *vt* to disorganize.

désorienté, e [dāzoryáɲtā] *a* disorientated; (*fig*) bewildered.

désormais [dāzorme] *ad* in the future, from now on.

désosser [dāzosā] *vt* to bone.

despote [despot] *nm* despot; (*fig*) tyrant.

despotique [despotēk] *a* despotic.

despotisme [despotēsm(ə)] *nm* despotism.

desquamer [deskwámā]: **se** ~ *vi* to flake off.

desquels, desquelles [dākel] *prép* + *pronom voir* **lequel**.

DESS *sigle m* (= *Diplôme d'études supérieures spécialisées*) *post-graduate diploma*.

dessaisir [dāsāzēr] *vt*: ~ **un tribunal d'une affaire** to remove a case from a court; **se** ~ **de** *vt* to give up, part with.

dessaler [dāsálā] *vt* (*eau de mer*) to desalinate; (*CULIN: morue etc*) to soak; (*fig fam: délurer*): ~ **qn** to teach sb a thing or two ♦ *vi* (*voilier*) to capsize.

Desse *abr* = **duchesse**.

desséché, e [dāsāshā] *a* dried up.

dessèchement [dāseshmáɲ] *nm* drying out; dryness; hardness.

dessécher [dāsāshā] *vt* (*terre, plante*) to dry out, parch; (*peau*) to dry out; (*volontairement: aliments etc*) to dry, dehydrate; (fig: cœur) to harden; **se** ~ vi to dry out; (peau, lèvres) to go dry.

dessein [dāsań] nm design; **dans le** ~ **de** with the intention of; **à** ~ intentionally, deliberately.

desserrer [dāsārā] vt to loosen; (frein) to release; (poing, dents) to unclench; (objets alignés) to space out; **ne pas** ~ **les dents** not to open one's mouth.

dessert [dāser] vb voir **desservir ♦** nm dessert.

desserte [dāsert(ə)] nf (table) serving table; (transport): **la** ~ **du village est assurée par autocar** there is a bus service to the village; **chemin** ou **voie de** ~ service road.

desservir [dāservēr] vt (ville, quartier) to serve; (: suj: voie de communication) to lead into; (suj: vicaire: paroisse) to serve; (nuire à: personne) to do a disservice to; (débarrasser): ~ **(la table)** to clear the table.

dessiller [dāsēyā] vt (fig): ~ **les yeux à qn** to open sb's eyes.

dessin [dāsań] nm (œuvre, art) drawing; (motif) pattern, design; (contour) (out)line; **le** ~ **industriel** draftsmanship (US), draughtsmanship (Brit); ~ **animé** cartoon (film); ~ **humoristique** cartoon.

dessinateur, trice [dāsēnátœr, -trēs] nm/f drawer; (de bandes dessinées) cartoonist; (industriel) draftsman (US), draughtsman (Brit); **dessinatrice de mode** fashion designer.

dessiner [dāsēnā] vt to draw; (concevoir: carrosserie, maison) to design; (suj: robe: taille) to show off; **se** ~ vi (forme) to be outlined; (fig: solution) to emerge.

dessouler [dāsōōlā] vt, vi to sober up.

dessous [dəsōō] ad underneath, beneath ♦ nm underside; (étage inférieur): **les voisins du** ~ the downstairs neighbors ♦ nmpl (sous-vêtements) underwear sg; (fig) hidden aspects; **en** ~ underneath; below; (fig: en catamini) slyly, on the sly; **par** ~ underneath; below; **de** ~ **le lit** from under the bed; **au-** ad below; **au-** ~ **de** prép below; (peu digne de) beneath; **au-** ~ **de tout** the (absolute) limit; **avoir le** ~ to get the worst of it.

dessous-de-bouteille [dəsōōdbōōtey] nm inv coaster.

dessous-de-plat [dəsōōdplá] nm inv hot pad (US), tablemat (Brit).

dessous-de-table [dəsōōdtábl(ə)] nm inv (fig) bribe, under-the-counter payment.

dessus [dəsü] ad on top; (collé, écrit) on it ♦ nm top; (étage supérieur): **les voisins/ l'appartement du** ~ the upstairs neighbors/ apartment; **en** ~ above; **par** ~ ad over it ♦ prép over; **au-** ~ above; **au-** ~ **de** above; **avoir/prendre le** ~ to have/get the upper hand; **reprendre le** ~ to get over it; **bras** ~ **bras dessous** arm in arm; **sens** ~ **dessous** upside down; voir **ci-, là-**.

dessus-de-lit [dəsüdlē] nm inv bedspread.

déstabiliser [dāstábēlēzā] vt (POL) to destabilize.

destin [destań] nm fate; (avenir) destiny.

destinataire [destēnáter] nm/f (POSTES) addressee; (d'un colis) consignee; (d'un mandat) payee; **aux risques et périls du** ~ at owner's risk.

destination [destēnâsyóń] nf (lieu) destination; (usage) purpose; **à** ~ **de** (avion etc) bound for; (voyageur) bound for, traveling to.

destinée [destēnā] nf fate; (existence, avenir) destiny.

destiner [destēnā] vt: ~ **qn à** (poste, sort) to destine sb for, intend sb to + verbe; ~ **qn/ qch à** (prédestiner) to mark sb/sth out for, destine sb/sth to + verbe; ~ **qch à** (envisager d'affecter) to intend to use sth for; ~ **qch à qn** (envisager de donner) to intend to give sth to sb, intend sb to have sth; (adresser) to intend sth for sb; **se** ~ **à l'enseignement** to intend to become a teacher; **être destiné à** (sort) to be destined to + verbe; (usage) to be intended ou meant for; (suj: sort) to be in store for.

destituer [destētüā] vt to depose; ~ **qn de ses fonctions** to relieve sb of his duties.

destitution [destētüsyóń] nf deposition.

destructeur, trice [destrüktœr, -trēs] a destructive.

destructif, ive [destrüktēf, -ēv] a destructive.

destruction [destrüksyóń] nf destruction.

déstructuré, e [dāstrüktürā] a: **vêtements** ~s casual clothes.

déstructurer [dāstrüktürā] vt to break down, take to pieces.

désuet, ète [dāsüe, -et] a outdated, outmoded.

désuétude [dāsüātüd] nf: **tomber en** ~ to fall into disuse, become obsolete.

désuni, e [dāzünē] a divided, disunited.

désunion [dāzünyóń] nf disunity.

désunir [dāzünēr] vt to disunite; **se** ~ vi (athlète) to break one's stride.

détachable [dātáshábl(ə)] a (coupon etc) tear-off cpd; (capuche etc) detachable.

détachant [dātásháń] nm stain remover.

détaché, e [dātáshā] a (fig) detached ♦ nm/f (représentant) person on an assignment.

détachement [dātáshmáń] nm detachment; (fonctionnaire, employé): **être en** ~ to be on an assignment.

détacher [dātáshā] vt (enlever) to detach, remove; (délier) to untie; (ADMIN): ~ **qn (auprès de ou à)** to assign sb (to); (MIL) to detail; (vêtement: nettoyer) to remove the stains from; **se** ~ vi (tomber) to come off; to come out; (se défaire) to come undone; (SPORT) to pull ou break away; (se délier: chien, prisonnier) to break loose; **se** ~ **sur** to stand out against; **se** ~ **de** (se désintéresser) to grow away from.

détail [dātáy] nm detail; (COMM): **le** ~ retail; **prix de** ~ retail price; **au** ~ ad (COMM) retail; (: individuellement) separately; **donner le** ~ **de** to give a detailed account of; (compte) to give a breakdown of; **en** ~ in detail.

détaillant, e [dātáyáń, -áńt] nm/f retailer.

détaillé, e [dātáyā] a (récit) detailed.

détailler [dātáyā] vt (COMM) to sell retail; to sell separately; (expliquer) to explain in detail; to detail; (examiner) to look over, examine.

détaler [dātálā] vi (lapin) to scamper off; (fam: personne) to make off, skedaddle *(fam)*.

détartrant |dātártráṅ| *nm* scale remover.

détartrer |dātártrā| *vt* to scale *(US)*, descale *(Brit)*; *(dents)* to remove the tartar from.

détaxe |dātáks(ə)| *nf (réduction)* reduction in tax; *(suppression)* removal of tax; *(remboursement)* tax refund.

détaxer |dātáksā| *vt (réduire)* to reduce the tax on; *(ôter)* to remove the tax on.

détecter |dātcktā| *vt* to detect.

détecteur |dātcktœr| *nm* detector, sensor; ~ **de mensonges** lie detector; ~ **(de mines)** mine detector.

détection |dātcksyóṅ| *nf* detection.

détective |dātcktēv| *nm (Brit: policier)* detective; ~ **(privé)** private detective *ou* investigator.

déteindre |dātaṅdr(ə)| *vi* to fade; *(fig)*: ~ **sur** to rub off on.

déteint, e |dātaṅ, -aṅt| *pp de* **déteindre**.

dételer |dctlā| *vt* to unharness; *(voiture, wagon)* to unhitch ♦ *vi (fig: s'arrêter)* to stop (working).

détendeur |dātaṅdœr| *nm (de bouteille à gaz)* regulator.

détendre |dātaṅdr(ə)| *vt (fil)* to slacken, loosen; *(relaxer: personne, atmosphère)* to relax; *(: situation)* to relieve; **se** ~ to lose its tension; to relax.

détendu, e |dātaṅdü| *a* relaxed.

détenir |dātnēr| *vt (fortune, objet, secret)* to be in possession of, have (in one's possession); *(prisonnier)* to detain, hold; *(record)* to hold; ~ **le pouvoir** to be in power.

détente |dātaṅt| *nf* relaxation; *(POL)* détente; *(d'une arme)* trigger; *(d'un athlète qui saute)* spring.

détenteur, trice |dātaṅtœr, -trēs| *nm/f* holder.

détention |dātaṅsyóṅ| *nf (voir détenir)* possession; detention; holding; ~ **préventive** (pre-trial) custody.

détenu, e |dātnü| *pp de* **détenir** ♦ *nm/f* prisoner.

détergent |dātcrzháṅ| *nm* detergent.

détérioration |dātāryorásyóṅ| *nf* damaging; deterioration.

détériorer |dātāryorā| *vt* to damage; **se** ~ *vi* to deteriorate.

déterminant, e |dātcrmēnáṅ, -aṅt| *a*: **un facteur** ~ a determining factor ♦ *nm (LING)* determiner.

détermination |dātcrmēnásyóṅ| *nf* determining; *(résolution)* decision; *(fermeté)* determination.

déterminé, e |dātcrmēnā| *a (résolu)* determined; *(précis)* specific, definite.

déterminer |dātcrmēnā| *vt* - *(fixer)* to determine; *(décider)*: ~ **qn à faire** to decide sb to do; **se** ~ **à faire** to make up one's mind to do.

déterminisme |dātcrmēnēsm(ə)| *nm* determinism.

déterré, e |dātārā| *nm/f*: **avoir une mine de** ~ to look like death warmed over *(US)* ou up *(Brit)*.

déterrer |dātārā| *vt* to dig up.

détersif, ive |dātcrsēf, -ēv| *a*, *nm* detergent.

détestable |dātcstábl(ə)| *a* foul, detestable.

détester |dātcstā| *vt* to hate, detest.

détiendrai |dātyaṅdrā|, **détiens** |dātyaṅ| *etc vb* *voir* **détenir**.

détonant, e |dātonáṅ, -áṅt| *a*: **mélange** ~ explosive mixture.

détonateur |dātonátœr| *nm* detonator.

détonation |dātonásyóṅ| *nf* detonation, bang, report (of a gun).

détoner |dātonā| *vi* to detonate, explode.

détonner |dātonā| *vi (MUS)* to go out of tune; *(fig)* to clash.

détordre |dātordr(ə)| *vt* to untwist, unwind.

détour |dātōōr| *nm* detour; *(tournant)* bend, curve; *(fig: subterfuge)* roundabout means; **au** ~ **de chemin** at the bend in the path; **sans** ~ *(fig)* plainly.

détourné, e |dātōōrnā| *a (sentier, chemin, moyen)* roundabout.

détournement |dātōōrnəmáṅ| *nm* diversion, rerouting; ~ **d'avion** hijacking; ~ **(de fonds)** embezzlement *ou* misappropriation (of funds); ~ **de mineur** corruption of a minor.

détourner |dātōōrnā| *vt* to divert; *(avion)* to divert, reroute; *(: par la force)* to hijack; *(yeux, tête)* to turn away; *(de l'argent)* to embezzle, misappropriate; **se** ~ to turn away; ~ **la conversation** to change the subject; ~ **qn de son devoir** to divert sb from his duty; ~ **l'attention (de qn)** to distract *ou* divert (sb's) attention.

détracteur, trice |dātráktœr, -trēs| *nm/f* disparager, critic.

détraqué, e |dātrákā| *a (machine, santé)* broken-down ♦ *nm/f (fam)*: **c'est un** ~ he's unhinged.

détraquer |dātrákā| *vt* to put out of order; *(estomac)* to upset; **se** ~ *vi* to go wrong.

détrempe |dātráṅp| *nf (ART)* tempera.

détrempé, e |dātráṅpā| *a (sol)* sodden, waterlogged.

détremper |dātráṅpā| *vt (peinture)* to water down.

détresse |dātrcs| *nf* distress; **en** ~ *(avion etc)* in distress; **appel/signal de** ~ distress call/ signal.

détriment |dātrcmáṅ| *nm*: **au** ~ **de** to the detriment of.

détritus |dātrētüs| *nmpl* rubbish *sg*, refuse *sg*, garbage *sg (US)*.

détroit |dātrwá| *nm* strait; **le** ~ **de Bering** *ou* **Behring** the Bering Strait; **le** ~ **de Gibraltar** the Strait of Gibraltar; **le** ~ **du Bosphore** the Bosphorus; **le** ~ **de Magellan** the Strait of Magellan, the Magellan Strait.

détromper |dātróṅpā| *vt* to disabuse; **se** ~: **détrompez-vous** don't believe it.

détrôner |dātrónā| *vt* to dethrone, depose; *(fig)* to oust, dethrone.

détrousser |dātrōōsā| *vt* to rob.

détruire |dātrüēr| *vt* to destroy; *(fig: santé, réputation)* to ruin; *(documents)* to shred.

détruit, e |dātrüē, -ēt| *pp de* **détruire**.

dette |dct| *nf* debt; ~ **publique** *ou* **de l'État** national debt.

DEUG |dœg| *sigle m* = *Diplôme d'études universitaires générales.*

deuil |dœy| *nm (perte)* bereavement; *(période)* mourning; *(chagrin)* grief; **porter le** ~ to wear mourning; **prendre le/être en** ~ to go into/be in mourning.

DEUST [dœst] *sigle m* = *Diplôme d'études universitaires scientifiques et techniques.*

deux [dœ] *num* two; **les ~** both; **ses ~ mains** both his hands, his two hands; **à ~ pas** a short distance away; **tous les ~ mois** every two months, every other month; **~ points** colon *sg*.

deuxième [dœzyem] *num* second.

deuxièmement [dœzyemmáṅ] *ad* secondly, in the second place.

deux-pièces [dœpyes] *nm inv* (*tailleur*) two-piece (suit); (*de bain*) two-piece (swimsuit); (*appartement*) two-room apartment.

deux-roues [dœrōō] *nm* two-wheeled vehicle.

deux-temps [dœtáṅ] *a* two-stroke.

devais [dəve] *etc vb voir* **devoir**.

dévaler [dāválā] *vt* to hurtle down.

dévaliser [dāvālēzā] *vt* to rob, burglarize (*US*), burgle (*Brit*).

dévalorisant, e [dāválorēzáṅ, -áṅt] *a* depreciatory.

dévalorisation [dāválorēzásyòṅ] *nf* depreciation.

dévaloriser [dāválorēzā] *vt*, **se ~** *vi* to depreciate.

dévaluation [dāválüásyòṅ] *nf* depreciation; (*ÉCON: mesure*) devaluation.

dévaluer [dāválüā] *vt*, **se ~** *vi* to devalue.

devancer [dəváṅsā] *vt* to be ahead of; (*distancer*) to get ahead of; (*arriver avant*) to arrive before; (*prévenir*) to anticipate; **~ l'appel** (*MIL*) to enlist before call-up.

devancier, ière [dəváṅsyā, -yer] *nm/f* precursor.

devant [dəváṅ] *vb voir* **devoir** ♦ *ad* in front; (*à distance: en avant*) ahead ♦ *prép* in front; ahead of; (*avec mouvement: passer*) past; (*fig*) before, in front of; (*: face à*) faced with, in the face of; (*: vu*) in view of ♦ *nm* front; **prendre les ~s** to make the first move; **de ~** (*roue, porte*) front; **les pattes de ~** the front legs, the forelegs; **par ~** (*boutonner*) at the front; (*entrer*) the front way; **par-~** **notaire** in the presence of a notary; **aller au-~ de qn** to go out to meet sb; **aller au-~ de** (*désirs de qn*) to anticipate; **aller au-~ des ennuis** *ou* **difficultés** to be asking for trouble.

devanture [dəváṅtür] *nf* (*façade*) storefront (*US*), (*shop*) front (*Brit*); (*étalage*) display; (*store (US) ou shop (Brit*)) window.

dévastateur, trice [dāvástátœr, -trēs] *a* devastating.

dévastation [dāvástásyòṅ] *nf* devastation.

dévaster [dāvástā] *vt* to devastate.

déveine [dāven] *nf* rotten luck *q*.

développement [dāvlopmáṅ] *nm* development.

développer [dāvlopā] *vt*, **se ~** *vi* to develop.

devenir [dəvnēr] *vb avec attribut* to become; **~ instituteur** to become a teacher; **que sont-ils devenus?** what has become of them?

devenu, e [dəvnü] *pp de* **devenir**.

dévergondé, e [dāvergòṅdā] *a* wild, shameless.

dévergonder [dāvergòṅdā] *vt*, **se ~** *vi* to run wild.

déverminer [dāvermēnā] *vt* (*INFORM*) to debug.

déverrouiller [dāverōōyā] *vt* to unbolt.

devers [dəver] *ad*: **par ~ soi** to oneself.

déverser [dāversā] *vt* (*liquide*) to pour (out); (*ordures*) to dump; **se ~ dans** (*fleuve, mer*) to flow into.

déversoir [dāverswár] *nm* overflow.

dévêtir [dāvātēr] *vt*, **se ~** *vi* to undress.

devez [dəvā] *vb voir* **devoir**.

déviation [dāvyâsyòṅ] *nf* deviation; (*AUTO*) detour (*US*), diversion (*Brit*); **~ de la colonne (vertébrale)** curvature of the spine.

dévider [dāvēdā] *vt* to unwind.

dévidoir [dāvēdwár] *nm* reel.

deviendrai [dəvyaṅdrā], **deviens** [dəvyaṅ] *etc vb voir* **devenir**.

dévier [dāvyā] *vt* (*fleuve, circulation*) to divert; (*coup*) to deflect ♦ *vi* to veer (off course); (*faire*) **~** (*projectile*) to deflect; (*véhicule*) to push off course.

devin [dəvaṅ] *nm* soothsayer, seer.

deviner [dəvēnā] *vt* to guess; (*prévoir*) to foretell, foresee; (*apercevoir*) to distinguish.

devinette [dəvēnet] *nf* riddle.

devint [dəvaṅ] *etc vb voir* **devenir**.

devis [dəvē] *nm* estimate, quote; **~ descriptif/estimatif** detailed/preliminary estimate.

dévisager [dāvēzázhā] *vt* to stare at.

devise [dəvēz] *nf* (*formule*) motto, watchword; (*ÉCON: monnaie*) currency; **~s** *nfpl* (*argent*) currency *sg*.

deviser [dəvēzā] *vi* to converse.

dévisser [dāvēsā] *vt* to unscrew, undo; **se ~** *vi* to come unscrewed.

de visu [dāvēzü] *ad*: **se rendre compte de qch ~** to see sth for o.s.

dévitaliser [dāvētálēzā] *vt* (*dent*) to kill the nerve of.

dévoiler [dāvwálā] *vt* to unveil.

devoir [dəvwár] *nm* duty; (*SCOL*) homework assignment, homework *q*; (*: en classe*) exercise ♦ *vt* (*argent, respect*): **~ qch (à qn)** to owe (sb) sth; (*suivi de l'infinitif: obligation*): **il doit le faire** he has to do it, he must do it; (*: fatalité*): **cela devait arriver un jour** it was bound to happen; (*: intention*): **il doit partir demain** he is (due) to leave tomorrow; (*: probabilité*): **il doit être tard** it must be late; **se faire un ~ de faire qch** to make it one's duty to do sth; **~s de vacances** homework assigned for the holidays; **se ~ de faire qch** to be duty bound to do sth; **je devrais faire** I ought to *ou* should do; **tu n'aurais pas dû** you ought not to have *ou* shouldn't have; **comme il se doit** (*comme il faut*) as is right and proper.

dévolu, e [dāvolü] *a*: **~ à** allotted to ♦ *nm*: **jeter son ~ sur** to fix one's choice on.

devons [dəvòṅ] *vb voir* **devoir**.

dévorant, e [dāvoráṅ, -áṅt] *a* (*faim, passion*) raging.

dévorer [dāvorā] *vt* to devour; (*suj: feu, soucis*) to consume; **~ qn/qch des yeux** *ou* **du regard** (*fig*) to eye sb/sth intently; (*: convoitise*) to eye sb/sth greedily.

dévot, e [dāvō, -ot] *a* devout, pious ♦ *nm/f* devout person; **un faux ~** a falsely pious person.

dévotion [dāvōsyòṅ] *nf* devoutness; **être à la ~ de qn** to be totally devoted to sb; **avoir**

une ~ **pour qn** to worship sb.

dévoué, e [dǽvwā] *a* devoted.

dévouement [dāvōōmáǹ] *nm* devotion, dedication.

dévouer [dǽvwā]: **se ~** *vi* (*se sacrifier*): **se ~ (pour)** to sacrifice o.s. (for); (*se 'consacrer*): **se ~ à** to devote *ou* dedicate o.s. to.

dévoyé, e [dǽvwáyā] *a* delinquent.

dévoyer [dǽvwáyā] *vt* to lead astray; **se ~** *vi* to go off the rails; **~ l'opinion publique** to influence public opinion.

devrai [dəvrā] *etc vb voir* **devoir**.

dextérité [dekstārētā] *nf* skill, dexterity.

dfc *abr* (= *désire faire connaissance*) *in personal column of newspaper*.

DG *sigle m* = **directeur général**.

dg. *abr* (= *décigramme*) dg.

DGE *sigle f* (= *Dotation globale d'équipement*) *state contribution to local government budget*.

DGSE *sigle f* (= *Direction générale des services extérieurs*) ≈ CIA (*US*), ≈ MI6 (*Brit*).

DI *sigle f* (*MIL*) = *division d'infanterie*.

dia [dyá] *abr* = **diapositive**.

diabète [dyábet] *nm* diabetes *sg*.

diabétique [dyábātēk] *nm/f* diabetic.

diable [dyábl(ə)] *nm* devil; **une musique du ~** an unholy racket; **il fait une chaleur du ~** it's fiendishly hot; **avoir le ~ au corps** to be the very devil.

diablement [dyáblɔmáǹ] *ad* fiendishly.

diableries [dyáblɔrē] *nfpl* (*d'enfant*) devilment *sg*, mischief *sg*.

diablesse [dyábles] *nf* (*petite fille*) little devil.

diablotin [dyáblotaǹ] *nm* imp; (*pétard*) cracker.

diabolique [dyábolēk] *a* diabolical.

diabolo [dyábolō] *nm* (*jeu*) diabolo; (*boisson*) lemonade and fruit cordial; **~(-menthe)** lemonade and mint cordial.

diacre [dyákr(ə)] *nm* deacon.

diadème [dyádem] *nm* diadem.

diagnostic [dyágnostēk] *nm* diagnosis *sg*.

diagnostiquer [dyágnostēkā] *vt* to diagnose.

diagonal, e, aux [dyágonál, -ō] *a*, *nf* diagonal; **en ~e** diagonally; **lire en ~e** (*fig*) to skim through.

diagramme [dyágràm] *nm* chart, graph.

dialecte [dyálekt(ə)] *nm* dialect.

dialogue [dyálog] *nm* dialogue; **~ de sourds** dialogue of the deaf.

dialoguer [dyáloga] *vi* to converse; (*POL*) to have a dialogue.

dialoguiste [dyálogēst(ə)] *nm/f* dialogue writer.

diamant [dyámáǹ] *nm* diamond.

diamantaire [dyámáǹter] *nm* diamond dealer.

diamétralement [dyámātrálmáǹ] *ad* diametrically; **~ opposés** (*opinions*) diametrically opposed.

diamètre [dyámetr(ə)] *nm* diameter.

diapason [dyápázóǹ] *nm* tuning fork; (*fig*): **être/se mettre au ~ (de)** to be/get in tune (with).

diaphane [dyáfán] *a* diaphanous.

diaphragme [dyáfràgm(ə)] *nm* (*ANAT*, *PHOTO*) diaphragm; (*contraceptif*) diaphragm; **ouverture du ~** (*PHOTO*) aperture.

diapo [dyápō], **diapositive** [dyápōzētēv] *nf* transparency, slide.

diaporama [dyápорáмá] *nm* slide show.

diapré, e [dyáprā] *a* many-colored (*US*), many-coloured (*Brit*).

diarrhée [dyárā] *nf* diarrhea (*US*), diarrhoea (*Brit*).

diatribe [dyátrēb] *nf* diatribe.

dichotomie [dēkotomē] *nf* dichotomy.

dictaphone [dēktáfon] *nm* Dictaphone ®.

dictateur [dēktátœr] *nm* dictator.

dictatorial, e, aux [dēktátoryál, -ō] *a* dictatorial.

dictature [dēktátür] *nf* dictatorship.

dictée [dēktā] *nf* dictation; **prendre sous ~** to take down (*sth dictated*).

dicter [dēktā] *vt* to dictate.

diction [dēksyóǹ] *nf* diction, delivery; **cours de ~** speech production lesson(s).

dictionnaire [dēksyoner] *nm* dictionary; **~ géographique** gazetteer.

dicton [dēktóǹ] *nm* saying, dictum.

didacticiel [dēdáktēsyel] *nm* educational software.

didactique [dēdáktēk] *a* didactic.

dièse [dyez] *nm* (*MUS*) sharp.

diesel [dyázel] *nm, a inv* diesel.

diète [dyet] *nf* diet; **être à la ~** to be on a diet.

diététicien, ne [dyātātēsyaǹ, -en] *nm/f* dietician.

diététique [dyātātēk] *nf* dietetics *sg* ♦ *a*: **magasin ~** health food store (*US*) *ou* shop (*Brit*).

dieu, x [dyǣ] *nm* god; **D~** God; **le bon D~** the good Lord; **mon D~!** good heavens!

diffamant, e [dēfámáǹ, -áǹt] *a* slanderous, defamatory; libellous.

diffamation [dēfámásyóǹ] *nf* slander; (*écrite*) libel; **attaquer qn en ~** to sue sb for slander (*ou* libel).

diffamatoire [dēfámátwár] *a* slanderous, defamatory; libellous.

diffamer [dēfámā] *vt* to slander, defame; to libel.

différé [dēfárā] *a* (*INFORM*): **traitement ~** batch processing; **crédit ~** deferred credit ♦ *nm* (*TV*): **en ~** (pre-)recorded.

différemment [dēfárámáǹ] *ad* differently.

différence [dēfáráǹs] *nf* difference; **à la ~ de** unlike.

différencier [dēfáráǹsyā] *vt* to differentiate; **se ~** *vi* (*organisme*) to become differentiated; **se ~ de** to differentiate o.s. from; (*être différent*) to differ from.

différend [dēfáráǹ] *nm* difference (of opinion), disagreement.

différent, e [dēfáráǹ, -áǹt] *a*: **~ (de)** different (from); **~s objets** different *ou* various objects; **à ~es reprises** on various occasions.

différentiel, le [dēfáráǹsyel] *a, nm* differential.

différer [dēfárā] *vt* to postpone, put off ♦ *vi*: **~ (de)** to differ (from); **~ de faire** (*tarder*) to delay doing.

difficile [dēfēsēl] *a* difficult; (*exigeant*) hard to please, difficult (to please); **faire le** *ou* **la ~** to be hard to please, be difficult.

difficilement [dēfēsēlmáǹ] *ad* (*marcher, s'expliquer etc*) with difficulty; **~ lisible/compréhensible** difficult *ou* hard to read/

understand.

difficulté [dēfēkültā] *nf* difficulty; **en ~** (*bateau, alpiniste*) in trouble *ou* difficulties; **avoir de la ~ à faire** to have difficulty (in) doing.

difforme [dēform(ə)] *a* deformed, misshapen.

difformité [dēformētā] *nf* deformity.

diffracter [dēfrāktā] *vt* to diffract.

diffus, e [dēfü, -üz] *a* diffuse.

diffuser [dēfüzā] *vt* (*chaleur, bruit, lumière*) to diffuse; (*émission, musique*) to broadcast; (*nouvelle, idée*) to circulate; (*COMM: livres, journaux*) to distribute.

diffuseur [dēfüzœr] *nm* diffuser; distributor.

diffusion [dēfüzyôń] *nf* diffusion; broadcast(ing); circulation; distribution.

digérer [dēzhārā] *vt* (*suj: personne*) to digest; (: *machine*) to process; (*fig: accepter*) to stomach, put up with.

digeste [dēzhest(ə)] *a* easily digestible.

digestible [dēzhestēbl(ə)] *a* digestible.

digestif, ive [dēzhestēf, -ēv] *a* digestive ♦ *nm* (after-dinner) liqueur.

digestion [dēzhestyôń] *nf* digestion.

digit [dēdzhēt] *nm*: **~ binaire** binary digit.

digital, e, aux [dēzhētāl, -ō] *a* digital.

digitale [dēzhētāl] *nf* digitalis, foxglove.

digne [dēny] *a* dignified; **~ de** worthy of; **~ de foi** trustworthy.

dignitaire [dēnyēter] *nm* dignitary.

dignité [dēnyētā] *nf* dignity.

digression [dēgrāsyôń] *nf* digression.

digue [dēg] *nf* dike, dyke; (*pour protéger la côte*) sea wall.

dijonnais, e [dēzhone, -ez] *a* of *ou* from Dijon ♦ *nm/f:* **D~, e** inhabitant *ou* native of Dijon.

dilapider [dēlāpēdā] *vt* to squander, waste; (*détourner: biens, fonds publics*) to embezzle, misappropriate.

dilater [dēlātā] *vt* to dilate; (*gaz, métal*) to cause to expand; (*ballon*) to distend; **se ~** *vi* to expand.

dilemme [dēlem] *nm* dilemma.

dilettante [dēlātānt] *nm/f* dilettante [dilətant'];
en ~ in a dilettantish way.

diligence [dēlēzhâńs] *nf* stagecoach, diligence; (*empressement*) dispatch; **faire ~** to make haste.

diligent, e [dēlēzhâń, -âńt] *a* prompt and efficient; diligent.

diluant [dēlüâń] *nm* thinner(s).

diluer [dēlüā] *vt* to dilute.

diluvien, ne [dēlüvyań, -en] *a*: **pluie ~ne** torrential rain.

dimanche [dēmâńsh] *nm* Sunday; **le ~ des Rameaux/de Pâques** Palm/Easter Sunday; *voir aussi* **lundi.**

dîme [dēm] *nf* tithe.

dimension [dēmâńsyôń] *nf* (*grandeur*) size; (*gén pl: cotes, MATH: de l'espace*) dimension.

diminué, e [dēmēnüā] *a* (*personne: physiquement*) run-down; (: *mentalement*) less alert.

diminuer [dēmēnüā] *vt* to reduce, decrease; (*ardeur etc*) to lessen; (*personne: physiquement*) to undermine; (*dénigrer*) to belittle ♦ *vi* to decrease, diminish.

diminutif [dēmēnütēf] *nm* (*LING*) diminutive; (*surnom*) pet name.

diminution [dēmēnüsyôń] *nf* decreasing, diminishing.

dînatoire [dēnátwār] *a*: **apéritif ~ ≈** evening buffet.

dinde [dańd] *nf* turkey; (*femme stupide*) goose.

dindon [dańdôń] *nm* turkey.

dindonneau, x [dańdonō] *nm* turkey poult.

dîner [dēnā] *nm* dinner ♦ *vi* to have dinner; **~ d'affaires/de famille** business/family dinner.

dînette [dēnet] *nf* (*jeu*): **jouer à la ~** to play at having a tea party.

dingue [dańg] *a* (*fam*) crazy.

dinosaure [dēnōzor] *nm* dinosaur.

diode [dyod] *nf* diode.

diphasé, e [dēfâzā] *a* (*ÉLEC*) two-phase.

diphtérie [dēftārē] *nf* diphtheria.

diphtongue [dēftôńg] *nf* diphthong.

diplomate [dēplomát] *a* diplomatic ♦ *nm* diplomat; (*fig: personne habile*) diplomatist; (*CULIN*): *gâteau*) dessert made of sponge cake, candied fruit and custard, ≈ trifle (*Brit*).

diplomatie [dēplomāsē] *nf* diplomacy.

diplomatique [dēplomátēk] *a* diplomatic.

diplôme [dēplôm] *nm* diploma; (*examen*) (diploma) examination.

diplômé, e [dēplômā] *a* qualified.

dire [dēr] *nm*: **au ~ de** according to; **leur ~s** what they say ♦ *vt* to say; (*secret, mensonge*) to tell; **~ l'heure/la vérité** to tell the time/the truth; **dis pardon/merci** say ''I'm sorry''/thank you; **~ qch à qn** to tell sb sth; **~ à qn qu'il fasse** *ou* **de faire** to tell sb to do; **~ que** to say that; **on dit que** they say that; **comme on dit** as they say; **on dirait que** it looks (*ou* sounds *etc*) as though; **on dirait du vin** you'd *ou* one would think it was wine; **que dites-vous de** (*penser*) what do you think of; **si cela lui dit** if he feels like it, if it appeals to him; **cela ne me dit rien** that doesn't appeal to me; **à vrai ~ ... to** tell the truth ...; **pour ainsi ~** so to speak; **cela va sans ~** that goes without saying; **dis donc!, dites donc!** (*pour attirer l'attention*) hey!; (*au fait*) by the way; **et ~ que ...** and to think that ...; **ceci** *ou* **cela dit** that being said; (*à ces mots*) whereupon; **c'est dit, voilà qui est dit** so that's settled; **il n'y a pas à ~** there's no getting away from it; **c'est ~ si ...** that just shows that ...; **c'est beaucoup/peu ~** that's saying a lot/not saying much; **se ~** (*à soi-même*) to say to oneself; (*se prétendre*): **se ~ malade** *etc* to say (that) one is ill *etc*; **ça se dit ... en anglais** that is ... in English; **cela ne se dit pas comme ça** you don't say it like that; **se ~ au revoir** to say goodbye (to each other).

direct, e [dērekt] *a* direct ♦ *nm* (*train*) through train; **en ~** (*émission*) live; **train/bus ~** express train/bus.

directement [dērektəmâń] *ad* directly.

directeur, trice [dērektœr, -trēs] *nm/f* (*d'entreprise*) director; (*de service*) manager/eress; (*d'école*) principal; **comité ~** executive (*US*) *ou* management (*Brit*) committee; **~ général** general manager; **~ de thèse ≈** dissertation advisor (*US*), Ph.D. supervisor (*Brit*).

direction [dērɛksyôǹ] *nf* management; conducting; supervision; (*AUTO*) steering; (*sens*) direction; **sous la ~ de** (*MUS*) conducted by; **en ~ de** (*avion, train, bateau*) for; "**toutes ~s**" (*AUTO*) "all routes".

directive [dērɛktēv] *nf* directive, instruction.

directorial, e, aux [dērɛktoryál, -ō] *a* (*bureau*) director's; manager's; principal's.

directrice [dērɛktrēs] *af*, *nf voir* **directeur**.

dirent [dēr] *vb voir* **dire**.

dirigeable [dērēzhábl(ə)] *a, nm*: (**ballon**) ~ dirigible.

dirigeant, e [dērēzhàǹ, -áǹt] *a* managerial; (*classes*) ruling ♦ *nm/f* (*d'un parti etc*) leader; (*d'entreprise*) manager, member of the management.

diriger [dērēzhā] *vt* (*entreprise*) to manage, run; (*véhicule*) to steer; (*orchestre*) to conduct; (*recherches, travaux*) to supervise, be in charge of; (*braquer: regard, arme*): ~ **sur** to point *ou* level *ou* aim at; (*fig: critiques*): ~ **contre** to aim at; **se** ~ (*s'orienter*) to find one's way; **se ~ vers** *ou* **sur** to make *ou* head for.

dirigisme [dērēzhēsm(ə)] *nm* (*ÉCON*) government intervention, interventionism.

dirigiste [dērēzhēst(ə)] *a* interventionist.

dis [dē], **disais** [dēze] *etc vb voir* **dire**.

discal, e, aux [dēskál, -ō] *a* (*MÉD*): **hernie ~e** slipped disk.

discernement [dēsɛrnəmáǹ] *nm* discernment, judgment.

discerner [dēsɛrnā] *vt* to discern, make out.

disciple [dēsēpl(ə)] *nm/f* disciple.

disciplinaire [dēsēplēnɛr] *a* disciplinary.

discipline [dēsēplēn] *nf* discipline.

discipliné, e [dēsēplēnā] *a* (well-)disciplined.

discipliner [dēsēplēnā] *vt* to discipline; (*cheveux*) to control.

discobole [dēskobol] *nm/f* discus thrower.

discontinu, e [dēskôǹtēnü] *a* intermittent; (*bande: sur la route*) broken.

discontinuer [dēskôǹtēnüā] *vi*: **sans ~** without stopping, without a break.

disconvenir [dēskôǹvnēr] *vi*: **ne pas ~ de** qch/que not to deny sth/that.

discophile [dēskofēl] *nm/f* record enthusiast.

discordance [dēskordáǹs] *nf* discordance; conflict.

discordant, e [dēskordáǹ, -áǹt] *a* discordant; conflicting.

discorde [dēskord(ə)] *nf* discord, dissension.

discothèque [dēskotek] *nf* (*disques*) record collection; (: *dans une bibliothèque*): ~ (**de prêt**) record library; (*boîte de nuit*) disco(thèque).

discourais [dēskōōre] *etc vb voir* **discourir**.

discourir [dēskōōrēr] *vi* to discourse, hold forth.

discours [dēskōōr] *vb voir* **discourir** ♦ *nm* speech; ~ **direct/indirect** (*LING*) direct/indirect *ou* reported speech.

discrédit [dēskrādē] *nm*: **jeter le ~ sur** to discredit.

discréditer [dēskrādētā] *vt* to discredit.

discret, ète [dēskre, -et] *a* discreet; (*fig: musique, style*) unobtrusive; (: *endroit*) quiet.

discrètement [dēskretmáǹ] *ad* discreetly.

discrétion [dēskrāsyôǹ] *nf* discretion; **à la ~ de qn** at sb's discretion; in sb's hands; **à ~** (*boisson etc*) unlimited, as much as one wants.

discrétionnaire [dēskrāsyoner] *a* discretionary.

discrimination [dēskrēmēnâsyôǹ] *nf* discrimination; **sans ~** indiscriminately.

discriminatoire [dēskrēmēnâtwár] *a* discriminatory.

disculper [dēskülpā] *vt* to exonerate.

discussion [dēsküsyôǹ] *nf* discussion.

discutable [dēskütábl(ə)] *a* (*contestable*) doubtful; (*à débattre*) debatable.

discuté, e [dēskütā] *a* controversial.

discuter [dēskütā] *vt* (*contester*) to question, dispute; (*débattre: prix*) to discuss ♦ *vi* to talk; (*ergoter*) to argue; ~ **de** to discuss.

dise [dēz] *etc vb voir* **dire**.

disert, e [dēzer, -ert(ə)] *a* loquacious.

disette [dēzet] *nf* food shortage.

diseuse [dēzœz] *nf*: ~ **de bonne aventure** fortuneteller.

disgrâce [dēsgrás] *nf* disgrace; **être en ~** to be in disgrace.

disgracieux, euse [dēsgrásyœ, -œz] *a* ungainly, awkward.

disjoindre [dēszhwaǹdr(ə)] *vt* to take apart; **se** ~ *vi* to come apart.

disjoint, e [dēszhwaǹ, -waǹt] *pp de* **disjoindre** ♦ *a* loose.

disjoncteur [dēszhôǹktœr] *nm* (*ÉLEC*) circuit breaker.

dislocation [dēslokásyôǹ] *nf* dislocation.

disloquer [dēslokā] *vt* (*membre*) to dislocate; (*chaise*) to dismantle; (*troupe*) to disperse; **se** ~ *vi* (*parti, empire*) to break up; **se ~ l'épaule** to dislocate one's shoulder.

disparaître [dēspáretr(ə)] *vi* to disappear; (*à la vue*) to vanish, disappear; to be hidden *ou* concealed; (*être manquant*) to be missing, disappear; (*se perdre: traditions etc*) to die out; (*personne: mourir*) to die; **faire ~** (*objet, tache, trace*) to remove; (*personne*) to get rid of.

disparate [dēspárát] *a* disparate; (*couleurs*) ill-assorted.

disparité [dēspárētā] *nf* disparity.

disparition [dēspárēsyôǹ] *nf* disappearance.

disparu, e [dēspárü] *pp de* **disparaître** ♦ *nm/f* missing person; (*défunt*) departed; **être porté ~** to be reported missing.

dispendieux, euse [dēspáǹdyœ, -œz] *a* extravagant, expensive.

dispensaire [dēspáǹser] *nm* free (*US*) *ou* community (*Brit*) clinic.

dispense [dēspáǹs] *nf* exemption; (*permission*) special permission; ~ **d'âge** special exemption from age limit.

dispenser [dēspáǹsā] *vt* (*donner*) to lavish, bestow; (*exempter*): ~ **qn de** to exempt sb from; **se ~ de** *vt* to avoid, get out of.

disperser [dēspersā] *vt* to scatter; (*fig: son attention*) to dissipate; **se** ~ *vi* to scatter; (*fig*) to dissipate one's efforts.

disponibilité [dēsponēbēlētā] *nf* availability; (*ADMIN*): **être en ~** to be on leave of absence; ~**s** *nfpl* (*COMM*) liquid assets.

disponible [dēsponēbl(ə)] *a* available.

dispos [dēspō] *am*: (**frais et**) ~ fresh (as a daisy).

disposé, e [dēspōzā] *a* (*d'une certaine manière*) arranged, laid-out; **bien/mal** ~ (*humeur*) in a good/bad mood; **bien/mal** ~ **pour** *ou* **envers qn** well/badly disposed towards sb; ~ **à** (*prêt à*) willing *ou* prepared to.

disposer [dēspōzā] *vt* (*arranger, placer*) to arrange; (*inciter*): ~ **qn à qch/faire qch** to dispose *ou* incline sb towards sth/to do sth ♦ *vi*: **vous pouvez** ~ you may leave; ~ **de** *vt* to have (at one's disposal); **se** ~ **à faire** to prepare to do, be about to do.

dispositif [dēspōzētēf] *nm* device; (*fig*) system, plan of action; set-up; (*d'un texte de loi*) operative part; ~ **de sûreté** safety device.

disposition [dēspōzēsyôn] *nf* (*arrangement*) arrangement, layout; (*humeur*) mood; (*tendance*) tendency; **~s** *nfpl* (*mesures*) steps, measures; (*préparatifs*) arrangements; (*de loi, testament*) provisions; (*aptitudes*) bent *sg*, aptitude *sg*; **à la** ~ **de qn** at sb's disposal.

disproportion [dēsproporsyôn] *nf* disproportion.

disproportionné, e [dēsproporsyonā] *a* disproportionate, out of all proportion.

dispute [dēspüt] *nf* quarrel, argument.

disputer [dēspütā] *vt* (*match*) to play; (*combat*) to fight; (*course*) to run; **se** ~ *vi* to quarrel, have a quarrel; (*match, combat, course*) to take place; ~ **qch à qn** to fight with sb for *ou* over sth.

disquaire [dēsker] *nm/f* record dealer.

disqualification [dēskálēfēkâsyôn] *nf* disqualification.

disqualifier [dēskálēfyā] *vt* to disqualify; **se** ~ *vi* to bring discredit on o.s.

disque [dēsk(ə)] *nm* (*MUS*) record; (*INFORM*) disk, disc; (*forme, pièce*) disc; (*SPORT*) discus; ~ **compact** compact disc; ~ **dur** hard disk; ~ **d'embrayage** (*AUTO*) clutch plate; ~ **laser** compact disc; ~ **de stationnement** parking disk; ~ **système** system disk.

disquette [dēsket] *nf* diskette, floppy (disk); ~ (**à**) **simple/double densité** single/double density disk; ~ **une face/double face** single-/double-sided disk.

dissection [dēseksyôn] *nf* dissection.

dissemblable [dēsânblábl(ə)] *a* dissimilar.

dissemblance [dēsânblâns] *nf* dissimilarity, difference.

disséminer [dēsāmēnā] *vt* to scatter; (*chasser*) to disperse.

dissension [dēsânsyôn] *nf* dissension; **~s** *nfpl* dissension.

disséquer [dēsākā] *vt* to dissect.

dissertation [dēsertâsyôn] *nf* (*SCOL*) essay.

disserter [dēsertā] *vi*: ~ **sur** to discourse upon.

dissident, e [dēsēdân, -ânt] *a, nm/f* dissident.

dissimilitude [dēsēmēlētüd] *nf* dissimilarity.

dissimulateur, trice [dēsēmültœr, -trēs] *a* dissembling ♦ *nm/f* dissembler.

dissimulation [dēsēmülâsyôn] *nf* concealing; (*duplicité*) dissimulation; ~ **de bénéfices/de revenus** concealment of profits/income.

dissimulé, e [dēsēmülā] (*personne: secret*) secretive; (*: fourbe, hypocrite*) deceitful.

dissimuler [dēsēmülā] *vt* to conceal; **se** ~ to conceal o.s.; to be concealed.

dissipation [dēsēpásyôn] *nf* squandering; unruliness; (*débauche*) dissipation.

dissipé, e [dēsēpā] *a* (*indiscipliné*) unruly.

dissiper [dēsēpā] *vt* to dissipate; (*fortune*) to squander, fritter away; **se** ~ *vi* (*brouillard*) to clear, disperse; (*doutes*) to disappear, melt away; (*élève*) to become undisciplined *ou* unruly.

dissociable [dēsosyábl(ə)] *a* separable.

dissocier [dēsosyā] *vt* to dissociate; **se** ~ *vi* (*éléments, groupe*) to break up, split up; **se** ~ **de** (*groupe, point de vue*) to dissociate o.s. from.

dissolu, e [dēsolü] *a* dissolute.

dissoluble [dēsolübl(ə)] *a* (*POL: assemblée*) dissolvable.

dissolution [dēsolüsyôn] *nf* dissolving; (*POL, JUR*) dissolution.

dissolvant, e [dēsolvân, -ânt] *vb voir* **dissoudre** ♦ *nm* (*CHIMIE*) solvent; ~ (**gras**) nail polish remover.

dissonant, e [dēsonân, -ânt] *a* discordant.

dissoudre [dēsōōdr(ə)] *vt*, **se** ~ *vi* to dissolve.

dissous, oute [dēsōō, -ōōt] *pp de* **dissoudre**.

dissuader [dēsüádā] *vt*: ~ **qn de faire/de qch** to dissuade sb from doing/from sth.

dissuasion [dēsüázyôn] *nf* dissuasion; **force de** ~ deterrent power.

distance [dēstâns] *nf* distance; (*fig: écart*) gap; **à** ~ at *ou* from a distance; (*mettre en marche, commander*) by remote control; (*situé*) **à** ~ (*INFORM*) remote; **tenir qn à** ~ to keep sb at a distance; **se tenir à** ~ to keep one's distance; **à une** ~ **de 10 km, à 10 km de** ~ 10 km away, at a distance of 10 km; **à 2 ans de** ~ with a gap of 2 years; **prendre ses ~s** to spread out; **garder ses ~s** to keep one's distance; **tenir la** ~ (*SPORT*) to cover the distance, last the course; ~ **focale** (*PHOTO*) focal length.

distancer [dēstânsā] *vt* to outdistance, leave behind.

distancier [dēstânsyā]: **se** ~ *vi* to distance o.s.

distant, e [dēstân, -ânt] *a* (*réservé*) distant, aloof; (*éloigné*) distant, far away; ~ **de** (*lieu*) far away *ou* a long way from; ~ **de 5 km** (*d'un lieu*) 5 km away (from a place).

distendre [dēstândr(ə)] *vt*, **se** ~ *vi* to distend.

distillation [dēstēlâsyôn] *nf* distillation, distilling.

distillé, e [dēstēlā] *a*: **eau** ~**e** distilled water.

distiller [dēstēlā] *vt* to distill (*US*) *ou* distil (*Brit*); (*fig*) to exude; to elaborate.

distillerie [dēstēlrē] *nf* distillery.

distinct, e [dēstan(kt), dēstankt(ə)] *a* distinct.

distinctement [dēstanktəmân] *ad* distinctly.

distinctif, ive [dēstanktēf, -ēv] *a* distinctive.

distinction [dēstanksyôn] *nf* distinction.

distingué, e [dēstangā] *a* distinguished.

distinguer [dēstangā] *vt* to distinguish; **se** ~ *vi* (*s'illustrer*) to distinguish o.s.; (*différer*): **se** ~ (**de**) to distinguish o.s. *ou* be distinguished (from).

distinguo [dēstangō] *nm* distinction.

distraction [dēstráksyôn] *nf* (*manque*

d'attention) absent-mindedness; (*oubli*) lapse (in concentration *ou* attention); (*détente*) diversion, recreation; (*passe-temps*) distraction, entertainment.

distraire [dēstrer] *vt* (*déranger*) to distract; (*divertir*) to entertain, divert; (*détourner: somme d'argent*) to divert, misappropriate; **se ~** to amuse *ou* enjoy o.s.

distrait, e [dēstre, -et] *pp de* **distraire** ♦ *a* absent-minded.

distraitement [dēstretmáň] *ad* absent-mindedly.

distrayant, e [dēstreyáň, -áňt] *vb voir* **distraire** ♦ *a* entertaining.

distribanque [dēstrēbáňk] *nm* automated teller machine (ATM).

distribuer [dēstrēbüä] *vt* to distribute; to hand out; (*CARTES*) to deal (out); (*courrier*) to deliver.

distributeur [dēstrēbütœr] *nm* (*AUTO, COMM*) distributor; (*automatique*) (vending) machine; **~ de billets** (*RAIL*) ticket machine; (*BANQUE*) automated teller machine (ATM).

distribution [dēstrēbüsyóň] *nf* distribution; (*postale*) delivery; (*choix d'acteurs*) casting; **circuits de ~** (*COMM*) distribution network; **~ des prix** (*SCOL*) awards ceremony (*US*), prize giving (*Brit*).

district [dēstrēk(t)] *nm* district.

dit, e [dē, dēt] *pp de* **dire** ♦ *a* (*fixé*): **le jour ~** the appointed day; (*surnommé*): **X, ~ Pierrot** X, known as *ou* called Pierrot.

dites [dēt] *vb voir* **dire**.

dithyrambique [dētēráňbēk] *a* eulogistic.

DIU *sigle m* (= *dispositif intra-utérin*) IUD.

diurétique [dyürātēk] *a, nm* diuretic.

diurne [dyürn(ə)] *a* diurnal, daytime *cpd*.

divagations [dēvágásyóň] *nfpl* ramblings; ravings.

divaguer [dēvágá] *vi* to ramble; (*malade*) to rave.

divan [dēváň] *nm* divan.

divan-lit [dēváňlē] *nm* divan (bed).

divergent, e [dēverzháň, -áňt] *a* divergent.

diverger [dēverzhá] *vi* to diverge.

divers, e [dēver, -ers(ə)] *a* (*varié*) diverse, varied; (*différent*) different, various ♦ *dét* (*plusieurs*) various, several; (**frais**) **~** (*COMM*) sundries, miscellaneous (expenses); **"~"** (*rubrique*) "miscellaneous".

diversement [dēversəmáň] *ad* in various *ou* diverse ways.

diversification [dēversēfēkásyóň] *nf* diversification.

diversifier [dēversēfyá] *vt,* **se ~** *vi* to diversify.

diversion [dēversyóň] *nf* diversion; **faire ~** to create a diversion.

diversité [dēversētá] *nf* diversity, variety.

divertir [dēvertēr] *vt* to amuse, entertain; **se ~** to amuse *ou* enjoy o.s.

divertissant, e [dēvertēsáň, -áňt] *a* entertaining.

divertissement [dēvertēsmáň] *nm* entertainment; (*MUS*) divertimento, divertissement.

dividende [dēvēdáňd] *nm* (*MATH, COMM*) dividend.

divin, e [dēvaň, -ēn] *a* divine; (*fig: excellent*) heavenly, divine.

divinateur, trice [dēvēnátœr, -trēs] *a* perspicacious.

divinatoire [dēvēnátwár] *a* (*art, science*) divinatory; **baguette ~** divining rod.

diviniser [dēvēnēzá] *vt* to deify.

divinité [dēvēnētá] *nf* divinity.

divisé, e [dēvēzá] *a* divided.

diviser [dēvēzá] *vt* (*gén, MATH*) to divide; (*morceler, subdiviser*) to divide (up), split (up); **se ~ en** to divide into; **~ par** to divide by.

diviseur [dēvēzœr] *nm* (*MATH*) divisor.

divisible [dēvēzēbl(ə)] *a* divisible.

division [dēvēzyóň] *nf* (*gén*) division; **~ du travail** (*ÉCON*) division of labor.

divisionnaire [dēvēzyoner] *a*: **commissaire ~** ≈ police chief (*US*), ≈ chief superintendent (*Brit*).

divorce [dēvors(ə)] *nm* divorce.

divorcé, e [dēvorsá] *nm/f* divorcee.

divorcer [dēvorsá] *vi* to get a divorce, get divorced; **~ de** *ou* **d'avec qn** to divorce sb.

divulgation [dēvülgásyóň] *nf* disclosure.

divulguer [dēvülgá] *vt* to divulge, disclose.

dix [dē, dēs, dēz] *num* ten.

dix-huit [dēzüēt] *num* eighteen.

dix-huitième [dēzüētyem] *num* eighteenth.

dixième [dēzyem] *num* tenth.

dix-neuf [dēznœf] *num* nineteen.

dix-neuvième [dēznœvyem] *num* nineteenth.

dix-sept [dēset] *num* seventeen.

dix-septième [dēsetyem] *num* seventeenth.

dizaine [dēzen] *nf* (*10*) ten; (*environ 10*): **une ~ (de)** about ten, ten *ou* so.

Djakarta [dzhákártá] *n* Djakarta.

Djibouti [dzhēbōōtē] *n* Djibouti.

DM *abr* (= *Deutschmark*) DM.

dm. *abr* (= *décimètre*) dm.

do [dō] *nm* (*note*) C; (*en chantant la gamme*) do(h).

docile [dosēl] *a* docile.

docilité [dosēlētá] *nf* docility.

dock [dok] *nm* dock; (*hangar, bâtiment*) warehouse.

docker [doker] *nm* docker.

docte [dokt(ə)] *a* (*péj*) learned.

docteur [doktœr] *nm* doctor; **~ en médecine** doctor of medicine.

doctoral, e, aux [doktorál, -ō] *a* pompous, bombastic.

doctorat [doktorá] *nm*: **~ (d'Université)** ≈ doctorate; **~ d'État** ≈ PhD; **~ de troisième cycle** ≈ doctorate.

doctoresse [doktores] *nf* lady doctor.

doctrinaire [doktrēner] *a* doctrinaire; (*sentencieux*) pompous, sententious.

doctrinal, e, aux [doktrēnál, ō] *a* doctrinal.

doctrine [doktrēn] *nf* doctrine.

document [dokümáň] *nm* document.

documentaire [dokümáňter] *a, nm* documentary.

documentaliste [dokümáňtálēst(ə)] *nm/f* archivist; (*PRESSE, TV*) researcher.

documentation [dokümáňtásyóň] *nf* documentation, literature; (*PRESSE, TV: service*) research.

documenté, e [dokümáňtá] *a* well-informed, well-documented; well-researched.

documenter [dokümåntā] *vt*: **se ~ (sur)** to gather information *ou* material (on *ou* about).

Dodécanèse [dodākánez] *nm* Dodecanese (Islands).

dodeliner [dodlēnā] *vi*: **~ de la tête** to nod one's head gently.

dodo [dodō] *nm*: **aller faire ~** to go to beddy-bye.

dodu, e [dodü] *a* plump.

dogmatique [dogmátēk] *a* dogmatic.

dogme [dogm(ə)] *nm* dogma.

dogue [dog] *nm* mastiff.

doigt [dwá] *nm* finger; **à deux ~s de** within an ace *ou* an inch of; **un ~ de lait/whisky** a drop of milk/whiskey; **désigner** *ou* **montrer du ~** to point at; **au ~ et à l'œil** to the letter; **connaître qch sur le bout du ~** to know sth backwards; **mettre le ~ sur la plaie** (*fig*) to find the sensitive spot; **~ de pied** toe.

doigté [dwátā] *nm* (*MUS*) fingering; (*fig: habileté*) diplomacy, tact.

doigtier [dwátyā] *nm* fingerstall.

dois [dwá], **doive** [dwáv] *etc vb voir* **devoir**.

doléances [dolããs] *nfpl* complaints; (*réclamations*) grievances.

dolent, e [dolåñ, -åñt] *a* doleful, mournful.

dollar [dolár] *nm* dollar.

dolmen [dolmen] *nm* dolmen.

DOM [dāōem, dom] *sigle m ou mpl =* Département(*s*) d'outre-mer.

domaine [domen] *nm* estate, property; (*fig*) domain, field; **tomber dans le ~ public** (*livre etc*) to be out of copyright; **dans tous les ~s** in all areas.

domanial, e, aux [dományál, -ō] *a* national, state *cpd*.

dôme [dōm] *nm* dome.

domestication [domestēkâsyóñ] *nf* (*voir domestiquer*) domestication; harnessing.

domesticité [domestēsētā] *nf* (domestic) staff.

domestique [domestēk] *a* domestic ♦ *nm/f* servant, domestic.

domestiquer [domestēkā] *vt* to domesticate; (*vent, marées*) to harness.

domicile [domēsēl] *nm* home, place of residence; **à ~** at home; **élire ~ à** to take up residence in; **sans ~ fixe** of no fixed abode; **~ conjugal** marital home; **~ légal** domicile.

domicilié, e [domēsēlyā] *a*: **être ~ à** to have one's home in *ou* at.

dominant, e [domēnåñ, -åñt] *a* dominant; (*plus important*) predominant.

dominateur, trice [domēnátœr, -trēs] *a* dominating; (*qui aime à dominer*) domineering.

domination [domēnâsyóñ] *nf* domination.

dominer [domēnā] *vt* to dominate; (*passions etc*) to control, master; (*surpasser*) to outclass, surpass; (*surplomber*) to tower above, dominate ♦ *vi* to be in the dominant position; **se ~** to control o.s.

dominicain, e [domēnēkañ, -en] *a* Dominican.

dominical, e, aux [domēnēkál, -ō] *a* Sunday *cpd*, dominical.

Dominique [domēnēk] *nf*: **la ~** Dominica.

domino [domēnō] *nm* domino; **~s** *nmpl* (*jeu*) dominoes *sg*.

dommage [domázh] *nm* (*préjudice*) harm, in-

jury; (*dégâts, pertes*) damage *q*; **c'est ~ de faire/que** it's a shame *ou* pity to do/that; **~s corporels** physical injury.

dommages-intérêts [domázh(əz)añtāre] *nmpl* damages.

dompter [dóñtā] *vt* to tame.

dompteur, euse [dóñtœr, -ēz] *nm/f* trainer; (*de lion*) liontamer.

DOM-TOM [domtom] *sigle m ou mpl =* Département(*s*) d'outre-mer/Territoire(*s*) d'outre-mer.

don [dóñ] *nm* (*cadeau*) gift; (*charité*) donation; (*aptitude*) gift, talent; **avoir des ~s pour** to have a gift *ou* talent for; **faire ~ de** to make a gift of; **~ en argent** cash donation.

donateur, trice [donátœr, -trēs] *nm/f* donor.

donation [donâsyóñ] *nf* donation.

donc [dóñk] *cj* therefore, so; (*après une digression*) so, then; (*intensif*): **voilà ~ la solution** so there's the solution; **je disais ~ que ...** as I was saying, ...; **venez ~ dîner à la maison** do come for dinner; **allons ~!** come now!; **faites ~** go ahead.

donjon [dóñzhóñ] *nm* keep.

donnant, e [donáñ, -áñt] *a*: **~, ~** fair's fair.

donne [don] *nf* (*CARTES*): **il y a mauvaise** *ou* **fausse ~** there's been a misdeal.

donné, e [donā] *a* (*convenu*) given; (*pas cher*) dirt cheap, very cheap ♦ *nf* (*MATH, INFORM, gén*) datum (*pl* data); **c'est ~** it's a gift; **étant ~ ... given ....**

donner [donā] *vt* to give; (*vieux habits etc*) to give away; (*spectacle*) to put on; (*film*) to show; **~ qch à qn** to give sb sth, give sth to sb; **~ sur** (*suj: fenêtre, chambre*) to look (out) onto; **~ dans** (*piège etc*) to fall into; **faire ~ l'infanterie** (*MIL*) to send in the infantry; **~ l'heure à qn** to tell sb the time; **~ le ton** (*fig*) to set the tone; **~ à penser/entendre que ...** to make one think/give one to understand that ...; **se ~ à fond** (à son travail) to give one's all (to one's work), devote o.s. heart and soul (to one's work); **se ~ du mal** *ou* **de la peine (pour faire qch)** to go to a lot of trouble (to do sth); **s'en ~ à cœur joie** (*fam*) to have a great time.

donneur, euse [donœr, -ēz] *nm/f* (*MÉD*) donor; (*CARTES*) dealer; **~ de sang** blood donor.

dont [dóñ] *pronom relatif*: **la maison ~ je vois le toit** the house whose roof I can see, the house I can see the roof of; **la maison ~ le toit est rouge** the house whose roof is red *ou* the roof of which is red; **l'homme ~ je connais la sœur** the man whose sister I know; **10 blessés, ~ 2 grièvement** 10 injured, 2 of them seriously; **2 livres, ~ l'un est ...** 2 books, one of which is ...; **il y avait plusieurs personnes, dont Gabrielle** there were several people, among them Gabrielle; **le fils ~ il est si fier** the son he's so proud of; **ce ~ je parle** what I'm talking about; *voir adjectifs et verbes à complément prépositionnel*: **responsable de, souffrir de** *etc*.

donzelle [dóñzel] *nf* (*péj*) young madam.

dopage [dopázh] *nm* doping.

dopant [dopáñ] *nm* dope.

doper [dopā] *vt* to dope; **se** ~ to take dope.
doping [dopēng] *nm* doping; *(excitant)* dope.
dorade [dorád] *nf* = **daurade**.
doré, e [dorā] *a* golden; *(avec dorure)* gilt, gilded.
dorénavant [dorānáváň] *ad* from now on, henceforth.
dorer [dorā] *vt* *(cadre)* to gild; **(faire)** ~ *(CULIN)* to brown; *(: gâteau)* to glaze; **se** ~ **au soleil** to sunbathe; ~ **la pilule à qn** to sugarcoat *(US)* ou sugar *(Brit)* the pill for sb.
dorloter [dorlotā] *vt* to pamper, cosset *(Brit)*; **se faire** ~ to be pampered *ou* cosseted.
dormant, e [dormáň, -áňt] *a*: **eau** ~**e** still water.
dorme [dorm(ə)] *etc vb voir* **dormir**.
dormeur, euse [dormœr, -œz] *nm/f* sleeper.
dormir [dormēr] *vi* to sleep; *(être endormi)* to be asleep; ~ **à poings fermés** to sleep very soundly.
dorsal, e, aux [dorsál, -ō] *a* dorsal; *voir* **rouleau.**
dortoir [dortwár] *nm* dormitory.
dorure [dorür] *nf* gilding.
doryphore [dorēfor] *nm* Colorado beetle.
dos [dō] *nm* back; *(de livre)* spine; "**voir au** ~" "see other side"; **robe décolletée dans le** ~ low-backed dress; **de** ~ from the back, from behind; ~ **à** ~ back to back; **sur le** ~ on one's back; **à** ~ **de chameau** riding on a camel; **avoir bon** ~ to be a good excuse; **se mettre qn à** ~ to turn sb against one.
dosage [dōzàzh] *nm* mixture.
dos-d'âne [dōdán] *nm* humpback; **pont en** ~ humpbacked bridge.
dose [dōz] *nf* *(MÉD)* dose; **forcer la** ~ *(fig)* to overstep the mark.
doser [dōzā] *vt* to measure out; *(mélanger)* to mix in the correct proportions; *(fig)* to expend in the right amounts *ou* proportions; to strike a balance between.
doseur [dōzœr] *nm* measure; **bouchon** ~ measuring cap.
dossard [dōsár] *nm* number *(worn by competitor)*.
dossier [dōsyā] *nm* *(renseignements, fichier)* file; *(enveloppe)* folder, file; *(de chaise)* back; *(PRESSE)* feature; **le** ~ **social/ monétaire** *(fig)* the social/financial question; ~ **suspendu** suspension file.
dot [dot] *nf* dowry.
dotation [dotásyóň] *nf* block grant; endowment.
doté, e [dotā] *a*: ~ **de** equipped with.
doter [dotā] *vt*: ~ **qn/qch de** to equip sb/sth with.
douairière [dweryer] *nf* dowager.
douane [dwán] *nf* *(poste, bureau)* customs *pl*; *(taxes)* (customs) duty; **passer la** ~ to go through customs; **en** ~ *(marchandises, entre-pôt)* bonded.
douanier, ière [dwányā, -yer] *a* customs *cpd* ♦ *nm* customs officer.
doublage [dōōblázh] *nm* *(CINÉMA)* dubbing.
double [dōōbl(ə)] *a*, *ad* double ♦ *nm* *(2 fois plus)*: **le** ~ **(de)** twice as much *(ou* many) (as), double the amount *(ou* number) (of); *(autre exemplaire)* duplicate, copy; *(sosie)*

double; *(TENNIS)* doubles *sg*; **voir** ~ to see double; **en** ~ **(exemplaire)** in duplicate; **faire** ~ **emploi** to be redundant; **à** ~ **sens** with a double meaning; **à** ~ **tranchant** two-edged; ~ **carburateur** twin carburetor; **à** ~**s commandes** dual-control; ~ **messieurs/ mixte** men's/mixed doubles *sg*; ~ **toit** *(de tente)* rainfly *(US)*, fly sheet *(Brit)*; ~ **vue** second sight.
doublé, e [dōōblā] *a* *(vêtement)*: ~ **(de)** lined (with).
doublement [dōōbləmáň] *nm* doubling; two-fold increase ♦ *ad* doubly; *(pour deux raisons)* in two ways, on two counts.
doubler [dōōblā] *vt* *(multiplier par 2)* to double; *(vêtement)* to line; *(dépasser)* to overtake, pass; *(film)* to dub; *(acteur)* to stand in for ♦ *vi* to double, increase twofold; **se** ~ **de** to be coupled with; ~ **(la classe)** *(SCOL)* to repeat a year; ~ **un cap** *(NAVIG)* to round a cape; *(fig)* to get over a hurdle.
doublure [dōōblür] *nf* lining; *(CINÉMA)* stand-in.
douce [dōōs] *af voir* **doux.**
douceâtre [dōōsâtr(ə)] *a* sickly sweet.
doucement [dōōsmáň] *ad* gently; *(à voix basse)* softly; *(lentement)* slowly.
doucereux, euse [dōōsrœ, -œz] *a* *(péj)* sugary.
douceur [dōōsœr] *nf* softness; sweetness; mildness; gentleness; ~**s** *nfpl* *(friandises)* candy *sg* *(US)*, sweets *(Brit)*; **en** ~ gently.
douche [dōōsh] *nf* shower; ~**s** *nfpl* shower room *sg*; **prendre une** ~ to have *ou* take a shower; ~ **écossaise** *(fig)*, ~ **froide** *(fig)* letdown.
doucher [dōōshā] *vt*: ~ **qn** to give sb a shower; *(mouiller)* to drench sb; *(fig)* to tell sb off; **se** ~ to have *ou* take a shower.
doudoune [dōōdōōn] *nf* padded jacket; *(fam)* boob.
doué, e [dwā] *a* gifted, talented; ~ **de** endowed with; **être** ~ **pour** to have a gift for.
douille [dōōy] *nf* *(ÉLEC)* socket; *(de projectile)* case.
douillet, te [dōōye, -et] *a* cosy; *(péj)* soft.
douleur [dōōlœr] *nf* pain; *(chagrin)* grief, distress; **ressentir des** ~**s** to feel pain; **il a eu la** ~ **de perdre son père** he suffered the grief of losing his father.
douloureux, euse [dōōlōōrœ, -œz] *a* painful.
doute [dōōt] *nm* doubt; **sans** ~ *ad* no doubt; *(probablement)* probably; **sans nul** *ou* **aucun** ~ without (a) doubt; **hors de** ~ beyond doubt; **nul** ~ **que** there's no doubt that; **mettre en** ~ to call into question; **mettre en** ~ **que** to question whether.
douter [dōōtā] *vt* to doubt; ~ **de** *vt* *(allié)* to doubt, have (one's) doubts about; *(résultat)* to be doubtful of; ~ **que** to doubt whether *ou* if; **j'en doute** I have my doubts; **se** ~ **de qch/que** to suspect sth/that; **je m'en doutais** I suspected as much; **il ne se doutait de rien** he didn't suspect a thing.
douteux, euse [dōōtœ, -œz] *a* *(incertain)* doubtful; *(discutable)* dubious, questionable; *(péj)* dubious-looking.
douve [dōōv] *nf* *(de château)* moat; *(de tonneau)* stave.

Douvres [dōovr(ə)] *n* Dover.

doux, douce [dōo, dōos] *a* (*lisse, moelleux, pas vif: couleur, non calcaire: eau*) soft; (*sucré, agréable*) sweet; (*peu fort: moutarde etc, clément: climat*) mild; (*pas brusque*) gentle; **en douce** (*partir etc*) on the q.t.

douzaine [dōozen] *nf* (*12*) dozen; (*environ 12*): **une ~ (de)** a dozen or so, twelve or so.

douze [dōoz] *num* twelve; **les D~** (*membres de la CEE*) the Twelve.

douzième [dōozyem] *num* twelfth.

doyen, ne [dwáyań, -en] *nm/f* (*en âge, ancienneté*) most senior member; (*de faculté*) dean.

DPLG *sigle* (= *diplômé par le gouvernement*) extra certificate for architects, engineers etc.

Dr *abr* (= *docteur*) Dr.

dr. *abr* (= *droit(e)*) R, r.

draconien, ne [drákonyań, -en] *a* draconian, stringent.

dragage [drágàzh] *nm* dredging.

dragée [dràzhā] *nf* sugared almond; (*MÉD*) (sugar-coated) pill.

dragéifié, e [dràzhāēfyā] *a* (*MÉD*) sugar-coated.

dragon [drágôń] *nm* dragon.

drague [dràg] *nf* (*filet*) dragnet; (*bateau*) dredger.

draguer [drágā] *vt* (*rivière: pour nettoyer*) to dredge; (*: pour trouver qch*) to drag; (*fam*) to try and pick up ♦ *vi* (*fam*) to try and pick sb up.

dragueur [drágœr] *nm* (*aussi:* **~ de mines**) minesweeper; (*fam*): **quel ~!** he's a great one for picking up girls!

drain [drań] *nm* (*MÉD*) drain.

drainage [drenàzh] *nm* drainage.

drainer [drānā] *vt* to drain; (*fig: visiteurs, région*) to drain off.

dramatique [drámátēk] *a* dramatic; (*tragique*) tragic ♦ *nf* (*TV*) (television) drama.

dramatiser [dràmàtēzā] *vt* to dramatize.

dramaturge [dràmátürzh(ə)] *nm* dramatist, playwright.

drame [drám] *nm* (*THÉÂTRE*) drama; (*catastrophe*) drama, tragedy; **~ familial** family drama.

drap [drá] *nm* (*de lit*) sheet; (*tissu*) woolen (*US*) *ou* woollen (*Brit*) fabric; **~ de plage** beach towel.

drapé [drápā] *nm* (*d'un vêtement*) hang.

drapeau, x [drápō] *nm* flag; **sous les ~x** in the army.

draper [drápā] *vt* to drape; (*robe, jupe*) to arrange.

draperies [dráprē] *nfpl* hangings.

drap-housse, *pl* **draps-housses** [dráōos] *nm* fitted sheet.

drapier [drápyā] *nm* (woolen (*US*) *ou* woollen (*Brit*)) cloth manufacturer; (*marchand*) clothier.

drastique [dràstēk] *a* drastic.

dressage [dresàzh] *nm* training.

dresser [drāsā] *vt* (*mettre vertical, monter: tente*) to put up, erect; (*fig: liste, bilan, contrat*) to draw up; (*animal*) to train; **se ~** *vi* (*falaise, obstacle*) to stand; (*avec grandeur, menace*) to tower (up); (*personne*) to draw

o.s. up; **~ l'oreille** to prick up one's ears; **~ la table** to set the table; **~ qn contre qn d'autre** to set sb against sb else; **~ un procès-verbal** *ou* **une contravention à qn** to book sb, give sb a ticket.

dresseur, euse [dresœr, -ēz] *nm/f* trainer.

dressoir [dreswár] *nm* dresser.

dribbler [drēblā] *vt, vi* (*SPORT*) to dribble.

drille [drēy] *nm*: **joyeux ~** cheerful sort.

drogue [drog] *nf* drug; **la ~** drugs *pl*; **~ dure/douce** hard/soft drugs *pl*.

drogué, e [drogā] *nm/f* drug addict.

droguer [drogā] *vt* (*victime*) to drug; (*malade*) to give drugs to; **se ~** (*aux stupéfiants*) to take drugs; (*péj: de médicaments*) to dose o.s. up.

droguerie [drogrē] *nf* ≈ hardware store (*US*) *ou* shop (*Brit*).

droguiste [drogēst(ə)] *nm* ≈ manager (*ou* owner) of a hardware store.

droit, e [drwá, drwát] *a* (*non courbe*) straight; (*vertical*) upright, straight; (*fig: loyal, franc*) upright, straight(forward); (*opposé à gauche*) right, right-hand ♦ *ad* straight ♦ *nm* (*prérogative, BOXE*) right; (*taxe*) duty, tax; (*: d'inscription*) fee; (*lois, branche*): **le ~** law ♦ *nf* (*POL*) right (wing); (*ligne*) straight line; **~ au but** *ou* **au fait/cœur** straight to the point/heart; **avoir le ~ de** to be allowed to; **avoir ~ à** to be entitled to; **être en ~ de** to have a *ou* the right to; **faire ~ à** to grant, accede to; **être dans son ~** to be within one's rights; **à bon ~** (*justement*) with good reason; **de quel ~?** by what right?; **à qui de ~** to whom it may concern; **à ~e** on the right; (*direction*) (to the) right; **à ~e de** to the right of; **de ~e** (*POL*) right-wing; **~ d'auteur** copyright; **avoir ~ de cité (dans)** (*fig*) to belong (to); **~ coutumier** common law; **~ de regard** right of access *ou* inspection; **~ de réponse** right to reply; **~ de visite** (right of) access; **~ de vote** (right to) vote; **~s d'auteur** royalties; **~s de douane** customs duties; **~s d'inscription** enrolment *ou* registration fees.

droitement [drwátmáń] *ad* (*agir*) uprightly.

droitier, ière [drwátyā, -yer] *nm/f* right-handed person.

droiture [drwátür] *nf* uprightness, straightness.

drôle [drōl] *a* (*amusant*) funny, amusing; (*bizarre*) funny, peculiar; **un ~ de ...** (*bizarre*) a strange *ou* funny ...; (*intensif*) an incredible ..., a terrific ....

drôlement [drōlmáń] *ad* funnily; peculiarly; (*très*) terribly, awfully; **il fait ~ froid** it's awfully cold.

drôlerie [drōlrē] *nf* funniness; funny thing.

dromadaire [dromáder] *nm* dromedary.

dru, e [drü] *a* (*cheveux*) thick, bushy; (*pluie*) heavy ♦ *ad* (*pousser*) thickly; (*tomber*) heavily.

drugstore [drœgstor] *nm* drugstore.

druide [drüēd] *nm* Druid.

ds *abr* = **dans**.

DST *sigle f* (= *Direction de la surveillance du territoire*) internal security service, ≈ CIA (*US*), ≈ MI5 (*Brit*).

DT *sigle m* (= *diphtérie tétanos*) vaccine.

DTCP *sigle m* (= *diphtérie tétanos coqueluche*

polio) vaccine.
DTP *sigle m* (= *diphtérie tétanos polio)*
vaccine.
DTTAB *sigle m* (= *diphtérie tétanos typhoïde
A et B) vaccine.*
du |dü| *prép* + *dét, dét voir* **de.**
dû, due |dü| *pp de* **devoir ♦** *a (somme)* owing,
owed; (: *venant à échéance)* due; *(causé
par)*: ~ **à** due to **♦** *nm* due; *(somme)* dues
pl.
Dubaï, Dubay |dübáy| *n* Dubai.
dubitatif, ive |dübĕtátĕf, -ĕv| *a* doubtful,
dubious.
Dublin |düblañ| *n* Dublin.
duc |dük| *nm* duke.
duché |düshá| *nm* dukedom, duchy.
duchesse |düshɛs| *nf* duchess.
DUEL |düɛl| *sigle m* = *Diplôme universitaire
d'études littéraires.*
duel |düɛl| *nm* duel.
DUES |düɛs| *sigle m* = *Diplôme universitaire
d'études scientifiques.*
duffel-coat |dœfœlkŏt| *nm* duffelcoat.
dûment |dümáñ| *ad* duly.
dune |dün| *nf* dune.
Dunkerque |dœñkɛrk| *n* Dunkirk.
duo |düŏ| *nm* (*MUS*) duet; *(fig: couple)* duo,
pair.
dupe |düp| *nf* dupe **♦** *a*: **(ne pas) être** ~ **de**
(not) to be taken in by.
duper |düpá| *vt* to dupe, deceive.
duperie |düprē| *nf* deception, dupery.
duplex |düplɛks| *nm (appartement)* split-level
apartment, duplex; *(TV)*: **émission en** ~
link-up.
duplicata |düplēkátá| *nm* duplicate.
duplicateur |düplēkátœr| *nm* duplicator; ~ **à
alcool** spirit duplicator.
duplicité |düplēsĕtá| *nf* duplicity.
duquel |dükɛl| *prép* + *pronom voir* **lequel.**
dur, e |dür| *a (pierre, siège, travail, problème)*
hard; *(lumière, voix, climat)* harsh; *(sévère)*
hard, harsh; *(cruel)* hard(-hearted); *(porte,
col)* stiff; *(viande)* tough **♦** *ad* hard **♦** *nf*: **à la**
~**e** rough; **mener la vie** ~**e à qn** to give sb a
hard time; ~ **d'oreille** hard of hearing.
durabilité |dürábĕlĕtá| *nf* durability.
durable |dürábl(ə)| *a* lasting.
durablement |düráblэmáñ| *ad* for the long
term.
durant |düráñ| *prép (au cours de)* during;
(pendant) for; ~ **des mois, des mois** ~ for
months.
durcir |dürsēr| *vt, vi,* **se** ~ *vi* to harden.
durcissement |dürsēsmáñ| *nm* hardening.
durée |dürā| *nf* length; *(d'une pile etc)* life;
(déroulement: des opérations etc) duration;
pour une ~ **illimitée** for an unlimited length
of time; **de courte** ~ *(séjour, répit)* brief,
short-term; **de longue** ~ *(effet)* long-term;
pile de longue ~ long-life battery.
durement |dürmáñ| *ad* harshly.
durent |dür| *vb voir* **devoir.**
durer |dürá| *vi* to last.
dureté |dürtá| *nf (voir dur)* hardness; harsh-
ness; stiffness; toughness.
durillon |dürēyóñ| *nm* callus.
durit |dürēt| *nf* ® (car radiator) hose.
DUT *sigle m* = *Diplôme universitaire de*

technologie.
dut |dü| *etc vb voir* **devoir.**
duvet |düve| *nm* down; **(sac de couchage en)**
~ down-filled sleeping bag.
duveteux, euse |düvtœ, -œz| *a* downy.
dynamique |dēnámēk| *a* dynamic.
dynamiser |dēnámēzá| *vt* to pep up, enliven;
(équipe, service) to inject some dynamism
into.
dynamisme |dēnámēsm(ə)| *nm* dynamism.
dynamite |dēnámēt| *nf* dynamite.
dynamiter |dēnámētá| *vt* to (blow up with)
dynamite.
dynamo |dēnámŏ| *nf* dynamo.
dynastie |dēnástē| *nf* dynasty.
dysenterie |dēsáñtrē| *nf* dysentery.
dyslexie |dēslɛksē| *nf* dyslexia, word-blindness.
dyslexique |dēslɛksĕk| *a* dyslexic.
dyspepsie |dēspɛpsē| *nf* dyspepsia.

E

E, e |ə| *nm inv* E, e **♦** *abr* (= *Est)* E; **E
comme Eugène** E for Easy.
EAO *sigle m* (= *enseignement assisté par
ordinateur)* CAL (= *computer-aided learning).*
EAU *sigle mpl* (= *Émirats arabes unis)* UAE
(= *United Arab Emirates).*
eau, x |ŏ| *nf* water **♦** *nfpl* waters; **prendre l'**~
(chaussure etc) to leak, let in water; **prendre
les** ~**x** to visit a spa; **faire** ~ to leak; **tomber
à l'**~ *(fig)* to fall through; **à l'**~ **de rose**
slushy, sentimental; ~ **bénite** holy water; ~
de Cologne eau de Cologne; ~ **courante**
running water; ~ **distillée** distilled water; ~
douce fresh water; ~ **de Javel** bleach; ~
lourde heavy water; ~ **minérale** mineral
water; ~ **oxygénée** hydrogen peroxide; ~
plate still water; ~ **de pluie** rainwater; ~
salée salt water; ~ **de toilette** toilet water;
~**x ménagères** dirty water *(from washing up
etc)*; ~**x territoriales** territorial waters; ~**x
usées** liquid waste.
eau-de-vie, *pl* **eaux-de-vie** |ŏdvē| *nf* brandy.
eau-forte, *pl* **eaux-fortes** |ŏfort(ə)| *nf* etching.
ébahi, e |ábáĕ| *a* dumbfounded, flabbergasted.
ébahir |ábáĕr| *vt* to astonish, astound.
ébats |ábá| *vb voir* **ébattre ♦** *nmpl* frolics,
gambols.
ébattre |ábátr(ə)|: **s'**~ *vi* to frolic.
ébauche |ábŏsh| *nf* (rough) outline, sketch.
ébaucher |ábŏshá| *vt* to sketch out, outline;
(fig): ~ **un sourire/geste** to give a hint of a
smile/make a slight gesture; **s'**~ *vi* to take
shape.
ébène |ábɛn| *nf* ebony.
ébéniste |ábánĕst(ə)| *nm* cabinetmaker.
ébénisterie |ábánĕstrē| *nf* cabinetmaking;
(bâti) cabinetwork.
éberlué, e |ábɛrlüá| *a* astounded,
flabbergasted.

éblouir [ābloōēr] *vt* to dazzle.

éblouissant, e [ābloōēsáṅ, -áṅt] *a* dazzling.

éblouissement [ābloōēsmáṅ] *nm* dazzle; *(faiblesse)* dizzy turn.

ébonite [ābonēt] *nf* vulcanite.

éborgner [ābornyā] *vt*: ~ **qn** to blind sb in one eye.

éboueur [ābwœr] *nm* garbageman *(US)*, dustman *(Brit)*.

ébouillanter [āboōyáṅtā] *vt* to scald; *(CULIN)* to blanch; **s'**~ to scald o.s.

éboulement [āboōlmáṅ] *nm* falling rocks *pl*, rock fall; *(amas)* heap of boulders *etc*.

ébouler [āboōlā]: **s'**~ *vi* to crumble, collapse.

éboulis [āboōlē] *nmpl* fallen rocks.

ébouriffé, e [āboōrēfā] *a* tousled, ruffled.

ébouriffer [āboōrēfā] *vt* to tousle, ruffle.

ébranlement [ābráṅlmáṅ] *nm* shaking.

ébranler [ābráṅlā] *vt* to shake; *(rendre instable: mur, santé)* to weaken; **s'**~ *vi (partir)* to move off.

ébrécher [ābrāshā] *vt* to chip.

ébriété [ābrēyātā] *nf*: **en état d'**~ in a state of intoxication.

ébrouer [ābroōā]: **s'**~ *vi (souffler)* to snort; *(s'agiter)* to shake o.s.

ébruiter [ābrüētā] *vt*, **s'**~ *vi* to spread.

ébullition [ābülēsyóṅ] *nf* boiling point; **en** ~ boiling; *(fig)* in an uproar.

écaille [ākáy] *nf (de poisson)* scale; *(de coquillage)* shell; *(matière)* tortoiseshell; *(de roc etc)* flake.

écaillé, e [ākāyā] *a (peinture)* flaking.

écailler [ākāyā] *vt (poisson)* to scale; *(huître)* to open; **s'**~ *vi* to flake *ou* peel (off).

écarlate [ākárlát] *a* scarlet.

écarquiller [ākárkēyā] *vt*: ~ **les yeux** to stare wide-eyed.

écart [ākár] *nm* gap; *(embardée)* swerve; *(saut)* sideways leap; *(fig)* departure, deviation; **à l'**~ *ad* out of the way; **à l'**~ **de** *prép* away from; *(fig)* out of; **faire le grand** ~ *(DANSE, GYM)* to do the splits; ~ **de conduite** misdemeanor.

écarté, e [ākártā] *a (lieu)* out-of-the-way, remote; *(ouvert)*: **les jambes** ~**es** legs apart; **les bras** ~**s** arms outstretched.

écarteler [ākártəlā] *vt* to quarter; *(fig)* to tear.

écartement [ākártəmáṅ] *nm* space, gap; *(RAIL)* gauge.

écarter [ākártā] *vt (séparer)* to move apart, separate; *(éloigner)* to push back, move away; *(ouvrir: bras, jambes)* to spread, open; *(: rideau)* to draw (back); *(éliminer: candidat, possibilité)* to dismiss; *(CARTES)* to discard; **s'**~ *vi* to part; *(personne)* to move away; **s'**~ **de** to wander from.

ecchymose [ākēmōz] *nf* bruise.

ecclésiastique [āklāzyástēk] *a* ecclesiastical ♦ *nm* ecclesiastic.

écervelé, e [āservəlā] *a* scatterbrained, featherbrained.

échafaud [āsháfō] *nm* scaffold.

échafaudage [āsháfōdázh] *nm* scaffolding; *(fig)* heap, pile.

échafauder [āsháfōdā] *vt (plan)* to construct.

échalas [āshálá] *nm* stake, pole; *(personne)* beanpole.

échalote [āshálot] *nf* shallot.

échancré, e [āsháṅkrā] *a (robe, corsage)* low-necked; *(côte)* indented.

échancrure [āsháṅkrür] *nf (de robe)* scoop neckline; *(de côte, arête rocheuse)* indentation.

échange [āsháṅzh] *nm* exchange; **en** ~ in exchange; **en** ~ **de** in exchange *ou* return for; **libre** ~ free trade; ~ **de lettres/politesses/vues** exchange of letters/civilities/views; ~**s commerciaux** trade; ~**s culturels** cultural exchanges.

échangeable [āsháṅzhábl(ə)] *a* exchangeable.

échanger [āsháṅzhā] *vt*: ~ **qch (contre)** to exchange sth (for).

échangeur [āsháṅzhœr] *nm (AUTO)* interchange.

échantillon [āsháṅtēyóṅ] *nm* sample.

échantillonnage [āsháṅtēyonázh] *nm* selection of samples.

échappatoire [āshápátwár] *nf* way out.

échappée [āshápā] *nf (vue)* vista; *(CYCLISME)* breakaway.

échappement [āshápmáṅ] *nm (AUTO)* exhaust; ~ **libre** cutout.

échapper [āshápā]: ~ **à** *vt (gardien)* to escape (from); *(punition, péril)* to escape; ~ **à qn** *(détail, sens)* to escape sb; *(objet qu'on tient: aussi: ~ **des mains de qn)** to slip out of sb's hands; **laisser** ~ to let fall; *(cri etc)* to let out; **s'**~ *vi* to escape; **l'**~ **belle** to have a narrow escape.

écharde [āshárd(ə)] *nf* splinter (of wood).

écharpe [āshárp(ə)] *nf* scarf *(pl* scarves); *(de maire)* sash; *(MÉD)* sling; **prendre en** ~ *(dans une collision)* to hit sideways on.

écharper [āshárpā] *vt* to tear to pieces.

échasse [āshás] *nf* stilt.

échassier [āshásyā] *nm* wader.

échauder [āshōdā] *vt*: **se faire** ~ *(fig)* to get one's fingers burnt.

échauffement [āshōfmáṅ] *nm* overheating; *(SPORT)* warm-up.

échauffer [āshōfā] *vt (métal, moteur)* to overheat; *(fig: exciter)* to fire, excite; **s'**~ *vi (SPORT)* to warm up; *(discussion)* to become heated.

échauffourée [āshōfoōrā] *nf* clash, brawl; *(MIL)* skirmish.

échéance [āshāáṅs] *nf (d'un paiement: date)* due date; *(: somme due)* financial commitment(s); *(fig)* deadline; **à brève/longue** ~ *a* short-/long-term ♦ *ad* in the short/long term.

échéancier [āshāáṅsyā] *nm* schedule.

échéant [āshāáṅ]: **le cas** ~ *ad* if the case arises.

échec [āshek] *nm* failure; *(ÉCHECS)*: ~ **et mat/au roi** checkmate/check; ~**s** *nmpl (jeu)* chess *sg*; **mettre en** ~ to put in check; **tenir en** ~ to hold in check; **faire** ~ **à** to foil, thwart.

échelle [āshel] *nf* ladder; *(fig, d'une carte)* scale; **à l'**~ **de** on the scale of; **sur une grande/petite** ~ on a large/small scale; **faire la courte** ~ **à qn** to give sb a boost *(US)* ou leg up *(Brit)*; ~ **de corde** rope ladder.

échelon [āshlóṅ] *nm (d'échelle)* rung; *(ADMIN)* grade.

échelonner [āshlonā] *vt* to space out, spread out; **(versement) échelonné** (payment) by instal(l)ments.

écheveau, x [ɛʃvō] *nm* skein, hank.

échevelé, e [āshəvlā] *a* tousled, dishevelled; *(fig)* wild, frenzied.

échine [āshēn] *nf* backbone, spine.

échiner [āshēnā]: **s'~** *vi (se fatiguer)* to work o.s. to the bone.

échiquier [āshēkyā] *nm* chessboard.

écho [ākō] *nm* echo; **~s** *nmpl (potins)* gossip *sg,* rumors *(US),* rumours *(Brit)*; *(PRESSE: rubrique)* "news in brief"; **rester sans ~** *(suggestion etc)* to come to nothing; **se faire l'~ de** to repeat, spread around.

échographie [ākogrāfē] *nf* ultrasound (scan).

échoir [āshwár] *vi (dette)* to fall due; *(délais)* to expire; **~ à** *vt* to fall to.

échoppe [āshop] *nf* stall, booth.

échouer [āshwā] *vi* to fail; *(débris etc: sur la plage)* to be washed up; *(aboutir: personne dans un café etc)* to arrive ♦ *vt (bateau)* to ground; **s'~** *vi* to run aground.

échu, e [āshü] *pp de* **échoir** ♦ *a* due, mature.

échut [āshü] *etc vb voir* **échoir**.

éclabousser [āklábōōsā] *vt* to splash; *(fig)* to tarnish.

éclaboussure [āklábōōsür] *nf* splash; *(fig)* stain.

éclair [ākler] *nm (d'orage)* flash of lightning, lightning *q; (PHOTO: de flash)* flash; *(fig)* flash, spark; *(gâteau)* éclair.

éclairage [āklerázh] *nm* lighting.

éclairagiste [āklerázhēst(ə)] *nm/f* lighting technician.

éclaircie [āklersē] *nf* bright *ou* sunny interval.

éclaircir [āklersēr] *vt* to lighten; *(fig)* to clear up, clarify; *(CULIN)* to thin (down); **s'~** *vi (ciel)* to brighten up, clear; *(cheveux)* to go thin; *(situation etc)* to become clearer; **s'~ la voix** to clear one's throat.

éclaircissement [āklersēsmáṅ] *nm* clearing up, clarification.

éclairer [āklārā] *vt (lieu)* to light (up); *(personne: avec une lampe de poche etc)* to light the way for; *(fig: instruire)* to enlighten; *(: rendre compréhensible)* to shed light on ♦ *vi:* **~ mal/bien** to give a poor/good light; **s'~** *vi (phare, rue)* to light up; *(situation etc)* to become clearer; **s'~ à la bougie/l'électricité** to use candlelight/have electric lighting.

éclaireur, euse [āklercœr, -œz] *nm/f (scout)* (boy) scout/girl scout *(US) ou* (girl) guide *(Brit)* ♦ *nm (MIL)* scout; **partir en ~** to go off to reconnoitre.

éclat [āklá] *nm (de bombe, de verre)* fragment; *(du soleil, d'une couleur etc)* brightness, brilliance; *(d'une cérémonie)* splendor *(US),* splendour *(Brit)*; *(scandale)*: **faire un ~** to cause a commotion; **action d'~** outstanding action; **voler en ~s** to shatter; **des ~s de verre** broken glass; flying glass; **~ de rire** burst *ou* roar of laughter; **~ de voix** shout.

éclatant, e [āklátáṅ, -áṅt] *a* brilliant, bright; *(succès)* resounding; *(revanche)* devastating.

éclater [āklátā] *vi (pneu)* to blow out; *(bombe)* to explode; *(guerre, épidémie)* to break out; *(groupe, parti)* to break up; **~ de rire/en sanglots** to burst out laughing/sobbing.

éclectique [āklɛktēk] *a* eclectic.

éclipse [āklēps(ə)] *nf* eclipse.

éclipser [āklēpsā] *vt* to eclipse; **s'~** *vi* to slip away.

éclopé, e [āklopā] *a* lame.

éclore [āklor] *vi (œuf)* to hatch; *(fleur)* to open (out).

éclosion [āklōzyóṅ] *nf* blossoming.

écluse [āklüz] *nf* lock.

éclusier [āklüzyā] *nm* lock keeper.

écœurant, e [ākœráṅ, -áṅt] *a* sickening; *(gâteau etc)* sickly.

écœurement [ākœrmáṅ] *nm* disgust.

écœurer [ākœrā] *vt:* **~ qn** to make sb feel sick; *(fig: démoraliser)* to disgust sb.

école [ākol] *nf* school; **aller à l'~** to go to school; **faire ~** to collect a following; **les grandes ~s** *prestige university-level colleges with competitive entrance examinations;* **~ maternelle** nursery school; **~ primaire** grade *(US) ou* primary *(Brit)* school; **~ secondaire** high *(US) ou* secondary *(Brit)* school; **~ privée/publique/élémentaire** private/public *(US) ou* state *(Brit)*/ elementary school; **~ de dessin/danse/ musique** art/dancing/music school; **~ hôtelière** hotel management school; **~ normale (d'instituteurs) (ENI)** *elementary school teachers' training college;* **~ normale supérieure (ENS)** *grande école for training high school teachers;* **~ de secrétariat** secretarial school.

écolier, ière [ākolyā, -yer] *nm/f* schoolboy/girl.

écolo [ākolō] *nm/f (fam)* ecologist ♦ *a* ecological.

écologie [ākolozhē] *nf* ecology; *(sujet scolaire)* environmental studies *pl.*

écologique [ākolozhēk] *a* ecological; environmental.

écologiste [ākolozhēst(ə)] *nm/f* ecologist; environmentalist.

éconduire [ākóṅdüēr] *vt* to dismiss.

économat [ākonomá] *nm (fonction)* treasurership *(US),* bursarship *(Brit)*; *(bureau)* bursar's office.

économe [ākonom] *a* thrifty ♦ *nm/f (de lycée etc)* bursar.

économétrie [ākonomātrē] *nf* econometrics *sg.*

économie [ākonomē] *nf (vertu)* economy, thrift; *(gain: d'argent, de temps etc)* saving; *(science)* economics *sg; (situation économique)* economy; **~s** *nfpl (pécule)* savings; **une ~ de temps/d'argent** a saving in time/of money; **~ dirigée** planned economy.

économique [ākonomēk] *a (avantageux)* economical; *(ÉCON)* economic.

économiquement [ākonomēkmáṅ] *ad* economically; **les ~ faibles** *(ADMIN)* the low-paid, people on low incomes.

économiser [ākonomēzā] *vt, vi* to save.

économiste [ākonomēst(ə)] *nm/f* economist.

écoper [ākopā] *vi* to bail out; *(fig)* to catch it; **~ (de)** *vt* to get.

écorce [ākors(ə)] *nf* bark; *(de fruit)* peel.

écorcer [ākorsā] *vt* to bark.

écorché, e [ākorshā] *a:* **~ vif** flayed alive ♦ *nm* cut-away drawing.

écorcher [ākorshā] *vt (animal)* to skin;

(*égratigner*) to graze; ~ **une langue** to speak a language brokenly; **s'~ le genou** *etc* to scrape *ou* graze one's knee *etc*.

écorchure [ākorshür] *nf* graze.

écorner [ākornā] *vt* (*taureau*) to dehorn; (*livre*) to dog-ear.

écossais, e [ākose, -ez] *a* (*lacs, tempérament*) Scottish, Scots; (*whisky, confiture*) Scotch; (*écharpe, tissu*) tartan ♦ *nm* (*LING*) Scots; (: *gaélique*) Gaelic; (*tissu*) tartan (cloth); É~ Scot, Scotsman; **les É~** the Scots ♦ *nf*: É~e Scot, Scotswoman.

Écosse [ākos] *nf*: **l'~** Scotland.

écosser [ākosā] *vt* to shell.

écosystème [ākosēstem] *nm* ecosystem.

écot [ākō] *nm*: **payer son ~** to pay one's share.

écoulement [ākōōlmāṅ] *nm* (*de faux billets*) circulation; (*de stock*) selling.

écouler [ākōōlā] *vt* to dispose of; **s'~** *vi* (*eau*) to flow (out); (*foule*) to drift away; (*jours, temps*) to pass (by).

écourter [ākōōrtā] *vt* to curtail, cut short.

écoute [ākōōt] *nf* (*NAVIG*: *cordage*) sheet; (*RADIO, TV*): **temps/heure d'~** listening (*ou* viewing) time/hour; **heure de grande ~** prime time; **prendre l'~** to tune in; **rester à l'~ (de)** to keep listening (to), stay tuned in (to); **~s téléphoniques** phone tapping *sg*.

écouter [ākōōtā] *vt* to listen to.

écouteur [ākōōtœr] *nm* (*TÉL*) (additional) earphone; **~s** *nmpl* (*RADIO*) headphones, headset *sg*.

écoutille [ākōōtēy] *nf* hatch.

écr. *abr* = **écrire**.

écrabouiller [ākrábōōyā] *vt* to squash, crush.

écran [ākrāṅ] *nm* screen; (*INFORM*) VDU, screen; **~ de fumée/d'eau** curtain of smoke/water; **porter à l'~** (*CINÉMA*) to adapt for the screen; **le petit ~** television, the small screen.

écrasant, e [ākrázāṅ, -āṅt] *a* overwhelming.

écraser [ākrázā] *vt* to crush; (*piéton*) to run over; (*INFORM*) to overwrite; **se faire ~** to be run over; **écrase(-toi)!** shut up!; **s'~ (au sol)** to crash; **s'~ contre** to crash into.

écrémer [ākrāmā] *vt* to skim.

écrevisse [ākrəvēs] *nf* crayfish *inv*.

écrier [ākrēyā]: **s'~** *vi* to exclaim.

écrin [ākraṅ] *nm* case, box.

écrire [ākrēr] *vt, vi* to write; ~ **à qn que** to write and tell sb that; **s'~** to write to one another ♦ *vi*: **ça s'écrit comment?** how is it spelled?

écrit, e [ākrē, -ēt] *pp de* **écrire** ♦ *a*: **bien/mal ~** well/badly written ♦ *nm* document; (*examen*) written exam; **par ~** in writing.

écriteau, x [ākrētō] *nm* notice, sign.

écritoire [ākrētwár] *nf* desk folder (*US*), writing case (*Brit*).

écriture [ākrētür] *nf* writing; (*COMM*) entry; **~s** *nfpl* (*COMM*) accounts, books; **l'É~ (sainte), les É~s** the Scriptures.

écrivain [ākrēvaṅ] *nm* writer.

écrivais [ākrēve] *etc vb voir* **écrire**.

écrou [ākrōō] *nm* nut.

écrouer [ākrōōā] *vt* to imprison; (*provisoirement*) to remand in custody.

écroulé, e [ākrōōlā] *a* (*de fatigue*) exhausted; (*par un malheur*) overwhelmed; ~ **(de rire)** in stitches.

écroulement [ākrōōlmāṅ] *nm* collapse.

écrouler [ākrōōlā]: **s'~** *vi* to collapse.

écru, e [ākrü] *a* (*toile*) raw, unbleached; (*couleur*) off white, écru.

écu [ākü] *nm* (*bouclier*) shield; (*monnaie: ancienne*) crown; (: *de la CEE*) ECU.

écueil [ākœy] *nm* reef; (*fig*) pitfall; stumbling block.

écuelle [āküel] *nf* bowl.

éculé, e [ākülā] *a* (*chaussure*) down at the heel(s) (*US*), down-at-heel (*Brit*); (*fig: péj*) hackneyed.

écume [āküm] *nf* foam; (*CULIN*) scum; ~ **de mer** meerschaum.

écumer [ākümā] *vt* (*CULIN*) to skim; (*fig*) to plunder ♦ *vi* (*mer*) to foam; (*fig*) to boil with rage.

écumoire [ākümwár] *nf* skimmer.

écureuil [ākürœy] *nm* squirrel.

écurie [ākürē] *nf* stable.

écusson [āküsóṅ] *nm* badge.

écuyer, ère [āküēyā, -er] *nm/f* rider.

eczéma [egzāmá] *nm* eczema.

éd. *abr* = **édition**.

édam [ādám] *nm* (*fromage*) Edam.

édelweiss [ādelváys] *nm inv* edelweiss.

éden [āden] *nm* Eden.

édenté, e [ādāṅtā] *a* toothless.

EDF *sigle f* (= *Electricité de France*) *national electricity company*.

édifiant, e [ādēfyáṅ, -áṅt] *a* edifying.

édifice [ādēfēs] *nm* building, edifice.

édifier [ādēfyā] *vt* to build, erect; (*fig*) to edify.

édiles [ādēl] *nmpl* city fathers.

Edimbourg [ādaṅbōōr] *n* Edinburgh.

édit [ādē] *nm* edict.

édit. *abr* = **éditeur**.

éditer [ādētā] *vt* (*publier*) to publish; (: *disque*) to produce; (*préparer: texte, INFORM*) to edit.

éditeur, trice [ādētœr, -trēs] *nm/f* publisher; editor.

édition [ādēsyóṅ] *nf* editing *q*; (*série d'exemplaires*) edition; (*industrie du livre*): **l'~** publishing; ~ **sur écran** (*INFORM*) screen editing.

édito [ādētō] *nm* (*fam* = *éditorial*) editorial.

éditorial, aux [ādētoryál, -ō] *nm* editorial.

éditorialiste [ādētoryálēst(ə)] *nm/f* editorial writer.

édredon [ādrədóṅ] *nm* eiderdown, comforter (*US*).

éducateur, trice [ādükátœr, -trēs] *nm/f* teacher; ~ **spécialisé** specialist teacher.

éducatif, ive [ādükátēf, -ēv] *a* educational.

éducation [ādükâsyóṅ] *nf* education; (*familiale*) upbringing; (*manières*) (good) manners *pl*; **bonne/mauvaise ~** good/bad upbringing; **sans ~** bad-mannered, ill-bred; **l'É~ (nationale)** the education department; ~ **permanente** continuing education; ~ **physique** physical education.

édulcorer [ādülkorā] *vt* to sweeten; (*fig*) to tone down.

éduquer [ādükā] *vt* to educate; (*élever*) to

bring up; *(faculté)* to train; **bien/mal éduqué** well/badly brought up.

effacé, e [ăfásă] *a (fig)* retiring, unassuming.

effacer [ăfásă] *vt* to erase, rub out; *(bande magnétique)* to erase; *(INFORM: fichier, fiche)* to delete, erase; **s'~** *vi (inscription etc)* to wear off; *(pour laisser passer)* to step aside; **~ le ventre** to pull one's stomach in.

effarant, e [ăfárăn̂, -ăn̂t] *a* alarming.

effaré, e [ăfáră] *a* alarmed.

effarement [ăfármăn̂] *nm* alarm.

effarer [ăfárā] *vt* to alarm.

effarouchement [ăfárōōshmăn̂] *nm* alarm.

effaroucher [ăfárōōshă] *vt* to frighten *ou* scare away; *(personne)* to alarm.

effectif, ive [ăfektĕf, -ēv] *a* real; effective ♦ *nm (MIL)* strength; *(SCOL)* total number of pupils, size; **~s** numbers, strength *sg*; *(COMM)* manpower *sg*.

effectivement [ăfektēvmăn̂] *ad* effectively; *(réellement)* actually, really; *(en effet)* indeed.

effectuer [ăfektüă] *vt (opération, mission)* to carry out; *(déplacement, trajet)* to make, complete; *(mouvement)* to execute, make; **s'~** to be carried out.

efféminé, e [ăfāmēnă] *a* effeminate.

effervescence [ăfervăsăn̂s] *nf (fig)*: **en ~** in a turmoil.

effervescent, e [ăfervăsăn̂, -ăn̂t] *a (cachet, boisson)* effervescent; *(fig)* agitated, in a turmoil.

effet [ăfe] *nm (résultat, artifice)* effect; *(impression)* impression; *(COMM)* bill; *(JUR: d'une loi, d'un jugement)*: **avec ~ rétroactif** applied retroactively; **~s** *nmpl (vêtements etc)* things; **~ de style/couleur/lumière** stylistic/color/lighting effect; **~s de voix** dramatic effects with one's voice; **faire de l'~** *(médicament, menace)* to have an effect, be effective; **sous l'~ de** under the effect of; **donner de l'~ à une balle** *(TENNIS)* to put some spin on a ball; **à cet ~** to that end; **en ~** *ad* indeed; **~ (de commerce)** bill of exchange; **~s spéciaux** *(CINÉMA)* special effects.

effeuiller [ăfœyă] *vt* to remove the leaves *(ou* petals) from.

efficace [ăfēkás] *a (personne)* efficient; *(action, médicament)* effective.

efficacité [ăfēkăsētă] *nf* efficiency; effectiveness.

effigie [ăfēzhē] *nf* effigy; **brûler qn en ~** to burn sb in effigy.

effilé, e [ăfēlā] *a* slender; *(pointe)* sharp; *(carrosserie)* streamlined.

effiler [ăfēlă] *vt (cheveux)* to thin (out); *(tissu)* to fray.

effilocher [ăfēloshă]: **s'~** *vi* to fray.

efflanqué, e [ăflăn̂kă] *a* emaciated.

effleurement [ăflœrmăn̂] *nm*: **touche à ~** touch-sensitive control *ou* key.

effleurer [ăflœră] *vt* to brush (against); *(sujet)* to touch upon; *(suj: idée, pensée)*: **~ qn** to cross sb's mind.

effluves [ăflüv] *nmpl* exhalation(s).

effondré, e [ăfôn̂drā] *a (abattu: par un malheur, échec)* overwhelmed.

effondrement [ăfôn̂drəmăn̂] *nm* collapse.

effondrer [ăfôn̂drā]: **s'~** *vi* to collapse.

efforcer [ăforsă]: **s'~ de** *vt*: **s'~ de faire** to try hard to do.

effort [ăfor] *nm* effort; **faire un ~** to make an effort; **faire tous ses ~s** to try one's hardest; **faire l'~ de ...** to make the effort to ...; **sans ~** *a* effortless ♦ *ad* effortlessly; **~ de mémoire** attempt to remember; **~ de volonté** effort of will.

effraction [ăfráksyôn̂] *nf* breaking-in; **s'introduire par ~ dans** to break into.

effrangé, e [ăfrăn̂zhă] *a* fringed; *(effiloché)* frayed.

effrayant, e [ăfreyăn̂, -ăn̂t] *a* frightening, fearsome; *(sens affaibli)* dreadful.

effrayer [ăfrāyă] *vt* to frighten, scare; *(rebuter)* to put off; **s'~ (de)** to be frightened *ou* scared (by).

effréné, e [ăfrānă] *a* wild.

effritement [ăfrētmăn̂] *nm* crumbling; erosion; slackening off.

effriter [ăfrētă]: **s'~** *vi* to crumble; *(monnaie)* to be eroded; *(valeurs)* to slacken off.

effroi [ăfrwă] *nm* terror, dread *q*.

effronté, e [ăfrôn̂tă] *a* insolent.

effrontément [ăfrôn̂tămăn̂] *ad* insolently.

effronterie [ăfrôn̂trē] *nf* insolence.

effroyable [ăfrwáyábl(ə)] *a* horrifying, appalling.

effusion [ăfüzyôn̂] *nf* effusion; **sans ~ de sang** without bloodshed.

égailler [ăgáyă]: **s'~** *vi* to scatter, disperse.

égal, e, aux [ăgál, -ō] *a (identique, ayant les mêmes droits)* equal; *(plan: surface)* even, level; *(constant: vitesse)* steady; *(équitable)* even ♦ *nm/f* equal; **être ~ à** *(prix, nombre)* to be equal to; **ça lui est ~** it's all the same to him, it doesn't matter to him, he doesn't mind; **c'est ~, ...** all the same, ...; **sans ~** matchless, unequalled; **à l'~ de** *(comme)* just like; **d'~ à ~** as equals.

également [ăgálmăn̂] *ad* equally; evenly; steadily; *(aussi)* too, as well.

égaler [ăgálă] *vt* to equal.

egalisateur, trice [ăgálēzátœr, -trēs] *a (SPORT)*: **but ~** tying goal *ou* score *(US)*, equalizer *(Brit)*.

egalisation [ăgálēzăsyôn̂] *nf (SPORT)* tying *(US)*, equalization *(Brit)*.

égaliser [ăgálēză] *vt (sol, salaires)* to level (out); *(chances)* to equalize ♦ *vi (SPORT)* to tie *(US)*, equalize *(Brit)*.

égalitaire [ăgálēter] *a* egalitarian.

égalitarisme [ăgálētárēsm(ə)] *nm* egalitarianism.

égalité [ăgálētă] *nf* equality; evenness; steadiness; *(MATH)* equality; **être à ~ (de points)** to be even; **~ de droits** equality of rights; **~ d'humeur** evenness of temper.

égard [ăgár] *nm*: **~s** *nmpl* consideration *sg*; **à cet ~** in this respect; **à certains ~s/tous ~s** in certain respects/all respects; **eu ~ à** in view of; **par ~ pour** out of consideration for; **sans ~ pour** without regard for; **à l'~ de** *prép* towards; *(en ce qui concerne)* concerning, as regards.

égaré, e [ăgáră] *a* lost.

égarement [ăgármăn̂] *nm* distraction; aberration.

égarer [āgàrā] *vt* (*objet*) to mislay; (*morale-ment*) to lead astray; **s'~** *vi* to get lost, lose one's way; (*objet*) to go astray; (*fig: dans une discussion*) to wander.

égayer [āgāyā] *vt* (*personne*) to amuse; (*: remonter*) to cheer up; (*récit, endroit*) to brighten up, liven up.

Égée [āzhā] *a*: **la mer ~** the Aegean (Sea).

égéen, ne [āzhāàn, -en] *a* Aegean.

égérie [āzhārē] *nf*: **l'~ de qn/qch** the brains behind sb/sth.

égide [āzhēd] *nf*: **sous l'~ de** under the aegis of.

églantier [āglàntyā] *nm* wild *ou* dog rose(-bush).

églantine [āglàntēn] *nf* wild *ou* dog rose.

églefin [āglàfàn] *nm* haddock.

église [āglēz] *nf* church.

égocentrique [āgosàntrēk] *a* egocentric, self-centered (*US*), self-centred (*Brit*).

égocentrisme [āgosàntrēsm(ǝ)] *nm* egocentricity.

égoïne [āgoēn] *nf* handsaw.

égoïsme [āgoēsm(ǝ)] *nm* selfishness, egoism.

égoïste [āgoēst(ǝ)] *a* selfish, egoistic ♦ *nm/f* egoist.

égoïstement [āgoēstǝmàn] *ad* selfishly.

égorger [āgorzhā] *vt* to cut the throat of.

égosiller [āgōzēyā]: **s'~** *vi* to shout o.s. hoarse.

égotisme [āgotēsm(ǝ)] *nm* egotism, egoism.

égout [āgōō] *nm* sewer; **eaux d'~** sewage.

égoutier [āgōōtyā] *nm* sewer worker.

égoutter [āgōōtā] *vt* (*linge*) to wring out; (*vaisselle, fromage*) to drain ♦ *vi*, **s'~** *vi* to drip.

égouttoir [āgōōtwàr] *nm* drainboard (*US*), draining board (*Brit*); (*mobile*) (dish) drainer.

égratigner [āgràtēnyā] *vt* to scratch; **s'~** to scratch o.s.

égratignure [āgràtēnyür] *nf* scratch.

égrener [āgrǝnā] *vt*: **~ une grappe**, **~ des raisins** to pick grapes off a bunch; **s'~** *vi* (*fig: heures etc*) to pass by; (*: notes*) to chime out.

égrillard, e [āgrēyàr, -àrd(ǝ)] *a* ribald, bawdy.

Egypte [āzhēpt] *nf*: **l'~** Egypt.

égyptien, ne [āzhēpsyàn, -en] *a* Egyptian ♦ *nm/f*: **É~, ne** Egyptian.

égyptologue [āzhēptolog] *nm/f* Egyptologist.

eh [ā] *excl* hey!; **~ bien** well.

éhonté, e [āōntā] *a* shameless, brazen.

éjaculation [āzhàkülàsyôn] *nf* ejaculation.

éjaculer [āzhàkülā] *vi* to ejaculate.

éjectable [āzhektábl(ǝ)] *a*: **siège ~** ejector seat.

éjecter [āzhektā] *vt* (*TECH*) to eject; (*fam*) to kick *ou* chuck out.

éjection [āzheksyôn] *nf* ejection.

élaboration [ālàbōràsyôn] *nf* elaboration.

élaboré, e [ālàborā] *a* (*complexe*) elaborate.

élaborer [ālàborā] *vt* to elaborate; (*projet, stratégie*) to work out; (*rapport*) to draft.

élagage [ālágàzh] *nm* pruning.

élaguer [ālágā] *vt* to prune.

élan [ālàn] *nm* (*ZOOL*) elk, moose; (*SPORT: avant le saut*) run-up; (*de véhicule ou objet en mouvement*) momentum; (*fig: de ten-*

dresse etc) surge; **prendre son ~/de l'~** to make (*US*) *ou* take (*Brit*) a run-up/gather speed; **perdre son ~** to lose one's momentum.

élancé, e [ālànsā] *a* slender.

élancement [ālànsmàn] *nm* shooting pain.

élancer [ālànsā]: **s'~** *vi* to dash, hurl o.s.; (*fig: arbre, clocher*) to soar (upwards).

élargir [ālàrzhēr] *vt* to widen; (*vêtement*) to let out; (*JUR*) to release; **s'~** *vi* to widen; (*vêtement*) to stretch.

élargissement [ālàrzhēsmàn] *nm* widening; letting out.

élasticité [ālàstēsētā] *nf* (*aussi ÉCON*) elasticity; **~ de l'offre/de la demande** flexibility of supply/demand.

élastique [ālàstēk] *a* elastic ♦ *nm* (*de bureau*) rubber band; (*pour la couture*) elastic *q*.

élastomère [ālàstomer] *nm* elastomer.

Elbe [elb] *nf*: **l'île d'~** (the Island of) Elba; (*fleuve*): **l'~** the Elbe.

eldorado [eldorádō] *nm* Eldorado.

électeur, trice [ālektœr, -trēs] *nm/f* elector, voter.

électif, ive [ālektēf, -ēv] *a* elective.

élection [āleksyôn] *nf* election; **~s** *nfpl* (*POL*) election(s); **sa terre/patrie d'~** one's chosen land/country, the land/country of one's choice; **~ partielle** by-election; **~s législatives** general election *sg*.

électoral, e, aux [ālektorál, -ō] *a* electoral, election *cpd*.

électoralisme [ālektorálēsm(ǝ)] *nm* electioneering.

électorat [ālektorá] *nm* electorate.

électricien, ne [ālektrēsyàn, -en] *nm/f* electrician.

électricité [ālektrēsētā] *nf* electricity; **allumer/éteindre l'~** to turn on/off the light; **~ statique** static electricity.

électrification [ālektrēfēkàsyôn] *nf* (*RAIL*) electrification; **l'~ d'un village** bringing electric power to a village.

électrifier [ālektrēfyā] *vt* (*RAIL*) to electrify.

électrique [ālektrēk] *a* electric(al).

électriser [ālektrēzā] *vt* to electrify.

électro... [ālektro] *préfixe* electro....

électro-aimant [ālektroemàn] *nm* electromagnet.

électrocardiogramme [ālektrokárdyográm] *nm* electrocardiogram.

électrocardiographe [ālektrokárdyográf] *nm* electrocardiograph.

électrochoc [ālektroshok] *nm* electroshock therapy.

électrocuter [ālektrokütā] *vt* to electrocute.

électrocution [ālektrokūsyôn] *nf* electrocution.

électrode [ālektrod] *nf* electrode.

électro-encéphalogramme [ālektroànsáfálográm] *nm* electroencephalogram.

électrogène [ālektrozhen] *a*: **groupe ~** electrical power unit, generator.

électrolyse [ālektrolēz] *nf* electrolysis *sg*.

électromagnétique [ālektromán—yátēk] *a* electromagnetic.

électroménager [ālektrománázhā] *a*: **appareils ~s** household (electrical) appliances ♦ *nm*: **l'~** household appliances.

électron [ālektrôn] *nm* electron.

électronicien, ne [ālektronēsyań, -en] *nm/f* electrical (US) *ou* electronics (Brit) engineer.

électronique [ālektronēk] *a* electronic ♦ *nf* (science) electronics *sg*.

électronucléaire [ālektronüklāer] *a* nuclear power *cpd* ♦ *nm*: **l'~** nuclear power.

électrophone [ālektrofon] *nm* record player.

élégamment [ālāgàmàń] *ad* elegantly.

élégance [ālāgàńs] *nf* elegance.

élégant, e [ālāgàń, -àńt] *a* elegant; (solution) neat, elegant; (attitude, procédé) courteous, civilized.

élément [ālāmàń] *nm* element; (pièce) component, part; **~s** *nmpl* (aussi: rudiments) elements.

élémentaire [ālāmàńter] *a* elementary; (CHIMIE) elemental.

éléphant [ālāfàń] *nm* elephant; **~ de mer** elephant seal.

éléphanteau, x [ālāfàńtō] *nm* baby elephant.

éléphantesque [ālāfàńtesk(ə)] *a* elephantine.

élevage [elvázh] *nm* breeding; (de bovins) cattle breeding *ou* rearing; (ferme) cattle farm.

élévateur [ālāvátœr] *nm* elevator.

élévation [ālāvásyoń] *nf* (gén) elevation; (voir élever) raising; (voir s'élever) rise.

élevé, e [elvā] *a* (prix, sommet) high; (fig: noble) elevated; **bien/mal ~** well-/ill-mannered.

élève [ālev] *nm/f* pupil; **~ infirmière** student nurse.

élever [elvā] *vt* (enfant) to bring up, raise; (bétail, volaille) to breed; (abeilles) to keep; (hausser: taux, niveau) to raise; (fig: âme, esprit) to elevate; (édifier: monument) to put up, erect; **s'~** *vi* (avion, alpiniste) to go up; (niveau, température, aussi: cri etc) to rise; (survenir: difficultés) to arise; **s'~ à** (suj: frais, dégâts) to amount to, add up to; **s'~ contre** to rise up against; **~ une protestation/critique** to raise a protest/make a criticism; **~ la voix** to raise one's voice; **~ qn au rang de** to raise *ou* elevate sb to the rank of; **~ un nombre au carré/au cube** to square/cube a number.

éleveur, euse [ālvœr, -œz] *nm/f* stock breeder.

elfe [elf(ə)] *nm* elf.

élidé, e [ālēdā] *a* elided.

élider [ālēdā] *vt* to elide.

éligibilité [ālēzhēbēlētā] *nf* eligibility.

éligible [ālēzhēbl(ə)] *a* eligible.

élimé, e [ālēmā] *a* worn (thin), threadbare.

élimination [ālēmēnásyoń] *nf* elimination.

éliminatoire [ālēmēnátwár] *a* eliminatory; (SPORT) disqualifying ♦ *nf* (SPORT) heat.

éliminer [ālēmēnā] *vt* to eliminate.

élire [ālēr] *vt* to elect; **~ domicile à** to take up residence in *ou* at.

élision [ālēzyoń] *nf* elision.

élite [ālēt] *nf* elite; **tireur d'~** crack rifleman; **chercheur d'~** top-notch researcher.

élitiste [ālētēst(ə)] *a* elitist.

élixir [ālēksēr] *nm* elixir.

elle [el] *pronom* (sujet) she; (: chose) it; (complément) her; it; **~s** (sujet) they; (complément) them; **~-même** herself; itself; **~s-mêmes** themselves; *voir* **il**.

ellipse [ālēps(ə)] *nf* ellipse; (LING) ellipsis *sg*.

elliptique [ālēptēk] *a* elliptical.

élocution [āloküsyoń] *nf* delivery; **défaut d'~** speech impediment.

éloge [ālozh] *nm* praise (gén q); **faire l'~ de** to praise.

élogieusement [ālozhyœzmàń] *ad* very favorably (US) *ou* favourably (Brit).

élogieux, euse [ālozhyœ, -œz] *a* laudatory, full of praise.

éloigné, e [ālwányā] *a* distant, far-off.

éloignement [ālwánymàń] *nm* removal; putting off; estrangement; (fig: distance) distance.

éloigner [ālwányā] *vt* (objet): **~ qch (de)** to move *ou* take sth away (from); (personne): **~ qn (de)** to take sb away *ou* remove sb (from); (échéance) to put off, postpone; (soupçons, danger) to ward off; **s'~ (de)** (personne) to go away (from); (véhicule) to move away (from); (affectivement) to become estranged (from).

élongation [ālońgásyoń] *nf* strained muscle.

éloquence [ālokàńs] *nf* eloquence.

éloquent, e [ālokàń, -àńt] *a* eloquent.

élu, e [ālü] *pp de* **élire** ♦ *nm/f* (POL) elected representative.

élucider [ālüsēdā] *vt* to elucidate.

élucubrations [ālükübrásyoń] *nfpl* wild imaginings.

éluder [ālüdā] *vt* to evade.

élus [ālü] *etc vb voir* **élire**.

élusif, ive [ālüzēf, -ēv] *a* elusive.

Élysée [ālēzā] *nm*: **(le palais de) l'~** the Élysée palace (the French president's residence and offices); **les Champs ~s** the Champs Élysées.

émacié, e [āmásyā] *a* emaciated.

émail, aux [āmáy, -ō] *nm* enamel.

émaillé, e [āmáyā] *a* enameled (US), enamelled (Brit); (fig): **~ de** dotted with.

émailler [āmáyā] *vt* to enamel.

émanation [āmánásyoń] *nf* emanation; **être l'~ de** to emanate from; to proceed from.

émancipation [āmàńsēpásyoń] *nf* emancipation.

émancipé, e [āmàńsēpā] *a* emancipated.

émanciper [āmàńsēpā] *vt* to emancipate; **s'~** (fig) to become emancipated *ou* liberated.

émaner [āmánā]: **~ de** *vt* to emanate from; (ADMIN) to proceed from.

émarger [āmárzhā] *vt* to sign; **~ de 1000 F à un budget** to receive 1000 F out of a budget.

émasculer [āmáskülā] *vt* to emasculate.

emballage [àńbálázh] *nm* wrapping; packing; (papier) wrapping; (carton) packaging.

emballer [àńbálā] *vt* to wrap (up); (dans un carton) to pack (up); (fig: fam) to thrill (to pieces); **s'~** *vi* (moteur) to race; (cheval) to bolt; (fig: personne) to get carried away.

emballeur, euse [àńbálœr, -œz] *nm/f* packer.

embarcadère [àńbárkáder] *nm* wharf, pier.

embarcation [àńbárkásyoń] *nf* (small) boat, (small) craft *inv*.

embardée [àńbárdā] *nf* swerve; **faire une ~** to swerve.

embargo [àńbàrgō] *nm* embargo; **mettre l'~ sur** to put an embargo on, embargo.

embarquement [àńbárkəmàń] *nm* embarkation; loading; boarding.

embarquer [åṅbárkā] *vt* (*personne*) to embark; (*marchandise*) to load; (*fam*) to cart off; (*: arrêter*) to nab ♦ *vi* (*passager*) to board; (*NAVIG*) to ship water; **s'~** *vi* to board; **s'~ dans** (*affaire, aventure*) to embark upon.

embarras [åṅbárà] *nm* (*obstacle*) hindrance; (*confusion*) embarrassment; (*ennuis*): **être dans l'~** to be in a predicament *ou* an awkward position; (*gêne financière*) to be having financial difficulties; **~ gastrique** stomach upset.

embarrassant, e [åṅbárásåṅ, -åṅt] *a* cumbersome; embarrassing; awkward.

embarrassé, e [åṅbárásā] *a* (*encombré*) encumbered; (*gêné*) embarrassed; (*explications etc*) awkward.

embarrasser [åṅbárásā] *vt* (*encombrer*) to clutter (up); (*gêner*) to hinder, hamper; (*fig*) to cause embarrassment to; to put in an awkward position; **s'~ de** to burden o.s. with.

embauche [åṅbōsh] *nf* hiring; **bureau d'~** employment *ou* hiring (*US*) office.

embaucher [åṅbōshā] *vt* to take on, hire; **s'~ comme** to get (o.s.) a job as.

embauchoir [åṅbōshwàr] *nm* shoetree.

embaumer [åṅbōmā] *vt* to embalm; (*parfumer*) to fill with its fragrance; **~ la lavande** to be fragrant with (the scent of) lavender.

embellie [åṅbālē] *nf* bright spell, brighter period.

embellir [åṅbālēr] *vt* to make more attractive; (*une histoire*) to embellish ♦ *vi* to grow lovelier *ou* more attractive.

embellissement [åṅbālēsmåṅ] *nm* embellishment.

embêtant, e [åṅbetåṅ, -åṅt] *a* annoying.

embêtement [åṅbetmåṅ] *nm* problem, difficulty; **~s** *nmpl* trouble *sg*.

embêter [åṅbātā] *vt* to bother; **s'~** *vi* (*s'ennuyer*) to be bored; **il ne s'embête pas!** (*ironique*) he does all right for himself!

emblée [åṅblā]: **d'~** *ad* right away.

emblème [åṅblem] *nm* emblem.

embobiner [åṅbōbēnā] *vt* (*enjôler*): **~ qn** to get around sb.

emboîtable [åṅbwátábl(ə)] *a* interlocking.

emboîter [åṅbwátā] *vt* to fit together; **s'~ dans** to fit into; **s'~ (l'un dans l'autre)** to fit together; **~ le pas à qn** to follow in sb's footsteps.

embolie [åṅbolē] *nf* embolism.

embonpoint [åṅbôṅpwaṅ] *nm* stoutness, corpulence; **prendre de l'~** to grow stout *ou* corpulent.

embouché, e [åṅbōōshā] *a*: **mal ~** foulmouthed.

embouchure [åṅbōōshür] *nf* (*GÉO*) mouth; (*MUS*) mouthpiece.

embourber [åṅbōōrbā]: **s'~** *vi* to get stuck in the mud; (*fig*): **s'~ dans** to sink into.

embourgeoiser [åṅbōōrzhwàzā]: **s'~** *vi* to adopt a middle-class outlook.

embout [åṅbōō] *nm* (*de canne*) tip; (*de tuyau*) nozzle.

embouteillage [åṅbōōteyàzh] *nm* traffic jam.

embouteiller [åṅbōōtāyā] *vt* (*suj: véhicules etc*) to block.

emboutir [åṅbōōtēr] *vt* (*TECH*) to stamp; (*heurter*) to crash into, ram.

embranchement [åṅbråṅshmåṅ] *nm* (*routier*) junction; (*classification*) branch.

embrancher [åṅbråṅshā] *vt* (*tuyaux*) to join; **~ qch sur** to join sth to.

embraser [åṅbrázā]: **s'~** *vi* to flare up.

embrassades [åṅbrásàd] *nfpl* hugging and kissing *sg*.

embrasse [åṅbràs] *nf* (*de rideau*) tie-back, loop.

embrasser [åṅbrásā] *vt* to kiss; (*sujet, période*) to embrace, encompass; (*carrière*) to embark on; (*métier*) to go in for, take up; **~ du regard** to take in (*with eyes*); **s'~** to kiss (each other).

embrasure [åṅbrázür] *nf*: **dans l'~ de la porte** in the door(way).

embrayage [åṅbreyàzh] *nm* clutch.

embrayer [åṅbrāyā] *vi* (*AUTO*) to let in the clutch ♦ *vt* (*fig: affaire*) to set in motion; **~ sur qch** to begin on sth.

embrigader [åṅbrēgàdā] *vt* to recruit.

embrocher [åṅbroshā] *vt* to (put on a) spit (*ou* skewer).

embrouillamini [åṅbrōōyámēnē] *nm* (*fam*) muddle.

embrouillé, e [åṅbrōōyā] *a* (*affaire*) confused, muddled.

embrouiller [åṅbrōōyā] *vt* (*fils*) to tangle (up); (*fiches, idées, personne*) to muddle up; **s'~** *vi* to get in a muddle.

embroussaillé, e [åṅbrōōsâyā] *a* overgrown; scrubby; (*cheveux*) bushy, shaggy.

embruns [åṅbrœṅ] *nmpl* sea spray *sg*.

embryologie [åṅbrēyolozhē] *nf* embryology.

embryon [åṅbrēyôṅ] *nm* embryo.

embryonnaire [åṅbrēyoner] *a* embryonic.

embûches [åṅbüsh] *nfpl* pitfalls, traps.

embué, e [åṅbüā] *a* misted up; **yeux ~s de larmes** eyes misty with tears.

embuscade [åṅbüskàd] *nf* ambush; **tendre une ~ à** to lay an ambush for.

embusqué, e [åṅbüskā] *a* in ambush ♦ *nm* (*péj*) shirker.

embusquer [åṅbüskā] *vt*: **s'~** *vi* to take up position (for an ambush).

éméché, e [āmāshā] *a* tipsy.

émeraude [emrōd] *nf* emerald ♦ *a inv* emerald-green.

émergence [āmerzhåṅs] *nf* (*fig*) emergence.

émerger [āmerzhā] *vi* to emerge; (*faire saillie, aussi fig*) to stand out.

émeri [emrē] *nm*: **toile** *ou* **papier ~** emery paper.

émérite [āmārēt] *a* highly skilled.

émerveillement [āmerveymåṅ] *nm* wonderment.

émerveiller [āmervāyā] *vt* to fill with wonder; **s'~ de** to marvel at.

émet [āme] *etc vb voir* **émettre**.

émétique [āmātēk] *nm* emetic.

émetteur, trice [āmetœr, -trēs] *a* transmitting; (*poste*) **~** transmitter.

émettre [āmetr(ə)] *vt* (*son, lumière*) to give out, emit; (*message etc: RADIO*) to transmit; (*billet, timbre, emprunt, chèque*) to issue;

(*hypothèse, avis*) to voice, put forward; (*vœu*) to express ♦ *vi*: ~ **sur ondes courtes** to broadcast on short wave.

émeus [āmœ̄] *etc vb voir* **émouvoir**.

émeute [āmœ̄t] *nf* riot.

émeutier, ière [āmœ̄tyā, -yer] *nm/f* rioter.

émeuve [āmœv] *etc vb voir* **émouvoir**.

émietter [āmyātā] *vt* (*pain, terre*) to crumble; (*fig*) to split up, disperse; **s'~** *vi* (*pain, terre*) to crumble.

émigrant, e [āmēgrāṅ, -āṅt] *nm/f* emigrant.

émigration [āmēgrásyóṅ] *nf* emigration.

émigré, e [āmēgrā] *nm/f* expatriate.

émigrer [āmēgrā] *vi* to emigrate.

émincer [āmaṅsā] *vt* (*CULIN*) to slice thinly.

éminemment [āmēnámáṅ] *ad* eminently.

éminence [āmēnáṅs] *nf* distinction; (*colline*) knoll, hill; **Son É~** His Eminence; ~ **grise** éminence grise.

éminent, e [āmēnáṅ, -áṅt] *a* distinguished.

émir [āmēr] *nm* emir.

émirat ·[āmērá] *nm* emirate; **les É~s arabes unis (EAU)** the United Arab Emirates (UAE).

émis, e [āmē, -ēz] *pp de* **émettre**.

émissaire [āmēser] *nm* emissary.

émission [āmēsyóṅ] *nf* (*voir émettre*) emission; transmission; issue; (*RADIO, TV*) program (*US*), programme (*Brit*), broadcast.

émit [āmē] *etc vb voir* **émettre**.

emmagasinage [āṅmágázēnázh] *nm* storage; storing away.

emmagasiner [āṅmágázēnā] *vt* to (put into) store; (*fig*) to store up.

emmailloter [āṅmáyotā] *vt* to wrap up.

emmanchure [āṅmáṅshür] *nf* armhole.

emmêlement [āṅmelmáṅ] *nm* (*état*) tangle.

emmêler [āṅmālā] *vt* to tangle (up); (*fig*) to muddle up; **s'~** to get into a tangle.

emménagement [āṅmānázhmáṅ] *nm* settling in.

emménager [āṅmānázhā] *vi* to move in; ~ **dans** to move into.

emmener [āṅmnā] *vt* to take (with one); (*comme otage, capture*) to take away; ~ **qn au concert** to take sb to a concert.

emment(h)al [āmaṅtál] *nm* (*fromage*) Emmenthal.

emmerder [āṅmerdā] (*fam!*) *vt* to bug, bother; **s'~** *vi* (*s'ennuyer*) to be bored stiff; **je t'emmerde!** to hell with you!

emmitoufler [āṅmētōōflā] *vt* to wrap up (warmly); **s'~** to wrap (o.s.) up (warmly).

emmurer [āṅmürā] *vt* to wall up, immure.

émoi [āmwá] *nm* (*agitation, effervescence*) commotion; (*trouble*) agitation; **en ~** (*sens*) excited, stirred.

émollient, e [āmolyáṅ, -áṅt] *a* (*MÉD*) emollient.

émoluments [āmolümáṅ] *nmpl* remuneration *sg*, fee *sg*.

émonder [āmóṅdā] *vt* (*arbre etc*) to prune; (*amande etc*) to blanch.

émotif, ive [āmotēf, -ēv] *a* emotional.

émotion [āmōsyóṅ] *nf* emotion; **avoir des ~s** (*fig*) to have a fright; **donner des ~s à** to give a fright to; **sans ~** without emotion, coldly.

émotionnant, e [āmōsyonáṅ, -áṅt] *a* upsetting.

émotionnel, le [āmōsyonel] *a* emotional.

émotionner [āmōsyonā] *vt* to upset.

émoulu, e [āmōōlü] *a*: **frais ~ de** fresh from, just out of.

émoussé, e [āmōōsā] *a* blunt.

émousser [āmōōsā] *vt* to blunt; (*fig*) to dull.

émoustiller [āmōōstēyā] *vt* to titillate, arouse.

émouvant, e [āmōōváṅ, -áṅt] *a* moving.

émouvoir [āmōōvwár] *vt* (*troubler*) to stir, affect; (*toucher, attendrir*) to move; (*indigner*) to rouse; (*effrayer*) to disturb, worry; **s'~** *vi* to be affected; to be moved; to be roused; to be disturbed *ou* worried.

empailler [āṅpāyā] *vt* to stuff.

empailleur, euse [āṅpāyœr, -ēz] *nm/f* (*d'animaux*) taxidermist.

empaler [āṅpálā] *vt* to impale.

empaquetage [āṅpáktázh] *nm* packing, packaging.

empaqueter [āṅpāktā] *vt* to pack up.

emparer [āṅpárā]: **s'~ de** *vt* (*objet*) to seize, grab; (*comme otage, MIL*) to seize; (*suj: peur etc*) to take hold of.

empâter [āṅpātā]: **s'~** *vi* to thicken out.

empattement [āṅpátmáṅ] *nm* (*AUTO*) wheelbase; (*TYPO*) serif.

empêché, e [āṅpāshā] *a* detained.

empêchement [āṅpeshmáṅ] *nm* (unexpected) obstacle, hitch.

empêcher [āṅpāshā] *vt* to prevent; ~ **qn de faire** to prevent *ou* stop sb (from) doing; ~ **que qch (n')arrive/qn (ne) fasse** to prevent sth from happening/sb from doing; **il n'empêche que** nevertheless, be that as it may; **il n'a pas pu s'~ de rire** he couldn't help laughing.

empêcheur [āṅpāshœr] *nm*: ~ **de danser en rond** spoilsport, killjoy.

empeigne [āṅpeny] *nf* upper (*of shoe*).

empennage [āṅpenázh] *nm* (*AVIAT*) tail assembly (*US*), tailplane (*Brit*).

empereur [āṅprœr] *nm* emperor.

empesé, e [āṅpǝzā] *a* (*fig*) stiff, starchy.

empeser [āṅpǝzā] *vt* to starch.

empester [āṅpestā] *vt* (*lieu*) to stink up (*US*) *ou* out (*Brit*) ♦ *vi* to stink, reek; ~ **le tabac/ le vin** to stink *ou* reek of tobacco/wine.

empêtrer [āṅpātrā] *vt*: **s'~ dans** (*fils etc, aussi fig*) to get tangled up in.

emphase [āṅfáz] *nf* pomposity, bombast; **avec ~** pompously.

emphatique [āṅfátēk] *a* emphatic.

empiècement [āṅpyesmáṅ] *nm* (*COUTURE*) yoke.

empierrer [āṅpyārā] *vt* (*route*) to gravel (*US*), metal (*Brit*).

empiéter [āṅpyātā]: ~ **sur** *vt* to encroach upon.

empiffrer [āṅpēfrā]: **s'~** *vi* (*péj*) to stuff o.s.

empiler [āṅpēlā] *vt* to pile (up), stack (up); **s'~** *vi* to pile up.

empire [āṅpēr] *nm* empire; (*fig*) influence; **style E~** Empire style; **sous l'~ de** in the grip of.

empirer [āṅpērā] *vi* to worsen, deteriorate.

empirique [āṅpērēk] *a* empirical.

empirisme [áṅpērēsm(ǝ)] *nm* empiricism.

emplacement [āṅplásmáṅ] *nm* site; **sur l'~ de** on the site of.

emplâtre [ãⁿplâtr(ə)] *nm* plaster; (*fam*) clod.
emplette [ãⁿplet] *nf*: **faire l'~ de** to purchase; **~s** shopping *sg*; **faire des ~s** to go shopping.
emplir [ãⁿplēr] *vt* to fill; **s'~ (de)** to fill (with).
emploi [ãⁿplwá] *nm* use; (*COMM, ÉCON*): **l'~** employment; (*poste*) job, situation; **d'~ facile** easy to use; **le plein ~** full employment; **~ du temps** timetable, schedule.
emploie [ãⁿplwá] *etc vb voir* **employer**.
employé, e [ãⁿplwáyã] *nm/f* employee; **~ de bureau/banque** office/bank employee *ou* clerk; **~ de maison** domestic (servant).
employer [ãⁿplwáyã] *vt* (*outil, moyen, méthode, mot*) to use; (*ouvrier, main-d'œuvre*) to employ; **s'~ à qch/à faire** to apply *ou* devote o.s. to sth/to doing.
employeur, euse [ãⁿplwàyœr, -ēz] *nm/f* employer.
empocher [ãⁿposhã] *vt* to pocket.
empoignade [ãⁿpwányàd] *nf* row, set-to.
empoigne [ãⁿpwány] *nf*: **foire d'~** free-for-all.
empoigner [ãⁿpwányã] *vt* to grab; **s'~** (*fig*) to have a row *ou* set-to.
empois [ãⁿpwá] *nm* starch.
empoisonnement [ãⁿpwàzonmãⁿ] *nm* poisoning; (*fam: ennui*) annoyance, irritation.
empoisonner [ãⁿpwàzonã] *vt* to poison; (*empester: air, pièce*) to stink up (*US*) *ou* out (*Brit*); (*fam*): **~ qn** to drive sb mad; **s'~** to poison o.s.; **~ l'atmosphère** (*aussi fig*) to poison the atmosphere; **il nous empoisonne l'existence** he's the bane of our life.
empoissonner [ãⁿpwàsonã] *vt* (*étang, rivière*) to stock with fish.
emporté, e [ãⁿportã] *a* (*personne, caractère*) fiery.
emportement [ãⁿportəmãⁿ] *nm* fit of rage, anger *q*.
emporte-pièce [ãⁿportəpyes] *nm inv* (*TECH*) punch; **à l'~** *a* (*fig*) incisive.
emporter [ãⁿportã] *vt* to take (with one); (*en dérobant ou enlevant, emmener: blessés, voyageurs*) to take away; (*entraîner*) to carry away *ou* along; (*arracher*) to tear off; (*suj: rivière, vent*) to carry away; (*MIL: position*) to take; (*avantage, approbation*) to win; **s'~** *vi* (*de colère*) to fly into a rage, lose one's temper; **la maladie qui l'a emporté** the illness which caused his death; **l'~** to win; **l'~ (sur)** to get the upper hand (of); (*méthode etc*) to prevail (over); **boissons à ~** drinks to go (*US*), take-away drinks (*Brit*).
empoté, e [ãⁿpotã] *a* (*maladroit*) clumsy.
empourpré, e [ãⁿpŏŏrprã] *a* crimson.
empreint, e [ãⁿpraⁿ, -aⁿt] *a*: **~ de** marked with; tinged with ♦ *nf* (*de pied, main*) print; (*fig*) stamp, mark; **~e (digitale)** fingerprint.
empressé, e [ãⁿprãsã] *a* attentive; (*péj*) overanxious to please, overattentive.
empressement [ãⁿpresmãⁿ] *nm* eagerness.
empresser [ãⁿprãsã]: **s'~** *vi*: **s'~ auprès de qn** to surround sb with attentions; **s'~ de faire** to hasten to do.
emprise [ãⁿprēz] *nf* hold, ascendancy; **sous l'~ de** under the influence of.
emprisonnement [ãⁿprēzonmãⁿ] *nm* imprisonment.
emprisonner [ãⁿprēzonã] *vt* to imprison, jail.
emprunt [ãⁿprœⁿ] *nm* borrowing *q*, loan

(*from debtor's point of view*); (*LING etc*) borrowing; **nom d'~** assumed name; **~ d'État** government *ou* state loan; **~ public à 5%** 5% public loan.
emprunté, e [ãⁿprœⁿtã] *a* (*fig*) ill-at-ease, awkward.
emprunter [ãⁿprœⁿtã] *vt* to borrow; (*itinéraire*) to take, follow; (*style, manière*) to adopt, assume.
emprunteur, euse [ãⁿprœⁿtœr, -ēz] *nm/f* borrower.
empuantir [ãⁿpüãⁿtēr] *vt* to stink up (*US*) *ou* out (*Brit*).
EMT *sigle f* (= *éducation manuelle et technique*) *handwork as a school subject.*
ému, e [ãmü] *pp de* **émouvoir** ♦ *a* excited; touched; moved.
émulation [ãmülãsyŏⁿ] *nf* emulation.
émule [ãmül] *nm/f* imitator.
émulsion [ãmülsyŏⁿ] *nf* emulsion; (*cosmétique*) (water-based) lotion.
émut [ãmü] *etc vb voir* **émouvoir**.
en [ãⁿ] *prép* in; (*avec direction*) to; (*temps: durée*): **~ 3 jours/20 ans** in 3 days/20 years; (*: moment*): **~ mars/hiver** in March/winter; (*moyen*): **~ avion/taxi** by plane/taxi; (*composition*): **~ verre** made of glass, glass *cpd*; **~ deux volumes/une pièce** in two volumes/one piece; **se casser ~ deux/plusieurs morceaux** to break in two/into several pieces; **~ dormant** while sleeping, as one sleeps; **~ sortant** on going out, as he *etc* went out; **fort ~ maths** good at math; **~ bonne santé** in good *ou* sound health; **~ réparation** being repaired, under repair; **~ T/étoile** T-/star-shaped; **~ chemise/chaussettes** in one's shirt/socks; **partir ~ vacances/voyage** to go (off) on vacation/on a trip; **peindre qch ~ rouge** to paint sth red; **~ soldat** as a soldier; **~ bon diplomate, il n'a rien dit** tactful as he is, he said nothing; **le même ~ plus grand** the same only *ou* but bigger ♦ *pronom* (*provenance*): **j'~ viens** I've come from there; (*cause*): **il ~ est malade** he's ill because of it; (*agent*): **il ~ est aimé** he's loved by her; (*complément de nom*): **j'~ connais les dangers** I know its dangers; (*indéfini*): **j'~ ai/veux** I have/want some; **~ as-tu?** have you got any?; **je n'~ veux pas** I don't want any; **j'~ ai assez** I've got enough (of it *ou* them); (*fig*) I've had enough; **j'~ ai 2** I've got 2 (of them); **combien y ~ a-t-il?** how many (of them) are there?; **j'~ suis fier/ai besoin** I am proud of it/need it; **où ~ étais-je?** where was I?, where had I got to? : *voir le verbe ou l'adjectif lorsque 'en' correspond à 'de' introduisant un complément prépositionnel.*
ENA [ãnã] *sigle f* (= *École nationale d'administration*) *grande école for training civil servants.*
énarque [ãnárk(ə)] *nm/f* former ENA student.
encablure [ãⁿkâblür] *nf* (*NAVIG*) cable's length.
encadrement [ãⁿkâdrəmãⁿ] *nm* framing; training; (*de porte*) frame; **~ du crédit** credit regulation.
encadrer [ãⁿkâdrã] *vt* (*tableau, image*) to frame; (*fig: entourer*) to surround;

(*personnel, soldats etc*) to train; (*COMM*: *crédit*) to regulate.

encadreur [ãnkádrœr] *nm* (picture) framer.

encaisse [ãnkes] *nf* cash in hand; ~ **or/ métallique** gold/gold and silver reserves.

encaissé, e [ãnkãsã] *a* (*vallée*) steep-sided; (*rivière*) with steep banks.

encaisser [ãnkãsã] *vt* (*chèque*) to cash; (*argent*) to collect; (*fig: coup, défaite*) to take.

encaisseur [ãnkesœr] *nm* collector (*of debts etc*).

encan [ãnkãn]: **à l'~** *ad* by auction.

encanailler [ãnkánáyã]: **s'~** *vi* to become vulgar *ou* common; to mix with the riff-raff.

encart [ãnkár] *nm* insert; ~ **publicitaire** advertising insert.

encarter [ãnkártã] *vt* to insert.

en-cas [ãnká] *nm inv* snack.

encastrable [ãnkástrábl(ə)] *a* (*four, élément*) that can be built in.

encastré, e [ãnkástrã] *a* (*four, baignoire*) built-in.

encastrer [ãnkástrã] *vt*: ~ **qch dans** (*mur*) to embed sth in(to); (*boîtier*) to fit sth into; **s'~ dans** to fit into; (*heurter*) to crash into.

encaustiquage [ãnkostẽkázh] *nm* polishing, waxing.

encaustique [ãnkostẽk] *nf* polish, wax.

encaustiquer [ãnkostẽkã] *vt* to polish, wax.

enceinte [ãnsãnt] *af*: ~ **(de 6 mois)** (6 months) pregnant ♦ *nf* (*mur*) wall; (*espace*) enclosure; ~ **(acoustique)** speaker.

encens [ãnsãn] *nm* incense.

encenser [ãnsãnsã] *vt* to (in)cense; (*fig*) to praise to the skies.

encensoir [ãnsãnswár] *nm* thurible (*Brit*), censer.

encercler [ãnserklã] *vt* to surround.

enchaîné [ãnshãnã] *nm* (*CINÉMA*) lap dissolve.

enchaînement [ãnshenmãn] *nm* (*fig*) linking.

enchaîner [ãnshãnã] *vt* to chain up; (*mouvements, séquences*) to link (together) ♦ *vi* to carry on.

enchanté, e [ãnshãntã] *a* (*ravi*) delighted; (*ensorcelé*) enchanted; ~ **(de faire votre connaissance)** pleased to meet you, how do you do?

enchantement [ãnshãntmãn] *nm* delight; (*magie*) enchantment; **comme par** ~ as if by magic.

enchanter [ãnshãntã] *vt* to delight.

enchanteur, teresse [ãnshãntœr, -tres] *a* enchanting.

enchâsser [ãnshãsã] *vt*: ~ **qch (dans)** to set sth (in).

enchère [ãnsher] *nf* bid; **faire une** ~ to (make a) bid; **mettre/vendre aux** ~s to put up for (sale by)/sell by auction; **les** ~s **montent** the bids are rising; **faire monter les** ~s (*fig*) to raise the bidding.

enchérir [ãnshãrẽr] *vi*: ~ **sur qn** (*aux enchères, aussi fig*) to outbid sb.

enchérisseur, euse [ãnshãrẽsœr, -ẽz] *nm/f* bidder.

enchevêtrement [ãnshvetrəmãn] *nm* tangle.

enchevêtrer [ãnshvãtrã] *vt* to tangle (up).

enclave [ãnklãv] *nf* enclave.

enclaver [ãnklãvã] *vt* to enclose, hem in.

enclencher [ãnklãnshã] *vt* (*mécanisme*) to engage; (*fig: affaire*) to set in motion; **s'~** *vi* to engage.

enclin, e [ãnklãn, -ẽn] *a*: ~ **à qch/à faire** inclined *ou* prone to sth/to do.

enclore [ãnklor] *vt* to enclose.

enclos [ãnklõ] *nm* enclosure; (*clôture*) fence.

enclume [ãnklüm] *nf* anvil.

encoche [ãnkosh] *nf* notch.

encoder [ãnkodã] *vt* to encode.

encodeur [ãnkodœr] *nm* encoder.

encoignure [ãnkonyür] *nf* corner.

encoller [ãnkolã] *vt* to paste.

encolure [ãnkolür] *nf* (*tour de cou*) collar size; (*col, cou*) neck.

encombrant, e [ãnkõnbrãn, -ãnt] *a* cumbersome, bulky.

encombre [ãnkõnbr(ə)]: **sans** ~ *ad* without mishap *ou* incident.

encombré, e [ãnkõnbrã] *a* (*pièce, passage*) cluttered; (*lignes téléphoniques*) busy; (*marché*) saturated.

encombrement [ãnkõnbrəmãn] *nm* (*d'un lieu*) cluttering (up); (*d'un objet: dimensions*) bulk.

encombrer [ãnkõnbrã] *vt* to clutter (up); (*gêner*) to hamper; **s'~ de** (*bagages etc*) to load *ou* burden o.s. with; ~ **le passage** to block *ou* obstruct the way.

encontre [ãnkõntr(ə)]: **à l'~ de** *prép* against, counter to.

encorbellement [ãnkorbelmãn] *nm*: **fenêtre en** ~ oriel window.

encorder [ãnkordã] *vt*: **s'~** (*ALPINISME*) to rope up.

encore [ãnkor] *ad* (*continuation*) still; (*de nouveau*) again; (*restriction*) even then *ou* so; (*intensif*): ~ **plus fort/mieux** even louder/better; ~**!** (*insatisfaction*) not again!; **pas** ~ not yet; ~ **que** even though; ~ **une fois** (once) again; ~ **deux jours** still two days, two more days; ~ **un effort** just a little more effort; **hier** ~ ... even yesterday ...; **non seulement ... mais** ~ not only ... but also; **(et puis) quoi** ~**?** what else?; **si** ~ if only.

encourageant, e [ãnkōōrázhãn, -ãnt] *a* encouraging.

encouragement [ãnkōōrázhmãn] *nm* encouragement; (*récompense*) incentive.

encourager [ãnkōōrázhã] *vt* to encourage; ~ **qn à faire qch** to encourage sb to do sth.

encourir [ãnkōōrẽr] *vt* to incur.

encrasser [ãnkrãsã] *vt* to dirty; (*AUTO etc*) to soot up.

encre [ãnkr(ə)] *nf* ink; ~ **de Chine** India (*US*) *ou* Indian (*Brit*) ink; ~ **indélébile** indelible ink; ~ **sympathique** invisible ink.

encrer [ãnkrã] *vt* to ink.

encreur [ãnkrœr] *am*: **rouleau** ~ inking roller.

encrier [ãnkrẽyã] *nm* inkwell.

encroûter [ãnkrōōtã]: **s'~** *vi* (*fig*) to get into a rut, get set in one's ways.

encyclique [ãnsẽklẽk] *nf* encyclical.

encyclopédie [ãnsẽklopãdẽ] *nf* encyclopedia (*US*), encyclopaedia (*Brit*).

encyclopédique [ãnsẽklopãdẽk] *a* encyclopedic (*US*), encyclopaedic (*Brit*).

endémique [ãndãmẽk] *a* endemic.

endetté, e [ăṅdātā] *a* in debt; (*fig*): **très ~ envers qn** deeply indebted to sb.

endettement [ăṅdetmăṅ] *nm* debts *pl.*

endetter [ăṅdātā] *vt*, **s'~** *vi* to get into debt.

endeuiller [ăṅdœyā] *vt* to plunge into mourning; **manifestation endeuillée par** event over which a tragic shadow was cast by.

endiablé, e [ăṅdyáblā] *a* furious; (*enfant*) boisterous.

endiguer [ăṅdēgā] *vt* to dike (up); (*fig*) to check, hold back.

endimancher [ăṅdēmăṅshā] *vt*: **s'~** to put on one's Sunday best; **avoir l'air endimanché** to be all dressed up to the nines (*fam*).

endive [ăṅdēv] *nf* chicory *q.*

endocrine [ăṅdokrēn] *af*: **glande ~** endocrine (gland).

endoctrinement [ăṅdoktrēnmăṅ] *nm* indoctrination.

endoctriner [ăṅdoktrēnā] *vt* to indoctrinate.

endolori, e [ăṅdolorē] *a* painful.

endommager [ăṅdomázhā] *vt* to damage.

endormant, e [ăṅdormăṅ, -ăṅt] *a* dull, boring.

endormi, e [ăṅdormē] *pp de* **endormir ♦** *a* (*personne*) asleep; (*fig: indolent, lent*) sluggish; (*engourdi: main, pied*) numb.

endormir [ăṅdormēr] *vt* to put to sleep; (*MÉD: dent, nerf*) to anesthetize (*US*), anaesthetize (*Brit*); (*fig: soupçons*) to allay; **s'~** *vi* to fall asleep, go to sleep.

endoscope [ăṅdoskop] *nm* (*MÉD*) endoscope.

endoscopie [ăṅdoskopē] *nf* endoscopy.

endosser [ăṅdōsā] *vt* (*responsabilité*) to take, shoulder; (*chèque*) to endorse; (*uniforme, tenue*) to put on, don.

endroit [ăṅdrwá] *nm* place; (*localité*): **les gens de l'~** the local people; (*opposé à l'envers*) right side; **à cet ~** in this place; **à l'~** right side out; the right way up; (*vêtement*) the right side out; **à l'~ de** *prép* regarding, with regard to; **par ~s** in places.

enduire [ăṅdüēr] *vt* to coat; **~ qch de** to coat sth with.

enduit, e [ăṅdüē, -ēt] *pp de* **enduire ♦** *nm* coating.

endurance [ăṅdürăṅs] *nf* endurance.

endurant, e [ăṅdürăṅ, -ăṅt] *a* tough, hardy.

endurcir [ăṅdürsēr] *vt* (*physiquement*) to toughen; (*moralement*) to harden; **s'~** *vi* to become tougher; to become hardened.

endurer [ăṅdürā] *vt* to endure, bear.

énergétique [ānerzhātēk] *a* (*ressources etc*) energy *cpd*; (*aliment*) energizing.

énergie [ānerzhē] *nf* (*PHYSIQUE*) energy; (*TECH*) power; (*fig: physique*) energy; (: *morale*) vigor (*US*), vigour (*Brit*), spirit.

énergique [ānerzhēk] *a* energetic; vigorous; (*mesures*) drastic, stringent.

énergiquement [ānerzhēkmăṅ] *ad* energetically; drastically.

énergisant, e [ānerzhēzăṅ, -ăṅt] *a* energizing.

énergumène [ānergümen] *nm* rowdy character *ou* customer.

énervant, e [ānervăṅ, -ăṅt] *a* irritating.

énervé, e [ānervā] *a* on edge; (*agacé*) irritated.

énervement [ānervəmăṅ] *nm* edginess; irritation.

énerver [ānervā] *vt* to irritate, annoy; **s'~** *vi*

to get excited, get worked up.

enfance [ăṅfăṅs] *nf* (*âge*) childhood; (*fig*) infancy; (*enfants*) children *pl*; **c'est l'~ de l'art** it's child's play; **petite ~** infancy; **souvenir/ami d'~** childhood memory/friend; **retomber en ~** to lapse into one's second childhood.

enfant [ăṅfăṅ] *nm/f* child (*pl* children); **~ adoptif/naturel** adopted/natural child; **bon ~** *a* good-natured, easy-going; **~ de chœur** *nm* (*REL*) altar boy; **~ prodige** child prodigy; **~ unique** only child.

enfanter [ăṅfăṅtā] *vi* to give birth ♦ *vt* to give birth to.

enfantillage [ăṅfăṅtēyázh] *nm* (*péj*) childish behavior *q* (*US*) *ou* behaviour *q* (*Brit*).

enfantin, e [ăṅfăṅtaṅ, -ēn] *a* childlike; (*péj*) childish; (*langage*) child *cpd.*

enfer [ăṅfer] *nm* hell; **allure/bruit d'~** horrendous speed/noise.

enfermer [ăṅfermā] *vt* to shut up; (*à clef, interner*) to lock up; **s'~** to shut o.s. away; **s'~ à clé** to lock o.s. in; **s'~ dans la solitude/le mutisme** to retreat into solitude/ silence.

enferrer [ăṅfārā] **s'~** *vi*: **s'~ dans** to tangle o.s. up in.

enfiévré, e [ăṅfyāvrā] *a* (*fig*) feverish.

enfilade [ăṅfēlad] *nf*: **une ~ de** a series *ou* line of; **prendre des rues en ~** to cross directly from one street into the next.

enfiler [ăṅfēlā] *vt* (*vêtement*): **~ qch** to slip sth on, slip into sth; (*insérer*): **~ qch dans** to stick sth into; (*rue, couloir*) to take; (*perles*) to string; (*aiguille*) to thread; **s'~ dans** to disappear into.

enfin [ăṅfaṅ] *ad* at last; (*en énumérant*) lastly; (*de restriction, résignation*) still; (*eh bien*) well; (*pour conclure*) in a word.

enflammé, e [ăṅflămā] *a* (*torche, allumette*) burning; (*MÉD: plaie*) inflamed; (*fig: nature, discours, déclaration*) fiery.

enflammer [ăṅflămā] *vt* to set fire to; (*MÉD*) to inflame; **s'~** *vi* to catch fire; to become inflamed.

enflé, e [ăṅflā] *a* swollen; (*péj: style*) bombastic, turgid.

enfler [ăṅflā] *vi* to swell (up); **s'~** *vi* to swell.

enflure [ăṅflür] *nf* swelling.

enfoncé, e [ăṅfôṅsā] *a* staved-in, smashed-in; (*yeux*) deep-set.

enfoncement [ăṅfôṅsmăṅ] *nm* (*recoin*) nook.

enfoncer [ăṅfôṅsā] *vt* (*clou*) to drive in; (*faire pénétrer*): **~ qch dans** to push (*ou* drive) sth into; (*forcer: porte*) to break open; (: *plancher*) to cause to cave in; (*défoncer: côtes etc*) to smash; (*fam: surpasser*) to lick, beat (hollow) ♦ *vi* (*dans la vase etc*) to sink in; (*sol, surface porteuse*) to give way; **s'~** *vi* to sink; **s'~ dans** to sink into; (*forêt, ville*) to disappear into; **~ un chapeau sur la tête** to ram a hat on one's head; **~ qn dans la dette** to drag sb into debt.

enfouir [ăṅfwēr] *vt* (*dans le sol*) to bury; (*dans un tiroir etc*) to tuck away; **s'~ dans/sous** to bury o.s. in/under.

enfourcher [ăṅfōōrshā] *vt* to mount; **~ son dada** (*fig*) to get on one's hobby-horse.

enfourner [ăṅfōōrnā] *vt* to put in the oven;

(*poterie*) to put in the kiln; ~ **qch dans** to shove *ou* stuff sth into; **s'~ dans** (*suj: personne*) to dive into.

enfreignais [ȧṅfrɛnyɛ] *etc vb voir* **enfreindre**.

enfreindre [ȧṅfraṅdr(ə)] *vt* to infringe, break.

enfuir [ȧṅfüɛ̈r]: **s'~** *vi* to run away *ou* off.

enfumer [ȧṅfümā] *vt* to smoke out.

enfuyais [ȧṅfüɛ̈yɛ] *etc vb voir* **enfuir**.

engagé, e [ȧṅgȧzhā] *a* (*littérature etc*) engagé, committed.

engageant, e [ȧṅgȧzhȧṅ, -ȧṅt] *a* attractive, appealing.

engagement [ȧṅgȧzhmȧṅ] *nm* taking on, engaging; starting; investing; (*prŏmesse*) commitment; (*MIL: combat*) engagement; (*: recrutement*) enlistment; (*SPORT*) entry; **prendre l'~ de faire** to undertake to do; **sans ~** (*COMM*) without obligation.

engager [ȧṅgȧzhā] *vt* (*embaucher*) to take on, engage; (*commencer*) to start; (*lier*) to bind, commit; (*impliquer, entraîner*) to involve; (*investir*) to invest, lay out; (*faire intervenir*) to engage; (*SPORT: concurrents, chevaux*) to enter; (*inciter*): ~ **qn à faire** to urge sb to do; (*faire pénétrer*): ~ **qch dans** to insert sth into; ~ **qn à qch** to urge sth on sb; **s'~** to take a job; (*MIL*) to enlist; (*promettre, politiquement*) to commit o.s.; (*débuter*) to start (up); **s'~ à faire** to undertake to do; **s'~ dans** (*rue, passage*) to enter, turn into; (*s'emboîter*) to engage *ou* fit into; (*fig: affaire, discussion*) to enter into, embark on.

engazonner [ȧṅgȧzonā] *vt* to turf.

engeance [ȧṅzhȧṅs] *nf* mob.

engelure [ȧṅzhlür] *nf* chilblain.

engendrer [ȧṅzhȧṅdrā] *vt* to father; (*fig*) to create, breed.

engin [ȧṅzhaṅ] *nm* machine; instrument; vehicle; (*péj*) gadget; (*AVIAT: avion*) aircraft *inv*; (*: missile*) missile; ~ **blindé** armored vehicle; ~ (**explosif**) (explosive) device; ~**s** (**spéciaux**) missiles.

englober [ȧṅglobā] *vt* to include.

engloutir [ȧṅglōōtēr] *vt* to swallow up; (*fig: dépenses*) to devour; **s'~** to be engulfed.

engoncé, e [ȧṅgôṅsā] *a*: ~ **dans** cramped in.

engorgement [ȧṅgorzhəmȧṅ] *nm* blocking; (*MÉD*) engorgement.

engorger [ȧṅgorzhā] *vt* to obstruct, block; **s'~** *vi* to become blocked.

engouement [ȧṅgōōmȧṅ] *nm* (sudden) passion.

engouffrer [ȧṅgōōfrā] *vt* to swallow up, devour; **s'~ dans** to rush into.

engourdi, e [ȧṅgōōrdē] *a* numb.

engourdir [ȧṅgōōrdēr] *vt* to numb; (*fig*) to dull, blunt; **s'~** *vi* to go numb.

engrais [ȧṅgrɛ] *nm* manure; ~ (**chimique**) (chemical) fertilizer; ~ **organique/ inorganique** organic/inorganic fertilizer.

engraisser [ȧṅgrȧsā] *vt* to fatten (up); (*terre: fertiliser*) to fertilize ♦ *vi* (*péj*) to get fat(ter).

engranger [ȧṅgrȧṅzhā] *vt* (*foin*) to bring in; (*fig*) to store away.

engrenage [ȧṅgrənázh] *nm* gears *pl*, gearing; (*fig*) chain.

engueuler [ȧṅgœlā] *vt* (*fam*) to bawl out.

enguirlander [ȧṅgērlȧṅdā] *vt* (*fam*) to give sb a bawling out.

enhardir [ȧṅȧrdēr]: **s'~** *vi* to grow bolder.

ENI [ȧnē] *sigle f* = **école normale** (**d'instituteurs**).

énième [ȧnyɛm] *a* = **nième**.

énigmatique [ȧnēgmátēk] *a* enigmatic.

énigmatiquement [ȧnēgmátēkmȧṅ] *ad* enigmatically.

énigme [ȧnēgm(ə)] *nf* riddle.

enivrant, e [ȧṅnēvrȧṅ, -ȧṅt] *a* intoxicating.

enivrer [ȧṅnēvrā] *vt*: **s'~** to get drunk; **s'~ de** (*fig*) to become intoxicated with.

enjambée [ȧṅzhȧṅbā] *nf* stride; **d'une ~** with one stride.

enjamber [ȧṅzhȧṅbā] *vt* to stride over; (*suj: pont etc*) to span, straddle.

enjeu, x [ȧṅzhœ̈] *nm* stakes *pl*.

enjoindre [ȧṅzhwaṅdr(ə)] *vt*: ~ **à qn de faire** to enjoin *ou* order sb to do.

enjôler [ȧṅzhōlā] *vt* to coax, wheedle.

enjôleur, euse [ȧṅzhōlœr, -œ̈z] *a* (*sourire, paroles*) winning.

enjolivement [ȧṅzholēvmȧṅ] *nm* embellishment.

enjoliver [ȧṅzholēvā] *vt* to embellish.

enjoliveur [ȧṅzholēvœr] *nm* (*AUTO*) hub cap.

enjoué, e [ȧṅzhwā] *a* playful.

enlacer [ȧṅlȧsā] *vt* (*étreindre*) to embrace, hug; (*suj: lianes*) to wind around, entwine.

enlaidir [ȧṅlȧdēr] *vt* to make ugly ♦ *vi* to become ugly.

enlevé, e [ȧṅlvā] *a* (*morceau de musique*) played brightly.

enlèvement [ȧṅlevmȧṅ] *nm* removal; (*rapt*) abduction, kidnapping; **l'~ des ordures ménagères** garbage (*US*) *ou* refuse (*Brit*) collection.

enlever [ȧṅlvā] *vt* (*ôter: gén*) to remove; (*: vêtement, lunettes*) to take off; (*: MÉD: organe*) to remove; (*emporter: ordures etc*) to collect, take away; (*prendre*): ~ **qch à qn** to take sth (away) from sb; (*kidnapper*) to abduct, kidnap; (*obtenir: prix, contrat*) to win; (*MIL: position*) to take; (*morceau de piano etc*) to execute with spirit *ou* brio; **s'~** *vi* (*tache*) to come out *ou* off; **la maladie qui nous l'a enlevé** (*euphémisme*) the illness which took him from us.

enliser [ȧṅlēzā]: **s'~** *vi* to sink, get stuck; (*dialogue etc*) to get bogged down.

enluminure [ȧṅlümēnür] *nf* illumination.

ENM *sigle f* (= *École nationale de la magistrature*) *grande école for law students*.

enneigé, e [ȧṅnȧzhā] *a* snowy; (*col*) snowbound; (*maison*) snowed-in.

enneigement [ȧṅnezhmȧṅ] *nm* depth of snow, snowfall; **bulletin d'~** snow report.

ennemi, e [enmē] *a* hostile; (*MIL*) enemy *cpd* ♦ *nm/f* enemy; **être ~ de** to be strongly averse *ou* opposed to.

ennième [enyem] *a* = **nième**.

ennoblir [ȧṅnoblēr] *vt* to ennoble.

ennui [ȧṅnüē] *nm* (*lassitude*) boredom; (*difficulté*) trouble *q*; **avoir des ~s** to have problems; **s'attirer des ~s** to cause problems for o.s.

ennuie [ȧṅnüē] *etc vb voir* **ennuyer**.

ennuyé, e [ȧṅnüēyā] *a* (*air, personne*) preoccupied, worried.

ennuyer [ăṅnüēyā] *vt* to bother; *(lasser)* to bore; **s'~** *vi* to be bored; **s'~ de** *(regretter)* to miss; **si cela ne vous ennuie pas** if it's no trouble to you.

ennuyeux, euse [ăṅnüēyœ̄, -ēz] *a* boring, tedious; *(agaçant)* annoying.

énoncé [ānóṅsā] *nm* terms *pl*; wording; *(LING)* utterance.

énoncer [ānóṅsā] *vt* to say, express; *(conditions)* to set out, lay down, state.

énonciation [ānóṅsyâsyóṅ] *nf* statement.

enorgueillir [ăṅnorgœyēr]: **s'~ de** *vt* to pride o.s. on; to boast.

énorme [ānorm(ə)] *a* enormous, huge.

énormément [ānormāmăṅ] *ad* enormously, tremendously; **~ de neige/gens** an enormous amount of snow/number of people.

énormité [ānormētā] *nf* enormity, hugeness; *(propos)* outrageous remark.

enquérir [ăṅkārēr]: **s'~ de** *vt* to inquire about.

enquête [ăṅket] *nf* *(de journaliste, de police)* investigation; *(judiciaire, administrative)* inquiry; *(sondage d'opinion)* survey.

enquêter [ăṅkātā] *vi* to investigate; to hold an inquiry; *(faire un sondage)*: **~ (sur)** to do a survey (on), carry out an opinion poll (on).

enquêteur, euse *ou* **trice** [ăṅketœr, -ēz, -trēs] *nm/f* officer in charge of an investigation; person conducting a survey; pollster.

enquiers, enquière [ăṅkyer] *etc vb voir* **enquérir**.

enquiquiner [ăṅkēkēnā] *vt* to rile, irritate.

enquis, e [ăṅkē, -ēz] *pp de* **enquérir**.

enraciné, e [ăṅrāsēnā] *a* deep-rooted.

enragé, e [ăṅrázhā] *a* *(MÉD)* rabid, with rabies; *(furieux)* furiously angry; *(fig)* fanatical; **~ de** wild about.

enrageant, e [ăṅrázhăṅ, -ăṅt] *a* infuriating.

enrager [ăṅrázhā] *vi* to be furious, be in a rage; **faire ~ qn** to make sb wild with anger.

enrayer [ăṅrāyā] *vt* to check, stop; **s'~** *vi* *(arme à feu)* to jam.

enrégimenter [ăṅrāzhēmăṅtā] *vt* *(péj)* to enlist.

enregistrement [ăṅrzhēstrəmăṅ] *nm* recording; *(ADMIN)* registration; **~ des bagages** *(à l'aéroport)* baggage check-in; **~ magnétique** tape-recording.

enregistrer [ăṅrzhēstrā] *vt* *(MUS, INFORM etc)* to record; *(remarquer, noter)* to note, record; *(COMM: commande)* to note, enter; *(fig: mémoriser)* to make a mental note of; *(ADMIN)* to register; *(aussi:* **faire ~**: *bagages: par train)* to register; *(: à l'aéroport)* to check in.

enregistreur, euse [ăṅrzhēstrœr, -ēz] *a* *(machine)* recording *cpd* ♦ *nm* *(appareil)*: **~ de vol** *(AVIAT)* flight recorder.

enrhumé, e [ăṅrümā] *a*: **il est ~** he has a cold.

enrhumer [ăṅrümā]: **s'~** *vi* to catch a cold.

enrichir [ăṅrēshēr] *vt* to make rich(er); *(fig)* to enrich; **s'~** to get rich(er).

enrichissement [ăṅrēshēsmăṅ] *nm* enrichment.

enrober [ăṅrobā] *vt*: **~ qch de** to coat sth with; *(fig)* to wrap sth up in.

enrôlement [ăṅrōlmăṅ] *nm* enlistment.

enrôler [ăṅrōlā] *vt* to enlist; **s'~ (dans)** to en-list (in).

enroué, e [ăṅrwā] *a* hoarse.

enrouer [ăṅrwā]: **s'~** *vi* to go hoarse.

enrouler [ăṅrōōlā] *vt* *(fil, corde)* to wind (up); **s'~** to coil up; **~ qch autour de** to wind sth (a)round.

enrouleur, euse [ăṅrōōlœr, -ēz] *a* *(TECH)* winding ♦ *nm voir* **ceinture**.

enrubanné, e [ăṅrübánā] *a* trimmed with ribbon.

ENS *sigle f* = **école normale supérieure**.

ensabler [ăṅsâblā] *vt* *(port, canal)* to silt up, sand up; *(embarcation)* to strand (on a sandbank); **s'~** *vi* to silt up; to get stranded.

ensacher [ăṅsáshā] *vt* to pack into bags.

ENSAM *sigle f* (= *École nationale supérieure des arts et métiers) grande école for engineering students*.

ensanglanté, e [ăṅsăṅglăṅtā] *a* covered with blood.

enseignant, e [ăṅsenyăṅ, -ăṅt] *a* teaching ♦ *nm/f* teacher.

enseigne [ăṅseny] *nf* sign ♦ *nm*: **~ de vaisseau** ensign *(US)*, lieutenant *(Brit)*; **à telle ~ que** so much so that; **être logés à la même ~** *(fig)* to be in the same boat; **~ lumineuse** neon sign.

enseignement [ăṅsenymăṅ] *nm* teaching; **~ ménager** home economics; **~ primaire** grade school *(US)* ou primary *(Brit)* education; **~ secondaire** high school *(US)* ou secondary *(Brit)* education.

enseigner [ăṅsānyā] *vt*, *vi* to teach; **~ qch à qn/à qn que** to teach sb sth/sb that.

ensemble [ăṅsăṅbl(ə)] *ad* together ♦ *nm* *(assemblage, MATH)* set; *(totalité)*: **l'~ du/ de la** the whole ou entire; *(vêtement féminin)* ensemble, suit; *(unité, harmonie)* unity; *(résidentiel)* housing development; **aller ~** to go together; **impression/idée d'~** overall ou general impression/idea; **dans l'~** *(en gros)* on the whole; **dans son ~** overall, in general; **~ vocal/musical** vocal/musical ensemble.

ensemblier [ăṅsăṅblēyā] *nm* interior designer.

ensemencer [ăṅsmăṅsā] *vt* to sow.

enserrer [ăṅsārā] *vt* to hug (tightly).

ENSET [enset] *sigle f* (= *École normale supérieure de l'enseignement technique) grande école for training technical teachers*.

ensevelir [ăṅsəvlēr] *vt* to bury.

ensilage [ăṅsēlázh] *nm* *(aliment)* silage.

ensoleillé, e [ăṅsolāyā] *a* sunny.

ensoleillement [ăṅsoleymăṅ] *nm* period ou hours *pl* of sunshine.

ensommeillé, e [ăṅsomāyā] *a* sleepy, drowsy.

ensorceler [ăṅsorsəlā] *vt* to enchant, bewitch.

ensuite [ăṅsüēt] *ad* then, next; *(plus tard)* afterwards, later; **~ de quoi** after which.

ensuivre [ăṅsüēvr(ə)]: **s'~** *vi* to follow, ensue; **il s'ensuit que ...** it follows that ...; **et tout ce qui s'ensuit** and all that goes with it.

entaché, e [ăṅtáshā] *a*: **~ de** marred by; **~ de nullité** null and void.

entacher [ăṅtáshā] *vt* to soil.

entaille [ăṅtáy] *nf* *(encoche)* notch; *(blessure)* cut; **se faire une ~** to cut o.s.

entailler [ăṅtáyā] *vt* to notch; to cut; **s'~ le doigt** to cut one's finger.

entamer [åṅtåmå] *vt* to start; (*hostilités, pourparlers*) to open; (*fig: altérer*) to make a dent in; to damage.

entartrer [åṅtårtrå]: **s'~** *vi* to fur up; (*dents*) to become covered with plaque.

entassement [åṅtåsmåṅ] *nm* (*tas*) pile, heap.

entasser [åṅtåså] *vt* (*empiler*) to pile up, heap up; (*tenir à l'étroit*) to cram together; **s'~** *vi* to pile up; to cram; **s'~ dans** to cram into.

entendement [åṅtåṅdmåṅ] *nm* understanding.

entendre [åṅtåṅdr(ə)] *vt* to hear; (*comprendre*) to understand; (*vouloir dire*) to mean; (*vouloir*): **~ être obéi/que** to intend *ou* mean to be obeyed/that; **j'ai entendu dire que** I've heard (it said) that; **je suis heureux de vous l'~ dire** I'm pleased to hear you say it; **~ parler de** to hear of; **laisser ~ que**, **donner à ~ que** to let it be understood that; **~ raison** to listen to reason; **qu'est-ce qu'il ne faut pas ~!** what next!; **j'ai mal entendu** I didn't catch what was said; **je vous entends très mal** I can hardly hear you; **s'~** *vi* (*sympathiser*) to get along; (*se mettre d'accord*) to agree; **s'~ à qch/à faire** (*être compétent*) to be good at sth/doing; **ça s'entend** (*est audible*) it's audible; **je m'entends** I mean; **entendons-nous!** let's be clear what we mean.

entendu, e [åṅtåṅdü] *pp de* **entendre** ♦ *a* (*réglé*) agreed; (*au courant: air*) knowing; **étant ~ que** since (it's understood *ou* agreed that); **(c'est) ~** all right, agreed; **c'est ~** (*concession*) all right, granted; **bien ~** of course.

entente [åṅtåṅt] *nf* (*entre amis, pays*) understanding, harmony; (*accord, traité*) agreement, understanding; **à double ~** (*sens*) with a double meaning.

entériner [åṅtårɛ̄nå] *vt* to ratify, confirm.

entérite [åṅtårɛ̄t] *nf* enteritis *q*.

enterrement [åṅtɛrmåṅ] *nm* burying; (*cérémonie*) funeral, burial; (*cortège funèbre*) funeral procession.

enterrer [åṅtårå] *vt* to bury.

entêtant, e [åṅtɛtåṅ, -åṅt] *a* heady.

entêté, e [åṅtåtå] *a* stubborn.

en-tête [åṅtɛt] *nm* heading; (*de papier à lettres*) letterhead; **papier à ~** letterhead (*US*), headed notepaper (*Brit*).

entêtement [åṅtɛtmåṅ] *nm* stubbornness.

entêter [åṅtåtå]: **s'~** *vi*: **s'~ (à faire)** to persist (in doing).

enthousiasmant, e [åṅtōōzyåsmåṅ, -åṅt] *a* exciting.

enthousiasme [åṅtōōzyåsm(ə)] *nm* enthusiasm; **avec ~** enthusiastically.

enthousiasmé, e [åṅtōōzyåsmå] *a* filled with enthusiasm.

enthousiasmer [åṅtōōzyåsmå] *vt* to fill with enthusiasm; **s'~ (pour qch)** to get enthusiastic (about sth).

enthousiaste [åṅtōōzyåst(ə)] *a* enthusiastic.

enticher [åṅtēshå]: **s'~ de** *vt* to become infatuated with.

entier, ière [åṅtyå, -yer] *a* (*non entamé, en totalité*) whole; (*total, complet*) complete; (*fig: caractère*) unbending, averse to compromise ♦ *nm* (*MATH*) whole; **en ~** totally; in its entirety; **se donner tout ~ à qch**

to devote o.s. completely to sth; **lait ~** whole (*US*) *ou* full-cream (*Brit*) milk; **pain ~** whole wheat (*US*) *ou* wholemeal (*Brit*) bread; **nombre ~** whole number.

entièrement [åṅtycrmåṅ] *ad* entirely, completely, wholly.

entité [åṅtētå] *nf* entity.

entomologie [åṅtomolozhē] *nf* entomology.

entonner [åṅtonå] *vt* (*chanson*) to strike up.

entonnoir [åṅtonwår] *nm* (*ustensile*) funnel; (*trou*) shell-hole, crater.

entorse [åṅtors(ə)] *nf* (*MÉD*) sprain; (*fig*): **~ à la loi/au règlement** infringement of the law/rule; **se faire une ~ à la cheville/au poignet** to sprain one's ankle/wrist.

entortiller [åṅtortēyå] *vt* (*envelopper*): **~ qch dans/avec** to wrap sth in/with; (*enrouler*): **~ qch autour de** to twist *ou* wind sth (a)round; (*fam*): **~ qn** to get (a)round sb; (: *duper*) to hoodwink *ou* trick sb; **s'~ dans** (*draps*) to roll o.s. up in; (*fig: réponses*) to get tangled up in.

entourage [åṅtōōrázh] *nm* circle; family (circle); (*d'une vedette etc*) entourage; (*ce qui enclôt*) border, frame.

entouré, e [åṅtōōrå] *a* (*recherché, admiré*) popular; **~ de** surrounded by.

entourer [åṅtōōrå] *vt* to surround; (*apporter son soutien à*) to rally round; **~ de** to surround with; (*trait*) to encircle with; **s'~ de** to surround o.s. with; **s'~ de précautions** to take all possible precautions.

entourloupette [åṅtōōrlōōpet] *nf* mean trick.

entournures [åṅtōōrnür] *nfpl*: **gêné aux ~** in financial difficulties; (*fig*) a bit awkward.

entracte [åṅtråkt(ə)] *nm* interval.

entraide [åṅtred] *nf* mutual aid *ou* assistance.

entraider [åṅtrådå]: **s'~** *vi* to help each other.

entrailles [åṅtråy] *nfpl* entrails; (*humaines*) bowels.

entrain [åṅtraṅ] *nm* spirit; **avec ~** (*répondre, travailler*) energetically; **faire qch sans ~** to do sth half-heartedly *ou* without enthusiasm.

entraînant, e [åṅtrenåṅ, -åṅt] *a* (*musique*) stirring, rousing.

entraînement [åṅtrenmåṅ] *nm* training; (*TECH*): **~ à chaîne/galet** chain/wheel drive; **manquer d'~** to be unfit; **~ par ergots/friction** (*INFORM*) tractor/friction feed.

entraîner [åṅtrånå] *vt* (*tirer: wagons*) to pull; (*charrier*) to carry *ou* drag along; (*TECH*) to drive; (*emmener: personne*) to take (off); (*mener à l'assaut, influencer*) to lead; (*SPORT*) to train; (*impliquer*) to entail; (*causer*) to lead to, bring about; **~ qn à faire** (*inciter*) to lead sb to do; **s'~** (*SPORT*) to train; **s'~ à qch/à faire** to train o.s. for sth/to do.

entraîneur [åṅtrencœr] *nm* (*SPORT*) coach, trainer; (*HIPPISME*) trainer.

entraîneuse [åṅtrencœz] *nf* (*de bar*) B-girl (*US*), hostess (*Brit*).

entrapercevoir [åṅtråpersəvwår] *vt* to catch a glimpse of.

entrave [åṅtråv] *nf* hindrance.

entraver [åṅtråvå] *vt* (*circulation*) to hold up; (*action, progrès*) to hinder, hamper.

entre [åṅtr(ə)] *prép* between; (*parmi*) among(st); **l'un d'~ eux/nous** one of them/

us; **le meilleur d'~ eux/nous** the best of them/us; **ils préfèrent rester ~ eux** they prefer to keep to themselves; **~ autres (choses)** among other things; **~ nous, ...** between ourselves ..., between you and me ...; **ils se battent ~ eux** they are fighting among(st) themselves.

entrebâillé, e [ȧntrəbâyā] *a* half-open, ajar.

entrebâillement [ȧntrəbâymáṅ] *nm*: **dans l'~ (de la porte)** in the half-open door.

entrebâiller [ȧntrəbâyā] *vt* to half open.

entrechat [ȧntrəshá] *nm* leap.

entrechoquer [ȧntrəshokā]: **s'~** *vi* to knock *ou* bang together.

entrecôte [ȧntrəkōt] *nf* entrecôte *ou* rib steak.

entrecoupé, e [ȧntrəkōōpā] *a* (*paroles, voix*) broken.

entrecouper [ȧntrəkōōpā] *vt*: **~ qch de** to intersperse sth with; **~ un récit/voyage de** to interrupt a story/journey with; **s'~** (*traits, lignes*) to cut across each other.

entrecroiser [ȧntrəkrwázā] *vt*, **s'~** *vi* to intertwine.

entrée [ȧntrā] *nf* entrance; (*accès: au cinéma etc*) admission; (*billet*) (admission) ticket; (*CULIN*) first course; (*COMM: de marchandises*) entry; (*INFORM*) entry, input; **~s** *nfpl*: **avoir ses ~s chez** *ou* **auprès de** to be a welcome visitor to; **d'~** *ad* from the outset; **erreur d'~** input error; **"~ interdite"** "no admittance *ou* entry"; **~ des artistes** stage door; **~ en matière** introduction; **~ en scène** entrance; **~ de service** service entrance.

entrefaites [ȧntrəfet]: **sur ces ~** *ad* at this juncture.

entrefilet [ȧntrəfēle] *nm* (*article*) paragraph, short report.

entregent [ȧntrəzháṅ] *nm*: **avoir de l'~** to have an easy manner.

entre-jambes [ȧntrəzháṅb] *nm inv* crotch.

entrelacement [ȧntrəlásmáṅ] *nm*: **un ~ de ...** a network of ....

entrelacer [ȧntrəlásā] *vt*, **s'~** *vi* to intertwine.

entrelarder [ȧntrəlárdā] *vt* to lard; (*fig*): **entrelardé de** interspersed with.

entremêler [ȧntrəmālā] *vt*: **~ qch de** to (inter)mingle sth with.

entremets [ȧntrəme] *nm* (cream) dessert.

entremetteur, euse [ȧntrəmetœr, -ēz] *nm/f* go-between.

entremettre [ȧntrəmetr(ə)]: **s'~** *vi* to intervene.

entremise [ȧntrəmēz] *nf* intervention; **par l'~ de** through.

entrepont [ȧntrəpóṅ] *nm* steerage; **dans l'~** in steerage.

entreposer [ȧntrəpōzā] *vt* to store, put into storage.

entrepôt [ȧntrəpō] *nm* warehouse.

entreprenant, e [ȧntrəprənáṅ, -áṅt] *vb voir* **entreprendre ♦** *a* (*actif*) enterprising; (*trop galant*) forward.

entreprendre [ȧntrəprάndr(ə)] *vt* (*se lancer dans*) to undertake; (*commencer*) to begin *ou* start (upon); (*personne*) to buttonhole; **~ qn sur un sujet** to tackle sb on a subject; **~ de faire** to undertake to do.

entrepreneur [ȧntrəprənœr] *nm*: **~ (en**

bâtiment) (building) contractor; **~ de pompes funèbres** funeral director, undertaker.

entreprenne [ȧntrəpren] *etc vb voir* **entreprendre**.

entrepris, e [ȧntrəprē, -ēz] *pp de* **entreprendre ♦** *nf* (*société*) firm, business; (*action*) undertaking, venture.

entrer [ȧntrā] *vi* to go (*ou* come) in, enter **♦** *vt* (*INFORM*) to input, enter; (**faire**) **~ qch dans** to get sth into; **~ dans** (*gén*) to enter; (*pièce*) to go (*ou* come) into, enter; (*club*) to join; (*heurter*) to run into; (*partager: vues, craintes de qn*) to share; (*être une composante de*) to go into; (*faire partie de*) to form part of; **~ au couvent** to enter a convent; **~ à l'hôpital** to go into the hospital; **~ dans le système** (*INFORM*) to log in; **~ en fureur** to become angry; **~ en ébullition** to start to boil; **~ en scène** to come on stage; **laisser ~ qn/qch** to let sb/sth in; **faire ~** (*visiteur*) to show in.

entresol [ȧntrəsol] *nm* entresol, mezzanine.

entre-temps [ȧntrətáṅ] *ad* meanwhile, (in the) meantime.

entretenir [ȧntrətnēr] *vt* to maintain; (*amitié*) to keep alive; (*famille, maîtresse*) to support, keep; **~ qn (de)** to speak to sb (about); **s'~ (de)** to converse (about); **~ qn dans l'erreur** to let sb remain in ignorance.

entretenu, e [ȧntrətnü] *pp de* **entretenir ♦** *a* (*femme*) kept; **bien/mal ~** (*maison, jardin*) well/badly kept.

entretien [ȧntrətyaṅ] *nm* maintenance; (*discussion*) discussion, talk; (*audience*) interview; **frais d'~** maintenance charges.

entretiendrai [ȧntrətyaṅdrā], **entretiens** [ȧntrətyaṅ] *etc vb voir* **entretenir**.

entre-tuer [ȧntrətüā]: **s'~** *vi* to kill one another.

entreverrai [ȧntrəverā], **entrevit** [ȧntrəvē] *etc vb voir* **entrevoir**.

entrevoir [ȧntrəvwár] *vt* (*à peine*) to make out; (*brièvement*) to catch a glimpse of.

entrevu, e [ȧntrəvü] *pp de* **entrevoir ♦** *nf* meeting; (*audience*) interview.

entrouvert, e [ȧntrōōver, -ert(ə)] *pp de* **entrouvrir ♦** *a* half-open.

entrouvrir [ȧntrōōvrēr] *vt*, **s'~** *vi* to half open.

énumération [ānümārȧsyóṅ] *nf* enumeration.

énumérer [ānümārā] *vt* to list, enumerate.

énurésie [ānürāzē] *nf* enuresis.

envahir [ȧnvȧēr] *vt* to invade; (*suj: inquiétude, peur*) to come over.

envahissant, e [ȧnvȧēsáṅ, -áṅt] *a* (*péj: personne*) interfering, intrusive.

envahissement [ȧnvȧēsmáṅ] *nm* invasion.

envahisseur [ȧnvȧēsœr] *nm* (*MIL*) invader.

envasement [ȧnnvȧzmáṅ] *nm* silting up.

envaser [ȧnvȧzā]: **s'~** *vi* to get bogged down (in the mud).

enveloppe [ȧnvlop] *nf* (*de lettre*) envelope; (*TECH*) casing; outer layer; **mettre sous ~** to put in an envelope; **~ autocollante** self-seal envelope; **~ budgétaire** budget; **~ à fenêtre** window envelope.

envelopper [ȧnvlopā] *vt* to wrap; (*fig*) to envelop, shroud; **s'~ dans un châle/une couverture** to wrap o.s. in a shawl/blanket.

envenimer [ȧṅvnēmā] *vt* to aggravate; **s'~** *vi* (*plaie*) to fester; (*situation, relations*) to worsen.

envergure [ȧṅvergür] *nf* (*d'un oiseau, avion*) wingspan; (*fig: étendue*) scope; (: *valeur*) calibre.

enverrai [ȧṅverā] *etc vb voir* **envoyer**.

envers [ȧṅver] *prép* towards, to ♦ *nm* other side; (*d'une étoffe*) wrong side; **à l'~** upside down; back to front; (*vêtement*) inside out; **~ et contre tous** *ou* **tout** against all opposition.

enviable [ȧṅvyábl(ə)] *a* enviable; **peu ~** unenviable.

envie [ȧṅvē] *nf* (*sentiment*) envy; (*souhait*) desire, wish; (*tache sur la peau*) birthmark; (*filet de peau*) hangnail; **avoir ~ de** to feel like; (*désir plus fort*) to want; **avoir ~ de faire** to feel like doing; to want to do; **avoir ~ que** to wish that; **donner à qn l'~ de faire** to make sb want to do; **ça lui fait ~** he would like that.

envier [ȧṅvyā] *vt* to envy; **~ qch à qn** to envy sb sth; **n'avoir rien à ~ à** to have no cause to be envious of.

envieux, euse [ȧṅvyœ̄, -ēz] *a* envious.

environ [ȧṅvērȯṅ] *ad*: **~ 3 h/2 km, 3 h/2 km ~** (around) about 3 o'clock/2 km, 3 o'clock/2 km or so.

environnant, e [ȧṅvēronȧṅ, -ȧṅt] *a* surrounding.

environnement [ȧṅvēronmȧṅ] *nm* environment.

environnementaliste [ȧṅvēronmȧṅtȧlēst(ə)] *nm/f* environmentalist.

environner [ȧṅvēronā] *vt* to surround.

environs [ȧṅvērȯṅ] *nmpl* surroundings; **aux ~ de** around.

envisageable [ȧṅvēzȧzhȧbl(ə)] *a* conceivable.

envisager [ȧṅvēzȧzhā] *vt* (*examiner, considérer*) to view, contemplate; (*avoir en vue*) to envisage; **~ de faire** to consider *ou* contemplate doing.

envoi [ȧṅvwȧ] *nm* sending; (*paquet*) parcel, consignment; **~ contre remboursement** (*COMM*) cash on delivery.

envoie [ȧṅvwȧ] *etc vb voir* **envoyer**.

envol [ȧṅvol] *nm* takeoff.

envolée [ȧṅvolā] *nf* (*fig*) flight.

envoler [ȧṅvolā]: **s'~** *vi* (*oiseau*) to fly away *ou* off; (*avion*) to take off; (*papier, feuille*) to blow away; (*fig*) to vanish (into thin air).

envoûtement [ȧṅvōōtmȧṅ] *nm* bewitchment.

envoûter [ȧṅvōōtā] *vt* to bewitch.

envoyé, e [ȧṅvwáyā] *nm/f* (*POL*) envoy; (*PRESSE*) correspondent ♦ *a*: **bien ~** (*remarque, réponse*) well-aimed.

envoyer [ȧṅvwáyā] *vt* to send; (*lancer*) to hurl, throw; **~ une gifle/un sourire à qn** to aim a blow/flash a smile at sb; **~ les couleurs** to run up the colors; **~ chercher** to send for; **~ par le fond** (*bateau*) to send to the bottom.

envoyeur, euse [ȧṅvwáyœr, -ēz] *nm/f* sender.

enzyme [ȧṅzēm] *nm* enzyme.

éolien, ne [āolyȧṅ, -en] *a* wind *cpd*; **pompe ~ne** windmill.

EOR *sigle m* (= *élève officier de réserve*) ≈ military cadet.

éosine [āozēn] *nf* eosin (*antiseptic used in France to treat skin ailments*).

épagneul, e [āpȧnyœl] *nm/f* spaniel.

épais, se [āpe, -es] *a* thick.

épaisseur [āpesœr] *nf* thickness.

épaissir [āpāsēr] *vt*, **s'~** *vi* to thicken.

épaississement [āpāsēsmȧṅ] *nm* thickening.

épanchement [āpȧṅshmȧṅ] *nm*: **un ~ de sinovie** water on the knee; **~s** *nmpl* (*fig*) (sentimental) outpourings.

épancher [āpȧṅshā] *vt* to give vent to; **s'~** *vi* to open one's heart; (*liquide*) to pour out.

épandage [āpȧṅdȧzh] *nm* manure spreading.

épanoui, e [āpȧnwē] *a* (*éclos, ouvert, développé*) blooming; (*radieux*) radiant.

épanouir [āpȧnwēr]: **s'~** *vi* (*fleur*) to bloom, open out; (*visage*) to light up; (*fig: se développer*) to blossom (out); (: *mentalement*) to open up.

épanouissement [āpȧnwēsmȧṅ] *nm* blossoming; opening up.

épargnant, e [āpȧrnyȧṅ, -ȧṅt] *nm/f* saver, investor.

épargne [āpȧrny(ə)] *nf* saving; **l'~-logement** property investment.

épargner [āpȧrnyā] *vt* to save; (*ne pas tuer ou endommager*) to spare ♦ *vi* to save; **~ qch à qn** to spare sb sth.

éparpiller [āpȧrpēyā] *vt* to scatter; (*pour répartir*) to disperse; (*fig: efforts*) to dissipate; **s'~** *vi* to scatter; (*fig*) to dissipate one's efforts.

épars, e [āpár, -árs(ə)] *a* (*maisons*) scattered; (*cheveux*) sparse.

épatant, e [āpátȧṅ, -ȧṅt] *a* (*fam*) super, splendid.

épaté, e [āpátā] *a*: **nez ~** flat nose (with wide nostrils).

épater [āpátā] *vt* to amaze; (*impressionner*) to impress.

épaule [āpōl] *nf* shoulder.

épaulé-jeté, pl épaulés-jetés [āpōlāzhətā] *nm* (*SPORT*) clean-and-jerk.

épaulement [āpōlmȧṅ] *nm* escarpment; (*mur*) retaining wall.

épauler [āpōlā] *vt* (*aider*) to back up, support; (*arme*) to raise (to one's shoulder) ♦ *vi* to (take) aim.

épaulette [āpōlet] *nf* (*MIL, d'un veston*) epaulette; (*de combinaison*) shoulder strap.

épave [āpáv] *nf* wreck.

épée [āpā] *nf* sword.

épeler [āplā] *vt* to spell.

éperdu, e [āperdü] *a* (*personne*) overcome; (*sentiment*) passionate; (*fuite*) frantic.

éperdument [āperdümȧṅ] *ad* (*aimer*) wildly; (*espérer*) fervently.

éperlan [āperlȧṅ] *nm* (*ZOOL*) smelt.

éperon [āprȯṅ] *nm* spur.

éperonner [āpronā] *vt* to spur (on); (*navire*) to ram.

épervier [āpervyā] *nm* (*ZOOL*) sparrowhawk; (*PÊCHE*) casting net.

éphèbe [āfeb] *nm* beautiful young man.

éphémère [āfāmer] *a* ephemeral, fleeting.

éphéméride [āfāmārēd] *nf* block *ou* tear-off calendar.

épi [āpē] *nm* (*de blé, d'orge*) ear; **~ de cheveux** tuft of hair; **stationnement/se garer**

en ~ parking/to park at an angle to the curb.
épice [āpēs] *nf* spice.
épicé, e [āpēsā] *a* highly spiced, spicy; (*fig*)
spicy.
épicéa [āpēsāá] *nm* spruce.
épicentre [āpēsântr(ə)] *nm* epicenter (*US*),
epicentre (*Brit*).
épicer [āpēsā] *vt* to spice; (*fig*) to add spice to.
épicerie [āpēsrē] *nf* (*magasin*) grocery,
grocer's store (*US*) *ou* shop (*Brit*); (*denrées*)
groceries *pl*; ~ **fine** delicatessen (shop).
épicier, ière [āpēsyā, -yer] *nm/f* grocer.
épidémie [āpēdāmē] *nf* epidemic.
épidémique [āpēdāmēk] *a* epidemic.
épiderme [āpēderm(ə)] *nm* skin, epidermis.
épidermique [āpēdermēk] *a* skin *cpd*,
epidermic.
épier [āpyā] *vt* to spy on, watch closely; (*occasion*) to look out for.
épieu, x [āpyœ] *nm* (hunting-)spear.
épigramme [āpēgrám] *nf* epigram.
épilation [āpēlásyôn] *nf* removal of unwanted
hair.
épilatoire [āpēlátwár] *a* depilatory, hair-
removing.
épilepsie [āpēlepsē] *nf* epilepsy.
épileptique [āpēleptēk] *a*, *nm/f* epileptic.
épiler [āpēlā] *vt* (*jambes*) to remove the hair
from; (*sourcils*) to pluck; **s'~ les jambes** to
remove the hair from one's legs; **s'~ les
sourcils** to pluck one's eyebrows; **se faire ~**
to get unwanted hair removed; **crème à ~**
hair-removing *ou* depilatory cream; **pince à
~** eyebrow tweezers.
épilogue [āpēlog] *nm* (*fig*) conclusion, dénouement.
épiloguer [āpēlogā] *vi*: ~ **sur** to hold forth on.
épinard [āpēnár] *nm* (*aussi*: ~**s**) spinach *sg*.
épine [āpēn] *nf* thorn, prickle; (*d'oursin etc*)
spine, prickle; ~ **dorsale** backbone.
épineux, euse [āpēnœ, -œz] *a* thorny, prickly.
épinglage [āpanglázh] *nm* pinning.
épingle [āpangl(ə)] *nf* pin; **tirer son ~ du jeu**
to play one's game well; **tiré à quatre ~s**
well turned-out; **monter qch en ~** to build
sth up, make a thing of sth (*fam*); ~ **à
chapeau** hatpin; ~ **à cheveux** hairpin;
virage en ~ à cheveux hairpin curve (*US*)
ou bend (*Brit*); ~ **de cravate** stickpin (*US*),
tiepin; ~ **de nourrice** *ou* **de sûreté** *ou* **double
safety pin**, diaper (*US*) *ou* nappy (*Brit*) pin.
épingler [āpanglā] *vt* (*badge, décoration*): ~
qch sur to pin sth on(to); (*COUTURE*: *tissu,
robe*) to pin together; (*fam*) to catch, nab.
épinière [āpēnyer] *af voir* **moelle**.
Epiphanie [āpēfánē] *nf* Epiphany.
épique [āpēk] *a* epic.
épiscopal, e, aux [āpēskopál, -ō] *a* episcopal.
épiscopat [āpēskopá] *nm* bishopric,
episcopate.
épisiotomie [āpēzyotōmē] *nf* (*MÉD*)
episiotomy.
épisode [āpēzod] *nm* episode; **film/roman à
~s** serialized film/novel, serial.
épisodique [āpēzodēk] *a* occasional.
épissure [āpēsür] *nf* splice.
épistémologie [āpēstāmolozhē] *nf* epistemol-
ogy.
épistolaire [āpēstoler] *a* epistolary; **être en**

relations ~s avec qn to correspond with sb.
épitaphe [āpētáf] *nf* epitaph.
épithète [āpētet] *nf* (*nom, surnom*) epithet;
adjectif ~ attributive adjective.
épître [āpētr(ə)] *nf* epistle.
éploré, e [āplorā] *a* in tears, tearful.
épluchage [āplüsházh] *nm* peeling; (*de dossier
etc*) careful reading *ou* analysis.
épluche-légumes [āplüshlāgüm] *nm inv*
potato peeler.
éplucher [āplüshā] *vt* (*fruit, légumes*) to peel;
(*comptes, dossier*) to go over with a fine-tooth
comb.
éplucheur [āplüshœr] *nm* (automatic) peeler.
épluchures [āplüshür] *nfpl* peelings.
épointer [āpwantā] *vt* to blunt.
éponge [āpônzh] *nf* sponge; **passer l'~ (sur)**
(*fig*) to let bygones be bygones (with regard
to); **jeter l'~** (*fig*) to throw in the towel; ~
métallique scouring pad.
éponger [āpônzhā] *vt* (*liquide*) to mop *ou*
sponge up; (*surface*) to sponge; (*fig: déficit*)
to soak up, absorb; **s'~ le front** to mop one's
brow.
épopée [āpopā] *nf* epic.
époque [āpok] *nf* (*de l'histoire*) age, era; (*de
l'année, la vie*) time; **d'~** *a* (*meuble*) period
cpd; **à cette ~** at this (*ou* that) time *ou*
period; **faire ~** to make history.
épouiller [āpōōyā] *vt* to pick lice off; (*avec un
produit*) to delouse.
époumoner [āpōōmonā]: **s'~** *vi* to shout (*ou*
sing) o.s. hoarse.
épouse [āpōōz] *nf* wife (*pl* wives).
épouser [āpōōzā] *vt* to marry; (*fig: idées*) to
espouse; (*: forme*) to fit.
époussetage [āpōōstázh] *nm* dusting.
épousseter [āpōōstā] *vt* to dust.
époustouflant, e [āpōōstōōflàn, -ánt] *a*
staggering, mind-boggling.
époustoufler [āpōōstōōflā] *vt* to flabbergast,
astound.
épouvantable [āpōōvântábl(ə)] *a* appalling,
dreadful.
épouvantail [āpōōvântáy] *nm* (*à moineaux*)
scarecrow; (*fig*) bog(e)y; bugbear.
épouvante [āpōōvânt] *nf* terror; **film d'~**
horror film.
épouvanter [āpōōvântā] *vt* to terrify.
époux [āpōō] *nm* husband ♦ *nmpl*: **les ~** the
(married) couple, the husband and wife.
éprendre [āprándr(ə)]: **s'~ de** *vt* to fall in
love with.
épreuve [āprœv] *nf* (*d'examen*) test;
(*malheur, difficulté*) trial, ordeal; (*PHOTO*)
print; (*TYPO*) proof; (*SPORT*) event; **à l'~
des balles/du feu** (*vêtement*) bulletproof/
fireproof; **à toute ~** unfailing; **mettre à l'~**
to put to the test; ~ **de force** test of
strength; (*fig*) showdown; ~ **de résistance**
test of resistance; ~ **de sélection** (*SPORT*)
heat.
épris, e [āprē, -ēz] *vb voir* **éprendre** ♦ *a*: ~ **de**
in love with.
éprouvant, e [āprōōvàn, -ánt] *a* trying.
éprouvé, e [āprōōvā] *a* tested, proven.
éprouver [āprōōvā] *vt* (*tester*) to test; (*mettre
à l'épreuve*) to put to the test; (*marquer,
faire souffrir*) to afflict, distress; (*ressentir*)

to experience.

éprouvette [āp͞r͞o͞ovet] *nf* test tube.

EPS *sigle f* (= *Education physique et sportive*) ≈ PE.

épuisant, e [āp͞ūēzáṅ, -áṅt] *a* exhausting.

épuisé, e [āp͞ūēzā] *a* exhausted; (*livre*) out of print.

épuisement [āp͞ūēzmáṅ] *nm* exhaustion; **jusqu'à ~ des stocks** while stocks last.

épuiser [āp͞ūēzā] *vt* (*fatiguer*) to exhaust, wear *ou* tire out; (*stock, sujet*) to exhaust; **s'~** *vi* to wear *ou* tire o.s. out, exhaust o.s.; (*stock*) to run out.

épuisette [āp͞ūēzet] *nf* landing net; shrimp(ing) net.

épuration [āp͞ūrāsyóṅ] *nf* purification; purging; refinement.

épurer [āp͞ūrā] *vt* (*liquide*) to purify; (*parti, administration*) to purge; (*langue, texte*) to refine.

équarrir [ākárēr] *vt* (*pierre, arbre*) to square (off); (*animal*) to quarter.

équateur [ākwátœr] *nm* equator; **(la république de) l'É~** Ecuador.

équation [ākwásyóṅ] *nf* equation; **mettre en ~ to equate; ~ du premier/second degré** linear/quadratic equation.

équatorial, e, aux [ākwátoryál, -ō] *a* equatorial.

équatorien, ne [ākwátoryaṅ, -en] *a* Ecuadorian ♦ *nm/f:* **É~, ne** Ecuadorian.

équerre [āker] *nf* (*à dessin*) (set) square; (*pour fixer*) brace; **en ~** at right angles; **à l'~, d'~** straight; **double ~** T-square.

équestre [ākestr(ə)] *a* equestrian.

équeuter [ākœtā] *vt* (CULIN) to remove the stalk(s) from.

équidé [ākēdā] *nm* (ZOOL) member of the horse family.

équidistance [ākūēdēstáṅs] *nf:* **à ~ (de)** equidistant (from).

équidistant, e [ākūēdēstáṅ, -áṅt] *a:* **~ (de)** equidistant (from).

équilatéral, e, aux [ākūēlátārál, -ō] *a* equilateral.

équilibrage [ākēlēbrázh] *nm* (AUTO): **~ des roues** wheel balancing.

équilibre [ākēlēbr(ə)] *nm* balance; (*d'une balance*) equilibrium; **~ budgétaire** balanced budget; **garder/perdre l'~** to keep/lose one's balance; **être en ~** to be balanced; **mettre en ~** to make steady; **avoir le sens de l'~** to be well-balanced.

équilibré, e [ākēlēbrā] *a* (*fig*) well-balanced, stable.

équilibrer [ākēlēbrā] *vt* to balance; **s'~** (*poids*) to balance; (*fig: défauts etc*) to balance each other out.

équilibriste [ākēlēbrēst(ə)] *nm/f* tightrope walker.

équinoxe [ākēnoks] *nm* equinox.

équipage [ākēpázh] *nm* crew; **en grand ~** in great array.

équipe [ākēp] *nf* team; (*bande: parfois péj*) bunch; **travailler par ~s** to work in shifts; **travailler en ~** to work as a team; **faire ~ avec** to team up with; **~ de chercheurs** research team; **~ de secours** *ou* **de sauvetage** rescue team.

équipé, e [ākēpā] *a* (*cuisine etc*) equipped, fitted(-out) ♦ *nf* escapade.

équipement [ākēpmáṅ] *nm* equipment; **~s** *nmpl* amenities, facilities; installations; **biens/dépenses d'~** capital goods/expenditure; **ministère de l'É~** department of public works; **~s sportifs/collectifs** sports/community facilities *ou* resources.

équiper [ākēpā] *vt* to equip; (*voiture, cuisine*) to equip, fit out; **~ qn/qch de** to equip sb/sth with; **s'~** (*sportif*) to equip o.s.

équipier, ière [ākēpyā, -yer] *nm/f* team member.

équitable [ākētábl(ə)] *a* fair.

équitation [ākētásyóṅ] *nf* (horse-)riding; **faire de l'~** to go (horse-)riding.

équité [ākētā] *nf* equity.

équivaille [ākēváy] *etc vb voir* **équivaloir.**

équivalence [ākēválāṅs] *nf* equivalence.

équivalent, e [ākēválāṅ, -áṅt] *a, nm* equivalent.

équivaloir [ākēválwár]: **~ à** *vt* to be equivalent to; (*représenter*) to amount to.

équivaut [ākēvō] *etc vb voir* **équivaloir.**

équivoque [ākēvok] *a* equivocal, ambiguous; (*louche*) dubious ♦ *nf* ambiguity.

érable [ārábl(ə)] *nm* maple.

éradiquer [ārádēkā] *vt* to eradicate.

érafler [āráflā] *vt* to scratch; **s'~ la main/les jambes** to scrape *ou* scratch one's hand/legs.

éraflure [āráflūr] *nf* scratch.

éraillé, e [āráyā] *a* (*voix*) rasping, hoarse.

ère [er] *nf* era; **en l'an 1050 de notre ~** in the year 1050 A.D.

érection [ārēksyóṅ] *nf* erection.

éreintant, e [āraṅtáṅ, -áṅt] *a* exhausting.

éreinté, e [āraṅtā] *a* exhausted.

éreintement [āraṅtmáṅ] *nm* exhaustion.

éreinter [āraṅtā] *vt* to exhaust, wear out; (*fig: critiquer*) to pan; **s'~ (à faire qch/à qch)** to wear o.s. out (doing sth/with sth).

ergonomie [ergonomē] *nf* ergonomics *sg.*

ergonomique [ergonomēk] *a* ergonomic.

ergot [ergō] *nm* (*de coq*) spur; (TECH) lug.

ergoter [ergotā] *vi* to split hairs, argue over details.

ergoteur, euse [ergotœr, -œz] *nm/f* hairsplitter.

ériger [ārēzhā] *vt* (*monument*) to erect; **~ qch en principe/loi** to make sth a principle/law; **s'~ en critique (de)** to set o.s. up as a critic (of).

ermitage [ermētázh] *nm* retreat.

ermite [ermēt] *nm* hermit.

éroder [ārodā] *vt* to erode.

érogène [ārozhen] *a* erogenous.

érosion [ārōzyóṅ] *nf* erosion.

érotique [ārotēk] *a* erotic.

érotiquement [ārotēkmáṅ] *ad* erotically.

érotisme [ārotēsm(ə)] *nm* eroticism.

errance [eráṅs] *nf* wandering.

errant, e [eráṅ, -áṅt] *a:* **un chien ~** a stray dog.

erratum, a [erátom, -á] *nm* erratum (*pl* -a).

errements [ermáṅ] *nmpl* misguided ways.

errer [erā] *vi* to wander.

erreur [erœr] *nf* mistake, error; (INFORM: *de programme*) bug; (*morale*): **~s** *nfpl* errors; **être dans l'~** to be wrong; **induire qn en ~**

to mislead sb; **par** ~ by mistake; **sauf** ~ unless I'm mistaken; **faire** ~ to be mistaken; ~ **de date** mistake in the date; ~ **de fait** error of fact; ~ **d'impression** (*TYPO*) misprint; ~ **judiciaire** miscarriage of justice; ~ **de jugement** error of judgment; ~ **matérielle** *ou* **d'écriture** clerical error; ~ **tactique** tactical error.

erroné, e [eronā] *a* wrong, erroneous.
éructer [ārüktā] *vi* to belch.
érudit, e [ārüdē, -ēt] *a* erudite, learned ♦ *nm/f* scholar.
érudition [ārüdēsyóń] *nf* erudition, scholarship.
éruptif, ive [ārüptēf, -ēv] *a* eruptive.
éruption [ārüpsyóń] *nf* eruption; (*cutanée*) outbreak; (: *boutons*) rash; (*fig: de joie, colère, folie*) outburst.
es [e] *vb voir* **être.**
ès [es] *prép:* **licencié** ~ **lettres/sciences** ≈ Bachelor of Arts/Science; **docteur** ~ **lettres** ≈ doctor of philosophy, PhD.
E/S *abr* (= *entrée/sortie*) I/O (= *in/out*).
esbroufe [esbrōōf] *nf:* **faire de l'**~ to put (*US*) *ou* have (*Brit*) people on.
escabeau, x [eskábō] *nm* (*tabouret*) stool; (*échelle*) stepladder.
escadre [eskádr(ə)] *nf* (*NAVIG*) squadron; (*AVIAT*) wing.
escadrille [eskádrēy] *nf* (*AVIAT*) flight.
escadron [eskádróń] *nm* squadron.
escalade [eskálád] *nf* climbing *q*; (*POL etc*) escalation.
escalader [eskáládā] *vt* to climb, scale.
escale [eskál] *nf* (*NAVIG*) call; (: *port*) port of call; (*AVIAT*) stop(over); **faire** ~ **à** to put in at, call in at; to stop over at; ~ **technique** (*AVIAT*) refuelling stop.
escalier [eskályā] *nm* stairs *pl*; **dans l'**~ *ou* **les** ~**s** on the stairs; **descendre l'**~ *ou* **les** ~**s** to go downstairs; ~ **mécanique** *ou* **roulant** escalator; ~ **de secours** fire escape; ~ **de service** backstairs; ~ **à vis** *ou* **en colimaçon** spiral staircase.
escalope [eskálop] *nf* cutlet (*US*), escalope (*Brit*).
escamotable [eskámotábl(ə)] *a* (*train d'atterrissage, antenne*) retractable; (*table, lit*) fold-away.
escamoter [eskámotā] *vt* (*esquiver*) to get around, evade; (*faire disparaître*) to conjure away; (*dérober: portefeuille etc*) to snatch; (*train d'atterrissage*) to retract; (*mots*) to leave out, skip.
escapade [eskápád] *nf:* **faire une** ~ to go on a jaunt; (*s'enfuir*) to run away *ou* off.
escarbille [eskárbēy] *nf* cinder.
escarcelle [eskársel] *nf:* **faire tomber dans l'**~ (*argent*) to bring in.
escargot [eskárgō] *nm* snail.
escarmouche [eskármōōsh] *nf* (*MIL*) skirmish; (*fig: propos hostiles*) angry exchange.
escarpé, e [eskárpā] *a* steep.
escarpement [eskárpəmáń] *nm* steep slope.
escarpin [eskárpań] *nm* flat(-heeled) shoe.
escarre [eskár] *nf* bedsore.
Escaut [eskō] *nm:* **l'**~ the Scheldt.
escient [āsyáń] *nm:* **à bon** ~ advisedly.
esclaffer [esklâfā] **s'**~ *vi* to guffaw.
esclandre [esklándr(ə)] *nm* scene, fracas.

esclavage [esklávázh] *nm* slavery.
esclave [eskláv] *nm/f* slave; **être** ~ **de** (*fig*) to be a slave of.
escogriffe [eskogrēf] *nm* (*péj*) beanpole.
escompte [eskóńt] *nm* discount.
escompter [eskóńtā] *vt* (*COMM*) to discount; (*espérer*) to expect, anticipate; ~ **que** to reckon *ou* expect that.
escorte [eskort(ə)] *nf* escort; **faire** ~ **à** to escort.
escorter [eskortā] *vt* to escort.
escorteur [eskortœr] *nm* (*NAVIG*) escort (ship).
escouade [eskwàd] *nf* squad; (*fig: groupe de personnes*) group.
escrime [eskrēm] *nf* fencing; **faire de l'**~ to fence.
escrimer [eskrēmā]: **s'**~ *vi:* **s'**~ **à faire** to wear o.s. out doing.
escrimeur, euse [eskrēmœr, -œz] *nm/f* fencer.
escroc [eskrō] *nm* swindler, con-man.
escroquer [eskrokā] *vt:* ~ **qn (de qch)/qch à qn** to swindle sb (out of sth)/sth out of sb.
escroquerie [eskrokrē] *nf* swindle.
ésotérique [āzotārēk] *a* esoteric.
espace [espás] *nm* space; ~ **publicitaire** advertising space; ~ **vital** living space.
espacé, e [espásā] *a* spaced out.
espacement [espásmáń] *nm:* ~ **proportionnel** proportional spacing (*on printer*).
espacer [espásā] *vt* to space out; **s'**~ *vi* (*visites etc*) to become less frequent.
espadon [espádóń] *nm* swordfish *inv*.
espadrille [espádrēy] *nf* rope-soled sandal.
Espagne [espány(ə)] *nf:* **l'**~ Spain.
espagnol, e [espányol] *a* Spanish ♦ *nm* (*LING*) Spanish ♦ *nm/f:* **E**~, **e** Spaniard.
espagnolette [espányolet] *nf* (*window*) catch; **fermé à l'**~ half-shut (*resting on the catch*).
espalier [espályā] *nm* (*arbre fruitier*) espalier.
espèce [espes] *nf* (*BIO, BOT, ZOOL*) species *inv*; (*gén: sorte*) sort, kind, type; (*péj*): ~ **de maladroit/de brute!** you clumsy oaf/you brute!; ~**s** *nfpl* (*COMM*) cash *sg*; (*REL*) species; **de toute** ~ of all kinds *ou* sorts; **en l'**~ *ad* in the case in point; **payer en** ~**s** to pay (in) cash; **cas d'**~ individual case; **l'**~ **humaine** humankind.
espérance [espāráńs] *nf* hope; ~ **de vie** life expectancy.
espéranto [espāráńtō] *nm* Esperanto.
espérer [espārā] *vt* to hope for; **j'espère (bien)** I hope so; ~ **que/faire** to hope that/to do; ~ **en** to trust in.
espiègle [espyegl(ə)] *a* mischievous.
espièglerie [espyeglərē] *nf* mischievousness; (*tour, farce*) piece of mischief, prank.
espion, ne [espyóń, -on] *nm/f* spy; **avion** ~ spy plane.
espionnage [espyonázh] *nm* espionage, spying; **film/roman d'**~ spy film/novel.
espionner [espyonā] *vt* to spy (up)on.
esplanade [esplánád] *nf* esplanade.
espoir [espwár] *nm* hope; **l'**~ **de qch/de faire qch** the hope of sth/of doing sth; **avoir bon** ~ **que ...** to have high hopes that ...; **garder l'**~ **que ...** to remain hopeful that ...; **un** ~ **de la boxe/du ski** one of boxing's/skiing's hopefuls, one of the hopes of boxing/skiing;

sans ~ *a* hopeless.
esprit [esprē] *nm* (*pensée, intellect*) mind; (*humour, ironie*) wit; (*mentalité, d'une loi etc, fantôme etc*) spirit; **l'**~ **d'équipe/de compétition** team/competitive spirit; **faire de l'**~ to try to be witty; **reprendre ses** ~**s** to come to; **perdre l'**~ to lose one's mind; **avoir bon/mauvais** ~ to be of a good/bad disposition; **avoir l'**~ **à faire qch** to have a mind to do sth; **avoir l'**~ **critique** to be critical; ~ **de contradiction** contrariness; ~ **de corps** esprit de corps; ~ **de famille** family loyalty; **l'**~ **malin** (*le diable*) the Evil One; ~**s cha-grins** faultfinders.
esquif [eskēf] *nm* skiff.
esquimau, de, x [eskēmō, -ōd] *a* Eskimo ♦ *nm* (*LING*) Eskimo; (*glace*): **E**~ ® Popsicle ® (*US*), ice lolly (*Brit*) ♦ *nm/f*: **E**~, **de** Eskimo; **chien** ~ husky.
esquinter [eskàntā] *vt* (*fam*) to mess up; **s'**~ *vi*: **s'**~ **à faire qch** to knock o.s. out doing sth.
esquisse [eskēs] *nf* sketch; **l'**~ **d'un sourire/ changement** a hint of a smile/of change.
esquisser [eskēsā] *vt* to sketch; **s'**~ *vi* (*amélioration*) to begin to be detectable; ~ **un sourire** to give a hint of a smile.
esquive [eskēv] *nf* (*BOXE*) dodging; (*fig*) side-stepping.
esquiver [eskēvā] *vt* to dodge; **s'**~ *vi* to slip away.
essai [āse] *nm* trying; (*tentative*) attempt, try; (*RUGBY*) try; (*LITTÉRATURE*) essay; ~**s** *nmpl* (*AUTO*) trials; **à l'**~ on a trial basis; ~ **gratuit** (*COMM*) free trial.
essaim [āsaǹ] *nm* swarm.
essaimer [āsāmā] *vi* to swarm; (*fig*) to spread, expand.
essayage [āseyàzh] *nm* (*d'un vêtement*) trying on, fitting; **salon d'**~ fitting room; **cabine d'**~ fitting room (*cubicle*).
essayer [āsāyā] *vt* (*gén*) to try; (*vêtement, chaussures*) to try (on); (*restaurant, mé-thode, voiture*) to try (out) ♦ *vi* to try; ~ **de faire** to try *ou* attempt to do; **s'**~ **à faire** to try one's hand at doing; **essayez un peu!** (*menace*) just you try!
essayeur, euse [āseyœr, -ēz] *nm/f* (*chez un tailleur etc*) fitter.
ESSEC [esek] *sigle f* (= *École supérieure des sciences économiques et sociales*) *grande école for management and business studies.*
essence [āsàǹs] *nf* (*de voiture*) gas(oline) (*US*), petrol (*Brit*); (*extrait de plante, PHILOSOPHIE*) essence; (*espèce: d'arbre*) species *inv*; **prendre de l'**~ to get (some) gas; **par** ~ (*essentiellement*) essentially; ~ **de citron/rose** lemon/rose oil; ~ **de térében-thine** turpentine.
essentiel, le [āsàǹsyel] *a* essential ♦ *nm*: **l'**~ **d'un discours/d'une œuvre** the essence of a speech/work of art; **emporter l'**~ to take the essentials; **c'est l'**~ (*ce qui importe*) that's the main thing; **l'**~ **de** (*la majeure partie*) the main part of.
essentiellement [āsàǹsyelmàǹ] *ad* essentially.
esseulé, e [āsœlā] *a* forlorn.
essieu, x [āsyœ] *nm* axle.
essor [āsor] *nm* (*de l'économie etc*) rapid

expansion; **prendre son** ~ (*oiseau*) to fly off.
essorage [āsoràzh] *nm* wringing out; spin-drying; spinning; shaking.
essorer [āsorā] *vt* (*en tordant*) to wring (out); (*par la force centrifuge*) to spin-dry; (*salade*) to spin; (*: en secouant*) to shake dry.
essoreuse [āsorœz] *nf* mangle, wringer; (*à tambour*) spin-dryer.
essouffler [āsōōflā] *vt* to make breathless; **s'**~ *vi* to get out of breath; (*fig: économie*) to run out of steam.
essuie [āsüē] *etc vb voir* **essuyer**.
essuie-glace [āsüēglás] *nm* windshield (*US*) *ou* windscreen (*Brit*) wiper.
essuie-mains [āsüēmaǹ] *nm inv* hand towel.
essuierai [āsüērā] *etc vb voir* **essuyer**.
essuie-tout [āsüētōō] *nm inv* paper towel.
essuyer [āsüēyā] *vt* to wipe; (*fig: subir*) to suffer; **s'**~ (*après le bain*) to dry o.s.; ~ **la vaisselle** to dry the dishes.
est [e] *vb voir* **être** ♦ *nm* [est]: **l'**~ the east ♦ *a inv* east; (*région*) east(ern); **à l'**~ in the east; (*direction*) to the east, east(wards); **à l'**~ **de** (to the) east of; **les pays de l'E**~ the eastern countries.
estafette [estáfet] *nf* (*MIL*) courier (*US*), dis-patch rider (*Brit*).
estafilade [estáfēlàd] *nf* gash, slash.
est-allemand, e [estálmàǹ, -àǹd] *a* East Ger-man.
estaminet [estámēne] *nm* tavern.
estampe [estàǹp] *nf* print, engraving.
estamper [estàǹpā] *vt* (*monnaies etc*) to stamp; (*fam: escroquer*) to swindle.
estampille [estàǹpēy] *nf* stamp.
est-ce que [eska] *ad*: ~ **c'est cher/c'était bon?** is it expensive/was it good?; **quand est-ce qu'il part?** when does he leave?, when is he leaving?; **où est-ce qu'il va?** where's he going?; **qui est-ce qui le connaît/a fait ça?** who knows him/did that?; *voir aussi* **que**.
este [est(ə)] *a* Estonian ♦ *nm/f*: **E**~ Estonian.
esthète [estet] *nm/f* aesthete.
esthéticienne [estātēsyen] *nf* beautician.
esthétique [estātēk] *a* (*sens, jugement*) aesthetic; (*beau*) attractive, aesthetically pleasing ♦ *nf* aesthetics *sg*; **l'**~ **industrielle** industrial design.
esthétiquement [estātēkmàǹ] *ad* aestheti-cally.
estimable [estēmàbl(ə)] *a* respected.
estimatif, ive [estēmátēf, -ēv] *a* estimated.
estimation [estēmàsyôǹ] *nf* valuation; assess-ment; **d'après mes** ~**s** according to my calculations.
estime [estēm] *nf* esteem, regard; **avoir de l'**~ **pour qn** to think highly of sb.
estimer [estēmā] *vt* (*respecter*) to esteem, hold in high regard; (*expertiser*) to value; (*évaluer*) to assess, estimate; (*penser*): ~ **que/être** to consider that/o.s. to be; **s'**~ **satisfait/heureux** to feel satisfied/happy; **j'estime la distance à 10 km** I reckon the distance to be 10 km.
estival, e, aux [estēvàl, -ō] *a* summer *cpd*; **station** ~**e** (summer) vacation (*US*) *ou* holi-day (*Brit*) resort.
estivant, e [estēvàǹ, -àǹt] *nm/f* (summer) vacationer (*US*) *ou* holiday-maker (*Brit*).

estoc [estok] *nm*: **frapper d'~ et de taille** to cut and thrust.

estocade [estokád] *nf* death-blow.

estomac [estomá] *nm* stomach; **avoir mal à l'~** to have stomach ache; **avoir l'~ creux** to have an empty stomach.

estomaqué, e [estomáká] *a* flabbergasted.

estompe [estònp] *nf* stump; (*dessin*) stump-drawing.

estompé, e [estònpá] *a* blurred.

estomper [estònpá] *vt* (*ART*) to shade off; (*fig*) to blur, dim; **s'~** *vi* (*sentiments*) to soften; (*contour*) to become blurred.

Estonie [estoné] *nf*: **l'~** Estonia.

estonien, ne [estonyań, -en] *a* Estonian.

estrade [estrád] *nf* platform, rostrum.

estragon [estrágóń] *nm* tarragon.

estropié, e [estropyá] *nm/f* cripple.

estropier [estropyá] *vt* to cripple, maim; (*fig*) to twist, distort.

estuaire [estüer] *nm* estuary.

estudiantin, e [estüdyáńtań, -ēn] *a* student *cpd*.

esturgeon [estürzhóń] *nm* sturgeon.

et [ā] *cj* and; **~ lui?** what about him?; **~ alors?**, **~ (puis) après?** so what?; (*ensuite*) and then?

ét. *abr* = **étage**.

ETA [ātá] *sigle m* (*POL*: = *Euzkadi ta Askatsuna*) ETA (*Basque separatist movement*).

étable [ātábl(ə)] *nf* cowshed.

établi, e [ātáblē] *a* established ♦ *nm* (*work*)bench.

établir [ātáblēr] *vt* (*papiers d'identité, facture*) to make out; (*liste, programme*) to draw up; (*gouvernement, artisan etc: aider à s'installer*) to set up, establish; (*entreprise, atelier, camp*) to set up; (*réputation, usage, fait, culpabilité, relations*) to establish; (*SPORT: record*) to set; **s'~** *vi* (*se faire: entente etc*) to be established; **s'~** (**à son compte**) to set up in business; **s'~ à/près de** to settle in/near.

établissement [ātáblēsmáń] *nm* making out; drawing up; setting up, establishing; (*entreprise, institution*) establishment; **~ de crédit** credit institution; **~ hospitalier** hospital complex; **~ industriel** industrial plant, factory; **~ scolaire** school, educational establishment.

étage [ātázh] *nm* (*d'immeuble*) story (*US*), storey (*Brit*), floor; (*de fusée*) stage; (*GÉO: de culture, végétation*) level; **au 2ème ~** on the 3rd (*US*) *ou* 2nd (*Brit*) floor; **à l'~** upstairs; **maison à deux ~s** two-story house; **de bas ~** *a* low-born; (*médiocre*) inferior.

étager [ātázhá] *vt* (*cultures*) to lay out in tiers; **s'~** *vi* (*prix*) to range; (*zones, cultures*) to lie on different levels.

étagère [ātázher] *nf* (*rayon*) shelf; (*meuble*) shelves *pl*, set of shelves.

étai [āte] *nm* stay, prop.

étain [ātań] *nm* tin; (*ORFÈVRERIE*) pewter *q*.

étais [āte] *etc vb voir* **être**.

étal [ātál] *nm* stall.

étalage [ātálázh] *nm* display; (*vitrine*) display window; **faire ~ de** to show off, parade.

étalagiste [ātálázhēst(ə)] *nm/f* window-dresser.

étale [ātál] *a* (*mer*) slack.

étalement [ātálmáń] *nm* spreading; (*échelonnement*) staggering.

étaler [ātálá] *vt* (*carte, nappe*) to spread (out); (*peinture, liquide*) to spread; (*échelonner: paiements, dates, vacances*) to spread, stagger; (*exposer: marchandises*) to display; (*richesses, connaissances*) to parade; **s'~** *vi* (*liquide*) to spread out; (*fam*) to fall flat on one's face; **s'~ sur** (*suj: paiements etc*) to be spread over.

étalon [ātálóń] *nm* (*mesure*) standard; (*cheval*) stallion; **l'~-or** the gold standard.

étalonner [ātálóná] *vt* to calibrate.

étamer [ātámá] *vt* (*casserole*) to tin(plate); (*glace*) to silver.

étamine [ātámēn] *nf* (*BOT*) stamen; (*tissu*) cheesecloth.

étanche [ātáńsh] *a* (*récipient; aussi fig*) watertight; (*montre, vêtement*) waterproof; **~ à l'air** airtight.

étanchéité [ātáńshāētá] *nf* watertightness; airtightness.

étancher [ātáńshá] *vt* (*liquide*) to stop (flowing); **~ sa soif** to quench *ou* slake one's thirst.

étançon [ātáńsóń] *nm* (*TECH*) prop.

étançonner [ātáńsoná] *vt* to prop up.

étang [ātáń] *nm* pond.

étant [ātáń] *vb voir* **être, donné**.

étape [ātáp] *nf* stage; (*lieu d'arrivée*) stopping place; (: *CYCLISME*) staging point; **faire ~ à** to stop off at; **brûler les ~s** (*fig*) to cut corners.

état [ātá] *nm* (*POL, condition*) state; (*d'un article d'occasion etc*) condition, state; (*liste*) inventory, statement; (*condition professionnelle*) profession, trade; (: *sociale*) status; **en mauvais ~** in poor condition; **en ~ (de marche)** in (working) order; **remettre en ~** to repair; **hors d'~** out of order; **être en ~/hors d'~ de faire** to be in a state/in no fit state to do; **en tout ~ de cause** in any event; **être dans tous ses ~s** to be in a state; **faire ~ de** (*alléguer*) to put forward; **en ~ d'arrestation** under arrest; **~ de grâce** (*REL*) state of grace; (*fig*) honeymoon period; **en ~ de grâce** (*fig*) inspired; **en ~ d'ivresse** under the influence of drink; **~ de choses** (*situation*) state of affairs; **~ civil** civil status; (*bureau*) registry office; **~ d'esprit** frame of mind; **~ des lieux** inventory of fixtures; **~ de santé** state of health; **~ de siège/d'urgence** state of siege/emergency; **~ de veille** (*PSYCH*) waking state; **~s d'âme** moods; **les É~s barbaresques** the Barbary States; **les É~s du Golfe** the Gulf States; **~s de service** service record *sg*.

étatique [ātátēk] *a* state *cpd*, State *cpd*.

étatiser [ātátēzá] *vt* to bring under state control.

étatisme [ātátēsm(ə)] *nm* state control.

étatiste [ātátēst(ə)] *a* (*doctrine etc*) of state control ♦ *nm/f* partisan of state control.

état-major, *pl* **états-majors** [ātámázhor] *nm* (*MIL*) staff; (*d'un parti etc*) top advisers *pl*; (*d'une entreprise*) top management.

État-providence [ātáprovēdáńs] *nm* welfare state.

États-Unis [ātázünē] *nmpl*: **les ~ (d'Amérique)** the United States (of America).

étau, x [ātō] *nm* vise (*US*), vice (*Brit*).

étayer [ātāyā] *vt* to prop *ou* shore up; (*fig*) to back up.

et c(a)etera [etsātārā], **etc.** *ad* et cetera, and so on, etc.

été [ātā] *pp de* **être ♦** *nm* summer; **en ~** in summer.

éteignais [ātenye] *etc vb voir* **éteindre**.

éteignoir [ātenywár] *nm* (candle) snuffer; (*péj*) killjoy, wet blanket.

éteindre [ātāndr(ə)] *vt* (*lampe, lumière, radio, chauffage*) to turn *ou* switch off; (*cigarette, incendie, bougie*) to put out, extinguish; (*JUR: dette*) to extinguish; **s'~** *vi* to go off; to go out; (*mourir*) to pass away.

éteint, e [ātān, -ánt] *pp de* **éteindre ♦** *a* (*fig*) lackluster (*US*), lacklustre (*Brit*), dull; (*volcan*) extinct; **tous feux ~s** (*AUTO: rouler*) without lights.

étendard [ātāndár] *nm* standard.

étendre [ātāndr(ə)] *vt* (*appliquer: pâte, liquide*) to spread; (*déployer: carte etc*) to spread out; (*sur un fil: lessive, linge*) to hang up *ou* out; (*bras, jambes, par terre: blessé*) to stretch out; (*diluer*) to dilute, thin; (*fig: agrandir*) to extend; (*fam: adversaire*) to floor; **s'~** *vi* (*augmenter, se propager*) to spread; (*terrain, forêt etc*): **s'~ jusqu'à/de ... à** to stretch as far as/from ... to; **s'~ (sur)** (*s'allonger*) to stretch out (upon); (*se coucher*) to lie down (on); (*fig: expliquer*) to elaborate *ou* enlarge (upon).

étendu, e [ātāndü] *a* extensive ♦ *nf* (*d'eau, de sable*) stretch, expanse; (*importance*) extent.

éternel, le [āternel] *a* eternal; **les neiges ~les** perpetual snow.

éternellement [āternelmán] *ad* eternally.

éterniser [āternēzā]: **s'~** *vi* to last for ages; (*personne*) to stay for ages.

éternité [āternētā] *nf* eternity; **il y a** *ou* **ça fait une ~ que** it's ages since; **de toute ~** from time immemorial.

éternuement [āternümán] *nm* sneeze.

éternuer [āternüā] *vi* to sneeze.

êtes [et] *vb voir* **être**.

étêter [ātātā] *vt* (*arbre*) to poll(ard); (*clou, poisson*) to cut the head off.

éther [āter] *nm* ether.

éthéré, e [ātārā] *a* ethereal.

Éthiopie [ātyopē] *nf*: **l'~** Ethiopia.

éthiopien, ne [ātyopyań, -en] *a* Ethiopian.

éthique [ātēk] *a* ethical ♦ *nf* ethics *sg*.

ethnie [etnē] *nf* ethnic group.

ethnique [etnēk] *a* ethnic.

ethnographe [etnográf] *nm/f* ethnographer.

ethnographique [etnográfēk] *a* ethnographic(al).

ethnologique [etnolozhēk] *a* ethnological.

ethnologue [etnolog] *nm/f* ethnologist.

éthylique [ātēlēk] *a* alcoholic.

éthylisme [ātēlēsm(ə)] *nm* alcoholism.

étiage [ātyázh] *nm* low water.

étiez [ātyā] *vb voir* **être**.

étincelant, e [ātanslán, -ánt] *a* sparkling.

étinceler [ātanslā] *vi* to sparkle.

étincelle [ātansel] *nf* spark.

étioler [ātyolā]: **s'~** *vi* to wilt.

étions [ātyón] *vb voir* **être**.

étique [ātēk] *a* skinny, bony.

étiqueter [ātēktā] *vt* to label.

étiquette [ātēket] *vb voir* **étiqueter ♦** *nf* label; (*protocole*): **l'~** etiquette.

étirer [ātērā] *vt* to stretch; (*ressort*) to stretch out; **s'~** *vi* (*personne*) to stretch; (*convoi, route*): **s'~ sur** to stretch out over.

étoffe [ātof] *nf* material, fabric; **avoir l'~ d'un chef** *etc* to be cut out to be a leader *etc*; **avoir de l'~** to be a forceful personality.

étoffer [ātofā] *vt*, **s'~** *vi* to fill out.

étoile [ātwál] *nf* star ♦ *a*: **danseuse** *ou* **danceur ~** leading dancer; **la bonne/ mauvaise ~ de qn** sb's lucky/unlucky star; **à la belle ~** (out) in the open; **~ filante** shooting star; **~ de mer** starfish; **~ polaire** pole star.

étoilé, e [ātwálā] *a* starry.

étole [ātol] *nf* stole.

étonnant, e [ātonán, -ánt] *a* surprising.

étonné, e [ātonā] *a* surprised.

étonnement [ātonmán] *nm* surprise; **à mon grand ~ ...** to my great surprise *ou* amazement ....

étonner [ātonā] *vt* to surprise; **s'~ que/de** to be surprised that/at; **cela m'étonnerait (que)** (*j'en doute*) I'd be (very) surprised (if).

étouffant, e [ātōōfán, -ánt] *a* stifling.

étouffé, e [ātōōfā] *a* (*asphyxié*) suffocated; (*assourdi: cris, rires*) smothered ♦ *nf*: **à l'~e** (*CULIN: poisson, légumes*) steamed; (: *viande*) braised.

étouffement [ātōōfmán] *nm* suffocation.

étouffer [ātōōfā] *vt* to suffocate; (*bruit*) to muffle; (*scandale*) to hush up ♦ *vi* to suffocate; (*avoir trop chaud; aussi fig*) to feel stifled; **s'~** *vi* (*en mangeant etc*) to choke.

étouffoir [ātōōfwár] *nm* (*MUS*) damper.

étourderie [ātōōrdərē] *nf* heedlessness *q*; thoughtless blunder; **faute d'~** careless mistake.

étourdi, e [ātōōrdē] *a* (*distrait*) scatterbrained, heedless.

étourdir [ātōōrdēr] *vt* (*assommer*) to stun, daze; (*griser*) to make dizzy *ou* giddy.

étourdissant, e [ātōōrdēsán, -ánt] *a* staggering.

étourdissement [ātōōrdēsmán] *nm* dizzy spell.

étourneau, x [ātōōrnō] *nm* starling.

étrange [ātrânzh] *a* strange.

étrangement [ātrânzhmán] *ad* strangely.

étranger, ère [ātrânzhā, -er] *a* foreign; (*pas de la famille, non familier*) strange ♦ *nm/f* foreigner; stranger ♦ *nm*: **l'~** foreign countries; **à l'~** abroad; **de l'~** from abroad; **~ à** (*mal connu*) unfamiliar to; (*sans rapport*) irrelevant to.

étrangeté [ātrânzhtā] *nf* strangeness.

étranglé, e [ātrânglā] *a*: **d'une voix ~e** in a strangled voice.

étranglement [ātrângləmán] *nm* (*d'une vallée etc*) constriction, narrow passage.

étrangler [ātrânglā] *vt* to strangle; (*fig: presse, libertés*) to stifle; **s'~** *vi* (*en mangeant etc*) to choke; (*se resserrer*) to make a bottleneck.

étrave [ātráv] *nf* stem.

être |ctr(ə)| *nm* being ♦ *vb avec attribut*, *vi* to be ♦ *vb auxiliaire* to have *(ou parfois* be*)*; **il est instituteur** he is a teacher; ~ **à qn** *(appartenir)* to be sb's, to belong to sb; **c'est à moi/eux** it is *ou* it's mine/theirs; **c'est à lui de le faire** it's up to him to do it; **il est à Paris/au salon** he is *ou* he's in Paris/the sitting room; ~ **de** *(provenance, origine)* to be from; *(appartenance)* to belong to; ~ **de Genève/de la même famille** to come from Geneva/belong to the same family; **nous sommes le 10 janvier** it's the 10th of January (today); **il est 10 heures, c'est 10 heures** it is *ou* it's 10 o'clock; **c'est à réparer** it needs repairing; **c'est à essayer** it should be tried; **il est à espérer que** it is to be hoped that; ~ **fait par** to be made by; **il a été promu** he has been promoted; ~ **humain** human being; *voir aussi* **est-ce que, n'est-ce pas, c'est-à-dire, ce.**

étreindre [ātrańdr(ə)] *vt* to clutch, grip; *(amoureusement, amicalement)* to embrace; **s'**~ to embrace.

étreinte [ātrańt] *nf* clutch, grip; embrace; **resserrer son** ~ **autour de** *(fig)* to tighten one's grip on *ou* around.

étrenner [ātrānā] *vt* to use *(ou* wear) for the first time.

étrennes [ātren] *nfpl (cadeaux)* New Year's present; *(gratifications)* ≈ Christmas bonus.

étrier [ātrēyā] *nm* stirrup.

étriller [ātrēyā] *vt (cheval)* to curry; *(fam: battre)* to slaughter *(fig)*.

étriper [ātrēpā] *vt* to gut; *(fam)*: ~ **qn** to tear sb's guts out.

étriqué, e [ātrēkā] *a* skimpy.

étroit, e [ātrwà, -wàt] *a* narrow; *(vêtement)* tight; *(fig: serré)* close, tight; **à l'**~ cramped; ~ **d'esprit** narrow-minded.

étroitement [ātrwàtmáń] *ad* closely.

étroitesse [ātrwátes] *nf* narrowness; ~ **d'esprit** narrow-mindedness.

Étrurie [ātrürē] *nf*: **l'**~ Etruria.

étrusque [ātrüsk(ə)] *a* Etruscan.

étude [ātüd] *nf* studying; *(ouvrage, rapport, MUS)* study; *(de notaire: bureau)* office; *(: charge)* practice; *(SCOL: salle de travail)* study hall *(US) ou* room *(Brit)*; ~**s** *nfpl (SCOL)* studies; **être à l'**~ *(projet etc)* to be under consideration; **faire des** ~**s (de droit/médecine)** to study (law/medicine); ~**s secondaires/supérieures** secondary/higher education; ~ **de cas** case study; ~ **de faisabilité** feasibility study; ~ **de marché** *(ÉCON)* market research.

étudiant, e [ātüdyáń, -áńt] *a, nm/f* student.

étudié, e [ātüdyā] *a (démarche)* studied; *(système)* carefully designed; *(prix)* competitive.

étudier [ātüdyā] *vt, vi* to study.

étui [ātüē] *nm* case.

étuve [ātüv] *nf* steamroom; *(appareil)* sterilizer.

étuvée [ātüvā]: **à l'**~ *ad* braised.

étymologie [ātēmolozhē] *nf* etymology.

étymologique [ātēmolozhēk] *a* etymological.

eu, eue [ü] *pp de* **avoir.**

EU(A) *sigle mpl* (= *États-Unis (d'Amérique)*) US(A).

eucalyptus [œkálēptüs] *nm* eucalyptus.

Eucharistie [œkárēstē] *nf*: **l'**~ the Eucharist, the Lord's Supper.

eugénique [œzhānēk] *a* eugenic ♦ *nf* eugenics *sg*.

eugénisme [œzhānēsm(ə)] *nm* eugenics *sg*.

euh [œ] *excl* er.

eunuque [œnük] *nm* eunuch.

euphémique [œfāmēk] *a* euphemistic.

euphémisme [œfāmēsm(ə)] *nm* euphemism.

euphonie [œfonē] *nf* euphony.

euphorbe [œforb(ə)] *nf (BOT)* spurge.

euphorie [œforē] *nf* euphoria.

euphorique [œforēk] *a* euphoric.

euphorisant, e [œforēzáń, -áńt] *a* exhilarating.

Euphrate [œfrát] *nm*: **l'**~ the Euphrates *sg*.

eurafricain, e [œráfrēkáń, -en] *a* Eurafrican.

eurasiatique [œrázyátēk] *a* Eurasiatic.

Eurasie [œrázē] *nf*: **l'**~ Eurasia.

eurasien, ne [œrázyáń, -en] *a* Eurasian.

EURATOM [œrátom] *sigle f* Euratom.

eurent [ür(ə)] *vb voir* **avoir.**

eurocrate [œrokrát] *nm/f (péj)* Eurocrat.

eurodevise [œrodəvēz] *nf* Eurocurrency.

euromonnaie [œromone] *nf* Eurocurrency.

Europe [œrop] *nf*: **l'**~ Europe; **l'**~ **centrale** Central Europe; **l'**~ **verte** European agriculture.

européaniser [œropáánēzā] *vt* to Europeanize.

européen, ne [œropáań, -en] *a* European ♦ *nm/f*: **E**~, **ne** European.

eus [ü] *etc vb voir* **avoir.**

euthanasie [œtánázē] *nf* euthanasia.

eux [œ] *pronom (sujet)* they; *(objet)* them; ~, **ils ont fait ...** THEY did ....

EV *abr* (= *en ville*) *used on mail to be delivered by hand, courier etc within the same town.*

évacuation [āvàküàsyóń] *nf* evacuation.

évacuer [āvàküā] *vt (salle, région)* to evacuate, clear; *(occupants, population)* to evacuate; *(toxine etc)* to evacuate, discharge.

évadé, e [āvàdā] *a* escaped ♦ *nm/f* escapee.

évader [āvàdā]: **s'**~ *vi* to escape.

évaluation [āvàlüàsyóń] *nf* assessment, evaluation.

évaluer [āvàlüā] *vt* to assess, evaluate.

évanescent, e [āvànèsáń, -áńt] *a* evanescent.

évangélique [āvánzhālēk] *a* evangelical.

évangéliser [āvánzhālēzā] *vt* to evangelize.

évangéliste [āvánzhālēst(ə)] *nm* evangelist.

évangile [āvánzhēl] *nm* gospel; *(texte de la Bible)*: **É**~ Gospel; **ce n'est pas l'É**~ *(fig)* it's not gospel.

évanoui, e [āvànwē] *a* in a faint; **tomber** ~ to faint.

évanouir [āvànwēr]: **s'**~ *vi* to faint, pass out; *(disparaître)* to vanish, disappear.

évanouissement [āvànwèsmáń] *nm (syncope)* fainting spell; *(MÉD)* loss of consciousness.

évaporation [āvàporásyóń] *nf* evaporation.

évaporé, e [āvàporā] *a* giddy, scatterbrained.

évaporer [āvàporā]: **s'**~ *vi* to evaporate.

évasé, e [āvàzā] *a (jupe etc)* flared.

évaser [āvàzā] *vt (tuyau)* to widen, open out; *(jupe, pantalon)* to flare; **s'**~ *vi* to widen, open out.

évasif, ive [āvàzēf, -ēv] *a* evasive.

évasion [āvàzyóń] *nf* escape; **littérature d'**~

escapist literature; ~ **des capitaux** (*ÉCON*) flight of capital; ~ **fiscale** tax avoidance.

évasivement [āvázĕvmáń] *ad* evasively.

évêché [āvāshā] *nm* (*fonction*) bishopric; (*palais*) bishop's palace.

éveil [āvey] *nm* awakening; **être en** ~ to be alert; **mettre qn en** ~, **donner l'**~ **à qn** to arouse sb's suspicions; **activités d'**~ early-learning activities.

éveillé, e [āvāyā] *a* awake; (*vif*) alert, sharp.

éveiller [āvāyā] *vt* to (a)waken; **s'**~ *vi* to (a)waken; (*fig*) to be aroused.

événement [āvenmáń] *nm* event.

éventail [āváńtáy] *nm* fan; (*choix*) range; **en** ~ fanned out; fan-shaped.

éventaire [āváńter] *nm* stall, stand.

éventé, e [āváńtā] *a* (*parfum, vin*) stale.

éventer [āváńtā] *vt* (*secret, complot*) to uncover; (*avec un éventail*) to fan; **s'**~ *vi* (*parfum, vin*) to go stale.

éventrer [āváńtrā] *vt* to disembowel; (*fig*) to tear *ou* rip open.

éventualité [āváńtüálētā] *nf* eventuality; possibility; **dans l'**~ **de** in the event of; **parer à toute** ~ to guard against all eventualities.

éventuel, le [āváńtüel] *a* possible.

éventuellement [āváńtüelmáń] *ad* possibly.

évêque [āvek] *nm* bishop.

Everest [evrest] *nm*: **(mont)** ~ (Mount) Everest.

évertuer [āvertüā]: **s'**~ *vi*: **s'**~ **à faire** to try very hard to do.

éviction [āvĕksyóń] *nf* ousting, supplanting; (*de locataire*) eviction.

évidemment [āvĕdámáń] *ad* obviously.

évidence [āvĕdáńs] *nf* obviousness; (*fait*) obvious fact; **se rendre à l'**~ to bow before the evidence; **nier l'**~ to deny the evidence; **à l'**~ evidently; **de toute** ~ quite obviously *ou* evidently; **en** ~ conspicuous; **mettre en** ~ to bring to the fore.

évident, e [āvĕdáń, -áńt] *a* obvious, evident; **ce n'est pas** ~ (*cela pose des problèmes*) it's not (all that) straightforward, it's not as simple as all that.

évider [āvĕdā] *vt* to scoop out.

évier [āvyā] *nm* (kitchen) sink.

évincement [āváńsmáń] *nm* ousting.

évincer [āváńsā] *vt* to oust, supplant.

évitable [āvĕtábl(ǝ)] *a* avoidable.

évitement [āvĕtmáń] *nm*: **place d'**~ (*AUTO*) passing place.

éviter [āvĕtā] *vt* to avoid; ~ **de faire/que qch ne se passe** to avoid doing/sth happening; ~ **qch à qn** to spare sb sth.

évocateur, trice [āvokátœr, -trēs] *a* evocative, suggestive.

évocation [āvokásyóń] *nf* evocation.

évolué, e [āvolüā] *a* advanced; (*personne*) broad-minded.

évoluer [āvolüā] *vi* (*enfant, maladie*) to develop; (*situation, moralement*) to evolve, develop; (*aller et venir: danseur etc*) to move about, circle.

évolutif, ive [āvolütēf, -ēv] *a* evolving.

évolution [āvolüsyóń] *nf* development; evolution; ~**s** *nfpl* movements.

évoquer [āvokā] *vt* to call to mind, evoke; (*mentionner*) to mention.

ex. *abr* (= *exemple*) ex.

ex- [eks] *préfixe* ex-.

exacerber [egzáserbā] *vt* to exacerbate.

exact, e [egzákt] *a* (*précis*) exact, accurate, precise; (*correct*) correct; (*ponctuel*) punctual; **l'heure** ~**e** the right *ou* exact time.

exactement [egzáktǝmáń] *ad* exactly, accurately, precisely; correctly; (*c'est cela même*) exactly.

exactions [egzáksyóń] *nfpl* exactions.

exactitude [egzáktētüd] *nf* exactitude, accurateness, precision.

ex aequo [egzākō] *a* tied; **classé 1er** ~ tied for first place.

exagération [egzázhārásyóń] *nf* exaggeration.

exagéré, e [egzázhārā] *a* (*prix etc*) excessive.

exagérément [egzázhārāmáń] *ad* excessively.

exagérer [egzázhārā] *vt* to exaggerate ♦ *vi* (*abuser*) to go too far; (*dépasser les bornes*) to overstep the mark; (*déformer les faits*) to exaggerate; **s'**~ **qch** to exaggerate sth.

exaltation [egzáltásyóń] *nf* exaltation.

exalté, e [egzáltā] *a* (over)excited ♦ *nm/f* (*péj*) fanatic.

exalter [egzáltā] *vt* (*enthousiasmer*) to excite, elate; (*glorifier*) to exalt.

examen [egzámań] *nm* examination; (*SCOL*) exam, examination; **à l'**~ (*dossier, projet*) under consideration; (*COMM*) on approval; ~ **blanc** practice test; ~ **de la vue** eye test.

examinateur, trice [egzámēnátœr, -trēs] *nm/f* examiner.

examiner [egzámēnā] *vt* to examine.

exaspération [egzáspārásyóń] *nf* exasperation.

exaspéré, e [egzáspārā] *a* exasperated.

exaspérer [egzáspārā] *vt* to exasperate; (*aggraver*) to exacerbate.

exaucer [egzōsā] *vt* (*vœu*) to grant, fulfil; ~ **qn** to grant sb's wishes.

excavateur [ekskávátœr] *nm* excavator, steam shovel.

excavation [ekskávásyóń] *nf* excavation.

excavatrice [ekskávátrēs] *nf* = **excavateur**.

excédent [eksádáń] *nm* surplus; **en** ~ surplus; **payer 600 F d'**~ (*de bagages*) to pay 600 F excess luggage; ~ **de bagages** excess luggage; ~ **commercial** trade surplus.

excédentaire [eksádáńter] *a* surplus, excess.

excéder [eksádā] *vt* (*dépasser*) to exceed; (*agacer*) to exasperate; **excédé de fatigue** exhausted; **excédé de travail** worn out with work.

excellence [ekselấńs] *nf* excellence; (*titre*) Excellency; **par** ~ par excellence.

excellent, e [ekselấń, -ấńt] *a* excellent.

exceller [ekselā] *vi*: ~ **(dans)** to excel (in).

excentricité [eksáńtrēsētā] *nf* eccentricity.

excentrique [eksáńtrēk] *a* eccentric; (*quartier*) outlying ♦ *nm/f* eccentric.

excepté, e [eksẽptā] *a, prép*: **les élèves ~s, ~ les élèves** except for *ou* apart from the pupils; ~ **si/quand** except if/when; ~ **que** except that.

excepter [eksẽptā] *vt* to except.

exception [eksepsyóń] *nf* exception; **faire** ~ to be an exception; **faire une** ~ to make an exception; **sans** ~ without exception; **à l'**~ **de** except for, with the exception of; **d'**~ (*mesure, loi*) special, exceptional.

exceptionnel, le |cksɛpsyoncl| *a* exceptional; (*prix*) special.

exceptionnellement |cksɛpsyonclmáṅ| *ad* exceptionally; (*par exception*) by way of exception, on this occasion.

excès |cksɛ| *nm* surplus ♦ *nmpl* excesses; **à l'~** (*méticuleux, généreux*) to excess; **avec ~** to excess; **sans ~** in moderation; **tomber dans l'~ inverse** to go to the opposite extreme; **~ de langage** immoderate language; **~ de pouvoir** abuse of power; **~ de vitesse** speeding *q*, exceeding the speed limit; **~ de zèle** overzealousness *q*.

excessif, ive |cksāsɛf, -ɛv| *a* excessive.

exciper |cksɛpā| **~ de** *vt* to plead.

excipient |cksɛpyáṅ| *nm* (*MÉD*) inert base, excipient.

exciser |cksēzā| *vt* (*MÉD*) to excise.

excitant, e |cksɛtáṅ, -áṅt| *a* exciting ♦ *nm* stimulant.

excitation |cksɛtásyóṅ| *nf* (*état*) excitement.

excité, e |cksɛtā| *a* excited.

exciter |cksɛtā| *vt* to excite; (*suj: café etc*) to stimulate; **s'~** *vi* to get excited; **~ qn à** (*révolte etc*) to incite sb to.

exclamation |cksklámásyóṅ| *nf* exclamation.

exclamer |cksklámā|: **s'~** *vi* to exclaim.

exclu, e |cksklü| *pp de* **exclure** ♦ *a*: **il est/n'est pas ~ que ...** it's out of the question/not impossible that ...; **ce n'est pas exclu** it's not impossible, I don't rule that out.

exclure |cksklür| *vt* (*faire sortir*) to expel; (*ne pas compter*) to exclude, leave out; (*rendre impossible*) to exclude, rule out.

exclusif, ive |cksklüzɛf, -ɛv| *a* exclusive; **avec la mission exclusive/ dans le but ~ de ...** with the sole mission/aim of ...; **agent ~** sole agent.

exclusion |cksklüzyóṅ| *nf* expulsion; **à l'~ de** with the exclusion *ou* exception of.

exclusivement |cksklüzēvmáṅ| *ad* exclusively.

exclusivité |cksklüzēvɛtā| *nf* exclusiveness; (*COMM*) exclusive rights *pl*; **film passant en ~ à** film showing only at.

excommunier |ckskomünyā| *vt* to excommunicate.

excréments |ckskrāmáṅ| *nmpl* excrement *sg*, feces (*US*), faeces (*Brit*).

excroissance |ckskrwásáṅs| *nf* excrescence, outgrowth.

excursion |ckskürsyóṅ| *nf* (*en autocar*) excursion, trip; (*à pied*) walk, hike; **faire une ~** to go on an excursion *ou* a trip; to go on a walk *ou* hike.

excursionniste |ckskürsyonɛst(ə)| *nm/f* traveler (*US*), tripper, tourist; hiker.

excuse |cksküz| *nf* excuse; **~s** *nfpl* apology *sg*, apologies; **faire des ~s** to apologize; **faire ses ~s** to offer one's apologies; **mot d'~** (*SCOL*) note from one's parent(s) (*to explain absence etc*); **lettre d'~s** letter of apology.

excuser |cksküzā| *vt* to excuse; **~ qn de qch** (*dispenser*) to excuse sb from sth; **s'~ (de)** to apologize (for); **"excusez-moi"** "I'm sorry"; (*pour attirer l'attention*) "excuse me"; **se faire ~** to ask to be excused.

exécrable |cgzākrábl(ə)| *a* atrocious.

exécrer |cgzākrā| *vt* to loathe, abhor.

exécutant, e |cgzākütáṅ, -áṅt| *nm/f* performer.

exécuter |cgzākütā| *vt* (*prisonnier*) to execute; (*tâche etc*) to execute, carry out; (*MUS: jouer*) to perform, execute; (*INFORM*) to run; **s'~** *vi* to comply.

exécuteur, trice |cgzākütœr, -trɛs| *nm/f* (*testamentaire*) executor ♦ *nm* (*bourreau*) executioner.

exécutif, ive |cgzākütɛf, -ɛv| *a, nm* (*POL*) executive.

exécution |cgzāküsyóṅ| *nf* execution; carrying out; **mettre à ~** to carry out.

exécutoire |cgzākütwár| *a* (*JUR*) (legally) binding.

exégèse |cgzāzhɛz| *nf* exegesis.

exemplaire |cgzáṅplɛr| *a* exemplary ♦ *nm* copy.

exemple |cgzáṅpl(ə)| *nm* example; **par ~** for instance, for example; (*valeur intensive*) really!; **sans ~** (*bêtise, gourmandise etc*) unparalleled; **donner l'~** to set an example; **prendre ~ sur** to take as a model; **à l'~ de** just like; **pour l'~** (*punir*) as an example.

exempt, e |cgzáṅ, -áṅt| *a*: **~ de** (*dispensé de*) exempt from; (*sans*) free from; **~ de taxes** tax-free.

exempter |cgzáṅtā| *vt*: **~ de** to exempt from.

exercé, e |cgzersā| *a* trained.

exercer |cgzersā| *vt* (*pratiquer*) to exercise, practice (*US*), practise (*Brit*); (*faire usage de: prérogative*) to exercise; (*effectuer: influence, contrôle, pression*) to exert; (*former*) to exercise, train ♦ *vi* (*médecin*) to be in practice; **s'~** (*sportif, musicien*) to practice (*US*), practise (*Brit*); (*se faire sentir: pression etc*): **s'~** (*sur ou* **contre**) to be exerted (on); **s'~ à faire qch** to train o.s. to do sth.

exercice |cgzersɛs| *nm* practice; exercising; (*tâche, travail*) exercise; (*COMM, ADMIN: période*) accounting period; **l'~** (*sportive etc*) exercise; (*MIL*) drill; **en ~** (*juge*) in office; (*médecin*) practicing (*US*), practising (*Brit*); **dans l'~ de ses fonctions** in the discharge of his duties; **~s d'assouplissement** limbering-up (exercises).

exergue |cgzerg(ə)| *nm*: **mettre en ~** (*inscription*) to inscribe; **porter en ~** to be inscribed with.

exhalaison |cgzálezóṅ| *nf* exhalation.

exhaler |cgzálā| *vt* (*parfum*) to exhale; (*souffle, son, soupir*) to utter, breathe; **s'~** *vi* to rise (up).

exhausser |cgzōsā| *vt* to raise (up).

exhaustif, ive |cgzōstɛf, -ɛv| *a* exhaustive.

exhiber |cgzēbā| *vt* (*montrer: papiers, certificat*) to present, produce; (*péj*) to display, flaunt; **s'~** (*personne*) to parade; (*suj: exhibitionniste*) to expose o.s.

exhibitionnisme |cgzēbēsyonɛsm(ə)| *nm* exhibitionism.

exhibitionniste |cgzēbēsyonɛst(ə)| *nm/f* exhibitionist.

exhorter |cgzortā| *vt*: **~ qn à faire** to urge sb to do.

exhumer |cgzümā| *vt* to exhume.

exigeant, e |cgzēzháṅ, -áṅt| *a* demanding; (*péj*) hard to please.

exigence |cgzēzháṅs| *nf* demand, requirement.

exiger |cgzēzhā| *vt* to demand, require.

exigible [egzēzhēbl(ə)] *a* (*COMM, JUR*) payable.

exigu, ë [egzēgü] *a* cramped, tiny.

exil [egzēl] *nm* exile; **en ~** in exile.

exilé, e [egzēlā] *nm/f* exile.

exiler [egzēlā] *vt* to exile; **s'~** to go into exile.

existant, e [egzēstáñ, -áñt] *a* (*actuel, présent*) existing.

existence [egzēstáñs] *nf* existence; **dans l'~** in life.

existentialisme [egzēstáñsyálēsm(ə)] *nm* existentialism.

existentiel, le [egzēstáñsyel] *a* existential.

exister [egzēstā] *vi* to exist; **il existe un/des** there is a/are (some).

exode [egzod] *nm* exodus.

exonération [egzonārásyóñ] *nf* exemption.

exonéré, e [egzonārā] *a*: **~ de TVA** exempt from value-added tax.

exonérer [egzonārā] *vt*: **~ de** to exempt from.

exorbitant, e [egzorbētáñ, -áñt] *a* exorbitant.

exorbité, e [egzorbētā] *a*: **yeux ~s** bulging eyes.

exorciser [egzorsēzā] *vt* to exorcize.

exorde [egzord(ə)] *nm* introduction.

exotique [egzotēk] *a* exotic.

exotisme [egzotēsm(ə)] *nm* exoticism.

expansif, ive [ekspáñsēf, -ēv] *a* expansive, communicative.

expansion [ekspáñsyóñ] *nf* expansion.

expansionniste [ekspáñsyonēst(ə)] *a* expansionist.

expatrié, e [ekspátrēyā] *nm/f* expatriate.

expatrier [ekspátrēyā] *vt* (*argent*) to take *ou* send out of the country; **s'~** to leave one's country.

expectative [ekspektátēv] *nf*: **être dans l'~** to be waiting to see.

expectorant, e [ekspektoráñ, -áñt] *a*: **sirop ~** expectorant (syrup).

expédient [ekspādyáñ] *nm* (*parfois péj*) expedient; **vivre d'~s** to live by one's wits.

expédier [ekspādyā] *vt* (*lettre, paquet*) to send; (*troupes, renfort*) to dispatch; (*péj*: *travail etc*) to dispose of, dispatch.

expéditeur, trice [ekspādētœr, -trēs] *nm/f* (*POSTES*) sender.

expéditif, ive [ekspādētēf, -ēv] *a* quick, expeditious.

expédition [ekspādēsyóñ] *nf* sending; (*scientifique, sportive, MIL*) expedition; **~ punitive** punitive raid.

expéditionnaire [ekspādēsyoner] *a*: **corps ~** (*MIL*) task force.

expérience [ekspāryáñs] *nf* (*de la vie, des choses*) experience; (*scientifique*) experiment; **avoir de l'~** to have experience, be experienced; **avoir l'~ de** to have experience of; **faire l'~ de qch** to experience sth; **~ de chimie/d'électricité** chemical/electrical experiment.

expérimental, e, aux [ekspārēmántál, -ō] *a* experimental.

expérimenté, e [ekspārēmántā] *a* experienced.

expérimenter [ekspārēmántā] *vt* (*machine, technique*) to test out, experiment with.

expert, e [eksper, -ert(ə)] *a*: **~ en** expert in ♦ *nm* (*spécialiste*) expert; **~ en assurances** insurance appraiser.

expert-comptable, *pl* **experts-comptables** [eksperkóñtábl(ə)] *nm* ≈ certified public (*US*) *ou* chartered (*Brit*) accountant.

expertise [ekspertēz] *nf* valuation; assessment; valuer's (*ou* assessor's) report; (*JUR*) (forensic) examination.

expertiser [ekspertēzā] *vt* (*objet de valeur*) to value; (*voiture accidentée etc*) to assess damage to.

expier [ekspyā] *vt* to expiate, atone for.

expiration [ekspērásyóñ] *nf* expiration; breathing out *q*.

expirer [ekspērā] *vi* (*prendre fin, littéraire*: *mourir*) to expire; (*respirer*) to breathe out.

explétif, ive [eksplātēf, -ēv] *a* (*LING*) expletive.

explicable [eksplēkábl(ə)] *a*: **pas ~** inexplicable.

explicatif, ive [eksplēkátēf, -ēv] *a* (*mot, texte, note*) explanatory.

explication [eksplēkásyóñ] *nf* explanation; (*discussion*) discussion; **~ de texte** (*SCOL*) critical analysis (of a text).

explicite [eksplēsēt] *a* explicit.

explicitement [eksplēsētmáñ] *ad* explicitly.

expliciter [eksplēsētā] *vt* to make explicit.

expliquer [eksplēkā] *vt* to explain; **~ (à qn) comment/que** to point out *ou* explain (to sb) how/that; **s'~** (*se faire comprendre*: *personne*) to explain o.s.; (*discuter*) to discuss things; (*se disputer*) to have it out; (*comprendre*): **je m'explique son retard/absence** I understand his lateness/absence; **son erreur s'explique** one can understand his mistake.

exploit [eksplwá] *nm* exploit, feat.

exploitable [eskplwátábl(ə)] *a* (*gisement etc*) that can be exploited; **~ par une machine** machine-readable.

exploitant [eksplwátáñ] *nm* farmer.

exploitation [eksplwátásyóñ] *nf* exploitation; running; (*entreprise*): **~ agricole** farming concern.

exploiter [eksplwátā] *vt* to exploit; (*entreprise, ferme*) to run, operate.

exploiteur, euse [eksplwátœr, -œz] *nm/f* (*péj*) exploiter.

explorateur, trice [eksplorátœr, -trēs] *nm/f* explorer.

exploration [eksplorásyóñ] *nf* exploration.

explorer [eksplorā] *vt* to explore.

exploser [eksplōzā] *vi* to explode, blow up; (*engin explosif*) to go off; (*fig*: *joie, colère*) to burst out, explode; (: *personne*: *de colère*) to explode, flare up; **faire ~** (*bombe*) to explode, detonate; (*bâtiment, véhicule*) to blow up.

explosif, ive [eksplōzēf, -ēv] *a, nm* explosive.

explosion [eksplōzyóñ] *nf* explosion; **~ de joie/colère** outburst of joy/rage; **~ démographique** population explosion.

exponentiel, le [eksponáñsyel] *a* exponential.

exportateur, trice [eksportátœr, -trēs] *a* exporting ♦ *nm* exporter.

exportation [eksportásyóñ] *nf* export.

exporter [eksportā] *vt* to export.

exposant [ekspōzáñ] *nm* exhibitor; (*MATH*) exponent.

exposé, e [ekspōzā] *nm* (*écrit*) exposé; (*oral*) talk ♦ *a*: **~ au sud** facing south, with a southern exposure; **bien** ~ well situated; **très** ~ very exposed.

exposer [ekspōzā] *vt* (*montrer: marchandise*) to display; (*: peinture*) to exhibit, show; (*parler de: problème, situation*) to explain, expose, set out; (*mettre en danger, orienter: maison etc*) to expose; ~ **qn/qch à** to expose sb/sth to; ~ **sa vie** to risk one's life; **s'~ à** (*soleil, danger*) to expose o.s. to; (*critiques, punition*) to lay o.s. open to.

exposition [ekspōzēsyôň] *nf* (*voir exposer*) displaying; exhibiting; explanation, exposition; exposure; (*voir exposé*) exposure, situation; (*manifestation*) exhibition; (*PHOTO*) exposure; (*introduction*) exposition.

exprès [ekspre] *ad* (*délibérément*) on purpose; (*spécialement*) specially; **faire** ~ **de faire qch** to do sth on purpose.

exprès, esse [ekspres] *a* (*ordre, défense*) express, formal ♦ *a inv, ad* (*POSTES*) special delivery (*US*), express (*Brit*); **envoyer qch en** ~ to send sth special delivery (*US*) *ou* express (*Brit*).

express [ekspres] *a, nm*: (**café**) ~ espresso; (**train**) ~ express (train).

expressément [ekspresāmāň] *ad* expressly, specifically.

expressif, ive [ekspräsēf, -ēv] *a* expressive.

expression [ekspresyôň] *nf* expression; **réduit à sa plus simple** ~ reduced to its simplest terms; **liberté/moyens d'~** freedom/means of expression; ~ **toute faite** set phrase.

exprimer [eksprēmā] *vt* (*sentiment, idée*) to express; (*faire sortir: jus, liquide*) to press out; **s'~** *vi* (*personne*) to express o.s.

expropriation [ekspropreyâsyôň] *nf* expropriation; **frapper d'~** to expropriate.

exproprier [eksopreyā] *vt* to expropriate.

expulser [ekspülsā] *vt* (*d'une salle, d'un groupe*) to expel; (*locataire*) to evict; (*FOOT-BALL*) to send off.

expulsion [ekspülsyôň] *nf* expulsion; eviction; sending off.

expurger [ekspürzhā] *vt* to expurgate, bowdler-ize.

exquis, e [ekskē, -ēz] *a* (*gâteau, parfum, élégance*) exquisite; (*personne, temps*) delightful.

exsangue [eksâňg] *a* bloodless, drained of blood.

exsuder [eksüdā] *vt* to exude.

extase [ekstâz] *nf* ecstasy; **être en** ~ to be in raptures.

extasier [ekstâzyā]: **s'~** *vi*: **s'~ sur** to go into raptures over.

extatique [ekstátēk] *a* ecstatic.

extenseur [ekstâňsœr] *nm* (*SPORT*) chest expander.

extensible [ekstâňsēbl(ə)] *a* extensible.

extensif, ive [ekstâňsēf, -ēv] *a* extensive.

extension [ekstâňsyôň] *nf* (*d'un muscle, res-sort*) stretching; (*MÉD*): **à l'~** in traction; (*fig*) extension; expansion.

exténuant [ekstānüâň, -âňt] *a* exhausting.

exténuer [ekstānüā] *vt* to exhaust.

extérieur, e [ekstāryœr] *a* (*de dehors: porte, mur etc*) outer, outside; (*: commerce, politique*) foreign; (*: influences, pressions*) external; (*au dehors: escalier, w.-c.*) outside;

(*apparent: calme, gaieté etc*) outer ♦ *nm* (*d'une maison, d'un récipient etc*) outside, exterior; (*d'une personne: apparence*) exterior; (*d'un pays, d'un groupe social*): **l'~** the outside world; **à l'~** (*dehors*) outside; (*fig: à l'étranger*) abroad.

extérieurement [ekstāryœrmâň] *ad* (*de dehors*) on the outside; (*en apparence*) on the surface.

extérioriser [ekstāryorēzā] *vt* to exteriorize.

exterminer [ekstermēnā] *vt* to exterminate, wipe out.

externat [eksternâ] *nm* day school.

externe [ekstern(ə)] *a* external, outer ♦ *nm/f* (*MÉD*) non-resident medical student, extern (*US*); (*SCOL*) day pupil.

extincteur [ekstaňktœr] *nm* (*fire*) extinguisher.

extinction [ekstaňksyôň] *nf* extinction; (*JUR*: *d'une dette*) extinguishment; ~ **de voix** (*MÉD*) loss of voice.

extirper [ekstērpā] *vt* (*tumeur*) to extirpate; (*plante*) to root out, pull up; (*préjugés*) to eradicate.

extorquer [ekstorkā] *vt* (*de l'argent, un ren-seignement*): ~ **qch à qn** to extort sth from sb.

extorsion [ekstorsyôň] *nf*: ~ **de fonds** extor-tion of money.

extra [ekstrá] *a inv* first-rate; (*marchandises*) top-quality ♦ *nm inv* extra help ♦ *préfixe* extra-(-).

extraction [ekstráksyôň] *nf* extraction.

extrader [ekstrádā] *vt* to extradite.

extradition [ekstrádēsyôň] *nf* extradition.

extra-fin, e [ekstráfaň, -ēn] *a* extra-fine.

extra-fort, e [ekstráfor, -fort(ə)] *a* extra strong.

extraire [ekstrer] *vt* to extract.

extrait, e [ekstre, -et] *pp de* **extraire** ♦ *nm* (*de plante*) extract; (*de film, livre*) extract, excerpt; ~ **de naissance** birth certificate.

extra-lucide [ekstrálüsēd] *a*: **voyante** ~ clairvoyant.

extraordinaire [ekstráordēner] *a* extraor-dinary; (*POL, ADMIN*) special; **ambassadeur** ~ ambassador extraordinary; **assemblée** ~ special meeting; **par** ~ by some unlikely chance.

extraordinairement [ekstráordēnermâň] *ad* extraordinarily.

extrapoler [ekstrápolā] *vt, vi* to extrapolate.

extra-sensoriel, le [ekstrásâňsoryel] *a* extra-sensory.

extra-terrestre [ekstráterestr(ə)] *nm/f* extra-terrestrial.

extra-utérin, e [ekstráütāraň, -ēn] *a* extra-uterine.

extravagance [ekstrávágâňs] *nf* extravagance *q*; extravagant behavior *q* (*US*) *ou* behaviour *q* (*Brit*).

extravagant, e [ekstrávágâň, -âňt] *a* (*personne, attitude*) extravagant; (*idée*) wild.

extraverti, e [ekstrávertē] *a* extrovert.

extrayais [ekstreye] *etc vb voir* **extraire**.

extrême [ekstrem] *a, nm* extreme; (*intensif*): **d'une** ~ **simplicité/brutalité** extremely simple/brutal; **d'un** ~ **à l'autre** from one extreme to another; **à l'~** in the extreme; **à l'~ rigueur** in the absolute extreme.

extrêmement [ekstremmâň] *ad* extremely.

extrême-onction, *pl* **extrêmes-onctions** [ekstremôṅksyôṅ] *nf* (*REL*) last rites *pl,* Extreme Unction.

Extrême-Orient [ekstremoryáṅ] *nm:* **l'~** the Far East.

extrême-oriental, e, aux [ekstremoryáṅtál, -ō] *a* Far Eastern.

extrémiste [ekstrámēst(ə)] *a, nm/f* extremist.

extrémité [ekstrámētá] *nf* (*bout*) end; (*situation*) straits *pl,* plight; (*geste désespéré*) extreme action; **~s** *nfpl* (*pieds et mains*) extremities; **à la dernière ~** (*à l'agonie*) on the point of death.

extroverti, e [ekstrovertē] *a* = **extraverti.**

exubérant, e [egzübāráṅ, -áṅt] *a* exuberant.

exulter [egzültā] *vi* to exult.

exutoire [egzütwár] *nm* outlet, release.

ex-voto [eksvotō] *nm inv* ex-voto.

eye-liner [áyláynœr] *nm* eyeliner.

F

F, f [ef] *nm inv* **F, f** ♦ *abr* = **féminin; femme;** (= *franc*) fr.; (= *Fahrenheit*) F; (= *frère*) Br(o).; (*appartement*): **un F2/F3** a 2-/3-roomed apartment; **F comme François** F for Fox.

fa [fá] *nm inv* (*MUS*) F; (*en chantant la gamme*) fa.

fable [fábl(ə)] *nf* fable; (*mensonge*) story, tale.

fabricant [fábrēkáṅ] *nm* manufacturer, maker.

fabrication [fábrēkásyôṅ] *nf* manufacture, making.

fabrique [fábrēk] *nf* factory.

fabriquer [fábrēkā] *vt* to make; (*industriellement*) to manufacture, make; (*construire: voiture*) to manufacture, build; (*: maison*) to build; (*fig: inventer: histoire, alibi*) to make up; (*fam*): **qu'est-ce qu'il fabrique?** what is he up to?; **~ en série** to mass-produce.

fabulateur, trice [fábülátœr, -trēs] *nm/f:* **c'est un ~** he fantasizes, he makes up stories.

fabulation [fábülásyôṅ] *nf* (*PSYCH*) fantasizing.

fabuleusement [fábülœzmáṅ] *ad* fabulously, fantastically.

fabuleux, euse [fábülœ, -œz] *a* fabulous, fantastic.

fac [fák] *abr f* (*fam:* = *faculté*) ≈ college (*US*), Uni (*Brit fam*).

façade [fásád] *nf* front, façade; (*fig*) façade.

face [fás] *nf* face; (*fig: aspect*) side ♦ *a:* **le côté ~** heads; **perdre/sauver la ~** to lose/save face; **regarder qn en ~** to look sb in the face; **la maison/le trottoir d'en ~** the house/sidewalk opposite; **en ~ de** *prép* opposite; (*fig*) in front of; **de ~** *ad* from the front; head-on; **~ à** *prép* facing; (*fig*) faced with, in the face of; **faire ~ à** to face; **faire ~ à la demande** (*COMM*) to meet the demand; **~ à ~** *ad* facing each other ♦ *nm inv* encounter.

face-à-main, *pl* **faces-à-main** [fásámáṅ] *nm* lorgnette.

facéties [fásāsē] *nfpl* jokes, pranks.

facétieux, euse [fásāsyœ, -œz] *a* mischievous.

facette [fáset] *nf* facet.

fâché, e [fáshā] *a* angry; (*désolé*) sorry.

fâcher [fáshā] *vt* to anger; **se ~** *vi* to get angry; **se ~ avec** (*se brouiller*) to fall out with.

fâcherie [fáshrē] *nf* quarrel.

fâcheusement [fáshœzmáṅ] *ad* unpleasantly; (*impressionné etc*) badly; **avoir ~ tendance à** to have an irritating tendency to.

fâcheux, euse [fáshœ, -œz] *a* unfortunate, regrettable.

facho [fáshō] *a, nm/f* (*fam:* = *fasciste*) fascist.

facial, e, aux [fásyál, -ō] *a* facial.

faciès [fásyes] *nm* (*visage*) features *pl.*

facile [fásēl] *a* easy; (*accommodant*) easygoing; **~ d'emploi** (*INFORM*) user-friendly.

facilement [fásēlmáṅ] *ad* easily.

facilité [fásēlētá] *nf* easiness; (*disposition, don*) aptitude; (*moyen, occasion, possibilité*): **il a la ~ de rencontrer les gens** he has every opportunity to meet people; **~s** *nfpl* facilities; (*COMM*) terms; **~s de crédit** credit terms; **~s de paiement** easy terms.

faciliter [fásēlētá] *vt* to make easier.

façon [fásôṅ] *nf* (*manière*) way; (*d'une robe etc*) tailoring; cut; (*: main-d'œuvre*) labor (*US*), labour (*Brit*); (*imitation*): **châle ~ cachemire** cashmere-style shawl; **~s** *nfpl* (*péj*) fuss *sg*; **faire des ~s** (*péj: être affecté*) to be affected; (*: faire des histoires*) to make a fuss; **de quelle ~?** (in) what way?; **sans ~** *ad* without fuss ♦ *a* unaffected; **d'une autre ~** in another way; **en aucune ~** in no way; **de ~ à** so as to; **de ~ à ce que, de (telle) ~ que** so that; **de toute ~** anyway, in any case; **(c'est une) ~ de parler** it's a way of putting it; **travail à ~** tailoring.

façonner [fásoná] *vt* (*fabriquer*) to manufacture; (*travailler: matière*) to shape, fashion; (*fig*) to mold (*US*), mould (*Brit*), shape.

fac-similé [fáksēmēlā] *nm* facsimile.

facteur, trice [fáktœr, -trēs] *nm/f* mailman/woman (*US*), postman/woman (*Brit*) ♦ *nm* (*MATH, gén*) factor; **~ d'orgues** organ builder; **~ de pianos** piano maker; **~ rhésus** Rh *ou* rhesus factor.

factice [fáktēs] *a* artificial.

faction [fáksyôṅ] *nf* (*groupe*) faction; (*MIL*) guard *ou* sentry (duty); watch; **en ~** on guard; standing watch.

factionnaire [fáksyoner] *nm* guard, sentry.

factoriel, le [fáktoryel] *a, nf* factorial.

factotum [fáktotom] *nm* odd-job man, gofer.

factuel, le [fáktüel] *a* factual.

facturation [fáktürásyôṅ] *nf* invoicing; (*bureau*) invoicing (office).

facture [fáktür] *nf* (*à payer: gén*) bill; (*: COMM*) invoice; (*d'un artisan, artiste*) technique, workmanship.

facturer [fáktürā] *vt* to invoice.

facturier, ière [fáktüryā, -yer] *nm/f* invoice clerk.

facultatif, ive [fákültátēf, -ēv] *a* optional; (*arrêt de bus*) request *cpd.*

faculté [fákültá] *nf* (*intellectuelle, d'université*) faculty; (*pouvoir, possibilité*) power.

fadaises [fádez] *nfpl* twaddle *sg.*

fade [fàd] *a* insipid.

fading [fádēng] *nm* (*RADIO*) fading.

fagot [fágō] *nm* (*de bois*) bundle of sticks.

fagoté, e [fàgotā] *a* (*fam*): **drôlement ~ oddly dressed.**

faible [febl(ə)] *a* weak; (*voix, lumière, vent*) faint; (*élève, copie*) poor; (*rendement, intensité, revenu etc*) low ♦ *nm* weak point; (*pour quelqu'un*) weakness, soft spot; **~ d'esprit** feeble-minded.

faiblement [feblǝmâǹ] *ad* weakly; (*peu: éclairer etc*) faintly.

faiblesse [febles] *nf* weakness.

faiblir [fāblēr] *vi* to weaken; (*lumière*) to dim; (*vent*) to drop.

faïence [fàyâǹs] *nf* earthenware *q*; (*objet*) piece of earthenware.

faignant, e [fenyâǹ, -âǹt] *nm/f* = **fainéant, e.**

faille [fày] *vb voir* **falloir** ♦ *nf* (*GÉO*) fault; (*fig*) flaw, weakness.

failli, e [fàyē] *a, nm/f* bankrupt.

faillible [fàyēbl(ə)] *a* fallible.

faillir [fàyēr] *vi*: **j'ai failli tomber/lui dire** I almost *ou* nearly fell/told him; **~ à une promesse/un engagement** to break a promise/an agreement.

faillite [fàyēt] *nf* bankruptcy; (*échec: d'une politique etc*) collapse; **être en ~** to be bankrupt; **faire ~** to go bankrupt.

faim [faǹ] *nf* hunger; (*fig*): **~ d'amour/de richesse** hunger *ou* yearning for love/wealth; **avoir ~** to be hungry; **rester sur sa ~** (*aussi fig*) to be left wanting more.

fainéant, e [fenââǹ, -âǹt] *nm/f* idler, loafer.

fainéantise [fānââǹtēz] *nf* idleness, laziness.

faire [fer] *vt* to do; (*fabriquer, préparer*) to make; (*maison*) to build; (*produire*) to produce; **"vraiment?" fit-il** "really?" he said; **je n'ai pas pu ~ autrement** I couldn't do otherwise; **fait à la main/machine** hand-/machine-made; **~ du bruit/des taches** to make a noise/marks; **~ du droit/du français** to study law/French; **~ du rugby/du piano** to play rugby/play the piano; **~ le malade/l'ignorant** to act the invalid/the fool; **~ du diabète** to suffer from *ou* have diabetes; **~ de la tension** to have high blood pressure; **~ de la fièvre** to run a temperature; **~ les magasins** to make the rounds of the stores; **~ de qn un frustré/avocat** to make sb frustrated/a lawyer; **ça ne me fait rien, ça ne me fait ni chaud ni froid** (*m'est égal*) I don't care *ou* mind; (*me laisse froid*) it has no effect on me; **ça ne fait rien** it doesn't matter; **qu'est-ce que ça peut ~?** what does it matter?; **je vous le fais 10 F** I'll let you have it for 10 F; **2 et 2 font 4** 2 and 2 are *ou* make 4; **9 divisé par 3 fait 3** 9 divided by 3 makes *ou* gives *ou* is 3; **~ que** (*impliquer*) to mean that ♦ *vi* (*agir,*

s'y prendre) to act; (*faire ses besoins*) to go (to the bathroom); **faites comme chez vous** make yourself at home ♦ *vb avec attribut*: **ça fait 10 m/15 F** it's 10 m/15 F; **~ vieux/démodé** to look old/old-fashioned ♦ *vb substitut*: **remets-le en place — je viens de le ~** put it back in its place — I've just done so *ou* I just did; **faites!** please do!; **il ne fait que critiquer** (*sans cesse*) all he (*ever*) does is criticize; (*seulement*) he's only criticizing ♦ *vb impersonnel*: **il fait beau** *etc* the weather is fine *etc*; *voir* **jour, froid** *etc*; **ça fait 2 ans qu'il est parti** it's 2 years since he left; **ça fait 2 ans qu'il y est** he's been there for 2 years ♦ **~ faire**: **~ réparer qch** to get *ou* have sth repaired; **~ tomber/bouger qch** to make sth fall/move; **cela fait dormir** it makes you sleep; **~ travailler les enfants** to make the children work, get the children to work; **~ punir les enfants** to have the children punished; **il m'a fait traverser la rue** (*aidé*) he helped me (to) cross the road, he helped me across the road; **~ démarrer un moteur/chauffer de l'eau** to start up an engine/heat some water; **se ~ couper les cheveux** to get *ou* have one's hair cut; **se ~ examiner la vue/opérer** to have one's eyes tested/have an operation; **il s'est fait aider (par qn)** he got sb to help him; **il va se ~ tuer/punir** he's going to get himself killed/get (himself) punished; **elle s'est fait expliquer le problème** she had the problem explained to her; **se ~ faire un vêtement** to get a garment made for o.s. ♦ **se ~** *vi* (*fromage, vin*) to mature; **se ~ à** (*s'habituer*) to get used to; **cela se fait beaucoup/ne se fait pas** it's done a lot/not done; **comment se fait-il que ...?** how is it that ...?; **il peut se ~ que ...** it can happen that ...; **se ~ vieux** to be getting old; **se ~ beau** to make o.s. beautiful; **se ~ les yeux/ongles** to do one's eyes/nails; **se ~ une jupe** to make o.s. a skirt; **se ~ des amis** to make friends; **se ~ du souci** to worry; **il ne s'en fait pas** he doesn't worry; **sans s'en ~** without worrying.

faire-part [ferpàr] *nm inv* announcement (*of birth, marriage etc*).

fair-play [ferple] *a inv* fair.

fais [fe] *vb voir* **faire.**

faisable [fǝzàbl(ə)] *a* feasible.

faisais [fǝze] *etc vb voir* **faire.**

faisan, e [fǝzâǹ, -âǹ] *nm/f* pheasant.

faisandé, e [fǝzâǹdā] *a* high (*bad*); (*fig péj*) corrupt, decadent.

faisceau, x [fesō] *nm* (*de lumière etc*) beam; (*de branches etc*) bundle.

faiseur, euse [fǝzœr, -œ̄z] *nm/f* (*gén: péj*): **~ de** maker of ♦ *nm* (*custom* (*US*) *ou* bespoke (*Brit*)) tailor; **~ d'embarras** fusspot; **~ de projets** schemer.

fait [fe] *vb voir* **faire** ♦ *nm* (*événement*) event, occurrence; (*réalité, donnée*) fact; **le ~ que/de manger** the fact that/of eating; **être le ~ de** (*causé par*) to be the work of; **être au ~ (de)** to be informed (of); **mettre qn au ~** to inform sb; **au ~** (*à propos*) by the way; **en venir au ~** to get to the point; **de ~** *a* (*opposé à: de droit*) de facto ♦ *ad* in fact; **du ~ de ceci/qu'il a menti** because of *ou* on account of this/his having lied; **de ce ~** therefore, for this reason; **en ~** in fact; **en ~ de repas** by way of a meal; **prendre ~ et cause pour qn** to support sb, side with sb; **prendre qn sur le ~** to catch sb in the act; **dire à qn son ~** to give sb a piece of one's mind; **hauts ~s** (*exploits*) exploits; **~ d'armes** feat of arms; **~ divers** (short) news item; **les ~s et gestes de qn** sb's actions *ou* doings.

fait, e [fɛ, fɛt] *pp de* **faire ♦** *a* (*mûr: fromage, melon*) ripe; (*maquillé: yeux*) made-up; (*vernis: ongles*) painted, polished; **un homme ~** a grown man; **tout(e) ~(e)** (*préparé à l'avance*) ready-made; **c'en est ~ de notre tranquillité** that's the end of our peace; **c'est bien ~ (pour lui** *ou* **eux** *etc*) it serves him (*ou* them *etc*) right.

faîte [fɛt] *nm* top; (*fig*) pinnacle, height.

faites [fɛt] *vb voir* **faire**.

faîtière [fɛtyɛr] *nf* (*de tente*) ridge pole.

fait-tout *nm inv*, **faitout** *nm* [fɛtu] stewpan (*US*), stewpot (*Brit*).

fakir [fakir] *nm* (*THÉÂTRE*) wizard.

falaise [falɛz] *nf* cliff.

falbalas [falbala] *nmpl* fripperies, frills.

fallacieux, euse [falasjø, -øz] *a* (*raisonnement*) fallacious; (*apparences*) deceptive; (*espoir*) illusory.

falloir [falwar] *vb impersonnel*: **il faut faire les lits we** (*ou* you *etc*) have to *ou* must make the beds; **il faut que je fasse les lits** I have to *ou* must make the beds; **il a fallu qu'il parte** he had to leave; **il faudrait qu'elle rentre** she ought to go home; **il va ~ 100 F** we'll (*ou* I'll *etc*) need 100 F; **il doit ~ du temps** that must take time; **il vous faut tourner à gauche après l'église** you have to turn left past the church; **nous avons ce qu'il (nous) faut** we have what we need; **il faut qu'il ait oublié** he must have forgotten; **il a fallu qu'il l'apprenne** he would have to hear about it; **il ne fallait pas** (*pour remercier*) you shouldn't have (done it); **faut le faire!** (it) takes some doing! **♦ s'en ~**: **il s'en est fallu de 100 F/5 minutes we** (*ou* they *etc*) were 100 F short/5 minutes late (*ou* early); **il s'en faut de beaucoup qu'il soit** ... he is far from being ...; **il s'en est fallu de peu que cela n'arrive** it very nearly happened; **ou peu s'en faut** or just about, or as good as; **comme il faut** *a* proper **♦** *ad* properly.

fallu [faly] *pp de* **falloir**.

falot, e [falo, -ot] *a* dreary, colorless (*US*), colourless (*Brit*) **♦** *nm* lantern.

falsifier [falsifje] *vt* to falsify; to doctor.

famé, e [fame] *a*: **mal ~** disreputable, of ill repute.

famélique [famelik] *a* half-starved.

fameux, euse [famø, -øz] *a* (*illustre: parfois péj*) famous; (*bon: repas, plat etc*) first-rate, first-class; (*intensif*): **un ~ problème** *etc* a real problem *etc*; **pas ~** not great, not much good.

familial, e, aux [familjal, -o] *a* family *cpd* **♦** *nf* (*AUTO*) station wagon (*US*), estate car (*Brit*).

familiariser [familjarize] *vt*: **~ qn avec** to familiarize sb with; **se ~ avec** to familiarize

o.s. with.

familiarité [familjarite] *nf* familiarity; informality; **~s** *nfpl* familiarities; **~ avec** (*sujet, science*) familiarity with.

familier, ière [familje, -jɛr] *a* (*connu, impertinent*) familiar; (*dénotant une certaine intimité*) informal, friendly; (*LING*) informal, colloquial **♦** *nm* regular (visitor).

famille [famij] *nf* family; **il a de la ~ à Paris** he has relatives in Paris.

famine [famin] *nf* famine.

fan [fan] *nm/f* fan.

fana [fana] *a, nm/f* (*fam*) = **fanatique**.

fanal, aux [fanal, -o] *nm* beacon; lantern.

fanatique [fanatik] *a*: **~ (de)** fanatical (about) **♦** *nm/f* fanatic.

fanatisme [fanatism(ə)] *nm* fanaticism.

fane [fan] *nf* top.

fané, e [fane] *a* faded.

faner [fane]: **se ~** *vi* to fade.

faneur, euse [fanœr, -øz] *nm/f* haymaker **♦** *nf* (*TECH*) tedder.

fanfare [fɑ̃far] *nf* (*orchestre*) brass band; (*musique*) fanfare; **en ~** (*avec bruit*) noisily.

fanfaron, ne [fɑ̃farɔ̃, -on] *nm/f* braggart.

fanfaronnades [fɑ̃faronad] *nfpl* bragging *q*.

fanfreluches [fɑ̃frəlyʃ] *nfpl* trimming *q*.

fange [fɑ̃ʒ] *nf* mire.

fanion [fanjɔ̃] *nm* pennant.

fanon [fanɔ̃] *nm* (*de baleine*) plate of baleen; (*repli de peau*) dewlap, wattle.

fantaisie [fɑ̃tezi] *nf* (*spontanéité*) fancy, imagination; (*caprice*) whim; extravagance; (*MUS*) fantasia **♦** *a*: **bijou (de) ~** (piece of) costume jewelry (*US*) *ou* jewellery (*Brit*); **pain (de) ~** fancy bread.

fantaisiste [fɑ̃tezist(ə)] *a* (*péj*) unorthodox, eccentric **♦** *nm/f* (*de music-hall*) variety artist *ou* entertainer.

fantasme [fɑ̃tasm(ə)] *nm* fantasy.

fantasmer [fɑ̃tasme] *vi* to fantasize.

fantasque [fɑ̃task(ə)] *a* whimsical, capricious; fantastic.

fantassin [fɑ̃tasɛ̃] *nm* infantryman.

fantastique [fɑ̃tastik] *a* fantastic.

fantoche [fɑ̃tɔʃ] *nm* (*péj*) puppet.

fantomatique [fɑ̃tomatik] *a* ghostly.

fantôme [fɑ̃tom] *nm* ghost, phantom.

FAO *sigle f* (= *Food and Agricultural Organization*) FAO.

faon [fɑ̃] *nm* fawn (*deer*).

faramineux, euse [faraminø, -øz] *a* (*fam*) fantastic.

farce [fars(ə)] *nf* (*viande*) stuffing; (*blague*) (practical) joke; (*THÉÂTRE*) farce; **faire une ~ à qn** to play a (practical) joke on sb; **~s et attrapes** jokes and novelties.

farceur, euse [farsœr, -øz] *nm/f* practical joker; (*fumiste*) clown.

farci, e [farsi] *a* (*CULIN*) stuffed.

farcir [farsir] *vt* (*viande*) to stuff; (*fig*): **~ qch de** to stuff sth with; **se ~** (*fam*): **je me suis farci la vaisselle** I've been stuck with (doing) the dishes.

fard [far] *nm* make-up; **~ à joues** blusher.

fardeau, x [fardo] *nm* burden.

farder [farde] *vt* to make up; (*vérité*) to disguise; **se ~** to make o.s. up.

farfelu, e [farfəly] *a* wacky (*fam*), harebrained.

farfouiller [fàrfōōyā] *vi* (*péj*) to rummage around.

fariboles [fàrēbol] *nfpl* nonsense *q*.

farine [fàrēn] *nf* flour; ~ **de blé** wheat flour; ~ **de maïs** cornstarch (*US*), cornflour (*Brit*); ~ **lactée** (*pour bouillie*) gruel.

fariner [fàrēnā] *vt* to flour.

farineux, euse [fàrēnœ̄, -œ̄z] *a* (*sauce, pomme*) floury ♦ *nmpl* (*aliments*) starchy foods.

farniente [fàrnyentā] *nm* idleness.

farouche [fàrōōsh] *a* shy, timid; (*sauvage*) savage, wild; (*violent*) fierce.

farouchement [fàrōōshmâṅ] *ad* fiercely.

fart [fàr(t)] *nm* (ski) wax.

farter [fàrtā] *vt* to wax.

fascicule [fàsēkül] *nm* volume.

fascinant, e [fàsēnâṅ, -âṅt] *a* fascinating.

fascination [fàsēnâsyóṅ] *nf* fascination.

fasciner [fàsēnā] *vt* to fascinate.

fascisant, e [fàshēzàṅ, -âṅt] *a* fascistic.

fascisme [fàshēsm(ə)] *nm* fascism.

fasciste [fàshēst(ə)] *a, nm/f* fascist.

fasse [fàs] *etc vb voir* **faire**.

faste [fàst(ə)] *nm* splendor (*US*), splendour (*Brit*) ♦ *a*: **c'est un jour** ~ it's his (*ou* our *etc*) lucky day.

fastidieux, euse [fàstēdyœ̄, -œ̄z] *a* tedious, tiresome.

fastueux, euse [fàstüœ̄, -œ̄z] *a* sumptuous, luxurious.

fat [fà] *am* conceited, smug.

fatal [fàtál] *a* fatal; (*inévitable*) inevitable.

fatalement [fàtálmâṅ] *ad* inevitably.

fatalisme [fàtálēsm(ə)] *nm* fatalism.

fataliste [fàtálēst(ə)] *a* a fatalistic.

fatalité [fàtálētā] *nf* (*destin*) fate; (*coïncidence*) fateful coincidence; (*caractère inévitable*) inevitability.

fatidique [fàtēdēk] *a* fateful.

fatigant, e [fàtēgâṅ, -âṅt] *a* tiring; (*agaçant*) tiresome.

fatigue [fàtēg] *nf* tiredness, fatigue; (*détérioration*) fatigue; **les ~s du voyage** the wear and tear of the journey.

fatigué, e [fàtēgā] *a* tired.

fatiguer [fàtēgā] *vt* to tire, make tired; (*TECH*) to put a strain on, strain; (*fig: importuner*) to wear out ♦ *vi* (*moteur*) to labor (*US*), labour (*Brit*), strain; **se ~** *vi* to get tired; to tire o.s. (out); **se ~ à faire qch** to tire o.s. out doing sth.

fatras [fàtrà] *nm* jumble, hodgepodge.

fatuité [fàtüētā] *nf* conceitedness, smugness.

faubourg [fōbōōr] *nm* suburb.

faubourien, ne [fōbōōryaṅ, -en] *a* (*accent*) working-class.

fauché, e [fōshā] *a* (*fam*) broke.

faucher [fōshā] *vt* (*herbe*) to cut; (*champs, blés*) to reap; (*fig*) to cut down; to mow down; (*fam: voler*) to swipe.

faucheur, euse [fōshœr, -œ̄z] *nm/f* reaper, mower.

faucille [fōsēy] *nf* sickle.

faucon [fōkóṅ] *nm* falcon, hawk.

faudra [fōdrà] *etc vb voir* **falloir**.

faufil [fōfēl] *nm* (*COUTURE*) basting thread.

faufilage [fōfēlàzh] *nm* (*COUTURE*) basting.

faufiler [fōfēlā] *vt* to tack, baste; **se ~** *vi*: **se ~ dans** to edge one's way into; **se ~ parmi/ entre** to thread one's way among/between.

faune [fōn] *nf* (*ZOOL*) wildlife, fauna; (*fig péj*) set, crowd ♦ *nm* faun; ~ **marine** marine (animal) life.

faussaire [fōser] *nm/f* forger.

fausse [fōs] *af voir* **faux**.

faussement [fōsmâṅ] *ad* (*accuser*) wrongly, wrongfully; (*croire*) falsely, erroneously.

fausser [fōsā] *vt* (*objet*) to bend, buckle; (*fig*) to distort; ~ **compagnie à qn** to give sb the slip.

fausset [fōse] *nm*: **voix de ~** falsetto voice.

fausseté [fōstā] *nf* wrongness; falseness.

faut [fō] *vb voir* **falloir**.

faute [fōt] *nf* (*erreur*) mistake, error; (*péché, manquement*) misdemeanor (*US*), misdemeanour (*Brit*); (*FOOTBALL etc*) foul, infraction (*US*); (*TENNIS*) fault; (*responsabilité*): **par la ~ de** through the fault of, because of; **c'est de sa/ma** ~ it's his/my fault; **être en ~** to be in the wrong; **prendre qn en ~** to catch *ou* trap sb; ~. **de** (*temps, argent*) for *ou* through lack of; ~ **de mieux** for want of anything *ou* something better; **sans ~** *ad* without fail; ~ **de frappe** typing error; ~ **d'inattention** careless mistake; ~ **d'orthographe** spelling mistake; ~ **professionnelle** professional misconduct *q*.

fauteuil [fōtœy] *nm* armchair; ~ **à bascule** rocking chair; ~ **club** (big) easy chair; ~ **d'orchestre** seat in the orchestra (*US*) *ou* the front stalls (*Brit*); ~ **roulant** wheelchair.

fauteur [fōtœr] *nm*: ~ **de troubles** troublemaker.

fautif, ive [fōtēf, -ēv] *a* (*incorrect*) incorrect, inaccurate; (*responsable*) at fault, in the wrong; (*coupable*) guilty ♦ *nm/f* culprit.

fauve [fōv] *nm* wildcat; (*peintre*) Fauve ♦ *a* (*couleur*) fawn.

fauvette [fōvet] *nf* warbler.

faux [fō] *nf* scythe.

faux, fausse [fō, fōs] *a* (*inexact*) wrong; (*piano, voix*) out of tune; (*falsifié*) fake, forged; (*sournois, postiche*) false ♦ *ad* (*MUS*) out of tune ♦ *nm* (*copie*) fake, forgery; (*opposé au vrai*): **le ~** falsehood; **le ~ numéro/la fausse clé** the wrong number/key; **faire fausse route** to go the wrong way; **faire ~ bond à qn** to let sb down; ~ **ami** (*LING*) deceptive cognate; ~ **col** detachable collar; ~ **départ** (*SPORT, fig*) false start; ~ **frais** *nmpl* extras, incidental expenses; ~ **frère** (*fig péj*) false friend; ~ **mouvement** awkward movement; ~ **nez** false nose; ~ **nom** assumed name; ~ **pas** tripping *q*; (*fig*) faux pas; ~ **témoignage** (*délit*) perjury; **fausse alerte** false alarm; **fausse clé** skeleton key; **fausse couche** (*MÉD*) miscarriage; **fausse joie** vain joy; **fausse note** wrong note.

faux-filet [fōfēle] *nm* sirloin.

faux-fuyant [fōfüėyâṅ] *nm* equivocation.

faux-monnayeur [fōmoneyœr] *nm* counterfeiter, forger.

faux-semblant [fōsâṅblâṅ] *nm* pretense (*US*), pretence (*Brit*).

faux-sens [fōsâṅs] *nm* mistranslation.

faveur [fàvœr] *nf* favor (*US*), favour (*Brit*);

traitement de ~ preferential treatment; **à la** ~ **de** under cover of; *(grâce à)* thanks to; **en** ~ **de** in favor of.

favorable [fávorábl(ə)] *a* favorable *(US)*, favourable *(Brit)*.

favori, te [fávorē, -ēt] *a, nm/f* favorite *(US)*, favourite *(Brit)*.

favoris [fávorē] *nmpl (barbe)* sideburns.

favoriser [fávorēzā] *vt* to favor *(US)*, favour *(Brit)*.

favoritisme [fávorētēsm(ə)] *nm (péj)* favoritism *(US)*, favouritism *(Brit)*.

fayot [fáyō] *nm (fam)* bootlicker.

FB *abr (= franc belge)* BF, FB.

FBI *sigle m* FBI.

FC *sigle m = Football Club.*

fébrile [fābrēl] *a* feverish, febrile; **capitaux ~s** *(ÉCON)* hot money.

fébrilement [fābrēlmáṅ] *ad* feverishly.

fécal, e, aux [fākál, -ō] *a voir* **matière.**

fécond, e [fākôṅ, -ôṅd] *a* fertile.

fécondation [fākôṅdásyóṅ] *nf* fertilization.

féconder [fākôṅdā] *vt* to fertilize.

fécondité [fākôṅdētā] *nf* fertility.

fécule [fākül] *nf* potato flour.

féculent [fākülāṅ] *nm* starchy food.

fédéral, e, aux [fādārál, -ō] *a* federal.

fédéralisme [fādārálēsm(ə)] *nm* federalism.

fédération [fādārásyóṅ] *nf* federation.

fée [fā] *nf* fairy.

féerie [fārē] *nf* enchantment.

féerique [fārēk] *a* magical, fairytale *cpd.*

feignant, e [fenyáṅ, -áṅt] *nm/f* = **fainéant, e.**

feindre [faṅdr(ə)] *vt* to feign ♦ *vi* to dissemble; ~ **de faire** to pretend to do.

feint, e [faṅ, faṅt] *pp de* **feindre** ♦ *a* feigned ♦ *nf (SPORT)* dummy.

fêler [fālā] *vt* to crack.

félicitations [fālēsētásyôṅ] *nfpl* congratulations.

félicité [fālēsētā] *nf* bliss.

féliciter [fālēsētā] *vt:* ~ **qn (de)** to congratulate sb (on).

félin, e [fālaṅ, -ēn] *a* feline ♦ *nm* (big) cat.

félon, ne [fālôṅ, -on] *a* perfidious, treacherous.

félonie [fālonē] *nf* treachery.

fêlure [fālür] *nf* crack.

femelle [fəmel] *a (aussi ÉLEC, TECH)* female ♦ *nf* female.

féminin, e [fāmēnaṅ, -ēn] *a* feminine; *(sexe)* female; *(équipe, vêtements etc)* women's; *(parfois péj: homme)* effeminate ♦ *nm (LING)* feminine.

féminiser [fāmēnēzā] *vt* to feminize; *(rendre efféminé)* to make effeminate; **se** ~ *vi:* **cette profession se féminise** this profession is attracting more women.

féminisme [fāmēnēsm(ə)] *nm* feminism.

féministe [fāmēnēst(ə)] *a, nf* feminist.

féminité [fāmēnētā] *nf* femininity.

femme [fàm] *nf* woman; *(épouse)* wife *(pl* wives); **être très** ~ to be very much a woman; **devenir** ~ to attain womanhood; ~ **d'affaires** businesswoman; ~ **de chambre** chambermaid; ~ **fatale** femme fatale; ~ **au foyer** housewife; ~ **d'intérieur** (real) homemaker; ~ **de ménage** domestic help, cleaning lady; ~ **du monde** society woman; ~ **de tête** determined, intellectual woman.

fémur [fāmür] *nm* femur, thighbone.

FEN [fen] *sigle f (= Fédération de l'éducation nationale)* teachers' union.

fenaison [fənezóṅ] *nf* haymaking.

fendillé, e [fáṅdēyā] *a (terre etc)* crazed.

fendre [fáṅdr(ə)] *vt (couper en deux)* to split; *(fissurer)* to crack; *(fig: traverser)* to cut through; to push one's way through; **se** ~ *vi* to crack.

fendu, e [fáṅdü] *a (sol, mur)* cracked; *(jupe)* slit.

fenêtre [fənetr(ə)] *nf* window; ~ **à guillotine** sash window.

fenouil [fənōōy] *nm* fennel.

fente [fáṅt] *nf* slit; *(fissure)* crack.

féodal, e, aux [fāodál, -ō] *a* feudal.

féodalisme [fāodálēsm(ə)] *nm* feudalism.

fer [fer] *nm* iron; *(de cheval)* shoe; ~**s** *pl (MÉD)* forceps; **mettre aux** ~**s** *(enchaîner)* to put in chains; **au** ~ **rouge** with a red-hot iron; **santé/main de** ~ iron constitution/ hand; ~ **à cheval** horseshoe; **en** ~ **à cheval** *(fig)* horseshoe-shaped; ~ **forgé** wrought iron; ~ **à friser** curling iron *(US)* ou tongs *pl (Brit)*; ~ **de lance** spearhead; ~ **(à repasser)** iron; ~ **à souder** soldering iron.

ferai [fərā] *etc vb voir* **faire.**

fer-blanc [ferblâṅ] *nm* tin(plate).

ferblanterie [ferblâṅtrē] *nf* tinplate making; *(produit)* tinware.

ferblantier [ferblâṅtyā] *nm* tinsmith.

férié, e [fāryā] *a:* **jour** ~ public holiday.

férir [fārēr]: **sans coup** ~ *ad* without meeting any opposition.

fermage [fermázh] *nm* tenant farming.

ferme [ferm(ə)] *a* firm ♦ *ad (travailler etc)* hard; *(discuter)* ardently ♦ *nf (exploitation)* farm; *(maison)* farmhouse; **tenir** ~ to stand firm.

fermé, e [fermā] *a* closed, shut; *(gaz, eau etc)* off; *(fig: personne)* uncommunicative; *(: milieu)* exclusive.

fermement [ferməmáṅ] *ad* firmly.

ferment [fermáṅ] *nm* ferment.

fermentation [fermáṅtásyóṅ] *nf* fermentation.

fermenter [fermáṅtā] *vi* to ferment.

fermer [fermā] *vt* to close, shut; *(cesser l'exploitation de)* to close down, shut down; *(eau, lumière, électricité, robinet)* to turn off; *(aéroport, route)* to close ♦ *vi* to close, shut; to close down, shut down; **se** ~ *vi (yeux)* to close, shut; *(fleur, blessure)* to close up; ~ **à clef** to lock; ~ **au verrou** to bolt; ~ **les yeux (sur qch)** *(fig)* to close one's eyes (to sth); **se** ~ **à** *(pitié, amour)* to close one's heart ou mind to.

fermeté [fermətā] *nf* firmness.

fermette [fermet] *nf* farmhouse.

fermeture [fermətür] *nf (voir fermer)* closing; shutting; closing ou shutting down; turning off; *(dispositif)* catch; fastening; fastener; **heure de** ~ *(COMM)* closing time; **jour de** ~ *(COMM)* day on which the shop *(etc)* is closed; ~ **éclair** ® *ou* **à glissière** zipper.

fermier, ière [fermyā, -yer] *nm/f* farmer ♦ *nf (femme de fermier)* farmer's wife ♦ *a:* **beurre/cidre** ~ farm butter/cider.

fermoir [fermwár] *nm* clasp.

féroce [fāros] *a* ferocious, fierce.

férocement [fãrosmáñ] *ad* ferociously.

férocité [fãrosētã] *nf* ferocity, ferociousness.

ferons [fərôñ] *etc vb voir* **faire**.

ferraille [fɛrãy] *nf* scrap iron; **mettre à la** ~ to scrap; **bruit de** ~ clanking.

ferrailler [fɛrãyã] *vi* to clank.

ferrailleur [fɛrãyœr] *nm* scrap iron dealer.

ferrant [fɛrãñ] *am voir* **maréchal-ferrant**.

ferré, e [fɛrã] *a* (*chaussure*) hobnailed; (*canne*) steel-tipped; ~ **sur** (*fam: savant*) well up on.

ferrer [fɛrã] *vt* (*cheval*) to shoe; (*chaussure*) to nail; (*canne*) to tip; (*poisson*) to strike.

ferreux, euse [fɛrœ̃, -œ̃z] *a* ferrous.

ferronnerie [fɛronrē] *nf* ironwork; ~ **d'art** wrought iron work.

ferronnier [fɛronyã] *nm* craftsman in wrought iron; (*marchand*) ironware merchant.

ferroviaire [fɛrovyɛr] *a* rail *cpd*, railroad *cpd* (*US*), railway *cpd* (*Brit*).

ferrure [fɛrür] *nf* (*ornamental*) hinge.

ferry(-boat) [fɛrã(bôt)] *nm* ferry.

fertile [fɛrtēl] *a* fertile; ~ **en incidents** eventful, packed with incidents.

fertilisant [fɛrtēlēzãñ] *nm* fertilizer.

fertiliser [fɛrtēlēzã] *vt* to fertilize.

fertilité [fɛrtēlētã] *nf* fertility.

féru, e [fãrü] *a:* ~ **de** with a keen interest in.

férule [fãrül] *nf:* **être sous la** ~ **de qn** to be under sb's (iron) rule.

fervent, e [fɛrvãñ, -ãñt] *a* fervent.

ferveur [fɛrvœr] *nf* fervor (*US*), fervour (*Brit*).

fesse [fɛs] *nf* buttock; **les** ~**s** the bottom *sg*, the buttocks.

fessée [fɛsã] *nf* spanking.

fessier [fɛsyã] *nm* (*fam*) behind.

festin [fɛstáñ] *nm* feast.

festival [fɛstēvãl] *nm* festival.

festivalier [fɛstēvãlyã] *nm* festival-goer.

festivités [fɛstēvētã] *nfpl* festivities, merrymaking *sg*.

feston [fɛstôñ] *nm* (*ARCHIT*) festoon; (*COUTURE*) scallop.

festoyer [fɛstwãyã] *vi* to feast.

fêtard [fɛtãr] *nm* (*péj*) high liver, merry-maker.

fête [fɛt] *nf* (*religieuse*) feast; (*publique*) holiday; (*en famille etc*) celebration; (*kermesse*) fête, fair, festival; (*du nom*) feast day, name day; **faire la** ~ to live it up; **faire** ~ **à qn** to give sb a warm welcome; **se faire une** ~ **de** to look forward to; to enjoy; **ça va être sa** ~**!** (*fam*) he's going to get it!; **jour de** ~ holiday; **les** ~**s** (**de fin d'année**) the holiday (*US*) *ou* festive (*Brit*) season; **la salle/le comité des** ~**s** the (village) hall/festival committee; **la** ~ **des Mères/Pères** Mother's/Father's Day; ~ **de charité** charity bazaar; ~ **foraine** carnival (*US*), (fun)fair (*Brit*); ~ **mobile** movable holiday; **la F**~ **Nationale** the national holiday.

Fête-Dieu [fɛtdyœ̃] *nf:* **la** ~ Corpus Christi.

fêter [fɛtã] *vt* to celebrate; (*personne*) to have a celebration for.

fétiche [fãtēsh] *nm* fetish; **animal** ~, **objet** ~ mascot.

fétichisme [fãtēshēsm(ə)] *nm* fetishism.

fétide [fãtēd] *a* fetid.

fétu [fãtü] *nm:* ~ **de paille** wisp of straw.

feu [fœ̃] *a inv:* ~ **son père** his late father.

feu, x [fœ̃] *nm* (*gén*) fire; (*signal lumineux*) light; (*de cuisinière*) burner (*US*), ring (*Brit*); (*sensation de brûlure*) burning (sensation); ~**x** *nmpl* fire *sg*; (*AUTO*) (traffic) lights; **tous** ~**x éteints** (*NAVIG, AUTO*) without lights; **au** ~**!** (*incendie*) fire!; **à** ~ **doux/vif** over a slow/brisk heat; **à petit** ~ (*CULIN*) over a gentle heat; (*fig*) slowly; **faire** ~ to fire; **ne pas faire long** ~ (*fig*) not to last long; **commander le** ~ (*MIL*) to give the order to (open) fire; **tué au** ~ (*MIL*) killed in action; **mettre à** ~ (*fusée*) to fire; **pris entre deux** ~**x** caught in the crossfire; **en** ~ on fire; **être tout** ~ **tout flammes (pour)** (*passion*) to be aflame with passion (for); (*enthousiasme*) to be fired with enthusiasm (for); **prendre** ~ to catch fire; **mettre le** ~ **à** to set fire to, set on fire; **faire du** ~ to make a fire; **avez-vous du** ~**?** (*pour cigarette*) have you (got) a light?; ~ **rouge/vert/orange** (*AUTO*) red/green/yellow (*US*) *ou* amber (*Brit*) light; **donner le** ~ **vert à qch/qn** (*fig*) to give sth/sb the go-ahead *ou* green light; ~ **arrière** (*AUTO*) taillight; ~ **d'artifice** firework; (*spectacle*) fireworks *pl*; ~ **de camp** campfire; ~ **de cheminée** chimney fire; ~ **de joie** bonfire; ~ **de paille** (*fig*) flash in the pan; ~**x de brouillard** (*AUTO*) fog lights *ou* lamps; ~**x de croisement** (*AUTO*) dimmed (*US*) *ou* dipped (*Brit*) headlights; ~**x de position** (*AUTO*) parking lights (*US*), sidelights (*Brit*); ~**x de route** (*AUTO*) headlights on high (*US*) *ou* full (*Brit*) beam); ~**x de stationnement** parking lights.

feuillage [fœyãzh] *nm* foliage, leaves *pl*.

feuille [fœy] *nf* (*d'arbre*) leaf (*pl* leaves); ~ (**de papier**) sheet (of paper); **rendre** ~ **blanche** (*SCOL*) to hand *ou* turn in a blank paper; ~ **d'or/de métal** gold/metal leaf; ~ **de chou** (*péj: journal*) rag; ~ **d'impôts** tax form; ~ **de maladie** medical expenses claim form; ~ **morte** dead leaf; ~ **de paye** check stub (*US*), pay slip (*Brit*); ~ **de présence** attendance sheet; ~ **de température** temperature chart; ~ **de vigne** (*BOT*) vine leaf; (*sur statue*) fig leaf; ~ **volante** loose sheet.

feuillet [fœye] *nm* leaf (*pl* leaves), page.

feuilletage [fœytãzh] *nm* (*aspect feuilleté*) flakiness.

feuilleté, e [fœytã] *a* (*CULIN*) flaky; (*verre*) laminated.

feuilleter [fœytã] *vt* (*livre*) to leaf through.

feuilleton [fœytôñ] *nm* serial.

feuillette [fœyet] *etc vb voir* **feuilleter**.

feuillu, e [fœyü] *a* leafy ♦ *nm* broad-leaved tree.

feulement [fœlmãñ] *nm* growl.

feutre [fœtr(ə)] *nm* felt; (*chapeau*) felt hat; (*stylo*) felt-tip(ped pen).

feutré, e [fœtrã] *a* feltlike; (*pas, voix*) muffled.

feutrer [fœtrã] *vt* to felt; (*fig: bruits*) to muffle ♦ *vi*, **se** ~ *vi* (*tissu*) to felt.

feutrine [fœtrēn] *nf* (lightweight) felt.

fève [fɛv] *nf* broad bean; (*dans la galette des Rois*) charm (*hidden in cake eaten on Twelfth Night*).

février [fãvrēyã] *nm* February; *voir aussi*

juillet.

fez [fez] *nm* fez.

FF *abr* (= *franc français*) FF.

FFA *sigle fpl* (= *Forces françaises en Allemagne*) French forces in Germany.

FFI *sigle fpl* = *Forces françaises de l'intérieur (1942-45)* ♦ *sigle m* member of the FFI.

FFL *sigle fpl* (= *Forces françaises libres*) Free French Army.

Fg *abr* = **faubourg**.

FGA *sigle m* (= *Fonds de garantie automobile*) fund financed through insurance premiums, to compensate victims of uninsured losses.

FGEN *sigle f* (= *Fédération générale de l'éducation nationale*) *teachers' union*.

fi [fē] *excl*: **faire ~ de** to snap one's fingers at.

fiabilité [fyàbēlētā] *nf* reliability.

fiable [fyàbl(ə)] *a* reliable.

fiacre [fyàkr(ə)] *nm* (hackney) cab *ou* carriage.

fiançailles [fyàṅsây] *nfpl* engagement *sg*.

fiancé, e [fyàṅsā] *nm/f* fiancé/fiancée ♦ *a*: **être ~ (à)** to be engaged (to).

fiancer [fyàṅsā]: **se ~** *vi*: **se ~ (avec)** to become engaged (to).

fiasco [fyàskō] *nm* fiasco.

fibranne [fēbrán] *nf* bonded fiber (*US*) *ou* fibre.

fibre [fēbr(ə)] *nf* fiber (*US*), fibre; **avoir la ~ paternelle/militaire** to be a born father/soldier; **~ optique** optical fiber *ou* fibre; **~ de verre** fiberglass (*US*), fibreglass (*Brit*), glass fiber *ou* fibre.

fibreux, euse [fēbrœ̄, -œ̄z] *a* fibrous; (*viande*) stringy.

fibrome [fēbrōm] *nm* (*MÉD*) fibroma.

ficelage [fēslázh] *nm* tying (up).

ficeler [fēslā] *vt* to tie up.

ficelle [fēsel] *nf* string *q*; (*morceau*) piece *ou* length of string; (*pain*) stick of French bread; **~s** *pl* (*fig*) strings; **tirer sur la ~** (*fig*) to go too far.

fiche [fēsh] *nf* (*carte*) (index) card; (*INFORM*) record; (*formulaire*) form; (*ÉLEC*) plug; **~ de paye** check stub (*US*), pay slip (*Brit*); **~ signalétique** (*POLICE*) description sheet; **~ technique** data sheet, specification *ou* spec sheet.

ficher [fēshā] *vt* (*dans un fichier*) to file; (: *POLICE*) to put on file; (*planter*): **~ qch dans** to stick *ou* drive sth into; (*fam*) to do; (: *donner*) to give; (: *mettre*) to stick *ou* shove; **~ qn à la porte** (*fam*) to kick *ou* throw sb out; **fiche(-moi) le camp** (*fam*) clear out, beat it; **fiche-moi la paix** (*fam*) leave me alone; **se ~ dans** (*s'enfoncer*) to get stuck in, embed itself in; **se ~ de** (*fam*) to make fun of; not to care about.

fichier [fēshyā] *nm* (*gén*, *INFORM*) file; (*à cartes*) card index; **~ actif** *ou* **en cours d'utilisation** (*INFORM*) active file; **~ d'adresses** mailing list; **~ d'archives** (*INFORM*) archive file.

fichu, e [fēshü] *pp de* **ficher** (*fam*) ♦ *a* (*fam*: *fini, inutilisable*) done for; (: *intensif*) wretched, darned ♦ *nm* (*foulard*) (head)scarf (*pl* -scarves); **être ~ de** to be capable of; **mal ~** feeling lousy; useless; **bien ~** great.

fictif, ive [fēktēf, -ēv] *a* fictitious.

fiction [fēksyôṅ] *nf* fiction; (*fait imaginé*) invention.

fictivement [fēktēvmáṅ] *ad* fictitiously.

fidèle [fēdel] *a*: **~ (à)** faithful (to) ♦ *nm/f* (*REL*): **les ~s** the faithful; (*à l'église*) the congregation.

fidèlement [fēdelmáṅ] *ad* faithfully.

fidélité [fēdālētā] *nf* faithfulness.

Fidji [fēdzhē] *nfpl*: (**les îles**) **~** Fiji.

fief [fyef] *nm* fief; (*fig*) preserve; stronghold.

fieffé, e [fyāfā] *a* (*ivrogne, menteur*) arrant, out-and-out.

fiel [fyel] *nm* gall.

fiente [fyáṅt] *nf* (*bird*) droppings *pl*.

fier [fyā]: **se ~ à** *vt* to trust.

fier, fière [fyer] *a* proud; **~ de** proud of; **avoir fière allure** to cut a fine figure.

fièrement [fyermáṅ] *ad* proudly.

fierté [fyertā] *nf* pride.

fièvre [fyevr(ə)] *nf* fever; **avoir de la ~/39 de ~** to have a high temperature/a temperature of 39°C; **~ typhoïde** typhoid fever.

fiévreusement [fyāvrœ̄zmáṅ] *ad* (*fig*) feverishly.

fiévreux, euse [fyāvrœ̄, -œ̄z] *a* feverish.

FIFA [fēfá] *sigle f* (= *Fédération internationale de Football Association*) FIFA.

fifre [fēfr(ə)] *nm* fife; (*personne*) fife-player.

figer [fēzhā] *vt* to congeal; (*fig*: *personne*) to freeze, root to the spot; **se ~** *vi* to congeal; to freeze; (*institutions etc*) to become set, stop evolving.

fignoler [fēnyolā] *vt* to put the finishing touches to.

figue [fēg] *nf* fig.

figuier [fēgyā] *nm* fig tree.

figurant, e [fēgüráṅ, -áṅt] *nm/f* (*THÉÂTRE*) walk-on actor; (*CINÉMA*) extra.

figuratif, ive [fēgürátēf, -ēv] *a* representational, figurative.

figuration [fēgürásyôṅ] *nf* walk-on parts *pl*; extras *pl*.

figure [fēgür] *nf* (*visage*) face; (*image, tracé, forme, personnage*) figure; (*illustration*) picture, diagram; **faire ~ de** to look like; **faire bonne ~** to put up a good show; **faire triste ~** to be a sorry sight; **~ de rhétorique** figure of speech.

figuré, e [fēgürā] *a* (*sens*) figurative.

figurer [fēgürā] *vi* to appear ♦ *vt* to represent; **se ~ que** to imagine that; **figurez-vous que** ... would you believe that ...?

figurine [fēgürēn] *nf* figurine.

fil [fēl] *nm* (*brin, fig*: *d'une histoire*) thread; (*du téléphone*) cable, wire; (*textile de lin*) linen; (*d'un couteau*: *tranchant*) edge; **au ~ des années** with the passing of the years; **au ~ de l'eau** with the stream *ou* current; **de ~ en aiguille** one thing leading to another; **ne tenir qu'à un ~** (*vie, réussite etc*) to hang by a thread; **donner du ~ à retordre à qn** to make life difficult for sb; **donner/recevoir un coup de ~** to make/get a phone call; **~ à coudre** (*sewing*) thread *ou* yarn; **~ électrique** electric wire; **~ de fer** wire; **~ de fer barbelé** barbed wire; **~ à pêche** fishing line; **~ à plomb** plumbline; **~ à souder** soldering wire.

filament [fēlámáṅ] *nm* (*ÉLEC*) filament; (*de*

liquide) trickle, thread.

filandreux, euse [fēlándrœ̄, -œ̄z] *a* stringy.

filant, e [fēláṅ, -áṅt] *a*: **étoile ~e** shooting star.

filasse [fēlás] *a inv* white blond.

filature [fēlátür] *nf* (*fabrique*) mill; (*policière*) shadowing *q*, tailing *q*; **prendre qn en ~** to shadow *ou* tail sb.

fildefériste [fēldəfārēst(ə)] *nm/f* high-wire artist.

file [fēl] *nf* line; (**d'attente**) line (*US*), queue (*Brit*); **prendre la ~** to join the (end of the) line; **prendre la ~ de droite** (*AUTO*) to move into the right-hand lane; **se mettre en ~** to form a line; (*AUTO*) to get into the correct lane; **stationner en double ~** (*AUTO*) to double-park; **à la ~** *ad* (**d'affilée**) in succession; (*à la suite*) one after another; **à la** *ou* **en ~ indienne** in single file.

filer [fēlā] *vt* (*tissu, toile, verre*) to spin; (*dérouler: câble etc*) to pay *ou* let out; (*prendre en filature*) to shadow, tail; (*fam: donner*): **~ qch à qn** to slip sb sth ♦ *vi* (*bas, maille, liquide, pâte*) to run; (*aller vite*) to fly past *ou* by; (*fam: partir*) to make off; **~ à l'anglaise** to take French leave; **~ doux** to behave o.s., toe the line; **~ un mauvais coton** to be in a bad way.

filet [fēle] *nm* net; (*CULIN*) fillet; (*d'eau, de sang*) trickle; **tendre un ~** (*suj: police*) to set a trap; **~ (à bagages)** (*RAIL*) luggage rack; **~ (à provisions)** string bag.

filetage [fēltázh] *nm* threading; thread.

fileter [fēltā] *vt* to thread.

filial, e, aux [fēlyál, -ō] *a* filial ♦ *nf* (*COMM*) subsidiary; affiliate.

filiation [fēlyásyōṅ] *nf* filiation.

filière [fēlyer] *nf*: **passer par la ~** to go through the (administrative) channels; **suivre la ~** to work one's way up (through the hierarchy).

filiforme [fēlēform(ə)] *a* spindly; threadlike.

filigrane [fēlēgrán] *nm* (*d'un billet, timbre*) watermark; **en ~** (*fig*) showing just beneath the surface.

filin [fēláṅ] *nm* (*NAVIG*) rope.

fille [fēy] *nf* girl; (*opposé à fils*) daughter; **vieille ~** old maid; **~ de joie** prostitute; **~ de salle** waitress.

fille-mère, *pl* **filles-mères** [fēymer] *nf* unmarried mother.

fillette [fēyet] *nf* (little) girl.

filleul, e [fēyœl] *nm/f* godchild, godson/ daughter.

film [fēlm] *nm* (*pour photo*) (roll of) film; (*œuvre*) film, picture, movie; (*couche*) film; **~ muet/parlant** silent/talking picture *ou* movie; **~ d'animation** animated film; **~ policier** thriller.

filmer [fēlmā] *vt* to film.

filon [fēlóṅ] *nm* vein, lode; (*fig*) lucrative line, moneymaker.

filou [fēlōō] *nm* (*escroc*) swindler.

fils [fēs] *nm* son; **~ de famille** moneyed young man; **~ à papa** (*péj*) daddy's boy.

filtrage [fēltrázh] *nm* filtering.

filtrant, e [fēltráṅ, -áṅt] *a* (*huile solaire etc*) filtering.

filtre [fēltr(ə)] *nm* filter; "**~ ou sans ~?**"

(*cigarettes*) "filter-tipped or plain?"; **~ à air** air filter.

filtrer [fēltrā] *vt* to filter; (*fig: candidats, visiteurs*) to screen ♦ *vi* to filter (through).

fin [faṅ] *nf* end; **~s** *nfpl* (*but*) ends; **à (la) ~ mai, ~ mai** at the end of May; **en ~ de semaine** at the end of the week; **prendre ~** to come to an end; **toucher à sa ~** to be drawing to a close; **mettre ~ à** to put an end to; **mener à bonne ~** to bring to a successful conclusion; **à cette ~** to this end; **à toutes ~s utiles** for your information; **à la ~** in the end, eventually; **sans ~** *a* endless ♦ *ad* endlessly; **~ de non-recevoir** (*JUR, ADMIN*) objection; **~ de section** (*de ligne d'autobus*) (fare) stage.

fin, e [faṅ, fēn] *a* (*papier, couche, fil*) thin; (*cheveux, poudre, pointe, visage*) fine; (*taille*) neat, slim; (*esprit, remarque*) subtle; shrewd ♦ *ad* (*moudre, couper*) finely ♦ *nm*: **vouloir jouer au plus ~ (avec qn)** to try to outsmart sb ♦ *nf* (*alcool*) liqueur brandy; **c'est ~!** (*ironique*) how clever!; **~ prêt/soûl** quite ready/drunk; **un ~ gourmet** a gourmet; **un ~ tireur** a crack shot; **avoir la vue/l'ouïe ~e** to have sharp eyes/ears, have keen eyesight/hearing; **or/linge/vin ~** fine gold/linen/wine; **le ~ fond de** the very depths of; **le ~ mot de** the real story behind; **la ~e fleur de** the flower of; **une ~e mouche** (*fig*) a sharp customer; **~es herbes** mixed herbs.

final, e [fēnál] *a, nf* final ♦ *nm* (*MUS*) finale; **quarts de ~e** quarter finals; **8èmes/16èmes de ~e** 2nd/1st round (*in 5 round knock-out competition*).

finalement [fēnálmáṅ] *ad* finally, in the end; (*après tout*) after all.

finaliste [fēnálēst(ə)] *nm/f* finalist.

finance [fēnáṅs] *nf* finance; **~s** *nfpl* (*situation financière*) finances; (*activités financières*) finance *sg*; **moyennant ~** for a fee *ou* consideration.

financement [fēnáṅsmáṅ] *nm* financing.

financer [fēnáṅsā] *vt* to finance.

financier, ière [fēnáṅsyā, -yer] *a* financial ♦ *nm* financier.

financièrement [fēnáṅsyermáṅ] *ad* financially.

finasser [fēnásā] *vi* (*péj*) to wheel and deal.

finaud, e [fēnō, -ōd] *a* wily.

fine [fēn] *af, nf voir* **fin, e**.

finement [fēnmáṅ] *ad* thinly; finely; neatly, slimly; subtly; shrewdly.

finesse [fēnes] *nf* thinness; fineness; neatness, slimness; subtlety; shrewdness; **~s** *nfpl* (*subtilités*) niceties; finer points.

fini, e [fēnē] *a* finished; (*MATH*) finite; (*intensif*): **un menteur ~** a liar through and through ♦ *nm* (*d'un objet manufacturé*) finish.

finir [fēnēr] *vt* to finish ♦ *vi* to finish, end; **~ quelque part** to end *ou* finish up somewhere; **~ de faire** to finish doing; (*cesser*) to stop doing; **~ par faire** to end *ou* finish up doing; **il finit par m'agacer** he's beginning to get on my nerves; **~ en pointe/tragédie** to end in a point/in tragedy; **en ~ avec** to be *ou* have done with; **à n'en plus ~** (*route, discussions*) never-ending; **il va mal ~** he will come to a bad end; **c'est bientôt fini?** (*reproche*) have

you quite finished?
finish [fēnēsh] *nm* (*SPORT*) finish.
finissage [fēnēsàzh] *nm* finishing.
finisseur, euse [fēnēsœr, -œz] *nm/f* (*SPORT*) strong finisher.
finition [fēnēsyôn] *nf* finishing; finish.
finlandais, e [fanlánde, -ez] *a* Finnish ♦ *nm/f*: F~, e Finn.
Finlande [fanlánd] *nf*: la ~ Finland.
finnois, e [fēnwà, -wàz] *a* Finnish ♦ *nm* (*LING*) Finnish.
fiole [fyol] *nf* phial.
fiord [fyor(d)] *nm* = **fjord**.
fioriture [fyorētür] *nf* embellishment, flourish.
fioul [fyōol] *nm* fuel oil.
firent [fēr] *vb voir* **faire**.
firmament [fērmámán] *nm* firmament, skies *pl*.
firme [fērm(ə)] *nf* firm.
fis [fē] *vb voir* **faire**.
fisc [fēsk] *nm* tax authorities *pl*, ≈ Internal Revenue Service (*US*), ≈ Inland Revenue (*Brit*).
fiscal, e, aux [fēskál, -ō] *a* tax *cpd*, fiscal.
fiscaliser [fēskálēzá] *vt* to subject to tax.
fiscaliste [fēskálēst(ə)] *nm/f* tax specialist.
fiscalité [fēskálētá] *nf* tax system; (*charges*) taxation.
fission [fēsyôn] *nf* fission.
fissure [fēsür] *nf* crack.
fissurer [fēsürá] *vt*, **se** ~ *vi* to crack.
fiston [fēstôn] *nm* (*fam*) son, lad.
fit [fē] *vb voir* **faire**.
fixage [fēksàzh] *nm* (*PHOTO*) fixing.
fixateur [fēksátœr] *nm* (*PHOTO*) fixer; (*pour cheveux*) hair cream.
fixatif [fēksátēf] *nm* fixative.
fixation [fēksâsyôn] *nf* fixing; fastening; setting; (*de ski*) binding; (*PSYCH*) fixation.
fixe [fēks(ə)] *a* fixed; (*emploi*) steady, regular ♦ *nm* (*salaire*) basic salary; **à heure** ~ at a set time; **menu à prix** ~ table d'hôte.
fixé, e [fēksá] *a* (*heure, jour*) appointed; **être** ~ **(sur)** to have made up one's mind (about); to know for certain (about).
fixement [fēksəmán] *ad* fixedly, steadily.
fixer [fēksá] *vt* (*attacher*): ~ **qch (à/sur)** to fix *ou* fasten sth (to/onto); (*déterminer*) to fix, set; (*CHIMIE, PHOTO*) to fix; (*poser son regard sur*) to look hard at, stare at; **se** ~ (*s'établir*) to settle down; ~ **son choix sur** **qch** to decide on sth; **se** ~ **sur** (*suj: attention*) to focus on.
fixité [fēksētá] *nf* fixedness.
fjord [fyor(d)] *nm* fjord, fiord.
fl. *abr* (= *fleuve*) r, R; (= *florin*) fl.
flacon [flákôn] *nm* bottle.
flagellation [flàzhelàsyôn] *nf* flogging.
flageller [flàzhālá] *vt* to flog, scourge.
flageoler [flàzholá] *vi* to have knees like jelly.
flageolet [flàzhole] *nm* (*MUS*) flageolet; (*CULIN*) dwarf kidney bean.
flagornerie [flàgornərē] *nf* toadying, fawning.
flagorneur, euse [flàgornœr, -œz] *nm/f* toady, fawner.
flagrant, e [flàgrán, -ánt] *a* flagrant, blatant; **en** ~ **délit** in the act, in flagrante delicto.
flair [fler] *nm* sense of smell; (*fig*) intuition.
flairer [flārá] *vt* (*humer*) to sniff (at);

. (*détecter*) to scent.
flamand, e [flámán, -ánd] *a* Flemish ♦ *nm* (*LING*) Flemish ♦ *nm/f*: F~, e Fleming; **les** F~s the Flemish.
flamant [flámán] *nm* flamingo.
flambant [flánbán] *ad*: ~ **neuf** brand new.
flambé, e [flánbá] *a* (*CULIN*) flambé ♦ *nf* blaze; (*fig*) flaring-up, explosion.
flambeau, x [flánbō] *nm* (flaming) torch; **se passer le** ~ (*fig*) to hand down the (*ou* a) tradition.
flambée [flánbá] *nf* (*feu*) blaze; (*COMM*): ~ **des prix** (sudden) shooting up of prices.
flamber [flánbá] *vi* to blaze (up) ♦ *vt* (*poulet*) to singe; (*aiguille*) to sterilize.
flamboyant, e [flánbwáyán, -ánt] *a* blazing; flaming.
flamboyer [flánbwáyá] *vi* to blaze (up); (*fig*) to flame.
flamingant, e [flámangán, -ánt] *a* Flemish-speaking ♦ *nm/f*: F~, e Flemish speaker; (*POL*) Flemish nationalist.
flamme [flám] *nf* flame; (*fig*) fire, fervor (*US*), fervour (*Brit*); **en** ~**s** on fire, ablaze.
flammèche [flámesh] *nf* (flying) spark.
flammerole [flámrol] *nf* will-o'-the-wisp.
flan [flán] *nm* (*CULIN*) baked custard (*US*), custard tart *ou* pie (*Brit*).
flanc [flán] *nm* side; (*MIL*) flank; **à** ~ **de colline** on the hillside; **prêter le** ~ **à** (*fig*) to lay o.s. open to.
flancher [flánshá] *vi* (*cesser de fonctionner*) to fail, pack up; (*armée*) to quit.
Flandre [flándr(ə)] *nf*: la ~ (*aussi*: les ~s) Flanders.
flanelle [flánel] *nf* flannel.
flâner [fláná] *vi* to stroll.
flânerie [flánrē] *nf* stroll.
flâneur, euse [flánœr, -œz] *a* idle ♦ *nm/f* stroller.
flanquer [flánká] *vt* to flank; (*fam: jeter*): ~ **par terre/à la porte** to fling to the ground/ throw *ou* kick out; (: *donner*): ~ **la frousse à qn** to give sb an awful fright.
flapi, e [flápē] *a* dog-tired.
flaque [flák] *nf* (*d'eau*) puddle; (*d'huile, de sang etc*) pool.
flash, pl flashes [flásh] *nm* (*PHOTO*) flash; ~ **(d'information)** newsflash.
flasque [flásk(ə)] *a* flabby ♦ *nf* (*flacon*) flask.
flatter [flátá] *vt* to flatter; (*caresser*) to stroke; **se** ~ **de qch** to pride o.s. on sth.
flatterie [flátrē] *nf* flattery.
flatteur, euse [flátœr, -œz] *a* flattering ♦ *nm/f* flatterer.
flatulence [flátüláns], **flatuosité** [flátüōzētá] *nf* (*MÉD*) flatulence, wind.
FLB *abr* (= *franco long du bord*) FAS ♦ *sigle* *m* (*POL*) = *Front de libération de la Bretagne*.
FLC *sigle m* = *Front de libération de la Corse*.
fléau, x [flāō] *nm* scourge, curse; (*de balance*) beam; (*pour le blé*) flail.
fléchage [flāsházh] *nm* (*d'un itinéraire*) sign-posting.
flèche [flesh] *nf* arrow; (*de clocher*) spire; (*de grue*) jib; (*trait d'esprit, critique*) shaft; **monter en** ~ (*fig*) to soar, rocket; **partir en** ~ (*fig*) to be off like a shot; **à** ~ **variable**

(avion) variable geometry wing *cpd* *(US)*, swing-wing *cpd* *(Brit)*.

flécher [flāshā] *vt* to mark with arrows.

fléchette [flāshet] *nf* dart; **~s** *nfpl* *(jeu)* darts *sg*.

fléchir [flāshēr] *vt* *(corps, genou)* to bend; *(fig)* to sway, weaken ♦ *vi* *(poutre)* to sag, bend; *(fig)* to weaken, flag; *(: baisser: prix)* to fall off.

fléchissement [flāshēsmáń] *nm* bending; sagging; flagging; *(de l'économie)* dullness.

flegmatique [flĕgmátēk] *a* phlegmatic.

flegme [flĕgm(ə)] *nm* composure.

flemmard, e [flāmár, -árd(ə)] *nm/f* lazybones *sg*, loafer.

flemme [flĕm] *nf* *(fam)*: **j'ai la ~ de faire** I can't be bothered to do.

flétan [flātáń] *nm* *(ZOOL)* halibut.

flétrir [flātrēr] *vt* to wither; *(stigmatiser)* to condemn (in the most severe terms); **se ~** *vi* to wither.

fleur [flœr] *nf* flower; *(d'un arbre)* blossom; **être en ~** *(arbre)* to be in blossom; **tissu à ~s** flowered *ou* flowery fabric; **la (fine) ~ de** *(fig)* the flower of; **être ~ bleue** to be soppy *ou* sentimental; **à ~ de terre** just above the ground; **faire une ~ à qn** to do sb a favor; **~ de lis** fleur-de-lis.

fleurer [flœrā] *vt*: **~ la lavande** to have the scent of lavender.

fleuret [flœrc] *nm* *(arme)* foil; *(sport)* fencing.

fleurette [flœrct] *nf*: **conter ~ à qn** to whisper sweet nothings to sb.

fleuri, e [flœrē] *a* in flower *ou* bloom; surrounded by flowers; *(fig: style)* flowery; *(: teint)* glowing.

fleurir [flœrēr] *vi* *(rose)* to flower; *(arbre)* to blossom; *(fig)* to flourish ♦ *vt* *(tombe)* to put flowers on; *(chambre)* to decorate with flowers.

fleuriste [flœrēst(ə)] *nm/f* florist.

fleuron [flœróń] *nm* jewel *(fig)*.

fleuve [flœv] *nm* river; **roman-~** saga; **discours-~** interminable speech.

flexibilité [flĕksēbēlētā] *nf* flexibility.

flexible [flĕksēbl(ə)] *a* flexible.

flexion [flĕksyóń] *nf* flexing, bending; *(LING)* inflection.

flibustier [flēbüstyā] *nm* buccaneer.

flic [flēk] *nm* *(fam: péj)* cop.

flipper *nm* [flēpœr] pinball (machine) ♦ *vi* [flēpā] *(fam: être déprimé)* to feel down, be on a downer; *(: être exalté)* to freak out.

flirt [flœrt] *nm* flirting; *(personne)* boyfriend, girlfriend.

flirter [flœrtā] *vi* to flirt.

FLN *sigle m* = *Front de libération nationale (during the Algerian war)*.

FLNKS *sigle m* (= *Front de libération nationale kanak et socialiste)* political movement in New Caledonia*.

flocon [flokóń] *nm* flake; *(de laine etc: boulette)* flock; **~s d'avoine** oatflakes.

floconneux, euse [flokonœ̄, -œ̄z] *a* fluffy, fleecy.

flonflons [flóńflóń] *nmpl* blare *sg*.

flopée [flopā] *nf*: **une ~ de** loads of.

floraison [florczóń] *nf* *(voir fleurir)* flowering; blossoming; flourishing.

floral, e, aux [florál, -ō] *a* floral, flower *cpd*.

floralies [florálē] *nfpl* flower show *sg*.

flore [flor] *nf* flora.

Florence [floráńs] *n* *(ville)* Florence.

florentin, e [floráńtań, -ēn] *a* Florentine.

floriculture [florēkültür] *nf* flower-growing.

florissant, e [florēsáń, -áńt] *vb voir* **fleurir** ♦ *a* flourishing; *(santé, teint, mine)* blooming.

flot [flō] *nm* flood, stream; *(marée)* flood tide; **~s** *nmpl* *(de la mer)* waves; **être à ~** *(NAVIG)* to be afloat; *(fig)* to be on an even keel; **à ~s** *(couler)* in torrents; **entrer à ~s** to stream *ou* pour in.

flottage [flotázh] *nm* *(du bois)* floating.

flottaison [flotczóń] *nf*: **ligne de ~** waterline.

flottant, e [flotáń, -áńt] *a* *(vêtement)* loose(-fitting); *(cours, barème)* floating.

flotte [flot] *nf* *(NAVIG)* fleet; *(fam)* water; rain.

flottement [flotmáń] *nm* *(fig)* wavering, hesitation; *(ÉCON)* floating.

flotter [flotā] *vi* to float; *(nuage, odeur)* to drift; *(drapeau)* to fly; *(vêtements)* to hang loose ♦ *vb impersonnel* *(fam: pleuvoir)*: **il flotte** it's raining ♦ *vt* to float; **faire ~** to float.

flotteur [flotœr] *nm* float.

flottille [flotēy] *nf* flotilla.

flou, e [flōō] *a* fuzzy, blurred; *(fig)* vague; *(non ajusté: robe)* loose(-fitting).

flouer [flōōā] *vt* to swindle.

FLQ *abr* (= *franco long du quai)* FAQ.

fluctuation [flüktüásyóń] *nf* fluctuation.

fluctuer [flüktüā] *vi* to fluctuate.

fluet, te [flüe, -et] *a* thin, slight; *(voix)* thin.

fluide [flüēd] *a* fluid; *(circulation etc)* flowing freely ♦ *nm* fluid; *(force)* (mysterious) power.

fluidifier [flüēdēfyā] *vt* to make fluid.

fluidité [flüēdētā] *nf* fluidity; free flow.

fluor [flüor] *nm* fluorine.

fluoré, e [flüorā] *a* fluoridated.

fluorescent, e [flüorāsáń, -áńt] *a* fluorescent.

flûte [flüt] *nf* *(aussi: ~ traversière)* flute; *(verre)* flute glass; *(pain)* long loaf *(pl* loaves)*; **petite ~** piccolo *(pl* -s)*; **~!** drat it!; **~ (à bec)** recorder; **~ de Pan** panpipes *pl*.

flûtiste [flütēst(ə)] *nm/f* flautist, flute player.

fluvial, e, aux [flüvyál, -ō] *a* river *cpd*, fluvial.

flux [flü] *nm* incoming tide; *(écoulement)* flow; **le ~ et le reflux** the ebb and flow.

fluxion [flüksyóń] *nf*: **~ de poitrine** pneumonia.

FM *sigle f* (= *frequency modulation)* FM.

Fme *abr* = *femme*.

FMI *sigle m* (= *Fonds monétaire international)* IMF.

FN *sigle m* (= *Front national)* political party.

FNAC [fnák] *sigle f* (= *Fédération nationale des achats des cadres)* chain of discount shops *(hi-fi, photo etc)*.

FNAH *sigle m* = *Fonds national d'amélioration de l'habitat*.

FNEF [fnef] *sigle f* (= *Fédération nationale des étudiants de France)* student union.

FNSEA *sigle f* (= *Fédération nationale des syndicats d'exploitants agricoles)* farmers' union.

FO *sigle f* (= *Force ouvrière)* labor union.

foc [fɔk] *nm* jib.

focal, e, aux [fɔkál, -ō] *a* focal ♦ *nf* focal length.

focaliser [fɔkálēzā] *vt* to focus.

foehn [fœn] *nm* foehn, föhn.

fœtal, e, aux [fātál, -ō] *a* fetal, foetal (*Brit*).

fœtus [fātüs] *nm* fetus, foetus (*Brit*).

foi [fwá] *nf* faith; **sous la ~ du serment** under *ou* on oath; **ajouter ~ à** to lend credence to; **faire ~** (*prouver*) to be evidence; **digne de ~** reliable; **sur la ~ de** on the word *ou* strength of; **être de bonne/mauvaise ~** to be in good faith/not to be in good faith; **ma ~!** well!

foie [fwá] *nm* liver; **~ gras** foie gras.

foin [fwáṅ] *nm* hay; **faire les ~s** to make hay; **faire du ~** (*fam*) to kick up a row.

foire [fwár] *nf* fair; (*fête foraine*) carnival (*US*), (fun)fair (*Brit*); (*fig: désordre, confusion*) bear garden; **faire la ~** to whoop it up; **~ (exposition)** trade fair.

fois [fwá] *nf* time; **une/deux ~** once/twice; **trois/vingt ~** three/twenty times; **2 ~ 2** 2 times 2; **deux/quatre ~ plus grand (que)** twice/four times as big (as); **une ~** (*passé*) once; (*futur*) sometime; **une (bonne) ~ pour toutes** once and for all; **encore une ~** again, once more; **il était une ~** once upon a time; **une ~ que c'est fait** once it's done; **une ~ parti** once he (*ou* I *etc*) had left; **des ~** (*parfois*) sometimes; **si des ~ ...** (*fam*) if ever ...; **non mais des ~!** (*fam*) (now) look here!; **à la ~** (*ensemble*) (all) at once; **à la ~ grand et beau** both tall and handsome.

foison [fwázôṅ] *nf*: **une ~ de** an abundance of; **à ~** *ad* in plenty.

foisonnant, e [fwázonâṅ, -âṅt] *a* teeming.

foisonnement [fwázonmáṅ] *nm* profusion, abundance.

foisonner [fwázonā] *vi* to abound; **~ en** *ou* **de** to abound in.

fol [fɔl] *am voir* **fou**.

folâtre [fɔlâtr(ə)] *a* playful.

folâtrer [fɔlâtrā] *vi* to frolic (around).

folichon, ne [fɔlēshôṅ, -on] *a*: **ça n'a rien de ~** it's not a lot of fun.

folie [fɔlē] *nf* (*d'une décision, d'un acte*) madness, folly; (*état*) madness, insanity; (*acte*) folly; **la ~ des grandeurs** delusions of grandeur; **faire des ~s** (*en dépenses*) to be extravagant.

folklore [fɔlklor] *nm* folklore.

folklorique [fɔlklorēk] *a* folk *cpd*; (*fam*) weird.

folle [fɔl] *af*, *nf voir* **fou**.

follement [fɔlmáṅ] *ad* (*très*) madly, wildly.

follet [fɔle] *am*: **feu ~** will-o'-the-wisp.

fomentateur, trice [fɔmâṅtátœr, -trēs] *nm/f* agitator.

fomenter [fɔmâṅtā] *vt* to stir up, foment.

foncé, e [fôṅsā] *a* dark; **bleu ~** dark blue.

foncer [fôṅsā] *vt* to make darker; (*CULIN: moule etc*) to line ♦ *vi* to go darker; (*fam: aller vite*) to tear *ou* belt along; **~ sur** to charge at.

fonceur, euse [fôṅsœr, -œz] *nm/f* whizz kid.

foncier, ière [fôṅsyá, -yer] *a* (*honnêteté etc*) basic, fundamental; (*malhonnêteté*) deep-rooted; (*COMM*) real estate *cpd*.

foncièrement [fôṅsyermáṅ] *ad* basically; (*absolument*) thoroughly.

fonction [fôṅksyôṅ] *nf* (*rôle*, MATH, LING) function; (*emploi, poste*) post, position; **~s** (*professionnelles*) duties; **entrer en ~s** to take up one's post *ou* duties; to take up office; **voiture de ~** company car; **être ~ de** (*dépendre de*) to depend on; **en ~ de** (*par rapport à*) according to; **faire ~ de** to serve as; **la ~ publique** the civil service.

fonctionnaire [fôṅksyoner] *nm/f* state employee *ou* official; (*dans l'administration*) ≈ civil servant.

fonctionnariser [fôṅksyonárēzā] *vt* (ADMIN: *personne*) to give the status of a state employee to.

fonctionnel, le [fôṅksyonel] *a* functional.

fonctionnellement [fôṅksyonelmáṅ] *ad* functionally.

fonctionnement [fôṅksyonmáṅ] *nm* working; functioning; operation.

fonctionner [fôṅksyonā] *vi* to work, function; (*entreprise*) to operate, function; **faire ~** to work, operate.

fond [fôṅ] *nm voir aussi* **fonds**; (*d'un récipient, trou*) bottom; (*d'une salle, scène*) back; (*d'un tableau, décor*) background; (*opposé à la forme*) content; (*petite quantité*): **un ~ de verre** a drop; (SPORT): **le ~** long distance (running); **course/épreuve de ~** long-distance race/trial; **au ~ de** at the bottom of; at the back of; **aller au ~ des choses** to get to the root of things; **le ~ de sa pensée** his (*ou* her) true thoughts *ou* feelings; **sans ~** a bottomless; **envoyer par le ~** (NAVIG: *couler*) to sink, scuttle; **à ~** *ad* (*connaître, soutenir*) thoroughly; (*appuyer, visser*) right down *ou* home; **à ~ (de train)** *ad* (*fam*) full tilt; **dans le ~, au ~** *ad* (*en somme*) basically, really; **de ~ en comble** *ad* from top to bottom; **~ sonore** background noise; background music; **~ de teint** (make-up) foundation.

fondamental, e, aux [fôṅdámâṅtál, -ō] *a* fundamental.

fondamentalement [fôṅdámâṅtálmáṅ] *ad* fundamentally.

fondamentalisme [fôṅdámâṅtálēsm(ə)] *nm* fundamentalism.

fondant, e [fôṅdâṅ, -âṅt] *a* (*neige*) melting; (*poire*) that melts in the mouth; (*chocolat*) fondant.

fondateur, trice [fôṅdátœr, -trēs] *nm/f* founder; **membre ~** founding (*US*) *ou* founder (*Brit*) member.

fondation [fôṅdásyôṅ] *nf* founding; (*établissement*) foundation; **~s** *nfpl* (*d'une maison*) foundations; **travail de ~** foundation works *pl*.

fondé, e [fôṅdā] *a* (*accusation etc*) well-founded; **mal ~** unfounded; **être ~ à croire** to have grounds for believing *ou* good reason to believe ♦ *nm*: **~ de pouvoir** authorized representative.

fondement [fôṅdmáṅ] *nm* (*derrière*) behind; **~s** *nmpl* foundations; **sans ~** a (*rumeur etc*) groundless, unfounded.

fonder [fôṅdā] *vt* to found; (*fig*): **~ qch sur** to base sth on; **se ~ sur** (*suj: personne*) to base o.s. on; **~ un foyer** (*se marier*) to set up house.

fonderie [fôṅdrē] *nf* smelting works *sg*.

fondeur, euse [fôṅdœr, -œz] *nm/f* (*skieur*) long-distance skier ♦ *nm*: (**ouvrier**) ~ caster.

fondre [fôṅdr(ə)] *vt* to melt; (*dans l'eau: sucre, sel*) to dissolve; (*fig: mélanger*) to merge, blend ♦ *vi* to melt; to dissolve; (*fig*) to melt away; (*se précipiter*): ~ **sur** to swoop down on; **se ~** *vi* (*se combiner, se confondre*) to merge into each other; to dissolve; ~ **en larmes** to dissolve into tears.

fondrière [fôṅdrēyer] *nf* rut.

fonds [fôṅ] *nm* (*de bibliothèque*) collection; (*COMM*): ~ (**de commerce**) business; (*fig*): ~ **de probité** *etc* fund of integrity *etc* ♦ *nmpl* (*argent*) funds; **à ~ perdus** *ad* with little or no hope of getting the money back; **être en** ~ to be in funds; **mise de ~** investment, (capital) outlay; **F~ Monétaire International (FMI)** International Monetary Fund (IMF); ~ **de roulement** *nm* working capital.

fondu, e [fôṅdü] *a* (*beurre, neige*) melted; (*métal*) molten ♦ *nm* (*CINÉMA*): ~ (**enchaîné**) dissolve ♦ *nf* (*CULIN*) fondue.

fongicide [fôṅzhēsēd] *nm* fungicide.

font [fôṅ] *vb voir* **faire**.

fontaine [fôṅten] *nf* fountain; (*source*) spring.

fonte [fôṅt] *nf* melting; (*métal*) cast iron; **la** ~ **des neiges** (the spring) thaw.

fonts baptismaux [fôṅbátēsmō] *nmpl* (baptismal) font *sg*.

foot(ball) [fōōt(bōl)] *nm* football, soccer.

footballeur, euse [fōōtbôlœr, -œz] *nm/f* football *ou* soccer player.

footing [fōōtēng] *nm* jogging; **faire du** ~ to go jogging.

for [for] *nm*: **dans** *ou* **en son** ~ **intérieur** in one's heart of hearts.

forage [forázh] *nm* drilling, boring.

forain, e [foraṅ, -en] *a* fairground *cpd* ♦ *nm* (*marchand*) boothkeeper (*US*), stallkeeper (*US*), stallholder (*Brit*); (*acteur etc*) fairground entertainer.

forban [forbáṅ] *nm* (*pirate*) pirate; (*escroc*) crook.

forçat [forsá] *nm* convict.

force [fors(ə)] *nf* strength; (*puissance: surnaturelle etc*) power; (*PHYSIQUE, MÉCANIQUE*) force; ~**s** *nfpl* (*physiques*) strength *sg*; (*MIL*) forces; (*effectifs*): **d'importantes** ~**s de police** big contingents of police; **avoir de la** ~ to be strong; **être à bout de** ~ to have no strength left; **à la** ~ **du poignet** (*fig*) by the sweat of one's brow; **à** ~ **de faire** by dint of doing; **arriver en** ~ (*nombreux*) to arrive in force; **cas de** ~ **majeure** case of absolute necessity; (*ASSURANCES*) act of God; ~ **de la nature** natural force; **de** ~ *ad* forcibly, by force; **de toutes mes/ses** ~**s** with all my/his strength; **par la** ~ using force; **par la** ~ **des choses/d'habitude** by force of circumstances/habit; **à toute** ~ (*absolument*) at all costs; **faire** ~ **de rames/voiles** to ply the oars/crowd on sail; **être de** ~ **à faire** to be up to doing; **de première** ~ first class; **la** ~ **armée** (*les troupes*) the army; ~ **d'âme** fortitude; ~ **de frappe** strike force; ~ **d'inertie** force of inertia; **la** ~ **publique** the authorities respon-

sible for public order; ~**s d'intervention** (*MIL, POLICE*) peace-keeping force *sg*; **les** ~**s de l'ordre** the police.

forcé, e [forsā] *a* forced; (*bain*) unintended; (*inevitable*): **c'est** ~! it's inevitable!, it HAS to be!

forcément [forsāmáṅ] *ad* necessarily; inevitably; (*bien sûr*) of course.

forcené, e [forsənā] *a* frenzied ♦ *nm/f* maniac.

forceps [forseps] *nm* forceps *pl*.

forcer [forsā] *vt* (*contraindre*): ~ **qn à faire** to force sb to do; (*porte, serrure, plante*) to force; (*moteur, voix*) to strain ♦ *vi* (*SPORT*) to overtax o.s.; **se** ~ **à faire qch** to force o.s. to do sth; ~ **la dose/l'allure** to overdo it/ increase the pace; ~ **l'attention/le respect** to command attention/respect; ~ **la consigne** to bypass orders.

forcing [forsēng] *nm* (*SPORT*): **faire le** ~ to pile on the pressure.

forcir [forsēr] *vi* (*grossir*) to broaden out; (*vent*) to freshen.

forclore [forklor] *vt* (*JUR: personne*) to debar.

forclusion [forklüzyôṅ] *nf* (*JUR*) debarment.

forer [forā] *vt* to drill, bore.

forestier, ière [forestyā, -yer] *a* forest *cpd*.

foret [fore] *nm* drill.

forêt [fore] *nf* forest; **Office National des F~s** (*ADMIN*) ≈ National Forest Service (*US*), ≈ Forestry Commission (*Brit*); **la F~ Noire** the Black Forest.

foreuse [forœz] *nf* (electric) drill.

forfait [forfe] *nm* (*COMM*) fixed *ou* set price; package deal, all-inclusive price; (*crime*) infamy; **déclarer** ~ to withdraw; **gagner par** ~ to win by default; **travailler à** ~ to work for a lump sum.

forfaitaire [forfeter] *a* set; inclusive.

forfait-vacances, *pl* **forfaits-vacances** [forfevákáṅs] *nm* package tour.

forfanterie [forfáṅtrē] *nf* boastfulness *q*.

forge [forzh(ə)] *nf* forge, smithy.

forger [forzhā] *vt* to forge; (*fig: personnalité*) to form; (: *prétexte*) to contrive, make up; **être forgé de toutes pièces** to be a complete fabrication.

forgeron [forzhərôṅ] *nm* (black)smith.

formaliser [formálēzá]: **se** ~ *vi*: **se** ~ (**de**) to take offense (*US*) *ou* offence (*Brit*) (at).

formalisme [formálēsm(ə)] *nm* formality.

formalité [formálētá] *nf* formality.

format [formá] *nm* size; **petit** ~ small size; (*PHOTO*) 35 mm (film).

formater [formátá] *vt* (*disque*) to format; **non formaté** unformatted.

formateur, trice [formátœr, -trēs] *a* formative.

formation [formásyôṅ] *nf* forming; (*éducation*) training; (*MUS*) group; (*MIL, AVIAT, GÉO*) formation; **la** ~ **permanente** *ou* **continue** continuing education; **la** ~ **professionnelle** vocational training.

forme [form(ə)] *nf* (*gén*) form; (*d'un objet*) shape, form; ~**s** *nfpl* (*bonnes manières*) proprieties; (*d'une femme*) figure *sg*; **en** ~ **de poire** pear-shaped, in the shape of a pear; **sous** ~ **de** in the form of; in the guise of; **sous** ~ **de cachets** in the form of tablets; **être en (bonne** *ou* **pleine)** ~, **avoir la** ~ (*SPORT etc*) to be in good shape; **en bonne et**

due ~ in due form; **pour la ~** for the sake of form; **sans autre ~ de procès** (*fig*) without further ado; **prendre ~** to take shape.

formel, le [formɛl] *a* (*preuve, décision*) definite, positive; (*logique*) formal.

formellement [formɛlmɑ̃] *ad* (*interdit*) strictly.

former [formɑ̃] *vt* (*gén*) to form; (*éduquer: soldat, ingénieur etc*) to train; **se ~** to form; to train.

formidable [formidabl(ə)] *a* tremendous.

formidablement [formidabləmɑ̃] *ad* tremendously.

formol [formɔl] *nm* formalin, formol.

formosan, e [formozɑ̃, -an] *a* Formosan.

Formose [formoz] *nm* Formosa.

formulaire [formyler] *nm* form.

formule [formyl] *nf* (*gén*) formula; (*formulaire*) form; **selon la ~ consacrée** as one says; **~ de politesse** polite phrase; (*en fin de lettre*) letter ending.

formuler [formyle] *vt* (*émettre: réponse, vœux*) to formulate; (*expliciter: sa pensée*) to express.

forniquer [fornike] *vi* to fornicate.

fort, e [for, fort(ə)] *a* strong; (*intensité, rendement*) high, great; (*corpulent*) large; (*doué*): **être ~ (en)** to be good (at) ♦ *ad* (*serrer, frapper*) hard; (*sonner*) loud(ly); (*beaucoup*) greatly, very much; (*très*) very ♦ *nm* (*édifice*) fort; (*point fort*) strong point, forte; (*gén pl: personne, pays*): **le ~, les ~s** the strong; **c'est un peu ~!** it's a bit much!; **à plus ~e raison** even more so, all the more reason; **avoir ~ à faire avec qn** to have one's work cut out with sb; **se faire ~ de faire** to claim one can do; **bien/peu** very well/few; **au plus ~ de** (*au milieu de*) in the thick of, at the height of; **~e tête** rebel.

fortement [fortəmɑ̃] *ad* strongly; (*s'intéresser*) deeply.

forteresse [fortərɛs] *nf* fortress.

fortifiant [fortifjɑ̃] *nm* tonic.

fortifications [fortifikɑsjɔ̃] *nfpl* fortifications.

fortifier [fortifje] *vt* to strengthen, fortify; (*MIL*) to fortify; **se ~** *vi* (*personne, santé*) to grow stronger.

fortin [fortɛ̃] *nm* (small) fort.

fortiori [forsjori]: **à ~** *ad* all the more so.

FORTRAN [fortrɑ̃] *nm* FORTRAN.

fortuit, e [fortɥi, -ɛt] *a* fortuitous, chance *cpd*.

fortuitement [fortɥitmɑ̃] *ad* fortuitously.

fortune [fortyn] *nf* fortune; **faire ~** to make one's fortune; **de ~** *a* makeshift; (*compagnon*) chance *cpd*.

fortuné, e [fortyne] *a* wealthy, well-off.

forum [forom] *nm* forum.

fosse [fos] *nf* (*grand trou*) pit; (*tombe*) grave; **la ~ aux lions/ours** the lions' den/bear pit; **~ commune** common *ou* communal grave; **~ (d'orchestre)** (orchestra) pit; **~ à purin** cesspit; **~ septique** septic tank; **~s nasales** nasal fossae.

fossé [fose] *nm* ditch; (*fig*) gulf, gap.

fossette [fosɛt] *nf* dimple.

fossile [fosil] *nm* fossil ♦ *a* fossilized, fossil *cpd*.

fossoyeur [foswayœr] *nm* gravedigger.

fou (fol), folle [fu, fol] *a* mad, crazy; (*déréglé etc*) wild, erratic; (*mèche*) stray; (*herbe*) wild; (*fam: extrême, très grand*) terrific, tremendous ♦ *nm/f* madman/woman ♦ *nm* (*du roi*) jester, fool; (*ÉCHECS*) bishop; **~ à lier, ~ furieux (folle furieuse)** raving mad; **être ~ de** to be mad *ou* crazy about; (*chagrin, joie, colère*) to be wild with; **faire le ~** to play *ou* act the fool; **avoir le ~ rire** to have the giggles.

foucade [fukad] *nf* caprice.

foudre [fudr(ə)] *nf* lightning; **~s** *nfpl* (*fig: colère*) wrath *sg*.

foudroyant, e [fudrwayɑ̃, -ɑ̃t] *a* devastating; (*maladie, poison*) violent.

foudroyer [fudrwaye] *vt* to strike down; **~ qn du regard** to look daggers at sb; **il a été foudroyé** he was struck by lightning.

fouet [fwe] *nm* whip; (*CULIN*) whisk; **de plein ~** *ad* head on.

fouettement [fwɛtmɑ̃] *nm* lashing *q*.

fouetter [fwɛte] *vt* to whip; to whisk.

fougasse [fugas] *nf* type of flat pastry.

fougère [fuʒer] *nf* fern.

fougue [fug] *nf* ardor (*US*), ardour (*Brit*).

fougueusement [fugøzmɑ̃] *ad* ardently.

fougueux, euse [fugø, -øz] *a* fiery, ardent.

fouille [fuj] *nf* search; **~s** *nfpl* (*archéologiques*) excavations; **passer à la ~** to be searched.

fouillé, e [fuje] *a* detailed.

fouiller [fuje] *vt* to search; (*creuser*) to dig; (: *suj: archéologue*) to excavate; (*approfondir: étude etc*) to go into ♦ *vi* (*archéologue*) to excavate; **~ dans/parmi** to rummage in/among.

fouillis [fuji] *nm* jumble, muddle.

fouine [fwin] *nf* stone marten.

fouiner [fwine] *vi* (*péj*): **~ dans** to nose around *ou* about in.

fouineur, euse [fwinœr, -øz] *a* nosey ♦ *nm/f* nosey parker, snooper.

fouir [fwir] *vt* to dig.

fouisseur, euse [fwisœr, -øz] *a* burrowing.

foulage [fulaʒ] *nm* pressing.

foulant, e [fulɑ̃, -ɑ̃t] *a*: **pompe ~** force pump.

foulard [fular] *nm* scarf (*pl* scarves).

foule [ful] *nf* crowd; **une ~ de** masses of; **venir en ~s** to come in droves.

foulée [fule] *nf* stride; **dans la ~ de** on the heels of.

fouler [fule] *vt* to press; (*sol*) to tread upon; **se ~** *vi* (*fam*) to overexert o.s.; **se ~ la cheville** to sprain one's ankle; **~ aux pieds** to trample underfoot.

foulure [fulyr] *nf* sprain.

four [fur] *nm* oven; (*de potier*) kiln; (*THÉÂTRE: échec*) flop; **allant au ~** ovenproof.

fourbe [furb(ə)] *a* deceitful.

fourberie [furbəri] *nf* deceit.

fourbi [furbi] *nm* (*fam*) gear, junk.

fourbir [furbir] *vt*: **~ ses armes** (*fig*) to get ready for the fray.

fourbu, e [furby] *a* exhausted.

fourche [furʃ(ə)] *nf* pitchfork; (*de bicyclette*) fork.

fourcher [furʃe] *vi*: **ma langue a fourché** it was a slip of the tongue.

fourchette [fōōrshet] *nf* fork; (*STATISTIQUE*) bracket, margin.

fourchu, e [fōōrshü] *a* split; (*arbre etc*) forked.

fourgon [fōōrgóń] *nm* truck, van; (*RAIL*) wag(g)on; ~ **mortuaire** hearse.

fourgonnette [fōōrgonet] *nf* (delivery) truck.

fourmi [fōōrmē] *nf* ant; **avoir des** ~**s** (*fig*) to have pins and needles.

fourmilière [fōōrmēlyer] *nf* anthill; (*fig*) hive of activity.

fourmillement [fōōrmēymáń] *nm* (*démangeaison*) pins and needles *pl*; (*grouillement*) swarming *q*.

fourmiller [fōōrmēyā] *vi* to swarm; ~ **de** to be teeming with, be swarming with.

fournaise [fōōrnez] *nf* blaze; (*fig*) furnace, oven.

fourneau, x [fōōrnō] *nm* stove.

fournée [fōōrnā] *nf* batch.

fourni, e [fōōrnē] *a* (*barbe, cheveux*) thick; (*magasin*): **bien** ~ **(en)** well stocked (with).

fournil [fōōrnē] *nm* bakery.

fournir [fōōrnēr] *vt* to supply; (*preuve, exemple*) to provide, supply; (*effort*) to put in; ~ **qch à qn** to supply sth to sb, supply *ou* provide sb with sth; ~ **qn en** (*COMM*) to supply sb with; **se** ~ **chez** to shop at.

fournisseur, euse [fōōrnēsœr, -ēz] *nm/f* supplier.

fourniture [fōōrnētür] *nf* supply(ing); ~**s** *nfpl* supplies; ~**s de bureau** office supplies, stationery; ~**s scolaires** school supplies.

fourrage [fōōrázh] *nm* fodder.

fourrager [fōōrázhā] *vi*: ~ **dans/parmi** to rummage through/among.

fourrager, ère [fōōrázhā, -er] *a* fodder *cpd* ♦ *nf* (*MIL*) fourragère.

fourré, e [fōōrā] *a* (*bonbon, chocolat*) filled; (*manteau, botte*) fur-lined ♦ *nm* thicket.

fourreau, x [fōōrō] *nm* sheath; (*de parapluie*) cover; **robe/jupe** ~ figure-hugging dress/ skirt.

fourrer [fōōrā] *vt* (*fam*): ~ **qch dans** to stick *ou* shove sth into; **se** ~ **dans/sous** to get into/under; **se** ~ **dans** (*une mauvaise situation*) to land o.s. in.

fourre-tout [fōōrtōō] *nm inv* (*sac*) tote bag, carryall (*US*); (*péj*) junk room (*ou* closet); (*fig*) rag-bag.

fourreur [fōōrœr] *nm* furrier.

fourrière [fōōryer] *nf* pound.

fourrure [fōōrür] *nf* fur; (*sur l'animal*) coat; **manteau/col de** ~ fur coat/collar.

fourvoyer [fōōrvwáyā]: **se** ~ *vi* to go astray, stray; **se** ~ **dans** to stray into.

foutre [fōōtr(ə)] *vt* (*fam!*) = **ficher** (*fam*).

foutu, e [fōōtü] *a* (*fam!*) = **fichu**.

foyer [fwàyā] *nm* (*de cheminée*) hearth; (*fig*) seat, center (*US*), centre (*Brit*); (*famille*) family; (*domicile*) home; (*local de réunion*) (social) club; (*résidence*) hostel; (*salon*) foyer; (*OPTIQUE, PHOTO*) focus; **lunettes à double** ~ bifocal glasses.

FP *sigle f* (= *franchise postale*) *exemption from postage*.

FPA *sigle f* (= *Formation professionnelle pour adultes*) adult education.

FPLP *sigle m* = *Front populaire de la*

libération de la Palestine.

FR3 [efertrwà] *sigle f* (= *France Régions 3*) *TV channel.*

fracas [fràká] *nm* din; crash.

fracassant, e [fràkásáń, -áńt] *a* sensational, staggering.

fracasser [fràkásā] *vt* to smash; **se** ~ **contre** *ou* **sur** to crash against.

fraction [fràksyóń] *nf* fraction.

fractionnement [fràksyonmáń] *nm* division.

fractionner [fràksyonā] *vt* to divide (up), split (up).

fracture [fràktür] *nf* fracture; ~ **du crâne** fractured skull; ~ **de la jambe** broken leg.

fracturer [fràktürā] *vt* (*coffre, serrure*) to break open; (*os, membre*) to fracture.

fragile [fràzhēl] *a* fragile, delicate; (*fig*) frail.

fragiliser [fràzhēlēzā] *vt* to weaken, make fragile.

fragilité [fràzhēlētā] *nf* fragility.

fragment [fràgmáń] *nm* (*d'un objet*) fragment, piece; (*d'un texte*) passage, extract.

fragmentaire [fràgmáńter] *a* sketchy.

fragmenter [fràgmáńtā] *vt* to split up.

frai [fre] *nm* spawn; (*ponte*) spawning.

fraîche [fresh] *af voir* **frais**.

fraîchement [freshmáń] *ad* (*sans en- thousiasme*) coolly; (*récemment*) freshly, newly.

fraîcheur [freshœr] *nf* (*voir frais*) coolness; freshness.

fraîchir [freshēr] *vi* to get cooler; (*vent*) to freshen.

frais, fraîche [fre, fresh] *a* (*air, eau, accueil*) cool; (*petit pois, œufs, nouvelles, couleur, troupes*) fresh; **le voilà** ~**!** he's in a (real) mess! ♦ *ad* (*récemment*) newly, fresh(ly); **il fait** ~ it's cool; **servir** ~ chill before serving, serve chilled ♦ *nm*: **mettre au** ~ to put in a cool place; **prendre le** ~ to take a breath of cool air ♦ *nmpl* (*débours*) expenses; (*COMM*) costs; charges; **faire des** ~ to spend; to go to a lot of expense; **faire les** ~ **de** to bear the brunt of; **faire les** ~ **de la conversation** (*parler*) to do most of the talking; (*en être le sujet*) to be the topic of conversation; **il en a été pour ses** ~ he could have spared himself the trouble; **rentrer dans ses** ~ to recover one's expenses; ~ **de déplacement** travel(ling) expenses; ~ **d'entretien** upkeep; ~ **généraux** overhead charges *ou* costs; ~ **de scolarité** school fees, tuition (*US*).

fraise [frez] *nf* strawberry; (*TECH*) countersink (bit); (*de dentiste*) drill; ~ **des bois** wild strawberry.

fraiser [frezā] *vt* to countersink; (*CULIN: pâte*) to knead.

fraiseuse [frezœz] *nf* (*TECH*) milling machine.

fraisier [frāzyā] *nm* strawberry plant.

framboise [fráńbwáz] *nf* raspberry.

framboisier [fráńbwázyā] *nm* raspberry bush.

franc, franche [fráń, fráńsh] *a* (*personne*) frank, straightforward; (*visage*) open; (*net: refus, couleur*) clear; (: *coupure*) clean; (*in- tensif*) downright; (*exempt*): ~ **de port** post free, postage paid; (*zone, port*) free; (*boutique*) duty-free ♦ *ad*: **parler** ~ to be frank *ou* candid ♦ *nm* franc.

français, e [fráńse, -ez] *a* French ♦ *nm* (*LING*)

French ♦ *nm/f*: F~, e Frenchman/woman; **les F~** the French.

franc-comtois, e, *mpl* **francs-comtois** [frãŋkôñtwà, -wàz] *a* of *ou* from (the) Franche-Comté.

France [frãs] *nf*: **la ~** France; **en ~** in France.

Francfort [frãŋkfor] *n* Frankfurt.

franche [frãsh] *af voir* **franc**.

franchement [frãshmãñ] *ad* (*voir franc*) frankly; clearly; (*tout à fait*) downright ♦ *excl* well, really!

franchir [frãshēr] *vt* (*obstacle*) to clear, get over; (*seuil, ligne, rivière*) to cross; (*distance*) to cover.

franchisage [frãshēzàzh] *nm* (*COMM*) franchising.

franchise [frãshēz] *nf* frankness; (*douanière, d'impôt*) exemption; (*ASSURANCES*) deductible (*US*), excess (*Brit*); (*COMM*) franchise; **~ de bagages** baggage allowance.

franchissable [frãshēsàbl(ə)] *a* (*obstacle*) surmountable.

franciscain, e [frãsēskañ, -en] *a* Franciscan.

franciser [frãsēzà] *vt* to gallicize, Frenchify.

franc-jeu [frãñzhœ] *nm*: **jouer ~** to play fair.

franc-maçon, *pl* **francs-maçons** [frãñmásóñ] *nm* Freemason.

franc-maçonnerie [frãñmásonrē] *nf* Freemasonry.

franco [frãŋkō] *ad* (*COMM*): **~ (de port)** postage paid.

franco... [frãŋkō] *préfixe* franco-.

franco-canadien [frãŋkokànàdyañ] *nm* (*LING*) Canadian French.

francophile [frãŋkofēl] *a* francophile.

francophone [frãŋkofon] *a* French-speaking ♦ *nm/f* French speaker.

francophonie [frãŋkofonē] *nf* French-speaking communities *pl*.

franco-québécois [frãŋkokābākwà] *nm* (*LING*) Quebec French.

franc-parler [frãñpàrlà] *nm inv* outspokenness.

franc-tireur [frãñtērœr] *nm* (*MIL*) irregular; (*fig*) freelance.

frange [frãñzh] *nf* fringe; (*cheveux*) bangs (*US*), fringe (*Brit*).

frangipane [frãñzhēpàn] *nf* almond paste.

franglais [frãñgle] *nm* Franglais.

franquette [frãŋkãt]: **à la bonne ~** *ad* without any fuss.

frappant, e [fràpàñ, -àñt] *a* striking.

frappe [fràp] *nf* (*d'une dactylo, pianiste, machine à écrire*) touch; (*BOXE*) punch; (*péj*) hood, thug.

frappé, e [fràpà] *a* (*CULIN*) chilled; **~ de panique** panic-stricken; **~ de stupeur** thunderstruck, dumbfounded.

frapper [fràpà] *vt* to hit, strike; (*étonner*) to strike; (*monnaie*) to strike, stamp; **se ~** *vi* (*s'inquiéter*) to get worked up; **~ à la porte** to knock at the door; **~ dans ses mains** to clap one's hands; **~ du poing sur** to bang one's fist on; **~ un grand coup** (*fig*) to strike a blow.

frasques [fràsk(ə)] *nfpl* escapades; **faire des ~s** to get up to mischief.

fraternel, le [fràternel] *a* brotherly, fraternal.

fraternellement [fràternelmãñ] *ad* in a brotherly way.

fraterniser [fràternēzà] *vi* to fraternize.

fraternité [fràternētà] *nf* brotherhood.

fratricide [fràtrēsēd] *a* fratricidal.

fraude [frōd] *nf* fraud; (*SCOL*) cheating; **passer qch en ~** to smuggle sth in (*ou* out); **~ fiscale** tax evasion.

frauder [frōdà] *vi, vt* to cheat; **~ le fisc** to evade paying tax(es).

fraudeur, euse [frōdœr, -œz] *nm/f* person guilty of fraud; (*candidat*) examinee who cheats; (*au fisc*) tax evader.

frauduleux, euse [frōdülœ, -œz] *a* fraudulent.

frayer [frāyà] *vt* to open up, clear ♦ *vi* to spawn; (*fréquenter*): **~ avec** to mix *ou* associate with; **se ~ un passage dans** to clear o.s. a path through, force one's way through.

frayeur [freyœr] *nf* fright.

fredaines [frədɛn] *nfpl* mischief *sg*, escapades.

fredonner [frədonà] *vt* to hum.

freezer [frēzœr] *nm* freezer compartment.

frégate [frāgàt] *nf* frigate.

frein [frañ] *nm* brake; **mettre un ~ à** (*fig*) to put a brake on, check; **sans ~** (*sans limites*) unchecked; **~ à main** handbrake; **~ moteur** engine braking; **~s à disques** disc brakes; **~s à tambour** drum brakes.

freinage [frenàzh] *nm* braking; **distance de ~** braking distance; **traces de ~** tire (*US*) *ou* tyre (*Brit*) marks.

freiner [frenà] *vi* to brake ♦ *vt* (*progrès etc*) to check.

frelaté, e [frəlàtà] *a* adulterated; (*fig*) tainted.

frêle [frel] *a* frail, fragile.

frelon [frəlóñ] *nm* hornet.

freluquet [frəlükɛ] *nm* (*péj*) whippersnapper.

frémir [frāmēr] *vi* (*de froid, de peur*) to tremble, shiver; (*de joie*) to quiver; (*eau*) to (begin to) bubble.

frémissement [frāmēsmãñ] *nm* shiver; quiver; bubbling *q*.

frêne [fren] *nm* ash (tree).

frénésie [frānāzē] *nf* frenzy.

frénétique [frānātēk] *a* frenzied, frenetic.

fréquemment [frākàmãñ] *ad* frequently.

fréquence [frākãs] *nf* frequency.

fréquent, e [frākã, -ãt] *a* frequent.

fréquentable [frākãtàbl(ə)] *a*: **il est peu ~** he's not the type one can associate oneself with.

fréquentation [frākãtàsyôñ] *nf* frequenting; seeing; **~s** *nfpl* company *sg*.

fréquenté, e [frākãtà] *a*: **très ~** (very) busy; **mal ~** patronized by disreputable elements.

fréquenter [frākãtà] *vt* (*lieu*) to frequent; (*personne*) to see; **se ~** to see a lot of each other.

frère [frer] *nm* brother ♦ *a*: **partis/pays ~s** sister parties/countries.

fresque [fresk(ə)] *nf* (*ART*) fresco.

fret [fre] *nm* freight.

fréter [frātà] *vt* to charter.

frétiller [frātēyà] *vi* to wriggle; to quiver; **~ de la queue** to wag its tail.

fretin [frətañ] *nm*: **le menu ~** the small fry.

freux [frœ] *nm* (*ZOOL*) rook.

friable [frēyàbl(ə)] *a* crumbly.

friand, e [frēyàñ, -àñd] *a*: **~ de** very fond of ♦

nm (*CULIN*) small ground-meat (*US*) *ou* minced-meat (*Brit*) pie; (: *sucré*) small almond cake.

friandise [frĕyândēz] *nf* sweet.

fric [frĕk] *nm* (*fam*) cash, bread.

fricassée [frĕkàsā] *nf* fricassee.

fric-frac [frĕkfràk] *nm* break-in.

friche [frĕsh]: **en ~** *a*, *ad* (lying) fallow.

friction [frĕksyôń] *nf* (*massage*) rub, rub-down; (*chez le coiffeur*) scalp massage; (*TECH*, *fig*) friction.

frictionner [frĕksyonā] *vt* to rub (down); to massage.

frigidaire [frĕzhēder] *nm* ® refrigerator.

frigide [frĕzhēd] *a* frigid.

frigidité [frĕzhēdētā] *nf* frigidity.

frigo [frĕgō] *nm* (= *frigidaire*) fridge.

frigorifier [frĕgorēfyā] *vt* to refrigerate; (*fig*: *personne*) to freeze.

frigorifique [frĕgorēfēk] *a* refrigerating.

frileusement [frĕlœzmâń] *ad* with a shiver.

frileux, euse [frĕlœ̄, -œ̄z] *a* sensitive to (the) cold; (*fig*) overcautious.

frimas [frĕmà] *nmpl* wintry weather *sg*.

frime [frĕm] *nf* (*fam*): **c'est de la ~** it's all put on; **pour la ~** just for show.

frimer [frĕmā] *vi* to put on an act.

frimeur, euse [frĕmœr, -œ̄z] *nm/f* poser.

frimousse [frĕmōōs] *nf* (sweet) little face.

fringale [frańgàl] *nf*: **avoir la ~** to be ravenous.

fringant, e [frańgâń, -âńt] *a* dashing.

fringues [frańg] *nfpl* (*fam*) clothes, gear *q*.

fripé, e [frĕpā] *a* crumpled.

friperie [frĕprē] *nf* (*commerce*) secondhand clothes shop; (*vêtements*) secondhand clothes.

fripes [frĕp] *nfpl* secondhand clothes.

fripier, ière [frĕpyā, -yer] *nm/f* secondhand clothes dealer.

fripon, ne [frĕpôń, -on] *a* roguish, mischievous ♦ *nm/f* rascal, rogue.

fripouille [frĕpōōy] *nf* scoundrel.

frire [frĕr] *vt* (*aussi*: **faire ~**), *vi* to fry.

frise [frĕz] *nf* frieze.

frisé, e [frĕzā] *a* curly, curly-haired ♦ *nf*: (**chicorée**) **~e** curly endive.

friser [frĕzā] *vt* to curl; (*fig*: *surface*) to skim, graze; (: *mort*) to come within a hair's breadth of; (: *hérésie*) to verge on ♦ *vi* (*cheveux*) to curl; (*personne*) to have curly hair; **se faire ~** to have one's hair curled.

frisette [frĕzet] *nf* little curl.

frisotter [frĕzotā] *vi* (*cheveux*) to curl tightly.

frisquet [frĕske] *am* chilly.

frisson [frĕsôń], **frissonnement** [frĕsonmâń] *nm* shudder, shiver; quiver.

frissonner [frĕsonā] *vi* (*personne*) to shudder, shiver; (*feuilles*) to quiver.

frit, e [frĕ, frĕt] *pp de* **frire** ♦ *a* fried ♦ *nf*: (**pommes**) **~es** French fries, chips (*Brit*).

friterie [frĕtrē] *nf* ≈ hamburger stand (*US*), ≈ chip shop (*Brit*).

friteuse [frĕtœ̄z] *nf* deep (fat) fryer.

friture [frĕtür] *nf* (*huile*) (deep) fat; (*plat*): **~** (**de poissons**) fried fish; (*RADIO*) crackle, crackling *q*; **~s** *nfpl* (*aliments frits*) fried food *sg*.

frivole [frĕvol] *a* frivolous.

frivolité [frĕvolētā] *nf* frivolity.

froc [frok] *nm* (*REL*) habit; (*fam*: *pantalon*) pants *pl* (*US*), trousers *pl* (*Brit*).

froid, e [frwà, frwàd] *a* cold ♦ *nm* cold; (*absence de sympathie*) coolness *q*; **il fait ~** it's cold; **avoir ~** to be cold; **prendre ~** to catch a chill *ou* cold; **à ~** *ad* (*démarrer*) (from) cold; (**pendant**) **les grands ~s** (in) the depths of winter, (during) the cold season; **jeter un ~** (*fig*) to cast a chill; **être en ~ avec** to be on bad terms with; **battre ~ à qn** to give sb the cold shoulder.

froidement [frwàdmâń] *ad* (*accueillir*) coldly; (*décider*) coolly.

froideur [frwàdœr] *nf* coolness *q*.

froisser [frwàsā] *vt* to crumple (up), crease; (*fig*) to hurt, offend; **se ~** *vi* to crumple, crease; to take offense (*US*) *ou* offence (*Brit*); **se ~ un muscle** to strain a muscle.

frôlement [frōlmâń] *nm* (*contact*) light touch.

frôler [frōlā] *vt* to brush against; (*suj*: *projectile*) to skim past; (*fig*) to come within a hair's breadth of, come very close to.

fromage [fromázh] *nm* cheese; **~ blanc** soft white cheese; **~ de tête** headcheese (*US*), pork brawn (*Brit*).

fromager, ère [fromàzhā, -er] *nm/f* cheese merchant ♦ *a* (*industrie*) cheese *cpd*.

fromagerie [fromàzhrē] *nf* cheese dairy.

froment [fromâń] *nm* wheat.

fronce [frôńs] *nf* (*de tissu*) gather.

froncement [frôńsmâń] *nm*: **~ de sourcils** frown.

froncer [frôńsā] *vt* to gather; **~ les sourcils** to frown.

frondaison [frôńdezôń] *nf* foliage.

fronde [frôńd] *nf* sling; (*fig*) rebellion, rebelliousness.

frondeur, euse [frôńdœr, -œ̄z] *a* rebellious.

front [frôń] *nm* forehead, brow; (*MIL*, *MÉTÉOROLOGIE*, *POL*) front; **avoir le ~ de faire** to have the effrontery *ou* front to do; **de ~** *ad* (*se heurter*) head-on; (*rouler*) together (*i.e. 2 or 3 abreast*); (*simultanément*) at once; **faire ~ à** to face up to; **~ de mer** (sea) front.

frontal, e, aux [frôńtàl, -ō] *a* frontal.

frontalier, ière [frôńtàlyā, -yer] *a* border *cpd*, frontier *cpd* ♦ *nm/f*: (**travailleurs**) **~s** workers who cross the border to go to work, commuters from across the border.

frontière [frôńtyer] *nf* (*GÉO*, *POL*) frontier, border; (*fig*) frontier, boundary.

frontispice [frôńtēspēs] *nm* frontispiece.

fronton [frôńtôń] *nm* pediment; (*de pelote basque*) (front) wall.

frottement [frotmâń] *nm* rubbing, scraping; **~s** *nmpl* (*fig*: *difficultés*) friction *sg*.

frotter [frotā] *vi* to rub, scrape ♦ *vt* to rub; (*pour nettoyer*) to polish; (: *avec une brosse*) to scrub; **~ une allumette** to strike a match; **se ~ à qn** to cross swords with sb; **se ~ à qch** to come up against sth; **se ~ les mains** (*fig*) to rub one's hands (gleefully).

frottis [frotē] *nm* (*MÉD*) smear.

frottoir [frotwàr] *nm* (*d'allumettes*) friction strip; (*pour encaustiquer*) (long-handled) brush.

frou-frou, *pl* **frous-frous** [frōōfrōō] *nm* rustle.

frousse [frōōs] *nf* (*fam*: *peur*): **avoir la ~** to

be in a blue funk.

fructifier |früktĬfyā| vi to yield a profit; **faire** ~ to turn to good account.

fructueux, euse [früktüœ̄, -œ̄z] a fruitful; profitable.

frugal, e, aux |frügàl, -ō] a frugal.

fruit [früē] nm fruit gén q; ~**s de mer** (CULIN) seafood(s); ~**s secs** dried fruit sg.

fruité, e [früētā] a (vin) fruity.

fruiterie [früētrē] nf (boutique) fruit (and vegetable) store (US), greengrocer's (Brit).

fruitier, ière [früētyā, -yer| a: **arbre** ~ fruit tree ♦ nm/f fruit merchant (US), fruiterer (Brit).

fruste [früst(ə)] a unpolished, uncultivated.

frustrant, e [früstrâṅ, -âṅt] a frustrating.

frustration [früstràsyóṅ] nf frustration.

frustré, e [früstrā] a frustrated.

frustrer [früstrā] vt to frustrate; (priver): ~ **qn de qch** to deprive sb of sth.

FS abr (= franc suisse) FS, SF.

FSE sigle m (= foyer socio-éducatif) community home.

FTP sigle mpl (= Francs-tireurs et partisans) Communist Resistance in 1940-45.

fuel(-oil) [fyōōl(oyl)] nm fuel oil; (pour chauffer) heating oil.

fugace [fügàs] a fleeting.

fugitif, ive [füzhētĬf, -ēv] a (lueur, amour) fleeting; (prisonnier etc) runaway ♦ nm/f fugitive, runaway.

fugue [füg] nf (d'un enfant) running away q; (MUS) fugue; **faire une** ~ to run away, abscond.

fuir [füēr] vt to flee from; (éviter) to shun ♦ vi to run away; (gaz, robinet) to leak.

fuite [füēt] nf flight; (écoulement) leak, leakage; (divulgation) leak; **être en** ~ to be on the run; **mettre en** ~ to put to flight; **prendre la** ~ to take flight.

fulgurant, e [fülgüràṅ, -âṅt] a lightning cpd, dazzling.

fulminant, e [fülmēnâṅ, -âṅt] a (lettre, regard) furious; ~ **de colère** raging with anger.

fulminer [fülmēnā] vi: ~ **(contre)** to thunder forth (against).

fumant, e [fümâṅ, -âṅt] a smoking; (liquide) steaming; **un coup** ~ (fam) a master stroke.

fumé, e [fümā] a (CULIN) smoked; (verre) tinted ♦ nf smoke; **partir en** ~**e** to go up in smoke.

fume-cigarette [fümsēgàret] nm inv cigarette holder.

fumer [fümā] vi to smoke; (liquide) to steam ♦ vt to smoke; (terre, champ) to manure.

fumerie [fümrē] nf: ~ **d'opium** opium den.

fumerolles [fümrol] nfpl gas and smoke (from volcano).

fûmes [füm] vb voir **être**.

fumet [füme] nm aroma.

fumeur, euse [fümœr, -œ̄z] nm/f smoker; **(compartiment)** ~**s** smoking compartment.

fumeux, euse [fümœ̄, -œ̄z] a (péj) hazy.

fumier [fümyā] nm manure.

fumigation [fümēgàsyóṅ] nf fumigation.

fumigène [fümēzhen] a smoke cpd.

fumiste [fümēst(ə)] nm (ramoneur) chimney sweep ♦ nm/f (péj: paresseux) shirker;

(charlatan) phoney.

fumisterie [fümēstərē] nf (péj) fraud, con.

fumoir [fümwàr] nm smoking room.

funambule [fünàṅbül] nm tightrope walker.

funèbre [fünebr(ə)] a funeral cpd; (fig) doleful; funereal.

funérailles [fünâray] nfpl funeral sg.

funéraire [fünārer] a funeral cpd, funerary.

funeste [fünest(ə)] a disastrous; deathly.

funiculaire [fünēküler] nm funicular (railway).

FUNU [fünü] sigle f (= Force d'urgence des Nations Unies) UNEF (= United Nations Emergency Forces).

fur [für]: **au** ~ **et à mesure** ad as one goes along; **au** ~ **et à mesure que** as; **au** ~ **et à mesure de leur progression** as they advance (ou advanced).

furax [füràks] a inv (fam) livid.

furent [für] vb voir **être**.

furet [füre] nm ferret.

fureter [fürtā] vi (péj) to nose about.

fureur [fürœr] nf fury; (passion): ~ **de** passion for; **faire** ~ to be all the rage.

furibard, e [fürēbàr, -àrd(ə)] a (fam) livid, absolutely furious.

furibond, e [fürēbóṅ, -óṅd] a livid, absolutely furious.

furie [fürē] nf fury; (femme) shrew, vixen; **en** ~ (mer) raging.

furieusement [füryœ̄zmâṅ] ad furiously.

furieux, euse [füryœ̄, -œ̄z] a furious.

furoncle [füróṅkl(ə)] nm boil.

furtif, ive [fürtĬf, -ēv] a furtive.

fus [fü] vb voir **être**.

fusain [füzaṅ] nm (BOT) spindle-tree; (ART) charcoal.

fuseau, x [füzō] nm (pantalon) (ski-)pants pl; (pour filer) spindle; (en jambes) tapering; (colonne) bulging; ~ **horaire** time zone.

fusée [füzā] nf rocket; ~ **éclairante** flare.

fuselage [füzlàzh] nm fuselage.

fuselé, e [füzlā] a slender; (galbé) tapering.

fuser [füzā] vi (rires etc) to burst forth.

fusible [füzēbl(ə)] nm (ÉLEC: fil) fuse wire; (: fiche) fuse.

fusil [füzē] nm (de guerre, à canon rayé) rifle, gun; (de chasse, à canon lisse) shotgun, gun; ~ **à deux coups** double-barreled rifle ou shotgun; ~ **sous-marin** spear-gun.

fusilier [füzēlyā] nm (MIL) rifleman.

fusillade [füzēyàd] nf gunfire q, shooting q; (combat) gun battle.

fusiller [füzēyā] vt to shoot; ~ **qn du regard** to look daggers at sb.

fusil-mitrailleur, pl **fusils-mitrailleurs** [füzēmētràyœr] nm machine gun.

fusion [füzyóṅ] nf fusion, melting; (fig) merging; (COMM) merger; **en** ~ (métal, roches) molten.

fusionnement [füzyonmâṅ] nm merger.

fusionner [füzyonā] vi to merge.

fustiger [füstēzhā] vt to denounce.

fut [fü] vb voir **être**.

fût [fü] vb voir **être** ♦ nm (tonneau) barrel, cask; (de canon) stock; (d'arbre) bole, trunk; (de colonne) shaft.

futaie [füte] nf forest, plantation.

futé, e [fütā] a crafty.

fûtes [füt] vb voir **être**.

futile [fütēl] *a* (*inutile*) futile; (*frivole*) frivolous.

futilité [fütēlētā] *nf* futility; frivolousness; (*chose futile*) futile pursuit (*ou* thing *etc*).

futur, e [fütür] *a, nm* future; **son ~ époux** her husband-to-be; **au ~** (*LING*) in the future.

futuriste [fütürēst(ə)] *a* futuristic.

fuyant, e [füċyáṅ, -áṅt] *vb voir* **fuir** ♦ *a* (*regard etc*) evasive; (*lignes etc*) receding; (*perspective*) vanishing.

fuyard, e [füċyár, -árd(ə)] *nm/f* runaway.

fuyons [füċyóṅ] *etc vb voir* **fuir**.

G

G, g [zhā] *nm inv* G, g ♦ *abr* (= *gramme*) g; (= *gauche*) L, l; **G comme Gaston** G for George.

gabardine [gábárdēn] *nf* gabardine.

gabarit [gábárē] *nm* (*fig: dimension, taille*) size; (*: valeur*) calibre; (*TECH*) template; **du même ~** (*fig*) of the same type, of that ilk.

gabegie [gábzhē] *nf* (*péj*) chaos.

Gabon [gábóṅ] *nm*: **le ~** Gabon.

gabonais, e [gábone, -cz] *a* Gabonese.

gâcher [gáshā] *vt* (*gâter*) to spoil, ruin; (*gaspiller*) to waste; (*plâtre*) to temper; (*mortier*) to mix.

gâchette [gáshct] *nf* trigger.

gâchis [gáshē] *nm* (*désordre*) mess; (*gaspillage*) waste *q*.

gadget [gádzhct] *nm* thingumajig; (*nouveauté*) gimmick.

gadoue [gádōō] *nf* sludge.

gaélique [gáālēk] *a* Gaelic ♦ *nm* (*LING*) Gaelic.

gaffe [gáf] *nf* (*instrument*) boat hook; (*fam: erreur*) blunder; **faire ~** (*fam*) to watch out.

gaffer [gáfā] *vi* to blunder.

gaffeur, euse [gáfœr, -œz] *nm/f* blunderer.

gag [gág] *nm* gag.

gaga [gágá] *a* (*fam*) gaga.

gage [gázh] *nm* (*dans un jeu*) forfeit; (*fig: de fidélité*) token; **~s** *nmpl* (*salaire*) wages; (*garantie*) guarantee *sg*; **mettre en ~** to pawn; **laisser en ~** to leave as security.

gager [gázhā] *vt*: **~ que** to bet *ou* wager that.

gageure [gázhür] *nf*: **c'est une ~** it's attempting the impossible.

gagnant, e [gáṅyáṅ, -áṅt] *a*: **billet/numéro ~** winning ticket/number ♦ *ad*: **jouer ~** (*aux courses*) to be bound to win ♦ *nm/f* winner.

gagne-pain [gáṅypáṅ] *nm inv* job.

gagne-petit [gáṅypətē] *nm inv* low wage earner.

gagner [gáṅyā] *vt* (*concours, procès, pari*) to win; (*somme d'argent, revenu*) to earn; (*aller vers, atteindre*) to reach; (*s'emparer de*) to overcome; (*envahir*) to spread to; (*se concilier*): **~ qn** to win sb over ♦ *vi* to win; (*fig*) to gain; **~ du temps/de la place** to gain time/save space; **~ sa vie** to earn one's liv-

ing; **~ du terrain** (*aussi fig*) to gain ground; **~ qn de vitesse** (*aussi fig*) to outstrip sb; **~ à faire** (*s'en trouver bien*) to be better off doing; **il y gagne** it's in his interest, it's to his advantage.

gagneur [gáṅyœr] *nm* winner.

gai, e [gā] *a* cheerful; (*livre, pièce de théâtre*) light-hearted; (*un peu ivre*) tipsy.

gaieté [gātā] *nf* cheerfulness; **~s** *nfpl* (*souvent ironique*) delights; **de ~ de cœur** with a light heart.

gaillard, e [gáyár, -árd(ə)] *a* (*robuste*) sprightly; (*grivois*) bawdy, ribald ♦ *nm/f* (*strapping*) fellow/wench.

gaillardement [gáyárdəmáṅ] *ad* cheerfully.

gain [gáṅ] *nm* (*revenu*) earnings *pl*; (*bénéfice: gén pl*) profits *pl*; (*au jeu: gén pl*) winnings *pl*; (*fig: de temps, place*) saving; (*: avantage*) benefit; (*: lucre*) gain; **avoir ~ de cause** to win the case; (*fig*) to be proved right; **obtenir ~ de cause** (*fig*) to win out.

gaine [gen] *nf* (*corset*) girdle; (*fourreau*) sheath; (*de fil électrique etc*) outer covering.

gaine-culotte, *pl* **gaines-culottes** [genkülot] *nf* panty girdle.

gainer [gānā] *vt* to cover.

gala [gálá] *nm* official reception; **soirée de ~** gala evening.

galant, e [gáláṅ, -áṅt] *a* (*courtois*) courteous, gentlemanly; (*entreprenant*) flirtatious, gallant; (*aventure, poésie*) amorous; **en ~e compagnie** (*homme*) with a lady friend; (*femme*) with a gentleman friend.

Galapagos [gálápágos] *nfpl*: **les (îles) ~** the Galapagos Islands.

galaxie [gáláksē] *nf* galaxy.

galbe [gálb(ə)] *nm* curve(s); shapeliness.

gale [gál] *nf* (*MÉD*) scabies *sg*; (*de chien*) mange.

galéjade [gálāzhád] *nf* tall story.

galère [gáler] *nf* galley.

galérer [gálārā] *vi* (*fam*) to work hard, slave (away).

galerie [gálrē] *nf* gallery; (*THÉÂTRE*) circle; (*de voiture*) roof rack; (*fig: spectateurs*) audience; **~ marchande** shopping mall; **~ de peinture** (*private*) art gallery.

galérien [gálāryáṅ] *nm* galley slave.

galet [gále] *nm* pebble; (*TECH*) wheel; **~s** *nmpl* pebbles, shingle *sg*.

galette [gálet] *nf* (*gâteau*) flat pastry cake; (*crêpe*) savory (*US*) *ou* savoury (*Brit*) pancake; **la ~ des Rois** *cake traditionally eaten on Twelfth Night*.

galeux, euse [gálœ, -œz] *a*: **un chien ~** a mangy dog.

Galice [gáles] *nf*: **la ~** Galicia (*in Spain*).

Galicie [gálēsē] *nf*: **la ~** Galicia (*in Central Europe*).

galiléen, ne [gálēlāáṅ, -en] *a* Galilean.

galimatias [gálēmátyá] *nm* (*péj*) gibberish.

galipette [gálēpct] *nf*: **faire des ~s** to turn somersaults.

Galles [gál] *nfpl*: **le pays de ~** Wales.

gallicisme [gálēsēsm(ə)] *nm* French idiom; (*tournure fautive*) gallicism.

gallois, e [gálwá, -wáz] *a* Welsh ♦ *nm* (*LING*) Welsh ♦ *nm/f*: **G~, e** Welshman/woman.

galoche [gálosh] *nf* clog.

galon [gàlôǹ] *nm* (*MIL*) stripe; (*décoratif*) piece of braid; **prendre du** ~ to be promoted.

galop [gàlō] *nm* gallop; **au** ~ at a gallop; ~ **d'essai** (*fig*) trial run.

galopade [gàlopàd] *nf* stampede.

galopant, e [gàlopàǹ, -àǹt] *a*: **inflation** ~**e** galloping inflation; **démographie** ~**e** exploding population.

galoper [gàlopā] *vi* to gallop.

galopin [gàlopaǹ] *nm* urchin, ragamuffin.

galvaniser [gàlvànēzā] *vt* to galvanize.

galvauder [gàlvōdā] *vt* to debase.

gambade [gàǹbàd] *nf*: **faire des** ~**s** to skip *ou* frisk around.

gambader [gàǹbàdā] *vi* to skip *ou* frisk around.

gamberger [gàǹberzhā] (*fam*) *vi* to (have a) think ♦ *vt* to dream up.

Gambie [gàǹbē] *nf*: **la** ~ (*pays*) Gambia; (*fleuve*) the Gambia.

gamelle [gàmel] *nf* mess tin; billy can; (*fam*): **ramasser une** ~ to fall flat on one's face.

gamin, e [gàmaǹ, -ēn] *nm/f* kid ♦ *a* mischievous, playful.

gaminerie [gàmēnrē] *nf* mischievousness, playfulness.

gamme [gàm] *nf* (*MUS*) scale; (*fig*) range.

gammé, e [gàmā] *a*: **croix** ~**e** swastika.

Gand [gàǹ] *n* Ghent.

gang [gàǹg] *nm* gang.

Gange [gàǹzh] *nm*: **le** ~ the Ganges.

ganglion [gàǹglēyôǹ] *nm* ganglion; (*lymphatique*) gland; **avoir des** ~**s** to have swollen glands.

gangrène [gàǹgren] *nf* gangrene; (*fig*) corruption; corrupting influence.

gangster [gàǹgster] *nm* gangster.

gangue [gàǹg] *nf* coating.

ganse [gàǹs] *nf* braid.

gant [gàǹ] *nm* glove; **prendre des** ~**s** (*fig*) to handle the situation with kid gloves; **relever le** ~ (*fig*) to take up the gauntlet; ~ **de crin** massage glove; ~ **de toilette** face cloth; ~**s de boxe** boxing gloves; ~**s de caoutchouc** rubber gloves.

ganté, e [gàǹtā] *a*: ~ **de blanc** wearing white gloves.

ganterie [gàǹtrē] *nf* glove trade; (*magasin*) glove shop.

garage [gàràzh] *nm* garage; ~ **à vélos** bicycle shed.

garagiste [gàràzhēst(ə)] *nm/f* (*propriétaire*) garage owner; (*mécanicien*) garage mechanic.

garant, e [gàràǹ, -àǹt] *nm/f* guarantor ♦ *nm* guarantee; **se porter** ~ **de** to vouch for; to be answerable for.

garantie [gàràǹtē] *nf* guarantee, warranty; (*gage*) security, surety; **(bon de)** ~ guarantee *ou* warranty slip; ~ **de bonne exécution** performance bond.

garantir [gàràǹtēr] *vt* to guarantee; (*protéger*): ~ **de** to protect from; **je vous garantis que** I can assure you that; **garanti pure laine/2 ans** guaranteed pure wool/for 2 years.

garce [gàrs(ə)] *nf* (*péj*) bitch.

garçon [gàrsôǹ] *nm* boy; (*célibataire*) bachelor; (*jeune homme*) boy, lad; (*aussi*: ~ **de café**) waiter; ~ **boucher/coiffeur** butcher's/hairdresser's assistant; ~ **de courses** messenger; ~ **d'écurie** stableboy; ~ **manqué** tomboy.

garçonnet [gàrsone] *nm* small boy.

garçonnière [gàrsonyer] *nf* bachelor apartment.

garde [gàrd(ə)] *nm* (*de prisonnier*) guard; (*de domaine etc*) warden; (*soldat, sentinelle*) guardsman ♦ *nf* guarding; looking after; (*soldats, BOXE, ESCRIME*) guard; (*faction*) watch; (*d'une arme*) hilt; (*TYPO*: *aussi*: **page** *ou* **feuille de** ~) flyleaf; (: *collée*) endpaper; **de** ~ *a, ad* on duty; **monter la** ~ to stand guard; **être sur ses** ~**s** to be on one's guard; **mettre en** ~ to warn; **mise en** ~ warning; **prendre** ~ **(à)** to be careful (of); **avoir la** ~ **des enfants** (*après divorce*) to have custody of the children; ~ **champêtre** *nm* rural policeman; ~ **du corps** *nm* bodyguard; ~ **d'enfants** *nf* child tender (*US*) *ou* minder (*Brit*); ~ **forestier** *nm* forest ranger (*US*) *ou* warden (*Brit*); ~ **mobile** *nm*, *nf* mobile guard; ~ **des Sceaux** *nm* ≈ Attorney General (*US*), ≈ Lord Chancellor (*Brit*); ~ **à vue** *nf* (*JUR*) ≈ police custody.

garde-à-vous [gàrdàvōō] *nm inv*: **être/se mettre au** ~ to be at/stand to attention; ~ **(fixe)!** (*MIL*) attention!

garde-barrière, *pl* **gardes-barrière(s)** [gàrdəbáryer] *nm/f* gatekeeper (*at a grade crossing*) (*US*), level-crossing keeper (*Brit*).

garde-boue [gàrdəbōō] *nm inv* mudguard, fender (*US*).

garde-chasse, *pl* **gardes-chasse(s)** [gàrdəshàs] *nm* gamekeeper.

garde-côte [gàrdəkōt] *nm* (*vaisseau*) coastguard boat.

garde-feu [gàrdəfœ̄] *nm inv* fire screen, fireguard.

garde-fou [gàrdəfōō] *nm* railing, parapet.

garde-malade, *pl* **gardes-malade(s)** [gàrdəmàlàd] *nf* home nurse.

garde-manger [gàrdmàǹzhā] *nm inv* (*boîte*) cooler (*US*), meat safe (*Brit*); (*placard*) pantry, larder.

garde-meuble [gàrdəmœbl(ə)] *nm* furniture storehouse.

garde-pêche [gàrdəpesh] *nm inv* (*personne*) fish warden (*US*), water bailiff (*Brit*); (*navire*) fisheries protection ship.

garder [gàrdā] *vt* (*conserver*) to keep; (: *sur soi*: *vêtement, chapeau*) to keep on; (*surveiller: enfants*) to look after; (: *immeuble, lieu, prisonnier*) to guard; **se** ~ *vi* (*aliment: se conserver*) to keep; **se** ~ **de faire** to be careful not to do; ~ **le lit/la chambre** to stay in bed/indoors; ~ **le silence** to keep silent *ou* quiet; ~ **la ligne** to keep one's figure; ~ **à vue** to keep in custody; **pêche/chasse gardée** private fishing/hunting (ground).

garderie [gàrdərē] *nf* day-care center (*US*), day nursery (*Brit*).

garde-robe [gàrdərob] *nf* wardrobe.

gardeur, euse [gàrdœr, -œz] *nm/f* (*de vaches*) cowherd; (*de chèvres*) goatherd.

gardian [gàrdyàǹ] *nm* cowboy (*in the Camargue*).

gardien, ne [gàrdyàǹ, -en] *nm/f* (*garde*) guard;

(de prison) guard, warder *(Brit)*; *(de domaine, réserve)* warden; *(de musée etc)* attendant; *(de phare, cimetière)* keeper; *(d'immeuble)* caretaker; *(fig)* guardian; ~ **de but** goalkeeper; ~ **de nuit** night watchman; ~ **de la paix** policeman.

gare [gàr] *nf* (railway) station, train station *(US)* ♦ *excl*: ~ **à** ... watch out for ...!; ~ **à ne pas** ... make sure you don't ...; ~ **à toi!** watch out!; **sans crier** ~ without warning; ~ **maritime** harbor *(US)* ou harbour *(Brit)* station; ~ **routière** bus station; *(camions)* trucking *(US)* ou haulage *(Brit)* depot; ~ **de triage** marshal(l)ing yard.

garenne [gàren] *nf voir* **lapin**.

garer [gàrā] *vt* to park; **se** ~ to park; *(pour laisser passer)* to pull over.

gargantuesque [gàrgàṅtüesk(ə)] *a* gargantuan.

gargariser [gàrgàrēzā]: **se** ~ *vi* to gargle; **se** ~ **de** *(fig)* to revel in.

gargarisme [gàrgàrēsm(ə)] *nm* gargling *q*; *(produit)* gargle.

gargote [gàrgot] *nf* cheap restaurant, greasy spoon *(fam)*.

gargouille [gàrgōōy] *nf* gargoyle.

gargouiller [gàrgōōyā] *vi* *(estomac)* to rumble; *(eau)* to gurgle.

garnement [gàrnəmàṅ] *nm* rascal, scallywag.

garni, e [gàrnē] *a* *(plat)* served with vegetables *(and French fries or pasta or rice)* ♦ *nm* *(appartement)* furnished accommodations *pl* *(US)* ou accommodation *q* *(Brit)*.

garnir [gàrnēr] *vt* to decorate; *(remplir)* to fill; *(recouvrir)* to cover; **se** ~ *vi* *(pièce, salle)* to fill up; ~ **qch de** *(orner)* to decorate sth with; to trim sth with; *(approvisionner)* to fill ou stock sth with; *(protéger)* to fit sth with; *(CULIN)* to garnish sth with.

garnison [gàrnēzòṅ] *nf* garrison.

garniture [gàrnētür] *nf* *(CULIN: légumes)* vegetables *pl*; *(: persil etc)* garnish; *(: farce)* filling; *(décoration)* trimming; *(protection)* fittings *pl*; ~ **de cheminée** mantelpiece ornaments *pl*; ~ **de frein** *(AUTO)* brake lining; ~ **intérieure** *(AUTO)* interior trim; ~ **périodique** sanitary napkin *(US)* ou towel *(Brit)*.

garrigue [gàrēg] *nf* scrubland.

garrot [gàrō] *nm* *(MÉD)* tourniquet; *(torture)* garrotte.

garrotter [gàrotā] *vt* to tie up; *(fig)* to muzzle.

gars [gà] *nm* lad; *(type)* guy.

Gascogne [gàskony] *nf*: **la** ~ Gascony.

gascon, ne [gàskòṅ, -on] *a* Gascon ♦ *nm*: **G**~ *(hâbleur)* braggart.

gas-oil [gàzoyl] *nm* diesel oil.

gaspillage [gàspēyàzh] *nm* waste.

gaspiller [gàspēyā] *vt* to waste.

gaspilleur, euse [gàspēyœr, -œz] *a* wasteful.

gastrique [gàstrēk] *a* gastric, stomach *cpd*.

gastro-entérite [gàstroàṅtàrēt] *nf* *(MÉD)* gastro-enteritis.

gastronome [gàstronom] *nm/f* gourmet.

gastronomie [gàstronomē] *nf* gástronomy.

gastronomique [gàstronomēk] *a*: **menu** ~ gourmet menu.

gâteau, x [gàtō] *nm* cake ♦ *a inv* *(fam: trop indulgent)*: **papa-/maman-**~ doting father/

mother; ~ **d'anniversaire** birthday cake; ~ **de riz** ≈ rice pudding; ~ **sec** cookie *(US)*, biscuit *(Brit)*.

gâter [gàtā] *vt* to spoil; **se** ~ *vi* *(dent, fruit)* to go bad; *(temps, situation)* to change for the worse.

gâterie [gàtrē] *nf* little treat.

gâteux, euse [gàtœ, -œz] *a* senile.

gâtisme [gàtēsm(ə)] *nm* senility.

GATT [gàt] *sigle m* (= *General Agreement on Tariffs and Trade*) GATT.

gauche [gōsh] *a* left, left-hand; *(maladroit)* awkward, clumsy ♦ *nf* *(POL)* left (wing); *(BOXE)* left; **à** ~ on the left; *(direction)* (to the) left; **à** ~ **de** (on *ou* to the) left of; **à la** ~ **de** to the left of; **de** ~ *(POL)* left-wing.

gauchement [gōshmàṅ] *ad* awkwardly, clumsily.

gaucher, ère [gōshā, -cr] *a* left-handed.

gaucherie [gōshrē] *nf* awkwardness, clumsiness.

gauchir [gōshēr] *vt* *(planche, objet)* to warp; *(fig: fait, idée)* to distort.

gauchisant, e [gōshēzàṅ, -àṅt] *a* with left-wing tendencies.

gauchisme [gōshēsm(ə)] *nm* leftism.

gauchiste [gōshēst(ə)] *a*, *nm/f* leftist.

gaufre [gōfr(ə)] *nf* *(pâtisserie)* waffle; *(de cire)* honeycomb.

gaufrer [gōfrā] *vt* *(papier)* to emboss; *(tissu)* to goffer.

gaufrette [gōfret] *nf* wafer.

gaufrier [gōfrēyā] *nm* *(moule)* waffle iron.

Gaule [gōl] *nf*: **la** ~ Gaul.

gaule [gōl] *nf* *(perche)* (long) pole; *(canne à pêche)* fishing rod.

gaulliste [gōlēst(ə)] *a*, *nm/f* Gaullist.

gaulois, e [gōlwà, -wàz] *a* Gallic; *(grivois)* bawdy ♦ *nm/f*: **G**~, **e** Gaul.

gauloiserie [gōlwàzrē] *nf* bawdiness.

gausser [gōsā]: **se** ~ **de** *vt* to deride.

gaver [gàvā] *vt* to force-feed; *(fig)*: ~ **de** to cram with, fill up with; *(personne)*: **se** ~ **de** to stuff o.s. with.

gaz [gàz] *nm inv* gas; **mettre les** ~ *(AUTO)* to step on the gas *(US)*, put one's foot down *(Brit)*; **chambre/masque à** ~ gas chamber/mask; ~ **en bouteilles** bottled gas; ~ **butane** butane; ~ **carbonique** carbon dioxide; ~ **hilarant** laughing gas; ~ **lacrymogène** tear gas; ~ **naturel** natural gas; ~ **de ville** manufactured domestic gas.

gaze [gàz] *nf* gauze.

gazéifié, e [gàzāēfyā] *a* carbonated, aerated.

gazelle [gàzel] *nf* gazelle.

gazer [gàzā] *vt* to gas ♦ *vi* *(fam)* to be going ou working well.

gazette [gàzet] *nf* newsletter.

gazeux, euse [gàzœ, -œz] *a* gaseous; *(eau)* sparkling; *(boisson)* fizzy.

gazoduc [gàzodük] *nm* gas pipeline.

gazole [gàzol] *nm* = **gas-oil.**

gazomètre [gàzometr(ə)] *nm* gasometer.

gazon [gàzòṅ] *nm* *(herbe)* turf, grass; *(pelouse)* lawn.

gazonner [gàzonā] *vt* *(terrain)* to grass over.

gazouiller [gàzōōyā] *vi* *(oiseau)* to chirp; *(enfant)* to babble.

gazouillis [gàzōōyē] *nmpl* chirp *sg*.

GB *sigle f* (= *Grande Bretagne*) GB.
gd *abr* (= *grand*) L.
GDF *sigle m* (= *Gaz de France*) national gas company.
geai [ʒhɛ] *nm* jay.
géant, e [ʒhāāṅ, -āṅt] *a* gigantic, giant; (*COMM*) giant-size ♦ *nm/f* giant.
geignement [ʒhɛnymāṅ] *nm* groaning, moaning.
geindre [ʒhaṅdr(ə)] *vi* to groan, moan.
gel [ʒhɛl] *nm* frost; (*de l'eau*) freezing; (*fig: des salaires, prix*) freeze; freezing; (*produit de beauté*) gel.
gélatine [ʒhālātēn] *nf* gelatine.
gélatineux, euse [ʒhālātēnœ̄, -œ̄z] *a* jelly-like, gelatinous.
gelé, e [ʒhəlā] *a* frozen ♦ *nf* jelly; (*gel*) frost; ~ **blanche** hoarfrost, white frost.
geler [ʒhəlā] *vt*, *vi* to freeze; **il gèle** it's freezing.
gélule [ʒhālül] *nf* capsule.
gelures [ʒhəlür] *nfpl* frostbite *sg*.
Gémeaux [ʒhāmō] *nmpl*: **les** ~ Gemini, the Twins; **être des** ~ to be Gemini.
gémir [ʒhāmēr] *vi* to groan, moan.
gémissement [ʒhāmēsmāṅ] *nm* groan, moan.
gemme [ʒhem] *nf* gem(stone).
gémonies [ʒhāmonē] *nfpl*: **vouer qn aux** ~ to subject sb to public scorn.
gênant, e [ʒhɛnāṅ, -āṅt] *a* (*objet*) awkward, in the way; (*histoire, personne*) embarrassing.
gencive [ʒhāṅsēv] *nf* gum.
gendarme [ʒhāṅdārm(ə)] *nm* gendarme.
gendarmer [ʒhāṅdārmā]: **se** ~ *vi* to kick up a fuss.
gendarmerie [ʒhāṅdārmərē] *nf* military police force in countryside and small towns; their police station or barracks.
gendre [ʒhāṅdr(ə)] *nm* son-in-law.
gène [ʒhen] *nm* (*BIO*) gene.
gêne [ʒhen] *nf* (*à respirer, bouger*) discomfort, difficulty; (*dérangement*) bother, trouble; (*manque d'argent*) financial difficulties *pl ou* straits *pl*; (*confusion*) embarrassment; **sans** ~ *a* inconsiderate.
gêné, e [ʒhānā] *a* embarrassed; (*dépourvu d'argent*) short (of money).
généalogie [ʒhānāālozhē] *nf* genealogy.
généalogique [ʒhānāālozhēk] *a* genealogical.
gêner [ʒhānā] *vt* (*incommoder*) to bother; (*encombrer*) to hamper; (*bloquer le passage*) to be in the way of; (*déranger*) to bother; (*embarrasser*): ~ **qn** to make sb feel ill-at-ease; **se** ~ to put o.s. out; **ne vous gênez pas!** (*ironique*) go right ahead!, don't mind me!; **je vais me** ~! (*ironique*) why should I care?
général, e, aux [ʒhānārál, -ō] *a*, *nm* general ♦ *nf*: (**répétition**) ~**e** final dress rehearsal; **en** ~ usually, in general; **à la satisfaction** ~**e** to everyone's satisfaction.
généralement [ʒhānārálmāṅ] *ad* generally.
généralisable [ʒhānārálēzábl(ə)] *a* generally applicable.
généralisation [ʒhānārálēzásyóṅ] *nf* generalization.
généraliser [ʒhānārálēzā] *vt*, *vi* to generalize; **se** ~ *vi* to become widespread.
généraliste [ʒhānārálēst(ə)] *nm/f* (*MÉD*) gen-

eral practitioner, GP.
généralité [ʒhānārálētā] *nf*: **la** ~ **des** ... the majority of ...; ~**s** *nfpl* generalities; (*introduction*) general points.
générateur, trice [ʒhānārátœr, -trēs] *a*: ~ **de** which causes *ou* brings about ♦ *nf* (*ÉLEC*) generator.
génération [ʒhānārásyóṅ] *nf* (*aussi INFORM*) generation.
généreusement [ʒhānārœ̄zmáṅ] *ad* generously.
généreux, euse [ʒhānārœ̄, -œ̄z] *a* generous.
générique [ʒhānārēk] *a* generic ♦ *nm* (*CINÉMA, TV*) credits *pl*, credit titles *pl*.
générosité [ʒhānārōzētā] *nf* generosity.
Gênes [ʒhen] *n* Genoa.
genèse [ʒhənɛz] *nf* genesis.
genêt [ʒhəne] *nm* (*BOT*) broom *q*.
généticien, ne [ʒhānātēsyáṅ, -en] *nm/f* geneticist.
génétique [ʒhānātēk] *a* genetic ♦ *nf* genetics *sg*.
gêneur, euse [ʒhɛnœr, -œ̄z] *nm/f* (*personne qui gêne*) obstacle; (*importun*) intruder.
Genève [ʒhənɛv] Geneva.
genevois, e [ʒhənəvwá, -wáz] *a* Genevan.
genévrier [ʒhənāvrēyā] *nm* juniper.
génial, e, aux [ʒhānyál, -ō] *a* of genius; (*fam*) fantastic, brilliant.
génie [ʒhānē] *nm* genius; (*MIL*): **le** ~ ≈ the Corps of Engineers; **avoir du** ~ to have genius; ~ **civil** civil engineering.
genièvre [ʒhənyevr(ə)] *nm* (*BOT*) juniper (tree); (*boisson*) ≈ gin; **grain de** ~ juniper berry.
génisse [ʒhānēs] *nf* heifer; **foie de** ~ ox liver.
génital, e, aux [ʒhānētál, -ō] *a* genital.
génitif [ʒhānētēf] *nm* genitive.
génocide [ʒhānōsēd] *nm* genocide.
génois, e [ʒhānwá, -wáz] *a* Genoese ♦ *nf* (*gâteau*) ≈ sponge cake.
genou, x [ʒhnōō] *nm* knee; **à** ~**x** on one's knees; **se mettre à** ~**x** to kneel down.
genouillère [ʒhənōōyer] *nf* (*SPORT*) kneepad.
genre [ʒháṅr] *nm* (*espèce, sorte*) kind, type, sort; (*allure*) manner; (*LING*) gender; (*ART*) genre; (*ZOOL etc*) genus; **se donner du** ~ to put on airs; **avoir bon** ~ to have style; **avoir mauvais** ~ to be ill-mannered.
gens [ʒháṅ] *nmpl (f in some phrases)* people *pl*; **les** ~ **d'Église** the clergy; **les** ~ **du monde** society people; ~ **de maison** domestics.
gentiane [ʒháṅsyáṅ] *nf* gentian.
gentil, le [ʒháṅtē, -ēy] *a* kind; (*enfant: sage*) good; (*sympa: endroit etc*) nice; **c'est très** ~ **à vous** it's very kind *ou* good *ou* nice of you.
gentilhommière [ʒháṅtēyomyer] *nf* (small) manor house.
gentillesse [ʒháṅtēyes] *nf* kindness.
gentillet, te [ʒháṅtēye, -et] *a* nice little.
gentiment [ʒháṅtēmáṅ] *ad* kindly.
génuflection [ʒhānüfleksyóṅ] *nf* genuflexion.
géodésique [ʒhāodāzēk] *a* geodesic.
géographe [ʒhāográf] *nm/f* geographer.
géographie [ʒhāográfē] *nf* geography.
géographique [ʒhāográfēk] *a* geographical.
geôlier [ʒhōlyā] *nm* jailer.
géologie [ʒhāolozhē] *nf* geology.

géologique [zhãolozhĕk] *a* geological.
géologue [zhãolog] *nm/f* geologist.
géomètre [zhãometr(ə)] *nm/f*: **(arpenteur-)**~ (land) surveyor.
géométrie [zhãomãtrē] *nf* geometry; **à** ~ **variable** (*AVIAT*) variable geometry (*US*), swing-wing (*Brit*).
géométrique [zhãomãtrēk] *a* geometric.
géophysique [zhãofēzĕk] *nf* geophysics *sg*.
géopolitique [zhãopolētĕk] *nf* geopolitics *sg*.
Géorgie [gãorzhē] *nf*: **la** ~ (*URSS, USA*) Georgia; **la** ~ **du Sud** South Georgia.
géorgien, ne [gãorzhyań, -en] *a* Georgian.
géothermique [zhãotermēk] *a*: **énergie** ~ geothermal energy.
gérance [zhãrâńs] *nf* management; **mettre en** ~ to appoint a manager for; **prendre en** ~ to take over (the management of).·
géranium [zhãrãnyom] *nm* geranium.
gérant, e [zhãrâń, -âńt] *nm/f* manager/manageress; ~ **d'immeuble** managing agent.
gerbe [zherb(ə)] *nf* (*de fleurs, d'eau*) spray; (*de blé*) sheaf (*pl* sheaves); (*fig*) shower, burst.
gercé, e [zhersā] *a* chapped.
gercer [zhersā] *vi*, **se** ~ *vi* to chap.
gerçure [zhersür] *nf* crack.
gérer [zhãrā] *vt* to manage.
gériatrie [zhãryàtrē] *nf* geriatrics *sg*.
gériatrique [zhãryátrēk] *a* geriatric.
germain, e [zhermań, -en] *a*: **cousin** ~ first cousin.
germanique [zhermánēk] *a* Germanic.
germaniste [zhermánēst(ə)] *nm/f* German scholar.
germe [zherm(ə)] *nm* germ.
germer [zhermā] *vi* to sprout; (*semence, aussi fig*) to germinate.
gérondif [zhãrôńdēf] *nm* gerund; (*en latin*) gerundive.
gérontologie [zherôńtolozhē] *nf* gerontology.
gésier [zhãzyā] *nm* gizzard.
gésir [zhãzēr] *vi* to be lying (down); *voir aussi* ci-gît.
gestation [zhestâsyôń] *nf* gestation.
geste [zhest(ə)] *nm* gesture; move; motion; **il fit un** ~ **de la main pour m'appeler** he signed to me to come over, he waved me over; **ne faites pas un** ~ (*ne bouger pas*) don't move.
gesticuler [zhestēkülā] *vi* to gesticulate.
gestion [zhestyôń] *nf* management; ~ **des disques** (*INFORM*) housekeeping; ~ **de fichier(s)** (*INFORM*) file management.
gestionnaire [zhestyoner] *nm/f* administrator; ~ **de fichier** (*INFORM*) file manager.
geyser [zhezer] *nm* geyser.
Ghana [gáná] *nm*: **le** ~ Ghana.
ghanéen, ne [gánáań, -en] *a* Ghanaian.
ghetto [getō] *nm* ghetto.
gibecière [zhēbsyer] *nf* (*de chasseur*) gamebag; (*sac en bandoulière*) shoulder bag.
gibet [zhēbe] *nm* gallows *pl*.
gibier [zhēbyā] *nm* (*animaux*) game; (*fig*) prey.
giboulée [zhēbōōlā] *nf* sudden shower.
giboyeux, euse [zhēbwáyœ̄, -œ̄z] *a* well-stocked·with game.
Gibraltar [zhēbráltár] *nm* Gibraltar.

gibus [zhēbüs] *nm* opera hat.
giclée [zhēklā] *nf* spurt, squirt.
gicler [zhēklā] *vi* to spurt, squirt.
gicleur [zhēklœr] *nm* (*AUTO*) spray nozzle.
GIE *sigle m* = **groupement d'intérêt économique**.
gifle [zhēfl(ə)] *nf* slap (in the face).
gifler [zhēflā] *vt* to slap (in the face).
gigantesque [zhēgáńtesk(ə)] *a* gigantic.
gigogne [zhēgony] *a*: **lits** ~s trundle (*US*) *ou* truckle (*Brit*) beds; **tables/poupées** ~s nest of tables/dolls.
gigot [zhēgō] *nm* leg (of mutton *ou* lamb).
gigoter [zhēgotā] *vi* to wriggle (about).
gilet [zhēle] *nm* vest (*US*), waistcoat (*Brit*); (*pull*) cardigan; (*de corps*) undershirt (*US*), vest (*Brit*); ~ **pare-balles** bulletproof vest (*US*) *ou* jacket (*Brit*); ~ **de sauvetage** life jacket.
gin [dzhēn] *nm* gin.
gingembre [zhańskĩńbr(ə)] *nm* ginger.
girafe [zhēráf] *nf* giraffe.
giratoire [zhērátwár] *a*: **sens** ~ traffic circle (*US*), roundabout (*Brit*).
girofle [zhērofl(ə)] *nm*: **clou de** ~ clove.
giroflée [zhēroflā] *nf* wallflower.
girolle [zhērol] *nf* chanterelle.
giron [zhērôń] *nm* (*genoux*) lap; (*fig: sein*) bosom.
Gironde [zhērôńd] *nf*: **la** ~ the Gironde.
girophare [zhērofár] *nm* revolving (flashing) light.
girouette [zhērwet] *nf* weather vane *ou* cock.
gis [zhē], **gisais** [zhēze] *etc vb voir* **gésir**.
gisement [zhēzmáń] *nm* deposit.
gît [zhē] *vb voir* **gésir**.
gitan, e [zhētáń, -áń] *nm/f* gipsy.
gîte [zhēt] *nm* home; shelter; (*du lièvre*) form; ~ **(rural)** (country) vacation cottage *ou* apartment.
gîter [zhētā] *vi* (*NAVIG*) to list.
givrage [zhēvrázh] *nm* icing.
givrant, e [zhēvrâń, -âńt] *a*: **brouillard** ~ freezing fog.
givre [zhēvr(ə)] *nm* (hoar) frost.
givré, e [zhēvrā] *a*: **citron** ~/**orange** ~e lemon/orange sorbet (*served in fruit skin*).
glabre [glâbr(ə)] *a* hairless; (*menton*) clean-shaven.
glace [glás] *nf* ice; (*crème glacée*) ice cream; (*verre*) sheet of glass; (*miroir*) mirror; (*de voiture*) window; ~s *nfpl* (*GÉO*) ice sheets, ice *sg*; **de** ~ (*fig: accueil, visage*) frosty, icy; **rester de** ~ to remain unmoved.
glacé, e [glásā] *a* icy; (*boisson*) iced.
glacer [glásā] *vt* to freeze; (*boisson*) to chill, ice; (*gâteau*) to ice, frost (*US*); (*papier, tissu*) to glaze; (*fig*): ~ **qn** to chill sb; (*fig*) to make sb's blood run cold.
glaciaire [glásyer] *a* (*période*) ice *cpd*; (*relief*) glacial.
glacial, e [glásyál] *a* icy.
glacier [glásyā] *nm* (*GÉO*) glacier; (*marchand*) ice-cream maker.
glacière [glásyer] *nf* icebox.
glaçon [glásôń] *nm* icicle; (*pour boisson*) ice

cube.

gladiateur [glàdyàtœr] *nm* gladiator.
glaïeul [glàyœl] *nm* gladiola.
glaire [glɛr] *nf* (*MÉD*) phlegm *q*.
glaise [glɛz] *nf* clay.
glaive [glɛv] *nm* two-edged sword.
gland [glɑ̃] *nm* (*de chêne*) acorn; (*décoration*) tassel; (*ANAT*) glans.
glande [glɑ̃d] *nf* gland.
glaner [glàne] *vt, vi* to glean.
glapir [glàper] *vi* to yelp.
glas [glɑ] *nm* knell, toll.
glauque [glok] *a* dull blue-green.
glissade [glɛsàd] *nf* (*par jeu*) slide; (*chute*) slip; (*dérapage*) skid; **faire des ~s** to slide.
glissant, e [glɛsɑ̃, -ɑ̃t] *a* slippery.
glissement [glɛsmɑ̃] *nm* sliding; (*fig*) shift; **~ de terrain** landslide.
glisser [glɛse] *vi* (*avancer*) to glide *ou* slide along; (*coulisser, tomber*) to slide; (*déraper*) to slip; (*être glissant*) to be slippery ♦ *vt*: **~ qch sous/dans/à** to slip sth under/into/to; **~ sur** (*fig: détail etc*) to skate over; **se ~ dans/entre** to slip into/between.
glissière [glɛsyɛr] *nf* slide channel; **à ~** (*porte, fenêtre*) sliding; **~ de sécurité** (*AUTO*) crash barrier.
glissoire [glɛswàr] *nf* slide.
global, e, aux [globàl, -o] *a* overall.
globalement [globàlmɑ̃] *ad* taken as a whole.
globe [glob] *nm* globe; **sous ~** under glass; **~ oculaire** eyeball; **le ~ terrestre** the globe.
globule [globül] *nm* (*du sang*): **~ blanc/rouge** white/red corpuscle.
globuleux, euse [globülœ, -œz] *a*: **yeux ~** protruding eyes.
gloire [glwàr] *nf* glory; (*mérite*) distinction, credit; (*personne*) celebrity.
glorieux, euse [gloryœ, -œz] *a* glorious.
glorifier [glorefyà] *vt* to glorify, extol; **se ~ de** to glory in.
gloriole [gloryol] *nf* vainglory.
glose [gloz] *nf* gloss.
glossaire [gloser] *nm* glossary.
glotte [glot] *nf* (*ANAT*) glottis.
glouglouter [glooglootà] *vi* to gurgle.
glousser [gloosà] *vi* to cluck; (*rire*) to chuckle.
glouton, ne [glootɔ̃, -on] *a* gluttonous, greedy.
gloutonnerie [glootonre] *nf* gluttony.
glu [glü] *nf* birdlime.
gluant, e [glüɑ̃, -ɑ̃t] *a* sticky, gummy.
glucose [glükoz] *nm* glucose.
gluten [glüten] *nm* gluten.
glycérine [glɛsaren] *nf* glycerine.
glycine [glɛsɛn] *nf* wisteria.
GMT *sigle a* (= *Greenwich Mean Time*) GMT.
GNL *sigle m* (= *gaz naturel liquéfié*) LNG (= *liquefied natural gas*).
gnôle [nyol] *nf* (*fam*) booze *q*; **un petit verre de ~** a drop of the hard stuff.
gnome [gnom] *nm* gnome.
GO *sigle fpl* (= *grandes ondes*) LW ♦ *sigle m* (= *gentil organisateur*) title given to leaders on Club Méditerranée vacations; extended to refer to easy-going leader of any group.
go [go]: **tout de ~** *ad* straight out.
goal [gol] *nm* goalkeeper.

gobelet [goble] *nm* (*en métal*) tumbler; (*en plastique*) beaker; (*à dés*) cup.
gober [gobà] *vt* to swallow.
goberger [goberzhà]: **se ~** *vi* to pamper o.s.
Gobi [gobe] *n*: **désert de ~** Gobi Desert.
godasse [godàs] *nf* (*fam*) shoe.
godet [gode] *nm* pot; (*COUTURE*) unpressed pleat.
godiller [godeyà] *vi* (*NAVIG*) to scull; (*SKI*) to wedeln.
goéland [goàlɑ̃] *nm* (sea)gull.
goélette [goàlet] *nf* schooner.
goémon [goàmɔ̃] *nm* wrack.
gogo [gogo] *nm* (*péj*) sucker; **à ~** *ad* galore.
goguenard, e [gognàr, -àrd(ə)] *a* mocking.
goguette [goget] *nf*: **en ~** on the binge.
goinfre [gwɑ̃fr(ə)] *nm* glutton.
goinfrer [gwɑ̃frà]: **se ~** *vi* to make a pig of o.s.; **se ~ de** to guzzle.
goitre [gwàtr(ə)] *nm* goiter (*US*), goitre (*Brit*).
golf [golf] *nm* (*jeu*) golf; (*terrain*) golf course; **~ miniature** crazy *ou* miniature golf.
golfe [golf(ə)] *nm* gulf; bay; **le ~ d'Aden** the Gulf of Aden; **le ~ de Gascogne** the Bay of Biscay; **le ~ du Lion** the Gulf of Lions; **le ~ Persique** the Persian Gulf.
gominé, e [gomenà] *a* slicked down.
gomme [gom] *nf* (*à effacer*) eraser; (*résine*) gum; **boule** *ou* **pastille de ~** throat pastille.
gommé, e [gomà] *a*: **papier ~** gummed paper.
gommer [gomà] *vt* (*effacer*) to erase; (*enduire de gomme*) to gum.
gond [gɔ̃] *nm* hinge; **sortir de ses ~s** (*fig*) to fly off the handle.
gondole [gɔ̃dol] *nf* gondola; (*pour l'étalage*) shelves *pl*, gondola.
gondoler [gɔ̃dolà]: **se ~** *vi* to warp, buckle; (*fam: rire*) to hoot with laughter; to be in stitches.
gondolier [gɔ̃dolyà] *nm* gondolier.
gonflable [gɔ̃flàbl(ə)] *a* inflatable.
gonflage [gɔ̃flàzh] *nm* inflating, blowing up.
gonflé, e [gɔ̃flà] *a* swollen; (*ventre*) bloated; (*fam: culotté*): **être ~** to have a nerve.
gonfler [gɔ̃flà] *vt* (*pneu, ballon*) to inflate, blow up; (*nombre, importance*) to inflate ♦ *vi* (*pied etc*) to swell (up); (*CULIN: pâte*) to rise.
gonfleur [gɔ̃flœr] *nm* air pump.
gong [gɔ̃g] *nm* gong.
gonzesse [gɔ̃zes] *nf* (*fam*) chick.
goret [gore] *nm* piglet.
gorge [gorzh(ə)] *nf* (*ANAT*) throat; (*poitrine*) breast; (*GÉO*) gorge; (*rainure*) groove; **avoir mal à la ~** to have a sore throat; **avoir la ~ serrée** to have a lump in one's throat.
gorgé, e [gorzhà] *a*: **~ de** filled with; (*eau*) saturated with ♦ *nf* mouthful; sip; gulp; **boire à petites/grandes ~es** to take little sips/big gulps.
gorille [goreÿ] *nm* gorilla; (*fam*) bodyguard.
gosier [gozyà] *nm* throat.
gosse [gos] *nm/f* kid.
gothique [gotek] *a* gothic.
gouaille [gwày] *nf* street wit, cocky humor (*US*) *ou* humour (*Brit*).
goudron [goodrɔ̃] *nm* (*asphalte*) asphalt; (*du tabac*) tar.

goudronner [gōōdronā] *vt* to asphalt.
gouffre [gōōfr(ə)] *nm* abyss, gulf.
goujat [gōōzhá] *nm* boor.
goujon [gōōzhóń] *nm* gudgeon.
goulée [gōōlā] *nf* gulp.
goulet [gōōle] *nm* bottleneck.
goulot [gōōlō] *nm* neck; **boire au ~** to drink from the bottle.
goulu, e [gōōlü] *a* greedy.
goupille [gōōpēy] *nf* (metal) pin.
goupiller [gōōpēyā] *vt* to pin (together).
goupillon [gōōpēyóń] *nm* (REL) sprinkler; (*brosse*) bottle brush; **le ~** (*fig*) the cloth, the clergy.
gourd, e [gōōr, gōōrd(ə)] *a* numb (with cold); (*fam*) oafish.
gourde [gōōrd(ə)] *nf* (*récipient*) flask; (*fam*) dumbbell, (clumsy) oaf.
gourdin [gōōrdań] *nm* club, bludgeon.
gourmand, e [gōōrmáń, -áńd] *a* greedy.
gourmandise [gōōrmáńdēz] *nf* greed; (*bonbon*) piece of candy (US), sweet (Brit).
gourmet [gōōrme] *nm* epicure.
gourmette [gōōrmet] *nf* chain bracelet.
gourou [gōōrōō] *nm* guru.
gousse [gōōs] *nf* (*de vanille etc*) pod; **~ d'ail** clove of garlic.
gousset [gōōse] *nm* (*de gilet*) fob.
goût [gōō] *nm* taste; (*fig: appréciation*) taste, liking; **le (bon) ~** good taste; **de bon ~** in good taste, tasteful; **de mauvais ~** in bad taste, tasteless; **avoir bon/mauvais ~** (*aliment*) to taste good/bad; (*personne*) to have good/bad taste; **avoir du/manquer de ~** to have/lack taste; **avoir du ~ pour** to have a liking for; **prendre ~ à** to develop a taste *ou* a liking for.
goûter [gōōtā] *vt* (*essayer*) to taste; (*apprécier*) to enjoy ♦ *vi* to have an afternoon snack ♦ *nm* afternoon snack; **~ à** to taste, sample; **~ de** to have a taste of; **~ d'enfants/d'anniversaire** children's tea/birthday party.
goutte [gōōt] *nf* drop; (MÉD) gout; (*alcool*) drop (US), nip (Brit); **~s** *nfpl* (MÉD) drops; **~ à ~** *ad* a drop at a time; **tomber ~ à ~** to drip.
goutte-à-goutte [gōōtágōōt] *nm inv* (MÉD) I.V. (US), drip (Brit); **alimenter au ~** to put on an I.V. (US), drip-feed (Brit).
gouttelette [gōōtlet] *nf* droplet.
goutter [gōōtā] *vi* to drip.
gouttière [gōōtyer] *nf* gutter.
gouvernail [gōōvernáy] *nm* rudder; (*barre*) helm, tiller.
gouvernant, e [gōōvernáń, -áńt] *a* ruling *cpd* ♦ *nf* housekeeper; (*d'un enfant*) governess.
gouverne [gōōvern(ə)] *nf*: **pour sa ~** for his guidance.
gouvernement [gōōvernəmáń] *nm* government.
gouvernemental, e, aux [gōōvernəmáńtál, -ō] *a* (*politique*) government *cpd*; (*journal, parti*) pro-government.
gouverner [gōōvernā] *vt* to govern; (*diriger*) to steer; (*fig*) to control.
gouverneur [gōōvernœr] *nm* governor; (MIL) commanding officer.
goyave [goyáv] *nf* guava.

GPL *sigle m* (= *gaz de pétrole liquéfié*) LPG (= *liquefied petroleum gas*).
GQG *sigle m* (= *grand quartier général*) GHQ.
grabataire [grábáter] *a* bedridden ♦ *nm/f* bed-ridden invalid.
grâce [grâs] *nf* grace; (*faveur*) favor (US), favour (Brit); (JUR) pardon; **~s** *nfpl* (REL) grace *sg*; **de bonne/mauvaise ~** with (a) good/bad grace; **dans les bonnes ~s de qn** in favor with sb; **faire ~ à qn de qch** to spare sb sth; **rendre ~(s) à** to give thanks to; **demander ~** to beg for mercy; **droit de ~** right of reprieve; **recours en ~** plea for pardon; **~ à** *prép* thanks to.
gracier [grásyā] *vt* to pardon.
gracieusement [grásyœzmáń] *ad* graciously, kindly; (*gratuitement*) freely; (*avec grâce*) gracefully.
gracieux, euse [grásyœ, -œz] *a* (*charmant, élégant*) graceful; (*aimable*) gracious, kind; **à titre ~** free of charge.
gracile [grásēl] *a* slender.
gradation [grádâsyóń] *nf* gradation.
grade [grád] *nm* (MIL) rank; (SCOL) degree; **monter en ~** to be promoted.
gradé [grádā] *nm* (MIL) (noncommissioned) officer.
gradin [grádań] *nm* (*dans un théâtre*) tier; (*de stade*) step; **~s** *nmpl* (*de stade*) stands (US), terracing *q* (Brit); **en ~s** terraced.
graduation [grádüásyóń] *nf* graduation.
gradué, e [grádüā] *a* (*exercices*) graded (for difficulty); (*thermomètre, verre*) graduated.
graduel, le [grádüel] *a* gradual; progressive.
graduer [grádüā] *vt* (*effort etc*) to increase gradually; (*règle, verre*) to graduate; (*exercices*) to increase in difficulty.
graffiti [gráfētē] *nmpl* graffiti.
grain [grań] *nm* (*gén*) grain; (*de chapelet*) bead; (NAVIG) squall; (*averse*) heavy shower; (*fig: petite quantité*): **un ~ de** a touch of; **~ de beauté** beauty spot; **~ de café** coffee bean; **~ de poivre** peppercorn; **~ de poussière** speck of dust; **~ de raisin** grape.
graine [gren] *nf* seed; **mauvaise ~** (*mauvais sujet*) bad lot; **une ~ de voyou** a hooligan in the making.
grainetier, -ière [grentyā, -yer] seed merchant.
graissage [gresázh] *nm* lubrication, greasing.
graisse [gres] *nf* fat; (*lubrifiant*) grease.
graisser [grásā] *vt* to lubricate, grease; (*tacher*) to make greasy.
graisseux, euse [gresœ, -œz] *a* greasy; (ANAT) fatty.
grammaire [grámer] *nf* grammar.
grammatical, e, aux [grámátēkál, -ō] *a* grammatical.
gramme [grám] *nm* gram (US), gramme (Brit).
grand, e [grań, gráńd] *a* (*haut*) tall; (*gros, vaste, large*) big, large; (*long*) long; (*sens abstraits*) great ♦ *ad*: **~ ouvert** wide open; **un ~ buveur** a heavy drinker; **un ~ homme** a great man; **son ~ frère** his big *ou* older brother; **avoir ~ besoin de** to be in dire *ou* desperate need of; **il est ~ temps de** it's high time to; **il est assez ~ pour** he's big *ou* old enough to; **voir ~** to think big; **en ~** on a

large scale; **au ~ air** in the open (air); **les ~s blessés/brûlés** the severely injured/ burned; **de ~ matin** at the crack of dawn; **~ écart** splits *pl*; **~ ensemble** housing project (*US*) *ou* scheme (*Brit*); **~ jour** broad daylight; **~ livre** (*COMM*) ledger; **~ magasin** department store; **~ malade** very sick person; **~ public** general public; **~e personne** grown-up; **~e surface** superstore; **~es écoles** *prestige university-level colleges with competitive entrance examinations*; **~es lignes** (*RAIL*) main lines; **~es vacances** summer vacation *sg* (*US*) *ou* holidays (*Brit*).

grand-angle, *pl* **grands-angles** [grântângl(ə)] *nm* (*PHOTO*) wide-angle lens.

grand-angulaire, *pl* **grands-angulaires** [grântângüler] *nm* (*PHOTO*) wide-angle lens.

grand-chose [grânshōz] *nm/f inv*: **pas ~** not much.

Grande-Bretagne [grândbrətâny] *nf*: **la ~** (Great) Britain; **en ~** in (Great) Britain.

grandement [grândmân] *ad* (*tout à fait*) greatly; (*largement*) easily; (*généreusement*) lavishly.

grandeur [grândœr] *nf* (*dimension*) size; (*fig: ampleur, importance*) magnitude; (*: gloire, puissance*) greatness; **~ nature** *a* life-size.

grand-guignolesque [grângēnyolesk(ə)] *a* gruesome.

grandiloquent, e [grândēlokân, -ânt] *a* bombastic, grandiloquent.

grandir [grândēr] *vi* (*enfant, arbre*) to grow; (*bruit, hostilité*) to increase, grow ♦ *vt*: **~ qn** (*suj: vêtement, chaussure*) to make sb look taller; (*fig*) to make sb grow in stature.

grandissant, e [grândēsân, -ânt] *a* growing.

grand-mère [grânmer] *nf* grandmother.

grand-messe [grânmes] *nf* high mass.

grand-peine [grânpen]: **à ~** *ad* with (great) difficulty.

grand-père, *pl* **grands-pères** [grânper] *nm* grandfather.

grand-route [grânrōot] *nf* main road.

grand-rue [grânrü] *nf* main street.

grands-parents [grânpârân] *nmpl* grandparents.

grand-voile [grânvwál] *nf* mainsail.

grange [grânzh] *nf* barn.

granit(e) [grânēt] *nm* granite.

granule [grânül] *nm* small pill.

granulé [grânülā] *nm* granule.

granuleux, euse [grânülœ, -œz] *a* granular.

graphe [gráf] *nm* graph.

graphie [gráfē] *nf* written form.

graphique [gráfēk] *a* graphic ♦ *nm* graph.

graphisme [gráfēsm(ə)] *nm* graphic arts *pl*; graphics *sg*; (*écriture*) handwriting.

graphiste [gráfēst(ə)] *nm/f* graphic designer.

graphologue [gráfolog] *nm/f* graphologist.

grappe [gráp] *nf* cluster; **~ de raisin** bunch of grapes.

grappiller [grápēyā] *vt* to glean.

grappin [grápân] *nm* grapnel; **mettre le ~ sur** (*fig*) to get one's claws on.

gras, se [grâ, grâs] *a* (*viande, soupe*) fatty; (*personne*) fat; (*surface, main, cheveux*) greasy; (*terre*) sticky; (*toux*) loose, phlegmy; (*rire*) throaty; (*plaisanterie*) coarse; (*crayon*) soft-lead; (*TYPO*) bold ♦ *nm*

(*CULIN*) fat; **faire la ~se matinée** to sleep late; **matière ~se** fat (content).

gras-double [grâdōobl(ə)] *nm* (*CULIN*) tripe.

grassement [grâsmân] *ad* (*généreusement*): **~ payé** handsomely paid; (*grossièrement: rire*) coarsely.

grassouillet, te [grâsōōye, -et] *a* pudgy, plump.

gratifiant, e [grátēfyân, -ânt] *a* gratifying, rewarding.

gratification [grátēfēkâsyôn] *nf* bonus.

gratifier [grátēfyā] *vt*: **~ qn de** to favor (*US*) *ou* favour (*Brit*) sb with; to reward sb with; (*sourire etc*) to favor sb with.

gratin [grátân] *nm* (*CULIN*) cheese- (*ou* crumb-)topped dish; (*: croûte*) topping; **au ~** au gratin; **tout le ~ parisien** all the best people of Paris.

gratiné, e [grátēnā] *a* (*CULIN*) au gratin; (*fam*) hellish ♦ *nf* (*soupe*) onion soup au gratin.

gratis [grátēs] *ad, a* free.

gratitude [grátētüd] *nf* gratitude.

gratte-ciel [grátsyel] *nm inv* skyscraper.

grattement [grátmân] *nm* (*bruit*) scratching (noise).

gratte-papier [grátpâpyā] *nm inv* (*péj*) pencil pusher (*US*), penpusher (*Brit*).

gratter [grátā] *vt* (*frotter*) to scrape; (*enlever*) to scrape off; (*bras, bouton*) to scratch; **se ~** to scratch o.s.

grattoir [grátwár] *nm* scraper.

gratuit, e [grátüē, -üēt] *a* (*entrée*) free; (*billet*) free, complimentary; (*fig*) gratuitous.

gratuité [grátüētā] *nf* being free (of charge); gratuitousness.

gratuitement [grátüētmân] *ad* (*sans payer*) free; (*sans preuve, motif*) gratuitously.

gravats [grávâ] *nmpl* rubble *sg*.

grave [gráv] *a* (*dangereux: maladie, accident*) serious, bad; (*sérieux: sujet, problème*) serious, grave; (*personne, air*) grave, solemn; (*voix, son*) deep, low-pitched ♦ *nm* (*MUS*) low register; **ce n'est pas ~!** it's all right, don't worry; **blessé ~** seriously injured person.

graveleux, euse [grávlœ, -œz] *a* (*terre*) gravelly; (*fruit*) gritty; (*contes, propos*) smutty.

gravement [grávmân] *ad* seriously; badly; gravely.

graver [grávā] *vt* (*plaque, nom*) to engrave; (*fig*): **~ qch dans son esprit/sa mémoire** to etch sth in one's mind/memory.

graveur [grávœr] *nm* engraver.

gravier [grávyā] *nm* (loose) gravel *q*.

gravillons [grávēyôn] *nmpl* gravel *sg*.

gravir [grávēr] *vt* to climb (up).

gravité [grávētā] *nf* (*voir grave*) seriousness; gravity; (*PHYSIQUE*) gravity.

graviter [grávētā] *vi*: **~ autour de** to revolve around.

gravure [grávür] *nf* engraving; (*reproduction*) print; plate.

GRE *sigle f* = *garantie contre les risques à l'exportation*.

gré [grā] *nm*: **à son ~** *a* to his liking ♦ *ad* as he pleases; **au ~ de** according to, following; **contre le ~ de qn** against sb's will; **de son (plein) ~** of one's own free will; **de ~ ou de**

force whether one likes it or not; **de bon ~** willingly; **bon ~ mal ~** like it or not; willy-nilly; **de ~ à ~** (*COMM*) by mutual agreement; **savoir (bien) ~ à qn de qch** to be (most) grateful to sb for sth.

grec, grecque [grek] *a* Greek; (*classique: vase etc*) Grecian ♦ *nm* (*LING*) Greek ♦ *nm/f*: **G~, Grecque** Greek.

Grèce [gres] *nf*: **la ~** Greece.

gredin, e [grədaṅ, -ēn] *nm/f* rogue, rascal.

gréement [grāmáṅ] *nm* rigging.

greffe [gref] *nf* graft; transplant ♦ *nm* (*JUR*) office.

greffer [grāfā] *vt* (*BOT*, *MÉD*: *tissu*) to graft; (*MÉD*: *organe*) to transplant.

greffier [grāfyā] *nm* clerk of the court.

grégaire [grāger] *a* gregarious.

grège [grezh] *a*: **soie ~** raw silk.

grêle [grel] *a* (very) thin ♦ *nf* hail.

grêlé, e [grālā] *a* pockmarked.

grêler [grālā] *vb impersonnel*: **il grêle** it's hailing ♦ *vt*: **la région a été grêlée** the region was damaged by hail.

grêlon [grəlóṅ] *nm* hailstone.

grelot [grəlō] *nm* little bell.

grelotter [grəlotā] *vi* (*trembler*) to shiver.

Grenade [grənád] *n* Granada ♦ *nf* (*île*) Grenada.

grenade [grənád] *nf* (*explosive*) grenade; (*BOT*) pomegranate; **~ lacrymogène** teargas grenade.

grenadier [grənádyā] *nm* (*MIL*) grenadier; (*BOT*) pomegranate tree.

grenadine [grənádēn] *nf* grenadine.

grenat [grəná] *a inv* dark red.

grenier [grənyā] *nm* (*de maison*) attic; (*de ferme*) loft.

grenouille [grənooy] *nf* frog.

grenouillère [grənooyer] *nf* (*de bébé*) leggings; (: *combinaison*) sleeper (*US*), sleepsuit (*Brit*).

grenu, e [grənü] *a* grainy, grained.

grès [gre] *nm* (*roche*) sandstone; (*poterie*) stoneware.

grésil [grāzē] *nm* (fine) hail.

grésillement [grāzēymáṅ] *nm* sizzling; crackling.

grésiller [grāzēyā] *vi* to sizzle; (*RADIO*) to crackle.

grève [grev] *nf* (*d'ouvriers*) strike; (*plage*) shore; **se mettre en/faire ~** to go on/be on strike; **~ bouchon** partial strike (*in key areas of a company*); **~ de la faim** hunger strike; **~ perlée** slowdown (*US*), go-slow (*Brit*); **~ sauvage** wildcat strike; **~ de solidarité** sympathy strike; **~ sur le tas** sit-down strike; **~ tournante** strike staggered; **~ du zèle** slowdown (*US*), work-to-rule (*Brit*).

grever [grəvā] *vt* (*budget, économie*) to put a strain on; **grevé d'impôts** crippled by taxes; **grevé d'hypothèques** heavily mortgaged.

gréviste [grāvēst(ə)] *nm/f* striker.

gribouillage [grēbooyázh] *nm* scribble, scrawl.

gribouiller [grēbooyā] *vt* to scribble, scrawl ♦ *vi* to doodle.

grief [grēyef] *nm* grievance; **faire ~ à qn de** to reproach sb for.

grièvement [grēyevmáṅ] *ad* seriously.

griffe [grēf] *nf* claw; (*fig*) signature; (: *d'un couturier, parfumeur*) label, signature.

griffé, e [grēfā] *a* designer(-label) *cpd*.

griffer [grēfā] *vt* to scratch.

griffonnage [grēfonázh] *nm* scribble.

griffonner [grēfonā] *vt* to scribble.

griffure [grēfür] *nf* scratch.

grignoter [grēnyotā] *vt*, *vi* to nibble.

gril [grēl] *nm* steak *ou* grill pan.

grillade [grēyád] *nf* grill.

grillage [grēyázh] *nm* (*treillis*) wire netting; (*clôture*) wire fencing.

grille [grēy] *nf* (*portail*) (metal) gate; (*clôture*) railings *pl*; (*d'égout*) (metal) grate; (*fig*) grid.

grille-pain [grēypaṅ] *nm inv* toaster.

griller [grēyā] *vt* (*aussi*: **faire ~**: *pain*) to toast; (: *viande*) to broil (*US*), grill (*Brit*); (: *café*) to roast; (*fig*: *ampoule etc*) to burn out, blow ♦ *vi* (*brûler*) to be roasting; **~ un feu rouge** to run a stoplight (*US*), jump the lights (*Brit*).

grillon [grēyóṅ] *nm* (*ZOOL*) cricket.

grimace [grēmás] *nf* grimace; (*pour faire rire*): **faire des ~s** to pull *ou* make faces.

grimacer [grēmásā] *vi* to grimace.

grimer [grēmā] *vt* to make up.

grimpant, e [graṅpáṅ, -áṅt] *a*: **plante ~e** climbing plant, climber.

grimper [graṅpā] *vi*, *vt* to climb ♦ *nm*: **le ~** (*SPORT*) rope-climbing; **~ à/sur** to climb (up)/climb onto.

grimpeur, euse [graṅpœr, -ēz] *nm/f* climber.

grinçant, e [graṅsáṅ, -áṅt] *a* grating.

grincement [graṅsmáṅ] *nm* grating (noise); creaking (noise).

grincer [graṅsā] *vi* (*porte, roue*) to grate; (*plancher*) to creak; **~ des dents** to grind one's teeth.

grincheux, euse [graṅshē, -ēz] *a* grumpy.

gringalet [graṅgále] *am* puny ♦ *nm* weakling.

griotte [grēyot] *nf* Morello cherry.

grippe [grēp] *nf* flu, influenza; **avoir la ~** to have (the) flu; **prendre qn/qch en ~** (*fig*) to take a sudden dislike to sb/sth.

grippé, e [grēpā] *a*: **être ~** to have (the) flu; (*moteur*) to have jammed.

gripper [grēpā] *vt*, *vi* to jam.

gris, e [grē, grēz] *a* gray (*US*), grey (*Brit*); (*ivre*) tipsy ♦ *nm* (*couleur*) gray (*US*), grey (*Brit*); **il fait ~** it's a dull *ou* gray day; **faire ~e mine** to look miserable *ou* morose; **faire ~e mine à qn** to give sb a cool reception.

grisaille [grēzáy] *nf* grayness (*US*), greyness (*Brit*), dullness.

grisant, e [grēzáṅ, -áṅt] *a* intoxicating, exhilarating.

grisâtre [grēzátr(ə)] *a* grayish (*US*), greyish (*Brit*).

griser [grēzā] *vt* to intoxicate; **se ~ de** (*fig*) to become intoxicated with.

grisonnant, e [grēzonáṅ, -áṅt] *a* graying (*US*), greying (*Brit*).

grisonner [grēzonā] *vi* to be going gray (*US*) *ou* grey (*Brit*).

grisou [grēzoo] *nm* firedamp.

grive [grēv] *nf* (*ZOOL*) thrush.

grivois, e [grēvwá, -wáz] *a* saucy.

Groenland [groenláṅd] *nm*: **le ~** Greenland.

groenlandais, e [grœnlâṅde, -ez] *a* of *ou* from Greenland ♦ *nm/f*: **G~, e** Greenlander.

grog [grɔg] *nm* grog.

grogne [grɔny] *nf* grumble.

grogner [grɔnyā] *vi* to growl; *(fig)* to grumble.

grognon, ne [grɔ́ṅnyôṅ, -on] *a* grumpy, grouchy.

groin [grwaṅ] *nm* snout.

grommeler [grɔmlā] *vi* to mutter to o.s.

grondement [grôṅdmâṅ] *nm* rumble; growl.

gronder [grôṅdā] *vi (canon, moteur, tonnerre)* to rumble; *(animal)* to growl; *(fig: révolte)* to be brewing ♦ *vt* to scold.

groom [grōōm] *nm* page, bellhop *(US)*.

gros, se [grō, grōs] *a* big, large; *(obèse)* fat; *(problème, quantité)* great; *(travaux, dégâts)* extensive; *(large: trait, fil)* thick, heavy ♦ *ad*: **risquer/gagner ~** to risk/win a lot ♦ *nm (COMM)*: **le ~** the wholesale business; **écrire ~** to write in big letters; **prix de ~** wholesale price; **par ~ temps/~se mer** in rough weather/heavy seas; **le ~ de** the main body of; *(du travail etc)* the bulk of; **en avoir ~ sur le cœur** to be upset; **en ~** roughly; *(COMM)* wholesale; **~ intestin** large intestine; **~ lot** jackpot; **~ mot** coarse word, vulgarity; **~ œuvre** shell (of building); **~ plan** *(PHOTO)* close-up; **~ porteur** wide-bodied aircraft, jumbo (jet); **~ sel** cooking salt; **~ titre** headline; **~se caisse** bass drum.

groseille [grōzey] *nf*: **~ (rouge)/(blanche)** red/white currant; **~ à maquereau** gooseberry.

groseillier [grōzāyā] *nm* red *ou* white currant bush; gooseberry bush.

grosse [grōs] *af voir* **gros** ♦ *nf (COMM)* gross.

grossesse [grōses] *nf* pregnancy; **~ nerveuse** phantom pregnancy.

grosseur [grōsœr] *nf* size; fatness; *(tumeur)* lump.

grossier, ière [grōsyā, -yer] *a* coarse; *(travail)* rough, crude; *(évident: erreur)* gross.

grossièrement [grōsyermâṅ] *ad* coarsely; roughly; crudely; *(en gros)* roughly.

grossièreté [grōsyertā] *nf* coarseness; rudeness.

grossir [grōsēr] *vi (personne)* to put on weight; *(fig)* to grow, get bigger; *(rivière)* to swell ♦ *vt* to increase; *(exagérer)* to exaggerate; *(au microscope)* to magnify, enlarge; *(suj: vêtement)*: **~ qn** to make sb look fatter.

grossissant, e [grōsêsâṅ, -âṅt] *a* magnifying, enlarging.

grossissement [grōsēsmâṅ] *nm (optique)* magnification.

grossiste [grōsêst(ə)] *nm/f* wholesaler.

grosso modo [grōsōmodō] *ad* roughly.

grotesque [grotesk(ə)] *a* grotesque.

grotte [grɔt] *nf* cave.

grouiller [grōōyā] *vi (foule)* to mill about; *(fourmis)* to swarm about; **~ de** to be swarming with.

groupe [grōōp] *nm* group; **cabinet de ~** group practice; **médecine de ~** group practice; **~ électrogène** generator; **~ de pression** pressure group; **~ sanguin** blood group; **~ scolaire** school complex.

groupement [grōōpmâṅ] *nm* grouping;

(groupe) group; **~ d'intérêt économique (GIE)** ≈ trade association.

grouper [grōōpā] *vt* to group; *(ressources, moyens)* to pool; **se ~** to get together.

groupuscule [grōōpüskül] *nm* clique.

gruau [grüō] *nm*: **pain de ~** wheaten bread.

grue [grü] *nf* crane; **faire le pied de ~** *(fam)* to hang around (waiting), cool one's heels.

gruger [grüzhā] *vt* to cheat, dupe.

grumeaux [grümō] *nmpl (CULIN)* lumps.

grumeleux, euse [grümlœ, -œz] *a (sauce etc)* lumpy; *(peau etc)* bumpy.

grutier [grütyā] *nm* crane driver.

gruyère [grüyer] *nm* Swiss cheese.

Guadeloupe [gwádlōōp] *nf*: **la ~** Guadeloupe.

guadeloupéen, ne [gwádlōōpāaṅ, -en] *a* Guadelupian.

Guatémala [gwátámálá] *nm*: **le ~** Guatemala.

guatémalien, ne [gwátāmályaṅ, -en] *a* Guatemalan.

guatémaltèque [gwátámáltek] *a* Guatemalan.

GUD [güd] *sigle m (= Groupe Union Défense)* student union.

gué [gā] *nm* ford; **passer à ~** to ford.

guenilles [gənēy] *nfpl* rags.

guenon [gənôṅ] *nf* female monkey.

guépard [gāpár] *nm* cheetah.

guêpe [gep] *nf* wasp.

guêpier [gāpyā] *nm (fig)* trap.

guère [ger] *ad (avec adjectif, adverbe)*: **ne ... ~** hardly; *(avec verbe)*: **ne ... ~** *tournure négative* + much; hardly ever; *tournure négative* + (very) long; **il n'y a ~ que/de** there's hardly anybody *(ou* anything) but/ hardly any.

guéridon [gārēdôṅ] *nm* pedestal table.

guérilla [gārēyá] *nf* guerrilla warfare.

guérillero [gārēyárō] *nm* guerrilla.

guérir [gārēr] *vt (personne, maladie)* to cure; *(membre, plaie)* to heal ♦ *vi (personne)* to recover, be cured; *(plaie, chagrin)* to heal; **~ de** to be cured of, recover from; **~ qn de** to cure sb of.

guérison [gārēzôṅ] *nf* curing; healing; recovery.

guérissable [gārēsábl(ə)] *a* curable.

guérisseur, euse [gārēsœr, -œz] *nm/f* healer.

guérite [gārēt] *nf (MIL)* sentry box; *(sur un chantier)* (workman's) hut.

Guernesey [gernəze] *nf* Guernsey.

guernesiais, e [gernəzye, -ez] *a* of *ou* from Guernsey.

guerre [ger] *nf* war; *(méthode)*: **~ atomique/ de tranchées** atomic/trench warfare *q*; **en ~** at war; **faire la ~ à** to wage war against; **de ~ lasse** *(fig)* tired of fighting *ou* resisting; **de bonne ~** fair and square; **~ civile/mondiale** civil/world war; **~ froide/sainte** cold/holy war; **~ d'usure** war of attrition.

guerrier, ière [geryā, -yer] *a* warlike ♦ *nm/f* warrior.

guerroyer [gerwáyā] *vi* to wage war.

guet [ge] *nm*: **faire le ~** to be on the watch *ou* look-out.

guet-apens, pl guets-apens [getápâṅ] *nm* ambush.

guêtre [getr(ə)] *nf* gaiter.

guetter [gātā] *vt (épier)* to watch (intently); *(attendre)* to watch (out) for; *(: pour* *surprendre)* to be lying in wait for.

guetteur [gɛtœr] *nm* look-out.

gueule [gœl] *nf* mouth; *(fam: visage)* mug; *(: bouche)* trap *(!)*, mouth; **ta ~!** *(fam)* shut up!; **~ de bois** *(fam)* hangover.

gueule-de-loup, *pl* **gueules-de-loup** [gœldəlōō] *nf* snapdragon.

gueuler [gœlā] *vi (fam)* to bawl.

gueux [gœ̈] *nm* beggar; *(coquin)* rogue.

gui [gē] *nm* mistletoe.

guichet [gēshc] *nm (de bureau, banque)* counter, window; *(d'une porte)* wicket, hatch; **les ~s** *(à la gare, au théâtre)* the ticket office; **jouer à ~s fermés** to play to a full house.

guichetier, ière [gēshtyā, -ycr] *nm/f* counter clerk.

guide [gēd] *nm* guide; *(livre)* guide(book) **♦** *nf (fille scout)* girl scout *(US)*, (girl) guide *(Brit)*; **~s** *nfpl (d'un cheval)* reins.

guider [gēdā] *vt* to guide.

guidon [gēdóń] *nm* handlebars *pl*.

guignol [gēnyol] *nm* ≈ Punch and Judy show; *(fig)* clown.

guillemets [gēyme] *nmpl:* **entre ~** in quotation marks; **~ de répétition** ditto marks.

guilleret, te [gēyrc, -et] *a* perky, bright.

guillotine [gēyotēn] *nf* guillotine.

guillotiner [gēyotēnā] *vt* to guillotine.

guimauve [gēmōv] *nf (BOT)* marshmallow; *(fig)* sentimentality, sloppiness.

guimbarde [gańbárd(ə)] *nf* jalopy, clunker *(US)*.

guindé, e [gańdā] *a* stiff, starchy.

Guinée [gēnā] *nf:* **la (République de) ~** (the Republic of) Guinea; **la ~ équatoriale** Equatorial Guinea.

Guinée-Bissau [gēnābēsō] *nf:* **la ~** Guinea-Bissau.

guinéen, ne [gēnāań, -en] *a* Guinean.

guingette [gańgct] *nf* open-air café *or* dance-hall.

guingois [gańgwá]: **de ~** *ad* askew.

guirlande [gērlåńd] *nf* garland; *(de papier)* paper chain; **~ lumineuse** string of Christmas tree lights; **~ de Noël** tinsel *q*.

guise [gēz] *nf:* **à votre ~** as you wish *ou* please; **en ~ de** by way of.

guitare [gētár] *nf* guitar.

guitariste [gētárɛ̈st(ə)] *nm/f* guitarist, guitar player.

gustatif, ive [güstátēf, -ēv] *a* gustatory; *voir* **papille.**

guttural, e, aux [gütürál, -ō] *a* guttural.

guyanais, e [güēyáńc, -ez] *a* Guyanese, Guyanan; *(français)* Guianese, Guianan.

Guyane [güēyáń] *nf:* **la ~** Guyana; **la ~ (française)** (French) Guiana.

gvt *abr (= gouvernement)* govt.

gym [zhēm] *abr f* = **gymnastique.**

gymkhana [zhēmkáná] *nm* rally; **~ motocycliste** motocross.

gymnase [zhēmnáz] *nm* gym(nasium).

gymnaste [zhēmnást(ə)] *nm/f* gymnast.

gymnastique [zhēmnástēk] *nf* gymnastics *sg*; *(au réveil etc)* stay-fit *(US)* ou keep-fit *(Brit)* exercises *pl*; **~ corrective** remedial gymnastics.

gynécologie [zhēnākolozhē] *nf* gynecology

(US), gynaecology *(Brit)*.

gynécologue [zhēnākolog] *nm/f* gynecologist *(US)*, gynaecologist *(Brit)*.

gypse [zhēps(ə)] *nm* gypsum.

gyrophare [zhērofár] *nm (sur une voiture)* revolving (flashing) light.

H

H, h [ásh] *nm inv* H, h **♦** *abr (= homme)* M; *(= hydrogène)* H; **bombe ~** H bomb; *(= heure):* **à l'heure ~** at zero hour; **H comme Henri** H for How.

ha. *abr (= hectare)* ha.

hab. *abr* = **habitant.**

habile [ábēl] *a* skillful *(US)*, skilful *(Brit)*; *(malin)* clever.

habilement [ábēlmáń] *ad* skillfully *(US)*, skilfully *(Brit)*; cleverly.

habileté [ábēltā] *nf* skill, skillfulness *(US)*, skilfulness *(Brit)*; cleverness.

habilité, e [ábēlētā] *a:* **~ à faire** entitled to do, empowered to do.

habiliter [ábēlētā] *vt* empower, entitle.

habillage [ábēyázh] *nm* dressing.

habillé, e [ábēyā] *a* dressed; *(chic)* dressy; *(TECH):* **~ de** covered with; encased in.

habillement [ábēymáń] *nm* clothes *pl*; *(profession)* clothing industry.

habiller [ábēyā] *vt* to dress; *(fournir en vête-ments)* to clothe; **s'~** to dress (o.s.); *(se déguiser, mettre des vêtements chic)* to dress up; **s'~ de/en** to dress in/dress up as; **s'~ chez/à** to buy one's clothes from/at.

habilleuse [ábēyœ̈z] *nf (CINÉMA, THÉÂTRE)* dresser.

habit [ábē] *nm* outfit; **~s** *nmpl (vêtements)* clothes; **~ (de soirée)** tails *pl*; evening dress; **prendre l'~** *(REL: entrer en religion)* to enter (holy) orders.

habitable [ábētábl(ə)] *a* (in)habitable.

habitacle [ábētákl(ə)] *nm* cockpit; *(AUTO)* passenger cell.

habitant, e [ábētáń, -áńt] *nm/f* inhabitant; *(d'une maison)* occupant, occupier; **loger chez l'~** to stay with local residents.

habitat [ábētá] *nm* housing conditions *pl*; *(BOT, ZOOL)* habitat.

habitation [ábētásyóń] *nf* living; *(demeure)* residence, home; *(maison)* house; **~s à loyer modéré (HLM)** low-rent, state-owned housing, ≈ public housing units *(US)*, ≈ council housing *sg (Brit)*.

habité, e [ábētā] *a* inhabited; lived in.

habiter [ábētā] *vt* to live in; *(suj: sentiment)* to dwell in **♦** *vi:* **~ à/dans** to live in *ou* at/in; **~ chez** *ou* **avec qn** to live with sb; **~ 16 rue Montmartre** to live at number 16 rue Montmartre; **~ rue Montmartre** to live on rue Montmartre.

habitude [ábētüd] *nf* habit; **avoir l'~ de faire** to be in the habit of doing; **avoir l'~ des**

-enfants to be used to children; **prendre l'~ de faire qch** to get into the habit of doing sth; **perdre une ~** to get out of a habit; **d'~** usually; **comme d'~** as usual; **par ~** out of habit.

habitué, e [ábētüã] *a*: **être ~ à** to be used *ou* accustomed to ♦ *nm/f* regular visitor; (*client*) regular (customer).

habituel, le [ábētüel] *a* usual.

habituellement [ábētüelmâṅ] *ad* usually.

habituer [ábētüã] *vt*: **~ qn à** to get sb used to; **s'~ à** to get used to.

'hâbleur, euse ['ábloer, -œz] *a* boastful.

'hache ['ásh] *nf* axe.

'haché, e ['áshã] *a* ground (*US*), minced (*Brit*); (*persil*) chopped; (*fig*) jerky.

'hache-légumes ['áshlãgüm] *nm inv* vegetable chopper.

'hacher ['áshã] *vt* (*viande*) to grind (*US*), mince (*Brit*); (*persil*) to chop; **~ menu** to grind finely; to chop finely.

'hachette ['áshet] *nf* hatchet.

'hache-viande ['áshvyáṅd] *nm inv* (meat) grinder (*US*) *ou* mincer (*Brit*); (*couteau*) (meat) cleaver.

'hachis ['áshē] *nm* hamburger meat (*US*), mince *q* (*Brit*); **~ de viande** ground (*US*) *ou* minced (*Brit*) meat.

'hachisch ['áshēsh] *nm* hashish.

'hachoir ['áshwár] *nm* chopper; (meat) grinder (*US*) *ou* mincer (*Brit*); (*planche*) chopping board.

'hachurer ['áshürã] *vt* to hatch.

'hachures ['áshür] *nfpl* hatching *sg*.

'hagard, e ['ágár, -árd(ə)] *a* wild, distraught.

'haie ['e] *nf* hedge; (*SPORT*) hurdle; (*fig: rang*) line, row; **200 m ~s** 200 m hurdles; **~ d'honneur** guard of honor.

'haillons ['áyôṅ] *nmpl* rags.

'haine ['en] *nf* hatred.

'haineux, euse ['enœ, -œz] *a* full of hatred.

'haïr ['áēr] *vt* to detest, hate; **se ~** to hate each other.

'hais ['e], **'haïs** ['áē] *etc vb voir* **haïr**.

'haïssable ['áēsábl(ə)] *a* detestable.

Haïti [áētē] *n* Haiti.

haïtien, ne [áēsyaṅ, -en] *a* Haitian.

'halage ['álázh] *nm*: **chemin de ~** towpath.

'hâle ['ál] *nm* (sun)tan.

'hâlé, e ['álã] *a* (sun)tanned, sunburned.

haleine [álen] *nf* breath; **perdre ~** to get out of breath; **à perdre ~** until one is gasping for breath; **avoir mauvaise ~** to have bad breath; **reprendre ~** to get one's breath back; **hors d'~** out of breath; **tenir en ~** to hold spellbound; (*en attente*) to keep in suspense; **de longue ~** *a* long-term.

'haler ['álã] *vt* to haul in; (*remorquer*) to tow.

'haleter ['áltã] *vi* to pant.

'hall ['ōl] *nm* hall.

hallali [álálē] *nm* kill.

'halle ['ál] *nf* (covered) market; **~s** *nfpl* central food market *sg*.

hallucinant, e [álüsēnáṅ, -áṅt] *a* staggering.

hallucination [álüsēnásyôṅ] *nf* hallucination.

hallucinatoire [álüsēnátwár] *a* hallucinatory.

halluciné, e [álüsēnã] *nm/f* person suffering from hallucinations; (*fou*) (raving) lunatic.

'halo ['álō] *nm* halo.

halogène [álozhen] *nm*: **lampe (à) ~** halogen lamp.

'halte ['ált(ə)] *nf* stop, break; (*escale*) stopping place; (*RAIL*) halt ♦ *excl* stop!; **faire ~** to stop.

'halte-garderie, *pl* **'haltes-garderies** ['áltgárdərē] *nf* child-care facility.

haltère [álter] *nm* (*à boules, disques*) dumbbell, barbell; **(poids et) ~s** weightlifting.

haltérophile [áltārofēl] *nm/f* weightlifter.

haltérophilie [áltārofēlē] *nf* weightlifting.

'hamac ['ámák] *nm* hammock.

'Hambourg ['áṅbōōr] *n* Hamburg.

'hameau, x ['ámō] *nm* hamlet.

hameçon [ámsôṅ] *nm* (fish) hook.

'hampe ['áṅp] *nf* (*de drapeau etc*) pole; (*de lance*) shaft.

'hamster ['ámster] *nm* hamster.

'hanche ['áṅsh] *nf* hip.

'hand-ball ['áṅdbál] *nm* handball.

'handicap ['áṅdēkáp] *nm* handicap.

'handicapé, e ['áṅdēkápã] *a* handicapped ♦ *nm/f* physically (*ou* mentally) handicapped person; **~ moteur** spastic.

'handicaper ['áṅdēkápã] *vt* to handicap.

'hangar ['áṅgár] *nm* shed; (*AVIAT*) hangar.

'hanneton ['ántôṅ] *nm* cockchafer.

'Hanovre ['ánovr(ə)] *n* Hanover.

'hanovrien, ne ['ánovryaṅ, -en] *a* Hanoverian.

'hanter ['ántã] *vt* to haunt.

'hantise ['ántēz] *nf* obsessive fear.

'happer ['ápã] *vt* to snatch; (*suj: train etc*) to hit.

'haranguer ['áráṅgã] *vt* to harangue.

'haras ['árá] *nm* stud farm.

'harassant, e ['árásáṅ, -áṅt] *a* exhausting.

'harceler ['ársəlã] *vt* (*MIL, CHASSE*) to harass, harry; (*importuner*) to plague.

'hardes ['árd(ə)] *nfpl* rags.

'hardi, e ['árdē] *a* bold, daring.

'hareng ['áráṅ] *nm* herring.

'hargne ['árny(ə)] *nf* aggressivity, aggressiveness.

'haricot ['árēkō] *nm* bean; **~ blanc/rouge** haricot/kidney bean; **~ vert** green bean.

harmonica [ármonēká] *nm* harmonica.

harmonie [ármonē] *nf* harmony.

harmonieux, euse [ármonyœ, -œz] *a* harmonious.

harmonique [ármonēk] *a, nm ou nf* harmonic.

harmoniser [ármonēzã] *vt* to harmonize; **s'~** (*couleurs, teintes*) to go well together.

harmonium [ármonyom] *nm* harmonium.

'harnaché, e ['árnáshã] *a* (*fig*) rigged out.

'harnachement ['árnáshmáṅ] *nm* (*habillement*) rig-out; (*équipement*) harness, equipment.

'harnacher ['árnáshã] *vt* to harness.

'harnais ['árne] *nm* harness.

'haro ['árō] *nm*: **crier ~ sur qn/qch** to inveigh against sb/sth.

'harpe ['árp(ə)] *nf* harp.

'harpiste ['árpēst(ə)] *nm/f* harpist.

'harpon ['árpôṅ] *nm* harpoon.

'harponner ['árponã] *vt* to harpoon; (*fam*) to collar.

'hasard ['ázár] *nm*: **le ~** chance, fate; **un ~** a coincidence; (*aubaine, chance*) a stroke of luck; **au ~** (*sans but*) aimlessly; (*à* *l'aveuglette*) at random, haphazardly; **par ~** by chance; **comme par ~** as if by chance; **à tout ~** on the off chance; (*en cas de besoin*) just in case.

'**hasarder** ['àzàrdā] *vt* (*mot*) to venture; (*fortune*) to risk; **se ~ à faire** to risk doing, venture to do.

'**hasardeux, euse** ['àzàrdœ̄, -œ̄z] *a* hazardous, risky; (*hypothèse*) rash.

'**haschisch** ['àshēsh] *nm* hashish.

'**hâte** ['àt] *nf* haste; **à la ~** hurriedly, hastily; **en ~** posthaste, with all possible speed; **avoir ~ de** to be eager *ou* anxious to.

'**hâter** ['àtā] *vt* to hasten; **se ~** to hurry; **se ~ de** to hurry *ou* hasten to.

'**hâtif, ive** ['àtēf, -ēv] *a* (*travail*) hurried; (*décision*) hasty; (*légume*) early.

'**hâtivement** ['àtēvmàn] *ad* hurriedly; hastily.

'**hauban** ['ōbàn] *nm* (*NAVIG*) shroud.

'**hausse** ['ōs] *nf* rise, increase; (*de fusil*) backsight adjuster; **à la ~** upwards; **en ~** rising.

'**hausser** ['ōsā] *vt* to raise; **~ les épaules** to shrug (one's shoulders); **se ~ sur la pointe des pieds** to stand (up) on tiptoe *ou* tippy-toe (*US*).

'**haut, e** ['ō, 'ōt] *a* high; (*grand*) tall; (*son, voix*) high(-pitched) ♦ *ad* high ♦ *nm* top (part); **de 3m de ~, ~ de 3m** 3m high, 3m in height; **en ~e montagne** high up in the mountains; **en ~ lieu** in high places; **à ~e voix, (tout) ~** aloud, out loud; **des ~s et des bas** ups and downs; **du ~ de** from the top of; **tomber de ~** to fall from a height; (*fig*) to have one's hopes dashed; **dire qch bien ~** to say sth plainly; **prendre qch de (très) ~** to react haughtily to sth; **traiter qn de ~** to treat sb with disdain; **de ~ en bas** from top to bottom; downwards; **~ en couleur** (*chose*) highly colored; (*personne*): **un personnage ~ en couleur** a colorful character; **plus ~** higher up, further up; (*dans un texte*) above; (*parler*) louder; **en ~** up above; **at** (*ou* to) the top; (*dans une maison*) upstairs; **en ~ de** at the top of; **~ les mains!** hands up!, stick 'em up!; **la ~e couture/ coiffure** haute couture/coiffure; **de ~e fidélité** hi-fi, high fidelity; **la ~e finance** high finance; **~e trahison** high treason.

'**hautain, e** ['ōtàn, -en] *a* (*personne, regard*) haughty.

'**hautbois** ['ōbwà] *nm* oboe.

'**hautboïste** ['ōboēst(ə)] *nm/f* oboist.

'**haut-de-forme**, *pl* '**hauts-de-forme** ['ōdform(ə)] *nm* top hat.

'**haute-contre**, *pl* '**hautes-contre** ['ōtkôntr(ə)] *nf* counter-tenor.

'**hauteur** ['ōtœr] *nf* height; (*GÉO*) height, hill; (*fig*) loftiness; haughtiness; **à ~ de** up to (the level of); **à ~ des yeux** at eye level; **à la ~ de** (*sur la même ligne*) level with; by; (*fig*) equal to; **à la ~** (*fig*) up to it, equal to the task.

'**Haute-Volta** ['ōtvoltá] *nf*: **la ~** Upper Volta.

'**haut-fond**, *pl* '**hauts-fonds** ['ōfôn] *nm* shallow.

'**haut-fourneau**, *pl* '**hauts-fourneaux** ['ōfōōrnō] *nm* blast *ou* smelting furnace.

'**haut-le-cœur** ['ōlkœr] *nm inv* retch, heave.

'**haut-le-corps** ['ōlkor] *nm inv* start, jump.

'**haut-parleur**, *pl* '**haut-parleurs** ['ōpàrlœr] *nm* (loud)speaker.

'**hauturier, ière** ['ōtüryā, -yer] *a* (*NAVIG*) deep-sea.

'**havanais, e** ['àváne, -ez] *a* of *ou* from Havana.

'**Havane** ['àván] *nf*: **la ~** Havana ♦ *nm*: '**h~** (*cigare*) Havana.

'**hâve** ['àv] *a* gaunt.

'**havrais, e** ['àvre, -ez] *a* of *ou* from Le Havre.

'**havre** ['àvr(ə)] *nm* haven.

'**havresac** ['àvrosàk] *nm* haversack.

Hawaï *ou* **Hawaii** [àwáē] *n* Hawaii; **les îles ~** the Hawaiian Islands.

hawaïen, ne [àwáyàn, -en] *a* Hawaiian ♦ *nm* (*LING*) Hawaiian.

'**Haye** ['e] *n*: **la ~** the Hague.

'**hayon** ['eyôn] *nm* tailgate.

hdb. *abr* (= *heures de bureau*) o.h. (= *office hours*).

'**hé** ['ā] *excl* hey!

hebdo [ebdō] *nm* (*fam*) weekly.

hebdomadaire [ebdomáder] *a, nm* weekly.

hébergement [āberzhəmàn] *nm* accommodations *pl* (*US*), accommodation (*Brit*), lodging; taking in.

héberger [āberzhā] *vt* to accommodate, lodge; (*réfugiés*) to take in.

hébété, e [ābātā] *a* dazed.

hébétude [ābātüd] *nf* stupor.

hébraïque [ābráēk] *a* Hebrew, Hebraic.

hébreu, x [ābrœ̄] *am, nm* Hebrew.

Hébrides [ābrēd] *nf*: **les ~** the Hebrides.

HEC *sigle fpl* (= *École des hautes études commerciales*) *grande école for management and business studies.*

hécatombe [ākàtônb] *nf* slaughter.

hectare [ektár] *nm* hectare, 10,000 square meters.

hecto... [ektō] *préfixe* hecto....

hectolitre [ektolētr(ə)] *nm* hectoliter (*US*), hectolitre (*Brit*).

hédoniste [ādonēst(ə)] *a* hedonistic.

hégémonie [āzhāmonē] *nf* hegemony.

'**hein** ['àn] *excl* eh?; (*sollicitant l'approbation*): **tu m'approuves, ~?** so I did the right thing then?; **Paul est venu, ~?** Paul came, did he?; **que fais-tu, ~?** hey! what are you doing?

'**hélas** ['ālás] *excl* alas! ♦ *ad* unfortunately.

'**héler** ['ālā] *vt* to hail.

hélice [ālēs] *nf* propeller.

hélicoïdal, e, aux [ālēkoēdàl, -ō] *a* helical; helicoid.

hélicoptère [ālēkopter] *nm* helicopter.

hélio(gravure) [ālyo(grávür)] *nf* heliogravure.

héliomarin, e [ālyomáràn, -ēn] *a*: **centre ~** center offering sea and sun therapy.

héliotrope [ālyotrop] *nm* (*BOT*) heliotrope.

héliport [ālēpor] *nm* heliport.

héliporté, e [ālēportā] *a* transported by helicopter.

hélium [ālyom] *nm* helium.

hellénique [ālānēk] *a* Hellenic.

hellénisant, e [ālānēzàn, -ànt], **helléniste** [ālānēst(ə)] *nm/f* Hellenist.

Helsinki [elzēnkē] *n* Helsinki.

helvète [elvet] *a* Helvetian ♦ *nm/f*: **H~** Helvetian.

Helvétie [elvāsē] *nf*: **la ~** Helvetia.

helvétique [elvātēk] *a* Swiss.

hématologie [āmátolozhē] *nf* (*MÉD*) hematology (*US*), haematology (*Brit*).

hématome [āmátōm] *nm* hematoma (*US*), haematoma (*Brit*).

hémicycle [āmēsēkl(ə)] *nm* semicircle; (*POL*): **l'~** the benches (*in French parliament*).

hémiplégie [āmēplāzhē] *nf* paralysis of one side, hemiplegia.

hémisphère [āmēsfer] *nf*: **~ nord/sud** northern/southern hemisphere.

hémisphérique [āmēsfārēk] *a* hemispherical.

hémoglobine [āmoglobēn] *nf* hemoglobin (*US*), haemoglobin (*Brit*).

hémophile [āmofēl] *a* hemophiliac (*US*), haemophiliac (*Brit*).

hémophilie [āmofēlē] *nf* hemophilia (*US*), haemophilia (*Brit*).

hémorragie [āmorázhē] *nf* bleeding *q*, hemorrhage (*US*), haemorrhage (*Brit*); **~ cérébrale** cerebral hemorrhage; **~ interne** internal bleeding *ou* hemorrhage.

hémorroïdes [āmoroēd] *nfpl* piles, hemorrhoids (*US*), haemorrhoids (*Brit*).

hémostatique [āmostátēk] *a* hemostatic (*US*), haemostatic (*Brit*).

'henné ['ānā] *nm* henna.

'hennir ['ānēr] *vi* to neigh, whinny.

'hennissement ['ānēsmáń] *nm* neighing, whinnying.

'hep ['ep] *excl* hey!

hépatite [āpátēt] *nf* hepatitis, liver infection.

héraldique [ārāldēk] *a* heraldry.

herbacé, e [erbásā] *a* herbaceous.

herbage [erbázh] *nm* pasture.

herbe [erb(ə)] *nf* grass; (*CULIN, MÉD*) herb; **en ~** unripe; (*fig*) budding; **touffe/brin d'~** clump/blade of grass.

herbeux, euse [erbœ, -œz] *a* grassy.

herbicide [erbēsēd] *nm* weed-killer.

herbier [erbyā] *nm* herbarium.

herbivore [erbēvor] *nm* herbivore.

herboriser [erborēzā] *vi* to collect plants.

herboriste [erborēst(ə)] *nm/f* herbalist.

herboristerie [erborēstrē] *nf* (*magasin*) herbalist's shop; (*commerce*) herb trade.

herculéen, ne [erkülāaǹ, -en] *a* (*fig*) herculean.

'hère ['er] *nm*: **pauvre ~** poor wretch.

héréditaire [ārādēter] *a* hereditary.

hérédité [ārādētā] *nf* heredity.

hérésie [ārāzē] *nf* heresy.

hérétique [ārātēk] *nm/f* heretic.

'hérissé, e ['ārēsā] *a* bristling; **~ de** spiked with; (*fig*) bristling with.

'hérisser ['ārēsā] *vt*: **~ qn** (*fig*) to ruffle sb; **se ~** *vi* to bristle, bristle up.

'hérisson ['ārēsóǹ] *nm* hedgehog.

héritage [ārētázh] *nm* inheritance; (*fig*) heritage; (*: legs*) legacy; **faire un (petit) ~** to come into (a little) money.

hériter [ārētā] *vi*: **~ de qch (de qn)** to inherit sth (from sb); **~ de qn** to inherit sb's property.

héritier, ière [ārētyā, -yer] *nm/f* heir/heiress.

hermaphrodite [ermáfrodēt] *a* (*BOT, ZOOL*) hermaphrodite.

hermétique [ermātēk] *a* (*à l'air*) airtight; (*à*

l'eau) watertight; (*fig*: *écrivain, style*) abstruse; (*: visage*) impenetrable.

hermétiquement [ermātēkmáǹ] *ad* hermetically.

hermine [ermēn] *nf* ermine.

'hernie ['ernē] *nf* hernia.

héroïne [āroēn] *nf* heroine; (*drogue*) heroin.

héroïnomane [āroēnomán] *nm/f* heroin addict.

héroïque [āroēk] *a* heroic.

héroïquement [āroēkmáǹ] *ad* heroically.

héroïsme [āroēsm(ə)] *nm* heroism.

'héron ['āróǹ] *nm* heron.

'héros ['ārō] *nm* hero.

herpès [erpes] *nm* herpes.

'herse ['ers(ə)] *nf* harrow; (*de château*) portcullis.

hertz [erts] *nm* (*ÉLEC*) hertz.

hertzien, ne [ertsyaǹ, -en] *a* (*ÉLEC*) Hertzian.

hésitant, e [āzētáǹ, -áǹt] *a* hesitant.

hésitation [āzētâsyóǹ] *nf* hesitation.

hésiter [āzētā] *vi*: **~ (à faire)** to hesitate (to do); **~ sur qch** to hesitate over sth.

hétéro [ātārō] *a inv* (= *hétérosexuel(le)*) hetero.

hétéroclite [ātāroklēt] *a* heterogeneous; (*objets*) sundry.

hétérogène [ātārozhen] *a* heterogeneous.

hétérosexuel, le [ātāroseküel] *a* heterosexual.

'hêtre ['etr(ə)] *nm* beech.

heure [œr] *nf* hour; (*SCOL*) period; (*moment, moment fixé*) time; **c'est l'~** it's time; **pourriez-vous me donner l'~, s'il vous plaît?** could you tell me the time, please?; **quelle ~ est-il?** what time is it?; **2 ~s (du matin)** 2 o'clock (in the morning); **à la bonne ~!** (*parfois ironique*) splendid!; **être à l'~** to be on time; (*montre*) to be right; **le bus passe à l'~** the bus runs on the hour; **mettre à l'~** to set right; **100km à l'~** ≈ 60 miles an *ou* per hour; **à toute ~** at any time; **24 ~s sur 24** around the clock, 24 hours a day; **à l'~ qu'il est** at this time (of day); (*fig*) now; **à l'~ actuelle** at the present time; **sur l'~** at once; **pour l'~** for the time being; **d'~ en ~** from one hour to the next; (*régulièrement*) hourly; **d'une ~ à l'autre** from hour to hour; **de bonne ~** early; **2 ~s de marche/travail** 2 hours' walking/work; **une ~ d'arrêt** an hour's break *ou* stop; **~ d'été** daylight saving time; **~ de pointe** rush hour; **~s de bureau** office hours; **~s supplémentaires** overtime *sg*.

heureusement [œrœzmáǹ] *ad* (*par bonheur*) fortunately, luckily; **~ que** ... it's a good thing that ..., fortunately ....

heureux, euse [œrœ, -œz] *a* happy; (*chanceux*) lucky, fortunate; (*judicieux*) felicitous, fortunate; **être ~ de qch** to be pleased *ou* happy about sth; **être ~ de faire/que** to be pleased *ou* happy to do/that; **s'estimer ~ de qch/que** to consider o.s. fortunate with/that; **encore ~ que** ... just as well that ....

'heurt ['œr] *nm* (*choc*) collision; **~s** *nmpl* (*fig*) clashes.

'heurté, e ['œrtā] *a* (*fig*) jerky, uneven; (*: couleurs*) clashing.

'heurter ['œrtā] *vt* (*mur*) to strike, hit; (*personne*) to collide with; (*fig*) to go against, upset; **se ~** (*couleurs, tons*) to clash; **se ~ à**

to collide with; *(fig)* to come up against; ~ **qn de front** to clash head-on with sb.

'heurtoir ['œrtwàr] *nm* door knocker.

hévéa [āvāá] *nm* rubber tree.

hexagonal, e, aux [egzágonàl. -ō] *a* hexagonal; *(français)* French *(see note at hexagone)*.

hexagone [egzágon] *nm* hexagon; *(la France)* France *(because of its roughly hexagonal shape)*.

HF *sigle f* (= *haute fréquence*) HF.

hiatus [yátüs] *nm* hiatus.

hibernation [ēbernâsyôñ] *nf* hibernation.

hiberner [ēbernā] *vi* to hibernate.

hibiscus [ēbēskūs] *nm* hibiscus.

'hibou, x ['ēbōō] *nm* owl.

'hic ['ēk] *nm (fam)* snag.

'hideusement ['ēdœzmâñ] *ad* hideously.

'hideux, euse ['ēdœ̄. -œ̄z] *a* hideous.

hier [yer] *ad* yesterday; ~ **matin/soir/midi** yesterday morning/evening/at midday; **toute la journée d'**~ all day yesterday; **toute la matinée d'**~ all yesterday morning.

'hiérarchie ['yārárshē] *nf* hierarchy.

'hiérarchique ['yārárshēk] *a* hierarchic.

'hiérarchiquement ['yārárshēkmâñ] *ad* hierarchically.

'hiérarchiser ['yārárshēzà] *vt* to organize into a hierarchy.

'hiéroglyphe ['yāroglēf] *nm* hieroglyphic.

'hiéroglyphique ['yāroglēfēk] *a* hieroglyphic.

hilarant, e [ēlárâñ. -âñt] *a* hilarious.

hilare [ēlár] *a* mirthful.

hilarité [ēlárētā] *nf* hilarity, mirth.

Himalaya [ēmáláyá] *nm*: **l'**~ the Himalayas *pl*.

himalayen, ne [ēmáláyañ, -en] *a* Himalayan.

hindou, e [añdōō] *a*, *nm/f* Hindu; *(Indien)* Indian.

hindouisme [añdōōēsm(ə)] *nm* Hinduism.

Hindoustan [añdōōstâñ] *nm*: **l'**~ Hindustan.

hippique [ēpēk] *a* equestrian, horse *cpd*.

hippisme [ēpēsm(ə)] *nm* (horse) riding.

hippocampe [ēpokâñp] *nm* sea horse.

hippodrome [ēpodrōm] *nm* racecourse.

hippophagique [ēpofázhēk] *a*: **boucherie** ~ horse butcher's.

hippopotame [ēpopotám] *nm* hippopotamus.

hirondelle [ērôñdel] *nf* swallow.

hirsute [ērsüt] *a (personne)* hairy; *(barbe)* shaggy; *(tête)* tousled.

hispanique [ēspánēk] *a* Hispanic.

hispanisant, e [ēspánēzáñ, -âñt], **hispaniste** [ēspánēst(ə)] *nm/f* Hispanist.

hispano-américain, e [ēspánoâmārēkañ, -en] *a* Spanish-American.

hispano-arabe [ēspánoàráb] *a* Hispano-Moresque.

'hisser ['ēsā] *vt* to hoist, haul up; **se** ~ **sur** to haul o.s. up onto.

histoire [ēstwár] *nf (science, événements)* history; *(anecdote, récit, mensonge)* story; *(affaire)* business *q*; *(chichis: gén pl)* fuss *q*; ~**s** *nfpl (ennuis)* trouble *sg*; **l'**~ **de France** French history, the history of France; **l'**~ **sainte** biblical history; **une** ~ **de** *(fig)* a question of.

histologie [ēstolozhē] *nf* histology.

historien, ne [ēstoryañ, -en] *nm/f* historian.

historique [ēstorēk] *a* historical; *(important)*

historic ♦ *nm (exposé, récit)*: **faire l'**~ **de** to give the background to.

historiquement [ēstorēkmâñ] *ad* historically.

hiver [ēver] *nm* winter; **en** ~ in winter.

hivernal, e, aux [ēvernàl. -ō] *a (de l'hiver)* winter *cpd*; *(comme en hiver)* wintry.

hivernant, e [ēvernâñ. -âñt] *n* winter vacationer *(US)* ou holidaymaker *(Brit)*.

hiverner [ēvernā] *vi* to winter.

HLM *sigle m ou f* (= *habitations à loyer modéré*) low-rent, state-owned housing; **un(e)** ~ ≈ a public housing unit *(US)*, ≈ a council flat *(ou house)* *(Brit)*.

Hme *abr* (= *homme*) M.

HO *abr* (= *hors œuvre*) labor *(US)* ou labour *(Brit)* not included *(on invoices)*.

'hobby ['obē] *nm* hobby.

'hochement ['oshmâñ] *nm*: ~ **de tête** nod; shake of the head.

'hocher ['oshā] *vt*: ~ **la tête** to nod; *(signe négatif ou dubitatif)* to shake one's head.

'hochet ['oshe] *nm* rattle.

'hockey ['oke] *nm*: ~ **(sur glace/gazon)** (ice/field) hockey.

'hockeyeur, euse ['okeyœr. -œ̄z] *nm/f* hockey player.

'hola ['olá] *nm*: **mettre le** ~ **à qch** to put a stop to sth.

'holding ['oldēng] *nm* holding company.

'hold-up ['oldœp] *nm inv* hold-up.

'hollandais, e ['olàñde, -ez] *a* Dutch ♦ *nm (LING)* Dutch ♦ *nm/f*: **H**~, **e** Dutchman/woman; **les H**~ the Dutch.

'Hollande ['olàñd] *nf*: **la** ~ Holland ♦ *nm*: **h**~ *(fromage)* Dutch cheese.

holocauste [olokōst(ə)] *nm* holocaust.

hologramme [ologràm] *nm* hologram.

'homard ['omár] *nm* lobster.

homéopathe [omāopát] *n* homeopath, homoeopath *(Brit)*.

homéopathie [omāopátē] *nf* homeopathy, homoeopathy *(Brit)*.

homéopathique [omāopátēk] *a* homeopathic, homoeopathic *(Brit)*.

homérique [omárēk] *a* Homeric.

homicide [omēsēd] *nm* murder ♦ *nm/f* murderer/eress; ~ **involontaire** manslaughter.

hommage [omázh] *nm* tribute; ~**s** *nmpl*: **présenter ses** ~**s** to pay one's respects; **rendre** ~ **à** to pay tribute *ou* homage to; **en** ~ **de** as a token of; **faire** ~ **de qch à qn** to present sb with sth.

homme [om] *nm* man; *(espèce humaine)*: **l'**~ man, mankind; ~ **d'affaires** businessman; ~ **des cavernes** caveman; ~ **d'Église** churchman, clergyman; ~ **d'État** statesman; ~ **de loi** lawyer; ~ **de main** hired man; ~ **de paille** stooge; **l'**~ **de la rue** the man in the street; ~ **à tout faire** odd-job man.

homme-grenouille, *pl* **hommes-grenouilles** [omgrənōōy] *nm* frogman.

homme-orchestre, *pl* **hommes-orchestres** [omorkestr(ə)] *nm* one-man band.

homme-sandwich, *pl* **hommes-sandwichs** [omsâñdwētsh] *nm* sandwich (board) man.

homogène [omozhen] *a* homogeneous.

homogénéisé, e [omozhānāēzā] *a*: **lait** ~ homogenized milk.

homogénéité |omozhānāĕtā| *nf* homogeneity.
homologation |omologâsyôṅ| *nf* ratification; official recognition.
homologue |omolog| *nm/f* counterpart, opposite number.
homologué, e |omologā| *a* (*SPORT*) officially recognized, ratified; (*tarif*) authorized.
homologuer |omologā| *vt* (*JUR*) to ratify; (*SPORT*) to recognize officially, ratify.
homonyme |omonēm| *nm* (*LING*) homonym; (*d'une personne*) namesake.
homosexualité |omoseksüálētā| *nf* homosexuality.
homosexuel, le |omoseksüel| *a* homosexual.
'**Honduras** |'ôṅdüràs| *nm*: **le ~** Honduras.
'**hondurien, ne** |'ôṅdüryaṅ, -en| *a* Honduran.
'**Hong-Kong** |'ôṅgkôṅg| *n* Hong Kong.
'**hongre** |'ôṅgr(ǝ)| *a* (*cheval*) gelded ♦ *nm* gelding.
'**Hongrie** |'ôṅgrē| *nf*: **la ~** Hungary.
'**hongrois, e** |'ôṅgrwà, -wàz| *a* Hungarian ♦ *nm* (*LING*) Hungarian ♦ *nm/f*: '**H~, e** Hungarian.
honnête |onet| *a* (*intègre*) honest; (*juste, satisfaisant*) fair.
honnêtement |onetmâṅ| *ad* honestly.
honnêteté |onettā| *nf* honesty.
honneur |onœr| *nm* honor (*US*), honour (*Brit*); (*mérite*): **l'~ lui revient** the credit is his; **à qui ai-je l'~?** to whom have I the pleasure of speaking?; "**j'ai l'~ de ...**" "I have the honor of ..."; **en l'~ de** (*personne*) in honor of; (*événement*) on the occasion of; **faire ~ à** (*engagements*) to honor; (*famille, professeur*) to be a credit to; (*fig: repas etc*) to do justice to; **être à l'~** to be in the place of honor; **être en ~** to be in favor; **membre d'~** honorary member; **table d'~** top table.
Honolulu |onolülü| *n* Honolulu.
honorable |onoràbl(ǝ)| *a* worthy, honorable (*US*), honourable (*Brit*); (*suffisant*) decent.
honorablement |onoràblǝmâṅ| *ad* honorably (*US*), honourably (*Brit*); decently.
honoraire |onorer| *a* honorary; **~s** *nmpl* fees; **professeur ~** professor emeritus.
honorer |onorā| *vt* to honor (*US*), honour (*Brit*); (*estimer*) to hold in high regard; (*faire honneur à*) to do credit to; **~ qn de** to honor sb with; **s'~ de** to pride o.s. upon.
honorifique |onorēfēk| *a* honorary.
'**honte** |'ôṅt| *nf* shame; **avoir ~ de** to be ashamed of; **faire ~ à qn** to make sb (feel) ashamed.
'**honteusement** |'ôṅtœzmâṅ| *ad* ashamedly, shamefully.
'**honteux, euse** |'ôṅtœ, -œz| *a* ashamed; (*conduite, acte*) shameful, disgraceful.
hôpital, aux |opētàl, -ō| *nm* hospital.
'**hoquet** |'oke| *nm* hiccough; **avoir le ~** to have (the) hiccoughs.
'**hoqueter** |'oktā| *vi* to hiccough.
horaire |orer| *a* hourly ♦ *nm* timetable, schedule; **~s** *nmpl* (*heures de travail*) hours; **~ flexible** *ou* **mobile** *ou* **à la carte** *ou* **souple** flex(i)time.
'**horde** |'ord(ǝ)| *nf* horde.
'**horions** |'oryôṅ| *nmpl* blows.
horizon |orēzôṅ| *nm* horizon; (*paysage*) landscape, view; **sur l'~** on the skyline *ou* horizon.
horizontal, e, aux |orēzôṅtál, -ō| *a* horizontal ♦ *nf*: **à l'~~e** on the horizontal.
horizontalement |orēzôṅtálmâṅ| *ad* horizontally.
horloge |orlozh| *nf* clock; **l'~ parlante** Time (*US*), the speaking clock (*Brit*); **~ normande** grandfather clock.
horloger, ère |orlozhā, -er| *nm/f* watchmaker; clockmaker.
horlogerie |orlozhrē| *nf* watch-making; watchmaker's (shop); clockmaker's (shop); **pièces d'~** watch parts *ou* components.
'**hormis** |'ormē| *prép* save.
hormonal, e, aux |ormonál, -ō| *a* hormonal.
hormone |ormon| *nf* hormone.
horodaté, e |orodátā| *a* (*ticket*) time- and date-stamped; (*stationnement*) automatically timed.
horodateur, trice |orodàtœr, -trēs| *a* (*appareil*) for stamping the time and date ♦ *nm/f* (parking) ticket machine.
horoscope |oroskop| *nm* horoscope.
horreur |orœr| *nf* horror; **avoir ~ de** to loathe, detest; **quelle ~!** how awful!; **cela me fait ~** I find that awful.
horrible |orēbl(ǝ)| *a* horrible.
horriblement |orēblǝmâṅ| *ad* horribly.
horrifiant, e |orēfyâṅ, -âṅt| *a* horrifying.
horrifier |orēfyā| *vt* to horrify.
horrifique |orēfēk| *a* horrific.
horripiler |orēpēlā| *vt* to exasperate.
'**hors** |'or| *prép* except (for); **~ de** out of; **~ ligne, ~ pair** outstanding; **~ de propos** inopportune; **~ série** (*sur mesure*) made-to-order; (*exceptionnel*) exceptional; **~ service** (**HS**), **~ d'usage** out of use; **~ taxe** (**HT**) (*article, boutique*) duty-free; (*prix*) before tax; **être ~ de soi** to be beside o.s.
'**hors-bord** |'orbor| *nm inv* outboard motor; (*canot*) speedboat (with outboard motor).
'**hors-concours** |'orkôṅkōōr| *a inv* ineligible to compete; (*fig*) in a class of one's own.
'**hors-d'œuvre** |'ordœvr(ǝ)| *nm inv* hors d'œuvre.
'**hors-jeu** |'orzhœ| *nm inv* being offside *q*.
'**hors-la-loi** |'orlàlwà| *nm inv* outlaw.
'**hors-piste(s)** |'orpēst| *nm inv* (*SKI*) cross-country.
'**hors-texte** |'ortekst(ǝ)| *nm inv* plate.
hortensia |ortáṅsyà| *nm* hydrangea.
horticole |ortēkol| *a* horticultural.
horticulteur, trice |ortēkültœr, -trēs| *nm/f* horticulturist (*US*), horticulturalist (*Brit*).
horticulture |ortēkültür| *nf* horticulture.
hospice |ospēs| *nm* (*de vieillards*) home; (*asile*) hospice.
hospitalier, ière |ospētályā, -yer| *a* (*accueillant*) hospitable; (*MÉD: service, centre*) hospital *cpd*.
hospitalisation |ospētálēzâsyôṅ| *nf* hospitalization.
hospitaliser |ospētálēzā| *vt* to take (*ou* send) to the hospital, hospitalize.
hospitalité |ospētálētā| *nf* hospitality.
hospitalo-universitaire |ospētáloũnēversēter| *a*: **centre ~** (**CHU**) ≈ (teaching) hospital.
hostie |ostē| *nf* host (*REL*).
hostile |ostēl| *a* hostile.

hostilité [ostēlētā] *nf* hostility; **~s** *nfpl* hostilities.

hôte [ōt] *nm* (*maître de maison*) host; (*invité*) guest; (*client*) patron; (*fig*) inhabitant, occupant; **~ payant** paying guest.

hôtel [ōtel] *nm* hotel; **aller à l'~** to stay in a hotel; **~ (particulier)** (private) mansion; **~ de ville** town hall.

hôtelier, ière [ōtəlyā, -yer] *a* hotel *cpd* ♦ *nm/f* hotelier, hotel-keeper.

hôtellerie [ōtelrē] *nf* (*profession*) hotel business; (*auberge*) inn.

hôtesse [ōtes] *nf* hostess; **~ de l'air** stewardess; **~ (d'accueil)** receptionist.

'**hotte** ['ot] *nf* (*panier*) basket (*carried on the back*); (*de cheminée*) hood; **~ aspirante** range (*US*) *ou* exhaust (*US*) *ou* cooker (*Brit*) hood.

'**houblon** ['ōōblôñ] *nm* (*BOT*) hop; (*pour la bière*) hops *pl*.

'**houe** ['ōō] *nf* hoe.

'**houille** ['ōōy] *nf* coal; **~ blanche** hydroelectric power.

'**houiller, ère** ['ōōyā, -er] *a* coal *cpd*; (*terrain*) coal-bearing ♦ *nf* coal mine.

'**houle** ['ōōl] *nf* swell.

'**houlette** ['ōōlet] *nf*: **sous la ~ de** under the guidance of.

'**houleux, euse** ['ōōlœ, -œz] *a* heavy, swelling; (*fig*) stormy, turbulent.

'**houppe** ['ōōp] *nf*, '**houppette** ['ōōpet] *nf* powder puff; (*cheveux*) tuft.

'**hourra** ['ōōrā] *nm* cheer ♦ *excl* hurrah!

'**houspiller** ['ōōspēyā] *vt* to scold.

'**housse** ['ōōs] *nf* cover; (*pour protégér provisoirement*) dust cover; (*pour recouvrir à neuf*) loose *ou* stretch cover; **~ (penderie)** garment bag (*US*), hanging wardrobe (*Brit*).

'**houx** ['ōō] *nm* holly.

HS *abr* = **hors service**.

HT *abr* = **hors taxe**.

'**hublot** ['üblō] *nm* porthole.

'**huche** ['üsh] *nf*: **~ à pain** bread box (*US*) *ou* bin (*Brit*).

'**huées** ['üā] *nfpl* boos.

'**huer** ['üā] *vt* to boo; (*hibou, chouette*) to hoot.

huile [üēl] *nf* oil; (*ART*) oil painting; (*fam*) bigwig; **mer d'~** (*très calme*) glassy sea, sea of glass; **faire tache d'~** (*fig*) to spread; **~ d'arachide** peanut oil; **~ essentielle** essential oil; **~ de foie de morue** cod-liver oil; **~ de ricin** castor oil; **~ solaire** suntan oil; **~ de table** salad oil.

huiler [üēlā] *vt* to oil.

huilerie [üēlrē] *nf* (*usine*) oil-works.

huileux, euse [üēlœ, -œz] *a* oily.

huilier [üēlyā] *nm* (oil and vinegar) cruet.

huis [üē] *nm*: **à ~ clos** in camera.

huissier [üēsyā] *nm* usher; (*JUR*) ≈ bailiff.

'**huit** ['üē(t)] *num* eight; **samedi en ~** a week from Saturday; **dans ~ jours** in a week('s time).

'**huitaine** ['üēten] *nf*: **une ~ de** about eight, eight or so; **une ~ de jours** a week or so.

'**huitante** ['üētâñt] *num* (*Suisse*) eighty.

'**huitième** ['üētyem] *num* eighth.

huître [üētr(ə)] *nf* oyster.

'**hululer** ['ülülā] *vi* to hoot.

humain, e [ümañ, -en] *a* human; (*compatissant*) humane ♦ *nm* human (being).

humainement [ümenmâñ] *ad* humanly; humanely.

humaniser [ümánēzā] *vt* to humanize.

humaniste [ümánēst(ə)] *nm/f* (*LING*) classicist; humanist.

humanitaire [ümánēter] *a* humanitarian.

humanitarisme [ümánētárēsm(ə)] *nm* humanitarianism.

humanité [ümánētā] *nf* humanity.

humanoïde [ümánoēd] *nm/f* humanoid.

humble [œñbl(ə)] *a* humble.

humblement [œñbləmâñ] *ad* humbly.

humecter [ümektā] *vt* to dampen; **s'~ les lèvres** to moisten one's lips.

'**humer** ['ümā] *vt* to inhale; (*pour sentir*) to smell.

humérus [ümārüs] *nf* (*ANAT*) humerus.

humeur [ümœr] *nf* mood; (*tempérament*) temper; (*irritation*) bad temper; **de bonne/mauvaise ~** in a good/bad mood; **être d'~ à faire qch** to be in the mood for doing sth.

humide [ümēd] *a* (*linge*) damp; (*main, yeux*) moist; (*climat, chaleur*) humid; (*saison, route*) wet.

humidificateur [ümēdēfēkátœr] *nm* humidifier.

humidifier [ümēdēfyā] *vt* to humidify.

humidité [ümēdētā] *nf* humidity; dampness; **traces d'~** traces of moisture *ou* damp.

humiliant, e [ümēlyâñ, -âñt] *a* humiliating.

humiliation [ümēlyásyôñ] *nf* humiliation.

humilier [ümēlyā] *vt* to humiliate; **s'~ devant qn** to humble o.s. before sb.

humilité [ümēlētā] *nf* humility.

humoriste [ümorēst(ə)] *nm/f* humorist.

humoristique [ümorēstēk] *a* humorous; humoristic.

humour [ümōōr] *nm* humor (*US*), humour (*Brit*); **avoir de l'~** to have a sense of humor; **~ noir** sick humor.

humus [ümüs] *nm* humus.

'**huppé, e** ['üpā] *a* crested; (*fam*) posh.

'**hurlement** ['ürləmâñ] *nm* howling *q*, howl; yelling *q*, yell.

'**hurler** ['ürlā] *vi* to howl, yell; (*fig: vent*) to howl; (: *couleurs etc*) to clash; **~ à la mort** (*suj: chien*) to bay at the moon.

hurluberlu [ürlüberlü] *nm* (*péj*) crank ♦ *a* cranky.

'**hutte** ['üt] *nf* hut.

hybride [ēbrēd] *a* hybrid.

hydratant, e [ēdrátâñ, -âñt] *a* (*crème*) moisturizing.

hydrate [ēdrát] *nm*: **~s de carbone** carbohydrates.

hydrater [ēdrátā] *vt* to hydrate.

hydraulique [ēdrōlēk] *a* hydraulic.

hydravion [ēdrávyôñ] *nm* seaplane, hydroplane.

hydro... [ēdro] *préfixe* hydro....

hydrocarbure [ēdrokárbür] *nm* hydrocarbon.

hydrocution [ēdroküsyôñ] *nf* immersion syncope.

hydro-électrique [ēdroálektrēk] *a* hydroelectric.

hydrogène [ēdrozhen] *nm* hydrogen.

hydroglisseur [ēdroglēsœr] *nm* hydroplane.

hydrographie [ēdrográfē] *nf* (*fleuves*) hydrog-

raphy.
hydrophile [ēdrofēl] *a voir* **coton.**
hyène [yen] *nf* hyena.
hygiène [ēzhyen] *nf* hygiene; ~ **intime** personal hygiene.
hygiénique [ēzhānēk] *a* hygienic.
hymne [ēmn(ǝ)] *nm* hymn; ~ **national** national anthem.
hyper... [ēper] *préfixe* hyper....
hypermarché [ēpermárshā] *nm* superstore.
hypermétrope [ēpermātrop] *a* farsighted, longsighted.
hypernerveux, euse [ēpernervœ̄, -œ̄z] *a* highstrung (*US*), highly-strung (*Brit*).
hypersensible [ēpersânsēbl(ǝ)] *a* hypersensitive.
hypertendu, e [ēpertâńdü] *a* having high blood pressure, hypertensive.
hypertension [ēpertâńsyôń] *nf* high blood pressure, hypertension.
hypertrophié, e [ēpertrofyā] *a* hypertrophic.
hypnose [ēpnōz] *nf* hypnosis.
hypnotique [ēpnotēk] *a* hypnotic.
hypnotiser [ēpnotēzā] *vt* to hypnotize.
hypnotiseur [ēpnotēzœr] *nm* hypnotist.
hypnotisme [ēpnotēsm(ǝ)] *nm* hypnotism.
hypocondriaque [ēpokôńdrēyák] *a* hypochondriac.
hypocrisie [ēpokrēzē] *nf* hypocrisy.
hypocrite [ēpokrēt] *a* hypocritical ♦ *nm/f* hypocrite.
hypocritement [ēpokrētmâń] *ad* hypocritically.
hypotendu, e [ēpotâńdü] *a* having low blood pressure, hypotensive.
hypotension [ēpotâńsyôń] *nf* low blood pressure, hypotension.
hypoténuse [ēpotānüz] *nf* hypotenuse.
hypothécaire [ēpotāker] *a* hypothecary; **garantie/prêt** ~ mortgage security/loan.
hypothèque [ēpotek] *nf* mortgage.
hypothéquer [ēpotākā] *vt* to mortgage.
hypothermie [ēpotermē] *nf* hypothermia.
hypothèse [ēpotez] *nf* hypothesis; **dans l'~ où** assuming that.
hypothétique [ēpotātēk] *a* hypothetical.
hystérectomie [ēstārektomē] *nf* hysterectomy.
hystérie [ēstārē] *nf* hysteria; ~ **collective** mass hysteria.
hystérique [ēstārēk] *a* hysterical.
Hz *abr* (= *Hertz*) Hz.

I

I, i [ē] *nm inv* I, i; **I comme Irma** I for Item.
IAC *sigle f* (= *insémination artificielle entre conjoints*) AIH.
IAD *sigle f* (= *insémination artificielle par donneur extérieur*) AID.
ibère [ēber] *a* Iberian ♦ *nm/f:* **I~** Iberian.
ibérique [ēbārēk] *a:* **la péninsule** ~ the Iberian peninsula.

iceberg [ēsberg] *nm* iceberg.
ici [ēsē] *ad* here; **jusqu'~** as far as this; (*temporel*) until now; **d'~ là** by then; (*en attendant*) in the meantime; **d'~ peu** before long.
icône [ēkōn] *nf* (*aussi INFORM*) icon.
iconoclaste [ēkonoklást(ǝ)] *nm/f* iconoclast.
iconographie [ēkonográfē] *nf* iconography; (*illustrations*) (collection of) illustrations.
idéal, e, aux [ēdāál, -ō] *a* ideal ♦ *nm* ideal; (*système de valeurs*) ideals *pl*.
idéalement [ēdāálmâń] *ad* ideally.
idéalisation [ēdāálēzásyôń] *nf* idealization.
idéaliser [ēdāálēzā] *vt* to idealize.
idéalisme [ēdāálēsm(ǝ)] *nm* idealism.
idéaliste [ēdāálēst(ǝ)] *a* idealistic ♦ *nm/f* idealist.
idée [ēdā] *nf* idea; (*illusion*): **se faire des ~s** to imagine things, get ideas into one's head; **avoir dans l'~ que** to have an idea that; **mon ~, c'est que ...** I suggest that ..., I think that ...; **à l'~ de/que** at the idea of/that, at the thought of/that; **je n'ai pas la moindre ~** I haven't the faintest idea; **avoir ~ que** to have an idea that; **avoir des ~s larges/étroites** to be broad-/narrow-minded; **venir à l'~ de qn** to occur to sb; **en voilà des ~s!** the very idea!; ~ **fixe** idée fixe, obsession; **~s noires** black *ou* dark thoughts; **~s reçues** accepted ideas *ou* wisdom.
identification [ēdâńtēfēkâsyôń] *nf* identification.
identifier [ēdâńtēfyā] *vt* to identify; ~ **qch/qn à** to identify sth/sb with; **s'~ avec** *ou* **à qn/qch** (*héros etc*) to identify with sb/sth.
identique [ēdâńtēk] *a:* ~ **(à)** identical (to).
identité [ēdâńtētā] *nf* identity; ~ **judiciaire** (*POLICE*) ≈ Criminal Records Office.
idéologie [ēdāolozhē] *nf* ideology.
idéologique [ēdāolozhēk] *a* ideological.
idiomatique [ēdyomátēk] *a:* **expression ~** idiom, idiomatic expression.
idiome [ēdyōm] *nm* (*LING*) idiom.
idiot, e [ēdyō, ēdyot] *a* idiotic ♦ *nm/f* idiot.
idiotie [ēdyosē] *nf* idiocy; (*propos*) idiotic remark *etc*.
idiotisme [ēdyotēsm(ǝ)] *nm* idiom, idiomatic phrase.
idoine [ēdwán] *a* fitting.
idolâtrer [ēdolátrā] *vt* to idolize.
idolâtrie [ēdolátrē] *nf* idolatry.
idole [ēdol] *nf* idol.
IDS *sigle f* (= *Initiative de défense stratégique*) SDI.
idylle [ēdēl] *nf* idyll.
idyllique [ēdēlēk] *a* idyllic.
if [ēf] *nm* yew.
IFOP [ēfop] *sigle m* (= *Institut français d'opinion publique*) French market research institute.
IGF *sigle m* (= *Impôt sur les grandes fortunes*) wealth tax.
IGH *sigle m* = *immeuble de grande hauteur*.
igloo [ēglōō] *nm* igloo.
IGN *sigle m* = *Institut géographique national*.
ignare [ēnyár] *a* ignorant.
ignifuge [ēgnēfüzh] *a* fireproofing ♦ *nm* fireproofing (substance).
ignifuger [ēgnēfüzhā] *vt* to fireproof.

ignoble [ĕnyobl(ə)] *a* vile.

ignominie [ĕnyomēnē] *nf* ignominy; *(acte)* ignominious *ou* base act.

ignominieux, euse [ĕnyomēnyœ̃, œ̃z] *a* ignominious.

ignorance [ĕnyoráns] *nf* ignorance; **dans l'~ de** in ignorance of, ignorant of.

ignorant, e [ĕnyoráń, -ánt] *a* ignorant ♦ *nm/f:* **faire l'~** to pretend one doesn't know; **~ de** ignorant of, not aware of; **~ en** ignorant of, knowing nothing of.

ignoré, e [ĕnyorā] *a* unknown.

ignorer [ĕnyorā] *vt (ne pas connaître)* not to know, be unaware *ou* ignorant of; *(être sans expérience de: plaisir, guerre etc)* not to know about, have no experience of; *(bouder: personne)* to ignore; **j'ignore comment/si** I do not know how/if; **~ que** to be unaware that, not to know that; **je n'ignore pas que ...** I'm not forgetting that ..., I'm not unaware that ...; **je l'ignore** I don't know.

IGPN *sigle f* (= *Inspection générale de la police nationale*) police disciplinary body.

IGS *sigle f* (= *Inspection générale des services*) police disciplinary body for Paris.

iguane [ĕgwán] *nm* iguana.

il [ĕl] *pronom* he; *(animal, chose, en tournure impersonnelle)* it; *NB: en anglais les navires et les pays sont en général assimilés aux femelles, et les bébés aux choses, si le sexe n'est pas spécifié;* **~s** they; **~ neige** it's snowing; *voir aussi* **avoir.**

iliaque [ĕlyák] *a* (ANAT): **os/artère ~** iliac bone/artery.

illégal, e, aux [ĕlāgál, -ō] *a* illegal, unlawful (ADMIN).

illégalement [ĕlāgálmáń] *ad* illegally.

illégalité [ĕlāgálētā] *nf* illegality; unlawfulness; **être dans l'~** to be outside the law.

illégitime [ĕlāzhētēm] *a* illegitimate; *(optimisme, sévérité)* unjustified, unwarranted.

illégitimement [ĕlāzhētēmmáń] *ad* illegitimately.

illégitimité [ĕlāzhētēmētā] *nf* illegitimacy; **gouverner dans l'~** to rule illegally.

illettré, e [ĕlātrā] *a, nm/f* illiterate.

illicite [ĕlēsēt] *a* illicit.

illicitement [ĕlēsētmáń] *ad* illicitly.

illico [ĕlēkō] *ad (fam)* pronto.

illimité, e [ĕlēmētā] *a (immense)* boundless, unlimited; *(congé, durée)* indefinite, unlimited.

illisible [ĕlēzēbl(ə)] *a* illegible; *(roman)* unreadable.

illisiblement [ĕlēzēblǝmáń] *ad* illegibly.

illogique [ĕlozhēk] *a* illogical.

illogisme [ĕlozhēsm(ə)] *nm* illogicality.

illumination [ĕlümēnásyóń] *nf* illumination, floodlighting; *(inspiration)* flash of inspiration; **~s** *nfpl* illuminations, lights.

illuminé, e [ĕlümēnā] *a* lit up; illuminated, floodlit ♦ *nm/f (fig: péj)* crank.

illuminer [ĕlümēnā] *vt* to light up; *(monument, rue: pour une fête)* to illuminate, floodlight; **s'~** *vi* to light up.

illusion [ĕlüzyóń] *nf* illusion; **se faire des ~s** to delude o.s.; **faire ~** to delude *ou* fool people; **~ d'optique** optical illusion.

illusionner [ĕlüzyonā] *vt* to delude; **s'~ (sur qn/qch)** to delude o.s. (about sb/sth).

illusionnisme [ĕlüzyonēsm(ə)] *nm* conjuring.

illusionniste [ĕlüzyonēst(ə)] *nm/f* conjuror.

illusoire [ĕlüzwár] *a* illusory, illusive.

illustrateur [ĕlüstrátœr] *nm* illustrator.

illustratif, ive [ĕlüstrátēf, -ēv] *a* illustrative.

illustration [ĕlüstrásyóń] *nf* illustration; *(d'un ouvrage: photos)* illustrations *pl.*

illustre [ĕlüstr(ə)] *a* illustrious, renowned.

illustré, e [ĕlüstrā] *a* illustrated ♦ *nm* illustrated magazine; *(pour enfants)* comic.

illustrer [ĕlüstrā] *vt* to illustrate; **s'~** to become famous, win fame.

ils [ĕl] *pronom voir* **il.**

image [ĕmázh] *nf* (gén) picture; *(comparaison, ressemblance,* OPTIQUE*)* image; **~ de** picture *ou* image of; **~ d'Épinal** (social) stereotype; **~ de marque** brand image; *(d'une personne)* (public) image; *(d'une entreprise)* corporate image; **~ pieuse** holy picture.

imagé, e [ĕmázhā] *a* full of imagery.

imaginable [ĕmázhēnábl(ə)] *a* imaginable; **difficilement ~** hard to imagine.

imaginaire [ĕmázhēner] *a* imaginary.

imaginatif, ive [ĕmázhēnátēf, -ēv] *a* imaginative.

imagination [ĕmázhēnásyóń] *nf* imagination; *(chimère)* fancy, imagining; **avoir de l'~** to be imaginative, have a good imagination.

imaginer [ĕmázhēnā] *vt* to imagine; *(croire)*: **qu'allez-vous ~ là?** what on earth are you thinking of?; *(inventer: expédient, mesure)* to devise, think up; **s'~** *vt (se figurer: scène etc)* to imagine, picture; **s'~ à 60 ans** to picture *ou* imagine o.s. at 60; **s'~ que** to imagine that; **s'~ pouvoir faire qch** to think one can do sth; **j'imagine qu'il a voulu plaisanter** I suppose he was joking; **~ de faire** *(se mettre dans l'idée de)* to dream up the idea of doing.

imbattable [ańbátábl(ə)] *a* unbeatable.

imbécile [ańbāsēl] *a* idiotic ♦ *nm/f* idiot; *(MÉD)* imbecile.

imbécillité [ańbāsēlētā] *nf* idiocy; imbecility; idiotic action *(ou* remark *etc)*.

imberbe [ańbɛrb(ə)] *a* beardless.

imbiber [ańbēbā] *vt:* **~ qch de** to moisten *ou* wet sth with; **s'~ de** to become saturated with; **imbibé(e) d'eau** *(chaussures, étoffe)* saturated; *(terre)* waterlogged.

imbriqué, e [ańbrēkā] *a* overlapping.

imbriquer [ańbrēkā]: **s'~** *vi* to overlap (each other); *(fig)* to become interlinked *ou* interwoven.

imbu, e [ańbü] *a:* **~ de** full of; **~ de soi-même/sa supériorité** full of oneself/one's superiority.

imbuvable [ańbüvábl(ə)] *a* undrinkable.

imitable [ĕmētábl(ə)] *a* imitable; **facilement ~** easily imitated.

imitateur, trice [ĕmētátœr, -trēs] *nm/f (gén)* imitator; *(*MUSIC-HALL*: d'une personnalité)* impersonator.

imitation [ĕmētásyóń] *nf* imitation; impersonation; **sac ~ cuir** bag in imitation *ou* simulated leather; **à l'~ de** in imitation of.

imiter [ĕmētā] *vt* to imitate; *(personne)* to

imitate, impersonate; (*contrefaire: signature, document*) to forge, copy; (*ressembler à*) to look like; **il se leva et je l'imitai** he got up and I did likewise.

imm. *abr* = **immeuble.**

immaculé, e [ēmákülā] *a* spotless, immaculate; **l'I~e Conception** (*REL*) the Immaculate Conception.

immanent, e [ēmánáñ, -áñt] *a* immanent.

immangeable [añmáñzhábl(ə)] *a* inedible, uneatable.

immanquable [añmáñkábl(ə)] *a* (*cible*) impossible to miss; (*fatal, inévitable*) bound to happen, inevitable.

immanquablement [añmáñkábləmáñ] *ad* inevitably.

immatériel, le [ēmátāryel] *a* ethereal; (*PHILOSOPHIE*) immaterial.

immatriculation [ēmátrēkülâsyóñ] *nf* registration.

immatriculer [ēmátrēkülā] *vt* to register; **faire/se faire ~** to register; **voiture immatriculée dans la Seine** car with a Seine registration (number).

immature [ēmátür] *a* immature.

immaturité [ēmátürētā] *nf* immaturity.

immédiat, e [ēmādyá, -át] *a* immediate ♦ *nm:* **dans l'~** for the time being; **dans le voisinage ~ de** in the immediate vicinity of.

immédiatement [ēmādyàtmáñ] *ad* immediately.

immémorial, e, aux [ēmāmoryál, -ō] *a* ancient, age-old.

immense [ēmáñs] *a* immense.

immensément [ēmáñsāmáñ] *ad* immensely.

immensité [ēmáñsētā] *nf* immensity.

immerger [ēmerzhā] *vt* to immerse, submerge; (*câble etc*) to lay under water; (*déchets*) to dump at sea; **s'~** *vi* (*sous-marin*) to dive, submerge.

immérité, e [ēmārētā] *a* undeserved.

immersion [ēmersyóñ] *nf* immersion.

immettable [añmetábl(ə)] *a* unwearable.

immeuble [ēmœbl(ə)] *nm* building ♦ *a* (*JUR*) immovable, real; **~ locatif** rental building (*US*), block of rented flats (*Brit*); **~ de rapport** investment property.

immigrant, e [ēmēgráñ, -áñt] *nm/f* immigrant.

immigration [ēmēgrásyóñ] *nf* immigration.

immigré, e [ēmēgrā] *nm/f* immigrant.

immigrer [ēmēgrā] *vi* to immigrate.

imminence [ēmēnáñs] *nf* imminence.

imminent, e [ēmēnáñ, -áñt] *a* imminent, impending.

immiscer [ēmēsā]: **s'~** *vi:* **s'~ dans** to interfere in *ou* with.

immixtion [ēmēksyóñ] *nf* interference.

immobile [ēmobēl] *a* still, motionless; (*pièce de machine*) fixed; (*fig*) unchanging; **rester/se tenir ~** to stay/keep still.

immobilier, ière [ēmobēlyā, -yer] *a* property *cpd*, in real property ♦ *nm:* **l'~** the property *ou* the real estate business.

immobilisation [ēmobēlēzâsyóñ] *nf* immobilization; **~s** *nfpl* (*JUR*) fixed assets.

immobiliser [ēmobēlēzā] *vt* (*gén*) to immobilize; (*circulation, affaires*) to bring to a standstill; **s'~** (*personne*) to stand still; (*machine, véhicule*) to come to a

halt *ou* a standstill.

immobilisme [ēmobēlēsm(ə)] *nm* strong resistance *ou* opposition to change.

immobilité [ēmobēlētā] *nf* immobility.

immodéré, e [ēmodārā] *a* immoderate, inordinate.

immodérément [ēmodārāmáñ] *ad* immoderately.

immoler [ēmolā] *vt* to sacrifice.

immonde [ēmóñd] *a* foul; (*sale: ruelle, taudis*) squalid.

immondices [ēmóñdēs] *nmpl* (*ordures*) refuse *sg*; (*saletés*) filth *sg*.

immoral, e, aux [ēmoràl, -ō] *a* immoral.

immoralité [ēmoràlētā] *nf* immorality.

immortaliser [ēmortálēzā] *vt* to immortalize.

immortel, le [ēmortel] *a* immortal ♦ *nf* (*BOT*) everlasting (flower).

immuable [ēmüábl(ə)] *a* (*inébranlable*) immutable; (*qui ne change pas*) unchanging; (*personne*): **~ dans ses convictions** immoveable (in one's convictions).

immunisation [ēmünēzásyóñ] *nf* immunization.

immuniser [ēmünēzā] *vt* (*MÉD*) to immunize; **~ qn contre** to immunize sb against; (*fig*) to make sb immune to.

immunité [ēmünētā] *nf* immunity; **~ diplomatique** diplomatic immunity; **~ parlementaire** parliamentary privilege.

immunologie [ēmünolozhē] *nf* immunology.

impact [añpákt] *nm* impact; **point d'~** point of impact.

impair, e [añper] *a* odd ♦ *nm* faux pas, blunder; **numéros ~s** odd numbers.

impaludation [añpálüdâsyóñ] *nf* inoculation against malaria.

imparable [añpárábl(ə)] *a* unstoppable.

impardonnable [añpárdonábl(ə)] *a* unpardonable, unforgivable; **vous êtes ~ d'avoir fait cela** it's unforgivable of you to have done that.

imparfait, e [añpárfe, -et] *a* imperfect ♦ *nm* (*LING*) imperfect (tense).

imparfaitement [añpárfetmáñ] *ad* imperfectly.

impartial, e, aux [añpársyál, -ō] *a* impartial, unbiased.

impartialité [añpársyálētā] *nf* impartiality.

impartir [añpártēr] *vt:* **~ qch à qn** to assign sth to sb; (*dons*) to bestow sth upon sb; **dans les délais impartis** in the time allowed.

impasse [añpás] *nf* dead end, cul-de-sac; (*fig*) deadlock; **être dans l'~** (*négociations*) to have reached deadlock; **~ budgétaire** budget deficit.

impassibilité [añpásēbēlētā] *nf* impassiveness.

impassible [añpásēbl(ə)] *a* impassive.

impatiemment [añpásyámáñ] *ad* impatiently.

impatience [añpásyáñs] *nf* impatience.

impatient, e [añpásyáñ, -áñt] *a* impatient; **~ de faire qch** impatient to do sth.

impatienter [añpásyáñtā] *vt* to irritate, annoy; **s'~** *vi* to get impatient; **s'~ de/contre** to lose patience at/with, grow impatient at/with.

impayable [añpeyábl(ə)] *a* (*drôle*) priceless.

impayé, e [añpáyā] *a* unpaid, outstanding.

impeccable [añpākábl(ə)] *a* faultless, impeccable; (*propre*) spotlessly clean; (*chic*) impeccably dressed; *(fam)* great, neat.

impeccablement [aṅpākábləmáṅ] *ad* impeccably.

impénétrable [aṅpānātrábl(ə)] *a* impenetrable.

impénitent, e [aṅpāṅctáṅ, -áṅt] *a* unrepentant.

impensable [aṅpáṅsábl(ə)] *a* unthinkable, unbelievable.

imper [aṅpcr] *nm* (= *imperméable*) raincoat.

impératif, ive [aṅpārátēf, -ēv] *a* imperative; *(JUR)* mandatory ♦ *nm (LING)* imperative; **~s** *nmpl* requirements; demands.

impérativement [aṅpārátēvmáṅ] *ad* imperatively.

impératrice [aṅpārátrēs] *nf* empress.

imperceptible [aṅpcrscptēbl(ə)] *a* imperceptible.

imperceptiblement [aṅpcrscptēbləmáṅ] *ad* imperceptibly.

imperdable [aṅperdábl(ə)] *a* that cannot be lost.

imperfectible [aṅpcrfcktēbl(ə)] *a* which cannot be perfected.

imperfection [aṅpcrfcksyóṅ] *nf* imperfection.

impérial, e, aux [aṅpāryál, -ō] *a* imperial ♦ *nf* upper deck; **autobus à ~e** double-decker bus.

impérialisme [aṅpāryálēsm(ə)] *nm* imperialism.

impérialiste [aṅpāryálēst(ə)] *a* imperialist.

impérieusement [aṅpāryœzmáṅ] *ad*: **avoir ~ besoin de qch** to have urgent need of sth.

impérieux, euse [aṅpāryœ̄, -œ̄z] *a (caractère, ton)* imperious; *(obligation, besoin)* pressing, urgent.

impérissable [aṅpārēsábl(ə)] *a* undying, imperishable.

imperméabilisation [aṅpermāābēlēzásyóṅ] *nf* waterproofing.

imperméabiliser [aṅpermāābēlēzā] *vt* to waterproof.

imperméable [aṅpermāābl(ə)] *a* waterproof; *(GÉO)* impermeable; *(fig)*: **~ à** impervious to ♦ *nm* raincoat; **~ à l'air** airtight.

impersonnel, le [aṅpersonel] *a* impersonal.

impertinemment [aṅpcrtēnámáṅ] *ad* impertinently.

impertinence [aṅpcrtēnáṅs] *nf* impertinence.

impertinent, e [aṅpcrtēnáṅ, -áṅt] *a* impertinent.

imperturbable [aṅpcrtürbábl(ə)] *a (personne)* imperturbable; *(sang-froid)* unshakeable; **rester ~** to remain unruffled.

imperturbablement [aṅpcrtürbábləmáṅ] *ad* imperturbably; unshakeably.

impétrant, e [aṅpātráṅ, -áṅt] *nm/f (JUR)* applicant.

impétueux, euse [aṅpātüœ̄, -œ̄z] *a* fiery.

impétuosité [aṅpātüōzētā] *nf* fieriness.

impie [aṅpē] *a* impious, ungodly.

impiété [aṅpyātā] *nf* impiety.

impitoyable [aṅpētwáyábl(ə)] *a* pitiless, merciless.

impitoyablement [aṅpētwáyábləmáṅ] *ad* mercilessly.

implacable [aṅplákábl(ə)] *a* implacable.

implacablement [aṅplákábləmáṅ] *ad* implacably.

implant [aṅpláṅ] *nm (MÉD)* implant.

implantation [aṅplàṅtásyóṅ] *nf* establishment;

settling; implantation.

implanter [aṅplàṅtā] *vt (usine, industrie, usage)* to establish; *(colons etc)* to settle; *(idée, préjugé)* to implant; **s'~ dans** to be established in; to settle in; to become implanted in.

implication [aṅplēkásyóṅ] *nf* implication.

implicite [aṅplēsēt] *a* implicit.

implicitement [aṅplēsētmáṅ] *ad* implicitly.

impliquer [aṅplēkā] *vt* to imply; **~ qn (dans)** to implicate sb (in).

implorer [aṅplorā] *vt* to implore.

imploser [aṅplōzā] *vi* to implode.

implosion [aṅplōzyóṅ] *nf* implosion.

impoli, e [aṅpolē] *a* impolite, rude.

impoliment [aṅpolēmáṅ] *ad* impolitely.

impolitesse [aṅpolētēs] *nf* impoliteness, rudeness; *(propos)* impolite *ou* rude remark.

impondérable [aṅpòṅdārábl(ə)] *nm* imponderable.

impopulaire [aṅpopüler] *a* unpopular.

impopularité [aṅpopülárētā] *nf* unpopularity.

importable [aṅportábl(ə)] *a (COMM: marchandise)* importable; *(vétement: immettable)* unwearable.

importance [aṅportáṅs] *nf* importance; **avoir de l'~** to be important; **sans ~** unimportant; **d'~** important, considerable; **quelle ~?** what does it matter?

important, e [aṅportáṅ, -áṅt] *a* important; *(en quantité)* considerable, sizeable; *(: gamme, dégâts)* extensive; *(péj: airs, ton)* self-important ♦ *nm*: **l'~** the important thing.

importateur, trice [aṅportátœr, -trēs] *a* importing ♦ *nm/f* importer; **pays ~ de blé** wheat-importing country.

importation [aṅportásyóṅ] *nf* import; introduction; *(produit)* import.

importer [aṅportā] *vt (COMM)* to import; *(maladies, plantes)* to introduce ♦ *vi (être important)* to matter; **~ à qn** to matter to sb; **il importe de** it is important to; **il importe qu'il fasse** he must do, it is important that he should do; **peu m'importe** I don't mind, I don't care; **peu importe** it doesn't matter; **peu importe (que)** it doesn't matter (if); **peu importe le prix** never mind the price; *voir aussi* **n'importe**.

import-export [aṅporekspor] *nm* import-export business.

importun, e [aṅportœṅ, -üṅ] *a* irksome, importunate; *(arrivée, visite)* inopportune, ill-timed ♦ *nm* intruder.

importuner [aṅportünā] *vt* to bother.

imposable [aṅpōzábl(ə)] *a* taxable.

imposant, e [aṅpōzáṅ, -áṅt] *a* imposing.

imposé, e [aṅpōzā] *a (soumis à l'impôt)* taxed; *(GYM etc: figures)* set.

imposer [aṅpōzā] *vt (taxer)* to tax; *(REL)*: **~ les mains** to lay on hands; **~ qch à qn** to impose sth on sb; **s'~** *(être nécessaire)* to be imperative; *(montrer sa proéminence)* to stand out, emerge; *(artiste: se faire connaître)* to win recognition, come to the fore; **en ~** to be imposing; **en ~ à** to impress; **ça s'impose** it's essential, it's vital.

imposition [aṅpōzēsyóṅ] *nf (ADMIN)* taxation.

impossibilité [aṅposēbēlētā] *nf* impossibility; **être dans l'~ de faire** to be unable to do, find it impossible to do.

impossible [aṅposēbl(ə)] *a* impossible ♦ *nm:* **l'~** the impossible; **~ à faire** impossible to do; **il m'est ~ de le faire** it is impossible for me to do it, I can't possibly do it; **faire l'~ (pour que)** to do one's utmost (so that); **si, par ~** ... if, by some miracle ....

imposteur [aṅpostœr] *nm* impostor.

imposture [aṅpostür] *nf* imposture, deception.

impôt [aṅpō] *nm* tax; *(taxes)* taxation, taxes *pl;* **~s** *nmpl (contributions)* (income) tax *sg;* **payer 1.000 F d'~s** to pay 1,000 F in tax; **~ direct/indirect** direct/indirect tax; **~ sur le chiffre d'affaires** tax on turnover; **~ foncier** property tax; **~ sur la fortune** wealth tax; **~ sur les plus-values** capital gains tax; **~ sur le revenu** income tax; **~ sur le RPP** personal income tax; **~ sur les sociétés** corporate tax; **~s locaux** rates.

impotence [aṅpotāṅs] *nf* disability.

impotent, e [aṅpotāṅ, -āṅt] *a* disabled.

impraticable [aṅprátēkàbl(ə)] *a (projet)* impracticable, unworkable; *(piste)* impassable.

imprécation [aṅprākàsyôṅ] *nf* imprecation.

imprécis, e [aṅprāsē, -ēz] *a (contours, souvenir)* imprecise, vague; *(tir)* inaccurate, imprecise.

imprécision [aṅprāsēzyôṅ] *nf* imprecision.

imprégner [aṅprānyā] *vt (tissu, tampon):* **~ (de)** to soak *ou* impregnate (with); *(lieu, air):* **~ (de)** to fill (with); *(suj: amertume, ironie)* to pervade; **s'~ de** to become impregnated with; to be filled with; *(fig)* to absorb.

imprenable [aṅprənàbl(ə)] *a (forteresse)* impregnable; **vue ~** unrestricted view.

impresario [aṅprāsàryō] *nm* manager, impresario.

impression [aṅprāsyôṅ] *nf* impression; *(d'un ouvrage, tissu)* printing; *(PHOTO)* exposure; **faire bonne ~** to make a good impression; **donner une ~ de/l'~ que** to give the impression of/that; **avoir l'~ de/que** to have the impression of/that; **faire ~** to make an impression; **~s de voyage** impressions of one's journey.

impressionnable [aṅprāsyonàbl(ə)] *a* impressionable.

impressionnant, e [aṅprāsyonāṅ, -āṅt] *a* impressive; upsetting.

impressionner [aṅprāsyonā] *vt (frapper)* to impress; *(troubler)* to upset; *(PHOTO)* to expose.

impressionnisme [aṅprāsyonēsm(ə)] *nm* impressionism.

impressionniste [aṅprāsyonēst(ə)] *a, nm/f* impressionist.

imprévisible [aṅprāvēzēbl(ə)] *a* unforeseeable; *(réaction, personne)* unpredictable.

imprévoyance [aṅprāvwàyāṅs] *nf* lack of foresight.

imprévoyant, e [aṅprāvwàyāṅ, -āṅt] *a* lacking in foresight; *(en matière d'argent)* improvident.

imprévu, e [aṅprāvü] *a* unforeseen, unexpected ♦ *nm* unexpected incident; **l'~** the unexpected; **en cas d'~** if anything unexpected happens; **sauf ~** barring anything unexpected.

imprimante [aṅprēmāṅt] *nf (INFORM)* printer; **~ à jet d'encre** ink-jet printer; **~ à laser** laser printer; **~ (ligne par)** ligne line printer; **~ à marguerite** daisy-wheel printer; **~ matricielle** dot-matrix printer; **~ thermique** thermal printer.

imprimé [aṅprēmā] *nm (formulaire)* printed form; *(POSTES)* printed matter *q; (tissu)* printed fabric; **un ~ à fleurs/pois** *(tissu)* a floral/polka-dot print.

imprimer [aṅprēmā] *vt* to print; *(INFORM)* to print (out); *(apposer: visa, cachet)* to stamp; *(empreinte etc)* to imprint; *(publier)* to publish; *(communiquer: mouvement, impulsion)* to impart, transmit.

imprimerie [aṅprēmrē] *nf* printing; *(établissement)* printing works *sg; (atelier)* print shop, printery.

imprimeur [aṅprēmœr] *nm* printer; **imprimeur-éditeur/-libraire** printer and publisher/bookseller.

improbable [aṅprobàbl(ə)] *a* unlikely, improbable.

improductif, ive [aṅprodüktēf, -ēv] *a* unproductive.

impromptu, e [aṅprôṅptü] *a* impromptu; *(départ)* sudden.

imprononçable [aṅpronôṅsàbl(ə)] *a* unpronounceable.

impropre [aṅpropr(ə)] *a* inappropriate; **~ à** unsuitable for.

improprement [aṅpropræmāṅ] *ad* improperly.

impropriété [aṅproprēyātā] *nf:* **~ (de langage)** incorrect usage *q.*

improvisation [aṅprovēzàsyôṅ] *nf* improvisation.

improvisé, e [aṅprovēzā] *a* makeshift, improvised; *(jeu etc)* scratch, improvised; **avec des moyens ~s** using whatever is on *ou* at hand.

improviser [aṅprovēzā] *vt, vi* to improvise; **s'~** *(secours, réunion)* to be improvised; **s'~ cuisinier** to (decide to) act as cook; **~ qn cuisinier** to get sb to act as cook.

improviste [aṅprovēst(ə)]: **à l'~** *ad* unexpectedly, without warning.

imprudemment [aṅprüdàmāṅ] *ad* carelessly; unwisely, imprudently.

imprudence [aṅprüdāṅs] *nf* carelessness *q;* imprudence *q;* act of carelessness; foolish *ou* unwise action.

imprudent, e [aṅprüdāṅ, -āṅt] *a (conducteur, geste, action)* careless; *(remarque)* unwise, imprudent; *(projet)* foolhardy.

impubère [aṅpüber] *a* below the age of puberty.

impudemment [aṅpüdàmāṅ] *ad* impudently.

impudence [aṅpüdāṅs] *nf* impudence.

impudent, e [aṅpüdāṅ, -āṅt] *a* impudent.

impudeur [aṅpüdœr] *nf* shamelessness.

impudique [aṅpüdēk] *a* shameless.

impuissance [aṅpüēsāṅs] *nf* helplessness; ineffectualness; impotence.

impuissant, e [aṅpüēsāṅ, -āṅt] *a* helpless; *(sans effet)* ineffectual; *(sexuellement)* impotent ♦ *nm* impotent man; **~ à faire qch** powerless to do sth.

impulsif, ive [aṅpülsēf, -ēv] *a* impulsive.

impulsion [aṅpülsyôṅ] *nf* (*ÉLEC*, *instinct*) impulse; (*élan*, *influence*) impetus.

impulsivement [aṅpülsēvmâṅ] *ad* impulsively.

impulsivité [aṅpülsēvētā] *nf* impulsiveness.

impunément [aṅpünāmâṅ] *ad* with impunity.

impuni, e [aṅpünē] *a* unpunished.

impunité [aṅpünētā] *nf* impunity.

impur, e [aṅpür] *a* impure.

impureté [aṅpürtā] *nf* impurity.

imputable [aṅpütábl(ə)] *a* (*attribuable*): ~ **à** imputable to, ascribable to; (*COMM*: *somme*): ~ **sur** chargeable to.

imputation [aṅpütāsyôṅ] *nf* imputation, charge.

imputer [aṅpütā] *vt* (*attribuer*): ~ **qch à** to ascribe *ou* impute sth to; (*COMM*): ~ **qch à** *ou* **sur** to charge sth to.

imputrescible [aṅpütrāsēbl(ə)] *a* rotproof.

in [ēn] *a inv* in, trendy.

INA [ēnà] *sigle m* (= *Institut national de l'audio-visuel*) library of television archives.

inabordable [ēnábordábl(ə)] *a* (*lieu*) inaccessible; (*cher*) prohibitive.

inaccentué, e [ēnáksâṅtüā] *a* (*LING*) unstressed.

inacceptable [ēnákseptábl(ə)] *a* unacceptable.

inaccessible [ēnáksāsēbl(ə)] *a* inaccessible; (*objectif*) unattainable; (*insensible*): ~ **à** impervious to.

inaccoutumé, e [ēnákōōtümā] *a* unaccustomed.

inachevé, e [ēnáshvā] *a* unfinished.

inactif, ive [ēnáktēf, -ēv] *a* inactive, idle.

inaction [ēnáksyôṅ] *nf* inactivity.

inactivité [ēnáktēvētā] *nf* (*ADMIN*): **en** ~ out of active service.

inadaptation [ēnádáptāsyôṅ] *nf* (*PSYCH*) maladjustment.

inadapté, e [ēnádáptā] *a* (*PSYCH*: *adulte*, *enfant*) maladjusted ♦ *nm/f* (*péj*: *adulte*: *asocial*) misfit; ~ **à** not adapted to, unsuited to.

inadéquat, e [ēnádākwà, wát] *a* inadequate.

inadéquation [ēnádākwâsyôṅ] *nf* inadequacy.

inadmissible [ēnádmēsēbl(ə)] *a* inadmissible.

inadvertance [ēnádvertâṅs]: **par** ~ *ad* inadvertently.

inaliénable [ēnályānábl(ə)] *a* inalienable.

inaltérable [ēnáltārábl(ə)] *a* (*matière*) stable; (*fig*) unchanging; ~ **à** unaffected by; **couleur** ~ (**au lavage/à la lumière**) fast color/fade-resistant color.

inamovible [ēnámovēbl(ə)] *a* fixed; (*JUR*) irremovable.

inanimé, e [ēnánēmā] *a* (*matière*) inanimate; (*évanoui*) unconscious; (*sans vie*) lifeless.

inanité [ēnánētā] *nf* futility.

inanition [ēnánēsyôṅ] *nf*: **tomber d'**~ to faint with hunger (and exhaustion).

inaperçu, e [ēnápersü] *a*: **passer** ~ to go unnoticed.

inappétence [ēnápātâṅs] *nf* lack of appetite.

inapplicable [ēnáplēkábl(ə)] *a* inapplicable.

inapplication [ēnáplēkâsyôṅ] *nf* lack of application.

inappliqué, e [ēnáplēkā] *a* lacking in application.

inappréciable [ēnáprāsyábl(ə)] *a* (*service*) invaluable; (*différence*, *nuance*) inappreciable.

inapte [ēnápt(ə)] *a*: ~ **à** incapable of; (*MIL*) unfit for.

inaptitude [ēnáptētüd] *nf* inaptitude; unfitness.

inarticulé, e [ēnártēkülā] *a* inarticulate.

inassimilable [ēnásēmēlábl(ə)] *a* that cannot be assimilated.

inassouvi, e [ēnásōōvē] *a* unsatisfied, unfulfilled.

inattaquable [ēnátákábl(ə)] *a* (*MIL*) unassailable; (*texte*, *preuve*) irrefutable.

inattendu, e [ēnátâṅdü] *a* unexpected ♦ *nm*: **l'**~ the unexpected.

inattentif, ive [ēnátâṅtēf, -ēv] *a* inattentive; ~ **à** (*dangers*, *détails*) heedless of.

inattention [ēnátâṅsyôṅ] *nf* inattention; (*inadvertance*): **une minute d'**~ a minute of inattention, a minute's carelessness; **par** ~ inadvertently; **faute d'**~ careless mistake.

inaudible [ēnōdēbl(ə)] *a* inaudible.

inaugural, e, aux [ēnogürál, -ō] *a* (*cérémonie*) inaugural, opening; (*vol*, *voyage*) maiden.

inauguration [ēnogürâsyôṅ] *nf* unveiling; opening; **discours/cérémonie d'**~ inaugural speech/ceremony.

inaugurer [ēnogürā] *vt* (*monument*) to unveil; (*exposition*, *usine*) to open; (*fig*) to inaugurate.

inauthenticité [ēnotâṅtēsētā] *nf* inauthenticity.

inavouable [ēnávwábl(ə)] *a* undisclosable; (*honteux*) shameful.

inavoué, e [ēnávwā] *a* unavowed.

INC *sigle m* (= *Institut national de la consommation*) consumer research organization.

inca [aṅká] *a inv* Inca ♦ *nm/f*: **l'**~ Inca.

incalculable [aṅkálkülábl(ə)] *a* incalculable; **un nombre** ~ **de** countless numbers of.

incandescence [aṅkâṅdāsâṅs] *nf* incandescence; **en** ~ incandescent, white-hot; **porter à** ~ to heat white-hot; **lampe/manchon à** ~ incandescent lamp/(gas) mantle.

incandescent, e [aṅkâṅdāsâṅ, -âṅt] *a* incandescent, white-hot.

incantation [aṅkâṅtâsyôṅ] *nf* incantation.

incapable [aṅkápábl(ə)] *a* incapable; ~ **de faire** incapable of doing; (*empêché*) unable to do.

incapacitant, e [aṅkápásētâṅ, -âṅt] *a* (*MIL*) incapacitating.

incapacité [aṅkápásētā] *nf* incapability; (*JUR*) incapacity; **être dans l'**~ **de faire** to be unable to do; ~ **permanente/de travail** permanent/industrial disablement; ~ **électorale** ineligibility to vote.

incarcération [aṅkârsārásyôṅ] *nf* incarceration.

incarcérer [aṅkârsārā] *vt* to incarcerate.

incarnat, e [aṅkárná, -át] *a* (*rosy*) pink.

incarnation [aṅkárnâsyôṅ] *nf* incarnation.

incarné, e [aṅkárnā] *a* incarnate; (*ongle*) ingrown.

incarner [aṅkárnā] *vt* to embody, personify; (*THÉÂTRE*) to play; (*REL*) to incarnate; **s'**~ **dans** (*REL*) to be incarnate in.

incartade [aṅkártád] *nf* prank, escapade.

incassable [aṅkásábl(ə)] *a* unbreakable.

incendiaire [aṅsâṅdyer] *a* incendiary; (*fig*: *discours*) inflammatory ♦ *nm/f* arsonist.

incendie [aṅsâṅdē] *nm* fire; ~ **criminel** arson

q; ~ **de forêt** forest fire.
incendier [ɑ̃sɑ̃dyā] *vt* (*mettre le feu à*) to set fire to; (*brûler complètement*) to burn down.
incertain, e [ɑ̃sertɑ̃, -en] *a* uncertain; (*temps*) uncertain, unsettled; (*imprécis: contours*) indistinct, blurred.
incertitude [ɑ̃sertētüd] *nf* uncertainty.
incessamment [ɑ̃sesámɑ̃] *ad* very shortly.
incessant, e [ɑ̃sesɑ̃, -ɑ̃t] *a* incessant, unceasing.
incessible [ɑ̃sāsēbl(ə)] *a* (*JUR*) nontransferable.
inceste [ɑ̃sest(ə)] *nm* incest.
incestueux, euse [ɑ̃sestüœ, -œz] *a* incestuous.
inchangé, e [ɑ̃shɑ̃nzhā] *a* unchanged, unaltered.
inchauffable [ɑ̃shōfábl(ə)] *a* impossible to heat.
incidemment [ɑ̃sēdámɑ̃] *ad* in passing.
incidence [ɑ̃sēdɑ̃s] *nf* (*effet, influence*) effect; (*PHYSIQUE*) incidence.
incident [ɑ̃sēdɑ̃] *nm* incident; ~ **de frontière** border incident; ~ **de parcours** minor hitch *ou* setback; ~ **technique** technical difficulties *pl*, technical hitch.
incinérateur [ɑ̃sēnārátœr] *nm* incinerator.
incinération [ɑ̃sēnārásyɔ̃] *nf* (*d'ordures*) incineration; (*crémation*) cremation.
incinérer [ɑ̃sēnārā] *vt* (*ordures*) to incinerate; (*mort*) to cremate.
incise [ɑ̃sēz] *nf* (*LING*) interpolated clause.
inciser [ɑ̃sēzā] *vt* to make an incision in; (*abcès*) to lance.
incisif, ive [ɑ̃sēzēf, -ēv] *a* incisive, cutting ♦ *nf* incisor.
incision [ɑ̃sēzyɔ̃] *nf* incision; (*d'un abcès*) lancing.
incitation [ɑ̃sētásyɔ̃] *nf* (*encouragement*) incentive; (*provocation*) incitement.
inciter [ɑ̃sētā] *vt*: ~ **qn à (faire) qch** to prompt *ou* encourage sb to do sth; (*à la révolte etc*) to incite sb to do sth.
incivil, e [ɑ̃sēvēl] *a* uncivil.
incivilité [ɑ̃sēvēlētā] *nf* incivility.
inclinable [ɑ̃klēnábl(ə)] *a* (*dossier etc*) tilting; **siège à dossier** ~ reclining seat.
inclinaison [ɑ̃klēnezɔ̃] *nf* (*déclivité: d'une route etc*) incline; (: *d'un toit*) slope; (*état penché: d'un mur*) lean; (: *de la tête*) tilt; (: *d'un navire*) list.
inclination [ɑ̃klēnásyɔ̃] *nf* (*penchant*) inclination, tendency; **montrer de l'~ pour les sciences** *etc* to show an inclination for the sciences *etc*; ~s **égoïstes/altruistes** egoistic/altruistic tendencies; ~ **de (la) tête** nod (of the head); ~ **(de buste)** bow.
incliner [ɑ̃klēnā] *vt* (*bouteille*) to tilt; (*tête*) to incline; (*inciter*): ~ **qn à qch/à faire** to encourage sb towards sth/to do ♦ *vi*: ~ **à qch/à faire** (*tendre à, pencher pour*) to incline towards sth/doing, tend towards sth/to do; **s'~** (*route*) to slope; (*toit*) to be sloping; **s'~ (devant)** to bow (before).
inclure [ɑ̃klür] *vt* to include; (*joindre à un envoi*) to enclose; **jusqu'au 10 mars inclus** until March 10(th) inclusive.
inclus, e [ɑ̃klü, -üz] *pp de* **inclure** ♦ *a* (*joint à un envoi*) enclosed; (*compris: frais, dépense*)

included; (*MATH: ensemble*): ~ **dans** included in; **jusqu'au troisième chapitre** ~ up to and including the third chapter.
inclusion [ɑ̃klüzyɔ̃] *nf* (*voir inclure*) inclusion; enclosing.
inclusivement [ɑ̃klüzēvmɑ̃] *ad* inclusively.
inclut [ɑ̃klü] *vb voir* **inclure**.
incoercible [ɑ̃koersēbl(ə)] *a* uncontrollable.
incognito [ɑ̃konyētō] *ad* incognito ♦ *nm*: **garder l'~** to remain incognito.
incohérence [ɑ̃koārɑ̃s] *nf* inconsistency; incoherence.
incohérent, e [ɑ̃koārɑ̃, -ɑ̃t] *a* inconsistent; incoherent.
incollable [ɑ̃kolábl(ə)] *a* (*riz*) that does not stick; (*fam: personne*): **il est** ~ he's got all the answers.
incolore [ɑ̃kolor] *a* colorless (*US*), colourless (*Brit*).
incomber [ɑ̃kɔ̃bā]: ~ **à** *vt* (*suj: devoirs, responsabilité*) to rest *ou* be incumbent upon; (: *frais, travail*) to be the responsibility of.
incombustible [ɑ̃kɔ̃büstēbl(ə)] *a* incombustible.
incommensurable [ɑ̃komɑ̃sürábl(ə)] *a* immeasurable.
incommodant, e [ɑ̃komodɑ̃, -ɑ̃t] *a* (*bruit*) annoying; (*chaleur*) uncomfortable.
incommode [ɑ̃komod] *a* inconvenient; (*posture, siège*) uncomfortable.
incommodément [ɑ̃komodāmɑ̃] *ad* (*installé, assis*) uncomfortably; (*logé, situé*) inconveniently.
incommoder [ɑ̃komodā] *vt*: ~ **qn** to bother *ou* inconvenience sb; (*embarrasser*) to make sb feel uncomfortable *ou* ill at ease.
incommodité [ɑ̃komodētā] *nf* inconvenience.
incomparable [ɑ̃kɔ̃párábl(ə)] *a* not comparable; (*inégalable*) incomparable, matchless.
incomparablement [ɑ̃kɔ̃párábləmɑ̃] *ad* incomparably.
incompatibilité [ɑ̃kɔ̃pátēbēlētā] *nf* incompatibility; ~ **d'humeur** (*mutual*) incompatibility.
incompatible [ɑ̃kɔ̃pátēbl(ə)] *a* incompatible.
incompétence [ɑ̃kɔ̃pātɑ̃s] *nf* lack of expertise; incompetence.
incompétent, e [ɑ̃kɔ̃pātɑ̃, -ɑ̃t] *a* (*ignorant*) inexpert; (*incapable*) incompetent, not competent.
incomplet, ète [ɑ̃kɔ̃ple, -et] *a* incomplete.
incomplètement [ɑ̃kɔ̃pletmɑ̃] *ad* not completely, incompletely.
incompréhensible [ɑ̃kɔ̃prāɑ̃sēbl(ə)] *a* incomprehensible.
incompréhensif, ive [ɑ̃kɔ̃prāɑ̃sēf, -ēv] *a* lacking in understanding, unsympathetic.
incompréhension [ɑ̃kɔ̃prāɑ̃syɔ̃] *nf* lack of understanding.
incompressible [ɑ̃kɔ̃prāsēbl(ə)] *a* (*PHYSIQUE*) incompressible; (*fig: dépenses*) that cannot be reduced; (*JUR: peine*) irreducible.
incompris, e [ɑ̃kɔ̃prē, -ēz] *a* misunderstood.
inconcevable [ɑ̃kɔ̃svábl(ə)] *a* (*conduite etc*) inconceivable; (*mystère*) incredible.
inconciliable [ɑ̃kɔ̃sēlyábl(ə)] *a* irreconcilable.
inconditionnel, le [ɑ̃kɔ̃dēsyonel] *a* uncondi-

tional; (*partisan*) unquestioning ♦ *nm/f* (*partisan*) unquestioning supporter.

incondítionnellement [aṅkôṅdēsyonelmâṅ] *ad* unconditionally.

inconduite [aṅkôṅdüēt] *nf* bad *ou* unsuitable behavior *q* (*US*) *ou* behaviour *q* (*Brit*).

inconfort [aṅkôṅfor] *nm* lack of comfort, discomfort.

inconfortable [aṅkôṅfortábl(ə)] *a* uncomfortable.

inconfortablement [aṅkôṅfortábləmâṅ] *ad* uncomfortably.

incongru, e [aṅkôṅgrü] *a* unseemly; (*remarque*) ill-chosen, incongruous.

incongruité [aṅkôṅgrüētā] *nf* unseemliness; incongruity; (*parole incongrue*) ill-chosen remark.

inconnu, e [aṅkonü] *a* unknown; (*sentiment, plaisir*) new, strange ♦ *nm/f* stranger; unknown person (*ou* artist *etc*) ♦ *nm*: **l'~** the unknown ♦ *nf* (*MATH*) unknown; (*fig*) unknown factor.

inconsciemment [aṅkôṅsyámâṅ] *ad* unconsciously.

inconscience [aṅkôṅsyâṅs] *nf* unconsciousness; recklessness.

inconscient, e [aṅkôṅsyâṅ, -âṅt] *a* unconscious; (*irréfléchi*) reckless ♦ *nm* (*PSYCH*): **l'~** the subconscious, the unconscious; **~ de** unaware of.

inconséquence [aṅkôṅsākâṅs] *nf* inconsistency; thoughtlessness; (*action, parole*) thoughtless thing to do (*ou* say).

inconséquent, e [aṅkôṅsākâṅ, -âṅt] *a* (*illogique*) inconsistent; (*irréfléchi*) thoughtless.

inconsidéré, e [aṅkôṅsēdārā] *a* ill-considered.

inconsidérément [aṅkôṅsēdārāmâṅ] *ad* thoughtlessly.

inconsistant, e [aṅkôṅsēstâṅ, -âṅt] *a* flimsy, weak; (*crème etc*) runny.

inconsolable [aṅkôṅsolábl(ə)] *a* inconsolable.

inconstance [aṅkôṅstâṅs] *nf* inconstancy, fickleness.

inconstant, e [aṅkôṅstâṅ, -âṅt] *a* inconstant, fickle.

inconstitutionnel, le [aṅkôṅstētüsyonel] *a* unconstitutional.

incontestable [aṅkôṅtestábl(ə)] *a* unquestionable, indisputable.

incontestablement [aṅkôṅtestábləmâṅ] *ad* unquestionably, indisputably.

incontesté, e [aṅkôṅtestā] *a* undisputed.

incontinence [aṅkôṅtēnâṅs] *nf* (*MÉD*) incontinence.

incontinent, e [aṅkôṅtēnâṅ, -âṅt] *a* (*MÉD*) incontinent ♦ *ad* (*tout de suite*) forthwith.

incontournable [aṅkôṅtōōrnábl(ə)] *a* unavoidable.

incontrôlable [aṅkôṅtrōlábl(ə)] *a* unverifiable.

incontrôlé, e [aṅkôṅtrōlā] *a* uncontrolled.

inconvenance [aṅkôṅvnâṅs] *nf* (*parole, action*) impropriety.

inconvenant, e [aṅkôṅvnâṅ, -âṅt] *a* unseemly, improper.

inconvénient [aṅkôṅvānyâṅ] *nm* (*d'une situation, d'un projet*) disadvantage, drawback; (*d'un remède, changement etc*) risk, inconvenience; **si vous n'y voyez pas d'~** if

you have no objections; **y a-t-il un ~ à ...?** (*risque*) isn't there a risk in ...?; (*objection*) is there any objection to ...?

inconvertible [aṅkôṅvertēbl(ə)] *a* inconvertible.

incorporation [aṅkorporâsyôṅ] *nf* (*MIL*) induction (*US*), call-up (*Brit*).

incorporé, e [aṅkorporā] *a* (*micro etc*) built-in.

incorporel, le [aṅkorporel] *a* (*JUR*): **biens ~s** intangible property.

incorporer [aṅkorporā] *vt*: **~ (à)** to mix in (with); (*paragraphe etc*): **~ (dans)** to incorporate (in); (*territoire, immigrants*): **~ (dans)** to incorporate (into); (*MIL: appeler*) to induct (*US*), call up (*Brit*); (: *affecter*): **~ qn dans** to enlist sb into.

incorrect, e [aṅkorekt] *a* (*impropre, inconvenant*) improper; (*défectueux*) faulty; (*inexact*) incorrect; (*impoli*) impolite; (*déloyal*) underhand.

incorrectement [aṅkorektəmâṅ] *ad* improperly; faultily; incorrectly; impolitely; in an underhand way.

incorrection [aṅkoreksyôṅ] *nf* impropriety; incorrectness; underhand nature; (*terme impropre*) impropriety; (*action, remarque*) improper behavior (*US*) *ou* behaviour (*Brit*) (*ou* remark).

incorrigible [aṅkorēzhēbl(ə)] *a* incorrigible.

incorruptible [aṅkorüptēbl(ə)] *a* incorruptible.

incrédibilité [aṅkrādēbēlētā] *nf* incredibility.

incrédule [aṅkrādül] *a* incredulous; (*REL*) unbelieving.

incrédulité [aṅkrādülētā] *nf* incredulity; **avec ~** incredulously.

increvable [aṅkrəvábl(ə)] *a* (*pneu*) punctureproof; (*fam*) tireless.

incriminer [aṅkrēmēnā] *vt* (*personne*) to incriminate; (*action, conduite*) to bring under attack; (*bonne foi, honnêteté*) to call into question; **livre/article incriminé** offending book/article.

incrochetable [aṅkroshtábl(ə)] *a* (*serrure*) that can't be picked, burglarproof.

incroyable [aṅkrwáyábl(ə)] *a* incredible, unbelievable.

incroyablement [aṅkrwáyábləmâṅ] *ad* incredibly, unbelievably.

incroyant, e [aṅkrwáyâṅ, -âṅt] *nm/f* nonbeliever.

incrustation [aṅkrüstâsyôṅ] *nf* inlaying *q*; inlay; (*dans une chaudière etc*) fur *q*, scale *q*.

incruster [aṅkrüstā] *vt* (*ART*): **~ qch dans/ qch de** to inlay sth into/sth with; (*radiateur etc*) to coat with scale *ou* fur; **s'~** *vi* (*invité*) to take root; (*radiateur etc*) to become coated with fur *ou* scale; **s'~ dans** (*suj: corps étranger, caillou*) to become embedded in.

incubateur [aṅkübátœr] *nm* incubator.

incubation [aṅkübâsyôṅ] *nf* incubation.

inculpation [aṅkülpâsyôṅ] *nf* charging *q*; charge; **sous l'~ de** on a charge of.

inculpé, e [aṅkülpā] *nm/f* accused.

inculper [aṅkülpā] *vt*: **~ (de)** to charge (with).

inculquer [aṅkülkā] *vt*: **~ qch à** to inculcate sth in, instill (*US*) *ou* instil (*Brit*) sth into.

inculte [aṅkült(ə)] *a* uncultivated; (*esprit,*

peuple) uncultured; (*barbe*) unkempt.
incultivable [aṅkültēvábl(ə)] *a* (*terrain*) unworkable.
inculture [aṅkültür] *nf* lack of education.
incurable [aṅkürábl(ə)] *a* incurable.
incurie [aṅkürē] *nf* carelessness.
incursion [aṅkürsyóṅ] *nf* incursion, foray.
incurvé, e [aṅkürvā] *a* curved.
incurver [aṅkürvā] *vt* (*barre de fer*) to bend into a curve; **s'~** *vi* (*planche, route*) to bend.
Inde [aṅd] *nf:* **l'~** India.
indécemment [aṅdāsámáṅ] *ad* indecently.
indécence [aṅdāsáṅs] *nf* indecency; (*propos, acte*) indecent remark (*ou* act *etc*).
indécent, e [aṅdāsáṅ, -áṅt] *a* indecent.
indéchiffrable [aṅdāshēfrábl(ə)] *a* indecipherable.
indéchirable [aṅdāshērábl(ə)] *a* tearproof.
indécis, e [aṅdāsē, -ēz] *a* indecisive; (*perplexe*) undecided.
indécision [aṅdāsēzyóṅ] *nf* indecision, indecisiveness.
indéclinable [aṅdāklēnábl(ə)] *a* (*LING*: *mot*) indeclinable.
indécomposable [aṅdākóṅpōzábl(ə)] *a* that cannot be broken down.
indéfectible [aṅdāfcktēbl(ə)] *a* (*attachement*) indestructible.
indéfendable [aṅdāfáṅdábl(ə)] *a* indefensible.
indéfini, e [aṅdāfēnē] *a* (*imprécis, incertain*) undefined; (*illimité, LING*) indefinite.
indéfiniment [aṅdāfēnēmáṅ] *ad* indefinitely.
indéfinissable [aṅdāfēnēsábl(ə)] *a* indefinable.
indéformable [aṅdāformábl(ə)] *a* that keeps its shape.
indélébile [aṅdālābēl] *a* indelible.
indélicat, e [aṅdālēkà, -àt] *a* tactless; (*malhonnête*) dishonest.
indélicatesse [aṅdālēkátcs] *nf* tactlessness; dishonesty.
indémaillable [aṅdāmáyábl(ə)] *a* run resistant, runproof.
indemne [aṅdcmn(ə)] *a* unharmed.
indemnisable [aṅdcmnēzábl(ə)] *a* entitled to compensation.
indemnisation [aṅdcmnēzásyóṅ] *nf* (*somme*) indemnity, compensation.
indemniser [aṅdcmnēzā] *vt:* **~ qn (de)** to compensate sb (for); **se faire ~** to get compensation.
indemnité [aṅdcmnētā] *nf* (*dédommagement*) compensation *q*; (*allocation*) allowance; **~ de licenciement** severance pay; **~ de logement** housing allowance; **~ parlementaire** ≈ Congressman's (*US*) *ou* M.P.'s (*Brit*) salary.
indémontable [aṅdāmóṅtábl(ə)] *a* (*meuble etc*) that cannot be dismantled, in one piece.
indéniable [aṅdānyábl(ə)] *a* undeniable, indisputable.
indéniablement [aṅdānyábləmáṅ] *ad* undeniably.
indépendamment [aṅdāpáṅdàmáṅ] *ad* independently; **~ de** independently of; (*abstraction faite de*) irrespective of; (*en plus de*) over and above.
indépendance [aṅdāpáṅdáṅs] *nf* independence; **~ matérielle** financial independence.

indépendant, e [aṅdāpáṅdáṅ, -áṅt] *a* independent; **~ de** independent of; **chambre ~e** room with private entrance; **travailleur ~** self-employed worker.
indépendantiste [aṅdāpáṅdáṅtēst(ə)] *a, nm/f* separatist.
indéracinable [aṅdārásēnábl(ə)] *a* (*fig: croyance etc*) ineradicable.
indéréglable [aṅdārāglábl(ə)] *a* which will not break down.
indescriptible [aṅdeskrēptēbl(ə)] *a* indescribable.
indésirable [aṅdāzērábl(ə)] *a* undesirable.
indestructible [aṅdestrüktēbl(ə)] *a* indestructible; (*marque, impression*) indelible.
indéterminable [aṅdātermēnábl(ə)] *a* indeterminable.
indétermination [aṅdātermēnásyóṅ] *nf* indecision, indecisiveness.
indéterminé, e [aṅdātermēnā] *a* unspecified; indeterminate; indeterminable.
index [aṅdeks] *nm* (*doigt*) index finger; (*d'un livre etc*) index; **mettre à l'~** to blacklist.
indexation [aṅdeksásyóṅ] *nf* indexing.
indexé, e [aṅdeksā] *a·* (*ÉCON*): **~ (sur)** index-linked (to).
indexer [aṅdeksā] *vt* (*salaire, emprunt*): **~ (sur)** to index (on).
indicateur [aṅdēkátœr] *nm* (*POLICE*) informer; (*livre*) guide; (*: liste*) directory; (*TECH*) gauge; indicator; (*ÉCON*) indicator ♦ *a:* **poteau ~** signpost; **tableau ~** indicator (board); **~ des chemins de fer** railroad (*US*) *ou* railway (*Brit*) timetable; **~ de direction** (*AUTO*) indicator; **~ immobilier** real estate directory (*US*), property gazette (*Brit*); **~ de niveau** level, gauge; **~ de pression** pressure gauge; **~ de rues** street directory; **~ de vitesse** speedometer.
indicatif, ive [aṅdēkátēf, -ēv] *a:* **à titre ~** for (your) information ♦ *nm* (*LING*) indicative; (*d'une émission*) theme song, signature (tune (*Brit*)); (*TÉL*) area code; **~ d'appel** (*RADIO*) call letters *pl* (*US*) *ou* sign (*Brit*).
indication [aṅdēkásyóṅ] *nf* indication; (*renseignement*) information *q*; **~s** *nfpl* (*directives*) instructions; **~ d'origine** (*COMM*) place of origin.
indice [aṅdēs] *nm* (*marque, signe*) indication, sign; (*POLICE: lors d'une enquête*) clue; (*JUR: présomption*) piece of evidence; (*SCIENCE, ÉCON, TECH*) index; (*ADMIN*) grading; rating; **~ du coût de la vie** cost-of-living index; **~ inférieur** subscript; **~ d'octane** octane rating; **~ des prix** price index; **~ de traitement** salary scale.
indicible [aṅdēsēbl(ə)] *a* inexpressible.
indien, ne [aṅdyaṅ, -en] *a* Indian ♦ *nm/f:* **l~, ne** (*d'Amérique*) (American *ou* Red) Indian; (*d'Inde*) Indian.
indifféremment [aṅdēfārámáṅ] *ad* (*sans distinction*) equally; indiscriminately.
indifférence [aṅdēfāráṅs] *nf* indifference.
indifférencié, e [aṅdēfāráṅsyā] *a* undifferentiated.
indifférent, e [aṅdēfāráṅ, -áṅt] *a* (*peu intéressé*) indifferent; **~ à** (*insensible à*) indifferent to, unconcerned about; (*peu intéressant pour*) indifferent to; immaterial to; **ça m'est**

~ **(que ...)** it doesn't matter to me (whether ...).

indifférer [aṅdēfārā] *vt*: **cela m'indiffère** I'm indifferent about it.

indigence [aṅdēzháns] *nf* poverty; **être dans l'~** to be destitute.

indigène [aṅdēzhen] *a* native, indigenous; *(de la région)* local ♦ *nm/f* native.

indigent, e [aṅdēzháṅ, -áṅt] *a* destitute, poverty-stricken; *(fig)* poor.

indigeste [aṅdēzhest(ə)] *a* indigestible.

indigestion [aṅdēzhestyôṅ] *nf* indigestion *q*; **avoir une** ~ to have indigestion.

indignation [aṅdēnyásyôṅ] *nf* indignation; **avec** ~ indignantly.

indigne [aṅdēny] *a*: ~ **(de)** unworthy (of).

indigné, e [aṅdēnyā] *a* indignant.

indignement [aṅdēnymáṅ] *ad* shamefully.

indigner [aṅdēnyā] *vt* to make indignant; **s'~ (de/contre)** to be (*ou* become) indignant (at).

indignité [aṅdēnyētā] *nf* unworthiness *q*; *(acte)* shameful act.

indigo [aṅdēgō] *nm* indigo.

indiqué, e [aṅdēkā] *a* *(date, lieu)* given, appointed; *(adéquat)* appropriate, suitable; *(conseillé)* advisable; *(remède, traitement)* appropriate.

indiquer [aṅdēkā] *vt* *(désigner)*: ~ **qch/qn à qn** to point sth/sb out to sb; *(suj: pendule, aiguille)* to show; *(suj: étiquette, plan)* to show, indicate; *(faire connaître: médecin, restaurant)*: ~ **qch/qn à qn** to tell sb of sth/ sb; *(renseigner sur)* to point out, tell; *(déterminer: date, lieu)* to give, state; *(dénoter)* to indicate, point to; ~ **du doigt** to point out; ~ **de la main** to indicate with one's hand; ~ **du regard** to glance towards *ou* in the direction of; **pourriez-vous m'~ les toilettes/l'heure?** could you direct me to the toilets/tell me the time?

indirect, e [aṅdērekt] *a* indirect.

indirectement [aṅdērektəmáṅ] *ad* indirectly; *(apprendre)* in a roundabout way.

indiscernable [aṅdēsernábl(ə)] *a* indiscernible.

indiscipline [aṅdēsēplēn] *nf* lack of discipline.

indiscipliné, e [aṅdēsēplēnā] *a* undisciplined; *(fig)* unmanageable.

indiscret, ète [aṅdēskre, -et] *a* indiscreet.

indiscrétion [aṅdēskrāsyôṅ] *nf* indiscretion; **sans** ~, ... without wishing to be indiscreet, ...

indiscutable [aṅdēskütábl(ə)] *a* indisputable.

indiscutablement [aṅdēskütábləmáṅ] *ad* indisputably.

indiscuté, e [aṅdēstütā] *a* *(incontesté: droit, chef)* undisputed.

indispensable [aṅdēspáṅsábl(ə)] *a* indispensable, essential; ~ **à qn/pour faire qch** essential for sb/to do sth.

indisponibilité [aṅdēsponēbēlētā] *nf* unavailability.

indisponible [aṅdēsponēbl(ə)] *a* unavailable.

indisposé, e [aṅdēspōzā] *a* indisposed, unwell.

indisposer [aṅdēspōzā] *vt* *(incommoder)* to upset; *(déplaire à)* to antagonize.

indisposition [aṅdēspōzēsyôṅ] *nf* (slight) illness, indisposition.

indistinct, e [aṅdēstaṅ, -aṅkt(ə)] *a* indistinct.

indistinctement [aṅdēstaṅktəmáṅ] *ad* *(voir,*

prononcer) indistinctly; *(sans distinction)* without distinction, indiscriminately.

individu [aṅdēvēdü] *nm* individual.

individualiser [aṅdēvēdüálēzā] *vt* to individualize; *(personnaliser)* to tailor to individual requirements; **s'~** to develop one's own identity.

individualisme [aṅdēvēdüálēsm(ə)] *nm* individualism.

individualiste [aṅdēvēdüálēst(ə)] *nm/f* individualist.

individualité [aṅdēvēdüálētā] *nf* individuality.

individuel, le [aṅdēvēdüel] *a* *(gén)* individual; *(opinion, livret, contrôle, avantages)* personal; **chambre** ~**le** single room; **maison** ~**le** detached house; **propriété** ~**le** personal *ou* private property.

individuellement [aṅdēvēdüelmáṅ] *ad* individually.

indivis, e [aṅdēvē, -ēz] *a* *(JUR: bien, propriété, succession)* indivisible; *(: cohéritiers, propriétaires)* joint.

indivisible [aṅdēvēzēbl(ə)] *a* indivisible.

Indochine [aṅdoshēn] *nf*: **l'~** Indochina.

indochinois, e [aṅdoshēnwá, -wáz] *a* Indochinese.

indocile [aṅdosēl] *a* unruly.

indo-européen, ne [aṅdo͞eeuropáaṅ, -en] *a* Indo-European ♦ *nm* *(LING)* Indo-European.

indolence [aṅdoláṅs] *nf* indolence.

indolent, e [aṅdoláṅ, -áṅt] *a* indolent.

indolore [aṅdolor] *a* painless.

indomptable [aṅdôṅtábl(ə)] *a* untameable; *(fig)* invincible, indomitable.

indompté, e [aṅdôṅtā] *a* *(cheval)* unbroken.

Indonésie [aṅdōnāzē] *nf*: **l'~** Indonesia.

indonésien, ne [aṅdōnāzyaṅ, -en] *a* Indonesian ♦ *nm/f*: **l~, ne** Indonesian.

indu, e [aṅdü] *a*: **à des heures** ~**es** at an ungodly hour.

indubitable [aṅdübētábl(ə)] *a* indubitable.

indubitablement [aṅdübētábləmáṅ] *ad* indubitably.

induire [aṅdüēr] *vt*: ~ **qch de** to induce sth from; ~ **qn en erreur** to lead sb astray, mislead sb.

indulgence [aṅdülzháṅs] *nf* indulgence; leniency; **avec** ~ indulgently; leniently.

indulgent, e [aṅdülzháṅ, -áṅt] *a* *(parent, regard)* indulgent; *(juge, examinateur)* lenient.

indûment [aṅdümáṅ] *ad* without due cause; *(: légitimement)* wrongfully.

industrialisation [aṅdüstrēyálēzâsyôṅ] *nf* industrialization.

industrialiser [aṅdüstrēyálēzā] *vt* to industrialize; **s'~** to become industrialized.

industrie [aṅdüstrē] *nf* industry; ~ **automobile/textile** car/textile industry; ~ **du spectacle** entertainment business.

industriel, le [aṅdüstrēyel] *a* industrial; *(produit industriellement: pain etc)* mass-produced, factory-produced ♦ *nm* industrialist; *(fabricant)* manufacturer.

industriellement [aṅdüstrēyelmáṅ] *ad* industrially.

industrieux, euse [aṅdüstrēyœ, -ēz] *a* industrious.

inébranlable [ēnābráṅlábl(ə)] *a* *(masse, colonne)* solid; *(personne, certitude, foi)* steadfast, unwavering.

inédit, e [ēnādē, -ēt] *a* (*correspondance etc*) (hitherto) unpublished; (*spectacle, moyen*) novel, original.

ineffable [ēnāfábl(ǝ)] *a* inexpressible, ineffable.

ineffaçable [ēnāfásábl(ǝ)] *a* indelible.

inefficace [ēnāfēkás] *a* (*remède, moyen*) ineffective; (*machine, employé*) inefficient.

inefficacité [ēnāfēkásētā] *nf* ineffectiveness; inefficiency.

inégal, e, aux [ēnāgál, -ō] *a* unequal; (*irrégulier*) uneven.

inégalable [ēnāgálábl(ǝ)] *a* matchless.

inégalé, e [ēnāgálā] *a* unmatched, unequalled.

inégalement [ēnāgálmáń] *ad* unequally.

inégalité [ēnāgálētā] *nf* inequality; unevenness *q*; ~ **de 2 hauteurs** difference *ou* disparity between 2 heights; ~**s de terrain** uneven ground.

inélégance [ēnālāgáńs] *nf* inelegance.

inélégant, e [ēnālāgáń, -áńt] *a* inelegant; (*indélicat*) discourteous.

inéligible [ēnālēzhēbl(ǝ)] *a* ineligible.

inéluctable [ēnālüktábl(ǝ)] *a* inescapable.

inéluctablement [ēnālüktáblǝmáń] *ad* inescapably.

inemployable [ēnáńplwáyábl(ǝ)] *a* unusable.

inemployé, e [ēnáńplwáyā] *a* unused.

inénarrable [ēnānárábl(ǝ)] *a* hilarious.

inepte [ēnept(ǝ)] *a* inept.

ineptie [ēnepsē] *nf* ineptitude; (*propos*) nonsense *q*.

inépuisable [ēnāpüēzábl(ǝ)] *a* inexhaustible.

inéquitable [ēnākētábl(ǝ)] *a* inequitable.

inerte [ēnert(ǝ)] *a* lifeless; (*apathique*) passive, inert; (*PHYSIQUE, CHIMIE*) inert.

inertie [ēnersē] *nf* inertia.

inescompté, e [ēneskóńtā] *a* unexpected, unhoped-for.

inespéré, e [ēnespārā] *a* unhoped-for, unexpected.

inesthétique [ēnestātēk] *a* unsightly.

inestimable [ēnestēmábl(ǝ)] *a* priceless; (*fig: bienfait*) invaluable.

inévitable [ēnāvētábl(ǝ)] *a* unavoidable; (*fatal, habituel*) inevitable.

inévitablement [ēnāvētáblǝmáń] *ad* inevitably.

inexact, e [ēnegzákt] *a* inaccurate, inexact; (*non ponctuel*) unpunctual.

inexactement [ēnegzáktǝmáń] *ad* inaccurately.

inexactitude [ēnegzáktētüd] *nf* inaccuracy.

inexcusable [ēneksküzábl(ǝ)] *a* inexcusable, unforgivable.

inexécutable [ēnegzākütábl(ǝ)] *a* impracticable, unworkable; (*MUS*) unplayable.

inexistant, e [ēnegzēstáń, -áńt] *a* non-existent.

inexorable [ēnegzorábl(ǝ)] *a* inexorable; (*personne: dur*): ~ (**à**) unmoved (by).

inexorablement [ēnegzoráblǝmáń] *ad* inexorably.

inexpérience [ēnekspāryáńs] *nf* inexperience, lack of experience.

inexpérimenté, e [ēnekspārēmáńtā] *a* inexperienced; (*arme, procédé*) untested.

inexplicable [ēneksplēkábl(ǝ)] *a* inexplicable.

inexpliqué, e [ēneksplēkā] *a* unexplained.

inexploité, e [ēneksplwátā] *a* unexploited, untapped.

inexploré, e [ēneksplorā] *a* unexplored.

inexpressif, ive [ēnekspräsēf, -ēv] *a* inexpressive; (*regard etc*) expressionless.

inexpressivité [ēnekspräsēvētā] *nf* expressionlessness.

inexprimable [ēneksprēmábl(ǝ)] *a* inexpressible.

inexprimé, e [ēneksprēmā] *a* unspoken, unexpressed.

inexpugnable [ēnekspügnábl(ǝ)] *a* impregnable.

inextensible [ēnekstáńsēbl(ǝ)] *a* (*tissu*) non-stretch.

in extenso [ēnekstańsō] *ad* in full.

inextinguible [ēnekstáńgēbl(ǝ)] *a* (*soif*) unquenchable; (*rire*) uncontrollable.

in extremis [ēnekstrāmēs] *ad* at the last minute ◊ *a* last-minute; (*testament*) death bed *cpd*.

inextricable [ēnekstrēkábl(ǝ)] *a* inextricable.

inextricablement [ēnekstrēkáblǝmáń] *ad* inextricably.

infaillible [áńfáyēbl(ǝ)] *a* infallible; (*instinct*) infallible, unerring.

infailliblement [áńfáyēblǝmáń] *ad* (*certainement*) without fail.

infaisable [áńfǝzábl(ǝ)] *a* (*travail etc*) impossible, impractical.

infamant, e [áńfámáń, -áńt] *a* libel(l)ous (*US*), libellous (*Brit*), defamatory.

infâme [áńfám] *a* vile.

infamie [áńfámē] *nf* infamy.

infanterie [áńfáńtrē] *nf* infantry.

infanticide [áńfáńtēsēd] *nm/f* child-murderer/ eress ◊ *nm* (*meurtre*) infanticide.

infantile [áńfáńtēl] *a* (*MÉD*) infantile, child *cpd*; (*péj: ton, réaction*) infantile, childish.

infantilisme [áńfáńtēlēsm(ǝ)] *nm* infantilism.

infarctus [áńfárktüs] *nm*: ~ (**du myocarde**) coronary (thrombosis).

infatigable [áńfátēgábl(ǝ)] *a* tireless, indefatigable.

infatué, e [áńfátüā] *a* conceited; ~ **de** full of.

infécond, e [áńfākóń, -óńd] *a* infertile, barren.

infect, e [áńfekt] *a* vile, foul; (*repas, vin*) revolting, foul.

infecter [áńfektā] *vt* (*atmosphère, eau*) to contaminate; (*MÉD*) to infect; **s'~** to become infected *ou* septic.

infectieux, euse [áńfeksyœ, -œz] *a* infectious.

infection [áńfeksyóń] *nf* infection.

inféoder [áńfāodā] *vt*: **s'~ à** to pledge allegiance to.

inférer [áńfārā] *vt*: ~ **qch de** to infer sth from.

inférieur, e [áńfāryœr] *a* lower; (*en qualité, intelligence*) inferior ◊ *nm/f* inferior; ~ **à** (*somme, quantité*) less *ou* smaller than; (*moins bon que*) inferior to; (*tâche: pas à la hauteur de*) unequal to.

infériorité [áńfāryorētā] *nf* inferiority; ~ **en nombre** inferiority in numbers.

infernal, e, aux [áńfernál, -ō] *a* (*chaleur, rythme*) infernal; (*méchanceté, complot*) diabolical.

infester [áńfestā] *vt* to infest; **infesté de moustiques** infested with mosquitoes, mosquito-ridden.

infidèle [áńfēdel] *a* unfaithful; (*REL*) infidel.

infidélité [aṅfēdālētā] *nf* unfaithfulness *q*.

infiltration [aṅfēltrásyóṅ] *nf* infiltration.

infiltrer [aṅfēltrā]: **s'~** *vi*: **s'~ dans** to penetrate into; (*liquide*) to seep into; (*fig: noyauter*) to infiltrate.

infime [aṅfēm] *a* minute, tiny; (*inférieur*) lowly.

infini, e [aṅfēnē] *a* infinite ♦ *nm* infinity; **à l'~** (*MATH*) to infinity; (*discourir*) ad infinitum, endlessly; (*agrandir, varier*) infinitely; (*à perte de vue*) endlessly (into the distance).

infiniment [aṅfēnēmáṅ] *ad* infinitely; **~ grand/petit** (*MATH*) infinitely great/ infinitesimal.

infinité [aṅfēnētā] *nf*: **une ~ de** an infinite number of.

infinitésimal, e, aux [aṅfēnētāzēmál, -ō] *a* infinitesimal.

infinitif, ive [aṅfēnētēf, -ēv] *a, nm* infinitive.

infirme [aṅfērm(ə)] *a* disabled ♦ *nm/f* disabled person; **~ mental** mentally handicapped person; **~ moteur** spastic; **~ de guerre** handicapped veteran (*US*), war cripple (*Brit*); **~ du travail** industrially disabled person.

infirmer [aṅfērmā] *vt* to invalidate.

infirmerie [aṅfērmərē] *nf* sick bay.

infirmier, ière [aṅfērmyā, -yer] *nm/f* nurse ♦ *a*: **élève ~** student nurse; **infirmière chef** head nurse (*US*), sister (*Brit*); **infirmière diplômée** registered nurse; **infirmière visiteuse** visiting nurse (*US*), ≈ district nurse (*Brit*).

infirmité [aṅfērmētā] *nf* disability.

inflammable [aṅflāmábl(ə)] *a* (in)flammable.

inflammation [aṅflāmāsyóṅ] *nf* inflammation.

inflammatoire [aṅflāmátwár] *a* (*MÉD*) inflammatory.

inflation [aṅflāsyóṅ] *nf* inflation; **~ rampante/galopante** creeping/galloping inflation.

inflationniste [aṅflāsyonēst(ə)] *a* inflationist.

infléchir [aṅflāshēr] *vt* (*fig: politique*) to reorientate, redirect; **s'~** *vi* (*poutre, tringle*) to bend, sag.

inflexibilité [aṅflēksēbēlētā] *nf* inflexibility.

inflexible [aṅflēksēbl(ə)] *a* inflexible.

inflexion [aṅflēksyóṅ] *nf* inflection; **~ de la tête** slight nod (of the head).

infliger [aṅflēzhā] *vt*: **~ qch (à qn)** to inflict sth (on sb); (*amende, sanction*) to impose sth (on sb).

influençable [aṅflüáṅsábl(ə)] *a* easily influenced.

influence [aṅflüáṅs] *nf* influence; (*d'un médicament*) effect.

influencer [aṅflüáṅsā] *vt* to influence.

influent, e [aṅflüáṅ, -áṅt] *a* influential.

influer [aṅflüā]: **~ sur** *vt* to have an influence upon.

influx [aṅflü] *nm*: **~ nerveux** (nervous) impulse.

infographie [aṅfogrāfē] *nf* computer graphics *sg*.

informateur, trice [aṅformátœr, -trēs] *nm/f* informant.

informaticien, ne [aṅformátēsyaṅ, -en] *nm/f* computer scientist.

informatif, ive [aṅformátēf, -ēv] *a* informative.

information [aṅformāsyóṅ] *nf* (*renseignement*) piece of information; (*PRESSE, TV: nouvelle*) item of news; (*diffusion de renseignements, INFORM*) information; (*JUR*) inquiry, investigation; **~s** *nfpl* (*TV*) news *sg*; **voyage d'~** fact-finding trip; **agence d'~** news agency; **journal d'~** serious newspaper.

informatique [aṅformátēk] *nf* (*technique*) data processing; (*science*) computer science ♦ *a* computer *cpd*.

informatisation [aṅformātēzásyóṅ] *nf* computerization.

informatiser [aṅformátēzā] *vt* to computerize.

informe [aṅform(ə)] *a* shapeless.

informé, e [aṅformā] *a*: **jusqu'à plus ample ~** until further information is available.

informer [aṅformā] *vt*: **~ qn (de)** to inform sb (of) ♦ *vi* (*JUR*): **~ contre qn/sur qch** to initiate inquiries about sb/sth; **s'~ (sur)** to inform o.s. (about); **s'~ (de qch/si)** to inquire *ou* find out (about sth/whether *ou* if).

informulé, e [aṅformülā] *a* unformulated.

infortune [aṅfortün] *nf* misfortune.

infos [aṅfō] *nfpl* (= *informations*) news.

infraction [aṅfráksyóṅ] *nf* offence; **~ à** violation *ou* breach of; **être en ~** to be in breach of the law.

infranchissable [aṅfráṅshēsábl(ə)] *a* impassable; (*fig*) insuperable.

infrarouge [aṅfrárōōzh] *a, nm* infrared.

infrason [aṅfrásóṅ] *nm* infrasonic vibration.

infrastructure [aṅfrástrüktür] *nf* (*d'une route etc*) substructure; (*AVIAT, MIL*) ground installations *pl*; (*touristique etc*) facilities.

infréquentable [aṅfrākáṅtábl(ə)] *a* not to be associated with.

infroissable [aṅfrwásábl(ə)] *a* crease-resistant.

infructueux, euse [aṅfrüktüœ, -œz] *a* fruitless, unfruitful.

infus, e [aṅfü, -üz] *a*: **avoir la science ~e** to have innate knowledge.

infuser [aṅfüzā] *vt* (*aussi*: **faire ~**: *thé*) to brew; (: *tisane*) to infuse ♦ *vi* to brew; to infuse; **laisser ~** (to leave) to brew.

infusion [aṅfüzyóṅ] *nf* (*tisane*) infusion, herb tea.

ingambe [aṅgáṅb] *a* spry, nimble.

ingénier [aṅzhānyā]: **s'~** *vi*: **s'~ à faire** to strive to do.

ingénierie [aṅzhānērē] *nf* engineering.

ingénieur [aṅzhānycer] *nm* engineer; **~ agronome/chimiste** agricultural/chemical engineer; **~ conseil** consulting engineer; **~ du son** sound engineer.

ingénieusement [aṅzhānyœzmáṅ] *ad* ingeniously.

ingénieux, euse [aṅzhānyœ, -œz] *a* ingenious, clever.

ingéniosité [aṅzhānyōzētā] *nf* ingenuity.

ingénu, e [aṅzhānü] *a* ingenuous, artless ♦ *nf* (*THÉÂTRE*) ingénue.

ingénuité [aṅzhānüētā] *nf* ingenuousness.

ingénument [aṅzhānümáṅ] *ad* ingenuously.

ingérence [aṅzhāráṅs] *nf* interference.

ingérer [aṅzhārā]: **s'~** *vi*: **s'~ dans** to interfere in.

ingouvernable [aṅgōōvernábl(ə)] *a* ungovernable.

ingrat, e [aṅgrá, -át] *a* (*personne*) ungrateful; (*sol*) poor; (*travail, sujet*) arid, thankless; (*visage*) unprepossessing.

ingratitude [aṅgràtɛtüd] *nf* ingratitude.
ingrédient [aṅgrādyáṅ] *nm* ingredient.
inguérissable [aṅgārēsábl(ə)] *a* incurable.
ingurgiter [aṅgürzhētā] *vt* to swallow; **faire ~ qch à qn** to make sb swallow sth; (*fig: connaissances*) to force sth into sb.
inhabile [ēnábēl] *a* clumsy; (*fig*) inept.
inhabitable [ēnábētábl(ə)] *a* uninhabitable.
inhabité, e [ēnábētā] *a* (*régions*) uninhabited; (*maison*) unoccupied.
inhabituel, le [ēnábētüel] *a* unusual.
inhalateur [ēnálátœr] *nm* inhaler; ~ **d'oxygène** oxygen mask.
inhalation [ēnálásyóṅ] *nf* (*MÉD*) inhalation; **faire des ~s** to use an inhalation bath.
inhaler [ēnálā] *vt* to inhale.
inhérent, e [ēnāráṅ, -áṅt] *a*: ~ **à** inherent in.
inhiber [ēnēbā] *vt* to inhibit.
inhibition [ēnēbēsyóṅ] *nf* inhibition.
inhospitalier, ière [ēnospētályā, -yer] *a* inhospitable.
inhumain, e [ēnümaṅ, -en] *a* inhuman.
inhumation [ēnümásyóṅ] *nf* interment, burial.
inhumer [ēnümā] *vt* to inter, bury.
inimaginable [ēnēmázhēnábl(ə)] *a* unimaginable.
inimitable [ēnēmētábl(ə)] *a* inimitable.
inimitié [ēnēmētyā] *nf* enmity.
ininflammable [ēnaṅflámábl(ə)] *a* nonflammable.
inintelligent, e [ēnaṅtālēzhâṅ, áṅt] *a* unintelligent.
inintelligible [ēnaṅtālēzhēbl(ə)] *a* unintelligible.
inintéressant, e [ēnaṅtāresáṅ, -áṅt] *a* uninteresting.
ininterrompu, e [ēnaṅtcrôṅpü] *a* (*file, série*) unbroken; (*flot, vacarme*) uninterrupted, non-stop; (*effort*) unremitting, continuous.
iniquité [ēnēkētā] *nf* iniquity.
initial, e, aux [ēnēsyál, -ō] *a, nf* initial; ~**es** *nfpl* initials.
initialement [ēnēsyálmáṅ] *ad* initially.
initialiser [ēnēsyálēzā] *vt* to initialize.
initiateur, trice [ēnēsyátœr, -trēs] *nm/f* initiator; (*d'une mode, technique*) innovator, pioneer.
initiation [ēnēsyásyóṅ] *nf* initiation.
initiatique [ēnēsyátēk] *a* (*rites, épreuves*) initiatory.
initiative [ēnēsyátēv] *nf* initiative; **prendre l'~ de qch/de faire** to take the initiative for sth/of doing; **avoir de l'~** to have initiative, show enterprise; **esprit/qualités d'~** spirit/qualities of initiative; **à** *ou* **sur l'~ de qn** on sb's initiative; **de sa propre ~** on one's own initiative.
initié, e [ēnēsyā] *a* initiated ♦ *nm/f* initiate.
initier [ēnēsyā] *vt* to initiate; ~ **qn à** to initiate sb into; (*faire découvrir: art, jeu*) to introduce sb to; **s'~ à** (*métier, profession, technique*) to become initiated into.
injecté, e [aṅzhektā] *a*: **yeux ~s de sang** bloodshot eyes.
injecter [aṅzhektā] *vt* to inject.
injection [aṅzhɛksyóṅ] *nf* injection; **à ~** (*AUTO*) fuel injection *cpd*.
injonction [aṅzhóṅksyóṅ] *nf* injunction, order; ~ **de payer** (*JUR*) order to pay.

injouable [aṅywábl(ə)] *a* unplayable.
injure [aṅzhür] *nf* insult, abuse *q*.
injurier [aṅzhüryā] *vt* to insult, abuse.
injurieux, euse [aṅzhüryœ̄, -œ̄z] *a* abusive, insulting.
injuste [aṅzhüst(ə)] *a* unjust, unfair.
injustement [aṅyüstəmáṅ] *ad* unjustly, unfairly.
injustice [aṅzhüstēs] *nf* injustice.
injustifiable [aṅyüstēfyábl(ə)] *a* unjustifiable.
injustifié, e [aṅyüstēfyā] *a* unjustified, unwarranted.
inlassable [aṅlásábl(ə)] *a* tireless, indefatigable.
inné, e [ēnā] *a* innate, inborn.
innocemment [ēnosámáṅ] *ad* innocently.
innocence [ēnosáṅs] *nf* innocence.
innocent, e [ēnosáṅ, -áṅt] *a* innocent ♦ *nm/f* innocent person; **faire l'~** to play *ou* come the innocent.
innocenter [ēnosáṅtā] *vt* to clear, prove innocent.
innocuité [ēnoküētā] *nf* innocuousness.
innombrable [ēnóṅbrábl(ə)] *a* innumerable.
innommable [ēnomábl(ə)] *a* unspeakable.
innovateur, trice [ēnóvátœr, -trēs] *a* innovatory.
innovation [ēnovásyóṅ] *nf* innovation.
innover [ēnóvā] *vi*: ~ **en matière d'art** to break new ground in the field of art.
inobservance [ēnopservà́ns] *nf* nonobservance.
inobservation [ēnopservásyóṅ] *nf* nonobservation, inobservance.
inoccupé, e [ēnóküpā] *a* unoccupied.
inoculer [ēnokülā] *vt*: ~ **qch à qn** (*volontairement*) to inoculate sb with sth; (*accidentellement*) to infect sb with sth; ~ **qn contre** to inoculate sb against.
inodore [ēnodor] *a* (*gaz*) odorless (*US*), odourless (*Brit*); (*fleur*) scentless.
inoffensif, ive [ēnofáṅsēf, -ēv] *a* harmless, innocuous.
inondable [ēnóṅdábl(ə)] *a* (*zone etc*) liable to flooding.
inondation [ēnóṅdâsyóṅ] *nf* flooding *q*; (*torrent, eau*) flood.
inonder [ēnóṅdā] *vt* to flood; (*fig*) to inundate, overrun; ~ **de** (*fig*) to flood *ou* swamp with.
inopérable [ēnopárábl(ə)] *a* inoperable.
inopérant, e [ēnopáráṅ, -áṅt] *a* inoperative, ineffective.
inopiné, e [ēnopēnā] *a* unexpected, sudden.
inopinément [ēnopēnámáṅ] *ad* unexpectedly.
inopportun, e [ēnoportœṅ, -ün] *a* ill-timed, untimely; inappropriate; (*moment*) inopportune.
inorganisation [ēnorgánēzâsyóṅ] *nf* lack of organization.
inorganisé, e [ēnorgánēzā] *a* (*travailleurs*) unorganized.
inoubliable [ēnōōblēyábl(ə)] *a* unforgettable.
inouï, e [ēnwē] *a* unheard-of, extraordinary.
inox [ēnoks] *a, nm* (= *inoxydable*) stainless (steel).
inoxydable [ēnoksēdábl(ə)] *a* stainless; (*couverts*) stainless steel *cpd*.
inqualifiable [aṅkálēfyábl(ə)] *a* unspeakable.
inquiet, ète [aṅkye, -et] *a* (*par nature*)

anxious; *(momentanément)* worried; ~ **de qch/au sujet de qn** worried about sth/sb.

inquiétant, e [aṅkyātāṅ, -āṅt] *a* worrying, disturbing.

inquiéter [aṅkyātā] *vt* to worry, disturb; *(harceler)* to harass; **s'**~ to worry, become anxious; **s'**~ **de** to worry about; *(s'enquérir de)* to inquire about.

inquiétude [aṅkyātüd] *nf* anxiety; **donner de l'**~ *ou* **des** ~**s à** to worry; **avoir de l'**~ *ou* **des** ~**s au sujet de** to feel anxious *ou* worried about.

inquisiteur, trice [aṅkēzētœr, -trēs] *a (regards, questions)* inquisitive, prying.

inquisition [aṅkēzēsyóṅ] *nf* inquisition.

INR *sigle m* = *Institut national (belge) de radiodiffusion*.

INRA [ēnrá] *sigle m* = *Institut national de la recherche agronomique*.

insaisissable [aṅsāzēsábl(ə)] *a* elusive.

insalubre [aṅsálübr(ə)] *a* insalubrious, unhealthy.

insanité [aṅsánētā] *nf* madness *q*, insanity *q*.

insatiable [aṅsásyábl(ə)] *a* insatiable.

insatisfaction [aṅsátēsfáksyóṅ] *nf* dissatisfaction.

insatisfait, e [aṅsátēsfe, -et] *a (non comblé)* unsatisfied; *(: passion, envie)* unfulfilled; *(mécontent)* dissatisfied.

inscription [aṅskrēpsyóṅ] *nf (sur un mur, écriteau etc)* inscription; *(à une institution: voir s'inscrire)* enrollment *(US)*, enrolment *(Brit)*; registration.

inscrire [aṅskrēr] *vt (marquer: sur son calepin etc)* to note *ou* write down; *(: sur un mur, une affiche etc)* to write; *(: dans la pierre, le métal)* to inscribe; *(mettre: sur une liste, un budget etc)* to put down; *(enrôler: soldat)* to enlist; ~ **qn à** *(club, école etc)* to enroll *(US)* ou enrol *(Brit)* sb at; **s'**~ *(pour une excursion etc)* to put one's name down; **s'**~ **(à)** *(club, parti)* to join; *(université)* to register *ou* enroll (at); *(examen, concours)* to register *ou* enter (for); **s'**~ **dans** *(se situer: négociations etc)* to come within the scope of; **s'**~ **en faux contre** to deny (strongly); *(JUR)* to challenge.

inscrit, e [aṅskrē, ēt] *pp de* **inscrire** ♦ *a (étudiant, électeur etc)* registered.

insecte [aṅsekt(ə)] *nm* insect.

insecticide [aṅsektēsēd] *nm* insecticide.

insécurité [aṅsākürētā] *nf* insecurity, lack of security.

INSEE [ēnsā] *sigle m* (= *Institut national de la statistique et des études économiques*) *national institute of statistical and economic information*.

insémination [aṅsāmēnásyóṅ] *nf* insemination.

insensé, e [aṅsáṅsā] *a* insane, mad.

insensibiliser [aṅsáṅsēbēlēzā] *vt* to anesthetize *(US)*, anaesthetize *(Brit)*; *(à une allergie)* to desensitize; ~ **à qch** *(fig)* to cause to become insensitive to sth.

insensibilité [aṅsáṅsēbēlētā] *nf* insensitivity.

insensible [aṅsáṅsēbl(ə)] *a (nerf, membre)* numb; *(dur, indifférent)* insensitive; *(imperceptible)* imperceptible.

insensiblement [aṅsáṅsēbləmáṅ] *ad (doucement, peu à peu)* imperceptibly.

inséparable [aṅsāpáráb l(ə)] *a:* ~ **(de)** inseparable (from) ♦ *nmpl:* ~**s** *(oiseaux)* lovebirds.

insérer [aṅsārā] *vt* to insert; **s'**~ **dans** to fit into; *(fig)* to come within.

INSERM [aṅserm] *sigle m* (= *Institut national de la santé et de la recherche médicale*) *national institute for medical research*.

insert [aṅser] *nm* enclosed fireplace burning solid fuel.

insertion [aṅsersyóṅ] *nf (d'une personne)* integration.

insidieusement [aṅsēdyœzmáṅ] *ad* insidiously.

insidieux, euse [aṅsēdyœ, -œz] *a* insidious.

insigne [aṅsēny] *nm (d'un parti, club)* badge ♦ *a* distinguished; ~**s** *nmpl (d'une fonction)* insignia *pl*.

insignifiant, e [aṅsēnyēfyáṅ, -áṅt] *a* insignificant; *(somme, affaire, détail)* trivial, insignificant.

insinuant, e [aṅsēnüáṅ, -áṅt] *a* ingratiating.

insinuation [aṅsēnüásyóṅ] *nf* innuendo, insinuation.

insinuer [aṅsēnüā] *vt* to insinuate, imply; **s'**~ **dans** to seep into; *(fig)* to worm one's way into, creep into.

insipide [aṅsēpēd] *a* insipid.

insistance [aṅsēstáṅs] *nf* insistence; **avec** ~ insistently.

insistant, e [aṅsēstáṅ, -áṅt] *a* insistent.

insister [aṅsēstā] *vi* to insist; *(s'obstiner)* to keep on; ~ **sur** *(détail, note)* to stress; ~ **pour qch/pour faire qch** to be insistent about sth/about doing sth.

insociable [aṅsosyábl(ə)] *a* unsociable.

insolation [aṅsolásyóṅ] *nf (MÉD)* sunstroke *q*; *(ensoleillement)* period of sunshine.

insolence [aṅsoláṅs] *nf* insolence *q*; **avec** ~ insolently.

insolent, e [aṅsoláṅ, -áṅt] *a* insolent.

insolite [aṅsolēt] *a* strange, unusual.

insoluble [aṅsolübl(ə)] *a* insoluble.

insolvable [aṅsolvábl(ə)] *a* insolvent.

insomniaque [aṅsomnyák] *a, nm/f* insomniac.

insomnie [aṅsomnē] *nf* insomnia *q*, sleeplessness *q*; **avoir des** ~**s** to suffer from insomnia.

insondable [aṅsóṅdábl(ə)] *a* unfathomable.

insonore [aṅsonor] *a* soundproof.

insonorisation [aṅsonorēzásyóṅ] *nf* soundproofing.

insonoriser [aṅsonorēzā] *vt* to soundproof.

insouciance [aṅsōōsyáṅs] *nf* carefree attitude; heedless attitude.

insouciant, e [aṅsōōsyáṅ, -áṅt] *a* carefree; *(imprévoyant)* heedless.

insoumis, e [aṅsōōmē, -ēz] *a (caractère, enfant)* rebellious, refractory; *(contrée, tribu)* unsubdued; *(MIL: soldat)* AWOL, absent without leave ♦ *nm (MIL: soldat)* AWOL *(US)*, absentee *(Brit)*.

insoumission [aṅsōōmēsyóṅ] *nf* rebelliousness; *(MIL)* absence without leave.

insoupçonnable [aṅsōōpsonábl(ə)] *a* above suspicion.

insoupçonné, e [aṅsōōpsonā] *a* unsuspected.

insoutenable [aṅsōōtnábl(ə)] *a (argument)* untenable; *(chaleur)* unbearable.

inspecter [aṅspektā] *vt* to inspect.

inspecteur, trice [añspektœr, -trēs] *nm/f* inspector; *(des assurances)* assessor; ~ **d'Académie** ≈ accreditation officer *(US)*, (regional) director of education; ~ **des finances** ≈ Internal Revenue Service agent *(US)*, ≈ tax inspector *(Brit)*; ~ **(de police)** (police) inspector.

inspection [añspeksyôñ] *nf* inspection.

inspirateur, trice [añspērátœr, -trēs] *nm/f (instigateur)* instigator; *(animateur)* inspirer.

inspiration [añspērâsyôñ] *nf* inspiration; breathing in *q*; *(idée)* flash of inspiration, brain wave; **sous l'~ de** prompted by.

inspiré, e [añspērā] *a*: **être bien/mal ~ de faire qch** to be well-advised/ill-advised to do sth.

inspirer [añspērā] *vt (gén)* to inspire ♦ *vi (aspirer)* to breathe in; **s'~ de** *(suj: artiste)* to draw one's inspiration from; *(suj: tableau)* to be inspired by; ~ **qch à qn** *(œuvre, project, action)* to inspire sb with sth; *(dégoût, crainte, honneur)* to fill sb with sth; **ça ne m'inspire pas** I'm not crazy about the idea.

instabilité [añstábēlētā] *nf* instability.

instable [añstábl(ə)] *a (meuble, équilibre)* unsteady; *(population, temps)* unsettled; *(paix, régime, caractère)* unstable.

installateur [añstálátœr] *nm* fitter.

installation [añstálâsyôñ] *nf* installation; putting in *ou* up; fitting out; settling in; *(appareils etc)* fittings *pl*, installations *pl*; ~**s** *nfpl* installations; *(industrielles)* plant *sg*; *(de loisirs)* facilities.

installé, e [añstálā] *a*: **bien/mal ~** well/poorly equipped; *(personne)* well/not very well set up *ou* organized.

installer [añstálā] *vt (loger)*: ~ **qn** to get sb settled, install sb; *(asseoir, coucher)* to settle (down); *(placer)* to put, place; *(meuble)* to put in; *(rideau, étagère, tente)* to put up; *(gaz, électricité etc)* to put in, install; **s'~** *(s'établir: artisan, dentiste etc)* to set o.s. up; *(se loger)*: **s'~ à l'hôtel/chez qn** to move into a hotel/in with sb; *(emménager)* to settle in; *(sur un siège, à un emplacement)* to settle (down); *(fig: maladie, grève)* to take a firm hold *ou* grip.

instamment [añstámáñ] *ad* urgently.

instance [añstáñs] *nf (JUR: procédure)* (legal) proceedings *pl*; *(ADMIN: autorité)* authority; ~**s** *nfpl (prières)* entreaties; **affaire en ~** matter pending; **courrier en ~** mail ready for mailing *(US)* ou posting *(Brit)*; **être en ~ de divorce** to be awaiting a divorce; **train en ~ de départ** train on the point of departure; **tribunal de première ~** court of first instance; **en seconde ~** on appeal.

instant [añstáñ] *nm* moment, instant; **dans un ~** in a moment; **à l'~** this instant; **je l'ai vu à l'~** I've just this minute seen him, I saw him a moment ago; **à l'~ (même) où** at the (very) moment that *ou* when, (just) as; **à chaque ~, à tout ~** at any moment; constantly; **pour l'~** for the moment, for the time being; **par ~s** at times; **de tous les ~s** perpetual; **dès l'~ où** *ou* **que ...** from the moment when ..., since that moment when ....

instantané, e [añstáñtánā] *a (lait, café)* instant; *(explosion, mort)* instantaneous ♦ *nm* snapshot.

instantanément [añstáñtánāmáñ] *ad* instantaneously.

instar [añstár]: **à l'~ de** *prép* following the example of, like.

instaurer [añstorā] *vt* to institute; **s'~** *vi* to set o.s. up; *(collaboration etc)* to be established.

instigateur, trice [añstēgátœr, -trēs] *nm/f* instigator.

instigation [añstēgásyôñ] *nf*: **à l'~ de qn** at sb's instigation.

instiller [añstēlā] *vt* to instill *(US)*, instil *(Brit)*, apply.

instinct [añstañ] *nm* instinct; **d'~** *(spontanément)* instinctively; ~ **grégaire** herd instinct; ~ **de conservation** instinct of self-preservation.

instinctif, ive [añstañktēf, -ēv] *a* instinctive.

instinctivement [añstañktēvmáñ] *ad* instinctively.

instituer [añstētüā] *vt* to institute, set up; **s'~ défenseur d'une cause** to set o.s up as defender of a cause.

institut [añstētü] *nm* institute; ~ **de beauté** beauty salon; ~ **médico-légal** mortuary; **I~ universitaire de technologie (IUT)** technical college.

instituteur, trice [añstētütœr, -trēs] *nm/f* (grade *(US)* ou primary *(Brit)* school) teacher.

institution [añstētüsyôñ] *nf* institution; *(collège)* private school.

institutionnaliser [añstētüsyonálēzā] *vt* to institutionalize.

instructeur, trice [añstrüktœr, -trēs] *a (MIL)*: **sergent ~** drill sergeant; *(JUR)*: **juge ~** committing *(US)* ou examining *(Brit)* magistrat ♦ *nm/f* instructor.

instructif, ive [añstrüktēf, -ēv] *a* instructive.

instruction [añstrüksyôñ] *nf (enseignement, savoir)* education; *(JUR)* (preliminary) investigation and hearing; *(directive)* instruction; *(ADMIN: document)* directive; ~**s** *nfpl* instructions; *(mode d'emploi)* directions, instructions; ~ **civique** civics *sg*; ~ **primaire/ publique** elementary/public education; ~ **religieuse** religious instruction; ~ **professionnelle** vocational training.

instruire [añstrüēr] *vt (élèves)* to teach; *(recrues)* to train; *(JUR: affaire)* to conduct the investigation for; **s'~** to educate o.s.; **s'~ auprès de qn de qch** *(s'informer)* to find sth out from sb; ~ **qn de qch** *(informer)* to inform *ou* advise sb of sth; ~ **contre qn** *(JUR)* to investigate sb.

instruit, e [añstrüē, -ēt] *pp de* **instruire** ♦ *a* educated.

instrument [añstrümáñ] *nm* instrument; ~ **à cordes/vent** stringed/wind instrument; ~ **de mesure** measuring instrument; ~ **de musique** musical instrument; ~ **de travail** (working) tool.

instrumental, e, aux [añstrümáñtál, -ō] *a* instrumental.

instrumentation [añstrümáñtâsyôñ] *nf* instrumentation.

instrumentiste [añstrümáñtēst(ə)] *nm/f* instrumentalist.

insu [ańsü] *nm*: **à l'~ de qn** without sb knowing.

insubmersible [ańsübmersẽbl(ə)] *a* unsinkable.

insubordination [ańsübordẽnåsyôń] *nf* rebelliousness; (*MIL*) insubordination.

insubordonné, e [ańsübordonā] *a* insubordinate.

insuccès [ańsükse] *nm* failure.

insuffisamment [ańsüfēzàmáń] *ad* insufficiently.

insuffisance [ańsüfēzáńs] *nf* insufficiency; inadequacy; **~s** *nfpl* (*lacunes*) inadequacies; **~ cardiaque** cardiac insufficiency *q*; **~ hépatique** liver deficiency.

insuffisant, e [ańsüfēzáń, -áńt] *a* insufficient; (*élève, travail*) inadequate.

insuffler [ańsüflā] *vt*: **~ qch dans** to blow sth into; **~ qch à qn** to inspire sb with sth.

insulaire [ańsüler] *a* island *cpd*; (*attitude*) insular.

insularité [ańsülárētā] *nf* insularity.

insuline [ańsülēn] *nf* insulin.

insultant, e [ańsültáń, -áńt] *a* insulting.

insulte [ańsült(ə)] *nf* insult.

insulter [ańsültā] *vt* to insult.

insupportable [ańsüportåbl(ə)] *a* unbearable.

insurgé, e [ańsürzhā] *a*, *nm/f* insurgent, rebel.

insurger [ańsürzhā]: **s'~** *vi*: **s'~ (contre)** to rise up *ou* rebel (against).

insurmontable [ańsürmôńtåbl(ə)] *a* (*difficulté*) insuperable; (*aversion*) unconquerable.

insurpassable [ańsürpåsåbl(ə)] *a* unsurpassable, unsurpassed.

insurrection [ańsüreksyôń] *nf* insurrection, revolt.

insurrectionnel, le [ańsüreksyonel] *a* insurrectionary.

intact, e [ańtåkt] *a* intact.

intangible [ańtåńzhēbl(ə)] *a* intangible; (*principe*) inviolable.

intarissable [ańtårēsåbl(ə)] *a* inexhaustible.

intégral, e, aux [ańtågrál, -ō] *a* complete ♦ *nf* (*MATH*) integral; (*œuvres complètes*) complete works.

intégralement [ańtågrálmáń] *ad* in full, fully.

intégralité [ańtågrálētā] *nf* (*d'une somme, d'un revenu*) whole (*ou* full) amount; **dans son ~** in its entirety.

intégrant, e [ańtågráń, -áńt] *a*: **faire partie ~e de** to be an integral part of, be part and parcel of.

intégration [ańtågråsyôń] *nf* integration.

intégrationniste [ańtågråsyonēst(ə)] *a*, *nm/f* integrationist.

intègre [ańtegr(ə)] *a* perfectly honest, upright.

intégré, e [ańtågrā] *a*: **circuit ~** integrated circuit.

intégrer [ańtågrā] *vt*: **~ qch à** *ou* **dans** to integrate sth into; **s'~ à** *ou* **dans** to become integrated into.

intégrisme [ańtågrēsm(ə)] *nm* fundamentalism.

intégriste [ańtågrēst(ə)] *a*, *nm/f* fundamentalist.

intégrité [ańtågrētā] *nf* integrity.

intellect [ańtālekt] *nm* intellect.

intellectualisme [ańtāleküálēsm(ə)] *nm* intellectualism.

intellectuel, le [ańtālektüel] *a*, *nm/f* intellectual; (*péj*) highbrow.

intellectuellement [ańtālektüelmáń] *ad* intellectually.

intelligemment [ańtālēzhámáń] *ad* intelligently.

intelligence [ańtālēzháńs] *nf* intelligence; (*compréhension*): **l'~ de** the understanding of; (*complicité*): **regard d'~** glance of complicity, meaningful *ou* knowing look; (*accord*): **vivre en bonne ~ avec qn** to be on good terms with sb; **~s** *nfpl* (*MIL*, *fig*) secret contacts; **être d'~** to have an understanding; **~ artificielle** artificial intelligence (A.I.).

intelligent, e [ańtālēzháń, -áńt] *a* intelligent; (*capable*): **~ en affaires** competent in business.

intelligentsia [ańtālēdzhensyá] *nf* intelligentsia.

intelligible [ańtālēzhēbl(ə)] *a* intelligible.

intello [ańtālō] *a*, *nm/f* (*fam*) highbrow.

intempérance [ańtáńpāráńs] *nf* overindulgence *q*; intemperance *q*.

intempérant, e [ańtáńpāráń, -áńt] *a* overindulgent; (*moralement*) intemperate.

intempéries [ańtáńpārē] *nfpl* bad weather *sg*.

intempestif, ive [ańtáńpestēf, -ēv] *a* untimely.

intenable [ańtnåbl(ə)] *a* unbearable.

intendance [ańtáńdáńs] *nf* (*MIL*) army materiel command (*US*), supply corps (*Brit*); (: *bureau*) supplies office; (*SCOL*) bursar's office.

intendant, e [ańtáńdáń, -áńt] *nm/f* (*MIL*) quartermaster; (*SCOL*) bursar; (*d'une propriété*) steward.

intense [ańtáńs] *a* intense.

intensément [ańtásámáń] *ad* intensely.

intensif, ive [ańtáńsēf, -ēv] *a* intensive; **cours ~** crash course; **~ en main-d'œuvre** labor-intensive; **~ en capital** capital-intensive.

intensifier [ańtáńsēfyā] *vt*, **s'~** *vi* to intensify.

intensité [ańtáńsētā] *nf* intensity.

intensivement [ańtáńsēvmáń] *ad* intensively.

intenter [ańtáńtā] *vt*: **~ un procès contre** *ou* **à qn** to start proceedings against sb.

intention [ańtáńsyoń] *nf* intention; (*JUR*) intent; **avoir l'~ de faire** to intend to do, have the intention of doing; **dans l'~ de faire qch** with a view to doing sth; **à l'~ de** *prép* for; (*renseignement*) for the benefit *ou* information of; (*film, ouvrage*) aimed at; **à cette ~** with this aim in view; **sans ~** unintentionally; **faire qch sans mauvaise ~** to do sth without ill intent; **agir dans une bonne ~** to act with good intentions.

intentionné, e [ańtáńsyonā] *a*: **bien ~** well-meaning *ou* -intentioned; **mal ~** ill-intentioned.

intentionnel, le [ańtáńsyonel] *a* intentional, deliberate.

intentionnellement [ańtáńsyonelmáń] *ad* intentionally, deliberately.

inter [ańter] *nm* (*TÉL*: = *interurbain*) long-distance call service; (*SPORT*): **~ gauche/droit** inside-left/right.

interactif, ive [ańteráktēf, -ēv] *a* (*aussi IN-FORM*) interactive.

interaction [ańteráksyôń] *nf* interaction.

interarmées [aṅterármã] *a inv* inter-army, combined.

interbancaire [aṅterbáṅker] *a* interbank.

intercalaire [aṅterkáler] *a, nm:* **(feuillet)** ~ insert; **(fiche)** ~ divider.

intercaler [aṅterkálã] *vt* to insert; **s'~ entre** to come in between; to slip in between.

intercéder [aṅtersãdã] *vi:* ~ **(pour qn)** to intercede (on behalf of sb).

intercepter [aṅterseptã] *vt* to intercept; *(lumière, chaleur)* to cut off.

intercepteur [aṅterseptœr] *nm (AVIAT)* interceptor.

interception [aṅtersepsyóṅ] *nf* interception; **avion d'~** interceptor.

intercession [aṅtersãsyóṅ] *nf* intercession.

interchangeable [aṅtershãṅzhábl(ə)] *a* interchangeable.

interclasse [aṅterklás] *nm (SCOL)* break (between classes).

interclubs [aṅterklœb] *a inv* interclub.

intercommunal, e, aux [aṅterkomünál, -õ] *a* intervillage, intercommunity.

intercommunautaire [aṅterkomünõter] *a* intercommunity.

interconnexion [aṅterkoneksyóṅ] *nf (INFORM)* networking.

intercontinental, e, aux [aṅterkõṅtẽnãṅtál, -õ] *a* intercontinental.

intercostal, e, aux [aṅterkostál, -õ] *a* intercostal, between the ribs.

interdépartemental, e, aux [aṅterdãpártə- mãṅtál, -õ] interdepartmental.

interdépendance [aṅterdãpãṅdáṅs] *nf* interdependence.

interdépendant, e [aṅterdãpãṅdáṅ, -áṅt] *a* interdependent.

interdiction [aṅterdẽksyóṅ] *nf* ban; ~ **de faire qch** ban on doing sth; ~ **de séjour** *(JUR) order banning ex-prisoner from frequenting specified places.*

interdire [aṅterdẽr] *vt* to forbid; *(ADMIN: stationnement, meeting, passage)* to ban, prohibit; *(: journal, livre)* to ban; ~ **qch à qn** to forbid sb sth; ~ **à qn de faire** to forbid sb to do, prohibit sb from doing; *(suj: empêchement)* to prevent *ou* preclude sb from doing; **s'~ qch** *(éviter)* to refrain *ou* abstain from sth; *(se refuser)*: **il s'interdit d'y penser** he doesn't allow himself to think about it.

interdisciplinaire [aṅterdẽsãplẽner] *a* interdisciplinary.

interdit, e [aṅterdẽ, -ẽt] *pp de* **interdire** ♦ *a (stupéfait)* taken aback; *(défendu)* forbidden, prohibited ♦ *nm* interdict, prohibition; **film ~ aux moins de 18/13 ans** ≈ X-/R-rated *(US) ou* 18-/PG-rated *(Brit)* film; **sens ~** one way; **stationnement ~** no parking; ~ **de chéquier** having checking account *(US) ou* cheque book facilities *(Brit)* suspended; ~ **de séjour** subject to an *interdiction de séjour.*

intéressant, e [aṅtãresáṅ, -áṅt] *a* interesting; **faire l'~** to draw attention to o.s.

intéressé, e [aṅtãrãsã] *a (parties)* involved, concerned; *(amitié, motifs)* self-interested ♦ *nm:* **l'~** the interested party; **les ~s** those concerned *ou* involved.

intéressement [aṅtãresmáṅ] *nm (COMM)*

profit-sharing.

intéresser [aṅtãrãsã] *vt* to interest; *(toucher)* to be of interest *ou* concern to; *(ADMIN: concerner)* to affect, concern; *(COMM: travailleur)* to give a share in the profits to; *(: partenaire)* to interest (in the business); **s'~ à** to take an interest in, be interested in; ~ **qn à qch** to get sb interested in sth.

intérêt [aṅtãre] *nm (aussi COMM)* interest; *(égoïsme)* self-interest; **porter de l'~ à qn** to take an interest in sb; **agir par ~** to act out of self-interest; **avoir des ~s dans** *(COMM)* to have a financial interest *ou* a stake in; **avoir ~ à faire** to do well to do; **il y a ~ à ...** it would be a good thing to ...; ~ **composé** compound interest.

interface [aṅterfás] *nf (INFORM)* interface.

interférence [aṅterfãráṅs] *nf* interference.

interférer [aṅterfãrã] *vi:* ~ **(avec)** to interfere (with).

intergouvernemental, e, aux [aṅtergõõvernə- mãṅtál, -õ] *a* intergovernmental.

intérieur, e [aṅtãryœr] *a (mur, escalier, poche)* inside; *(commerce, politique)* domestic; *(cour, calme, vie)* inner; *(navigation)* inland ♦ *nm (d'une maison, d'un récipient etc)* inside; *(d'un pays, aussi: décor, mobilier)* interior; *(POL):* **l'I~** (the Department of the Interior); **à l'~ (de)** inside; *(fig)* within; **de l'~** *(fig)* from the inside; **en ~** *(CINÉMA)* in the studio; **vêtement d'~** indoor garment.

intérieurement [aṅtãryœrmáṅ] *ad* inwardly.

intérim [aṅterẽm] *nm* interim period; **assurer l'~ (de)** to deputize (for); **par ~** *a* interim ♦ *ad* in a temporary capacity.

intérimaire [aṅterẽmer] *a* temporary, interim ♦ *nm/f (secrétaire etc)* temporary; *(suppléant)* deputy.

intérioriser [aṅtãryorẽzã] *vt* to internalize.

interjection [aṅterzheksyóṅ] *nf* interjection.

interjeter [aṅterzhətã] *vt (JUR):* ~ **appel** to file *(US) ou* lodge *(Brit)* an appeal.

interligne [aṅterlẽny] *nm* interline space ♦ *nf (TYPO)* lead, leading; **simple/double** ~ single/double spacing.

interlocuteur, trice [aṅterlokütœr, -trẽs] *nm/f* speaker; *(POL):* ~ **valable** valid representative; **son** ~ the person he *ou* she was speaking to.

interlope [aṅterlop] *a* illicit; *(milieu, bar)* shady.

interloquer [aṅterlokã] *vt* to take aback.

interlude [aṅterlüd] *nm* interlude.

intermède [aṅtermed] *nm* interlude.

intermédiaire [aṅtermãdyer] *a* intermediate; middle; half-way ♦ *nm/f* intermediary; *(COMM)* middleman; **sans** ~ directly; **par l'~ de** through.

interminable [aṅtermẽnábl(ə)] *a* never-ending.

interminablement [aṅtermẽnáblemáṅ] *ad* interminably.

interministériel, le [aṅtermẽnẽstáryel] *a:* **comité** ~ interdepartmental committee.

intermittence [aṅtermãtáṅs] *nf:* **par** ~ intermittently, sporadically.

intermittent, e [aṅtermãtáṅ, -áṅt] *a* intermittent, sporadic.

internat [aṅternã] *nm (SCOL)* boarding school.

international, e, aux [aṅternãsyonál, -õ] *a,*

nm/f international.

internationaliser [aṅternȧsyonȧlēzȧ] *vt* to internationalize.

internationalisme [aṅternȧsyonȧlēsm(ǝ)] *nm* internationalism.

interne [aṅtern(ǝ)] *a* internal ♦ *nm/f* (*SCOL*) boarder; (*MÉD*) intern (*US*), houseman (*Brit*).

internement [aṅternǝmȧṅ] *nm* (*POL*) internment; (*MÉD*) confinement.

interner [aṅternȧ] *vt* (*POL*) to intern; (*MÉD*) to confine to a mental institution.

interparlementaire [aṅterpȧrlǝmȧṅter] *a* interparliamentary.

interpellation [aṅterpȧlȧsyóṅ] *nf* interpellation; (*POL*) question.

interpeller [aṅterpȧlȧ] *vt* (*appeler*) to call out to; (*apostropher*) to shout at; (*POLICE*) to take in for questioning; (*POL*) to question; **s'~** to exchange insults.

interphone [aṅterfon] *nm* intercom.

interplanétaire [aṅterplȧnȧter] *a* interplanetary.

INTERPOL [aṅterpol] *sigle m* Interpol.

interpoler [aṅterpolȧ] *vt* to interpolate.

interposer [aṅterpōzȧ] *vt* to interpose; **s'~** *vi* to intervene; **par personnes interposées** through a third party.

interprétariat [aṅterprȧtȧryȧ] *nm* interpreting.

interprétation [aṅterprȧtȧsyóṅ] *nf* interpretation.

interprète [aṅterpret] *nm/f* interpreter; (*porte-parole*) spokesman.

interpréter [aṅterprȧtȧ] *vt* to interpret.

interprofessionnel, le [aṅterprofȧsyonel] *a* interprofessional.

interrogateur, trice [aṅtȧrogȧtœr, -trēs] *a* questioning, inquiring ♦ *nm/f* (*SCOL*) (oral) examiner.

interrogatif, ive [aṅtȧrogȧtēf, -ēv] *a* (*LING*) interrogative.

interrogation [aṅtȧrogȧsyóṅ] *nf* question; (*SCOL*) (written *ou* oral) test.

interrogatoire [aṅtȧrogȧtwȧr] *nm* (*POLICE*) questioning *q*; (*JUR*) cross-examination, interrogation.

interroger [aṅtȧrozhȧ] *vt* to question; (*INFORM*) to interrogate; (*SCOL*: *candidat*) to test; **~ qn (sur qch)** to question sb (about sth); **~ qn du regard** to look questioningly at sb, give sb a questioning look; **s'~ sur qch** to ask o.s. about sth, ponder (about) sth.

interrompre [aṅtȧróṅpr(ǝ)] *vt* (*gén*) to interrupt; (*travail, voyage*) to break off, interrupt; **s'~** to break off.

interrupteur [aṅtȧrüptœr] *nm* switch; **~ à bascule** (*INFORM*) toggle switch.

interruption [aṅtȧrüpsyóṅ] *nf* interruption; **sans ~** without a break; **~ de grossesse** termination of pregnancy; **~ volontaire de grossesse** voluntary termination of pregnancy, abortion.

interscolaire [aṅterskoler] *a* interschool(s).

intersection [aṅterseksyóṅ] *nf* intersection.

intersidéral, e, aux [aṅtersēdȧrȧl, -ō] *a* intersidereal, interstellar.

interstice [aṅterstēs] *nm* crack, slit.

intersyndical, e, aux [aṅtersȧndēkȧl, -ō] *a* interunion.

interurbain [aṅterürbaṅ] (*TÉL*) *nm* long-distance call service ♦ *a* long-distance.

intervalle [aṅtervȧl] *nm* (*espace*) space; (*de temps*) interval; **dans l'~** in the meantime; **à 2 mois d'~** after a space of 2 months; **à ~s rapprochés** at close intervals; **par ~s** at intervals.

intervenant, e [aṅtervǝnȧṅ, -ȧṅt] *vb voir* **intervenir** ♦ *nm/f* speaker (*at conference*).

intervenir [aṅtervǝnēr] *vi* (*gén*) to intervene; (*survenir*) to take place; (*faire une conférence*) to give a talk *ou* lecture; **~ auprès de/en faveur de qn** to intervene with/on behalf of sb; **la police a dû ~** police had to step in *ou* intervene; **les médecins ont dû ~** the doctors had to operate.

intervention [aṅtervȧṅsyóṅ] *nf* intervention; (*conférence*) talk, paper; **~ (chirurgicale)** operation.

interventionnisme [aṅtervȧṅsyonēsm(ǝ)] *nm* interventionism.

intervenu, e [aṅtervǝnü] *pp de* **intervenir**.

intervertible [aṅtervertēbl(ǝ)] *a* interchangeable.

intervertir [aṅtervertēr] *vt* to invert (the order of), reverse.

interviendrai [aṅtervyaṅdrȧ], **interviens** [aṅtervyaṅ] *etc vb voir* **intervenir**.

interview [aṅtervyōō] *nf* interview.

interviewer [aṅtervyōōvȧ] *vt* to interview ♦ *nm* [aṅtervyōōvœr] (*journaliste*) interviewer.

intervins [aṅtervaṅ] *etc vb voir* **intervenir**.

intestat [aṅtestȧ] *a* (*JUR*): **décéder ~** to die intestate.

intestin, e [aṅtestaṅ, -ēn] *a* internal ♦ *nm* intestine; **~ grêle** small intestine.

intestinal, e, aux [aṅtestēnȧl, -ō] *a* intestinal.

intime [aṅtēm] *a* intimate; (*vie, journal*) private; (*convictions*) inmost; (*dîner, cérémonie*) held among friends, quiet ♦ *nm/f* close friend.

intimement [aṅtēmmȧṅ] *ad* (*profondément*) deeply, firmly; (*étroitement*) intimately.

intimer [aṅtēmȧ] *vt* (*JUR*) to notify; **~ à qn l'ordre de faire** to order sb to do.

intimider [aṅtēmēdȧ] *vt* to intimidate.

intimité [aṅtēmētȧ] *nf* intimacy; (*vie privée*) privacy; private life; **dans l'~** in private; (*sans formalités*) with only a few friends, quietly.

intitulé [aṅtētülȧ] *nm* title.

intituler [aṅtētülȧ] *vt*: **comment a-t-il intitulé son livre?** what title did he give his book?; **s'~** to be entitled; (*personne*) to call o.s.

intolérable [aṅtolȧrȧbl(ǝ)] *a* intolerable.

intolérant, e [aṅtolȧrȧṅ, -ȧṅt] *a* intolerant.

intonation [aṅtonȧsyóṅ] *nf* intonation.

intouchable [aṅtōōshȧbl(ǝ)] *a* (*fig*) above the law, sacrosanct; (*REL*) untouchable.

intoxication [aṅtoksēkȧsyóṅ] *nf* poisoning *q*; (*toxicomanie*) drug addiction; (*fig*) brainwashing; **~ alimentaire** food poisoning.

intoxiqué, e [aṅtoksēkȧ] *nm/f* addict.

intoxiquer [aṅtoksēkȧ] *vt* to poison; (*fig*) to brainwash; **s'~** to poison o.s.

intraduisible [aṅtrȧdüēzēbl(ǝ)] *a* untranslatable; (*fig*) inexpressible.

intraitable [aṅtretȧbl(ǝ)] *a* inflexible, uncompromising.

intransigeance [aṅtrȧṅzēzhȧṅs] *nf* intransigence.

intransigeant, e [aṅtrȧṅzēzhȧṅ, -ȧṅt] *a* intransigent; (*morale, passion*) uncompromising.

intransitif, ive [aṅtrȧṅzētēf, -ēv] *a* (*LING*) intransitive.

intransportable [aṅtrȧṅsportȧbl(ə)] *a* (*blessé*) unable to travel.

intraveineux, euse [aṅtrȧvenœ̄, -œ̄z] *a* intravenous.

intrépide [aṅtrȧpēd] *a* dauntless, intrepid.

intrigant, e [aṅtrēgȧṅ, -ȧṅt] *nm/f* schemer.

intrigue [aṅtrēg] *nf* intrigue; (*scénario*) plot.

intriguer [aṅtrēgȧ] *vi* to scheme ♦ *vt* to puzzle, intrigue.

intrinsèque [aṅtraṅsek] *a* intrinsic.

introductif, ive [aṅtrodüktēf, -ēv] *a* introductory.

introduction [aṅtrodüksyôṅ] *nf* introduction; **paroles/chapitre d'~** introductory words/chapter; **lettre/mot d'~** letter/note of introduction.

introduire [aṅtrodüēr] *vt* to introduce; (*visiteur*) to show in; (*aiguille, clef*): ~ **qch dans** to insert *ou* introduce sth into; (*personne*): ~ **à qch** to introduce to sth; (: *présenter*): ~ **qn à qn/dans un club** to introduce sb to sb/to a club; (*INFORM*) to input, enter; **s'~** (*techniques, usages*) to be introduced; **s'~ dans** to gain entry into; to get o.s. accepted into; (*eau, fumée*) to get into; ~ **au clavier** to key in.

introduit, e [aṅtrodüē, -ēt] *pp de* **introduire** ♦ *a*: **bien ~** (*personne*) well-received.

introniser [aṅtronēzȧ] *vt* to enthrone.

introspection [aṅtrospeksyôṅ] *nf* introspection.

introuvable [aṅtrōōvȧbl(ə)] *a* which cannot be found; (*COMM*) unobtainable.

introverti, e [aṅtrovertē] *nm/f* introvert.

intrus, e [aṅtrü, -üz] *nm/f* intruder.

intrusion [aṅtrüzyôṅ] *nf* intrusion; (*ingérence*) interference.

intuitif, ive [aṅtüētēf, -ēv] *a* intuitive.

intuition [aṅtüēsyôṅ] *nf* intuition; **avoir une ~** to have a feeling; **avoir l'~ de qch** to have an intuition of sth; **avoir de l'~** to have intuition.

intuitivement [aṅtüētēvmȧṅ] *ad* intuitively.

inusable [ēnüzȧbl(ə)] *a* wear-resistant.

inusité, e [ēnüzētȧ] *a* rarely used.

inutile [ēnütēl] *a* useless; (*superflu*) unnecessary.

inutilement [ēnütēlmȧṅ] *ad* needlessly.

inutilisable [ēnütēlēzȧbl(ə)] *a* unusable.

inutilisé, e [ēnütēlēzȧ] *a* unused.

inutilité [ēnütēlētȧ] *nf* uselessness.

invaincu, e [aṅvaṅkü] *a* unbeaten; (*armée, peuple*) unconquered.

invalide [aṅvȧlēd] *a* disabled ♦ *nm/f*: ~ **de guerre** disabled veteran (*US*) *ou* ex-serviceman (*Brit*); ~ **du travail** industrially disabled person.

invalider [aṅvȧlēdȧ] *vt* to invalidate.

invalidité [aṅvȧlēdētȧ] *nf* disability.

invariable [aṅvȧryȧbl(ə)] *a* invariable.

invariablement [aṅvȧryȧbləmȧṅ] *ad* invariably.

invasion [aṅvȧzyôṅ] *nf* invasion.

invective [aṅvektēv] *nf* invective.

invectiver [aṅvektēvȧ] *vt* to hurl abuse at ♦ *vi*: ~ **contre** to rail against.

invendable [aṅvȧṅdȧbl(ə)] *a* unsaleable, unmarketable.

invendu, e [aṅvȧṅdü] *a* unsold ♦ *nm* return; **~s** *nmpl* unsold goods.

inventaire [aṅvȧṅter] *nm* inventory; (*COMM*: *liste*) stocklist; (: *opération*) stocktaking *q*; (*fig*) survey; **faire un ~** to make an inventory; (*COMM*) to take stock; **faire** *ou* **procéder à l'~** to take stock.

inventer [aṅvȧṅtȧ] *vt* to invent; (*subterfuge*) to devise, invent; (*histoire, excuse*) to make up, invent; ~ **de faire** to hit on the idea of doing.

inventeur, trice [aṅvȧṅtœr, -trēs] inventor.

inventif, ive [aṅvȧṅtēf, -ēv] *a* inventive.

invention [aṅvȧṅsyôṅ] *nf* invention; (*imagination, inspiration*) inventiveness.

inventivité [aṅvȧṅtēvētȧ] *nf* inventiveness.

inventorier [aṅvȧṅtoryȧ] *vt* to make an inventory of.

invérifiable [aṅvȧrēfyȧbl(ə)] *a* unverifiable.

inverse [aṅvers(ə)] *a* (*ordre*) reverse; (*sens*) opposite; (*rapport*) inverse ♦ *nm* reverse; inverse; **en proportion ~** in inverse proportion; **dans le sens ~ des aiguilles d'une montre** counterclockwise (*US*), anticlockwise (*Brit*); **en sens ~** in (*ou* from) the opposite direction; **à l'~** conversely.

inversement [aṅversəmȧṅ] *ad* conversely.

inverser [aṅversȧ] *vt* to reverse, invert; (*ÉLEC*) to reverse.

inversion [aṅversyôṅ] *nf* reversal; inversion.

invertébré, e [aṅvertȧbrȧ] *a, nm* invertebrate.

inverti, e [aṅvertē] *nm/f* homosexual.

investigation [aṅvestēgȧsyôṅ] *nf* investigation, inquiry.

investir [aṅvestēr] *vt* to invest; **s'~** *vi* (*PSYCH*) to involve o.s.; ~ **qn de** to vest *ou* invest sb with.

investissement [aṅvestēsmȧṅ] *nm* investment; (*PSYCH*) involvement.

investiture [aṅvestētür] *nf* investiture; (*à une élection*) nomination.

invétéré, e [aṅvȧtȧrȧ] *a* (*habitude*) ingrained; (*bavard, buveur*) inveterate.

invincible [aṅvaṅsēbl(ə)] *a* invincible, unconquerable.

invinciblement [aṅvaṅsēbləmȧṅ] *ad* (*fig*) invincibly.

inviolabilité [aṅvyolȧbēlētȧ] *nf*: ~ **parlementaire** parliamentary immunity.

inviolable [aṅvyolȧbl(ə)] *a* inviolable.

invisible [aṅvēzēbl(ə)] *a* invisible; (*fig*: *personne*) not available.

invitation [aṅvētȧsyôṅ] *nf* invitation; **à/sur l'~ de qn** at/on sb's invitation; **carte/lettre d'~** invitation card/letter.

invite [aṅvēt] *nf* invitation.

invité, e [aṅvētȧ] *nm/f* guest.

inviter [aṅvētȧ] *vt* to invite; ~ **qn à faire qch** to invite sb to do sth; (*suj: chose*) to induce *ou* tempt sb to do sth.

invivable [aṅvēvȧbl(ə)] *a* unbearable, impossible.

involontaire [aṅvolôṅter] *a* (*mouvement*) involuntary; (*insulte*) unintentional; (*complice*) unwitting.

involontairement [aṅvolôṅtermâṅ] *ad* involuntarily.

invoquer [aṅvokā] *vt* (*Dieu, muse*) to call upon, invoke; (*prétexte*) to put forward (as an excuse); (*témoignage*) to call upon; (*loi, texte*) to refer to; ~ **la clémence de qn** to beg sb *ou* appeal to sb for clemency.

invraisemblable [aṅvresâṅblábl(ə)] *a* unlikely, improbable; (*bizarre*) incredible.

invraisemblance [aṅvresâṅblâṅs] *nf* unlikelihood *q*, improbability.

invulnérable [aṅvülnārábl(ə)] *a* invulnerable.

iode [yod] *nm* iodine.

iodé, e [yodā] *a* iodized.

ion [yôṅ] *nm* ion.

ionique [yonēk] *a* (*ARCHIT*) Ionic; (*SCIENCE*) ionic.

IPC *sigle m* (= *Indice des prix à la consommation*) CPI.

IR. *abr* = **infrarouge**.

IRA *sigle f* (= *Irish Republican Army*) IRA.

irai [ērā] *etc vb voir* **aller**.

Irak [ērák] *nm*: **l'**~ Iraq *ou* Irak.

irakien, ne [ērákyaṅ, -en] *a* Iraqi ♦ *nm* (*LING*) Iraqi ♦ *nm/f*: **l'**~, **ne** Iraqi.

Iran [ērâṅ] *nm*: **l'**~ Iran.

iranien, ne [ērányaṅ, -en] *a* Iranian ♦ *nm* (*LING*) Iranian ♦ *nm/f*: **l'**~, **ne** Iranian.

Iraq [ērák] = **Irak**.

iraquien, ne [ērákyaṅ, -en] = **irakien, ne**.

irascible [ērásēbl(ə)] *a* short-tempered, irascible.

irions [ēryôṅ] *etc vb voir* **aller**.

iris [ērēs] *nm* iris.

irisé, e [ērēzā] *a* iridescent.

irlandais, e [ērlâṅde, -ez] *a, nm* (*LING*) Irish ♦ *nm/f*: **l'**~, **e** Irishman/woman; **les l'**~ the Irish.

Irlande [ērlâṅd] *nf*: **l'**~ (*pays*) Ireland; (*état*) the Irish Republic, the Republic of Ireland, Eire; ~ **du Nord** Northern Ireland, Ulster; ~ **du Sud** Southern Ireland, Irish Republic, Eire; **la mer d'**~ the Irish Sea.

ironie [ēronē] *nf* irony.

ironique [ēronēk] *a* ironical.

ironiquement [ēronēkmáṅ] *ad* ironically.

ironiser [ēronēzā] *vi* to be ironical.

irons [ērôṅ] *etc vb voir* **aller**.

IRPP *sigle m* (= *impôt sur le revenu des personnes physiques*) income tax.

irradiation [ērádyásyôṅ] *nf* irradiation.

irradier [ērádyā] *vi* to radiate ♦ *vt* to irradiate.

irraisonné, e [ērezonā] *a* irrational, unreasoned.

irrationnel, le [ērásyonel] *a* irrational.

irrattrapable [ērátrápábl(ə)] *a* (*retard*) that cannot be made up; (*bévue*) that cannot be made good.

irréalisable [ērāálēzábl(ə)] *a* unrealizable; (*projet*) impracticable.

irréalisme [ērāálēsm(ə)] *nm* lack of realism.

irréaliste [ērāálēst(ə)] *a* unrealistic.

irréalité [ērāálētā] *nf* unreality.

irrecevable [ērsəvábl(ə)] *a* unacceptable.

irréconciliable [ērākôṅsēlyábl(ə)] *a* irreconcilable.

irrécouvrable [ērākōōvrábl(ə)] *a* irrecover-

able.

irrécupérable [ērāküpārábl(ə)] *a* unreclaimable, beyond repair; (*personne*) beyond redemption *ou* recall.

irrécusable [ērāküzábl(ə)] *a* (*témoignage*) unimpeachable; (*preuve*) incontestable, indisputable.

irréductible [ērādüktēbl(ə)] *a* indomitable, implacable; (*MATH*: *fraction, équation*) irreducible.

irréductiblement [ērādüktēbləmáṅ] *ad* implacably.

irréel, le [ērāel] *a* unreal.

irréfléchi, e [ērāflāshē] *a* thoughtless.

irréfutable [ērāfütábl(ə)] *a* irrefutable.

irréfutablement [ērāfütábləmáṅ] *ad* irrefutably.

irrégularité [ērágulárētā] *nf* irregularity; unevenness *q*.

irrégulier, ière [ērāgülyā, -yer] *a* irregular; (*surface, rythme, écriture*) uneven, irregular; (*élève, athlète*) erratic.

irrégulièrement [ērāgülyermáṅ] *ad* irregularly.

irrémédiable [ērāmādyábl(ə)] *a* irreparable.

irrémédiablement [ērāmādyábləmáṅ] *ad* irreparably.

irremplaçable [ērāṅplásábl(ə)] *a* irreplaceable.

irréparable [ērāpárábl(ə)] *a* beyond repair, irreparable; (*fig*) irreparable.

irrépréhensible [ērāprāáṅsēbl(ə)] *a* irreprehensible.

irrépressible [ērāprásēbl(ə)] *a* irrepressible.

irréprochable [ērāproshábl(ə)] *a* irreproachable, beyond reproach; (*tenue, toilette*) impeccable.

irrésistible [ērāzēstēbl(ə)] *a* irresistible; (*preuve, logique*) compelling.

irrésistiblement [ērāzēstēbləmáṅ] *ad* irresistibly.

irrésolu, e [ērāzolü] *a* irresolute.

irrésolution [ērāzolüsyôṅ] *nf* irresoluteness.

irrespectueux, euse [ērespektüœ, -œz] *a* disrespectful.

irrespirable [ērespērábl(ə)] *a* unbreathable; (*fig*) oppressive, stifling.

irresponsabilité [ērespôṅsábēlētā] *nf* irresponsibility.

irresponsable [ērespôṅsábl(ə)] *a* irresponsible.

irrévérencieux, euse [ērāvārâṅsyœ, -œz] *a* irreverent.

irréversible [ērāversēbl(ə)] *a* irreversible.

irréversiblement [ērāversēbləmáṅ] *ad* irreversibly.

irrévocable [ērāvokábl(ə)] *a* irrevocable.

irrévocablement [ērāvokábləmáṅ] *ad* irrevocably.

irrigation [ērēgásyôṅ] *nf* irrigation.

irriguer [ērēgā] *vt* to irrigate.

irritabilité [ērētábēlētā] *nf* irritability.

irritable [ērētábl(ə)] *a* irritable.

irritant, e [ērētáṅ, -áṅt] *a* irritating; (*MÉD*) irritant.

irritation [ērētásyôṅ] *nf* irritation.

irrité, e [ērētā] *a* irritated.

irriter [ērētā] *vt* (*agacer*) to irritate, annoy; (*MÉD*: *enflammer*) to irritate; **s'**~ **contre qn/de qch** to get annoyed *ou* irritated with sb/at sth.

irruption [ērüpsyóṅ] *nf* irruption *q*; **faire ~ dans** to burst into.

ISBN *sigle m* (= *International Standard Book Number*) ISBN.

Islam [ēslám] *nm* Islam.

islamique [ēslámēk] *a* Islamic.

islandais, e [ēslâṅde, -ez] *a* Icelandic ♦ *nm* (*LING*) Icelandic ♦ *nm/f*: **I~, e** Icelander.

Islande [ēslâṅd] *nf*: **l'~** Iceland.

ISMH *sigle m* (= *Inventaire supplémentaire des monuments historiques*): **monument inscrit à l'~** ≈ historical monument.

isocèle [ēzosel] *a* isoceles.

isolant, e [ēzolâṅ, -âṅt] *a* insulating; (*insonorisant*) soundproofing ♦ *nm* insulator.

isolateur [ēzolátœr] *nm* (*ÉLEC*) insulator.

isolation [ēzolâsyóṅ] *nf* insulation; **~ acoustique/thermique** sound/thermal insulation.

isolationnisme [ēzolâsyonēsm(ə)] *nm* isolationism.

isolé, e [ēzolā] *a* isolated; (*ÉLEC*) insulated.

isolement [ēzolmâṅ] *nm* isolation; solitary confinement.

isolément [ēzolāmâṅ] *ad* in isolation.

isoler [ēzolā] *vt* to isolate; (*prisonnier*) to put in solitary confinement; (*ville*) to cut off, isolate; (*ÉLEC*) to insulate.

isoloir [ēzolwár] *nm* polling *ou* voting (*US*) booth.

isorel [ēzorel] *nm* ® hardboard.

isotherme [ēzoterm(ə)] *a* (*camion*) refrigerated.

Israël [ēsráel] *nm*: **l'~** Israel.

israélien, ne [ēsrāālyaṅ, -en] *a* Israeli ♦ *nm/f*: **I~, ne** Israeli.

israélite [ēsrāālēt] *a* Jewish; (*dans l'Ancien Testament*) Israelite ♦ *nm/f*: **I~** Jew/Jewess; Israelite.

issu, e [ēsü] *a*: **~ de** descended from; (*fig*) stemming from ♦ *nf* (*ouverture, sortie*) exit; (*solution*) way out, solution; (*dénouement*) outcome; **à l'~e de** at the conclusion *ou* close of; **rue sans ~e** dead end, no through road; **~e de secours** emergency exit.

Istamboul *ou* **Istanbul** [ēstâṅbōōl] *n* Istanbul.

isthme [ēsm(ə)] *nm* isthmus.

Italie [ētálē] *nf*: **l'~** Italy.

italien, ne [ētályaṅ, -en] *a* Italian ♦ *nm* (*LING*) Italian ♦ *nm/f*: **I~, ne** Italian.

italique [ētálēk] *nf*: **en ~(s)** in italics.

item [ētem] *nm* item; (*question*) question, test.

itinéraire [ētēnārer] *nm* itinerary, route.

itinérant, e [ētēnārâṅ, -âṅt] *a* itinerant, travelling (*US*), travelling (*Brit*).

ITP *sigle m* (= *ingénieur des travaux publics*) civil engineer.

IUT *sigle m* = **Institut universitaire de technologie.**

IVG *sigle f* (= *interruption volontaire de grossesse*) abortion.

ivoire [ēvwár] *nm* ivory.

ivoirien, ne [ēvwáryaṅ, -en] *a* of *ou* from the Ivory Coast.

ivraie [ēvre] *nf*: **séparer l'~ du bon grain** (*fig*) to separate the wheat from the chaff.

ivre [ēvr(ə)] *a* drunk; **~ de** (*colère*) wild with; (*bonheur*) drunk *ou* intoxicated with; **~ mort** dead drunk.

ivresse [ēvres] *nf* drunkenness; (*euphorie*) intoxication.

ivrogne [ēvrony] *nm/f* drunkard.

J

J, j [zhē] *nm inv* J, j ♦ *abr* (= *jour*): **jour ~ D**-day; (= *Joule*) J; **J comme Joseph** J for Jig.

j' [zh] *pronom voir* **je.**

jabot [zhábō] *nm* (*ZOOL*) crop; (*de vêtement*) jabot.

JAC [zhák] *sigle f* (= *Jeunesse agricole catholique*) youth organization.

jacasser [zhákásā] *vi* to chatter.

jachère [zhásher] *nf*: **(être) en ~** (to lie) fallow.

jacinthe [zhásaṅt] *nf* hyacinth; **~ des bois** bluebell.

jack [dzhák] *nm* jack plug.

jacquerie [zhákrē] *nf* riot.

jade [zhád] *nm* jade.

jadis [zhádēs] *ad* in times past, formerly.

jaguar [zhágwár] *nm* (*ZOOL*) jaguar.

jaillir [zhàyēr] *vi* (*liquide*) to spurt out, gush out; (*lumière*) to flood out; (*fig*) to rear up; to burst out.

jaillissement [zháyēsmâṅ] *nm* spurt, gush.

jais [zhe] *nm* jet; **(d'un noir) de ~** jet-black.

jalon [zhálóṅ] *nm* range pole; (*fig*) milestone; **poser des ~s** (*fig*) to pave the way.

jalonner [zhálonā] *vt* to mark out; (*fig*) to mark, punctuate.

jalousement [zhálōōzmâṅ] *ad* jealously.

jalouser [zhálōōzā] *vt* to be jealous of.

jalousie [zhálōōzē] *nf* jealousy; (*store*) (venetian) blind.

jaloux, ouse [zhálōō, -ōōz] *a* jealous; **être ~ de qn/qch** to be jealous of sb/sth.

jamaïquain, e [zhámáēkaṅ, -en] *a* Jamaican.

Jamaïque [zhámáēk] *nf*: **la ~** Jamaica.

jamais [zháme] *ad* never; (*sans négation*) ever; **ne ... ~** never; **~ de la vie!** never!; **si ~ ...** if ever ...; **à (tout) ~, pour ~** for ever, for ever and ever.

jambage [zhâṅbázh] *nm* (*de lettre*) downstroke; (*de porte*) jamb.

jambe [zhâṅb] *nf* leg; **à toutes ~s** as fast as one's legs can carry one.

jambières [zhâṅbyer] *nfpl* legwarmers; (*SPORT*) shin pads.

jambon [zhâṅbóṅ] *nm* ham.

jambonneau, x [zhâṅbonō] *nm* knuckle of ham.

jante [zhâṅt] *nf* (wheel) rim.

janvier [zhâṅvyā] *nm* January; *voir aussi* **juillet.**

Japon [zhápóṅ] *nm*: **le ~** Japan.

japonais, e [zhápone, -ez] *a* Japanese ♦ *nm* (*LING*) Japanese ♦ *nm/f*: **J~, e** Japanese.

japonaiserie [zháponezrē] *nf* (*bibelot*) Japanese curio.

jappement [zhápmáṅ] *nm* yap, yelp.

japper [zhápā] *vi* to yap, yelp.

jaquette [zháket] *nf* (*de cérémonie*) morning coat; (*de femme*) jacket; (*de livre*) dust cover, (dust) jacket.

jardin [zhárdaṅ] *nm* garden; ~ **d'acclimatation** zoological gardens *pl*; ~ **botanique** botanical gardens *pl*; ~ **d'enfants** nursery school; ~ **potager** vegetable garden; ~ **public** (public) park, public gardens *pl*; ~**s suspendus** hanging gardens.

jardinage [zhárdēnázh] *nm* gardening.

jardiner [zhárdēnā] *vi* to garden, do some gardening.

jardinet [zhárdēne] *nm* little garden.

jardinier, ière [zhárdēnyā, -yer] *nm/f* gardener ♦ *nf* (*de fenêtre*) window box; **jardinière d'enfants** nursery school teacher; **jardinière (de légumes)** (*CULIN*) mixed vegetables.

jargon [zhárgóṅ] *nm* (*charabia*) gibberish; (*publicitaire, scientifique etc*) jargon.

jarre [zhár] *nf* (earthenware) jar.

jarret [zháre] *nm* back of knee; (*CULIN*) knuckle, shin.

jarretelle [zhártel] *nf* garter (*US*), suspender (*Brit*).

jarretière [zhártyer] *nf* garter.

jars [zhár] *nm* (*ZOOL*) gander.

jaser [zházā] *vi* to chatter, prattle; (*indiscrètement*) to gossip.

jasmin [zhásmaṅ] *nm* jasmin.

jaspe [zhásp(ə)] *nm* jasper.

jaspé, e [zháspā] *a* marbled, mottled.

jatte [zhát] *nf* basin, bowl.

jauge [zhōzh] *nf* (*capacité*) capacity, tonnage; (*instrument*) gauge; ~ **(de niveau) d'huile** dipstick.

jauger [zhōzhā] *vt* to gauge the capacity of; (*fig*) to size up; ~ **3000 tonneaux** to measure 3,000 tons.

jaunâtre [zhōnâtr(ə)] *a* (*couleur, teint*) yellowish.

jaune [zhōn] *a*, *nm* yellow ♦ *nm/f* Asiatic; (*briseur de grève*) scab ♦ *ad* (*fam*): **rire** ~ to laugh out of the other side of one's mouth (*US*), laugh on the other side of one's face; ~ **d'œuf** (egg) yolk.

jaunir [zhōnēr] *vi*, *vt* to turn yellow.

jaunisse [zhōnēs] *nf* jaundice.

Java [zhává] *nf* Java.

javanais, e [zhávàne, -ez] *a* Javanese.

Javel [zhável] *nf voir* **eau.**

javelliser [zhávēlēsā] *vt* (*eau*) to chlorinate.

javelot [zhávlō] *nm* javelin; (*SPORT*): **faire du** ~ to throw the javelin.

jazz [dzház] *nm* jazz.

J.-C. *abr* = **Jésus-Christ.**

JCR *sigle f* (= *Jeunesse communiste révolutionnaire*) communist youth movement.

je, j' [zh(ə)] *pronom* I.

jean [dzhēn] *nm* jeans *pl*.

jeannette [zhánet] *nf* (*planchette*) sleeveboard; (*petite fille scout*) Brownie.

JEC [zhek] *sigle f* (= *Jeunesse étudiante chrétienne*) youth organization.

jérémiades [zhārāmyád] *nfpl* moaning *sg*.

jerrycan [zhārēkán] *nm* jerrycan.

Jersey [zherze] *nf* Jersey.

jersey [zherze] *nm* jersey; (*TRICOT*): **pointe de** ~ stocking stitch.

jersiais, e [zherzye, -ez] *a* Jersey *cpd*, of *ou* from Jersey.

Jérusalem [zhārüzálem] *n* Jerusalem.

jésuite [zhāzüēt] *nm* Jesuit.

Jésus-Christ [zhāzükrē(st)] *n* Jesus Christ; **600 avant/après** ~ *ou* **J.-C.** 600 B.C./A.D.

jet [zhe] *nm* (*lancer*) throwing *q*, throw; (*jaillissement*) jet; spurt; (*de tuyau*) nozzle; (*avion*) [dzhet] jet; (*fig*): **premier** ~ (*ébauche*) rough outline; **arroser au** ~ to hose; **d'un (seul)** ~ (*d'un seul coup*) at (*ou* in) one try; **du premier** ~ at the first attempt *or* shot; ~ **d'eau** spray; (*fontaine*) fountain.

jetable [zhətábl(ə)] *a* disposable.

jeté [zhətā] *nm*: ~ **de table** (table) runner; ~ **de lit** bedspread.

jetée [zhətā] *nf* jetty; pier.

jeter [zhətā] *vt* (*gén*) to throw; (*se défaire de*) to throw away *ou* out; (*son, lueur etc*) to give out; ~ **qch à qn** to throw sth to sb; (*de façon agressive*) to throw sth at sb; (*NAVIG*): ~ **l'ancre** to drop anchor; ~ **un coup d'œil (à)** to take a look (at); ~ **les bras en avant/la tête en arrière** to throw one's arms forward/one's head back(ward); ~ **l'effroi parmi** to spread fear among; ~ **un sort à qn** to cast a spell on sb; ~ **qn dans la misère** to reduce sb to poverty; ~ **qn dehors/en prison** to throw sb out/into prison; ~ **l'éponge** (*fig*) to throw in the towel; ~ **des fleurs à qn** (*fig*) to say lovely things to sb; ~ **la pierre à qn** (*accuser, blâmer*) to accuse sb; **se** ~ **sur** to throw o.s. onto; **se** ~ **dans** (*suj: fleuve*) to flow into; **se** ~ **par la fenêtre** to jump out of the window; **se** ~ **à l'eau** (*fig*) to take the plunge.

jeton [zhətóṅ] *nm* (*au jeu*) counter; (*de téléphone*) token; ~**s de présence** (director's) fees.

jette [zhet] *etc vb voir* **jeter.**

jeu, x [zhœ] *nm* (*divertissement*, *TECH*: *d'une pièce*) play; (*défini par des règles*, *TENNIS*: *partie*, *FOOTBALL etc*: *façon de jouer*) game; (*THÉÂTRE etc*) acting; (*au casino*): **le** ~ gambling; (*fonctionnement*) working, interplay; (*série d'objets, jouet*) set; (*CARTES*) hand; **cacher son** ~ (*fig*) to keep one's cards hidden, conceal one's hand; **c'est un** ~ **d'enfant!** (*fig*) it's child's play!; **en** ~ at stake; at work; (*FOOTBALL*) in play; **remettre en** ~ to throw in; **entrer/mettre en** ~ to come/bring into play; **par** ~ (*pour s'amuser*) for fun; **d'entrée de** ~ (*tout de suite, dès le début*) from the outset; **entrer dans le** ~**/le** ~ **de qn** (*fig*) to play the game/sb's game; **jouer gros** ~ to play for high stakes; **se piquer/se prendre au** ~ to get excited over/get caught up in *ou* involved in the game; ~ **de boules** game of bowls; (*endroit*) bowling ground; (*boules*) set of bowls; ~ **de cartes** card game; (*paquet*) deck of cards; ~ **de construction** building set; ~ **d'échecs** chess set; ~ **d'écritures** (*COMM*) paper transaction; ~ **de hasard** game of chance; ~ **de mots** pun; ~ **d'orgue(s)** organ stop; ~ **de patience** puzzle; ~ **de physionomie** facial expressions *pl*; ~ **de société** parlor (*US*) *ou* parlour (*Brit*) game; **~x de lumière** lighting effects; **J~x olympiques (JO)** Olympic Games.

jeu-concours, *pl* **jeux-concours** [yœ̄kôṅkōōr] *nm* competition.

jeudi [zhœ̄dē] *nm* Thursday; **~ saint** Maundy Thursday; *voir aussi* **lundi.**

jeun [zhœ̄ṅ]: **à ~** *ad* on an empty stomach.

jeune [zhœn] *a* young ♦ *ad*: **faire/s'habiller ~** to look/dress young; **les ~s** young people, the young; **~ fille** *nf* girl; **~ homme** *nm* young man; **~ loup** *nm* (*POL, ÉCON*) young go-getter; **~ premier** leading man; **~s gens** *nmpl* young people; **~s mariés** *nmpl* newlyweds.

jeûne [zhœ̄n] *nm* fast.

jeûner [zhœ̄nā] *vt* to fast, go without food.

jeunesse [zhœnes] *nf* youth; (*aspect*) youthfulness; (*jeunes*) young people *pl*, youth.

JF *sigle f* = **jeune fille.**

JH *sigle m* = **jeune homme.**

JI *sigle m* = **juge d'instruction.**

jiu-jitsu [zhüzhētsü] *nm inv* (*SPORT*) jujitsu.

JMF *sigle f* (= *Jeunesses musicales de France*) *association to promote music among the young.*

JO *sigle m* = **Journal officiel** ♦ *sigle mpl* = **Jeux Olympiques.**

joaillerie [zhoâyrē] *nf* jewel trade; jewelry (*US*), jewellery (*Brit*).

joaillier, ière [zhoâyā, -yer] *nm/f* jeweler (*US*), jeweller (*Brit*).

job [dzhob] *nm* job.

jobard [zhobár] *nm* (*péj*) sucker.

JOC [zhok] *sigle f* (= *Jeunesse ouvrière chrétienne*) *youth organization.*

jockey [zhoke] *nm* jockey.

jodler [zhodlā] *vi* to yodel.

jogging [dzhogēng] *nm* sweatsuit (*US*), tracksuit (*Brit*); **faire du ~** to jog, go jogging.

joie [zhwà] *nf* joy.

joignais [zhwàne] *etc vb voir* **joindre.**

joindre [zhwàṅdr(ə)] *vt* to join; (*à une lettre*): **~ qch à** to enclose sth with; (*contacter*) to contact, get in touch with; **~ les mains/talons** to put one's hands/heels together; **~ les deux bouts** (*fig: du mois*) to make ends meet; **se ~** (*mains etc*) to come together; **se ~ à qn** to join sb; **se ~ à qch** to join in sth.

joint, e [zhwàn, -àṅt] *pp de* **joindre** ♦ *a*: **~ (à)** (*lettre, paquet*) attached (to), enclosed (with); **pièce ~e** enclosure ♦ *nm* joint; (*ligne*) join; (*de ciment etc*) pointing *q*; **chercher/trouver le ~** (*fig*) to look for/come up with the answer; **~ de cardan** cardan joint; **~ de culasse** cylinder head gasket; **~ de robinet** washer; **~ universel** universal joint.

jointure [zhwàntür] *nf* (*ANAT: articulation*) joint; (*TECH: assemblage*) joint; (*: ligne*) join.

joker [zhoker] *nm* (*CARTES*) joker.

joli, e [zholē] *a* pretty, attractive; **une ~e somme/situation** a nice little sum/situation; **un ~ gâchis** *etc* a nice mess *etc*; **c'est du ~!** that's very nice!; **tout ça, c'est bien ~ mais** ... that's all very well but ....

joliment [zholēmàṅ] *ad* prettily, attractively; (*fam: très*) pretty.

jonc [zhôṅ] *nm* (*bul*)rush; (*bague, bracelet*) band.

joncher [zhôṅshā] *vt* (*suj: choses*) to be strewed on; **jonché de** strewn with.

jonction [zhôṅksyôṅ] *nf* joining; (**point de**) **~** (*de routes*) junction; (*de fleuves*) confluence; **opérer une ~** (*MIL etc*) to rendezvous.

jongler [zhôṅglā] *vi* to juggle; (*fig*): **~ avec** to juggle with, play with.

jongleur, euse [zhôṅglœr, -œ̄z] *nm/f* juggler.

jonquille [zhôṅkēy] *nf* daffodil.

Jordanie [zhordánē] *nf*: **la ~** Jordan.

jordanien, ne [zhordányaṅ, -en] *a* Jordanian ♦ *nm/f*: **J~, ne** Jordanian.

jouable [zhwàbl(ə)] *a* playable.

joue [zhōō] *nf* cheek; **mettre en ~** to take aim at.

jouer [zhwā] *vt* (*partie, carte, coup, MUS: morceau*) to play; (*somme d'argent, réputation*) to stake, wager; (*pièce, rôle*) to perform; (*film*) to show; (*simuler: sentiment*) to affect, feign ♦ *vi* to play; (*THÉÂTRE, CINÉMA*) to act, perform; (*bois, porte: se voiler*) to warp; (*clef, pièce: avoir du jeu*) to be loose; (*entrer ou être en jeu*) to come into play, come into it; **~ sur** (*miser*) to gamble on; **~ de** (*MUS*) to play; **~ du couteau/des coudes** to use knives/one's elbows; **~ à** (*jeu, sport, roulette*) to play; **~ au héros** to act *ou* play the hero; **~ avec** (*risquer*) to gamble with; **se ~ de** (*difficultés*) to make light of; **se ~ de qn** to deceive *ou* dupe sb; **~ un tour à qn** to play a trick on sb; **~ la comédie** (*fig*) to put on an act, put it on; **~ aux courses** to back horses, bet on horses; **~ à la baisse/hausse** (*BOURSE*) to bear/bull the market (*US*), play for a fall/rise (*Brit*); **~ serré** to play a close game; **~ de malchance** to be dogged with ill-luck; **~ sur les mots** to play with words; **à toi/nous de ~** it's your/our go *ou* turn.

jouet [zhwe] *nm* toy; **être le ~ de** (*illusion etc*) to be the victim of.

joueur, euse [zhwœr, -œ̄z] *nm/f* player ♦ *a* (*enfant, chat*) playful; **être beau/mauvais ~** to be a good/bad loser.

joufflu, e [zhōōflü] *a* chubby(-cheeked).

joug [zhōō] *nm* yoke.

jouir [zhwēr]: **~ de** *vt* to enjoy.

jouissance [zhwēsáṅs] *nf* pleasure; (*JUR*) use.

jouisseur, euse [zhwēsœr, -œ̄z] *nm/f* sensualist.

joujou [zhōōzhōō] *nm* (*fam*) toy.

jour [zhōōr] *nm* day; (*opposé à la nuit*) day, daytime; (*clarté*) daylight; (*fig: aspect*): **sous un ~ favorable/nouveau** in a favorable/new light; (*ouverture*) opening; (*COUTURE*) openwork *q*; **au ~ le ~** from day to day; **de nos ~s** these days, nowadays; **tous les ~s** every day; **de ~ en ~** day by day; **d'un ~ à l'autre** from one day to the next; **du ~ au lendemain** overnight; **il fait ~** it's daylight; **en plein ~** in broad daylight; **au ~** in daylight; **au petit ~** at daybreak; **au grand ~** (*fig*) in the open; **mettre au ~** to uncover, disclose; **être à ~** to be up to date; **mettre à ~** to bring up to date, update; **mise à ~** updating; **donner le ~ à** to give birth to; **voir le ~** to be born; **se faire ~** (*fig*) to become clear; ~ **férié** legal (*US*) *ou* public (*Brit*) holiday; **le** ~ **J** D-day.

Jourdain [zhŏŏrdań] *nm*: **le** ~ the (River) Jordan.

journal, aux [zhŏŏrnál, -ō] *nm* (news)paper; (*personnel*) journal, diary; ~ **de bord** log; ~ **de mode** fashion magazine; **le J~ officiel (de la République française) (JO)** *bulletin giving details of laws and official announcements*; ~ **parlé/télévisé** radio/television news *sg*.

journalier, ière [zhŏŏrnályă, -yer] *a* daily; (*banal*) everyday ♦ *nm* day laborer (*US*) *ou* labourer (*Brit*).

journalisme [zhŏŏrnálĕsm(ə)] *nm* journalism.

journaliste [zhŏŏrnálĕst(ə)] *nm/f* journalist.

journalistique [zhŏŏrnálĕstĕk] *a* journalistic.

journée [zhŏŏrnă] *nf* day; **la** ~ **continue** the 9 to 5 working day (*with short lunch break*).

journellement [zhŏŏrnelmáń] *ad* (*tous les jours*) daily; (*souvent*) every day.

joute [zhŏŏt] *nf* (*tournoi*) duel; (*verbale*) duel, battle of words.

jouvence [zhŏŏváńs] *nf*: **bain de** ~ rejuvenating experience.

jouxter [zhŏŏkstă] *vt* to adjoin.

jovial [zhovyál] *a* jovial, jolly.

jovialité [zhovyálĕtă] *nf* joviality.

joyau, x [zhwáyō] *nm* gem, jewel.

joyeusement [zhwáyœzmáń] *ad* joyfully, gladly.

joyeux, euse [zhwáyœ, -œz] *a* joyful, merry; ~ **Noël!** merry *ou* happy Christmas!; ~ **anniversaire!** many happy returns!

JT *sigle m* = **journal télévisé.**

jubilation [zhübĕlásyóń] *nf* jubilation.

jubilé [zhübĕlă] *nm* jubilee.

jubiler [zhübĕlă] *vi* to be jubilant, exult.

jucher [zhüshă] *vt*: ~ **qch sur** to perch sth (up)on ♦ *vi* (*oiseau*): ~ **sur** to perch (up)on; **se** ~ **sur** to perch o.s. (up)on.

judaïque [zhüdáĕk] *a* (*loi*) Judaic; (*religion*) Jewish.

judaïsme [zhüdáĕsm(ə)] *nm* Judaism.

judas [zhüdá] *nm* (*trou*) judas hole, peephole.

Judée [zhüdă] *nf*: **la** ~ Jud(a)ea.

judéo- [zhüdăo] *préfixe* Judeo-.

judéo-allemand, e [zhüdăoálmáń, -áńd] *a, nm* Yiddish.

judiciaire [zhüdĕsyer] *a* judicial.

judicieusement [zhüdĕsyœzmáń] *ad* judiciously.

judicieux, euse [zhüdĕsyœ, -œz] *a* judicious.

judo [zhüdō] *nm* judo.

judoka [zhüdoká] *nm/f* judoka.

juge [zhüzh] *nm* judge; ~ **des enfants** children's judge, ≈ juvenile magistrate; ~ **d'instruction** committing (*US*) *ou* examining (*Brit*) magistrate; ~ **de paix** justice of the peace; ~ **de touche** linesman.

jugé [zhüzhă]: **au** ~ *ad* by guesswork.

jugement [zhüzhmáń] *nm* judgment; (*JUR*: *au pénal*) sentence; (: *au civil*) decision; ~ **de valeur** value judgment.

jugeote [zhüzhot] *nf* (*fam*) gumption.

juger [zhüzhă] *vt* to judge ♦ *nm*: **au** ~ by guesswork; ~ **qn/qch satisfaisant** to consider sb/sth (to be) satisfactory; ~ **que** to think *ou* consider that; ~ **bon de faire** to consider it a

good idea to do, see fit to do; ~ **de** *vt* to judge; **jugez de ma surprise** imagine my surprise.

jugulaire [zhügüler] *a* jugular ♦ *nf* (*MIL*) chinstrap.

juguler [zhügülă] *vt* (*maladie*) to halt; (*révolte*) to suppress, put down; (*inflation etc*) to control, curb.

juif, ive [zhüĕf, -ĕv] *a* Jewish ♦ *nm/f*: **J~, ive** Jew/Jewess *ou* Jewish woman.

juillet [zhüĕye] *nm* July; **le premier** ~ July first (*US*), the first of July (*Brit*); **le deux/ onze** ~ the second/eleventh of July, July second/eleventh; **il est venu le 5** ~ he came on 5th July *ou* July 5th; **en** ~ in July; **début/fin** ~ at the beginning/end of July.

juin [zhüań] *nm* June; *voir aussi* **juillet.**

juive [zhüĕv] *voir* **juif.**

jumeau, elle, x [zhümō, -el] *a, nm/f* twin; **maisons jumelles** duplexes (*US*), semidetached houses (*Brit*).

jumelage [zhümlázh] *nm* twinning.

jumeler [zhümlă] *vt* to twin; **roues jumelées** double wheels; **billets de loterie jumelés** double series lottery tickets; **pari jumelé** double bet.

jumelle [zhümel] *af, nf voir* **jumeau** ♦ *vb voir* **jumeler.**

jumelles [zhümel] *nfpl* binoculars.

jument [zhümáń] *nf* mare.

jungle [zhóńgl(ə)] *nf* jungle.

junior [zhünyor] *a* junior.

junte [zhœńt] *nf* junta.

jupe [zhüp] *nf* skirt.

jupe-culotte, *pl* **jupes-culottes** [zhüpkülot] *nf* divided skirt, culotte(s).

jupette [zhüpet] *nf* short skirt.

jupon [zhüpóń] *nm* waist slip *ou* petticoat.

Jura [zhürá] *nm*: **le** ~ the Jura (Mountains).

jurassien, ne [zhürásyań, -en] *a* of *ou* from the Jura Mountains.

juré, e [zhüră] *nm/f* juror ♦ *a*: **ennemi** ~ sworn *ou* avowed enemy.

jurer [zhüră] *vt* (*obéissance etc*) to swear, vow (*dire des jurons*) to swear, curse; (*dissoner*): ~ (**avec**) to clash (with); (*s'engager*): ~ **de faire/que** to swear *ou* vow to do/that; (*affirmer*): ~ **que** to swear *ou* vouch that; ~ **de qch** (*s'en porter garant*) to swear to sth; **ils ne jurent que par lui** they swear by him; **je vous jure!** honestly!

juridiction [zhürĕdĕksyóń] *nf* jurisdiction; (*tribunal, tribunaux*) court(s) of law.

juridique [zhürĕdĕk] *a* legal.

juridiquement [zhürĕdĕkmáń] *ad* (*devant la justice*) juridically; (*du point de vue du droit*) legally.

jurisconsulte [zhürĕskóńsült(ə)] *nm* jurisconsult.

jurisprudence [zhürĕsprüdáńs] *nf* (*JUR*: *décisions*) (legal) precedents; (*principes juridiques*) jurisprudence; **faire** ~ (*faire autorité*) to set a precedent.

juriste [zhürĕst(ə)] *nm/f* jurist; lawyer.

juron [zhüróń] *nm* curse, swearword.

jury [zhürē] *nm* (*JUR*) jury; (*SCOL*) board (of examiners), jury.

jus [zhü] *nm* juice; (*de viande*) gravy, (meat) juice; ~ **de fruits** fruit juice; ~ **de raisin/**

tomates grape/tomato juice.
jusant [zhüzáń] *nm* ebb (tide).
jusqu'au-boutiste [zhüskŏbŏŏtēst(ə)] *nm/f* extremist, hardliner.
jusque [zhüsk(ə)]: **jusqu'à** *prép* (*endroit*) as far as, (up) to; (*moment*) until, till; (*limite*) up to; ~ **sur/dans** up to, as far as; (*y compris*) even on/in; **jusque vers** until about; **jusqu'à ce que** *cj* until; **jusque-là** (*temps*) until then; (*espace*) up to there; **jusqu'ici** (*temps*) until now; (*espace*) up to here; **jusqu'à présent** until now, so far.
justaucorps [zhüstŏkor] *nm inv* (*DANSE*, *SPORT*) leotard.
juste [zhüst(ə)] *a* (*équitable*) just, fair; (*légitime*) just, justified; (*exact*, *vrai*) right; (*étroit*, *insuffisant*) tight ♦ *ad* right; tight; (*chanter*) in tune; (*seulement*) just; ~ **assez/au-dessus** just enough/above; **pouvoir tout** ~ **faire** to be only just able to do; **au** ~ exactly, actually; **comme de** ~ of course, naturally; **le** ~ **milieu** the happy medium; **à** ~ **titre** rightfully.
justement [zhüstəmáń] *ad* rightly; justly; (*précisément*): **c'est** ~ **ce qu'il fallait faire** that's just *ou* precisely what needed doing.
justesse [zhüstes] *nf* (*précision*) accuracy; (*d'une remarque*) aptness; (*d'une opinion*) soundness; **de** ~ just, by a narrow margin.
justice [zhüstēs] *nf* (*équité*) fairness, justice; (*ADMIN*) justice; **rendre la** ~ to dispense justice; **traduire en** ~ to bring before the courts; **obtenir** ~ to obtain justice; **rendre** ~ **à qn** to do sb justice; **se faire** ~ to take the law into one's own hands; (*se suicider*) to take one's life.
justiciable [zhüstēsyábl(ə)] *a*: ~ **de** (*JUR*) answerable to.
justicier, ière [zhüstēsyā, -yer] *nm/f* judge, righter of wrongs.
justifiable [zhüstēfyábl(ə)] *a* justifiable.
justificatif, ive [zhüstēfēkátēf, -ēv] *a* (*document etc*) supporting ♦ *nm* supporting proof.
justification [zhüstēfēkásyóń] *nf* justification.
justifier [zhüstēfyā] *vt* to justify; ~ **de** *vt* to prove; **non justifié** unjustified; **justifié à droite/gauche** justified right/left.
jute [zhüt] *nm* jute.
juteux, euse [zhütœ̄, -œ̄z] *a* juicy.
juvénile [zhüvānēl] *a* young, youthful.
juxtaposer [zhükstápŏzā] *vt* to juxtapose.
juxtaposition [zhükstápŏzēsyóń] *nf* juxtaposition.

K

K, k [ká] *nm inv* K, k ♦ *abr* (= *kilo*) kg; (= *kilooctet*) K; **K comme Kléber** K for King.
Kaboul *ou* **Kabul** [kábŏŏl] *n* Kabul.
kabyle [kábēl] *a* Kabyle ♦ *nm* (*LING*) Kabyle ♦ *nm/f*: **K~** Kabyle.

Kabylie [kábēlē] *nf*: **la** ~ Kabylia.
kaki [kákē] *a inv* khaki.
Kalahari [káláárē] *n*: **désert de** ~ Kalahari Desert.
kaléidoscope [káláēdoskop] *nm* kaleidoscope.
Kampala [káńpálá] *n* Kampala.
Kampuchéa [káńpŏŏtshāá] *nm*: **le** ~ **(démocratique)** (the People's Republic of) Kampuchea.
kangourou [káńgŏŏrŏŏ] *nm* kangaroo.
kaolin [káolań] *nm* kaolin.
kapok [kápok] *nm* kapok.
karaté [kárátā] *nm* karate.
kart [kárt] *nm* go-cart.
karting [kártēng] *nm* go-carting, karting.
kascher [kásher] *a inv* kosher.
kayac, kayak [káyák] *nm* kayak.
Kenya [kānyá] *nm*: **le** ~ Kenya.
kenyan, e [kānyáń, -áń] *a* Kenyan ♦ *nm/f*: **K~**, **ne** Kenyan.
képi [kāpē] *nm* kepi.
Kerguelen [kergālen] *n*: **les (îles)** ~ Kerguelen.
kermesse [kermes] *nf* charity bazaar; village fair.
kérosène [kārŏzen] *nm* jet fuel; rocket fuel.
kg *abr* (= *kilogramme*) kg.
KGB *sigle m* KGB.
khmer, ère [kmer] *a* Khmer ♦ *nm* (*LING*) Khmer.
khôl [kōl] *nm* kohl.
kibboutz [kēbŏŏts] *nm* kibbutz.
kidnapper [kēdnápā] *vt* to kidnap.
kidnappeur, euse [kēdnápœr, -œ̄z] *nm/f* kidnapper.
Kilimandjaro [kēlēmáńdzhárŏ] *nm*: **le** ~ Mount Kilimanjaro.
kilo [kēlŏ] *nm* kilo.
kilogramme [kēlográm] *nm* kilogram (*US*), kilogramme (*Brit*).
kilométrage [kēlŏmātrázh] *nm* number of kilometers traveled, ≈ mileage.
kilomètre [kēlŏmetr(ə)] *nm* kilometer (*US*), kilometre (*Brit*); **~s-heure** kilometers per hour.
kilométrique [kēlŏmātrēk] *a* (*distance*) in kilometers; **compteur** ~ odometer (*US*), ≈ mileage indicator (*Brit*).
kilooctet [kēlooktē] *nm* kilobyte.
kilowatt [kēlowát] *nm* kilowatt.
kinésithérapeute [kēnāzētāráp̄ēt] *nm/f* physical therapist (*US*), physiotherapist (*Brit*).
kiosque [kyosk(ə)] *nm* kiosk, stall; (*TÉL etc*) telephone and/or videotext information service.
kirsch [kērsh] *nm* kirsch.
kiwi [kēwē] *nm* (*ZOOL*) kiwi; (*BOT*) kiwi fruit.
klaxon [klákson] *nm* horn.
klaxonner [kláksonā] *vi*, *vt* to honk (one's horn) (*US*), hoot (*Brit*).
kleptomane [kleptomán] *nm/f* kleptomaniac.
km *abr* (= *kilomètre*) km.
km/h *abr* (= *kilomètres/heure*) km/h.
knock-out [nokáwt] *nm* knockout.
Ko *abr* (*INFORM*: = *kilooctet*) K.
K.-O. [káŏ] *a inv* (knocked) out, out for the count.
kolkhoze [kolkōz] *nm* kolkhoz.

Koweit *ou* **Kuweit** [kowet] *nm:* **le** ~ Kuwait.
koweïtien, ne [kowetyañ, -en] *a* Kuwaiti ♦ *nm/f:* **K~, ne** Kuwaiti.
krach [kråk] *nm (ÉCON)* crash.
kraft [kråft] *nm* brown *ou* kraft paper.
Kremlin [kremlañ] *nm:* **le** ~ the Kremlin.
Kuala Lumpur [kwålálümpōōr] *n* Kuala Lumpur.
kurde [kürd(ə)] *a* Kurdish ♦ *nm (LING)* Kurdish ♦ *nm/f:* **K~** Kurd.
Kurdistan [kürdēståñ] *nm:* **le** ~ Kurdistan.
Kuweit [kowet] = **Koweit.**
kW *abr* (= *kilowatt*) kW.
kW/h *abr* (= *kilowatt/heure*) kW/h.
kyrielle [kēryel] *nf:* **une** ~ **de** a stream of.
kyste [kēst(ə)] *nm* cyst.

L

L, I [el] *nm inv* L, l ♦ *abr* (= *litre*) l; *(SCOL):* **L ès L = Licence ès Lettres; L en D = Licence en Droit; L comme Louis** L for Love.
l' [l] *dét voir* **le.**
la [lå] *dét, pronom voir* **le** ♦ *nm (MUS)* A; *(en chantant la gamme)* la.
là [lå] *ad (voir aussi* **-ci, celui)** there; *(ici)* here; *(dans le temps)* then; **est-ce que Catherine est** ~**?** is Catherine there *(ou* here)?; **c'est** ~ **que** this is where; ~ **où** where; **de** ~ *(fig)* hence; **par** ~ *(fig)* by that; **tout est** ~ *(fig)* that's what it's all about.
là-bas [låbå] *ad* there.
label [låbel] *nm* stamp, seal.
labeur [låbœr] *nm* toil *q,* toiling *q.*
labo [låbō] *nm* (= *laboratoire*) lab.
laborantin, e [låboråñtañ, -ēn] *nm/f* laboratory assistant.
laboratoire [låboråtwår] *nm* laboratory; ~ **de langues/d'analyses** language/(medical) analysis laboratory.
laborieux, euse [låboryœ̄, -œ̄z] *a (tâche)* laborious; **classes** ~**euses** working classes.
labour [låbōōr] *nm* plowing *q (US),* ploughing *q (Brit);* ~**s** *nmpl (champs)* plowed fields; **cheval de** ~ plow- *ou* cart-horse; **bœuf de** ~ ox *(pl* oxen).
labourage [låbōōråzh] *nm* plowing *(US),* ploughing *(Brit).*
labourer [låbōōrå] *vt* to plow *(US),* plough *(Brit);* *(fig)* to make deep gashes *ou* furrows in.
laboureur [låbōōrœr] *nm* plowman *(US),* ploughman *(Brit).*
labrador [låbrådor] *nm (chien)* labrador; *(GÉO):* **le L~** Labrador.
labyrinthe [låbērañt] *nm* labyrinth, maze.
lac [låk] *nm* lake; **le** ~ **Léman** Lake Geneva; **les Grands L~s** the Great Lakes; *voir aussi* **lacs.**
lacer [låså] *vt* to lace *ou* do up.
lacérer [låsårå] *vt* to tear to shreds.
lacet [låse] *nm (de chaussure)* lace; *(de route)*

sharp curve *(US) ou* bend *(Brit);* *(piège)* snare; **chaussures à** ~**s** lace-up *ou* lacing shoes.
lâche [låsh] *a (poltron)* cowardly; *(desserré)* loose, slack; *(morale, mœurs)* lax ♦ *nm/f* coward.
lâcher [låshå] *nm (de ballons, oiseaux)* release ♦ *vt* to let go of; *(ce qui tombe, abandonner)* to drop; *(oiseau, animal: libérer)* to release, set free; *(fig: mot, remarque)* to let slip, come out with; *(SPORT: distancer)* to leave behind ♦ *vi (fil, amarres)* to break, give way; *(freins)* to fail; ~ **les amarres** *(NAVIG)* to cast off (the moorings); ~ **prise** to let go.
lâcheté [låshtå] *nf* cowardice; *(bassesse)* baseness.
lacis [låsē] *nm (de ruelles)* maze.
laconique [låkonēk] *a* laconic.
lacrymal, e, aux [låkrēmål, -ō] *a (canal, glande)* tear *cpd.*
lacrymogène [låkrēmozheñ] *a:* **grenade/gaz** ~ tear gas grenade/tear gas.
lacs [lå] *nm (piège)* snare.
lactation [låktåsyōñ] *nf* lactation.
lacté, e [låktå] *a* milk *cpd.*
lactose [låktōz] *nm* lactose, milk sugar.
lacune [låkün] *nf* gap.
lacustre [låküstr(ə)] *a* lake *cpd,* lakeside *cpd.*
lad [låd] *nm* stableboy.
là-dedans [lådədåñ] *ad* inside (there), in it; *(fig)* in that.
là-dehors [lådəor] *ad* out there.
là-derrière [låderyer] *ad* behind there; *(fig)* behind that.
là-dessous [lådsōō] *ad* underneath, under there; *(fig)* behind that.
là-dessus [lådsü] *ad* on there; *(fig)* at that point; *(: à ce sujet)* about that.
là-devant [lådvåñ] *ad* there (in front).
ladite [lådēt] *dét voir* **ledit.**
ladre [lådr(ə)] *a* miserly.
lagon [lågôñ] *nm* lagoon.
Lagos [lågos] *n* Lagos.
lagune [lågün] *nf* lagoon.
là-haut [låō] *ad* up there.
laïc [låēk] *a, nm/f* = **laïque.**
laïcité [låēsētå] *nf* secularity, secularism.
laid, e [le, led] *a* ugly; *(fig: acte)* mean, cheap.
laideron [ledrôñ] *nm* ugly girl.
laideur [ledœr] *nf* ugliness *q;* meanness *q.*
laie [le] *nf* wild sow.
lainage [lenåzh] *nm* woolen *(US) ou* woollen *(Brit)* garment; *(étoffe)* woolen *ou* woollen material.
laine [len] *nf* wool; ~ **peignée** worsted (wool); ~ **à tricoter** knitting wool; ~ **de verre** glass wool; ~ **vierge** virgin *(US) ou* new *(Brit)* wool.
laineux, euse [lenœ̄, -œ̄z] *a* woolly.
lainier, ière [lenyå, -yer] *a (industrie etc)* woolen *(US),* woollen *(Brit).*
laïque [låēk] *a* lay, civil; *(SCOL)* public *cpd (US),* state *cpd (Brit) (as opposed to private and Roman Catholic)* ♦ *nm/f* layman/woman.
laisse [les] *nf (de chien)* lead, leash; **tenir en** ~ to keep on a lead *ou* leash.
laissé-pour-compte, laissée-, laissés- [låsåpōōrkôñt] *a (COMM)* unsold; *(: refusé)*

returned ♦ *nm/f* (*fig*) reject; **les laissés-pour-compte de la reprise économique** those who are left out of the economic upturn.

laisser [lesā] *vt* to leave ♦ *vb auxiliaire*: ~ **qn faire** to let sb do; **se** ~ **exploiter** to let o.s. be exploited; **se** ~ **aller** to let o.s. go; ~ **qn tranquille** to let *ou* leave sb alone; **laisse-toi faire** let me (*ou* him) do it; **rien ne laisse penser que ...** there is no reason to think that ...; **cela ne laisse pas de surprendre** nonetheless it is surprising.

laisser-aller [lāsāálā] *nm* carelessness, slovenliness.

laisser-faire [lāsāfer] *nm* laissez-faire.

laissez-passer [lāsāpāsā] *nm inv* pass.

lait [le] *nm* milk; **frère/sœur de** ~ foster brother/sister; ~ **écrémé/concentré/condensé** skimmed/condensed/evaporated milk; ~ **en poudre** powdered milk, milk powder; ~ **de chèvre/vache** goat's/cow's milk; ~ **maternel** mother's milk; ~ **démaquillant/de beauté** cleansing/beauty lotion.

laitage [letázh] *nm* milk product.

laiterie [lctrē] *nf* dairy.

laiteux, euse [letœ̄, -œ̄z] *a* milky.

laitier, ière [lātyā, -yer] *a* dairy ♦ *nm/f* milkman/dairywoman.

laiton [letóń] *nm* brass.

laitue [lātü] *nf* lettuce.

laïus [lâyüs] *nm* (*péj*) spiel.

lama [lámá] *nm* llama.

lambeau, x [lâńbō] *nm* scrap; **en** ~**x** in tatters, tattered.

lambin, e [lâńbań, -ēn] *a* (*péj*) slow.

lambiner [lâńbēnā] *vi* (*péj*) to dawdle.

lambris [lâńbrē] *nm* paneling *q* (*US*), panelling *q* (*Brit*).

lambrissé, e [lâńbrēsā] *a* paneled (*US*), panelled (*Brit*).

lame [lám] *nf* blade; (*vague*) wave; (*lamelle*) strip; ~ **de fond** ground swell *q*; ~ **de rasoir** razor blade.

lamé [lámā] *nm* lamé.

lamelle [lámel] *nf* (*lame*) small blade; (*morceau*) sliver; (*de champignon*) gill; **couper en** ~**s** to slice thinly.

lamentable [lámáńtábl(ə)] *a* (*déplorable*) appalling; (*pitoyable*) pitiful.

lamentation [lámáńtâsyóń] *nf* wailing *q*, lamentation; moaning *q*.

lamenter [lámáńtā]: **se** ~ *vi*: **se** ~ (**sur**) to moan (over).

laminage [lámēnázh] *nm* lamination.

laminer [lámēnā] *vt* to laminate; (*fig: écraser*) to wipe out.

laminoir [lámēnwár] *nm* rolling mill; **passer au** ~ (*fig*) to go (*ou* put) through the mill.

lampadaire [lâńpáder] *nm* (*de salon*) floor (*US*) *ou* standard (*Brit*) lamp; (*dans la rue*) streetlight.

lampe [lâńp(ə)] *nf* lamp; (*TECH*) valve; ~ **à alcool** spirit lamp; ~ **à bronzer** sunlamp; ~ **de poche** flashlight, torch (*Brit*); ~ **à souder** blowtorch; ~ **témoin** warning light.

lampée [lâńpā] *nf* gulp, swig.

lampe-tempête [lâńptâńpet] *pl* **lampes-tempête** *nf* storm lantern.

lampion [lâńpyóń] *nm* Chinese lantern.

lampiste [lâńpēst(ə)] *nm* light (maintenance) man; (*fig*) underling.

lamproie [lâńprwá] *nf* lamprey.

lance [lâńs] *nf* spear; ~ **d'arrosage** garden hose; ~ **à eau** water hose; ~ **d'incendie** fire hose.

lancée [lâńsā] *nf*: **être/continuer sur sa** ~ to be under way/keep going.

lance-flammes [lâńsflâm] *nm inv* flamethrower.

lance-fusées [lâńsfüzā] *nm inv* rocket launcher.

lance-grenades [lâńsgrənád] *nm inv* grenade launcher.

lancement [lâńsmáń] *nm* launching *q*, launch; **offre de** ~ introductory offer.

lance-missiles [lâńsmēsēl] *nm inv* missile launcher.

lance-pierres [lâńspyer] *nm inv* slingshot.

lancer [lâńsā] *nm* (*SPORT*) throwing *q*, throw; (*PÊCHE*) rod and reel fishing ♦ *vt* to throw; (*émettre, projeter*) to throw out, send out; (*produit, fusée, bateau, artiste*) to launch; (*injure*) to hurl, fling; (*proclamation, mandat d'arrêt*) to issue; (*emprunt*) to float; (*moteur*) to send roaring away; ~ **qch à qn** to throw sth to sb; (*de façon agressive*) to throw sth at sb; ~ **un cri** *ou* **un appel** to shout *ou* call out; **se** ~ *vi* (*prendre de l'élan*) to build up speed; (*se précipiter*): **se** ~ **sur** *ou* **contre** to rush at; **se** ~ **dans** (*discussion*) to launch into; (*aventure*) to embark on; (*les affaires, la politique*) to go into; ~ **du poids** *nm* putting the shot.

lance-roquettes [lâńsroket] *nm inv* rocket launcher.

lance-torpilles [lâństorpēy] *nm inv* torpedo tube.

lanceur, euse [lâńscœr, -œ̄z] *nm/f* bowler; (*BASEBALL*) pitcher ♦ *nm* (*ESPACE*) launcher.

lancinant, e [lâńsēnâń, -âńt] *a* (*regrets etc*) haunting; (*douleur*) shooting.

lanciner [lâńsēnā] *vi* to throb; (*fig*) to nag.

landais, e [lâńde, -ez] *a* of *ou* from the Landes.

landau [lâńdō] *nm* baby carriage (*US*), pram (*Brit*).

lande [lâńd] *nf* moor.

Landes [lâńd] *nfpl*: **les** ~ the Landes.

langage [lâńgázh] *nm* language; ~ **d'assemblage** (*INFORM*) assembly language; ~ **évolué/machine** (*INFORM*) high-level/machine language; ~ **de programmation** (*INFORM*) programming language.

lange [lâńzh] *nm* flannel blanket; ~**s** *nmpl* swaddling clothes.

langer [lâńzhā] *vt* to change (the diaper (*US*) *ou* nappy (*Brit*) of); **table à** ~ changing table.

langoureux, euse [lâńgōōrœ̄, -œ̄z] *a* languorous.

langouste [lâńgōōst(ə)] *nf* crayfish *inv*.

langoustine [lâńgōōstēn] *nf* prawn (*US*), Dublin Bay prawn (*Brit*).

langue [lâńg] *nf* (*ANAT, CULIN*) tongue; (*LING*) language; (*bande*): ~ **de terre** spit of land; **tirer la** ~ (**à**) to stick out one's tongue (at); **donner sa** ~ **au chat** to give up; **de** ~ **française** French-speaking; ~ **de bois** officialese; ~ **maternelle** native language, mother tongue; ~ **verte** slang; ~ **vivante** modern language.

langue-de-chat [lăṅgdəshá] *nf* ladyfinger (*US*), finger biscuit (*Brit*).

languedocien, ne [lăṅgdosyaṅ, -en] *a* of *ou* from the Languedoc.

languette [lăṅget] *nf* tongue.

langueur [lăṅgœr] *nf* languidness.

languir [lăṅgēr] *vi* to languish; (*conversation*) to flag; **se** ~ *vi* to be languishing; **faire** ~ **qn** to keep sb waiting.

languissant, e [lăṅgēsaṅ, -àṅt] *a* languid.

lanière [lănyer] *nf* (*de fouet*) lash; (*de valise, bretelle*) strap.

lanoline [lănolēn] *nf* lanolin.

lanterne [lăṅtern(ə)] *nf* (*portable*) lantern; (*électrique*) light, lamp; (*de voiture*) (side)light; ~ **rouge** (*fig*) tail-ender; ~ **vénitienne** Chinese lantern.

lanterneau, x [lăṅternō] *nm* skylight.

lanterner [lăṅternā] *vi*: **faire** ~ **qn** to keep sb hanging around.

Laos [làos] *nm*: **le** ~ Laos.

laotien, ne [làosyaṅ, -en] *a* Laotian.

lapalissade [lăpálēsàd] *nf* statement of the obvious.

La Paz [lápáz] *n* La Paz.

laper [lăpā] *vt* to lap up.

lapereau, x [lăprō] *nm* young rabbit.

lapidaire [lăpēder] *a* stone *cpd*; (*fig*) terse.

lapider [lăpēdā] *vt* to stone.

lapin [lăpaṅ] *nm* rabbit; (*fourrure*) cony; **coup du** ~ rabbit punch; **poser un** ~ **à qn** to stand sb up; ~ **de garenne** wild rabbit.

lapon, e [lăpôṅ, -on] *a* Lapp, Lappish ♦ *nm* (*LING*) Lapp, Lappish ♦ *nm/f*: **L~, e** Lapp, Laplander.

Laponie [lăponē] *nf*: **la** ~ Lapland.

laps [lăps] *nm*: ~ **de temps** space of time, time *q*.

lapsus [lăpsüs] *nm* slip.

laquais [lăke] *nm* lackey.

laque [lăk] *nf* lacquer; (*brute*) shellac; (*pour cheveux*) hair spray ♦ *nm* lacquer; piece of lacquer ware.

laqué, e [lăkā] *a* lacquered.

laquelle [lăkel] *pronom voir* **lequel**.

larbin [lărbaṅ] *nm* (*péj*) flunkey.

larcin [lărsaṅ] *nm* theft.

lard [lăr] *nm* (*graisse*) fat; (*bacon*) (streaky) bacon.

larder [lărdā] *vt* (*CULIN*) to lard.

lardon [lărdôṅ] *nm* (*CULIN*) piece of chopped bacon; (*fam: enfant*) kid.

large [lărzh(ə)] *a* wide; broad; (*fig*) generous ♦ *ad*: **calculer/voir** ~ to allow extra/think big ♦ *nm* (*largeur*): **5 m de** ~ 5 m wide *ou* in width; (*mer*): **le** ~ the open sea; **en** ~ *ad* sideways; **au** ~ **de** off; ~ **d'esprit** broad-minded; **ne pas en mener** ~ to have one's heart in one's boots.

largement [lărzhəmàṅ] *ad* widely; (*de loin*) greatly; (*amplement, au minimum*) easily; (*sans compter: donner etc*) generously.

largesse [lărzhes] *nf* generosity; ~**s** *nfpl* liberalities.

largeur [lărzhœr] *nf* (*qu'on mesure*) width; (*impression visuelle*) wideness, width; breadth; broadness.

larguer [lărgā] *vt* to drop; (*fam: se débarrasser de*) to get rid of; ~ **les amarres** to cast off (the moorings).

larme [lărm(ə)] *nf* tear; (*fig*): **une** ~ **de** a drop of; **en** ~**s** in tears; **pleurer à chaudes** ~**s** to cry one's eyes out, cry bitterly.

larmoyant, e [lărmwáyàṅ, -àṅt] *a* tearful.

larmoyer [lărmwáyā] *vi* (*yeux*) to water; (*se plaindre*) to whimper.

larron [lărôṅ] *nm* thief (*pl* thieves).

larve [lărv(ə)] *nf* (*ZOOL*) larva (*pl* -ae); (*fig*) worm.

larvé, e [lărvā] *a* (*fig*) latent.

laryngite [lărăṅzhēt] *nf* laryngitis.

laryngologiste [lărăṅgolozhēst(ə)] *nm/f* throat specialist.

larynx [lărăṅks] *nm* larynx.

las, lasse [lâ, lâs] *a* weary.

lasagne [lăzány] *nf* lasagne.

lascar [lăskár] *nm* character; (*malin*) rogue.

lascif, ive [lăsēf, -ēv] *a* lascivious.

laser [lăzer] *nm*: **(rayon)** ~ laser (beam); **chaîne** *ou* **platine** ~ compact disc (player); **disque** ~ compact disc.

lassant, e [lâsàṅ, -àṅt] *a* tiresome, wearisome.

lasse [lâs] *af voir* **las**.

lasser [lâsā] *vt* to weary, tire; **se** ~ **de** to grow weary *ou* tired of.

lassitude [lâsētüd] *nf* lassitude, weariness.

lasso [lâsō] *nm* lasso; **prendre au** ~ to lasso.

latent, e [lătàṅ, -àṅt] *a* latent.

latéral, e, aux [lătārál, -ō] *a* side *cpd*, lateral.

latéralement [lătārálmàṅ] *ad* edgeways; (*arriver, souffler*) from the side.

latex [lăteks] *nm inv* latex.

latin, e [lătaṅ, -ēn] *a* Latin ♦ *nm* (*LING*) Latin ♦ *nm/f*: **L~, e** Latin; **j'y perds mon** ~ it's all Greek to me.

latiniste [lătēnēst(ə)] *nm/f* Latin scholar (*ou* student).

latino-américain, e [lătēnoàmārēkaṅ, -en] *a* Latin-American.

latitude [lătētüd] *nf* latitude; (*fig*): **avoir la** ~ **de faire** to be left free *ou* be at liberty to do; **à 48° de** ~ **Nord** at latitude 48° North; **sous toutes les** ~**s** (*fig*) worldwide, throughout the world.

latrines [lătrēn] *nfpl* latrines.

latte [lăt] *nf* lath, slat; (*de plancher*) board.

lattis [lătē] *nm* lathwork.

laudatif, ive [lōdátēf, -ēv] *a* laudatory.

lauréat, e [lorāà, -àt] *nm/f* winner.

laurier [loryā] *nm* (*BOT*) laurel; (*CULIN*) bay leaves *pl*; ~**s** *nmpl* (*fig*) laurels.

laurier-rose, *pl* **lauriers-rose** [loryārōz] *nm* oleander.

lavable [lăvábl(ə)] *a* washable.

lavabo [lăvábō] *nm* washbasin; ~**s** *nmpl* toilet *sg*.

lavage [lăvázh] *nm* washing *q*, wash; ~ **d'estomac/d'intestin** stomach/intestinal wash; ~ **de cerveau** brainwashing *q*.

lavande [lăvàṅd] *nf* lavender.

lavandière [lăvàṅdyer] *nf* washerwoman.

lave [lăv] *nf* lava *q*.

lave-glace [lăvglás] *nm* (*AUTO*) windshield (*US*) *ou* windscreen (*Brit*) washer.

lave-linge [lăvlàṅzh] *nm inv* washing machine.

lavement [lăvmàṅ] *nm* (*MÉD*) enema.

laver [làvā] *vt* to wash; *(tache)* to wash off; *(fig: affront)* to avenge; **se** ~ to have a wash, wash; **se** ~ **les mains/dents** to wash one's hands/brush one's teeth; ~ **la vaisselle/le linge** to wash the dishes/clothes; ~ **qn de** *(accusation)* to clear sb of.

laverie [làvrē] *nf:* ~ **(automatique)** laundromat *(US)*, launderette *(Brit)*.

lavette [làvct] *nf (chiffon)* dishcloth; *(brosse)* dish mop; *(fam: homme)* wimp, drip.

laveur, euse [làvœr, -œz] *nm/f* cleaner.

lave-vaisselle [làvvcscl] *nm inv* dishwasher.

lavis [làvē] *nm (technique)* washing; *(dessin)* wash drawing.

lavoir [làvwàr] *nm* wash house; *(bac)* washtub.

laxatif, ive [làksátēf, -ēv] *a*, *nm* laxative.

laxisme [làksēsm(ə)] *nm* laxity.

laxiste [làksēst(ə)] *a* lax.

layette [lcyct] *nf* layette.

layon [lcyôn] *nm* trail.

lazaret [làzàrc] *nm* quarantine area.

lazzi [làdzē] *nm* gibe.

LCR *sigle f (= Ligue communiste révolutionnaire) political party*.

le (**l'**), **la** (**l'**), **les** [l(ə), là, lā] *dét* the ♦ *pronom (personne: mâle)* him; (: *femelle)* her; *(animal, chose)* it; *(remplaçant une phrase)* it *ou non traduit; (indique la possession)*: **je me casser la jambe** *etc* to break one's leg *etc*; *voir note sous* **il**; **les** them; **je ne le savais pas** I didn't know (about it); **il était riche et ne l'est plus** he was once rich but no longer is; **levez la main** put your hand up; **avoir les yeux gris/le nez rouge** to have gray eyes/a red nose; **le jeudi** *etc ad (d'habitude)* on Thursdays *etc; (ce jeudi-là)* on the Thursday *etc;* **le matin/soir** *ad* in the morning/evening; mornings/evenings; **nous venons le 3 décembre** *(parlé)* we're coming (on) December 3 *ou* 3 December; *(écrit)* we're coming (on) 3rd *ou* 3 December; **10 F le mètre/kilo** 10 F a *ou* per meter/kilo; **le tiers/quart de** a third/quarter of.

lé [lā] *nm (de tissu)* width; *(de papier peint)* strip, length.

leader [lēdœr] *nm* leader.

lèche-bottes [lcshbot] *nm inv* bootlicker.

lèchefrite [lcshfrēt] *nf* dripping pan *ou* tray.

lécher [làshā] *vt* to lick; *(laper: lait, eau)* to lick *ou* lap up; *(finir, polir)* to over-refine; ~ **les vitrines** to go window-shopping; **se** ~ **les doigts/lèvres** to lick one's fingers/lips.

leçon [ləsôn] *nf* lesson; **faire la** ~ to teach; **faire la** ~ **à** *(fig)* to give a lecture to; **~s de conduite** driving lessons; **~s particulières** private lessons *ou* tuition *sg (Brit)*.

lecteur, trice [lcktœr, -trēs] *nm/f* reader; *(d'université)* (foreign) teaching assistant *(US)*, (foreign language) assistant *(Brit)* ♦ *nm (TECH)*: ~ **de cassettes** cassette player; *(INFORM)*: ~ **de disquette(s)** *ou* **de disque** disk drive; ~ **compact-disc** *ou* **CD** compact disc (player).

lectorat [lcktorà] *nm* (foreign language *ou* teaching) assistantship.

lecture [lcktür] *nf* reading.

LED [lcd] *sigle f (= light emitting diode)* LED; **affichage** ~ LED display.

ledit [lədē], **ladite** [làdēt], *mpl* **lesdits** [lādē], *fpl*

lesdites [lādēt] *dét* the aforesaid.

légal, e, aux [lāgàl, -ō] *a* legal.

légalement [lāgàlmán] *ad* legally.

légaliser [lāgàlēzā] *vt* to legalize.

légalité [lāgàlētā] *nf* legality, lawfulness; **être dans/sortir de la** ~ to be within/step outside the law.

légat [lāgà] *nm (REL)* legate.

légataire [lāgáter] *nm* legatee.

légendaire [lāzhánder] *a* legendary.

légende [lāzhánd] *nf (mythe)* legend; *(de carte, plan)* key, legend; *(de dessin)* caption, legend.

léger, ère [lāzhā, -er] *a* light; *(bruit, retard)* slight; *(boisson, parfum)* weak; *(couche, étoffe)* thin; *(superficiel)* thoughtless; *(volage)* free and easy; flighty; *(peu sérieux)* lightweight; **blessé** ~ slightly injured person; **à la légère** *ad (parler, agir)* rashly, thoughtlessly.

légèrement [lāzhermán] *ad* lightly; thoughtlessly, rashly; ~ **plus grand** slightly bigger.

légèreté [lāzhertā] *nf* lightness; thoughtlessness.

légiférer [lāzhēfārā] *vi* to legislate.

légion [lāzhyôn] *nf* legion; **la L~ étrangère** the Foreign Legion; **la L~ d'honneur** the Legion of Honor.

légionnaire [lāzhyoner] *nm (MIL)* legionnaire; *(de la Légion d'honneur)* holder of the Legion of Honor.

législateur [lāzhēslátœr] *nm* legislator, lawmaker.

législatif, ive [lāzhēslátēf, -ēv] *a* legislative; **législatives** *nfpl* general election *sg.*

législation [lāzhēslásyôn] *nf* legislation.

législature [lāzhēslátür] *nf* legislature; *(période)* term (of office).

légiste [lāzhēst(ə)] *nm* jurist ♦ *a:* **médecin** ~ medical examiner *(US)*, forensic scientist *(Brit)*.

légitime [lāzhētēm] *a (JUR)* lawful, legitimate; *(enfant)* legitimate; *(fig)* rightful, legitimate; **en état de** ~ **défense** in self-defense.

légitimement [lāzhētēmmán] *ad* lawfully; legitimately; rightfully.

légitimer [lāzhētēmā] *vt (enfant)* to legitimize; *(justifier: conduite etc)* to justify.

légitimité [lāzhētēmētā] *nf (JUR)* legitimacy.

legs [lcg] *nm* legacy.

léguer [lāgā] *vt:* ~ **qch à qn** *(JUR)* to bequeath sth to sb; *(fig)* to hand sth down *ou* pass sth on to sb.

légume [lāgüm] *nm* vegetable; **~s verts** green vegetables; **~s secs** pulses.

légumier [lāgümyā] *nm* vegetable dish.

Léman [lāmán] *nm voir* **lac**.

lendemain [lándmán] *nm:* **le** ~ the next *ou* following day; **le** ~ **matin/soir** the next *ou* following morning/evening; **le** ~ **de** the day after; **au** ~ **de** in the days following; in the wake of; **penser au** ~ to think of the future; **sans** ~ short-lived; **de beaux ~s** bright prospects; **des ~s qui chantent** a rosy future.

lénifiant, e [lānēfyán, -ánt] *a* soothing.

léniniste [lānēnēst(ə)] *a, nm/f* Leninist.

lent, e [lán, lánt] *a* slow.

lente [lánt] *nf* nit.

lentement [lå̃tmå̃] *ad* slowly.
lenteur [lå̃tœr] *nf* slowness *q*; ~**s** *nfpl*
(*actions, décisions lentes*) slowness *sg*.
lentille [lå̃tēy] *nf* (*OPTIQUE*) lens *sg*; (*BOT*)
lentil; ~ **d'eau** duckweed; ~**s de contact**
contact lenses.
léonin, e [lāonań, -ēn] *a* (*fig: contrat etc*) one-
sided.
léopard [lāopár] *nm* leopard.
LEP [lep] *sigle m* (= *lycée d'enseignement
professionnel*) *secondary school for vocational
training, pre-1986.*
lèpre [lepr(ə)] *nf* leprosy.
lépreux, euse [lāprœ̄, -œ̄z] *nm/f* leper ♦ *a* (*fig*)
flaking, peeling.
lequel [ləkel], **laquelle** [lákel], *mpl* **lesquels**,
fpl **lesquelles** [lākel] (*avec à, de:* **auquel**,
duquel *etc*) *pronom* (*interrogatif*) which,
which one; (*relatif: personne: sujet*) who; (:
objet, après préposition) whom; (: *chose*)
which ♦ *a:* **auquel cas** in which case.
les [lā] *dét voir* **le**.
lesbienne [lesbyen] *nf* lesbian.
lesdits [lādē], **lesdites** [lādēt] *dét voir* **ledit**.
léser [lāzā] *vt* to wrong; (*MÉD*) to injure.
lésiner [lāzēnā] *vt:* ~ (**sur**) to skimp (on).
lésion [lāzyôń] *nf* lesion, damage *q*; ~**s céré-
brales** brain damage.
Lesotho [lāzotō] *nm:* **le** ~ Lesotho.
lesquels, lesquelles [lākel] *pronom voir*
lequel.
lessivable [lāsēvábl(ə)] *a* washable.
lessive [lāsēv] *nf* (*poudre*) washing powder;
(*linge*) washing *q*, wash; (*opération*) washing
q; **faire la** ~ to do the washing.
lessivé, e [lāsēvā] *a* (*fam*) washed out.
lessiver [lāsēvā] *vt* to wash.
lessiveuse [lāsēvœ̄z] *nf* (*récipient*) (laundry)
boiler.
lessiviel [lāsēvyel] *a* detergent.
lest [lest] *nm* ballast; **jeter** *ou* **lâcher du** ~
(*fig*) to make concessions.
leste [lest(ə)] *a* (*personne, mouvement*)
sprightly, nimble; (*désinvolte: manières*) off-
hand; (*osé: plaisanterie*) risqué.
lestement [lestəmå̃] *ad* nimbly.
lester [lestā] *vt* to ballast.
letchi [letshē] *nm* = **litchi**.
léthargie [lātárzhē] *nf* lethargy.
léthargique [lātárzhēk] *a* lethargic.
letton, ne [letôń, -on] *a* Latvian, Lett.
Lettonie [letonē] *nf:* **la** ~ Latvia.
lettre [letr(ə)] *nf* letter; ~**s** *nfpl* (*étude,
culture*) literature *sg*; (*SCOL*) arts (sub-
jects); **à la** ~ (*au sens propre*) literally;
(*ponctuellement*) to the letter; **en** ~**s
majuscules** *ou* **capitales** in capital letters, in
capitals; **en toutes** ~**s** in words, in full; ~
de change bill of exchange; ~ **piégée** letter
bomb; ~ **de voiture (aérienne)** (air) waybill,
(air) bill of lading; ~**s de noblesse** pedigree.
lettré, e [lātrā] *a* well-read, scholarly.
lettre-transfert, *pl* **lettres-transferts**
[letrətrå̃sfer] *nf* (*pressure*) transfer.
leu [lœ] *voir* **queue**.
leucémie [lœsāmē] *nf* leukemia (*US*),
leukaemia (*Brit*).
leur [lœr] *dét* their ♦ *pronom* them; **le (la)** ~,
les ~**s** theirs; **à** ~ **approche** as they came

near; **à** ~ **vue** at the sight of them.
leurre [lœr] *nm* (*appât*) lure; (*fig*) delusion; (:
piège) snare.
leurrer [lœrā] *vt* to delude, deceive.
levain [ləvań] *nm* leaven; **sans** ~ unleavened.
levant, e [ləvåń, -åńt] *a:* **soleil** ~ rising sun ♦
nm: **le L**~ the Levant; **au soleil** ~ at sunrise.
levantin, e [ləvåńtań, -ēn] *a* Levantine ♦ *nm/f:*
L~, e Levantine.
levé, e [ləvā] *a:* **être** ~ to be up ♦ *nm:* ~ **de
terrain** land survey; **à mains** ~**es** (*vote*) by a
show of hands; **au pied** ~ at a moment's
notice.
levée [ləvā] *nf* (*POSTES*) collection; (*CARTES*)
trick; ~ **de boucliers** general outcry; ~ **du
corps** *collection of the body from house of the
deceased, before funeral;* ~ **d'écrou** release
from custody; ~ **de terre** levee; ~ **de
troupes** levy.
lever [ləvā] *vt* (*vitre, bras etc*) to raise;
(*soulever de terre, supprimer: interdiction,
siège*) to lift; (: *difficulté*) to remove;
(*séance*) to close; (*impôts, armée*) to levy;
(*CHASSE: lièvre*) to start; (: *perdrix*) to
flush; (*fam: fille*) to pick up ♦ *vi* (*CULIN*) to
rise ♦ *nm:* **au** ~ on getting up; **se** ~ *vi* to get
up; (*soleil*) to rise; (*jour*) to break;
(*brouillard*) to lift; **ça va se** ~ the weather
will clear; ~ **du jour** daybreak; ~ **du rideau**
(*THÉÂTRE*) curtain; ~ **de rideau** (*pièce*)
curtain raiser; ~ **de soleil** sunrise.
lève-tard [levtár] *nm/f inv* late riser.
lève-tôt [levtō] *nm/f inv* early riser, early
bird.
levier [ləvyā] *nm* lever; **faire** ~ **sur** to lever up
(*ou* off); ~ **de changement de vitesse** gear-
shift.
levraut [ləvrō] *nm* (*ZOOL*) leveret.
lèvre [levr(ə)] *nf* lip; ~**s** *nfpl* (*d'une plaie*)
edges; **petites/grandes** ~**s** labia minora/
majora; **du bout des** ~**s** half-heartedly.
lévrier [lāvrēyā] *nm* greyhound.
levure [ləvür] *nf* yeast; ~ **chimique** baking
powder.
lexicographe [leksēkográf] *nm/f* lexicographer.
lexicographie [leksēkográfē] *nf* lexicography,
dictionary writing.
lexique [leksēk] *nm* vocabulary, lexicon;
(*glossaire*) vocabulary.
lézard [lāzár] *nm* lizard; (*peau*) lizard skin.
lézarde [lāzárd(ə)] *nf* crack.
lézarder [lāzárdā]: **se** ~ *vi* to crack.
liaison [lyezôń] *nf* (*rapport*) connection, link;
(*RAIL, AVIAT etc*) link; (*relation: d'amitié*)
friendship; (: *d'affaires*) relationship; (:
amoureuse) affair; (*CULIN, PHONÉTIQUE*)
liaison; **entrer/être en** ~ **avec** to get/be in
contact with; ~ **radio** radio contact; ~ **(de
transmission de données)** (*INFORM*) data
link.
liane [lyán] *nf* creeper.
liant, e [lyåń, -åńt] *a* sociable.
liasse [lyás] *nf* wad, bundle.
Liban [lēbáń] *nm:* **le** ~ (the) Lebanon.
libanais, e [lēbáne, -ez] *a* Lebanese ♦ *nm/f:* **L**~,
e Lebanese.
libations [lēbásyôń] *nfpl* libations.

libelle [lēbɛl] *nm* lampoon.
libellé [lēbālā] *nm* wording.
libeller [lēbālā] *vt* (*chèque, mandat*): ~ **(au nom de)** to make out (to); (*lettre*) to word.
libellule [lēbālül] *nf* dragonfly.
libéral, e, aux [lēbārál, -ō] *a, nm/f* liberal; **les professions** ~**es** the professions.
libéralement [lēbérálmáṅ] *ad* liberally.
libéralisation [lēbārálēzásyôṅ] *nf* liberalization; ~ **du commerce** easing of trade restrictions.
libéraliser [lēbārálēzā] *vt* to liberalize.
libéralisme [lēbārálēsm(ə)] *nm* liberalism.
libéralité [lēbārálētā] *nf* liberality *q*, generosity *q*.
libérateur, trice [lēbārátœr, -trēs] *a* liberating ♦ *nm/f* liberator.
libération [lēbārásyóṅ] *nf* liberation, freeing; release; discharge; ~ **conditionnelle** release on parole.
libéré, e [lēbārā] *a* liberated; ~ **de** freed from; **être** ~ **sous caution/sur parole** to be released on bail/on parole.
libérer [lēbārā] *vt* (*délivrer*) to free, liberate; (: *moralement,* PSYCH) to liberate; (*relâcher: prisonnier*) to release; (: *soldat*) to discharge; (*dégager: gaz, cran d'arrêt*) to release; (ÉCON: *échanges commerciaux*) to ease restrictions on; **se** ~ (*de rendez-vous*) to try and be free, get out of previous engagements; ~ **qn de** (*liens, dette*) to free sb from; (*promesse*) to release sb from.
Libéria [lēbáryá] *nm*: **le** ~ Liberia.
libérien, ne [lēbāryaṅ, -en] *a* Liberian ♦ *nm/f*: **L**~, **ne** Liberian.
libertaire [lēberter] *a* libertarian.
liberté [lēbertā] *nf* freedom; (*loisir*) free time; ~**s** *nfpl* (*privautés*) liberties; **mettre/être en** ~ to set/be free; **en** ~ **provisoire/surveillée/conditionnelle** on bail/probation/parole; ~ **d'association** right of association; ~ **de conscience** freedom of conscience; ~ **du culte** freedom of worship; ~ **d'esprit** independence of mind; ~ **d'opinion** freedom of thought; ~ **de la presse** freedom of the press; ~ **de réunion** right of assembly; ~ **syndicale** union rights *pl*; ~**s individuelles** personal freedom *sg*; ~**s publiques** civil rights.
libertin, e [lēbertaṅ, -ēn] *a* libertine, licentious.
libertinage [lēbertēnázh] *nm* licentiousness.
libidineux, euse [lēbēdēnœ̄, -œ̄z] *a* libidinous, lustful.
libido [lēbēdō] *nf* libido.
libraire [lēbrer] *nm/f* bookseller.
libraire-éditeur, *pl* **libraires-éditeurs** [lēbrerādētœr] *nm* publisher and bookseller.
librairie [lēbrārē] *nf* bookstore (US), bookshop (*Brit*).
librairie-papeterie, *pl* **librairies-papeteries** [lēbrārēpápátrē] bookseller's and stationer's.
libre [lēbr(ə)] *a* free; (*route*) clear; (*place etc*) vacant, free; (*fig: propos, manières*) open; (SCOL) private and Roman Catholic (*as opposed to "laïque"*); **de** ~ (*place*) free; ~ **de qch/de faire** free from sth/to do; **vente** ~ (COMM) unrestricted sale; ~ **arbitre** free will; ~ **concurrence** free-market economy; ~ **entreprise** free enterprise.

libre-échange [lēbrāshâṅzh] *nm* free trade.
librement [lēbrəmáṅ] *ad* freely.
libre-penseur, euse [lēbrəpáṅsœr, -œ̄z] *nm/f* freethinker.
libre-service [lēbrəservēs] *nm inv* (*magasin*) self-service store; (*restaurant*) self-service restaurant.
librettiste [lēbrātēst(ə)] *nm/f* librettist.
Libye [lēbē] *nf*: **la** ~ Libya.
libyen, ne [lēbyaṅ, -en] *a* Libyan ♦ *nm/f*: **L**~, **ne** Libyan.
lice [lēs] *nf*: **entrer en** ~ (*fig*) to enter the lists.
licence [lēsáṅs] *nf* (*permis*) permit; (*diplôme*) (first) degree; (*liberté*) liberty; (*poétique, orthographique*) license (US), licence (*Brit*); (*des mœurs*) licentiousness; ~ **ès lettres/en droit** arts/law degree.
licencié, e [lēsáṅsyā] *nm/f* (SCOL): ~ **ès lettres/en droit** ≈ Master (US) *ou* Bachelor (*Brit*) of Arts/Law, arts/law graduate; (SPORT) permit holder.
licenciement [lēsáṅsēmáṅ] *nm* dismissal; laying off *q*.
licencier [lēsáṅsyā] *vt* (*renvoyer*) to dismiss; to lay off.
licencieux, euse [lēsáṅsyœ̄, -œ̄z] *a* licentious.
lichen [lēken] *nm* lichen.
licite [lēsēt] *a* lawful.
licorne [lēkorn(ə)] *nf* unicorn.
licou [lēkōō] *nm* halter.
lie [lē] *nf* dregs *pl*, sediment.
lié, e [lyā] *a*: **très** ~ **avec** (*fig*) very friendly with *ou* close to; ~ **par** (*serment, promesse*) bound by; **avoir partie** ~**e (avec qn)** to be involved (with sb).
Liechtenstein [lēshtenshtáyn] *nm*: **le** ~ Liechtenstein.
lie-de-vin [lēdvaṅ] *a inv* wine(-colored).
liège [lyezh] *nm* cork.
liégeois, e [lyāzhwá, -wáz] *a* of *ou* from Liège ♦ *nm/f*: **L**~, **e** inhabitant *ou* native of Liège; **café/chocolat** ~ *coffee/chocolate ice cream topped with whipped cream.*
lien [lyaṅ] *nm* (*corde, fig: affectif, culturel*) bond; (*rapport*) link, connection; (*analogie*) link; ~ **de parenté** family tie.
lier [lyā] *vt* (*attacher*) to tie up; (*joindre*) to link up; (*fig: unir, engager*) to bind; (CULIN) to thicken; ~ **qch à** (*attacher*) to tie sth to; (*associer*) to link sth to; ~ **amitié/conversation (avec)** to strike up a friendship/conversation (with); **se** ~ **avec** to make friends with.
lierre [lyer] *nm* ivy.
liesse [lyes] *nf*: **être en** ~ to be jubilant.
lieu, x [lyœ̄] *nm* place; ~**x** *nmpl* (*locaux*) premises; (*endroit: d'un accident etc*) scene *sg*; **en** ~ **sûr** in a safe place; **en haut** ~ in high places; **vider** *ou* **quitter les** ~**x** to leave the premises; **arriver/être sur les** ~**x** to arrive/be on the scene; **en premier** ~ in the first place; **en dernier** ~ lastly; **avoir** ~ to take place; **avoir** ~ **de faire** to have grounds *ou* good reason for doing; **tenir** ~ **de** to take the place of; (*servir de*) to serve as; **donner** ~ **à** to give rise to, give cause for; **au** ~ **de** instead of; **au** ~ **qu'il y aille** instead of him going; ~ **commun** commonplace; ~ **géomé-**

trique locus; ~ **de naissance** place of birth; ~ **de rendez-vous** venue, meeting place.

lieu-dit, *pl* **lieux-dits** [lyœ̃dē] *nm* locality.

lieue [lyœ̃] *nf* league.

lieutenant [lyœ̃tnáń] *nm* lieutenant; ~ **de vaisseau** (*NAVIG*) lieutenant.

lièvre [lyevr(ə)] *nm* hare; (*coureur*) pacemaker; **lever un** ~ (*fig*) to bring up a touchy subject.

liftier, ière [lēftyā, -yer] elevator (*US*) *ou* lift (*Brit*) attendant.

lifting [lēftēng] *nm* face lift.

ligament [lēgámáń] *nm* ligament.

ligature [lēgátür] *nf* ligature.

lige [lēzh] *a*: **homme** ~ (*péj*) henchman.

ligne [lēny] *nf* (*gén*) line; (*TRANSPORTS*: *liaison*) service; (: *trajet*) route; (*silhouette*): **garder la** ~ to keep one's figure; **en** ~ (*INFORM*) on line; **en** ~ **droite** as the crow flies; **"à la** ~" "new paragraph"; **entrer en** ~ **de compte** to be taken into account; to come into it; ~ **de but/médiane** goal/halfway line; ~ **d'arrivée/de départ** finish (*US*) *ou* finishing (*Brit*)/starting line; ~ **de conduite** course of action; ~ **directrice** guiding line; ~ **d'horizon** skyline; ~ **de mire** line of sight; ~ **de touche** touchline.

ligné, e [lēnyā] *a*: **papier** ~ ruled paper ♦ *nf* (*race, famille*) line, lineage; (*postérité*) descendants *pl*.

ligneux, euse [lēnyœ̃, -œ̃z] *a* ligneous, woody.

lignite [lēnyēt] *nm* lignite.

ligoter [lēgotā] *vt* to tie up.

ligue [lēg] *nf* league.

liguer [lēgā]: **se** ~ *vi* to form a league; **se** ~ **contre** (*fig*) to combine against.

lilas [lēlá] *nm* lilac.

lillois, e [lēlwá, -wáz] *a* of *ou* from Lille.

Lima [lēmá] *n* Lima.

limace [lēmás] *nf* slug.

limaille [lēmáy] *nf*: ~ **de fer** iron filings *pl*.

limande [lēmáńd] *nf* dab.

limande-sole [lēmáńdsōl] *nf* lemon sole.

limbes [lāńb] *nmpl* limbo *sg*; **être dans les** ~ (*fig: projet etc*) to be up in the air.

lime [lēm] *nf* (*TECH*) file; (*BOT*) lime; ~ **à ongles** nail file.

limer [lēmā] *vt* (*bois, métal*) to file (down); (*ongles*) to file; (*fig: prix*) to pare down.

limier [lēmyā] *nm* (*ZOOL*) bloodhound; (*détective*) sleuth.

liminaire [lēmēner] *a* (*propos*) introductory.

limitatif, ive [lēmētátēf, -ēv] *a* restrictive.

limitation [lēmētásyóń] *nf* limitation, restriction; **sans** ~ **de temps** with no time limit; ~ **des naissances** birth control; ~ **de vitesse** speed limit.

limite [lēmēt] *nf* (*de terrain*) boundary; (*partie ou point extrême*) limit; **dans la** ~ **de** within the limits of; **à la** ~ (*au pire*) if the worst comes (*ou* came) to the worst; **sans** ~**s** (*bêtise, richesse, pouvoir*) limitless, boundless; **vitesse/charge** ~ maximum speed/load; **cas** ~ borderline case; **date** ~ deadline; **date** ~ **de vente/consommation** sell-by/best-before date; **prix** ~ upper price limit; ~ **d'âge** maximum age, age limit.

limiter [lēmētā] *vt* (*restreindre*) to limit, restrict; (*délimiter*) to border, form the boundary of; **se** ~ (**à qch/à faire**) (*personne*) to limit *ou* confine o.s. (to sth/to doing sth); **se** ~ **à** (*chose*) to be limited to.

limitrophe [lēmētrof] *a* border *cpd*; ~ **de** bordering on.

limogeage [lēmozházh] *nm* dismissal.

limoger [lēmozhā] *vt* to dismiss.

limon [lēmóń] *nm* silt.

limonade [lēmonád] *nf* lemonade.

limonadier, ière [lēmonádyā, -yer] *nm/f* (*commerçant*) café owner; (*fabricant de limonade*) soft drinks manufacturer.

limoneux, euse [lēmonœ̃, -œ̃z] *a* muddy.

limousin, e [lēmōōzań, -ēn] *a* of *ou* from Limousin ♦ *nm* (*région*): **le L**~ the Limousin.

limpide [lańpēd] *a* limpid.

lin [lań] *nm* (*BOT*) flax; (*tissu, toile*) linen.

linceul [lańsœl] *nm* shroud.

linéaire [lēnāer] *a* linear ♦ *nm*: ~ (**de vente**) shelves *pl*.

linéament [lēnāámáń] *nm* outline.

linge [lańzh] *nm* (*serviettes etc*) linen; (*pièce de tissu*) cloth; (*aussi*: ~ **de corps**) underwear; (*aussi*: ~ **de toilette**) towel; (*lessive*) washing; ~ **sale** dirty linen.

lingerie [lańzhrē] *nf* lingerie, underwear.

lingot [lańgō] *nm* ingot.

linguiste [lańgüēst(ə)] *nm/f* linguist.

linguistique [lańgüēstēk] *a* linguistic ♦ *nf* linguistics *sg*.

lino(léum) [lēno(lāom)] *nm* linoleum.

linotte [lēnot] *nf*: **tête de** ~ bird brain.

linteau, x [lańtō] *nm* lintel.

lion, ne [lyóń, lyon] *nm* lion/lioness; (*signe*): **le L**~ Leo, the Lion; **être du L**~ to be Leo; ~ **de mer** sea lion.

lionceau, x [lyóńsō] *nm* lion cub.

lippu, e [lēpü] *a* thick-lipped.

liquéfier [lēkāfyā] *vt* to liquefy; **se** ~ *vi* (*gaz etc*) to liquefy; (*fig: personne*) to succumb.

liqueur [lēkœr] *nf* liqueur.

liquidateur, trice [lēkēdátœr, -trēs] *nm/f* (*JUR*) receiver; ~ **judiciaire** official liquidator.

liquidation [lēkēdásyóń] *nf* liquidation; (*COMM*) clearance (sale); ~ **judiciaire** compulsory liquidation.

liquide [lēkēd] *a* liquid ♦ *nm* liquid; (*COMM*): **en** ~ in ready money *ou* cash.

liquider [lēkēdā] *vt* (*société, biens, témoin gênant*) to liquidate; (*compte, problème*) to settle; (*COMM: articles*) to clear, sell off.

liquidités [lēkēdētā] *nfpl* (*COMM*) liquid assets.

liquoreux, euse [lēkorœ̃, -œ̃z] *a* syrupy.

lire [lēr] *nf* (*monnaie*) lira ♦ *vt, vi* to read; ~ **qch à qn** to read sth (out) to sb.

lis *vb* [lē] *voir* **lire** ♦ *nm* [lēs] = **lys**.

lisais [lēze] *etc vb voir* **lire**.

Lisbonne [lēzbon] *n* Lisbon.

lise [lēz] *etc vb voir* **lire**.

liseré [lēzrā] *nm* border, edging.

liseron [lēzróń] *nm* bindweed.

liseuse [lēzœ̃z] *nf* book cover; (*veste*) bed jacket.

lisible [lēzēbl(ə)] *a* legible; (*digne d'être lu*) readable.

lisiblement [lēzēbləmáń] *ad* legibly.

lisière [lēzyer] *nf* (*de forêt*) edge; (*de tissu*) selvage.

lisons [lēzóń] *vb voir* **lire.**
lisse [lēs] *a* smooth.
lisser [lēsā] *vt* to smooth.
listage [lēstázh] *nm* (*INFORM*) listing.
liste [lēst(ǝ)] *nf* list; (*INFORM*) listing; **faire la** ~ **de** to list, make out a list of; ~ **d'attente** waiting list; ~ **civile** civil list; ~ **électorale** electoral roll; ~ **de mariage** wedding (present) list.
lister [lēstā] *vt* (*aussi INFORM*) to list; ~ **la mémoire** to dump.
listing [lēstēng] *nm* (*INFORM*) listing; **qualité** ~ draft quality.
lit [lē] *nm* (*gén*) bed; **faire son** ~ to make one's bed; **aller/se mettre au** ~ to go to/get into bed; **prendre le** ~ to take to one's bed; **d'un premier** ~ (*JUR*) of a first marriage; ~ **de camp** cot (*US*), campbed (*Brit*); ~ **d'enfant** crib (*US*), cot (*Brit*).
litanie [lētānē] *nf* litany.
lit-cage, *pl* **lits-cages** [lēkázh] *nm* folding bed.
litchi [lētshē] *nm* litchi (*US*), lychee (*Brit*).
literie [lētrē] *nf* bedding; (*linge*) bedding, bedclothes *pl*.
litho [lētō], **lithographie** [lētográfē] *nf* litho(graphy); (*épreuve*) litho(graph).
litière [lētyer] *nf* litter.
litige [lētēzh] *nm* dispute; **en** ~ in contention.
litigieux, euse [lētēzhyœ̄, -œ̄z] *a* litigious, contentious.
litote [lētot] *nf* understatement.
litre [lētr(ǝ)] *nm* liter (*US*), litre (*Brit*); (*récipient*) liter *ou* litre measure.
littéraire [lētārer] *a* literary.
littéral, e, aux [lētārál, -ō] *a* literal.
littérature [lētārátür] *nf* literature.
littoral, e, aux [lētorál, -ō] *a* coastal ♦ *nm* coast.
Lituanie [lētüánē] *nf:* **la** ~ Lithuania.
lituanien, ne [lētüányań, -en] *a* Lithuanian.
liturgie [lētürzhē] *nf* liturgy.
liturgique [lētürzhēk] *a* liturgical.
livide [lēvēd] *a* livid, pallid.
living(-room) [lēvēng(rōōm)] *nm* living room.
livrable [lēvrábl(ǝ)] *a* (*COMM*) that can be delivered.
livraison [lēvrezóń] *nf* delivery; ~ **à domicile** home delivery (service).
livre [lēvr(ǝ)] *nm* book; (*imprimerie etc*): **le** ~ the book industry ♦ *nf* (*poids, monnaie*) pound; **traduire qch à** ~ **ouvert** to translate sth off the cuff *ou* at sight; ~ **blanc** official report (*prepared by independent body, following war, natural disaster etc*); ~ **de bord** (*NAVIG*) logbook; ~ **de comptes** account(s) book; ~ **de cuisine** cookbook; ~ **de messe** mass *ou* prayer book; ~ **d'or** guest book; ~ **de poche** paperback (*cheap and pocket size*); ~ **verte** unit of account used in calculating contributions to and payments from the Community Agricultural Fund of the ECM, green pound (*Brit*).
livré, e [lēvrá] *nf* livery ♦ *a:* ~ **à** (*l'anarchie etc*) given over to; ~ **à soi-même** left to oneself *ou* one's own devices.
livrer [lēvrā] *vt* (*COMM*) to deliver; (*otage, coupable*) to hand over; (*secret, information*) to give away; **se** ~ **à** (*se confier*) to confide in; (*se rendre*) to give o.s. up to;

(*s'abandonner à: débauche etc*) to give o.s. up *ou* over to; (*faire: pratiques, actes*) to indulge in; (*travail*) to be engaged in, engage in; (*: sport*) to practice (*US*), practise (*Brit*); (*: enquête*) to carry out; ~ **bataille** to give battle.
livresque [lēvresk(ǝ)] *a* (*péj*) bookish.
livret [lēvre] *nm* booklet; (*d'opéra*) libretto (*pl* -s); ~ **de caisse d'épargne** (savings) bankbook; ~ **de famille** (official) family record book; ~ **scolaire** ≈ (school) record (*US*), report book (*Brit*).
livreur, euse [lēvrœr, -œ̄z] *nm/f* delivery boy *ou* man/girl *ou* woman.
LO *sigle f* (= *Lutte ouvrière*) political party.
lobe [lob] *nm:* ~ **de l'oreille** ear lobe.
lobé, e [lobá] *a* (*ARCHIT*) foiled.
lober [lobā] *vt* to lob.
local, e, aux [lokál, -ō] *a* local ♦ *nm* (*salle*) premises *pl* ♦ *nmpl* premises.
localement [lokálmáń] *ad* locally.
localisé, e [lokálēzá] *a* localized.
localiser [lokálēzá] *vt* (*repérer*) to locate, place; (*limiter*) to localize, confine.
localité [lokálētá] *nf* locality.
locataire [lokáter] *nm/f* tenant; (*de chambre*) lodger.
locatif, ive [lokátēf, -ēv] *a* (*charges, réparations*) incumbent upon the tenant; (*valeur*) rental; (*immeuble*) with rented apartments, used as a letting *ou* rental (*US*) concern.
location [lokásyóń] *nf* (*par le locataire*) renting; (*par l'usager: de voiture etc*) renting (*US*), hiring (*Brit*); (*par le propriétaire*) renting out, letting; (*de billets, places*) booking; (*bureau*) box *ou* ticket office; "~ **de voitures**" "car rental (*US*) *ou* hire (*Brit*)".
location-vente [lokásyóńváńt] *nf* form of installment plan (*US*) *ou* hire purchase (*Brit*).
lock-out [lokáwt] *nm inv* lockout.
locomoteur, trice [lokomotœr, -trēs] *a, nf* locomotive.
locomotion [lokomōsyóń] *nf* locomotion.
locomotive [lokomotēv] *nf* locomotive, engine; (*fig*) pacesetter, pacemaker.
locuteur, trice [lokütœr, -trēs] *nm/f* (*LING*) speaker.
locution [loküsyóń] *nf* phrase.
loden [loden] *nm* loden.
lofer [lofá] *vi* (*NAVIG*) to luff.
logarithme [logárētm(ǝ)] *nm* logarithm.
loge [lozh] *nf* (*THÉÂTRE:* d'artiste) dressing room; (*: de spectateurs*) box; (*de concierge, franc-maçon*) lodge.
logeable [lozhábl(ǝ)] *a* habitable; (*spacieux*) roomy.
logement [lozhmáń] *nm* apartment (*US*), flat (*Brit*); accommodations *q* (*US*), accommodation *q* (*Brit*); **le** ~ housing; **chercher un** ~ to look for an apartment, look for accommodation(s); **construire des** ~**s bon marché** to build cheap housing *sg*; **crise du** ~ housing shortage; ~ **de fonction** (*ADMIN*) company flat *ou* apartment, accommodation(s) provided with one's job.
loger [lozhá] *vt* to accommodate ♦ *vi* to live; **se** ~: **trouver à se** ~ to find accommodations (*US*) *ou* accommodation (*Brit*); **se** ~

dans (*suj: balle, flèche*) to lodge itself in.

logeur, euse [lozhœr, -œz] *nm/f* landlord/landlady.

loggia [lodzhyà] *nf* loggia.

logiciel [lozhēsyčl] *nm* software.

logique [lozhčk] *a* logical ♦ *nf* logic; **c'est** ~ **it** stands to reason.

logiquement [lozhčkmáñ] *ad* logically.

logis [lozhē] *nm* home; abode, dwelling.

logistique [lozhēstčk] *nf* logistics *sg* ♦ *a* logistic.

logo [logō], **logotype** [logotēp] *nm* logo.

loi [lwà] *nf* law; **faire la** ~ to lay down the law; **les** ~**s de la mode** (*fig*) the dictates of fashion; **proposition de** ~ (private member's) bill; **projet de** ~ (government) bill.

loin [lwañ] *ad* far; (*dans le temps: futur*) a long way off; (*: passé*) a long time ago; **plus** ~ further; **moins** ~ (**que**) not as far (as); ~ **de** far from; **pas** ~ **de 1000 F** not far off 1000 F; **au** ~ far off; **de** ~ *ad* from a distance; (*fig: de beaucoup*) by far; **il vient de** ~ he's come a long way; he comes from a long way away; **de** ~ **en** ~ here and there; (*de temps en temps*) (every) now and then; ~ **de là** (*au contraire*) far from it.

lointain, e [lwañtañ, -en] *a* faraway, distant; (*dans le futur, passé*) distant, far-off; (*cause, parent*) remote, distant ♦ *nm:* **dans le** ~ in the distance.

loi-programme, *pl* **lois-programmes** [lwàprogràm] *nf* (*POL*) *act providing framework for government program.*

loir [lwàr] *nm* dormouse (*pl* -mice).

Loire [lwàr] *nf:* **la** ~ the Loire.

loisible [lwàzēbl] *a:* **il vous est** ~ **de** ... you are free to ....

loisir [lwàzēr] *nm:* **heures de** ~ spare time; ~**s** *nmpl* leisure *sg*; (*activités*) leisure activities; **avoir le** ~ **de faire** to have the time *ou* opportunity to do; (**tout**) **à** ~ (*en prenant son temps*) at leisure; (*autant qu'on le désire*) at one's pleasure.

lombaire [lôñber] *a* lumbar.

lombalgie [lôñbàlzhē] *nf* back pain.

lombard, e [lôñbàr, -àrd(ə)] *a* Lombard.

Lombardie [lôñbàrdē] *nf:* **la** ~ Lombardy.

londonien, ne [lôñdonyañ, -en] *a* London *cpd*, of London ♦ *nm/f:* **L**~, **ne** Londoner.

Londres [lôñdr(ə)] *n* London.

long, longue [lôñ, lôñg] *a* a long ♦ *ad:* **en savoir** ~ to know a great deal ♦ *nm:* **de 3 m de** ~ 3 m long, 3 m in length ♦ *nf:* **à la longue** in the end; **faire** ~ **feu** to fizzle out; **ne pas faire** ~ **feu** not to last long; **au** ~ **cours** (*NAVIG*) ocean *cpd*, oceangoing; **de longue date** *a* long-standing; **longue durée** *a* long-term; **de longue haleine** *a* long-term; **être** ~ **à faire** to take a long time to do; **en** ~ *ad* lengthwise, lengthways; (**tout**) **le** ~ **de** (all) along; **tout au** ~ **de** (*année, vie*) throughout; **de** ~ **en large** (*marcher*) to and fro, up and down; **en** ~ **et en large** (*fig*) in every detail.

longanimité [lôñgànēmētà] *nf* forbearance.

long-courrier [lôñkōōryà] *nm* (*AVIAT*) long-haul aircraft.

longe [lôñzh] *nf* (*corde: pour attacher*) tether; (*pour mener*) lead; (*CULIN*) loin.

longer [lôñzhā] *vt* to go (*ou* walk *ou* drive) along(side); (*suj: mur, route*) to border.

longévité [lôñzhāvētà] *nf* longevity.

longiligne [lôñzhčlēny] *a* long-limbed.

longitude [lôñzhčtüd] *nf* longitude; **à 45° de** ~ **ouest** at 45° longitude west.

longitudinal, e, aux [lôñzhčtüdēnàl, -ō] *a* longitudinal, lengthways; (*entaille, vallée*) running lengthways.

longtemps [lôñtáñ] *ad* (for) a long time, (for) long; **ça ne va pas durer** ~ it won't last long; **avant** ~ before long; **pour/pendant** ~ for a long time; **je n'en ai pas pour** ~ I shan't be long; **mettre** ~ **à faire** to take a long time to do; **il en a pour** ~ he'll be a long time; **il y a** ~ **que je travaille** I have been working (for) a long time; **il n'y a pas** ~ **que je l'ai rencontré** it's not long since I met him.

longue [lôñg] *af voir* **long.**

longuement [lôñgmáñ] *ad* (*longtemps: parler, regarder*) for a long time; (*en détail: expliquer, raconter*) at length.

longueur [lôñgœr] *nf* length; ~**s** *nfpl* (*fig: d'un film etc*) tedious parts; **sur une** ~ **de 10 km** for *ou* over 10 km; **en** ~ *ad* lengthwise, lengthways; **tirer en** ~ to drag on; **à** ~ **de journée** all day long; **d'une** ~ (*gagner*) by a length; ~ **d'onde** wavelength.

longue-vue [lôñgvü] *nf* telescope.

looping [lōōpēng] *nm* (*AVIAT*): **faire des** ~**s** to loop the loop.

lopin [lopañ] *nm:* ~ **de terre** patch of land.

loquace [lokàs] *a* talkative, loquacious.

loque [lok] *nf* (*personne*) wreck; ~**s** *nfpl* (*habits*) rags; **être** *ou* **tomber en** ~**s** to be in rags.

loquet [loke] *nm* latch.

lorgner [lornyā] *vt* to eye; (*convoiter*) to have one's eye on.

lorgnette [lornyet] *nf* opera glasses *pl*.

lorgnon [lornyôñ] *nm* (*face-à-main*) lorgnette; (*pince-nez*) pince-nez.

loriot [loryō] *nm* (golden) oriole.

lorrain, e [lorañ, -en] *a* of *ou* from Lorraine; **quiche** ~**e** quiche lorraine.

lors [lor]: ~ **de** *prép* (*au moment de*) at the time of; (*pendant*) during; ~ **même que** even though.

lorsque [lorsk(ə)] *cj* when, as.

losange [lozàñzh] *nm* diamond; (*GÉOM*) lozenge; **en** ~ diamond-shaped.

lot [lō] *nm* (*part*) share; (*de loterie*) prize; (*fig: destin*) fate, lot; (*COMM, INFORM*) batch; ~ **de consolation** consolation prize.

loterie [lotrē] *nf* lottery; (*tombola*) raffle; **L**~ **nationale** *French national lottery.*

loti, e [lotē] *a:* **bien/mal** ~ well-/badly off, lucky/unlucky.

lotion [lōsyôñ] *nf* lotion; ~ **après rasage** after-shave (lotion); ~ **capillaire** hair tonic.

lotir [lotēr] *vt* (*terrain: diviser*) to divide into plots; (*: vendre*) to sell by lots.

lotissement [lotēsmáñ] *nm* (*groupe de maisons, d'immeubles*) housing development; (*parcelle*) (building) plot, lot.

loto [lotō] *nm* lotto.

lotte [lot] *nf* (*ZOOL: de rivière*) burbot; (*: de mer*) monkfish.

louable [lwábl(ə)] a (appartement, garage) rentable; (action, personne) praiseworthy, commendable.

louage [lwàzh] nm: **voiture de** ~ rented (US) ou hired (Brit) car; (à louer) rental (US) ou hire (Brit) car.

louange [lwânzh] nf: **à la** ~ **de** in praise of; ~**s** nfpl praise sg.

loubar(d) [lōōbár] nm (fam) hoodlum.

louche [lōōsh] a shady, fishy, dubious ♦ nf ladle.

loucher [lōōshā] vi to squint; (fig): ~ **sur** to have one's (beady) eye on.

louer [lwā] vt (maison: suj: propriétaire) to let, rent (out); (: locataire) to rent; (voiture etc) to rent (out); (: réserver) to book; (faire l'éloge de) to praise; **"à** ~**"** "for rent" (US), "to let" (Brit); ~ **qn de** to praise sb for; **se** ~ **de** to congratulate o.s. on.

loufoque [lōōfok] a (fam) crazy, zany.

loukoum [lōōkōōm] nm Turkish delight.

loulou [lōōlōō] nm (chien) spitz; ~ **de Poméranie** Pomeranian (dog).

loup [lōō] nm wolf (pl wolves); (poisson) bass; (masque) (eye) mask; **jeune** ~ young go-getter; ~ **de mer** (marin) old sea dog.

loupe [lōōp] nf magnifying glass; ~ **de noyer** burr walnut; **à la** ~ (fig) in minute detail.

louper [lōōpā] vt (fam: manquer) to miss; (: gâcher) to mess up, bungle.

lourd, e [lōōr, lōōrd(ə)] a heavy; (chaleur, temps) sultry; (fig: personne, style) heavy-handed ♦ ad: **peser** ~ to be heavy; ~ **de** (menaces) charged with; (conséquences) fraught with; **artillerie/industrie** ~**e** heavy artillery/industry.

lourdaud, e [lōōrdō, -ōd] a oafish.

lourdement [lōōrdəmân] ad heavily; **se tromper** ~ to make a big mistake.

lourdeur [lōōrdœr] nf heaviness; ~ **d'estomac** indigestion q.

loustic [lōōstēk] nm (fam péj) joker.

loutre [lōōtr(ə)] nf otter; (fourrure) otter skin.

louve [lōōv] nf she-wolf.

louveteau, x [lōōvtō] nm (ZOOL) wolf cub; (scout) cub (scout).

louvoyer [lōōvwàyā] vi (NAVIG) to tack; (fig) to hedge, evade the issue.

lover [lovā]: **se** ~ vi to coil up.

loyal, e, aux [lwàyàl, -ō] a (fidèle) loyal, faithful; (fair-play) fair.

loyalement [lwàyàlmân] ad loyally, faithfully; fairly.

loyalisme [lwàyàlēsm(ə)] nm loyalty.

loyauté [lwàyōtā] nf loyalty, faithfulness; fairness.

loyer [lwàyā] nm rent; ~ **de l'argent** interest rate.

LP sigle m (= lycée professionnel) secondary school for vocational training.

LPO sigle f (= Ligue pour la protection des oiseaux) bird protection society.

LSD sigle m (= Lyserg Säure Diäthylamid) LSD.

lu, e [lü] pp de **lire**.

lubie [lübē] nf whim, craze.

lubricité [lübrēsētā] nf lust.

lubrifiant [lübrēfyâñ] nm lubricant.

lubrifier [lübrēfyā] vt to lubricate.

lubrique [lübrēk] a lecherous.

lucarne [lükárn(ə)] nf skylight.

lucide [lüsēd] a (conscient) lucid, conscious; (perspicace) clear-headed.

lucidité [lüsēdētā] nf lucidity.

luciole [lüsyol] nf firefly.

lucratif, ive [lükrátēf, -ēv] a lucrative; profitable; **à but non** ~ non profit-making.

ludique [lüdēk] a play cpd, playing.

ludothèque [lüdotek] nf toy library.

luette [lüet] nf uvula.

lueur [lüœr] nf (chatoyante) glimmer q; (métallique, mouillée) gleam q; (rougeoyante, chaude) glow q; (pâle) (faint) light; (fig) spark; (: d'espérance) glimmer, gleam.

luge [lüzh] nf sled (US), sledge (Brit); **faire de la** ~ to sled (US), sledge (Brit), toboggan.

lugubre [lügübr(ə)] a gloomy; dismal.

lui [lüē] pp de **luire** ♦ pronom (chose, animal) it; (personne: mâle) him; (: femelle) her; (: femelle) her; voir note sous **il**; ~, **il** ... HE ... (emphatic); **je la connais mieux que** ~ (que je ne le connais) I know her better than (I know) him; (qu'il ne la connaît) I know her better than he does.

lui-même [lüēmem] pronom (personne) himself; (chose) itself.

luire [lüēr] vi (gén) to shine, gleam; (surface mouillée) to glisten; (reflets chauds, cuivrés) to glow.

luisant, e [lüēzâñ, -âñt] vb voir **luire** ♦ a shining, gleaming.

lumbago [lôñbágō] nm lumbago.

lumière [lümyer] nf light; ~**s** nfpl (d'une personne) knowledge sg, wisdom sg; **à la** ~ **de** by the light of; (fig: événements) in the light of; **fais de la** ~ let's have some light, give us some light; **faire (toute) la** ~ **sur** (fig) to clarify (completely); **mettre en** ~ (fig) to highlight; ~ **du jour/soleil** day/sunlight.

luminaire [lümēner] nm lamp, light.

lumineux, euse [lümēnœ, -œz] a (émettant de la lumière) luminous; (éclairé) illuminated; (ciel, journée, couleur) bright; (relatif à la lumière: rayon etc) of light, light cpd; (fig: regard) radiant.

luminosité [lümēnozētā] nf (TECH) luminosity.

lump [lœñp] nm: **œufs de** ~ lumpfish roe.

lunaire [lüner] a lunar, moon cpd.

lunatique [lünátēk] a whimsical, temperamental.

lunch [lœntsh] nm (réception) buffet lunch.

lundi [lœñdē] nm Monday; **on est** ~ it's Monday; **le** ~ **20 août** Monday 20th August; **il est venu** ~ he came on Monday; **le(s)** ~**(s)** on Mondays; **à** ~! see you (on) Monday!; ~ **de Pâques** Easter Monday; ~ **de Pentecôte** Whitmonday.

lune [lün] nf moon; **pleine/nouvelle** ~ full/new moon; **être dans la** ~ (distrait) to have one's head in the clouds; ~ **de miel** honeymoon.

luné, e [lünā] a: **bien/mal** ~ in a good/bad mood.

lunette [lünet] nf: ~**s** nfpl glasses, spectacles; (protectrices) goggles; ~ **d'approche** telescope; ~ **arrière** (AUTO) rear window; ~**s**

noires dark glasses; ~s de soleil sunglasses.
lurent [lür] *vb voir* **lire.**
lurette [lüret] *nf*: **il y a belle** ~ ages ago.
luron, ne [lürôn, -on] *nm/f* lad/lass; **joyeux** *ou* **gai** ~ gay dog.
lus [lü] *etc vb voir* **lire.**
lustre [lüstr(ə)] *nm* (*de plafond*) chandelier; (*fig: éclat*) luster (*US*), lustre (*Brit*).
lustrer [lüstrā] *vt*: ~ **qch** (*faire briller*) to make sth shine; (*user*) to make sth shiny.
lut [lü] *vb voir* **lire.**
luth [lüt] *nm* lute.
luthier [lütyā] *nm* (stringed-)instrument maker.
lutin [lütan] *nm* imp, goblin.
lutrin [lütran] *nm* lectern.
lutte [lüt] *nf* (*conflit*) struggle; (*SPORT*): **la** ~ wrestling; **de haute** ~ after a hard-fought struggle; ~ **des classes** class struggle; ~ **libre** (*SPORT*) freestyle (*US*) *ou* all-in (*Brit*) wrestling.
lutter [lütā] *vi* to fight, struggle; (*SPORT*) to wrestle.
lutteur, euse [lütœr, -ēz] *nm/f* (*SPORT*) wrestler; (*fig*) battler, fighter.
luxation [lüksāsyôn] *nf* dislocation.
luxe [lüks(ə)] *nm* luxury; **un** ~ **de** (*détails, précautions*) a wealth of; **de** ~ *a* luxury *cpd*.
Luxembourg [lüksânbōōr] *nm*: **le** ~ Luxembourg.
luxembourgeois, e [lüksânbōōrzhwà, -wáz] *a* of *ou* from Luxembourg ♦ *nm/f*: **L~, e** inhabitant *ou* native of Luxembourg.
luxer [lüksā] *vt*: **se** ~ **l'épaule** to dislocate one's shoulder.
luxueux, euse [lüksüœ̃, -œ̃z] *a* luxurious.
luxure [lüksür] *nf* lust.
luxuriant, e [lüksüryân, -ânt] *a* luxuriant, lush.
luzerne [lüzern(ə)] *nf* alfalfa.
lycée [lēsā] *nm* (public (*US*) *ou* state (*Brit*)) high school; ~ **technique** technical high school.
lycéen, ne [lēsāan, -en] *nm/f* high school pupil.
lymphatique [lanfátēk] *a* (*fig*) lethargic, sluggish.
lymphe [lanf] *nf* lymph.
lyncher [lanshā] *vt* to lynch.
lynx [lanks] *nm* lynx.
Lyon [lyôn] *n* Lyons.
lyonnais, e [lyone, -ez] *a* of *ou* from Lyons; (*CULIN*) Lyonnaise.
lyophilisé, e [lyofēlēzā] *a* freeze-dried.
lyre [lēr] *nf* lyre.
lyrique [lērēk] *a* lyrical; (*OPÉRA*) lyric; **artiste** ~ opera singer; **comédie** ~ comic opera; **théâtre** ~ opera house (*for light opera*).
lyrisme [lērēsm(ə)] *nm* lyricism.
lys [lēs] *nm* lily.

M

M, m [em] *nm inv* M, m ♦ *abr* = **majeur, masculin, mètre, Monsieur;** (= *million*) M;

M comme Marcel M for Mike.
m' [m] *pronom voir* **me.**
MA *sigle m* = **maître auxiliaire.**
ma [mà] *dét voir* **mon.**
maboul, e [mábōōl] *a* (*fam*) loony.
macabre [mákàbr(ə)] *a* macabre, gruesome.
macadam [mákàdàm] *nm* tarmac (*Brit*), asphalt.
Macao [mákáō] *nf* Macao.
macaron [mákàrôn] *nm* (*gâteau*) macaroon; (*insigne*) (round) badge.
macaroni(s) [mákárōnē] *nm(pl)* macaroni *sg*; ~ **au fromage** *ou* **au gratin** macaroni and cheese (*US*), macaroni cheese (*Brit*).
macédoine [másādwán] *nf*: ~ **de fruits** fruit salad; ~ **de légumes** mixed vegetables *pl*.
macérer [másārā] *vi, vt* to macerate; (*dans du vinaigre*) to pickle.
mâchefer [máshfer] *nm* clinker, cinders *pl*.
mâcher [máshā] *vt* to chew; **ne pas** ~ **ses mots** not to mince one's words; ~ **le travail à qn** (*fig*) to spoonfeed sb, do half sb's work for him.
machiavélique [mákyàvālēk] *a* Machiavellian.
machin [máshan] *nm* (*fam*) thingamajig, thing; (*personne*): **M~** what's-his(*ou*-her)-name.
machinal, e, aux [máshēnál, -ō] *a* mechanical, automatic.
machination [máshēnàsyôn] *nf* scheming, frame-up.
machine [máshēn] *nf* machine; (*locomotive; de navire etc*) engine; (*fig: rouages*) machinery; (*fam: personne*): **M~** what's-her-name; **faire** ~ **arrière** (*NAVIG*) to go astern; (*fig*) to back-pedal; ~ **à laver/coudre/tricoter** washing/sewing/knitting machine; ~ **à écrire** typewriter; ~ **à sous** slot machine; ~ **à vapeur** steam engine.
machine-outil, *pl* **machines-outils** [máshēnōōtē] *nf* machine tool.
machinerie [máshēnrē] *nf* machinery, plant; (*d'un navire*) engine room.
machinisme [máshēnēsm(ə)] *nm* mechanization.
machiniste [máshēnēst(ə)] *nm* (*THÉÂTRE*) stage hand; (*de bus, métro*) driver.
mâchoire [máshwár] *nf* jaw; ~ **de frein** brake shoe.
mâchonner [máshonā] *vt* to chew (at).
mâcon [mákôn] *nm* Mâcon wine.
maçon [másôn] *nm* bricklayer; (*constructeur*) builder.
maçonner [másonā] *vt* (*revêtir*) to face, render (with cement); (*boucher*) to brick up.
maçonnerie [másonrē] *nf* (*murs: de brique*) brickwork; (: *de pierre*) masonry, stonework; (*activité*) bricklaying; building; ~ **de béton** concrete.
maçonnique [másonēk] *a* masonic.
macramé [mákràmā] *nm* macramé.
macrobiotique [mákrobyotēk] *a* macrobiotic.
macro-économie [mákroākonomē] *nf* macroeconomics *sg*.
maculer [mákülā] *vt* to stain; (*TYPO*) to mackle.
Madagascar [mádàgáskàr] *nf* Madagascar.

Madame [mádàm], *pl* **Mesdames** [mādàm] *nf*:
~ X Mrs X ['mɪsɪz]; **occupez-vous de ~/**
Monsieur/Mademoiselle please help this
lady/gentleman/(young) lady; **bonjour** ~/
Monsieur/Mademoiselle good morning; (*ton
déférent*) good morning Madam/Sir/Madam;
(*le nom est connu*) good morning Mrs X/Mr
X/Miss X; **~/Monsieur/Mademoiselle!** (*pour
appeler*) excuse me!; (*ton déférent*) Madam/
Sir/Miss!; **~/Monsieur/Mademoiselle** (*sur
lettre*) Dear Madam/Sir/Madam; **chère ~/**
cher Monsieur/chère Mademoiselle Dear
Mrs X/Mr X/Miss X; **~ la Directrice** the director; the manageress; the principal;
Mesdames Ladies.

Madeleine [mádlen]: **îles de la ~** *nfpl*
Magdalen Islands.

madeleine [mádlen] *nf* madeleine, ≈ sponge
finger cake.

Madelinot, e [mádlēnō, -ot] *nm/f* inhabitant *ou*
native of the Magdalen Islands.

Mademoiselle [mádmwázel], *pl*
Mesdemoiselles [mādmwázel] *nf* Miss; *voir
aussi* **Madame**.

Madère [máder] *nf* Madeira ♦ *nm*: **m~**
Madeira (wine).

madone [mádon] *nf* madonna.

madré, e [mádrā] *a* crafty, wily.

Madrid [mádrēd] *n* Madrid.

madrier [mádrēyā] *nm* beam.

madrilène [mádrēlen] *a* of *ou* from Madrid.

maestria [máestrēyá] *nf* (masterly) skill.

maf(f)ia [máfyá] *nf* Maf(f)ia.

magasin [mágázań] *nm* (*boutique*) shop; (*entrepôt*) warehouse; (*d'arme, appareil-photo*)
magazine; **en ~** (*COMM*) in stock; **faire les
~s** to make the rounds of the stores; **~
d'alimentation** grocery store (*US*), grocer's
shop (*Brit*).

magasinier [mágázēnyā] *nm* warehouseman.

magazine [mágázēn] *nm* magazine.

mage [mázh] *nm*: **les Rois M~s** the Magi, the
(Three) Wise Men.

Maghreb [mágreb] *nm*: **le ~** the Maghreb,
North(-West) Africa.

maghrébin, e [mágrābań, -ēn] *a* of *ou* from
the Maghreb ♦ *nm/f*: **M~, e** North African,
Maghrebi.

magicien, ne [mázhēsyań, -en] *nm/f* magician.

magie [mázhē] *nf* magic; **~ noire** black
magic.

magique [mázhēk] *a* (*occulte*) magic; (*fig*)
magical.

magistral, e, aux [mázhēstrál, -ō] *a* (*œuvre,
addresse*) masterly; (*ton*) authoritative;
(*gifle etc*) sound, resounding; (*ex cathedra*):
enseignement ~ lecturing, lectures *pl*; **cours
~** lecture.

magistrat [mázhēstrá] *nm* magistrate.

magistrature [mázhēstrátür] *nf* magistracy,
magistrature; **~ assise** judges *pl*, bench; **~
debout** state prosecutors *pl*.

magma [mágmá] *nm* (*GÉO*) magma; (*fig*)
jumble.

magnanerie [mányánrē] *nf* silk farm.

magnanime [mányánēm] *a* magnanimous.

magnat [mágná] *nm* tycoon, magnate; **~ de la
presse** press baron.

magner [mányā]: **se ~** *vi* (*fam*) to get a move
on.

magnésie [mányázē] *nf* magnesia.

magnésium [mányázyom] *nm* magnesium.

magnétique [mányátēk] *a* magnetic.

magnétiser [mányātēzā] *vt* to magnetize; (*fig*)
to mesmerize, hypnotize.

magnétisme [mányātēsm(ə)] *nm* magnetism.

magnéto [mányātō] *nm* (= *magnétocassette*)
cassette deck; (= *magnétophone*) tape recorder.

magnétocassette [mányātokáset] *nm* cassette
deck.

magnétophone [mányátofon] *nm* tape recorder; **~ à cassettes** cassette recorder.

magnétoscope [mányátoskop] *nm*: **~ (à
cassette)** video (recorder).

magnificence [mányēfēsáns] *nf* (*faste*)
magnificence, splendor (*US*), splendour
(*Brit*); (*générosité, prodigalité*) munificence,
lavishness.

magnifier [mányēfyā] *vt* (*glorifier*) to glorify;
(*idéaliser*) to idealize.

magnifique [mányēfēk] *a* magnificent.

magnolia [mányolyá] *nm* magnolia.

magnum [mágnom] *nm* magnum.

magot [mágō] *nm* (*argent*) pile (of money);
(*économies*) nest egg.

magouille [mágōōy] *nf* (*fam*) scheming.

mahométan, e [máomātáń, -án] *a*
Mohammedan, Mahometan.

mai [me] *nm* May; *voir aussi* **juillet**.

maigre [megr(ə)] *a* (very) thin, skinny;
(*viande*) lean; (*fromage*) low-fat; (*végétation*) thin, sparse; (*fig*) poor, meager (*US*),
meagre (*Brit*), skimpy ♦ *ad*: **faire ~** not to
eat meat; **jours ~s** days of abstinence, fish
days.

maigrelet, te [megrəle, -et] *a* skinny, scrawny;

maigreur [megrœr] *nf* thinness.

maigrichon, ne [mågrēshóń, -on] *a* = **maigrelet, te**.

maigrir [māgrēr] *vi* to get thinner, lose weight
♦ *vt*: **~ qn** (*suj: vêtement*) to make sb look
slim(mer).

mailing [melēng] *nm* direct mail *q*; **un ~** a
mailing.

maille [máy] *nf* (*boucle*) stitch; (*ouverture*)
hole (in the mesh); **avoir ~ à partir avec qn**
to have a bone to pick with sb; **~ à
l'endroit/à l'envers** knit one/purl one;
(*boucle*) plain/purl stitch.

maillechort [máyshor] *nm* nickel silver.

maillet [máyc] *nm* mallet.

maillon [máyóń] *nm* link.

maillot [máyō] *nm* (*aussi*: **~ de corps**) undershirt (*US*), vest (*Brit*); (*de danseur*) leotard;
(*de sportif*) jersey; **~ de bain** bathing suit,
swimsuit; (*d'homme*) bathing trunks *pl*; **~
une pièce** one-piece swimsuit; **~ deux pièces**
two-piece swimsuit, bikini.

main [mań] *nf* hand; **la ~ dans la ~** hand in
hand; **à deux ~s** with both hands; **à une ~**
with one hand; **à la ~** (*tenir, avoir*) in one's
hand; (*faire, tricoter etc*) by hand; **se
donner la ~** to hold hands; **donner** *ou* **tendre
la ~ à qn** to hold out one's hand to sb; **se
serrer la ~** to shake hands; **serrer la ~ à qn**
to shake hands with sb; **sous la ~** to *ou* at
hand; **haut les ~s!** hands up!; **à ~ levée**

(ART) freehand; **à ~s levées** (voter) with a show of hands; **attaque à ~ armée** armed attack; **à ~ droite/gauche** to the right/left; **à remettre en ~s propres** to be delivered personally; **de première ~** (renseignement) first-hand; (COMM: voiture etc) with only one previous owner; **faire ~ basse sur** to help o.s. to; **mettre la dernière ~ à** to put the finishing touches to; **mettre la ~ à la pâte** (fig) to lend a hand; **prendre qch en ~** (fig) to take sth in hand; **avoir/passer la ~** (CARTES) to lead/hand over the lead; **s'en laver les ~s** (fig) to wash one's hands of it; **se faire/perdre la ~** to get one's hand in/lose one's touch; **avoir qch bien en ~** to have got the hang of sth; **en un tour de ~** (fig) in the twinkling of an eye; **~ courante** handrail.

mainate [menát] nm myna(h) bird.

main-d'œuvre [mandœvr(ə)] nf manpower, labor (US), labour (Brit).

main-forte [manfort(ə)] nf: **prêter ~ à qn** to come to sb's assistance.

mainmise [manmēz] nf seizure; (fig): **avoir la ~ sur** to have a complete hold on.

maint, e [man, mant] a many a; **~s** many; **à ~es reprises** time and (time) again.

maintenance [mantnáns] nf maintenance.

maintenant [mantnán] ad now; (actuellement) nowadays.

maintenir [mantnēr] vt (retenir, soutenir) to support; (contenir: foule etc) to keep in check, hold back; (conserver) to maintain, uphold; (affirmer) to maintain; **se ~** vi (paix, temps) to hold; (préjugé) to persist; (malade) to remain stable.

maintien [mantyan] nm maintaining, upholding; (attitude) bearing; **~ de l'ordre** maintenance of law and order.

maintiendrai [mantyandrā], **maintiens** [mantyan] etc vb voir **maintenir**.

maire [mer] nm mayor.

mairie [mārē] nf (endroit) town hall; (administration) town council.

mais [me] cj but; **~ non!** of course not!; **~ enfin** but after all; (indignation) look here!; **~ encore?** is that all?

maïs [máēs] nm corn (US), maize (Brit).

maison [mezón] nf (bâtiment) house; (chez-soi) home; (COMM) firm; (famille): **ami de la ~** friend of the family ♦ a inv (CULIN) home-made; (: au restaurant) made by the chef; (COMM) in-house, own; (fam) first-rate; **à la ~** at home; (direction) home; **~ d'arrêt** (short-stay) prison; **~ de campagne** country cottage; **~ centrale** prison; **~ close ou de passe** brothel; **~ de correction** ≈ reformatory (US), ≈ remand home (Brit); **~ de la culture** ≈ arts center; **~ des jeunes** ≈ youth club; **~ mère** parent company; **~ de passe** = **~ close**; **~ de repos** convalescent home; **~ de retraite** old people's home; **~ de santé** mental home.

Maison-Blanche [mezónblánsh] nf: **la ~** the White House.

maisonnée [mezonā] nf household, family.

maisonnette [mezonet] nf small house, cottage.

maître, esse [metr(ə), metres] nm/f master/ mistress; (SCOL) teacher, schoolmaster/

mistress ♦ nm (peintre etc) master; (titre): **M~ (Me)** Maître, term of address for lawyers etc ♦ nf (amante) mistress ♦ a (principal, essentiel) main; **maison de ~** family seat; **être ~ de** (soi-même, situation) to be in control of; **se rendre ~ de** (pays, ville) to gain control of; (situation, incendie) to bring under control; **être passé ~ dans l'art de** to be a (past) master in the art of; **une maîtresse femme** a forceful woman; **~ d'armes** fencing master; **~ auxiliaire (MA)** (SCOL) substitute (US) ou temporary (Brit) teacher; **~ chanteur** blackmailer; **~ de chapelle** choirmaster; **~ de conférences** ≈ associate professor (US), ≈ senior lecturer (Brit); **~/ maîtresse d'école** teacher, schoolmaster/ mistress; **~ d'hôtel** (domestique) butler; (d'hôtel) headwaiter, maître d'; **~ de maison** host; **~ nageur** lifeguard; **~ d'œuvre** (CONSTR) project manager; **~ d'ouvrage** (CONSTR) client; **~ à penser** intellectual leader; **~ queux** chef; **maîtresse de maison** hostess; (ménagère) housewife (pl -wives).

maître-assistant, e, pl **maîtres-assistants, es** [metrásēstán, -ánt] nm/f ≈ assistant professor (US), ≈ lecturer (Brit).

maître-autel, pl **maîtres-autels** [metrōtel] nm high altar.

maîtrise [mātrēz] nf (aussi: **~ de soi**) self-control, self-possession; (habileté) skill, mastery; (suprématie) mastery, command; (diplôme) ≈ master's degree; (chefs d'équipe) supervisory staff.

maîtriser [mātrēzā] vt (cheval, incendie) to (bring under) control; (sujet) to master; (émotion) to control; **se ~** to control o.s.

majesté [mázhestā] nf majesty.

majestueux, euse [mázhestüœ̄, -œ̄z] a majestic.

majeur, e [mázhœr] a (important) major; (JUR) of age; (fig) adult ♦ nm/f (JUR) person who has come of age ou attained his (ou her) majority ♦ nm (doigt) middle finger; **en ~e partie** for the most part; **la ~e partie de** the major part of.

major [mázhor] nm adjutant; (SCOL): **~ de la promotion** first in one's ou at the head of one's class.

majoration [mázhorâsyôn] nf increase.

majorer [mázhorā] vt to increase.

majorette [mázhoret] nf majorette.

majoritaire [mázhorēter] a majority cpd; **système/scrutin ~** majority system/ballot.

majorité [mázhorētā] nf (gén) majority; (parti) party in power; **en ~** (composé etc) mainly.

Majorque [mázhork(ə)] nf Majorca.

majorquin, e [mázhorkan, -ēn] a Majorcan ♦ nm/f: **M~, e** Majorcan.

majuscule [mázhüskül] a, nf: **(lettre) ~** capital (letter).

MAL [mál] sigle f (= Maison d'animation et des loisirs) cultural center.

mal, maux [mál, mō] nm (opposé au bien) evil; (tort, dommage) harm; (douleur physique) pain, ache; (maladie) illness, sickness q; (difficulté, peine) trouble; (souffrance morale) pain ♦ ad badly ♦ a: **c'est ~ (de faire)** it's bad ou wrong (to do); **être ~** to be uncomfortable; **être ~ avec qn** to be on bad terms with sb; **être au plus ~** (*malade*) to be very bad; (*brouillé*) to be at sword's points (*US*) *ou* daggers drawn (*Brit*); **il comprend ~** he has difficulty in understanding; **il a ~ compris** he misunderstood; **~ tourner** to go wrong; **dire/penser du ~ de** to speak/think ill of; **ne vouloir de ~ à personne** to wish nobody any ill; **il n'a rien fait de ~** he has done nothing wrong; **avoir du ~ à faire qch** to have trouble doing sth; **se donner du ~ pour faire qch** to go to a lot of trouble to do sth; **ne voir aucun ~ à** to see no harm in, see nothing wrong in; **craignant ~ faire** fearing he *etc* was doing the wrong thing; **sans penser** *ou* **songer à ~** without meaning any harm; **faire du ~ à qn** to hurt sb; to harm sb; **se faire ~** to hurt o.s.; **se faire ~ au pied** to hurt one's foot; **ça fait ~** it hurts; **j'ai ~ (ici)** it hurts (here); **j'ai ~ au dos** my back aches, I've got a pain in my back; **avoir ~ à la tête/à la gorge/aux dents** to have a headache/a sore throat/ toothache; **avoir le ~ de l'air** to be airsick; **avoir le ~ du pays** to be homesick; **~ de mer** seasickness; **~ de la route** carsickness; **~ en point** *a inv* in a bad state; **maux de ventre** stomach ache *sg*; *voir* **cœur**.

Malabar [màlàbár] *nm*: **le ~, la côte de ~** the Malabar (Coast).

malade [màlàd] *a* ill, sick; (*poitrine, jambe*) bad; (*plante*) diseased; (*fig: entreprise, monde*) ailing ♦ *nm/f* invalid, sick person; (*à l'hôpital etc*) patient; **tomber ~** to fall ill; **être ~ du cœur** to have heart trouble *ou* a bad heart; **grand ~** seriously ill person; **~ mental** mentally sick *ou* ill person.

maladie [màlàdē] *nf* (*spécifique*) disease, illness; (*mauvaise santé*) illness, sickness; (*fig: manie*) **être rongé par la ~** to be wasting away (through illness); **~ de peau** skin disease.

maladif, ive [màlàdēf, -ēv] *a* sickly; (*curiosité, besoin*) pathological.

maladresse [màlàdres] *nf* clumsiness *q*; (*gaffe*) blunder.

maladroit, e [màlàdrwà, -wàt] *a* clumsy.

maladroitement [màlàdrwàtmáñ] *ad* clumsily.

malais, e [màle, -ez] *a* Malay, Malayan ♦ *nm* (*LING*) Malay ♦ *nm/f*: **M~,** e Malay, Malayan.

malaise [màlez] *nm* (*MÉD*) feeling of faintness; feeling of discomfort; (*fig*) uneasiness, malaise; **avoir un ~** to feel faint *ou* dizzy.

malaisé, e [màlàzā] *a* difficult.

Malaisie [màlezē] *nf*: **la ~** Malaya, West Malaysia; **la péninsule de ~** the Malay Peninsula.

malappris, e [màlàprē, -ēz] *nm/f* ill-mannered *ou* boorish person.

malaria [màlàryà] *nf* malaria.

malavisé, e [màlàvēzā] *a* ill-advised, unwise.

Malawi [màlàwē] *nm*: **le ~** Malawi.

malaxer [màlàksā] *vt* (*pétrir*) to knead; (*mêler*) to mix.

Malaysia [màlezyà] *nf*: **la ~** Malaysia.

malchance [màlshàns] *nf* misfortune, bad luck *q*; **par ~** unfortunately; **quelle ~!** what bad luck!

malchanceux, euse [màlshàñsœ̄, -ēz] *a* unlucky.

malcommode [màlkomod] *a* impractical, inconvenient.

Maldives [màldēv] *nfpl*: **les ~** the Maldive Islands.

maldonne [màldon] *nf* (*CARTES*) misdeal; **il y a ~** (*fig*) there's been a misunderstanding.

mâle [mâl] *a* (*aussi ÉLEC, TECH*) male; (*viril: voix, traits*) manly ♦ *nm* male.

malédiction [màlādēksyóñ] *nf* curse.

maléfice [màlāfēs] *nm* evil spell.

maléfique [màlāfēk] *a* evil, baleful.

malencontreux, euse [màláñkóñtrœ̄, -ēz] *a* unfortunate, untoward.

malentendant, e [màláñtáñdâñ, -âñt] *nm/f*: **les ~s** the hard of hearing.

malentendu [màláñtáñdü] *nm* misunderstanding.

malfaçon [màlfàsóñ] *nf* fault.

malfaisant, e [màlfəzáñ, -âñt] *a* evil, harmful.

malfaiteur [màlfetœr] *nm* lawbreaker, criminal; (*voleur*) thief (*pl* thieves).

malfamé, e [màlfàmā] *a* disreputable, of ill repute.

malfrat [màlfrâ] *nm* villain, crook.

malgache [màlgàsh] *a* Malagasy, Madagascan ♦ *nm* (*LING*) Malagasy ♦ *nm/f*: **M~** Malagasy, Madagascan.

malgré [màlgrā] *prép* in spite of, despite; **~ tout** *ad* in spite of everything.

malhabile [màlàbēl] *a* clumsy.

malheur [màlœr] *nm* (*situation*) adversity, misfortune; (*événement*) misfortune; (*: plus fort*) disaster, tragedy; **par ~** unfortunately; **quel ~!** what a shame *ou* pity!; **faire un ~** (*fam: un éclat*) to do something desperate; (*: avoir du succès*) to be a smash hit.

malheureusement [màlœrœ̄zmáñ] *ad* unfortunately.

malheureux, euse [màlœrœ̄, -ēz] *a* (*triste*) unhappy, miserable; (*infortuné, regrettable*) unfortunate; (*malchanceux*) unlucky; (*insignifiant*) wretched ♦ *nm/f* (*infortuné, misérable*) poor soul; (*indigent, miséreux*) unfortunate creature; **les ~** the destitute; **avoir la main malheureuse** (*au jeu*) to be unlucky; (*tout casser*) to be ham-handed.

malhonnête [màlonct] *a* dishonest; (*impoli*) rude.

malhonnêteté [màlonettā] *nf* dishonesty; rudeness *q*.

Mali [màlē] *nm*: **le ~** Mali.

malice [màlēs] *nf* mischievousness; (*méchanceté*): **par ~** out of malice *ou* spite; **sans ~** guileless.

malicieux, euse [màlēsyœ̄, -ēz] *a* mischievous.

malien, ne [màlyañ, -en] *a* Malian.

malignité [màlēnyētā] *nf* (*d'une tumeur, d'un mal*) malignancy.

malin, igne [màlañ, -ēny] *a* (*futé: f gén:* **maligne**) smart, shrewd; (*: sourire*) knowing; (*MÉD, influence*) malignant; **faire le ~** to show off; **éprouver un ~ plaisir à** to take malicious pleasure in.

malingre [màláñgr(ə)] *a* puny.

malintentionné, e [màláñtáñsyonā] *a* ill-intentioned, malicious.

malle [mál] *nf* trunk; (*AUTO*): **~ (arrière)**

trunk (*US*), boot (*Brit*).

malléable [málãäbl(ə)] *a* malleable.

malle-poste, *pl* **malles-poste** [málpost(ə)] *nf* mail car (*US*) *ou* coach (*Brit*).

mallette [málet] *nf* (*valise*) (small) suitcase; (*aussi:* ~ **de voyage**) overnight case; (*pour documents*) attaché case.

malmener [málmənã] *vt* to manhandle; (*fig*) to give a rough ride to.

malodorant, e [málodorãṅ, -ãṅt] *a* a foul- *ou* bad-smelling.

malotru [málotrü] *nm* lout, boor.

malouin, e [málwaṅ, -ēn] *a* of *ou* from Saint Malo.

Malouines [málwēn] *nfpl:* **les** ~ the Falklands, the Falkland Islands.

malpoli, e [málpolē] *nm/f* rude individual.

malpropre [málpropr(ə)] *a* (*personne, vêtement*) dirty; (*travail*) slovenly; (*histoire, plaisanterie*) unsavory (*US*), unsavoury (*Brit*), smutty; (*malhonnête*) dishonest.

malpropreté [málproprətã] *nf* dirtiness.

malsain, e [málsaṅ, -en] *a* unhealthy.

malséant, e [málsãäṅ, -ãṅt] *a* unseemly, unbecoming.

malsonnant, e [málsonãṅ, -ãṅt] *a* offensive.

malt [mált] *nm* malt; **pur** ~ (*whisky*) malt (whisky).

maltais, e [málte, -ez] *a* Maltese.

Malte [mált(ə)] *nf* Malta.

malté, e [máltã] *a* (*lait etc*) malted.

maltraiter [máltrãtã] *vt* (*brutaliser*) to manhandle, ill-treat; (*critiquer, éreinter*) to pan, roast.

malus [málüs] *nm* (*ASSURANCES*) car insurance surcharge, penalty.

malveillance [málveyãṅs] *nf* (*animosité*) ill will; (*intention de nuire*) malevolence; (*JUR*) malicious intent *q*.

malveillant, e [málveyãṅ, -ãṅt] *a* malevolent, malicious.

malvenu, e [málvənü] *a*: **être** ~ **de** *ou* **à faire qch** not to be in a position to do sth.

malversation [málversãsyóṅ] *nf* embezzlement, misappropriation (of funds).

maman [mámãṅ] *nf* mom (*US*), mum(my) (*Brit*).

mamelle [mámel] *nf* teat.

mamelon [mámlóṅ] *nm* (*ANAT*) nipple; (*colline*) knoll, hillock.

mamie [mámē] *nf* (*fam*) granny.

mammifère [mámēfer] *nm* mammal.

mammouth [mámōöt] *nm* mammoth.

manager [mánãdzher] *nm* (*SPORT*) manager; (*COMM*): ~ **commercial** commercial director.

manceau, elle, x [mãṅsō, -el] *a* of *ou* from Le Mans.

manche [mãṅsh] *nf* (*de vêtement*) sleeve; (*d'un jeu, tournoi*) round; (*GÉO*): **la M**~ the (English) Channel ♦ *nm* (*d'outil, casserole*) handle; (*de pelle, pioche etc*) shaft; (*de violon, guitare*) neck; (*fam*) clumsy oaf; **faire la** ~ to pass the hat; ~ **à air** *nf* (*AVIAT*) windsock; ~ **à balai** *nm* broomstick; (*AVIAT, INFORM*) joystick.

manchette [mãṅshet] *nf* (*de chemise*) cuff; (*coup*) forearm blow; (*titre*) headline.

manchon [mãṅshóṅ] *nm* (*de fourrure*) muff;

~ **à incandescence** incandescent (gas) mantle.

manchot [mãṅshō] *nm* one-armed man; armless man; (*ZOOL*) penguin.

mandarine [mãṅdárēn] *nf* mandarin (orange), tangerine.

mandat [mãṅdá] *nm* (*postal*) postal *ou* money order; (*d'un député etc*) mandate; (*procuration*) power of attorney, proxy; (*POLICE*) warrant; ~ **d'amener** summons *sg*; ~ **d'arrêt** warrant for arrest; ~ **de dépôt** committal order; ~ **de perquisition** (*POLICE*) search warrant.

mandataire [mãṅdáter] *nm/f* (*représentant, délégué*) representative; (*JUR*) proxy.

mandat-carte, *pl* **mandats-cartes** [mãṅdákárt(ə)] *nm* money order (*in postcard form*).

mandater [mãṅdátã] *vt* (*personne*) to appoint; (*POL: député*) to elect.

mandat-lettre, *pl* **mandats-lettres** [mãṅdáletr(ə)] *nm* money order (*with space for correspondence*).

mandchou, e [mãṅtshōō] *a* Manchu, Manchurian ♦ *nm* (*LING*) Manchu ♦ *nm/f:* **M**~, **e** Manchu.

Mandchourie [mãṅtshōōrē] *nf:* **la** ~ Manchuria.

mander [mãṅdã] *vt* to summon.

mandibule [mãṅdēbül] *nf* mandible.

mandoline [mãṅdolēn] *nf* mandolin(e).

manège [mánezh] *nm* riding school; (*à la foire*) merry-go-round; (*fig*) game, ploy; **faire un tour de** ~ to go for a ride on a *ou* the roundabout *etc*; ~ (**de chevaux de bois**) merry-go-round.

manette [mánet] *nf* lever, tap; ~ **de jeu** (*INFORM*) joystick.

manganèse [mãṅgánez] *nm* manganese.

mangeable [mãṅzhábl(ə)] *a* edible, eatable.

mangeaille [mãṅzhây] *nf* (*péj*) grub.

mangeoire [mãṅzhwár] *nf* trough, manger.

manger [mãṅzhã] *vt* to eat; (*ronger: suj: rouille etc*) to eat into *ou* away; (*utiliser, consommer*) to eat up ♦ *vi* to eat.

mange-tout [mãṅzhtōō] *nm inv* sugar pea (*US*), mange-tout (*Brit*).

mangeur, euse [mãṅzhœr, -ēz] *nm/f* eater.

mangouste [mãṅgōōst(ə)] *nf* mongoose.

mangue [mãṅg] *nf* mango.

maniable [mányábl(ə)] *a* (*outil*) handy; (*voiture, voilier*) easy to handle, maneuverable (*US*), manœuvrable (*Brit*); (*fig: personne*) easily influenced, manipulable.

maniaque [mányák] *a* (*pointilleux, méticuleux*) finicky, fussy; (*atteint de manie*) suffering from a mania ♦ *nm/f* maniac.

manie [mánē] *nf* mania; (*tic*) odd habit.

maniement [mánēmãṅ] *nm* handling; ~ **d'armes** arms drill.

manier [mányã] *vt* to handle; **se** ~ *vi* (*fam*) to get a move on.

manière [mányer] *nf* (*façon*) way, manner; (*genre, style*) style; ~**s** *nfpl* (*attitude*) manners; (*chichis*) fuss *sg*; **de** ~ **à** so as to; **de telle** ~ **que** in such a way that; **de cette** ~ in this way *ou* manner; **d'une** ~ **générale** generally speaking, as a general rule; **de toute** ~ in any case; **d'une certaine** ~ in a (certain) way; **faire des ~s** to put on airs; **employer la ~ forte** to use strong-arm tactics; **adverbe de ~** adverb of manner.

maniéré, e [mányārā] *a* affected.

manif [mȧnēf] *nf* (= *manifestation*) demo (*pl -s*).

manifestant, e [mȧnēfestȧṅ, -ȧṅt] *nm/f* demonstrator.

manifestation [mȧnēfestȧsyȯṅ] *nf* (*de joie, mécontentement*) expression, demonstration; (*symptôme*) outward sign; (*fête etc*) event; (*POL*) demonstration.

manifeste [mȧnēfest(ǝ)] *a* obvious, evident ♦ *nm* manifesto (*pl -s*).

manifester [mȧnēfestā] *vt* (*volonté, intentions*) to show, indicate; (*joie, peur*) to express, show ♦ *vi* (*POL*) to demonstrate; **se ~** *vi* (*émotion*) to show *ou* express itself; (*difficultés*) to arise; (*symptômes*) to appear; (*témoin etc*) to come forward.

manigance [mȧnēgȧṅs] *nf* scheme.

manigancer [mȧnēgȧṅsā] *vt* to plot, devise.

Manille [mȧnēy] *n* Manila.

manioc [mányok] *nm* cassava, manioc.

manipulateur, trice [mȧnēpülȧtœr, -trēs] *a* (*technicien*) technician, operator; (*prestidigitateur*) conjurer; (*péj*) manipulator.

manipulation [mȧnēpülȧsyȯṅ] *nf* handling; manipulation.

manipuler [mȧnēpülā] *vt* to handle; (*fig*) to manipulate.

manivelle [mȧnēvel] *nf* crank.

manne [mȧn] *nf* (*REL*) manna; (*fig*) godsend.

mannequin [mȧnkȧṅ] *nm* (*COUTURE*) dummy; (*MODE*) model.

manœuvrable [mȧnœvrȧbl(ǝ)] *a* (*bateau, véhicule*) maneuverable (*US*), manœuvrable (*Brit*).

manœuvre [mȧnœvr(ǝ)] *nf* (*gén*) maneuver (*US*), manœuvre (*Brit*) ♦ *nm* (*ouvrier*) laborer (*US*), labourer (*Brit*).

manœuvrer [mȧnœvrā] *vt* to maneuver (*US*), manœuvre (*Brit*); (*levier, machine*) to operate; (*personne*) to manipulate ♦ *vi* to maneuvre *ou* manœuvrer.

manoir [mȧnwȧr] *nm* manor *ou* country house.

manomètre [mȧnometr(ǝ)] *nm* gauge, manometer.

manquant, e [mȧṅkȧṅ, -ȧṅt] *a* missing.

manque [mȧṅk] *nm* (*insuffisance*): **~ de** lack of; (*vide*) emptiness, gap; (*MÉD*) withdrawal; **~s** *nmpl* (*lacunes*) faults, defects; **par ~ de** for want of; **~ à gagner** loss of profit *ou* earnings.

manqué, e [mȧṅkā] *a* failed; **garçon ~** tomboy.

manquement [mȧṅkmȧṅ] *nm*: **~ à** (*discipline, règle*) breach of.

manquer [mȧṅkā] *vi* (*faire défaut*) to be lacking; (*être absent*) to be missing; (*échouer*) to fail ♦ *vt* to miss ♦ *vb impersonnel*: **il (nous) manque encore 100 F** we are still 100 F short; **il manque des pages (au livre)** there are some pages missing *ou* some pages are missing (from the book); **l'argent qui leur manque** the money they need *ou* are short of; **le pied/la voix lui manqua** he missed his footing/his voice failed him; **~ à qn** (*absent etc*): **il/cela me manque** I miss him/that; **~ à** *vt* (*règles etc*) to be in breach of, fail to observe; **~ de** *vt* to lack; (*COMM*) to be out of (stock of); **ne pas ~ de faire: il n'a pas manqué de le dire** he certainly said it; **~ (de) faire: il a manqué (de) se tuer** he very nearly got killed; **il ne manquerait plus qu'il fasse** all we need now is for him to do; **je n'y manquerai pas** leave it to me, I'll definitely do it.

mansarde [mȧṅsȧrd(ǝ)] *nf* attic.

mansardé, e [mȧṅsȧrdā] *a* attic *cpd*.

mansuétude [mȧṅsüātüd] *nf* leniency.

mante [mȧṅt] *nf*: **~ religieuse** praying mantis.

manteau, x [mȧṅtō] *nm* coat; **~ de cheminée** mantelpiece; **sous le ~** (*fig*) under cover.

mantille [mȧṅtēy] *nf* mantilla.

Mantoue [mȧṅtōō] *n* Mantua.

manucure [mȧnükür] *nf* manicurist.

manuel, le [mȧnüel] *a* manual ♦ *nm/f* manually gifted pupil *etc* (*as opposed to intellectually gifted*) ♦ *nm* (*ouvrage*) manual, handbook.

manuellement [mȧnüelmȧṅ] *ad* manually.

manufacture [mȧnüfȧktür] *nf* (*établissement*) factory; (*fabrication*) manufacture.

manufacturé, e [mȧnüfȧktürā] *a* manufactured.

manufacturier, ière [mȧnüfȧktüryā, -yer] *nm/f* factory owner.

manuscrit, e [mȧnüskrē, -ēt] *a* handwritten ♦ *nm* manuscript.

manutention [mȧnütȧṅsyȯṅ] *nf* (*COMM*) handling; (*local*) storehouse.

manutentionnaire [mȧnütȧṅsyoner] *nm/f* warehouseman/woman, packer.

manutentionner [mȧnütȧṅsyonā] *vt* to handle.

MAP *sigle f* (*PHOTO*: = *mise au point*) focusing.

mappemonde [mȧpmȯṅd] *nf* (*plane*) map of the world; (*sphère*) globe.

maquereau, x [mȧkrō] *nm* mackerel *inv*; (*fam: proxénète*) pimp.

maquerelle [mȧkrel] *nf* (*fam*) madam.

maquette [mȧket] *nf* (*d'un décor, bâtiment, véhicule*) (scale) model; (*TYPO*) mock-up; (: *d'une page illustrée, affiche*) paste-up; (: *prêt à la réproduction*) artwork.

maquignon [mȧkēnȯṅ] *nm* horse dealer.

maquillage [mȧkēyȧzh] *nm* making up; faking; (*produits*) make-up.

maquiller [mȧkēyā] *vt* (*personne, visage*) to make up; (*truquer: passeport, statistique*) to fake; (: *voiture volée*) to do over (*respray etc*); **se ~** to make o.s. up.

maquilleur, euse [mȧkēyœr, -ēz] *nm/f* make-up artist.

maquis [mȧkē] *nm* (*GÉO*) scrub; (*fig*) tangle; (*MIL*) maquis, underground fighting *q*.

maquisard, e [mȧkēzȧr, -ȧrd(ǝ)] *nm/f* maquis, member of the Resistance.

marabout [mȧrȧbōō] *nm* (*ZOOL*) marabou(t).

maraîcher, ère [mȧrāshā, mȧresher] *a*: **cultures maraîchères** truck farming *sg* (*US*), market gardening *sg* (*Brit*) ♦ *nm/f* truck farmer (*US*), market gardener (*Brit*).

marais [mȧre] *nm* marsh, swamp; **~ salant** saltworks.

marasme [mȧrȧsm(ǝ)] *nm* (*POL*, *ÉCON*)

stagnation, sluggishness; (*accablement*) dejection, depression.

marathon [màràtóǹ] *nm* marathon.

marâtre [màràtr(ə)] *nf* cruel mother.

maraude [màrōd] *nf* pilfering, thieving (*of poultry, crops*); (*dans un verger*) fruitstealing; (*vagabondage*) prowling; **en ~** on the prowl; (*taxi*) cruising.

maraudeur, euse [màrōdœr, -œz] *nm/f* marauder; prowler.

marbre [màrbr(ə)] *nm* (*pierre, statue*) marble; (*d'une table, commode*) marble top; (*TYPO*) stone, bed; **rester de ~** to remain stonily indifferent.

marbrer [màrbrā] *vt* to mottle, blotch; (*TECH*: *papier*) to marble.

marbrier [màrbrēyā] *nm* monumental mason.

marbrière [màrbrēyɛr] *nf* marble quarry.

marbrures [màrbrür] *nfpl* blotches *pl*; (*TECH*) marbling *sg*.

marc [màr] *nm* (*de raisin, pommes*) marc; **~ de café** coffee grounds *pl ou* dregs *pl*.

marcassin [màrkàsaǹ] *nm* young wild boar.

marchand, e [màrshāǹ, -āǹd] *nm/f* shopkeeper, tradesman/woman; (*au marché*) stallholder; (*spécifique*): **~ de cycles/tapis** bicycle/carpet dealer; **~ de charbon/vins** coal/wine merchant ♦ *a*: **prix/valeur ~(e)** market price/value; **qualité ~e** standard quality; **~ en gros/au détail** wholesaler/retailer; **~ de biens** real estate agent; **~ de canons** (*péj*) arms dealer; **~ de couleurs** hardware dealer (*US*), ironmonger (*Brit*); **~/e de fruits** fruit seller (*US*), fruiterer (*Brit*); **~/e de journaux** newsagent; **~/e de légumes** produce dealer (*US*), greengrocer (*Brit*); **~/e de poisson** fish seller (*US*), fishmonger (*Brit*); **~e de quatre saisons** street vendor (selling fresh fruit and vegetables); **~ de sable** (*fig*) sandman; **~ de tableaux** art dealer.

marchander [màrshāǹdā] *vt* (*article*) to bargain *ou* haggle over; (*éloges*) to be sparing with ♦ *vi* to bargain, haggle.

marchandise [màrshāǹdēz] *nf* goods *pl*, merchandise *q*.

marche [màrsh(ə)] *nf* (*d'escalier*) step; (*activité*) walking; (*promenade, trajet, allure*) walk; (*démarche*) walk, gait; (*MIL etc, MUS*) march; (*fonctionnement*) running; (*progression*) progress; course; **à une heure de ~** an hour's walk (away); **ouvrir/fermer la ~** to lead the way/bring up the rear; **dans le sens de la ~** (*RAIL*) facing the engine; **en ~** (*monter etc*) while the vehicle is moving *ou* in motion; **mettre en ~** to start; **remettre qch en ~** to set *ou* start sth going again; **se mettre en ~** (*personne*) to get moving; (*machine*) to start; **~ arrière** (*AUTO*) reverse (gear); **faire ~ arrière** (*AUTO*) to reverse; (*fig*) to backtrack, back-pedal; **~ à suivre** (correct) procedure; (*sur notice*) (step by step) instructions *pl*.

marché [màrshā] *nm* (*lieu, COMM, ÉCON*) market; (*ville*) trading center (*US*) *ou* centre (*Brit*); (*transaction*) bargain, deal; **par-dessus le ~** into the bargain; **faire son ~** to do one's shopping; **mettre le ~ en main à qn** to tell sb to take it or leave it; **~ au comptant** (*BOURSE*) spot market; **M~**

commun Common Market; **~ aux fleurs** flower market; **~ noir** black market; **faire du ~ noir** to buy and sell on the black market; **~ aux puces** flea market; **~ à terme** (*BOURSE*) forward market; **~ du travail** labor (*US*) *ou* labour (*Brit*) market.

marchepied [màrshəpyā] *nm* (*RAIL*) step; (*AUTO*) running board; (*fig*) stepping stone.

marcher [màrshā] *vi* to walk; (*MIL*) to march; (*aller: voiture, train, affaires*) to go; (*prospérer*) to go well; (*fonctionner*) to work, run; (*fam*) to go along, agree; (*: croire naivement*) to be taken in; **~ sur** to walk on; (*mettre le pied sur*) to step on *ou* in; (*MIL*) to march upon; **~ dans** (*herbe etc*) to walk in *ou* on; (*flaque*) to step in; **faire ~ qn** (*pour rire*) to pull sb's leg; (*pour tromper*) to lead sb up the garden path.

marcheur, euse [màrshœr, -œz] *nm/f* walker.

marcotter [màrkotā] *vt* to layer.

mardi [màrdē] *nm* Tuesday; **M~ gras** Shrove Tuesday; *voir aussi* **lundi**.

mare [màr] *nf* pond; **~ de sang** pool of blood.

marécage [màrākàzh] *nm* marsh, swamp.

marécageux, euse [màrākàzhœ, -œz] *a* marshy, swampy.

maréchal, aux [màrāshàl, -ō] *nm* marshal; **~ des logis** (*MIL*) sergeant.

maréchal-ferrant, *pl* **maréchaux-ferrants** [màrāshàlferàǹ, màràshō-] *nm* blacksmith.

maréchaussée [màrāshōsā] *nf* (*humoristique*: *gendarmes*) police.

marée [màrā] *nf* tide; (*poissons*) fresh (sea) fish; **~ haute/basse** high/low tide; **~ montante/descendante** rising/ebb tide; **~ noire** oil slick.

marelle [màrel] *nf*: **(jouer à) la ~** (to play) hopscotch.

marémotrice [màrāmotrēs] *af* tidal.

mareyeur, euse [màrɛyœr, -œz] *nm/f* wholesale (sea) fish merchant.

margarine [màrgàrēn] *nf* margarine.

marge [màrzh(ə)] *nf* margin; **en ~** in the margin; **en ~ de** (*fig*) on the fringe of; (*en dehors de*) cut off from; (*qui se rapporte à*) connected with; **~ bénéficiaire** profit margin, markup; **~ de sécurité** safety margin.

margelle [màrzhel] *nf* coping.

margeur [màrzhœr] *nm* margin stop.

marginal, e, aux [màrzhēnàl, -ō] *a* marginal ♦ *nm/f* dropout.

marguerite [màrgərēt] *nf* marguerite, (oxeye) daisy; (*INFORM*) daisy wheel.

marguillier [màrgēyā] *nm* churchwarden.

mari [màrē] *nm* husband.

mariage [màryàzh] *nm* (*union, état, fig*) marriage; (*noce*) wedding; **~ civil/religieux** civil/church wedding; **un ~ de raison/d'amour** a marriage of convenience/a love match; **~ blanc** unconsummated marriage; **~ en blanc** white wedding.

marié, e [màryā] *a* married ♦ *nm/f* (bride)groom/bride; **les ~s** the bride and groom; **les (jeunes) ~s** the newlyweds.

marier [màryā] *vt* to marry; (*fig*) to blend; **se ~ (avec)** to marry, get married (to); (*fig*) to blend (with).

marijuana [màrēzhwànà] *nf* marijuana.

marin, e [màraǹ, -ēn] *a* sea *cpd*, marine ♦ *nm*

sailor ♦ *nf* navy; (*ART*) seascape; (*couleur*) navy (blue); **avoir le pied** ~ to be a good sailor; (*garder son équilibre*) to have one's sea legs; ~**e de guerre** navy; ~**e marchande** merchant marine (*US*) *ou* navy (*Brit*); ~**e à voiles** sailing ships *pl*.

marinade [màrēnàd] *nf* marinade.

marine [màrēn] *af*, *nf voir* **marin** ♦ *a inv* navy (blue) ♦ *nm* (*MIL*) marine.

mariner [màrēnā] *vi*, *vt* to marinate, marinade.

marinier [màrēnyā] *nm* bargeman (*US*), bargee (*Brit*).

marinière [màrēnyer] *nf* (*blouse*) smock ♦ *a inv*: **moules** ~ (*CULIN*) mussels in white wine.

marionnette [màryonet] *nf* puppet.

marital, e, aux [màrētàl, -ō] *a*: **autorisation** ~e husband's permission.

maritalement [màrētàlmâṅ] *ad*: **vivre** ~ to live together (as husband and wife).

maritime [màrētēm] *a* sea *cpd*, maritime; (*ville*) coastal, seaside; (*droit*) shipping, maritime.

marjolaine [màrzholen] *nf* marjoram.

mark [màrk] *nm* (*monnaie*) mark.

marketing [màrkətēng] *nm* (*COMM*) marketing.

marmaille [màrmây] *nf* (*péj*) (gang of) brats *pl*.

marmelade [màrməlàd] *nf* (*compote*) stewed fruit, compote; ~ **d'oranges** (orange) marmalade; **en** ~ (*fig*) crushed (to a pulp).

marmite [màrmēt] *nf* (cooking-)pot.

marmiton [màrmētóṅ] *nm* kitchen boy.

marmonner [màrmonā] *vt*, *vi* to mumble, mutter.

marmot [màrmō] *nm* (*fam*) brat.

marmotte [màrmot] *nf* marmot.

marmotter [màrmotā] *vt* (*prière*) to mumble, mutter.

marne [màrn(ə)] *nf* (*GÉO*) marl.

Maroc [màrok] *nm*: **le** ~ Morocco.

marocain, e [màrokàṅ, -en] *a* Moroccan ♦ *nm/f*: **M**~, **e** Moroccan.

maroquin [màrokàṅ] *nm* (*peau*) morocco (leather); (*fig*) (minister's) portfolio.

maroquinerie [màrokēnrē] *nf* (*industrie*) leather craft; (*commerce*) leather shop; (*articles*) fine leather goods *pl*.

marotte [màrot] *nf* fad.

marquant, e [màrkâṅ, -âṅt] *a* outstanding.

marque [màrk(ə)] *nf* mark; (*SPORT, JEU*: *décompte des points*) score; (*COMM*: *de produits*) brand, make; (*: de disques*) label; (*insigne: d'une fonction*) badge; (*fig*): ~ **d'affection** token of affection; ~ **de joie** sign of joy; **à vos** ~**s!** (*SPORT*) on your marks!; **de** ~ *a* (*COMM*) brand-name *cpd*; proprietary; (*fig*) high-class; (*: personnage, hôte*) distinguished; **produit de** ~ (*COMM*) quality product; ~ **déposée** registered trademark; ~ **de fabrique** trademark.

marqué, e [màrkā] *a* marked.

marquer [màrkā] *vt* to mark; (*inscrire*) to write down; (*bétail*) to brand; (*SPORT*: *but etc*) to score; (*: joueur*) to mark; (*accentuer*: *taille etc*) to emphasize; (*manifester*: *refus, intérêt*) to show ♦ *vi*

(*événement, personnalité*) to stand out, be outstanding; (*SPORT*) to score; ~ **qn de son influence/empreinte** to have an influence/leave its impression on sb; ~ **un temps d'arrêt** to pause momentarily; ~ **le pas** (*fig*) to mark time; **il a marqué ce jour-là d'une pierre blanche** that was a red-letter day for him; ~ **les points** (*tenir la marque*) to keep the score.

marqueté, e [màrkətā] *a* inlaid.

marqueterie [màrkətrē] *nf* inlaid work, marquetry.

marqueur, euse [màrkœr, -ēz] *nm/f* (*SPORT*: *de but*) scorer ♦ *nm* (*crayon feutre*) marker pen.

marquis, e [màrkē, -ēz] *nm/f* marquis *ou* marquess/marchioness ♦ *nf* (*auvent*) glass canopy *ou* awning.

Marquises [màrkēz] *nfpl*: **les (îles)** ~ the Marquesas Islands.

marraine [màren] *nf* godmother; (*d'un navire, d'une rose etc*) namer.

Marrakech [màràkesh] *n* Marrakech *ou* Marrakesh.

marrant, e [màràṅ, -âṅt] *a* (*fam*) funny.

marre [màr] *ad* (*fam*): **en avoir** ~ **de** to be fed up with.

marrer [màrā]: **se** ~ *vi* (*fam*) to have a (good) laugh.

marron, ne [màróṅ, -on] *nm* (*fruit*) chestnut ♦ *a inv* brown ♦ *a* (*péj*) crooked; (*: faux*) bogus; ~**s glacés** marrons glacés.

marronnier [màronyā] *nm* chestnut (tree).

Mars [màrs] *nm ou nf* Mars.

mars [màrs] *nm* March; *voir aussi* **juillet**.

marseillais, e [màrseye, -ez] *a* of *ou* from Marseilles ♦ *nf*: **la M**~**e** the French national anthem.

Marseille [màrsey] *n* Marseilles.

marsouin [màrswàṅ] *nm* porpoise.

marsupiaux [màrsüpyō] *nmpl* marsupials.

marteau, x [màrtō] *nm* hammer; (*de porte*) knocker; ~ **pneumatique** pneumatic drill.

marteau-pilon, *pl* **marteaux-pilons** [màrtōpēlóṅ] *nm* drop (*US*) *ou* power (*Brit*) hammer.

marteau-piqueur, *pl* **marteaux-piqueurs** [màrtōpēkœr] *nm* pneumatic drill.

martel [màrtel] *nm*: **se mettre** ~ **en tête** to worry o.s.

martèlement [màrtelmâṅ] *nm* hammering.

marteler [màrtəlā] *vt* to hammer; (*mots, phrases*) to rap out.

martial, e, aux [màrsyàl, -ō] *a* martial; **cour** ~**e** court-martial.

martien, ne [màrsyaṅ, -en] *a* Martian, of *ou* from Mars.

martinet [màrtēne] *nm* (*fouet*) small whip; (*ZOOL*) swift.

martingale [màrtaṅgàl] *nf* (*COUTURE*) half-belt; (*JEU*) winning formula.

martiniquais, e [màrtēnēke, -ez] *a* of *ou* from Martinique.

Martinique [màrtēnēk] *nf*: **la** ~ Martinique.

martin-pêcheur, *pl* **martins-pêcheurs** [màrtaṅpeshœr] *nm* kingfisher.

martre [màrtr(ə)] *nf* marten; ~ **zibeline** sable.

martyr, e [màrtēr] *nm/f* martyr ♦ *a* martyred; **enfants** ~**s** battered children.

martyre [mártĕr] *nm* martyrdom; *(fig: sens affaibli)* agony, torture; **souffrir le ~** to suffer agonies.

martyriser [mártĕrĕzã] *vt* (*REL*) to martyr; *(fig)* to bully; (: *enfant*) to batter.

marxisme [márksĕsm(ə)] *nm* Marxism.

marxiste [márksĕst(ə)] *a, nm/f* Marxist.

mas [mâ(s)] *nm traditional house or farm in Provence.*

mascarade [máskárád] *nf* masquerade.

mascotte [máskot] *nf* mascot.

masculin, e [máskülań, -ēn] *a* masculine; *(sexe, population)* male; *(équipe, vêtements)* men's; *(viril)* manly ♦ *nm* masculine.

masochisme [mázoshĕsm(ə)] *nm* masochism.

masque [másk(ə)] *nm* mask; **~ de beauté** face pack; **~ à gaz** gas mask; **~ de plongée** diving mask.

masqué, e [máskã] *a* masked.

masquer [máskã] *vt* (*cacher: porte, goût*) to hide, conceal; *(dissimuler: vérité, projet)* to mask, obscure.

massacrant, e [másákrań, -áňt] *a*: **humeur ~e** foul temper.

massacre [másákr(ə)] *nm* massacre, slaughter; *jeu de ~ (fig)* wholesale slaughter.

massacrer [másákrã] *vt* to massacre, slaughter; *(fig: adversaire)* to slaughter; (: *texte etc*) to murder.

massage [másázh] *nm* massage.

masse [más] *nf* mass; *(péj)*: **la ~** the masses *pl*; (*ÉLEC*) earth; *(maillet)* sledgehammer; **~s** *nfpl* masses; **une ~ de, des ~s de** *(fam)* masses *ou* loads of; **en ~** *ad* (*en bloc*) in bulk; *(en foule)* en masse ♦ *a* (*exécutions, production*) mass *cpd*; **~ monétaire** (*ÉCON*) money supply; **~ salariale** (*COMM*) wage(s) bill.

massepain [máspań] *nm* marzipan.

masser [másã] *vt* (*assembler*) to gather; *(pétrir)* to massage; **se ~** *vi* to gather.

masseur, euse [másœr, -œ̄z] *nm/f* (*personne*) masseur/masseuse ♦ *nm* (*appareil*) massager.

massicot [másĕkō] *nm* (*TYPO*) guillotine.

massif, ive [másĕf, -ēv] *a* (*porte*) solid, massive; *(visage)* heavy, large; *(bois, or)* solid; *(dose)* massive; *(déportations etc)* mass *cpd* ♦ *nm* (*montagneux*) massif; *(de fleurs)* clump, bank.

massue [mású] *nf* club, bludgeon ♦ *a inv*: **argument ~** sledgehammer argument.

mastic [mástĕk] *nm* (*pour vitres*) putty; *(pour fentes)* filler.

mastication [mástĕkásyôń] *nf* chewing, mastication.

mastiquer [mástĕkã] *vt* (*aliment*) to chew, masticate; *(fente)* to fill; *(vitre)* to putty.

mastoc [mástok] *a inv* hefty.

mastodonte [mástodôńt] *nm* monster *(fig)*.

masturbation [mástürbásyôń] *nf* masturbation.

masturber [mástürbã] *vt*: **se ~** to masturbate.

m'as-tu-vu [mátüvü] *nm/f inv* show-off.

masure [mázür] *nf* tumbledown cottage.

mat, e [mát] *a* (*couleur, métal*) mat(t); *(bruit, son)* dull ♦ *a inv* (*ÉCHECS*): **être ~** to be checkmated.

mât [mâ] *nm* (*NAVIG*) mast; *(poteau)* pole, post.

matamore [mátámor] *nm* braggart, blusterer.

match [mátsh] *nm* match; **~ nul** draw, tie (*US*); **faire ~ nul** to tie (*US*), draw (*Brit*); **~ aller** first leg; **~ retour** second leg, return match.

matelas [mátlá] *nm* mattress; **~ pneumatique** air bed *ou* mattress; **~ à ressorts** innerspring (*US*) *ou* interior-sprung (*Brit*) mattress.

matelasser [mátlásã] *vt* to pad.

matelot [mátlō] *nm* sailor, seaman.

mater [mátã] *vt* (*personne*) to bring to heel, subdue; *(révolte)* to put down; *(fam)* to watch, look at.

matérialiser [mátáryálĕzã]: **se ~** *vi* to materialize.

matérialisme [mátáryálĕsm(ə)] *nm* materialism.

matérialiste [mátáryálĕst(ə)] *a* materialistic ♦ *nm/f* materialist.

matériau, x [mátáryō] *nm* material; **~x** *nmpl* material(s); **~x de construction** building materials.

matériel, le [mátáryel] *a* material; *(organisation, aide, obstacle)* practical; *(fig: péj: personne)* materialistic ♦ *nm* equipment *q*; *(de camping etc)* gear *q*; **il n'a pas le temps ~ de le faire** he doesn't have the time (needed) to do it; **~ d'exploitation** (*COMM*) plant; **~ roulant** rolling stock.

maternel, le [mátĕrnel] *a* (*amour, geste*) motherly, maternal; *(grand-père, oncle)* maternal ♦ *nf* (*aussi*: **école ~le**) (state) nursery school.

materner [mátĕrnã] *vt* (*personne*) to mother.

maternité [mátĕrnĕtã] *nf* (*établissement*) maternity hospital; *(état de mère)* motherhood, maternity; *(grossesse)* pregnancy.

math [mát] *nfpl* math (*US*), maths (*Brit*).

mathématicien, ne [mátămátĕsyań, -en] *nm/f* mathematician.

mathématique [mátămátĕk] *a* mathematical.

mathématiques [mátămátĕk] *nfpl* mathematics *sg*.

matheux, euse [mátœ̄, -œ̄z] *nm/f* (*fam*) math (*US*) *ou* maths (*Brit*) student; *(fort en math)* mathematical genius.

maths [mát] *nfpl* math (*US*), maths (*Brit*).

matière [mátyer] *nf* (*PHYSIQUE*) matter; *(COMM, TECH)* material, matter *q*; *(fig: d'un livre etc)* subject matter; *(SCOL)* subject; **en ~ de** as regards; **donner ~ à** to give cause to; **~ grise** gray (*US*) *ou* grey (*Brit*) matter; **~ plastique** plastic; **~s fécales** feces (*US*), faeces (*Brit*); **~s grasses** fat (content) *sg*; **~s premières** raw materials.

MATIF [mátĕf] *sigle m* (= *Marché à terme des instruments financiers*) *body which regulates the activities of the French Stock Exchange.*

Matignon [mátēñôń] *n French prime minister's offices.*

matin [mátań] *nm, ad* morning; **le ~** *(pendant le ~)* in the morning; **demain ~** tomorrow morning; **le lendemain ~** (the) next morning; **du ~ au soir** from morning till night; **une heure du ~** one o'clock in the morning; **de grand** *ou* **bon ~** early in the morning.

matinal, e, aux [mátĕnál, -ō] *a* (*toilette,*

gymnastique) morning *cpd*; (*de bonne heure*) early; **être** ~ (*personne*) to be up early; (*: habituellement*) to be an early riser.

mâtiné, e [mâtēnā] *a* crossbred, mixed race *cpd*.

matinée [mâtēnā] *nf* morning; (*spectacle*) matinée, afternoon performance.

matois, e [mâtwá, -wáz] *a* wily.

matou [mâtōō] *nm* tom(cat).

matraquage [mátrâkázh] *nm* beating up; ~ **publicitaire** plug, plugging.

matraque [mátrák] *nf* (*de malfaiteur*) club; (*de policier*) billy (*US*), truncheon (*Brit*).

matraquer [mátrákā] *vt* to beat up (with a truncheon *ou* billy); to club; (*fig: touristes etc*) to rip off; (*: disque*) to plug.

matriarcal, e, aux [mátrēyárkál, -ō] *a* matriarchal.

matrice [mátrēs] *nf* (*ANAT*) womb; (*TECH*) mold (*US*), mould (*Brit*); (*MATH etc*) matrix.

matricule [mátrēkül] *nf* (*aussi:* **registre** ~) roll, register ♦ *nm* (*aussi:* **numéro** ~: *MIL*) regimental number; (*: ADMIN*) reference number.

matrimonial, e, aux [mátrēmonyál, -ō] *a* marital, marriage *cpd*.

matrone [mátron] *nf* matron.

mâture [mâtür] *nf* masts *pl*.

maturité [mátürētā] *nf* maturity; (*d'un fruit*) ripeness, maturity.

maudire [mōdēr] *vt* to curse.

maudit, e [mōdē, -ēt] *a* (*fam: satané*) blasted, confounded.

maugréer [mōgrāā] *vi* to grumble.

mauresque [moresk(ə)] *a* Moorish.

Maurice [morēs] *nf*: (**l'île**) ~ Mauritius.

mauricien, ne [morēsyań, -en] *a* Mauritian.

Mauritanie [morētánē] *nf*: **la** ~ Mauritania.

mauritanien, ne [morētányań, -en] *a* Mauritanian.

mausolée [mōzolā] *nm* mausoleum.

maussade [mōsád] *a* (*air, personne*) sullen; (*ciel, temps*) dismal.

mauvais, e [move, -ez] *a* bad; (*faux*): **le** ~ **numéro/moment** the wrong number/moment; (*méchant, malveillant*) malicious, spiteful ♦ *nm*: **le** ~ the bad side ♦ *ad*: **il fait** ~ the weather is bad; **sentir** ~ to have a nasty smell, smell bad *ou* nasty; **la mer est** ~**e** the sea is rough; ~ **coucheur** tough customer; ~ **coup** (*fig*) criminal venture; ~ **garçon** tough; ~ **pas** tight spot; ~ **plaisant** hoaxer; ~ **traitements** ill treatment *sg*; ~**e herbe** weed; ~**e langue** gossip, scandalmonger; ~**e passe** difficult situation; (*période*) rough time; ~**e tête** rebellious *ou* headstrong customer.

mauve [mōv] *a* (*couleur*) mauve ♦ *nf* (*BOT*) mallow.

mauviette [mōvyet] *nf* (*péj*) weakling.

maux [mō] *nmpl voir* **mal**.

max. *abr* (= *maximum*) max.

maximal, e, aux [máksēmál, -ō] *a* maximal.

maxime [máksēm] *nf* maxim.

maximum [máksēmom] *a, nm* maximum; **atteindre un/son** ~ to reach a/his peak; **au** ~ *ad* (*le plus possible*) to the full; as much as one can; (*tout au plus*) at the (very) most *ou* maximum.

Mayence [máyâńs] *n* Mainz.

mayonnaise [máyonez] *nf* mayonnaise.

Mayotte [máyot] *nf* Mayotte.

mazout [mázōōt] *nm* (fuel) oil; **chaudière/poêle à** ~ oil-fired boiler/stove.

mazouté, e [mázōōtā] *a* oil-polluted.

MDM *sigle mpl* (= *Médecins du Monde*) *medical association for aid to Third World countries*.

Me *abr* = **Maître**.

me, m' [m(ə)] *pronom* me; (*réfléchi*) myself.

méandres [māâńdr(ə)] *nmpl* meanderings.

mec [mek] *nm* (*fam*) guy.

mécanicien, ne [mākánēsyań, -en] *nm/f* mechanic; (*RAIL*) engineer (*US*), (train *ou* engine) driver (*Brit*); ~ **navigant** *ou* **de bord** (*AVIAT*) flight engineer.

mécanicien-dentiste [mākánēsyańdâńtēst(ə)], **mécanicienne-dentiste** [mākánēsyen-] (*pl* ~**s**-~**s**) *nm/f* dental technician.

mécanique [mākánēk] *a* mechanical ♦ *nf* (*science*) mechanics *sg*; (*technologie*) mechanical engineering; (*mécanisme*) mechanism; engineering; works *pl*; **ennui** ~ engine trouble *q*; **s'y connaître en** ~ to be mechanically inclined; ~ **hydraulique** hydraulics *sg*; ~ **ondulataire** wave mechanics *sg*.

mécaniquement [mākánēkmáń] *ad* mechanically.

mécanisation [mākánēzâsyóń] *nf* mechanization.

mécaniser [mākánēzā] *vt* to mechanize.

mécanisme [mākánēsm(ə)] *nm* mechanism.

mécano [mākánō] *nm* (*fam*) mechanic.

mécanographie [mākánogrâfē] *nf* (mechanical) data processing.

mécène [māsen] *nm* patron.

méchamment [māshámáń] *ad* nastily, maliciously, spitefully; viciously.

méchanceté [māshâństā] *nf* (*d'une personne, d'une parole*) nastiness, maliciousness, spitefulness; (*parole, action*) nasty *ou* spiteful *ou* malicious remark (*ou* action).

méchant, e [māsháń, -âńt] *a* nasty, malicious, spiteful; (*enfant: pas sage*) naughty; (*animal*) vicious; (*avant le nom: valeur péjorative*) nasty; miserable; (*: intensive*) terrific.

mèche [mesh] *nf* (*de lampe, bougie*) wick; (*d'un explosif*) fuze (*US*), fuse (*Brit*); (*MÉD*) pack, dressing; (*de vilebrequin, perceuse*) bit; (*de dentiste*) drill; (*de fouet*) lash; (*de cheveux*) lock; **se faire faire des** ~**s** (*chez le coiffeur*) to have one's hair streaked, have highlights put in one's hair; **vendre la** ~ to give the game away; **de** ~ **avec** in league with.

méchoui [māshwē] *nm whole sheep barbecue*.

mécompte [mākóńt] *nm* (*erreur*) miscalculation; (*déception*) disappointment.

méconnais [mākonc] *etc vb voir* **méconnaître**.

méconnaissable [mākonesábl(ə)] *a* unrecognizable.

méconnaissais [mākonese] *etc vb voir* **méconnaître**.

méconnaissance [mākonesâńs] *nf* ignorance.

méconnaître [mākonetr(ə)] *vt* (*ignorer*) to be unaware of; (*mésestimer*) to misjudge.

méconnu, e [mākonü] *pp de* **méconnaître** ♦ *a* (*génie etc*) unrecognized.

mécontent, e [mākôṅtàṅ, -àṅt] *a*: ~ **(de)** (*insatisfait*) discontented *ou* dissatisfied *ou* displeased (with); (*contrarié*) annoyed (at) ♦ *nm/f* malcontent, dissatisfied person.

mécontentement [mākôṅtàṅtmàṅ] *nm* dissatisfaction, discontent, displeasure; annoyance.

mécontenter [mākôṅtàṅtā] *vt* to displease.

Mecque [mɛk] *nf*: **la** ~ Mecca.

mécréant, e [mākrāàṅ, -àṅt] *a* (*peuple*) infidel; (*personne*) atheistic.

méd. *abr* = **médecin.**

médaille [mādáy] *nf* medal.

médaillé, e [mādāyā] *nm/f* (*SPORT*) medalholder.

médaillon [mādáyôṅ] *nm* (*portrait*) medallion; (*bijou*) locket; (*CULIN*) thin, round slice (*of meat etc*), médaillon (*Brit*); **en** ~ *a* (*carte etc*) inset.

médecin [medsaṅ] *nm* doctor; ~ **du bord** (*NAVIG*) ship's doctor; ~ **généraliste** general practitioner, GP; ~ **légiste** medical examiner (*US*), forensic scientist (*Brit*); ~ **traitant** family doctor, GP.

médecine [medsēn] *nf* medicine; ~ **générale** general medicine; ~ **infantile** pediatrics *sg* (*US*), paediatrics *sg* (*Brit*); ~ **légale** forensic medicine; ~ **préventive** preventive medicine; ~ **du travail** occupational *ou* industrial medicine.

médian, e [mādyàṅ, -àn] *a* median.

médias [mādyà] *nmpl*: **les** ~ the media.

médiateur, trice [mādyàtœr, -trēs] *nm/f* (*voir médiation*) mediator; arbitrator.

médiathèque [mādyátɛk] *nf* media library.

médiation [mādyâsyôṅ] *nf* mediation; (*dans conflit social etc*) arbitration.

médiatique [mādyátɛk] *a* media *cpd*.

médiator [mādyátor] *nm* plectrum.

médical, e, aux [mādēkál, -ō] *a* medical; **visiteur** *ou* **délégué** ~ medical rep *ou* representative.

médicament [mādēkámàṅ] *nm* medicine, drug.

médicamenteux, euse [mādēkámàṅtœ, -œz] *a* medicinal.

médication [mādēkásyôṅ] *nf* medication.

médicinal, e, aux [mādēsēnál, -ō] *a* medicinal.

médico-légal, e, aux [mādēkolāgál, -ō] *a* forensic.

médiéval, e, aux [mādyāvál, -ō] *a* medieval.

médiocre [mādyokr(ə)] *a* mediocre, poor.

médiocrité [mādyokrētā] *nf* mediocrity.

médire [mādēr] *vi*: ~ **de** to speak ill of.

médisance [mādēzàṅs] *nf* scandalmongering *q*, mudslinging *q*; (*propos*) piece of scandal *ou* malicious gossip.

médisant, e [mādēzàṅ, -àṅt] *vb voir* **médire** ♦ *a* slanderous, malicious.

médit, e [mādē, -ēt] *pp de* **médire.**

méditatif, ive [mādētàtēf, -ēv] *a* thoughtful.

méditation [mādētàsyôṅ] *nf* meditation.

méditer [mādētā] *vt* (*approfondir*) to meditate on, ponder (over); (*combiner*) to meditate ♦ *vi* to meditate; ~ **de faire** to contemplate doing, plan to do.

Méditerranée [mādēteràná] *nf*: **la (mer)** ~ the Mediterranean (Sea).

méditerranéen, ne [mādēteràṅàaṅ, -en] *a*

Mediterranean ♦ *nm/f*: **M~, ne** Mediterranean.

médium [mādyom] *nm* medium (*spiritualist*).

médius [mādyüs] *nm* middle finger.

méduse [mādüz] *nf* jellyfish.

méduser [mādüzā] *vt* to dumbfound.

meeting [mētēng] *nm* (*POL*) rally, meeting; (*SPORT*) meet (*US*), meeting (*Brit*); ~ **d'aviation** air show.

méfait [māfe] *nm* (*faute*) misdemeanor (*US*), misdemeanour (*Brit*), wrongdoing; ~**s** *nmpl* (*ravages*) ravages.

méfiance [māfyàṅs] *nf* mistrust, distrust.

méfiant, e [māfyàṅ, -àṅt] *a* mistrustful, distrustful.

méfier [māfyā]: **se** ~ *vi* to be wary; (*faire attention*) to be careful; **se** ~ **de** *vt* to mistrust, distrust, be wary of; to be careful about.

mégalomane [māgálomán] *a* megalomaniac.

mégalomanie [māgálománē] *nf* megalomania.

méga-octet [māgáokte] *nm* megabyte.

mégarde [māgárd(ə)] *nf*: **par** ~ accidentally; (*par erreur*) by mistake.

mégatonne [māgáton] *nf* megaton.

mégère [māzher] *nf* (*péj: femme*) shrew.

mégot [māgō] *nm* cigarette end *ou* butt.

mégoter [māgotā] *vi* to nitpick.

meilleur, e [meyœr] *a, ad* better; (*valeur superlative*) best ♦ *nm*: **le** ~ (*celui qui ...*) the best (one); (*ce qui ...*) the best ♦ *nf*: **la** ~**e** the best (one); **le** ~ **des deux** the better of the two; **de** ~**e heure** earlier; ~ **marché** cheaper.

méjuger [māzhüzhā] *vt* to misjudge.

mélancolie [mālàṅkolē] *nf* melancholy, gloom.

mélancolique [mālàṅkolēk] *a* melancholy, gloomy.

mélange [mālàṅzh] *nm* (*opération*) mixing; blending; (*résultat*) mixture; blend; **sans** ~ unadulterated.

mélanger [mālàṅzhā] *vt* (*substances*) to mix; (*vins, couleurs*) to blend; (*mettre en désordre, confondre*) to mix up, muddle (up); **se** ~ (*liquides, couleurs*) to blend, mix.

mélanine [mālánēn] *nf* melanin.

mélasse [mālás] *nf* treacle, molasses *sg*.

mêlée [mālā] *nf* (*bataille, cohue*) mêlée, scramble; (*lutte, conflit*) tussle, scuffle; (*RUGBY*) scrum(mage).

mêler [mālā] *vt* (*substances, odeurs, races*) to mix; (*embrouiller*) to muddle (up), mix up; **se** ~ to mix; (*se joindre, s'allier*) to mingle; **se** ~ **à** (*suj: personne*) to join; to mix with; (: *odeurs etc*) to mingle with; **se** ~ **de** (*suj: personne*) to meddle with, interfere in; **mêle-toi de tes affaires!** mind your own business!; ~ **à** *ou* **avec** *ou* **de** to mix with; to mingle with; ~ **qn à** (*affaire*) to get sb mixed up *ou* involved in.

mélo [mālō] *nm, a* = **mélodrame, mélodramatique.**

mélodie [mālodē] *nf* melody.

mélodieux, euse [mālodyœ, -œz] *a* melodious, tuneful.

mélodique [mālodēk] *a* melodic.

mélodramatique [mālodrámátēk] *a* melodramatic.

mélodrame [mālodrám] *nm* melodrama.

mélomane [mālomán] *nm/f* music lover.

melon [mǝlóṅ] *nm* (*BOT*) (honeydew) melon; (*aussi*: **chapeau** ~) derby (*US*) *ou* bowler (*Brit*) (hat); ~ **d'eau** watermelon.

mélopée [mālopā] *nf* monotonous chant.

membrane [máṅbrán] *nf* membrane.

membre [máṅbr(ǝ)] *nm* (*ANAT*) limb; (*personne, pays, élément*) member ♦ *a* member; **être** ~ **de** to be a member of; ~ (**viril**) (male) organ.

mémé [māmā] *nf* (*fam*) granny; (*: vieille femme*) old dear.

même [mem] *a* same ♦ *pronom*: **le** (**la**) ~ the same (one) ♦ *ad* even; **en** ~ **temps** at the same time; **ils ont les** ~**s goûts** they have the same tastes; **ce sont ses paroles/celles-là** ~**s** they are his very words/the very ones; **il est la loyauté** ~ he is loyalty itself, he is loyalty personified; **il n'a** ~ **pas pleuré** he didn't even cry; **ici** ~ at this very place; ~ **lui a ...** even he has ...; **à** ~ **la bouteille** straight from the bottle; **à** ~ **la peau** next to the skin; **être à** ~ **de faire** to be in a position *ou* be able to do; **mettre qn à** ~ **de faire** to enable sb to do; **faire de** ~ to do likewise; **lui de** ~ so does (*ou* did *ou* is) he; **de lui-**~ on his own initiative; **de** ~ **que** just as; **il en va/est allé de** ~ **pour** the same goes/ happened for; ~ **si** even if.

mémento [māmáṅtō] *nm* (*agenda*) appointment book; (*ouvrage*) summary.

mémoire [māmwár] *nf* memory ♦ *nm* (*ADMIN, JUR*) memorandum (*pl* -a); (*SCOL*) dissertation, paper; **avoir la** ~ **des visages/chiffres** to have a (good) memory for faces/figures; **n'avoir aucune** ~ to have a terrible memory; **avoir de la** ~ to have a good memory; **à la** ~ **de** to the *ou* in memory of; **pour** ~ *ad* for the record; **de** ~ *ad* from memory; **de** ~ **d'homme** in living memory; **mettre en** ~ (*INFORM*) to store; ~ **morte** ROM; ~ **rémanente** *ou* **non volatile** non-volatile memory; ~ **vive** RAM.

mémoires [māmwár] *nmpl* memoirs.

mémorable [māmorábl(ǝ)] *a* memorable.

mémorandum [māmoráṅdom] *nm* memorandum (*pl* -a); (*carnet*) notebook.

mémorial, aux [māmoryál, -ō] *nm* memorial.

mémoriser [māmorēzā] *vt* to memorize; (*INFORM*) to store.

menaçant, e [mǝnásáṅ, -áṅt] *a* threatening, menacing.

menace [mǝnás] *nf* threat; ~ **en l'air** empty threat.

menacer [mǝnásā] *vt* to threaten; ~ **qn de qch/de faire qch** to threaten sb with sth/to do sth.

ménage [mānázh] *nm* (*travail*) housekeeping, housework; (*couple*) (married) couple; (*famille, ADMIN*) household; **faire le** ~ to do the housework; **faire des** ~**s** to work as a housekeeper (*US*) *ou* cleaner (*Brit*) (*in people's homes*); **monter son** ~ to set up house; **se mettre en** ~ (**avec**) to set up house (with); **heureux en** ~ happily married; **faire bon** ~ **avec** to get along well with; ~ **de poupée** doll's kitchen set; ~ **à trois** love triangle.

ménagement [mānázhmáṅ] *nm* care and

attention; ~**s** *nmpl* (*égards*) consideration *sg*, attention *sg*.

ménager [mānázhā] *vt* (*traiter avec mesure*) to handle with tact; to treat considerately; (*utiliser*) to use with care; (*: avec économie*) to use sparingly; (*prendre soin de*) to take (great) care of, look after; (*organiser*) to arrange; (*installer*) to put in; to make; **se** ~ to look after o.s.; ~ **qch à qn** (*réserver*) to have sth in store for sb.

ménager, ère [mānázhā, -er] *a* household *cpd*, domestic ♦ *nf* (*femme*) housewife (*pl* -wives); (*couverts*) silverware tray (*US*), canteen (of cutlery) (*Brit*).

ménagerie [mānázhrē] *nf* menagerie.

mendiant, e [māndēsáṅt] *nm/f* beggar.

mendicité [máṅdēsētā] *nf* begging.

mendier [máṅdyā] *vi* to beg ♦ *vt* to beg (for); (*fig: éloges, compliments*) to fish for.

menées [mǝnā] *nfpl* intrigues, maneuvers (*US*), manœuvres (*Brit*); (*COMM*) activities.

mener [mǝnā] *vt* to lead; (*enquête*) to conduct; (*affaires*) to manage, conduct, run ♦ *vi*: ~ (**à la marque**) to lead, be in the lead; ~ **à/dans** (*emmener*) to take to/into; ~ **qch à bonne fin** *ou* **à terme** *ou* **à bien** to see sth through (to a successful conclusion), complete sth successfully.

meneur, euse [mǝnœr, -ēz] *nm/f* leader; (*péj: agitateur*) ringleader; ~ **d'hommes** born leader; ~ **de jeu** host, quizmaster.

menhir [mānēr] *nm* standing stone.

méningite [mānáṅzhēt] *nf* meningitis *q*.

ménopause [mānopōz] *nf* menopause.

menotte [mǝnot] *nf* (*langage enfantin*) little hand; ~**s** *nfpl* handcuffs; **passer les** ~**s à** to handcuff.

mens [máṅ] *vb voir* **mentir**.

mensonge [máṅsôṅzh] *nm*: **le** ~ lying *q*; **un** ~ a lie.

mensonger, ère [máṅsôṅzhā, -er] *a* false.

menstruation [máṅstrüásyóṅ] *nf* menstruation.

menstruel, le [máṅstrüel] *a* menstrual.

mensualiser [máṅsüálēzā] *vt* to pay monthly.

mensualité [máṅsüálētā] *nf* (*somme payée*) monthly payment; (*somme perçue*) monthly salary.

mensuel, le [máṅsüel] *a* monthly ♦ *nm/f* (*employé*) employee paid monthly ♦ *nm* (*PRESSE*) monthly.

mensuellement [máṅsüelmáṅ] *ad* monthly.

mensurations [máṅsürásyóṅ] *nfpl* measurements.

mentais [máṅte] *etc vb voir* **mentir**.

mental, e, aux [máṅtál, -ō] *a* mental.

mentalement [máṅtálmáṅ] *ad* in one's head, mentally.

mentalité [máṅtálētā] *nf* mentality.

menteur, euse [máṅtœr, -ēz] *nm/f* liar.

menthe [máṅt] *nf* mint; ~ (**à l'eau**) mint-flavored water (*drink*).

mentholé, e [máṅtolā] *a* menthol *cpd*, mentholated.

mention [máṅsyóṅ] *nf* (*note*) note, comment; (*SCOL*): ~ (**très**) **bien/passable** (*very*) *good/ satisfactory passmark*; **faire** ~ **de** to mention; **"rayer la** ~ **inutile"** "delete as appropriate".

mentionner [mãsyonã] *vt* to mention.
mentir [mãtēr] *vi* to lie.
menton [mãtôn] *nm* chin.
mentonnière [mãntonyer] *nf* chin strap.
menu, e [mənü] *a* (*mince*) thin; (*petit*) tiny; (*frais, difficulté*) minor ♦ *ad* (*couper, hacher*) very fine ♦ *nm* menu; **par le ~** (*raconter*) in minute detail; **~ touristique** popular *ou* tourist menu; **~e monnaie** small change.
menuet [mənüe] *nm* minuet.
menuiserie [mənüēzrē] *nf* (*travail*) joinery, carpentry; (*d'amateur*) woodwork; (*local*) joiner's workshop; (*ouvrages*) woodwork *q*.
menuisier [mənüēzyã] *nm* joiner, carpenter.
méprendre [māprãndr(ə)]: **se ~** *vi*: **se ~ sur** to be mistaken about.
mépris, e [māprē, -ēz] *pp de* **méprendre** ♦ *nm* (*dédain*) contempt, scorn; (*indifférence*): **le ~ de** contempt *ou* disregard for; **au ~ de** regardless of, in defiance of.
méprisable [māprēzābl(ə)] *a* contemptible, despicable.
méprisant, e [māprēzãn, -ãnt] *a* contemptuous, scornful.
méprise [māprēz] *nf* mistake, error; (*malentendu*) misunderstanding.
mépriser [māprēzã] *vt* to scorn, despise; (*gloire, danger*) to scorn, spurn.
mer [mer] *nf* sea; (*marée*) tide; **~ fermée** inland sea; **en ~** at sea; **prendre la ~** to put out to sea; **en haute** *ou* **pleine ~** off shore, on the open sea; **la ~ Adriatique** the Adriatic (Sea); **la ~ des Antilles** *ou* **des Caraïbes** the Caribbean (Sea); **la ~ Baltique** the Baltic (Sea); **la ~ Caspienne** the Caspian Sea; **la ~ de Corail** the Coral Sea; **la ~ Égée** the Aegean (Sea); **la ~ Ionienne** the Ionian Sea; **la ~ Morte** the Dead Sea; **la ~ Noire** the Black Sea; **la ~ du Nord** the North Sea; **la ~ Rouge** the Red Sea; **la ~ des Sargasses** the Sargasso Sea; **les ~s du Sud** the South Seas; **la ~ Tyrrhénienne** the Tyrrhenian Sea.
mercantile [merkãntēl] *a* (*péj*) mercenary.
mercenaire [mersəner] *nm* mercenary.
mercerie [mersərē] *nf* (*COUTURE*) notions *pl* (*US*), haberdashery (*Brit*); (*boutique*) notions store (*US*), haberdasher's shop (*Brit*).
merci [mersē] *excl* thank you ♦ *nf*: **à la ~ de qn/qch** at sb's mercy/the mercy of sth; **~ beaucoup** thank you very much; **~ de** *ou* **pour** thank you for; **sans ~** *a* merciless ♦ *ad* mercilessly.
mercier, ière [mersyā, -yer] *nm/f* notions dealer (*US*), haberdasher (*Brit*).
mercredi [merkrədē] *nm* Wednesday; **~ des Cendres** Ash Wednesday; *voir aussi* **lundi**.
mercure [merkür] *nm* mercury.
merde [merd(ə)] (*fam!*) *nf* shit (*!*) ♦ *excl* hell (*!*).
merdeux, euse [merdø, -øz] *nm/f* (*fam!*) little devil.
mère [mer] *nf* mother ♦ *a inv* mother *cpd*; **~ célibataire** single parent, unmarried mother.
merguez [mergez] *nf* spicy North African sausage.
méridien [mārēdyãn] *nm* meridian.
méridional, e, aux [mārēdyonãl, -ō] *a* southern; (*du midi de la France*) Southern (French) ♦ *nm/f* Southerner.

meringue [mərãng] *nf* meringue.
mérinos [mārēnōs] *nm* merino.
merisier [mərēzyã] *nm* wild cherry (tree).
méritant, e [mārētãn, -ãnt] *a* deserving.
mérite [mārēt] *nm* merit; **le ~ (de ceci) lui revient** the credit (for this) is his.
mériter [mārētã] *vt* to deserve; **~ de réussir** to deserve to succeed; **il mérite qu'on fasse ...** he deserves people to do ....
méritocratie [mārētokrãsē] *nf* meritocracy.
méritoire [mārētwár] *a* praiseworthy, commendable.
merlan [merlãn] *nm* whiting.
merle [merl(ə)] *nm* blackbird.
mérou [mārōō] *nm* grouper (*fish*).
merveille [mervey] *nf* marvel, wonder; **faire ~** *ou* **des ~s** to work wonders; **à ~** perfectly, wonderfully.
merveilleux, euse [merveyø, -øz] *a* marvellous, wonderful.
mes [mā] *dét voir* **mon**.
mésalliance [māzalyãns] *nf* misalliance, mismatch.
mésallier [māzalyã]: **se ~** *vi* to marry beneath (*ou* above) o.s.
mésange [māzãnzh] *nf* tit(mouse) (*pl* -mice); **~ bleue** bluetit.
mésaventure [māzávãntür] *nf* misadventure, misfortune.
Mesdames [mādám] *nfpl voir* **Madame**.
Mesdemoiselles [mādmwàzel] *nfpl voir* **Mademoiselle**.
mésentente [māzãntãnt] *nf* dissension, disagreement.
mésestimer [māzestēmã] *vt* to underestimate, underrate.
Mésopotamie [māzopotámē] *nf*: **la ~** Mesopotamia.
mésopotamien, ne [māzopotámyãn, -en] *a* Mesopotamian.
mesquin, e [meskãn, -ēn] *a* mean, petty.
mesquinerie [meskēnrē] *nf* meanness *q*, pettiness *q*.
mess [mes] *nm* mess.
message [māsàzh] *nm* message; **~ d'erreur** (*INFORM*) error message; **~ (de guidage)** (*INFORM*) prompt; **~ publicitaire** ad, advertisement; **~ téléphoné** telegram dictated by telephone.
messager, ère [māsàzhã, -er] *nm/f* messenger.
messagerie [māsàzhrē] *nf*: **~ (électronique)** (electronic) bulletin board; **~ rose** *lonely hearts and contact service on videotext*; **~s aériennes/ maritimes** air freight/shipping service *sg*; **~s de presse** press distribution service.
messe [mes] *nf* mass; **aller à la ~** to go to mass; **~ de minuit** midnight mass; **faire des ~s basses** (*fig, péj*) to mutter.
messie [māsē] *nm*: **le M~** the Messiah.
Messieurs [māsyø] *nmpl voir* **Monsieur**.
mesure [məzür] *nf* (*évaluation, dimension*) measurement; (*étalon, récipient, contenu*) measure; (*MUS: cadence*) time, tempo; (: *division*) bar; (*retenue*) moderation; (*disposition*) measure, step; **unité/système de ~** unit/system of measurement; **sur ~** (*costume*) made-to-order (*US*), made-to-measure (*Brit*); (*fig*) personally adapted; **à**

la ~ de (*fig: personne*) worthy of; (*chambre etc*) on the same scale as; **dans la ~ où** insofar as, inasmuch as; **dans une certaine ~** to some *ou* a certain extent; **à ~ que** as; **en ~** (*MUS*) in time *ou* tempo; **être en ~ de** to be in a position to; **dépasser la ~** (*fig*) to overstep the bounds (*US*) *ou* mark (*Brit*).

mesuré, e [məzürā] *a* (*ton, effort*) measured; (*personne*) restrained.

mesurer [məzürā] *vt* to measure; (*juger*) to weigh, assess; (*limiter*) to limit, ration; (*modérer*) to moderate; (*proportionner*): **~ qch à** to match sth to, gear sth to; **se ~ avec** to have a confrontation with; to tackle; **il mesure 1 m 80** he's 1 m 80 tall.

met [me] *vb voir* **mettre**.

métabolisme [mātábolēsm(ə)] *nm* metabolism.

métairie [mātārē] *nf* small farm.

métal, aux [mātál, -ō] *nm* metal.

métalangage [mātálâṅgázh] *nm* metalanguage.

métallique [mātálēk] *a* metallic.

métallisé, e [mātálēzā] *a* metallic.

métallurgie [mātálürzhē] *nf* metallurgy.

métallurgiste [mātálürzhēst(ə)] *nm/f* (*ouvrier*) steel *ou* metal worker; (*industriel*) metallurgist.

métamorphose [mātámorfōz] *nf* metamorphosis (*pl* -oses).

métaphore [mātáfor] *nf* metaphor.

métaphorique [mātáforēk] *a* metaphorical, figurative.

métaphysique [mātáfēzēk] *nf* metaphysics *sg* ♦ *a* metaphysical.

métapsychique [mātápsēshēk] *a* psychic, parapsychological.

métayer, ère [mātāyā, mātcyer] *nm/f* sharecropper (*US*), (tenant) farmer (*Brit*).

météo [mātāō] *nf* (*bulletin*) (weather) forecast; (*service*) ≈ National Weather Service (*US*), ≈ Met Office (*Brit*).

météore [mātáor] *nm* meteor.

météorite [mātáorēt] *nf* meteorite.

météorologie [mātáorolozhē] *nf* (*étude*) meteorology; (*service*) ≈ National Weather Service (*US*), ≈ Meteorological Office (*Brit*).

météorologique [mātáorolozhēk]' *a* meteorological, weather *cpd*.

météorologue [mātáorolog] *nm/f*, **météorologiste** [mātáorolozhēst(ə)] *nm/f* meteorologist, weather forecaster.

métèque [mātēk] *nm* (*péj*) wop.

méthane [mātán] *nm* methane.

méthanier [mātányā] *nm* (*bateau*) (liquefied) gas carrier *ou* tanker.

méthode [mātod] *nf* method; (*livre, ouvrage*) manual, primer.

méthodique [mātodēk] *a* methodical.

méthodiste [mātodēst(ə)] *a, nm/f* (*REL*) Methodist.

méthylène [mātēlen] *nm*: **bleu de ~** *nm* methylene blue.

méticuleux, euse [mātēkülœ̄, -œ̄z] *a* meticulous.

métier [mātyā] *nm* (*profession: gén*) job; (*: manuel*) trade; (*: artisanal*) craft; (*technique, expérience*) (acquired) skill *ou* technique; (*aussi:* **~ à tisser**) (weaving)

loom; **être du ~** to be in the trade *ou* profession.

métis, se [mātēs] *a, nm/f* half-caste, half-breed.

métisser [mātēsā] *vt* to cross(breed).

métrage [mātrázh] *nm* (*de tissu*) length; (*CINÉMA*) footage, length; **long/moyen ~** feature *ou* full-length/medium-length film; **court ~** short (film (*Brit*)).

mètre [metr(ə)] *nm* meter (*US*), metre (*Brit*); (*règle*) (meter *ou* metre) rule; (*ruban*) tape measure; **~ carré/cube** square/cubic meter *ou* metre.

métrer [mātrā] *vt* (*TECH*) to measure (in meters *ou* metres); (*CONSTR*) to survey.

métreur, euse [mātrœr, -œ̄z] *nm/f*: **~ (vérificateur), métreuse (vérificatrice)** (quantity) surveyor.

métrique [mātrēk] *a* metric ♦ *nf* metrics *sg*.

métro [mātrō] *nm* subway (*US*), underground (*Brit*).

métronome [mātronom] *nm* metronome.

métropole [mātropol] *nf* (*capitale*) metropolis; (*pays*) mother country.

métropolitain, e [mātropolētaṅ, -en] *a* metropolitan.

mets [me] *nm* dish ♦ *vb voir* **mettre**.

mettable [metábl(ə)] *a* fit to be worn, decent.

metteur [metœr] *nm*: **~ en scène** (*THÉÂTRE*) producer; (*CINÉMA*) director; **~ en ondes** (*RADIO*) producer.

mettre [metr(ə)] *vt* (*placer*) to put; (*vêtement: revêtir*) to turn on; (*: porter*) to wear; (*installer: gaz, électricité*) to put in; (*faire fonctionner: chauffage, électricité*) to turn on; (*: réveil*) to set; (*noter, écrire*) to say, put down; (*dépenser*) to lay out, give; (*supposer*): **mettons que** let's suppose *ou* say that; **~ en bouteille/en sac** to bottle/put in bags *ou* sacks; **~ qn/qch en terre** to bury sb/plant sth; **~ à la poste** to mail; **~ une note gaie/amusante** to inject a cheerful/an amusing note; **y ~ du sien** to pull one's weight; **~ du temps/2 heures à faire** to take time/2 hours to do; **~ qn debout** to stand sb up; **se ~: n'avoir rien à se ~** to have nothing to wear; **se ~ de l'encre sur les doigts** to get ink on one's fingers; **se ~ au lit** to get into bed; **se ~ au piano** (*s'asseoir*) to sit down at the piano; (*apprendre*) to start learning the piano; **se ~ à l'eau** to get into the water; **se ~ bien/mal avec qn** to get on sb's good/bad side; **se ~ qn à dos** to alienate sb, turn sb against one; **se ~ avec qn** (*prendre parti*) to side with *ou* go along with sb; (*en ménage*) to move in with sb; **se ~ à faire** to begin *ou* start doing *ou* to do; **se ~ au travail/à l'étude** to get down to work/one's studies.

meublant, e [mœblâṅ, -âṅt] *a* (*tissus etc*) effective (in the room).

meuble [mœbl(ə)] *nm* (*objet*) piece of furniture; (*ameublement*) furniture *q* ♦ *a* (*terre*) loose, friable; (*JUR*): **biens ~s** movables.

meublé [mœblā] *nm* (*pièce*) furnished room; (*appartement*) furnished apartment.

meubler [mœblā] *vt* to furnish; (*fig*): **~ qch (de)** to fill sth (with); **se ~** to furnish one's house.

meugler [mœglā] *vi* to low, moo.

meule [mœl] *nf* (*à broyer*) millstone; (*à aiguiser*) grindstone; (*à polir*) buffwheel; (*de foin, blé*) stack; (*de fromage*) round.

meunerie [mœnrē] *nf* (*industrie*) flour trade; (*métier*) milling.

meunier, ière [mœnyā, -yer] *nm* miller ♦ *nf* miller's wife ♦ *af* (*CULIN*) meunière.

meurs [mœr] *etc vb voir* **mourir**.

meurtre [mœrtr(ə)] *nm* murder.

meurtrier, ière [mœrtrēyā, -yer] *a* (*arme, épidémie, combat*) deadly; (*accident*) fatal; (*carrefour, route*) lethal; (*fureur, instincts*) murderous ♦ *nm/f* murderer/murderess ♦ *nf* (*ouverture*) loophole.

meurtrir [mœrtrēr] *vt* to bruise; (*fig*) to wound.

meurtrissure [mœrtrēsür] *nf* bruise; (*fig*) scar.

meus [mœ] *etc vb voir* **mouvoir**.

Meuse [mœz] *nf*: **la ~** the Meuse:

meute [mœt] *nf* pack.

meuve [mœv] *etc vb voir* **mouvoir**.

mévente [māvânt] *nf* slump (in sales).

mexicain, e [meksēkaṅ, -en] *a* Mexican ♦ *nm/f*: **M~, e** Mexican.

Mexico [meksēkō] *n* Mexico City.

Mexique [meksēk] *nm*: **le ~** Mexico.

mezzanine [medzánēn] *nf* mezzanine (floor).

MF *sigle mpl* = *millions de francs* ♦ *sigle f* (*RADIO*: = *modulation de fréquence*) FM.

Mgr *abr* = **Monseigneur**.

mi [mē] *nm* (*MUS*) E; (*en chantant la gamme*) mi.

mi... [mē] *préfixe* half(-); mid-; **à la ~-janvier** in mid-January; **~-bureau, ~-chambre** half office, half bedroom; **à ~-jambes/-corps** (up *ou* down) to the knees/waist; **à ~-hauteur/-pente** halfway up (*ou* down)/up (*ou* down) the hill.

miaou [myȧōō] *nm* miaow.

miauler [mēyōlā] *vi* to mew.

mi-bas [mēbá] *nm inv* knee-length sock.

mica [mēká] *nm* mica.

mi-carême [mēkárem] *nf*: **la ~** the third Thursday in Lent.

miche [mēsh] *nf* round loaf.

mi-chemin [mēshmaṅ]: **à ~** *ad* halfway, midway.

mi-clos, e [mēklō, -klōz] *a* half-closed.

micmac [mēkmák] *nm* (*péj*) fuss.

mi-côte [mēkōt]: **à ~** *ad* halfway up (*ou* down) the hill.

mi-course [mēkōōrs]: **à ~** *ad* halfway through the race.

micro [mēkrō] *nm* mike, microphone; (*IN-FORM*) micro; **~ cravate** lapel mike.

microbe [mēkrob] *nm* germ, microbe.

microbiologie [mēkrobyolozhē] *nf* microbiology.

microchirurgie [mēkroshērürzhē] *nf* microsurgery.

microcosme [mēkrokosm(ə)] *nm* microcosm.

micro-édition [mēkroādēsyōn] *nf* desktop publishing.

micro-électronique [mēkroālektronēk] *nf* microelectronics *sg*.

microfiche [mēkrofēsh] *nf* microfiche.

microfilm [mēkrofēlm] *nm* microfilm.

micro-onde [mēkroônd] *nf*: **four à ~s** microwave oven.

micro-ordinateur [mēkroordēnátœr] *nm* microcomputer.

microphone [mēkrofon] *nm* microphone.

microplaquette [mēkropláket] *nf* microchip.

microprocesseur [mēkroprosesœr] *nm* microprocessor.

microscope [mēkroskop] *nm* microscope; **au ~** under *ou* through the microscope.

microsillon [mēkrosēyōn] *nm* long-playing record.

MIDEM [mēdem] *sigle m* (= *Marché international du disque et de l'édition musicale*) music industry trade fair.

midi [mēdē] *nm* (*milieu du jour*) midday, noon; (*moment du déjeuner*) lunchtime; (*sud*) south; .(: *de la France*): **le M~** the South (of France), the Midi; **à ~** at 12 (o'clock) *ou* midday *ou* noon; **tous les ~s** every lunchtime; **le repas de ~** lunch; **en plein ~** (right) in the middle of the day; (*sud*) facing south.

midinette [mēdēnet] *nf* silly young townie.

mie [mē] *nf* inside (of the loaf).

miel [myel] *nm* honey; **être tout ~** (*fig*) to be all sweetness and light.

mielleux, euse [myelœ, -œz] *a* (*péj*) sugary, honeyed.

mien, ne [myan, myen] *a, pronom*: **le (la) ~(ne), les ~s** mine; **les ~s** (*ma famille*) my family.

miette [myet] *nf* (*de pain, gâteau*) crumb; (*fig: de la conversation etc*) scrap; **en ~s** (*fig*) in pieces *ou* bits.

mieux [myœ] *ad* better ♦ *a* better; (*plus joli*) better-looking ♦ *nm* (*progrès*) improvement; **le ~** the best (thing); **le (la) ~, les ~** the best; **le ~ des deux** the better of the two; **les livres les ~ faits** the best made books; **de mon/ton ~** as best I/you can (*ou* could); **faire de son ~** to do one's best; **vous feriez ~ de faire ...** you would be better to do ...; **aimer ~** to prefer; **de ~ en ~** better and better; **pour le ~** for the best; **crier à qui ~ ~** to try to shout each other down *ou* outshout each other; **du ~ qu'il peut** the best he can; **au ~** at best; **au ~ avec** on the best of terms with; **qui ~ est** even better, better still; **faute de ~** for lack of anything better.

mieux-être [myœzetr(ə)] *nm* greater well-being; (*financier*) improved standard of living.

mièvre [myevr(ə)] *a* sickly sentimental.

mignon, ne [mēnyoṅ, -on] *a* sweet, cute.

migraine [mēgren] *nf* headache; migraine.

migrant, e [mēgrâṅ, -âṅt] *a, nm/f* migrant.

migrateur, trice [mēgrátœr, -trēs] *a* migratory.

migration [mēgrásyōṅ] *nf* migration.

mijaurée [mēzhorā] *nf* pretentious (young) madam.

mijoter [mēzhotā] *vt* to simmer; (*préparer avec soin*) to cook lovingly; (*affaire, projet*) to plot, cook up ♦ *vi* to simmer.

mil [mēl] *num* = **mille**.

Milan [mēlâṅ] *n* Milan.

milanais, e [mēlâne, -ez] *a* Milanese.

mildiou [mēldyōō] *nm* mildew.

milice [mēlēs] *nf* militia.

milicien, ne [mēlēsyañ, -en] *nm/f* militiaman/woman.

milieu, x [mēlyœ̄] *nm (centre)* middle; *(fig)* middle course *ou* way; *(aussi:* **juste ~**) happy medium; *(BIO, GÉO)* environment; *(entourage social)* milieu; *(familial)* background; circle; *(pègre):* **le ~** the underworld; **au ~ de** in the middle of; **au beau** *ou* **en plein ~ (de)** right in the middle (of); **~ de terrain** *(FOOTBALL: joueur)* midfield player; *(: joueurs)* midfield.

militaire [mēlēter] *a* military ♦ *nm* serviceman; **service ~** military service.

militant, e [mēlētāñ, -āñt] *a, nm/f* militant.

militantisme [mēlētāñtēsm(ə)] *nm* militancy.

militariser [mēlētárēzā] *vt* to militarize.

militer [mēlētā] *vi* to be a militant; **~ pour/contre** to militate in favor of/against.

mille [mēl] *num* a *ou* one thousand ♦ *nm (mesure):* **~ (marin)** nautical mile; **mettre dans le ~** to hit the bull's-eye; *(fig)* to be right on (target).

millefeuille [mēlfœy] *nm* napoleon *(US)*, cream *ou* vanilla slice *(Brit)*.

millénaire [mēlāner] *nm* millennium ♦ *a* thousand-year-old; *(fig)* ancient.

mille-pattes [mēlpát] *nm inv* centipede.

millésime [mēlāzēm] *nm* year.

millésimé, e [mēlāzēmā] *a* vintage *cpd*.

millet [mēye] *nm* millet.

milliard [mēlyár] *nm* milliard, billion *(US)*, thousand million *(Brit)*.

milliardaire [mēlyárder] *nm/f* billionaire *(US)*, multimillionaire *(Brit)*.

millième [mēlyem] *num* thousandth.

millier [mēlyā] *nm* thousand; **un ~ (de)** a thousand or so, about a thousand; **par ~s** in (their) thousands, by the thousand.

milligramme [mēlēgràm] *nm* milligram *(US)*, milligramme *(Brit)*.

millimètre [mēlēmetr(ə)] *nm* millimeter *(US)*, millimetre *(Brit)*.

millimétré, e [mēlēmātrā] *a:* **papier ~** graph paper.

million [mēlyôñ] *nm* million; **deux ~s de** two million; **riche à ~s** worth millions.

millionième [mēlyonyem] *num* millionth.

millionnaire [mēlyoner] *nm/f* millionaire.

mi-lourd [mēlōōr] *am, nm* light heavyweight.

mime [mēm] *nm/f (acteur)* mime(r); *(imitateur)* mimic ♦ *nm (art)* mime, miming.

mimer [mēmā] *vt* to mime; *(singer)* to mimic, take off.

mimétisme [mēmātēsm(ə)] *nm (BIO)* mimicry.

mimique [mēmēk] *nf (funny)* face; *(signes)* gesticulations *pl*, sign language *q*.

mimosa [mēmōzá] *nm* mimosa.

mi-moyen [mēmwàyañ] *am, nm* welterweight.

MIN *sigle m (= Marché d'intérêt national)* wholesale market for fruit, vegetables and agricultural produce.

min. *abr (= minimum)* min.

minable [mēnábl(ə)] *a (personne)* shabby(-looking); *(travail)* pathetic.

minaret [mēnáre] *nm* minaret.

minauder [mēnōdā] *vi* to mince, simper.

minauderies [mēnōdrē] *nfpl* simperings.

mince [mañs] *a* thin; *(personne, taille)* slim, slender; *(fig: profit, connaissances)* slight, small; *(: prétexte)* weak ♦ *excl:* **~ (alors)!** darn it!

minceur [mañsœr] *nf* thinness; slimness, slenderness.

mincir [mañsēr] *vi* to get slimmer *ou* thinner.

mine [mēn] *nf (physionomie)* expression, look; *(extérieur)* exterior, appearance; *(de crayon)* lead; *(gisement, exploitation, explosif)* mine; **~s** *nfpl (péj)* simpering airs; **les M~s** *(ADMIN)* the national mining and geological service; the government vehicle testing department; **avoir bonne ~** *(personne)* to look well; *(ironique)* to look like an utter idiot; **avoir mauvaise ~** to look unwell *ou* poorly; **faire ~ de faire** to make a pretense *(US)* ou pretence *(Brit)* of doing; to make as if to do; **ne pas payer de ~** to be not much to look at; **~ de rien** *ad* with a casual air; although you wouldn't think so; **~ de charbon** coal mine; **~ à ciel ouvert** opencut *(US)* ou opencast *(Brit)* mine.

miner [mēnā] *vt (saper)* to undermine, erode; *(MIL)* to mine.

minerai [mēnrc] *nm* ore.

minéral, e, aux [mēnārál, -ō] *a* mineral; *(CHIMIE)* inorganic ♦ *nm* mineral.

minéralier [mēnárályā] *nm (bateau)* ore tanker.

minéralisé, e [mēnárálēzā] *a* mineralized.

minéralogie [mēnárálozhē] *nf* mineralogy.

minéralogique [mēnárálozhēk] *a* mineralogical; **plaque ~** license *(US)* ou number *(Brit)* plate; **numéro ~** license *(US)* ou registration *(Brit)* number.

minet, te [mēnc, -et] *nm/f (chat)* pussycat; *(péj)* young trendy.

mineur, e [mēncer] *a* minor ♦ *nm/f (JUR)* minor ♦ *nm (travailleur)* miner; *(MIL)* sapper; **~ de fond** underground *(US)* ou face *(Brit)* worker.

miniature [mēnyátür] *a, nf* miniature.

miniaturiser [mēnyátürēzā] *vt* to miniaturize.

minibus [mēnēbüs] *nm* minibus.

mini-cassette [mēnēkáset] *nf* cassette (recorder).

minier, ière [mēnyā, -yer] *a* mining.

mini-jupe [mēnēzhüp] *nf* miniskirt.

minimal, e, aux [mēnēmál, -ō] *a* minimum.

minime [mēnēm] *a* minor, minimal ♦ *nm/f (SPORT)* junior.

minimiser [mēnēmēzā] *vt* to minimize; *(fig)* to play down.

minimum [mēnēmom] *a, nm* minimum; **au ~** at the very least; **~ vital** *(salaire)* living wage; *(niveau de vie)* subsistence level.

mini-ordinateur [mēnēordēnátœr] *nm* minicomputer.

ministère [mēnēster] *nm (cabinet)* government; *(département)* department; *(REL)* ministry; **~ public** *(JUR)* Prosecution, State Prosecutor.

ministériel, le [mēnēstáryel] *a* government *cpd*; ministerial, departmental; *(partisan)* pro-government.

ministre [mēnēstr(ə)] *nm* secretary; *(REL)* minister; **~ d'État** senior secretary.

Minitel [mēnētel] *nm* ® *videotext terminal and service.*

minium [mēnyom] *nm* red lead paint.

minois [mēnwá] *nm* little face.

minorer [mēnorā] *vt* to cut, reduce.

minoritaire [mēnorēter] *a* minority *cpd*.

minorité [mēnorētā] *nf* minority; **être en ~** to be in the *ou* a minority; **mettre en ~** (*POL*) to defeat.

Minorque [mēnork] *nf* Minorca.

minorquin, e [mēnorkań, -ēn] *a* Minorcan.

minoterie [mēnotrē] *nf* flour mill.

minuit [mēnüē] *nm* midnight.

minuscule [mēnüskül] *a* minute, tiny ♦ *nf:* (*lettre*) ~ small letter.

minutage [mēnütázh] *nm* timing.

minute [mēnüt] *nf* minute; (*JUR:* *original*) minute, draft ♦ *excl* just a minute!, hang on!; **à la ~** (*présent*) (just) this instant; (*passé*) there and then; **entrecôte** *ou* **steak ~** minute steak.

minuter [mēnütā] *vt* to time.

minuterie [mēnütrē] *nf* time switch.

minuteur [mēnütœr] *nm* timer.

minutie [mēnüsē] *nf* meticulousness; minute detail; **avec ~** meticulously; in minute detail.

minutieux, euse [mēnüsyœ̄, -œ̄z] *a* (*personne*) meticulous; (*inspection*) minutely detailed; (*travail*) requiring painstaking attention to detail.

mioche [myosh] *nm* (*fam*) brat.

mirabelle [mērábel] *nf* (*fruit*) (cherry) plum; (*eau-de-vie*) plum brandy.

miracle [mērákl(ə)] *nm* miracle.

miraculé, e [mērákülā] *a* who has been miraculously cured (*ou* rescued).

miraculeux, euse [mērákülœ̄, -œ̄z] *a* miraculous.

mirador [mērádor] *nm* (*MIL*) watchtower.

mirage [mērázh] *nm* mirage.

mire [mēr] *nf* (*d'un fusil*) sight; (*TV*) test pattern (*US*) *ou* card (*Brit*); **point de ~** target; (*fig*) focal point; **ligne de ~** line of sight.

mirent [mēr] *vb* voir **mettre**.

mirer [mērā] *vt* (*œufs*) to candle; **se ~** *vi:* **se ~ dans** (*suj: personne*) to gaze at one's reflection in; (*: chose*) to be mirrored in.

mirifique [mērēfēk] *a* wonderful.

mirobolant, e [mērobolāń, -áńt] *a* fantastic.

miroir [mērwár] *nm* mirror.

miroiter [mērwátā] *vi* to sparkle, shimmer; **faire ~ qch à qn** to paint sth in glowing colors for sb, dangle sth in front of sb's eyes.

miroiterie [mērwátrē] *nf* (*usine*) mirror factory; (*magasin*) mirror dealer's (shop).

mis, e [mē, mēz] *pp de* **mettre** ♦ *a* (*couvert, table*) set, laid; (*personne*): **bien ~** well dressed ♦ *nf* (*argent: au jeu*) stake; (*tenue*) clothing; attire; **être de ~e** to be acceptable *ou* in season; **~e en bouteilles** bottling; **~e à feu** blast-off; **~e de fonds** capital outlay; **~e à jour** updating; **~e à mort** kill; **~e à pied** (*d'un employé*) suspension; layoff; **~e sur pied** (*d'une affaire, entreprise*) setting up; **~e en plis** set; **~e au point** (*PHOTO*) focusing; (*fig*) clarification; **~e à prix** upset *ou* reserve (*Brit*) price; **~e en scène** production.

misaine [mēzen] *nf:* **mât de ~** foremast.

misanthrope [mēzáńtrop] *nm/f* misanthropist.

Mis(e) *abr* = **marquis(e)**.

mise [mēz] *af*, *nf* voir **mis**.

miser [mēzā] *vt* (*enjeu*) to stake, bet; **~ sur** *vt* (*cheval, numéro*) to bet on; (*fig*) to bank *ou* count on.

misérable [mēzārábl(ə)] *a* (*lamentable, malheureux*) pitiful, wretched; (*pauvre*) poverty-stricken; (*insignifiant, mesquin*) miserable ♦ *nm/f* wretch; (*miséreux*) poor wretch.

misère [mēzer] *nf* (*pauvreté*) (extreme) poverty, destitution; **~s** *nfpl* (*malheurs*) woes, miseries; (*ennuis*) little troubles; **être dans la ~** to be destitute *ou* poverty-stricken; **salaire de ~** starvation wage; **faire des ~s à qn** to torment sb; **~ noire** utter destitution, abject poverty.

miséreux, euse [mēzārœ̄, -œ̄z] *a* poverty-stricken ♦ *nm/f* down-and-out.

miséricorde [mēzārēkord(ə)] *nf* mercy, forgiveness.

miséricordieux, euse [mēzārēkordyœ̄, -œ̄z] *a* merciful, forgiving.

misogyne [mēzozhēn] *a* misogynous ♦ *nm/f* misogynist.

missel [mēsel] *nm* missal.

missile [mēsēl] *nm* missile.

mission [mēsyoń] *nf* mission; **partir en ~** (*ADMIN, POL*) to go on an assignment.

missionnaire [mēsyoner] *nm/f* missionary.

missive [mēsēv] *nf* missive.

mistral [mēstrál] *nm* mistral (wind).

mit [mē] *vb* voir **mettre**.

mitaine [mēten] *nf* mitt(en).

mite [mēt] *nf* clothes moth.

mité, e [mētā] *a* moth-eaten.

mi-temps [mētāń] *nf inv* (*SPORT: période*) half (*pl* halves); (*: pause*) half-time; **à ~ a, ad** part-time.

miteux, euse [mētœ̄, -œ̄z] *a* seedy, shabby.

mitigé, e [mētēzhā] *a* (*conviction, ardeur*) lukewarm; (*sentiments*) mixed.

mitonner [mētonā] *vt* (*préparer*) to cook with loving care; (*fig*) to cook up quietly.

mitoyen, ne [mētwàyań, -en] *a* common, party *cpd*; **maisons ~nes** duplex (*US*) *ou* semi-detached (*Brit*) houses; (*plus de deux*) town (*US*) *ou* terraced (*Brit*) houses.

mitraille [mētráy] *nf* (*balles de fonte*) grapeshot; (*décharge d'obus*) shellfire.

mitrailler [mētráyā] *vt* to machine-gun; (*fig: photographier*) to snap away at; **~ qn de** to pelt *ou* bombard sb with.

mitraillette [mētráyet] *nf* submachine gun.

mitrailleur [mētráyœr] *nm* machine gunner ♦ *am:* **fusil ~** machine gun.

mitrailleuse [mētráyœ̄z] *nf* machine gun.

mitre [mētr(ə)] *nf* miter (*US*), mitre (*Brit*).

mitron [mētroń] *nm* baker's boy.

mi-voix [mēvwá]: **à ~** *ad* in a low *ou* hushed voice.

mixage [mēksázh] *nm* (*CINÉMA*) (sound) mixing.

mixer, mixeur [mēksœr] *nm* (*CULIN*) (food) mixer.

mixité [mēksētā] *nf* (*SCOL*) coeducation.

mixte [mēkst(ə)] *a* (*gén*) mixed; (*SCOL*) mixed, coeducational; **à usage ~** dual-purpose; **cuisinière ~** combined gas and electric cooker; **équipe ~** combined team.

mixture [mĕkstür] *nf* mixture; *(fig)* concoction.

MLF *sigle m* (= *Mouvement de libération de la femme*) Women's Lib(eration) Movement.

Mlle, *pl* **Mlles** *abr* = **Mademoiselle**.

MM *abr* = **Messieurs**; *voir* **Monsieur**.

Mme, *pl* **Mmes** *abr* = **Madame**.

mn. *abr* (= *minute*) min.

mnémotechnique [mnāmoteknĕk] *a* mnemonic.

MNS *sigle m* (= *maître nageur sauveteur*) ≈ lifeguard.

MO *sigle f* (= *main-d'œuvre*) labor costs *(on invoices)*.

Mo *abr* = **métro, méga-octet**.

mobile [mobĕl] *a* mobile; *(amovible)* loose, removable; *(pièce de machine)* moving; *(élément de meuble etc)* movable ♦ *nm (motif)* motive; *(œuvre d'art)* mobile; *(PHYSIQUE)* moving object *ou* body.

mobilier, ière [mobēlyā, -yer] *a (JUR)* personal ♦ *nm (meubles)* furniture; **valeurs mobilières** transferable securities; **vente mobilière** sale of personal property *ou* chattels.

mobilisation [mobēlēzâsyôn] *nf* mobilization.

mobiliser [mobēlēzā] *vt (MIL, gén)* to mobilize.

mobilité [mobēlētā] *nf* mobility.

mobylette [mobēlet] *nf* ® moped.

mocassin [mokásan] *nm* moccasin.

moche [mosh] *a (fam: laid)* ugly; *(: mauvais, méprisable)* rotten.

modalité [modálētā] *nf* form, mode; **~s** *nfpl (d'un accord etc)* clauses, terms; **~s de paiement** methods of payment.

mode [mod] *nf* fashion; *(commerce)* fashion trade *ou* industry ♦ *nm (manière)* form, mode, method; *(LING)* mood; *(INFORM, MUS)* mode; **travailler dans la ~** to be in the fashion business; **à la ~** fashionable, in fashion; **~ dialogué** *(INFORM)* interactive *ou* conversational mode; **~ d'emploi** directions *pl* (for use); **~ de vie** way of life.

modelage [modlázh] *nm* modeling *(US)*, modelling *(Brit)*.

modelé [modlā] *nm (GÉO)* relief; *(du corps etc)* contours *pl*.

modèle [model] *a* model ♦ *nm* model; *(qui pose: de peintre)* sitter; *(type)* type; *(gabarit, patron)* pattern; **~ courant** *ou* **de série** *(COMM)* production model; **~ déposé** registered design; **~ réduit** small-scale model.

modeler [modlā] *vt (ART)* to model, mold *(US)*, mould *(Brit)*; *(suj: vêtement, érosion)* to mold *ou* mould, shape; **~ qch sur/d'après** to model sth on.

modélisation [modālēzâsyôn] *nf (MATH)* modeling *(US)*, modelling *(Brit)*.

modéliste [modālēst(ə)] *nm/f (COUTURE)* designer; *(de modèles réduits)* model maker.

modem [modem] *nm* modem.

Modène [moden] *n* Modena.

modérateur, trice [modārátœr, -trēs] *a* moderating ♦ *nm/f* moderator.

modération [modārāsyôn] *nf* moderation; **~ de peine** reduction of sentence.

modéré, e [modārā] *a, nm/f* moderate.

modérément [modārāmân] *ad* moderately, in moderation.

modérer [modārā] *vt* to moderate; **se ~** *vi* to restrain o.s.

moderne [modern(ə)] *a* modern ♦ *nm (ART)* modern style; *(ameublement)* modern furniture.

moderniser [modernēzā] *vt* to modernize.

modeste [modest(ə)] *a* modest; *(origine)* humble, lowly.

modestie [modestē] *nf* modesty; **fausse ~** false modesty.

modicité [modēsētā] *nf*: **la ~ des prix** *etc* the low prices *etc*.

modificatif, ive [modēfēkátēf, -ēv] *a* modifying.

modification [modēfēkâsyôn] *nf* modification.

modifier [modēfyā] *vt* to modify, alter; *(LING)* to modify; **se ~** *vi* to alter.

modique [modēk] *a (salaire, somme)* modest.

modiste [modēst(ə)] *nf* milliner.

modulaire [modüler] *a* modular.

modulation [modülâsyôn] *nf* modulation; **~ de fréquence (FM** *ou* **MF)** frequency modulation (FM).

module [modül] *nm* module.

moduler [modülā] *vt* to modulate; *(air)* to warble.

moelle [mwál] *nf* marrow; *(fig)* pith, core; **~ épinière** spinal chord.

moelleux, euse [mwálœ, -œz] *a* soft; *(au goût, à l'ouïe)* mellow; *(gracieux, souple)* smooth.

moellon [mwálôn] *nm* rubble stone.

mœurs [mœr] *nfpl (conduite)* morals; *(manières)* manners; *(pratiques sociales)* habits; *(mode de vie)* life style *sg*; *(d'une espèce animale)* behavior *sg (US)*, behaviour *sg (Brit)*; **femme de mauvaises ~** loose woman; **passer dans les ~** to become the custom; **contraire aux bonnes ~** contrary to proprieties.

mohair [moer] *nm* mohair.

moi [mwá] *pronom* me; *(emphatique)*: **~, je ...** for my part, I ..., I myself ... ♦ *nm inv (PSYCH)* ego, self; **à ~!** *(à l'aide)* help (me)!

moignon [mwányôn] *nm* stump.

moi-même [mwámem] *pronom* myself; *(emphatique)* I myself.

moindre [mwandr(ə)] *a* lesser; lower; **le(la) ~, les ~s** the least; the slightest; **le(la) ~ de** the least of; **c'est la ~ des choses** it's nothing at all.

moindrement [mwandrəmân] *ad*: **pas le ~** not in the least.

moine [mwán] *nm* monk, friar.

moineau, x [mwánō] *nm* sparrow.

moins [mwan] *ad* less ♦ *cj*: **~ 2** minus 2 ♦ *prép*: **dix heures ~ cinq** five to ten ♦ *nm*: **(le signe) ~** the minus sign; **~ je travaille, mieux je me porte** the less I work, the better I feel; **~ grand que** not as tall as, less tall than; **le (la) ~ doué(e)** the least gifted; **le ~** the least; **~ de** *(sable, eau)* less; *(livres, gens)* fewer; **~ de 2 ans/100 F** less than 2 years/100 F; **~ de midi** not yet midday; **100 F/3 jours de ~** 100 F/3 days less; **3 livres en ~ 3** books fewer; 3 books too few; **de l'argent en ~** less money; **le soleil en ~** but for the sun, minus the sun; **à ~ que** *cj* unless; **à ~**

de faire unless we do (*ou* he does); **à ~ de** (*imprévu, accident*) barring any; **au ~ at** least; **il a 3 ans de ~ que moi** he is 3 years younger than I; **de ~ en ~** less and less; **pour le ~** at the very least; **du ~** at least; **il fait ~ cinq** it's five below (freezing), it's minus five.

moins-value [mwaṅválü] *nf* (*ÉCON, COMM*) depreciation.

moire [mwár] *nf* moiré.

moiré, e [mwárā] *a* (*tissu, papier*) moiré, watered; (*reflets*) shimmering.

mois [mwá] *nm* month; (*salaire, somme dû*) (monthly) pay *ou* salary; **treizième ~**, **double ~** extra month's salary.

moïse [moćz] *nm* wicker cradle.

moisi, e [mwázē] *a* moldy (*US*), mouldy (*Brit*), mildewed ♦ *nm* mold (*US*), mould (*Brit*) mildew; **odeur de ~** musty smell.

moisir [mwázēr] *vi* to go moldy (*US*) *ou* mouldy (*Brit*); (*fig*) to rot; (*personne*) to hang about ♦ *vt* to make moldy *ou* mouldy.

moisissure [mwázēsür] *nf* mold *q* (*US*), mould *q* (*Brit*).

moisson [mwásóṅ] *nf* harvest; (*époque*) harvest (time); (*fig*): **faire une ~ de** to gather a wealth of.

moissonner [mwásonā] *vt* to harvest, reap; (*fig*) to collect.

moissonneur, euse [mwásonœr, -ōēz] *nm/f* harvester, reaper ♦ *nf* (*machine*) harvester.

moissonneuse-batteuse, ** *pl* **moisson-neuses-batteuses [mwásonozbátōēz] *nf* combine harvester.

moite [mwát] *a* (*peau, mains*) sweaty, sticky; (*atmosphère*) muggy.

moitié [mwátyā] *nf* half (*pl* halves); (*épouse*): **sa ~** his better half; **la ~** half; **la ~ de** half (of), half the amount (*ou* number) of; **la ~ du temps/des gens** half the time/the people; **à la ~ de** halfway through; **~ moins grand** half as tall; **~ plus long** half as long again, longer by half; **à ~** half (*avant le verbe*), half- (*avant l'adjectif*); **à ~ prix** (at) half price, half-price; **de ~** by half; **~ ~** half-and-half.

moka [mokà] *nm* (*café*) mocha coffee; (*gâteau*) mocha cake.

mol [mol] *am voir* **mou**.

molaire [moler] *nf* molar.

moldave [moldáv] *a* Moldavian.

Moldavie [moldávē] *nf*: **la ~** Moldavia.

môle [mōl] *nm* jetty.

moléculaire [molāküler] *a* molecular.

molécule [molākül] *nf* molecule.

moleskine [moleskēn] *nf* imitation leather.

molester [molestā] *vt* to manhandle, maul (about).

molette [molet] *nf* toothed *ou* cutting wheel.

mollasse [molàs] *a* (*péj: sans énergie*) sluggish; (*: flasque*) flabby.

molle [mol] *af voir* **mou**.

mollement [molmáṅ] *ad* softly; (*péj*) sluggishly; (*protester*) feebly.

mollesse [moles] *nf* (*voir mou*) softness; flabbiness; limpness; sluggishness; feebleness.

mollet [mole] *nm* calf (*pl* calves) ♦ *am*: **œuf ~** soft-boiled egg.

molletière [moltyer] *af*: **bande ~** puttee.

molleton [moltôṅ] *nm* (*TEXTILES*) felt.

molletonné, e [moltonā] *a* (*gants etc*) fleece-lined.

mollir [molēr] *vi* (*jambes*) to give way; (*NAVIG: vent*) to drop, die down; (*fig: personne*) to relent; (*: courage*) to fail, flag.

mollusque [molüsk(ə)] *nm* (*ZOOL*) mollusk (*US*), mollusc; (*fig: personne*) lazy lump.

molosse [molos] *nm* big ferocious dog.

môme [mōm] *nm/f* (*fam: enfant*) brat; (*: fille*) chick.

moment [momáṅ] *nm* moment; (*occasion*): **profiter du ~** to take (advantage of) the opportunity; **ce n'est pas le ~** this is not the right time; **à un certain ~** at some point; **à un ~ donné** at a certain point; **à quel ~?** when exactly?; **au même ~** at the same time; (*instant*) at the same moment; **pour un bon ~** for a good while; **pour le ~** for the moment, for the time being; **au ~ de** at the time of; **au ~ où** as; at a time when; **à tout ~** at any time *ou* moment; (*continuellement*) constantly, continually; **en ce ~** at the moment; (*aujourd'hui*) at present; **sur le ~** at the time; **par ~s** now and then, at times; **d'un ~ à l'autre** any time (now); **du ~ où** *ou* **que** seeing that, since; **n'avoir pas un ~ à soi** not to have a minute to oneself.

momentané, e [momáṅtánā] *a* temporary, momentary.

momie [momē] *nf* mummy.

mon [môṅ], **ma** [má], *pl* **mes** [mā] *dét* my.

monacal, e, aux [monákál, -ō] *a* monastic.

Monaco [monákō] *nm*: **le ~** Monaco.

monarchie [monárshē] *nf* monarchy.

monarchiste [monárshēst(ə)] *a, nm/f* monarchist.

monarque [monárk(ə)] *nm* monarch.

monastère [monáster] *nm* monastery.

monastique [monástēk] *a* monastic.

monceau, x [mônsō] *nm* heap.

mondain, e [môṅdaṅ, -en] *a* (*soirée, vie*) society *cpd*; (*obligations*) social; (*peintre, écrivain*) fashionable; (*personne*) society *cpd* ♦ *nm/f* society man/woman, socialite ♦ *nf*: **la M~e, la police ~e** ≈ the vice squad.

mondanités [môṅdánētā] *nfpl* (*vie mondaine*) society life *sg*; (*paroles*) (society) small talk *sg*; (*PRESSE*) (society) gossip column *sg*.

monde [môṅd] *nm* world; (*personnes mondaines*): **le ~** (high) society; (*milieu*): **être du même ~** to move in the same circles; (*gens*): **il y a du ~** (*beaucoup de gens*) there are a lot of people; (*quelques personnes*) there are some people; **y a-t-il du ~ dans la cuisine?** is there anybody in the kitchen?; **beaucoup/peu de ~** many/few people; **le meilleur** *etc* **du ~** the best *etc* in the world *ou* on earth; **mettre au ~** to bring into the world; **pas le moins du ~** not in the least; **se faire un ~ de qch** to make a great deal of fuss about sth; **tour du ~** round-the-world trip; **homme/femme du ~** society man/woman.

mondial, e, aux [môṅdyál, -ō] *a* (*population*) world *cpd*; (*influence*) worldwide.

mondialement [môṅdyálmáṅ] *ad* throughout the world.

mondialisation [môndyálēzâsyôn] *nf* (*d'une technique*) global application; (*d'un conflit*) global spread.

mondovision [môndovēzyôn] *nf* (world coverage by) satellite television.

monégasque [monāgásk(ə)] *a* Monegasque, of *ou* from Monaco ♦ *nm/f*: **M~** Monegasque.

monétaire [monāter] *a* monetary.

monétarisme [monātárēsm(ə)] *nm* monetarism.

monétique [monātēk] *nf* electronic money.

mongol, e [môngol] *a* Mongol, Mongolian ♦ *nm* (*LING*) Mongolian ♦ *nm/f*: **M~, e** (*MÉD*) Mongol, Mongoloid; (*de la Mongolie*) Mongolian.

Mongolie [môngolē] *nf*: **la ~** Mongolia.

mongolien, ne [môngolyăn, -en] *a*, *nm/f* mongol.

mongolisme [môngolēsm(ə)] *nm* mongolism, Down's syndrome.

moniteur, trice [monētœr, -trēs] *nm/f* (*SPORT*) instructor/instructress; (*de colonie de vacances*) supervisor ♦ *nm* (*écran*) monitor; **~ cardiaque** cardiac monitor; **~ d'auto-école** driving instructor.

monitorat [monētorá] *nm* (*formation*) instructor's training (course); (*fonction*) instructorship.

monnaie [mone] *nf* (*pièce*) coin; (*ÉCON, gén: moyen d'échange*) currency; (*petites pièces*): **avoir de la ~** to have (some) change; **faire de la ~** to get (some) change; **avoir/faire la ~ de 20 F** to have change for/get change for 20 F; **faire** *ou* **donner à qn la ~ de 20 F** to give sb change for 20 F, change 20 F for sb; **rendre à qn la ~** (**sur 20 F**) to give sb the change (from *ou* out of 20 F); **servir de ~ d'échange** (*fig*) to be used as a bargaining token *ou* as bargaining tokens; **payer en ~ de singe** to fob (sb) off with empty promises; **c'est ~ courante** it's a common occurrence; **~ légale** legal tender.

monnayer [monāyā] *vt* to convert into cash; (*talent*) to capitalize on.

monnayeur [moneyœr] *nm voir* **faux**.

mono [monō] *nf* (= *monophonie*) mono ♦ *nm* (= *monoski*) monoski.

monochrome [monokrôm] *a* monochrome.

monocle [monokl(ə)] *nm* monocle, eyeglass.

monocoque [monokok] *a* (*voiture*) monocoque ♦ *nm* (*voilier*) monohull.

monocorde [monokord(ə)] *a* monotonous.

monoculture [monokültür] *nf* single-crop farming, monoculture.

monogramme [monográm] *nm* monogram.

monokini [monokēnē] *nm* one-piece bikini, bikini pants *pl*.

monolingue [monolăng] *a* monolingual.

monologue [monolog] *nm* monologue, soliloquy; **~ intérieur** stream of consciousness.

monologuer [monologā] *vi* to soliloquize.

monôme [monôm] *nm* (*MATH*) monomial; (*d'étudiants*) students' procession.

monoparental, e, aux [monopárăntál, -ō] *a* one-parent *cpd*; **famille ~e** one-parent family *cpd*.

monophasé, e [monofázā] *a* single-phase *cpd*.

monoplace [monoplás] *a*, *nm*, *nf* single-seater, one-seater.

monoplan [monoplăn] *nm* monoplane.

monopole [monopol] *nm* monopoly.

monopoliser [monopolēzā] *vt* to monopolize.

monorail [monoráy] *nm* monorail; monorail train.

monoski [monoskē] *nm* monoski.

monosyllabe [monosēláb] *nm* monosyllable, word of one syllable.

monotone [monoton] *a* monotonous.

monotonie [monotonē] *nf* monotony.

monseigneur [mônsenyœr] *nm* (*archevêque, évêque*) Your (*ou* His) Grace; (*cardinal*) Your (*ou* His) Eminence; **Mgr Thomas** Bishop Thomas; Cardinal Thomas.

Monsieur [məsyœ], *pl* **Messieurs** [māsyœ] *titre* Mr [mis'tûr] ♦ *nm* (*homme quelconque*): **un/le m~** a/the gentleman; *voir aussi* **Madame**.

monstre [mônstr(ə)] *nm* monster ♦ *a* (*fam: effet, publicité*) massive; **un travail ~** a fantastic amount of work; an enormous job; **~ sacré** superstar.

monstrueux, euse [mônstrüœ, -œz] *a* monstrous.

monstruosité [mônstrüözētā] *nf* monstrosity.

mont [môn] *nm*: **par ~s et par vaux** over hill and dale; **le M~ Blanc** Mont Blanc; **~ de Vénus** mons veneris.

montage [môntázh] *nm* putting up; (*d'un bijou*) mounting, setting; (*d'une machine etc*) assembly; (*PHOTO*) photomontage; (*CINÉMA*) editing; **~ sonore** sound editing.

montagnard, e [môntányár, -árd(ə)] *a* mountain *cpd* ♦ *nm/f* mountaindweller.

montagne [môntány] *nf* (*cime*) mountain; (*région*): **la ~** the mountains *pl*; **la haute ~** the high mountains; **les ~s Rocheuses** the Rocky Mountains, the Rockies; **~s russes** roller coaster *sg*.

montagneux, euse [môntányœ, -œz] *a* mountainous; hilly.

montant, e [môntăn, -ănt] *a* (*mouvement, marée*) rising; (*chemin*) uphill; (*robe, corsage*) high-necked ♦ *nm* (*somme, total*) (sum) total, (total) amount; (*de fenêtre*) upright; (*de lit*) post.

mont-de-piété, *pl* **monts-de-piété** [môndpyātā] *nm* pawnshop.

monte [mônt] *nf* (*accouplement*): **la ~** stud; (*d'un jockey*) seat.

monté, e [môntā] *a*: **être ~ contre qn** to be angry with sb; (*fourni, équipé*): **~ en** equipped with.

monte-charge [môntshárzh(ə)] *nm inv* freight elevator (*US*), goods lift (*Brit*), hoist.

montée [môntā] *nf* rising, rise; (*escalade*) ascent, climb; (*chemin*) way up; (*côte*) hill; **au milieu de la ~** halfway up; **le moteur chauffe dans les ~s** the engine overheats going uphill.

monte-plats [môntplá] *nm inv* dumb waiter.

monter [môntā] *vt* (*escalier, côte*) to go (*ou* come) up; (*valise, paquet*) to take (*ou* bring) up; (*cheval*) to mount; (*femelle*) to cover, serve; (*tente, échafaudage*) to put up; (*machine*) to assemble; (*bijou*) to mount, set; (*COUTURE*) to sew on; (: *manche*) to set in; (*CINÉMA*) to edit; (*THÉÂTRE*) to put on, stage; (*société, coup etc*) to set up; (*fournir, équiper*) to equip ♦ *vi* to go (*ou* come) up;

(*avion, voiture*) to climb, go up; (*chemin, niveau, température, voix, prix*) to go up, rise; (*brouillard, bruit*) to rise, come up; (*passager*) to get on; (*à cheval*): ~ **bien/mal** to ride well/badly; ~ **à cheval/bicyclette** to get on *ou* mount a horse/bicycle; (*faire du cheval etc*) to ride (a horse); to (ride a) bicycle; ~ **à pied/en voiture** to walk/drive up, go up on foot/by car; ~ **dans le train/ l'avion** to get into the train/plane, board the train/plane; ~ **sur** to climb up onto; ~ **sur** *ou* **à un arbre/une échelle** to climb (up) a tree/ ladder; ~ **à bord** to (get on) board; ~ **à la tête de qn** to go to sb's head; ~ **sur les planches** to go on the stage; ~ **en grade** to be promoted; **se ~** (*s'équiper*) to equip o.s.; **se ~ à** (*frais etc*) to add up to, come to; ~ **qn contre qn** to set sb against sb; ~ **la tête à qn** to give sb ideas.

monteur, euse [mõtœr, -ēz] *nm/f* (*TECH*) fitter; (*CINÉMA*) (film) editor.

monticule [mõtēkül] *nm* mound.

montmartrois, e [mõṁartrwà, -wáz] *a* of *ou* from Montmartre.

montre [mõtr(ə)] *nf* watch; (*ostentation*): **pour la ~** for show; ~ **en main** exactly, to the minute; **faire ~ de** to show, display; **contre la ~** (*SPORT*) against the clock; ~ **de plongée** diver's watch.

Montréal [mõrēàl] *n* Montreal.

montréalais, e [mṍrēàle, -ez] *a* of *ou* from Montreal ♦ *nm/f*: **M~, e** Montrealer.

montre-bracelet, *pl* **montres-bracelets** [mṍtrəbràsle] *nf* wristwatch.

montrer [mõtrā] *vt* to show; **se ~** to appear; ~ **qch à qn** to show sb sth; ~ **qch du doigt** to point to sth, point one's finger at sth; **se ~ intelligent** to prove (to be) intelligent.

montreur, euse [mõtrœr, -ēz] *nm/f*: ~ **de marionnettes** puppeteer.

monture [mõtür] *nf* (*bête*) mount; (*d'une bague*) setting; (*de lunettes*) frame.

monument [monümáṅ] *nm* monument; ~ **aux morts** war memorial.

monumental, e, aux [monümáṅtál, -ō] *a* monumental.

moquer [mokā]: **se ~ de** *vt* to make fun of, laugh at; (*fam: se désintéresser de*) not to care about; (*tromper*): **se ~ de qn** to take sb for a ride.

moquerie [mokrē] *nf* mockery *q*.

moquette [moket] *nf* fitted carpet, wall-to-wall carpeting *q*.

moquetter [mokātā] *vt* to carpet.

moqueur, euse [mokœr, -ēz] *a* mocking.

moral, e, aux [morál, -ō] *a* moral ♦ *nm* morale ♦ *nf* (*conduite*) morals *pl*; (*règles*) moral code, ethic; (*valeurs*) moral standards *pl*, morality; (*science*) ethics *sg*, moral philosophy; (*conclusion: d'une fable etc*) moral; **au ~, sur le plan ~** morally; **avoir le ~ à zéro** to be really down; **faire la ~e à** to lecture, preach at.

moralement [morálmáṅ] *ad* morally.

moralisateur, trice [morálēzàtœr, -trēs] *a* moralizing, sanctimonious ♦ *nm/f* moralizer.

moraliser [morálēzā] *vt* (*sermonner*) to lecture, preach at.

moraliste [morálēst(ə)] *nm/f* moralist ♦ *a* mor-

alistic.

moralité [morálētā] *nf* (*d'une action, attitude*) morality; (*conduite*) morals *pl*; (*conclusion, enseignement*) moral.

moratoire [morátwár] *am*: **intérêts ~s** (*ÉCON*) interest on arrears.

morave [moráv] *a* Moravian.

Moravie [morávē] *nf*: **la ~** Moravia.

morbide [morbēd] *a* morbid.

morceau, x [morsō] *nm* piece, bit; (*d'une œuvre*) passage, extract; (*MUS*) piece; (*CULIN: de viande*) cut; **mettre en ~x** to pull to pieces *ou* bits.

morceler [morsəlā] *vt* to break up, divide up.

mordant, e [mordáṅ, -áṅt] *a* scathing, cutting; (*froid*) biting ♦ *nm* (*dynamisme, énergie*) spirit; (*fougue*) bite, punch.

mordicus [mordēküs] *ad* (*fam*) obstinately, stubbornly.

mordiller [mordēyā] *vt* to nibble at, chew at.

mordoré, e [mordorā] *a* lustrous bronze.

mordre [mordr(ə)] *vt* to bite; (*suj: lime, vis*) to bite into ♦ *vi* (*poisson*) to bite; ~ **dans** to bite into; ~ **sur** (*fig*) to go over into, overlap into; ~ **à qch** (*comprendre, aimer*) to take to; ~ **à l'hameçon** to bite, rise to the bait.

mordu, e [mordü] *pp de* **mordre** ♦ *a* (*amoureux*) smitten ♦ *nm/f*: **un ~ du jazz/de la voile** a jazz/sailing fanatic *ou* buff.

morfondre [morfõdr(ə)]: **se ~** *vi* to mope.

morgue [morg(ə)] *nf* (*arrogance*) haughtiness; (*lieu: de la police*) morgue; (: *à l'hôpital*) mortuary.

moribond, e [morēbṍ, -ṍd] *a* dying, moribund.

morille [morēy] *nf* morel (mushroom).

mormon, e [mormṍ, -on] *a, nm/f* Mormon.

morne [morn(ə)] *a* (*personne, visage*) glum, gloomy; (*temps, vie*) dismal, dreary.

morose [morōz] *a* sullen, morose; (*marché*) sluggish.

morphine [morfēn] *nf* morphine.

morphinomane [morfēnomán] *nm/f* morphine addict.

morphologie [morfolozhē] *nf* morphology.

mors [mor] *nm* bit.

morse [mors(ə)] *nm* (*ZOOL*) walrus; (*TÉL*) Morse (code).

morsure [morsür] *nf* bite.

mort [mor] *nf* death; **se donner la ~** to take one's own life; **de ~** (*silence, pâleur*) deathly; **blessé à ~** fatally wounded *ou* injured; **à la vie, à la ~** for better, for worse; ~ **clinique** brain death.

mort, e [mor, mort(ə)] *pp de* **mourir** ♦ *a* dead ♦ *nm/f* (*défunt*) dead man/woman; (*victime*): **il y a eu plusieurs ~s** several people were killed, there were several killed ♦ *nm* (*CARTES*) dummy; ~ **ou vif** dead or alive; ~ **de peur/fatigue** frightened to death/dead tired; **~s et blessés** casualties; **faire le ~** to play dead; (*fig*) to lie low.

mortadelle [mortádel] *nf* mortadella (*type of luncheon meat*).

mortalité [mortálētā] *nf* mortality, death rate.

mort-aux-rats [mortōrá] *nf inv* rat poison.

mortel, le [mortel] *a* (*poison etc*) deadly, lethal; (*accident, blessure*) fatal; (*REL, danger, frayeur*) mortal; (*fig: froid*) deathly;

(: *ennui, soirée*) deadly (boring) ♦ *nm/f* mor-tal.

mortellement [mortelmáṅ] *ad* (*blessé etc*) fa-tally, mortally; (*pâle etc*) deathly; (*fig: ennuyeux etc*) deadly.

morte-saison, *pl* **mortes-saisons** [mortəsezóṅ] *nf* slack *ou* off season.

mortier [mortyā] *nm* (*gén*) mortar.

mortifier [mortēfyā] *vt* to mortify.

mort-né, e [mornā] *a* (*enfant*) stillborn; (*fig*) abortive.

mortuaire [mortüer] *a* funeral *cpd*; **avis ~s** death announcements, intimations; **chapelle ~** mortuary chapel; **couronne ~** (funeral) wreath; **domicile ~** house of the deceased; **drap ~** pall.

morue [morü] *nf* (*ZOOL*) cod *inv*; (*CULIN: salée*) salt-cod.

morutier [morütyā] *nm* (*pêcheur*) cod fisher-man; (*bateau*) cod fishing boat.

morvandeau, elle, x [morváṅdō, -el] *a* of *ou* from the Morvan region.

morveux, euse [morvœ̄, -œ̄z] *a* (*fam*) snotty-nosed.

mosaïque [mozáĕk] *nf* (*ART*) mosaic; (*fig*) patchwork.

Moscou [moskōō] *n* Moscow.

moscovite [moskovēt] *a* of *ou* from Moscow, Moscow *cpd* ♦ *nm/f*: **M~** Muscovite.

mosquée [moskā] *nf* mosque.

mot [mō] *nm* word; (*message*) line, note; (*bon mot etc*) saying; **le ~ de la fin** the last word; **~ à ~** *a, ad* word for word; **~ pour ~** word for word, verbatim; **sur** *ou* **à ces ~s** with these words; **en un ~** in a word; **à ~s couverts** in veiled terms; **prendre qn au ~** to take sb at his word; **se donner le ~** to send the word around; **avoir son ~ à dire** to have a say; **~ d'ordre** watchword; **~ de passe** password; **~s croisés** crossword (puzzle) *sg*.

motard [motár] *nm* biker; (*policier*) motor-cycle cop.

motel [motel] *nm* motel.

moteur, trice [motœr, -trēs] *a* (*ANAT, PHYSIOL*) motor; (*TECH*) driving; (*AUTO*): **à 4 roues motrices** 4-wheel drive ♦ *nm* engine, motor; (*fig*) mover, mainspring; **à ~** power-driven, motor *cpd*; **~ à deux temps** two-stroke engine; **~ à explosion** internal combustion engine; **~ à réaction** jet engine; **~ thermique** heat engine.

motif [motēf] *nm* (*cause*) motive; (*décoratif*) design, pattern, motif; (*d'un tableau*) subject, motif; (*MUS*) figure, motif; **~s** *nmpl* (*JUR*) grounds *pl*; **sans ~** *a* groundless.

motion [mōsyóṅ] *nf* motion; **~ de censure** motion of censure, vote of no confidence.

motivation [motēvâsyóṅ] *nf* motivation.

motivé, e [motēvā] *a* (*acte*) justified; (*personne*) motivated.

motiver [motēvā] *vt* (*justifier*) to justify, account for; (*ADMIN, JUR, PSYCH*) to motivate.

moto [motō] *nf* (motor)bike; **~ verte** *ou* **de trial** [US] *ou* trail (*Brit*) bike.

moto-cross [motokros] *nm* motocross.

motoculteur [motokültœr] *nm* (motorized) cultivator.

motocyclette [motosēklet] *nf* motorbike, motorcycle.

motocyclisme [motosēklēsm(ə)] *nm* motor-cycle racing.

motocycliste [motosēklēst(ə)] *nm/f* motor-cyclist.

motoneige [motonezh] *nf* snowmobile.

motorisé, e [motorēzā] *a* (*troupe*) motorized; (*personne*) having one's own transport.

motrice [motrēs] *af voir* **moteur**.

motte [mot] *nf*: **~ de terre** lump of earth, clod (of earth); **~ de gazon** turf, sod; **~ de beurre** lump of butter.

motus [motüs] *excl*: **~ (et bouche cousue)!** mum's the word!

mou (mol), molle [mōō, mol] *a* soft; (*péj: visage, traits*) flabby; (: *geste*) limp; (: *personne*) sluggish; (: *résistance, protestations*) feeble ♦ *nm* (*homme mou*) wimp; (*abats*) lights *pl*, lungs *pl*; (*de la corde*): **avoir du ~** to be slack; **donner du ~** to slacken, loosen; **avoir les jambes molles** to be weak at the knees.

mouchard, e [mōōshár, -árd(ə)] *nm/f* (*péj: SCOL*) snitch (*US*), squealer; (: *POLICE*) stool pigeon ♦ *nm* (*appareil*) control device; (: *de camion*) tachograph.

mouche [mōōsh] *nf* fly; (*ESCRIME*) button; (*de taffetas*) patch; **prendre la ~** to go into a huff; **faire ~** to score a bull's-eye.

moucher [mōōshā] *vt* (*enfant*) to blow the nose of; (*chandelle*) to snuff (out); **se ~** to blow one's nose.

moucheron [mōōshróṅ] *nm* midge.

moucheté, e [mōōshtā] *a* (*cheval*) dappled; (*laine*) flecked; (*ESCRIME*) buttoned.

mouchoir [mōōshwár] *nm* handkerchief, hanky; **~ en papier** tissue, paper hanky.

moudre [mōōdr(ə)] *vt* to grind.

moue [mōō] *nf* pout; **faire la ~** to pout; (*fig*) to make a face.

mouette [mwet] *nf* (sea)gull.

mouf(f)ette [mōōfet] *nf* skunk.

moufle [mōōfl(ə)] *nf* (*gant*) mitt(en); (*TECH*) pulley block.

mouflon [mōōflóṅ] *nm* mouf(f)lon.

mouillage [mōōyázh] *nm* (*NAVIG*: *lieu*) anchorage, moorings *pl*.

mouillé, e [mōōyā] *a* wet.

mouiller [mōōyā] *vt* (*humecter*) to wet, moisten; (*tremper*): **~ qn/qch** to make sb/ sth wet; (*CULIN: ragoût*) to add stock *ou* wine to; (*couper, diluer*) to water down; (*mine etc*) to lay ♦ *vi* (*NAVIG*) to lie *ou* be at anchor; **se ~** to get wet; (*fam*) to commit o.s.; to get (o.s.) involved; **~ l'ancre** to drop *ou* cast anchor.

mouillette [mōōyet] *nf* sippet (*US*), (bread) finger (*Brit*).

mouillure [mōōyür] *nf* wet *q*; (*tache*) wet spot.

moulage [mōōlázh] *nm* molding (*US*), mould-ing (*Brit*); casting; (*objet*) cast.

moulais [mōōle] *etc vb voir* **moudre**.

moulant, e [mōōláṅ, -áṅt] *a* snug-fitting.

moule [mōōl] *vb voir* **moudre** ♦ *nf* (*mollusque*) mussel ♦ *nm* (*creux, CULIN*) mold (*US*), mould (*Brit*); (*modèle plein*) cast; **~ à gâteau** *nm* cake pan (*US*) *ou* tin

(*Brit*); ~ **à gaufre** *nm* waffle iron; ~ **à tarte** *nm* pie *ou* flan plate (*US*) *ou* dish (*Brit*).
moulent [mo͞ol] *vb voir* **moudre, mouler.**
mouler [mo͞olā] *vt* (*brique*) to mold (*US*), mould (*Brit*); (*statue*) to cast; (*visage, bas-relief*) to make a cast of; (*lettre*) to shape with care; (*suj: vêtement*) to hug, fit closely round; ~ **qch sur** (*fig*) to model sth on.
moulin [mo͞olaṅ] *nm* mill; (*fam*) engine; ~ **à café** coffee mill; ~ **à eau** watermill; ~ **à légumes** (vegetable) shredder; ~ **à paroles** (*fig*) chatterbox; ~ **à poivre** pepper mill; ~ **à prières** prayer wheel; ~ **à vent** windmill.
mouliner [mo͞olēnā] *vt* to shred.
moulinet [mo͞olēne] *nm* (*de treuil*) winch; (*de canne à pêche*) reel; (*mouvement*): **faire des ~s avec qch** to whirl sth around.
moulinette [mo͞olēnet] *nf* ® (vegetable) shredder.
moulons [mo͞olôṅ] *etc vb voir* **moudre.**
moulu, e [mo͞olü] *pp de* **moudre** ♦ *a* (*café*) ground.
moulure [mo͞olür] *nf* (*ornement*) molding (*US*), moulding (*Brit*).
mourant, e [mo͞orâṅ, -âṅt] *vb voir* **mourir** ♦ *a* dying ♦ *nm/f* dying man/woman.
mourir [mo͞orēr] *vi* to die; (*civilisation*) to die out; ~ **assassiné** to be murdered; ~ **de froid/faim/vieillesse** to die of exposure/hunger/old age; ~ **de faim/d'ennui** (*fig*) to be starving/be bored to death; ~ **d'envie de faire** to be dying to do; **s'ennuyer à** ~ to be bored to death.
mousquetaire [mo͞oskəter] *nm* musketeer.
mousqueton [mo͞oskətôṅ] *nm* (*fusil*) carbine; (*anneau*) snap-link, karabiner.
moussant, e [mo͞osâṅ, -âṅt] *a* foaming; **bain** ~ foam *ou* bubble bath, bath foam.
mousse [mo͞os] *nf* (*BOT*) moss; (*écume: sur eau, bière*) froth, foam; (*: shampooing*) lather; (*de champagne*) bubbles *pl*; (*CULIN*) mousse; (*en caoutchouc etc*) foam ♦ *nm* (*NAVIG*) ship's boy; **bain de** ~ bubble bath; **bas** ~ stretch stockings; **balle** ~ rubber ball; ~ **carbonique** (fire-fighting) foam; ~ **de nylon** nylon foam; (*tissu*) stretch nylon; ~ **à raser** shaving foam.
mousseline [mo͞oslēn] *nf* (*TEXTILES*) muslin; chiffon; **pommes** ~ (*CULIN*) creamed potatoes.
mousser [mo͞osā] *vi* to foam; to lather.
mousseux, euse [mo͞osœ, -œz] *a* (*chocolat*) frothy; (*eau*) foamy, frothy; (*vin*) sparkling ♦ *nm*: **(vin)** ~ sparkling wine.
mousson [mo͞osôṅ] *nf* monsoon.
moussu, e [mo͞osü] *a* mossy.
moustache [mo͞ostásh] *nf* moustache; **~s** *nfpl* (*d'animal*) whiskers *pl*.
moustachu, e [mo͞ostáshü] *a* wearing a moustache.
moustiquaire [mo͞ostēker] *nf* (*rideau*) mosquito net; (*chassis*) mosquito screen.
moustique [mo͞ostēk] *nm* mosquito.
moutarde [mo͞otárd(ə)] *nf* mustard ♦ *a inv* mustard(-colored).
moutardier [mo͞otárdyā] *nm* mustard jar.
mouton [mo͞otôṅ] *nm* (*ZOOL, péj*) sheep *inv*; (*peau*) sheepskin; (*CULIN*) mutton.
mouture [mo͞otür] *nf* grinding; (*péj*) rehash.
mouvant, e [mo͞ovâṅ, -âṅt] *a* unsettled; changing; shifting.
mouvement [mo͞ovmâṅ] *nm* (*gén, aussi: mécanisme*) movement; (*ligne courbe*) contours *pl*; (*fig: tumulte, agitation*) activity, bustle; (*: impulsion*) impulse; reaction; (*geste*) gesture; (*MUS: rythme*) tempo (*pl* -s *ou* tempi); **en** ~ in motion; on the move; **mettre qch en** ~ to set sth in motion, set sth going; ~ **d'humeur** fit *ou* burst of temper; ~ **d'opinion** trend of (public) opinion; **le** ~ **perpétuel** perpetual motion.
mouvementé, e [mo͞ovmâṅtā] *a* (*vie, poursuite*) eventful; (*réunion*) turbulent.
mouvoir [mo͞ovwår] *vt* (*levier, membre*) to move; (*machine*) to drive; **se** ~ to move.
moyen, ne [mwáyaṅ, -en] *a* average; (*tailles, prix*) medium; (*de grandeur moyenne*) medium-sized ♦ *nm* (*façon*) means *sg*, way ♦ *nf* average; (*STATISTIQUE*) mean; (*SCOL: à l'examen*) pass mark; (*AUTO*) average speed; **~s** *nmpl* (*capacités*) means; **au** ~ **de** by means of; **y a-t-il** ~ **de ...?** is it possible to ...?, can one ...?; **par quel ~?** how?, which way?, by which means?; **par tous les ~s** by every possible means, every possible way; **avec les ~s du bord** (*fig*) with what's available *ou* what comes to hand; **employer les grands ~s** to resort to drastic measures; **par ses propres ~s** all by oneself; **en ~ne** on (an) average; **faire la ~ne** to work out the average; ~ **de locomotion/d'expression** means of transport/expression; ~ **âge** Middle Ages; ~ **de transport** means of transport; **~ne d'âge** average age; **~ne entreprise** (*COMM*) medium-sized firm.
moyen-courrier [mwáyaṅko͞oryā] *nm* (*AVIAT*) medium-haul aircraft.
moyennant [mwáyenâṅ] *prép* (*somme*) for; (*service, conditions*) in return for; (*travail, effort*) with.
moyennement [mwáyenmâṅ] *ad* fairly, moderately; (*faire qch*) fairly *ou* moderately well.
Moyen-Orient [mwáyenoryâṅ] *nm*: **le** ~ the Middle East.
moyeu, x [mwáyœ] *nm* hub.
mozambicain, e [mozâṅbēkaṅ, -en] *a* Mozambican.
Mozambique [mozâṅbēk] *nm*: **le** ~ Mozambique.
MRAP *sigle m = Mouvement contre le racisme, l'antisémitisme et pour la paix.*
MRG *sigle m (= Mouvement des radicaux de gauche) political party.*
MRP *sigle m (= Mouvement républicain populaire) political party.*
ms *abr* (= *manuscrit*) MS., ms.
MST *sigle f* (= *maladie sexuellement transmissible*) STD (= *sexually transmitted disease*).
mû, mue [mü] *pp de* **mouvoir.**
mucosité [mükōzētā] *nf* mucus *q*.
mucus [mükü s] *nm* mucus *q*.
mue [mü] *pp de* **mouvoir** ♦ *nf* molting (*US*), moulting (*Brit*); sloughing; breaking of the voice.
muer [müā] *vi* (*oiseau, mammifère*) to molt (*US*), moult (*Brit*); (*serpent*) to slough;

(jeune garçon): **il mue** his voice is breaking; **se ~ en** to transform into.

muet, te [müe, -et] *a* dumb; *(fig)*: **~ d'admiration** *etc* speechless with admiration *etc*; *(joie, douleur, CINÉMA)* silent; *(LING: lettre)* silent, mute; *(carte)* blank ♦ *nm/f* mute ♦ *nm*: **le ~** *(CINÉMA)* the silent cinema *ou* movies.

mufle [müfl(ə)] *nm* muzzle; *(goujat)* boor ♦ *a* boorish.

mugir [müzhēr] *vi (bœuf)* to bellow; *(vache)* to low, moo; *(fig)* to howl.

mugissement [müzhēsmåṅ] *nm (voir mugir)* bellowing; lowing, mooing; howling.

muguet [müge] *nm (BOT)* lily of the valley; *(MÉD)* thrush.

mulâtre, tresse [mülâtr(ə), -tres] *nm/f* mulatto.

mule [mül] *nf (ZOOL)* (she-)mule.

mules [mül] *nfpl (pantoufles)* mules.

mulet [müle] *nm (ZOOL)* (he-)mule; *(poisson)* mullet.

muletier, ière [mültyā, -yer] *a*: **sentier** *ou* **chemin ~** mule track.

mulot [mülō] *nm* fieldmouse *(pl* -mice).

multicolore [mültēkolor] *a* multicolored *(US)*, multicoloured *(Brit)*.

multicoque [mültēkok] *nm* multihull.

multidisplinaire [mültēdēsēplēner] *a* multidisciplinary.

multiforme [mültēform(ə)] *a* many-sided.

multilatéral, e, aux [mültēlátārál, -ō] *a* multilateral.

multimilliardaire [mültēmēlyárdɛr], **multimillionnaire** [mültēmēlyoner] *a, nm/f* multimillionaire.

multinational, e, aux [mültēnásyonál, -ō] *a, nf* multinational.

multiple [mültēpl(ə)] *a* multiple, numerous; *(varié)* many, manifold ♦ *nm (MATH)* multiple.

multiplicateur [mültēplēkátœr] *nm* multiplier.

multiplication [mültēplēkásyóṅ] *nf* multiplication.

multiplicité [mültēplēsētā] *nf* multiplicity.

multiplier [mültēplēyā] *vt* to multiply; **se ~** *vi* to multiply; *(fig: personne)* to be everywhere at once.

multiprogrammation [mültēprográmásyóṅ] *nf (INFORM)* multiprogramming.

multipropriété [mültēproprēyātā] *nf* timesharing *q*.

multitraitement [mültētrɛtmåṅ] *nm (INFORM)* multiprocessing.

multitude [mültētüd] *nf* multitude; mass; **une ~ de** a vast number of, a multitude of.

Munich [münēk] *n* Munich.

munichois, e [münēkwà, -wáz] *a* of *ou* from Munich.

municipal, e, aux [münēsēpàl, -ō] *a* municipal; town *cpd*.

municipalité [münēsēpàlētā] *nf (corps municipal)* town council, corporation; *(commune)* town, municipality.

munir [münēr] *vt*: **~ qn/qch de** to equip sb/sth with; **se ~ de** to provide o.s. with.

munitions [münēsyóṅ] *nfpl* ammunition *sg*.

muqueuse [mükœz] *nf* mucous membrane.

mur [mür] *nm* wall; *(fig)* stone *ou* brick wall; **faire le ~** *(interne, soldat)* to sneak out (over

the wall); **~ du son** sound barrier.

mûr, e [mür] *a* ripe; *(personne)* mature ♦ *nf (de la ronce)* blackberry; *(du mûrier)* mulberry.

muraille [müráy] *nf* (high) wall.

mural, e, aux [mürál, -ō] *a* wall *cpd* ♦ *nm (ART)* mural.

mûre [mür] *nf voir* **mûr.**

mûrement [mürmåṅ] *ad*: **ayant ~ réfléchi** having given the matter much thought.

murène [müren] *nf* moray (eel).

murer [mürā] *vt (enclos)* to wall (in); *(porte, issue)* to wall up; *(personne)* to wall up *ou* in.

muret [müre] *nm* low wall.

mûrier [müryā] *nm* mulberry tree; *(ronce)* blackberry bush.

mûrir [mürēr] *vi (fruit, blé)* to ripen; *(abcès, furoncle)* to come to a head; *(fig: idée, personne)* to mature; *(projet)* to develop ♦ *vt (fruit, blé)* to ripen; *(personne)* to (make) mature; *(pensée, projet)* to nurture.

murmure [mürmür] *nm* murmur; **~s** *nmpl (plaintes)* murmurings, mutterings.

murmurer [mürmürā] *vi* to murmur; *(se plaindre)* to mutter, grumble.

mus [mü] *etc vb voir* **mouvoir.**

musaraigne [müzáreny] *nf* shrew.

musarder [müzárdā] *vi* to idle (about); *(en marchant)* to dawdle (along).

musc [müsk] *nm* musk.

muscade [müskàd] *nf (aussi:* **noix ~)** nutmeg.

muscat [müskà] *nm (raisin)* muscat grape; *(vin)* muscatel (wine).

muscle [müskl(ə)] *nm* muscle.

musclé, e [müsklā] *a (personne, corps)* muscular; *(fig: politique, régime etc)* strong-arm *cpd*.

muscler [müsklā] *vt* to develop the muscles of.

musculaire [müskülɛr] *a* muscular.

musculation [müskülásyóṅ] *nf*: **exercices de ~** muscle-developing exercises.

musculature [müskülátür] *nf* muscle structure, muscles *pl*, musculature.

muse [müz] *nf* muse.

museau, x [müzō] *nm* muzzle.

musée [müzā] *nm* museum; *(de peinture)* art gallery.

museler [müzlā] *vt* to muzzle.

muselière [müzəlyer] *nf* muzzle.

musette [müzet] *nf (sac)* lunchbag ♦ *a inv (orchestre etc)* accordion *cpd*.

muséum [müzāom] *nm* museum.

musical, e, aux [müzēkál, -ō] *a* musical.

music-hall [müzēkōl] *nm* variety theater *(US) ou* theatre *(Brit)*; *(genre)* variety.

musicien, ne [müzēsyaṅ, -en] *a* musical ♦ *nm/f* musician.

musique [müzēk] *nf* music; *(fanfare)* band; **faire de la ~** to make music; *(jouer d'un instrument)* to play an instrument; **~ de chambre** chamber music; **~ de fond** background music.

musqué, e [müskā] *a* musky.

must [mœst] *nm* must.

musulman, e [müzülmåṅ, -àn] *a, nm/f* Moslem, Muslim.

mutant, e [mütåṅ, -åṅt] *nm/f* mutant.

mutation [mütásyóṅ] *nf (ADMIN)* transfer; *(BIO)* mutation.

muter [müté] *vt* (*ADMIN*) to transfer.
mutilation [mütélâsyôñ] *nf* mutilation.
mutilé, e [mütélá] *nm/f* disabled person (*through loss of limbs*); ~ **de guerre** disabled veteran (*US*) *ou* ex-serviceman (*Brit*); **grand** ~ severely disabled person.
mutiler [mütélá] *vt* to mutilate, maim; (*fig*) to mutilate, deface.
mutin, e [mütañ, -ēn] *a* (*enfant, air, ton*) mischievous, impish ♦ *nm/f* (*MIL*, *NAVIG*) mutineer.
mutiner [mütēná]: **se** ~ *vi* to mutiny.
mutinerie [mütēnrē] *nf* mutiny.
mutisme [mütēsm(ə)] *nm* silence.
mutualité [mütüálētá] *nf* (*assurance*) mutual (*benefit*) insurance plan (*US*) *ou* scheme (*Brit*).
mutuel, le [mütüel] *a* mutual ♦ *nf* mutual benefit society.
myocarde [myokárd(ə)] *nm voir* **infarctus.**
myope [myop] *a* nearsighted, shortsighted.
myopie [myopē] *nf* nearsightedness, shortsightedness, myopia.
myosotis [myôzotēs] *nm* forget-me-not.
myriade [mēryád] *nf* myriad.
myrtille [mērtēy] *nf* blueberry (*US*), bilberry (*Brit*), whortleberry.
mystère [mēster] *nm* mystery.
mystérieusement [mēstáryœzmáñ] *ad* mysteriously.
mystérieux, euse [mēstáryœ̄, -œ̄z] *a* mysterious.
mysticisme [mēstēsēsm(ə)] *nm* mysticism.
mystificateur, trice [mēstēfēkátœr, -trēs] *nm/f* hoaxer, practical joker.
mystification [mēstēfēkásyôñ] *nf* (*tromperie, mensonge*) hoax; (*mythe*) mystification.
mystifier [mēstēfyá] *vt* to fool, take in; (*tromper*) to mystify.
mystique [mēstēk] *a* mystic, mystical ♦ *nm/f* mystic.
mythe [mēt] *nm* myth.
mythifier [mētēfyá] *vt* to turn into a myth, mythologize.
mythique [mētēk] *a* mythical.
mythologie [mētolozhē] *nf* mythology.
mythologique [mētolozhēk] *a* mythological.
mythomane [mētomán] *a, nm/f* mythomaniac.

N

N, n [en] *nm inv* N, n ♦ *abr* (= *nord*) N; **N comme Nicolas** N for Nan.
n' [n] *ad voir* **ne.**
nabot [nábō] *nm* dwarf.
nacelle [násel] *nf* (*de ballon*) basket.
nacre [nákr(ə)] *nf* mother-of-pearl.
nacré, e [nákrá] *a* pearly.
nage [názh] *nf* swimming; (*manière*) style of swimming, stroke; **traverser/s'éloigner à la** ~ to swim across/away; **en** ~ bathed in perspiration; ~ **indienne** sidestroke; ~ **libre**
freestyle; ~ **papillon** butterfly.
nageoire [názhwár] *nf* fin.
nager [názhá] *vi* to swim; (*fig: ne rien comprendre*) to be all at sea; ~ **dans** to be swimming in; (*vêtements*) to be lost in; ~ **dans le bonheur** to be overjoyed.
nageur, euse [názhœr, -œ̄z] *nm/f* swimmer.
naguère [náger] *ad* (*il y a peu de temps*) not long ago; (*autrefois*) formerly.
naïf, ïve [náēf, náēv] *a* naïve.
nain, e [nañ, nen] *a, nm/f* dwarf.
Nairobi [náērobē] *n* Nairobi.
nais [ne], **naissais** [nese] *etc vb voir* **naître.**
naissance [nesáñs] *nf* birth; **donner** ~ **à** to give birth to; (*fig*) to give rise to; **prendre** ~ to originate; **aveugle de** ~ born blind; **Français de** ~ French by birth; **à la** ~ **des cheveux** at the roots of the hair; **lieu de** ~ place of birth.
naissant, e [nesáñ, -áñt] *vb voir* **naître** ♦ *a* budding, incipient; (*jour*) dawning.
naît [ne] *vb voir* **naître.**
naître [netr(ə)] *vi* to be born; (*conflit, complications*) ~ **de** to arise from, be born out of; ~ **à** (*amour, poésie*) to awaken to; **il est né en 1960** he was born in 1960; **il naît plus de filles que de garçons** there are more girls born than boys; **faire** ~ (*fig*) to give rise to, arouse.
naïvement [náēvmáñ] *ad* naïvely.
naïveté [náēvtá] *nf* naïvety.
Namibie [námēbē] *nf*: **la** ~ Namibia.
nana [náná] *nf* (*fam: fille*) chick.
nancéien, ne [náñsáyañ, -en] *a* of *ou* from Nancy.
nantais, e [náñte, -ez] *a* of *ou* from Nantes.
nantir [náñtēr] *vt*: ~ **qn de** to provide sb with; **les nantis** (*péj*) the well-to-do.
NAP *sigle a* (= *Neuilly Auteuil Passy*) ≈ preppy.
napalm [nápálm] *nm* napalm.
naphtaline [náftálēn] *nf*: **boules de** ~ mothballs.
Naples [nápl(ə)] *n* Naples.
napolitain, e [nápoletañ, -en] *a* Neapolitan; **tranche** ~**e** Neapolitan ice cream.
nappe [náp] *nf* tablecloth; (*fig*) sheet; layer; ~ **de mazout** oil slick; ~ (**phréatique**) water table.
napper [nápá] *vt*: ~ **qch de** to coat sth with.
napperon [náprôñ] *nm* table-mat; ~ **individuel** place mat.
naquis [nákē] *etc vb voir* **naître.**
narcisse [nársēs] *nm* narcissus.
narcissique [nársēsēk] *a* narcissistic.
narcotique [nárkotēk] *a, nm* narcotic.
narguer [nárgá] *vt* to taunt.
narine [nárēn] *nf* nostril.
narquois, e [nárkwá, -wáz] *a* derisive, mocking.
narrateur, trice [nárátœr, -trēs] *nm/f* narrator.
narration [nárásyôñ] *nf* narration, narrative; (*SCOL*) essay.
narrer [nárá] *vt* to tell the story of, recount.
NASA [násá] *sigle f* (= *National Aeronautics and Space Administration*) NASA.
nasal, e, aux [názál, -ō] *a* nasal.
naseau, x [názō] *nm* nostril.
nasillard, e [názēyár, -árd(ə)] *a* nasal.

nasiller [názēyā] *vi* to speak with a (nasal) twang.

Nassau [nàsō] *n* Nassau.

nasse [nàs] *nf* fish trap.

natal, e [nàtál] *a* native.

nataliste [nàtálēst(ə)] *a* supporting a rising birth rate.

natalité [nàtálētā] *nf* birth rate.

natation [nàtàsyóń] *nf* swimming; **faire de la** ~ to go swimming (*regularly*).

natif, ive [nàtĕf, -ēv] *a* native.

nation [nàsyóń] *nf* nation; **les N~s Unies (NU)** the United Nations (UN).

national, e, aux [nàsyonàl, -ō] *a* national ♦ *nf:* **(route) ~e** ≈ state highway (*US*), ≈ A road (*Brit*); **obsèques ~es** state funeral.

nationalisation [nàsyonálēzâsyóń] *nf* nationalization.

nationaliser [nàsyonálēzā] *vt* to nationalize.

nationalisme [nàsyonálēsm(ə)] *nm* nationalism.

nationaliste [nàsyonálēst(ə)] *a, nm/f* nationalist.

nationalité [nàsyonálētā] *nf* nationality; **de ~ française** of French nationality.

natte [nàt] *nf* (*tapis*) mat; (*cheveux*) plait.

natter [nàtā] *vt* (*cheveux*) to plait.

naturalisation [nàtürálēzàsyóń] *nf* naturalization.

naturaliser [nàtürálēzā] *vt* to naturalize; (*empailler*) to stuff.

naturaliste [nàtürálēst(ə)] *nm/f* naturalist; (*empailleur*) taxidermist.

nature [nàtür] *nf* nature ♦ *a, ad* (*CULIN*) plain, without seasoning or sweetening; (*café, thé: sans lait*) black; (*: sans sucre*) without sugar; **payer en** ~ to pay in kind; **peint d'après** ~ painted from life; **être de** ~ **à faire qch** (*propre à*) to be the sort of thing (*ou* person) to do sth; ~ **morte** still life.

naturel, le [nàtürel] *a* (*gén, aussi: enfant*) natural ♦ *nm* naturalness; (*caractère*) disposition, nature; (*autochtone*) native; **au ~** (*CULIN*) in water; in its own juices.

naturellement [nàtürelmâń] *ad* naturally; (*bien sûr*) of course.

naturisme [nàtürĕsm(ə)] *nm* naturism.

naturiste [nàtürĕst(ə)] *nm/f* naturist.

naufrage [nōfràzh] *nm* (*ship*)wreck; (*fig*) wreck; **faire** ~ to be shipwrecked.

naufragé, e [nōfràzhā] *nm/f* shipwreck victim, castaway.

Nauru [norü] *nm* Nauru.

nauséabond, e [nōzāàbóń, -óńd] *a* foul, nauseous.

nausée [nōzā] *nf* nausea; **avoir la** ~ to feel sick; **avoir des ~s** to have waves of nausea, feel nauseous *ou* sick.

nautique [nōtĕk] *a* nautical, water *cpd*; **sports ~s** water sports.

nautisme [nōtĕsm(ə)] *nm* water sports *pl*.

naval, e [nàvàl] *a* naval.

navarrais, e [nàvàre, -ez] *a* Navarrian.

navet [nàve] *nm* turnip; (*péj*) third-rate film.

navette [nàvet] *nf* shuttle; (*en car etc*) shuttle (*service*); **faire la ~ (entre)** to go to and fro (*between*), shuttle (*between*); ~ **spatiale** space shuttle.

navigabilité [nàvēgàbēlētā] *nf* (*d'un navire*) seaworthiness; (*d'un avion*) airworthiness.

navigable [nàvēgàbl(ə)] *a* navigable.

navigant, e [nàvēgáń, -âńt] *a* (*AVIAT: personnel*) flying ♦ *nm/f:* **les ~s** the flying staff *ou* personnel.

navigateur [nàvēgàtœr] *nm* (*NAVIG*) seafarer, sailor; (*AVIAT*) navigator.

navigation [nàvēgàsyóń] *nf* navigation, sailing; (*COMM*) shipping; **compagnie de ~** shipping company; ~ **spatiale** space navigation.

naviguer [nàvēgā] *vi* to navigate, sail.

navire [nàvĕr] *nm* ship; ~ **de guerre** warship; ~ **marchand** merchantman.

navire-citerne, *pl* **navires-citernes** [nàvērsētern(ə)] *nm* tanker.

navire-hôpital, *pl* **navires-hôpitaux** [nàvēropētàl, -tō] *nm* hospital ship.

navrant, e [nàvráń, -âńt] *a* (*affligeant*) upsetting; (*consternant*) annoying.

navrer [nàvrā] *vt* to upset, distress; **je suis navré (de/de faire/que)** I'm so sorry (for/for doing/that).

nazaréen, ne [nàzàràáń, -en] *a* Nazarene.

Nazareth [nàzàret] *n* Nazareth.

NB *abr* (= *nota bene*) NB.

nbr. *abr* = **nombreux.**

nbses *abr* = **nombreuses.**

n.c. *abr* = *non communiqué, non coté*.

ND *sigle f* = *Notre Dame*.

n.d. *abr* = *non daté, non disponible*.

NDA *sigle f* = *note de l'auteur*.

NDE *sigle f* = *note de l'éditeur*.

NDLR *sigle f* = *note de la rédaction*.

ne, n' [n(ə)] *ad voir* **pas, plus, jamais** *etc*; (*explétif*) *non traduit*.

né, e [nā] *pp de* **naître;** ~ **en 1960** born in 1960; **~e Scott** née Scott; **~(e) de ... et de ...** son/daughter of ... and of ...; ~ **d'une mère française** having a French mother; ~ **pour commander** born to lead ♦ *a:* **un comédien** ~ a born comedian.

néanmoins [nāáńmwań] *ad* nevertheless, yet.

néant [nāáń] *nm* nothingness; **réduire à** ~ to bring to nought; (*espoir*) to dash.

nébuleux, euse [nābülœ, -œz] *a* (*ciel*) cloudy; (*fig*) nebulous.

nébuliser [nābülēzā] *vt* (*liquide*) to spray.

nébulosité [nābülōzētā] *nf* cloud cover; ~ **variable** cloudy in places.

nécessaire [nāsāser] *a* necessary ♦ *nm* necessary; (*sac*) kit; **faire le** ~ to do the necessary; **n'emporter que le strict** ~ to take only what is strictly necessary; ~ **de couture** sewing kit; ~ **de toilette** toilet case (*US*) *ou* bag (*Brit*); ~ **de voyage** overnight bag.

nécessairement [nāsāsermâń] *ad* necessarily.

nécessité [nāsāsētā] *nf* necessity; **se trouver dans la** ~ **de faire qch** to find it necessary to do sth; **par** ~ out of necessity.

nécessiter [nāsāsētā] *vt* to require.

nécessiteux, euse [nāsāsētœ, -œz] *a* needy.

nec plus ultra [nākplüsültrà] *nm:* **le** ~ **de** the last word in.

nécrologie [nākrolozhē] *nf* obituary.

nécrologique [nākrolozhēk] *a:* **article** ~ obituary; **rubrique** ~ obituary column.

nécromancie [nākromáńsē] *nf* necromancy.

nécromancien, ne [nākromáńsyań, -en] *nm/f* necromancer.

nécrose [nākrōz] *nf* necrosis.

nectar [nektár] *nm* nectar.

nectarine [nektárēn] *nf* nectarine.

néerlandais, e [nāerlâńde, -ez] *a* Dutch, of the Netherlands ♦ *nm* (*LING*) Dutch ♦ *nm/f*: **N~,** **e** Dutchman/woman; **les N~** the Dutch.

nef [nef] *nf* (*d'église*) nave.

néfaste [nāfást(ə)] *a* baneful; ill-fated.

négatif, ive [nāgátēf, ēv] *a* negative ♦ *nm* (*PHOTO*) negative.

négativement [nāgátēvmáń] *ad*: **répondre ~** to give a negative response.

négligé, e [nāglēzhā] *a* (*en désordre*) slovenly ♦ *nm* (*tenue*) negligee.

négligeable [nāglēzhábl(ə)] *a* insignificant, negligible.

négligemment [nāglēzhámáń] *ad* carelessly.

négligence [nāglēzháńs] *nf* carelessness *q*; (*faute*) careless omission.

négligent, e [nāglēzháń, -áńt] *a* careless; (*JUR etc*) negligent.

négliger [nāglēzhā] *vt* (*épouse, jardin*) to neglect; (*tenue*) to be careless about; (*avis, précautions*) to disregard, overlook; **~ de faire** to fail to do, not bother to do; **se ~** to neglect o.s.

négoce [nāgos] *nm* trade.

négociable [nāgosyábl(ə)] *a* negotiable.

négociant [nāgosyáń] *nm* merchant.

négociateur [nāgosyátœr] *nm* negotiator.

négociation [nāgosyásyóń] *nf* negotiation; **~s collectives** collective bargaining *sg*.

négocier [nāgosyā] *vi, vt* to negotiate.

nègre [negr(ə)] *nm* (*péj*) Negro; (*péj*: *écrivain*) ghost writer ♦ *a* Negro.

négresse [nāgres] *nf* (*péj*) Negress.

négrier [nāgrēyā] *nm* (*fig*) slave driver.

négroïde [nāgroēd] *a* negroid.

neige [nezh] *nf* snow; **battre les œufs en ~** (*CULIN*) to whip *ou* beat the egg whites until stiff; **~ carbonique** dry ice; **~ fondue** (*par terre*) slush; (*qui tombe*) sleet; **~ poudreuse** powder snow.

neiger [nāzhā] *vi* to snow.

neigeux, euse [nezhœ, -œz] *a* snowy, snow-covered.

nénuphar [nānüfár] *nm* water lily.

néo-calédonien, ne [nāokálādonyań, -en] *a* New Caledonian ♦ *nm/f*: **N~, ne** native of New Caledonia.

néologisme [nāolozhēsm(ə)] *nm* neologism.

néon [nāóń] *nm* neon.

néo-natal, e [nāonátál] *a* neonatal.

néophyte [nāofēt] *nm/f* novice.

néo-zélandais, e [nāozālâńde, -ez] *a* New Zealand *cpd* ♦ *nm/f*: **N~,** **e** New Zealander.

Népal [nāpál] *nm*: **le ~** Nepal.

népalais, e [nāpále, -ez] *a* Nepalese, Nepali ♦ *nm* (*LING*) Nepalese, Nepali ♦ *nm/f*: **N~, e** Nepalese, Nepali.

néphrétique [nāfrātēk] *a* (*MÉD*: *colique*) nephritic.

néphrite [nāfrēt] *nf* (*MÉD*) nephritis.

nerf [ner] *nm* nerve; (*fig*) spirit; (*: forces*) stamina; **~s** *nmpl* nerves; **être** *ou* **vivre sur les ~s** to be a bundle of nerves; **être à bout de ~s** to be at the end of one's rope; **passer**

ses ~s sur qn to take it out on sb.

nerveusement [nervœzmáń] *ad* nervously.

nerveux, euse [nervœ, -œz] *a* nervous; (*cheval*) high-strung (*US*), highly-strung (*Brit*); (*voiture*) responsive; (*tendineux*) sinewy.

nervosité [nervōzētā] *nf* nervousness; (*émotivité*) excitability.

nervure [nervür] *nf* (*de feuille*) vein; (*ARCHIT, TECH*) rib.

n'est-ce pas [nespâ] *ad* isn't it?, won't you? *etc, selon le verbe qui précède*; **c'est bon, ~?** it's good, isn't it?; **il a peur, ~?** he's afraid, isn't he?; **~ que c'est bon?** don't you think it's good?; **lui, ~, il peut se le permettre** he, of course, can afford to do that, can't he?

net, nette [net] *a* (*sans équivoque, distinct*) clear; (*photo*) sharp; (*évident*) definite; (*propre*) neat, clean; (*COMM*: *prix, salaire, poids*) net ♦ *ad* (*refuser*) flatly ♦ *nm*: **mettre au ~** to copy out; **s'arrêter ~** to stop dead; **la lame a cassé ~** the blade snapped clean through; **faire place nette** to make a clean sweep; **~ d'impôt** tax free.

nettement [netmáń] *ad* (*distinctement*) clearly; (*évidemment*) definitely; (*avec comparatif, superlatif*): **~ mieux** definitely *ou* clearly better.

netteté [nettā] *nf* clearness.

nettoie [netwá] *etc vb voir* **nettoyer.**

nettoiement [nātwámáń] *nm* (*ADMIN*) cleaning; **service du ~** garbage (*US*) *ou* refuse (*Brit*) collection.

nettoierai [netwārā] *etc vb voir* **nettoyer.**

nettoyage [netwàyázh] *nm* cleaning; **~ à sec** dry cleaning.

nettoyant [nātwáyáń] *nm* (*produit*) cleaning agent.

nettoyer [netwáyā] *vt* to clean; (*fig*) to clean out.

neuf [nœf] *num* nine.

neuf, neuve [nœf, nœv] *a* new ♦ *nm*: **repeindre à ~** to redecorate; **remettre à ~** to renovate, refurbish; **n'acheter que du ~** to buy everything new; **quoi de ~?** what's new?

neurasthénique [nœrástānēk] *a* neurasthenic.

neurochirurgien [nœroshērürzhyań] *nm* neurosurgeon.

neuroleptique [nœroleptēk] *a* neuroleptic.

neurologique [nœrolozhēk] *a* neurological.

neurologue [nœrolog] *nm/f* neurologist.

neuropsychiatre [nœropsēkyátr(ə)] *nm/f* neuropsychiatrist.

neutralisation [nœtrálēzásyóń] *nf* neutralization.

neutraliser [nœtrálēzā] *vt* to neutralize.

neutraliste [nœtrálēst(ə)] *a* neutralist.

neutralité [nœtrálētā] *nf* neutrality.

neutre [nœtr(ə)] *a, nm* (*aussi LING*) neutral.

neutron [nœtróń] *nm* neutron.

neuve [nœv] *af voir* **neuf.**

neuvième [nœvyem] *num* ninth.

névé [nāvā] *nm* permanent snowpatch.

neveu, x [nəvœ] *nm* nephew.

névralgie [nāvrálzhē] *nf* neuralgia.

névralgique [nāvrálzhēk] *a* (*fig*: *sensible*) sensitive; **centre ~** nerve center (*US*) *ou* centre (*Brit*).

névrite [nāvrēt] *nf* neuritis.

névrose [nãvrōz] *nf* neurosis.
névrosé, e [nãvrōzā] *a, nmf* neurotic.
névrotique [nãvrotĕk] *a* neurotic.
New York [nyōōyork] *n* New York.
new yorkais, e [nyōōyorke, -ez] *a* of *ou* from New York, New York *cpd* ♦ *nm/f:* **New Yorkais, e** New Yorker.
nez [nã] *nm* nose; **rire au ~ de qn** to laugh in sb's face; **avoir du ~** to have flair; **avoir le ~ fin** to have foresight; **~ à ~ avec** face to face with; **à vue de ~** roughly.
NF *sigle mpl = nouveaux francs* ♦ *sigle f (IN-DUSTRIE: = norme française) industrial standard.*
ni [nē] *cj:* **~ l'un ~ l'autre ne sont** *ou* **n'est** neither one nor the other is; **il n'a rien dit ~ fait** he hasn't said or done anything.
Niagara [nyágárá] *nm:* **les chutes du ~** the Niagara Falls.
niais, e [nye, -ez] *a* silly, thick.
niaiserie [nyezrē] *nf* gullibility; *(action, propos, futilité)* silliness.
Nicaragua [nēkârágwá] *nm:* **le ~** Nicaragua.
nicaraguayen, ne [nēkârágwáyań, -en] *a* Nicaraguan ♦ *nm/f:* **N~, ne** Nicaraguan.
Nice [nēs] *n* Nice.
niche [nēsh] *nf (du chien)* kennel; *(de mur)* recess, niche; *(farce)* trick.
nichée [nēshā] *nf* brood, nest.
nicher [nēshā] *vi* to nest; **se ~ dans** *(personne: se blottir)* to snuggle into; *(: se cacher)* to hide in; *(objet)* to lodge itself in.
nichon [nēshóń] *nm (fam)* boob, tit.
nickel [nēkel] *nm* nickel.
niçois, e [nēswá, -wáz] *a* of *ou* from Nice; *(CULIN)* Nicoise.
Nicosie [nēkosē] *n* Nicosia.
nicotine [nēkotēn] *nf* nicotine.
nid [nē] *nm* nest; *(fig: repaire etc)* den, lair; **~ d'abeilles** *(COUTURE, TEXTILE)* honeycomb stitch; **~ de poule** pothole.
nièce [nyes] *nf* niece.
nième [enyem] *a:* **la ~ fois** the nth *ou* umpteenth time.
nier [nyā] *vt* to deny.
nigaud, e [nēgō, -ōd] *nm/f* booby, fool.
Niger [nēzher] *nm:* **le ~** Niger; *(fleuve)* the Niger.
Nigéria [nēzhāryá] *nm ou nf* Nigeria.
nigérian, e [nēzhāryáń, -án] *a* Nigerian ♦ *nm/f:* **N~, e** Nigerian.
nigérien, ne [nēzhāryań, -en] *a* of *ou* from Niger.
Nil [nēl] *nm:* **le ~** the Nile.
n'importe [nańport(ə)] *ad:* **~!** no matter!; **~ qui/quoi/où** anybody/anything/ anywhere; **~ quoi!** *(fam: désapprobation)* what rubbish!; **~ quand** any time; **~ quel/quelle** any; **~ lequel/laquelle** any (one); **~ comment** *(sans soin)* carelessly; **~ comment, il part ce soir** he's leaving tonight in any case.
nippes [nēp] *nfpl (fam)* duds *(US)*, togs *(Brit)*.
nippon, e *ou* **ne** [nēpóń, -on] *a* Japanese.
nique [nēk] *nf:* **faire la ~ à** to thumb one's nose at *(fig)*.
nitouche [nētōōsh] *nf (péj):* **c'est une sainte ~** she looks as if butter wouldn't melt in her mouth.

nitrate [nētrát] *nm* nitrate.
nitrique [nētrēk] *a:* **acide ~** nitric acid.
nitroglycérine [nētroglēsārēn] *nf* nitro-glycerin(e).
niveau, x [nēvō] *nm* level; *(des élèves, études)* standard; **au ~ de** at the level of; *(personne)* on a level with; **de ~ (avec)** level (with); **le ~ de la mer** sea level; **~ (à bulle)** spirit level; **~ (d'eau)** water level; **~ de vie** standard of living.
niveler [nēvlā] *vt* to level.
niveleuse [nēvlœz] *nf (TECH)* grader.
nivellement [nēvelmáń] *nm* leveling *(US)*, levelling *(Brit)*.
nivernais, e [nēverne, -ez] *a* of *ou* from Nevers (and region) ♦ *nm/f:* **N~, e** inhabitant *ou* native of Nevers (and region).
NL *sigle f = nouvelle lune.*
NN *abr (= nouvelle norme) revised standard of hotel classification.*
n° *abr (= numéro)* no.
nobiliaire [nobēlyer] *af voir* **particule.**
noble [nobl(ə)] *a* noble; *(de qualité: métal etc)* precious ♦ *nm/f* noble(man/woman).
noblesse [nobles] *nf (classe sociale)* nobility; *(d'une action etc)* nobleness.
noce [nos] *nf* wedding; *(gens)* wedding party *(ou guests pl)*; **il a épousée en secondes ~s** she was his second wife; **faire la ~** *(fam)* to go on a binge; **~s d'or/d'argent/de diamant** golden/silver/diamond wedding.
nocif, ive [nosēf, -ēv] *a* harmful, noxious.
noctambule [noktáńbül] *nm* night owl.
nocturne [noktürn(ə)] *a* nocturnal ♦ *nf (SPORT)* floodlit fixture; *(d'un magasin)* late opening.
Noël [noel] *nm* Christmas; **la (fête de) ~** Christmas time.
nœud [nœ] *nm (de corde, du bois, NAVIG)* knot; *(ruban)* bow; *(fig: liens)* bond, tie; *(fig: d'une question)* crux; *(THÉÂTRE etc):* **le ~ de l'action** the web of events; **~ coulant** noose; **~ gordien** Gordian knot; **~ papillon** bow tie.
noie [nwá] *etc vb voir* **noyer.**
noir, e [nwár] *a* black; *(obscur, sombre)* dark ♦ *nm/f* black man/woman, Negro/Negro woman ♦ *nm:* **dans le ~** in the dark ♦ *nf (MUS)* quarter note *(US)*, crotchet *(Brit)*; **il fait ~** it is dark; **au ~** *ad (acheter, vendre)* on the black market; **travail au ~** moonlight-ing.
noirâtre [nwárâtr(ə)] *a (teinte)* blackish.
noirceur [nwársœr] *nf* blackness; darkness.
noircir [nwársēr] *vt, vi* to blacken.
noise [nwáz] *nf:* **chercher ~ à** to try and pick a quarrel with.
noisetier [nwáztyā] *nm* hazel (tree).
noisette [nwázet] *nf* hazelnut; *(morceau: de beurre etc)* small knob ♦ *a (yeux)* hazel.
noix [nwá] *nf* walnut; *(fam)* twit; *(CULIN):* **une ~ de beurre** a lump of butter; **à la ~** *(fam)* worthless; **~ de cajou** cashew nut; **~ de coco** coconut; **~ muscade** nutmeg; **~ de veau** *(CULIN)* round fillet of veal.
nom [nóń] *nm* name; *(LING)* noun; **connaître qn de ~** to know sb by name; **au ~ de** in the name of; **~ d'une pipe** *ou* **d'un chien!** *(fam)* for goodness' sake!; **~ de Dieu!** *(fam!)* my

God!; ~ **commun/propre** common/proper
noun; ~ **composé** (*LING*) compound noun; ~
déposé trade name; ~ **d'emprunt** assumed
name; ~ **de famille** surname; ~ **de fichier**
file name; ~ **de jeune fille** maiden name.
nomade |nomád| *a* nomadic ♦ *nm/f* nomad.
nombre |nóñbr(ə)| *nm* number; **venir en** ~ to
come in large numbers; **depuis** ~ **d'années**
for many years; **ils sont au** ~ **de 3** there are
3 of them; **au** ~ **de mes amis** among my
friends; **sans** ~ countless; **(bon)** ~ **de**
(*beaucoup, plusieurs*) a (large) number of; ~
premier/entier prime/whole number.
nombreux, euse |nóñbrœ̄, -œ̄z| *a* many,
numerous; (*avec nom sg: foule etc*) large;
peu ~ few; small; **de** ~ **cas** many cases.
nombril |nóñbrē| *nm* navel.
nomenclature |nomáñklátür| *nf* wordlist; list
of items.
nominal, e, aux |nomēnál, -ō| *a* nominal;
(*appel, liste*) of names.
nominatif, ive |nomēnátēf, -ēv| *nm* (*LING*)
nominative ♦ *a*: **liste** ~**ive** list of names;
carte ~**ive** calling card; **titre** ~ registered
name.
nomination |nomēnásyóñ| *nf* nomination.
nommément |nomámáñ| *ad* (*désigner*) by
name.
nommer |nomā| *vt* (*baptiser*) to name, give a
name to; (*qualifier*) to call; (*mentionner*) to
name, give the name of; (*élire*) to appoint,
nominate; **se** ~: **il se nomme Pascal** his
name's Pascal, he's called Pascal.
non |nóñ| *ad* (*réponse*) no; (*suivi d'un
adjectif, adverbe*) not; **Paul est venu,** ~**?**
Paul came, didn't he?; **répondre** *ou* **dire que**
~ to say no; ~ **pas que** not that; ~ **plus:
moi** ~ **plus** neither do I, I don't either; **je
préférerais que** ~ I would prefer not; **il se
trouve que** ~ perhaps not; **je pense que** ~ I
don't think so; ~ **mais!** well really!; ~ **mais
des fois!** you must be joking!; ~ **alcoolisé**
non-alcoholic; ~ **loin/seulement** not far/only.
nonagénaire |nonázhānœr| *nm/f* nonagenarian.
non-agression |nonágrãsyóñ| *nf*: **pacte de** ~
non-aggression pact.
non-aligné, e |nonálēnyā| *a* nonaligned.
nonante |nonáñt| *num* (*Belgique, Suisse*) nine-
ty.
nonce |nóñs| *nm* (*REL*) nuncio.
nonchalance |nóñsháláñs| *nf* nonchalance,
casualness.
nonchalant, e |nóñshálāñ, -áñt| *a* nonchalant,
casual.
non-conformiste |nóñkóñformēst(ə)| *a, nm/f*
nonconformist.
non-croyant, e |nóñkrwáyáñ, -áñt| *nm/f* (*REL*)
nonbeliever.
non(-)engagé, e |nonáñgázhā| *a* nonaligned.
non-fumeur |nóñfümœr| *nm* nonsmoker.
non-ingérence |nonáñzhāráñs| *nf* noninterfer-
ence.
non-inscrit, e |nonáñskrē, -ēt| *nm/f* (*POL*:
député) independent.
non-intervention |nonáñtervấñsyóñ| *nf* non-
intervention.
non-lieu |nóñlyœ̄| *nm*: **il y a eu** ~ the case
was dismissed.
nonne |non| *nf* nun.

nonobstant |nonopstáñ| *prép* notwithstanding.
non-paiement |nóñpemáñ| *nm* nonpayment.
non-prolifération |nóñprolēfârâsyóñ| *nf* non-
proliferation.
non-résident |nóñrāsēdáñ| *nm* (*ÉCON*) non-
resident.
non-retour |nóñrətōōr| *nm*: **point de** ~ point
of no return.
non-sens |nóñsáñs| *nm* absurdity.
non-syndiqué, e |nóñsañdēkā| *nm/f* nonunion
member.
non-violent, e |nóñvyoláñ, -áñt| *a* nonviolent.
nord |nor| *nm* North ♦ *a* northern; north; **au**
~ (*situation*) in the north; (*direction*) to the
north; **au** ~ **de** north of, to the north of; **perdre le** ~ to lose the place (*fig*).
nord-africain, e |noráfrēkañ, -en| *a* North
African ♦ *nm/f*: **Nord-Africain, e** North
African.
nord-américain, e |norámārēkañ, -en| *a* North
American ♦ *nm/f*: **Nord-Américain, e** North
American.
nord-coréen, ne |norkorāañ, -en| *a* North Ko-
rean ♦ *nm/f*: **Nord-Coréen, ne** North Korean.
nord-est |norest| *nm* northeast.
nordique |nordēk| *a* (*pays, race*) Nordic;
(*langues*) Scandinavian, Nordic ♦ *nm/f*: **N**~
Scandinavian.
nord-ouest |norwest| *nm* northwest.
nord-vietnamien, ne |norvyetnámyañ, -en| *a*
North Vietnamese ♦ *nm/f*: **Nord-Vietnamien,
ne** North Vietnamese.
normal, e, aux |normál, -ō| *a* normal ♦ *nf*: **la**
~**e** the norm, the average.
normalement |normálmáñ| *ad* (*en général*)
normally; (*comme prévu*): ~, **il le fera
demain** he should be doing it tomorrow, he's
supposed to do it tomorrow.
normalien, ne |normályañ, -en| *nm/f student
of École normale supérieure*.
normalisation |normálēzásyóñ| *nf* standardiza-
tion; normalization.
normaliser |normálēzā| *vt* (*COMM, TECH*) to
standardize; (*POL*) to normalize.
normand, e |normáñ, -áñd| *a* (*de Normandie*)
Norman ♦ *nm/f*: **N**~, **e** (*de Normandie*) Norman.
Normandie |normáñdē| *nf*: **la** ~ Normandy.
norme |norm(ə)| *nf* norm; (*TECH*) standard.
Norvège |norvezh| *nf*: **la** ~ Norway.
norvégien, ne |norvāzhyañ, -en| *a* Norwegian
♦ *nm* (*LING*) Norwegian ♦ *nm/f*: **N**~, **ne**
Norwegian.
nos |nō| *dét voir* **notre**.
nostalgie |nostálzhē| *nf* nostalgia.
nostalgique |nostálzhēk| *a* nostalgic.
notabilité |notábēlētā| *nf* notability.
notable |notábl(ə)| *a* notable, noteworthy;
(*marqué*) noticeable, marked ♦ *nm*
prominent citizen.
notablement |notáblǝmáñ| *ad* notably;
(*sensiblement*) noticeably.
notaire |noter| *nm* notary; solicitor.
notamment |notámáñ| *ad* in particular,
among others.
notariat |notáryá| *nm* profession of notary.
notarié, e |notáryā| *a*: **acte** ~ deed drawn up
by a notary.
notation |notâsyóñ| *nf* notation.

note [not] *nf* (*écrite*, *MUS*) note; (*SCOL*) grade; (*facture*) bill; **prendre des** ~**s** to take notes; **prendre** ~ **de** to note; (*par écrit*) to note, write down; **dans la** ~ exactly right; **forcer la** ~ to exaggerate; **une** ~ **de tristesse/de gaieté** a sad/happy note; ~ **de service** memorandum.

noté, e [notā] *a*: **être bien/mal** ~ (*employé etc*) to have a good/bad record.

noter [notā] *vt* (*écrire*) to write down, note; (*remarquer*) to note, notice; (*SCOL*, *ADMIN*: *donner une appréciation*) to mark, give a grade to; **notez bien que ...** (please) note that ....

notice [notēs] *nf* summary, short article; (*brochure*): ~ **explicative** explanatory leaflet, instruction booklet.

notification [notēfēkásyôñ] *nf* notification.

notifier [notēfyā] *vt*: ~ **qch à qn** to notify sb of sth, notify sth to sb.

notion [nōsyóñ] *nf* notion, idea; ~**s** *nfpl* (*rudiments*) rudiments.

notoire [notwár] *a* widely known; (*en mal*) notorious; **le fait est** ~ the fact is common knowledge.

notoriété [notoryātā] *nf*: **c'est de** ~ **publique** it's common knowledge.

notre, nos [notr(ə), nō] *dét* our.

nôtre [nōtr(ə)] *pronom*: **le/la** ~ ours; **les** ~**s** ours; (*alliés etc*) our own people; **soyez des** ~**s** join us ♦ *a* ours.

nouer [nwā] *vt* to tie, knot; (*fig: alliance etc*) to strike up; ~ **la conversation** to start a conversation; **se** ~ *vi*: **c'est là où l'intrigue se noue** it's at that point that the strands of the plot come together; **ma gorge se noua** a lump came to my throat.

noueux, euse [nwœ̄, -œ̄z] *a* gnarled.

nougat [nōōgá] *nm* nougat.

nouille [nōōy] *nf* (*pâtes*): ~**s** noodles; pasta *sg*; (*fam*) noodle, fathead.

nounou [nōōnōō] *nf* nanny.

nounours [nōōnōōrs] *nm* teddy (bear).

nourri, e [nōōrē] *a* (*feu etc*) sustained.

nourrice [nōōrēs] *nf* ≈ nanny; (*autrefois*) wet nurse.

nourrir [nōōrēr] *vt* to feed; (*fig: espoir*) to harbor (*US*), harbour (*Brit*), nurse; **logé nourri** with room and board; ~ **au sein** to breast-feed; **se** ~ **de légumes/rêves** to live on vegetables/dreams.

nourrissant, e [nōōrēsáñ, -áñt] *a* nourishing, nutritious.

nourrisson [nōōrēsóñ] *nm* (*unweaned*) infant.

nourriture [nōōrētür] *nf* food.

nous [nōō] *pronom* (*sujet*) we; (*objet*) us.

nous-mêmes [nōōmem] *pronom* ourselves.

nouveau (**nouvel**, **elle**, **x** [nōōvō, -el] *a* new; (*original*) novel ♦ *nm/f* new pupil (*ou* employee) ♦ *nm*: **il y a du** ~ there's something new ♦ *nf* (piece of) news *sg*; (*LITTÉRATURE*) short story; **nouvelles** *nfpl* (*PRESSE*, *TV*) news; **de** ~, **à** ~ again; **je suis sans nouvelles de lui** I haven't heard from him; **Nouvel An** New Year; ~ **riche** nouveau riche; ~ **venu**, **nouvelle venue** newcomer; ~**x mariés** newlyweds; **nouvelle vague** new wave.

nouveau-né, e [nōōvōnā] *nm/f* newborn (baby).

nouveauté [nōōvōtā] *nf* novelty; (*chose nouvelle*) innovation, something new; (*COMM*) new film (*ou* book *ou* creation *etc*).

nouvel *am*, **nouvelle** *af*, *nf* [nōōvel] *voir* nouveau.

Nouvelle-Angleterre [nōōveláñglətər] *nf*: **la** ~ New England.

Nouvelle-Calédonie [nōōvelkálādonē] *nf*: **la** ~ New Caledonia.

Nouvelle-Écosse [nōōvelākos] *nf*: **la** ~ Nova Scotia.

Nouvelle-Galles du Sud [nōōvelgáldüsüd] *nf*: **la** ~ New South Wales.

Nouvelle-Guinée [nōōvelgēnā] *nf*: **la** ~ New Guinea.

nouvellement [nōōvelmáñ] *ad* (*arrivé etc*) recently, newly.

Nouvelle-Orléans [nōōvelorlāáñ] *nf*: **la** ~ New Orleans.

Nouvelles-Hébrides [nōōvelsābrēd] *nfpl*: **les** ~ the New Hebrides.

Nouvelle-Zélande [nōōvelzāláñd] *nf*: **la** ~ New Zealand.

nouvelliste [nōōvālēst(ə)] *nm/f* editor *ou* writer of short stories.

novateur, trice [novátœr, -trēs] *a* innovative ♦ *nm/f* innovator.

novembre [novâñbr(ə)] *nm* November; *voir aussi* juillet.

novice [novēs] *a* inexperienced ♦ *nm/f* novice.

noviciat [novēsyá] *nm* (*REL*) novitiate.

noyade [nwáyád] *nf* drowning *q*.

noyau, x [nwáyō] *nm* (*de fruit*) pit (*US*), stone; (*BIO, PHYSIQUE*) nucleus; (*ÉLEC, GÉO, fig: centre*) core; (*fig: d'artistes etc*) group; (*: de résistants etc*) cell.

noyautage [nwáyōtázh] *nm* (*POL*) infiltration.

noyauter [nwáyōtā] *vt* (*POL*) to infiltrate.

noyé, e [nwáyā] *nm/f* drowning (*ou* drowned) man/woman ♦ *a* (*fig: dépassé*) out of one's depth.

noyer [nwáyā] *nm* walnut (tree); (*bois*) walnut ♦ *vt* to drown; (*fig*) to flood; to submerge; (*AUTO*: *moteur*) to flood; **se** ~ to be drowned, drown; (*suicide*) to drown o.s; ~ **son chagrin** to drown one's sorrows; ~ **le poisson** to duck the issue.

NSP *sigle m* (*REL*) = *Notre Saint Père*; (*dans les sondages*: = *ne sais pas*) don't know.

NT *sigle m* (= *Nouveau Testament*) NT.

NU *sigle fpl* (= *Nations Unies*) UN.

nu, e [nü] *a* naked; (*membres*) naked, bare; (*chambre, fil, plaine*) bare ♦ *nm* (*ART*) nude; **le** ~ **intégral** total nudity; **à mains** ~**es** with one's bare hands; **se mettre** ~ to strip; **mettre à** ~ to bare.

nuage [nüázh] *nm* cloud; **être dans les** ~**s** (*distrait*) to have one's head in the clouds; ~ **de lait** drop of milk.

nuageux, euse [nüázhœ̄, -œ̄z] *a* cloudy.

nuance [nüáñs] *nf* (*de couleur, sens*) shade; **il y a une** ~ (**entre**) there's a slight difference (between); **une** ~ **de tristesse** a tinge of sadness.

nuancé, e [nüáñsā] *a* (*opinion*) finely-shaded, subtly differing; **être** ~ **dans ses opinions** to have finely-shaded opinions.

nuancer [nüáñsā] *vt* (*pensée, opinion*) to qualify.

nubile [nübēl] *a* nubile.
nucléaire [nüklāer] *a* nuclear ♦ *nm* nuclear power.
nudisme [nüdēsm(ə)] *nm* nudism.
nudiste [nüdēst(ə)] *a*, *nm/f* nudist.
nudité [nüdētā] *nf* (*voir nu*) nudity, nakedness; bareness.
nuée [nüā] *nf*: **une ~ de** a cloud *ou* host *ou* swarm of.
nues [nü] *nfpl*: **tomber des ~** to be taken aback; **porter qn aux ~** to praise sb to the skies.
nui [nüē] *pp de* **nuire**.
nuire [nüēr] *vi* to be harmful; **~ à** to harm, do damage to.
nuisance [nüēzáńs] *nf* nuisance; **~s** *nfpl* pollution *sg*.
nuisible [nüēzēbl(ə)] *a* harmful; **(animal) ~** pest.
nuisis [nüēzē] *etc vb voir* **nuire**.
nuit [nüē] *nf* night; **payer sa ~** to pay for one's overnight accommodations (*US*) *ou* accommodation (*Brit*); **il fait ~** it's dark; **cette ~** (*hier*) last night; (*aujourd'hui*) tonight; **de ~** (*vol, service*) night *cpd*; **~ blanche** sleepless night; **~ de noces** wedding night; **~ de Noël** Christmas Eve.
nuitamment [nüētámáń] *ad* by night.
nuitées [nüētā] *nfpl* overnight stays, beds occupied (*in statistics*).
nul, nulle [nül] *a* (*aucun*) no; (*minime*) nil, nonexistent; (*non valable*) null; (*péj*) useless, hopeless ♦ *pronom* none, no one; **résultat ~**, **match ~** draw; **nulle part** *ad* nowhere.
nullement [nülmáń] *ad* by no means.
nullité [nülētā] *nf* nullity; (*péj*) hopelessness; (*: personne*) hopeless individual, nonentity.
numéraire [nümārer] *nm* cash; metal currency.
numéral, e, aux [nümārál, -ō] *a* numeral.
numérateur [nümārátœr] *nm* numerator.
numération [nümārásyóń] *nf*: **~ décimale/binaire** decimal/binary notation.
numérique [nümārēk] *a* numerical; (*INFORM*) digital.
numériquement [nümārēkmáń] *ad* numerically.
numériser [nümārēzā] *vt* (*INFORM*) to digitize.
numéro [nümārō] *nm* number; (*spectacle*) act, turn; **faire** *ou* **composer un ~** to dial a number; **~ d'identification personnel** personal identification number (PIN); **~ d'immatriculation** *ou* **minéralogique** *ou* **de police** license (*US*) *ou* registration (*Brit*) number; **~ de téléphone** (tele)phone number; **~ vert** ≈ toll-free number (*US*), ≈ Freefone ® number (*Brit*).
numérotage [nümārotázh] *nm* numbering.
numérotation [nümārotásyóń] *nf* numeration.
numéroter [nümārotā] *vt* to number.
numerus clausus [nümārüsklōzüs] *nm inv* restriction *ou* limitation of numbers.
numismate [nümēsmát] *nm/f* numismatist, coin collector.
nu-pieds [nüpyā] *nm inv* sandal ♦ *a inv* barefoot.
nuptial, e, aux [nüpsyál, -ō] *a* nuptial; wedding *cpd*.
nuptialité [nüpsyálētā] *nf*: **taux de ~** marriage rate.
nuque [nük] *nf* nape of the neck.
nu-tête [nütet] *a inv* bareheaded.
nutritif, ive [nütrētēf, -ēv] *a* nutritional; (*aliment*) nutritious, nourishing.
nutrition [nütrēsyóń] *nf* nutrition.
nutritionnel, le [nütrēsyonel] *a* nutritional.
nutritionniste [nütrēsyonēst(ə)] *nm/f* nutritionist.
nylon [nēlóń] *nm* nylon.
nymphomane [nańfomán] *a*, *nf* nymphomaniac.

O

O, o [ō] *nm inv* O, o ♦ *abr* (= *ouest*) W; **O comme Oscar** O for Oboe.
OAS *sigle f* (= *Organisation de l'armée secrète*) *organization opposed to Algerian independence (1961-63)*.
oasis [oázēs] *nf* oasis (*pl* oases).
obédience [obādyáńs] *nf* allegiance.
obéir [obāēr] *vi* to obey; **~ à** to obey; (*suj: moteur, véhicule*) to respond to.
obéissance [obāēsáńs] *nf* obedience.
obéissant, e [obāēsáń, -áńt] *a* obedient.
obélisque [obālēsk(ə)] *nm* obelisk.
obèse [obez] *a* obese.
obésité [obāzētā] *nf* obesity.
objecter [obzhektā] *vt* (*prétexter*) to plead, put forward as an excuse; **~ qch à** (*argument*) to put forward sth against; **~ (à qn) que** to object (to sb) that.
objecteur [obzhektœr] *nm*: **~ de conscience** conscientious objector.
objectif, ive [obzhektēf, -ēv] *a* objective ♦ *nm* (*OPTIQUE, PHOTO*) lens *sg*; (*MIL, fig*) objective; **~ grand angulaire/à focale variable** wide-angle/zoom lens.
objection [obzheksyóń] *nf* objection; **~ de conscience** conscientious objection.
objectivement [obzhektēvmáń] *ad* objectively.
objectivité [obzhektēvētā] *nf* objectivity.
objet [obzhe] *nm* (*chose*) object; (*d'une discussion, recherche*) subject; **être** *ou* **faire l'~ de** (*discussion*) to be the subject of; (*soins*) to be given *ou* shown; **sans ~** *a* purposeless; (*sans fondement*) groundless; **~ d'art** objet d'art; **~s personnels** personal items; **~s de toilette** toiletries; **~s trouvés** lost-and-found *sg* (*US*), lost property *sg* (*Brit*).
objurgations [obzhürgásyóń] *nfpl* objurgations; (*prières*) entreaties.
obligataire [oblēgáter] *a* bond *cpd* ♦ *nm/f* bondholder, debenture holder.
obligation [oblēgásyóń] *nf* obligation; (*gén pl: devoir*) duty; (*COMM*) bond, debenture; **sans ~ d'achat** with no obligation (to buy); **être dans l'~ de faire** to be obliged to do; **avoir l'~ de faire** to be under an obligation to do; **~s familiales** family obligations *ou* re-

sponsibilities; ~**s militaires** military obligations *ou* duties.

obligatoire [oblēgátwàr] *a* compulsory, obligatory.

obligatoirement [oblēgátwàrmáň] *ad* compulsorily; (*fatalement*) necessarily.

obligé, e [oblēzhā] *a* (*redevable*): **être très ~ à qn** to be most obliged to sb; (*contraint*): **je suis (bien) ~ (de le faire)** I have to (do it); (*nécessaire: conséquence*) necessary; **c'est ~!** it's inevitable.

obligeamment [oblēzhámáň] *ad* obligingly.

obligeance [oblēzhàns] *nf*: **avoir l'~ de** to be kind *ou* good enough to.

obligeant, e [oblēzhàn, -àňt] *a* obliging; kind.

obliger [oblēzhā] *vt* (*contraindre*): **~ qn à faire** to force *ou* oblige sb to do; (*JUR: engager*) to bind; (*rendre service à*) to oblige.

oblique [oblēk] *a* oblique; **regard ~** sidelong glance; **en ~** *ad* diagonally.

obliquer [oblēkā] *vi*: **~ vers** to turn off towards.

oblitération [oblētárásyóň] *nf* canceling q (*US*), cancelling q (*Brit*), cancellation; obstruction.

oblitérer [oblētárā] *vt* (*timbre-poste*) to cancel; (*MÉD: canal, vaisseau*) to obstruct.

oblong, oblongue [oblóň, oblóňg] *a* oblong.

obnubiler [obnübēlā] *vt* to obsess.

obole [obol] *nf* offering.

obscène [opsen] *a* obscene.

obscénité [opsánētā] *nf* obscenity.

obscur, e [opskür] *a* (*sombre*) dark; (*fig: raisons*) obscure; (*: sentiment, malaise*) vague; (*: personne, vie*) humble, lowly.

obscurcir [opskürsēr] *vt* to darken; (*fig*) to obscure; **s'~** *vi* to grow dark.

obscurité [opskürētā] *nf* darkness; **dans l'~** in the dark, in darkness; (*anonymat, médiocrité*) in obscurity.

obsédant, e [opsādáň, -àňt] *a* obsessive.

obsédé, e [opsādā] *nm/f* fanatic; ~**(e) sexuel(le)** sex maniac.

obséder [opsādā] *vt* to obsess, haunt.

obsèques [opsek] *nfpl* funeral *sg*.

obséquieux, euse [opsākyœ̄, -ēz] *a* obsequious.

observance [opservàns] *nf* observance.

observateur, trice [opservátœr, -trēs] *a* observant, perceptive ♦ *nm/f* observer.

observation [opservásyóň] *nf* observation; (*d'un règlement etc*) observance; (*commentaire*) observation, remark; (*reproche*) reproof; **en ~** (*MÉD*) under observation.

observatoire [opservátwár] *nm* observatory; (*lieu élevé*) observation post, vantage point.

observer [opservā] *vt* (*regarder*) to observe, watch; (*examiner*) to examine; (*scientifiquement, aussi: règlement, jeûne etc*) to observe; (*surveiller*) to watch; (*remarquer*) to observe, notice; **faire ~ qch à qn** (*dire*) to point out sth to sb; **s'~** (*se surveiller*) to keep a check on o.s.

obsession [opsāsyóň] *nf* obsession; **avoir l'~ de** to have an obsession with.

obsessionnel, le [opsāsyonel] *a* obsessive.

obsolescent, e [opsolāsáň, -áňt] *a* obsolescent.

obstacle [opstákl(ə)] *nm* obstacle; (*ÉQUITA-*

TION) jump, hurdle; **faire ~ à** (*lumière*) to block out; (*projet*) to hinder, put obstacles in the path of; ~**s antichars** tank defenses (*US*) *ou* defences (*Brit*).

obstétricien, ne [obstātrēsyaň, -en] *nm/f* obstetrician.

obstétrique [opstātrēk] *nf* obstetrics *sg*.

obstination [opstēnásyóň] *nf* obstinacy.

obstiné, e [opstēnā] *a* obstinate.

obstinément [opstēnāmáň] *ad* obstinately.

obstiner [opstēnā]: **s'~** *vi* to insist, dig one's heels in; **s'~ à faire** to persist (obstinately) in doing; **s'~ sur qch** to keep working at sth, labor away at sth.

obstruction [opstrüksyóň] *nf* obstruction, blockage; (*SPORT*) obstruction; **faire de l'~** (*fig*) to be obstructive.

obstruer [opstrüā] *vt* to block, obstruct; **s'~** *vi* to become blocked.

obtempérer [optáňpārā] *vi* to obey; **~ à** to obey, comply with.

obtenir [optənēr] *vt* to obtain, get; (*total*) to arrive at, reach; (*résultat*) to achieve, obtain; **~ de pouvoir faire** to obtain permission to do; **~ qch à qn** to obtain sth for sb; **~ de qn qu'il fasse** to get sb to agree to do(ing).

obtention [optáňsyóň] *nf* obtaining.

obtenu, e [opt(ə)nü] *pp de* **obtenir**.

obtiendrai [optyaňdrā], **obtiens** [optyaň], **obtint** [optaň] *etc vb voir* **obtenir**.

obturateur [optürátœr] *nm* (*PHOTO*) shutter; **~ à rideau** focal plane shutter.

obturation [optürásyóň] *nf* closing (up); ~ **(dentaire)** filling; **vitesse d'~** (*PHOTO*) shutter speed.

obturer [optürā] *vt* to close (up); (*dent*) to fill.

obtus, e [optü, -üz] *a* obtuse.

obus [obü] *nm* shell; ~ **explosif** high-explosive shell; ~ **incendiaire** incendiary device, fire bomb.

obvier [obvyā]: **~ à** *vt* to obviate.

OC *sigle fpl* (= *ondes courtes*) SW.

occasion [okázyóň] *nf* (*aubaine, possibilité*) opportunity; (*circonstance*) occasion; (*COMM: article non neuf*) secondhand buy; (*: acquisition avantageuse*) bargain; **à plusieurs ~s** on several occasions; **à la première ~** at the first *ou* earliest opportunity; **avoir l'~ de faire** to have the opportunity to do; **être l'~ de** to occasion, give rise to; **à l'~** *ad* sometimes, on occasions; (*un jour*) sometime; **à l'~ de** on the occasion of; **d'~** *a, ad* secondhand.

occasionnel, le [okázyonel] *a* (*fortuit*) chance *cpd*; (*non régulier*) occasional; (*: travail*) casual.

occasionner [okázyonā] *vt* to cause, bring about; **~ qch à qn** to cause sb sth.

occident [oksēdáň] *nm*: **l'O~** the West.

occidental, e, aux [oksēdáňtál, -ō] *a* western; (*POL*) Western ♦ *nm/f* Westerner.

occidentaliser [oksēdáňtálēzā] *vt* (*coutumes, mœurs*) to westernize.

occiput [oksēpüt] *nm* back of the head, occiput.

occire [oksēr] *vt* to slay.

occitan, e [oksētáň, -áň] *a* of the langue d'oc, of Provençal French.

occlusion [oklüzyôñ] *nf:* ~ **intestinale** obstruction of the bowel.

occulte [okült(ə)] *a* occult, supernatural.

occulter [okültā] *vt* (*fig*) to overshadow.

occupant, e [oküpáñ, -áñt] *a* occupying ♦ *nm/f* (*d'un appartement*) occupier, occupant; (*d'un véhicule*) occupant ♦ *nm* (*MIL*) occupying forces *pl*; (*POL: d'usine etc*) occupier.

occupation [oküpâsyôñ] *nf* occupation; **l'O~** the Occupation (of France).

occupationnel, le [oküpâsyonel] *a:* **thérapie** ~**le** occupational therapy.

occupé, e [oküpā] *a* (*MIL, POL*) occupied; (*personne: affairé, pris*) busy; (*esprit: absorbé*) occupied; (*place, sièges*) taken; (*toilettes, ligne*) engaged.

occuper [oküpā] *vt* to occupy; (*poste, fonction*) to hold; (*main-d'œuvre*) to employ; **s'~** (**à qch**) to occupy o.s. (with sth); **s'~ de** (*être responsable de*) to be in charge of; (*se charger de: affaire*) to take charge of, deal with; (*: clients etc*) to attend to; (*s'intéresser à, pratiquer: politique etc*) to be involved in; **ça occupe trop de place** it takes up too much room.

occurrence [oküráñs] *nf:* **en l'~** in this case.

OCDE *sigle f* (= *Organisation de coopération et de développement économique*) OECD.

océan [osáâñ] *nm* ocean; **l'~ Indien** the Indian Ocean.

Océanie [osáânē] *nf:* **l'~** Oceania, South Sea Islands.

océanique [osáânēk] *a* oceanic.

océanographe [osáânográf] *nm/f* oceanographer.

océanographie [osáânográfē] *nf* oceanography.

océanologie [osáânolozhē] *nf* oceanology.

ocelot [oslō] *nm* (*ZOOL*) ocelot; (*fourrure*) ocelot fur.

ocre [okr(ə)] *a inv* ocher (*US*), ochre (*Brit*).

octane [oktán] *nm* octane.

octante [oktáñt] *num* (*Belgique, Suisse*) eighty.

octave [oktáv] *nf* octave.

octet [okte] *nm* byte.

octobre [oktobr(ə)] *nm* October; *voir aussi* **juillet.**

octogénaire [oktozhäner] *a, nm/f* octogenarian.

octogonal, e, aux [oktogonál, -ō] *a* octagonal.

octogone [oktogon] *nm* octagon.

octroi [oktrwá] *nm* granting.

octroyer [oktrwáyā] *vt:* ~ **qch à qn** to grant sth to sb, grant sb sth.

oculaire [oküler] *a* ocular, eye *cpd* ♦ *nm* (*de microscope*) eyepiece.

oculiste [okülēst(ə)] *nm/f* eye specialist, oculist.

ode [od] *nf* ode.

odeur [odœr] *nf* smell.

odieusement [odyœzmáñ] *ad* odiously.

odieux, euse [odyœ̃, -œ̃z] *a* odious, hateful.

odontologie [odôñtolozhē] *nf* odontology.

odorant, e [odoráñ, -áñt] *a* sweet-smelling, fragrant.

odorat [odorá] *nm* (sense of) smell; **avoir l'~ fin** to have a keen sense of smell.

odoriférant, e [odorēfáráñ, -áñt] *a* sweet-smelling, fragrant.

odyssée [odēsā] *nf* odyssey.

OEA *sigle f* (= *Organisation des états américains*) OAS.

œcuménique [ākümánēk] *a* ecumenical.

œdème [ādem] *nm* edema (*US*), oedema (*Brit*).

œil [œy], *pl* **yeux** [yœ̃] *nm* eye; **avoir un** ~ **poché** *ou* **au beurre noir** to have a black eye; **à l'~** (*fam*) for free; **à l'~ nu** with the naked eye; **tenir qn à l'~** to keep an eye *ou* a watch on sb; **avoir l'~ à** to keep an eye on; **faire de l'~ à qn** to make eyes at sb; **voir qch d'un bon/mauvais** ~ to view sth in a favorable/an unfavorable light; **à l'~ vif** with a lively expression; **à mes/ses yeux** in my/his eyes; **de ses propres yeux** with his own eyes; **fermer les yeux (sur)** (*fig*) to shut one's eyes (to); **les yeux fermés** (*aussi fig*) with one's eyes shut; **fermer l'~** to get a moment's sleep; ~ **pour** ~, **dent pour dent** an eye for an eye, a tooth for a tooth; **pour les beaux yeux de qn** (*fig*) for love of sb; ~ **de verre** glass eye.

œil-de-bœuf, *pl* **œils-de-bœuf** [œydəbœf] *nm* bull's-eye (window).

œillade [œyád] *nf:* **lancer une** ~ **à qn** to wink at sb, give sb a wink; **faire des** ~**s à** to make eyes at.

œillères [œyer] *nfpl* blinders (*US*), blinkers (*Brit*); **avoir des** ~ (*fig*) to wear blinders (*US*), be blinkered (*Brit*).

œillet [œye] *nm* (*BOT*) carnation; (*trou*) eyelet.

œnologue [ānolog] *nm/f* wine expert.

œsophage [āzofázh] *nm* esophagus (*US*), oesophagus (*Brit*).

œstrogène [estrozhen] *a* estrogen (*US*), oestrogen (*Brit*).

œuf [œf, *pl* œ̃] *nm* egg; **étouffer dans l'~** to nip in the bud; ~ **à la coque/dur/mollet** boiled/hard-boiled/soft-boiled egg; ~ **au plat/ poché** fried/poached egg; ~**s brouillés** scrambled eggs; ~ **de Pâques** Easter egg; ~ **à repriser** darning egg.

œuvre [œvr(ə)] *nf* (*tâche*) task, undertaking; (*ouvrage achevé, livre, tableau etc*) work; (*ensemble de la production artistique*) works *pl*; (*organisation charitable*) charity ♦ *nm* (*d'un artiste*) works *pl*; (*CONSTR*): **le gros** ~ the shell; ~**s** *nfpl* (*actes*) deeds, works; **être/se mettre à l'**~ to be at/get (down) to work; **mettre en** ~ (*moyens*) to make use of; (*plan, loi, projet etc*) to implement; ~ **d'art** work of art; **bonnes** ~**s** good works *ou* deeds; ~**s de bienfaisance** charitable works.

OFCE *sigle m* (= *Observatoire français des conjonctures économiques*) economic research institute.

offensant, e [ofáñsáñ, -áñt] *a* offensive, insulting.

offense [ofáñs] *nf* (*affront*) insult; (*REL: péché*) transgression, trespass.

offenser [ofáñsā] *vt* to offend, hurt; (*principes, Dieu*) to offend against; **s'~ de** to take offense (*US*) *ou* offence (*Brit*) at.

offensif, ive [ofáñsēf, -ēv] *a* (*armes, guerre*) offensive ♦ *nf* offensive; (*fig: du froid, de l'hiver*) onslaught; **passer à l'offensive** to go into the attack *ou* offensive.

offert, e [ɔfɛr, -ɛrt(ə)] *pp de* **offrir**.

offertoire [ɔfɛrtwár] *nm* offertory.

office [ɔfēs] *nm* (*charge*) office; (*agence*) bureau, agency; (*REL*) service ♦ *nm ou nf* (*pièce*) pantry; **faire ~ de** to act as; to do duty as; **d'~** *ad* automatically; **bons ~s** (*POL*) good offices; **~ du tourisme** tourist bureau.

officialiser [ɔfēsyálēzā] *vt* to make official.

officiel, le [ɔfēsyɛl] *a*, *nm/f* official.

officiellement [ɔfēsyɛlmáń] *ad* officially.

officier [ɔfēsyā] *nm* officer ♦ *vi* (*REL*) to officiate; **~ de l'état-civil** registrar; **~ ministériel** member of the legal profession; **~ de police** ≈ police officer.

officieusement [ɔfēsyœ̄zmáń] *ad* unofficially.

officieux, euse [ɔfēsyœ̄, -œ̄z] *a* unofficial.

officinal, e, aux [ɔfēsēnál, -ō] *a*: **plantes ~es** medicinal plants.

officine [ɔfēsēn] *nf* (*de pharmacie*) dispensary; (*ADMIN*: *pharmacie*) pharmacy; (*gén péj*: *bureau*) agency, office.

offrais [ɔfrɛ] *etc vb voir* **offrir**.

offrande [ɔfráńd] *nf* offering.

offrant [ɔfráń] *nm*: **au plus ~** to the highest bidder.

offre [ɔfr(ə)] *vb voir* **offrir** ♦ *nf* offer; (*aux enchères*) bid; (*ADMIN*: *soumission*) tender; (*ÉCON*): **l'~** supply; **~ d'emploi** job advertised; **"~s d'emploi"** "help wanted" (*US*), "situations vacant" (*Brit*); **~ publique d'achat (OPA)** takeover bid; **~s de service** offer of service.

offrir [ɔfrēr] *vt*: **~ (à qn)** to offer (to sb); (*faire cadeau*) to give to (sb); **s'~** *vi* (*se présenter*: *occasion*, *paysage*) to present itself ♦ *vt* (*se payer*: *vacances*, *voiture*) to treat o.s. to; **~ (à qn) de faire qch** to offer to do sth (for sb); **~ à boire à qn** to offer sb a drink; **s'~ à faire qch** to offer *ou* volunteer to do sth; **s'~ comme guide/en otage** to offer one's services as (a) guide/offer o.s. as (a) hostage; **s'~ aux regards** (*suj*: *personne*) to expose o.s. to the public gaze.

offset [ɔfsɛt] *nm* offset (printing).

offusquer [ɔfüskā] *vt* to offend; **s'~ de** to take offense (*US*) *ou* offence (*Brit*) at, be offended by.

ogive [ɔzhēv] *nf* (*ARCHIT*) diagonal rib; (*d'obus, de missile*) nose cone; **voûte en ~** rib vault; **arc en ~** lancet arch; **~ nucléaire** nuclear warhead.

ogre [ɔgr(ə)] *nm* ogre.

oh [ō] *excl* oh!; **~ la la!** oh (dear)!; **pousser des ~! et des ah!** to gasp with admiration.

oie [wà] *nf* (*ZOOL*) goose (*pl* geese); **~ blanche** (*fig*) young innocent.

oignon [ɔnyóń] *nm* (*CULIN*) onion; (*de tulipe etc*: *bulbe*) bulb; (*MÉD*) bunion; **ce ne sont pas tes ~s** (*fam*) that's none of your business.

oindre [wáńdr(ə)] *vt* to anoint.

oiseau, x [wàzō] *nm* bird; **~ de proie** bird of prey.

oiseau-mouche, *pl* **oiseaux-mouches** [wàzōmōōsh] *nm* hummingbird.

oiseleur [wàzlœr] *nm* bird catcher.

oiselier, ière [wàzəlyā, -ycr] *nm/f* bird seller.

oisellerie [wàzɛlrē] *nf* bird shop.

oiseux, euse [wàzœ̄, -œ̄z] *a* pointless, idle; (*sans valeur, importance*) trivial.

oisif, ive [wàzēf, -ēv] *a* idle ♦ *nm/f* (*péj*) man/lady of leisure.

oisillon [wàzēyóń] *nm* little *ou* baby bird.

oisiveté [wàzēvtā] *nf* idleness.

OIT *sigle f* (= *Organisation internationale du travail*) ILO.

OK [ōke] *excl* OK!, all right!

OL *sigle fpl* (= *ondes longues*) LW.

oléagineux, euse [ɔlāàzhēnœ̄, -œ̄z] *a* oleaginous, oil-producing.

oléiculture [ɔlāēkültür] *nm* olive growing.

oléoduc [ɔlāodük] *nm* (oil) pipeline.

olfactif, ive [ɔlfáktēf, -ēv] *a* olfactory.

olibrius [ɔlēbrēyüs] *nm* oddball.

oligarchie [ɔlēgárshē] *nf* oligarchy.

oligo-élément [ɔlēgoàlāmáń] *nm* trace element.

oligopole [ɔlēgopol] *nm* oligopoly.

olivâtre [ɔlēvâtr(ə)] *a* olive-greenish; (*teint*) sallow.

olive [ɔlēv] *nf* (*BOT*) olive ♦ *a inv* olive (-green).

oliveraie [ɔlēvrɛ] *nf* olive grove.

olivier [ɔlēvyā] *nm* olive (tree); (*bois*) olive (wood).

olographe [ɔlográf] *a*: **testament ~** will written, dated and signed by the testator.

OLP *sigle f* (= *Organisation de libération de la Palestine*) PLO.

olympiade [ɔláńpyád] *nf* (*période*) Olympiad; **les ~s** (*jeux*) the Olympiad *sg*.

olympien, ne [ɔláńpyàn, -cn] *a* Olympian, of Olympian aloofness.

olympique [ɔláńpēk] *a* Olympic.

OM *sigle fpl* (= *ondes moyennes*) MW.

Oman [ɔmáń] *nm*: **l'~, le sultanat d'~** (the Sultanate of) Oman.

ombilical, e, aux [ɔńbēlēkál, -ō] *a* umbilical.

ombrage [ɔńbrázh] *nm* (*ombre*) (leafy) shade; (*fig*): **prendre ~ de** to take umbrage at; **faire *ou* porter ~ à qn** to offend sb.

ombragé, e [ɔńbrázhā] *a* shaded, shady.

ombrageux, euse [ɔńbrázhœ̄, -œ̄z] *a* (*cheval*) skittish, nervous; (*personne*) touchy, easily offended.

ombre [ɔńbr(ə)] *nf* (*espace non ensoleillé*) shade; (*ombre portée, tache*) shadow; **à l'~** in the shade; (*fam*: *en prison*) behind bars; **à l'~ de** in the shade of; (*tout près de, fig*) in the shadow of; **tu me fais de l'~** you're in my light; **ça nous donne de l'~** it gives us (some) shade; **il n'y a pas l'~ d'un doute** there's not the shadow of a doubt; **dans l'~** in the shade; **vivre dans l'~** (*fig*) to live in obscurity; **laisser dans l'~** (*fig*) to leave in the dark; **~ à paupières** eyeshadow; **~ portée** shadow; **~s chinoises** (*spectacle*) shadow show *sg*.

ombrelle [ɔńbrɛl] *nf* parasol, sunshade.

ombrer [ɔńbrā] *vt* to shade.

omelette [ɔmlct] *nf* omelette; **~ baveuse** runny omelette; **~ au fromage/au jambon** cheese/ham omelette; **~ aux herbes** omelette with herbs; **~ norvégienne** baked Alaska.

omettre [ɔmctr(ə)] *vt* to omit, leave out; **~ de faire** to fail *ou* omit to do.

omis, e |omē. -ēz| *pp de* **omettre.**

omission |omēsyón| *nf* omission.

omnibus |omnēbüs| *nm* slow *ou* local train.

omnipotent, e |omnēpotán, -ánt| *a* omnipotent.

omnipraticien, ne |omnēprátēsyaṅ, -en| *nm/f* (*MÉD*) general practitioner.

omniprésent, e |omnēprāzáṅ, -áṅt| *a* omnipresent.

omniscient, e |omnēsyáṅ, -áṅt| *a* omniscient.

omnisports |omnēspor| *a inv* (*club*) general sports *cpd*; (*salle*) multi-purpose *cpd*; (*terrain*) all-purpose *cpd*.

omnium |omnyom| *nm* (*COMM*) corporation; (*CYCLISME*) mixed race (*US*), omnium (*Brit*); (*COURSES*) open handicap.

omnivore |omnēvor| *a* omnivorous.

omoplate |omoplát| *nf* shoulder blade.

OMS *sigle f* (= *Organisation mondiale de la santé*) WHO.

on |óṅ| *pronom* (*indéterminé*): ~ **peut le faire ainsi** you *ou* one can do it like this, it can be done like this; (*quelqu'un*): ~ **les a attaqués** they were attacked; (*nous*): ~ **va y aller demain** we're going tomorrow; (*les gens*): **autrefois,** ~ **croyait aux fantômes** they used to believe in ghosts years ago; (*ironiquement, affectueusement*): **alors,** ~ **se promène?** off for a stroll then, are we?; ~ **y va!** let's go!; ~ **y va?** are we going?; ~ **vous demande au téléphone** there's a phone call for you, there's somebody on the phone for you; ~ **ne peut plus** *ad*: ~ **ne peut plus stupide** as stupid as can be.

once |óṅs| *nf*: **une** ~ **de** an ounce of.

oncle |óṅkl(ə)| *nm* uncle.

onction |óṅksyóṅ| *nf voir* **extrême-onction.**

onctueux, euse |óṅktüœ̄. -ēz| *a* creamy, smooth; (*fig*) smooth, unctuous.

onde |óṅd| *nf* (*PHYSIQUE*) wave; **sur l'**~ on the waters; **sur les** ~**s** on the radio; **mettre en** ~**s** to produce for the radio; ~ **de choc** shock wave; ~**s courtes (OC)** short wave *sg*; **petites** ~**s (PO),** ~**s moyennes (OM)** medium wave *sg*; **grandes** ~**s (GO),** ~**s longues (OL)** long wave *sg*; ~**s sonores** sound waves.

ondée |óṅdā| *nf* shower.

on-dit |óṅdē| *nm inv* rumor (*US*), rumour (*Brit*).

ondoyer |óṅdwáyā| *vi* to ripple, wave ♦ *vt* (*REL*) to baptize (*in an emergency*).

ondulant, e |óṅdülāṅ, -áṅt| *a* (*démarche*) swaying; (*ligne*) undulating.

ondulation |óṅdülásyóṅ| *nf* undulation; wave.

ondulé, e |óṅdülā| *a* undulating; wavy.

onduler |óṅdülā| *vi* to undulate; (*cheveux*) to wave.

onéreux, euse |onārœ̄. -ēz| *a* costly; **à titre** ~ in return for payment.

ONF *sigle m* (= *Office national des forêts*) ≈ National Forest Service (*US*), ≈ Forestry Commission (*Brit*).

ongle |óṅgl(ə)| *nm* (*ANAT*) nail; **manger** *ou* **ronger ses** ~**s** to bite one's nails; **se faire les** ~**s** to do one's nails.

onglet |óṅgle| *nm* (*rainure*) (thumbnail) groove; (*bande de papier*) tab.

onguent |óṅgáṅ| *nm* ointment.

onirique |onērēk| *a* dreamlike, dream *cpd*.

onirisme |onērēsm(ə)| *nm* dreams *pl*.

onomatopée |onomátopā| *nf* onomatopoeia.

ont |óṅ| *vb voir* **avoir.**

ontarien, ne |óṅtáryaṅ, -en| *a* Ontarian.

ONU |onü| *sigle f* (= *Organisation des Nations Unies*) UN(O).

onusien, ne |onüzyaṅ, -en| *a* of the UN(O), of the United Nations (Organization).

onyx |onēks| *nm* onyx.

onze |óṅz| *num* eleven.

onzième |óṅzyem| *num* eleventh.

op |op| *nf* (= *opération*): **salle d'**~ operating room (*US*), (operating) theatre (*Brit*).

OPA *sigle f* = **offre publique d'achat.**

opacité |opásētā| *nf* opaqueness.

opale |opál| *nf* opal.

opalescent, e |opálāsáṅ, -áṅt| *a* opalescent.

opalin, e |opálaṅ, -ēn| *a*, *nf* opaline.

opaque |opák| *a* (*vitre, verre*) opaque; (*brouillard, nuit*) impenetrable.

OPE *sigle f* (= *offre publique d'échange*) take-over bid where bidder offers shares in his company in exchange for shares in target company.

OPEP |opep| *sigle f* (= *Organisation des pays exportateurs de pétrole*) OPEC.

opéra |opárá| *nm* opera; (*édifice*) opera house.

opérable |opārábl(ə)| *a* operable.

opéra-comique, *pl* **opéras-comiques** |opārákomēk| *nm* light opera, opéra comique.

opérant, e |opāráṅ, -áṅt| *a* (*mesure*) effective.

opérateur, trice |opārátœr, -trēs| *nm/f* operator; ~ **(de prise de vues)** cameraman.

opération |opārásyóṅ| *nf* operation; (*COMM*) dealing; **salle/table d'**~ operating room (*US*) *ou* theatre (*Brit*)/table; ~ **de sauvetage** rescue operation; ~ **à cœur ouvert** open-heart surgery *q*.

opérationel, le |opārásyonāl| *a* operational.

opératoire |opārátwár| *a* (*manœuvre, méthode*) operating; (*choc etc*) post-operative.

opéré, e |opārā| *nm/f* post-operative patient.

opérer |opārā| *vt* (*MÉD*) to operate on; (*faire, exécuter*) to carry out, make ♦ *vi* (*remède: faire effet*) to act, work; (*procéder*) to proceed; (*MÉD*) to operate; **s'**~ *vi* (*avoir lieu*) to occur, take place; **se faire** ~ to have an operation; **se faire** ~ **des amygdales/du cœur** to have one's tonsils out/have a heart operation.

opérette |opāret| *nf* operetta, light opera.

ophtalmique |oftálmēk| *a* ophthalmic.

ophtalmologie |oftálmolozhē| *nf* ophthalmology.

ophtalmologue |oftálmolog| *nm/f* ophthalmologist.

opiacé, e |opyásā| *a* opiate.

opiner |opēnā| *vi*: ~ **de la tête** to nod assent ♦ *vt*: ~ **à** to consent to.

opiniâtre |opēnyátr(ə)| *a* stubborn.

opiniâtreté |opēnyátrətā| *nf* stubbornness.

opinion |opēnyóṅ| *nf* opinion; **l'**~ **(publique)** public opinion; **avoir bonne/mauvaise** ~ **de** to have a high/low opinion of.

opiomane |opyomán| *nm/f* opium addict.

opium |opyom| *nm* opium.

OPJ *sigle m* = *officier de police judiciaire*.

opportun, e [ɔpɔrtœ̃, -ün] *a* timely, opportune; **en temps ~** at the appropriate time.

opportunément [ɔpɔrtünåmåṅ] *ad* opportunely.

opportunisme [ɔpɔrtünɛsm(ə)] *nm* opportunism.

opportuniste [ɔpɔrtünɛst(ə)] *a, nm/f* opportunist.

opportunité [ɔpɔrtünētå] *nf* timeliness, opportuneness.

opposant, e [ɔpōzåṅ, -åṅt] *a* opposing ♦ *nm/f* opponent.

opposé, e [ɔpōzå] *a* (*direction, rive*) opposite; (*faction*) opposing; (*couleurs*) contrasting; (*opinions, intérêts*) conflicting; (*contre*): **~ à** opposed to, against ♦ *nm*: **l'~** the other *ou* opposite side (*ou* direction); (*contraire*) the opposite; **être ~ à** to be opposed to; **à l'~** (*fig*) on the other hand; **à l'~ de** on the other *ou* opposite side from; (*fig*) contrary to, unlike.

opposer [ɔpōzå] *vt* (*meubles, objets*) to place opposite each other; (*personnes, armées, équipes*) to oppose; (*couleurs, termes, tons*) to contrast; (*comparer: livres, avantages*) to contrast; **~ qch à** (*comme obstacle, défense*) to set sth against; (*comme objection*) to put sth forward against; (*en contraste*) to set sth opposite; to match sth with; **s'~** (*sens réciproque*) to conflict; to clash; to face each other; to contrast; **s'~ à** (*interdire, empêcher*) to oppose; (*tenir tête à*) to rebel against; **sa religion s'y oppose** it's against his religion; **s'~ à ce que qn fasse** to be opposed to sb's doing.

opposition [ɔpōzēsyóṅ] *nf* opposition; **par ~** in contrast; **par ~ à** as opposed to, in contrast with; **entrer en ~ avec** to come into conflict with; **être en ~ avec** (*idées, conduite*) to be at variance with; **faire ~ à un chèque** to stop a check.

oppressant, e [ɔprāsåṅ, -åṅt] *a* oppressive.

oppresser [ɔprāså] *vt* to oppress; **se sentir oppressé** to feel breathless.

oppresseur [ɔprāsœr] *nm* oppressor.

oppressif, ive [ɔprāsēf, -ēv] *a* oppressive.

oppression [ɔprāsyóṅ] *nf* oppression; (*malaise*) feeling of suffocation.

opprimer [ɔprēmå] *vt* (*asservir: peuple, faibles*) to oppress; (*étouffer: liberté, opinion*) to suppress, stifle; (*suj: chaleur etc*) to suffocate, oppress.

opprobre [ɔprɔbr(ə)] *nm* disgrace.

opter [ɔptå] *vi*: **~ pour** to opt for; **~ entre** to choose between.

opticien, ne [ɔptēsyaṅ, -ɛn] *nm/f* optician.

optimal, e, aux [ɔptēmål, -ō] *a* optimal.

optimisation [ɔptēmēzåsyóṅ] *nf* optimization.

optimiser [ɔptēmēzå] *vt* to optimize.

optimisme [ɔptēmēsm(ə)] *nm* optimism.

optimiste [ɔptēmēst(ə)] *a* optimistic ♦ *nm/f* optimist.

optimum [ɔptēmom] *a, nm* optimum.

option [ɔpsyóṅ] *nf* option; (*AUTO: supplément*) optional extra; **matière à ~** (*SCOL*) elective (*US*), optional subject (*Brit*); **prendre une ~ sur** to take (out) an option on; **~ par défaut** (*INFORM*) default (option).

optionnel, le [ɔpsyonɛl] *a* optional.

optique [ɔptēk] *a* (*nerf*) optic; (*verres*) optical ♦ *nf* (*PHOTO: lentilles etc*) optics *pl*; (*science, industrie*) optics *sg*; (*fig: manière de voir*) perspective.

opulence [ɔpülåṅs] *nf* wealth, opulence.

opulent, e [ɔpülåṅ, -åṅt] *a* wealthy, opulent; (*formes, poitrine*) ample, generous.

or [ɔr] *nm* gold ♦ *cj* now, but; **d'~** (*fig*) golden; **en ~** gold *cpd*; (*occasion*) golden; **un mari/enfant en ~** a treasure; **une affaire en ~** (*achat*) a real bargain; (*commerce*) a gold mine; **plaqué ~** gold-plated; **~ noir** black gold.

oracle [ɔråkl(ə)] *nm* oracle.

orage [ɔråzh] *nm* (thunder)storm.

orageux, euse [ɔråzhœ̈, -ēz] *a* stormy.

oraison [ɔrezóṅ] *nf* orison, prayer; **~ funèbre** funeral oration.

oral, e, aux [ɔrål, -ō] *a* (*déposition, promesse*) oral, verbal; (*MÉD*): **par voie ~e** by mouth, orally ♦ *nm* (*SCOL*) oral.

oralement [ɔrålmåṅ] *ad* orally.

orange [ɔråṅzh] *a inv, nf* orange; **~ sanguine** blood orange; **~ pressée** freshly-squeezed orange juice.

orangé, e [ɔråṅzhå] *a* orangey, orange-colored (*US*), orange-coloured (*Brit*).

orangeade [ɔråṅzhåd] *nf* orangeade.

oranger [ɔråṅzhå] *nm* orange tree.

orangeraie [ɔråṅzhrɛ] *nf* orange grove.

orangerie [ɔråṅzhrē] *nf* orangery.

orang-outan(g) [ɔråṅōōtåṅ] *nm* orangutan.

orateur [ɔråtœr] *nm* speaker; orator.

oratoire [ɔråtwår] *nm* (*lieu, chapelle*) oratory; (*au bord du chemin*) wayside shrine ♦ *a* oratorical.

oratorio [ɔråtoryō] *nm* oratorio.

orbital, e, aux [ɔrbētål, -ō] *a* orbital; **station ~e** space station.

orbite [ɔrbēt] *nf* (*ANAT*) (eye-)socket; (*PHYSIQUE*) orbit; **mettre sur ~** to put into orbit; (*fig*) to launch; **dans l'~ de** (*fig*) within the sphere of influence of.

Orcades [ɔrkåd] *nfpl*: **les ~** the Orkneys, the Orkney Islands.

orchestral, e, aux [ɔrkestrål, -ō] *a* orchestral.

orchestrateur, trice [ɔrkestråtœr, -trēs] *nm/f* orchestrator.

orchestration [ɔrkestråsyóṅ] *nf* orchestration.

orchestre [ɔrkestr(ə)] *nm* orchestra; (*de jazz, danse*) band; (*places*) orchestra (*US*), stalls *pl* (*Brit*).

orchestrer [ɔrkestrå] *vt* (*MUS*) to orchestrate; (*fig*) to mount, stage-manage.

orchidée [ɔrkēdå] *nf* orchid.

ordinaire [ɔrdēnɛr] *a* ordinary; (*coutumier: maladresse etc*) usual; (*de tous les jours*) everyday; (*modèle, qualité*) standard ♦ *nm* ordinary; (*menus*) everyday fare ♦ *nf* (*essence*) ≈ regular (gas) (*US*), ≈ two-star (petrol) (*Brit*); **d'~** usually, normally; **à l'~** usually, ordinarily.

ordinairement [ɔrdēnermåṅ] *ad* ordinarily, usually.

ordinal, e, aux [ɔrdēnål, -ō] *a* ordinal.

ordinateur [ɔrdēnåtœr] *nm* computer; **mettre sur ~** to computerize, put on computer; **~ domestique** home computer; **~ individuel** *ou*

personnel personal computer.

ordination [ordĕnásyôn] *nf* ordination.

ordonnance [ordonáns] *nf* organization; (*groupement, disposition*) layout; (*MÉD*) prescription; (*JUR*) order; (*MIL*) orderly; **d'~** (*MIL*) regulation *cpd*; **officier d'~** aide-de-camp.

ordonnateur, trice [ordonátœr, -trĕs] *nm/f* (*d'une cérémonie, fête*) organizer; **~ des pompes funèbres** funeral director.

ordonné, e [ordonā] *a* tidy, orderly;. (*MATH*) ordered ♦ *nf* (*MATH*) Y-axis, ordinate.

ordonner [ordonā] *vt* (*agencer*) to organize, arrange; (: *meubles, appartement*) to lay out, arrange; (*donner un ordre*): **~ à qn de faire** to order sb to do; (*MATH*) (arrange in) order; (*REL*) to ordain; (*MÉD*) to prescribe; (*JUR*) to order; **s'~** (*faits*) to organize themselves.

ordre [ordr(ə)] *nm* (*gén*) order; (*propreté et soin*) orderliness, tidiness; (*association professionnelle, honorifique*) association; (*COMM*): **à l'~ de** payable to; (*nature*): **d'~ pratique** of a practical nature; **~s** *nmpl* (*REL*) holy orders; **avoir de l'~** to be tidy *ou* orderly; **mettre en ~** to tidy (up), put in order; **mettre bon ~ à** to put to rights, sort out; **procéder par ~** to take things one at a time; **être aux ~s de qn/sous les ~s de qn** to be at sb's disposal/under sb's command; **rappeler qn à l'~** to call sb to order; **jusqu'à nouvel ~** until further notice; **dans le même ~ d'idées** in this connection; **par ~ d'entrée en scène** in order of appearance; **un ~ de grandeur** some idea of the size (*ou* amount); **de premier ~** first-rate; **~ de grève** strike call; **~ du jour** (*d'une réunion*) agenda; (*MIL*) order of the day; **à l'~ du jour** on the agenda; (*fig*) topical; (*MIL*) **citer**) in dispatches; **~ de mission** (*MIL*) orders *pl*; **~ public** law and order; **~ de route** marching orders *pl*.

ordure [ordür] *nf* filth *q*; (*propos, écrit*) obscenity, (piece of) filth; **~s** *nfpl* (*balayures, déchets*) garbage *sg* (*US*), trash *sg* (*US*), rubbish *sg* (*Brit*), refuse *sg* (*Brit*); **~s ménagères** household garbage (*US*) *ou* refuse (*Brit*).

ordurier, ière [ordüryā. -yer] *a* lewd, filthy.

oreille [orey] *nf* (*ANAT*) ear; (*de marmite, tasse*) handle; (*TECH*: *d'un écrou*) wing; **avoir de l'~** to have a good ear (for music); **avoir l'~ fine** to have good *ou* sharp ears; **l'~ basse** crestfallen, dejected; **se faire tirer l'~** to take a lot of persuading; **dire qch à l'~ de qn** to have a word in sb's ear (about sth).

oreiller [orāyā] *nm* pillow.

oreillette [oreyet] *nf* (*ANAT*) auricle.

oreillons [oreyôn] *nmpl* mumps *sg*.

ores [or]: **d'~ et déjà** *ad* already.

orfèvre [orfevr(ə)] *nm* goldsmith; silversmith.

orfèvrerie [orfevrərē] *nf* (*art, métier*) goldsmith's (*ou* silversmith's) trade; (*ouvrage*) (silver *ou* gold) plate.

orfraie [orfre] *nm* white-tailed eagle; **pousser des cris d'~** to yell at the top of one's voice.

organe [organ] *nm* organ; (*véhicule, instrument*) instrument; (*voix*) voice; (*porte-parole*) representative, mouthpiece; **~s de**

commande (*TECH*) controls; **~s de transmission** (*TECH*) transmission system *sg*.

organigramme [organēgram] *nm* (*hiérarchique, structurel*) organization chart; (*des opérations*) flow chart.

organique [organēk] *a* organic.

organisateur, trice [organēzátœr, -trĕs] *nm/f* organizer.

organisation [organēzásyôn] *nf* organization; **O~ des Nations Unies (ONU)** United Nations (Organization) (UN, UNO); **O~ mondiale de la santé (OMS)** World Health Organization (WHO); **O~ du traité de l'Atlantique Nord (OTAN)** North Atlantic Treaty Organization (NATO).

organisationnel, le [organēzásyonel] *a* organizational.

organiser [organēzā] *vt* to organize; (*mettre sur pied: service etc*) to set up; **s'~** to get organized.

organisme [organēsm(ə)] *nm* (*BIO*) organism; (*corps humain*) body; (*ADMIN, POL etc*) body, organism.

organiste [organēst(ə)] *nm/f* organist.

orgasme [orgásm(ə)] *nm* orgasm, climax.

orge [orzh(ə)] *nf* barley.

orgeat [orzhá] *nm*: **sirop d'~** barley water.

orgelet [orzhəle] *nm* sty(e).

orgie [orzhē] *nf* orgy.

orgue [org(ə)] *nm* organ; **~s** *nfpl* organ *sg*; **~ de Barbarie** barrel *ou* street organ.

orgueil [orgœy] *nm* pride.

orgueilleux, euse [orgœyœ̄, -œ̄z] *a* proud.

Orient [oryán] *nm*: **l'~** the East, the Orient.

orientable [oryántábl(ə)] *a* (*phare, lampe etc*) adjustable.

oriental, e, aux [oryántál, -ō] *a* oriental, eastern; (*frontière*) eastern ♦ *nm/f*: **O~, e** Oriental.

orientation [oryántásyôn] *nf* positioning; adjustment; orientation; direction; (*d'une maison etc*) exposure; (*d'un journal*) leanings *pl*; **avoir le sens de l'~** to have a (good) sense of direction; **course d'~** orienteering exercise; **~ professionnelle** careers advice *ou* guidance; (*service*) careers advisory service.

orienté, e [oryántā] *a* (*fig: article, journal*) slanted; **bien/mal ~** (*appartement*) well/badly positioned; **~ au sud** facing south, with a southern exposure.

orienter [oryántā] *vt* (*situer*) to position; (*placer, disposer: pièce mobile*) to adjust, position; (*tourner*) to direct, turn; (*voyageur, touriste, recherches*) to direct; (*fig: élève*) to orientate; **s'~** (*se repérer*) to find one's bearings; **s'~ vers** (*fig*) to turn towards.

orienteur, euse [oryántœr, -œ̄z] *nm/f* (*SCOL*) careers adviser.

orifice [orēfēs] *nm* opening, orifice.

oriflamme [orēflám] *nf* banner, standard.

origan [orēgán] *nm* oregano.

originaire [orēzhēner] *a* original; **être ~ de** (*pays, lieu*) to be a native of; (*provenir de*) to originate from; to be native to.

original, e, aux [orēzhēnál, -ō] *a* original; (*bizarre*) eccentric ♦ *nm/f* (*fam: excentrique*) eccentric; (: *fantaisiste*) joker ♦ *nm* (*document etc, ART*) original; (*dactylo-*

graphie) original (*US*), top copy (*Brit*).

originalité [orēzhēnálētā] *nf* (*d'un nouveau modèle*) originality *q*; (*excentricité, bizarrerie*) eccentricity.

origine [orēzhēn] *nf* origin; (*d'un message, appel téléphonique*) source; (*d'une révolution, réussite*) root; ~**s** *nfpl* (*d'une personne*) origins; **d'~** of origin; (*pneus etc*) original; (*bureau postal*) dispatching; **d'~ française** of French origin; **dès l'~** at *ou* from the outset; **à l'~** originally; **avoir son ~ dans** to have its origins in, originate in.

originel, le [orēzhēnel] *a* original.

originellement [orēzhēnelmáń] *ad* (*à l'origine*) originally; (*dès l'origine*) from the beginning.

oripeaux [orēpō] *nmpl* rags.

ORL *sigle f* (= *oto-rhino-laryngologie*) ENT ♦ *sigle m/f* (= *oto-rhino-laryngologiste*) ENT specialist; **être en ~** (*malade*) to be in the ENT hospital *ou* department.

orme [orm(ə)] *nm* elm.

orné, e [ornā] *a* ornate; ~ **de** adorned *ou* decorated with.

ornement [ornəmáń] *nm* ornament; (*fig*) embellishment, adornment; ~**s sacerdotaux** vestments.

ornemental, e, aux [ornəmáńtál, -ō] *a* ornamental.

ornementer [ornəmáńtā] *vt* to ornament.

orner [ornā] *vt* to decorate, adorn; ~ **qch de** to decorate sth with.

ornière [ornyer] *nf* rut; (*fig*): **sortir de l'~** (*routine*) to get out of the rut; (*impasse*) to get out of a spot.

ornithologie [ornētolozhē] *nf* ornithology.

ornithologue [ornētolog] *nm/f* ornithologist; ~ **amateur** birdwatcher.

orphelin, e [orfəlań, -ēn] *a* orphan(ed) ♦ *nm/f* orphan; ~ **de père/mère** fatherless/ motherless.

orphelinat [orfəlēná] *nm* orphanage.

ORSEC [orsek] *sigle f* (= *Organisation des secours*): **le plan ~** disaster contingency plan.

ORSECRAD [orsekrád] *sigle m* = *ORSEC en cas d'accident nucléaire*.

orteil [ortey] *nm* toe; **gros ~** big toe.

ORTF *sigle m* (= *Office de radio-diffusion télévision française*) (*formerly*) French broadcasting corporation.

orthodontiste [ortodóńtēst(ə)] *nm/f* orthodontist.

orthodoxe [ortodoks(ə)] *a* orthodox.

orthodoxie [ortodoksē] *nf* orthodoxy.

orthogénie [ortozhānē] *nf* family planning.

orthographe [ortográf] *nf* spelling.

orthographier [ortográfyā] *vt* to spell; **mal orthographié** misspelled.

orthopédie [ortopādē] *nf* orthopedics *sg* (*US*), orthopaedics *sg* (*Brit*).

orthopédique [ortopādēk] *a* orthopedic (*US*), orthopaedic (*Brit*).

orthopédiste [ortopādēst(ə)] *nm/f* orthopedic (*US*) *ou* orthopaedic (*Brit*) specialist.

orthophonie [ortofonē] *nf* (*MÉD*) speech therapy; (*LING*) correct pronunciation.

orthophoniste [ortofonēst(ə)] *nm/f* speech therapist.

ortie [ortē] *nf* (stinging) nettle; ~ **blanche** white dead-nettle.

OS *sigle m* = **ouvrier spécialisé**.

os [os, *pl* ō] *nm* bone; **sans ~** (*BOUCHERIE*) off the bone, boned; ~ **à moelle** marrowbone.

oscillation [osēlásyóń] *nf* oscillation; ~**s** *nfpl* (*fig*) fluctuations.

osciller [osēlā] *vi* (*pendule*) to swing; (*au vent etc*) to rock; (*TECH*) to oscillate; (*fig*): ~ **entre** to waver *ou* fluctuate between.

osé, e [ōzā] *a* daring, bold.

oseille [ōzey] *nf* sorrel.

oser [ōzā] *vi, vt* to dare; ~ **faire** to dare (to) do.

osier [ōzyā] *nm* (*BOT*) willow; **d'~, en ~** wicker(work) *cpd*.

Oslo [oslō] *n* Oslo.

osmose [osmōz] *nf* osmosis.

ossature [osátür] *nf* (*ANAT*: *squelette*) frame, skeletal structure; (: *du visage*) bone structure; (*fig*) framework.

osselet [osle] *nm* (*ANAT*) ossicle; **jouer aux ~s** to play jacks.

ossements [osmáń] *nmpl* bones.

osseux, euse [osœ̄, -œ̄z] *a* bony; (*tissu, maladie, greffe*) bone *cpd*.

ossifier [osēfyā]: **s'~** *vi* to ossify.

ossuaire [osüer] *nm* ossuary.

Ostende [ostáńd] *n* Ostend.

ostensible [ostáńsēbl(ə)] *a* conspicuous.

ostensiblement [ostáńsēbləmáń] *ad* conspicuously.

ostensoir [ostáńswár] *nm* monstrance.

ostentation [ostáńtásyóń] *nf* ostentation; **faire ~ de** to parade, make a display of.

ostentatoir [ostáńtátwár] *a* ostentatious.

ostracisme [ostrásēsm(ə)] *nm* ostracism; **frapper d'~** to ostracize.

ostréicole [ostrăēkol] *a* oyster *cpd*.

ostréiculture [ostrăēkültür] *nf* oyster farming.

otage [otázh] *nm* hostage; **prendre qn comme ~** to take sb hostage.

OTAN [otáń] *sigle f* (= *Organisation du traité de l'Atlantique Nord*) NATO.

otarie [otárē] *nf* sea lion.

OTASE [otáz] *sigle f* (= *Organisation du traité de l'Asie du Sud-Est*) SEATO (= *Southeast Asia Treaty Organization*).

ôter [ōtā] *vt* to remove; (*soustraire*) to take away; ~ **qch à qn** to take sth (away) from sb; ~ **qch de** to remove sth from; **6 ôté de 10 égale 4** 6 from 10 equals *ou* is 4.

otite [otēt] *nf* ear infection.

oto-rhino(-laryngologiste) [otorēno(láráńgolozhēst(ə))] *nm/f* ear, nose and throat specialist.

ottomane [otomán] *nf* ottoman.

ou [ōō] *cj* or; ~ ... ~ either ... or; ~ **bien** or (else).

où [ōō] *ad, pronom* where; (*dans lequel*) in which, into which; from which, out of which; (*hors duquel, duquel*) from which; (*sur lequel*) on which; (*sens de 'que'*): **au train ~ ça va/prix ~ c'est** at the rate it's going/price it is; **le jour ~ il est parti** the day (that) he left; **par ~ passer?** which way should we go?; **les villes par ~ il est passé** the towns he went through; **le village d'~ je viens** the village I come from; **la chambre ~ il était**

the room he was in; **d'~ vient qu'il est parti?** how is it that he left?, how come he left?

OUA *sigle f* (= *Organisation de l'unité africaine*) OAU (= *Organization of African Unity*).

ouais [wɛ] *excl* yeah.

ouate [wát] *nf* cotton (*US*), cotton wool (*Brit*); (*bourre*) padding, wadding; **~ (hydrophile)** (absorbent) cotton (*US*), cotton wool (*Brit*).

ouaté, e [wátā] *a* cotton (*US*), cotton-wool (*Brit*); (*doublé*) padded; (*fig: atmosphère*) cocoon-like; (*: pas, bruit*) muffled.

oubli [ōōblē] *nm* (*acte*): **l'~ de** forgetting; (*étourderie*) forgetfulness *q*; (*négligence*) omission, oversight; (*absence de souvenirs*) oblivion; **~ de soi** self-effacement, self-negation.

oublier [ōōblēyā] *vt* (*gén*) to forget; (*ne pas voir: erreurs etc*) to miss; (*ne pas mettre: virgule, nom*) to leave out, forget; (*laisser quelque part: chapeau etc*) to leave behind; **s'~** to forget o.s.; (*enfant, animal*) to have an accident (*euphemism*); **~ l'heure** to forget (about) the time.

oubliettes [ōōblēyɛt] *nfpl* dungeon *sg*; **(jeter) aux ~** (*fig*) (to put) completely out of mind.

oublieux, euse [ōōblēyø̄, -ø̄z] *a* forgetful.

oued [wɛd] *nm* wadi.

ouest [wɛst] *nm* west ♦ *a inv* west; (*région*) western; **à l'~** in the west; (*to the*) west, westwards; **à l'~ de** (to the) west of; **vent d'~** westerly wind.

ouest-allemand, e [wɛstálmáṅ, -áṅd] *a* West German.

ouf [ōōf] *excl* phew!

Ouganda [ōōgáṅdá] *nm*: **l'~** Uganda.

ougandais, e [ōōgáṅdɛ, -ɛz] *a* Ugandan.

oui [wē] *ad* yes; **répondre (par) ~** to answer yes; **mais ~, bien sûr** yes, of course; **je pense que ~** I think so; **pour un ~ ou pour un non** for no apparent reason.

ouï-dire [wēdēr]: **par ~** *ad* by hearsay.

ouïe [wē] *nf* hearing; **~s** *nfpl* (*de poisson*) gills; (*de violon*) sound hole *sg*.

ouïr [wēr] *vt* to hear; **avoir ouï dire que** to have heard it said that.

ouistiti [wēstētē] *nm* marmoset.

ouragan [ōōrágáṅ] *nm* hurricane; (*fig*) storm.

Oural [ōōrál] *nm*: **l'~** (*fleuve*) the Ural; (*aussi*: **les monts ~**) the Urals, the Ural Mountains.

ouralo-altaïque [ōōráloáltáēk] *a, nm* Ural-Altaic.

ourdir [ōōrdēr] *vt* (*complot*) to hatch.

ourdou [ōōrdōō] *a inv* Urdu ♦ *nm* (*LING*) Urdu.

ourlé, e [ōōrlā] *a* hemmed; (*fig*) rimmed.

ourler [ōōrlā] *vt* to hem.

ourlet [ōōrlɛ] *nm* hem; (*de l'oreille*) rim; **faire un ~ à** to hem.

ours [ōōrs] *nm* bear; **~ brun/blanc** brown/polar bear; **~ marin** fur seal; **~ mal léché** uncouth fellow; **~ (en peluche)** teddy (bear).

ourse [ōōrs(ə)] *nf* (*ZOOL*) she-bear; **la Grande/Petite O~** the Great/Little Bear, Ursa Major/Minor.

oursin [ōōrsaṅ] *nm* sea urchin.

ourson [ōōrsóṅ] *nm* (bear) cub.

ouste [ōōst(ə)] *excl* hop it!

outil [ōōtē] *nm* tool.

outillage [ōōtēyázh] *nm* set of tools; (*d'atelier*) equipment *q*.

outiller [ōōtēyā] *vt* (*ouvrier, usine*) to equip.

outrage [ōōtrázh] *nm* insult; **faire subir les derniers ~s à** (*femme*) to rape; **~ aux bonnes mœurs** (*JUR*) outrage to public decency; **~ à magistrat** (*JUR*) contempt of court; **~ à la pudeur** (*JUR*) indecent behavior *q* (*US*) *ou* behaviour *q* (*Brit*).

outragé, e [ōōtrázhā] *a* offended; outraged.

outrageant, e [ōōtrázháṅ, -áṅt] *a* offensive.

outrager [ōōtrázhā] *vt* to offend gravely; (*fig: contrevenir à*) to outrage, insult.

outrageusement [ōōtrázhœ̄zmáṅ] *ad* outrageously.

outrance [ōōtráṅs] *nf* excessiveness *q*, excess; **à ~** ad excessively, to excess.

outrancier, ière [ōōtráṅsyā, -yɛr] *a* extreme.

outre [ōōtr(ə)] *nf* goatskin bottle ♦ *prép* besides ♦ *ad*: **passer ~** to carry on regardless; **passer ~ à** to disregard, take no notice of; **en ~** besides, moreover; **~ que** apart from the fact that; **~ mesure** immoderately; unduly.

outré, e [ōōtrā] *a* (*flatterie, éloge*) excessive, exaggerated; (*indigné, scandalisé*) outraged.

outre-Atlantique [ōōtrátláṅtēk] *ad* across the Atlantic.

outrecuidance [ōōtrəküēdáṅs] *nf* presumptuousness *q*.

outre-Manche [ōōtrəmáṅsh] *ad* across the Channel.

outremer [ōōtrəmɛr] *a inv* ultramarine.

outre-mer [ōōtrəmɛr] *ad* overseas; **d'~** overseas.

outrepasser [ōōtrəpásā] *vt* to go beyond, exceed.

outrer [ōōtrā] *vt* (*pensée, attitude*) to exaggerate; (*indigner: personne*) to outrage.

outre-Rhin [ōōtrəraṅ] *ad* across the Rhine, in Germany.

outsider [àwtsáydɛr] *nm* outsider.

ouvert, e [ōōver, -ert(ə)] *pp de* **ouvrir** ♦ *a* open; (*robinet, gaz etc*) on; **à bras ~s** with open arms.

ouvertement [ōōvertəmáṅ] *ad* openly.

ouverture [ōōvertür] *nf* opening; (*MUS*) overture; (*POL*): **l'~** the widening of the political spectrum; (*PHOTO*): **~ (du diaphragme)** aperture; **~s** *nfpl* (*propositions*) overtures; **~ d'esprit** open-mindedness; **heures d'~** (*COMM*) opening hours; **jours d'~** (*COMM*) days of opening.

ouvrable [ōōvrábl(ə)] *a*: **jour ~** working day, weekday; **heures ~s** business hours.

ouvrage [ōōvrázh] *nm* (*tâche, de tricot etc, MIL*) work *q*; (*objet: COUTURE, ART*) (piece of) work; (*texte, livre*) work; **panier** *ou* **corbeille à ~** work basket; **~ d'art** (*GÉNIE CIVIL*) bridge or tunnel etc.

ouvragé, e [ōōvrázhā] *a* finely embroidered (*ou* worked *ou* carved).

ouvrant, e [ōōvráṅ, -áṅt] *vb voir* **ouvrir** ♦ *a*: **toit ~** sunroof.

ouvré, e [ōōvrā] *a* finely-worked; **jour ~** working day.

ouvre-boîte(s) [ōōvrəbwát] *nm inv* can

opener.

ouvre-bouteille(s) [ōōvrəbōōtey] *nm inv* bottle opener.

ouvreuse [ōōvrȫz] *nf* usherette.

ouvrier, ière [ōōvrēyā, -yer] *nm/f* worker ♦ *nf* (*ZOOL*) worker (bee) ♦ *a* working-class; (*problèmes, conflit*) industrial, labor *cpd* (*US*), labour *cpd* (*Brit*); (*revendications*) workers'; **classe ouvrière** working class; ~ **agricole** farmworker; ~ **qualifié** skilled worker; ~ **spécialisé (OS)** semiskilled worker; ~ **d'usine** factory worker.

ouvrir [ōōvrēr] *vt* (*gén*) to open; (*brèche, passage*) to open up; (*commencer l'exploitation de, créer*) to open (up); (*eau, électricité, chauffage, robinet*) to turn on; (*MÉD: abcès*) to open up, cut open ♦ *vi* to open; to open up; (*CARTES*): ~ **à trèfle** to open with clubs; **s'**~ *vi* to open; **s'**~ **à** (*art etc*) to open one's mind to; **s'**~ **à qn (de qch)** to open one's heart to sb (about sth); **s'**~ **les veines** to slash *ou* cut one's wrists; ~ **sur** to open onto; ~ **l'appétit à qn** to whet sb's appetite; ~ **des horizons** to open up new horizons; ~ **l'esprit** to broaden one's horizons; ~ **une session** (*INFORM*) to log in.

ouvroir [ōōvrwár] *nm* workroom, sewing room.

ovaire [over] *nm* ovary.

ovale [ovál] *a* oval.

ovation [ovâsyóń] *nf* ovation.

ovationner [ovâsyonā] *vt*: ~ **qn** to give sb an ovation.

ovin, e [ovań, -ēn] *a* ovine.

OVNI [ovnē] *sigle m* (= *objet volant non identifié*) UFO.

ovoïde [ovoēd] *a* egg-shaped.

ovulation [ovülâsyóń] *nf* (*PHYSIOL*) ovulation.

ovule [ovül] *nm* (*PHYSIOL*) ovum (*pl* ova); (*MÉD*) pessary.

oxfordien, ne [oksfordyań, -en] *a* Oxonian ♦ *nm/f*: **O**~, **ne** Oxonian.

oxydable [oksēdábl(ə)] *a* liable to rust.

oxyde [oksēd] *nm* oxide; ~ **de carbone** carbon monoxide.

oxyder [oksēdā]: **s'**~ *vi* to become oxidized.

oxygène [oksēzhen] *nm* oxygen; (*fig*): **cure d'**~ fresh air cure.

oxygéné, e [oksēzhānā] *a*: **eau** ~**e** hydrogen peroxide; **cheveux** ~**s** bleached hair.

ozone [ōzon] *nm* ozone.

P

P, p [pā] *nm inv* P, p ♦ *abr* (= *Père*) Fr; (= *page*) p; **P comme Pierre** P for Peter.

PA *sigle fpl* = **petites annonces**.

PAC *sigle f* (= *Politique agricole commune*) CAP.

pacage [pákázh] *nm* grazing, pasture.

pace-maker [pesmekœr] *nm* pacemaker.

pachyderme [páshēderm(ə)] *nm* pachyderm; elephant.

pacificateur, trice [pásēfēkátœr, -trēs] *a* pacificatory.

pacifier [pásēfyā] *vt* to pacify.

pacifique [pásēfēk] *a* (*personne*) peaceable; (*intentions, coexistence*) peaceful ♦ *nm*: **le P**~, **l'océan P**~ the Pacific (Ocean).

pacifiquement [pásēfēkmáń] *ad* peaceably; peacefully.

pacifiste [pásēfēst(ə)] *nm/f* pacifist.

pack [pák] *nm* pack.

pacotille [pákotēy] *nf* (*péj*) cheap goods *pl*; **de** ~ cheap.

pacte [pákt(ə)] *nm* pact, treaty.

pactiser [páktēzā] *vi*: ~ **avec** to come to terms with.

pactole [páktol] *nm* gold mine (*fig*).

paddock [pádok] *nm* paddock.

Padoue [pádōō] *n* Padua.

PAF *sigle f* (= *Police de l'air et des frontières*) police authority responsible for civil aviation, border control etc.

pagaie [páge] *nf* paddle.

pagaille [págáy] *nf* mess, shambles *sg*; **il y en a en** ~ there are loads *ou* heaps of them.

paganisme [págánēsm(ə)] *nm* paganism.

pagayer [págāyā] *vi* to paddle.

page [pázh] *nf* page; (*passage: d'un roman*) passage ♦ *nm* page (boy); **mettre en** ~**s** to make up (into pages); **mise en** ~ layout; **à la** ~ (*fig*) up-to-date; ~ **blanche** blank page; ~ **de garde** endpaper.

page-écran, *pl* **pages-écrans** [pázhākráń] *nf* (*INFORM*) screen page.

pagination [pázhēnásyóń] *nf* pagination.

paginer [pázhēnā] *vt* to paginate.

pagne [pány] *nm* loincloth.

pagode [págod] *nf* pagoda.

paie [pe] *nf* = **paye**.

paiement [pemáń] *nm* = **payement**.

païen, ne [páyań, -en] *a*, *nm/f* pagan, heathen.

paillard, e [páyár, -árd(ə)] *a* bawdy.

paillasse [páyás] *nf* (*matelas*) straw mattress; (*d'un évier*) drainboard (*US*), draining board (*Brit*).

paillasson [páyásóń] *nm* doormat.

paille [páy] *nf* straw; (*défaut*) flaw; **être sur la** ~ to be ruined; ~ **de fer** steel wool.

paillé, e [páyā] *a*, with a straw seat.

pailleté, e [páytā] *a* sequined.

paillette [páyet] *nf* speck, flake; ~**s** *nfpl* (*décoratives*) sequins, spangles; **lessive en** ~**s** soapflakes *pl*.

pain [pań] *nm* (*substance*) bread; (*unité*) loaf (*pl* loaves) (of bread); (*morceau*): ~ **de cire** *etc* bar of wax *etc*; (*CULIN*): ~ **de poisson/légumes** fish/vegetable loaf; **petit** ~ (bread) roll; ~ **bis/complet** brown/wholewheat (*US*) *ou* wholemeal (*Brit*) bread; ~ **de campagne** farmhouse bread; ~ **d'épice** ≈ gingerbread; ~ **grillé** toast; ~ **de mie** sandwich loaf; ~ **perdu** French toast; ~ **de seigle** rye bread; ~ **de sucre** sugar loaf.

pair, e [per] *a* (*nombre*) even ♦ *nm* peer; **aller de** ~ (**avec**) to go hand in hand *ou* together (with); **au** ~ (*FINANCE*) at par; **valeur au** ~ par value; **jeune fille au** ~ au pair.

paire [per] *nf* pair; **une** ~ **de lunettes/tenailles** a pair of glasses/pincers; **faire la** ~: **les deux font la** ~ they are two of a kind.

pais [pe] *vb voir* **paître**.

paisible [pāzēbl(ə)] *a* peaceful, quiet.

paisiblement [pāzēbləmáṅ] *ad* peacefully, quietly.

paître [petr(ə)] *vi* to graze.

paix [pe] *nf* peace; *(fig)* peacefulness, peace; **faire la ~ avec** to make peace with; **avoir la ~** to have peace (and quiet).

Pakistan [pákēstáṅ] *nm:* **le ~** Pakistan.

pakistanais, e [pákēstáne, -ez] *a* Pakistani.

PAL *sigle m* (= *Phase Alternation Line*) PAL.

palabrer [pálábrā] *vi* to argue endlessly.

palabres [pálábr(ə)] *nfpl* endless discussions.

palace [pálás] *nm* luxury hotel.

palais [pále] *nm* palace; *(ANAT)* palate; **le P~ Bourbon** the seat of the French National Assembly; **le P~ de l'Élysée** the Élysée Palace; **~ des expositions** exhibition center (*US*) *ou* centre (*Brit*); **le P~ de Justice** the Law Courts *pl*.

palan [páláṅ] *nm* hoist.

Palatin [pálátaṅ]: **le (mont) ~** the Palatine (Hill).

pale [pál] *nf* (*d'hélice, de rame*) blade; (*de roue*) paddle.

pâle [pál] *a* pale; *(fig)*: **une ~ imitation** a pale imitation; **bleu ~** pale blue; **~ de colère** white *ou* pale with anger.

palefrenier [pálfrənyā] *nm* groom.

paléontologie [pálāóṅtolozhē] *nf* paleontology.

Palerme [pálerm(ə)] *n* Palermo.

Palestine [pálestēn] *nf:* **la ~** Palestine.

palestinien, ne [pálestēnyaṅ, -en] *a* Palestinian ♦ *nm/f:* **P~, ne** Palestinian.

palet [pále] *nm* disc; (*HOCKEY*) puck.

paletot [páltō] *nm* (short) coat.

palette [pálet] *nf* palette; (*produits*) range.

palétuvier [pálātüvyā] *nm* mangrove.

pâleur [pálœr] *nf* paleness.

palier [pályā] *nm* (*d'escalier*) landing; *(fig)* level, plateau; (: *phase stable*) leveling (*US*) *ou* levelling (*Brit*) off, new level; (*TECH*) bearing; **nos voisins de ~** our neighbors across the hall (*US*) *ou* the landing (*Brit*); **en ~** *ad* level; **par ~s** in stages.

palière [pályer] *af* landing *cpd*.

pâlir [pálēr] *vi* to turn *ou* go pale; (*couleur*) to fade; **faire ~ qn** (*de jalousie*) to make sb green (with envy).

palissade [pálēsád] *nf* fence.

palissandre [pálēsáṅdr(ə)] *nm* rosewood.

palliatif [pályátēf] *nm* palliative; (*expédient*) stopgap measure.

pallier [pályā] *vt*, **~ à** *vt* to offset, make up for.

palmarès [pálmáres] *nm* record (of achievements); (*SCOL*) prize list; (*SPORT*) list of winners.

palme [pálm(ə)] *nf* (*BOT*) palm leaf (*pl* leaves); (*symbole*) palm; (*de plongeur*) flipper; **~s (académiques)** decoration for services to education.

palmé, e [pálmā] *a* (*pattes*) webbed.

palmeraie [pálməre] *nf* palm grove.

palmier [pálmyā] *nm* palm tree.

palmipède [pálmēped] *nm* palmiped, webfooted bird.

palois, e [pálwá, -wáz] *a* of *ou* from Pau ♦ *nm/f:* **P~, e** inhabitant *ou* native of Pau.

palombe [pálôṅb] *nf* woodpigeon, ringdove.

pâlot, te [pálō, -ot] *a* pale, peaky.

palourde [pálōōrd(ə)] *nf* clam.

palpable [pálpábl(ə)] *a* tangible, palpable.

palper [pálpā] *vt* to feel, finger.

palpitant, e [pálpētáṅ, -áṅt] *a* thrilling, gripping.

palpitation [pálpētâsyôṅ] *nf* palpitation.

palpiter [pálpētā] *vi* (*cœur, pouls*) to beat; (: *plus fort*) to pound, throb; (*narines, chair*) to quiver.

paludisme [pálüdēsm(ə)] *nm* malaria.

palustre [pálüstr(ə)] *a* (*coquillage etc*) marsh *cpd*; (*fièvre*) malarial.

pâmer [pámā]: **se ~** *vi* to swoon; *(fig)*: **se ~ devant** to go into raptures over.

pâmoison [pámwàzôṅ] *nf:* **tomber en ~** to swoon.

pampa [páṅpá] *nf* pampas *pl.*

pamphlet [páṅfle] *nm* lampoon, satirical tract.

pamphlétaire [páṅflāter] *nm/f* lampoonist.

pamplemousse [páṅpləmōōs] *nm* grapefruit.

pan [páṅ] *nm* section, piece; (*côté: d'un prisme, d'une tour*) side, face ♦ *excl* bang!; **~ de chemise** shirt tail; **~ de mur** section of wall.

panacée [pánásā] *nf* panacea.

panachage [pánásházh] *nm* blend, mix; (*POL*) voting for candidates from different parties instead of for the set list of one party.

panache [pánásh] *nm* plume; *(fig)* spirit, panache.

panaché, e [pánáshā] *a:* **œillet ~** variegated carnation; **glace ~e** mixed ice cream; **salade ~e** mixed salad; **bière ~e** shandy.

panais [páne] *nm* parsnip.

Panama [pánámá] *nm:* **le ~** Panama.

panaméen, ne [pánámāaṅ, -en] *a* Panamanian ♦ *nm/f:* **P~, ne** Panamanian.

panaris [pánárē] *nm* whitlow.

pancarte [páṅkárt(ə)] *nf* sign, notice; (*dans un défilé*) placard.

pancréas [páṅkrãás] *nm* pancreas.

panda [páṅdá] *nm* panda.

pané, e [pánā] *a* fried in breadcrumbs.

panégyrique [pánāzhērēk] *nm:* **faire le ~ de qn** to extol sb's merits *ou* virtues.

panier [pányā] *nm* basket; (*à diapositives*) magazine; **mettre au ~** to chuck away; **~ de crabes: c'est un ~ de crabes** *(fig)* they're constantly at one another's throats; **~ percé** *(fig)* spendthrift; **~ à provisions** shopping basket; **~ à salade** (*CULIN*) salad shaker; (*POLICE*) paddy wagon, police van.

panier-repas, *pl* **paniers-repas** [pányār(ə)pá] *nm* packed lunch.

panification [pánēfēkásyôṅ] *nf* bread-making.

panique [pánēk] *a* panicky ♦ *nf* panic.

paniquer [pánēkā] *vi* to panic.

panne [pán] *nf* (*d'un mécanisme, moteur*) breakdown; **être/tomber en ~** to have broken down/break down; **être en ~ d'essence** *ou* **en ~ sèche** to have run out of gas (*US*) *ou* petrol (*Brit*); **mettre en ~** (*NAVIG*) to bring to; **~ d'électricité** *ou* **de courant** power *ou* electrical failure.

panneau, x [pánō] *nm* (*écriteau*) sign, notice; (*de boiserie, de tapisserie etc*) panel; **tomber dans le ~** *(fig)* to walk into the trap; **~**

d'affichage bulletin board; ~ **électoral** board for election poster; ~ **indicateur** signpost; ~ **publicitaire** billboard (*US*), hoarding (*Brit*); ~ **de signalisation** roadsign.

panneau-réclame, *pl* **panneaux-réclame** [pànōràklám] *nm* billboard (*US*), hoarding (*Brit*).

panonceau, x [pànóǹsō] *nm* (*de magasin etc*) sign; (*de médecin etc*) plaque.

panoplie [pànoplē] *nf* (*jouet*) outfit; (*d'armes*) display; (*fig*) array.

panorama [pànoràmá] *nm* (*vue*) all-round view, panorama; (*peinture*) panorama; (*fig: étude complète*) complete overview.

panoramique [pànoràmēk] *a* panoramic; (*carrosserie*) with panoramic windows ♦ *nm* (*CINÉMA, TV*) panoramic shot.

panse [pàǹs] *nf* paunch.

pansement [pàǹsmáǹ] *nm* dressing, bandage; ~ **adhésif** bandaid ® (*US*), sticking plaster (*Brit*).

panser [pàǹsā] *vt* (*plaie*) to dress, bandage; (*bras*) to put a dressing on, bandage; (*cheval*) to groom.

pantalon [pàǹtálóǹ] *nm* (*aussi*: ~**s, paire de** ~**s**) pants *pl* (*US*), trousers *pl* (*Brit*), pair of trousers *ou* pants; ~ **de ski** ski pants *pl*.

pantalonnade [pàǹtálonàd] *nf* slapstick (comedy).

pantelant, e [pàǹtláǹ, -áǹt] *a* gasping for breath, panting.

panthère [pàǹter] *nf* panther.

pantin [pàǹtàǹ] *nm* (*jouet*) jumping jack; (*péj: personne*) puppet.

pantois [pàǹtwá] *am*: **rester** ~ to be flabbergasted.

pantomime [pàǹtomēm] *nf* mime; (*pièce*) mime show; (*péj*) fuss, carrying-on (*US*), carry-on (*Brit*).

pantouflard, e [pàǹtōōflàr, -árd(ə)] *a* (*péj*) stay-at-home.

pantoufle [pàǹtōōfl(ə)] *nf* slipper.

panure [pànür] *nf* breadcrumbs *pl*.

PAO *sigle f* (= *publication assistée par ordinateur*) desktop publishing.

paon [pàǹ] *nm* peacock.

papa [pàpà] *nm* dad(dy).

papauté [pàpōtā] *nf* papacy.

papaye [pàpáy] *nf* pawpaw.

pape [pàp] *nm* pope.

paperasse [pàprás] *nf* (*péj*) useless papers *pl*; forms *pl*.

paperasserie [pàprásrē] *nf* (*péj*) red tape *q*; paperwork *q*.

papeterie [pàpàtrē] *nf* (*fabrication du papier*) paper-making (industry); (*usine*) paper mill; (*magasin*) stationer's; (*articles*) stationery.

papetier, ière [pàptyā, -yer] *nm/f* paper-maker; stationer.

papetier-libraire, *pl* **papetiers-libraires** [pàptyelēbrēr] *nm* bookseller and stationer.

papier [pàpyā] *nm* paper; (*feuille*) sheet *ou* piece of paper; (*article*) article; (*écrit officiel*) document; ~**s** *nmpl* (*aussi*: ~**s d'identité**) (identity) papers; **sur le** ~ (*théoriquement*) on paper; **noircir du** ~ to write page after page; ~ **couché/glacé** art/glazed paper; ~ **(d')aluminium** aluminum (*US*) *ou* aluminium (*Brit*) foil, tinfoil; ~

d'Arménie incense paper; ~ **bible** India *ou* bible paper; ~ **de brouillon** rough *ou* scrap paper; ~ **bulle** manil(l)a paper; ~ **buvard** blotting paper; ~ **calque** tracing paper; ~ **carbone** carbon paper; ~ **collant** Scotch ® (*US*), Sellotape ® (*Brit*) *ou* sticky tape; ~ **en continu** continuous stationery; ~ **à dessin** drawing paper; ~ **d'emballage** wrapping paper; ~ **gommé** gummed paper; ~ **hygiénique** toilet paper; ~ **journal** newsprint; (*pour emballer*) newspaper; ~ **à lettres** writing paper, notepaper; ~ **mâché** papier-mâché; ~ **machine** typing paper; ~ **peint** wallpaper; ~ **pelure** India paper; ~ **à pliage accordéon** fanfold paper; ~ **de soie** tissue paper; ~ **thermique** thermal paper; ~ **de tournesol** litmus paper; ~ **de verre** sandpaper.

papier-filtre, *pl* **papiers-filtres** [pàpyāfēltr(ə)] *nm* filter paper.

papier-monnaie, *pl* **papiers-monnaies** [pàpyāmone] *nm* paper money.

papille [pàpēy] *nf*: ~**s gustatives** taste buds.

papillon [pàpēyóǹ] *nm* butterfly; (*fam: contravention*) (parking) ticket; (*TECH: écrou*) wing *ou* butterfly nut; ~ **de nuit** moth.

papillonner [pàpēyonā] *vi* to flit from one thing (*ou* person) to another.

papillote [pàpēyot] *nf* (*pour cheveux*) curlpaper; (*de gigot*) (paper) frill.

papilloter [pàpēyotā] *vi* (*yeux*) to blink; (*paupières*) to flutter; (*lumière*) to flicker.

papotage [pàpotázh] *nm* chitchat.

papoter [pàpotá] *vi* to chatter.

papou, e [pàpōō] *a* Papuan.

Papouasie-Nouvelle-Guinée [pàpwàzēnōōvelgēnā] *nf*: **la** ~ Papua-New-Guinea.

paprika [pàprēká] *nm* paprika.

papyrus [pàpērüs] *nm* papyrus.

Pâque [pàk] *nf*: **la** ~ Passover; *voir aussi* **Pâques**.

paquebot [pàkbō] *nm* liner.

pâquerette [pàkret] *nf* daisy.

Pâques [pàk] *nm*, *nfpl* Easter; **faire ses** ~ to do one's Easter duties; **l'île de** ~ Easter Island.

paquet [pàke] *nm* packet; (*colis*) parcel; (*ballot*) bundle; (*dans négociations*) package (deal); (*fig: tas*): ~ **de** pile *ou* heap of; ~**s** *nmpl* (*bagages*) bags; **mettre le** ~ (*fam*) to give one's all; ~ **de mer** big wave.

paquetage [pàktázh] *nm* (*MIL*) kit, pack.

paquet-cadeau, *pl* **paquets-cadeaux** [pàkekádō] *nm* gift-wrapped parcel.

par [pàr] *prép* by; **finir** *etc* ~ to end *etc* with; ~ **amour** out of love; **passer** ~ **Lyon/la côte** to go via *ou* through Lyons/along by the coast; ~ **la fenêtre** (*jeter, regarder*) out of the window; **3** ~ **jour/personne** 3 a *ou* per day/head; **2** ~ **2** two at a time; (*marcher etc*) in twos; ~ **où?** which way?; ~ **ici** this way; (*dans le coin*) around here; ~**-ci, **~**-là** here and there.

para [pàrá] *nm* = **parachutiste**.

parabole [pàràbol] *nf* (*REL*) parable; (*GÉOM*) parabola.

parabolique [pàràbolēk] *a* parabolic.

parachever [pàràshvā] *vt* to perfect.

parachute [pàràshüt] *nm* parachute.

parachuter [párảshütā] *vt* (*soldat etc*) to parachute; (*fig*) to pitchfork.

parachutisme [párảshütēsm(ǝ)] *nm* parachuting.

parachutiste [párảshütēst(ǝ)] *nm/f* parachutist; (*MIL*) paratrooper.

parade [párảd] *nf* (*spectacle, défilé*) parade; (*ESCRIME, BOXE*) parry; (*ostentation*): **faire ~ de** to display, show off; (*défense, riposte*): **trouver la ~ à une attaque** to find the answer to an attack; **de ~** *a* ceremonial; (*superficiel*) superficial, outward.

parader [párảdā] *vi* to swagger (around), show off.

paradis [párảdē] *nm* heaven, paradise; **P~ terrestre** (*REL*) Garden of Eden; (*fig*) heaven on earth.

paradisiaque [párảdēzyák] *a* heavenly, divine.

paradoxal, e, aux [párảdoksál, -ō] *a* paradoxical.

paradoxe [párảdoks(ǝ)] *nm* paradox.

parafe [páráf] *nm*, **parafer** [páráfā] *vt* = **paraphe, parapher**.

paraffine [páráfēn] *nf* paraffin; paraffin wax.

paraffiné, e [páráfēnā] *a*: **papier ~** wax(ed) paper.

parafoudre [párảfōōdr(ǝ)] *nm* (*ÉLEC*) lightning rod (*US*) *ou* conductor (*Brit*).

parages [párảzh] *nmpl* (*NAVIG*) waters; **dans les ~ (de)** in the area *ou* vicinity (of).

paragraphe [párảgráf] *nm* paragraph.

Paraguay [párảgwe] *nm*: **le ~** Paraguay.

paraguayen, ne [párảgwáyáñ, -en] *a* Paraguayan ♦ *nm/f*: **P~, ne** Paraguayan.

paraître [páretr(ǝ)] *vb avec attribut* to seem, look, appear ♦ *vi* to appear; (*être visible*) to show; (*PRESSE, ÉDITION*) to be published, come out, appear; (*briller*) to show off; **laisser ~ qch** to let (sth) show ♦ *vb impersonnel*: **il paraît que** it seems *ou* appears that; **il me paraît que** it seems to me that; **il paraît absurde de** it seems absurd to; **il ne paraît pas son âge** he doesn't look his age; **~ en justice** to appear before the court(s); **~ en scène/en public/à l'écran** to appear on stage/in public/on the screen.

parallèle [párálel] *a* parallel; (*police, marché*) unofficial; (*société, énergie*) alternative ♦ *nm* (*comparaison*): **faire un ~ entre** to draw a parallel between; (*GÉO*) parallel ♦ *nf* parallel (line); **en ~** in parallel; **mettre en ~** (*choses opposées*) to compare; (*choses semblables*) to parallel.

parallèlement [párálelmáñ] *ad* in parallel; (*fig: en même temps*) at the same time.

parallélisme [párálālēsm(ǝ)] *nm* parallelism; (*AUTO*) wheel alignment.

parallélogramme [párálālográm] *nm* parallelogram.

paralyser [párálēzā] *vt* to paralyze.

paralysie [párálēzē] *nf* paralysis.

paralytique [párálētēk] *a, nm/f* paralytic.

paramédical, e, aux [párámādēkál, -ō] *a* paramedical.

paramètre [párámetr(ǝ)] *nm* parameter.

paramilitaire [párámēlēter] *a* paramilitary.

paranoïaque [párảnoyák] *nm/f* paranoiac.

paranormal, e, aux [párảnormál, -ō] *a* para-

normal.

parapet [párảpe] *nm* parapet.

paraphe [páráf] *nm* (*trait*) flourish; (*signature*) initials *pl*; signature.

parapher [páráfā] *vt* to initial; to sign.

paraphrase [páráfráz] *nf* paraphrase.

paraphraser [páráfrázā] *vt* to paraphrase.

paraplégique [páráplảzhēk] *a, nm/f* paraplegic.

parapluie [párảplüē] *nm* umbrella; **~ atomique** *ou* **nucléaire** nuclear umbrella; **~ pliant** telescopic umbrella.

parapsychique [párápsēshēk] *a* parapsychological.

parapsychologie [párápsēkolozhē] *nf* parapsychology.

parapublic, ique [párápüblēk] *a partly state-controlled*.

parascolaire [párảskoler] *a* extracurricular.

parasitaire [párázēter] *a* parasitic(al).

parasite [párázēt] *nm* parasite ♦ *a* (*BOT, BIO*) parasitic(al); **~s** *nmpl* (*TÉL*) interference *sg*.

parasol [párásol] *nm* parasol, sunshade.

paratonnerre [párátoner] *nm* lightning rod (*US*) *ou* conductor (*Brit*).

paravent [párảváñ] *nm* folding screen; (*fig*) screen.

parc [párk] *nm* (*public*) park, gardens *pl*; (*de château etc*) grounds *pl*; (*pour le bétail*) pen, enclosure; (*d'enfant*) playpen; (*MIL*: *entrepôt*) depot; (*ensemble d'unités*) stock; (*de voitures etc*) fleet; **~ d'attractions** amusement park; **~ automobile** (*d'un pays*) number of cars on the roads; **~ à huîtres** oyster bed; **~ national** national park; **~ naturel** nature reserve; **~ de stationnement** parking lot (*US*), car park (*Brit*); **~ zoologique** zoological gardens *pl*.

parcelle [pársel] *nf* fragment, scrap; (*de terrain*) plot, parcel.

parcelliser [pársālēzā] *vt* to divide *ou* split up.

parce que [pársk(ǝ)] *cj* because.

parchemin [párshǝmáñ] *nm* parchment.

parcheminé, e [párshǝmēnā] *a* wrinkled; (*papier*) with a parchment finish.

parcimonie [pársēmonē] *nf* parsimony, parsimoniousness.

parcimonieux, euse [pársēmonyœ̄, -œ̄z] *a* parsimonious, miserly.

parc(o)mètre [párk(o)metr(ǝ)] *nm* parking meter.

parcotrain [párkotráñ] *nm* station parking lot (*US*) *ou* car park (*Brit*).

parcourir [párkōōrēr] *vt* (*trajet, distance*) to cover; (*article, livre*) to skim *ou* glance through; (*lieu*) to go all over, travel up and down; (*suj: frisson, vibration*) to run through; **~ des yeux** to run one's eye over.

parcours [párkōōr] *vb voir* **parcourir** ♦ *nm* (*trajet*) journey; (*itinéraire*) route; (*SPORT: terrain*) course; (*: tour*) round; run; lap; **~ du combattant** assault course.

parcouru, e [párkōōrü] *pp de* **parcourir**.

par-delà [párdǝlá] *prép* beyond.

par-dessous [párdǝsōō] *prép*, *ad* under(neath).

pardessus [párdǝsü] *nm* overcoat.

par-dessus [párdǝsü] *prép* over (the top of) ♦ *ad* over (the top); **~ le marché** on top of it all.

par-devant [párdəváň] *prép* in the presence of, before ♦ *ad* at the front; around (*US*) *ou* round (*Brit*) the front.

pardon [párdôň] *nm* forgiveness *q* ♦ *excl* (*excuses*) (I'm) sorry; (*pour interpeller etc*) excuse me; (*demander de répéter*) pardon me? (*US*), (I beg your) pardon? (*Brit*).

pardonnable [párdonábl(ə)] *a* forgivable, excusable.

pardonner [párdoná] *vt* to forgive; ~ **qch à qn** to forgive sb for sth; **qui ne pardonne pas** (*maladie, erreur*) fatal.

paré, e [párá] *a* ready, prepared.

pare-balles [párbál] *a inv* bulletproof.

pare-boue [párbōō] *nm inv* mudflap.

pare-brise [párbrēz] *nm inv* windshield (*US*), windscreen (*Brit*).

pare-chocs [párshok] *nm inv* bumper.

pare-étincelles [párātǎnscl] *nm inv* fireguard.

pare-feu [párfœ̄] *nm inv* firebreak ♦ *a inv*: **portes** ~ fire (resistant) doors.

pareil, le [pàrcy] *a* (*identique*) the same, alike; (*similaire*) similar; (*tel*): **un courage/livre** ~ such courage/a book, courage/a book like this; **de** ~**s livres** such books ♦ *ad*: **habillés** ~ dressed the same (way), dressed alike; **faire** ~ to do the same (thing); **j'en veux un** ~ I'd like one just like it; **rien de** ~ no (*ou* any) such thing, nothing (*ou* anything) like it; **ses** ~**s** one's fellow men; one's peers; **ne pas avoir son (sa)** ~**(le)** to be second to none; ~ **à** the same as; similar to; **sans** ~ unparalleled, unequaled (*US*), unequalled (*Brit*); **c'est du** ~ **au même** it comes to the same thing, it's six (of one) and half-a-dozen (of the other); **en** ~ **cas** in such a case; **rendre la** ~**le à qn** to pay sb back in his own coin.

pareillement [pàrcymáň] *ad* the same, alike; in such a way; (*également*) likewise.

parement [pàrmáň] *nm* (*CONSTR, revers d'un col, d'une manche*) facing; (*REL*): ~ **d'autel** antependium.

parent, e [pàráň, -áňt] *nm/f*: **un/une** ~**/e** *a* relative *ou* relation ♦ *a*: **être** ~ **de** to be related to; ~**s** *nmpl* (*père et mère*) parents; (*famille, proches*) relatives, relations; ~**s par alliance** relatives *ou* relations by marriage; ~**s en ligne directe** blood relations.

parental, e, aux [pàráňtál, -ō] *a* parental.

parenté [pàráňtá] *nf* (*lien*) relationship; (*personnes*) relatives *pl*, relations *pl*.

parenthèse [pàráňtez] *nf* (*ponctuation*), parenthesis; (*MATH*) parenthesis (*US*), bracket (*Brit*); (*digression*) parenthesis, digression; **ouvrir/fermer la** ~ to open/close the parentheses; **entre** ~**s** in parentheses; (*fig*) incidentally.

parer [pàrá] *vt* to adorn; (*CULIN*) to dress, trim; (*éviter*) to ward off; ~ **à** (*danger*) to ward off; (*inconvénient*) to deal with; **se** ~ **de** (*fig: qualité, titre*) to assume; ~ **à toute éventualité** to be ready for every eventuality; ~ **au plus pressé** to attend to what's most urgent.

pare-soleil [pàrsolcy] *nm inv* sun visor.

paresse [pàrcs] *nf* laziness.

paresser [párásā] *vi* to laze around.

paresseusement [páresœ̄zmáň] *ad* lazily; sluggishly.

paresseux, euse [páresœ̄, -œ̄z] *a* lazy; (*fig*) slow, sluggish ♦ *nm* (*ZOOL*) sloth.

parfaire [pàrfer] *vt* to perfect, complete.

parfait, e [pàrfe, -et] *pp de* **parfaire** ♦ *a* perfect ♦ *nm* (*LING*) perfect (tense); (*CULIN*) parfait ♦ *excl* fine, excellent.

parfaitement [pàrfetmáň] *ad* perfectly ♦ *excl* (most) certainly.

parfaites [pàrfet], **parfasse** [pàrfàs], **parferai** [pàrfrā] *etc vb voir* **parfaire**.

parfois [pàrfwá] *ad* sometimes.

parfum [pàrfœň] *nm* (*produit*) perfume, scent; (*odeur: de fleur*) scent, fragrance; (: *de tabac, vin*) aroma; (*goût: de glace, milkshake*) flavor (*US*), flavour (*Brit*).

parfumé, e [pàrfūmā] *a* (*fleur, fruit*) fragrant; (*papier à lettres etc*) scented; (*femme*) wearing perfume *ou* scent, perfumed; (*aromatisé*): ~ **au café** coffee-flavored (*US*) *ou* -flavoured (*Brit*).

parfumer [pàrfūmā] *vt* (*suj: odeur, bouquet*) to perfume; (*mouchoir*) to put scent *ou* perfume on; (*crème, gâteau*) to flavor (*US*), flavour (*Brit*); **se** ~ to put on (some) perfume *ou* scent; (*d'habitude*) to use perfume *ou* scent.

parfumerie [pàrfūmrē] *nf* (*commerce*) perfumery; (*produits*) perfumes *pl*; (*boutique*) perfume store (*US*) *ou* shop (*Brit*).

pari [pàrē] *nm* bet, wager; (*SPORT*) bet; ~ **mutuel urbain (PMU)** *system of betting on horses*.

paria [pàryà] *nm* outcast.

parier [pàryā] *vt* to bet; **j'aurais parié que si/non** I'd have said he (*ou* you *etc*) would/wouldn't.

parieur [pàryœr] *nm* (*turfiste etc*) punter.

Paris [pàrē] *n* Paris.

parisien, ne [pàrēzyaň, -en] *a* Parisian; (*GÉO, ADMIN*) Paris *cpd* ♦ *nm/f*: **P~, ne** Parisian.

paritaire [pàrēter] *a*: **commission** ~ joint commission.

parité [pàrētá] *nf* parity; ~ **de change** (*ÉCON*) exchange parity.

parjure [pàrzhür] *nm* (*faux serment*) false oath, perjury; (*violation de serment*) breach of oath, perjury ♦ *nm/f* perjurer.

parjurer [pàrzhürā]: **se** ~ *vi* to perjure o.s.

parka [pàrkà] *nf* parka.

parking [pàrkēng] *nm* (*lieu*) parking lot (*US*), car park (*Brit*).

parlant, e [pàrlàň, -áňt] *a* (*fig*) graphic, vivid; (: *comparaison, preuve*) eloquent; (*CINÉMA*) talking ♦ *ad*: **généralement** ~ generally speaking.

parlé, e [pàrlā] *a*: **langue** ~**e** spoken language.

parlement [pàrləmáň] *nm* parliament.

parlementaire [pàrləmáňter] *a* parliamentary ♦ *nm/f* (*député*) ≈ Member of Congress (*US*) *ou* Parliament (*Brit*); parliamentarian; (*négociateur*) negotiator, mediator.

parlementarisme [pàrləmáňtárēsm(ə)] *nm* parliamentary government.

parlementer [pàrləmáňtā] *vi* (*ennemis*) to negotiate, parley; (*s'entretenir, discuter*) to argue at length, have lengthy talks.

parler [pàrlā] *nm* speech; dialect ♦ *vi* to speak, talk; (*avouer*) to talk; ~ (**à qn**) **de** to talk *ou* speak (to sb) about; ~ **pour qn** (*intercéder*) to speak for sb; ~ **en l'air** to say the first thing that comes into one's head; ~ **le/en français** to speak French/in French; ~ **affaires** to talk business; ~ **en dormant/du nez** to talk in one's sleep/through one's nose; **sans** ~ **de** (*fig*) not to mention, to say nothing of; **tu parles!** you must be joking!; **n'en parlons plus!** let's forget it!

parleur [pàrlœr] *nm*: **beau** ~ fine talker.

parloir [pàrlwàr] *nm* (*d'une prison, d'un hôpital*) visiting room; (*REL*) parlor (*US*), parlour (*Brit*).

parlote [pàrlot] *nf* chitchat.

Parme [pàrm(ə)] *n* Parma.

parme [pàrm(ə)] *a* violet (blue).

parmesan [pàrməzàñ] *nm* Parmesan (cheese).

parmi [pàrmē] *prép* among(st).

parodie [pàrodē] *nf* parody.

parodier [pàrodyā] *vt* (*œuvre, auteur*) to parody.

paroi [pàrwá] *nf* wall; (*cloison*) partition; ~ **rocheuse** rock face.

paroisse [pàrwás] *nf* parish.

paroissial, e, aux [pàrwàsyàl, -ō] *a* parish *cpd*.

paroissien, ne [pàrwàsyañ, -en] *nm/f* parishioner ♦ *nm* prayer book.

parole [pàrol] *nf* (*faculté*): **la** ~ speech; (*mot, promesse*) word; (*REL*): **la bonne** ~ the word of God; **~s** *nfpl* (*MUS*) words, lyrics; **tenir** ~ to keep one's word; **avoir la** ~ to have the floor; **n'avoir qu'une** ~ to be true to one's word; **donner la** ~ **à qn** to hand over to sb; **prendre la** ~ to speak; **demander la** ~ to ask for permission to speak; **perdre la** ~ to lose the power of speech; (*fig*) to lose one's tongue; **je le crois sur** ~ I'll take his word for it, I'll take him at his word; **temps de** ~ (*TV, RADIO etc*) discussion time; **ma** ~**!** my word!, good heavens!; ~ **d'honneur** word of honor.

parolier, ière [pàrolyā, -yer] *nm/f* lyricist; (*OPÉRA*) librettist.

paroxysme [pàroksēsm(ə)] *nm* height, paroxysm.

parpaing [pàrpañ] *nm* bondstone.

parquer [pàrkā] *vt* (*voiture, matériel*) to park; (*bestiaux*) to pen (in *ou* up); (*prisonniers*) to pack in.

parquet [pàrke] *nm* (parquet) floor; (*JUR*: *bureau*) public prosecutor's office; **le** ~ (**général**) (*magistrats*) ≈ the Bench.

parqueter [pàrkətā] *vt* to lay a parquet floor in.

parrain [pàrañ] *nm* godfather; (*d'un navire*) namer; (*d'un nouvel adhérent*) sponsor, proposer.

parrainage [pàrenázh] *nm* sponsorship.

parrainer [pàrānā] *vt* (*nouvel adhérent*) to sponsor, propose; (*entreprise*) to promote, sponsor.

parricide [pàrēsēd] *nm, nf* parricide.

pars [pàr] *vb voir* **partir**.

parsemer [pàrsəmā] *vt* (*suj: feuilles, papiers*) to be scattered over; ~ **qch de** to scatter sth with.

parsi, e [pàrsē] *a* Parsee.

part [pàr] *vb voir* **partir** ♦ *nf* (*qui revient à qn*) share; (*fraction, partie*) part; (*de gâteau, fromage*) portion; (*FINANCE*) (non-voting) share; **prendre** ~ **à** (*débat etc*) to take part in; (*soucis, douleur de qn*) to share in; **faire** ~ **de qch à qn** to announce sth to sb, inform sb of sth; **pour ma** ~ as for me, as far as I'm concerned; **à** ~ **entière** *a* full; **de la** ~ **de** (*au nom de*) on behalf of; (*donné par*) from; **c'est de la** ~ **de qui?** (*au téléphone*) who's calling *ou* speaking (please)?; **de toute(s)** ~**(s)** from all sides *ou* quarters; **de** ~ **et d'autre** on both sides, on either side; **de** ~ **en** ~ right through; **d'une** ~ **... d'autre** ~ on the one hand ... on the other hand; **nulle/ autre/quelque** ~ nowhere/elsewhere/ somewhere; **à** ~ *ad* separately; (*de côté*) aside ♦ *prép* apart from, except for ♦ *a* exceptional, special; **pour une large** *ou* **bonne** ~ to a great extent; **prendre qch en bonne/mauvaise** ~ to take sth well/badly; **faire la** ~ **des choses** to make allowances; **faire la** ~ **du feu** (*fig*) to cut one's losses; **faire la** ~ (**trop**) **belle à qn** to give sb more than his (*ou* her) share.

part. *abr* = **particulier**.

partage [pàrtàzh] *nm* (*voir partager*) sharing (out) *q*, share-out (*Brit*); sharing; dividing up; (*POL*: *de suffrages*) share; **recevoir qch en** ~ to receive sth as one's share (*ou* lot); **sans** ~ undivided.

partagé, e [pàrtàzhā] *a* (*opinions etc*) divided; (*amour*) shared; **temps** ~ (*INFORM*) time sharing; **être** ~ **entre** to be shared between; **être** ~ **sur** to be divided about.

partager [pàrtàzhā] *vt* to share; (*distribuer, répartir*) to share (out); (*morceler, diviser*) to divide (up); **se** ~ *vt* (*héritage etc*) to share between themselves (*ou* ourselves *etc*).

partance [pàrtãns]: **en** ~ *ad* outbound, due to leave; **en** ~ **pour** (bound) for.

partant, e [pàrtañ, -ãnt] *vb voir* **partir** ♦ *a*: **être** ~ **pour qch** (*d'accord pour*) to be quite ready for sth ♦ *nm* (*SPORT*) starter; (*HIPPISME*) runner.

partenaire [pàrtəner] *nm/f* partner; ~**s sociaux** management and workforce.

parterre [pàrter] *nm* (*de fleurs*) (flower) bed, border; (*THÉÂTRE*) orchestra (*US*), stalls *pl* (*Brit*).

parti [pàrtē] *nm* (*POL*) party; (*décision*) course of action; (*personne à marier*) match; **tirer** ~ **de** to take advantage of, turn to good account; **prendre le** ~ **de faire** to make up one's mind to do, resolve to do; **prendre le** ~ **de qn** to stand up for sb, side with sb; **prendre** ~ (**pour/contre**) to take sides *ou* a stand (for/against); **prendre son** ~ **de** to come to terms with; ~ **pris** bias.

partial, e, aux [pàrsyàl, -ō] *a* biased, partial.

partialement [pàrsyàlmãñ] *ad* in a biased way.

partialité [pàrsyàlētā] *nf* bias, partiality.

participant, e [pàrtēsēpãñ, -ãnt] *nm/f* participant; (*à un concours*) entrant; (*d'une société*) member.

participation [pàrtēsēpàsyôñ] *nf* participation; sharing; (*COMM*) interest; **la** ~ **aux bénéfices** profit-sharing; **la** ~ **ouvrière** worker participation; **"avec la ~ de ..."** "featuring ...".

participe [pártēsēp] *nm* participle; **~ passé/présent** past/present participle.

participer [pártēsēpā]: **~ à** *vt* (*course, réunion*) to take part in; (*profits etc*) to share in; (*frais etc*) to contribute to; (*entreprise: financièrement*) to cooperate in; (*chagrin, succès de qn*) to share (in); **~ de** *vt* to partake of.

particulariser [pártēkülárēzā] *vt*: **se ~** to mark o.s. (*ou* itself) out.

particularisme [pártēkülárēsm(ə)] *nm* sense of identity.

particularité [pártēkülárētā] *nf* particularity; (*distinctive*) characteristic, feature.

particule [pártēkül] *nf* particle; **~ (nobiliaire)** nobiliary particle.

particulier, ière [pártēkülyā, -yer] *a* (*personnel, privé*) private; (*spécial*) special, particular; (*caractéristique*) characteristic, distinctive; (*spécifique*) particular ♦ *nm* (*individu:* ADMIN) private individual; **"~ vend ..."** (COMM) "for sale privately ...", "for sale by owner ..." (*US*); **~ à** peculiar to; **en ~** *ad* (*surtout*) in particular, particularly; (*à part*) separately; (*en privé*) in private.

particulièrement [pártēkülyermáṅ] *ad* particularly.

partie [pártē] *nf* (*gén*) part; (*profession, spécialité*) field, subject; (*JUR etc: protagonistes*) party; (*de cartes, tennis etc*) game; (*fig: lutte, combat*) struggle, fight; **une ~ de campagne/de pêche** an outing in the country/a fishing party *ou* trip; **en ~** *ad* partly, in part; **faire ~ de** to belong to; (*suj: chose*) to be part of; **prendre qn à ~** to take sb to task; (*malmener*) to set on sb; **en grande ~** largely, in the main; **ce n'est que ~ remise** it will be for another time *ou* the next time; **avoir ~ liée avec qn** to be in league with sb; **~ civile** (JUR) party claiming damages in a criminal case.

partiel, le [pársyel] *a* partial ♦ *nm* (SCOL) class exam.

partiellement [pársyelmáṅ] *ad* partially, partly.

partir [pártēr] *vi* (*gén*) to go; (*quitter*) to go, leave; (*s'éloigner*) to go (*ou* drive *etc*) away *ou* off; (*moteur*) to start; (*pétard*) to go off; (*bouchon*) to come out; (*bouton*) to come off; **~ de** (*lieu: quitter*) to leave; (: *commencer à*) to start from; (*date*) to run *ou* start from; **~ pour/à** (*lieu, pays etc*) to leave for/go off to; **à ~ de** from.

partisan, e [pártēzáṅ, -áṅ] *nm/f* partisan; (*d'un parti, régime etc*) supporter ♦ *a* (*lutte, querelle*) partisan, one-sided; **être ~ de qch/faire** to be in favor of sth/doing.

partitif, ive [pártētēf, -ēv] *a*: **article ~** partitive article.

partition [pártēsyóṅ] *nf* (MUS) score.

partout [pártoō] *ad* everywhere; **~ où il allait** everywhere *ou* wherever he went; **trente ~** (TENNIS) thirty all.

paru [párü] *pp de* **paraître**.

parure [párür] *nf* (*bijoux etc*) finery *q*; jewelry *q* (*US*), jewellery *q* (*Brit*); (*assortiment*) set.

parus [párü] *etc vb voir* **paraître**.

parution [párüsyóṅ] *nf* publication, appearance.

parvenir [párvənēr]: **~ à** *vt* (*atteindre*) to reach; (*obtenir, arriver à*) to attain; (*réussir*): **~ à faire** to manage to do, succeed in doing; **faire ~ qch à qn** to have sth sent to sb.

parvenu, e [párvənü] *pp de* **parvenir** ♦ *nm/f* (*péj*) parvenu, upstart.

parviendrai [párvyaṅdrā], **parviens** [párvyaṅ] *etc voir* **parvenir**.

parvis [párvē] *nm* square (*in front of a church*).

pas [pâ] *nm voir le mot suivant* ♦ *ad* not; **~ de** no; **ne ... ~:** **il ne le voit ~/ne l'a ~ vu/ne le verra ~** he doesn't see it/hasn't seen it *ou* didn't see it/won't see it; **ils n'ont ~ de voiture/d'enfants** they haven't got a car/any children, they have no car/children; **~ de sucre, merci** no sugar, thank you; **il m'a dit de ne ~ le faire** he told me not to do it; **il n'est ~ plus grand** he isn't bigger, he's no bigger; **... lui ~ ou ~ lui** he doesn't (*ou* isn't *etc*); **ceci est à vous ou ~?** is this yours or not?; **non ~ que** ... not that ...; **une pomme ~ mûre** an unripe apple, an apple which isn't ripe; **~ du tout** not at all; **~ encore** not yet; **~ plus tard qu'hier** only yesterday; **~ mal** a not bad, quite good (*ou* pretty *ou* nice) ♦ *ad* quite well; (*beaucoup*) quite a lot; **~ mal de** quite a lot of.

pas [pâ] *ad voir le mot précédent* ♦ *nm* (*allure, mesure*) pace; (*démarche*) tread; (*enjambée, DANSE, fig: étape*) step; (*bruit*) (foot)step; (*trace*) footprint; (*allure*) pace; (*d'un cheval*) walk; (*mesure*) pace; (TECH: *de vis, d'écrou*) thread; **~ à ~** step by step; **au ~** at walking pace; **de ce ~** (*à l'instant même*) straightaway, at once; **marcher à grands ~** to stride along; **mettre qn au ~** to bring sb to heel; **au ~ de gymnastique/de course** at a jog trot/at a run; **à ~ de loup** stealthily; **faire les cent ~** to pace up and down; **faire les premiers ~** to make the first move; **retourner** *ou* **revenir sur ses ~** to retrace one's steps; **se tirer d'un mauvais ~** to get o.s. out of a tight spot; **sur le ~ de la porte** on the doorstep; **le ~ de Calais** (*détroit*) the Straits *pl* of Dover.

pascal, e, aux [páskál, -ō] *a* Easter *cpd*.

passable [pâsábl(ə)] *a* passable, tolerable.

passablement [pâsábləmáṅ] *ad* (*pas trop mal*) reasonably well; (*beaucoup*) quite a lot.

passade [pâsád] *nf* passing fancy, whim.

passage [pâsázh] *nm* (*fait de passer*) *voir* **passer**; (*lieu, prix de la traversée, extrait de livre etc*) passage; (*chemin*) way; (*itinéraire*) **: sur le ~ du cortège** along the route of the procession; **"laissez/n'obstruez pas le ~"** "keep clear/do not block"; **au ~** (*en passant*) as I (*ou* he *etc*) went by; **de ~** (*touristes*) passing through; (*amants etc*) casual; **~ clouté** pedestrian crossing; **"~ interdit"** "do not enter", "no thoroughfare"; **~ à niveau** grade (*US*) *ou* level (*Brit*) crossing; **"~ protégé"** right of way over secondary road(s) on your right; **~ souterrain** underpass, subway (*Brit*); **~ à tabac** beating; **~ à vide** (*fig*) rough spot.

passager, ère [pàsàzhã, -er] *a* passing; (*hôte*) short-stay *cpd*; (*oiseau*) migratory ♦ *nm/f* passenger; ~ **clandestin** stowaway.

passagèrement [pàsàzhermâñ] *ad* temporarily, for a short time.

passant, e [pàsâñ, -âñt] *a* (*rue, endroit*) busy ♦ *nm/f* passer-by ♦ *nm* (*pour ceinture etc*) loop; **en ~: remarquer qch en ~** to notice sth in passing.

passation [pàsâsyôñ] *nf* (*JUR: d'un acte*) signing; ~ **des pouvoirs** transfer *ou* handover of power.

passe [pàs] *nf* (*SPORT, magnétique*) pass; (*NAVIG*) channel ♦ *nm* (*passe-partout*) master *ou* skeleton key; **être en ~ de faire** to be on the way to doing; **être dans une bonne ~** (*fig*) to be in a healthy situation; **être dans une mauvaise ~** (*fig*) to be having a rough time; ~ **d'armes** (*fig*) heated exchange.

passé, e [pàsã] *a* (*événement, temps*) past; (*couleur, tapisserie*) faded; (*précédent*): **dimanche ~** last Sunday ♦ *prép* after ♦ *nm* past; (*LING*) past (tense); **il est ~ midi** *ou* **midi ~** it's past twelve; ~ **de mode** out of fashion; ~ **composé** perfect (tense); ~ **simple** past historic.

passe-droit [pàsdrwà] *nm* special privilege.

passéiste [pàsãëst(ə)] *a* backward-looking.

passementerie [pàsmâñtrẽ] *nf* trimmings *pl*.

passe-montagne [pàsmôñtàny] *nm* balaclava.

passe-partout [pàspàrtōō] *nm inv* master *ou* skeleton key ♦ *a inv* all-purpose.

passe-passe [pàspàs] *nm*: **tour de ~** trick, sleight of hand *q*.

passe-plat [pàsplà] *nm* serving hatch.

passeport [pàspor] *nm* passport.

passer [pàsã] *vi* (*se rendre, aller*) to go; (*voiture, piétons: défiler*) to pass (by), go by; (*faire une halte rapide: facteur, laitier etc*) to come, call; (: *pour rendre visite*) to call *ou* drop in; (*courant, air, lumière, franchir un obstacle etc*) to get through; (*accusé, projet de loi*): ~ **devant** to come before; (*film, émission*) to be on; (*temps, jours*) to pass, go by; (*liquide, café*) to go through; (*être digéré, avalé*) to go down; (*couleur, papier*) to fade; (*mode*) to die out; (*douleur*) to pass, go away; (*CARTES*) to pass; (*SCOL*) to be promoted (to the next grade) (*US*), go up (to the next class) (*Brit*); (*devenir*): ~ **président** to be appointed *ou* become president ♦ *vt* (*frontière, rivière etc*) to cross; (*douane*) to go through; (*examen*) to take; (*visite médicale etc*) to have; (*journée, temps*) to spend; (*donner*): ~ **qch à qn** to pass sth to sb; to give sb sth; (*transmettre*): ~ **qch à qn** to pass sth on to sb; (*enfiler: vêtement*) to slip on; (*faire entrer, mettre*): **(faire) ~ qch dans/par** to get sth into/ through; (*café*) to pour the water on; (*thé, soupe*) to strain; (*film, pièce*) to show, put on; (*disque*) to play, put on; (*marché, accord*) to agree on; (*tolérer*): ~ **qch à qn** to let sb get away with sth; **se ~** *vi* (*avoir lieu: scène, action*) to take place; (*se dérouler: entretien etc*) to go; (*arriver*): **que s'est-il passé?** what happened?; (*s'écouler: semaine etc*) to pass, go by; **se ~ de** *vt* to go *ou* do

without; **se ~ les mains sous l'eau/de l'eau sur le visage** to put one's hands under the tap/run water over one's face; **en passant** in passing; ~ **par** to go through; **passez devant/par ici** go in front/this way; ~ **sur** *vt* (*faute, détail inutile*) to pass over; ~ **dans les mœurs/l'usage** to become the custom/ normal usage; ~ **avant qch/qn** (*fig*) to come before sth/sb; **laisser ~** (*air, lumière, personne*) to let through; (*occasion*) to let slip, miss; (*erreur*) to overlook; **faire ~** (*message*) to get over *ou* across; **faire ~ à qn le goût de qch** to cure sb of his (*ou* her) taste for sth; ~ **à la radio/fouille** to be X-rayed/searched; ~ **à la radio/télévision** to be on the radio/on television; ~ **à table** to sit down to eat; ~ **au salon** to go into the living room; ~ **à l'opposition** to go over to the opposition; ~ **aux aveux** to confess, make a confession; ~ **à l'action** to go into action; ~ **pour riche** to be taken for a rich man; **il passait pour avoir** he was said to have; **faire ~ qn/qch pour** to make sb/sth out to be; **passe encore de le penser, mais de le dire!** it's one thing to think it, but to say it!; **passons!** let's say no more (about it); **et j'en passe!** and that's not all!; ~ **en seconde,** ~ **la seconde** (*AUTO*) to shift into second; ~ **qch en fraude** to smuggle sth in (*ou* out); ~ **la main par la portière** to stick one's hand out of the door; ~ **le balai/l'aspirateur** to sweep up/vacuum; ~ **commande/la parole à qn** to hand over to sb; **je vous passe M X** (*je vous mets en communication avec lui*) I'm putting you through to Mr X; (*je lui passe l'appareil*) here is Mr X, I'll hand you over to Mr X; ~ **prendre** to (come and) get.

passereau, x [pàsrō] *nm* sparrow.

passerelle [pàsrel] *nf* footbridge; (*de navire, avion*) gangway; (*NAVIG*): ~ **(de commandement)** bridge.

passe-temps [pàstâñ] *nm inv* pastime.

passette [pàset] *nf* (tea-)strainer.

passeur, euse [pàsœr, -œz] *nm/f* smuggler.

passible [pàsēbl(ə)] *a*: ~ **de** liable to.

passif, ive [pàsēf, -ēv] *a* passive ♦ *nm* (*LING*) passive; (*COMM*) liabilities *pl*.

passion [pàsyôñ] *nf* passion; **avoir la ~ de** to have a passion for; **fruit de la ~** passion fruit.

passionnant, e [pàsyonâñ, -âñt] *a* fascinating.

passionné, e [pàsyonã] *a* (*personne, tempérament*) passionate; (*description*) impassioned ♦ *nm/f*: **c'est un ~ d'échecs** he's a chess fanatic; **être ~ de** *ou* **pour qch** to have a passion for sth.

passionnel, le [pàsyonel] *a* of passion.

passionnément [pàsyonãmâñ] *ad* passionately.

passionner [pàsyonã] *vt* (*personne*) to fascinate, grip; (*débat, discussion*) to inflame; **se ~ pour** to take an avid interest in; to have a passion for.

passivement [pàsēvmâñ] *ad* passively.

passivité [pàsēvētã] *nf* passivity, passiveness.

passoire [pàswár] *nf* sieve; (*à légumes*) colander; (*à thé*) strainer.

pastel [pàstel] *nm, a inv* (*ART*) pastel.

pastèque [pàstek] *nf* watermelon.

pasteur [pástœr] *nm* (*protestant*) minister, pastor.

pasteuriser [pástœrēzā] *vt* to pasteurize.

pastiche [pástēsh] *nm* pastiche.

pastille [pástēy] *nf* (*à sucer*) lozenge, pastille; (*de papier etc*) (small) disc; ~**s pour la toux** cough drops *ou* lozenges.

pastis [pástēs] *nm* anise-flavored alcoholic drink.

pastoral, e, aux [pástorál, -ō] *a* pastoral.

patagon, ne [pátágóń, -on] *a* Patagonian.

Patagonie [pátágonē] *nf*: **la** ~ Patagonia.

patate [pátát] *nf* spud; ~ **douce** sweet potato.

pataud, e [pátō, -ōd] *a* lumbering.

patauger [pátōzhā] *vi* (*pour s'amuser*) to splash about; (*avec effort*) to wade about; (*fig*) to flounder; ~ **dans** (*en marchant*) to wade through.

pâte [pát] *nf* (*à tarte*) pastry; (*à pain*) dough; (*à frire*) batter; (*substance molle*) paste; cream; ~**s** *nfpl* (*macaroni etc*) pasta *sg*; **fromage à** ~ **dure/molle** hard/soft cheese; ~ **d'amandes** almond paste; ~ **brisée** pie crust (*US*) *ou* shortcrust (*Brit*) pastry; ~ **à choux/feuilletée** choux/puff pastry; ~ **de fruits** candied fruit *q*; ~ **à modeler** modeling (*US*) *ou* modelling (*Brit*) clay; ~ **à papier** paper pulp.

pâté [pátā] *nm* (*charcuterie: terrine*) pâté; (*tache*) ink blot; (*de sable*) sand pie; ~ **(en croûte)** ≈ meat pie; ~ **de foie** liver pâté; ~ **de maisons** block (of houses).

pâtée [pátā] *nf* mash, feed.

patelin [pátlań] *nm* little place.

patente [pátáńt] *nf* (*COMM*) trading license (*US*) *ou* licence (*Brit*).

patenté, e [pátáńtā] *a* (*COMM*) licensed; (*fig: attitré*) registered, (officially) recognized.

patère [páter] *nf* (coat) peg.

paternaliste [páternálēst(ə)] *a* paternalistic.

paternel, le [pátärnel] *a* (*amour, soins*) fatherly; (*ligne, autorité*) paternal.

paternité [páternētā] *nf* paternity, fatherhood.

pâteux, euse [pátœ̄, -œz] *a* thick; pasty; **avoir la bouche** *ou* **langue pâteuse** to have a coated tongue.

pathétique [pátátēk] *a* pathetic, moving.

pathologie [pátolozhē] *nf* pathology.

pathologique [pátolozhēk] *a* pathological.

patibulaire [pátēbüler] *a* sinister.

patiemment [pásyámáń] *ad* patiently.

patience [pásyáńs] *nf* patience; **être à bout de** ~ to have run out of patience; **perdre/prendre** ~ to lose (one's)/have patience.

patient, e [pásyáń, -áńt] *a, nm/f* patient.

patienter [pásyáńtā] *vi* to wait.

patin [pátáń] *nm* skate; (*sport*) skating; (*de traîneau, luge*) runner; (*pièce de tissu*) cloth pad (*used as slippers to protect polished floor*); ~ **(de frein)** brake shoe; ~**s (à glace)** (ice) skates; ~**s à roulettes** roller skates.

patinage [pátēnázh] *nm* skating; ~ **artistique/de vitesse** figure/speed skating.

patine [pátēn] *nf* sheen.

patiner [pátēnā] *vi* to skate; (*embrayage*) to slip; (*roue, voiture*) to spin; **se** ~ *vi* (*meuble, cuir*) to acquire a sheen, become polished.

patineur, euse [pátēnœr, -œz] *nm/f* skater.

patinoire [pátēnwár] *nf* skating rink, (ice) rink.

patio [pátyō] *nm* patio.

pâtir [pátēr]: ~ **de** *vt* to suffer because of.

pâtisserie [pátēsrē] *nf* (*boutique*) pastry (*US*) *ou* cake (*Brit*) shop; (*métier*) confectionery; (*à la maison*) pastry *ou* cake making, baking; ~**s** *nfpl* (*gâteaux*) pastries, cakes.

pâtissier, ière [pátēsyā, -yer] *nm/f* pastry cook; confectioner.

patois [pátwá] *nm* dialect, patois.

patriarche [pátrēyársh(ə)] *nm* patriarch.

patrie [pátrē] *nf* homeland.

patrimoine [pátrēmwáń] *nm* inheritance, patrimony; (*culture*) heritage; ~ **génétique** *ou* **héréditaire** genetic inheritance.

patriote [pátrēyot] *a* patriotic ♦ *nm/f* patriot.

patriotique [pátrēyotēk] *a* patriotic.

patron, ne [pátróń, -on] *nm/f* (*chef*) boss, manager/eress; (*propriétaire*) owner, proprietor/tress; (*employeur*) employer; (*MÉD*) ≈ senior consultant; (*REL*) patron saint ♦ *nm* (*COUTURE*) pattern; ~ **de thèse** supervisor (of postgraduate thesis).

patronage [pátronázh] *nm* patronage; (*organisation, club*) (parish) youth club; (parish) children's club.

patronal, e, aux [pátronál, -ō] *a* (*syndicat, intérêts*) employers'.

patronat [pátroná] *nm* employers *pl*.

patronner [pátroná] *vt* to sponsor, support.

patronnesse [pátrones] *af*: **dame** ~ patroness.

patronyme [pátronēm] *nm* name.

patronymique [pátronēmēk] *a*: **nom** ~ patronymic (name).

patrouille [pátrōōy] *nf* patrol.

patrouiller [pátrōōyā] *vi* to patrol, be on patrol.

patrouilleur [pátrōōyœr] *nm* (*AVIAT*) scout (plane); (*NAVIG*) patrol boat.

patte [pát] *nf* (*jambe*) leg; (*pied: de chien, chat*) paw; (: *d'oiseau*) foot; (*languette*) strap; (: *de poche*) flap; (*favoris*): ~**s (de lapin)** (short) sideburns; **à** ~**s d'éléphant** *a* (*pantalon*) flared; ~**s de mouche** (*fig*) spidery scrawl *sg*; ~**s d'oie** (*fig*) crow's feet.

pattemouille [pátmōōy] *nf* damp cloth (*for ironing*).

pâturage [pátürázh] *nm* pasture.

pâture [pátür] *nf* food.

paume [pōm] *nf* palm.

paumé, e [pōmā] *nm/f* (*fam*) dropout.

paumer [pōmā] *vt* (*fam*) to lose.

paupière [pōpyer] *nf* eyelid.

paupiette [pōpyet] *nf*: ~**s de veau** veal olives.

pause [pōz] *nf* (*arrêt*) break; (*en parlant*) pause; (*MUS*) rest, pause.

pause-café, *pl* **pauses-café** [pōzkáfá] *nf* coffee break.

pauvre [pōvr(ə)] *a* poor ♦ *nm/f* poor man/woman; **les** ~**s** the poor; ~ **en calcium** low in calcium.

pauvrement [pōvrəmáń] *ad* poorly.

pauvreté [pōvrətā] *nf* (*état*) poverty.

pavage [pávázh] *nm* paving; cobblestones *pl*.

pavaner [pávánā]: **se** ~ *vi* to strut about.

pavé, e [pávā] *a* (*cour*) paved; (*rue*) cobbled ♦

nm (*bloc*) paving stone; cobblestone; (*pavage*) paving; (*bifteck*) slab of steak; (*fam: livre*) hefty tome; **être sur le ~** (*sans domicile*) to be on the streets; (*sans emploi*) to be out of a job; **~ numérique** (*INFORM*) keypad.

pavillon [pàvēyóñ] *nm* (*de banlieue*) small (detached) house; (*kiosque*) lodge; pavilion; (*d'hôpital*) ward; (*MUS: de cor etc*) bell; (*ANAT: de l'oreille*) pavilion, pinna; (*NAVIG*) flag; **~ de complaisance** flag of convenience.

pavoiser [pàvwàzā] *vt* to deck with flags ♦ *vi* to put out flags; (*fig*) to rejoice, exult.

pavot [pàvō] *nm* poppy.

payable [pcyàbl(ə)] *a* payable.

payant, e [pcyàñ, -àñt] *a* (*spectateurs etc*) paying; (*billet*) that you pay for, to be paid for; (*fig: entreprise*) profitable; **c'est ~** you have to pay, there is a charge.

paye [pcy] *nf* pay, wages *pl.*

payement [pcymàñ] *nm* payment.

payer [pāyā] *vt* (*créancier, employé, loyer*) to pay; (*achat, réparations, fig: faute*) to pay for ♦ *vi* to pay; (*métier*) to pay, be well-paid; (*effort, tactique etc*) to pay off; **il me l'a fait ~ 10 F** he charged me 10 F for it; **~ qn de** (*ses efforts, peines*) to reward sb for; **~ qch à qn** to buy sth for sb, buy sb sth; **ils nous ont payé le voyage** they paid for our trip; **~ de sa personne** to give of oneself; **~ d'audace** to act with great daring; **~ cher qch** to pay dear(ly) for sth; **cela ne paie pas de mine** it doesn't look like much, it's not much to look at; **se ~ qch** to buy o.s. sth; **se ~ de mots** to shoot one's mouth off; **se ~ la tête de qn** to make a fool of sb; (*duper*) to take sb for a ride.

payeur, euse [pcyœr, -œz] *a* (*organisme, bureau*) payments *cpd* ♦ *nm/f* payer.

pays [pāē] *nm* (*territoire, habitants*) country, land; (*région*) region; (*village*) village; **du ~** a local; **le ~ de Galles** Wales.

paysage [pāēzàzh] *nm* landscape.

paysagiste [pāēzàzhēst(ə)] *nm/f* (*de jardin*) landscape gardener; (*ART*) landscapist, landscape painter.

paysan, ne [pāēzàñ, -àn] *nm/f* countryman/woman; farmer; (*péj*) peasant ♦ *a* country *cpd*, farming; farmers'.

paysannat [pāēzànà] *nm* peasantry.

Pays-Bas [pāēbá] *nmpl*: **les ~** the Netherlands.

PC *sigle m* (*POL*) = *Parti communiste*; (*INFORM: = personal computer*) PC; (= *prêt conventionné*) *type of loan for house purchase*; (*CONSTR*) = **permis de construire**; (*MIL*) = **poste de commandement**.

pcc *abr* (= *pour copie conforme*) c.c.

Pce *abr* = **prince**.

Pcesse *abr* = **princesse**.

PCV *abr* (= *percevoir*) *voir* **communication**.

p de p *abr* = **pas de porte**.

PDG *sigle m* = **président directeur général**.

p.ê. *abr* = **peut-être**.

péage [pāàzh] *nm* toll; (*endroit*) tollgate; **pont à ~** toll bridge.

peau, x [pō] *nf* skin; (*cuir*): **gants de ~** leather gloves; **être bien/mal dans sa ~** to be at ease/odds with oneself; **se mettre dans**

la ~ de qn to put o.s. in sb's place *ou* shoes; **faire ~ neuve** (*se renouveler*) to change one's image; **~ de chamois** (*chiffon*) chamois leather, shammy; **~ d'orange** orange peel.

peaufiner [pōfēnā] *vt* to polish (up).

Peau-Rouge [pōrōōzh] *nm/f* Red Indian, redskin.

peccadille [pākàdēy] *nf* trifle, peccadillo.

péché [pāshā] *nm* sin; **~ mignon** weakness.

pêche [pesh] *nf* (*sport, activité*) fishing; (*poissons péchés*) catch; (*fruit*) peach; **aller à la ~** to go fishing; **avoir la ~** (*fam*) to be in (top) form; **~ à la ligne** (*en rivière*) angling; **~ sous-marine** deep-sea fishing.

pêche-abricot, *pl* **pêches-abricots** [peshàbrēkō] *nf* yellow peach.

pécher [pāshā] *vi* (*REL*) to sin; (*fig: personne*) to err; (: *chose*) to be flawed; **~ contre la bienséance** to break the rules of good behavior.

pêcher [pāshā] *nm* peach tree ♦ *vi* to go fishing; (*en rivière*) to go angling ♦ *vt* (*attraper*) to catch, land; (*chercher*) to fish for; **~ au chalut** to trawl.

pécheur, eresse [pāshœr, pāshres] *nm/f* sinner.

pêcheur [peshœr] *nm* (*voir pêcher*) fisherman; angler; **~ de perles** pearl diver.

pectine [pektēn] *nf* pectin.

pectoral, e, aux [pektorál, -ō] *a* (*ANAT*) pectoral; (*sirop*) throat *cpd*, cough *cpd* ♦ *nmpl* pectoral muscles.

pécule [pākül] *nm* savings *pl*, nest egg; (*d'un détenu*) earnings *pl* (*paid on release*).

pécuniaire [pākünyer] *a* financial.

pédagogie [pādàgozhē] *nf* educational methods *pl*, pedagogy.

pédagogique [pādàgozhēk] *a* educational; **formation ~** teacher training.

pédagogue [pādàgog] *nm/f* teacher; education(al)ist.

pédale [pādàl] *nf* pedal; **mettre la ~ douce** to soft-pedal.

pédaler [pādàlā] *vi* to pedal.

pédalier [pādàlyā] *nm* pedal and gear mechanism.

pédalo [pādàlō] *nm* pedalo, pedal boat.

pédant, e [pādàñ, -àñt] *a* (*péj*) pedantic ♦ *nm/f* pedant.

pédantisme [pādàñtēsm(ə)] *nm* pedantry.

pédéraste [pādārást(ə)] *nm* homosexual, pederast.

pédérastie [pādārástē] *nf* homosexuality, pederasty.

pédestre [pādestr(ə)] *a*: **tourisme ~** hiking; **randonnée ~** (*activité*) rambling; (*excursion*) ramble.

pédiatre [pādyàtr(ə)] *nm/f* pediatrician *ou* pediatrist (*US*), paediatrician (*Brit*), child specialist.

pédiatrie [pādyàtrē] *nf* pediatrics *sg* (*US*), paediatrics *sg* (*Brit*).

pédicure [pādēkür] *nm/f* chiropodist.

pedigree [pādēgrā] *nm* pedigree.

peeling [pēlēñg] *nm* exfoliation treatment.

PEEP *sigle f* = *Fédération des parents d'élèves de l'enseignement public*.

pègre [pegr(ə)] *nf* underworld.

peigne [peny] *vb voir* **peindre, peigner** ♦ *nm*

comb.

peigné, e [pānyā] *a*: **laine** ~**e** worsted wool; combed wool.

peigner [pānyā] *vt* to comb (the hair of); **se** ~ to comb one's hair.

peignez [penyā] *etc vb voir* **peindre**.

peignoir [penywár] *nm* dressing gown; ~ **de bain** bathrobe; ~ **de plage** beach robe.

peignons [penyóń] *vb voir* **peindre**.

peinard, e [penár, -árd(ə)] *a* (*emploi*) easy; (*personne*): **on est** ~ **ici** we're left in peace here.

peindre [paṅdr(ə)] *vt* to paint; (*fig*) to portray, depict.

peine [pen] *nf* (*affliction*) sorrow, sadness *q*; (*mal, effort*) trouble *q*, effort; (*difficulté*) difficulty; (*punition, châtiment*) punishment; (*JUR*) sentence; **faire de la** ~ **à qn** to distress *ou* upset sb; **prendre la** ~ **de faire** to go to the trouble of doing; **se donner de la** ~ to make an effort; **ce n'est pas la** ~ **de faire** there's no point in doing, it's not worth doing; **ce n'est pas la** ~ **que vous fassiez** there's no point (in) you doing; **avoir de la** ~ **à faire** to have difficulty doing; **donnez-vous** *ou* **veuillez vous donner la** ~ **d'entrer** please do come in; **c'est** ~ **perdue** it's a waste of time (and effort); **à** ~ *ad* scarcely, hardly, barely; **à** ~ ... **que** hardly ... than; **c'est à** ~ **si** ... it's (*ou* it was) a job to ...; **sous** ~: **sous** ~ **d'être puni** for fear of being punished; **défense d'afficher sous** ~ **d'amende** billposters will be fined; ~ **de mort** death sentence *ou* penalty.

peiner [pānā] *vi* to work hard; to struggle; (*moteur, voiture*) to labor (*US*), labour (*Brit*) ♦ *vt* to grieve, sadden.

peint, e [paṅ, paṅt] *pp de* **peindre**.

peintre [paṅtr(ə)] *nm* painter; ~ **en bâtiment** house painter, painter and decorator; ~ **d'enseignes** signwriter, sign painter (*US*).

peinture [paṅtür] *nf* painting; (*couche de couleur, couleur*) paint; (*surfaces peintes: aussi:* ~**s**) paintwork; **je ne peux pas le voir en** ~ I can't stand the sight of him; ~ **mate/brillante** matt/gloss paint; "~ **fraîche**" "wet paint".

péjoratif, ive [pāzhorátēf, -ēv] *a* pejorative, derogatory.

Pékin [pākaṅ] *n* Peking.

pékinois, e [pākēnwá, -wáz] *a* Pekin(g)ese ♦ *nm* (*chien*) peke, pekin(g)ese; (*LING*) Mandarin, Pekin(g)ese ♦ *nm/f*: **P~, e** Pekin(g)ese.

PEL *sigle m* (= *Plan d'épargne logement*) savings plan providing lower-interest mortgages.

pelade [pəlád] *nf* alopecia.

pelage [pəlázh] *nm* coat, fur.

pelé, e [pəlā] *a* (*chien*) hairless; (*vêtement*) threadbare; (*terrain*) bare.

pêle-mêle [pelmel] *ad* higgledy-piggledy.

peler [pəlā] *vt, vi* to peel.

pèlerin [pelraṅ] *nm* pilgrim.

pèlerinage [pelrēnázh] *nm* (*voyage*) pilgrimage; (*lieu*) place of pilgrimage, shrine.

pèlerine [pelrēn] *nf* cape.

pélican [pālēkáṅ] *nm* pelican.

pelle [pel] *nf* shovel; (*d'enfant, de terrassier*) spade; ~ **à gâteau** cake slice; ~ **mécanique** power shovel (*US*), mechanical digger (*Brit*).

pelletée [peltā] *nf* shovelful; spadeful.

pelleter [peltā] *vt* to shovel (up).

pelleteuse [peltœz] *nf* power shovel (*US*), mechanical digger (*Brit*), excavator.

pelletier [peltyā] *nm* furrier.

pellicule [pālēkül] *nf* film; ~**s** *nfpl* (*MÉD*) dandruff *sg*.

Péloponnèse [pāloponez] *nm*: **le** ~ the Peloponnese.

pelote [pəlot] *nf* (*de fil, laine*) ball; (*d'épingles*) pin cushion; ~ **basque** pelota.

peloter [pəlotā] *vt* (*fam*) to feel (up); **se** ~ to pet.

peloton [pəlotóń] *nm* (*groupe: personnes*) group; (: *pompiers, gendarmes*) squad; (: *SPORT*) pack; (*de laine*) ball; ~ **d'exécution** firing squad.

pelotonner [pəlotonā]: **se** ~ *vi* to curl (o.s.) up.

pelouse [pəloōz] *nf* lawn; (*HIPPISME*) spectating area inside racetrack.

peluche [pəlüsh] *nf* (bit of) fluff; **animal en** ~ soft toy, stuffed animal.

pelucher [p(ə)lüshā] *vi* to become fluffy, fluff up.

pelucheux, euse [p(ə)lüshœ̄, -œ̄z] *a* fluffy.

pelure [pəlür] *nf* peeling, peel *q*; ~ **d'oignon** onion skin.

pénal, e, aux [pānál, -ō] *a* penal.

pénaliser [pānálēzā] *vt* to penalize.

pénalité [pānálētā] *nf* penalty.

penalty, ies [pānáltē, -z] *nm* (*SPORT*) penalty (kick).

pénard, e [pānár, -árd(ə)] *a* = **peinard**.

pénates [pānát] *nmpl*: **regagner ses** ~ to return to the bosom of one's family.

penaud, e [pənō, -ōd] *a* sheepish, contrite.

penchant [páṅsháṅ] *nm*: **un** ~ **à faire/à qch** a tendency to do/to sth; **un** ~ **pour qch** a liking *ou* fondness for sth.

penché, e [páṅshā] *a* slanting.

pencher [páṅshā] *vi* to tilt, lean over ♦ *vt* to tilt; **se** ~ *vi* to lean over; (*se baisser*) to bend down; **se** ~ **sur** to bend over; (*fig: problème*) to look into; **se** ~ **au dehors** to lean out; ~ **pour** to be inclined to favor.

pendable [páṅdábl(ə)] *a*: **tour** ~ rotten trick; **c'est un cas** ~! he (*ou* she) deserves to be shot!

pendaison [páṅdezóń] *nf* hanging.

pendant, e [páṅdáṅ, -áṅt] *a* hanging (out); (*ADMIN, JUR*) pending ♦ *nm* counterpart; matching piece ♦ *prép* during; **faire** ~ **à** to match; to be the counterpart of; ~ **que** while; ~**s d'oreilles** drop *ou* pendant earrings.

pendeloque [páṅdlok] *nf* pendant.

pendentif [páṅdáṅtēf] *nm* pendant.

penderie [páṅdrē] *nf* wardrobe; (*placard*) walk-in closet (*US*) *ou* cupboard (*Brit*).

pendiller [páṅdēyā] *vi* to flap (about).

pendre [páṅdr(ə)] *vt, vi* to hang; **se** ~ **(à)** (*se suicider*) to hang o.s. (on); **se** ~ **à** (*se suspendre*) to hang from; ~ **à** to hang (down) from; ~ **qch à** (*mur*) to hang sth (up) on; (*plafond*) to hang sth (up) from.

pendu, e [pãndü] *pp de* **pendre ♦** *nm/f* hanged man (*ou* woman).

pendulaire [pãndüler] *a* pendular, of a pendulum.

pendule [pãndül] *nf* clock **♦** *nm* pendulum.

pendulette [pãndület] *nf* small clock.

pêne [pen] *nm* bolt.

pénétrant, e [pãnãtrãn, -ãnt] *a* (*air, froid*) biting; (*pluie*) that soaks right through you; (*fig: odeur*) noticeable; (*œil, regard*) piercing; (*clairvoyant, perspicace*) perceptive **♦** *nf* (*route*) expressway.

pénétration [pãnãtrãsyôn] *nf* (*fig: d'idées etc*) penetration; (*perspicacité*) perception.

pénétré, e [pãnãtrã] *a* (*air, ton*) earnest; **être ~ de soi-même/son importance** to be full of oneself/one's own importance.

pénétrer [pãnãtrã] *vi* to come *ou* get in **♦** *vt* to penetrate; **~ dans** to enter; (*suj: froid, projectile*) to penetrate; (*: air, eau*) to come into, get into; (*mystère, secret*) to fathom; **se ~ de qch** to get sth firmly set in one's mind.

pénible [pãnēbl(ə)] *a* (*astreignant*) hard; (*affligeant*) painful; (*personne, caractère*) tiresome; **il m'est ~ de ...** I'm sorry to ....

péniblement [pãnēbləmãn] *ad* with difficulty.

péniche [pãnēsh] *nf* barge; **~ de débarquement** landing craft *inv*.

pénicilline [pãnēsēlēn] *nf* penicillin.

péninsule [pãnaṅsül] *nf* peninsula.

pénis [pãnēs] *nm* penis.

pénitence [pãnētãns] *nf* (*repentir*) penitence; (*peine*) penance; (*punition, châtiment*) punishment; **mettre un enfant en ~ ≈** to make a child stand in the corner; **faire ~** to do a penance.

pénitencier [pãnētãnsyã] *nm* prison, penitentiary (*US*).

pénitent, e [pãnētãn, -ãnt] *a* penitent.

pénitentiaire [pãnētãnsyer] *a* prison *cpd*, penitentiary (*US*).

pénombre [pãnônbr(ə)] *nf* half-light.

pensable [pãnsãbl(ə)] *a*: **ce n'est pas ~** it's unthinkable.

pensant, e [pãnsãn, -ãnt] *a*: **bien ~** right-thinking.

pense-bête [pãnsbet] *nm* aide-mémoire, mnemonic device.

pensée [pãnsã] *nf* thought; (*démarche, doctrine*) thinking *q*; (*BOT*) pansy; **se représenter qch par la ~** to conjure up a mental picture of sth; **en ~** in one's mind.

penser [pãnsã] *vi* to think **♦** *vt* to think; (*concevoir: problème, machine*) to think out; **~ à** to think of; (*songer à: ami, vacances*) to think of *ou* about; (*réfléchir à: problème, offre*): **~ à qch** to think about sth, think sth over; **~ à faire qch** to think of doing sth; **~ faire qch** to be thinking of doing sth, intend to do sth; **faire ~ à** to remind one of; **n'y pensons plus** let's forget it; **vous n'y pensez pas!** don't let it bother you!; **sans ~ à mal** without meaning any harm; **je le pense aussi** I think so too; **je pense que oui/non** I think so/don't think so.

penseur [pãnsœr] *nm* thinker; **libre ~** free-thinker.

pensif, ive [pãnsēf, -ēv] *a* pensive, thoughtful.

pension [pãnsyôn] *nf* (*allocation*) pension; (*prix du logement*) board and lodging, bed and board; (*maison particulière*) boarding house; (*hôtel*) guesthouse, hotel; (*école*) boarding school; **prendre ~ chez** to take board and lodging at; **prendre qn en ~** to take sb (in) as a lodger; **mettre en ~** to send to boarding school; **~ alimentaire** (*d'étudiant*) living allowance; (*de divorcée*) maintenance allowance; alimony; **~ complète** full board; **~ de famille** boarding house, guesthouse; **~ de guerre/d'invalidité** war/disablement pension.

pensionnaire [pãnsyoner] *nm/f* boarder; guest.

pensionnat [pãnsyonã] *nm* boarding school.

pensionné, e [pãnsyonã] *nm/f* pensioner.

pensivement [pãnsēvmãn] *ad* pensively, thoughtfully.

pensum [pãnsom] *nm* (*SCOL*) punishment exercise; (*fig*) chore.

pentagone [pãntãgon] *nm* pentagon; **le P~** the Pentagon.

pentathlon [pãntãtlôn] *nm* pentathlon.

pente [pãnt] *nf* slope; **en ~** *a* sloping.

Pentecôte [pãntkōt] *nf*: **la ~** Pentecost, Whitsun; (*dimanche*) Whitsunday; **lundi de ~** Whitmonday.

pénurie [pãnürē] *nf* shortage; **~ de main-d'œuvre** undermanning.

pépé [pãpã] *nm* (*fam*) grandad.

pépère [pãper] *a* (*fam*) cushy (*fam*), quiet **♦** *nm* (*fam*) grandad.

pépier [pãpyã] *vi* to chirp, tweet.

pépin [pãpaṅ] *nm* (*BOT: graine*) pip; (*fam: ennui*) snag, hitch; (*: parapluie*) umbrella.

pépinière [pãpēnyer] *nf* nursery; (*fig*) nest, breeding ground.

pépiniériste [pãpēnyãrēst(ə)] *nm* nurseryman.

pépite [pãpēt] *nf* nugget.

PEPS *abr* (= *premier entré premier sorti*) first in first out.

PER [per] *sigle m* (= *plan d'épargne retraite*) type of personal pension plan.

perçant, e [persãn, -ãnt] *a* (*vue, regard, yeux*) sharp, keen; (*cri, voix*) piercing, shrill.

percée [persã] *nf* (*trouée*) opening; (*MIL, COMM, fig*) breakthrough; (*SPORT*) break.

perce-neige [persənezh] *nm ou f inv* snowdrop.

perce-oreille [persorey] *nm* earwig.

percepteur [perseptœr] *nm* tax collector.

perceptible [perseptēbl(ə)] *a* (*son, différence*) perceptible; (*impôt*) payable, collectable.

perception [persepsyôn] *nf* perception; (*d'impôts etc*) collection; (*bureau*) tax (collector's) office.

percer [persã] *vt* to pierce; (*ouverture etc*) to make; (*mystère, énigme*) to penetrate **♦** *vi* to come through; (*réussir*) to break through; **~ une dent** to cut a tooth.

perceuse [persœz] *nf* drill; **~ à percussion** hammer drill.

percevable [persəvãbl(ə)] *a* collectable, payable.

percevoir [persəvwãr] *vt* (*distinguer*) to perceive, detect; (*taxe, impôt*) to collect; (*revenu, indemnité*) to receive.

perche [persh(ə)] *nf* (*ZOOL*) perch; (*bâton*)

pole; ~ **à son** (sound) boom.
percher [pershā] *vt*: ~ **qch sur** to perch sth on
♦ *vi*, **se** ~ *vi* (*oiseau*) to perch.
perchiste [pershēst(ə)] *nm/f* (*SPORT*) pole
vaulter; (*TV etc*) boom operator.
perchoir [pershwár] *nm* perch; (*fig*)
presidency of the French National Assembly.
perclus, e [perklū, -üz] *a*: ~ **de**
(*rhumatismes*) crippled with.
perçois [perswá] *etc vb voir* **percevoir.**
percolateur [perkolátœr] *nm* percolator.
perçu, e [persü] *pp de* **percevoir.**
percussion [perküsyóń] *nf* percussion.
percussionniste [perküsyonēst(ə)] *nm/f*
percussionist.
percutant, e [perkütáń, -áńt] *a* (*article etc*) resounding, forceful.
percuter [perkütā] *vt* to strike; (*suj: véhicule*)
to crash into ♦ *vi*: ~ **contre** to crash into.
percuteur [perkütœr] *nm* firing pin, hammer.
perdant, e [perdáń, -áńt] *nm/f* loser ♦ *a* losing.
perdition [perdēsyóń] *nf* (*morale*) ruin; **en** ~
(*NAVIG*) in distress; **lieu de** ~ den of vice.
perdre [perdr(ə)] *vt* to lose; (*gaspiller: temps,
argent*) to waste; (: *occasion*) to waste,
miss; (*personne: moralement etc*) to ruin ♦
vi to lose; (*sur une vente etc*) to lose out;
(*récipient*) to leak; **se** ~ *vi* (*s'égarer*) to get
lost, lose one's way; (*fig: se gâter*) to go to
waste; (*disparaître*) to disappear, vanish; **il
ne perd rien pour attendre** it can wait, it'll
keep.
perdreau, x [perdrō] *nm* (young) partridge.
perdrix [perdrē] *nf* partridge.
perdu, e [perdü] *pp de* **perdre** ♦ *a* (*enfant,
cause, objet*) lost; (*isolé*) out-of-the-way;
(*COMM: emballage*) non returnable; (*récolte
etc*) ruined; (*malade*): **il est** ~ there's no
hope left for him; **à vos moments** ~**s** in
your spare time.
père [per] *nm* father; ~**s** *nmpl* (*ancêtres*) forefathers; **de** ~ **en fils** from father to son; ~
de famille father; family man; **mon** ~ (*REL*)
Father; **le** ~ **Noël** Santa Claus.
pérégrinations [pārāgrēnásyóń] *nfpl* travels.
péremption [pāráńpsyóń] *nf*: **date de** ~
expiry date.
péremptoire [pāráńptwár] *a* peremptory.
pérennité [pārānētā] *nf* durability, lasting
quality.
péréquation [pārākwásyóń] *nf* (*des salaires*)
realignment; (*des prix, impôts*) equalization.
perfectible [perfektēbl(ə)] *a* perfectible.
perfection [perfeksyóń] *nf* perfection; **à la** ~
ad to perfection.
perfectionné, e [perfeksyonā] *a* sophisticated.
perfectionnement [perfeksyonmáń] *nm*
improvement.
perfectionner [perfeksyonā] *vt* to improve,
perfect; **se** ~ **en anglais** to improve one's
English.
perfectionniste [perfeksyonēst(ə)] *nm/f*
perfectionist.
perfide [perfēd] *a* perfidious, treacherous.
perfidie [perfēdē] *nf* treachery.
perforant, e [perforáń, -áńt] *a* (*balle*) armor-
piercing (*US*), armour-piercing (*Brit*).
perforateur, trice [perforátœr, -trēs] *nm/f*
punch-card operator ♦ *nm* (*perceuse*) borer;

drill ♦ *nf* (*perceuse*) borer; drill; (*pour
cartes*) card punch; (*de bureau*) punch.
perforation [perforásyóń] *nf* perforation;
punching; (*trou*) hole.
perforatrice [perforátrēs] *nf voir* **perforateur.**
perforé, e [perforā] *a*: **bande** ~ punched tape;
carte ~ punch card.
perforer [perforā] *vt* to perforate, punch a hole
(*ou* holes) in; (*ticket, bande, carte*) to punch.
perforeuse [perforœz] *nf* (*machine*) (card)
punch; (*personne*) card punch operator.
performance [performáńs] *nf* performance.
performant, e [performáń, -áńt] *a* (*ÉCON:
produit, entreprise*) high-return *cpd*; (*TECH:
appareil, machine*) high-performance *cpd*.
perfusion [perfüzyóń] *nf* perfusion; **faire une**
~ **à qn** to put sb on an I.V. (*US*) *ou* on a drip
(*Brit*).
péricliter [pārēklētā] *vi* to go downhill.
péridurale [pārēdürál] *nf* epidural.
périgourdin, e [pārēgōōrdań, -ēn] *a* of *ou* from
the Perigord.
péril [pārēl] *nm* peril; **au** ~ **de sa vie** at the
risk of his life; **à ses risques et** ~**s** at his (*ou*
her) own risk.
périlleux, euse [pārēyœ̄, -œ̄z] *a* perilous.
périmé, e [pārēmā] *a* (out)dated; (*ADMIN*)
out-of-date, expired.
périmètre [pārēmetr(ə)] *nm* perimeter.
périnatal, e [pārēnátál] *a* perinatal.
période [pāryod] *nf* period.
périodique [pāryodēk] *a* (*phases*) periodic;
(*publication*) periodical; (*MATH: fraction*) re-
curring ♦ *nm* periodical; **garniture** *ou*
serviette ~ sanitary napkin (*US*) *ou* towel
(*Brit*).
périodiquement [pāryodēkmáń] *ad* periodically.
péripéties [pārēpāsē] *nfpl* events, episodes.
périphérie [pārēfārē] *nf* periphery; (*d'une
ville*) outskirts *pl*.
périphérique [pārēfārēk] *a* (*quartiers*) outlying; (*ANAT, TECH*) peripheral; (*station de
radio*) operating from a neighboring country
♦ *nm* (*INFORM*) peripheral; (*AUTO*):
(**boulevard**) ~ beltway (*US*), ring road
(*Brit*).
périphrase [pārēfráz] *nf* circumlocution.
périple [pārēpl(ə)] *nm* journey.
périr [pārēr] *vi* to die, perish.
périscolaire [pārēskoler] *a* extracurricular.
périscope [pārēskop] *nm* periscope.
périssable [pārēsábl(ə)] *a* perishable.
péritonite [pārētonēt] *nf* peritonitis.
perle [perl(ə)] *nf* pearl; (*de plastique, métal,
sueur*) bead; (*personne, chose*) gem,
treasure; (*erreur*) gem, howler.
perlé, e [perlā] *a* (*rire*) rippling, tinkling;
(*travail*) exquisite; (*orge*) pearl *cpd*; **grève**
~**e** slowdown (*US*), go-slow (*Brit*), selective
strike (action).
perler [perlā] *vi* to form in droplets.
perlier, ière [perlyā, -yer] *a* pearl *cpd*.
permanence [permánáńs] *nf* permanence;
(*local*) (duty) office; strike headquarters;
(*service des urgences*) emergency service;
(*SCOL*) study hall (*US*) *ou* room (*Brit*);
assurer une ~ (*service public, bureaux*) to
operate *ou* maintain a basic service; **être de**

~ to be on call *ou* duty; **en** ~ *ad* (*toujours*) permanently; (*continûment*) continuously.

permanent, e [permánáń, -áńt] *a* permanent; (*spectacle*) continuous; (*armée, comité*) standing ◆ *nf* perm ◆ *nm/f* (*d'un syndicat, parti*) paid official.

perméable [permáábl(ə)] *a* (*terrain*) permeable; ~ **à** (*fig*) receptive *ou* open to.

permettre [permetr(ə)] *vt* to allow, permit; ~ **à qn de faire/qch** to allow sb to do/sth; **se** ~ **de faire qch** to take the liberty of doing sth; **permettez!** excuse me!

permis, e [permē, -ēz] *pp de* **permettre** ◆ *nm* permit, license (*US*), licence (*Brit*); ~ **de chasse** hunting permit; ~ (**de conduire**) (driver's) license (*US*), (driving) licence (*Brit*); ~ **de construire** building permit (*US*), planning permission (*Brit*); ~ **d'inhumer** burial certificate; ~ **poids lourds** ≈ class E (driver's) license (*US*), ≈ HGV (driving) licence (*Brit*); ~ **de séjour** residence permit; ~ **de travail** work permit.

permissif, ive [permēsēf, -ēv] *a* permissive.

permission [permēsyóń] *nf* permission; (*MIL*) leave; (: *papier*) pass; **en** ~ on leave; **avoir la** ~ **de faire** to have permission to do, be allowed to do.

permissionnaire [permēsyoner] *nm* soldier on leave.

permutable [permütábl(ə)] *a* which can be changed *ou* switched around.

permuter [permütā] *vt* to change around, permutate ◆ *vi* to change, swap.

pernicieux, euse [pernēsyœ̄, -œ̄z] *a* pernicious.

péroné [pāronā] *nm* fibula.

pérorer [pārorā] *vi* to hold forth.

Pérou [pārōō] *nm*: **le** ~ Peru.

perpendiculaire [perpáńdēküler] *a*, *nf* perpendicular.

perpète [perpet] *nf* (*fam*: *loin*): **à** ~ miles away; (: *longtemps*) forever.

perpétrer [perpātrā] *vt* to perpetrate.

perpétuel, le [perpātüel] *a* perpetual; (*ADMIN etc*) permanent; for life.

perpétuellement [perpātüelmáń] *ad* perpetually, constantly.

perpétuer [perpātüā] *vt* to perpetuate; **se** ~ (*usage, injustice*) to be perpetuated; (*espèces*) to survive.

perpétuité [perpātüētā] *nf*: **à** ~ *a*, *ad* for life; **être condamné à** ~ to be sentenced to life imprisonment, receive a life sentence.

perplexe [perpleks(ə)] *a* perplexed, puzzled.

perplexité [perpleksētā] *nf* perplexity.

perquisition [perkēzēsyóń] *nf* (police) search.

perquisitionner [perkēzēsyonā] *vi* to carry out a search.

perron [peróń] *nm* steps *pl* (*in front of mansion etc*).

perroquet [peroke] *nm* parrot.

perruche [pārüsh] *nf* parakeet (*US*), budgerigar (*Brit*), budgie (*Brit*).

perruque [pārük] *nf* wig.

persan, e [persáń, -áń] *a* Persian ◆ *nm* (*LING*) Persian.

perse [pers(ə)] *a* Persian ◆ *nm* (*LING*) Persian ◆ *nm/f*: **P**~ Persian ◆ *nf*: **la P**~ Persia.

persécuter [persākütā] *vt* to persecute.

persécution [persāküsyóń] *nf* persecution.

persévérance [persāvāráńs] *nf* perseverance.

persévérant, e [persāvāráń, -áńt] *a* persevering.

persévérer [persāvārā] *vi* to persevere; ~ **à croire que** to continue to believe that.

persiennes [persyen] *nfpl* (slatted) shutters.

persiflage [persēflázh] *nm* mockery *q*.

persifleur, euse [persēflœr, -œ̄z] *a* mocking.

persil [persē] *nm* parsley.

persillé, e [persēyā] *a* (sprinkled) with parsley; (*fromage*) veined; (*viande*) marbled, with fat running through.

Persique [persēk] *a*: **le golfe** ~ the (Persian) Gulf.

persistance [persēstáńs] *nf* persistence.

persistant, e [persēstáń, -áńt] *a* persistent; (*feuilles*) evergreen; **à feuillage** ~ evergreen.

persister [persēstā] *vi* to persist; ~ **à faire qch** to persist in doing sth.

personnage [personázh] *nm* (*notable*) personality; figure; (*individu*) character, individual; (*THÉÂTRE*) character; (*PEINTURE*) figure.

personnaliser [personálēzā] *vt* to personalize; (*appartement*) to give a personal touch to.

personnalité [personálētā] *nf* personality; (*personnage*) prominent figure.

personne [person] *nf* person ◆ *pronom* nobody, no one; (*quelqu'un*) anybody, anyone; ~**s** *nfpl* people *pl*; **il n'y a** ~ there's nobody in *ou* there, there isn't anybody in *ou* there; **10 F par** ~ 10 F per person, 10 F a head; **en** ~ personally, in person; ~ **âgée** elderly person; ~ **à charge** (*JUR*) dependent; ~ **morale** *ou* **civile** (*JUR*) legal entity.

personnel, le [personel] *a* personal; (*égoïste*: *personne*) selfish, self-centered (*US*), self-centred (*Brit*); (*idée, opinion*): **j'ai des idées** ~**les à ce sujet** I have my own ideas about that ◆ *nm* personnel, staff; **service du** ~ personnel department.

personnellement [personelmáń] *ad* personally.

personnifier [personēfyā] *vt* to personify; to typify; **c'est l'honnêteté personifiée** he (*ou* she *etc*) is honesty personified.

perspective [perspektēv] *nf* (*ART*) perspective; (*vue, coup d'œil*) view; (*point de vue*) viewpoint, angle; (*chose escomptée, envisagée*) prospect; **en** ~ in prospect.

perspicace [perspēkás] *a* clear-sighted, gifted with (*ou* showing) insight.

perspicacité [perspēkásētā] *nf* insight, perspicacity.

persuader [persüádā] *vt*: ~ **qn (de/de faire)** to persuade sb (of/to do); **j'en suis persuadé** I'm quite sure *ou* convinced (of it).

persuasif, ive [persüázēf, -ēv] *a* persuasive.

persuasion [persüázyóń] *nf* persuasion.

perte [pert(ə)] *nf* loss; (*de temps*) waste; (*fig*: *morale*) ruin; ~**s** *nfpl* losses; **à** ~ (*COMM*) at a loss; **à** ~ **de vue** as far as the eye can (*ou* could) see; (*fig*) interminably; **en pure** ~ for absolutely nothing; **courir à sa** ~ to be on the road to ruin; **être en** ~ **de vitesse** (*fig*) to be losing momentum; **avec** ~ **et fracas** forcibly; ~ **de chaleur** heat loss; ~ **sèche** dead loss; ~**s blanches** (vaginal) discharge *sg*.

pertinemment [pertēnámáń] *ad* to the point;

(savoir) perfectly well, full well.

pertinence [pɛrtɛ̃nɑ̃s] *nf* pertinence, relevance; discernment.

pertinent, e [pɛrtɛ̃nɑ̃, -ɑ̃t] *a (remarque)* apt, pertinent, relevant; *(analyse)* discerning, judicious.

perturbateur, trice [pɛrtürbátœr, -trēs] *a* disruptive.

perturbation [pɛrtürbãsyôñ] *nf (dans un service public)* disruption; *(agitation, trouble)* perturbation; **~ (atmosphérique)** atmospheric disturbance.

perturber [pɛrtürbã] *vt* to disrupt; *(PSYCH)* to perturb, disturb.

péruvien, ne [pärüvyañ, -en] *a* Peruvian ♦ *nm/f:* **P~, ne** Peruvian.

pervenche [pɛrvãñsh] *nf* periwinkle; *(fam)* meter maid *(US)*, traffic warden *(Brit)*.

pervers, e [pɛrver, -ers(ə)] *a* perverted, depraved; *(malfaisant)* perverse.

perversion [pɛrversyôñ] *nf* perversion.

perversité [pɛrversētã] *nf* depravity; perversity.

perverti, e [pɛrvertē] *nm/f* pervert.

pervertir [pɛrvertēr] *vt* to pervert.

pesage [pəzazh] *nm* weighing; *(HIPPISME: action)* weigh-in; *(: salle)* weighing room; *(: enceinte)* enclosure.

pesamment [pəzãmãñ] *ad* heavily.

pesant, e [pəzãñ, -ãñt] *a* heavy; *(fig)* burdensome ♦ *nm:* **valoir son ~ de** to be worth one's weight in.

pesanteur [pəzãñtœr] *nf* gravity.

pèse-bébé [pezbābã] *nm* (baby) scales *pl.*

pesée [pəzã] *nf* weighing; *(BOXE)* weigh-in; *(pression)* pressure.

pèse-lettre [pezletr(ə)] *nm* letter scales *pl.*

pèse-personne [pezperson] *nm* (bathroom) scales *pl.*

peser [pəzã] *vt, vb avec attribut* to weigh; *(considérer, comparer)* to weigh ♦ *vi* to be heavy; *(fig)* to carry weight; **~ sur** *(levier, bouton)* to press, push; *(fig: accabler)* to lie heavy on; *(: influencer)* to influence; **~ à qn** to weigh heavy on sb.

pessaire [peser] *nm* pessary.

pessimisme [pāsēmēsm(ə)] *nm* pessimism.

pessimiste [pāsēmēst(ə)] *a* pessimistic ♦ *nm/f* pessimist.

peste [pest(ə)] *nf* plague; *(fig)* pest, nuisance.

pester [pestã] *vi:* **~ contre** to curse.

pesticide [pestēsēd] *nm* pesticide.

pestiféré, e [pestēfãrã] *nm/f* plague victim.

pestilentiel, le [pestēlãñsyel] *a* foul.

pet [pe] *nm (fam!)* fart *(!).*

pétale [pātál] *nm* petal.

pétanque [pātãñk] *nf type of* bowls.

pétarader [pātãrádã] *vi* to backfire.

pétard [pātár] *nm (feu d'artifice)* firecracker; *(de cotillon)* cracker; *(RAIL)* detonator.

pet-de-nonne, *pl* **pets-de-nonne** [pednon] *nm* ≈ fritter *(US)*, ≈ choux bun *(Brit)*.

péter [pātã] *vi (fam: casser, sauter)* to burst; to bust; *(fam!)* to fart *(!).*

pète-sec [pɛtsek] *a inv* abrupt, sharp(-tongued).

pétillant, e [pātēyãñ, -ãñt] *a* sparkling.

pétiller [pātēyã] *vi (flamme, bois)* to crackle; *(mousse, champagne)* to bubble; *(pierre,*

métal) to glisten; *(yeux)* to sparkle; *(fig):* **~ d'esprit** to sparkle with wit.

petit, e [pətē, -ēt] *a (gén)* small; *(main, objet, colline, en âge: enfant)* small, little; *(mince, fin: personne, taille, pluie)* slight; *(voyage)* short, little; *(bruit etc)* faint, slight; *(mesquin)* mean; *(peu important)* minor ♦ *nm/f (petit enfant)* little one, child ♦ *nmpl (d'un animal)* young *pl;* **faire des ~s** to have kittens *(ou* puppies *etc)*; **en ~** in miniature; **mon ~** son; little one; **ma ~e** dear; little one; **pauvre ~** poor little thing; **la classe des ~s** the infant class; **pour ~s et grands** for children and adults; **les tout-~s** the little ones, the tiny tots; **~ à ~** bit by bit, gradually; **~(e) ami/e** boyfriend/girlfriend; **les ~es annonces** the classified ads; **~ déjeuner** breakfast; **~ doigt** little finger; **le ~ écran** the small screen; **~ four** petit four; **~ pain** (bread) roll; **~e monnaie** small change; **~e vérole** smallpox; **~s pois** petit pois *pl,* garden peas; **~es gens** people of modest means.

petit-beurre, *pl* **petits-beurre** [pətēbœr] *nm* sweet butter cookie *(US) ou* biscuit *(Brit)*.

petit(e)-bourgeois(e), *pl* **petit(e)s-bourgeois(es)** [pətē(t)bōōrzhwá(z)] *a (péj)* petit-bourgeois, middle-class.

petite-fille, *pl* **petites-filles** [pətētfēy] *nf* granddaughter.

petitement [pətētmãñ] *ad* poorly; meanly; **être logé ~** to be in cramped accommodations *(US) ou* accommodation *(Brit)*.

petitesse [pətētes] *nf* smallness; *(d'un salaire, de revenus)* modestness; *(mesquinerie)* meanness.

petit-fils, *pl* **petits-fils** [pətēfēs] *nm* grandson.

pétition [pātēsyôñ] *nf* petition; **faire signer une ~** to get up a petition.

pétitionner [pātēsyonã] *vt* to petition.

petit-lait, *pl* **petits-laits** [pətēle] *nm* whey *q.*

petit-nègre [pətēnegr(ə)] *nm (péj)* pidgin French.

petits-enfants [pətēzãñfãñ] *nmpl* grandchildren.

petit-suisse, *pl* **petits-suisses** [pətēsüēs] *nm* small individual pot of cream cheese.

pétoche [pātosh] *nf (fam):* **avoir la ~** to be scared out of one's wits.

pétri, e [pātrē] *a:* **~ d'orgueil** filled with pride.

pétrifier [pātrēfyã] *vt* to petrify; *(fig)* to paralyze, transfix.

pétrin [pātrañ] *nm* kneading trough; *(fig):* **dans le ~** in a jam *ou* fix.

pétrir [pātrēr] *vt* to knead.

pétrochimie [pātroshēmē] *nf* petrochemistry.

pétrochimique [pātroshēmēk] *a* petrochemical.

pétrodollar [pātrōdolár] *nm* petrodollar.

pétrole [pātrol] *nm* oil; *(aussi:* **~ lampant)** kerosene *(US)*, paraffin *(Brit)*.

pétrolier, ière [pātrolyã, -yer] *a* oil *cpd; (pays)* oil-producing ♦ *nm (navire)* oil tanker; *(financier)* oilman; *(technicien)* petroleum engineer.

pétrolifère [pātrolēfer] *a* oil(-bearing).

P et T *sigle fpl = postes et télécommunications.*

pétulant, e [pātülâṅ, -âṅt] *a* exuberant.

pétunia [pātünyá] *nm* petunia.

peu [pœ̄] *ad* little, *tournure négative* + much; (*avec adjectif*) *tournure négative* + very; (*avec adverbe*) a little, slightly ◊ *pronom* few ◊ *nm* little; **le ~ de courage qui nous restait** what little courage we still had; **~ avant/ après** shortly before/afterwards; **~ de** (*nombre*) few, *négation* + (very) many; (*quantité*) little, *négation* + (very) much; **pour ~ de temps** for (only) a short while; **le ~ de gens qui** the few people who; **le ~ de sable qui** what little sand, the little sand which; **un (petit) ~** a little (bit); **un ~ de** a little; **un ~ plus/moins de** slightly more/less (*ou* fewer); **pour ~ qu'il fasse** if he should do, if by any chance he does; **pour un ~, il** ... he very nearly ...; **de ~** (only) just; **~ à ~** little by little; **à ~ près** *ad* just about, more or less; **à ~ près 10 kg/10 F** approximately 10 kg/10 F; **sous ou avant ~** before long, shortly; **depuis ~** for a short *ou* little while; **c'est ~ de chose** it's nothing; **c'est si ~ de chose** it's such a small thing; **essayez un ~!** have a go!, just try it!

peuplade [pœplád] *nf* (*horde, tribu*) tribe, people.

peuple [pœpl(ə)] *nm* people; (*masse indifférenciée*): **un ~ de vacanciers** a crowd of vacationers (*US*) *ou* holiday-makers (*Brit*); **il y a du ~** there are a lot of people.

peuplé, e [pœplā] *a*: **très/peu ~** densely/ sparsely populated.

peupler [pœplā] *vt* (*pays, région*) to populate; (*étang*) to stock; (*suj: hommes, poissons*) to inhabit; (*fig: imagination, rêves*) to fill; **se ~** *vi* (*ville, région*) to become populated; (*fig: s'animer*) to fill (up), be filled.

peuplier [pœ̄plēyā] *nm* poplar (tree).

peur [pœr] *nf* fear; **avoir ~ (de/de faire/que)** to be frightened *ou* afraid (of/of doing/that); **prendre ~** to take fright; **faire ~ à** to frighten; **de ~ de/que** for fear of/that; **j'ai ~ qu'il ne soit trop tard** I'm afraid it might be too late; **j'ai ~ qu'il (ne) vienne (pas)** I'm afraid he may (not) come.

peureux, euse [pœrœ̄, -œ̄z] *a* fearful, timorous.

peut [pœ̄] *vb voir* **pouvoir**.

peut-être [pœ̄tetr(ə)] *ad* perhaps, maybe; **~ que** perhaps, maybe; **~ bien qu'il fera/est** he may well do/be.

peuvent [pœv], **peux** [pœ̄] *etc vb voir* **pouvoir**.

p. ex. *abr* (= *par exemple*) e.g.

phalange [fálâṅzh] *nf* (*ANAT*) phalanx (*pl* phalanges); (*MIL, fig*) phalanx (*pl* -es).

phallique [fálēk] *a* phallic.

phallocrate [fálokrát] *nm* male chauvinist.

phallocratie [fálokrásē] *nf* male chauvinism.

phallus [fálüs] *nm* phallus.

pharaon [fáráóṅ] *nm* Pharaoh.

phare [fár] *nm* (*en mer*) lighthouse; (*d'aéroport*) beacon; (*de véhicule*) headlight ◊ *a*: **produit ~** leading product; **se mettre en ~s, mettre ses ~s** to put on one's headlights; **~s de recul** back-up (*US*) *ou* reversing (*Brit*) lights.

pharmaceutique [fàrmásœ̄tēk] *a* pharmaceutic(al).

pharmacie [fàrmásē] *nf* (*science*) pharmacology; (*magasin*) pharmacy, chemist's (*Brit*); (*officine*) dispensary; (*produits*) pharmaceuticals *pl*; (*armoire*) medicine chest *ou* cupboard, first-aid cupboard.

pharmacien, ne [fàrmásyaṅ, -en] *nm/f* pharmacist, chemist (*Brit*).

pharmacologie [fàrmákolozhē] *nf* pharmacology.

pharyngite [fàraṅzhēt] *nf* pharyngitis *q*.

pharynx [fàraṅks] *nm* pharynx.

phase [fáz] *nf* phase.

phénoménal, e, aux [fānomānál, -ō] phenomenal.

phénomène [fānomen] *nm* phenomenon (*pl* -a); (*monstre*) freak.

philanthrope [fēlâṅtrop] *nm/f* philanthropist.

philanthropie [fēlâṅtropē] *nf* philanthropy.

philatélie [fēlátālē] *nf* philately, stamp collecting.

philatéliste [fēlátālēst(ə)] *nm/f* philatelist, stamp collector.

philharmonique [fēlàrmonēk] *a* philharmonic.

philippin, e [fēlēpaṅ, -ēn] *a* Filipino.

Philippines [fēlēpēn] *nfpl*: **les ~** the Philippines.

philistin [fēlēstaṅ] *nm* philistine.

philo [fēlō] *nf* (*fam*: = *philosophie*) philosophy.

philosophe [fēlozof] *nm/f* philosopher ◊ *a* philosophical.

philosopher [fēlozofā] *vi* to philisophize.

philosophie [fēlozofē] *nf* philosophy.

philosophique [fēlozofēk] *a* philosophical.

philtre [fēltr(ə)] *nm* philter (*US*), philtre (*Brit*), love potion.

phlébite [flābēt] *nf* phlebitis.

phlébologue [flābolog] *nm/f* vein specialist.

phobie [fobē] *nf* phobia.

phonétique [fonātēk] *a* phonetic ◊ *nf* phonetics *sg*.

phonographe [fonográf] *nm* (wind-up) phonograph (*US*) *ou* gramophone (*Brit*).

phoque [fok] *nm* seal; (*fourrure*) sealskin.

phosphate [fosfát] *nm* phosphate.

phosphaté, e [fosfátā] *a* phosphate-enriched.

phosphore [fosfor] *nm* phosphorus.

phosphoré, e [fosforā] *a* phosphorous.

phosphorescent, e [fosforāsâṅ, -âṅt] *a* luminous.

phosphorique [fosforēk] *a*: **acide ~** phosphoric acid.

photo [fotō] *nf* (= *photographie*) photo ◊ *a*: **appareil/pellicule ~** camera/film; **en ~** in *ou* on a photo; **prendre en ~** to take a photo of; **aimer la/faire de la ~** to like taking/take photos; **~ en couleurs** color photo; **~ d'identité** passport photo.

photo... [foto] *préfixe* photo....

photocopie [fotokopē] *nf* (*procédé*) photocopying; (*document*) photocopy.

photocopier [fotokopyā] *vt* to photocopy.

photocopieur [fotokopyœr] *nm*, **photocopieuse** [fotokopyœz] *nf* (photo)copier.

photo-électrique [fotoālektrēk] *a* photoelectric.

photogénique [fotozhānēk] *a* photogenic.

photographe [fotográf] *nm/f* photographer.

photographie [fotográfē] *nf* (*procédé, technique*) photography; (*cliché*) photograph;

faire de la ~ to have photography as a hobby; (*comme métier*) to be a photographer.

photographier [fotográfyā] *vt* to photograph, take.

photographique [fotográfēk] *a* photographic.

photogravure [fotográvür] *nf* photoengraving.

photomaton [fotomátôn] *nm* photo booth, photomat.

photomontage [fotomôntàzh] *nm* photomontage.

photo-robot [fotorobō] *nf* Identikit ® (picture).

photosensible [fotosânsēbl(ə)] *a* photosensitive.

photostat [fotostá] *nm* photostat.

phrase [fráz] *nf* (*LING*) sentence; (*propos, MUS*) phrase; ~**s** *nfpl* (*péj*) flowery language *sg*.

phraséologie [frázāolozhē] *nf* phraseology; (*rhétorique*) flowery language.

phraseur, euse [frázœr, -œz] *nm/f*: **c'est un** ~ he uses such flowery language.

phrygien, ne [frēzhyań, -en] *a*: **bonnet** ~ Phrygian cap.

phtisie [ftēzē] *nf* consumption.

phylloxéra [fēloksárá] *nm* phylloxera.

physicien, ne [fēzēsyań, -en] *nm/f* physicist.

physiologie [fēzyolozhē] *nf* physiology.

physiologique [fēzyolozhēk] *a* physiological.

physiologiquement [fēzyolozhēkmâń] *ad* physiologically.

physionomie [fēzyonomē] *nf* face; (*d'un paysage etc*) physiognomy.

physionomiste [fēzyonomēst(ə)] *nm/f* good judge of faces; person who has a good memory for faces.

physiothérapie [fēzyotàrápē] *nf* natural medicine, alternative medicine.

physique [fēzēk] *a* physical ♦ *nm* physique ♦ *nf* physics *sg*; **au** ~ physically.

physiquement [fēzēkmâń] *ad* physically.

phytothérapie [fētotàrápē] *nf* herbal medicine.

p.i. *abr* = **par intérim**; *voir* **intérim**.

piaffer [pyáfá] *vi* to stamp.

piailler [pyáyá] *vi* to squawk.

pianiste [pyánēst(ə)] *nm/f* pianist.

piano [pyánō] *nm* piano; ~ **à queue** grand piano.

pianoter [pyánotá] *vi* to tinkle away (at the piano); (*tapoter*): ~ **sur** to drum one's fingers on.

piaule [pyōl] *nf* (*fam*) pad.

piauler [pyōlá] *vi* (*enfant*) to whimper; (*oiseau*) to cheep.

PIB *sigle m* (= *produit intérieur brut*) GDP.

pic [pēk] *nm* (*instrument*) pick(ax) (*US*); pick(axe) (*Brit*); (*montagne*) peak; (*ZOOL*) woodpecker; **à** ~ *ad* vertically; (*fig*) just at the right time; **couler à** ~ (*bateau*) to go straight down; ~ **à glace** ice pick.

picard, e [pēkár, -árd(ə)] *a* of *ou* from Picardy.

Picardie [pēkárdē] *nf*: **la** ~ Picardy.

piccolo [pēkolō] *nm* piccolo.

pichenette [pēshnet] *nf* flick.

pichet [pēshe] *nm* jug.

pickpocket [pēkpoket] *nm* pickpocket.

pick-up [pēkœp] *nm inv* record player.

picorer [pēkorá] *vt* to peck.

picot [pēkō] *nm* sprocket; **entraînement par roue à** ~**s** sprocket feed.

picotement [pēkotmâń] *nm* smarting *q*, prickling *q*.

picoter [pēkotá] *vt* (*suj: oiseau*) to peck ♦ *vi* (*irriter*) to smart, prickle.

pictural, e, aux [pēktürál, -ō] *a* pictorial.

pie [pē] *nf* magpie; (*fig*) chatterbox ♦ *a inv*: **cheval** ~ piebald; **vache** ~ black and white cow.

pièce [pyes] *nf* (*d'un logement*) room; (*THÉÀTRE*) play; (*de mécanisme, machine*) part; (*de monnaie*) coin; (*COUTURE*) patch; (*document*) document; (*de drap, fragment, d'une collection*) piece; (*de bétail*) head; **mettre en** ~**s** to smash to pieces; **dix francs** ~ ten francs each; **vendre à la** ~ to sell separately *ou* individually; **travailler/payer à la** ~ to do piecework/pay piece rate; **de toutes** ~**s**: **c'est inventé de toutes** ~**s** it's a complete fabrication; **un maillot une** ~ a one-piece swimsuit; **un deux-**~**s cuisine** a two-room(ed) apartment (*US*) with kitchen; **tout d'une** ~ (*personne: franc*) blunt; (: *sans souplesse*) inflexible; ~ **à conviction** exhibit; ~ **d'eau** ornamental lake *ou* pond; ~ **d'identité: avez-vous une** ~ **d'identité?** have you got any (means of) identification?; ~ **montée** tiered cake; ~ **de rechange** spare (part); ~ **de résistance** pièce de résistance; (*plat*) main dish; ~**s détachées** spares, (spare) parts; **en** ~**s détachées** (*à monter*) in kit form; ~**s justificatives** supporting documents.

pied [pyā] *nm* foot (*pl* feet); (*de verre*) stem; (*de table*) leg; (*de lampe*) base; (*plante*) plant; ~**s nus** barefoot; **à** ~ on foot; **à** ~ **sec** without getting one's feet wet; **à** ~ **d'œuvre** ready to start (work); **au** ~ **de la lettre** literally; **au** ~ **levé** at a moment's notice; **de** ~ **en cap** from head to foot; **en** ~ (*portrait*) full-length; **avoir** ~ to be able to touch the bottom, not to be out of one's depth; **avoir le** ~ **marin** to be a good sailor; **perdre** ~ to lose one's footing; (*fig*) to get out of one's depth; **sur** ~ (*AGR*) on the stalk, uncut; (*debout, rétabli*) up and about; **mettre sur** ~ (*entreprise*) to set up; **mettre à** ~ to suspend; to lay off; **mettre qn au** ~ **du mur** to get sb with his (*ou* her) back to the wall; **sur le** ~ **de guerre** ready for action; **sur un** ~ **d'égalité** on an equal footing; **sur** ~ **d'intervention** on standby; **faire du** ~ **à qn** (*prévenir*) to give sb a (warning) kick; (*galamment*) to play footsy with sb; **mettre les** ~**s quelque part** to set foot somewhere; **faire des** ~**s et des mains** (*fig*) to move heaven and earth, pull out all the stops; **c'est le** ~**!** (*fam*) it's terrific!; **se lever du bon** ~**/du** ~ **gauche** to get out of bed on the right/wrong side; ~ **de lit** footboard; ~ **de nez: faire un** ~ **de nez à** to thumb one's nose at; ~ **de vigne** vine.

pied-à-terre [pyātáter] *nm inv* pied-à-terre.

pied-bot, *pl* **pieds-bots** [pyābō] *nm* person with a club foot.

pied-de-biche, *pl* **pieds-de-biche** [pyādbēsh] *nm* claw; (*COUTURE*) presser foot.

pied-de-poule [pyădpōōl] *a inv* hound's-tooth.
piédestal, aux [pyădestál, -ō] *nm* pedestal.
pied-noir, *pl* **pieds-noirs** [pyănwàr] *nm* Algerian-born Frenchman.
piège [pyezh] *nm* trap; **prendre au** ~ to trap.
piéger [pyăzhā] *vt* (*animal, fig*) to trap; (*avec une bombe*) to booby-trap; **lettre/voiture piégée** letter-/car-bomb.
pierraille [pyeráy] *nf* loose stones *pl.*
pierre [pyer] *nf* stone; **première** ~ (*d'un édifice*) foundation stone; **mur de** ~**s sèches** drystone wall; **faire d'une** ~ **deux coups** to kill two birds with one stone; ~ **à briquet** flint; ~ **fine** semiprecious stone; ~ **ponce** pumice stone; ~ **de taille** freestone *q*; ~ **tombale** tombstone, gravestone; ~ **de touche** touchstone.
pierreries [pyerrē] *nfpl* gems, precious stones.
pierreux, euse [pyerœ, -ōēz] *a* stony.
piété [pyătā] *nf* piety.
piétinement [pyătēnmáń] *nm* stamping *q.*
piétiner [pyătēnā] *vi* (*trépigner*) to stamp (one's foot); (*marquer le pas*) to stand around; (*fig*) to be at a standstill ♦ *vt* to trample on.
piéton, ne [pyătôń, -on] *nm/f* pedestrian ♦ *a* pedestrian *cpd.*
piétonnier, ière [pyătonyā, -yer] *a* pedestrian *cpd.*
piètre [pyetr(ə)] *a* poor, mediocre.
pieu, x [pyœ] *nm* (*piquet*) post; (*pointu*) stake; (*fam: lit*) bed.
pieusement [pyœzmáń] *ad* piously.
pieuvre [pyœvr(ə)] *nf* octopus.
pieux, euse [pyœ, -ōēz] *a* pious.
pif [pēf] *nm* (*fam*) beak; **au** ~ = **au pifomètre.**
piffer [pēfā] *vt* (*fam*): **je ne peux pas le** ~ I can't stand him.
pifomètre [pēfometr(ə)] *nm* (*fam*): **choisir** *etc* **au** ~ to follow one's nose when choosing *etc.*
pige [pēzh] *nf* piecework rate.
pigeon [pēzhóń] *nm* pigeon; ~ **voyageur** homing pigeon.
pigeonnant, e [pēzhonáń, -áńt] *a* full, well-developed.
pigeonnier [pēzhonyā] *nm* pigeon house, dovecot(e).
piger [pēzhā] *vi* (*fam*) to get it ♦ *vt* (*fam*) to get, understand.
pigiste [pēzhēst(ə)] *nm/f* (*typographe*) type-setter on piecework; (*journaliste*) freelance journalist (*paid by the line*).
pigment [pēgmáń] *nm* pigment.
pignon [pēnyóń] *nm* (*de mur*) gable; (*d'engrenage*) cog(wheel), gearwheel; (*graine*) pine kernel; **avoir** ~ **sur rue** (*fig*) to have a prosperous business.
pile [pēl] *nf* (*tas, pilier*) pile; (*ÉLEC*) battery ♦ *a*: **le côté** ~ **tails** ♦ *ad* (*net, brusquement*) dead; (*à temps, à point nommé*) just at the right time; **à deux heures** ~ at two on the dot; **jouer à** ~ **ou face** to toss up (for it); ~ **ou face?** heads or tails?
piler [pēlā] *vt* to crush, pound.
pileux, euse [pēlœ, -ōēz] *a*: **système** ~ (body) hair.
pilier [pēlyā] *nm* (*colonne, support*) pillar; (*personne*) mainstay; (*RUGBY*) prop (for-

ward).
pillage [pēyázh] *nm* pillaging, plundering, looting.
pillard, e [pēyàr, -àrd(ə)] *nm/f* looter; plunderer.
piller [pēyā] *vt* to pillage, plunder, loot.
pilon [pēlôń] *nm* (*instrument*) pestle; (*de volaille*) drumstick; **mettre un livre au** ~ to pulp a book.
pilonner [pēlonā] *vt* to pound.
pilori [pēlorē] *nm*: **mettre** *ou* **clouer au** ~ to pillory.
pilotage [pēlotázh] *nm* piloting; flying; ~ **automatique** automatic piloting; ~ **sans visibilité** blind flying.
pilote [pēlot] *nm* pilot; (*de char, voiture*) driver ♦ *a* pilot *cpd*; **usine/ferme** ~ experimental factory/farm; ~ **de chasse/d'essai/de ligne** fighter/test/airline pilot; ~ **de course** racing driver.
piloter [pēlotā] *vt* (*navire*) to pilot; (*avion*) to fly; (*automobile*) to drive; (*fig*): ~ **qn** to guide sb round; **piloté par menu** (*INFORM*) menu-driven.
pilotis [pēlotē] *nm* pile; stilt.
pilule [pēlül] *nf* pill; **prendre la** ~ to be on the pill.
pimbêche [pańbesh] *nf* (*péj*) stuck-up girl.
piment [pēmáń] *nm* (*BOT*) pepper, capsicum; (*fig*) spice, piquancy; ~ **rouge** (*CULIN*) chilli.
pimenté, e [pēmáńtā] *a* hot and spicy.
pimenter [pēmáńtā] *vt* (*plat*) to season (with peppers *ou* chillis); (*fig*) to add *ou* give spice to.
pimpant, e [pańpáń, -áńt] *a* spruce.
pin [pań] *nm* pine (tree); (*bois*) pine(wood).
pinacle [pēnàkl(ə)] *nm*: **porter qn au** ~ (*fig*) to praise sb to the skies.
pinard [pēnàr] *nm* (*fam*) (cheap) wine.
pince [pańs] *nf* (*outil*) pliers *pl*; (*de homard, crabe*) pincer, claw; (*COUTURE*: *pli*) dart; ~ **à sucre/glace** sugar/ice tongs *pl*; ~ **à épiler** tweezers *pl*; ~ **à linge** clothes pin (*US*) *ou* peg (*Brit*); ~ **universelle** (universal) pliers *pl*; ~**s de cycliste** bicycle clips.
pincé, e [pańsā] *a* (*air*) stiff; (*mince: bouche*) pinched ♦ *nf*: **une** ~**e de** a pinch of.
pinceau, x [pańsō] *nm* (paint)brush.
pince-monseigneur, *pl* **pinces-monseigneur** [pańsmôńsenyœr] *nf* crowbar.
pince-nez [pańsnā] *nm inv* pince-nez.
pincer [pańsā] *vt* to pinch; (*MUS*: *cordes*) to pluck; (*COUTURE*) to dart, put darts in; (*fam*) to nab; **se** ~ **le doigt** to squeeze *ou* nip one's finger; **se** ~ **le nez** to hold one's nose.
pince-sans-rire [pańssáńrēr] *a inv* deadpan.
pincettes [pańset] *nfpl* tweezers; (*pour le feu*) (fire) tongs.
pinçon [pańsóń] *nm* pinch mark.
pinède [pēned] *nf* pinewood, pine forest.
pingouin [pańgwań] *nm* penguin.
ping-pong [pēŋpóŋg] *nm* table tennis.
pingre [pańgr(ə)] *a* niggardly.
pinson [pańsóń] *nm* chaffinch.
pintade [pańtád] *nf* guinea fowl.
pin up [pēnœp] *nf inv* pinup (girl).
pioche [pyosh] *nf* pickaxe, pickax (*US*).
piocher [pyoshā] *vt* to dig up (with a pickaxe);

(*fam*) to grind (*US*) *ou* swot (*Brit*) at; ~ **dans** to dig into.

piolet [pyolɛ] *nm* ice axe *ou* ax (*US*).

pion, ne [pyɔ̃, pyɔn] *nm/f* (*SCOL*: *péj*) *student paid to supervise schoolchildren* ♦ *nm* (*ÉCHECS*) pawn; (*DAMES*) piece, checker (*US*), draught (*Brit*).

pionnier [pyɔnye] *nm* pioneer.

pipe [pip] *nf* pipe; **fumer la** *ou* **une** ~ to smoke a pipe; ~ **de bruyère** briar pipe.

pipeau, x [pipo] *nm* (reed) pipe.

pipe-line [piplɛn] *nm* pipeline.

piper [pipe] *vt* (*dé*) to load; (*carte*) to mark; **sans** ~ **mot** (*fam*) without a peep; **les dés sont pipés** (*fig*) the dice are loaded.

pipette [pipɛt] *nf* pipette.

pipi [pipi] *nm* (*fam*): **faire** ~ to have a pee.

piquant, e [pikɑ̃, -ɑ̃t] *a* (*barbe, rosier etc*) prickly; (*saveur, sauce*) hot, pungent; (*fig: description, style*) racy; (: *mordant, caustique*) biting ♦ *nm* (*épine*) thorn, prickle; (*de hérisson*) quill, spine; (*fig*) spiciness, spice.

pique [pik] *nf* (*arme*) pike; (*fig*): **envoyer** *ou* **lancer des** ~**s à qn** to make cutting remarks to sb ♦ *nm* (*CARTES*: *couleur*) spades *pl*; (: *carte*) spade.

piqué, e [pike] *a* (*COUTURE*) (machine-) stitched; quilted; (*livre, glace*) mildewed; (*vin*) sour; (*MUS*: *note*) staccato; (*fam: personne*) nuts ♦ *nm* (*AVIAT*) dive; (*TEXTILE*) piqué.

pique-assiette [pikasyɛt] *nm/f inv* (*péj*) scrounger, sponger.

pique-fleurs [pikflœr] *nm inv* flower holder.

pique-nique [piknik] *nm* picnic.

pique-niquer [piknike] *vi* to (have a) picnic.

pique-niqueur, euse [piknikœr, -øz] *nm/f* picnicker.

piquer [pike] *vt* (*percer*) to prick; (*planter*): ~ **qch dans** to stick sth into; (*fixer*): ~ **qch à** *ou* **sur** to pin sth onto; (*MÉD*) to give an injection to; (: *animal blessé etc*) to put to sleep; (*suj: insecte, fumée, ortie*) to sting; (: *poivre*) to burn; (: *froid*) to bite; (*COUTURE*) to machine (stitch); (*intérêt etc*) to arouse; (*fam: prendre*) to pick up; (: *voler*) to pinch; (: *arrêter*) to nab ♦ *vi* (*oiseau, avion*) to go into a dive; (*saveur*) to be pungent; to be sour; **se** ~ (*avec une aiguille*) to prick o.s.; (*se faire une piqûre*) to inject o.s.; (*se vexer*) to get annoyed; **se** ~ **de faire** to pride o.s. on doing; **se** ~ **sur** to swoop down on; to head straight for; ~ **du nez** (*avion*) to go into a nose-dive; ~ **une tête** (*plonger*) to dive headfirst; ~ **un galop/un cent mètres** to break into a gallop/put on a sprint; ~ **une crise** to throw a fit; ~ **au vif** (*fig*) to sting.

piquet [pikɛ] *nm* (*pieu*) post, stake; (*de tente*) peg; **mettre un élève au** ~ to make a pupil stand in the corner; ~ **de grève** (strike-)picket; ~ **d'incendie** fire-fighting squad.

piqueté, e [pikte] *a*: ~ **de** dotted with.

piquette [pikɛt] *nf* (*fam*) cheap wine.

piqûre [pikyr] *nf* (*d'épingle*) prick; (*d'ortie*) sting; (*de moustique*) bite; (*MÉD*) injection, shot (*US*); (*COUTURE*) (straight) stitch; straight stitching; (*de ver*) hole; (*tache*)

(spot of) mildew; **faire une** ~ **à qn** to give sb an injection.

piranha [pirana] *nm* piranha.

piratage [pirataʒ] *nm* piracy.

pirate [pirat] *a* pirate *cpd* ♦ *nm* pirate; (*fig: escroc*) crook, shark; ~ **de l'air** hijacker.

pirater [pirate] *vt* to pirate.

piraterie [piratri] *nf* (act of) piracy; ~ **aérienne** hijacking.

pire [pir] *a* (*comparatif*) worse; (*superlatif*): **le (la)** ~ ... the worst ... ♦ *nm*: **le** ~ **(de)** the worst (of).

Pirée [pire] *n* Piraeus.

pirogue [pirog] *nf* dugout (canoe).

pirouette [pirwɛt] *nf* pirouette; (*fig: volte-face*) about-face (*US*), about-turn (*Brit*).

pis [pi] *nm* (*de vache*) udder; (*pire*): **le** ~ the worst ♦ *a, ad* worse; **qui** ~ **est** what is worse; **au** ~ **aller** if the worst comes to the worst, at worst.

pis-aller [pizale] *nm inv* stopgap.

pisciculture [pisikyltyr] *nf* fish farming.

piscine [pisin] *nf* (swimming) pool; ~ **couverte** indoor (swimming) pool.

Pise [piz] *n* Pisa.

pissenlit [pisɑ̃li] *nm* dandelion.

pisser [pise] *vi* (*fam!*) to pee.

pissotière [pisotyɛr] *nf* (*fam*) public urinal.

pistache [pistaʃ] *nf* pistachio (nut).

pistard [pistar] *nm* (*CYCLISME*) track cyclist.

piste [pist(ə)] *nf* (*d'un animal, sentier*) track, trail; (*indice*) lead; (*de stade, de magnétophone, INFORM*) track; (*de cirque*) ring; (*de danse*) floor; (*de patinage*) rink; (*de ski*) run; (*AVIAT*) runway; ~ **cavalière** bridle path; ~ **cyclable** bicycle path, bikeway (*US*); ~ **sonore** sound track.

pister [piste] *vt* to track, trail.

pisteur [pistœr] *nm* (*SKI*) member of the ski patrol.

pistil [pistil] *nm* pistil.

pistolet [pistolɛ] *nm* (*arme*) pistol, gun; (*à peinture*) spray gun; ~ **à bouchon/air comprimé** popgun/airgun; ~ **à eau** water pistol.

pistolet-mitrailleur, *pl* **pistolets-mitrailleurs** [pistolɛmitrajœr] *nm* submachine gun.

piston [pistɔ̃] *nm* (*TECH*) piston; (*MUS*) valve; (*fig: appui*) string-pulling.

pistonner [pistone] *vt* (*candidat*) to pull strings for.

pitance [pitɑ̃s] *nf* (*péj*) (means of) sustenance.

piteux, euse [pitø, -øz] *a* pitiful, sorry (*avant le nom*); **en** ~ **état** in a sorry state.

pitié [pitye] *nf* pity; **sans** ~ *a* pitiless, merciless; **faire** ~ to inspire pity; **il me fait** ~ I pity him, I feel sorry for him; **avoir** ~ **de** (*compassion*) to pity, feel sorry for; (*merci*) to have pity *ou* mercy on; **par** ~! for pity's sake!

piton [pitɔ̃] *nm* (*clou*) peg, bolt; ~ **rocheux** rocky outcrop.

pitoyable [pitwayabl(ə)] *a* pitiful.

pitre [pitr(ə)] *nm* clown.

pitrerie [pitrəri] *nf* tomfoolery *q*.

pittoresque [pitoresk(ə)] *a* picturesque; (*expression, détail*) colorful (*US*), colourful (*Brit*).

pivert [pĕver] *nm* green woodpecker.
pivoine [pĕvwán] *nf* peony.
pivot [pĕvõ] *nm* pivot; (*d'une dent*) post.
pivoter [pĕvotá] *vi* (*fauteuil*) to swivel; (*porte*) to revolve; ~ **sur ses talons** to swing around.
pixel [pĕksel] *nm* pixel.
pizza [pĕdzà] *nf* pizza.
PJ *sigle f* = **police judiciaire** ♦ *sigle fpl* (= *pièces jointes*) encl.
PL *sigle m* (*AUTO*) = **poids lourd**.
Pl. *abr* = **place**.
placage [plákázh] *nm* (*bois*) veneer.
placard [plákár] *nm* (*armoire*) closet (*US*), cupboard (*Brit*); (*affiche*) poster, notice; (*TYPO*) galley; ~ **publicitaire** display advertisement.
placarder [plákárdá] *vt* (*affiche*) to put up; (*mur*) to stick posters on.
place [plás] *nf* (*emplacement, situation, classement*) place; (*de ville, village*) square; (*ÉCON*): ~ **financière/boursière** money/stock market; (*espace libre*) room, space; (*de parking*) space; (*siège: de train, cinéma, voiture*) seat; (*prix: au cinéma etc*) price; (: *dans un bus, taxi*) fare; (*emploi*) job; **en** ~ (*mettre*) in its place; **de** ~ **en** ~, **par** ~**s** here and there, in places; **sur** ~ on the spot; **faire** ~ **à** to give way to; **faire de la** ~ **à** to make room for; **ça prend de la** ~ it takes up a lot of room *ou* space; **prendre** ~ to take one's place; **remettre qn à sa** ~ to put sb in his (*ou* her) place; **ne pas rester** *ou* **tenir en** ~ to be always on the go; **à la** ~ **de** in place of, instead of; **une quatre** ~**s** (*AUTO*) a four-seater; **il y a 20** ~**s assises/debout** there are 20 seats/there is standing room for 20; ~ **forte** fortified town; ~ **d'honneur** place (*ou* seat) of honor.
placé, e [plásá] *a* (*HIPPISME*) placed; **haut** ~ (*fig*) high-ranking; **être bien/mal** ~ to be well/badly placed; (*spectateur*) to have a good/bad seat; **être bien/mal** ~ **pour faire** to be in/not to be in a position to do.
placebo [plásábõ] *nm* placebo.
placement [plásmáň] *nm* placing; (*FINANCE*) investment; **agence** *ou* **bureau de** ~ employment agency.
placenta [plásáňtá] *nm* placenta.
placer [plásá] *vt* to place, put; (*convive, spectateur*) to seat; (*capital, argent*) to place, invest; (*dans la conversation*) to put *ou* get in; ~ **qn chez** to get sb a job at (*ou* with); **se** ~ **au premier rang** to go and stand (*ou* sit) in the first row.
placide [plásĕd] *a* placid.
placier, ière [plásyá, -yer] *nm/f* commercial rep(resentative), salesman/woman.
plafond [pláfóň] *nm* ceiling.
plafonner [pláfoná] *vt* (*pièce*) to put a ceiling (up) in ♦ *vi* to reach one's (*ou* a) ceiling.
plafonnier [pláfonyá] *nm* ceiling light; (*AUTO*) interior light.
plage [plázh] *nf* beach; (*station*) (seaside) resort; (*fig*) band, bracket; (*de disque*) track, band; ~ **arrière** (*AUTO*) rear window shelf (*US*), parcel *ou* back shelf (*Brit*).
plagiaire [plázhyer] *nm/f* plagiarist.
plagiat [plázhyá] *nm* plagiarism.
plagier [plázhyá] *vt* to plagiarize.

plagiste [plázhĕst(ə)] *nm/f* beach attendant.
plaid [pled] *nm* (tartan) car rug, lap robe (*US*).
plaidant, e [pledáň, -áňt] *a* litigant.
plaider [pládá] *vi* (*avocat*) to plead; (*plaignant*) to go to court, litigate ♦ *vt* to plead; ~ **pour** (*fig*) to speak for.
plaideur, euse [pledœr, -øz] *nm/f* litigant.
plaidoirie [pledwárĕ] *nf* (*JUR*) speech for the defense (*US*) *ou* defence (*Brit*).
plaidoyer [pledwáyá] *nm* (*JUR*) speech for the defense (*US*) *ou* defence (*Brit*); (*fig*) plea.
plaie [ple] *nf* wound.
plaignant, e [plenyáň, -áňt] *vb voir* **plaindre** ♦ *nm/f* plaintiff.
plaindre [plaňdr(ə)] *vt* to pity, feel sorry for; **se** ~ *vi* (*gémir*) to moan; (*protester, rouspéter*): **se** ~ (**à qn**) (**de**) to complain (to sb) (about); (*souffrir*): **se** ~ **de** to complain of.
plaine [plen] *nf* plain.
plain-pied [plaňpyá]: **de** ~ *ad* at street level; (*fig*) straight; **de** ~ (**avec**) on the same level (as).
plaint, e [plaň, -áňt] *pp de* **plaindre** ♦ *nf* (*gémissement*) moan, groan; (*doléance*) complaint; **porter** ~**e** to lodge a complaint.
plaintif, ive [plaňtĕf, -ĕv] *a* plaintive.
plaire [pler] *vi* to be a success, be successful; to please; ~ **à**: **cela me plaît** I like it; **essayer de** ~ **à qn** (*en étant serviable etc*) to try and please sb; **elle plaît aux hommes** she's a success with men, men like her; **se** ~ **quelque part** to like being somewhere, like it somewhere; **se** ~ **à faire** to take pleasure in doing; **ce qu'il vous plaira** what(ever) you like *ou* wish; **s'il vous plaît** please.
plaisamment [plezámáň] *ad* pleasantly.
plaisance [plezáňs] *nf* (*aussi*: **navigation de** ~) (pleasure) sailing, yachting.
plaisancier [plezáňsyá] *nm* amateur sailor, yachting enthusiast.
plaisant, e [plezáň, -áňt] *a* pleasant; (*histoire, anecdote*) amusing.
plaisanter [plezáňtá] *vi* to joke ♦ *vt* (*personne*) to tease, make fun of; **pour** ~ for a joke; **on ne plaisante pas avec cela** that's no joking matter; **tu plaisantes!** you're joking *ou* kidding!
plaisanterie [plezáňtrĕ] *nf* joke; joking *q*.
plaisantin [plezáňtaň] *nm* joker; (*fumiste*) fly-by-night.
plaise [plez] *etc vb voir* **plaire**.
plaisir [plázĕr] *nm* pleasure; **faire** ~ **à qn** (*délibérément*) to be nice to sb, please sb; (*suj: cadeau, nouvelle etc*): **ceci me fait** ~ I'm delighted *ou* very pleased with this; **prendre** ~ **à/à faire** to take pleasure in/in doing; **j'ai le** ~ **de** ... it is with great pleasure that I ...; **M. et Mme X ont le** ~ **de vous faire part de** ... M. and Mme X are pleased to announce ...; **se faire un** ~ **de faire qch** to be (only too) pleased to do sth; **faites-moi le** ~ **de** ... would you mind ..., would you be kind enough to ...; **à** ~ freely; for the sake of it; **au** ~ (**de vous revoir**) (I hope to) see you again; **pour le** *ou* **pour son** *ou* **par** ~ for pleasure.
plaît [ple] *vb voir* **plaire**.

plan, e [plåñ, -àn] *a* flàt ◊ *nm* plan; (*GÉOM*) plane; (*fig*) level, plane; (*CINÉMA*) shot; **au premier/second ~** in the foreground/middle distance; **à l'arrière ~** in the background; **mettre qch au premier ~** (*fig*) to consider sth to be of primary importance; **sur le ~ sexuel** sexually, as far as sex is concerned; **laisser/rester en ~** to abandon/be abandoned; **~ d'action** plan of action; **~ directeur** (*ÉCON*) master plan; **~ d'eau** lake; pond; **~ de travail** work-top, work surface; **~ de vol** (*AVIAT*) flight plan.

planche [plåñsh] *nf* (*pièce de bois*) plank, (wooden) board; (*illustration*) plate; (*de salades, radis, poireaux*) bed; (*d'un plongeur*) (diving) board; **les ~s** (*THÉÂTRE*) the boards; **en ~s** *a* wooden; **faire la ~** (*dans l'eau*) to float on one's back; **avoir du pain sur la ~** to have one's work cut out; **~ à découper** chopping board; **~ à dessin** drawing board; **~ à pain** breadboard; **~ à repasser** ironing board; **~ (à roulettes)** (*planche*) skateboard; (*sport*) skateboarding; **~ de salut** (*fig*) sheet anchor; **~ à voile** (*planche*) windsurfer, sailboard; (*sport*) windsurfing.

plancher [plåñshā] *nm* floor; (*planches*) floorboards *pl*; (*fig*) minimum level ◊ *vi* to work hard.

planchiste [plåñshēst(ə)] *nm/f* windsurfer.

plancton [plåñktóñ] *nm* plankton.

planer [plånā] *vi* (*oiseau, avion*) to glide; (*fumée, vapeur*) to float, hover; (*drogué*) to be (on a) high; **~ sur** (*fig*) to hang over; to hover above.

planétaire [plånāter] *a* planetary.

planétarium [plånātáryom] *nm* planetarium.

planète [plånet] *nf* planet.

planeur [plåncer] *nm* glider.

planification [plånēfēkàsyóñ] *nf* (economic) planning.

planifier [plånēfyā] *vt* to plan.

planning [plånēng] *nm* program (*US*), programme (*Brit*), schedule; **~ familial** family planning.

planque [plåñk] *nf* (*fam: combine, filon*) easy number; (*: cachette*) hideout.

planquer [plåñkā] *vt* (*fam*) to hide (away), stash away; **se ~** to hide.

plant [plåñ] *nm* seedling, young plant.

plantaire [plåñter] *a voir* **voûte**.

plantation [plåñtàsyóñ] *nf* planting; (*de fleurs, légumes*) bed; (*exploitation*) plantation.

plante [plåñt] *nf* plant; **~ d'appartement** house *ou* pot plant; **~ du pied** sole (of the foot); **~ verte** house plant.

planter [plåñtā] *vt* (*plante*) to plant; (*enfoncer*) to hammer *ou* drive in; (*tente*) to put up, pitch; (*drapeau, échelle, décors*) to put up; (*fam: mettre*) to dump; (*: abandonner*): **~ là** to ditch; **se ~** *vi* (*fam: se tromper*) to get it wrong; **~ qch dans** to hammer *ou* drive sth into; to stick sth into; **se ~ dans** to sink into; to get stuck in; **se ~ devant** to plant o.s. in front of.

planteur [plåñtcer] *nm* planter.

planton [plåñtóñ] *nm* orderly.

plantureux, euse [plåñtürœ̄, -œ̄z] *a* (*repas*) copious, lavish; (*femme*) buxom.

plaquage [plåkàzh] *nm* (*RUGBY*) tackle.

plaque [plåk] *nf* plate; (*de verre*) sheet; (*de verglas, d'eczéma*) patch; (*dentaire*) plaque; (*avec inscription*) plaque; **~ (minéralogique ou de police ou d'immatriculation)** license (*US*) *ou* number (*Brit*) plate; **~ de beurre** slab of butter; **~ chauffante** hotplate; **~ de chocolat** bar of chocolate; **~ de cuisson** hob; **~ d'identité** identification tag; **~ tournante** (*fig*) center (*US*), centre (*Brit*).

plaqué, e [plåkā] *a*: **~ or/argent** gold-/silver-plated ◊ *nm*: **~ or/argent** gold/silver plate; **~ acajou** with a mahogany veneer.

plaquer [plåkā] *vt* (*bijou*) to plate; (*bois*) to veneer; (*aplatir*): **~ qch sur/contre** to make sth stick *ou* cling to; (*RUGBY*) to bring down; (*fam: laisser tomber*) to drop, ditch; **se ~ contre** to flatten o.s. against; **~ qn contre** to pin sb to.

plaquette [plåket] *nf* tablet; (*de chocolat*) bar; (*de beurre*) slab; (*livre*) small volume; (*MÉD: de pilules, gélules*) pack, packet; (*INFORM*) circuit board; **~ de frein** (*AUTO*) brake pad.

plasma [plåsmà] *nm* plasma.

plastic [plåstēk] *nm* plastic explosive.

plastifié, e [plåstēfyā] *a* plastic-coated.

plastiquage [plåstēkàzh] *nm* bombing, bomb attack.

plastique [plåstēk] *a* plastic ◊ *nm* plastic ◊ *nf* plastic arts *pl*; (*d'une statue*) modeling (*US*), modelling (*Brit*).

plastiquer [plåstēkā] *vt* to blow up.

plastiqueur [plåstēkœr] *nm* terrorist (*planting a plastic bomb*).

plastron [plåstróñ] *nm* shirt front.

plastronner [plåstronā] *vi* to swagger.

plat, e [plå, -àt] *a* flat; (*fade: vin*) flat-tasting, insipid; (*personne, livre*) dull ◊ *nm* (*récipient, CULIN*) dish; (*d'un repas*): **le premier ~** the first course; (*partie plate*): **le ~ de la main** the flat of the hand; (*: d'une route*) flat (part); **à ~ ventre** *ad* face down; (*tomber*) flat on one's face; **à ~** *a* (*pneu*) flat; (*batterie*) dead; (*fam: fatigué*) dead tired, tired out; **~ cuisiné** pre-cooked meal (*ou* dish); **~ du jour** special (*US*) *ou* dish (*Brit*) of the day; **~ de résistance** main course; **~s préparés** convenience food(s).

platane [plåtàn] *nm* plane tree.

plateau, x [plåtō] *nm* (*support*) tray; (*d'une table*) top; (*d'une balance*) pan; (*GÉO*) plateau; (*de tourne-disques*) turntable; (*CINÉMA*) set; (*TV*): **nous avons 2 journalistes sur le ~ ce soir** we have 2 journalists with us tonight; **~ à fromages** cheeseboard.

plateau-repas, *pl* **plateaux-repas** [plåtōrəpå] *nm* tray meal, TV dinner (*US*).

plate-bande, *pl* **plates-bandes** [plåtbåñd] *nf* flower bed.

platée [plåtā] *nf* dish(ful).

plate-forme, *pl* **plates-formes** [plåtform(ə)] *nf* platform; **~ de forage/pétrolière** drilling/oil rig.

platine [plåtēn] *nm* platinum ◊ *nf* (*d'un tourne-disque*) turntable; **~ disque/cassette** record/cassette deck; **~ laser** *ou* **compact-disc** compact disc (player).

platitude [plátētüd] *nf* platitude.
platonique [plátonēk] *a* platonic.
plâtras [plâträ] *nm* rubble *q*.
plâtre [plâtr(ə)] *nm* (*matériau*) plaster; (*statue*) plaster statue; (*MÉD*) (plaster) cast; ~s *nmpl* plasterwork *sg*; **avoir un bras dans le** ~ to have an arm in plaster.
plâtrer [plâträ] *vt* to plaster; (*MÉD*) to set *ou* put in a (plaster) cast.
plâtrier [plâtrēyä] *nm* plasterer.
plausible [plōzēbl(ə)] *a* plausible.
play-back [plebák] *nm* miming.
plébiscite [plābēsēt] *nm* plebiscite.
plébisciter [plābēsētä] *vt* (*approuver*) to give overwhelming support to; (*élire*) to elect by an overwhelming majority.
plectre [plɛktr(ə)] *nm* plectrum.
plein, e [plań, -en] *a* full; (*porte, roue*) solid; (*chienne, jument*) big (with young) ♦ *nm*: **faire le** ~ **(d'essence)** to fill up (with gas (*US*) *ou* petrol (*Brit*)) ♦ *prép*: **avoir de l'argent** ~ **les poches** to have loads of money; ~ **de** full of; **avoir les mains** ~es to have one's hands full; **à** ~es **mains** (*ramasser*) in handfuls; (*empoigner*) firmly; **à** ~ **régime** at maximum revs; (*fig*) at full speed; **à** ~ **temps** full-time; **en** ~ **air** in the open air; **jeux en** ~ **air** outdoor games; **en** ~**e mer** on the open sea; **en** ~ **soleil** in direct sunlight; **en** ~**e nuit/rue** in the middle of the night/street; **en** ~ **milieu** right in the middle; **en** ~ **jour** in broad daylight; **les** ~**s** the downstrokes (*in handwriting*); **faire le** ~ **des voix** to get the maximum number of votes possible; **en** ~ **sur** right on; **en avoir** ~ **le dos** (*fam*) to have had it up to here.
pleinement [plenmań] *ad* fully; to the full.
plein-emploi [plenäńplwä] *nm* full employment.
plénière [plänyɛr] *af*: **assemblée** ~ plenary assembly.
plénipotentiaire [plänēpotáńsyer] *nm* plenipotentiary.
plénitude [plänētüd] *nf* fullness.
pléthore [plātor] *nf*: ~ **de** overabundance *ou* plethora of.
pleurer [plœrä] *vi* to cry; (*yeux*) to water ♦ *vt* to mourn (for); ~ **sur** *vt* to lament (over), bemoan; ~ **de rire** to laugh till one cries.
pleurésie [plœrāzē] *nf* pleurisy.
pleureuse [plœrœz] *nf* professional mourner.
pleurnicher [plœrnēshä] *vi* to snivel, whine.
pleurs [plœr] *nmpl*: **en** ~ in tears.
pleut [plœ] *vb voir* **pleuvoir**.
pleutre [plœtr(ə)] *a* cowardly.
pleuvait [plœve] *etc vb voir* **pleuvoir**.
pleuviner [plœvēnä] *vb impersonnel* to drizzle.
pleuvoir [plœvwár] *vb impersonnel* to rain ♦ *vi* (*fig*): ~ **(sur)** to shower down (upon), be showered upon; **il pleut** it's raining; **il pleut des cordes** *ou* **à verse** *ou* **à torrents** it's pouring (down), it's raining cats and dogs.
pleuvra [plœvrá] *etc vb voir* **pleuvoir**.
Plexiglas [pleksēglâs] *nm* ® acrylic glass, Plexiglas ® (*US*).
pli [plē] *nm* fold; (*de jupe*) pleat; (*de pantalon*) crease; (*aussi*: **faux** ~) crease; (*enveloppe*) envelope; (*lettre*) letter; (*CARTES*) trick; **prendre le** ~ **de faire** to get

into the habit of doing; **ça ne fait pas un** ~! don't you worry!; ~ **d'aisance** inverted pleat.
pliable [plēyábl(ə)] *a* pliable, flexible.
pliage [plēyázh] *nm* folding; (*ART*) origami.
pliant, e [plēyáń, -áńt] *a* folding ♦ *nm* folding stool, campstool.
plier [plēyä] *vt* to fold; (*pour ranger*) to fold up; (*table pliante*) to fold down; (*genou, bras*) to bend ♦ *vi* to bend; (*fig*) to yield; **se** ~ **à** to submit to; ~ **bagages** (*fig*) to pack up (and go).
plinthe [plańt] *nf* baseboard (*US*), skirting board (*Brit*).
plissé, e [plēsā] *a* (*jupe, robe*) pleated; (*peau*) wrinkled; (*GÉO*) folded ♦ *nm* (*COUTURE*) pleats *pl*.
plissement [plēsmáń] *nm* (*GÉO*) fold.
plisser [plēsä] *vt* (*chiffonner: papier, étoffe*) to crease; (*rider: front*) to furrow, wrinkle; (: *bouche*) to pucker; (*jupe*) to put pleats in; **se** ~ *vi* (*vêtement, étoffe*) to crease.
pliure [plēyür] *nf* (*du bras, genou*) bend; (*d'un ourlet*) fold.
plomb [plóń] *nm* (*métal*) lead; (*d'une cartouche*) (lead) shot; (*PÊCHE*) sinker; (*sceau*) (lead) seal; (*ÉLEC*) fuse; **de** ~ (*soleil*) blazing; **sommeil de** ~ heavy *ou* very deep sleep; **mettre à** ~ to plumb.
plombage [plóńbázh] *nm* (*de dent*) filling.
plomber [plóńbä] *vt* (*canne, ligne*) to weight (with lead); (*colis, wagon*) to put a lead seal on; (*TECH: mur*) to plumb; (*dent*) to fill; (*INFORM*) to protect.
plomberie [plóńbrē] *nf* plumbing.
plombier [plóńbyä] *nm* plumber.
plonge [plóńzh] *nf*: **faire la** ~ to be a dishwasher (*person*).
plongeant, e [plóńzháń, -áńt] *a* (*vue*) from above; (*tir, décolleté*) plunging.
plongée [plóńzhā] *nf* (*SPORT*) diving *q*; (: *sans scaphandre*) skin diving; (*de sous-marin*) submersion, dive; **en** ~ (*sous-marin*) submerged; (*prise de vue*) high angle.
plongeoir [plóńzhwár] *nm* diving board.
plongeon [plóńzhóń] *nm* dive.
plonger [plóńzhä] *vi* to dive ♦ *vt*: ~ **qch dans** to plunge sth into; ~ **dans un sommeil profond** to sink straight into a deep sleep; ~ **qn dans l'embarras** to throw sb into a state of confusion.
plongeur, euse [plóńzhœr, -œz] *nm/f* diver; (*de café*) dishwasher (*person*).
plot [plō] *nm* (*ÉLEC*) contact.
ploutocratie [plōōtokrásē] *nf* plutocracy.
ployer [plwáyä] *vt* to bend ♦ *vi* to bend; (*plancher*) to sag.
plu [plü] *pp de* **plaire, pleuvoir**.
pluie [plüē] *nf* rain; (*averse, ondée*): **une** ~ **brève** a shower; (*fig*): ~ **de** shower of; **une** ~ **fine fine** rain; **retomber en** ~ to shower down; **sous la** ~ in the rain.
plumage [plümázh] *nm* plumage *q*, feathers *pl*.
plume [plüm] *nf* feather; (*pour écrire*) (pen) nib; (*fig*) pen; **dessin à la** ~ pen and ink drawing.
plumeau, x [plümō] *nm* feather duster.
plumer [plümä] *vt* to pluck.
plumet [plüme] *nm* plume.

plumier [plümyā] *nm* pencil box.
plupart [plüpár]: **la ~** *pronom* the majority, most (of them); **la ~ des** most, the majority of; **la ~ du temps/d'entre nous** most of the time/of us; **pour la ~** *ad* for the most part, mostly.
pluralisme [plürálēsm(ə)] *nm* pluralism.
pluralité [plürálētā] *nf* plurality.
pluridisciplinaire [plürēdēsēplēner] *a* multidisciplinary.
pluriel [plüryel] *nm* plural; **au ~** in the plural.
plus *vb* [plü] *voir* **plaire ♦** *ad* (plü, plüz + *vowel*) (*comparatif*) more, *adjectif court* + ...er; (*davantage*) [plüs] more; (*négatif*): **ne ... ~** no more, *tournure négative* + any more, no longer **♦** *cj* [plüs]: **~ 2** plus 2; **~ que** more than; **~ grand que** bigger than; **~ de 10 personnes** more than 10 people, over 10 people; **~ de minuit** after *ou* past midnight; **~ de pain** more bread; **~ il travaille, ~ il est heureux** the more he works, the happier he is; **le ~ intelligent/grand** the most intelligent/biggest; **3 heures/kilos de ~ que** 3 hours/kilos more than; **il a 3 ans de ~ que moi** he is 3 years older than I; **de ~** (*en outre*) what's more, moreover; **3 kilos en ~** 3 kilos more, 3 extra kilos; **en ~ de** in addition to; **de ~ en ~** more and more; **d'autant ~ que** all the more so since *ou* because; **(tout) au ~** at the (very) most; **sans ~** (but) no more than that, (but) that's all; **~ ou moins** more or less; **ni ~ ni moins** no more, no less; **qui ~ est** what is more.
plusieurs [plüzyœr] *dét, pronom* several; **ils sont ~** there are several of them.
plus-que-parfait [plüskəpárfe] *nm* pluperfect, past perfect.
plus-value [plüvalü] *nf* (*d'un bien*) appreciation; (*bénéfice*) capital gain; (*budgétaire*) surplus.
plut [plü] *vb voir* **plaire, pleuvoir.**
plutonium [plütonyom] *nm* plutonium.
plutôt [plütō] *ad* rather; **je ferais ~ ceci** I'd rather *ou* sooner do this; **fais ~ comme ça** try this way instead, you'd better try this way; **~ que (de) faire** rather than *ou* instead of doing.
pluvial, e, aux [plüvyál, -ō] *a* (*eaux*) rain *cpd*.
pluvieux, euse [plüvyœ̄, -œz] *a* rainy, wet.
pluviosité [plüvyozētā] *nf* rainfall.
PM *sigle f = Police militaire.*
p.m. *abr* (= *pour mémoire*) for the record.
PME *sigle fpl* = *petites et moyennes entreprises.*
PMI *sigle fpl* = *petites et moyennes industries* **♦** *sigle f* = **protection maternelle et infantile.**
PMU *sigle m* (= *pari mutuel urbain*) *system of betting on horses;* (*café*) betting agency.
PNB *sigle m* (= *produit national brut*) GNP.
pneu [pnœ̄] *nm* (*de roue*) tire (*US*), tyre (*Brit*); (*message*) letter sent by pneumatic tube.
pneumatique [pnœ̄mátēk] *a* pneumatic; (*gonflable*) inflatable **♦** *nm* tire (*US*), tyre (*Brit*).
pneumonie [pnœ̄monē] *nf* pneumonia.
PO *sigle fpl* (= *petites ondes*) MW.
Pô [pō] *nm*: **le ~** the Po.
po [pō] *abr voir* **science.**
p.o. *abr* (= *par ordre*) p.p. (*on letters etc*).

poche [posh] *nf* pocket; (*déformation*): **faire une/des ~(s)** to bag; (*sous les yeux*) bag, pouch; (*ZOOL*) pouch **♦** *nm* (= *livre de ~*) (pocket-size) paperback; **de ~** pocket *cpd*; **en être de sa ~** to be out of pocket; **c'est dans la ~** it's in the bag.
poché, e [poshā] *a*: **œuf ~** poached egg; **œil ~** black eye.
pocher [poshā] *vt* (*CULIN*) to poach; (*ART*) to sketch **♦** *vi* (*vêtement*) to bag.
poche-revolver, *pl* **poches-revolver** [poshrəvolver] *nf* hip pocket.
pochette [poshet] *nf* (*de timbres*) folder, envelope; (*d'aiguilles etc*) case; (*sac: de femme*) clutch bag, purse; (*: d'homme*) bag; (*sur veston*) breast pocket; (*mouchoir*) breast pocket handkerchief; **~ d'allumettes** book of matches; **~ de disque** record jacket (*US*) *ou* sleeve (*Brit*); **~ surprise** surprise package.
pochoir [poshwár] *nm* (*ART: cache*) stencil; (*: tampon*) transfer.
podium [podyom] *nm* podium (*pl* -ia).
poêle [pwál] *nm* stove **♦** *nf*: **~ (à frire)** frying pan.
poêlon [pwálôn] *nm* casserole.
poème [poem] *nm* poem.
poésie [poāzē] *nf* (*poème*) poem; (*art*): **la ~** poetry.
poète [poet] *nm* poet; (*fig*) dreamer **♦** *a* poetic.
poétique [poātēk] *a* poetic.
pognon [ponyôn] *nm* (*fam: argent*) dough.
poids [pwá] *nm* weight; (*SPORT*) shot; **vendre au ~** to sell by weight; **de ~** *a* (*argument etc*) weighty; **prendre du ~** to put on weight; **faire le ~** (*fig*) to measure up; **~ plume/mouche/coq/moyen** (*BOXE*) feather/fly/bantam/ middleweight; **~ et haltères** *nmpl* weight lifting *sg*; **~ lourd** (*BOXE*) heavyweight; (*camion: aussi*: **PL**) (big) truck (*US*), lorry (*Brit*); (*: ADMIN*) truck (*US*), heavy goods vehicle (*Brit*); **~ mort** dead weight; **~ utile** net weight.
poignant, e [pwányân, -ânt] *a* poignant, harrowing.
poignard [pwányár] *nm* dagger.
poignarder [pwányárdā] *vt* to stab, knife.
poigne [pwány] *nf* grip; (*fig*) firm-handedness; **à ~** firm-handed.
poignée [pwányā] *nf* (*de sel etc, fig*) handful; (*de couvercle, porte*) handle; **~ de main** handshake.
poignet [pwánye] *nm* (*ANAT*) wrist; (*de chemise*) cuff.
poil [pwál] *nm* (*ANAT*) hair; (*de pinceau, brosse*) bristle; (*de tapis, tissu*) strand; (*pelage*) coat; (*ensemble des poils*): **avoir du ~ sur la poitrine** to have hair(s) on one's chest, have a hairy chest; **à ~** *a* (*fam*) stark naked; **au ~** *a* (*fam*) hunky-dory; **de tout ~** of all kinds; **être de bon/mauvais ~** to be in a good/bad mood; **~ à gratter** itching powder.
poilu, e [pwálü] *a* hairy.
poinçon [pwánsôn] *nm* awl; bodkin; (*marque*) hallmark.
poinçonner [pwánsonā] *vt* (*marchandise*) to stamp; (*bijou etc*) to hallmark; (*billet, tick-*

et) to clip, punch.

poinçonneuse [pwaṅsonœz] *nf* (*outil*) punch.

poindre [pwaṅdr(ə)] *vi* (*fleur*) to come up; (*aube*) to break; (*jour*) to dawn.

poing [pwaṅ] *nm* fist; **dormir à ~s fermés** to sleep soundly.

point [pwaṅ] *vb voir* **poindre** ♦ *nm* (*marque*, *signe*) dot; (: *de ponctuation*) full stop, period (*US*); (*moment, de score etc, fig*: *question*) point; (*endroit*) spot; (*COUTURE*, *TRICOT*) stitch ♦ *ad* = **pas**; **ne ... ~** not (at all); **faire le ~** (*NAVIG*) to take a bearing; (*fig*) to take stock (of the situation); **faire le ~ sur** to review; **en tout ~** in every respect; **sur le ~ de faire** (just) about to do; **au ~ que, à tel ~ que** so much so that; **mettre au ~** (*mécanisme*, *procédé*) to develop; (*appareil-photo*) to focus; (*affaire*) to settle; **à ~** (*CULIN*) just right; (: *viande*) medium; **à ~ (nommé)** just at the right time; **~ de croix/tige/chaînette** (*COUTURE*) cross/stem/chain stitch; **~ mousse/jersey** (*TRICOT*) garter/stocking stitch; **~ de départ/d'arrivée/d'arrêt** departure/arrival/stopping point; **~ chaud** (*MIL*, *POL*) hot spot; **~ de chute** landing place; (*fig*) stopping-off point; **~ (de côté)** stitch (*pain*); **~ culminant** summit; (*fig*) height, climax; **~ d'eau** spring; water hole; **~ d'exclamation** exclamation mark; **~ faible** weak spot; **~ final** full stop, period (*US*); **~ d'interrogation** question mark; **~ mort** (*FINANCE*) break-even point; **au ~ mort** (*AUTO*) in neutral; (*affaire, entreprise*) at a standstill; **~ noir** (*sur le visage*) blackhead; (*AUTO*) deathtrap (*US*), accident black spot (*Brit*); **~ de non-retour** point of no return; **~ de repère** landmark; (*dans le temps*) point of reference; **~ de vente** retail outlet; **~ de vue** viewpoint; (*fig: opinion*) point of view; **du ~ de vue de** from the point of view of; **~s cardinaux** points of the compass, cardinal points; **~s de suspension** ellipsis *sg* suspension.

pointage [pwaṅtazh] *nm* ticking off; checking in.

pointe [pwaṅt] *nf* point; (*de la côte*) headland; (*allusion*) dig; sally; (*fig*): **une ~ d'ail/d'accent** a touch *ou* hint of garlic/of an accent; **~s** *nfpl* (*DANSE*) points, point shoes; **être à la ~ de** (*fig*) to be in the forefront of; **faire** *ou* **pousser une ~ jusqu'à ...** to press on as far as ...; **sur la ~ des pieds** on tiptoe; **en ~** *ad* (*tailler*) into a point ♦ *a* pointed, tapered; **de ~** *a* (*technique etc*) leading; (*vitesse*) maximum, top; **heures/jours de ~** peak hours/days; **faire du 180 en ~** (*AUTO*) to have a top *ou* maximum speed of 180; **faire des ~s** (*DANSE*) to dance on points; **~ d'asperge** asparagus tip; **~ de courant** surge (of current); **~ de tension** (*INFORM*) spike; **~ de vitesse** burst of speed.

pointer [pwaṅte] *vt* (*cocher*) to tick *ou* check (*US*) off; (*employés etc*) to check in; (*diriger: canon, longue-vue, doigt*): **~ vers qch** to point at sth; (*MUS: note*) to dot ♦ *vi* (*employé*) to clock in; (*pousses*) to come through; (*jour*) to break; **~ les oreilles** (*chien*) to prick up its ears.

pointeur, euse [pwaṅtœr, -œz] *nm/f* time-

keeper ♦ *nf* timeclock.

pointillé [pwaṅtēyā] *nm* (*trait*) dotted line; (*ART*) stippling *q*.

pointilleux, euse [pwaṅtēyœ, -œz] *a* particular, pernickety.

pointu, e [pwaṅtü] *a* pointed; (*clou*) sharp; (*voix*) shrill; (*analyse*) precise.

pointure [pwaṅtür] *nf* size.

point-virgule, *pl* **points-virgules** [pwaṅvērgül] *nm* semicolon.

poire [pwár] *nf* pear; (*fam: péj*) mug; **~ électrique** (*pear-shaped*) switch; **~ à injections** syringe.

poireau, x [pwárō] *nm* leek.

poireauter [pwárōtā] *vi* (*fam*) to hang around (waiting).

poirier [pwáryā] *nm* pear tree; (*GYM*): **faire le ~** to do a headstand.

pois [pwá] *nm* (*BOT*) pea; (*sur une étoffe*) dot, spot; **à ~** (*cravate etc*) spotted, polka-dot *cpd*; **~ chiche** chickpea; **~ de senteur** sweet pea; **~ cassés** split peas.

poison [pwázôṅ] *nm* poison.

poisse [pwás] *nf* rotten luck.

poisser [pwásā] *vt* to make sticky.

poisseux, euse [pwásœ, -œz] *a* sticky.

poisson [pwásôṅ] *nm* fish *gén inv*; **les P~s** (*signe*) Pisces, the Fish; **être des P~s** to be Pisces; **pêcher** *ou* **prendre du ~** *ou* **des ~s** to fish; **~ d'avril** April fool; (*blague*) April fool's day trick; **~ rouge** goldfish.

poisson-chat, *pl* **poissons-chats** [pwásôṅshà] *nm* catfish.

poissonnerie [pwásonrē] *nf* fishmonger's, fish market (*US*).

poissonneux, euse [pwásonœ, -œz] *a* abounding in fish.

poissonnier, ière [pwásonyā, -yer] *nm/f* fishmonger, fish merchant (*US*) ♦ *nf* (*ustensile*) fish kettle.

poisson-scie, *pl* **poissons-scies** [pwásôṅsē] *nm* sawfish.

poitevin, e [pwátvaṅ, -ēn] *a* (*région*) of *ou* from Poitou; (*ville*) of *ou* from Poitiers.

poitrail [pwátrày] *nm* (*d'un cheval etc*) breast.

poitrine [pwátrēn] *nf* (*ANAT*) chest; (*seins*) bust, bosom; (*CULIN*) breast; **~ de bœuf** brisket.

poivre [pwávr(ə)] *nm* pepper; **~ en grains/moulu** whole/ground pepper; **~ de cayenne** cayenne (pepper); **~ et sel** *a* (*cheveux*) pepper-and-salt.

poivré, e [pwávrā] *a* peppery.

poivrer [pwávrā] *vt* to pepper.

poivrier [pwávrēyā] *nm* (*BOT*) pepper plant.

poivrière [pwávrēyer] *nf* pepperpot, pepper shaker (*US*).

poivron [pwávrôṅ] *nm* pepper, capsicum; **~ vert/rouge** green/red pepper.

poix [pwá] *nf* pitch (*tar*).

poker [poker] *nm*: **le ~** poker; **partie de ~** (*fig*) gamble; **~ d'as** four aces.

polaire [poler] *a* polar.

polariser [polárēzā] *vt* to polarize; (*fig: attirer*) to attract; (: *réunir, concentrer*) to focus; **être polarisé sur** (*personne*) to be completely bound up with *ou* absorbed by.

pôle [pōl] *nm* (*GÉO, ÉLEC*) pole; **le ~ Nord/Sud** the North/South Pole; **~ d'attraction**

(fig) center of attraction.

polémique [polămēk] *a* controversial, polemic(al) ♦ *nf* controversy.

polémiquer [polămēkă] *vi* to be involved in controversy.

polémiste [polămēst(ə)] *nm/f* polemist, polemicist.

poli, e [polē] *a* polite; *(lisse)* smooth; polished.

police [polēs] *nf* police; *(discipline)*: **assurer la ~ de** *ou* **dans** to keep order in; **peine de simple ~** *sentence given by a magistrates' or police court*; **~ (d'assurance)** (insurance) policy; **~ (de caractères)** *(TYPO, INFORM)* typeface; **~ judiciaire (PJ)** ≈ Federal Bureau of Investigation (FBI) *(US)*, ≈ Criminal Investigation Department (CID) *(Brit)*; **~ des mœurs** ≈ vice squad; **~ secours** ≈ emergency services *pl*.

polichinelle [polēshēncl] *nm* Punch; *(péj)* buffoon; **secret de ~** open secret.

policier, ière [polēsyā, -yer] *a* police *cpd* ♦ *nm* policeman; *(aussi:* **roman ~**) detective novel.

policlinique [polēklēnēk] *nf* ≈ outpatients (clinic).

poliment [polēmăn] *ad* politely.

polio(myélite) [polyo(myălēt)] *nf* polio(myelitis).

polio(myélitique) [polyo(myălētēk)] *nm/f* polio patient *ou* case.

polir [polēr] *vt* to polish.

polisson, ne [polēsŏn, -on] *a* naughty.

politesse [polētes] *nf* politeness; **~s** *nfpl* (exchange of) courtesies; **rendre une ~ à qn** to return sb's favor.

politicard [polētēkăr] *nm* *(péj)* politico, political schemer.

politicien, ne [polētēsyăn, -en] *a* political ♦ *nm/f* politician.

politique [polētēk] *a* political ♦ *nf (science, activité)* politics *sg*; *(principes, tactique)* policy, policies *pl* ♦ *nm (politicien)* politician; **~ étrangère/intérieure** foreign/domestic policy.

politique-fiction [polētēkfēksyŏn] *nf* political fiction.

politiquement [polētēkmăn] *ad* politically.

politiser [polētēză] *vt* to politicize; **~ qn** to make sb politically aware.

pollen [polen] *nm* pollen.

polluant, e [polüăn, -ănt] *a* polluting ♦ *nm* polluting agent, pollutant.

polluer [polüă] *vt* to pollute.

pollution [polüsyŏn] *nf* pollution.

polo [polŏ] *nm (sport)* polo; *(tricot)* polo shirt.

Pologne [polony] *nf*: **la ~** Poland.

polonais, e [polone, -ez] *a* Polish ♦ *nm (LING)* Polish ♦ *nm/f*: **P~, e** Pole.

poltron, ne [poltrŏn, -on] *a* cowardly.

poly... [polē] *préfixe* poly....

polyamide [polēămēd] *nf* polyamide.

polychrome [polēkrŏm] *a* polychrome, polychromatic.

polyclinique [polēklēnēk] *nf* (private) clinic *(treating different illnesses)*.

polycopié, e [polēkopyā] *a* duplicated ♦ *nm* handout, duplicated notes *pl*.

polycopier [polēkopyā] *vt* to duplicate.

polyculture [polēkültür] *nf* mixed farming.

polyester [polēester] *nm* polyester.

polyéthylène [polēātēlen] *nm* polyethylene.

polygame [polēgăm] *a* polygamous.

polygamie [polēgămē] *nf* polygamy.

polyglotte [polēglot] *a* polyglot.

polygone [polēgon] *nm* polygon.

Polynésie [polēnāzē] *nf*: **la ~** Polynesia; **la ~ française** French Polynesia.

polynésien, ne [polēnāzyăn, -en] *a* Polynesian.

polype [polēp] *nm* polyp.

polystyrène [polēstēren] *nm* polystyrene.

polytechnicien, ne [polēteknēsyăn, -en] *nm/f* student or former student of the École Polytechnique.

polyvalent, e [polēvălăn, -ănt] *a (vaccin)* polyvalent; *(personne)* versatile; *(salle)* multipurpose ♦ *nm* ≈ tax inspector.

pomélo [pomălŏ] *nm* grapefruit.

Poméranie [pomărănē] *nf*: **la ~** Pomerania.

pommade [pomăd] *nf* ointment, cream.

pomme [pom] *nf (BOT)* apple; *(boule décorative)* knob; *(pomme de terre)*: **steak ~s (frites)** steak and (French) fries *ou* chips *(Brit)*; **tomber dans les ~s** *(fam)* to pass out; **~ d'Adam** Adam's apple; **~s allumettes** French fries *(thin-cut)*; **~ d'arrosoir** (sprinkler) rose; **~ de pin** pine *ou* fir cone; **~ de terre** potato; **~s vapeur** boiled potatoes.

pommé, e [pomā] *a (chou etc)* firm, with a firm heart.

pommeau, x [pomŏ] *nm (boule)* knob; *(de selle)* pommel.

pommelé, e [pomlā] *a*: **gris ~** dapple grey.

pommette [pomet] *nf* cheekbone.

pommier [pomyā] *nm* apple tree.

pompe [pŏnp] *nf* pump; *(faste)* pomp (and ceremony); **~ de bicyclette** bicycle pump; **~ à eau/essence** water/gas(oline) *(US)* ou petrol *(Brit)* pump; **~ à huile** oil pump; **~ à incendie** fire engine *(apparatus)*; **~s funèbres** undertaker's *sg*, mortician's *sg (US)*, funeral parlour *sg (Brit)*.

Pompéi [pŏnpāē] *n* Pompeii.

pompéien, ne [pŏnpāyăn, -en] *a* Pompeiian.

pomper [pŏnpā] *vt* to pump; *(évacuer)* to pump out; *(aspirer)* to pump up; *(absorber)* to soak up ♦ *vi* to pump.

pompeusement [pŏnpœzmăn] *ad* pompously.

pompeux, euse [pŏnpœ, -œz] *a* pompous.

pompier [pŏnpyā] *nm* fireman ♦ *am (style)* pretentious, pompous.

pompiste [pŏnpēst(ə)] *nm/f* gas *(US)* ou petrol *(Brit)* pump attendant.

pompon [pŏnpŏn] *nm* pompom, bobble.

pomponner [pŏnponā] *vt* to dress up.

ponce [pŏns] *nf*: **pierre ~** pumice stone.

poncer [pŏnsā] *vt* to sand (down).

ponceuse [pŏnsœz] *nf* sander.

poncif [pŏnsēf] *nm* cliché.

ponction [pŏnksyŏn] *nf (d'argent etc)* withdrawal; **~ lombaire** lumbar puncture.

ponctualité [pŏnktüălētā] *nf* punctuality.

ponctuation [pŏnktüāsyŏn] *nf* punctuation.

ponctuel, le [pŏnktüel] *a (à l'heure, aussi TECH)* punctual; *(fig: opération etc)* one-shot *(US)*, one-off *(Brit)*, single; *(scrupuleux)* punctilious, meticulous.

ponctuellement [pŏnktüelmăn] *ad* punctually; punctiliously, meticulously.

ponctuer [pɔ́ŋktüä] *vt* to punctuate; (*MUS*) to phrase.

pondéré, e [pɔ́ŋdārā] *a* levelheaded, composed.

pondérer [pɔ́ŋdārā] *vt* to balance.

pondeuse [pɔ́ŋdœ̄z] *nf* layer, laying hen.

pondre [pɔ́ŋdr(ə)] *vt* to lay; (*fig*) to produce ♦ *vi* to lay.

poney [pone] *nm* pony.

pongiste [pɔ́ŋzhēst(ə)] *nm/f* table tennis player.

pont [pɔ́ŋ] *nm* bridge; (*AUTO*): ~ **arrière/avant** rear/front axle; (*NAVIG*) deck; **faire le** ~ to take the extra day off; **faire un** ~ **d'or à qn** to offer sb a fortune to take a job; ~ **aérien** airlift; ~ **basculant** bascule bridge; ~ **d'envol** flight deck; ~ **élévateur** hydraulic ramp; ~ **de graissage** ramp (*in garage*); ~ **à péage** tollbridge; ~ **roulant** traveling crane; ~ **suspendu** suspension bridge; ~ **tournant** swing bridge; **P~s et Chaussées** highways department.

ponte [pɔ́ŋt] *nf* laying; (*œufs pondus*) clutch ♦ *nm* (*fam*) big shot.

pontife [pɔ́ŋtēf] *nm* pontiff.

pontifier [pɔ́ŋtēfyā] *vi* to pontificate.

pont-levis, *pl* **ponts-levis** [pɔ́ŋlvē] *nm* drawbridge.

ponton [pɔ́ŋtɔ́ŋ] *nm* pontoon (*on water*).

pop [pop] *a inv* pop ♦ *nm*: **le** ~ pop (music).

pop-corn [popkorn] *nm* popcorn.

popeline [poplēn] *nf* poplin.

populace [popülás] *nf* (*péj*) rabble.

populaire [popüler] *a* popular; (*manifestation*) mass *cpd*, of the people; (*milieux, clientèle*) working-class; (*LING*: *mot etc*) used by the lower classes (of society).

populariser [popülárēzā] *vt* to popularize.

popularité [popülárētā] *nf* popularity.

population [popülásyɔ́ŋ] *nf* population; ~ **active/agricole** working/farming population.

populeux, euse [popülœ̄, -œ̄z] *a* densely populated.

porc [por] *nm* (*ZOOL*) pig; (*CULIN*) pork; (*peau*) pigskin.

porcelaine [porsəlen] *nf* (*substance*) porcelain, china; (*objet*) piece of china(ware).

porcelet [porsəle] *nm* piglet.

porc-épic, *pl* **porcs-épics** [porkāpēk] *nm* porcupine.

porche [porsh(ə)] *nm* porch.

porcher, ère [porshā, -er] *nm/f* swineherd.

porcherie [porshərē] *nf* pigsty.

porcin, e [porsaŋ, -ēn] *a* (*race*) porcine; (*élevage*) pig *cpd*; (*fig*) piglike.

pore [por] *nm* pore.

poreux, euse [porœ̄, -œ̄z] *a* porous.

porno [pornɔ́] *a* porno ♦ *nm* porn.

pornographie [pornográfē] *nf* pornography.

pornographique [pornográfēk] *a* pornographic.

port [por] *nm* (*NAVIG*) harbor (*US*), harbour (*Brit*), port; (*ville, aussi INFORM*) port; (*de l'uniforme etc*) wearing; (*pour lettre*) postage; (*pour colis, aussi: posture*) carriage; ~ **de commerce/de pêche** commercial/fishing port; **arriver à bon** ~ to arrive safe and sound; ~ **d'arme** (*JUR*) carrying of a

firearm; ~ **d'attache** (*NAVIG*) port of registry; (*fig*) home base; ~ **d'escale** port of call; ~ **franc** free port.

portable [portábl(ə)] *a* (*vêtement*) wearable; (*portatif*) transportable.

portail [portáy] *nm* gate; (*de cathédrale*) portal.

portant, e [portáŋ, -âŋt] *a* (*murs*) structural, supporting; (*roues*) running; **bien/mal** ~ in good/poor health.

portatif, ive [portátēf, -ēv] *a* portable.

porte [port(ə)] *nf* door; (*de ville, forteresse, SKI*) gate; **mettre à la** ~ to throw out; **prendre la** ~ to leave, go away; **à ma/sa** ~ (*tout près*) on my/his (*ou* her) doorstep; ~ **(d'embarquement)** (*AVIAT*) (departure) gate; ~ **d'entrée** front door; ~ **à** ~ *nm* door-to-door selling; ~ **de secours** emergency exit; ~ **de service** service entrance.

porté, e [portā] *a*: **être** ~ **à faire qch** to be apt to do sth, tend to do sth; **être** ~ **sur qch** to be partial to sth.

porte-à-faux [portáfɔ́] *nm*: **en** ~ cantilevered; (*fig*) in an awkward position.

porte-aiguilles [portāgüēy] *nm inv* needle case.

porte-avions [portávyɔ́ŋ] *nm inv* aircraft carrier.

porte-bagages [portbágázh] *nm inv* luggage rack (*ou* basket *etc*).

porte-bébé [portbābā] *nm* baby sling *ou* carrier.

porte-bonheur [portbonœr] *nm inv* lucky charm.

porte-bouteilles [portbōōtey] *nm inv* bottle carrier; (*à casiers*) wine rack.

porte-cartes [portkárt(ə)] *nm inv* (*de cartes d'identité*) card holder; (*de cartes géographiques*) map holder *ou* case.

porte-cigarettes [portsēgáret] *nm inv* cigarette case.

porte-clefs [portəklā] *nm inv* key ring.

porte-conteneurs [portəkɔ́ŋtnœr] *nm inv* container ship.

porte-couteau, x [portkōōtɔ́] *nm* knife rest.

porte-crayon [portkreyɔ́ŋ] *nm* pencil holder.

porte-documents [portdokümáŋ] *nm inv* attaché *ou* document case.

porte-drapeau, x [portdrápɔ́] *nm* standard-bearer.

portée [portā] *nf* (*d'une arme*) range; (*fig: importance*) impact, import; (*: capacités*) scope, capability; (*de chatte etc*) litter; (*MUS*) stave, staff (*pl* staves); **à/hors de** ~ **(de)** within/out of reach (of); **à** ~ **de (la) main** within (arm's) reach; **à** ~ **de voix** within earshot; **à la** ~ **de qn** (*fig*) at sb's level, within sb's capabilities; **à la** ~ **de toutes les bourses** to suit every pocket, within everyone's means.

portefaix [portəfe] *nm inv* porter.

porte-fenêtre, *pl* **portes-fenêtres** [portfənetr(ə)] *nf* French window.

portefeuille [portəfœy] *nm* wallet; (*POL, BOURSE*) portfolio; **faire un lit en** ~ to short-sheet a bed (*US*), make an apple-pie bed (*Brit*).

porte-jarretelles [portzhártel] *nm inv* garter (*US*) *ou* suspender (*Brit*) belt.

porte-jupe [portəzhüp] *nm* skirt hanger.
portemanteau, x [portmáṅtō] *nm* coat rack.
porte-mine [portəmēn] *nm* mechanical (*US*) *ou* propelling (*Brit*) pencil.
porte-monnaie [portmone] *nm inv* coin purse.
porte-parapluies [portpáráplüē] *nm inv* umbrella stand.
porte-parole [portpárol] *nm inv* spokesperson.
porte-plume [portəplüm] *nm inv* penholder.
porter [portā] *vt* (*charge ou sac etc, aussi: fœtus*) to carry; (*sur soi: vêtement, barbe, bague*) to wear; (*fig: responsabilité etc*) to bear, carry; (*inscription, marque, titre, patronyme, suj: arbre: fruits, fleurs*) to bear; (*jugement*) to pass; (*apporter*): ~ **qch quelque part/à qn** to take sth somewhere/to sb; (*inscrire*): ~ **qch sur** to put sth down on; to enter sth in ♦ *vi* (*voix, regard, canon*) to carry; (*coup, argument*) to hit home; **se** ~ *vi* (*se sentir*): **se** ~ **bien/mal** to be well/unwell; (*aller*): **se** ~ **vers** to go towards; ~ **sur** (*peser*) to rest on; (*accent*) to fall on; (*conférence etc*) to concern; (*heurter*) to strike; **être porté à faire** to be apt *ou* inclined to do; **elle portait le nom de Rosalie** she was called Rosalie; ~ **qn au pouvoir** to bring sb to power; ~ **bonheur à qn** to bring sb luck; ~ **qn à croire** to lead sb to believe; ~ **son âge** to look one's age; ~ **un toast** to drink a toast; ~ **de l'argent au crédit d'un compte** to credit an account with some money; **se** ~ **partie civile** *to associate in a court action with the public prosecutor;* **se** ~ **garant de qch** to guarantee sth, vouch for sth; **se** ~ **candidat à la députation** ≈ to run for Congress (*US*), ≈ stand for Parliament (*Brit*); **se faire** ~ **malade** to report sick; ~ **la main à son chapeau** to raise one's hand to one's hat; ~ **son effort sur** to direct one's efforts towards; ~ **un fait à la connaissance de qn** to bring a fact to sb's attention *ou* notice.
porte-savon [portsávóṅ] *nm* soap dish.
porte-serviettes [portservyet] *nm inv* towel rack (*US*) *ou* rail (*Brit*).
portes-ouvertes [portōōvert(ə)] *a inv:* **journée** ~ open house, open day (*Brit*).
porteur, euse [portœr, -ēz] *a* (*COMM*) strong, promising; (*nouvelle, chèque etc*): **être** ~ **de** to be the bearer of ♦ *nm/f* (*de messages*) bearer ♦ *nm* (*de bagages*) porter; (*COMM: de chèque*) bearer; (*: d'actions*) holder; (*avion*) **gros** ~ wide-bodied aircraft, jumbo (jet).
porte-voix [portəvwá] *nm inv* megaphone.
portier [portyā] *nm* doorman.
portière [portyer] *nf* door.
portillon [portēyóṅ] *nm* gate.
portion [porsyóṅ] *nf* (*part*) portion, share; (*partie*) portion, section.
portique [portēk] *nm* (*GYM*) crossbar; (*ARCHIT*) portico; (*RAIL*) gantry.
porto [portō] *nm* port (wine).
portoricain, e [portorēkaṅ, -en] *a* Puerto Rican.
Porto Rico [portorēkō] *nf* Puerto Rico.
portrait [portre] *nm* portrait; (*photographie*) photograph; (*fig*): **elle est le** ~ **de sa mère** she's the image of her mother.
portraitiste [portrātēst(ə)] *nm/f* portrait painter.
portrait-robot [portrerobō] *nm* Identikit ® picture.
portuaire [portüer] *a* port *cpd*, harbor *cpd* (*US*), harbour *cpd* (*Brit*).
portugais, e [portüge, -ez] *a* Portuguese ♦ *nm* (*LING*) Portuguese ♦ *nm/f:* **P~, e** Portuguese.
Portugal [portügál] *nm:* **le** ~ Portugal.
pose [pōz] *nf* (*de moquette*) laying; (*de rideaux, papier peint*) hanging; (*attitude, d'un modèle*) pose; (*PHOTO*) exposure.
posé, e [pōzā] *a* calm, unruffled.
posément [pōzāmáṅ] *ad* calmly.
posemètre [pōzmetr(ə)] *nm* exposure meter.
poser [pōzā] *vt* (*déposer*): ~ **qch (sur)/qn à** to put sth down (on)/drop sb at; (*placer*): ~ **qch sur/quelque part** to put sth on/somewhere; (*installer: moquette, carrelage*) to lay; (*rideaux, papier peint*) to hang; (*MATH: chiffre*) to put (down); (*question*) to ask; (*principe, conditions*) to lay *ou* set down; (*problème*) to formulate; (*difficulté*) to pose; (*personne: mettre en valeur*) to give standing to ♦ *vi* (*modèle*) to pose; to sit; **se** ~ (*oiseau, avion*) to land; (*question*) to arise; **se** ~ **en** to pass o.s. off as, pose as; ~ **son** *ou* **un regard sur qn/qch** to turn one's gaze on sb/sth; ~ **sa candidature** to apply; (*POL*) to put o.s. up for election.
poseur, euse [pōzœr, -ēz] *nm/f* (*péj*) show-off, poseur; ~ **de parquets/ carrelages** floor/tile layer.
positif, ive [pōzētēf, -ēv] *a* positive.
position [pōzēsyóṅ] *nf* position; **prendre** ~ (*fig*) to take a stand.
positionner [pōzēsyonā] *vt* to position; (*compte en banque*) to calculate the balance of.
positivement [pōzētēvmáṅ] *ad* positively.
posologie [posolozhē] *nf* directions *pl* for use, dosage.
possédant, e [posādáṅ, -áṅt] *a* (*classe*) wealthy ♦ *nm/f:* **les** ~**s** the haves, the wealthy.
possédé, e [posādā] *nm/f* person possessed.
posséder [posādā] *vt* to own, possess; (*qualité, talent*) to have, possess; (*bien connaître: métier, langue*) to have mastered, have a thorough knowledge of; (*sexuellement, aussi: suj: colère etc*) to possess; (*fam: duper*) to take in.
possesseur [posāsœr] *nm* owner.
possessif, ive [posāsēf, -ēv] *a, nm* (*aussi LING*) possessive.
possession [posāsyóṅ] *nf* ownership *q*; possession; **être/entrer en** ~ **de qch** to be in/take possession of sth.
possibilité [posēbēlētā] *nf* possibility; ~**s** *nfpl* (*moyens*) means; (*potentiel*) potential *sg*; **avoir la** ~ **de faire** to be in a position to do; to have the opportunity to do.
possible [posēbl(ə)] *a* possible; (*projet, entreprise*) feasible ♦ *nm:* **faire son** ~ to do all one can, do one's utmost; (**ce n'est**) **pas** ~**!** impossible!; **le plus/moins de livres** ~ as many/few books as possible; **dès que** ~ as soon as possible; **gentil** *etc* **au** ~ as nice *etc* as it is possible to be.
postal, e, aux [postál, -ō] *a* postal, post office

cpd; **sac** ~ mailbag.
postdater [postdàtá] *vt* to postdate.
poste [post(ə)] *nf* (*service*) post, postal service; (*administration, bureau*) post office ♦ *nm* (*fonction*, MIL) post; (*TÉL*) extension; (*de radio etc*) set; (*de budget*) item; ~**s** *nfpl* post office *sg*; **P~s télécommunications et télédiffusion (PTT)** *postal and telecommunications service*; **agent** *ou* **employé des** ~**s** post office worker; **mettre à la** ~ to mail; ~ **de commandement (PC)** *nm* (*MIL etc*) headquarters; ~ **de contrôle** *nm* checkpoint; ~ **de douane** *nm* customs post; ~ **émetteur** *nm* transmitting set; ~ **d'essence** *nm* filling station; ~ **d'incendie** *nm* fire station (*US*) *ou* point (*Brit*); ~ **de péage** *nm* tollgate; ~ **de pilotage** *nm* cockpit; ~ **(de police)** *nm* police station; ~ **de radio** *nm* radio set; ~ **restante (PR)** *nf* general delivery (*US*), poste restante (*Brit*); ~ **de secours** *nm* first-aid post; ~ **de télévision** *nm* television set; ~ **de travail** *nm* work station.
poster *vt* [postá] to post ♦ *nm* [poster] poster; **se** ~ to position o.s.
postérieur, e [postáryœr] *a* (*date*) later; (*partie*) back ♦ *nm* (*fam*) behind.
postérieurement [postáryœrmáń] *ad* later, subsequently; ~ **à** after.
posteriori [postáryorē]: **a** ~ *ad* with hindsight, a posteriori.
postérité [postārētá] *nf* posterity.
postface [postfás] *nf* appendix.
posthume [postüm] *a* posthumous.
postiche [postēsh] *a* false ♦ *nm* hairpiece.
postier, ière [postyá, -yer] *nm/f* post office worker.
postillonner [postēyonã] *vi* to sp(l)utter.
post-natal, e [postnátál] *a* postnatal.
postopératoire [postopărátwár] *a* postoperative.
postscolaire [postskoler] *a* further, continuing.
post-scriptum [postskrēptom] *nm inv* postscript.
postsynchroniser [postsáńkronēzá] *vt* to dub.
postulant, e [postüláń, -áńt] *nm/f* (*candidat*) applicant; (*REL*) postulant.
postulat [postülá] *nm* postulate.
postuler [postülá] *vt* (*emploi*) to apply for, put in for.
posture [postür] *nf* posture, position; (*fig*) position.
pot [põ] *nm* jar, pot; (*en plastique, carton*) carton; (*en métal*) tin; (*fam*): **avoir du** ~ to be lucky; **boire** *ou* **prendre un** ~ (*fam*) to have a drink; **découvrir le** ~ **aux roses** to find out what's been going on; ~ **(de chambre)** (chamber)pot; ~ **d'échappement** exhaust pipe; ~ **de fleurs** plant pot, flowerpot; (*plante*) pot plant; ~ **à tabac** tobacco jar.
potable [potábl(ə)] *a* (*fig: boisson*) drinkable; (: *travail, devoir*) decent; **eau (non)** ~ (not) drinking water.
potache [potásh] *nm* schoolboy.
potage [potázh] *nm* soup.
potager, ère [potázhã, -er] *a* (*plante*) edible, vegetable *cpd*; (**jardin**) ~ kitchen *ou* vegetable garden.
potasse [potás] *nf* potassium hydroxide; (*engrais*) potash.

potasser [potásá] *vt* (*fam*) to cram.
potassium [potásyom] *nm* potassium.
pot-au-feu [potõfœ] *nm inv* (beef) stew; (*viande*) stewing beef ♦ *a* (*fam: personne*) stay-at-home.
pot-de-vin, *pl* **pots-de-vin** [põdvań] *nm* bribe.
pote [pot] *nm* (*fam*) pal.
poteau, x [potõ] *nm* post; ~ **de départ/arrivée** starting/finish (*US*) *ou* finishing (*Brit*) post; ~ **(d'exécution)** execution post, stake; ~ **indicateur** signpost; ~ **télégraphique** telegraph pole; ~**x (de but)** goal posts.
potée [potá] *nf* baked stew (*of pork and cabbage*).
potelé, e [potlá] *a* plump, chubby.
potence [potáńs] *nf* gallows *sg*; **en** ~ T-shaped.
potentat [potáńtá] *nm* potentate; (*fig, péj*) despot.
potentiel, le [potáńsyel] *a, nm* potential.
poterie [potrē] *nf* (*fabrication*) pottery; (*objet*) piece of pottery.
potiche [potēsh] *nf* large vase.
potier [potyá] *nm* potter.
potins [potań] *nmpl* gossip *sg*.
potion [põsyoń] *nf* potion.
potiron [potēróń] *nm* pumpkin.
pot-pourri, *pl* **pots-pourris** [põpōōrē] *nm* (*MUS*) potpourri, medley.
pou, x [põō] *nm* louse (*pl* lice).
pouah [pwá] *excl* ugh!, yuk!
poubelle [pōōbel] *nf* trash *ou* garbage can (*US*), (dust)bin (*Brit*).
pouce [pōōs] *nm* thumb; **se tourner** *ou* **se rouler les** ~**s** (*fig*) to twiddle one's thumbs; **manger sur le** ~ to eat on the run, grab something to eat.
poudre [pōōdr(ə)] *nf* powder; (*fard*) (face) powder; (*explosif*) gunpowder; **en** ~: **café en** ~ instant coffee; **savon en** ~ soap powder; **lait en** ~ dried *ou* powdered milk; ~ **à canon** gunpowder; ~ **à éternuer** sneezing powder; ~ **à récurer** scouring powder; ~ **de riz** face powder.
poudrer [pōōdrá] *vt* to powder.
poudrerie [pōōdrərē] *nf* gunpowder factory.
poudreux, euse [pōōdrœ, -œz] *a* dusty; (*neige*) powdery, powder *cpd*.
poudrier [pōōdrēyá] *nm* (powder) compact.
poudrière [pōōdrēyer] *nf* powder magazine; (*fig*) powder keg.
poudroyer [pōōdrwáyá] *vi* to rise in clouds *ou* a flurry.
pouf [pōōf] *nm* pouffe.
pouffer [pōōfá] *vi*: ~ **(de rire)** to snigger; to giggle.
pouffiasse [pōōfyás] *nf* (*fam*) fat cow; (*prostituée*) tart.
pouilleux, euse [pōōyœ, -œz] *a* flea-ridden; (*fig*) seedy.
poulailler [pōōláyá] *nm* henhouse; (*THÉÂTRE*): **le** ~ the peanut gallery (*US*), the gods *sg* (*Brit*).
poulain [pōōlań] *nm* foal; (*fig*) protégé.
poularde [pōōlárd(ə)] *nf* fatted chicken.
poule [pōōl] *nf* (*ZOOL*) hen; (*CULIN*) (boiling) fowl; (*SPORT*) (round-robin) tournament; (*RUGBY*) group; (*fam*) chick, broad (*US*),

bird (*Brit*); (*prostituée*) tart; ~ **d'eau** moorhen; ~ **mouillée** coward; ~ **pondeuse** laying hen, layer; ~ **au riz** chicken and rice.

poulet [pōōle] *nm* chicken; (*fam*) cop.

poulette [pōōlet] *nf* (*jeune poule*) pullet.

pouliche [pōōlēsh] *nf* filly.

poulie [pōōlē] *nf* pulley.

poulpe [pōōlp(ə)] *nm* octopus.

pouls [pōō] *nm* pulse (*ANAT*); **prendre le ~ de qn** to feel sb's pulse.

poumon [pōōmoṅ] *nm* lung; ~ **d'acier** *ou* **artificiel** iron *ou* artificial lung.

poupe [pōōp] *nf* stern; **en ~** astern.

poupée [pōōpā] *nf* doll; **jouer à la ~** to play with one's doll (*ou* dolls); **de ~** (*très petit*): **jardin de ~** doll's garden, pocket-handkerchief-sized garden.

poupin, e [pōōpaṅ, -ēn] *a* chubby.

poupon [pōōpoṅ] *nm* babe-in-arms.

pouponner [pōōponā] *vi* to fuss (around).

pouponnière [pōōponyer] *nf* day nursery.

pour [pōōr] *prép* for ♦ *nm*: **le ~ et le contre** the pros and cons; ~ **faire** (so as) to do, in order to do; ~ **avoir fait** for having done; ~ **que** so that, in order that; ~ **moi** (*à mon avis, pour ma part*) for my part, personally; ~ **riche qu'il soit** rich though he may be; ~ **100 francs d'essence** 100 francs' worth of gas (*US*) *ou* petrol (*Brit*); ~ **cent** per cent; ~ **ce qui est de** as for; **y être ~ quelque chose** to have something to do with it.

pourboire [pōōrbwàr] *nm* tip.

pourcentage [pōōrsâṅtàzh] *nm* percentage; **travailler au ~** to work on commission.

pourchasser [pōōrshàsà] *vt* to pursue.

pourfendeur [pōōrfâṅdœr] *nm* sworn opponent.

pourfendre [pōōrfâṅdr(ə)] *vt* to assail.

pourlécher [pōōrlāshā]: **se ~** *vi* to smack one's lips.

pourparlers [pōōrpàrlā] *nmpl* talks, negotiations; **être en ~ avec** to be having talks with.

pourpre [pōōrpr(ə)] *a* crimson.

pourquoi [pōōrkwà] *ad*, *cj* why ♦ *nm inv*: **le ~ (de)** the reason (for).

pourrai [pōōrā] *etc vb voir* **pouvoir**.

pourri, e [pōōrē] *a* rotten; (*roche, pierre*) crumbling; (*temps, climat*) filthy, foul ♦ *nm*: **sentir le ~** to smell rotten.

pourrir [pōōrēr] *vi* to rot; (*fruit*) to go rotten *ou* bad; (*fig: situation*) to deteriorate ♦ *vt* to rot; (*fig: corrompre: personne*) to corrupt; (*: gâter: enfant*) to spoil thoroughly.

pourrissement [pōōrēsmâṅ] *nm* deterioration.

pourriture [pōōrētūr] *nf* rot.

pourrons [pōōroṅ] *etc vb voir* **pouvoir**.

poursuis [pōōrsüē] *etc vb voir* **poursuivre**.

poursuite [pōōrsüēt] *nf* pursuit, chase; ~**s** *nfpl* (*JUR*) legal proceedings; (**course**) ~ track race; (*fig*) chase.

poursuivant, e [pōōrsüēvâṅ, -âṅt] *vb voir* **poursuivre** ♦ *nm/f* pursuer; (*JUR*) plaintiff.

poursuivre [pōōrsüēvr(ə)] *vt* to pursue, chase (after); (*relancer*) to hound, harry; (*obséder*) to haunt; (*JUR*) to bring proceedings against, prosecute; (*: au civil*) to sue; (*but*) to strive towards; (*voyage, études*) to carry on with, continue ♦ *vi* to carry on, go

on; **se ~** *vi* to go on, continue.

pourtant [pōōrtâṅ] *ad* yet; **mais ~** but nevertheless, but even so; **c'est ~ facile** (and) yet it's easy.

pourtour [pōōrtōōr] *nm* perimeter.

pourvoi [pōōrvwà] *nm* appeal.

pourvoir [pōōrvwàr] *nm* (*COMM*) supply ♦ *vt*: ~ **qch/qn de** to equip sth/sb with ♦ *vi*: ~ **à** to provide for; (*emploi*) to fill; **se ~** (*JUR*): **se ~ en cassation** to take one's case to the Court of Appeal.

pourvoyeur, euse [pōōrvwàyœr, -ēz] *nm/f* supplier.

pourvu, e [pōōrvü] *pp de* **pourvoir** ♦ *a*: ~ **de** equipped with; ~ **que** (*si*) provided that, so long as; (*espérons que*) let's hope (that).

pousse [pōōs] *nf* growth; (*bourgeon*) shoot.

poussé, e [pōōsā] *a* sophisticated, advanced; (*moteur*) souped-up.

pousse-café [pōōskàfā] *nm inv* (after-dinner) liqueur.

poussée [pōōsā] *nf* thrust; (*coup*) push; (*MÉD*) eruption; (*fig*) upsurge.

pousse-pousse [pōōspōōs] *nm inv* rickshaw.

pousser [pōōsā] *vt* to push; (*inciter*): ~ **qn à** to urge *ou* press sb to + *infinitif*; (*acculer*): ~ **qn à** to drive sb to; (*moteur, voiture*) to drive hard; (*émettre: cri etc*) to give; (*stimuler*) to urge on; to drive hard; (*poursuivre*) to carry on ♦ *vi* to push; (*croître*) to grow; (*aller*): ~ **plus loin** to push on a bit further; **se ~** *vi* to move over; **faire ~** (*plante*) to grow; ~ **le dévouement** *etc* **jusqu'à ...** to take devotion *etc* as far as ....

poussette [pōōset] *nf* (*voiture d'enfant*) stroller (*US*), pushchair (*Brit*).

poussette-canne, *pl* **poussettes-cannes** [pōōsetkàn] *nf* (folding) stroller (*US*), baby buggy (*Brit*).

poussier [pōōsyā] *nm* coal dust.

poussière [pōōsyer] *nf* dust; (*grain*) speck of dust; **et des ~s** (*fig*) and a bit; ~ **de charbon** coal dust.

poussiéreux, euse [pōōsyārœ, -ēz] *a* dusty.

poussif, ive [pōōsēf, -ēv] *a* wheezy, wheezing.

poussin [pōōsaṅ] *nm* chick.

poussoir [pōōswàr] *nm* button.

poutre [pōōtr(ə)] *nf* beam; (*en fer, ciment armé*) girder; ~**s apparentes** exposed beams.

poutrelle [pōōtrel] *nf* (*petite poutre*) small beam; (*barre d'acier*) girder.

pouvoir [pōōvwàr] *nm* power; (*POL: dirigeants*): **le ~** those in power, the government ♦ *vb + infinitif* can; (*suj: personne*) can, to be able to; (*permission*) can, may; (*probabilité, hypothèse*) may; **il peut arriver que** it may happen that; **il pourrait pleuvoir** it might rain; **déçu de ne pas ~ le faire** disappointed not to be able to do it *ou* that he *etc* couldn't do it; **il aurait pu le dire!** he could *ou* might have said!; **il se peut que** it may be that; **je n'en peux plus** (*épuisé*) I'm exhausted; (*accablé*) I can't take any more; **tu ne peux pas savoir!** you have no idea!; **tu peux le dire!** you can say that again!; **on ne peut mieux** as well as it is possible to; **donner ~ de faire qch** (*JUR*) to give proxy to do sth; ~ **absolu** absolute power; ~ **d'achat** purchasing power; **les** ~**s publics** the authorities.

PP *sigle f* (= *préventive de la pellagre: vitamine*) niacin ♦ *abr* (= *pages*) pp.

p.p. *abr* (= *par procuration*) p.p.

p.p.c.m. *sigle m* (MATH: = *plus petit commun multiple*) LCM (= *lowest common multiple*).

PR *sigle m* = *Parti républicain* ♦ *sigle f* = **poste restante.**

pr *abr* = **pour.**

pragmatique [prágmátĕk] *a* pragmatic.

Prague [pràg] *n* Prague.

prairie [prărĕ] *nf* meadow.

praline [prálĕn] *nf* (*bonbon*) sugared almond; (*au chocolat*) praline.

praliné, e [prálĕná] *a* (*amande*) sugared; (*chocolat, glace*) praline *cpd*.

praticable [prátĕkábl(ə)] *a* (*route etc*) passable, practicable; (*projet*) practicable.

praticien, ne [prátĕsyàn, -en] *nm/f* practitioner.

pratiquant, e [prátĕkân, -ânt] *a* practicing (*US*), practising (*Brit*).

pratique [prátĕk] *nf* practice ♦ *a* practical; (*commode: horaire etc*) convenient; (: *outil*) handy, useful; **dans la** ~ **in** (actual) practice; **mettre en** ~ to put into practice.

pratiquement [prátĕkmán] *ad* (*dans la pratique*) in practice; (*pour ainsi dire*) practically, virtually.

pratiquer [prátĕká] *vt* to practice (*US*), practise (*Brit*); (*SPORT etc*) to go (in for), play; (*appliquer: méthode, théorie*) to apply; (*intervention, opération*) to carry out; (*ouverture, abri*) to make ♦ *vi* (*REL*) to be a churchgoer.

pré [prá] *nm* meadow.

préalable [prăálábl(ə)] *a* preliminary; **condition** ~ (**de**) precondition (for), prerequisite (for); **sans avis** ~ without prior *ou* previous notice; **au** ~ first, beforehand.

préalablement [prăálábləmán] *ad* first, beforehand.

Préalpes [prăálp(ə)] *nfpl*: **les** ~ the Pre-Alps.

préalpin, e [prăálpàn, -en] *a* of the Pre-Alps.

préambule [prăánbül] *nm* preamble; (*fig*) prelude; **sans** ~ straight away.

préau, x [prăŏ] *nm* (*d'une cour d'école*) covered playground; (*d'un monastère, d'une prison*) inner courtyard.

préavis [prăávĕ] *nm* notice; ~ **de congé** notice; **communication avec** ~ (*TÉL*) person-to-person call.

prébende [prábánd] *nf* (*péj*) remuneration.

précaire [prăker] *a* precarious.

précaution [prăkŏsyón] *nf* precaution; **avec** ~ cautiously; **prendre des** *ou* **ses** ~**s** to take precautions; **par** ~ as a precaution; **pour plus de** ~ to be on the safe side; ~**s oratoires** carefully phrased remarks.

précautionneux, euse [prăkŏsyonœ, -œz] *a* cautious, careful.

précédemment [prăsădámán] *ad* before, previously.

précédent, e [prăsădàn, -ânt] *a* previous ♦ *nm* precedent; **sans** ~ unprecedented; **le jour** ~ the day before, the previous day.

précéder [prăsădá] *vt* to precede; (*marcher ou*

rouler devant) to be in front of; (*arriver avant*) to get ahead of.

précepte [prăsept(ə)] *nm* precept.

précepteur, trice [prăsepttœr, -trĕs] *nm/f* (*private*) tutor.

préchauffer [prăshŏfá] *vt* to preheat.

prêcher [prăshá] *vt, vi* to preach.

prêcheur, euse [preshœr, -œz] *a* moralizing ♦ *nm/f* (*REL*) preacher; (*fig*) moralizer.

précieusement [prăsyœzmán] *ad* (*avec soin*) carefully; (*avec préciosité*) preciously.

précieux, euse [prăsyœ, -œz] *a* precious; (*collaborateur, conseils*) invaluable; (*style, écrivain*) précieux, precious.

préciosité [prăsyŏzătá] *nf* preciosity, preciousness.

précipice [prăsĕpĕs] *nm* drop, chasm; (*fig*) abyss; **au bord du** ~ at the edge of the precipice.

précipitamment [prăsĕpĕtámán] *ad* hurriedly, hastily.

précipitation [prăsĕpĕtâsyón] *nf* (*hâte*) haste; ~**s (atmosphériques)** *nfpl* precipitation *sg*.

précipité, e [prăsĕpĕtá] *a* (*respiration*) fast; (*pas*) hurried; (*départ*) hasty.

précipiter [prăsĕpĕtá] *vt* (*faire tomber*): ~ **qn/qch du haut de** to throw *ou* hurl sb/sth off *ou* from; (*hâter: marche*) to quicken; (: *départ*) to hasten; **se** ~ *vi* (*événements*) to move faster; (*respiration*) to speed up; **se** ~ **sur/vers** to rush at/towards; **se** ~ **au-devant de qn** to throw o.s. before sb.

précis, e [prăsĕ, -ĕz] *a* precise; (*tir, mesures*) accurate, precise ♦ *nm* handbook.

précisément [prăsĕzámán] *ad* precisely; **ma vie n'est pas** ~ **distrayante** my life is not exactly entertaining.

préciser [prăsĕzá] *vt* (*expliquer*) to be more specific about, clarify; (*spécifier*) to state, specify; **se** ~ *vi* to become clear(er).

précision [prăsĕzyón] *nf* precision; accuracy; (*détail*) point *ou* detail (*made clear or to be clarified*); ~**s** *nfpl* further details.

précoce [prăkos] *a* early; (*enfant*) precocious; (*calvitie*) premature.

précocité [prăkosĕtá] *nf* earliness; precociousness.

préconçu, e [prăkónsü] *a* preconceived.

préconiser [prăkonĕzá] *vt* to advocate.

précontraint, e [prăkóntràn, -ânt] *a*: **béton** ~ prestressed concrete.

précuit, e [prăküĕ, -ĕt] *a* precooked.

précurseur [prăkürscer] *am* precursory ♦ *nm* forerunner, precursor.

prédateur [prădátœr] *nm* predator.

prédécesseur [prădăsăscer] *nm* predecessor.

prédestiner [prădestĕná] *vt*: ~ **qn à qch/à faire** to predestine sb for sth/to do.

prédicateur [prădĕkátœr] *nm* preacher.

prédiction [prădĕksyón] *nf* prediction.

prédilection [prădĕleksyón] *nf*: **avoir une** ~ **pour** to be partial to; **de** ~ favorite (*US*), favourite (*Brit*).

prédire [prădĕr] *vt* to predict.

prédisposer [prădĕspŏzá] *vt*: ~ **qn à qch/à faire** to predispose sb to sth/to do.

prédit, e [prădĕ, -ĕt] *pp* de **prédire.**

prédominant, e [prădomĕnán, -ânt] *a* predominant; prevailing.

prédominer [prādomēnā] *vi* to predominate; (*avis*) to prevail.

pré-électoral, e, aux [prāālektorál, -ō] *a* pre-election *cpd*.

pré-emballé, e [prāáṅbálā] *a* pre-packed.

prééminent, e [prāāmēnáṅ, -áṅt] *a* pre-eminent.

préemption [prāáṅpsyóṅ] *nf*: **droit de ~** (*JUR*) pre-emptive right.

pré-encollé, e [prāáṅkolā] *a* pre-pasted.

préétabli, e [prāātáblē] *a* pre-established.

préexistant, e [prāegzēstáṅ, -áṅt] *a* pre-existing.

préfabriqué, e [prāfábrēkā] *a* prefabricated; (*péj: sourire*) artificial ♦ *nm* prefabricated material.

préface [prāfás] *nf* preface.

préfacer [prāfásā] *vt* to write a preface for.

préfectoral, e, aux [prāfektorál, -ō] *a* pre-fectorial.

préfecture [prāfektür] *nf* prefecture; **~ de police** police headquarters.

préférable [prāfārábl(ə)] *a* preferable.

préféré, e [prāfārā] *a*, *nm/f* favorite (*US*), favourite (*Brit*).

préférence [prāfāráṅs] *nf* preference; **de ~** preferably; **de** *ou* **par ~ à** in preference to, rather than; **donner la ~ à qn** to give preference to sb; **par ordre de ~** in order of preference; **obtenir la ~ sur** to have preference over.

préférentiel, le [prāfāráṅsyel] *a* preferential.

préférer [prāfārā] *vt*: **~ qn/qch (à)** to prefer sb/sth (to), like sb/sth better (than); **~ faire** to prefer to do; **je préférerais du thé** I would rather have tea, I'd prefer tea.

préfet [prāfe] *nm* prefect; **~ de police** ≈ Police Commissioner (*US*), ≈ Chief Constable (*Brit*).

préfigurer [prāfēgürā] *vt* to prefigure.

préfixe [prāfēks(ə)] *nm* prefix.

préhistoire [prāēstwár] *nf* prehistory.

préhistorique [prāēstorēk] *a* prehistoric.

préjudice [prāzhüdēs] *nm* (*matériel*) loss; (*moral*) harm *q*; **porter ~ à** to harm, be detrimental to; **au ~ de** at the expense of.

préjudiciable [prāzhüdēsyábl(ə)] *a*: **~ à** preju-dicial *ou* harmful to.

préjugé [prāzhüzhā] *nm* prejudice; **avoir un ~ contre** to be prejudiced *ou* biased against; **bénéficier d'un ~ favorable** to be viewed favorably.

préjuger [prāzhüzhā]: **~ de** *vt* to prejudge.

prélasser [prālásā]: **se ~** *vi* to lounge.

prélat [prālá] *nm* prelate.

prélavage [prālávázh] *nm* pre-wash.

prélèvement [prālevmáṅ] *nm* deduction; withdrawal; **faire un ~ de sang** to take a blood sample.

prélever [prālvā] *vt* (*échantillon*) to take; (*argent*): **~ (sur)** to deduct (from); (*: sur son compte*): **~ (sur)** to withdraw (from).

préliminaire [prālēmēner] *a* preliminary; **~s** *nmpl* preliminaries; (*négociations*) pre-liminary talks.

prélude [prālüd] *nm* prelude; (*avant le con-cert*) warm-up.

prématuré, e [prāmátürā] *a* premature; (*re-traite*) early ♦ *nm* premature baby.

prématurément [prāmátürāmáṅ] *ad* prema-turely.

préméditation [prāmādētâsyóṅ] *nf*: **avec ~** *a* premeditated ♦ *ad* with intent.

préméditer [prāmādētā] *vt* to premeditate, plan.

prémices [prāmēs] *nfpl* beginnings.

premier, ière [prəmyā, -yer] *a* first; (*branche, marche, grade*) bottom; (*fig: fondamental*) basic; prime; (*en importance*) first, foremost ♦ *nm* (~ *étage*) second (*US*) *ou* first (*Brit*) floor ♦ *nf* (*AUTO*) first (gear); (*RAIL, AVIAT etc*) first class; (*SCOL: classe*) penultimate school year (*age 16-17*); (*THÉÂTRE*) first night; (*CINÉMA*) première; (*exploit*) first; **au ~ abord** at first sight; **au** *ou* **du ~ coup** at the first attempt; **de ~ ordre** first-class, first-rate; **de première qualité, de ~ choix** best *ou* top quality; **de première importance** of the highest importance; **de première nécessité** absolutely essential; **le ~ venu** the first person to come along; **jeune ~** leading man; **le ~ de l'an** New Year's Day; **enfant du ~ lit** child of a first marriage; **en ~ lieu** in the first place; **~ âge** (*d'un enfant*) the first 3 months (of life); **P~ Ministre** Prime Minister.

premièrement [prəmyermáṅ] *ad* firstly.

première-née, *pl* **premières-nées** [prəmyernā] *nf* firstborn.

premier-né, *pl* **premiers-nés** [prəmyānā] *nm* firstborn.

prémisse [prāmēs] *nf* premise.

prémolaire [prāmoler] *nf* premolar.

prémonition [prāmonēsyóṅ] *nf* premonition.

prémonitoire [prāmonētwár] *a* premonitory.

prémunir [prāmünēr]: **se ~** *vi*: **se ~ contre** to protect o.s. from, guard against.

prenant, e [prənáṅ, -áṅt] *vb voir* **prendre** ♦ *a* absorbing, engrossing.

prénatal, e [prānátál] *a* (*MÉD*) antenatal; (*allocation*) maternity *cpd*.

prendre [prăndr(ə)] *vt* to take; (*ôter*): **~ qch à** to take sth from; (*aller chercher*) to get, fetch; (*se procurer*) to get; (*réserver: place*) to reserve; (*acquérir: du poids, de la valeur*) to put on, gain; (*malfaiteur, poisson*) to catch; (*passager*) to pick up; (*personnel, aussi: couleur, goût*) to take on; (*locataire*) to take in; (*traiter: enfant, problème*) to handle; (*voix, ton*) to put on; (*prélever: pourcentage, argent*) to take off; (*coincer*): **se ~ les doigts dans** to get one's fingers caught in ♦ *vi* (*liquide, ciment*) to set; (*greffe, vaccin*) to take; (*mensonge*) to be successful; (*feu: foyer*) to go; (*: incendie*) to start; (*allumette*) to light; (*se diriger*): **~ à gauche** to turn (to the) left; **~ son origine** *ou* **sa source** (*mot, rivière*) to have its source; **~ qn pour** to take sb for; **se ~ pour** to think one is; **~ sur soi de faire qch** to take it upon o.s. to do sth; **~ qn en sympathie/horreur** to get to like/loathe sb; **à tout ~** all things considered; **s'en ~ à** (*agresser*) to set about; (*passer sa colère sur*) to take it out on; (*critiquer*) to attack; (*remettre en question*) to challenge; **se ~ d'amitié/d'affection pour** to befriend/become fond of; **s'y ~** (*procéder*) to set about it; **s'y**

~ **à l'avance** to see to it in advance; **s'y** ~ **à deux fois** to try twice, make two attempts.

preneur [prənœr] nm: **être** ~ to be willing to buy; **trouver** ~ to find a buyer.

prénom [prānôn] nm first name.

prénommer [prānomā] vt: **elle se prénomme Claude** her (first) name is Claude.

prénuptial, e, aux [prānüpsyál, -ō] a premarital.

préoccupant, e [prāokūpán, -ánt] a worrying.

préoccupation [prāokūpásyôn] nf (souci) concern; (idée fixe) preoccupation.

préoccupé, e [prāokūpā] a concerned; preoccupied.

préoccuper [prāokūpā] vt (tourmenter, tracasser) to concern; (absorber, obséder) to preoccupy; **se** ~ **de qch** to be concerned about sth; to show concern about sth.

préparateur, trice [prāpárátœr, -trēs] nm/f assistant.

préparatifs [prāpárátēf] nmpl preparations.

préparation [prāpárásyôn] nf preparation; (SCOL) homework assignment.

préparatoire [prāpárátwár] a preparatory.

préparer [prāpárā] vt to prepare; (café, repas) to make; (examen) to prepare for; (voyage, entreprise) to plan; **se** ~ vi (orage, tragédie) to brew, be in the air; **se** ~ **(à qch/à faire)** to prepare (o.s.) ou get ready (for sth/to do); ~ **qch à qn** (surprise etc) to have sth in store for sb; ~ **qn à qch** (nouvelle etc) to prepare sb for sth.

prépondérant, e [prāpôndárán, -ánt] a major, dominating; **voix** ~**e** deciding vote.

préposé, e [prāpōzā] a: ~ **à** in charge of ♦ nm/f (gén: employé) employee; (ADMIN: facteur) mailman/woman (US), postman/woman (Brit); (de la douane etc) official; (de vestiaire) hatcheck person (US), attendant (Brit).

préposer [prāpōzā] vt: ~ **qn à qch** to appoint sb to sth.

préposition [prāpōzēsyôn] nf preposition.

préretraite [prārətret] nf early retirement.

prérogative [prārogátēv] nf prerogative.

près [pre] ad near, close; ~ **de** prép near (to), close to; (environ) nearly, almost; **de** ~ ad closely; **à 5 kg** ~ to within about 5 kg; **à cela** ~ apart from the fact that; **je ne suis pas** ~ **de lui pardonner** I'm nowhere near ready to forgive him; **on n'est pas à un jour** ~ one day (either way) won't make any difference, we're not going to quibble over one day.

présage [prāzázh] nm omen.

présager [prāzázhā] vt (prévoir) to foresee; (annoncer) to portend.

pré-salé, e, pl **prés-salés** [prāsálā] nm (CULIN) salt-meadow lamb.

presbyte [presbēt] a farsighted, longsighted.

presbytère [presbēter] nm presbytery.

presbytérien, ne [presbētáryán, -en] a, nm/f Presbyterian.

presbytie [presbēsē] nf farsightedness, longsightedness.

prescience [prāsyáns] nf prescience, foresight.

préscolaire [prāskoler] a preschool cpd.

prescription [preskrēpsyôn] nf (instruction) order, instruction; (MÉD, JUR) prescription.

prescrire [preskrēr] vt to prescribe; **se** ~ vi (JUR) to lapse.

prescrit, e [preskrē, -ēt] pp de **prescrire** ♦ a (date etc) stipulated.

préséance [prāsááns] nf precedence q.

présélectionner [prāsáleksyonā] vt to preselect; (dispositif) to preset; (candidats) to screen (US), short-list (Brit).

présence [prāzáns] nf presence; (au bureau etc) attendance; **en** ~ face to face; **en** ~ **de** in (the) presence of; (fig) in the face of; **faire acte de** ~ to put in a token appearance; ~ **d'esprit** presence of mind.

présent, e [prāzán, -ánt] a, nm present; (ADMIN, COMM): **la** ~**e lettre/loi** this letter/law ♦ nm/f: **les** ~**s** (personnes) those present ♦ nf (COMM: lettre): **la** ~**e** this letter; **à** ~ now, at present; **dès à** ~ here and now; **jusqu'à** ~ up till now, until now; **à** ~ **que** now that.

présentateur, trice [prāzántátœr, -trēs] nm/f (TV) announcer, presenter.

présentation [prāzántásyôn] nf presentation; introduction; (allure) appearance.

présenter [prāzántā] vt to present; (invité, candidat) to introduce; (félicitations, condoléances) to offer; (montrer: billet, pièce d'identité) to show, produce; (faire inscrire: candidat) to put forward; (soumettre) to submit ♦ vi: ~ **mal/bien** to have an unattractive/a pleasing appearance; **se** ~ vi (sur convocation) to report, come; (se faire connaître) to come forward; (à une élection) to run (US), stand (Brit), be a candidate; (occasion) to arise; **se** ~ **à un examen** to take an exam; **se** ~ **bien/mal** to look good/not too good.

présentoir [prāzántwár] nm (étagère) display shelf (pl shelves); (vitrine) showcase; (étal) display stand.

préservatif [prāzervátēf] nm condom, prophylactic (US), sheath (Brit).

préservation [prāzervásyôn] nf protection, preservation.

préserver [prāzervā] vt: ~ **de** (protéger) to protect from; (sauver) to save from.

présidence [prāzēdáns] nf presidency; chairmanship.

président [prāzēdán] nm (POL) president; (d'une assemblée, COMM) chairman; ~ **directeur général (PDG)** chairman and chief executive officer, ~ **du jury** (JUR) foreman of the jury; (d'examen) chairman (US), chief examiner (Brit).

présidente [prāzēdánt] nf president; (femme du président) president's wife; (d'une réunion) chairwoman.

présidentiable [prāzēdánsyábl(ə)] a, nm/f potential president.

présidentiel, le [prāzēdánsyel] a presidential; ~**les** nfpl presidential election(s).

présider [prāzēdā] vt to preside over; (dîner) to be the guest of honor (US) ou honour (Brit) at; ~ **à** vt to direct; to govern.

présomption [prāzônpsyôn] nf presumption.

présomptueux, euse [prāzônptüœ, -œz] a presumptuous.

presque [presk(ə)] ad almost, nearly; ~ **rien** hardly anything; ~ **pas** hardly (at all); ~

pas de hardly any; **personne, ou** ~ next to nobody, hardly anyone; **la** ~ **totalité (de)** almost *ou* nearly all.

presqu'île [preskēl] *nf* peninsula.

pressant, e [presán, -ánt] *a* urgent; (*personne*) insistent; **se faire** ~ to become insistent.

presse [pres] *nf* press; (*affluence*): **heures de** ~ busy times; **sous** ~ gone to press; **mettre sous** ~ to send to press; **avoir une bonne/ mauvaise** ~ to have a good/bad press; ~ **féminine** women's magazines *pl*; ~ **d'information** quality newspapers *pl*.

pressé, e [prāsā] *a* in a hurry; (*air*) hurried; (*besogne*) urgent ♦ *nm*: **aller au plus** ~ to see to first things first; **être** ~ **de faire qch** to be in a hurry to do sth; **orange** ~**e** freshly squeezed orange juice.

presse-citron [pressētrón] *nm inv* lemon squeezer.

pressentiment [prāsántēmán] *nm* foreboding, premonition.

pressentir [prāsántēr] *vt* to sense; (*prendre contact avec*) to approach.

presse-papiers [prespápyā] *nm inv* paperweight.

presse-purée [prespürā] *nm inv* potato masher.

presser [prāsā] *vt* (*fruit, éponge*) to squeeze; (*interrupteur, bouton*) to press, push; (*allure, affaire*) to speed up; (*débiteur etc*) to press; (*inciter*): ~ **qn de faire** to urge *ou* press sb to do ♦ *vi* to be urgent; **se** ~ (*se hâter*) to hurry (up); (*se grouper*) to crowd; **rien ne presse** there's no hurry; **se** ~ **contre qn** to squeeze up against sb; ~ **le pas** to quicken one's step; ~ **qn entre ses bras** to squeeze sb tight.

pressing [prāsēng] *nm* (*repassage*) steampressing; (*magasin*) dry cleaner's.

pression [presyón] *nf* pressure; (*bouton*) snap fastener; **faire** ~ **sur** to put pressure on; **sous** ~ pressurized, under pressure; (*fig*) keyed up; ~ **artérielle** blood pressure.

pressoir [preswár] *nm* (wine *ou* oil *etc*) press.

pressurer [prāsürā] *vt* (*fig*) to squeeze.

pressurisé, e [prāsürēzā] *a* pressurized.

prestance [prestáns] *nf* presence, imposing bearing.

prestataire [prestáter] *nm/f* person receiving benefits; (*COMM*): ~ **de services** provider of services.

prestation [prestásyón] *nf* (*allocation*) benefit; (*d'une assurance*) coverage *q* (*US*), cover *q* (*Brit*); (*d'une entreprise*) service provided; (*d'un joueur, artiste*) performance; ~ **de serment** taking the oath; ~ **de service** provision of a service; ~**s familiales** ≈ child benefit.

preste [prest(ə)] *a* nimble.

prestement [prestəmán] *ad* nimbly.

prestidigitateur, trice [prestēdēzhētátœr, -trēs] *nm/f* conjurer.

prestidigitation [prestēdēzhētásyón] *nf* conjuring.

prestige [prestēzh] *nm* prestige.

prestigieux, euse [prestēzhyœ, -œz] *a* prestigious.

présumer [prāzümā] *vt*: ~ **que** to presume *ou* assume that; ~ **de** to overrate; ~ **qn coupa-**

ble to presume sb guilty.

présupposé [prāsüpōzā] *nm* presupposition.

présupposer [prāsüpōzā] *vt* to presuppose.

présure [prāzür] *nf* rennet.

prêt, e [pre, pret] *a* ready ♦ *nm* lending *q*; (*somme prêtée*) loan; ~ **à faire** ready to do; ~ **à tout** ready for anything; ~ **sur gages** pawnbroking *q*.

prêt-à-porter, *pl* **prêts-à-porter** [pretáportā] *nm* ready-to-wear clothes *pl*.

prétendant [prātándán] *nm* pretender; (*d'une femme*) suitor.

prétendre [prātándr(ə)] *vt* (*affirmer*): ~ **que** to claim that; (*avoir l'intention de*): ~ **faire qch** to mean *ou* intend to do sth; ~ **à** *vt* (*droit, titre*) to lay claim to.

prétendu, e [prātándü] *a* (*supposé*) so-called.

prétendument [prātándümán] *ad* allegedly.

prête-nom [pretnón] *nm* (*péj*) figurehead; (*COMM etc*) dummy.

prétentieux, euse [prātánsyœ, -œz] *a* pretentious.

prétention [prātánsyón] *nf* pretentiousness; (*exigence, ambition*) claim; **sans** ~ unpretentious.

prêter [prātā] *vt* (*livres, argent*): ~ **qch (à)** to lend sth (to); (*supposer*): ~ **à qn** (*caractère, propos*) to attribute to sb ♦ *vi* (*aussi*: **se** ~: *tissu, cuir*) to give; ~ **à** (*commentaires etc*) to be open to, give rise to; **se** ~ **à** to lend o.s. (*ou* itself) to; (*manigances etc*) to go along with; ~ **assistance à** to give help to; ~ **attention** to pay attention; ~ **serment** to take the oath; ~ **l'oreille** to listen.

prêteur, euse [pretœr, -œz] *nm/f* moneylender; ~ **sur gages** pawnbroker.

prétexte [prātekst(ə)] *nm* pretext, excuse; **sous aucun** ~ on no account; **sous (le)** ~ **que/de** on the pretext that/of.

prétexter [prātekstā] *vt* to give as a pretext *ou* an excuse.

prêtre [pretr(ə)] *nm* priest.

prêtre-ouvrier, *pl* **prêtres-ouvriers** [pretrōōvrēyā] *nm* worker-priest.

prêtrise [pretrēz] *nf* priesthood.

preuve [prœv] *nf* proof; (*indice*) proof, evidence *q*; **jusqu'à** ~ **du contraire** until proved otherwise; **faire** ~ **de** to show; **faire ses** ~**s** to prove o.s. (*ou* itself); ~ **matérielle** material evidence.

prévaloir [prāvàlwár] *vi* to prevail; **se** ~ **de** *vt* to take advantage of; (*tirer vanité de*) to pride o.s. on.

prévarication [prāvàrēkásyón] *nf* maladministration.

prévaut [prāvō] *etc vb voir* **prévaloir.**

prévenances [prevnáns] *nfpl* thoughtfulness *sg*, kindness *sg*.

prévenant, e [prevnán, -ánt] *a* thoughtful, kind.

prévenir [prevnēr] *vt* (*avertir*): ~ **qn (de)** to warn sb (about); (*informer*): ~ **qn (de)** to tell *ou* inform sb (about); (*éviter*) to avoid, prevent; (*anticiper*) to anticipate; (*influencer*): ~ **qn contre** to prejudice sb against.

préventif, ive [prāvántēf, -ēv] *a* preventive.

prévention [prāvánsyón] *nf* prevention; (*préjugé*) prejudice; (*JUR*) custody, detention; ~

routière road safety.

prévenu, e [prevnü] *nm/f* (*JUR*) defendant, accused.

prévisible [prăvēzēbl(ə)] *a* foreseeable.

prévision [prăvēzyôn] *nf*: **~s** predictions; (*météorologiques, économiques*) forecast *sg*; **en ~ de** in anticipation of; **~s météorologiques** *ou* **du temps** weather forecast *sg*.

prévisionnel, le [prăvēzyonel] *a* concerned with future requirements.

prévit [prăvē] *etc vb voir* **prévoir**.

prévoir [prăvwár] *vt* (*deviner*) to foresee; (*s'attendre à*) to expect, reckon on; (*prévenir*) to anticipate; (*organiser*) to plan; (*préparer, réserver*) to allow; **prévu pour 4 personnes** designed for 4 people; **prévu pour 10h** scheduled for 10 o'clock.

prévoyance [prăvwáyáns] *nf* foresight; **société/caisse de ~** provident society/ contingency fund.

prévoyant, e [prăvwáyán, -ánt] *vb voir* **prévoir** ♦ *a* gifted with (*ou* showing) foresight, farsighted.

prévu, e [prăvü] *pp de* **prévoir**.

prier [preyă] *vi* to pray ♦ *vt* (*Dieu*) to pray to; (*implorer*) to beg; (*demander*): **~ qn de faire** to ask sb to do; (*inviter*): **~ qn à dîner** to invite sb to dinner; **se faire ~** to need coaxing *ou* persuading; **je vous en prie** (*allez-y*) please do; (*de rien*) don't mention it; **je vous prie de faire** please (would you) do.

prière [preyer] *nf* prayer; (*demande instante*) plea, entreaty; "**~ de faire ...**" "please do ...".

primaire [premer] *a* primary; (*péj: personne*) simple-minded; (*: idées*) simplistic ♦ *nm* (*SCOL*) elementary (*US*) *ou* primary (*Brit*) education.

primauté [premōtă] *nf* (*fig*) primacy.

prime [prem] *nf* (*bonification*) bonus; (*subside*) allowance; (*COMM: cadeau*) free gift; (*ASSURANCES, BOURSE*) premium ♦ *a*: **de ~ abord** at first glance; **~ de risque** hazard pay *q* (*US*), danger money *q* (*Brit*); **~ de transport** travel allowance.

primer [premă] *vt* (*l'emporter sur*) to prevail over; (*récompenser*) to award a prize to ♦ *vi* to dominate, prevail.

primesautier, ière [premsōtyă, -yer] *a* impulsive.

primeur [premœr] *nf*: **avoir la ~ de** to be the first to hear (*ou* see *etc*); **~s** *nfpl* (*fruits, légumes*) early fruits and vegetables; **marchand de ~** produce dealer (*US*), greengrocer (*Brit*).

primevère [premver] *nf* primrose.

primitif, ive [premētēf, -ēv] *a* primitive; (*originel*) original ♦ *nm/f* primitive.

primo [premō] *ad* first (of all), firstly.

primordial, e, aux [premordyál, -ō] *a* essential, primordial.

prince [prans] *nm* prince; **~ charmant** Prince Charming; **~ de Galles** *nm inv* (*tissu*) check cloth; **~ héritier** crown prince.

princesse [pranses] *nf* princess.

princier, ière [pransyă, -yer] *a* princely.

principal, e, aux [pransēpál, -ō] *a* principal,

main ♦ *nm* (*SCOL*) principal (*US*), head(teacher) (*Brit*); (*essentiel*) main thing ♦ *nf* (*LING*): (**proposition**) **~e** main clause.

principalement [pransēpálmán] *ad* principally, mainly.

principauté [pransēpōtă] *nf* principality.

principe [pransēp] *nm* principle; **partir du ~ que** to work on the principle *ou* assumption that; **pour le ~** on principle, for the sake of it; **de ~** *a* (*hostilité*) automatic; (*accord*) in principle; **par ~** on principle; **en ~** (*habituellement*) as a rule; (*théoriquement*) in principle.

printanier, ière [prantányă, -yer] *a* spring *cpd*; spring-like.

printemps [prantán] *nm* spring; **au ~** in spring.

priori [preyorē]: **a ~** *ad* at first glance; initially; a priori.

prioritaire [preyorēter] *a* having priority; (*AUTO*) having right of way; (*INFORM*) foreground.

priorité [preyorētă] *nf* (*AUTO*): **avoir la ~ (sur)** to have right of way (over); **~ à droite** right of way to vehicles coming from the right; **en ~** as a (matter of) priority.

pris, e [pre, prez] *pp de* **prendre** ♦ *a* (*place*) taken; (*billets*) sold; (*journée, mains*) full; (*personne*) busy; (*crème, ciment*) set; (*MÉD: enflammé*): **avoir le nez/la gorge ~(e)** to have a stuffy nose/a bad throat; (*saisi*): **être ~ de peur/de fatigue** to be stricken with fear/overcome with fatigue.

prise [prez] *nf* (*d'une ville*) capture; (*PÊCHE, CHASSE*) catch; (*de judo ou catch, point d'appui ou pour empoigner*) hold; (*ÉLEC: fiche*) plug; (*: femelle*) socket; (*: au mur*) (wall) outlet (*US*), point (*Brit*); **en ~** (*AUTO*) in gear; **être aux ~s avec** to be grappling with; to be battling with; **lâcher ~** to let go; **donner ~ à** (*fig*) to give rise to; **avoir ~ sur qn** to have a hold over sb; **~ en charge** (*taxi*) ≈ minimum fare; (*par la sécurité sociale*) undertaking to reimburse costs; **~ de contact** initial meeting, first contact; **~ de courant** outlet (*US*), power point (*Brit*); **~ d'eau** hydrant, water (supply) point; tap; **~ multiple** adaptor; **~ d'otages** hostage-taking; **~ à partie** (*JUR*) action against a judge; **~ de sang** blood test; **~ de son** sound recording; **~ de tabac** pinch of snuff; **~ de terre** earth; **~ de vue** (*photo*) shot; (*action*): **~ de vue(s)** filming, shooting.

priser [preză] *vt* (*tabac, héroïne*) to take; (*estimer*) to prize, value ♦ *vi* to take snuff.

prisme [prēsm(ə)] *nm* prism.

prison [prēzôn] *nf* prison; **aller/être en ~** to go to/be in prison *ou* jail; **faire de la ~** to serve time; **être condamné à 5 ans de ~** to be sentenced to 5 years' imprisonment *ou* 5 years in prison.

prisonnier, ière [prēzonyă, -yer] *nm/f* prisoner ♦ *a* captive; **faire qn ~** to take sb prisoner.

prit [pre] *vb voir* **prendre**.

privatif, ive [prēvătēf, -ēv] *a* (*jardin etc*) private; (*peine*) which deprives one of one's liberties.

privations [prēvâsyôn] *nfpl* privations, hardships.

privatisation [prĕvátēzásyóñ] *nf* privatization.
privatiser [prĕvátēzā] *vt* to privatize.
privautés [prĕvōtā] *nfpl* liberties.
privé, e [prĕvā] *a* private; (*dépourvu*): ~ **de** without, lacking; **en ~, dans le ~** in private.
priver [prĕvā] *vt*: ~ **qn de** to deprive sb of; **se ~ de** to go on *ou* do without; **ne pas se ~ de faire** not to refrain from doing.
privilège [prĕvēlezh] *nm* privilege.
privilégié, e [prĕvēlāzhyā] *a* privileged.
privilégier [prĕvēlāzhyā] *vt* to favor (*US*), favour (*Brit*).
prix [prē] *nm* (*valeur*) price; (*récompense, SCOL*) prize; **mettre à ~** to set an upset (*US*) *ou* a reserve (*Brit*) price on; **au ~ fort** at a very high price; **acheter qch à ~ d'or** to pay a (small) fortune for sth; **hors de ~** exorbitantly priced; **à aucun ~** not at any price; **à tout ~** at all costs; **grand ~** (*SPORT*) Grand Prix; ~ **d'achat/de vente/de revient** purchasing/selling/cost price; ~ **conseillé** manufacturer's recommended price (MRP).
pro [prō] *nm* (= *professionnel*) pro.
probabilité [prōbábēlētā] *nf* probability; **selon toute ~** in all probability.
probable [prōbábl(ə)] *a* likely, probable.
probablement [prōbábləmáñ] *ad* probably.
probant, e [prōbáñ, -áñt] *a* convincing.
probatoire [prōbátwár] *a* (*examen, test*) preliminary; (*stage*) probationary, trial *cpd*.
probité [prōbētā] *nf* integrity, probity.
problématique [prōblāmátēk] *a* problematic(al) ♦ *nf* problematics *sg*; (*problème*) problem.
problème [prōblem] *nm* problem.
procédé [prōsādā] *nm* (*méthode*) process; (*comportement*) behavior *q* (*US*), behaviour *q* (*Brit*).
procéder [prōsādā] *vi* to proceed; to behave; ~ **à** *vt* to carry out.
procédure [prōsādür] *nf* (*ADMIN, JUR*) procedure.
procès [prose] *nm* (*JUR*) trial; (*: poursuites*) proceedings *pl*; **être en ~ avec** to be involved in a lawsuit with; **faire le ~ de qn/qch** (*fig*) to put sb/sth on trial; **sans autre forme de ~** without further ado.
processeur [prōsăsœr] *nm* processor.
procession [prōsāsyóñ] *nf* procession.
processus [prōsāsüs] *nm* process.
procès-verbal, aux [prōseverbál, -ō] *nm* (*constat*) statement; (*aussi:* **PV**): **avoir un ~** to get a parking ticket; (*de réunion*) minutes *pl*.
prochain, e [prōshañ, -en] *a* next; (*proche*) impending; near ♦ *nm* fellow man; **la ~e fois/semaine** ~e next time/week; **à la ~e!** (*fam*), **à la ~e fois** see you!, till the next time!; **un ~ jour** (some day) soon.
prochainement [proshenmáñ] *ad* soon, shortly.
proche [prosh] *a* nearby; (*dans le temps*) imminent; close at hand; (*parent, ami*) close; ~**s** *nmpl* (*parents*) close relatives, next of kin; (*amis*): **l'un de ses ~s** one of those close to him (*ou* her); **être ~ (de)** to be near, be close (to); **de ~ en ~** gradually.
Proche-Orient [proshoryáñ] *nm*: **le ~** the Near East.

proclamation [proklámásyóñ] *nf* proclamation.
proclamer [proklámā] *vt* to proclaim; (*résultat d'un examen*) to announce.
procréer [prokrāā] *vt* to procreate.
procuration [prokürásyóñ] *nf* proxy; power of attorney; **voter par ~** to vote by proxy.
procurer [prokürā] *vt* (*fournir*): ~ **qch à qn** to get *ou* obtain sth for sb; (*causer: plaisir etc*): ~ **qch à qn** to bring *ou* give sb sth; **se ~** *vt* to get.
procureur [prokürœr] *nm* public prosecutor; ~ **général** attorney general (*US*), public prosecutor (*in appeal court*) (*Brit*).
prodigalité [prodēgálētā] *nf* (*générosité*) generosity; (*extravagance*) extravagance, wastefulness.
prodige [prodēzh] *nm* (*miracle, merveille*) marvel, wonder; (*personne*) prodigy.
prodigieux, euse [prodēzhyœ, -œz] *a* prodigious; phenomenal.
prodigue [prodēg] *a* (*généreux*) generous; (*dépensier*) extravagant, wasteful; **fils ~** prodigal son.
prodiguer [prodēgā] *vt* (*argent, biens*) to be lavish with; (*soins, attentions*): ~ **qch à qn** to lavish sth on sb.
producteur, trice [prodüktœr, -trēs] *a*: ~ **de blé** wheat-producing; (*CINÉMA*): **société productrice** film *ou* movie company ♦ *nm/f* producer.
productif, ive [prodüktēf, -ēv] *a* productive.
production [prodüksyóñ] *nf* (*gén*) production; (*rendement*) output; (*produits*) products *pl*, goods *pl*; (*œuvres*): **la ~ dramatique du XVIIe siècle** the plays of the 17th century.
productivité [prodüktēvētā] *nf* productivity.
produire [prodüēr] *vt, vi* to produce; **se ~** *vi* (*acteur*) to perform, appear; (*événement*) to happen, occur.
produit, e [prodüē, -ēt] *pp de* **produire** ♦ *nm* (*gén*) product; ~ **d'entretien** cleaning product; ~ **national brut (PNB)** gross national product (GNP); ~ **net** net profit; ~ **pour la vaisselle** dish-washing (*US*) *ou* washing-up (*Brit*) liquid; ~ **des ventes** income from sales; ~**s agricoles** farm produce *sg*; ~**s alimentaires** foodstuffs; ~**s de beauté** beauty products, cosmetics.
proéminent, e [proāmēnáñ, -áñt] *a* prominent.
prof [prof] *nm* (*fam*: = *professeur*) teacher; professor; lecturer.
prof. [prof] *abr* = **professeur, professionnel.**
profane [profán] *a* (*REL*) secular; (*ignorant, non initié*) uninitiated ♦ *nm/f* layman.
profaner [profánā] *vt* to desecrate; (*fig: sentiment*) to defile; (*: talent*) to debase.
proférer [profārā] *vt* to utter.
professer [profāsā] *vt* to profess.
professeur [profesœr] *nm* teacher; (*titulaire d'une chaire*) professor; ~ **(de faculté)** instructor (*US*), (university) lecturer (*Brit*).
profession [profesyóñ] *nf* (*libérale*) profession; (*gén*) occupation; **faire ~ de** (*opinion, religion*) to profess; **de ~** by profession; **"sans ~"** "unemployed"; (*femme mariée*) "housewife".
professionnel, le [profesyonel] *a* professional ♦ *nm/f* professional; (*ouvrier qualifié*) skilled

worker.
professoral, e, aux [profɛsorál, -ō] *a*
professorial; **le corps** ~ the teaching profession.
professorat [profɛsorá] *nm*: **le** ~ the teaching
profession.
profil [profēl] *nm* profile; *(d'une voiture)* line,
contour; **de** ~ in profile.
profilé, e [profēlā] *a* shaped; *(aile etc)*
streamlined.
profiler [profēlā] *vt* to streamline; **se** ~ *vi (arbre, tour)* to stand out, be silhouetted.
profit [profē] *nm (avantage)* benefit, advantage; *(COMM, FINANCE)* profit; **au** ~ **de** in
aid of; **tirer** *ou* **retirer** ~ **de** to profit from;
mettre à ~ to take advantage of; to turn to
good account; **~s et pertes** *(COMM)* profit
and loss(es).
profitable [profētábl(ə)] *a* beneficial; profitable.
profiter [profētā] *vi*: ~ **de** to take advantage
of; to make the most of; ~ **de ce que** ... to
take advantage of the fact that ...; ~ **à** to be
of benefit to, benefit; to be profitable to.
profiteur, euse [profētœr, -ēz] *nm/f (péj)*
profiteer.
profond, e [profóṅ, -óṅd] *a* deep; *(méditation,
mépris)* profound; **au plus** ~ **de** in the
depths of, at the (very) bottom of; **la France**
~**e** the heartlands of France.
profondément [profóṅdāmáṅ] *ad* deeply;
profoundly.
profondeur [profóṅdœr] *nf* depth.
profusément [profüzāmáṅ] *ad* profusely.
profusion [profüzyóṅ] *nf* profusion; **à** ~ in
plenty.
progéniture [prozhānētür] *nf* offspring *inv*.
progiciel [prozhēsyel] *nm (INFORM)* (software)
package; ~ **d'application** applications package, applications software *q*.
progouvernemental, e, aux
[progōōvernəmáṅtál, -ō] *a* pro-government
cpd.
programmable [prográmábl(ə)] *a* programmable.
programmateur, trice [prográmátœr, -trēs]
nm/f (CINÉMA, TV) program *(US) ou* programme *(Brit)* planner ♦ *nm (de machine à
laver etc)* timer.
programmation [prográmásyóṅ] *nf* programming.
programme [prográm] *nm* program *(US)*, programme *(Brit)*; *(TV, RADIO)* program(me)s
pl; *(SCOL)* syllabus, curriculum; *(INFORM)*
program; **au** ~ **de ce soir** *(TV)* among
tonight's program(me)s.
programmé, e [prográmā] *a*: **enseignement**
~ programmed learning.
programmer [prográmā] *vt (TV, RADIO)* to
put on, show; *(organiser, prévoir)* to
schedule; *(INFORM)* to program.
programmeur, euse [prográmœr, -ēz] *nm/f*
(computer) programmer.
progrès [progre] *nm* progress *q*; **faire des/
être en** ~ to make/be making progress.
progresser [progrāsā] *vi* to progress; *(troupes
etc)* to make headway *ou* progress.
progressif, ive [progrāsēf, -ēv] *a* progressive.
progression [progrāsyóṅ] *nf* progression;

(d'une troupe etc) advance, progress.
progressiste [progrāsēst(ə)] *a* progressive.
progressivement [progrāsēvmáṅ] *ad* progressively.
prohiber [proēbā] *vt* to prohibit, ban.
proie [prwá] *nf* prey *q*; **être la** ~ **de** to fall
prey to; **être en** ~ **à** *(doutes, sentiment)* to
be prey to; *(douleur, mal)* to be suffering.
projecteur [prozhektœr] *nm* projector; *(de
théâtre, cirque)* spotlight.
projectile [prozhektēl] *nm* missile; *(d'arme)*
projectile, bullet *(ou* shell *etc)*.
projection [prozheksyóṅ] *nf* projection; showing; **conférence avec** ~**s** lecture with slides
(ou a film).
projectionniste [prozheksyonēst(ə)] *nm/f*
(CINÉMA) projectionist.
projet [prozhe] *nm* plan; *(ébauche)* draft;
faire des ~**s** to make plans; ~ **de loi** bill.
projeter [prozhtā] *vt (envisager)* to plan;
(film, photos) to project; *(passer)* to show;
(ombre, lueur) to throw, cast, project; *(jeter)*
to throw up *(ou* off *ou* out); ~ **de faire qch** to
plan to do sth.
prolétaire [prolāter] *a, nm/f* proletarian.
prolétariat [prolātáryá] *nm* proletariat.
proliférer [prolēfārā] *vi* to proliferate.
prolifique [prolēfēk] *a* prolific.
prolixe [prolēks(ə)] *a* verbose.
prolo [prolō] *nm/f (fam)* = **prolétaire**.
prologue [prolog] *nm* prologue.
prolongateur [prolóṅgátœr] *nm (ÉLEC)* extension cable.
prolongation [prolóṅgásyóṅ] *nf* prolongation;
extension; ~**s** *nfpl (FOOTBALL)* overtime *sg
(US)*, extra time *sg (Brit)*.
prolongement [prolóṅzhmáṅ] *nm* extension;
~**s** *nmpl (fig)* repercussions, effects; **dans le**
~ **de** running on from.
prolonger [prolóṅzhā] *vt (débat, séjour)* to
prolong; *(délai, billet, rue)* to extend; *(suj:
chose)* to be a continuation *ou* an extension
of; **se** ~ *vi* to go on.
promenade [promnád] *nf* walk *(ou* drive *ou*
ride); **faire une** ~ to go for a walk; **une** ~ **(à
pied)/en voiture/à vélo** a walk/drive/
(bicycle) ride.
promener [promnā] *vt (personne, chien)* to
take out for a walk; *(fig)* to carry around;
(doigts, regard): ~ **qch sur** to run sth over;
se ~ *vi (à pied)* to go for *(ou* be out for) a
walk; *(en voiture)* to go for *(ou* be out for) a
drive; *(fig)*: **se** ~ **sur** to wander over.
promeneur, euse [promnœr, -ēz] *nm/f* walker, stroller.
promenoir [promənwár] *nm* gallery, (covered)
walkway.
promesse [promes] *nf* promise; ~ **d'achat**
commitment to buy.
prometteur, euse [prometœr, -ēz] *a* promising.
promettre [prometr(ə)] *vt* to promise ♦ *vi
(récolte, arbre)* to look promising; *(enfant,
musicien)* to be promising; **se** ~ **de faire** to
resolve *ou* mean to do; ~ **à qn de faire** to
promise sb that one will do.
promeus [promœ] *etc vb voir* **promouvoir**.
promis, e [promē, -ēz] *pp de* **promettre** ♦ *a*:
être ~ **à qch** *(destiné)* to be destined for sth.

promiscuité [prɔmɛsküɛtā] *nf* crowding; lack of privacy.

promit [prɔmɛ] *vb voir* **promettre**.

promontoire [prɔmôṅtwár] *nm* headland.

promoteur, trice [prɔmotœr, -trɛ̄s] *nm/f (instigateur)* instigator, promoter; ~ **(immobilier)** real estate promoter (*US*), property developer (*Brit*).

promotion [prɔmosyôṅ] *nf (avancement)* promotion; (*SCOL*) class; **en** ~ (*COMM*) on special (offer) (*US*) *ou* (special) offer (*Brit*).

promotionnel, le [prɔmosyonel] *a (article)* on special (offer) (*US*) *ou* (special) offer (*Brit*); (*vente*) promotional.

promouvoir [prɔmōōvwár] *vt* to promote.

prompt, e [prôṅ, prôṅt] *a* swift, rapid; (*intervention, changement*) sudden; ~ **à faire qch** quick to do sth.

prompteur [prôṅtœr] *nm* ® teleprompter ®.

promptitude [prôṅtɛtüd] *nf* swiftness, rapidity.

promu, e [prɔmü] *pp de* **promouvoir**.

promulguer [prɔmülgā] *vt* to promulgate.

prôner [prônā] *vt (louer)* to laud, extol; (*préconiser*) to advocate, commend.

pronom [prɔnôṅ] *nm* pronoun.

pronominal, e, aux [prɔnɔmɛ̄nàl, -ō] *a* pronominal; (*verbe*) reflexive, pronominal.

prononcé, e [prɔnôṅsā] *a* pronounced, marked.

prononcer [prɔnôṅsā] *vt (son, mot, jugement)* to pronounce; (*dire*) to utter; (*allocution*) to deliver ♦ *vi* (*JUR*) to deliver *ou* give a verdict; ~ **bien/mal** to have a good/poor pronunciation; **se** ~ *vi* to reach a decision, give a verdict; **se** ~ **sur** to give an opinion on; **se** ~ **contre** to come down against; **ça se prononce comment?** how do you pronounce this?

prononciation [prɔnôṅsyâsyôṅ] *nf* pronunciation.

pronostic [prɔnostɛ̄k] *nm* (*MÉD*) prognosis (*pl* -oses); (*fig: aussi:* ~**s**) forecast.

pronostiquer [prɔnostɛ̄kā] *vt* (*MÉD*) to prognosticate; (*annoncer, prévoir*) to forecast, foretell.

pronostiqueur, euse [prɔnostɛ̄kœr, -œ̄z] *nm/f* forecaster.

propagande [prɔpágâṅd] *nf* propaganda; **faire de la** ~ **pour qch** to plug *ou* push sth.

propager [prɔpázhā] *vt* to spread; **se** ~ *vi* to spread; (*PHYSIQUE*) to be propagated.

propane [prɔpán] *nm* propane.

propension [prɔpâṅsyôṅ] *nf:* ~ **à (faire) qch** propensity to (do) sth.

prophète [prɔfet], **prophétesse** [prɔfātes] *nm/f* prophet(ess).

prophétie [prɔfāsɛ̄] *nf* prophecy.

prophétiser [prɔfātɛ̄zā] *vt* to prophesy.

prophylactique [prɔfɛ̄láktɛ̄k] *a* prophylactic.

propice [prɔpɛ̄s] *a* favorable (*US*), favourable (*Brit*).

proportion [prɔporsyôṅ] *nf* proportion; **il n'y a aucune** ~ **entre le prix demandé et le prix réel** the asking price bears no relation to the real price; **à** ~ **de** proportionally to, in proportion to; **en** ~ **(de)** in proportion (to); **hors de** ~ out of proportion; **toute(s)** ~**(s) gardée(s)** making due allowance(s)

proportionné, e [prɔporsyonā] *a:* **bien** ~ well-proportioned; ~ **à** proportionate to.

proportionnel, le [prɔporsyonel] *a* proportional; ~ **à** proportional to.

proportionner [prɔporsyonā] *vt:* ~ **qch à** to proportion *ou* adjust sth to.

propos [prɔpō] *nm (paroles)* talk *q*, remark; (*intention, but*) intention, aim; (*sujet*): **à quel** ~**?** what about?; **à** ~ **de** about, regarding; **à tout** ~ for no reason at all; **à ce** ~ on that subject, in this connection; **à** ~ *ad* by the way; (*opportunément*) (just) at the right moment; **hors de** ~, **mal à** ~ *ad* at the wrong moment.

proposer [prɔpōzā] *vt (suggérer)*: ~ **qch (à qn)/de faire** to suggest sth (to sb)/doing, propose sth (to sb)/to do; (*offrir*): ~ **qch à qn/de faire** to offer sb sth/to do; (*candidat*) to nominate, put forward; (*loi, motion*) to propose; **se** ~ **(pour faire)** to offer one's services (to do); **se** ~ **de faire** to intend *ou* propose to do.

proposition [prɔpōzɛ̄syôṅ] *nf* suggestion; proposal; offer; (*LING*) clause; **sur la** ~ **de** at the suggestion of; ~ **de loi** private bill.

propre [prɔpr(ə)] *a* clean; (*net*) neat, tidy; (*qui ne salit pas: chien, chat*) house-broken; (: *enfant*) toilet-trained; (*fig: honnête*) honest; (*possessif*) own; (*sens*) literal; (*particulier*): ~ **à** peculiar to, characteristic of; (*approprié*): ~ **à** suitable *ou* appropriate for; (*de nature à*): ~ **à faire** likely to do, that will do ♦ *nm:* **recopier au** ~ to make a fair copy of; (*particularité*): **le** ~ **de** the peculiarity of, the distinctive feature of; **au** ~ (*LING*) literally; **appartenir à qn en** ~ to belong to sb (exclusively); ~ **à rien** *nm/f* (*péj*) good-for-nothing.

proprement [prɔprəmâṅ] *ad* cleanly; neatly, tidily; **à** ~ **parler** strictly speaking; **le village** ~ **dit** the actual village, the village itself.

propret, te [prɔpre, -et] *a* neat and tidy, spick-and-span.

propreté [prɔprətā] *nf* cleanliness, cleanness; neatness, tidiness.

propriétaire [prɔprɛ̄yāter] *nm/f* owner; (*d'hôtel etc*) proprietor/tress, owner; (*pour le locataire*) landlord/lady; ~ **(immobilier)** house owner; householder; ~ **récoltant** grower; ~ **(terrien)** landowner.

propriété [prɔprɛ̄yātā] *nf (droit)* ownership; (*objet, immeuble etc*) property *gén q*; (*villa*) residence, property; (*terres*) property *gén q*, land *gén q*; (*qualité, CHIMIE, MATH*) property; (*correction*) appropriateness, suitability; ~ **artistique et littéraire** artistic and literary copyright; ~ **industrielle** patent rights *pl*.

propulser [prɔpülsā] *vt (missile)* to propel; (*projeter*) to hurl, fling.

propulsion [prɔpülsyôṅ] *nf* propulsion.

prorata [prɔrátá] *nm inv:* **au** ~ **de** in proportion to, on the basis of.

prorogation [prɔrogâsyôṅ] *nf* deferment; extension; adjournment.

proroger [prɔrozhā] *vt* to postpone, defer; (*prolonger*) to extend; (*assemblée*) to adjourn, prorogue.

prosaïque [prɔzàɛ̄k] *a* mundane, prosaic.

proscription [proskrĕpsyôṅ] *nf* banishment; (*interdiction*) banning; prohibition.

proscrire [proskrĕr] *vt* (*bannir*) to banish; (*interdire*) to ban, prohibit.

prose [prōz] *nf* prose (*style*).

prosélyte [prozălĕt] *nm/f* proselyte, convert.

prospecter [prospektă] *vt* to prospect; (*COMM*) to canvass.

prospecteur-placier, *pl* **prospecteurs-placiers** [prospektœrplásyă] *nm* placement officer.

prospectif, ive [prospektĕf, -ĕv] *a* prospective.

prospectus [prospektüs] *nm* (*feuille*) leaflet; (*dépliant*) brochure, leaflet.

prospère [prosper] *a* prosperous; (*santé, entreprise*) thriving, flourishing.

prospérer [prospără] *vi* to thrive.

prospérité [prospărĕtă] *nf* prosperity.

prostate [prostát] *nf* prostate (gland).

prosterner [prosternă]: **se ~** *vi* to bow low, prostrate o.s.

prostituée [prostĕtüă] *nf* prostitute.

prostitution [prostĕtüsyôṅ] *nf* prostitution.

prostré, e [prostră] *a* prostrate.

protagoniste [protăgonĕst(ə)] *nm* protagonist.

protecteur, trice [protektœr, -trĕs] *a* protective; (*air, ton*: *péj*) patronizing ♦ *nm/f* (*défenseur*) protector; (*des arts*) patron.

protection [proteksyôṅ] *nf* protection; (*d'un personnage influent*: *aide*) patronage; **écran de ~** protective screen; **~ civile** state-financed civilian rescue service; **maternelle et infantile (PMI)** social service concerned with child welfare.

protectionniste [proteksyonĕst(ə)] *a* protectionist.

protégé, e [protăzhă] *nm/f* protégé/e.

protège-cahier [protezhkáyă] *nm* notebook cover.

protéger [protăzhă] *vt* to protect; (*aider, patronner*: *personne, arts*) to be a patron of; (: *carrière*) to further; **se ~ de/contre** to protect o.s. from.

protéine [protăĕn] *nf* protein.

protestant, e [protestáṅ, -áṅt] *a*, *nm/f* Protestant.

protestantisme [protestáṅtĕsm(ə)] *nm* Protestantism.

protestataire [protestáter] *nm/f* protestor.

protestation [protestásyôṅ] *nf* (*plainte*) protest; (*déclaration*) protestation, profession.

protester [protestă] *vi*: **~ (contre)** to protest (against *ou* about); **~ de** (*son innocence, sa loyauté*) to protest.

prothèse [protez] *nf* artificial limb, prosthesis (*pl* -ses); **~ dentaire** (*appareil*) denture; (*science*) dental engineering.

protocolaire [protokoler] *a* formal; (*questions, règles*) of protocol.

protocole [protokol] *nm* protocol; (*fig*) etiquette; **~ d'accord** draft treaty; **~ opératoire** (*MÉD*) operating procedure.

prototype [prototĕp] *nm* prototype.

protubérance [protübăráṅs] *nf* bulge, protuberance.

protubérant, e [protübăráṅ, -áṅt] *a* protruding, bulging, protuberant.

proue [prōō] *nf* bow(s *pl*), prow.

prouesse [prōōes] *nf* feat.

prouver [prōōvă] *vt* to prove.

provenance [provnáṅs] *nf* origin; (*de mot, coutume*) source; **avion en ~ de** plane (arriving) from.

provençal, e, aux [provâṅsál, -ō] *a* Provençal ♦ *nm* (*LING*) Provençal.

Provence [provâṅs] *nf*: **la ~** Provence.

provenir [provnĕr]: **~ de** *vt* to come from; (*résulter de*) to be due to, be the result of.

proverbe [proverb(ə)] *nm* proverb.

proverbial, e, aux [proverbyál, -ō] *a* proverbial.

providence [provĕdáṅs] *nf*: **la ~** providence.

providentiel, le [provĕdáṅsyel] *a* providential.

province [provâṅs] *nf* province.

provincial, e, aux [provâṅsyál, -ō] *a*, *nm/f* provincial.

proviseur [provĕzœr] *nm* ≈ principal (*US*), ≈ head(teacher) (*Brit*).

provision [provĕzyôṅ] *nf* (*réserve*) stock, supply; (*avance*: *à un avocat, avoué*) retainer, retaining fee; (*COMM*) funds *pl* (in account); reserve; **~s** *nfpl* (*vivres*) provisions, food *q*; **faire ~ de** to stock up with; **placard** *ou* **armoire à ~s** food closet (*US*) *ou* cupboard (*Brit*).

provisoire [provĕzwár] *a* temporary; (*JUR*) provisional; **mise en liberté ~** release on bail.

provisoirement [provĕzwármáṅ] *ad* temporarily, for the time being.

provocant, e [provokáṅ, -áṅt] *a* provocative.

provocateur, trice [provokátœr, -trĕs] *a* provocative ♦ *nm* (*meneur*) agitator.

provocation [provokásyôṅ] *nf* provocation.

provoquer [provokă] *vt* (*défier*) to provoke; (*causer*) to cause, bring about; (: *curiosité*) to arouse, give rise to; (: *aveux*) to prompt, elicit; (*inciter*): **~ qn à** to incite sb to.

prox. *abr* = **proximité.**

proxénète [proksănĕt] *nm* procurer.

proximité [proksĕmĕtă] *nf* nearness, closeness, proximity; (*dans le temps*) imminence, closeness; **à ~** near *ou* close by; **à ~ de** near (to), close to.

prude [prüd] *a* prudish.

prudemment [prüdámáṅ] *ad* (*voir prudent*) carefully; cautiously; prudently; wisely, sensibly.

prudence [prüdáṅs] *nf* carefulness; caution; prudence; **avec ~** carefully; cautiously; wisely; **par (mesure de) ~** as a precaution.

prudent, e [prüdáṅ, -áṅt] *a* (*pas téméraire*) careful, cautious, prudent; (: *en général*) safety-conscious; (*sage, conseillé*) wise, sensible; (*réservé*) cautious; **ce n'est pas ~** it's risky; it's not sensible; **soyez ~** take care, be careful.

prune [prün] *nf* plum.

pruneau, x [prünō] *nm* prune.

prunelle [prünel] *nf* pupil; (*œil*) eye; (*BOT*) sloe; (*eau de vie*) sloe gin.

prunier [prünyă] *nm* plum tree.

PS *sigle m* = Parti socialiste; (= *post-scriptum*) PS.

psalmodier [psálmodyă] *vt* to chant; (*fig*) to drone out.

psaume [psōm] *nm* psalm.

pseudonyme [psœdonēm] *nm* (*gén*) fictitious name; (*d'écrivain*) pseudonym, pen name; (*de comédien*) stage name.

PSIG *sigle m* (= *Peloton de surveillance et d'intervention de gendarmerie*) *type of police commando squad.*

PSU *sigle m* = *Parti socialiste unifié.*

psy [psē] *nm/f* (*fam, péj*: = *psychiatre, psychologue*) shrink.

psychanalyse [psēkánálēz] *nf* psychoanalysis.

psychanalyser [psēkánálēzā] *vt* to psychoanalyze; **se faire** ~ to undergo (psycho)analysis.

psychanalyste [psēkánálēst(ə)] *nm/f* psychoanalyst.

psychédélique [psēkādālēk] *a* psychedelic.

psychiatre [psēkyátr(ə)] *nm/f* psychiatrist.

psychiatrie [psēkyátrē] *nf* psychiatry.

psychiatrique [psēkyátrēk] *a* psychiatric; (*hôpital*) mental, psychiatric.

psychique [psēshēk] *a* psychological.

psychisme [psēshēsm(ə)] *nm* psyche.

psychologie [psēkolozhē] *nf* psychology.

psychologique [psēkolozhēk] *a* psychological.

psychologue [psēkolog] *nm/f* psychologist; **être** ~ (*fig*) to be a good psychologist.

psychopathe [psēkopát] *nm/f* psychopath.

psychopédagogie [psēkopādágozhē] *nf* educational psychology.

psychose [psēkōz] *nf* (*MÉD*) psychosis (*pl* -ses); (*obsession, idée fixe*) obsessive fear.

psychosomatique [psēkosomátēk] *a* psychosomatic.

psychothérapie [psēkotārápē] *nf* psychotherapy.

psychotique [psēkotēk] *a* psychotic.

PTCA *sigle m* = *poids total en charge autorisé.*

Pte *abr* = **Porte**.

pte *abr* (= *pointe*) pt.

PTMA *sigle m* (= *poids total maximum autorisé*) maximum loaded weight.

PTT *sigle fpl voir* **poste**.

pu [pü] *pp de* **pouvoir**.

puanteur [püántœr] *nf* stink, stench.

pub [püb] *nf* (*fam*: = *publicité*): **la** ~ advertising.

pubère [püber] *a* pubescent.

puberté [pübertā] *nf* puberty.

pubis [pübēs] *nm* (*bas-ventre*) pubes *pl*; (*os*) pubis.

public, ique [püblēk] *a* public; (*école, instruction*) state *cpd*; (*scrutin*) open ♦ *nm* public; (*assistance*) audience; **en** ~ in public; **le grand** ~ the general public.

publication [püblēkásyôǹ] *nf* publication.

publiciste [püblēsēst(ə)] *nm/f* adman.

publicitaire [püblēsēter] *a* advertising *cpd*; (*film, voiture*) publicity *cpd*; (*vente*) promotional ♦ *nm* adman; **rédacteur** ~ copywriter.

publicité [püblēsētā] *nf* (*méthode, profession*) advertising; (*annonce*) advertisement; (*révélations*) publicity.

publier [püblēyā] *vt* to publish; (*nouvelle*) to publicize, make public.

publipostage [püblēpostázh] *nm* mailing.

publique [püblēk] *af voir* **public**.

publiquement [püblēkmáǹ] *ad* publicly.

puce [püs] *nf* flea; (*INFORM*) chip; (**marché aux**) ~**s** flea market *sg*; **mettre la** ~ **à**

l'oreille de qn to give sb something to think about.

puceau, x [püsō] *am*: **être** ~ to be a virgin.

pucelle [püsel] *af*: **être** ~ to be a virgin.

puceron [püsrôǹ] *nm* aphid.

pudeur [püdœr] *nf* modesty.

pudibond, e [püdēbôǹ, -ôǹd] *a* prudish.

pudique [püdēk] *a* (*chaste*) modest; (*discret*) discreet.

puer [püā] (*péj*) *vi* to stink ♦ *vt* to stink of, reek of.

puériculture [püārēkültür] *nf* infant care.

puéricultrice [püārēkültrēs] *nf* ≈ nursery nurse.

puéril, e [püārēl] *a* childish.

pugilat [püzhēlà] *nm* (*fist*) fight.

puis [püē] *vb voir* **pouvoir** ♦ *ad* (*ensuite*) then; (*dans une énumération*) next; (*en outre*): **et** ~ and (then); **et** ~ (**après** *ou* **quoi**)? so (what)?

puisard [püēzár] *nm* (*égout*) cesspool.

puiser [püēzā] *vt*: ~ (**dans**) to draw (from); ~ **dans qch** to dip into sth.

puisque [püēsk(ə)] *cj* since; (*valeur intensive*): ~ **je te le dis!** I'm telling you!

puissamment [püēsámáǹ] *ad* powerfully.

puissance [püēsáǹs] *nf* power; **en** ~ *a* potential; **2 (à la)** ~ **5** 2 to the power (of) 5.

puissant, e [püēsáǹ, -áǹt] *a* powerful.

puisse [püēs] *etc vb voir* **pouvoir**.

puits [püē] *nm* well; ~ **artésien** artesian well; ~ **de mine** mine shaft; ~ **de science** font of knowledge.

pull(-over) [pül(ovœr)] *nm* sweater.

pulluler [pülülā] *vi* to swarm; (*fig: erreurs*) to abound, proliferate.

pulmonaire [pülmoner] *a* lung *cpd*; (*artère*) pulmonary.

pulpe [pülp(ə)] *nf* pulp.

pulsation [pülsásyôǹ] *nf* (*MÉD*) beat.

pulsion [pülsyôǹ] *nf* (*PSYCH*) drive, urge.

pulvérisateur [pülvārēzátœr] *nm* spray.

pulvérisation [pülvārēzásyôǹ] *nf* spraying.

pulvériser [pülvārēzā] *vt* (*solide*) to pulverize; (*liquide*) to spray; (*fig: anéantir: adversaire*) to pulverize; (*: record*) to smash, shatter; (*: argument*) to demolish.

puma [pümá] *nm* puma, cougar.

punaise [pünez] *nf* (*ZOOL*) bug; (*clou*) thumbtack (*US*), drawing pin (*Brit*).

punch [pôǹsh] *nm* (*boisson*) punch; [pœǹsh] (*BOXE*) punching ability; (*fig*) punch.

punching-ball [pœǹshēngbōl] *nm* punching bag.

punir [pünēr] *vt* to punish; ~ **qn de qch** to punish sb for sth.

punitif, ive [pünētēf, -ēv] *a* punitive.

punition [pünēsyôǹ] *nf* punishment.

pupille [püpēy] *nf* (*ANAT*) pupil ♦ *nm/f* (*enfant*) ward; ~ **de l'État** ward of the state *ou* court (*US*), child in care (*Brit*); ~ **de la Nation** war orphan.

pupitre [püpētr(ə)] *nm* (*SCOL*) desk; (*REL*) lectern; (*de chef d'orchestre*) podium; (*INFORM*) console; ~ **de commande** control panel.

pupitreur, euse [püpētrœr, -œz] *nm/f* (*INFORM*) (computer) operator, keyboarder.

pur, e [pür] *a* pure; (*vin*) undiluted; (*whisky*)

neat; (*intentions*) honorable (*US*), honourable (*Brit*) ♦ *nm* (*personne*) hard-liner; **en ~e perte** fruitlessly, to no avail.

purée [püră] *nf*: **~ (de pommes de terre)** ≈ mashed potatoes *pl*; **~ de marrons** chestnut purée; **~ de pois** (*fig*) pea soup.

purement [pürmáň] *ad* purely.

pureté [pürtă] *nf* purity.

purgatif [pürgátĕf] *nm* purgative, purge.

purgatoire [pürgátwăr] *nm* purgatory.

purge [pürzh(ə)] *nf* (*POL*) purge; (*MÉD*) purging *q*; purge.

purger [pürzhă] *vt* (*radiateur*) to flush (out), drain; (*circuit hydraulique*) to bleed; (*MÉD, POL*) to purge; (*JUR*: *peine*) to serve.

purifier [pürĕfyă] *vt* to purify; (*TECH*: *métal*) to refine.

purin [püraň] *nm* liquid manure.

puriste [pürĕst(ə)] *nm/f* purist.

puritain, e [pürĕtaň, -en] *a*, *nm/f* Puritan.

puritanisme [pürĕtánĕsm(ə)] *nm* Puritanism.

pur-sang [pürsáň] *nm inv* thoroughbred, purebred.

purulent, e [pürüláň, -áňt] *a* purulent.

pus [pü] *vb voir* **pouvoir** ♦ *nm* pus.

pusillanime [püzĭlánĕm] *a* fainthearted.

putain [pütaň] *nf* (*fam!*) whore (*!*); **ce/cette ~ de ...** this goddamn (*US*) *ou* bloody (*Brit*) ... (*!*).

putois [pütwá] *nm* polecat; **crier comme un ~** to yell one's head off.

putréfier [pütrăfyă] *vt*, **se ~** *vi* to putrefy, rot.

putride [pütrĕd] *a* putrid.

puzzle [pœzl(ə)] *nm* jigsaw (puzzle).

PV *sigle m* = **procès-verbal**.

PVC *sigle f* (= *polychlorure de vinyle*) PVC.

PVD *sigle mpl* (= *pays en voie de développement*) developing countries.

Px *abr* = **prix**.

pygmée [pĕgmă] *nm* pygmy.

pyjama [pĕzhámá] *nm* pajamas *pl* (*US*), pyjamas *pl* (*Brit*), pair of pajamas *ou* pyjamas.

pylône [pĕlōn] *nm* pylon.

pyramide [pĕrámĕd] *nf* pyramid.

pyrénéen, ne [pĕránăaň, -en] *a* Pyrenean.

Pyrénées [pĕránă] *nfpl*: **les ~** the Pyrenees.

pyrex [pĕreks] *nm* ® Pyrex ®.

pyrogravure [pĕrográvür] *nf* poker-work.

pyromane [pĕrománe] *nm/f* arsonist.

python [pĕtoň] *nm* python.

Q

Q, q [kü] *nm inv* Q, q ♦ *abr* (= *quintal*) q; **Q comme Quintal** Q for Queen.

Qatar [kátár] *nm*: **le ~** Qatar.

QCM *sigle fpl* (= *questions à choix multiples*) multiple choice *sg*.

QG *sigle m* (= *quartier général*) HQ.

QHS *sigle m* (= *quartier de haute sécurité*) high-security wing *ou* prison.

QI *sigle m* (= *quotient intellectuel*) IQ.

qqch. *abr* (= *quelque chose*) sth.

qqe(s) *abr* = **quelque(s)**.

qqn *abr* (= *quelqu'un*) sb., s.o.

quadragénaire [kádrázhăner] *nm/f* (*de quarante ans*) forty-year-old; (*de quarante à cinquante ans*) man/woman in his/her forties.

quadrangulaire [kwádráňgüler] *a* quadrangular.

quadrature [kwádrátür] *nf*: **c'est la ~ du cercle** it's like trying to square the circle.

quadrichromie [kwádrĭkromĕ] *nf* four-color (*US*) *ou* -colour (*Brit*) printing.

quadrilatère [k(w)ádrĕláter] *nm* (*GÉOM, MIL*) quadrilateral; (*terrain*) four-sided area.

quadrillage [kádrĕyázh] *nm* (*lignes etc*) square pattern, crisscross pattern.

quadrillé, e [kádrĕyă] *a* (*papier*) squared.

quadriller [kádrĕyă] *vt* (*papier*) to mark out in squares; (*POLICE*: *ville, région etc*) to keep under tight control, be positioned throughout.

quadrimoteur [k(w)ádrĕmotœr] *nm* four-engined plane.

quadripartite [kwádrĕpártĕt] *a* (*entre pays*) four-power; (*entre partis*) four-party.

quadriphonie [kádrĕfonĕ] *nf* quadraphony.

quadriréacteur [k(w)ádrĕrăáktœr] *nm* four-engined jet.

quadrupède [k(w)ádrüped] *nm* quadruped.

quadruple [k(w)ádrüpl(ə)] *nm*: **le ~ de** four times as much as.

quadrupler [k(w)ádrüplă] *vt*, *vi* to quadruple, increase fourfold.

quadruplés, ées [k(w)ádrüplă] *nm/fpl* quadruplets, quads.

quai [kă] *nm* (*de port*) quay; (*de gare*) platform; (*de cours d'eau, canal*) embankment; **être à ~** (*navire*) to be alongside; (*train*) to be in the station; **le Q~ d'Orsay** offices of the French Ministry for Foreign Affairs; **le Q~ des Orfèvres** central police headquarters.

qualifiable [kálĕfyábl(ə)] *a*: **ce n'est pas ~** it defies description.

qualificatif, ive [kálĕfēkátĕf, -ēv] *a* (*LING*) qualifying ♦ *nm* (*terme*) term; (*LING*) qualifier.

qualification [kálĕfēkásyóň] *nf* qualification.

qualifier [kálĕfyă] *vt* to qualify; (*appeler*): **~ qch/qn de** to describe sth/sb as; **se ~** *vi* (*SPORT*) to qualify; **être qualifié pour** to be qualified for.

qualitatif, ive [kálĕtátĕf, -ēv] *a* qualitative.

qualité [kálĕtă] *nf* quality; (*titre, fonction*) position; **en ~ de** in one's capacity as; **ès ~s** in an official capacity; **avoir ~ pour** to have authority to; **de ~** *a* quality *cpd*; **rapport ~-prix** value (for money).

quand [káň] *cj*, *ad* when; **~ je serai riche** when I'm rich; **~ même** (*cependant, pourtant*) nevertheless; (*tout de même*) all the same; really; **~ bien même** even though.

quant [káň]: **~ à** *prép* (*pour ce qui est de*) as for, as to; (*au sujet de*) regarding.

quant-à-soi [káňtáswá] *nm*: **rester sur son ~** to remain aloof.

quantième [káňtyem] *nm* date, day (of the month).

quantifiable [káňtĕfyábl(ə)] *a* quantifiable.

quantifier [káňtĕfyă] *vt* to quantify.

quantitatif, ive [kȧṅtētȧtēf, -ēv] *a* quantitative.

quantitativement [kȧṅtētȧtēvmȧṅ] *ad* quantitatively.

quantité [kȧṅtētā] *nf* quantity, amount; (*SCIENCE*) quantity; (*grand nombre*): **une** *ou* **des ~(s) de** a great deal of; a lot of; **en grande ~** in large quantities; **en ~s industrielles** in vast amounts; **du travail en ~** a great deal of work; **~ de** many.

quarantaine [kȧrȧṅten] *nf* (*isolement*) quarantine; (*âge*): **avoir la ~** to be around forty; (*nombre*): **une ~ (de)** forty or so, about forty; **mettre en ~** to put into quarantine; (*fig*) to ostracize.

quarante [kȧrȧṅt] *num* forty.

quarantième [kȧrȧṅtyem] *num* fortieth.

quart [kȧr] *nm* (*fraction*) quarter; (*surveillance*) watch; (*partie*): **un ~ de poulet/fromage** a chicken quarter/a quarter of a cheese; **un ~ de beurre** a quarter kilo of butter, ≈ a half pound of butter; **un ~ de vin** a quarter liter of wine; **une livre un ~** *ou* **et ~** one and a quarter pounds; **le ~ de** a quarter of; **~ d'heure** quarter of an hour; **2h et** *ou* **un ~** (a) quarter past two, (a) quarter after two (*US*); **il est le ~** it's (a) quarter past *ou* after (*US*); **1h moins le ~** (a) quarter to one, (a) quarter of one (*US*); **il est moins le ~** it's (a) quarter to; **être de/ prendre le ~** to keep/take the watch; **~ de tour** quarter turn; **au ~ de tour** (*fig*) straight off; **~s de finale** (*SPORT*) quarter finals.

quarté [kȧrtā] *nm* (*COURSES*) system of forecast betting giving first four horses.

quarternaire [kwȧterner] *a* (*GÉO*) Quaternary.

quarteron [kȧrtərȯṅ] *nm* (*péj*) small bunch, handful.

quartette [kwȧrtet] *nm* quartet(te).

quartier [kȧrtyā] *nm* (*de ville*) district, area; (*de bœuf, de la lune*) quarter; (*de fruit, fromage*) piece; **~s** *nmpl* (*MIL, BLASON*) quarters; **cinéma/salle de ~** local cinema/hall; **avoir ~ libre** to be free; (*MIL*) to have leave from barracks; **ne pas faire de ~** to spare no one, give no quarter; **~ commerçant/résidentiel** shopping/residential area; **~ général (QG)** headquarters (HQ).

quartier-maître [kȧrtyȧmetr(ə)] *nm* ≈ leading seaman.

quartz [kwȧrts] *nm* quartz.

quasi [kȧzē] *ad* almost, nearly ♦ *préfixe*: **~-certitude** near certainty.

quasiment [kȧzēmȧṅ] *ad* almost, very nearly.

quatorze [kȧtorz(ə)] *num* fourteen.

quatorzième [kȧtorzyem] *num* fourteenth.

quatrain [kȧtraṅ] *nm* quatrain.

quatre [kȧtr(ə)] *num* four; **à ~ pattes** on all fours; **tiré à ~ épingles** dressed up to the nines; **faire les ~ cent coups** to be a bit wild; **se mettre en ~ pour qn** to go out of one's way for sb; **~ à ~** (*monter, descendre*) four at a time; **à ~ mains** (*jouer*) four-handed.

quatre-vingt-dix [kȧtrəvȧṅdēs] *num* ninety.

quatre-vingts [kȧtrəvȧṅ] *num* eighty.

quatrième [kȧtrēyem] *num* fourth.

quatuor [kwȧtüor] *nm* quartet(te).

que [kə] *cj* (*gén*) that; (*après comparatif*) than; as: *voir* **plus, aussi, autant** *etc*; (*seulement*): **ne ... ~** only; **il sait ~ tu es là** he knows (that) you're here; **je veux ~ tu acceptes** I want you to accept; **il a dit ~ oui** he said he would (*ou* it was *etc, suivant le contexte*); **si vous y allez** *ou* **~ vous lui téléphoniez** if you go there or (if you) phone him; **quand il rentrera et qu'il aura mangé** when he gets back and (when he) has eaten; **qu'il le veuille** *ou* **non** whether he likes it or not; **tenez-le qu'il ne tombe pas** hold it so (that) it doesn't fall; **qu'il fasse ce qu'il voudra** let him do as he pleases; **il ne boit ~ de l'eau** he only drinks water; *voir* **avant, pour, tel,** *à* **peine** *etc* ♦ *ad*: **qu'il** *ou* **qu'est-ce qu'il est bête/court vite** he's so silly/he runs so fast; **~ de** what a lot of ♦ *pronom*: **l'homme ~ je vois** the man (whom) I see; **le livre ~ tu vois** the book (that *ou* which) you see; **un jour ~ j'étais** a day when I was; **c'est une erreur ~ de croire** it's a mistake to believe; **qu'est-ce que c'est?** (*ceci*) what is it?; (*cela*) what's that?; **~ fais-tu?, qu'est-ce ~ tu fais?** what are you doing?; **~ préfères-tu, celui-ci** *ou* **celui-là?** which do you prefer, this one or that one?; **~ faire?** what can one do?

Québec [kābek] *n* (*ville*) Quebec ♦ *nm*: **le ~** Quebec (Province).

québécois, e [kābȧkwȧ, -wȧz] *a* Quebec *cpd* ♦ *nm* (*LING*) Quebec French ♦ *nm/f*: **Q~, e** Quebecois, Quebec(k)er.

quel, quelle [kel] *a*: **~ livre/homme?** what book/man?; (*parmi un certain choix*) which book/man?; **~ est cet homme?** who is this man?; **~ est ce livre?** what is this book?; **~ est le plus petit?** which is the smallest?; **~s acteurs préférez-vous?** which actors do you prefer?; **dans ~s pays êtes-vous allé?** which *ou* what countries did you go to?; **~le surprise!** what a surprise!; **~ que soit le coupable** whoever is guilty; **~ que soit votre avis** whatever your opinion; whichever is your opinion.

quelconque [kelkȯṅk] *a* (*médiocre*) indifferent, poor; (*sans attrait*) ordinary, plain; (*indéfini*): **un ami/prétexte ~** some friend/pretext or other; **un livre ~ suffira** any book will do; **pour une raison ~** for some reason (or other).

quelque [kelk(ə)] *dét* some; a few, *tournure interrogative* + any ♦ *ad* (*environ*): **~ 100 mètres** some 100 meters; **~ espoir** some hope; **il a ~s amis** he has a few *ou* some friends; **a-t-il ~s amis?** has he any friends?; **les ~s livres qui** the few books which; **~ livre qu'il choisisse** whatever (*ou* whichever) book he chooses; **20 kg et ~(s)** a bit over 20 kg; **~ chose** something, *tournure interrogative* + anything; **~ chose d'autre** something else; anything else; **~ part** somewhere; **~ peu** rather, somewhat; **en ~ sorte** as it were.

quelquefois [kelkəfwȧ] *ad* sometimes.

quelques-uns, -unes [kelkəzœṅ, -ün] *pronom* some, a few; **~ des lecteurs** some of the readers.

quelqu'un [kelkœṅ] *pronom* someone, somebody, *tournure interrogative ou négative* + anyone *ou* anybody; **~ d'autre** someone *ou* somebody else; anybody else.

quémander [kāmâńdā] *vt* to beg for.

qu'en dira-t-on [kâńdērátóń] *nm inv*: **le ~** gossip, what people say.

quenelle [kənel] *nf* quenelle.

quenouille [kənōōy] *nf* distaff.

querelle [kərel] *nf* quarrel; **chercher ~ à qn** to pick a quarrel with sb.

quereller [kərālā]: **se ~** *vi* to quarrel.

querelleur, euse [kərelœr, -œz] *a* quarrelsome.

qu'est-ce que (*ou* **qui**) [keskə(kē)] *voir* **que, qui.**

question [kestyóń] *nf* (*gén*) question; (*fig*) matter; issue; **il a été ~ de** we (*ou* they) spoke about; **il est ~ de les emprisonner** there's talk of them being jailed; **c'est une ~ de temps** it's a matter *ou* question of time; **de quoi est-il ~?** what is it about?; **il n'en est pas ~** there's no question of it; **en ~** in question; **hors de ~** out of the question; **je ne me suis jamais posé la ~** I've never thought about it; **(re)mettre en ~** (*autorité, science*) to question; **poser la ~ de confiance** (*POL*) to ask for a vote of confidence; **~ piège** (*d'apparence facile*) trick question; (*pour nuire*) loaded question; **~ subsidiaire** tiebreaker.

questionnaire [kestyoner] *nm* questionnaire.

questionner [kestyonā] *vt* to question.

quête [ket] *nf* (*collecte*) collection; (*recherche*) quest, search; **faire la ~** (*à l'église*) to take the collection; (*artiste*) to pass the hat around; **se mettre en ~ de qch** to go in search of sth.

quêter [kātā] *vi* (*à l'église*) to take the collection; (*dans la rue*) to collect money (for charity) ♦ *vt* to seek.

quetsche [kwetsh(ə)] *nf* damson.

queue [kœ] *nf* tail; (*fig: du classement*) bottom; (*: de poêle*) handle; (*: de fruit, feuille*) stalk; (*: de train, colonne, file*) rear; (*file: de personnes*) line (*US*), queue (*Brit*); **en ~ (de train)** at the rear (of the train); **faire la ~** to line up (*US*), queue (up) (*Brit*); **se mettre à la ~** to join the line (*US*) *ou* queue (*Brit*); **histoire sans ~ ni tête** cock and bull story; **à la ~ leu leu** in single file; (*fig*) one after the other; **~ de cheval** pony-tail; **~ de poisson: faire une ~ de poisson à qn** (*AUTO*) to cut in front of sb; **finir en ~ de poisson** (*film*) to come to an abrupt end.

queue-de-pie, *pl* **queues-de-pie** [kœdpē] *nf* (*habit*) tails *pl*, tail coat.

queux [kœ] *am voir* **maître.**

qui [kē] *pronom* (*personne*) who, *prép* + whom; (*chose, animal*) which, that; (*interrogatif indirect: sujet*): **je me demande ~ est là?** I wonder who is there?; (*: objet*): **elle ne sait à ~ se plaindre** she doesn't know who to complain to *ou* to whom to complain; **qu'est-ce ~ est sur la table?** what is on the table?; **à ~ est ce sac?** whose bag is this?; **à ~ parlais-tu?** who were you talking to?, to whom were you talking?; **chez ~ allez-vous?** whose house are you going to?; **amenez ~ vous voulez** bring who(ever) you like; **~ est-ce ~ ...?** who?; **~ est-ce que ...?** who?; whom?; **~ que ce soit** whoever it may be.

quiche [kēsh] *nf* quiche; **~ lorraine** quiche

Lorraine.

quiconque [kēkôńk] *pronom* (*celui qui*) whoever, anyone who; (*n'importe qui, personne*) anyone, anybody.

quidam [küēdám] *nm* (*hum*) fellow.

quiétude [kyātüd] *nf* (*d'un lieu*) quiet, tranquillity; (*d'une personne*) peace (of mind), serenity; **en toute ~** in complete peace; (*mentale*) with complete peace of mind.

quignon [kēnyóń] *nm*: **~ de pain** (*croûton*) crust of bread; (*morceau*) hunk of bread.

quille [kēy] *nf* ninepin; (*NAVIG: d'un bateau*) keel; **(jeu de) ~s** ninepins *sg*.

quincaillerie [kańkáyrē] *nf* (*ustensiles, métier*) hardware; (*magasin*) hardware store (*US*) *ou* shop (*Brit*).

quincaillier, ière [kańkâyā, -yer] *nm/f* hardware dealer, ironmonger (*Brit*).

quinconce [kańkôńs] *nm*: **en ~** in staggered rows.

quinine [kēnēn] *nf* quinine.

quinquagénaire [kańkázhāner] *nm/f* (*de cinquante ans*) fifty-year old; (*de cinquante à soixante ans*) man/woman in his/her fifties.

quinquennal, e, aux [kańkānál, -ō] *a* five-year, quinquennial.

quintal, aux [kańtál, -ō] *nm* quintal (*100 kg*).

quinte [kańt] *nf*: **~ (de toux)** coughing fit.

quintessence [kańtāsáńs] *nf* quintessence, very essence.

quintette [kańtet] *nm* quintet(te).

quintuple [kańtüpl(ə)] *nm*: **le ~ de** five times as much as.

quintupler [kańtüplā] *vt, vi* to increase five-fold.

quintuplés, ées [kańtüplā] *nm/fpl* quintuplets, quins.

quinzaine [kańzen] *nf*: **une ~ (de)** about fifteen, fifteen or so; **une ~ (de jours)** (*deux semaines*) two weeks; **~ publicitaire** *ou* **commerciale** (two-week) sale.

quinze [kańz] *num* fifteen; **demain en ~** two weeks tomorrow; **dans ~ jours** in two weeks(' time).

quinzième [kańzyem] *num* fifteenth.

quiproquo [kēprokō] *nm* (*méprise sur une personne*) mistake; (*malentendu sur un sujet*) misunderstanding; (*THÉÂTRE*) (case of) mistaken identity.

Quito [kētō] *n* Quito.

quittance [kētáńs] *nf* (*reçu*) receipt; (*facture*) bill.

quitte [kēt] *a*: **être ~ envers qn** to be no longer in sb's debt; (*fig*) to be quits with sb; **être ~ de** (*obligation*) to be clear of; **en être ~ à bon compte** to have got off lightly; **~ à faire** even if it means doing; **~ ou double** (*jeu*) double or nothing (*US*), double or quits (*Brit*); (*fig*): **c'est du ~ ou double** it's a big risk.

quitter [kētā] *vt* to leave; (*espoir, illusion*) to give up; (*vêtement*) to take off; **se ~** (*couples, interlocuteurs*) to part; **ne quittez pas** (*au téléphone*) hold the line; **ne pas ~ qn d'une semelle** to stick to sb like glue.

quitus [kētüs] *nm* final discharge; **donner ~ à** to discharge.

qui-vive [kēvēv] *nm inv*: **être sur le ~** to be

on the alert.

quoi [kwá] *pronom* (*interrogatif*) what; ~ **de
neuf** *ou* **de nouveau?** what's new *ou* the
news?; **as-tu de** ~ **écrire?** have you anything
to write with?; **il n'a pas de** ~ **se l'acheter**
he can't afford it, he hasn't got the money to
buy it; **il y a de** ~ **être fier** that's something
to be proud of; **"il n'y a pas de** ~**"** "(please)
don't mention it", "not at all"; ~ **qu'il arrive**
whatever happens; ~ **qu'il en soit** be that as
it may; ~ **que ce soit** anything at all; **en** ~
puis-je vous aider? how can I help you?; **à** ~
bon? what's the use *ou* point?; **et puis** ~
encore! what(ever) next!; ~ **faire?** what's to
be done?; **sans** ~ (*ou sinon*) otherwise.
quoique [kwák(ə)] *cj* (al)though.
quolibet [kolēbe] *nm* gibe, jeer.
quorum [korom] *nm* quorum.
quota [kwotá] *nm* quota.
quote-part [kotpár] *nf* share.
quotidien, ne [kotēdyań, -en] *a* (*journalier*)
daily; (*banal*) ordinary, everyday ♦ *nm*
(*journal*) daily (paper); (*vie quotidienne*)
daily life, day-to-day existence; **les grands**
~**s** the big (national) dailies.
quotidiennement [kotēdyenmáń] *ad* daily,
every day.
quotient [kosyáń] *nm* (MATH) quotient; ~
intellectuel (QI) intelligence quotient (IQ).
quotité [kotētá] *nf* (FINANCE) quota.

R

R, r [er] *nm inv* R, r ♦ *abr* = **route, rue; R
comme Raoul** R for Roger.
rab [ráb] (*fam*), **rabiot** [rábyō] *nm* extra, more.
rabâcher [rábáshā] *vi* to harp on ♦ *vt* keep on
repeating.
rabais [rábe] *nm* reduction, discount; **au** ~ at
a reduction *ou* discount.
rabaisser [rábāsā] *vt* (*rabattre*) to reduce;
(*dénigrer*) to belittle.
rabane [rábán] *nf* raffia (matting).
Rabat [rábá(t)] *n* Rabat.
rabat [rábá] *vb voir* **rabattre** ♦ *nm* flap.
rabat-joie [rábázhwá] *nm/f inv* killjoy, spoilsport.
rabatteur, euse [rábátœr, -œz] *nm/f* (*de
gibier*) beater; (*péj*) tout.
rabattre [rábátr(ə)] *vt* (*couvercle, siège*) to
pull down; (*col*) to turn down; (*couture*) to
stitch down; (*gibier*) to drive; (*somme d'un
prix*) to deduct, take off; (*orgueil, prétentions*) to humble; (TRICOT) to decrease; **se** ~
vi (*bords, couvercle*) to fall shut; (*véhicule,
coureur*) to cut in; **se** ~ **sur** (*accepter*) to
fall back on.
rabattu, e [rábátü] *pp de* **rabattre** ♦ *a* turned
down.
rabbin [rábáń] *nm* rabbi.
rabique [rábēk] *a* rabies *cpd*.
râble [rábl(ə)] *nm* back; (CULIN) saddle.

râblé, e [ráblā] *a* broad-backed, stocky.
rabot [rábō] *nm* plane.
raboter [rábotā] *vt* to plane (down).
raboteux, euse [rábotœ, -œz] *a* uneven, rough.
rabougri, e [rábōōgrē] *a* stunted.
rabrouer [rábrōōā] *vt* to snub, rebuff.
racaille [rákáy] *nf* (*péj*) rabble, riffraff.
raccommodage [rákomodázh] *nm* mending *q*,
repairing *q*; darning *q*.
raccommoder [rákomodā] *vt* to mend, repair;
(*chaussette etc*) to darn; (*fam: réconcilier:
amis, ménage*) to bring together again; **se** ~
(**avec**) (*fam*) to patch it up (with).
raccompagner [rákôńpáńyā] *vt* to take *ou* see
back.
raccord [rákor] *nm* link; ~ **de maçonnerie**
pointing *q*; ~ **de peinture** join; touch-up.
raccordement [rákordəmáń] *nm* joining up;
connection.
raccorder [rákordā] *vt* to join (up), link up;
(*suj: pont etc*) to connect, link; **se** ~ **à** to
join up with; (*fig: se rattacher à*) to tie in
with; ~ **au réseau du téléphone** to connect
to the telephone service.
raccourci [rákōōrsē] *nm* short cut; **en** ~ in
brief.
raccourcir [rákōōrsēr] *vt* to shorten ♦ *vi* (*vêtement*) to shrink.
raccroc [rákrō] : **par** ~ *ad* by chance.
raccrocher [rákroshā] *vt* (*tableau, vêtement*)
to hang back up; (*récepteur*) to put down;
(*fig: affaire*) to save ♦ *vi* (TÉL) to hang up;
se ~ **à** *vt* to cling to, hang on to; **ne raccrochez pas** (TÉL) hold on, don't hang up.
race [rás] *nf* race; (*d'animaux, fig: espèce*)
breed; (*ascendance, origine*) stock, race; **de**
~ *a* purebred, pedigree.
racé, e [rásā] *a* thoroughbred.
rachat [ráshá] *nm* buying; buying back; redemption; atonement.
racheter [ràshtā] *vt* (*article perdu*) to buy
another; (*davantage*): ~ **du lait/3 œufs** to
buy more milk/another 3 eggs *ou* 3 more
eggs; (*après avoir vendu*) to buy back;
(*d'occasion*) to buy; (COMM: *part, firme*) to
buy up; (: *pension, rente*) to redeem; (REL:
pécheur) to redeem; (: *péché*) to atone for,
expiate; (*mauvaise conduite, oubli, défaut*) to
make up for; **se** ~ (REL) to redeem o.s.;
(*gén*) to make amends, make up for it.
rachidien, ne [ráshēdyań, -en] *a* rachidian, of
the spine.
rachitique [ráshētēk] *a* suffering from rickets;
(*fig*) scraggy, scrawny.
rachitisme [ráshētēsm(ə)] *nm* rickets *sg*.
racial, e, aux [rásyál, -ō] *a* racial.
racine [rásēn] *nf* root; (*fig: attache*) roots *pl*;
~ **carrée/cubique** square/cube root; **prendre**
~ (*fig*) to take root; to put down roots.
racisme [rásēsm(ə)] *nm* racism, racialism.
raciste [rásēst(ə)] *a, nm/f* racist, racialist.
racket [ráket] *nm* racketeering *q*.
racketteur [ráketœr] *nm* racketeer.
raclée [ráklā] *nf* (*fam*) hiding, thrashing.
raclement [ráklə máń] *nm* (*bruit*) scraping
(noise).
racler [ráklā] *vt* (*os, plat*) to scrape; (*tache,
boue*) to scrape off; (*fig: instrument*) to
scrape on; (*suj: chose: frotter contre*) to

scrape (against).

raclette [råklɛt] *nf* (*CULIN*) raclette (*Swiss cheese dish*).

racloir [råklwår] *nm* (*outil*) scraper.

racolage [råkolázh] *nm* soliciting; touting.

racoler [råkolá] *vt* (*attirer: suj: prostituée*) to solicit; (: *parti, marchand*) to tout for; (*attraper*) to pick up.

racoleur, euse [råkolœr, -œ̄z] *a* (*péj: publicité*) cheap and alluring ♦ *nm* (*péj: de clients etc*) tout ♦ *nf* streetwalker.

racontars [råkôñtår] *nmpl* stories, gossip *sg*.

raconter [råkôñtá] *vt*: ~ **(à qn)** (*décrire*) to relate (to sb), tell (sb) about; (*dire*) to tell (sb).

racorni, e [råkornē] *a* hard(ened).

racornir [råkornēr] *vt* to harden.

radar [rådår] *nm* radar; **système** ~ radar system; **écran** ~ radar screen.

rade [råd] *nf* (natural) harbor (*US*) *ou* harbour (*Brit*); **en** ~ **de Toulon** in Toulon harbor; **rester en** ~ (*fig*) to be left stranded.

radeau, x [rådō] *nm* raft; ~ **de sauvetage** life raft.

radial, e, aux [rådyál, -ō] *a* radial; **pneu à carcasse** ~**e** radial tire (*US*) *ou* tyre (*Brit*).

radiant, e [rådyâñ, -âñt] *a* radiant.

radiateur [rådyátœr] *nm* radiator, heater (*AUTO*) radiator; ~ **électrique/à gaz** electric/gas heater.

radiation [rådyåsyôñ] *nf* (*voir radier*) striking off *q*; (*PHYSIQUE*) radiation.

radical, e, aux [rådēkál, -ō] *a* radical ♦ *nm* (*LING*) stem; (*MATH*) root sign; (*POL*) radical.

radicalement [rådēkálmâñ] *ad* radically, completely.

radicaliser [rådēkálēzá] *vt* (*durcir: opinions etc*) to harden; **se** ~ *vi* (*mouvement etc*) to become more radical.

radicalisme [rådēkálēsm(ə)] *nm* (*POL*) radical-ism.

radier [rådyá] *vt* to strike off.

radiesthésie [rådyestázē] *nf* divination (by radiation).

radiesthésiste [rådyestázēst(ə)] *nm/f* diviner.

radieux, euse [rådyœ̄, -œ̄z] *a* (*visage, personne*) radiant; (*journée, soleil*) brilliant, glorious.

radin, e [rådañ, -ēn] *a* (*fam*) stingy.

radio [rådyō] *nf* radio; (*MÉD*) X-ray ♦ *nm* (*personne*) radio operator; **à la** ~ on the radio; **avoir la** ~ to have a radio; **passer à la** ~ to be on the radio; **se faire faire une** ~**/une** ~ **des poumons** to have an X-ray/a chest X-ray.

radio... [rådyo] *préfixe* radio....

radioactif, ive [rådyoáktēf, -ēv] *a* radioactive.

radioactivité [rådyoáktēvētá] *nf* radioactivity.

radioamateur [rådyoámátœr] *nm* (radio) ham.

radiobalise [rådyobálēz] *nf* radio beacon.

radiocassette [rådyokásɛt] *nf* cassette radio.

radiodiffuser [rådyodēfüzá] *vt* to broadcast.

radiodiffusion [rådyodēfüzyôñ] *nf* (radio) broadcasting.

radioélectrique [rådyoálektrēk] *a* radio *cpd*.

radiogoniomètre [rådyogonyometr(ə)] *nm* direction finder, radiogoniometer.

radiographie [rådyográfē] *nf* radiography;

(*photo*) X-ray photograph, radiograph.

radiographier [rådyográfyá] *vt* to X-ray; **se faire** ~ to have an X-ray.

radioguidage [rådyogēdázh] *nm* (*NAVIG, AVIAT*) radio control; (*AUTO*) (broadcast of) traffic information.

radioguider [rådyogēdá] *vt* (*NAVIG, AVIAT*) to guide by radio, control by radio.

radiologie [rådyolozhē] *nf* radiology.

radiologique [rådyolozhēk] *a* radiological.

radiologue [rådyolog] *nm/f* radiologist.

radionavigant [rådyonávēgáñ] *nm* radio of-ficer.

radiophare [rådyofår] *nm* radio beacon.

radiophonique [rådyofonēk] *a*: **programme/émission/jeu** ~ radio program (*US*) *ou* pro-gramme (*Brit*)/broadcast/game.

radioreportage [rådyorəportázh] *nm* radio re-port.

radio(-)réveil [rådyorávey] *nm* clock radio.

radioscopie [rådyoskopē] *nf* radioscopy.

radio-taxi [rådyotáksē] *nm* radiotaxi.

radiotélégraphie [rådyotálágráfē] *nf* radiotelegraphy.

radiotéléphone [rådyotáláfon] *nm* radiotele-phone.

radiotélescope [rådyotáleskop] *nm* radiotele-scope.

radiotélévisé, e [rådyotálávēzá] *a* broadcast on radio and television.

radiothérapie [rådyotárápē] *nf* radiotherapy.

radis [rådē] *nm* radish; ~ **noir** horseradish *q*.

radium [rådyom] *nm* radium.

radoter [rådotá] *vi* to ramble on.

radoub [rådōō] *nm*: **bassin** *ou* **cale de** ~ dry dock.

radouber [rådōōbá] *vt* to repair, refit.

radoucir [rådōōsēr]: **se** ~ *vi* (*se réchauffer*) to become milder; (*se calmer*) to calm down; to soften.

radoucissement [rådōōsēsmâñ] *nm* milder period, better weather.

rafale [råfál] *nf* (*vent*) gust (of wind); (*de balles, d'applaudissements*) burst; ~ **de mi-trailleuse** burst of machine-gun fire.

raffermir [råfermēr] *vt*, **se** ~ *vi* (*tissus, muscle*) to firm up; (*fig*) to strengthen.

raffermissement [råfermēsmâñ] *nm* (*fig*) strengthening.

raffinage [råfēnázh] *nm* refining.

raffiné, e [råfēná] *a* refined.

raffinement [råfēnmâñ] *nm* refinement.

raffiner [råfēná] *vt* to refine.

raffinerie [råfēnrē] *nf* refinery.

raffoler [råfolá]: ~ **de** *vt* to be very fond of.

raffut [råfü] *nm* (*fam*) row, racket.

rafiot [råfyō] *nm* tub.

rafistoler [råfēstolá] *vt* (*fam*) to patch up.

rafle [råfl(ə)] *nf* (*de police*) roundup, raid.

rafler [råflá] *vt* (*fam*) to swipe.

rafraîchir [råfrāshēr] *vt* (*atmosphère, température*) to cool (down); (*aussi:* **mettre à** ~) to chill; (*suj: air, eau*) to freshen up; (: *boisson*) to refresh; (*fig: rénover*) to brighten up ♦ *vi*: **mettre du vin/une boisson à** ~ to chill wine/a drink; **se** ~ to grow cooler; to freshen up; (*personne: en buvant etc*) to re-fresh o.s.; ~ **la mémoire** *ou* **les idées à qn** to refresh sb's memory.

rafraîchissant, e [ráfrāshēsáń, -áńt] a refreshing.

rafraîchissement [ráfrāshēsmáń] nm cooling; (boisson) cool drink; ~s nmpl (boissons, fruits etc) refreshments.

ragaillardir [rágáyárdēr] vt (fam) to perk ou buck up.

rage [rázh] nf (MÉD): **la** ~ rabies; (fureur) rage, fury; **faire** ~ to rage; ~ **de dents** (raging) toothache.

rager [rázhā] vi to fume (with rage); **faire** ~ **qn** to enrage sb, get sb mad.

rageur, euse [rázhœr, -ēz] a snarling; ill-tempered.

raglan [rágláń] a inv raglan.

ragot [rágō] nm (fam) malicious gossip q.

ragoût [rágōō] nm (plat) stew.

ragoûtant, e [rágōōtáń, -áńt] a: **peu** ~ unpalatable.

rai [re] nm: **un** ~ **de soleil/lumière** a shaft of sunshine/light.

raid [red] nm (MIL) raid; (attaque aérienne) air raid; (SPORT) long-distance trek.

raide [red] a (tendu) taut, tight; (escarpé) steep; (droit: cheveux) straight; (ankylosé, dur, guindé) stiff; (fam: cher) steep, stiff; (: sans argent) flat broke; (osé, licencieux) daring ♦ ad (en pente) steeply; ~ **mort** stone dead.

raideur [redœr] nf steepness; stiffness.

raidir [rēdēr] vt (muscles) to stiffen; (câble) to pull taut, tighten; **se** ~ vi to stiffen; to become taut; (personne: se crisper) to tense up; (: devenir intransigeant) to harden.

raidissement [rēdēsmáń] nm stiffening; tightening; hardening.

raie [re] nf (ZOOL) skate, ray; (rayure) stripe; (des cheveux) part (US), parting (Brit).

raifort [refor] nm horseradish.

rail [ráy] nm (barre d'acier) rail; (chemins de fer) railroads pl (US), railways pl (Brit); **les** ~s (la voie ferrée) the rails, the track sg; **par** ~ by rail; ~ **conducteur** live ou conductor rail.

railler [ráyā] vt to scoff at, jeer at.

raillerie [ráyrē] nf mockery.

railleur, euse [ráyœr, -ēz] a mocking.

rail-route [ráyrōōt] nm road-rail.

rainurage [ránürázh] nm (AUTO) uneven road surface.

rainure [ránür] nf groove; slot.

rais [re] nm inv = **rai.**

raisin [rezáń] nm (aussi: ~s) grapes pl; (variété): ~ **blanc/noir** white (ou green)/black grape; ~ **muscat** muscat grape; ~s **secs** raisins.

raison [rezóń] nf reason; **avoir** ~ to be right; **donner** ~ **à qn** (personne) to agree with sb; (fait) to prove sb right; **avoir** ~ **de qn/qch** to get the better of sb/sth; **se faire une** ~ to learn to live with it; **perdre la** ~ to become insane; (fig) to take leave of one's senses; **recouvrer la** ~ to come to one's senses; **ramener qn à la** ~ to make sb see sense; **demander** ~ **à qn de** (affront etc) to demand satisfaction from sb for; **entendre** ~ to listen to reason, see reason; **plus que de** ~ too much, more than is reasonable; ~ **de plus** all the more reason; **à plus forte** ~ all the

more so; **en** ~ **de** (à cause de) because of; (à proportion de) in proportion to; **à** ~ **de** at the rate of; ~ **d'État** reason of state; ~ **d'être** raison d'être; ~ **sociale** corporate name.

raisonnable [rezonábl(ə)] a reasonable, sensible.

raisonnablement [rezonábləmáń] ad reasonably.

raisonné, e [rezoná] a reasoned.

raisonnement [rezonmáń] nm reasoning; arguing; argument.

raisonner [rezoná] vi (penser) to reason; (argumenter, discuter) to argue ♦ vt (personne) to reason with; (attitude: justifier) to reason out; **se** ~ to reason with oneself.

raisonneur, euse [rezonœr, -ēz] a (péj) quibbling.

rajeunir [rázhœnēr] vt (suj: coiffure, robe): ~ **qn** to make sb look younger; (suj: cure etc) to rejuvenate; (fig: rafraîchir) to brighten up; (: moderniser) to give a new look to; (: en recrutant) to inject new blood into ♦ vi (personne) to become (ou look) younger; (entreprise, quartier) to be modernized.

rajout [rázhōō] nm addition.

rajouter [rázhōōtā] vt (commentaire) to add; ~ **du sel/un œuf** to add some more salt/another egg; ~ **que** to add that; **en** ~ to lay it on thick.

rajustement [rázhüstəmáń] nm adjustment.

rajuster [rázhüstā] vt (vêtement) to straighten, tidy; (salaires) to adjust; (machine) to re-adjust; **se** ~ to tidy ou straighten o.s. up.

râle [rál] nm groan; ~ **d'agonie** death rattle.

ralenti [rálántē] nm: **au** ~ (AUTO): **tourner au** ~ to idle; (CINÉMA) in slow motion; (fig) at a slower pace.

ralentir [rálántēr] vt, vi, **se** ~ vi to slow down.

ralentissement [rálántēsmáń] nm slowing down.

râler [rálā] vi to groan; (fam) to grouse, moan (and groan).

ralliement [rálēmáń] nm (rassemblement) rallying; (adhésion: à une cause, une opinion) winning over; **point/signe de** ~ rallying point/sign.

rallier [rályā] vt (rassembler) to rally; (rejoindre) to rejoin; (gagner à sa cause) to win over; **se** ~ **à** (avis) to come over ou round to.

rallonge [rálóńzh] nf (de table) (extra) leaf (pl leaves); (argent etc) extra q; (ÉLEC) extension (cable); (fig: de crédit etc) extension.

rallonger [rálóńzhā] vt to lengthen.

rallumer [rálümā] vt to light up again, relight; (fig) to revive; **se** ~ vi (lumière) to come on again.

rallye [rálē] nm rally; (POL) march.

ramages [rámázh] nmpl (dessin) leaf pattern sg; (chants) songs.

ramassage [rámásázh] nm: ~ **scolaire** school bus service.

ramassé, e [rámásā] a (trapu) squat, stocky; (concis: expression etc) compact.

ramasse-miettes [rámásmyet] nm inv silent butler (US), table-tidy (Brit).

ramasse-monnaie [ràmásmone] *nm inv* change-tray.

ramasser [ràmâsē] *vt (objet tombé ou par terre, fam)* to pick up; *(recueillir)* to collect; *(récolter)* to gather; *(: pommes de terre)* to lift; **se ~** *vi (sur soi-même)* to huddle up; to crouch.

ramasseur, euse [ràmâsœr, -ēz] *nm/f:* **~ de balles** ballboy/girl.

ramassis [ràmâsē] *nm (péj: de gens)* bunch; *(: de choses)* jumble.

rambarde [ràñbárd(ə)] *nf* guardrail.

rame [ràm] *nf (aviron)* oar; *(de métro)* train; *(de papier)* ream; **~ de haricots** bean support; **faire force de ~s** to row hard.

rameau, x [ràmō] *nm* (small) branch; *(fig)* branch; **les R~x** *(REL)* Palm Sunday *sg.*

ramener [ràmnā] *vt* to bring back; *(reconduire)* to take back; *(rabattre: couverture, visière):* **~ qch sur** to pull sth back over; **~ qch à** *(réduire à, aussi MATH)* to reduce sth to; **~ qn à la vie/raison** to bring sb back to life/bring sb to his *(ou* her*)* senses; **se ~** *vi (fam)* to roll *ou* turn up; **se ~ à** *(se réduire à)* to come *ou* boil down to.

ramequin [ràmkàñ] *nm* ramekin.

ramer [ràmā] *vi* to row.

rameur, euse [ràmœr, -ēz] *nm/f* rower.

rameuter [ràmœtā] *vt* to gather together.

ramier [ràmyā] *nm:* **(pigeon) ~** woodpigeon.

ramification [ràmēfēkâsyôñ] *nf* ramification.

ramifier [ràmēfyā]: **se ~** *vi (tige, secte, réseau):* **se ~ (en)** to branch out (into); *(veines, nerfs)* to ramify.

ramolli, e [ràmolē] *a* soft.

ramollir [ràmolēr] *vt* to soften; **se ~** *vi (os, tissus)* to get *(ou* go*)* soft; *(beurre, asphalte)* to soften.

ramonage [ràmonàzh] *nm* (chimney-) sweeping.

ramoner [ràmonā] *vt (cheminée)* to sweep; *(pipe)* to clean.

ramoneur [ràmonœr] *nm* (chimney) sweep.

rampe [ràñp] *nf (d'escalier)* banister(s *pl*); *(dans un garage, d'un terrain)* ramp; *(THÉÂTRE):* **la ~** the footlights *pl*; *(lampes: lumineuse, de balisage)* floodlights *pl*; **passer la ~** *(toucher le public)* to get across to the audience; **~ de lancement** launching pad.

ramper [ràñpā] *vi (reptile, animal)* to crawl; *(plante)* to creep.

rancard [ràñkár] *nm (fam)* date; tip.

rancart [ràñkár] *nm:* **mettre au ~** *(article, projet)* to scrap; *(personne)* to put on the scrapheap.

rance [ràñs] *a* rancid.

rancir [ràñsēr] *vi* to go off, go rancid.

rancœur [ràñkœr] *nf* rancor *(US)*, rancour *(Brit)*, resentment.

rançon [ràñsôñ] *nf* ransom; *(fig):* **la ~ du succès** *etc* the price of success *etc.*

rançonner [ràñsonā] *vt* to hold for *(US)* ou to ransom *(Brit)*.

rancune [ràñkün] *nf* grudge, rancor *(US)*, rancour *(Brit)*; **garder ~ à qn (de qch)** to bear sb a grudge (for sth); **sans ~!** no hard feelings!

rancunier, ière [ràñkünyā, -yer] *a* vindictive, spiteful.

randonnée [ràñdonā] *nf* ride; *(à pied)* walk, ramble; hike, hiking *q.*

randonneur, euse [ràñdonœr, -ēz] *nm/f* hiker.

rang [ràñ] *nm (rangée)* row; *(de perles)* row, string, rope; *(grade, condition sociale, classement)* rank; **~s** *nmpl (MIL)* ranks; **se mettre en ~s/sur un ~** to get into *ou* form rows/a line; **sur 3 ~s** (lined up) 3 deep; **se mettre en ~s par 4** to form rows of 4; **se mettre sur les ~s** *(fig)* to get into the running; **au premier ~** in the first row; *(fig)* ranking first; **rentrer dans le ~** to get into line; **au ~ de** *(au nombre de)* among (the ranks of); **avoir ~ de** to hold the rank of.

rangé, e [ràñzhā] *a (sérieux)* orderly, steady.

rangée [ràñzhā] *nf* row.

rangement [ràñzhmàñ] *nm* tidying-up, putting-away; **faire des ~s** to tidy up.

ranger [ràñzhā] *vt (classer, grouper)* to order, arrange; *(mettre à sa place)* to put away; *(voiture dans la rue)* to park; *(mettre de l'ordre dans)* to tidy up; *(arranger, disposer: en cercle etc)* to arrange; *(fig: classer):* **~ qn/qch parmi** to rank sb/sth among; **se ~** *vi (se placer, se disposer: autour d'une table etc)* to take one's place, sit around; *(véhicule, conducteur: s'écarter)* to pull over; *(: s'arrêter)* to pull in; *(piéton)* to step aside; *(s'assagir)* to settle down; **se ~ à** *(avis)* to come around to, fall in with.

ranimer [rànēmā] *vt (personne évanouie)* to bring around *(US)* ou round *(Brit)*; *(revigorer: forces, courage)* to restore; *(réconforter: troupes etc)* to kindle new life in; *(douleur, souvenir)* to revive; *(feu)* to rekindle.

rapace [ràpás] *nm* bird of prey ♦ *a (péj)* rapacious, grasping; **~ diurne/nocturne** diurnal/nocturnal bird of prey.

rapatrié, e [ràpátrēyā] *nm/f* repatriate *(esp French North African settler)*.

rapatriement [ràpátrēmàñ] *nm* repatriation.

rapatrier [ràpátrēyā] *vt* to repatriate; *(capitaux)* to bring (back) into the country.

râpe [ràp] *nf (CULIN)* grater; *(à bois)* rasp.

râpé, e [ràpā] *a (tissu)* threadbare; *(CULIN)* grated.

râper [ràpā] *vt (CULIN)* to grate; *(gratter, râcler)* to rasp.

rapetasser [ràptàsā] *vt (fam)* to patch up.

rapetisser [ràptēsā] *vt:* **~ qch** to shorten sth; to make sth look smaller ♦ *vi,* **se ~** *vi* to shrink.

râpeux, euse [ràpœ, -ēz] *a* rough.

raphia [ràfyá] *nm* raffia.

rapide [ràpēd] *a* fast; *(prompt)* quick; *(intelligence)* quick ♦ *nm* express (train); *(de cours d'eau)* rapid.

rapidement [ràpēdmàñ] *ad* fast; quickly.

rapidité [ràpēdētā] *nf* speed; quickness.

rapiécer [ràpyàsā] *vt* to patch.

rappel [ràpel] *nm (d'un ambassadeur, MIL)* recall; *(THÉÂTRE)* curtain call; *(MÉD: vaccination)* booster; *(ADMIN: de salaire)* back pay *q*; *(d'une aventure, d'un nom)* reminder; *(de limitation de vitesse: sur écriteau)* speed limit sign *(reminder)*; *(TECH)* return; *(ALPINISME: aussi:* **~ de corde)** rappelling *q (US)*; rappel *(US)*; abseiling *q (Brit)*; abseil

(*Brit*); ~ **à l'ordre** call to order.

rappeler [ràplā] *vt* (*pour faire revenir, retéléphoner*) to call back; (*ambassadeur, MIL, INFORM*) to recall; (*acteur*) to call back (onto the stage); (*faire se souvenir*): ~ **qch à qn** to remind sb of sth; **se ~** *vt* (*se souvenir de*) to remember, recall; ~ **qn à la vie** to bring sb back to life; ~ **qn à la décence** to recall sb to a sense of decency; **ça rappelle la Provence** it's reminiscent of Provence, it reminds you of Provence; **se ~ que** ... to remember that ....

rappelle [ràpel] *etc vb voir* **rappeler**.

rappliquer [ràplēkā] *vi* (*fam*) to turn up.

rapport [ràpor] *nm* (*compte rendu*) report; (*profit*) yield, return; revenue; (*lien, analogie*) relationship; (*corrélation*) connection; (*proportion*: MATH, TECH) ratio (*pl* -s); **~s** *nmpl* (*entre personnes, pays*) relations; **avoir ~ à** to have something to do with, concern; **être en ~ avec** (*idée de corrélation*) to be related to; **être/se mettre en ~ avec qn** to be/get in touch with sb; **par ~ à** (*comparé à*) in relation to; (*à propos de*) with regard to; **sous le ~ de** from the point of view of; **sous tous (les) ~s** in all respects; **~s (sexuels)** (sexual) intercourse *sg*; ~ **qualité-prix** value (for money).

rapporté, e [ràportā] *a*: **pièce ~e** (*COUTURE*) patch.

rapporter [ràportā] *vt* (*rendre, ramener*) to bring back; (*apporter davantage*) to bring more; (*COUTURE*) to sew on; (*suj: investissement*) to yield; (*: activité*) to bring in; (*relater*) to report; (*JUR: annuler*) to revoke ♦ *vi* (*investissement*) to give a good return *ou* yield; (*activité*) to be very profitable; (*péj: moucharder*) to tell; ~ **qch à** (*fig: rattacher*) to relate sth to; **se ~ à** (*correspondre à*) to relate to; **s'en ~ à** to rely on.

rapporteur, euse [ràportœr, -ēz] *nm/f* (*de procès, commission*) reporter; (*péj*) telltale ♦ *nm* (*GÉOM*) protractor.

rapproché, e [ràproshā] *a* (*proche*) near, close at hand; **~s** (*l'un de l'autre*) at close intervals.

rapprochement [ràproshmâṅ] *nm* (*réconciliation: de nations, familles*) reconciliation; (*analogie, rapport*) parallel.

rapprocher [ràproshā] *vt* (*chaise d'une table*): ~ **qch (de)** to bring sth closer (to); (*deux objets*) to bring closer together; (*réunir*) to bring together; (*comparer*) to establish a parallel between; **se ~** *vi* to draw closer *ou* nearer; (*fig: familles, pays*) to come together; to come closer together; **se ~ de** to come closer to; (*présenter une analogie avec*) to be close to.

rapt [ràpt] *nm* abduction.

raquette [ràket] *nf* (*de tennis*) racket; (*de ping-pong*) paddle (*US*), racket (*US*), bat (*Brit*); (*à neige*) snowshoe.

rare [ràr] *a* rare; (*main-d'œuvre, denrées*) scarce; (*cheveux, herbe*) sparse; **il est ~ que** it's rare that, it's unusual that; **se faire ~** to become scarce; (*fig: personne*) to make oneself scarce.

raréfaction [ràrāfáksyôṅ] *nf* scarcity; (*de l'air*) rarefaction.

(*air*) to rarefy.

rarement [ràrmâṅ] *ad* rarely, seldom.

rareté [ràrtā] *nf* (*voir rare*) rarity; scarcity.

rarissime [ràrēsēm] *a* extremely rare.

RAS *abr* = *rien à signaler*.

ras, e [rá, ráz] *a* (*tête, cheveux*) close-cropped; (*poil, herbe*) short; (*mesure, cuillère*) level ♦ *ad* short; **faire table ~e** to make a clean sweep; **en ~e campagne** in open country; **à ~ bords** to the brim; **au ~ de** level with; **en avoir ~ le bol** (*fam*) to be fed up; ~ **du cou** *a* (*pull, robe*) crew-neck.

rasade [ràzàd] *nf* glassful.

rascasse [ràskàs] *nf* (*ZOOL*) scorpion fish.

rasé, e [ràzā] *a*: ~ **de frais** freshly shaven; ~ **de près** close-shaven.

rase-mottes [ràzmot] *nm inv*: **faire du ~** to hedgehop; **vol en ~** hedgehopping.

raser [ràzā] *vt* (*barbe, cheveux*) to shave off; (*menton, personne*) to shave; (*fam: ennuyer*) to bore; (*démolir*) to raze (to the ground); (*frôler*) to graze, skim; **se ~** to shave; (*fam*) to be bored (to tears).

rasoir [ràzwàr] *nm* razor; ~ **électrique** electric shaver *ou* razor; ~ **mécanique** *ou* **de sûreté** safety razor.

rassasier [ràsázyā] *vt* to satisfy; **être rassasié** (*dégoûté*) to be sated; to have had more than enough.

rassemblement [ràsâṅbləmâṅ] *nm* (*groupe*) gathering; (*POL*) union; association; (*MIL*): **le ~** parade.

rassembler [ràsâṅblā] *vt* (*réunir*) to assemble, gather; (*regrouper, amasser*) to gather together, collect; **se ~** *vi* to gather; ~ **ses idées/ses esprits/son courage** to collect one's thoughts/gather one's wits/screw up one's courage.

rasseoir [ràswàr]: **se ~** *vi* to sit down again.

rasséréner [ràsārānā] *vt*: **se ~** *vi* to recover one's serenity.

rassir [ràsēr] *vi* to go stale.

rassis, e [ràsē, -ēz] *a* (*pain*) stale.

rassurant, e [ràsüràṅ, -âṅt] *a* (*nouvelles etc*) reassuring.

rassuré, e [ràsürā] *a*: **ne pas être très ~** to be rather ill at ease.

rassurer [ràsürā] *vt* to reassure; **se ~** to be reassured; **rassure-toi** don't worry.

rat [rà] *nm* rat; ~ **d'hôtel** hotel thief (*pl* thieves); ~ **musqué** muskrat.

ratatiné, e [ràtátēnā] *a* shrivelled (up), wrinkled.

ratatiner [ràtátēnā] *vt* to shrivel; (*peau*) to wrinkle; **se ~** *vi* to shrivel; to become wrinkled.

ratatouille [ràtátōōy] *nf* (*CULIN*) ratatouille.

rate [ràt] *nf* female rat; (*ANAT*) spleen.

raté, e [ràtā] *a* (*tentative*) unsuccessful, failed ♦ *nm/f* failure ♦ *nm* misfiring *q*.

râteau, x [ràtō] *nm* rake.

râtelier [ràtəlyā] *nm* rack; (*fam*) false teeth *pl*.

rater [ràtā] *vi* (*ne pas partir: coup de feu*) to fail to go off; (*affaire, projet etc*) to go wrong, fail ♦ *vt* (*cible, train, occasion*) to miss; (*démonstration, plat*) to spoil; (*examen*) to fail; ~ **son coup** to fail, not to bring it off.

raticide [rátēsēd] *nm* rat poison.
ratification [rátēfēkâsyóñ] *nf* ratification.
ratifier [rátēfyā] *vt* to ratify.
ratio [rásyō] *nm* ratio (*pl* -s).
ration [râsyóñ] *nf* ration; (*fig*) share; ~ **alimentaire** food intake.
rationalisation [rásyonálēzâsyóñ] *nf* rationalization.
rationaliser [rásyonálēzā] *vt* to rationalize.
rationellement [rásyonelmáñ] *ad* rationally.
rationnel, le [rásyonel] *a* rational.
rationnement [rásyonmáñ] *nm* rationing; **ticket de** ~ ration coupon.
rationner [rásyonā] *vt* to ration; (*personne*) to put on rations; **se** ~ to ration o.s.
ratisser [rátēsā] *vt* (*allée*) to rake; (*feuiller*) to rake up; (*suj: armée, police*) to comb; ~ **large** to cast one's nets wide.
raton [rátóñ] *nm*: ~ **laveur** raccoon.
RATP *sigle f* (= *Régie autonome des transports parisiens*) Paris transport authority.
rattacher [rátáshā] *vt* (*animal, cheveux*) to tie up again; (*incorporer*: ADMIN *etc*): ~ **qch à** to join sth to, unite sth with; (*fig: relier*): ~ **qch à** to link sth with, relate sth to; (: *lier*): ~ **qn à** to bind *ou* tie sb to; **se** ~ **à** (*fig: avoir un lien avec*) to be linked (*ou* connected) with.
rattrapage [rátrápázh] *nm* (SCOL) remedial classes *pl*; (ÉCON) catching up.
rattraper [rátrápā] *vt* (*fugitif*) to recapture; (*retenir, empêcher de tomber*) to catch (hold of); (*atteindre, rejoindre*) to catch up with; (*réparer: imprudence, erreur*) to make up for; **se** ~ *vi* (*regagner: du temps*) to make up for lost time; (: *de l'argent etc*) to make good one's losses; (*réparer une gaffe etc*) to make up for it; **se** ~ **(à)** (*se raccrocher*) to stop o.s. falling (by catching hold of); ~ **son retard/le temps perdu** to make up (for) lost time.
rature [rátür] *nf* deletion, erasure.
raturer [rátürā] *vt* to cross out, delete, erase.
rauque [rōk] *a* raucous; hoarse.
ravagé, e [rávázhā] *a* (*visage*) harrowed.
ravager [rávázhā] *vt* to devastate, ravage.
ravages [rávázh] *nmpl* ravages; **faire des** ~ to wreak havoc; (*fig: séducteur*) to break hearts.
ravalement [ráválmáñ] *nm* restoration.
ravaler [ráválā] *vt* (*mur, façade*) to restore; (*déprécier*) to lower; (*avaler de nouveau*) to swallow again; ~ **sa colère/son dégoût** to stifle one's anger/distaste.
ravaudage [rávōdázh] *nm* repairing, mending.
ravauder [rávōdā] *vt* to repair, mend.
rave [ráv] *nf* (BOT) rape.
ravi, e [rávē] *a* delighted; **être** ~ **de/que** to be delighted with/that.
ravier [rávyā] *nm* hors d'œuvre dish.
ravigote [rávēgot] *a*: **sauce** ~ *oil and vinegar dressing with shallots*.
ravigoter [rávēgotā] *vt* (*fam*) to buck up.
ravin [ráváñ] *nm* gully, ravine.
raviner [rávēnā] *vt* to furrow, gully.
ravir [rávēr] *vt* (*enchanter*) to delight; (*enlever*): ~ **qch à qn** to rob sb of sth; **à** ~ *ad* delightfully, beautifully; **être beau à** ~ to be

ravishingly beautiful.
raviser [rávēzā]: **se** ~ *vi* to change one's mind.
ravissant, e [rávēsáñ, -áñt] *a* delightful.
ravissement [rávēsmáñ] *nm* (*enchantement, délice*) rapture.
ravisseur, euse [rávēsœr, -ēz] *nm/f* abductor, kidnapper.
ravitaillement [rávētáymáñ] *nm* resupplying; refuelling; (*provisions*) supplies *pl*; **aller au** ~ to go for fresh supplies; ~ **en vol** (AVIAT) in-flight refuelling.
ravitailler [rávētáyā] *vt* to resupply; (*véhicule*) to refuel; **se** ~ *vi* to get fresh supplies.
raviver [rávēvā] *vt* (*feu, douleur*) to revive; (*couleurs*) to brighten up.
ravoir [rávwár] *vt* to get back.
rayé, e [rāyā] *a* (*à rayures*) striped; (*éraflé*) scratched.
rayer [rāyā] *vt* (*érafler*) to scratch; (*barrer*) to cross *ou* score out; (*d'une liste: radier*) to cross *ou* strike off.
rayon [reyóñ] *nm* (*de soleil etc*) ray; (GÉOM) radius; (*de roue*) spoke; (*étagère*) shelf (*pl* shelves); (*de grand magasin*) department; (*fig: domaine*) responsibility, concern; (*de ruche*) (honey)comb; **dans un** ~ **de** within a radius of; ~**s** *nmpl* (*radiothérapie*) radiation; ~ **d'action** range; ~ **de braquage** (AUTO) turning radius; ~ **laser** laser beam; ~ **de soleil** sunbeam, ray of sunshine; ~**s X** X-rays.
rayonnage [reyonázh] *nm* set of shelves.
rayonnant, e [reyonáñ, -áñt] *a* radiant.
rayonne [reyon] *nf* rayon.
rayonnement [reyonmáñ] *nm* radiation; (*fig: éclat*) radiance; (: *influence*) influence.
rayonner [reyonā] *vi* (*chaleur, énergie*) to radiate; (*fig: émotion*) to shine forth; (: *visage*) to be radiant; (*avenues, axes etc*) to radiate; (*touriste*) to go touring (*from one base*).
rayure [rāyür] *nf* (*motif*) stripe; (*éraflure*) scratch; (*rainure, d'un fusil*) groove; **à** ~**s** striped.
raz-de-marée [rádmárā] *nm inv* tidal wave.
razzia [rázyá] *nf* raid, foray.
RBE *sigle m* (= *revenu brut d'exploitation*) gross profit (*of a farm*).
R-D *sigle f* (= *Recherche-Développement*) R & D.
RDA *sigle f* (= *République démocratique allemande*) GDR.
RDB *sigle m* (STATISTIQUES: = *revenu disponible brut*) total income (*of a family etc*).
RdC. *abr* = **rez-de-chaussée**.
ré [rā] *nm* (MUS) D; (*en chantant la gamme*) re.
réabonnement [rāäbonmáñ] *nm* renewal of subscription.
réabonner [rāäbonā] *vt*: ~ **qn à** to renew sb's subscription to; **se** ~ **(à)** to renew one's subscription (to).
réac [rāäk] *a*, *nm/f* (*fam*: = *réactionnaire*) reactionary.
réacteur [rāäktœr] *nm* jet engine; ~ **nucléaire** nuclear reactor.
réactif [rāäktēf] *nm* reagent.
réaction [rāäksyóñ] *nf* reaction; **par** ~ jet-propelled; **avion/moteur à** ~ jet (plane)/jet

engine; ~ **en chaîne** chain reaction.

réactionnaire [rǎǎksyoner] *a, nm/f* reactionary.

réadaptation [rǎǎdáptâsyôṅ] *nf* readjustment, rehabilitation.

réadapter [rǎǎdàptā] *vt* to readjust; (*MÉD*) to rehabilitate; **se ~ (à)** to readjust (to).

réaffirmer [rǎǎfěrmā] *vt* to reaffirm, reassert.

réagir [rǎǎzhěr] *vi* to react.

réajuster [rǎǎzhüstā] *vt* = **rajuster.**

réalisable [rǎǎlēzábl(ə)] *a* (*projet, plan*) feasible; (*COMM: valeur*) realizable.

réalisateur, trice [rǎǎlēzàtœr, -trēs] *nm/f* (*TV, CINÉMA*) director.

réalisation [rǎǎlēzâsyôṅ] *nf* carrying out; realization; fulfillment (*US*), fulfilment (*Brit*); achievement; production; (*œuvre*) production, work; (*création*) creation.

réaliser [rǎǎlēzā] *vt* (*projet, opération*) to carry out, realize; (*rêve, souhait*) to realize, fulfill (*US*), fulfil (*Brit*); (*exploit*) to achieve; (*achat, vente*) to make; (*film*) to produce; (*se rendre compte de, COMM: bien, capital*) to realize; **se ~** *vi* to be realized.

réalisme [rǎǎlēsm(ə)] *nm* realism.

realiste [rǎǎlēst(ə)] *a* realistic; (*peintre, roman*) realist ♦ *nm/f* realist.

réalité [rǎǎlētā] *nf* reality; **en ~** in (actual) fact; **dans la ~** in reality.

réanimation [rǎǎnēmâsyôṅ] *nf* resuscitation; **service de ~** intensive care unit.

réanimer [rǎǎnēmā] *vt* (*MÉD*) to resuscitate.

réapparaître [rǎápárétr(ə)] *vi* to reappear.

réapparition [rǎápárēsyôṅ] *nf* reappearance.

réarmer [rǎǎrmā] *vt* (*arme*) to reload ♦ *vi* (*état*) to rearm.

réassortiment [rǎásortēmáṅ] *nm* (*COMM*) restocking.

réassortir [rǎásortēr] *vt* to match up.

réassurance [rǎásüráńs] *nf* reinsurance.

rébarbatif, ive [rābárbátēf, -ēv] *a* forbidding; (*style*) crabbed.

rebattre [rəbátr(ə)] *vt*: ~ **les oreilles à qn de qch** to keep harping on (about (*Brit*)) sth to sb.

rebattu, e [rəbátü] *pp de* **rebattre** ♦ *a* hackneyed.

rebelle [rəbel] *nm/f* rebel ♦ *a* (*troupes*) rebel; (*enfant*) rebellious; (*mèche etc*) unruly; ~ **à qch** unamenable to sth; ~ **à faire** unwilling to do.

rebeller [rəbālā]: **se ~** *vi* to rebel.

rébellion [rābālyôṅ] *nf* rebellion; (*rebelles*) rebel forces *pl*.

reboiser [rəbwázā] *vt* to replant with trees, reforest.

rebond [rəbôṅ] *nm* (*voir rebondir*) bounce; rebound.

rebondi, e [rəbôṅdē] *a* (*ventre*) rounded; (*joues*) chubby, well-rounded.

rebondir [rəbôṅdēr] *vi* (*ballon: au sol*) to bounce; (*: contre un mur*) to rebound; (*fig: procès, action, conversation*) to get moving again, be suddenly revived.

rebondissement [rəbôṅdēsmáṅ] *nm* new development.

rebord [rəbor] *nm* edge.

reboucher [rəbōōshā] *vt* (*flacon*) to put the stopper (*ou* top) back on, recork; (*trou*) to stop up.

rebours [rəbōōr]: **à ~** *ad* the wrong way.

rebouteux, euse [rəbōōtœ, -œz] *nm/f* (*péj*) bonesetter.

reboutonner [rəbōōtonā] *vt* (*vêtement*) to button up (again).

rebrousse-poil [rəbrōōspwál]: **à ~** *ad* the wrong way.

rebrousser [rəbrōōsā] *vt* (*cheveux, poils*) to brush back, brush up; ~ **chemin** to turn back.

rebuffade [rəbüfád] *nf* rebuff.

rébus [rābüs] *nm inv* (*jeu d'esprit*) rebus; (*fig*) puzzle.

rebut [rəbü] *nm*: **mettre au ~** to scrap, discard.

rebutant, e [rəbütâṅ, -âṅt] *a* (*travail, démarche*) disagreeable.

rebuter [rəbütā] *vt* to put off.

récalcitrant, e [rākálsētrâṅ, -âṅt] *a* refractory, recalcitrant.

recaler [rəkàlā] *vt* (*SCOL*) to fail.

récapitulatif, ive [rākápētülátēf, -ēv] *a* (*liste, tableau*) summary *cpd*, that sums up.

récapituler [rākápētülā] *vt* to recapitulate; (*résumer*) to sum up.

recel [rəsel] *nm* fencing.

receler [rəsəlā] *vt* (*produit d'un vol*) to fence; (*malfaiteur*) to harbor (*US*), harbour (*Brit*); (*fig*) to conceal.

receleur, euse [rəsəlœr, -œz] *nm/f* receiver.

récemment [rāsámáṅ] *ad* recently.

recensement [rəsáṅsmáṅ] *nm* census; inventory.

recenser [rəsáṅsā] *vt* (*population*) to take a census of; (*inventorier*) to make an inventory of; (*dénombrer*) to list.

récent, e [rāsâṅ, -âṅt] *a* recent.

recentrer [rəsáṅtrā] *vt* (*POL*) to move towards the center (*US*) *ou* centre (*Brit*).

récépissé [rāsāpēsā] *nm* receipt.

récepteur, trice [rāsɛptœr, -trēs] *a* receiving ♦ *nm* receiver; ~ **(de papier)** (*INFORM*) stacker; ~ **(de radio)** radio set *ou* receiver.

réceptif, ive [rāsɛptēf, -ēv] *a*: ~ **(à)** receptive (to).

réception [rāsepsyôṅ] *nf* receiving *q*; (*d'une marchandise, commande*) receipt; (*accueil*) reception, welcome; (*bureau*) reception (desk); (*réunion mondaine*) reception, party; (*pièces*) reception rooms *pl*; (*SPORT: après un saut*) landing; (*du ballon*) catching *q*; **jour/heures de ~** day/hours for receiving visitors (*ou* students *etc*).

réceptionnaire [rāsepsyoner] *nm/f* receiving clerk.

réceptionner [rāsepsyonā] *vt* (*COMM*) to take delivery of; (*SPORT: ballon*) to catch (and control).

réceptionniste [rāsepsyonēst(ə)] *nm/f* receptionist.

récession [rāsāsyôṅ] *nf* recession.

recette [rəset] *nf* (*CULIN*) recipe; (*fig*) formula, recipe; (*COMM*) takings *pl*; (*ADMIN: bureau*) tax *ou* revenue office; ~**s** *nfpl* (*COMM: rentrées*) receipts; **faire ~** (*spectacle, exposition*) to be a winner.

receveur, euse [rəsvœr, -œz] *nm/f* (*des contributions*) tax collector; (*des postes*)

postmaster/mistress; (*d'autobus*) conductor/
conductress; (*MÉD*: *de sang, organe*) recipient.

recevoir [rəsvwár] *vt* to receive; (*lettre,
prime*) to receive, get; (*client, patient, représentant*) to see; (*jour, soleil: suj: pièce*)
to get; (*SCOL*: *candidat*) to pass ♦ *vi* to
receive visitors; to give parties; to see
patients *etc*; **se ~** *vi* (*athlète*) to land; **~ qn
à diner** to invite sb to dinner; **il reçoit de 8 à
10** he's at home from 8 to 10, he will see
visitors from 8 to 10; (*docteur, dentiste etc*)
he sees patients from 8 to 10; **être reçu** (*à un
examen*) to pass; **être bien/mal reçu** to be
well/badly received.

rechange [rəshâńzh]: **de ~** *a* (*pièces, roue*)
spare; (*fig: solution*) alternative; **des
vêtements de ~** a change of clothes.

rechaper [rəshápá] *vt* to remold (*US*), remould
(*Brit*), retread.

réchapper [rāshápā]: **~ de** *ou* **à** *vt* (*accident,
maladie*) to come through; **va-t-il en ~?** is he
going to get over it?, is he going to come
through (it)?

recharge [rəshárzh(ə)] *nf* refill.

rechargeable [rəshárzhábl(ə)] *a* refillable; rechargeable.

recharger [rəshárzhā] *vt* (*camion, fusil,
appareil-photo*) to reload; (*briquet, stylo*) to
refill; (*batterie*) to recharge.

réchaud [rāshō] *nm* (portable) stove; hotplate.

réchauffé [rāshōfā] *nm* (*nourriture*) reheated
food; (*fig*) stale news (*ou* joke *etc*).

réchauffer [rāshōfā] *vt* (*plat*) to reheat;
(*mains, personne*) to warm; **se ~** *vi* to get
warmer; **se ~ les doigts** to warm (up) one's
fingers.

rêche [resh] *a* rough.

recherche [rəshersh(ə)] *nf* (*action*): **la ~ de**
the search for; (*raffinement*) affectedness,
studied elegance; (*scientifique etc*): **la ~ research; ~s** *nfpl* (*de la police*) investigations;
(*scientifiques*) research *sg*; **être/se mettre à
la ~ de** to be/go in search of.

recherché, e [rəshershā] *a* (*rare, demandé*)
much sought-after; (*entouré: acteur, femme*)
in demand; (*raffiné*) studied, affected.

rechercher [rəshershā] *vt* (*objet égaré,
personne*) to look for, search for; (*témoins,
coupable, main-d'œuvre*) to look for; (*causes
d'un phénomène, nouveau procédé*) to try to
find; (*bonheur etc, l'amitié de qn*) to seek;
"~ et remplacer" (*INFORM*) "search and replace".

rechigner [rəshēnyā] *vi*: **~ (à)** to balk (at).

rechute [rəshüt] *nf* (*MÉD*) relapse; (*dans le
péché, le vice*) lapse; **faire une ~** to have a
relapse.

rechuter [rəshütā] *vi* (*MÉD*) to relapse.

récidive [rāsēdēv] *nf* (*JUR*) second (*ou* subsequent) offense (*US*) *ou* offence (*Brit*); (*fig*)
repetition; (*MÉD*) recurrence.

récidiver [rāsēdēvā] *vi* to commit a second (*ou*
subsequent) offense (*US*) *ou* offence (*Brit*);
(*fig*) to do it again.

récidiviste [rāsēdēvēst] *nm/f* second (*ou*
habitual) offender, recidivist.

récif [rāsēf] *nm* reef.

récipiendaire [rāsēpyáńder] *nm* recipient (*of*

diploma *etc*); (*d'une societé*) newly elected
member.

récipient [rāsēpyáń] *nm* container.

réciproque [rāsēprok] *a* reciprocal ♦ *nf*: **la ~**
(*l'inverse*) the converse.

réciproquement [rāsēprokmáń] *ad* recipro-
cally; **et ~** and vice versa.

récit [rāsē] *nm* (*action de narrer*) telling;
(*conte, histoire*) story.

récital [rāsētál] *nm* recital.

récitant, e [rāsētáń, -áńt] *nm/f* narrator.

récitation [rāsētásyóń] *nf* recitation.

réciter [rāsētā] *vt* to recite.

réclamation [rāklámásyóń] *nf* complaint; **~s**
nfpl (*bureau*) complaints department *sg*.

réclame [rāklám] *nf*: **la ~** advertising; **une ~**
an ad(vertisement); **faire de la ~ (pour
qch/qn)** to advertise (sth/sb); **article en ~**
special offer.

réclamer [rāklámā] *vt* (*aide, nourriture etc*) to
ask for; (*revendiquer: dû, part, indemnité*) to
claim, demand; (*nécessiter*) to demand, require ♦ *vi* to complain; **se ~ de** to give as
one's authority; to claim filiation with.

reclassement [rəklásmáń] *nm* reclassifying;
regrading; rehabilitation.

reclasser [rəklásā] *vt* (*fiches, dossiers*) to re-
classify; (*fig: fonctionnaire etc*) to regrade;
(*: ouvrier licencié*) to place, rehabilitate.

reclus, e [rəklü, -üz] *nm/f* recluse.

réclusion [rāklüzyóń] *nf* imprisonment; **~ à
perpétuité** life imprisonment.

recoiffer [rəkwáfā] *vt*: **~ un enfant** to do a
child's hair again; **se ~** to do one's hair
again.

recoin [rəkwáń] *nm* nook, corner; (*fig*) hidden
recess.

reçois [rəswá] *etc vb voir* **recevoir**.

reçoive [rəswáv] *etc vb voir* **recevoir**.

recoller [rəkolā] *vt* (*enveloppe*) to stick back
down.

récolte [rākolt(ə)] *nf* harvesting, gathering;
(*produits*) harvest, crop; (*fig*) crop, collection; (*: d'observations*) findings.

récolter [rākoltā] *vt* to harvest, gather (in);
(*fig*) to get.

recommandable [rəkomáńdábl(ə)] *a*
commendable; **peu ~** not very commendable.

recommandation [rəkomáńdásyóń] *nf* recommendation.

recommandé [rəkomáńdā] *nm* (*méthode etc*)
recommended; (*POSTES*): **en ~** by registered
mail.

recommander [rəkomáńdā] *vt* to recommend;
(*suj: qualités etc*) to commend; (*POSTES*) to
register; **~ qch à qn** to recommend sth to
sb; **~ à qn de faire** to recommend sb to do;
~ qn auprès de qn *ou* **à qn** to recommend
sb to sb; **il est recommandé de faire ...** it is
recommended that one do ...; **se ~ à qn** to
commend o.s. to sb; **se ~ de qn** to give sb's
name as a reference.

recommencer [rəkomáńsā] *vt* (*reprendre:
lutte, séance*) to resume, start again;
(*refaire: travail, explications*) to start afresh,
start (over) again; (*récidiver: erreur*) to
make again ♦ *vi* to start again; (*récidiver*) to
do it again; **~ à faire** to start doing again;

ne recommence pas! don't do that again!

récompense [rākôṅpâṅs] *nf* reward; (*prix*) award; **recevoir qch en ~** to get sth as a reward, be rewarded with sth.

récompenser [rākôṅpâṅsā] *vt:* ~ **qn (de** *ou* **pour)** to reward sb (for).

réconciliation [rākôṅsēlyâsyôṅ] *nf* reconciliation.

réconcilier [rākôṅsēlyā] *vt* to reconcile; ~ **qn avec qn** to reconcile sb with sb; ~ **qn avec qch** to reconcile sb to sth; **se ~ (avec)** to be reconciled (with).

reconductible [rəkôṅdüktēbl(ə)] *a* (*JUR:* *contrat, bail*) renewable.

reconduction [rəkôṅdüksyôṅ] *nf* renewal; (*POL: d'une politique*) continuation.

reconduire [rəkôṅdüēr] *vt* (*raccompagner*) to take *ou* see back; (: *à la porte*) to show out; (: *à son domicile*) to see home, take home; (*JUR, POL: renouveler*) to renew.

réconfort [rākôṅfor] *nm* comfort.

réconfortant, e [rākôṅfortâṅ, -âṅt] *a* (*idée, paroles*) comforting; (*boisson*) fortifying.

réconforter [rākôṅfortā] *vt* (*consoler*) to comfort; (*revigorer*) to fortify.

reconnais [r(ə)kone] *etc vb voir* **reconnaître**.

reconnaissable [rəkonesàbl(ə)] *a* recognizable.

reconnaissais [r(ə)konese] *etc vb voir* **reconnaître**.

reconnaissance [rəkonesâṅs] *nf* recognition; acknowledgement; (*gratitude*) gratitude, gratefulness; (*MIL*) reconnaissance, recce; **en ~** (*MIL*) on reconnaissance; ~ **de dette** acknowledgement of a debt, IOU.

reconnaissant, e [rəkonesâṅ, -âṅt] *vb voir* **reconnaître** ♦ *a* grateful; **je vous serais ~ de bien vouloir** I should be most grateful if you would (kindly).

reconnaître [rəkonetr(ə)] *vt* to recognize; (*MIL: lieu*) to reconnoiter (*US*), reconnoitre (*Brit*); (*JUR: enfant, dette, droit*) to acknowledge; ~ **que** to admit *ou* acknowledge that; ~ **qn/qch à** (*l'identifier grâce à*) to recognize sb/sth by; ~ **à qn: je lui reconnais certaines qualités** I recognize certain qualities in him; **se ~ quelque part** (*s'y retrouver*) to find one's way around (a place).

reconnu, e [r(ə)konü] *pp de* **reconnaître** ♦ *a* (*indiscuté, connu*) recognized.

reconquérir [rəkôṅkārēr] *vt* (*aussi fig*) to reconquer, recapture; (*sa dignité etc*) to recover.

reconquête [rəkôṅket] *nf* recapture; recovery.

reconsidérer [rəkôṅsēdārā] *vt* to reconsider.

reconstituant, e [rəkôṅstētüâṅ, -âṅt] *a* (*régime*) strength-building ♦ *nm* tonic, pick-me-up.

reconstituer [rəkôṅstētüā] *vt* (*monument ancien*) to recreate, build a replica of; (*fresque, vase brisé*) to piece together, reconstitute; (*événement, accident*) to reconstruct; (*fortune, patrimoine*) to rebuild; (*BIO: tissus etc*) to regenerate.

reconstitution [rəkôṅstētüsyôṅ] *nf* (*d'un accident etc*) reconstruction.

reconstruction [rəkôṅstrüksyôṅ] *nf* rebuilding, reconstruction.

reconstruire [rəkôṅstrüēr] *vt* to rebuild, reconstruct.

reconversion [rəkôṅversyôṅ] *nf* (*du personnel*) redeployment.

reconvertir [rəkôṅvertēr] *vt* (*usine*) to reconvert; (*personnel, troupes etc*) to redeploy; **se ~ dans** (*un métier, une branche*) to move into, be redeployed into.

recopier [rəkopyā] *vt* (*transcrire*) to copy out again, write out again; (*mettre au propre: devoir*) to make a clean *ou* fair copy of.

record [rəkor] *nm, a* record; ~ **du monde** world record.

recoucher [rəkōōshā] *vt* (*enfant*) to put back to bed.

recoudre [rəkōōdr(ə)] *vt* (*bouton*) to sew back on; (*plaie, incision*) to sew (back) up, stitch up.

recoupement [rəkōōpmâṅ] *nm:* **faire un ~** *ou* **des ~s** to cross-check; **par ~** by cross-checking.

recouper [rəkōōpā] *vt* (*tranche*) to cut again; (*vêtement*) to recut ♦ *vi* (*CARTES*) to cut again; **se ~** *vi* (*témoignages*) to tie *ou* match up.

recourais [rəkōōre] *etc vb voir* **recourir**.

recourbé, e [rəkōōrbā] *a* curved; hooked; bent.

recourber [rəkōōrbā] *vt* (*branche, tige de métal*) to bend.

recourir [rəkōōrēr] *vi* (*courir de nouveau*) to run again; (*refaire une course*) to race again; ~ **à** *vt* (*ami, agence*) to turn *ou* appeal to; (*force, ruse, emprunt*) to resort to, have recourse to.

recours [rəkōōr] *vb voir* **recourir** ♦ *nm* (*JUR*) appeal; **avoir ~ à** = **recourir à; en dernier ~** as a last resort; **sans ~** final; with no way out; ~ **en grâce** plea for clemency (*ou* pardon).

recouru, e [rəkōōrü] *pp de* **recourir**.

recousu, e [rəkōōzü] *pp de* **recoudre**.

recouvert, e [rəkōōver, -ert(ə)] *pp de* **recouvrir**.

recouvrable [rəkōōvrábl(ə)] *a* (*somme*) recoverable.

recouvrais [rəkōōvre] *etc vb voir* **recouvrer, recouvrir**.

recouvrement [rəkōōvrəmâṅ] *nm* recovery.

recouvrer [rəkōōvrā] *vt* (*vue, santé etc*) to recover, regain; (*impôts*) to collect; (*créance*) to recover.

recouvrir [rəkōōvrēr] *vt* (*couvrir à nouveau*) to re-cover; (*couvrir entièrement, aussi fig*) to cover; (*cacher, masquer*) to conceal, hide; **se ~** (*se superposer*) to overlap.

recracher [rəkrāshā] *vt* to spit out.

récréatif, ive [rākrāātēf, -ēv] *a* of entertainment; recreational.

récréation [rākrāāsyôṅ] *nf* recreation, entertainment; (*SCOL*) break.

recréer [rəkrāā] *vt* to recreate.

récrier [rākrēyā]: **se ~** *vi* to exclaim.

récriminations [rākrēmēnâsyôṅ] *nfpl* remonstrations, complaints.

récriminer [rākrēmēnā] *vi:* ~ **contre qn/qch** to remonstrate against sb/sth.

recroqueviller [rəkrokvēyā]: **se ~** *vi* (*feuilles*) to curl *ou* shrivel up; (*personne*) to huddle up.

recru, e [rəkrü] a: ~ **de fatigue** exhausted ♦ nf recruit.

recrudescence [rəkrüdāsâṅs] nf fresh outbreak.

recrutement [rəkrütmâṅ] nm recruiting, recruitment.

recruter [rəkrütā] vt to recruit.

rectal, e, aux [rektál, -ō] a: **par voie** ~e rectally.

rectangle [rektâṅgl(ə)] nm rectangle; ~ **blanc** (TV) "adults only" symbol.

rectangulaire [rektâṅgüler] a rectangular.

recteur [rektœr] nm ≈ state superintendent of education (US), ≈ (regional) director of education (Brit).

rectificatif, ive [rektēfēkátēf, -ēv] a corrected ♦ nm correction.

rectification [rektēfēkâsyôṅ] nf correction.

rectifier [rektēfyā] vt (tracé, virage) to straighten; (calcul, adresse) to correct; (erreur, faute) to rectify, put right.

rectiligne [rektēlēny] a straight; (GÉOM) rectilinear.

rectitude [rektētüd] nf rectitude, uprightness.

recto [rektō] nm front (of a sheet of paper).

reçu, e [rəsü] pp de **recevoir** ♦ a (admis, consacré) accepted ♦ nm (COMM) receipt.

recueil [rəkœy] nm collection.

recueillement [rəkœymâṅ] nm meditation, contemplation.

recueilli, e [rəkœyē] a contemplative.

recueillir [rəkœyēr] vt to collect; (voix, suffrages) to win; (accueillir: réfugiés, chat) to take in; **se** ~ vi to gather one's thoughts; to meditate.

recuire [rəküēr] vi: **faire** ~ to recook.

recul [rəkül] nm retreat; recession; decline; (d'arme à feu) recoil, kick; **avoir un mouvement de** ~ to recoil, start back; **prendre du** ~ to stand back; **avec le** ~ with the passing of time, in retrospect.

reculade [rəkülád] nf (péj) retreat.

reculé, e [rəkülā] a remote.

reculer [rəkülā] vi to move back, back away; (AUTO) to reverse, back (up); (fig: civilisation, épidémie) to (be on the) decline; (: se dérober) to shrink back ♦ vt to move back; to reverse, back (up); (fig: possibilités, limites) to extend; (: date, décision) to postpone; ~ **devant** (danger, difficulté) to shrink from; ~ **pour mieux sauter** (fig) to delay the day of reckoning.

reculons [rəkülôṅ]: **à** ~ ad backwards.

récupérable [rāküpārábl(ə)] a (créance) recoverable; (heures) which can be made up; (ferraille) salvageable.

récupération [rāküpārâsyôṅ] nf (de vieux métaux etc) salvage, reprocessing; (POL) bringing into line.

récupérer [rāküpārā] vt (rentrer en possession de) to recover, get back; (: forces) to recover; (déchets etc) to salvage (for reprocessing); (remplacer: journée, heures de travail) to make up; (délinquant etc) to rehabilitate; (POL) to bring into line ♦ vi to recover.

récurer [rākürā] vt to scour; **poudre à** ~ scouring powder.

reçus [rəsü] etc vb voir **recevoir**.

récuser [rāküzā] vt to challenge; **se** ~ to decline to give an opinion.

recyclage [rəsēklázh] nm reorientation; retraining; recycling; **cours de** ~ retraining course.

recycler [rəsēklā] vt (SCOL) to reorientate; (employés) to retrain; (matériau) to recycle; **se** ~ to retrain; to take a retraining course.

rédacteur, trice [rādáktœr, -trēs] nm/f (journaliste) writer; subeditor; (d'ouvrage de référence) editor, compiler; ~ **en chef** editor in chief; ~ **publicitaire** copywriter.

rédaction [rādáksyôṅ] nf writing; (rédacteurs) editorial staff; (bureau) editorial office(s); (SCOL: devoir) essay, composition.

reddition [rādēsyôṅ] nf surrender.

redéfinir [rədāfēnēr] vt to redefine.

redemander [rədmâṅdā] vt (renseignement) to ask again for; (nourriture): ~ **de** to ask for more (ou another); (objet prêté): ~ **qch** to ask for sth back.

redémarrer [rədāmárā] vi (véhicule) to start again, get going again; (fig: industrie etc) to get going again.

rédemption [rādâṅpsyôṅ] nf redemption.

redéploiement [rədāplwámâṅ] nm redeployment.

redescendre [rədāsâṅdr(ə)] vi (à nouveau) to go back down; (après la montée) to go down (again) ♦ vt (pente etc) to go down.

redevable [rədvábl(ə)] a: **être** ~ **de qch à qn** (somme) to owe sb sth; (fig) to be indebted to sb for sth.

redevance [rədvâṅs] nf (TÉL) leasing (US) ou rental (Brit) charge; (TV) ≈ cable (US) ou licence (Brit) fee.

redevenir [rədvənēr] vi to become again.

rediffuser [rədēfüzā] vt (RADIO, TV) to rerun, broadcast again.

rediffusion [rədēfüzyôṅ] nf rerun.

rédiger [rādēzhā] vt to write; (contrat) to draw up.

redire [rədēr] vt to repeat; **trouver à** ~ **à** to find fault with.

redistribuer [rədēstrēbüā] vt (cartes etc) to deal again; (richesses, tâches, revenus) to redistribute.

redite [rədēt] nf (needless) repetition.

redondance [rədôṅdâṅs] nf redundancy.

redonner [rədonā] vt (restituer) to give back, return; (du courage, des forces) to restore.

redoublé, e [rədōōblā] a: **à coups** ~**s** even harder, twice as hard.

redoubler [rədōōblā] vi (tempête, violence) to intensify, get even stronger ou fiercer etc; (SCOL) to repeat a grade (US) ou year (Brit) ♦ vt (SCOL: classe) to repeat; (LING: lettre) to double; ~ **de** vt to be twice as + adjectif; **le vent redouble de violence** the wind is blowing twice as hard.

redoutable [rədōōtábl(ə)] a formidable, fearsome.

redouter [rədōōtā] vt to fear; (appréhender) to dread; ~ **de faire** to dread doing.

redoux [rədōō] nm milder spell.

redressement [rədresmâṅ] nm (de l'économie etc) recovery, upturn; **maison de** ~ reformatory; ~ **fiscal** repayment of back taxes.

redresser [rədrāsā] *vt* (*arbre, mât*) to set upright, right; (*pièce tordue*) to straighten out; (*AVIAT, AUTO*) to straighten up; (*situation, économie*) to straighten out; **se ~** *vi* (*objet penché*) to right itself; to straighten up; (*personne*) to sit (*ou* stand) up; to sit (*ou* stand) up straight; (*fig: pays, situation*) to recover; **~ (les roues)** (*AUTO*) to straighten up.

redresseur [rədrescœr] *nm*: **~ de torts** righter of wrongs.

réducteur, trice [rādüktœr, -trēs] *a* simplistic.

réduction [rādüksyôn] *nf* reduction; **en ~** *ad* in miniature, scaled-down.

réduire [rādüēr] *vt* (*gén, aussi CULIN, MATH*) to reduce; (*prix, dépenses*) to cut, reduce; (*carte*) to scale down, reduce; (*MÉD: fracture*) to set; **~ qn/qch à** to reduce sb/sth to; **se ~ à** (*revenir à*) to boil down to; **se ~ en** (*se transformer en*) to be reduced to; **en être réduit à** to be reduced to.

réduit, e [rādüē, -ēt] *pp de* **réduire ♦** *a* (*prix, tarif, échelle*) reduced; (*mécanisme*) scaled-down; (*vitesse*) reduced **♦** *nm* tiny room; recess.

rééchelonner [rāāshlonā] *vt* to reschedule.

rééditer [rāādētā] *vt* to republish.

réédition [rāādēsyôn] *nf* new edition.

rééducation [rāādükâsyôn] *nf* (*d'un membre*) re-education; (*de délinquants, d'un blessé*) rehabilitation; **~ de la parole** speech therapy; **centre de ~** physical therapy center (*US*), physiotherapy centre (*Brit*).

rééduquer [rāādükā] *vt* to reeducate; to rehabilitate.

réel, le [rāel] *a* real **♦** *nm*: **le ~** reality.

réélection [rāāleksyôn] *nf* re-election.

réélire [rāālēr] *vt* to re-elect.

réellement [rāelmân] *ad* really.

réembaucher [rāânbōshā] *vt* to take on again.

réemploi [rāânplwā] *nm* = **remploi**.

réemployer [rāânplwâyā] *vt* (*méthode, produit*) to re-use; (*argent*) to reinvest; (*personnel, employé*) to re-employ.

rééquilibrer [rāākēlēbrā] *vt* (*budget*) to balance (again).

réescompte [rāeskônt] *nm* rediscount.

réessayer [rāesāyā] *vt* to try on again.

réévaluer [rāāválüā] *vt* to revalue.

réexaminer [rāegzámēnā] *vt* to re-examine.

réexpédier [rāekspādyā] *vt* (*à l'envoyeur*) to return, send back; (*au destinataire*) to send on, forward.

réexporter [rāeksportā] *vt* to re-export.

réf. *abr* (= *référence(s)*): **V/~** Your ref.

refaire [rəfer] *vt* (*faire de nouveau, recommencer*) to do again; (*réparer, restaurer*) to renovate, redecorate; **se ~** *vi* (*en argent*) to make up one's losses; **se ~ une santé** to recuperate; **se ~ à qch** (*se réhabituer à*) to get used to sth again.

refasse [rəfás] *etc vb voir* **refaire**.

réfection [rāfeksyôn] *nf* repair; **en ~** under repair.

réfectoire [rāfektwár] *nm* refectory.

referai [r(ə)frā] *etc vb voir* **refaire**.

référé [rāfārā] *nm* (*JUR*) emergency interim proceedings *ou* ruling.

référence [rāfārâns] *nf* reference; **~s** *nfpl* (*re-*

commandations*) reference *sg*; **faire ~ à to refer to; **ouvrage de ~** reference work; **ce n'est pas une ~** (*fig*) that's no recommendation.

référendum [rāfārandom] *nm* referendum.

référer [rāfārā]: **se ~ à** *vt* to refer to; **en ~ à qn** to refer the matter to sb.

refermer [rəfermā] *vt* to close again, shut again.

refiler [rəfēlā] *vt* (*fam*): **~ qch à qn** to palm *ou* fob sth off on sb; to pass sth on to sb.

refit [rəfē] *etc vb voir* **refaire**.

réfléchi, e [rāflāshē] *a* (*caractère*) thoughtful; (*action*) well-thought-out; (*LING*) reflexive.

réfléchir [rāflāshēr] *vt* to reflect **♦** *vi* to think; **~ à** *ou* **sur** to think about; **c'est tout réfléchi** my mind's made up.

réflecteur [rāflektœr] *nm* (*AUTO*) reflector.

reflet [rəflē] *nm* reflection; (*sur l'eau etc*) sheen *q*, glint; **~s** *nmpl* gleam *sg*.

refléter [rəflātā] *vt* to reflect; **se ~** *vi* to be reflected.

réflex [rāfleks] *a inv* (*PHOTO*) reflex.

réflexe [rāfleks(ə)] *a, nm* reflex; **~ conditionné** conditioned reflex.

réflexion [rāfleksyôn] *nf* (*de la lumière etc, pensée*) reflection; (*fait de penser*) thought; (*remarque*) remark; **~s** *nfpl* (*méditations*) thought *sg*, reflection *sg*; **sans ~** without thinking; **~ faite, à la ~, après ~** on reflection; **délai de ~** cooling-off period; **groupe de ~** think tank.

refluer [rəflüā] *vi* to flow back; (*foule*) to surge back.

reflux [rəflü] *nm* (*de la mer*) ebb; (*fig*) backward surge.

refondre [rəfôndr(ə)] *vt* (*texte*) to recast.

refont [r(ə)fôn] *vb voir* **refaire**.

reformater [rəformátā] *vt* to reformat.

réformateur, trice [rāformátœr, -trēs] *nm/f* reformer **♦** *a* (*mesures*) reforming.

Réformation [rāformâsyôn] *nf*: **la ~** the Reformation.

réforme [rāform(ə)] *nf* reform; (*MIL*) declaration of unfitness for service; discharge (*on health grounds*); (*REL*): **la R~** the Reformation.

réformé, e [rāformā] *a, nm/f* (*REL*) Protestant.

reformer [rəformā] *vt*, **se ~** *vi* to reform; **~ les rangs** (*MIL*) to fall in again.

réformer [rāformā] *vt* to reform; (*MIL: recrue*) to declare unfit for service; (*: soldat*) to discharge; (*matériel*) to scrap.

réformisme [rāformēsm(ə)] *nm* reformism, policy of reform.

réformiste [rāformēst(ə)] *a, nm/f* (*POL*) reformist.

refoulé, e [rəfōōlā] *a* (*PSYCH*) repressed.

refoulement [rəfōōlmân] *nm* (*d'une armée*) driving back; (*PSYCH*) repression.

refouler [rəfōōlā] *vt* (*envahisseurs*) to drive back, repulse; (*liquide*) to force back; (*fig*) to suppress; (*PSYCH*) to repress.

réfractaire [rāfrákter] *a* (*minerai*) refractory; (*brique*) fire *cpd*; (*maladie*) which is resistant to treatment; (*prêtre*) non-juring; **soldat ~** draft dodger; **être ~ à** to resist.

réfracter [rāfráktā] *vt* to refract.

réfraction [rāfráksyôn] *nf* refraction.

refrain [rəfraṅ] *nm* (*MUS*) refrain, chorus; (*air, fig*) tune.

refréner, réfréner [rəfrénā, rāfrānā] *vt* to curb, check.

réfrigérant, e [rāfrēzhāràṅ, -àṅt] *a* refrigerant, cooling.

réfrigérateur [rāfrēzhārātœr] *nm* refrigerator.

réfrigération [rāfrēzhārásyóṅ] *nf* refrigeration.

réfrigérer [rāfrēzhārā] *vt* to refrigerate; (*fam: glacer, aussi fig*) to cool.

refroidir [rəfrwàdēr] *vt* to cool; (*fig*) to have a cooling effect on ♦ *vi* to cool (down); **se ~** *vi* (*prendre froid*) to catch a chill; (*temps*) to get cooler *ou* colder; (*fig*) to cool (off).

refroidissement [rəfrwàdēsmàṅ] *nm* cooling; (*grippe etc*) chill.

refuge [rəfüzh] *nm* refuge; (*pour piétons*) (traffic) island; **demander ~ à qn** to ask sb for refuge.

réfugié, e [rāfüzhyā] *a, nm/f* refugee.

réfugier [rāfüzhyā]: **se ~** *vi* to take refuge.

refus [rəfü] *nm* refusal; **ce n'est pas de ~** I won't say no, it's very welcome.

refuser [rəfüzā] *vt* to refuse; (*SCOL: candidat*) to fail ♦ *vi* to refuse; **~ qch à qn/de faire** to refuse sb sth/to do; **~ du monde** to have to turn people away; **se ~ à qch** *ou* **à faire qch** to refuse to do sth; **il ne se refuse rien** he doesn't deny himself (anything); **se ~ à qn** to refuse sb.

réfuter [rāfütā] *vt* to refute.

regagner [rəgàṅyā] *vt* (*argent, faveur*) to win back; (*lieu*) to get back to; **~ le temps perdu** to make up (for) lost time; **~ du terrain** to regain ground.

regain [rəgaṅ] *nm* (*herbe*) second crop of hay; (*renouveau*): **un ~ de** renewed + *nom*.

régal [rāgál] *nm* treat; **un ~ pour les yeux** a pleasure *ou* delight to look at.

régalade [rāgàlàd] *ad*: **à la ~** from the bottle (held away from the lips).

régaler [rāgàlā] *vt*: **~ qn** to treat sb to a delicious meal; **~ qn de** to treat sb to; **se ~** *vi* to have a delicious meal; (*fig*) to enjoy o.s.

regard [rəgàr] *nm* (*coup d'œil*) look, glance; (*expression*) look (in one's eye); **parcourir/menacer du ~** to cast an eye over/look threateningly at; **au ~ de** (*loi, morale*) from the point of view of; **en ~** (*vis à vis*) opposite; **en ~ de** in comparison with.

regardant, e [rəgàrdàṅ, -àṅt] *a*: **très/peu ~ (sur)** quite fussy/very free (about); (*économe*) very tight-fisted/quite generous (with).

regarder [rəgàrdā] *vt* (*examiner, observer, lire*) to look at; (*film, télévision, match*) to watch; (*envisager: situation, avenir*) to view; (*considérer: son intérêt etc*) to be concerned with; (*être orienté vers*): **~ (vers)** to face; (*concerner*) to concern ♦ *vi* to look; **~ à qch** (*dépense, qualité, détails*) to be fussy with *ou* over; **~ à faire** to hesitate to do; **dépenser sans ~** to spend freely; **~ qn/qch comme** to regard sb/sth as; **~ (qch) dans le dictionnaire/l'annuaire** to look (sth up) in the dictionary/directory; **~ par la fenêtre** to look out of the window; **cela me regarde** it concerns me, it's my business.

régate(s) [rāgát] *nf(pl)* regatta.

régénérer [rāzhānārā] *vt* to regenerate; (*fig*) to revive.

régent [rāzhàṅ] *nm* regent.

régenter [rāzhàṅtā] *vt* to rule over; to dictate to.

régie [rāzhē] *nf* (*COMM, INDUSTRIE*) state-owned company; (*THÉÂTRE, CINÉMA*) production; (*RADIO, TV*) control room; **la ~ de l'État** state control.

regimber [rəzhaṅbā] *vi* to balk, jib.

régime [rāzhēm] *nm* (*POL*) régime; (*ADMIN: carcéral, fiscal etc*) system; (*MÉD*) diet; (*GÉO*) régime; (*TECH*) (engine) speed; (*fig*) rate, pace; (*de bananes, dattes*) bunch; **se mettre au/suivre un ~** to go on/be on a diet; **~ sans sel** salt-free diet; **à bas/haut ~** (*AUTO*) at low/high revs; **à plein ~** flat out, at full speed; **~ matrimonial** marriage settlement.

régiment [rāzhēmàṅ] *nm* (*MIL: unité*) regiment; (*fig: fam*): **un ~ de** an army of; **un copain de ~** a pal from military service *ou* (one's) army days.

région [rāzhyóṅ] *nf* region; **la ~ parisienne** the Paris area.

régional, e, aux [rāzhyonál, -ō] *a* regional.

régionalisation [rāzhyonálēzāsyóṅ] *nf* regionalization.

régionalisme [rāzhyonálēsm(ə)] *nm* regionalism.

régir [rāzhēr] *vt* to govern.

régisseur [rāzhēsœr] *nm* (*d'un domaine*) steward; (*CINÉMA, TV*) assistant director; (*THÉÂTRE*) stage manager.

registre [rəzhēstr(ə)] *nm* (*livre*) register; log-book; ledger; (*MUS, LING*) register; (*d'orgue*) stop; **~ de comptabilité** ledger; **~ de l'état civil** register of births, marriages and deaths.

réglable [rāglábl(ə)] *a* (*siège, flamme etc*) adjustable; (*achat*) payable.

réglage [rāglázh] *nm* (*d'une machine*) adjustment; (*d'un moteur*) tuning.

règle [regl(ə)] *nf* (*instrument*) ruler; (*loi, prescription*) rule; **~s** *nfpl* (*PHYSIOL*) period *sg*; **avoir pour ~ de** to make it a rule that *ou* to; **en ~** (*papiers d'identité*) in order; **être/se mettre en ~** to be/put o.s. in order with the authorities; **en ~ générale** as a (general) rule; **être la ~** to be the rule; **être de ~** to be usual; **~ à calcul** slide rule; **~ de trois** (*MATH*) rule of three.

réglé, e [rāglā] *a* well-ordered; stable, steady; (*papier*) ruled; (*arrangé*) settled; (*femme*): **bien ~e** whose periods are regular.

règlement [reglmàṅ] *nm* settling; (*paiement*) settlement; (*arrêté*) regulation; (*règles, statuts*) regulations *pl*, rules *pl*; **~ à la commande** cash with order; **~ de compte(s)** settling of scores; **~ en espèces/par chèque** payment in cash/by check; **~ intérieur** (*SCOL*) school rules *pl*; (*ADMIN*) by-laws *pl*; **~ judiciaire** compulsory liquidation.

réglementaire [reglmàṅter] *a* conforming to the regulations; (*tenue, uniforme*) regulation *cpd*.

réglementation [reglmàṅtāsyóṅ] *nf* regulation, control; (*règlements*) regulations *pl*.

réglementer [reglmàṅtā] *vt* to regulate, control.

régler [rāglā] vt (mécanisme, machine) to regulate, adjust; (moteur) to tune; (thermostat etc) to set, adjust; (emploi du temps etc) to organize, plan; (question, conflit, facture, dette) to settle; (fournisseur) to settle up with, pay; (papier) to rule; ~ qch sur to model sth on; ~ son compte à qn to fix sb; ~ un compte avec qn to settle a score with sb.

réglisse [rāglēs] nf licorice, liquorice (Brit); bâton de ~ licorice stick.

règne [reny] nm (d'un roi etc, fig) reign; (BIO): le ~ végétal/animal the vegetable/animal kingdom.

régner [rānyā] vi (roi) to rule, reign; (fig) to reign.

regonfler [r(ə)gôṅflā] vt (ballon, pneu) to reinflate, blow up again.

regorger [rəgorzhā] vi to overflow; ~ de to overflow with, be bursting with.

régresser [rāgrāsā] vi (phénomène) to decline; (enfant, malade) to regress.

régressif, ive [rāgrāsēf, -ēv] a regressive.

régression [rāgrāsyôṅ] nf decline; regression; être en ~ to be on the decline.

regret [rəgre] nm regret; à ~ with regret; avec ~ regretfully; être au ~ de devoir/ne pas pouvoir faire to regret to have to/that one is unable to do; j'ai le ~ de vous informer que ... I regret to inform you that ....

regrettable [rəgretábl(ə)] a regrettable.

regretter [rəgrātā] vt to regret; (personne) to miss; ~ d'avoir fait to regret doing; ~ que to regret that, be sorry that; non, je regrette no, I'm sorry.

regroupement [r(ə)grōōpmáṅ] nm grouping together; (groupe) group.

regrouper [rəgrōōpā] vt (grouper) to group together; (contenir) to include, comprise; se ~ vi to gather (together).

régulariser [rāgülárēzā] vt (fonctionnement, trafic) to regulate; (passeport, papiers) to put in order; (sa situation) to straighten out, regularize.

régularité [rāgülárētā] nf regularity.

régulateur, trice [rāgülátœr, -trēs] a regulating ♦ nm (TECH): ~ de vitesse/de température speed/temperature regulator.

régulation [rāgülásyôṅ] nf (du trafic) regulation; ~ des naissances birth control.

régulier, ière [rāgülyā, -yer] a (gén) regular; (vitesse, qualité) steady; (répartition, pression, paysage) even; (TRANSPORTS: ligne, service) scheduled, regular; (légal, réglementaire) lawful, in order; (fam: correct) straight, on the level.

régulièrement [rāgülyermáṅ] ad regularly; steadily; evenly; normally.

réhabiliter [rāábēlētā] vt to rehabilitate; (fig) to restore to favor.

réhabituer [rāábētüā] vt: se ~ à qch/à faire qch to get used to sth again/to doing sth again.

rehausser [rəōsā] vt to heighten, raise; (fig) to set off, enhance.

réimporter [rāáṅportā] vt to reimport.

réimposer [rāáṅpōzā] vt (FINANCE) to re-impose; to tax again.

réimpression [rāáṅpresyôṅ] nf reprinting; (ouvrage) reprint.

réimprimer [rāáṅprēmā] vt to reprint.

Reims [raṅs] n Rheims.

rein [raṅ] nm kidney; ~s nmpl (dos) back sg; avoir mal aux ~s to have backache; ~ artificiel kidney machine.

reine [ren] nf queen.

reine-claude [renklōd] nf greengage.

reinette [renet] nf rennet, pippin.

réinitialisation [rāēnēsyálēzásyôṅ] nf (INFORM) reset.

réinsérer [rāáṅsārā] vt (délinquant, handicapé etc) to rehabilitate.

réinsertion [rāáṅsersyôṅ] nf rehabilitation.

réintégrer [rāáṅtāgrā] vt (lieu) to return to; (fonctionnaire) to reinstate.

réitérer [rāētārā] vt to repeat, reiterate.

rejaillir [rəzháyēr] vi to splash up; ~ sur to splash up onto; (fig) to rebound on; to fall upon.

rejet [rəzhe] nm (action, aussi MÉD) rejection; (POÉSIE) enjambement, rejet; (BOT) shoot.

rejeter [rəzhtā] vt (relancer) to throw back; (vomir) to bring ou throw up; (écarter) to reject; (déverser) to throw out, discharge; (reporter): ~ un mot à la fin d'une phrase to transpose a word to the end of a sentence; se ~ sur qch (accepter faute de mieux) to fall back on sth; ~ la tête/les épaules en arrière to throw one's head/pull one's shoulders back; ~ la responsabilité de qch sur qn to lay the responsibility for sth at sb's door.

rejeton [rəzhtôṅ] nm offspring.

rejette [r(ə)zhet] etc vb voir **rejeter.**

rejoignais [r(ə)zhwánye] etc vb voir **rejoindre.**

rejoindre [rəzhwaṅdr(ə)] vt (famille, régiment) to rejoin, return to; (lieu) to get (back) to; (suj: route etc) to meet, join; (rattraper) to catch up (with); se ~ vi to meet; je te rejoins au café I'll see ou meet you at the café.

réjoui, e [rāzhwē] a joyous.

réjouir [rāzhwēr] vt to delight; se ~ vi to be delighted; se ~ de qch/de faire to be delighted about sth/to do; se ~ que to be delighted that.

réjouissances [rāzhwēsáṅs] nfpl (joie) rejoicing sg; (fête) festivities, merry-making sg.

réjouissant, e [rāzhwēsáṅ, -áṅt] a heartening, delightful.

relâche [rəlásh]: faire ~ vi (navire) to put into port; (CINÉMA) it's to be closed; c'est le jour de ~ (CINÉMA) it's closed today; sans ~ ad without respite ou a break.

relâché, e [rəlâshā] a loose, lax.

relâcher [rəláshā] vt (ressort, prisonnier) to release; (étreinte, cordes) to loosen; (discipline) to relax ♦ vi (NAVIG) to put into port; se ~ vi to loosen; (discipline) to become slack ou lax; (élève etc) to slacken off.

relais [rəle] nm (SPORT): (course de) ~ relay (race); (RADIO, TV) relay; (intermédiaire) go-between; équipe de ~ shift team; (SPORT) relay team; prendre le ~ (de) to take over (from); ~ de poste post house; ~ routier ≈ truck stop (US), ≈ transport café (Brit).

relance [rəlãns] *nf* boosting, revival; (*ÉCON*) reflation.

relancer [rəlãsã] *vt* (*balle*) to throw back (again); (*moteur*) to restart; (*fig*) to boost, revive; (*personne*): ~ **qn** to pester sb.

relater [rəlãtã] *vt* to relate, recount.

relatif, ive [rəlãtéf, -ēv] *a* relative.

relation [rəlãsyôn] *nf* (*récit*) account, report; (*rapport*) relation(ship); **~s** *nfpl* (*rapports*) relations; relationship; (*connaissances*) connections; **être/entrer en ~(s) avec** to be in contact *ou* be dealing/get in contact with; **mettre qn en ~(s) avec** to put sb in touch with; **~s internationales** international relations; **~s publiques (RP)** public relations (PR); **~s (sexuelles)** sexual relations, (sexual) intercourse *sg*.

relativement [rəlãtēvmãn] *ad* relatively; ~ **à** in relation to.

relativiser [rəlãtēvēzã] *vt* to see in relation to; to put into context.

relativité [rəlãtēvētã] *nf* relativity.

relax [rəlãks] *a inv*, **relaxe** [rəlãks(ə)] *a* relaxed, informal, casual; easy-going; **(fauteuil-)~** *nm* reclining chair.

relaxant, e [rəlãksãn, -ãnt] *a* (*cure, médicament*) relaxant; (*ambiance*) relaxing.

relaxation [r(ə)lãksãsyôn] *nf* relaxation.

relaxer [rəlãksã] *vt* to relax; (*JUR*) to discharge; **se ~** *vi* to relax.

relayer [rəlãyã] *vt* (*collaborateur, coureur etc*) to relieve, take over from; (*RADIO, TV*) to relay; **se ~** (*dans une activité*) to take it in turns.

relecture [r(ə)lektür] *nf* rereading.

relégation [rəlãgãsyôn] *nf* (*SPORT*) relegation.

reléguer [rəlãgã] *vt* to relegate; ~ **au second plan** to push into the background.

relent(s) [rəlãn] *nm(pl)* stench *sg*.

relevé, e [rəlvã] *a* (*bord de chapeau*) turned-up; (*manches*) rolled-up; (*fig: style*) elevated; (: *sauce*) highly-seasoned ♦ *nm* (*lecture*) reading; (*de cotes*) plotting; (*liste*) statement; list; (*facture*) account; ~ **de compte** bank statement; ~ **d'identité bancaire (RIB)** (bank) account number.

relève [rəlev] *nf* relief; (*équipe*) relief team (*ou* troops *pl*); **prendre la ~** to take over.

relèvement [rəlevmãn] *nm* (*d'un taux, niveau*) raising.

relever [rəlvã] *vt* (*statue, meuble*) to stand up again; (*personne tombée*) to help up; (*vitre, plafond, niveau de vie*) to raise; (*pays, économie, entreprise*) to put back on its feet; (*col*) to turn up; (*style, conversation*) to elevate; (*plat, sauce*) to season; (*sentinelle, équipe*) to relieve; (*souligner: fautes, points*) to pick out; (*constater: traces etc*) to find, pick up; (*répliquer à: remarque*) to react to, reply to; (: *défi*) to accept, take up; (*noter: adresse etc*) to take down, note; (: *plan*) to sketch; (: *cotes etc*) to plot; (*compteur*) to read; (*ramasser: cahiers, copies*) to collect, take up ♦ *vi* (*jupe, bord*) to ride up; ~ **de** *vt* (*maladie*) to be recovering from; (*être du ressort de*) to be a matter for; (*ADMIN: dépendre de*) to come under; (*fig*) to pertain to; **se ~** *vi* (*se remettre debout*) to get up; (*fig*): **se ~ (de)** to recover (from); ~ **qn de**

(*vœux*) to release sb from; (*fonctions*) to relieve sb of; ~ **la tête** to look up; to hold up one's head.

relief [rəlyef] *nm* relief; (*de pneu*) tread pattern; **~s** *nmpl* (*restes*) remains; **en ~** in relief; (*photographie*) three-dimensional; **mettre en ~** (*fig*) to bring out, highlight.

relier [rəlyã] *vt* to link up; (*livre*) to bind; ~ **qch à** to link sth to; **livre relié cuir** leather-bound book.

relieur, euse [rəlyœr, -œz] *nm/f* (book)binder.

religieusement [r(ə)lēzhyœzmãn] *ad* religiously; (*enterré, mariés*) in church; **vivre ~** to lead a religious life.

religieux, euse [rəlēzhyœ, -œz] *a* religious ♦ *nm* monk ~ *nf* nun; (*gâteau*) cream puff.

religion [rəlēzhyôn] *nf* religion; (*piété, dévotion*) faith; **entrer en ~** to take one's vows.

reliquaire [rəlēker] *nm* reliquary.

reliquat [rəlēkã] *nm* (*d'une somme*) balance; (*JUR: de succession*) residue.

relique [rəlēk] *nf* relic.

relire [rəlēr] *vt* (*à nouveau*) to reread, read again; (*vérifier*) to read over; **se ~** to read through what one has written.

reliure [rəlyür] *nf* binding; (*art, métier*): **la ~** bookbinding.

reloger [r(ə)lozhã] *vt* (*locataires, sinistrés*) to rehouse.

relu, e [rəlü] *pp de* **relire**.

reluire [rəlüēr] *vi* to gleam.

reluisant, e [rəlüēzãn, -ãnt] *vb voir* **reluire** ♦ *a* gleaming; **peu ~** (*fig*) unattractive; unsavoury (*US*), unsavoury (*Brit*).

reluquer [r(ə)lükã] *vt* (*fam*) to eye, ogle.

remâcher [rəmãshã] *vt* to chew *ou* ruminate over.

remailler [rəmãyã] *vt* (*tricot*) to darn; (*filet*) to mend.

remaniement [rəmãnēmãn] *nm*: ~ **ministériel** Cabinet reshuffle.

remanier [rəmãnyã] *vt* to reshape, recast; (*POL*) to reshuffle.

remarier [r(ə)mãryã]: **se ~** *vi* to remarry, get married again.

remarquable [rəmãrkãbl(ə)] *a* remarkable.

remarquablement [r(ə)mãrkãbləmãn] *ad* remarkably.

remarque [rəmãrk(ə)] *nf* remark; (*écrite*) note.

remarquer [rəmãrkã] *vt* (*voir*) to notice; (*dire*): ~ **que** to remark that; **se ~** to be noticeable; **se faire ~** to draw attention to o.s.; **faire ~ (à qn) que** to point out (to sb) that; **faire ~ qch (à qn)** to point sth out (to sb); **remarquez, ...** mind you, ...

remballer [rãnbãlã] *vt* to wrap up (again); (*dans un carton*) to pack up (again).

rembarrer [rãnbãrã] *vt*: ~ **qn** (*repousser*) to rebuff sb; (*remettre à sa place*) to put sb in his (*ou* her) place.

remblai [rãnble] *nm* embankment.

remblayer [rãnblãyã] *vt* to bank up; (*fossé*) to fill in.

rembobiner [rãnbobēnã] *vt* to rewind.

rembourrage [rãnbōōrãzh] *nm* stuffing; padding.

rembourré, e [rãnbōōrã] *a* padded.

rembourrer [rãnbōōrã] *vt* to stuff; (*dossier,*

vêtement, souliers) to pad.

remboursable [rånbŏōrsábl(ə)] *a* repayable.

remboursement [rånbŏōrsəmåń] *nm* repayment; **envoi contre** ~ cash on delivery.

rembourser [rånbŏōrsã] *vt* to pay back, repay.

rembrunir [rånbrünẽr]: **se** ~ *vi* to grow somber (*US*) *ou* sombre (*Brit*).

remède [rəmed] *nm* (*médicament*) medicine; (*traitement, fig*) remedy, cure; **trouver un** ~ **à** (*MÉD, fig*) to find a cure for.

remédier [rəmãdyã]: ~ **à** *vt* to remedy.

remembrement [rəmåńbrəmåń] *nm* (*AGR*) regrouping of lands.

remémorer [rəmãmorã]: **se** ~ *vt* to recall, recollect.

remerciements [rəmersẽmåń] *nmpl* thanks; (**avec**) **tous mes** ~ (with) grateful *ou* many thanks.

remercier [rəmersyã] *vt* to thank; (*congédier*) to dismiss; ~ **qn de/d'avoir fait** to thank sb for/for having done; **non, je vous remercie** no, thank you.

remettre [rəmetr(ə)] *vt* (*vêtement*): ~ **qch** to put sth back on, put sth on again; (*replacer*): ~ **qch quelque part** to put sth back somewhere; (*ajouter*): ~ **du sel/un sucre** to add more salt/another lump of sugar; (*rétablir: personne*): ~ **qn** to set sb back on his (*ou* her) feet; (*rendre, restituer*): ~ **qch à qn** to give sth back to sb, return sth to sb; (*donner, confier: paquet, argent*): ~ **qch à qn** to hand sth over to sb, deliver sth to sb; (*prix, décoration*): ~ **qch à qn** to present sb with sth; (*ajourner*): ~ **qch (à)** to postpone sth *ou* put sth off (until); **se** ~ *vi* to get better, recover; **se** ~ **de** to recover from, get over; **s'en** ~ **à** to leave it (up) to; **se** ~ **à faire/qch** to start doing/sth again; ~ **une pendule à l'heure** to set a clock right; ~ **un moteur/une machine en marche** to get an engine/a machine going again; ~ **en état/en ordre** to repair/sort out; ~ **en cause/question** to challenge/question again; ~ **sa démission** to hand in one's notice; ~ **qch à neuf** to make sth as good as new; ~ **qn à sa place** (*fig*) to put sb in his (*ou* her) place.

remis, e [rəmĩ, -ẽz] *pp de* **remettre** ♦ *nf* delivery; presentation; (*rabais*) discount; (*local*) shed; ~ **en marche/en ordre** starting up again/sorting out; ~ **en cause/question** calling into question/challenging; ~ **de fonds** remittance; ~ **en jeu** (*FOOTBALL*) throw-in; ~ **à neuf** restoration; ~ **de peine** reduction *ou* commutation (*US*) of sentence.

remiser [rəmẽzã] *vt* to put away.

rémission [rãmẽsyóń]: **sans** ~ *a* irremediable ♦ *ad* unremittingly.

remodeler [rəmodlã] *vt* to remodel; (*fig: restructurer*) to restructure.

rémois, e [rãmwá, -wáz] *a ou* from Rheims ♦ *nm/f*: **R~, e** inhabitant *ou* native of Rheims.

remontant [rəmóńtåń] *nm* tonic, pick-me-up.

remontée [rəmóńtã] *nf* rising; ascent; ~**s mécaniques** (*SKI*) ski lifts, ski tows.

remonte-pente [rəmóńtpåńt] *nm* ski lift, (ski) tow.

remonter [rəmóńtã] *vi* (*à nouveau*) to go back

up; (*sur un cheval*) to remount; (*après une descente*) to go up (again); (*dans une voiture*) to get back in; (*jupe*) to ride up ♦ *vt* (*pente*) to go up; (*fleuve*) to sail (*ou* swim etc) up; (*manches, pantalon*) to roll up; (*col*) to turn up; (*niveau, limite*) to raise; (*fig: personne*) to buck up; (*moteur, meuble*) to put back together, reassemble; (*garde-robe etc*) to renew, replenish; (*montre, mécanisme*) to wind up; ~ **le moral à qn** to raise sb's spirits; ~ **à** (*dater de*) to date *ou* go back to; ~ **en voiture** to get back into the car.

remontoir [rəmóńtwàr] *nm* winding mechanism, winder.

remontrance [rəmóńtråńs] *nf* reproof, reprimand.

remontrer [rəmóńtrã] *vt* (*montrer de nouveau*): ~ **qch (à qn)** to show sth again (to sb); (*fig*): **en** ~ **à** to prove one's superiority over.

remords [rəmor] *nm* remorse *q*; **avoir des** ~ to feel remorse, be conscience-stricken.

remorque [rəmork(ə)] *nf* trailer; **prendre/être en** ~ to tow/be on tow; **être à la** ~ (*fig*) to tag along (behind).

remorquer [rəmorkã] *vt* to tow.

remorqueur [rəmorkœr] *nm* tug(boat).

rémoulade [rãmŏōlàd] *nf* dressing with mustard and herbs.

rémouleur [rãmŏōlœr] *nm* (knife- *ou* scissor-) grinder.

remous [rəmŏō] *nm* (*d'un navire*) (back)wash *q*; (*de rivière*) swirl, eddy ♦ *nmpl* (*fig*) stir *sg*.

rempailler [rånpåyã] *vt* to reseat (with straw).

remparts [rånpár] *nmpl* walls, ramparts.

rempiler [rånpẽlã] *vt* (*dossiers, livres etc*) to pile up again ♦ *vi* (*MIL, fam*) to join up again.

remplaçant, e [rånplásåń, -åńt] *nm/f* replacement, substitute, stand-in; (*THÉÂTRE*) understudy; (*SCOL*) substitute (*US*) *ou* supply (*Brit*) teacher.

remplacement [rånplásmåń] *nm* replacement; (*job*) replacement work *q*; (*suppléance: SCOL*) substitute (*US*) *ou* supply (*Brit*) teacher; **assurer le** ~ **de qn** (*suj: remplaçant*) to stand in *ou* substitute for sb; **faire des** ~**s** (*professeur*) to do supply *ou* substitute teaching; (*médecin*) to do locum work.

remplacer [rånplásã] *vt* to replace; (*prendre temporairement la place de*) to stand in for; (*tenir lieu de*) to take the place of, act as a substitute for; ~ **qch/qn par** to replace sth/sb with.

rempli, e [rånplẽ] *a* (*emploi du temps*) full, busy; ~ **de** full of, filled with.

remplir [rånplẽr] *vt* to fill (up); (*questionnaire*) to fill out *ou* in; (*obligations, fonction, condition*) to fulfill (*US*), fulfil (*Brit*); **se** ~ *vi* to fill up; ~ **qch de** to fill sth with.

remplissage [rånplẽsàzh] *nm* (*fig: péj*) padding.

remploi [rånplwá] *nm* re-use.

rempocher [rånposhã] *vt* to put back into one's pocket.

remporter [rånportã] *vt* (*marchandise*) to take

away; (*fig*) to win, achieve.
rempoter [rɑ̃pɔtā] *vt* to repot.
remuant, e [rəmüäṅ, -äṅt] *a* restless.
remue-ménage [rəmümānázh] *nm inv* commotion.
remuer [rəmüä] *vt* to move; (*café, sauce*) to stir ♦ *vi* to move; (*fig: opposants*) to show signs of unrest; **se** ~ *vi* to move; (*se démener*) to stir o.s.; (*fam*) to get a move on.
rémunérateur, trice [rāmünārátœr, -trēs] *a* remunerative, lucrative.
rémunération [rāmünārâsyôṅ] *nf* remuneration.
rémunérer [rāmünārā] *vt* to remunerate, pay.
renâcler [rənáklā] *vi* to snort; (*fig*) to grumble, balk.
renaissance [rənesáṅs] *nf* rebirth, revival; **la R~** the Renaissance.
renaître [rənetr(ə)] *vi* to be revived; ~ **à la vie** to take on a new lease of life; ~ **à l'espoir** to find fresh hope.
rénal, e, aux [rānál, -ō] *a* renal, kidney *cpd*.
renard [rənár] *nm* fox.
renardeau [rənárdō] *nm* fox cub.
rencard [ráṅkár] *nm* = **rancard**.
rencart [ráṅkár] *nm* = **rancart**.
renchérir [ráṅshārēr] *vi* to become more expensive; (*fig*): ~ **(sur)** to add something (to).
renchérissement [ráṅshārēsmáṅ] *nm* increase (in the cost *ou* price of).
rencontre [ráṅkôṅtr(ə)] *nf* (*de cours d'eau*) confluence; (*véhicules*) collision; (*entrevue, congrès, match etc*) meeting; (*imprévue*) encounter; **faire la** ~ **de qn** to meet sb; **aller à la** ~ **de qn** to go and meet sb; **amours de** ~ casual love affairs.
rencontrer [ráṅkôṅtrā] *vt* to meet; (*mot, expression*) to come across; (*difficultés*) to meet with; **se** ~ to meet; (*véhicules*) to collide.
rendement [rāndmáṅ] *nm* (*d'un travailleur, d'une machine*) output; (*d'une culture*) yield; (*d'un investissement*) return; **à plein** ~ at full capacity.
rendez-vous [rándāvōō] *nm* (*rencontre*) appointment; (: *d'amoureux*) date; (*lieu*) meeting place; **donner** ~ **à qn** to arrange to meet sb; **recevoir sur** ~ to have an appointment system; **fixer un** ~ **à qn** to give sb an appointment; **avoir/prendre** ~ **(avec)** to have/make an appointment (with); **prendre** ~ **chez le médecin** to make an appointment with the doctor; ~ **spatial** *ou* **orbital** docking (in space).
rendre [rándr(ə)] *vt* (*livre, argent etc*) to give back, return; (*otages, visite, politesse, JUR: verdict*) to return; (*honneurs*) to pay; (*sang, aliments*) to bring up; (*sons: suj: instrument*) to produce, make; (*exprimer, traduire*) to render; (*jugement*) to pronounce, render; (*faire devenir*): ~ **qn célèbre/qch possible** to make sb famous/sth possible; **se** ~ *vi* (*capituler*) to surrender, give o.s. up; (*aller*): **se** ~ **quelque part** to go somewhere; **se** ~ **à** (*arguments etc*) to bow to; (*ordres*) to comply with; **se** ~ **compte de qch** to realize sth; ~ **la vue/la santé à qn** to restore

sb's sight/health; ~ **la liberté à qn** to set sb free; ~ **la monnaie** to give change; **se** ~ **insupportable/malade** to become unbearable/make o.s. ill.
rendu, e [rándü] *pp de* **rendre** ♦ *a* (*fatigué*) exhausted.
renégat, e [rənāgá, -át] *nm/f* renegade.
renégocier [rənāgosyā] *vt* to renegociate.
rênes [ren] *nfpl* reins.
renfermé, e [ráṅfermā] *a* (*fig*) withdrawn ♦ *nm*: **sentir le** ~ to smell stuffy.
renfermer [ráṅfermā] *vt* to contain; **se** ~ **(sur soi-même)** to withdraw into o.s.
renfiler [ráṅfēlā] *vt* (*collier*) to rethread; (*pull*) to slip on.
renflé, e [ráṅflā] *a* bulging, bulbous.
renflement [ráṅfləmáṅ] *nm* bulge.
renflouer [ráṅflōōā] *vt* to refloat; (*fig*) to set back on its (*ou* his/her *etc*) feet (again).
renfoncement [ráṅfôṅsmáṅ] *nm* recess.
renforcer [ráṅforsā] *vt* to reinforce; ~ **qn dans ses opinions** to confirm sb's opinion.
renfort [ráṅfor]: ~**s** *nmpl* reinforcements; **en** ~ as a back-up; **à grand** ~ **de** with a great deal of.
renfrogné, e [ráṅfronyā] *a* sullen, scowling.
renfrogner [ráṅfronyā]: **se** ~ *vi* to scowl.
rengager [ráṅgázhā] *vt* (*personnel*) to take on again; **se** ~ (*MIL*) to re-enlist.
rengaine [ráṅgen] *nf* (*péj*) old tune.
rengainer [ráṅgānā] *vt* (*revolver*) to put back in its holster; (*épée*) to sheathe; (*fam: compliment, discours*) to save, withhold.
rengorger [ráṅgorzhā]: **se** ~ *vi* (*fig*) to puff o.s. up.
renier [rənyā] *vt* (*parents*) to disown, repudiate; (*engagements*) to go back on; (*foi*) to renounce.
renifler [rənēflā] *vi* to sniff ♦ *vt* (*tabac*) to sniff up; (*odeur*) to sniff.
rennais, e [rene, -ez] *a* of *ou* from Rennes ♦ *nm/f*: **R~, e** inhabitant *ou* native of Rennes.
renne [ren] *nm* reindeer *inv*.
renom [rənôṅ] *nm* reputation; (*célébrité*) renown; **vin de grand** ~ celebrated *ou* highly renowned wine.
renommé, e [r(ə)nomā] *a* celebrated, renowned ♦ *nf* fame.
renoncement [rənôṅsmáṅ] *nm* abnegation, renunciation.
renoncer [rənôṅsā] *vi*: ~ **à** *vt* to give up; ~ **à faire** to give up the idea of doing; **j'y renonce!** I give up!
renouer [rənwā] *vt* (*cravate etc*) to retie; (*fig: conversation, liaison*) to renew, resume; ~ **avec** (*tradition*) to revive; (*habitude*) to take up again; ~ **avec qn** to take up with sb again.
renouveau, x [rənōōvō] *nm* revival; ~ **de succès** renewed success.
renouvelable [r(ə)nōōvlábl(ə)] *a* (*contrat, bail*) renewable; (*expérience*) which can be renewed.
renouveler [rənōōvlā] *vt* to renew; (*exploit, méfait*) to repeat; **se** ~ *vi* (*incident*) to recur, happen again, be repeated; (*cellules etc*) to be renewed *ou* replaced; (*artiste, écrivain*) to try something new.
renouvellement [r(ə)nōōvelmáṅ] *nm* renewal;

recurrence.

rénovation [rānovâsyôn] *nf* renovation; restoration; reform(ing); redevelopment.

rénover [rānovā] *vt* (*immeuble*) to renovate, do up; (*meuble*) to restore; (*enseignement*) to reform; (*quartier*) to redevelop.

renseignement [rānsenymân] *nm* information *q*, piece of information; (*MIL*) intelligence *q*; **prendre des ~s sur** to make inquiries about, ask for information about; **(guichet des)** ~s information desk; **(service des)** ~s (*TÉL*) information (*US*), directory inquiries (*Brit*); **service/agent de** ~s (*MIL*) intelligence service/agent; **les** ~s **généraux** ≈ the secret police.

renseigner [rānsānyā] *vt*: ~ **qn (sur)** to give information to sb (about); **se** ~ *vi* to ask for information, make inquiries.

rentabiliser [rāntābēlēzā] *vt* (*capitaux, production*) to make profitable.

rentabilité [rāntābēlētā] *nf* profitability; cost-effectiveness; (*d'un investissement*) return; **seuil de** ~ break-even point.

rentable [rāntābl(ə)] *a* profitable; cost-effective.

rente [rānt] *nf* income; (*pension*) pension; (*titre*) government stock *ou* bond; ~ **viagère** life annuity.

rentier, ière [rāntyā, -yer] *nm/f* person of private *ou* independent means.

rentrée [rāntrā] *nf*: ~ **(d'argent)** cash *q* coming in; **la** ~ **(des classes)** the start of the new school year; **la** ~ **(parlementaire)** the reopening *ou* reassembly of parliament; **faire sa** ~ (*artiste, acteur*) to make a comeback.

rentrer [rāntrā] *vi* (*entrer de nouveau*) to go (*ou* come) back in; (*entrer*) to go (*ou* come) in; (*revenir chez soi*) to go (*ou* come) (back) home; (*air, clou: pénétrer*) to go in; (*revenu, argent*) to come in ♦ *vt* (*foins*) to bring in; (*véhicule*) to put away; (*chemise dans pantalon etc*) to tuck in; (*griffes*) to draw in; (*train d'atterrissage*) to raise; (*fig: larmes, colère etc*) to hold back; ~ **le ventre** to pull in one's stomach; ~ **dans** to go (*ou* come) back into; to go (*ou* come) into; (*famille, patrie*) to go back *ou* return to; (*heurter*) to crash into; (*appartenir à*) to be included in; (*: catégorie etc*) to fall into; ~ **dans l'ordre** to get back to normal; ~ **dans ses frais** to recover one's expenses (*ou* initial outlay).

renverrai [rānverā] *etc vb voir* **renvoyer**.

renversant, e [rānversān, -ānt] *a* amazing, astounding.

renverse [rānvers(ə)]: **à la** ~ *ad* backwards.

renversé, e [rānversā] *a* (*écriture*) backhand; (*image*) reversed; (*stupéfait*) staggered.

renversement [rānversəmân] *nm* (*d'un régime, des traditions*) overthrow; ~ **de la situation** reversal of the situation.

renverser [rānversā] *vt* (*faire tomber: chaise, verre*) to knock over, overturn; (*piéton*) to knock down; (*liquide, contenu*) to spill, upset; (*retourner: verre, image*) to turn upside down, invert; (*: ordre des mots etc*) to reverse; (*fig: gouvernement etc*) to overthrow; (*stupéfier*) to bowl over, stagger; **se** ~ *vi* to fall over; to overturn; to spill; **se** ~ **(en arrière)** to lean back; ~ **la tête/le corps**

(en arrière) to tip one's head back/throw oneself back; ~ **la vapeur** (*fig*) to change course.

renvoi [rānvwā] *nm* dismissal; return; reflection; postponement; (*référence*) cross-reference; (*éructation*) belch.

renvoyer [rānvwāyā] *vt* to send back; (*congédier*) to dismiss; (*TENNIS*) to return; (*lumière*) to reflect; (*son*) to echo; (*ajourner*): ~ **qch (à)** to put sth off *ou* postpone sth (until); ~ **qch à qn** (*rendre*) to return sth to sb; ~ **qn à** (*fig*) to refer sb to.

réorganisation [rāorgānēzāsyôn] *nf* reorganization.

réorganiser [rāorgānēzā] *vt* to reorganize.

réorienter [rāoryāntā] *vt* to reorient(ate), redirect.

réouverture [rāōōvertür] *nf* reopening.

repaire [rəper] *nm* den.

repaître [rəpetr(ə)] *vt* to feast; to feed; **se** ~ **de** *vt* (*animal*) to feed on; (*fig*) to wallow *ou* revel in.

répandre [rāpāndr(ə)] *vt* (*renverser*) to spill; (*étaler, diffuser*) to spread; (*lumière*) to shed; (*chaleur, odeur*) to give off; **se** ~ *vi* to spill; to spread; **se** ~ **en** (*injures etc*) to pour out.

répandu, e [rāpāndü] *pp de* **répandre** ♦ *a* (*opinion, usage*) widespread.

réparable [rāpárábl(ə)] *a* (*montre etc*) repairable; (*perte etc*) which can be made up for.

reparaître [rəpáretr(ə)] *vi* to reappear.

réparateur, trice [rāpárátœr, -trēs] *nm/f* repairer.

réparation [rāpárâsyôn] *nf* repairing *q*, repair; **en** ~ (*machine etc*) under repair; **demander à qn** ~ **de** (*offense etc*) to ask sb to make amends for.

réparer [rāpárā] *vt* to repair; (*fig: offense*) to make up for, atone for; (*: oubli, erreur*) to make *ou* set right.

reparler [rəpárlā] *vi*: ~ **de qn/qch** to talk about sb/sth again; ~ **à qn** to speak to sb again.

repars [rəpár] *etc vb voir* **repartir**.

repartie [rəpártē] *nf* retort; **avoir de la** ~ to be quick at repartee.

repartir [rəpártēr] *vi* to set off again; to leave again; (*fig*) to get going again, pick up again; ~ **à zéro** to start from scratch (again).

répartir [rāpártēr] *vt* (*pour attribuer*) to divide up, share out (*Brit*); (*pour disperser, disposer*) to divide up; (*poids, chaleur*) to distribute; (*étaler: dans le temps*): ~ **sur** to spread over; (*classer, diviser*): ~ **en** to divide into, split up into; **se** ~ *vt* (*travail, rôles*) to divide up between themselves.

répartition [rāpártēsyôn] *nf* dividing up; distribution.

repas [rəpâ] *nm* meal; **à l'heure des** ~ at mealtimes.

repassage [rəpásázh] *nm* ironing.

repasser [rəpásā] *vi* to come (*ou* go) back ♦ *vt* (*vêtement, tissu*) to iron; (*examen*) to retake; (*film*) to show again; (*lame*) to sharpen; (*leçon, rôle: revoir*) to go over (again); (*plat, pain*): ~ **qch à qn** to pass sth back to sb.

repasseuse |rəpâsœz| *nf* (*machine*) ironing machine.

repayer |rəpāyā| *vt* to pay again.

repêchage |rəpeshäzh| *nm* (*SCOL*): **question de** ~ question to give students (*ou* examinees) a second chance.

repêcher |rəpâshā| *vt* (*noyé*) to recover the body of, fish out; (*fam: candidat*) to pass (*by inflating grades*); to give a second chance to.

repeindre |rəpaṅdr(ə)| *vt* to repaint.

repentir |rəpáṅtēr| *nm* repentance; **se** ~ *vi*: **se** ~ (**de**) to repent (of).

répercussions |rāperküsyóṅ| *nfpl* repercussions.

répercuter |rāperkütā| *vt* (*réfléchir, renvoyer: son, voix*) to reflect; (*faire transmettre: consignes, charges etc*) to pass on; **se** ~ *vi* (*bruit*) to reverberate; (*fig*): **se** ~ **sur** to have repercussions on.

repère |rəper| *nm* mark; (*monument etc*) landmark; (**point de**) ~ point of reference.

repérer |rəpārā| *vt* (*erreur, connaissance*) to spot; (*abri, ennemi*) to locate; **se** ~ *vi* to get one's bearings; **se faire** ~ to be spotted.

répertoire |rāpertwàr| *nm* (*liste*) (alphabetical) list; (*carnet*) index notebook; (*INFORM*) directory; (*de carnet*) thumb index; (*indicateur*) directory, index; (*d'un théâtre, artiste*) repertoire.

répertorier |rāpārtoryā| *vt* to itemize, list.

répéter |rāpātā| *vt* to repeat; (*préparer: leçon: aussi vi*) to learn, go over; (*THÉÂTRE*) to rehearse; **se** ~ (*redire*) to repeat o.s.; (*se reproduire*) to be repeated, recur.

répéteur |rāpātœr| *nm* (*TÉL*) repeater.

répétitif, ive |rāpātētēf, -ēv| *a* repetitive.

répétition |rāpātēsyóṅ| *nf* repetition; (*THÉÂTRE*) rehearsal; ~**s** *nfpl* (*leçons*) private tutoring *sg*; **armes à** ~ repeater weapons; ~ **générale** final dress rehearsal.

repeupler |rəpœplā| *vt* to repopulate; (*forêt, rivière*) to restock.

repiquage |rəpēkázh| *nm* pricking out, planting out; re-recording.

repiquer |rəpēkā| *vt* (*plants*) to prick out, plant out; (*enregistrement*) to re-record.

répit |rāpē| *nm* respite; **sans** ~ without letting up.

replacer |rəplásā| *vt* to replace, put back.

replanter |rəplàṅtā| *vt* to replant.

replat |rəplá| *nm* ledge.

replâtrer |rəplátrā| *vt* (*mur*) to replaster; (*fig*) to patch up.

replet, ète |rəple, -et| *a* chubby, fat.

repli |rəplē| *nm* (*d'une étoffe*) fold; (*MIL, fig*) withdrawal.

replier |rəplēyā| *vt* (*rabattre*) to fold down *ou* over; **se** ~ *vi* (*troupes, armée*) to withdraw, fall back; **se** ~ **sur soi-même** to withdraw into oneself.

réplique |rāplēk| *nf* (*repartie, fig*) reply; (*objection*) retort; (*THÉÂTRE*) line; (*copie*) replica, copy; **donner la** ~ **à** to play opposite; **sans** ~ *a* no-nonsense; irrefutable.

répliquer |rāplēkā| *vi* to reply; (*avec impertinence*) to answer back; (*riposter*) to retaliate.

replonger |rəplóṅzhā| *vt*: ~ **qch dans** to plunge sth back into; **se** ~ **dans** (*journal etc*)

to immerse o.s. in again.

répondant, e |rāpóṅdàṅ, -àṅt| *nm/f* (*garant*) guarantor, surety.

répondeur |rāpóṅdœr| *nm*: ~ (**automatique**) (*TÉL*) (telephone) answering machine.

répondre |rāpóṅdr(ə)| *vi* to answer, reply; (*freins, mécanisme*) to respond; ~ **à** *vt* to reply to, answer; (*avec impertinence*): ~ **à qn** to answer sb back; (*invitation, convocation*) to reply to; (*affection, salut*) to return; (*provocation, suj: mécanisme etc*) to respond to; (*correspondre à: besoin*) to answer; (*: conditions*) to meet; (*: description*) to match; ~ **que** to answer *ou* reply that; ~ **de** to answer for.

réponse |rāpóṅs| *nf* answer, reply; **avec** ~ **payée** (*POSTES*) reply-paid, post-paid (*US*); **avoir** ~ **à tout** to have an answer for everything; **en** ~ **à** in reply to; **carte-** /**bulletin-**~ reply card/slip.

report |rəpor| *nm* postponement; transfer; ~ **d'incorporation** (*MIL*) deferment.

reportage |rəportázh| *nm* (*bref*) report; (*écrit: documentaire*) story; article; (*en direct*) commentary; (*genre, activité*): **le** ~ reporting.

reporter *nm* |rəporter| reporter ♦ *vt* |rəportā| (*total*): ~ **qch sur** to carry sth forward *ou* over to; (*ajourner*): ~ **qch (à)** to postpone sth (until); (*transférer*): ~ **qch sur** to transfer sth to; **se** ~ **à** (*époque*) to think back to; (*document*) to refer to.

repos |rəpó| *nm* rest; (*fig*) peace (and quiet); (*mental*) peace of mind; (*MIL*): ~**!** (stand) at ease!; **en** ~ at rest; **au** ~ at rest; (*soldat*) at ease; **de tout** ~ safe.

reposant, e |r(ə)pōzàṅ, -àṅt| *a* restful; (*sommeil*) refreshing.

repose |rəpōz| *nf* refitting.

reposé, e |rəpōzā| *a* fresh, rested; **à tête** ~**e** in a leisurely way, taking time to think.

repose-pied |rəpōzpyā| *nm inv* footrest.

reposer |rəpōzā| *vt* (*verre, livre*) to put down; (*rideaux, carreaux*) to put back; (*délasser*) to rest; (*problème*) to reformulate ♦ *vi* (*liquide, pâte*) to settle, rest; (*personne*): **ici repose** ... here lies ...; ~ **sur** to be built on; (*fig*) to rest on; **se** ~ *vi* to rest; **se** ~ **sur qn** to rely on sb.

repoussant, e |rəpōōsàṅ, -àṅt| *a* repulsive.

repoussé, e |rəpōōsā| *a* (*cuir*) embossed (by hand).

repousser |rəpōōsā| *vi* to grow again ♦ *vt* to repel, repulse; (*offre*) to turn down, reject; (*tiroir, personne*) to push back; (*différer*) to put off, defer.

répréhensible |rāprāāṅsēbl(ə)| *a* reprehensible.

reprendre |rəpràṅdr(ə)| *vt* (*prisonnier, ville*) to recapture; (*objet prêté, donné*) to take back; (*chercher*): **je viendrai te** ~ **à 4h** I'll come back for you at 4; (*se resservir de*): ~ **du pain/un œuf** to take (*ou* eat) more bread/another egg; (*COMM: article usagé*) to take back; to take as a trade-in; (*firme, entreprise*) to take over; (*travail, promenade*) to resume; (*emprunter: argument, idée*) to take up, use; (*refaire: article etc*) to go over again; (*jupe etc*) to alter; (*émission, pièce*) to put on again; (*réprimander*) to tell off; (*corriger*) to correct ♦ *vi* (*classes, pluie*) to start (up) again; (*activités, travaux, combats*) to resume, start (up) again; (*affaires, industrie*) to pick up; (*dire*): **reprit-il** he went on; **se ~** (*se ressaisir*) to recover, pull o.s. together; **s'y ~** to make another attempt; **~ des forces** to recover one's strength; **~ courage** to take new courage; **~ ses habitudes/sa liberté** to get back into one's old habits/regain one's freedom; **~ la route** to resume one's journey, set off again; **~ connaissance** to come to, regain consciousness; **~ haleine** *ou* **son souffle** to get one's breath back; **~ la parole** to speak again.

repreneur [rəprənœr] *nm* company fixer *ou* doctor.

reprenne [rəpren] *etc vb voir* **reprendre**.

représailles [rəprāzây] *nfpl* reprisals, retaliation *sg*.

représentant, e [rəprāzàn̄tàn̄, -àn̄t] *nm/f* representative.

représentatif, ive [rəprāzàn̄tàtēf, -ēv] *a* representative.

représentation [rəprāzàn̄tàsyôn̄] *nf* representation; performing; (*symbole, image*) representation; (*spectacle*) performance; (*COMM*): **la ~** commercial traveling (*US*) *ou* travelling (*Brit*); sales representation; **frais de ~** (*d'un diplomate*) entertainment allowance.

représenter [rəprāzàn̄tà] *vt* to represent; (*donner: pièce, opéra*) to perform; **se ~** *vt* (*se figurer*) to imagine; to visualize ♦ *vi*: **se ~ à** (*POL*) to run again for; (*SCOL*) to retake.

répressif, ive [rāprāsēf, -ēv] *a* repressive.

répression [rāprāsyôn̄] *nf* (*voir réprimer*) suppression; repression; (*POL*): **la ~** repression; **mesures de ~** repressive measures.

réprimande [rāprēmàn̄d] *nf* reprimand, rebuke.

réprimander [rāprēmàn̄dà] *vt* to reprimand, rebuke.

réprimer [rāprēmà] *vt* (*émotions*) to suppress; (*peuple etc*) repress.

repris, e [rəprē, -ēz] *pp de* **reprendre** ♦ *nm*: **~ de justice** ex-prisoner, ex-convict.

reprise [rəprēz] *nf* (*recommencement*) resumption; (*économique*) recovery; (*TV*) rerun; (*CINÉMA*) rerun; (*BOXE etc*) round; (*AUTO*) acceleration *q*; (*COMM*) trade-in; (*de location*) sum asked for any extras or improvements made to the property; (*raccommodage*) darn; mend; **la ~ des hostilités** the resumption of hostilities; **à plusieurs ~s** on several occasions, several times.

repriser [rəprēzà] *vt* to darn; to mend; **aiguille/coton à ~** darning needle/thread.

réprobateur, trice [rāprobátœr, -trēs] *a* reproving.

réprobation [rāprobàsyôn̄] *nf* reprobation.

reproche [rəprosh] *nm* (*remontrance*) reproach; **ton/air de ~** reproachful tone/look; **faire des ~s à qn** to reproach sb; **faire ~ à qn de qch** to reproach sb for sth; **sans ~(s)** beyond *ou* above reproach.

reprocher [rəproshà] *vt*: **~ qch à qn** to reproach *ou* blame sb for sth; **~ qch à** (*machine, théorie*) to have sth against; **se ~ qch/d'avoir fait qch** to blame o.s. for sth/for doing sth.

reproducteur, trice [rəprodüktœr, -trēs] *a* reproductive.

reproduction [rəprodüksyôn̄] *nf* reproduction; **~ interdite** all rights (of reproduction) reserved.

reproduire [rəproduēr] *vt* to reproduce; **se ~** *vi* (*BIO*) to reproduce; (*recommencer*) to recur, re-occur.

réprouvé, e [rāprōōvā] *nm/f* reprobate.

réprouver [rāprōōvà] *vt* to reprove.

reptation [rəptàsyôn̄] *nf* crawling.

reptile [rəptēl] *nm* reptile.

repu, e [rəpü] *pp de* **repaître** ♦ *a* satisfied, sated.

républicain, e [rāpüblēkàn̄, -en] *a, nm/f* republican.

république [rāpüblēk] *nf* republic; **R~ arabe du Yémen** Yemen Arab Republic; **R~ Centrafricaine** Central African Republic; **R~ de Corée** South Korea; **R~ démocratique allemande (RDA)** German Democratic Republic (GDR); **R~ dominicaine** Dominican Republic; **R~ fédérale d'Allemagne (RFA)** Federal Republic of Germany; **R~ d'Irlande** Irish Republic, Eire; **R~ populaire de Chine** People's Republic of China; **R~ populaire démocratique de Corée** Democratic People's Republic of Korea; **R~ populaire du Yémen** People's Democratic Republic of Yemen.

répudier [rāpüdyà] *vt* (*femme*) to repudiate; (*doctrine*) to renounce.

répugnance [rāpünyàn̄s] *nf* repugnance, loathing; **avoir** *ou* **éprouver de la ~ pour** (*médicament, comportement, travail etc*) to have an aversion to; **avoir** *ou* **éprouver de la ~ à faire qch** to be reluctant to do sth.

répugnant, e [rāpünyàn̄, -àn̄t] *a* repulsive, loathsome.

répugner [rāpünyà]: **~ à** *vt*: **~ à qn** to repel *ou* disgust sb; **~ à faire** to be loath *ou* reluctant to do.

répulsion [rāpülsyôn̄] *nf* repulsion.

réputation [rāpütàsyôn̄] *nf* reputation; **avoir la ~ d'être ...** to have a reputation for being ...; **connaître qn/qch de ~** to know sb/sth by repute; **de ~ mondiale** world-renowned.

réputé, e [rāpütà] *a* renowned; **être ~ pour** to have a reputation for, be renowned for.

requérir [rəkārēr] *vt* (*nécessiter*) to require, call for; (*au nom de la loi*) to call upon; (*JUR: peine*) to call for, demand.

requête [rəket] *nf* request, petition; (*JUR*) petition.

requiem [rāküēyem] *nm* requiem.

requiers [rəkyer] *etc vb voir* **requérir**.

requin [rəkàn̄] *nm* shark.

requinquer [rəkàn̄kà] *vt* to set up, pep up.

requis, e [rəkē, -ēz] *pp de* **requérir** ♦ *a* required.

réquisition [rākēzēsyôn̄] *nf* requisition.

réquisitionner [rākēzēsyonà] *vt* to requisition.

réquisitoire [rākēzētwàr] *nm* (*JUR*) closing speech for the prosecution; (*fig*): **~ contre** indictment of.

RER *sigle m* (= *Réseau express régional*) *Greater Paris high speed train service.*

rescapé, e [rɛskápā] *nm/f* survivor.

rescousse [rɛskōōs] *nf*: **aller à la ~ de qn** to go to sb's aid *ou* rescue; **appeler qn à la ~** to call on sb for help.

réseau, x [rāzō] *nm* network.

réséda [rāzādá] *nm* (*BOT*) reseda, mignonette.

réservation [rāzɛrvásyôǹ] *nf* reservation; booking.

réserve [rāzɛrv(ə)] *nf* (*retenue*) reserve; (*entrepôt*) storeroom; (*restriction, aussi: d'Indiens*) reservation; (*de pêche, chasse*) preserve; (*restrictions*): **faire des ~s** to have reservations; **officier de ~** reserve officer; **sous toutes ~s** with all reserve; (*dire*) with reservations; **sous ~ de** subject to; **sans ~** *ad* unreservedly; **en ~** in reserve; **de ~** (*provisions etc*) in reserve.

réservé, e [rāzɛrvā] *a* (*discret*) reserved; (*chasse, pêche*) private; **~ à** *ou* **pour** reserved for.

réserver [rāzɛrvā] *vt* (*gén*) to reserve; (*chambre, billet etc*) to book, reserve; (*mettre de côté, garder*): **~ qch pour** *ou* **à** to keep *ou* save sth for; **~ qch à qn** to reserve (*ou* book) sth for sb; (*fig: destiner*) to have sth in store for sb; **se ~ le droit de faire** to reserve the right to do.

réserviste [rāzɛrvēst(ə)] *nm* reservist.

réservoir [rāzɛrvwár] *nm* tank.

résidence [rāzēdáǹs] *nf* residence; **~ principale/secondaire** main/second home; **~ universitaire** residence hall (*US*), dormitory (*US*), hall of residence (*Brit*); **(en) ~ surveillée** (under) house arrest.

résident, e [rāzēdáǹ, -áǹt] *nm/f* (*ressortissant*) foreign resident; (*d'un immeuble*) resident ◆ *a* (*INFORM*) resident.

résidentiel, le [rāzēdáǹsyɛl] *a* residential.

résider [rāzēdā] *vi*: **~ à** *ou* **dans** *ou* **en** to reside in; **~ dans** (*fig*) to lie in.

résidu [rāzēdü] *nm* residue *q*.

résiduel, le [rāzēdüɛl] *a* residual.

résignation [rāzēnyásyôǹ] *nf* resignation.

résigné, e [rāzēnyā] *a* resigned.

résigner [rāzēnyā] *vt* to relinquish, resign; **se ~** *vi*: **se ~ (à qch/à faire)** to resign o.s. (to sth/to doing).

résilier [rāzēlyā] *vt* to terminate.

résille [rāzēy] *nf* (*hair*)net.

résine [rāzēn] *nf* resin.

résiné, e [rāzēnā] *a*: **vin ~** retsina.

résineux, euse [rāzēnœ̄, -œ̄z] *a* resinous ◆ *nm* coniferous tree.

résistance [rāzēstáǹs] *nf* resistance; (*de réchaud, bouilloire: fil*) element.

résistant, e [rāzēstáǹ, -áǹt] *a* (*personne*) robust, tough; (*matériau*) strong, hard-wearing ◆ *nm/f* (*patriote*) Resistance worker *ou* fighter.

résister [rāzēstā] *vi* to resist; **~ à** *vt* (*assaut, tentation*) to resist; (*effort, souffrance*) to withstand; (*suj: matériau, plante*) to stand up to, withstand; (*personne: désobéir à*) to stand up to, oppose.

résolu, e [rāzolü] *pp de* **résoudre** ◆ *a* (*ferme*) resolute; **être ~ à qch/faire** to be set upon sth/doing.

résolution [rāzolüsyôǹ] *nf* solving; (*fermeté, décision, INFORM*) resolution; **prendre la ~ de** to make a resolution to.

résolvais [rāzolvɛ] *etc vb voir* **résoudre**.

résonance [rāzonáǹs] *nf* resonance.

résonner [rāzonā] *vi* (*cloche, pas*) to reverberate, resound; (*salle*) to be resonant; **~ de** to resound with.

résorber [rāzorbā]: **se ~** *vi* (*MÉD*) to be resorbed; (*fig*) to be absorbed.

résoudre [rāzōōdr(ə)] *vt* to solve; **~ qn à faire qch** to get sb to make up his (*ou* her) mind to do sth; **~ de faire** to resolve to do; **se ~ à faire** to bring o.s. to do.

respect [rɛspɛ] *nm* respect; **tenir en ~** to keep at bay.

respectabilité [rɛspɛktábēlētā] *nf* respectability.

respectable [rɛspɛktábl(ə)] *a* respectable.

respecter [rɛspɛktā] *vt* to respect; **faire ~** to enforce; **le lexicographe qui se respecte** (*fig*) any self-respecting lexicographer.

respectif, ive [rɛspɛktēf, -ēv] *a* respective.

respectivement [rɛspɛktēvmáǹ] *ad* respectively.

respectueusement [rɛspɛktüœ̄zmáǹ] *ad* respectfully.

respectueux, euse [rɛspɛktüœ̄, -œ̄z] *a* respectful; **~ de** respectful of.

respirable [rɛspērábl(ə)] *a*: **peu ~** unbreathable.

respiration [rɛspērásyôǹ] *nf* breathing *q*; **faire une ~ complète** to breathe in and out; **retenir sa ~** to hold one's breath; **~ artificielle** artificial respiration.

respiratoire [rɛspērátwár] *a* respiratory.

respirer [rɛspērā] *vi* to breathe; (*fig: se reposer*) to get one's breath, have a break; (*: être soulagé*) to breathe again ◆ *vt* to breathe (in), inhale; (*manifester: santé, calme etc*) to exude.

resplendir [rɛsplándēr] *vi* to shine; (*fig*): **~ (de)** to be radiant (with).

resplendissant, e [rɛsplándēsáǹ, -áǹt] *a* radiant.

responsabilité [rɛspôǹsábēlētā] *nf* responsibility; (*légale*) liability; **refuser la ~ de** to deny responsibility (*ou* liability) for; **prendre ses ~s** to assume responsibility for one's actions; **~ civile** civil liability; **~ pénale/morale/collective** criminal/moral/collective responsibility.

responsable [rɛspôǹsábl(ə)] *a* responsible ◆ *nm/f* (*du ravitaillement etc*) person in charge; (*de parti, syndicat*) official; **~ de** responsible for; (*légalement: de dégâts etc*) liable for; (*chargé de*) in charge of, responsible for.

resquiller [rɛskēyā] *vi* (*au cinéma, au stade*) to sneak in (without paying); (*dans le train*) to grab a free ride.

resquilleur, euse [rɛskēyœr, -œ̄z] *nm/f* (*qui n'est pas invité*) gate-crasher; (*qui ne paie pas*) fare dodger.

ressac [rəsák] *nm* backwash.

ressaisir [rəsāzēr]: **se ~** *vi* to regain one's self-control; (*équipe sportive*) to rally.

ressasser [rəsásā] *vt* (*remâcher*) to keep turning over; (*redire*) to keep trotting out.

ressemblance [rəsáñbláñs] *nf* (*visuelle*) resemblance, similarity, likeness; (: *ART*) likeness; (*analogie, trait commun*) similarity.

ressemblant, e [rəsáñblàñ, -àñt] *a* (*portrait*) lifelike, true to life.

ressembler [rəsáñblā]: ~ **à** *vt* to be like, resemble; (*visuellement*) to look like; **se** ~ to be (*ou* look) alike.

ressemeler [rəsəmlā] *vt* to (re)sole.

ressens [r(ə)sáñ] *etc vb voir* **ressentir**.

ressentiment [rəsáñtēmáñ] *nm* resentment.

ressentir [rəsáñtēr] *vt* to feel; **se** ~ **de** to feel (*ou* show) the effects of.

resserre [rəsɛr] *nf* shed.

resserrement [r(ə)sɛrmáñ] *nm* narrowing; strengthening; (*goulet*) narrow part.

resserrer [rəsārā] *vt* (*pores*) to close; (*nœud, boulon*) to tighten (up); (*fig: liens*) to strengthen; **se** ~ *vi* (*route, vallée*) to narrow; (*liens*) to strengthen; **se** ~ (**autour de**) to draw closer (around); to close in (on).

ressers [r(ə)sɛr] *etc vb voir* **resservir**.

resservir [rəsɛrvēr] *vi* to do *ou* serve again ♦ *vt*: ~ **qch** (**à qn**) to serve sth up again (to sb); ~ **de qch** (**à qn**) to give (sb) a second helping of sth; ~ **qn** (**d'un plat**) to give sb a second helping (of a dish); **se** ~ **de** (*plat*) to take a second helping of; (*outil etc*) to use again.

ressort [rəsɔr] *vb voir* **ressortir** ♦ *nm* (*pièce*) spring; (*force morale*) spirit; (*recours*): **en dernier** ~ as a last resort; (*compétence*): **être du** ~ **de** to fall within the competence of.

ressortir [rəsɔrtēr] *vi* to go (*ou* come) out (again); (*contraster*) to stand out; ~ **de** (*résulter de*): **il ressort de ceci que** it emerges from this that; ~ **à** (*JUR*) to come under the jurisdiction of; (*ADMIN*) to be the concern of; **faire** ~ (*fig: souligner*) to bring out.

ressortissant, e [rəsɔrtēsáñ, -àñt] *nm/f* national.

ressouder [rəsōōdā] *vt* to solder together again.

ressource [rəsōōrs(ə)] *nf*: **avoir la** ~ **de** to have the possibility of; ~**s** *nfpl* resources; (*fig*) possibilities; **leur seule** ~ **était de** the only course open to them was to; ~**s d'énergie** energy resources.

ressusciter [rāsüsētā] *vt* to resuscitate, restore to life; (*fig*) to revive, bring back ♦ *vi* to rise (from the dead); (*fig: pays*) to come back to life.

restant, e [rɛstáñ, -àñt] *a* remaining ♦ *nm*: **le** ~ (**de**) the remainder (of); **un** ~ **de** (*de trop*) some leftover; (*fig: vestige*) a remnant *ou* last trace of.

restaurant [rɛstoráñ] *nm* restaurant; **manger au** ~ to eat out; ~ **d'entreprise** staff canteen *ou* cafeteria (*US*); ~ **universitaire** (**RU**) university refectory *ou* cafeteria (*US*).

restaurateur, trice [rɛstorátœr, -trēs] *nm/f* restaurant owner, restaurateur; (*de tableaux*) restorer.

restauration [rɛstorásyōñ] *nf* restoration; (*hôtellerie*) catering; ~ **rapide** fast food.

restaurer [rɛstorā] *vt* to restore; **se** ~ *vi* to have something to eat.

restauroute [rɛstorōōt] *nm* = **restoroute**.

reste [rɛst(ə)] *nm* (*restant*): **le** ~ (**de**) the rest (of); (*de trop*): **un** ~ (**de**) some leftover; (*vestige*): **un** ~ **de** a remnant *ou* last trace of; (*MATH*) remainder; ~**s** *nmpl* leftovers; (*d'une cité etc, dépouille mortelle*) remains; **avoir du temps de** ~ to have time to spare; **ne voulant pas être en** ~ not wishing to be outdone; **partir sans attendre** *ou* **demander son** ~ (*fig*) to leave without waiting to hear more; **du** ~, **au** ~ *ad* besides, moreover; **pour le reste, quant au** ~ *ad* as for the rest.

rester [rɛstā] *vi* (*dans un lieu, un état, une position*) to stay, remain; (*subsister*) to remain, be left; (*durer*) to last, live on ♦ *vb impersonnel*: **il reste du pain/2 œufs** there's some bread/there are 2 eggs left (over); **il reste du temps/10 minutes** there's some time/there are 10 minutes left; **il me reste assez de temps** I have enough time left; **voilà tout ce qui (me) reste** that's all I've got left; **ce qui reste à faire** what remains to be done; **ce qui me reste à faire** what remains for me to do; (**il**) **reste à savoir/établir si** ... it remains to be seen/established if *ou* whether ...; **il n'en reste pas moins que** ... the fact remains that ..., it's nevertheless a fact that ...; **en** ~ **à** (*stade, menaces*) to go no further than, only go as far as; **restons-en là** let's leave it at that; ~ **sur une impression** to retain an impression; **y** ~: **il a failli y** ~ he nearly met his end.

restituer [rɛstĭtüā] *vt* (*objet, somme*): ~ **qch** (**à qn**) to return *ou* restore sth (to sb); (*énergie*) to release; (*son*) to reproduce.

restitution [rɛstĭtüsyóñ] *nf* restoration.

restoroute [rɛstorōōt] *nm* highway (*US*) *ou* motorway (*Brit*) restaurant.

restreindre [rɛstráñdr(ə)] *vt* to restrict, limit; **se** ~ (*dans ses dépenses etc*) to cut down; (*champ de recherches*) to narrow.

restreint, e [rɛstráñ, -àñt] *pp de* **restreindre** ♦ *a* restricted, limited.

restrictif, ive [rɛstrēktēf, -ēv] *a* restrictive, limiting.

restriction [rɛstrēksyóñ] *nf* restriction; (*condition*) qualification; ~**s** *nfpl* (*mentales*) reservations; **sans** ~ *ad* unreservedly.

restructuration [rəstrüktürásyóñ] *nf* restructuring.

restructurer [rəstrüktürā] *vt* to restructure.

résultante [rāzültáñt] *nf* (*conséquence*) result, consequence.

résultat [rāzültá] *nm* result; (*conséquence*) outcome *q*, result; (*d'élection etc*) results *pl*; ~**s** *nmpl* (*d'une enquête*) findings; ~**s sportifs** sports results.

résulter [rāzültā]: ~ **de** *vt* to result from, be the result of; **il résulte de ceci que** ... the result of this is that ....

résumé [rāzümā] *nm* summary, résumé; **faire le** ~ **de** to summarize; **en** ~ *ad* in brief; (*pour conclure*) to sum up.

résumer [rāzümā] *vt* (*texte*) to summarize; (*récapituler*) to sum up; (*fig*) to epitomize, typify; **se** ~ *vi* (*personne*) to sum up (one's ideas); **se** ~ **à** to come down to.

resurgir [rəsürzhēr] *vi* to reappear, re-emerge.

résurrection [rāzüreksyóñ] *nf* resurrection;

(fig) revival.

rétablir [rātáblēr] *vt* to restore, re-establish; *(personne: suj: traitement)*: ~ **qn** to restore sb to health, help sb recover; *(ADMIN)*: ~ **qn dans son emploi/ses droits** to reinstate sb in his post/restore sb's rights; **se** ~ *vi (guérir)* to recover; *(silence, calme)* to return, be restored; *(GYM etc)*: **se** ~ **(sur)** to pull o.s. up (onto).

rétablissement [rātáblēsmáň] *nm* restoring; recovery; pull-up.

rétamer [rātámā] *vt* to re-coat, re-tin.

rétameur [rātámœr] *nm* tinker.

retaper [rətāpā] *vt (maison, voiture etc)* to renovate; *(fam: revigorer)* to buck up; *(redactylographier)* to retype.

retard [rətár] *nm (d'une personne attendue)* lateness *q*; *(sur l'horaire, un programme, une échéance)* delay; *(fig: scolaire, mental etc)* backwardness; **être en** ~ *(pays)* to be backward; *(dans paiement, travail)* to be behind; **en** ~ **(de 2 heures)** (2 hours) late; **avoir un** ~ **de 2 km** *(SPORT)* to be 2 km behind; **rattraper son** ~ to catch up; **avoir du** ~ to be late; *(sur un programme)* to be behind (schedule); **prendre du** ~ *(train, avion)* to be delayed; *(montre)* to lose (time); **sans** ~ *ad* without delay; ~ **à l'allumage** *(AUTO)* retarded ignition; ~ **scolaire** backwardness at school.

retardataire [rətárdátɛr] *a* late; *(enfant, idées)* backward ♦ *nm/f* latecomer; backward child.

retardé, e [rətárdā] *a* backward.

retardement [rətárdəmáň]: **à** ~ *a* delayed action *cpd*; **bombe à** ~ time bomb.

retarder [rətárdā] *vt (sur un horaire)*: ~ **qn (d'une heure)** to delay sb (an hour); *(sur un programme)*: ~ **qn (de 3 mois)** to set sb back *ou* delay sb (3 months); *(départ, date)*: ~ **qch (de 2 jours)** to delay sth (for *ou* by 2 days); *(horloge)* to set back ♦ *vi (montre)* to be slow; *(: habituellement)* to lose (time); **je retarde (d'une heure)** I'm (an hour) slow.

retendre [rətáňdr(ə)] *vt (câble etc)* to stretch again; *(MUS: cordes)* to retighten.

retenir [rətnēr] *vt (garder, retarder)* to keep, detain; *(maintenir: objet qui glisse, fig: colère, larmes, rire)* to hold back; *(: objet suspendu)* to hold; *(: chaleur, odeur)* to retain; *(fig: empêcher d'agir)*: ~ **qn (de faire)** to hold sb back (from doing); *(se rappeler)* to retain; *(réserver)* to reserve; *(accepter)* to accept; *(prélever)*: ~ **qch (sur)** to deduct sth (from); **se** ~ *(euphémisme)* to hold on; *(se raccrocher)*: **se** ~ **à** to hold onto; *(se contenir)*: **se** ~ **de faire** to restrain o.s. from doing; ~ **son souffle** *ou* **haleine** to hold one's breath; ~ **qn à dîner** to ask sb to stay for dinner; **je pose 3 et je retiens 2** put down 3 and carry 2.

rétention [rātáňsyóň] *nf*: ~ **d'urine** urine retention.

retentir [rətáňtēr] *vi* to ring out; *(salle)*: ~ **de** to ring *ou* resound with; ~ **sur** *vt (fig)* to have an effect upon.

retentissant, e [rətáňtēsáň, -áňt] *a* resounding; *(fig)* impact-making.

retentissement [rətáňtēsmáň] *nm (re-tombées)* repercussions *pl*; effect, impact.

retenu, e [rətnü] *pp de* **retenir** ♦ *a (place)* reserved; *(personne: empêché)* held up; *(propos: contenu, discret)* restrained ♦ *nf (prélèvement)* deduction; *(MATH)* number to carry over; *(SCOL)* detention; *(modération)* (self-)restraint; *(réserve)* reserve, reticence; *(AUTO)* (traffic) backup *(US)*, tailback *(Brit)*.

réticence [rātēsáňs] *nf* reticence *q*, reluctance *q*; **sans** ~ without hesitation.

réticent, e [rātēsáň, -áňt] *a* reticent, reluctant.

retiendrai [rətyaňdrā], **retiens** [rətyaň] *etc vb voir* **retenir**.

rétif, ive [rātēf, -ēv] *a* restive.

rétine [rātēn] *nf* retina.

retint [rətaň] *etc vb voir* **retenir**.

retiré, e [rətērā] *a (solitaire)* secluded; *(éloigné)* remote.

retirer [rətērā] *vt* to withdraw; *(vêtement, lunettes)* to take off, remove; *(enlever)*: ~ **qch à qn** to take sth from sb; *(extraire)*: ~ **qn/qch de** to take sb away from/sth out of, remove sb/sth from; *(reprendre: bagages, billets)* to collect, pick up; ~ **des avantages de** to derive advantages from; **se** ~ *vi (partir, reculer)* to withdraw; *(prendre sa retraite)* to retire; **se** ~ **de** to withdraw from; to retire from.

retombées [rətóňbā] *nfpl (radioactives)* fallout *sg*; *(fig)* fallout; spin-offs.

retomber [rətóňbā] *vi (à nouveau)* to fall again; *(rechuter)*: ~ **malade/dans l'erreur** to fall ill again/fall back into error; *(atterrir: après un saut etc)* to land; *(tomber, redescendre)* to fall back; *(pendre)* to fall, hang (down); *(échoir)*: ~ **sur qn** to fall on sb.

retordre [rətordr(ə)] *vt*: **donner du fil à** ~ **à qn** to make life difficult for sb.

rétorquer [rātorkā] *vt*: ~ **(à qn) que** to retort (to sb) that.

retors, e [rətor, -ors(ə)] *a* wily.

rétorsion [rātorsyóň] *nf*: **mesures de** ~ reprisals.

retouche [rətōōsh] *nf* touching up *q*; alteration; **faire une** ~ *ou* **des** ~**s à** to touch up.

retoucher [rətōōshā] *vt (photographie, tableau)* to touch up; *(texte, vêtement)* to alter.

retour [rətōōr] *nm* return; **au** ~ *(en arrivant)* when we *(ou they etc)* get *(ou got)* back; *(en route)* on the way back; **pendant le** ~ on the way *ou* journey back; **à mon/ton** ~ on my/ your return; **au** ~ **de** on the return of; **être de** ~ **(de)** to be back (from); **de** ~ **à .../chez moi** back at .../back home; **en** ~ *ad* in return; **par** ~ **du courrier** by return mail; **par un juste** ~ **des choses** by a favorable twist of fate; **match** ~ return match; ~ **en arrière** *(CINÉMA)* flashback; *(mesure)* backward step; ~ **de bâton** kickback; ~ **de chariot** carriage return; ~ **à l'envoyeur** *(POSTES)* return to sender; ~ **de flamme** backfire; ~ **(automatique) à la ligne** *(INFORM)* wordwrap; ~ **de manivelle** *(fig)* backfire; ~ **offensif** renewed attack; ~ **aux sources** *(fig)* return to basics.

retournement [rətōōrnəmáň] *nm (d'une personne: revirement)* turning (around); ~

de la situation reversal of the situation.

retourner |rətōōrnā| *vt* (*dans l'autre sens: matelas, crêpe*) to turn (over); (: *caisse*) to turn upside down; (: *sac, vêtement*) to turn inside out; (*fig: argument*) to turn back; (*en remuant: terre, sol, foin*) to turn over; (*émouvoir: personne*) to shake; (*renvoyer, restituer*): ~ **qch à qn** to return sth to sb ♦ *vi* (*aller, revenir*): ~ **quelque part/à** to go back *ou* return somewhere/to; ~ **à** (*état, activité*) to return to, go back to; **se** ~ *vi* to turn over; (*tourner la tête*) to turn around; **s'en** ~ to go back; **se** ~ **contre** (*fig*) to turn against; **savoir de quoi il retourne** to know what it is all about; ~ **sa veste** (*fig*) to be a turncoat; ~ **en arrière** *ou* **sur ses pas** to turn back, retrace one's steps; ~ **aux sources** to go back to basics.

retracer |rətrȧsā| *vt* to relate, recount.

rétracter |rātrȧktā| *vt*, **se** ~ *vi* to retract.

retraduire |rətrȧdüēr| *vt* to translate again; (*dans la langue de départ*) to translate back.

retrait |rətre| *nm* (*voir retirer*) withdrawal; collection; (*voir se retirer*) withdrawal; (*rétrécissement*) shrinkage; **en** ~ *a* set back; **écrire en** ~ to indent; ~ **du permis (de conduire)** revocation of driver's license (*US*), disqualification from driving (*Brit*).

retraite |rətret| *nf* (*d'une armée*, REL, *refuge*) retreat; (*d'un employé*) retirement; (*revenu*) (retirement) pension; **être/mettre à la** ~ to be retired/pension off *ou* retire; **prendre sa** ~ to retire; ~ **anticipée** early retirement; ~ **aux flambeaux** torchlight procession.

retraité, e |rətrātā| *a* retired ♦ *nm/f* (old age) pensioner.

retraitement |rətretmȧ́n| *nm* reprocessing.

retraiter |rətretā| *vt* to reprocess.

retranchement |rətrȧ́nshmȧ́n| *nm* entrenchment; **poursuivre qn dans ses derniers ~s** to drive sb into a corner.

retrancher |rətrȧ́nshā| *vt* (*passage, détails*) to take out, remove; (*nombre, somme*): ~ **qch de** to take *ou* deduct sth from; (*couper*) to cut off; **se** ~ **derrière/dans** to entrench o.s. behind/in; (*fig*) to take refuge behind/in.

retranscrire |rətrȧ́nskrēr| *vt* to retranscribe.

retransmettre |rətrȧ́nsmetr(ə)| *vt* (RADIO) to broadcast, relay; (TV) to show.

retransmission |rətrȧ́nsmēsyȯ́n| *nf* broadcast; showing.

retravailler |rətrȧvȧyā| *vi* to start work again ♦ *vt* to work on again.

retraverser |rətrȧversā| *vt* (*dans l'autre sens*) to cross back over.

rétréci, e |rātrāsē| *a* (*idées, esprit*) narrow.

rétrécir |rātrāsēr| *vt* (*vêtement*) to take in ♦ *vi* to shrink; **se** ~ *vi* to narrow.

rétrécissement |rātrāsēsmȧ́n| *nm* narrowing.

retremper |rətrȧ́npā| *vt*: **se** ~ **dans** (*fig*) to reimmerse o.s. in.

rétribuer |rātrēbüā| *vt* (*travail*) to pay for; (*personne*) to pay.

rétribution |rātrēbüsyȯ́n| *nf* payment.

rétro |rātrō| *a inv* old-style ♦ *nm* (= *rétroviseur*) (rear-view) mirror; **la mode** ~ the nostalgia vogue.

rétroactif, ive |rātroȧktēf, -ēv| *a* retroactive.

rétrocéder |rātrosādā| *vt* to retrocede.

rétrocession |rātrosȧsyȯ́n| *nf* retrocession.

rétrofusée |rātrofüzā| *nf* retrorocket.

rétrograde |rātrogrȧd| *a* reactionary, backward-looking.

rétrograder |rātrogrȧdā| *vi* (*élève*) to fall back; (*économie*) to regress; (AUTO) to shift to a lower gear.

rétroprojecteur |rātroprozhektœr| *nm* overhead projector.

rétrospectif, ive |rātrospektēf, -ēv| *a*, *nf* retrospective.

rétrospectivement |rātrospektēvmȧ́n| *ad* in retrospect.

retroussé, e |rətrōōsā| *a*: **nez** ~ turned-up nose.

retrousser |rətrōōsā| *vt* to roll up; (*fig: nez*) to wrinkle; (: *lèvres*) to curl up.

retrouvailles |rətrōōvȧy| *nfpl* reunion *sg*.

retrouver |rətrōōvā| *vt* (*fugitif, objet perdu*) to find; (*occasion*) to find again; (*calme, santé*) to regain; (*reconnaître: expression, style*) to recognize; (*revoir*) to see again; (*rejoindre*) to meet (again), join; **se** ~ *vi* to meet; (*s'orienter*) to find one's way; **se** ~ **quelque part** to find o.s. somewhere; to end up somewhere; **se** ~ **seul/sans argent** to find o.s. alone/with no money; **se** ~ **dans** (*calculs, dossiers, désordre*) to make sense of; **s'y** ~ (*rentrer dans ses frais*) to break even.

rétroviseur |rātrovēzœr| *nm* (rear-view) mirror.

Réunion |rāünyȯ́n| *nf*: **la** ~, **l'île de la** ~ Réunion.

réunion |rāünyȯ́n| *nf* bringing together; joining; (*séance*) meeting.

réunionnais, e |rāünyone, -ez| *a* of *ou* from Réunion.

réunir |rāünēr| *vt* (*convoquer*) to call together; (*rassembler*) to gather together; (*cumuler*) to combine; (*rapprocher*) to bring together (again), reunite; (*rattacher*) to join (together); **se** ~ *vi* (*se rencontrer*) to meet; (*s'allier*) to unite.

réussi, e |rāüsē| *a* successful.

réussir |rāüsēr| *vi* to succeed, be successful; (*à un examen*) to pass; (*plante, culture*) to thrive, do well ♦ *vt* to make a success of; to bring off; ~ **à faire** to succeed in doing; ~ **à qn** to go right for sb; (*aliment*) to agree with sb; **le travail/le mariage lui réussit** work/married life agrees with him.

réussite |rāüsēt| *nf* success; (CARTES) solitaire (*US*), patience (*Brit*).

réutiliser |rāütēlēzā| *vt* to re-use.

revaloir |rəvȧlwȧr| *vt*: **je vous revaudrai cela** I'll repay you some day; (*en mal*) I'll pay you back for this.

revalorisation |rəvȧlorēzȧsyȯ́n| *nf* revaluation; raising.

revaloriser |rəvȧlorēzȧ| *vt* (*monnaie*) to revalue; (*salaires, pensions*) to raise the level of; (*institution, tradition*) to reassert the value of.

revanche |rəvȧ́nsh| *nf* revenge; **prendre sa** ~ (**sur**) to take one's revenge (on); **en** ~ (*par contre*) on the other hand; (*en compensation*) in return.

rêvasser |revȧsā| *vi* to daydream.

rêve |rev| *nm* dream; (*activité psychique*): **le**

~ dreaming; **paysage/silence de** ~ dreamlike landscape/silence; ~ **éveillé** daydreaming *q*, daydream.

rêvé, e [rĕvā] *a* (*endroit, mari etc*) ideal.

revêche [rəvesh] *a* surly, sour-tempered.

réveil [rāvey] *nm* (*d'un dormeur*) waking up *q*; (*fig*) awakening; (*pendule*) alarm (clock); **au** ~ when I (*ou* you *etc*) wake (*ou* woke) up, on waking (up); **sonner le** ~ (*MIL*) to sound the reveille.

réveille-matin [rāveymátań] *nm inv* alarm clock.

réveiller [rāvāyā] *vt* (*personne*) to wake up; (*fig*) to awaken, revive; **se** ~ *vi* to wake up; (*fig*) to be revived, reawaken.

réveillon [rāveyóń] *nm* Christmas Eve; (*de la Saint-Sylvestre*) New Year's Eve; Christmas Eve (*ou* New Year's Eve) party *ou* dinner.

réveillonner [rāveyonā] *vi* to celebrate Christmas Eve (*ou* New Year's Eve).

révélateur, trice [rāvālátœr, -trēs] *a*: ~ **(de qch)** revealing (sth) ♦ *nm* (*PHOTO*) developer.

révélation [rāvālâsyóń] *nf* revelation.

révéler [rāvālā] *vt* (*gén*) to reveal; (*divulguer*) to disclose, reveal; (*dénoter*) to reveal, show; (*faire connaître au public*): ~ **qn/qch** to make sb/sth widely known, bring sb/sth to the public's notice; **se** ~ *vi* to be revealed, reveal itself ♦ *vb avec attribut*: **se** ~ **facile/ faux** to prove (to be) easy/false; **se** ~ **cruel/ un allié sûr** to show o.s. to be cruel/a trustworthy ally.

revenant, e [rəvnáń, -áńt] *nm/f* ghost.

revendeur, euse [rəváńdœr, -ēz] *nm/f* (*détaillant*) retailer; (*d'occasions*) secondhand dealer.

revendicatif, ive [rəváńdēkátēf, -ēv] *a* (*mouvement*) of protest.

revendication [rəváńdēkásyóń] *nf* claim, demand; **journée de** ~ day of protest (in support of one's claims).

revendiquer [rəváńdēkā] *vt* to claim, demand; (*responsabilité*) to claim ♦ *vi* to agitate in favor of one's claims.

revendre [rəváńdr(ə)] *vt* (*d'occasion*) to resell; (*détailler*) to sell; (*vendre davantage de*): ~ **du sucre/un foulard/deux bagues** to sell more sugar/another scarf/another two rings; **à** ~ *ad* (*en abondance*) to spare.

revenir [rəvnēr] *vi* to come back; (*CULIN*): **faire** ~ to brown; (*coûter*): ~ **cher/à 100 F (à qn)** to cost (sb) a lot/100 F; ~ **à** (*études, projet*) to return to, go back to; (*équivaloir à*) to amount to; ~ **à qn** (*rumeur, nouvelle*) to get back to sb, reach sb's ears; (*part, honneur*) to go to sb, be sb's; (*souvenir, nom*) to come back to sb; ~ **de** (*fig: maladie, étonnement*) to recover from; ~ **sur** (*question, sujet*) to go back over; (*engagement*) to go back on; ~ **à la charge** to return to the attack; ~ **à soi** to come around (*US*) *ou* round (*Brit*); **n'en pas** ~: **je n'en reviens pas** I can't get over it; ~ **sur ses pas** to retrace one's steps; **cela revient à dire que/au même** it amounts to saying that/to the same thing; ~ **de loin** (*fig*) to have been at death's door.

revente [rəváńt] *nf* resale.

revenu, e [rəvnü] *pp de* **revenir** ♦ *nm* income; (*de l'État*) revenue; (*d'un capital*) yield; ~**s** *nmpl* income *sg*; ~ **national brut** gross national income.

rêver [rāvā] *vi, vt* to dream; (*rêvasser*) to (day)dream; ~ **de** (*voir en rêve*) to dream of *ou* about; ~ **de qch/de faire** to dream of sth/of doing; ~ **à** to dream of.

réverbération [rāverbārâsyóń] *nf* reflection.

réverbère [rāverber] *nm* street lamp *ou* light.

réverbérer [rāverbārā] *vt* to reflect.

reverdir [rəverdēr] *vi* (*arbre etc*) to turn green again.

révérence [rāvāráńs] *nf* (*vénération*) reverence; (*salut: d'homme*) bow; (*: de femme*) curtsey.

révérencieux, euse [rāvāráńsyœ̄, -ēz] *a* reverent.

révérend, e [rāvāráń, -áńd] *a*: **le** ~ **père Pascal** the Reverend Father Pascal.

révérer [rāvārā] *vt* to revere.

rêverie [revrē] *nf* daydreaming *q*, daydream.

reverrai [rəverā] *etc vb voir* **revoir**.

revers [rəver] *nm* (*de feuille, main*) back; (*d'étoffe*) wrong side; (*de pièce, médaille*) back, reverse; (*TENNIS, PING-PONG*) backhand; (*de veston*) lapel; (*de pantalon*) cuff (*US*), turn-up (*Brit*); (*fig: échec*) setback; ~ **de fortune** reverse of fortune; **d'un** ~ **de main** with the back of one's hand; **le** ~ **de la médaille** (*fig*) the other side of the coin; **prendre à** ~ (*MIL*) to take from the rear.

reverser [rəversā] *vt* (*reporter: somme etc*): ~ **sur** to put back into; (*liquide*): ~ **(dans)** to pour some more (into).

réversible [rāversēbl(ə)] *a* reversible.

revêtement [rəvetmáń] *nm* (*de paroi*) facing; (*des sols*) flooring; (*de chaussée*) surface; (*de tuyau etc: enduit*) coating.

revêtir [rəvetēr] *vt* (*habit*) to don, put on; (*fig*) to take on; ~ **qn de** to dress sb in; (*fig*) to endow *ou* invest sb with; ~ **qch de** to cover sth with; (*fig*) to cloak sth in; ~ **d'un visa** to append a visa to.

rêveur, euse [revœr, -ēz] *a* dreamy ♦ *nm/f* dreamer.

reviendrai [rəvyańdrā] *etc vb voir* **revenir**.

revienne [rəvyen] *etc vb voir* **revenir**.

revient [rəvyań] *vb voir* **revenir** ♦ *nm*: **prix de** ~ cost price.

revigorer [rəvēgorā] *vt* to invigorate, revive, buck up.

revint [rəvań] *etc vb voir* **revenir**.

revirement [rəvērmáń] *nm* change of mind; (*d'une situation*) reversal.

revis [rəvē] *etc vb voir* **revoir**.

révisable [rāvēzábl(ə)] *a* (*procès, taux etc*) reviewable, subject to review.

réviser [rāvēzā] *vt* (*texte*) to revise; (*SCOL: matière*) to review (*US*), revise (*Brit*); (*comptes*) to audit; (*machine, installation, moteur*) to overhaul, service; (*JUR: procès*) to review.

révision [rāvēzyóń] *nf* revision; auditing *q*; overhaul, servicing *q*; review; **conseil de** ~ (*MIL*) draft (*US*) *ou* recruiting (*Brit*) board; **faire ses** ~**s** (*SCOL*) to review (*US*), revise (*Brit*); **la** ~ **des 10000 km** (*AUTO*) the 10,000 km service.

révisionnisme [rāvēzyonēsm(ə)] *nm* revisionism.

revisser [rəvēsā] *vt* to screw back again.

revit [rəvē] *vb voir* **revoir**.

revitaliser [rəvētálēzā] *vt* to revitalize.

revivifier [rəvēvēfyā] *vt* to revitalize.

revivre [rəvēvr(ə)] *vi* (*reprendre des forces*) to come alive again; (*traditions*) to be revived ♦ *vt* (*épreuve, moment*) to relive; **faire** ~ (*mode, institution, usage*) to bring back to life.

révocable [rāvokábl(ə)] *a* (*délégué*) dismissible; (*contrat*) revocable.

révocation [rāvokásyōn] *nf* dismissal; revocation.

revoir [rəvwár] *vt* to see again; (*réviser*) to review (*US*), revise (*Brit*) ♦ *nm*: **au** ~ goodbye; **dire au** ~ **à qn** to say goodbye to sb; **se** ~ (*amis*) to meet (again), see each other again.

révoltant, e [rāvoltán, -ánt] *a* revolting.

révolte [rāvolt(ə)] *nf* rebellion, revolt.

révolter [rāvoltā] *vt* to revolt, outrage; **se** ~ *vi*: **se** ~ **(contre)** to rebel (against); **se** ~ **(à)** to be outraged (by).

révolu, e [rāvolü] *a* past; (*ADMIN*): **âgé de 18 ans** ~**s** over 18 years of age; **après 3 ans** ~**s** when 3 full years have passed.

révolution [rāvolüsyón] *nf* revolution; **être en** ~ (*pays etc*) to be in revolt; **la** ~ **industrielle** the industrial revolution.

révolutionnaire [rāvolüsyoner] *a, nm/f* revolutionary.

révolutionner [rāvolüsyonā] *vt* to revolutionize; (*fig*) to stir up.

revolver [rāvolver] *nm* gun; (*à barillet*) revolver.

révoquer [rāvokā] *vt* (*fonctionnaire*) to dismiss, remove from office; (*arrêt, contrat*) to revoke.

revoyais [rəvwáyɛ] *etc vb voir* **revoir**.

revu, e [rəvü] *pp de* **revoir** ♦ *nf* (*inventaire, examen*) review; (*MIL*: *défilé*) review, march-past; (*: inspection*) inspection, review; (*périodique*) review, magazine; (*pièce satirique*) revue; (*de music-hall*) variety show; **passer en** ~ to review, inspect; (*fig*) to review; ~ **de (la) presse** press review.

révulsé, e [rāvülsā] *a* (*yeux*) rolled upwards; (*visage*) contorted.

Reykjavik [rākyávēk] *n* Reykjavik.

rez-de-chaussée [rādshōsā] *nm inv* ground floor.

rez-de-jardin [rādzhárdan] *nm inv* garden level.

RF *sigle f = République française*.

RFA *sigle f* (= *République fédérale d'Allemagne*) FRG.

RFO *sigle f* (= *Radio-Télévision Française d'Outre-mer*) French overseas broadcasting service.

RG *sigle mpl* (= *renseignements généraux*) security section of the police force.

rhabiller [rábēyā] *vt*: **se** ~ to get dressed again, put one's clothes on again.

rhapsodie [rápsodē] *nf* rhapsody.

rhénan, e [rānán, -án] *a* Rhine *cpd*, of the Rhine.

Rhénanie [rānánē] *nf*: **la** ~ the Rhineland.

rhésus [rāzüs] *a, nm* rhesus; ~ **positif/négatif** Rh- *ou* rhesus positive/negative.

rhétorique [rātorēk] *nf* rhetoric ♦ *a* rhetorical.

rhéto-roman, e [rātoromán, -án] *a* Rhaeto-Romanic.

Rhin [ran] *nm*: **le** ~ the Rhine.

rhinite [rēnēt] *nf* rhinitis.

rhinocéros [rēnosáros] *nm* rhinoceros.

rhinopharyngite [rēnofáranzhēt] *nf* throat infection.

rhodanien, ne [rodányan, -en] *a* Rhône *cpd*, of the Rhône.

Rhodes [rod] *n*: **(l'île de)** ~ (the island of) Rhodes.

Rhodésie [rodāzē] *nf*: **la** ~ Rhodesia.

rhodésien, ne [rodāzyan, -en] *a* Rhodesian.

rhododendron [rododandrón] *nm* rhododendron.

Rhône [rōn] *nm*: **le** ~ the Rhône.

rhubarbe [rübárb(ə)] *nf* rhubarb.

rhum [rom] *nm* rum.

rhumatisant, e [rümátēzán, -ánt] *a, nm/f* rheumatic.

rhumatismal, e, aux [rümátēsmál, -ō] *a* rheumatic.

rhumatisme [rümátēsm(ə)] *nm* rheumatism *q*.

rhumatologue [rümátolog] *nm/f* rheumatologist.

rhume [rüm] *nm* cold; ~ **de cerveau** head cold; **le** ~ **des foins** hay fever.

rhumerie [romrē] *nf* (*distillerie*) rum distillery.

RI *sigle m* (*MIL*) = *régiment d'infanterie* ♦ *sigle mpl* (= *Républicains indépendants*) *political party*.

ri [rē] *pp de* **rire**.

riant, e [ryán, -ánt] *vb voir* **rire** ♦ *a* smiling, cheerful; (*campagne, paysage*) pleasant.

RIB *sigle m* = **relevé d'identité bancaire**.

ribambelle [rēbánbel] *nf*: **une** ~ **de** a herd *ou* swarm of.

ricain, e [rēkan, -en] *a* (*fam*) Yank, Yankee.

ricanement [rēkánmán] *nm* snigger; giggle.

ricaner [rēkánā] *vi* (*avec méchanceté*) to snigger; (*bêtement, avec gêne*) to giggle.

riche [rēsh] *a* (*gén*) rich; (*personne, pays*) rich, wealthy; ~ **en** rich in; ~ **de** full of; rich in.

richement [rēshmán] *ad* richly.

richesse [rēshes] *nf* wealth; (*fig*) richness; ~**s** *nfpl* wealth *sg*; treasures; ~ **en vitamines** high vitamin content.

richissime [rēshēsēm] *a* extremely rich *ou* wealthy.

ricin [rēsan] *nm*: **huile de** ~ castor oil.

ricocher [rēkoshā] *vi*: ~ **(sur)** to rebound (off); (*sur l'eau*) to bounce (on *ou* off); **faire** ~ (*galet*) to skim.

ricochet [rēkoshe] *nm* rebound; bounce; **faire** ~ to rebound, bounce; (*fig*) to rebound; **faire des** ~**s** to skip stones; **par** ~ *ad* on the rebound; (*fig*) as an indirect result.

rictus [rēktüs] *nm* grin; (*snarling*) grimace.

ride [rēd] *nf* wrinkle; (*fig*) ripple.

ridé, e [rēdā] *a* wrinkled.

rideau, x [rēdō] *nm* curtain; **tirer/ouvrir les** ~**x** to draw/open the curtains; ~ **de fer** metal shutter; (*POL*): **le** ~ **de fer** the Iron Curtain.

ridelle [rēdel] *nf* slatted side (*of truck*).

rider [rēdā] *vt* to wrinkle; (*fig*) to ripple, ruffle the surface of; **se ~** *vi* to become wrinkled.

ridicule [rēdēkül] *a* ridiculous ♦ *nm* ridiculousness *q*; **le ~** ridicule; (*travers: gén pl*) absurdities *pl*; **tourner en ~** to ridicule.

ridiculement [rēdēkülmân] *ad* ridiculously.

ridiculiser [rēdēkülēzā] *vt* to ridicule; **se ~** to make a fool of o.s.

ridule [rēdül] *nf* (*euph: ride*) little wrinkle.

rie [rē] *etc vb voir* **rire**.

rien [ryań] *pronom* nothing; (*quelque chose*) anything; **ne ... ~** nothing, *tournure négative* + anything; **~ d'autre** nothing else; **~ du tout** nothing at all; **~ que** just, only; nothing but; **~ que cela/qu'à faire cela** just that/just doing that; **a-t-il jamais ~ fait pour nous?** has he ever done anything for us?; **il n'a ~** (*n'est pas blessé*) he's all right; **il n'a ~ d'un champion** he has nothing of the champion about him; **il n'y est pour ~** he's got nothing to do with it; **il n'en est ~!** nothing of the sort!; **ça ne fait ~** it doesn't matter; **~ à faire!** it's no good!; **il n'y ~ à faire ...** whatever I (*ou* you *etc*) do ...; **de ~!** (*formule*) not at all!, don't mention it!; **comme si de ~ n'était** as if nothing had happened; **un petit ~** (*cadeau*) a little something; **un ~ de** a hint of; **des ~s** trivia *pl*; **avoir peur d'un ~** to be frightened of every little thing.

rieur, euse [ryœr, -œz] *a* cheerful.

rigide [rēzhēd] *a* stiff; (*fig*) rigid; (*moralement*) strict.

rigidité [rēzhēdētā] *nf* stiffness; **la ~ cadavérique** rigor mortis.

rigolade [rēgolád] *nf*: **la ~** fun; (*fig*): **c'est de la ~** it's a big farce; (*c'est facile*) it's a cinch.

rigole [rēgol] *nf* (*conduit*) channel; (*filet d'eau*) rivulet.

rigoler [rēgolā] *vi* (*rire*) to laugh; (*s'amuser*) to have (some) fun; (*plaisanter*) to be joking *ou* kidding.

rigolo, ote [rēgolō, -ot] *a* (*fam*) funny ♦ *nm/f* comic; (*péj*) fraud, phoney.

rigoureusement [rēgōōrœzmân] *ad* rigorously; **~ vrai/interdit** strictly true/forbidden.

rigoureux, euse [rēgōōrœ, -œz] *a* (*morale*) rigorous, strict; (*personne*) stern, strict; (*climat, châtiment*) rigorous, harsh, severe; (*interdiction, neutralité*) strict; (*preuves, analyse, méthode*) rigorous.

rigueur [rēgœr] *nf* rigor (*US*), rigour (*Brit*); strictness; harshness; **"tenue de soirée de ~"** "evening dress (to be worn)"; **être de ~** to be the usual thing, be the rule; **à la ~** in (*US*) *ou* at (*Brit*) a pinch; possibly; **tenir ~ à qn de qch** to hold sth against sb.

riions [rēyôń] *etc vb voir* **rire**.

rillettes [rēyet] *nfpl* ≈ potted meat *sg*.

rime [rēm] *nf* rhyme; **n'avoir ni ~ ni raison** to have neither rhyme nor reason.

rimer [rēmā] *vi*: **~ (avec)** to rhyme (with); **ne ~ à rien** not to make sense.

Rimmel [rēmel] *nm* ® mascara.

rinçage [rańsázh] *nm* rinsing (out); (*opération*) rinse.

rince-doigts [rańsdwá] *nm inv* finger bowl.

rincer [rańsā] *vt* to rinse; (*récipient*) to rinse out; **se ~ la bouche** to rinse out one's mouth.

ring [rēng] *nm* (boxing) ring; **monter sur le ~** (*aussi fig*) to enter the ring; (: *faire carrière de boxeur*) to take up boxing.

ringard, e [rańgár, -árd(ə)] *a* (*péj*) old-fashioned.

Rio de Janeiro [rēōdzháner(ō)] *n* Rio de Janeiro.

rions [rēoń] *vb voir* **rire**.

ripaille [rēpáy] *nf*: **faire ~** to feast.

riper [rēpā] *vi* to slip, slide.

ripoliné, e [rēpolēnā] *a* enamel-painted.

riposte [rēpost(ə)] *nf* retort, riposte; (*fig*) counter-attack, reprisal.

riposter [rēpostā] *vi* to retaliate ♦ *vt*: **~ que** to retort that; **~ à** *vt* to counter; to reply to.

rire [rēr] *vi* to laugh; (*se divertir*) to have fun; (*plaisanter*) to joke ♦ *nm* laugh; **le ~** laughter; **~ de** *vt* to laugh at; **se ~ de** to make light of; **tu veux ~!** you must be joking!; **~ aux éclats/aux larmes** to roar with laughter/laugh until one cries; **~ jaune** to force oneself to laugh; **~ sous cape** to laugh up one's sleeve; **~ au nez de qn** to laugh in sb's face; **pour ~** (*pas sérieusement*) for a joke *ou* a laugh.

ris [rē] *vb voir* **rire** ♦ *nm*: **~ de veau** (calf) sweetbread.

risée [rēzā] *nf*: **être la ~ de** to be the laughing stock of.

risette [rēzet] *nf*: **faire ~ (à)** to give a nice little smile (to).

risible [rēzēbl(ə)] *a* laughable, ridiculous.

risque [rēsk(ə)] *nm* risk; **l'attrait du ~** the lure of danger; **prendre des ~s** to take risks; **à ses ~s et périls** at his own risk; **au ~ de** at the risk of; **~ d'incendie** fire risk; **~ calculé** calculated risk.

risqué, e [rēskā] *a* risky; (*plaisanterie*) risqué, daring.

risquer [rēskā] *vt* to risk; (*allusion, question*) to venture, hazard; **tu risques qu'on te renvoie** you risk being dismissed; **ça ne risque rien** it's quite safe; **~ de: il risque de se tuer** he could get *ou* risks getting himself killed; **il a risqué de se tuer** he almost got himself killed; **ce qui risque de se produire** what might *ou* could well happen; **il ne risque pas de recommencer** there's no chance of him doing that again; **se ~ dans** (*s'aventurer*) to venture into; **se ~ à faire** (*tenter*) to venture *ou* dare to do; **~ le tout pour le tout** to risk the lot.

risque-tout [rēskətōō] *nm/f inv* daredevil.

rissoler [rēsolā] *vi, vt*: **(faire) ~** to brown.

ristourne [rēstōōrn(ə)] *nf* rebate; discount.

rit [rē] *etc vb voir* **rire**.

rite [rēt] *nm* rite; (*fig*) ritual; **~s d'initiation** initiation rites.

ritournelle [rētōōrnel] *nf* (*fig*) tune; **c'est toujours la même ~** (*fam*) it's always the same old story.

rituel, le [rētüel] *a, nm* ritual.

rituellement [rētüelmâń] *ad* religiously.

riv. *abr* (= *rivière*) R.

rivage [rēvázh] *nm* shore.

rival, e, aux [rēvál, -ō] *a, nm/f* rival; **sans ~** *a* unrivalled.

rivaliser [rēválēzā] *vi*: **~ avec** to rival, vie

with; (*être comparable*) to hold its own against, compare with; ~ **avec qn de** (*élégance etc*) to vie with *ou* rival sb in.

rivalité [rēválētā] *nf* rivalry.

rive [rēv] *nf* shore; (*de fleuve*) bank.

river [rēvā] *vt* (*clou, pointe*) to clinch; (*plaques*) to rivet together; **être rivé sur/à** to be riveted on/to.

riverain, e [rēvrań, -en] *a* riverside *cpd*; lakeside *cpd*; roadside *cpd* ♦ *nm/f* riverside (*ou* lakeside) resident; local *ou* roadside resident.

rivet [rēvc] *nm* rivet.

riveter [rēvtā] *vt* to rivet (together).

Riviera [rēvycrā] *nf*: **la ~ (italienne)** the Italian Riviera.

rivière [rēvycr] *nf* river; **~ de diamants** diamond rivière.

rixe [rēks(ə)] *nf* brawl, scuffle.

Riyad [rēyád] *n* Riyadh.

riz [rē] *nm* rice; **~ au lait** ≈ rice pudding.

rizière [rēzyer] *nf* rice paddy.

RMC *sigle f = Radio Monte Carlo*.

RN *sigle f = route nationale*.

robe [rob] *nf* dress; (*de juge, d'ecclésiastique*) robe; (*de professeur*) gown; (*pelage*) coat; **~ de soirée/de mariée** evening/wedding dress; **~ de baptême** christening robe; **~ de chambre** dressing gown; **~ de grossesse** maternity dress.

robinet [robēnc] *nm* tap, faucet (*US*); **~ du gaz** gas tap; **~ mélangeur** mixer tap.

robinetterie [robēnetrē] *nf* plumbing.

roboratif, ive [roborátēf, -ēv] *a* bracing, invigorating.

robot [robō] *nm* robot; **~ de cuisine** food processor.

robotique [robotēk] *nf* robotics *sg*.

robotiser [robotēzā] *vt* (*personne, travailleur*) to turn into a robot; (*monde, vie*) to automate.

robuste [robüst(ə)] *a* robust, sturdy.

robustesse [robüstes] *nf* robustness, sturdiness.

roc [rok] *nm* rock.

rocade [rokád] *nf* (*AUTO*) bypass.

rocaille [rokáy] *nf* (*pierres*) loose stones *pl*; (*terrain*) rocky *ou* stony ground; (*jardin*) rockery, rock garden ♦ *a* (*style*) rocaille.

rocailleux, euse [rokáyœ̄, -œ̄z] *a* rocky, stony; (*voix*) harsh.

rocambolesque [rokáṅbolesk(ə)] *a* fantastic, incredible.

roche [rosh] *nf* rock.

rocher [roshā] *nm* rock; (*ANAT*) petrosal bone.

rochet [roshe] *nm*: **roue à ~** ratchet wheel.

rocheux, euse [roshœ̄, -œ̄z] *a* rocky; **les (montagnes) Rocheuses** the Rockies, the Rocky Mountains.

rock (and roll) [rok(enrol)] *nm* (*musique*) rock(-'n'-roll); (*danse*) rock.

rocker [rokœr] *nm* (*chanteur*) rock musician; (*adepte*) rock fan.

rodage [rodázh] *nm* breaking in (*US*), running in (*Brit*); **en ~** (*AUTO*) running *ou* breaking in.

rodé, e [rodā] *a* broken in (*US*), run in (*Brit*); (*personne*): **~ à qch** having got the hang of sth.

rodéo [rodāō] *nm* rodeo (*pl* -s).

roder [rodā] *vt* (*moteur, voiture*) to break in (*US*), run in (*Brit*); **~ un spectacle/service** to iron out the initial problems of a show/service.

rôder [rodā] *vi* to roam *ou* wander about; (*de façon suspecte*) to lurk (about *ou* around).

rôdeur, euse [rodœr, -œ̄z] *nm/f* prowler.

rodomontades [rodomôntád] *nfpl* bragging *sg*; saber (*US*) *ou* sabre (*Brit*) rattling *sg*.

rogatoire [rogátwár] *a*: **commission ~** letters rogatory.

rogne [rony] *nf*: **être en ~** to be mad *ou* in a temper; **se mettre en ~** to get mad *ou* in a temper.

rogner [ronyā] *vt* to trim; (*fig*) to whittle down; **~ sur** (*fig*) to cut down *ou* back on.

rognons [ronyôṅ] *nmpl* kidneys.

rognures [ronyür] *nfpl* trimmings.

rogue [rog] *a* arrogant.

roi [rwá] *nm* king; **les R~s mages** the Three Wise Men, the Magi; **le jour** *ou* **la fête des R~s, les R~s** Twelfth Night.

roitelet [rwátlc] *nm* wren; (*péj*) kinglet.

rôle [rōl] *nm* role; (*contribution*) part.

rollmops [rolmops] *nm* rollmop.

romain, e [romaṅ, -cn] *a* Roman ♦ *nm/f*: **R~, e** Roman ♦ *nf* (*CULIN*) romaine (*US*) *ou* cos (*Brit*) (lettuce).

roman, e [romáṅ, -án] *a* (*ARCHIT*) Romanesque; (*LING*) Romance *cpd*, Romanic ♦ *nm* novel; **~ policier** detective novel; **~ d'espionnage** spy novel *ou* story; **~ noir** thriller.

romance [romáṅs] *nf* ballad.

romancer [romáṅsā] *vt* to romanticize.

romanche [romáṅsh] *a, nm* Romansh.

romancier, ière [romáṅsyā, -ycr] *nm/f* novelist.

romand, e [romáṅ, -áṅd] *a* of *ou* from French-speaking Switzerland ♦ *nm/f*: **R~, e** French-speaking Swiss.

romanesque [románcsk(ə)] *a* (*fantastique*) fantastic; storybook *cpd*; (*sentimental*) romantic; (*LITTÉRATURE*) novelistic.

roman-feuilleton, *pl* **romans-feuilletons** [romáṅfœytôṅ] *nm* serialized novel.

roman-fleuve, *pl* **romans-fleuves** [romáṅflœv] *nm* saga, roman-fleuve.

romanichel, le [romáṅshcl] *nm/f* gipsy.

roman-photo, *pl* **romans-photos** [romáṅfotō] *nm* photo romance.

romantique [romáṅtēk] *a* romantic.

romantisme [romáṅtēsm(ə)] *nm* romanticism.

romarin [romáráṅ] *nm* rosemary.

rombière [rôṅbyer] *nf* (*péj*) old bag.

Rome [rom] *n* Rome.

rompre [rôṅpr(ə)] *vt* to break; (*entretien, fiançailles*) to break off ♦ *vi* (*fiancés*) to break it off; **se ~** *vi* to break; (*MÉD*) to burst, rupture; **se ~ les os** *ou* **le cou** to break one's neck; **~ avec** to break with; **à tout ~** *ad* wildly; **applaudir à tout ~** to bring down the house, applaud wildly; **~ la glace** (*fig*) to break the ice; **rompez (les rangs)!** (*MIL*) dismiss!, fall out!

rompu, e [rôṅpü] *pp de* **rompre** ♦ *a* (*fourbu*) exhausted, worn out; **~ à** with wide experience in; inured to.

romsteck [rôṅmstck] *nm* rump steak *q*.

ronce [rôṅs] *nf* (*BOT*) bramble branch;

(*MENUISERIE*): ~ **de noyer** burr walnut; ~**s** *nfpl* brambles, thorns.

ronchonner [rôṅshonā] *vi* (*fam*) to grouse, grouch.

rond, e [rôṅ, rôṅd] *a* round; (*joues, mollets*) well-rounded; (*fam:* *ivre*) tight; (*sincère, décidé*): **être** ~ **en affaires** to be on the level in business, do an honest deal ♦ *nm* (*cercle*) ring; (*fam: sou*): **je n'ai plus un** ~ I haven't a penny left ♦ *nf* (*gén: de surveillance*) rounds *pl*, patrol; (*danse*) round (dance); (*MUS*) whole note (*US*), semibreve (*Brit*) ♦ *ad:* **tourner** ~ (*moteur*) to run smoothly; **ça ne tourne pas** ~ (*fig*) there's something not quite right about it; **pour faire un compte** ~ to make (it) a round figure, to round (it) off; **avoir le dos** ~ to be round-shouldered; **en** ~ (*s'asseoir, danser*) in a ring; **à la** ~**e** (*alentour*): **à 10 km à la** ~**e** within a 10 km radius; (*à chacun son tour*): **passer qch à la** ~**e** to pass sth (a)round; **faire des** ~**s de jambe** to bow and scrape; ~ **de serviette** napkin ring.

rond-de-cuir, *pl* **ronds-de-cuir** [rôṅdküēr] *nm* (*péj*) pencil pusher (*US*), penpusher (*Brit*).

rondelet, te [rôṅdle, -et] *a* plump; (*fig: somme*) tidy; (*: bourse*) well-lined, fat.

rondelle [rôṅdel] *nf* (*TECH*) washer; (*tranche*) slice, round.

rondement [rôṅdmāṅ] *ad* (*avec décision*) briskly; (*loyalement*) frankly.

rondeur [rôṅdœr] *nf* (*d'un bras, des formes*) plumpness; (*bonhomie*) friendly straight-forwardness; ~**s** *nfpl* (*d'une femme*) curves.

rondin [rôṅdaṅ] *nm* log.

rond-point, *pl* **ronds-points** [rôṅpwaṅ] *nm* traffic circle (*US*), roundabout (*Brit*).

ronéotyper [ronāotēpā] *vt* to duplicate, roneo ®.

ronflant, e [rôṅflāṅ, -āṅt] *a* (*péj*) high-flown, grand.

ronflement [rôṅfləmāṅ] *nm* snore, snoring *q*.

ronfler [rôṅflā] *vi* to snore; (*moteur, poêle*) to hum; (*: plus fort*) to roar.

ronger [rôṅzhā] *vt* to gnaw (at); (*suj: vers, rouille*) to eat into; ~ **son frein** to champ (at) the bit (*fig*); **se** ~ **de souci, se** ~ **les sangs** to worry o.s. sick, fret; **se** ~ **les on-gles** to bite one's nails.

rongeur, euse [rôṅzhœr, -œēz] *nm/f* rodent.

ronronnement [rôṅronmāṅ] *nm* purring; (*bruit*) purr.

ronronner [rôṅronā] *vi* to purr.

roque [rok] *nm* (*ÉCHECS*) castling.

roquer [rokā] *vi* to castle.

roquet [roke] *nm* nasty little lap-dog.

roquette [roket] *nf* rocket; ~ **antichar** anti-tank rocket.

rosace [rōzàs] *nf* (*vitrail*) rose window, rosace; (*motif: de plafond etc*) rose.

rosaire [rōzer] *nm* rosary.

rosbif [rosbēf] *nm:* **du** ~ roasting beef; (*cuit*) roast beef; **un** ~ a joint of (roasting) beef.

rose [rōz] *nf* rose; (*vitrail*) rose window ♦ *a* pink; ~ **bonbon** *a inv* candy pink; ~ **des vents** compass card.

rosé, e [rōzā] *a* pinkish; (*vin*) ~ rosé (wine).

roseau, x [rōzō] *nm* reed.

rosée [rōzā] *af voir* **rosé** ♦ *nf:* **goutte de** ~ dewdrop.

roseraie [rōzre] *nf* rose garden; (*plantation*) rose nursery.

rosette [rōzet] *nf* rosette (*gen of the Légion d'honneur*).

rosier [rōzyā] *nm* rosebush, rose tree.

rosir [rōzēr] *vi* to go pink.

rosse [ros] *nf* (*péj: cheval*) nag ♦ *a* nasty, vicious.

rosser [rosā] *vt* (*fam*) to thrash.

rossignol [rosēnyol] *nm* (*ZOOL*) nightingale; (*crochet*) picklock.

rot [rō] *nm* belch; (*de bébé*) burp.

rotatif, ive [rotàtēf, -ēv] *a* rotary ♦ *nf* rotary press.

rotation [rotàsyôṅ] *nf* rotation; (*fig*) rotation, swap-around; (*renouvellement*) turnover; **par** ~ on a rotation (*US*) *ou* rota (*Brit*) basis; ~ **des cultures** rotation of crops; ~ **des stocks** stock turnover.

rotatoire [rotàtwàr] *a:* **mouvement** ~ rotary movement.

roter [rotā] *vi* (*fam*) to burp, belch.

rôti [rōtē] *nm:* **du** ~ roasting meat; (*cuit*) roast meat; **un** ~ **de bœuf/porc** a joint of (roasting) beef/pork.

rotin [rotaṅ] *nm* rattan (cane); **fauteuil en** ~ cane (arm)chair.

rôtir [rōtēr] *vt* (*aussi:* **faire** ~) to roast ♦ *vi* to roast; **se** ~ **au soleil** to bask in the sun.

rôtisserie [rōtēsrē] *nf* (*restaurant*) steakhouse; (*comptoir, magasin*) roast meat counter (*ou* shop).

rôtissoire [rōtēswàr] *nf* (roasting) spit.

rotonde [rotôṅd] *nf* (*ARCHIT*) rotunda; (*RAIL*) engine shed.

rotondité [rotôṅdētā] *nf* roundness.

rotor [rotor] *nm* rotor.

Rotterdam [roterdàm] *n* Rotterdam.

rotule [rotül] *nf* kneecap, patella.

roturier, ière [rotüryā, -yer] *nm/f* commoner.

rouage [rwàzh] *nm* cog(wheel), gearwheel; (*de montre*) part; (*fig*) cog; ~**s** *nmpl* (*fig*) internal structure *sg*.

Rouanda [rwâṅdá] *nm:* **le** ~ Rwanda.

roubaisien, ne [rōōbāzyaṅ, -en] *a* of *ou* from Roubaix.

roublard, e [rōōblár, -àrd(ə)] *a* (*péj*) crafty, wily.

rouble [rōōbl(ə)] *nm* ruble.

roucouler [rōōkōōlā] *vi* to coo; (*fig: péj*) to warble; (*: amoureux*) to bill and coo.

roue [rōō] *nf* wheel; **faire la** ~ (*paon*) to spread *ou* fan its tail; (*GYM*) to do a cart-wheel; **descendre en** ~ **libre** to freewheel *ou* coast down; **pousser à la** ~ to put one's shoulder to the wheel; **grande** ~ (*à la foire*) Ferris wheel; ~ **à aubes** paddle wheel; ~ **dentée** cogwheel; ~ **de secours** spare wheel.

roué, e [rwā] *a* wily.

rouennais, e [rwàne, -ez] *a* of *ou* from Rouen.

rouer [rwā] *vt:* ~ **qn de coups** to give sb a thrashing.

rouet [rwe] *nm* spinning wheel.

rouge [rōōzh] *a, nm/f* red ♦ *nm* red; (*fard*) rouge; (*vin*) ~ red wine; **passer au** ~ (*signal*) to turn red; (*automobiliste*) to go through a red light; **porter au** ~ (*métal*) to bring to red heat; **sur la liste** ~ (*TÉL*) unlisted (*US*), ex-directory (*Brit*); ~ **de honte/colère** red with shame/anger; **se fâcher tout/voir** ~ to blow one's top/see red; ~ **(à lèvres)** lipstick.

rougeâtre [roozhâtr(ə)] *a* reddish.

rougeaud, e [roozhō, -ōd] *a* (*teint*) red; (*personne*) red-faced.

rouge-gorge [roozhgorzh(ə)] *nm* robin (redbreast).

rougeoiement [roozhwâmâń] *nm* reddish glow.

rougeole [roozhol] *nf* measles *sg*.

rougeoyer [roozhwâyâ] *vi* to glow red.

rouget [roozhe] *nm* mullet.

rougeur [roozhœr] *nf* redness; (*du visage*) red face; ~**s** *nfpl* (*MÉD*) red blotches.

rougir [roozhēr] *vi* (*de honte, timidité*) to blush, flush; (*de plaisir, colère*) to flush; (*fraise, tomate*) to go *ou* turn red; (*ciel*) to redden.

rouille [rooy] *a inv* rust-colored (*US*) *ou* -coloured (*Brit*), rusty ♦ *nf* rust; (*CULIN*) *spicy* (*Provençal*) *sauce served with fish dishes.*

rouillé, e [rooyâ] *a* rusty.

rouiller [rooyâ] *vt* to rust ♦ *vi* to rust, get rusty; **se** ~ *vi* to rust; (*fig: mentalement*) to become rusty; (*: physiquement*) to grow stiff.

roulade [roolâd] *nf* (*GYM*) roll; (*CULIN*) meat roll; (*MUS*) roulade, run.

roulant, e [roolâń, -âńt] *a* (*meuble*) on wheels; (*surface, trottoir*) moving; **matériel** ~ (*RAIL*) rolling stock; **personnel** ~ (*RAIL*) train crews *pl*.

roulé, e [roolâ] *a*: **bien** ~**e** (*fam: femme*) shapely, curvy.

rouleau, x [roolō] *nm* (*de papier, tissu, pièces de monnaie, SPORT*) roll; (*de machine à écrire*) roller, platen; (*à mise en plis, à peinture, vague*) roller; **être au bout du** ~ (*fig*) to be at the end of one's rope; ~ **compresseur** steamroller; ~ **à pâtisserie** rolling pin; ~ **de pellicule** roll of film.

roulé-boulé, *pl* **roulés-boulés** [roolâboolâ] (*SPORT*) roll.

roulement [roolmâń] *nm* (*bruit*) rumbling *q*, rumble; (*rotation*) rotation; turnover; (*: de capitaux*) circulation; **par** ~ on a rotation (*US*) *ou* rota (*Brit*) basis; ~ **(à billes)** ball bearings *pl*; ~ **de tambour** drum roll; ~ **d'yeux** roll(ing) of the eyes.

rouler [roolâ] *vt* to roll; (*papier, tapis*) to roll up; (*CULIN: pâte*) to roll out; (*fam*) to con ♦ *vi* (*bille, boule*) to roll; (*voiture, train*) to go, run; (*automobiliste*) to drive; (*cycliste*) to ride; (*bateau*) to roll; (*tonnerre*) to rumble, roll; (*dégringoler*): ~ **en bas de** to roll down; ~ **sur** (*suj: conversation*) to turn on; **se** ~ **dans** (*boue*) to roll in; (*couverture*) to roll o.s. (up) in; ~ **dans la farine** (*fam*) to con; ~ **les épaules/hanches** to sway one's shoulders/wiggle one's hips; ~ **les "r"** to roll one's r's; ~ **sur l'or** to be rolling in money, be rolling in it; ~ **(sa bosse)** to get around.

roulette [roolet] *nf* (*de table, fauteuil*) castor; (*de pâtissier*) pastry wheel; (*jeu*): **la** ~ roulette; **à** ~**s** on castors; **la** ~ **russe** Russian roulette.

roulis [roolē] *nm* roll(ing).

roulotte [roolot] *nf* trailer (*US*), caravan (*Brit*).

roumain, e [roomań, -en] *a* Rumanian, Romanian ♦ *nm* (*LING*) Rumanian, Romanian ♦ *nm/f*: **R~, e** Rumanian, Romanian.

Roumanie [roomanē] *nf*: **la** ~ Rumania, Romania.

roupiller [roopēyâ] *vi* (*fam*) to sleep.

rouquin, e [rookań, -ēn] *nm/f* (*péj*) redhead.

rouspéter [roospâtâ] *vi* (*fam*) to moan, grouse.

rousse [roos] *af voir* **roux**.

rousseur [roosœr] *nf*: **tache de** ~ freckle.

roussi [roosē] *nm*: **ça sent le** ~ there's a smell of burning; (*fig*) I can smell trouble.

roussir [roosēr] *vt* to scorch ♦ *vi* (*feuilles*) to go *ou* turn brown; (*CULIN*): **faire** ~ to brown.

routage [rootâzh] *nm* (*collective*) mailing.

routard, e [rootâr, -ârd(ə)] *nm/f* travel(l)er.

route [root] *nf* road; (*fig: chemin*) way; (*itinéraire, parcours*) route; (*fig: voie*) road, path; **par (la)** ~ by road; **il y a 3h de** ~ it's a 3-hour ride *ou* journey; **en** ~ *ad* on the way; **en** ~**!** let's go!; **en cours de** ~ en route; **mettre en** ~ to start up; **se mettre en** ~ to set off; **faire** ~ **vers** to head towards; **faire fausse** ~ (*fig*) to be on the wrong track; ~ **nationale (RN)** ≈ state highway (*US*), ≈ A-road (*Brit*).

routier, ière [rootyâ, -ycr] *a* road *cpd* ♦ *nm* (*camionneur*) (long-distance) truck driver; (*restaurant*) ≈ truck stop (*US*), ≈ transport café (*Brit*); (*scout*) ≈ Explorer (*US*), ~ rover (*Brit*); (*cycliste*) road racer ♦ *nf* (*voiture*) touring car; **vieux** ~ old hand; **carte routière** road map.

routine [rootēn] *nf* routine; **visite/contrôle de** ~ routine visit/check.

routinier, ière [rootēnyâ, -ycr] *a* (*péj: travail*) humdrum, routine; (*: personne*) addicted to routine.

rouvert, e [roover, -ert(ə)] *pp de* **rouvrir**.

rouvrir [roovrēr] *vt, vi* to reopen, open again; **se** ~ *vi* (*blessure*) to open up again.

roux, rousse [roo, roos] *a* red; (*personne*) red-haired ♦ *nm/f* redhead ♦ *nm* (*CULIN*) roux.

royal, e, aux [rwâyâl, -ō] *a* royal; (*fig*) fit for a king, princely; blissful; thorough.

royalement [rwâyâlmâń] *ad* royally.

royaliste [rwâyâlēst(ə)] *a, nm/f* royalist.

royaume [rwâyōm] *nm* kingdom; (*fig*) realm; **le** ~ **des cieux** the kingdom of heaven.

Royaume-Uni [rwâyōmünē] *nm*: **le** ~ the United Kingdom.

royauté [rwâyōtâ] *nf* (*dignité*) kingship; (*régime*) monarchy.

RP *sigle f* (= *recette principale*) ≈ main post office; = *région parisienne* ♦ *sigle fpl* (= *relations publiques*) PR.

RPR *sigle m* (= *Rassemblement pour la République*) *political party.*

R.S.V.P. *abr* (= *répondez s'il vous plaît*) R.S.V.P.

RTB *sigle f* = *Radio-Télévision belge.*

Rte *abr* = **route**.

RTL *sigle f* = *Radio-Télévision Luxembourg.*

RTVE *sigle f* = Radio-Télévision espagnole.
RU [rü] *sigle m* = **restaurant universitaire**.
ruade [rüád] *nf* kick.
Ruanda [rwǎṅdá] *nm*: **le ~** Rwanda.
ruban [rübǎṅ] *nm* (*gén*) ribbon; (*pour ourlet, couture*) binding; (*de téléscripteur etc*) tape; (*d'acier*) strip; **~ adhésif** sticky tape; **~ carbone** carbon ribbon.
rubéole [rübǎol] *nf* German measles *sg*, rubella.
rubicond, e [rübēkôṅ, -ôṅd] *a* rubicund, ruddy.
rubis [rübē] *nm* ruby; (*HORLOGERIE*) jewel; **payer ~ sur l'ongle** to pay cash on the line.
rubrique [rübrēk] *nf* (*titre, catégorie*) heading, rubric; (*PRESSE*: *article*) column.
ruche [rüsh] *nf* hive.
rucher [rüshā] *nm* apiary.
rude [rüd] *a* (*barbe, toile*) rough; (*métier, tâche*) hard, tough; (*climat*) severe, harsh; (*bourru*) harsh, rough; (*fruste*) rugged, tough; (*fam*) real good; **être mis à ~ épreuve** to be put through the mill.
rudement [rüdmǎṅ] *ad* (*tomber, frapper*) hard; (*traiter, reprocher*) harshly; (*fam*: *très*) terribly; (: *beaucoup*) terribly hard.
rudesse [rüdes] *nf* roughness; toughness; severity; harshness.
rudimentaire [rüdēmǎṅter] *a* rudimentary, basic.
rudiments [rüdēmǎṅ] *nmpl* rudiments; basic knowledge *sg*; basic principles.
rudoyer [rüdwáyā] *vt* to treat harshly.
rue [rü] *nf* street; **être/jeter qn à la ~** to be on the streets/throw sb out onto the street.
ruée [rüā] *nf* rush; **la ~ vers l'or** the gold rush.
ruelle [rüel] *nf* alley(-way).
ruer [rüā] *vi* (*cheval*) to kick out; **se ~** *vi*: **~ sur** to pounce on; **se ~ vers/dans/hors de** to rush *ou* dash towards/into/out of; **~ dans les brancards** to become rebellious.
rugby [rügbē] *nm* Rugby (football); **~ à treize/quinze** Rugby League/Union.
rugir [rüzhēr] *vi* to roar.
rugissement [rüzhēsmǎṅ] *nm* roar, roaring *q*.
rugosité [rügōzētā] *nf* roughness; (*aspérité*) rough spot.
rugueux, euse [rügœ̄, -œ̄z] *a* rough.
ruine [rüēn] *nf* ruin; **~s** *nfpl* ruins; **tomber en ~** to fall into ruin(s).
ruiner [rüēnā] *vt* to ruin.
ruineux, euse [rüēnœ̄, -œ̄z] *a* terribly expensive to buy (*ou* run), ruinous; extravagant.
ruisseau, x [rüēsō] *nm* stream, brook; (*caniveau*) gutter; (*fig*): **~x de larmes/sang** floods of tears/streams of blood.
ruisselant, e [rüēslǎṅ, -ǎṅt] *a* streaming.
ruisseler [rüēslā] *vi* to stream; **~ (d'eau)** to be streaming (with water); **~ de lumière** to stream with light.
ruissellement [rüēselmǎṅ] *nm* streaming; **~ de lumière** stream of light.
rumeur [rümœr] *nf* (*bruit confus*) rumbling; hubbub *q*; (*protestation*) murmur(ing); (*nouvelle*) rumor (*US*), rumour (*Brit*).
ruminer [rümēnā] *vt* (*herbe*) to ruminate; (*fig*) to ruminate on *ou* over, chew over ♦ *vi*

(*vache*) to chew the cud, ruminate.
rumsteck [rômstek] *nm* = **romsteck**.
rupestre [rüpestr(ə)] *a* (*plante*) rock *cpd*; (*art*) cave *cpd*.
rupture [rüptür] *nf* (*de câble, digue*) breaking; (*de tendon*) rupture, tearing; (*de négociations etc*) breakdown; (*de contrat*) breach; (*séparation, désunion*) break-up, split; **en ~ de ban** at odds with authority; **en ~ de stock** (*COMM*) out of stock.
rural, e, aux [rürál, -ō] *a* rural, country *cpd* ♦ *nmpl*: **les ruraux** country people.
ruse [rüz] *nf*: **la ~** cunning, craftiness; trickery; **une ~** a trick, a ruse; **par ~** by trickery.
rusé, e [rüzā] *a* cunning, crafty.
russe [rüs] *a* Russian ♦ *nm* (*LING*) Russian ♦ *nm/f*: **R~** Russian.
Russie [rüsē] *nf*: **la ~** Russia; **la ~ blanche** White Russia; **la ~ soviétique** Soviet Russia.
rustine [rüstēn] *nf* repair patch (*for bicycle inner tube*).
rustique [rüstēk] *a* rustic; (*plante*) hardy.
rustre [rüstr(ə)] *nm* boor.
rut [rüt] *nm*: **être en ~** (*animal domestique*) to be in *ou* on heat; (*animal sauvage*) to be rutting.
rutabaga [rütábágá] *nm* rutabaga (*US*), swede (*Brit*).
rutilant, e [rütēlǎṅ, -ǎṅt] *a* gleaming.
RV *sigle m* = **rendez-vous**.
Rwanda [rwǎṅdá] *nm*: **le ~** Rwanda.
rythme [rētm(ə)] *nm* rhythm; (*vitesse*) rate; (: *de la vie*) pace, tempo; **au ~ de 10 par jour** at the rate of 10 a day.
rythmé, e [rētmā] *a* rhythmic(al).
rythmer [rētmā] *vt* to give rhythm to.
rythmique [rētmēk] *a* rhythmic(al) ♦ *nf* rhythmics *sg*.

S

S, s [es] *nm inv* S, s ♦ *abr* (= *sud*) S; **S comme Suzanne** S for Sugar.
s' [s] *pronom voir* **se**.
s/ *abr* = **sur**.
SA *sigle f* = **société anonyme**; (= *Son Altesse*) HH.
sa [sá] *dét voir* **son**.
sabbatique [sábátēk] *a*: **année ~** sabbatical year.
sable [sábl(ə)] *nm* sand; **~s mouvants** quicksand(s).
sablé [sáblā] *a* (*allée*) sandy ♦ *nm* shortbread cookie (*US*) *ou* biscuit (*Brit*); **pâte ~e** (*CULIN*) shortbread dough.
sabler [sáblā] *vt* to sand; (*contre le verglas*) to sand; **~ le champagne** to drink champagne.
sableux, euse [sáblœ̄, -œ̄z] *a* sandy.
sablier [sáblēyā] *nm* hourglass; (*de cuisine*) egg timer.
sablière [sáblēyer] *nf* sand quarry.

sablonneux, euse [sáblonœ̃, -œ̃z] *a* sandy.
saborder [sábordā] *vt* (*navire*) to scuttle; (*fig*) to wind up, shut down.
sabot [sábō] *nm* clog; (*de cheval, bœuf*) hoof; ~ **(de Denver)** (wheel) clamp; ~ **de frein** brake shoe.
sabotage [sábotázh] *nm* sabotage.
saboter [sábotā] *vt* (*travail, morceau de musique*) to botch, make a mess of; (*machine, installation, négociation etc*) to sabotage.
saboteur, euse [sábotœr, -œ̃z] *nm/f* saboteur.
sabre [sábr(ə)] *nm* saber (*US*), sabre (*Brit*); **le** ~ (*fig*) the sword, the army.
sabrer [sábrā] *vt* to cut down.
SAC [sák] *sigle m* (= *Service d'action civile*) *former Gaullist parapolice.*
sac [sák] *nm* bag; (*à charbon etc*) sack; (*pillage*) sack(ing); **mettre à** ~ to sack; ~ **à provisions/de voyage** shopping/overnight bag; ~ **de couchage** sleeping bag; ~ **à dos** backpack; ~ **à main** handbag; ~ **de plage** beach bag.
saccade [sákád] *nf* jerk; **par** ~s jerkily; haltingly.
saccadé, e [sákádā] *a* jerky.
saccage [sákázh] *nm* havoc.
saccager [sákázhā] *vt* (*piller*) to sack, lay waste; (*dévaster*) to create havoc in, wreck.
saccharine [sákárēn] *nf* saccharin(e).
SACEM [sásem] *sigle f* (= *Société des auteurs, compositeurs et éditeurs de musique*) *body responsible for collecting and distributing royalties.*
sacerdoce [sáserdos] *nm* priesthood; (*fig*) calling, vocation.
sacerdotal, e, aux [sáserdotál, -ō] *a* priestly, sacerdotal.
sachant [sáshâṅ] *etc vb voir* **savoir.**
sachet [sáshe] *nm* (small) bag; (*de lavande, poudre, shampooing*) sachet; **thé en** ~s tea bags; ~ **de thé** tea bag.
sacoche [sákosh] *nf* (*gén*) bag; (*de bicyclette*) saddlebag; (*du facteur*) mailbag; (*d'outils*) toolbag.
sacquer [sákā] *vt* (*fam: candidat, employé*) to fire; (*: réprimander, mal noter*) to flunk.
sacraliser [sákrálēzā] *vt* to make sacred.
sacre [sákr(ə)] *nm* coronation; consecration.
sacré, e [sákrā] *a* sacred; (*fam: satané*) blasted; (*: fameux*): **un** ~ ... a heck of a ...; (*ANAT*) sacral.
sacrement [sákrəmâṅ] *nm* sacrament; **les derniers** ~s the last rites.
sacrer [sákrā] *vt* (*roi*) to crown; (*évêque*) to consecrate ♦ *vi* to curse, swear.
sacrifice [sákrēfēs] *nm* sacrifice; **faire le** ~ **de** to sacrifice.
sacrificiel, le [sákrēfēsyel] *a* sacrificial.
sacrifier [sákrēfyā] *vt* to sacrifice; ~ **à** *vt* to conform to; **se** ~ to sacrifice o.s.; **articles sacrifiés** (*COMM*) items sold at rock-bottom *ou* give-away prices.
sacrilège [sákrēlezh] *nm* sacrilege ♦ *a* sacrilegious.
sacristain [sákrēstaṅ] *nm* sexton; sacristan.
sacristie [sákrēstē] *nf* sacristy; (*culte protestant*) vestry.
sacro-saint, e [sákrosaṅ, -aṅt] *a* sacrosanct.

sadique [sádēk] *a* sadistic ♦ *nm/f* sadist.
sadisme [sádēsm(ə)] *nm* sadism.
sadomasochiste [sádomázoshēst(ə)] *nm/f* sadomasochist.
safari [sáfárē] *nm* safari; **faire un** ~ to go on safari.
safari-photo [sáfárēfotō] *nm* photographic safari.
SAFER [sáfer] *sigle f* (= *société d'aménagement foncier et d'établissement rural*) *organization with the right to buy land in order to retain it for agricultural use.*
safran [sáfrâṅ] *nm* saffron.
sagace [ságás] *a* sagacious, shrewd.
sagacité [ságásētā] *nf* sagacity, shrewdness.
sagaie [ságe] *nf* assegai.
sage [sázh] *a* wise; (*enfant*) good ♦ *nm* wise man; sage.
sage-femme [sázhfám] *nf* midwife (*pl* -wives).
sagement [sázhmâṅ] *ad* (*raisonnablement*) wisely, sensibly; (*tranquillement*) quietly.
sagesse [sázhes] *nf* wisdom.
Sagittaire [sázhēter] *nm*: **le** ~ Sagittarius, the Archer; **être du** ~ to be Sagittarius.
Sahara [sáárá] *nm*: **le** ~ the Sahara (Desert); **le** ~ **occidental** (*pays*) Western Sahara.
saharien, ne [sááryaṅ, -en] *a* Saharan ♦ *nf* safari jacket.
sahélien, ne [sáályaṅ, -en] *a* Sahelian.
saignant, e [senyâṅ, -âṅt] *a* (*viande*) rare; (*blessure, plaie*) bleeding.
saignée [sānyā] *nf* (*MÉD*) bleeding *q*; bloodletting *q*; (*ANAT*): **la** ~ **du bras** the bend of the arm; (*fig: MIL*) heavy losses *pl*; (*: prélèvement*) deep cut.
saignement [senymâṅ] *nm* bleeding; ~ **de nez** nosebleed.
saigner [sānyā] *vi* to bleed ♦ *vt* to bleed; (*animal*) to bleed to death; ~ **qn à blanc** (*fig*) to bleed sb white; ~ **du nez** to have a nosebleed.
Saigon [sáygóṅ] *n* Saigon.
saillant, e [sáyáṅ, -âṅt] *a* (*pommettes, menton*) prominent; (*corniche etc*) projecting; (*fig*) salient, outstanding.
saillie [sáyē] *nf* (*sur un mur etc*) projection; (*trait d'esprit*) witticism; (*accouplement*) covering, serving; **faire** ~ to project, stick out; **en** ~, **formant** ~ projecting, overhanging.
saillir [sáyēr] *vi* to project, stick out; (*veine, muscle*) to bulge ♦ *vt* (*ÉLEVAGE*) to cover, serve.
sain, e [saṅ, sen] *a* healthy; (*dents, constitution*) healthy, sound; (*lectures*) wholesome; ~ **et sauf** safe and sound, unharmed; ~ **d'esprit** sound in mind, sane.
saindoux [saṅdōō] *nm* lard.
sainement [senmâṅ] *ad* (*vivre*) healthily; (*raisonner*) soundly.
saint, e [saṅ, saṅt] *a* holy; (*fig*) saintly ♦ *nm/f* saint; **le S**~ **Esprit** the Holy Spirit *ou* Ghost; **la S**~**e Vierge** the Blessed Virgin.
saint-bernard [saṅbernár] *nm inv* (*chien*) St Bernard.
Sainte-Hélène [saṅtālen] *nf* St Helena.
Sainte-Lucie [saṅtlüsē] *nf* Saint Lucia.
sainteté [saṅttā] *nf* holiness; saintliness.
Saint-Laurent [saṅloráṅ] *nm*: **le** ~ the St

Lawrence.

Saint-Marin [sańmárań] *nm*: **le** ~ San Marino.

Saint-Père [sańper] *nm*: **le** ~ the Holy Father, the Pontiff.

Saint-Pierre [sańpyer] *nm* Saint Peter; (*église*) Saint Peter's.

Saint-Pierre-et-Miquelon [sańpyerāmēklóń] *nm* Saint Pierre and Miquelon.

Saint-Siège [sańsyezh] *nm*: **le** ~ the Holy See.

Saint-Sylvestre [sańsēlvestr(ə)] *nf*: **la** ~ New Year's Eve.

Saint-Thomas [sańtomá] *nf* Saint Thomas.

Saint-Vincent et les Grenadines [sańvańsáńálāgrənádēn] *nm* St Vincent and the Grenadines.

sais [se] *etc vb voir* **savoir**.

saisie [sāzē] *nf* seizure; **à la** ~ (*texte*) being keyed; ~ **(de données)** (data) capture.

saisine [sāzēn] *nf* (JUR) *submission of a case to the court*.

saisir [sāzēr] *vt* to take hold of, grab; (*fig: occasion*) to seize; (*comprendre*) to grasp; (*entendre*) to get, catch; (*suj: émotions*) to take hold of, come over; (INFORM) to capture, keyboard; (CULIN) to fry quickly; (JUR: *biens, publication*) to seize; (: *juridiction*): ~ **un tribunal d'une affaire** to refer a case to a court; **se** ~ **de** *vt* to seize; **être saisi** (*frappé de*) to be overcome.

saisissant, e [sāzēsáń, -áńt] *a* startling, striking; (*froid*) biting.

saisissement [sāzēsmáń] *nm*: **muet/figé de** ~ speechless/frozen with emotion.

saison [sezóń] *nf* season; **la belle/mauvaise** ~ the summer/winter months; **être de** ~ to be in season; **en/hors** ~ in/out of season; **haute/basse/morte** ~ high/low/slack season; **la** ~ **des pluies/des amours** the rainy/mating season.

saisonnier, ière [sezonyā, -yer] *a* seasonal ♦ *nm* (*travailleur*) seasonal worker; (*vacancier*) seasonal vacationer (US) *ou* holidaymaker (*Brit*).

sait [se] *vb voir* **savoir**.

salace [sálás] *a* salacious.

salade [sálád] *nf* (BOT) lettuce *etc* (*generic term*); (CULIN) (green) salad; (*fam*) tangle, muddle; ~**s** *nfpl* (*fam*): **raconter des** ~**s** to tell tales (*fam*); **haricots en** ~ bean salad; ~ **de concombres** cucumber salad; ~ **de fruits** fruit salad; ~ **niçoise** salade niçoise; ~ **russe** Russian salad.

saladier [sáládyā] *nm* (salad) bowl.

salaire [sáler] *nm* (*annuel, mensuel*) salary; (*hebdomadaire, journalier*) pay, wages *pl*; (*fig*) reward; ~ **de base** base pay (US), basic salary (*ou* wage) (*Brit*); ~ **de misère** starvation wage; ~ **minimum interprofessionnel de croissance (SMIC)** index-linked guaranteed minimum wage.

salaison [sálezóń] *nf* salting; ~**s** *nfpl* salt meat *sg*.

salamandre [sálámáńdr(ə)] *nf* salamander.

salami [sálámē] *nm* salami *q*, salami sausage.

salant [sáláń] *am*: **marais** ~ salt pan.

salarial, e, aux [sáláryál, -ō] *a* salary *cpd*, wage(s) *cpd*.

salariat [sáláryá] *nm* salaried staff.

salarié, e [sáláryā] *a* salaried; wage-earning ♦

nm/f salaried employee; wage-earner.

salaud [sálō] *nm* (*fam!*) bastard (*!*).

sale [sál] *a* dirty; (*fig: avant le nom*) nasty.

salé, e [sálā] *a* (*liquide, saveur*) salty; (CULIN) salted, salt *cpd*; (*fig*) spicy, juicy; (: *note, facture*) steep, stiff ♦ *nm* (*porc salé*) salt pork; **petit** ~ ≈ pickled pork.

salement [sálmáń] *ad* (*manger etc*) dirtily, messily.

saler [sálā] *vt* to salt.

saleté [sáltā] *nf* (*état*) dirtiness; (*crasse*) dirt, filth; (*tache etc*) dirt *q*, something dirty, dirty mark; (*fig: tour*) dirty trick; (: *chose sans valeur*) rubbish *q*; (: *obscénité*) filth *q*; (: *microbe etc*) bug; **vivre dans la** ~ to live in squalor.

salière [sályer] *nf* salt shaker (US), saltcellar (*Brit*).

saligaud [sálēgō] *nm* (*fam!*) bastard (*!*).

salin, e [sálań, -ēn] *a* saline ♦ *nf* saltworks *sg*.

salinité [sálēnētā] *nf* salinity, salt-content.

salir [sálēr] *vt* to (make) dirty; (*fig*) to soil the reputation of; **se** ~ to get dirty.

salissant, e [sálēsáń, -áńt] *a* (*tissu*) which shows the dirt; (*métier*) dirty, messy.

salissure [sálēsür] *nf* dirt *q*; (*tache*) dirty mark.

salive [sálēv] *nf* saliva.

saliver [sálēvā] *vi* to salivate.

salle [sál] *nf* room; (*d'hôpital*) ward; (*de restaurant*) dining room; (*d'un cinéma*) auditorium; (: *public*) audience; **faire** ~ **comble** to have a full house; ~ **d'armes** (*pour l'escrime*) fencing room; ~ **d'attente** waiting room; ~ **de bain(s)** bathroom; ~ **de bal** ballroom; ~ **de cinéma** cinema; ~ **de classe** classroom; ~ **commune** (*d'hôpital*) ward; ~ **de concert** concert hall; ~ **de consultation** office (US), consulting room (*Brit*); ~ **de danse** dance hall; ~ **de douches** shower-room; ~ **d'eau** shower-room; ~ **d'embarquement** (*à l'aéroport*) departure lounge; ~ **d'exposition** showroom; ~ **de jeux** games room; playroom; ~ **des machines** engine room; ~ **à manger** dining room; (*mobilier*) dining room suite; ~ **obscure** movie theater (US), cinema (*Brit*); ~ **d'opération** (*d'hôpital*) operating room (US) *ou* theatre (*Brit*); ~ **de projection** movie auditorium (US), film theatre (*Brit*); ~ **de séjour** living room; ~ **de spectacle** theater (US), theatre (*Brit*); cinema; ~ **des ventes** salesroom.

salmonellose [sálmonálōz] *nf* (MÉD) salmonella poisoning.

Salomon [sálomóń]: **les îles** ~ the Solomon Islands.

salon [sálóń] *nm* lounge, living room; (*mobilier*) living room suite; (*exposition*) exhibition, show; (*mondain, littéraire*) salon; ~ **de coiffure** hairdressing salon; ~ **de thé** tearoom.

salopard [sálopár] *nm* (*fam!*) bastard (*!*).

salope [sálop] *nf* (*fam!*) bitch (*!*).

saloper [sálopā] *vt* (*fam!*) to botch, bungle, mess up.

saloperie [sáloprē] *nf* (*fam!*) filth *q*; dirty trick; rubbish *q*.

salopette [sálopet] *nf* dungarees *pl*;

(*d'ouvrier*) overall(s).

salpêtre [sàlpɛtr(ə)] *nm* saltpetre.

salsifis [sàlsɛ̄fē] *nm* salsify, oyster-plant.

SALT [sàlt] *sigle* (= *Strategic Arms Limitation Talks*) SALT.

saltimbanque [sàltàñbàñk] *nm/f* (travel(l)ing) acrobat.

salubre [sàlübr(ə)] *a* healthy, salubrious.

salubrité [sàlübrɛ̄tà] *nf* healthiness, salubrity; ~ **publique** public health.

saluer [sàlüà] *vt* (*pour dire bonjour, fig*) to greet; (*pour dire au revoir*) to take one's leave; (*MIL*) to salute.

salut [sàlü] *nm* (*sauvegarde*) safety; (*REL*) salvation; (*geste*) wave; (*parole*) greeting; (*MIL*) salute ♦ *excl* (*fam: pour dire bonjour*) hi (there); (*: pour dire au revoir*) see you!, 'bye!; (*style relevé*) (all) hail.

salutaire [sàlütɛr] *a* (*remède*) beneficial; (*conseils*) salutary.

salutations [sàlütàsyóñ] *nfpl* greetings; **recevez mes ~ distinguées** *ou* **respectueuses** yours truly (*US*) *ou* faithfully (*Brit*).

salutiste [sàlütēst(ə)] *nm/f* Salvationist.

Salvador [sàlvàdor] *nm*: **le ~** El Salvador.

salve [sàlv(ə)] *nf* salvo; volley of shots; ~ **d'applaudissements** burst of applause.

Samarie [sàmàrē] *nf*: **la ~** Samaria.

samaritain [sàmàrɛ̄tañ] *nm*: **le bon S~** the Good Samaritan.

samedi [sàmdē] *nm* Saturday; *voir aussi* **lundi.**

Samoa [sàmoà] *nfpl*: **les (îles) ~** Samoa, the Samoa Islands.

SAMU [sàmü] *sigle m* (= *service d'assistance médicale d'urgence*) ≈ paramedics (*US*), ≈ ambulance (service) (*Brit*).

sanatorium [sànàtoryom] *nm* sanatorium (*pl* -a).

sanctifier [sàñktɛ̄fyà] *vt* to sanctify.

sanction [sàñksyóñ] *nf* sanction; (*fig*) penalty; **prendre des ~s contre** to impose sanctions on.

sanctionner [sàñksyonà] *vt* (*loi, usage*) to sanction; (*punir*) to punish.

sanctuaire [sàñktüɛr] *nm* sanctuary.

sandale [sàñdàl] *nf* sandal.

sandalette [sàñdàlɛt] *nf* sandal.

sandow [sàñdō] *nm* ® bungee cord (*US*), luggage elastic (*Brit*).

sandwich [sàñdwɛtsh] *nm* sandwich; **pris en ~** sandwiched.

sang [sàñ] *nm* blood; **en ~** covered in blood; **jusqu'au ~** (*mordre, pincer*) till the blood comes; **se faire du mauvais ~** to fret, get in a state.

sang-froid [sàñfrwà] *nm* calm, sangfroid; **garder/perdre/reprendre son ~** to keep/lose/regain one's cool; **de ~** in cold blood.

sanglant, e [sàñglàñ, -àñt] *a* bloody, covered in blood; (*combat*) bloody; (*fig: reproche, affront*) cruel.

sangle [sàñgl(ə)] *nf* strap; ~**s** *nfpl* (*pour lit etc*) webbing *sg*.

sangler [sàñglà] *vt* to strap up; (*animal*) to girth.

sanglier [sàñglēyà] *nm* (wild) boar.

sanglot [sàñglō] *nm* sob.

sangloter [sàñglotà] *vi* to sob.

sangsue [sàñsü] *nf* leech.

sanguin, e [sàñgañ, -ēn] *a* blood *cpd*; (*fig*) fiery ♦ *nf* blood orange; (*ART*) red pencil drawing.

sanguinaire [sàñgēnɛr] *a* (*animal, personne*) bloodthirsty; (*lutte*) bloody.

sanguinolent, e [sàñgēnolàñ, -àñt] *a* streaked with blood.

sanisette [sànēzɛt] *nf* (automatic) public toilet.

sanitaire [sànētɛr] *a* health *cpd*; ~**s** *nmpl* (*salle de bain et w.-c.*) bathroom *sg*; **installation/appareil ~** bathroom plumbing/appliance.

sans [sàñ] *prép* without; ~ **qu'il s'en aperçoive** without him *ou* his noticing; ~ **scrupules** unscrupulous; ~ **manches** sleeveless.

sans-abri [sàñzàbrē] *nmpl* homeless.

sans-emploi [sàñzàñplwà] *nmpl* jobless.

sans-façon [sàñfàsóñ] *a inv* fuss-free; free and easy.

sans-gêne [sàñzhɛn] *a inv* inconsiderate ♦ *nm inv* (*attitude*) lack of consideration.

sans-logis [sàñlozhē] *nmpl* homeless.

sans-souci [sàñsōōsē] *a inv* carefree.

sans-travail [sàñtràvày] *nmpl* unemployed, jobless.

santal [sàñtàl] *nm* sandal(wood).

santé [sàñtà] *nf* health; **avoir une ~ de fer** to have an iron constitution; **être en bonne ~** to be in good health, be healthy; **boire à la ~ de qn** to drink (to) sb's health; **"à la ~ de"** "here's to"; **à ta** *ou* **votre ~!** cheers!; **service de ~** (*dans un port etc*) quarantine service; **la ~ publique** public health.

Santiago (du Chili) [sàñtyàgō(düshēlē)] *n* Santiago (de Chile).

santon [sàñtóñ] *nm ornamental figure at a Christmas crib.*

saoudien, ne [sàōōdyañ, -ɛn] *a* Saudi (Arabian) ♦ *nm/f*: **S~, ne** Saudi (Arabian).

saoul, e [sōō, sōōl] *a* = **soûl, e.**

sape [sàp] *nf*: **travail de ~** (*MIL*) sap; (*fig*) insidious undermining process *ou* work; ~**s** *nfpl* (*fam*) gear *sg*, togs.

saper [sàpà] *vt* to undermine, sap; **se ~** *vi* (*fam*) to dress.

sapeur [sàpœr] *nm* sapper.

sapeur-pompier [sàpœrpóñpyà] *nm* fireman.

saphir [sàfɛr] *nm* sapphire; (*d'électrophone*) needle, sapphire needle.

sapin [sàpañ] *nm* fir (tree); (*bois*) fir; ~ **de Noël** Christmas tree.

sapinière [sàpɛnyɛr] *nf* fir plantation *ou* forest.

SAR *sigle f* (= *Son Altesse Royale*) HRH.

sarabande [sàràbàñd] *nf* saraband; (*fig*) hullabaloo; whirl.

sarbacane [sàrbàkàn] *nf* blowpipe, blowgun; (*jouet*) peashooter.

sarcasme [sàrkàsm(ə)] *nm* sarcasm *q*; (*propos*) piece of sarcasm.

sarcastique [sàrkàstēk] *a* sarcastic.

sarcastiquement [sàrkàstēkmàñ] *ad* sarcastically.

sarclage [sàrklàzh] *nm* weeding.

sarcler [sàrklà] *vt* to weed.

sarcloir [sàrklwàr] *nm* (weeding) hoe, spud.

sarcophage [sȧrkofȧzh] *nm* sarcophagus (*pl* -i).

Sardaigne [sȧrdeny] *nf*: **la** ~ Sardinia.

sarde [sȧrd(ə)] *a* Sardinian.

sardine [sȧrdēn] *nf* sardine; ~**s à l'huile** sardines in oil.

sardinier, ière [sȧrdēnyā, -ycr] *a* (*pêche, industrie*) sardine *cpd* ◆ *nm* (*bateau*) sardine boat.

sardonique [sȧrdonēk] *a* sardonic.

sari [sȧrē] *nm* sari.

SARL [sȧrl] *sigle f* = **société à responsabilité limitée**.

sarment [sȧrmǡ] *nm*: ~ **(de vigne)** vine shoot.

sarrasin [sȧrázaṅ] *nm* buckwheat.

sarrau [sȧrō] *nm* smock.

Sarre [sȧr] *nf*: **la** ~ the Saar.

sarriette [sȧryet] *nf* savory.

sarrois, e [sȧrwȧ, -wȧz] *a* Saar *cpd* ◆ *nm/f*: **S~, e** inhabitant *ou* native of the Saar.

sas [sȧs] *nm* (*de sous-marin, d'engin spatial*) airlock; (*d'écluse*) lock.

satané, e [sȧtȧnȧ] *a* confounded.

satanique [sȧtȧnēk] *a* satanic, fiendish.

satelliser [sȧtȧlēzȧ] *vt* (*fusée*) to put into orbit; (*fig: pays*) to make into a satellite.

satellite [sȧtȧlēt] *nm* satellite; **pays** ~ satellite country.

satellite-espion, *pl* **satellites-espions** [sȧtȧlētespyóṅ] *nm* spy satellite.

satellite-observatoire, *pl* **satellites-observatoires** [sȧtȧlētopservȧtwȧr] *nm* observation satellite.

satellite-relais, *pl* **satellites-relais** [sȧtȧlētrəlc] *nm* (*TV*) relay satellite.

satiété [sȧsyȧtȧ]: **à** ~ *ad* to satiety *ou* satiation; (*répéter*) ad nauseam.

satin [sȧtaṅ] *nm* satin.

satiné, e [sȧtēnȧ] *a* satiny; (*peau*) satin-smooth.

satinette [sȧtēnet] *nf* satinet, sateen.

satire [sȧtēr] *nf* satire; **faire la** ~ to satirize.

satirique [sȧtērēk] *a* satirical.

satiriser [sȧtērēzȧ] *vt* to satirize.

satiriste [sȧtērēst(ə)] *nm/f* satirist.

satisfaction [sȧtēsfȧksyóṅ] *nf* satisfaction; **à ma grande** ~ to my great satisfaction; **obtenir** ~ to obtain *ou* get satisfaction; **donner** ~ **(à)** to give satisfaction (to).

satisfaire [sȧtēsfer] *vt* to satisfy; **se** ~ **de** to be satisfied *ou* content with; ~ **à** *vt* (*engagement*) to fulfill (*US*), fulfil (*Brit*); (*revendications, conditions*) to satisfy, meet.

satisfaisant, e [sȧtēsfəzǡ, -ǡt] *vb voir* **satisfaire** ◆ *a* satisfactory; (*qui fait plaisir*) satisfying.

satisfait, e [sȧtēsfe, -et] *pp de* **satisfaire** ◆ *a* satisfied; ~ **de** happy *ou* satisfied with.

satisfasse [sȧtēsfȧs], **satisferai** [sȧtēsfrȧ] *etc vb voir* **satisfaire**.

saturation [sȧtürȧsyóṅ] *nf* saturation; **arriver à** ~ to reach saturation point.

saturer [sȧtürȧ] *vt* to saturate; ~ **qn/qch de** to saturate sb/sth with.

saturnisme [sȧtürnēsm(ə)] *nm* (*MÉD*) lead poisoning.

satyre [sȧtēr] *nm* satyr; (*péj*) lecher.

sauce [sōs] *nf* sauce; (*avec un rôti*) gravy; **en** ~ in a sauce; ~ **blanche** white sauce; ~ **chasseur** sauce chasseur; ~ **tomate** tomato sauce.

saucer [sōsȧ] *vt* (*assiette*) to soak up the sauce from.

saucière [sōsyer] *nf* gravy boat.

saucisse [sōsēs] *nf* sausage.

saucisson [sōsēsóṅ] *nm* (slicing) sausage; ~ **à l'ail** garlic sausage.

saucissonner [sōsēsonȧ] *vt* to cut up, slice ◆ *vi* to picnic.

sauf [sōf] *prép* except; ~ **si** (*à moins que*) unless; ~ **avis contraire** unless you hear to the contrary; ~ **empêchement** barring (any) problems; ~ **erreur** if I'm not mistaken; ~ **imprévu** unless anything unforeseen arises, barring accidents.

sauf, sauve [sōf, sōv] *a* unharmed, unhurt; (*fig: honneur*) intact, saved; **laisser la vie sauve à qn** to spare sb's life.

sauf-conduit [sōfkóṅdüē] *nm* safe-conduct.

sauge [sōzh] *nf* sage.

saugrenu, e [sōgrənü] *a* preposterous, ludicrous.

saule [sōl] *nm* willow (tree); ~ **pleureur** weeping willow.

saumâtre [sōmȧtr(ə)] *a* briny; (*désagréable: plaisanterie*) unsavory (*US*), unsavoury (*Brit*).

saumon [sōmóṅ] *nm* salmon *inv* ◆ *a inv* salmon (pink).

saumoné, e [sōmonȧ] *a*: **truite saumonée** salmon trout.

saumure [sōmür] *nf* brine.

sauna [sōnȧ] *nm* sauna.

saupoudrer [sōpōōdrȧ] *vt*: ~ **qch de** to sprinkle sth with.

saupoudreuse [sōpōōdrœz] *nf* dredger.

saur [sor] *am*: **hareng** ~ smoked *ou* red herring, kipper.

saurai [sorȧ] *etc vb voir* **savoir**.

saut [sō] *nm* jump; (*discipline sportive*) jumping; **faire un** ~ to (make a) jump *ou* leap; **faire un** ~ **chez qn** to pop over to sb's (place); **au** ~ **du lit** on getting out of bed; ~ **en hauteur/longueur** high/long jump; ~ **à la corde** jumping rope (*US*), skipping (*Brit*); ~ **de page** (*INFORM*) page break; ~ **en parachute** parachuting *q*; ~ **à la perche** pole vaulting; ~ **périlleux** somersault.

saute [sōt] *nf*: ~ **de vent/température** sudden change of wind direction/in the temperature; **avoir des** ~**s d'humeur** to have sudden changes of mood.

sauté, e [sōtȧ] *a* (*CULIN*) sauté ◆ *nm*: ~ **de veau** sauté of veal.

saute-mouton [sōtmōōtóṅ] *nm*: **jouer à** ~ to play leapfrog.

sauter [sōtȧ] *vi* to jump, leap; (*exploser*) to blow up, explode; (*: fusibles*) to blow; (*se rompre*) to snap, burst; (*se détacher*) to pop out (*ou* off) ◆ *vt* to jump (over), leap (over); (*fig: omettre*) to jump rope (*US*), skip (*Brit*), miss (out); **faire** ~ to blow up; to burst open; (*CULIN*) to sauté; ~ **à pieds joints/à cloche-pied** to make a standing jump/to hop; ~ **en parachute** to make a parachute jump; ~ **à la corde** to jump rope (*US*), skip (*Brit*); ~ **de joie** to jump for joy; ~ **de colère** to be hopping with rage *ou* hopping mad; ~ **au cou de qn** to fly into sb's arms; ~ **aux yeux** to be quite obvious; ~ **au plafond** (*fig*) to hit the roof.

sauterelle [sōtrel] *nf* grasshopper.

sauterie [sōtrē] *nf* party, hop.

sauteur, euse [sōtœr, -œz] *nm/f* (*athlète*) jumper ♦ *nf* (*casserole*) shallow pan, frying pan; ~ **à la perche** pole vaulter; ~ **à skis** skijumper.

sautiller [sōtēyā] *vi* to hop; to skip.

sautoir [sōtwár] *nm* chain; (*SPORT: emplacement*) jumping pit; ~ **(de perles)** string of pearls.

sauvage [sōvázh] *a* (*gén*) wild; (*peuplade*) savage; (*farouche*) unsociable; (*barbare*) wild, savage; (*non officiel*) unauthorized, unofficial ♦ *nm/f* savage; (*timide*) unsociable type, recluse.

sauvagement [sōvázhmáṅ] *ad* savagely.

sauvageon, ne [sōvázhȯṅ, -on] *nm/f* little savage.

sauvagerie [sōvázhrē] *nf* wildness; savagery; unsociability.

sauve [sōv] *af voir* **sauf**.

sauvegarde [sōvgárd(ə)] *nf* safeguard; **sous la** ~ **de** under the protection of; **disquette/ fichier de** ~ (*INFORM*) backup disk/file.

sauvegarder [sōvgárdā] *vt* to safeguard; (*INFORM: enregistrer*) to save; (: *copier*) to back up.

sauve-qui-peut [sōvkēpœ̄] *nm inv* stampede, mad rush ♦ *excl* run for your life!

sauver [sōvā] *vt* to save; (*porter secours à*) to rescue; (*récupérer*) to salvage, rescue; **se** ~ *vi* (*s'enfuir*) to run away; (*fam: partir*) to be off; ~ **qn de** to save sb from; ~ **la vie à qn** to save sb's life; ~ **les apparences** to keep up appearances.

sauvetage [sōvtázh] *nm* rescue; ~ **en montagne** mountain rescue; **ceinture de** ~ life preserver (*US*), life belt (*Brit*); **brassière** *ou* **gilet de** ~ life jacket, life preserver (*US*).

sauveteur [sōvtœr] *nm* rescuer.

sauvette [sōvet]: **à la** ~ *ad* (*vendre*) without authorization; (*se marier etc*) hastily, hurriedly; **vente à la** ~ (unauthorized) street selling, (street) peddling.

sauveur [sōvœr] *nm* savior (*US*), saviour (*Brit*).

SAV *sigle m* = **service après vente**.

savais [sávā] *etc vb voir* **savoir**.

savamment [sávámáṅ] *ad* (*avec érudition*) learnedly; (*habilement*) skillfully (*US*), skilfully (*Brit*), cleverly.

savane [sáván] *nf* savannah.

savant, e [sáváṅ, -áṅt] *a* scholarly, learned; (*calé*) clever ♦ *nm* scientist; **animal** ~ performing animal.

savate [sávát] *nf* worn-out shoe; (*SPORT*) (*type of*) boxing.

saveur [sávœr] *nf* flavor (*US*), flavour (*Brit*); (*fig*) savor (*US*), savour (*Brit*).

Savoie [sávwá] *nf*: **la** ~ Savoy.

savoir [sávwár] *vt* to know; (*être capable de*): **il sait nager** he knows how to swim, he can swim ♦ *nm* knowledge; **se** ~ (*être connu*) to be known; **se** ~ **malade/incurable** to know that one is ill/incurably ill; **il est petit: tu ne**

peux pas ~! you won't believe how small he is!; **vous n'êtes pas sans** ~ **que** you are not *ou* will not be unaware of the fact that; **je crois** ~ **que** ... I believe that ..., I think I know that ...; **je n'en sais rien** I (really) don't know; **à** ~ **(que)** that is, namely; **faire** ~ **qch à qn** to inform sb about sth, let sb know sth; **pas que je sache** not as far as I know; **sans le** ~ *ad* unknowingly, unwittingly; **en** ~ **long** to know a lot.

savoir-faire [sávwárfer] *nm inv* savoir-faire, know-how.

savoir-vivre [sávwárvēvr(ə)] *nm inv*: **le** ~ savoir-faire, good manners *pl*.

savon [sávȯṅ] *nm* (*produit*) soap; (*morceau*) bar *ou* tablet of soap; (*fam*): **passer un** ~ **à qn** to give sb a good dressing-down.

savonner [sávonā] *vt* to soap.

savonnerie [sávonrē] *nf* soap factory.

savonnette [sávonet] *nf* bar *ou* tablet of soap.

savonneux, euse [sávonœ̄, -œz] *a* soapy.

savons [sávȯṅ] *vb voir* **savoir**.

savourer [sávōōrā] *vt* to savor (*US*), savour (*Brit*).

savoureux, euse [sávōōrœ̄, -œz] *a* tasty; (*fig*) spicy, juicy.

savoyard, e [sávwáyár, -árd(ə)] *a* Savoyard.

sax [sáks] *nm* sax.

Saxe [sáks(ə)] *nf*: **la** ~ Saxony.

saxo(phone) [sákso(fon)] *nm* sax(ophone).

saxophoniste [sáksofonēst(ə)] *nm/f* saxophonist, sax(ophone) player.

saynète [senet] *nf* playlet.

SBB *sigle f* (= *Schweizerische Bundesbahn*) *Swiss federal railways*.

sbire [sbēr] *nm* (*péj*) henchman.

sc. *abr* = **scène**.

s/c *abr* (= *sous couvert de*) ≈ c/o.

scabreux, euse [skábrœ̄, -œz] *a* risky; (*indécent*) improper, shocking.

scalpel [skálpel] *nm* scalpel.

scalper [skálpā] *vt* to scalp.

scampi [skáṅpē] *nmpl* scampi.

scandale [skáṅdál] *nm* scandal; (*tapage*): **faire du** ~ to make a scene, create a disturbance; **faire** ~ to scandalize people; **au grand** ~ **de** ... to the great indignation of ....

scandaleusement [skáṅdálœzmáṅ] *ad* scandalously, outrageously.

scandaleux, euse [skáṅdálœ̄, -œz] *a* scandalous, outrageous.

scandaliser [skáṅdálēzā] *vt* to scandalize; **se** ~ **(de)** to be scandalized (by).

scander [skáṅdā] *vt* (*vers*) to scan; (*mots, syllabes*) to stress separately; (*slogans*) to chant.

scandinave [skáṅdēnáv] *a* Scandinavian ♦ *nm/ f*: **S**~ Scandinavian.

Scandinavie [skáṅdēnávē] *nf*: **la** ~ Scandinavia.

scanner [skáner] *nm* (*MÉD*) scanner.

scanographie [skánográfē] *nf* (*MÉD*) scanning; (*image*) scan.

scaphandre [skáfáṅdr(ə)] *nm* (*de plongeur*) diving suit; (*de cosmonaute*) space-suit; ~ **autonome** aqualung.

scaphandrier [skáfáṅdrēyā] *nm* diver.

scarabée [skárábā] *nm* beetle.

scarlatine [skárlátēn] *nf* scarlet fever.

scarole [skȧrol] *nf* endive.
scatologique [skȧtolozhēk] *a* scatological, lavatorial.
sceau, x [sō] *nm* seal; *(fig)* stamp, mark; **sous le ~ du secret** under the seal of secrecy.
scélérat, e [sālȧrȧ, -ȧt] *nm/f* villain, blackguard ♦ *a* villainous, blackguardly.
sceller [sālā] *vt* to seal.
scellés [sālā] *nmpl* seals.
scénario [sānȧryō] *nm* *(CINÉMA)* screenplay, script; *(: idée, plan)* scenario; *(fig)* pattern; scenario.
scénariste [sānȧrēst(ə)] *nm/f* scriptwriter.
scène [sɛn] *nf* *(gén)* scene; *(estrade, fig: théâtre)* stage; **entrer en ~** to come on stage; **mettre en ~** *(THÉÂTRE)* to stage; *(CINÉMA)* to direct; *(fig)* to present, introduce; **sur le devant de la ~** *(en pleine actualité)* in the forefront; **porter à la ~** to adapt for the stage; **faire une ~ (à qn)** to make a scene (with sb); **~ de ménage** domestic fight *ou* scene.
scénique [sānēk] *a* *(effets)* theatrical; *(art)* scenic.
scepticisme [septēsēsm(ə)] *nm* skepticism *(US)*, scepticism *(Brit)*.
sceptique [septēk] *a* skeptical *(US)*, sceptical *(Brit)* ♦ *nm/f* skeptic *(US)*, sceptic *(Brit)*.
sceptre [septr(ə)] *nm* skepter *(US)*, sceptre *(Brit)*.
schéma [shāmȧ] *nm* *(diagramme)* diagram, sketch; *(fig)* outline.
schématique [shāmȧtēk] *a* diagrammatic(al), schematic; *(fig)* oversimplified.
schématiquement [shāmȧtēkmȧṅ] *ad* schematically, diagrammatically.
schématiser [shāmȧtēzā] *vt* to schematize; to (over)simplify.
schismatique [shēsmȧtēk] *a* schismatic.
schisme [shēsm(ə)] *nm* schism; rift, split.
schiste [shēst(ə)] *nm* schist.
schizophrène [skēzofren] *nm/f* schizophrenic.
schizophrénie [skēzofrānē] *nf* schizophrenia.
sciatique [syȧtēk] *a*: **nerf ~** sciatic nerve ♦ *nf* sciatica.
scie [sē] *nf* saw; *(fam: rengaine)* catchword, catch phrase; *(: personne)* bore; **~ à bois** wood saw; **~ circulaire** circular saw; **~ à découper** fretsaw; **~ à métaux** hacksaw; **~ sauteuse** jigsaw.
sciemment [syȧmȧṅ] *ad* knowingly, wittingly.
science [syȧṅs] *nf* science; *(savoir)* knowledge; *(savoir-faire)* art, skill; **~s humaines/ sociales** social sciences; **~s naturelles** natural science *sg*, biology *sg*; **~s po** political studies.
science-fiction [syȧṅsfēksyóṅ] *nf* science fiction.
scientifique [syȧṅtēfēk] *a* scientific ♦ *nm/f* (savant) scientist; *(étudiant)* science student.
scientifiquement [syȧṅtēfēkmȧṅ] *ad* scientifically.
scier [syā] *vt* to saw; *(retrancher)* to saw off.
scierie [sērē] *nf* sawmill.
scieur [syœr] *nm*: **~ de long** pit sawyer.
Scilly [sēlē]: **les îles ~** the Scilly Isles, the Scillies, the Isles of Scilly.
scinder [saṅdā] *vt*, **se ~** *vi* to split (up).

scintillant, e [saṅtēyȧṅ, -ȧṅt] *a* sparkling.
scintillement [saṅtēymȧṅ] *nm* sparkling *q*.
scintiller [saṅtēyā] *vi* to sparkle.
scission [sēsyóṅ] *nf* split.
sciure [syür] *nf*: **~ (de bois)** sawdust.
sclérose [sklārōz] *nf* sclerosis; *(fig)* ossification; **~ en plaques (SEP)** multiple sclerosis (MS).
sclérosé, e [sklārōzā] *a* sclerosed, sclerotic; ossified.
scléroser [sklārōzā]: **se ~** *vi* to become sclerosed; *(fig)* to become ossified.
scolaire [skoler] *a* school *cpd*; *(péj)* schoolish; **l'année ~** the school year; *(à l'université)* the academic year; **en âge ~** of school age.
scolariser [skolȧrēzā] *vt* to provide with schooling *(ou* schools).
scolarité [skolȧrētā] *nf* schooling; **frais de ~** tuition *(US)*, school fees *(Brit)*.
scolastique [skolȧstēk] *a* *(péj)* scholastic.
scoliose [skolyōz] *nf* curvature of the spine, scoliosis.
scoop [skōōp] *nm* *(PRESSE)* scoop, exclusive.
scooter [skōōtœr] *nm* (motor) scooter.
scorbut [skorbüt] *nm* scurvy.
score [skor] *nm* score; *(électoral etc)* result.
scories [skorē] *nfpl* scoria *pl*.
scorpion [skorpyóṅ] *nm* *(signe)*: **le S~** Scorpio, the Scorpion; **être du S~** to be Scorpio.
scotch [skotsh] *nm* *(whisky)* scotch, whisky; *(adhésif)* Scotch tape ® *(US)*, Sellotape ® *(Brit)*.
scotcher [skotshā] *vt* to scotchtape ® *(US)*, sellotape ® *(Brit)*.
scout, e [skōōt] *a, nm* scout.
scoutisme [skōōtēsm(ə)] *nm* (boy) scout movement; *(activités)* scouting.
scribe [skrēb] *nm* scribe; *(péj)* pencil pusher *(US)*, penpusher *(Brit)*.
scribouillard [skrēbōōyȧr] *nm* pencil pusher *(US)*, penpusher *(Brit)*.
script [skrēpt] *nm* printing; *(CINÉMA)* (shooting) script.
script-girl [skrēptgœrl] *nf* continuity girl.
scriptural, e, aux [skrēptürȧl, -ō] *a*: **monnaie ~e** bank money.
scrupule [skrüpül] *nm* scruple; **être sans ~s** to be unscrupulous; **se faire un ~ de qch** to have scruples *ou* qualms about doing sth.
scrupuleusement [skrüpülœzmȧṅ] *ad* scrupulously.
scrupuleux, euse [skrüpülœ, -œz] *a* scrupulous.
scrutateur, trice [skrütȧtœr, -trēs] *a* searching ♦ *nm/f* canvasser *(US)*, scrutineer *(Brit)*.
scruter [skrütā] *vt* to search, scrutinize; *(l'obscurité)* to peer into; *(motifs, comportement)* to examine, scrutinize.
scrutin [skrütaṅ] *nm* *(vote)* ballot; *(ensemble des opérations)* poll; **~ proportionnel/ majoritaire** election on a proportional/ majority basis; **~ à deux tours** poll with two ballots *ou* rounds; **~ de liste** list system.
sculpter [skültā] *vt* to sculpt; *(suj: érosion)* to carve.
sculpteur [skültœr] *nm* sculptor.
sculptural, e, aux [skültürȧl, -ō] *a* sculptural; *(fig)* statuesque.

sculpture [skültür] *nf* sculpture; ~ **sur bois** wood carving.

sdb. *abr* = **salle de bain**.

SDN *sigle f* (= *Société des Nations*) League of Nations.

SE *sigle f* (= *Son Excellence*) HE.

se, s' [s(ə)] *pronom* (*emploi réfléchi*) oneself, *m* himself, *f* herself, *sujet non humain* itself; *pl* themselves; (: *réciproque*) one another, each other; (: *passif*): **cela se répare facilement** it is easily repaired; (: *possessif*): ~ **casser la jambe/laver les mains** to break one's leg/wash one's hands; *autres emplois pronominaux: voir le verbe en question*.

séance [sããs] *nf* (*d'assemblée, récréative*) meeting, session; (*de tribunal*) sitting, session; (*musicale, CINÉMA, THÉÂTRE*) performance; **ouvrir/lever la** ~ to open/close the meeting; ~ **tenante** forthwith.

séant, e [sãã, -ãt] *a* seemly, fitting ♦ *nm* posterior.

seau, x [sõ] *nm* bucket, pail; ~ **à glace** ice-bucket.

sébum [sãbom] *nm* sebum.

sec, sèche [sɛk, sɛʃ] *a* dry; (*raisins, figues*) dried; (*cœur, personne: insensible*) hard, cold; (*maigre, déchaîné*) spare, lean; (*réponse, ton*) sharp, curt; (*démarrage*) sharp, sudden ♦ *nm*: **tenir au** ~ to keep in a dry place ♦ *ad* hard; (*démarrer*) sharply; **boire** ~ to be a heavy drinker; **je le bois** ~ I drink it straight ou neat; **à pied** ~ without getting one's feet wet; **à** ~ a dried up; (*à court d'argent*) broke.

SECAM [sãkám] *sigle m* (= *procédé séquentiel à mémoire*) SECAM.

sécateur [sãkátœr] *nm* shears *pl*, pair of shears.

sécession [sãsãsyõ] *nf*: **faire** ~ to secede; **la guerre de S~** the American Civil War.

séchage [sãʃãzh] *nm* drying; (*de bois*) seasoning.

sèche [sɛʃ] *af voir* **sec** ♦ *nf* (*fam*) cigarette.

sèche-cheveux [sɛʃʃəvœ] *nm inv* hair dryer.

sèche-linge [sɛʃlãʒ] *nm inv* (*machine*) clothes dryer.

sèche-mains [sɛʃmã] *nm inv* hand dryer.

sèchement [sɛʃmã] *ad* (*frapper etc*) sharply; (*répliquer etc*) dryly, sharply.

sécher [sãʃã] *vt* to dry; (*dessécher: peau, blé*) to dry (out); (: *étang*) to dry up; (*bois*) to season; (*fam: classe, cours*) to skip, miss ♦ *vi* to dry; to dry out; to dry up; (*fam: candidat*) to be stumped; **se** ~ (*après le bain*) to dry o.s.

sécheresse [sɛʃrɛs] *nf* dryness; (*absence de pluie*) drought.

séchoir [sãʃwár] *nm* dryer.

second, e [səgõ, -õd] *a* second ♦ *nm* (*assistant*) second in command; (*étage*) third floor (*US*), second floor (*Brit*); (*NAVIG*) first mate ♦ *nf* second; (*SCOL: degré*) ≈ tenth grade (*US*), ≈ fifth form (*Brit*); **en** ~**e** (*en second rang*) in second place; **voyager en** ~**e** to travel second-class; **doué de** ~**e vue** having (the gift of) second sight; **trouver son** ~ **souffle** (*SPORT, fig*) to get one's second wind;

être dans un état ~ to be in a daze (*ou* trance); **de** ~**e main** second-hand.

secondaire [səgõdɛr] *a* secondary.

seconder [səgõdã] *vt* to assist; (*favoriser*) to back.

secouer [səkwã] *vt* to shake; (*passagers*) to rock; (*traumatiser*) to shake (up); **se** ~ (*chien*) to shake itself; (*fam: se démener*) to shake o.s. up; ~ **la poussière d'un tapis** to shake the dust off a carpet; ~ **la tête** to shake one's head.

secourable [səkōōrábl(ə)] *a* helpful.

secourir [səkōōrēr] *vt* (*aller sauver*) to (go and) rescue; (*prodiguer des soins à*) to help, assist; (*venir en aide à*) to assist, aid.

secourisme [səkōōrēsm(ə)] *nm* (*premiers soins*) first aid; (*sauvetage*) lifesaving.

secouriste [səkōōrēst(ə)] *nm/f* first-aid worker.

secourons [səkōōrõ] *etc vb voir* **secourir**.

secours [səkōōr] *vb voir* **secourir** ♦ *nm* help, aid, assistance ♦ *nmpl* aid *sg*; **cela lui a été d'un grand** ~ this was a great help to him; **au** ~! help!; **appeler au** ~ to shout ou call for help; **appeler qn à son** ~ to call sb to one's assistance; **porter** ~ **à qn** to give sb assistance, help sb; **les premiers** ~ first aid *sg*; **le** ~ **en montagne** mountain rescue.

secouru, e [səkōōrü] *pp de* **secourir**.

secousse [səkōōs] *nf* jolt, bump; (*électrique*) shock; (*fig: psychologique*) jolt, shock; ~ **sismique** ou **tellurique** earth tremor.

secret, ète [səkrɛ, -ɛt] *a* secret; (*fig: renfermé*) reticent, reserved ♦ *nm* secret; (*discrétion absolue*): **le** ~ secrecy; **en** ~ in secret, secretly; **au** ~ in solitary confinement; ~ **de fabrication** trade secret; ~ **professionnel** professional secrecy.

secrétaire [səkrãtɛr] *nm/f* secretary ♦ *nm* (*meuble*) secretary (*US*), writing desk; ~ **d'ambassade** embassy secretary; ~ **de direction** private ou personal secretary; ~ **d'État** ≈ Secretary of State (*US*), junior minister (*Brit*); ~ **général (SG)** Secretary-General; (*COMM*) company secretary; ~ **de mairie** town clerk; ~ **médicale** medical secretary; ~ **de rédaction** sub-editor.

secrétariat [s(ə)krãtãryã] *nm* (*profession*) secretarial work; (*bureau: d'entreprise, d'école*) (secretary's) office; (: *d'organisation internationale*) secretariat; (*POL etc: fonction*) secretaryship, office of Secretary.

secrètement [səkrɛtmã] *ad* secretly.

sécréter [sãkrãtã] *vt* to secrete.

sécrétion [sãkrãsyõ] *nf* secretion.

sectaire [sɛktɛr] *a* sectarian, bigoted.

sectarisme [sɛktãrɛsm(ə)] *nm* sectarianism.

secte [sɛkt(ə)] *nf* sect.

secteur [sɛktœr] *nm* sector; (*ADMIN*) district; (*ÉLEC*): **branché sur le** ~ plugged into the mains (supply); **fonctionne sur pile et** ~ operates on DC or AC (*US*), battery or mains operated (*Brit*); **le** ~ **privé/public** (*ÉCON*) the private/public sector; **le** ~ **primaire/tertiaire** the primary/tertiary sector.

section [sɛksyõ] *nf* section; (*de parcours d'autobus*) fare zone (*US*) ou stage (*Brit*); (*MIL: unité*) platoon; ~ **rythmique** rhythm section.

sectionner [sɛksyonã] *vt* to sever; **se** ~ *vi* to

be severed.

sectionneur [sɛksyonœr] *nm* (*ÉLEC*) isolation switch.

sectoriel, le [sektoryɛl] *a* sector-based.

sectoriser [sektorēzā] *vt* to divide into sectors.

sécu [sākü] *nf* (*fam*: = *sécurité sociale*) ≈ dole, ≈ Welfare (*US*).

séculaire [sākūler] *a* secular; (*très vieux*) age-old.

séculariser [sākūlárēzā] *vt* to secularize.

séculier, ière [sākülyā, -yer] *a* secular.

sécurisant, e [sākürēzáń, -áńt] *a* secure, giving a sense of security.

sécuriser [sākürēzā] *vt* to give a sense of security to.

sécurité [sākürētā] *nf* security; (*absence de danger*) safety; **impression de** ~ sense of security; **la** ~ **internationale** international security; **système de** ~ security (*ou* safety) system; **être en** ~ to be safe; **la** ~ **de l'emploi** job security; **la** ~ **routière** road safety; **la** ~ **sociale** ≈ (the) Welfare (*US*), ≈ (the) Social Security (*Brit*).

sédatif, ive [sādátēf, -ēv] *a*, *nm* sedative.

sédentaire [sādáńter] *a* sedentary.

sédiment [sādēmáń] *nm* sediment; ~**s** *nmpl* (*alluvions*) sediment *sg*.

sédimentaire [sādēmáńter] *a* sedimentary.

séditieux, euse [sādēsyœ̄, -œ̄z] *a* insurgent; seditious.

sédition [sādēsyóń] *nf* insurrection; sedition.

séducteur, trice [sādüktœr, -trēs] *a* seductive ♦ *nm/f* seducer/seductress.

séduction [sādüksyóń] *nf* seduction; (*charme, attrait*) appeal, charm.

séduire [sādüēr] *vt* to charm; (*femme: abuser de*) to seduce; (*suj: chose*) to appeal to.

séduisant, e [sādüēzáń, -áńt] *vb voir* **séduire** ♦ *a* (*femme*) seductive; (*homme, offre*) very attractive.

séduit, e [sādüē, -ēt] *pp de* **séduire**.

segment [segmáń] *nm* segment; (*AUTO*): ~ **(de piston)** piston ring; ~ **de frein** brake shoe.

segmenter [segmáńtā] *vt*, **se** ~ *vi* to segment.

ségrégation [sāgrāgásyóń] *nf* segregation.

ségrégationniste [sāgrāgásyonēst(ə)] *a* segregationist.

seiche [sesh] *nf* cuttlefish.

séide [sāēd] *nm* (*péj*) henchman.

seigle [segl(ə)] *nm* rye.

seigneur [senyœr] *nm* lord; **le S**~ the Lord.

seigneurial, e, aux [senyœryál, -ō] *a* lordly, stately.

sein [sań] *nm* breast; (*entrailles*) womb; **au** ~ **de** *prép* (*équipe, institution*) within; (*flots, bonheur*) in the midst of; **donner le** ~ **à** (*bébé*) to feed (at the breast); to breast-feed; **nourrir au** ~ to breast-feed.

Seine [sen] *nf*: **la** ~ the Seine.

séisme [sāēsm(ə)] *nm* earthquake.

séismique *etc* [seismik] *voir* **sismique** *etc*.

SEITA [sāētá] *sigle f* = *Société d'exploitation industrielle des tabacs et allumettes*.

seize [sez] *num* sixteen.

seizième [sezyem] *num* sixteenth.

séjour [sāzhōōr] *nm* stay; (*pièce*) living room.

séjourner [sāzhōōrnā] *vi* to stay.

sel [sel] *nm* salt; (*fig*) wit; spice; ~ **de**

cuisine/de table cooking/table salt; ~ **gemme** rock salt; ~**s de bain** bath salts.

sélect, e [sālckt] *a* select.

sélectif, ive [sālcktēf, -ēv] *a* selective.

sélection [sālcksyóń] *nf* selection; **faire/opérer une** ~ **parmi** to make a selection from among; **épreuve de** ~ (*SPORT*) trial (for selection); ~ **naturelle** natural selection; ~ **professionnelle** professional recruitment.

selectionné, e [sālcksyonā] *a* (*joueur*) selected; (*produit*) specially selected.

sélectionner [sālcksyonā] *vt* to select.

sélectionneur, euse [sālcksyonœr, -œ̄z] *nm/f* selector.

sélectivement [sālcktēvmáń] *ad* selectively.

sélénologie [sālānolozhē] *nf* study of the moon, selenology.

self [self] *nm* (*fam*) self-service.

self-service [selfservēs] *a* self-service ♦ *nm* self-service (*restaurant*); (*magasin*) self-service shop.

selle [sel] *nf* saddle; ~**s** *nfpl* (*MÉD*) stools; **aller à la** ~ (*MÉD*) to have a bowel movement; **se mettre en** ~ to mount, get into the saddle.

seller [sālā] *vt* to saddle.

sellette [selet] *nf*: **être sur la** ~ to be on the carpet (*fig*).

sellier [sālyā] *nm* saddler.

selon [səlóń] *prép* according to; (*en se conformant à*) in accordance with; ~ **moi** as I see it; ~ **que** according to, depending on whether.

SEm *sigle f* (= *Son Éminence*) HE.

semailles [səmáy] *nfpl* sowing *sg*.

semaine [səmen] *nf* week; (*salaire*) week's wages *ou* pay, weekly wages *ou* pay; **en** ~ during the week, on weekdays; **à la petite** ~ from day to day; **la** ~ **sainte** Holy Week.

semainier [səmānyā] *nm* (*bracelet*) bracelet made up of seven bands; (*calendrier*) desk calendar (*US*) *ou* diary (*Brit*); (*meuble*) chest of (seven) drawers.

sémantique [sāmáńtēk] *a* semantic ♦ *nf* semantics *sg*.

sémaphore [sāmáfor] *nm* (*RAIL*) semaphore signal.

semblable [sáńblábl(ə)] *a* similar; (*de ce genre*): **de** ~**s mésaventures** such mishaps ♦ *nm* fellow creature *ou* man; ~ **à** similar to, like.

semblant [sáńbláń] *nm*: **un** ~ **de vérité** a semblance of truth; **faire** ~ **(de faire)** to pretend (to do).

sembler [sáńblā] *vb avec attribut* to seem ♦ *vb impersonnel*: **il semble (bien) que/inutile de** it (really) seems *ou* appears that/useless to; **il me semble (bien) que** it (really) seems to me that, I (really) think (that); **il me semble le connaître** I think *ou* I've a feeling I know him; ~ **être** to seem to be; **comme bon lui semble** as he sees fit; **me semble- t-il, à ce qu'il me semble** it seems to me, to my mind.

semelle [səmel] *nf* sole; (*intérieure*) insole, inner sole; **battre la** ~ to stamp one's feet (to keep them warm); (*fig*) to hang around (waiting); ~**s compensées** platform soles.

semence [səmáńs] *nf* (*graine*) seed; (*clou*) tack.

semer [səmā] *vt* to sow; (*fig: éparpiller*) to scatter; (*confusion*) to spread; (: *poursuivants*) to lose, shake off; ~ **la discorde/terreur parmi** to sow discord/terror among; **semé de** (*difficultés*) riddled with.

semestre [səmestr(ə)] *nm* half-year; (*SCOL*) semester.

semestriel, le [səmestrēyel] *a* half-yearly; semestral.

semeur, euse [səmœr, -ēz] *nm/f* sower.

semi-automatique [səmēotomátēk] *a* semi-automatic.

semiconducteur [səmēkôńdüktœr] *nm* (*IN-FORM*) semiconductor.

sémillant, e [sāmēyáń, -áńt] *a* vivacious; dashing.

séminaire [sāmēner] *nm* seminar; (*REL*) seminary.

séminariste [sāmēnárēst(ə)] *nm* seminarist.

sémiologie [sāmyolozhē] *nf* semiology.

semi-public, ique [səmēpüblēk] *a* (*JUR*) semi-public.

semi-remorque [səmērəmork(ə)] *nf* trailer ♦ *nm* semi(trailer) (*US*), articulated lorry (*Brit*).

semis [səmē] *nm* (*terrain*) seedbed, seed plot; (*plante*) seedling.

sémite [sāmēt] *a* Semitic.

sémitique [sāmētēk] *a* Semitic.

semoir [səmwár] *nm* seed-bag; seeder.

semonce [səmôńs] *nf*: **un coup de** ~ a warning shot.

semoule [səmōōl] *nf* semolina; ~ **de riz** ground rice.

sempiternel, le [sańpēternel] *a* eternal, neverending.

sénat [sānà] *nm* senate.

sénateur [sānátœr] *nm* senator.

Sénégal [sānāgál] *nm*: **le** ~ Senegal.

sénégalais, e [sānāgàle, -ez] *a* Senegalese.

sénevé [senvā] *nm* (*BOT*) mustard; (*graine*) mustard seed.

sénile [sānēl] *a* senile.

sénilité [sānēlētā] *nf* senility.

senior [sānyor] *nm/f* (*SPORT*) senior.

sens [sáń] *vb voir* **sentir** ♦ *nm* [sáńs] (*PHYSIOL, instinct*) sense; (*signification*) meaning, sense; (*direction*) direction, way ♦ *nmpl* (*sensualité*) senses; **reprendre ses** ~ to regain consciousness; **avoir le** ~ **des affaires/de la mesure** to have business sense/a sense of moderation; **ça n'a pas de** ~ that doesn't make (any) sense; **en dépit du bon** ~ contrary to all good sense; **tomber sous le** ~ to stand to reason, be perfectly obvious; **en un** ~, **dans un** ~ in a way; **en ce** ~ **que** in the sense that; **à mon** ~ to my mind; **dans le** ~ **des aiguilles d'une montre** clockwise; **dans le** ~ **de la longeur/largeur** lengthwise/widthwise; **dans le mauvais** ~ the wrong way; in the wrong direction; **bon** ~ good sense; ~ **commun** common sense; ~ **dessus dessous** upside down; ~ **interdit,** ~ **unique** one-way street.

sensass [sáńsás] *a* (*fam*) fantastic.

sensation [sáńsásyôń] *nf* sensation; **faire** ~ to cause a sensation, create a stir; **à** ~ (*péj*) sensational.

sensationnel, le [sáńsásyonel] *a* sensational.

sensé, e [sáńsā] *a* sensible.

sensibiliser [sáńsēbēlēzā] *vt* to sensitize; ~ **qn** **(à)** to make sb sensitive (to).

sensibilité [sáńsēbēlētā] *nf* sensitivity; (*affectivité, émotivité*) sensitivity, sensibility.

sensible [sáńsēbl(ə)] *a* sensitive; (*aux sens*) perceptible; (*appréciable: différence, progrès*) appreciable, noticeable; ~ **à** sensitive to.

sensiblement [sáńsēbləmáń] *ad* (*notablement*) appreciably, noticeably; (*à peu près*): **ils ont** ~ **le même poids** they weigh approximately the same.

sensiblerie [sáńsēblərē] *nf* sentimentality; squeamishness.

sensitif, ive [sáńsētēf, -ēv] *a* (*nerf*) sensory; (*personne*) oversensitive.

sensoriel, le [sáńsoryel] *a* sensory, sensorial.

sensualité [sáńsüálētā] *nf* sensuality, sensuousness.

sensuel, le [sáńsüel] *a* sensual; sensuous.

sent [sáń] *vb voir* **sentir**.

sente [sáńt] *nf* path.

sentence [sáńtáńs] *nf* (*jugement*) sentence; (*adage*) maxim.

sentencieux, euse [sáńtáńsyœ̄, -ēz] *a* sententious.

senteur [sáńtœr] *nf* scent, perfume.

senti, e [sáńtē] *a*: **bien** ~ (*mots etc*) well-chosen.

sentier [sáńtyā] *nm* path.

sentiment [sáńtēmáń] *nm* feeling; (*conscience, impression*): **avoir le** ~ **de/que** to be aware of/have the feeling that; **recevez mes** ~**s respectueux** yours truly (*US*) *ou* faithfully (*Brit*); **faire du** ~ (*péj*) to be sentimental; **si vous me prenez par les** ~**s** if you appeal to my feelings.

sentimental, e, aux [sáńtēmáńtál, -ō] *a* sentimental; (*vie, aventure*) love *cpd*.

sentimentalisme [sáńtēmáńtálēsm(ə)] *nm* sentimentalism.

sentimentalité [sáńtēmáńtálētā] *nf* sentimentality.

sentinelle [sáńtēnel] *nf* sentry; **en** ~ standing guard; (*soldat: en faction*) on sentry duty.

sentir [sáńtēr] *vt* (*par l'odorat*) to smell; (*par le goût*) to taste; (*au toucher, fig*) to feel; (*répandre une odeur de*) to smell of; (: *ressemblance*) to smell like; (*avoir la saveur de*) to taste of; to taste like; (*fig: dénoter, annoncer*) to be indicative of; to smack of; to foreshadow ♦ *vi* to smell; ~ **mauvais** to smell bad; **se** ~ **bien** to feel good; **se** ~ **mal** (*être indisposé*) to feel unwell *ou* ill; **se** ~ **le courage/la force de faire** to feel brave/strong enough to do; **ne plus se** ~ **de joie** to be beside o.s. with joy; **il ne peut pas le** ~ (*fam*) he can't stand him.

seoir [swár]: ~ **à** *vt* to become, befit; **comme il (leur) sied** as it is fitting (to them).

Seoul [sāōōl] *n* Seoul.

SEP *sigle f* (= *sclérose en plaques*) MS.

séparation [sāpárásyôń] *nf* separation; (*cloison*) division, partition; ~ **de biens** division of property (*in marriage settlement*); ~ **de corps** legal separation.

séparatiste [sāpárátēst(ə)] *a, nm/f* (*POL*) separatist.

séparé, e [sāpárā] *a (appartements, pouvoirs)* separate; *(époux)* separated; ~ **de** separate from; separated from.

séparément [sāpárāmáǹ] *ad* separately.

séparer [sāpárā] *vt (gén)* to separate; *(suj: divergences etc)* to divide; to drive apart; *(: différences, obstacles)* to stand between; *(détacher):* ~ **qch de** to pull sth (off) from; *(dissocier)* to distinguish between; *(diviser):* ~ **qch par** to divide sth (up) with; ~ **une pièce en deux** to divide a room into two; **se** ~ *(époux)* to separate, part; *(prendre congé: amis etc)* to part, leave each other; *(adversaires)* to separate; *(se diviser: route, tige etc)* to divide; *(se détacher):* **se** ~ **(de)** to split off (from); to come off; **se** ~ **de** *(époux)* to separate *ou* part from; *(employé, objet personnel)* to part with.

sépia [sāpyá] *nf* sepia.

sept [set] *num* seven.

septante [septáǹt] *num (Belgique, Suisse)* seventy.

septembre [septáǹbr(ə)] *nm* September; *voir aussi* **juillet**.

septennal, e, aux [septānál, -ō] *a* seven-year; *(festival)* seven-year, septennial.

septennat [septānā] *nm* seven-year term (of office); seven-year reign.

septentrional, e, aux [septáǹtrēyonál, -ō] *a* northern.

septicémie [septēsāmē] *nf* blood poisoning, septicemia *(US)*, septicaemia *(Brit)*.

septième [setyem] *num* seventh; **être au** ~ **ciel** to be on cloud nine.

septique [septēk] *a:* **fosse** ~ septic tank.

septuagénaire [septüázhāner] *a, nm/f* septuagenarian.

sépulcral, e, aux [sāpülkrál, -ō] *a (voix)* sepulchral.

sépulcre [sāpülkr(ə)] *nm* sepulcher *(US)*, sepulchre *(Brit)*.

sépulture [sāpültür] *nf* burial; *(tombeau)* burial place, grave.

séquelles [sākel] *nfpl* after-effects; *(fig)* aftermath *sg*; consequences.

séquence [sākáǹs] *nf* sequence.

séquentiel, le [sākáǹsyel] *a* sequential.

séquestration [sākestrásyóǹ] *nf* illegal confinement; impounding.

séquestre [sākestr(ə)] *nm* impoundment; **mettre sous** ~ to impound.

séquestrer [sākestrā] *vt (personne)* to confine illegally; *(biens)* to impound.

serai [sorā] *etc vb voir* **être**.

sérail [sāráy] *nm* seraglio; harem; **rentrer au** ~ to return to the fold.

serbe [serb(ə)] *a* Serbian ♦ *nm (LING)* Serbian ♦ *nm/f:* **S**~ Serb.

Serbie [serbē] *nf:* **la** ~ Serbia.

serbo-croate [serbokroát] *a* Serbo-Croat, Serbo-Croatian ♦ *nm (LING)* Serbo-Croatian.

serein, e [soraǹ, -en] *a* serene; *(jugement)* dispassionate.

sereinement [sorenmáǹ] *ad* serenely.

sérénade [sārānád] *nf* serenade; *(fam)* hullabaloo.

sérénité [sārānētā] *nf* serenity.

serez [sorā] *vb voir* **être**.

serf, serve [scr, scrv(ə)] *nm/f* serf.

serfouette [serfwet] *nf* weeding hoe.

serge [serzh(ə)] *nf* serge.

sergent [serzháǹ] *nm* sergeant.

sergent-chef [serzháǹshef] *nm* staff sergeant.

sergent-major [serzháǹmázhor] *nm* ≈ quartermaster sergeant.

sériciculture [sārēsēkültür] *nf* silkworm breeding, sericiculture.

série [sārē] *nf (de questions, d'accidents, TV)* series *inv*; *(de clés, casseroles, outils)* set; *(catégorie: SPORT)* rank; class; **en** ~ in quick succession; *(COMM)* mass *cpd*; **de** ~ *a* standard; **hors** ~ *(COMM)* custom-built; *(fig)* outstanding; **imprimante** ~ *(INFORM)* serial printer; **soldes de fin de** ~**s** end of line special offers; ~ **noire** *nm* (crime) thriller ♦ *nf (suite de malheurs)* run of bad luck.

sérier [sāryā] *vt* to classify, sort out.

sérieusement [sāryœzmáǹ] *ad* seriously; reliably; responsibly; **il parle** ~ he's serious, he means it; ~**?** are you serious?, do you mean it?

sérieux, euse [sāryœ, -œz] *a* serious; *(élève, employé)* reliable, responsible; *(client, maison)* reliable, dependable; *(offre, proposition)* genuine, serious; *(grave, sévère)* serious, solemn; *(maladie, situation)* serious, grave; *(important)* considerable ♦ *nm* seriousness; reliability; **ce n'est pas** ~ *(raisonnable)* that won't do; **garder son** ~ to keep a straight face; **manquer de** ~ not to be very responsible *(ou* reliable); **prendre qch/qn au** ~ to take sth/sb seriously.

sérigraphie [sārēgráfē] *nf* silk screen printing.

serin [soraǹ] *nm* canary.

seriner [sorēnā] *vt:* ~ **qch à qn** to drum sth into sb.

seringue [soraǹg] *nf* syringe.

serions [soryóǹ] *etc vb voir* **être**.

serment [sermáǹ] *nm (juré)* oath; *(promesse)* pledge, vow; **prêter** ~ to take the *ou* an oath; **faire le** ~ **de** to take a vow to, swear to; **sous** ~ on *ou* under oath.

sermon [scrmóǹ] *nm* sermon; *(péj)* sermon, lecture.

sermonner [scrmonā] *vt* to lecture.

SERNAM [scrnám] *sigle m (= Service national de messageries)* rail delivery service.

sérologie [sārolozhē] *nf* serology.

serpe [serp(ə)] *nf* billhook.

serpent [serpáǹ] *nm* snake; ~ **à sonnettes** rattlesnake; ~ **monétaire (européen)** (European) monetary snake.

serpenter [serpáǹtā] *vi* to wind.

serpentin [serpáǹtaǹ] *nm (tube)* coil; *(ruban)* streamer.

serpillière [serpēyer] *nf* floorcloth.

serrage [scrázh] *nm* tightening; **collier de** ~ clamp.

serre [scr] *nf (AGR)* greenhouse; ~ **chaude** hothouse; ~ **froide** unheated greenhouse.

serré, e [sārā] *a (tissu)* closely woven; *(réseau)* dense; *(écriture)* close; *(habits)* tight; *(fig: lutte, match)* tight, close-fought; *(passagers etc)* (tightly) packed; *(café)* strong ♦ *ad:* **jouer** ~ to play it close, play a close game; **écrire** ~ to write a cramped hand; **avoir la gorge** ~**e** to have a lump in one's throat.

serre-livres [sɛrlēvr(ə)] *nm inv* bookends *pl*.
serrement [sɛrmâṅ] *nm*: ~ **de main** handshake; ~ **de cœur** pang of anguish.
serrer [sārā] *vt* (*tenir*) to grip *ou* hold tight; (*comprimer, coincer*) to squeeze; (*poings, mâchoires*) to clench; (*suj: vêtement*) to be too tight for; to fit tightly; (*rapprocher*) to close up, move closer together; (*ceinture, nœud, frein, vis*) to tighten ♦ *vi*: ~ **à droite** to keep to the right; to move into the right-hand lane; **se** ~ (*se rapprocher*) to squeeze up; **se** ~ **contre qn** to huddle up to sb; **se** ~ **les coudes** to stick together, back one another up; **se** ~ **la ceinture** to tighten one's belt; ~ **la main à qn** to shake sb's hand; ~ **qn dans ses bras** to hug sb, clasp sb in one's arms; ~ **la gorge à qn** (*suj: chagrin*) to bring a lump to sb's throat; ~ **les dents** to clench *ou* grit one's teeth; ~ **qn de près** to follow close behind sb; ~ **le trottoir** to hug the curb; ~ **sa droite** to keep well to the right; ~ **la vis à qn** to crack down harder on sb; ~ **les rangs** to close ranks.
serres [sɛr] *nfpl* (*griffes*) claws, talons.
serre-tête [sɛrtet] *nm inv* (*bandeau*) headband; (*bonnet*) skullcap.
serrure [sārür] *nf* lock.
serrurerie [sārürrē] *nf* (*métier*) locksmith's trade; (*ferronnerie*) ironwork; ~ **d'art** ornamental ironwork.
serrurier [sārüryā] *nm* locksmith.
sers, sert [sɛr] *vb voir* **servir**.
sertir [sɛrtēr] *vt* (*pierre*) to set; (*pièces métalliques*) to crimp.
sérum [sārom] *nm* serum; ~ **antivenimeux** snakebite serum; ~ **sanguin** (blood) serum; ~ **de vérité** truth serum.
servage [sɛrvázh] *nm* serfdom.
servant [sɛrvâṅ] *nm* server.
servante [sɛrvâṅt] *nf* (maid)servant.
serve [sɛrv] *nf voir* **serf** ♦ *vb voir* **servir**.
serveur, euse [sɛrvœr, -œz] *nm/f* waiter/waitress ♦ *a*: **centre** ~ (*INFORM*) service center.
servi, e [sɛrvē] *a*: **être bien** ~ to get a large helping (*ou* helpings); **vous êtes** ~? are you being helped? (*US*) *ou* served? (*Brit*).
serviable [sɛrvyábl(ə)] *a* obliging, willing to help.
service [sɛrvēs] *nm* (*gén*) service; (*série de pas*): **premier** ~ first sitting; (*pourboire*) service (charge); (*assortiment de vaisselle*) set, service; (*linge de table*) set; (*bureau: de la vente etc*) department, section; (*travail*): **pendant le** ~ on duty; ~**s** *nmpl* (*travail, ÉCON*) services; ~ **compris/non compris** service included/not included; **faire le** ~ to serve; **être en** ~ **chez qn** to be in sb's service; **être au** ~ **de** (*patron, patrie*) to be in the service of; **être au** ~ **de qn** (*collaborateur, voiture*) to be at sb's service; **porte de** ~ service (*US*) *ou* tradesman's (*Brit*) entrance; **rendre** ~ **à** to help; **il aime rendre** ~ he likes to help; **rendre un** ~ **à qn** to do sb a favor; **heures de** ~ hours of duty; **être de** ~ to be on duty; **reprendre du** ~ to get back into action; **avoir 25 ans de** ~ to have completed 25 years' service; **être/mettre en** ~ to be in/put into service *ou*

operation; **hors** ~ not in use; out of order; ~ **à thé/café** tea/coffee set *ou* service; ~ **après vente (SAV)** after-sales service; **en** ~ **commandé** on an official assignment; ~ **funèbre** funeral service; ~ **militaire** military service; ~ **d'ordre** police (*ou* stewards) in charge of maintaining order; ~**s publics** public services, (public) utilities; ~**s secrets** secret service *sg*; ~**s sociaux** social services.
serviette [sɛrvyet] *nf* (*de table*) (table) napkin, serviette; (*de toilette*) towel; (*porte-documents*) briefcase; ~ **éponge** terry towel; ~ **hygiénique** sanitary napkin (*US*) *ou* towel (*Brit*).
servile [sɛrvēl] *a* servile.
servir [sɛrvēr] *vt* (*gén*) to serve; (*dîneur: au restaurant*) to wait on; (*client: au magasin*) to serve, attend to; (*fig: aider*): ~ **qn** to aid sb; to serve sb's interests; to stand sb in good stead; (*COMM: rente*) to pay ♦ *vi* (*TENNIS*) to serve; (*CARTES*) to deal; (*être militaire*) to serve; ~ **qch à qn** to serve sb with sth; **qu'est-ce que je vous sers?** what can I get you?; **se** ~ (*prendre d'un plat*) to help o.s.; (*s'approvisionner*): **se** ~ **chez** to shop at; **se** ~ **de** (*plat*) to help o.s. to; (*voiture, outil, relations*) to use; ~ **à qn** (*diplôme, livre*) to be of use to sb; **ça m'a servi pour faire** it was useful to me when I did; I used it to do; ~ **à qch/à faire** (*outil etc*) to be used for sth/for doing; **ça peut** ~ it may come in handy; **ça peut encore** ~ it can still be used (*ou* of use); **à quoi cela sert-il (de faire)?** what's the use (of doing?); **cela ne sert à rien** it's no use; ~ (**à qn**) **de** to serve as (for sb); ~ **à dîner (à qn)** to serve dinner (to sb).
serviteur [sɛrvētœr] *nm* servant.
servitude [sɛrvētüd] *nf* servitude; (*fig*) constraint; (*JUR*) easement.
servofrein [sɛrvofraṅ] *nm* power brake.
servomécanisme [sɛrvomākánēsm(ə)] *nm* servo mechanism.
ses [sā] *dét voir* **son**.
sésame [sāzám] *nm* (*BOT*) sesame; (*graine*) sesame seed.
session [sāsyóṅ] *nf* session.
set [sɛt] *nm* set; (*napperon*) placemat; ~ **de table** set of placemats.
seuil [sœy] *nm* doorstep; (*fig*) threshold; **sur le** ~ **de sa maison** in the doorway of his house, on his doorstep; **au** ~ **de** (*fig*) on the threshold *ou* brink *ou* edge of; ~ **de rentabilité** (*COMM*) breakeven point.
seul, e [sœl] *a* (*sans compagnie*) alone; (*avec nuance affective: isolé*) lonely; (*unique*): **un** ~ **livre** only one book, a single book; **le** ~ **livre** the only book; ~ **ce livre, ce livre** ~ this book alone, only this book; **d'un** ~ **coup** (*soudainement*) all at once; (*à la fois*) at one blow ♦ *ad* (*vivre*) alone, on one's own; **parler tout** ~ to talk to oneself; **faire qch (tout)** ~ to do sth (all) on one's own *ou* (all) by oneself ♦ *nm, nf*: **il en reste un(e)** ~(**e**) there's only one left; **pas un(e)** ~(**e**) not a single; **à lui (tout)** ~ single-handed, on his own; ~ **à** ~ in private.
seulement [sœlmâṅ] *ad* (*pas davantage*): ~ **5, 5** ~ only 5; (*exclusivement*): ~ **eux** only

them, them alone; (*pas avant*): ~ **hier/à 10h** only yesterday/at 10 o'clock; (*mais, toutefois*): **il consent, ~ il demande des garanties** he agrees, only he wants guarantees; **non ~ ... mais aussi** *ou* **encore** not only ... but also.

sève [sɛv] *nf* sap.

sévère [sãvɛr] *a* severe.

sévèrement [sãvɛrmãn] *ad* severely.

sévérité [sãvãrētã] *nf* severity.

sévices [sãvēs] *nmpl* (physical) cruelty *sg*, ill treatment *sg*.

Séville [sãvēl] *n* Seville.

sévir [sãvɛr] *vi* (*punir*) to use harsh measures, crack down; (*suj: fléau*) to rage, be rampant; **~ contre** (*abus*) to deal ruthlessly with, crack down on.

sevrage [səvraz̧] *nm* weaning; deprivation; (*d'un toxicomane*) withdrawal.

sevrer [səvrā] *vt* to wean; (*fig*): **~ qn de** to deprive sb of.

sexagénaire [sɛgzãz̧hänɛr] *a, nm/f* sexagenarian.

SExc *sigle f* (= *Son Excellence*) HE.

sexe [sɛks(ə)] *nm* sex; (*organe mâle*) member.

sexisme [sɛksēsm(ə)] *nm* sexism.

sexiste [sɛksēst(ə)] *a, nm* sexist.

sexologue [sɛksolog] *nm/f* sexologist, sex specialist.

sextant [sɛkstãn] *nm* sextant.

sexualité [sɛksüālētã] *nf* sexuality.

sexué, e [sɛksüā] *a* sexual.

sexuel, le [sɛksüɛl] *a* sexual; **acte ~** sex act.

sexuellement [sɛksüɛlmãn] *ad* sexually.

seyant, e [sɛyãn, -ãnt] *vb voir* **seoir** ♦ *a* becoming.

Seychelles [sãshɛl] *nfpl*: **les ~** the Seychelles.

SFIO *sigle f* (= *Section française de l'internationale ouvrière*) *former name of French Socialist Party*.

SG *sigle m* = **secrétaire général**.

SGEN *sigle m* (= *Syndicat général de l'éducation nationale*) *labor union*.

shaker [shɛkœr] *nm* (cocktail) shaker.

shampooiner [shãnpwēnā] *vt* to shampoo.

shampooineur, euse [shãnpwēnœr, -œz] *nm/f* (*personne*) shampooer.

shampooing [shãnpwan] *nm* shampoo; **se faire un ~** to shampoo one's hair; **~ colorant** color rinse; **~ traitant** medicated shampoo.

Shetland [shetlãnd] *n*: **les îles ~** the Shetland Islands, Shetland.

shooter [shōōtā] *vi* (*FOOTBALL*) to shoot; **se ~** (*drogué*) to mainline.

short [short] *nm* (pair of) shorts *pl*.

SI *sigle m* = **syndicat d'initiative**.

si [sē] *nm* (*MUS*) B; (*en chantant la gamme*) ti, te ♦ *ad* (*oui*) yes; (*tellement*) so ♦ *cj* if; (*d'opposition*): **s'il est amiable, eux par contre** ... whereas he's nice, they on the other hand ...; **Paul n'est pas venu, ~?** Paul didn't come, did he?; **je vous assure que ~** I can assure you that it is (*ou* he did *etc*); **~ seulement** if only; (*tant et*) **~ bien que** so much so that; **~ rapide qu'il soit** however fast he may be, fast though he is; **je me demande ~** I wonder if *ou* whether.

siamois, e [syãmwà, -wàz̧] *a* Siamese; **frères/sœurs ~(es)** Siamese twins.

Sibérie [sēbārē] *nf*: **la ~** Siberia.

sibérien, ne [sēbāryan̄, -en] *a* Siberian ♦ *nm/f*: **S~, ne** Siberian.

sibyllin, e [sēbēlan̄, -ēn] *a* sibylline.

SICAV [sēkáv] *sigle f* (= *société d'investissement à capital variable*) open-ended investment trust; *share in such a trust*.

Sicile [sēsēl] *nf*: **la ~** Sicily.

sicilien, ne [sēsēlyan̄, -en] *a* Sicilian.

SIDA, sida [sēdá] *nm* (= *syndrome immuno-déficitaire acquis*) AIDS *sg*.

sidéral, e, aux [sēdārál, -ō] *a* sidereal.

sidéré, e [sēdārā] *a* staggered.

sidérurgie [sēdārürzhē] *nf* steel industry.

sidérurgique [sēdārürzhēk] *a* steel *cpd*.

sidérurgiste [sēdārürzhēst(ə)] *nm/f* steel worker.

siècle [syɛkl(ə)] *nm* century; (*époque*): **le ~ des lumières/de l'atome** the age of enlightenment/atomic age; (*REL*): **le ~** the world.

sied [syã] *vb voir* **seoir**.

siège [syɛz̧h] *nm* seat; (*d'entreprise*) head office; (*d'organisation*) headquarters *pl*; (*MIL*) siege; **lever le ~** to raise the siege; **mettre le ~ devant** to besiege; **présentation par le ~** (*MÉD*) breech position; `~ avant/arrière` (*AUTO*) front/back seat; **~ baquet** bucket seat; **~ social** head office.

siéger [syãz̧hā] *vi* (*assemblée, tribunal*) to sit; (*résider, se trouver*) to lie, be located.

sien, ne [syan̄, syen] *pronom*: **le(la) ~(ne), les ~s(~nes)** *m* his; *f* hers; *non humain* its; **y mettre du ~** to pull one's weight; **faire des ~nes** (*fam*) to be up to one's (usual) tricks; **les ~s** (*sa famille*) one's family.

siérait [syãrɛ] *etc vb voir* **seoir**.

Sierra Leone [syɛrãlãon] *nf*: **la ~** Sierra Leone.

sieste [syɛst(ə)] *nf* (afternoon) snooze *ou* nap, siesta; **faire la ~** to have a snooze *ou* nap.

sieur [syœr] *nm*: **le ~ Thomas** Mr. Thomas; (*en plaisantant*) Master Thomas.

sifflant, e [sēflan̄, -ãnt] *a* (*bruit*) whistling; (*toux*) wheezing; (**consonne**) **~e** sibilant.

sifflement [sēflomãn] *nm* whistle, whistling *q*; wheezing *q*; hissing *q*.

siffler [sēflā] *vi* (*gén*) to whistle; (*avec un sifflet*) to blow (on) one's whistle; (*en respirant*) to wheeze; (*serpent, vapeur*) to hiss ♦ *vt* (*chanson*) to whistle; (*chien etc*) to whistle for; (*fille*) to whistle at; (*pièce, orateur*) to hiss, boo; (*faute*) to blow one's whistle at; (*fin du match, départ*) to blow one's whistle for; (*fam: verre, bouteille*) to guzzle.

sifflet [sēflɛ] *nm* whistle; **~s** *nmpl* (*de mécontentement*) whistles, boos; **coup de ~** whistle.

siffloter [sēflotā] *vi, vt* to whistle.

sigle [sēgl(ə)] *nm* acronym, (set of) initials *pl*.

signal, aux [sēnyál, -ō] *nm* (*signe convenu, appareil*) signal; (*indice, écriteau*) sign; **donner le ~ de** to give the signal for; **~ d'alarme** alarm signal; **~ d'alerte/de détresse** warning/distress signal; **~ horaire** time signal; **~ optique/sonore** warning light/sound; visual/acoustic signal; **signaux (lumineux)** (*AUTO*) traffic signals; **signaux routiers** road signs; (*lumineux*) traffic lights.

signalement [sĕnyálmáń] *nm* description, particulars *pl*.

signaler [sĕnyálá] *vt* to indicate; to announce; to report; (*être l'indice de*) to indicate; (*faire remarquer*): ~ **qch à qn/à qn que** to point out sth to sb/to sb that; (*appeler l'attention sur*): ~ **qn à la police** to bring sb to the attention of the police; **se ~ par** to distinguish o.s. by; **se ~ à l'attention de qn** to attract sb's attention.

signalétique [sĕnyálátĕk] *a*: **fiche ~** description sheet.

signalisation [sĕnyálĕzâsyôń] *nf* signalling, signposting; **signals** *pl*; **roadsigns** *pl*; **panneau de ~** roadsign.

signaliser [sĕnyálĕzá] *vt* to put up roadsigns on; to put signals on.

signataire [sĕnyátcr] *nm/f* signatory.

signature [sĕnyátür] *nf* signature; (*action*) signing.

signe [sĕny] *nm* sign; (*TYPO*) mark; **ne pas donner ~ de vie** to give no sign of life; **c'est bon ~** it's a good sign; **c'est ~ que** it's a sign that; **faire un ~ de la main/tête** to give a sign with one's hand/shake one's head; **faire ~ à qn** (*fig*) to get in touch with sb; **faire ~ à qn d'entrer** to motion (to) sb to come in; **en ~ de** as a sign *ou* mark of; **le ~ de la croix** the sign of the Cross; **~ de ponctuation** punctuation mark; **~ du zodiaque** sign of the zodiac; **~s particuliers** distinguishing marks.

signer [sĕnyá] *vt* to sign; **se ~** *vi* to cross o.s.

signet [sĕnyc] *nm* bookmark.

significatif, ive [sĕnyčfĕkátĕf, -ĕv] *a* significant.

signification [sĕnyčfĕkâsyôń] *nf* meaning.

signifier [sĕnyčfyá] *vt* (*vouloir dire*) to mean, signify; (*faire connaître*): ~ **qch (à qn)** to make sth known (to sb); (*JUR*): ~ **qch à qn** to serve notice of sth on sb.

silence [sĕláńs] *nm* silence; (*MUS*) rest; **garder le ~ (sur qch)** to keep silent (about sth), say nothing (about sth); **passer sous ~** to pass over (in silence); **réduire au ~** to silence.

silencieusement [sĕláńsyŏēzmáń] *ad* silently.

silencieux, euse [sĕláńsyŏē, -ēz] *a* quiet, silent ♦ *nm* (*d'arme à feu*) silencer; (*AUT*) muffler (*US*), silencer (*Brit*).

silex [sĕlcks] *nm* flint.

silhouette [sĕlwct] *nf* outline, silhouette; (*lignes, contour*) outline; (*figure*) figure.

silice [sĕlēs] *nf* silica.

siliceux, euse [sĕlēsŏē, -ēz] *a* (*terrain*) chalky.

silicium [sĕlēsyom] *nm* silicon; **plaquette de ~** silicon chip.

silicone [sĕlĕkŏn] *nf* silicone.

silicose [sĕlĕkŏz] *nf* silicosis, dust disease.

sillage [sĕyázh] *nm* wake; (*fig*) trail; **dans le ~ de** (*fig*) in the wake of.

sillon [sĕyôń] *nm* (*d'un champ*) furrow; (*de disque*) groove.

sillonner [sĕyoná] *vt* (*creuser*) to furrow; (*traverser*) to cross, criss-cross.

silo [sĕlŏ] *nm* silo.

simagrées [sĕmágrá] *nfpl* fuss *sg*; airs and graces.

simiesque [sĕmycsk(ə)] *a* monkey-like, ape-like.

similaire [sĕmēler] *a* similar.

similarité [sĕmēlárĕtá] *nf* similarity.

simili [sĕmēlē] *nm* imitation; (*TYPO*) halftone ♦ *nf* halftone engraving.

simili... [sĕmēlē] *préfixe* imitation *cpd*, artificial.

similicuir [sĕmēlĕküčr] *nm* imitation leather.

similigravure [sĕmēlĕgrávür] *nf* halftone engraving.

similitude [sĕmēlĕtüd] *nf* similarity.

simple [sáńpl(ə)] *a* (*gén*) simple; (*non multiple*) single; **~s** *nmpl* (*MÉD*) medicinal plants; **~ messieurs** *nm* (*TENNIS*) men's singles *sg*; **un ~ particulier** an ordinary citizen; **une ~ formalité** a mere formality; **cela varie du ~ au double** it can double, it can double the price *etc*; **dans le plus ~ appareil** in one's birthday suit; **~ course** *a* single; **~ d'esprit** *nm/f* simpleton; **~ soldat** private.

simplement [sáńpləmáń] *ad* simply.

simplet, te [sáńplc, -ct] *a* (*personne*) simple-minded.

simplicité [sáńplĕsĕtá] *nf* simplicity; **en toute ~** quite simply.

simplification [sáńplĕfĕkâsyôń] *nf* simplification.

simplifier [sáńplĕfyá] *vt* to simplify.

simpliste [sáńplĕst(ə)] *a* simplistic.

simulacre [sĕmülákr(ə)] *nm* enactment; (*péj*): **un ~ de** a pretense (*US*) *ou* pretence (*Brit*) of, a sham.

simulateur, trice [sĕmülátœr, -trēs] *nm/f* shammer, pretender; (*qui se prétend malade*) malingerer ♦ *nm*: **~ de vol** flight simulator.

simulation [sĕmülâsyôń] *nf* shamming, simulation; malingering.

simuler [sĕmülá] *vt* to sham, simulate.

simultané, e [sĕmültáná] *a* simultaneous.

simultanéité [sĕmültánáĕtá] *nf* simultaneity.

simultanément [sĕmültánámáń] *ad* simultaneously.

Sinaï [sĕnáč] *nm*: **le ~** Sinai.

sinapisme [sĕnápĕsm(ə)] *nm* (*MÉD*) mustard plaster (*US*) *ou* poultice (*Brit*).

sincère [sáńscr] *a* sincere; genuine; heartfelt; **mes ~s condoléances** my deepest sympathy.

sincèrement [sáńscrmáń] *ad* sincerely; genuinely.

sincérité [sáńsárĕtá] *nf* sincerity; **en toute ~** in all sincerity.

sinécure [sĕnákür] *nf* sinecure.

sine die [sĕnádyá] *ad* sine die, indefinitely.

sine qua non [sĕnákwánon] *a*: **condition ~** indispensable condition.

Singapour [sáńgápŏōr] *nm*: **le ~** Singapore.

singe [sańzh] *nm* monkey; (*de grande taille*) ape.

singer [sańzhá] *vt* to ape, mimic.

singeries [sańzhrĕ] *nfpl* antics; (*simagrées*) airs and graces.

singulariser [sáńgülárĕzá] *vt* to mark out; **se ~** to call attention to o.s.

singularité [sáńgülárĕtá] *nf* peculiarity.

singulier, ière [scgülyá, -ycr] *a* remarkable, singular; (*LING*) singular ♦ *nm* singular.

singulièrement [sáńgülycrmáń] *ad* singularly, remarkably.

sinistre [sēnēstr(ə)] *a* sinister; *(intensif)*: **un ~ imbécile** an incredible idiot ♦ *nm (incendie)* blaze; *(catastrophe)* disaster; *(ASSURANCES)* damage *(giving rise to a claim)*.

sinistré, e [sēnēstrā] *a* disaster-stricken ♦ *nm/f* disaster victim.

sinistrose [sēnēstrōz] *nf* pessimism.

sino... [sēnō] *préfixe*: **~-indien** Sino-Indian, Chinese-Indian.

sinon [sēnōñ] *cj (autrement, sans quoi)* otherwise, or else; *(sauf)* except, other than; *(si ce n'est)* if not.

sinueux, euse [sēnüœ̄, -œ̄z] *a* winding; *(fig)* tortuous.

sinuosités [sēnüōzētā] *nfpl* winding *sg*, curves.

sinus [sēnüs] *nm (ANAT)* sinus; *(GÉOM)* sine.

sinusite [sēnüzēt] *nf* sinusitis, sinus infection.

sionisme [syonēsm(ə)] *nm* Zionism.

sioniste [syonēst(ə)] *a, nm/f* Zionist.

siphon [sēfōñ] *nm (tube, d'eau gazeuse)* siphon; *(d'évier etc)* trap, U-bend *(Brit)*.

siphonner [sēfonā] *vt* to siphon.

sire [sēr] *nm (titre)*: **S~** Sire; **un triste ~** an unsavory individual.

sirène [sēren] *nf* siren; **~ d'alarme** fire alarm; *(pendant la guerre)* air-raid siren.

sirop [sērō] *nm (à diluer: de fruit etc)* syrup; *(boisson)* fruit drink; *(pharmaceutique)* syrup, mixture; **~ de menthe** mint syrup *ou* cordial; **~ contre la toux** cough syrup *ou* mixture.

siroter [sērotā] *vt* to sip.

sirupeux, euse [sērüpœ̄, -œ̄z] *a* syrupy.

sis, e [sē, sēz] *a*: **~ rue de la Paix** located in the rue de la Paix.

sisal [sēzál] *nm (BOT)* sisal.

sismique [sēsmēk] *a* seismic.

sismographe [sēsmogrắf] *nm* seismograph.

sismologie [sēsmolozhē] *nf* seismology.

site [sēt] *nm (paysage, environnement)* setting; *(d'une ville etc: emplacement)* site; **~ (pittoresque)** beauty spot; **~s touristiques** places of interest; **~s naturels/historiques** natural/historic sites.

sitôt [sētō] *ad*: **~ parti** as soon as he *etc* had left; **~ après** straight after; **pas de ~** not for a long time; **~ (après) que** as soon as.

situation [sētüāsyōñ] *nf (gén)* situation; *(d'un édifice, d'une ville)* situation, position; *(emplacement)* location; **être en ~ de faire qch** to be in a position to do sth; **~ de famille** marital status.

situé, e [sētüā] *a*: **bien ~** well situated, in a good location; **~ à/près de** situated at/near.

situer [sētüā] *vt* to site, situate; *(en pensée)* to set, place; **se ~** *vi*: **se ~ à/près de** to be situated at/near.

SIVOM [sēvom] *sigle m (= syndicat intercommunal à vocation multiple)* association of "communes".

six [sēs] *num* six.

sixième [sēzyem] *num* sixth.

skate (board) [skắt(bord)] *nm (SPORT)* skateboarding; *(planche)* skateboard.

sketch [sketsh] *nm (variety)* sketch.

ski [skē] *nm (objet)* ski; *(sport)* skiing; **faire du ~** to ski; **~ alpin** Alpine skiing; **~ courts** short skis; **~ évolutif** short ski method; **~ de fond** cross-country skiing; **~ nautique**

water-skiing; **~ de piste** downhill skiing; **~ de randonnée** cross-country skiing.

ski-bob [skēbob] *nm* skibob.

skier [skyā] *vi* to ski.

skieur, euse [skyœr, -œ̄z] *nm/f* skier.

skif(f) [skēf] *nm* skiff.

slalom [slálom] *nm* slalom; **faire du ~ entre** to slalom between; **~ géant/spécial** giant/special slalom.

slave [slắv] *a* Slav(onic), Slavic ♦ *nm (LING)* Slavonic ♦ *nm/f*: **S~** Slav.

slip [slēp] *nm (sous-vêtement)* underpants *pl*, briefs *pl*; *(de bain: d'homme)* (bathing *ou* swimming) trunks *pl*; (: *du bikini)* (bikini) briefs *pl ou* bottoms *pl*.

slogan [slogắñ] *nm* slogan.

slovaque [slovák] *a* Slovak ♦ *nm (LING)* Slovak ♦ *nm/f*: **S~** Slovak.

Slovaquie [slovákē] *nf*: **la ~** Slovakia.

slovène [sloven] *a* Slovene.

Slovénie [slovănē] *nf*: **la ~** Slovenia.

SM *sigle f (= Sa Majesté)* HM.

SMAG [smắg] *sigle m = salaire minimum agricole garanti*.

smasher [smắshā] *vi* to smash the ball ♦ *vt (balle)* to smash.

SME *sigle m (= Système monétaire européen)* EMS.

SMIC [smēk] *sigle m = salaire minimum interprofessionnel de croissance*.

smicard, e [smēkắr, -ắrd(ə)] *nm/f* minimum wage earner.

smocks [smok] *nmpl (COUTURE)* smocking *q*.

smoking [smokēng] *nm* tuxedo.

SMUR [smür] *sigle m (= service médical d'urgence et de réanimation)* specialist mobile emergency unit.

snack [snák] *nm* snack bar.

SNC *abr = service non compris*.

SNCB *sigle f (= Société nationale des chemins de fer belges)* Belgian railroad.

SNCF *sigle f (= Société nationale des chemins de fer français)* French railroad.

SNES [snes] *sigle m (= Syndicat national de l'enseignement secondaire)* secondary teachers' union.

SNE-sup [csenəsüp] *sigle m (= Syndicat national de l'enseignement supérieur)* university teachers' union.

SNI *sigle m (= Syndicat national des instituteurs)* elementary teachers' union.

SNJ *sigle m (= Syndicat national des journalistes)* journalists' union.

snob [snob] *a* snobbish ♦ *nm/f* snob.

snober [snobā] *vt*: **~ qn** to give sb the cold shoulder, treat sb with disdain.

snobinard, e [snobēnắr, -ắrd(ə)] *nm/f* snooty *ou* stuck-up person.

snobisme *nm* snobbery.

SNSM *sigle f (= Société nationale de sauvetage en mer)* national sea-rescue association.

s.o. *abr (= sans objet)* no longer applicable.

sobre [sobr(ə)] *a* temperate, abstemious; *(élégance, style)* restrained, sober; **~ de** *(gestes, compliments)* sparing of.

sobrement [sobrəmáñ] *ad* in moderation, abstemiously; soberly.

sobriété [sobrēyātā] *nf* temperance, abstemiousness; sobriety.

sobriquet |sobrĕke| *nm* nickname.

soc |sok| *nm* plowshare (*US*), ploughshare (*Brit*).

sociable |sosyàbl(ə)| *a* sociable.

social, e, aux |sosyàl, -ō| *a* social.

socialement |sosyàlmàň| *ad* socially.

socialisant, e |sosyàlēzàň, -àňt| *a* with socialist tendencies.

socialisation |sosyàlēzàsyôň| *nf* socialization.

socialiser |sosyàlēzà| *vt* to socialize.

socialisme |sosyàlēsm(ə)| *nm* socialism.

socialiste |sosyàlēst(ə)| *a, nm/f* socialist.

sociétaire |sosyàter| *nm/f* member.

société |sosyàtā| *nf* society; (*d'abeilles, de fourmis*) colony; (*sportive*) club; (*COMM*) company; **la bonne ~** polite society; **se plaire dans la ~ de** to enjoy the society of; **l'archipel de la S~** the Society Islands; **la ~ d'abondance/de consommation** the affluent/ consumer society; **~ par actions** joint stock company; **~ anonyme (SA)** ≈ incorporated company (Inc.) (*US*), ≈ limited company (Ltd) (*Brit*); **≈ d'investissement à capital variable (SICAV)** ≈ mutual fund (*US*), ≈ investment trust (*Brit*); **~ à responsabilité limitée (SARL)** *type of limited liability company (with non-negotiable shares)*; **~ savante** learned society; **~ de services** service company.

socio-économique |sosyoàkonomĕk| *a* socioeconomic.

sociolinguistique |sosyolàňgüĕstĕk| *a* sociolinguistic.

sociologie |sosyolozhē| *nf* sociology.

sociologique |sosyolozhĕk| *a* sociological.

sociologue |sosyolog| *nm/f* sociologist.

socio-professionnel, le |sosyoprofesyonel| *a* socioprofessional.

socle |sokl(ə)| *nm* (*de colonne, statue*) plinth, pedestal; (*de lampe*) base.

socquette |soket| *nf* ankle sock.

soda |sodà| *nm* (*boisson*) fizzy drink, soda (*US*).

sodium |sodyom| *nm* sodium.

sodomie |sodomē| *nf* sodomy.

sœur |sœr| *nf* sister; (*religieuse*) nun, sister; **~ Élisabeth** (*REL*) Sister Elizabeth; **~ de lait** foster sister.

sofa |sofà| *nm* sofa.

Sofia |sofyà| *n* Sofia.

SOFRES |sofres| *sigle f* (= *Société française d'enquête par sondage*) *company which conducts opinion polls.*

soi |swà| *pronom* oneself; **cela va de ~** that *ou* it goes without saying, it stands to reason.

soi-disant |swàdēzàň| *a inv* so-called ♦ *ad* supposedly.

soie |swà| *nf* silk; (*de porc, sanglier: poil*) bristle.

soient |swà| *vb voir* **être**.

soierie |swàrē| *nf* (*industrie*) silk trade; (*tissu*) silk.

soif |swàf| *nf* thirst; (*fig*): **~ de** thirst *ou* craving for; **avoir ~** to be thirsty; **donner ~ à qn** to make sb thirsty.

soigné, e |swànyā| *a* (*tenue*) well-groomed, neat; (*travail*) careful, meticulous; (*fam*) whopping; stiff.

soigner |swànyā| *vt* (*malade, maladie: suj: docteur*) to treat; (: *suj: infirmière, mère*) to nurse, look after; (*blessé*) to tend; (*travail, détails*) to take care over; (*jardin, chevelure, invités*) to look after.

soigneur |swànyœr| *nm* (*CYCLISME, FOOT-BALL*) trainer; (*BOXE*) second.

soigneusement |swànyœzmàň| *ad* carefully.

soigneux, euse |swànyœ, -œz| *a* (*propre*) tidy, neat; (*méticuleux*) painstaking, careful; **~ de** careful with.

soi-même |swàmem| *pronom* oneself.

soin |swàň| *nm* (*application*) care; (*propreté, ordre*) tidiness, neatness; (*responsabilité*): **le ~ de qch** the care of sth; **~s** *nmpl* (*à un malade, blessé*) treatment *sg*, medical attention *sg*; (*attentions, prévenance*) care and attention *sg*; (*hygiène*) care *sg*; **~s de la chevelure/de beauté** hair/beauty care; **~s du corps/ménage** care of one's body/the home; **avoir** *ou* **prendre ~ de** to take care of, look after; **avoir** *ou* **prendre ~ de faire** to take care to do; **sans ~** *a* careless; untidy; **les premiers ~s** first aid *sg*; **aux bons ~s de** c/o, care of; **être aux petits ~s pour qn** to wait on sb hand and foot, see to sb's every need; **confier qn aux ~s de qn** to hand sb over to sb's care.

soir |swàr| *nm, ad* evening; **le ~** in the evening(s); **ce ~** this evening, tonight; **à ce ~!** see you this evening (*ou* tonight)!; **la veille au ~** the previous evening; **sept/dix heures du ~** seven in the evening/ten at night; **le repas/journal du ~** the evening meal/ newspaper: **dimanche ~** Sunday evening; **hier ~** yesterday evening; **demain ~** tomorrow evening, tomorrow night.

soirée |swàrā| *nf* evening; (*réception*) party; **donner en ~** (*film, pièce*) to give an evening performance of.

soit |swà| *vb voir* **être**; **~ un triangle ABC** let ABC be a triangle ♦ *cj* (*à savoir*) namely, to wit; (*ou*): **~ ... ~ ...** either ... or ♦ *ad* so be it, very well; **~ que ... ~ que** *ou* **ou que** whether ... or whether.

soixantaine |swàsàňten| *nf*: **une ~ (de)** sixty or so, about sixty; **avoir la ~** to be around sixty.

soixante |swàsàňt| *num* sixty.

soixante-dix |swàsàňtdēs| *num* seventy.

soixante-dixième |swàsàňtdēzyem| *num* seventieth.

soixante-huitard, e |swàzàňtüĕtàr, -àrd(ə)| *a* relating to the demonstrations of May 1968 ♦ *nm/f* participant in the demonstrations of May 1968.

soixantième |swàsàňtyem| *num* sixtieth.

soja |sozhà| *nm*, soy, soya (*Brit*); (*graines*) soybeans *pl* (*US*), soya beans *pl* (*Brit*); **germes de ~** beansprouts.

sol |sol| *nm* ground; (*de logement*) floor; (*revêtement*) flooring *q*; (*territoire, AGR, GÉO*) soil; (*MUS*) G; (: *en chantant la gamme*) so(h).

solaire |soler| *a* solar, sun *cpd*.

solarium |solàryom| *nm* solarium.

soldat |soldà| *nm* soldier; **S~ inconnu** Unknown Warrior *ou* Soldier; **~ de plomb** tin *ou* toy soldier.

solde [sold(ə)] *nf* pay ♦ *nm* (*COMM*) balance;
~**s** *nmpl ou nfpl* (*COMM*) sales; (*articles*)
sale goods; **à la ~ de qn** (*péj*) in sb's pay; ~
créditeur/débiteur credit/debit balance; ~ **à**
payer balance outstanding; **en** ~ at sale
price; **aux** ~**s** at the sales.

solder [soldā] *vt* (*compte*) to settle;
(*marchandise*) to sell at sale price, sell off;
se ~ **par** (*fig*) to end in; **article soldé (à) 10**
F item reduced to 10 F.

soldeur, euse [soldœr, -ēz] *nm/f* (*COMM*) dis-
counter.

sole [sol] *nf* sole *inv* (*fish*).

soleil [soley] *nm* sun; (*lumière*) sun(light);
(*temps ensoleillé*) sun(shine); (*feu d'artifice*)
pinwheel (*US*), Catherine wheel (*Brit*);
(*ACROBATIE*) grand circle; (*BOT*) sunflower;
il y a *ou* **il fait du** ~ it's sunny; **au** ~ in the
sun; **en plein** ~ in full sun; **le** ~ **levant/**
couchant the rising/setting sun; **le** ~ **de**
minuit the midnight sun.

solennel, le [solánel] *a* solemn; ceremonial.

solennellement [solánelmáň] *ad* solemnly.

solenniser [solánēzā] *vt* to solemnize.

solennité [solánētā] *nf* (*d'une fête*) solemnity;
~**s** *nfpl* (*formalités*) formalities.

solénoïde [solānoēd] *nm* (*ÉLEC*) solenoid.

solfège [solfezh] *nm* rudiments *pl* of music;
(*exercices*) ear training *q*.

solfier [solfyā] *vt*: ~ **un morceau** to sing a
piece using the sol-fa.

soli [solē] *pl de* **solo**.

solidaire [solēder] *a* (*personnes*) who stand
together, who show solidarity; (*pièces*
mécaniques) interdependent; (*JUR: engage-*
ment) binding on all parties; (*: débiteurs*)
jointly liable; **être** ~ **de** (*collègues*) to stand
by; (*mécanisme*) to be bound up with, be
dependent on.

solidairement [solēdermáň] *ad* jointly.

solidariser [solēdárēzā]: **se** ~ **avec** *vt* to show
solidarity with.

solidarité [solēdárētā] *nf* (*entre personnes*)
solidarity; (*de mécanisme, phénomènes*)
interdependence; **par** ~ **(avec)** (*cesser le*
travail etc) in sympathy (with).

solide [solēd] *a* solid; (*mur, maison, meuble*)
solid, sturdy; (*connaissances, argument*)
sound; (*personne*) robust, sturdy; (*estomac*)
strong ♦ *nm* solid; **avoir les reins** ~**s** (*fig*) to
be in a good financial position; to have sound
financial backing.

solidement [solēdmáň] *ad* solidly; (*ferme-*
ment) firmly.

solidifier [solēdēfyā] *vt*, **se** ~ *vi* to solidify.

solidité [solēdētā] *nf* solidity; sturdiness.

soliloque [solēlok] *nm* soliloquy.

soliste [solēst(ə)] *nm/f* soloist.

solitaire [solēter] *a* (*sans compagnie*) solitary,
lonely; (*isolé*) solitary, isolated, lone; (*lieu*)
lonely ♦ *nm/f* recluse; loner ♦ *nm* (*diamant,*
jeu) solitaire.

solitude [solētüd] *nf* loneliness; '(*paix*)
solitude.

solive [solēv] *nf* joist.

sollicitations [solēsētâsyóň] *nfpl* (*requêtes*) entreaties, appeals; (*attractions*) enticements;
(*TECH*) stress *sg*.

solliciter [solēsētā] *vt* (*personne*) to appeal to;

(*emploi, faveur*) to seek; (*moteur*) to
prompt; (*suj: occupations, attractions etc*):
~ **qn** to appeal to sb's curiosity *etc*; to entice
sb; to make demands on sb's time; ~ **qn de**
faire to appeal to sb *ou* request sb to do.

sollicitude [solēsētüd] *nf* concern.

solo [solō] *nm, pl* **soli** [solē] (*MUS*) solo (*pl* -s
ou soli).

solstice [solstēs] *nm* solstice; ~ **d'hiver/d'été**
winter/summer solstice.

solubilisé, e [solübēlēzā] *a* soluble.

soluble [solübl(ə)] *a* (*sucre, cachet*) soluble;
(*problème etc*) soluble, solvable.

soluté [solütā] *nm* solution.

solution [solüsyóň] *nf* solution; ~ **de**
continuité gap, break; ~ **de facilité** easy
way out.

solutionner [solüsyonā] *vt* to solve, find a solution for.

solvabilité [solvábēlētā] *nf* solvency.

solvable [solvábl(ə)] *a* solvent.

solvant [solváň] *nm* solvent.

Somalie [somálē] *nf*: **la** ~ Somalia.

somalien, ne [somályaň, -en] *a* Somalian.

sombre [sóňbr(ə)] *a* dark; (*fig*) somber (*US*),
sombre (*Brit*), gloomy; (*sinistre*) awful,
dreadful.

sombrer [sóňbrā] *vi* (*bateau*) to sink, go
down; ~ **corps et biens** to go down with all
hands; ~ **dans** (*misère, désespoir*) to sink into.

sommaire [somer] *a* (*simple*) basic;
(*expéditif*) summary ♦ *nm* summary; **faire le**
~ **de** to make a summary of, summarize;
exécution ~ summary execution.

sommairement [somermáň] *ad* basically;
summarily.

sommation [somásyóň] *nf* (*JUR*) summons *sg*;
(*avant de faire feu*) warning.

somme [som] *nf* (*MATH*) sum; (*fig*) amount;
(*argent*) sum, amount ♦ *nm*: **faire un** ~ to
have a (short) nap; **faire la** ~ **de** to add up;
en ~, ~ **toute** *ad* all in all.

sommeil [somey] *nm* sleep; **avoir** ~ to be
sleepy; **avoir le** ~ **léger** to be a light sleeper;
en ~ (*fig*) dormant.

sommeiller [somāyā] *vi* to doze; (*fig*) to lie
dormant.

sommelier [somətyā] *nm* wine waiter.

sommer [somā] *vt*: ~ **qn de faire** to
command *ou* order sb to do; (*JUR*) to
summon sb to do.

sommes [som] *vb voir* **être**; *voir aussi*
somme.

sommet [some] *nm* top; (*d'une montagne*)
summit, top; (*fig: de la perfection, gloire*)
height; (*GÉOM: d'angle*) vertex (*pl* vertices);
(*conférence*) summit (conference).

sommier [somyā] *nm* bedspring (*US*), bed
base (*Brit*); (*ADMIN: registre*) register; ~ **à**
ressorts box spring (*US*), (interior sprung)
divan base (*Brit*); ~ **à lattes** slatted bedspring *ou* bed base.

sommité [somētā] *nf* prominent person, leading light.

somnambule [somnáňbül] *nm/f* sleepwalker.

somnambulisme [somnáňbülēsm(ə)] *nm*
sleepwalking.

somnifère [somnēfer] *nm* sleeping drug;
(*comprimé*) sleeping pill *ou* tablet.

somnolence [somnolâńs] *nf* drowsiness.

somnolent, e [somnolâń, -âńt] *a* sleepy, drowsy.

somnoler [somnolā] *vi* to doze.

somptuaire [sôńptüer] *a*: **lois ~s** sumptuary laws; **dépenses ~s** extravagant expenditure *sg*.

somptueusement [sôńptüœ̄zmâń] *ad* sumptuously.

somptueux, euse [sôńptüœ̄, -œ̄z] *a* sumptuous; (*cadeau*) lavish.

son [sôń], **sa** [sà], *pl* **ses** [sā] *dét* (*antécédent humain mâle*) his; (: *femelle*) her; (: *valeur indéfinie*) one's, his/her; (: *non humain*) its; *voir note sous* **il.**

son [sôń] *nm* sound; (*de blé etc*) bran; **~ et lumière** *a inv* son et lumière.

sonar [sonár] *nm* (*NAVIG*) sonar.

sonate [sonát] *nf* sonata.

sondage [sôńdázh] *nm* (*de terrain*) boring, drilling; (*mer, atmosphère*) sounding; probe; (*enquête*) survey, sounding out of opinion; **~ (d'opinion)** (opinion) poll.

sonde [sôńd] *nf* (*NAVIG*) lead *ou* sounding line; (*MÉTÉOROLOGIE*) sonde; (*MÉD*) probe; catheter; (*d'alimentation*) feeding tube; (*TECH*) borer, driller; (*de forage, sondage*) drill; (*pour fouiller etc*) probe; **~ à avalanche** pole (*for probing snow and locating victims*); **~ spatiale** probe.

sonder [sôńdā] *vt* (*NAVIG*) to sound; (*atmosphère, plaie, bagages etc*) to probe; (*TECH*) to bore, drill; (*fig: personne*) to sound out; (: *opinion*) to probe; **~ le terrain** (*fig*) to see how the land lies.

songe [sôńzh] *nm* dream.

songer [sôńzhā] *vi* to dream; **~ à** (*rêver à*) to muse over, think over; (*penser à*) to think of; (*envisager*) to contemplate, think of, consider; **~ que** to consider that; to think that.

songerie [sôńzhrē] *nf* reverie.

songeur, euse [sôńzhœr, -œ̄z] *a* pensive; **ça me laisse ~** that makes me wonder.

sonnailles [sonáy] *nfpl* jingle of bells.

sonnant, e [sonâń,́ -âńt] *a*: **en espèces ~es et trébuchantes** in coin of the realm; **à 8 heures ~es** on the stroke of 8.

sonné, e [sonā] *a* (*fam*) cracked; (*passé*): **il est midi ~** it's past twelve; **il a quarante ans bien ~s** he's well into his forties.

sonner [sonā] *vi* (*retentir*) to ring; (*donner une impression*) to sound ♦ *vt* (*cloche*) to ring; (*glas, tocsin*) to sound; (*portier, infirmière*) to ring for; (*messe*) to ring the bell for; (*fam: suj: choc, coup*) to knock out; **~ du clairon** to sound the bugle; **~ bien/mal/creux** to sound good/bad/hollow; **~ faux** (*instrument*) to sound out of tune; (*rire*) to ring false; **~ les heures** to strike the hours; **minuit vient de ~** midnight has just struck; **~ chez qn** to ring sb's doorbell, ring at sb's door.

sonnerie [sonrē] *nf* (*son*) ringing; (*sonnette*) bell; (*mécanisme d'horloge*) striking mechanism; **~ d'alarme** alarm bell; **~ de clairon** bugle call.

sonnet [sone] *nm* sonnet.

sonnette [sonet] *nf* bell; **~ d'alarme** alarm bell; **~ de nuit** night-bell.

sono [sonō] *nf* (= *sonorisation*) PA (system).

sonore [sonor] *a* (*voix*) sonorous, ringing; (*salle, métal*) resonant; (*ondes, film, signal*) sound *cpd*; (*LING*) voiced; **effets ~s** sound effects.

sonorisation [sonorēzâsyôń] *nf* (*installations*) public address system.

sonoriser [sonorēzā] *vt* (*film, spectacle*) to add the sound track to; (*salle*) to fit with a public address system.

sonorité [sonorētā] *nf* (*de piano, violon*) tone; (*de voix, mot*) sonority; (*d'une salle*) resonance; acoustics *pl*.

sonothèque [sonotek] *nf* sound library.

sont [sôń] *vb voir* **être.**

sophistication [sofēstēkâsyôń] *nf* sophistication.

sophistiqué, e [sofēstēkā] *a* sophisticated.

soporifique [soporēfēk] *a* soporific.

soprano [sopranō] *nm/f* soprano (*pl* -s).

sorbet [sorbe] *nm* sherbet (*US*), sorbet (*Brit*).

sorbetière [sorbətyer] *nf* ice-cream maker.

sorbier [sorbyā] *nm* service tree.

sorcellerie [sorselrē] *nf* witchcraft *q*, sorcery *q*.

sorcier, ière [sorsyā, -yer] *nm/f* sorcerer/witch *ou* sorceress ♦ *a*: **ce n'est pas ~** (*fam*) it's as easy as pie.

sordide [sordēd] *a* sordid; squalid.

Sorlingues [sorlańg] *nfpl*: **les (îles) ~** the Scilly Isles, the Isles of Scilly, the Scillies.

sornettes [sornet] *nfpl* twaddle *sg*.

sort [sor] *vb voir* **sortir** ♦ *nm* (*fortune, destinée*) fate; (*condition, situation*) lot; (*magique*): **jeter un ~** to cast a spell; **un coup du ~** a blow dealt by fate; **le ~ en est jeté** the die is cast; **tirer au ~** to draw lots; **tirer qch au ~** to draw lots for sth.

sortable [sortábl(ə)] *a*: **il n'est pas ~** he doesn't know how to behave.

sortant, e [sortâń, -âńt] *vb voir* **sortir** ♦ *a* (*numéro*) which comes up (*in a draw etc*); (*député, président*) outgoing.

sorte [sort(ə)] *vb voir* **sortir** ♦ *nf* sort, kind; **de la ~** *ad* in that way; **en quelque ~** in a way; **de ~ à** so as to, in order to; **de (telle) ~ que, en ~ que** (*de manière que*) so that; (*si bien que*) so much so that; **faire en ~ que** to see to it that.

sortie [sortē] *nf* (*issue*) way out, exit; (*MIL*) sortie; (*fig: verbale*) outburst; sally; (: *parole incongrue*) odd remark; (*d'un gaz, de l'eau*) outlet; (*promenade*) outing; (*le soir: au restaurant etc*) night out; (*de produits*) export; (*de capitaux*) outflow; (*COMM: somme*): **~s** items of expenditure; outgoings *sans sg*; (*INFORM*) output; (*d'imprimante*) printout; **à sa ~** as he went out *ou* left; **à la ~ de l'école/l'usine** (*moment*) after school/work; when school/the factory finishes; (*lieu*) at the school/factory gates; **à la ~ de ce nouveau modèle** when this new model comes (*ou* came) out, when they bring (*ou* brought) out this new model; **~ de bain** (*vêtement*) bathrobe; **"~ de camions"** "vehicle exit"; **~ papier** hard copy; **~ de secours** emergency exit.

sortilège [sortēlezh] *nm* (magic) spell.

sortir [sortēr] *vi* (*gén*) to come out; (*partir, se*

promener, aller au spectacle etc) to go out; (bourgeon, plante, numéro gagnant) to come up ♦ vt (gén) to take out; (produit, ouvrage, modèle) to bring out; (boniments, incongruités) to come out with; (INFORM) to output; (: sur papier) to print out; (fam: expulser) to throw out ♦ nm: **au ~ de l'hiver/l'enfance** as winter/childhood nears its end; **~ qch de** to take sth out of; **~ qn d'embarras** to get sb out of trouble; **~ de** (gén) to leave; (endroit) to go (ou come) out of, leave; (rainure etc) to come out of; (maladie) to get over; (époque) to get through; (cadre, compétence) to be outside; (provenir de: famille etc) to come from; **~ de table** to leave the table; **~ du système** (INFORM) to log out; **~ de ses gonds** (fig) to fly off the handle; **se ~ de** (affaire, situation) to get out of; **s'en ~** (malade) to pull through; (d'une difficulté etc) to come through all right; to get through, be able to manage.

SOS sigle m mayday, SOS.

sosie [sozē] nm double.

sot, sotte [so, sot] a silly, foolish ♦ nm/f fool.

sottement [sotmáň] ad foolishly.

sottise [sotēz] nf silliness q, foolishness q; (propos, acte) silly ou foolish thing (to do ou say).

sou [sōō] nm: **près de ses ~s** tight-fisted; **sans le ~** penniless; **~ à ~** penny by penny; **pas un ~ de bon sens** not a scrap ou an ounce of good sense; **de quatre ~s** worthless.

souahéli, e [swááēlē] a Swahili ♦ nm (LING) Swahili.

soubassement [sōōbásmáň] nm base.

soubresaut [sōōbrəsō] nm (de peur etc) start; (cahot: d'un véhicule) jolt.

soubrette [sōōbret] nf soubrette, maidservant.

souche [sōōsh] nf (d'arbre) stump; (de carnet) stub; **dormir comme une ~** to sleep like a log; **de vieille ~** of old stock.

souci [sōōsē] nm (inquiétude) worry; (préoccupation) concern; (BOT) marigold; **se faire du ~** to worry; **avoir (le) ~ de** to have concern for; **par ~ de** for the sake of, out of concern for.

soucier [sōōsyā]: **se ~ de** vt to care about.

soucieux, euse [sōōsyœ, -œz] a concerned, worried; **~ de** concerned about; **peu ~ de/que** caring little about/whether.

soucoupe [sōōkōōp] nf saucer; **~ volante** flying saucer.

soudain, e [sōōdaň, -en] a (douleur, mort) sudden ♦ ad suddenly, all of a sudden.

soudainement [sōōdenmáň] ad suddenly.

soudaineté [sōōdentā] nf suddenness.

Soudan [sōōdáň] nm: **le ~** the Sudan.

soudanais, e [sōōdáne, -ez] a Sudanese.

soude [sōōd] nf soda.

soudé, e [sōōdā] a (fig: pétales, organes) joined (together).

souder [sōōdā] vt (avec fil à souder) to solder; (par soudure autogène) to weld; (fig) to bind ou knit together; to fuse (together); **se ~** vi (os) to knit (together).

soudeur, euse [sōōdœr, -œz] nm/f (ouvrier) welder.

soudoyer [sōōdwáyā] vt (péj) to bribe, buy over.

soudure [sōōdür] nf soldering; welding; (joint) soldered joint; weld; **faire la ~** (COMM) to fill a gap; (fig: assurer une transition) to bridge the gap.

souffert, e [sōōfer, -ert(ə)] pp de **souffrir**.

soufflage [sōōflázh] nm (du verre) glassblowing.

souffle [sōōfl(ə)] nm (en expirant) breath; (en soufflant) puff, blow; (respiration) breathing; (d'explosion, de ventilateur) blast; (du vent) blowing; (fig) inspiration; **retenir son ~** to hold one's breath; **avoir du/manquer de ~** to have a lot of/be short of breath; **être à bout de ~** to be out of breath; **avoir le ~ court** to be short-winded; **un ~ d'air** ou **de vent** a breath of air, a puff of wind; **~ au cœur** (MÉD) heart murmur.

soufflé, e [sōōflā] a (CULIN) soufflé; (fam: ahuri, stupéfié) staggered ♦ nm (CULIN) soufflé.

souffler [sōōflā] vi (gén) to blow; (haleter) to puff (and blow) ♦ vt (feu, bougie) to blow out; (chasser: poussière etc) to blow away; (TECH: verre) to blow; (suj: explosion) to destroy (with its blast); (dire): **~ qch à qn** to whisper sth to sb; (fam: voler): **~ qch à qn** to pinch sth from sb; **~ son rôle à qn** to prompt sb; **ne pas ~ mot** not to breathe a word; **laisser ~ qn** (fig) to give sb a breather.

soufflet [sōōfle] nm (instrument) bellows pl; (entre wagons) vestibule; (COUTURE) gusset; (gifle) slap (in the face).

souffleur, euse [sōōflœr, -œz] nm/f (THÉÂTRE) prompter; (TECH) glass-blower.

souffrance [sōōfráns] nf suffering; **en ~** (marchandise) awaiting delivery; (affaire) pending.

souffrant, e [sōōfráň, -áňt] a unwell.

souffre-douleur [sōōfrədōōlœr] nm inv whipping boy, butt, underdog.

souffreteux, euse [sōōfrətœ, -œz] a sickly.

souffrir [sōōfrēr] vi to suffer; (éprouver des douleurs) to be in pain ♦ vt to suffer, endure; (supporter) to bear, stand; (admettre: exception etc) to allow ou admit of; **~ de** (maladie, froid) to suffer from; **~ des dents** to have trouble with one's teeth; **ne pas pouvoir ~ qch/que** ... not to be able to endure ou bear sth/that ...; **faire ~ qn** (suj: personne) to make sb suffer; (: dents, blessure etc) to hurt sb.

soufre [sōōfr(ə)] nm sulfur (US), sulphur (Brit).

soufrer [sōōfrā] vt (vignes) to treat with sulphur ou sulfur.

souhait [swe] nm wish; **tous nos ~s de** good wishes ou our best wishes for; **riche** etc **à ~** as rich etc as one could wish; **à vos ~s!** bless you!

souhaitable [swetábl(ə)] a desirable.

souhaiter [swātā] vt to wish for; **~ le bonjour à qn** to bid sb good day; **~ la bonne année à qn** to wish sb a happy New Year; **il est à ~ que** it is to be hoped that.

souiller [sōōyā] vt to dirty, soil; (fig) to sully, tarnish.

souillure [sōōyür] nf stain.

soûl, e [sōō, sōōl] a drunk; (fig): **~ de**

musique/plaisirs drunk with music/pleasure ♦ *nm*: **tout son** ~ to one's heart's content.
soulagement [sōōlázhmáń] *nm* relief.
soulager [sōōlázhā] *vt* to relieve; ~ **qn de** to relieve sb of.
soûler [sōōlā] *vt*: ~ **qn** to get sb drunk; (*suj*: *boisson*) to make sb drunk; (*fig*) to make sb's head spin *ou* reel; **se** ~ to get drunk; **se** ~ **de** (*fig*) to intoxicate o.s. with.
soûlerie [sōōlrē] *nf* (*péj*) drunken binge.
soulèvement [sōōlevmáń] *nm* uprising; (*GÉO*) upthrust.
soulever [sōōlvā] *vt* to lift; (*vagues*, *poussière*) to send up; (*peuple*) to stir up (to revolt); (*enthousiasme*) to arouse; (*question*, *débat*, *protestations*, *difficultés*) to raise; **se** ~ *vi* (*peuple*) to rise up; (*personne couchée*) to lift o.s. up; (*couvercle etc*) to lift; **cela me soulève le cœur** it makes me feel sick.
soulier [sōōlyā] *nm* shoe; ~**s bas** low-heeled shoes; ~**s plats/à talons** flat/heeled shoes.
souligner [sōōlēnyā] *vt* to underline; (*fig*) to emphasize, stress.
soumettre [sōōmetr] *vt* (*pays*) to subject, subjugate; (*rebelles*) to put down, subdue; ~ **qn/qch à** to subject sb/sth to; ~ **qch à qn** (*projet etc*) to submit sth to sb; **se** ~ (**à**) (*se rendre*, *obéir*) to submit (to); **se** ~ **à** (*formalités etc*) to submit to; (*régime etc*) to submit o.s. to.
soumis, e [sōōmē, -ēz] *pp de* **soumettre** ♦ *a* submissive; **revenus** ~ **à l'impôt** taxable income.
soumission [sōōmēsyóń] *nf* (*voir se soumettre*) submission; (*docilité*) submissiveness; (*COMM*) tender.
soumissionner [sōōmēsyonā] *vt* (*COMM*: *travaux*) to bid for, tender for.
soupape [sōōpáp] *nf* valve; ~ **de sûreté** safety valve.
soupçon [sōōpsóń] *nm* suspicion; (*petite quantité*): **un** ~ **de** a hint *ou* touch of; **avoir** ~ **de** to suspect; **au dessus de tout** ~ above (all) suspicion.
soupçonner [sōōpsonā] *vt* to suspect; ~ **qn de qch/d'être** to suspect sb of sth/of being.
soupçonneux, euse [sōōpsonœ̄, -ēz] *a* suspicious.
soupe [sōōp] *nf* soup; ~ **au lait** *a inv* quick-tempered; ~ **à l'oignon/de poisson** onion/fish soup; ~ **populaire** soup kitchen.
soupente [sōōpáńt] *nf* (*mansarde*) attic; (*placard*) closet (*US*) *ou* cupboard (*Brit*) under the stairs.
souper [sōōpā] *vi* to have supper ♦ *nm* supper; **avoir soupé de** (*fam*) to be sick and tired of.
soupeser [sōōpəzā] *vt* to weigh in one's hand(s), feel the weight of; (*fig*) to weigh (up) (*Brit*)).
soupière [sōōpyer] *nf* (soup) tureen.
soupir [sōōpēr] *nm* sigh; (*MUS*) quarter rest (*US*), crotchet rest (*Brit*); **rendre le dernier** ~ to breathe one's last.
soupirail, aux [sōōpērày, -ō] *nm* (small) basement window.
soupirant [sōōpēráń] *nm* (*péj*) suitor, wooer.
soupirer [sōōpērā] *vi* to sigh; ~ **après qch** to yearn for sth.
souple [sōōpl(ə)] *a* supple; (*col*) soft; (*fig*: rè-

glement, caractère) flexible; (: *démarche*, *taille*) lithe, supple; **disque(tte)** ~ (*INFORM*) floppy disk, diskette.
souplesse [sōōples] *nf* suppleness; flexibility.
source [sōōrs(ə)] *nf* (*point d'eau*) spring; (*d'un cours d'eau*, *fig*) source; **prendre sa** ~ **à/dans** (*suj*: *cours d'eau*) to have its source at/in; **tenir qch de bonne** ~/**de** ~ **sûre** to have sth on good authority/from a reliable source; ~ **thermale/d'eau minérale** hot *ou* thermal/mineral spring.
sourcier, ière [sōōrsyā, -yer] *nm* water diviner.
sourcil [sōōrsē] *nm* (eye)brow.
sourcilière [sōōrsēlyer] *af voir* **arcade**.
sourciller [sōōrsēyā] *vi*: **sans** ~ without turning a hair *ou* batting an eyelid.
sourcilleux, euse [sōōrsēyœ̄, -ēz] *a* (*hautain*, *sévère*) haughty, supercilious; (*pointilleux*) finicky, pernickety.
sourd, e [sōōr, sōōrd(ə)] *a* deaf; (*bruit, voix*) muffled; (*couleur*) muted; (*douleur*) dull; (*lutte*) silent, hidden; (*LING*) voiceless ♦ *nm/f* deaf person; **être** ~ **à** to be deaf to.
sourdement [sōōrdəmáń] *ad* (*avec un bruit sourd*) dully; (*secrètement*) silently.
sourdine [sōōrdēn] *nf* (*MUS*) mute; **en** ~ *ad* softly, quietly; **mettre une** ~ **à** (*fig*) to tone down.
sourd-muet, sourde-muette [sōōrmüe, sōōrdmüet] *a* deaf-and-dumb ♦ *nm/f* deaf-mute.
sourdre [sōōrdr(ə)] *vi* (*eau*) to spring up; (*fig*) to rise.
souriant, e [sōōryáń, -áńt] *vb voir* **sourire** ♦ *a* cheerful.
souricière [sōōrēsyer] *nf* mousetrap; (*fig*) trap.
sourie [sōōrē] *etc vb voir* **sourire**.
sourire [sōōrēr] *nm* smile ♦ *vi* to smile; ~ **à qn** to smile at sb; (*fig*) to appeal to sb; (: *chance*) to smile on sb; **faire un** ~ **à qn** to give sb a smile; **garder le** ~ to keep smiling.
souris [sōōrē] *nf* mouse (*pl* mice); (*INFORM*) mouse.
sournois, e [sōōrnwá, -wáz] *a* deceitful, underhand.
sournoisement [sōōrnwázmáń] *ad* deceitfully.
sous [sōō] *prép* (*gén*) under; ~ **la pluie/le soleil** in the rain/sunshine; ~ **mes yeux** before my eyes; ~ **terre** *a, ad* underground; ~ **vide** *a, ad* vacuum-packed; ~ **l'influence/l'action de** under the influence of/by the action of; ~ **antibiotiques/perfusion** on antibiotics/an I.V. (*US*) *ou* a drip (*Brit*); ~ **cet angle/ce rapport** from this angle/in this respect; ~ **peu** *ad* shortly, before long.
sous... [sōō, sōōz + *vowel*] *préfixe* sub-; under....
sous-alimenté, e [sōōzálēmáńtā] *a* undernourished.
sous-bois [sōōbwá] *nm inv* undergrowth.
sous-catégorie [sōōkátāgorē] *nf* sub-category.
sous-chef [sōōshef] *nm* deputy chief, second in command; ~ **de bureau** deputy head of department.
sous-comité [sōōkomētā] *nm* subcommittee.
sous-commission [sōōkomēsyóń] *nf* sub-committee.
sous-continent [sōōkóńtēnáń] *nm* sub-

continent.

sous-couche [sookoosh] *nf* (*de peinture*) undercoat.

souscripteur, trice [sooskrẽptœr, -trẽs] *nm/f* subscriber.

souscription [sooskrẽpsyóń] *nf* subscription; **offert en** ~ available on subscription.

souscrire [sooskrēr]: ~ **à** *vt* to subscribe to.

sous-cutané, e [sookütáná] *a* subcutaneous.

sous-développé, e [soodávlopá] *a* underdeveloped.

sous-directeur, trice [soodērektœr, -trẽs] *nm/f* assistant manager/manageress, sub-manager/manageress.

sous-emploi [soozáńplwá] *nm* underemployment.

sous-employé, e [soozáńplwáyá] *a* underemployed.

sous-ensemble [soozáńsáńbl(ə)] *nm* subset.

sous-entendre [soozáńtáńdr(ə)] *vt* to imply, infer.

sous-entendu, e [soozáńtáńdü] *a* implied; (*LING*) understood ♦ *nm* innuendo, insinuation.

sous-equipé, e [soozākēpá] *a* underequipped.

sous-estimer [soozestēmá] *vt* to underestimate.

sous-exploiter [soozāksplwátá] *vt* to underexploit.

sous-exposer [soozekspōzá] *vt* to underexpose.

sous-fifre [soofēfr(ə)] *nm* (*péj*) underling.

sous-groupe [soogroop] *nm* subgroup.

sous-homme [soozom] *nm* subhuman.

sous-jacent, e [soozhásáń, -áńt] *a* underlying.

sous-lieutenant [soolyœtnáń] *nm* second lieutenant (*US*), sub-lieutenant (*Brit*).

sous-locataire [soolokátēr] *nm/f* subtenant.

sous-location [soolokásyóń] *nf* subletting.

sous-louer [soolwá] *vt* to sublet.

sous-main [soomań] *nm inv* desk blotter; **en** ~ *ad* secretly.

sous-marin, e [soomáráń, -ēn] *a* (*flore, volcan*) submarine; (*navigation, pêche, explosif*) underwater ♦ *nm* submarine.

sous-médicalisé, e [soomādēkálēzá] *a* lacking adequate medical care.

sous-nappe [soonáp] *nf* table pad (*US*), undercloth (*Brit*).

sous-officier [soozofēsyá] *nm* ≈ non-commissioned officer (NCO).

sous-ordre [soozordr(ə)] *nm* subordinate; **créancier en** ~ creditor's creditor.

sous-payé, e [soopáyá] *a* underpaid.

sous-préfecture [sooprāfektür] *nf* sub-prefecture.

sous-préfet [sooprāfe] *nm* sub-prefect.

sous-production [sooprodüksyóń] *nf* underproduction.

sous-produit [sooprodüē] *nm* by-product; (*fig: péj*) pale imitation.

sous-programme [sooprográm] *nm* (*INFORM*) subroutine.

sous-pull [soopool] *nm* thin poloneck sweater.

sous-secrétaire [soosəkrāter] *nm*: ~ **d'État** Under Secretary of State.

soussigné, e [soosēnyá] *a*: **je** ~ I the undersigned.

sous-sol [soosol] *nm* basement; (*GÉO*) subsoil.

sous-tasse [sootás] *nf* saucer.

sous-tendre [sootáńdr(ə)] *vt* to underlie.

sous-titre [sootētr(ə)] *nm* subtitle.

sous-titré, e [sootētrá] *a* with subtitles.

soustraction [sootráksyóń] *nf* subtraction.

soustraire [sootrer] *vt* to subtract, take away; (*dérober*): ~ **qch à qn** to remove sth from sb; ~ **qn à** (*danger*) to shield sb from; **se** ~ **à** (*autorité, obligation, devoir*) to elude, escape from.

sous-traitance [sootretáńs(ə)] *nf* subcontracting.

sous-traitant [sootretáń] *nm* subcontractor.

sous-traiter [sootrātá] *vt*, *vi* to subcontract.

soustrayais [sootreye] *etc vb voir* **soustraire**.

sous-verre [soover] *nm inv* glass mount.

sous-vêtement [soovetmáń] *nm* undergarment, item of underwear; ~**s** *nmpl* underwear *sg*.

soutane [sootán] *nf* cassock, soutane.

soute [soot] *nf* hold; ~ **à bagages** baggage hold.

soutenable [sootnábl(ə)] *a* (*opinion*) tenable, defensible.

soutenance [sootnáńs] *nf*: ~ **de thèse** ≈ defense (*US*), ≈ viva (voce) (*Brit*).

soutènement [sootenmáń] *nm*: **mur de** ~ retaining wall.

souteneur [sootnœr] *nm* procurer.

soutenir [sootnēr] *vt* to support; (*assaut, choc, regard*) to stand up to, withstand; (*intérêt, effort*) to keep up; (*assurer*): ~ **que** to maintain that; **se** ~ (*dans l'eau etc*) to hold o.s. up; (*être soutenable: point de vue*) to be tenable; (*s'aider mutuellement*) to stand by each other; ~ **la comparaison avec** to bear *ou* stand comparison with; ~ **le regard de qn** to be able to look sb in the face.

soutenu, e [sootnü] *pp de* **soutenir** ♦ *a* (*efforts*) sustained, unflagging; (*style*) elevated; (*couleur*) strong.

souterrain, e [sooteráń, -en] *a* underground; (*fig*) subterranean ♦ *nm* underground passage.

soutien [sootyań] *nm* support; **apporter son** ~ **à** to lend one's support to; ~ **de famille** breadwinner.

soutiendrai [sootyańdrá] *etc vb voir* **soutenir**.

soutien-gorge, *pl* **soutiens-gorge** [sootyańgorzh(ə)] *nm* bra; (*de maillot de bain*) top.

soutiens [sootyań], **soutint** [sootáń] *etc vb voir* **soutenir**.

soutirer [sootērá] *vt*: ~ **qch à qn** to squeeze *ou* get sth out of sb.

souvenance [soovnáńs] *nf*: **avoir** ~ **de** to recollect.

souvenir [soovnēr] *nm* (*réminiscence*) memory; (*cadeau*) souvenir, keepsake; (*de voyage*) souvenir ♦ *vb*: **se** ~ **de** *vt* to remember; **se** ~ **que** to remember that; **garder le** ~ **de** to retain the memory of; **en** ~ **de** in memory *ou* remembrance of; **avec mes affectueux/meilleurs** ~**s,** ... with love from, .../regards, ...

souvent [soováń] *ad* often; **peu** ~ seldom, infrequently; **le plus** ~ more often than not, most often.

souvenu, e [soovənü] *pp de* **se souvenir**.

souverain, e [sŏŏvrań, -en] *a* sovereign; *(fig: mépris)* supreme ♦ *nm/f* sovereign, monarch.

souverainement [sŏŏvrenmáń] *ad (sans appel)* with sovereign power; *(extrêmement)* supremely, intensely.

souveraineté [sŏŏvrentā] *nf* sovereignty.

souviendrai [sŏŏvyańdrā], **souviens** [sŏŏvyań], **souvint** [sŏŏvań] *etc vb voir* **se souvenir**.

soviétique [sovyātēk] *a* Soviet ♦ *nm/f*: **S~** Soviet citizen.

soviétiser [sovyātēzā] *vt* to sovietize.

soviétologue [sovyātolog] *nm/f* Kremlinologist.

soyeux, euse [swàyœ̄, -œ̄z] *a* silky.

soyez [swàyā] *etc vb voir* **être**.

SPA *sigle f* (= *Société protectrice des animaux*) ≈ SPCA *(US)*, ≈ RSPCA *(Brit)*.

spacieux, euse [spásyœ̄, -œ̄z] *a* spacious; roomy.

spaciosité [spásyozētā] *nf* spaciousness.

spaghettis [spágātē] *nmpl* spaghetti *sg*.

sparadrap [spárádrá] *nm* adhesive tape *(US)*, adhesive *ou* sticking plaster *(Brit)*.

Sparte [spárt(ə)] *nf* Sparta.

spartiate [spársyát] *a* Spartan; **~s** *nfpl (sandales)* Roman sandals.

spasme [spázm(ə)] *nm* spasm.

spasmodique [spázmodēk] *a* spasmodic.

spatial, e, aux [spásyál, -ō] *a (AVIAT)* space *cpd*; *(PSYCH)* spatial.

spatule [spátül] *nf (ustensile)* slice; spatula; *(bout)* tip.

speaker, ine [spēkœr, -krēn] *nm/f* announcer.

spécial, e, aux [spásyál, -ō] *a* special; *(bizarre)* peculiar.

spécialement [spásyálmáń] *ad* especially, particularly; *(tout exprès)* specially; **pas ~** not particularly.

spécialisation [spásyálēzásyóń] *nf* specialization.

spécialisé, e [spásyálēzā] *a* specialized; **ordinateur ~** dedicated computer.

spécialiser [spásyálēzā]: **se ~** *vi* to specialize.

spécialiste [spásyálēst(ə)] *nm/f* specialist.

spécialité [spásyálētā] *nf* specialty *(US)*, speciality *(Brit)*; *(SCOL)* major *(US)*, special field *(Brit)*; **~ pharmaceutique** patent medicine.

spécieux, euse [spásyœ̄, -œ̄z] *a* specious.

spécification [spásēfēkásyóń] *nf* specification.

spécifier [spásēfyā] *vt* to specify, state.

spécifique [spásēfēk] *a* specific.

spécifiquement [spásēfēkmáń] *ad (typiquement)* typically; *(tout exprès)* specifically.

spécimen [spásēmen] *nm* specimen; *(revue etc)* specimen *ou* sample copy.

spectacle [spektákl(ə)] *nm (tableau, scène)* sight; *(représentation)* show; *(industrie)* show business, entertainment; **se donner en ~** *(péj)* to make a spectacle *ou* an exhibition of o.s; **pièce/revue à grand ~** spectacular (play/revue); **au ~ de ...** at the sight of ....

spectaculaire [spektáküler] *a* spectacular.

spectateur, trice [spektátœr, -trēs] *nm/f (CINÉMA etc)* member of the audience; *(SPORT)* spectator; *(d'un événement)* onlooker, witness.

spectre [spektr(ə)] *nm (fantôme, fig)* specter *(US)*, spectre *(Brit)*; *(PHYSIQUE)* spectrum

(pl -a); **~ solaire** solar spectrum.

spéculateur, trice [spākülátœr, -trēs] *nm/f* speculator.

spéculatif, ive [spākülátēf, -ēv] *a* speculative.

spéculation [spākülásyóń] *nf* speculation.

spéculer [spākülā] *vi* to speculate; **~ sur** *(COMM)* to speculate in; *(réfléchir)* to speculate on; *(tabler sur)* to bank *ou* rely on.

spéléologie [spālāolozhē] *nf (étude)* speleology; *(activité)* spelunking *(US)*, potholing *(Brit)*.

spéléologue [spālāolog] *nm/f* speleologist; spelunker *(US)*, potholer *(Brit)*.

spermatozoïde [spermátōzoēd] *nm* sperm, spermatozoon *(pl -zoa)*.

sperme [sperm(ə)] *nm* semen, sperm.

spermicide [spermēsēd] *a, nm* spermicide.

sphère [sfer] *nf* sphere.

sphérique [sfārēk] *a* spherical.

sphincter [sfańkter] *nm* sphincter.

sphinx [sfańks] *nm inv* sphinx; *(ZOOL)* hawkmoth.

spiral, aux [spērál, -ō] *nm* hairspring.

spirale [spērál] *nf* spiral; **en ~** in a spiral.

spire [spēr] *nf (d'une spirale)* turn; *(d'une coquille)* whorl.

spiritisme [spērētēsm(ə)] *nm* spiritualism, spiritism.

spirituel, le [spērētüel] *a* spiritual; *(fin, piquant)* witty; **musique ~le** sacred music; **concert ~** concert of sacred music.

spirituellement [spērētüelmáń] *ad* spiritually; wittily.

spiritueux [spērētüœ̄] *nm* spirit.

splendeur [splándœr] *nf* splendor *(US)*, splendour *(Brit)*.

splendide [splándēd] *a* splendid, magnificent.

spolier [spolyā] *vt*: **~ qn (de)** to despoil sb (of).

spongieux, euse [spóńzhyœ̄, -œ̄z] *a* spongy.

sponsor [spóńsor] *nm* sponsor.

sponsoriser [spóńsorēzā] *vt* to sponsor.

spontané, e [spóńtánā] *a* spontaneous.

spontanément [spóńtánámáń] *ad* spontaneously.

sporadique [sporádēk] *a* sporadic.

sport [spor] *nm* sport ♦ *a inv (vêtement)* casual; *(fair-play)* sporting; **faire du ~** to engage in sports; **~ individuel/d'équipe** individual/team sport; **~ de combat** combative sport; **~s d'hiver** winter sports.

sportif, ive [sportēf, -ēv] *a (journal, association, épreuve)* sports *cpd*; *(allure, démarche)* athletic; *(attitude, esprit)* sporting; **les résultats ~s** the sports results.

sportivement [sportēvmáń] *ad* sportingly.

sportivité [sportēvētā] *nf* sportsmanship.

spot [spot] *nm (lampe)* spot(light); *(annonce)*: **~ (publicitaire)** commercial (break).

spray [spre] *nm* spray, aerosol.

sprint [sprēnt] *nm* sprint; **piquer un ~** to put on a (final) spurt.

squale [skwál] *nm (type of)* shark.

square [skwár] *nm* public garden(s).

squash [skwásh] *nm* squash.

squatter *nm* [skwátœr] squatter ♦ *vt* [skwátā] to squat.

squelette [skəlet] *nm* skeleton.

squelettique [skəlātēk] *a* scrawny; *(fig)*

skimpy.
Sri Lanka [srēlåṅká] *nm* Sri Lanka.
sri-lankais, e [srēlåṅke, -ez] *a* Sri Lankan.
SS *sigle f* = **sécurité sociale**; (= *Sa Sainteté*)
HH.
ss *abr* = **sous.**
S/S *sigle m* (= *steamship*) SS.
SSR *sigle f* (= *Société suisse romande*) *the
Swiss   French-language   broadcasting
company.*
stabilisateur, trice [ståbēlēzàtœr, -trēs] *a*
stabilizing ♦ *nm* stabilizer; (*véhicule*) anti-
roll device; (*avion*) stabilizer (*US*), tailplane
(*Brit*).
stabiliser [ståbēlēzā] *vt* to stabilize; (*terrain*)
to consolidate.
stabilité [ståbēlētā] *nf* stability.
stable [ståbl(ə)] *a* stable, steady.
stade [ståd] *nm* (*SPORT*) stadium; (*phase,
niveau*) stage.
stage [ståzh] *nm* training period; training
course.
stagiaire [ståzhyer] *nm/f, a* trainee *(cpd)*.
stagnant, e [stågnåṅ, -åṅt] *a* stagnant.
stagner [stågnā] *vi* to stagnate.
stalactite [ståláktēt] *nf* stalactite.
stalagmite [stålágmēt] *nf* stalagmite.
stalle [stål] *nf* stall, box.
stand [ståṅd] *nm* (*d'exposition*) stand; (*de
foire*) stall; ~ **de tir** (*à la foire, SPORT*)
shooting gallery; ~ **de ravitaillement** pit.
standard [ståṅdár] *a inv* standard ♦ *nm* (*type,
norme*) standard; (*téléphonique*) switchboard.
standardiser [ståṅdárdēzā] *vt* to standardize.
standardiste [ståṅdárdēst(ə)] *nm/f* switchboard operator.
standing [ståṅdēng] *nm* standing; **immeuble
de grand** ~ luxury apartment building (*US*),
block of luxury flats (*Brit*).
star [står] *nf* star.
starlette [stárlet] *nf* starlet.
starter [stárter] *nm* (*AUTO*) choke; (*SPORT*:
personne) starter; **mettre le** ~ to pull out the
choke.
station [ståsyóṅ] *nf* station; (*de bus*) stop; (*de
villégiature*) resort; (*posture*): **la** ~ **debout**
standing, an upright posture; ~ **balnéaire**
seaside resort; ~ **de graissage** lubrication
bay; ~ **de lavage** carwash; ~ **de ski** ski resort; ~ **de sports d'hiver** winter sports resort; ~ **de taxis** taxi stand (*US*) *ou* rank
(*Brit*); ~ **thermale** thermal spa.
stationnaire [ståsyoner] *a* stationary.
stationnement   [ståsyonmåṅ]   *nm*   parking;
zone de ~ **interdit** no parking area; ~
alterné parking on alternate sides.
stationner [ståsyonā] *vi* to park.
station-service [ståsyóṅservēs] *nf* service
station.
statique [ståtēk] *a* static.
statisticien, ne [ståtēstēsyaṅ, -en] *nm/f*
statistician.
statistique [ståtēstēk] *nf* (*science*) statistics
sg; (*rapport, étude*) statistic ♦ *a* statistical;
~**s** *nfpl* (*données*) statistics *pl*.
statistiquement [ståtēstēkmåṅ] *ad* statisti-
cally.
statue [ståtü] *nf* statue.

statuer [ståtüā] *vi*: ~ **sur** to rule on, give a
ruling on.
statuette [ståtüet] *nf* statuette.
statu quo [ståtükwō] *nm* status quo.
stature [ståtür] *nf* stature; **de haute** ~ of
great stature.
statut [ståtü] *nm* status; ~**s** *nmpl* (*JUR,
ADMIN*) statutes.
statutaire [ståtüter] *a* statutory.
Sté *abr* (= *société*) soc.
St(e) *abr* (= *Saint(e)*) St.
steak [stek] *nm* steak.
stèle [stel] *nf* stela, stele.
stellaire [ståler] *a* stellar.
stencil [stensēl] *nm* stencil.
sténodactylo [stånodáktēlō] *nf* stenographer
(*US*), shorthand typist (*Brit*).
sténodactylographie [stånodáktēlográfē] *nf*
stenography (*US*), shorthand typing (*Brit*).
sténo(graphie) [ståno(gráfē)] *nf* shorthand;
prendre en ~ to take down in shorthand.
sténographier [stånográfyā] *vt* to take down
in shorthand.
sténographique   [stånográfēk]   *a*   shorthand
cpd.
stentor [ståṅtor] *nm*: **voix de** ~ stentorian
voice.
stéphanois, e [ståfånwá, -wáz] *a* of *ou* from
Saint-Étienne.
steppe [step] *nf* steppe.
stère [ster] *nm* stere.
stéréo(phonie)   [stårāo(fonē)]   *nf*
stereo(phony); **émission en** ~ stereo broadcast.
stéréo(phonique)   [stårāo(fonēk)]   *a*
stereo(phonic).
stéréoscope [stårāoskop] *nm* stereoscope.
stéréoscopique [stårāoskopēk] *a* stereoscopic.
stéréotype [stårāotēp] *nm* stereotype.
stéréotypé, e [stårāotēpā] *a* stereotyped.
stérile [stårēl] *a* sterile; (*terre*) barren; (*fig*)
fruitless, futile.
stérilement [stårēlmåṅ] *ad* fruitlessly.
stérilet [stårēle] *nm* coil, loop.
stérilisateur [stårēlēzàtœr] *nm* sterilizer.
stérilisation [stårēlēzàsyóṅ] *nf* sterilization.
stériliser [stårēlēzā] *vt* to sterilize.
stérilité [stårēlētā] *nf* sterility.
sternum [sternom] *nm* breastbone, sternum.
stéthoscope [ståtoskop] *nm* stethoscope.
stick [stēk] *nm* stick.
stigmates [stēgmát] *nmpl* scars, marks;
(*REL*) stigmata *pl*.
stigmatiser [stēgmátēzā] *vt* to denounce,
stigmatize.
stimulant, e [stēmülåṅ, -åṅt] *a* stimulating ♦
nm (*MÉD*) stimulant; (*fig*) stimulus (*pl* -i),
incentive.
stimulateur [stēmülátœr] *nm*: ~ **cardiaque**
pacemaker.
stimulation [stēmülásyóṅ] *nf* stimulation.
stimuler [stēmülā] *vt* to stimulate.
stimulus, i [stēmülüs, -ē] *nm* stimulus (*pl* -i).
stipulation [stēpülásyóṅ] *nf* stipulation.
stipuler [stēpülā] *vt* to stipulate, specify.
stock [stok] *nm* stock; **en** ~ in stock.
stockage [stokázh] *nm* stocking; storage.
stocker [stokā] *vt* to stock; (*déchets*) to store.
Stockholm [stokolm] *n* Stockholm.

stockiste |stokēst(ə)| *nm* dealer.
stoïcisme |stoēsēsm(ə)| *nm* stoicism.
stoïque |stoēk| *a* stoic, stoical.
stomacal, e, aux |stomákál, -ō| *a* gastric, stomach *cpd*.
stomatologie |stomátolozhē| *nf* stomatology.
stop |stop| *nm* (AUTO: *écriteau*) stop sign; (: *signal*) brake light; (*dans un télégramme*) stop ♦ *excl* stop!
stoppage |stopázh| *nm* invisible mending.
stopper |stopā| *vt* to stop, halt; (COUTURE) to mend ♦ *vi* to stop, halt.
store |stor| *nm* blind; (*de magasin*) shade, awning.
strabisme |stràbēsm(ə)| *nm* squint(ing).
strangulation |stràṅgülásyôṅ| *nf* strangulation.
strapontin |stràpôṅtàṅ| *nm* jump *ou* foldaway seat.
Strasbourg |stràzbōōr| *n* Strasbourg.
strass |stràs| *nm* paste, strass.
stratagème |stràtázhem| *nm* stratagem.
strate |stràt| *nf* (GÉO) stratum, layer.
stratège |stràtezh| *nm* strategist.
stratégie |stràtāzhē| *nf* strategy.
stratégique |stràtāzhēk| *a* strategic.
stratégiquement |stràtāzhēkmáṅ| *ad* strategically.
stratifié, e |stràtēfyā| *a* (GÉO) stratified; (TECH) laminated.
stratosphère |stràtosfer| *nf* stratosphere.
stress |stres| *nm inv* stress.
stressant, e |stresàṅ, -àṅt| *a* stressful.
stresser |stresā| *vt* to stress, cause stress in.
strict, e |strēkt(ə)| *a* strict; (*tenue, décor*) severe, plain; **son droit le plus ~** his most basic right; **dans la plus ~e intimité** strictly in private; **le ~ nécessaire/minimum** the bare essentials/minimum.
strictement |strēktəmáṅ| *ad* strictly; plainly.
strident, e |strēdàṅ, -àṅt| *a* shrill, strident.
stridulations |strēdülásyôṅ| *nfpl* stridulations, chirrings.
strie |strē| *nf* streak; (ANAT, GÉO) stria (*pl* -ae).
strier |strēyā| *vt* to streak; to striate.
strip-tease |strēptēz| *nm* striptease.
strip-teaseuse |strēptēzœz| *nf* stripper, striptease artist.
striures |strēyür| *nfpl* streaking *sg*.
strophe |strof| *nf* verse, stanza.
structure |strüktür| *nf* structure; **~s d'accueil/touristiques** reception/tourist facilities.
structurer |strüktürā| *vt* to structure.
strychnine |strēknēn| *nf* strychnine.
stuc |stük| *nm* stucco.
studieusement |stüdyœzmáṅ| *ad* studiously.
studieux, euse |stüdyœ, -œz| *a* (*élève*) studious; (*vacances*) study *cpd*.
studio |stüdyō| *nm* (*logement*) studio apartment; (*d'artiste*, TV *etc*) studio (*pl* -s).
stupéfaction |stüpāfáksyôṅ| *nf* stupefaction, astonishment.
stupéfait, e |stüpáfe, -ct| *a* astonished.
stupéfiant, e |stüpáfyáṅ, -àṅt| *a* stunning, astonishing ♦ *nm* (MÉD) drug, narcotic.
stupéfier |stüpáfyā| *vt* to stupefy; (*étonner*) to stun, astonish.
stupeur |stüpœr| *nf* (*inertie, insensibilité*)

stupor; (*étonnement*) astonishment, amazement.
stupide |stüpēd| *a* stupid; (*hébété*) stunned.
stupidement |stüpēdmáṅ| *ad* stupidly.
stupidité |stüpēdētā| *nf* stupidity *q*; (*propos, action*) stupid thing (to say *ou* do).
stups |stüp| *nmpl* (= *stupéfiants*): **brigade des ~** narcotics bureau *ou* squad.
style |stēl| *nm* style; **meuble/robe de ~** piece of period furniture/period dress; **~ de vie** lifestyle.
stylé, e |stēlā| *a* well-trained.
stylet |stēle| *nm* (*poignard*) stiletto; (CHIRURGIE) stylet.
stylisé, e |stēlēzā| *a* stylized.
styliste |stēlēst(ə)| *nm/f* designer; stylist.
stylistique |stēlēstēk| *nf* stylistics *sg* ♦ *a* stylistic.
stylo |stēlō| *nm*: **~ (à encre)** (fountain) pen; **~ (à) bille** ballpoint pen.
stylo-feutre |stēlofœtr(ə)| *nm* felt-tip pen.
su, e |sü| *pp de* **savoir** ♦ *nm*: **au ~ de** with the knowledge of.
suaire |süer| *nm* shroud.
suant, e |süàṅ, -àṅt| *a* sweaty.
suave |süàv| *a* (*odeur*) sweet; (*voix*) suave, smooth; (*coloris*) soft, mellow.
subalterne |sübàltern(ə)| *a* (*employé, officier*) junior; (*rôle*) subordinate, subsidiary ♦ *nm/f* subordinate, inferior.
subconscient |sübkôṅsyàṅ| *nm* subconscious.
subdiviser |sübdēvēzā| *vt* to subdivide.
subdivision |sübdēvēzyôṅ| *nf* subdivision.
subir |sübēr| *vt* (*affront, dégâts, mauvais traitements*) to suffer; (*influence, charme*) to be under, be subjected to; (*traitement, opération, châtiment*) to undergo; (*personne*) to suffer, be subjected to.
subit, e |sübē, -ēt| *a* sudden.
subitement |sübētmáṅ| *ad* suddenly, all of a sudden.
subjectif, ive |sübzhektēf, -ēv| *a* subjective.
subjectivement |sübzhektēvmáṅ| *ad* subjectively.
subjonctif |sübzhôṅktēf| *nm* subjunctive.
subjuguer |sübzhügā| *vt* to subjugate.
sublime |süblēm| *a* sublime.
sublimer |süblēmā| *vt* to sublimate.
submergé, e |sübmerzhā| *a* submerged; (*fig*): **~ de** snowed under with; overwhelmed with.
submerger |sübmerzhā| *vt* to submerge; (*suj: foule*) to engulf; (*fig*) to overwhelm.
submersible |sübmersēbl(ə)| *nm* submarine.
subordination |sübordēnásyôṅ| *nf* subordination.
subordonné, e |sübordonā| *a, nm/f* subordinate; **~ à** (*personne*) subordinate to; (*résultats etc*) subject to, depending on.
subordonner |sübordonā| *vt*: **~ qn/qch à** to subordinate sb/sth to.
subornation |sübornásyôṅ| *nf* bribing.
suborner |sübornā| *vt* to bribe.
subrepticement |sübreptēsmáṅ| *ad* surreptitiously.
subroger |sübrozhā| *vt* (JUR) to subrogate.
subside |süpsēd| *nm* grant.
subsidiaire |süpsēdycr| *a* subsidiary; **question ~** deciding question.
subsistance |sübzēstàṅs| *nf* subsistence;

pourvoir à la ~ de qn to keep sb, provide for sb's subsistence *ou* keep.

subsister [sübzĕstā] *vi (rester)* to remain, subsist; *(vivre)* to live; *(survivre)* to live on.

substance [süpstâns] *nf* substance; **en ~** in substance.

substantiel, le [süpstânsyel] *a* substantial.

substantif [süpstântēf] *nm* noun, substantive.

substantiver [süpstântēvā] *vt* to nominalize.

substituer [süpstĕtüā] *vt*: **~ qn/qch à** to substitute sb/sth for; **se ~ à qn** *(représenter)* to substitute for sb; *(évincer)* to substitute o.s. for sb.

substitut [süpstĕtü] *nm (JUR)* assistant district attorney *(US)*, deputy public prosecutor *(Brit)*; *(succédané)* substitute.

substitution [süpstĕtüsyón] *nf* substitution.

subterfuge [süpterfüzh] *nm* subterfuge.

subtil, e [süptĕl] *a* subtle.

subtilement [süptĕlmán] *ad* subtly.

subtiliser [süptĕlēzā] *vt*: **~ qch (à qn)** to spirit sth away (from sb).

subtilité [süptēlētā] *nf* subtlety.

suburbain, e [sübürbań, -en] *a* suburban.

subvenir [sübvənēr]: **~ à** *vt* to meet.

subvention [sübvânsyón] *nf* subsidy, grant.

subventionner [sübvânsyonā] *vt* to subsidize.

subversif, ive [sübversĕf, -ēv] *a* subversive.

subversion [sübversyón] *nf* subversion.

suc [sük] *nm (BOT)* sap; *(de viande, fruit)* juice; **~s gastriques** gastric juices.

succédané [süksādānā] *nm* substitute.

succéder [süksādā]: **~ à** *vt (directeur, roi etc)* to succeed; *(venir après: dans une série)* to follow, succeed; **se ~** *vi (accidents, années)* to follow one another.

succès [sükse] *nm* success; **avec ~** successfully; **sans ~** unsuccessfully; **avoir du ~** to be a success, be successful; **à ~** successful; **livre à ~** bestseller; **~ de librairie** bestseller; **~ (féminins)** conquests.

successeur [süksäsœr] *nm* successor.

successif, ive [süksäsĕf, -ēv] *a* successive.

succession [süksäsyón] *nf (série, POL)* succession; *(JUR: patrimoine)* estate, inheritance; **prendre la ~ de** *(directeur)* to succeed, take over from; *(entreprise)* to take over.

successivement [süksäsēvmán] *ad* successively.

succinct, e [süksań, -ańt] *a* succinct.

succinctement [süksańtmán] *ad* succinctly.

succion [süksyón] *nf*: **bruit de ~** sucking noise.

succomber [sükónbā] *vi* to die, succumb; *(fig)*: **~ à** to give way to, succumb to.

succulent, e [sükülán, -ánt] *a* succulent.

succursale [sükürsál] *nf* branch; **magasin à ~s multiples** chain store.

sucer [süsā] *vt* to suck.

sucette [süset] *nf (bonbon)* lollipop; *(de bébé)* pacifier *(US)*, dummy *(Brit)*.

suçoter [süsotā] *vt* to suck.

sucre [sükr(ə)] *nm (substance)* sugar; *(morceau)* lump of sugar, sugar lump *ou* cube; **~ de canne/betterave** cane/beet sugar; **~ en morceaux/cristallisé/en poudre** lump *ou* cube/granulated/powdered *(US) ou* caster *(Brit)* sugar; **~ glace** confectioners' *(US) ou* icing *(Brit)* sugar; **~ d'orge** barley sugar.

sucré, e [sükrā] *a (produit alimentaire)* sweetened; *(au goût)* sweet; *(péj)* sugary, honeyed.

sucrer [sükrā] *vt (thé, café)* to sweeten, put sugar in; **~ qn** to put sugar in sb's tea *(ou* coffee *etc)*; **se ~** to help o.s. to sugar, have some sugar; *(fam)* to line one's pocket(s).

sucrerie [sükrərē] *nf (usine)* sugar refinery; **~s** *nfpl (bonbons)* sweets, sweet things.

sucrier, ière [sükrēyā, -ycr] *a (industrie)* sugar *cpd; (région)* sugar-producing ♦ *nm (fabricant)* sugar producer; *(récipient)* sugar bowl.

sud [süd] *nm*: **le ~** the south ♦ *a inv* south; *(côte)* south, southern; **au ~** *(situation)* in the south; *(direction)* to the south; **au ~ de** (to the) south of.

sud-africain, e [südáfrēkań, -en] *a* South African ♦ *nm/f*: **Sud-Africain, e** South African.

sud-américain, e [südámārēkań, -en] *a* South American ♦ *nm/f*: **Sud-Américain, e** South American.

sudation [südâsyón] *nf* sweating, sudation.

sud-coréen, ne [südkorāań, -en] *a* South Korean ♦ *nm/f*: **Sud-Coréen, ne** South Korean.

sud-est [südest] *nm, a inv* southeast.

sud-ouest [südwest] *nm, a inv* southwest.

sud-vietnamien, ne [südvyetnámyań, -en] *a* South Vietnamese ♦ *nm/f*: **Sud-Vietnamien, ne** South Vietnamese.

Suède [süed] *nf*: **la ~** Sweden.

suédois, e [süādwā, -wàz] *a* Swedish ♦ *nm (LING)* Swedish ♦ *nm/f*: **S~, e** Swede.

suer [süā] *vi* to sweat; *(suinter)* to ooze ♦ *vt (fig)* to exude; **~ à grosses gouttes** to sweat profusely.

sueur [süœr] *nf* sweat; **en ~** sweating, in a sweat; **avoir des ~s froides** to be in a cold sweat.

suffire [süfēr] *vi (être assez)*: **~ (à qn/pour qch/pour faire)** to be enough *ou* sufficient (for sb/for sth/to do); *(satisfaire)*: **cela lui suffit** he's content with this, this is enough for him; **se ~** *vi* to be self-sufficient; **cela suffit pour les irriter/qu'ils se fâchent** it's enough to annoy them/for them to get angry; **il suffit d'une négligence/qu'on oublie pour que ...** it only takes one act of carelessness/one only needs to forget for ...; **ça suffit!** that's enough!, that'll do!

suffisamment [süfēzámán] *ad* sufficiently, enough; **~ de** sufficient, enough.

suffisance [süfēzáns] *nf (vanité)* self-importance, bumptiousness; *(quantité)*: **en ~** in plenty.

suffisant, e [süfēzáń, -áńt] *a (temps, ressources)* sufficient; *(résultats)* satisfactory; *(vaniteux)* self-important, bumptious.

suffisons [süfēzóń] *etc vb voir* **suffire**.

suffixe [süfēks(ə)] *nm* suffix.

suffocant, e [süfokáń, -áńt] *a (étouffant)* suffocating; *(stupéfiant)* staggering.

suffocation [süfokásyóń] *nf* suffocation.

suffoquer [süfokā] *vt* to choke, suffocate; *(stupéfier)* to stagger, astound ♦ *vi* to choke, suffocate; **~ de colère/d'indignation** to choke with anger/indignation.

suffrage [süfrázh] *nm* (*POL: voix*) vote; (*: méthode*): ~ **universel/direct/indirect** universal/direct/indirect suffrage; (*du public etc*) approval *q*; ~s **exprimés** cast (*US*) *ou* valid (*Brit*) votes.

suggérer [sügzhārā] *vt* to suggest; ~ **que/de faire** to suggest that/doing.

suggestif, ive [sügzhestēf, -ēv] *a* suggestive.

suggestion [sügzhestyóṅ] *nf* suggestion.

suicidaire [süēsēder] *a* suicidal.

suicide [süēsēd] *nm* suicide ♦ *a*: **opération** ~ suicide mission.

suicidé, e [süēsēdā] *nm/f* suicide.

suicider [süēsēdā]: **se** ~ *vi* to commit suicide.

suie [süē] *nf* soot.

suif [süēf] *nm* tallow.

suinter [süàṅtā] *vi* to ooze.

suis [süē] *vb voir* **être, suivre**.

suisse [süēs] *a* Swiss ♦ *nm* (*bedeau*) ≈ verger ♦ *nm/f*: **S~** Swiss *pl inv* ♦ *nf*: **la S~** Switzerland; **la S~ romande/allemande** French-speaking/German-speaking Switzerland; ~ **romand** Swiss French.

suisse-allemand, e [süēsálmàṅ, -àṅd] *a*, *nm/f* Swiss German.

Suissesse [süēses] *nf* Swiss (woman *ou* girl).

suit [süē] *vb voir* **suivre**.

suite [süēt] *nf* (*continuation: d'énumération etc*) rest, remainder; (*: de feuilleton*) continuation; (*: second film etc sur le même thème*) sequel; (*série: de maisons, succès*): **une** ~ **de** a series *ou* succession of; (*MATH*) series *sg*; (*conséquence*) result; (*ordre, liaison logique*) coherence; (*appartement, MUS*) suite; (*escorte*) retinue, suite; ~s *nfpl* (*d'une maladie etc*) effects; **prendre la** ~ **de** (*directeur etc*) to succeed, take over from; **donner** ~ **à** (*requête, projet*) to follow up; **faire** ~ **à** to follow; (**faisant**) ~ **à votre lettre du ...** with reference to your letter of the ...; **sans** ~ *a* incoherent, disjointed ♦ *ad* incoherently, disjointedly; **de** ~ *ad* (*d'affilée*) in succession; (*immédiatement*) at once; **par la** ~ afterwards, subsequently; **à la** ~ *ad* one after the other; **à la** ~ **de** (*derrière*) behind; (*en conséquence de*) following; **par** ~ **de** owing to, as a result of; **avoir de la** ~ **dans les idées** to show great singleness of purpose; **attendre la** ~ **des événements** to (wait and see) what happens.

suivant, e [süēvàṅ, -àṅt] *vb voir* **suivre** ♦ *a* next, following; (*ci-après*): **l'exercice** ~ the following exercise ♦ *prép* (*selon*) according to; ~ **que** according to whether; **au** ~! next!

suive [süēv] *etc vb voir* **suivre**.

suiveur [süēvɐr] *nm* (*CYCLISME*) (official) follower; (*péj*) (camp) follower.

suivi, e [süēvē] *pp de* **suivre** ♦ *a* (*régulier*) regular; (*COMM: article*) in general production; (*cohérent*) consistent; coherent ♦ *nm* follow-up; **très/peu** ~ (*cours*) well-/poorly-attended; (*mode*) widely/not widely adopted; (*feuilleton etc*) widely/not widely followed.

suivre [süēvr(ə)] *vt* (*gén*) to follow; (*SCOL: cours*) to attend; (*: leçon*) to follow, attend to; (*: programme*) to keep up with; (*COMM: article*) to continue to stock ♦ *vi* to follow; (*élève: écouter*) to attend, pay attention; (*: assimiler le programme*) to keep up, follow;

se ~ (*accidents, personnes, voitures etc*) to follow one after the other; (*raisonnement*) to be coherent; ~ **des yeux** to follow with one's eyes; **faire** ~ (*lettre*) to forward; ~ **son cours** (*suj: enquête etc*) to run *ou* take its course; **"à** ~**"** "to be continued".

sujet, te [süzhe, -et] *a*: **être** ~ **à** (*accidents*) to be prone to; (*vertige etc*) to be liable *ou* subject to ♦ *nm/f* (*d'un souverain*) subject ♦ *nm* subject; **un** ~ **de dispute/discorde/mécontentement** a cause for argument/dissension/dissatisfaction; **c'est à quel** ~? what is it about?; **avoir** ~ **de se plaindre** to have cause for complaint; **au** ~ **de** *prép* about; ~ **à caution** *a* questionable; ~ **de conversation** topic *ou* subject of conversation; ~ **d'examen** (*SCOL*) examination question; examination paper; ~ **d'expérience** (*BIO etc*) experimental subject.

sujétion [süzhāsyóṅ] *nf* subjection; (*fig*) constraint.

sulfater [sülfátā] *vt* to spray with copper sulphate.

sulfureux, euse [sülfürœ̄, -œ̄z] *a* sulfurous (*US*), sulphurous (*Brit*).

sulfurique [sülfürēk] *a*: **acide** ~ sulfuric (*US*) *ou* sulphuric (*Brit*) acid.

sulfurisé, e [sülfürēzā] *a*: **papier** ~ wax (*US*) *ou* greaseproof (*Brit*) paper.

Sumatra [sümátrá] *nf* Sumatra.

summum [somom] *nm*: **le** ~ **de** the height of.

super [süper] *a inv* great, fantastic ♦ *nm* (= **supercarburant**) ≈ premium (*US*), ≈ 4-star (*Brit*).

superbe [süperb(ə)] *a* magnificent, superb ♦ *nf* arrogance.

superbement [süperbəmàṅ] *ad* superbly.

supercarburant [süperkárbüràṅ] *nm* ≈ premium gas (*US*), ≈ 4-star petrol (*Brit*).

supercherie [süpersharē] *nf* trick, trickery *q*; (*fraude*) fraud.

supérette [süpāret] *nf* minimarket.

superfétatoire [süperfātátwár] *a* superfluous.

superficie [süperfēsē] *nf* (*surface*) area; (*fig*) surface.

superficiel, le [süperfēsyel] *a* superficial.

superficiellement [süperfēsyelmàṅ] *ad* superficially.

superflu, e [süperflü] *a* superfluous ♦ *nm*: **le** ~ the superfluous.

superforme [süperform(ə)] *nf* (*fam*) top form, excellent shape.

super-grand [süpergràṅ] *nm* superpower.

super-huit [süperüēt] *a*: **camera/film** ~ super-eight camera/film.

supérieur, e [süpāryɐr] *a* (*lèvre, étages, classes*) upper; (*plus élevé: température, niveau*): ~ **(à)** higher (than); (*meilleur: qualité, produit*): ~ **(à)** superior (to); (*excellent, hautain*) superior ♦ *nm*, *nf* superior; **Mère** ~e Mother Superior; **à l'étage** ~ on the next floor up; ~ **en nombre** superior in number.

supérieurement [süpāryɐrmàṅ] *ad* exceptionally well, exceptionally + *adj*.

supériorité [süpāryorētā] *nf* superiority.

superlatif [süperlátēf] *nm* superlative.

supermarché [süpermárshā] *nm* supermarket.

superposable [süperpōzábl(ə)] *a* (*figures*) that

may be superimposed; (*lits*) stackable.
superposer [süperpōzā] *vt* to superpose;
(*meubles, caisses*) to stack; (*faire
chevaucher*) to superimpose; **se ~** (*images,
souvenirs*) to be superimposed; **lits
superposés** bunk beds.
superposition [süperpōzēsyôn] *nf* superposition; superimposition.
superpréfet [süperprăfe] *nm* prefect in charge
of a region.
superproduction [süperprodüksyôn] *nf* (*film*)
spectacular.
superpuissance [süperpüēsáns] *nf* superpower.
supersonique [süpersonēk] *a* supersonic.
superstitieux, euse [süperstēsyœ̄, -œ̄z] *a*
superstitious.
superstition [süperstēsyôn] *nf* superstition.
superstructure [süperstrüktür] *nf* superstructure.
supertanker [süpertánkœr] *nm* supertanker.
superviser [süpervēzā] *vt* to supervise.
supervision [süpervēzyôn] *nf* supervision.
supplanter [süplántā] *vt* to supplant.
suppléance [süplāáns] *nf* (*poste*) substitute
teacher's post (*US*), supply post (*Brit*).
suppléant, e [süplāán, -ánt] *a* (*juge,
fonctionnaire*) deputy *cpd*; (*professeur*) substitute *cpd* (*US*), supply *cpd* (*Brit*) ♦ *nm/f*
deputy; substitute *ou* supply teacher;
médecin ~ locum tenens.
suppléer [süplāā] *vt* (*ajouter: mot manquant
etc*) to supply, provide; (*compenser: lacune*)
to fill in; (*: défaut*) to make up for; (*remplacer: professeur*) to stand in for; (*: juge*)
to deputize for; **~ à** *vt* to make up for; to
substitute for.
supplément [süplāmán] *nm* supplement; **un ~
de travail** extra *ou* additional work; **un ~ de
frites** *etc* an extra portion of French fries
etc; **un ~ de 100 F** a supplement of 100 F;
an extra *ou* additional 100 F; **ceci est en ~**
(*au menu etc*) this is extra, there is an extra
charge for this; **~ d'information** additional
information.
supplémentaire [süplāmántėr] *a* additional,
further; (*train, bus*) relief *cpd*, extra.
supplétif, ive [süplātēf, -ēv] *a* (*MIL*) auxiliary.
suppliant, e [süplēyán, -ánt] *a* imploring.
supplication [süplēkásyôn] *nf* (*REL*) supplication; **~s** *nfpl* (*adjurations*) pleas, entreaties.
supplice [süplēs] *nm* (*peine corporelle*) torture
q; form of torture; (*douleur physique, morale*) torture, agony; **être au ~** to be in
agony.
supplier [süplēyā] *vt* to implore, beseech.
supplique [süplēk] *nf* petition.
support [süpor] *nm* support; (*pour livre, outils*) stand; **~ audio-visuel** audio-visual aid;
~ publicitaire advertising medium.
supportable [süportábl(ə)] *a* (*douleur,
température*) bearable; (*procédé, conduite*)
tolerable.
supporter *nm* [süporter] supporter, fan ♦ *vt*
[süportā] (*poids, poussée, SPORT: concurrent,
équipe*) to support; (*conséquences, épreuve*)
to bear, endure; (*défauts, personne*) to tolerate, put up with; (*suj: chose: chaleur etc*) to
withstand; (*suj: personne: chaleur, vin*) to

take.
supposé, e [süpōzā] *a* (*nombre*) estimated;
(*auteur*) supposed.
supposer [süpōzā] *vt* to suppose; (*impliquer*)
to presuppose; **en supposant** *ou* **à ~ que**
supposing (that).
supposition [süpōzēsyôn] *nf* supposition.
suppositoire [süpōzētwár] *nm* suppository.
suppôt [süpō] *nm* (*péj*) henchman.
suppression [süprāsyôn] *nf* (*voir supprimer*)
removal; deletion; cancellation; suppression.
supprimer [süprēmā] *vt* (*cloison, cause,
anxiété*) to remove; (*clause, mot*) to delete;
(*congés, service d'autobus etc*) to cancel;
(*publication, article*) to suppress; (*emplois,
privilèges, témoin gênant*) to do away with;
~ qch à qn to deprive sb of sth.
suppurer [süpürā] *vi* to suppurate.
supputations [süpütásyôn] *nfpl* calculations,
reckonings.
supputer [süpütā] *vt* to calculate, reckon.
supranational, e, aux [süpránásyonál, -ō] *a*
supranational.
suprématie [süprāmásē] *nf* supremacy.
suprême [süprem] *a* supreme.
suprêmement [süpremmán] *ad* supremely.
sur, e [sür] *prép* (*gén*) on; (*par-dessus*) over;
(*au-dessus*) above; (*direction*) towards; (*à
propos de*) about, on; **un ~ 10** one out of 10,
one in 10; (*SCOL*) one out of 10; **4m ~ 2** 4m
by 2; **~ sa recommandation/leur invitation**
on his (*ou* her) recommendation/their invitation; **avoir accident ~ accident** to have
accident after accident; **je n'ai pas d'argent
~ moi** I haven't got any money with *ou* on
me; **~ ce** *ad* hereupon.
sur, e [sür] *a* sour.
sûr, e [sür] *a* sure, certain; (*digne de confiance*) reliable; (*sans danger*) safe; **peu ~**
unreliable; **~ de qch** sure *ou* certain of sth;
être ~ de qn to be sure of sb; **~ et certain**
absolutely certain; **~ de soi** self-assured,
self-confident; **le plus ~ est de** the safest
thing is to.
surabondant, e [sürábôndán, -ánt] *a* over-
abundant.
surabonder [sürábôndā] *vi* to be over-
abundant; **~ de** to abound with, have an
overabundance of.
suractivité [süráktēvētā] *nf* hyperactivity.
suraigu, ë [sürágü] *a* very shrill.
surajouter [süràzhōōtā] *vt*: **~ qch à** to add sth
to.
suralimenté, e [sürálēmántā] *a* (*personne*)
overfed; (*moteur*) turbocharged.
suranné, e [süránā] *a* outdated, outmoded.
surarmement [sürárməmán] *nm* (excess)
stockpiling of arms (*ou* weapons).
surbaissé, e [sürbāsā] *a* lowered, low.
surcharge [sürshárzh(ə)] *nf* (*de passagers,
marchandises*) excess load; (*de détails,
d'ornements*) overabundance, excess;
(*correction*) alteration; (*POSTES*) surcharge;
prendre des passagers en ~ to take on
excess *ou* extra passengers; **~ de bagages**
excess luggage; **~ de travail** extra work.
surchargé, e [sürshárzhā] *a* (*décoration, style*)
over-elaborate, overfussy; (*voiture, emploi du
temps*) overloaded.

surcharger [sürshárzhā] *vt* to overload; (*timbre-poste*) to surcharge; (*décoration*) to overdo.

surchauffe [sürshōf] *nf* overheating.

surchauffé, e [sürshōfā] *a* overheated; (*fig: imagination*) overactive.

surchoix [sürshwá] *a inv* top-quality.

surclasser [sürklásā] *vt* to outclass.

surconsommation [sürkônsomásyôn] *nf* (*ÉCON*) overconsumption.

surcoté, e [sürkotā] *a* overpriced.

surcouper [sürkōōpā] *vt* to overtrump.

surcroît [sürkrwá] *nm*: **un ~ de** additional + *nom*; **par** *ou* **de ~** moreover; **en ~** in addition.

surdi-mutité [sürdēmütētā] *nf*: **atteint de ~** deaf and dumb.

surdité [sürdētā] *nf* deafness; **atteint de ~ totale** profoundly deaf.

surdoué, e [sürdwā] *a* gifted.

sureau, x [sürō] *nm* elder (tree).

sureffectif [süräfektēf] *nm* overmanning.

surélever [sürelvā] *vt* to raise, heighten.

sûrement [sürmán] *ad* reliably; safely, securely; (*certainement*) certainly; **~ pas** certainly not.

suremploi [süránplwá] *nm* (*ÉCON*) overemployment.

surenchère [süránsher] *nf* (*aux enchères*) higher bid; (*sur prix fixe*) overbid; (*fig*) overstatement; outbidding tactics *pl*; **~ de violence** build-up of violence; **~ électorale** political (*ou* electoral) one-upmanship.

surenchérir [süránshārēr] *vi* to bid higher; to raise one's bid; (*fig*) to try and outbid each other.

surent [sür] *vb voir* **savoir**.

suréquipé, e [sürākēpā] *a* overequipped.

surestimer [sürestēmā] *vt* (*tableau*) to overvalue; (*possibilité, personne*) to overestimate.

sûreté [sürtā] *nf* (*voir sûr*) reliability; safety; (*JUR*) guaranty; surety; **mettre en ~** to put in a safe place; **pour plus de ~** as an extra precaution; **to be on the safe side**; **la ~ de l'État** State security; **la S~ (nationale)** *division of the Ministère de l'Intérieur heading all police forces except the gendarmerie and the Paris préfecture de police.*

surexcité, e [süreksētā] *a* overexcited.

surexploiter [süreksplwátā] *vt* to overexploit.

surexposer [sürekspōzā] *vt* to overexpose.

surf [sœrf] *nm* surfing; **faire du ~** to go surfing.

surface [sürfás] *nf* surface; (*superficie*) surface area; **faire ~** to surface; **en ~** *ad* near the surface; (*fig*) superficially; **la pièce fait 100m² de ~** the room has a surface area of 100m²; **~ de réparation** (*SPORT*) penalty area; **~ porteuse** *ou* **de sustentation** (*AVIAT*) airfoil (*US*), aerofoil (*Brit*).

surfait, e [sürfe, -et] *a* overrated.

surfiler [sürfēlā] *vt* (*COUTURE*) to oversew.

surfin, e [sürfañ, -ēn] *a* superfine.

surgélateur [sürzhālátœr] *nm* deep freeze.

surgelé, e [sürzhǝlā] *a* (deep-)frozen.

surgeler [sürzhǝlā] *vt* to (deep-)freeze.

surgir [sürzhēr] *vi* (*personne, véhicule*) to appear suddenly; (*jaillir*) to shoot up;

(*montagne etc*) to rise up, loom up; (*fig: problème, conflit*) to arise.

surhomme [sürom] *nm* superman.

surhumain, e [sürümañ, -en] *a* superhuman.

surimposer [süránpōzā] *vt* to overtax.

surimpression [süránprāsyôn] *nf* (*PHOTO*) double exposure; **en ~** superimposed.

surimprimer [süránprēmā] *vt* to overstrike, overprint.

Surinam [sürēnám] *nm*: **le ~** Surinam.

surinfection [süránfeksyôn] *nf* (*MÉD*) secondary infection.

surjet [sürzhe] *nm* (*COUTURE*) overcast seam.

sur-le-champ [sürlǝshán] *ad* immediately.

surlendemain [sürlándmañ] *nm*: **le ~ (soir)** two days later (in the evening); **le ~ de** two days after.

surligneur [sürlēnyœr] *nm* (*feutre*) highlighter (pen).

surmenage [sürmǝnázh] *nm* overwork; **le ~ intellectuel** mental fatigue.

surmené, e [sürmǝnā] *a* overworked.

surmener [sürmǝnā] *vt*, **se ~** *vi* to overwork.

surmonter [sürmôntā] *vt* (*suj: coupole etc*) to surmount, top; (*vaincre*) to overcome, surmount.

surmultiplié, e [sürmültēplēyā] *a*, *nf*: **(vitesse) ~e** overdrive.

surnager [sürnázhā] *vi* to float.

surnaturel, le [sürnátürel] *a*, *nm* supernatural.

surnom [sürnôn] *nm* nickname.

surnombre [sürnônbr(ǝ)] *nm*: **être en ~** to be too many (*ou* one too many).

surnommer [sürnomā] *vt* to nickname.

surnuméraire [sürnümārer] *nm/f* supernumerary.

suroît [sürwá] *nm* sou'wester.

surpasser [sürpásā] *vt* to surpass; **se ~** to surpass o.s., excel o.s.

surpayer [sürpāyā] *vt* (*personne*) to overpay; (*article etc*) to pay too much for.

surpeuplé, e [sürpœplā] *a* overpopulated.

surpeuplement [sürpœplǝmán] *nm* overpopulation.

surpiquer [sürpēkā] *vt* (*COUTURE*) to topstitch.

surpiqûre [sürpēkür] *nf* (*COUTURE*) topstitching.

surplace [sürplás] *nm*: **faire du ~** to mark time.

surplis [sürplē] *nm* surplice.

surplomb [sürplôn] *nm* overhang; **en ~** overhanging.

surplomber [sürplônbā] *vi* to be overhanging ♦ *vt* to overhang; (*dominer*) to tower above.

surplus [sürplü] *nm* (*COMM*) surplus; (*reste*): **~ de bois** wood left over; **au ~** moreover; **~ américains** American army surplus *sg*.

surpopulation [sürpopülásyôn] *nf* overpopulation.

surprenant, e [sürprǝnáñ, -áñt] *vb voir* **surprendre** ♦ *a* amazing.

surprendre [sürpráñdr(ǝ)] *vt* (*étonner, prendre à l'improviste*) to amaze, surprise; (*secret*) to discover; (*tomber sur: intrus etc*) to catch; (*fig*) to detect; to chance *ou* happen upon; (*clin d'œil*) to intercept; (*conversation*) to overhear; (*suj: orage, nuit etc*) to catch (out (*Brit*)), take by surprise; **~ la**

vigilance/bonne foi de qn to catch sb off guard/betray sb's good faith; **se ~ à faire** to catch *ou* find o.s. doing.

surprime [sürprēm] *nf* additional premium.

surpris, e [sürprē, -ēz] *pp de* **surprendre ♦** *a*: **~ (de/que)** amazed *ou* surprised (at/that).

surprise [sürprēz] *nf* surprise; **faire une ~ à qn** to give sb a surprise; **voyage sans ~s** uneventful journey; **par ~** *ad* by surprise.

surprise-partie [sürprēzpàrtē] *nf* party.

surprit [sürprē] *vb voir* **surprendre.**

surproduction [sürprodüksyôň] *nf* overproduction.

surréaliste [sürrāàlēst(ə)] *a, nm/f* surrealist.

sursaut [sürsō] *nm* start, jump; **~ de** (*énergie, indignation*) sudden fit *ou* burst of; **en ~** *ad* with a start.

sursauter [sürsōtā] *vi* to (give a) start, jump.

surseoir [sürswàr]: **~ à** *vt* to defer; (*JUR*) to stay.

sursis [sürsē] *nm* (*JUR*: *gén*) suspended sentence; (*à l'exécution capitale, aussi fig*) reprieve; (*MIL*): **~ (d'appel *ou* d'incorporation)** deferment; **condamné à 5 mois (de prison) avec ~** given a 5-month suspended (prison) sentence.

sursitaire [sürsēter] *nm* (*MIL*) deferred draftee.

sursois [sürswà], **sursoyais** [sürswàyā] *etc vb voir* **surseoir.**

surtaxe [sürtàks(ə)] *nf* surcharge.

surtout [sürtōō] *ad* (*avant tout, d'abord*) above all; (*spécialement, particulièrement*) especially; **il aime le sport, ~ le football** he likes sports, especially football; **cet été, il a ~ fait de la pêche** this summer he went fishing more than anything (else); **~ pas d'histoires!** no fuss now!; **~, ne dites rien!** whatever you do - don't say anything!; **~ pas!** certainly *ou* definitely not!; **~ que ...** especially as ....

survécu, e [sürvākü] *pp de* **survivre.**

surveillance [sürveyàňs] *nf* watch; (*POLICE, MIL*) surveillance; **sous ~ médicale** under medical supervision; **la ~ du territoire** internal security; *voir aussi* **DST.**

surveillant, e [sürveyàň, -àňt] *nm/f* (*de prison*) guard, warder (*Brit*); (*SCOL*) monitor; (*de travaux*) supervisor, overseer.

surveiller [sürvāyā] *vt* (*enfant, élèves, bagages*) to watch, keep an eye on; (*malade*) to watch over; (*prisonnier, suspect*) to keep (a) watch on; (*territoire, bâtiment*) to (keep) watch over; (*travaux, cuisson*) to supervise; (*SCOL*: *examen*) to proctor (*US*), invigilate (*Brit*); **se ~** to keep a check *ou* watch on o.s.; **~ son langage/sa ligne** to watch one's language/figure.

survenir [sürvənēr] *vi* (*incident, retards*) to occur, arise; (*événement*) to take place; (*personne*) to appear, arrive.

survenu, e [sürv(ə)nü] *pp de* **survenir.**

survêt(ement) [sürvet(màň)] *nm* sweat suit (*US*), tracksuit (*Brit*).

survie [sürvē] *nf* survival; (*REL*) afterlife; **équipement de ~** survival equipment; **une ~ de quelques mois** a few more months of life.

surviens [sürvyàň], **survint** [sürvàň] *etc vb voir*

survenir.

survit [sōōrvē] *etc vb voir* **survivre.**

survitrage [sürvētràzh] *nm* insulating (window) (*US*), double-glazing (*Brit*).

survivance [sürvēvàňs] *nf* relic.

survivant, e [sürvēvàň, -àňt] *vb voir* **survivre ♦** *nm/f* survivor.

survivre [sürvēvr(ə)] *vi* to survive; **~ à** *vt* (*accident etc*) to survive; (*personne*) to outlive; **la victime a peu de chance de ~** the victim has little hope of survival.

survol [sürvol] *nm* flying over.

survoler [sürvolā] *vt* to fly over; (*fig: livre*) to skim through; (*: question, problèmes*) to skim over.

survolté, e [sürvoltā] *a* (*ÉLEC*) stepped up, boosted; (*fig*) worked up.

sus [sü(s)]: **en ~ de** *prép* in addition to, over and above; **en ~** *ad* in addition; **~ à** *excl*: **~ au tyran!** at the tyrant! **♦** *vb* [sü] *voir* **savoir.**

susceptibilité [süseptēbēlētā] *nf* sensitivity *q*.

susceptible [süseptēbl(ə)] *a* touchy, sensitive; **~ d'amélioration** *ou* **d'être amélioré** that can be improved, open to improvement; **~ de faire** (*capacité*) able to do; (*probabilité*) liable to do.

susciter [süsētā] *vt* (*admiration*) to arouse; (*obstacles, ennuis*): **~ (à qn)** to create (for sb).

susdit, e [süsdē, -dēt] *a* aforesaid.

susmentionné, e [süsmàňsyonā] *a* above-mentioned.

susnommé, e [süsnomā] *a* above-named.

suspect, e [süspe(kt), -ekt(ə)] *a* suspicious; (*témoignage, opinions, vin etc*) suspect **♦** *nm/f* suspect; **peu ~ de** most unlikely to be suspected of.

suspecter [süspektā] *vt* to suspect; (*honnêteté de qn*) to question, have one's suspicions about; **~ qn d'être/d'avoir fait qch** to suspect sb of being/having done sth.

suspendre [süspàňdr(ə)] *vt* (*accrocher: vêtement*): **~ qch (à)** to hang sth up (on); (*fixer: lustre etc*): **~ qch à** to hang sth from; (*interrompre, démettre*) to suspend; (*remettre*) to defer; **se ~ à** to hang from.

suspendu, e [süspàňdü] *pp de* **suspendre ♦** *a* (*accroché*): **~ à** hanging on (*ou* from); (*perché*): **~ au-dessus de** suspended over; (*AUTO*): **bien/mal ~** with good/poor suspension; **être ~ aux lèvres de qn** to hang upon sb's every word.

suspens [süspàň]: **en ~** *ad* (*affaire*) in abeyance; **tenir en ~** to keep in suspense.

suspense [süspàňs] *nm* suspense.

suspension [süspàňsyôň] *nf* suspension; deferment; (*AUTO*) suspension; (*lustre*) pendant lamp; **en ~** in suspension, suspended; **~ d'audience** adjournment.

suspicieux, euse [süspēsyœ, -œz] *a* suspicious.

suspicion [süspēsyôň] *nf* suspicion.

sustenter [süstàňtā]: **se ~** *vi* to take sustenance.

susurrer [süsürā] *vt* to whisper.

sut [sü] *vb voir* **savoir.**

suture [sütür] *nf*: **point de ~** stitch.

suturer [sütürā] *vt* to stitch up, suture.

suzeraineté [süzrentā] *nf* suzerainty.

svelte [svelt(ə)] *a* slender, svelte.

SVP *sigle* (= *s'il vous plaît*) please.

Swaziland [swázēlând] *nm*: **le** ~ Swaziland.

syllabe [sēláb] *nf* syllable.

syllaber [sēlábā] *vi* to pronounce syllable by syllable.

sylvestre [sēlvestr(ə)] *a*: **pin** ~ Scots pine, Scotch fir.

sylvicole [sēlvēkol] *a* forestry *cpd*.

sylviculteur [sēlvēkültœr] *nm* forester.

sylviculture [sēlvēkültür] *nf* forestry, silviculture.

symbole [sanbol] *nm* symbol; ~ **graphique** (*INFORM*) icon.

symbolique [sanbolēk] *a* symbolic; (*geste, offrande*) token *cpd*; (*salaire, dommages-intérêts*) nominal.

symboliquement [sanbolēkmân] *ad* symbolically.

symboliser [sanbolēzā] *vt* to symbolize.

symétrie [sēmātrē] *nf* symmetry.

symétrique [sēmātrēk] *a* symmetrical.

symétriquement [sēmātrēkmân] *ad* symmetrically.

sympa [sanpá] *a inv* (= *sympathique*) nice; friendly; good.

sympathie [sanpátē] *nf* (*inclination*) liking; (*affinité*) fellow feeling; (*condoléances*) sympathy; **accueillir avec** ~ (*projet*) to receive favorably; **avoir de la** ~ **pour qn** to like sb, have a liking for sb; **témoignages de** ~ expressions of sympathy; **croyez à toute ma** ~ you have my deepest sympathy.

sympathique [sanpátēk] *a* (*personne, figure*) nice, friendly, likeable; (*geste*) friendly; (*livre*) good; (*déjeuner*) nice; (*réunion, endroit*) pleasant, nice.

sympathisant, e [sanpátēzân, -ânt] *nm/f* sympathizer.

sympathiser [sanpátēzā] *vi* (*voisins etc: s'entendre*) to get along (well); (*: se fréquenter*) to socialize, see each other; ~ **avec** to get on *ou* along (well) with; to see, socialize with.

symphonie [sanfonē] *nf* symphony.

symphonique [sanfonēk] *a* (*orchestre, concert*) symphony *cpd*; (*musique*) symphonic.

symposium [sanpōzyom] *nm* symposium.

symptomatique [sanptomátēk] *a* symptomatic.

symptôme [sanptōm] *nm* symptom.

synagogue [sēnágog] *nf* synagogue.

synchrone [sankron] *a* synchronous.

synchronique [sankronēk] *a*: **tableau** ~ synchronic table of events.

synchronisation [sankronēzâsyōn] *nf* synchronization.

synchronisé, e [sankronēzā] *a* synchronized.

synchroniser [sankronēzā] *vt* to synchronize.

syncope [sankop] *nf* (*MÉD*) blackout; (*MUS*) syncopation; **tomber en** ~ to faint, pass out.

syncopé, e [sankopā] *a* syncopated.

syndic [sandēk] *nm* managing agent.

syndical, e, aux [sandēkál, -ō] *a* (labor) union *cpd* (*US*), (trade-)union *cpd* (*Brit*); **centrale** ~e group of affiliated labor unions.

syndicalisme [sandēkálēsm(ə)] *nm* (*mouvement*) labor *ou* trade (*Brit*) unionism; (*activités*) union(ist) activities *pl*.

syndicaliste [sandēkálēst(ə)] *nm/f* labor (*US*)

ou trade (*Brit*) unionist.

syndicat [sandēká] *nm* (*d'ouvriers, employés*) (labor (*US*) *ou* trade(s) (*Brit*)) union; (*autre association d'intérêts*) union, association; ~ **d'initiative (SI)** tourist office *ou* bureau; ~ **patronal** employers' association, federation of employers; ~ **de propriétaires** association of property owners.

syndiqué, e [sandēkā] *a* belonging to a union; **non** ~ non-union.

syndiquer [sandēkā]: **se** ~ *vi* to form a labor (*US*) *ou* trade (*Brit*) union; (*adhérer*) to join a labor *ou* trade union.

syndrome [sandrōm] *nm* syndrome; ~ **prémenstruel** premenstrual syndrome (PMS).

synergie [sēnerzhē] *nf* synergy.

synode [sēnod] *nm* synod.

synonyme [sēnonēm] *a* synonymous ♦ *nm* synonym; ~ **de** synonymous with.

synopsis [sēnopsēs] *nm ou nf* synopsis.

synoptique [sēnoptēk] *a*: **tableau** ~ synoptic table.

synovie [sēnovē] *nf* synovia; **épanchement de** ~ water on the knee.

syntaxe [santáks(ə)] *nf* syntax.

synthèse [santez] *nf* synthesis (*pl* -es); **faire la** ~ **de** to synthesize.

synthétique [santātēk] *a* synthetic.

synthétiser [santātēzā] *vt* to synthesize.

synthétiseur [santātēzœr] *nm* (*MUS*) synthesizer.

syphilis [sēfēlēs] *nf* syphilis.

Syrie [sērē] *nf*: **la** ~ Syria.

syrien, ne [sēryan, -en] *a* Syrian ♦ *nm/f*: **S**~, **ne** Syrian.

systématique [sēstāmátēk] *a* systematic.

systématiquement [sēstāmátēkmân] *ad* systematically.

systématiser [sēstāmátēzā] *vt* to systematize.

système [sēstem] *nm* system; **le** ~ **D** resourcefulness; ~ **décimal** decimal system; ~ **expert** expert system; ~ **d'exploitation à disques** (*INFORM*) disk operating system; ~ **métrique** metric system; ~ **solaire** solar system.

T

T, t [tā] *nm inv* T, t ♦ *abr* (= *tonne*) t; **T comme Thérèse** T for Tommy.

t' [t(ə)] *pronom voir* **te**.

ta [tá] *dét voir* **ton**.

tabac [tábá] *nm* tobacco; (*aussi*: **débit** *ou* **bureau de** ~) tobacco shop (*US*), tobacconist's (shop) (*Brit*) ♦ *a inv*: (**couleur**) ~ buff, tobacco *cpd*; **passer qn à** ~ to beat sb up; **faire un** ~ (*fam*) to be a big hit; ~ **blond/brun** light/dark tobacco; ~ **gris** shag; ~ **à priser** snuff.

tabagie [tábázhē] *nf* smoke den.

tabagisme [tábázhēsm(ə)] *nm* nicotine addiction.

tabasser [tåbásā] *vt* to beat up.
tabatière [tåbátyer] *nf* snuffbox.
tabernacle [tåbernákl(ə)] *nm* tabernacle.
table [tåbl(ə)] *nf* table; **avoir une bonne ~** to keep a good table; **à ~!** dinner *etc* is ready!; **se mettre à ~** to sit down to eat; (*fig: fam*) to come clean; **mettre** *ou* **dresser/desservir la ~** to lay *ou* set/clear the table; **faire ~ rase de** to make a clean sweep of; **~ basse** coffee table; **~ de cuisson** (*à l'électricité*) hotplate; (*au gas*) gas burner; **~ d'écoute** wire-tapping set; **~ d'harmonie** sounding board; **~ d'hôte** set menu; **~ de lecture** turntable; **~ des matières** (table of) contents *pl*; **~ de multiplication** multiplication table; **~ de nuit** *ou* **de chevet** bedside table; **~ ronde** (*débat*) round table; **~ roulante** serving cart (*US*), (tea) trolley (*Brit*); **~ de toilette** washstand; **~ traçante** (*INFORM*) plotter.
tableau, x [tåblō] *nm* (*ART*) painting; (*reproduction, fig*) picture; (*panneau*) board; (*schéma*) table, chart; **~ d'affichage** bulletin board; **~ de bord** dashboard; (*AVIAT*) instrument panel; **~ de chasse** tally; **~ de contrôle** console, control panel; **~ de maître** masterpiece; **~ noir** blackboard.
tablée [tåblā] *nf* (*personnes*) table.
tabler [tåblā] *vi*: **~ sur** to count *ou* bank on.
tablette [tåblet] *nf* (*planche*) shelf (*pl* shelves); **~ de chocolat** bar of chocolate.
tableur [tåblœr] *nm* (*INFORM*) spreadsheet.
tablier [tåblēyā] *nm* apron; (*de pont*) roadway; (*de cheminée*) (flue-)shutter.
tabou, e [tåbōō] *a*, *nm* taboo.
tabouret [tåbōōre] *nm* stool.
tabulateur [tåbülátœr] *nm* (*TECH*) tabulator.
TAC *sigle m* (= *train-auto-couchettes*) car-sleeper train.
tac [tåk] *nm*: **du ~ au ~** tit for tat.
tache [tåsh] *nf* (*saleté*) stain, mark; (*ART, de couleur, lumière*) spot; splash, patch; **faire ~ d'huile** to spread, gain ground; **~ de rousseur** *ou* **de son** freckle; **~ de vin** (*sur la peau*) strawberry mark.
tâche [tåsh] *nf* task; **travailler à la ~** to do piecework.
tacher [tåshā] *vt* to stain, mark; (*fig*) to sully, stain; **se ~** *vi* (*fruits*) to become marked.
tâcher [tåshā] *vi*: **~ de faire** to try to do, endeavor (*US*) *ou* endeavour (*Brit*) to do.
tâcheron [tåshrôn] *nm* (*fig*) drudge.
tacheté, e [tåshtā] *a*: **~ de** speckled *ou* spotted with.
tachisme [tåshēsm(ə)] *nm* (*PEINTURE*) tachisme.
tachygraphe [tåkēgráf] *nm* tachograph.
tachymètre [tåkēmetr(ə)] *nm* tachometer.
tacite [tåsēt] *a* tacit.
tacitement [tåsētmán] *ad* tacitly.
taciturne [tåsētürn(ə)] *a* taciturn.
tacot [tåkō] *nm* (*péj: voiture*) clunker (*US*), banger (*Brit*).
tact [tåkt] *nm* tact; **avoir du ~** to be tactful, have tact.
tacticien, ne [tåktēsyań, -en] *nm/f* tactician.
tactile [tåktēl] *a* tactile.
tactique [tåktēk] *a* tactical ♦ *nf* (*technique*) tactics *sg*; (*plan*) tactic.

taffetas [tåftá] *nm* taffeta.
Tage [tåzh] *nm*: **le ~** the (river) Tagus.
Tahiti [tåētē] *nf* Tahiti.
tahitien, ne [tåētsyań, -en] *a* Tahitian.
taie [te] *nf*: **~ (d'oreiller)** pillowslip, pillowcase.
taillader [tåyádā] *vt* to gash.
taille [tåy] *nf* cutting; pruning; (*milieu du corps*) waist; (*hauteur*) height; (*grandeur*) size; **de ~ à faire** capable of doing; **de ~ à** sizeable; **quelle ~ faites-vous?** what size are you?
taillé, e [tåyā] *a* (*moustache, ongles, arbre*) trimmed; **~ pour** (*fait pour, apte à*) cut out for; tailor-made for; **~ en pointe** sharpened to a point.
taille-crayon(s) [tåykreyôn] *nm inv* pencil sharpener.
tailler [tåyā] *vt* (*pierre, diamant*) to cut; (*arbre, plante*) to prune; (*vêtement*) to cut out; (*crayon*) to sharpen; **se ~** *vt* (*ongles, barbe*) to trim, cut; (*fig: réputation*) to gain, win ♦ *vi* (*fam: s'enfuir*) to beat it; **~ dans** (*chair, bois*) to cut into; **~ grand/petit** to be on the large/small side.
tailleur [tåyœr] *nm* (*couturier*) tailor; (*vêtement*) suit, costume; **en ~** (*assis*) cross-legged; **~ de diamants** diamond-cutter.
tailleur-pantalon [tåyœrpâńtálôn] *nm* pant(s) (*US*) *ou* trouser (*Brit*) suit.
taillis [tåye] *nm* copse.
tain [tań] *nm* silvering; **glace sans ~** two-way mirror.
taire [ter] *vt* to keep to o.s., conceal ♦ *vi*: **faire ~ qn** to make sb be quiet; (*fig*) to silence sb; **se ~** *vi* (*s'arrêter de parler*) to fall silent, stop talking; (*ne pas parler*) to be silent *ou* quiet; (*s'abstenir de s'exprimer*) to keep quiet; (*bruit, voix*) to disappear; **tais-toi!, taisez-vous!** be quiet!
Taiwan [tåywàn] *nf* Taiwan.
talc [tålk] *nm* talc, talcum powder.
talé, e [tålā] *a* (*fruit*) bruised.
talent [tålåń] *nm* talent; **avoir du ~** to be talented, have talent.
talentueux, euse [tålántüœ, -œz] *a* talented.
talion [tålyôń] *nm*: **la loi du ~** an eye for an eye.
talisman [tålēsmáń] *nm* talisman.
talkie-walkie [tokēwokē] *nm* walkie-talkie.
taloche [tålosh] *nf* (*fam: claque*) slap; (*TECH*) plaster float.
talon [tålôń] *nm* heel; (*de chèque, billet*) stub; **~s plats/aiguilles** flat/stiletto heels; **être sur les ~s de qn** to be on sb's heels; **tourner les ~s** to turn on one's heel; **montrer les ~s** (*fig*) to show a clean pair of heels.
talonner [tålonā] *vt* to follow hard behind; (*fig*) to hound; (*RUGBY*) to heel.
talonnette [tålonet] *nf* (*de chaussure*) heel-piece; (*de pantalon*) stirrup.
talquer [tålkā] *vt* to put talc(um powder) on.
talus [tålü] *nm* embankment; **~ de remblai/déblai** embankment/excavation slope.
tamarin [tåmáráń] *nm* (*BOT*) tamarind.
tambour [tåńbōōr] *nm* (*MUS, aussi TECH*) drum; (*musicien*) drummer; (*porte*) revolving door(s *pl*); **sans ~ ni trompette** unobtrusively.

tambourin [tânbŏŏrań] *nm* tambourine.
tambouriner [tânbŏŏrēnā] *vi*: ~ **contre** to drum against *ou* on.
tambour-major, *pl* **tambours-majors** [tânbŏŏrmázhor] *nm* drum major.
tamis [támē] *nm* sieve.
Tamise [támēz] *nf*: **la** ~ the Thames.
tamisé, e [támēzā] *a* (*fig*) subdued, soft.
tamiser [támēzā] *vt* to sieve, sift.
tampon [tânpôn] *nm* (*de coton, d'ouate*) pad; (*aussi*: ~ **hygiénique** *ou* **périodique**) tampon; (*amortisseur*, *INFORM*: *aussi*: **mémoire** ~) buffer; (*bouchon*) plug, stopper; (*cachet, timbre*) stamp; (*CHIMIE*) buffer; ~ **buvard** blotter; ~ **encreur** inking pad; ~ (**à récurer**) scouring pad.
tamponné, e [tânponā] *a*: **solution** ~**e** buffer solution.
tamponner [tânponā] *vt* (*timbres*) to stamp; (*heurter*) to crash *ou* ram into; (*essuyer*) to mop up; **se** ~ (*voitures*) to crash (into each other).
tamponneuse [tânponœz] *af*: **autos** ~**s** dodgems, bumper cars.
tam-tam [támtám] *nm* tomtom.
tancer [tânsā] *vt* to scold.
tanche [tânsh] *nf* tench.
tandem [tândɛm] *nm* tandem; (*fig*) duo, pair.
tandis [tâńdɛ̃]: ~ **que** *cj* while.
tangage [tâńgázh] *nm* pitching (and tossing).
tangent, e [tâńzhâń, -âńt] *a* (*MATH*): ~ **à** tangential to; (*fam: de justesse*) close ♦ *nf* (*MATH*) tangent.
Tanger [tâńzhā] *n* Tangier.
tangible [tâńzhēbl(ə)] *a* tangible, concrete.
tango [tâńgō] *nm* (*MUS*) tango ♦ *a inv* (*couleur*) bright orange.
tanguer [tâńgā] *vi* to pitch (and toss).
tanière [tányer] *nf* lair, den.
tanin [tânań] *nm* tannin.
tank [tâńk] *nm* tank.
tanker [tâńker] *nm* tanker.
tanné, e [tânā] *a* a weather-beaten.
tanner [tânā] *vt* to tan.
tannerie [tânrē] *nf* tannery.
tanneur [tânœr] *nm* tanner.
tant [tâń] *ad* so much; ~ **de** (*sable, eau*) so much; (*gens, livres*) so many; ~ **que** *cj* as long as; ~ **que** (*comparatif*) as much as; ~ **mieux** that's great; so much the better; ~ **mieux pour lui** good for him; ~ **pis** too bad; **un** ~ **soit peu** (*un peu*) a little bit; (*même un peu*) (even) remotely; ~ **bien que mal** as well as can be expected; ~ **s'en faut** far from it, not by a long way.
tante [tâńt] *nf* aunt.
tantinet [tâńtēne]: **un** ~ *ad* a tiny bit.
tantôt [tâńtō] *ad* (*parfois*): ~ ... ~ now ... now; (*cet après-midi*) this afternoon.
Tanzanie [tâńzánē] *nf*: **la** ~ Tanzania.
tanzanien, ne [tâńzányań, -en] *a* Tanzanian.
TAO *sigle f* (= *traduction assistée par ordinateur*) MAT (= *machine-aided translation*).
taon [tâń] *nm* horsefly, gadfly.
tapage [tápázh] *nm* uproar, din; (*fig*) fuss, row; ~ **nocturne** (*JUR*) disturbance of the peace (*at night*).
tapageur, euse [tápázhœr, -œz] *a* (*bruyant*:

enfants etc) noisy; (*toilette*) loud, flashy; (*publicité*) obtrusive.
tape [táp] *nf* slap.
tape-à-l'œil [tápálœy] *a inv* flashy, showy.
taper [tápā] *vt* (*personne*) to clout; (*porte*) to bang, slam; (*dactylographier*) to type (out); (*INFORM*) to key(board); (*fam: emprunter*): ~ **qn de 10 F** to touch sb for 10 F, cadge 10 F off sb ♦ *vi* (*soleil*) to beat down; **se** ~ *vt* (*fam: travail*) to get landed with; (*: boire, manger*) to down; ~ **sur qn** to thump sb; (*fig*) to run sb down; ~ **sur qch** (*clou etc*) to hit sth; (*table etc*) to bang on sth; ~ **à** (*porte etc*) to knock on; ~ **dans** (*se servir*) to dig into; ~ **des mains/pieds** to clap one's hands/ stamp one's feet; ~ (**à la machine**) to type.
tapi, e [tápē] *a*: ~ **dans/derrière** (*blotti*) crouching *ou* cowering in/behind; (*caché*) hidden away in/behind.
tapinois [tápēnwá]: **en** ~ *ad* stealthily.
tapioca [tápyoká] *nm* tapioca.
tapir [tápēr]: **se** ~ *vi* to hide away.
tapis [tápē] *nm* carpet; (*de table*) cloth; **mettre sur le** ~ (*fig*) to bring up for discussion; **aller au** ~ (*BOXE*) to go down; **envoyer au** ~ (*BOXE*) to floor; ~ **roulant** conveyor belt; ~ **de sol** (*de tente*) groundsheet.
tapis-brosse [tápēbros] *nm* doormat.
tapisser [tápēsā] *vt* (*avec du papier peint*) to paper; (*recouvrir*): ~ **qch (de)** to cover sth (with).
tapisserie [tápēsrē] *nf* (*tenture, broderie*) tapestry; (*: travail*) tapestry-making; (*: ouvrage*) tapestry work; (*papier peint*) wallpaper; (*fig*): **faire** ~ to sit out, be a wallflower.
tapissier, ière [tápēsyā, -yer] *nm/f*: ~(**-décorateur**) upholsterer (and decorator).
tapoter [tápotā] *vt* to pat, tap.
taquet [táke] *nm* (*cale*) wedge; (*cheville*) peg.
taquin, e [tákań, -ēn] *a* teasing.
taquiner [tákēnā] *vt* to tease.
taquinerie [tákēnrē] *nf* teasing *q*.
tarabiscoté, e [tárábēskotā] *a* over-ornate, fussy.
tarabuster [tárábüstā] *vt* to bother, worry.
tarama [tárámá] *nm* (*CULIN*) taramasalata.
tarauder [tárōdā] *vt* (*TECH*) to tap; to thread; (*fig*) to pierce.
tard [tár] *ad* late; **au plus** ~ at the latest; **plus** ~ later (on) ♦ *nm*: **sur le** ~ (*à une heure avancée*) late in the day; (*vers la fin de la vie*) late in life.
tarder [tárdā] *vi* (*chose*) to be a long time coming; (*personne*): ~ **à faire** to delay doing; **il me tarde d'être** I am longing to be; **sans (plus)** ~ without (further) delay.
tardif, ive [tárdēf, -ēv] *a* (*heure, repas, fruit*) late; (*talent, goût*) late in developing.
tardivement [tárdēvmâń] *ad* late.
tare [tár] *nf* (*COMM*) tare; (*fig*) defect; taint, blemish.
targette [tárzhet] *nf* (*verrou*) bolt.
targuer [tárgā]: **se** ~ **de** *vt* to boast about.
tarif [tárēf] *nm* (*liste*) price list; (*barème*) rate, rates *pl*; (*: de taxis etc*) fares *pl*; **voyager à plein** ~/**à** ~ **réduit** to travel at full/reduced fare.
tarifaire [tárēfer] *a* (*voir tarif*) relating to

price lists *etc.*

tarifé, e [tárēfā] *a*: ~ **10 F** priced at 10 F.

tarifer [tárēfā] *vt* to fix the price *ou* rate for.

tarir [tárēr] *vi* to dry up, run dry ♦ *vt* to dry up.

tarot(s) [tárō] *nm (pl)* tarot cards.

tartare [tártár] *a (CULIN)* tartar(e).

tarte [tárt(ə)] *nf* tart; ~ **aux pommes/à la crème** apple/custard tart.

tartelette [tártəlet] *nf* tartlet.

tartine [tártēn] *nf* slice of bread (and butter (*ou* jam)); ~ **de miel** slice of bread and honey; ~ **beurrée** slice of bread and butter.

tartiner [tártēnā] *vt* to spread; **fromage à** ~ cheese spread.

tartre [tártr(ə)] *nm (des dents)* tartar; *(de chaudière)* fur, scale.

tas [tâ] *nm* heap, pile; *(fig)*: **un** ~ **de** heaps of, lots of; **en** ~ in a heap *ou* pile; **dans le** ~ *(fig)* in the crowd; among them; **formé sur le** ~ trained on the job.

Tasmanie [tàsmánē] *nf*: **la** ~ Tasmania.

tasmanien, ne [tàsmányań, -en] *a* Tasmanian.

tasse [tâs] *nf* cup; **boire la** ~ *(en se baignant)* to swallow a mouthful; ~ **à café/thé** coffee/teacup.

tassé, e [tâsā] *a*: **bien** ~ *(café etc)* strong.

tasseau, x [tàsō] *nm* length of wood.

tassement [tásmáń] *nm (de vertèbres)* compression; *(ÉCON, POL): ralentissement)* fall-off, slowdown; *(BOURSE)* dullness.

tasser [tâsā] *vt (terre, neige)* to pack down; *(entasser)*: ~ **qch dans** to cram sth into; *(INFORM)* to pack; **se** ~ *vi (terrain)* to settle; *(personne: avec l'âge)* to shrink; *(fig)* to sort itself out, settle down.

tâter [tâtā] *vt* to feel; *(fig)* to sound out; ~ **de** *(prison etc)* to have a taste of; **se** ~ *(hésiter)* to be of *(US)* ou in *(Brit)* two minds; ~ **le terrain** *(fig)* to test the ground.

tatillon, ne [tátēyóń, -on] *a* pernickety.

tâtonnement [tátonmáń] *nm*: **par ~s** *(fig)* by trial and error.

tâtonner [tátonā] *vi* to grope one's way along; *(fig)* to grope around (in the dark).

tâtons [tátóń]: **à** ~ *ad*: **chercher/avancer à** ~ to grope around for/grope one's way forward.

tatouage [tàtwázh] *nm* tattooing; *(dessin)* tattoo.

tatouer [tàtwā] *vt* to tattoo.

taudis [tōdē] *nm* hovel, slum.

taule [tōl] *nf (fam)* jail.

taupe [tōp] *nf* mole; *(peau)* moleskin.

taupinière [tōpēnyer] *nf* molehill.

taureau, x [torō] *nm* bull; *(signe)*: **le T~** Taurus, the Bull; **être du T~** to be Taurus.

taurillon [torēyóń] *nm* bull-calf.

tauromachie [toromáshē] *nf* bullfighting.

taux [tō] *nm* rate; *(d'alcool)* level; ~ **d'escompte** discount rate; ~ **d'intérêt** interest rate; ~ **de mortalité** mortality rate.

tavelé, e [távlā] *a* marked.

taverne [tàvern(ə)] *nf* inn, tavern.

taxable [táksábl(ə)] *a* taxable.

taxation [táksásyóń] *nf* taxation; *(TÉL)* charges *pl*.

taxe [táks(ə)] *nf* tax; *(douanière)* duty; **toutes ~s comprises (TTC)** inclusive of tax; ~ **de base** *(TÉL)* unit charge; ~ **de séjour** tourist

tax; ~ **à** *ou* **sur la valeur ajoutée (TVA)** value added tax (VAT).

taxer [táksā] *vt (personne)* to tax; *(produit)* to put a tax on, tax; *(fig)*: ~ **qn de** *(qualifier de)* to call sb + *attribut*; *(accuser de)* to accuse sb of, tax sb with.

taxi [táksē] *nm* taxi.

taxidermie [táksēdermē] *nf* taxidermy.

taximètre [táksēmetr(ə)] *nm* (taxi)meter.

taxiphone [táksēfon] *nm* pay phone.

tb *abr* (= *très bien,* = *très bon*) VG.

tbe *abr* (= *très bon état*) VGC, vgc.

TCA *sigle f* (= *taxe sur le chiffre d'affaires*) tax on turnover.

TCF *sigle m* (= *Touring Club de France*) ≈ AAA (*US*), ≈ AA *ou* RAC (*Brit*).

Tchad [tshád] *nm*: **le** ~ Chad.

tchadien, ne [tshádyań, -en] *a* Chad(ian), of *ou* from Chad.

tchao [tshâō] *excl (fam)* bye(-bye)!

tchécoslovaque [tshākoslovák] *a* Czechoslovak(ian) ♦ *nm/f*: **T~** Czechoslovak(ian).

Tchécoslovaquie [tshākoslovákē] *nf*: **la** ~ Czechoslovakia.

tchèque [tshek] *a* Czech ♦ *nm (LING)* Czech ♦ *nm/f*: **T~** Czech.

TCS *sigle m* (= *Touring Club de Suisse*) ≈ AAA (*US*), ≈ AA *ou* RAC (*Brit*).

TD *sigle mpl* = **travaux dirigés.**

TDF *sigle f* (= *Télévision de France*) French broadcasting authority.

te, t' [t(ə)] *pronom* you; *(réfléchi)* yourself.

té [tā] *nm* T-square.

technicien, ne [teknēsyań, -en] *nm/f* technician.

technicité [teknēsētā] *nf* technical nature.

technique [teknēk] *a* technical ♦ *nf* technique.

techniquement [teknēkmáń] *ad* technically.

technocrate [teknokrát] *nm/f* technocrat.

technocratie [teknokrásē] *nf* technocracy.

technologie [teknolozhē] *nf* technology.

technologique [teknolozhēk] *a* technological.

technologue [teknolog] *nm/f* technologist.

teck [tek] *nm* teak.

teckel [tākel] *nm* dachshund.

TEE *sigle m* = *Trans-Europ-Express.*

tee-shirt [tēshœrt] *nm* T-shirt, tee-shirt.

Téhéran [tāáráń] *n* Teheran.

teigne [teny] *vb voir* **teindre** ♦ *nf (ZOOL)* moth; *(MÉD)* ringworm.

teigneux, euse [tenyœ, -œz] *a (péj)* nasty, scabby.

teindre [tańdr(ə)] *vt* to dye; **se** ~ **(les cheveux)** to dye one's hair.

teint, e [tań, tańt] *pp de* **teindre** ♦ *a* dyed ♦ *nm (du visage: permanent)* complexion, coloring (*US*), colouring (*Brit*); *(momentané)* color (*US*), colour (*Brit*) ♦ *nf* shade, color, colour; *(fig: petite dose)*: **une ~e de** a hint of; **grand** ~ *a inv* colorfast (*US*), colourfast (*Brit*); **bon** ~ *a inv (couleur)* fast; *(tissu)* colorfast (*US*), colourfast (*Brit*); *(personne)* staunch, firm.

teinté, e [tańtā] *a (verres)* tinted; *(bois)* stained; ~ **acajou** mahogany-stained; ~ **de** *(fig)* tinged with.

teinter [tańtā] *vt* to tint; *(bois)* to stain; *(fig: d'ironie etc)* to tinge.

teinture [tańtür] *nf* dyeing; *(substance)* dye;

(*MÉD*): ~ **d'iode** tincture of iodine.
teinturerie [taǹtürrē] *nf* dry cleaner's.
teinturier, ière [taǹtüryā, -ycr] *nm/f* dry cleaner.
tel, telle [tcl] *a* (*pareil*) such; (*comme*): ~ **un/des** ... like a/like ...; (*indéfini*) such-and-such a, a given; (*intensif*): **un ~/de ~s** ... such (a)/such ...; **rien de** ~ nothing like it, no such thing; ~ **que** *cj* like, such as; ~ **quel** as it is *ou* stands (*ou* was *etc*).
tél. *abr* = *téléphone*.
Tel Aviv [tclávēv] *n* Tel Aviv.
télé [tālā] *nf* (= *télévision*) TV; **à la** ~ on TV *ou* telly.
télébenne [tālābcn] *nm*, *nf* cable car, gondola.
télécabine [tālākábēn] *nm*, *nf* cable car, gondola.
télécarte [tālākárt(ə)] *nf* phonecard.
télécharger [tālāshárzhā] *vt* (*INFORM*) to download.
télécommande [tālākomáǹd] *nf* remote control.
télécommander [tālākomáǹdā] *vt* to operate by remote control, radio-control.
télécommunications [tālākomünēkásyóǹ] *nfpl* telecommunications.
télécopie [tālākopē] *nf* fax, telefax.
télécopieur [tālākopycœr] *nm* fax (machine).
télédétection [tālādātcksyóǹ] *nf* remote sensing.
télédiffuser [tālādēfüzā] *vt* to broadcast (on television).
télédiffusion [tālādēfüzyóǹ] *nf* television broadcasting.
télédistribution [tālādēstrēbüsyóǹ] *nf* cable TV.
téléenseignement [tālāáǹscnymáǹ] *nm* educational television (*US*), ≈ distance teaching (*ou* learning) (*Brit*).
téléférique [tālāfārēk] *nm* = **téléphérique**.
téléfilm [tālāfēlm] *nm* film made for TV, TV film.
télégramme [tālāgràm] *nm* telegram.
télégraphe [tālāgráf] *nm* telegraph.
télégraphie [tālāgráfē] *nf* telegraphy.
télégraphier [tālāgráfyā] *vt* to telegraph, cable.
télégraphique [tālāgráfēk] *a* telegraph *cpd*, telegraphic; (*fig*) telegraphic.
télégraphiste [tālāgráfēst(ə)] *nm/f* telegraphist.
téléguider [tālāgēdā] *vt* to operate by remote control, radio-control.
téléinformatique [tālāáǹformátēk] *nf* remote access computing.
téléjournal, aux [tālāzhōōrnál, -ō] *nm* television news magazine program (*US*) *ou* programme (*Brit*).
télématique [tālāmátēk] *nf* telematics *sg* ♦ *a* telematic.
téléobjectif [tālāobzhcktēf] *nm* telephoto lens *sg*.
télépathie [tālāpátē] *nf* telepathy.
téléphérique [tālāfārēk] *nm* cable-car.
téléphone [tālāfon] *nm* telephone; **avoir le** ~ to have a (tele)phone; **au** ~ on the phone; **les T~s** the (tele)phone service *sg*; ~ **arabe** bush telegraph; ~ **manuel** manually-operated telephone system; ~ **rouge** hot line.

téléphoner [tālāfonā] *vt* to telephone ♦ *vi* to telephone; to make a phone call; ~ **à qn** to phone sb, give sb a ring.
téléphonique [tālāfonēk] *a* telephone *cpd*, phone *cpd*; **cabine** ~ (tele)phone booth *ou* box (*Brit*); **conversation/appel** ~ (tele)phone conversation/call.
téléphoniste [tālāfonēst(ə)] *nm/f* telephone operator; (*d'entreprise*) switchboard operator.
téléport [tālāpor] *nm* teleport.
téléprospection [tālāprospeksyóǹ] *nf* telephone selling.
télescope [tālcskop] *nm* telescope.
télescoper [tālcskopā] *vt* to smash up; **se** ~ (*véhicules*) to telescope.
télescopique [tālcskopēk] *a* telescopic.
téléscripteur [tālāskrēptcœr] *nm* teleprinter.
télésiège [tālāsyezh] *nm* chairlift.
téléski [tālāskē] *nm* ski lift; ~ **à archets** T-bar tow; ~ **à perche** button lift.
téléspectateur, trice [tālāspcktátœr, -trēs] *nm/f* (television) viewer.
télétraitement [tālātrctmáǹ] *nm* remote processing.
télétransmission [tālātráǹsmēsyóǹ] *nf* remote transmission.
télétype [tālātēp] *nm* teleprinter.
téléviser [tālāvēzā] *vt* to televise.
téléviseur [tālāvēzœr] *nm* television set.
télévision [tālāvēzyóǹ] *nf* television; (**poste de**) ~ television (set); **avoir la** ~ to have a television; **à la** ~ on television; ~ **par câble** cable television.
télex [tālcks] *nm* telex.
télexer [tālcksā] *vt* to telex.
télexiste [tālcksēst(ə)] *nm/f* telex operator.
telle [tcl] *af voir* **tel**.
tellement [tclmáǹ] *ad* (*tant*) so much; (*si*) so; ~ **plus grand** (**que**) so much bigger (than); ~ **de** (*sable, eau*) so much; (*gens, livres*) so many; **il s'est endormi** ~ **il était fatigué** he was so tired (that) he fell asleep; **pas** ~ not really; **pas** ~ **fort/lentement** not (all) that strong/slowly; **il ne mange pas** ~ he doesn't eat (all that) much.
tellurique [tālürēk] *a*: **secousse** ~ earth tremor.
téméraire [tāmārcr] *a* reckless, rash.
témérité [tāmārētā] *nf* recklessness, rashness.
témoignage [tāmwányázh] *nm* (*JUR*: *déclaration*) testimony *q*, evidence *q*; (: *faits*) evidence *q*; (*gén*: *rapport, récit*) account; (*fig*: *d'affection etc*) token, mark; expression.
témoigner [tāmwányā] *vt* (*manifester*: *intérêt, gratitude*) to show ♦ *vi* (*JUR*) to testify, give evidence; ~ **que** to testify that; (*fig*: *démontrer*) to reveal that, testify to the fact that; ~ **de** *vt* (*confirmer*) to bear witness to, testify to.
témoin [tāmwaǹ] *nm* witness; (*fig*) testimony; (*SPORT*) baton; (*CONSTR*) telltale ♦ *a* control *cpd*, test *cpd* ♦ *ad*: ~ **le fait que** ... (*as*) witness the fact that ...; **appartement-~** model apartment (*US*), show flat (*Brit*); **être** ~ **de** (*voir*) to witness; **prendre à** ~ to call to witness; ~ **à charge** witness for the prosecution; **T~ de Jehovah** Jehovah's Witness; ~ **de moralité** character reference; ~ **oculaire**

eyewitness.

tempe [tãp] *nf* (*ANAT*) temple.

tempérament [tãpãrãmãn] *nm* temperament, disposition; (*santé*) constitution; **à ~** (*vente*) on deferred (payment) terms; (*achat*) on the installment plan (*US*), by instalments; **avoir du ~** to be hot-blooded.

tempérance [tãpãrãns] *nf* temperance; **société de ~** temperance society.

tempérant, e [tãpãrãn, -ãnt] *a* temperate.

température [tãpãrãtür] *nf* temperature; **prendre la ~ de** to take the temperature of; (*fig*) to gauge the feeling of; **avoir** *ou* **faire de la ~** to be running *ou* have a temperature.

tempéré, e [tãpãrã] *a* temperate.

tempérer [tãpãrã] *vt* to temper.

tempête [tãpet] *nf* storm; **~ de sable/neige** sand/snowstorm; **vent de ~** gale.

tempêter [tãpãtã] *vi* to rant and rave.

temple [tãpl(ə)] *nm* temple; (*protestant*) church.

tempo [tempõ] *nm* tempo (*pl* -s).

temporaire [tãporer] *a* temporary.

temporairement [tãporermãn] *ad* temporarily.

temporel, le [tãporel] *a* temporal.

temporisateur, trice [tãporẽzãtœr, -trẽs] *a* temporizing, delaying.

temporiser [tãporẽzã] *vi* to temporize, play for time.

temps [tãn] *nm* (*atmosphérique*) weather; (*durée*) time; (*époque*) time, times *pl*; (*LING*) tense; (*MUS*) beat; (*TECH*) stroke; **les ~ changent/sont durs** times are changing/hard; **il fait beau/mauvais ~** the weather is fine/bad; **avoir le ~/tout le ~/juste le ~** to have time/plenty of time/just enough time; **avoir fait son ~** (*fig*) to have had its (*ou* his *etc*) day; **en ~ de paix/guerre** in peacetime/wartime; **en ~ utile** *ou* **voulu** in due time *ou* course; **de ~ en ~, de ~ à autre** from time to time, now and again; **en même ~** at the same time; **à ~** (*partir, arriver*) in time; **à plein/mi-~** *ad, a* full-/part-time; **à ~ partiel** *ad, a* part-time; **dans le ~** at one time; **de tout ~** always; **du ~ que** at the time when, in the days when; **dans le** *ou* **du** *ou* **au ~ où** at the time when; **pendant ce ~** in the meantime; **~ d'accès** (*INFORM*) access time; **~ d'arrêt** pause, halt; **~ mort** (*SPORT*) time-out (*US*), stoppage (time) (*Brit*); (*COMM*) slack period; **~ partagé** (*INFORM*) time-sharing; **~ réel** (*INFORM*) real time.

tenable [tǝnãbl(ə)] *a* bearable.

tenace [tǝnãs] *a* tenacious, persistent.

ténacité [tãnãsẽtã] *nf* tenacity, persistence.

tenailler [tǝnãyã] *vt* (*fig*) to torment, torture.

tenailles [tǝnãy] *nfpl* pincers.

tenais [t(ǝ)ne] *etc vb voir* **tenir.**

tenancier, ière [tǝnãnsyã, -yer] *nm/f* (*d'hôtel, de bistro*) manager/manageress.

tenant, e [tǝnãn, -ãnt] *af voir* **séance** ♦ *nm/f* (*SPORT*): **~ du titre** title-holder ♦ *nm*: **d'un seul ~** in one piece; **les ~s et les aboutissants** (*fig*) the ins and outs.

tendance [tãdãns] *nf* (*opinions*) leanings *pl*, sympathies *pl*; (*inclination*) tendency; (*évolution*) trend; **~ à la hausse/baisse** upward/downward trend; **avoir ~ à** to have a

tendency to, tend to.

tendancieux, euse [tãdãnsyœ, -œz] *a* tendentious.

tendeur [tãdœr] *nm* (*de vélo*) tension pulley (*US*), chain-adjuster (*Brit*); (*de câble*) wire-strainer; (*de tente*) runner; (*attache*) elastic strap.

tendon [tãdõn] *nm* tendon, sinew; **~ d'Achille** Achilles' tendon.

tendre [tãdr(ə)] *a* (*viande, légumes*) tender; (*bois, roche, couleur*) soft; (*affectueux*) tender, loving ♦ *vt* (*élastique, peau*) to stretch, draw tight; (*muscle*) to tense; (*donner*): **~ qch à qn** to hold sth out to sb; to offer sb sth; (*fig: piège*) to set, lay; (*tapisserie*): **tendu de soie** hung with silk, with silk hangings; **se ~** *vi* (*corde*) to tighten; (*relations*) to become strained; **~ à qch/à faire** to tend towards sth/to do; **~ l'oreille** to prick up one's ears; **~ la main/le bras** to hold out one's hand/stretch out one's arm; **~ la perche à qn** (*fig*) to throw sb a line.

tendrement [tãdrəmãn] *ad* tenderly, lovingly.

tendresse [tãdres] *nf* tenderness; **~s** *nfpl* (*caresses etc*) tenderness *q*, caresses.

tendu, e [tãdü] *pp de* **tendre** ♦ *a* tight; tensed; strained.

ténèbres [tãnebr(ə)] *nfpl* darkness *sg*.

ténébreux, euse [tãnãbrœ, -œz] *a* obscure, mysterious; (*personne*) saturnine.

Ténérife [tãnãrẽf] *nf* Tenerife.

teneur [tǝnœr] *nf* content, substance; (*d'une lettre*) terms *pl*, content; **~ en cuivre** copper content.

ténia [tãnyã] *nm* tapeworm.

tenir [tǝnẽr] *vt* to hold; (*magasin, hôtel*) to run; (*promesse*) to keep ♦ *vi* to hold; (*neige, gel*) to last; (*survivre*) to survive; **se ~** *vi* (*avoir lieu*) to be held, take place; (*être: personne*) to stand; **se ~ droit** to stand up (*ou* sit up) straight; **bien se ~** to behave well; **se ~ à qch** to hold on to sth; **s'en ~ à qch** to confine o.s. to sth; to stick to sth; **~ à** *vt* to be attached to, care about (*ou* for); (*avoir pour cause*) to be due to, stem from; **~ à faire** to want to do, be keen to do; **~ à ce que qn fasse qch** to be anxious that sb should do sth; **~ de** *vt* to partake of; (*ressembler à*) to take after; **ça ne tient qu'à lui** it is entirely up to him; **~ qn pour** to take sb for; **~ qch de qn** (*histoire*) to have heard *ou* learned sth from sb; (*qualité, défaut*) to have inherited *ou* got sth from sb; **~ les comptes** to keep the books; **~ un rôle** to play a part; **~ de la place** to take up space *ou* room; **~ l'alcool** to be able to hold a drink; **~ le coup** to hold out; **~ bon** to stand *ou* hold fast; **~ 3 jours/2 mois** (*résister*) to hold out *ou* last 3 days/2 months; **~ au chaud/à l'abri** to keep hot/under shelter *ou* cover; **~ prêt** to have ready; **~ sa langue** (*fig*) to hold one's tongue; **tiens** (*ou* **tenez**), **voilà le stylo** there's the pen!; **tiens, Alain!** look, here's Alain!; **tiens?** (*surprise*) really?; **tiens-toi bien!** (*pour informer*) brace yourself!, take a deep breath!

tennis [tãnẽs] *nm* tennis; (*aussi*: **court de ~**) tennis court ♦ *nmpl ou fpl* (*aussi*: **chaussures de ~**) tennis *ou* gym shoes; **~ de table** table tennis.

tennisman [tānēsmán] *nm* tennis player.

ténor [tānor] *nm* tenor.

tension [tânsyón] *nf* tension; (*fig: des relations, de la situation*) tension; (: *concentration, effort*) strain; (*MÉD*) blood pressure; **faire** *ou* **avoir de la ~** to have high blood pressure; **~ nerveuse/raciale** nervous/racial tension.

tentaculaire [tântáküler] *a* (*fig*) sprawling.

tentacule [tântákül] *nm* tentacle.

tentant, e [tântân, -ânt] *a* tempting.

tentateur, trice [tântátœr, -trēs] *a* tempting ♦ *nm* (*REL*) tempter.

tentation [tântâsyón] *nf* temptation.

tentative [tântátēv] *nf* attempt, bid; **~ d'évasion** escape attempt; **~ de suicide** suicide attempt.

tente [tânt] *nf* tent; **~ à oxygène** oxygen tent.

tenter [tântā] *vt* (*éprouver, attirer*) to tempt; (*essayer*): **~ qch/de faire** to attempt *ou* try sth/to do; **être tenté de** to be tempted to; **~ sa chance** to try one's luck.

tenture [tântür] *nf* hanging.

tenu, e [tānü] *pp de* **tenir** ♦ *a* (*maison, comptes*): **bien ~** well-kept; (*obligé*): **~ de faire** under an obligation to do ♦ *nf* (*action de tenir*) running; keeping; holding; (*vêtements*) clothes *pl*, gear; (*allure*) dress *q*, appearance; (*comportement*) manners *pl*, behavior (*US*), behaviour (*Brit*); **être en ~e** to be dressed (up); **se mettre en ~e** to dress (up); **en grande ~e** in full dress; **en petite ~e** scantily dressed *ou* clad; **avoir de la ~e** to have good manners; (*journal*) to have a high standard; **~e de combat** combat gear *ou* dress; **~e de pompier** fireman's uniform; **~e de route** (*AUTO*) road-holding; **~e de soirée** evening dress; **~e de sport/voyage** sports/traveling clothes *pl ou* gear *q*.

ténu, e [tānü] *a* (*indice, nuance*) tenuous, subtle; (*fil, objet*) fine; (*voix*) thin.

TEP *sigle m* = *Théâtre de l'Est parisien*.

ter [ter] *a*: **16 ~ 16b** *ou* B.

térébenthine [tārābântēn] *nf*: **(essence de) ~** (oil of) turpentine.

tergal [tergál] *nm* ® Terylene ®.

tergiversations [terzhēversâsyón] *nfpl* shilly-shallying *q*.

tergiverser [terzhēversā] *vi* to shilly-shally.

terme [term(ə)] *nm* term; (*fin*) end; **être en bons/mauvais ~s avec qn** to be on good/bad terms with sb; **vente/achat à ~** (*COMM*) forward sale/purchase; **au ~ de** at the end of; **en d'autres ~s** in other words; **moyen ~** (*solution intermédiaire*) middle course; **à court/long ~** *a* short-/long-term *ou* -range ♦ *ad* in the short/long term; **à ~** *a* (*MÉD*) full-term ♦ *ad* sooner or later, eventually; (*MÉD*) at term; **avant ~** (*MÉD*) *a* premature ♦ *ad* prematurely; **mettre un ~ à** to put an end *ou* a stop to; **toucher à son ~** to be nearing its end.

terminaison [termēnezón] *nf* (*LING*) ending.

terminal, e, aux [termēnál, -ō] *a* (*partie, phase*) final; (*MÉD*) terminal ♦ *nm* terminal ♦ *nf* (*SCOL*) ≈ twelfth grade (*US*), ≈ sixth form *ou* year (*Brit*).

terminer [termēnā] *vt* to end; (*travail, repas*) to finish; **se ~** *vi* to end; **se ~ par** to end with.

terminologie [termēnolozhē] *nf* terminology.

terminus [termēnüs] *nm* terminal (*US*), terminus (*pl* -i) (*Brit*); **~!** last stop!, end of the line!

termite [termēt] *nm* termite, white ant.

termitière [termētyer] *nf* anthill.

ternaire [terner] *a* compound.

terne [tern(ə)] *a* dull.

ternir [ternēr] *vt* to dull; (*fig*) to sully, tarnish; **se ~** *vi* to become dull.

terrain [terań] *nm* (*sol, fig*) ground; (*COMM*) land *q*, plot (of land); (: *à bâtir*) site; **sur le ~** (*fig*) on the field; **~ de football/rugby** football/rugby field (*US*) *ou* pitch (*Brit*); **~ d'atterrissage** landing strip; **~ d'aviation** airfield; **~ de camping** campsite; **un ~ d'entente** an area of agreement; **~ de golf** golf course; **~ de jeu** playground; (*SPORT*) games field; **~ de sport** sports ground; **~ vague** waste ground *q*.

terrasse [terás] *nf* terrace; (*de café*) sidewalk (*US*) *ou* pavement (*Brit*) area, terrace; **à la ~** (*café*) outside.

terrassement [terásmân] *nm* earth-moving, earthworks *pl*; embankment.

terrasser [terásā] *vt* (*adversaire*) to floor, bring down; (*suj: maladie etc*) to lay low.

terrassier [terásyā] *nm* roadworker.

terre [ter] *nf* (*gén, aussi ÉLEC*) earth; (*substance*) soil, earth; (*opposé à mer*) land *q*; (*contrée*) land; **~s** *nfpl* (*terrains*) lands, land *sg*; **travail de la ~** work on the land; **en ~** (*pipe, poterie*) clay *cpd*; **mettre en ~** (*plante etc*) to plant; (*personne: enterrer*) to bury; **à ou par ~** (*mettre, être*) on the ground (*ou* floor); (*jeter, tomber*) to the ground, down; **~ à ~** *a inv* down-to-earth, matter-of-fact; **la T~ Adélie** Adélie Coast *ou* Land; **~ de bruyère** (heath-)peat; **~ cuite** earthenware; terracotta; **la ~ ferme** dry land, terra firma; **la T~ de feu** Tierra del Fuego; **~ glaise** clay; **la T~ promise** the Promised Land; **la T~ Sainte** the Holy Land.

terreau [terō] *nm* compost.

Terre-Neuve [ternœv] *nf*: **la ~** (*aussi*: **l'île de ~**) Newfoundland.

terre-plein [terplań] *nm* platform.

terrer [terā]: **se ~** *vi* to hide away; to go into hiding.

terrestre [terestr(ə)] *a* (*surface*) earth's, of the earth; (*BOT, ZOOL, MIL*) land *cpd*; (*REL*) earthly, worldly.

terreur [terœr] *nf* terror *q*, fear.

terreux, euse [terœ, -œz] *a* muddy; (*goût*) earthy.

terrible [terēbl(ə)] *a* terrible, dreadful; (*fam: fantastique*) terrific.

terriblement [terēbləmân] *ad* (*très*) terribly, awfully.

terrien, ne [teryań, -en] *a*: **propriétaire ~** landowner ♦ *nm/f* countryman/woman, man/woman of the soil; (*non martien etc*) earthling; (*non marin*) landsman.

terrier [teryā] *nm* burrow, hole; (*chien*) terrier.

terrifiant, e [terēfyân, -ânt] *a* (*effrayant*) terrifying; (*extraordinaire*) terrible, awful.

terrifier [terēfyā] *vt* to terrify.
terril [terēl] *nm* slag heap.
terrine [terēn] *nf* (*récipient*) terrine; (*CULIN*) pâté.
territoire [terētwár] *nm* territory; **T~ des Afars et des Issas** French Territory of Afars and Issas.
territorial, e, aux [terētoryàl, -ō] *a* territorial; **eaux ~es** territorial waters; **armée ~e** regional defense force; **collectivités ~es** local and regional authorities.
terroir [terwár] *nm* (*AGR*) soil; (*région*) region; **accent du ~** country *ou* rural accent.
terroriser [terorēzā] *vt* to terrorize.
terrorisme [terorēsm(ə)] *nm* terrorism.
terroriste [terorēst(ə)] *nm/f* terrorist.
tertiaire [tersyer] *a* tertiary ♦ *nm* (*ÉCON*) tertiary sector, service industries *pl*.
tertre [tertr(ə)] *nm* hillock, mound.
tes [tā] *dét voir* **ton.**
tesson [tāsôn] *nm*: **~ de bouteille** piece of broken bottle.
test [test] *nm* test.
testament [testámán] *nm* (*JUR*) will; (*fig*) legacy; (*REL*): **T~** Testament; **faire son ~** to make one's will.
testamentaire [testámánter] *a* of a will.
tester [testā] *vt* to test.
testicule [testēkül] *nm* testicle.
tétanos [tātánōs] *nm* tetanus.
têtard [tetár] *nm* tadpole.
tête [tet] *nf* head; (*cheveux*) hair *q*; (*visage*) face; (*longueur*): **gagner d'une (courte) ~** to win by a (short) head; (*FOOTBALL*) header; **de ~** *a* (*wagon etc*) front *cpd*; (*concurrent*) leading ♦ *ad* (*calculer*) in one's head, mentally; **par ~** (*par personne*) per head; **se mettre en ~ que** to get it into one's head that; **se mettre en ~ de faire** to take it into one's head to do; **prendre la ~ de qch** to take the lead in sth; **perdre la ~** (*fig*: *s'affoler*) to lose one's head; (: *devenir fou*) to go crazy; **ça ne va pas, la ~?** (*fam*) are you crazy?; **tenir ~ à qn** to stand up to *ou* defy sb; **la ~ en bas** with one's head down; **la ~ la première** (*tomber*) headfirst; **la ~ basse** hanging one's head; **avoir la ~ dure** (*fig*) to be thickheaded; **faire une ~** (*FOOTBALL*) to head the ball; **faire la ~** (*fig*) to sulk; **en ~** (*SPORT*) in the lead; at the front *ou* head; **de la ~ aux pieds** from head to toe; **~ d'affiche** (*THÉÂTRE etc*) headliner (*US*), top of the bill (*Brit*); **~ de bétail** head *inv* of cattle; **~ brulée** desperado; **~ chercheuse** homing device; **~ d'enregistrement** recording head; **~ de lecture** (playback) head; **~ de ligne** (*TRANSPORTS*) terminal (*US*), start of the line (*Brit*); **~ de liste** (*POL*) chief candidate; **~ de mort** skull and crossbones; **~ de pont** (*MIL*) bridge- *ou* beachhead; **~ de série** (*TENNIS*) seeded player, seed; **~ de Turc** (*fig*) whipping boy, butt; **~ de veau** (*CULIN*) calf's head.
tête-à-queue [tetákœ] *nm inv*: **faire un ~** to spin around.
tête-à-tête [tetátet] *nm inv* tête-à-tête; (*service*) breakfast set for two; **en ~** in private, alone together.
tête-bêche [tetbesh] *ad* head to tail.

tétée [tātā] *nf* (*action*) sucking; (*repas*) nursing (*US*), feed (*Brit*).
téter [tātā] *vt*: **~ (sa mère)** to suck at one's mother's breast.
tétine [tātēn] *nf* teat; (*sucette*) pacifier (*US*), dummy (*Brit*).
téton [tātôn] *nm* breast.
têtu, e [tātü] *a* stubborn, pigheaded.
texte [tekst(ə)] *nm* text; (*SCOL*: *d'un devoir*) subject, topic; **apprendre son ~** (*THÉÂTRE*) to learn one's lines; **un ~ de loi** the wording of a law.
textile [tekstēl] *a* textile *cpd* ♦ *nm* textile; (*industrie*) textile industry.
textuel, le [tekstüel] *a* literal, word for word.
textuellement [tekstüelmán] *ad* literally.
texture [tekstür] *nf* texture; (*fig*: *d'un texte, livre*) feel.
TF1 *sigle f* (= *Télévision française 1*) *TV channel.*
TG *sigle f* = **Trésorerie générale.**
TGI *sigle m* = **tribunal de grande instance.**
TGV *sigle m* = **train à grande vitesse.**
thaï, e [tàē] *a* Thai ♦ *nm* (*LING*) Thai.
thaïlandais, e [tàēlánde, -ez] *a* Thai.
Thaïlande [tàēlánd] *nf*: **la ~** Thailand.
thalassothérapie [tàlásotárápē] *nf* sea-water therapy.
thé [tā] *nm* tea; (*réunion*) tea party; **prendre le ~** to have tea; **~ au lait/citron** tea with milk/lemon.
théâtral, e, aux [tāátrál, -ō] *a* theatrical.
théâtre [tāátr(ə)] *nm* theater (*US*), theatre (*Brit*); (*techniques, genre*) drama, theater; (*activité*) stage, theater; (*œuvres*) plays *pl*, dramatic works *pl*; (*fig*: *lieu*): **le ~ de** the scene of; (*péj*) histrionics *pl*, playacting; **faire du ~** (*en professionnel*) to be on the stage; (*en amateur*) to do some acting; **~ filmé** filmed stage productions *pl*.
thébain, e [tābàn, -en] *a* Theban.
Thèbes [teb] *n* Thebes.
théière [tāyer] *nf* teapot.
théine [tāēn] *nf* theine.
théisme [tāēsm(ə)] *nm* theism.
thématique [tāmátēk] *a* thematic.
thème [tem] *nm* theme; (*SCOL*: *traduction*) translation (*into the foreign language*); **~ astral** birth chart.
théocratie [tāokrásē] *nf* theocracy.
théologie [tāolozhē] *nf* theology.
théologien, ne [tāolozhyàn, -en] *nm* theologian.
théologique [tāolozhēk] *a* theological.
théorème [tāorem] *nm* theorem.
théoricien, ne [tāorēsyàn, -en] *nm/f* theoretician, theorist.
théorie [tāorē] *nf* theory; **en ~** in theory.
théorique [tāorēk] *a* theoretical.
théoriser [tāorēzā] *vi* to theorize.
thérapeutique [tārápœtēk] *a* therapeutic ♦ *nf* (*MÉD*: *branche*) therapeutics *sg*; (: *traitement*) therapy.
thérapie [tārápē] *nf* therapy.
thermal, e, aux [termál, -ō] *a* thermal; **station ~e** spa; **cure ~e** water cure.
thermes [term(ə)] *nmpl* thermal baths; (*romains*) thermae *pl*.
thermique [termēk] *a* (*énergie*) thermic;

(unité) thermal.

thermodynamique [termodēnámēk] *nf* thermodynamics *sg*.

thermomètre [termometr(ə)] *nm* thermometer.

thermonucléaire [termonüklāer] *a* thermonuclear.

thermos [termōs] *nm ou nf* ®: **(bouteille)** ~ vacuum *ou* Thermos ® bottle *(US) ou* flask *(Brit)*.

thermostat [termostá] *nm* thermostat.

thésauriser [tāzorēzā] *vi* to hoard money.

thèse [tez] *nf* thesis *(pl* theses).

Thessalie [tesálē] *nf*: **la** ~ Thessaly.

thessalien, ne [tesályań, -en] *a* Thessalian.

thibaude [tēbōd] *nf* carpet underlay.

thon [tóń] *nm* tuna (fish).

thoracique [toráscēk] *a* thoracic.

thorax [toráks] *nm* thorax.

thrombose [trônbōz] *nf* thrombosis.

thym [tań] *nm* thyme.

thyroïde [tēroēd] *nf* thyroid (gland).

TI *sigle m* = **tribunal d'instance.**

tiare [tyár] *nf* tiara.

Tibet [tēbe] *nm*: **le** ~ Tibet.

tibétain, e [tēbātań, -en] *a* Tibetan.

tibia [tēbyá] *nm* shin; *(os)* shinbone, tibia.

Tibre [tēbr(ə)] *nm*: **le** ~ the Tiber.

tic [tēk] *nm* tic, (nervous) twitch; *(de langage etc)* mannerism.

ticket [tēke] *nm* ticket; ~ **de caisse** sales slip *ou* receipt; ~ **modérateur** *patient's contribution towards medical costs*; ~ **de quai** platform ticket; ~ **repas** luncheon voucher.

tic-tac [tēkták] *nm inv* tick-tock.

tictaquer [tēktákā] *vi* to tick (away).

tiède [tyed] *a (bière etc)* lukewarm; *(thé, café etc)* tepid; *(bain, accueil, sentiment)* lukewarm; *(vent, air)* mild, warm ♦ *ad*: **boire** ~ to drink things lukewarm.

tièdement [tyedmáń] *ad* coolly, half-heartedly.

tiédir [tyādēr] *vi (se réchauffer)* to grow warmer; *(refroidir)* to cool.

tien, tienne [tyań, tyen] *pronom*: **le** ~ **(la tienne), les** ~**s (tiennes)** yours; **à la tienne!** cheers!

tiendrai [tyańdrā] *etc vb voir* tenir.

tienne [tyen] *vb voir* tenir ♦ *pronom voir* tien.

tiens [tyań] *vb, excl voir* tenir.

tierce [tyers(ə)] *af, nf voir* tiers.

tiercé [tyersā] *nm* system of forecast betting giving first 3 horses.

tiers, tierce [tyer, tyers(ə)] *a* third ♦ *nm (JUR)* third party; *(fraction)* third ♦ *nf (MUS)* third; *(CARTES)* tierce; **une tierce personne** a third party; **assurance au** ~ third-party insurance; **le** ~ **monde** the third world; ~ **payant** *direct payment by insurers of medical expenses*; ~ **provisionnel** *interim payment of tax*.

tiersmondisme [tyermóńdēsm(ə)] *nm* support for the Third World.

TIG *sigle m* = **travail d'intérêt général.**

tige [tēzh] *nf* stem; *(baguette)* rod.

tignasse [tēnyás] *nf (péj)* shock *ou* mop of hair.

Tigre [tēgr(ə)] *nm*: **le** ~ the Tigris.

tigre [tēgr(ə)] *nm* tiger.

tigré, e [tēgrā] *a (rayé)* striped; *(tacheté)* spotted.

tigresse [tēgres] *nf* tigress.

tilleul [tēyœl] *nm* lime (tree), linden (tree); *(boisson)* lime(-blossom) tea.

tilt [tēlt(ə)] *nm*: **faire** ~ *(fig: échouer)* to miss the target; *(: inspirer)* to ring a bell.

timbale [tańbál] *nf* (metal) tumbler; ~**s** *nfpl (MUS)* timpani, kettledrums.

timbrage [tańbrázh] *nm*: **dispensé de** ~ post(age) paid.

timbre [tańbr(ə)] *nm (tampon)* stamp; *(aussi:* ~**-poste)** (postage) stamp; *(cachet de la poste)* postmark; *(sonnette)* bell; *(MUS: de voix, instrument)* timbre, tone; ~ **dateur** date stamp.

timbré, e [tańbrā] *a (enveloppe)* stamped; *(voix)* resonant; *(fam: fou)* cracked, nuts.

timbrer [tańbrā] *vt* to stamp.

timide [tēmēd] *a (emprunté)* shy, timid; *(timoré)* timid, timorous.

timidement [tēmēdmáń] *ad* shyly; timidly.

timidité [tēmēdētā] *nf* shyness; timidity.

timonerie [tēmonrē] *nf* wheelhouse.

timonier [tēmonyá] *nm* helmsman.

timoré, e [tēmorā] *a* timorous.

tint [tań] *etc vb voir* tenir.

tintamarre [tańtámár] *nm* din, uproar.

tintement [tańtmáń] *nm* ringing, chiming; ~**s d'oreilles** ringing in the ears.

tinter [tańtā] *vi* to ring, chime; *(argent, clefs)* to jingle.

Tipp-Ex [tēpeks] *nm* ® Liquid Paper ®, Tipp-Ex ® *(Brit)*.

tique [tēk] *nf* tick *(insect)*.

tiquer [tēkā] *vi (personne)* to make a face.

TIR *sigle mpl* (= *Transports internationaux routiers*) TIR.

tir [tēr] *nm (sport)* shooting; *(fait ou manière de tirer)* firing *q; (FOOTBALL)* shot; *(stand)* shooting gallery; ~ **d'obus/de mitraillette** shell/machine gun fire; ~ **à l'arc** archery; ~ **de barrage** barrage fire; ~ **au fusil** (rifle) shooting; ~ **au pigeon** *(d'argile)* trapshooting *(US)*, clay pigeon shooting *(Brit)*.

tirade [tērád] *nf* tirade.

tirage [tērázh] *nm (action)* printing; *(PHOTO)* print; *(INFORM)* printout; *(de journal)* circulation; *(de livre)* (print-)run; edition; *(de cheminée)* draft *(US)*, draught *(Brit)*; *(de loterie)* drawing *(US)*, draw *(Brit); (fig: désaccord)* friction; ~ **au sort** drawing lots.

tiraillement [tēráymáń] *nm (douleur)* sharp pain; *(fig: doutes)* agony *q* of indecision; *(conflits)* friction *q*.

tirailler [tēráyā] *vt* to pull at, tug at; *(fig)* to gnaw at ♦ *vi* to fire at random.

tirailleur [tēráycœr] *nm* skirmisher.

tirant [tēráń] *nm*: ~ **d'eau** draft *(US)*, draught *(Brit)*.

tire [tēr] *nf*: **vol à la** ~ pickpocketing *(fam)*.

tiré [tērā] *a (visage, traits)* drawn ♦ *nm (COMM)* drawee; ~ **par les cheveux** far-fetched; ~ **à part** offprint.

tire-au-flanc [tērōfláń] *nm inv (péj)* shirker.

tire-bouchon [tērbōōshóń] *nm* corkscrew.

tire-bouchonner [tērbōōshonā] *vt* to twirl.

tire-d'aile [tērdel]: **à** ~ *ad* swiftly.

tire-fesses [tērfes] *nm inv* ski tow.

tire-lait [tērle] *nm inv* breast pump.

tire-larigot [tĕrlárēgō]: **à ~** *ad* as much as one likes, to one's heart's content.

tirelire [tĕrlēr] *nf* moneybox.

tirer [tĕrā] *vt* (*gén*) to pull; (*extraire*): **~ qch de** to take *ou* pull sth out of; to get sth out of; to extract sth from; (*tracer: ligne, trait*) to draw, trace; (*fermer: volet, porte, trappe*) to pull to, close; (*: rideau*) to draw; (*choisir: carte, conclusion, aussi COMM: chèque*) to draw; (*en faisant feu: balle, coup*) to fire; (*: animal*) to shoot; (*journal, livre, photo*) to print; (*FOOTBALL: corner etc*) to take ♦ *vi* (*faire feu*) to fire; (*faire du tir, FOOTBALL*) to shoot; (*cheminée*) to draw; **se ~** *vi* (*fam*) to push off; **s'en ~** to pull through; **~ sur** (*corde, poignée*) to pull on *ou* at; (*faire feu sur*) to shoot *ou* fire at; (*pipe*) to draw on; (*fig: avoisiner*) to verge *ou* border on; **~ 6 mètres** (*NAVIG*) to draw 6 meters of water; **~ son nom de** to take *ou* get its name from; **~ la langue** to stick out one's tongue; **~ qn de** (*embarras etc*) to help *ou* get sb out of; **~ à l'arc/la carabine** to shoot with a bow and arrow/with a rifle; **~ en longueur** to drag on; **~ à sa fin** to be drawing to an end; **~ les cartes** to read *ou* tell the cards.

tiret [tĕre] *nm* dash; (*en fin de ligne*) hyphen.

tireur, euse [tĕrœr, -ēz] *nm/f* gunman; (*COMM*) drawer; **bon ~** good shot; **~ d'élite** marksman; **~ des cartes** fortuneteller.

tiroir [tĕrwár] *nm* drawer.

tiroir-caisse [tĕrwárkes] *nm* till.

tisane [tĕzán] *nf* herb tea.

tison [tĕzóñ] *nm* brand.

tisonner [tĕzoná] *vt* to poke.

tisonnier [tĕzonyá] *nm* poker.

tissage [tĕsázh] *nm* weaving *q*.

tisser [tĕsá] *vt* to weave.

tisserand, e [tĕsráñ, -áñd] *nm/f* weaver.

tissu [tĕsü] *nm* fabric, material, cloth *q*; (*fig*) fabric; (*ANAT, BIO*) tissue; **~ de mensonges** web of lies.

tissu, e [tĕsü] *a*: **~ de** woven through with.

tissu-éponge [tĕsüápôñzh] *nm* terry cloth (*US*), (terry) towelling *q* (*Brit*).

titane [tĕtán] *nm* titanium.

titanesque [tĕtánesk(ə)] *a* titanic.

titiller [tĕtēlá] *vt* to titillate.

titre [tĕtr(ə)] *nm* (*gén*) title; (*de journal*) headline; (*diplôme*) qualification; (*COMM*) security; (*CHIMIE*) titer (*US*), titre (*Brit*); **en ~** (*champion, responsable*) official, recognized; **à juste ~** with just cause, rightly; **à quel ~?** on what grounds?; **à aucun ~** on no account; **au même ~ (que)** in the same way (as); **au ~ de la coopération** *etc* in the name of cooperation *etc*; **à ~ d'exemple** as an *ou* by way of an example; **à ~ exceptionnel** exceptionally; **à ~ d'information** for (your) information; **à ~ gracieux** free of charge; **à ~ d'essai** on a trial basis; **à ~ privé** in a private capacity; **~ courant** running head; **~ de propriété** title deed; **~ de transport** ticket.

titré, e [tĕtrá] *a* (*livre, film*) entitled; (*personne*) titled.

titrer [tĕtrá] *vt* (*CHIMIE*) to titrate; to assay; (*PRESSE*) to run as a headline; (*suj: vin*): **~ 10°** to be 10° proof.

titubant, e [tĕtübáñ, -áñt] *a* staggering, reeling.

tituber [tĕtübá] *vi* to stagger *ou* reel (along).

titulaire [tĕtüler] *a* (*ADMIN*) appointed, with tenure ♦ *nm* (*ADMIN*) incumbent; **être ~ de** to hold.

titulariser [tĕtülárēzá] *vt* to give tenure to.

TNP *sigle m* = *Théâtre national populaire*.

TNT *sigle m* (= *Trinitrotoluène*) TNT.

toast [tōst] *nm* slice *ou* piece of toast; (*de bienvenue*) (welcoming) toast; **porter un ~ à qn** to propose *ou* drink a toast to sb.

toboggan [tobogáñ] *nm* toboggan; (*jeu*) slide; (*AUTO*) overpass (*US*), flyover (*Brit*); **~ de secours** (*AVIAT*) escape chute.

toc [tok] *nm*: **en ~** imitation *cpd*.

tocsin [toksáñ] *nm* alarm (bell).

toge [tozh] *nf* toga; (*de juge*) gown.

Togo [togō] *nm*: **le ~** Togo.

togolais, e [togolɛ, -cz] *a* Togolese.

tohu-bohu [toüboü] *nm* (*désordre*) confusion; (*tumulte*) commotion.

toi [twá] *pronom* you; **~, tu l'as fait?** did YOU do it?

toile [twál] *nf* (*matériau*) cloth *q*; (*bâche*) piece of canvas; (*tableau*) canvas; **grosse ~** canvas; **tisser sa ~** (*araignée*) to spin its web; **~ d'araignée** spider's web; (*au plafond etc: à enlever*) cobweb; **~ cirée** oilcloth; **~ émeri** emery cloth; **~ de fond** (*fig*) backdrop; **~ de jute** hessian; **~ de lin** linen; **~ de tente** canvas.

toilettage [twáletázh] *nm* grooming *q*; (*d'un texte*) tidying up.

toilette [twálet] *nf* wash; (*s'habiller et se préparer*) getting ready, washing and dressing; (*habits*) outfit, dress *q*; **~s** *nfpl* toilet *sg*; **les ~s des dames/messieurs** the ladies'/mens' (rest)room (*US*), the ladies'/gents' (toilets) (*Brit*); **faire sa ~** to get washed; **faire la ~ de** (*animal*) to groom; (*voiture etc*) to clean, wash; (*texte*) to tidy up; **articles de ~** toiletries; **~ intime** personal hygiene.

toi-même [twámem] *pronom* yourself.

toise [twáz] *nf*: **passer à la ~** to have one's height measured.

toiser [twázá] *vt* to eye up and down.

toison [twázóñ] *nf* (*de mouton*) fleece; (*cheveux*) mane.

toit [twá] *nm* roof; **~ ouvrant** sun roof.

toiture [twátür] *nf* roof.

Tokyo [tokyō] *n* Tokyo.

tôle [tōl] *nf* sheet metal *q*; (*plaque*) steel (*ou* iron) sheet; **~s** *nfpl* (*carrosserie*) body *sg*; panels; **~ d'acier** sheet steel *q*; **~ ondulée** corrugated iron.

Tolède [toled] *n* Toledo.

tolérable [tolārábl(ə)] *a* tolerable, bearable.

tolérance [tolāráñs] *nf* tolerance; (*hors taxe*) allowance.

tolérant, e [tolāráñ, -áñt] *a* tolerant.

tolérer [tolārá] *vt* to tolerate; (*ADMIN: hors taxe etc*) to allow.

tôlerie [tōlrē] *nf* sheet metal manufacture; (*atelier*) sheet metal workshop; (*ensemble des tôles*) panels *pl*.

tollé [tolá] *nm*: **un ~ (de protestations)** a general outcry.

TOM [parfois: tom] *sigle m(pl)* = *territoire(s)*

d'outre-mer.

tomate [tomát] *nf* tomato.

tombal, e [tôṅbál] *a*: **pierre** ~**e** tombstone, gravestone.

tombant, e [tôṅbâṅ, -âṅt] *a* (*fig*) drooping, sloping.

tombe [tôṅb] *nf* (*sépulture*) grave; (*avec monument*) tomb.

tombeau, x [tôṅbō] *nm* tomb; **à** ~ **ouvert** at breakneck speed.

tombée [tôṅbā] *nf*: **à la** ~ **du jour** *ou* **de la nuit** at the close of day, at nightfall.

tomber [tôṅbā] *vi* to fall ♦ *vt*: ~ **la veste** to slip off one's jacket; **laisser** ~ to drop; ~ **sur** *vt* (*rencontrer*) to come across; (*attaquer*) to set about; ~ **de fatigue/sommeil** to drop from exhaustion/be falling asleep on one's feet; ~ **à l'eau** (*fig*: *projet etc*) to fall through; ~ **en panne** to break down; ~ **juste** (*opération, calcul*) to come out right; ~ **en ruine** to fall into ruins; **ça tombe bien/mal** (*fig*) that's come at the right/wrong time; **il est bien/mal tombé** (*fig*) he's been lucky/unlucky.

tombereau, x [tôṅbrō] *nm* tipcart.

tombeur [tôṅbœr] *nm* (*péj*) Casanova.

tombola [tôṅbolá] *nf* raffle, tombola (*Brit*).

Tombouctou [tôṅbōōktōō] *n* Timbuktu.

tome [tom] *nm* volume.

tommette [tomet] *nf* hexagonal floor tile.

ton, ta, *pl* **tes** [tôṅ, tá, tā] *dét* your.

ton [tôṅ] *nm* (*gén*) tone; (*MUS*) key; (*couleur*) shade, tone; (*de la voix*: *hauteur*) pitch; **donner le** ~ to set the tone; **élever** *ou* **hausser le** ~ to raise one's voice; **de bon** ~ in good taste; **si vous le prenez sur ce** ~ if you're going to take it like that; ~ **sur** ~ in matching shades.

tonal, e [tonál] *a* tonal.

tonalité [tonálētā] *nf* (*au téléphone*) dial tone; (*MUS*) tonality; (: *ton*) key; (*fig*) tone.

tondeuse [tôṅdœz] *nf* (*à gazon*) (lawn)mower; (*du coiffeur*) clippers *pl*; (*pour la tonte*) shears *pl*.

tondre [tôṅdr(ə)] *vt* (*pelouse, herbe*) to mow; (*haie*) to cut, clip; (*mouton, toison*) to shear; (*cheveux*) to crop.

tondu, e [tôṅdü] *pp de* **tondre** ♦ *a* (*cheveux*) cropped; (*mouton, crâne*) shorn.

Tonga [tôṅgá]: **les îles** ~ Tonga.

tonicité [tonēsētā] *nf* (*MÉD*: *des tissus*) tone; (*fig*: *de l'air, la mer*) bracing effect.

tonifiant, e [tonēfyâṅ, -âṅt] *a* invigorating, revivifying.

tonifier [tonēfyā] *vt* (*air, eau*) to invigorate; (*peau, organisme*) to tone up.

tonique [tonēk] *a* fortifying; (*personne*) dynamic ♦ *nm, nf* tonic.

tonitruant, e [tonētrüâṅ, -âṅt] *a*: **voix** ~**e** thundering voice.

Tonkin [tôṅkáṅ] *nm*: **le** ~ Tonkin, Tongking.

tonkinois, e [tôṅkēnwá, -wáz] *a* Tonkinese.

tonnage [tonázh] *nm* tonnage.

tonnant, e [tonáṅ, -âṅt] *a* thunderous.

tonne [ton] *nf* metric ton, ton (*US*), tonne (*Brit*).

tonneau, x [tonō] *nm* (*à vin, cidre*) barrel; (*NAVIG*) ton; **faire des** ~**x** (*voiture, avion*) to roll over.

tonnelet [tonle] *nm* keg.

tonnelier [tonəlyā] *nm* cooper.

tonnelle [tonel] *nf* bower, arbor (*US*), arbour (*Brit*).

tonner [tonā] *vi* to thunder; (*parler avec véhémence*): ~ **contre qn/qch** to inveigh against sb/sth; **il tonne** it is thundering, there's some thunder.

tonnerre [toner] *nm* thunder; **coup de** ~ (*fig*) thunderbolt, bolt from the blue; **un** ~ **d'applaudissements** thunderous applause; **du** ~ *a* (*fam*) terrific.

tonsure [tôṅsür] *nf* bald patch; (*de moine*) tonsure.

tonte [tôṅt] *nf* shearing.

tonus [tonüs] *nm* (*des muscles*) tone; (*d'une personne*) dynamism.

top [top] *nm*: **au 3ème** ~ at the 3rd stroke ♦ *a*: ~ **secret** top secret ♦ *excl* go!

topaze [topáz] *nf* topaz.

toper [topā] *vi*: **tope-/topez-là** it's a deal!, you're on!

topinambour [topēnâṅbōōr] *nm* Jerusalem artichoke.

topo [topō] *nm* (*discours, exposé*) talk; (*fam*) spiel.

topographie [topográfē] *nf* topography.

topographique [topográfēk] *a* topographical.

toponymie [toponēmē] *nf* study of place-names, toponymy.

toquade [tokád] *nf* fad, craze.

toque [tok] *nf* (*de fourrure*) fur hat; ~ **de jockey/juge** jockey's/judge's cap; ~ **de cuisinier** chef's hat.

toqué, e [tokā] *a* (*fam*) touched, cracked.

torche [torsh(ə)] *nf* torch; **se mettre en** ~ (*parachute*) to fail to open.

torcher [torshā] *vt* (*fam*) to wipe.

torchère [torsher] *nf* flare.

torchon [torshôṅ] *nm* cloth, duster; (*à vaisselle*) dish (*US*) *ou* tea (*Brit*) towel.

tordre [tordr(ə)] *vt* (*chiffon*) to wring; (*barre, fig*: *visage*) to twist; **se** ~ *vi* (*barre*) to bend; (*roue*) to twist, buckle; (*ver, serpent*) to writhe; **se** ~ **le pied/bras** to twist one's foot/arm; **se** ~ **de douleur/rire** to writhe in pain/be doubled up with laughter.

tordu, e [tordü] *pp de* **tordre** ♦ *a* (*fig*) warped, twisted.

torero [torārō] *nm* bullfighter.

tornade [tornád] *nf* tornado.

toron [torôṅ] *nm* strand (of rope).

Toronto [torôṅtō] *n* Toronto.

torontois, e [torôṅtwá, -wáz] *a* Torontonian ♦ *nm/f*: **T**~, **e** Torontonian.

torpeur [torpœr] *nf* torpor, drowsiness.

torpille [torpēy] *nf* torpedo.

torpiller [torpēyā] *vt* to torpedo.

torpilleur [torpēyœr] *nm* torpedo boat.

torréfaction [torāfáksyôṅ] *nf* roasting.

torréfier [torāfyā] *vt* to roast.

torrent [toráṅ] *nm* torrent, mountain stream; (*fig*): **un** ~ **de** a torrent *ou* flood of; **il pleut à** ~**s** the rain is lashing down.

torrentiel, le [torâṅsyel] *a* torrential.

torride [torēd] *a* torrid.

tors, torse *ou* **torte** [tor, tors(ə) *ou* tort(ə)] *a* twisted.

torsade [torsád] *nf* twist; (*ARCHIT*) cable

molding (*US*) *ou* moulding (*Brit*).
torsader [torsådå] *vt* to twist.
torse [tors(ə)] *nm* torso; (*poitrine*) chest.
torsion [torsyôń] *nf* (*action*) twisting; (*TECH, PHYSIQUE*) torsion.
tort [tor] *nm* (*défaut*) fault; (*préjudice*) wrong *q*; ~s *nmpl* (*JUR*) fault *sg*; **avoir** ~ to be wrong; **être dans son** ~ to be in the wrong; **donner** ~ **à qn** to lay the blame on sb; (*fig*) to prove sb wrong; **causer du** ~ **à** to harm; to be harmful *ou* detrimental to; **en** ~ in the wrong, at fault; **à** ~ wrongly; **à** ~ **ou à raison** rightly or wrongly; **à** ~ **et à travers** wildly.
torte [tort(ə)] *af voir* **tors**.
torticolis [tortēkolē] *nm* stiff neck.
tortiller [tortēyå] *vt* (*corde, mouchoir*) to twist; (*doigts*) to twiddle; **se** ~ *vi* to wriggle, squirm.
tortionnaire [torsyoner] *nm* torturer.
tortue [tortü] *nf* tortoise; (*fig*) slowpoke (*US*), slowcoach (*Brit*).
tortueux, euse [tortüœ̄, -œ̄z] *a* (*rue*) twisting; (*fig*) tortuous.
torture [tortür] *nf* torture.
torturer [tortürå] *vt* to torture; (*fig*) to torment.
torve [torv(ə)] *a*: **regard** ~ menacing *ou* grim look.
toscan, e [toskåń, -ån] *a* Tuscan.
Toscane [toskån] *nf*: **la** ~ Tuscany.
tôt [tō] *ad* early; ~ **ou tard** sooner or later; **si** ~ so early; (*déjà*) so soon; **au plus** ~ at the earliest, as soon as possible; **plus** ~ earlier; **il eut** ~ **fait de faire** ... he soon did ....
total, e, aux [totål, -ō] *a, nm* total; **au** ~ in total *ou* all; (*fig*) all in all; **faire le** ~ to work out the total.
totalement [totålmåń] *ad* totally, completely.
totalisateur [totålēzåtœr] *nm* adding machine.
totaliser [totålēzå] *vt* to total (up).
totalitaire [totålēter] *a* totalitarian.
totalitarisme [totålētårēsm(ə)] *nm* totalitarianism.
totalité [totålētå] *nf*: **la** ~ **de**: **la** ~ **des élèves** all (of) the pupils; **la** ~ **de la population/classe** the whole population/class; **en** ~ entirely.
totem [totem] *nm* totem.
toubib [tōōbēb] *nm* (*fam*) doctor.
touchant, e [tōōshåń, -åńt] *a* touching.
touche [tōōsh] *nf* (*de piano, de machine à écrire*) key; (*de violon*) fingerboard; (*de télécommande etc*) key, button; (*PEINTURE etc*) stroke, touch; (*fig: de couleur, nostalgie*) touch, hint; (*RUGBY*) line-out; (*FOOTBALL: aussi:* **remise en** ~) throw-in; (*aussi:* **ligne de** ~) touchline; (*ESCRIME*) hit; **en** ~ in (*ou* into) touch; **avoir une drôle de** ~ to look a sight; ~ **de commande/de fonction/de retour** (*INFORM*) control/function/return key; ~ **à effleurement** *ou* **sensitive** touch-sensitive control *ou* key.
touche-à-tout [tōōshåtōō] *nm inv* (*péj: gén: enfant*) meddler; (: *fig: inventeur etc*) dabbler.
toucher [tōōshå] *nm* touch ◊ *vt* to touch; (*palper*) to feel; (*atteindre: d'un coup de feu etc*) to hit; (*affecter*) to touch, affect;

(*concerner*) to concern, affect; (*contacter*) to reach, contact; (*recevoir: récompense*) to receive, get; (: *salaire*) to draw, get; (*chèque*) to cash; (*aborder: problème, sujet*) to touch on; **au** ~ to the touch; by the feel; **se** ~ (*être en contact*) to touch; ~ **à** to touch; (*modifier*) to touch, tamper *ou* meddle with; (*traiter de, concerner*) to have to do with, concern; **je vais lui en** ~ **un mot** I'll have a word with him about it; ~ **au but** (*fig*) to near one's goal; ~ **à sa fin** to be drawing to a close.
touffe [tōōf] *nf* tuft.
touffu, e [tōōfü] *a* thick, dense; (*fig*) complex, involved.
toujours [tōōzhōōr] *ad* always; (*encore*) still; (*constamment*) forever; **depuis** ~ always; **essaie** ~ (you can) try anyway; **pour** ~ forever; ~ **est-il que** the fact remains that; ~ **plus** more and more.
toulonnais, e [tōōlone, -ez] of *ou* from Toulon.
toulousain, e [tōōlōōzåń, -en] *a* of *ou* from Toulouse.
toupet [tōōpe] *nm* tuft; (*fam*) nerve.
toupie [tōōpē] *nf* (spinning) top.
tour [tōōr] *nf* tower; (*immeuble*) high-rise building (*US*) *ou* block (*Brit*); (*ÉCHECS*) castle, rook ◊ *nm* (*excursion: à pied*) stroll, walk; (: *en voiture etc*) run, ride; (: *plus long*) trip; (*SPORT: aussi:* ~ **de piste**) lap; (*d'être servi ou de jouer etc, tournure, de vis ou clef*) turn; (*de roue etc*) revolution; (*circonférence*): **de 3 m de** ~ 3 m around, with a circumference *ou* girth of 3 m; (*POL: aussi:* ~ **de scrutin**) ballot; (*ruse, de prestidigitation, de cartes*) trick; (*de potier*) wheel; (*à bois, métaux*) lathe; **faire le** ~ **de** to go (a)round; (*à pied*) to walk (a)round; (*fig*) to review; **faire le** ~ **de l'Europe** to tour Europe; **faire un** ~ to go for a walk; (*en voiture etc*) to go for a ride; **faire 2** ~s to go (a)round twice; (*hélice etc*) to turn *ou* revolve twice; **fermer à double** ~ *vi* to double-lock the door; **c'est au** ~ **de Renée** it's Renée's turn; **à** ~ **de rôle**, ~ **à** ~ in turn; **à** ~ **de bras** with all one's strength; (*fig*) nonstop, relentlessly; ~ **de taille/tête** waist/head measurement; ~ **de chant** song recital; ~ **de contrôle** *nf* control tower; ~ **de garde** turn of duty; ~ **d'horizon** (*fig*) general survey; ~ **de lit** valance; ~ **de main** dexterity, knack; **en un** ~ **de main** (as) quick as a flash; ~ **de passe-passe** trick, sleight of hand; ~ **de reins** sprained back.
tourangeau, elle, x [tōōrånzhō, -el] *a* (*de la région*) of *ou* from Touraine; (*de la ville*) of *ou* from Tours.
tourbe [tōōrb(ə)] *nf* peat.
tourbière [tōōrbyer] *nf* peat bog.
tourbillon [tōōrbēyôń] *nm* whirlwind; (*d'eau*) whirlpool; (*fig*) whirl, swirl.
tourbillonner [tōōrbēyonå] *vi* to whirl, swirl; (*objet, personne*) to whirl *ou* twirl round.
tourelle [tōōrel] *nf* turret.
tourisme [tōōrēsm(ə)] *nm* tourism; **agence de** ~ travel agency; **avion/voiture de** ~ private plane/car; **faire du** ~ to do some sightseeing, go touring.
touriste [tōōrēst(ə)] *nm/f* tourist.

touristique [tōōrēstēk] *a* tourist *cpd*; (*région*) touristic (*péj*), with tourist appeal.
tourment [tōōrmáń] *nm* torment.
tourmente [tōōrmáńt] *nf* storm.
tourmenté, e [tōōrmáńtā] *a* tormented, tortured; (*mer, période*) turbulent, tempestuous.
tourmenter [tōōrmáńtā] *vt* to torment; **se ~** *vi* to fret, worry o.s.
tournage [tōōrnäzh] *nm* (*d'un film*) shooting.
tournant, e [tōōrnáń, -áńt] *a* (*feu, scène*) revolving; (*chemin*) winding; (*escalier*) spiral *cpd*; (*mouvement*) circling; *voir* **plaque**, **grève ♦** *nm* (*de route*) curve (*US*), bend (*Brit*); (*fig*) turning point.
tourné, e [tōōrnā] *a* (*lait, vin*) sour; (*MENUISERIE*: *bois*) turned; (*fig*: *compliment*) well-phrased; **bien ~** (*personne*) shapely; **mal ~** (*lettre*) badly expressed; **avoir l'esprit mal ~** to have a dirty mind.
tournebroche [tōōrnəbrosh] *nm* roasting spit.
tourne-disque [tōōrnədēsk(ə)] *nm* record player.
tournedos [tōōrnədō] *nm* tournedos.
tournée [tōōrnā] *nf* (*du facteur etc*) round; (*d'artiste, politicien*) tour; (*au café*) round (of drinks); **~ électorale/musicale** election/concert tour; **faire la ~ de** to go (a)round.
tournemain [tōōrnəmáń]: **en un ~** *ad* in a flash.
tourner [tōōrnā] *vt* to turn; (*sauce, mélange*) to stir; (*contourner*) to get (a)round; (*CINÉMA*) to shoot; to make ♦ *vi* to turn; (*moteur*) to run; (*compteur*) to tick away; (*lait etc*) to turn (sour); (*fig*: *chance, vie*) to turn out; **se ~** *vi* to turn (a)round; **se ~ vers** to turn to; to turn towards; **bien ~** to turn out well; **~ autour de** to go (a)round; (*planète*) to revolve (a)round; (*péj*) to hang (a)round; **~ autour du pot** (*fig*) to go (a)round in circles; **~ à/en** to turn into; **~ à la pluie/au rouge** to turn rainy/red; **~ en ridicule** to ridicule; **~ le dos à** (*mouvement*) to turn one's back on; (*position*) to have one's back to; **~ court** to come to a sudden end; **se ~ les pouces** to twiddle one's thumbs; **~ la tête** to look away; **~ la tête à qn** (*fig*) to go to sb's head; **~ de l'œil** to pass out; **~ la page** (*fig*) to turn the page.
tournesol [tōōrnəsol] *nm* sunflower.
tourneur [tōōrnœr] *nm* turner; lathe-operator.
tournevis [tōōrnəvēs] *nm* screwdriver.
tourniquer [tōōrnēkā] *vi* to go (a)round in circles.
tourniquet [tōōrnēke] *nm* (*pour arroser*) sprinkler; (*portillon*) turnstile; (*présentoir*) revolving stand, spinner; (*CHIRURGIE*) tourniquet.
tournis [tōōrnē] *nm*: **avoir/donner le ~** to feel/make dizzy.
tournoi [tōōrnwä] *nm* tournament.
tournoyer [tōōrnwàyā] *vi* (*oiseau*) to wheel (a)round; (*fumée*) to swirl (a)round.
tournure [tōōrnür] *nf* (*LING*: *syntaxe*) turn of phrase; form; (: *d'une phrase*) phrasing; (*évolution*): **la ~ de qch** the way sth is developing; (*aspect*): **la ~ de** the look of; **la ~ des événements** the turn of events; **prendre ~** to take shape; **~ d'esprit** turn *ou* cast of mind.

tour-opérateur [tōōropārátœr] *nm* tour operator.
tourte [tōōrt(ə)] *nf* pie.
tourteau, x [tōōrtō] *nm* (*AGR*) oil cake, cattle-cake; (*ZOOL*) edible crab.
tourtereaux [tōōrtərō] *nmpl* lovebirds.
tourterelle [tōōrtərel] *nf* turtledove.
tourtière [tōōrtyer] *nf* pie tin (*US*) *ou* dish (*Brit*).
tous *dét* [tōō] , *pronom* [tōōs] *voir* **tout**.
Toussaint [tōōsań] *nf*: **la ~** All Saints' Day.
tousser [tōōsā] *vi* to cough.
toussoter [tōōsotā] *vi* to have a slight cough; to cough a little; (*pour avertir*) to give a slight cough.
tout, e, *pl* **tous, toutes** [tōō, tōōs, tōōt] *dét* all; **~ le lait** all the milk, the whole of the milk; **~e la nuit** all night, the whole night; **~ le livre** the whole book; **~ un pain** a whole loaf; **tous les livres** all the books; **toutes les nuits** every night; **à ~ âge** at any age; **toutes les fois** every time; **toutes les 3/2 semaines** every third/other *ou* second week; **tous les 2** both *ou* each of us (*ou* them); **toutes les 3** all 3 of us (*ou* them); **~ le temps** *ad* all the time; (*sans cesse*) the whole time; **c'est ~ le contraire** it's quite the opposite; **il avait pour ~e nourriture** his only food was ♦ *pronom* everything, all; **tous, toutes** all (of them); **je les vois tous** I can see them all *ou* all of them; **nous y sommes tous allés** all of us went, we all went; **en ~** in all; **en ~ et pour ~** all in all ♦ *ad* (*assez*) quite; (*très*) very; **en haut** right at the top; **le ~ premier** the very first; **le livre ~ entier** the whole book; **~ court** quite simply; **~ seul** all alone; **~ droit** straight ahead; **~ en travaillant/mangeant** while working/eating, as *ou* while he *etc* works/eats ♦ *nm* whole; **le ~** all of it (*ou* them), the whole lot; **le ~ est de** the main thing is to; **du ~ au ~** (*complètement*) utterly; **avoir ~ de**: **elle a ~ d'une mère** she's a real mother; **~ ce que ...** all that ...; **~ ce qu'il y a de plus aimable** the nicest possible, as nice as possible; **~ ou rien** all or nothing; **~ d'abord** first of all; **~ à coup** suddenly; **~ à fait** absolutely; **~ à l'heure** (*passé*) a short while ago; (*futur*) in a short while, shortly; **à ~ à l'heure!** see you later!; **~ de même** all the same; **~ le monde** everybody, everyone; **~ de suite** immediately, straightaway; **~ terrain** *ou* **tous terrains** *a inv* all-terrain.
tout-à-l'égout [tōōtálāgōō] *nm inv* sewer system.
toutefois [tōōtfwä] *ad* however.
toutou [tōōtōō] *nm* (*fam*) doggie.
tout-petit [tōōp(ə)tē] *nm* toddler.
tout-puissant, toute-puissante [tōōpüēsáń, tōōtpüēsáńt] *a* all-powerful, omnipotent.
tout-venant [tōōvnáń] *nm*: **le ~** everyday stuff.
toux [tōō] *nf* cough.
toxémie [toksāmē] *nf* toxemia (*US*), toxaemia (*Brit*).
toxicité [toksēsētā] *nf* toxicity.
toxicomane [toksēkomán] *nm/f* drug addict.
toxicomanie [toksēkománē] *nf* drug addiction.

toxine [toksēn] *nf* toxin.

toxique [toksēk] *a* toxic, poisonous.

TP *sigle mpl* = **travaux pratiques, travaux publics** ♦ *sigle m* = **trésor public**.

TPG *sigle m* = **Trésorier-payeur général**.

tps *abr* = **temps**.

trac [tràk] *nm* nerves *pl*; (*THÉÂTRE*) stage fright; **avoir le ~** to get an attack of nerves; to have stage fright; **tout à ~** all of a sudden.

traçant, e [tràsàǹ, -àǹt] *a*: **table ~e** (*INFORM*) (graph) plotter.

tracas [tràkà] *nm* bother *q*, worry *q*.

tracasser [tràkàsà] *vt* to worry, bother; (*harceler*) to harass; **se ~** *vi* to worry o.s., fret.

tracasserie [tràkàsrē] *nf* annoyance *q*; harassment *q*.

tracassier, ière [tràkàsyà, -yer] *a* irksome.

trace [tràs] *nf* (*empreintes*) tracks *pl*; (*marques, aussi fig*) mark; (*restes, vestige*) trace; (*indice*) sign; **suivre à la ~** to track; **~s de pas** footprints.

tracé [tràsà] *nm* (*contour*) line; (*plan*) layout.

tracer [tràsà] *vt* to draw; (*mot*) to trace; (*piste*) to open up; (*fig: chemin*) to show.

traceur [tràsœr] *nm* (*INFORM*) plotter.

trachée(-artère) [tràshà(àrter)] *nf* windpipe, trachea.

trachéite [tràkàēt] *nf* tracheitis.

tract [tràkt] *nm* tract, pamphlet; (*publicitaire*) handout.

tractations [tràktàsyòǹ] *nfpl* dealings, bargaining *sg*.

tracter [tràktà] *vt* to tow.

tracteur [tràktœr] *nm* tractor.

traction [tràksyòǹ] *nf* traction; (*GYM*) pull-up; **~ avant/arrière** front-wheel/rear-wheel drive; **~ électrique** electric(al) traction *ou* haulage.

tradition [tràdēsyòǹ] *nf* tradition.

traditionaliste [tràdēsyonàlēst(ə)] *a, nm/f* traditionalist.

traditionnel, le [tràdēsyonel] *a* traditional.

traditionnellement [tràdēsyonelmàǹ] *ad* traditionally.

traducteur, trice [tràdüktœr, -trēs] *nm/f* translator.

traduction [tràdüksyòǹ] *nf* translation.

traduire [tràdüēr] *vt* to translate; (*exprimer*) to render, convey; **se ~ par** to find expression in; **~ en français** to translate into French; **~ en justice** to bring before the courts.

traduis [tràdüē] *etc vb voir* **traduire**.

traduisible [tràdüēzēbl(ə)] *a* translatable.

traduit, e [tràdüē, -ēt] *pp de* **traduire**.

trafic [tràfēk] *nm* traffic; **~ d'armes** arms dealing; **~ de drogue** drug peddling.

trafiquant, e [tràfēkàǹ, -àǹt] *nm/f* trafficker; dealer.

trafiquer [tràfēkà] *vt* (*péj*) to doctor, tamper with ♦ *vi* to traffic, be engaged in trafficking.

tragédie [tràzhàdē] *nf* tragedy.

tragédien, ne [tràzhàdyaǹ, -en] *nm/f* tragedian/tragedienne.

tragi-comique [tràzhēkomēk] *a* tragi-comic.

tragique [tràzhēk] *a* tragic ♦ *nm*: **prendre qch au ~** to make a tragedy out of sth.

tragiquement [tràzhēkmàǹ] *ad* tragically.

trahir [tràēr] *vt* to betray; (*fig*) to give away, reveal; **se ~** to betray o.s., give o.s. away.

trahison [tràēzòǹ] *nf* betrayal; (*JUR*) treason.

traie [tre] *etc vb voir* **traire**.

train [traǹ] *nm* (*RAIL*) train; (*allure*) pace; (*fig: ensemble*) set; **être en ~ de faire qch** to be doing sth; **mettre qch en ~** to get sth under way; **mettre qn en ~** to put sb in good spirits; **se mettre en ~** (*commencer*) to get started; (*faire de la gymnastique*) to warm up; **se sentir en ~** to feel in good form; **aller bon ~** to make good progress; **~ avant/arrière** front-wheel/rear-wheel axle assembly; **~ à grande vitesse (TGV)** high-speed train; **~ d'atterrissage** landing gear; **~-autos-couchettes** car-sleeper train; **~ électrique** (*jouet*) (electric) train set; **~ de pneus** set of tires (*US*) *ou* tyres (*Brit*); **~ de vie** style of living.

traînailler [trenàyà] *vi* = **traînasser**.

traînant, e [trenàǹ, -àǹt] *a* (*voix, ton*) drawling.

traînard, e [trenàr, -àrd(ə)] *nm/f* (*péj*) slowpoke (*US*), slowcoach (*Brit*).

traînasser [trenàsà] *vi* to dawdle.

traîne [tren] *nf* (*de robe*) train; **être à la ~** to be in tow; (*en arrière*) to lag behind; (*en désordre*) to be lying around.

traîneau, x [trenò] *nm* sleigh, sledge.

traînée [trenà] *nf* streak, trail; (*péj*) slut.

traîner [trenà] *vt* (*remorque*) to pull; (*enfant, chien*) to drag *ou* trail along; (*maladie*): **il traîne un rhume depuis l'hiver** he has a cold which has been dragging on since winter ♦ *vi* (*être en désordre*) to lie around; (*marcher lentement*) to dawdle (along); (*vagabonder*) to hang about; (*agir lentement*) to idle about; (*durer*) to drag on; **se ~** *vi* (*ramper*) to crawl along; (*marcher avec difficulté*) to drag o.s. along; (*durer*) to drag on; **se ~ par terre** to crawl (on the ground); **~ qn au cinéma** to drag sb to the cinema; **~ les pieds** to drag one's feet; **~ par terre** to trail on the ground; **~ en longueur** to drag out.

training [trenēng] *nm* (*pull*) tracksuit top; (*chaussure*) sneaker (*US*), trainer (*Brit*).

train-train [traǹtraǹ] *nm* humdrum routine.

traire [trer] *vt* to milk.

trait, e [tre, -et] *pp de* **traire** ♦ *nm* (*ligne*) line; (*de dessin*) stroke; (*caractéristique*) feature, trait; (*flèche*) dart, arrow; shaft; **~s** *nmpl* (*du visage*) features; **d'un ~** (*boire*) in one gulp; **de ~** *a* (*animal*) draft (*US*), draught (*Brit*); **avoir ~ à** to concern; **~ pour ~** line for line; **~ de caractère** characteristic, trait; **~ d'esprit** flash of wit; **~ de génie** brain wave; **~ d'union** hyphen; (*fig*) link.

traitable [tretàbl(ə)] *a* (*personne*) accommodating; (*sujet*) manageable.

traitant, e [tretàǹ, -àǹt] *a*: **votre médecin ~** your usual *ou* family doctor; **shampooing ~** medicated shampoo; **crème ~e** conditioning cream, conditioner.

traite [tret] *nf* (*COMM*) draft; (*AGR*) milking; (*trajet*) stretch; **d'une (seule) ~** without stopping (once); **la ~ des noirs** the slave trade; **la ~ des blanches** the white slave trade.

traité [tràtà] *nm* treaty.

traitement [tretmɑ̃] *nm* treatment; process-ing; (*salaire*) salary; **suivre un** ~ to undergo treatment; **mauvais** ~ ill-treatment; ~ **de données** *ou* **de l'information** (*INFORM*) data processing; ~ **par lots** (*INFORM*) batch processing; ~ **de texte** (*INFORM*) word processing.

traiter [trɛtā] *vt* (*gén*) to treat; (*TECH*: *maté-riaux*) to process, treat; (*INFORM*) to pro-cess; (*affaire*) to deal with, handle; (*quali-fier*): ~ **qn d'idiot** to call sb a fool ♦ *vi* to deal; ~ **de** *vt* to deal with; **bien/mal** ~ to treat well/ill-treat.

traiteur [trɛtœr] *nm* caterer.

traître, esse [trɛtr(ə), -trɛs] *a* (*dangereux*) treacherous ♦ *nm* traitor; **prendre qn en** ~ to make an insidious attack on sb.

traîtrise [trɛtriz] *nf* treachery.

trajectoire [traʒɛktwar] *nf* trajectory, path.

trajet [traʒe] *nm* journey; (*itinéraire*) route; (*fig*) path, course. /

tralala [tralala] *nm* (*péj*) fuss.

tram [tram] *nm* streetcar (*US*), tram (*Brit*).

trame [tram] *nf* (*de tissu*) weft; (*fig*) frame-work; texture; (*TYPO*) screen.

tramer [trame] *vt* to plot, hatch.

trampoline [trɑ̃polen], **trampolino** [trɑ̃polēnō] *nm* trampoline; (*SPORT*) trampolining.

tramway [tramwɛ] *nm* tram(way); (*voiture*) streetcar (*US*), tram(car) (*Brit*).

tranchant, e [trɑ̃ʃɑ̃, -ɑ̃t] *a* sharp; (*fig*: *personne*) peremptory; (: *couleurs*) striking ♦ *nm* (*d'un couteau*) cutting edge; (*de la main*) edge; **à double** ~ (*argument*, *procédé*) double-edged.

tranche [trɑ̃ʃ] *nf* (*morceau*) slice; (*arête*) edge; (*partie*) section; (*série*) block; (*d'impôts, revenus etc*) bracket; (*loterie*) issue; ~ **d'âge** age bracket; ~ (**de silicium**) wafer.

tranché, e [trɑ̃ʃā] *a* (*couleurs*) distinct, sharply contrasted; (*opinions*) clear-cut, definite ♦ *nf* trench.

trancher [trɑ̃ʃā] *vt* to cut, sever; (*fig*: ré-soudre) to settle ♦ *vi* to be decisive; (*entre deux choses*) to settle the argument; ~ **avec** to contrast sharply with.

tranchet [trɑ̃ʃe] *nm* knife.

tranchoir [trɑ̃ʃwar] *nm* chopper.

tranquille [trɑ̃kēl] *a* calm, quiet; (*enfant*, *élève*) quiet; (*rassuré*) easy in one's mind, with one's mind at rest; **se tenir** ~ (*enfant*) to be quiet; **avoir la conscience** ~ to have an easy conscience; **laisse-moi/laisse-ça** ~ leave me/it alone.

tranquillement [trɑ̃kēlmɑ̃] *ad* calmly.

tranquillisant, e [trɑ̃kēlēzɑ̃, -ɑ̃t] *a* (*nouvelle*) reassuring ♦ *nm* tranquillizer.

tranquilliser [trɑ̃kēlēzā] *vt* to reassure; **se** ~ to calm (o.s.) down.

tranquillité [trɑ̃kēlētā] *nf* quietness; peace (and quiet); **en toute** ~ with complete peace of mind; ~ **d'esprit** peace of mind.

transaction [trɑ̃záksyɔ̃] *nf* (*COMM*) transac-tion, deal.

transafricain, e [trɑ̃sáfrēkaṅ, -cn] *a* transafrican.

transalpin, e [trɑ̃zálpaṅ, -ēn] *a* transalpine.

transaméricain, e [trɑ̃zámārēkaṅ, -en] *a* transamerican.

transat [trɑ̃zát] *nm* deck chair ♦ *nf* = *course transatlantique*.

transatlantique [trɑ̃zátlàntēk] *a* transatlantic ♦ *nm* transatlantic liner.

transborder [trɑ̃sbordā] *vt* to tran(s)ship.

transcendant, e [trɑ̃sɑ̃dɑ̃, -ɑ̃t] *a* (*PHILOSOPHIE*, *MATH*) transcendental; (*supérieur*) transcendent.

transcodeur [trɑ̃skodœr] *nm* compiler.

transcription [trɑ̃skrēpsyɔ̃] *nf* transcription.

transcrire [trɑ̃skrēr] *vt* to transcribe.

transe [trɑ̃s] *nf*: **entrer en** ~ to go into a trance; ~**s** *nfpl* agony *sg*.

transfèrement [trɑ̃sfɛrmɑ̃] *nm* transfer.

transférer [trɑ̃sfārā] *vt* to transfer.

transfert [trɑ̃sfer] *nm* transfer.

transfigurer [trɑ̃sfēgürā] *vt* to transform.

transfo [trɑ̃sfō] *nm* (= *transformateur*) transformer.

transformable [trɑ̃sformábl(ə)] *a* convertible.

transformateur [trɑ̃sformátœr] *nm* transformer.

transformation [trɑ̃sformásyɔ̃] *nf* transformation; (*RUGBY*) conversion; **indus-tries de** ~ processing industries.

transformer [trɑ̃sformā] *vt* to transform, alter ('*alter*' *implique un changement moins radical*); (*matière première, appartement*, *RUGBY*) to convert; ~ **en** to transform into; to turn into; to convert into; **se** ~ *vi* to be transformed; to alter.

transfuge [trɑ̃sfüzh] *nm* renegade.

transfuser [trɑ̃sfüzā] *vt* to transfuse.

transfusion [trɑ̃sfüzyɔ̃] *nf*: ~ **sanguine** blood transfusion.

transgresser [trɑ̃sgrāsā] *vt* to contravene, disobey.

transhumance [trɑ̃zümɑ̃s] *nf* transhumance, seasonal move to new pastures.

transi, e [trɑ̃zē] *a* numb (with cold), chilled to the bone.

transiger [trɑ̃zēzhā] *vi* to compromise, come to an agreement; ~ **sur** *ou* **avec qch** to compromise on sth.

transistor [trɑ̃zēstor] *nm* transistor.

transistorisé, e [trɑ̃zēstorēzā] *a* transistorized.

transit [trɑ̃zēt] *nm* transit; **de** ~ transit *cpd*; **en** ~ in transit.

transitaire [trɑ̃zēter] *nm/f* forwarding agent.

transiter [trɑ̃zētā] *vi* to pass in transit.

transitif, ive [trɑ̃zētēf, -ēv] *a* transitive.

transition [trɑ̃zēsyɔ̃] *nf* transition; **de** ~ transitional.

transitoire [trɑ̃zētwar] *a* (*mesure, gouverne-ment*) transitional, provisional; (*fugitif*) transient.

translucide [trɑ̃slüsēd] *a* translucent.

transmet [trɑ̃smɛ] *etc vb voir* **transmettre**.

transmettais [trɑ̃smɛte] *etc vb voir* **transmettre**.

transmetteur [trɑ̃smɛtœr] *nm* transmitter.

transmettre [trɑ̃smɛtr(ə)] *vt* (*passer*): ~ **qch à qn** to pass sth on to sb; (*TECH, TÉL, MÉD*) to transmit; (*TV, RADIO*: *retransmettre*) to broadcast.

transmis, e [trɑ̃smē, -ēz] *pp de* **transmettre**.

transmissible [trầnsmēsēbl(ǝ)] *a* transmissible.

transmission [trầnsmēsyôṅ] *nf* transmission, passing on; (*AUTO*) transmission; **~s** *nfpl* (*MIL*) ≈ signals corps; **~ de données** (*INFORM*) data transmission; **~ de pensée** thought transmission.

transocéanien, ne [trầnzosǎányaṅ, -en] *a*, **transocéanique** [trầnzosǎánēk] *a* transoceanic.

transparaître [trầnspárétr(ǝ)] *vi* to show (through).

transparence [trầnspáráṅs] *nf* transparence; **par ~** (*regarder*) against the light; (*voir*) showing through.

transparent, e [trầnspáráṅ, -áṅt] *a* transparent.

transpercer [trầnspersǎ] *vt* to go through, pierce.

transpiration [trầnspērásyôṅ] *nf* perspiration.

transpirer [trầnspērá] *vi* to perspire; (*information, nouvelle*) to come to light.

transplant [trầnspláṅ] *nm* transplant.

transplantation [trầnspláṅtásyôṅ] *nf* transplant.

transplanter [trầnspláṅtá] *vt* (*MÉD*, *BOT*) to transplant; (*personne*) to uproot, move.

transport [trầnspor] *nm* transport; (*émotions*): **~ de colère** fit of rage; **~ de joie** transport of delight; **~ de voyageurs/ marchandises** passenger/goods transportation; **~s en commun** public transport *sg*; **~s routiers** trucking (*US*), haulage (*Brit*).

transportable [trầnsportábl(ǝ)] *a* (*marchandises*) transportable; (*malade*) fit (enough) to be moved.

transporter [trầnsportá] *vt* to carry, move; (*COMM*) to transport, convey; (*fig*): **~ qn (de joie)** to send sb into raptures; **se ~ quelque part** (*fig*) to let one's imagination carry one away (somewhere); **~ qn à l'hôpital** to take sb to hospital.

transporteur [trầnsportœr] *nm* trucker (*US*), haulage contractor (*Brit*).

transposer [trầnspŏzá] *vt* to transpose.

transposition [trầnspŏzēsyôṅ] *nf* transposition.

transrhénan, e [trầnsránáṅ, -áṅ] *a* beyond the Rhine.

transsaharien, ne [trầnssǎáryaṅ, -en] *a* trans-Saharan.

transsexuel, le [trầnsseksüel] *a*, *nm/f* transsexual.

transsibérien, ne [trầnssēbǎryaṅ, -en] *a* trans-Siberian.

transvaser [trầnsvázá] *vt* to decant.

transversal, e, aux [trầnsversál, -ŏ] *a* transverse, cross(-); (*route etc*) cross-country; (*mur, chemin, rue*) running at right angles; (*AUTO*): **axe ~** main cross-country highway (*US*) *ou* road (*Brit*).

transversalement [trầnsversálmáṅ] *ad* crosswise.

trapèze [trápez] *nm* (*GÉOM*) trapezoid (*US*), trapezium (*Brit*); (*au cirque*) trapeze.

trapéziste [trápǎzēst(ǝ)] *nm/f* trapeze artist.

trappe [tráp] *nf* (*de cave, grenier*) trap door; (*piège*) trap.

trappeur [trápœr] *nm* trapper, fur trader.

trapu, e [trápü] *a* squat, stocky.

traquenard [tráknár] *nm* trap.

traquer [tráká] *vt* to track down; (*harceler*) to hound.

traumatisant, e [trŏmátēzáṅ, -áṅt] *traumatic.

traumatiser [trŏmátēzá] *vt* to traumatize.

traumatisme [trŏmátēsm(ǝ)] *nm* traumatism; **~ crânien** cranial traumatism.

traumatologie [trŏmátolozhē] *nf branch of medicine concerned with accidents*.

travail, aux [trávày, -ŏ] *nm* (*gén*) work; (*tâche, métier*) work *q*, job; (*ÉCON, MÉD*) labor (*US*), labour (*Brit*); (*INFORM*) job ♦ *nmpl* (*de réparation, agricoles etc*) work *sg*; (*sur route*) road construction (*US*) *ou* repairs, roadworks (*Brit*); (*de construction*) building (work) *sg*; **être/entrer en ~** (*MÉD*) to be in/ go into labor; **être sans ~** (*employé*) to be out of work, be unemployed; **~ d'intérêt général (TIG)** ≈ community service; **~ (au) noir** moonlighting; **~ posté** shiftwork; **travaux des champs** farmwork *sg*; **travaux dirigés (TD)** (*SCOL*) supervised practical work *sg*; **travaux forcés** hard labor *sg*; **travaux manuels** (*SCOL*) handicrafts; **travaux ménagers** housework *sg*; **travaux pratiques (TP)** (*gén*) practical work; (*en laboratoire*) lab (*US*), lab work (*Brit*); **travaux publics (TP)** ≈ public works *sg*.

travaillé, e [trávàyá] *a* (*style*) polished.

travailler [trávàyá] *vi* to work; (*bois*) to warp ♦ *vt* (*bois, métal*) to work; (*pâte*) to knead; (*objet d'art, discipline, fig: influencer*) to work on; **cela le travaille** it is on his mind; **~ la terre** to work the land; **~ son piano** to do one's piano practice; **~ à** to work on; (*fig: contribuer à*) to work towards; **~ à faire** to endeavor to do.

travailleur, euse [trávàyœr, -œz] *a* hardworking ♦ *nm/f* worker; **~ de force** laborer (*US*), labourer (*Brit*); **~ intellectuel** non-manual worker; **~ social** social worker; **travailleuse familiale** *social welfare worker in the home*.

travailliste [trávàyēst(ǝ)] *a* ≈ Labour *cpd* (*Brit*) ♦ *nm/f* member of the Labour party (*Brit*).

travée [trává] *nf* row; (*ARCHIT*) bay; span.

travelling [trávlēng] *nm* (*chariot*) dolly; (*technique*) tracking; **~ optique** zoom shots *pl*.

travelo [trávlŏ] *nm* (*fam*) (drag) queen.

travers [tráver] *nm* fault, failing; **en ~ (de)** across; **au ~ (de)** through; **de ~** a askew ♦ *ad* sideways; (*fig*) the wrong way; **à ~** through; **regarder de ~** (*fig*) to look askance at.

traverse [trávers(ǝ)] *nf* (*de voie ferrée*) tie (*US*), sleeper (*Brit*); **chemin de ~** shortcut.

traversée [tráversá] *nf* crossing.

traverser [tráversá] *vt* (*gén*) to cross; (*ville, tunnel, aussi: percer, fig*) to go through; (*suj: ligne, trait*) to run across.

traversin [tráversaṅ] *nm* bolster.

travesti [trávestē] *nm* (*costume*) costume; (*artiste de cabaret*) female impersonator, drag artist; (*pervers*) transvestite.

travestir [trávestēr] *vt* (*vérité*) to misrepresent; **se ~** (*se costumer*) to dress up; (*artiste*) to put on drag; (*PSYCH*) to dress as a woman.

trayais |trcyc| *etc vb voir* **traire**.

trayeuse |trcyœ̄z| *nf* milking machine.

trébucher |trābüshā| *vi*: ~ **(sur)** to stumble (over), trip (over).

trèfle |trefl(ə)| *nm* (*BOT*) clover; (*CARTES: couleur*) clubs *pl*; (: *carte*) club; ~ **à quatre feuilles** four-leaf clover.

treillage |treyàzh| *nm* latticework.

treille |trey| *nf* (*tonnelle*) vine arbor (*US*) *ou* arbour (*Brit*); (*vigne*) climbing vine.

treillis |trāyē| *nm* (*métallique*) wire netting; (*toile*) canvas; (*uniforme*) battle-dress.

treize |trez| *num* thirteen.

treizième |trezyem| *num* thirteenth.

tréma |trāmà| *nm* dieresis (*US*), diaeresis (*Brit*).

tremblant, e |tràṅblàṅ, -àṅt| *a* trembling, shaking.

tremble |tràṅbl(ə)| *nm* (*BOT*) aspen.

tremblé, e |tràṅblā| *a* shaky.

tremblement |tràṅbləmàṅ| *nm* trembling *q*, shaking *q*, shivering *q*; ~ **de terre** earthquake.

trembler |tràṅblā| *vi* to tremble, shake; ~ **de** (*froid, fièvre*) to shiver *ou* tremble with; (*peur*) to shake *ou* tremble with; ~ **pour qn** to fear for sb.

trembloter |tràṅblotā| *vi* to tremble *ou* shake slightly.

trémolo |trāmolō| *nm* (*d'un instrument*) tremolo; (*de la voix*) quaver.

trémousser |trāmōōsā|: **se** ~ *vi* to jig about, wriggle about.

trempe |tràṅp| *nf* (*fig*): **de cette/sa** ~ of this/his caliber (*US*) *ou* calibre (*Brit*).

trempé, e |tràṅpā| *a* soaking (wet), drenched; (*TECH*): **acier** ~ tempered steel.

tremper |tràṅpā| *vt* to soak, drench; (*aussi:* **faire** ~, **mettre à** ~) to soak; (*plonger*): ~ **qch dans** to dip sth in(to) ♦ *vi* to soak; (*fig*): ~ **dans** to be involved *ou* have a hand in; **se** ~ *vi* to have a quick dip; **se faire** ~ to get soaked *ou* drenched.

trempette |tràṅpet| *nf*: **faire** ~ to go paddling.

tremplin |tràṅplàṅ| *nm* springboard; (*SKI*) ski jump.

trentaine |tràṅten| *nf* (*âge*): **avoir la** ~ to be around thirty; **une** ~ **(de)** thirty or so, about thirty.

trente |tràṅt| *num* thirty; **voir** ~**-six chandelles** (*fig*) to see stars; **être/se mettre sur son** ~ **et un** to be/get dressed to kill; ~**-trois tours** *nm* long-playing record, LP.

trentième |tràṅtyem| *num* thirtieth.

trépaner |trāpánā| *vt* to trepan, trephine.

trépasser |trāpàsā| *vi* to pass away.

trépidant, e |trāpēdàṅ, -àṅt| *a* (*fig: rythme*) pulsating; (: *vie*) hectic.

trépidation |trāpēdàsyóṅ| *nf* (*d'une machine, d'un moteur*) vibration; (*fig: de la vie*) whirl.

trépider |trāpēdā| *vi* to vibrate.

trépied |trāpyā| *nm* (*d'appareil*) tripod; (*meuble*) trivet.

trépigner |trāpēnyā| *vi* to stamp (one's feet).

très |tre| *ad* very; much + *pp*, highly + *pp*; ~ **beau/bien** very beautiful/well; ~ **critiqué** much criticized; ~ **industrialisé** highly industrialized; **j'ai** ~ **faim** I'm very hungry.

trésor |trāzor| *nm* treasure; (*ADMIN*) finances

pl; (*d'un organisation*) funds *pl*; ~ **(public) (TP)** public revenue; (*service*) public revenue office.

trésorerie |trāzorrē| *nf* (*fonds*) funds *pl*; (*gestion*) accounts *pl*; (*bureaux*) accounts department; (*poste*) treasurership; **difficultés de** ~ cash problems, shortage of cash *ou* funds; ~ **générale (TG)** *local government finance office*.

trésorier, ière |trāzoryā, -yer| *nm/f* treasurer.

trésorier-payeur |trāzoryāpeyœr| *nm*: ~ **général (TPG)** paymaster.

tressaillement |trāsàymàṅ| *nm* shiver, shudder; quiver.

tressaillir |trāsàyēr| *vi* (*de peur etc*) to shiver, shudder; (*de joie*) to quiver.

tressauter |trāsōtā| *vi* to start, jump.

tresse |tres| *nf* (*de cheveux*) braid, plait; (*cordon, galon*) braid.

tresser |trāsā| *vt* (*cheveux*) to braid, plait; (*fil, jonc*) to plait; (*corbeille*) to weave; (*corde*) to twist.

tréteau, x |trātō| *nm* trestle; **les** ~**x** (*fig: THÉÂTRE*) the boards.

treuil |trœy| *nm* winch.

trêve |trev| *nf* (*MIL, POL*) truce; (*fig*) respite; **sans** ~ unremittingly; ~ **de** ... enough of this ...; **les États de la T**~ the Trucial States.

tri |trē| *nm* (*voir trier*) sorting (out) *q*; selection; screening; (*INFORM*) sort; (*POSTES: action*) sorting; (: *bureau*) sorting office.

triage |trēyàzh| *nm* (*RAIL*) shunting; (*gare*) marshalling yard.

triangle |trēyàṅgl(ə)| *nm* triangle; ~ **isocèle/ équilatéral** isosceles/equilateral triangle; ~ **rectangle** right (*US*) *ou* right-angled (*Brit*) triangle.

triangulaire |trēyàṅgüler| *a* triangular.

tribal, e, aux |trēbál, -ō| *a* tribal.

tribord |trēbor| *nm*: **à** ~ to starboard, on the starboard side.

tribu |trēbü| *nf* tribe.

tribulations |trēbülàsyóṅ| *nfpl* tribulations, trials.

tribunal, aux |trēbünál, -ō| *nm* (*JUR*) court; (*MIL*) tribunal; ~ **de police/pour enfants** police/juvenile court; ~ **d'instance (TI)** ≈ district court (*US*), ≈ magistrates' court (*Brit*); ~ **de grande instance (TGI)** ≈ Supreme Court (*US*), ≈ High Court (*Brit*).

tribune |trēbün| *nf* (*estrade*) platform, rostrum; (*débat*) forum; (*d'église, de tribunal*) gallery; (*de stade*) stand; ~ **libre** (*PRESSE*) opinion column.

tribut |trēbü| *nm* tribute.

tributaire |trēbüter| *a*: **être** ~ **de** to be dependent on; (*GÉO*) to be a tributary of.

tricentenaire |trēsàṅtner| *nm* tercentenary, tricentennial.

tricher |trēshā| *vi* to cheat.

tricherie |trēshrē| *nf* cheating *q*.

tricheur, euse |trēshœr, -œ̄z| *nm/f* cheat.

trichromie |trēkromē| *nf* three-color (*US*) *ou* -colour (*Brit*) printing.

tricolore |trēkolor| *a* three-colored (*US*), three-coloured (*Brit*); (*français: drapeau*) red, white and blue; (: *équipe etc*) French.

tricot |trēkō| *nm* (*technique, ouvrage*) knitting *q*; (*tissu*) knitted fabric; (*vêtement*) jersey, sweater; ~ **de corps** undershirt (*US*), vest (*Brit*).

tricoter [trēkotā] *vt* to knit; **machine/aiguille à** ~ knitting machine/needle.

trictrac [trēktrák] *nm* backgammon.

tricycle [trēsēkl(ə)] *nm* tricycle.

triennal, e, aux [trēenál, -ō] *a* (*prix, foire, élection*) triennial; (*charge, mandat, plan*) three-year.

trier [trēyā] *vt* (*classer*) to sort (out); (*choisir*) to select; (*visiteurs*) to screen; (*POSTES, INFORM*) to sort.

trieur, euse [trēyœr, -ēz] *nm/f* sorter.

trigonométrie [trēgonomātrē] *nf* trigonometry.

trilingue [trēlañg] *a* trilingual.

trilogie [trēlozhē] *nf* trilogy.

trimbaler [trañbálā] *vt* to cart around, trail along.

trimer [trēmā] *vi* to slave away.

trimestre [trēmestr(ə)] *nm* (*SCOL*) term; (*COMM*) quarter.

trimestriel, le [trēmestrēyel] *a* quarterly; (*SCOL*) final (*US*), end-of-term (*Brit*).

tringle [trañgl(ə)] *nf* rod.

Trinité [trēnētā] *nf* Trinity.

Trinité et Tobago [trēnētāātobágō] *nf* Trinidad and Tobago.

trinquer [trañkā] *vi* to clink glasses; (*fam*) to take the rap; ~ **à qch/la santé de qn** to drink to sth/sb.

trio [trēyō] *nm* trio.

triolet [trēyole] *nm* (*MUS*) triplet.

triomphal, e, aux [trēyōñfál, -ō] *a* triumphant, triumphal.

triomphant, e [trēyōñfàñ, -áñt] *a* triumphant.

triomphateur, trice [trēyōñfátœr, -trēs] *nm/f* (*triumphant*) victor.

triomphe [trēyōñf] *nm* triumph; **être reçu/porté en** ~ to be given a triumphant welcome/be carried shoulder-high in triumph.

triompher [trēyōñfā] *vi* to triumph; ~ **de** to triumph over, overcome.

triparti, e [trēpártē] *a* (*aussi:* **tripartite**: *réunion, assemblée*) tripartite, three-party.

triperie [trēprē] *nf* tripe shop.

tripes [trēp] *nfpl* (*CULIN*) tripe *sg*; (*fam*) guts.

triplace [trēplás] *a* three-seater *cpd*.

triple [trēpl(ə)] *a* (*à trois éléments*) triple; (*trois fois plus grand*) treble ♦ *nm*: **le** ~ **(de)** (*comparaison*) three times as much (as); **en** ~ **exemplaire** in triplicate.

triplé [trēplā] *nm* triple success, hat-trick (*Brit*).

triplement [trēpləmáñ] *ad* (*à un degré triple*) three times over; (*de trois façons*) in three ways; (*pour trois raisons*) on three counts ♦ *nm* trebling, threefold increase.

tripler [trēplā] *vi, vt* to triple, treble, increase threefold.

triplés, es [trēplā] *nm/fpl* triplets.

Tripoli [trēpolē] *n* Tripoli.

tripot [trēpō] *nm* (*péj*) dive.

tripotage [trēpotázh] *nm* (*péj*) hanky-panky.

tripoter [trēpotā] *vt* to fiddle with, finger ♦ *vi* (*fam*) to rummage about.

trique [trēk] *nf* cudgel.

trisannuel, le [trēzánüel] *a* triennial.

triste [trēst(ə)] *a* sad; (*péj*): ~ **personnage/**

affaire sorry individual/affair; **c'est pas** ~! (*fam*) it's something else!

tristement [trēstəmáñ] *ad* sadly.

tristesse [trēstes] *nf* sadness.

triton [trētōñ] *nm* triton.

triturer [trētürā] *vt* (*pâte*) to knead; (*objets*) to manipulate.

trivial, e, aux [trēvyál, -ō] *a* coarse, crude; (*commun*) mundane.

trivialité [trēvyálētā] *nf* coarseness, crudeness; mundaneness.

troc [trok] *nm* (*ÉCON*) barter; (*transaction*) exchange, swap.

troène [troen] *nm* privet.

troglodyte [troglodēt] *nm/f* cave dweller, troglodyte.

trognon [tronyōñ] *nm* (*de fruit*) core; (*de légume*) stalk.

trois [trwâ] *num* three.

trois-huit [trwäüēt] *nm inv*: **faire les** ~ to work eight-hour shifts (round the clock).

troisième [trwâzyem] *num* third; **le** ~ **âge** years of retirement.

troisièmement [trwâzyemmáñ] *ad* thirdly.

trois-quarts [trwäkár] *nmpl*: **les** ~ **de** three-quarters of.

trolleybus [trolebüs] *nm* trolley bus.

trombe [trōñb] *nf* waterspout; **des** ~**s d'eau** a downpour; **en** ~ (*arriver, passer*) like a whirlwind.

trombone [trōñbon] *nm* (*MUS*) trombone; (*de bureau*) paper clip; ~ **à coulisse** slide trombone.

tromboniste [trōñbonēst(ə)] *nm/f* trombonist.

trompe [trōñp] *nf* (*d'éléphant*) trunk; (*MUS*) trumpet, horn; ~ **d'Eustache** Eustachian tube; ~**s utérines** Fallopian tubes.

trompe-l'œil [trōñplœy] *nm*: **en** ~ in trompe l'œil style.

tromper [trōñpā] *vt* to deceive; (*fig: espoir, attente*) to disappoint; (*vigilance, poursuivants*) to elude; **se** ~ *vi* to make a mistake, be mistaken; **se** ~ **de voiture/jour** to take the wrong car/get the day wrong; **se** ~ **de 3 cm/20 F** to be off by 3 cm/20 F.

tromperie [trōñprē] *nf* deception, trickery *q*.

trompette [trōñpet] *nf* trumpet; **en** ~ (*nez*) turned-up.

trompettiste [trōñpātēst(ə)] *nm/f* trumpet player.

trompeur, euse [trōñpœr, -ēz] *a* deceptive, misleading.

tronc [trōñ] *nm* (*BOT, ANAT*) trunk; (*d'église*) collection box; ~ **d'arbre** tree trunk; ~ **commun** (*SCOL*) common-core syllabus; ~ **de cône** truncated cone.

tronche [trōñsh] *nf* (*fam*) mug, face.

tronçon [trōñsōñ] *nm* section.

tronçonner [trōñsonā] *vt* (*arbre*) to saw up; (*pierre*) to cut up.

tronçonneuse [trōñsonēz] *nf* chain saw.

trône [trōn] *nm* throne; **monter sur le** ~ to ascend the throne.

trôner [trōnā] *vi* (*fig*) to have the place of honor (*US*) *ou* honour (*Brit*).

tronquer [trōñkā] *vt* to truncate; (*fig*) to curtail.

trop [trō] *ad vb* + too much, too + *adjectif, adverbe*; ~ **(nombreux)** too many; ~ **peu**

(nombreux) too few; ~ **(souvent)** too often; ~ **(longtemps)** (for) too long; ~ **de** *(nombre)* too many; *(quantité)* too much; **de** ~, **en** ~: **des livres en** ~ a few books too many, a few extra books; **du lait en** ~ too much milk; **3 livres/5 F de** ~ 3 books too many/5 F too much.

trophée [trofã] *nm* trophy.

tropical, e, aux [tropēkál, -ō] *a* tropical.

tropique [tropēk] *nm* tropic; ~**s** *nmpl* tropics; ~ **du Cancer/Capricorne** Tropic of Cancer/ Capricorn.

trop-plein [troplañ] *nm (tuyau)* overflow *ou* outlet (pipe); *(liquide)* overflow.

troquer [trokã] *vt*: ~ **qch contre** to barter *ou* trade sth for; *(fig)* to swap sth for.

trot [trō] *nm* trot; **aller au** ~ to trot along; **partir au** ~ to set off at a trot.

trotter [trotã] *vi* to trot; *(fig)* to scamper along *(ou* about).

trotteuse [trotãēz] *nf (de montre)* second hand.

trottiner [trotēnã] *vi (fig)* to scamper along *(ou* about).

trottinette [trotēnet] *nf* (child's) scooter.

trottoir [trotwár] *nm* sidewalk *(US)*, pavement *(Brit)*; **faire le** ~ *(péj)* to walk the streets; ~ **roulant** moving walkway.

trou [trōō] *nm* hole; *(fig)* gap; *(COMM)* deficit; ~ **d'aération** (air) vent; ~ **d'air** air pocket; ~ **de mémoire** blank, lapse of memory; ~ **noir** black hole; ~ **de la serrure** keyhole.

troublant, e [trōōblãñ, -âñt] *a* disturbing.

trouble [trōōbl(ǝ)] *a (liquide)* cloudy; *(image, mémoire)* indistinct, hazy; *(affaire)* shady, murky ♦ *ad* indistinctly ♦ *nm (désarroi)* distress, agitation; *(émoi sensuel)* turmoil, agitation; *(embarras)* confusion; *(zizanie)* unrest, discord; ~**s** *nmpl (POL)* disturbances, troubles, unrest *sg*; *(MÉD)* trouble *sg*, disorders; ~**s de la personnalité** personality problems; ~**s de la vision** eye trouble.

trouble-fête [trōōblafet] *nm/f inv* spoilsport.

troubler [trōōblã] *vt (embarrasser)* to confuse, disconcert; *(émouvoir)* to agitate; to disturb; to perturb; *(perturber: ordre etc)* to disrupt, disturb; *(liquide)* to make cloudy; **se** ~ *vi (personne)* to become flustered *ou* confused; ~ **l'ordre public** to cause a breach of the peace.

troué, e [trōōã] *a* with a hole *(ou* holes) in it ♦ *nf* gap; *(MIL)* breach.

trouer [trōōã] *vt* to make a hole *(ou* holes) in; *(fig)* to pierce.

trouille [trōōy] *nf (fam)*: **avoir la** ~ to be scared stiff, be scared out of one's wits.

troupe [trōōp] *nf (MIL)* troop; *(groupe)* troop, group; **la** ~ *(MIL: l'armée)* the army; *(: les simples soldats)* the troops *pl*; ~ **(de théâtre)** (theatrical) company; ~**s de choc** shock troops.

troupeau, x [trōōpō] *nm (de moutons)* flock; *(de vaches)* herd.

trousse [trōōs] *nf* case, kit; *(d'écolier)* pencil case; *(de docteur)* doctor's bag; **aux** ~**s de** *(fig)* on the heels *ou* tail of; ~ **à outils** toolkit; ~ **de toilette** toilet *ou* sponge *(Brit)* bag.

trousseau, x [trōōsō] *nm (de mariée)* trousseau; ~ **de clefs** bunch of keys.

trouvaille [trōōváy] *nf* find; *(fig: idée, expression etc)* brainwave.

trouvé, e [trōōvã] *a*: **tout** ~ ready-made.

trouver [trōōvã] *vt* to find; *(rendre visite)*: **aller/venir** ~ **qn** to go/come and see sb; **je trouve que** I find *ou* think that; ~ **à boire/ critiquer** to find something to drink/criticize; ~ **asile/refuge** to find refuge/shelter; **se** ~ *vi (être)* to be; *(être soudain)* to find o.s.; **se** ~ **être/avoir** to happen to be/have; **il se trouve que** it happens that, it turns out that; **se** ~ **bien** to feel well; **se** ~ **mal** to pass out.

truand [trüäñ] *nm* villain, crook.

truander [trüäñdã] *vi (fam)* to cheat, swindle.

trublion [trüblēyôñ] *nm* troublemaker.

truc [trük] *nm (astuce)* way, device; *(de cinéma, prestidigitateur)* trick effect; *(chose)* thing; *(machin)* thingummyjig; **avoir le** ~ to have the knack; **c'est pas son** *(ou* **mon** *etc)* ~ *(fam)* it's not really his *(ou* my *etc)* thing.

truchement [trüshmâñ] *nm*: **par le** ~ **de qn** through (the intervention of) sb.

trucider [trüsēdã] *vt (fam)* to do in, bump off.

truculent, e [trükülâñ, -âñt] *a* colorful *(US)*, colourful *(Brit)*.

truelle [trüel] *nf* trowel.

truffe [trüf] *nf* truffle; *(nez)* nose.

truffer [trüfã] *vt (CULIN)* to garnish with truffles; **truffé de** *(fig: citations)* peppered with; *(: pièges)* bristling with.

truie [trüē] *nf* sow.

truite [trüēt] *nf* trout *inv*.

truquage [trükázh] *nm* fixing; *(CINÉMA)* special effects *pl*.

truquer [trükã] *vt (élections, serrure, dés)* to fix; *(CINÉMA)* to use special effects in.

trust [trœst] *nm (COMM)* trust.

truster [trœstã] *vt (COMM)* to monopolize.

ts *abr* = **tous**.

tsar [dzár] *nm* tsar.

tsé-tsé [tsätsã] *nf*: **mouche** ~ tsetse fly.

TSF *sigle f* = télégraphie sans fil.

tsigane [tsēgán] *a, nm/f* = **tzigane**.

TSVP *abr (= tournez s'il vous plaît)* PTO.

tt *abr* = **tout**.

TT(A) *sigle m (= transit temporaire (autorisé))* vehicle registration for cars etc bought in France for export tax-free by non-residents.

TTC *abr* = **toutes taxes comprises**.

ttes *abr* = **toutes**.

TU *sigle m = temps universel*.

tu [tü] *pronom* you ♦ *nm*: **employer le** ~ to use the "tu" form.

tu, e [tü] *pp de* taire.

tuant, e [tüäñ, -âñt] *a (épuisant)* killing; *(énervant)* infuriating.

tuba [tübá] *nm (MUS)* tuba; *(SPORT)* snorkel.

tube [tüb] *nm* tube; *(de canalisation, métallique etc)* pipe; *(chanson, disque)* hit song *ou* record; ~ **digestif** alimentary canal, digestive tract; ~ **à essai** test tube.

tuberculeux, euse [tüberkülœ, -œz] *a* tubercular ♦ *nm/f* tuberculosis *ou* TB patient.

tuberculose [tüberkülōz] *nf* tuberculosis, TB.

tubulaire [tübülaire] *a* tubular.

tubulure [tübülür] *nf* pipe; piping *q*; *(AUTO)*: ~ **d'échappement/d'admission** exhaust/inlet manifold.

TUC |tük| *sigle m* (= *travail d'utilité collective*) *community work plan for the young unemployed.*

tuciste |tüsēst(ə)| *nm/f young person on a community work plan.*

tué, e |tüä| *nm/f:* **5 ~s** 5 killed *ou* dead.

tue-mouche |tümōōsh| *a:* **papier ~(s)** flypaper.

tuer |tüä| *vt* to kill; **se ~** (*se suicider*) to kill o.s.; (*dans un accident*) to be killed; **se ~ au travail** (*fig*) to work o.s. to death.

tuerie |türē| *nf* slaughter *q*, massacre.

tue-tête |tütet|: **à ~** *ad* at the top of one's voice.

tueur |tüœr| *nm* killer; **~ à gages** hired killer.

tuile |tüēl| *nf* tile; (*fam*) bit of bad luck, blow.

tulipe |tülēp| *nf* tulip.

tuméfié, e |tümāfyä| *a* puffy, swollen.

tumeur |tümœr| *nf* growth, tumor (*US*), tumour (*Brit*).

tumulte |tümült(ə)| *nm* commotion, hubbub.

tumultueux, euse |tümültüœ̄, -œ̄z| *a* stormy, turbulent.

tuner |tünœr| *nm* tuner.

tungstène |tœńksten| *nm* tungsten.

tunique |tünēk| *nf* tunic; (*de femme*) smock, tunic.

Tunis |tünēs| *n* Tunis.

Tunisie |tünēzē| *nf:* **la ~** Tunisia.

tunisien, ne |tünēzyań, -en| *a* Tunisian ♦ *nm/f:* **T~, ne** Tunisian.

tunisois, e |tünēzwä, -wäz| *a* of *ou* from Tunis.

tunnel |tünel| *nm* tunnel.

TUP *sigle m* (= *titre universel de paiement*) ≈ payment slip.

turban |türbåń| *nm* turban.

turbin |türbań| *nm* (*fam*) work *q*.

turbine |türbēn| *nf* turbine.

turbomoteur |türbomotœr| *nm* turbo(-boosted) engine.

turbopropulseur |türbopropülsœr| *nm* turboprop.

turboréacteur |türborääktœr| *nm* turbojet.

turbot |türbō| *nm* turbot.

turbotrain |türbotrań| *nm* turbotrain.

turbulences |türbüläńs| *nfpl* (*AVIAT*) turbulence *sg*.

turbulent, e |türbüläń, -åńt| *a* boisterous, unruly.

turc, turque |türk(ə)| *a* Turkish; (*w.-c.*) seatless ♦ *nm* (*LING*) Turkish ♦ *nm/f:* **T~, Turque** Turk/Turkish woman; **à la turque** *ad* (*assis*) cross-legged.

turf |türf| *nm* racing.

turfiste |türfēst(ə)| *nm/f* racegoer.

Turks et Caïques *ou* **Caicos** |türkākäēk(os)| *nfpl* Turks and Caicos Islands.

turpitude |türpētüd| *nf* base act, baseness *q*.

turque |türk(ə)| *af*, *nf voir* **turc.**

Turquie |türkē| *nf:* **la ~** Turkey.

turquoise |türkwäz| *nf*, *a inv* turquoise.

tut |tü| *etc vb voir* **taire.**

tutelle |tütel| *nf* (*JUR*) guardianship; (*POL*) trusteeship; **sous la ~ de** (*fig*) under the supervision of.

tuteur, trice |tütœr, -trēs| *nm/f* (*JUR*) guardian; (*de plante*) stake, support.

tutoiement |tütwåmåń| *nm* use of familiar "tu" form.

tutoyer |tütwåyä| *vt:* **~ qn** to address sb as "tu".

tutti quanti |tōōtēkwåńtē| *nmpl:* **et ~** and all the rest (of them).

tutu |tütü| *nm* (*DANSE*) tutu.

Tuvalu |tüvälü| *nm:* **le ~** Tuvalu.

tuyau, x |tüēyō| *nm* pipe; (*flexible*) tube; (*fam: conseil*) tip; (*: mise au courant*) gen *q*; **~ d'arrosage** garden hose; **~ d'échappement** exhaust pipe; **~ d'incendie** fire hose.

tuyauté, e |tüēyōtä| *a* fluted.

tuyauterie |tüēyōtrē| *nf* piping *q*.

tuyère |tüēyer| *nf* nozzle.

TV |tävä| *nf* TV.

TVA *sigle f* = **taxe à** *ou* **sur la valeur ajoutée.**

tweed |twēd| *nm* tweed.

tympan |tańpåń| *nm* (*ANAT*) eardrum.

type |tēp| *nm* type; (*personne, chose: représentant*) classic example, epitome; (*fam*) chap, guy ♦ *a* typical, standard; **avoir le ~ nordique** to be Nordic-looking.

typé, e |tēpä| *a* ethnic (*euph*).

typhoïde |tēfoēd| *nf* typhoid (fever).

typhon |tēfóń| *nm* typhoon.

typhus |tēfüs| *nm* typhus (fever).

typique |tēpēk| *a* typical.

typiquement |tēpēkmåń| *ad* typically.

typographe |tēpográf| *nm/f* typographer.

typographie |tēpográfē| *nf* typography; (*procédé*) letterpress (printing).

typographique |tēpográfēk| *a* typographical; letterpress *cpd*.

typologie |tēpolozhē| *nf* typology.

tyran |tēråń| *nm* tyrant.

tyrannie |tēránē| *nf* tyranny.

tyrannique |tēránēk| *a* tyrannical.

tyranniser |tēránēzä| *vt* to tyrannize.

Tyrol |tērol| *nm:* **le ~** the Tyrol.

tyrolien, ne |tērolyań, -en| *a* Tyrolean.

tzar |dzär| *nm* = **tsar.**

tzigane |dzēgán| *a* gypsy, tzigane ♦ *nm/f* (Hungarian) gypsy, Tzigane.

U

U, u |ü| *nm inv* U, u ♦ *abr* (= *unité*) *10,000 francs*; **maison à vendre 50 U** house for sale: 500,000 francs; **U comme Ursule** U for Uncle.

ubiquité |übēküētä| *nf:* **avoir le don d'~** to be everywhere at once, be ubiquitous.

UDF *sigle f* (= *Union pour la démocratie française*) *political party.*

UEFA *sigle f* (= *Union of European Football Associations*) UEFA.

UER *sigle f* (= *unité d'enseignement et de recherche*) *old title of* UFR; (= *Union européenne de radiodiffusion*) EBU (= *European Broadcasting Union*).

UFC *sigle f* (= *Union fédérale des*

consommateurs) national consumer group.

UFR *sigle f* (= *unité de formation et de recherche*) ≈ university department.

UHF *sigle f* (= *ultra-haute fréquence*) UHF.

UHT *sigle* (= *ultra-haute température*) UHT.

UIT *sigle f* (= *Union internationale des télécommunications*) ITU (= *International Telecommunications Union*).

UJP *sigle f* (= *Union des jeunes pour le progrès*) *political party.*

Ukraine [ükren] *nf*: **l'~** the Ukraine.

ukrainien, ne [ükrenyań, -en] *a* Ukrainian.

ulcère [ülser] *nm* ulcer; **~ à l'estomac** stomach ulcer.

ulcérer [ülsārā] *vt* (*MÉD*) to ulcerate; (*fig*) to sicken, appall (*US*), appal (*Brit*).

ulcéreux, euse [ülsārœ̄, -ēz] *a* (*plaie, lésion*) ulcerous; (*membre*) ulcerated.

ULM *sigle m* (= *ultra léger motorisé*) ultralight (*US*), microlight (*Brit*).

ultérieur, e [ültāryœr] *a* later, subsequent; **remis à une date ~e** postponed to a later date.

ultérieurement [ültāryœrmāń] *ad* later.

ultimatum [ültēmátom] *nm* ultimatum.

ultime [ültēm] *a* final.

ultra... [ültrá] *préfixe* ultra....

ultramoderne [ültrámodern(ə)] ultramodern.

ultra-rapide [ültrárápēd] *a* ultrafast.

ultra-sensible [ültrásáńsēbl(ə)] *a* (*PHOTO*) high-speed.

ultra-sons [ültrásóń] *nmpl* ultrasonics *sg.*

ultra-violet, te [ültrávyole, -et] *a* ultraviolet.

ululer [ülülā] *vi* = **hululer.**

un, une [œ́ń, ün] *dét* a, an + *voyelle* ♦ *pronom, num, a* one; **l'~ l'autre, les ~s les autres** each other, one another; **l'~ ..., l'autre** (the) one ..., the other; **les ~s ..., les autres** some ..., others; **l'~ et l'autre** both (of them); **l'~ ou l'autre** either (of them); **l'~ des meilleurs** one of the best; **la une** (*PRESSE*) the front page.

unanime [ünánēm] *a* unanimous; **ils sont ~s (à penser que)** they are unanimous (in thinking that).

unanimement [ünánēmmáń] *ad* (*par tous*) unanimously; (*d'un commun accord*) with one accord.

unanimité [ünánēmētā] *nf* unanimity; **à l'~** unanimously; **faire l'~** to be approved unanimously.

UNEF [ünef] *sigle f* = *Union nationale des étudiants de France.*

UNESCO [üneskō] *sigle f* (= *United Nations Educational, Scientific and Cultural Organization*) UNESCO.

unetelle [üntel] *nf voir* **untel.**

UNI *sigle f* = *Union nationale interuniversitaire.*

uni, e [ünē] *a* (*ton, tissu*) plain; (*surface*) smooth, even; (*famille*) close(-knit); (*pays*) united.

UNICEF [ünēsef] *sigle m* (= *United Nations International Children's Emergency Fund*) UNICEF.

unième [ünyem] *num*: **vingt/trente et ~** twenty-/thirty-first; **cent ~** (one) hundred and first.

unificateur, trice [ünēfēkátœr, -trēs] *a* unify-

ing.

unification [ünēfēkâsyóń] *nf* uniting; unification; standardization.

unifier [ünēfyā] *vt* to unite, unify; (*systèmes*) to standardize, unify; **s'~** to become united.

uniforme [ünēform(ə)] *a* (*mouvement*) regular, uniform; (*surface, ton*) even; (*objets, maisons*) uniform; (*fig: vie, conduite*) unchanging ♦ *nm* uniform; **être sous l'~** (*MIL*) to be serving in the military.

uniformément [ünēformāmáń] *ad* uniformly.

uniformiser [ünēformēzā] *vt* to make uniform; (*systèmes*) to standardize.

uniformité [ünēformētā] *nf* regularity; uniformity; evenness.

unijambiste [ünēzhâńbēst(ə)] *nm/f* one-legged man/woman.

unilatéral, e, aux [ünēlátārál, -ō] *a* unilateral; **stationnement ~** parking on one side only.

unilatéralement [ünēlátārálmáń] *ad* unilaterally.

uninominal, e, aux [ünēnomēnál, -ō] *a* uncontested.

union [ünyóń] *nf* union; **~ conjugale** union of marriage; **~ de consommateurs** consumers' association; **~ libre** free love; **l'U~ des Républiques socialistes soviétiques (URSS)** the Union of Soviet Socialist Republics (USSR); **l'U~ soviétique** the Soviet Union.

unique [ünēk] *a* (*seul*) only; (*le même*): **un prix/système ~** a single price/system; (*exceptionnel*) unique; **ménage à salaire ~** one-salary family; **route à voie ~** single-lane road; **fils/fille ~** only son/daughter, only child; **~ en France** the only one of its kind in France.

uniquement [ünēkmáń] *ad* only, solely; (*juste*) only, merely.

unir [ünēr] *vt* (*nations*) to unite; (*éléments, couleurs*) to combine; (*en mariage*) to unite, join together; **~ qch à** to unite sth with; to combine sth with; **s'~** to unite; (*en mariage*) to be joined together; **s'~ à** *ou* **avec** to unite with.

unisexe [ünēseks] *a* unisex.

unisson [ünēsóń]: **à l'~** *ad* in unison.

unitaire [ünēter] *a* unitary; (*POL*) unitarian; **prix ~** unit price.

unité [ünētā] *nf* (*harmonie, cohésion*) unity; (*COMM, MIL, de mesure, MATH*) unit; **~ centrale (de traitement)** central processing unit (CPU); **~ de valeur (UV)** (university) course, credit.

univers [ünēver] *nm* universe.

universaliser [ünēversálēzā] *vt* to universalize.

universel, le [ünēversel] *a* universal; (*esprit*) all-embracing.

universellement [ünēverselmáń] *ad* universally.

universitaire [ünēversēter] *a* university *cpd*; (*diplôme, études*) academic, university *cpd* ♦ *nm/f* academic.

université [ünēversētā] *nf* university.

univoque [ünēvok] *a* unambiguous; (*MATH*) one-to-one.

UNR *sigle f* (= *Union pour la nouvelle ré-publique*) *former political party.*

UNSS *sigle f* = *Union nationale de sport scolaire.*

untel, unetelle [œntel, üntel] *nm/f* so-and-so.
uranium [üranyom] *nm* uranium.
urbain, e [ürbaṅ, -en] *a* urban, city *cpd*, town *cpd*; (*poli*) urbane.
urbanisation [ürbánēzásyóṅ] *nf* urbanization.
urbaniser [ürbánēzá] *vt* to urbanize.
urbanisme [ürbánēsm(ə)] *nm* town planning.
urbaniste [ürbánēst(ə)] *nm/f* town planner.
urbanité [ürbánētá] *nf* urbanity.
urée [ürā] *nf* urea.
urémie [ürāmē] *nf* uremia (*US*), uraemia (*Brit*).
urgence [ürzháṅs] *nf* urgency; (*MÉD etc*) emergency; **d'~** *a* emergency *cpd* ♦ *ad* as a matter of urgency; **en cas d'~** in case of emergency; **service des ~s** emergency service.
urgent, e [ürzháṅ, -áṅt] *a* urgent.
urinaire [ürēner] *a* urinary.
urinal, aux [ürēnál, -ō] *nm* (bed) urinal.
urine [ürēn] *nf* urine.
uriner [ürēná] *vi* to urinate.
urinoir [ürēnwár] *nm* (public) urinal.
urne [ürn(ə)] *nf* (*électorale*) ballot box; (*vase*) urn; **aller aux ~s** (*voter*) to go to the polls.
urologie [ürolozhē] *nf* urology.
URSS [*parfois*: ürs] *sigle f* (= *Union des Républiques Socialistes Soviétiques*) USSR.
URSSAF [ürsáf] *sigle f* (= *Union pour le recouvrement de la sécurité sociale et des allocations familiales*) *administrative body responsible for social security funds and payments*.
urticaire [ürtēker] *nf* nettle rash, urticaria.
Uruguay [ürügwe] *nm*: **l'~** Uruguay.
uruguayen, ne [ürügwàyaṅ, -en] *a* Uruguayan ♦ *nm/f*: **U~, ne** Uruguayan.
us [üs] *nmpl*: **~ et coutumes** (habits and) customs.
US(A) *sigle mpl* (= *United States (of America)*) US(A).
usage [üzàzh] *nm* (*emploi, utilisation*) use; (*coutume*) custom; (*éducation*) (good) manners *pl*, (good) breeding; (*LING*): **l'~** usage; **faire ~ de** (*pouvoir, droit*) to exercise; **avoir l'~ de** to have the use of; **à l'~** *ad* with use; **à l'~ de** (*pour*) (for use of); **en ~** in use; **hors d'~** out of service; **à ~ interne** to be taken; **à ~ externe** for external use only.
usagé, e [üzàzhā] *a* (*usé*) worn; (*d'occasion*) used.
usager, ère [üzàzhā, -er] *nm/f* user.
usé, e [üzā] *a* worn (down *ou* out *ou* away); ruined; (*banal*) hackneyed.
user [üzā] *vt* (*outil*) to wear down; (*vêtement*) to wear out; (*matière*) to wear away; (*consommer: charbon etc*) to use; (*fig: santé*) to ruin; (: *personne*) to wear out; **s'~** *vi* to wear; to wear out; (*fig*) to decline; **s'~ à la tâche** to wear o.s. out with work; **~ de** *vt* (*moyen, procédé*) to use, employ; (*droit*) to exercise.
usine [üzēn] *nf* factory; **~ atomique** nuclear power plant; **~ à gaz** gasworks *sg*; **~ marémotrice** tidal power station.
usiner [üzēnā] *vt* (*TECH*) to machine; (*fabriquer*) to manufacture.
usité, e [üzētā] *a* in common use, common;

peu ~ rarely used.
ustensile [üstâṅsēl] *nm* implement; **~ de cuisine** kitchen utensil.
usuel, le [üzüel] *a* everyday, common.
usufruit [üzüfrüē] *nm* usufruct.
usuraire [üzürer] *a* usurious.
usure [üzür] *nf* wear; worn state; (*de l'usurier*) usury; **avoir qn à l'~** to wear sb down; **~ normale** normal wear and tear.
usurier, ière [üzüryā, -yer] *nm/f* usurer.
usurpateur, trice [üzürpátœr, -trēs] *nm/f* usurper.
usurper [üzürpā] *vt* to usurp.
ut [üt] *nm* (*MUS*) C.
UTA *sigle f* = *Union des transporteurs aériens*.
utérin, e [ütāraṅ, -ēn] *a* uterine.
utérus [ütārüs] *nm* uterus, womb.
utile [ütēl] *a* useful; **~ à qn/qch** of use to sb/sth.
utilement [ütēlmáṅ] *ad* usefully.
utilisable [ütēlēzábl(ə)] *a* usable.
utilisateur, trice [ütēlēzátœr, -trēs] *nm/f* user.
utilisation [ütēlēzásyóṅ] *nf* use.
utiliser [ütēlēzá] *vt* to use.
utilitaire [ütēlēter] *a* utilitarian; (*objets*) practical ♦ *nm* (*INFORM*) utility.
utilité [ütēlētá] *nf* usefulness *q*; use; **jouer les ~s** (*THÉÂTRE*) to play bit parts; **reconnu d'~ publique** state-approved; **c'est d'une grande ~** it's extremely useful; **il n'y a aucune ~ à ...** there's no use in ....
utopie [ütopē] *nf* (*idée, conception*) utopian idea *ou* view; (*société etc idéale*) utopia.
utopiste [ütopēst(ə)] *nm/f* utopian.
UV *sigle f* (*SCOL*) = **unité de valeur**.
uvule [üvül] *nf* uvula.

V

V, v [vā] *nm inv* V, v ♦ *abr* (= *voir, verset*) v.; (= *vers: de poésie*) l.; (: *en direction de*) toward(s); **V comme Victor** V for Victor; **en ~** V-shaped; **encolure en ~** V-neck; **décolleté en ~** plunging neckline.
va [và] *vb voir* **aller**.
vacance [vàkâṅs] *nf* (*ADMIN*) vacancy; **~s** *nfpl* vacation *sg* (*US*), holiday(s *pl*) (*Brit*); **les grandes ~s** the summer vacation *ou* holidays; **prendre des/ses ~s** to take a vacation *ou* holiday/one's vacation *ou* holiday(s); **aller en ~s** to go on vacation *ou* holiday.
vacancier, ière [vàkâṅsyā, -yer] *nm/f* vacationer (*US*), holiday-maker (*Brit*).
vacant, e [vàkâṅ, -âṅt] *a* vacant.
vacarme [vàkárm(ə)] *nm* row, din.
vacataire [vàkáter] *nm/f* temporary (employee); (*enseignement*) substitute (*US*) *ou* supply (*Brit*) teacher; (*UNIVERSITÉ*) part-time temporary lecturer.
vaccin [vàksaṅ] *nm* vaccine; (*opération*) vaccination.
vaccination [vàksēnâsyóṅ] *nf* vaccination.

vacciner [våksēnā] *vt* to vaccinate; (*fig*) to make immune; **être vacciné** (*fig*) to be immune.

vache [våsh] *nf* (*ZOOL*) cow; (*cuir*) cowhide ♦ *a* (*fam*) rotten, mean; ~ **à eau** (*canvas*) water bag; **(manger de la)** ~ **enragée** (to go through) hard times; ~ **à lait** (*péj*) sucker; ~ **laitière** dairy cow; **période des** ~**s maigres** lean times *pl*, lean period.

vachement [våshmåṅ] *ad* (*fam*) damned, fantastically.

vacher, ère [våshā, -er] *nm/f* cowherd.

vacherie [våshrē] *nf* (*fam*) meanness *q*; (*action*) dirty trick; (*propos*) nasty remark.

vacherin [våshraṅ] *nm* (*fromage*) vacherin cheese; (*gâteau*): ~ **glacé** vacherin (*type of cream gâteau*).

vachette [våshet] *nf* calfskin.

vacillant, e [våsēyåṅ, -åṅt] *a* wobbly; flickering; failing, faltering.

vaciller [våsēyā] *vi* to sway, wobble; (*bougie, lumière*) to flicker; (*fig*) to be failing, falter; ~ **dans ses réponses** to falter in one's replies; ~ **dans ses résolutions** to waver in one's resolutions.

vacuité [våküĕtā] *nf* emptiness, vacuity.

vade-mecum [vådāmåkom] *nm inv* pocketbook.

vadrouille [vådrōōy] *nf*: **être/partir en** ~ to be/go rambling around.

vadrouiller [vådrōōyā] *vi* to wander around *ou* about.

va-et-vient [vååvyaṅ] *nm inv* (*de pièce mobile*) to and fro (*ou* up and down) movement; (*de personnes, véhicules*) comings and goings *pl*, to-ings and fro-ings *pl*; (*ÉLEC*) two-way switch.

vagabond, e [vågåbôṅ, -ôṅd] *a* wandering; (*imagination*) roaming, roving ♦ *nm* (*rôdeur*) tramp, vagrant; (*voyageur*) wanderer.

vagabondage [vågåbôṅdåzh] *nm* roaming, wandering; (*JUR*) vagrancy.

vagabonder [vågåbôṅdā] *vi* to roam, wander.

vagin [våzhaṅ] *nm* vagina.

vaginal, e, aux [våzhēnål, -ō] *a* vaginal.

vagissement [våzhēsmåṅ] *nm* cry (*of newborn baby*).

vague [våg] *nf* wave ♦ *a* vague; (*regard*) faraway; (*manteau, robe*) loose(-fitting); (*quelconque*): **un** ~ **bureau/cousin** some office/cousin or other ♦ *nm*: **être dans le** ~ to be rather in the dark; **rester dans le** ~ to keep things rather vague; **regarder dans le** ~ to gaze into space; ~ **à l'âme** *nm* vague melancholy; ~ **d'assaut** *nf* (*MIL*) wave of assault; ~ **de chaleur** *nf* heat wave; ~ **de fond** *nf* ground swell; ~ **de froid** *nf* cold spell.

vaguelette [våglet] *nf* ripple.

vaguement [vågmåṅ] *ad* vaguely.

vaillamment [våyåmåṅ] *ad* bravely, gallantly.

vaillant, e [våyåṅ, -åṅt] *a* (*courageux*) brave, gallant; (*robuste*) vigorous, hale and hearty; **n'avoir plus un sou** ~ to be penniless.

vaille [våy] *vb voir* **valoir**.

vain, e [vaṅ, ven] *a* vain; **en** ~ *ad* in vain.

vaincre [vaṅkr(ə)] *vt* to defeat; (*fig*) to conquer, overcome.

vaincu, e [vaṅkü] *pp de* **vaincre** ♦ *nm/f*

defeated party.

vainement [venmåṅ] *ad* vainly.

vainquais [vaṅke] *etc vb voir* **vaincre**.

vainqueur [vaṅkœr] *nm* victor; (*SPORT*) winner ♦ *am* victorious.

vais [ve] *vb voir* **aller**.

vaisseau, x [vesō] *nm* (*ANAT*) vessel; (*NAVIG*) ship, vessel; ~ **spatial** spaceship.

vaisselier [vesəlyā] *nm* sideboard.

vaisselle [vesel] *nf* (*service*) dishes; (*plats etc à laver*) (dirty) dishes *pl*; **faire la** ~ to do the dishes.

val, vaux *ou* **vals** [vål, vō] *nm* valley.

valable [vålåbl(ə)] *a* valid; (*acceptable*) decent, worthwhile.

valablement [vålåbləmåṅ] *ad* legitimately; (*de façon satisfaisante*) satisfactorily.

Valence [vålåṅs] *n* (*en Espagne*) Valencia; (*en France*) Valence.

valent [vål] *etc vb voir* **valoir**.

valet [våle] *nm* valet; (*péj*) lackey; (*CARTES*) jack; ~ **de chambre** manservant, valet; ~ **de ferme** farmhand; ~ **de pied** footman.

valeur [vålœr] *nf* (*gén*) value; (*mérite*) worth, merit; (*COMM*: *titre*) security; **mettre en** ~ (*bien*) to exploit; (*terrain, région*) to develop; (*fig*) to highlight; to show off to advantage; **avoir de la** ~ to be valuable; **prendre de la** ~ to go up *ou* gain in value; **sans** ~ worthless; ~ **absolue** absolute value; ~ **d'échange** exchange value; ~ **nominale** face value; ~**s mobilières** transferable securities.

valeureux, euse [vålœrœ̄, -œ̄z] *a* valorous.

valide [vålēd] *a* (*en bonne santé*) fit, well; (*indemne*) able-bodied, fit; (*valable*) valid.

valider [vålēdā] *vt* to validate.

validité [vålēdētā] *nf* validity.

valions [vålyôṅ] *etc vb voir* **valoir**.

valise [vålēz] *nf* (*suit*)case; **faire sa** ~ to pack one's (suit)case; **la** ~ (**diplomatique**) the diplomatic pouch (*US*) *ou* bag (*Brit*).

vallée [vålā] *nf* valley.

vallon [vålôṅ] *nm* small valley.

vallonné, e [vålonā] *a* undulating.

valoir [vålwår] *vi* (*être valable*) to hold, apply ♦ *vt* (*prix, valeur, effort*) to be worth; (*causer*): ~ **qch à qn** to earn sb sth; **se** ~ to be of equal merit; (*péj*) to be two of a kind; **faire** ~ (*droits, prérogatives*) to assert; (*domaine, capitaux*) to exploit; **faire** ~ **que** to point out that; **se faire** ~ to make the most of o.s.; **à** ~ on account; **à** ~ **sur** to be deducted from; **vaille que vaille** somehow or other; **cela ne me dit rien qui vaille** I don't like the look of it at all; **ce climat ne me vaut rien** this climate doesn't suit me; ~ **la peine** to be worth the trouble, be worth it; ~ **mieux**: **il vaut mieux se taire** it's better to say nothing; **il vaut mieux que je fasse/comme ceci** it's better if I do/like this; **ça ne vaut rien** it's worthless; **que vaut ce candidat?** how good is this applicant?

valorisation [vålorēzåsyôṅ] *nf* (economic) development; increased standing.

valoriser [vålorēzā] *vt* (*ÉCON*) to develop (the economy of); (*produit*) to increase the value of; (*PSYCH*) to increase the standing of; (*fig*) to highlight, bring out.

valse [vȧls(ə)] *nf* waltz; **c'est la ~ des étiquettes** the prices don't stay the same from one moment to the next.

valser [vȧlsȧ] *vi* to waltz; *(fig)*: **aller ~ to go flying.**

valu, e [vȧlü] *pp de* **valoir**.

valve [vȧlv(ə)] *nf* valve.

vamp [vȧ̃p] *nf* vamp.

vampire [vȧ̃pēr] *nm* vampire.

van [vȧ̃] *nm* horse trailer (*US*) *ou* box (*Brit*).

vandale [vȧ̃dȧl] *nm/f* vandal.

vandalisme [vȧ̃dȧlēsm(ə)] *nm* vandalism.

vanille [vȧnēy] *nf* vanilla; **glace à la ~** vanilla ice cream.

vanillé, e [vȧnēyȧ] *a* vanilla *cpd*.

vanité [vȧnētȧ] *nf* vanity.

vaniteux, euse [vȧnētœ̄, -œ̄z] *a* vain, conceited.

vanne [vȧn] *nf* gate; *(fam: remarque)* dig, (nasty) crack; **lancer une ~ à qn** to knock sb.

vanneau, x [vȧnō] *nm* lapwing.

vanner [vȧnȧ] *vt* to winnow.

vannerie [vȧnrē] *nf* basketwork.

vantail, aux [vȧ̃tȧy, -ō] *nm* door, leaf (*pl* leaves).

vantard, e [vȧ̃tȧr, -ȧrd(ə)] *a* boastful.

vantardise [vȧ̃tȧrdēz] *nf* boastfulness *q*; boast.

vanter [vȧ̃tȧ] *vt* to speak highly of, vaunt; **se ~** *vi* to boast, brag; **se ~ de** to pride o.s. on; *(péj)* to boast of.

Vanuatu [vȧnwȧtōō] *nm*: **le ~** Vanuatu.

va-nu-pieds [vȧnüpyȧ] *nm/f inv* tramp, beggar.

vapeur [vȧpœr] *nf* steam; *(émanation)* vapor (*US*), vapour (*Brit*), fumes *pl*; *(brouillard, buée)* haze; **~s** *nfpl (bouffées)* vapours, vapors; **à ~** steam-powered, steam *cpd*; **à toute ~** full steam ahead; *(fig)* at full tilt; **renverser la ~** to reverse engines; *(fig)* to backtrack, backpedal; **cuit à la ~** steamed.

vapocuisuer [vȧpokǖzœr] *nm* pressure cooker.

vaporeux, euse [vȧporœ̄, -œ̄z] *a (flou)* hazy, misty; *(léger)* filmy, gossamer *cpd*.

vaporisateur [vȧporēzȧtœr] *nm* spray.

vaporiser [vȧporēzȧ] *vt (CHIMIE)* to vaporize; *(parfum etc)* to spray.

vaquer [vȧkȧ] *vi (ADMIN)* to be on vacation; **~ à ses occupations** to attend to one's affairs, go about one's business.

varappe [vȧrȧp] *nf* rock climbing.

varappeur, euse [vȧrȧpœr, -œ̄z] *nm/f* (rock) climber.

varech [vȧrek] *nm* wrack, kelp.

vareuse [vȧrœ̄z] *nf (blouson)* pea jacket; *(d'uniforme)* tunic.

variable [vȧryȧbl(ə)] *a* variable; *(temps, humeur)* changeable; *(TECH: à plusieurs positions etc)* adaptable; *(LING)* inflectional; *(divers: résultats)* varied, various ♦ *nf (INFORM, MATH)* variable.

variante [vȧryȧ̃t] *nf* variant.

variation [vȧryȧsyȱ] *nf* variation; changing *q*, change; *(MUS)* variation.

varice [vȧrēs] *nf* varicose vein.

varicelle [vȧrēsel] *nf* chickenpox.

varié, e [vȧryȧ] *a* varied; *(divers)* various;

hors-d'œuvre **~s** selection of hors d'œuvres.

varier [vȧryȧ] *vi* to vary; *(temps, humeur)* to change ♦ *vt* to vary.

variété [vȧryȧtȧ] *nf* variety; **spectacle de ~s** variety show.

variole [vȧryol] *nf* smallpox.

variqueux, euse [vȧrēkœ̄, -œ̄z] *a* varicose.

Varsovie [vȧrsovē] *n* Warsaw.

vas [vȧ] *vb voir* **aller**; **~-y!** [vȧzi] go on!

vasculaire [vȧskülɛr] *a* vascular.

vase [vȧz] *nm* vase ♦ *nf* silt, mud; **en ~ clos** in isolation; **~ de nuit** chamber pot; **~s communicants** communicating vessels.

vasectomie [vȧzektomē] *nf* vasectomy.

vaseline [vȧzlēn] *nf* Vaseline ®.

vaseux, euse [vȧzœ̄, -œ̄z] *a* silty, muddy; *(fig: confus)* woolly, hazy; *(: fatigué)* peaky; *(: étourdi)* woozy.

vasistas [vȧzēstȧs] *nm* transom (*US*), fanlight (*Brit*).

vasque [vȧsk(ə)] *nf (bassin)* basin; *(coupe)* bowl.

vaste [vȧst(ə)] *a* vast, immense.

Vatican [vȧtēkȧ̃] *nm*: **le ~** the Vatican.

vaticiner [vȧtēsēnȧ] *vi (péj)* to make pompous predictions.

va-tout [vȧtōō] *nm*: **jouer son ~** to stake one's all.

vaudeville [vōdvēl] *nm* vaudeville, light comedy.

vaudrai [vōdrȧ] *etc vb voir* **valoir**.

vau-l'eau [vōlō]: **à ~** *ad* with the current; **s'en aller à ~** *(fig: projets)* to be adrift.

vaurien, ne [vōryȧ̃, -en] *nm/f* good-for-nothing, guttersnipe.

vaut [vō] *vb voir* **valoir**.

vautour [vōtōōr] *nm* vulture.

vautrer [vōtrȧ]: **se ~** *vi*: **se ~ dans** to wallow in; **se ~ sur** to sprawl on.

vaux [vō] *pl de* **val** ♦ *vb voir* **valoir**.

va-vite [vȧvēt]: **à la ~** *ad* in a rush.

vd *abr = vend*.

VDQS *abr* (= *vin délimité de qualité supérieure*) *label guaranteeing quality of wine*.

vds *abr = vends*.

veau, x [vō] *nm (ZOOL)* calf (*pl* calves); *(CULIN)* veal; *(peau)* calfskin; **tuer le ~ gras** to kill the fatted calf.

vecteur [vektœr] *nm* vector; *(MIL, BIO)* carrier.

vécu, e [vȧkü] *pp de* **vivre** ♦ *a (aventure)* real(-life).

vedettariat [vədetȧryȧ] *nm* stardom; *(attitude)* acting like a star.

vedette [vədet] *nf (artiste etc)* star; *(canot)* patrol boat; launch; **avoir la ~** to get star billing; **mettre qn en ~** *(CINÉMA etc)* to give sb the starring role; *(fig)* to push sb into the limelight.

végétal, e, aux [vȧzhȧtȧl, -ō] *a* vegetable ♦ *nm* vegetable, plant.

végétalien, ne [vȧzhȧtȧlyȧ̃, -en] *a, nm/f* vegan.

végétarien, ne [vȧzhȧtȧryȧ̃, -en] *a, nm/f* vegetarian.

végétarisme [vȧzhȧtȧrēsm(ə)] *nm* vegetarianism.

végétatif, ive [vȧzhȧtȧtēf, -ēv] *a*: **une vie ~ive** a vegetable existence.

végétation [vāzhātâsyôṅ] nf vegetation; ~s nfpl (MÉD) adenoids.

végéter [vāzhātā] vi (fig) to vegetate; to stagnate.

véhémence [vāāmâṅs] nf vehemence.

véhément, e [vāāmâṅ, -âṅt] a vehement.

véhicule [vāĕkül] nm vehicle; ~ **utilitaire** commercial vehicle.

véhiculer [vāĕkülā] vt (personnes, marchandises) to transport, convey; (fig: idées, substances) to convey, serve as a vehicle for.

veille [vey] nf (garde) watch; (PSYCH) wakefulness; (jour): **la** ~ the day before, the previous day; **la** ~ **au soir** the previous evening; **la** ~ **de** the day before; **à la** ~ **de** on the eve of; **l'état de** ~ the waking state.

veillée [vāyā] nf (soirée) evening; (réunion) evening gathering; ~ **d'armes** night before combat; (fig) vigil; ~ **(mortuaire)** watch.

veiller [vāyā] vi (rester debout) to stay ou sit up; (ne pas dormir) to be awake; (être de garde) to be on watch; (être vigilant) to be watchful ♦ vt (malade, mort) to watch over, sit up with; ~ **à** vt to attend to, see to; ~ **à ce que** to make sure that, see to it that; ~ **sur** vt to keep a watch ou an eye on.

veilleur [veyœr] nm: ~ **de nuit** night watchman.

veilleuse [veyŏ̄z] nf (lampe) night light; (AUTO) sidemarker light (US), sidelight (Brit); (flamme) pilot light; **en** ~ a (lampe) dimmed; (fig: affaire) shelved, set aside.

veinard, e [venâr, -ârd(ə)] nm/f (fam) lucky devil.

veine [ven] nf (ANAT, du bois etc) vein; (filon) vein, seam; (fam: chance): **avoir de la** ~ to be lucky; (inspiration) inspiration.

veiné, e [vānā] a veined; (bois) grained.

veineux, euse [vānŏ̄, -ŏ̄z] a venous.

vêler [vālā] vi to calve.

vélin [vālaṅ] nm: **(papier)** ~ vellum (paper).

véliplanchiste [vālēplâṅshēst(ə)] nm/f windsurfer.

velléitaire [vālāĕter] a irresolute, indecisive.

velléités [vālāĕtā] nfpl vague impulses.

vélo [vālō] nm bike, cycle; **faire du** ~ to go cycling.

véloce [vālos] a swift.

vélocité [vālosētā] nf (MUS) nimbleness, swiftness; (vitesse) velocity.

vélodrome [vālodrom] nm velodrome.

vélomoteur [vālomotœr] nm moped.

velours [vəlŏōr] nm velvet; ~ **côtelé** corduroy.

velouté, e [vəlŏōtā] a (au toucher) velvety; (à la vue) soft, mellow; (au goût) smooth, mellow ♦ nm: ~ **d'asperges/de tomates** cream of asparagus/tomato soup.

velu, e [vəlü] a hairy.

venaison [vənezôṅ] nf venison.

vénal, e, aux [vānál, -ō] a venal.

vénalité [vānálētā] nf venality.

venant [vənâṅ]: **à tout** ~ ad to all and sundry.

vendable [vâṅdâbl(ə)] a saleable, marketable.

vendange [vâṅdâṅzh] nf (opération, période: aussi: ~s) grape harvest; (raisins) grape crop, grapes pl.

vendanger [vâṅdâṅzhā] vi to harvest the grapes.

vendangeur, euse [vâṅdâṅzhœr, -ŏ̄z] nm/f grape-picker.

vendéen, ne [vâṅdāaṅ, -en] a of ou from the Vendée.

vendeur, euse [vâṅdœr, -ŏ̄z] nm/f (de magasin) sales clerk (US), shop ou sales assistant (Brit); (COMM) salesman/woman ♦ nm (JUR) vendor, seller; ~ **de journaux** newspaper seller.

vendre [vâṅdr(ə)] vt to sell; ~ **qch à qn** to sell sb sth; **cela se vend à la douzaine** these are sold by the dozen; **cela se vend bien** it's selling well; **"à** ~**"** "for sale".

vendredi [vâṅdrədē] nm Friday; **V~ saint** Good Friday; voir aussi **lundi.**

vendu, e [vâṅdü] pp de **vendre** ♦ a (péj) corrupt.

venelle [vənel] nf alley.

vénéneux, euse [vānānŏ̄, -ŏ̄z] a poisonous.

vénérable [vānārâbl(ə)] a venerable.

vénération [vānārâsyôṅ] nf veneration.

vénérer [vānārā] vt to venerate.

vénerie [venrē] nf hunting.

vénérien, ne [vānāryaṅ, -en] a venereal.

Venezuela [vānāzüelà] nm: **le** ~ Venezuela.

vénézuélien, ne [vānāzüālyaṅ, -en] a Venezuelan ♦ nm/f: **V~, ne** Venezuelan.

vengeance [vâṅzhâṅs] nf vengeance q, revenge q; (acte) act of vengeance ou revenge.

venger [vâṅzhā] vt to avenge; **se** ~ vi to avenge o.s.; (par rancune) to take revenge; **se** ~ **de qch** to avenge o.s. for sth; to take one's revenge for sth; **se** ~ **de qn** to take revenge on sb; **se** ~ **sur** to wreak vengeance upon; to take revenge on ou through; to take it out on.

vengeur, eresse [vâṅzhœr, -zhres] a vengeful ♦ nm/f avenger.

véniel, le [vānycl] a venial.

venimeux, euse [vənēmŏ̄, -ŏ̄z] a poisonous, venomous; (fig: haineux) venomous, vicious.

venin [vənaṅ] nm venom, poison; (fig) venom.

venir [vənēr] vi to come; ~ **de** to come from; ~ **de faire: je viens d'y aller/de le voir** I've just been there/seen him; **s'il vient à pleuvoir** if it should rain, if it happens to rain; **en** ~ **à faire: j'en viens à croire que** I am coming to believe that; **où veux-tu en** ~? what are you getting at?; **il en est venu à mendier** he has been reduced to begging; **en** ~ **aux mains** to come to blows; **les années/générations à** ~ the years/generations to come; **il me vient une idée** an idea has just occurred to me; **il me vient des soupçons** I'm beginning to be suspicious; **je te vois** ~ I know what you're after; **faire** ~ (docteur, plombier) to call (out); **d'où vient que ...?** how is it that ...?; ~ **au monde** to come into the world.

Venise [vənēz] n Venice.

vénitien, ne [vānēsyaṅ, -en] a Venetian.

vent [vâṅ] nm wind; **il y a du** ~ it's windy; **c'est du** ~ it's all hot air; **au** ~ to windward; **sous le** ~ to leeward; **avoir le** ~ **debout/arrière** to head into the wind/have the wind astern; **dans le** ~ (fam) trendy; **prendre le** ~ (fig) to see which way the wind blows; **avoir** ~ **de** to get wind of; **contre** ~s

et marées come hell or high water.
vente [vãnt] *nf* sale; **la ~** (*activité*) selling; (*secteur*) sales *pl*; **mettre en ~** to put on sale; (*objets personnels*) to put up for sale; **~ de charité** rummage (*US*) *ou* jumble (*Brit*) sale; **~ par correspondance (VPC)** mail-order selling; **~ aux enchères** auction.
venté, e [vãntā] *a* windswept, windy.
venter [vãntā] *vb impersonnel*: **il vente** the wind is blowing.
venteux, euse [vãntœ̄, -œ̄z] *a* windswept, windy.
ventilateur [vãntēlátœr] *nm* fan.
ventilation [vãntēlásyôṅ] *nf* ventilation.
ventiler [vãntēlā] *vt* to ventilate; (*total, statistiques*) to break down.
ventouse [vãntōōz] *nf* (*ampoule*) cupping glass; (*de caoutchouc*) suction cup (*US*) *ou* pad (*Brit*); (*ZOOL*) sucker.
ventre [vãntr(ə)] *nm* (*ANAT*) stomach; (*fig*) belly; **prendre du ~** to be getting a paunch; **avoir mal au ~** to have (a) stomach ache.
ventricule [vãntrēkül] *nm* ventricle.
ventriloque [vãntrēlok] *nm/f* ventriloquist.
ventripotent, e [vãntrēpotãṅ, -ãṅt] *a* potbellied.
ventru, e [vãntrü] *a* potbellied.
venu, e [vənü] *pp* de **venir ♦** *a*: **être mal ~ à ou de faire** to have no grounds for doing, be in no position to do; **mal ~** ill-timed, unwelcome; **bien ~** timely, welcome ♦ *nf* coming.
vêpres [vepr(ə)] *nfpl* vespers.
ver [ver] *nm voir aussi* **vers**; worm; (*des fruits etc*) maggot; (*du bois*) woodworm *q*; **~ blanc** May beetle grub; **~ luisant** glow-worm; **~ à soie** silkworm; **~ solitaire** tapeworm; **~ de terre** earthworm.
véracité [vārásētā] *nf* veracity.
véranda [vārãndá] *nf* veranda(h).
verbal, e, aux [verbál, -ō] *a* verbal.
verbalement [verbálmãṅ] *ad* verbally.
verbaliser [verbálēzā] *vi* (*POLICE*) to report an offender; (*PSYCH*) to verbalize.
verbe [verb(ə)] *nm* (*LING*) verb; (*voix*): **avoir le ~ sonore** to have a sonorous tone (of voice); (*expression*): **la magie du ~** the magic of language *ou* the word; (*REL*): **le V~** the Word.
verbeux, euse [verbœ̄, -œ̄z] *a* verbose, wordy.
verbiage [verbyázh] *nm* verbiage.
verdâtre [verdátr(ə)] *a* greenish.
verdeur [verdœr] *nf* (*vigueur*) vigor (*US*), vigour (*Brit*), vitality; (*crudité*) forthrightness; (*défaut de maturité*) tartness, sharpness.
verdict [verdēk(t)] *nm* verdict.
verdir [verdēr] *vi, vt* to turn green.
verdoyant, e [verdwáyãṅ, -ãṅt] *a* green, verdant.
verdure [verdür] *nf* (*arbres, feuillages*) greenery; (*légumes verts*) green vegetables *pl*, greens *pl*.
véreux, euse [vārœ̄, -œ̄z] *a* worm-eaten; (*malhonnête*) shady, corrupt.
verge [verzh(ə)] *nf* (*ANAT*) penis; (*baguette*) stick, cane.
verger [verzhā] *nm* orchard.
vergeture [verzhətür] *nf gén pl* stretch mark.
verglacé, e [verglásā] *a* icy, iced-over.

verglas [verglá] *nm* (black) ice.
vergogne [vergony]: **sans ~** *ad* shamelessly.
véridique [vārēdēk] *a* truthful.
vérificateur, trice [vcrēfēkátœr, -trēs] *nm/f* controller, checker ♦ *nf* (*machine*) verifier; **~ des comptes** (*FINANCE*) auditor.
vérification [vārēfēkásyôṅ] *nf* checking *q*, check; **~ d'identité** identity check.
vérifier [vārēfyā] *vt* to check; (*corroborer*) to confirm, bear out; (*INFORM*) to verify; **se ~** *vi* to be confirmed *ou* verified.
vérin [vārań] *nm* jack.
véritable [vārētábl(ə)] *a* real; (*ami, amour*) true; **un ~ désastre** an absolute disaster; **que le ~ X sorte du rang!** ≈ will the real X (please) stand up!
veritablement [verētábləmãṅ] *ad* (*effectivement*) really; (*absolument*) absolutely.
vérité [vārētā] *nf* truth; (*d'un portrait*) lifelikeness; (*sincérité*) truthfulness, sincerity; **en ~, à la ~** to tell the truth.
vermeil, le [vermey] *a* bright red, ruby red ♦ *nm* (*substance*) vermeil.
vermicelles [vermēsel] *nmpl* vermicelli *sg*.
vermifuge [vermēfüzh] *nm*: **poudre ~** worm powder.
vermillon [vermēyôṅ] *a inv* vermilion, scarlet.
vermine [vermēn] *nf* vermin *pl*.
vermoulu, e [vermōōlü] *a* worm-eaten, with woodworm.
vermout(h) [vermōōt] *nm* vermouth.
verni, e [vernē] *a* varnished; glazed; (*fam*) lucky; **cuir ~** patent leather; **souliers ~s** patent (leather) shoes.
vernir [vernēr] *vt* (*bois, tableau, ongles*) to varnish; (*poterie*) to glaze.
vernis [vernē] *nm* (*enduit*) varnish; glaze; (*fig*) veneer; **~ à ongles** nail polish.
vernissage [vernēsázh] *nm* varnishing; glazing; (*d'une exposition*) preview.
vernisser [vernēsā] *vt* to glaze.
vérole [vārol] *nf* (*variole*) smallpox; (*fam: syphilis*) pox.
Vérone [vāron] *n* Verona.
verrai [verā] *etc vb voir* **voir**.
verre [verr] *nm* glass; (*de lunettes*) lens *sg*; **~s** *nmpl* (*lunettes*) glasses; **boire** *ou* **prendre un ~** to have a drink; **~ à vin/à liqueur** wine/liqueur glass; **~ à dents** tooth mug; **~ dépoli** frosted glass; **~ de lampe** lamp glass *ou* chimney; **~ de montre** watch crystal (*US*) *ou* glass (*Brit*); **~ à pied** stemmed glass; **~s de contact** contact lenses; **~s fumés** tinted lenses.
verrerie [verrē] *nf* (*fabrique*) glassworks *sg*; (*activité*) glass-making, glass-working; (*objets*) glassware.
verrier [veryā] *nm* glass-blower.
verrière [veryer] *nf* (*grand vitrage*) window; (*toit vitré*) glass roof.
verrons [verôṅ] *etc vb voir* **voir**.
verroterie [verotrē] *nf* glass beads *pl*, glass jewelry (*US*) *ou* jewellery (*Brit*).
verrou [verōō] *nm* (*targette*) bolt; (*fig*) constriction; **mettre le ~** to bolt the door; **mettre qn sous les ~s** to put sb behind bars.
verrouillage [verōōyázh] *nm* (*dispositif*) locking mechanism; (*AUTO*): **~ central** central locking.

verrouiller [verōōyā] *vt* to bolt; to lock; (MIL: *brèche*) to close.

verrue [verü] *nf* wart; (*plantaire*) verruca; (*fig*) eyesore.

vers [ver] *nm* line ♦ *nmpl* (*poésie*) verse *sg* ♦ *prép* (*en direction de*) toward(s); (*près de*) around (about); (*temporel*) about, around.

versant [versåñ] *nm* slopes *pl*, side.

versatile [versátēl] *a* fickle, changeable.

verse [vers(ə)]: **à ~** *ad*: **il pleut à ~** it's pouring (with rain).

versé, e [versā] *a*: **être ~ dans** (*science*) to be (well-)versed in.

Verseau [versō] *nm*: **le ~** Aquarius, the water carrier; **être du ~** to be Aquarius.

versement [versəmåñ] *nm* payment; (*sur un compte*) deposit, remittance; **en 3 ~s** in 3 installments (US) *ou* instalments (*Brit*).

verser [versā] *vt* (*liquide, grains*) to pour; (*larmes, sang*) to shed; (*argent*) to pay; (*soldat: affecter*): **~ qn dans** to assign sb to ♦ *vi* (*véhicule*) to overturn; (*fig*): **~ dans** to lapse into; **~ à un compte** to pay into an account.

verset [verse] *nm* verse; versicle.

verseur [versœr] *am voir* **bec, bouchon.**

versifier [versēfyā] *vt* to put into verse ♦ *vi* to versify, write verse.

version [versyōñ] *nf* version; (SCOL) translation (*into the mother tongue*); **film en ~ originale** film in the original language.

verso [versō] *nm* back; **voir au ~** see over(leaf).

vert, e [ver, vert(ə)] *a* green; (*vin*) young; (*vigoureux*) sprightly; (*cru*) forthright ♦ *nm* green; **dire des ~es (et des pas mûres)** to say some pretty spicy things; **il en a vu des ~es** he's seen a thing or two; **~ bouteille** *a inv* bottle-green; **~ d'eau** *a inv* sea-green; **~ pomme** *a inv* apple-green.

vert-de-gris [verdəgrē] *nm* verdigris ♦ *a inv* gray(ish)- (US) *ou* grey(ish)- (*Brit*) green.

vertébral, e, aux [vertābrál, -ō] *a* back *cpd*; *voir* **colonne.**

vertèbre [vertebr(ə)] *nf* vertebra (*pl* -ae).

vertébré, e [vertābrā] *a, nm* vertebrate.

vertement [vertəmåñ] *ad* (*réprimander*) sharply.

vertical, e, aux [vertēkál, -ō] *a, nf* vertical; **à la ~e** *ad* vertically.

verticalement [vertēkálmåñ] *ad* vertically.

verticalité [vertēkálētā] *nf* verticalness, verticality.

vertige [vertēzh] *nm* (*peur du vide*) vertigo; (*étourdissement*) dizzy spell; (*fig*) fever; **ça me donne le ~** it makes me dizzy; (*fig*) it makes my head spin *ou* reel.

vertigineux, euse [vertēzhēnœ̄, -œ̄z] *a* (*hausse, vitesse*) breathtaking; (*altitude, gorge*) breathtakingly high (*ou* deep).

vertu [vertü] *nf* virtue; **une ~** a saint, a paragon of virtue; **avoir la ~ de faire** to have the virtue of doing; **en ~ de** *prép* in accordance with.

vertueusement [vertüœ̄zmåñ] *ad* virtuously.

vertueux, euse [vertüœ̄, -œ̄z] *a* virtuous.

verve [verv(ə)] *nf* witty eloquence; **être en ~** to be in brilliant form.

verveine [verven] *nf* (BOT) verbena, vervain;

(*infusion*) verbena tea.

vésicule [vāzēkül] *nf* vesicle; **~ biliaire** gallbladder.

vespasienne [vespázyen] *nf* urinal.

vespéral, e, aux [vespārál, -ō] *a* vespertine, evening *cpd*.

vessie [vāsē] *nf* bladder.

veste [vãst(ə)] *nf* jacket; **~ droite/croisée** single-/double-breasted jacket; **retourner sa ~** (*fig*) to turn one's coat.

vestiaire [vestyer] *nm* (*au théâtre etc*) cloakroom; (*de stade etc*) locker room (US), changing-room (*Brit*); (*métallique*): (**armoire**) **~** locker.

vestibule [vestēbül] *nm* hall.

vestige [vestēzh] *nm* (*objet*) relic; (*fragment*) trace; (*fig*) remnant, vestige; **~s** *nmpl* (*d'une ville*) remains; (*d'une civilisation, du passé*) remnants, relics.

vestimentaire [vestēmåñter] *a* (*dépenses*) clothing; (*détail*) of dress; (*élégance*) sartorial.

veston [vestōñ] *nm* jacket.

Vésuve [vāzüv] *nm*: **le ~** Vesuvius.

vêtais [vete] *etc vb voir* **vêtir.**

vêtement [vetmåñ] *nm* garment, item of clothing; (COMM): **le ~** the clothing industry; **~s** *nmpl* clothes; **~s de sport** sportswear *sg*, sports clothes.

vétéran [vātāråñ] *nm* veteran.

vétérinaire [vātārēner] *a* veterinary ♦ *nm/f* vet, veterinarian (US), veterinary surgeon (*Brit*).

vétille [vātēy] *nf* trifle, triviality.

vétilleux, euse [vātēyœ̄, -œ̄z] *a* punctilious.

vêtir [vātēr] *vt* to clothe, dress; **se ~** to dress (o.s.).

vêtit [vātē] *etc vb voir* **vêtir.**

veto [vātō] *nm* veto; **opposer un ~ à** to veto.

vêtu, e [vetü] *pp de* **vêtir** ♦ *a*: **~ de** dressed in, wearing; **chaudement ~** warmly dressed.

vétuste [vātüst(ə)] *a* ancient, timeworn.

vétusté [vātüstā] *nf* age, delapidation.

veuf, veuve [vœf, vœv] *a* widowed ♦ *nm* widower ♦ *nf* widow.

veuille [vœy], **veuillez** [vœyā] *etc vb voir* **vouloir.**

veule [vœl] *a* spineless.

veulent [vœl] *etc vb voir* **vouloir.**

veulerie [vœlrē] *nf* spinelessness.

veut [vœ] *vb voir* **vouloir.**

veuvage [vœvázh] *nm* widowhood.

veuve [vœv] *af, nf voir* **veuf.**

veux [vœ] *vb voir* **vouloir.**

vexant, e [veksåñ, -åñt] *a* (*contrariant*) annoying; (*blessant*) upsetting.

vexations [veksâsyōñ] *nfpl* humiliations.

vexatoire [veksátwár] *a*: **mesures ~s** harassment *sg*.

vexer [veksā] *vt* to hurt, upset; **se ~** *vi* to be hurt, get upset.

VF *sigle f* (CINÉMA) = *version française.*

VHF *sigle f* (= *Very High Frequency*) VHF.

via [vyá] *prép* via.

viabiliser [vyábēlēzā] *vt* to provide with services (*water etc*).

viabilité [vyábēlētā] *nf* viability; (*d'un chemin*) practicability.

viable [vyábl(ə)] *a* viable.

viaduc [vyàdük] *nm* viaduct.

viager, ère [vyàzhǎ, -er] *a*: **rente ~ère** life annuity ♦ *nm*: **mettre en ~** to sell in return for a life annuity.

viande [vyâ̂d] *nf* meat.

viatique [vyàtēk] *nm* (*REL*) viaticum; (*fig*) provisions *pl ou* money for the journey.

vibrant, e [vēbrâ̂, -â̂t] vibrating; (*voix*) vibrant; (*émouvant*) emotive.

vibraphone [vēbràfon] *nm* vibraphone, vibes *pl*.

vibration [vēbràsyô̂] *nf* vibration.

vibratoire [vēbràtwár] *a* vibratory.

vibrer [vēbrǎ] *vi* to vibrate; (*son, voix*) to be vibrant; (*fig*) to be stirred; **faire ~** to (cause to) vibrate; to stir, thrill.

vibromasseur [vēbromàsœr] *nm* vibrator.

vicaire [vēker] *nm* curate.

vice... [vēs] *préfixe* vice-.

vice [vēs] *nm* vice; (*défaut*) fault; **~ caché** (*COMM*) latent *ou* inherent defect; **~ de forme** legal flaw *ou* irregularity.

vice-consul [vēskô̂sül] *nm* vice-consul.

vice-président, e [vēsprázēdâ̂, -â̂t] *nm/f* vice-president; vice-chairman.

vice-roi [vēsrwá] *nm* viceroy.

vice versa [vēsàversá] *ad* vice versa.

vichy [vēshē] *nm* (*toile*) gingham; (*eau*) Vichy water; **carottes V~** boiled carrots.

vichyssois, e [vēshēswà, -wàz] *a* of *ou* from Vichy, Vichy *cpd* ♦ *nf* (*soupe*) vichyssoise (soup), *cream of leek and potato soup* ♦ *nm/f*: **V~, e** native *ou* inhabitant of Vichy.

vicié, e [vēsyá] *a* (*air*) polluted, tainted; (*JUR*) invalidated.

vicier [vēsyá] *vt* (*JUR*) to invalidate.

vicieux, euse [vēsyœ̂, -œ̂z] *a* (*pervers*) dirty(-minded); (*méchant*) nasty; (*fautif*) incorrect, wrong.

vicinal, e, aux [vēsēnàl, -ō] *a*: **chemin ~** by-road, byway.

vicissitudes [vēsēsētüd] *nfpl* (trials and) tribulations.

vicomte [vēkô̂t] *nm* viscount.

vicomtesse [vēkô̂tes] *nf* viscountess.

victime [vēktēm] *nf* victim; (*d'accident*) casualty; **être (la) ~ de** to be the victim of; **être ~ d'une attaque/d'un accident** to suffer a stroke/be involved in an accident.

victoire [vēktwár] *nf* victory.

victorieux, euse [vēktoryœ̂, -œ̂z] *a* victorious; (*sourire, attitude*) triumphant.

victuailles [vēktüày] *nfpl* provisions.

vidange [vēdâ̂zh] *nf* (*d'un fossé, réservoir*) emptying; (*AUTO*) oil change; (*de lavabo: bonde*) drain; **~s** *nfpl* (*matières*) sewage *sg*; **faire la ~** (*AUTO*) to change the oil, do an oil change; **tuyau de ~** drain pipe.

vidanger [vēdâ̂zhá] *vt* to empty; **faire ~ la voiture** to have the oil changed in one's car.

vide [vēd] *a* empty ♦ *nm* (*PHYSIQUE*) vacuum; (*espace*) (empty) space, gap; (*sous soi: dans une falaise etc*) drop; (*futilité, néant*) void; **~ de** empty of; (*de sens etc*) devoid of; **sous ~** *ad* in a vacuum; **emballé sous ~** vacuum packed; **regarder dans le ~** to stare into space; **avoir peur du ~** to be afraid of heights; **parler dans le ~** to waste one's breath; **faire le ~** (*dans son esprit*) to make

one's mind go blank; **faire le ~ autour de qn** to isolate sb; **à ~** *ad* (*sans occupants*) empty; (*sans charge*) unladen; (*TECH*) without gripping *ou* being in gear.

vidé, e [vēdá] *a* (*épuisé*) done in, all in.

vidéo [vēdāō] *nf*, *a inv* video; **~ inverse** reverse video.

vidéocassette [vēdāokàsét] *nf* video cassette.

vidéoclub [vēdāoklœb] *nm* video club.

vidéodisque [vēdāodēsk] *nm* videodisc.

vide-ordures [vēdordür] *nm inv* (garbage (*US*) *ou* rubbish (*Brit*)) chute.

vidéotex [vēdāoteks] *nm* ® teletext.

vide-poches [vēdposh] *nm inv* tidy; (*AUTO*) glove compartment.

vide-pomme [vēdpom] *nm inv* apple corer.

vider [vēdá] *vt* to empty; (*CULIN: volaille, poisson*) to gut, clean; (*régler: querelle*) to settle; (*fatiguer*) to wear out; (*fam: expulser*) to throw out, chuck out; **se ~** *vi* to empty; **~ les lieux** to quit *ou* vacate the premises.

videur [vēdœr] *nm* (*de boîte de nuit*) bouncer.

vie [vē] *nf* life (*pl* lives); **être en ~** to be alive; **sans ~** lifeless; **à ~** for life; **membre à ~** life member; **dans la ~ courante** in everyday life; **avoir la ~ dure** to have nine lives;· to die hard; **mener la ~ dure à qn** to make life miserable for sb.

vieil [vyey] *am voir* **vieux**.

vieillard [vyeyár] *nm* old man; **les ~s** old people, the elderly.

vieille [vyey] *af*, *nf voir* **vieux**.

vieilleries [vyeyrē] *nfpl* old things *ou* stuff *sg*.

vieillesse [vyeyes] *nf* old age; (*vieillards*): **la ~** the old *pl*, the elderly *pl*.

vieilli, e [vyāyē] *a* (*marqué par l'âge*) aged; (*suranné*) dated.

vieillir [vyāyēr] *vi* (*prendre de l'âge*) to grow old; (*population, vin*) to age; (*doctrine, auteur*) to become dated ♦ *vt* to age; **il a beaucoup vieilli** he has aged a lot; **se ~** to make o.s. older.

vieillissement [vyāyēsmâ̂] *nm* growing old; aging.

vieillot, te [vyeyō, -ot] *a* antiquated, quaint.

vielle [vyel] *nf* hurdy-gurdy.

viendrai [vyâ̂drá] *etc vb voir* **venir**.

Vienne [vyen] *n* (*en Autriche*) Vienna.

vienne [vyen], **viens** [vyâ̂] *etc vb voir* **venir**.

viennois, e [vyenwà, -wàz] *a* Viennese.

vierge [vyerzh(ə)] *a* virgin; (*film*) blank; (*page*) clean, blank; (*jeune fille*): **être ~** to be a virgin ♦ *nf* virgin; (*signe*): **la V~** Virgo, the Virgin; **être de la V~** to be Virgo; **~ de** (*sans*) free from, unsullied by.

Viet-Nam, Vietnam [vyetnám] *nm*: **le ~** Vietnam; **le ~ du Nord/du Sud** North/South Vietnam.

vietnamien, ne [vyetnàmyâ̂, -en] *a* Vietnamese ♦ *nm* (*LING*) Vietnamese ♦ *nm/f*: **V~, ne** Vietnamese; **V~, ne du Nord/Sud** North/South Vietnamese.

vieux (vieil), vieille [vyœ̂, vyey] *a* old ♦ *nm/f* old man/woman ♦ *nmpl*: **les ~** the old, old people; (*fam: parents*) the old folk *ou* ones; **un petit ~** a little old man; **mon ~/ma vieille** (*fam*) old man/girl; **pauvre ~** poor old soul; **prendre un coup de ~** to put years on;

se faire ~ to make o.s. look older; **un** ~ **de la vieille** one of the old brigade; ~ **garçon** *nm* bachelor; ~ **jeu** *a inv* old-fashioned; ~ **rose** *a inv* old rose; **vieil or** *a inv* old gold; **vieille fille** *nf* spinster.

vif, vive [vēf, vēv] *a* (*animé*) lively; (*alerte*) sharp, quick; (*brusque*) sharp, brusque; (*aigu*) sharp; (*lumière, couleur*) brilliant; (*air*) crisp; (*vent, émotion*) keen; (*froid*) bitter; (*fort: regret, déception*) great, deep; (*vivant*): **brûlé** ~ burned alive; **eau vive** running water; **de vive voix** personally; **piquer qn au** ~ to cut sb to the quick; **tailler dans le** ~ to cut into the living flesh; **à** ~ (*plaie*) open; **avoir les nerfs à** ~ to be on edge; **sur le** ~ (*ART*) from life; **entrer dans le** ~ **du sujet** to get to the very heart of the matter.

vif-argent [vēfárzháň] *nm inv* quicksilver.

vigie [vēzhē] *nf* (*matelot*) lookout; (*poste*) look-out post, crow's nest.

vigilance [vēzhēláñs] *nf* vigilance.

vigilant, e [vēzhēláñ, -áñt] *a* vigilant.

vigile [vēzhēl] *nm* (*veilleur de nuit*) (night) watchman; (*police privée*) vigilante.

vigne [vēny] *nf* (*plante*) vine; (*plantation*) vineyard; ~ **vierge** Virginia creeper.

vigneron [vēnyoróň] *nm* wine grower.

vignette [vēnyet] *nf* (*motif*) vignette; (*de marque*) manufacturer's label *ou* seal; (*petite illustration*) (small) illustration; (*ADMIN*) ≈ (road) license plate sticker (*US*), ≈ tax disc (*Brit*); (*: sur médicament*) price label (*on medicines for reimbursement by Social Security*).

vignoble [vēnyobl(ə)] *nm* (*plantation*) vineyard; (*vignes d'une région*) vineyards *pl*.

vigoureusement [vēgōōrōēzmáň] *ad* vigorously.

vigoureux, euse [vēgōōrōē, -ēz] *a* vigorous, robust.

vigueur [vēgœr] *nf* vigor (*US*), vigour (*Brit*); **être/entrer en** ~ to be in/come into force; **en** ~ current.

vil, e [vēl] *a* vile, base; **à** ~ **prix** at a very low price.

vilain, e [vēlaň, -en] *a* (*laid*) ugly; (*affaire, blessure*) nasty; (*pas sage: enfant*) naughty ♦ *nm* (*paysan*) villein, villain; **ça va tourner au** ~ things are going to turn nasty; ~ **mot** bad word.

vilebrequin [vēlbrəkaň] *nm* (*outil*) (bit-)brace; (*AUTO*) crankshaft.

vilenie [vēlnē] *nf* vileness *q*, baseness *q*.

vilipender [vēlēpáňdá] *vt* to revile, vilify.

villa [vēlá] *nf* (detached) house.

village [vēlázh] *nm* village; ~ **de toile** tent village; ~ **de vacances** vacation (*US*) *ou* holiday (*Brit*) village.

villageois, e [vēlázhwá, -wáz] *a* village *cpd* ♦ *nm/f* villager.

ville [vēl] *nf* town; (*importante*) city; (*administration*): **la** ~ ≈ the Corporation; ≈ the (town) council; **aller en** ~ to go to town; **habiter en** ~ to live in town; ~ **nouvelle** new town.

ville-champignon, *pl* **villes-champignons** [vēlsháňpēnyôň] *nf* boom town.

ville-dortoir, *pl* **villes-dortoirs** [vēldortwár] *nf* bedroom community (*US*), dormitory town (*Brit*).

villégiature [vēlázhyátür] *nf* (*séjour*) vacation (*US*), holiday (*Brit*); (*lieu*) (vacation *ou* holiday) resort.

vin [vaň] *nm* wine; **avoir le** ~ **gai/triste** to get happy/miserable after a few drinks; ~ **blanc/rosé/rouge** white/rosé/red wine; ~ **d'honneur** reception (*with wine and snacks*); ~ **de messe** communion wine; ~ **ordinaire** *ou* **de table** table wine; ~ **de pays** local wine.

vinaigre [vēnegr(ə)] *nm* vinegar; **tourner au** ~ (*fig*) to turn sour; ~ **de vin/d'alcool** wine/spirit vinegar.

vinaigrette [vēnegret] *nf* vinaigrette, French dressing.

vinaigrier [vēnegrēyá] *nm* (*fabricant*) vinegar-maker; (*flacon*) vinegar cruet *ou* bottle.

vinasse [vēnás] *nf* (*péj*) cheap wine.

vindicatif, ive [vaňdēkátēf, -ēv] *a* vindictive.

vindicte [vaňdēkt(ə)] *nf*: **désigner qn à la** ~ **publique** to expose sb to public condemnation.

vineux, euse [vēnœ, -ēz] *a* win(e)y.

vingt [vaň, vaňt + *vowel and in* 22, 23 *etc*] *num* twenty; ~**-quatre heures sur** ~**-quatre** twenty-four hours a day, round the clock.

vingtaine [vaňten] *nf*: **une** ~ **(de)** around twenty, twenty or so.

vingtième [vaňtyem] *num* twentieth.

vinicole [vēnēkol] *a* (*production*) wine *cpd*; (*région*) wine-growing.

vinification [vēnēfēkásyôň] *nf* wine-making, wine production; (*des sucres*) vinification.

vinyle [vēnēl] *nm* vinyl.

viol [vyol] *nm* (*d'une femme*) rape; (*d'un lieu sacré*) violation.

violacé, e [vyolásá] *a* purplish, mauvish.

violation [vyolásyôň] *nf* desecration; violation; (*d'un droit*) breach.

violemment [vyolámáň] *ad* violently.

violence [vyoláns] *nf* violence; ~**s** *nfpl* acts of violence; **faire** ~ **à qn** to do violence to sb; **se faire** ~ to force o.s.

violent, e [vyoláň, -áňt] *a* violent; (*remède*) drastic; (*besoin, désir*) intense, urgent.

violenter [vyolάňtá] *vt* to assault (sexually).

violer [vyolá] *vt* (*femme*) to rape; (*sépulture*) to desecrate, violate; (*loi, traité*) to violate.

violet, te [vyole, -et] *a, nm* purple, mauve ♦ *nf* (*fleur*) violet.

violeur [vyolœr] *nm* rapist.

violon [vyolôň] *nm* violin; (*dans la musique folklorique etc*) fiddle; (*fam: prison*) lockup; **premier** ~ first violin; ~ **d'Ingres** (artistic) hobby.

violoncelle [vyolôňsel] *nm* cello.

violoncelliste [vyolôňsālēst(ə)] *nm/f* cellist.

violoniste [vyolonēst(ə)] *nm/f* violinist, violin player; (*folklorique etc*) fiddler.

VIP *sigle m* (= *Very Important Person*) VIP.

vipère [vēper] *nf* viper, adder.

virage [vērázh] *nm* (*d'un véhicule*) turn; (*d'une route, piste*) curve (*US*), turn (*US*), bend (*Brit*); (*CHIMIE*) change in color (*US*) *ou* colour (*Brit*); (*de cuti-réaction*) positive reaction; (*PHOTO*) toning; (*fig: POL*) about-face (*US*), about-turn (*Brit*); **prendre un** ~

to go into a curve *ou* bend, take a curve *ou* bend; ~ **sans visibilité** blind curve *ou* bend.

viral, e, aux [vēràl, -ō] *a* viral.

virée [vērā] *nf* (*courte*) run; (: *à pied*) walk; (*longue*) trip; hike, walking tour.

virement [vērmáń] *nm* (*COMM*) transfer; ~ **bancaire** (bank) credit transfer, ≈ (bank) giro transfer (*Brit*); ~ **postal** Post office credit transfer, ≈ Girobank ® transfer (*Brit*).

virent [vēr] *vb voir* **voir**.

virer [vērā] *vt* (*COMM*): ~ **qch (sur)** to transfer sth (into); (*PHOTO*) to tone; (*fam: renvoyer*) to sack, boot out ♦ *vi* to turn; (*CHIMIE*) to change color (*US*) *ou* colour (*Brit*); (*cuti-réaction*) to come up positive; (*PHOTO*) to tone; ~ **au bleu** to turn blue; ~ **de bord** to tack; (*fig*) to change tack; ~ **sur l'aile** to bank.

virevolte [vērvolt(ə)] *nf* twirl; (*d'avis, d'opinion*) about-face (*US*), about-turn (*Brit*).

virevolter [vērvoltā] *vi* to twirl around.

virginal, e, aux [vērzhēnàl, -ō] *a* virginal.

virginité [vērzhēnētā] *nf* virginity; (*fig*) purity.

virgule [vērgül] *nf* comma; (*MATH*) point; **4** ~ **2** 4 point 2; ~ **flottante** floating decimal.

viril, e [vērēl] *a* (*propre à l'homme*) masculine; (*énergique, courageux*) manly, virile.

viriliser [vērēlēzā] *vt* to make (more) manly *ou* masculine.

virilité [vērēlētā] *nf* (*attributs masculins*) masculinity; (*fermeté, courage*) manliness; (*sexuelle*) virility.

virologie [vērolozhē] *nf* virology.

virtualité [vērtüàlētā] *nf* virtuality; potentiality.

virtuel, le [vērtüel] *a* potential; (*théorique*) virtual.

virtuellement [vērtüelmáń] *a* potentially; (*presque*) virtually.

virtuose [vērtüōz] *nm/f* (*MUS*) virtuoso; (*gén*) master.

virtuosité [vērtüōzētā] *nf* virtuosity; masterliness, masterful skills *pl*.

virulence [vērülâńs] *nf* virulence.

virulent, e [vērülâń, -áńt] *a* virulent.

virus [vērüs] *nm* virus.

vis *vb* [vē] *voir* **voir**, **vivre** ♦ *nf* [vēs] screw; ~ **à tête plate/ronde** flat-headed/round-headed screw; ~ **platinées** (*AUTO*) (contact) points; ~ **sans fin** worm, endless screw.

visa [vēzà] *nm* (*sceau*) stamp; (*validation de passeport*) visa; ~ **de censure** (censor's) certificate.

visage [vēzàzh] *nm* face; **à** ~ **découvert** (*franchement*) openly.

visagiste [vēzàzhēst(ə)] *nm/f* beautician.

vis-à-vis [vēzàvē] *ad* face to face ♦ *nm* person opposite; house *etc* opposite; ~ **de** *prép* opposite; (*fig*) towards, vis-à-vis; **en** ~ facing *ou* opposite each other; **sans** ~ (*immeuble*) with an open view.

viscéral, e, aux [vēsāràl, -ō] *a* (*fig*) deep-seated, deep-rooted.

viscères [vēser] *nmpl* intestines, entrails.

viscose [vēskōz] *nf* viscose.

viscosité [vēskōzētā] *nf* viscosity.

visée [vēzā] *nf* (*avec une arme*) aiming; (*ARPENTAGE*) sighting; ~**s** *nfpl* (*intentions*)

designs; **avoir des** ~**s sur qn/qch** to have designs on sb/sth.

viser [vēzā] *vi* to aim ♦ *vt* to aim at; (*concerner*) to be aimed *ou* directed at; (*apposer un visa sur*) to stamp, visa; ~ **à qch/faire** to aim at sth/at doing *ou* to do.

viseur [vēzœr] *nm* (*d'arme*) sight(s) (*pl*); (*PHOTO*) viewfinder.

visibilité [vēzēbēlētā] *nf* visibility; **sans** ~ (*pilotage, virage*) blind *cpd*.

visible [vēzēbl(ə)] *a* visible; (*disponible*): **est-il** ~? can he see me?, will he see visitors?

visiblement [vēzēbləmáń] *ad* visibly, obviously.

visière [vēzyer] *nf* (*de casquette*) peak; (*qui s'attache*) eyeshade.

vision [vēzyóń] *nf* vision; (*sens*) (eye)sight, vision; (*fait de voir*): **la** ~ **de** the sight of; **première** ~ (*CINÉMA*) first showing.

visionnaire [vēzyoner] *a, nm/f* visionary.

visionner [vēzyonā] *vt* to view.

visionneuse [vēzyonœz] *nf* viewer.

visite [vēzēt] *nf* visit; (*visiteur*) visitor; (*touristique: d'un musée etc*) tour; (*COMM: de représentant*) call; (*expertise, d'inspection*) inspection; (*médicale, à domicile*) visit, call; **la** ~ (*MÉD*) medical examination; (*MIL*): **d'entrée** physical (examination); (: *quotidienne*) sick call (*US*) *ou* parade (*Brit*); **faire une** ~ **à qn** to call on sb, pay sb a visit; **rendre** ~ **à qn** to visit sb, pay sb a visit; **être en** ~ (**chez qn**) to be visiting (sb); **heures de** ~ (*hôpital, prison*) visiting hours; **le droit de** ~ (*JUR: aux enfants*) right of access, access; ~ **de douane** customs inspection *ou* examination.

visiter [vēzētā] *vt* to visit; (*musée, ville*) to visit, tour.

visiteur, euse [vēzētœr, -ēz] *nm/f* visitor; ~ **des douanes** customs inspector; ~ **médical** medical rep(resentative); ~ **de prison** prison visitor.

vison [vēzóń] *nm* mink.

visqueux, euse [vēskœ, -ēz] *a* viscous; (*péj*) gooey; (: *manières*) slimy.

visser [vēsā] *vt*: ~ **qch** (*fixer, serrer*) to screw sth on.

visu [vēzü]: **de** ~ *ad* with one's own eyes.

visualisation [vēzüàlēzàsyóń] *nf* (*INFORM*) display; **écran de** ~ visual display unit (VDU).

visualiser [vēzüàlēzā] *vt* to visualize; (*INFORM*) to display, bring up on screen.

visuel, le [vēzüel] *a* visual ♦ *nm* (visual) display; (*INFORM*) visual display unit (VDU).

visuellement [vēzüelmáń] *ad* visually.

vit [vē] *vb voir* **voir**, **vivre**.

vital, e, aux [vētàl, -ō] *a* vital.

vitalité [vētàlētā] *nf* vitality.

vitamine [vētàmēn] *nf* vitamin.

vitaminé, e [vētàmēnā] *a* with (added) vitamins.

vitaminique [vētàmēnēk] *a* vitamin *cpd*.

vite [vēt] *ad* (*rapidement*) quickly, fast; (*sans délai*) quickly; soon; **faire** ~ (*agir rapidement*) to act fast; (*se dépêcher*) to be quick; **ce sera** ~ **fini** this will soon be finished; **viens** ~ come quick(ly).

vitesse [vētes] *nf* speed; (*AUTO: dispositif*) gear; **faire de la** ~ to speed, drive fast;

prendre qn de ~ to outstrip sb, get ahead of sb; **prendre de la** ~ to pick up *ou* gather speed; **à toute** ~ at full *ou* top speed; **en perte de** ~ (*avion*) losing lift; (*fig*) losing momentum; **changer de** ~ (*AUTO*) to change gear; ~ **acquise** momentum; ~ **de croisière** cruising speed; ~ **de pointe** top speed; ~ **du son** speed of sound.

viticole [větěkɔl] *a* (*industrie*) wine *cpd*; (*région*) wine-growing.

viticulteur [větěkültœr] *nm* wine grower.

viticulture [větěkültür] *nf* wine growing.

vitrage [větràʒ] *nm* (*cloison*) glass partition; (*toit*) glass roof; (*rideau*) net curtain.

vitrail, aux [větráy, -ō] *nm* stained-glass window.

vitre [větr(ə)] *nf* (window) pane; (*de portière, voiture*) window.

vitré, e [větrā] *a* glass *cpd*.

vitrer [větrā] *vt* to glaze.

vitreux, euse [větrœ̄, - œ̄z] *a* vitreous; (*terne*) glassy.

vitrier [větrēyā] *nm* glazier.

vitrifier [větrēfyā] *vt* to vitrify; (*parquet*) to glaze.

vitrine [větrēn] *nf* (*devanture*) show (*US*) *ou* shop (*Brit*) window; (*étalage*) display; (*petite armoire*) display cabinet; **en** ~ in the window, on display; ~ **publicitaire** display case, showcase.

vitriol [větrēyɔl] *nm* vitriol; **au** ~ (*fig*) vitriolic.

vitupérations [větüpàràsyôn] *nfpl* invective *sg*.

vitupérer [větüpàrā] *vi* to rant and rave; ~ **contre** to rail against.

vivable [věvàbl(ə)] *a* (*personne*) livable-with; (*endroit*) fit to live in.

vivace *a* [věvàs] (*arbre, plante*) hardy; (*fig*) enduring ♦ *ad* [věvàtshā] (*MUS*) vivace.

vivacité [věvàsětā] *nf* (*voir vif*) liveliness, vivacity; sharpness; brilliance.

vivant, e [věvàn, -ânt] *vb voir* **vivre** ♦ *a* (*qui vit*) living, alive; (*animé*) lively; (*preuve, exemple*) living; (*langue*) modern ♦ *nm*: **du** ~ **de qn** in sb's lifetime; **les** ~**s et les morts** the living and the dead.

vivarium [věvàryom] *nm* vivarium.

vivats [věvà] *nmpl* cheers.

vive [věv] *af voir* **vif** ♦ *vb voir* **vivre** ♦ *excl*: ~ **le roi!** long live the king!; ~ **les vacances!** hurrah for the vacation! (*US*) *ou* holidays! (*Brit*).

vivement [věvmân] *ad* vivaciously; sharply ♦ *excl*: ~ **les vacances!** I can't wait for the vacation! (*US*) *ou* holidays! (*Brit*), bring on vacation (time)!

vivier [věvyā] *nm* (*au restaurant etc*) fish tank; (*étang*) fishpond.

vivifiant, e [věvēfyàn, -ânt] *a* invigorating.

vivifier [věvēfyā] *vt* to invigorate; (*fig*: *souvenirs, sentiments*) to liven up, enliven.

vivisection [věvěsɛksyôn] *nf* vivisection.

vivoter [věvotā] *vi* (*personne*) to scrape a living, get by; (*fig*: *affaire etc*) to struggle along.

vivre [věvr(ə)] *vi, vt* to live ♦ *nm*: **le** ~ **et le logement** room and board ♦ ~**s** *nmpl* provisions, food supplies; **il vit encore** he is still alive; **se laisser** ~ to take life as it comes;

ne plus ~ (*être anxieux*) to be a bundle of nerves; **il a vécu** (*eu une vie aventureuse*) he has seen life; **ce régime a vécu** this regime has had its day; **être facile à** ~ to be easy to get along with; **faire** ~ **qn** (*pourvoir à sa subsistance*) to provide (a living) for sb; ~ **mal** (*chichement*) to have a meager existence; ~ **de** (*salaire etc*) to live on.

vivrier, ière [věvrēyā, -yer] *a* food-producing *cpd*.

vlan [vlân] *excl* wham!, bang!

VO *sigle f* (*CINÉMA*: = *version originale*): **voir un film en** ~ to see a film in its original language.

v° *abr* = **verso**.

vocable [vokábl(ə)] *nm* term.

vocabulaire [vokábüler] *nm* vocabulary.

vocal, e, aux [vokál, -ō] *a* vocal.

vocalique [vokálěk] *a* vocalic, vowel *cpd*.

vocalise [vokálēz] *nf* singing exercise.

vocaliser [vokálēzā] *vi* (*LING*) to vocalize; (*MUS*) to do one's singing exercises.

vocation [vokásyôn] *nf* vocation, calling; **avoir la** ~ to have a vocation.

vociférations [vosēfàràsyôn] *nfpl* cries of rage, screams.

vociférer [vosēfàrā] *vi, vt* to scream.

vodka [vodká] *nf* vodka.

vœu, x [vœ̄] *nm* wish; (*à Dieu*) vow; **faire** ~ **de** to take a vow of; **avec tous nos** ~**x** with every good wish *ou* our best wishes; ~**x de bonheur** best wishes for your future happiness; ~**x de bonne année** best wishes for the New Year.

vogue [vog] *nf* fashion, vogue; **en** ~ in fashion, in vogue.

voguer [vogā] *vi* to sail.

voici [vwàsē] *prép* (*pour introduire, désigner*) here is + *sg*, here are + *pl*; **et** ~ **que** ... and now it (*ou* he) ...; **il est parti** ~ **3 ans** he left 3 years ago; ~ **une semaine que je l'ai vue** it's a week since I've seen her; **me** ~ here I am; *voir aussi* **voilà**.

voie [vwà] *vb voir* **voir** ♦ *nf* way; (*RAIL*) track, line; (*AUTO*) lane; **par** ~ **buccale** *ou* **orale** orally; **par** ~ **rectale** rectally; **suivre la** ~ **hiérarchique** to go through official channels; **ouvrir/montrer la** ~ to open up/show the way; **être en bonne** ~ to be shaping up *ou* going well; **mettre qn sur la** ~ to put sb on the right track; **être en** ~ **d'achèvement/de rénovation** to be nearing completion/in the process of renovation; **à** ~ **étroite** narrow-gauge; **à** ~ **unique** single-track; **route à 2/3** ~**s** 2-/3-lane road; **par la** ~ **aérienne/maritime** by air/sea; ~ **d'eau** (*NAVIG*) leak; ~ **express** expressway; ~ **de fait** (*JUR*) assault (and battery); ~ **ferrée** track; railroad (*US*), railway line (*Brit*); **par** ~ **ferrée** by rail, by railroad; ~ **de garage** (*RAIL*) siding; **la** ~ **lactée** the Milky Way; ~ **navigable** waterway; ~ **prioritaire** (*AUTO*) road with right of way; ~ **privée** private road; **la** ~ **publique** the public highway.

voilà [vwàlá] *prép* (*en désignant*) there is + *sg*, there are + *pl*; **les** ~ *ou* **voici** here *ou* there they are; **en** ~ *ou* **voici un** here's one, there's one; ~ *ou* **voici deux ans** two years ago; ~ *ou* **voici deux ans que** it's two years since; **et ~!** there we are!; **~ tout** that's all; **"~ ou voici"** (*en offrant etc*) "there *ou* here you are".

voilage [vwálázh] *nm* (*rideau*) sheer (curtain) (*US*), net curtain (*Brit*); (*tissu*) net.

voile [vwál] *nm* veil; (*tissu léger*) sheer (*US*), net (*Brit*) ♦ *nf* sail; (*sport*) sailing; **prendre le ~** to take the veil; **mettre à la ~** to set sail; **~ du palais** *nm* soft palate, velum; **~ au poumon** *nm* shadow on the lung.

voiler [vwálā] *vt* to veil; (*PHOTO*) to fog; (*fausser: roue*) to buckle; (*: bois*) to warp; **se ~** *vi* (*lune, regard*) to mist over; (*ciel*) to grow hazy; (*voix*) to become husky; (*roue, disque*) to buckle; (*planche*) to warp; **se ~ la face** to hide one's face.

voilette [vwálet] *nf* (hat) veil.

voilier [vwályā] *nm* sailing ship; (*de plaisance*) sailboat (*US*), sailing boat (*Brit*).

voilure [vwálür] *nf* (*de voilier*) sails *pl*; (*d'avion*) airfoils *pl* (*US*), aerofoils *pl* (*Brit*); (*de parachute*) canopy.

voir [vwár] *vi, vt* to see; **se ~:** **se ~ critiquer/ transformer** to be criticized/transformed; **cela se voit** (*cela arrive*) it happens; (*c'est visible*) that's obvious, it shows; **~ à faire qch** to see to it that sth is done; **~ loin** (*fig*) to be farsighted; **~ venir** (*fig*) to wait and see; **faire ~ qch à qn** to show sb sth; **en faire ~ à qn** (*fig*) to give sb a hard time; **ne pas pouvoir ~ qn** (*fig*) not to be able to stand sb; **regardez ~** just look; **montrez ~** show (me); **dites ~** tell me; **voyons!** let's see now; (*indignation etc*) come (on) now!; **c'est à ~!** we'll see!; **c'est ce qu'on va ~!** we'll see about that!; **avoir quelque chose à ~ avec** to have something to do with; **ça n'a rien à ~ avec lui** that has nothing to do with him.

voire [vwár] *ad* indeed; nay; or even.

voirie [vwárē] *nf* highway maintenance; (*administration*) highway (*US*) *ou* highways (*Brit*) department; (*enlèvement des ordures*) garbage (*US*) *ou* refuse (*Brit*) collection.

vois [vwá] *vb voir* **voir.**

voisin, e [vwázañ, -ēn] *a* (*proche*) neighboring (*US*), neighbouring (*Brit*); (*contigu*) next; (*ressemblant*) connected ♦ *nm/f* neighbor (*US*), neighbour (*Brit*); (*de table, de dortoir etc*) person next to me (*ou* him *etc*); **~ de palier** neighbor across the hall (*US*) *ou* landing (*Brit*).

voisinage [vwázēnázh] *nm* (*proximité*) proximity; (*environs*) vicinity; (*quartier, voisins*) neighborhood (*US*), neighbourhood (*Brit*); **relations de bon ~** neighborly terms.

voisiner [vwázēnā] *vi:* **~ avec** to be side by side with.

voit [vwá] *vb voir* **voir.**

voiture [vwátür] *nf* car; (*wagon*) car (*US*), carriage (*Brit*); **en ~!** all aboard!; **~ à bras** handcart; **~ d'enfant** baby carriage (*US*), pram (*Brit*); **~ d'infirme** wheelchair; **~ de sport** sports car.

voiture-lit, *pl* **voitures-lits** [vwátürlē] *nf* Pullman (*US*), sleeper (*Brit*).

voiture-restaurant, *pl* **voitures-restaurants** [vwátürrestorāñ] *nf* dining car.

voix [vwá] *nf* voice; (*POL*) vote; **la ~ de la**

conscience/raison the voice of conscience/ reason; **à haute ~** aloud; **à ~ basse** in a low voice; **faire la grosse ~** to speak gruffly; **avoir de la ~** to have a good voice; **rester sans ~** to be speechless; **~ de basse/ténor** *etc* bass/tenor *etc* voice; **à 2/4 ~** (*MUS*) in 2/4 parts; **avoir ~ au chapitre** to have a say in the matter; **mettre aux ~** to put to the vote.

vol [vol] *nm* (*mode de locomotion*) flying; (*trajet, voyage, groupe d'oiseaux*) flight; (*mode d'appropriation*) theft, stealing; (*larcin*) theft; **à ~ d'oiseau** as the crow flies; **au ~: attraper qch au ~** to catch sth as it flies past; **saisir une remarque au ~** to pick up a passing remark; **prendre son ~** to take flight; **de haut ~** (*fig*) of the highest order; **en ~** in flight; **~ avec effraction** breaking and entering *q*, break-in; **~ à l'étalage** shoplifting *q*; **~ libre** hang-gliding; **~ à main armée** armed robbery; **~ de nuit** night flight; **~ plané** (*AVIAT*) glide, gliding *q*; **~ à la tire** pickpocketing *q*; **~ à voile** gliding.

vol. *abr* (= *volume*) vol.

volage [volázh] *a* fickle.

volaille [voláy] *nf* (*oiseaux*) poultry *pl*; (*viande*) poultry *q*; (*oiseau*) fowl.

volailler [voláyā] *nm* poulterer.

volant, e [volāñ, -āñt] *a voir* **feuille** *etc* ♦ *nm* (*d'automobile*) (steering) wheel; (*de commande*) wheel; (*objet lancé*) shuttlecock; (*jeu*) battledore and shuttlecock; (*bande de tissu*) flounce; (*feuillet détachable*) tear-off portion; **le personnel ~, les ~s** (*AVIAT*) the flight crew; **~ de sécurité** (*fig*) reserve, margin, safeguard.

volatil, e [volátēl] *a* volatile.

volatile [volátēl] *nm* (*volaille*) bird; (*tout oiseau*) winged creature.

volatiliser [volátēlēzā]: **se ~** *vi* (*CHIMIE*) to volatilize; (*fig*) to vanish into thin air.

vol-au-vent [volōvāñ] *nm inv* vol-au-vent.

volcan [volkáñ] *nm* volcano; (*fig: personne*) hothead.

volcanique [volkánēk] *a* volcanic; (*fig: tempérament*) volatile.

volcanologue [volkánolog] *nm/f* vulcanologist.

volée [volā] *nf* (*groupe d'oiseaux*) flight, flock; (*TENNIS*) volley; **~ de coups/de flèches** volley of blows/arrows; **à la ~: rattraper à la ~** to catch in midair; **lancer à la ~** to fling about; **semer à la ~** to (sow) broadcast; **à toute ~** (*sonner les cloches*) vigorously; (*lancer un projectile*) with full force; **de haute ~** (*fig*) of the highest order.

voler [volā] *vi* (*avion, oiseau, fig*) to fly; (*voleur*) to steal ♦ *vt* (*objet*) to steal; (*personne*) to rob; **~ en éclats** to smash to smithereens; **~ de ses propres ailes** (*fig*) to stand on one's own two feet; **~ au vent** to fly in the wind; **~ qch à qn** to steal sth from sb.

volet [vole] *nm* (*de fenêtre*) shutter; (*AVIAT*) flap; (*de feuillet, document*) section; (*fig: d'un plan*) facet; **trié sur le ~** hand-picked.

voleter [voltā] *vi* to flutter (about).

voleur, euse [volœr, -œz] *nm/f* thief (*pl* thieves) ♦ *a* thieving.

volière [volyer] *nf* aviary.

volley(-ball) [vole(bōl)] *nm* volleyball.

volleyeur, euse [voleyœr, -œz] *nm/f* volleyball

player.

volontaire [volôńter] *a* (*acte, activité*) voluntary; (*délibéré*) deliberate; (*caractère, personne: décidé*) self-willed ♦ *nm/f* volunteer.

volontairement [volôńtermáń] *ad* voluntarily; deliberately.

volontariat [volôńtáryá] *nm* voluntary service.

volontariste [volôńtárēst(ə)] *a, nm/f* voluntarist.

volonté [volôńtā] *nf* (*faculté de vouloir*) will; (*énergie, fermeté*) will(power); (*souhait, désir*) wish; **se servir/boire à** ~ to take/drink as much as one likes; **bonne** ~ goodwill, willingness; **mauvaise** ~ lack of goodwill, unwillingness.

volontiers [volôńtyā] *ad* (*de bonne grâce*) willingly; (*avec plaisir*) willingly, gladly; (*habituellement, souvent*) readily, willingly; "~" "with pleasure", "I'd be glad to".

volt [volt] *nm* volt.

voltage [voltázh] *nm* voltage.

volte-face [voltəfás] *nf inv* about-face (*US*), about-turn (*Brit*); (*fig*) about-turn, U-turn; **faire** ~ to do an about-face *ou* about-turn; to make a U-turn.

voltige [voltēzh] *nf* (*ÉQUITATION*) trick riding; (*au cirque*) acrobatics *sg*; (*AVIAT*) (aerial) acrobatics *sg*; **numéro de haute** ~ acrobatic act.

voltiger [voltēzhā] *vi* to flutter (about).

voltigeur [voltēzhœr] *nm* (*au cirque*) acrobat; (*MIL*) light infantryman.

voltmètre [voltmetr(ə)] *nm* voltmeter.

volubile [volübēl] *a* voluble.

volubilis [volübēlēs] *nm* convolvulus.

volume [volüm] *nm* volume; (*GÉOM: solide*) solid.

volumineux, euse [volümēnœ, -œz] *a* voluminous, bulky.

volupté [volüptā] *nf* sensual delight *ou* pleasure.

voluptueusement [volüptüœzmáń] *ad* voluptuously.

voluptueux, euse [volüptüœ, -œz] *a* voluptuous.

volute [volüt] *nf* (*ARCHIT*) volute; ~ **de fumée** curl of smoke.

vomi [vomē] *nm* vomit.

vomir [vomēr] *vi* to vomit, be sick ♦ *vt* to vomit, bring up; (*fig*) to belch out, spew out; (*exécrer*) to loathe, abhor.

vomissement [vomēsmáń] *nm* (*action*) vomiting *q*; **des** ~**s** vomit.

vomissure [vomēsür] *nf* vomit *q*.

vomitif [vomētēf] *nm* emetic.

vont [vóń] *vb voir* **aller**.

vorace [vorás] *a* voracious.

voracement [vorásmáń] *ad* voraciously.

vos [vō] *dét voir* **votre**.

Vosges [vōzh] *nfpl:* **les** ~ the Vosges.

vosgien, ne [vōzhyań, -en] *a* of *ou* from the Vosges ♦ *nm/f* inhabitant *ou* native of the Vosges.

VOST *sigle f* (*CINÉMA:* = *version originale sous-titrée*) subtitled version.

votant, e [votáń, -áńt] *nm/f* voter.

vote [vot] *nm* vote; ~ **par correspondance** absentee ballot (*US*), postal vote (*Brit*); ~

par procuration proxy vote; ~ **à main levée** vote by show of hands; ~ **secret,** ~ **à bulletins secrets** secret ballot.

voter [votā] *vi* to vote ♦ *vt* (*loi, décision*) to vote for.

votre [votr(ə)], *pl* **vos** [vō] *dét* your.

vôtre [vōtr(ə)] *pronom:* **le** ~, **la** ~, **les** ~**s** yours; **les** ~**s** (*fig*) your family *ou* folks; **à la** ~ (*toast*) your (good) health!

voudrai [vōōdrā] *etc vb voir* **vouloir**.

voué, e [vwā] *a:* ~ **à** doomed to, destined for.

vouer [vwā] *vt:* ~ **qch à** (*Dieu/un saint*) to dedicate sth to; ~ **sa vie/son temps à** (*étude, cause etc*) to devote one's life/time to; ~ **une haine/amitié éternelle à qn** to vow undying hatred/friendship to sb.

vouloir [vōōlwār] *vi* to show will, have willpower ♦ *vt* to want ♦ *nm:* **le bon** ~ **de qn** sb's goodwill; sb's pleasure; ~ **que qn fasse** to want sb to do; ~ **faire** to want to do; **je voudrais ceci** I would like this; **il voudrait que l'on vienne** he would like us to come; **le hasard a voulu que** fate decreed that; **la tradition veut que** tradition requires that; ... **qui se veut moderne** ... which purports to be modern; **veuillez attendre** please wait; **je veux bien** (*bonne volonté*) I'll be happy to; (*concession*) fair enough, that's fine; **si on veut, comme vous voudrez** as you wish; (*en quelque sorte*) if you like; **que me veut-il?** what does he want with me?; ~ **dire (que)** (*signifier*) to mean (that); **sans le** ~ (*involontairement*) without meaning to, unintentionally; ~ **qch à qn** to wish sth for sb; **en** ~ **à qn** to bear sb a grudge; **en** ~ **à qch** (*avoir des visées sur*) to be after sth; **s'en** ~ **de** to be annoyed with o.s. for; ~ **de qch/qn** (*accepter*) to want sth/sb.

voulu, e [vōōlü] *pp de* **vouloir** ♦ *a* (*requis*) required, requisite; (*délibéré*) deliberate, intentional.

voulus [vōōlü] *etc vb voir* **vouloir**.

vous [vōō] *pronom* you; (*objet indirect*) (to) you; (*réfléchi*) yourself (*pl* yourselves); (*réciproque*) each other ♦ *nm:* **employer le** ~ (*vouvoyer*) to use the "vous" form; ~-**même** yourself; ~-**mêmes** yourselves.

voûte [vōōt] *nf* vault; **la** ~ **céleste** the vault of heaven; ~ **du palais** (*ANAT*) roof of the mouth; ~ **plantaire** arch (of the foot).

voûté, e [vōōtā] *a* vaulted, arched; (*dos, personne*) bent, stooped.

voûter [vōōtā] *vt* (*ARCHIT*) to arch, vault; **se** ~ *vi* (*dos, personne*) to become stooped.

vouvoiement [vōōvwámáń] *nm* use of formal "vous" form.

vouvoyer [vōōvwáyā] *vt:* ~ **qn** to address sb as "vous".

voyage [vwáyázh] *nm* journey, trip; (*fait de voyager*): **le** ~ travel, traveling (*US*), travelling (*Brit*); **partir/être en** ~ to go off/be away on a journey *ou* trip; **faire un** ~ to go on *ou* make a trip *ou* journey; **faire bon** ~ to have a good journey; **les gens du** ~ traveling people; ~ **d'agrément/d'affaires** pleasure/business trip; ~ **de noces** honeymoon; ~ **organisé** package tour.

voyager [vwáyázhā] *vi* to travel.

voyageur, euse [vwáyázhœr, -œz] *nm/f*

traveler (*US*), traveller (*Brit*); (*passager*) passenger ♦ *a* (*tempérament*) nomadic, wayfaring; ~ **(de commerce)** traveling (*US*) *ou* travelling (*Brit*) salesman.

voyagiste [vwàyázhĕst(ə)] *nm* tour operator.

voyais [vwàye] *etc vb voir* **voir.**

voyance [vwàyáńs] *nf* clairvoyance.

voyant, e [vwàyáń, -áńt] *a* (*couleur*) loud, gaudy ♦ *nm/f* (*personne qui voit*) sighted person ♦ *nm* (*signal*) (warning) light ♦ *nf* clairvoyant.

voyelle [vwàyel] *nf* vowel.

voyeur, euse [vwàyœr, -ēz] *nm/f* voyeur; peeping Tom.

voyons [vwàyóń] *etc vb voir* **voir.**

voyou [vwàyōō] *nm* lout, hoodlum; (*enfant*) guttersnipe.

VPC *sigle f* (= *vente par correspondance*) mail-order selling.

vrac [vràk]: **en** ~ *ad* higgledy-piggledy; (*COMM*) in bulk.

vrai, e [vre] *a* (*véridique: récit, faits*) true; (*non factice, authentique*) real ♦ *nm*: **le** ~ the truth; **à** ~ **dire** to tell the truth; **il est** ~ **que** it is true that; **être dans le** ~ to be right.

vraiment [vrémáń] *ad* really.

vraisemblable [vresáńblábl(ə)] *a* (*plausible*) likely, plausible; (*probable*) likely, probable.

vraisemblablement [vresáńblábləmáń] *ad* in all likelihood, very likely.

vraisemblance [vresáńbláńs] *nf* likelihood, plausibility; (*romanesque*) verisimilitude; **selon toute** ~ in all likelihood.

vraquier [vràkyá] *nm* freighter.

vrille [vrēy] *nf* (*de plante*) tendril; (*outil*) gimlet; (*spirale*) spiral; (*AVIAT*) spin.

vriller [vrēyá] *vt* to bore into, pierce.

vrombir [vróńbēr] *vi* to hum.

vrombissant, e [vróńbēsáń, -áńt] *a* humming.

vrombissement [vróńbēsmáń] *nm* hum(ming).

VRP *sigle m* (= *voyageur, représentant, placier*) (sales) rep.

vu [vü] *prép* (*en raison de*) in view of; ~ **que** in view of the fact that.

vu, e [vü] *pp de* **voir** ♦ *a*: **bien/mal** ~ (*personne*) well/poorly thought of; (*conduite*) good/bad form ♦ *nm*: **au** ~ **et au su de tous** openly and publicly; **ni** ~ **ni connu** what the eye doesn't see ...!, no one will be any the wiser; **c'est tout** ~ it's a foregone conclusion.

vue [vü] *nf* (*fait de voir*): **la** ~ **de** the sight of; (*sens, faculté*) (eye)sight; (*panorama, image, photo*) view; (*spectacle*) sight; ~**s** *nfpl* (*idées*) views; (*dessein*) designs; **perdre la** ~ to lose one's (eye)sight; **perdre de** ~ to lose sight of; **à la** ~ **de tous** in full view of everybody; **hors de** ~ out of sight; **à première** ~ at first sight; **connaître de** ~ to know by sight; **à** ~ (*COMM*) at sight; **tirer à** ~ to shoot on sight; **à** ~ **d'œil** *ad* visibly; (*à première vue*) at a quick glance; **avoir** ~ **sur** to have a view of; **en** ~ (*visible*) in sight; (*COMM*) in the public eye; **avoir qch en** ~ (*intentions*) to have one's sights on sth; **en** ~ **de faire** with the intention of doing, with a view to doing; ~ **d'ensemble** overall view; ~

de l'esprit theoretical view.

vulcaniser [vülkánēzá] *vt* to vulcanize.

vulcanologue [vülkánolog] *nm/f* = **volcanologue.**

vulgaire [vülger] *a* (*grossier*) vulgar, coarse; (*trivial*) commonplace, mundane; (*péj: quelconque*): **de** ~**s touristès/chaises de cuisine** common tourists/kitchen chairs; (*BOT, ZOOL*: *non latin*) common.

vulgairement [vülgermáń] *ad* vulgarly, coarsely; (*communément*) commonly.

vulgarisation [vülgárēzásyóń] *nf*: **ouvrage de** ~ popularizing work, popularization.

vulgariser [vülgárēzá] *vt* to popularize.

vulgarité [vülgárētá] *nf* vulgarity, coarseness.

vulnérable [vülnárábl(ə)] *a* vulnerable.

vulve [vülv(ə)] *nf* vulva.

Vve *abr* = **veuve.**

VVF *sigle m* (= *village vacances famille*) state-subsidized vacation village.

vx *abr* = **vieux.**

W

W, w [dōōbləvá] *nm inv* W, w ♦ *abr* (= *watt*) W; **W comme William** W for William.

wagon [vágóń] *nm* (*de voyageurs*) car (*US*), carriage (*Brit*); (*de marchandises*) truck, wagon.

wagon-citerne, *pl* **wagons-citernes** [vágóńsĕtern(ə)] *nm* tanker.

wagon-lit, *pl* **wagons-lits** [vágóńlē] *nm* Pullman (*US*), sleeper (*Brit*).

wagonnet [vágone] *nm* small truck.

wagon-poste, *pl* **wagons-postes** [vágóńpost(ə)] *nm* mail car (*US*) *ou* van (*Brit*).

wagon-restaurant, *pl* **wagons-restaurants** [vágóńrestoráń] *nm* restaurant *ou* dining car.

walkman [wokmáń] *nm* ® walkman ®, personal stereo.

Wallis et Futuna [wálēsáfütúná]: **les îles** ~ the Wallis and Futuna Islands.

wallon, ne [wálóń, -on] *a* Walloon ♦ *nm* (*LING*) Walloon ♦ *nm/f*: **W**~, **ne** Walloon.

waters [wáter] *nmpl* toilet *sg*.

watt [wát] *nm* watt.

w.-c. [vásá] *nmpl* toilet *sg*, lavatory *sg*.

week-end [wĕkend] *nm* weekend.

western [western] *nm* western.

Westphalie [vesfálē] *nf*: **la** ~ Westphalia.

whisky, *pl* **whiskies** [wĕskē] *nm* whiskey (*US, Ireland*), whisky (*Brit*).

Winchester [wĕntshester]: **disque** ~ Winchester disk.

X

X, x [ēks] *nm inv* X, x ♦ *sigle m* = *École Polytechnique*; **plainte contre X** (*JUR*) action against person or persons unknown; **X comme Xavier** X for Xmas.
xénophobe [ksănofob] *a* xenophobic ♦ *nm/f* xenophobe.
xérès [gzāres] *nm* sherry.
xylographie [ksēlográfē] *nf* xylography; (*image*) xylograph.
xylophone [ksēlofon] *nm* xylophone.

Y

Y, y [ēgrek] *nm inv* Y, y; **Y comme Yvonne** Y for Yoke.
y [ē] *ad* (*à cet endroit*) there; (*dessus*) on it (*ou* them); (*dedans*) in it (*ou* them) ♦ *pronom* (*about* ou *on* ou *of*) it : *vérifier la syntaxe du verbe employé*; **j'~ pense** I'm thinking about it; *voir aussi* **aller, avoir**.
yacht [yot] *nm* yacht.
yaourt [yáōōrt] *nm* yoghurt.
yaourtière [yáōōrtyer] *nf* yoghurt maker.
Yémen [yāmen] *nm*: **le ~** Yemen.
yéménite [yāmānēt] *a* Yemeni.
yeux [yœ̄] *pl de* **œil**.
yoga [yogá] *nm* yoga.
yoghourt [yogōōrt] *nm* = **yaourt**.
yole [yol] *nf* skiff.
yougoslave [yōōgoslàv] *a* Yugoslav(ian) ♦ *nm/f*: **Y~** Yugoslav(ian).
Yougoslavie [yōōgoslávē] *nf*: **la ~** Yugoslavia.
youyou [yōōyōō] *nm* dinghy.
yo-yo [yōyō] *nm inv* yo-yo.
yucca [yōōká] *nm* yucca (tree *ou* plant).

Z

Z, z [zed] *nm inv* Z, z; **Z comme Zoé** Z for Zebra.
ZAC [zák] *sigle f* (= *zone d'aménagement concerté*) urban development zone.
ZAD [zàd] *sigle f* (= *zone d'aménagement différé*) future development zone.

Zaïre [záēr] *nm*: **le ~** Zaire.
zaïrois, e [záērwà, -wáz] *a* Zairian (*US*), Zairese (*Brit*).
Zambèze [zánbez] *nm*: **le ~** the Zambezi.
Zambie [zánbē] *nf*: **la ~** Zambia.
zambien, ne [zánbyań, -en] *a* Zambian.
zèbre [zebr(ə)] *nm* (*ZOOL*) zebra.
zébré, e [zābrā] *a* striped, streaked.
zébrure [zābrür] *nf* stripe, streak.
zélateur, trice [zālátœr, -trēs] *nm/f* partisan, zealot.
zèle [zel] *nm* diligence, assiduousness; **faire du ~** (*péj*) to be overzealous.
zélé, e [zālā] *a* zealous.
zénith [zānēt] *nm* zenith.
ZEP [zep] *sigle f* (= *zone d'éducation prioritaire*) *area targeted for special help in education.*
zéro [zārō] *nm* zero; **au-dessous de ~** below zero (Centigrade), below freezing; **partir de ~** to start from scratch; **réduire à ~** to reduce to nothing; **trois (buts) à ~** three (goals to) nothing.
zeste [zest(ə)] *nm* peel, zest; **un ~ de citron** a piece of lemon peel.
zézaiement [zāzemáń] *nm* lisp.
zézayer [zāzāyā] *vi* to have a lisp.
ZI *sigle f* = **zone industrielle.**
zibeline [zēblēn] *nf* sable.
ZIF [zēf] *sigle f* (= *zone d'intervention foncière*) intervention zone.
zigouiller [zēgōōyā] *vt* (*fam*) to do in.
zigzag [zēgzàg] *nm* zigzag.
zigzaguer [zēgzàgā] *vi* to zigzag (along).
Zimbabwe [zēmbábwā] *nm*: **le ~** Zimbabwe.
zimbabwéen, ne [zēmbábwāań, -en] *nm* Zimbabwean.
zinc [zañg] *nm* (*CHIMIE*) zinc; (*comptoir*) bar, counter.
zinguer [zañgā] *vt* to cover with zinc.
zircon [zērkóñ] *nm* zircon.
zizanie [zēzánē] *nf*: **semer la ~** to stir up ill feeling.
zizi [zēzē] *nm* (*fam*) peter (*US*), willy (*Brit*).
zodiaque [zodyák] *nm* zodiac.
zona [zōná] *nm* shingles *sg*.
zonage [zōnàzh] *nm* (*ADMIN*) zoning.
zonard, e [zōnàr, -àrd] *nm/f* (*fam*) (young) hooligan *ou* thug.
zone [zōn] *nf* zone, area; (*INFORM*) field; (*quartiers*): **la ~** the slum belt; **de seconde ~** (*fig*) second-rate; **~ d'action** (*MIL*) sphere of activity; **~ bleue** ≈ restricted parking area; **~ d'extension** *ou* **d'urbanisation** urban development area; **~ franche** free zone; **~ industrielle** (**ZI**) industrial park (*US*) *ou* estate (*Brit*); **~ résidentielle** residential area.
zoner [zōnā] *vi* (*fam*) to hang around.
zoo [zōō] *nm* zoo.
zoologie [zoolozhē] *nf* zoology.
zoologique [zoolozhēk] *a* zoological.
zoologiste [zoolozhēst(ə)] *nm/f* zoologist.
zoom [zōōm] *nm* (*PHOTO*) zoom (lens).
ZUP [züp] *sigle f* (= *zone à urbaniser en priorité*) = **ZAC.**
Zurich [zürēk] *n* Zurich.
zut [züt] *excl* nuts! (*US*), dash (it)! (*Brit*).

ENGLISH-FRENCH
ANGLAIS-FRANÇAIS

A

A, a [ā] *n* (*letter*) A, a *m*; (*SCOL: mark*) A;
(*MUS*): **A la** *m*; **A for Able** A comme Anatole; **A road** *n* (*Brit AUT*) route nationale; **A
shares** *npl* (*Brit STOCK EXCHANGE*) actions
fpl prioritaires.

a, an [ā, ə, an, ən] *definite article* un(e); **an
apple** une pomme; **I haven't got ~ car** je
n'ai pas de voiture; **he's ~ doctor** il est médecin; **3 ~ day/week** 3 par jour/semaine; **10
km an hour** 10 km à l'heure.

a. *abbr* = **acre.**

AA *n abbr* (*US*: = *Associate in/of Arts*) diplôme universitaire; (= *Alcoholics Anonymous*) AA; (= *anti-aircraft*) AA; (*Brit*: =
Automobile Association) ≈ ACF *m*.

AAA [trip'əlā] *n abbr* (= *American Automobile
Association*) ≈ ACF *m*; (*Brit*) = *Amateur
Athletics Association*.

AAUP *n abbr* (= *American Association of University Professors*) *syndicat universitaire*.

AB *abbr* = **able-bodied seaman**; (*Canada*) =
Alberta.

ABA *n abbr* = *American Bankers Association*;
American Bar Association.

aback [əbak'] *ad*: **to be taken ~** être décontе-
nancé(e).

abacus, *pl* **abaci** [ab'əkəs, ab'əsī] *n* boulier *m*.

abandon [əban'dən] *vt* abandonner ♦ *n*
abandon *m*; **to ~ ship** évacuer le navire.

abandoned [əban'dənd] *a* (*child, house etc*)
abandonné(e); (*unrestrained*) sans retenue.

abase [əbās'] *vt*: **to ~ o.s. (so far as to do)**
s'abaisser (à faire).

abashed [əbasht'] *a* confus(e), embarrassé(e).

abate [əbāt'] *vi* s'apaiser, se calmer.

abatement [əbāt'mənt] *n*: **noise ~** lutte *f*
contre le bruit.

abattoir [abətwâr'] *n* (*Brit*) abattoir *m*.

abbey [ab'ē] *n* abbaye *f*.

abbot [ab'ət] *n* père supérieur.

abbreviate [əbrē'vēāt] *vt* abréger.

abbreviation [əbrēvēā'shən] *n* abréviation *f*.

ABC [ābēsē'] *n abbr* (= *American Broadcasting
Company*) chaîne de télévision.

abdicate [ab'dikāt] *vt, vi* abdiquer.

abdication [abdikā'shən] *n* abdication *f*.

abdomen [ab'dəmən] *n* abdomen *m*.

abdominal [abdâm'ənəl] *a* abdominal(e).

abduct [abdukt'] *vt* enlever.

abduction [abduk'shən] *n* enlèvement *m*.

aberration [abərā'shən] *n* anomalie *f*; **in a
moment of mental ~** dans un moment d'égarement.

abet [əbet'] *vt see* **aid.**

abeyance [əbā'əns] *n*: **in ~** (*law*) en désuétude; (*matter*) en suspens.

abhor [abhôr'] *vt* abhorrer, exécrer.

abhorrent [abhôr'ənt] *a* odieux(euse), exécra-

ble.

abide [əbīd'] *vt* souffrir, supporter.
　abide by *vt fus* observer, respecter.

ability [əbil'itē] *n* compétence *f*; capacité *f*;
(*skill*) talent *m*; **to the best of my ~** de mon
mieux.

abject [ab'jckt] *a* (*poverty*) sordide; (*coward*)
méprisable; **an ~ apology** les excuses les
plus plates.

ablaze [əblāz'] *a* en feu, en flammes; **~ with
light** resplendissant de lumière.

able [ā'bəl] *a* compétent(e); **to be ~ to do sth**
pouvoir faire qch, être capable de faire qch.

able-bodied [ā'bəlbâd'ēd] *a* robuste; **~ seaman** matelot breveté.

ably [ā'blē] *ad* avec compétence *or* talent, habilement.

ABM *n abbr* = *anti-ballistic missile.*

abnormal [abnôr'məl] *a* anormal(e).

abnormality [abnôrmal'ətē] *n* (*condition*) caractère anormal; (*instance*) anomalie *f*.

aboard [əbôrd'] *ad* à bord ♦ *prep* à bord de;
(*train*) dans.

abode [əbōd'] *n* (*old*) demeure *f*; (*LAW*): **of
no fixed ~** sans domicile fixe.

abolish [əbâl'ish] *vt* abolir.

abolition [abəlish'ən] *n* abolition *f*.

abominable [əbâm'inəbəl] *a* abominable.

aborigine [abərij'ənē] *n* aborigène *m/f*.

abort [əbôrt'] *vt* (*MED, fig*) faire avorter;
(*COMPUT*) abandonner.

abortion [əbôr'shən] *n* avortement *m*; **to have
an ~** se faire avorter.

abortive [əbôr'tiv] *a* manqué(e).

abound [əbound'] *vi* abonder; **to ~ in** abonder
en, regorger de.

about [əbout'] *prep* au sujet de, à propos de ♦
ad environ; (*here and there*) de côté et d'autre, çà et là; **do something ~ it!** faites
quelque chose!; **it takes ~ 10 hours** ça
prend environ *or* à peu près 10 heures, ça
prend une dizaine d'heures; **at ~ 2 o'clock**
vers 2 heures; **it's just ~ finished** c'est
presque fini; **it's ~ here** c'est par ici, c'est
dans les parages; **to walk ~ the town** se
promener dans *or* à travers la ville; **they left
all their things lying ~** ils ont laissé traîner
toutes leurs affaires; **to be ~ to: he was ~
to cry** il allait pleurer, il était sur le point de
pleurer; **I'm not ~ to do all that for nothing**
(*col*) je ne vais quand même pas faire tout ça
pour rien; **what** *or* **how ~ doing this?** et si
on faisait ça?

about-face [əbout'fās] *n* (*US: MIL*) demi-tour
m; (: *fig*) volte-face *f*.

about-turn [əbout'tûrn] *n* (*Brit*) = **about-face.**

above [əbuv'] *ad* au-dessus ♦ *prep* au-dessus
de; **mentioned ~** mentionné ci-dessus;

costing ~ $10 coûtant plus de 10 dollars; **~ all** par-dessus tout, surtout.

aboveboard [əbuv'bōrd] *a* franc(franche), loyal(e); honnête.

abrasion [əbrā'zhən] *n* frottement *m*; (*on skin*) écorchure *f*.

abrasive [əbrā'siv] *a* abrasif(ive); (*fig*) caustique, agressif(ive).

abreast [əbrest'] *ad* de front; **to keep ~ of** se tenir au courant de.

abridge [əbrij'] *vt* abréger.

abroad [əbrôd'] *ad* à l'étranger; **there is a rumor ~ that...** (*fig*) le bruit court que....

abrupt [əbrupt'] *a* (*steep, blunt*) abrupt(e); (*sudden, gruff*) brusque.

abscess [ab'ses] *n* abcès *m*.

abscond [abskând'] *vi* disparaître, s'enfuir.

absence [ab'səns] *n* absence *f*; **in the ~ of** (*person*) en l'absence de; (*thing*) faute de.

absent [ab'sənt] *a* absent(e); **~ without leave (AWOL)** (*MIL*) en absence irrégulière.

absentee [absəntē'] *n* absent/e.

absentee ballot *n* (*US*) vote *m* par correspondance.

absenteeism [absəntē'izəm] *n* absentéisme *m*.

absent-minded [ab'səntmīn'did] *a* distrait(e).

absent-mindedness [ab'səntmīn'didnis] *n* distraction *f*.

absolute [ab'səlōōt] *a* absolu(e).

absolutely [absəlōōt'lē] *ad* absolument.

absolve [abzâlv'] *vt*: **to ~ sb (from)** (*sin etc*) absoudre qn (de); **to ~ sb from** (*oath*) délier qn de.

absorb [absôrb'] *vt* absorber; **to be ~ed in a book** être plongé(e) dans un livre.

absorbent [absôr'bənt] *a* absorbant(e).

absorbent cotton *n* (*US*) coton *m* hydrophile.

absorbing [absôr'bing] *a* absorbant(e); (*book, film etc*) captivant(e).

absorption [absôrp'shən] *n* absorption *f*.

abstain [abstān'] *vi*: **to ~ (from)** s'abstenir (de).

abstemious [abstē'mēəs] *a* sobre, frugal(e).

abstention [absten'shən] *n* abstention *f*.

abstinence [ab'stənəns] *n* abstinence *f*.

abstract *a, n* [ab'strakt] *a* abstrait(e) ♦ *n* (*summary*) résumé *m* ♦ *vt* [abstrakt'] extraire.

absurd [absûrd'] *a* absurde.

absurdity [absûr'dətē] *n* absurdité *f*.

Abu Dhabi [âb'ōō dâ'bē] *n* Ab(o)u Dhabi *m*.

abundance [əbun'dəns] *n* abondance *f*.

abundant [əbun'dənt] *a* abondant(e).

abuse *n* [əbyōōs'] insultes *fpl*, injures *fpl*; (*of power etc*) abus *m* ♦ *vt* [əbyōōz'] abuser de; **to be open to ~** se prêter à des abus.

abusive [əbyōō'siv] *a* grossier(ière), injurieux(euse).

abysmal [əbiz'məl] *a* exécrable; (*ignorance etc*) sans bornes.

abyss [əbis'] *n* abîme *m*, gouffre *m*.

AC *abbr* (= *alternating current*) courant alternatif ♦ *n abbr* (*US*) = *athletic club*.

a/c *abbr* (*BANKING etc*) = *account, account current*.

academic [akədem'ik] *a* universitaire; (*pej: issue*) oiseux(euse), purement théorique ♦ *n* universitaire *m/f*; **~ freedom** liberté *f* académique.

academic year *n* année *f* universitaire.

academy [əkad'əmē] *n* (*learned body*) académie *f*; (*school*) collège *m*; **military/naval ~** école militaire/navale; **~ of music** conservatoire *m*.

accede [aksēd'] *vi*: **to ~ to** (*request, throne*) accéder à.

accelerate [aksel'ərāt] *vt, vi* accélérer.

acceleration [akselərā'shən] *n* accélération *f*.

accelerator [aksel'ərātûr] *n* accélérateur *m*.

accent [ak'sent] *n* accent *m*.

accentuate [aksen'chōōāt] *vt* (*syllable*) accentuer; (*need, difference etc*) souligner.

accept [aksept'] *vt* accepter.

acceptable [aksep'təbəl] *a* acceptable.

acceptance [aksep'təns] *n* acceptation *f*; **to meet with general ~** être favorablement accueilli par tous.

access [ak'ses] *n* accès *m* ♦ *vt* (*COMPUT*) accéder à; **to have ~ to** (*information, library etc*) avoir accès à, pouvoir utiliser *or* consulter; (*person*) avoir accès auprès de; **the burglars gained ~ through a window** les cambrioleurs sont entrés par une fenêtre.

accessible [akses'əbəl] *a* accessible.

accession [aksesh'ən] *n* accession *f*; (*of king*) avènement *m*; (*to library*) acquisition *f*.

accessory [akses'ûrē] *n* accessoire *m*; **toilet accessories** (*Brit*) articles *mpl* de toilette.

access road *n* (*Brit*) voie *f* d'accès; (: *to freeway*) bretelle *f* de raccordement.

access time *n* (*COMPUT*) temps *m* d'accès.

accident [ak'sidənt] *n* accident *m*; (*chance*) hasard *m*; **to meet with** *or* **to have an ~** avoir un accident; **~s at work** accidents du travail; **by ~** par hasard; (*not deliberately*) accidentellement.

accidental [aksiden'təl] *a* accidentel(le).

accidentally [aksiden'təlē] *ad* accidentellement.

accident insurance *n* assurance *f* accident.

accident-prone [ak'sidəntprōn'] *a* sujet(te) aux accidents.

acclaim [əklām'] *vt* acclamer ♦ *n* acclamation *f*.

acclamation [akləmā'shən] *n* (*approval*) acclamation *f*; (*applause*) ovation *f*.

acclimate [əklī'mit] *vt* (*US*): **to become ~d** s'acclimater.

acclimatize [əklī'mətīz] *vt* (*Brit*) = **acclimate**.

accolade [akəlād'] *n* accolade *f*; (*fig*) marque *f* d'honneur.

accommodate [əkâm'ədāt] *vt* loger, recevoir; (*oblige, help*) obliger; (*adapt*): **to ~ one's plans to** adapter ses projets à; **this car ~s 4 people comfortably** on tient confortablement à 4 dans cette voiture.

accommodating [əkâm'ədāting] *a* obligeant(e), arrangeant(e).

accommodations, (*Brit*) **accommodation** [əkâmədā'shən(z)] *n(pl)* logement *m*; **he's found ~** il a trouvé à se loger; **they have ~ for 500** ils peuvent recevoir 500 personnes, il y a de la place pour 500 personnes.

accompaniment [əkum'pənimənt] *n* accompagnement *m*.

accompanist [əkum'pənist] *n* accompagnateur/trice.

accompany [əkum'pənē] *vt* accompagner.
accomplice [əkâm'plis] *n* complice *m/f*.
accomplish [əkâm'plish] *vt* accomplir.
accomplished [əkâm'plisht] *a* accompli(e).
accomplishment [əkâm'plishmənt] *n* accomplissement *m*; (*achievement*) réussite *f*; ~s *npl* (*skills*) talents *mpl*.
accord [əkôrd'] *n* accord *m* ♦ *vt* accorder; **of his own** ~ de son plein gré; **with one** ~ d'un commun accord.
accordance [əkôr'dəns] *n*: **in** ~ **with** conformément à.
according [əkôr'ding] : ~ **to** *prep* selon; ~ **to plan** comme prévu.
accordingly [əkôr'dinglē] *ad* en conséquence.
accordion [əkôr'dēən] *n* accordéon *m*.
accost [əkôst'] *vt* accoster, aborder.
account [əkount'] *n* (*COMM*) compte *m*; (*report*) compte rendu, récit *m*; ~s *npl* (*BOOK-KEEPING*) comptabilité *f*, comptes; **to keep an** ~ **of** noter; **to bring sb to** ~ **for having done sth** amener qn à rendre compte de qch/d'avoir fait qch; **by all** ~s au dire de tous; **of little** ~ de peu d'importance; **to pay $5 on** ~ verser un acompte de 5 dollars; **to buy sth on** ~ acheter qch à crédit; **on no** ~ en aucun cas; **on** ~ **of** à cause de; **to take into** ~, **take** ~ **of** tenir compte de.
account for *vt fus* expliquer, rendre compte de; **all the children were** ~**ed for** aucun enfant ne manquait; **4 people are still not** ~**ed for** on n'a toujours pas retrouvé 4 personnes.
accountability [əkountəbil'ətē] *n* responsabilité *f*; (*financial, political*) transparence *f*.
accountable [əkoun'təbəl] *a* responsable.
accountancy [əkoun'tənsē] *n* comptabilité *f*.
accountant [əkoun'tənt] *n* comptable *m/f*.
accounting [əkoun'ting] *n* comptabilité *f*.
accounting period *n* exercice financier, période *f* comptable.
account number *n* numéro *m* de compte.
account payable *n* compte *m* fournisseurs.
account receivable *n* compte *m* clients.
accredited [əkred'itid] *a* (*person*) accrédité(e).
accretion [əkrē'shən] *n* accroissement *m*.
accrue [əkrōō'] *vi* s'accroître; (*mount up*) s'accumuler; **to** ~ **to** s'ajouter à; ~**d interest** intérêt couru.
acct. *abbr* = **account; accountant**.
accumulate [əkyōōm'yəlāt] *vt* accumuler, amasser ♦ *vi* s'accumuler, s'amasser.
accumulation [əkyōōmyəlā'shən] *n* accumulation *f*.
accuracy [ak'yûrəsē] *n* exactitude *f*, précision *f*.
accurate [ak'yûrit] *a* exact(e), précis(e).
accurately [ak'yûritlē] *ad* avec précision.
accusation [akyōōzā'shən] *n* accusation *f*.
accusative [əkyōō'zətiv] *n* (*LING*) accusatif *m*.
accuse [əkyōōz'] *vt* accuser.
accused [əkyōōzd'] *n* accusé/e.
accustom [əkus'təm] *vt* accoutumer, habituer; **to** ~ **o.s. to sth** s'habituer à qch.
accustomed [əkus'təmd] *a* (*usual*) habituel(le); ~ **to** habitué(e) or accoutumé(e) à.
AC/DC *abbr* = **alternating current/direct current**.

ACE [ās] *n abbr* = *American Council on Education*.
ace [ās] *n* as *m*; **within an** ~ **of** à deux doigts *or* un cheveu de.
Ace bandage *n* ® (*US*) bande *f* Velpeau ®.
acerbic [əsûr'bik] *a* (*also fig*) acerbe.
acetate [as'itāt] *n* acétate *m*.
ache [āk] *n* mal *m*, douleur *f* ♦ *vi* (*be sore*) faire mal, être douloureux(euse); (*yearn*): **to** ~ **to do sth** mourir d'envie de faire qch; **I've got a stomach**~ *or* (*Brit*) **stomach** ~ j'ai mal à l'estomac; **my head** ~s j'ai mal à la tête; **I'm aching all over** j'ai mal partout.
achieve [əchēv'] *vt* (*aim*) atteindre; (*victory, success*) remporter, obtenir; (*task*) accomplir.
achievement [əchēv'mənt] *n* exploit *m*, réussite *f*; (*of aims*) réalisation *f*.
acid [as'id] *a, n* acide (*m*).
acidity [əsid'itē] *n* acidité *f*.
acid rain *n* pluie(s) *f(pl)* acide(s).
acknowledge [aknâl'ij] *vt* (*also*: ~ **receipt of**) accuser réception de; (*fact*) reconnaître.
acknowledgement [aknâl'ijmənt] *n* accusé *m* de réception; ~s (*in book*) remerciements *mpl*.
ACLU *n abbr* (= *American Civil Liberties Union*) ligue des droits de l'homme.
acme [ak'mē] *n* point culminant.
acne [ak'nē] *n* acné *m*.
acorn [ā'kôrn] *n* gland *m*.
acoustic [əkōōs'tik] *a* acoustique.
acoustic coupler [əkōōs'tik kup'lûr] *n* (*COMPUT*) coupleur *m* acoustique.
acoustics [əkōōs'tiks] *n, npl* acoustique *f*.
acoustic screen *n* panneau *m* d'isolation phonique.
acquaint [əkwānt'] *vt*: **to** ~ **sb with sth** mettre qn au courant de qch; **to be** ~**ed with** (*person*) connaître; (*fact*) savoir.
acquaintance [əkwān'təns] *n* connaissance *f*; **to make sb's** ~ faire la connaissance de qn.
acquiesce [akwēs'] *vi* (*agree*): **to** ~ (**in**) acquiescer (à).
acquire [əkwī'ûr] *vt* acquérir.
acquired [əkwī'ûrd] *a* acquis(e); **an** ~ **taste** un goût acquis.
acquisition [akwizish'ən] *n* acquisition *f*.
acquisitive [əkwiz'ətiv] *a* qui a l'instinct de possession *or* le goût de la propriété.
acquit [əkwit'] *vt* acquitter; **to** ~ **o.s. well** s'en tirer très honorablement.
acquittal [əkwit'əl] *n* acquittement *m*.
acre [ā'kûr] *n* acre *f* (= *4047 m²*).
acreage [ā'kûrij] *n* superficie *f*.
acrid [ak'rid] *a* (*smell*) âcre; (*fig*) mordant(e).
acrimonious [akrəmō'nēəs] *a* acrimonieux(euse), aigre.
acrobat [ak'rəbat] *n* acrobate *m/f*.
acrobatic [akrəbat'ik] *a* acrobatique.
acrobatics [akrəbat'iks] *n, npl* acrobatie *f*.
Acropolis [əkrâp'əlis] *n*: **the** ~ l'Acropole *f*.
across [əkrôs'] *prep* (*on the other side*) de l'autre côté de; (*crosswise*) en travers de ♦ *ad* de l'autre côté; en travers; **to walk** ~ (**the road**) traverser (la route); **to take sb** ~ **the road** faire traverser la route à qn; **a road** ~ **the wood** une route qui traverse le

bois; **the lake is 12 km ~** le lac fait 12 km
de large; **~ from** en face de; **to get sth ~
(to sb)** faire comprendre qch (à qn).

acrylic [ǝkril'ik] *a, n* acrylique *(m).*

ACT *n abbr* (= *American College Test)*
examen de fin d'études secondaires.

act [akt] *n* acte *m,* action *f;* (*THEATER*: *part of
play*) acte; (: *of performer*) numéro *m;*
(*LAW*) loi *f* ♦ *vi* agir; (*THEATER*) jouer; (*pretend*) jouer la comédie ♦ *vt* (*rôle*) jouer, tenir; **~ of God** (*LAW*) catastrophe naturelle;
to catch sb in the ~ prendre qn sur le fait;
it's only an ~ c'est du cinéma; **to ~ Hamlet**
tenir *or* jouer le rôle d'Hamlet; **to ~ the fool**
(*Brit*) faire l'idiot; **to ~ as** servir de; **it ~s
as a deterrent** cela a un effet dissuasif; **~ing
in my capacity as chairman, I** '... en ma qualité de président, je ....
   act on *vt:* **to ~ on sth** agir sur la base de
qch.
   act out *vt* (*event*) raconter en mimant;
(*fantasies*) réaliser.
   act up *vi* (*cause trouble*) faire des siennes.

acting [ak'ting] *a* suppléant(e), par intérim ♦ *n*
(*of actor*) jeu *m;* (*activity*): **to do some ~**
faire du théâtre (*or* du cinéma); **he is the ~
manager** il remplace (provisoirement) le directeur.

action [ak'shǝn] *n* action *f;* (*MIL*) combat(s)
m(pl); (*LAW*) procès *m,* action en justice; **to
bring an ~ against sb** (*LAW*) poursuivre qn
en justice, intenter un procès contre qn;
killed in ~ (*MIL*) tué au champ d'honneur;
out of ~ hors de combat; (*machine etc*) hors
d'usage; **to take ~** agir, prendre des mesures; **to put a plan into ~** mettre un projet à
exécution.

action replay *n* (*Brit TV*) retour *m* sur une
séquence.

activate [ak'tǝvāt] *vt* (*mechanism*) actionner,
faire fonctionner; (*CHEMISTRY, PHYSICS*) activer.

active [ak'tiv] *a* actif(ive); (*volcano*) en activité; **to play an ~ part in** jouer un rôle actif
dans.

active duty (AD) *n* (*US MIL*) campagne *f.*

actively [ak'tivlē] *ad* activement.

active partner *n* (*COMM*) associé(e).

active service *n* (*Brit MIL*) campagne *f.*

activist [ak'tivist] *n* activiste *m/f.*

activity [aktiv'ǝtē] *n* activité *f.*

actor [ak'tûr] *n* acteur *m.*

actress [ak'tris] *n* actrice *f.*

actual [ak'chōōǝl] *a* réel(le), véritable.

actually [ak'chōōǝlē] *ad* réellement, véritable-
ment; (*in fact*) en fait.

actuary [ak'chōōārē] *n* actuaire *m.*

actuate [ak'chōōāt] *vt* déclencher, actionner.

acuity [ǝkyōō'itē] *n* acuité *f.*

acumen [ǝkyōō'mǝn] *n* perspicacité *f;* **business ~** sens *m* des affaires.

acupuncture [ak'yōōpungkchûr] *n* acuponcture
f.

acute [ǝkyōōt'] *a* aigu(ë); (*mind, observer*) pé-
nétrant(e).

AD *ad abbr* (= *Anno Domini*) ap. J.-C. ♦ *n
abbr* (*US MIL*) = **active duty.**

ad [ad] *n abbr* = **advertisement.**

adamant [ad'ǝmǝnt] *a* inflexible.

Adam's apple [ad'ǝms ap'ǝl] *n* pomme *f*
d'Adam.

adapt [ǝdapt'] *vt* adapter ♦ *vi:* **to ~ (to)**
s'adapter (à).

adaptability [ǝdaptǝbil'ǝtē] *n* faculté *f*
d'adaptation.

adaptable [ǝdap'tǝbǝl] *a* (*device*) adaptable;
(*person*) qui s'adapte facilement.

adaptation [adǝptā'shǝn] *n* adaptation *f.*

adapter [ǝdap'tûr] *n* (*ELEC*) adapteur *m.*

ADC *n abbr* (*MIL*) = *aide-de-camp;* (*US:* =
Aid to Dependent Children) aide pour enfants
assistés.

add [ad] *vt* ajouter; (*figures*) additionner ♦ *vi:*
to ~ to (*increase*) ajouter à, accroître.
   add on *vt* ajouter.
   add up *vt* (*figures*) additionner ♦ *vi* (*fig*): **it
doesn't ~** cela ne rime à rien; **it doesn't
~ up to much** ça n'est pas grand'chose.

adder [ad'ûr] *n* vipère *f.*

addict [ad'ikt] *n* toxicomane *m/f;* (*fig*) fanatique *m/f;* **heroin ~** héroïnomane *m/f;* **drug ~**
drogué/e *m/f.*

addicted [ǝdik'tid] *a:* **to be ~ to** (*drink etc*)
être adonné(e) à; (*fig:* football etc) être
un(e) fanatique de.

addiction [ǝdik'shǝn] *n* (*MED*) dépendance *f.*

adding machine [ad'ing mashēn'] *n* machine *f*
à calculer.

Addis Ababa [ad'is âb'ǝbá] *n* Addis Abeba,
Addis Ababa.

addition [ǝdish'ǝn] *n* addition *f;* **in ~** de plus,
de surcroît; **in ~ to** en plus de.

additional [ǝdish'ǝnǝl] *a* supplémentaire.

additive [ad'ǝtiv] *n* additif *m.*

addled [ad'ǝld] *a* (*Brit: egg*) pourri(e).

address [adres'] *n* adresse *f;* (*talk*) discours
m, allocution *f* ♦ *vt* adresser; (*speak to*)
s'adresser à; **form of ~** titre *m;* **what form
of ~ do you use for...?** comment s'adresse-t-
on à...?; **to ~ (o.s. to)** (*problem, issue*)
aborder qch; **absolute/relative ~** (*COMPUT*)
adresse absolue/relative.

Aden [ā'dǝn] *n:* **Gulf of ~** Golfe *m* d'Aden.

adenoids [ad'ǝnoidz] *npl* végétations *fpl.*

adept [ǝdept'] *a:* **~ at** expert(e) à *or* en.

adequate [ad'ǝkwit] *a* (*enough*) suffisant(e);
to feel ~ to the task se sentir à la hauteur
de la tâche.

adequately [ad'ǝkwitlē] *ad* de façon adéquate.

adhere [adhēr'] *vi:* **to ~ to** adhérer à; (*fig:
rule, decision*) se tenir à.

adhesion [adhē'zhǝn] *n* adhésion *f.*

adhesive [adhē'siv] *a* adhésif(ive) ♦ *n* adhésif
m; **~ tape** (*US*) sparadrap *m;* (*Brit*) ruban
adhésif.

ad hoc [ad hâk'] *a* (*decision*) de circonstance;
(*committee*) ad hoc.

ad infinitum [ad infǝnī'tǝm] *ad* à l'infini.

adjacent [ǝjā'sǝnt] *a* adjacent(e), contigu(ë);
~ to adjacent à.

adjective [aj'iktiv] *n* adjectif *m.*

adjoin [ǝjoin'] *vt* jouxter.

adjoining [ǝjoi'ning] *a* voisin(e), adjacent(e),
attenant(e) ♦ *prep* voisin de, adjacent de.

adjourn [ǝjûrn'] *vt* ajourner ♦ *vi* suspendre la
séance; lever la séance; clore la session;
(*go*) se retirer; **to ~ a meeting till the
following week** reporter une réunion à la se-

maine suivante.

adjournment |əjûrn'mənt| *n* (*period*) ajournement *m*.

Adjt *abbr* (MIL: = *adjutant*) Adj.

adjudicate |əjōō'dikāt| *vt* (*contest*) juger; (*claim*) statuer (sur) ♦ *vi* se prononcer.

adjudication |əjōōdikā'shən| *n* (LAW) jugement *m*.

adjust |əjust'| *vt* ajuster, régler; rajuster ♦ *vi*: **to ~ (to)** s'adapter (à).

adjustable |əjust'əbəl| *a* réglable.

adjuster |əjust'ûr| *n see* **loss**.

adjustment |əjust'mənt| *n* ajustage *m*, réglage *m*; (*of prices, wages*) rajustement *m*; (*of person*) adaptation *f*.

adjutant |aj'ətənt| *n* adjudant *m*.

ad-lib |adlib'| *vt, vi* improviser ♦ *n* improvisation *f* ♦ *ad*: **ad lib** à volonté, à discrétion.

adman |ad'man| *n* (*col*) publicitaire *m*.

admin |ad'min| *n abbr* (*col*) = **administration**.

administer |admin'istûr| *vt* administrer; (*justice*) rendre.

administration |administrā'shən| *n* administration *f*; **the A~** (US) le gouvernement.

administrative |admin'istrātiv| *a* administratif(ive).

administrator |admin'istrātûr| *n* administrateur/trice.

admirable |ad'mûrəbəl| *a* admirable.

admiral |ad'mûrəl| *n* amiral *m*.

Admiralty |ad'mûrəltē| *n* (*Brit: also:* **~ Board**) ministère *m* de la Marine.

admiration |admərā'shən| *n* admiration *f*.

admire |admī'ûr| *vt* admirer.

admirer |admī'ərûr| *n* admirateur/trice.

admission |admish'ən| *n* admission *f*; (*to exhibition, night club etc*) entrée *f*; (*confession*) aveu *m*; **"~ free"**, **"free ~"** "entrée libre"; **by his own ~** de son propre aveu.

admit |admit'| *vt* laisser entrer; admettre; (*agree*) reconnaître, admettre; **"children not ~ted"** "entrée interdite aux enfants"; **this ticket ~s two** ce billet est valable pour deux personnes; **I must ~ that...** je dois admettre *or* reconnaître que....

admit of *vt fus* admettre, permettre.

admit to *vt fus* reconnaître, avouer.

admittance |admit'əns| *n* admission *f*, (droit *m* d')entrée *f*; **"no ~"** "défense d'entrer".

admittedly |admit'idlē| *ad* il faut en convenir.

admonish |admán'ish| *vt* donner un avertissement à; réprimander.

ad nauseam |ad nô'zēəm| *ad* à satiété.

ado |ədōō'| *n*: **without further ~** sans plus de cérémonies.

adolescence |adəlcs'əns| *n* adolescence *f*.

adolescent |adəlcs'ənt| *a, n* adolescent(e).

adopt |ədåpt'| *vt* adopter.

adopted |ədåp'tid| *a* adoptif(ive), adopté(e).

adoption |ədåp'shən| *n* adoption *f*.

adore |ədôr| *vt* adorer.

adoringly |ədôr'inglē| *ad* avec adoration.

adorn |ədôrn'| *vt* orner.

adornment |ədôrn'mənt| *n* ornement *m*.

ADP *n abbr* = **automatic data processing**.

adrenalin |ədrcn'əlin| *n* adrénaline *f*; **to get the ~ going** faire monter le taux d'adrénaline.

Adriatic (Sea) |ādrēat'ik (sē')| *n* Adriatique *f*.

adrift |ədrift'| *ad* à la dérive; **to come ~** (*boat*) aller à la dérive; (*wire, rope, fastening etc*) se défaire.

adroit |ədroit'| *a* adroit(e), habile.

adult |ədult'| *n* adulte *m/f*.

adult education *n* éducation *f* des adultes.

adulterate |ədul'tûrāt| *vt* frelater, falsifier.

adultery |ədul'tûrē| *n* adultère *m*.

adulthood |ədult'hōōd| *n* âge *m* adulte.

advance |advans'| *n* avance *f* ♦ *vt* avancer ♦ *vi* s'avancer; **in ~** en avance, d'avance; **to make ~s to sb** (*gen*) faire des propositions à qn; (*amorously*) faire des avances à qn.

advanced |advanst'| *a* avancé(e); (SCOL: *studies*) supérieur(e); **~ in years** d'un âge avancé.

advancement |advans'mənt| *n* avancement *m*.

advance notice *n* préavis *m*.

advantage |advan'tij| *n* (*also* TENNIS) avantage *m*; **to take ~ of** profiter de; **it's to our ~** c'est notre intérêt; **it's to our ~ to ...** nous avons intérêt à ....

advantageous |advəntā'jəs| *a* avantageux(euse).

advent |ad'vcnt| *n* avènement *m*, venue *f*; **A~** (REL) Avent *m*.

Advent calendar *n* calendrier *m* de l'avent.

adventure |advcn'chûr| *n* aventure *f*.

adventurous |advcn'chûrəs| *a* aventureux(euse).

adverb |ad'vûrb| *n* adverbe *m*.

adversary |ad'vûrsârē| *n* adversaire *m/f*.

adverse |advûrs'| *a* contraire, adverse; **~ to** hostile à; **in ~ circumstances** dans l'adversité.

adversity |advûr'sitē| *n* adversité *f*.

advert |ad'vûrt| *n abbr* (*Brit*) = **advertisement**.

advertise |ad'vûrtīz| *vi* (*vt*) faire de la publicité *or* de la réclame (pour); (*in classified ads etc*) mettre une annonce (pour vendre); **to ~ for** (*staff*) recruter par (voie d')annonce.

advertisement |advûrtīz'mənt| *n* (COMM) réclame *f*, publicité *f*; (*in classified ads etc*) annonce *f*.

advertiser |ad'vûrtīzûr| *n* annonceur *m*.

advertising |ad'vûrtīzing| *n* publicité *f*.

advertising agency *n* agence *f* de publicité.

advertising campaign *n* campagne *f* de publicité.

advice |advīs'| *n* conseils *mpl*; (*notification*) avis *m*; **piece of ~** conseil; **to ask (sb) for ~** demander conseil (à qn); **to seek legal ~** consulter un avocat.

advice slip *n* avis *m* d'expédition.

advisable |advī'zəbəl| *a* recommandable, indiqué(e).

advise |advīz'| *vt* conseiller; **to ~ sb of sth** aviser *or* informer qn de qch; **to ~ sb against sth** déconseiller qch à qn; **to ~ sb against doing sth** conseiller à qn de ne pas faire qch; **you would be well/ill ~d to go** vous feriez mieux d'y aller/de ne pas y aller, vous auriez intérêt à y aller/à ne pas y aller.

advisedly |advī'zidlē| *ad* (*deliberately*) délibérément.

adviser |advī'zûr| *n* conseiller/ère.

advisory |advī'zûrē| *a* consultatif(ive); **in an ~ capacity** à titre consultatif.

advocate *n* [ad'vəkit] (*upholder*) défenseur *m*, avocat/e ♦ *vt* [ad'vəkāt] recommander, prôner; **to be an ~ of** être partisan/e de.

advt. *abbr* = **advertisement.**

AEA *n* *abbr* (*Brit*: = *Atomic Energy Authority*) ≈ AEN *f* (= *Agence pour l'énergie nucléaire*).

AEC *n* *abbr* (*US*: = *Atomic Energy Commission*) ≈ AEN *f* (= *Agence pour l'énergie nucléaire*).

Aegean (Sea) [ijē'ən (sē')] *n* mer *f* Égée.

aegis [ē'jis] *n*: **under the ~ of** sous l'égide de.

aeon [ē'ən] *n* (*Brit*) = **eon.**

aerial [är'ēəl] *n* antenne *f* ♦ *a* aérien(ne).

aerie [är'ē] *n* aire *f*.

aerobatics [ärəbat'iks] *npl* acrobaties aériennes.

aerobics [ärō'biks] *n* aérobic *m*.

aerodrome [är'ədrōm] *n* (*Brit*) aérodrome *m*.

aerodynamic [ärōdīnam'ik] *a* aérodynamique.

aerogramme [är'əgram] *n* aérogramme *m*.

aeronautics [ärənô'tiks] *n* aéronautique *f*.

aeroplane [är'əplān] *n* (*Brit*) avion *m*.

aerosol [är'əsòl] *n* aérosol *m*.

aerospace industry [är'əspās in'dəstrē] *n* (industrie) aérospatiale.

aesthetic [esthet'ik] *a* (*Brit*) = **esthetic.**

afar [əfär'] *ad*: **from ~** de loin.

AFB *n* *abbr* (*US*) = *Air Force Base*.

AFDC *n* *abbr* (*US*: = *Aid to Families with Dependent Children*) aide pour enfants assistés.

affable [af'əbəl] *a* affable.

affair [əfär'] *n* affaire *f*; (*also*: **love ~**) liaison *f*; aventure *f*; **~s** (*business*) affaires *f*.

affect [əfekt'] *vt* affecter.

affectation [afektā'shən] *n* affectation *f*.

affected [əfek'tid] *a* affecté(e).

affection [əfek'shən] *n* affection *f*.

affectionate [əfek'shənit] *a* affectueux(euse).

affectionately [əfek'shənitlē] *ad* affectueusement.

affidavit [afidā'vit] *n* (*LAW*) déclaration écrite sous serment.

affiliated [əfil'ēātid] *a* affilié(e); **~ company** filiale *f*.

affinity [əfin'ətē] *n* affinité *f*.

affirm [əfûrm'] *vt* affirmer.

affirmation [afûrmā'shən] *n* affirmation *f*, assertion *f*.

affirmative [əfûr'mətiv] *a* affirmatif(ive) ♦ *n*: **in the ~** dans or par l'affirmative.

affix [əfiks'] *vt* apposer, ajouter.

afflict [əflikt'] *vt* affliger.

affliction [əflik'shən] *n* affliction *f*.

affluence [af'lōōəns] *n* aisance *f*, opulence *f*.

affluent [af'lōōənt] *a* opulent(e); (*person*) dans l'aisance, riche; **the ~ society** la société d'abondance.

afford [əfôrd'] *vt* (*goods etc*) avoir les moyens d'acheter or d'entretenir; (*behavior*) se permettre; (*provide*) fournir, procurer; **can we ~ a car?** avons-nous de quoi acheter or les moyens d'acheter une voiture?; **I can't ~ the time** je n'ai vraiment pas le temps.

affront [əfrunt'] *n* affront *m*.

affronted [əfrun'tid] *a* insulté(e).

Afghan [af'gan] *n* afghan(e) ♦ *n* Afghan/e.

Afghanistan [afgan'istan] *n* Afghanistan *m*.

afield [əfēld'] *ad*: **far ~** loin.

AFL-CIO *n* *abbr* (= *American Federation of Labor and Congress of Industrial Organizations*) confédération syndicale.

afloat [əflōt'] *a* à flot ♦ *ad*: **to stay ~** surnager; **to keep/get a business ~** maintenir à flot/lancer une affaire.

afoot [əfōōt'] *ad*: **there is something ~** il se prépare quelque chose.

aforementioned [əfôr'menshənd] *a*, **aforesaid** [əfôr'sed] *a* susdit(e), susmentionné(e).

afraid [əfrād'] *a* effrayé(e); **to be ~ of** or **to** avoir peur de; **I am ~ that** je crains que + *sub*; **I'm ~ so/not** oui/non, malheureusement.

afresh [əfresh'] *ad* de nouveau.

Africa [af'rikə] *n* Afrique *f*.

African [af'rikən] *a* africain(e) ♦ *n* Africain/e.

Afrikaans [afrikäns'] *n* afrikaans *m*.

Afrikaner [afrikä'nûr] *n* Afrikaner or Afrikander *m/f*.

Afro-American [af'rōəmär'ikən] *a* afro-américain(e).

AFT *n* *abbr* (= *American Federation of Teachers*) syndicat enseignant.

aft [aft] *ad* à l'arrière, vers l'arrière.

after [af'tûr] *prep*, *ad* après ♦ *cj* après que, après avoir or être + *pp*; **~ dinner** après (le) dîner; **the day ~ tomorrow** après demain; **quarter ~ two** (*US*) deux heures et quart; **what/who are you ~?** que/qui cherchez-vous?; **the police are ~ him** la police est à ses trousses; **~ you!** après vous!; **~ all** après tout.

aftercare [af'tûrkär] *n* (*MED*) post-cure *f*.

after-effects [af'tûrifekts] *npl* répercussions *fpl*; (*of illness*) séquelles *fpl*, suites *fpl*.

afterlife [af'tûrlīf] *n* vie future.

aftermath [af'tûrmath] *n* conséquences *fpl*; **in the ~ of** dans les mois or années etc qui suivirent, au lendemain de.

afternoon [aftûrnōōn'] *n* après-midi *m* or *f*; **good ~!** bonjour!; (*goodbye*) au revoir!

after-sales service [af'tûrsālz sûr'vis] *n* (*Brit*) service *m* après-vente, SAV *m*.

after-shave (lotion) [af'tûrshāv (lō'shən)] *n* lotion *f* après-rasage.

aftershock [af'tûrshâk] *n* réplique *f* (sismique).

afterthought [af'tûrthôt] *n*: **I had an ~** il m'est venu une idée après coup.

afterwards [af'tûrwûrdz] *ad* après.

again [əgen'] *ad* de nouveau, encore une fois; **to begin/see ~** recommencer/revoir; **not ... ~ ne ... plus**; **~ and ~** à plusieurs reprises; **he's opened it ~** il l'a rouvert, il l'a de nouveau or l'a encore ouvert; **now and ~** de temps à autre.

against [əgenst'] *prep* contre; **~ a blue background** sur un fond bleu; (*over*) **~** contre.

age [āj] *n* âge *m* ♦ *vt*, *vi* vieillir; **what ~ is he?** quel âge a-t-il?; **he is 20 years of ~** il a 20 ans; **under ~** mineur(e); **to come of ~** atteindre sa majorité; **it's been ~s since** ça fait une éternité que ... ne.

aged [ājd] *a* âgé(e); **~ 10** âgé de 10 ans; **the ~** [ā'jid] *npl* les personnes âgées.

age group *n* tranche *f* d'âge; **the 40 to 50 ~** la tranche d'âge des 40 à 50 ans.

ageless [āj'lis] *a* sans âge.

age limit *n* limite *f* d'âge.

agency [ā'jənsē] *n* agence *f*; **through** *or* **by the ~ of** par l'entremise *or* l'action de.

agenda [əjen'də] *n* ordre *m* du jour; **on the ~** à l'ordre du jour.

agent [ā'jənt] *n* agent *m*.

aggravate [ag'rəvāt] *vt* aggraver; (*annoy*) exaspérer, agacer.

aggravation [agrəvā'shən] *n* agacements *mpl*.

aggregate [ag'rəgit] *n* ensemble *m*, total *m*; **on ~** (*SPORT*) au total des points.

aggression [əgresh'ən] *n* agression *f*.

aggressive [əgres'iv] *a* agressif(ive).

aggressiveness [əgres'ivnis] *n* agressivité *f*.

aggrieved [əgrēvd'] *a* chagriné(e), affligé(e).

aghast [əgast'] *a* consterné(e), atterré(e).

agile [aj'əl] *a* agile.

agitate [aj'ətāt] *vt* rendre inquiet(ète) *or* agité(e) ♦ *vi* faire de l'agitation (politique); **to ~ for** faire campagne pour.

agitator [aj'itātûr] *n* agitateur/trice (politique).

AGM *n abbr* (*Brit*) = **annual general meeting**.

ago [əgō'] *ad*: **2 days ~** il y a 2 jours; **not long ~** il n'y a pas longtemps; **as long ~ as 1960** déjà en 1960; **how long ~?** il y a combien de temps (de cela)?

agog [əgâg'] *a*: **(all) ~** en émoi.

agonize [ag'ənīz] *vi*: **he ~d over the problem** ce problème lui a causé bien du tourment.

agonizing [ag'ənīzing] *a* angoissant(e); (*cry*) déchirant(e).

agony [ag'ənē] *n* grande souffrance *or* angoisse; **to be in ~** souffrir le martyre.

agony column *n* courrier *m* du cœur.

agree [əgrē'] *vt* (*price*) convenir de ♦ *vi*: **to ~ (with)** (*person*) être d'accord (avec); (*statements etc*) concorder (avec); (*LING*) s'accorder (avec); **to ~ to do** accepter de *or* consentir à faire; **to ~ to sth** consentir à qch; **to ~ that** (*admit*) convenir *or* reconnaître que; **it was ~d that ...** il a été convenu que ...; **they ~ on this** ils sont d'accord sur ce point; **they ~d on going/a price** ils se mirent d'accord pour y aller/sur un prix; **garlic doesn't ~ with me** je ne supporte pas l'ail.

agreeable [əgrē'əbəl] *a* (*pleasant*) agréable; (*willing*) consentant(e), d'accord; **are you ~ to this?** est-ce que vous êtes d'accord?

agreed [əgrēd'] *a* (*time, place*) convenu(e); **to be ~** être d'accord.

agreement [əgrē'mənt] *n* accord *m*; **in ~** d'accord; **by mutual ~** d'un commun accord.

agricultural [agrəkul'chûrəl] *a* agricole.

agriculture [ag'rəkulchûr] *n* agriculture *f*.

aground [əground'] *ad*: **to run ~** s'échouer.

agt. *abbr* = **agent**.

ahead [əhed'] *ad* en avant; devant; **go right** *or* **straight ~** allez tout droit; **go ~!** (*fig*) allez-y!; **~ of** devant; (*fig: schedule etc*) en avance sur; **~ of time** en avance; **they were (right) ~ of us** ils nous précédaient (de peu), ils étaient (juste) devant nous.

AI *n abbr* = *Amnesty International*; (*COMPUT*) = **artificial intelligence**.

AID *n abbr* (= *artificial insemination by donor*) IAD *f*; (*US*: = *Agency for International Development*) agence pour le développement international.

aid [ād] *n* aide *f* ♦ *vt* aider; **with the ~ of**

avec l'aide de; **in ~ of** en faveur de; **to ~ and abet** (*LAW*) se faire le complice de.

aide [ād] *n* (*person*) assistant/e.

AIDS [ādz] *n abbr* (= *acquired immune deficiency syndrome*) SIDA *m*.

AIH *n abbr* (= *artificial insemination by husband*) IAC *f*.

ailment [āl'mənt] *n* affection *f*.

aim [ām] *n* but *m* ♦ *vt*: **to ~ sth at** (*gun, camera*) braquer *or* pointer qch sur, diriger qch contre; (*missile*) pointer qch vers *or* sur; (*remark, blow*) destiner *or* adresser qch à ♦ *vi* (*also*: **to take ~**) viser; **to ~ at** viser; (*fig*) viser (à); avoir pour but *or* ambition; **to ~ to do** avoir l'intention de faire.

aimless [ām'lis] *a* sans but.

aimlessly [ām'lislē] *ad* sans but.

ain't [ānt] (*col*) = **am not, aren't, isn't**.

air [är] *n* air *m* ♦ *vt* aérer; (*idea, grievance, views*) mettre sur le tapis; (*knowledge*) faire étalage de ♦ *cpd* (*currents, attack etc*) aérien(ne); **by ~** par avion; **to be on the ~** (*RADIO, TV: program*) être diffusé(e); (: *station*) émettre.

air base *n* base aérienne.

air bed *n* (*Brit*) matelas *m* pneumatique.

airborne [är'bôrn] *a* (*plane*) en vol; (*troops*) aeroporté(e); (*particles*) dans l'air; **as soon as the plane was ~** dès que l'avion eut décollé.

air cargo *n* fret aérien.

air-conditioned [är'kəndishənd] *a* climatisé(e), à air conditionné.

air conditioning [är' kəndish'əning] *n* climatisation *f*.

air-cooled [är'kōōld] *a* à refroidissement à air.

aircraft [är'kraft] *n* (*pl inv*) avion *m*.

aircraft carrier *n* porte-avions *m inv*.

air cushion *n* coussin *m* d'air.

airdrome [är'drōm] *n* (*US*) aérodrome *m*.

airfield [är'fēld] *n* terrain *m* d'aviation.

Air Force *n* Armée *f* de l'air.

air freight *n* fret aérien.

air gun *n* fusil *m* à air comprimé.

air hostess *n* (*Brit*) hôtesse *f* de l'air.

airily [är'ilē] *ad* d'un air dégagé.

airing [är'ing] *n*: **to give an ~ to** aérer; (*fig: ideas, views etc*) mettre sur le tapis.

air letter *n* aérogramme *m*.

airlift [är'lift] *n* pont aérien.

airline [är'līn] *n* ligne aérienne, compagnie aérienne.

airliner [är'līnûr] *n* avion *m* de ligne.

airlock [är'lâk] *n* sas *m*.

airmail [är'māl] *n*: **by ~** par avion.

air mattress *n* matelas *m* pneumatique.

airplane [är'plān] *n* (*US*) avion *m*.

airport [är'pôrt] *n* aéroport *m*.

air raid *n* attaque aérienne.

airsick [är'sik] *a*: **to be ~** avoir le mal de l'air.

airstrip [är'strip] *n* terrain *m* d'atterrissage.

air terminal *n* aérogare *f*.

airtight [är'tit] *a* hermétique.

air traffic control *n* contrôle *m* de la navigation aérienne.

air traffic controller *n* aiguilleur *m* du ciel.

air waybill [är' wā'bil] *n* lettre *f* de transport aérien.

airy [är'ē] *a* bien aéré(e); (*manners*) dégagé(e).

aisle [īl] *n* (*of church*) allée centrale; nef latérale; (*in theater*) allée *f*; (*on plane*) couloir *m*.

ajar [əjâr'] *a* entrouvert(e).

AK *abbr* (*US MAIL*) = *Alaska*.

aka *abbr* (= *also known as*) alias.

akin [əkin'] *a*: ~ **to** semblable à, du même ordre que.

AL *abbr* (*US MAIL*) = *Alabama*.

ALA *n abbr* = *American Library Association*.

Ala. *abbr* (*US*) = *Alabama*.

alacrity [əlak'ritē] *n*: **with** ~ avec empressement, promptement.

alarm [əlârm'] *n* alarme *f* ♦ *vt* alarmer.

alarm clock *n* réveille-matin *m*, réveil *m*.

alarming [əlâr'ming] *a* alarmant(e).

alarmist [əlâr'mist] *n* alarmiste *m/f*.

Alas. *abbr* (*US*) = *Alaska*.

alas [əlas'] *excl* hélas.

Alaska [əlas'kə] *n* Alaska *m*.

Albania [albā'nēə] *n* Albanie *f*.

Albanian [albā'nēən] *a* albanais(e) ♦ *n* Albanais/e; (*LING*) albanais *m*.

albeit [ôlbē'it] *cj* bien que + *sub*, encore que + *sub*.

album [al'bəm] *n* album *m*.

albumen [albyōō'mən] *n* albumine *f*; (*of egg*) albumen *m*.

alchemy [al'kəmē] *n* alchimie *f*.

alcohol [al'kəhôl] *n* alcool *m*.

alcoholic [alkəhôl'ik] *a*, *n* alcoolique *(m/f)*.

alcoholism [al'kəhôlizəm] *n* alcoolisme *m*.

alcove [al'kōv] *n* alcôve *f*.

ald. *abbr* = **alderman**.

alderman [ôl'dûrmən] *n* conseiller municipal (*en Angleterre*).

ale [āl] *n* bière *f*.

alert [əlûrt'] *a* alerte, vif(vive); (*watchful*) vigilant(e) ♦ *n* alerte *f* ♦ *vt*: **to** ~ **sb (to sth)** attirer l'attention de qn (sur qch); **to** ~ **sb to the dangers of sth** avertir qn des dangers de qch; **on the** ~ sur le qui-vive; (*MIL*) en état d'alerte.

Aleutian Islands [əlōō'shən ī'ləndz] *npl* îles Aléoutiennes.

Alexandria [aligzan'drēə] *n* Alexandrie.

alfresco [alfres'kō] *a*, *ad* en plein air.

algebra [al'jəbrə] *n* algèbre *m*.

Algeria [aljē'rēə] *n* Algérie *f*.

Algerian [aljə'rēən] *a* algérien(ne) ♦ *n* Algérien/ne.

Algiers [aljērz'] *n* Alger.

algorithm [al'gəriťhəm] *n* algorithme *m*.

alias [ā'lēəs] *ad* alias ♦ *n* faux nom, nom d'emprunt.

alibi [al'əbī] *n* alibi *m*.

alien [āl'yən] *n* étranger/ère ♦ *a*: ~ **(to)** étranger(ère) (à).

alienate [āl'yənāt] *vt* aliéner; (*subj: person*) s'aliéner.

alienation [ālyənā'shən] *n* aliénation *f*.

alight [əlīt'] *a*, *ad* en feu ♦ *vi* mettre pied à terre; (*passenger*) descendre; (*bird*) se poser.

align [əlīn'] *vt* aligner.

alignment [əlīn'mənt] *n* alignement *m*; **it's out of** ~ **(with)** ce n'est pas aligné (avec).

alike [əlīk'] *a* semblable, pareil(le) ♦ *ad* de même; **to look** ~ se ressembler.

alimony [al'əmōnē] *n* (*payment*) pension *f* alimentaire.

alive [əlīv'] *a* vivant(e); (*active*) plein(e) de vie; ~ **with** grouillant(e) de; ~ **to** sensible à.

alkali [al'kəlī] *n* alcali *m*.

all [ôl] *a* tout(e), tous(toutes) *pl* ♦ *pronoun* tout *m*; (*pl*) tous(toutes) ♦ *ad* tout; ~ **wrong/alone** tout faux/seul; ~ **the time/his life** tout le temps/toute sa vie; ~ **five** (**of them**) tous les cinq; ~ **five girls** les cinq filles; ~ **of them** tous, toutes; ~ **of it** tout; ~ **of us went** nous y sommes tous allés; ~ **day** toute la journée; **is that** ~? c'est tout?; (*in store*) ce sera tout?; **for** ~ **their efforts** malgré tous leurs efforts; **as hard** *etc* **as** ~ **that** pas si dur *etc* que ça; **at** ~: **not at** ~ (*in answer to question*) pas du tout; (*in answer to thanks*) je vous en prie!; **I'm not at** ~ **tired** je ne suis pas du tout fatigué; **anything at** ~ **will do** n'importe quoi fera l'affaire; ~ **but** presque, pratiquement; **to be** ~ **in** (*col*) être complètement à plat; ~ **in** = en somme, somme toute, finalement; ~ **out** *ad* à fond.

all-around [ôl'əround] *a* compétent(e) dans tous les domaines; (*athlete etc*) complet (ète).

allay [əlā'] *vt* (*fears*) apaiser, calmer.

all clear *n* (*also fig*) fin *f* d'alerte.

allegation [aləgā'shən] *n* allégation *f*.

allege [əlej'] *vt* alléguer, prétendre; **he is** ~**d to have said** il aurait dit.

alleged [əlejd'] *a* prétendu(e).

allegedly [əlej'idlē] *ad* à ce que l'on prétend, paraît-il.

allegiance [əlē'jəns] *n* fidélité *f*, obéissance *f*.

allegory [al'əgôrē] *n* allégorie *f*.

all-embracing [ôl'embrās'ing] *a* universel(le).

allergic [əlûr'jik] *a*: ~ **to** allergique à.

allergy [al'ûrjē] *n* allergie *f*.

alleviate [əlē'vēāt] *vt* soulager, adoucir.

alley [al'ē] *n* ruelle *f*; (*in garden*) allée *f*.

alliance [əlī'əns] *n* alliance *f*.

allied [əlīd'] *a* allié(e).

alligator [al'əgātûr] *n* alligator *m*.

all-important [ôl'impôr'tənt] *a* capital(e), crucial(e).

all-inclusive [ôl'inklōō'siv] *a* (*also ad: charge*) tout compris.

all-in wrestling [ôl'in res'ling] *n* (*Brit*) catch *m*.

alliteration [əlitərā'shən] *n* allitération *f*.

all-night [ôl'nīt] *a* ouvert(e) *or* qui dure toute la nuit.

allocate [al'əkāt] *vt* (*share out*) répartir, distribuer; (*duties*): **to** ~ **sth to** assigner *or* attribuer qch à; (*sum, time*): **to** ~ **sth to** allouer qch à; **to** ~ **sth for** affecter qch à.

allocation [aləkā'shən] *n* (*see vb*) répartition *f*; attribution *f*; allocation *f*; affectation *f*; (*money*) crédit(s) *m(pl)*, somme(s) allouée(s).

allot [əlât'] *vt* (*share out*) répartir, distribuer; (*time*): **to** ~ **sth to** allouer qch à; (*duties*): **to** ~ **sth to** assigner qch à; **in the** ~**ted time** dans le temps imparti.

allotment [əlât'mənt] *n* (*share*) part *f*; (*Brit*:

garden) lopin *m* de terre (*loué à la municipalité*).

all-out |ôl'out'| *a* (*effort etc*) total(e).

allow |əlou'| *vt* (*practice, behavior*) permettre, autoriser; (*sum to spend etc*) accorder, allouer; (*sum, time estimated*) compter, prévoir; (*concede*): **to ~ that** convenir que; **to ~ sb to do** permettre à qn de faire, autoriser qn à faire; **he is ~ed to ...** on lui permet de ...; **smoking is not ~ed** il est interdit de fumer; **we must ~ 3 days for the journey** il faut compter 3 jours pour le voyage.
 allow for *vt fus* tenir compte de.

allowance |əlou'əns| *n* (*money received*) allocation *f*; (: *from parent etc*) subside *m*; (: *for expenses*) indemnité *f*; (*TAX*) somme *f* déductible du revenu imposable, abattement *m*; **to make ~s for** tenir compte de.

alloy |al'oi| *n* alliage *m*.

all right *ad* (*feel, work*) bien; (*as answer*) d'accord.

all-rounder |ôlroun'dûr| *n* (*Brit*): **to be a good ~** être doué(e) en tout.

allspice |ôl'spīs| *n* poivre *m* de la Jamaïque.

all-time |ôl'tīm| *a* (*record*) sans précédent, absolu(e).

allude |əlōōd'| *vi*: **to ~ to** faire allusion à.

alluring |əlōō'ring| *a* séduisant(e), alléchant(e).

allusion |əlōō'zhən| *n* allusion *f*.

alluvium |əlōō'vēəm| *n* alluvions *fpl*.

ally *n* |al'ī| allié *m* ♦ *vt* |əlī|: **to ~ o.s. with** s'allier avec.

almighty |ôlmī'tē| *a* tout-puissant.

almond |â'mənd| *n* amande *f*.

almost |ôl'mōst| *ad* presque; **he ~ fell** il a failli tomber.

alms |âmz| *n* aumône(s) *f(pl)*.

aloft |əlôft'| *ad* en haut, en l'air; (*NAUT*) dans la mâture.

alone |əlōn'| *a*, *ad* seul(e); **to leave sb ~** laisser qn tranquille; **to leave sth ~** ne pas toucher à qch; **let ~ ...** sans parler de ...; encore moins ....

along |əlông'| *prep* le long de ♦ *ad*: **is he coming ~?** vient-il avec nous?; **he was hopping/limping ~** il venait *or* avançait en sautillant/boitant; **~ with** avec, en plus de; (*person*) en compagnie de.

alongside |əlông'sīd'| *prep* le long de; au côté de ♦ *ad* bord à bord; côte à côte; **we brought our boat ~** (*of a pier, shore etc*) nous avons accosté.

aloof |əlōōf'| *a*, *ad* à distance, à l'écart; **to stand ~** se tenir à l'écart *or* à distance.

aloofness |əlōōf'nis| *n* réserve (hautaine), attitude distante.

aloud |əloud'| *ad* à haute voix.

alphabet |al'fəbet| *n* alphabet *m*.

alphabetical |alfəbet'ikəl| *a* alphabétique; **in ~ order** par ordre alphabétique.

alphanumeric |alfənōōmâr'ik| *a* alphanumérique.

alpine |al'pīn| *a* alpin(e), alpestre; **~ hut** cabane *f or* refuge *m* de montagne; **~ pasture** pâturage *m* (de montagne); **~ skiing** ski alpin.

Alps |alps| *npl*: **the ~** les Alpes *fpl*.

already |ôlred'ē| *ad* déjà.

alright |ôlrīt'| *ad* = **all right**.

Alsace |alsâs'| *n* Alsace *f*.

Alsatian |alsā'shən| *a* alsacien(ne), d'Alsace ♦ *n* Alsacien/ne; (*Brit: dog*) berger allemand.

also |ôl'sō| *ad* aussi.

Alta. *abbr* (*Canada*) = *Alberta*.

altar |ôl'tûr| *n* autel *m*.

alter |ôl'tûr| *vt*, *vi* changer, modifier.

alteration |ôltərā'shən| *n* changement *m*, modification *f*; **~s** (*SEWING*) retouches *fpl*; (*ARCHIT*) modifications *fpl*; **timetable subject to ~** horaires sujets à modifications.

alternate *a* |ôl'tûrnit| alterné(e), alternant(e), alternatif(ive) ♦ *vi* |ôl'tûrnāt| alterner; **on ~ days** un jour sur deux, tous les deux jours.

alternately |ôl'tûrnitlē| *ad* alternativement, en alternant.

alternating |ôl'tûrnāting| *a* (*current*) alternatif(ive).

alternative |ôltûr'nətiv| *a* (*solutions*) interchangeable, possible; (*solution*) autre, de remplacement; (*energy*) doux(douce); (*society*) parallèle ♦ *n* (*choice*) alternative *f*; (*other possibility*) autre possibilité *f*.

alternatively |ôltûr'nətivlē| *ad*: **~ one could** une autre *or* l'autre solution serait de.

alternator |ôl'tûrnātûr| *n* (*AUT*) alternateur *m*.

although |ôlthō'| *cj* bien que + *sub*.

altitude |al'tətōōd| *n* altitude *f*.

alto |al'tō| *n* (*female*) contralto *m*; (*male*) haute-contre *f*.

altogether |ôltəgeth'ûr| *ad* entièrement, tout à fait; (*on the whole*) tout compte fait; (*in all*) en tout; **how much is that ~?** ça fait combien en tout?

altruistic |altrōōis'tik| *a* altruiste.

aluminium *etc* |alōōmin'ēəm| (*Brit*) = **aluminum** *etc*.

aluminum |əlōō'mənəm| *n* (*US*) aluminium *m*.

aluminum foil *n* papier *m* d'alu.

alumnus |əlum'nəs| *n* (*US*) ancien(ne) élève.

always |ôl'wāz| *ad* toujours.

AM *abbr* = *amplitude modulation*.

am |am| *vb see* **be**.

a.m. *ad abbr* (= *ante meridiem*) du matin.

AMA *n abbr* = *American Medical Association*.

amalgam |əmal'gəm| *n* amalgame *m*.

amalgamate |əmal'gəmāt| *vt*, *vi* fusionner.

amalgamation |əmalgəmā'shən| *n* fusion *f*; (*COMM*) fusionnement *m*.

amass |əmas'| *vt* amasser.

amateur |am'əchûr| *n* amateur *m* ♦ *a* (*SPORT*) amateur *inv*; **~ dramatics** le théâtre amateur.

amateurish |aməchōō'rish| *a* (*pej*) d'amateur, un peu amateur.

amaze |əmāz'| *vt* surprendre, étonner; **to be ~d (at)** être surpris *or* étonné (de).

amazement |əmāz'mənt| *n* surprise *f*, étonnement *m*.

amazing |əmā'zing| *a* étonnant(e), incroyable; (*bargain, offer*) exceptionnel(le).

amazingly |əmā'zinglē| *ad* incroyablement.

Amazon |am'əzän| *n* (*GEO, MYTHOLOGY*) Amazone *f* ♦ *cpd* amazonien(ne), de l'Amazone; **the ~ basin** le bassin de l'Amazone; **the ~ jungle** la forêt amazonienne.

Amazonian |aməzō'nēən| *a* amazonien(ne).

ambassador |ambas'ədûr| *n* ambassadeur *m*.

amber [am'bûr] *n* ambre *m*; **at ~** (*Brit AUT*) à l'orange.

ambidextrous [ambidɛk'strəs] *a* ambidextre.

ambience [am'bēəns] *n* ambiance *f*.

ambiguity [ambəgyōō'itē] *n* ambiguïté *f*.

ambiguous [ambig'yōōəs] *a* ambigu(ë).

ambition [ambish'ən] *n* ambition *f*.

ambitious [ambish'əs] *a* ambitieux(euse).

ambivalent [ambiv'ələnt] *a* (*attitude*) ambivalent(e).

amble [am'bəl] *vi* (*also:* **to ~ along**) aller d'un pas tranquille.

ambulance [am'byələns] *n* ambulance *f*.

ambush [am'bōōsh] *n* embuscade *f* ♦ *vt* tendre une embuscade à.

ameba [əmē'bə] *n* (*US*) = **amoeba.**

ameliorate [əmēl'yərāt] *vt* améliorer.

amen [ā'men'] *excl* amen.

amenable [əmē'nəbəl] *a:* **~ to** (*advice etc*) disposé(e) à écouter *or* suivre; **~ to the law** responsable devant la loi.

amend [əmend'] *vt* (*law*) amender; (*text*) corriger; (*habits*) réformer ♦ *vi* s'amender, se corriger; **to make ~s** réparer ses torts, faire amende honorable.

amendment [əmend'mənt] *n* (*to law*) amendement *m*; (*to text*) correction *f*.

amenities [əmen'itēz] *npl* aménagements *mpl*, équipements *mpl*.

amenity [əmen'itē] *n* charme *m*, agrément *m*.

America [əmär'ikə] *n* Amérique *f*.

American [əmär'ikən] *a* américain(e) ♦ *n* Américain/e.

americanize [əmär'ikənīz] *vt* américaniser.

Amerindian [amərin'dēən] *a* amérindien(ne) ♦ *n* Amérindien/ne.

amethyst [am'ithist] *n* améthyste *f*.

Amex [am'eks] *n abbr* = *American Stock Exchange.*

amiable [ā'mēəbəl] *a* aimable, affable.

amicable [am'ikəbəl] *a* amical(e).

amid(st) [əmid(st)'] *prep* parmi, au milieu de.

amiss [əmis'] *a, ad:* **there's something ~** il y a quelque chose qui ne va pas *or* qui cloche; **to take sth ~** prendre qch mal *or* de travers.

ammo [am'ō] *n abbr* (*col*) = **ammunition.**

ammonia [əmōn'yə] *n* (*gas*) ammoniac *m*; (*liquid*) ammoniaque *f*.

ammunition [amyənish'ən] *n* munitions *fpl*; (*fig*) arguments *mpl*.

ammunition dump *n* dépôt *m* de munitions.

amnesia [amnē'zhə] *n* amnésie *f*.

amnesty [am'nistē] *n* amnistie *f*; **to grant an ~ to** accorder une amnistie à.

amoeba [əmē'bə] *n* amibe *f*.

amok [əmuk'] *ad:* **to run ~** être pris(e) d'un accès de folie furieuse.

among(st) [əmung(st)'] *prep* parmi, entre.

amoral [āmôr'əl] *a* amoral(e).

amorous [am'ûrəs] *a* amoureux(euse).

amorphous [əmôr'fəs] *a* amorphe.

amortization [amûrtəzā'shən] *n* (*COMM*) amortissement *m*.

amount [əmount'] *n* (*sum of money*) somme *f*; (*total*) montant *m*; (*quantity*) quantité *f*; nombre *m* ♦ *vi:* **to ~ to** (*total*) s'élever à; (*be same as*) équivaloir à, revenir à; **this ~s to a refusal** cela équivaut à un refus; **the total ~** (*of money*) le montant total.

amp(ere) [am'pēr] *n* ampère *m*; **a 13 amp plug** une fiche de 13 A.

ampersand [am'pûrsand] *n* signe &, "et" commercial.

amphibian [amfib'ēən] *n* batracien *m*.

amphibious [amfib'ēəs] *a* amphibie.

amphitheater, (*Brit*) **amphitheatre** [am'fəthēətûr] *n* amphithéâtre *m*.

ample [am'pəl] *a* ample; spacieux(euse); (*enough*): **this is ~** c'est largement suffisant; **to have ~ time/room** avoir bien assez de temps/place, avoir largement le temps/la place.

amplifier [am'pləfûr] *n* amplificateur *m*.

amplify [am'pləfī] *vt* amplifier.

amply [am'plē] *ad* amplement, largement.

ampule, (*Brit*) **ampoule** [am'pyōōl] *n* (*MED*) ampoule *f*.

amputate [am'pyōōtāt] *vt* amputer.

Amsterdam [am'stûrdam] *n* Amsterdam.

amt *abbr* = **amount.**

amuck [əmuk'] *ad* = **amok.**

amuse [əmyōōz'] *vt* amuser; **to ~ o.s. with sth/by doing sth** se divertir avec qch/à faire qch; **to be ~d at** être amusé par; **he was not ~d** il n'a pas apprécié.

amusement [əmyōōz'mənt] *n* amusement *m*.

amusement arcade *n* salle *f* de jeu.

amusement park *n* parc *m* d'attractions.

amusing [əmyōō'zing] *a* amusant(e), divertissant(e).

an [an, ən, n] *definite article see* **a.**

ANA *n abbr* = *American Newspaper Association; American Nurses Association.*

anachronism [ənak'rənizəm] *n* anachronisme *m*.

anaemia [ənē'mēə] *etc* (*Brit*) = **anemia.**

anaesthetic [anisthet'ik] (*Brit*) *a, n* = **anesthetic.**

anaesthetist [ənēs'thətist] *n* (*Brit*) anesthésiste *m/f*.

anagram [an'əgram] *n* anagramme *m*.

analgesic [ənəljē'zik] *a, n* analgésique (*m*).

analog(ue) [an'əlôg] *a* (*watch, computer*) analogique.

analogy [ənal'əjē] *n* analogie *f*; **to draw an ~ between** établir une analogie entre.

analyse [an'əlīz] *vt* (*Brit*) = **analyze.**

analysis, *pl* **analyses** [ənal'isis, -sēz] *n* analyse *f*; **in the last ~** en dernière analyse.

analyst [an'əlist] *n* (*political ~ etc*) analyste *m/f*; (*US*) psychanalyste *m/f*.

analytic(al) [ənəlit'ik(əl)] *a* analytique.

analyze [an'əlīz] *vt* (*US*) analyser.

anarchist [an'ûrkist] *a, n* anarchiste (*m/f*).

anarchy [an'ûrkē] *n* anarchie *f*.

anathema [ənath'əmə] *n:* **it is ~ to him** il a cela en abomination.

anatomical [anətâm'ikəl] *a* anatomique.

anatomy [ənat'əmē] *n* anatomie *f*.

ANC *n abbr* (= *African National Congress*) ANC *m*.

ancestor [an'sestûr] *n* ancêtre *m*, aïeul *m*.

ancestral [anses'trəl] *a* ancestral(e).

ancestry [an'sestrē] *n* ancêtres *mpl*; ascendance *f*.

anchor [ang'kûr] *n* ancre *f* ♦ *vi* (*also:* **to drop ~**) jeter l'ancre, mouiller ♦ *vt* mettre à l'ancre.

anchorage [ang'kûrij] *n* mouillage *m*, ancrage *m*.

anchovy [an'chōvē] *n* anchois *m*.

ancient [ān'shənt] *a* ancien(ne), antique; (*fig*) d'un âge vénérable, antique; ~ **monument** monument *m* historique.

ancillary [an'səlärē] *a* auxiliaire.

and [and] *cj* et; ~ **so on** et ainsi de suite; **try** ~ **come** tâchez de venir; **come** ~ **sit here** venez vous asseoir ici; **better** ~ **better** de mieux en mieux; **more** ~ **more** de plus en plus.

Andes [an'dēz] *npl:* **the** ~ les Andes *fpl.*

anecdote [an'ikdōt] *n* anecdote *f.*

anemia [ənē'mēə] *n* (*US*) anémie *f.*

anemic [ənē'mik] *a* (*US*) anémique.

anemone [ənem'ənē] *n* (*BOT*) anémone *f;* **sea** ~ anémone de mer.

anesthesiologist [an'isthēzēâl'əjist] *n* (*US*) anesthésiste *m/f.*

anesthetic [anisthet'ik] (*US*) *a, n* anesthésique (*m*); **under the** ~ sous anesthésie; **local/general** ~ anesthésie locale/générale.

anew [ənōō'] *ad* à nouveau.

angel [ān'jəl] *n* ange *m.*

anger [ang'gûr] *n* colère *f* ♦ *vt* mettre en colère, irriter.

angina [anjī'nə] *n* angine *f* de poitrine.

angle [ang'gəl] *n* angle *m* ♦ *vi:* **to** ~ **for** (*trout*) pêcher; (*compliments*) chercher, quêter; **from their** ~ de leur point de vue.

angler [ang'glûr] *n* pêcheur/euse à la ligne.

Anglican [ang'glikən] *a, n* anglican(e).

anglicize [ang'gləsīz] *vt* angliciser.

angling [ang'gling] *n* pêche *f* à la ligne.

Anglo- [an'glō] *prefix* anglo(-).

Anglo-French [an'glōfrench'] *a* anglo-français(e).

Anglo-Saxon [an'glōsak'sən] *a, n* anglo-saxon(ne).

Angola [anggō'lə] *n* Angola *m.*

Angolan [anggō'lən] *a* angolais(e) ♦ *n* Angolais/e.

angrily [ang'grilē] *ad* avec colère.

angry [ang'grē] *a* en colère, furieux(euse); **to be** ~ **with sb/at sth** être furieux contre qn/de qch; **to get** ~ se fâcher, se mettre en colère; **to make sb** ~ mettre qn en colère.

anguish [ang'gwish] *n* angoisse *f.*

angular [ang'gyəlûr] *a* anguleux(euse).

animal [an'əməl] *n* animal *m* ♦ *a* animal(e).

animal spirits *npl* entrain *m*, vivacité *f.*

animate *vt* [an'əmāt] animer ♦ *a* [an'əmit] animé(e), vivant(e).

animated [an'əmātid] *a* animé(e).

animosity [anəmâs'ətē] *n* animosité *f.*

aniseed [an'isēd] *n* anis *m.*

Ankara [ang'kûrə] *n* Ankara.

ankle [ang'kəl] *n* cheville *f.*

ankle socks *npl* socquettes *fpl.*

annex *n* [an'eks] (*also: Brit:* **annexe**) annexe *f* ♦ *vt* [əneks'] annexer.

annexation [anəksā'shən] *n* annexion *f.*

annihilate [ənī'əlāt] *vt* annihiler, anéantir.

anniversary [anəvûr'sûrē] *n* anniversaire *m.*

anniversary dinner *n* dîner commémoratif *or* anniversaire.

annotate [an'ōtāt] *vt* annoter.

announce [ənouns'] *vt* annoncer; (*birth,*

death) faire part de; **he** ~**d that he wasn't going** il a déclaré qu'il n'irait pas.

announcement [ənouns'mənt] *n* annonce *f;* (*for births etc: in newspaper*) avis *m* de faire-part; (*: letter, card*) faire-part *m;* **I'd like to make an** ~ j'ai une communication à faire.

announcer [ənoun'sûr] *n* (*RADIO, TV: between programs*) speaker/ine; (*: in a program*) présentateur/trice.

annoy [ənoi'] *vt* agacer, ennuyer, contrarier; **to be** ~**ed (at sth/with sb)** être en colère *or* irrité (contre qch/qn); **don't get** ~**ed!** ne vous fâchez pas!

annoyance [ənoi'əns] *n* mécontentement *m*, contrariété *f.*

annoying [ənoi'ing] *a* ennuyeux(euse), agaçant(e), contrariant(e).

annual [an'yōōəl] *a* annuel(le) ♦ *n* (*BOT*) plante annuelle; (*book*) album *m.*

annual general meeting (AGM) *n* (*Brit*) assemblée générale annuelle (AGA).

annually [an'yōōəlē] *ad* annuellement.

annual report *n* rapport annuel.

annuity [ənōō'itē] *n* rente *f;* **life** ~ rente viagère.

annul [ənul'] *vt* annuler; (*law*) abroger.

annulment [ənul'mənt] *n* (*see vb*) annulation *f;* abrogation *f.*

annum [an'əm] *n see* **per annum.**

Annunciation [ənunsēā'shən] *n* Annonciation *f.*

anode [an'ōd] *n* anode *f.*

anoint [ənoint'] *vt* oindre.

anomalous [ənâm'ələs] *a* anormal(e).

anomaly [ənâm'əlē] *n* anomalie *f.*

anon. [ənân'] *abbr* = **anonymous.**

anonymity [anənim'itē] *n* anonymat *m.*

anonymous [ənân'əməs] *a* anonyme; **to remain** ~ garder l'anonymat.

anorak [ân'ərāk] *n* anorak *m.*

anorexia [anərek'sēə] *n* (*also:* ~ **nervosa**) anorexie *f.*

another [ənuth'ûr] *a:* ~ **book** (*one more*) un autre livre, encore un livre, un livre de plus; (*a different one*) un autre livre; ~ **drink?** encore un verre?; **in** ~ **5 years** dans 5 ans ♦ *pronoun* un(e) autre, encore un(e), un(e) de plus; **some actor or** ~ un certain acteur, je ne sais quel acteur; *see also* **one.**

ANSI *n abbr* (= *American National Standards Institute*) association de normalisation.

answer [an'sûr] *n* réponse *f;* (*to problem*) solution *f* ♦ *vi* répondre ♦ *vt* (*reply to*) répondre à; (*problem*) résoudre; (*prayer*) exaucer; **to** ~ **the phone** répondre (au téléphone); **in** ~ **to your letter** suite à *or* en réponse à votre lettre; **to** ~ **the bell** *or* **the door** aller *or* venir ouvrir (la porte).

answer back *vi* répondre, répliquer.

answer for *vt fus* répondre de, se porter garant de; (*crime, one's actions*) répondre de.

answer to *vt fus* (*description*) répondre *or* correspondre à.

answerable [an'sûrəbəl] *a:* ~ **(to sb/for sth)** responsable (devant qn/de qch); **I am** ~ **to no one** je n'ai de comptes à rendre à personne.

answering machine [an'sûring məshēn'] *n* répondeur *m*.

ant [ant] *n* fourmi *f*.

ANTA *n abbr* = *American National Theatre and Academy*.

antagonism [antag'ənizəm] *n* antagonisme *m*.

antagonist [antag'ənist] *n* antagoniste *m/f*, adversaire *m/f*.

antagonistic [antagənis'tik] *a* (*attitude, feelings*) hostile.

antagonize [antag'ənīz] *vt* éveiller l'hostilité de, contrarier.

Antarctic [antárk'tik] *a* antarctique, austral(e) ♦ *n*: **the ~** l'Antarctique *m*.

Antarctica [antárk'tikə] *n* Antarctique *m*, Terres Australes.

Antarctic Circle *n* cercle *m* Antarctique.

Antarctic Ocean *n* océan *m* Antarctique *or* Austral.

ante [an'tē] *n*: **to up the ~** faire monter les enjeux.

ante... *prefix* anté..., anti..., pré....

anteater [ant'ētûr] *n* fourmilier *m*, tamanoir *m*.

antecedent [antisē'dənt] *n* antécédent *m*.

antechamber [an'tēchāmbûr] *n* antichambre *f*.

antelope [an'tәlōp] *n* antilope *f*.

antenatal [antēnā'təl] *a* (*Brit*) = **prenatal**.

antenna, *pl* **~e** [anten'ə, -ē] *n* antenne *f*; (*US TV*) antenne intérieure.

anthem [an'thəm] *n* motet *m*; **national ~** hymne national.

anthill [ant·hil'] *n* fourmilière *f*.

anthology [anthál'əjē] *n* anthologie *f*.

anthropologist [anthrəpál'əjist] *n* anthropologue *m/f*.

anthropology [anthrəpál'əjē] *n* anthropologie *f*.

anti- [an'tī] *prefix* anti-.

antiaircraft [antiär'kraft] *a* antiaérien(ne).

antiaircraft defense *n* défense *f* contre avions, DCA *f*.

antiballistic [antēbəlis'tik] *a* antibalistique.

antibiotic [antēbīat'ik] *a, n* antibiotique (*m*).

antibody [an'tēbâdē] *n* anticorps *m*.

anticipate [antis'əpāt] *vt* s'attendre à, prévoir; (*wishes, request*) aller au devant de, devancer; **this is worse than I ~d** c'est pire que je ne pensais; **as ~d** comme prévu.

anticipation [antisəpā'shən] *n* attente *f*; **thanking you in ~** en vous remerciant d'avance, avec mes remerciements anticipés.

anticlimax [antēklī'maks] *n* réalisation décevante d'un événement que l'on escomptait important, intéressant etc.

anticlockwise [antēkläk'wīz] *a* (*Brit*) dans le sens inverse des aiguilles d'une montre.

antics [an'tiks] *npl* singeries *fpl*.

anticyclone [antēsī'klōn] *n* anticyclone *m*.

antidote [an'tidōt] *n* antidote *m*, contrepoison *m*.

antifreeze [an'tēfrēz] *n* antigel *m*.

antihistamine [antēhis'təmēn] *n* antihistaminique *m*.

Antilles [antil'ēz] *npl*: **the ~** les Antilles *fpl*.

antipathy [antip'əthē] *n* antipathie *f*.

Antipodean [antipədē'ən] *a* australien(ne) et néozélandais(e), d'Australie et de Nouvelle-Zélande.

Antipodes [antip'ədēz] *npl*: **the ~** l'Australie *f* et la Nouvelle-Zélande.

antiquarian [antəkwär'ēən] *a*: **~ bookshop** librairie *f* d'ouvrages anciens ♦ *n* expert *m* en objets *or* livres anciens; amateur *m* d'antiquités.

antiquated [an'təkwātid] *a* vieilli(e), suranné(e), vieillot(te).

antique [antēk'] *n* objet *m* d'art ancien, meuble ancien *or* d'époque, antiquité *f* ♦ *a* ancien(ne); (*pre-medieval*) antique.

antique dealer *n* antiquaire *m/f*.

antique shop *n* magasin *m* d'antiquités.

antiquity [antik'witē] *n* antiquité *f*.

anti-Semitic [an'tīsəmit'ik] *a* antisémite.

anti-Semitism [antīsem'itizəm] *n* antisémitisme *m*.

antiseptic [antēsep'tik] *a, n* antiseptique (*m*).

antisocial [antēsō'shəl] *a* peu liant(e), sauvage, insociable; (*against society*) antisocial(e).

antitank [antētangk'] *a* antichar.

antithesis, *pl* **antitheses** [antith'əsis, -sēz] *n* antithèse *f*.

antitrust [antētrust'] *a*: **~ legislation** loi *f* anti-trust.

antlers [ant'lûrz] *npl* bois *mpl*, ramure *f*.

Antwerp [ant'wûrp] *n* Anvers.

anus [ā'nəs] *n* anus *m*.

anvil [an'vil] *n* enclume *f*.

anxiety [angzī'ətē] *n* anxiété *f*; (*keenness*): **~ to do** grand désir *or* impatience *f* de faire.

anxious [angk'shəs] *a* anxieux(euse), (très) inquiet(ète); (*keen*): **~ to do/that** qui tient beaucoup à faire/à ce que; impatient(e) de faire/que; **I'm very ~ about you** je me fais beaucoup de souci pour toi.

anxiously [angk'shəslē] *ad* anxieusement.

any [en'ē] *a* (*in negative and interrogative sentences* = *some*) de, d'; du, de l', de la, des; (*no matter which*) n'importe quel(le), quelconque; (*each and every*) tout(e), chaque; **I haven't ~ money/books** je n'ai pas d'argent/de livres; **have you ~ butter/children?** avez-vous du beurre/des enfants?; **without ~ difficulty** sans la moindre difficulté; **come (at) ~ time** venez à n'importe quelle heure; **at ~ moment** à tout moment, d'un instant à l'autre; **~ day now** d'un jour à l'autre; **in ~ case** de toute façon; (*at least*) en tout cas; **at ~ rate** de toute façon ♦ *pronoun* n'importe lequel(laquelle); (*anybody*) n'importe qui; (*in negative and interrogative sentences*): **I haven't ~** je n'en ai pas, je n'en ai aucun; **have you got ~?** en avez-vous?; **can ~ of you sing?** est-ce que l'un d'entre vous *or* quelqu'un parmi vous sait chanter? ♦ *ad* (*in negative sentences*) nullement, aucunement; (*in interrogative and conditional constructions*) un peu; tant soit peu; **I can't hear him ~ more** je ne l'entends plus; **are you feeling ~ better?** vous sentez-vous un peu mieux?; **do you want ~ more soup?** voulez-vous encore un peu de soupe?

anybody [en'ēbâdē] *pronoun* n'importe qui; (*in interrogative sentences*) quelqu'un; (*in negative sentences*): **I don't see ~** je ne vois personne.

anyhow [en'ēhou] *ad* quoi qu'il en soit; (*haphazardly*) n'importe comment; **I shall go ~**

j'irai de toute façon.

anyone [en'ēwun] = **anybody**.

anyplace [en'ēplās] *ad* (*US*) = **anywhere**.

anything [en'ēthing] *pronoun* n'importe quoi; (*in interrogative sentences*) quelque chose; (*in negative sentences*): **I don't want** ~ je ne veux rien; ~ **else?** (*in store*) et avec ça?

anytime [en'ētīm] *ad* n'importe quand.

anyway [en'ēwā] *ad* de toute façon.

anywhere [en'ēhwär] *ad* n'importe où; (*in interrogative sentences*) quelque part; (*in negative sentences*): **I don't see him** ~ je ne le vois nulle part; ~ **in the world** n'importe où dans le monde.

Anzac [an'zak] *n abbr* (= *Australia-New Zealand Army Corps*) soldat du corps ANZAC.

apart [əpârt'] *ad* (*to one side*) à part; de côté; à l'écart; (*separately*) séparément; **10 miles/a long way** ~ à 10 milles/très éloignés l'un de l'autre; **they are living** ~ ils sont séparés; ~ **from** *prep* à part, excepté.

apartheid [əpârt'hīt] *n* apartheid *m*.

apartment [əpârt'mənt] *n* appartement *m*, logement *m*.

apartment building *or* **block** *or* **house** *n* immeuble *m*; maison divisée en appartements.

apathetic [apəthet'ik] *a* apathique, indifférent(e).

apathy [ap'əthē] *n* apathie *f*, indifférence *f*.

APB *n abbr* (*US*: = *all points bulletin*) expression de la police signifiant 'découvrir et appréhender le suspect'.

ape [āp] *n* (grand) singe ♦ *vt* singer.

Apennines [ap'ənīnz] *npl*: **the** ~ les Apennins *mpl*.

aperitif [əpārētēf'] *n* apéritif *m*.

aperture [ap'ûrchûr] *n* orifice *m*, ouverture *f*; (*PHOT*) ouverture (du diaphragme).

APEX [ā'peks] *n abbr* (*AVIAT*: = *advance purchase excursion*) APEX *m*.

apex [ā'peks] *n* sommet *m*.

aphid [ā'fid] *n* puceron *m*.

aphrodisiac [afrədiz'ēak] *a, n* aphrodisiaque (*m*).

API *n abbr* = *American Press Institute*.

apiece [əpēs'] *ad* (*for each person*) chacun(e), par tête; (*for each item*) chacun(e), (la) pièce.

aplomb [əplâm'] *n* sang-froid *m*, assurance *f*.

APO *n abbr* (*US*: = *Army Post Office*) service postal de l'armée.

apocalypse [əpâk'əlips] *n* apocalypse *f*.

apolitical [āpəlit'ikəl] *a* apolitique.

apologetic [əpâləjet'ik] *a* (*tone, letter*) d'excuse; **to be very** ~ **about** s'excuser vivement de.

apologetically [əpâləjet'iklē] *ad* (*say*) en s'excusant.

apologize [əpâl'əjīz] *vi*: **to** ~ (**for sth to sb**) s'excuser (de qch auprès de qn), présenter des excuses (à qn pour qch).

apology [əpâl'əjē] *n* excuses *fpl*; **to send one's apologies** envoyer une lettre *or* un mot d'excuse, s'excuser (de ne pas pouvoir venir); **please accept my apologies** vous voudrez bien m'excuser.

apoplectic [apəplek'tik] *a* (*MED*) apoplectique;

(*col*): ~ **with rage** fou(folle) de rage.

apoplexy [ap'əpleksē] *n* apoplexie *f*.

apostle [əpâs'əl] *n* apôtre *m*.

apostrophe [əpâs'trəfē] *n* apostrophe *f*.

Appalachian Mountains [apəlā'chēən moun'tənz] *npl*: **the** ~ les (monts *mpl*) Appalaches.

appall, (*Brit*) **appal** [əpôl'] *vt* consterner, atterrer; horrifier.

appalling [əpôl'ing] *a* épouvantable; (*stupidity*) consternant(e); **she's an** ~ **cook** c'est une très mauvaise cuisinière.

apparatus [apərat'əs] *n* appareil *m*, dispositif *m*; (*in gymnasium*) agrès *mpl*.

apparel [əpar'əl] *n* (*US*) habillement *m*, confection *f*.

apparent [əpar'ənt] *a* apparent(e); **it is** ~ **that** il est évident que.

apparently [əpar'əntlē] *ad* apparemment.

apparition [apərish'ən] *n* apparition *f*.

appeal [əpēl'] *vi* (*LAW*) faire *or* interjeter appel ♦ *n* (*LAW*) appel *m*; (*request*) appel; prière *f*; (*charm*) attrait *m*, charme *m*; **to** ~ **for** demander (instamment); implorer; **to** ~ **to** (*subj: person*) faire appel à; (*subj: thing*) plaire à; **to** ~ **to sb for mercy** implorer la pitié de qn, prier *or* adjurer qn d'avoir pitié; **it doesn't** ~ **to me** cela ne m'attire pas; **right of** ~ droit *m* de recours.

appealing [əpē'ling] *a* (*nice*) attrayant(e); (*touching*) attendrissant(e).

appear [əpēr'] *vi* apparaître, se montrer; (*LAW*) comparaître; (*publication*) paraître, sortir, être publié(e); (*seem*) paraître, sembler; **it would** ~ **that** il semble que; **to** ~ **in Hamlet** jouer dans Hamlet; **to** ~ **on TV** passer à la télé.

appearance [əpē'rəns] *n* apparition *f*; parution *f*; (*look, aspect*) apparence *f*, aspect *m*; **to put in** *or* **make an** ~ faire acte de présence; (*THEATER*): **by order of** ~ par ordre d'entrée en scène; **to keep up** ~**s** sauver les apparences; **to all** ~**s** selon toute apparence.

appease [əpēz'] *vt* apaiser, calmer.

appeasement [əpēz'mənt] *n* (*POL*) apaisement *m*.

appellate court [əpel'it kôrt] *n* (*US*) cour *f* d'appel.

append [əpend'] *vt* (*COMPUT*) ajouter (à la fin d'un fichier).

appendage [əpen'dij] *n* appendice *m*.

appendicitis [əpendisī'tis] *n* appendicite *f*.

appendix, *pl* **appendices** [əpen'diks, -disēz] *n* appendice *m*; **to have one's** ~ **out** se faire opérer de l'appendicite.

appetite [ap'itit] *n* appétit *m*; **that walk has given me an** ~ cette promenade m'a ouvert l'appétit.

appetizer [ap'itīzûr] *n* (*food*) amuse-gueule *m*; (*drink*) apéritif *m*.

appetizing [ap'itīzing] *a* appétissant(e).

applaud [əplôd'] *vt, vi* applaudir.

applause [əplôz'] *n* applaudissements *mpl*.

apple [ap'əl] *n* pomme *f*; (*also*: ~ **tree**) pommier *m*; **it's the** ~ **of my eye** j'y tiens comme à la prunelle de mes yeux.

apple turnover *n* chausson *m* aux pommes.

appliance [əplī'əns] *n* appareil *m*; **electrical** ~**s** l'électroménager *m*.

applicable [ap'likəbəl] *a* applicable; **the law is ~ from January** la loi entre en vigueur au mois de janvier; **to be ~ to** valoir pour.

applicant [ap'likənt] *n*: **~ (for)** (*ADMIN*: *for benefit etc*) demandeur/euse (de); (*for post*) candidat/e (à).

application [aplikā'shən] *n* application *f*; (*for a job, a grant etc*) demande *f*; candidature *f*; **on ~** sur demande.

application form *n* formulaire *m* de demande.

application program *n* (*COMPUT*) programme *m* d'application.

applications package [aplikā'shənz pak'ij] *n* (*COMPUT*) progiciel *m* d'application.

applied [əplīd'] *a* appliqué(e); **~ arts** *npl* arts décoratifs.

apply [əplī'] *vt*: **to ~ (to)** (*paint, ointment*) appliquer (sur); (*theory, technique*) appliquer (à) ♦ *vi*: **to ~ to** (*ask*) s'adresser à; (*be suitable for, relevant to*) s'appliquer à, être valable pour; **to ~ (for)** (*permit, grant*) faire une demande (en vue d'obtenir); (*job*) poser sa candidature (pour), faire une demande d'emploi (concernant); **to ~ the brakes** actionner les freins, freiner; **to ~ o.s. to** s'appliquer à.

appoint [əpoint'] *vt* nommer, engager; (*date, place*) fixer, désigner.

appointee [əpointē'] *n* personne nommée; candidat retenu.

appointment [əpoint'mənt] *n* (*to post*) nomination *f*; (*arrangement to meet*) rendez-vous *m*; **to make an ~ (with)** prendre rendez-vous (avec); **by ~** sur rendez-vous.

appointment book *n* agenda *m*.

apportion [əpôr'shən] *vt* (*share out*) répartir, distribuer; **to ~ sth to sb** attribuer *or* assigner *or* allouer qch à qn.

appraisal [əprā'zəl] *n* évaluation *f*.

appraise [əprāz'] *vt* (*value*) estimer; (*situation etc*) évaluer.

appreciable [əprē'shēəbəl] *a* appréciable.

appreciate [əprē'shēāt] *vt* (*like*) apprécier, faire cas de; (*be grateful for*) être reconnaissant(e) de; (*assess*) évaluer; (*be aware of*) comprendre, se rendre compte de ♦ *vi* (*FINANCE*) prendre de la valeur; **I ~ your help** je vous remercie pour votre aide.

appreciation [əprēshēā'shən] *n* appréciation *f*; (*gratitude*) reconnaissance *f*; (*FINANCE*) hausse *f*, valorisation *f*.

appreciative [əprē'shətiv] *a* (*person*) sensible; (*comment*) élogieux(euse).

apprehend [aprihend'] *vt* appréhender, arrêter; (*understand*) comprendre.

apprehension [aprihen'shən] *n* appréhension *f*, inquiétude *f*.

apprehensive [aprihen'siv] *a* inquiet(ète), appréhensif(ive).

apprentice [əpren'tis] *n* apprenti *m* ♦ *vt*: **to be ~d to** être en apprentissage chez.

apprenticeship [əpren'tisship] *n* apprentissage *m*; **to serve one's ~** faire son apprentissage.

approach [əprōch'] *vi* approcher ♦ *vt* (*come near*) approcher de; (*ask, apply to*) s'adresser à; (*subject, passer-by*) aborder ♦ *n* approche *f*; accès *m*, abord *m*; démarche *f* (*auprès de qn*); démarche (*intellectuelle*); **to**

~ sb about sth aller *or* venir voir qn pour qch.

approachable [əprō'chəbəl] *a* accessible.

approbation [aprəbā'shən] *n* approbation *f*.

appropriate *vt* [əprōp'rēāt] (*take*) s'approprier; (*allot*): **to ~ sth for** affecter qch à ♦ *a* [əprōp'rēit] qui convient, approprié(e); (*timely*) opportun(e); **~ for** *or* **to** approprié à; **it would not be ~ for me to comment** il ne me serait pas approprié de commenter.

appropriately [əprōp'rēitlē] *ad* pertinemment, avec à-propos.

appropriation [əprōprēā'shən] *n* dotation *f*, affectation *f*.

approval [əprōō'vəl] *n* approbation *f*; **to meet with sb's ~** (*proposal etc*) recueillir l'assentiment de qn; **on ~** (*COMM*) à l'examen.

approve [əprōōv'] *vt* approuver.

approve of *vt fus* approuver.

approvingly [əprōō'vinglē] *ad* d'un air approbateur.

approx. *abbr* (= *approximately*) env.

approximate *a* [əprāk'səmit] approximatif(ive) ♦ *vt* [əprāk'səmāt] se rapprocher de; être proche de.

approximation [əprāksəmā'shən] *n* approximation *f*.

appt. *abbr* (*US*) = **appointment**.

Apr. *abbr* = **April**.

apr *n abbr* (= *annual percentage rate*) taux (d'intérêt) annuel.

apricot [ap'rikāt] *n* abricot *m*.

April [āp'rəl] *n* avril *m*; **~ fool!** poisson d'avril!; *for phrases see also* **July.**

April Fool's Day *n* le premier avril.

apron [ā'prən] *n* tablier *m*; (*AVIAT*) aire *f* de stationnement.

apse [aps] *n* (*ARCHIT*) abside *f*.

Apt. *abbr* (= *apartment*) appt.

apt [apt] *a* (*suitable*) approprié(e); (*able*): **~ (at)** doué(e) (pour); apte (à); (*likely*): **~ to do** susceptible de faire; ayant tendance à faire.

aptitude [ap'tətōōd] *n* aptitude *f*.

aptitude test *n* test *m* d'aptitude.

aptly [apt'lē] *ad* (fort) à propos.

aqualung [ak'wəlung] *n* scaphandre *m* autonome.

aquarium [əkwär'ēəm] *n* aquarium *m*.

Aquarius [əkwär'ēəs] *n* le Verseau; **to be ~** être du Verseau.

aquatic [əkwat'ik] *a* aquatique; (*sport*) nautique.

aqueduct [ak'widukt] *n* aqueduc *m*.

AR *abbr* (*US MAIL*) = *Arkansas.*

Arab [ar'əb] *n* Arabe *m/f* ♦ *a* arabe.

Arabia [ərā'bēə] *n* Arabie *f*.

Arabian [ərā'bēən] *a* arabe.

Arabian Desert *n* désert *m* d'Arabie.

Arabian Sea *n* mer *f* d'Arabie.

Arabic [ar'əbik] *a*, *n* arabe (*m*).

Arabic numerals *npl* chiffres *mpl* arabes.

arable [ar'əbəl] *a* arable.

arbiter [ār'bitûr] *n* arbitre *m*.

arbitrary [ār'biträrē] *a* arbitraire.

arbitrate [ār'bitrāt] *vi* arbitrer; trancher.

arbitration [ārbitrā'shən] *n* arbitrage *m*; **the dispute went to ~** le litige a été soumis à

arbitrage.
arbitrator [âr'bitrātûr] *n* arbitre *m*, médiateur/trice.
ARC *n abbr* = *American Red Cross.*
arc [ârk] *n* arc *m*.
arcade [ârkād'] *n* arcade *f*; (*passage with stores*) passage *m*, galerie *f*.
arch [ârch] *n* arche *f*; (*of foot*) cambrure *f*, voûte *f* plantaire ♦ *vt* arquer, cambrer ♦ *a* malicieux(euse) ♦ *prefix*: ~(-) achevé(e); par excellence; **pointed** ~ ogive *f*.
archaeology [ârkēâl'əjē] *etc* = **archeology** *etc*.
archaic [ârkā'ik] *a* archaïque.
archangel [ârkān'jəl] *n* archange *m*.
archbishop [ârchbish'əp] *n* archevêque *m*.
archenemy [ârch'en'əmē] *n* ennemi *m* de toujours *or* par excellence.
archeological [ârkēəlâj'ikəl] *a* archéologique.
archeologist [ârkēâl'əjist] *n* archéologue *m/f*.
archeology [ârkēâl'əjē] *n* archéologie *f*.
archer [âr'chûr] *n* archer *m*.
archery [âr'chûrē] *n* tir *m* à l'arc.
archetypal [âr'kitīpəl] *a* archétype.
archetype [âr'kitīp] *n* prototype *m*, archétype *m*.
archipelago [ârkəpel'əgō] *n* archipel *m*.
architect [âr'kitekt] *n* architecte *m*.
architectural [âr'kitekchûrəl] *a* architectural(e).
architecture [âr'kitekchûr] *n* architecture *f*.
archive file [âr'kīv fīl'] *n* (*COMPUT*) fichier *m* d'archives.
archives [âr'kīvz] *npl* archives *fpl*.
archivist [âr'kəvist] *n* archiviste *m/f*.
archway [ârch'wā] *n* voûte *f*, porche voûté *or* cintré.
Arctic [ârk'tik] *a* arctique ♦ *n*: **the** ~ l'Arctique *m*.
Arctic Circle *n* cercle *m* Arctique.
Arctic Ocean *n* océan *m* Arctique.
ARD *n abbr* (*US MED*) = *acute respiratory disease.*
ardent [âr'dənt] *a* fervent(e).
ardor, (*Brit*) **ardour** [âr'dûr] *n* ardeur *f*.
arduous [âr'jōōəs] *a* ardu(e).
are [âr] *vb see* **be**.
area [är'ēə] *n* (*GEOM*) superficie *f*; (*zone*) région *f*; (: *smaller*) secteur *m*; **dining** ~ coin *m* salle à manger; **the New York** ~ la région new-yorkaise.
area code *n* (*TEL*) indicatif *m* de zone.
arena [ərē'nə] *n* arène *f*.
aren't [ärnt] = **are not**.
Argentina [ârjəntē'nə] *n* Argentine *f*.
Argentinian [ârjəntin'ēən] *a* argentin(e) ♦ *n* Argentin/e.
arguable [âr'gyōōəbəl] *a* discutable, contestable; **it is** ~ **whether** on peut se demander si.
arguably [âr'gyōōəblē] *ad*: **it is** ~ ... on peut soutenir que c'est ....
argue [âr'gyōō] *vi* (*quarrel*) se disputer; (*reason*) argumenter ♦ *vt* (*debate: case, matter*) débattre; **to** ~ **about sth (with sb)** se disputer (avec qn) au sujet de qch; **to** ~ **that** objecter *or* alléguer que, donner comme argument que.
argument [âr'gyəmənt] *n* (*reasons*) argument *m*; (*quarrel*) dispute *f*, discussion *f*; (*debate*) discussion, controverse *f*; ~ **for/against** argument pour/contre.
argumentative [ârgyəmen'tətiv] *a* ergoteur(euse), raisonneur(euse).
aria [âr'ēə] *n* aria *f*.
arid [ar'id] *a* aride.
aridity [ərid'itē] *n* aridité *f*.
Aries [är'ēz] *n* le Bélier; **to be** ~ être du Bélier.
arise, *pt* **arose**, *pp* **arisen** [ərīz', ərōz', əriz'ən] *vi* survenir, se présenter; **to** ~ **from** résulter de; **should the need** ~ en cas de besoin.
aristocracy [aristâk'rəsē] *n* aristocratie *f*.
aristocrat [əris'təkrat] *n* aristocrate *m/f*.
aristocratic [əristəkrat'ik] *a* aristocratique.
arithmetic [ərith'mətik] *n* arithmétique *f*.
arithmetical [arithmet'ikəl] *a* arithmétique.
Ariz. *abbr* (*US*) = *Arizona.*
Ark. *abbr* (*US*) = *Arkansas.*
ark [ârk] *n*: **Noah's A~** l'Arche *f* de Noé.
arm [ârm] *n* bras *m* ♦ *vt* armer; ~ **in** ~ bras dessus bras dessous.
armaments [âr'məmənts] *npl* (*weapons*) armement *m*.
armband [ârm'band] *n* brassard *m*.
armchair [ârm'chär] *n* fauteuil *m*.
armed [ârmd] *a* armé(e); **the** ~ **forces** les forces armées.
armed robbery *n* vol *m* à main armée.
Armenia [ârmē'nēə] *n* Arménie *f*.
Armenian [ârmē'nēən] *a* arménien(ne) ♦ *n* Arménien/ne; (*LING*) arménien *m*.
armful [ârm'fəl] *n* brassée *f*.
armistice [âr'mistis] *n* armistice *m*.
armor [âr'mûr] *n* (*US*) armure *f*; (*also:* ~ **plating**) blindage *m*; (*MIL: tanks*) blindés *mpl*.
armored car [ârmûrd kâr'] *n* véhicule blindé.
armory [âr'mûrē] *n* arsenal *m*.
armour *etc* [âr'mûr] (*Brit*) = **armor** *etc*.
armpit [ârm'pit] *n* aisselle *f*.
armrest [ârm'rest] *n* accoudoir *m*.
arms [ârmz] *npl* (*weapons, HERALDRY*) armes *fpl*.
arms control *n* contrôle *m* des armements.
arms race *n* course *f* aux armements.
army [âr'mē] *n* armée *f*.
aroma [ərō'mə] *n* arôme *m*.
aromatic [arəmat'ik] *a* aromatique.
arose [ərōz'] *pt of* **arise**.
around [əround'] *ad* (tout) autour; (*nearby*) dans les parages ♦ *prep* autour de; (*fig: about*) environ; vers; **is he** ~? est-il dans les parages *or* là?; **it's the other way** ~ c'est l'inverse; **all** ~ tout autour; **the long way** ~ (par) le chemin le plus long; **it's just** ~ **the corner** c'est juste après le coin; (*fig*) c'est tout près; **to ask sb** ~ inviter qn (chez soi); **I'll be** ~ **at 6 o'clock** je serai là à six heures; **to go** ~ faire le tour *or* un détour; **to go** ~ **to sb's (house)** aller chez qn; **to go** ~ **an obstacle** contourner un obstacle; **go** ~ **the back** passez par derrière; **to go** ~ **a house** visiter une maison, faire le tour d'une maison; **enough to go** ~ assez pour tout le monde; ~ **the clock** 24 heures sur 24.
arouse [ərouz'] *vt* (*sleeper*) éveiller; (*curiosity, passions*) éveiller, susciter; exciter.
arpeggio [ârpej'ēō] *n* arpège *m*.

arrange [ərănj'] *vt* arranger; (*program*) arrêter, convenir de ♦ *vi*: **we have ~d for a car to pick you up** nous avons prévu qu'une voiture viendra vous prendre; **it was ~d that...** il a été convenu que..., il a été décidé que...; **to ~ to do sth** prévoir de faire qch.

arrangement [ərānj'mənt] *n* arrangement *m*; (*plans etc*): **~s** dispositions *fpl*; **to come to an ~ (with sb)** se mettre d'accord (avec qn); **home deliveries by ~** livraison à domicile sur demande; **I'll make ~s for you to be met** je vous enverrai chercher.

array [ərā'] *n* (*of objects*) déploiement *m*, étalage *m*; (*MATH, COMPUT*) tableau *m*.

arrears [ərērz'] *npl* arriéré *m*; **to be in ~ with one's rent** devoir un arriéré de loyer, être en retard pour le paiement de son loyer.

arrest [ərest'] *vt* arrêter; (*sb's attention*) retenir, attirer ♦ *n* arrestation *f*; **under ~** en état d'arrestation.

arresting [əres'ting] *a* (*fig: beauty*) saisissante(e); (*: charm, candor*) désarmant(e).

arrival [ərī'vəl] *n* arrivée *f*; (*COMM*) arrivage *m*; (*person*) arrivant/e; **new ~** nouveau venu/nouvelle venue.

arrive [ərīv'] *vi* arriver.
  arrive at *vt fus* (*fig*) parvenir à.

arrogance [ar'əgəns] *n* arrogance *f*.

arrogant [ar'əgənt] *a* arrogant(e).

arrow [ar'ō] *n* flèche *f*.

arse [ârs] *n* (*Brit col!*) cul *m* (*!*).

arsenal [âr'sənəl] *n* arsenal *m*.

arsenic [âr'sənik] *n* arsenic *m*.

arson [âr'sən] *n* incendie criminel.

art [ârt] *n* art *m*; (*craft*) métier *m*; **work of ~** œuvre *f* d'art.

artefact [âr'təfakt] *n* (*Brit*) = **artifact**.

arterial [ârtē'rēəl] *a* (*ANAT*) artériel(le); (*road etc*) à grande circulation.

artery [âr'tûrē] *n* artère *f*.

artful [ârt'fəl] *a* rusé(e).

art gallery *n* musée *m* d'art; (*small and private*) galerie *f* de peinture.

arthritis [ârthrī'tis] *n* arthrite *f*.

artichoke [âr'tichōk] *n* artichaut *m*; **Jerusalem ~** topinambour *m*.

article [âr'tikəl] *n* article *m*; (*Brit LAW: training*): **~s** *npl* ≈ stage *m*; **~s of clothing** vêtements *mpl*.

articles of association *npl* (*COMM*) statuts *mpl* d'une société.

articulate *a* [ârtik'yəlit] (*person*) qui s'exprime clairement et aisément; (*speech*) bien articulé(e), prononcé(e) clairement ♦ *vi* [ârtik'yəlāt] articuler, parler distinctement.

articulated lorry [ârtik'yəlātid lôr'ē] *n* (*Brit*) (camion *m*) semi-remorque *m*.

artifact [âr'təfakt] *n* (*US*) objet fabriqué.

artifice [âr'təfis] *n* ruse *f*.

artificial [ârtəfish'əl] *a* artificiel(le).

artificial insemination [ârtəfish'əl insemənā'shən] *n* insémination artificielle.

artificial intelligence (AI) *n* intelligence artificielle (IA).

artificial respiration *n* respiration artificielle.

artillery [ârtil'ûrē] *n* artillerie *f*.

artisan [âr'tizən] *n* artisan/e.

artist [âr'tist] *n* artiste *m/f*.

artistic [ârtis'tik] *a* artistique.

artistry [âr'tistrē] *n* art *m*, talent *m*.

artless [ârt'lis] *a* naïf(naïve), simple, ingénu(e).

arts [ârts] *npl* (*SCOL*) lettres *fpl*.

art school *n* ≈ école *f* des beaux-arts.

ARV *n abbr* (= *American Revised Version*) traduction américaine de la Bible.

AS *n abbr* (*US SCOL*: = *Associate in/of Science*) diplôme universitaire ♦ *abbr* (*US MAIL*) = *American Samoa*.

as [az] *cj* (*cause*) comme, puisque; (*time: moment*) alors que, comme; (*: duration*) tandis que; (*manner*) comme ♦ *prep* (*in the capacity of*) en tant que, en qualité de; **~ big ~** aussi grand que; **twice ~ big ~** deux fois plus grand que; **big ~ it is** si grand que ce soit; **much ~ I like them, I ...** je les aime bien, mais je ...; **~ the years went by** à mesure que les années passaient; **~ she said** comme elle l'avait dit; **he gave it to me ~ a present** il m'en a fait cadeau; **~ if** *or* **though** comme si; **~ for** *or* **to** en ce qui concerne, quant à; **~ or so long ~** *cj* à condition que; si; **~ much/many (~)** autant (que); **~ soon ~** *cj* aussitôt que, dès que; **~ soon ~ possible** aussitôt *or* dès que possible; **~ such** *ad* en tant que tel(le); **~ well** *ad* aussi; **~ well ~** *cj* et en plus de, en même temps que; *see also* **so, such.**

ASA *n abbr* (= *American Standards Association*) association de normalisation.

a.s.a.p. *abbr* = **as soon as possible.**

asbestos [asbes'təs] *n* asbeste *m*, amiante *m*.

ascend [əsend'] *vt* gravir.

ascendancy [əsen'dənsē] *n* ascendant *m*.

ascendant [əsen'dənt] *n*: **to be in the ~** monter.

ascension [əsen'shən] *n*: **the A~** (*REL*) l'Ascension *f*.

Ascension Island *n* île *f* de l'Ascension.

ascent [əsent'] *n* ascension *f*.

ascertain [asûrtān'] *vt* s'assurer de, vérifier; établir.

ascetic [əset'ik] *a* ascétique.

asceticism [əset'isizəm] *n* ascétisme *m*.

ASCII [as'kē] *n abbr* (= *American Standard Code for Information Interchange*) ASCII.

ascribe [əskrīb'] *vt*: **to ~ sth to** attribuer qch à; (*blame*) imputer qch à.

ASCU *n abbr* (*US*) = *Association of State Colleges and Universities.*

ASE *n abbr* = *American Stock Exchange.*

ash [ash] *n* (*dust*) cendre *f*; (*also*: **~ tree**) frêne *m*.

ashamed [əshāmd'] *a* honteux(euse), confus(e); **to be ~ of** avoir honte de; **to be ~ (of o.s.) for having done** avoir honte d'avoir fait.

ashen [ash'ən] *a* (*pale*) cendreux(euse), blême.

ashore [əshôr'] *ad* à terre; **to go ~** aller à terre, débarquer.

ashtray [ash'trā] *n* cendrier *m*.

Ash Wednesday *n* mercredi *m* des Cendres.

Asia [ā'zhə] *n* Asie *f*.

Asia Minor *n* Asie Mineure.

Asian [ā'zhən] *n* Asiatique *m/f* ♦ *a* asiatique.

Asiatic [āzhēat'ik] *a* asiatique.

aside [əsīd'] *ad* de côté; à l'écart ♦ *n* aparté

m; ~ **from** *prep* à part, excepté.

ask [ask] *vt* demander; (*invite*) inviter; **to ~ sb sth/to do sth** demander à qn qch/de faire qch; **to ~ sb the time** demander l'heure à qn; **to ~ sb about sth** questionner qn au sujet de qch; se renseigner auprès de qn au sujet de qch; **to ~ about the price** s'informer du prix, se renseigner au sujet du prix; **to ~ (sb) a question** poser une question (à qn); **to ~ sb out to dinner** inviter qn au restaurant.

ask after *vt fus* demander des nouvelles de.

ask for *vt fus* demander; **it's just ~ing for trouble** *or* **for it** ce serait chercher des ennuis.

askance [əskans'] *ad*: **to look ~ at sb** regarder qn de travers *or* d'un œil désapprobateur.

askew [əskyōō'] *ad* de travers, de guinguois.

asking price [as'king prīs] *n* prix demandé.

asleep [əslēp'] *a* endormi(e); **to be ~** dormir, être endormi; **to fall ~** s'endormir.

asp [asp] *n* aspic *m*.

asparagus [əspar'əgəs] *n* asperges *fpl*.

asparagus tips *npl* pointes *fpl* d'asperges.

ASPCA *n abbr* (= *American Society for the Prevention of Cruelty to Animals*) ≈ SPA *f*.

aspect [as'pekt] *n* aspect *m*; (*direction in which a building etc faces*) orientation *f*, exposition *f*.

aspersions [əspûr'zhənz] *npl*: **to cast ~ on** dénigrer.

asphalt [as'fôlt] *n* asphalte *m*.

asphyxiate [asfik'sēāt] *vt* asphyxier.

asphyxiation [asfiksēā'shən] *n* asphyxie *f*.

aspirate *vt* [as'pûrāt] aspirer ♦ *a* [as'pûrit] aspiré(e).

aspiration [aspərā'shən] *n* aspiration *f*.

aspire [əspī'ûr] *vi*: **to ~ to** aspirer à.

aspirin [as'pûrin] *n* aspirine *f*.

ass [as] *n* âne *m*; (*col*) imbécile *m/f*; (*US col!*) cul *m* (!); **kiss my ~!** (*US col!*) va te faire foutre (!).

assail [əsāl'] *vt* assaillir.

assailant [əsā'lənt] *n* agresseur *m*; assaillant *m*.

assassin [əsas'in] *n* assassin *m*.

assassinate [əsas'ənāt] *vt* assassiner.

assassination [əsasinā'shən] *n* assassinat *m*.

assault [əsôlt'] *n* (*MIL*) assaut *m*; (*gen: attack*) agression *f*; (*LAW*): **~ (and battery)** voies *fpl* de fait, coups *mpl* et blessures *fpl* ♦ *vt* attaquer; (*sexually*) violenter.

assemble [əsem'bəl] *vt* assembler ♦ *vi* s'assembler, se rassembler.

assembly [əsem'blē] *n* (*meeting*) rassemblement *m*; (*construction*) assemblage *m*.

assembly language *n* (*COMPUT*) langage *m* d'assemblage.

assembly line *n* chaîne *f* de montage.

assent [əsent'] *n* assentiment *m*, consentement *m* ♦ *vi*: **to ~ (to sth)** donner son assentiment (à qch), consentir (à qch).

assert [əsûrt'] *vt* affirmer, déclarer; établir; **to ~ o.s.** s'imposer.

assertion [əsûr'shən] *n* assertion *f*, affirmation *f*.

assertive [əsûr'tiv] *a* assuré(e); péremptoire.

assess [əses'] *vt* évaluer, estimer; (*tax, damages*) établir *or* fixer le montant de; (*property etc: for tax*) calculer la valeur imposable de.

assessment [əses'mənt] *n* évaluation *f*, estimation *f*; (*judgment*): **~ (of)** jugement *m* or opinion *f* (sur).

assessor [əses'ûr] *n* expert *m* (*en matière d'impôt et d'assurance*).

asset [as'et] *n* avantage *m*, atout *m*; (*person*) atout; **~s** *npl* (*COMM*) capital *m*; avoir(s) *m(pl)*; actif *m*.

asset-stripping [as'ctstriping] *n* (*COMM*) récupération *f* (et démantèlement *m*) d'une entreprise en difficulté.

assiduous [əsij'ōōəs] *a* assidu(e).

assign [əsīn'] *vt* (*date*) fixer, arrêter; (*task*): **to ~ sth to** assigner qch à; (*resources*): **to ~ sth to** affecter qch à; (*cause, meaning*): **to ~ sth to** attribuer qch à.

assignment [əsīn'mənt] *n* tâche *f*, mission *f*; (*SCOL*) devoir *m*.

assimilate [əsim'əlāt] *vt* assimiler.

assimilation [əsiməlā'shən] *n* assimilation *f*.

assist [əsist'] *vt* aider, assister; (*injured person etc*) secourir.

assistance [əsis'təns] *n* aide *f*, assistance *f*; secours *mpl*.

assistant [əsis'tənt] *n* assistant/e, adjoint/e; (*Brit: also*: **shop ~**) vendeur/euse.

assistant manager *n* sous-directeur *m*.

assizes [əsī'ziz] *npl* assises *fpl*.

associate *a*, *n* [əsō'shēit] associé(e) ♦ *vb* [əsō'shēāt] *vt* associer ♦ *vi*: **to ~ with sb** fréquenter qn; **~ director** directeur adjoint; **~d company** société affiliée.

association [əsōsēā'shən] *n* association *f*; **in ~ with** en collaboration avec.

association football *n* (*Brit*) football *m*.

assorted [əsôr'tid] *a* assorti(e); **in ~ sizes** en plusieurs tailles.

assortment [əsôrt'mənt] *n* assortiment *m*.

Asst. *abbr* = **assistant**.

assuage [əswāj'] *vt* (*grief, pain*) soulager; (*thirst, appetite*) assouvir.

assume [əsōōm'] *vt* supposer; (*responsibilities etc*) assumer; (*attitude, name*) prendre, adopter.

assumed name [əsōōmd' nām'] *n* nom *m* d'emprunt.

assumption [əsump'shən] *n* supposition *f*, hypothèse *f*; **on the ~ that** dans l'hypothèse où; (*on condition that*) à condition que.

assurance [əshōōr'əns] *n* assurance *f*; **I can give you no ~s** je ne peux rien vous garantir.

assure [əshōōr'] *vt* assurer.

AST *abbr* (*US*: = *Atlantic Standard Time*) heure d'hiver de la Nouvelle-Ecosse.

asterisk [as'tûrisk] *n* astérisque *m*.

astern [əstûrn'] *ad* à l'arrière.

asteroid [as'təroid] *n* astéroïde *m*.

asthma [az'mə] *n* asthme *m*.

asthmatic [azmat'ik] *a*, *n* asthmatique (*m/f*).

astigmatism [əstig'mətizəm] *n* astigmatisme *m*.

astir [əstûr'] *ad* en émoi.

ASTM *abbr* = *American Society for Testing Materials*.

astonish [əstán'ish] *vt* étonner, stupéfier.

astonishing [əstán'ishing] *a* étonnant(e), stupéfiant(e); **I find it ~ that** ... je trouve incroyable que ....

astonishingly [əstân'ishinglē] *ad* incroyablement.

astonishment [əstân'ishmənt] *n* (grand) étonnement, stupéfaction *f*.

astound [əstound'] *vt* stupéfier, sidérer.

astray [əstrā'] *ad:* **to go ~** s'égarer; *(fig)* quitter le droit chemin; **to go ~ in one's calculations** faire fausse route dans ses calculs.

astride [əstrīd'] *ad* à cheval ♦ *prep* à cheval sur.

astringent [əstrin'jənt] *a* astringent(e) ♦ *n* astringent *m*.

astrologer [əstrâl'əjûr] *n* astrologue *m*.

astrology [əstrâl'əjē] *n* astrologie *f*.

astronaut [as'trənôt] *n* astronaute *m/f*.

astronomer [əstrân'əmûr] *n* astronome *m*.

astronomical [astrənâm'ikəl] *a* astronomique.

astronomy [əstrân'əmē] *n* astronomie *f*.

astrophysics [astrōfiz'iks] *n* astrophysique *f*.

astute [əstōōt'] *a* astucieux(euse), malin(igne).

asunder [əsun'dûr] *ad:* **to tear ~** déchirer.

ASV *n abbr* (= *American Standard Version*) *traduction de la Bible.*

asylum [əsī'ləm] *n* asile *m*; **to seek political ~** demander l'asile politique.

asymmetric(al) [āsəmet'rik(əl)] *a* asymétrique.

at [at] *prep* à; *(because of: following surprised, annoyed etc)* de; par; **~ the top** au sommet; **~ Pierre's** chez Pierre; **~ the baker's** chez le boulanger, à la boulangerie; **~ times** parfois; **~ 4 o'clock** à 4 heures; **~ night** la nuit; *(in the evening)* le soir; **~ $1 a kilo** un dollar le kilo; **two ~ a time** deux à la fois; **~ full speed** à toute vitesse.

ate [āt] *pt of* **eat**.

atheism [ā'thēizəm] *n* athéisme *m*.

atheist [ā'thēist] *n* athée *m/f*.

Athenian [əthē'nēən] *a* athénien(ne) ♦ *n* Athénien/ne.

Athens [ath'ənz] *n* Athènes *f*.

athlete [ath'lēt] *n* athlète *m/f*.

athletic [athlet'ik] *a* athlétique.

athletics [athlet'iks] *n* athlétisme *m*.

Atlantic [atlan'tik] *a* atlantique ♦ *n:* **the ~ (Ocean)** l'Atlantique *m*, l'océan *m* Atlantique.

atlas [at'ləs] *n* atlas *m*.

Atlas Mountains *npl:* **the ~** les monts *mpl* de l'Atlas, l'Atlas *m*.

A.T.M. *abbr* (= *Automated Teller Machine*) guichet *m* automatique.

atmosphere [at'məsfēr] *n* atmosphère *f*; *(air)* air *m*.

atmospheric [atməsfär'ik] *a* atmosphérique.

atmospherics [atməsfär'iks] *n* (RADIO) parasites *mpl*.

atoll [at'ôl] *n* atoll *m*.

atom [at'əm] *n* atome *m*.

atomic [ətâm'ik] *a* atomique.

atom(ic) bomb *n* bombe *f* atomique.

atomizer [at'əmīzûr] *n* atomiseur *m*.

atone [ətōn'] *vi:* **to ~ for** expier, racheter.

atonement [ətōn'mənt] *n* expiation *f*.

ATP *n abbr* (= *Association of Tennis Professionals*) ATP *f* (= *Association des tennismen professionnels*).

atrocious [ətrō'shəs] *a* (*very bad*) atroce, exécrable.

atrocity [ətrâs'itē] *n* atrocité *f*.

atrophy [at'rəfē] *n* atrophie *f* ♦ *vt* atrophier ♦ *vi* s'atrophier.

attach [ətach'] *vt* (*gen*) attacher; (*document, letter*) joindre; (*employee, troops*) affecter; **to be ~ed to sb/sth** (*to like*) être attaché à qn/qch; **the ~ed letter** la lettre ci-jointe.

attaché [atashā'] *n* attaché *m*.

attaché case *n* mallette *f*, attaché-case *m*.

attachment [ətach'mənt] *n* (*tool*) accessoire *m*; (*love*): **~ (to)** affection *f* (pour), attachement *m* (à).

attack [ətak'] *vt* attaquer; (*task etc*) s'attaquer à ♦ *n* attaque *f*; (*also:* **heart ~**) crise *f* cardiaque.

attacker [ətak'ûr] *n* attaquant *m*; agresseur *m*.

attain [ətān'] *vt* (*also:* **to ~ to**) parvenir à, atteindre; acquérir.

attainments [ətān'mənts] *npl* connaissances *fpl*, résultats *mpl*.

attempt [ətempt'] *n* tentative *f* ♦ *vt* essayer, tenter; **~ed theft** *etc* (*LAW*) tentative de vol *etc*; **to make an ~ on sb's life** attenter à la vie de qn; **he made no ~ to help** il n'a rien fait pour m'aider (*or* l'aider *etc*).

attend [ətend'] *vt* (*course*) suivre; (*meeting, talk*) assister à; (*school, church*) aller à, fréquenter; (*patient*) soigner, s'occuper de; **to ~ (up)on** servir; être au service de.

attend to *vt fus* (*needs, affairs etc*) s'occuper de; (*customer*) s'occuper de, servir.

attendance [əten'dəns] *n* (*being present*) présence *f*; (*people present*) assistance *f*.

attendant [əten'dənt] *n* employé/e; gardien/ne ♦ *a* concomitant(e), qui accompagne *or* s'ensuit.

attention [əten'shən] *n* attention *f*; **~s** attentions *fpl*, prévenances *fpl*; **~!** (*MIL*) garde-à-vous!; **at ~** (*MIL*) au garde-à-vous; **for the ~ of** (*ADMIN*) à l'attention de; **it has come to my ~ that ...** je constate que ....

attentive [əten'tiv] *a* attentif(ive); (*kind*) prévenant(e).

attentively [əten'tivlē] *ad* attentivement, avec attention.

attenuate [əten'yōōāt] *vt* atténuer ♦ *vi* s'atténuer.

attest [ətest'] *vi:* **to ~ to** témoigner de, attester (de).

attic [at'ik] *n* grenier *m*, combles *mpl*.

attire [ətīûr'] *n* habit *m*, atours *mpl*.

attitude [at'ətōōd] *n* (*behavior*) attitude *f*, manière *f*; (*posture*) pose *f*, attitude; (*view*): **~ (to)** attitude (envers).

attorney [ətûr'nē] *n* (*US: lawyer*) avocat *m*; (*having proxy*) mandataire *m*; **power of ~** procuration *f*.

Attorney General *n* (*US*) ≈ garde *m* des Sceaux, ministre *m* de la Justice; (*Brit*) ≈ procureur général.

attract [ətrakt'] *vt* attirer.

attraction [ətrak'shən] *n* (*gen pl: pleasant things*) attraction *f*; attrait *m*; (*PHYSICS*) attraction; (*fig: towards sth*) attirance *f*.

attractive [ətrak'tiv] *a* séduisant(e), at-

trayant(e).
attribute *n* [at'rəbyōōt] attribut *m* ♦ *vt* [ətrib'yōōt]: **to ~ sth to** attribuer qch à.
attrition [ətrish'ən] *n*: **war of ~** guerre *f* d'usure.
atty *abbr* (*US*) = **attorney**.
Atty. Gen. *abbr* = **Attorney General.**
ATV *n abbr* (= *all terrain vehicle*) véhicule *m* tout-terrain.
aubergine [ō'bûrzhēn] *n* aubergine *f*.
auburn [ô'bûrn] *a* auburn *inv*, châtain roux *inv*.
auction [ôk'shən] *n* (*also*: **sale by ~**) vente *f* aux enchères ♦ *vt* (*also*: **to sell by ~**) vendre aux enchères; (*also*: **to put up for ~**) mettre aux enchères.
auctioneer [ôkshənēr'] *n* commissaire-priseur *m*.
auction room *n* salle *f* des ventes.
aud. *abbr* = **audit; auditor.**
audacious [ôdā'shəs] *a* impudent(e); audacieux(euse), intrépide.
audacity [ôdas'itē] *n* impudence *f*; audace *f*.
audible [ôd'əbəl] *a* audible.
audience [ôd'ēəns] *n* (*people*) assistance *f*, auditoire *m*; auditeurs *mpl*; spectateurs *mpl*; (*interview*) audience *f*.
audiovisual [ôd'ēōvizh'ōōəl] *a* audiovisuel(le); **~ aids** supports *or* moyens audiovisuels.
audit [ôd'it] *n* vérification *f* des comptes, apurement *m* ♦ *vt* vérifier, apurer.
audition [ôdish'ən] *n* audition *f* ♦ *vi* auditionner.
auditor [ô'ditûr] *n* vérificateur *m* des comptes; (*US*: *SCOL*) auditeur/trice libre.
auditorium [ôditôr'ēəm] *n* auditorium *m*, salle *f* de concert *or* de spectacle; (*US*: *SCOL*) amphithéâtre *m*.
Aug. *abbr* = **August.**
augment [ôgment'] *vt*, *vi* augmenter.
augur [ô'gûr] *vt* (*be a sign of*) présager, annoncer ♦ *vi*: **it ~s well** c'est bon signe *or* de bon augure, cela s'annonce bien.
August [ôg'əst] *n* août *m*; *for phrases see also* **July.**
august [ôgust'] *a* majestueux(euse), imposant(e).
aunt [ant] *n* tante *f*.
auntie, aunty [an'tē] *n diminutive* of **aunt.**
au pair [ô pär'] *n* (*also*: **~ girl**) jeune fille *f* au pair.
aura [ô'rə] *n* atmosphère *f*.
auspices [ôs'pisiz] *npl*: **under the ~ of** sous les auspices de.
auspicious [ôspish'əs] *a* de bon augure, propice.
austere [ôstēr'] *a* austère.
austerity [ôstär'itē] *n* austérité *f*.
Australasia [ôstrəlā'zhə] *n* Australasie *f*.
Australia [ôstrāl'yə] *n* Australie *f*.
Australian [ôstrāl'yən] *a* australien(ne) ♦ *n* Australien/ne.
Austria [ôs'trēə] *n* Autriche *f*.
Austrian [ôs'trēən] *a* autrichien(ne) ♦ *n* Autrichien/ne.
authentic [ôthen'tik] *a* authentique.
authenticate [ôthen'tikāt] *vt* établir l'authenticité de.

authenticity [ôthəntis'itē] *n* authenticité *f*.
author [ô'thûr] *n* auteur *m*.
authoritarian [əthôritär'ēən] *a* autoritaire.
authoritative [əthôr'itātiv] *a* (*account*) digne de foi; (*study, treatise*) qui fait autorité; (*manner*) autoritaire.
authority [əthôr'itē] *n* autorité *f*; (*permission*) autorisation (formelle); **the authorities** les autorités, l'administration *f*; **to have ~ to do sth** être habilité à faire qch.
authorization [ôthûrəzā'shən] *n* autorisation *f*.
authorize [ô'thərīz] *vt* autoriser.
authorized capital [ô'thərīzd kap'ətəl] *n* (*COMM*) capital social.
authorship [ô'thûrship] *n* paternité *f* (*littéraire etc*).
autistic [ôtis'tik] *a* autistique.
autobiography [ôtəbīāg'rəfē] *n* autobiographie *f*.
autocratic [ôtəkrat'ik] *a* autocratique.
autograph [ô'təgraf] *n* autographe *m* ♦ *vt* signer, dédicacer.
automat [ô'təmat] *n* (*vending machine*) distributeur *m* (automatique); (*US*: *place*) cafétéria *f* avec distributeurs automatiques.
automated [ô'təmātid] *a* automatisé(e).
automatic [ôtəmat'ik] *a* automatique ♦ *n* (*gun*) automatique *m*; (*washing machine*) lave-linge *m* automatique; (*AUT*) voiture *f* à transmission automatique.
automatically [ôtəmat'iklē] *ad* automatiquement.
automatic data processing (ADP) *n* traitement *m* automatique des données.
automation [ôtəmā'shən] *n* automatisation *f*.
automaton, pl automata [ôtăm'ətăn, -tə] *n* automate *m*.
automobile [ôtəməbēl'] *n* (*US*) automobile *f*.
autonomous [ôtän'əməs] *a* autonome.
autonomy [ôtän'əmē] *n* autonomie *f*.
autopsy [ô'tăpsē] *n* autopsie *f*.
autumn [ô'təm] *n* automne *m*.
auxiliary [ôgzil'yûrē] *a*, *n* auxiliaire *(m/f)*.
AV *n abbr* (= *Authorized Version*) *traduction anglaise de la Bible* ♦ *abbr* = **audiovisual.**
Av. *abbr* (= *avenue*) Av.
avail [əvāl'] *vt*: **to ~ o.s. of** user de; profiter de ♦ *n*: **to no ~** sans résultat, en vain, en pure perte.
availability [əvāləbil'ətē] *n* disponibilité *f*.
available [əvā'ləbəl] *a* disponible; **every ~ means** tous les moyens possibles *or* à sa (*or* notre *etc*) disposition; **is the manager ~?** est-ce que le directeur peut (me) recevoir?; (*on phone*) pourrais-je parler au directeur?; **to make sth ~ to sb** mettre qch à la disposition de qn.
avalanche [av'əlanch] *n* avalanche *f*.
avant-garde [avàntgárd'] *a* d'avant-garde.
avaricious [avərish'əs] *a* âpre au gain.
avdp. *abbr* = *avoirdupoids*.
Ave. *abbr* (= *avenue*) Av.
avenge [əvenj'] *vt* venger.
avenue [av'ənōō] *n* avenue *f*.
average [av'ûrij] *n* moyenne *f* ♦ *a* moyen(ne) ♦ *vt* (*a certain figure*) atteindre *or* faire *etc* en moyenne; **on (the) ~** en moyenne; **above/below (the) ~** au-dessus/en-dessous de la moyenne.

average out *vi*: **to ~ out at** représenter en moyenne, donner une moyenne de.

averse |əvûrs'| *a*: **to be ~ to sth/doing** éprouver une forte répugnance envers qch/à faire; **I wouldn't be ~ to a drink** un petit verre ne serait pas de refus, je ne dirais pas non à un petit verre.

aversion |əvûr'zhən| *n* aversion *f*, répugnance *f*.

avert |əvûrt'| *vt* prévenir, écarter; *(one's eyes)* détourner.

aviary |ā'vēărē| *n* volière *f*.

aviation |āvēā'shən| *n* aviation *f*.

avid |av'id| *a* avide.

avidly |av'idlē| *ad* avidement, avec avidité.

avocado |avəkäd'ō| *n* avocat *m*.

avoid |əvoid'| *vt* éviter.

avoidable |əvoid'əbəl| *a* évitable.

avoidance |əvoid'əns| *n* le fait d'éviter.

avowed |əvoud'| *a* déclaré(e).

AVP *n abbr* (US) = *assistant vice-president*.

AWACS |ā'waks| *n abbr* (= *airborne warning and control system*) AWACS (*système aéroporté d'alerte et de contrôle*).

await |əwāt'| *vt* attendre; **~ing attention/ delivery** (*COMM*) en souffrance; **long ~ed** tant attendu(e).

awake |əwāk'| *a* éveillé(e); *(fig)* en éveil ♦ *vb* (*pt* **awoke** |əwōk'|, *pp* **awaked, awoken** |əwō'kən|) *vt* éveiller ♦ *vi* s'éveiller; **~ to** conscient de; **he was still ~** il ne dormait pas encore.

awakening |əwā'kəning| *n* réveil *m*.

award |əwôrd'| *n* récompense *f*, prix *m* ♦ *vt* (*prize*) décerner; (*LAW*: *damages*) accorder.

aware |əwär'| *a*: **~ of** (*conscious*) conscient(e) de; (*informed*) au courant de; **to become ~ of** avoir conscience de, prendre conscience de; **se rendre compte de; politically/socially ~ sensibilisé(e)** aux *or* ayant pris conscience des problèmes politiques/sociaux; **I am fully ~ that** je me rends parfaitement compte que.

awareness |əwär'nis| *n* conscience *f*, connaissance *f*; **to develop people's ~ (of)** sensibiliser le public (à).

awash |əwâsh'| *a* recouvert(e) (d'eau); **~ with** inondé(e) de.

away |əwā'| *a*, *ad* (au) loin; absent(e); **two kilometers ~** à (une distance de) deux kilomètres, à deux kilomètres de distance; **two hours ~ by car** à deux heures de voiture *or* de route; **the vacation was two weeks ~** il restait deux semaines jusqu'aux vacances; **~ from** loin de; **he's ~ for a week** il est parti (pour) une semaine; **he's ~ in Milan** il est (parti) à Milan; **to take ~** *vt* emporter; **to pedal/work/laugh** *etc* **~** *la particule indique la constance et l'énergie de l'action*: il pédalait *etc* tant qu'il pouvait; **to fade/wither** *etc* **~** *la particule renforce l'idée de la disparition, l'éloignement*.

away game *n* (*SPORT*) match *m* à l'extérieur.

awe |ô| *n* respect mêlé de crainte, effroi mêlé d'admiration.

awe-inspiring |ô'inspīuring|, **awesome** |ô'səm| *a* impressionnant(e).

awestruck |ô'struk| *a* frappé(e) d'effroi.

awful |ô'fəl| *a* affreux(euse); **an ~ lot of** énormément de.

awfully |ô'fəlē| *ad* (*very*) terriblement, vraiment.

awhile |əhwīl'| *ad* un moment, quelque temps.

awkward |ôk'wûrd| *a* (*clumsy*) gauche, maladroit(e); (*inconvenient*) malaisé(e), d'emploi malaisé, peu pratique; (*embarrassing*) gênant(e), délicat(e); (*difficult: problem, task*) délicat, difficile.

awkwardness |ôk'wûrdnis| *n* (*embarrassment*) gêne *f*.

awl |ôl| *n* alêne *f*.

awning |ô'ning| *n* (*of tent*) auvent *m*; (*of store*) store *m*; (*of hotel etc*) marquise *f* (de toile).

awoke |əwōk'| *pt of* **awake**.

awoken |əwō'kən| *pp of* **awake**.

AWOL |ā'wôl| *abbr* (*MIL*) = **absent without leave**.

awry |ərī'| *ad*, *a* de travers; **to go ~** mal tourner.

ax, (*Brit*) **axe** |aks| *n* hache *f* ♦ *vt* (*employee*) renvoyer; (*project etc*) abandonner; (*jobs*) supprimer; **to have an ~ to grind** (*fig*) prêcher pour son saint.

axes |ak'sēz| *npl of* **axis**.

axiom |ak'sēəm| *n* axiome *m*.

axiomatic |aksēəmat'ik| *a* axiomatique.

axis, *pl* **axes** |ak'sis, -sēz| *n* axe *m*.

axle |ak'səl| *n* (*also*: **~-tree**) essieu *m*.

ay(e) |ī'| *excl* (*yes*) oui ♦ *n*: **the ~s** les oui.

AYH *n abbr* = *American Youth Hostels*.

AZ *abbr* (*US MAIL*) = *Arizona*.

azalea |əzāl'yə| *n* azalée *f*.

Azores |əzôrz'| *npl*: **the ~** les Açores *fpl*.

Aztec |az'tek| *a* aztèque ♦ *n* Aztèque *m/f*.

azure |azh'ûr| *a* azuré(e).

B

B, b |bē| *n* (*letter*) B, b *m*; (*SCOL*: *mark*) B; (*MUS*): **B** si *m*; **B for Baker** B comme Berthe; **B road** *n* (*Brit AUT*) route départementale.

b. *abbr* = **born**.

BA *n abbr* (*SCOL*) = **Bachelor of Arts**.

babble |bab'əl| *vi* babiller ♦ *n* babillage *m*.

baboon |baboon'| *n* babouin *m*.

baby |bā'bē| *n* bébé *m*.

baby buggy |bā'bē bug'ē| *n* voiture *f* d'enfant.

baby carriage *n* (*US*) voiture *f* d'enfant.

baby grand *n* (*also*: **~ piano**) (piano *m*) demi-queue *m*.

babyhood |bā'bēhood| *n* petite enfance.

babyish |bā'bēish| *a* enfantin(e), de bébé.

baby-minder |bā'bēmīndûr| *n* (*Brit*) gardienne *f* (d'enfants).

baby-sit |bā'bēsit| *vi* garder les enfants.

baby-sitter |bā'bēsitûr| *n* baby-sitter *m/f*.

bachelor |bach'əlûr| *n* célibataire *m*; **B~ of Arts/Science (BA/BSc)** ≈ licencié/e ès *or* en lettres/sciences; **B~ of Arts/Science degree**

(BA/BSc) *n* ≈ licence *f* ès *or* en lettres/sciences.

bachelorhood [bach'əlûrhŏŏd] *n* célibat *m*.

bachelor party *n* (*US*) enterrement *m* de vie de garçon.

back [bak] *n* (*of person, horse*) dos *m*; (*of hand*) dos, revers *m*; (*of house*) derrière *m*; (*of car, train*) arrière *m*; (*of chair*) dossier *m*; (*of page*) verso *m*; (*SPORT*) arrière *m*; **to have one's ~ to the wall** (*fig*) être au pied du mur; **~ to front** à l'envers ♦ *vt* (*financially*) soutenir (financièrement); (*candidate: also:* **~ up**) soutenir, appuyer; (*horse: at races*) parier *or* miser sur; (*car*) (faire) reculer ♦ *vi* reculer; (*car etc*) faire marche arrière ♦ *a* (*in compounds*) de derrière, à l'arrière; **~ seats/wheels** (*AUT*) sièges *mpl*/roues *fpl* arrière; **~ payments/rent** arriéré *m* de paiements/loyer; **~ garden/room** jardin/pièce sur l'arrière; **to take a ~ seat** (*fig*) se contenter d'un second rôle, être relégué(e) au second plan ♦ *ad* (*not forward*) en arrière; (*returned*): **he's ~** il est rentré, il est de retour; **when will you be ~?** quand seras-tu de retour?; **he ran ~** il est revenu en courant; (*restitution*): **throw the ball ~** renvoie la balle; **can I have it ~?** puis-je le ravoir?, peux-tu me le rendre?; (*again*): **he called ~** il a rappelé.

back down *vi* rabattre de ses prétentions.

back on to *vt fus*: **the house ~s on to the golf course** la maison donne derrière sur le terrain de golf.

back out *vi* (*of promise*) se dédire.

back up *vt* (*COMPUT*) faire une copie de sauvegarde de.

backache [bak'āk] *n* maux *mpl* de reins.

backbencher [bak'benchûr] *n* (*Brit*) membre du parlement sans portefeuille.

backbiting [bak'bīting] *n* médisance(s) *f(pl)*.

backbone [bak'bōn] *n* colonne vertébrale, épine dorsale; **he's the ~ of the organization** c'est sur lui que repose l'organisation.

back burner *n*: **to put sth on the ~** mettre qch en veilleuse *or* en attente.

backcomb [bak'kōm] *vt* (*Brit*) crêper.

backdate [bakdāt'] *vt* (*letter*) antidater; **~d pay raise** augmentation *f* avec effet rétroactif.

backdrop [bak'dráp] *n* toile *f* de fond.

backer [bak'ûr] *n* partisan *m*; (*COMM*) commanditaire *m*.

backfire [bak'fîûr] *vi* (*AUT*) pétarader; (*plans*) mal tourner.

backgammon [bak'gamən] *n* trictrac *m*.

background [bak'ground] *n* arrière-plan *m*; (*of events*) situation *f*, conjoncture *f*; (*basic knowledge*) éléments *mpl* de base; (*experience*) formation *f* ♦ *cpd* (*noise, music*) de fond; **~ reading** lecture(s) générale(s) (sur un sujet); **family ~** milieu familial.

backhand [bak'hand] *n* (*TENNIS: also:* **~hand stroke**) revers *m*.

backhanded [bak'handid] *a* (*fig*) déloyal(e); équivoque.

backhander [bak'handûr] *n* (*Brit: bribe*) pot-de-vin *m*.

backing [bak'ing] *n* (*fig*) soutien *m*, appui *m*; (*COMM*) soutien (financier); (*MUS*) accompa-

gnement *m*.

backlash [bak'lash] *n* contre-coup *m*, répercussion *f*.

backlog [bak'lôg] *n*: **~ of work** travail *m* en retard.

back number *n* (*of magazine etc*) vieux numéro.

backpack [bak'pak] *n* sac *m* à dos.

backpacker [bak'pakûr] *n* randonneur/euse.

back pay *n* rappel *m* de salaire.

backpedal [bak'pedəl] *vi* (*fig*) faire marche arrière.

backside [bak'sīd] *n* (*col*) derrière *m*, postérieur *m*.

backslash [bak'slash] *n* barre oblique inversée.

backslide [bak'slīd] *vi* retomber dans l'erreur.

backspace [bak'spās] *vi* (*in typing*) appuyer sur la touche retour.

backstage [bak'stāj'] *ad* dans les coulisses.

back-street [bak'strēt] *a* (*abortion*) clandestin(e); **~ abortionist** avorteur/euse (clandestin).

backstroke [bak'strōk] *n* dos crawlé.

backtalk [bak'tôk] *n* (*col*) impertinences *fpl*.

backtrack [bak'trak] *vi* (*Brit fig*) = **backpedal**.

backup [bak'up] *a* (*train, plane*) supplémentaire, de réserve; (*COMPUT*) de sauvegarde ♦ *n* (*support*) appui *m*, soutien *m*; (*COMPUT: also:* **~ file**) sauvegarde *f*.

back-up lights [bak'up lītz] *npl* (*US AUT*) feux *mpl* de marche arrière *or* de recul.

backward [bak'wûrd] *a* (*movement*) en arrière; (*measure*) rétrograde; (*person, country*) arriéré(e); attardé(e); (*shy*) hésitant(e); **~ and forward movement** mouvement de va-et-vient.

backwards [bak'wûrdz] *ad* (*move, go*) en arrière; (*read a list*) à l'envers, à rebours; (*fall*) à la renverse; (*walk*) à reculons; (*in time*) en arrière, vers le passé; **to know sth ~ and forwards** *or* (*Brit*) **~** (*col*) connaître qch sur le bout des doigts.

backwater [bak'wôtûr] *n* (*fig*) coin reculé; bled perdu.

backyard [bak'yârd] *n* arrière-cour *f*.

bacon [bā'kən] *n* bacon *m*, lard *m*.

bacteria [baktē'reə] *npl* bactéries *fpl*.

bacteriology [baktērēâl'əjē] *n* bactériologie *f*.

bad [bad] *a* mauvais(e); (*child*) vilain(e); (*meat, food*) gâté(e), avarié(e); **his ~ leg** sa jambe malade; **to go ~** (*meat, food*) se gâter; (*milk*) tourner; **to have a ~ time of it** traverser une mauvaise passe; **I feel ~ about it** (*guilty*) j'ai un peu mauvaise conscience; **~ debt** créance douteuse; **in ~ faith** de mauvaise foi.

bade [bad] *pt of* **bid**.

bad feeling *n* ressentiment *m*, rancune *f*.

badge [baj] *n* insigne *m*; (*of policeman*) plaque *f*; (*stick-on, sew-on*) badge *m*.

badger [baj'ûr] *n* blaireau *m* ♦ *vt* harceler.

badly [bad'lē] *ad* (*work, dress etc*) mal; **~ wounded** grièvement blessé; **he needs it ~** il en a absolument besoin; **things are going ~** les choses vont mal; **~ off** *a, ad* dans la gêne.

bad-mannered [badman'ûrd] *a* mal élevé(e).

badminton [bad'mintən] *n* badminton *m*.

bad-mouth [bad'mouth'] *vt* (*US*) critiquer, dé-

nigrer.
bad-smelling [bad'smɛ'ling] a malodorant(e).
bad-tempered [bad'tɛm'púrd] a (by nature) ayant mauvais caractère; (on one occasion) de mauvaise humeur.
baffle [baf'əl] vt (puzzle) déconcerter.
baffling [baf'ling] a déroutant(e), déconcertant(e).
bag [bag] n sac m; (of hunter) gibecière f, chasse f ♦ vt (col: take) empocher; s'approprier; (TECH) mettre en sacs; ~s of (col: lots of) des masses de; **to pack one's ~s** faire ses valises or bagages; (: for meat) plat m pour le four.
bagful [bag'fəl] n plein sac.
baggage [bag'ij] n bagages mpl.
baggage check n bulletin m de consigne.
baggage claim n (at airport) livraison f des bagages.
baggy [bag'ē] a avachi(e), qui fait des poches.
Baghdad [bag'dad] n Baghdâd, Bagdad.
bagpipes [bag'pīps] npl cornemuse f.
bag-snatcher [bag'snachûr] n (Brit) voleur m à l'arraché.
Bahamas [bəhâm'əz] npl: **the ~** les Bahamas fpl.
Bahrain [bârân'] n Bahreïn m.
bail [bāl] n caution f ♦ vt (prisoner: also: **grant ~ to**) mettre en liberté sous caution; (boat: also: ~ **out**) écoper; **to be released on ~** être libéré(e) sous caution.
bail out vt (prisoner) payer la caution de; (NAUT: water, boat) écoper ♦ vi (of a plane) sauter en parachute.
bailiff [bā'lif] n huissier m.
bait [bāt] n appât m ♦ vt appâter; (fig) tourmenter.
bake [bāk] vt (faire) cuire au four ♦ vi (bread etc) cuire (au four); (make cakes etc) faire de la pâtisserie.
baked beans [bākt bēnz] npl haricots blancs à la sauce tomate.
baker [bā'kûr] n boulanger m.
bakery [bā'kûrē] n boulangerie f; boulangerie industrielle.
baking [bā'king] n cuisson f.
baking dish, baking pan n (US) plat m pour le four.
baking powder n levure f (chimique).
baking sheet n plaque f à gâteaux.
baking tin n (Brit: for cake) moule m à gâteaux; (: for meat) plat m pour le four.
baking tray n (Brit) = **baking sheet**.
balaclava [baləklâv'ə] n (also: ~ **helmet**) passe-montagne m.
balance [bal'əns] n équilibre m; (COMM: sum) solde m; (scales) balance f ♦ vt mettre or faire tenir en équilibre; (pros and cons) peser; (budget) équilibrer; (account) balancer; (compensate) compenser, contrebalancer; ~ **of trade/payments** balance commerciale/des comptes or paiements; ~ **carried forward** solde m à reporter; ~ **brought forward** solde reporté; **to ~ the books** arrêter les comptes, dresser le bilan.
balanced [bal'ənst] a (personality, diet) équilibré(e).
balance sheet n bilan m.
balance wheel n balancier m.

balcony [bal'kənē] n balcon m; **first ~** (US) premier balcon.
bald [bôld] a chauve; (tire) lisse.
baldness [bôld'nis] n calvitie f.
bale [bāl] n balle f, ballot m.
bale out vt (Brit) vi (of a plane) sauter en parachute ♦ vt (NAUT: water, boat) écoper.
Balearic Islands [balēâr'ək ī'ləndz] npl: **the ~** les (îles fpl) Baléares.
baleful [bāl'fəl] a funeste, maléfique.
balk [bôk] vi: **to ~ (at)** (person) regimber (contre); (horse) se dérober (devant).
Balkan [bôl'kən] a balkanique ♦ n: **the ~s** les Balkans mpl.
ball [bôl] n boule f; (football) ballon m; (for tennis, golf) balle f; (dance) bal m; **to play ~ (with sb)** jouer au ballon (or à la balle) (avec qn); (fig) coopérer (avec qn); **to be on the ~** (fig: competent) être à la hauteur; (: alert) être éveillé(e), être vif(vive); **to start the ~ rolling** (fig) commencer; **the ~ is in their court** (fig) la balle est dans leur camp.
ballad [bal'əd] n ballade f.
ballast [bal'əst] n lest m.
ball bearing n roulement m à billes.
ball cock n robinet m à flotteur.
ballerina [balərē'nə] n ballerine f.
ballet [balā'] n ballet m; (art) danse f (classique).
ballet dancer n danseur/euse de ballet.
ballistic [bəlis'tik] a balistique.
ballistics [bəlis'tiks] n balistique f.
balloon [bəlōōn'] n ballon m; (in comic strip) bulle f ♦ vi gonfler.
balloonist [bəlōō'nist] n aéronaute m/f.
ballot [bal'ət] n scrutin m; (US: ~ paper) bulletin m de vote.
ballot box n urne f (électorale).
ballot paper n bulletin m de vote.
ballpark [bôl'pârk] n (US) stade m de baseball.
ballpark figure n (col) chiffre approximatif.
ball-point (pen) [bôl'point (pen)'] n stylo m à bille.
ballroom [bôl'rōōm] n salle f de bal.
balls [bôlz] npl (col!) couilles fpl (!).
balm [bâm] n baume m.
balmy [bâ'mē] a (breeze, air) doux(douce).
balsam [bôl'səm] n baume m.
balsa (wood) [bôl'sə (wōōd)] n balsa m.
Baltic [bôl'tik] a, n: **the ~ (Sea)** la (mer) Baltique.
balustrade [bal'əstrād] n balustrade f.
bamboo [bambōō'] n bambou m.
bamboozle [bambōō'zəl] vt (col) embobiner.
ban [ban] n interdiction f ♦ vt interdire.
banal [bənal'] a banal(e).
banana [bənan'ə] n banane f.
band [band] n bande f; (at a dance) orchestre m; (MIL) musique f, fanfare f.
band together vi se liguer.
bandage [ban'dij] n bandage m, pansement m ♦ vt (wound, leg) mettre un pansement or un bandage sur; (person) mettre un pansement or un bandage à.
Band-Aid [band'ād] n ® (US) pansement adhésif.
bandit [ban'dit] n bandit m.

bandstand [band'stand] *n* kiosque *m* (à musique).

bandwagon [band'wagən] *n*: **to jump on the ~** (*fig*) monter dans *or* prendre le train en marche.

bandy [ban'dē] *vt* (*jokes, insults*) échanger.
bandy about *vt* employer à tout bout de champ *or* à tort et à travers.

bandy-legged [ban'dēlegid] *a* aux jambes arquées.

bane [bān] *n*: **it** (*or* **he** *etc*) **is the ~ of my life** c'est (*or* il est *etc*) le drame de ma vie.

bang [bang] *n* détonation *f*; (*of door*) claquement *m*; (*blow*) coup (violent) ♦ *vt* frapper (violemment); (*door*) claquer ♦ *vi* détoner; claquer; **to ~ at the door** cogner à la porte; **to ~ into sth** se cogner contre qch.

banger [bang'ûr] *n* (*Brit*: *car*: *also*: **old ~**) (vieux) tacot; (*Brit col*: *sausage*) saucisse *f*; (*firework*) pétard *m*.

Bangkok [bang'kák] *n* Bangkok.

Bangladesh [banggladesh'] *n* Bangladesh *m*.

bangle [bang'gəl] *n* bracelet *m*.

bangs [bangz] *npl* (*US: hair*) frange *f*.

banish [ban'ish] *vt* bannir.

banister(s) [ban'istûr(z)] *n(pl)* rampe *f* (d'escalier).

banjo, **~es** *or* **~s** [ban'jō] *n* banjo *m*.

bank [bangk] *n* banque *f*; (*of river, lake*) bord *m*, rive *f*; (*of earth*) talus *m*, remblai *m* ♦ *vi* (*AVIAT*) virer sur l'aile; (*COMM*): **they ~ with Pitt's** leur banque *or* banquier est Pitt's.
bank on *vt fus* miser *or* tabler sur.

bank account *n* compte *m* en banque.

bank card *n* carte d'identité bancaire.

bank charges *npl* frais *mpl* de banque.

bank draft *n* traite *f* bancaire.

banker [bangk'ûr] *n* banquier *m*; **~'s order** (*Brit*) ordre *m* de virement.

Bank holiday *n* (*Brit*) jour férié (*où les banques sont fermées*).

banking [bangk'ing] *n* opérations *fpl* bancaires; profession *f* de banquier.

banking hours *npl* heures *fpl* d'ouverture des banques.

bank loan *n* prêt *m* bancaire.

bank manager *n* directeur *m* d'agence (bancaire).

banknote [bangk'nōt] *n* billet *m* de banque.

bank rate *n* taux *m* de l'escompte.

bankrupt [bangk'rupt] *n* failli/e ♦ *a* en faillite; **to go ~** faire faillite.

bankruptcy [bangk'ruptsē] *n* faillite *f*.

bank statement *n* relevé *m* de compte.

banner [ban'ûr] *n* bannière *f*.

bannister(s) [ban'istûr(z)] *n(pl)* = **banister(s)**.

banns [banz] *npl* bans *mpl* (de mariage).

banquet [bang'kwit] *n* banquet *m*, festin *m*.

bantamweight [ban'təmwāt] *n* poids *m* coq *inv*.

banter [ban'tûr] *n* badinage *m*.

BAOR *n abbr* (= *British Army of the Rhine*) forces britanniques en Allemagne.

baptism [bap'tizəm] *n* baptême *m*.

Baptist [bap'tist] *n* baptiste *m/f*.

baptize [baptīz'] *vt* baptiser.

bar [bâr] *n* barre *f*; (*of window etc*) barreau *m*; (*of chocolate*) tablette *f*, plaque *f*; (*fig*) obstacle *m*; mesure *f* d'exclusion; (*place*)

bar *m*; (*counter*) comptoir *m*, bar; (*MUS*) mesure *f* ♦ *vt* (*road*) barrer; (*window*) munir de barreaux; (*person*) exclure; (*activity*) interdire; **~ of soap** savonnette *f*; **behind ~s** (*prisoner*) derrière les barreaux; **the B~** (*LAW*) le barreau; **~ none** sans exception.

Barbados [bârbā'dōs] *n* Barbade *f*.

barbaric [bârbar'ik] *a* barbare.

barbarous [bâr'bûrəs] *a* barbare, cruel(le).

barbecue [bâr'bəkyōō] *n* barbecue *m*.

barbed wire [bârbd wīûr] *n* fil *m* de fer barbelé.

barber [bâr'bûr] *n* coiffeur *m* (pour hommes).

barbiturate [bârbich'ûrit] *n* barbiturique *m*.

Barcelona [bârsəlō'nə] *n* Barcelone.

bar chart *n* diagramme *m* en bâtons.

bar code *n* code *m* à barres.

bare [bär] *a* nu(e) ♦ *vt* mettre à nu, dénuder; (*teeth*) montrer; **the ~ essentials** le strict nécessaire.

bareback [bär'bak] *ad* à cru, sans selle.

barefaced [bär'fāst] *a* impudent(e), effronté(e).

barefoot [bär'fŏŏt] *a*, *ad* nu-pieds, (les) pieds nus.

bareheaded [bär'hedid] *a*, *ad* nu-tête, (la) tête nue.

barely [bär'lē] *ad* à peine.

Barents Sea [bär'ənts sē] *n*: **the ~** la mer de Barents.

bargain [bâr'gin] *n* (*transaction*) marché *m*; (*good buy*) affaire *f*, occasion *f* ♦ *vi* (*haggle*) marchander; (*trade*) négocier, traiter; **into the ~** par-dessus le marché.
bargain for *vi* (*col*): **he got more than he ~ed for!** il en a eu pour son argent!

bargaining [bâr'gining] *n* marchandage *m*; négociations *fpl*.

barge [bârj] *n* péniche *f*.
barge in *vi* (*walk in*) faire irruption; (*interrupt talk*) intervenir mal à propos.
barge into *vt fus* rentrer dans.

baritone [bar'itōn] *n* baryton *m*.

barium meal [bar'ēəm mēl'] *n* (bouillie *f* de) sulfate *m* de baryum.

bark [bârk] *n* (*of tree*) écorce *f*; (*of dog*) aboiement *m* ♦ *vi* aboyer.

barley [bâr'lē] *n* orge *f*.

barley sugar *n* sucre *m* d'orge.

barmaid [bâr'mād] *n* serveuse *f* (de bar), barmaid *f*.

barman [bâr'mən] *n* serveur *m* (de bar), barman *m*.

barn [bârn] *n* grange *f*.

barnacle [bâr'nəkəl] *n* anatife *m*, bernacle *f*.

barometer [bərâm'itûr] *n* baromètre *m*.

baron [bar'ən] *n* baron *m*; **the press/oil ~s** les magnats *mpl* *or* barons *mpl* de la presse/du pétrole.

baroness [bar'ənis] *n* baronne *f*.

barracks [bar'əks] *npl* caserne *f*.

barrage [bərâzh'] *n* (*MIL*) tir *m* de barrage; (*dam*) barrage *m*; **a ~ of questions** un feu roulant de questions.

barrel [bar'əl] *n* tonneau *m*; (*of gun*) canon *m*.

barrel organ *n* orgue *m* de Barbarie.

barren [bar'ən] *a* stérile; (*hills*) aride.

barrette [bəret'] *n* (*US*) barrette *f*.

barricade [bar'əkād] *n* barricade *f* ♦ *vt* barricader.

barrier [bar'ēûr] *n* barrière *f*; (*Brit: also:* **crash ~**) rail *m* de sécurité.

barring [bâr'ing] *prep* sauf.

barrister [bar'istûr] *n* (*Brit*) avocat (plaidant).

barrow [bar'ō] *n* (*cart*) charrette *f* à bras.

barstool [bâr'stŏŏl] *n* tabouret *m* de bar.

bartender [bâr'tendûr] *n* (*US*) serveur *m* (de bar), barman *m*.

barter [bâr'tûr] *n* échange *m*, troc *m* ♦ *vt*: **to ~ sth for** échanger qch contre.

base [bās] *n* base *f* ♦ *vt* (*troops*): **to be ~d at** être basé(e) à; (*opinion, belief*): **to ~ sth on** baser *or* fonder qch sur ♦ *a* vil(e), bas(se); **coffee-~d** à base de café; **a Paris-~d firm** une maison opérant de Paris *or* dont le siège est à Paris; **I'm ~d in New York** je suis basé(e) à New York.

baseball [bās'bôl] *n* base-ball *m*.

baseboard [bās'bôrd] *n* (*US*) plinthe *f*.

base camp *n* camp *m* de base.

Basel [bäz'əl] *n* = **Basle**.

basement [bās'mənt] *n* sous-sol *m*.

base pay *n* (*US*) salaire *m* de base.

base rate *n* taux *m* de base.

bases [bā'sēz] *npl of* **basis**; [bā'siz] *npl of* **base**.

bash [bash] *vt* (*col*) frapper, cogner ♦ *n*: **I'll have a ~** (**at it**) (*col*) je vais essayer un coup; **~ed in** *a* enfoncé(e), défoncé(e).
  bash up *vt* (*col: car*) bousiller; (: *Brit: person*) tabasser.

bashful [bash'fəl] *a* timide; modeste.

bashing [bash'ing] *n* (*col*) raclée *f*; **Paki-~** (*Brit*) ≈ ratonnade *f*.

BASIC [bā'sik] *n* (*COMPUT*) BASIC *m*.

basic [bā'sik] *a* (*precautions, rules*) élémentaire; (*principles, research*) fondamental(e); (*vocabulary, salary*) de base; réduit(e) au minimum, rudimentaire.

basically [bā'siklē] *ad* (*really*) en fait; (*essentially*) fondamentalement.

basic rate *n* (*of tax*) première tranche d'imposition.

basil [baz'əl] *n* basilic *m*.

basin [bā'sin] *n* (*vessel, also GEO*) cuvette *f*, bassin *m*; (*Brit: for food*) bol *m*; (: *bigger*) saladier *m*; (*also:* **wash~**) lavabo *m*.

basis, *pl* **bases** [bā'sis, -sēz] *n* base *f*; **on the ~ of what you've said** d'après ce que *or* compte tenu de ce que vous dites.

bask [bask] *vi*: **to ~ in the sun** se chauffer au soleil.

basket [bas'kit] *n* corbeille *f*; (*with handle*) panier *m*.

basketball [bas'kitbôl] *n* basket-ball *m*.

basketball player *n* basketteur/euse.

Basle [baz'əl] *n* Bâle.

Basque [bask] *a* basque ♦ *n* Basque *m/f*.

bass [bās] *n* (*MUS*) basse *f*.

bass clef [bās klef] *n* clé *f* de fa.

bassoon [basōōn'] *n* basson *m*.

bastard [bas'tûrd] *n* enfant naturel(le), bâtard/e; (*col!*) salaud *m* (!).

baste [bāst] *vt* (*CULIN*) arroser; (*SEWING*) bâtir, faufiler.

bastion [bas'chən] *n* bastion *m*.

bat [bat] *n* chauve-souris *f*; (*for baseball etc*) batte *f*; (*Brit: for table tennis*) raquette *f* ♦ *vt*: **he didn't ~ an eyelid** il n'a pas sourcillé

or bronché; **to take off like a ~ out of hell** filer comme un zèbre.

batch [bach] *n* (*of bread*) fournée *f*; (*of papers*) liasse *f*; (*of applicants, letters*) paquet *m*; (*of work*) monceau *m*; (*of goods*) lot *m*.

batch processing *n* (*COMPUT*) traitement *m* par lot.

bated [bā'tid] *a*: **with ~ breath** en retenant son souffle.

bath [bath, *pl* bathz] *n* bain *m*; (*bathtub*) baignoire *f* ♦ *vt* baigner, donner un bain à; **to have a ~** prendre un bain; *see also* **baths**.

bathe [bāth] *vi* se baigner ♦ *vt* baigner; (*wound etc*) laver.

bather [bāth'ûr] *n* baigneur/euse.

bathing [bā'thing] *n* baignade *f*.

bathing cap *n* bonnet *m* de bain.

bathing suit *n* maillot *m* (de bain).

bathmat [bath'mat] *n* tapis *m* de bain.

bathrobe [bath'rōb] *n* peignoir *m* de bain.

bathroom [bath'rōōm] *n* salle *f* de bains.

baths [bathz] *npl* établissement *m* de bains(-douches).

bath towel [bath' toul] *n* serviette *f* de bain.

bathtub [bath'tub] *n* baignoire *f*.

baton [batán'] *n* bâton *m*; (*MUS*) baguette *f*; (*club*) matraque *f*.

battalion [batal'yən] *n* bataillon *m*.

batten [bat'ən] *n* (*CARPENTRY*) latte *f*; (*NAUT: on sail*) latte de voile.
  batten down *vt* (*NAUT*): **to ~ down the hatches** fermer les écoutilles.

batter [bat'ûr] *vt* battre ♦ *n* pâte *f* à frire.

battered [bat'ûrd] *a* (*hat, pan*) cabossé(e); **~ wife/child** épouse/enfant maltraité(e) *or* martyr(e).

battering ram [bat'ûring ram] *n* bélier *m* (*fig*).

battery [bat'ûrē] *n* batterie *f*; (*of torch*) pile *f*.

battery charger *n* chargeur *m*.

battery farming *n* élevage *m* en batterie.

battle [bat'əl] *n* bataille *f*, combat *m* ♦ *vi* se battre, lutter; **that's half the ~** (*fig*) c'est déjà bien; **it's a** *or* **we're fighting a losing ~** (*fig*) c'est perdu d'avance, c'est peine perdue.

battle dress *n* tenue *f* de campagne *or* d'assaut.

battlefield [bat'əlfēld] *n* champ *m* de bataille.

battlements [bat'əlmənts] *npl* remparts *mpl*.

battleship [bat'əlship] *n* cuirassé *m*.

bauble [bô'bəl] *n* babiole *f*.

baud [bôd] *n* (*COMPUT*) baud *m*.

baud rate *n* (*COMPUT*) vitesse *f* de transmission.

baulk [bôk] *vi* = **balk**.

bauxite [bôk'sit] *n* bauxite *f*.

Bavaria [bəvär'ēə] *n* Bavière *f*.

Bavarian [bəvär'ēən] *a* bavarois(e) ♦ *n* Bavarois/e.

bawdy [bô'dē] *a* paillard(e).

bawl [bôl] *vi* hurler, brailler.
  bawl out *vt fus* (*col*) engueuler.

bay [bā] *n* (*of sea*) baie *f*; (*Brit: for parking*) place *f* de stationnement; (: *for loading*) aire *f* de chargement; (*horse*) bai/e *m/f*; **to hold sb at ~** tenir qn à distance *or* en échec.

bay leaf *n* laurier *m*.

bayonet [bā'ənet] *n* baïonnette *f*.

bay tree *n* laurier *m*.

bay window n baie vitrée.
bazaar [bəzâr'] n bazar m; vente f de charité.
bazooka [bəzōō'kə] n bazooka m.
B & B n abbr = **bed and breakfast**.
BBA n abbr (US: = Bachelor of Business Administration) licencié/e en administration des affaires.
BBB n abbr (US: = Better Business Bureau) organisme de défense du consommateur.
BBC n abbr (= British Broadcasting Corporation) office de la radiodiffusion et télévision britannique.
BC ad abbr (= before Christ) av. J.-C. ♦ abbr (Canada) = British Columbia ♦ n abbr (US) = Bachelor of Commerce.
BCG n abbr (= Bacillus Calmette-Guérin) BCG m.
BD n abbr (= Bachelor of Divinity) diplôme universitaire.
B/D abbr = **bank draft**.
BDS n abbr (= Bachelor of Dental Surgery) diplôme universitaire.
be, pt **was, were**, pp **been** [bē, wuz, wûr, bēn] vi être; **how are you?** comment allez-vous?; **I am warm** j'ai chaud; **it is cold** il fait froid; **how much is it?** combien ça coûte?; **what are you doing?** que faites-vous?; **he is four (years old)** il a quatre ans; **it's 8 o'clock** il est 8 heures; **2 and 2 are 4** 2 et 2 font 4; **where have you been?** où êtes-vous allé(s)?; où étiez-vous?; **I've been waiting for her for two hours** cela fait deux heures que je l'attends, je l'attends depuis deux heures; **to ~ killed** être tué, se faire tuer; **he is nowhere to ~ found** on ne sait pas où il se trouve; **the car is to ~ sold** la voiture est à vendre; **he was to have come yesterday** il devait venir hier; **if I were you, I ...** à votre place, je ..., si j'étais vous, je ...; **am I to understand that ...?** dois-je comprendre que ...?
B/E abbr = **bill of exchange**.
beach [bēch] n plage f ♦ vt échouer.
beachcomber [bēch'kōmûr] n ramasseur m d'épaves; (fig) glandeur m.
beachwear [bēch'wär] n tenues fpl de plage.
beacon [bē'kən] n (lighthouse) fanal m; (marker) balise f; (also: **radio ~**) radiophare m.
bead [bēd] n perle f; (of dew, sweat) goutte f; **~s** (necklace) collier m.
beady [bē'dē] a: **~ eyes** yeux mpl de fouine.
beagle [bē'gəl] n beagle m.
beak [bēk] n bec m; (US col: nose) blair m.
beaker [bē'kûr] n gobelet m.
beam [bēm] n poutre f; (of light) rayon m; (RADIO) faisceau m radio ♦ vi rayonner; **to drive on high** or (Brit) **full ~** rouler en pleins phares.
beaming [bē'ming] a (sun, smile) radieux(euse).
bean [bēn] n haricot m; (of coffee) grain m.
bean sprouts npl pousses fpl (de soja).
bear [bär] n ours m; (STOCK EXCHANGE) baissier m ♦ vb (pt **bore**, pp **borne** [bôr, bôrn]) vt porter; (endure) supporter; (traces, signs) porter; (COMM: interest) rapporter ♦ vi: **to ~ right/left** obliquer à droite/gauche, se diriger vers la droite/gauche; **to ~ the re-**

sponsibility of assumer la responsabilité de; **to ~ comparison with** soutenir la comparaison avec; **I can't ~ him** je ne peux pas le supporter or souffrir; **to bring pressure to ~ on sb** faire pression sur qn.
bear out vt (theory, suspicion) confirmer.
bear up vi supporter, tenir le coup; **he bore up well** il a tenu le coup.
bear with vt fus (sb's moods, temper) supporter; **~ with me a minute** un moment, s'il vous plaît.
bearable [bär'əbəl] a supportable.
beard [bērd] n barbe f.
bearded [bērd'id] a barbu(e).
bearer [bär'ûr] n porteur m; (of passport etc) titulaire m/f.
bearing [bär'ing] n maintien m, allure f; (connection) rapport m; (TECH): (**ball**) **~s** npl roulement m (à billes); **to take a ~** faire le point; **to find one's ~s** s'orienter.
beast [bēst] n bête f; (col): **he's a ~** c'est une brute.
beastly [bēst'lē] a infect(e).
beat [bēt] n battement m; (MUS) temps m, mesure f; (of policeman) ronde f ♦ vt (pt **beat**, pp **beaten**) battre ♦ a (US col) crevé(e); **off the ~en track** hors des chemins or sentiers battus; **to ~ around the bush** tourner autour du pot; **to ~ time** battre la mesure; **that ~s everything!** c'est le comble!
beat down vt (door) enfoncer; (price) faire baisser; (seller) faire descendre ♦ vi (rain) tambouriner; (sun) taper.
beat off vt repousser.
beat up vt (eggs) battre; (col: person) tabasser.
beater [bē'tûr] n (for eggs, cream) fouet m, batteur m.
beating [bē'ting] n raclée f.
beat-up [bēt'up] a (col) déglingué(e).
beautician [byōōtish'ən] n esthéticien/ne.
beautiful [byōō'təfəl] a beau(belle).
beautifully [byōō'təfəlē] ad admirablement.
beautify [byōō'təfī] vt embellir.
beauty [byōō'tē] n beauté f; **the ~ of it is that ...** le plus beau, c'est que ....
beauty contest n concours m de beauté.
beauty queen n reine f de beauté.
beauty salon [byōō'tē sal'ân] n institut m de beauté.
beauty spot n grain m de beauté; (Brit TOURISM) site naturel (d'une grande beauté).
beaver [bē'vûr] n castor m.
becalmed [bikâmd'] a immobilisé(e) par le calme plat.
became [bikām'] pt of **become**.
because [bikôz'] cj parce que; **~ of** prep à cause de.
beck [bck] n: **to be at sb's ~ and call** être à l'entière disposition de qn.
beckon [bck'ən] vt (also: **~ to**) faire signe (de venir) à.
become [bikum'] vt (irg: like **come**) devenir; **to ~ fat/thin** grossir/maigrir; **to ~ angry** se mettre en colère; **it became known that** on apprit que; **what has ~ of him?** qu'est-il devenu?
becoming [bikum'ing] a (behavior) convena-

ble, bienséant(e); (*clothes*) seyant(e).

BEd *n abbr* (= *Bachelor of Education*) diplôme d'aptitude à l'enseignement.

bed [bed] *n* lit *m*; (*of flowers*) parterre *m*; (*of coal, clay*) couche *f*; (*of sea, lake*) fond *m*; **to go to ~** aller se coucher.
bed down *vi* se coucher.

bed and breakfast (B & B) *n* (*terms*) chambre et petit déjeuner; (*place*) ≈ chambre *f* d'hôte.

bedbug [bed'bug] *n* punaise *f*.

bedclothes [bed'klōz] *npl* couvertures *fpl* et draps *mpl*.

bedcover [bed'kuvûr] *n* couvre-lit *m*, dessus-de-lit *m*.

bedding [bed'ing] *n* literie *f*.

bedevil [bidev'əl] *vt* (*harass*) harceler; **to be ~led by** être victime de.

bedfellow [bed'felō] *n*: **they are strange ~s** (*fig*) ça fait un drôle de mélange.

bedlam [bed'ləm] *n* chahut *m*, cirque *m*.

bedpan [bed'pan] *n* bassin *m* (hygiénique).

bedpost [bed'pōst] *n* colonne *f* de lit.

bedraggled [bidrag'əld] *a* dépenaillé(e), les vêtements en désordre.

bedridden [bed'ridən] *a* cloué(e) au lit.

bedrock [bed'râk] *n* (*fig*) principes essentiels *or* de base, essentiel *m*; (*GEO*) roche *f* en place, socle *m*.

bedroom [bed'rōōm] *n* chambre *f* (à coucher).

Beds [bedz] *abbr* (*Brit*) = *Bedfordshire*.

bedside [bed'sīd] *n*: **at sb's ~** au chevet de qn ♦ *cpd* (*book, lamp*) de chevet.

bedsit(ter) [bed'sit(ûr)] *n* (*Brit*) chambre meublée, studio *m*.

bedspread [bed'spred] *n* couvre-lit *m*, dessus-de-lit *m*.

bedtime [bed'tīm] *n*: **it's ~** c'est l'heure de se coucher.

bee [bē] *n* abeille *f*; **to have a ~ in one's bonnet (about sth)** être obnubilé(e) (par qch).

beech [bēch] *n* hêtre *m*.

beef [bēf] *n* bœuf *m*.
beef up *vt* (*col: support*) renforcer; (: *essay*) étoffer.

beefburger [bēf'bûrgûr] *n* hamburger *m*.

beefeater [bēf'ētûr] *n* hallebardier *m* (de la tour de Londres).

beehive [bē'hīv] *n* ruche *f*.

beeline [bē'līn] *n*: **to make a ~ for** se diriger tout droit vers.

been [bin] *pp of* **be**.

beeper [bēp'ûr] *n* (*of doctor etc*) bip *m*.

beer [bēr] *n* bière *f*.

beer can *n* canette *f* de bière.

beet [bēt] *n* (*US*) betterave *f*.

beetle [bēt'əl] *n* scarabée *m*, coléoptère *m*.

beetroot [bēt'rōōt] *n* (*Brit*) betterave *f*.

befall [bifôl'] *vi*(*vt*) (*irg: like* **fall**) advenir (à).

befit [bifit'] *vt* seoir à.

before [bifôr'] *prep* (*of time*) avant; (*of space*) devant ♦ *cj* avant que + *sub*; avant de ♦ *ad* avant; **~ going** avant de partir; **~ she goes** avant qu'elle (ne) parte; **the week ~** la semaine précédente *or* d'avant; **I've seen it ~** je l'ai déjà vu; **I've never seen it ~** c'est la première fois que je le vois.

beforehand [bifôr'hand] *ad* au préalable, à

l'avance.

befriend [bifrend'] *vt* venir en aide à; traiter en ami.

befuddled [bifud'əld] *a*: **to be ~** avoir les idées brouillées.

beg [beg] *vi* mendier ♦ *vt* mendier; (*favor*) quémander, solliciter; (*entreat*) supplier; **I ~ your pardon** (*apologizing*) excusez-moi; (: *not hearing*) pardon?; **that ~s the question of** ... cela soulève la question de ..., cela suppose réglée la question de ....

began [bigan'] *pt of* **begin**.

beggar [beg'ûr] *n* (*also:* **~man, ~woman**) mendiant/e.

begin, *pt* **began**, *pp* **begun** [bigin', bigan', bigun'] *vt, vi* commencer; **to ~ doing** *or* **to do sth** commencer à faire qch; **~ning (from) Monday** à partir de lundi; **I can't ~ to thank you** je ne saurais vous remercier; **to ~ with** d'abord, pour commencer.

beginner [bigin'ûr] *n* débutant/e.

beginning [bigin'ing] *n* commencement *m*, début *m*; **right from the ~** dès le début.

begrudge [bigruj'] *vt*: **to ~ sb sth** envier qch à qn; donner qch à contrecœur *or* à regret à qn.

beguile [bigīl'] *vt* (*enchant*) enjôler.

beguiling [bigī'ling] *a* (*charming*) séduisant(e), enchanteur(eresse).

begun [bigun'] *pp of* **begin**.

behalf [bihaf'] *n*: **in ~ of**, (*Brit*) **on ~ of** de la part de; au nom de; pour le compte de.

behave [bihāv'] *vi* se conduire, se comporter; (*well: also:* **~ o.s.**) se conduire bien *or* comme il faut.

behavior, (*Brit*) **behaviour** [bihāv'yûr] *n* comportement *m*, conduite *f*.

behead [bihed'] *vt* décapiter.

beheld [biheld'] *pt, pp of* **behold**.

behind [bihīnd'] *prep* derrière; (*time*) en retard sur ♦ *ad* derrière; en retard ♦ *n* derrière *m*; **~ the scenes** dans les coulisses; **to leave sth ~** (*forget*) oublier de prendre qch; **to be ~ (schedule) with sth** être en retard dans qch.

behold [bihōld'] *vt* (*irg: like* **hold**) apercevoir, voir.

beige [bāzh] *a* beige.

being [bē'ing] *n* être *m*; **to come into ~** prendre naissance.

Beirut [bārōōt'] *n* Beyrouth.

belated [bilā'tid] *a* tardif(ive).

belch [belch] *vi* avoir un renvoi, roter ♦ *vt* (*also:* **~ out**: *smoke etc*) vomir, cracher.

beleaguered [bilē'gûrd] *a* (*city*) assiégé(e); (*army*) cerné(e); (*fig*) sollicité(e) de toutes parts.

Belfast [bel'fast] *n* Belfast.

belfry [bel'frē] *n* beffroi *m*.

Belgian [bel'jən] *a* belge, de Belgique ♦ *n* Belge *m/f*.

Belgium [bel'jəm] *n* Belgique *f*.

Belgrade [belgrād'] *n* Belgrade.

belie [bilī'] *vt* démentir; (*give false impression of*) occulter.

belief [bilēf'] *n* (*opinion*) conviction *f*; (*trust, faith*) foi *f*; (*acceptance as true*) croyance *f*; **it's beyond ~** c'est incroyable; **in the ~ that** dans l'idée que.

believable [bilēv'əbəl] *a* croyable.

believe [bilēv'] *vt, vi* croire, estimer; **to ~ in** (*God*) croire en; (*ghosts, method*) croire à; **I don't ~ in corporal punishment** je ne suis pas partisan des châtiments corporels; **he is ~d to be abroad** il serait à l'étranger.

believer [bilēv'ûr] *n* (*in idea, activity*): **~ in** partisan/e de; (*REL*) croyant/e.

belittle [bilit'əl] *vt* déprécier, rabaisser.

Belize [bəlēz'] *n* Bélize *m*.

bell [bel] *n* cloche *f*; (*small*) clochette *f*, grelot *m*; (*on door*) sonnette *f*; (*electric*) sonnerie *f*; **that rings a ~** (*fig*) cela me rappelle qch.

bell-bottoms [bel'bátəmz] *npl* pantalon *m* à pattes d'éléphant.

bellhop [bel'hâp] (*Brit*) **bellboy** [bel'boi] *n* groom *m*, chasseur *m*.

belligerent [bəlij'ûrənt] *a* (*at war*) belligérant(e); (*fig*) agressif(ive).

bellow [bel'ō] *vi* mugir; beugler ♦ *vt* (*orders*) hurler.

bellows [bel'ōz] *npl* soufflet *m*.

belly [bel'ē] *n* ventre *m*.

bellyache [bel'ēāk] *n* (*col*) colique *f* ♦ *vi* ronchonner.

bellybutton [bel'ēbutən] *n* nombril *m*.

belong [bilông'] *vi*: **to ~ to** appartenir à; (*club etc*) faire partie de; **this book ~s here** ce livre va ici, la place de ce livre est ici.

belongings [bilông'ingz] *npl* affaires *fpl*, possessions *fpl*; **personal ~** effets personnels.

beloved [biluv'id] *a* (bien-)aimé(e), chéri(e) ♦ *n* bien-aimé/e.

below [bilō'] *prep* sous, au-dessous de ♦ *ad* en dessous; en contre-bas; **see ~** voir plus bas *or* plus loin *or* ci-dessous; **temperatures ~ normal** températures inférieures à la normale.

belt [belt] *n* ceinture *f*; (*TECH*) courroie *f* ♦ *vt* (*thrash*) donner une raclée à; **industrial ~** zone industrielle.

belt out *vt* (*song*) chanter à tue-tête *or* à pleins poumons.

belt up *vi* (*Brit col*) la boucler.

beltway [belt'wā] *n* (*US AUT*) route *f* de ceinture; (: *freeway*) périphérique *m*.

bemoan [bimōn'] *vt* se lamenter sur.

bemused [bimyōōzd'] *a* médusé(e).

bench [bench] *n* banc *m*; (*in workshop*) établi *m*; **the B~** (*LAW*) la magistrature, la Cour.

bench mark *n* repère *m*.

bend [bend] *vb* (*pt, pp* **bent** [bent]) *vt* courber; (*leg, arm*) plier ♦ *vi* se courber ♦ *n* (*Brit: in road*) virage *m*, tournant *m*; (*in pipe, river*) coude *m*.

bend down *vi* se baisser.

bend over *vi* se pencher.

bends [bendz] *npl* (*MED*) maladie *f* des caissons.

beneath [binēth'] *prep* sous, au-dessous de; (*unworthy of*) indigne de ♦ *ad* dessous, au-dessous, en bas.

benefactor [ben'əfaktûr] *n* bienfaiteur *m*.

benefactress [ben'əfaktris] *n* bienfaitrice *f*.

beneficial [benəfish'əl] *a*: **~ (to)** salutaire (pour), bénéfique (à).

beneficiary [benəfish'ēârē] *n* (*LAW*) bénéficiaire *m/f*.

benefit [ben'əfit] *n* avantage *m*, profit *m*; (*allowance of money*) allocation *f* ♦ *vt* faire du bien à, profiter à ♦ *vi*: **he'll ~ from it** cela lui fera du bien, il y gagnera *or* s'en trouvera bien.

benefit performance *n* représentation *f or* gala *m* de bienfaisance.

benefit society *n* (*US*) société *f* mutualiste.

Benelux [ben'əluks] *n* Bénélux *m*.

benevolent [bənev'ələnt] *a* bienveillant(e).

BEng *n abbr* (= *Bachelor of Engineering*) *diplôme universitaire.*

benign [binīn'] *a* (*person, smile*) bienveillant(e), affable; (*MED*) bénin(igne).

bent [bent] *pt, pp of* **bend** ♦ *n* inclination *f*, penchant *m* ♦ *a* (*wire, pipe*) coudé(e); (*col: dishonest*) véreux(euse); **to be ~ on** être résolu(e) à.

bequeath [bikwēth'] *vt* léguer.

bequest [bikwest'] *n* legs *m*.

bereaved [birēvd'] *n*: **the ~** la famille du disparu ♦ *a* endeuillé(e).

bereavement [birēv'mənt] *n* deuil *m*.

beret [bərā'] *n* béret *m*.

Bering Sea [bar'ing sē] *n*: **the ~** la mer de Béring.

Berks *abbr* (*Brit*) = *Berkshire.*

Berlin [bûrlin'] *n* Berlin; **East/West ~** Berlin Est/Ouest.

berm [bûrm] *n* (*US AUT*) accotement *m*.

Bermuda [bûrmōō'də] *n* Bermudes *fpl*.

Bermuda shorts *npl* bermuda *m*.

Bern [bûrn] *n* Berne.

berry [bär'ē] *n* baie *f*.

berserk [bûrsûrk'] *a*: **to go ~** être pris(e) d'une rage incontrôlable; se déchaîner.

berth [bûrth] *n* (*bed*) couchette *f*; (*for ship*) poste *m* d'amarrage, mouillage *m* ♦ *vi* (*in harbor*) venir à quai; (*at anchor*) mouiller; **to give sb a wide ~** (*fig*) éviter qn.

beseech, *pt, pp* **besought** [bisēch', bisôt'] *vt* implorer, supplier.

beset, *pt, pp* **beset** [biset'] *vt* assaillir ♦ *a*: **~ with** semé(e) de.

besetting [biset'ing] *a*: **his ~ sin** son vice, son gros défaut.

beside [bisid'] *prep* à côté de; (*compared with*) par rapport à; **that's ~ the point** ça n'a rien à voir; **to be ~ o.s. (with anger)** être hors de soi.

besides [bisīdz'] *ad* en outre, de plus ♦ *prep* en plus de; (*except*) excepté.

besiege [bisēj'] *vt* (*town*) assiéger; (*fig*) assaillir.

besotted [bisät'id] *a*: **~ with** entiché(e) de.

besought [bisôt'] *pt, pp of* **beseech**.

bespectacled [bispek'təkəld] *a* à lunettes.

best [best] *a* meilleur(e) ♦ *ad* le mieux; **the ~ part of** (*quantity*) le plus clair de, la plus grande partie de; **at ~** au mieux; **to make the ~ of sth** s'accommoder de qch (du mieux que l'on peut); **to do one's ~** faire de son mieux; **to the ~ of my knowledge** pour autant que je sache; **to the ~ of my ability** du mieux que je pourrai; **he's not exactly patient at the ~ of times** il n'est jamais spécialement patient; **the ~ thing to do is ...** le mieux, c'est de ....

best man *n* garçon *m* d'honneur.

bestow [bistō'] *vt* accorder; (*title*) conférer.

best seller *n* bestseller *m*, succès *m* de librairie.

bet [bet] *n* pari *m* ♦ *vt*, *vi* (*pt*, *pp* **bet** *or* **betted**) parier; **it's a safe ~** (*fig*) il y a de fortes chances.

Bethlehem [beth'lēəm] *n* Bethléem.

betray [bitrā'] *vt* trahir.

betrayal [bitrā'əl] *n* trahison *f*.

better [bet'ûr] *a* meilleur(e) ♦ *ad* mieux ♦ *vt* améliorer ♦ *n*: **to get the ~ of** triompher de, l'emporter sur; **a change for the ~** une amélioration; **I had ~ go** il faut que je m'en aille; **you had ~ do it** vous feriez mieux de le faire; **he thought ~ of it** il s'est ravisé; **to get ~** aller mieux; s'améliorer; **that's ~!** c'est mieux!; **~ off** *a* plus à l'aise financièrement; (*fig*): **you'd be ~ off this way** vous vous en trouveriez mieux ainsi, ce serait mieux *or* plus pratique ainsi.

betting [bet'ing] *n* paris *mpl*.

betting shop *n* (*Brit*) bureau *m* de paris.

between [bitwēn'] *prep* entre ♦ *ad* au milieu, dans l'intervalle; **the road ~ here and Chicago** la route d'ici à Chicago; **we only had 5 ~ us** nous n'en avions que 5 en tout.

bevel [bev'əl] *n* (*also:* **~ edge**) biseau *m*.

beverage [bev'ûrij] *n* boisson *f* (*gén sans alcool*).

bevy [bev'ē] *n*: **a ~ of** un essaim *or* une volée de.

bewail [biwāl'] *vt* se lamenter sur.

beware [biwär'] *vt*, *vi*: **to ~ (of)** prendre garde (à).

bewildered [biwil'dûrd] *a* dérouté(e), ahuri(e).

bewildering [biwil'dûring] *a* déroutant(e), ahurissant(e).

bewitching [biwich'ing] *a* enchanteur(teresse).

beyond [bēänd'] *prep* (*in space*) au-delà de; (*exceeding*) au-dessus de ♦ *ad* au-delà; **~ doubt** hors de doute; **~ repair** irréparable.

b/f *abbr* = brought forward.

BFPO *n abbr* (= *British Forces Post Office*) service postal de l'armée.

bhp *n abbr* (*AUT*: = *brake horsepower*) puissance *f* aux freins.

bi... [bī] *prefix* bi....

biannual [bīan'yōōəl] *a* semestriel(le).

bias [bī'əs] *n* (*prejudice*) préjugé *m*, parti pris; (*preference*) prévention *f*.

bias(s)ed [bī'əst] *a* partial(e), montrant un parti pris; **to be ~ against** avoir un préjugé contre.

bib [bib] *n* bavoir *m*, bavette *f*.

Bible [bī'bəl] *n* Bible *f*.

bibliography [biblēäg'rəfē] *n* bibliographie *f*.

bicarbonate of soda [bīkâr'bənit əv sō'də] *n* bicarbonate *m* de soude.

bicentenary [bīsen'tənärē] *n* bicentenaire *m*.

bicentennial [bīsenten'ēəl] *n* = **bicentenary.**

biceps [bī'seps] *n* biceps *m*.

bicker [bik'ûr] *vi* se chamailler.

bicycle [bī'sikəl] *n* bicyclette *f*.

bicycle path *n* piste *f* cyclable.

bicycle pump *n* pompe *f* à vélo.

bicycle track *n* piste *f* cyclable.

bid [bid] *n* offre *f*; (*at auction*) enchère *f*; (*attempt*) tentative *f* ♦ *vb* (*pt* **bid** *or* **bade** [bad], *pp* **bid** *or* **bidden** [bid'n]) *vi* faire une enchère *or* offre ♦ *vt* faire une enchère *or* offre de; **to ~ sb good day** souhaiter le bonjour à qn.

bidder [bid'ûr] *n*: **the highest ~** le plus offrant.

bidding [bid'ing] *n* enchères *fpl*.

bide [bīd] *vt*: **to ~ one's time** attendre son heure.

bidet [bēdā'] *n* bidet *m*.

bidirectional [bīdirek'shənəl] *a* bidirectionnel(le).

biennial [bīen'ēəl] *a* biennal(e), bisannuel(le) ♦ *n* biennale *f*; (*plant*) plante bisannuelle.

bier [bēr] *n* bière *f* (*cercueil*).

bifocals [bīfō'kəlz] *npl* lunettes *fpl* à double foyer.

big [big] *a* grand(e); gros(se); **to do things in a ~ way** faire les choses en grand.

bigamy [big'əmē] *n* bigamie *f*.

big dipper [big dip'ûr] *n* (*Brit*) montagnes *fpl* russes.

big end *n* (*Brit AUT*) tête *f* de bielle.

bigheaded [big'hedid] *a* prétentieux(euse).

big-hearted [big'hârtid] *a* au grand cœur.

bigot [big'ət] *n* fanatique *m/f*, sectaire *m/f*.

bigoted [big'ətid] *a* fanatique, sectaire.

bigotry [big'ətrē] *n* fanatisme *m*, sectarisme *m*.

big toe *n* gros orteil.

big top *n* grand chapiteau.

big wheel *n* (*Brit*: *at fair*) grande roue.

bigwig [big'wig] *n* (*col*) grosse légume, huile *f*.

bike [bīk] *n* vélo *m*, bécane *f*.

bike rack *n* (*US*) râtelier *m* á bicyclette.

bikeway [bīk'wā] *n* (*US*) piste *f* cyclable.

bikini [bikē'nē] *n* bikini *m*.

bilateral [bīlat'ûrəl] *a* bilatéral(e).

bile [bīl] *n* bile *f*.

bilingual [bīling'gwəl] *a* bilingue.

bilious [bil'yəs] *a* bilieux(euse); (*fig*) maussade, irritable.

bill [bil] *n* note *f*, facture *f*; (*POL*) projet *m* de loi; (*US*: *bank note*) billet *m* (de banque); (*in restaurant*) addition *f*, note *f*; (*notice*) affiche *f*; (*THEATER*): **on the ~** à l'affiche; (*of bird*) bec *m* ♦ *vt* (*item*) facturer; (*customer*) remettre la facture à; **may I have the ~ please?** (est-ce que je peux avoir) l'addition, s'il vous plaît?; **"post no ~s"** "défense d'afficher"; **to fit** *or* **fill the ~** (*fig*) faire l'affaire; **~ of exchange** lettre *f* de change; **~ of lading** connaissement *m*; **~ of sale** contrat *m* de vente.

billboard [bil'bôrd] *n* panneau *m* d'affichage.

billet [bil'it] *n* cantonnement *m* (chez l'habitant) ♦ *vt* (*troops*) cantonner.

billfold [bil'fōld] *n* (*US*) portefeuille *m*.

billiards [bil'yûrdz] *n* (jeu *m* de) billard *m*.

billion [bil'yən] *n* (*US*) milliard *m*; (*Brit*) billion *m* (*million de millions*).

billionaire [bilyənär'] *n* ≈ milliardaire *m/f*.

billow [bil'ō] *n* nuage *m* ♦ *vi* (*smoke*) s'élever en nuage; (*sail*) se gonfler.

billy [bil'ē] *n* (*US*) matraque *f*.

billy goat [bil'ē gōt] *n* bouc *m*.

bin [bin] *n* boîte *f*; (*Brit*: *also:* **dust~, litter~**) poubelle *f*; (*for coal*) coffre *m*.

binary [bī'nûrē] *a* binaire.

bind, ** *pt*, *pp* **bound [bīnd, bound] *vt* attacher;

(*book*) relier; (*oblige*) obliger, contraindre.
bind over *vt* (*LAW*) mettre en liberté conditionnelle.
bind up *vt* (*wound*) panser; **to be bound up in** (*work, research etc*) être complètement absorbé par, être accroché par; **to be bound up with** (*person*) être accroché à.
binder [bīn'dûr] *n* (*file*) classeur *m*.
binding [bīn'ding] *n* (*of book*) reliure *f* ♦ *a* (*contract*) qui constitue une obligation.
binge [binj] *n* (*col*): **to go on a** ~ faire la bringue.
bingo [bing'gō] *n sorte de jeu de loto pratiqué dans des établissements publics.*
binoculars [bənák'yəlûrz] *npl* jumelles *fpl.*
biochemistry [bīōkem'istrē] *n* biochimie *f.*
biodegradable [bīōdigrā'dəbəl] *a* biodégradable.
biographer [bīâg'rəfûr] *n* biographe *m/f.*
biographic(al) [bīəgraf'ik(əl)] *a* biographique.
biography [bīâg'rəfē] *n* biographie *f.*
biological [bīəlâj'ikəl] *a* biologique.
biologist [bīál'əjist] *n* biologiste *m/f.*
biology [bīál'əjē] *n* biologie *f.*
biophysics [bīōfiz'iks] *n* biophysique *f.*
biopsy [bī'âpsē] *n* biopsie *f.*
biorhythm [bī'ōrithəm] *n* biorythme *m.*
biotechnology [bīōteknâl'əjē] *n* biotechnologie *f.*
birch [bûrch] *n* bouleau *m.*
bird [bûrd] *n* oiseau *m*; (*Brit col: girl*) nana *f.*
bird's-eye view [bûrdz'ī vyōō'] *n* vue *f* à vol d'oiseau; (*fig*) vue d'ensemble *or* générale.
bird watcher [bûrd' wâch'ûr] *n* ornithologue *m/f* amateur.
Biro [bē'rō] *n* ® (*Brit*) stylo *m* à bille.
birth [bûrth] *n* naissance *f*; **to give** ~ **to** donner naissance à, mettre au monde; (*animal*) mettre bas.
birth certificate *n* acte *m* de naissance.
birth control *n* limitation *f* des naissances; méthode(s) contraceptive(s).
birthday [bûrth'dā] *n* anniversaire *m.*
birthmark [bûrth'mârk] *n* envie *f*, tache *f* de vin.
birthplace [bûrth'plās] *n* lieu *m* de naissance.
birth rate [bûrth rāt] *n* (taux *m* de) natalité *f.*
Biscay [bis'kā] *n*: **the Bay of** ~ le golfe de Gascogne.
biscuit [bis'kit] *n* (*US*) petit pain au lait; (*Brit*) biscuit *m.*
bisect [bīsekt'] *vt* couper *or* diviser en deux.
bishop [bish'əp] *n* évêque *m*; (*CHESS*) fou *m.*
bison [bī'sən] *n* bison *m.*
bit [bit] *pt of* **bite** ♦ *n* morceau *m*; (*of tool*) mèche *f*; (*of horse*) mors *m*; (*COMPUT*) bit *m*, élément *m* binaire; **a** ~ **of** un peu de; **a** ~ **mad/dangerous** un peu fou/risqué; ~ **by** ~ petit à petit; . **to come to** ~**s** (*break*) tomber en morceaux, se déglinguer; **bring all your** ~**s and pieces** apporte toutes tes affaires; **to do one's** ~ y mettre du sien.
bitch [bich] *n* (*dog*) chienne *f*; (*col!*) salope *f* (!), garce *f.*
bite [bīt] *vt, vi* (*pt* **bit**, *pp* **bitten** [bit, bit'ən]) mordre ♦ *n* morsure *f*; (*insect* ~) piqûre *f*; (*mouthful*) bouchée *f*; **let's have a** ~ **(to eat)** mangeons un morceau; **to** ~ **one's nails** se ronger les ongles.

biting [bī'ting] *a* mordant(e).
bit part *n* (*THEATER*) petit rôle.
bitten [bit'ən] *pp of* **bite.**
bitter [bit'ûr] *a* amer(ère); (*criticism*) cinglant(e); (*icy: weather, wind*) glacial(e) ♦ *n* (*Brit: beer*) bière *f* (*à forte teneur en houblon*); **to the** ~ **end** jusqu'au bout.
bitterly [bit'ûrlē] *ad* (*complain, weep*) amèrement; (*oppose, criticize*) durement, âprement; (*jealous, disappointed*) horriblement; **it's** ~ **cold** il fait un froid de loup.
bitterness [bit'ûrnis] *n* amertume *f*; goût amer.
bittersweet [bit'ûrswēt] *a* aigre-doux(douce).
bitty [bit'ē] *a* (*US: tiny*) minuscule; (*Brit col*) décousu(e).
bitumen [bitōō'mən] *n* bitume *m.*
bivouac [biv'ōōak] *n* bivouac *m.*
bizarre [bizâr'] *a* bizarre.
bk *abbr* = **bank, book.**
BL *n abbr* (= *Bachelor of Law(s), Bachelor of Letters*) diplôme universitaire.
b/l *abbr* = **bill of lading.**
blab [blab] *vi* jaser, trop parler ♦ *vt* (*also:* ~ **out**) laisser échapper, aller raconter.
black [blak] *a* noir(e) ♦ *n* (*color*) noir *m*; (*person*): **B**~ noir/e ♦ *vt* (*shoes*) cirer; (*Brit INDUSTRY*) boycotter; **to give sb a** ~ **eye** pocher l'œil à qn, faire un œil au beurre noir à qn; ~ **coffee** café noir; **there it is in** ~ **and white** (*fig*) c'est écrit noir sur blanc; **to be in the** ~ (*in credit*) avoir un compte créditeur; ~ **and blue** *a* couvert(e) de bleus.
black out *vi* (*faint*) s'évanouir.
black belt *n* (*US*) *région à forte population noire.*
blackberry [blak'bärē] *n* mûre *f.*
blackbird [blak'bûrd] *n* merle *m.*
blackboard [blak'bôrd] *n* tableau noir.
black box *n* (*AVIAT*) boîte noire.
blackcurrant [blakkur'ənt] *n* cassis *m.*
black economy *n* (*Brit*) travail *m* au noir.
blacken [blak'ən] *vt* noircir.
Black Forest *n*: **the** ~ la Forêt Noire.
blackhead [blak'hed] *n* point noir.
black ice *n* verglas *m.*
blackjack [blak'jak] *n* (*CARDS*) vingt-et-un *m*; (*US: billy*) matraque *f.*
blackleg [blak'leg] *n* (*Brit*) briseur *m* de grève, jaune *m.*
blacklist [blak'list] *n* liste noire ♦ *vt* mettre sur la liste noire.
blackmail [blak'māl] *n* chantage *m* ♦ *vt* faire chanter, soumettre au chantage.
blackmailer [blak'mālûr] *n* maître-chanteur *m.*
black market *n* marché noir.
blackout [blak'out] *n* panne *f* d'électricité; (*in wartime*) black-out *m*; (*TV*) interruption *f* d'émission; (*fainting*) syncope *f.*
Black Sea *n*: **the** ~ la mer Noire.
black sheep *n* brebis galeuse.
blacksmith [blak'smith] *n* forgeron *m.*
black spot *n* (*Brit AUT*) point noir.
bladder [blad'ûr] *n* vessie *f.*
blade [blād] *n* lame *f*; (*of oar*) plat *m*; ~ **of grass** brin *m* d'herbe.
blame [blām] *n* faute *f*, blâme *m* ♦ *vt*: **to** ~ **sb/sth for sth** attribuer à qn/qch la responsabilité de qch; reprocher qch à qn/qch; **who's**

to ~? qui est le fautif or coupable or responsable?; **I'm not to ~** ce n'est pas ma faute.

blameless |blām'lis| a irréprochable.

blanch |blanch| vi (person, face) blêmir ♦ vt (CULIN) blanchir.

bland |bland| a affable; (taste) doux(douce), fade.

blank |blangk| a blanc(blanche); (look) sans expression, dénué(e) d'expression ♦ n espace m vide, blanc m; (cartridge) cartouche f à blanc; **we drew a ~** (fig) nous n'avons abouti à rien.

blank check n chèque m en blanc; **to give sb a ~ to do ...** (fig) donner carte blanche à qn pour faire ....

blanket |blang'kit| n couverture f ♦ a (statement, agreement) global(e), de portée générale.

blare |blār| vi (brass band, horns, radio) beugler.

blarney |blár'nē| n boniment m.

blasé |blázā'| a blasé(e).

blasphemous |blas'fəməs| a (words) blasphématoire; (person) blasphémateur(trice).

blasphemy |blas'fəmē| n blasphème m.

blast |blast| n explosion f; (shock wave) souffle m; (of air, steam) bouffée f ♦ vt faire sauter or exploser ♦ excl (Brit col) zut!; **(at) full ~** (play music etc) à plein volume.

blast off vi (SPACE) décoller.

blast-off |blast'ôf| n (SPACE) lancement m.

blatant |blā'tənt| a flagrant(e), criant(e).

blatantly |blā'təntlē| ad (lie) ouvertement; **it's ~ obvious** c'est l'évidence même.

blaze |blāz| n (fire) incendie m; (flames: of fire, sun etc) embrasement m; (: in hearth) flamme f, flambée f; (fig) flamboiement m ♦ vi (fire) flamber; (fig) flamboyer, resplendir ♦ vt: **to ~ a trail** (fig) montrer la voie; **in a ~ of publicity** à grand renfort de publicité.

blazer |blā'zûr| n blazer m.

bleach |blēch| n (also: **household ~**) eau f de Javel ♦ vt (linen) blanchir.

bleached |blēcht| a (hair) oxygéné(e), décoloré(e).

bleachers |blē'chûrz| npl (US SPORT) gradins mpl (en plein soleil).

bleak |blēk| a morne, désolé(e); (weather) triste, maussade; (smile) lugubre; (prospect, future) morose.

bleary-eyed |blē'rēid| a aux yeux pleins de sommeil.

bleat |blēt| n bêlement m ♦ vi bêler.

bleed, pt, pp **bled** |blēd, bled| vt saigner; (brakes, radiator) purger ♦ vi saigner; **my nose is ~ing** je saigne du nez.

bleeper |blē'pûr| n (Brit: of doctor etc) bip m.

blemish |blem'ish| n défaut m; (on reputation) tache f.

blend |blend| n mélange m ♦ vt mélanger ♦ vi (colors etc) se mélanger, se fondre, s'allier.

blender |blen'dûr| n (CULIN) mixeur m.

bless, pt, pp **blessed** or **blest** |bles, blest| vt bénir; **to be ~ed with** avoir le bonheur de jouir de or d'avoir.

blessed |bles'id| a (REL: holy) béni(e); (happy) bienheureux(euse); **it rains every ~ day** il ne se passe pas de jour sans qu'il ne

pleuve.

blessing |bles'ing| n bénédiction f; bienfait m; **to count one's ~s** s'estimer heureux; **it was a ~ in disguise** c'est un bien pour un mal.

blew |bloo| pt of **blow.**

blight |blīt| n (of plants) rouille f ♦ vt (hopes etc) anéantir, briser.

blind |blīnd| a aveugle ♦ n (for window) store m ♦ vt aveugler; **to turn a ~ eye (on or to)** fermer les yeux (sur).

blind alley n impasse f.

blind corner n virage m sans visibilité.

blinders |blīn'dûrz| npl (US) œillères fpl.

blindfold |blīnd'fōld| n bandeau m ♦ a, ad les yeux bandés ♦ vt bander les yeux à.

blindly |blīnd'lē| ad aveuglément.

blindness |blīnd'nis| n cécité f; (fig) aveuglement m.

blind spot n (AUT etc) angle m aveugle; (fig) angle mort.

blink |blingk| vi cligner des yeux; (light) clignoter ♦ n: **the TV's on the ~** (col) la télé ne va pas tarder à nous lâcher.

blinkers |blingk'ûrz| npl (Brit) œillères fpl.

bliss |blis| n félicité f, bonheur m sans mélange.

blissful |blis'fəl| a (event, day) merveilleux(euse); (smile) de bonheur; **a ~ sigh** un soupir d'aise; **in ~ ignorance** dans une ignorance béate.

blissfully |blis'fəlē| ad (smile) béatement; (happy) merveilleusement.

blister |blis'tûr| n (on skin) ampoule f, cloque f; (on paintwork) boursouflure f ♦ vi (paint) se boursoufler, se cloquer.

blithely |blīth'lē| ad (unconcernedly) tranquillement; (joyfully) gaiement.

blithering |blith'ûring| a (col): **this ~ idiot** cet espèce d'idiot.

BLit(t) n abbr (= Bachelor of Literature) diplôme universitaire.

blitz |blits| n bombardement (aérien); **to have a ~ on sth** (fig) s'attaquer à qch.

blizzard |bliz'ûrd| n blizzard m, tempête f de neige.

BLM n abbr (US: = Bureau of Land Management) ≈ les domaines.

bloated |blō'tid| a (face) bouffi(e); (stomach) gonflé(e).

blob |blâb| n (drop) goutte f; (stain, spot) tache f.

bloc |blâk| n (POL) bloc m.

block |blâk| n bloc m; (in pipes) obstruction f; (toy) cube m; (of buildings) pâté m (de maisons) ♦ vt bloquer; (COMPUT) grouper; **~ of flats** (Brit) immeuble (locatif); **3 ~s from here** à trois rues d'ici; **mental ~** blocage m; **~ and tackle** (TECH) palan m.

block up vt boucher.

blockade |blâkād'| n blocus m ♦ vt faire le blocus de.

blockage |blâk'ij| n obstruction f.

block booking n réservation f en bloc.

blockbuster |blâk'bustûr| n (film, book) grand succès.

block capitals npl (Brit) majuscules fpl d'imprimerie.

blockhead |blâk'hed| n imbécile m/f.

block letters npl majuscules fpl.

block release n (*Brit*) congé m de formation.
block vote n (*Brit*) vote m de délégation.
bloke [blōk] n (*Brit col*) type m.
blonde [blånd] a, n blond(e).
blood [blud] n sang m.
bloodcurdling [blud'kûrdling] a à vous glacer le sang.
blood donor n donneur/euse de sang.
blood group n groupe sanguin.
bloodhound [blud'hound] n limier m.
bloodless [blud'lis] a (*victory*) sans effusion de sang; (*pale*) anémié(e).
bloodletting [blud'leting] n (*MED*) saignée f; (*fig*) effusion f de sang, représailles fpl.
blood poisoning n empoisonnement m du sang.
blood pressure n tension (artérielle); **to have high/low** ~ faire de l'hypertension/ l'hypotension.
blood sausage n (*US*) boudin m.
bloodshed [blud'shed] n effusion f de sang, carnage m.
bloodshot [blud'shât] a: ~ **eyes** yeux injectés de sang.
bloodstained [blud'stānd] a taché(e) de sang.
bloodstream [blud'strēm] n sang m, système sanguin.
blood test n analyse f de sang.
bloodthirsty [blud'thûrstē] a sanguinaire.
blood transfusion n transfusion f de sang.
blood vessel n vaisseau sanguin.
bloody [blud'ē] a sanglant(e); (*Brit col!*): **this** ~ ... ce foutu ..., ce putain de ... (!); ~ **strong/good** (*col!*) vachement or sacrément fort/bon.
bloody-minded [blud'ēmīn'did] a (*Brit col*) contrariant(e), obstiné(e).
bloom [blōōm] n fleur f; (*fig*) épanouissement m ♦ vi être en fleur; (*fig*) s'épanouir; être florissant(e).
blossom [blâs'əm] n fleur(s) f(pl) ♦ vi être en fleurs; (*fig*) s'épanouir; **to** ~ **into** (*fig*) devenir.
blot [blât] n tache f ♦ vt tacher; (*ink*) sécher; **to be a** ~ **on the landscape** gâcher le paysage.
  blot out vt (*memories*) effacer; (*view*) cacher, masquer; (*nation, city*) annihiler.
blotchy [blâch'ē] a (*complexion*) couvert(e) de marbrures.
blotter [blât'ûr] n, **blotting paper** [blât'ing pā'pûr] n buvard m.
blouse [blous] n (*feminine garment*) chemisier m, corsage m.
blow [blō] n coup m ♦ vb (*pt* **blew**, *pp* **blown** [blōō, bloun]) vi souffler ♦ vt (*glass*) souffler; (*fuse*) faire sauter; **to** ~ **one's nose** se moucher; **to** ~ **a whistle** siffler; **to come to** ~**s** en venir aux coups.
  blow away vi s'envoler ♦ vt chasser, faire s'envoler.
  blow down vt faire tomber, renverser.
  blow off vi s'envoler ♦ vt (*hat*) emporter; (*ship*): **to** ~ **off course** faire dévier.
  blow out vi (*tire*) éclater; (*fuse*) sauter.
  blow over vi s'apaiser.
  blow up vi exploser, sauter ♦ vt faire sauter; (*tire*) gonfler; (*PHOT*) agrandir.
blow-dry [blō'drī] n (*hairstyle*) brushing m ♦

vt faire un brushing à.
blowfly [blō'flī] n (*US*) mouche f á viande.
blowout [blō'out] n (*of tire*) éclatement m; (*col: big meal*) gueuleton m.
blowtorch [blō'tôrch] n chalumeau m.
BLS n abbr (*US*) = *Bureau of Labor Statistics*.
BLT n abbr = *bacon, lettuce and tomato* (*sandwich*).
blubber [blub'ûr] n blanc m de baleine ♦ vi (*pej*) pleurer comme un veau.
bludgeon [bluj'ən] n gourdin m, trique f.
blue [blōō] a bleu(e); ~ **film/joke** film m/ histoire f pornographique; (**only) once in a** ~ **moon** tous les trente-six du mois; **out of the** ~ (*fig*) à l'improviste, sans qu'on si attende.
blue baby n enfant bleu(e).
bluebell [blōō'bel] n jacinthe f des bois.
blueberry [blōō'bärē] n (*US*) myrtille f.
bluebottle [blōō'bâtəl] n mouche f à viande.
blue cheese n (fromage) bleu m.
blue-chip [blōō'chip] a: ~ **investment** investissement m de premier ordre.
blue-collar worker [blōō'kâl'ûr wûr'kûr] n ouvrier/ère, col bleu.
blue jeans npl blue-jeans mpl.
blueprint [blōō'print] n bleu m; (*fig*) projet m, plan directeur.
blues [blōōz] npl: **the** ~ (*MUS*) le blues; **to have the** ~ (*col: feeling*) avoir le cafard.
bluff [bluf] vi bluffer ♦ n bluff m; (*cliff*) promontoire m, falaise f ♦ a (*person*) bourru(e), brusque; **to call sb's** ~ mettre qn au défi d'exécuter ses menaces.
blunder [blun'dûr] n gaffe f, bévue f ♦ vi faire une gaffe or une bévue; **to** ~ **into sb/sth** buter contre qn/qch.
blunt [blunt] a émoussé(e), peu tranchant(e); (*pencil*) mal taillé(e); (*person*) brusque, ne mâchant pas ses mots ♦ vt émousser; ~ **instrument** (*LAW*) instrument contondant.
bluntly [blunt'lē] ad carrément, sans prendre de gants.
bluntness [blunt'nis] n (*of person*) brusquerie f, franchise brutale.
blur [blûr] n tache or masse floue or confuse ♦ vt brouiller, rendre flou(e).
blurb [blûrb] n (*for book*) texte m de présentation; (*pej*) baratin m.
blurred [blûrd] a flou(e).
blurt [blûrt] : **to** ~ **out** vt (*reveal*) lâcher; (*say*) balbutier, dire d'une voix entrecoupée.
blush [blush] vi rougir ♦ n rougeur f.
blusher [blush'ûr] n rouge m à joues.
bluster [blus'tûr] n paroles fpl en l'air; (*boasting*) fanfaronnades fpl; (*threats*) menaces fpl en l'air ♦ vi parler en l'air; fanfaronner.
blustering [blus'tûring] a fanfaron(ne).
blustery [blus'tûrē] a (*weather*) à bourrasques.
Blvd abbr (= *boulevard*) Bd.
BM n abbr (*SCOL*: = *Bachelor of Medicine*) diplôme universitaire.
BMA n abbr = *British Medical Association*.
BMus n abbr (= *Bachelor of Music*) diplôme universitaire.
BO n abbr (*col*: = *body odor*) odeurs corporelles; (*US*) = **box office**.
boar [bôr] n sanglier m.
board [bôrd] n planche f; (*on wall*) panneau

m; (*for chess etc*) plateau *m*; (*committee*) conseil *m*, comité *m*; (*in firm*) conseil d'administration; (*NAUT, AVIAT*): **on ~ à bord ∮** *vt* (*ship*) monter à bord de; (*train*) monter dans; **full ~** (*Brit*) pension complète; **half ~** (*Brit*) demi-pension *f*; **~ and lodging** *n* chambre *f* avec pension; **with ~ and lodging** logé nourri; **above ~** (*fig*) régulier(ère); **across the ~** (*fig: ad*) systématiquement; (*: a*) de portée générale; **to go by the ~** être abandonné(e); (*be unimportant*) compter pour rien, n'avoir aucune importance.

board up *vt* (*door*) condamner (*au moyen de planches, de tôle*).

boarder [bôr'dûr] *n* pensionnaire *m/f*; (*SCOL*) interne *m/f*, pensionnaire.

board game *n* jeu *m* de société.

boarding house [bôr'ding hous] *n* pension *f*.

boarding pass [bôr'ding pas] *n* (*AVIAT, NAUT*) carte *f* d'embarquement.

boarding school [bôr'ding skool] *n* internat *m*, pensionnat *m*.

board meeting *n* réunion *f* du conseil d'administration.

board room *n* salle *f* du conseil d'administration.

boardwalk [bôrd'wôk] *n* (*US*) cheminement *m* en planches.

boast [bôst] *vi*: **to ~ (about** *or* **of)** se vanter (de) ∮ *vt* s'enorgueillir de ∮ *n* vantardise *f*; sujet *m* d'orgueil *or* de fierté.

boastful [bôst'fəl] *a* vantard(e).

boastfulness [bôst'fəlnis] *n* vantardise *f*.

boat [bôt] *n* bateau *m*; (*small*) canot *m*; barque *f*; **to go by ~** aller en bateau; **to be in the same ~** (*fig*) être logé à la même enseigne.

boater [bô'tûr] *n* (*hat*) canotier *m*.

boating [bô'ting] *n* canotage *m*.

boatswain [bô'sən] *n* maître *m* d'équipage.

bob [bâb] *vi* (*boat, cork on water: also:* **~ up and down**) danser, se balancer ∮ *n* (*Brit col*) = **shilling**.

bob up *vi* surgir *or* apparaître brusquement.

bobbin [bâb'in] *n* bobine *f*; (*of sewing machine*) navette *f*.

bobby [bâb'ē] *n* (*Brit col*) ≈ agent *m* (de police).

bobby pin [bâb'ē pin] *n* pince *f* à cheveux.

bobsled [bâb'sled], (*Brit*) **bobsleigh** [bâb'slā] *n* bob *m*.

bode [bôd] *vi*: **to ~ well/ill (for)** être de bon/mauvais augure (pour).

bodice [bâd'is] *n* corsage *m*.

bodily [bâd'əlē] *a* corporel(le); (*pain, comfort*) physique; (*needs*) matériel(le) ∮ *ad* (*carry, lift*) dans ses bras.

body [bâd'ē] *n* corps *m*; (*of car*) carrosserie *f*; (*of plane*) fuselage *m*; (*fig: society*) organe *m*, organisme *m*; (*: quantity*) ensemble *m*, masse *f*; (*of wine*) corps *m*; (*also:* **~ stocking**) body *m*; **ruling ~** organe directeur; **in a ~** en masse, ensemble; (*speak*) comme un seul et même homme.

body-building [bâd'ēbil'ding] *n* body-building *m*, culturisme *m*.

bodyguard [bâd'ēgârd] *n* garde *m* du corps.

body repairs *npl* travaux *mpl* de carrosserie.

bodywork [bâd'ēwûrk] *n* carrosserie *f*.

boffin [bâf'in] *n* (*Brit*) savant *m*.

bog [bâg] *n* tourbière *f* ∮ *vt*: **to get ~ged down (in)** (*fig*) s'enliser (dans).

boggle [bâg'əl] *vi*: **the mind ~s** c'est incroyable, on en reste sidéré.

bogie [bô'gē] *n* bogie *m*.

Bogotá [bôgətâ'] *n* Bogotá.

bogus [bô'gəs] *a* bidon *inv*; fantôme.

Bohemia [bôhē'mēə] *n* Bohême *f*.

Bohemian [bôhē'mēən] *a* bohémien(ne) ∮ *n* Bohémien/ne; (*gipsy: also:* **b~**) bohémien/ne.

boil [boil] *vt* (faire) bouillir ∮ *vi* bouillir ∮ *n* (*MED*) furoncle *m*; **to come to a** *or* (*Brit*) **the ~** bouillir; **to bring to a** *or* (*Brit*) **the ~** porter à ébullition; **~ed egg** œuf *m* à la coque; **~ed potatoes** pommes *fpl* à l'anglaise *or* à l'eau.

boil down *vi* (*fig*): **to ~ down to** se réduire *or* ramener à.

boil over *vi* déborder.

boiler [boi'lûr] *n* chaudière *f*.

boiler suit *n* (*Brit*) bleu *m* de travail, combinaison *f*.

boiling [boi'ling] *a*: **I'm ~ (hot)** (*col*) je crève de chaud.

boiling point *n* point *m* d'ébullition.

boisterous [bois'tûrəs] *a* bruyant(e), tapageur(euse).

bold [bôld] *a* hardi(e), audacieux(euse); (*pej*) effronté(e); (*outline, color*) franc(franche), tranché(e), marqué(e).

boldness [bôld'nis] *n* hardiesse *f*, audace *f*; aplomb *m*, effronterie *f*.

bold type *n* (*TYP*) caractères *mpl* gras.

Bolivia [bôliv'ēə] *n* Bolivie *f*.

Bolivian [bôliv'ēən] *a* bolivien(ne) ∮ *n* Bolivien/ne.

bollard [bâl'ûrd] *n* (*NAUT*) bitte *f* d'amarrage; (*Brit AUT*) borne lumineuse *or* de signalisation.

bolster [bôl'stûr] *n* traversin *m*.

bolster up *vt* soutenir.

bolt [bôlt] *n* verrou *m*; (*with nut*) boulon *m* ∮ *ad*: **~ upright** droit(e) comme un piquet ∮ *vt* verrouiller; (*food*) engloutir ∮ *vi* se sauver, filer (comme une flèche); **a ~ from the blue** (*fig*) un coup de tonnerre dans un ciel bleu.

bomb [bâm] *n* bombe *f* ∮ *vt* bombarder.

bombard [bâmbârd'] *vt* bombarder.

bombardment [bâmbârd'mənt] *n* bombardement *m*.

bombastic [bâmbas'tik] *a* grandiloquent(e), pompeux(euse).

bomb disposal *n*: **~ unit** section *f* de déminage; **~ expert** artificier *m*.

bomber [bâm'ûr] *n* caporal *m* d'artillerie; (*AVIAT*) bombardier *m*; (*terrorist*) poseur *m* de bombes.

bombing [bâm'ing] *n* bombardement *m*.

bombshell [bâm'shel] *n* obus *m*; (*fig*) bombe *f*.

bomb site *n* zone *f* de bombardement.

bona fide [bô'nə fīd'] *a* de bonne foi; (*offer*) sérieux(euse).

bonanza [bənan'zə] *n* filon *m*.

bond [bând] *n* lien *m*; (*binding promise*) engagement *m*, obligation *f*; (*FINANCE*) obliga-

tion; **in ~** (*of goods*) en entrepôt.
bondage [bân'dij] *n* esclavage *m*.
bonded warehouse [bân'did wär'hous] *n* entrepôt *m* sous douanes.
bone [bōn] *n* os *m*; (*of fish*) arête *f* ♦ *vt* désosser; ôter les arêtes de.
  bone up on *vt* bûcher.
bone china *n* porcelaine *f* tendre.
bone-dry [bōn'drī'] *a* absolument sec(sèche).
bone idle *a* fainéant(e).
boner [bō'nûr] *n* (*US*) gaffe *f*, bourde *f*.
bonfire [bân'fīûr] *n* feu *m* (de joie); (*for garbage*) feu.
Bonn [bân] *n* Bonn.
bonnet [bân'it] *n* bonnet *m*; (*Brit: of car*) capot *m*.
bonny [bân'ē] *a* (*Scottish*) joli(e).
bonus [bō'nəs] *n* prime *f*, gratification *f*; (*on wages*) prime.
bony [bō'nē] *a* (*arm, face,* MED: *tissue*) osseux(euse); (*thin: person*) squelettique; (*meat*) plein(e) d'os; (*fish*) plein d'arêtes.
boo [boō] *excl* hou!, peuh! ♦ *vt* huer ♦ *n* huée *f*.
boob [boōb] *n* (*col: breast*) nichon *m*; (*: Brit: mistake*) gaffe *f*.
boo-boo [boō'boō] *n* gaffe *f*.
booby prize [boō'bē prīz] *n* timbale *f* (ironique).
booby trap [boō'bē trap] *n* guet-apens *m*.
booby-trapped [boō'bētrapt] *a* piégé(e).
book [boōk] *n* livre *m*; (*of stamps etc*) carnet *m*; (COMM): **~s** comptes *mpl*, comptabilité *f* ♦ *vt* (*ticket*) prendre; (*seat, room*) réserver; (*driver*) dresser un procès-verbal à; (*soccer player*) prendre le nom de, donner un carton à; **to keep the ~s** tenir la comptabilité; **by the ~** à la lettre, selon les règles; **to throw the ~ at sb** passer un savon à qn.
  book in *vi* (*Brit: at hotel*) prendre sa chambre.
  book up *vt* réserver; **all seats are ~ed up** tout est pris, c'est complet; **the hotel is ~ed up** l'hôtel est complet.
bookable [boōk'əbəl] *a*: **seats are ~** on peut réserver ses places.
bookcase [boōk'kās] *n* bibliothèque *f* (*meuble*).
book ends *npl* serre-livres *m inv*.
booking [boōk'ing] *n* (*Brit*) réservation *f*.
booking office [boōk'ing ôf'is] *n* (*Brit*) bureau *m* de location.
book-keeping [boōkkē'ping] *n* comptabilité *f*.
booklet [boōk'lit] *n* brochure *f*.
bookmaker [boōk'mākûr] *n* bookmaker *m*.
bookseller [boōk'selûr] *n* libraire *m/f*.
bookshop [boōk'shâp] *n* librairie *f*.
bookstall [boōk'stôl] *n* (*Brit*) kiosque *m* à journaux.
bookstore [boōk'stôr] *n* librairie *f*.
book token *n* (*Brit*) bon-cadeau *m* (pour un livre).
book value *n* valeur *f* comptable.
boom [boōm] *n* (*noise*) grondement *m*; (*busy period*) boom *m*, vague *f* de prospérité ♦ *vi* gronder; prospérer.
boomerang [boō'mərang] *n* boomerang *m*.
boom town *n* ville *f* en plein essor.
boon [boōn] *n* bénédiction *f*, grand avantage.

boorish [boō'rish] *a* grossier(ère), rustre.
boost [boōst] *n* stimulant *m*, remontant *m* ♦ *vt* stimuler; **to give a ~ to sb's spirits** *or* **to sb** remonter le moral à qn.
booster [boōs'tûr] *n* (*TV*) amplificateur *m* (de signal); (ELEC) survolteur *m*; (*also:* **~ rocket**) booster *m*; (MED: *vaccine*) rappel *m*.
booster seat *n* (*Brit* AUT: *for children*) siège *m* rehausseur.
boot [boōt] *n* botte *f*; (*for hiking*) chaussure *f* (de marche); (*for football etc*) soulier *m*; (*ankle ~*) bottine *f*; (US: *also:* **Denver ~**) sabot *m* (de Denver); (*Brit: of car*) coffre *m* ♦ *vt* (COMPUT) lancer, mettre en route; **to ~** (*in addition*) par-dessus le marché, en plus; **to give sb the ~** (*col*) flanquer qn dehors, virer qn.
booth [boōth] *n* (*at fair*) baraque (foraine); (*of cinema, telephone etc*) cabine *f*; (*also:* **voting ~**) isoloir *m*.
bootleg [boōt'leg] *a* de contrebande; **~ record** enregistrement *m* pirate.
bootlicker [boōt'likûr] *n* (*col*) fayot *m*.
booty [boō'tē] *n* butin *m*.
booze [boōz] (*col*) *n* boissons *fpl* alcooliques, alcool *m* ♦ *vi* boire, picoler.
boozer [boōz'ûr] *n* (*col: person*): **he's a ~** il picole pas mal.
border [bôr'dûr] *n* bordure *f*; bord *m*; (*of a country*) frontière *f*.
  border on *vt fus* être voisin(e) de, toucher à.
borderline [bôr'dûrlīn] *n* (*fig*) ligne *f* de démarcation ♦ *a*: **~ case** cas *m* limite.
bore [bôr] *pt of* **bear** ♦ *vt* (*hole*) percer; (*person*) ennuyer, raser ♦ *n* (*person*) raseur/euse; (*of gun*) calibre *m*; **he's ~d to tears** *or* **~d to death** *or* **~d stiff** il s'ennuie à mourir.
boredom [bôr'dəm] *n* ennui *m*.
boring [bôr'ing] *a* ennuyeux(euse).
born [bôrn] *a*: **to be ~** naître; **I was ~ in 1960** je suis né en 1960; **~ blind** aveugle de naissance; **a ~ comedian** un comédien-né.
borne [bôrn] *pp of* **bear**.
Borneo [bôr'nēo] *n* Bornéo *f*.
borough [bur'ə] *n* municipalité *f*.
borrow [bâr'ō] *vt*: **to ~ sth (from sb)** emprunter qch (à qn); **may I ~ your car?** est-ce que je peux vous emprunter votre voiture?
borrower [bâr'ōûr] *n* emprunteur/euse.
borrowing [bâr'ōing] *n* emprunt(s) *m(pl)*.
bosom [boōz'əm] *n* poitrine *f*; (*fig*) sein *m*.
bosom friend *n* ami/e intime.
boss [bôs] *n* patron/ne ♦ *vt* (*also:* **~ around**) mener à la baguette.
bossy [bôs'ē] *a* autoritaire.
bosun [bō'sən] *n* maître *m* d'équipage.
botanical [bətan'ikəl] *a* botanique.
botanist [bât'ənist] *n* botaniste *m/f*.
botany [bât'ənē] *n* botanique *f*.
botch [bâch] *vt* (*also:* **~ up**) saboter, bâcler.
both [bōth] *a* les deux, l'un(e) et l'autre ♦ *pronoun*: **~ (of them)** les deux, tous(toutes) (les) deux, l'un(e) et l'autre; **~ of us went, we ~ went** nous y sommes allés tous les deux ♦ *ad*: **they sell ~ the fabric and the finished curtains** ils vendent (et) le tissu et les rideaux (finis), ils vendent à la fois le

tissu et les rideaux (finis).

bother [báth'ûr] *vt* (*worry*) tracasser; (*needle, bait*) importuner, ennuyer; (*disturb*) déranger ♦ *vi* (*also*: ~ **o.s.**) se tracasser, se faire du souci ♦ *n*: **it is a ~ to have to do** c'est vraiment ennuyeux d'avoir à faire ♦ *excl* zut!; **to ~ doing** prendre la peine de faire; **I'm sorry to ~ you** excusez-moi de vous déranger; **please don't ~** ne vous dérangez pas; **don't ~** ce n'est pas la peine; **it's no ~** aucun problème.

Botswana [bắchwắn'ə] *n* Botswana *m*.

bottle [bắt'əl] *n* bouteille *f*; (*baby's*) biberon *m*; (*of perfume, medicine*) flacon *m* ♦ *vt* mettre en bouteille(s); ~ **of wine/milk** bouteille de vin/lait; **wine/milk ~** bouteille à vin/lait.

bottle up *vt* refouler, contenir.

bottleneck [bắt'əlnɛk] *n* étranglement *m*.

bottle opener *n* ouvre-bouteille *m*.

bottom [bắt'əm] *n* (*of container, sea etc*) fond *m*; (*buttocks*) derrière *m*; (*of page, list*) bas *m*; (*of chair*) siège *m*; (*of mountain, tree, hill*) pied *m* ♦ *a* du fond; du bas; **to get to the ~ of sth** (*fig*) découvrir le fin fond de qch.

bottomless [bắt'əmlis] *a* sans fond, insondable.

bottom line *n* (*fig*): **the ~ is** ... l'essentiel *m* est ....

bough [bou] *n* branche *f*, rameau *m*.

bought [bôt] *pt, pp of* **buy**.

bouillon cube [bool'yən kyōōb] *n* (*US CULIN*) bouillon-cube *m*.

boulder [bōl'dûr] *n* gros rocher (*gén lisse, arrondi*).

bounce [bouns] *vi* (*ball*) rebondir; (*check*) être refusé (*étant sans provision*); (*also*: **to ~ forward/out** *etc*) bondir, s'élancer ♦ *vt* faire rebondir ♦ *n* (*rebound*) rebond *m*; **he's got plenty of ~** (*fig*) il est plein d'entrain *or* d'allant.

bouncer [boun'sûr] *n* (*col*) videur *m*.

bound [bound] *pt, pp of* **bind** ♦ *n* (*gen pl*) limite *f*; (*leap*) bond *m* ♦ *vt* (*leap*) bondir; (*limit*) borner ♦ *a*: **to be ~ to do sth** (*obliged*) être obligé(e) *or* avoir obligation de faire qch; **he's ~ to fail** (*likely*) il est sûr d'échouer, son échec est inévitable *or* assuré; ~ **for** à destination de; **out of ~s** dont l'accès est interdit.

boundary [boun'dûrē] *n* frontière *f*.

boundless [bound'lis] *a* illimité(e), sans bornes.

bountiful [boun'təfəl] *a* (*person*) généreux(euse); (*God*) bienfaiteur(trice); (*supply*) ample.

bounty [boun'tē] *n* (*generosity*) générosité *f*.

bouquet [bōōkā'] *n* bouquet *m*.

bourbon [bûr'bən] *n* (*US: also*: ~ **whiskey**) bourbon *m*.

bourgeois [bōōr'zhwâ] *a, n* bourgeois(e).

bout [bout] *n* période *f*; (*of malaria etc*) accès *m*, crise *f*, attaque *f*; (*BOXING etc*) combat *m*, match *m*.

boutique [bōōtēk'] *n* boutique *f*.

bow *n* [bō] nœud *m*; (*weapon*) arc *m*; (*MUS*) archet *m*; [bou] (*with body*) révérence *f*, inclination *f* (du buste *or* corps); (*NAUT: also*: ~**s**) proue *f* ♦ *vi* [bou] faire une révérence,

s'incliner; (*yield*): **to ~ to** *or* **before** s'incliner devant, se soumettre à; **to ~ to the inevitable** accepter l'inévitable *or* l'inéluctable.

bowels [bou'əlz] *npl* intestins *mpl*; (*fig*) entrailles *fpl*.

bowl [bōl] *n* (*for eating*) bol *m*; (*for washing*) cuvette *f*; (*ball*) boule *f*; (*of pipe*) fourneau *m*; (*US: stadium*) stade *m* ♦ *vi* (*CRICKET*) lancer (la balle).

bowl over *vt* (*fig*) renverser.

bow-legged [bō'lɛgid] *a* aux jambes arquées.

bowler [bō'lûr] *n* joueur *m* de boules; (*CRICKET*) lanceur *m* (de la balle); (*Brit: also*: ~ **hat**) (chapeau *m*) melon *m*.

bowling [bō'ling] *n* (*game*) jeu *m* de boules; jeu de quilles.

bowling alley *n* bowling *m*.

bowling green *n* terrain *m* de boules (*gazonné et carré*).

bowls [bōlz] *n* (jeu *m* de) boules *fpl*.

bow tie [bō tī] *n* nœud *m* papillon.

box [bâks] *n* boîte *f*; (*also*: **cardboard ~**) carton *m*; (*crate*) caisse *f*; (*THEATER*) loge *f*; (*Brit AUT*) intersection *f* (*matérialisée par des marques au sol*) ♦ *vt* mettre en boîte; (*SPORT*) boxer avec ♦ *vi* boxer, faire de la boxe.

boxcar [bâks'kâr] *n* (*RAIL*) wagon couvert.

boxer [bâk'sûr] *n* (*person*) boxeur *m*; (*dog*) boxer *m*.

boxing [bâk'sing] *n* (*sport*) boxe *f*.

Boxing Day *n* (*Brit*) le lendemain de Noël.

boxing gloves *npl* gants *mpl* de boxe.

boxing ring *n* ring *m*.

box number *n* (*Brit: for advertisements*) numéro *m* d'annonce.

box office *n* bureau *m* de location.

boy [boi] *n* garçon *m*.

boycott [boi'kât] *n* boycottage *m* ♦ *vt* boycotter.

boyfriend [boi'frɛnd] *n* (petit) ami.

boyish [boi'ish] *a* d'enfant, de garçon.

Bp *abbr* = **bishop**.

BPOE *n abbr* (*US*: = *Benevolent and Protective Order of Elks*) association charitable.

BR *abbr* = **British Rail**.

bra [brâ] *n* soutien-gorge *m*.

brace [brās] *n* attache *f*, agrafe *f*; (*on teeth*) appareil *m* (dentaire); (*tool*) vilbrequin *m*; (*TYP: also*: *Brit*: ~ **bracket**) accolade *f* ♦ *vt* consolider, soutenir; **to ~ o.s.** (*fig*) se préparer mentalement.

bracelet [brās'lit] *n* bracelet *m*.

braces [brā'siz] *npl* (*on teeth*) appareil *m* (dentaire); (*Brit*) bretelles *fpl*.

bracing [brā'sing] *a* tonifiant(e), tonique.

bracken [brak'ən] *n* fougère *f*.

bracket [brak'it] *n* (*TECH*) tasseau *m*, support *m*; (*group*) classe *f*, tranche *f*; (*also*: *Brit*: **brace ~**) accolade *f*; (*also*: *Brit*: **round ~**) parenthèse *f*; (*also*: **square ~**) crochet *m* ♦ *vt* mettre entre parenthèses; (*fig: also*: ~ **together**) regrouper; **income ~** tranche *f* des revenus; **in ~s** entre parenthèses (*or* crochets).

brackish [brak'ish] *a* (*water*) saumâtre.

brag [brag] *vi* se vanter.

braid [brād] *n* (*trimming*) galon *m*; (*of hair*)

tresse *f*, natte *f*.

Braille [brāl] *n* braille *m*.

brain [brān] *n* cerveau *m*; **~s** *npl* cervelle *f*; he's got **~s** il est intelligent.

brainchild [brān'chīld] *n* trouvaille (personnelle), invention *f*.

brainless [brān'lis] *a* sans cervelle, stupide.

brainstorm [brān'stôrm] *n* (*fig*) moment *m* d'égarement; (*US: brain wave*) idée *f* de génie.

brainwash [brān'wâsh] *vt* faire subir un lavage de cerveau à.

brain wave *n* idée *f* de génie.

brainy [brā'nē] *a* intelligent(e), doué(e).

braise [brāz] *vt* braiser.

brake [brāk] *n* (*on vehicle*) frein *m* ♦ *vt*, *vi* freiner.

brake light *n* feu *m* de stop.

brake pedal *n* pédale *f* de frein.

bramble [bram'bəl] *n* ronces *fpl*; (*fruit*) mûre *f*.

bran [bran] *n* son *m*.

branch [branch] *n* branche *f*; (*COMM*) succursale *f*; (: *bank*) agence *f*; (*of association*) section locale ♦ *vi* bifurquer.

branch out *vi* diversifier ses activités; **to ~ out into** étendre ses activités à.

branch line *n* (*RAIL*) bifurcation *f*, embranchement *m*.

branch manager *n* directeur/trice de succursale (*or* d'agence).

brand [brand] *n* marque (commerciale) ♦ *vt* (*cattle*) marquer (au fer rouge); (*fig: pej*): **to ~ sb a communist** *etc* traiter *or* qualifier qn de communiste *etc*.

brandish [bran'dish] *vt* brandir.

brand name *n* nom *m* de marque.

brand-new [brand'nōō'] *a* tout(e) neuf(neuve), flambant neuf(neuve).

brandy [bran'dē] *n* cognac *m*, fine *f*.

brash [brash] *a* effronté(e).

Brasilia [brəzil'ēə] *n* Brasilia.

brass [bras] *n* cuivre *m* (jaune), laiton *m*; **the ~** (*MUS*) les cuivres.

brass band *n* fanfare *f*.

brassière [brəzēr'] *n* soutien-gorge *m*.

brass knuckles *npl* coup-de-poing américain.

brass tacks *npl*: **to get down to ~** en venir au fait.

brat [brat] *n* (*pej*) mioche *m/f*, môme *m/f*.

bravado [brəvâ'dō] *n* bravade *f*.

brave [brāv] *a* courageux(euse), brave ♦ *n* guerrier indien ♦ *vt* braver, affronter.

bravery [brā'vûrē] *n* bravoure *f*, courage *m*.

bravo [brá'vō] *excl* bravo!

brawl [brôl] *n* rixe *f*, bagarre *f* ♦ *vi* se bagarrer.

brawn [brôn] *n* muscle *m*; (*Brit: meat*) fromage *m* de tête.

brawny [brô'nē] *a* musclé(e), costaud(e).

bray [brā] *n* braiement *m* ♦ *vi* braire.

brazen [brā'zən] *a* impudent(e), effronté(e) ♦ *vt*: **to ~ it out** payer d'effronterie, crâner.

brazier [brā'zhûr] *n* brasero *m*.

Brazil [brəzil'] *n* Brésil *m*.

Brazilian [brəzil'ēən] *a* brésilien(ne) ♦ *n* Brésilien/ne.

Brazil nut *n* noix *f* du Brésil.

breach [brēch] *vt* ouvrir une brèche dans ♦ *n* (*gap*) brèche *f*; (*estrangement*) brouille *f*; (*breaking*): **~ of contract** rupture *f* de contrat; **~ of the peace** attentat *m* à l'ordre public; **~ of trust** abus *m* de confiance.

bread [bred] *n* pain *m*; (*col: money*) fric *m*; **~ and butter** *n* tartines (beurrées); (*fig*) subsistance *f*; **to earn one's daily ~** gagner son pain; **to know which side one's ~ is buttered (on)** savoir où est son avantage *or* intérêt.

breadbin [bred'bin] *n* (*Brit*) boîte *f* or huche *f* à pain.

breadboard [bred'bôrd] *n* planche *f* à pain; (*COMPUT*) montage expérimental.

breadbox [bred'bâks] *n* (*US*) boîte *f* or huche *f* à pain.

breadcrumbs [bred'krumz] *npl* miettes *fpl* de pain; (*CULIN*) chapelure *f*, panure *f*.

breadline [bred'līn] *n*: **to be on the ~** être sans le sou *or* dans l'indigence.

breadth [bredth] *n* largeur *f*.

breadwinner [bred'winûr] *n* soutien *m* de famille.

break [brāk] *vb* (*pt* **broke** [brōk], *pp* **broken** [brō'kən]) *vt* casser, briser; (*promise*) rompre; (*law*) violer ♦ *vi* (se) casser, se briser; (*weather*) tourner ♦ *n* (*gap*) brèche *f*; (*fracture*) cassure *f*; (*rest*) interruption *f*, arrêt *m*; (: *short*) pause *f*; (: *at school*) récréation *f*; (*chance*) chance *f*, occasion *f* favorable; **to ~ one's leg** *etc* se casser la jambe *etc*; **to ~ a record** battre un record; **to ~ the news to sb** annoncer la nouvelle à qn; **to ~ with sb** rompre avec qn; **to ~ even** *vi* rentrer dans ses frais; **to ~ free** *or* **loose** *vi* se dégager, s'échapper; **to take a ~** (*few minutes*) faire une pause, s'arrêter cinq minutes; (*vacation*) prendre un peu de repos; **without a ~** sans interruption, sans arrêt.

break down *vt* (*door etc*) enfoncer; (*resistance*) venir à bout de; (*figures, data*) décomposer, analyser ♦ *vi* s'effondrer; (*MED*) faire une dépression (nerveuse); (*AUT*) tomber en panne.

break in *vt* (*horse etc*) dresser; (*US: car*) roder ♦ *vi* (*burglar*) entrer par effraction.

break into *vt fus* (*house*) s'introduire *or* pénétrer par effraction dans.

break off *vi* (*speaker*) s'interrompre; (*branch*) se rompre ♦ *vt* (*talks, engagement*) rompre.

break open *vt* (*door etc*) forcer, fracturer.

break out *vi* éclater, se déclarer; **to ~ out in spots** se couvrir de boutons.

break through *vi*: **the sun broke through** le soleil a fait son apparition ♦ *vt fus* (*defenses, barrier*) franchir; (*crowd*) se frayer un passage à travers.

break up *vi* (*partnership*) cesser, prendre fin; (*marriage*) se briser; (*friends*) se séparer ♦ *vt* fracasser, casser; (*fight etc*) interrompre, faire cesser; (*marriage*) désunir.

breakable [brā'kəbəl] *a* cassable, fragile ♦ *n*: **~s** objets *mpl* fragiles.

breakage [brā'kij] *n* casse *f*; **to pay for ~s** payer la casse.

breakaway [brā'kəwā] *a* (*group etc*) dissident(e).

breakdown [brāk'doun] n (AUT) panne f; (in communications) rupture f; (MED: also: **nervous** ~) dépression (nerveuse); (of figures) ventilation f, répartition f.

breakdown service n (Brit) service m de dépannage.

breakdown van n (Brit) dépanneuse f.

breaker [brā'kûr] n brisant m.

breakeven [brākē'vən] cpd: ~ **chart** n graphique m de rentabilité; ~ **point** n seuil m de rentabilité.

breakfast [brek'fəst] n petit déjeuner m.

breakfast cereal n céréales fpl.

break-in [brāk'in] n cambriolage m.

breaking point [brā'king point] n limites fpl.

breakthrough [brāk'thrōō] n percée f.

break-up [brāk'up] n (of partnership, marriage) rupture f.

break-up value n (Brit COMM) valeur f de liquidation.

breakwater [brāk'wôtûr] n brise-lames m inv, digue f.

breast [brest] n (of woman) sein m; (chest) poitrine f.

breast-feed [brest'fēd] vt, vi (irg: like **feed**) allaiter.

breast pocket n poche f (de) poitrine.

breaststroke [brest'strōk] n brasse f.

breath [breth] n haleine f, souffle m; **to go out for a ~ of air** sortir prendre l'air; **out of ~** à bout de souffle, essoufflé(e).

Breathalyzer [breth'əlīzûr] n ® alcootest m.

breathe [brēth] vt, vi respirer; **I won't ~ a word about it** je n'en soufflerai pas mot, je n'en dirai rien à personne.

breathe in vi inspirer ♦ vt aspirer.

breathe out vt, vi expirer.

breather [brē'thûr] n moment m de repos or de répit.

breathing [brē'thing] n respiration f.

breathing space n (fig) (moment m de) répit m.

breathless [breth'lis] a essoufflé(e), haletant(e); oppressé(e); ~ **with excitement** le souffle coupé par l'émotion.

breathtaking [breth'tāking] a stupéfiant(e), à vous couper le souffle.

breed [brēd] vb (pt, pp **bred** [bred]) vt élever, faire l'élevage de; (fig: hate, suspicion) engendrer ♦ vi se reproduire ♦ n race f, variété f.

breeder [brē'dûr] n (person) éleveur m; (PHYSICS: also: ~ **reactor**) (réacteur m) surrégénérateur m.

breeding [brē'ding] n reproduction f; élevage m; (upbringing) éducation f.

breeze [brēz] n brise f.

breezeblock [brēz'blâk] n (Brit) parpaing m.

breezy [brē'zē] a frais(fraîche); aéré(e); désinvolte, jovial(e).

Breton [bret'ən] a breton(ne) ♦ n Breton/ne; (LING) breton m.

brevity [brev'itē] n brièveté f.

brew [brōō] vt (tea) faire infuser; (beer) brasser; (plot) tramer, préparer ♦ vi (tea) infuser; (beer) fermenter; (fig) se préparer, couver.

brewer [brōō'ûr] n brasseur m.

brewery [brōō'ûrē] n brasserie f (fabrique).

briar [brī'ûr] n (thorny bush) ronces fpl; (wild rose) églantine f.

bribe [brīb] n pot-de-vin m ♦ vt acheter; soudoyer; **to ~ sb to do sth** soudoyer qn pour qu'il fasse qch.

bribery [brī'bûrē] n corruption f.

bric-a-brac [brik'əbrak] n bric-à-brac m.

brick [brik] n brique f.

bricklayer [brik'lāûr] n maçon m.

brickwork [brik'wûrk] n briquetage m, maçonnerie f.

brickyard [brik'yârd] n briqueterie f.

bridal [brīd'əl] a nuptial(e); ~ **party** noce f.

bride [brīd] n mariée f, épouse f.

bridegroom [brīd'grōōm] n marié m, époux m.

bridesmaid [brīdz'mād] n demoiselle f d'honneur.

bridge [brij] n pont m; (NAUT) passerelle f (de commandement); (of nose) arête f; (CARDS, DENTISTRY) bridge m ♦ vt (river) construire un pont sur; (gap) combler.

bridge loan, (Brit) **bridging loan** [brij'ing lōn] n prêt m relais.

bridle [brīd'əl] n bride f ♦ vt refréner, mettre la bride à; (horse) brider.

bridle path n piste or allée cavalière.

brief [brēf] a bref(brève) ♦ n (LAW) dossier m; cause f ♦ vt (MIL etc) donner des instructions à; **in ~ ...** (en) bref ...; **to ~ sb (about sth)** mettre qn au courant (de qch).

briefcase [brēf'kās] n serviette f; porte-documents m inv.

briefing [brē'fing] n instructions fpl.

briefly [brēf'lē] ad brièvement; (visit) en coup de vent; **to glimpse ~** entrevoir.

briefness [brēf'nis] n brièveté f.

briefs [brēfs] npl slip m.

Brig. abbr = **brigadier**.

brigade [brigād'] n (MIL) brigade f.

brigadier [brigədi'ûr] n brigadier général.

bright [brīt] a brillant(e); (room, weather) clair(e); (person) intelligent(e), doué(e); (color) vif(vive); **to look on the ~ side** regarder le bon côté des choses.

brighten [brīt'ən] (also: ~ **up**) vt (room) éclaircir; égayer ♦ vi s'éclaircir; (person) retrouver un peu de sa gaieté.

brightly [brīt'lē] ad brillamment.

brilliance [bril'yəns] n éclat m; (fig: of person) brio m.

brilliant [bril'yənt] a brillant(e).

brim [brim] n bord m.

brimful [brim'fōōl'] a plein(e) à ras bord; (fig) débordant(e).

brine [brīn] n eau salée; (CULIN) saumure f.

bring [bring], pt, pp **brought** [brôt] vt (thing) apporter; (person) amener; **to ~ sth to an end** mettre fin à qch; **I can't ~ myself to fire him** je ne peux me résoudre à le mettre à la porte.

bring about vt provoquer, entraîner.

bring around vt (US: unconscious person) ranimer.

bring back vt rapporter; (person) ramener.

bring down vt (lower) abaisser; (shoot down) abattre; (government) faire s'effondrer.

bring forward vt avancer; (BOOK-

KEEPING) reporter.

bring in *vt* (*person*) faire entrer; (*object*) rentrer; (*POL*: *legislation*) introduire; (*LAW*: *verdict*) rendre; (*produce*: *income*) rapporter.

bring off *vt* (*task, plan*) réussir, mener à bien; (*deal*) mener à bien.

bring out *vt* (*meaning*) faire ressortir, mettre en relief; (*new product, book*) sortir.

bring round, bring to *vt* (*Brit*) = **bring around.**

bring up *vt* élever; (*question*) soulever; (*food: vomit*) vomir, rendre.

brink [bringk] *n* bord *m*; **on the ~ of doing** sur le point de faire, à deux doigts de faire; **she was on the ~ of tears** elle était au bord des larmes.

brisk [brisk] *a* vif(vive); (*abrupt*) brusque; (*trade etc*) actif(ive); **to go for a ~ walk** se promener d'un bon pas; **business is ~** les affaires marchent (bien).

bristle [bris'əl] *n* poil *m* ♦ *vi* se hérisser; **bristling with** hérissé(e) de.

bristly [bris'lē] *a* (*beard, hair*) hérissé(e); **your chin's all ~** ton menton gratte.

Brit [brit] *n abbr* (*col*: = *British person*) Britannique *m/f*.

Britain [brit'in] *n* (*also*: **Great ~**) la Grande-Bretagne; **in ~** en Grande-Bretagne.

British [brit'ish] *a* britannique; **the ~** *npl* les Britanniques *mpl*; **the ~ Isles** les îles *fpl* Britanniques.

British Rail (BR) *n compagnie ferroviaire britannique*, ≈ SNCF *f*.

Briton [brit'ən] *n* Britannique *m/f*.

Brittany [brit'ənē] *n* Bretagne *f*.

brittle [brit'əl] *a* cassant(e), fragile.

Br(o). *abbr* (*REL*) = **brother.**

broach [brōch] *vt* (*subject*) aborder.

broad [brôd] *a* large; (*distinction*) général(e); (*accent*) prononcé(e) ♦ *n* (*US col*) nana *f*; **~ hint** allusion transparente; **in ~ daylight** en plein jour; **the ~ outlines** les grandes lignes.

broad bean *n* fève *f*.

broadcast [brôd'kast] *n* émission *f* ♦ *vb* (*pt, pp* **broadcast**) *vt* radiodiffuser; téléviser ♦ *vi* émettre.

broadcasting [brôd'kasting] *n* radiodiffusion *f*; télévision *f*.

broadcasting station *n* station *f* de radio (*or* de télévision).

broaden [brôd'ən] *vt* élargir ♦ *vi* s'élargir.

broadly [brôd'lē] *ad* en gros, généralement.

broad-minded [brôd'mīn'did] *a* large d'esprit.

broccoli [brāk'əlē] *n* brocoli *m*.

brochure [brōshōōr'] *n* prospectus *m*, dépliant *m*.

brogue [brōg] *n* (*accent*) accent régional; (*shoe*) (*sorte de*) chaussure basse de cuir épais.

broil [broil] *vt* griller.

broiler [broi'lûr] *n* (*fowl*) poulet *m* (à rôtir).

broke [brōk] *pt of* **break** ♦ *a* (*col*) fauché(e); **to go ~** (*business*) faire faillite.

broken [brō'kən] *pp of* **break** ♦ *a* (*stick, leg etc*) cassé(e); (*promise, vow*) rompu(e); **a ~ marriage** un couple dissocié; **a ~ home** un foyer désuni; **in ~ French/English** dans un français/anglais approximatif *or* hésitant.

broken-down [brō'kəndoun'] *a* (*car*) en panne; (*machine*) fichu(e); (*house*) en ruines.

brokenhearted [brō'kənhâr'tid] *a* (ayant) le cœur brisé.

broker [brō'kûr] *n* courtier *m*.

brokerage [brō'kûrij] *n* courtage *m*; (*US: payment*) commission *f*.

brolly [brál'ē] *n* (*Brit col*) pépin *m*, parapluie *m*.

bronchitis [brāngkī'tis] *n* bronchite *f*.

bronze [brânz] *n* bronze *m*.

bronzed [brânzd] *a* bronzé(e), hâlé(e).

brooch [brōch] *n* broche *f*.

brood [brōōd] *n* couvée *f* ♦ *vi* (*hen, storm*) couver; (*person*) méditer (sombrement), ruminer.

broody [brōō'dē] *a* (*fig*) taciturne, mélancolique.

brook [brōōk] *n* ruisseau *m*.

broom [brōōm] *n* balai *m*.

broomstick [brōōm'stik] *n* manche *m* à balai.

Bros. *abbr* (*COMM*: = *brothers*) Frères.

broth [brôth] *n* bouillon *m* de viande et de légumes.

brothel [brāth'əl] *n* maison close, bordel *m*.

brother [bruth'ûr] *n* frère *m*.

brotherhood [bruth'ûrhōōd] *n* fraternité *f*.

brother-in-law [bruth'ûrinlô] *n* beau-frère *m*.

brotherly [bruth'ûrlē] *a* fraternel(le).

brought [brôt] *pt, pp of* **bring.**

brow [brou] *n* front *m*; (*rare: gen:* **eye~**) sourcil *m*; (*of hill*) sommet *m*.

browbeat [brou'bēt] *vt* intimider, brusquer.

brown [broun] *a* brun(e), marron *inv*; (*hair*) châtain *inv*; (*rice, bread, flour*) complet(ète) ♦ *n* (*color*) brun *m*, marron *m* ♦ *vt* brunir; (*CULIN*) faire dorer, faire roussir; **to go ~** (*person*) bronzer; (*leaves*) jaunir.

brownie [brou'nē] *n* jeannette *f*, éclaireuse (cadette); (*US: cake*) gâteau au chocolat et aux noix.

brownnose(r) [broun'nōz(ûr)] *n* (*US col*) fayot *m*.

brown paper *n* papier *m* d'emballage, papier kraft.

brown sugar *n* cassonade *f*.

browse [brouz] *vi* (*among books*) bouquiner, feuilleter les livres; (*animal*) paître; **to ~ through a book** feuilleter un livre.

bruise [brōōz] *n* bleu *m*, ecchymose *f*, contusion *f* ♦ *vt* contusionner, meurtrir ♦ *vi* (*fruit*) se taler, se meurtrir; **to ~ one's arm** se faire un bleu au bras.

brunch [brunch] *n* brunch *m*.

brunette [brōōnet'] *n* (*femme*) brune.

brunt [brunt] *n*: **the ~ of** (*attack, criticism etc*) le plus gros de.

brush [brush] *n* brosse *f*; (*quarrel*) accrochage *m*, prise *f* de bec ♦ *vt* brosser; (*also*: **~ past, ~ against**) effleurer, frôler; **to have a ~ with sb** s'accrocher avec qn; **to have a ~ with the police** avoir maille à partir avec la police.

brush aside *vt* écarter, balayer.

brush up *vt* (*knowledge*) rafraîchir, réviser.

brushed [brusht] *a* (*TECH*: *steel, chrome etc*) brossé(e); (*nylon, denim etc*) gratté(e).

brush-off [brush'ôf] *n* (*col*): **to give sb the ~** envoyer qn promener.

brushwood [brush'wʊd] *n* broussailles *fpl*, taillis *m*.

brusque [brusk] *a* (*person, manner*) brusque, cassant(e); (*tone*) sec(sèche), cassant(e).

Brussels [brus'əlz] *n* Bruxelles.

Brussels sprout *n* chou *m* de Bruxelles.

brutal [brōōt'əl] *a* brutal(e).

brutality [brōōtal'itē] *n* brutalité *f*.

brute [brōōt] *n* brute *f* ♦ *a*: **by ~ force** par la force.

brutish [brōō'tish] *a* grossier(ère), brutal(e).

BS *n abbr* (*US*: = *Bachelor of Science*) diplôme universitaire.

bs *abbr* = **bill of sale.**

BSc *n abbr* = **Bachelor of Science.**

BSI *n abbr* (= *British Standards Institution*) association de normalisation.

BST *abbr* (= *British Summer Time*) heure *f* d'été.

btu *n abbr* (= *British thermal unit*) btu (= 1054,2 *joules*).

bubble [bub'əl] *n* bulle *f* ♦ *vi* bouillonner, faire des bulles; (*sparkle, fig*) pétiller.

bubble bath *n* bain moussant.

Bucharest [bōō'kərest] *n* Bucarest.

buck [buk] *n* mâle *m* (*d'un lapin, lièvre, daim etc*); (*US col*) dollar *m* ♦ *vi* ruer, lancer une ruade; **to pass the ~ (to sb)** se décharger de la responsabilité (sur qn).

buck up *vi* (*cheer up*) reprendre du poil de la bête, se remonter ♦ *vt*: **to ~ one's ideas up** se reprendre.

bucket [buk'it] *n* seau *m*.

buckle [buk'əl] *n* boucle *f* ♦ *vt* boucler, attacher; (*warp*) tordre, gauchir; (: *wheel*) voiler.

buckle down *vi* s'y mettre.

buckle up *vi* (*AUT*) attacher sa ceinture.

Bucks *abbr* (*Brit*) = **Buckinghamshire.**

bud [bud] *n* bourgeon *m*; (*of flower*) bouton *m* ♦ *vi* bourgeonner; (*flower*) éclore.

Budapest [bōō'dəpest] *n* Budapest.

Buddha [bōō'də] *n* Bouddha *m*.

Buddhism [bōō'dizəm] *n* bouddhisme *m*.

Buddhist [bōō'dist] *a* bouddhiste ♦ *n* Bouddhiste *m/f*.

budding [bud'ing] *a* (*flower*) en bouton; (*poet etc*) en herbe; (*passion etc*) naissant(e).

buddy [bud'ē] *n* (*US*) copain *m*.

budge [buj] *vt* faire bouger ♦ *vi* bouger.

budgerigar [buj'ûrēgâr] *n* perruche *f*.

budget [buj'it] *n* budget *m* ♦ *vi*: **to ~ for sth** inscrire qch au budget; **I'm on a tight ~** je dois faire attention à mon budget.

budgie [buj'ē] *n* = **budgerigar.**

Buenos Aires [bwā'nəs ī'riz] *n* Buenos Aires.

buff [buf] *a* (*couleur f*) chamois *m* ♦ *n* (*enthusiast*) mordu(e).

buffalo, *pl* ~ *or* ~**es** [buf'əlō] *n* buffle *m*; (*US*) bison *m*.

buffer [buf'ûr] *n* tampon *m*; (*COMPUT*) mémoire *f* tampon.

buffering [buf'ûring] *n* (*COMPUT*) mise *f* en mémoire tampon.

buffer state *n* état *m* tampon.

buffet *n* [bōōfā'] (*food, Brit*: *bar*) buffet *m* ♦ *vt* [buf'it] gifler, frapper; secouer, ébranler.

buffet car [bōōfā' kâr] *n* (*Brit RAIL*) voiture-bar *f*.

buffet lunch [bōōfā' lunch] *n* lunch *m*.

buffoon [bufōōn'] *n* buffon *m*, pitre *m*.

bug [bug] *n* (*insect*) punaise *f*; (: *gen*) insecte *m*, bestiole *f*; (*fig*: *germ*) virus *m*, microbe *m*; (*spy device*) dispositif *m* d'écoute (électronique), micro clandestin; (*COMPUT*: *of program*) erreur *f*; (: *of equipment*) défaut *m* ♦ *vt* (*room*) poser des micros dans; (*col*: *annoy*) embêter; **I've got the travel ~** (*fig*) j'ai le virus du voyage.

bugbear [bug'bär] *n* cauchemar *m*, bête noire.

bugle [byōō'gəl] *n* clairon *m*.

build [bild] *n* (*of person*) carrure *f*, charpente *f* ♦ *vt* (*pt, pp* **built** [bilt]) construire, bâtir.

build on *vt fus* (*fig*) tirer parti de, partir de.

build up *vt* accumuler, amasser; (*business*) développer; (*reputation*) bâtir; (*increase*: *production*) développer, accroître.

builder [bil'dûr] *n* entrepreneur *m*.

building [bil'ding] *n* construction *f*; (*structure*) bâtiment *m*, construction; (: *residential, offices*) immeuble *m*.

building contractor *n* entrepreneur *m* (en bâtiment).

building industry *n* (industrie *f* du) bâtiment *m*.

building site *n* chantier *m* (de construction).

building society *n* (*Brit*) société *f* de crédit immobilier.

building trade *n* = **building industry.**

build-up [bild'up] *n* (*of gas etc*) accumulation *f*; (*publicity*): **to give sb/sth a good ~** faire de la pub pour qn/qch.

built [bilt] *pt, pp of* **build.**

built-in [bilt'in'] *a* (*closet*) encastré(e); (*device*) incorporé(e); intégré(e).

built-up area [bilt'up är'ēə] *n* agglomération (urbaine); zone urbanisée.

bulb [bulb] *n* (*BOT*) bulbe *m*, oignon *m*; (*ELEC*) ampoule *f*.

bulbous [bul'bəs] *a* bulbeux(euse).

Bulgaria [bulgär'ēə] *n* Bulgarie *f*.

Bulgarian [bulgär'ēən] *a* bulgare ♦ *n* Bulgare *m/f*; (*LING*) bulgare *m*.

bulge [bulj] *n* renflement *m*, gonflement *m*; (*in birth rate, sales*) brusque augmentation *f* ♦ *vi* faire saillie; présenter un renflement; **to be bulging with** être plein(e) à craquer de.

bulk [bulk] *n* masse *f*, volume *m*; **in ~** (*COMM*) en gros, en vrac; **the ~ of** la plus grande *or* grosse partie de.

bulk buying [bulk bī'ing] *n* achat *m* en gros.

bulkhead [bulk'hed] *n* cloison *f* (étanche).

bulky [bul'kē] *a* volumineux(euse), encombrant(e).

bull [bʊl] *n* taureau *m*; (*STOCK EXCHANGE*) haussier *m*; (*REL*) bulle *f*.

bulldog [bʊl'dôg] *n* bouledogue *m*.

bulldoze [bʊl'dōz] *vt* passer *or* raser au bulldozer; **I was ~d into doing it** (*fig col*) on m'a forcé la main.

bulldozer [bʊl'dōzûr] *n* bulldozer *m*.

bullet [bʊl'it] *n* balle *f* (*de fusil etc*).

bulletin [bʊl'itən] *n* bulletin *m*, communiqué *m*.

bulletin board *n* panneau *m* d'affichage;

(*COMPUT*) messagerie *f* (électronique).

bulletproof [bool'itproof] *a* à l'épreuve des balles; ~ **vest** gilet *m* pare-balles.

bullfight [bool'fīt] *n* corrida *f*, course *f* de taureaux.

bullfighter [bool'fītûr] *n* torero *m*.

bullfighting [bool'fīting] *n* tauromachie *f*.

bullhorn [bool'hôrn] *n* (*US*) porte-voix *m inv*.

bullion [bool'yən] *n* or *m* or argent *m* en lingots.

bullock [bool'ək] *n* bœuf *m*.

bullring [bool'ring] *n* arène *f*.

bull's-eye [boolz'ī] *n* centre *m* (*de la cible*).

bully [bool'ē] *n* brute *f*, tyran *m* ♦ *vt* tyranniser, rudoyer; (*frighten*) intimider.

bullying [bool'ēing] *n* brimades *fpl*.

bum [bum] *n* (*col*: *backside*) derrière *m*; (: *tramp*) vagabond/e, traîne-savates *m/f inv*; (: *idler*) glandeur *m*.

bum around *vi* (*col*) vagabonder.

bumblebee [bum'bəlbē] *n* bourdon *m*.

bumf [bumf] *n* (*Brit col*: *forms etc*) paperasses *fpl*.

bump [bump] *n* (*blow*) coup *m*, choc *m*; (*jolt*) cahot *m*; (*on road etc, on head*) bosse *f* ♦ *vt* heurter, cogner; (*car*) emboutir.

bump along *vi* avancer en cahotant.

bump into *vt fus* rentrer dans, tamponner; (*col*: *meet*) tomber sur.

bumper [bum'pûr] *n* pare-chocs *m inv* ♦ *a*: ~ **crop/harvest** récolte/moisson exceptionnelle.

bumper cars *npl* autos tamponneuses.

bumptious [bump'shəs] *a* suffisant(e), prétentieux(euse).

bumpy [bum'pē] *a* cahoteux(euse); **it was a ~ flight/ride** on a été secoués dans l'avion/la voiture.

bun [bun] *n* petit pain au lait; (*of hair*) chignon *m*.

bunch [bunch] *n* (*of flowers*) bouquet *m*; (*of keys*) trousseau *m*; (*of bananas*) régime *m*; (*of people*) groupe *m*; ~ **of grapes** grappe *f* de raisin.

bundle [bun'dəl] *n* paquet *m* ♦ *vt* (*also*: ~ **up**) faire un paquet de; (*put*): **to** ~ **sth/sb into** fourrer *or* enfourner qch/qn dans.

bundle off *vt* (*person*) faire sortir (en toute hâte); expédier.

bundle out *vt* éjecter, sortir (sans ménagements).

bung [bung] *n* bonde *f*, bouchon *m* ♦ *vt* (*Brit*: *throw*: *also*: ~ **into**) flanquer; (*also*: ~ **up**: *pipe, hole*) boucher.

bungalow [bung'gəlō] *n* bungalow *m*.

bungle [bung'gəl] *vt* bâcler, gâcher.

bunion [bun'yən] *n* oignon *m* (*au pied*).

bunk [bungk] *n* couchette *f*.

bunk beds *npl* lits superposés.

bunker [bung'kûr] *n* (*coal store*) soute *f* à charbon; (*MIL, GOLF*) bunker *m*.

bunny [bun'ē] *n* (*also*: ~ **rabbit**) Jeannot *m* lapin.

bunny girl *n* hôtesse de cabaret.

bunny hill *n* (*US SKI*) piste *f* pour débutants.

bunting [bun'ting] *n* pavoisement *m*, drapeaux *mpl*.

buoy [boo'ē] *n* bouée *f*.

buoy up *vt* faire flotter; (*fig*) soutenir, épauler.

buoyancy [boi'ənsē] *n* (*of ship*) flottabilité *f*.

buoyant [boi'ənt] *a* (*ship*) flottable; (*carefree*) gai(e), plein(e) d'entrain; (*COMM*: *market*) actif(ive); (: *prices, currency*) soutenu(e).

burden [bûr'dən] *n* fardeau *m*, charge *f* ♦ *vt* charger; (*oppress*) accabler, surcharger; **to be a ~ to sb** être un fardeau pour qn.

bureau, *pl* ~**x** [byoor'ō, z] *n* (*US*: *chest of drawers*) commode *f*; (*Brit*: *writing desk*) bureau *m*, secrétaire *m*; (*office*) bureau, office *m*.

bureaucracy [byoorák'rəsē] *n* bureaucratie *f*.

bureaucrat [byoor'əkrat] *n* bureaucrate *m/f*, rond-de-cuir *m*.

bureaucratic [byoorəkrat'ik] *a* bureaucratique.

burgeon [bûr'jən] *vi* (*fig*) être en expansion rapide.

burglar [bûr'glûr] *n* cambrioleur *m*.

burglar alarm *n* sonnerie *f* d'alarme.

burglarize [bûr'glərīz] *vt* (*US*) cambrioler.

burglary [bûr'glûrē] *n* cambriolage *m*.

burgle [bûr'gəl] *vt* cambrioler.

Burgundy [bûr'gəndē] *n* Bourgogne *f*.

burial [bär'ēəl] *n* enterrement *m*.

burial ground *n* cimetière *m*.

burlesque [bûrlesk'] *n* caricature *f*, parodie *f*.

burly [bûr'lē] *a* de forte carrure, costaud(e).

Burma [bûr'mə] *n* Birmanie *f*.

Burmese [bûrmēz'] *a* birman(e), de Birmanie ♦ *n* (*pl inv*) Birman/e; (*LING*) birman *m*.

burn [bûrn] *vt*, *vi* (*pt*, *pp* **burned** *or* **burnt** [bûrnt]) brûler ♦ *n* brûlure *f*; **the cigarette ~ed a hole in her dress** la cigarette a fait un trou dans sa robe; **I've ~ed myself!** je me suis brûlé(e)!

burn down *vt* incendier, détruire par le feu.

burn out *vt* (*subj*: *writer etc*): **to** ~ **o.s. out** s'user (à force de travailler).

burner [bûr'nûr] *n* brûleur *m*.

burning [bûr'ning] *a* (*building, forest*) en flammes; (*issue, question*) brûlant(e).

burnish [bûr'nish] *vt* polir.

burnt [bûrnt] *pt*, *pp of* **burn**.

burp [bûrp] (*col*) *n* rot *m* ♦ *vi* roter.

burrow [bûr'ō] *n* terrier *m* ♦ *vt* creuser.

bursar [bûr'sûr] *n* économe *m/f*; (*Brit*: *student*) boursier/ère.

bursary [bûr'sûrē] *n* (*Brit*) bourse *f* (d'études).

burst [bûrst] *vb* (*pt*, *pp* **burst**) *vt* faire éclater ♦ *vi* éclater ♦ *n* explosion *f*; (*also*: ~ **pipe**) fuite *f* (*due à une rupture*); ~ **of energy** déploiement soudain d'énergie, activité soudaine; ~ **of laughter** éclat *m* de rire; **a ~ of applause** une salve d'applaudissement; **a ~ of speed** une pointe de vitesse; ~ **blood vessel** rupture *f* de vaisseau sanguin; **the river has ~ its banks** le cours d'eau est sorti de son lit; **to ~ into flames** s'enflammer soudainement; **to ~ out laughing** éclater de rire; **to ~ into tears** fondre en larmes; **to ~ open** *vi* s'ouvrir violemment *or* soudainement; **to be ~ing with** être plein(e) (à craquer) de; regorger de.

burst into *vt fus* (*room etc*) faire irruption dans.

burst out of *vt fus* sortir précipitamment de.

bury [bär'ē] *vt* enterrer; **to ~ one's face in**

one's hands se couvrir le visage de ses mains; **to ~ one's head in the sand** (fig) pratiquer la politique de l'autruche; **to ~ the hatchet** (fig) enterrer la hache de guerre.

bus, ~**es** [bus] n autobus m; autocar m.

bush [bŏŏsh] n buisson m; (scrub land) brousse f.

bushel [bŏŏsh'əl] n boisseau m.

bushy [bŏŏsh'ē] a broussailleux(euse), touffu(e).

busily [biz'ilē] ad: **to be ~ doing sth** s'affairer à faire qch.

business [biz'nis] n (matter, firm) affaire f; (trading) affaires fpl; (job, duty) travail m; **to be away on ~** être en déplacement d'affaires; **I'm here on ~** je suis là pour affaires; **he's in the insurance/transport ~** il est dans les assurances/les transports; **to do ~ with sb** traiter avec qn; **it's none of my ~** cela ne me regarde pas, ce ne sont pas mes affaires; **he means ~** il ne plaisante pas, il est sérieux.

business address n adresse professionnelle or au bureau.

business card n carte f de visite (professionnelle).

business corporation n (US) ≈ société f anonyme (SA) (cotée en bourse).

business hours npl heures fpl ouvrables.

businesslike [biz'nislīk] a sérieux(euse); efficace.

businessman [biz'nisman] n homme m d'affaires.

business school n école f de commerce.

business suit n complet m.

business trip n voyage m d'affaires.

businesswoman [biz'niswŏŏmən] n femme f d'affaires.

busker [bus'kûr] n (Brit) artiste ambulant(e).

bus lane n voie réservée aux autobus.

bus shelter n abribus m.

bus station n gare routière.

bus stop n arrêt m d'autobus.

bust [bust] n buste m ♦ a (col: broken) fichu(e), fini(e) ♦ vt (col: POLICE: arrest) pincer; **to go ~** faire faillite.

bustle [bus'əl] n remue-ménage m, affairement m ♦ vi s'affairer, se démener.

bustling [bus'ling] a (person) affairé(e); (town) très animé(e).

bust-up [bust'up] n (Brit col) engueulade f.

busy [biz'ē] a occupé(e); (store, street) très fréquenté(e); (US: telephone, line) occupé ♦ vt: **to ~ o.s.** s'occuper; **he's a ~ man** (normally) c'est un homme très pris; (temporarily) il est très pris.

busybody [biz'ēbádē] n mouche f du coche, âme f charitable.

busy signal n (US) tonalité f occupé.

but [but] cj mais ♦ prep excepté, sauf; **nothing ~** rien d'autre que; **~ for** sans, si ce n'était pour; **no one ~ him** lui seul; **all ~ finished** pratiquement fini; **anything ~ finished** tout sauf fini, très loin d'être fini.

butane [byŏŏ'tãn] n (also: ~ **gas**) butane m.

butcher [bŏŏch'ûr] n boucher m ♦ vt massacrer; (cattle etc for meat) tuer; ~**'s (shop)** boucherie f.

butler [but'lûr] n maître m d'hôtel.

butt [but] n (cask) gros tonneau; (thick end) (gros) bout; (of gun) crosse f; (of cigarette) mégot m; (US col) derrière m; (Brit fig: target) cible f ♦ vt donner un coup de tête à.

butt in vi (interrupt) interrompre.

butter [but'ûr] n beurre m ♦ vt beurrer.

buttercup [but'ûrkup] n bouton m d'or.

butter dish n beurrier m.

butterfingers [but'ûrfinggûrz] n (col) maladroit/e.

butterfly [but'ûrflī] n papillon m; (SWIMMING: also: ~ **stroke**) brasse f papillon.

buttocks [but'əks] npl fesses fpl.

button [but'ən] n bouton m ♦ vt (also: ~ **up**) boutonner ♦ vi se boutonner.

buttonhole [but'ənhōl] n boutonnière f ♦ vt accrocher, arrêter, retenir.

buttress [but'tris] n contrefort m.

buxom [buk'səm] a aux formes avantageuses or épanouies, bien galbé(e).

buy [bī] vb (pt, pp **bought** [bôt]) vt acheter; (COMM: company) (r)acheter ♦ n: **that was a good/bad ~** c'était un bon/mauvais achat; **to ~ sb sth/sth from sb** acheter qch à qn; **to ~ sb a drink** offrir un verre or à boire à qn.

buy back vt racheter.

buy in vt (Brit: goods) acheter, faire venir.

buy into vt fus (COMM) acheter des actions de.

buy off vt (bribe) acheter.

buy out vt (partner) désintéresser; (business) racheter.

buy up vt acheter en bloc, rafler.

buyer [bī'ûr] n acheteur/euse; ~**'s market** marché m favorable aux acheteurs.

buzz [buz] n bourdonnement m; (col: phone call) coup m de fil ♦ vi bourdonner ♦ vt (call on intercom) appeler; (with buzzer) sonner; (AVIAT: plane, building) raser; **my head is** ~**ing** j'ai la tête qui bourdonne.

buzz off vi (col) s'en aller, ficher le camp.

buzzard [buz'ûrd] n buse f.

buzzer [buz'ûr] n timbre m électrique.

buzz word n (col) mot m à la mode or dans le vent.

by [bī] prep par; (beside) à côté de; au bord de; (before): ~ **4 o'clock** avant 4 heures, d'ici 4 heures; ~ **this time tomorrow** demain à la même heure ♦ ad see **pass, go** etc; **a picture ~ Picasso** un tableau de Picasso; **surrounded ~ enemies** entouré d'ennemis; ~ **bus/car** en autobus/voiture; **paid ~ the hour** payé à l'heure; **to increase** etc ~ **the hour** augmenter etc d'heure en heure; ~ **the kilo/meter** au kilo/mètre; **to pay ~ check** payer par chèque; ~ **a room 3 meters ~ 4** une pièce de 3 mètres sur 4; **the bullet missed him ~ inches** la balle est passée à quelques centimètres de lui; ~ **saving hard, he ... à** force d'économiser, il ...; **(all)** ~ **oneself** tout(e) seul(e); ~ **the way** à propos; ~ **and large** dans l'ensemble; ~ **and ~** bientôt.

bye(-bye) [bī'(bī')] excl au revoir!, salut!

by(e)-law [bī'lô] n arrêté municipal.

by-election [bī'ilekshən] n élection (législative) partielle.

bygone [bī'gôn] a passé(e) ♦ n: **let ~s be ~s** passons l'éponge, oublions le passé.

bypass [bī'pas] *n* (route *f* de) contournement *m*; (*MED*) pontage *m* ♦ *vt* éviter.

by-product [bī'prådəkt] *n* sous-produit *m*, dérivé *m*; (*fig*) conséquence *f* secondaire, retombée *f*.

bystander [bī'standûr] *n* spectateur/trice, badaud/e.

byte [bīt] *n* (*COMPUT*) octet *m*.

byway [bī'wā] *n* chemin détourné.

byword [bī'wûrd] *n*: **to be a ~ for** être synonyme de (*fig*).

by-your-leave [bīyōōrlēv'] *n*: **without so much as a ~** sans même demander la permission.

C

C, c [sē] *n* (*letter*) C, c *m*; (*SCOL*: *grade*) C; (*MUS*): **C do** *m*; **C for Charlie** C comme Célestin.

C *abbr* (= *Celsius, centigrade*) C.

c [sē] *abbr* (= *century*) s.; (= *circa*) v.; (*US etc*) = **cent(s)**.

CA *n abbr* = *Central America*; = **chartered accountant** ♦ *abbr* (*US MAIL*) = *California*.

ca. *abbr* (= *circa*) v.

c/a *abbr* = **capital account, credit account, current account.**

CAA *n abbr* (*Brit*: = *Civil Aviation Authority*) direction de l'aviation civile.

cab [kab] *n* taxi *m*; (*of train, truck*) cabine *f*; (*horse-drawn*) fiacre *m*.

cabaret [kabərā'] *n* attractions *fpl*, spectacle *m* de cabaret.

cabbage [kab'ij] *n* chou *m*.

cabin [kab'in] *n* cabane *f*, hutte *f*; (*on ship*) cabine *f*.

cabin cruiser *n* yacht *m* (à moteur).

cabinet [kab'ənit] *n* (*POL*) cabinet *m*; (*furniture*) petit meuble à tiroirs et rayons; (*also*: **display ~**) vitrine *f*, petite armoire vitrée.

cabinet-maker [kab'ənitmākûr] *n* ébéniste *m*.

cabinet minister *n* ministre *m* (*membre du cabinet*).

cable [kā'bəl] *n* câble *m* ♦ *vt* câbler, télégraphier.

cable car *n* téléphérique *m*.

cablegram [kā'bəlgram] *n* câblogramme *m*.

cable railway *n* (*Brit*) funiculaire *m*.

cable television *n* télévision *f* par câble.

caboose [kəbōōs'] *n* (*US*: *RAIL*) fourgon *m*.

cache [kash] *n* cachette *f*; **a ~ of food** *etc* un dépôt secret de provisions *etc*, une cachette contenant des provisions *etc*.

cackle [kak'əl] *vi* caqueter.

cactus [kak'əl], *pl* **cacti** [kak'təs, kak'tī] *n* cactus *m*.

CAD *n abbr* (= *computer-aided design*) CAO *f*.

caddie [kad'ē] *n* caddie *m*.

cadet [kədet'] *n* (*MIL*) élève *m* officier; **police ~** élève agent de police.

cadge [kaj] *vt* (*col*) se faire donner; **to ~ a meal (off sb)** se faire inviter à manger (par

qn).

cadger [kaj'ûr] *n* pique-assiette *m/f inv*, tapeur/euse.

cadre [kâd'rə] *n* cadre *m*.

Caesarean [sizär'ēən] *a* (*Brit*) = **Cesarean.**

CAF *abbr* (= *cost and freight*) C et F.

café [kafā'] *n* ≈ café(-restaurant) *m* (*sans alcool*).

cafeteria [kafītē'rēə] *n* cafétéria *f*.

caffein(e) [ka'fēn] *n* caféine *f*.

cage [kāj] *n* cage *f* ♦ *vt* mettre en cage.

cagey [kā'jē] *a* (*col*) réticent(e); méfiant(e).

cagoule [kəgōōl'] *n* K-way *m* ®.

CAI *n abbr* (= *computer-aided instruction*) EAO *m*.

Cairo [kī'rō] *n* le Caire.

cajole [kəjōl'] *vt* couvrir de flatteries *or* de gentillesses.

cake [kāk] *n* gâteau *m*; **~ of soap** savonnette *f*; **it's a piece of ~** (*col*) c'est un jeu d'enfant; **he wants to have his ~ and eat it too** (*fig*) il veut tout avoir.

caked [kākt] *a*: **~ with** raidi(e) par, couvert(e) d'une croûte de.

cake pan *n* (*US*) moule *m* à gâteaux.

Cal. *abbr* (*US*) = *California*.

calamitous [kəlam'itəs] *a* catastrophique, désastreux(euse).

calamity [kəlam'itē] *n* calamité *f*, désastre *m*.

calcium [kal'sēəm] *n* calcium *m*.

calculate [kal'kyəlāt] *vt* calculer; (*estimate: chances, effect*) évaluer.

calculate on *vt fus*: **to ~ on sth/on doing sth** compter sur qch/faire qch.

calculated [kal'kyəlātid] *a* (*insult, action*) délibéré(e); **a ~ risk** un risque pris en toute connaissance de cause.

calculating [kal'kyəlāting] *a* calculateur(trice).

calculation [kalkyəlā'shən] *n* calcul *m*.

calculator [kal'kyəlātûr] *n* machine *f* à calculer, calculatrice *f*.

calculus [kal'kyələs] *n* analyse *f* (mathématique), calcul infinitésimal; **integral/differential ~** calcul intégral/différentiel.

calendar [kal'əndûr] *n* calendrier *m*.

calendar month *n* mois *m* (de calendrier).

calendar year *n* année civile.

calf [kaf], *pl* **calves** [kaf, kavz] *n* (*of cow*) veau *m*; (*of other animals*) petit *m*; (*also*: **~skin**) veau *m*, vachette *f*; (*ANAT*) mollet *m*.

caliber [kal'əbûr] *n* (*US*) calibre *m*.

calibrate [kal'əbrāt] *vt* (*gun etc*) calibrer; (*scale of measuring instrument*) étalonner.

calibre [kal'əbûr] *n* (*Brit*) = **caliber.**

calico [kal'ikō] *n* (*US*) indienne *f*; (*Brit*) calicot *m*.

Calif. *abbr* (*US*) = *California*.

California [kaləfôr'nyə] *n* Californie *f*.

calipers [kal'əpûrz] *npl* (*US MATH*) compas *m*; (: *MED*) appareil *m* orthopédique; gouttière *f*; étrier *m*.

call [kôl] *vt* (*gen, also TEL*) appeler; (*announce: flight*) annoncer; (*meeting*) convoquer; (*strike*) lancer ♦ *vi* appeler; (*visit: also*: **~ in**): **to ~ (for)** passer (prendre) ♦ *n* (*shout*) appel *m*, cri *m*; (*summons: for flight etc, fig: lure*) appel *m*; (*visit*) visite *f*; (*also*: **telephone ~**) coup *m* de téléphone; communication *f*; **to be on ~** être de permanence; **she's ~ed Suzanne** elle s'appelle Suzanne; **who is ~ing?** (*TEL*) qui est à l'appareil?; **New York ~ing** (*RADIO*) ici New York; **please give me a ~ at 7** appelez-moi à 7 heures; **to make a ~** téléphoner, passer un coup de fil; **to pay a ~ on sb** rendre visite à qn, passer voir qn; **there's not much ~ for these items** ces articles ne sont pas très demandés.

call at *vt fus* (*subj: ship*) faire escale à; (: *train*) s'arrêter à.

call back *vi* (*return*) repasser; (*TEL*) rappeler ♦ *vt* (*TEL*) rappeler.

call for *vt fus* demander.

call in *vt* (*doctor, expert, police*) appeler, faire venir.

call off *vt* annuler; **the strike was ~ed off** l'ordre de grève a été rapporté.

call on *vt fus* (*visit*) rendre visite à, passer voir; (*request*): **to ~ on sb to do** inviter qn à faire.

call out *vi* pousser un cri *or* des cris ♦ *vt* (*doctor, police, troops*) appeler.

call up *vt* (*MIL*) appeler, mobiliser.

callbox [kôl'bâks] *n* (*Brit*) cabine *f* téléphonique.

caller [kôl'ûr] *n* personne *f* qui appelle; visiteur *m*; **hold the line, ~!** (*TEL*) ne quittez pas, Monsieur (*or* Madame)!

call girl *n* call-girl *f*.

call-in [kôl'in] *n* (*US RADIO, TV*) programme *m* à ligne ouverte.

calling [kôl'ing] *n* vocation *f*; (*trade, occupation*) état *m*.

calling card *n* (*US*) carte *f* de visite.

callipers [kal'əpûrz] *npl* (*Brit*) = **calipers.**

callous [kal'əs] *a* dur(e), insensible.

callousness [kal'əsnis] *n* dureté *f*, manque *m* de cœur, insensibilité *f*.

callow [kal'ō] *a* sans expérience (de la vie).

calm [kâm] *a* calme ♦ *n* calme *m* ♦ *vt* calmer, apaiser.

calm down *vi* se calmer, s'apaiser ♦ *vt* calmer, apaiser.

calmly [kâm'lē] *ad* calmement, avec calme.

calmness [kâm'nis] *n* calme *m*.

Calor gas [kā'lûr gas] *n* ® (*Brit*) butane *m*, butagaz *m* ®.

calorie [kal'ûrē] *n* calorie *f*; **low ~ product** produit *m* pauvre en calories.

calve [kav] *vi* vêler, mettre bas.

calves [kavz] *npl of* **calf.**

CAM *n abbr* (= *computer-aided manufacturing*) FAO *f*.

camber [kam'bûr] *n* (*of road*) bombement *m*.

Cambodia [kambō'dēə] *n* Cambodge *m*.

Cambodian [kambō'dēən] *a* cambodgien(ne) ♦ *n* Cambodgien/ne.

Cambs *abbr* (*Brit*) = *Cambridgeshire.*

camcorder [kam'kôrdûr] *n* caméscope *m*.

came [kām] *pt of* **come.**

camel [kam'əl] *n* chameau *m*.

cameo [kam'ēō] *n* camée *m*.

camera [kam'ûrə] *n* appareil-photo *m*; (*CINEMA, TV*) caméra *f*; **35mm ~** appareil 24 x 36 *or* petit format.

cameraman [kam'ûrəman] *n* caméraman *m*.

Cameroon, Cameroun [kamərōōn'] *n* Cameroun *m*.

camouflage [kam'əflâzh] *n* camouflage *m* ♦ *vt* camoufler.

camp [kamp] *n* camp *m* ♦ *vi* camper; **to go ~ing** faire du camping.

campaign [kampān'] *n* (*MIL, POL etc*) campagne *f* ♦ *vi* (*also fig*) faire campagne; **to ~ for/against** militer pour/contre.

campaigner [kampān'ûr] *n*: **~ for** partisan/e de; **~ against** opposant/e à.

camp bed *n* lit *m* de camp.

camper [kam'pûr] *n* campeur/euse; (*vehicle*) camping-car *m*.

camping [kam'ping] *n* camping *m*.

camp(ing) site *n* (terrain *m* de) camping *m*.

campus [kam'pəs] *n* campus *m*.

camshaft [kam'shaft] *n* arbre *m* à came.

can [kan] *auxiliary vb see next headword* ♦ *n* (*of milk, oil, water*) bidon *m*; (*of fruit, soup etc*) boîte *f* (de conserve) ♦ *vt* mettre en conserve; **a ~ of beer** une canette de bière; **he had to carry the ~** (*Brit col*) on lui a fait porter le chapeau.

can [kan] *n, vt see previous headword* ♦ *auxiliary vb* (*gen*) pouvoir; (*know how to*) savoir; **I ~ swim** *etc* je sais nager *etc*; **I ~ speak French** je parle français; **I ~'t see you** je ne vous vois pas; **could I have a word with you?** est-ce que je pourrais vous parler un instant?; **he could be in the library** il est peut-être dans la bibliothèque; **they could have forgotten** ils ont pu oublier.

Canada [kan'ədə] *n* Canada *m*.

Canadian [kənā'dēən] *a* canadien(ne) ♦ *n* Canadien/ne.

canal [kənal'] *n* canal *m*.

canary [kənär'ē] *n* canari *m*, serin *m*.

Canary Islands, Canaries [kənär'ēz] *npl*: **the ~** les (îles *fpl*) Canaries *fpl*.

Canberra [kan'bärə] *n* Canberra *m*.

cancel [kan'səl] *vt* annuler; (*train*) supprimer; (*party, appointment*) décommander; (*cross out*) barrer, rayer; (*stamp*) oblitérer; (*check*) faire opposition à.

cancel out *vt* annuler; **they ~ each other out** ils s'annulent.

cancellation [kansəlā'shən] *n* annulation *f*; suppression *f*; oblitération *f*; (*TOURISM*) réservation annulée, client *etc* qui s'est décommandé.

cancer [kan'sûr] *n* cancer *m*; **C~** (*sign*) le Cancer; **to be C~** être du Cancer.

cancerous [kan'sûrəs] *a* cancéreux(euse).

cancer patient *n* cancéreux/euse.

cancer research *n* recherche *f* contre le cancer.

C and F *abbr* (= *cost and freight*) C et F.

candid [kan'did] *a* (très) franc(franche), sincère.

candidacy [kan'didəsē] *n* candidature *f*.

candidate [kan'didāt] *n* candidat/e.

candied [kan'dēd] *a* confit(e); **~ apple** (*US*) pomme caramélisée.

candle [kan'dəl] *n* bougie *f*; (*of tallow*) chandelle *f*; (*in church*) cierge *m*.

candlelight [kan'dəlīt] *n*: **by ~** à la lumière d'une bougie; (*dinner*) aux chandelles.

candlestick [kan'dəlstik] *n* (*also:* **candle holder**) bougeoir *m*; (*bigger, ornate*) chandelier *m*.

candor, (Brit) **candour** [kan'dûr] n (grande) franchise or sincérité.
candy [kan'dē] n sucre candi; (US) bonbon m.
candy-floss [kan'dēflôs] n (Brit) barbe f à papa.
candy store n (US) confiserie f.
cane [kān] n canne f; (for baskets, chairs etc) rotin m ♦ vt (Brit SCOL) administrer des coups de bâton à.
canine [kā'nīn] a canin(e).
canister [kan'istûr] n boîte f (gén en métal).
cannabis [kan'əbis] n (drug) cannabis m; (also: ~ **plant**) chanvre indien.
canned [kand] a (food) en boîte, en conserve; (col: music) enregistré(e); (US col: worker) mis(e) à la porte; (Brit col: drunk) bourré(e).
cannibal [kan'əbəl] n cannibale m/f, anthropophage m/f.
cannibalism [kan'əbəlizəm] n cannibalisme m, anthropophagie f.
cannon, pl ~ or ~s [kan'ən] n (gun) canon m.
cannonball [kan'ənbôl] n boulet m de canon.
cannon fodder n chair f à canon.
cannot [kan'ât] = **can not.**
canny [kan'ē] a madré(e), finaud(e).
canoe [kənōō'] n pirogue f; (SPORT) canoë m.
canoeing [kənōō'ing] n (sport) canoë m.
canoeist [kənōō'ist] n canoéiste m/f.
canon [kan'ən] n (clergyman) chanoine m; (standard) canon m.
canonize [kan'ənīz] vt canoniser.
can opener [kan ō'pənûr] n ouvre-boîte m.
canopy [kan'əpē] n baldaquin m; dais m.
cant [kant] n jargon m ♦ vt, vi pencher.
can't [kant] = **can not.**
cantankerous [kantang'kûrəs] a querelleur(euse), acariâtre.
canteen [kantēn'] n cantine f; (Brit: of cutlery) ménagère f.
canter [kan'tûr] n petit galop ♦ vi aller au petit galop.
cantilever [kan'təlevûr] n porte-à-faux m inv.
canvas [kan'vəs] n (gen) toile f; (under ~ (camping) sous la tente; (NAUT) toutes voiles dehors.
canvass [kan'vəs] vt (POL: district) faire la tournée électorale dans; (: person) solliciter le suffrage de; (COMM: district) prospecter; (citizens, opinions) sonder.
canvasser [kan'vəsûr] n (POL) agent électoral; (COMM) démarcheur m.
canvassing [kan'vəsing] n (POL) prospection électorale, démarchage électoral; (COMM) démarchage, prospection.
canyon [kan'yən] n cañon m, gorge (profonde).
CAP n abbr (Brit: = Common Agricultural Policy) PAC f.
cap [kap] n casquette f; (for swimming) bonnet m de bain; (of pen) capuchon m; (of bottle) capsule f; (Brit: contraceptive: also: **Dutch** ~) diaphragme m; (: SOCCER) sélection f pour l'équipe nationale ♦ vt capsuler; (outdo) surpasser; ~**ped with** coiffé(e) de; **and to** ~ **it all, he ...** (Brit) pour couronner le tout, il ....
capability [kāpəbil'ətē] n aptitude f, capacité f.
capable [kā'pəbəl] a capable; ~ **of** (interpre-

tation etc) susceptible de.
capacious [kəpā'shəs] a vaste.
capacity [kəpas'itē] n (of container) capacité f, contenance f; (ability) aptitude f; **filled to** ~ plein(e); **in his** ~ **as** en sa qualité de; **this work is beyond my** ~ ce travail dépasse mes capacités; **in an advisory** ~ à titre consultatif; **to work at full** ~ travailler à plein rendement.
cape [kāp] n (garment) cape f; (GEO) cap m.
Cape of Good Hope n cap m de Bonne Espérance.
caper [kā'pûr] n (CULIN: also: ~**s**) câpre f.
Cape Town n Le Cap.
capita [kap'itə] see **per capita.**
capital [kap'itəl] n (also: ~ **city**) capitale f; (money) capital m; (also: ~ **letter**) majuscule f.
capital account n balance f des capitaux; (of country) compte capital.
capital allowance n provision f pour amortissement.
capital assets npl immobilisations fpl.
capital expenditure n dépenses fpl d'équipement.
capital gains tax n impôt m sur les plus-values.
capital goods n biens mpl d'équipement.
capital-intensive [kap'itəlinten'siv] a à forte proportion de capitaux.
capitalism [kap'itəlizəm] n capitalisme m.
capitalist [kap'itəlist] a, n capitaliste (m/f).
capitalize [kap'itəlīz] vt (provide with capital) financer.
capitalize on vt fus (fig) profiter de.
capital punishment n peine capitale.
capitulate [kəpich'ōōlāt] vi capituler.
capitulation [kəpichōōlā'shən] n capitulation f.
capricious [kəprish'əs] a capricieux(euse), fantasque.
Capricorn [kap'rikôrn] n le Capricorne; **to be** ~ être du Capricorne.
caps [kaps] abbr = **capital letters.**
capsize [kap'sīz] vt faire chavirer ♦ vi chavirer.
capstan [kap'stən] n cabestan m.
capsule [kap'səl] n capsule f.
Capt. abbr (= captain) Cne.
captain [kap'tin] n capitaine m ♦ vt commander, être le capitaine de.
caption [kap'shən] n légende f.
captivate [kap'təvāt] vt captiver, fasciner.
captive [kap'tiv] a, n captif(ive).
captivity [kaptiv'ətē] n captivité f.
captor [kap'tûr] n (unlawful) ravisseur m; (lawful): **his** ~**s** les gens (or ceux etc) qui l'ont arrêté.
capture [kap'chûr] vt capturer, prendre; (attention) capter ♦ n capture f.
car [kâr] n voiture f, auto f; (US RAIL) wagon m, voiture; **by** ~ en voiture.
Caracas [kərak'əs] n Caracas.
carafe [kəraf'] n carafe f.
carafe wine n (in restaurant) ≈ vin ouvert.
caramel [kar'əməl] n caramel m.
carat [kar'ət] n carat m; **18** ~ **gold** or m à 18 carats.
caravan [kar'əvan] n (Brit: camper) caravane f.

caravan site *n* (*Brit*) camping *m* pour caravanes.

caraway [kar'əwā] *n*: ~ **seed** graine *f* de cumin, cumin *m*.

carbohydrates [kârbōhī'drāts] *npl* (*foods*) aliments *mpl* riches en hydrate de carbone.

carbolic acid [kârbál'ik as'id] *n* phénol *m*.

carbon [kâr'bən] *n* carbone *m*.

carbonated [kâr'bənātid] *a* (*drink*) gazeux(euse).

carbon copy *n* carbone *m*.

carbon dioxide *n* gas *m* carbonique, dioxyde *m* de carbone.

carbon paper *n* papier *m* carbone.

carbon ribbon *n* ruban *m* carbone.

carburetor, (*Brit*) **carburettor** [kâr'bərātûr] *n* carburateur *m*.

carcass [kâr'kəs] *n* carcasse *f*.

carcinogenic [kârsinəjen'ik] *a* cancérigène.

card [kârd] *n* carte *f*; (*membership* ~) carte d'adhérent; **to play** ~**s** jouer aux cartes.

cardamom [kâr'dəməm] *n* cardamome *f*.

cardboard [kârd'bôrd] *n* carton *m*.

cardboard box *n* (boîte *f* en) carton *m*.

card-carrying member [kârd'karēing mem'bûr] *n* membre actif.

card game *n* jeu *m* de cartes.

cardiac [kâr'dēak] *a* cardiaque.

cardigan [kâr'digən] *n* cardigan *m*.

cardinal [kâr'dənəl] *a* cardinal(e) ♦ *n* cardinal *m*.

card index *n* fichier *m* (alphabétique).

Cards *abbr* (*Brit*) = *Cardiganshire*.

cardsharp [kârd'shârp] *n* tricheur/euse professionnel(le).

CARE *n abbr* (= *Cooperative for American Relief Everywhere*) association charitable.

care [kär] *n* soin *m*, attention *f*; (*worry*) souci *m* ♦ *vi*: **to** ~ **about** se soucier de, s'intéresser à; **would you** ~ **to/for ...?** voulez-vous ...?; **I wouldn't** ~ **to do it** je n'aimerais pas le faire; **in sb's** ~ à la garde de qn, confié à qn; ~ **of** (**c/o**) (*on letter*) aux bons soins de; "**handle with** ~" "fragile"; **to take** ~ (**to do**) faire attention (à faire); **to take** ~ **of** *vt* s'occuper de, prendre soin de; (*details, arrangements*) s'occuper de; **the child has been taken into** ~ l'enfant a été placé en institution; **I don't** ~ ça m'est bien égal, peu m'importe; **I could** ~ **less**, (*Brit*) **I couldn't** ~ **less** cela m'est complètement égal, je m'en fiche complètement.

care for *vt fus* s'occuper de; (*like*) aimer.

careen [kərēn'] *vi* (*ship*) donner de la bande ♦ *vt* caréner, mettre en carène.

career [kərēr'] *n* carrière *f* ♦ *vi* (*also*: ~ **along**) aller à toute allure.

career counselor *n* counseiller/ère d'orientation (professionnelle).

career girl *n* jeune fille *f* (*or* femme *f*) qui veut faire carrière.

careers officer *n* (*Brit*) conseiller/ère d'orientation (professionnelle).

carefree [kär'frē] *a* sans souci, insouciant(e).

careful [kär'fəl] *a* soigneux(euse); (*cautious*) prudent(e); (**be**) ~**!** (fais) attention!; **to be** ~ **with one's money** regarder à la dépense.

carefully [kär'fəlē] *ad* avec soin, soigneusement; prudemment.

careless [kär'lis] *a* négligent(e); (*heedless*) insouciant(e).

carelessly [kär'islē] *ad* négligemment; avec insouciance.

carelessness [kär'lisnis] *n* manque *m* de soin, négligence *f*; insouciance *f*.

caress [kəres'] *n* caresse *f* ♦ *vt* caresser.

caretaker [kär'tākûr] *n* gardien/ne, concierge *m/f*.

caretaker government *n* gouvernement *m* intérimaire.

car ferry *n* (*on sea*) ferry(-boat) *m*; (*on river*) bac *m*.

cargo, *pl* ~**es** [kâr'gō] *n* cargaison *f*, chargement *m*.

cargo boat *n* cargo *m*.

cargo plane *n* avion-cargo *m*.

car hire *n* (*Brit*) location *f* de voitures.

Caribbean [karəbē'ən] *a* des Caraïbes; **the** ~ (**Sea**) la mer des Antilles *or* des Caraïbes.

caricature [kar'əkəchûr] *n* caricature *f*.

caring [kär'ing] *a* (*person*) bienveillant(e); (*society, organization*) humanitaire.

carnage [kâr'nij] *n* carnage *m*.

carnal [kâr'nəl] *a* charnel(le).

carnation [kârnā'shən] *n* œillet *m*.

carnival [kâr'nəvəl] *n* (*public celebration*) carnaval *m*; (*US*) fête foraine.

carnivorous [kârniv'ûrəs] *a* carnivore, carnassier(ière).

carol [kar'əl] *n*: (**Christmas**) ~ chant *m* de Noël.

carouse [kərouz'] *vi* faire la bringue.

carousel [karəsel'] *n* (*US*) manège *m*.

carp [kârp] *n* (*fish*) carpe *f*.

carp at *vt fus* critiquer.

car park *n* (*Brit*) parking *m*, parc *m* de stationnement.

carpenter [kâr'pəntûr] *n* charpentier *m*.

carpentry [kâr'pəntrē] *n* charpenterie *f*, métier *m* de charpentier; (*woodwork: at school etc*) menuiserie *f*.

carpet [kâr'pit] *n* tapis *m* ♦ *vt* recouvrir (d'un tapis).

carpet slippers *npl* pantoufles *fpl*.

carpet sweeper [kâr'pit swē'pûr] *n* balai *m* mécanique.

car phone *n* téléphone *m* de voiture.

car rental *n* (*US*) location *f* de voitures.

carriage [kar'ij] *n* voiture *f*; (*of goods*) transport *m*; (: *cost*) port *m*; (*of typewriter*) chariot *m*; (*bearing*) maintien *m*, port *m*; ~ **forward** port dû; ~ **free** franco de port; ~ **paid** (en) port payé.

carriage return *n* retour *m* à la ligne.

carriageway [kar'ijwā] *n* (*Brit: part of road*) chaussée *f*.

carrier [kar'ēûr] *n* transporteur *m*, camionneur *m*; (*MED*) porteur/euse; (*NAUT*) porte-avions *m inv*.

carrier bag *n* (*Brit*) sac *m* en papier *or* en plastique.

carrier pigeon *n* pigeon voyageur.

carrion [kar'ēən] *n* charogne *f*.

carrot [kar'ət] *n* carotte *f*.

carry [kar'ē] *vt* (*subj: person*) porter; (: *vehicle*) transporter; (*a motion, bill*) voter, adopter; (*MATH: figure*) retenir; (*COMM: interest*) rapporter; (*involve: responsibilities* *etc)* comporter, impliquer ♦ *vi* (*sound*) porter; **to be carried away** (*fig*) s'emballer, s'enthousiasmer; **this loan carries 10% interest** ce prêt est à 10% (d'intérêt).

carry forward *vt* (*gen*, BOOK-KEEPING) reporter.

carry on *vi* (*continue*): **to ~ on with sth/doing** continuer qch/à faire; (*col: make a fuss*) faire des histoires ♦ *vt* entretenir, poursuivre.

carry out *vt* (*orders*) exécuter; (*investigation*) effectuer; (*idea, threat*) mettre à exécution.

carryall [kar'ēôl] *n* (*US*) fourre-tout *m inv*.

carrycot [kar'ēkät] *n* (*Brit*) porte-bébé *m*.

carry-on [kar'ēăn] *n* (*Brit col: fuss*) histoires *fpl*; (: *annoying behavior*) cirque *m*, cinéma *m*.

cart [kärt] *n* charrette *f*; (*US: for shopping*) chariot *m*, caddie *m* ♦ *vt* transporter.

carte blanche [kärt' blänsh'] *n*: **to give sb ~** donner carte blanche à qn.

cartel [kärtel'] *n* (COMM) cartel *m*.

cartilage [kär'təlij] *n* cartilage *m*.

cartographer [kärtäg'rəfûr] *n* cartographe *m/f*.

cartography [kärtäg'rəfē] *n* cartographie *f*.

carton [kär'tən] *n* (*box*) carton *m*; (*of yogurt*) pot *m* (en carton); (*of cigarettes*) cartouche *f*.

cartoon [kärtōōn'] *n* (PRESS) dessin *m* (humoristique); (*satirical*) caricature *f*; (*comic strip*) bande dessinée; (CINEMA) dessin animé.

cartoonist [kärtōō'nist] *n* dessinateur/trice humoristique; caricaturiste *m/f*; auteur *m* de dessins animés; auteur de bandes dessinées.

cartridge [kär'trij] *n* (*for gun, pen*) cartouche *f*; (*for camera*) chargeur *m*; (*music tape*) cassette *f*; (*of record player*) cellule *f*.

cartwheel [kärt'hwēl] *n* roue *f*; **to turn a ~** faire la roue.

carve [kärv] *vt* (*meat: also: ~ up*) découper; (*wood, stone*) tailler, sculpter.

carving [kär'ving] *n* (*in wood etc*) sculpture *f*.

carving knife *n* couteau *m* à découper.

car wash *n* station *f* de lavage (de voitures).

Casablanca [kasəblang'kə] *n* Casablanca.

cascade [kaskād'] *n* cascade *f* ♦ *vi* tomber en cascade.

case [kās] *n* cas *m*; (LAW) affaire *f*, procès *m*; (*box*) caisse *f*, boîte *f*, étui *m*; (*Brit: also: suit~*) valise *f*; (TYP): **lower/upper ~** minuscule *f*/majuscule *f*; **to have a good ~** avoir de bons arguments; **there's a strong ~ for reform** il y aurait lieu d'engager une réforme; **in ~ of** en cas de; **in ~ he** au cas où il; **just in ~** à tout hasard.

case-hardened [kās'här'dənd] *a* endurci(e).

case history *n* (MED) dossier médical, antécédents médicaux.

case study *n* étude *f* de cas.

cash [kash] *n* argent *m*; (COMM) argent liquide, numéraire *m*; liquidités *m*; (: *in payment*) argent comptant, espèces *fpl* ♦ *vt* encaisser; **to pay (in) ~** payer (en argent) comptant *or* en espèces; **~ on delivery (COD)** (COMM) payable *or* paiement à la livraison; **to be short of ~** être à court d'argent.

cash in *vt* (*insurance policy etc*) toucher.

cash in on *vt fus* profiter de.

cash account *n* compte *m* caisse.

cashbook [kash'bŏŏk] *n* livre *m* de caisse.

cash box *n* caisse *f*.

cash card *n* carte de retrait *or* accréditive.

cash desk *n* (*Brit*) caisse *f*.

cash discount *n* escompte *m* de caisse (pour paiement au comptant), remise *f* au comptant.

cash dispenser *n* distributeur *m* automatique de billets.

cashew [kash'ōō] *n* (*also: ~ nut*) noix *f* de cajou.

cash flow *n* cash-flow *m*, marge brute d'autofinancement.

cashier [kashi'ûr] *n* caissier/ère ♦ *vt* (MIL) destituer, casser.

cashmere [kazh'mēr] *n* cachemire *m*.

cash payment *n* paiement comptant, versement *m* en espèces.

cash price *n* prix comptant.

cash register *n* caisse enregistreuse.

cash sale *n* vente *f* au comptant.

casing [kā'sing] *n* revêtement (protecteur), enveloppe (protectrice).

casino [kəsē'nō] *n* casino *m*.

cask [kask] *n* tonneau *m*.

casket [kas'kit] *n* coffret *m*; (*US: coffin*) cercueil *m*.

Caspian Sea [kas'pēən sē'] *n*: **the ~** la mer Caspienne.

casserole [kas'ərōl] *n* cocotte *f*; (*food*) ragoût *m* (en cocotte).

cassette [kəset'] *n* cassette *f*, musicassette *f*.

cassette deck *n* platine *f* cassette.

cassette player *n* lecteur *m* de cassettes.

cassette recorder *n* magnétophone *m* à cassettes.

cast [kast] *vb* (*pt, pp* **cast**) *vt* (*throw*) jeter; (*shed*) perdre; se dépouiller de; (*metal*) couler, fondre; (THEATER): **to ~ sb as Hamlet** attribuer à qn le rôle d'Hamlet ♦ *n* (THEATER) distribution *f*; (*mold*) moule *m*; (*also: plaster ~*) plâtre *m*; **to ~ one's vote** voter, exprimer son suffrage.

cast aside *vt* (*reject*) rejeter.

cast off *vi* (NAUT) larguer les amarres; (KNITTING) arrêter les mailles ♦ *vt* (KNITTING) arrêter.

cast on (KNITTING) *vt* monter ♦ *vi* monter les mailles.

castanets [kastənets'] *npl* castagnettes *fpl*.

castaway [kas'təwā] *n* naufragé/e.

caste [kast] *n* caste *f*, classe sociale.

caster sugar [kas'tûr shŏŏg'ûr] *n* (*Brit*) sucre *m* semoule.

casting vote [kas'ting vōt'] *n* (*Brit*) voix prépondérante (*pour départager*).

cast iron *n* fonte *f* ♦ *a*: **cast-iron** (*fig: will*) de fer; (: *alibi*) en béton.

castle [kas'əl] *n* château-fort *m*; (*manor*) château *m*.

castor [kas'tûr] *n* (*wheel*) roulette *f*.

castor oil *n* huile *f* de ricin.

castrate [kas'trāt] *vt* châtrer.

casual [kazh'ōōəl] *a* (*by chance*) de hasard, fait(e) au hasard, fortuit(e); (*irregular: work etc*) temporaire; (*unconcerned*) désinvolte; **~ wear** vêtements *mpl* sport *inv*.

casual labor *n* main-d'œuvre *f* temporaire.
casually [kazh'ōōəlē] *ad* avec désinvolture, négligemment; (*by chance*) fortuitement.
casualty [kazh'ōōəltē] *n* accidenté/e, blessé/e;
(*dead*) victime *f*, mort/e; **heavy casualties**
lourdes pertes.
casualty ward *n* (*Brit*) service *m* des
urgences.
cat [kat] *n* chat *m*.
catacombs [kat'əkōmz] *npl* catacombes *fpl*.
catalog, (*Brit*) **catalogue** [kat'əlôg] *n* catalogue *m* ♦ *vt* cataloguer.
catalyst [kat'əlist] *n* catalyseur *m*.
catalytic converter [katəlit'ik kânvûrt'ûr] *n*
(*AUT*) pot *m* catalytique.
catapult [kat'əpult] *n* lance-pierres *m* inv,
fronde *m*; (*HIST*) catapulte *f*.
cataract [kat'ərakt] *n* (*also MED*) cataracte *f*.
catarrh [kətâr'] *n* rhume *m* chronique, catarrhe *f*.
catastrophe [kətas'trəfē] *n* catastrophe *f*.
catastrophic [katəstrâf'ik] *a* catastrophique.
catcall [kat'kôl] *n* (*at meeting etc*) sifflet *m*.
catch [kach] *vb* (*pt, pp* **caught** [kôt]) *vt* (*ball,
train, thief, cold*) attraper; (*person: by surprise*) prendre, surprendre; (*understand*) saisir; (*get entangled*) accrocher ♦ *vi* (*fire*)
prendre; (*get entangled*) s'accrocher ♦ *n* (*fish
etc caught*) prise *f*; (*thief etc caught*) capture
f; (*trick*) attrape *f*; (*TECH*) loquet *m*; cliquet
m; **to ~ sb's attention** or **eye** attirer
l'attention de qn; **to ~ fire** prendre feu; **to ~
sight of** apercevoir.
catch on *vi* (*become popular*) prendre;
(*understand*): **to ~ on (to sth)** saisir (qch).
catch out *vt* (*Brit fig: with trick question*)
prendre en défaut.
catch up *vi* se rattraper, combler son retard ♦ *vt* (*also*: **~ up with**) rattraper.
catching [kach'ing] *a* (*MED*) contagieux(euse).
catchment area [kach'mənt är'ēə] *n* (*Brit
SCOL*) aire *f* de recrutement; (*GEO*) bassin *m*
hydrographique.
catch phrase *n* slogan *m*; expression toute
faite.
catch-22 [kach'twentētōō'] *n*: **it's a ~ situation** c'est (une situation) sans issue.
catchy [kach'ē] *a* (*tune*) facile à retenir.
cat door *n* (*US*) chatière *f*.
catechism [kat'əkizəm] *n* catéchisme *m*.
categoric(al) [kat'əgôr'ik(əl)] *a* catégorique.
categorize [kat'əgəriz] *vt* classer par catégories.
category [kat'əgôrē] *n* catégorie *f*.
cater [kā'tûr] *vi* (*provide food*): **to ~ (for)** préparer des repas (pour), se charger de la
restauration (pour).
cater to *vt fus* (*needs*) satisfaire, pourvoir
à; (: *readers, consumers*) s'adresser à,
pourvoir aux besoins de.
caterer [kā'tûrûr] *n* traiteur *m*; fournisseur *m*.
catering [kā'tûring] *n* restauration *f*; approvisionnement *m*, ravitaillement *m*.
caterpillar [kat'ûrpilûr] *n* chenille *f* ♦ *cpd* (*vehicle*) à chenille; **~ track** *n* chenille *f*.
cathedral [kəthē'drəl] *n* cathédrale *f*.
cathode [kath'ōd] *n* cathode *f*.
cathode ray tube [kath'ōd rā' tōōb] *n* tube *m*
cathodique.

catholic [kath'əlik] *a* éclectique; universel(le);
libéral(e); **C~** *a, n* (*REL*) catholique (*m/f*).
cat's-eye [kats'ī'] *n* (*Brit AUT*) (clou *m* à) catadioptre *m*.
catsup [kat'səp] *n* (*US*) ketchup *m*.
cattle [kat'əl] *npl* bétail *m*, bestiaux *mpl*.
catty [kat'ē] *a* méchant(e).
CATV *n abbr* (*US*: = *community antenna television*) télédistribution *f*.
Caucasian [kôkā'zhən] *a, n* caucasien(ne).
Caucasus [kôk'əsəs] *n* Caucase *m*.
caucus [kô'kəs] *n* (*US POL*) comité électoral
(pour désigner des candidats); (*Brit POL*:
group) comité local (*d'un parti politique*).
caught [kôt] *pt, pp of* **catch**.
cauliflower [kô'ləflouûr] *n* chou-fleur *m*.
cause [kôz] *n* cause *f* ♦ *vt* causer; **there is no
~ for concern** il n'y a pas lieu de s'inquiéter;
to ~ sth to be done faire faire qch; **to ~ sb
to do sth** faire faire qch à qn.
causeway [kôz'wā] *n* chaussée (surélevée).
caustic [kôs'tik] *a* caustique.
caution [kô'shən] *n* prudence *f*; (*warning*)
avertissement *m* ♦ *vt* avertir, donner un
avertissement à.
cautious [kô'shəs] *a* prudent(e).
cautiously [kô'shəslē] *ad* prudemment, avec
prudence.
cautiousness [kô'shəsnis] *n* prudence *f*.
cavalier [kavəliûr'] *a* cavalier(ère), désinvolte
♦ *n* (*knight*) cavalier *m*.
cavalry [kav'əlrē] *n* cavalerie *f*.
cave [kāv] *n* caverne *f*, grotte *f* ♦ *vi*: **to go
caving** faire de la spéléo(logie).
cave in *vi* (*roof etc*) s'effondrer.
caveman [kāv'mən] *n* homme *m* des cavernes.
cavern [kav'ûrn] *n* caverne *f*.
caviar(e) [kav'ēâr] *n* caviar *m*.
cavity [kav'itē] *n* cavité *f*.
cavity wall insulation *n* isolation *f* des murs
creux.
cavort [kəvôrt'] *vi* cabrioler, faire des cabrio-
les.
cayenne [kīen'] *n* (*also*: **~ pepper**) poivre *m*
de cayenne.
CB *n abbr* (= *Citizens' Band (Radio)*) CB *f*
CBC *n abbr* (= *Canadian Broadcasting Corporation*) organisme *m* de radiodiffusion.
CBI *n abbr* (= *Confederation of British Industry*) ≈ CNPF *m* (= *Conseil national du patronat français*).
CBS *n abbr* (*US*: = *Columbia Broadcasting
System*) chaîne de télévision.
cc *abbr* (= *cubic centimeter*) cm³; (*on letter
etc*) = **carbon copy.**
CCA *n abbr* (*US*: = *Circuit Court of Appeals*)
cour d'appel itinérante.
CCC *n abbr* (*US*: = *Commodity Credit Corpo-
ration*) organisme *m* d'aide aux prix agrico-
les.
CCU *n abbr* (*US*: = *coronary care unit*) unité *f*
de soins cardiologiques.
CD *n abbr* (= *compact disc*) CD *m*; (*MIL*) =
Civil Defense (*US*), *Civil Defence (Corps)*
(*Brit*) ♦ *abbr* (*Brit*: = *Corps Diplomatique*)
CD.
CDC *n abbr* (*US*) = *center for disease control*.
Cdr. *abbr* (= *commander*) Cdt.
CDV *n abbr* (= *compact disc video*) CDV *m*.

CDW _n abbr_ = **collision damage waiver**.
cease [sēs] _vt, vi_ cesser.
ceasefire [sēs'fiûr'] _n_ cessez-le-feu _m_.
ceaseless [sēs'lis] _a_ incessant(e), continuel(le).
CED _n abbr (US)_ = _Committee for Economic Development_.
cedar [sē'dûr] _n_ cèdre _m_.
cede [sēd] _vt_ céder.
cedilla [sidil'ə] _n_ cédille _f_.
CEEB _n abbr (US: = College Entry Examination Board)_ commission d'admission dans l'enseignement supérieur.
ceiling [sē'ling] _n (also fig)_ plafond _m_.
celebrate [sel'əbrāt] _vt, vi_ célébrer.
celebrated [sel'əbrātid] _a_ célèbre.
celebration [seləbrā'shən] _n_ célébration _f_.
celebrity [səleb'ritē] _n_ célébrité _f_.
celeriac [səlär'ēak] _n_ céleri(-rave) _m_.
celery [sel'ûrē] _n_ céleri _m_ (en branches).
celestial [səles'chəl] _a_ céleste.
celibacy [sel'əbəsē] _n_ célibat _m_.
cell [sel] _n (gen)_ cellule _f_; (ELEC) élément _m_ (de pile).
cellar [sel'ûr] _n_ cave _f_.
cellophane [sel'əfān] _n_ ® cellophane _f_ ®.
cellular [sel'yəlûr] _a_ cellulaire.
Celluloid [sel'yəloid] _n_ ® celluloïd _m_ ®.
cellulose [sel'yəlōs] _n_ cellulose _f_.
Celsius [sel'sēəs] _a_ Celsius _inv_.
Celt [selt, kelt] _n_ Celte _m/f_.
Celtic [sel'tik, kel'tik] _a_ celte, celtique ♦ _n_ (LING) celtique _m_.
cement [siment'] _n_ ciment _m_ ♦ _vt_ cimenter.
cement mixer _n_ bétonnière _f_.
cemetery [sem'itärē] _n_ cimetière _m_.
cenotaph [sen'ətaf] _n_ cénotaphe _m_.
censor [sen'sûr] _n_ censeur _m_ ♦ _vt_ censurer.
censorship [sen'sûrship] _n_ censure _f_.
censure [sen'shûr] _vt_ blâmer, critiquer.
census [sen'səs] _n_ recensement _m_.
cent [sent] _n (US: coin)_ cent _m (= 1:100 du dollar)_; _see also_ **percent**.
centenary [sen'tənārē] _n_ centenaire _m_.
centennial [senten'ēəl] _n_ = **centenary**.
center [sen'tûr] (US) _n_ centre _m_ ♦ _vt_ centrer; (PHOT) cadrer; (concentrate): **to ~ on** centrer sur.
centerfold [sen'tûrfōld] _n_ (PRESS) pages centrales détachables _(avec photo de pin up)_.
center forward _n_ (SPORT) avant-centre _m_.
center half _n_ (SPORT) demi-centre _m_.
centerpiece [sen'tûrpēs] _n_ milieu _m_ de table; _(fig)_ pièce maîtresse.
centigrade [sen'tigrād] _a_ centigrade.
centiliter, _(Brit)_ **centilitre** [sen'təlētûr] _n_ centilitre _m_.
centimeter, _(Brit)_ **centimetre** [sen'təmētûr] _n_ centimètre _m_.
centipede [sen'təpēd] _n_ mille-pattes _m inv_.
central [sen'trəl] _a_ central(e).
Central African Republic _n_ République Centrafricaine.
central heating _n_ chauffage central.
centralize [sen'trəlīz] _vt_ centraliser.
central processing unit (CPU) _n_ (COMPUT) unité centrale (de traitement).
central reservation _n_ (Brit AUT) terre-plein central.

centre [sen'tûr] _etc (Brit)_ = **center** _etc_.
centrifugal [sentrif'əgəl] _a_ centrifuge.
centrifuge [sen'trəfyōōj] _n_ centrifugeuse _f_.
century [sen'chûrē] _n_ siècle _m_; **in the twentieth ~** au vingtième siècle.
CEO _n abbr_ = **chief executive officer**.
ceramic [səram'ik] _a_ céramique.
cereal [sēr'ēəl] _n_ céréale _f_.
cerebral [sär'əbrəl] _a_ cérébral(e).
ceremonial [särəmō'nēəl] _n_ cérémonial _m_; _(rite)_ rituel _m_.
ceremony [sär'əmōnē] _n_ cérémonie _f_; **to stand on ~** faire des façons.
certain [sûr'tən] _a_ certain(e); **to make ~ of** s'assurer de; **for ~** certainement, sûrement.
certainly [sûr'tənlē] _ad_ certainement.
certainty [sûr'təntē] _n_ certitude _f_.
certificate [sûrtif'əkit] _n_ certificat _m_.
certified letter [sûr'təfīd let'ûr] _n_ (US) lettre recommandée.
certified public accountant (CPA) _n_ (US) expert-comptable _m_.
certify [sûr'təfī] _vt_ certifier ♦ _vi_: **to ~ to** attester.
cervical [sûr'vikəl] _a_: **~ cancer** cancer _m_ du col de l'utérus; **~ smear** frottis vaginal.
cervix [sûr'viks] _n_ col _m_ de l'utérus.
Cesarean [sizär'ēən] _a_ (US): **~ (section)** césarienne _f_.
cessation [sesā'shən] _n_ cessation _f_, arrêt _m_.
cesspit [ses'pit] _n_ fosse _f_ d'aisance.
CET _abbr (= Central European Time)_ heure d'Europe centrale.
Ceylon [silän'] _n_ Ceylan _m_.
cf. _abbr (= compare)_ cf., voir.
C.F. _abbr (= cost and freight)_ coût _m_ et fret _m_.
c/f _abbr (COMM)_ = _carried forward_.
cfc _n abbr (= chlorofluorocarbon)_ CFC.
C.F.I. _abbr (= cost, freight and insurance)_ CAF.
CG _n abbr (US)_ = **coastguard**.
cg _abbr (= centigram)_ cg.
ch _abbr (Brit)_ = _central heating_ c.c.
ch. _abbr (= chapter)_ chap.
Chad [chad] _n_ Tchad _m_.
chafe [chāf] _vt_ irriter, frotter contre ♦ _vi (fig)_: **to ~ against** se rebiffer contre, regimber contre.
chaffinch [chaf'inch] _n_ pinson _m_.
chagrin [shəgrin'] _n_ contrariété _f_, déception _f_.
chain [chān] _n (gen)_ chaîne _f_ ♦ _vt (also: ~ up)_ enchaîner, attacher (avec une chaîne).
chain reaction _n_ réaction _f_ en chaîne.
chain-smoke [chān'smōk] _vi_ fumer cigarette sur cigarette.
chain store _n_ magasin _m_ à succursales multiples.
chair [chär] _n_ chaise _f_; _(armchair)_ fauteuil _m_; _(of university)_ chaire _f_ ♦ _vt (meeting)_ présider; **the ~** (US:. electric ~) la chaise électrique.
chairlift [chär'lift] _n_ télésiège _m_.
chairman [chär'mən] _n_ président _m_.
chairperson [chär'pûrsən] _n_ président/e.
chairwoman [chär'wōōmən] _n_ présidente _f_.
chalet [shalā'] _n_ chalet _m_.
chalice [chal'is] _n_ calice _m_.
chalk [chôk] _n_ craie _f_.

chalk up *vt* écrire à la craie; (*fig: success etc*) remporter.

challenge [chal'inj] *n* défi *m* ♦ *vt* défier; (*statement, right*) mettre en question, contester; **to ~ sb to a fight/game** inviter qn à se battre/à jouer (*sous forme d'un défi*); **to ~ sb to do** mettre qn au défi de faire.

challenger [chal'ınjûr] *n* (*SPORT*) challenger *m*.

challenging [chal'injing] *a* de défi, provocateur(trice).

chamber [chăm'bûr] *n* chambre *f*; **~ of commerce** chambre de commerce.

chambermaid [chăm'bûrmād] *n* femme *f* de chambre.

chamber music *n* musique *f* de chambre.

chamber pot *n* pot *m* de chambre.

chameleon [kəmē'lēən] *n* caméléon *m*.

chamois [sham'ē] *n* chamois *m*.

chamois leather [sham'ē leth'ûr] *n* peau *f* de chamois.

champagne [shampăn'] *n* champagne *m*.

champion [cham'pēən] *n* (*also of cause*) champion/ne ♦ *vt* défendre.

championship [cham'pēənship] *n* championnat *m*.

chance [chans] *n* hasard *m*; (*opportunity*) occasion *f*, possibilité *f*; (*hope, likelihood*) chance *f* ♦ *vt* (*risk*): **to ~ it** risquer (le coup), essayer; (*happen*): **to ~ to do** faire par hasard ♦ *a* fortuit(e), de hasard; **there is little ~ of his coming** il est peu probable *or* il y a peu de chances qu'il vienne; **to take a ~** prendre un risque; **it's the ~ of a lifetime** c'est une occasion unique; **by ~** par hasard.

chance (up)on *vt fus* (*person*) tomber sur, rencontrer par hasard; (*thing*) trouver par hasard.

chancel [chan'səl] *n* chœur *m*.

chancellor [chan'səlûr] *n* chancelier *m*; **C~ of the Exchequer** (*Brit*) chancelier de l'Échiquier.

chandelier [shandəliûr'] *n* lustre *m*.

change [chănj] *vt* (*alter, replace, COMM: money*) changer; (*switch, substitute: gear, hands, trains, clothes, one's name etc*) changer de; (*transform*): **to ~ sb into** changer *or* transformer qn en ♦ *vi* (*gen*) changer; (*change clothes*) se changer; (*be transformed*): **to ~ into** se changer *or* transformer en ♦ *n* changement *m*; (*money*) monnaie *f*; **to ~ one's mind** changer d'avis; **she ~d into an old skirt** elle (s'est changée et) a enfilé une vieille jupe; **a ~ of clothes** des vêtements de rechange; **for a ~** pour changer; **small ~** petite monnaie; **to give sb ~ for $10** faire à qn la monnaie de 10 dollars.

changeable [chăn'jəbəl] *a* (*weather*) variable; (*person*) d'humeur changeante.

change machine *n* distributeur *m* de monnaie.

changeover [chănj'ōvûr] *n* (*to new system*) changement *m*, passage *m*.

changing [chăn'jing] *a* changeant(e).

changing room *n* (*Brit: in store*) salon *m* d'essayage; (*: SPORT*) vestiaire *m*.

channel [chan'əl] *n* (*TV*) chaîne *f*; (*waveband, groove, fig: medium*) canal *m*; (*of river, sea*)

chenal *m* ♦ *vt* canaliser; (*fig: interest, energies*): **to ~ into** diriger vers; **through the usual ~s** en suivant la filière habituelle; **green/red ~** (*CUSTOMS*) couloir *m* or sortie *f* "rien à déclarer"/"marchandises à déclarer"; **the (English) C~** la Manche.

Channel Islands *npl*: **the ~** les îles de la Manche, les îles anglo-normandes.

chant [chant] *n* chant *m*; mélopée *f*; psalmodie *f* ♦ *vt* chanter, scander; psalmodier.

chaos [kā'ås] *n* chaos *m*.

chaotic [kāăt'ik] *a* chaotique.

chap [chap] *n* (*Brit col: man*) type *m*; (*term of address*): **old ~** mon vieux ♦ *vt* (*skin*) gercer, crevasser.

chapel [chap'əl] *n* chapelle *f*.

chaperon [shap'ərōn] *n* chaperon *m* ♦ *vt* chaperonner.

chaplain [chap'lin] *n* aumônier *m*.

chapter [chap'tûr] *n* chapitre *m*.

char [chär] *vt* (*burn*) carboniser ♦ *vi* (*Brit: cleaner*) faire des ménages ♦ *n* (*Brit*) = **charlady**.

character [kar'iktûr] *n* caractère *m*; (*in novel, film*) personnage *m*; (*eccentric*) numéro *m*, phénomène *m*; **a person of good ~** une personne bien.

character code *n* (*COMPUT*) code *m* de caractère.

characteristic [kariktəris'tik] *a*, *n* caractéristique (*f*).

characterize [kar'iktərīz] *vt* caractériser; **to ~ (as)** définir (comme).

charade [shərād'] *n* charade *f*.

charcoal [chär'kōl] *n* charbon *m* de bois.

charge [chärj] *n* accusation *f*; (*LAW*) inculpation *f*; (*cost*) prix (demandé); (*of gun, battery, MIL: attack*) charge *f* ♦ *vt* (*LAW*): **to ~ sb (with)** inculper qn (de); (*gun, battery, MIL: enemy*) charger; (*customer, sum*) faire payer ♦ *vi* (*gen with: up, along etc*) foncer; **~s** *npl*: **bank/labor ~s** frais *mpl* de banque/main-d'œuvre; **to ~ in/out** entrer/sortir en trombe; **to ~ down/up** dévaler/grimper à toute allure; **is there a ~?** doit-on payer?; **there's no ~** c'est gratuit, on ne fait pas payer; **extra ~** supplément *m*; **to take ~ of** se charger de; **to be in ~ of** être responsable de, s'occuper de; **to have ~ of sb** avoir la charge de qn; **they ~d us $10 for the meal** ils nous ont fait payer le repas 10 dollars, ils nous ont compté 10 dollars pour le repas; **how much do you ~ for this repair?** combien demandez-vous pour cette réparation?; **to ~ an expense (up) to sb** mettre une dépense sur le compte de qn; **~ it to my account** facturez-le sur mon compte.

charge account *n* compte *m* client.

charge card *n* carte *f* de client (*émise par un grand magasin*).

chargehand [chärj'hand] *n* (*Brit*) chef *m* d'équipe.

charger [chär'jûr] *n* (*also:* **battery ~**) chargeur *m*; (*old: warhorse*) cheval *m* de bataille.

charitable [char'itəbəl] *a* charitable.

charity [char'itē] *n* charité *f*; (*organization*) institution *f* charitable *or* de bienfaisance, œuvre *f* (de charité).

charlady [châr'lādē] *n* (*Brit*) femme *f* de ménage.

charm [chârm] *n* charme *m* ♦ *vt* charmer, enchanter.

charm bracelet *n* bracelet *m* à breloques.

charming [châr'ming] *a* charmant(e).

chart [chârt] *n* tableau *m*, diagramme *m*; graphique *m*; (*map*) carte marine; (*weather ~*) carte *f* du temps ♦ *vt* dresser *or* établir la carte de; (*sales, progress*) établir la courbe de; **to be on** *or* (*Brit*) **in the ~s** (*record, pop group*) figurer au hit-parade.

charter [châr'tûr] *vt* (*plane*) affréter ♦ *n* (*document*) charte *f*; **on ~** (*plane*) affrété(e).

chartered accountant (CA) [châr'tûrd əkoun'tənt] *n* expert-comptable *m*.

charter flight *n* charter *m*.

charwoman [châr'wo͞omən] *n* = **charlady**.

chase [chās] *vt* poursuivre, pourchasser ♦ *n* poursuite *f*, chasse *f*.

chase down *vt* (*US: person*) relancer; (: *information*) rechercher.

chase up *vt* (*Brit*) = **chase down**.

chasm [kaz'əm] *n* gouffre *m*, abîme *m*.

chassis [shas'ē] *n* châssis *m*.

chastened [chā'sənd] *a* assagi(e), rappelé(e) à la raison.

chastening [chā'səning] *a* qui fait réfléchir.

chastise [chastīz'] *vt* punir, châtier; corriger.

chastity [chas'titē] *n* chasteté *f*.

chat [chat] *vi* (*also*: **have a ~**) bavarder, causer ♦ *n* conversation *f*.

chat up *vt* (*Brit col: girl*) baratiner.

chat show *n* (*Brit*) entretien télévisé.

chattel [chat'əl] *see* **goods**.

chatter [chat'ûr] *vi* (*person*) bavarder, papoter ♦ *n* bavardage *m*, papotage *m*; **my teeth are ~ing** je claque des dents.

chatterbox [chat'ûrbâks] *n* moulin *m* à paroles, babillard/e.

chatty [chat'ē] *a* (*style*) familier(ière); (*person*) enclin(e) à bavarder *or* au papotage.

chauffeur [shō'fûr] *n* chauffeur *m* (de maître).

chauvinism [shō'vənizəm] *n* (*also*: **male ~**) phallocratie *f*, machisme *m*; (*nationalism*) chauvinisme *m*.

chauvinist [shō'vənist] *n* (*also*: **male ~**) phallocrate *m*, macho *m*; (*nationalist*) chauvin/e.

ChE *abbr* = **chemical engineer**.

cheap [chēp] *a* à bon marché *inv*, pas cher(chère); (*reduced: ticket*) à prix réduit; (: *fare*) réduit(e); (*joke*) facile, d'un goût douteux; (*poor quality*) à bon marché, de qualité médiocre ♦ *ad* à bon marché, pour pas cher; **~er** *a* moins cher(chère).

cheapen [chē'pən] *vt* rabaisser, déprécier.

cheaply [chēp'lē] *ad* à bon marché, à bon compte.

cheat [chēt] *vi* tricher; (*in exam*) copier ♦ *vt* tromper, duper; (*rob*) escroquer ♦ *n* tricheur/euse; escroc *m*; (*trick*) duperie *f*, tromperie *f*; **to ~ on sb** (*col: husband, wife etc*) tromper qn.

cheating [chē'ting] *n* tricherie *f*.

check [chek] *vt* vérifier; (*passport, ticket*) contrôler; (*halt*) enrayer; (*restrain*) maîtriser ♦ *vi* (*official etc*) se renseigner ♦ *n* vé-

rification *f*; contrôle *m*; (*curb*) frein *m*; (*bill*) addition *f*; (*pattern: gen pl*) carreaux *mpl*; (*US*) chèque *m* ♦ *a* (*also*: **~ed**: *pattern, cloth*) à carreaux; **to ~ with sb** demander à qn; **to keep a ~ on sb/sth** surveiller qn/qch; **to pay by ~** payer par chèque.

check in *vi* (*in hotel*) remplir sa fiche (d'hôtel); (*at airport*) se présenter à l'enregistrement ♦ *vt* (*baggage*) (faire) enregistrer.

check off *vt* cocher.

check out *vi* (*in hotel*) régler sa note ♦ *vt* (*baggage*) retirer; (*investigate: story*) vérifier; (*person*) prendre des renseignements sur.

check up *vi*: **to ~ up (on sth)** vérifier (qch); **to ~ up on sb** se renseigner sur le compte de qn.

checkbook [chek'bo͞ok] *n* chéquier *m*, carnet *m* de chèques.

checkerboard [chek'ərbôrd] *n* damier *m*.

checkered [chek'ûrd] *a* (*fig*) varié(e).

checkers [chek'ûrz] *n* (*US*) (jeu *m* de) dames.

check guarantee card *n* (*US*) carte *f* (d'identité) bancaire.

check-in [chek'in] *n* (*also*: **~ desk**: *at airport*) enregistrement *m*.

checking account [chek'ing əkount'] *n* (*US*) compte courant.

checklist [chek'list] *n* liste *f* de contrôle.

checkmate [chek'māt] *n* échec et mat *m*.

checkout [chek'out] *n* (*in supermarket*) caisse *f*.

checkpoint [chek'point] *n* contrôle *m*.

checkroom [chek'ro͞om] *n* (*US*) vestiaire *m*.

checkup [chek'up] *n* (*MED*) examen médical, check-up *m*.

cheek [chēk] *n* joue *f*; (*impudence*) toupet *m*, culot *m*.

cheekbone [chēk'bōn] *n* pommette *f*.

cheeky [chē'kē] *a* effronté(e), culotté(e).

cheep [chēp] *n* (*of bird*) piaulement *m* ♦ *vi* piauler.

cheer [chēr] *vt* acclamer, applaudir; (*gladden*) réjouir, réconforter ♦ *vi* applaudir ♦ *n* (*gen pl*) acclamations *fpl*, applaudissements *mpl*; bravos *mpl*, hourras *mpl*; **~s!** (à votre) santé!

cheer on *vt* encourager (par des cris *etc*).

cheer up *vi* se dérider, reprendre courage ♦ *vt* remonter le moral à *or* de, dérider, égayer.

cheerful [chēr'fəl] *a* gai(e), joyeux(euse).

cheerfulness [chēr'fəlnis] *n* gaieté *f*, bonne humeur.

cheerio [chēr'ēō] *excl* (*Brit*) salut!, au revoir!

cheerless [chēr'lis] *a* sombre, triste.

cheese [chēz] *n* fromage *m*.

cheeseboard [chēz'bôrd] *n* plateau *m* à fromages; (*with cheese on it*) plateau *m* de fromages.

cheesecake [chēz'kāk] *n* tarte *f* au fromage.

cheetah [chē'tə] *n* guépard *m*.

chef [shef] *n* chef (cuisinier).

chemical [kem'ikəl] *a* chimique ♦ *n* produit *m* chimique.

chemist [kem'ist] *n* (*Brit: pharmacist*) pharmacien/ne; (*scientist*) chimiste *m/f*; **~'s (shop)** *n* (*Brit*) pharmacie *f*.

chemistry [kem'istrē] *n* chimie *f*.

cheque [chck] *etc* (*Brit*) = **check.**
cheque card *n* (*Brit*) carte *f* (d'identité) bancaire.
chequered [chck'ûrd] *a* (*Brit*) = **checkered.**
cherish [chär'ish] *vt* chérir; (*hope etc*) entretenir.
cheroot [shərōōt'] *n* cigare *m* de Manille.
cherry [chär'ē] *n* cerise *f*.
Ches *abbr* (*Brit*) = *Cheshire.*
chess [ches] *n* échecs *mpl*.
chessboard [ches'bôrd] *n* échiquier *m*.
chessman [ches'man] *n* pièce *f* (de jeu d'échecs).
chessplayer [ches'plāûr] *n* joueur/euse d'échecs.
chest [chest] *n* poitrine *f*; (*box*) coffre *m*, caisse *f*; **to get sth off one's ~** (*col*) vider son sac; **~ of drawers** *n* commode *f*.
chest measurement *n* tour *m* de poitrine.
chestnut [ches'nut] *n* châtaigne *f*; (*also*: **~ tree**) châtaignier *m*; (*color*) châtain *m* ♦ *a* (*hair*) châtain *inv*; (*horse*) alezan.
chew [chōō] *vt* mâcher.
chewing gum [chōō'ing gum] *n* chewing-gum *m*.
chic [shēk] *a* chic *inv*, élégant(e).
chick [chik] *n* poussin *m*; (*col*) pépée *f*.
chicken [chik'ən] *n* poulet *m*; (*col: coward*) poule mouillée.
  chicken out *vi* (*col*) se dégonfler.
chicken feed *n* (*fig*) broutilles *fpl*, bagatelle *f*.
chickenpox [chik'ənpáks] *n* varicelle *f*.
chick pea [chik pē] *n* pois *m* chiche.
chicory [chik'ûrē] *n* (*for coffee*) chicorée *f*; (*salad*) endive *f*.
chide [chīd] *vt* réprimander, gronder.
chief [chēf] *n* chef *m* ♦ *a* principal(e); **C~ of Staff** (*MIL*) chef d'État-major.
chief constable *n* (*Brit*) ≈ préfet *m* de police.
chief executive officer, chief executive *n* directeur général.
chiefly [chēf'lē] *ad* principalement, surtout.
chiffon [shifan'] *n* mousseline *f* de soie.
chilblain [chil'blān] *n* engelure *f*.
child, *pl* **~ren** [chīld, chil'drən] *n* enfant *m/f*.
childbirth [chīld'bûrth] *n* accouchement *m*.
childhood [chīld'hōōd] *n* enfance *f*.
childish [chīl'dish] *a* puéril(e), enfantin(e).
childless [chīld'lis] *a* sans enfants.
childlike [chīld'līk] *a* innocent(e), pur(e).
child minder *n* (*Brit*) garde *f* d'enfants.
Chile [chil'ē] *n* Chili *m*.
Chilean [chēl'āən] *a* chilien(ne) ♦ *n* Chilien/ne.
chili, (*Brit*) **chilli** [chil'ē] *n* piment *m* (rouge).
chill [chil] *n* froid *m*; (*MED*) refroidissement *m*, coup *m* de froid ♦ *a* froid(e), glacial(e) ♦ *vt* faire frissonner; refroidir; (*CULIN*) mettre au frais, rafraîchir; **"serve ~ed"** "à servir frais".
chilly [chil'ē] *a* froid(e), glacé(e); (*sensitive to cold*) frileux(euse); **to feel ~** avoir froid.
chime [chīm] *n* carillon *m* ♦ *vi* carillonner, sonner.
chimney [chim'nē] *n* cheminée *f*.
chimney sweep *n* ramonneur *m*.
chimpanzee [chimpanzē'] *n* chimpanzé *m*.
chin [chin] *n* menton *m*.
China [chī'nə] *n* Chine *f*.

china *n* porcelaine *f*; (*vaisselle f en*) porcelaine.
Chinese [chīnēz'] *a* chinois(e) ♦ *n* (*pl inv*) Chinois/e; (*LING*) chinois *m*.
chink [chingk] *n* (*opening*) fente *f*, fissure *f*; (*noise*) tintement *m*.
chip [chip] *n* (*gen pl: US: also:* **potato ~**) chip *m*; (: *Brit CULIN*) frite *f*; (*of wood*) copeau *m*; (*of glass, stone*) éclat *m*; (*also:* **micro~**) puce *f*; (*in gambling*) fiche *f* ♦ *vt* (*cup, plate*) ébrécher; **when the ~s are down** (*fig*) au moment critique.
  chip in *vi* (*col*) mettre son grain de sel.
chipboard [chip'bôrd] *n* (*Brit*) aggloméré *m*, panneau *m* de particules.
chipmunk [chip'mungk] *n* suisse *m* (*animal*).
chiropodist [kirâp'ədist] *n* (*Brit*) pédicure *m/f*.
chiropody [kirâp'ədē] *n* (*Brit*) pédicurie *f*.
chirp [chûrp] *n* pépiement *m*, gazouillis *m*; (*of crickets*) stridulation *f* ♦ *vi* pépier, gazouiller; chanter, striduler.
chirpy [chûr'pē] *a* (*col*) plein(e) d'entrain, tout guilleret(te).
chisel [chiz'əl] *n* ciseau *m*.
chit [chit] *n* mot *m*, note *f*.
chitchat [chit'chat] *n* bavardage *m*, papotage *m*.
chivalrous [shiv'əlrəs] *a* chevaleresque.
chivalry [shiv'əlrē] *n* chevalerie *f*; esprit *m* chevaleresque.
chives [chīvz] *npl* ciboulette *f*, civette *f*.
chloride [klôr'īd] *n* chlorure *m*.
chlorinate [klôr'ənāt] *vt* chlorer.
chlorine [klôr'ēn] *n* chlore *m*.
chock [chák] *n* cale *f*.
chock-a-block [chák'əblâk'], **chock-full** [chák'fōōl] *a* plein(e) à craquer.
chocolate [chôk'əlit] *n* chocolat *m*.
choice [chois] *n* choix *m* ♦ *a* de choix; **by** *or* **from ~** par choix; **a wide ~** un grand choix.
choir [kwī'ûr] *n* chœur *m*, chorale *f*.
choirboy [kwîûr'boi] *n* jeune choriste *m*, petit chanteur.
choke [chōk] *vi* étouffer ♦ *vt* étrangler; étouffer; (*block*) boucher, obstruer ♦ *n* (*AUT*) starter *m*.
cholera [kál'ərə] *n* choléra *m*.
cholesterol [kəles'tərôl] *n* cholestérol *m*.
choose, *pt* **chose,** *pp* **chosen** [chōōz, chôz, chō'zən] *vt* choisir ♦ *vi*: **to ~ between** choisir entre; **to ~ from** choisir parmi; **to ~ to do** décider de faire, juger bon de faire.
choosy [chōō'zē] *a*: (**to be) ~** (faire le) difficile.
chop [châp] *vt* (*wood*) couper (à la hache); (*CULIN: also:* **~ up**) couper (fin), émincer, hacher (en morceaux) ♦ *n* coup *m* (*de hache, du tranchant de la main*); (*CULIN*) côtelette *f*; **to get the ~** (*Brit col: project*) tomber à l'eau; (: *person: be sacked*) se faire renvoyer.
  chop down *vt* (*tree*) abattre.
chopper [châp'ûr] *n* (*helicopter*) hélicoptère *m*, hélico *m*.
choppy [châp'ē] *a* (*sea*) un peu agité(e).
chops [châps] *npl* (*jaws*) mâchoires *fpl*; babines *fpl*.
chopsticks [châp'stiks] *npl* baguettes *fpl*.
choral [kôr'əl] *a* choral(e), chanté(e) en

chœur.

chord [kôrd] *n* (MUS) accord *m*.

chore [chôr] *n* travail *m* de routine; **household** ~**s** travaux *mpl* du ménage.

choreographer [kôrēăg'rəfûr] *n* chorégraphe *m/f*.

chorister [kôr'istûr] *n* choriste *m/f*.

chortle [chôr'təl] *vi* glousser.

chorus [kôr'əs] *n* chœur *m*; (*repeated part of song, also fig*) refrain *m*.

chose [chōz] *pt of* **choose**.

chosen [chō'zən] *pp of* **choose**.

chow [chou] *n* (*dog*) chow-chow *m*.

chowder [chou'dûr] *n* soupe *f* de poisson.

Christ [krīst] *n* Christ *m*.

christen [kris'ən] *vt* baptiser.

christening [kris'əning] *n* baptême *m*.

Christian [kris'chən] *a*, *n* chrétien(ne).

Christianity [krischēan'itē] *n* christianisme *m*; chrétienté *f*.

Christian name *n* prénom *m*.

Christmas [kris'məs] *n* Noël *m or f*; **happy or merry** ~**!** joyeux Noël!

Christmas card *n* carte *f* de Noël.

Christmas Day *n* le jour de Noël.

Christmas Eve *n* la veille de Noël; la nuit de Noël.

Christmas Island *n* île *f* Christmas.

Christmas tree *n* arbre *m* de Noël.

Christmas tree lights *npl* guirlande lumineuse.

chrome [krōm] *n* = **chromium**.

chromium [krō'mēəm] *n* chrome *m*; (*also:* ~ **plating**) chromage *m*.

chromosome [krō'məsōm] *n* chromosome *m*.

chronic [krân'ik] *a* chronique; (*fig: liar, smoker*) invétéré(e).

chronicle [krân'ikəl] *n* chronique *f*.

chronological [krânəlâj'ikəl] *a* chronologique.

chrysanthemum [krisan'thəməm] *n* chrysanthème *m*.

chubby [chub'ē] *a* potelé(e), rondelet(te).

chuck [chuk] *vt* lancer, jeter; **to** ~ (**up** *or* **in**) *vt* (*Brit: job*) lâcher; (: *person*) plaquer.
  chuck out *vt* flanquer dehors *or* à la porte.

chuckle [chuk'əl] *vi* glousser.

chug [chug] *vi* faire teuf-teuf; souffler.

chum [chum] *n* copain/copine.

chump [chump] *n* (*col*) imbécile *m/f*, crétin/e.

chunk [chungk] *n* gros morceau; (*of bread*) quignon *m*.

chunky [chung'kē] *a* (*furniture etc*) massif(ive); (*person*) trapu(e); (*knitwear*) en grosse laine.

church [chûrch] *n* église *f*; **the C**~ **of England** l'Église anglicane.

churchyard [chûrch'yârd] *n* cimetière *m*.

churlish [chûr'lish] *a* grossier(ère); hargneux(euse).

churn [chûrn] *n* (*for butter*) baratte *f*; (*for transport: also:* **milk** ~) (grand) bidon à lait.
  churn out *vt* débiter.

chute [shōōt] *n* glissoire *f*; (*also:* **garbage** ~) vide-ordures *m inv*; (*Brit: children's slide*) toboggan *m*.

chutney [chut'nē] *n* chutney *m*.

CIA *n abbr* (US: = *Central Intelligence Agency*) CIA *f*.

CID *n abbr* (*Brit:* = *Criminal Investigation De-*

partment) ≈ P.J. *f* (= *police judiciaire*).

cider [sī'dûr] *n* cidre *m*.

CIF *abbr* (= *cost, insurance and freight*) CAF.

cigar [sigâr'] *n* cigare *m*.

cigarette [sigəret'] *n* cigarette *f*.

cigarette butt, (*Brit*) **cigarette end** *n* mégot *m*.

cigarette case *n* étui *m* à cigarettes.

cigarette holder *n* fume-cigarettes *m inv*.

C in C *abbr* = **commander in chief**.

cinch [sinch] *n* (*col*): **it's a** ~ c'est du gâteau, c'est l'enfance de l'art.

cinder [sin'dûr] *n* cendre *f*.

cinder block [sindûr blâk] *n* (US) parpaing *m*.

Cinderella [sindərĕl'ə] *n* Cendrillon.

cine-camera [sin'ēkamûrə] *n* (*Brit*) caméra *f*.

cine-film [sin'ēfilm] *n* (*Brit*) film *m*.

cinema [sin'əmə] *n* cinéma *m*.

cinnamon [sin'əmən] *n* cannelle *f*.

cipher [sī'fûr] *n* code secret; (*fig: faceless employee etc*) numéro *m*; **in** ~ codé(e).

circa [sûr'kə] *prep* circa, environ.

circle [sûr'kəl] *n* cercle *m*; (*in cinema*) balcon *m* ♦ *vi* faire *or* décrire des cercles ♦ *vt* (*surround*) entourer, encercler; (*move around*) faire le tour de, tourner autour de.

circuit [sûr'kit] *n* circuit *m*.

circuit board *n* plaquette *f*.

circuit court *n* (US) ≈ Cour *f* d'assises.

circuitous [sûrkyōō'itəs] *a* indirect(e), qui fait un détour.

circular [sûr'kyəlûr] *a* circulaire ♦ *n* circulaire *f*; (*as advertisement*) prospectus *m*.

circulate [sûr'kyəlāt] *vi* circuler ♦ *vt* faire circuler.

circulation [sûrkyəlā'shən] *n* circulation *f*; (*of newspaper*) tirage *m*.

circumcise [sûr'kəmsīz] *vt* circoncire.

circumference [sûrkum'fûrəns] *n* circonférence *f*.

circumflex [sûr'kəmfleks] *n* (*also:* ~ **accent**) accent *m* circonflexe.

circumscribe [sûr'kəmskrīb'] *vt* circonscrire.

circumspect [sûr'kəmspekt] *a* circonspect(e).

circumstances [sûr'kəmstansiz] *npl* circonstances *fpl*; (*financial condition*) moyens *mpl*, situation financière; **under the** ~ dans ces conditions; **under no** ~ en aucun cas, sous aucun prétexte.

circumstantial [sûrkəmstan'shəl] *a* (*report, statement*) circonstancié(e); ~ **evidence** preuve indirecte.

circumvent [sûr'kəmvent'] *vt* (*rule etc*) tourner.

circus [sûr'kəs] *n* cirque *m*; (*also:* **C**~: *in place names*) place *f*.

cistern [sis'tûrn] *n* réservoir *m* (d'eau); (*Brit: in toilet*) réservoir de la chasse d'eau.

citation [sītā'shən] *n* citation *f*; (US) P.-V. *m*.

cite [sīt] *vt* citer.

citizen [sit'əzən] *n* (POL) citoyen/ne; (*resident*): **the** ~**s of this town** les habitants de cette ville.

citizenship [sit'əzənship] *n* citoyenneté *f*.

citric [sit'rik] *a*: ~ **acid** acide *m* citrique.

citrus fruit [sit'rəs frōōt] *n* agrume *m*.

city [sit'ē] *n* ville *f*, cité *f*.

city center *n* centre *m* de la ville, centre-ville *m*.

city hall n (US) hôtel m de ville.
city plan n plan m de ville.
city planner n (US) urbaniste m/f.
city planning n (US) urbanisme m.
civic [siv'ik] a civique.
civil [siv'əl] a civil(e); (polite) poli(e), civil.
civil disobedience n désobéissance civile.
civil engineer n ingénieur civil.
civil engineering n génie civil, travaux publics.
civilian [sivil'yən] a, n civil(e).
civilization [sivələzā'shən] n civilisation f.
civilized [siv'əlīzd] a civilisé(e); (fig) où règnent les bonnes manières, empreint(e) d'une courtoisie de bon ton.
civil law n code civil; (study) droit civil.
civil rights npl droits mpl civiques.
civil servant n fonctionnaire m/f.
Civil Service n fonction publique, administration f.
civil war n guerre civile.
cl abbr (= centiliter) cl.
clad [klad] a: ~ (in) habillé(e) de, vêtu(e) de.
claim [klām] vt (rights etc) revendiquer; (compensation) réclamer; **to ~ that/to be** prétendre que/être ♦ vi (for insurance) faire une déclaration de sinistre ♦ n revendication f; prétention f; (right) droit m; (for expenses) note f de frais; (insurance) ~ demande f d'indemnisation, déclaration f de sinistre; **to put in a ~ for** (pay raise etc) demander.
claimant [klā'mənt] n (ADMIN, LAW) requérant/e.
claim form n (gen) formulaire m de demande.
clairvoyant [klârvoi'ənt] n voyant/e, extralucide m/f.
clam [klam] n palourde f.
   clam up vi (col) la boucler.
clamber [klam'bûr] vi grimper, se hisser.
clammy [klam'ē] a humide et froid(e) (au toucher), moite.
clamor, (Brit) **clamour** [klam'ûr] n (noise) clameurs fpl; (protest) protestations bruyantes ♦ vi: **to ~ for sth** réclamer qch à grands cris.
clamp [klamp] n étau m à main; agrafe f, crampon m ♦ vt serrer; cramponner.
   clamp down on vt fus sévir contre, prendre des mesures draconiennes à l'égard de.
clan [klan] n clan m.
clandestine [klandes'tin] a clandestin(e).
clang [klang] n bruit m or fracas m métallique ♦ vi émettre un bruit or fracas métallique.
clansman [klanz'mən] n membre m d'un clan (écossais).
clap [klap] vi applaudir ♦ vt: **to ~ (one's hands)** battre des mains ♦ n claquement m; tape f; **a ~ of thunder** un coup de tonnerre.
clapping [klap'ing] n applaudissements mpl.
claret [klar'it] n (vin m de) bordeaux m (rouge).
clarification [klarəfəkā'shən] n (fig) clarification f, éclaircissement m.
clarify [klar'əfī] vt clarifier.
clarinet [klarənet'] n clarinette f.
clarity [klar'itē] n clarté f.
clash [klash] n (sound) choc m, fracas m;

(with police) affrontement m; (fig) conflit m
♦ vi se heurter; être or entrer en conflit; (dates, events) tomber en même temps.
clasp [klasp] n fermoir m ♦ vt serrer, étreindre.
class [klas] n (gen) classe f; (group, category) catégorie f ♦ vt classer, classifier.
class-conscious [klas'kân'shəs] a conscient(e) de son appartenance sociale.
class consciousness n conscience f de classe.
classic [klas'ik] a classique ♦ n (author) classique m; (race etc) classique f.
classical [klas'ikəl] a classique.
classics [klas'iks] npl (SCOL) lettres fpl classiques.
classification [klasəfəkā'shən] n classification f.
classified [klas'əfīd] a (information) secret(ète); ~ **ads** petites annonces.
classify [klas'əfī] vt classifier, classer.
classmate [klas'māt] n camarade m/f de classe.
classroom [klas'rōōm] n (salle f de) classe f.
clatter [klat'ûr] n cliquetis m ♦ vi cliqueter.
clause [klôz] n clause f; (LING) proposition f.
claustrophobia [klôstrəfō'bēə] n claustrophobie f.
claw [klô] n griffe f; (of bird of prey) serre f; (of lobster) pince f ♦ vt griffer; déchirer.
clay [klā] n argile f.
clean [klēn] a propre; (clear, smooth) net(te) ♦ vt nettoyer ♦ ad: **he ~ forgot** il a complètement oublié; **to come** (col: admit guilt) se mettre à table; **to ~ one's teeth** (Brit) se laver les dents; ~ **driving record** permis où n'est portée aucune indication de contravention.
   clean off vt enlever.
   clean out vt nettoyer (à fond).
   clean up vt nettoyer; (fig) remettre de l'ordre dans ♦ vi (fig: make profit): **to ~ up on** faire son beurre avec.
clean-cut [klēn'kut'] a (man) soigné; (situation etc) bien délimité(e), net(te), clair(e).
cleaner [klē'nûr] n (person) nettoyeur/euse, femme f de ménage; (also: **dry ~er**) teinturier/ière; (product) détachant m.
cleaning [klē'ning] n nettoyage m.
cleaning lady or **woman** n femme f de ménage.
cleanliness [klen'lēnis] n propreté f.
cleanly [klēn'lē] ad proprement; nettement.
cleanse [klenz] vt nettoyer; purifier.
cleanser [klen'zûr] n détergent m; (for face) démaquillant m.
clean-shaven [klēn'shā'vən] a rasé(e) de près.
cleansing department [klen'zing dipârt'mənt] n (Brit) service m de voirie.
clean-up [klēn'up] n nettoyage m.
clear [kli'ûr] a clair(e); (road, way) libre, dégagé(e); (profit, majority) net(te) ♦ vt dégager, déblayer, débarrasser; (room etc: of people) faire évacuer; (woodland) défricher; (check) compenser; (COMM: goods) liquider; (LAW: suspect) innocenter; (obstacle) franchir or sauter sans heurter ♦ vi (weather) s'éclaircir; (fog) se dissiper ♦ ad: ~ **of** à distance de, à l'écart de ♦ n: **to be in the ~**

(*out of debt*) être dégagé(e) de toute dette; (*out of suspicion*) être lavé(e) de tout soupçon; (*out of danger*) être hors de danger; **to ~ the table** débarrasser la table, desservir; **to ~ one's throat** s'éclaircir la gorge; **to ~ a profit** faire un bénéfice net; **to make o.s. ~** se faire bien comprendre; **to make it ~ to sb that ...** bien faire comprendre à qn que ...; **I have a ~ day tomorrow** (*Brit*) je n'ai rien de prévu demain; **to keep ~ of sb/sth** éviter qn/qch.

clear off *vi* (*Brit col*) = **clear out.**

clear out *vi* (*US col*) dégager.

clear up *vi* s'éclaircir, se dissiper ♦ *vt* ranger, mettre en ordre; (*mystery*) éclaircir, résoudre.

clearance [klē'rəns] *n* (*removal*) déblayage *m*; (*free space*) dégagement *m*; (*permission*) autorisation *f*.

clearance sale *n* (*COMM*) liquidation *f*.

clear-cut [kli'ûrkut'] *a* précise(e), nettement défini(e).

clearing [klē'ring] *n* (*in forest*) clairière *f*; (*Brit BANKING*) compensation *f*, clearing *m*.

clearing bank *n* (*Brit*) banque *f* qui appartient à une chambre de compensation.

clearly [kli'ûrlē] *ad* clairement; (*obviously*) de toute évidence.

clearway [klēr'wā] *n* (*Brit*) route *f* à stationnement interdit.

cleavage [klē'vij] *n* (*of dress*) décolleté *m*.

cleaver [klē'vûr] *n* fendoir *m*, couperet *m*.

clef [klef] *n* (*MUS*) clé *f*.

cleft [kleft] *n* (*in rock*) crevasse *f*, fissure *f*.

clemency [klem'ənsē] *n* clémence *f*.

clement [klem'ənt] *a* (*weather*) clément(e).

clench [klench] *vt* serrer.

clergy [klûr'jē] *n* clergé *m*.

clergyman [klûr'jēmən] *n* ecclésiastique *m*.

clerical [klär'ikəl] *a* de bureau, d'employé de bureau; (*REL*) clérical(e), du clergé.

clerk [klûrk] *n* employé·e de bureau; (*US: salesman/woman*) vendeur/euse; **C~ of Court** (*LAW*) greffier *m* (du tribunal).

clever [klev'ûr] *a* (*mentally*) intelligent(e); (*deft, crafty*) habile, adroit(e); (*device, arrangement*) ingénieux(euse), astucieux(euse).

clew [klōō] *n* (*US*) = **clue.**

cliché [klēshā'] *n* cliché *m*.

click [klik] *vi* faire un bruit sec *or* un déclic ♦ *vt*: **to ~ one's tongue** faire claquer sa langue; **to ~ one's heels** claquer des talons.

client [kli'ənt] *n* client/e.

clientele [klīəntel'] *n* clientèle *f*.

cliff [klif] *n* falaise *f*.

cliffhanger [klif'hangûr] *n* (*TV, fig*) histoire pleine de suspense.

climactic [klīmak'tik] *a* à son point culminant, culminant(e).

climate [kli'mit] *n* climat *m*.

climax [kli'maks] *n* apogée *m*, point culminant; (*sexual*) orgasme *m*.

climb [klīm] *vi* grimper, monter; (*plane*) prendre de l'altitude ♦ *vt* gravir, escalader, monter sur ♦ *n* montée *f*, escalade *f*; **to ~ over a wall** passer par dessus un mur.

climb down *vi* (re)descendre; (*Brit fig*) rabattre de ses prétentions.

climbdown [klīm'doun] *n* (*Brit*) reculade *f*.

climber [klī'mûr] *n* (*also:* **rock ~**) grimpeur/euse, varappeur/euse.

climbing [klī'ming] *n* (*also:* **rock ~**) escalade *f*, varappe *f*.

clinch [klinch] *vt* (*deal*) conclure, sceller.

cling [kling], *pt, pp* **clung** [kling, klung] *vi*: **to ~ (to)** se cramponner (à), s'accrocher (à); (*of clothes*) coller (à).

clinic [klin'ik] *n* clinique *f*; centre médical; (*session*: *MED*) consultation(s) *f(pl)*, séance(s) *f(pl)*; (*SPORT*) séance(s) de perfectionnement.

clinical [klin'ikəl] *a* clinique; (*fig*) froid(e).

clink [klingk] *vi* tinter, cliqueter.

clip [klip] *n* (*for hair*) barrette *f*; (*also:* **paper ~**) trombone *m*; (*clamp*) pince *f* de bureau; (*holding hose etc*) collier *m* or bague *f* (métallique) de serrage ♦ *vt* (*also:* **~ together**) (*papers*) attacher; (*hair, nails*) couper; (*hedge*) tailler.

clippers [klip'ûrz] *npl* tondeuse *f*; (*also:* **nail ~**) coupe-ongles *m inv*.

clipping [klip'ing] *n* (*from newspaper*) coupure *f* de journal.

clique [klēk] *n* clique *f*, coterie *f*.

cloak [klōk] *n* grande cape.

cloakroom [klōk'rōōm] *n* (*for coats etc*) vestiaire *m*; (*Brit: W.C.*) toilettes *fpl*.

clock [klák] *n* (*large*) horloge *f*; (*small*) pendule *f*; **around the ~** (*work etc*) vingt-quatre heures sur vingt-quatre; **to sleep around the ~** faire le tour du cadran; **30,000 on the ~** (*Brit AUT*) 30 000 km au compteur; **to work against the ~** faire la course contre la montre.

clock in, clock on *vi* pointer (en arrivant).

clock off, clock out *vi* pointer (en partant).

clock up *vt* (*miles, hours etc*) faire.

clockwise [klák'wīz] *ad* dans le sens des aiguilles d'une montre.

clockwork [klák'wûrk] *n* mouvement *m* (d'horlogerie); rouages *mpl*, mécanisme *m* ♦ *a* (*toy, train*) mécanique.

clod [klád] *n* (*col*) lourdaud *m*, balourd *m*.

clog [klág] *n* sabot *m* ♦ *vt* boucher, encrasser ♦ *vi* se boucher, s'encrasser.

cloister [klois'tûr] *n* cloître *m*.

clone [klōn] *n* clone *m*.

close *a, ad and derivatives* [klōs] *a* (*near*): **~ (to)** près (de), proche (de); (*writing, texture*) serré(e); (*watch*) étroit(e), strict(e); (*examination*) attentif(ive), minutieux(euse); (*weather*) lourd(e), étouffant(e); (*room*) mal aéré(e) ♦ *ad* près, à proximité; **~ to** *prep* près de; **~ by, ~ at hand** *a, ad* tout(e) près; **how ~ is Philadelphia to New York?** combien de kilomètres y-a-t-il entre Philadelphie et New York?; **a ~ friend** un ami intime; **to have a ~ shave** (*fig*) l'échapper belle; **at ~ quarters** tout près, à côté ♦ *vb and derivatives* [klōz] *vt* fermer; (*bargain, deal*) conclure ♦ *vi* (*store etc*) fermer; (*lid, door etc*) se fermer; (*end*) se terminer, se conclure ♦ *n* (*end*) conclusion *f*; **to bring sth to a ~** mettre fin à qch.

close down *vt, vi* fermer (définitivement).

close in *vi* (*hunters*) approcher; (*night, fog*) tomber; **the days are closing in** les jours

raccourcissent; **to** ~ **in on sb** cerner qn.
close off *vt* (*area*) boucler.
closed [klōzd] *a* (*store etc*) fermé(e); (*road*) fermé à la circulation.
closed-circuit [klōzdsûr'kit] *a*: ~ **television** télévision *f* en circuit fermé.
closed shop *n* organisation *f* qui n'admet que des travailleurs syndiqués.
close-knit [klōs'nit'] *a* (*family, community*) très uni(e).
closely [klōs'lē] *ad* (*examine, watch*) de près; **we are** ~ **related** nous sommes proches parents; **a** ~ **guarded secret** un secret bien gardé.
closet [klâz'it] *n* placard *m*, réduit *m*; (*for hanging clothes*) penderie *f*.
close-up [klōs'up] *n* gros plan.
closing [klō'zing] *a* (*stages, remarks*) final(e); ~ **price** (*STOCK EXCHANGE*) cours *m* de clôture.
closure [klō'zhûr] *n* fermeture *f*.
clot [klât] *n* (*gen: blood* ~) caillot *m*; (*col: person*) ballot *m* ♦ *vi* (*blood*) former des caillots; (*: external bleeding*) se coaguler.
cloth [klôth] *n* (*material*) tissu *m*, étoffe *f*; (*Brit: also:* **tea**~) torchon *m*; lavette *f*; (*also:* **table**~) nappe *f*.
clothe [klōth̲] *vt* habiller, vêtir.
clothes [klōz] *npl* vêtements *mpl*, habits *mpl*; **to put one's** ~ **on** s'habiller; **to take one's** ~ **off** enlever ses vêtements.
clothes brush *n* brosse *f* à habits.
clothes line *n* corde *f* (à linge).
clothes pin, (*Brit*) **clothes peg** *n* pince *f* à linge.
clothing [klō'thing] *n* = **clothes.**
clotted cream [klât'id krēm'] *n* (*Brit*) crème caillée.
cloud [kloud] *n* nuage *m* ♦ *vt* (*liquid*) troubler; **to** ~ **the issue** brouiller les cartes; **every** ~ **has a silver lining** (*proverb*) à quelque chose malheur est bon (*proverbe*).
cloud over *vi* se couvrir; (*fig*) s'assombrir.
cloudburst [kloud'bûrst] *n* violente averse.
cloudland [kloud'land] *n* (*US*) monde *m* imaginaire.
cloudy [klou'dē] *a* nuageux(euse), couvert(e); (*liquid*) trouble.
clout [klout] *n* (*blow*) taloche *f*; (*fig*) pouvoir *m* ♦ *vt* flanquer une taloche à.
clove [klōv] *n* clou *m* de girofle; ~ **of garlic** gousse *f* d'ail.
clover [klō'vûr] *n* trèfle *m*.
cloverleaf [klō'vûrlēf] *n* feuille *f* de trèfle; (*AUT*) croisement en trèfle.
clown [kloun] *n* clown *m* ♦ *vi* (*also:* ~ **around**) faire le clown.
cloying [kloi'ing] *a* (*taste, smell*) écœurant(e).
CLU *n abbr* (*US: = Chartered Life Underwriter*) spécialiste agréé en assurance-vie.
club [klub] *n* (*society*) club *m*; (*weapon*) massue *f*, matraque *f*; (*also:* **golf** ~) club ♦ *vt* matraquer ♦ *vi*: **to** ~ **together** s'associer; ~**s** *npl* (*CARDS*) trèfle *m*.
club car *n* (*US RAIL*) wagon-restaurant *m*.
clubhouse [klub'hous] *n* pavillon *m*.
cluck [kluk] *vi* glousser.
clue [klōō] *n* indice *m*; (*in crosswords*) définition *f*; **I haven't a** ~ je n'en ai pas la moin-

dre idée.
clued in [klōōd in] *a* (*US col*) (*vachement*) calé(e).
clued up [klōōd up] *a* (*Brit col*) = **clued in.**
clump [klump] *n*: ~ **of trees** bouquet *m* d'arbres.
clumsy [klum'zē] *a* (*person*) gauche, maladroit(e); (*object*) malcommode, peu maniable.
clung [klung] *pt, pp of* **cling.**
clunker [klunk'ûr] *n* (*US col: car*) (vieux) tacot.
cluster [klus'tûr] *n* (petit) groupe ♦ *vi* se rassembler.
clutch [kluch] *n* (*grip, grasp*) étreinte *f*, prise *f*; (*AUT*) embrayage *m* ♦ *vt* agripper, serrer fort; **to let out the** ~ (*AUT*) débrayer; **to** ~ **at** se cramponner à.
clutter [klut'ûr] *vt* (*also:* ~ **up**) encombrer ♦ *n* désordre *m*, fouillis *m*.
CM *abbr* (*US MAIL*) = *North Marianna Islands*.
cm *abbr* (= *centimeter*) cm.
CND *n abbr* = *Campaign for Nuclear Disarmament*.
CO *n abbr* (= *commanding officer*) Cdt ♦ *abbr* (*US MAIL*) = *Colorado*.
Co. *abbr* = **company, county.**
c/o *abbr* (= *care of*) c/o, aux bons soins de.
coach [kōch] *n* (*bus*) autocar *m*; (*horsedrawn*) diligence *f*; (*of train*) voiture *f*, wagon *m*; (*SPORT: trainer*) entraîneur/euse; (*school: tutor*) répétiteur/trice ♦ *vt* entraîner; donner des leçons particulières à.
coach trip *n* excursion *f* en car.
coagulate [kōag'yəlāt] *vt* coaguler ♦ *vi* se coaguler.
coal [kōl] *n* charbon *m*.
coalfield [kōl'fēld] *n* bassin houiller.
coalition [kōəlish'ən] *n* coalition *f*.
coalman [kōl'mən], **coal merchant** *n* charbonnier *m*, marchand *m* de charbon.
coal mine *n* mine *f* de charbon.
coal miner *n* mineur *m*.
coal mining *n* extraction *f* du charbon.
coarse [kôrs] *a* grossier(ère), rude; (*vulgar*) vulgaire.
coast [kōst] *n* côte *f* ♦ *vi* (*with cycle etc*) descendre en roue libre.
coastal [kōs'təl] *a* côtier(ère).
coaster [kōs'tûr] *n* (*NAUT*) caboteur *m*; (*for glass*) dessous *m* de verre.
coastguard [kōst'gârd] *n* garde-côte *m*.
coastline [kōst'līn] *n* côte *f*, littoral *m*.
coat [kōt] *n* manteau *m*; (*of animal*) pelage *m*, poil *m*; (*of paint*) couche *f* ♦ *vt* couvrir, enduire; ~ **of arms** *n* blason *m*, armoiries *fpl*.
coated [kō'tid] (*US*) *a*: **to have a** ~ **tongue** avoir la langue pâteuse.
coat hanger *n* cintre *m*.
coating [kō'ting] *n* couche *f*, enduit *m*.
co-author [kōôth'ûr] *n* co-auteur *m*.
coax [kōks] *vt* persuader par de cajoleries.
cob [kâb] *n see* **corn.**
cobbler [kâb'lûr] *n* cordonnier *m*.
cobbles [kâb'əlz], **cobblestones** [kâb'əlstōnz] *npl* pavés (ronds).
COBOL [kō'bôl] *n* COBOL *m*.

cobra [kōb'rə] *n* cobra *m*.
cobweb [kâb'web] *n* toile *f* d'araignée.
cocaine [kōkān'] *n* cocaïne *f*.
cock [kâk] *n* (*rooster*) coq *m*; (*male bird*) mâle *m* ♦ *vt* (*gun*) armer; **to ~ one's ears** (*fig*) dresser l'oreille.
cock-a-hoop [kâkəhōōp'] *a* jubilant(e).
cockerel [kâk'ûrəl] *n* jeune coq *m*.
cockeyed [kâk'īd] *a* (*fig*) de travers; qui louche; qui ne tient pas debout (*fig*).
cockle [kâk'əl] *n* coque *f*.
cockney [kâk'nē] *n* cockney *m/f* (*habitant des quartiers populaires de l'East End de Londres*), ≈ faubourien/ne.
cockpit [kâk'pit] *n* (*in aircraft*) poste *m* de pilotage, cockpit *m*.
cockroach [kâk'rōch] *n* cafard *m*, cancrelat *m*.
cocktail [kâk'tāl] *n* cocktail *m*; **shrimp ~**, (*Brit*) **prawn ~** cocktail de crevettes.
cocktail cabinet *n* (meuble-)bar *m*.
cocktail party *n* cocktail *m*.
cocktail shaker [kâk'tāl shā'kûr] *n* shaker *m*.
cocoa [kō'kō] *n* cacao *m*.
coconut [kō'kənut] *n* noix *f* de coco.
cocoon [kəkōōn'] *n* cocon *m*.
COD *abbr* = **cash on delivery, collect on delivery** (*US*).
cod [kâd] *n* morue (fraîche), cabillaud *m*.
code [kōd] *n* code *m*; **~ of behavior** règles *fpl* de conduite; **~ of practice** déontologie *f*.
codeine [kō'dēn] *n* codéine *f*.
codicil [kâd'isəl] *n* codicille *m*.
codify [kâd'əfī] *vt* codifier.
cod-liver oil [kâd'livûr oil] *n* huile *f* de foie de morue.
co-driver [kōdrī'vûr] *n* (*in race*) copilote *m*; (*of truck*) deuxième chauffeur *m*.
co-ed [kōed'] *a abbr* = **coeducational** ♦ *n abbr* (*US: female student*) étudiante d'une université mixte; (*Brit: school*) école *f* mixte.
coeducational [kōejōōkā'shənəl] *a* mixte.
coerce [kōûrs'] *vt* contraindre.
coercion [kōûr'shən] *n* contrainte *f*.
coexistence [kōigzis'təns] *n* coexistence *f*.
C. of C. *n abbr* = **chamber of commerce.**
C of E *abbr* = **Church of England.**
coffee [kôf'ē] *n* café *m*; **~ with cream** (café-)crème *m*.
coffee bar *n* (*Brit*) café *m*.
coffee bean *n* grain *m* de café.
coffee break *n* pause-café *f*.
coffeecake [kôf'ēkāk] *n* (*US*) ≈ petit pain aux raisins.
coffee cup *n* tasse *f* à café.
coffeepot [kôf'ēpât] *n* cafetière *f*.
coffee table *n* (petite) table basse.
coffin [kôf'in] *n* cercueil *m*.
cog [kâg] *n* dent *f* (d'engrenage).
cogent [kō'jənt] *a* puissant(e), convaincant(e).
cognac [kōn'yak] *n* cognac *m*.
cogwheel [kâg'hwēl] *n* roue dentée.
cohabit [kōhab'it] *vi* (*formal*): **to ~ (with sb)** cohabiter (avec qn).
coherent [kōhē'rənt] *a* cohérent(e).
cohesion [kōhē'zhən] *n* cohésion *f*.
cohesive [kōhē'siv] *a* (*fig*) cohésif(ive).
coil [koil] *n* rouleau *m*, bobine *f*; (*one loop*) anneau *m*, spire *f*; (*of smoke*) volute *f*;

(*contraceptive*) stérilet *m* ♦ *vt* enrouler.
coin [koin] *n* pièce *f* de monnaie ♦ *vt* (*word*) inventer.
coinage [koi'nij] *n* monnaie *f*, système *m* monétaire.
coincide [kōinsīd'] *vi* coïncider.
coincidence [kōin'sidəns] *n* coïncidence *f*.
coin-operated [koinâp'ərātid] *a* (*machine, launderette*) automatique.
coin purse *n* (*US*) porte-monnaie *m inv*.
coke [kōk] *n* coke *m*; (®: *Coca-Cola*) coca *m*.
Col. *abbr* (*US*) = *Colorado*; (= *colonel*) Col.
COLA *n abbr* (*US*: = *cost-of-living adjustment*) réajustement (*des salaires, indemnités etc*) *en fonction du coût de la vie*.
colander [kâl'əndûr] *n* passoire *f* (à légumes).
cold [kōld] *a* froid(e) ♦ *n* froid *m*; (*MED*) rhume *m*; **it's ~** il fait froid; **to be ~** avoir froid; **to catch ~** prendre *or* attraper froid; **to catch a ~** s'enrhumer, attraper un rhume; **in ~ blood** de sang-froid; **to have ~ feet** avoir froid aux pieds; (*fig*) avoir la frousse *or* la trouille; **to give sb the ~ shoulder** battre froid à qn.
cold-blooded [kōld'blud'id] *a* (*ZOOL*) à sang froid.
cold cream *n* crème *f* de soins.
cold cuts *npl* viandes froides.
coldly [kōld'lē] *ad* froidement.
cold sore *n* bouton *m* de fièvre.
coleslaw [kōl'slô] *n* sorte de salade de chou cru.
colic [kâl'ik] *n* colique(s) *f(pl)*.
collaborate [kəlab'ərāt] *vi* collaborer.
collaboration [kəlabərā'shən] *n* collaboration *f*.
collaborator [kəlab'ərātûr] *n* collaborateur/trice.
collage [kəlâzh'] *n* (*ART*) collage *m*.
collagen [kâl'əjən] *n* collagène *m*.
collapse [kəlaps'] *vi* s'effondrer, s'écrouler ♦ *n* effondrement *m*, écroulement *m*; (*of government*) chute *f*.
collapsible [kəlaps'əbəl] *a* pliant(e); télescopique.
collar [kâl'ûr] *n* (*of coat, shirt*) col *m*; (*for dog*) collier *m*; (*TECH*) collier, bague *f* ♦ *vt* (*col: person*) pincer.
collarbone [kâl'ûrbōn] *n* clavicule *f*.
collate [kəlāt'] *vt* collationner.
collateral [kəlat'ûrəl] *n* nantissement *m*.
collation [kəlā'shən] *n* collation *f*.
colleague [kâl'ēg] *n* collègue *m/f*.
collect [kəlekt'] *vt* rassembler; (*pick up*) ramasser; (*as a hobby*) collectionner; (*Brit: call for*) (passer) prendre; (*mail*) faire la levée de, ramasser; (*money owed*) encaisser; (*donations, subscriptions*) recueillir ♦ *vi* (*people*) se rassembler; (*dust, dirt*) s'amasser; **to ~ one's thoughts** réfléchir, réunir ses idées; **~ on delivery (COD)** (*US COMM*) payable *or* paiement à la livraison; **to call ~** (*US TEL*) téléphoner en PCV.
collect call *n* (*US TEL*) communication *f* en PCV.
collected [kəlek'tid] *a*: **~ works** œuvres complètes.
collection [kəlek'shən] *n* collection *f*; (*of mail*) levée *f*; (*for money*) collecte *f*, quête *f*.

collective [kəlek'tiv] *a* collectif(ive) ♦ *n* collectif *m*.

collective bargaining *n* convention collective.

collector [kəlek'tûr] *n* collectionneur *m*; *(of taxes)* percepteur *m*; *(of rent, cash)* encaisseur *m*; ~'s **item** *or* **piece** pièce *f* de collection.

college [kâl'ij] *n* collège *m*; *(of technology, agriculture etc)* institut *m*; **to go to** ~ faire des études supérieures; ~ **of education** ≈ école normale.

collide [kəlīd'] *vi*: **to** ~ **(with)** entrer en collision (avec).

collie [kâl'ē] *n (dog)* colley *m*.

colliery [kâl'yûrē] *n (Brit)* mine *f* de charbon, houillère *f*.

collision [kəlizh'ən] *n* collision *f*, heurt *m*; **to be on a** ~ **course** aller droit à la collision; *(fig)* aller vers l'affrontement.

collision damage waiver *n (INSURANCE)* rachat *m* de franchise.

colloquial [kəlō'kwēəl] *a* familier(ère).

collusion [kəlōō'zhən] *n* collusion *f*; **in** ~ **with** en complicité avec.

Colo. *abbr (US)* = *Colorado*.

cologne [kəlōn'] *n (also:* **eau de** ~) eau *f* de cologne.

Colombia [kəlum'bēə] *n* Colombie *f*.

Colombian [kəlum'bēən] *a* colombien(ne) ♦ *n* Colombien/ne.

colon [kō'lən] *n (sign)* deux-points *mpl*; *(MED)* côlon *m*.

colonel [kûr'nəl] *n* colonel *m*.

colonial [kəlō'nēəl] *a* colonial(e).

colonize [kâl'əniz] *vt* coloniser.

colony [kâl'ənē] *n* colonie *f*.

color [kul'ûr] *(US) n* couleur *f* ♦ *vt* colorer; peindre; *(with crayons)* colorier; *(news)* fausser, exagérer ♦ *vi* rougir ♦ *cpd (film, photograph, television)* en couleur; ~**s** *npl (of party, club)* couleurs *fpl*.

Colorado beetle [kâlərâd'ō bē'təl] *n* doryphore *m*.

color bar *n* discrimination raciale *(dans un établissement etc)*.

color-blind [kul'ûrblīnd] *a* daltonien(ne).

colored [kul'ûrd] *a* coloré(e); *(photo)* en couleur ♦ *n*: ~**s** personnes *fpl* de couleur.

colorful [kul'ûrfəl] *a* coloré(e), vif(vive); *(personality)* pittoresque, haut(e) en couleurs.

coloring [kul'ûring] *n* colorant *m*; *(complexion)* teint *m*.

color scheme *n* combinaison *f* de(s) couleur(s).

colossal [kəlâs'əl] *a* colossal(e).

colour [kul'ûr] *etc (Brit)* = **color** etc.

colt [kōlt] *n* poulain *m*.

column [kâl'əm] *n* colonne *f*; *(fashion* ~, *sports* ~ *etc)* rubrique *f*; **the editorial** ~ l'éditorial *m*.

columnist [kâl'əmist] *n* rédacteur/trice d'une rubrique.

coma [kō'mə] *n* coma *m*.

comb [kōm] *n* peigne *m* ♦ *vt (hair)* peigner; *(area)* ratisser, passer au peigne fin.

combat *n* [kâm'bat] combat *m* ♦ *vt* [kəmbat'] combattre, lutter contre.

combination [kâmbənā'shən] *n (gen)* combinaison *f*.

combination lock *n* serrure *f* à combinaison.

combine *vb* [kəmbīn'] *vt* combiner; *(one quality with another)*: **to** ~ **sth with sth** joindre qch à qch, allier qch à qch ♦ *vi* s'associer; *(CHEMISTRY)* se combiner ♦ *n* [kâm'bīn] association *f*; *(ECON)* trust *m*; **a** ~**d effort** un effort conjugué.

combine (harvester) *n* moissonneuse-batteuse(-lieuse) *f*.

combo [kâm'bō] *n (JAZZ etc)* groupe *m* de musiciens.

combustible [kəmbus'təbəl] *a* combustible.

combustion [kəmbus'chən] *n* combustion *f*.

come, *pt* **came**, *pp* **come** [kum, kām] *vi* venir; *(col: sexually)* jouir; ~ **with me** suivez-moi; **we've just** ~ **from Paris** nous arrivons de Paris; ... **what might** ~ **of it** ... ce qui pourrait en résulter, ... ce qui pourrait advenir *or* se produire; **to** ~ **into sight** *or* **view** apparaître; **to** ~ **to** *(decision etc)* parvenir *or* arriver à; **to** ~ **undone/loose** se défaire/desserrer; **coming!** j'arrive!; **if it** ~**s to it** s'il le faut, dans le pire des cas.

come about *vi* se produire, arriver.

come across *vt fus* rencontrer par hasard, tomber sur ♦ *vi*: **to** ~ **across well/badly** faire une bonne/mauvaise impression.

come along *vi (pupil, work)* faire des progrès, avancer; ~ **along!** viens!; allons!, allez!

come apart *vi* s'en aller en morceaux; se détacher.

come around *vi (US: after faint, operation)* revenir à soi, reprendre connaissance.

come away *vi* partir, s'en aller; *(become detached)* se détacher.

come back *vi* revenir; *(reply)*: **can I** ~ **back to you on that one?** est-ce qu'on peut revenir là-dessus plus tard?

come by *vt fus (acquire)* obtenir, se procurer.

come down *vi* descendre; *(prices)* baisser; *(buildings)* s'écrouler; *(: be demolished)* être démoli(e).

come forward *vi* s'avancer; *(make o.s. known)* se présenter, s'annoncer.

come from *vt fus* venir de; *(place)* venir de, être originaire de.

come in *vi* entrer.

come in for *vt fus (criticism etc)* être l'objet de.

come into *vt fus (money)* hériter de.

come off *vi (button)* se détacher; *(stain)* s'enlever; *(attempt)* réussir.

come on *vi (lights, electricity)* s'allumer; *(central heating)* se mettre en marche; *(pupil, work, project)* faire des progrès, avancer; ~ **on!** viens!; allons!, allez!

come out *vi* sortir; *(book)* paraître; *(strike)* cesser le travail, se mettre en grève.

come over *vt fus*: **I don't know what's** ~ **over him!** je ne sais pas ce qui lui a pris!

come round *vi (Brit)* = **come around**.

come through *vi (survive)* s'en sortir; *(telephone call)*: **the call came through** l'appel est bien parvenu.

come to *vi* revenir à soi; *(add up to:*

amount): **how much does it ~ to?** ça fait combien?
come under *vt fus (heading)* se trouver sous; *(influence)* subir.
come up *vi* monter.
come up against *vt fus (resistance, difficulties)* rencontrer.
come up to *vt fus* arriver à; **the film didn't ~ up to our expectations** le film nous a déçu.
come up with *vt fus*: **he came up with an idea** il a eu une idée, il a proposé quelque chose.
come upon *vt fus* tomber sur.
comeback [kum'bak] *n (reaction)* réaction *f*; *(response)* réponse *f*; *(THEATER etc)* rentrée *f*.
Comecon [kâm'əkân] *n abbr (= Council for Mutual Economic Aid)* COMECON *m*.
comedian [kəmē'dēən] *n (in music hall etc)* comique *m*; *(THEATER)* comédien *m*.
comedienne [kəmēdēen'] *n* comique *f*.
comedown [kum'doun] *n* déchéance *f*.
comedy [kâm'idē] *n* comédie *f*.
comet [kâm'it] *n* comète *f*.
comeuppance [kumup'əns] *n*: **to get one's ~** recevoir ce qu'on mérite.
comfort [kum'fûrt] *n* confort *m*, bien-être *m*; *(solace)* consolation *f*, réconfort *m* ♦ *vt* consoler, réconforter.
comfortable [kum'fûrtəbəl] *a* confortable; **I don't feel very ~ about it** cela m'inquiète un peu.
comfortably [kum'fûrtəblē] *ad (sit)* confortablement; *(live)* à l'aise.
comforter [kum'fûrtûr] *n (US)* édredon *m*.
comforts [kum'fûrts] *npl* aises *fpl*.
comfort station *n (US)* toilettes *fpl*.
comic [kâm'ik] *a* comique ♦ *n* comique *m*; *(magazine)* illustré *m*.
comical [kâm'ikəl] *a* amusant(e).
comic strip *n* bande dessinée.
coming [kum'ing] *n* arrivée *f* ♦ *a (next)* prochain(e); *(future)* à venir; **in the ~ weeks** dans les prochaines semaines.
coming(s) and going(s) *n(pl)* va-et-vient *m* *inv*.
Comintern [kâm'intûrn] *n* Comintern *m*.
comma [kâm'ə] *n* virgule *f*.
command [kəmand'] *n* ordre *m*, commandement *m*; *(MIL: authority)* commandement; *(mastery)* maîtrise *f*; *(COMPUT)* commande *f* ♦ *vt (troops)* commander; *(be able to get)* (pouvoir) disposer de, avoir à sa disposition; *(deserve)* avoir droit à; **to ~ sb to do** donner l'ordre *or* commander à qn de faire; **to have/take ~ of** avoir/prendre le commandement de; **to have at one's ~** *(money, resources etc)* disposer de.
commandeer [kâməndēr'] *vt* réquisitionner (par la force).
commander [kəman'dûr] *n* chef *m*; *(MIL)* commandant *m*.
commander in chief *n (MIL)* commandant *m* en chef.
commanding [kəman'ding] *a (appearance)* imposant(e); *(voice, tone)* autoritaire; *(lead, position)* dominant(e).
commanding officer *n* commandant *m*.

commandment [kəmand'mənt] *n (REL)* commandement *m*.
command module *n (SPACE)* module *m* de commande.
commando [kəman'dō] *n* commando *m*; membre *m* d'un commando.
commemorate [kəmem'ərāt] *vt* commémorer.
commemoration [kəmemərā'shən] *n* commémoration *f*.
commemorative [kəmem'ərātiv] *a* commémoratif(ive).
commence [kəmens'] *vt, vi* commencer.
commend [kəmend'] *vt* louer; recommander.
commendable [kəmend'əbəl] *a* louable.
commendation [kâməndā'shən] *n* éloge *m*; recommandation *f*.
commensurate [kəmen'sərit] *a*: **~ with/to** en rapport avec/selon.
comment [kâm'ent] *n* commentaire *m* ♦ *vi* faire des remarques *or* commentaires; **to ~ on** faire des remarques sur; **to ~ that** faire remarquer que; **"no ~"** "je n'ai rien à déclarer".
commentary [kâm'əntārē] *n* commentaire *m*; *(SPORT)* reportage *m* (en direct).
commentator [kâm'əntātûr] *n* commentateur *m*; *(SPORT)* reporter *m*.
commerce [kâm'ûrs] *n* commerce *m*.
commercial [kəmûr'shəl] *a* commercial(e) ♦ *n* *(TV: also: ~ break)* annonce *f* publicitaire, spot *m* (publicitaire).
commercial bank *n* banque *f* d'affaires.
commercialism [kəmûr'shəlizəm] *n* mercantilisme *m*.
commercialize [kəmûr'shəlīz] *vt* commercialiser.
commercial television *n* publicité *f* à la télévision; chaînes indépendantes (financées par la publicité).
commercial vehicle *n* véhicule *m* utilitaire.
commiserate [kəmiz'ərāt] *vi*: **to ~ with sb** témoigner de la sympathie pour qn.
commission [kəmish'ən] *n (committee; fee: also for salesman)* commission *f*; *(order for work of art etc)* commande *f* ♦ *vt (MIL)* nommer (à un commandement); *(work of art)* commander, charger un artiste de l'exécution de; **out of ~** *(NAUT)* hors de service; *(machine)* hors service; **I get 10% ~** je reçois une commission de 10%.
commissionaire [kəmishənār'] *n (Brit: at store, cinema etc)* portier *m* (en uniforme).
commissioner [kəmish'ənûr] *n* membre *m* d'une commission; *(POLICE)* préfet *m* (de police).
commit [kəmit'] *vt (act)* commettre; *(to sb's care)* confier (à); **to ~ o.s. (to do)** s'engager (à faire); **to ~ suicide** se suicider; **to ~ to writing** coucher par écrit; **to ~ sb for trial** traduire qn en justice.
commitment [kəmit'mənt] *n* engagement *m*; *(obligation)* responsabilité(s) *f(pl)*.
committed [kəmit'id] *a (writer, politician etc)* engagé(e).
committee [kəmit'ē] *n* comité *m*; commission *f*; **to be on a ~** siéger dans un comité (*or* une commission).
committee meeting *n* réunion *f* de comité *or* commission.

commodity [kəmâd'itē] *n* produit *m*, marchandise *f*, article *m*; (*food*) denrée *f*.

commodity exchange *n* bourse *f* de marchandises.

common [kâm'ən] *a* (*gen, also pej*) commun(e); (*usual*) courant(e) ♦ *n* terrain communal; **in ~ en commun; in ~ use** d'un usage courant; **it's ~ knowledge that** il est bien connu *or* notoire que; **to the ~ good** pour le bien de tous, dans l'intérêt général.

commoner [kâm'ənûr] *n* roturier/ière.

common ground *n* (*fig*) terrain *m* d'entente.

common law *n* droit coutumier.

common-law [kâm'ənlô'] *a*: **~ wife** épouse *f* de facto.

commonly [kâm'ənlē] *ad* communément, généralement; couramment.

Common Market *n* Marché commun.

commonplace [kâm'ənplās] *a* banal(e), ordinaire.

common room *n* (*Brit*) salle commune.

Commons [kâm'ənz] *npl* (*Brit POL*): **the (House of) ~** la chambre des Communes.

commons [kâm'ənz] *n sg* (*US UNIV*) réfectoire *m*.

common sense *n* bon sens.

common stock *n* (*US FINANCE*) actions *fpl* ordinaires.

Commonwealth [kâm'ənwelth] *n*: **the ~ le** Commonwealth.

commotion [kəmō'shən] *n* désordre *m*, tumulte *m*.

communal [kəmyōō'nəl] *a* (*life*) communautaire; (*for common use*) commun(e).

commune *n* [kâm'yōōn] (*group*) communauté *f* ♦ *vi* [kəmyōōn']: **to ~ with** converser intimement avec; communier avec.

communicate [kəmyōō'nikāt] *vt* communiquer, transmettre ♦ *vi*: **to ~ (with)** communiquer (avec).

communication [kəmyōōnikā'shən] *n* communication *f*.

communication cord *n* (*Brit*) sonnette *f* d'alarme.

communications network *n* réseau *m* de communications.

communications satellite *n* satellite *m* de télécommunications.

communicative [kəmyōō'nikātiv] *a* communicatif(ive).

communion [kəmyōōn'yən] *n* (*also*: **Holy C~**) communion *f*.

communiqué [kəmyōōnikā'] *n* communiqué *m*.

communism [kâm'yənizəm] *n* communisme *m*.

communist [kâm'yənist] *a, n* communiste (*m/ f*).

community [kəmyōō'nitē] *n* communauté *f*.

community center *n* foyer socio-éducatif, centre *m* de loisirs.

community chest *n* (*US*) fonds commun.

community health center *n* centre médico-social.

community spirit *n* solidarité *f*.

commutation ticket [kâmyətā'shən tik'it] *n* (*US*) carte *f* d'abonnement.

commute [kəmyōōt'] *vi* faire le trajet journalier (de son domicile à un lieu de travail

assez éloigné) ♦ *vt* (*LAW*) commuer; (*MATH: terms etc*) opérer la commutation de.

commuter [kəmyōōt'ûr] *n* banlieusard/e (qui ... *see vi*).

compact [kâm'pakt] *a* compact(e) ♦ *n* contrat *m*, entente *f*; (*also*: **powder ~**) poudrier *m*.

compact disc [kâm'pakt disk] *n* disque compact.

companion [kəmpan'yən] *n* compagnon/ compagne.

companionship [kəmpan'yənship] *n* camaraderie *f*.

companionway [kəmpan'yənwā] *n* (*NAUT*) escalier *m* des cabines.

company [kum'pənē] *n* (*also COMM, MIL, THEATER*) compagnie *f*; **he's good ~** il est d'une compagnie agréable; **we have ~** nous avons de la visite; **to keep sb ~** tenir compagnie à qn; **to part ~ with** se séparer de; **Smith and C~** Smith et Compagnie.

company car *n* voiture *f* de fonction.

company director *n* administrateur/trice.

company secretary *n* (*Brit COMM*) secrétaire général (*d'une société*).

comparable [kâm'pûrəbəl] *a* comparable.

comparative [kəmpar'ətiv] *a* comparatif(ive); (*relative*) relatif(ive).

comparatively [kəmpar'ətivlē] *ad* (*relatively*) relativement.

compare [kəmpär'] *vt*: **to ~ sth/sb with/to** comparer qch/qn avec *or* et/à ♦ *vi*: **to ~ (with)** se comparer (à); être comparable (à); **how do the prices ~?** comment sont les prix?, est-ce que les prix sont comparables?; **~d with** *or* **to** par rapport à.

comparison [kəmpar'isən] *n* comparaison *f*; **in ~ (with)** en comparaison (de).

compartment [kəmpârt'mənt] *n* (*also RAIL*) compartiment *m*.

compass [kum'pəs] *n* boussole *f*; **within the ~ of** dans les limites de.

compasses [kum'pəsiz] *npl* compas *m*.

compassion [kəmpash'ən] *n* compassion *f*, humanité *f*.

compassionate [kəmpash'ənit] *a* accessible à la compassion, au cœur charitable et bienveillant; **on ~ grounds** pour raisons personnelles *or* de famille.

compatibility [kəmpatəbil'ətē] *n* compatibilité *f*.

compatible [kəmpat'əbəl] *a* compatible.

compel [kəmpel'] *vt* contraindre, obliger.

compelling [kəmpel'ing] *a* (*fig: argument*) irrésistible.

compendium [kəmpen'dēəm] *n* (*summary*) abrégé *m*.

compensate [kâm'pənsāt] *vt* indemniser, dédommager ♦ *vi*: **to ~ for** compenser.

compensation [kâmpənsā'shən] *n* compensation *f*; (*money*) dédommagement *m*, indemnité *f*.

compère [kâm'pär] *n* (*Brit*) présentateur/trice, animateur/trice.

compete [kəmpēt'] *vi* (*take part*) concourir; (*vie*): **to ~ (with)** rivaliser (avec), faire concurrence (à).

competence [kâm'pitəns] *n* compétence *f*, aptitude *f*.

competent [kâm'pitənt] *a* compétent(e), capable.

competition [kâmpitish'ən] *n* compétition *f*, concours *m*; (*ECON*) concurrence *f*; **in ~ with** en concurrence avec.

competitive [kəmpet'ətiv] *a* (*ECON*) concurrentiel(le); (*sports*) de compétition.

competitive examination *n* concours *m*.

competitor [kəmpet'itûr] *n* concurrent/e.

compile [kəmpīl'] *vt* compiler.

complacency [kəmplā'sənsē] *n* contentement *m* de soi, autosatisfaction *f*.

complacent [kəmplā'sənt] *a* (trop) content(e) de soi.

complain [kəmplān'] *vi*: **to ~ (about)** se plaindre (de); (*in store etc*) réclamer (au sujet de).

complain of *vt fus* (*MED*) se plaindre de.

complaint [kəmplānt'] *n* plainte *f*; (*in store etc*) réclamation *f*; (*MED*) affection *f*.

complement *n* [kâm'pləmənt] complément *m*; (*esp of ship's crew etc*) effectif complet ♦ *vt* [kâm'pləmənt] compléter.

complementary [kâmpləmen'tûrē] *a* complémentaire.

complete [kəmplēt'] *a* complet(ète) ♦ *vt* achever, parachever; (*a form*) remplir.

completely [kəmplēt'lē] *ad* complètement.

completion [kəmplē'shən] *n* achèvement *m*; **to be nearing ~** être presque terminé; **on ~ of contract** dès signature du contrat.

complex [kəmpleks'] *a* complexe ♦ *n* (*PSYCH*, *buildings etc*) complexe *m*.

complexion [kəmplek'shən] *n* (*of face*) teint *m*; (*of event etc*) aspect *m*, caractère *m*.

complexity [kəmplek'sitē] *n* complexité *f*.

compliance [kəmplī'əns] *n* (*submission*) docilité *f*; (*agreement*): **~ with** le fait de se conformer à; **in ~ with** en conformité avec, conformément à.

compliant [kəmplī'ənt] *a* docile, très accommodant(e).

complicate [kâm'pləkāt] *vt* compliquer.

complicated [kâm'pləkātid] *a* compliqué(e).

complication [kâmpləkā'shən] *n* complication *f*.

complicity [kəmplis'ətē] *n* complicité *f*.

compliment *n* [kâm'pləmənt] compliment *m* ♦ *vt* [kâm'pləment] complimenter; **~s** *npl* compliments *mpl*, hommages *mpl*; vœux *mpl*; **to pay sb a ~** faire *or* adresser un compliment à qn; **to ~ sb (on sth/on doing sth)** féliciter qn (pour qch/de faire qch).

complimentary [kâmpləmen'tûrē] *a* flatteur(euse); (*free*) à titre gracieux.

complimentary ticket *n* billet *m* de faveur.

compliments card, (*Brit*) **compliments slip** *n* fiche *f* de transmission.

comply [kəmplī'] *vi*: **to ~ with** se soumettre à, se conformer à.

component [kəmpō'nənt] *a* composant(e), constituant(e) ♦ *n* composant *m*, élément *m*.

compose [kəmpōz'] *vt* composer; **to ~ o.s.** se calmer, se maîtriser; prendre une contenance.

composed [kəmpōzd'] *a* calme, posé(e).

composer [kəmpō'zûr] *n* (*MUS*) compositeur *m*.

composite [kəmpâz'it] *a* composite; (*BOT*, *MATH*) composé(e).

composition [kâmpəzish'ən] *n* composition *f*.

compost [kâm'pōst] *n* compost *m*.

composure [kəmpō'zhûr] *n* calme *m*, maîtrise *f* de soi.

compound [kâm'pound] *n* (*CHEM*, *LING*) composé *m*; (*enclosure*) enclos *m*, enceinte *f* ♦ *a* composé(e) ♦ *vt* [kəmpound'] (*fig: problem etc*) aggraver.

compound fracture *n* fracture compliquée.

compound interest *n* intérêt composé.

comprehend [kâmprihend'] *vt* comprendre.

comprehension [kâmprihen'shən] *n* compréhension *f*.

comprehensive [kâmprihen'siv] *a* (très) complet(ète).

comprehensive insurance policy *n* assurance *f* tous risques.

comprehensive (school) *n* (*Brit*) école secondaire non sélective avec libre circulation d'une section à l'autre, ≈ CES *m*.

compress *vt* [kəmpres'] comprimer ♦ *n* [kâm'pres] (*MED*) compresse *f*.

compression [kəmpresh'ən] *n* compression *f*.

comprise [kəmprīz'] *vt* (*also:* **be ~d of**) comprendre.

compromise [kâm'prəmīz] *n* compromis *m* ♦ *vt* compromettre ♦ *vi* transiger, accepter un compromis ♦ *cpd* (*decision, solution*) de compromis.

compulsion [kəmpul'shən] *n* contrainte *f*, force *f*; **under ~** sous la contrainte.

compulsive [kəmpul'siv] *a* (*PSYCH*) compulsif(ive); **he's a ~ smoker** c'est un fumeur invétéré.

compulsory [kəmpul'sûrē] *a* obligatoire.

compulsory purchase *n* (*Brit*) expropriation *f*.

compunction [kəmpungk'shən] *n* scrupule *m*; **to have no ~ about doing sth** n'avoir aucun scrupule à faire qch.

computer [kəmpyōō'tûr] *n* ordinateur *m*; (*mechanical*) calculatrice *f*.

computerize [kəmpyōō'tərīz] *vt* traiter *or* automatiser par ordinateur.

computer language *n* langage *m* machine *or* informatique.

computer peripheral *n* périphérique *m*.

computer program *n* programme *m* informatique.

computer programmer *n* programmeur/euse.

computer programming *n* programmation *f*.

computer science *n* informatique *f*.

computer scientist *n* informaticien/ne.

computing [kəmpyōō'ting] *n* informatique *f*.

comrade [kâm'rad] *n* camarade *m/f*.

comradeship [kâm'rədship] *n* camaraderie *f*.

comsat [kâm'sat] *n abbr* = **communications satellite**.

con [kân] *vt* duper; escroquer ♦ *n* escroquerie *f*; **to ~ sb into doing sth** tromper qn pour lui faire faire qch.

concave [kânkāv'] *a* concave.

conceal [kənsēl'] *vt* cacher, dissimuler.

concede [kənsēd'] *vt* concéder ♦ *vi* céder.

conceit [kənsēt'] *n* vanité *f*, suffisance *f*, prétention *f*.

conceited [kənsē'tid] *a* vaniteux(euse),

suffisant(e).

conceivable [kənsēv'əbəl] *a* concevable, imaginable; **it is ~ that** il est concevable que.

conceivably [kənsēv'əblē] *ad*: **he may ~ be right** il n'est pas impossible qu'il ait raison.

conceive [kənsēv'] *vt* concevoir ♦ *vi*: **to ~ of sth/of doing sth** imaginer qch/de faire qch.

concentrate [kân'səntrāt] *vi* se concentrer ♦ *vt* concentrer.

concentration [kânsəntrā'shən] *n* concentration *f*.

concentration camp *n* camp *m* de concentration.

concentric [kənsen'trik] *a* concentrique.

concept [kân'sept] *n* concept *m*.

conception [kənsep'shən] *n* conception *f*; (*idea*) idée *f*.

concern [kənsûrn'] *n* affaire *f*; (*COMM*) entreprise *f*, firme *f*; (*anxiety*) inquiétude *f*, souci *m* ♦ *vt* concerner; **to be ~ed (about)** s'inquiéter (de), être inquiet(ète) (au sujet de); **"to whom it may ~"** "à qui de droit"; **as far as I am ~ed** en ce qui me concerne; **to be ~ed with** (*person: involved with*) s'occuper de; **the department ~ed** (*under discussion*) le service en question; (*involved*) le service concerné.

concerning [kənsûr'ning] *prep* en ce qui concerne, à propos de.

concert [kân'sûrt] *n* concert *m*; **in ~** à l'unisson, en chœur; ensemble.

concerted [kənsûr'tid] *a* concerté(e).

concert hall *n* salle *f* de concert.

concertina [kânsûrtē'nə] *n* concertina *m* ♦ *vi* se télescoper, se caramboler.

concertmaster [kân'sûrtmastûr] *n* (*US*) premier violon.

concerto [kənchär'tō] *n* concerto *m*.

concession [kənsesh'ən] *n* concession *f*.

concessionaire [kənseshənär'] *n* concessionnaire *m/f*.

concessionary [kənsesh'ənārē] *a* (*ticket, fare*) à tarif réduit.

conciliation [kənsilēā'shən] *n* conciliation *f*, apaisement *m*.

conciliatory [kənsil'ēətôrē] *a* conciliateur(trice); conciliant(e).

concise [kənsīs'] *a* concis(e).

conclave [kân'klāv] *n* assemblée secrète; (*REL*) conclave *m*.

conclude [kənklōōd'] *vt* conclure ♦ *vi* (*speaker*) conclure; (*events*): **to ~ (with)** se terminer (par).

conclusion [kənklōō'zhən] *n* conclusion *f*; **to come to the ~ that** (en) conclure que.

conclusive [kənklōō'siv] *a* concluant(e), définitif(ive).

concoct [kənkâkt'] *vt* confectionner, composer.

concoction [kənkâk'shən] *n* (*food, drink*) mélange *m*.

concord [kân'kôrd] *n* (*harmony*) harmonie *f*; (*treaty*) accord *m*.

concourse [kân'kôrs] *n* (*hall*) hall *m*, salle *f* des pas perdus; (*crowd*) affluence *f*; multitude *f*.

concrete [kân'krēt] *n* béton *m* ♦ *a* concret(ète); (*CONSTR*) en béton.

concrete mixer *n* bétonnière *f*.

concur [kənkûr'] *vi* être d'accord.

concurrently [kənkûr'əntlē] *ad* simultanément.

concussion [kənkush'ən] *n* (*MED*) commotion (cérébrale).

condemn [kəndem'] *vt* condamner.

condemnation [kândemnā'shən] *n* condamnation *f*.

condensation [kândensā'shən] *n* condensation *f*.

condense [kəndens'] *vi* se condenser ♦ *vt* condenser.

condensed milk [kəndenst' milk'] *n* lait concentré (sucré).

condescend [kândisend'] *vi* condescendre, s'abaisser; **to ~ to do sth** daigner faire qch.

condescending [kândisen'ding] *a* condescendant(e).

condition [kəndish'ən] *n* condition *f*; (*disease*) maladie *f* ♦ *vt* déterminer, conditionner; **in good/poor ~** en bon/mauvais état; **a heart ~** une maladie cardiaque; **weather ~s** conditions *fpl* météorologiques; **on ~ that** à condition que + *sub*, à condition de.

conditional [kəndish'ənəl] *a* conditionnel(le); **to be ~ upon** dépendre de.

conditioner [kəndish'ənûr] *n* (*for hair*) baume démêlant.

condolences [kəndō'lənsiz] *npl* condoléances *fpl*.

condom [kân'dəm] *n* préservatif *m*.

condo(minium) [kân'dō(min'ēəm)] *n* (*US: building*) immeuble *m* (en copropriété); (: *rooms*) appartement *m* (dans un immeuble en copropriété).

condone [kəndōn'] *vt* fermer les yeux sur, approuver (tacitement).

conducive [kəndōō'siv] *a*: **~ to** favorable à, qui contribue à.

conduct *n* [kân'dukt] conduite *f* ♦ *vt* [kəndukt'] conduire; (*manage*) mener, diriger; (*MUS*) diriger; **to ~ o.s.** se conduire, se comporter.

conductor [kənduk'tûr] *n* (*of orchestra*) chef *m* d'orchestre; (*on bus*) receveur *m*; (*US: on train*) chef *m* de train; (*ELEC*) conducteur *m*.

conductress [kənduk'tris] *n* (*on bus*) receveuse *f*.

conduit [kân'dōōwit] *n* conduit *m*, tuyau *m*; tube *m*.

cone [kōn] *n* cône *m*; (*for ice-cream*) cornet *m*; (*BOT*) pomme *f* de pin, cône.

confectioner [kənfek'shənûr] *n* (*of cakes*) pâtissier/ière; (*of sweets*) confiseur/euse; **~'s (shop)** confiserie(-pâtisserie) *f*.

confectioner's sugar *n* (*US*) sucre *m* glace.

confectionery [kənfek'shənārē] *n* (*cakes*) pâtisserie *f*; (*sweets*) confiserie *f*.

confederate [kənfed'ûrit] *a* confédéré(e) ♦ (*pej*) acolyte *m*; (*US HIST*) confédéré/e.

confederation [kənfedərā'shən] *n* confédération *f*.

confer [kənfûr'] *vt*: **to ~ sth on** conférer qch à ♦ *vi* conférer, s'entretenir; **to ~ (with sb about sth)** s'entretenir (de qch avec qn).

conference [kân'fûrəns] *n* conférence *f*; **to be in ~** être en réunion *or* en conférence.

conference room *n* salle *f* de conférence.

confess [kənfes'] *vt* confesser, avouer ♦ *vi* se confesser.

confession [kənfesh'ən] *n* confession *f*.

confessional [kənfesh'ənəl] *n* confessional *m*.

confessor [kənfes'ûr] *n* confesseur *m.*
confetti [kənfet'ē] *n* confettis *mpl.*
confide [kənfīd'] *vi*: **to ~ in** s'ouvrir à, se confier à.
confidence [kân'fidəns] *n* confiance *f*; (*also*: **self-~**) assurance *f*, confiance en soi; (*secret*) confidence *f*; **to have (every) ~ that** être certain que; **motion of no ~** motion *f* de censure; **to tell sb sth in strict ~** dire qch à qn en toute confidence.
confidence game *n* escroquerie *f.*
confident [kân'fidənt] *a* sûr(e), assuré(e).
confidential [kânfiden'shəl] *a* confidentiel(le); (*secretary*) particulier(ère).
confidentiality [kânfidenshēal'itē] *n* confidentialité *f.*
configuration [kənfigyərā'shən] *n* (*also* COMPUT) configuration *f.*
confine [kənfīn'] *vt* limiter, borner; (*shut up*) confiner, enfermer; **to ~ o.s. to doing sth/ to sth** se contenter de faire qch/se limiter à qch.
confined [kənfīnd'] *a* (*space*) restreint(e), réduit(e).
confinement [kənfīn'mənt] *n* emprisonnement *m*, détention *f*; (MIL) consigne *f* (au quartier); (MED) accouchement *m.*
confines [kân'fīnz] *npl* confins *mpl*, bornes *fpl.*
confirm [kənfûrm'] *vt* (*report*, REL) confirmer; (*appointment*) ratifier.
confirmation [kânfûrmā'shən] *n* confirmation *f*; ratification *f.*
confirmed [kənfûrmd'] *a* invétéré(e), incorrigible.
confiscate [kân'fiskāt] *vt* confisquer.
confiscation [kânfiskā'shən] *n* confiscation *f.*
conflagration [kânfləgrā'shən] *n* incendie *m*; (*fig*) conflagration *f.*
conflict *n* [kân'flikt] conflit *m*, lutte *f* ♦ *vi* [kənflikt'] être *or* entrer en conflit; (*opinions*) s'opposer, se heurter.
conflicting [kənflik'ting] *a* contradictoire.
conform [kənfôrm'] *vi*: **to ~ (to)** se conformer (à).
conformist [kənfôr'mist] *n* conformiste *m/f.*
confound [kənfound'] *vt* confondre; (*amaze*) rendre perplexe.
confounded [kənfoun'did] *a* maudit(e), sacré(e).
confront [kənfrunt'] *vt* confronter, mettre en présence; (*enemy*, *danger*) affronter, faire face à.
confrontation [kânfrəntā'shən] *n* confrontation *f.*
confuse [kənfyōōz'] *vt* embrouiller; (*one thing with another*) confondre.
confused [kənfyōōzd'] *a* (*person*) dérouté(e), désorienté(e); (*situation*) embrouillé(e).
confusing [kənfyōō'zing] *a* peu clair(e), déroutant(e).
confusion [kənfyōō'zhən] *n* confusion *f.*
congeal [kənjēl'] *vi* (*oil*) se figer; (*blood*) se coaguler.
congenial [kənjēn'yəl] *a* sympathique, agréable.
congenital [kənjen'itəl] *a* congénital(e).
conger eel [kâng'gûr ēl] *n* congre *m.*
congested [kənjes'tid] *a* (MED) congestionné(e); (*fig*) surpeuplé(e); con-

gestionné; bloqué(e); (*telephone lines*) encombré(e).
congestion [kənjes'chən] *n* congestion *f*; (*fig*) encombrement *m.*
conglomerate [kənglâm'ûrit] *n* (COMM) conglomérat *m.*
conglomeration [kənglâmərā'shən] *n* groupement *m*; agglomération *f.*
Congo [kâng'gō] *n* (*state*) (république *f* du) Congo.
congratulate [kəngrach'ōōlāt] *vt*: **to ~ sb (on)** féliciter qn (de).
congratulations [kəngrachōōlā'shənz] *npl*: **~ (on)** félicitations *fpl* (pour) ♦ *excl*: **~!** (toutes mes) félicitations!
congregate [kâng'grəgāt] *vi* se rassembler, se réunir.
congregation [kânggrəgā'shən] *n* assemblée *f* (des fidèles).
congress [kâng'gris] *n* congrès *m.*
congressman [kâng'grismən], **congresswoman** [kâ'ng'griswōōmən] *n* (US) membre *m* du Congrès.
conical [kân'ikəl] *a* (de forme) conique.
conifer [kō'nifûr] *n* conifère *m.*
coniferous [kōnif'ûrəs] *a* (*forest*) de conifères.
conjecture [kənjek'chûr] *n* conjecture *f* ♦ *vt*, *vi* conjecturer.
conjugal [kân'jəgəl] *a* conjugal(e).
conjugate [kân'jəgāt] *vt* conjuguer.
conjugation [kânjəgā'shən] *n* conjugaison *f.*
conjunction [kənjungk'shən] *n* conjonction *f*; **in ~ with** (conjointement) avec.
conjunctivitis [kənjungktəvī'tis] *n* conjonctivite *f.*
conjure [kân'jûr] *vt* faire apparaître (par la prestidigitation); [kənjōōr'] conjurer, supplier ♦ *vi* faire des tours de passe-passe.
conjure up *vt* (*ghost*, *spirit*) faire apparaître; (*memories*) évoquer.
conjurer [kân'jûrûr] *n* prestidigitateur *m*, illusionniste *m/f.*
conjuring trick [kân'jûring trik] *n* tour *m* de prestidigitation.
conker [kâng'kûr] *n* (*Brit*) marron *m* (d'Inde).
conk out [kângk out] *vi* (*col*) tomber *or* rester en panne.
con man *n* escroc *m.*
Conn. *abbr* (US) = Connecticut.
connect [kənekt'] *vt* joindre, relier; (ELEC) connecter; (*fig*) établir un rapport entre, faire un rapprochement entre ♦ *vi* (*train*): **to ~ with** assurer la correspondance avec; **to be ~ed with** avoir un rapport avec; (*have dealings with*) avoir des rapports avec, être en relation avec; **I am trying to ~ you** (TEL) j'essaie d'obtenir votre communication.
connection [kənek'shən] *n* relation *f*, lien *m*; (ELEC) connexion *f*; (TEL) communication *f*; (*train etc*) correspondance *f*; **in ~ with** à propos de; **what is the ~ between them?** quel est le lien entre eux?; **business ~s** relations d'affaires; **to miss/get one's ~** (*train etc*) rater/avoir sa correspondance.
connexion [kənek'shən] *n* (*Brit*) = **connection.**
conning tower [kân'ing tou'ûr] *n* kiosque *m* (de sous-marin).
connive [kənīv'] *vi*: **to ~ at** se faire le compli-

ce de.
connoisseur [kânisûr'] *n* connaisseur *m*.
connotation [kânətā'shən] *n* connotation *f*, implication *f*.
connubial [kənōō'bēəl] *a* conjugal(e).
conquer [kâng'kûr] *vt* conquérir; *(feelings)* vaincre, surmonter.
conqueror [kâng'kûrûr] *n* conquérant *m*, vainqueur *m*.
conquest [kân'kwest] *n* conquête *f*.
cons [kânz] *npl see* **pro.**
conscience [kân'shəns] *n* conscience *f*; **in all** ~ en conscience.
conscientious [kânshēen'shəs] *a* consciencieux(euse); *(scruple, objection)* de conscience.
conscientious objector *n* objecteur *m* de conscience.
conscious [kân'shəs] *a* conscient(e); *(deliberate: insult, error)* délibéré(e); **to become ~ of sth/that** prendre conscience de qch/que.
consciousness [kân'shəsnis] *n* conscience *f*; *(MED)* connaissance *f*; **to lose/regain ~** perdre/reprendre connaissance.
conscript [kân'skript] *(Brit)* *n* conscrit *m*.
conscription [kənskrip'shən] *n* conscription *f*.
consecrate [kân'səkrāt] *vt* consacrer.
consecutive [kənsek'yətiv] *a* consécutif(ive); **on three ~ occasions** trois fois de suite.
consensus [kənsen'səs] *n* consensus *m*; **the ~ (of opinion)** le consensus (d'opinion).
consent [kənsent'] *n* consentement *m* ♦ *vi:* **to ~ (to)** consentir (à); **age of ~** âge nubile (légal); **by common ~** d'un commun accord.
consequence [kân'səkwens] *n* suites *fpl*, conséquence *f*; importance *f*; **in ~** en conséquence, par conséquent.
consequently [kân'səkwentlē] *ad* par conséquent, donc.
conservation [kânsûrvā'shən] *n* préservation *f*, protection *f*; *(also:* **nature ~)** défense *f* de l'environnement; **energy ~** économies *fpl* d'énergie.
conservationist [kânsûrvā'shənist] *n* protecteur/trice de la nature.
conservative [kənsûr'vətiv] *a* conservateur(trice); *(cautious)* prudent(e); **C~** *a, n (Brit POL)* conservateur(trice).
conservatory [kənsûr'vətôrē] *n (greenhouse)* serre *f*.
conserve *vt* [kənsûrv'] conserver, préserver; *(supplies, energy)* économiser ♦ *n* [kân'sûrv] confiture *f*, conserve *f* (de fruits).
consider [kənsid'ûr] *vt* considérer, réfléchir à; *(take into account)* penser à, prendre en considération; *(regard, judge)* considérer, estimer; **to ~ doing sth** envisager de faire qch; **~ yourself lucky** estimez-vous heureux; **all things ~ed** (toute) réflexion faite.
considerable [kənsid'ûrəbəl] *a* considérable.
considerably [kənsid'ûrəblē] *ad* nettement.
considerate [kənsid'ûrit] *a* prévenant(e), plein(e) d'égards.
consideration [kənsidərā'shən] *n* considération *f*; *(reward)* rétribution *f*, rémunération *f*; **out of ~ for** par égard pour; **under ~** à l'étude; **my first ~ is my family** ma famille passe avant tout le reste.
considering [kənsid'ûring] *prep:* ~ **(that)**

étant donné (que).
consign [kənsīn'] *vt* expédier, livrer.
consignee [kânsīnē'] *n* destinataire *m/f*.
consignment [kənsīn'mənt] *n* arrivage *m*, envoi *m*.
consignment note *n (Brit COMM)* bordereau *m* d'expédition.
consignor [kənsī'nûr] *n* expéditeur/trice.
consist [kənsist'] *vi:* **to ~ of** consister en, se composer de.
consistency [kənsis'tənsē] *n* consistance *f*; *(fig)* cohérence *f*.
consistent [kənsis'tənt] *a* logique, cohérent(e); ~ **with** compatible avec, en accord avec.
consolation [kânsəlā'shən] *n* consolation *f*.
console *vt* [kənsōl'] consoler ♦ *n* [kân'sōl] console *f*.
consolidate [kənsâl'idāt] *vt* consolider.
consommé [kânsəmā'] *n* consommé *m*.
consonant [kân'sənənt] *n* consonne *f*.
consort *n* [kân'sôrt] époux/épouse; **prince ~** prince *m* consort ♦ *vi* [kənsôrt'] *(often pej):* **to ~ with sb** frayer avec qn.
consortium [kənsôr'shēəm] *n* consortium *m*, comptoir *m*.
conspicuous [kənspik'yōōəs] *a* voyant(e), qui attire la vue *or* l'attention; **to make o.s. ~** se faire remarquer.
conspiracy [kənspir'əsē] *n* conspiration *f*, complot *m*.
conspiratorial [kənspirətôr'ēəl] *a (behavior)* de conspirateur; *(glance)* conspirateur(trice).
conspire [kənspī'ûr] *vi* conspirer, comploter.
constable [kân'stəbəl] *n (Brit)* ≈ agent *m* de police, gendarme *m*.
constabulary [kənstab'yəlärē] *n* ≈ police *f*, gendarmerie *f*.
constant [kân'stənt] *a* constant(e); incessant(e).
constantly [kân'stəntlē] *ad* constamment, sans cesse.
constellation [kânstəlā'shən] *n* constellation *f*.
consternation [kânstûrnā'shən] *n* consternation *f*.
constipated [kân'stəpātid] *a* constipé(e).
constipation [kânstəpā'shən] *n* constipation *f*.
constituency [kənstich'ōōənsē] *n* circonscription électorale; *(people)* électorat *m*.
constituency party *n* section locale (d'un parti).
constituent [kənstich'ōōənt] *n* électeur/trice; *(part)* élément constitutif, composant *m*.
constitute [kân'stitōōt] *vt* constituer.
constitution [kânstitōō'shən] *n* constitution *f*.
constitutional [kânstitōō'shənəl] *a* constitutionnel(le).
constrain [kənstrān'] *vt* contraindre, forcer.
constrained [kənstrānd'] *a* contraint(e), gêné(e).
constraint [kənstrānt'] *n* contrainte *f*; *(embarrassment)* gêne *f*.
constrict [kənstrikt'] *vt* rétrécir, resserrer; gêner, limiter.
construct [kənstrukt'] *vt* construire.
construction [kənstruk'shən] *n* construction *f*; *(fig: interpretation)* interprétation *f*; **under ~** *(building etc)* en construction.
construction industry *n* (industrie *f* du) bâtiment *m*.

constructive [kənstruk'tiv] *a* constructif(ive).
construe [kənstrōō'] *vt* analyser, expliquer.
consul [kân'səl] *n* consul *m*.
consulate [kân'səlit] *n* consulat *m*.
consult [kənsult'] *vt* consulter; **to ~ sb (about sth)** consulter qn (à propos de qch).
consultancy [kənsul'tənsē] *n* service *m* de conseils.
consultancy fee *n* honoraires *mpl* d'expert.
consultant [kənsul'tənt] *n* (*MED*) médecin consultant; (*other specialist*) consultant *m*, (expert-)conseil *m* ♦ *cpd*: **~ engineer** *n* ingénieur-conseil *m*; **~ pediatrician** *n* pédiatre *m*; **legal/management ~** conseiller *m* juridique/en gestion.
consultation [kânsəltā'shən] *n* consultation *f*; **in ~ with** en consultation avec.
consulting room [kənsul'ting rōōm] *n* cabinet *m* de consultation.
consume [kənsōōm'] *vt* consommer.
consumer [kənsōō'mûr] *n* consommateur/trice; (*of electricity, gas etc*) usager *m*.
consumer credit *n* crédit *m* aux consommateurs.
consumer durables *npl* biens *mpl* de consommation durables.
consumer goods *npl* biens *mpl* de consommation.
consumerism [kənsōō'mərizəm] *n* (*consumer protection*) défense *f* du consommateur; (*ECON*) consumérisme *m*.
consumer society *n* société *f* de consommation.
consummate [kân'səmāt] *vt* consommer.
consumption [kənsump'shən] *n* consommation *f*; (*MED*) consomption *f* (pulmonaire); **not fit for human ~** non comestible.
cont. *abbr* = **continued.**
contact [kân'takt] *n* contact *m*; (*person*) connaissance *f*, relation *f* ♦ *vt* se mettre en contact *or* en rapport avec; **to be in ~ with sb/sth** être en contact avec qn/qch; **business ~s** relations *fpl* d'affaires, contacts *mpl*.
contact lenses *npl* verres *mpl* de contact.
contagious [kəntā'jəs] *a* contagieux(euse).
contain [kəntān'] *vt* contenir; **to ~ o.s.** se contenir, se maîtriser.
container [kəntā'nûr] *n* récipient *m*; (*for shipping etc*) conteneur *m*.
containerize [kəntā'nəriz] *vt* conteneuriser.
contaminate [kəntam'ənāt] *vt* contaminer.
contamination [kəntamənā'shən] *n* contamination *f*.
cont'd *abbr* = **continued.**
contemplate [kân'təmplāt] *vt* contempler; (*consider*) envisager.
contemplation [kântəmplā'shən] *n* contemplation *f*.
contemporary [kəntem'pərārē] *a* contemporain(e); (*design, wallpaper*) moderne ♦ *n* contemporain/e.
contempt [kəntempt'] *n* mépris *m*, dédain *m*; **~ of court** (*LAW*) outrage *m* à l'autorité de la justice.
contemptible [kəntemp'təbəl] *a* méprisable, vil(e).
contemptuous [kəntemp'chōōəs] *a* dédaigneux(euse), méprisant(e).
contend [kəntend'] *vt*: **to ~ that** soutenir *or*

prétendre que ♦ *vi*: **to ~ with** (*compete*) lutter avec; **to have to ~ with** (*be faced with*) avoir affaire à, être aux prises avec.
contender [kəntend'ûr] *n* prétendant/e; candidat/e.
content [kəntent'] *a* content(e), satisfait(e) ♦ *vt* contenter, satisfaire ♦ *n* [kân'tent] contenu *m*; teneur *f*; **~s** *npl* contenu *m*; **(table of) ~s** table *f* des matières; **to be ~ with** se contenter de; **to ~ o.s. with sth/with doing sth** se contenter de qch/de faire qch.
contented [kəntent'id] *a* content(e), satisfait(e).
contentedly [kəntent'idlē] *ad* avec un sentiment de (profonde) satisfaction.
contention [kənten'shən] *n* dispute *f*, contestation *f*; (*argument*) assertion *f*, affirmation *f*; **bone of ~** sujet *m* de discorde.
contentious [kənten'shəs] *a* querelleur(euse); litigieux(euse).
contentment [kəntent'mənt] *n* contentement *m*, satisfaction *f*.
contest *n* [kân'test] combat *m*, lutte *f*; (*competition*) concours *m* ♦ *vt* [kəntest'] contester, discuter; (*compete for*) disputer; (*LAW*) attaquer.
contestant [kəntes'tənt] *n* concurrent/e; (*in fight*) adversaire *m/f*.
context [kân'tekst] *n* contexte *m*; **in/out of ~** dans le/hors contexte.
continent [kân'tənənt] *n* continent *m*; **the C~** l'Europe continentale; **on the C~** en Europe (continentale).
continental [kântənen'təl] *a* continental(e) ♦ *n* (*Brit*) Européen/ne (continental(e)).
continental breakfast *n* café (*or* thé) complet.
continental quilt *n* (*Brit*) couette *f*.
contingency [kəntin'jənsē] *n* éventualité *f*, événement imprévu.
contingency plan *n* plan *m* d'urgence.
contingent [kəntin'jənt] *a* contingent(e) ♦ *n* contingent *m*; **to be ~ upon** dépendre de.
continual [kəntin'yōōəl] *a* continuel(le).
continually [kəntin'yōōəlē] *ad* continuellement, sans cesse.
continuation [kəntinyōōā'shən] *n* continuation *f*; (*after interruption*) reprise *f*; (*of story*) suite *f*.
continue [kəntin'yōō] *vi* continuer ♦ *vt* continuer; (*start again*) reprendre; **to be ~d** (*story*) à suivre; **~d on page 10** suite page 10.
continuity [kântənōō'itē] *n* continuité *f*; (*CINEMA*) script *m*.
continuous [kəntin'yōōəs] *a* continu(e), permanent(e); **~ performance** (*CINEMA*) séance permanente.
continuously [kəntin'yōōəslē] *ad* (*repeatedly*) continuellement; (*uninterruptedly*) sans interruption.
contort [kəntôrt'] *vt* tordre, crisper.
contortion [kəntôr'shən] *n* crispation *f*, torsion *f*; (*of acrobat*) contorsion *f*.
contortionist [kəntôr'shənist] *n* contorsionniste *m/f*.
contour [kân'tōōr] *n* contour *m*, profil *m*; (*also*: **~ line**) courbe *f* de niveau.
contraband [kân'trəband] *n* contrebande *f* ♦ *a* de contrebande.

contraception [kȧntrəsep'shən] *n* contraception *f*.

contraceptive [kȧntrəsep'tiv] *a* contraceptif(ive), anticonceptionnel(le) ♦ *n* contraceptif *m*.

contract [kȧn'trakt] *n* contrat *m* ♦ *cpd* (*price, date*) contractuel(le); (*work*) à forfait ♦ *vb* [kȧntrakt'] *vi* (*become smaller*) se contracter, se resserrer; (*COMM*): **to ~ to do sth** s'engager (par contrat) à faire qch ♦ *vt* contracter; **~ of employment/service** contrat de travail/de service.

contraction [kȧntrak'shən] *n* contraction *f*; (*LING*) forme contractée.

contractor [kȧn'traktûr] *n* entrepreneur *m*.

contractual [kȧntrak'chōōəl] *a* contractuel(le).

contradict [kȧntrədikt'] *vt* contredire; (*be contrary to*) démentir, être en contradiction avec.

contradiction [kȧntrədik'shən] *n* contradiction *f*; **to be in ~ with** contredire, être en contradiction avec.

contradictory [kȧntrədik'tûrē] *a* contradictoire.

contralto [kȧntral'tō] *n* contralto *m*.

contraption [kȧntrap'shən] *n* (*pej*) machin *m*, truc *m*.

contrary [kȧn'trärē] *a* contraire, opposé(e); (*perverse*) contrariant(e), entêté(e) ♦ *n* contraire *m*; **on the ~** au contraire; **unless you hear to the ~** sauf avis contraire; **~ to what we thought** contrairement à ce que nous pensions.

contrast *n* [kȧn'trast] contraste *m* ♦ *vt* [kȧntrast'] mettre en contraste, contraster; **in ~ to** *or* **with** contrairement à, par opposition à.

contrasting [kȧntras'ting] *a* opposé(e), contrasté(e).

contravene [kȧntrəvēn'] *vt* enfreindre, violer, contrevenir à.

contravention [kȧntrəven'shən] *n*: **~ (of)** infraction *f* (à).

contribute [kȧntrib'yōōt] *vi* contribuer ♦ *vt*: **to ~ $10/an article** to donner 10 dollars/un article à; **to ~ to** (*gen*) contribuer à; (*newspaper*) collaborer à; (*discussion*) prendre part à.

contribution [kȧntrəbyōō'shən] *n* contribution *f*.

contributor [kȧntrib'yətûr] *n* (*to newspaper*) collaborateur/trice.

contributory [kȧntrib'yətôrē] *a* (*cause*) annexe; **it was a ~ factor in ...** ce facteur a contribué à ....

contributory pension plan *n* régime *m* de retraite salariale.

contrite [kȧntrīt'] *a* contrit(e).

contrivance [kȧntrī'vəns] *n* (*scheme*) machination *f*, combinaison *f*; (*device*) appareil *m*, dispositif *m*.

contrive [kȧntrīv'] *vt* combiner, inventer ♦ *vi*: **to ~ to do** s'arranger pour faire, trouver le moyen de faire.

control [kȧntrōl'] *vt* maîtriser; (*check*) contrôler ♦ *n* maîtrise *f*; **~s** *npl* commandes *fpl*; **to take ~ of** se rendre maître de; (*COMM*) acquérir une participation majoritaire dans; **to be in ~ of** être maître de, maîtriser; (*in*

charge of) être responsable de; **to ~ o.s.** se contrôler; **everything is under ~** j'ai (*or* il a *etc*) la situation en main; **the car went out of ~** j'ai (*or* il a *etc*) perdu le contrôle du véhicule; **beyond our ~** indépendant(e) de notre volonté.

control key *n* (*COMPUT*) touche *f* de commande.

controller [kȧntrō'lûr] *n* contrôleur *m*.

controlling interest [kȧntrō'ling in'trist] *n* (*COMM*) participation *f* majoritaire.

control panel *n* (*on aircraft, ship, TV etc*) tableau *m* de commandes.

control point *n* (*poste m de*) contrôle *m*.

control room *n* (*RADIO, TV*) régie *f*.

control tower *n* (*AVIAT*) tour *f* de contrôle.

control unit *n* (*COMPUT*) unité *f* de contrôle.

controversial [kȧntrəvûr'shəl] *a* discutable, controversé(e).

controversy [kȧn'trəvûrsē] *n* controverse *f*, polémique *f*.

conurbation [kȧnûrbā'shən] *n* conurbation *f*.

convalesce [kȧnvəles'] *vi* relever de maladie, se remettre (d'une maladie).

convalescence [kȧnvəles'əns] *n* convalescence *f*.

convalescent [kȧnvəles'ənt] *a, n* convalescent(e).

convector [kȧnvek'tûr] *n* radiateur *m* à convection, appareil *m* de chauffage par convection.

convene [kȧnvēn'] *vt* convoquer, assembler ♦ *vi* se réunir, s'assembler.

convener [kȧnvē'nûr] *n* organisateur *m*.

convenience [kȧnvēn'yəns] *n* commodité *f*; **at your ~** quand *or* comme cela vous convient; **at your earliest ~** (*COMM*) dans les meilleurs délais, le plus tôt possible; **all modern ~s** avec tout le confort moderne, tout confort.

convenience foods *npl* plats cuisinés.

convenient [kȧnvēn'yənt] *a* commode; **if it is ~ to you** si cela vous convient, si cela ne vous dérange pas.

conveniently [kȧnvēn'yəntlē] *ad* (*happen*) à pic; (*situated*) commodément.

convent [kȧn'vent] *n* couvent *m*.

convention [kȧnven'shən] *n* convention *f*.

conventional [kȧnven'shənəl] *a* conventionnel(le).

convent school *n* couvent *m*.

converge [kȧnvûrj'] *vi* converger.

conversant [kȧnvûr'sənt] *a*: **to be ~ with** s'y connaître en; être au courant de.

conversation [kȧnvûrsā'shən] *n* conversation *f*.

conversational [kȧnvûrsā'shənəl] *a* de la conversation; (*COMPUT*) conversationnel(le).

conversationalist [kȧnvûrsāsh'nəlist] *n* brillant(e) causeur/euse.

converse *n* [kȧn'vûrs] contraire *m*, inverse *m* ♦ *vi* [kȧnvûrs'] : **to ~ (with sb about sth)** s'entretenir (avec qn de qch).

conversely [kȧnvûrs'lē] *ad* inversement, réciproquement.

conversion [kȧnvûr'zhən] *n* conversion *f*; (*Brit: of house*) transformation *f*, aménagement *m*.

conversion table *n* table *f* de conversion.

convert vt [kənvûrt'] (REL, COMM) convertir; (alter) transformer, aménager; (RUGBY) transformer ♦ n [kân'vûrt] converti/e.

convertible [kənvûr'təbəl] a convertible ♦ n (voiture f) décapotable f.

convex [kânveks'] a convexe.

convey [kənvā'] vt transporter; (thanks) transmettre; (idea) communiquer.

conveyance [kənvā'əns] n (of goods) transport m de marchandises; (vehicle) moyen m de transport.

conveyancing [kənvā'ənsing] n (LAW) rédaction f des actes de cession de propriété.

conveyor belt [kənvā'ûr belt] n convoyeur m, tapis roulant.

convict vt [kənvikt'] déclarer (or reconnaître) coupable ♦ n [kân'vikt] forçat m, convict m.

conviction [kənvik'shən] n condamnation f; (belief) conviction f.

convince [kənvins'] vt convaincre, persuader; **to ~ sb (of sth/that)** persuader qn (de qch/que).

convincing [kənvin'sing] a persuasif(ive), convaincant(e).

convincingly [kənvin'singlē] ad de façon convaincante.

convivial [kənviv'ēəl] a joyeux(euse), plein(e) d'entrain.

convoluted [kân'vəlōōtid] a (shape) tarabiscoté(e); (argument) compliqué(e).

convoy [kân'voi] n convoi m.

convulse [kənvuls'] vt ébranler; **to be ~d with laughter** se tordre de rire.

convulsion [kənvul'shən] n convulsion f.

coo [kōō] vi roucouler.

cook [kook] vt (faire) cuire ♦ vi cuire; (person) faire la cuisine ♦ n cuisinier/ière.

cook up vt (col: excuse, story) inventer.

cookbook [kook'book] n livre m de cuisine.

cooker [kook'ûr] n cuisinière f.

cookery [kook'ûrē] n cuisine f.

cookery book n (Brit) = **cookbook**.

cookie [kook'ē] n (US) biscuit m, petit gâteau sec.

cookie sheet n (US) plaque f à gâteaux.

cooking [kook'ing] n cuisine f ♦ cpd (apples, chocolate) à cuire; (utensils, salt) de cuisine.

cookout [kook'out] n (US) barbecue m.

cool [kool] a frais(fraîche); (not afraid) calme; (unfriendly) froid(e); (impertinent) effronté(e) ♦ vt, vi rafraîchir, refroidir; **it's ~** (weather) il fait frais; **to keep sth ~ or in a ~ place** garder or conserver qch au frais.

cool down vi refroidir; (fig: person, situation) se calmer.

cooler [kool'ûr], (Brit) **cool box** n boîte f isotherme.

cooling tower [kool'ing tou'ûr] n refroidisseur m.

coolly [kool'lē] ad (calmly) calmement; (audaciously) sans se gêner; (unenthusiastically) froidement.

coolness [kool'nis] n fraîcheur f; sang-froid m, calme m; froideur f.

coop [koop] n poulailler m ♦ vt: **to ~ up** (fig) cloîtrer, enfermer.

co-op [kō'âp] n abbr (= cooperative society)) coop f.

cooperate [kōâp'ərāt] vi coopérer, collaborer.

cooperation [kōâpərā'shən] n coopération f, collaboration f.

cooperative [kōâp'rətiv] a coopératif(ive) ♦ n coopérative f.

co-opt [kōâpt'] vt: **to ~ sb onto a committee** coopter qn pour faire partie d'un comité.

coordinate vt [kōōr'dənāt] coordonner ♦ n [kōōr'dənit] (MATH) coordonnée f; **~s** npl (clothes) ensemble m, coordonnés mpl.

coordination [kōōrdənā'shən] n coordination f.

coot [koot] n foulque f.

co-ownership [kōō'nûrship] n copropriété f.

cop [kâp] n (col) flic m.

cope [kōp] vi s'en sortir, tenir le coup; **to ~ with** faire face à; (take care of) s'occuper de.

Copenhagen [kōpenhā'gən] n Copenhague.

copier [kâp'ēûr] n (also: **photo~**) copieur m.

copilot [kōpī'lət] n copilote m.

copious [kō'pēəs] a copieux(euse), abondant(e).

copper [kâp'ûr] n cuivre m; (col: policeman) flic m; **~s** npl petite monnaie.

copse [kâps] n taillis m.

copulate [kâp'yəlāt] vi copuler.

copy [kâp'ē] n copie f; (book etc) exemplaire m; (material: for printing) copie ♦ vt copier; (imitate) imiter; **to make good ~** (PRESS) faire un bon sujet d'article.

copy out vt copier.

copycat [kâp'ēkat] n (pej) copieur/euse.

copyright [kâp'ērīt] n droit m d'auteur, copyright m; **~ reserved** tous droits (de reproduction) réservés.

copy typist n dactylo m/f.

copywriter [kâp'ērītûr] n rédacteur/trice publicitaire.

coral [kôr'əl] n corail m.

coral reef n récif m de corail.

Coral Sea n: **the ~** la mer de Corail.

cord [kôrd] n corde f; (fabric) velours côtelé; whipcord m; corde f; (ELEC) cordon m (d'alimentation), fil m (électrique); **~s** npl (pants) pantalon m de velours côtelé.

cordial [kôr'jəl] a cordial(e), chaleureux(euse) ♦ n sirop m; cordial m.

cordless [kôrd'lis] a sans fil.

cordon [kôr'dən] n cordon m.

cordon off vt (area) interdire l'accès à; (crowd) tenir à l'écart.

corduroy [kôr'dəroi] n velours côtelé.

CORE n abbr (US) = Congress of Racial Equality.

core [kôr] n (of fruit) trognon m, cœur m; (TECH: also of earth) noyau m; (of nuclear reactor, fig: of problem etc) cœur ♦ vt enlever le trognon or le cœur de; **rotten to the ~** complètement pourri.

Corfu [kôr'fōō] n Corfou.

coriander [kôrēan'dûr] n coriandre f.

cork [kôrk] n liège m; (of bottle) bouchon m.

corkscrew [kôrk'skrōō] n tire-bouchon m.

corky [kôr'kē], (Brit) **corked** [kôrkt] a (wine) qui sent le bouchon.

corm [kôrm] n bulbe m.

cormorant [kôr'mûrənt] n cormoran m.

Corn abbr (Brit) = Cornwall.

corn [kôrn] n (US: maize) maïs m; (Brit: wheat) blé m; (on foot) cor m; **~ on the cob**

(CULIN) épi m de maïs au naturel.

cornea [kôr'nēə] n cornée f.

corned beef [kôrnd bēf] n corned-beef m.

corner [kôr'nûr] n coin m; (AUT) tournant m, virage m; (SOCCER: also: ~ **kick**) corner m ♦ vt acculer, mettre au pied du mur; coincer; (COMM: market) accaparer ♦ vi prendre un virage; **to cut ~s** (fig) prendre des raccourcis.

corner flag n (SOCCER) piquet m de coin.

corner kick n (SOCCER) corner m.

cornerstone [kôr'nûrstōn] n pierre f angulaire.

cornet [kôrnet'] n (MUS) cornet m à pistons; (Brit: of ice-cream) cornet (de glace).

cornflakes [kôrn'flāks] npl cornflakes mpl.

cornflour [kôrn'flouûr] n (Brit) farine f de maïs, maïzena f ®.

cornice [kôr'nis] n corniche f.

corn oil n huile f de maïs.

cornstarch [kôrn'stârch] n (US) farine f de maïs, maïzena f ®.

cornucopia [kôrnəkō'pēə] n corne f d'abondance.

corny [kôr'nē] a (col) rebattu(e), galvaudé(e).

corollary [kôr'əlärē] n corollaire m.

coronary [kôr'ənärē] n: ~ **(thrombosis)** infarctus m (du myocarde), thrombose f coronaire.

coronation [kôrənā'shən] n couronnement m.

coroner [kôr'ənûr] n coroner m.

coronet [kôr'ənit] n couronne f.

Corp. abbr = **corporation**.

corporal [kôr'pûrəl] n caporal m, brigadier m ♦ a: ~ **punishment** châtiment corporel.

corporate [kôr'pərit] a en commun; (COMM) constitué(e) (en corporation).

corporate identity, corporate image n (of organization) image f de l'entreprise.

corporation [kôrpərā'shən] n (of town) municipalité f, conseil municipal; (COMM) société f.

corporation tax n ≈ impôt m sur les bénéfices.

corps [kôr], pl **corps** [kôrz] n corps m; **the press** ~ la presse.

corpse [kôrps] n cadavre m.

corpuscle [kôr'pəsəl] n corpuscule m.

corral [kərol'] n corral m.

correct [kərekt'] a (accurate) correct(e), exact(e); (proper) correct, convenable ♦ vt corriger; **you are** ~ vous avez raison.

correction [kərek'shən] n correction f.

correlate [kôr'əlāt] vt mettre en corrélation ♦ vi: **to** ~ **with** correspondre à.

correlation [kôrəlā'shən] n corrélation f.

correspond [kôrəspând'] vi correspondre.

correspondence [kôrəspân'dəns] n correspondance f.

correspondence column n (PRESS) courrier m des lecteurs.

correspondence course n cours m par correspondance.

correspondent [kôrəspân'dənt] n correspondant/e.

corridor [kôr'idûr] n couloir m, corridor m.

corroborate [kəráb'ərāt] vt corroborer, confirmer.

corrode [kərōd'] vt corroder, ronger ♦ vi se corroder.

corrosion [kərō'zhən] n corrosion f.

corrosive [kərō'siv] a corrosif(ive).

corrugated [kôr'əgātid] a plissé(e); ondulé(e).

corrugated iron n tôle ondulée.

corrupt [kərupt'] a corrompu(e) ♦ vt corrompre; (data) altérer; ~ **practices** (dishonesty, bribery) malversation f.

corruption [kərup'shən] n corruption f; altération f (de données).

corset [kôr'sit] n corset m.

Corsica [kôr'sikə] n Corse f.

Corsican [kôr'sikən] a corse ♦ n Corse m/f.

cortège [kôrtezh'] n cortège m (gén funèbre).

cortisone [kôr'tisōn] n cortisone f.

coruscating [kôr'əskāting] a scintillant(e).

c.o.s. abbr (= cash on shipment) paiement m à l'expédition.

cosh [kâsh] n (Brit) matraque f.

cosignatory [kōsig'nətôrē] n cosignataire m/f.

cosiness [kō'zēnis] n (Brit) = **coziness**.

cos lettuce [kâs let'is] n (laitue f) romaine f.

cosmetic [kâzmet'ik] n produit m de beauté, cosmétique m ♦ a (preparation) cosmétique; (surgery) esthétique; (fig: reforms) symbolique, superficiel(le).

cosmic [kâz'mik] a cosmique.

cosmonaut [kâz'mənôt] n cosmonaute m/f.

cosmopolitan [kâzməpál'itən] a cosmopolite.

cosmos [kâz'məs] n cosmos m.

cosset [kâs'it] vt choyer, dorloter.

cost [kôst] n coût m ♦ vb (pt, pp **cost**) vi coûter ♦ vt établir or calculer le prix de revient de; ~s npl (LAW) dépens mpl; **how much does it** ~? combien ça coûte?; **it** ~s **$5/too much** cela coûte 5 dollars/trop cher; **what will it** ~ **to have it repaired?** combien cela coûtera de le faire réparer?; **it** ~ **him his life/job** ça lui a coûté la vie/son emploi; **the** ~ **of living** le coût de la vie; **at all** ~s coûte que coûte, à tout prix.

cost accountant n analyste m/f de coûts.

co-star [kō'stâr] n partenaire m/f.

Costa Rica [kâs'tə rē'kə] n Costa Rica m.

cost center n centre m de coût.

cost control n contrôle m des coûts.

cost-effective [kôstifek'tiv] a rentable.

cost-effectiveness [kôstifek'tivnis] n rentabilité f.

costing [kôs'ting] n calcul m du prix de revient.

costly [kôst'lē] a coûteux(euse).

cost-of-living [kôstəvliv'ing] a: ~ **allowance** indemnité f de vie chère; ~ **index** indice m du coût de la vie.

cost price n (Brit) prix coûtant or de revient.

costume [kâs'tōōm] n costume m; (lady's suit) tailleur m; (Brit: also: **swimming** ~) maillot m (de bain).

costume ball n bal masqué or costumé.

costume jewelry n bijoux mpl de fantaisie.

cosy [kō'zē] a (Brit) = **cozy**.

cot [kât] n (US: camp bed) lit de camp; (Brit: child's) lit m d'enfant, petit lit.

cottage [kât'ij] n petite maison (à la campagne), cottage m.

cottage cheese n fromage blanc (maigre).

cottage industry n industrie familiale or artisanale.

cottage pie n (Brit) ≈ hachis m Parmentier.
cotton [kát'ən] n coton m; (MED) ouate f, coton m hydrophile; ~ **dress** etc robe etc en or de coton.
  cotton on vi (Brit col): **to ~ on (to sth)** piger (qch).
cotton candy n (US) barbe f à papa.
cotton wool n (Brit) ouate f, coton m hydrophile.
couch [kouch] n canapé m; divan m; (doctor's) table f d'examen; (psychiatrist's) divan ♦ vt formuler, exprimer.
couchette [kōōshet'] n (Brit) couchette f.
cough [kôf] vi tousser ♦ n toux f.
cough drop n pastille f pour or contre la toux.
cough syrup n sirop m pour la toux.
could [kōōd] pt of **can.**
couldn't [kōōd'ənt] = **could not.**
council [koun'səl] n conseil m; **city** or **town** ~ conseil municipal; **C~ of Europe** Conseil de l'Europe.
council estate n (Brit) (quartier m or zone f de) logements loués à/par la municipalité.
council house n (Brit) maison f (à loyer modéré) louée par la municipalité.
councilor, (Brit) **councillor** [koun'səlûr] n conseiller/ère.
counsel [koun'səl] n consultation f, délibération f; (person) avocat/e ♦ vt: **to ~ sth/sb to do sth** conseiller qch/à qn de faire qch; ~ **for the defense/the prosecution** (avocat de la) défense/avocat du ministère public.
counselor, (Brit) **counsellor** [koun'səlûr] n conseiller/ère; (US LAW) avocat m.
count [kount] vt, vi compter ♦ n compte m; (nobleman) comte m; **to ~ (up) to 10** compter jusqu'à 10; **to keep ~ of sth** tenir le compte de qch; **not ~ing the children** sans compter les enfants; **10 ~ing him** 10 avec lui, 10 en le comptant; **to ~ the cost of** établir le coût de; **it ~s for very little** cela n'a pas beaucoup d'importance; ~ **yourself lucky** estimez-vous heureux.
  count on vt fus compter sur; **to ~ on doing sth** compter faire qch.
  count up vt compter, additionner.
countdown [kount'doun] n compte m à rebours.
countenance [koun'tənəns] n expression f ♦ vt approuver.
counter [koun'tûr] n comptoir m; (in post office, bank) guichet m; (in game) jeton m ♦ vt aller à l'encontre de, opposer; (blow) parer ♦ ad: ~ **to** à l'encontre de; contrairement à; **to buy under the ~** (fig) acheter sous le manteau or en sous-main; **to ~ sth with sth/by doing sth** contrer or riposter à qch par qch/en faisant qch.
counteract [kountûrakt'] vt neutraliser, contrebalancer.
counterattack n [koun'tûrətak] contre-attaque f ♦ vi [kountûrətak'] contre-attaquer.
counterbalance [kountûrbal'əns] vt contrebalancer, faire contrepoids à.
counterclockwise [kountûrklâk'wīz] ad dans le sens inverse des aiguilles d'une montre.
counterespionage [kountûres'pēənâzh] n contre-espionnage m.

counterfeit [koun'tûrfit] n faux m, contrefaçon f ♦ vt contrefaire ♦ a faux (fausse).
counterfoil [koun'tûrfoil] n talon m, souche f.
counterintelligence [kountûrintel'ijəns] n contre-espionnage m.
countermand [kountûrmand'] vt annuler.
countermeasure [koun'tûrmezhûr] n contre-mesure f.
counteroffensive [kountûrəfen'siv] n contre-offensive f.
counterpane [koun'tûrpān] n dessus-de-lit m.
counterpart [koun'tûrpârt] n (of document etc) double m; (of person) homologue m/f.
counterproductive [kountûrprəduk'tiv] a contre-productif(ive).
counterproposal [koun'tûrprəpōzəl] n contre-proposition f.
countersign [koun'tûrsīn] vt contresigner.
countersink [koun'tûrsingk] vt (hole) fraiser.
countess [koun'tis] n comtesse f.
countless [kount'lis] a innombrable.
countrified [kun'trəfīd] a rustique, à l'air campagnard.
country [kun'trē] n pays m; (native land) patrie f; (as opposed to town) campagne f; (region) région f, pays; **in the ~** à la campagne; **mountainous ~** pays de montagne, région montagneuse.
country and western (music) n musique f country.
country dancing n (Brit) danse f folklorique.
country house n manoir m, (petit) château.
countryman [kun'trēmən] n (national) compatriote m; (rural) habitant m de la campagne, campagnard m.
countryside [kun'trēsīd] n campagne f.
country-wide [kun'trēwīd] a s'étendant à l'ensemble du pays; (problem) à l'échelle du pays entier ♦ ad à travers or dans tout le pays.
county [koun'tē] n comté m.
county seat n chef-lieu m.
coup, ~**s** [kōō, -z] n beau coup; (also: ~ **d'état**) coup d'État.
coupé [kōōpā'] n (AUT) coupé m.
couple [kup'əl] n couple m ♦ vt (carriages) atteler; (TECH) coupler; (ideas, names) associer; **a ~ of** deux; (a few) deux ou trois.
couplet [kup'lit] n distique m.
coupling [kup'ling] n (RAIL) attelage m.
coupon [kōō'pân] n (voucher) bon-prime m, bon-réclame m; (detachable form) coupon m détachable, coupon-réponse m; (FINANCE) coupon.
courage [kûr'ij] n courage m.
courageous [kərā'jəs] a courageux(euse).
courgette [kōōrzhet'] n (Brit) courgette f.
courier [kûr'ēûr] n messager m, courrier m; (for tourists) accompagnateur/trice.
course [kôrs] n cours m; (of ship) route f; (of golf) terrain m; (part of meal) plat m; **first ~** entrée f; **of ~** ad bien sûr; **(no) of ~ not!** bien sûr que non!, évidemment que non!; **in the ~ of the next few days** au cours des prochains jours; **in due ~** en temps utile or voulu; ~ **(of action)** parti m, ligne f de conduite; **the best ~ would be to** ... le mieux serait de ...; **we have no other ~ but to** ... nous n'avons pas d'autre solution

que de ...; ~ **of lectures** série *f* de conférences; ~ **of treatment** (*MED*) traitement *m*.
court [kôrt] *n* cour *f*; (*LAW*) cour, tribunal *m*;
(*TENNIS*) court *m* ♦ *vt* (*woman*) courtiser,
faire la cour à; (*fig: favor, popularity*) rechercher; (: *death, disaster*) courir après,
flirter avec; **out of** ~ (*LAW: settle*) à l'amiable; **to take to** ~ actionner *or* poursuivre en
justice; ~ **of appeal** cour d'appel.
courteous [kûr'tēəs] *a* courtois(e), poli(e).
courtesan [kôr'tizən] *n* courtisane *f*.
courtesy [kûr'tisē] *n* courtoisie *f*, politesse *f*;
by ~ **of** avec l'aimable autorisation de.
courtesy bus *n* navette gratuite.
courtesy light *n* (*AUT*) plafonnier *m*.
courtesy van *n* (*US*) navette gratuite.
courthouse [kôrt'hous] *n* (*US*) palais *m* de
justice.
courtier [kôr'tēûr] *n* courtisan *m*, dame *f* de
cour.
court martial, *pl* **courts martial** *n* cour
martiale, conseil *m* de guerre.
courtroom [kôrt'rōōm] *n* salle *f* de tribunal.
court shoe *n* (*Brit*) escarpin *m*.
courtyard [kôrt'yârd] *n* cour *f*.
cousin [kuz'in] *n* cousin/e.
cove [kōv] *n* petite baie, anse *f*.
covenant [kuv'ənənt] *n* contrat *m*, engagement *m*.
Coventry [kuv'intrē] *n*: **to send sb to** ~ (*fig*)
mettre qn en quarantaine.
cover [kuv'ûr] *vt* couvrir; (*PRESS: report on*)
faire un reportage sur ♦ *n* (*for bed, of book,
COMM, INSURANCE*) couverture *f*; (*of pan*)
couvercle *m*; (*over furniture*) housse *f*;
(*shelter*) abri *m*; **to take** ~ se mettre à
l'abri; **under** ~ à l'abri; **under** ~ **of darkness** à la faveur de la nuit; **under separate**
~ (*COMM*) sous pli séparé; **$10 will** ~ **every-
thing** 10 dollars suffiront (pour tout payer).
cover up *vt* (*person, object*): **to** ~ **up
(with)** couvrir (de); (*fig: truth, facts*)
occulter; **to** ~ **up for sb** (*fig*) couvrir qn.
coverage [kuv'ûrij] *n* (*in media*) reportage *m*;
(*INSURANCE*) couverture *f*.
coveralls [kuv'ûrôlz] *npl* bleu *m* de travail,
combinaison *f*.
cover charge *n* couvert *m* (*supplément à
payer*).
covering [kuv'ûring] *n* couverture *f*, enveloppe
f.
cover letter, (*Brit*) **covering letter** *n* lettre
explicative.
cover note *n* (*INSURANCE*) police *f* provisoire.
cover price *n* prix *m* de l'exemplaire.
covert [kō'vûrt] *a* (*threat*) voilé(e), caché(e);
(*attack*) indirect(e); (*glance*) furtif(ive).
cover-up [kuv'ûrup] *n* tentative *f* pour étouffer
une affaire.
covet [kuv'it] *vt* convoiter.
cow [kou] *n* vache *f* ♦ *cpd* femelle ♦ *vt* effrayer, intimider.
coward [kou'ûrd] *n* lâche *m/f*.
cowardice [kou'ûrdis] *n* lâcheté *f*.
cowardly [kou'ûrdlē] *a* lâche.
cowboy [kou'boi] *n* cow-boy *m*.
cower [kou'ûr] *vi* se recroqueviller; trembler.
cowshed [kou'shed] *n* étable *f*.
cowslip [kou'slip] *n* (*BOT*) (fleur *f* de) coucou

m.
coxswain [kâk'sin] *n* (*abbr*: **cox**) barreur *m*;
(*of ship*) patron *m*.
coy [koi] *a* faussement effarouché(e) *or* timide.
coyote [kīōt'ē] *n* coyote *m*.
coziness [kō'zēnis] *n* (*US*) atmosphére
douillette, confort *m*.
cozy [kō'zē] *a* (*US: bed*) douillet(te); (: *scarf,
gloves*) bien chaud(e); (: *atmosphere*) cha-
leureux(euse); (: *room*) mignon(ne).
CP *n abbr* (= *Communist Party*) PC *m*.
cp. *abbr* (= *compare*) cf.
c/p *abbr* (*Brit*) = **carriage paid.**
CPA *n abbr* (*US*) = **certified public
accountant.**
CPI *n abbr* (= *Consumer Price Index*) IPC *m*.
Cpl. *abbr* (= *corporal*) C/C.
CP/M *n abbr* (= *Central Program for Micro-
processors*) CP/M *m*.
c.p.s. *abbr* (= *characters per second*)
caractères/seconde.
CPU *n abbr* = **central processing unit.**
cr. *abbr* = **credit, creditor.**
crab [krab] *n* crabe *m*.
crab apple *n* pomme *f* sauvage.
crack [krak] *n* fente *f*, fissure *f*; (*in bone, dish,
glass*) fêlure *f*; (*in wall*) lézarde *f*; (*noise*)
craquement *m*, coup (sec); (*joke*) plaisanterie *f*; (*col: attempt*): **to have a** ~ **(at sth)**
essayer (qch); (*DRUGS*) crack *m* ♦ *vt* fendre,
fissurer; fêler; lézarder; (*whip*) faire claquer; (*nut*) casser; (*solve*) résoudre, trouver
la clef de; déchiffrer ♦ *cpd* (*athlete*) de première classe, d'élite; **to** ~ **jokes** (*col*) raconter des blagues; **to get** ~**ing** (*col*) s'y
mettre, se magner.
crack down on *vt fus* (*crime*) sévir
contre, réprimer; (*spending*) mettre un frein
à.
crack up *vi* être au bout de son rouleau,
flancher.
crackdown [krak'doun] *n*: ~ **(on)** (*on crime*)
répression *f* (de); (*on spending*) restrictions
fpl (de).
cracked [krakt] *a* (*col*) toqué(e), timbré(e).
cracker [krak'ûr] *n* pétard *m*; (*cookie*) biscuit
(salé), craquelin *m*; (*Christmas* ~) diablotin
m.
crackle [krak'əl] *vi* crépiter, grésiller.
crackling [krak'ling] *n* crépitement *m*, grésillement *m*; (*on radio, telephone*) grésillement,
friture *f*; (*of pork*) couenne *f*.
cradle [krā'dəl] *n* berceau *m* ♦ *vt* (*child*)
bercer; (*object*) tenir dans ses bras.
craft [kraft] *n* métier (artisanal); (*cunning*)
ruse *f*, astuce *f*; (*boat*) embarcation *f*, barque
f.
craftsman [krafts'mən] *n* artisan *m*, ouvrier
(qualifié).
craftsmanship [krafts'mənship] *n* métier *m*,
habileté *f*.
crafty [kraf'tē] *a* rusé(e), malin(igne), astu-
cieux(euse).
crag [krag] *n* rocher escarpé.
craggy [krag'ē] *a* escarpé(e), rocheux(euse).
cram [kram] *vt* (*fill*): **to** ~ **sth with** bourrer
qch de; (*put*): **to** ~ **sth into** fourrer qch
dans.
cramming [kram'ing] *n* (*for exams*) bachotage

m.

cramp [kramp] *n* crampe *f* ♦ *vt* gêner, entraver.

cramped [krampt] *a* à l'étroit, très serré(e).

crampon [kram'pån] *n* crampon *m.*

cranberry [kran'bärē] *n* canneberge *f.*

crane [krān] *n* grue *f* ♦ *vt, vi:* **to ~ forward, to ~ one's neck** allonger le cou.

cranium, *pl* **crania** [krā'nēəm, krā'nēə] *n* boîte crânienne.

crank [krangk] *n* manivelle *f;* (*person*) excentrique *m/f.*

crankshaft [krangk'shaft] *n* vilebrequin *m.*

cranky [krang'kē] *a* excentrique, loufoque; (*bad-tempered*) grincheux(euse), revêche.

cranny [kran'ē] *n see* **nook.**

crap [krap] *n* (*col!*) conneries *fpl* (!); **to have a ~** chier (!).

crash [krash] *n* fracas *m;* (*of car, plane*) collision *f;* (*of business*) faillite *f;* (*STOCK EXCHANGE*) krach *m* ♦ *vt* (*plane*) écraser ♦ *vi* (*plane*) s'écraser; (*two cars*) se percuter, s'emboutir; (*fig*) s'effondrer; **to ~ into** se jeter *or* se fracasser contre; **he ~ed the car into a wall** il s'est écrasé contre un mur avec sa voiture.

crash barrier *n* (*Brit AUT*) rail *m* de sécurité.

crash course *n* cours intensif.

crash helmet *n* casque (protecteur).

crash landing *n* atterrissage forcé *or* en catastrophe.

crass [kras] *a* grossier(ière), crasse.

crate [krāt] *n* cageot *m.*

crater [krā'tûr] *n* cratère *m.*

cravat(e) [krəvat'] *n* foulard (noué autour du cou).

crave [krāv] *vt, vi:* **to ~ for** désirer violemment, avoir un besoin physiologique de, avoir une envie irrésistible de.

craving [krā'ving] *n:* **~ (for)** (*for food, cigarettes etc*) envie *f* irrésistible (de).

crawfish [krô'fish] *n* (*US*) = **crayfish.**

crawl [krôl] *vi* ramper; (*vehicle*) avancer au pas ♦ *n* (*SWIMMING*) crawl *m;* **to ~ to sb** (*col*) faire de la lèche à qn.

crayfish [krā'fish] *n* (*pl inv*) (*freshwater*) écrevisse *f;* (*saltwater*) langoustine *f.*

crayon [krā'ân] *n* crayon *m* (de couleur).

craze [krāz] *n* engouement *m.*

crazed [krāzd] *a* (*look, person*) affolé(e); (*pottery, glaze*) craquelé(e).

crazy [krā'zē] *a* fou(folle); **to go ~** devenir fou; **to be ~ about sb** (*col*) aimer qn à la folie; **he's ~ about skiing** (*col*) c'est un fana(tique) de ski.

crazy paving *n* (*Brit*) dallage irrégulier (en pierres plates).

CRC *n abbr* (*US*) = *Civil Rights Commission.*

creak [krēk] *vi* (*hinge*) grincer; (*floor, shoes*) craquer.

cream [krēm] *n* crème *f* ♦ *a* (*color*) crème *inv;* **whipped ~** crème fouettée.

cream cake *n* (*Brit*) (petit) gâteau à la crème.

cream cheese *n* fromage *m* à la crème, fromage blanc.

creamery [krē'mûrē] *n* (*store*) crémerie *f;* (*factory*) laiterie *f.*

creamy [krē'mē] *a* crémeux(euse).

crease [krēs] *n* pli *m* ♦ *vt* froisser, chiffonner ♦ *vi* se froisser, se chiffonner.

crease-resistant [krēsrizis'tənt] *a* infroissable.

create [krēāt'] *vt* créer; (*impression, fuss*) faire.

creation [krēā'shən] *n* création *f.*

creative [krēā'tiv] *a* créateur(trice).

creativity [krēātiv'ətē] *n* créativité *f.*

creator [krēā'tûr] *n* créateur/trice.

creature [krē'chûr] *n* créature *f.*

crèche, creche [kresh] *n* (*Brit*) garderie *f,* crèche *f.*

credence [krēd'əns] *n* croyance *f,* foi *f.*

credentials [kriden'shəlz] *npl* (*papers*) références *fpl;* (*letters of reference*) pièces justificatives.

credibility [kredəbil'ətē] *n* crédibilité *f.*

credible [kred'əbəl] *a* digne de foi, crédible.

credit [kred'it] *n* crédit *m;* (*SCOL*) unité *f* de valeur ♦ *vt* (*COMM*) créditer; (*believe: also:* **give ~ to**) ajouter foi à, croire; **to ~ sb with** (*fig*) prêter *or* attribuer à qn; **to ~ $50 to sb** créditer (le compte de) qn de 50 dollars; **to be in ~** (*person, bank account*) être créditeur(trice); **on ~** à crédit; **to one's ~** à son honneur; à son actif; **to take the ~ for** s'attribuer le mérite de; **it does him ~** cela lui fait honneur.

creditable [kred'itəbəl] *a* honorable, estimable.

credit account *n* compte *m* client.

credit agency *n* (*Brit*) agence *f* de renseignements commerciaux.

credit balance *n* solde créditeur.

credit bureau *n* (*US*) agence *f* de renseignements commerciaux.

credit card *n* carte *f* de crédit.

credit control *n* suivi *m* des factures.

credit facilities *npl* facilités *fpl* de paiement.

credit limit *n* limite *f* de crédit.

credit note *n* (*Brit*) avoir *m.*

creditor [kred'itûr] *n* créancier/ière.

credit rating *n* réputation *f* de solvabilité.

credits [kred'its] *npl* (*CINEMA*) générique *m.*

credit transfer *n* virement *m.*

creditworthy [kred'itwûrthē] *a* solvable.

credulity [krədōō'litē] *n* crédulité *f.*

creed [krēd] *n* croyance *f;* credo *m,* principes *mpl.*

creek [krēk] *n* crique *f,* anse *f;* (*US*) ruisseau *m,* petit cours d'eau.

creel [krēl] *n* panier *m* de pêche; (*also:* **lobster ~**) panier à homards.

creep, *pt, pp* **crept** [krēp, krept] *vi* ramper; (*fig*) se faufiler, se glisser; (*plant*) grimper ♦ *n* (*col*) saligaud *m;* **he's a ~** c'est un type puant; **it gives me the ~s** cela me fait froid dans le dos; **to ~ up on sb** s'approcher furtivement de qn.

creeper [krē'pûr] *n* plante grimpante.

creepers [krē'pûrz] *npl* (*US: for baby*) barboteuse *f.*

creepy [krē'pē] *a* (*frightening*) qui fait frissonner, qui donne la chair de poule.

creepy-crawly [krē'pēkrôl'ē] *n* (*col*) bestiole *f.*

cremate [krē'māt] *vt* incinérer.

cremation [krimā'shən] *n* incinération *f.*

crematorium, *pl* **crematoria** [krēmətôr'ēəm, -tôr'ēə] *n* four *m* crématoire.

creosote [krē'əsōt] *n* créosote *f.*

crêpe |krăp| n crêpe m.
crêpe bandage n (Brit) bande f Velpeau ®.
crêpe paper n papier m crépon.
crêpe sole n semelle f de crêpe.
crept |krept| pt, pp of **creep**.
crescendo |krishen'dō| n crescendo m.
crescent |kres'ənt| n croissant m; (street) rue f (en arc de cercle).
cress |kres| n cresson m.
crest |krest| n crête f; (of helmet) cimier m; (of coat of arms) timbre m.
crestfallen |krest'fölən| a déconfit(e), découragé(e).
Crete |krēt| n Crète f.
crevasse |krəvas'| n crevasse f.
crevice |krev'is| n fissure f, lézarde f, fente f.
crew |krōō| n équipage m; (CINEMA) équipe f (de tournage); (gang) bande f.
crew cut n: **to have a ~** avoir les cheveux en brosse.
crew neck n col ras.
crib |krib| n lit m d'enfant ♦ vt (col) copier.
cribbage |krib'ij| n sorte de jeu de cartes.
crick |krik| n crampe f; **~ in the neck** torticolis m.
cricket |krik'it| n (insect) grillon m, cri-cri m inv; (game) cricket m.
cricketer |krik'itûr| n joueur m de cricket.
crime |krīm| n crime m; **minor ~** délit m or infraction f mineur(e).
crime wave n poussée f de la criminalité.
criminal |krim'ənəl| a, n criminel(le).
crimp |krimp| vt friser, frisotter.
crimson |krim'zən| a cramoisi(e).
cringe |krinj| vi avoir un mouvement de recul; (fig) s'humilier, ramper.
crinkle |kring'kəl| vt froisser, chiffonner.
cripple |krip'əl| n boiteux/euse, infirme m/f ♦ vt estropier, paralyser; (ship, plane) immobiliser; (production, exports) paralyser; **~d with rheumatism** perclus(e) de rhumatismes.
crippling |krip'ling| a (disease) handicapant(e); (taxation, debts) écrasant(e).
crisis, pl **crises** |krī'sis, -sēz| n crise f.
crisp |krisp| a croquant(e); (fig) vif(vive); brusque.
crisps |krisps| npl (Brit) (pommes) chips fpl.
crisscross |kris'krôs| a entrecroisé(e), en croisillons ♦ vt sillonner; **~ pattern** croisillons mpl.
criterion, pl **criteria** |krītēr'ēən, -tēr'ēə| n critère m.
critic |krit'ik| n critique m/f.
critical |krit'ikəl| a critique; **to be ~ of sb/sth** critiquer qn/qch.
critical list n (MED): **on the ~** dans un état critique.
critically |krit'iklē| ad (examine) d'un œil critique; (speak) sévèrement; **~ ill** gravement malade.
criticism |krit'isizəm| n critique f.
criticize |krit'əsīz| vt critiquer.
croak |krōk| vi (frog) coasser; (raven) croasser.
crochet |krōshā'| n travail m au crochet.
crock |krák| n cruche f; (col: also: **old ~**) épave f.
crockery |krák'ûrē| n vaisselle f.

crocodile |krák'ədīl| n crocodile m.
crocus |krō'kəs| n crocus m.
croft |krôft| n (Brit) petite ferme.
crone |krōn| n vieille bique, (vieille) sorcière.
crony |krō'nē| n copain/copine.
crook |krōōk| n escroc m; (of shepherd) houlette f.
crooked |krōōk'id| a courbé(e), tordu(e); (action) malhonnête.
crop |krâp| n (produce) culture f; (amount produced) récolte f; (riding ~) cravache f; (of bird) jabot m ♦ vt (hair) tondre; (subj: animals: grass) brouter.
crop up vi surgir, se présenter, survenir.
cropper |krâp'ûr| n: **to come a ~** (col) faire la culbute, s'étaler.
crop spraying |krâp sprā'ing| n pulvérisation f des cultures.
croquet |krōkā'| n croquet m.
croquette |krōket'| n croquette f.
cross |krôs| n croix f; (BIOL) croisement m ♦ vt (street etc) traverser; (arms, legs, BIOL) croiser; (check) barrer; (thwart: person, plan) contrarier ♦ vi: **the boat ~es from ... to ...** le bateau fait la traversée de ... à ... ♦ a en colère, fâché(e); **to ~ o.s.** se signer, faire le signe de (la) croix; **we have a ~ed line** (Brit: on telephone) il y a des interférences; **they've got their wires ~ed** (fig) il y a un malentendu entre eux; **to be/get ~ with sb (about sth)** être en colère/se fâcher contre qn (à propos de qch).
cross out vt barrer, biffer.
cross over vi traverser.
crossbar |krôs'bár| n barre transversale.
crossbreed |krôs'brēd| n hybride m, métis/se.
cross-Channel ferry |krôs'chanəl fär'ē| n ferry m qui fait la traversée de la manche.
cross-check |krôs'chek| n recoupement m ♦ vi vérifier par recoupement.
cross-country (race) |krôs'kun'trē (rās)| n cross(-country) m.
cross-examination |krôs'igzamənə'shən| n (LAW) examen m contradictoire (d'un témoin).
cross-examine |krôs'igzam'in| vt (LAW) faire subir un examen contradictoire à.
cross-eyed |krôs'īd| a qui louche.
crossfire |krôs'fīúr| n feux croisés.
crossing |krôs'ing| n croisement m, carrefour m; (sea passage) traversée f; (also: **pedestrian ~**) passage clouté.
cross-purposes |krôs'pûr'pəsiz| npl: **to be at ~ with sb** comprendre qn de travers; **we're (talking) at ~** on ne parle pas de la même chose.
cross-reference |krôs'ref'ûrəns| n renvoi m, référence f.
crossroads |krôs'rōdz| n carrefour m.
cross section n (BIOL) coupe transversale; (in population) échantillon m.
crosswalk |krôs'wôk| n (US) passage clouté.
crosswind |krôs'wind| n vent m de travers.
crosswise |krôs'wīz| ad en travers.
crossword |krôs'wûrd| n mots croisés mpl.
crotch |krâch| n (of garment) entre-jambes m inv.
crotchet |krâch'it| n (MUS) noire f.
crotchety |krâch'ətē| a (person) grognon(ne),

grincheux(euse).

crouch [krouch] *vi* s'accroupir; se tapir; se ramasser.

croup [krōōp] *n* (*MED*) croup *m*.

crouton [krōō'tân] *n* croûton *m*.

crow [krō] *n* (*bird*) corneille *f*; (*of cock*) chant *m* du coq, cocorico *m* ♦ *vi* (*cock*) chanter; (*fig*) pavoiser, chanter victoire.

crowbar [krō'bâr] *n* levier *m*.

crowd [kroud] *n* foule *f* ♦ *vt* bourrer, remplir ♦ *vi* affluer, s'attrouper, s'entasser; ~**s of people** une foule de gens.

crowded [krou'did] *a* bondé(e), plein(e); ~ **with** plein de.

crowd scene *n* (*CINEMA. THEATER*) scène *f* de foule.

crown [kroun] *n* couronne *f*; (*of head*) sommet *m* de la tête, calotte crânienne; (*of hat*) fond *m*; (*of hill*) sommet *m* ♦ *vt* (*also tooth*) couronner.

crown court *n* (*Brit*) ≈ Cour *f* d'assises.

crowning [krou'ning] *a* (*achievement, glory*) suprême.

crown jewels *npl* joyaux *mpl* de la Couronne.

crown prince *n* prince héritier.

crow's-feet [krōz'fēt] *npl* pattes *fpl* d'oie (*fig*).

crow's-nest [krōz'nest] *n* (*on sailing-ship*) nid *m* de pie.

crucial [krōō'shəl] *a* crucial(e), décisif(ive); ~ **to** essentiel(le) à.

crucifix [krōō'səfiks] *n* crucifix *m*.

crucifixion [krōōsəfik'shən] *n* crucifiement *m*, crucifixion *f*.

crucify [krōō'səfī] *vt* crucifier, mettre en croix; (*fig*) crucifier.

crude [krōōd] *a* (*materials*) brut(e); non raffiné(e); (*basic*) rudimentaire, sommaire; (*vulgar*) cru(e), grossier(ière).

crude (oil) *n* (pétrole) brut *m*.

cruel [krōō'əl] *a* cruel(le).

cruelty [krōō'əltē] *n* cruauté *f*.

cruet [krōō'it] *n* huilier *m*; vinaigrier *m*.

cruise [krōōz] *n* croisière *f* ♦ *vi* (*ship*) croiser; (*car*) rouler; (*aircraft*) voler; (*taxi*) être en maraude.

cruise missile *n* missile *m* de croisière.

cruiser [krōō'zûr] *n* croiseur *m*.

cruise ship *n* vapeur *m* de plaisance.

cruising speed [krōō'zing spēd] *n* vitesse *f* de croisière.

crumb [krum] *n* miette *f*.

crumble [krum'bəl] *vt* émietter ♦ *vi* s'émietter; (*plaster etc*) s'effriter; (*land, earth*) s'ébouler; (*building*) s'écrouler, crouler; (*fig*) s'effondrer.

crumbly [krum'blē] *a* friable.

crummy [krum'ē] *a* (*col*) minable; (: *unwell*) mal fichu(e), patraque.

crumpet [krum'pit] *n* petite crêpe (épaisse).

crumple [krum'pəl] *vt* froisser, friper.

crunch [krunch] *vt* croquer; (*underfoot*) faire craquer, écraser; faire crisser ♦ *n* (*fig*) instant *m or* moment *m* critique, moment de vérité.

crunchy [krun'chē] *a* croquant(e), croustillant(e).

crusade [krōōsād'] *n* croisade *f* ♦ *vi* (*fig*): **to ~ for/against** partir en croisade pour/contre.

crusader [krōōsā'dûr] *n* croisé *m*; (*fig*): ~

(for) champion *m* (de).

crush [krush] *n* foule *f*, cohue *f*; (*love*): **to have a ~ on sb** avoir le béguin pour qn ♦ *vt* écraser; (*crumple*) froisser; (*grind, break up: garlic, ice*) piler; (: *grapes*) presser.

crushing [krush'ing] *a* écrasant(e).

crust [krust] *n* croûte *f*.

crustacean [krustā'shən] *n* crustacé *m*.

crusty [krus'tē] *a* (*loaf*) croustillant(e).

crutch [kruch] *n* béquille *f*; (*TECH*) support *m*; (*also*: **crotch**) entrejambe *m*.

crux [kruks] *n* point crucial.

cry [krī] *vi* pleurer; (*shout: also*: ~ **out**) crier ♦ *n* cri *m*; **what are you ~ing about?** pourquoi pleures-tu?; **to ~ for help** appeler à l'aide; **she had a good ~** elle a pleuré un bon coup; **it's a far ~ from ...** (*fig*) on est loin de ....

cry off *vi* (*Brit*) se dédire; se décommander.

crying [krī'ing] *a* (*fig*) criant(e), flagrant(e).

crypt [kript] *n* crypte *f*.

cryptic [krip'tik] *a* énigmatique.

crystal [kris'təl] *n* cristal *m*.

crystal-clear [kris'təlkli'ûr] *a* clair(e) comme de l'eau de roche.

crystallize [kris'təlīz] *vt* cristalliser ♦ *vi* (se) cristalliser; ~**d fruits** (*Brit*) fruits confits.

CSA *n abbr* = *Confederate States of America*.

CS gas [sē'es gas'] *n* (*Brit*) gaz *m* C.S.

CST *abbr* (*US*: = *Central Standard Time*) *fuseau horaire*.

CT *abbr* (*US MAIL*) = *Connecticut*.

ct *abbr* = **carat**.

Ct. *abbr* (*US*) = *Connecticut*.

cu. *abbr* = **cubic**.

cub [kub] *n* petit *m* (*d'un animal*); (*also*: ~ **scout**) louveteau *m*.

Cuba [kyōō'bə] *n* Cuba *m*.

Cuban [kyōō'bən] *a* cubain(e) ♦ *n* Cubain/e.

cubbyhole [kub'ēhōl] *n* cagibi *m*.

cube [kyōōb] *n* cube *m* ♦ *vt* (*MATH*) élever au cube.

cube root *n* racine *f* cubique.

cubic [kyōō'bik] *a* cubique; ~ **meter** *etc* mètre *m etc* cube; ~ **capacity** (*AUT*) cylindrée *f*.

cubicle [kyōō'bikəl] *n* box *m*, cabine *f*.

cuckoo [kōō'kōō] *n* coucou *m*.

cuckoo clock *n* (pendule *f* à) coucou *m*.

cucumber [kyōō'kumbûr] *n* concombre *m*.

cud [kud] *n*: **to chew the ~** ruminer.

cuddle [kud'əl] *vt* câliner, caresser ♦ *vi* se blottir l'un contre l'autre.

cuddly [kud'lē] *a* câlin(e).

cudgel [kuj'əl] *n* gourdin *m* ♦ *vt*: **to ~ one's brains** se creuser la tête.

cue [kyōō] *n* queue *f* de billard; (*THEATER etc*) signal *m*.

cuff [kuf] *n* (*of shirt, coat etc*) poignet *m*, manchette *f*; (*US*: *on pants*) revers *m*; (*blow*) gifle *f* ♦ *vt* gifler; **off the ~** *ad* de chic, à l'improviste.

cuff link *n* bouton *m* de manchette.

cu. in. *abbr* = *cubic inches*.

cuisine [kwizēn'] *n* cuisine *f*, art *m* culinaire.

cul-de-sac [kul'dəsak'] *n* cul-de-sac *m*, impasse *f*.

culinary [kyōō'lənãrē] *a* culinaire.

cull [kul] *vt* sélectionner; (*kill selectively*) pratiquer l'abattage sélectif de.

culminate [kul'mənāt] *vi*: **to ~ in** finir *or* se terminer par; (*lead to*) mener à.

culmination [kulmənā'shən] *n* point culminant.

culotte [kyōōlǎt'] *n* (*US*) jupe-culotte *f*.

culottes [kyōōlǎts'] *npl* (*Brit*) jupe-culotte *f*.

culpable [kul'pəbəl] *a* coupable.

culprit [kul'prit] *n* coupable *m/f*.

cult [kult] *n* culte *m*.

cult figure *n* idole *f*.

cultivate [kul'təvāt] *vt* (*also fig*) cultiver.

cultivation [kultəvā'shən] *n* culture *f*.

cultural [kul'chûrəl] *a* culturel(le).

culture [kul'chûr] *n* (*also fig*) culture *f*.

cultured [kul'chûrd] *a* cultivé(e) (*fig*).

cumbersome [kum'bûrsəm] *a* encombrant(e), embarrassant(e).

cumin [kyōōm'in] *n* (*spice*) cumin *m*.

cumulative [kyōōm'yələtiv] *a* cumulatif(ive).

cunning [kun'ing] *n* ruse *f*, astuce *f* ♦ *a* rusé(e), malin(igne); (*clever: device, idea*) astucieux(euse).

cup [kup] *n* tasse *f*; (*prize, event*) coupe *f*; (*of bra*) bonnet *m*; **a ~ of tea** une tasse de thé.

cupboard [kub'ûrd] *n* placard *m*.

Cupid [kyōō'pid] *n* Cupidon *m*; (*figurine*) amour *m*.

cupidity [kyōōpid'itē] *n* cupidité *f*.

cupola [kyōō'pələ] *n* coupole *f*.

curable [kyōō'rəbəl] *a* guérissable, curable.

curate [kyōō'rit] *n* vicaire *m*.

curator [kyōōrā'tûr] *n* conservateur *m* (*d'un musée etc*).

curb [kûrb] *vt* refréner, mettre un frein à; (*expenditure*) limiter, juguler ♦ *n* frein *m* (*fig*); (*US*) bordure *f* du trottoir.

curd cheese [kûrd chēz] *n* ≈ fromage blanc.

curdle [kûr'dəl] *vi* (se) cailler.

curds [kûrdz] *npl* lait caillé.

cure [kyōōr] *vt* guérir; (*CULIN*) saler; fumer; sécher ♦ *n* remède *m*; **to be ~d of sth** être guéri de qch.

cure-all [kyōōr'ôl] *n* (*also fig*) panacée *f*.

curfew [kûr'fyōō] *n* couvre-feu *m*.

curio [kyōō'rēō] *n* bibelot *m*, curiosité *f*.

curiosity [kyōōrēâs'ətē] *n* curiosité *f*.

curious [kyōō'rēəs] *a* curieux(euse); **I'm ~ about him** il m'intrigue.

curiously [kyōō'rēəslē] *ad* curieusement; (*inquisitively*) avec curiosité; **~ enough, ...** bizarrement ....

curl [kûrl] *n* boucle *f* (de cheveux); (*of smoke etc*) volute *f* ♦ *vt, vi* boucler; (*tightly*) friser. **curl up** *vi* s'enrouler; se pelotonner.

curler [kûr'lûr] *n* bigoudi *m*, rouleau *m*; (*SPORT*) joueur/euse de curling.

curlew [kûr'lōō] *n* courlis *m*.

curling [kûr'ling] *n* (*sport*) curling *m*.

curling iron *n* (*US*) fer *m* à friser.

curling tongs *npl* (*Brit*) = curling iron.

curly [kûr'lē] *a* bouclé(e); (*tightly curled*) frisé(e).

currant [kûr'ənt] *n* raisin *m* de Corinthe, raisin sec.

currency [kûr'ənsē] *n* monnaie *f*; **foreign ~** devises étrangères, monnaie étrangère; **to gain ~** (*fig*) s'accréditer.

current [kûr'ənt] *n* courant *m* ♦ *a* courant(e); (*tendency, price, event*) actuel(le); **direct/**

alternating ~ (*ELEC*) courant continu/ alternatif; **the ~ issue of a magazine** le dernier numéro d'un magazine; **in ~ use** d'usage courant.

current account *n* (*Brit*) compte courant.

current affairs *npl* (questions *fpl* d')actualité *f*.

current assets *npl* (*COMM*) actif *m* disponible.

current liabilities *npl* (*COMM*) passif *m* exigible.

currently [kûr'əntlē] *ad* actuellement.

curriculum, *pl* **~s** *or* **curricula** [kərik'yələm, -yələ] *n* programme *m* d'études.

curriculum vitae (CV) [kərik'yələm vē'tī] *n* curriculum vitae (CV) *m*.

curry [kûr'ē] *n* curry *m* ♦ *vt*: **to ~ favor with** chercher à gagner la faveur *or* à s'attirer les bonnes grâces de; **chicken ~** curry de poulet, poulet *m* au curry.

curry powder *n* poudre *f* de curry.

curse [kûrs] *vi* jurer, blasphémer ♦ *vt* maudire ♦ *n* malédiction *f*; fléau *m*; (*swearword*) juron *m*.

cursor [kûr'sûr] *n* (*COMPUT*) curseur *m*.

cursory [kûr'sûrē] *a* superficiel(le), hâtif(ive).

curt [kûrt] *a* brusque, sec(sèche).

curtail [kûrtāl'] *vt* (*visit etc*) écourter; (*expenses etc*) réduire.

curtain [kûr'tən] *n* rideau *m*; **to draw the ~s** (*together*) fermer *or* tirer les rideaux; (*apart*) ouvrir les rideaux.

curtain call *n* (*THEATER*) rappel *m*.

curts(e)y [kûrt'sē] *n* révérence *f* ♦ *vi* faire une révérence.

curvature [kûr'vəchûr] *n* courbure *f*.

curve [kûrv] *n* courbe *f*; (*in the road*) tournant *m*, virage *m* ♦ *vt* courber ♦ *vi* se courber; (*road*) faire une courbe.

curved [kûrvd] *a* courbe.

cushion [kōōsh'ən] *n* coussin *m* ♦ *vt* (*seat*) rembourrer; (*shock*) amortir.

cushy [kōōsh'ē] *a* (*col*): **a ~ job** un boulot de tout repos.

custard [kus'tûrd] *n* (*for pouring*) crème anglaise.

custodian [kustō'dēən] *n* gardien/ne; (*of collection etc*) conservateur/trice.

custody [kus'tədē] *n* (*of child*) garde *f*; (*for offenders*) détention préventive; **to take sb into ~** placer qn en détention préventive; **in the ~ of** sous la garde de.

custom [kus'təm] *n* coutume *f*, usage *m*; (*LAW*) droit coutumier, coutume; (*COMM*) clientèle *f*.

customary [kus'təmärē] *a* habituel(le); **it is ~ to do it** l'usage veut qu'on le fasse.

custom-built [kus'təmbilt'] *a* see **custom-made.**

customer [kus'təmûr] *n* client/e; **he's a tough ~** (*col*) ce n'est pas quelqu'un de facile.

customer profile *n* profil *m* du client.

customer service *n* service *m* après-vente, SAV *m*.

customized [kus'təmīzd] *a* personnalisé(e).

custom-made [kus'təmmād'] *a* (*clothes*) fait(e) sur mesure; (*other goods: also*: **custom-built**) hors série, fait(e) sur commande.

customs [kus'təmz] *npl* douane *f*; **to go through (the)** ~ passer la douane.
Customs and Excise *n* (*Brit*) administration *f* des douanes.
customs duty *n* droits *mpl* de douane.
customs officer *n* douanier *m*.
cut [kut] *vb* (*pt, pp* **cut**) *vt* couper; (*meat*) découper; (*shape, make*) tailler; couper; creuser; graver; (*reduce*) réduire; (*col: lecture, appointment*) manquer ♦ *vi* couper; (*intersect*) se couper ♦ *n* (*gen*) coupure *f*; (*of clothes*) coupe *f*; (*of jewel*) taille *f*; (*in salary etc*) réduction *f*; (*of meat*) morceau *m*; **cold** ~**s** *npl* viandes froides; **to** ~ **teeth** (*baby*) faire ses dents; **to** ~ **a tooth** percer une dent; **to** ~ **one's finger** se couper le doigt; **to get one's hair** ~ se faire couper les cheveux; **to** ~ **sth short** couper court à qch.
cut back *vt* (*plants*) tailler; (*production, expenditure*) réduire.
cut down *vt* (*tree*) abattre; (*reduce*) réduire; **to** ~ **sb down to size** (*fig*) remettre qn à sa place.
cut down on *vt fus* réduire.
cut in *vi* (*interrupt: conversation*): **to** ~ **in (on)** couper la parole (à); (*AUT*) faire une queue de poisson.
cut off *vt* couper; (*fig*) isoler; **we've been** ~ **off** (*TEL*) nous avons été coupés.
cut out *vt* (*picture etc*) découper; (*remove*) ôter; supprimer.
cut up *vt* découper.
cut-and-dried [kutəndrīd'] *a* (*also:* **cut-and-dry**) tout(e) fait(e), tout(e) décidé(e).
cutaway [kut'əwā] *a, n:* ~ **(drawing)** écorché *m*.
cutback [kut'bak] *n* réduction *f*.
cute [kyōōt] *a* mignon(ne), adorable; (*clever*) rusé(e), astucieux(euse).
cut glass *n* cristal taillé.
cuticle [kyōō'tikəl] *n* (*on nail*): ~ **remover** repousse-peaux *m inv*.
cutlery [kut'lûrē] *n* couverts *mpl*; (*trade*) coutellerie *f*.
cutlet [kut'lit] *n* côtelette *f*.
cutoff [kut'óf] *n* (*also:* ~ **point**) seuil-limite *m*.
cutoff switch *n* interrupteur *m*.
cutout [kut'out] *n* coupe-circuit *m inv*; (*paper figure*) découpage *m*.
cut-price [kut'prīs] *a* (*Brit*) = **cut-rate**.
cut-rate [kut'rāt] *a* (*US*) au rabais, à prix réduit.
cutthroat [kut'thrōt] *n* assassin *m* ♦ *a:* ~ **competition** concurrence *f* sauvage.
cutting [kut'ing] *a* tranchant(e), coupant(e); (*fig*) cinglant(e), mordant(e) ♦ *n* (*Brit: from newspaper*) coupure *f* (de journal); (: *RAIL*) tranchée *f*; (*CINEMA*) montage *m*.
cuttlefish [kut'əlfish] *n* seiche *f*.
CV *n abbr* = **curriculum vitae**.
C & W *n abbr* = **country and western (music)**.
cwt. *abbr* = **hundredweight**.
cyanide [sī'ənīd] *n* cyanure *m*.
cybernetics [sībûrnet'iks] *n* cybernétique *f*.
cyclamen [sik'ləmən] *n* cyclamen *m*.
cycle [sī'kəl] *n* cycle *m* ♦ *vi* faire de la bicyclette.
cycle race *n* course *f* cycliste.

cycle rack *n* (*Brit*) râtelier *m* à bicyclette.
cycling [sīk'ling] *n* cyclisme *m*; **to go on a** ~ **tour** faire du cyclotourisme.
cyclist [sīk'list] *n* cycliste *m/f*.
cyclone [sīk'lōn] *n* cyclone *m*.
cygnet [sig'nit] *n* jeune cygne *m*.
cylinder [sil'indûr] *n* cylindre *m*.
cylinder block *n* bloc-cylindres *m*.
cylinder capacity *n* cylindrée *f*.
cylinder head *n* culasse *f*.
cylinder-head gasket [sil'indûrhed gas'kit] *n* joint *m* de culasse.
cymbals [sim'bəlz] *npl* cymbales *fpl*.
cynic [sin'ik] *n* cynique *m/f*.
cynical [sin'ikəl] *a* cynique.
cynicism [sin'əsizəm] *n* cynisme *m*.
CYO *n abbr* (*US:* = *Catholic Youth Organization*) ≈ JC *f*.
cypress [sī'pris] *n* cyprès *m*.
Cypriot [sip'rēət] *a* cypriote, chypriote ♦ *n* Cypriote *m/f*, Chypriote *m/f*.
Cyprus [sīp'rəs] *n* Chypre *f*.
cyst [sist] *n* kyste *m*.
cystitis [sistī'tis] *n* cystite *f*.
CZ *n abbr* (*US:* = *Canal Zone*) zone du canal de Panama.
czar [zâr] *n* tsar *m*.
Czech [chek] *a* tchèque ♦ *n* Tchèque *m/f*; (*LING*) tchèque *m*.
Czechoslovak [chekəslō'vak] *a, n* = **Czechoslovakian**.
Czechoslovakia [chekəsləvàk'ēə] *n* Tchécoslovaquie *f*.
Czechoslovakian [chekəsləvàk'ēən] *a* tchécoslovaque ♦ *n* Tchécoslovaque *m/f*.

D

D, d [dē] *n* (*letter*) D, d *m*; (*MUS*): **D** ré *m*; **D for Dog** D comme Désirée.
D [dē] *abbr* (*US POL*) = **democrat(ic)**.
d. *abbr* = **died**.
DA *n abbr* (*US*) = **district attorney**.
dab [dab] *vt* (*eyes, wound*) tamponner; (*paint, cream*) appliquer (par petites touches *or* rapidement); **a** ~ **of paint** un petit coup de peinture.
dabble [dab'əl] *vi:* **to** ~ **in** faire *or* se mêler *or* s'occuper un peu de.
Dacca [dak'ə] *n* Dacca.
dachshund [dàks'ŏŏnd] *n* teckel *m*.
dad, daddy [dad, dad'ē] *n* papa *m*.
daddy-long-legs [dadēlóng'legz] *n* tipule *f*; faucheux *m*.
daffodil [daf'ədil] *n* jonquille *f*.
daft [daft] *a* (*col*) idiot(e), stupide; **to be** ~ **about** être toqué(e) *or* mordu(e) de.
dagger [dag'ûr] *n* poignard *m*; **to be at** ~**s drawn with sb** (*Brit*) être à couteaux tirés avec qn; **to look** ~**s at sb** foudroyer qn du regard.
dahlia [dal'yə] *n* dahlia *m*.

daily [dā'lē] *a* quotidien(ne), journalier(ière) ♦ *n* quotidien *m*; (*Brit: domestic help*) femme *f* de ménage (*à la journée*) ♦ *ad* tous les jours; **twice** ~ deux fois par jour.

dainty [dān'tē] *a* délicat(e), mignon(ne).

dairy [dâr'ē] *n* (*store*) crémerie *f*, laiterie *f*; (*on farm*) laiterie ♦ *a* laitier(ière).

dairy cow *n* vache laitière.

dairy farm *n* exploitation *f* pratiquant l'élevage laitier.

dairy produce *n* produits laitiers.

dais [dā'is] *n* estrade *f*.

daisy [dā'zē] *n* pâquerette *f*.

daisy wheel *n* (*on printer*) marguerite *f*.

daisy-wheel printer [dā'zēhwēl prin'tûr] *n* imprimante *f* à marguerite.

Dakar [dâkâr'] *n* Dakar.

dale [dāl] *n* vallon *m*.

dally [dal'ē] *vi* musarder, flâner.

dalmatian [dalmā'shən] *n* (*dog*) dalmatien/ne.

dam [dam] *n* barrage *m*; (*reservoir*) réservoir *m*, lac *m* de retenue ♦ *vt* endiguer.

damage [dam'ij] *n* dégâts *mpl*, dommages *mpl*; (*fig*) tort *m* ♦ *vt* endommager, abîmer; (*fig*) faire du tort à; ~ **to property** dégâts matériels.

damages [dam'ijiz] *npl* (*LAW*) dommages-intérêts *mpl*; **to pay $5000 in** ~ payer 5000 dollars de dommages-intérêts.

damaging [dam'ijing] *a*: ~ **(to)** préjudiciable (à), nuisible (à).

Damascus [dəmas'kəs] *n* Damas.

dame [dām] *n* (*title*) titre porté par une femme décorée de l'ordre de l'Empire Britannique ou d'un ordre de chevalerie; titre porté par la femme ou la veuve d'un chevalier ou baronnet; (*THEATER*) vieille dame (*rôle comique joué par un homme*).

damn [dam] *vt* condamner; (*curse*) maudire ♦ *n* (*col*): **I don't give a** ~ je m'en fous ♦ *a* (*col*): **this** ~ ... ce sacré *or* foutu ...; ~ **(it)!** zut!

damnable [dam'nəbəl] *a* (*col: behavior*) odieux(euse), détestable; (: *weather*) épouvantable, abominable.

damnation [damnā'shən] *n* (*REL*) damnation *f* ♦ *excl* (*col*) malédiction!, merde!

damning [dam'ing] *a* (*evidence*) accablant(e).

damp [damp] *a* humide ♦ *n* humidité *f* ♦ *vt* (*also*: ~**en**: *cloth, rag*) humecter; (: *enthusiasm etc*) refroidir.

dampcourse [damp'kôrs] *n* (*Brit*) couche isolante (contre l'humidité).

damper [dam'pûr] *n* (*MUS*) étouffoir *m*; (*of fire*) registre *m*; **to put a** ~ **on** (*fig: atmosphere, enthusiasm*) refroidir.

dampness [damp'nis] *n* humidité *f*.

damson [dam'zən] *n* prune *f* de Damas.

dance [dans] *n* danse *f*; (*ball*) bal *m* ♦ *vi* danser; **to** ~ **about** sautiller, gambader.

dance hall *n* salle *f* de bal, dancing *m*.

dancer [dan'sûr] *n* danseur/euse.

dancing [dan'sing] *n* danse *f*.

D and C *n abbr* (*Brit MED*: = *dilation and curettage*) curetage *m*.

dandelion [dan'dəlīən] *n* pissenlit *m*.

dandruff [dan'drəf] *n* pellicules *fpl*.

dandy [dan'dē] *n* dandy *m*, élégant *m* ♦ *a* (*US col*) fantastique, super.

Dane [dān] *n* Danois/e.

danger [dān'jûr] *n* danger *m*; **there is a** ~ **of fire** il y a (un) risque d'incendie; **in** ~ en danger; **he was in** ~ **of falling** il risquait de tomber; **out of** ~ hors de danger.

danger list *n* (*Brit MED*): **on the** ~ dans un état critique.

dangerous [dān'jûrəs] *a* dangereux(euse).

dangerously [dān'jûrəslē] *ad* dangereusement; ~ **ill** très gravement malade, en danger de mort.

danger zone *n* zone dangereuse.

dangle [dang'gəl] *vt* balancer; (*fig*) faire miroiter ♦ *vi* pendre, se balancer.

Danish [dā'nish] *a* danois(e) ♦ *n* (*LING*) danois *m*.

Danish pastry *n* feuilleté *m* (*recouvert d'un glaçage et fourré aux fruits etc*).

dank [dangk] *a* froid(e) et humide.

Danube [dan'yōōb] *n*: **the** ~ le Danube.

dapper [dap'ûr] *a* pimpant(e).

Dardanelles [dârdənelz'] *npl* Dardanelles *fpl*.

dare [dâr] *vt*: **to** ~ **sb to do** défier qn *or* mettre qn au défi de faire ♦ *vi*: **to** ~ **(to) do sth** oser faire qch; **I** ~**n't tell him** (*Brit*) je n'ose pas le lui dire; **I** ~ **say he'll turn up** il est probable qu'il viendra.

daredevil [dâr'devəl] *n* casse-cou *m inv*.

Dar es Salaam [dâr es səlâm'] *n* Dar-es-Salaam, Dar-es-Salam.

daring [dâr'ing] *a* hardi(e), audacieux(euse) ♦ *n* audace *f*, hardiesse *f*.

dark [dârk] *a* (*night, room*) obscur(e), sombre; (*color, complexion*) foncé(e), sombre; (*fig*) sombre ♦ *n*: **in the** ~ dans le noir; **in the** ~ **about** (*fig*) ignorant tout de; **after** ~ après la tombée de la nuit; **it is/is getting** ~ il fait nuit/commence à faire nuit.

dark chocolate *n* chocolat *m* à croquer.

darken [dâr'kən] *vt* obscurcir, assombrir ♦ *vi* s'obscurcir, s'assombrir.

dark glasses *npl* lunettes noires.

darkly [dârk'lē] *ad* (*gloomily*) mélancoliquement; (*in a sinister way*) lugubrement.

darkness [dârk'nis] *n* obscurité *f*.

darkroom [dârk'rōōm] *n* chambre noire.

darling [dâr'ling] *a*, *n* chéri(e).

darn [dârn] *vt* repriser.

dart [dârt] *n* fléchette *f* ♦ *vi*: **to** ~ **towards** (*also*: **make a** ~ **towards**) se précipiter *or* s'élancer vers; **to** ~ **away/along** partir/passer comme une flèche.

dartboard [dârt'bôrd] *n* cible *f* (de jeu de fléchettes).

darts [dârts] *n* jeu *m* de fléchettes.

dash [dash] *n* (*sign*) tiret *m*; (*small quantity*) goutte *f*, larme *f* ♦ *vt* (*missile*) jeter *or* lancer violemment; (*hopes*) anéantir ♦ *vi*: **to** ~ **towards** (*also*: **make a** ~ **towards**) se précipiter *or* se ruer vers; **a** ~ **of soda** un peu d'eau gazeuse.

dash away *vi* partir à toute allure.

dashboard [dash'bôrd] *n* (*AUT*) tableau *m* de bord.

dashing [dash'ing] *a* fringant(e).

dastardly [das'tûrdlē] *a* lâche.

data [dā'tə] *npl* données *fpl*.

database [dā'təbās] *n* base *f* de données.

data capture *n* saisie *f* de données.
data processing *n* traitement *m* (électronique) de l'information.
data transmission *n* transmission *f* de données.
date [dāt] *n* date *f*; (*appointment*) rendez-vous *m*; (*fruit*) datte *f* ♦ *vt* dater; (*col: girl etc*) sortir avec; **what's the ~ today?** quelle date sommes-nous aujourd'hui?; **~ of birth** date de naissance; **closing ~** date de clôture; **to ~** *ad* à ce jour; **out of ~** périmé(e); **up to ~** à la page; mis(e) à jour; moderne; **to bring up to ~** (*correspondence, information*) mettre à jour; (*method*) moderniser; (*person*) mettre au courant; **letter ~d July 5th** lettre (datée) du 5 juillet.
dated [dā'tid] *a* démodé(e).
dateline [dāt'līn] *n* ligne *f* de changement de date.
date stamp *n* timbre-dateur *m*.
daub [dôb] *vt* barbouiller.
daughter [dôt'ûr] *n* fille *f*.
daughter-in-law [dôt'ûrinlô] *n* belle-fille *f*, bru *f*.
daunt [dônt] *vt* intimider, décourager.
daunting [dôn'ting] *a* décourageant(e), intimidant(e).
dauntless [dônt'lis] *a* intrépide.
dawdle [dôd'əl] *vi* traîner, lambiner; **to ~ over one's work** traînasser *or* lambiner sur son travail.
dawn [dôn] *n* aube *f*, aurore *f* ♦ *vi* (*day*) se lever, poindre; (*fig*) naître, se faire jour; **at ~** à l'aube; **from ~ to dusk** du matin au soir; **it ~ed on him that** ... il lui vint à l'esprit que ....
day [dā] *n* jour *m*; (*as duration*) journée *f*; (*period of time, age*) époque *f*, temps *m*; **the ~ before** la veille, le jour précédent; **the after, the following ~** le lendemain, le jour suivant; **the ~ before yesterday** avant-hier; **the ~ after tomorrow** après-demain; (**on**) **the ~ that** ... le jour où ...; **~ by ~** jour après jour; **by ~** de jour; **paid by the ~** payé(e) à la journée; **these ~s, in the present ~** de nos jours, à l'heure actuelle.
daybreak [dā'brāk] *n* point *m* du jour.
day-care center [dā'kär sen'tûr] *n* garderie *f*, crèche *f*.
daydream [dā'drēm] *n* rêverie *f* ♦ *vi* rêver (tout éveillé).
daylight [dā'līt] *n* (lumière *f* du) jour *m*.
Daylight Saving Time *n* (*US*) heure *f* d'été.
day nursery *n* garderie *f*, crèche *f*.
day release *n* (*Brit*): **to be on ~** avoir une journée de congé pour formation professionnelle.
day return (ticket) *n* (*Brit*) billet *m* d'aller-retour (valable pour la journée).
day shift *n* équipe *f* de jour.
day student *n* (*at school*) externe *m/f*.
daytime [dā'tīm] *n* jour *m*, journée *f*.
day-to-day [dā'tōōdā'] *a* (*routine, expenses*) journalier(ière); **on a ~ basis** au jour le jour.
day trip *n* excursion *f* (d'une journée).
day-tripper [dā'trip'ûr] *n* excursionniste *m/f*.
daze [dāz] *vt* (*subj: drug*) hébéter; (: *blow*) étourdir ♦ *n*: **in a ~** hébété(e); étourdi(e).

dazzle [daz'əl] *vt* éblouir, aveugler.
dazzling [daz'ling] *a* (*light*) aveuglant(e), éblouissant(e); (*fig*) éblouissant(e).
DC *abbr* (*ELEC*) = **direct current**; (*US MAIL*) = *District of Columbia*.
DD *n* *abbr* (= *Doctor of Divinity*) titre universitaire.
D/D *abbr* = **demand draft**; = **direct debit**.
D-day [dē'dā] *n* le jour J.
DDS *n* *abbr* (*US*: = *Doctor of Dental Science, Doctor of Dental Surgery*) titres universitaires.
DDT *n* *abbr* (= *dichlorodiphenyl trichloroethane*) DDT *m*.
DE *abbr* (*US MAIL*) = *Delaware*.
DEA *n* *abbr* (*US*: = *Drug Enforcement Administration*) ≈ brigade *f* des stupéfiants.
deacon [dē'kən] *n* diacre *m*.
dead [ded] *a* mort(e); (*numb*) engourdi(e), insensible; (*battery*) plat(e) ♦ *ad* absolument, complètement; **the ~** *npl* les morts; **he was shot ~** il a été tué d'un coup de revolver; **~ on time** à l'heure pile; **~ tired** éreinté(e), complètement fourbu(e); **to stop ~** s'arrêter pile *or* net; **the line has gone ~** (*TEL*) on n'entend plus rien.
deaden [ded'ən] *vt* (*blow, sound*) amortir; (*make numb*) endormir, rendre insensible.
dead end *n* impasse *f*.
dead-end [dedend'] *a*: **a ~ job** un emploi *or* poste sans avenir.
dead heat *n* (*SPORT*): **to finish in a ~** terminer ex-aequo.
dead-letter office [ded'let'ûr ôf'is] *n* ≈ centre *m* de recherche du courrier.
deadline [ded'līn] *n* date *f* *or* heure *f* limite; **to work to a ~** avoir des délais stricts à respecter.
deadlock [ded'lâk] *n* impasse *f* (*fig*).
dead loss *n* (*col*): **to be a ~** (*person*) n'être bon(bonne) à rien; (*thing*) ne rien valoir.
deadly [ded'lē] *a* mortel(le); (*weapon*) meurtrier(ière); **~ dull** ennuyeux(euse) à mourir, mortellement ennuyeux.
deadpan [ded'pan] *a* impassible; (*humor*) pince-sans-rire *inv*.
Dead Sea *n*: **the ~** la mer Morte.
dead season *n* (*TOURISM*) morte saison.
deaf [def] *a* sourd(e); **to turn a ~ ear to sth** faire la sourde oreille à qch.
deaf-and-dumb [def'əndum'] *a* sourd(e)-muet(te); **~ alphabet** alphabet *m* des sourds-muets.
deafen [def'ən] *vt* rendre sourd(e); (*fig*) assourdir.
deafening [def'əning] *a* assourdissant(e).
deaf-mute [def'myōōt'] *n* sourd/e-muet/te.
deafness [def'nis] *n* surdité *f*.
deal [dēl] *n* affaire *f*, marché *m* ♦ *vt* (*pt, pp* **dealt** [delt]) (*blow*) porter; (*cards*) donner, distribuer; **to strike a ~ with sb** faire *or* conclure un marché avec qn; **it's a ~!** (*col*) marché conclu!, tope-là!, topez-là!; **he got a bad ~ from them** ils ont mal agi envers lui; **he got a fair ~ from them** ils ont agi loyalement envers lui; **a good ~** (*a lot*) beaucoup; **a good ~ of, a great ~ of** beaucoup de, énormément de.
deal in *vt fus* (*COMM*) faire le commerce

de, être dans le commerce de.

deal with vt fus (COMM) traiter avec; (handle) s'occuper or se charger de; (be about: book etc) traiter de.

dealer [dē'lûr] n marchand m.

dealership [dē'lûrship] n concession f.

dealings [dē'lingz] npl (in goods, shares) opérations fpl, transactions fpl; (relations) relations fpl, rapports mpl.

dean [dēn] n (US SCOL) conseiller/ère (principal(e)) d'éducation; (REL, Brit SCOL) doyen m.

dear [dēr] a cher(chère); (expensive) cher, coûteux(euse) ♦ n: **my ~** mon cher/ma chère; **~ me!** mon Dieu!; **D~ Sir/Madam** (in letter) Monsieur/Madame; **D~ Mr/Mrs X** Cher Monsieur/Chère Madame X.

dearly [dēr'lē] ad (love) tendrement; (pay) cher.

dearth [dûrth] n disette f, pénurie f.

death [deth] n mort f; (ADMIN) décès m.

deathbed [deth'bed] n lit m de mort.

death certificate n acte m de décès.

deathly [deth'lē] a de mort ♦ ad comme la mort.

death penalty n peine f de mort.

death rate n taux m de mortalité.

death sentence n condamnation f à mort.

deathtrap [deth'trap] n endroit (or véhicule etc) dangereux; (AUT) point noir.

debar [dibâr'] vt: **to ~ sb from a club** etc exclure qn d'un club etc; **to ~ sb from doing** interdire à qn de faire.

debase [dibās'] vt (currency) déprécier, dévaloriser; (person) abaisser, avilir.

debatable [dibā'təbəl] a discutable, contestable; **it is ~ whether** ... il est douteux que ....

debate [dibāt'] n discussion f, débat m ♦ vt discuter, débattre ♦ vi (consider): **to ~ whether** se demander si.

debauchery [debô'chûrē] n débauche f.

debenture [diben'chûr] n (COMM) obligation f.

debilitate [dibil'ətāt] vt débiliter.

debit [deb'it] n débit m ♦ vt: **to ~ a sum to sb** or **to sb's account** porter une somme au débit de qn, débiter qn d'une somme.

debit balance n solde débiteur.

debit note n note f de débit.

debrief [dēbrēf'] vt demander un compte rendu de fin de mission à.

debriefing [dēbrēf'ing] n compte rendu m.

debris [dəbrē'] n débris mpl, décombres mpl.

debt [det] n dette f; **to be in ~** avoir des dettes, être endetté(e); **bad ~** créance f irrécouvrable.

debt collector n agent m de recouvrements.

debtor [det'ûr] n débiteur/trice.

debug [dēbug'] vt (COMPUT) déverminer.

debunk [dibungk'] vt (theory, claim) montrer le ridicule de.

debut [dābyoo'] n début(s) m(pl).

debutante [debyootânt'] n débutante f.

Dec. abbr (= December) déc.

decade [dek'ād] n décennie f, décade f.

decadence [dek'ədəns] n décadence f.

decadent [dek'ədənt] a décadent(e).

decaffeinated [dēkaf'ənātid] a décaféiné(e).

decamp [dikamp'] vi (col) décamper, filer.

decant [dikant'] vt (wine) décanter.

decanter [dikan'tûr] n carafe f.

decarbonize [dēkâr'bənīz] vt (AUT) décalaminer.

decay [dikā'] n décomposition f, pourrissement m; (fig) déclin m, délabrement m; (also: **tooth ~**) carie f (dentaire) ♦ vi (rot) se décomposer, pourrir; (fig) se délabrer; décliner; se détériorer.

decease [disēs'] n décès m.

deceased [disēst'] n: **the ~** le/la défunt/e.

deceit [disēt'] n tromperie f, supercherie f.

deceitful [disēt'fəl] a trompeur(euse).

deceive [disēv'] vt tromper; **to ~ o.s.** s'abuser.

decelerate [dēsel'ərāt] vt, vi ralentir.

December [disem'bûr] n décembre m; for phrases see also **July.**

decency [dē'sənsē] n décence f.

decent [dē'sənt] a décent(e), convenable; **they were very ~ about it** ils se sont montrés très chics.

decently [dē'səntlē] ad (respectably) décemment, convenablement; (kindly) décemment.

decentralization [dēsentrəlizā'shən] n décentralisation f.

decentralize [dēsen'trəliz] vt décentraliser.

deception [disep'shən] n tromperie f.

deceptive [disep'tiv] a trompeur(euse).

decibel [des'əbəl] n décibel m.

decide [disīd'] vt (person) décider; (question, argument) trancher, régler ♦ vi se décider, décider; **to ~ to do/that** décider de faire/que; **to ~ on** décider, se décider pour; **to ~ on doing** décider de faire; **to ~ against doing** décider de ne pas faire.

decided [disī'did] a (resolute) résolu(e), décidé(e); (clear, definite) net(te), marqué(e).

decidedly [disī'didlē] ad résolument; incontestablement, nettement.

deciding [disī'ding] a décisif(ive); **~ vote** voix prépondérante (pour départager).

deciduous [disij'ōōəs] a à feuilles caduques.

decimal [des'əməl] a décimal(e) ♦ n décimale f; **to 3 ~ places** (jusqu')à la troisième décimale.

decimalize [des'əməlīz] vt décimaliser.

decimal point n ≈ virgule f.

decimate [des'əmāt] vt décimer.

decipher [disī'fûr] vt déchiffrer.

decision [disizh'ən] n décision f; **to make a ~** prendre une décision.

decisive [disī'siv] a décisif(ive); (influence) décisif, déterminant(e); (manner, person) décidé(e), catégorique; (reply) ferme, catégorique.

deck [dek] n (NAUT) pont m; (of bus): **top ~** impériale f; (of cards) jeu m; **to go up on ~** monter sur le pont; **below ~** dans l'entrepont; **record/cassette ~** platine-disques/-cassettes f.

deck chair n chaise longue.

deck hand n matelot m.

declaration [deklərā'shən] n déclaration f.

declare [diklär'] vt déclarer.

declassify [dēklas'əfī] vt rendre accessible au public or à tous.

decline [diklīn'] n (decay) déclin m; (lessening) baisse f ♦ vt refuser, décliner ♦ vi décliner; être en baisse, baisser; ~ **in living standards** baisse du niveau de vie; **to ~ to do sth** refuser (poliment) de faire qch.

declutch [dēkluch'] *vi* (*Brit*) débrayer.

decode [dēkōd'] *vt* décoder.

decoder [dēkō'dúr] *n* décodeur *m*.

decompose [dēkəmpōz'] *vi* se décomposer.

decomposition [dēkâmpəzish'ən] *n* décomposition *f*.

decompression [dēkəmpresh'ən] *n* décompression *f*.

decompression chamber *n* caisson *m* de décompression.

decongestant [dēkənjes'tənt] *n* décongestif *m*.

decontaminate [dēkəntam'ənāt] *vt* décontaminer.

decontrol [dēkəntrōl'] *vt* (*Brit: prices etc*) libérer.

décor [dākôr'] *n* décor *m*.

decorate [dek'ərāt] *vt* (*adorn, give a medal to*) décorer; (*paint and paper*) peindre et tapisser.

decoration [dekərā'shən] *n* (*medal etc, adornment*) décoration *f*.

decorative [dek'ûrətiv] *a* décoratif(ive).

decorator [dek'ərātûr] *n* peintre *m* en bâtiment.

decorum [dikôr'əm] *n* décorum *m*, bienséance *f*.

decoy [dē'koi] *n* piège *m*; **they used him as a ~ for the enemy** ils se sont servis de lui pour attirer l'ennemi.

decrease *n* [dē'krēs] diminution *f* ♦ *vt, vi* [dikrēs'] diminuer; **to be on the ~** diminuer, être en diminution.

decreasing [dikrēs'ing] *a* en voie de diminution.

decree [dikrē'] *n* (*POL, REL*) décret *m*; (*LAW*) arrêt *m*, jugement *m* ♦ *vt*: **to ~ (that)** décréter (que), ordonner (que); **~ absolute** jugement définitif (de divorce); **~ nisi** jugement provisoire de divorce.

decrepit [dikrep'it] *a* (*person*) décrépit(e); (*building*) délabré(e).

decry [dikrī'] *vt* condamner ouvertement, déplorer; (*disparage*) dénigrer, décrier.

dedicate [ded'ikāt] *vt* consacrer; (*book etc*) dédier.

dedicated [ded'ikātid] *a* (*person*) dévoué(e); (*COMPUT*) spécialisé(e), dédié(e); **~ word processor** station *f* de traitement de texte.

dedication [dedikā'shən] *n* (*devotion*) dévouement *m*; (*in book*) dédicace *f*.

deduce [didōōs'] *vt* déduire, conclure.

deduct [didukt'] *vt*: **to ~ sth (from)** déduire qch (de), retrancher qch (de); (*from wage etc*) prélever qch (sur), retenir qch (sur).

deduction [diduk'shən] *n* (*deducting*) déduction *f*; (*from wage etc*) prélèvement *m*, retenue *f*; (*deducing*) déduction, conclusion *f*.

deed [dēd] *n* action *f*, acte *m*; (*LAW*) acte notarié, contrat *m*; **~ of covenant** (acte *m* de) donation *f*.

deem [dēm] *vt* (*formal*) juger, estimer; **to ~ it wise to do** juger bon de faire.

deep [dēp] *a* (*water, sigh, sorrow, thoughts*) profond(e); (*voice*) grave ♦ *ad*: **~ in snow** recouvert(e) d'une épaisse couche de neige; **spectators stood 20 ~** il y avait 20 rangs de

spectateurs; **knee-~ in water** dans l'eau jusqu'aux genoux; **4 meters ~** de 4 mètres de profondeur; **he took a ~ breath** il inspira profondément, il prit son souffle.

deepen [dē'pən] *vt* (*hole*) approfondir ♦ *vi* s'approfondir; (*darkness*) s'épaissir.

deep-freeze [dēp'frēz'] *n* congélateur *m* ♦ *vt* surgeler.

deep-fry [dēp'frī'] *vt* faire frire (dans une friteuse).

deep fryer [dēp' frī'ûr] *n* friteuse *f*.

deeply [dēp'lē] *ad* profondément; (*dig*) en profondeur; (*regret, interest*) vivement.

deep-rooted [dēp'rōō'tid] *a* (*prejudice*) profondément enraciné(e); (*affection*) profond(e); (*habit*) invétéré(e).

deep-sea [dēp'sē'] *a*: **~ diver** plongeur sous-marin; **~ diving** *n* plongée sous-marine.

deep-sea fishing *n* pêche hauturière.

deep-seated [dēp'sē'tid] *a* (*beliefs*) profondément enraciné(e).

deep-set [dēp'set] *a* (*eyes*) enfoncé(e).

deer [dēr] *n* (*pl inv*): **the ~** les cervidés *mpl* (*ZOOL*); (**red**) **~** cerf *m*; (**fallow**) **~** daim *m*; (**roe**) **~** chevreuil *m*.

deerskin [dēr'skin] *n* peau *f* de daim.

deerstalker [dēr'stôkûr] *n* (*person*) chasseur *m* de cerf; (*hat*) casquette *f* à la Sherlock Holmes.

deface [difās'] *vt* dégrader; barbouiller; rendre illisible.

defamation [defəmā'shən] *n* diffamation *f*.

defamatory [difam'ətôrē] *a* diffamatoire, diffamant(e).

default [difôlt'] *vi* (*LAW*) faire défaut; (*gen*) manquer à ses engagements ♦ *n* (*COMPUT: also*: **~ value**) valeur *f* par défaut; **by ~** (*LAW*) par défaut, par contumace; (*SPORT*) par forfait; **to ~ on a debt** ne pas s'acquitter d'une dette.

defaulter [difôlt'ûr] *n* (*on debt*) débiteur défaillant.

default option *n* (*COMPUT*) option *f* par défaut.

defeat [difēt'] *n* défaite *f* ♦ *vt* (*team, opponents*) battre; (*fig: plans, efforts*) faire échouer.

defeatism [difē'tizəm] *n* défaitisme *m*.

defeatist [difē'tist] *a, n* défaitiste (*m/f*).

defect *n* [dē'fekt] défaut *m* ♦ *vi* [difekt']: **to ~ to the enemy/the West** passer à l'ennemi/l'Ouest; **physical ~** malformation *f*, vice *m* de conformation; **mental ~** anomalie *or* déficience mentale.

defective [difek'tiv] *a* défectueux(euse).

defector [difek'tûr] *n* transfuge *m/f*.

defence [difens'] *n* (*Brit*) = **defense**; **the Ministry of D~** le ministère de la Défense nationale.

defend [difend'] *vt* défendre; (*decision, action, opinion*) justifier, défendre.

defendant [difen'dənt] *n* défendeur/deresse; (*in criminal case*) accusé/e, prévenu/e.

defender [difen'dûr] *n* défenseur *m*.

defending champion [difen'ding cham'pēən] *n* (*SPORT*) champion/ne en titre.

defending counsel [difen'ding koun'səl] *n* (*Brit LAW*) avocat *m* de la défense.

defense [difens'] *n* (*US*) défense *f*; **in ~ of**

pour défendre; **the Department of D~** le ministère de la Défense nationale.

defense counsel *n* (*US*) avocat *m* de la défense.

defenseless [difens'lis] *a* sans défense.

defensive [difen'siv] *a* défensif(ive) ♦ *n* défensive *f*; **on the ~** sur la défensive.

defer [difûr'] *vt* (*postpone*) différer, ajourner ♦ *vi* (*submit*): **to ~ to sb/sth** déférer à qn/qch, s'en remettre à qn/qch.

deference [def'ûrəns] *n* déférence *f*, égards *mpl*; **out of** *or* **in ~ to** par déférence *or* égards pour.

defiance [difi'əns] *n* défi *m*; **in ~ of** au mépris de.

defiant [difi'ənt] *a* provocant(e), de défi.

defiantly [difi'əntlē] *ad* d'un air (*or* d'un ton) de défi.

deficiency [difish'ənsē] *n* insuffisance *f*, déficience *f*; carence *f*; (*COMM*) déficit *m*, découvert *m*.

deficiency disease *n* maladie *f* de carence.

deficient [difish'ənt] *a* insuffisant(e); défectueux(euse); déficient(e); **to be ~ in** manquer de.

deficit [def'isit] *n* déficit *m*.

defile [difil'] *vt* souiller ♦ *vi* défiler ♦ *n* défilé *m*.

define [difin'] *vt* définir.

definite [def'ənit] *a* (*fixed*) défini(e), (bien) déterminé(e); (*clear, obvious*) net(te), manifeste; (*LING*) défini(e); **he was ~ about it** il a été catégorique; il était sûr de son fait.

definitely [def'ənitlē] *ad* sans aucun doute.

definition [defənish'ən] *n* définition *f*.

definitive [difin'ətiv] *a* définitif(ive).

deflate [diflāt'] *vt* dégonfler; (*pompous person*) rabattre le caquet à; (*ECON*) provoquer la déflation de; (*: prices*) faire tomber *or* baisser.

deflation [diflā'shən] *n* (*ECON*) déflation *f*.

deflationary [diflā'shənārē] *a* (*ECON*) déflationniste.

deflect [diflekt'] *vt* détourner, faire dévier.

defog [dēfôg'] *vt* (*US AUT*) désembuer.

defogger [dēfôg'ûr] *n* (*US AUT*) dispositif *m* anti-buée *inv*.

deforestation [dēfôristā'shən] *n* déboisement *m*.

deform [difôrm'] *vt* déformer.

deformed [difôrmd'] *a* difforme.

deformity [difôr'mitē] *n* difformité *f*.

defraud [difrôd'] *vt* frauder; **to ~ sb of sth** soutirer qch malhonnêtement à qn; escroquer qch à qn; frustrer qn de qch.

defray [difrā'] *vt*: **to ~ sb's expenses** défrayer qn (de ses frais), rembourser *or* payer à qn ses frais.

defrost [difrôst'] *vt* (*fridge*) dégivrer; (*frozen food*) décongeler.

deft [deft] *a* adroit(e), preste.

defunct [difungkt'] *a* défunt(e).

defuse [dēfyōōz'] *vt* désamorcer.

defy [difi'] *vt* défier; (*efforts etc*) résister à.

degenerate *vi* [dijen'ûrāt] dégénérer ♦ *a* [dijen'ûrit] dégénéré(e).

degradation [degrədā'shən] *n* dégradation *f*.

degrade [digrād'] *vt* dégrader.

degrading [digrā'ding] *a* dégradant(e).

degree [digrē'] *n* degré *m*; (*SCOL*) diplôme *m* (universitaire); **10 ~s below (zero)** 10 degrés au-dessous de zéro; **a (first) ~ in math** une licence en maths; **a considerable ~ of risk** un considérable facteur *or* élément de risque; **by ~s** (*gradually*) par degrés; **to some ~, to a certain ~** jusqu'à un certain point, dans une certaine mesure.

dehydrated [dēhī'drātid] *a* déshydraté(e); (*milk, eggs*) en poudre.

dehydration [dēhīdrā'shən] *n* déshydratation *f*.

de-ice [dēīs'] *vt* (*windscreen*) dégivrer.

de-icer [dēī'sûr] *n* dégivreur *m*.

deign [dān] *vi*: **to ~ to do** daigner faire.

deity [dē'itē] *n* divinité *f*; dieu *m*, déesse *f*.

dejected [dijek'tid] *a* abattu(e), déprimé(e).

dejection [dijek'shən] *n* abattement *m*, découragement *m*.

Del. *abbr* (*US*) = *Delaware*.

del. *abbr* = **delete**.

delay [dilā'] *vt* (*journey, operation*) retarder, différer; (*travelers, trains*) retarder; (*payment*) différer ♦ *vi* s'attarder ♦ *n* délai *m*, retard *m*; **without ~** sans délai, sans tarder.

delayed-action [dilād'ak'shən] *a* à retardement.

delectable [dilek'təbəl] *a* délicieux(euse).

delegate *n* [del'əgit] délégué(e) ♦ *vt* [del'əgāt] déléguer; **to ~ sth to sb/sb to do sth** déléguer qch à qn/qn pour faire qch.

delegation [deləgā'shən] *n* délégation *f*.

delete [dilēt'] *vt* rayer, supprimer; (*COMPUT*) effacer.

Delhi [del'ē] *n* Delhi.

deliberate *a* [dilib'ûrit] (*intentional*) délibéré(e); (*slow*) mesuré(e) ♦ *vi* [dilib'ûrāt] délibérer, réfléchir.

deliberately [dilib'ûritlē] *ad* (*on purpose*) exprès, délibérément.

deliberation [dilibərā'shən] *n* délibération *f*, réflexion *f*; (*gen pl: discussion*) délibérations, débats *mpl*.

delicacy [del'əkəsē] *n* délicatesse *f*; (*choice food*) mets fin *or* délicat, friandise *f*.

delicate [del'əkit] *a* délicat(e).

delicately [del'əkitlē] *ad* délicatement; (*act, express*) avec délicatesse, avec tact.

delicatessen [deləkətes'ən] *n* épicerie fine.

delicious [dilish'əs] *a* délicieux(euse), exquis(e).

delight [dilīt'] *n* (grande) joie, grand plaisir ♦ *vt* enchanter; **a ~ to the eyes** un régal *or* plaisir pour les yeux; **to take ~ in** prendre grand plaisir à; **to be the ~ of** faire les délices *or* la joie de.

delighted [dilī'tid] *a*: **~ (at** *or* **with sth)** ravi(e) (de qch); **to be ~ to do sth/that** être enchanté(e) *or* ravi(e) de faire qch/que; **I'd be ~** j'en serais enchanté *or* ravi.

delightful [dilīt'fəl] *a* (*person, child*) absolument charmant(e), adorable; (*evening, view*) merveilleux(euse); (*meal*) délicieux(euse).

delimit [dilim'it] *vt* délimiter.

delineate [dilin'ēāt] *vt* tracer, esquisser; (*fig*) dépeindre, décrire.

delinquency [diling'kwənsē] *n* délinquance *f*.

delinquent [diling'kwint] *a*, *n* délinquant(e).

delirious [dilēr'ēəs] *a* (*MED, fig*) délirant(e); **to be ~** délirer.

delirium [dilēr'ēəm] n délire m.

deliver [diliv'ûr] vt (mail) distribuer; (goods) livrer; (message) remettre; (speech) prononcer; (warning, ultimatum) lancer; (free) délivrer; (MED) accoucher; **to ~ the goods** (fig) tenir ses promesses.

deliverance [diliv'ûrəns] n délivrance f, libération f.

delivery [diliv'ûrē] n (of mail) distribution f; (of goods) livraison f; (of speaker) élocution f; (MED) accouchement m; **to take ~ of** prendre livraison de.

delivery slip n bon m de livraison.

delivery truck n, (Brit) **delivery van** n fourgonnette f or camionnette f de livraison.

delouse [dēlous'] vt épouiller, débarrasser de sa (or leur etc) vermine.

delta [del'tə] n delta m.

delude [dilood'] vt tromper, leurrer; **to ~ o.s.** se leurrer, se faire des illusions.

deluge [del'yooj] n déluge m ♦ vt (fig): **to ~ (with)** inonder (de).

delusion [diloo'zhən] n illusion f; **to have ~s of grandeur** être un peu mégalomane.

de luxe [dəluks'] a de luxe.

delve [delv] vi: **to ~ into** fouiller dans.

Dem. abbr (US POL) = **democrat(ic)**.

demagogue [dem'əgôg] n démagogue m/f.

demand [dimand'] vt réclamer, exiger; (need) exiger, requérir ♦ n exigence f; (claim) revendication f; (ECON) demande f; **to ~ sth (from or of sb)** exiger qch (de qn), réclamer qch (à qn); **in ~** demandé(e), recherché(e); **on ~** sur demande.

demand draft n bon m à vue.

demanding [dimand'ing] a (person) exigeant(e); (work) astreignant(e).

demarcation [dēmârkā'shən] n démarcation f.

demarcation dispute n (INDUSTRY) conflit m d'attributions.

demean [dimēn'] vt: **to ~ o.s.** s'abaisser.

demeanor, (Brit) demeanour [dimē'nûr] n comportement m; maintien m.

demented [dimen'tid] a dément(e), fou(folle).

demilitarized zone [dēmil'itərīzd zōn'] n zone démilitarisée.

demise [dimīz'] n décès m.

demist [dēmist'] vt (Brit AUT) désembuer.

demister [dimis'tûr] n (Brit AUT) dispositif m anti-buée inv.

demo [dem'ō] n abbr (col: = demonstration) manif f.

demobilize [dēmō'bəlīz] vt démobiliser.

democracy [dimâk'rəsē] n démocratie f.

democrat [dem'əkrat] n (also: POL: **D~**) démocrate m/f.

democratic [deməkrat'ik] a démocratique.

demography [dimâg'rəfē] n démographie f.

demolish [dimâl'ish] vt démolir.

demolition [deməlish'ən] n démolition f.

demon [dē'mən] n démon m ♦ cpd: **a ~ squash player** un crack en squash; **a ~ driver** un fou du volant.

demonstrate [dem'ənstrāt] vt démontrer, prouver ♦ vi: **to ~ (for/against)** manifester (en faveur de/contre).

demonstration [demənstrā'shən] n démonstration f; (POL etc) manifestation f; **to hold a ~** (POL etc) organiser une manifestation, ma-

nifester.

demonstrative [dimân'strətiv] a démonstratif(ive).

demonstrator [dem'ənstrātûr] n (POL etc) manifestant/e; (COMM: sales person) vendeur/euse; (: car, computer etc) modèle m de démonstration.

demoralize [dimôr'əlīz] vt démoraliser.

demote [dimōt'] vt rétrograder.

demotion [dimō'shən] n rétrogradation f.

demur [dimûr'] vi: **to ~ (at sth)** hésiter (devant qch); (object) élever des objections (contre qch) ♦ n: **without ~** sans hésiter; sans faire de difficultés.

demure [dimyoor'] a sage, réservé(e); d'une modestie affectée.

demurrage [dimûr'ij] n droits mpl de magasinage; surestarie f.

den [den] n tanière f, antre m.

denationalization [dēnashnəlizā'shən] n dénationalisation f.

denationalize [dēnash'nəlīz] vt dénationaliser.

denial [dinī'əl] n (of accusation) démenti m; (of rights, guilt, truth) dénégation f.

denier [den'yûr] n denier m; **15 ~ stockings** bas de 15 deniers.

denigrate [den'əgrāt] vt dénigrer.

denim [den'əm] n coton émerisé.

denim jacket n veste f en jean.

denims [den'əmz] npl (blue-)jeans mpl.

denizen [den'izən] n (inhabitant) habitant/e; (foreigner) étranger/ère.

Denmark [den'mârk] n Danemark m.

denomination [dinâmənā'shən] n (money) valeur f; (REL) confession f; culte m.

denominator [dinâm'ənātûr] n dénominateur m.

denote [dinōt'] vt dénoter.

denounce [dinouns'] vt dénoncer.

dense [dens] a dense; (col: stupid) obtus(e), dur(e) or lent(e) à la comprenette.

densely [dens'lē] ad: **~ wooded** couvert(e) d'épaisses forêts; **~ populated** à forte densité (de population), très peuplé(e).

density [den'sitē] n densité f; **single/double ~ disk** (COMPUT) disquette f (à) simple/double densité.

dent [dent] n bosse f ♦ vt (also: **make a ~ in**) cabosser; **to make a ~ in** (fig) entamer.

dental [den'təl] a dentaire.

dental surgeon n (chirurgien/ne) dentiste.

dentifrice [den'təfris] n dentifrice m.

dentist [den'tist] n dentiste m/f; **~'s office** or (Brit) **surgery** cabinet m de dentiste.

dentistry [den'tistrē] n art m dentaire.

denture(s) [den'chûr(z)] n(pl) dentier m.

denunciation [dinunsēā'shən] n dénonciation f.

deny [dinī'] vt nier; (refuse) refuser; (disown) renier; **he denies having said it** il nie l'avoir dit.

deodorant [dēō'dûrənt] n désodorisant m, déodorant m.

depart [dipârt'] vi partir; **to ~ from** (leave) quitter, partir de; (fig: differ from) s'écarter de.

department [dipârt'mənt] n (COMM) rayon m; (SCOL) section f; (POL) ministère m, département m; **that's not my ~** (fig) ce n'est pas mon domaine or ma compétence, ce n'est pas mon rayon; **D~ of State** (*US*) Département d'État.

departmental |dēpârtmen'təl| *a* d'une *or* de la section; d'un *or* du ministère, d'un *or* du département; ~ **manager** chef *m* de service; (*in shop*) chef de rayon.

department store *n* grand magasin.

departure |dipâr'chûr| *n* départ *m*; (*fig*): ~ **from** écart *m* par rapport à; **a new** ~ une nouvelle voie.

departure lounge *n* salle *f* de départ.

depend |dipend'| *vi*: **to** ~ **(up)on** dépendre de; (*rely on*) compter sur; (*financially*) dépendre (financièrement) de, être à la charge de; **it ~s** cela dépend; **~ing on the result** ... selon le résultat ....

dependable |dipen'dəbəl| *a* sûr(e), digne de confiance.

dependant |dipen'dənt| *n* personne *f* à charge.

dependence |dipen'dəns| *n* dépendance *f*.

dependent |dipen'dənt| *a*: **to be** ~ **(on)** dépendre (de) ♦ *n* = **dependant**.

depict |dipikt'| *vt* (*in picture*) représenter; (*in words*) (dé)peindre, décrire.

depilatory |dipil'ətôrē| *n* (*also*: ~ **cream**) dépilatoire *m*, crème *f* à épiler.

deplane |dēplān'| *vi* (*US*) débarquer.

depleted |diplēt'id| *a* (considérablement) réduit(e) *or* diminué(e).

deplorable |diplôr'əbəl| *a* déplorable, lamentable.

deplore |diplôr'| *vt* déplorer.

deploy |diploi'| *vt* déployer.

depopulate |dipâp'yəlāt| *vt* dépeupler.

depopulation |dipâpyəlā'shən| *n* dépopulation *f*, dépeuplement *m*.

deport |dipôrt'| *vt* déporter, expulser.

deportation |dēpôrtā'shən| *n* déportation *f*, expulsion *f*.

deportation order *n* arrêté *m* d'expulsion.

deportment |dipôrt'mənt| *n* maintien *m*, tenue *f*.

depose |dipōz'| *vt* déposer.

deposit |dipâz'it| *n* (*CHEMISTRY*, *COMM*, *GEO*) dépôt *m*; (*of ore, oil*) gisement *m*; (*part payment*) arrhes *fpl*, acompte *m*; (*on bottle etc*) consigne *f*; (*for rented goods etc*) cautionnement *m*, garantie *f* ♦ *vt* déposer; (*valuables*) mettre *or* laisser en dépôt; **to put down a** ~ **of $50** verser 50 dollars d'arrhes *or* d'acompte; laisser 50 dollars en garantie.

deposit account *n* compte *m* de dépôt.

depositor |dipâz'itûr| *n* déposant/e.

depository |dipâz'itôrē| *n* (*person*) dépositaire *m/f*; (*place*) dépôt *m*.

depot |dē'pō| *n* dépôt *m*.

depraved |diprāvd'| *a* dépravé(e), perverti(e).

depravity |diprav'itē| *n* dépravation *f*.

deprecate |dep'rəkāt| *vt* désapprouver.

deprecating |dep'rəkāting| *a* (*disapproving*) désapprobateur(trice); (*apologetic*): **a** ~ **smile** un sourire d'excuse.

depreciate |diprē'shēāt| *vt* déprécier ♦ *vi* se déprécier, se dévaloriser.

depreciation |diprēshēā'shən| *n* dépréciation *f*.

depress |dipres'| *vt* déprimer; (*press down*) appuyer sur, abaisser.

depressant |dipres'ənt| *n* (*MED*) dépresseur *m*.

depressed |diprest'| *a* (*person*) déprimé(e), abattu(e); (*area*) en déclin, touché(e) par le sous-emploi; (*COMM*: *market, trade*) maussade; **to get** ~ se démoraliser, se laisser abattre.

depressing |dipres'ing| *a* déprimant(e).

depression |dipresh'ən| *n* (*also ECON*) dépression *f*.

deprivation |deprəvā'shən| *n* privation *f*; (*loss*) perte *f*.

deprive |diprīv'| *vt*: **to** ~ **sb of** priver qn de; enlever à qn.

deprived |diprīvd'| *a* déshérité(e).

dept. *abbr* (= *department*) dép., dépt.

depth |depth| *n* profondeur *f*; **in the ~s of** au fond de; au cœur de; au plus profond de; **at a** ~ **of 3 meters** à 3 mètres de profondeur; **to be out of one's** ~ (*swimmer*) ne plus avoir pied; (*fig*) être dépassé(e), nager; **to study sth in** ~ étudier qch en profondeur.

depth charge *n* grenade sous-marine.

deputation |depyətā'shən| *n* députation *f*, délégation *f*.

deputize |dep'yətīz| *vi*: **to** ~ **for** assurer l'intérim de.

deputy |dep'yətē| *a*: ~ **chairman** vice-président *m*; ~ **head** (*SCOL*) directeur/trice adjoint(e), sous-directeur/trice; ~ **leader** (*Brit POL*) vice-président/e, secrétaire adjoint(e) ♦ *n* (*replacement*) suppléant/e, intérimaire *m/f*; (*second in command*) adjoint/e.

derail |dirāl'| *vt* faire dérailler; **to be ~ed** dérailler.

derailment |dirāl'mənt| *n* déraillement *m*.

deranged |dirānjd'| *a*: **to be (mentally)** ~ avoir le cerveau dérangé.

derby (hat) |dûr'bē (hat)| *n* (*US*) (chapeau *m*) melon *m*.

Derbys *abbr* (*Brit*) = *Derbyshire*.

deregulate |dēreg'yəlāt| *vt* libérer, dérégler.

deregulation |dēregyəlā'shən| *n* libération *f*, déréglement *m*.

derelict |där'əlikt| *a* abandonné(e), à l'abandon.

deride |dirīd'| *vt* railler.

derision |dirizh'ən| *n* dérision *f*.

derisive |dirī'siv| *a* moqueur(euse), railleur(euse).

derisory |dirī'sûrē| *a* (*sum*) dérisoire; (*smile, person*) moqueur(euse), railleur(euse).

derivation |därəvā'shən| *n* dérivation *f*.

derivative |diriv'ətiv| *n* dérivé *m* ♦ *a* dérivé(e).

derive |dirīv'| *vt*: **to** ~ **sth from** tirer qch de; trouver qch dans ♦ *vi*: **to** ~ **from** provenir de, dériver de.

dermatitis |dûrmətī'tis| *n* dermatite *f*.

dermatology |dûrmətâl'əjē| *n* dermatologie *f*.

derogatory |dirâg'ətôrē| *a* désobligeant(e); péjoratif(ive).

derrick |där'ik| *n* mât *m* de charge; derrick *m*.

derv |dûrv| *n* (*Brit*) gas-oil *m*, diesel *m*.

DES *n abbr* (*Brit*: = *Department of Education and Science*) *ministère de l'éducation nationale et des sciences*.

desalination |dēsalənā'shən| *n* dessalement *m*, dessalage *m*.

descend |disend'| *vt, vi* descendre; **to** ~ **from**

descendre de, être issu(e) de; **in ~ing order of importance** par ordre d'importance décroissante.

descend on *vt fus* (*subj: enemy, angry person*) tomber *or* sauter sur; (: *misfortune*) s'abattre sur; (: *gloom, silence*) envahir; **visitors ~ed (up)on us** des gens sont arrivés chez nous à l'improviste.

descendant [disen'dənt] *n* descendant/e.

descent [disent'] *n* descente *f*; (*origin*) origine *f*.

describe [diskrīb'] *vt* décrire.

description [diskrip'shən] *n* description *f*; (*sort*) sorte *f*, espèce *f*; **of every ~** de toutes sortes.

descriptive [diskrip'tiv] *a* descriptif(ive).

desecrate [des'əkrāt] *vt* profaner.

desert *n* [dez'ûrt] désert *m* ♦ *vb* [dizûrt'] *vt* déserter, abandonner ♦ *vi* (*MIL*) déserter.

deserter [dizûr'tûr] *n* déserteur *m*.

desertion [dizûr'shən] *n* désertion *f*.

desert island *n* île déserte.

deserts [dizûrts'] *npl*: **to get one's just ~** n'avoir que ce qu'on mérite.

deserve [dizûrv'] *vt* mériter.

deservedly [dizûr'vidlē] *ad* à juste titre, à bon droit.

deserving [dizûr'ving] *a* (*person*) méritant(e); (*action, cause*) méritoire.

desiccated [des'əkātid] *a* séché(e).

design [dizīn'] *n* (*sketch*) plan *m*, dessin *m*; (*layout, shape*) conception *f*, ligne *f*; (*pattern*) dessin *m*, motif(s) *m(pl)*; (*of dress, car*) modèle *m*; (*art*) design *m*, stylisme *m*; (*intention*) dessein *m* ♦ *vt* dessiner; (*plan*) concevoir; **to have ~s on** avoir des visées sur; **well-~ed** *a* bien conçu(e); **industrial ~** esthétique industrielle.

designate *vt* [dez'ignāt] désigner ♦ *a* [dez'ignit] désigné(e).

designation [dezignā'shən] *n* désignation *f*.

designer [dizī'nûr] *n* (*ARCHIT, ART*) dessinateur/trice; (*INDUSTRY*) concepteur *m*, designer *m*; (*FASHION*) modéliste *m/f*.

desirability [dizīûrəbil'ətē] *n* avantage *m*; attrait *m*.

desirable [dizī'ûrəbəl] *a* désirable; **it is ~ that** il est souhaitable que.

desire [dizī'ûr] *n* désir *m* ♦ *vt* désirer, vouloir; **to ~ to do sth/that** désirer faire qch/que.

desirous [dizī'ûrəs] *a*: **~ of** désireux(euse) de.

desk [desk] *n* (*in office*) bureau *m*; (*for pupil*) pupitre *m*; (*Brit: in store, restaurant*) caisse *f*; (*in hotel, at airport*) réception *f*.

desktop publishing [desk'tâp pub'lishing] *n* publication assistée par ordinateur, PAO *f*.

desolate [des'əlit] *a* désolé(e).

desolation [desəlā'shən] *n* désolation *f*.

despair [dispär'] *n* désespoir *m* ♦ *vi*: **to ~ of** désespérer de; **to be in ~** être au désespoir.

despatch [dispach'] *n*, *vt* = **dispatch**.

desperate [des'pûrit] *a* désespéré(e); (*fugitive*) prêt(e) à tout; (*measures*) désespéré, extrême; **we are getting ~** nous commençons à désespérer.

desperately [des'pûritlē] *ad* désespérément; (*very*) terriblement, extrêmement; **~ ill** très gravement malade.

desperation [despərā'shən] *n* désespoir *m*; **in**

~ en désespoir de cause.

despicable [des'pikəbəl] *a* méprisable.

despise [dispīz'] *vt* mépriser, dédaigner.

despite [dispīt'] *prep* malgré, en dépit de.

despondent [dispân'dənt] *a* découragé(e), abattu(e).

despot [des'pət] *n* despote *m/f*.

dessert [dizûrt'] *n* dessert *m*.

dessertspoon [dizûrt'spōōn] *n* cuiller *f* à dessert.

destabilize [dēstā'bəlīz] *vt* déstabiliser.

destination [destənā'shən] *n* destination *f*.

destine [des'tin] *vt* destiner.

destined [des'tind] *a*: **to be ~ to do sth** être destiné(e) à faire qch; **~ for New York** à destination de New York.

destiny [des'tənē] *n* destinée *f*, destin *m*.

destitute [des'titōōt] *a* indigent(e), dans le dénuement; **~ of** dépourvu(e) *or* dénué(e) de.

destroy [distroi'] *vt* détruire.

destroyer [distroi'ûr] *n* (*NAUT*) contre-torpilleur *m*.

destruction [distruk'shən] *n* destruction *f*.

destructive [distruk'tiv] *a* destructeur(trice).

desultory [des'əltôrē] *a* (*reading, conversation*) décousu(e); (*contact*) irrégulier(ière).

detach [ditach'] *vt* détacher.

detachable [ditach'əbəl] *a* amovible, détachable.

detached [ditacht'] *a* (*attitude*) détaché(e).

detached house *n* (*Brit*) pavillon *m*, maison(nette) (individuelle).

detachment [ditach'mənt] *n* (*MIL*) détachement *m*; (*fig*) détachement, indifférence *f*.

detail [ditāl'] *n* détail *m*; (*MIL*) détachement *m* ♦ *vt* raconter en détail, énumérer; (*MIL*): **to ~ sb (for)** affecter qn (à), désigner qn (pour); **in ~** en détail; **to go into ~(s)** entrer dans les détails.

detailed [ditāld'] *a* détaillé(e).

detain [ditān'] *vt* retenir; (*in captivity*) détenir; (*in hospital*) hospitaliser.

detainee [dētānē'] *n* détenu/e.

detect [ditekt'] *vt* déceler, percevoir; (*MED, POLICE*) dépister; (*MIL, RADAR, TECH*) détecter.

detection [ditek'shən] *n* découverte *f*; (*MED, POLICE*) dépistage *m*; (*MIL, RADAR, TECH*) détection *f*; **to escape ~** échapper aux recherches, éviter d'être découvert(e); (*mistake*) passer inaperçu(e); **crime ~** le dépistage des criminels.

detective [ditek'tiv] *n* agent *m* de la sûreté, policier *m*; **private ~** détective privé.

detective story *n* roman policier.

detector [ditek'tûr] *n* détecteur *m*.

détente [dātânt'] *n* détente *f*.

detention [diten'chən] *n* détention *f*; (*SCOL*) retenue *f*, consigne *f*.

deter [ditûr'] *vt* dissuader.

detergent [ditûr'jənt] *n* détersif *m*, détergent *m*.

deteriorate [ditē'rēərāt] *vi* se détériorer, se dégrader.

deterioration [ditērēərā'shən] *n* détérioration *f*.

determination [ditûrmənā'shən] *n* détermination *f*.

determine [ditûr'min] *vt* déterminer; **to ~ to**

do résoudre de faire, se déterminer à faire.
determined [ditûr'mind] *a* (*person*) détermi-né(e), décidé(e); (*quantity*) déterminé, éta-bli(e); (*effort*) très gros(se).
deterrence [ditûr'əns] *n* dissuasion *f*.
deterrent [ditûr'ənt] *n* effet *m* de dissuasion; force *f* de dissuasion; **to act as a** ~ avoir un effet dissuasif.
detest [ditest'] *vt* détester, avoir horreur de.
detestable [dites'təbəl] *a* détestable, odieux(euse).
detonate [det'ənāt] *vi* exploser ♦ *vt* faire ex-ploser *or* détoner.
detonator [det'ənātûr] *n* détonateur *m*.
detour [dē'tōōr] *n* détour *m*; (*US AUT*: *di-version*) déviation *f*.
detract [ditrakt'] *vt*: **to** ~ **from** (*quality*, *pleasure*) diminuer; (*reputation*) porter atteinte à.
detractor [ditrak'tûr] *n* détracteur/trice.
detriment [det'rəmənt] *n*: **to the** ~ **of** au dé-triment de, au préjudice de; **without** ~ **to** sans porter atteinte *or* préjudice à, sans conséquences fâcheuses pour.
detrimental [detrəmen'təl] *a*: ~ **to** préjudicia-ble *or* nuisible à.
deuce [dōōs] *n* (*TENNIS*) égalité *f*.
devaluation [dēvalyōōā'shən] *n* dévaluation *f*.
devalue [dēval'yōō] *vt* dévaluer.
devastate [dev'əstāt] *vt* dévaster; **he was ~d by the news** cette nouvelle lui a porté un coup terrible.
devastating [dev'əstāting] *a* dévasta-teur(trice).
devastation [devəstā'shən] *n* dévastation *f*.
develop [divel'əp] *vt* (*gen*) développer; (*habit*) contracter; (*resources*) mettre en valeur, ex-ploiter; (*land*) aménager ♦ *vi* se développer; (*situation, disease: evolve*) évoluer; (*facts, symptoms: appear*) se manifester, se produi-re; **to** ~ **a taste for sth** prendre goût à qch; **to** ~ **into** devenir.
developer [divel'əpûr] *n* (*PHOT*) révélateur *m*; (*of land*) promoteur *m*; (*also*: **property** ~) promoteur immobilier.
developing country [divel'əping kun'trē] *n* pays *m* en voie de développement.
development [divel'əpmənt] *n* développement *m*; (*of affair, case*) rebondissement *m*, fait(s) nouveau(x).
development area *n* zone *f* à urbaniser.
deviate [dē'vēāt] *vi*: **to** ~ **(from)** dévier (de).
deviation [dēvēā'shən] *n* déviation *f*.
device [divīs'] *n* (*scheme*) moyen *m*, expédient *m*; (*apparatus*) engin *m*, dispositif *m*; **explo-sive** ~ engin explosif.
devil [dev'əl] *n* diable *m*; démon *m*.
devilish [dev'əlish] *a* diabolique.
devil-may-care [dev'əlmākâr'] *a* je-m'en-foutiste.
devious [dē'vēəs] *a* (*means*) détourné(e); (*person*) sournois(e), dissimulé(e).
devise [divīz'] *vt* imaginer, concevoir.
devoid [divoid'] *a*: ~ **of** dépourvu(e) de, dé-nué(e) de.
devolution [devəlōō'shən] *n* (*POL*) décentrali-sation *f*.
devolve [divâlv'] *vi*: **to** ~ **(up)on** retomber sur.

devote [divōt'] *vt*: **to** ~ **sth to** consacrer qch à.
devoted [divōt'id] *a* dévoué(e); **to be** ~ **to** être dévoué(e) *or* très attaché(e) à; (*subj: book etc*) être consacré(e) à.
devotee [devōtē'] *n* (*REL*) adepte *m/f*; (*MUS, SPORT*) fervent/e.
devotion [divō'shən] *n* dévouement *m*, atta-chement *m*; (*REL*) dévotion *f*, piété *f*.
devour [divou'ûr] *vt* dévorer.
devout [divout'] *a* pieux(euse), dévot(e).
dew [dōō] *n* rosée *f*.
dexterity [dekstär'itē] *n* dextérité *f*, adresse *f*.
dext(e)rous [dek'strəs] *a* adroit(e).
dg *abbr* (= *decigram*) dg.
diabetes [dīəbē'tis] *n* diabète *m*.
diabetic [dīəbet'ik] *n* diabétique *m/f* ♦ *a* (*person*) diabétique; (*chocolate, jam*) pour diabétiques.
diabolical [dīəbâl'ikəl] *a* diabolique; (*col: dreadful*) infernal(e), atroce.
diaeresis [diär'əsis] *n* tréma *m*.
diagnose [dīəgnōs'] *vt* diagnostiquer.
diagnosis, *pl* **diagnoses** [dīəgnō'sis, -sēz] *n* diagnostic *m*.
diagonal [dīag'ənəl] *a* diagonal(e) ♦ *n* dia-gonale *f*.
diagram [dī'əgram] *n* diagramme *m*, schéma *m*.
dial [dīl] *n* cadran *m* ♦ *vt* (*number*) faire, composer; **to** ~ **a wrong number** faire un faux numéro; **can I** ~ **New York direct?** puis-je *or* est-ce-que je peux avoir New York par l'automatique?
dial. *abbr* = **dialect**.
dial code, (*Brit*) **dialling code** [dī'ling kōd] *n* indicatif *m* (téléphonique).
dial tone, (*Brit*) **dialling tone** [dī'ling tōn] *n* tonalité *f*.
dialect [dī'əlekt] *n* dialecte *m*.
dialogue [dī'əlóg] *n* dialogue *m*.
dialysis [dīal'isis] *n* dialyse *f*.
diameter [dīam'itûr] *n* diamètre *m*.
diametrically [dīəmet'riklē] *ad*: ~ **opposed (to)** diamétralement opposé(e) (à).
diamond [dī'mənd] *n* diamant *m*; (*shape*) lo-sange *m*; ~**s** *npl* (*CARDS*) carreau *m*.
diamond ring *n* bague *f* de diamant(s).
diaper [dī'pûr] *n* (*US*) couche *f*.
diaphragm [dī'əfram] *n* diaphragme *m*.
diarrhea, (*Brit*) **diarrhoea** [dīərē'ə] *n* diarrhée *f*.
diary [dī'ûrē] *n* (*daily account*) journal *m*; (*book*) agenda *m*; **to keep a** ~ tenir un journal.
diatribe [dī'ətrīb] *n* diatribe *f*.
dice [dīs] *n* (*pl inv*) dé *m* ♦ *vt* (*CULIN*) couper en dés *or* en cubes.
dichotomy [dīkât'əmē] *n* dichotomie *f*.
Dictaphone [dik'təfōn] *n* ® Dictaphone *m* ®.
dictate *vt* [diktāt'] dicter ♦ *vi*: **to** ~ **to** (*person*) imposer sa volonté à, régenter; **I won't be** ~**d to** je n'ai d'ordres à recevoir de personne ♦ *n* [dik'tāt] injonction *f*.
dictation [diktā'shən] *n* dictée *f*; **at** ~ **speed** à une vitesse de dictée.
dictator [dik'tātûr] *n* dictateur *m*.
dictatorship [dik'tātûrship] *n* dictature *f*.
diction [dik'shən] *n* diction *f*, élocution *f*.

dictionary [dik'shənärē] *n* dictionnaire *m*.

did [did] *pt of* **do**.

didactic [dīdak'tik] *a* didactique.

die [dī] *n* (*pl:* **dice**) dé *m*; (*pl:* **dies**) coin *m*; matrice *f*; étampe *f* ♦ *vi:* **to ~ (of** *or* **from)** mourir (de); **to be dying** être mourant(e); **to be dying for sth** avoir une envie folle de qch; **to be dying to do sth** mourir d'envie de faire qch.
  die away *vi* s'éteindre.
  die down *vi* se calmer, s'apaiser.
  die out *vi* disparaître, s'éteindre.

diehard [dī'hârd] *n* réactionnaire *m/f*, jusqu'au-boutiste *m/f*.

dieresis [dīär'əsis] *n* tréma *m*.

diesel [dē'zəl] *n* diesel *m*.

diesel engine *n* moteur *m* diesel.

diesel fuel, diesel oil *n* carburant *m* diesel.

diet [dī'ət] *n* alimentation *f*; (*restricted food*) régime *m* ♦ *vi* (*also:* **be on a ~**) suivre un régime; **to live on a ~ of** se nourrir de.

dietician [dīətish'ən] *n* diététicien/ne.

differ [dif'ûr] *vi:* **to ~ from sth** être différent(e) de; différer de; **to ~ from sb over sth** ne pas être d'accord avec qn au sujet de qch.

difference [dif'ûrəns] *n* différence *f*; (*quarrel*) différend *m*, désaccord *m*; **it makes no ~ to me** cela m'est égal, cela m'est indifférent; **to settle one's ~s** résoudre la situation.

different [dif'ûrənt] *a* différent(e).

differential [difərcn'chəl] *n* (*AUT, wages*) différentiel *m*.

differentiate [difərcn'chēāt] *vt* différencier ♦ *vi* se différencier; **to ~ between** faire une différence entre.

differently [dif'ûrəntlē] *ad* différemment.

difficult [dif'əkult] *a* difficile; **~ to understand** difficile à comprendre.

difficulty [dif'əkultē] *n* difficulté *f*; **to have difficulties with** avoir des ennuis *or* problèmes avec; **to be in ~** avoir des difficultés, avoir des problèmes.

diffidence [dif'idəns] *n* manque *m* de confiance en soi, manque d'assurance.

diffident [dif'idənt] *a* qui manque de confiance *or* d'assurance, peu sûr(e) de soi.

diffuse *a* [difyōōs'] diffus(e) ♦ *vt* [difyōōz'] diffuser, répandre.

dig [dig] *vt* (*pt, pp* **dug** [dug]) (*hole*) creuser; (*garden*) bêcher ♦ *n* (*prod*) coup *m* de coude; (*fig*) coup de griffe *or* de patte; (*ARCHEOLOGY*) fouille *f*; **to ~ into** (*snow, soil*) creuser; **to ~ into one's pockets for sth** fouiller dans ses poches pour chercher *or* prendre qch; **to ~ one's nails into** enfoncer ses ongles dans.
  dig in *vi* (*also:* **~ o.s. in:** *MIL*) se retrancher; (: *fig*) tenir bon, se braquer; (*col: eat*) attaquer (un repas *or* un plat *etc*) ♦ *vt* (*compost*) bien mélanger à la bêche; (*knife, claw*) enfoncer; **to ~ in one's heels** (*fig*) se braquer, se buter.
  dig out *vt* (*survivors, car from snow*) sortir *or* dégager (à coups de pelles *or* pioches).
  dig up *vt* déterrer.

digest *vt* [dijest'] digérer ♦ *n* [dī'jest] sommaire *m*, résumé *m*.

digestible [dijes'təbəl] *a* digestible.

digestion [dijes'chən] *n* digestion *f*.

digestive [dijes'tiv] *a* digestif(ive).

digit [dij'it] *n* chiffre *m* (*de 0 à 9*); (*finger*) doigt *m*.

digital [dij'itəl] *a* digital(e); (*watch*) à affichage numérique *or* digital.

dignified [dig'nəfīd] *a* digne.

dignitary [dig'nitärē] *n* dignitaire *m*.

dignity [dig'nitē] *n* dignité *f*.

digress [digres'] *vi:* **to ~ from** s'écarter de, s'éloigner de.

digression [digresh'ən] *n* digression *f*.

digs [digz] *npl* (*Brit col*) piaule *f*, chambre meublée.

dike [dīk] *n* (*embankment*) digue *f*.

dilapidated [dilap'ədātid] *a* délabré(e).

dilate [dīlāt'] *vt* dilater ♦ *vi* se dilater.

dilatory [dil'ətôrē] *a* dilatoire.

dilemma [dilem'ə] *n* dilemme *m*; **to be in a ~** être pris dans un dilemme.

diligent [dil'ijənt] *a* appliqué(e), assidu(e).

dill [dil] *n* aneth *m*.

dilly-dally [dil'ēdalē] *vi* hésiter, tergiverser; traînasser, lambiner.

dilute [dilōōt'] *vt* diluer ♦ *a* dilué(e).

dim [dim] *a* (*light, eyesight*) faible; (*memory, outline*) vague, indécis(e); (*stupid*) borné(e), obtus(e) ♦ *vt* (*light*) réduire, baisser; (*US AUT*) mettre en code, baisser; **to take a ~ view of sth** voir qch d'un mauvais œil.

dime [dīm] *n* (*US*) = *10 cents*.

dimension [dimen'chən] *n* dimension *f*.

diminish [dimin'ish] *vt, vi* diminuer.

diminished [dimin'isht] *a:* **~ responsibility** (*LAW*) responsabilité atténuée.

diminutive [dimin'yətiv] *a* minuscule, tout(e) petit(e) ♦ *n* (*LING*) diminutif *m*.

dimly [dim'lē] *ad* faiblement; vaguement.

dimmers [dim'ûrz] *npl* (*US AUT*) phares *mpl* code *inv*; (: *parking lights*) feux *mpl* de position.

dimple [dim'pəl] *n* fossette *f*.

dim-witted [dim'witid] *a* (*col*) stupide, borné(e).

din [din] *n* vacarme *m* ♦ *vt:* **to ~ sth into sb** (*col*) enfoncer qch dans la tête *or* la caboche de qn.

dine [dīn] *vi* dîner.

diner [dīn'ûr] *n* (*person*) dîneur/euse; (*RAIL*) = **dining car**; (*US: eating place*) petit restaurant.

dinghy [ding'ē] *n* youyou *m*; (*inflatable*) canot *m* pneumatique; (*also:* **sailing ~**) voilier *m*, dériveur *m*.

dingy [din'jē] *a* miteux(euse), minable.

dining car [dīn'ing kâr] *n* voiture-restaurant *f*, wagon-restaurant *m*.

dining room [dīn'ing rōōm] *n* salle *f* à manger.

dinner [din'ûr] *n* dîner *m*; (*public*) banquet *m*; **~'s ready!** à table!

dinner jacket *n* smoking *m*.

dinner party *n* dîner *m*.

dinner time *n* heure *f* du dîner.

dinosaur [dī'nəsôr] *n* dinosaure *m*.

dint [dint] *n:* **by ~ of (doing) sth** à force de (faire) qch.

diocese [dī'əsēs] *n* diocèse *m*.

dioxide [dīāk'sid] *n* dioxyde *m*.

dioxin [dīāks'in] *n* dioxine *f*.

dip [dip] *n* déclivité *f*; (*in sea*) baignade *f*, bain *m* ♦ *vt* tremper, plonger; (*Brit AUT: lights*) mettre en code, baisser ♦ *vi* plonger.

diphtheria [dipthē'rēə] *n* diphtérie *f*.

diphthong [dif'thông] *n* diphtongue *f*.

diploma [diplō'mə] *n* diplôme *m*.

diplomacy [diplō'məsē] *n* diplomatie *f*.

diplomat [dip'ləmat] *n* diplomate *m*.

diplomatic [dipləmat'ik] *a* diplomatique; **to break off ~ relations (with)** rompre les relations diplomatiques (avec).

diplomatic corps *n* corps *m* diplomatique.

dipstick [dip'stik] *n* (*AUT*) jauge *f* de niveau d'huile.

dipswitch [dip'swich] *n* (*Brit AUT*) commutateur *m* de code.

dire [dī'ûr] *a* extrême, affreux(euse).

direct [direkt'] *a* direct(e); (*manner, person*) direct, franc(franche) ♦ *vt* diriger, orienter; **can you ~ me to ...?** pouvez-vous m'indiquer le chemin de ...?; **to ~ sb to do sth** ordonner à qn de faire qch.

direct cost *n* (*COMM*) coût *m* variable.

direct current *n* (*ELEC*) courant continu.

direct debit *n* (*BANKING*) prélèvement *m* automatique.

direct dialling [direkt' dī'ling] *n* (*TEL*) automatique *m*.

direct hit *n* (*MIL*) coup *m* au but, touché *m*.

direction [direk'shən] *n* direction *f*; (*THEATER*) mise *f* en scène; (*CINEMA, TV*) réalisation *f*; **~s** *npl* (*instructions: to a place*) indications *fpl*; **~s for use** mode *m* d'emploi; **to ask for ~s** demander sa route *or* son chemin; **sense of ~** sens *m* de l'orientation; **in the ~ of** dans la direction de, vers.

directive [direk'tiv] *n* directive *f*; **a government ~** une directive du gouvernement.

directly [direkt'lē] *ad* (*in straight line*) directement, tout droit; (*at once*) tout de suite, immédiatement.

direct mail *n* vente *f* par publicité directe.

direct mailshot *n* (*Brit*) publicité postale.

directness [direkt'nis] *n* (*of person, speech*) franchise *f*.

director [direk'tûr] *n* directeur *m*; (*board member*) administrateur *m*; (*THEATER*) metteur *m* en scène; (*CINEMA, TV*) réalisateur/trice; **D~ of Public Prosecutions** (*Brit*) ≈ procureur général.

directory [direk'tûrē] *n* annuaire *m*; (*also:* **street ~**) indicateur *m* de rues; (*also:* **trade ~**) annuaire du commerce; (*COMPUT*) répertoire *m*.

directory assistance, (*Brit*) **directory enquiries** *n* (*TEL: service*) renseignements *mpl*.

dirt [dûrt] *n* saleté *f*; (*mud*) boue *f*; **to treat sb like ~** traiter qn comme un chien.

dirt-cheap [dûrt'chēp'] *a* (ne) coûtant presque rien.

dirt road *n* chemin non macadamisé *or* non revêtu.

dirty [dûr'tē] *a* sale ♦ *vt* salir; **~ story** histoire cochonne; **~ trick** coup tordu.

disability [disəbil'ətē] *n* invalidité *f*, infirmité *f*.

disability allowance *n* allocation *f* d'invalidité *or* d'infirmité.

disable [disā'bəl] *vt* (*subj: illness, accident*) rendre *or* laisser infirme; (*tank, gun*) mettre hors d'action.

disabled [disā'bəld] *a* infirme, invalide; (*maimed*) mutilé(e); (*through illness, old age*) impotent(e).

disadvantage [disədvan'tij] *n* désavantage *m*, inconvénient *m*.

disadvantaged [disədvan'tijd] *a* (*person*) désavantagé(e).

disadvantageous [disadvəntā'jəs] *a* désavantageux(euse).

disaffected [disəfek'tid] *a*: **~ (to or towards)** mécontent(e) (de).

disaffection [disəfek'shən] *n* désaffection *f*, mécontentement *m*.

disagree [disəgrē'] *vi* (*differ*) ne pas concorder; (*be against, think otherwise*): **to ~ (with)** ne pas être d'accord (avec); **garlic ~s with me** l'ail ne me convient pas, je ne supporte pas l'ail.

disagreeable [disəgrē'əbəl] *a* désagréable.

disagreement [disəgrē'mənt] *n* désaccord *m*, différend *m*.

disallow [disəlou'] *vt* rejeter, désavouer.

disappear [disəpi'ûr] *vi* disparaître.

disappearance [disəpi'ûrəns] *n* disparition *f*.

disappoint [disəpoint'] *vt* décevoir.

disappointed [disəpoin'tid] *a* déçu(e).

disappointing [disəpoin'ting] *a* décevant(e).

disappointment [disəpoint'mənt] *n* déception *f*.

disapproval [disəprōō'vəl] *n* désapprobation *f*.

disapprove [disəprōōv'] *vi*: **to ~ of** désapprouver.

disapproving [disəprōō'ving] *a* désapprobateur(trice), de désapprobation.

disarm [disârm'] *vt* désarmer.

disarmament [disâr'məmənt] *n* désarmement *m*.

disarming [disârm'ing] *a* (*smile*) désarmant(e).

disarray [disərā'] *n* désordre *m*, confusion *f*; **in ~** (*troops*) en déroute; (*thoughts*) embrouillé(e); (*clothes*) en désordre; **to throw into ~** semer la confusion *or* le désordre dans (*or* parmi).

disaster [dizas'tûr] *n* catastrophe *f*, désastre *m*.

disastrous [dizas'trəs] *a* désastreux(euse).

disband [disband'] *vt* démobiliser; disperser ♦ *vi* se séparer; se disperser.

disbelief [disbilēf'] *n* incrédulité *f*; **in ~** avec incrédulité.

disbelieve [disbilēv'] *vt* (*person*) ne pas croire; (*story*) mettre en doute; **I don't ~ you** je veux bien vous croire.

disc [disk] *n* (*Brit*) disque *m*.

disc. *abbr* (*COMM*) = **discount**.

discard [diskârd'] *vt* (*old things*) se défaire de, mettre au rencart *or* au rebut; (*fig*) écarter, renoncer à.

disc brake [disk brāk] *n* frein *m* à disque.

discern [disûrn'] *vt* discerner, distinguer.

discernible [disûr'nəbəl] *a* discernable, perceptible; (*object*) visible.

discerning [disûr'ning] *a* judicieux(euse), perspicace.

discharge *vt* [dischârj'] (*duties*) s'acquitter de; (*settle: debt*) s'acquitter de, régler; (*waste etc*) déverser; décharger; (*ELEC, MED*) émettre; (*patient*) renvoyer (chez lui); (*employee, soldier*) congédier, licencier; (*defendant*) relaxer, élargir ♦ *n* [dis'chärj] (*ELEC, MED etc*) émission *f*; (*also:* **vaginal** ~) pertes blanches; (*dismissal*) renvoi *m*; licenciement *m*; élargissement *m*; **to** ~ **one's gun** faire feu; ~**d bankrupt** failli/e réhabilité(e).

disciple [disī'pəl] *n* disciple *m*.

disciplinary [dis'əplənärē] *a* disciplinaire; **to take** ~ **action against sb** prendre des mesures disciplinaires à l'encontre de qn.

discipline [dis'əplin] *n* discipline *f* ♦ *vt* discipliner; (*punish*) punir; **to** ~ **o.s. to do sth** s'imposer *or* s'astreindre à une discipline pour faire qch.

disc jockey (DJ) *n* disque-jockey *m* (DJ).

disclaim [disklām'] *vt* désavouer, dénier.

disclaimer [disklām'ûr] *n* démenti *m*, dénégation *f*; **to issue a** ~ publier un démenti.

disclose [disklōz'] *vt* révéler, divulguer.

disclosure [disklō'zhûr] *n* révélation *f*, divulgation *f*.

disco [dis'kō] *n abbr* = **discothèque**.

discolor [diskul'ûr] (*US*) *vt* décolorer; (*sth white*) jaunir ♦ *vi* se décolorer; jaunir.

discoloration [diskulərā'shən] *n* décoloration *f*; jaunissement *m*.

discolored [diskul'ûrd] *a* décoloré(e); jauni(e).

discolour [diskul'ûr] *etc* (*Brit*) = **discolor** *etc*.

discomfort [diskum'fûrt] *n* malaise *m*, gêne *f*; (*lack of comfort*) manque *m* de confort.

disconcert [diskənsûrt'] *vt* déconcerter, décontenancer.

disconnect [diskənekt'] *vt* détacher; (*ELEC, RADIO*) débrancher; (*gas, water*) couper.

disconnected [diskənekt'id] *a* (*speech, thoughts*) décousu(e), peu cohérent(e).

disconsolate [diskän'səlit] *a* inconsolable.

discontent [diskəntent'] *n* mécontentement *m*.

discontented [diskəntent'id] *a* mécontent(e).

discontinue [diskəntin'yōō] *vt* cesser, interrompre; **"~d"** (*COMM*) "fin de série".

discord [dis'kôrd] *n* discorde *f*, dissension *f*; (*MUS*) dissonance *f*.

discordant [diskôr'dənt] *a* discordant(e), dissonant(e).

discothèque [dis'kōtek] *n* discothèque *f*.

discount *n* [dis'kount] remise *f*, rabais *m* ♦ *vt* [diskount'] (*report etc*) ne pas tenir compte de; **to give sb a** ~ **on sth** faire une remise *or* un rabais à qn sur qch; ~ **for cash** escompte *f* au comptant; **at a** ~ avec une remise *or* réduction, au rabais.

discount house *n* (*FINANCE*) banque *f* d'escompte; (*COMM: also:* **discount store**) magasin *m* de discount.

discount rate *n* taux *m* de remise.

discourage [diskûr'ij] *vt* décourager; (*dissuade, deter*) dissuader, décourager.

discouragement [diskûr'ijmənt] *n* (*depression*) découragement *m*; **to act as a** ~ **to sb** dissuader qn.

discouraging [diskûr'ijing] *a* décourageant(e).

discourteous [diskûr'tēəs] *a* incivil(e), discourtois(e).

discover [diskuv'ûr] *vt* découvrir.

discovery [diskuv'ûrē] *n* découverte *f*.

discredit [diskred'it] *vt* mettre en doute; discréditer ♦ *n* discrédit *m*.

discreet [diskrēt'] *a* discret(ète).

discreetly [diskrēt'lē] *ad* discrètement.

discrepancy [diskrep'ənsē] *n* divergence *f*, contradiction *f*.

discretion [diskresh'ən] *n* discrétion *f*; **use your own** ~ à vous de juger.

discretionary [diskresh'ənärē] *a* (*powers*) discrétionnaire.

discriminate [diskrim'ənāt] *vi*: **to** ~ **between** établir une distinction entre, faire la différence entre; **to** ~ **against** pratiquer une discrimination contre.

discriminating [diskrim'ənāting] *a* qui a du discernement.

discrimination [diskrimənā'shən] *n* discrimination *f*; (*judgment*) discernement *m*; **racial/sexual** ~ discrimination raciale/sexuelle.

discus [dis'kəs] *n* disque *m*.

discuss [diskus'] *vt* discuter de; (*debate*) discuter.

discussion [diskush'ən] *n* discussion *f*; **under** ~ en discussion.

disdain [disdān'] *n* dédain *m*.

disease [dizēz'] *n* maladie *f*.

diseased [dizēzd'] *a* malade.

disembark [disembârk'] *vt, vi* débarquer.

disembarkation [disembârkā'shən] *n* débarquement *m*.

disembodied [disembâd'ēd] *a* désincarné(e).

disembowel [disembou'əl] *vt* éviscérer, étriper.

disenchanted [disenchan'tid] *a*: ~ **(with)** désenchanté(e) (de), désabusé(e) (de).

disenfranchise [disenfran'chīz] *vt* priver du droit de vote; (*COMM*) retirer la franchise à.

disengage [disengāj'] *vt* dégager; (*TECH*) déclencher; **to** ~ **the clutch** (*AUT*) débrayer.

disengagement [disengāj'mənt] *n* (*POL*) désengagement *m*.

disentangle [disentang'gəl] *vt* démêler.

disfavor, (*Brit*) **disfavour** [disfā'vûr] *n* défaveur *f*; disgrâce *f*.

disfigure [disfig'yûr] *vt* défigurer.

disgorge [disgôrj'] *vt* déverser.

disgrace [disgrās'] *n* honte *f*; (*disfavor*) disgrâce *f* ♦ *vt* déshonorer, couvrir de honte.

disgraceful [disgrās'fəl] *a* scandaleux(euse), honteux(euse).

disgruntled [disgrun'təld] *a* mécontent(e).

disguise [disgīz'] *n* déguisement *n* ♦ *vt* déguiser; (*voice*) déguiser, contrefaire; (*feelings etc*) masquer, dissimuler; **in** ~ déguisé(e); **to** ~ **o.s. as** se déguiser en; **there's no disguising the fact that ...** on ne peut pas se dissimuler que ....

disgust [disgust'] *n* dégoût *m*, aversion *f* ♦ *vt* dégoûter, écœurer.

disgusting [disgus'ting] *a* dégoûtant(e), révoltant(e).

dish [dish] *n* plat *m*; **to do** *or* **wash the** ~**es** faire la vaisselle.

dish out *vt* distribuer.

dish up *vt* servir; (*facts, statistics*) sortir, débiter.

dishcloth [dish'klôth] *n* (*for drying*) torchon *m*; (*for washing*) lavette *f*.

dishearten [dis·hâr'tən] *vt* décourager.

disheveled, (*Brit*) **dishevelled** [dishev'əld] *a* ébouriffé(e); décoiffé(e); débraillé(e).
dishonest [disân'ist] *a* malhonnête.
dishonesty [disân'istē] *n* malhonnêteté *f*.
dishonor [disân'ûr] *n* (*US*) déshonneur *m*.
dishonorable [disân'ûrəbəl] *a* déshonorant(e).
dishonour [disân'ûr] *etc* (*Brit*) = **dishonor** *etc*.
dish soap *n* (*US*) produit *m* pour la vaisselle.
dishtowel [dish'touəl] *n* torchon *m* (à vaisselle).
dishwasher [dish'wâshûr] *n* lave-vaisselle *m*; (*person*) plongeur/euse.
dishwashing liquid [dish'wâshing lik'wid] *n* produit *m* pour la vaiselle.
disillusion [disiloo'zhən] *vt* désabuser, désenchanter ♦ *n* désenchantement *m*; **to become ~ed (with)** perdre ses illusions (en ce qui concerne).
disillusionment [disiloo'zhənmənt] *n* désillusionnement *m*, désillusion *f*.
disincentive [disinsen'tiv] *n*: **it's a ~** c'est démotivant; **to be a ~ to sb** démotiver qn.
disinclined [disinklīnd'] *a*: **to be ~ to do sth** être peu disposé(e) *or* peu enclin(e) à faire qch.
disinfect [disinfekt'] *vt* désinfecter.
disinfectant [disinfek'tənt] *n* désinfectant *m*.
disinflation [disinflā'shən] *n* désinflation *f*.
disinherit [disinhär'it] *vt* déshériter.
disintegrate [disin'təgrāt] *vi* se désintégrer.
disinterested [disin'tristid] *a* désintéressé(e).
disjointed [disjoint'id] *a* décousu(e), incohérent(e).
disk [disk] *n* disque *m*; (*COMPUT*) disquette *f*; **single-/double-sided ~** disquette une face/double face.
disk drive *n* lecteur *m* de disquette.
diskette [disket'] *n* (*COMPUT*) disquette *f*.
disk operating system (DOS) *n* système *m* d'exploitation à disques (DOS).
dislike [dislīk'] *n* aversion *f*, antipathie *f* ♦ *vt* ne pas aimer; **to take a ~ to sb/sth** prendre qn/qch en grippe; **I ~ the idea** l'idée me déplaît.
dislocate [dis'lōkāt] *vt* disloquer, déboîter; (*services etc*) désorganiser; **he has ~d his shoulder** il s'est disloqué l'épaule.
dislodge [dislâj'] *vt* déplacer, faire bouger; (*enemy*) déloger.
disloyal [disloi'əl] *a* déloyal(e).
dismal [diz'məl] *a* lugubre, maussade.
dismantle [disman'təl] *vt* démonter; (*fort, warship*) démanteler.
dismast [dismast'] *vt* démâter.
dismay [dismā'] *n* consternation *f* ♦ *vt* consterner; **much to my ~** à ma grande consternation, à ma grande inquiétude.
dismiss [dismis'] *vt* congédier, renvoyer; (*idea*) écarter; (*LAW*) rejeter ♦ *vi* (*MIL*) rompre les rangs.
dismissal [dismis'əl] *n* renvoi *m*.
dismount [dismount'] *vi* mettre pied à terre.
disobedience [disəbē'dēəns] *n* désobéissance *f*.
disobedient [disəbē'dēənt] *a* désobéissant(e), indiscipliné(e).
disobey [disəbā'] *vt* désobéir à; (*rule*) transgresser, enfreindre.

disorder [disôr'dûr] *n* désordre *m*; (*rioting*) désordres *mpl*; (*MED*) troubles *mpl*.
disorderly [disôr'dûrlē] *a* (*room*) en désordre; (*behavior, retreat, crowd*) désordonné(e).
disorderly conduct *n* (*LAW*) conduite *f* contraire aux bonnes mœurs.
disorganized [disôr'gənīzd] *a* désorganisé(e).
disorientated [disô'rēintātid] *a* désorienté(e).
disown [disōn'] *vt* renier.
disparaging [dispar'ijing] *a* désobligeant(e); **to be ~ about sb/sth** faire des remarques désobligeantes sur qn/qch.
disparate [dis'pûrit] *a* disparate.
disparity [dispar'itē] *n* disparité *f*.
dispassionate [dispash'ənit] *a* calme, froid(e); impartial(e), objectif(ive).
dispatch [dispach'] *vt* expédier, envoyer; (*deal with: business*) régler, en finir avec ♦ *n* envoi *m*, expédition *f*; (*MIL, PRESS*) dépêche *f*.
dispatch department *n* service *m* des expéditions.
dispatch rider *n* (*MIL*) estafette *f*.
dispel [dispel'] *vt* dissiper, chasser.
dispensary [dispen'sûrē] *n* pharmacie *f*; (*in chemist's*) officine *f*.
dispense [dispens'] *vt* distribuer, administrer; (*medicine*) préparer (et vendre); **to ~ sb from** dispenser qn de.
dispense with *vt fus* se passer de; (*make unnecessary*) rendre superflu(e).
dispenser [dispen'sûr] *n* (*device*) distributeur *m*.
dispensing chemist [dispen'sing kem'ist] *n* (*Brit*) pharmacie *f*.
dispersal [dispûr'səl] *n* dispersion *f*; (*ADMIN*) déconcentration *f*.
disperse [dispûrs'] *vt* disperser; (*knowledge*) disséminer ♦ *vi* se disperser.
dispirited [dispir'itid] *a* découragé(e), déprimé(e).
displace [displās'] *vt* déplacer.
displaced person [displāst' pûr'sən] *n* (*POL*) personne déplacée.
displacement [displās'mənt] *n* déplacement *m*.
display [displā'] *n* (*of goods*) étalage *m*; affichage *m*; (*computer ~: information*) visualisation *f*; (*: device*) visuel *m*; (*of feeling*) manifestation *f*; (*pej*) ostentation *f*; (*show, spectacle*) spectacle *m*; (*military ~*) parade *f* militaire ♦ *vt* montrer; (*goods*) mettre à l'étalage, exposer; (*results, departure times*) afficher; (*pej*) faire étalage de; **on ~** (*exhibits*) exposé(e), exhibé(e); (*goods*) à l'étalage.
display advertising *n* publicité rédactionnelle.
displease [displēz'] *vt* mécontenter, contrarier; **~d with** mécontent(e) de.
displeasure [displezh'ûr] *n* mécontentement *m*.
disposable [dispō'zəbəl] *a* (*pack etc*) jetable; (*income*) disponible; **~ diaper** couche *f* à jeter, couche-culotte *f*.
disposal [dispō'zəl] *n* (*availability, arrangement*) disposition *f*; (*of property etc: by selling*) vente *f*; (*: by giving away*) cession *f*; (*of garbage*) évacuation *f*, destruction *f*; **at one's ~** à sa disposition; **to put sth at sb's**

~ mettre qch à la disposition de qn.
dispose [dispōz'] *vt* disposer.
  dispose of *vt fus* (*time, money*) disposer
  de; (*unwanted goods*) se débarrasser de, se
  défaire de; (COMM: *stock*) écouler, vendre;
  (*problem*) expédier.
disposed [dispōzd'] *a*: ~ **to do** disposé(e) à
  faire.
disposition [dispəzish'ən] *n* disposition *f*;
  (*temperament*) naturel *m*.
dispossess [dispəzes'] *vt*: **to** ~ **sb (of)** dé-
  posséder qn (de).
disproportion [disprəpôr'shən] *n* disproportion
  f.
disproportionate [disprəpôr'shənit] *a* dispro-
  portionné(e).
disprove [disprōōv'] *vt* réfuter.
dispute [dispyōōt'] *n* discussion *f*; (*also*: **industrial** ~) conflit *m* ♦ *vt* contester; (*matter*)
  discuter; (*victory*) disputer; **to be in** *or*
  under ~ (*matter*) être en discussion; (*territory*) être contesté(e).
disqualification [diskwâləfəkā'shən] *n* disqualification *f*; ~ **(from driving)** (*Brit*) retrait *m*
  du permis (de conduire).
disqualify [diskwâl'əfī] *vt* (SPORT) disqualifier;
  to ~ **sb for sth/from doing** (*status, situation*) rendre qn inapte à qch/à faire;
  (*authority*) signifier à qn l'interdiction de faire; **to** ~ **sb (from driving)** (*Brit*) retirer à qn
  son permis (de conduire).
disquiet [diskwī'it] *n* inquiétude *f*, trouble *m*.
disquieting [diskwī'iting] *a* inquiétant(e),
  alarmant(e).
disregard [disrigârd'] *vt* ne pas tenir compte
  de ♦ *n* (*indifference*): ~ **(for)** (*feelings*)
  indifférence *f* (pour), insensibilité *f* (à);
  (*danger, money*) mépris *m* (pour).
disrepair [disripär'] *n* mauvais état; **to fall
  into** ~ (*building*) tomber en ruine; (*street*)
  se dégrader.
disreputable [disrep'yətəbəl] *a* (*person*) de
  mauvaise réputation, peu recommandable;
  (*behavior*) déshonorant(e); (*area*) mal fa-
  mé(e), louche.
disrepute [disripyōōt'] *n* déshonneur *m*, discrédit *m*; **to bring into** ~ faire tomber dans le
  discrédit.
disrespectful   [disrispekt'fəl]   *a*
  irrespectueux(euse).
disrupt [disrupt'] *vt* (*plans, meeting, lesson*)
  perturber, déranger.
disruption [disrup'shən] *n* perturbation *f*, dérangement *m*.
disruptive [disrup'tiv] *a* perturbateur(trice).
dissatisfaction [dissatisfak'shən] *n* mécontentement *m*, insatisfaction *f*.
dissatisfied [dissat'isfīd] *a*: ~ **(with)** mé-
  content(e) *or* insatisfait(e) (de).
dissect [disekt'] *vt* disséquer; (*fig*) disséquer,
  éplucher.
disseminate [disem'ənāt] *vt* disséminer.
dissent [disent'] *n* dissentiment *m*, différence *f*
  d'opinion.
dissenter [disen'tûr] *n* (REL, POL *etc*)
  dissident/e.
dissertation [disûrtā'shən] *n* (SCOL) mémoire
  m.
disservice [dissûr'vis] *n*: **to do sb a** ~ rendre

un mauvais service à qn; desservir qn.
dissident [dis'idənt] *a, n* dissident(e).
dissimilar [disim'ilûr] *a*: ~ **(to)** dissemblable
  (à), différent(e) (de).
dissipate [dis'əpāt] *vt* dissiper; (*energy,
  efforts*) disperser.
dissipated [dis'əpātid] *a* dissolu(e); débau-
  ché(e).
dissociate [disō'shēāt] *vt* dissocier; **to** ~ **o.s.
  from** se désolidariser de.
dissolute [dis'əlōōt] *a* débauché(e), dissolu(e).
dissolution [disəlōō'shən] *n* dissolution *f*.
dissolve [dizâlv'] *vt* dissoudre ♦ *vi* se dissoudre, fondre; (*fig*) disparaître.
dissuade [diswād'] *vt*: **to** ~ **sb (from)** dissuader qn (de).
distaff [dis'taf] *n*: ~ **side** côté maternel.
distance [dis'təns] *n* distance *f*; **what's the** ~
  to Chicago? à quelle distance se trouve Chicago?; **it's within walking** ~ on peut y aller
  à pied; **in the** ~ au loin.
distant [dis'tənt] *a* lointain(e), éloigné(e);
  (*manner*) distant(e), froid(e).
distaste [distāst'] *n* dégoût *m*.
distasteful [distāst'fəl] *a* déplaisant(e), désagréable.
Dist. Atty. *abbr* (US) = **district attorney**.
distemper [distem'pûr] *n* (*paint*) détrempe *f*,
  badigeon *m*; (*of dogs*) maladie *f* de Carré.
distended [distend'id] *a* (*stomach*) dilaté(e).
distil(l) [distil'] *vt* distiller.
distillery [distil'ûrē] *n* distillerie *f*.
distinct [distingkt'] *a* distinct(e); (*preference,
  progress*) marqué(e); **as** ~ **from** par opposition à, en contraste avec.
distinction [distingk'shən] *n* distinction *f*; (*in
  exam*) mention *f* très bien; **to draw a** ~
  between faire une distinction entre; **a writer
  of** ~ un écrivain réputé.
distinctive [distingk'tiv] *a* distinctif(ive).
distinctly [distingkt'lē] *ad* distinctement;
  (*specify*) expressément.
distinguish [disting'gwish] *vt* distinguer; **to** ~
  between (*concepts*) distinguer entre, faire
  une distinction entre; **to** ~ **o.s.** se distinguer.
distinguished [disting'gwisht] *a* (*eminent,
  refined*) distingué(e); (*career*) remarquable,
  brillant(e).
distinguishing [disting'gwishing] *a* (*feature*)
  distinctif(ive), caractéristique.
distort [distôrt'] *vt* déformer.
distortion [distôr'shən] *n* déformation *f*.
distr. *abbr* = **distribution; distributor**.
distract [distrakt'] *vt* distraire, déranger.
distracted [distrak'tid] *a* (*look etc*) éperdu(e),
  égaré(e).
distraction [distrak'shən] *n* distraction *f*, dérangement *m*; **to drive sb to** ~ rendre qn
  fou(folle).
distraught [distrôt'] *a* éperdu(e).
distress [distres'] *n* détresse *f*; (*pain*) douleur *f*
  ♦ *vt* affliger; **in** ~ (*ship*) en perdition;
  (*plane*) en détresse.
distressing [distres'ing] *a* douloureux(euse),
  pénible, affligeant(e).
distress signal *n* signal *m* de détresse.
distribute [distrib'yōōt] *vt* distribuer.
distribution [distrəbyōō'shən] *n* distribution *f*.
distribution cost *n* coût *m* de distribution.

distributor [distrib'yətûr] *n* (*gen*, TECH) distributeur *m*; (COMM) concessionnaire *m/f*.

district [dis'trikt] *n* (*of country*) région *f*; (*of town*) quartier *m*; (ADMIN) district *m*.

district attorney *n* (*US*) ≈ procureur *m* de la République.

district council *n* (*Brit*) ≈ conseil municipal.

district nurse *n* (*Brit*) infirmière visiteuse.

distrust [distrust'] *n* méfiance *f*, doute *m* ♦ *vt* se méfier de.

distrustful [distrust'fəl] *a* méfiant(e).

disturb [distûrb'] *vt* troubler; (*inconvenience*) déranger; **sorry to ~ you** excusez-moi de vous déranger.

disturbance [distûr'bəns] *n* dérangement *m*; (*political etc*) troubles *mpl*; (*by drunks etc*) tapage *m*; **to cause a ~** troubler l'ordre public; **~ of the peace** (LAW) tapage injurieux *or* nocturne.

disturbed [distûrbd'] *a* agité(e), troublé(e); **to be mentally/emotionally ~** avoir des problèmes psychologiques/affectifs.

disturbing [distûrb'ing] *a* troublant(e), inquiétant(e).

disuse [disyōos'] *n*: **to fall into ~** tomber en désuétude.

disused [disyōozd'] *a* désaffecté(e).

ditch [dich] *n* fossé *m* ♦ *vt* (*col*) abandonner.

dither [dith'ûr] *vi* hésiter.

ditto [dit'ō] *ad* idem.

divan [divan'] *n* divan *m*.

divan bed *n* divan-lit *m*.

dive [dīv] *n* plongeon *m*; (*of submarine*) plongée *f*; (AVIAT) piqué *m*; (*pej*: *café, bar etc*) bouge *m* ♦ *vi* plonger.

diver [dī'vûr] *n* plongeur *m*.

diverge [divûrj'] *vi* diverger.

divergent [divûr'jənt] *a* divergent(e).

diverse [divûrs'] *a* divers(e).

diversification [divûrsəfəkā'shən] *n* diversification *f*.

diversify [divûr'səfī] *vt* diversifier.

diversion [divûr'zhən] *n* (*distraction*, MIL) diversion *f*; (*Brit* AUT) déviation *f*.

diversity [divûr'sitē] *n* diversité *f*, variété *f*.

divert [divûrt'] *vt* (*plane*) dérouter; (*train, river*) détourner; (*amuse*) divertir; (*Brit*: *traffic*) dévier.

divest [divest'] *vt*: **to ~ sb of** dépouiller qn de.

divide [divīd'] *vt* diviser; (*separate*) séparer ♦ *vi* se diviser; **to ~ (between** *or* **among)** répartir *or* diviser (entre); **40 ~d by 5** 40 divisé par 5.

divide out *vt*: **to ~ out (between** *or* **among)** distribuer *or* répartir (entre).

divided [divīd'id] *a* (*fig*: *country, couple*) désuni(e); (*opinions*) partagé(e).

dividend [div'idend] *n* dividende *m*.

dividend cover *n* rapport *m* dividendes-résultat.

dividers [divī'dûrz] *npl* compas *m* à pointes sèches; (*between pages*) feuillets *mpl* intercalaires.

divine [divīn'] *a* divin(e) ♦ *vt* (*future*) prédire; (*truth*) deviner, entrevoir; (*water, metal*) détecter la présence de (*par l'intermédiaire de la radiesthésie*).

diving [dī'ving] *n* plongée (sous-marine).

diving board [dī'ving bōrd] *n* plongeoir *m*.

diving suit *n* scaphandre *m*.

divinity [divin'ətē] *n* divinité *f*; (*as study*) théologie *f*.

division [divizh'ən] *n* (*also Brit* SOCCER) division *f*; (*separation*) séparation *f*; (*Brit* POL) vote *m*; **~ of labor** division du travail.

divisive [divī'siv] *a* qui entraîne la division, qui crée des dissensions.

divorce [divôrs'] *n* divorce *m* ♦ *vt* divorcer d'avec.

divorced [divôrst'] *a* divorcé(e).

divorcee [divôrsē'] *n* divorcé/e.

divulge [divulj'] *vt* divulguer, révéler.

DIY *a, n abbr* (*Brit*) = **do-it-yourself**.

dizziness [diz'ēnis] *n* vertige *m*, étourdissement *m*.

dizzy [diz'ē] *a* (*height*) vertigineux(euse); **to make sb ~** donner le vertige à qn; **I feel ~** la tête me tourne, j'ai la tête qui tourne.

DJ *n abbr* = **disc jockey**.

Djakarta [jəkâr'tə] *n* Djakarta.

DJIA *n abbr* (*US* STOCK EXCHANGE) = *Dow-Jones Industrial Average*.

dl *abbr* (= *decilitre*) dl.

DLit(t) *n abbr* (= *Doctor of Literature, Doctor of Letters*) *titre universitaire*.

DLO *n abbr* = **dead-letter office**.

dm *abbr* (= *decimetre*) dm.

DMus *n abbr* (= *Doctor of Music*) *titre universitaire*.

DMZ *n abbr* = **demilitarized zone**.

DNA *n abbr* (= *deoxyribonucleic acid*) ADN *m*.

do [dōō] *abbr* (= *ditto*) d°.

do [dōō] *vt, vi* (*pt* **did** [did], *pp* **done** [dun]) faire; (*visit*: *city, museum*) faire, visiter ♦ *n* (*col*: *party*) fête *f*, soirée *f*; (: *formal gathering*) réception *f*; **he didn't laugh** il n'a pas ri; **~ you want any?** en voulez-vous?, est-ce que vous en voulez?; **she swims better than I ~** elle nage mieux que moi; **he laughed, didn't he?** il a ri, n'est-ce pas?; **~ they?** ah oui?, vraiment?; **who broke it? - I did** qui l'a cassé? - (c'est) moi; **~ you agree? - I ~** êtes-vous d'accord? - oui; **you speak better than I ~** tu parles mieux que moi; **so does he** lui aussi; **DO come!** je t'en prie, viens, il faut absolument que tu viennes; **I DO wish I could go** j'aimerais tant y aller; **but I DO like it!** mais si, je l'aime!; **to ~ one's nails/teeth** se faire les ongles/brosser les dents; **to ~ one's hair** se coiffer; **will it ~?** est-ce que ça ira?; **that'll ~!** (*in annoyance*) ça suffit!, c'en est assez!; **to make ~ (with)** se contenter (de); **to ~ without sth** se passer de qch; **what did he ~ with the cat?** qu'a-t-il fait du chat?; **what has that got to ~ with it?** quel rapport y-a-t-il?, qu'est-ce que cela vient faire là-dedans?

do away with *vt fus* supprimer, abolir; (*kill*) supprimer.

do up *vt* remettre à neuf; **to ~ o.s. up** se faire beau(belle).

do with *vt fus*: **I could ~ with a drink** je prendrais bien un verre; **I could ~ with some help** j'aurais bien besoin d'un petit coup de main; **it could ~ with a wash** ça ne lui ferait pas de mal d'être lavé.

DOA *abbr* (= *dead on arrival*) décédé(e) à

l'admission.
d.o.b. *abbr* = **date of birth**.
docile [dâs'əl] *a* docile.
dock [dâk] *n* dock *m*; (*wharf*) quai *m*; (*LAW*) banc *m* des accusés ♦ *vi* se mettre à quai ♦ *vt*: **they ~ed a third of his wages** ils lui ont retenu *or* décompté un tiers de son salaire.
dock dues *npl* droits *mpl* de bassin.
docker [dâk'ûr] *n* docker *m*.
docket [dâk'it] *n* bordereau *m*; (*on parcel etc*) étiquette *f or* fiche *f* (*décrivant le contenu d'un paquet etc*).
dockyard [dâk'yârd] *n* chantier *m* de construction navale.
doctor [dâk'tûr] *n* médecin *m*, docteur *m*; (*PhD etc*) docteur ♦ *vt* (*cat*) couper; (*interfere with: food*) altérer; (*: drink*) frelater; (*: text, document*) arranger; **~'s office** *or* (*Brit*) **surgery** cabinet *m* de consultation; **D~ of Philosophy (PhD)** doctorat *m*; titulaire *m/f* d'un doctorat.
doctorate [dâk'tûrit] *n* doctorat *m*.
doctrine [dâk'trin] *n* doctrine *f*.
document *n* [dâk'yəmənt] document *m* ♦ *vt* [dâk'yəmənt] documenter.
documentary [dâkyəmen'tûrē] *a*, *n* documentaire *(m)*.
documentation [dâkyəməntā'shən] *n* documentation *f*.
DOD *n abbr* (*US*) = **Department of Defense**.
doddering [dâd'ûring] *a* (*senile*) gâteux(euse).
Dodecanese (Islands) [dōdekənēs' (ī'ləndz)] *n(pl)* Dodécanèse *m*.
dodge [dâj] *n* truc *m*; combine *f* ♦ *vt* esquiver, éviter ♦ *vi* faire un saut de côté; (*SPORT*) faire une esquive; **to ~ out of the way** s'esquiver; **to ~ through the traffic** se faufiler *or* faire de savantes manœuvres entre les voitures.
dodgems [dâj'əmz] *npl* autos tamponneuses.
DOE *n abbr* (*US*) = **Department of Energy**; (*Brit*) = **Department of the Environment**.
doe [dō] *n* (*deer*) biche *f*; (*rabbit*) lapine *f*.
does [duz] *see* **do**.
doesn't [duz'nt] = **does not**.
dog [dôg] *n* chien/ne ♦ *vt* (*follow closely*) suivre de près, ne pas lâcher d'une semelle; (*fig: memory etc*) poursuivre, harceler; **to go to the ~s** (*nation etc*) aller à vau-l'eau.
dog biscuits *npl* biscuits *mpl* pour chien.
dog collar *n* collier *m* de chien; (*fig*) faux-col *m* d'ecclésiastique.
dog-eared [dôg'ērd] *a* corné(e).
dog food *n* nourriture *f* pour les chiens *or* le chien.
dogged [dô'gid] *a* obstiné(e), opiniâtre.
dogma [dôg'mə] *n* dogme *m*.
dogmatic [dôgmat'ik] *a* dogmatique.
do-gooder [dōōgōōd'ûr] *n* (*pej*) faiseur/euse de bonnes œuvres.
dogsbody [dôgz'bâdē] *n* (*Brit*) bonne *f* à tout faire, tâcheron *m*.
dog tag *n* (*US*) plaque *f* d'identité.
doing [dōō'ing] *n*: **this is your ~** c'est votre travail, c'est vous qui avez fait ça.
doings [dōō'ingz] *npl* activités *fpl*.
do-it-yourself [dōō'ityōōrself'] *n* bricolage *m*.
do-it-yourselfer [dōō'ityōōrself'ûr] *n* bricoleur *m*, euse *f*.

doldrums [dōl'drəmz] *npl*: **to be in the ~** avoir le cafard; être dans le marasme.
dole [dōl] *n* (*payment*) allocation *f* de chômage; **on the ~** au chômage.
dole out *vt* donner au compte-goutte.
doleful [dōl'fəl] *a* triste, lugubre.
doll [dâl] *n* poupée *f*.
doll up *vt*: **to ~ o.s. up** se faire beau(belle).
dollar [dâl'ûr] *n* dollar *m*.
dollar area *n* zone *f* dollar.
dolphin [dâl'fin] *n* dauphin *m*.
domain [dōmān'] *n* (*also fig*) domaine *m*.
dome [dōm] *n* dôme *m*.
domestic [dəmes'tik] *a* (*duty, happiness*) familial(e); (*policy, affairs, flights*) intérieur(e); (*news*) national(e); (*animal*) domestique.
domesticated [dəmes'tikātid] *a* domestiqué(e); (*pej*) d'intérieur; **he's very ~** il participe volontiers aux tâches ménagères; question ménage, il est très organisé.
domesticity [dōmestis'itē] *n* vie *f* de famille.
domestic servant *n* domestique *m/f*.
domicile [dâm'isīl] *n* domicile *m*.
dominant [dâm'ənənt] *a* dominant(e).
dominate [dâm'ənāt] *vt* dominer.
domination [dâmənā'shən] *n* domination *f*.
domineering [dâmənēr'ing] *a* dominateur(trice), autoritaire.
Dominican Republic [dəmin'əkən ripub'lik] *n* République Dominicaine.
dominion [dəmin'yən] *n* domination *f*; territoire *m*; dominion *m*.
domino [dâm'ənō] *n* domino *m*; **~es** *n* (*game*) dominos *mpl*.
don [dân] *n* (*Brit*) professeur *m* d'université ♦ *vt* revêtir.
donate [dō'nāt] *vt* faire don de, donner.
donation [dōnā'shən] *n* donation *f*, don *m*.
done [dun] *pp of* **do**.
donkey [dâng'kē] *n* âne *m*.
donkey-work *n* (*Brit col*) le gros du travail, le plus dur (du travail).
donor [dō'nûr] *n* (*of blood etc*) donneur/euse; (*to charity*) donateur/trice.
don't [dōnt] = **do not**.
donut [dō'nut] *n* (*US*) = **doughnut**.
doodle [dōōd'əl] *n* griffonnage *m*, gribouillage *m* ♦ *vi* griffonner, gribouiller.
doom [dōōm] *n* (*fate*) destin *m*; (*ruin*) ruine *f* ♦ *vt*: **to be ~ed (to failure)** être voué(e) à l'échec.
doomsday [dōōmz'dā'] *n* le Jugement dernier.
door [dôr] *n* porte *f*; (*of vehicle*) portière *f*, porte; **to go from ~ to ~** aller de porte en porte.
doorbell [dôr'bel] *n* sonnette *f*.
door handle *n* poignée *f* de porte.
doorman [dôr'man] *n* (*in hotel*) portier *m*; (*in block of flats*) concierge *m*.
doormat [dôr'mat] *n* paillasson *m*.
doorpost [dôr'pōst] *n* montant *m* de porte.
doorstep [dôr'step] *n* pas *m* de (la) porte, seuil *m*.
door-to-door [dôr'tədôr'] *a*: **~ selling** vente *f* à domicile.
doorway [dôr'wā] *n* (*embrasure f de*) porte *f*.
dope [dōp] *n* (*col*) drogue *f*; (*: information*) tuyaux *mpl*, rancards *mpl*; (*: fool*) andouille

f ♦ *vt* (*horse etc*) doper.
dopey [dō'pē] *a* (*col*) à moitié endormi(e).
dormant [dôr'mənt] *a* assoupi(e), en veilleuse; (*rule, law*) inappliqué(e).
dormer [dôr'mûr] *n* (*also*: ~ **window**) lucarne *f.*
dormice [dôr'mīs] *npl of* **dormouse.**
dormitory [dôr'mitôrē] *n* dortoir *m*; (*US: for students*) foyer *m* d'étudiants.
dormouse, *pl* **dormice** [dôr'mous, -mīs] *n* loir *m.*
Dors *abbr* (*Brit*) = *Dorset.*
DOS [dôs] *n abbr* = **disk operating system.**
dosage [dō'sij] *n* dose *f*; dosage *m*; (*on label*) posologie *f.*
dose [dōs] *n* dose *f*; (*Brit*: *bout*) attaque *f* ♦ *vt*: **to ~ o.s.** se bourrer de médicaments; **a ~ of flu** une belle *or* bonne grippe.
doss house [dâs' hous] *n* (*Brit*) asile *m* de nuit.
dossier [dâs'ēā] *n* dossier *m.*
DOT *n abbr* (*US*) = **Department of Transportation.**
dot [dât] *n* point *m* ♦ *vt*: ~**ted with** parsemé(e) de; **on the ~** à l'heure tapante.
dot command *n* (*COMPUT*) commande précédée d'un point.
dote [dōt]: **to ~ on** *vt fus* être fou(folle) de.
dot-matrix printer [dâtmāt'riks prin'tûr] *n* imprimante matricielle.
dotted line [dât'id līn'] *n* ligne pointillée; (*AUT*) ligne discontinue; **to sign on the ~** signer à l'endroit indiqué *or* sur la ligne pointillée; (*fig*) donner son consentement.
dotty [dât'ē] *a* (*col*) loufoque, farfelu(e).
double [dub'əl] *a* double ♦ *ad* (*fold*) en deux; (*twice*): **to cost ~** (**sth**) coûter le double (de qch) *or* deux fois plus (que qch) ♦ *n* double *m*; (*CINEMA*) doublure *f* ♦ *vt* doubler; (*fold*) plier en deux ♦ *vi* doubler; (*have two uses*): **to ~ as** servir aussi de; **it's spelled with a ~ "l"** ça s'écrit avec deux ''l''; **on the ~** au pas de course.
   double back *vi* (*person*) revenir sur ses pas.
   double up *vi* (*bend over*) se courber, se plier; (*share room*) partager la chambre.
double bass *n* contrebasse *f.*
double bed *n* grand lit.
double bend *n* (*Brit*) virage *m* en S.
double-breasted [dub'əlbres'tid] *a* croisé(e).
double-check [dub'əlchek'] *vt, vi* revérifier.
double-clutch [dub'əlkluch'] *vi* (*US*) faire un double débrayage.
double cream *n* (*Brit*) crème fraîche épaisse.
doublecross [dub'əlkrôs'] *vt* doubler, trahir.
doubledecker [dub'əldek'ûr] *n* autobus *m* à impériale.
double-declutch [dub'əldēkluch'] *vi* (*Brit*) faire un double débrayage.
double exposure *n* (*PHOT*) surimpression *f.*
double glazing [dub'əl glāz'ing] *n* (*Brit*) double vitrage *m.*
double-page [dub'əlpāj] *a*: ~ **spread** publicité *f* en double page.
double parking *n* stationnement *m* en double file.
double room *n* chambre *f* pour deux.

doubles [dub'əlz] *n* (*TENNIS*) double *m.*
doubly [dub'lē] *ad* doublement, deux fois plus.
doubt [dout] *n* doute *m* ♦ *vt* douter de; **without (a) ~** sans aucun doute; **beyond ~** *ad* indubitablement ♦ *a* indubitable; **to ~ that** douter que; **I ~ it very much** j'en doute fort.
doubtful [dout'fəl] *a* douteux(euse); (*person*) incertain(e); **to be ~ about sth** avoir des doutes sur qch, ne pas être convaincu de qch; **I'm a bit ~** je n'en suis pas certain *or* sûr.
doubtless [dout'lis] *ad* sans doute, sûrement.
dough [dō] *n* pâte *f*; (*col*: *money*) fric *m*, pognon *m.*
doughnut [dō'nut] *n* beignet *m.*
dour [dōōr] *a* austère.
douse [dous] *vt* (*with water*) tremper, inonder; (*flames*) éteindre.
dove [duv] *n* colombe *f.*
Dover [dō'vûr] *n* Douvres.
dovetail [duv'tāl] *n*: ~ **joint** assemblage *m* à queue d'aronde ♦ *vi* (*fig*) concorder.
dowager [dou'əjûr] *n* douairière *f.*
dowdy [dou'dē] *a* démodé(e); mal fagoté(e).
Dow-Jones average [dou'jōnz' av'ûrij] *n* (*US*) indice boursier Dow-Jones.
down [doun] *n* (*fluff*) duvet *m*; (*hill*) colline (dénudée) ♦ *ad* en bas ♦ *prep* en bas de ♦ *vt* (*enemy*) abattre; (*col*: *drink*) siffler; ~ **there** là-bas (en bas), là au fond; ~ **here** ici en bas; **the price of meat is** ~ le prix de la viande a baissé; **I've got it** ~ **in my diary** c'est inscrit dans mon agenda; **to pay $2** ~ verser 2 dollars d'arrhes *or* en acompte; **England is two goals** ~ l'Angleterre a deux buts de retard; **to ~ tools** (*Brit*) cesser le travail; ~ **with X!** à bas X!
down-and-out [doun'ənout] *n* (*tramp*) clochard/e.
down-at-heel(s) [dounat·hēl(z)'] *a* (*fig*) miteux(euse).
downbeat [doun'bēt] *n* (*MUS*) temps frappé ♦ *a* sombre, négatif(ive).
downcast [doun'kast] *a* démoralisé(e).
downer [dou'nûr] *n* (*col*: *drug*) tranquillisant *m*; **to be on a** ~ (*depressed*) flipper.
downfall [doun'fôl] *n* chute *f*; ruine *f.*
downgrade [doun'grād] *vt* déclasser.
downhearted [doun'hâr'tid] *a* découragé(e).
downhill [doun'hil'] *ad* (*face, look*) en aval, vers l'aval; (*roll, go*) vers le bas, en bas ♦ *n* (*SKI*: *also*: ~ **race**) descente *f*; **to go** ~ descendre; (*business*) péricliter, aller à vau-l'eau.
Downing Street [dou'ning strēt] *n* (*Brit*): **10** ~ *résidence du Premier ministre.*
download [doun'lōd] *vt* télécharger.
down-market [doun'dmár'kıt] *a* (*Brit*: *product*) bas de gamme *inv.*
down payment *n* acompte *m.*
downplay [doun'plā] *vt* (*US*) minimiser (l'importance de).
downpour [doun'pôr] *n* pluie torrentielle, déluge *m.*
downright [doun'rīt] *a* franc(franche); (*refusal*) catégorique.
Down's syndrome [dounz' sin'drōm] *n* (*MED*) trisomie *f*, mongolisme *m.*
downstairs [doun'stärz'] *ad* (*on or to ground*

floor) au rez-de-chaussée; (*on or to floor below*) à l'étage inférieur; **to come ~, to go ~** descendre (l'escalier).

downstream [doun'strēm'] *ad* en aval.

downtime [doun'tīm] *n* (*of machine etc*) temps mort; (*of person*) temps d'arrêt.

down-to-earth [dountōōúrth'] *a* terre à terre *inv.*

downtown [doun'toun'] *ad* en ville ♦ *a* (*US*): **~ Chicago** le centre commerçant de Chicago.

downtrodden [doun'trâdən] *a* opprimé(e).

down under *ad* en Australie (*or* Nouvelle Zélande).

downward [doun'wûrd] *a* vers le bas; **a ~ trend** une tendance à la baisse, une diminution progressive.

downward(s) [doun'wûrd(z)] *ad* vers le bas.

dowry [dou'rē] *n* dot *f.*

doz. *abbr* (= *dozen*) douz.

doze [dōz] *vi* sommeiller.

doze off *vi* s'assoupir.

dozen [duz'ən] *n* douzaine *f*; **a ~ books** une douzaine de livres; **80¢ a ~** 80¢ la douzaine; **~s of times** des centaines de fois.

DPh, DPhil *n abbr* (= *Doctor of Philosophy*) *titre universitaire*.

DPP *n abbr* (*Brit*) = **Director of Public Prosecutions**.

DPT *n abbr* (*MED*: = *diphtheria, pertussis, tetanus*) DCT *m.*

DPW *n abbr* (*US*) = *Department of Public Works.*

Dr, Dr. *abbr* (= *doctor*) Dr.

Dr. *abbr* (*in street names*) = **drive.**

dr *abbr* (*COMM*) = **debtor.**

drab [drab] *a* terne, morne.

draft [draft] *n* brouillon *m*; (*of contract, document*) version *f* préliminaire; (*COMM*) traite *f*; (*US*: *MIL*) contingent *m*; (: *call-up*) conscription *f*; (: *of air*) courant m d air; (: *of chimney*) tirage *m*; (: *NAUT*) tirant *m* d'eau ♦ *vt* faire le brouillon de; (*document, report*) rédiger une version préliminaire de; **on ~** (*beer*) à la pression.

draftee [draftē'] *n* (*US MIL*) appelé *m.*

draftsman [drafts'mən] *n* (*US*) dessinateur/trice (industriel(le)).

draftsmanship [drafts'mənship] *n* (*US*: *technique*) dessin industriel; (: *art*) graphisme *m.*

drag [drag] *vt* traîner; (*river*) draguer ♦ *vi* traîner ♦ *n* (*AVIAT, NAUT*) résistance *f*, (*col*: *person*) raseur/euse; (: *task etc*) corvée *f*; (*women's clothing*): **in ~** (en) travesti.

drag away *vt*: **to ~ away (from)** arracher *or* emmener de force (de).

drag on *vi* s'éterniser.

dragnet [drag'net] *n* drège *f*; (*fig*) piège *m*, filets *mpl.*

dragon [drag'ən] *n* dragon *m.*

dragonfly [drag'ənflī] *n* libellule *f.*

dragoon [drəgōōn'] *n* (*cavalryman*) dragon *m* ♦ *vt*: **to ~ sb into doing sth** (*Brit*) forcer qn à faire qch.

drain [drān] *n* égout *m*; (*on resources*) saignée *f* ♦ *vt* (*land, marshes*) drainer, assécher; (*vegetables*) égoutter; (*reservoir etc*) vider ♦ *vi* (*water*) s'écouler; **to feel ~ed (of energy *or* emotion)** être miné(e).

drainage [drā'nij] *n* système *m* d'égouts.

drainboard [drān'bôrd], (*Brit*) **draining board** [drā'ning bôrd] *n* égouttoir *m.*

drainpipe [drān'pīp] *n* tuyau *m* d'écoulement.

drake [drāk] *n* canard *m* (mâle).

dram [dram] *n* petit verre.

drama [drám'ə] *n* (*art*) théâtre *m*, art *m* dramatique; (*play*) pièce *f*; (*event*) drame *m.*

dramatic [drəmat'ik] *a* (*THEATER*) dramatique; (*impressive*) spectaculaire.

dramatically [drəmat'iklē] *ad* de façon spectaculaire.

dramatist [dram'ətist] *n* auteur *m* dramatique.

dramatize [dram'ətīz] *vt* (*events etc*) dramatiser; (*adapt*) adapter pour la télévision (*or* pour l'écran).

drank [drangk] *pt of* **drink.**

drape [drāp] *vt* draper.

drapes [drāps] *npl* (*US*) rideaux *mpl.*

drastic [dras'tik] *a* (*measures*) d'urgence, énergique; (*change*) radical(e).

drastically [dras'tiklē] *ad* radicalement.

draught [draft] *n* courant m d'air; (*of chimney*) tirage *m*; (*NAUT*) tirant *m* d'eau; **on ~** (*beer*) à la pression.

draughtboard [draft'bôrd] *n* (*Brit*) damier *m.*

draughts [drafts] *n* (*Brit*) (jeu *m* de) dames *fpl.*

draughtsman [drafts'mən] *etc* (*Brit*) = **draftsman** *etc.*

draw [drô] *vb* (*pt* **drew**, *pp* **drawn** [drōō, drôn]) *vt* tirer; (*attract*) attirer; (*picture*) dessiner; (*line, circle*) tracer; (*money*) retirer; (*comparison, distinction*): **to ~ (between)** faire (entre) ♦ *vi* (*SPORT*) faire match nul ♦ *n* match nul; (*lottery*) loterie *f*; (: *picking of ticket*) tirage *m* au sort; **to ~ to a close** toucher à *or* tirer à sa fin; **to ~ near** *vi* s'approcher; approcher.

draw back *vi* (*move back*): **to ~ back (from)** reculer (de).

draw in *vi* (*Brit*: *car*) s'arrêter le long du trottoir; (: *train*) entrer en gare *or* dans la station.

draw on *vt* (*resources*) faire appel à; (*imagination, person*) avoir recours à, faire appel à.

draw out *vi* (*lengthen*) s'allonger ♦ *vt* (*money*) retirer.

draw up *vi* (*stop*) s'arrêter ♦ *vt* (*document*) établir, dresser; (*plans*) formuler, dessiner.

drawback [drô'bak] *n* inconvénient *m*, désavantage *m.*

drawbridge [drô'brij] *n* pont-levis *m.*

drawee [drôē'] *n* tiré *m.*

drawer [drôr] *n* tiroir *m*; [drô'ûr] (*of check*) tireur *m.*

drawing [drô'ing] *n* dessin *m.*

drawing board *n* planche *f* à dessin.

drawing pin *n* (*Brit*) punaise *f.*

drawing room *n* salon *m.*

drawl [drôl] *n* accent traînant.

drawn [drôn] *pp of* **draw** ♦ *a* (*haggard*) tiré(e), crispé(e).

drawstring [drô'string] *n* cordon *m.*

dread [dred] *n* épouvante *f*, effroi *m* ♦ *vt* redouter, appréhender.

dreadful [dred'fəl] *a* épouvantable, affreux(euse).

dream [drēm] *n* rêve *m* ♦ *vt, vi* (*pt, pp*

dreamed *or* **dreamt** [dremt]) rêver; **to have a ~ about sb/sth** rêver à qn/qch; **sweet ~s!** faites de beaux rêves!
dream up *vt* inventer.
dreamer [drē'mûr] *n* rêveur/euse.
dream world *n* monde *m* imaginaire.
dreamy [drē'mē] *a* (*absent-minded*) rêveur(euse).
dreary [drēr'ē] *a* triste; monotone.
dredge [drej] *vt* draguer.
  dredge up *vt* draguer; (*fig: unpleasant facts*) (faire) ressortir.
dredger [drej'ûr] *n* (*ship*) dragueur *m*; (*machine*) drague *f*; (*for sugar*) saupoudreuse *f*.
dregs [dregz] *npl* lie *f*.
drench [drench] *vt* tremper; **~ed to the skin** trempé(e) jusqu'aux os.
dress [dres] *n* robe *f*; (*clothing*) habillement *m*, tenue *f* ♦ *vt* habiller; (*wound*) panser; (*food*) préparer ♦ *vi*: **she ~es very well** elle s'habille très bien; **to ~ o.s., to get ~ed** s'habiller; **to ~ a shop window** faire l'étalage *or* la vitrine.
  dress up *vi* s'habiller; (*in fancy dress*) se déguiser.
dress circle *n* (*Brit*) premier balcon.
dress designer *n* modéliste *m/f*, dessinateur/trice de mode.
dresser [dres'ûr] *n* (*THEATER*) habilleur/euse; (*also*: **window ~**) étalagiste *m/f*; (*furniture*) vaisselier *m*.
dressing [dres'ing] *n* (*MED*) pansement *m*; (*CULIN*) sauce *f*, assaisonnement *m*.
dressing gown *n* (*Brit*) robe *f* de chambre.
dressing room *n* (*THEATER*) loge *f*; (*SPORT*) vestiaire *m*.
dressing table *n* coiffeuse *f*.
dressmaker [dres'mākûr] *n* couturière *f*.
dressmaking [dres'māking] *n* couture *f*; travaux *mpl* de couture.
dress rehearsal *n* (répétition *f*) générale.
dress shirt *n* chemise *f* à plastron.
dressy [dres'ē] *a* (*col: clothes*) (qui fait) habillé(e).
drew [drōō] *pt of* **draw**.
dribble [drib'əl] *vi* tomber goutte à goutte; (*baby*) baver ♦ *vt* (*ball*) dribbler.
dried [drīd] *a* (*fruit, beans*) sec(sèche); (*eggs, milk*) en poudre.
drier [drī'ûr] *n* = **dryer**.
drift [drift] *n* (*of current etc*) force *f*; direction *f*; (*of sand etc*) amoncellement *m*; (*of snow*) rafale *f*; coulée *f*; (: *on ground*) congère *f*; (*general meaning*) sens général ♦ *vi* (*boat*) aller à la dérive, dériver; (*sand, snow*) s'amonceler, s'entasser; **to let things ~** laisser les choses aller à la dérive; **to ~ apart** (*friends, lovers*) s'éloigner l'un de l'autre; **I get** *or* **catch your ~** je vois en gros ce que vous voulez dire.
drifter [drif'tûr] *n* personne *f* sans but dans la vie.
driftwood [drift'wōōd] *n* bois flotté.
drill [dril] *n* perceuse *f*; (*bit*) foret *m*; (*of dentist*) roulette *f*, fraise *f*; (*MIL*) exercice *m* ♦ *vt* percer; (*soldiers*) faire faire l'exercice à; (*pupils: in grammar*) faire faire des exercices à ♦ *vi* (*for oil*) faire un *or* des forage(s).

drilling [dril'ing] *n* (*for oil*) forage *m*.
drilling rig *n* (*on land*) tour *f* (de forage), derrick *m*; (*at sea*) plate-forme *f* de forage.
drily [drī'lē] *ad* = **dryly**.
drink [dringk] *n* boisson *f* ♦ *vt, vi* (*pt* **drank**, *pp* **drunk** [drangk, drungk]) boire; **to have a ~** boire quelque chose, boire un verre; **a ~ of water** un verre d'eau; **would you like something to ~?** aimeriez-vous boire quelque chose?; **we had ~s before lunch** on a pris l'apéritif.
  drink in *vt* (*fresh air*) inspirer profondément; (*story*) avaler, ne pas perdre une miette de; (*sight*) se remplir la vue de.
drinkable [dring'kəbəl] *a* (*not dangerous*) potable; (*palatable*) buvable.
drinker [dring'kûr] *n* buveur/euse.
drinking [dring'king] *n* (*drunkenness*) boisson *f*, alcoolisme *m*.
drinking fountain *n* (*in park etc*) fontaine publique; (*in building*) jet *m* d'eau potable.
drinking water *n* eau *f* potable.
drip [drip] *n* goutte *f*; (*sound: of water etc*) bruit *m* de l'eau qui tombe goutte à goutte; (*Brit MED*) goutte-à-goutte *m inv*, perfusion *f*; (*col: person*) lavette *f*, nouille *f* ♦ *vi* tomber goutte à goutte; (*washing*) s'égoutter; (*wall*) suinter.
drip-dry [drip'drī] *a* (*shirt*) sans repassage.
drip-feed [drip'fēd] *vt* (*Brit*) alimenter au goutte-à-goutte *or* par perfusion.
dripping [drip'ing] *n* graisse *f* de rôti ♦ *a*: **~ wet** trempé(e).
drive [drīv] *n* promenade *f or* trajet *m* en voiture; (*also*: **~way**) allée *f*; (*energy*) dynamisme *m*, énergie *f*; (*PSYCH*) besoin *m*; pulsion *f*; (*push*) effort (concerté) *m*; campagne *f*; (*SPORT*) drive *m*; (*TECH*) entraînement *m*; traction *f*; transmission *f* ♦ *vb* (*pt* **drove**, *pp* **driven** [drōv, driv'ən]) *vt* conduire; (*nail*) enfoncer; (*push*) chasser, pousser; (*TECH: motor*) actionner; entraîner; (*COMPUT: also*: **disk ~**) lecteur *m* de disquette ♦ *vi* (*be at the wheel*) conduire; (*travel by car*) aller en voiture; **to go for a ~** aller faire une promenade en voiture; **it's 3 hours' ~ from Philadelphia** Philadelphie est à 3 heures de route; **left-/right-hand ~** (*AUT*) conduite *f* à gauche/droite; **front-/rear-wheel ~** (*AUT*) traction *f* avant/arrière; **to ~ sb to (do) sth** pousser *or* conduire qn à (faire) qch; **to ~ sb mad** rendre qn fou(folle).
  drive at *vt fus* (*fig: intend, mean*) vouloir dire, en venir à.
  drive on *vi* poursuivre sa route, continuer; (*after stopping*) reprendre sa route, repartir ♦ *vt* (*incite, encourage*) inciter.
drive-in [drīv'in] *a, n* (*esp US*) drive-in (*m*).
drive-in window *n* (*US*) guichet-auto *m*.
drivel [driv'əl] *n* (*col*) idioties *fpl*, imbécillités *fpl*.
driven [driv'ən] *pp of* **drive**.
driver [drī'vûr] *n* conducteur/trice; (*of taxi, bus*) chauffeur *m*.
driver's license *n* (*US*) permis *m* de conduire.
driveway [drīv'wā] *n* allée *f*.
driving [drī'ving] *a*: **~ rain** *n* pluie battante ♦ *n* conduite *f*.

driving belt *n* courroie *f* de transmission.
driving force *n* locomotive *f*, élément *m* dynamique.
driving instructor *n* moniteur *m* d'auto-école.
driving lesson *n* leçon *f* de conduite.
driving licence *n* (*Brit*) permis *m* de conduire.
driving school *n* auto-école *f*.
driving test *n* examen *m* du permis de conduire.
drizzle [driz'əl] *n* bruine *f*, crachin *m* ♦ *vi* bruiner.
droll [drōl] *a* drôle.
dromedary [drâm'idärē] *n* dromadaire *m*.
drone [drōn] *vi* (*bee*) bourdonner; (*engine etc*) ronronner; (*also:* ~ **on**) parler d'une voix monocorde ♦ *n* bourdonnement *m*; ronronnement *m*; (*male bee*) faux-bourdon *m*.
drool [drool] *vi* baver; **to** ~ **over sb/sth** (*fig*) baver d'admiration *or* être en extase devant qn/qch.
droop [droop] *vi* s'affaisser; tomber.
drop [drâp] *n* goutte *f*; (*fall: also in price*) baisse *f*; (: *in salary*) réduction *f*; (*also:* **parachute** ~) saut *m*; (*of cliff*) dénivellation *f*; à-pic *m* ♦ *vt* laisser tomber; (*voice, eyes, price*) baisser; (*set down from car*) déposer ♦ *vi* (*wind, temperature, price, voice*) tomber; (*numbers, attendance*) diminuer; ~**s** *npl* (*MED*) gouttes; **cough** ~**s** pastilles *fpl* pour la toux; **a** ~ **of 10%** une baisse (*or* réduction) de 10%; **to** ~ **anchor** jeter l'ancre; **to** ~ **sb a line** mettre un mot à qn.
drop in *vi* (*col: visit*): **to** ~ **in (on)** faire un saut (chez), passer (chez).
drop off *vi* (*sleep*) s'assoupir ♦ *vt*: **to** ~ **sb off** déposer qn.
drop out *vi* (*withdraw*) se retirer; (*student etc*) abandonner, décrocher.
droplet [drâp'lit] *n* gouttelette *f*.
dropout [drâp'out] *n* (*from society*) marginal/e; (*from university*) drop-out *m/f*, dropé/e.
dropper [drâp'ûr] *n* (*MED etc*) compte-gouttes *m inv*.
droppings [drâp'ingz] *npl* crottes *fpl*.
dross [drôs] *n* déchets *mpl*; rebut *m*.
drought [drout] *n* sécheresse *f*.
drove [drōv] *pt of* **drive** ♦ *n*: ~**s of people** une foule de gens.
drown [droun] *vt* noyer; (*also:* ~ **out**: *sound*) couvrir, étouffer ♦ *vi* se noyer.
drowse [drouz] *vi* somnoler.
drowsy [drou'zē] *a* somnolent(e).
drudge [druj] *n* bête *f* de somme (*fig*).
drudgery [druj'ûrē] *n* corvée *f*.
drug [drug] *n* médicament *m*; (*narcotic*) drogue *f* ♦ *vt* droguer; **he's on** ~**s** il se drogue; (*MED*) il est sous médication.
drug addict *n* toxicomane *m/f*.
druggist [drug'ist] *n* (*US*) pharmacien/ne-droguiste.
drug peddler *n* revendeur/euse de drogue.
drugstore [drug'stôr] *n* pharmacie-droguerie *f*, drugstore *m*.
drum [drum] *n* tambour *m*; (*for oil, gasoline*) bidon *m* ♦ *vt*: **to** ~ **one's fingers on the table** pianoter *or* tambouriner sur la table; ~**s** *npl* (*MUS*) batterie *f*.

drum up *vt* (*enthusiasm, support*) susciter, rallier.
drummer [drum'ûr] *n* (joueur *m* de) tambour *m*.
drum roll *n* roulement *m* de tambour.
drumstick [drum'stik] *n* (*MUS*) baguette *f* de tambour; (*of chicken*) pilon *m*.
drunk [drungk] *pp of* **drink** ♦ *a* ivre, soûl(e) ♦ *n* soûlard/e; homme/femme soûl(e); **to get** ~ s'enivrer, se soûler.
drunkard [drung'kûrd] *n* ivrogne *m/f*.
drunken [drung'kən] *a* ivre, soûl(e); (*habitual*) ivrogne, d'ivrogne; ~ **driving** conduite *f* en état d'ivresse.
drunkenness [drung'kənnis] *n* ivresse *f*; ivrognerie *f*.
dry [drī] *a* sec(sèche); (*day*) sans pluie; (*humor*) pince-sans-rire; (*uninteresting*) aride, rébarbatif(ive) ♦ *vt* sécher; (*clothes*) faire sécher ♦ *vi* sécher; **on** ~ **land** sur la terre ferme; **to** ~ **one's hands/hair/eyes** se sécher les mains/les cheveux/les yeux.
dry up *vi* (*also fig: source of supply, imagination*) se tarir; (: *speaker*) sécher, rester sec.
dry-clean [drī'klēn'] *vt* nettoyer à sec.
dry-cleaner [drī'klē'nûr] *n* teinturier *m*.
dry-cleaner's [drī'klē'nûrz] *n* teinturerie *f*.
dry-cleaning [drī'klē'ning] *n* nettoyage *m* à sec.
dry dock *n* (*NAUT*) cale sèche, bassin *m* de radoub.
dryer [drī'ûr] *n* séchoir *m*; (*spin-*~) essoreuse *f*.
dry goods *npl* (*COMM*) textiles *mpl*, mercerie *f*.
dry goods store *n* (*US*) magasin *m* de nouveautés.
dry ice *n* neige *f* carbonique.
dryly [drī'lē] *ad* sèchement; d'un ton pince-sans-rire.
dryness [drī'nis] *n* sécheresse *f*.
dry rot *n* pourriture sèche (*du bois*).
dry run *n* (*fig*) essai *m*.
dry ski slope *n* piste (de ski) artificielle.
DSc *n abbr* (= *Doctor of Science*) *titre universitaire*.
DSS *n abbr* (*Brit*) = **Department of Social Security**.
DST *abbr* (*US:* = *Daylight Saving Time*) *heure d'été*.
DT *n abbr* (*COMPUT*) = **data transmission**.
DTI *n abbr* (*Brit*) = **Department of Trade and Industry**.
DT's *n abbr* (*col:* = *delirium tremens*) delirium tremens *m*.
dual [doo'əl] *a* double.
dual carriageway *n* (*Brit*) route *f* à quatre voies.
dual-control [doo'əlkəntrōl'] *a* à doubles commandes.
dual nationality *n* double nationalité *f*.
dual-purpose [doo'əlpûr'pəs] *a* à double emploi.
dubbed [dubd] *a* (*CINEMA*) doublé(e); (*nicknamed*) surnommé(e).
dubious [doo'bēəs] *a* hésitant(e), incertain(e); (*reputation, company*) douteux(euse); **I'm very** ~ **about it** j'ai des doutes sur la

question, je n'en suis pas sûr du tout.

Dublin [dub'lin] *n* Dublin.

Dubliner [dub'linûr] *n* habitant/e de Dublin; originaire *m/f* de Dublin.

duchess [duch'is] *n* duchesse *f*.

duck [duk] *n* canard *m* ♦ *vi* se baisser vivement, baisser subitement la tête ♦ *vt* plonger dans l'eau.

duckling [duk'ling] *n* caneton *m*.

duct [dukt] *n* conduite *f*, canalisation *f*; (*ANAT*) conduit *m*.

dud [dud] *n* (*shell*) obus non éclaté; (*object, tool*): **it's a ~** c'est de la camelote, ça ne marche pas ♦ *a* (*Brit: check*) sans provision; (*: note, coin*) faux(fausse).

dude [dōōd] *n* (*US col*) coco *m*.

due [dōō] *a* dû(due); (*expected*) attendu(e); (*fitting*) qui convient ♦ *n* dû *m* ♦ *ad*: **~ north** droit vers le nord; **~s** *npl* (*for club, union*) cotisation *f*; (*in harbor*) droits *mpl* (de port); **in ~ course** en temps utile *or* voulu; (*in the end*) finalement; **~ to** dû à; causé par; **the rent is ~ on the 30th** il faut payer le loyer le 30; **the train is ~ at 8** le train est attendu à 8h; **she is ~ back tomorrow** elle doit rentrer demain; **I am ~ 6 days' leave** j'ai droit à 6 jours de congé.

due date *n* date *f* d'échéance.

duel [dōō'əl] *n* duel *m*.

duet [dōōet'] *n* duo *m*.

duff [duf] *a* (*Brit col*) nullard(e), nul(le).

duffelbag, duffle bag [duf'əlbag] *n* sac marin.

duffelcoat, duffle coat [duf'əlkōt] *n* duffel-coat *m*.

duffer [duf'ûr] *n* (*col*) nullard/e.

dug [dug] *pt*, *pp of* **dig**.

duke [dōōk] *n* duc *m*.

dull [dul] *a* (*boring*) ennuyeux(euse); (*slow*) borné(e); (*lackluster*) morne, terne; (*sound, pain*) sourd(e); (*weather, day*) gris(e), maussade; (*blade*) émoussé(e) ♦ *vt* (*pain, grief*) atténuer; (*mind, senses*) engourdir.

duly [dōō'lē] *ad* (*on time*) en temps voulu; (*as expected*) comme il se doit.

dumb [dum] *a* muet(te); (*stupid*) bête; **to be struck ~** (*fig*) rester abasourdi(e), être sidéré(e).

dumbbell [dum'bel] *n* (*SPORT*) haltère *m*; (*fig*) gourde *f*.

dumbfounded [dumfound'id] *a* sidéré(e).

dummy [dum'ē] *n* (*tailor's model*) mannequin *m*; (*SPORT*) feinte *f*; (*Brit: for baby*) tétine *f* ♦ *a* faux(fausse), factice.

dummy run *n* essai *m*.

dump [dump] *n* tas *m* d'ordures; (*place*) décharge (publique); (*MIL*) dépôt *m*; (*COMPUT*) listage *m* (de la mémoire) ♦ *vt* (*put down*) déposer; déverser; (*get rid of*) se débarrasser de; (*COMPUT*) lister; (*COMM: goods*) vendre à perte (*sur le marché extérieur*); **to be (down) in the ~s** (*col*) avoir le cafard, broyer du noir.

dumping [dum'ping] *n* (*ECON*) dumping *m*; (*of garbage*): **"no ~"** "décharge interdite".

dumpling [dump'ling] *n* boulette *f* (de pâte).

dumpy [dump'ē] *a* courtaud(e), boulot(te).

dunce [duns] *n* âne *m*, cancre *m*.

dune [dōōn] *n* dune *f*.

dung [dung] *n* fumier *m*.

dungarees [dunggərēz'] *npl* bleu(s) *m(pl)*; (*for child, woman*) salopette *f*.

dungeon [dun'jən] *n* cachot *m*.

dunk [dungk] *vt* tremper.

Dunkirk [dun'kûrk] *n* Dunkerque.

duo [dōō'ō] *n* (*gen, MUS*) duo *m*.

duodenal [dōōədē'nəl] *a* duodénal(e); **~ ulcer** ulcère *m* du duodénum.

dupe [dōōp] *n* dupe *f* ♦ *vt* duper, tromper.

duplex [dōōp'leks] *n* (*US: also: ~ apartment*) duplex *m*.

duplicate [dōō'plikit] *n* double *m*, copie exacte; (*copy of letter etc*) duplicata *m* ♦ *a* (*copy*) en double ♦ *vt* [dōō'plikāt] faire un double de; (*on machine*) polycopier; **in ~** en deux exemplaires, en double; **~ key** double *m* de la (*or* d'une) clé.

duplicating machine [dōō'plikāting məshēn'], **duplicator** [dōō'plikātûr] *n* duplicateur *m*.

duplicity [dōōplis'ətē] *n* duplicité *f*, fausseté *f*.

Dur *abbr* (*Brit*) = *Durham*.

durability [dōōrəbil'ətē] *n* solidité *f*; durabilité *f*.

durable [dōōr'əbəl] *a* durable; (*clothes, metal*) résistant(e), solide.

duration [dōōrā'shən] *n* durée *f*.

duress [dōōres'] *n*: **under ~** sous la contrainte.

Durex [dōō'reks] *n* ® (*Brit*) préservatif (masculin).

during [dōōr'ing] *prep* pendant, au cours de.

dusk [dusk] *n* crépuscule *m*.

dusky [dus'kē] *a* sombre.

dust [dust] *n* poussière *f* ♦ *vt* (*furniture*) essuyer, épousseter; (*cake etc*): **to ~ with** saupoudrer de.

dust off *vt* (*also fig*) dépoussiérer.

dustbin [dust'bin] *n* (*Brit*) poubelle *f*.

duster [dus'tûr] *n* chiffon *m*.

dust jacket *n* jaquette *f*.

dustman [dust'man] *n* (*Brit*) boueux *m*, éboueur *m*.

dustpan [dust'pan] *n* pelle *f* à poussière.

dusty [dus'tē] *a* poussiéreux(euse).

Dutch [duch] *a* hollandais(e), néerlandais(e) ♦ *n* (*LING*) hollandais *m*, néerlandais *m* ♦ *ad*: **to go ~** *or* **d~** partager les frais; **the ~** *npl* les Hollandais, les Néerlandais.

Dutch auction *n* enchères *fpl* à la baisse.

Dutchman [duch'mən], **Dutchwoman** [duch'wŏomən] *n* Hollandais/e.

dutiable [dōō'tēəbəl] *a* taxable; soumis(e) à des droits de douane.

dutiful [dōō'tifəl] *a* (*child*) respectueux(euse); (*husband, wife*) plein(e) d'égards, prévenant(e); (*employee*) consciencieux(euse).

duty [dōō'tē] *n* devoir *m*; (*tax*) droit *m*, taxe *f*; **duties** *npl* fonctions *fpl*; **to make it one's ~ to do sth** se faire un devoir de faire qch; **to pay ~ on sth** payer un droit *or* une taxe sur qch; **on ~** de service; (*at night etc*) de garde; **off ~** libre, pas de service *or* de garde.

duty-free [dōō'tēfrē'] *a* exempté(e) de douane, hors-taxe; **~ shop** boutique *f* hors-taxe.

duty officer *n* (*MIL etc*) officier *m* de permanence.

duvet [dōō'vā] *n* (*Brit*) couette *f*.

DV *abbr* (= *Deo volente*) si Dieu le veut.

DVM *n abbr* (*US:* = *Doctor of Veterinary Medicine*) titre universitaire.

dwarf [dwôrf] *n* nain/e ♦ *vt* écraser.

dwell, *pt, pp* **dwelt** [dwel, dwelt] *vi* demeurer.
dwell on *vt fus* s'étendre sur.

dweller [dwel'úr] *n* habitant/e.

dwelling [dwel'ing] *n* habitation *f*, demeure *f*.

dwindle [dwin'dəl] *vi* diminuer, décroître.

dwindling [dwin'dling] *a* décroissant(e), en diminution.

dye [dī] *n* teinture *f* ♦ *vt* teindre; **hair ~** teinture pour les cheveux.

dyestuffs [dī'stufs] *npl* colorants *mpl*.

dying [dī'ing] *a* mourant(e), agonisant(e).

dyke [dīk] *n* (*embankment*) digue *f*.

dynamic [dīnam'ik] *a* dynamique.

dynamics [dīnam'iks] *n or npl* dynamique *f*.

dynamite [dī'nəmīt] *n* dynamite *f* ♦ *vt* dynamiter, faire sauter à la dynamite.

dynamo [dī'nəmō] *n* dynamo *f*.

dynasty [dī'nəstē] *n* dynastie *f*.

dysentery [dis'əntärē] *n* dysenterie *f*.

dyslexia [dislek'sēə] *n* dyslexie *f*.

dyslexic [dislek'sik] *a*, *n* dyslexique *m/f*.

dyspepsia [dispep'shə] *n* dyspepsie *f*.

dystrophy [dis'trəfē] *n* dystrophie *f*; **muscular ~** dystrophie musculaire.

E

E, e [ē] *n* (*letter*) E, e *m*; (*MUS*): **E** mi *m*; **E for Easy** E comme Eugène.

E [ē] *abbr* (= *east*) E.

E111 *n abbr* (*Brit: also:* **form ~**) formulaire *m* E111.

ea. *abbr* = **each.**

E.A. *n abbr* (*US:* = *educational age*) niveau scolaire.

each [ēch] *a* chaque ♦ *pronoun* chacun(e); **~ one** chacun(e); **~ other** se (*or* nous *etc*); **they hate ~ other** ils se détestent (mutuellement); **you are jealous of ~ other** vous êtes jaloux l'un de l'autre; **~ day** chaque jour, tous les jours; **they have 2 books ~** ils ont 2 livres chacun; **they cost $5 ~** ils coûtent 5 dollars (la) pièce; **~ of us** chacun(e) de nous.

eager [ē'gûr] *a* impatient(e); avide; ardent(e), passionné(e); (*keen: pupil*) plein(e) d'enthousiasme, qui se passionne pour les études; **to be ~ to do sth** être impatient de faire qch, brûler de faire qch; désirer vivement faire qch; **to be ~ for** désirer vivement, être avide de.

eagle [ē'gəl] *n* aigle *m*.

E and OE *abbr* = **errors and omissions excepted.**

ear [ēr] *n* oreille *f*; (*of corn*) épi *m*; **up to one's ~s in debt** endetté(e) jusqu'au cou.

earache [ēr'āk] *n* douleurs *fpl* aux oreilles.

eardrum [ēr'drum] *n* tympan *m*.

earl [ûrl] *n* comte *m*.

earlier [ûr'lēûr] *a* (*date etc*) plus rapproché(e); (*edition etc*) plus ancien(ne), antérieur(e) ♦ *ad* plus tôt.

early [ûr'lē] *ad* tôt, de bonne heure; (*ahead of time*) en avance ♦ *a* précoce; qui se manifeste (*or* se fait) tôt *or* de bonne heure; (*Christians, settlers*) premier(ière); **have an ~ night/start** couchez-vous/partez tôt *or* de bonne heure; **take the ~ train** prenez le premier train; **in the ~** *or* **~ in the spring/19th century** au début *or* commencement du printemps/19ème siècle; **you're ~!** tu es en avance!; **~ in the morning** tôt le matin; **she's in her ~ forties** elle a un peu plus de quarante ans *or* de la quarantaine; **at your earliest convenience** (*COMM*) dans les meilleurs délais.

early retirement *n* retraite anticipée.

early warning system *n* système *m* de première alerte.

earmark [ēr'márk] *vt*: **to ~ sth for** réserver *or* destiner qch à.

earn [ûrn] *vt* gagner; (*COMM: yield*) rapporter; **to ~ one's living** gagner sa vie; **this ~ed him much praise, he ~ed much praise for this** ceci lui a valu de nombreux éloges; **he's ~ed his rest/reward** il mérite *or* a bien mérité *or* a bien gagné son repos/sa récompense.

earned income [ûrnd' in'kum] *n* revenu *m* du travail.

earnest [ûr'nist] *a* sérieux(euse) ♦ *n* (*also:* **~ money**) acompte *m*, arrhes *fpl*; **in ~** *ad* sérieusement, pour de bon.

earnings [ûr'ningz] *npl* salaire *m*; gains *mpl*; (*of company etc*) profits *mpl*, bénéfices *mpl*.

ear, nose and throat specialist *n* otorhino-laryngologiste *m/f*.

earphones [ēr'fōnz] *npl* écouteurs *mpl*.

earplugs [ēr'plugz] *npl* boules *fpl* Quiès ®; (*to keep out water*) protège-tympans *mpl*.

earring [ēr'ring] *n* boucle *f* d'oreille.

earshot [ēr'shät] *n*: **out of/within ~** hors de portée/à portée de la voix.

earth [ûrth] *n* (*gen, also Brit ELEC*) terre *f*; (*of fox etc*) terrier *m* ♦ *vt* (*Brit ELEC*) relier à la terre.

earthenware [ûr'thənwär] *n* poterie *f*; faïence *f* ♦ *a* de *or* en faïence.

earthly [ûrth'lē] *a* terrestre; **~ paradise** paradis *m* terrestre; **there is no ~ reason to think ...** il n'y a absolument aucune raison *or* pas la moindre raison de penser ....

earthquake [ûrth'kwāk] *n* tremblement *m* de terre, séisme *m*.

earth tremor *n* secousse *f* sismique.

earthworks [ûrth'wûrks] *npl* travaux *mpl* de terrassement.

earthworm [ûrth'wûrm] *n* ver *m* de terre.

earthy [ûr'thē] *a* (*fig*) terre à terre *inv*; truculent(e).

earwax [ēr'waks] *n* cérumen *m*.

earwig [ēr'wig] *n* perce-oreille *m*.

ease [ēz] *n* facilité *f*, aisance *f* ♦ *vt* (*soothe*) calmer; (*loosen*) relâcher, détendre; (*help pass*): **to ~ sth in/out** faire pénétrer/sortir qch délicatement *or* avec douceur; faciliter la pénétration/la sortie de qch ♦ *vi* (*situation*) se détendre; **with** ~ sans difficulté, aisément; **life of** ~ vie oisive; **at** ~ à l'aise; (*MIL*) au repos.

ease off, ease up *vi* diminuer; (*slow down*) ralentir; (*relax*) se détendre.

easel [ē'zəl] *n* chevalet *m*.

easily [ē'zilē] *ad* facilement.

easiness [ē'zēnis] *n* facilité *f*; (*of manner*) aisance *f*; nonchalance *f*.

east [ēst] *n* est *m* ♦ *a* d'est ♦ *ad* à l'est, vers l'est; **the E~** l'Orient *m*; (*POL*) les pays *mpl* de l'Est.

Easter [ēs'tûr] *n* Pâques *fpl* ♦ *a* (*vacation*) de Pâques, pascal(e).

Easter egg *n* œuf *m* de Pâques.

Easter Island *n* île *f* de Pâques.

easterly [ēs'tûrlē] *a* d'est.

Easter Monday *n* le lundi de Pâques.

eastern [ēs'tûrn] *a* de l'est, oriental(e); **E~ Europe** l'Europe de l'Est; **the E~ bloc** (*POL*) les pays *mpl* de l'est.

Easter Sunday *n* le dimanche de Pâques.

East Germany *n* Allemagne *f* de l'Est.

eastward(s) [ēst'wûrd(z)] *ad* vers l'est, à l'est.

easy [ē'zē] *a* facile; (*manner*) aisé(e) ♦ *ad*: **to take it** *or* **things** ~ ne pas se fatiguer; (*not worry*) ne pas (trop) s'en faire; **payment on** ~ **terms** (*COMM*) facilités *fpl* de paiement; **that's easier said than done** c'est plus facile à dire qu'à faire, c'est vite dit; **I'm** ~ (*col*) ça m'est égal.

easy chair *n* fauteuil *m*.

easy-going [ē'zēgō'ing] *a* accommodant(e), facile à vivre.

eat, *pt* **ate**, *pp* **eaten** [ēt, āt, ē'tən] *vt*, *vi* manger.

eat away *vt* (*subj: sea*) saper, éroder; (*: acid*) ronger, corroder.

eat away at, eat into *vt fus* ronger, attaquer.

eat out *vi* manger au restaurant.

eat up *vt* (*food*) finir (de manger); **it ~s up electricity** ça bouffe du courant, ça consomme beaucoup d'électricité.

eatable [ē'təbəl] *a* mangeable; (*safe to eat*) comestible.

eau de Cologne [ō' də kəlōn'] *n* eau *f* de Cologne.

eaves [ēvz] *npl* avant-toit *m*.

eavesdrop [ēvz'dräp] *vi*: **to** ~ **(on)** écouter de façon indiscrète.

ebb [eb] *n* reflux *m* ♦ *vi* refluer; (*fig: also:* ~ **away**) décliner; **the ~ and flow** le flux et le reflux; **to be at a low** ~ (*fig*) être bien bas(se), ne pas aller bien fort.

ebb tide *n* marée descendante, reflux *m*.

ebony [eb'ənē] *n* ébène *f*.

ebullient [ibul'yənt] *a* exubérant(e).

EC *n abbr* (= *European Community*) CE *f* (= *Communauté européenne*).

eccentric [iksen'trik] *a*, *n* excentrique (*m/f*).

ecclesiastic(al) [iklēzēas'tik(əl)] *a* ecclésiastique.

ECG *n abbr* = **electrocardiogram**.

ECGD *n abbr* (= *Export Credits Guarantee Department*) service de garantie financière à l'exportation.

echo, ~**es** [ek'ō] *n* écho *m* ♦ *vt* répéter; faire chorus avec ♦ *vi* résonner; faire écho.

éclair [iklär'] *n* éclair *m* (*CULIN*).

eclipse [iklips'] *n* éclipse *f* ♦ *vt* éclipser.

ECM *n abbr* (*US*) = *European Common Market*.

ecologist [ikâl'əjist] *n* écologiste *m/f*.

ecology [ikâl'əjē] *n* écologie *f*.

economic [ēkənâm'ik] *a* économique; (*profitable*) rentable.

economical [ēkənâm'ikəl] *a* économique; (*person*) économe.

economically [ēkənâm'iklē] *ad* économiquement.

economics [ēkənâm'iks] *n* économie *f* politique ♦ *npl* côté *m or* aspect *m* économique.

economist [ikân'əmist] *n* économiste *m/f*.

economize [ikân'əmīz] *vi* économiser, faire des économies.

economy [ikân'əmē] *n* économie *f*; **economies of scale** économies d'échelle.

economy class *n* (*AVIAT etc*) classe *f* touriste.

economy size *n* taille *f* économique.

ecosystem [ek'ōsistəm] *n* écosystème *m*.

ECSC *n abbr* (= *European Coal & Steel Community*) CECA *f* (= *Communauté européenne du charbon et de l'acier*).

ecstasy [ek'stəsē] *n* extase *f*; **to go into ecstasies over** s'extasier sur.

ecstatic [ekstat'ik] *a* extatique, en extase.

ECT *n abbr* = **electroconvulsive therapy**.

ECU *n abbr* (= *European Currency Unit*) ECU *m*.

Ecuador [ek'wədōr] *n* Équateur *m*.

ecumenical [ekyōōmen'ikəl] *a* œcuménique.

eczema [ek'səmə] *n* eczéma *m*.

eddy [ed'ē] *n* tourbillon *m*.

edge [ej] *n* bord *m*; (*of knife etc*) tranchant *m*, fil *m* ♦ *vt* border ♦ *vi*: **to** ~ **forward** avancer petit à petit; **to** ~ **away from** s'éloigner furtivement de; **on** ~ (*fig*) = **edgy**; **to have the** ~ **on** (*fig*) l'emporter (de justesse) sur, être légèrement meilleur que.

edgeways [ej'wāz] *ad* latéralement; **he couldn't get a word in** ~ il ne pouvait pas placer un mot.

edging [ej'ing] *n* bordure *f*.

edgy [ej'ē] *a* crispé(e), tendu(e).

edible [ed'əbəl] *a* comestible; (*meal*) mangeable.

edict [ē'dikt] *n* décret *m*.

edifice [ed'əfis] *n* édifice *m*.

edifying [ed'əfīing] *a* édifiant(e).

Edinburgh [ed'ənbûrə] *n* Édimbourg.

edit [ed'it] *vt* éditer; (*magazine*) diriger; (*newspaper*) être le rédacteur *or* la rédactrice en chef de.

edition [idish'ən] *n* édition *f*.

editor [ed'itûr] *n* (*in newspaper*) rédacteur/trice; rédacteur/trice en chef; (*of sb's work*) éditeur/trice; (*also:* **film** ~) monteur/euse.

editorial [editôr'ēəl] *a* de la rédaction, éditorial(e) ♦ *n* éditorial *m*; **the** ~ **staff** la rédaction.

EDP *n abbr* = **electronic data processing**.

EDT *abbr* (*US:* = *Eastern Daylight Time*) heure d'été de New York.

educate [ej'ōōkāt] *vt* instruire; éduquer; ~**d at ...** qui a fait ses études à ....

education [ejōōkā'shən] *n* éducation *f*;

(*schooling*) enseignement *m*, instruction *f*; (*at university: subject etc*) pédagogie *f*; **elementary** or (*Brit*) **primary/secondary** ~ instruction *f* primaire/secondaire.

educational [cjŏōkā'shənəl] *a* pédagogique; scolaire; (*useful*) instructif(ive); (*games, toys*) éducatif(ive); ~ **technology** technologie *f* de l'enseignement.

Edwardian [edwôr'dēən] *a* de l'époque du roi Édouard VII, des années 1900.

EE *abbr* = **electrical engineer**.

EEC *n abbr* (= *European Economic Community*) C.E.E. *f* (= *Communauté économique européenne*).

EEG *n abbr* = **electroencephalogram**.

eel [ēl] *n* anguille *f*.

EENT *n abbr* (*US MED*) = *eye, ear, nose and throat*.

EEOC *n abbr* (*US*) = **Equal Employment Opportunity Commission**.

eerie [ē'rē] *a* inquiétant(e), spectral(e), surnaturel(le).

EET *abbr* (= *Eastern European Time*) HEO (= *heure d'Europe orientale*).

effect [ifekt'] *n* effet *m* ♦ *vt* effectuer; **to take** ~ (*LAW*) entrer en vigueur, prendre effet; (*drug*) agir, faire son effet; **to put into** ~ (*plan*) mettre en application or à exécution; **to have an** ~ **on sb/sth** avoir or produire un effet sur qn/qch; **in** ~ en fait; **his letter is to the** ~ **that** ... sa lettre nous apprend que ....

effective [ifek'tiv] *a* efficace; (*striking: display, outfit*) frappant(e), qui produit or fait de l'effet; **to become** ~ (*LAW*) entrer en vigueur, prendre effet; ~ **date** date *f* d'effet or d'entrée en vigueur.

effectively [ifek'tivlē] *ad* efficacement; (*strikingly*) d'une manière frappante, avec beaucoup d'effet; (*in reality*) effectivement, en fait.

effectiveness [ifek'tivnis] *n* efficacité *f*.

effects [ifekts'] *npl* (*THEATER*) effets *mpl*; (*property*) effets, affaires *fpl*.

effeminate [ifem'ənit] *a* efféminé(e).

effervescent [efûrves'ənt] *a* effervescent(e).

efficacy [ef'ikəsē] *n* efficacité *f*.

efficiency [ifish'ənsē] *n* efficacité *f*; rendement *m*.

efficiency apartment *n* (*US*) studio *m* avec coin cuisine.

efficient [ifish'ənt] *a* efficace; (*machine, car*) d'un bon rendement.

efficiently [ifish'əntlē] *ad* efficacement.

effigy [ef'ijē] *n* effigie *f*.

effluent [ef'lōōənt] *n* effluent *m*.

effort [ef'ûrt] *n* effort *m*; **to make an** ~ **to do sth** faire or fournir un effort pour faire qch.

effortless [ef'ûrtlis] *a* sans effort, aisé(e).

effrontery [ifrun'tûrē] *n* effronterie *f*.

effusive [ifyōō'siv] *a* (*person*) expansif(ive); (*welcome*) chaleureux(euse).

EFL *n abbr* (*SCOL*) = *English as a foreign language*.

EFT *n abbr* (*US*: = *electronic funds transfer*) transfert *m* électronique de fonds.

EFTA [ef'tə] *n abbr* (= *European Free Trade Association*) AELE *f* (= *Association européenne de libre échange*).

e.g. *ad abbr* (= *exempli gratia*) par exemple,

p. ex.

egalitarian [igalitär'ēən] *a* égalitaire.

egg [eg] *n* œuf *m*.
  egg on *vt* pousser.

eggcup [eg'kup] *n* coquetier *m*.

eggplant [eg'plant] *n* aubergine *f*.

eggshell [eg'shel] *n* coquille *f* d'œuf ♦ *a* (*color*) blanc cassé *inv*.

egg white *n* blanc *m* d'œuf.

egg yolk *n* jaune *m* d'œuf.

ego [ē'gō] *n* moi *m*.

egoism [ē'gōizəm] *n* égoïsme *m*.

egoist [ē'gōist] *n* égoïste *m/f*.

egotism [ē'gətizəm] *n* égotisme *m*.

egotist [ē'gətist] *n* égocentrique *m/f*.

Egypt [ē'jipt] *n* Egypte *f*.

Egyptian [ijip'shən] *a* égyptien(ne) ♦ *n* Egyptien/ne.

eiderdown [ī'dûrdoun] *n* édredon *m*.

eight [āt] *num* huit.

eighteen [ā'tēn'] *num* dix-huit.

eighth [ātth] *num* huitième.

eighth note *n* (*US*) croche *f*.

eighty [ā'tē] *num* quatre-vingt(s).

Eire [är'ə] *n* République *f* d'Irlande.

either [ē'thûr] *a* l'un ou l'autre; (*both, each*) chaque; **on** ~ **side** de chaque côté ♦ *pronoun*: ~ (**of them**) l'un ou l'autre; **I don't like** ~ je n'aime ni l'un ni l'autre ♦ *ad* non plus; **no, I don't** ~ moi non plus ♦ *cj*: ~ **good or bad** ou bon ou mauvais, soit bon soit mauvais; **I haven't seen** ~ **one or the other** je n'ai vu ni l'un ni l'autre.

ejaculation [ijakyəlā'shən] *n* (*PHYSIOL*) éjaculation *f*.

eject [ijekt'] *vt* expulser; éjecter ♦ *vi* (*pilot*) s'éjecter.

ejector seat [ijek'tûr sēt] *n* siège *m* éjectable.

eke [ēk]: **to** ~ **out** *vt* faire durer; augmenter.

EKG *n abbr* (*US*) = **electrocardiogram**.

el [el] *n abbr* (*US col*) = **elevated railroad**.

elaborate *a* [ilab'ûrit] compliqué(e), recherché(e), minutieux(euse) ♦ *vb* [ilab'ûrāt] *vt* élaborer ♦ *vi* entrer dans les détails.

elapse [ilaps'] *vi* s'écouler, passer.

elastic [ilas'tik] *a*, *n* élastique (*m*).

elastic band *n* (*Brit*) élastique *m*.

elasticity [ilastis'itē] *n* élasticité *f*.

elated [ilā'tid] *a* transporté(e) de joie.

elation [ilā'shən] *n* (grande) joie, allégresse *f*.

elbow [el'bō] *n* coude *m* ♦ *vt*: **to** ~ **one's way through the crowd** se frayer un passage à travers la foule (en jouant des coudes).

elder [el'dûr] *a* aîné(e) ♦ *n* (*tree*) sureau *m*; **one's** ~**s** ses aînés.

elderly [el'dûrlē] *a* âgé(e) ♦ *npl*: **the** ~ les personnes âgées.

eldest [el'dist] *a*, *n*: **the** ~ (**child**) l'aîné(e) (des enfants).

elect [ilekt'] *vt* élire; (*choose*): **to** ~ **to do** choisir de faire ♦ *a*: **the president** ~ le président désigné.

election [ilek'shən] *n* élection *f*; **to hold an** ~ procéder à une élection.

election campaign *n* campagne électorale.

electioneering [ilekshənē'ring] *n* propagande électorale, manœuvres électorales.

elective [ilek'tiv] *n* (*SCOL*) cours facultatif.

elector [ilek'tûr] *n* électeur/trice.

electoral [ilek'tûrəl] *a* électoral(e).
electoral college *n* collège électoral.
electoral roll *n* (*Brit*) liste électorale.
electorate [ilek'tûrit] *n* électorat *m*.
electric [ilek'trik] *a* électrique.
electrical [ilek'trikəl] *a* électrique.
electrical engineer *n* ingénieur électricien.
electrical failure *n* panne d'électricité *or* de courant.
electric blanket *n* couverture chauffante.
electric chair *n* chaise *f* électrique.
electric current *n* courant *m* électrique.
electrician [ilektrish'ən] *n* électricien *m*.
electricity [ilektris'ətē] *n* électricité *f*; **to switch on/off the** ~ rétablir/couper le courant.
electric light *n* lumière *f* électrique.
electric shock *n* choc *m* *or* décharge *f* électrique.
electrify [ilek'trəfī] *vt* (*RAIL*) électrifier; (*audience*) électriser.
electro... [ilek'trō] *prefix* électro....
electrocardiogram (ECG) [ilektrōkár'dēəgram] *n* électrocardiogramme *m* (ECG).
electro-convulsive therapy [ilek'trōkənvul'siv thär'əpē] *n* électrochocs *mpl*.
electrocute [ilek'trəkyōōt] *vt* électrocuter.
electrode [ilek'trōd] *n* électrode *f*.
electroencephalogram (EEG) [ilektrōensef'ələgram] *n* électroencéphalogramme *m* (EEG).
electrolysis [ilektrâl'isis] *n* électrolyse *f*.
electromagnetic [ilektrōmagnet'ik] *a* électromagnétique.
electron [ilek'trân] *n* électron *m*.
electronic [ilektrân'ik] *a* électronique.
electronic data processing (EDP) *n* traitement *m* électronique des données.
electronic mail *n* courrier *m* électronique.
electronics [ilektrân'iks] *n* électronique *f*.
electron microscope *n* microscope *m* électronique.
electroplated [ilek'trəplātid] *a* plaqué(e) *or* doré(e) *or* argenté(e) par galvanoplastie.
electrotherapy [ilektrōthär'əpē] *n* électrothérapie *f*.
elegance [el'əgəns] *n* élégance *f*.
elegant [el'əgənt] *a* élégant(e).
element [el'əmənt] *n* (*gen*) élément *m*; (*of heater, kettle etc*) résistance *f*.
elementary [elimen'tûrē] *a* élémentaire; (*school, education*) primaire.
elephant [el'əfənt] *n* éléphant *m*.
elevate [el'əvāt] *vt* élever.
elevated railroad [el'əvātid rāl'rōd] *n* (*US*) métro aérien.
elevation [eləvā'shən] *n* élévation *f*; (*height*) altitude *f*.
elevator [el'əvātûr] *n* élévateur *m*, montecharge *m inv*; (*US*) ascenseur *m*.
eleven [ilev'ən] *num* onze.
elevenses [ilev'ənziz] *npl* (*Brit*) ≈ pause-café *f*.
eleventh [ilev'ənth] *a* onzième; **at the** ~ **hour** (*fig*) à la dernière minute.
elf, *pl* **elves** [elf, elvz] *n* lutin *m*.
elicit [ilis'it] *vt*: **to** ~ (**from**) obtenir (de); tirer (de).
eligible [el'ijəbəl] *a* éligible; (*for membership*)

admissible; ~ **for a pension** ayant droit à la retraite.
eliminate [əlim'ənāt] *vt* éliminer.
elimination [əlimənā'shən] *n* élimination *f*; **by process of** ~ par élimination.
élite [ilēt'] *n* élite *f*.
élitist [ilē'tist] *a* (*pej*) élitiste.
elixir [ilik'sûr] *n* élixir *m*.
Elizabethan [ilizəbē'thən] *a* élisabéthain(e).
ellipse [ilips'] *n* ellipse *f*.
elliptical [ilip'tikəl] *a* elliptique.
elm [elm] *n* orme *m*.
elocution [eləkyōō'shən] *n* élocution *f*.
elongated [ilông'gātid] *a* étiré(e), allongé(e).
elope [ilōp'] *vi* (*lovers*) s'enfuir (ensemble).
elopement [ilōp'mənt] *n* fugue amoureuse.
eloquence [el'əkwəns] *n* éloquence *f*.
eloquent [el'əkwənt] *a* éloquent(e).
else [els] *ad* d'autre; **something** ~ quelque chose d'autre, autre chose; **somewhere** ~ ailleurs, autre part; **everywhere** ~ partout ailleurs; **everyone** ~ tous les autres; **nothing** ~ rien d'autre; **is there anything** ~ **I can do?** est-ce que je peux faire quelque chose d'autre?; **where** ~**?** à quel autre endroit?; **little** ~ pas grand-chose d'autre.
elsewhere [els'hwär] *ad* ailleurs, autre part.
ELT *n abbr* (*SCOL*) = *English Language Teaching*.
elucidate [ilōō'sidāt] *vt* élucider.
elude [ilōōd'] *vt* échapper à; (*question*) éluder.
elusive [ilōō'siv] *a* insaisissable; (*answer*) évasif(ive).
elves [elvz] *npl of* **elf**.
emaciated [imā'shēātid] *a* émacié(e), décharné(e).
emanate [em'ənāt] *vi*: **to** ~ **from** émaner de.
emancipate [iman'səpāt] *vt* émanciper.
emancipation [imansəpā'shən] *n* émancipation *f*.
emasculate [imas'kyəlāt] *vt* émasculer.
embalm [embâm'] *vt* embaumer.
embankment [embangk'mənt] *n* (*of road, railway*) remblai *m*, talus *m*; (*riverside*) berge *f*, quai *m*; (*dyke*) digue *f*.
embargo, ~**es** [embâr'gō] *n* (*COMM, NAUT*) embargo *m* ♦ *vt* frapper d'embargo, mettre l'embargo sur; **to put an** ~ **on sth** mettre l'embargo sur qch.
embark [embârk'] *vi*: **to** ~ (**on**) (s')embarquer (à bord de *or* sur) ♦ *vt* embarquer; **to** ~ **on** (*journey etc*) commencer, entreprendre; (*fig*) se lancer *or* s'embarquer dans.
embarkation [embârkā'shən] *n* embarquement *m*.
embarkation card *n* carte *f* d'embarquement.
embarrass [embar'əs] *vt* embarrasser, gêner; **to be** ~**ed** être gêné(e).
embarrassing [embar'əsing] *a* gênant(e), embarrassant(e).
embarrassment [embar'əsmənt] *n* embarras *m*, gêne *f*.
embassy [em'bəsē] *n* ambassade *f*; **the French E**~ l'ambassade de France.
embed [embed'] *vt* enfoncer; sceller.
embellish [embel'ish] *vt* embellir; enjoliver.
embers [em'bûrz] *npl* braise *f*.
embezzle [embez'əl] *vt* détourner.

embezzlement [embez'əlmənt] *n* détournement *m* (de fonds).

embezzler [embez'lûr] *n* escroc *m*.

embitter [embit'ûr] *vt* aigrir; envenimer.

emblem [em'bləm] *n* emblème *m*.

embodiment [embâd'ēmənt] *n* personification *f*, incarnation *f*.

embody [embâd'ē] *vt* (*features*) réunir, comprendre; (*ideas*) formuler, exprimer.

embolden [embōl'dən] *vt* enhardir.

embolism [em'bəlizəm] *n* embolie *f*.

embossed [embôst'] *a* repoussé(e); gaufré(e); ~ **with** où figure(nt) en relief.

embrace [embrās'] *vt* embrasser, étreindre; (*include*) embrasser, couvrir, comprendre ♦ *vi* s'embrasser, s'étreindre ♦ *n* étreinte *f*.

embroider [embroi'dûr] *vt* broder; (*fig: story*) enjoliver.

embroidery [embroi'dûrē] *n* broderie *f*.

embroil [embroil'] *vt*: **to become ~ed (in sth)** se retrouver mêlé(e) (à qch), se laisser entraîner (dans qch).

embryo [em'brēō] *n* (*also fig*) embryon *m*.

emcee [em'sē'] *n* (*US: col*) animateur/trice, présentateur/trice.

emend [imend'] *vt* (*text*) corriger.

emerald [em'ûrəld] *n* émeraude *f*.

emerge [imûrj'] *vi* apparaître, surgir; **it ~s that** (*Brit*) il ressort que.

emergence [imûr'jəns] *n* apparition *f*; (*of nation*) naissance *f*.

emergency [imûr'jənsē] *n* urgence *f*; **in an ~** en cas d'urgence; **state of ~** état *m* d'urgence.

emergency exit *n* sortie *f* de secours.

emergency flasher *n* (*US: AUT*) feux *mpl* de détresse.

emergency landing *n* atterrissage forcé.

emergency lane *n* (*US AUT*) accotement stabilisé.

emergency road service *n* (*US*) service *m* de dépannage.

emergency service *n* service *m* d'urgence.

emergency stop *n* (*AUT*) arrêt *m* d'urgence.

emergent [imûr'jənt] *a*: ~ **nation** pays *m* en voie de développement.

emery board [em'ûrē bôrd] *n* lime *f* à ongles (*en carton émerisé*).

emery paper [em'ûrē pāpûr] *n* papier *m* (d')émeri.

emetic [imet'ik] *n* vomitif *m*, émétique *m*.

emigrant [em'əgrənt] *n* émigrant/e.

emigrate [em'əgrāt] *vi* émigrer.

emigration [eməgrā'shən] *n* émigration *f*.

émigré [emigrā'] *n* émigré/e.

eminence [em'ənəns] *n* éminence *f*.

eminent [em'ənənt] *a* éminent(e).

eminently [em'ənəntlē] *ad* éminemment, admirablement.

emirate [emē'rit] *n* émirat *m*.

emission [imish'ən] *n* émission *f*.

emit [imit'] *vt* émettre.

emolument [imâl'yəmənt] *n* (*often pl: formal*) émoluments *mpl*; (*fee*) honoraires *mpl*; (*salary*) traitement *m*.

emotion [imō'shən] *n* sentiment *m*; (*as opposed to reason*) émotion *f*, sentiments.

emotional [imō'shənəl] *a* (*person*) émotif(ive), très sensible; (*scene*) émouvant(e); (*tone,*

speech) qui fait appel aux sentiments.

emotionally [imō'shənəlē] *ad* (*behave*) émotivement; (*be involved*) affectivement; (*speak*) avec émotion; ~ **disturbed** qui souffre de troubles de l'affectivité.

emotive [imō'tiv] *a* émotif(ive); ~ **power** capacité *f* d'émouvoir *or* de toucher.

empathy [em'pəthē] *n* communion *f* d'idées *or* de sentiments; empathie *f*; **to feel ~ with sb** se mettre à la place de qn.

emperor [em'pûrûr] *n* empereur *m*.

emphasis, *pl* **-ases** [em'fəsis, -sēz] *n* accent *m*; force *f*, insistance *f*; **to lay** *or* **place ~ on sth** (*fig*) mettre l'accent sur, insister sur; **the ~ is on reading** la lecture tient une place primordiale, on accorde une importance particulière à la lecture.

emphasize [em'fəsīz] *vt* (*syllable, word, point*) appuyer *or* insister sur; (*feature*) souligner, accentuer.

emphatic [əmfat'ik] *a* (*strong*) énergique, vigoureux(euse); (*unambiguous, clear*) catégorique.

emphatically [əmfat'iklē] *ad* avec vigueur *or* énergie; catégoriquement.

empire [em'pīûr] *n* empire *m*.

empirical [empir'ikəl] *a* empirique.

employ [emploi'] *vt* employer; **he's ~ed in a bank** il est employé de banque, il travaille dans une banque.

employee [emploi'ē] *n* employé/e.

employer [emploi'ûr] *n* employeur/euse.

employment [emploi'mənt] *n* emploi *m*; **to find ~** trouver un emploi *or* du travail; **without ~** au chômage, sans emploi; **place of ~** lieu *m* de travail.

employment agency *n* agence *f* or bureau *m* de placement.

empower [empou'ûr] *vt*: **to ~ sb to do** autoriser *or* habiliter qn à faire.

empress [em'pris] *n* impératrice *f*.

emptiness [emp'tēnis] *n* vide *m*.

empty [emp'tē] *a* vide; (*street, area*) désert(e); (*threat, promise*) en l'air, vain(e) ♦ *n* (*bottle*) bouteille *f* vide ♦ *vt* vider ♦ *vi* se vider; (*liquid*) s'écouler; **on an ~ stomach** à jeun; **to ~ into** (*river*) se jeter dans, se déverser dans.

empty-handed [emp'tēhan'did] *a* les mains vides.

empty-headed [emp'tēhed'id] *a* écervelé(e), qui n'a rien dans la tête.

EMT *n abbr* = *emergency medical technician*.

emulate [em'yəlāt] *vt* rivaliser avec, imiter.

emulsion [imul'shən] *n* émulsion *f*; (*also:* ~ **paint**) peinture mate.

enable [enā'bəl] *vt*: **to ~ sb to do** permettre à qn de faire, donner à qn la possibilité de faire.

enact [enakt'] *vt* (*LAW*) promulguer; (*play, scene*) jouer, représenter.

enamel [inam'əl] *n* émail *m*.

enamel paint *n* peinture émaillée.

enamored, (*Brit*) **enamoured** [enam'ûrd] *a*: ~ **of** amoureux(euse) de; (*idea*) enchanté(e) par.

encampment [enkamp'mənt] *n* campement *m*.

encased [enkāst'] *a*: ~ **in** enfermé(e) dans, recouvert(e) de.

enchant [enchant'] *vt* enchanter.
enchanting [enchan'ting] *a* ravissant(e), enchanteur(eresse).
encircle [ensûr'kəl] *vt* entourer, encercler.
enc(l). *abbr* (*on letters etc*: = enclosed, enclosure) PJ.
enclose [enklōz'] *vt* (*land*) clôturer; (*letter etc*): **to ~ (with)** joindre (à); **please find ~d** veuillez trouver ci-joint.
enclosure [enklō'zhûr] *n* enceinte *f*; (*in letter etc*) annexe *f*.
encoder [enkō'dûr] *n* (*COMPUT*) encodeur *m*.
encompass [enkum'pəs] *vt* encercler, entourer; (*include*) contenir, inclure.
encore [áng'kôr] *excl*, *n* bis *(m)*.
encounter [enkoun'tûr] *n* rencontre *f* ♦ *vt* rencontrer.
encourage [enkûr'ij] *vt* encourager; (*industry, growth*) favoriser; **to ~ sb to do sth** encourager qn à faire qch.
encouragement [enkûr'ijmənt] *n* encouragement *m*.
encouraging [enkûr'ijing] *a* encourageant(e).
encroach [enkrōch'] *vi*: **to ~ (up)on** empiéter sur.
encrust [enkrust'] *vt*: **~ed (with)** incrusté(e) (de).
encumber [enkum'bûr] *vt*: **to be ~ed with** (*luggage*) être encombré(e) de; (*debts*) être grevé(e) de.
encyclop(a)edia [ensīkləpē'dēa] *n* encyclopédie *f*.
end [end] *n* (*gen, also: aim*) fin *f*; (*of table, street, line, rope etc*) bout *m*, extrémité *f*; (*of pointed object*) pointe *f*; (*of town*) bout ♦ *vt* terminer; (*also*: **bring to an ~**, **put an ~ to**) mettre fin à ♦ *vi* se terminer, finir; **from ~ to ~** d'un bout à l'autre; **to come to an ~** prendre fin; **to be at an ~** être fini(e), être terminé(e); **in the ~** finalement; **on ~** (*object*) debout, dressé(e); **to stand on ~** (*hair*) se dresser sur la tête; **for 5 hours on ~** durant 5 heures d'affilée *or* de suite; **for hours on ~** pendant des heures (et des heures); **at the ~ of the day** (*Brit fig*) en fin de compte; **to this ~, with this ~ in view** à cette fin, dans ce but.
end up *vi*: **to ~ up in** finir *or* se terminer par; (*place*) finir *or* aboutir à.
endanger [endān'jûr] *vt* mettre en danger; **an ~ed species** une espèce en voie de disparition.
endear [endēr'] *vt*: **to ~ o.s. to sb** se faire aimer de qn.
endearing [endēr'ing] *a* attachant(e).
endearment [endēr'mənt] *n*: **to whisper ~s** murmurer des mots *or* choses tendres; **term of ~** terme *m* d'affection.
endeavor, (*Brit*) **endeavour** [endev'ûr] *n* tentative *f*, effort *m* ♦ *vi*: **to ~ to do** tenter *or* s'efforcer de faire.
endemic [endem'ik] *a* endémique.
ending [en'ding] *n* dénouement *m*, conclusion *f*; (*LING*) terminaison *f*.
endive [en'dīv] *n* (*curly*) chicorée *f*; (*smooth, flat*) endive *f*.
endless [end'lis] *a* sans fin, interminable; (*patience, resources*) inépuisable, sans limites; (*possibilities*) illimité(e).

endorse [endôrs'] *vt* (*check*) endosser; (*approve*) appuyer, approuver, sanctionner.
endorsee [endôrsē'] *n* bénéficiaire *m/f*, endossataire *m/f*.
endorsement [endôrs'mənt] *n* (*approval*) caution *f*, aval *m*; (*signature*) endossement *m*; (*Brit*: *on driver's license*) contravention *f* (*portée au permis de conduire*).
endorser [endôrs'ûr] *n* avaliste *m*, endosseur *m*.
endow [endou'] *vt* (*provide with money*) faire une donation à, doter; (*equip*): **to ~ with** gratifier de, doter de.
endowment [endou'mənt] *n* dotation *f*.
endowment insurance *n* assurance *f* mixte.
end product *n* (*INDUSTRY*) produit fini; (*fig*) résultat *m*, aboutissement *m*.
end result *n* résultat final.
endurable [endoo'rəbəl] *a* supportable.
endurance [endoor'əns] *n* endurance *f*, résistance *f*; patience *f*.
endurance test *n* test *m* d'endurance.
endure [endoor'] *vt* supporter, endurer ♦ *vi* durer.
end user *n* (*COMPUT*) utilisateur final.
enema [en'əmə] *n* (*MED*) lavement *m*.
enemy [en'əmē] *a*, *n* ennemi(e); **to make an ~ of sb** se faire un(e) ennemi(e) de qn, se mettre qn à dos.
energetic [enûrjet'ik] *a* énergique; (*activity*) très actif(ive), qui fait se dépenser (physiquement).
energy [en'ûrjē] *n* énergie *f*; **Department of E~** ministère *m* de l'Énergie.
energy crisis *n* crise *f* de l'énergie.
energy-saving [en'ûrjēsāving] *a* (*policy*) d'économie d'énergie; (*device*) qui permet de réaliser des économies d'énergie.
enervating [en'ûrvāting] *a* débilitant(e), affaiblissant(e).
enforce [enfôrs'] *vt* (*LAW*) appliquer, faire respecter.
enforced [enfôrst'] *a* forcé(e).
enfranchise [enfran'chīz] *vt* accorder le droit de vote à; (*set free*) affranchir.
engage [engāj'] *vt* engager; (*MIL*) engager le combat avec; (*lawyer*) prendre ♦ *vi* (*TECH*) s'enclencher, s'engrener; **to ~ in** se lancer dans; **to ~ sb in conversation** engager la conversation avec qn.
engaged [engājd'] *a* (*betrothed*) fiancé(e); (*Brit*: *busy, in use*) occupé(e); **to get ~** se fiancer; **he is ~ in research/a survey** il fait de la recherche/une enquête.
engaged tone *n* (*Brit TEL*) tonalité *f* occupé.
engagement [engāj'mənt] *n* obligation *f*, engagement *m*; (*appointment*) rendez-vous *m inv*; (*to marry*) fiançailles *fpl*; (*MIL*) combat *m*; **I have a previous ~** j'ai déjà un rendez-vous, je suis déjà prise(e).
engagement ring *n* bague *f* de fiançailles.
engaging [engā'jing] *a* engageant(e), attirant(e).
engender [enjen'dûr] *vt* produire, causer.
engine [en'jən] *n* (*AUT*) moteur *m*; (*RAIL*) locomotive *f*.
engine driver *n* (*Brit*: *of train*) mécanicien *m*.
engineer [enjənēr'] *n* ingénieur *m*; (*US RAIL*)

mécanicien *m*; (*Brit*: *for domestic appliances*) réparateur *m*; **civil/mechanical** ~ ingénieur des Travaux Publics *or* des Ponts et Chaussées/mécanicien.

engineering [enjənēr'ing] *n* engineering *m*, ingénierie *f*; (*of bridges, ships*) génie *m*; (*of machine*) mécanique *f* ♦ *cpd*: ~ **works** *or* **factory** atelier *m* de construction mécanique.

engine failure *n* panne *f*.

engine trouble *n* ennuis *mpl* mécaniques.

England [ing'glənd] *n* Angleterre *f*.

English [ing'glish] *a* anglais(e) ♦ *n* (*LING*) anglais *m*; **the** ~ *npl* les Anglais; **an** ~ **speaker** un anglophone.

English Channel *n*: **the** ~ la Manche.

English horn *n* (*US*) cor anglais.

Englishman [ing'glishmən], **Englishwoman** [ing'glishwŏŏmən] *n* Anglais/e.

English-speaking [ing'glishspē'king] *a* qui parle anglais; anglophone.

engrave [engrāv'] *vt* graver.

engraving [engrā'ving] *n* gravure *f*.

engrossed [engrōst'] *a*: ~ **in** absorbé(e) par, plongé(e) dans.

engulf [engulf'] *vt* engloutir.

enhance [enhans'] *vt* rehausser, mettre en valeur; (*position*) améliorer; (*reputation*) accroître.

enigma [ənig'mə] *n* énigme *f*.

enigmatic [enigmat'ik] *a* énigmatique.

enjoy [enjoi'] *vt* aimer, prendre plaisir à; (*have benefit of: health, fortune*) jouir de; (*: success*) connaître; **to** ~ **o.s.** s'amuser.

enjoyable [enjoi'əbəl] *a* agréable.

enjoyment [enjoi'mənt] *n* plaisir *m*.

enlarge [enlärj'] *vt* accroître; (*PHOT*) agrandir ♦ *vi*: **to** ~ **on** (*subject*) s'étendre sur.

enlarged [enlärjd'] *a* (*edition*) augmenté(e); (*MED*: *organ, gland*) anormalement gros(se), hypertrophié(e).

enlargement [enlärj'mənt] *n* (*PHOT*) agrandissement *m*.

enlighten [enlīt'ən] *vt* éclairer.

enlightened [enlīt'ənd] *a* éclairé(e).

enlightening [enlīt'əning] *a* instructif(ive), révélateur(trice).

enlightenment [enlīt'ənmənt] *n* édification *f*; éclaircissements *mpl*; (*HIST*): **the E**~ ≈ le Siècle des lumières.

enlist [enlist'] *vt* recruter; (*support*) s'assurer ♦ *vi* s'engager; ~**ed man** (*US MIL*) simple soldat *m*.

enliven [enlī'vən] *vt* animer, égayer.

enmity [en'mitē] *n* inimitié *f*.

ennoble [ennō'bəl] *vt* (*with title*) anoblir.

enormity [inôr'mitē] *n* énormité *f*.

enormous [inôr'məs] *a* énorme.

enormously [inôr'məslē] *ad* (*increase*) dans des proportions énormes; (*rich*) extrêmement.

enough [inuf'] *a, n*: ~ **time/books** assez *or* suffisamment de temps/livres; **have you got** ~**?** (en) avez-vous assez?; **will 5 be** ~**?** est-ce que 5 suffiront?, est-ce qu'il y en aura assez avec 5?; **that's** ~**!** ça suffit!, assez!; **that's** ~**, thanks** cela suffit *or* c'est assez, merci; **I've had** ~**!** je n'en peux plus! ♦ *ad*: **big** ~ assez *or* suffisamment grand; **he has not worked** ~ il n'a pas assez *or*

suffisamment travaillé, il n'a pas travaillé assez *or* suffisamment; ~**!** assez!, ça suffit!; **it's hot** ~ **(as it is)!** il fait assez chaud comme ça!; **he was kind** ~ **to lend me the money** il a eu la gentillesse de me prêter l'argent; **... which, funnily** ~ **...** qui, chose curieuse.

enquire [enkwī'ûr] *vt, vi* = **inquire**.

enrage [enrāj'] *vt* mettre en fureur *or* en rage, rendre furieux(euse).

enrich [enrich'] *vt* enrichir.

enroll, (*Brit*) **enrol** [enrōl'] *vt* inscrire ♦ *vi* s'inscrire.

enrol(l)ment [enrōl'mənt] *n* inscription *f*.

en route [ôn rōōt'] *ad* en route, en chemin; ~ **for** *or* **to** en route vers, à destination de.

ensconced [enskânst'] *a*: ~ **in** bien calé(e) dans.

enshrine [enshrīn'] *vt* (*fig*) préserver.

ensign [en'sən] *n* (*NAUT*) enseigne *f*, pavillon *m*.

enslave [enslāv'] *vt* asservir.

ensue [ensōō'] *vi* s'ensuivre, résulter.

ensure [enshōōr'] *vt* assurer, garantir; **to** ~ **that** s'assurer que.

ENT *n abbr* (= *Ear, Nose & Throat*) ORL *f*.

entail [entāl'] *vt* entraîner, nécessiter.

entangle [entang'gəl] *vt* emmêler, embrouiller; **to become** ~**d in sth** (*fig*) se laisser entraîner *or* empêtrer dans qch.

enter [en'tûr] *vt* (*room*) entrer dans, pénétrer dans; (*club, army*) entrer à; (*profession*) embrasser; (*competition*) s'inscrire à *or* pour; (*sb for a competition*) (faire) inscrire; (*write down*) inscrire, noter; (*COMPUT*) entrer, introduire ♦ *vi* entrer.

enter for *vt fus* s'inscrire à, se présenter pour *or* à.

enter into *vt fus* (*explanation*) se lancer dans; (*negotiations*) entamer; (*debate*) prendre part à; (*agreement*) conclure.

enter (up)on *vt fus* commencer.

enteritis [entərī'tis] *n* entérite *f*.

enterprise [en'tûrprīz] *n* (*company, undertaking*) entreprise *f*; (*initiative*) (esprit *m* d')initiative *f*.

enterprising [en'tûrprīzing] *a* entreprenant(e), dynamique.

entertain [entûrtān'] *vt* amuser, distraire; (*invite*) recevoir (à dîner); (*idea, plan*) envisager.

entertainer [entûrtān'ûr] *n* artiste *m/f* de variétés.

entertaining [entûrtā'ning] *a* amusant(e), distrayant(e) ♦ *n*: **to do a lot of** ~ beaucoup recevoir.

entertainment [entûrtān'mənt] *n* (*amusement*) distraction *f*, divertissement *m*, amusement *m*; (*show*) spectacle *m*.

entertainment allowance *n* frais *mpl* de représentation.

enthralling [enthrôl'ing] *a* captivant(e); enchanteur(eresse).

enthuse [enthōōz'] *vi*: **to** ~ **about** *or* **over** parler avec enthousiasme de.

enthusiasm [enthōō'zēazəm] *n* enthousiasme *m*.

enthusiast [enthōō'zēast] *n* enthousiaste *m/f*; **a jazz** *etc* ~ un fervent *or* passionné du jazz *etc.*

enthusiastic [enthōōzēas'tik] *a* enthousiaste; **to be ~ about** être enthousiasmé(e) par.

entice [entīs'] *vt* attirer, séduire.

enticing [enti'sing] *a* (*person, offer*) séduisant(e); (*food*) alléchant(e).

entire [enti'ûr] *a* (tout) entier(ère).

entirely [entūr'lē] *ad* entièrement, complètement.

entirety [entīr'tē] *n*: **in its ~** dans sa totalité.

entitle [entīt'əl] *vt* (*allow*): **to ~ sb to do** donner (le) droit à qn de faire; **to ~ sb to sth** donner droit à qch à qn.

entitled [entīt'əld] *a* (*book*) intitulé(e); **to be ~ to sth/to do sth** avoir droit à qch/le droit de faire qch.

entity [en'titē] *n* entité *f*.

entrails [en'trālz] *npl* entrailles *fpl*.

entrance *n* [en'trəns] entrée *f* ♦ *vt* [entrans'] enchanter, ravir; **to gain ~ to** (*university etc*) être admis à.

entrance examination *n* examen *m* d'entrée or d'admission.

entrance fee *n* droit *m* d'inscription; (*to museum etc*) prix *m* d'entrée.

entrance ramp *n* (*US AUT*) bretelle *f* d'accès.

entrancing [entrans'ing] *a* enchanteur-(teresse), ravissant(e).

entrant [en'trənt] *n* (*in race etc*) participant/e, concurrent/e; (*Brit: in exam*) candidat/e.

entreat [entrēt'] *vt* supplier.

entreaty [entrē'tē] *n* supplication *f*, prière *f*.

entrée [ántrā'] *n* (*CULIN*) entrée *f*.

entrenched [entrencht'] *a* retranché(e).

entrepreneur [ántrəprənûr'] *n* entrepreneur *m*.

entrepreneurial [ántrəprənûr'ēəl] *a* animé(e) d'un esprit d'entreprise.

entrust [entrust'] *vt*: **to ~ sth to** confier qch à.

entry [en'trē] *n* entrée *f*; (*in register, diary*) inscription *f*; (*in ledger*) écriture *f*; **"no ~"** "défense d'entrer", "entrée interdite"; (*AUT*) "sens interdit"; **single/double ~ bookkeeping** comptabilité *f* en partie simple/double.

entry form *n* feuille *f* d'inscription.

entry phone *n* (*Brit*) interphone *m* (*à l'entrée d'un immeuble*).

entwine [entwīn'] *vt* entrelacer.

enumerate [inōō'mərāt] *vt* énumérer.

enunciate [inun'sēāt] *vt* énoncer; prononcer.

envelop [envel'əp] *vt* envelopper.

envelope [en'vəlōp] *n* enveloppe *f*.

enviable [en'vēəbəl] *a* enviable.

envious [en'vēəs] *a* envieux(euse).

environment [envī'rənmənt] *n* milieu *m*; environnement *m*; **Department of the E~** (*Brit*) *ministère de l'équipement et de l'aménagement du territoire*.

environmental [envīrənmen'təl] *a* écologique, relatif(ive) à l'environnement; **~ studies** (*in school etc*) écologie *f*.

environmentalist [envīrənmen'təlist] *n* écologiste *m/f*.

Environmental Protection Agency (EPA) *n* (*US*) ≈ ministère *m* de l'Environnement.

envisage [enviz'ij] *vt* envisager; prévoir.

envision [envizh'ən] *vt* envisager, concevoir.

envoy [en'voi] *n* envoyé/e.

envy [en'vē] *n* envie *f* ♦ *vt* envier; **to ~ sb sth** envier qch à qn.

enzyme [en'zīm] *n* enzyme *m*.

eon [ē'ən] *n* (*US*) éternité *f*.

EPA *n abbr* (*US*) = **Environmental Protection Agency.**

ephemeral [ifem'ûrəl] *a* éphémère.

epic [ep'ik] *n* épopée *f* ♦ *a* épique.

epicenter, (*Brit*) **epicentre** [ep'isentûr] *n* épicentre *m*.

epidemic [epidem'ik] *n* épidémie *f*.

epilepsy [ep'əlepsē] *n* épilepsie *f*.

epileptic [epəlep'tik] *a, n* épileptique (*m/f*).

epilogue [ep'əlôg] *n* épilogue *m*.

episcopal [ipis'kəpəl] *a* épiscopal(e).

episode [ep'isōd] *n* épisode *m*.

epistle [ipis'əl] *n* épître *f*.

epitaph [ep'itaf] *n* épitaphe *f*.

epithet [ep'əthet] *n* épithète *f*.

epitome [ipit'əmē] *n* (*fig*) quintessence *f*, type *m*.

epitomize [ipit'əmīz] *vt* (*fig*) illustrer, incarner.

epoch [ep'ək] *n* époque *f*, ère *f*.

epoch-making [ep'əkmāking] *a* qui fait époque.

eponymous [epân'əməs] *a* de ce or du même nom, éponyme.

equable [ek'wəbəl] *a* égal(e); de tempérament égal.

equal [ē'kwəl] *a* égal(e) ♦ *n* égal/e ♦ *vt* égaler; **~ to** (*task*) à la hauteur de; **~ to doing** de taille à or capable de faire.

equality [ikwâl'itē] *n* égalité *f*.

equalize [ē'kwəlīz] *vt, vi* égaliser.

equalizer [ē'kwəlīzûr] *n* but égalisateur.

equally [ē'kwəlē] *ad* également; (*just as*) tout aussi; **they are ~ clever** ils sont tout aussi intelligents.

Equal Employment Opportunity Commission, (*Brit*) **Equal Opportunities Commission** *n commission pour la non discrimination dans l'emploi.*

equal(s) sign [ē'kwəl(z) sīn] *n* signe *m* d'égalité.

equanimity [ēkwanim'itē] *n* égalité *f* d'humeur.

equate [ikwāt'] *vt*: **to ~ sth with** comparer qch à; assimiler qch à; **to ~ sth to** mettre qch en équation avec; égaler qch à.

equation [ikwā'zhən] *n* (*MATH*) équation *f*.

equator [ikwā'tûr] *n* équateur *m*.

equatorial [ēkwətôr'ēəl] *a* équatorial(e).

Equatorial Guinea *n* Guinée équatoriale.

equestrian [ikwes'trēən] *a* équestre ♦ *n* écuyer/ère, cavalier/ère.

equilibrium [ēkwəlib'rēəm] *n* équilibre *m*.

equinox [ē'kwənâks] *n* équinoxe *m*.

equip [ikwip'] *vt* équiper; **to ~ sb/sth with** équiper or munir qn/qch de; **he is well ~ped for the job** il a les compétences or les qualités requises pour ce travail.

equipment [ikwip'mənt] *n* équipement *m*; (*electrical etc*) appareillage *m*, installation *f*.

equitable [ek'witəbəl] *a* équitable.

equities [ek'witēz] *npl* (*Brit COMM*) actions cotées en Bourse.

equity [ĕk'witē] *n* équité *f*.

equity capital *n* capitaux *mpl* propres.

equivalent [ikwiv'ələnt] *a* équivalent(e) ◊ *n* équivalent *m*; **to be ~ to** équivaloir à, être équivalent(e) à.

equivocal [ikwiv'əkəl] *a* équivoque; (*open to suspicion*) douteux(euse).

equivocate [ikwiv'əkāt] *vi* user de faux-fuyants; éviter de répondre.

equivocation [ikwivəkā'shən] *n* équivoque *f*.

ER *abbr* (*Brit*: = *Elizabeth Regina*) la reine Élisabeth.

ERA *n* *abbr* (*US POL*: = *Equal Rights Amendment*) amendement sur l'égalité des droits des femmes.

era [ē'rə] *n* ère *f*, époque *f*.

eradicate [irad'ikāt] *vt* éliminer.

erase [irās'] *vt* effacer.

eraser [irā'sûr] *n* gomme *f*.

erect [irekt'] *a* droit(e) ◊ *vt* construire; (*monument*) ériger, élever; (*tent etc*) dresser.

erection [irek'shən] *n* (*PHYSIOL*) érection *f*; (*of building*) construction *f*; (*of machinery etc*) installation *f*.

ergonomics [ûrgənâm'iks] *n* ergonomie *f*.

ERISA *n* *abbr* (*US*: = *Employee Retirement Income Security Act*) loi sur les pensions de retraite.

ermine [ûr'min] *n* hermine *f*.

erode [irōd'] *vt* éroder; (*metal*) ronger.

erosion [irō'zhən] *n* érosion *f*.

erotic [irât'ik] *a* érotique.

eroticism [irât'isizəm] *n* érotisme *m*.

err [ûr] *vi* se tromper; (*REL*) pécher.

errand [är'ənd] *n* course *f*, commission *f*; **to run ~s** faire des courses; **~ of mercy** mission *f* de charité, acte *m* charitable.

errand boy *n* garçon *m* de courses.

erratic [irat'ik] *a* irrégulier(ière); inconstant(e).

erroneous [irō'nēəs] *a* erroné(e).

error [är'ûr] *n* erreur *f*; **typing/spelling ~** faute *f* de frappe/d'orthographe; **in ~** par erreur, par méprise; **~s and omissions excepted** sauf erreur ou omission.

error message *n* (*COMPUT*) message *m* d'erreur.

erstwhile [ûrst'hwīl] *a* précédent(e), d'autrefois.

erudite [är'yōōdīt] *a* savant(e).

erupt [irupt'] *vi* entrer en éruption; (*fig*) éclater, exploser.

eruption [irup'shən] *n* éruption *f*; (*of anger, violence*) explosion *f*.

ESA *n* *abbr* (= *European Space Agency*) ASE *f* (= *Agence spatiale européenne*).

escalate [es'kəlāt] *vi* s'intensifier; (*costs*) monter en flèche.

escalation [es'kəlāshən] *n* escalade *f*.

escalation clause [eskəlā'shən klóz] *n* clause *f* d'indexation.

escalator [es'kəlātûr] *n* escalier roulant.

escapade [es'kəpād] *n* fredaine *f*; équipée *f*.

escape [eskāp'] *n* évasion *f*, fuite *f*; (*of gas etc*) fuite; (: *TECH*) échappement *m* ◊ *vi* s'échapper, fuir; (*from jail*) s'évader; (*fig*) s'en tirer, en réchapper; (*leak*) fuir; s'échapper ◊ *vt* échapper à; **to ~ from** (*person*) échapper à; (*place*) s'échapper de;

(*fig*) fuir; **to ~ to** (*another place*) fuir à, s'enfuir à; **to ~ to safety** se réfugier dans *or* gagner un endroit sûr; **to ~ notice** passer inaperçu(e).

escape artist *n* virtuose *m*/*f* de l'évasion.

escape clause *n* clause *f* dérogatoire.

escape key *n* (*COMPUT*) touche *f* d'échappement.

escape route *n* (*from fire*) issue *f* de secours; (*of prisoners etc*) voie empruntée pour s'échapper.

escapism [eskā'pizəm] *n* évasion *f* (*fig*).

escapist [eskā'pist] *a* (*literature*) d'évasion ◊ *n* personne *f* qui se réfugie hors de la réalité.

escapologist [eskəpâl'əjist] *n* (*Brit*) = **escape artist**.

escarpment [eskârp'mənt] *n* escarpement *m*.

eschew [eschōō'] *vt* éviter.

escort *vt* [eskôrt'] escorter ◊ *n* [es'kôrt] escorte *f*; (*to dance etc*): **her ~** son compagnon *or* cavalier; **his ~** sa compagne.

escort agency *n* bureau *m* d'hôtesses.

Eskimo [es'kəmō] *a* esquimau(de), eskimo ◊ *n* Esquimau/de; (*LING*) esquimau *m*.

ESL *n* *abbr* (*SCOL*) = *English as a Second Language*.

esophagus [isâf'əgəs] *n* (*US*) oesophage *m*.

esoteric [esətär'ik] *a* ésotérique.

ESP *n* *abbr* = **extrasensory perception**.

esp. *abbr* = **especially**.

especially [espesh'əlē] *ad* (*specifically*) spécialement, exprès; (*more than usually*) particulièrement; (*above all*) particulièrement, surtout.

espionage [es'pēənâzh] *n* espionnage *m*.

esplanade [esplənâd'] *n* esplanade *f*.

espouse [espouz'] *vt* épouser, embrasser.

Esquire [eskwīûr] *n* (*Brit*: *abbr* **Esq.**): **J. Brown, ~** Monsieur J. Brown.

essay [es'ā] *n* (*SCOL*) dissertation *f*; (*LITERATURE*) essai *m*; (*attempt*) tentative *f*.

essence [es'əns] *n* essence *f*; **in ~** en substance; **speed is of the ~** l'essentiel, c'est la rapidité.

essential [əsen'chəl] *a* essentiel(le); (*basic*) fondamental(e) ◊ *n* élément essentiel; **it is ~ that** il est essentiel *or* primordial que.

essentially [əsen'chəlē] *ad* essentiellement.

EST *abbr* (*US*: = *Eastern Standard Time*) heure d'hiver de New York.

est. *abbr* = *established*, *estimate(d)*.

establish [əstab'lish] *vt* établir; (*business*) fonder, créer; (*one's power etc*) asseoir, affermir.

establishment [əstab'lishmənt] *n* établissement *m*; création *f*; (*institution*) établissement; **the E~** les pouvoirs établis; l'ordre établi.

estate [əstāt'] *n* (*land*) domaine *m*, propriété *f*; (*LAW*) biens *mpl*, succession *f*; (*Brit*: *also*: **housing ~**) lotissement *m*.

estate agent *n* (*Brit*) agent immobilier.

estate car *n* (*Brit*) break *m*.

esteem [əstēm'] *n* estime *f* ◊ *vt* estimer; apprécier; **to hold sb in high ~** tenir qn en haute estime.

esthetic [esthet'ik] *a* (*US*) esthétique.

estimate *n* [es'təmit] estimation *f*; (*COMM*) devis *m* ◊ *vt* [es'təmāt] estimer; **to give sb an**

~ **of** faire *or* donner un devis à qn pour; **at a rough** ~ approximativement.

estimation [estəmā'shən] *n* opinion *f*; estime *f*; **in my** ~ à mon avis, selon moi.

estimator [es'təmātŭr] *n* personne *f* qui évalue.

Estonia [estō'nēə] *n* Estonie *f*.

estranged [estrānjd'] *a* (*couple*) séparé(e); (*husband, wife*) dont on s'est séparé(e).

estrangement [estrānj'mənt] *n* (*from wife, family*) séparation *f*.

estrogen [es'trəjən] *n* (*US*) oestrogène.

estuary [es'chōōārē] *n* estuaire *m*.

ETA *n abbr* (= *estimated time of arrival*) HPA *f* (= *heure probable d'arrivée*).

et al. [et ál] *abbr* (= *et alii: and others*) et coll.

etc. *abbr* (= *et cetera*) etc.

etch [ech] *vt* graver à l'eau forte.

etching [ech'ing] *n* eau-forte *f*.

ETD *n abbr* (= *estimated time of departure*) HPA *f* (= *heure probable de départ*).

eternal [itûr'nəl] *a* éternel(le).

eternity [itûr'nitē] *n* éternité *f*.

ether [ē'thûr] *n* éther *m*.

ethereal [ithēr'ēəl] *a* éthéré(e).

ethical [eth'ikəl] *a* moral(e).

ethics [eth'iks] *n* éthique *f* ♦ *npl* moralité *f*.

Ethiopia [ēthēō'pēə] *n* Ethiopie *f*.

Ethiopian [ēthēō'pēən] *a* éthiopien(ne) ♦ *n* Ethiopien/ne.

ethnic [eth'nik] *a* ethnique; (*clothes, food*) folklorique, exotique: *propre aux minorités ethniques non-occidentales*.

ethnology [ethnál'əjē] *n* ethnologie *f*.

ethos [ē'thás] *n* (*système m de*) valeurs *fpl*.

etiquette [et'əkit] *n* convenances *fpl*, étiquette *f*.

ETV *n abbr* (*US*: = *Educational Television*) télévision scolaire.

etymology [etəmál'əjē] *n* étymologie *f*.

eucalyptus [yōōkəlip'təs] *n* eucalyptus *m*.

eulogy [yōō'ləjē] *n* éloge *m*.

euphemism [yōō'fəmizəm] *n* euphémisme *m*.

euphemistic [yōōfəmis'tik] *a* euphémique.

euphoria [yōōfôr'ēə] *n* euphorie *f*.

Eurasia [yōōrā'zhə] *n* Eurasie *f*.

Eurasian [yōōrā'zhən] *a* eurasien(ne); (*continent*) eurasiatique ♦ *n* Eurasien/ne.

Euratom [yōōrat'əm] *n abbr* (= *European Atomic Energy Community*) EURATOM *f*.

Euro... [yōō'rō] *prefix* euro....

Eurocheque [yōō'rōchek] *n* (*Brit*) eurochèque *m*.

Eurocrat [yōō'rəkrat] *n* eurocrate *m/f*.

Eurodollar [yōō'rōdálûr] *n* eurodollar *m*.

Europe [yōō'rəp] *n* Europe *f*.

European [yōōrəpē'ən] *a* européen(ne) ♦ *n* Européen/ne.

European Court of Justice *n* Cour *f* de Justice de la CEE.

euthanasia [yōōthənā'zhə] *n* euthanasie *f*.

evacuate [ivak'yōōāt] *vt* évacuer.

evacuation [ivakyōōā'shən] *n* évacuation *f*.

evade [ivād'] *vt* échapper à; (*question etc*) éluder; (*duties*) se dérober à.

evaluate [ival'yōōāt] *vt* évaluer.

evangelist [ivan'jəlist] *n* évangéliste *m*.

evangelize [ivan'jəlīz] *vt* évangéliser, prêcher l'Évangile à.

evaporate [ivap'ərāt] *vi* s'évaporer ♦ *vt* faire évaporer.

evaporated milk [ivap'ərātid milk'] *n* lait condensé (non sucré).

evaporation [ivapərā'shən] *n* évaporation *f*.

evasion [ivā'zhən] *n* dérobade *f*; (*excuse*) faux-fuyant *m*.

evasive [ivā'siv] *a* évasif(ive).

eve [ēv] *n*: **on the** ~ **of** à la veille de.

even [ē'vən] *a* régulier(ière), égal(e); (*number*) pair(e) ♦ *ad* même; ~ **if** même si + *indicative*; ~ **though** quand (bien) même + *conditional*, alors même que + *conditional*; ~ **more** encore plus; ~ **faster** encore plus vite; ~ **so** quand même; **not** ~ pas même; **to break** ~ s'y retrouver, équilibrer ses comptes; **to get** ~ **with sb** prendre sa revanche sur qn.

even out *vi* s'égaliser.

evening [ēv'ning] *n* soir *m*; (*as duration, event*) soirée *f*; **in the** ~ le soir; **this** ~ ce soir; **tomorrow/yesterday** ~ demain/hier soir.

evening class *n* cours *m* du soir.

evening dress *n* (*man's*) habit *m* de soirée, smoking *m*; (*woman's*) robe *f* de soirée.

evenly [ē'vənlē] *ad* uniformément, également; (*space*) régulièrement.

evensong [ē'vənsông] *n* office *m* du soir.

event [ivent'] *n* événement *m*; (*SPORT*) épreuve *f*; **in the course of** ~**s** par la suite; **in the** ~ **of** en cas de; **in the** ~ en réalité, en fait; **in any** ~ en tout cas, de toute manière.

eventful [ivent'fəl] *a* mouvementé(e).

eventual [iven'chōōəl] *a* final(e).

eventuality [ivenchōōal'itē] *n* possibilité *f*, éventualité *f*.

eventually [iven'chōōəlē] *ad* finalement.

ever [ev'ûr] *ad* jamais; (*at all times*) toujours; **the best** ~ le meilleur qu'on ait jamais vu; **did you** ~ **meet him?** est-ce qu'il vous est arrivé de le rencontrer?; **have you** ~ **been there?** y êtes-vous déjà allé?; **for** ~ pour toujours; **hardly** ~ ne ... presque jamais; ~ **since** *ad* depuis ♦ *cj* depuis que; ~ **so pretty** si joli; **thank you** ~ **so much** merci mille fois; **yours** ~ (*Brit: in letters*) cordialement vôtre.

Everest [ev'ûrist] *n* (*also:* **Mount** ~) le mont Everest, l'Everest *m*.

evergreen [ev'ûrgrēn] *n* arbre *m* à feuilles persistantes.

everlasting [evûrlas'ting] *a* éternel(le).

every [ev'rē] *a* chaque; ~ **day** tous les jours, chaque jour; ~ **other/third day** tous les deux/trois jours; ~ **other car** une voiture sur deux; ~ **now and then** de temps en temps; **I have** ~ **confidence in him** j'ai entièrement *or* pleinement confiance en lui.

everybody [ev'rēbádē] *pronoun* tout le monde, tous *pl*; ~ **knows about it** tout le monde le sait; ~ **else** tous les autres.

everyday [ev'rēdā] *a* (*expression*) courant(e), d'usage courant; (*use*) courant; (*occurrence, experience*) de tous les jours, ordinaire.

everyone [ev'rēwun] = **everybody**.

everything [ev'rēthing] *pronoun* tout; ~ **is ready** tout est prêt; **he did** ~ **possible** il a fait tout son possible.

everywhere |ɛv'rēhwär| ad partout; ~ **you go you meet** ... où qu'on aille, on rencontre ....
evict |ivikt'| vt expulser.
eviction |ivik'shən| n expulsion f.
eviction notice n préavis m d'expulsion.
evidence |ɛv'idəns| n (proof) preuve(s) f(pl); (of witness) témoignage m; (sign): **to show ~ of** donner des signes de; **to give ~** témoigner, déposer; **in ~** (obvious) en évidence; en vue.
evident |ɛv'idənt| a évident(e).
evidently |ɛv'idəntlē| ad de toute évidence.
evil |ē'vəl| a mauvais(e) ♦ n mal m.
evince |ivins'| vt manifester.
evocative |ivăk'ətiv| a évocateur(trice).
evoke |ivōk'| vt évoquer; (admiration) susciter.
evolution |ɛvəlōō'shən| n évolution f.
evolve |ivălv'| vt élaborer ♦ vi évoluer, se transformer.
ewe |yōō| n brebis f.
ewer |yōō'ûr| n broc m.
ex- |ɛks| prefix (former: husband, president etc) ex-; (out of): **the price ~works** le prix départ usine.
exacerbate |igzas'ûrbāt| vt (pain) exacerber, accentuer; (fig) aggraver.
exact |igzakt'| a exact(e) ♦ vt: **to ~ sth (from)** extorquer qch (à); exiger qch (de).
exacting |igzak'ting| a exigeant(e); (work) fatigant(e).
exactitude |igzakt'ətōōd| n exactitude f, précision f.
exactly |igzakt'lē| ad exactement; **~!** parfaitement!, précisément!
exaggerate |igzaj'ərāt| vt, vi exagérer.
exaggeration |igzajərā'shən| n exagération f.
exalted |igzōl'tid| a (rank) élevé(e); (person) haut placé(e); (elated) exalté(e).
exam |igzam'| n abbr (SCOL) = **examination**.
examination |igzamənā'shən| n (SCOL, MED) examen m; **to take an ~** passer un examen; **the matter is under ~** la question est à l'examen.
examine |igzam'in| vt (gen) examiner; (SCOL, LAW: person) interroger; (inspect: machine, premises) inspecter; (passport) contrôler; (luggage) fouiller.
examiner |igzam'inûr| n examinateur/trice.
example |igzam'pəl| n exemple m; **for ~** par exemple; **to set a good/bad ~** donner le bon/mauvais exemple.
exasperate |igzas'pərāt| vt exaspérer, agacer.
exasperation |igzaspərā'shən| n exaspération f, irritation f.
excavate |ɛks'kəvāt| vt excaver; (object) mettre au jour.
excavation |ɛks'kəvā'shən| n excavation f.
excavator |ɛks'kəvātûr| n excavateur m, excavatrice f.
exceed |iksēd'| vt dépasser; (one's powers) outrepasser.
exceedingly |iksē'dinglē| ad excessivement.
excel |iksel'| vi exceller ♦ vt surpasser.
excellence |ɛk'sələns| n excellence f.
Excellency |ɛk'sələnsē| n: **His ~** son Excellence f.
excellent |ɛk'sələnt| a excellent(e).
except |iksɛpt'| prep (also: ~ **for**, ~**ing**) sauf,

excepté, à l'exception de ♦ vt excepter; **~ if/ when** sauf si/quand; **~ that** excepté que, si ce n'est que.
exception |iksep'shən| n exception f; **to take ~ to** s'offusquer de; **with the ~ of** à l'exception de.
exceptional |iksep'shənəl| a exceptionnel(le).
excerpt |ɛk'sûrpt| n extrait m.
excess |ɛkses'| n excès m; **in ~ of** plus de.
excess baggage n excédent m de bagages.
excess fare n supplément m.
excessive |ikses'iv| a excessif(ive).
excess supply n suroffre f, offre f excédentaire.
exchange |ikschānj'| n échange m; (also: **telephone ~**) central m ♦ vt: **to ~ (for)** échanger (contre); **in ~ for** en échange de; **foreign ~** (COMM) change m.
exchange control n contrôle m des changes.
exchange market n marché m des changes.
exchange rate n taux m de change.
exchequer |ɛks'chɛkûr| n (Brit) Échiquier m, ≈ ministère m des Finances.
excisable |iksī'zəbəl| a taxable.
excise n |ɛk'sīz| taxe f ♦ vt |iksīz'| exciser.
excise duties npl impôts indirects.
excitable |iksī'təbəl| a excitable, nerveux(euse).
excite |iksīt'| vt exciter; **to get ~d** s'exciter.
excitement |iksīt'mənt| n excitation f.
exciting |iksī'ting| a passionnant(e).
excl. abbr = **excluding, exclusive (of)**.
exclaim |iksklām'| vi s'exclamer.
exclamation |ɛkskləmā'shən| n exclamation f.
exclamation mark n point m d'exclamation.
exclude |iksklōōd'| vt exclure.
excluding |iksklōō'ding| prep: **~ VAT** la TVA non comprise.
exclusion |iksklōō'zhən| n exclusion f; **to the ~ of** à l'exclusion de.
exclusion clause n clause f d'exclusion.
exclusive |iksklōō'siv| a exclusif(ive); (club, district) sélect(e); (item of news) en exclusivité ♦ ad (COMM) exclusivement, non inclus; **~ of VAT** TVA non comprise; **~ of postage** (les) frais de poste non compris; **from 1st to 15th March ~** du 1er au 15 mars exclusivement or exclu; **~ rights** (COMM) exclusivité f.
exclusively |iksklōō'sivlē| ad exclusivement.
excommunicate |ɛkskəmyōō'nəkāt| vt excommunier.
excrement |ɛks'krəmənt| n excrément m.
excruciating |ikskrōō'shēāting| a atroce, déchirant(e).
excursion |ikskûr'zhən| n excursion f.
excursion ticket n billet m tarif excursion.
excusable |ikskyōō'zəbəl| a excusable.
excuse n |ikskyōōs'| excuse f ♦ vt |ikskyōōz'| excuser; (justify) justifier; **to ~ sb from** (activity) dispenser qn de; **~ me!** excusez-moi!, pardon!; **now if you will ~ me,** ... maintenant, si vous (le) permettez ...; **to make ~s for sb** trouver des excuses à qn; **to ~ o.s. for sth/for doing sth** s'excuser de/ d'avoir fait qch.
ex-directory |ɛksdirɛk'tûrē| a (Brit): **~ (phone) number** numéro m (de téléphone) sur la liste rouge.

exec. [igzɛk'] *abbr* = **executive.**
execute [ɛk'səkyōōt] *vt* exécuter.
execution [ɛksəkyōō'shən] *n* exécution *f.*
executioner [ɛksəkyōō'shənûr] *n* bourreau *m.*
executive [igzɛk'yətiv] *n* (COMM) cadre *m*; (POL) exécutif *m* ♦ *a* exécutif(ive); (position, job) de cadre; (secretary) de direction; (offices) de la direction; (car, plane) de fonction.
executive director *n* administrateur/trice.
executor [igzɛk'yətûr] *n* exécuteur/trice testamentaire.
exemplary [igzɛm'plûrē] *a* exemplaire.
exemplify [igzɛm'pləfī] *vt* illustrer.
exempt [igzɛmpt'] *a*: ~ **from** exempté(e) *or* dispensé(e) de ♦ *vt*: **to** ~ **sb from** exempter *or* dispenser qn de.
exemption [igzɛmp'shən] *n* exemption *f,* dispense *f.*
exercise [ɛk'sûrsīz] *n* exercice *m* ♦ *vt* exercer; (patience etc) faire preuve de; (dog) promener ♦ *vi* prendre de l'exercice.
exercise book *n* cahier *m.*
exert [igzûrt'] *vt* exercer, employer; (strength, force) employer; **to** ~ **o.s.** se dépenser.
exertion [igzûr'shən] *n* effort *m.*
ex gratia [ɛks grā'tēə] *a*: ~ **payment** gratification *f.*
exhale [ɛks·hāl'] *vt* expirer; exhaler ♦ *vi* expirer.
exhaust [igzóst'] *n* (also: ~ **fumes**) gaz *mpl* d'échappement; (also: ~ **pipe**) tuyau *m* d'échappement ♦ *vt* épuiser; **to** ~ **o.s.** s'épuiser.
exhausted [igzós'tid] *a* épuisé(e).
exhausting [igzós'ting] *a* épuisant(e).
exhaustion [igzós'chən] *n* épuisement *m*; **nervous** ~ fatigue nerveuse.
exhaustive [igzós'tiv] *a* très complet(ète).
exhibit [igzib'it] *n* (ART) pièce *f or* objet *m* exposé(e); (LAW) pièce à conviction ♦ *vt* exposer; (courage, skill) faire preuve de.
exhibition [ɛksəbish'ən] *n* exposition *f*; ~ **of temper** manifestation *f* de colère.
exhibitionist [ɛksəbish'ənist] *n* exhibitionniste *m/f.*
exhibitor [igzib'ətûr] *n* exposant/e.
exhilarating [igzil'ərāting] *a* grisant(e); stimulant(e).
exhilaration [igzilərā'shən] *n* euphorie *f,* ivresse *f.*
exhort [igzórt'] *vt* exhorter.
exile [ɛg'zīl] *n* exil *m*; (person) exilé/e ♦ *vt* exiler; **in** ~ en exil.
exist [igzist'] *vi* exister.
existence [igzis'təns] *n* existence *f*; **to be in** ~ exister.
existentialism [ɛgzisten'chəlizəm] *n* existentialisme *m.*
existing [igzis'ting] *a* (laws) existant(e); (system, regime) actuel(le).
exit [ɛg'zit] *n* sortie *f* ♦ *vi* (COMPUT, THEATER) sortir.
exit poll *n* (POL) sondage *m* à la sortie des bureaux de vote.
exit ramp *n* (US AUT) bretelle *f* d'accès.
exit visa *n* visa *m* de sortie.
exodus [ɛk'sədəs] *n* exode *m.*
ex officio [ɛks əfish'ēō] *a, ad* d'office, de droit.

exonerate [igzán'ərāt] *vt*: **to** ~ **from** disculper de.
exorbitant [igzór'bətənt] *a* (price) exorbitant(e), excessif(ive); (demands) exorbitant, démesuré(e).
exorcize [ɛk'sôrsīz] *vt* exorciser.
exotic [igzát'ik] *a* exotique.
exp. *abbr* = **expenses; expired; export; express.**
expand [ikspand'] *vt* (area) agrandir; (quantity) accroître; (influence etc) étendre ♦ *vi* (population, production) s'accroître; (trade, influence etc) se développer, s'étendre; (gas, metal) se dilater; **to** ~ **on** (notes, story etc) développer.
expanse [ikspans'] *n* étendue *f.*
expansion [ikspan'chən] *n* (see expand) développement *m*; accroissement *m*; extension *f*; dilatation *f.*
expansionism [ikspan'chənizəm] *n* expansionnisme *m.*
expansionist [ikspan'chənist] *a* expansionniste.
expatriate *n* [ɛkspā'trēit] expatrié/e ♦ *vt* [ɛkspā'trēāt] expatrier, exiler.
expect [ikspɛkt'] *vt* (anticipate) s'attendre à, s'attendre à ce que + sub; (count on) compter sur, escompter; (hope for) espérer; (require) demander, exiger; (suppose) supposer; (await, also baby) attendre ♦ *vi*: **to be** ~**ing** être enceinte; **to** ~ **sb to do** (anticipate) s'attendre à ce que qn fasse; (demand) attendre de qn qu'il fasse; **to** ~ **to do sth** penser *or* compter faire qch, s'attendre à faire qch; **as** ~**ed** comme prévu; **I** ~ **so** je crois que oui, je crois bien.
expectancy [ikspɛk'tənsē] *n* attente *f*; **life** ~ espérance *f* de vie.
expectant [ikspɛk'tənt] *a* qui attend (quelque chose); ~ **mother** future maman.
expectantly [ikspɛk'təntlē] *ad* (look, listen) avec l'air d'attendre quelque chose.
expectation [ikspɛktā'shən] *n* attente *f*, prévisions *fpl*; espérance(s) *f(pl)*; **in** ~ **of** dans l'attente de, en prévision de; **against** *or* **contrary to all** ~**(s)** contre toute attente, contrairement à ce qu'on attendait; **to come** *or* **live up to sb's** ~**s** répondre à l'attente *or* aux espérances de qn.
expedience, expediency [ikspē'dēəns, ikspē'dēənsē] *n* opportunité *f*; convenance *f* (du moment); **for the sake of** ~ parce que c'est (or c'était) plus simple *or* plus commode.
expedient [ikspē'dēənt] *a* indiqué(e), opportun(e); commode ♦ *n* expédient *m.*
expedite [ɛk'spidīt] *vt* hâter; expédier.
expedition [ɛkspidish'ən] *n* expédition *f.*
expeditionary force [ɛkspədish'ənārē fôrs] *n* corps *m* expéditionnaire.
expeditious [ɛkspidish'əs] *a* expéditif(ive), prompt(e).
expel [ikspel'] *vt* chasser, expulser; (SCOL) renvoyer, exclure.
expend [ikspend'] *vt* consacrer; (use up) dépenser.
expendable [ikspen'dəbəl] *a* remplaçable.
expenditure [ikspen'dichûr] *n* dépense *f*; dépenses *fpl.*
expense [ikspens'] *n* (cost) coût *m*; (spending)

dépense *f*, frais *mpl*; ~s *npl* frais *mpl*; dépenses; **to go to the** ~ **of** faire la dépense de; **at great/little** ~ à grands/peu de frais; **at the** ~ **of** aux frais de; (*fig*) aux dépens de.

expense account *n* (note *f* de) frais *mpl*.

expensive [ikspɛn'siv] *a* cher(chère), coûteux(euse); **to be** ~ coûter cher; ~ **tastes** goûts *mpl* de luxe.

experience [ikspēr'ēəns] *n* expérience *f* ♦ *vt* connaître; éprouver; **to know by** ~ savoir par expérience.

experienced [ikspēr'ēənst] *a* expérimenté(e).

experiment *n* [ikspär'əmənt] expérience *f* ♦ *vi* [ikspär'əment] faire une expérience; **to** ~ **with** expérimenter; **to perform** *or* **carry out an** ~ faire une expérience; **as an** ~ à titre d'expérience.

experimental [ikspärəmen'təl] *a* expérimental(e).

expert [ek'spûrt] *a* expert(e) ♦ *n* expert *m*; ~ **in** *or* **at doing sth** spécialiste de qch; **an** ~ **on sth** un spécialiste de qch; ~ **witness** (*LAW*) expert *m*.

expertise [ekspûrtēz'] *n* (grande) compétence.

expiration [eksperā'shən] *n* expiration *f*.

expire [ikspī'ûr] *vi* expirer.

expiry [ikspīûr'ē] *n* (*Brit*) expiration *f*.

explain [iksplān'] *vt* expliquer.

  explain away *vt* justifier, excuser.

explanation [eksplənā'shən] *n* explication *f*; **to find an** ~ **for sth** trouver une explication à qch.

explanatory [iksplan'ətôrē] *a* explicatif(ive).

explicit [iksplis'it] *a* explicite; (*definite*) formel(le).

explode [iksplōd'] *vi* exploser ♦ *vt* faire exploser; (*fig: theory*) démolir; **to** ~ **a myth** détruire un mythe.

exploit *n* [eks'ploit] exploit *m* ♦ *vt* [iksploit'] exploiter.

exploitation [eksploitā'shən] *n* exploitation *f*.

exploration [eksplərā'shən] *n* exploration *f*.

exploratory [iksplôr'ətôrē] *a* (*fig: talks*) préliminaire; ~ **operation** (*MED*) intervention *f* (à visée) exploratrice.

explore [iksplôr'] *vt* explorer; (*possibilities*) étudier, examiner.

explorer [iksplôr'ûr] *n* explorateur/trice.

explosion [iksplō'zhən] *n* explosion *f*.

explosive [iksplō'siv] *a* explosif(ive) ♦ *n* explosif *m*.

exponent [ekspō'nent] *n* (*of school of thought etc*) interprète *m*, représentant *m*; (*MATH*) exposant *m*.

export *vt* [ikspôrt'] exporter ♦ *n* [eks'pôrt] exportation *f* ♦ *cpd* d'exportation.

exportation [ekspôrtā'shən] *n* exportation *f*.

exporter [ekspôr'tûr] *n* exportateur *m*.

export license *n* licence *f* d'exportation.

expose [ikspōz'] *vt* exposer; (*unmask*) démasquer, dévoiler; **to** ~ **o.s.** (*LAW*) commettre un outrage à la pudeur.

exposed [ikspōzd'] *a* (*land, house*) exposé(e); (*ELEC: wire*) à nu; (*pipe, beam*) apparent(e).

exposition [ekspəzish'ən] *n* exposition *f*.

exposure [ikspō'zhûr] *n* exposition *f*; (*PHOT*) (temps *m* de) pose *f*; (*: shot*) pose; **suffering from** ~ (*MED*) souffrant des effets du froid et

de l'épuisement; **to die of** ~ (*MED*) mourir de froid.

exposure meter *n* posemètre *m*.

expound [ikspound'] *vt* exposer, expliquer.

express [ikspres'] *a* (*definite*) formel(le), exprès(esse); (*Brit: letter etc*) exprès *inv* ♦ *n* (*train*) rapide *m* ♦ *ad* (*send*) exprès ♦ *vt* exprimer; **to** ~ **o.s.** s'exprimer; **to send sth** ~ envoyer qch exprès.

expression [ikspresh'ən] *n* expression *f*.

expressionism [ikspresh'ənizəm] *n* expressionnisme *m*.

expressive [ikspres'iv] *a* expressif(ive).

expressly [ikspres'lē] *ad* expressément, formellement.

expressway [ikspres'wā] *n* voie *f* express (à plusieurs files).

expropriate [eksprōp'rēāt] *vt* exproprier.

expulsion [ikspul'shən] *n* expulsion *f*; renvoi *m*.

exquisite [ekskwiz'it] *a* exquis(e).

ex-serviceman [ekssûr'vismən] *n* (*Brit*) ancien combattant.

ext. *abbr* (*TEL*) = **extension**.

extemporize [ikstem'pərīz] *vi* improviser.

extend [ikstend'] *vt* (*visit, street*) prolonger; (*deadline*) reporter, remettre; (*building*) agrandir; (*offer*) présenter, offrir; (*COMM: credit*) accorder ♦ *vi* (*land*) s'étendre.

extension [iksten'chən] *n* (*see extend*) prolongation *f*; agrandissement *m*; (*building*) annexe *f*; (*to wire, table*) rallonge *f*; (*telephone: in offices*) poste *m*; (*: in private house*) téléphone *m* supplémentaire; ~ **3718** (*TEL*) poste 3718.

extension cord *n* (*ELEC*) rallonge *f*.

extensive [iksten'siv] *a* étendu(e), vaste; (*damage, alterations*) considérable; (*inquiries*) approfondi(e); (*use*) largement répandu(e).

extensively [iksten'sivlē] *ad* (*altered, damaged etc*) considérablement; **he's traveled** ~ il a beaucoup voyagé.

extent [ikstent'] *n* étendue *f*; (*degree: of damage, loss*) importance *f*; **to some** ~ dans une certaine mesure; **to a certain** ~ dans une certaine mesure, jusqu'à un certain point; **to a large** ~ en grande partie; **to what** ~? dans quelle mesure?, jusqu'à quel point?; **to such an** ~ **that** ... à tel point que ....

extenuating [iksten'yōōāting] *a*: ~ **circumstances** circonstances atténuantes.

exterior [ikstēr'ēûr] *a* extérieur(e), du dehors ♦ *n* extérieur *m*; dehors *m*.

exterminate [ikstûr'mənāt] *vt* exterminer.

extermination [ikstûrmənā'shən] *n* extermination *f*.

extern [eks'tûrn] *n* (*US*) externe *m/f*.

external [ikstûr'nəl] *a* externe ♦ *n*: **the** ~**s** les apparences *fpl*; **for** ~ **use only** (*MED*) à usage externe.

externally [ikstûr'nəlē] *ad* extérieurement.

extinct [ikstingkt'] *a* éteint(e).

extinction [ikstingk'shən] *n* extinction *f*.

extinguish [iksting'gwish] *vt* éteindre.

extinguisher [iksting'gwishûr] *n* extincteur *m*.

extoll, (*Brit*) **extol** [ikstōl'] *vt* (*merits*) chanter, prôner; (*person*) chanter les louanges de.

extort [ikstôrt'] *vt*: **to ~ sth (from)** extorquer qch (à).

extortion [ikstôr'shən] *n* extorsion *f*.

extortionate [ikstôr'shənit] *a* exorbitant(e).

extra [ek'strə] *a* supplémentaire, de plus ♦ *ad* (*in addition*) en plus ♦ *n* supplément *m*; (*THEATER*) figurant/e; **wine will cost ~ le** vin sera en supplément; **~ large sizes** très grandes tailles.

extra... *prefix* extra....

extract *vt* [ikstrakt'] extraire; (*tooth*) arracher; (*money, promise*) soutirer ♦ *n* [eks'trakt] extrait *m*.

extraction [ikstrak'shən] *n* (*also descent*) extraction *f*.

extracurricular [ekstrəkərik'yəlûr] *a* (*SCOL*) parascolaire.

extradite [eks'trədīt] *vt* extrader.

extradition [ekstrədish'ən] *n* extradition *f*.

extramarital [ekstrəmar'itəl] *a* extra-conjugal(e).

extramural [ekstrəmyōōr'əl] *a* hors-faculté *inv*.

extraneous [ikstrā'nēəs] *a*: **~ to** étranger(ère) à.

extraordinary [ikstrôr'dənärē] *a* extraordinaire; **the ~ thing is that ...** le plus étrange *or* étonnant c'est que ....

extraordinary general meeting *n* assemblée générale extraordinaire.

extrapolation [ikstrapəlā'shən] *n* extrapolation *f*.

extrasensory perception (ESP) [ekstrəsen'sûrē pûrsep'shən] *n* perception extra-sensorielle.

extra time *n* (*SOCCER*) prolongations *fpl*.

extravagance [ikstrav'əgəns] *n* (*excessive spending*) prodigalités *fpl*; (*thing bought*) folie *f*, dépense excessive *or* exagérée.

extravagant [ikstrav'əgənt] *a* extravagant(e); (*in spending: person*) prodigue, dépensier(ière); (*: tastes*) dispendieux(euse).

extreme [ikstrēm'] *a*, *n* extrême *(m)*; **the ~ left/right** (*POL*) l'extrême gauche *f*/droite *f*; **~s of temperature** différences *fpl* extrêmes de température.

extremely [ikstrēm'lē] *ad* extrêmement.

extremist [ikstrē'mist] *a*, *n* extrémiste *(m/f)*.

extremity [ikstrem'itē] *n* extrémité *f*.

extricate [ek'strikāt] *vt*: **to ~ sth (from)** dégager qch (de).

extrovert [ek'strōvûrt] *n* extraverti/e.

exuberance [igzōō'bûrəns] *n* exubérance *f*.

exuberant [igzōō'bûrənt] *a* exubérant(e).

exude [igzōōd'] *vt* exsuder; (*fig*) respirer; **the charm** *etc* **he ~s** le charme *etc* qui émane de lui.

exult [igzult'] *vi* exulter, jubiler.

exultant [igzul'tənt] *a* (*shout, expression*) de triomphe; **to be ~** jubiler, triompher.

exultation [egzultā'shən] *n* exultation *f*, jubilation *f*.

eye [ī] *n* œil *m* (*pl* yeux); (*of needle*) trou *m*, chas *m* ♦ *vt* examiner; **as far as the ~ can see** à perte de vue; **to keep an ~ on** surveiller; **to have an ~ for sth** avoir l'œil pour qch; **in the public ~** en vue; **there's more to this than meets the ~** ce n'est pas aussi simple que cela paraît.

eyeball [ī'bôl] *n* globe *m* oculaire.

eyebath [ī'bath] *n* (*Brit*) = **eye cup**.

eyebrow [ī'brou] *n* sourcil *m*.

eyebrow pencil *n* crayon *m* à sourcils.

eye-catching [ī'kaching] *a* voyant(e), accrocheur(euse).

eye cup *n* (*US*) œillère *f* (*pour bains d'œil*).

eyedrops [ī'drâps] *npl* gouttes *fpl* pour les yeux.

eyeglass [ī'glas] *n* monocle *m*.

eyelash [ī'lash] *n* cil *m*.

eyelet [ī'lit] *n* œillet *m*.

eye-level [ī'levəl] *a* en hauteur.

eyelid [ī'lid] *n* paupière *f*.

eyeliner [ī'līnûr] *n* eye-liner *m*.

eye-opener [ī'ōpənûr] *n* révélation *f*.

eyeshadow [ī'shadō] *n* ombre *f* à paupières.

eyesight [ī'sīt] *n* vue *f*.

eyesore [ī'sôr] *n* horreur *f*, chose *f* qui dépare *or* enlaidit.

eyestrain [ī'strān] *a*: **to get ~** se fatiguer la vue *or* les yeux.

eye test *n* examen *m* de la vue.

eyetooth, *pl* **-teeth** [ī'tōōth, -tēth] *n* canine supérieure; **to give one's eyeteeth for sth/to do sth** (*fig*) donner n'importe quoi pour qch/pour faire qch.

eyewash [ī'wâsh] *n* bain *m* d'œil; (*fig*) frime *f*.

eye witness *n* témoin *m* oculaire.

eyrie [är'ē] *n* aire *f*.

F

F, f [ef] *n* (*letter*) F, f *m*; (*MUS*): **F** fa *m*; **F for Fox** F comme François.

F [ef] *abbr* (= *Fahrenheit*) F.

FA *n abbr* (*Brit*: = *Football Association*) fédération de football.

FAA *n abbr* (*US*) = *Federal Aviation Administration*.

fable [fā'bəl] *n* fable *f*.

fabric [fab'rik] *n* tissu *m* ♦ *cpd*: **~ ribbon** *n* (*for typewriter*) ruban *m* (en) tissu.

fabricate [fab'rikāt] *vt* fabriquer, inventer.

fabrication [fabrikā'shən] *n* fabrication *f*, invention *f*.

fabulous [fab'yələs] *a* fabuleux(euse); (*col: super*) formidable, sensationnel(le).

façade [fəsâd'] *n* façade *f*.

face [fās] *n* visage *m*, figure *f*; expression *f*; grimace *f*; (*of clock*) cadran *m*; (*of building*) façade *f*; (*side, surface*) face *f*; (*in mine*) front *m* de taille ♦ *vt* faire face à; (*facts etc*) accepter; **~ down** (*person*) à plat ventre; (*card*) face en dessous; **to lose/save ~** perdre/sauver la face; **to make a ~** faire une grimace; **in the ~ of** (*difficulties etc*) face à, devant; **on the ~ of it** à première vue.

face up to *vt fus* faire face à, affronter.

facecloth [fās'klôth] *n* gant *m* de toilette.

face cream *n* crème *f* pour le visage.

face lift *n* lifting *m*; (*of façade etc*) ravale-

ment *m*, retapage *m*.
face powder *n* poudre *f* (pour le visage).
face-saving [fās'sāving] *a* qui sauve la face.
facet [fas'it] *n* facette *f*.
facetious [fəsē'shəs] *a* facétieux(euse).
face-to-face [fās'təfās'] *ad* face à face.
face value [fās val'yōō] *n* (*of coin*) valeur nominale; **to take sth at ~** (*fig*) prendre qch
pour argent comptant.
facia [fā'shēə] *n* = **fascia**.
facial [fā'shəl] *a* facial(e) ♦ *n* soin complet du
visage.
facile [fas'əl] *a* facile.
facilitate [fəsil'ətāt] *vt* faciliter.
facility [fəsil'ətē] *n* facilité *f*; **facilities** *npl*
installations *fpl*, équipement *m*; **credit facilities** facilités de paiement.
facing [fā'sing] *prep* face à, en face de ♦ *n* (*of
wall etc*) revêtement *m*; (*SEWING*) revers *m*.
facsimile [faksim'əlē] *n* (*exact replica*) fac-
similé *m*; (*also:* ~ **machine**) télécopieur *m*;
(*transmitted document*) télécopie *f*.
fact [fakt] *n* fait *m*; **in** ~ en fait; **to know for
a** ~ **that** ... savoir pertinemment que ....
fact-finding [fakt'fīnding] *a*: **a** ~ **tour** or
mission une mission d'enquête.
faction [fak'shən] *n* faction *f*.
factor [fak'tûr] *n* facteur *m*; (*COMM*) factor *m*,
société *f* d'affacturage; (*: agent*) dépositaire
m/f ♦ *vi* faire du factoring; **safety** ~ facteur
de sécurité.
factory [fak'tûrē] *n* usine *f*, fabrique *f*.
factory farming *n* (*Brit*) élevage industriel.
factory ship *n* navire-usine *m*.
factual [fak'chōōəl] *a* basé(e) sur les faits.
faculty [fak'əltē] *n* faculté *f*; (*US: teaching
staff*) corps enseignant.
fad [fad] *n* (*col*) manie *f*; engouement *m*.
fade [fād] *vi* se décolorer, passer; (*light,
sound, hope*) s'affaiblir, disparaître; (*flower*)
se faner.
   fade in *vt* (*picture*) ouvrir en fondu;
(*sound*) monter progressivement.
   fade out *vt* (*picture*) fermer en fondu;
(*sound*) baisser progressivement.
faeces [fē'sēz] *npl* (*Brit*) = **feces**.
fag [fag] *n* (*US col: homosexual*) pédé *m*; (*Brit
col: cigarette*) sèche *f*; (*: chore*): **what a** ~!
quelle corvée!
fag end *n* (*Brit col*) mégot *m*.
fail [fāl] *vt* (*exam*) échouer à; (*candidate*) recaler; (*subj: courage, memory*) faire défaut
à ♦ *vi* échouer; (*supplies*) manquer; (*eyesight, health, light: also:* **be ~ing**) baisser,
s'affaiblir; (*brakes*) lâcher; **to** ~ **to do sth**
(*neglect*) négliger de *or* ne pas faire qch; (*be
unable*) ne pas arriver *or* parvenir à faire
qch; **without** ~ à coup sûr; sans faute.
failing [fā'ling] *n* défaut *m* ♦ *prep* faute de; ~
that à défaut, sinon.
failsafe [fāl'sāf] *a* (*device etc*) à sûreté inté-
grée.
failure [fāl'yûr] *n* échec *m*; (*person*) raté/e;
(*mechanical etc*) défaillance *f*; **his** ~ **to turn
up** le fait de n'être pas venu *or* qu'il ne soit
pas venu.
faint [fānt] *a* faible; (*recollection*) vague;
(*mark*) à peine visible; (*smell, breeze, trace*)
léger(ère) ♦ *n* évanouissement *m* ♦ *vi* s'éva-

nouir; **to feel** ~ défaillir.
faint-hearted [fānt'hâr'tid] *a* pusillanime.
faintly [fānt'lē] *ad* faiblement; vaguement.
faintness [fānt'nis] *n* faiblesse *f*.
fair [fär] *a* équitable, juste; (*reasonable*)
correct(e), honnête; (*hair*) blond(e); (*skin,
complexion*) pâle, blanc(blanche); (*weather*)
beau(belle); (*good enough*) assez bon(ne) ♦
ad: **to play** ~ jouer franc jeu ♦ *n* foire *f*;
(*carnival*) fête (foraine); (*also:* **trade** ~)
foire(-exposition) commerciale; **it's not** ~!
ce n'est pas juste!; **a** ~ **amount of** une
quantité considérable de.
fairground [fär'ground] *n* champ *m* de foire.
fair-haired [fär'härd] *a* (*person*) aux cheveux
clairs, blond(e).
fairly [fär'lē] *ad* équitablement; (*quite*) assez;
I'm ~ **sure** j'en suis quasiment *or* presque
sûr.
fairness [fär'nis] *n* (*of trial etc*) justice *f*, équité *f*; (*of person*) sens *m* de la justice; **in all**
~ en toute justice.
fair play *n* fair play *m*.
fair trade *n* (*US*) *vente au détail á prix
imposé.*
fairy [fär'ē] *n* fée *f*.
fairy godmother *n* bonne fée.
fairy tale *n* conte *m* de fées.
faith [fāth] *n* foi *f*; (*trust*) confiance *f*; (*sect*)
culte *m*, religion *f*; **to have** ~ **in sb/sth**
avoir confiance en qn/qch.
faithful [fāth'fəl] *a* fidèle.
faithfully [fāth'fəlē] *ad* fidèlement; **yours** ~
(*Brit: in letters*) veuillez agréer l'expression
de mes salutations les plus distinguées.
faith healer [fāth' hē'lûr] *n* guérisseur/euse.
fake [fāk] *n* (*painting etc*) faux *m*; (*photo*) tru-
cage *m*; (*person*) imposteur *m* ♦ *a*
faux(fausse) ♦ *vt* (*emotions*) simuler; (*photo*)
truquer; (*story*) fabriquer; **his illness is a** ~
sa maladie est une comédie *or* de la simulation.
falcon [fal'kən] *n* faucon *m*.
Falkland Islands [fôlk'lənd ī'ləndz] *npl*: **the** ~
les Malouines *fpl*, les îles *fpl* Falkland.
fall [fôl] *n* chute *f*; (*decrease*) baisse *f*; (*US*)
automne *m* ♦ *vi* (*pt* **fell**, *pp* **fallen** [fel, fôl'ən])
tomber; **~s** *npl* (*waterfall*) chute *f* d'eau,
cascade *f*; **to** ~ **flat** *vi* (*on one's face*)
tomber de tout son long, s'étaler; (*joke*)
tomber à plat; (*plan*) échouer; **to** ~ **short of**
(*sb's expectations*) ne pas répondre à; **a** ~ **of
snow** (*Brit*) une chute de neige.
   fall apart *vi* tomber en morceaux; (*col:
emotionally*) craquer.
   fall back *vi* reculer, se retirer.
   fall back on *vt fus* se rabattre sur; **to have
something to** ~ **back on** (*money etc*) avoir
quelque chose en réserve; (*job etc*) avoir une
solution de rechange.
   fall behind *vi* prendre du retard.
   fall down *vi* (*person*) tomber; (*building,
hopes*) s'effondrer, s'écrouler.
   fall for *vt fus* (*trick*) se laisser prendre à;
(*person*) tomber amoureux(euse) de.
   fall in *vi* s'effondrer; (*MIL*) se mettre en
rangs.
   fall in with *vt fus* (*sb's plans etc*) accepter.
   fall off *vi* tomber; (*diminish*) baisser, dimi-

nuer.
fall out vi (*friends etc*) se brouiller.
fall over vi tomber (par terre).
fall through vi (*plan, project*) tomber à l'eau.
fallacy |fal'əsē| n erreur f, illusion f.
fallback |fôl'bak| a: ~ **position** position f de repli.
fallen |fôl'ən| pp of **fall**.
fallible |fal'əbəl| a faillible.
fallopian tube |fəlō'pēən tōōb'| n (*ANAT*) trompe f de Fallope.
fallout |fôl'out| n retombées (radioactives).
fallout shelter n abri m anti-atomique.
fallow |fal'ō| a en jachère; en friche.
false |fôls| a faux(fausse); **under ~ pretenses** sous un faux prétexte.
false alarm n fausse alerte.
falsehood |fôls'hōōd| n mensonge m.
falsely |fôls'lē| ad (*accuse*) à tort.
false teeth npl fausses dents.
falsify |fôl'səfī| vt falsifier; (*accounts*) maquiller.
falter |fôl'tûr| vi chanceler, vaciller.
fame |fām| n renommée f, renom m.
familiar |fəmil'yûr| a familier(ière); **to be ~ with sth** connaître qch; **to make o.s. ~ with sth** se familiariser avec qch; **to be on ~ terms with sb** bien connaître qn.
familiarity |fəmilēar'ətē| n familiarité f.
familiarize |fəmil'yərīz| vt familiariser.
family |fam'lē| n famille f.
family allowance n allocations familiales.
family business n entreprise familiale.
family doctor n médecin m de famille.
family life n vie f de famille.
family planning clinic n centre m de planning familial.
family tree n arbre m généalogique.
famine |fam'in| n famine f.
famished |fam'isht| a affamé(e); **I'm ~!** (*col*) je meurs de faim!
famous |fā'məs| a célèbre.
famously |fā'məslē| ad (*get on*) fameusement, à merveille.
fan |fan| n (*folding*) éventail m; (*ELEC*) ventilateur m; (*person*) fan m, admirateur/trice; (*SPORT*) supporter m/f ♦ vt éventer; (*fire, quarrel*) attiser.
fan out vi se déployer (en éventail).
fanatic |fənat'ik| n fanatique m/f.
fanatical |fənat'ikəl| a fanatique.
fan belt n courroie f de ventilateur.
fancied |fan'sēd| a imaginaire.
fanciful |fan'sifəl| a fantaisiste.
fancy |fan'sē| n fantaisie f, envie f; imagination f ♦ cpd (de) fantaisie inv ♦ vt (*feel like, want*) avoir envie de; (*imagine*) imaginer; **to take a ~ to** se prendre d'affection pour; s'enticher de; **it took** or **caught my ~** ça m'a plu; **when the ~ takes him** quand ça lui prend; **to ~ that ...** se figurer or s'imaginer que ...; **he fancies her** (*Brit*) elle lui plaît.
fancy dress n déguisement m, travesti m.
fancy-dress ball |fan'sedres bôl'| n (*Brit*) bal masqué or costumé.
fancy goods npl articles mpl (de) fantaisie.
fanfare |fan'fär| n fanfare f (*musique*).
fanfold paper |fan'fōld pā'pûr| n papier m à pliage accordéon.

fang |fang| n croc m; (*of snake*) crochet m.
fan heater n (*Brit*) radiateur soufflant.
fanlight |fan'lit| n imposte f.
fantasize |fan'təsīz| vi fantasmer.
fantastic |fantas'tik| a fantastique.
fantasy |fan'təsē| n imagination f, fantaisie f; fantasme m.
FAO n abbr (= *Food and Agriculture Organization*) FAO f.
far |fär| a: **the ~ side/end** l'autre côté/bout; **the ~ left/right** (*POL*) l'extrême gauche f/ droite f ♦ ad loin; **is it ~ to Boston?** est-ce qu'on est loin de Boston?; **it's not ~ (from here)** ce n'est pas loin (d'ici); **~ away, ~ off** au loin, dans le lointain; **~ better** beaucoup mieux; **~ from** loin de; **by ~** de loin, de beaucoup; **as ~ back as the 13th century** dès le 13e siècle; **go as ~ as the farm** allez jusqu'à la ferme; **as ~ as I know** pour autant que je sache; **as ~ as possible** dans la mesure du possible; **how ~ have you got with your work?** où en êtes-vous dans votre travail?
faraway |fär'əwā| a lointain(e); (*look*) absent(e).
farce |färs| n farce f.
farcical |fär'sikəl| a grotesque.
fare |fär| n (*on trains, buses*) prix m du billet; (*in taxi*) prix de la course; (*passenger in taxi*) client m; (*food*) table f, chère f ♦ vi se débrouiller.
Far East n: **the ~** l'Extrême-Orient m.
farewell |fär'wel'| excl, n adieu (m) ♦ cpd |fär'wel| (*party etc*) d'adieux.
far-fetched |fär'fecht'| a exagéré(e), poussé(e).
farm |färm| n ferme f ♦ vt cultiver.
farm out vt (*work etc*) distribuer.
farmer |fär'mûr| n fermier/ière; cultivateur/ trice.
farmhand |färm'hand| n ouvrier/ière agricole.
farmhouse |färm'hous| n (maison f de) ferme f.
farming |fär'ming| n agriculture f; **intensive ~** culture intensive; **sheep ~** élevage m du mouton.
farm laborer n = **farmhand**.
farmland |färm'land| n terres cultivées or arables.
farm produce n produits mpl agricoles.
farm worker n = **farmhand**.
farmyard |färm'yärd| n cour f de ferme.
Faroe Islands |farō' i'ləndz| npl, **Faroes** |farōz'| npl: **the ~** les îles fpl Féroé or Faeroe.
far-reaching |fär'rē'ching| a d'une grande portée.
farsighted |fär'sī'tid| a presbyte; (*fig*) prévoyant(e), qui voit loin.
fart |färt| (*col!*) n pet m ♦ vi péter.
farther |fär'thûr| ad plus loin ♦ a plus eloigné(e), plus lointain(e).
farthest |fär'thist| superlative of **far**.
FAS abbr (= *free alongside ship*) FLB.
fascia |fā'shēə| n (*AUT*) (garniture f du) tableau m de bord.
fascinate |fas'ənāt| vt fasciner, captiver.
fascinating |fas'ənāting| a fascinant(e).

fascination [fasənā'shən] *n* fascination *f*.
fascism [fash'izəm] *n* fascisme *m*.
fascist [fash'ist] *a*, *n* fasciste *(m/f)*.
fashion [fash'ən] *n* mode *f*; *(manner)* façon *f*, manière *f* ♦ *vt* façonner; **in** ~ à la mode; **out of** ~ démodé(e); **in the Greek** ~ à la grecque; **after a** ~ *(finish, manage etc)* tant bien que mal.
fashionable [fash'ənəbəl] *a* à la mode.
fashion designer *n* (grand(e)) couturier/ière.
fashion show *n* défilé *m* de mannequins *or* de mode.
fast [fast] *a* rapide; *(clock)*: **to be** ~ avancer; *(dye, color)* grand *or* bon teint *inv* ♦ *ad* vite, rapidement; *(stuck, held)* solidement ♦ *n* jeûne *m* ♦ *vi* jeûner; **my watch is 5 minutes** ~ ma montre avance de 5 minutes; ~ **asleep** profondément endormi; **as** ~ **as I can** aussi vite que je peux.
fasten [fas'ən] *vt* attacher, fixer; *(coat)* attacher, fermer ♦ *vi* se fermer, s'attacher.
fasten (up)on *vt fus (idea)* se cramponner à.
fastener [fas'ənûr], **fastening** [fas'əning] *n* fermeture *f*, attache *f*; *(Brit: zip ~)* fermeture éclair *inv* ® *or* à glissière.
fast food *n* fast food *m*, restauration *f* rapide.
fastidious [fastid'ēəs] *a* exigeant(e), difficile.
fast lane *n* *(AUT: in Britain)* voie *f* de droite.
fat [fat] *a* gros(se) ♦ *n* graisse *f*; *(on meat)* gras *m*; **to live off the** ~ **of the land** vivre grassement.
fatal [fāt'əl] *a* fatal(e); *(leading to death)* mortel(le).
fatalism [fāt'əlizəm] *n* fatalisme *m*.
fatality [fātal'itē] *n* *(road death etc)* victime *f*, décès *m*.
fatally [fāt'əlē] *ad* fatalement; mortellement.
fate [fāt] *n* destin *m*; *(of person)* sort *m*; **to meet one's** ~ trouver la mort.
fated [fā'tid] *a* *(person)* condamné(e); *(project)* voué(e) à l'échec.
fateful [fāt'fəl] *a* fatidique.
father [fâ'thûr] *n* père *m*.
Father Christmas *n* *(Brit)* le Père Noël.
fatherhood [fâ'thûrhoͦod] *n* paternité *f*.
father-in-law [fâ'thûrinlô] *n* beau-père *m*.
fatherland [fâ'thûrland] *n* *(mère f)* patrie *f*.
fatherly [fâ'thûrlē] *a* paternel(le).
fathom [fath'əm] *n* brasse *f* *(= 1828 mm)* ♦ *vt* *(mystery)* sonder, pénétrer.
fatigue [fətēg'] *n* fatigue *f*; *(MIL)* corvée *f*; **metal** ~ fatigue du métal.
fatness [fat'nis] *n* corpulence *f*, grosseur *f*.
fatten [fat'ən] *vt*, *vi* engraisser; **chocolate is** ~**ing** le chocolat fait grossir.
fatty [fat'ē] *a* *(food)* gras(se) ♦ *n* *(col)* gros/grosse.
fatuous [fach'ōōəs] *a* stupide.
faucet [fô'sit] *n* *(US)* robinet *m*.
fault [fôlt] *n* faute *f*; *(defect)* défaut *m*; *(GEO)* faille *f* ♦ *vt* trouver des défauts à, prendre en défaut; **it's my** ~ c'est de ma faute; **to find** ~ **with** trouver à redire *or* à critiquer à; **at** ~ fautif(ive), coupable; **to a** ~ à l'excès.
faultless [fôlt'lis] *a* impeccable; irréprochable.
faulty [fôl'tē] *a* défectueux(euse).
fauna [fôn'ə] *n* faune *f*.
faux pas [fō pá'] *n* impair *m*, bévue *f*, gaffe *f*.

favor [fā'vûr] *(US)* *n* faveur *f*; *(help)* service *m* ♦ *vt* *(proposition)* être en faveur de; *(pupil etc)* favoriser; *(team, horse)* donner gagnant; **to do sb a** ~ rendre un service à qn; **in** ~ **of** en faveur de; **to be in** ~ **of sth/of doing sth** être partisan de qch/de faire qch; **to find** ~ **with sb** trouver grâce aux yeux de qn.
favorable [fā'vûrəbəl] *a* favorable; *(price)* avantageux(euse).
favorably [fā'vûrəblē] *ad* favorablement.
favorite [fā'vûrit] *a*, *n* favori(te).
favoritism [fā'vûritizəm] *n* favoritisme *m*.
favour [fā'vûr] *etc (Brit)* = **favor** *etc*.
fawn [fôn] *n* faon *m* ♦ *a* *(also:* ~-**colored)** fauve ♦ *vi*: ~ **to** ~ **(up)on** flatter servilement.
fax [faks] *n* *(document)* télécopie *f*; *(machine)* télécopieur *m* ♦ *vt* envoyer par télécopie.
fazed [fāzd] *a* *(col)* déconcerté(e).
FBI *n abbr (US:* = *Federal Bureau of Investigation)* FBI *m*.
FCA *n abbr (US)* = *Farm Credit Administration*.
FCC *n abbr (US)* = *Federal Communications Commission*.
FCO *n abbr (Brit:* = *Foreign and Commonwealth Office)* ministère des Affaires étrangères et du Commonwealth.
FD *n abbr (US)* = **fire department**.
FDA *n abbr (US:* = *Food and Drug Administration)* office de contrôle des produits pharmaceutiques et alimentaires.
FDIC *n abbr (US:* = *Federal Deposit Insurance Corporation)* organisme fédéral assurant les dépôts des banques.
fear [fēr] *n* crainte *f*, peur *f* ♦ *vt* craindre ♦ *vi*: **to** ~ **for** craindre pour; **to** ~ **that** craindre que; ~ **of heights** vertige *m*; **for** ~ **of** de peur que + *sub or* de + *infinitive*.
fearful [fēr'fəl] *a* craintif(ive); *(sight, noise)* affreux(euse), épouvantable; **to be** ~ **of** avoir peur de, craindre.
fearfully [fēr'fəlē] *ad (timidly)* craintivement; *(col: very)* affreusement.
fearless [fēr'lis] *a* intrépide, sans peur.
fearsome [fēr'səm] *a* *(opponent)* redoutable; *(sight)* épouvantable.
feasibility [fēzəbil'ətē] *n* *(of plan)* possibilité *f* de réalisation, faisabilité *f*.
feasibility study *n* étude *f* de faisabilité.
feasible [fē'zəbəl] *a* faisable, réalisable.
feast [fēst] *n* festin *m*, banquet *m*; *(REL: also:* ~ **day)** fête *f* ♦ *vi* festoyer; **to** ~ **on** se régaler de.
feat [fēt] *n* exploit *m*, prouesse *f*.
feather [feth'ûr] *n* plume *f* ♦ *vt*: **to** ~ **one's nest** *(fig)* faire sa pelote ♦ *cpd (bed etc)* de plumes.
featherweight [feth'ûrwāt] *n* poids *m* plume *inv*.
feature [fē'chûr] *n* caractéristique *f*; *(article)* chronique *f*, rubrique *f* ♦ *vt* *(subj: film)* avoir pour vedette(s) ♦ *vi* figurer (en bonne place); ~**s** *npl (of face)* traits *mpl*; **a (special)** ~ **on sth/sb** un reportage sur qch/qn; **it** ~**d prominently in** ... cela a figuré en bonne place sur *or* dans ....
feature film *n* long métrage.
featureless [fē'chûrlis] *a* anonyme, sans traits

distinctifs.

Feb. *abbr* (= *February*) fév.

February [feb'yəwārē] *n* février *m*; *for phrases see also* **July**.

feces [fē'sēz] *npl* (*US*) féces *fpl*.

feckless [fek'lis] *a* inepte.

Fed *abbr* (*US*) = **federal, federation**.

fed [fed] *pt, pp of* **feed; to be ~ up** en avoir marre *or* plein le dos.

Fed. [fed] *n abbr* (*US col*) = **Federal Reserve Board**.

federal [fed'ûrəl] *a* fédéral(e).

Federal Republic of Germany (FRG) *n* République fédérale d'Allemagne (RFA).

Federal Reserve Board *n* (*US*) *organe de contrôle de la banque centrale américaine.*

Federal Trade Commission (FTC) *n* (*US*) *organisme de protection contre les pratiques commerciales abusives.*

federation [fedərā'shən] *n* fédération *f*.

fedora [fədôr'ə] *n* (*US*) chapeau mou, feutre *m*.

fee [fē] *n* rémunération *f*; (*of doctor, lawyer*) honoraires *mpl*; (*of school, college etc*) frais *mpl* de scolarité; (*for examination*) droits *mpl*; **entrance/membership ~** droit d'entrée/d'inscription; **for a small ~** pour une somme modique.

feeble [fē'bəl] *a* faible.

feeble-minded [fē'bəlmīndid] *a* faible d'esprit.

feed [fēd] *n* (*of baby*) tétée *f*; (*of animal*) fourrage *m*; pâture *f*; (*on printer*) mécanisme *m* d'alimentation ♦ *vt* (*pt, pp* **fed** [fed]) nourrir; (*horse etc*) donner à manger à; (*machine*) alimenter; (*data etc*): **to ~ sth into** fournir qch à, introduire qch dans.

feed back *vt* (*results*) donner en retour.

feed on *vt fus* se nourrir de.

feedback [fēd'bak] *n* feed-back *m*; (*from person*) réactions *fpl*.

feeder [fē'dûr] *n* (*bib*) bavette *f*.

feeding bottle [fē'ding bât'əl] *n* (*Brit*) biberon *m*.

feel [fēl] *n* sensation *f* ♦ *vt* (*pt, pp* **felt** [felt]) (*touch*) toucher; tâter, palper; (*cold, pain*) sentir; (*grief, anger*) ressentir, éprouver; (*think, believe*): **to ~ (that)** trouver que; **I ~ that you ought to do it** il me semble que vous devriez le faire; **to ~ hungry/cold** avoir faim/froid; **to ~ lonely/better** se sentir seul/mieux; **I don't ~ well** je ne me sens pas bien; **to ~ sorry for** avoir pitié de; **it ~s soft** c'est doux au toucher; **it ~s colder here** je trouve qu'il fait plus froid ici; **it ~s like velvet** on dirait du velours, ça ressemble au velours; **to ~ like** (*want*) avoir envie de; **to ~ around** fouiller, tâtonner; **to get the ~ of sth** (*fig*) s'habituer à qch.

feeler [fē'lûr] *n* (*of insect*) antenne *f*; (*fig*): **to put out a ~** *or* **~s** tâter le terrain.

feeling [fē'ling] *n* sensation *f*, sentiment *m*; (*impression*) sentiment; **to hurt sb's ~s** froisser qn; **~s ran high about it** cela a déchaîné les passions; **what are your ~s about the matter?** quel est votre sentiment sur cette question?; **my ~ is that** ... j'estime que ...; **I have a ~ that** ... j'ai l'impression que ....

feet [fēt] *npl of* **foot**.

feign [fān] *vt* feindre, simuler.

felicitous [filis'itəs] *a* heureux(euse).

fell [fel] *pt of* **fall** ♦ *vt* (*tree*) abattre ♦ *a*: **with one ~ blow** d'un seul coup.

fellow [fel'ō] *n* type *m*; (*comrade*) compagnon *m*; (*of learned society*) membre *m*; (*of university*) universitaire *m/f* (membre du conseil) ♦ *cpd*: **their ~ prisoners/students** leurs camarades prisonniers/étudiants; **his ~ workers** ses collègues *mpl* (de travail).

fellow citizen *n* concitoyen/ne.

fellow countryman *n* compatriote *m*.

fellow feeling *n* sympathie *f*.

fellow men *npl* semblables *mpl*.

fellowship [fel'ōship] *n* (*society*) association *f*; (*comradeship*) amitié *f*, camaraderie *f*; (*SCOL*) *sorte de bourse universitaire.*

fellow traveler *n* compagnon/compagne de route; (*POL*) communisant/e.

fell-walking [fel'wôking] *n* (*Brit*) randonnée *f* en montagne.

felon [fel'ən] *n* (*LAW*) criminel/le.

felony [fel'ənē] *n* (*LAW*) crime *m*, forfait *m*.

felt [felt] *pt, pp of* **feel** ♦ *n* feutre *m*.

felt-tip pen [felt'tip pen'] *n* stylo-feutre *m*.

female [fē'māl] *n* (*ZOOL*) femelle *f*; (*pej: woman*) bonne femme ♦ *a* (*BIOL, ELEC*) femelle; (*sex, character*) féminin(e); (*vote etc*) des femmes; (*child etc*) du sexe féminin; **male and ~ students** étudiants et étudiantes.

female impersonator *n* (*THEATER*) travesti *m*.

feminine [fem'ənin] *a* féminin(e) ♦ *n* féminin *m*.

femininity [femənin'ətē] *n* féminité *f*.

feminism [fem'ənizəm] *n* féminisme *m*.

feminist [fem'ənist] *n* féministe *m/f*.

fence [fens] *n* barrière *f*; (*SPORT*) obstacle *m*; (*col: person*) receleur/euse ♦ *vt* (*also:* **~ in**) clôturer ♦ *vi* faire de l'escrime; **to sit on the ~** (*fig*) ne pas se mouiller.

fencing [fen'sing] *n* (*sport*) escrime *m*.

fend [fend] *vi*: **to ~ for o.s.** se débrouiller (tout seul).

fend off *vt* (*attack etc*) parer.

fender [fen'dûr] *n* (*of fireplace*) garde-feu *m inv*; (*on boat*) défense *f*; (*US AUT*) garde-boue *m*.

fennel [fen'əl] *n* fenouil *m*.

FEPC *n abbr* (*US*: = *Fair Employment Practices Committee*) *commission f pour l'égalité des chances dans le travail.*

FERC *n abbr* (*US*) = *Federal Energy Regulatory Commission.*

ferment *vi* [fərment'] fermenter ♦ *n* [fûr'ment] agitation *f*, effervescence *f*.

fermentation [fûrmentā'shən] *n* fermentation *f*.

fern [fûrn] *n* fougère *f*.

ferocious [fərō'shəs] *a* féroce.

ferocity [fərâs'itē] *n* férocité *f*.

ferret [fär'it] *n* furet *m*.

ferret around *vi* fureter.

ferret out *vt* dénicher.

Ferris wheel [fär'is hwēl] *n* (*at fair*) grande roue.

ferry [fär'ē] *n* (*small*) bac *m*; (*large: also:* **~boat**) ferry(-boat) *m* ♦ *vt* transporter; **to ~**

sth/sb **across** or **over** faire traverser qch/qn.
ferryman [fär'ēmən] n passeur m.
fertile [fûr'təl] a fertile; (BIOL) fécond(e); ~
period période f de fécondité.
fertility [fûrtil'ətē] n fertilité f; fécondité f.
fertility drug n médicament m contre la stérilité.
fertilize [fûr'təlīz] vt fertiliser; féconder.
fertilizer [fûr'təlīzûr] n engrais m.
fervent [fûr'vənt] a fervent(e), ardent(e).
fervor, (Brit) **fervour** [fûr'vûr] n ferveur f.
fester [fes'tûr] vi suppurer.
festival [fes'təvəl] n (REL) fête f; (ART, MUS)
festival m.
festive [fes'tiv] a de fête; **the ~ season** (Brit:
Christmas) la période des fêtes.
festivities [festiv'itēz] npl réjouissances fpl.
festoon [festōōn'] vt: **to ~ with** orner de.
FET n abbr (US: = Federal Excise Tax) excise
fédérale.
fetal [fēt'l] a (US) fœtal(e).
fetch [fech] vt aller chercher; (Brit: sell for)
se vendre.
fetching [fech'ing] a charmant(e).
fête [fet] n fête f, kermesse f.
fetid [fet'id] a fétide.
fetish [fet'ish] n fétiche m.
fetter [fet'ûr] vt entraver.
fetters [fet'ûrz] npl chaînes fpl.
fettle [fet'əl] n (Brit): **in fine ~** en bonne
forme.
fetus [fē'təs] n (US) foetus m.
feud [fyōōd] n dispute f, dissension f ♦ vi se
disputer, se quereller; **a family ~** une querelle de famille.
feudal [fyōōd'əl] a féodal(e).
feudalism [fyōōd'dəlizəm] n féodalité f.
fever [fē'vûr] n fièvre f; **he has a ~** il a de la
fièvre.
feverish [fē'vûrish] a fiévreux(euse), fébrile.
few [fyōō] a peu de ♦ pronoun: **~ succeed** il y
en a peu qui réussissent, (bien) peu
réussissent; **they were ~** ils étaient peu
(nombreux), il y en avait peu; **a ~** ...
quelques ...; **I know a ~** j'en connais
quelques-uns; **quite a ~** ... un certain nombre
de ..., pas mal de ...; **in the next ~ days**
dans les jours qui viennent; **in the past ~
days** ces derniers jours; **every ~ days/
months** tous les deux ou trois jours/mois; **a
~ more** ... encore quelques ..., quelques ... de
plus.
fewer [fyōō'ûr] a moins de ♦ pronoun moins;
they are ~ now il y en a moins maintenant,
ils sont moins (nombreux) maintenant.
fewest [fyōō'ist] a le moins nombreux.
FFA n abbr = Future Farmers of America.
FHA n abbr (US: = Federal Housing Administration) office fédéral du logement.
fiancé [fēânsā'] n fiancé m.
fiancée [fēânsā'] n fiancée f.
fiasco [fēas'kō] n fiasco m.
fib [fib] n bobard m.
fiber [fī'bûr] n (US) fibre f.
fiberboard [fī'bûrbôrd] n panneau m de fibres.
fiber-glass [fī'bûrglas] n fibre de verre.
fibre [fī'bûr] etc (Brit) = fiber etc.
fibrositis [fībrəsī'tis] n aponévrosite f.
FIC n abbr (US: = Federal Information

Centers) centre fédéral d'information au public.
FICA n abbr (US) = Federal Insurance Contributions Act.
fickle [fik'əl] a inconstant(e), volage, capri-
cieux(euse).
fiction [fik'shən] n romans mpl, littérature f romanesque; (invention) fiction f.
fictional [fik'shənəl] a fictif(ive).
fictionalize [fik'shənəlīz] vt romancer.
fictitious [fiktish'əs] a fictif(ive), imaginaire.
fiddle [fid'əl] n (MUS) violon m; (cheating)
combine f; escroquerie f ♦ vt (Brit:
accounts) falsifier, maquiller; **to work a ~**
traficoter.
fiddle with vt fus tripoter.
fiddler [fid'lûr] n violoniste m/f.
fiddly [fid'lē] a (task) minutieux(euse).
fidelity [fidel'itē] n fidélité f.
fidget [fij'it] vi se trémousser, remuer.
fidgety [fij'itē] a agité(e), qui a la bougeotte.
fiduciary [fidōō'shēärē] n agent m fiduciaire.
field [fēld] n champ m; (fig) domaine m,
champ; (SPORT: ground) terrain m;
(COMPUT) champ, zone f; **to lead the ~**
(SPORT, COMM) dominer; **the children had a
~ day** (fig) c'était un grand jour pour les
enfants.
field glasses npl jumelles fpl.
field marshal n maréchal m.
fieldwork [fēld'wûrk] n travaux mpl pratiques
(or recherches fpl) sur le terrain.
fiend [fēnd] n démon m.
fiendish [fēn'dish] a diabolique.
fierce [fērs] a (look) féroce, sauvage; (wind,
attack) (très) violent(e); (fighting, enemy)
acharné(e).
fiery [fī'ûrē] a ardent(e), brûlant(e); fou-
gueux(euse).
FIFA [fē'fa] n abbr (= Fédération Internationale de Football Association) FIFA f.
fifteen [fif'tēn'] num quinze.
fifth [fifth] num cinquième.
fiftieth [fif'tēith] num cinquantième.
fifty [fif'tē] num cinquante.
fifty-fifty [fif'tēfif'tē] ad: **to share ~ with sb**
partager moitié-moitié avec qn ♦ a: **to have
a ~ chance (of success)** avoir une chance
sur deux (de réussir).
fig [fig] n figue f.
fight [fīt] n bagarre f; (MIL) combat m;
(against cancer etc) lutte f ♦ vb (pt, pp
fought [fôt]) vt se battre contre; (cancer,
alcoholism) combattre, lutter contre; (LAW:
case) défendre ♦ vi se battre; (fig): **to ~
(for/against)** lutter (pour/contre).
fighter [fī'tûr] n lutteur m (fig); (plane)
chasseur m.
fighter pilot n pilote m de chasse.
fighting [fī'ting] n combats mpl; (brawls) ba-
garres fpl.
figment [fig'mənt] n: **a ~ of the imagination**
une invention.
figurative [fig'yûrətiv] a figuré(e).
figure [fig'yûr] n (DRAWING, GEOM) figure f;
(number, cipher) chiffre m; (body, outline)
silhouette f, ligne f, formes fpl; (person)
personnage m ♦ vt (US) supposer ♦ vi
(appear) figurer; (US: make sense) s'expli-

quer; **public** ~ personnalité *f*; ~ **of speech** figure *f* de rhétorique.

figure on *vt fus* (*US*): **to** ~ **on doing** compter faire.

figure out *vt* arriver à comprendre; calculer.

figurehead [fig'yûrhed] *n* (*NAUT*) figure *f* de proue; (*pej*) prête-nom *m*.

figure skating *n* figures imposées (*en patinage*); patinage *m* artistique.

Fiji (Islands) [fē'jē (ī'lǝndz)] *n(pl)* (îles *fpl*) Fi(d)ji *fpl*.

filament [fil'ǝmǝnt] *n* filament *m*.

filch [filch] *vt* (*col: steal*) voler, chiper.

file [fīl] *n* (*tool*) lime *f*; (*dossier*) dossier *m*; (*folder*) dossier, chemise *f*; (*: binder*) classeur *m*; (*COMPUT*) fichier *m*; (*row*) file *f* ♦ *vt* (*nails, wood*) limer; (*papers*) classer; (*LAW: claim*) faire enregistrer; déposer ♦ *vi*: **to** ~ **in/out** entrer/sortir l'un derrière l'autre; **to** ~ **past** défiler devant; **to** ~ **a suit against sb** (*LAW*) intenter un procès à qn.

file name *n* (*COMPUT*) nom *m* de fichier.

filibuster [fil'ǝbustûr] (*esp US POL*) *n* (*also:* ~**er**) obstructionniste *m/f* ♦ *vi* faire de l'obstructionnisme.

filing [fī'ling] *n* (travaux *mpl* de) classement *m*; ~**s** *npl* limaille *f*.

filing cabinet *n* classeur *m* (*meuble*).

filing clerk *n* documentaliste *m/f*.

Filipino [filǝpē'nō] *n* (*person*) Philippin/e; (*LING*) tagalog *m*.

fill [fil] *vt* remplir; (*vacancy*) pourvoir à; (*tooth*) plomber ♦ *n*: **to eat one's** ~ manger à sa faim.

fill in *vt* (*hole*) boucher; (*form*) remplir; (*details, report*) compléter.

fill out *vt* (*form, receipt*) remplir.

fill up *vt* remplir ♦ *vi* (*AUT*) faire le plein; ~ **it up, please** (*AUT*) le plein, s'il vous plaît.

fillet [filā'] *n* filet *m* ♦ *vt* préparer en filets.

fillet steak *n* filet *m* de bœuf, tournedos *m*.

filling [fil'ing] *n* (*CULIN*) garniture *f*, farce *f*; (*for tooth*) plombage *m*.

filling station *n* station *f* d'essence.

fillip [fil'ǝp] *n* coup *m* de fouet (*fig*).

filly [fil'ē] *n* pouliche *f*.

film [film] *n* film *m*; (*PHOT*) pellicule *f*, film ♦ *vt* (*scene*) filmer.

film star *n* vedette *f* de cinéma.

filmstrip [film'strip] *n* (film *m* pour) projection *f* fixe.

film studio *n* studio *m* (de cinéma).

filter [fil'tûr] *n* filtre *m* ♦ *vt* filtrer.

filter coffee *n* café *m* filtre.

filter lane *n* (*Brit AUT*) voie *f* de sortie.

filter tip *n* bout *m* filtre.

filter-tipped [fil'tûrtipt] *a* à bout filtre.

filth [filth] *n* saleté *f*.

filthy [fil'thē] *a* sale, dégoûtant(e); (*language*) ordurier(ière), grossier(ière).

fin. *abbr* = **finance.**

fin [fin] *n* (*of fish*) nageoire *f*.

final [fī'nǝl] *a* final(e), dernier(ière); (*decision, answer*) définitif(ive) ♦ *n* (*SPORT*) finale *f*; ~**s** *npl* (*SCOL*) examens *mpl* de dernière année; ~ **demand** (*on invoice etc*) dernier rappel.

finale [final'ē] *n* finale *m*.

finalist [fī'nǝlist] *n* (*SPORT*) finaliste *m/f*.

finalize [fī'nǝlīz] *vt* mettre au point.

finally [fī'nǝlē] *ad* (*lastly*) en dernier lieu; (*eventually*) enfin, finalement; (*irrevocably*) définitivement.

finance *n* [fī'nans] finance *f* ♦ *vt* [finans'] financer; ~**s** *npl* finances *fpl*.

financial [finan'chǝl] *a* financier(ière); ~ **statement** bilan *m*, exercice financier.

financially [finan'chǝlē] *ad* financièrement.

financial year *n* année *f* budgétaire.

financier [finansiûr'] *n* financier *m*.

find [fīnd] *vt* (*pt, pp* **found** [found]) trouver; (*lost object*) retrouver ♦ *n* trouvaille *f*, découverte *f*; **to** ~ **sb guilty** (*LAW*) déclarer qn coupable; **to** ~ **(some) difficulty in doing sth** avoir du mal à faire qch.

find out *vt* se renseigner sur; (*truth, secret*) découvrir; (*person*) démasquer ♦ *vi*: **to** ~ **out about** se renseigner sur; (*by chance*) apprendre.

findings [fīn'dingz] *npl* (*LAW*) conclusions *fpl*, verdict *m*; (*of report*) constatations *fpl*.

fine [fīn] *a* beau(belle); excellent(e); (*subtle, not coarse*) fin(e) ♦ *ad* (*well*) très bien; (*small*) fin, finement ♦ *n* (*LAW*) amende *f*; contravention *f* ♦ *vt* (*LAW*) condamner à une amende; donner une contravention à; **he's** ~ il va bien; **the weather is** ~ il fait beau; **you're doing** ~ c'est bien, vous vous débrouillez bien; **to cut it** ~ calculer un peu juste.

fine arts *npl* beaux-arts *mpl*.

finery [fī'nûrē] *n* parure *f*.

finesse [fines'] *n* finesse *f*, élégance *f*.

fine-tooth comb [fīn'tōoth kōm] *n*: **to go through sth with a** ~ (*fig*) passer qch au peigne fin ou au crible.

finger [fing'gûr] *n* doigt *m* ♦ *vt* palper, toucher.

fingernail [fing'gûrnāl] *n* ongle *m* (de la main).

fingerprint [fing'gûrprint] *n* empreinte digitale ♦ *vt* (*person*) prendre les empreintes digitales de.

fingerstall [fing'gûrstôl] *n* doigtier *m*.

fingertip [fing'gûrtip] *n* bout *m* du doigt; (*fig*): **to have sth at one's** ~**s** avoir qch à sa disposition; (*knowledge*) savoir qch sur le bout du doigt.

finicky [fin'ikē] *a* tatillon(ne), méticuleux(euse); minutieux(euse).

finish [fin'ish] *n* fin *f*; (*SPORT*) arrivée *f*; (*polish etc*) finition *f* ♦ *vt* finir, terminer ♦ *vi* finir, se terminer; (*session*) s'achever; **to** ~ **doing sth** finir de faire qch; **to** ~ **third** arriver ou terminer troisième.

finish off *vt* finir, terminer; (*kill*) achever.

finish up *vi, vt* finir.

finished product [fin'isht prâd'ǝkt] *n* produit fini.

finishing line [fin'ishing līn] *n* ligne *f* d'arrivée.

finishing school [fin'ishing skōol] *n* institution privée (*pour jeunes filles*).

finite [fī'nīt] *a* fini(e); (*verb*) conjugué(e).

Finland [fin'lǝnd] *n* Finlande *f*.

Finn [fin] *n* Finnois/e; Finlandais/e.

Finnish [fin'ish] *a* finnois(e); finlandais(e) ♦ *n* (*LING*) finnois *m*.

fiord [fyôrd] *n* fjord *m*.

fir [fûr] n sapin m.

fire [fī'ûr] n feu m; incendie m ♦ vt (discharge): **to ~ a gun** tirer un coup de feu; (fig) enflammer, animer; (dismiss) mettre à la porte, renvoyer ♦ vi tirer, faire feu ♦ cpd: **~ hazard, ~ risk: that's a ~ hazard** or **risk** cela présente un risque d'incendie; **on ~** en feu; **to set ~ to sth, set sth on ~** mettre le feu à qch; **insured against ~** assuré contre l'incendie.

fire alarm n avertisseur m d'incendie.

firearm [fīûr'ärm] n arme f à feu.

fire brigade n (Brit) = **fire department**.

fire chief n (US) capitaine m des pompiers.

fire department n (US) (régiment m de sapeurs-)pompiers mpl.

fire engine n pompe f à incendie.

fire escape n escalier m de secours.

fire extinguisher n extincteur m.

fire insurance n assurance f incendie.

fireman [fīûr'mən] n pompier m.

fire master n (Brit) = **fire chief**.

fireplace [fīûr'plās] n cheminée f.

fireplug [fi'ûrplug] n (US) bouche f d'incendie.

fireproof [fīûr'prōōf] a ignifuge.

fire regulations npl consignes fpl en cas d'incendie.

fire screen n (decorative) écran m de cheminée; (for protection) garde-feu m inv.

fireside [fīûr'sīd] n foyer m, coin m du feu.

fire station n caserne f de pompiers.

firewood [fīûr'wōōd] n bois m de chauffage.

firework [fīûr'wûrk] n feu m d'artifice; **~s** npl (display) feu(x) d'artifice.

firing [fīûr'ing] n (MIL) feu m, tir m.

firing squad n peloton m d'exécution.

firm [fûrm] n ferme ♦ n compagnie f, firme f.

firmly [fûrm'lē] ad fermement.

firmness [fûrm'nis] n fermeté f.

first [fûrst] a premier(ière) ♦ ad (before others) le premier, la première; (before other things) en premier, d'abord; (when listing reasons etc) en premier lieu, premièrement ♦ n (person: in race) premier/ière; (AUT) première f; **the ~ of January** le premier janvier; **at ~** au commencement, au début; **~ of all** tout d'abord, pour commencer; **in the ~ instance** en premier lieu; **I'll do it ~ thing tomorrow** je le ferai tout de suite demain matin.

first aid n premiers secours or soins.

first-aid kit [fûrstād' kit] n trousse f à pharmacie.

first-class [fûrst'klas'] a de première classe.

first-class mail n courrier m rapide.

first-hand [fûrst'hand'] a de première main.

first lady n (US) femme f du président.

firstly [fûrst'lē] ad premièrement, en premier lieu.

first name n prénom m.

first night n (THEATER) première f.

first-rate [fûrst'rāt'] a excellent(e).

fir tree n sapin m.

fiscal [fis'kəl] a fiscal(e); **~ year** exercice financier.

fish [fish] n (pl inv) poisson m; poissons mpl ♦ vt, vi pêcher; **to ~ a river** pêcher dans une rivière; **to go ~ing** aller à la pêche.

fisherman [fish'ûrmən] n pêcheur m.

fishery [fish'ûrē] n pêcherie f.

fish factory n (Brit) conserverie f de poissons.

fish farm n établissement m piscicole.

fish fingers npl (Brit) = **fish sticks**.

fish hook n hameçon m.

fishing boat [fish'ing bōt] n barque f de pêche.

fishing industry n industrie f de la pêche.

fishing line n ligne f (de pêche).

fishing rod n canne f à pêche.

fishing tackle n attirail m de pêche.

fish market n marché m au poisson.

fishmonger [fish'munggûr] n marchand m de poisson; **~'s (shop)** poissonnerie f.

fish slice n (Brit) pelle f à poisson.

fish sticks npl bâtonnets de poisson (congelés).

fishy [fish'ē] a (fig) suspect(e), louche.

fission [fish'ən] n fission f; **atomic** or **nuclear ~** fission nucléaire.

fissure [fish'ûr] n fissure f.

fist [fist] n poing m.

fistfight [fist'fīt] n pugilat m, bagarre f (à coups de poing).

fit [fit] a (MED, SPORT) en (bonne) forme; (proper) convenable; approprié(e) ♦ vt (subj: clothes) aller à; (adjust) ajuster; (put in, attach) installer, poser; adapter; (equip) équiper, garnir, munir ♦ vi (clothes) aller; (parts) s'adapter; (in space, gap) entrer, s'adapter ♦ n (MED) accès m, crise f; (of coughing) quinte f; **~ to** en état de; **~ for** digne de; apte à; **to keep ~** se maintenir en forme; **this dress is a tight/good ~** cette robe est un peu juste/(me) va très bien; **a ~ of anger** un accès de colère; **to have a ~** (MED) faire or avoir une crise; (col) piquer une crise; **by ~s and starts** par à-coups.

fit in vi s'accorder; (person) s'adapter.

fit out vt équiper.

fitful [fit'fəl] a intermittent(e).

fitment [fit'mənt] n (Brit) meuble encastré, élément m.

fitness [fit'nis] n (MED) forme f physique; (of remark) à-propos m, justesse f.

fitted kitchen [fit'id kich'ən] n (Brit) cuisine équipée.

fitter [fit'ûr] n monteur m; (DRESSMAKING) essayeur/euse.

fitting [fit'ing] a approprié(e) ♦ n (of dress) essayage m; (of piece of equipment) pose f, installation f.

fitting room n (in shop) cabine f d'essayage.

fittings [fit'ingz] npl installations fpl.

five [fīv] num cinq.

five-day week [fīv'dā wēk'] n semaine f de cinq jours.

fiver [fi'vûr] n (col: US) billet de cinq dollars; (: Brit) billet m de cinq livres.

fix [fiks] vt fixer; (sort out) arranger; (mend) réparer; (make ready: meal, drink) préparer; (castrate) châtrer, castrer; (col: game etc) truquer ♦ n: **to be in a ~** être dans le pétrin.

fix up vt (meeting) arranger; **to ~ sb up with sth** faire avoir qch à qn.

fixation [fiksā'shən] n (PSYCH) fixation f; (fig) obsession f.

fixed [fikst] *a* (*prices etc*) fixe; **there's a ~ charge** il y a un prix forfaitaire; **how are you ~ for money?** (*col*) question fric, ça va?

fixed assets *npl* immobilisations *fpl*.

fixture [fiks'chûr] *n* installation *f* (fixe); (*SPORT*) rencontre *f* (au programme).

fizz [fiz] *vi* pétiller.

fizzle [fiz'əl] *vi* pétiller.

fizzle out *vi* rater.

fizzy [fiz'ē] *a* pétillant(e); gazeux(euse).

fjord [fyôrd] *n* = **fiord**.

FL *abbr* (*US MAIL*) = *Florida*.

Fla. *abbr* (*US*) = *Florida*.

flabbergasted [flab'ûrgastid] *a* sidéré(e), ahuri(e).

flabby [flab'ē] *a* mou(molle).

flag [flag] *n* drapeau *m*; (*also:* **~stone**) dalle *f* ♦ *vi* faiblir; fléchir; **~ of convenience** pavillon *m* de complaisance.

flag down *vt* héler, faire signe (de s'arrêter) à.

flagon [flag'ən] *n* bonbonne *f*.

flagpole [flag'pōl] *n* mât *m*.

flagrant [flā'grənt] *a* flagrant(e).

flag stop *n* (*US: for bus*) arrêt facultatif.

flair [flär] *n* flair *m*.

flak [flak] *n* (*MIL*) tir antiaérien; (*col: criticism*) critiques *fpl*.

flake [flāk] *n* (*of rust, paint*) écaille *f*; (*of snow, soap powder*) flocon *m* ♦ *vi* (*also: ~ off*) s'écailler.

flaky [flā'kē] *a* (*paintwork*) écaillé(e); (*skin*) desquamé(e); (*Brit: pastry*) feuilleté(e).

flamboyant [flamboi'ənt] *a* flamboyant(e), éclatant(e); (*person*) haut(e) en couleur.

flame [flām] *n* flamme *f*.

flamingo [fləming'gō] *n* flamant *m* (rose).

flammable [flam'əbəl] *a* inflammable.

flan [flan] *n* tarte *f*.

Flanders [flan'dûrz] *n* Flandre(s) *f(pl)*.

flange [flanj] *n* boudin *m*; collerette *f*.

flank [flangk] *n* flanc *m* ♦ *vt* flanquer.

flannel [flan'əl] *n* (*Brit: also:* **face ~**) gant *m* de toilette; (*fabric*) flanelle *f*; (*Brit col*) baratin *m*; **~s** *npl* pantalon *m* de flanelle.

flap [flap] *n* (*of pocket, envelope*) rabat *m* ♦ *vt* (*wings*) battre (de) ♦ *vi* (*sail, flag*) claquer; (*col: also:* **be in a ~**) paniquer.

flapjack [flap'jak] *n* (*US*) ≈ crêpe *f*; (*Brit: biscuit*) galette *f*.

flare [flär] *n* fusée éclairante; (*in skirt etc*) évasement *m*.

flare up *vi* s'embraser; (*fig: person*) se mettre en colère, s'emporter; (: *revolt*) éclater.

flared [flärd] *a* (*trousers*) à jambes évasées; (*skirt*) évasé(e).

flash [flash] *n* éclair *m*; (*also:* **news ~**) flash *m* (d'information); (*PHOT*) flash ♦ *vt* (*switch on*) allumer (brièvement); (*direct*): **to ~ sth at** braquer qch sur; (*flaunt*) étaler, exhiber; (*send: message*) câbler ♦ *vi* briller; jeter des éclairs; (*light on ambulance etc*) clignoter; **in a ~** en un clin d'œil; **to ~ one's headlights** faire un appel de phares; **he ~ed by or past** il passa (devant nous) comme un éclair.

flashback [flash'bak] *n* flashback *m*, retour *m* en arrière.

flashbulb [flash'bulb] *n* ampoule *f* de flash.

flash card *n* (*SCOL*) carte *f* (*support visuel*).

flashcube [flash'kyōōb] *n* cube-flash *m*.

flasher [flash'ûr] *n* (*AUT*) clignotant *m*.

flashlight [flash'lit] *n* lampe *f* de poche.

flash point *n* point *m* d'ignition; (*fig*): **to be at ~** être sur le point d'exploser.

flashy [flash'ē] *a* (*pej*) tape-à-l'œil *inv*, tapageur(euse).

flask [flask] *n* flacon *m*, bouteille *f*; (*CHEMISTRY*) ballon *m*; (*also:* **vacuum ~**) bouteille *f* thermos ®.

flat [flat] *a* plat(e); (*tire*) dégonflé(e), à plat; (*denial*) catégorique; (*MUS*) bémolisé(e); (*voice*) faux(fausse) ♦ *n* (*Brit: rooms*) appartement *m*; (*AUT*) crevaison *f*, pneu crevé; (*MUS*) bémol *m*; **~ out** (*work*) sans relâche; (*race*) à fond; **~ rate of pay** (*COMM*) (salaire *m*) fixe.

flat-footed [flat'fōōtid] *a*: **to be ~** avoir les pieds plats.

flatly [flat'lē] *ad* catégoriquement.

flatmate [flat'māt] *n* (*Brit*): **he's my ~** il partage l'appartement avec moi.

flatness [flat'nis] *n* (*of land*) absence *f* de relief, aspect plat.

flatten [flat'ən] *vt* (*also:* **~ten out**) aplatir; (*house, city*) raser.

flatter [flat'ûr] *vt* flatter.

flatterer [flat'ûrûr] *n* flatteur *m*.

flattering [flat'ûring] *a* flatteur(euse); (*clothes etc*) seyant(e).

flattery [flat'ûrē] *n* flatterie *f*.

flatulence [flach'ələns] *n* flatulence *f*.

flaunt [flônt] *vt* faire étalage de.

flavor [flā'vûr] (*US*) *n* goût *m*, saveur *f*; (*of ice cream etc*) parfum *m* ♦ *vt* parfumer, aromatiser; **vanilla-~ed** à l'arôme de vanille, vanillé(e); **to give** *or* **add ~ to** donner du goût à, relever.

flavoring [flā'vûring] *n* arôme *m* (synthétique).

flavour [flā'vûr] *etc* (*Brit*) = **flavor** *etc*.

flaw [flô] *n* défaut *m*.

flawless [flô'lis] *a* sans défaut.

flax [flaks] *n* lin *m*.

flaxen [flaks'ən] *a* blond(e).

flea [flē] *n* puce *f*.

flea market *n* marché *m* aux puces.

fleck [flek] *n* (*of dust*) particule *f*; (*of mud, paint, color*) tacheture *f*, moucheture *f* ♦ *vt* tacher, éclabousser; **brown ~ed with white** brun moucheté de blanc.

fledg(e)ling [flej'ling] *n* oisillon *m*.

flee, *pt, pp* **fled** [flē, fled] *vt* fuir, s'enfuir de ♦ *vi* fuir, s'enfuir.

fleece [flēs] *n* toison *f* ♦ *vt* (*col*) voler, filouter.

fleecy [flē'sē] *a* (*blanket*) moelleux(euse); (*cloud*) floconneux(euse).

fleet [flēt] *n* flotte *f*; (*of trucks, cars etc*) parc *m*; convoi *m*.

fleeting [flē'ting] *a* fugace, fugitif(ive); (*visit*) très bref(brève).

Flemish [flem'ish] *a* flamand(e) ♦ *n* (*LING*) flamand *m*; **the ~** *npl* les Flamands.

flesh [flesh] *n* chair *f*.

flesh wound *n* blessure superficielle.

flew [flōō] *pt of* **fly**.

flex [fleks] *n* fil *m or* câble *m* électrique (souple) ♦ *vt* fléchir; (*muscles*) tendre.

flexibility [fleksəbil'ətē] *n* flexibilité *f*.
flexible [flek'səbəl] *a* flexible; (*person, schedule*) souple.
flick [flik] *n* petite tape; chiquenaude *f*; sursaut *m*.
flick through *vt fus* feuilleter.
flicker [flik'ûr] *vi* vaciller ♦ *n* vacillement *m*; **a ~ of light** une brève lueur.
flick knife *n* (*Brit*) couteau *m* à cran d'arrêt.
flier [flī'ûr] *n* aviateur *m*.
flight [flīt] *n* vol *m*; (*escape*) fuite *f*; (*also*: **~ of steps**) escalier *m*; **to take ~** prendre la fuite; **to put to ~** mettre en fuite.
flight attendant *n* steward *m*, hôtesse *f* de l'air.
flight crew *n* équipage *m*.
flight deck *n* (*AVIAT*) poste *m* de pilotage; (*NAUT*) pont *m* d'envol.
flight recorder *n* enregistreur *m* de vol.
flimsy [flim'zē] *a* (*partition, fabric*) peu solide, mince; (*excuse*) pauvre, mince.
flinch [flinch] *vi* tressaillir; **to ~ from** se dérober à, reculer devant.
fling [fling] *vt* (*pt, pp* **flung** [flung]) jeter, lancer ♦ *n* (*love affair*) brève liaison, passade *f*.
flint [flint] *n* silex *m*; (*in lighter*) pierre *f* (à briquet).
flip [flip] *n* chiquenaude *f* ♦ *vt* donner une chiquenaude à; (*US: flapjack*) faire sauter ♦ *vi*: **to ~ for sth** (*US*) jouer qch à pile ou face.
flip through *vt fus* feuilleter.
flippant [flip'ənt] *a* désinvolte, irrévérencieux(euse).
flipper [flip'ûr] *n* (*of animal*) nageoire *f*; (*for swimmer*) palme *f*.
flip side *n* (*of record*) deuxième face *f*.
flirt [flûrt] *vi* flirter ♦ *n* flirteuse *f*.
flirtation [flûrtā'shən] *n* flirt *m*.
flit [flit] *vi* voleter.
float [flōt] *n* flotteur *m*; (*in procession*) char *m*; (*sum of money*) réserve *f* ♦ *vi* flotter; (*bather*) flotter, faire la planche ♦ *vt* faire flotter; (*loan, business, idea*) lancer.
floating [flō'ting] *a* flottant(e); **~ vote** voix flottante; **~ voter** électeur indécis.
flock [flâk] *n* troupeau *m*; (*of birds*) vol *m*; (*of people*) foule *f*.
floe [flō] *n* (*also*: **ice ~**) iceberg *m*.
flog [flâg] *vt* fouetter.
flood [flud] *n* inondation *f*; (*of words, tears etc*) flot *m*, torrent *m*; (*AUT: carburetor*) noyer; **to ~ the market** (*COMM*) inonder le marché; **in ~** en crue.
flooding [flud'ing] *n* inondation *f*.
floodlight [flud'līt] *n* projecteur *m* ♦ *vt* éclairer aux projecteurs, illuminer.
floodlit [flud'līt] *pt, pp of* **floodlight** ♦ *a* illuminé(e).
flood tide *n* marée montante.
floor [flôr] *n* sol *m*; (*story*) étage *m*; (*of sea, valley*) fond *m*; (*fig: at meeting*): **the ~** l'assemblée *f*, les membres *mpl* de l'assemblée ♦ *vt* terrasser; (*baffle*) désorienter; **on the ~** par terre; **first ~**, (*Brit*) **ground ~** rez-de-chaussée *m*; **second ~**, (*Brit*) **first ~** premier étage; **top ~** dernier étage; **to have the ~** (*speaker*) avoir la parole.
floorboard [flôr'bôrd] *n* planche *f* (du plan-

cher).
flooring [flôr'ing] *n* sol *m*; (*wooden*) plancher *m*; (*material to make floor*) matériau(x) *m(pl)* pour planchers; (*covering*) revêtement *m* de sol.
floor lamp *n* (*US*) lampadaire *m*.
floor show *n* spectacle *m* de variétés.
floorwalker [flôr'wôkûr] *n* (*esp US*) surveillant *m* (de grand magasin).
flop [flâp] *n* fiasco *m* ♦ *vi* (*fail*) faire fiasco.
flophouse [flâp'hous] *n* (*US*) asile *m* de nuit.
floppy [flâp'ē] *a* lâche, flottant(e); **~ hat** chapeau *m* à bords flottants.
floppy disk *n* disquette *f*, disque *m* souple.
flora [flôr'ə] *n* flore *f*.
floral [flôr'əl] *a* floral(e).
Florence [flâr'əns] *n* Florence.
florid [flôr'id] *a* (*complexion*) fleuri(e); (*style*) plein(e) de fioritures.
florist [flôr'ist] *n* fleuriste *m/f*; **~'s (shop)** magasin *m* or boutique *f* de fleuriste.
flotation [flōtā'shən] *n* (*of shares*) émission *f*; (*of company*) lancement *m* (en Bourse).
flounce [flouns] *n* volant *m*.
flounce out *vi* sortir dans un mouvement d'humeur.
flounder [floun'dûr] *n* (*ZOOL*) flet *m* ♦ *vi* patauger.
flour [flou'ûr] *n* farine *f*.
flourish [flûr'ish] *vi* prospérer ♦ *vt* brandir ♦ *n* fioriture *f*; (*of trumpets*) fanfare *f*.
flourishing [flûr'ishing] *a* prospère, florissant(e).
flout [flout] *vt* se moquer de, faire fi de.
flow [flō] *n* (*of water, traffic etc*) écoulement *m*; (*tide, influx*) flux *m*; (*of orders, letters etc*) flot *m*; (*of blood, ELEC*) circulation *f*; (*of river*) courant *m* ♦ *vi* couler; (*traffic*) s'écouler; (*robes, hair*) flotter.
flow chart, flow diagram *n* organigramme *m*.
flower [flou'ûr] *n* fleur *f* ♦ *vi* fleurir; **in ~** en fleur.
flower bed *n* plate-bande *f*.
flowerpot [flou'ûrpât] *n* pot *m* (à fleurs).
flowery [flou'ûrē] *a* fleuri(e).
flown [flōn] *pp of* **fly**.
flu [flōō] *n* grippe *f*.
fluctuate [fluk'chōōāt] *vi* varier, fluctuer.
fluctuation [flukchōōā'shən] *n* fluctuation *f*, variation *f*.
flue [flōō] *n* conduit *m*.
fluency [flōō'ənsē] *n* facilité *f*, aisance *f*.
fluent [flōō'ənt] *a* (*speech, style*) coulant(e), aisé(e); **he's a ~ speaker/reader** il s'exprime/lit avec aisance *or* facilité; **he speaks ~ French, he's ~ in French** il parle le français couramment.
fluently [flōō'əntlē] *ad* couramment; avec aisance *or* facilité.
fluff [fluf] *n* duvet *m*; peluche *f*.
fluffy [fluf'ē] *a* duveteux(euse); pelucheux(euse).
fluid [flōō'id] *n* fluide *m*; (*in diet*) liquide *m* ♦ *a* fluide.
fluid ounce *n* (*Brit*) = 0.028 l; 0.05 pints.
fluke [flōōk] *n* (*col*) coup *m* de veine.
flummox [flum'əks] *vt* dérouter, déconcerter.
flung [flung] *pt, pp of* **fling**.

flunky [flung'kē] *n* larbin *m*.
fluorescent [floōores'ǝnt] *a* fluorescent(e).
fluoride [floō'ǝrīd] *n* fluor *m*.
fluorine [floō'ǝrēn] *n* fluor *m*.
flurry [flûr'ē] *n* (*of snow*) rafale *f*, bourrasque *f*; ~ **of activity/excitement** affairement *m*/ excitation *f* soudain(e).
flush [flush] *n* rougeur *f*; (*fig*) éclat *m*; afflux *m* ♦ *vt* nettoyer à grande eau; (*also:* ~ **out**) débusquer ♦ *vi* rougir ♦ *a* (*col*) en fonds; (*level*): ~ **with** au ras de, de niveau avec; **to** ~ **the toilet** tirer la chasse (d'eau).
flushed [flusht] *a* (tout(e)) rouge.
fluster [flus'tûr] *n* agitation *f*, trouble *m*.
flustered [flus'tûrd] *a* énervé(e).
flute [floōt] *n* flûte *f*.
fluted [floō'tid] *a* cannelé(e).
flutter [flut'ûr] *n* agitation *f*; (*of wings*) battement *m* ♦ *vi* battre des ailes, voleter; (*person*) aller et venir dans une grande agitation.
flux [fluks] *n*: **in a state of** ~ fluctuant sans cesse.
fly [flī] *n* (*insect*) mouche *f*; (*on trousers: also:* **flies**) braguette *f* ♦ *vb* (*pt* **flew**, *pp* **flown** [floō, flōn]) *vt* (*plane*) piloter; (*passengers, cargo*) transporter (par avion); (*distances*) parcourir ♦ *vi* voler; (*passengers*) aller en avion; (*escape*) s'enfuir, fuir; (*flag*) se déployer; **to** ~ **open** s'ouvrir brusquement; **to** ~ **off the handle** s'énerver, s'emporter.
  fly away *vi* s'envoler.
  fly in *vi* (*plane*) atterrir; (*person*): **he flew in yesterday** il est arrivé hier (par avion).
  fly off *vi* s'envoler.
  fly out *vi* (*see fly in*) s'envoler; partir (par avion).
fly-fishing [flī'fishing] *n* pêche *f* à la mouche.
flying [flī'ing] *n* (*activity*) aviation *f* ♦ *a*: ~ **visit** visite *f* éclair *inv*; **with** ~ **colors** haut la main; **he doesn't like** ~ il n'aime pas voyager en avion.
flying buttress *n* arc-boutant *m*.
flying saucer *n* soucoupe volante.
flying squad *n* (*MIL etc*) brigade volante.
flying start *n*: **to get off to a** ~ faire un excellent départ.
flyleaf [flī'lēf] *n* page *f* de garde.
flyover [flī'ōvûr] *n* (*Brit*) défilé aérien; (*Brit: overpass*) saut-de-mouton *m*, pont autoroutier.
flypast [flī'past] *n* défilé aérien.
flysheet [flī'shēt] *n* (*for tent*) double toit *m*.
flywheel [flī'hwēl] *n* volant *m* (de commande).
FM *abbr* (*RADIO*) = **frequency modulation**; (*Brit MIL*) = **field marshal**.
FMB *n abbr* (*US*) = *Federal Maritime Board*.
FMCS *n abbr* (*US*) = *Federal Mediation and Conciliation Services*) *organisme de conciliation en cas de conflits du travail*.
foal [fōl] *n* poulain *m*.
foam [fōm] *n* écume *f*; (*on beer*) mousse *f*; (*also:* **plastic** ~) mousse cellulaire *or* de plastique ♦ *vi* écumer; (*soapy water*) mousser.
foam rubber *n* caoutchouc *m* mousse.
FOB *abbr* (= *free on board*) fob.
fob [fàb] *n* (*also:* **watch** ~) chaîne *f*, ruban *m* ♦ *vt*: **to** ~ **sb off with** refiler à qn; se dé-

barrasser de qn avec.
foc *abbr* (*Brit*) = **free of charge**.
focal [fō'kǝl] *a* (*also fig*) focal(e).
focal point *n* foyer *m*; (*fig*) centre *m* de l'attention, point focal.
focus [fō'kǝs] *n* (*pl*: ~**es**) foyer *m*; (*of interest*) centre *m* ♦ *vt* (*field glasses etc*) mettre au point; (*light rays*) faire converger ♦ *vi*: **to** ~ (**on**) (*with camera*) régler la mise au point (sur); (*person*) fixer son regard (sur); **in** ~ au point; **out of** ~ pas au point.
fodder [fàd'ûr] *n* fourrage *m*.
FOE *n abbr* (= *Friends of the Earth*) AT *mpl* (= *Amis de la Terre*); (*US*: = *Fraternal Order of Eagles*) *organisation charitable*.
foe [fō] *n* ennemi *m*.
foetus [fē'tǝs] *etc n* (*Brit*) = **fetus** *etc*.
fog [fòg] *n* brouillard *m*.
  fog up *vi* (*windows*) s'embuer.
fogbound [fòg'bound] *a* bloqué(e) par le brouillard.
foggy [fòg'ē] *a*: **it's** ~ il y a du brouillard.
fog light *n* (*AUT*) phare *m* anti-brouillard.
foible [foi'bǝl] *n* faiblesse *f*.
foil [foil] *vt* déjouer, contrecarrer ♦ *n* feuille *f* de métal; (*kitchen* ~) papier *m* d'alu(minium); (*FENCING*) fleuret *m*; **to act as a** ~ **to** (*fig*) servir de repoussoir *or* de faire valoir à.
foist [foist] *vt*: **to** ~ **sth on sb** imposer qch à qn.
fold [fōld] *n* (*bend, crease*) pli *m*; (*AGR*) parc *m* à moutons; (*fig*) bercail *m* ♦ *vt* plier; **to** ~ **one's arms** croiser les bras.
  fold up *vi* (*map etc*) se plier, se replier; (*business*) fermer boutique ♦ *vt* (*map etc*) plier, replier.
folder [fōl'dûr] *n* (*for papers*) chemise *f*; (: *binder*) classeur *m*; (*brochure*) dépliant *m*.
folding [fōl'ding] *a* (*chair, bed*) pliant(e).
foliage [fō'lēij] *n* feuillage *m*.
folk [fōk] *npl* gens *mpl* ♦ *cpd* folklorique; ~**s** *npl* famille *f*, parents *mpl*.
folklore [fōk'lôr] *n* folklore *m*.
folksong [fōk'sông] *n* chanson *f* folklorique; (*contemporary*) chanson folk *inv*.
follow [fàl'ō] *vt* suivre ♦ *vi* suivre; (*result*) s'ensuivre; **to** ~ **sb's advice** suivre les conseils de qn; **I don't quite** ~ **you** je ne vous suis plus; **to** ~ **in sb's footsteps** emboîter le pas à qn; (*fig*) suivre les traces de qn; **it** ~**s that ...** de ce fait, il s'ensuit que ...; **he** ~**ed suit** il fit de même.
  follow out *vt* (*idea, plan*) poursuivre, mener à terme.
  follow through *vt* = **follow out**.
  follow up *vt* (*victory*) tirer parti de; (*letter, offer*) donner suite à; (*case*) suivre.
follower [fàl'ōûr] *n* disciple *m*/*f*, partisan/e.
following [fàl'ōing] *a* suivant(e) ♦ *n* partisans *mpl*, disciples *mpl*.
follow-up [fàl'ōup] *n* suite *f*; suivi *m*.
folly [fàl'ē] *n* inconscience *f*; sottise *f*; (*building*) folie *f*.
fond [fànd] *a* (*memory, look*) tendre, affectueux(euse); **to be** ~ **of** aimer beaucoup.
fondle [fàn'dǝl] *vt* caresser.
fondly [fànd'lē] *ad* (*lovingly*) tendrement;

(*naïvely*) naïvement.

fondness [fând'nis] *n* (*for things*) attachement *m*; (*for people*) sentiments affectueux; **a special ~ for** une prédilection pour.

font [fânt] *n* (*REL*) fonts baptismaux; (*TYP*) police *f* de caractères.

food [fōōd] *n* nourriture *f*.

food mixer *n* mixeur *m*.

food poisoning *n* intoxication *f* alimentaire.

food processor [fōōd prâs'esûr] *n* robot *m* de cuisine.

foodstuffs [fōōd'stufs] *npl* denrées *fpl* alimentaires.

fool [fōōl] *n* idiot/e; (*HIST: of king*) bouffon *m*, fou *m*; (*CULIN*) purée *f* de fruits à la crème ♦ *vt* berner, duper ♦ *vi* (*also:* **~ around**) faire l'idiot *or* l'imbécile; **to make a ~ of sb** (*ridicule*) ridiculiser qn; (*trick*) avoir *or* duper qn; **to make a ~ of o.s.** se couvrir de ridicule; **you can't ~ me** vous (ne) me la ferez pas, on (ne) me la fait pas.

fool about, fool around *vi* (*pej: waste time*) traînailler, glandouiller; (: *behave foolishly*) faire l'imbécile.

foolhardy [fōōl'hârdē] *a* téméraire, imprudent(e).

foolish [fōō'lish] *a* idiot(e), stupide; (*rash*) imprudent(e).

foolishly [fōō'lishlē] *ad* stupidement.

foolishness [fōō'lishnis] *n* idiotie *f*, stupidité *f*.

foolproof [fōōl'prōōf] *a* (*plan etc*) infaillible.

foolscap [fōōlz'kap] *n* ≈ papier *m* ministre.

foot [fōōt] *n* (*pl:* **feet**) pied *m*; (*measure*) pied (*= 304 mm; 12 inches*); (*of animal*) patte *f* ♦ *vt* (*bill*) casquer, payer; **on ~** à pied; **to find one's feet** (*fig*) s'acclimater; **to put one's ~ down** (*AUT*) appuyer sur le champignon; (*say no*) s'imposer.

footage [fōōt'ij] *n* (*CINEMA: length*) ≈ métrage *m*; (: *material*) séquences *fpl*.

foot and mouth (disease) *n* fièvre aphteuse.

football [fōōt'bôl] *n* ballon *m* (de football); (*sport: US*) football américain; (: *Brit*) football *m*, foot *m*.

footballer [fōōt'bôlûr] *n* (*Brit*) = **football player**.

football field *n* terrain *m* de football.

football game *n* match *m* de football.

football player *n* footballeur *m*, joueur *m* de football.

footbrake [fōōt'brāk] *n* frein *m* à pied.

footbridge [fōōt'brij] *n* passerelle *f*.

foothills [fōōt'hilz] *npl* contreforts *mpl*.

foothold [fōōt'hōld] *n* prise *f* (de pied).

footing [fōōt'ing] *n* (*fig*) position *f*; **to lose one's ~** perdre pied; **on an equal ~** sur pied d'égalité.

footlights [fōōt'līts] *npl* rampe *f*.

footman [fōōt'mən] *n* laquais *m*.

footnote [fōōt'nōt] *n* note *f* (en bas de page).

footpath [fōōt'path] *n* sentier *m*; (*in street*) trottoir *m*.

footprint [fōōt'print] *n* trace *f* (de pied).

footrest [fōōt'rest] *n* marchepied *m*.

footsore [fōōt'sôr] *a* aux pieds endoloris.

footstep [fōōt'step] *n* pas *m*.

footwear [fōōt'weûr] *n* chaussure(s) *f(pl)* (*terme générique en anglais*).

FOR *abbr* (= *free on rail*) franco wagon.

for [fôr] *prep* pour; (*during*) pendant; (*in spite of*) malgré ♦ *cj* car; **I haven't seen him ~ a week** je ne l'ai pas vu depuis une semaine, cela fait une semaine que je ne l'ai pas vu; **I'll be away ~ 3 weeks** je serai absent pendant 3 semaines; **he went down ~ the paper** il est descendu chercher le journal; **I sold it for $5** je l'ai vendu 5 dollars; **~ sale** à vendre; **the train ~ Ohio** le train pour Ohio; **it's time ~ lunch** c'est l'heure de déjeuner; **what ~?** (*why*) pourquoi?; (*to what end*) pourquoi faire?, à quoi bon?; **what's this button ~?** à quoi sert ce bouton?; **~ all that** malgré cela, néamoins; **there's nothing ~ it but to jump** (*Brit*) il n'y a plus qu'à sauter.

forage [fôr'ij] *n* fourrage *m* ♦ *vi* fourrager, fouiller.

forage cap *n* (*Brit*) calot *m*.

foray [fôr'ā] *n* incursion *f*.

forbad(e) [fûrbād] *pt of* **forbid**.

forbearing [fôrbär'ing] *a* patient(e), tolérant(e).

forbid [fûrbid'] *pt* **forbad(e)**, *pp* **forbidden** [fûrbid', -bād', -bid'n] *vt* défendre, interdire; **to ~ sb to do** défendre *or* interdire à qn de faire.

forbidden [fûrbid'ən] *a* défendu(e).

forbidding [fûrbid'ing] *a* d'aspect *or* d'allure sévère *or* sombre.

force [fôrs] *n* force *f* ♦ *vt* forcer; **the Armed F~s** *npl* l'armée *f*; **to ~ sb to do sth** forcer qn à faire qch; **in ~** en force; **to come into ~** entrer en vigueur; **a ~ 5 wind** un vent de force 5; **the sales ~** (*COMM*) la force de vente; **to join ~s** unir ses forces.

force back *vt* (*crowd, enemy*) repousser; (*tears*) refouler.

force down *vt* (*food*) se forcer à manger.

forced [fôrst] *a* forcé(e).

force-feed [fôrs'fēd] *vt* nourrir de force.

forceful [fôrs'fəl] *a* énergique, volontaire.

forceps [fôr'səps] *npl* forceps *m*.

forcibly [fôr'səblē] *ad* par la force, de force; (*vigorously*) énergiquement.

ford [fôrd] *n* gué *m* ♦ *vt* passer à gué.

fore [fôr] *n*: **to the ~** en évidence.

forearm [fôr'ârm] *n* avant-bras *m inv*.

forebear [fôr'beûr] *n* ancêtre *m*.

foreboding [fôrbō'ding] *n* pressentiment *m* (néfaste).

forecast [fôr'kast] *n* prévision *f*; (*also:* **weather ~**) prévisions météorologiques, météo *f* ♦ *vt* (*irg: like* **cast**) prévoir.

foreclose [fôrklōz'] *vt* (*LAW: also:* **~ on**) saisir.

foreclosure [fôrklō'zhûr] *n* saisie *f* du bien hypothéqué.

forecourt [fôr'kôrt] *n* (*of garage*) devant *m*.

forefathers [fôr'fāthûrz] *npl* ancêtres *mpl*.

forefinger [fôr'finggûr] *n* index *m*.

forefront [fôr'frunt] *n*: **in the ~ of** au premier rang *or* plan de.

forego, *pt* **forewent**, *pp* **foregone** [fôrgō', -went', -gôn'] *vt* = **forgo**.

foregoing [fôrgō'ing] *a* susmentionné(e) ♦ *n*: **the ~** ce qui précède.

foregone [fôrgôn'] *a*: **it's a ~ conclusion** c'est à prévoir, c'est couru d'avance.

foreground [fôr'ground] n premier plan ♦ cpd (COMPUT) prioritaire.

forehand [fôr'hand] n (TENNIS) coup droit.

forehead [fôr'hed] n front m.

foreign [fôr'in] a étranger(ère); (trade) extérieur(e).

foreign body n corps étranger.

foreign currency n devises étrangères.

foreigner [fôr'ənûr] n étranger/ère.

foreign exchange n (system) change m; (money) devises fpl.

foreign exchange market n marché m des devises.

foreign exchange rate n cours m des devises.

foreign investment n investissement m à l'étranger.

Foreign Office n (Brit) ministère m des Affaires étrangères.

foreign secretary n (Brit) ministre m des Affaires étrangères.

foreleg [fôr'leg] n patte f de devant; jambe antérieure.

foreman [fôr'mən] n contremaître m; (LAW: of jury) président m (du jury).

foremost [fôr'mōst] a le(la) plus en vue; premier(ière) ♦ ad: **first and ~** avant tout, tout d'abord.

forename [fôr'nām] n prénom m.

forensic [fəren'sik] a: **~ medicine** médecine légale; **~ expert** expert m de la police, expert légiste.

forerunner [fôr'runûr] n précurseur m.

foresee, pt **foresaw**, pp **foreseen** [fôrsē', -sô', -sēn'] vt prévoir.

foreseeable [fôrsē'əbəl] a prévisible.

foreshadow [fôrshad'ō] vt présager, annoncer, laisser prévoir.

foreshorten [fôrshôr'tən] vt (figure, scene) réduire, faire en raccourci.

foresight [fôr'sīt] n prévoyance f.

foreskin [fôr'skin] n (ANAT) prépuce m.

forest [fôr'ist] n forêt f.

forestall [fôrstôl'] vt devancer.

forestry [fôr'istrē] n sylviculture f.

foretaste [fôr'tāst] n avant-goût m.

foretell, pt, pp **foretold** [fôrtel', -tōld'] vt prédire.

forethought [fôr'thôt] n prévoyance f.

forever [fôrev'ûr] ad pour toujours; (fig) continuellement.

forewarn [fôrwôrn'] vt avertir.

forewent [fôrwent'] pt of **forego**.

foreword [fôr'wûrd] n avant-propos m inv.

forfeit [fôr'fit] n prix m, rançon f ♦ vt perdre; (one's life, health) payer de.

forgave [fûrgāv'] pt of **forgive**.

forge [fôrj] n forge f ♦ vt (signature) contrefaire; (wrought iron) forger; **to ~ documents/ a will** fabriquer de faux papiers/un faux testament; **to ~ money** (Brit) fabriquer de la fausse monnaie.

forge ahead vi pousser de l'avant, prendre de l'avance.

forger [fôr'jûr] n faussaire m.

forgery [fôr'jûrē] n faux m, contrefaçon f.

forget, pt **forgot**, pp **forgotten** [fûrget', -gât', -gât'ən] vt, vi oublier.

forgetful [fûrget'fəl] a distrait(e), étourdi(e);

~ of oublieux(euse) de.

forgetfulness [fûrget'fəlnis] n tendance f aux oublis; (oblivion) oubli m.

forget-me-not [fûrget'mēnât] n myosotis m.

forgive, pt **forgave**, pp **forgiven** [fûrgiv', -gāv', -giv'ən] vt pardonner; **to ~ sb for sth/for doing sth** pardonner qch à qn/à qn de faire qch.

forgiveness [fûrgiv'nis] n pardon m.

forgiving [fûrgiv'ing] a indulgent(e).

forgo, pt **forwent**, pp **forgone** [fôrgō', -went', -gôn'] vt renoncer à.

forgot [fûrgât'] pt of **forget**.

forgotten [fûrgât'ən] pp of **forget**.

fork [fôrk] n (for eating) fourchette f; (for gardening) fourche f; (of roads) bifurcation f; (of railways) embranchement m ♦ vi (road) bifurquer.

fork out (col: pay) vt allonger, se fendre de ♦ vi casquer.

forked [fôrkt] a (lightning) en zigzags, ramifié(e).

forklift truck [fôrk'lift truk'] n chariot élévateur.

forlorn [fôrlôrn'] a abandonné(e), délaissé(e); (hope, attempt) désespéré(e).

form [fôrm] n forme f; (Brit SCOL) classe f; (questionnaire) formulaire m ♦ vt former; **in the ~ of** sous forme de; **to ~ part of sth** faire partie de qch; **to be in good ~** (SPORT, fig) être en forme; **in top ~** en pleine forme.

formal [fôr'məl] a (offer, receipt) en bonne et due forme; (person) cérémonieux(euse), à cheval sur les convenances; (occasion, dinner) officiel(le); (ART, PHILOSOPHY) formel(le); **~ dress** tenue f de cérémonie; (evening dress) tenue de soirée.

formality [fôrmal'itē] n formalité f; cérémonie(s) f(pl).

formalize [fôr'məlīz] vt officialiser.

formally [fôr'məlē] ad officiellement; formellement; cérémonieusement.

format [fôr'mat] n format m ♦ vt (COMPUT) formater.

formation [fôrmā'shən] n formation f.

formative [fôr'mətiv] a: **~ years** années fpl d'apprentissage (fig) or de formation (d'un enfant, d'un adolescent).

former [fôr'mûr] a ancien(ne) (before n), précédent(e); **the ~ ... the latter** le premier ... le second, celui-là ... celui-ci; **the ~ president** l'ex-président.

formerly [fôr'mûrlē] ad autrefois.

form feed n (on printer) alimentation f en feuilles.

formidable [fôr'midəbəl] a redoutable.

formula [fôr'myələ] n formule f; **F~ One** (AUT) Formule un.

formulate [fôr'myəlāt] vt formuler.

fornicate [fôr'nikāt] vi forniquer.

forsake, pt **forsook**, pp **forsaken** [fôrsāk', -sook, -sā'kən] vt abandonner.

fort [fôrt] n fort m; **to hold the ~** (fig) assurer la permanence.

forte [fôr'tā] n (point) fort m.

forth [fôrth] ad en avant; **to go back and ~** aller et venir; **and so ~** et ainsi de suite.

forthcoming [fôrth'kum'ing] a qui va paraître or avoir lieu prochainement; (character) ouvert(e), communicatif(ive).

forthright [fôrth'rīt] *a* franc(franche), direct(e).

forthwith [fôrthwith'] *ad* sur le champ.

fortieth [fôr'tēith] *num* quarantième.

fortification [fôrtəfəkā'shən] *n* fortification *f*.

fortified wine [fôr'təfīd wīn'] *n* vin liquoreux *or* de liqueur.

fortify [fôr'təfī] *vt* fortifier.

fortitude [fôr'tətōod] *n* courage *m*, force *f* d'âme.

fortnight [fôrt'nīt] *n* (*Brit*) quinzaine *f*, quinze jours *mpl*; **it's a ~ since** ... il y a quinze jours que ....

fortnightly [fôrt'nītlē] (*Brit*) *a* bimensuel(le) ♦ *ad* tous les quinze jours.

FORTRAN [fôr'tran] *n* FORTRAN *m*.

fortress [fôr'tris] *n* forteresse *f*.

fortuitous [fôrtōo'itəs] *a* fortuit(e).

fortunate [fôr'chənit] *a*: **to be ~** avoir de la chance; **it is ~ that** c'est une chance que, il est heureux que.

fortunately [fôr'chənitlē] *ad* heureusement, par bonheur.

fortune [fôr'chən] *n* chance *f*; (*wealth*) fortune *f*; **to make a ~** faire fortune.

fortuneteller [fôr'chəntelûr] *n* diseuse *f* de bonne aventure.

forty [fôr'tē] *num* quarante.

forum [fôr'əm] *n* forum *m*, tribune *f*.

forward [fôr'wûrd] *a* (*movement, position*) en avant, vers l'avant; (*not shy*) effronté(e); (*COMM: delivery, sales, exchange*) à terme ♦ *ad* en avant ♦ *n* (*SPORT*) avant *m* ♦ *vt* (*letter*) faire suivre; (*parcel, goods*) expédier; (*fig*) promouvoir, contribuer au développement *or* à l'avancement de; **to move ~** avancer; **"please ~"** "prière de faire suivre".

forward(s) [fôr'wûrd(z)] *ad* en avant.

forwent [fôrwent'] *pt of* **forgo**.

fossil [fâs'əl] *a, n* fossile (*m*); **~ fuel** combustible *m* fossile.

foster [fôs'tûr] *vt* encourager, favoriser.

foster brother *n* frère adoptif; frère de lait.

foster child *n* enfant adopté.

foster mother *n* mère adoptive; mère nourricière.

fought [fôt] *pt, pp of* **fight**.

foul [foul] *a* (*weather, smell, food*) infect(e); (*language*) ordurier(ière); (*deed*) infâme ♦ *n* (*SPORT*) faute *f* ♦ *vt* salir, encrasser; (*player*) commettre une faute sur; (*entangle: anchor, propeller*) emmêler.

foul play *n* (*SPORT*) jeu déloyal; **~ is not suspected** la mort (*or* l'incendie *etc*) n'a pas de causes suspectes, on écarte l'hypothèse d'un meurtre (*or* d'un acte criminel).

found [found] *pt, pp of* **find** ♦ *vt* (*establish*) fonder.

foundation [foundā'shən] *n* (*act*) fondation *f*; (*base*) fondement *m*; (*also*: **~ cream**) fond *m* de teint; **~s** *npl* (*of building*) fondations *fpl*; **to lay the ~s** (*fig*) poser les fondements.

foundation stone *n* première pierre.

founder [foun'dûr] *n* fondateur *m* ♦ *vi* couler, sombrer.

founding [foun'ding] *a*: **~ fathers** (*esp US*) pères *mpl* fondateurs; **~ member** membre *m*

fondateur.

foundry [foun'drē] *n* fonderie *f*.

fount [fount] *n* source *f*; (*Brit TYP*) fonte *f*.

fountain [foun'tin] *n* fontaine *f*.

fountain pen *n* stylo *m* (à encre).

four [fôr] *num* quatre; **on all ~s** à quatre pattes.

four-poster [fôr'pōs'tûr] *n* (*also*: **~ bed**) lit *m* à baldaquin.

foursome [fôr'səm] *n* partie *f* à quatre; sortie *f* à quatre.

fourteen [fôr'tēn'] *num* quatorze.

fourth [fôrth] *num* quatrième ♦ *n* (*AUT*: *also*: **~ gear**) quatrième *f*.

four-wheel drive [fôr'hwēl drīv'] *n* (*AUT*): **with ~** à quatre roues motrices.

fowl [foul] *n* volaille *f*.

fox [fâks] *n* renard *m* ♦ *vt* mystifier.

fox fur *n* renard *m*.

foxglove [fâks'gluv] *n* (*BOT*) digitale *f*.

fox-hunting [fâks'hunting] *n* chasse *f* au renard.

foyer [foi'ûr] *n* vestibule *m*; (*THEATER*) foyer *m*.

FP *n abbr* (*US*) = **fireplug**; (*Brit*) = *former pupil*.

Fr. *abbr* (= *father*: *REL*) P; (= *friar*) F.

fr. *abbr* (= *franc*) F.

fracas [frâ'kəs] *n* bagarre *f*.

fraction [frak'shən] *n* fraction *f*.

fractionally [frak'shənəlē] *ad*: **~ smaller** *etc* un poil plus petit *etc*.

fractious [frak'shəs] *a* grincheux(euse).

fracture [frak'chûr] *n* fracture *f* ♦ *vt* fracturer.

fragile [fraj'əl] *a* fragile.

fragment [frag'mənt] *n* fragment *m*.

fragmentary [frag'məntärē] *a* fragmentaire.

fragrance [frā'grəns] *n* parfum *m*.

fragrant [frā'grənt] *a* parfumé(e), odorant(e).

frail [frāl] *a* fragile, délicat(e).

frame [frām] *n* (*of building*) charpente *f*; (*of human, animal*) charpente, ossature *f*; (*of picture*) cadre *m*; (*of door, window*) encadrement *m*, chambranle *m*; (*of spectacles*: *also*: **~s**) monture *f* ♦ *vt* encadrer; (*theory, plan*) construire, élaborer; **to ~ sb** (*col*) monter un coup contre qn; **~ of mind** disposition *f* d'esprit.

framework [frām'wûrk] *n* structure *f*.

France [frans] *n* la France; **in ~** en France.

franchise [fran'chīz] *n* (*POL*) droit *m* de vote; (*COMM*) franchise *f*.

franchisee [franchizē'] *n* franchisé *m*.

franchiser [fran'chīzûr] *n* franchiseur *m*.

frank [frangk] *a* franc(franche) ♦ *vt* (*letter*) affranchir.

Frankfurt [frangk'fûrt] *n* Francfort.

frankly [frangk'lē] *ad* franchement.

frankness [frangk'nis] *n* franchise *f*.

frantic [fran'tik] *a* frénétique; (*desperate: need, desire*) effréné(e); (*person*) hors de soi.

frantically [fran'tiklē] *ad* frénétiquement.

fraternal [frətûr'nəl] *a* fraternel(le).

fraternity [frətûr'nitē] *n* (*club*) communauté *f*, confrérie *f*; (*spirit*) fraternité *f*.

fraternize [frat'ûrnīz] *vi* fraterniser.

fraud [frôd] *n* supercherie *f*, fraude *f*, tromperie *f*; (*person*) imposteur *m*.

fraudulent [frô'jələnt] *a* frauduleux(euse).
fraught [frôt] *a* (*tense: person*) très tendu(e); (: *situation*) pénible; ~ **with** (*difficulties etc*) chargé(e) de, plein(e) de.
fray [frā] *n* bagarre *f*; (*MIL*) combat *m* ♦ *vt* effilocher ♦ *vi* s'effilocher; **tempers were** ~**ed** les gens commençaient à s'énerver; **her nerves were** ~**ed** elle était à bout de nerfs.
FRB *n abbr* (*US*) = **Federal Reserve Board**.
freak [frēk] *n* (*also cpd*) phénomène *m*, *créature ou événement exceptionnel par sa rareté, son caractère d'anomalie*; (*pej: fanatic*): **health** ~ fana *m/f or* obsédé/e de l'alimentation saine (*or de la forme physique*).
  freak out *vi* (*col: drop out*) se marginaliser; (: *on drugs*) se défoncer.
freakish [frēk'ish] *a* insolite; anormal(e).
freckle [frek'əl] *n* tache *f* de rousseur.
free [frē] *a* libre; (*gratis*) gratuit(e); (*liberal*) généreux(euse), large ♦ *vt* (*prisoner etc*) libérer; (*jammed object or person*) dégager; **to give sb a** ~ **hand** donner carte blanche à qn; ~ **and easy** sans façon, décontracté(e); **admission** ~ entrée libre; ~ (**of charge**) *ad* gratuitement.
-free *suffix*: **additive**~ sans additif; **tax**~ exonéré(e) d'impôt.
freebie [frē'bē] *n* (*col*): **it's a** ~ c'est gratuit.
freedom [frē'dəm] *n* liberté *f*.
freedom fighter *n* combattant *m* de la liberté.
free enterprise *n* libre entreprise *f*.
free-for-all [frē'fûrôl'] *n* mêlée générale.
free gift *n* prime *f*.
freehold [frē'hōld] *n* propriété foncière libre.
free kick *n* (*SPORT*) coup franc.
freelance [frē'lans] *a* (*journalist etc*) indépendant(e); (*work*) à la pige, à la tâche.
freeloader [frē'lōdûr] *n* (*pej*) parasite *m*.
freely [frē'lē] *ad* librement; (*liberally*) libéralement.
freemason [frē'māsən] *n* franc-maçon *m*.
freemasonry [frē'māsənrē] *n* franc-maçonnerie *f*.
free-range [frē'rānj] *a* (*Brit: eggs*) de ferme.
free sample *n* échantillon gratuit.
free speech *n* liberté *f* d'expression.
freestyle wrestling [frē'stīl res'ling] *n* (*US*) catch *m*.
free trade *n* libre-échange *m*.
freeway [frē'wā] *n* (*US*) autoroute *f*.
freewheel [frē'hwēl'] *vi* descendre en roue libre.
freewheeling [frē'hwē'ling] *a* indépendant(e), libre.
free will *n* libre arbitre *m*; **of one's own** ~ de son plein gré.
freeze [frēz] *vb* (*pt* **froze**, *pp* **frozen** [frōz, frō'zən]) *vi* geler ♦ *vt* geler; (*food*) congeler; (*prices, salaries*) bloquer, geler ♦ *n* gel *m*; blocage *m*.
  freeze over *vi* (*river*) geler; (*windshield*) se couvrir de givre *or* de glace.
  freeze up *vi* geler.
freeze-dried [frēz'drīd'] *a* lyophilisé(e).
freezer [frē'zûr] *n* congélateur *m*.
freezing [frē'zing] *a*: ~ (**cold**) (*room etc*) glacial(e); (*person, hands*) gelé(e), glacé(e) ♦ *n*: **3 degrees below** ~ 3 degrés au-dessous

de zéro.
freezing point *n* point *m* de congélation.
freight [frāt] *n* (*goods*) fret *m*, cargaison *f*; (*money charged*) fret, prix *m* du transport; ~ **forward** port dû; ~ **inward** port payé par le destinataire.
freighter [frā'tûr] *n* (*NAUT*) cargo *m*.
freight forwarder [frāt' fôr'wûrdûr] *n* transitaire *m*.
freight train *n* (*US*) train *m* de marchandises.
French [french] *a* français(e) ♦ *n* (*LING*) français *m*; **the** ~ *npl* les Français.
French bean *n* (*Brit*) haricot vert.
French Canadian *a* canadien(ne) français(e) ♦ *n* Canadien/ne français(e); (*LING*) français canadien.
French dressing *n* (*CULIN*) vinaigrette *f*.
French fries [french frīz] *npl* (pommes de terre *fpl*) frites.
French Guiana [french gēan'ə] *n* Guyane française.
Frenchman [french'mən] *n* Français *m*.
French Riviera *n*: **the** ~ la Côte d'Azur.
French window *n* porte-fenêtre *f*.
Frenchwoman [french'wŏŏmən] *n* Française *f*.
frenetic [frənet'ik] *a* frénétique.
frenzy [fren'zē] *n* frénésie *f*.
frequency [frē'kwənsē] *n* fréquence *f*.
frequency modulation (FM) *n* modulation *f* de fréquence (FM, MF).
frequent *a* [frē'kwint] fréquent(e) ♦ *vt* [frikwent'] fréquenter.
frequently [frē'kwintlē] *ad* fréquemment.
fresco [fres'kō] *n* fresque *f*.
fresh [fresh] *a* frais(fraîche); (*new*) nouveau(nouvelle); (*cheeky*) familier(ière), culotté(e); **to make a** ~ **start** prendre un nouveau départ.
freshen [fresh'ən] *vi* (*wind, air*) fraîchir.
  freshen up *vi* faire un brin de toilette.
freshener [fresh'ənûr] *n*: **skin** ~ astringent *m*; **air** ~ désodorisant *m*.
fresher [fresh'ûr] *n* (*Brit SCOL: col*) = **freshman**.
freshly [fresh'lē] *ad* nouvellement, récemment.
freshman [fresh'mən] *n* (*SCOL*) bizuth *m*, étudiant/e de première année.
freshness [fresh'nis] *n* fraîcheur *f*.
freshwater [fresh'wôtûr] *a* (*fish*) d'eau douce.
fret [fret] *vi* s'agiter, se tracasser.
fretful [fret'fəl] *a* (*child*) grincheux(euse).
Freudian [froi'dēən] *a* freudien(ne); ~ **slip** lapsus *m*.
FRG *n abbr* (= *Federal Republic of Germany*) RFA *f*.
Fri. *abbr* (= *Friday*) ve.
friar [frī'ûr] *n* moine *m*, frère *m*.
friction [frik'shən] *n* friction *f*, frottement *m*.
friction feed *n* (*on printer*) entraînement *m* par friction.
Friday [frī'dā] *n* vendredi *m*; *for phrases see also* **Tuesday**.
fridge [frij] *n* (*Brit*) frigo *m*, frigidaire *m* ®.
fried [frīd] *pt, pp of* **fry** ♦ *a* frit(e); ~ **egg** œuf *m* sur le plat.
friend [frend] *n* ami/e; **to make** ~**s with** se lier (d'amitié) avec.

friendliness [frend'lēnis] *n* attitude amicale.
friendly [frend'lē] *a* amical(e); (*kind*) sympathique, gentil(le); (*POL*: *country, government*) ami(e) ♦ *n* (*also*: ~ **match**)
match amical; **to be** ~ **with** être ami(e)
avec; **to be** ~ **to** être bien disposé(e) à
l'égard de.
friendly society *n* (*Brit*) société *f* mutualiste.
friendship [frend'ship] *n* amitié *f*.
frieze [frēz] *n* frise *f*, bordure *f*.
frigate [frig'it] *n* (*NAUT: modern*) frégate *f*.
fright [frīt] *n* peur *f*, effroi *m*; **to take** ~ prendre peur, s'effrayer; **she looks a** ~ elle a
l'air d'un épouvantail.
frighten [frīt'ən] *vt* effrayer, faire peur à.
frighten away, frighten off *vt* (*birds,
children etc*) faire fuir, effaroucher.
frightened [frīt'ənd] *a*: **to be** ~ **(of)** avoir
peur (de).
frightening [frīt'ning] *a* effrayant(e).
frightful [frīt'fəl] *a* affreux(euse).
frightfully [frīt'fəlē] *ad* affreusement.
frigid [frij'id] *a* (*woman*) frigide.
frigidity [frijid'itē] *n* frigidité *f*.
frill [fril] *n* (*of dress*) volant *m*; (*of shirt*) jabot
m; **without** ~**s** (*fig*) sans manières.
fringe [frinj] *n* frange *f*; (*edge: of forest etc*)
bordure *f*; (*fig*): **on the** ~ en marge.
fringe benefits *npl* avantages sociaux *or* en
nature.
fringe theatre *n* (*Brit*) théâtre *m* d'avant-
garde.
frisk [frisk] *vt* fouiller.
frisky [fris'kē] *a* vif(vive), sémillant(e).
fritter [frit'ûr] *n* beignet *m*.
fritter away *vt* gaspiller.
frivolity [frəvål'itē] *n* frivolité *f*.
frivolous [friv'ələs] *a* frivole.
frizzy [friz'ē] *a* crépu(e).
fro [frō] *see* **to**.
frock [fråk] *n* robe *f*.
frog [frôg] *n* grenouille *f*; **to have a** ~ **in one's
throat** avoir un chat dans la gorge.
frogman [frôg'man] *n* homme-grenouille *m*.
frogmarch [frôg'mårch] *vt* (*Brit*): **to** ~ **sb in/
out** faire entrer/sortir qn de force.
frolic [frål'ik] *n* ébats *mpl* ♦ *vi* folâtrer, batifoler.
from [frum] *prep* de; **where is he** ~? d'où est-
il?; **where has he come** ~? d'où arrive-t-il?;
(as) ~ **Friday** à partir de vendredi; **a telephone call** ~ **Mr. Smith** un appel de M.
Smith; **prices range** ~ **$10 to $50** les prix
vont de 10 dollars à 50 dollars; ~ **what he
says** d'après ce qu'il dit.
frond [frånd] *n* fronde *f*.
front [frunt] *n* (*of house, dress*) devant *m*; (*of
coach, train*) avant *m*; (*of book*) couverture
f; (*promenade: also*: **sea** ~) bord *m* de mer;
(*MIL, POL, METEOROLOGY*) front *m*; (*fig:
appearances*) contenance *f*, façade *f* ♦ *a* de
devant; premier(ière) ♦ *vi*: **to** ~ **onto sth**
donner sur qch; **in** ~ **(of)** devant.
frontage [frun'tij] *n* façade *f*; (*of shop*) devanture *f*.
frontal [frun'təl] *a* frontal(e).
front bench *n* (*Brit POL*) les dirigeants du
parti au pouvoir ou de l'opposition.
front desk *n* (*in hotel, at doctor's*) réception

f.
front door *n* porte *f* d'entrée; (*of car*) portière *f* avant.
frontier [fruntêûr'] *n* frontière *f*.
frontispiece [frun'tispēs] *n* frontispice *m*.
front page *n* première page.
front room *n* pièce *f* de devant, salon *m*.
front runner *n* (*fig*) favori/te.
front-wheel drive [frunt'hwēl drīv] *n* traction
f avant.
frost [frôst] *n* gel *m*, gelée *f*; (*also*: **hoar**~) givre *m* ♦ *vt* (*cake*) glacer.
frostbite [frôst'bīt] *n* gelures *fpl*.
frosted [frôs'tid] *a* (*glass*) dépoli(e); (*esp US:
cake*) glacé(e).
frosting [frôs'ting] *n* (*esp US: on cake*) glaçage *m*.
frosty [frôs'tē] *a* (*window*) couvert(e) de givre; (*welcome*) glacial(e).
froth [frôth] *n* mousse *f*; écume *f*.
frown [froun] *n* froncement *m* de sourcils ♦ *vi*
froncer les sourcils.
frown on *vt* (*fig*) désapprouver.
froze [frōz] *pt of* **freeze**.
frozen [frō'zən] *pp of* **freeze** ♦ *a* (*food*) conge-
lé(e); (*COMM: assets*) gelé(e).
FRS *n abbr* (*US*: = *Federal Reserve System*)
banque centrale américaine.
frugal [frōō'gəl] *a* frugal(e).
fruit [frōōt] *n* (*pl inv*) fruit *m*.
fruiterer [frōōt'ərûr] *n* fruitier *m*, marchand/e
de fruits; ~**'s (shop)** fruiterie *f*.
fruitful [frōōt'fəl] *a* fructueux(euse); (*plant,
soil*) fécond(e).
fruition [frōōish'ən] *n*: **to come to** ~ se réaliser.
fruit juice *n* jus *m* de fruit.
fruitless [frōōt'lis] *a* (*fig*) vain(e), in-
fructueux(euse).
fruit machine *n* (*Brit*) machine *f* à sous.
fruit salad *n* salade *f* de fruits.
frump [frump] *n* mocheté *f*.
frustrate [frus'trāt] *vt* frustrer; (*plot, plans*)
faire échouer.
frustrated [frus'trātid] *a* frustré(e).
frustrating [frus'trāting] *a* (*job*) frustrant(e);
(*day*) démoralisant(e).
frustration [frustrā'shən] *n* frustration *f*.
fry, *pt, pp* **fried** [frī, frīd] *vt* (faire) frire; **the
small** ~ le menu fretin.
frying pan [frī'ing pan] *n* poêle *f* (à frire).
FSLIC *n abbr* (*US*: = *Federal Savings and
Loan Insurance Corporation*) *organisme
fédéral assurant les dépôts des associations
d'épargne et de prêt.*
FT *n abbr* (*Brit*: = *Financial Times*) *journal
financier*; **the** ~ **index** *l'indice boursier du
Financial Times.*
ft. *abbr* = **foot, feet**.
FTC *n abbr* (*US*) = **Federal Trade
Commission**.
fuchsia [fyōō'sha] *n* fuchsia *m*.
fuck [fuk] *vt, vi* (*col!*) baiser (*!*); ~ **off!** fous
le camp! (*!*).
fuddled [fud'əld] *a* (*muddled*) embrouillé(e),
confus(e).
fuddy-duddy [fud'ēdudē] *a* (*pej*) vieux jeu
inv, ringard(e).
fudge [fuj] *n* (*CULIN*) sorte de confiserie à

base de sucre, de beurre et de lait ♦ *vt* (*issue, problem*) esquiver.

fuel [fyōō'əl] *n* (*for heating*) combustible *m*; (*for propelling*) carburant *m*.

fuel oil *n* mazout *m*.

fuel pump *n* (*AUT*) pompe *f* d'alimentation.

fuel tank *n* cuve *f* à mazout, citerne *f*; (*in vehicle*) réservoir *m* de or à carburant.

fug [fug] *n* (*Brit*) puanteur *f*, odeur *f* de renfermé.

fugitive [fyōō'jətiv] *n* fugitif/ive.

fulfill, (*Brit*) **fulfil** [fōōlfil'] *vt* (*function*) remplir; (*order*) exécuter; (*wish, desire*) satisfaire, réaliser.

fulfilled [fōōlfild'] *a* (*person*) comblé(e), épanoui(e).

fulfillment [fōōlfil'mənt] *n* (*of wishes*) réalisation *f*.

full [fōōl] *a* plein(e); (*details, information*) complet(ète); (*price*) fort(e), normal(e); (*skirt*) ample, large ♦ *ad*: **to know** ~ **well that** savoir fort bien que; ~ (**up**) (*hotel etc*) complet(ète); **I'm** ~ (**up**) j'ai bien mangé; ~ **employment/fare** plein emploi/tarif; **a** ~ **two hours** deux bonnes heures; **at** ~ **speed** à toute vitesse; **in** ~ (*reproduce, quote, pay*) intégralement; (*write name etc*) en toutes lettres.

fullback [fōōl'bak] *n* (*RUGBY, SOCCER*) arrière *m*.

full-blooded [fōōl'blud'id] *a* (*vigorous*) vigoureux(euse).

full-cream [fōōl'krēm] *a*: ~ **milk** (*Brit*) lait entier.

full-fledged [fōōl'flejd'] *a* (*US: teacher, barrister*) diplômé(e); (: *citizen, member*) à part entière.

full-grown [fōōl'grōn'] *a* arrivé(e) à maturité, adulte.

full-length [fōōl'lengkth'] *a* (*portrait*) en pied; ~ **film** long métrage.

full moon *n* pleine lune.

full-scale [fōōl'skāl'] *a* (*model*) grandeur nature *inv*; (*search, retreat*) complet(ète), total(e).

full-sized [fōōl'sīzd'] *a* (*portrait etc*) grandeur nature *inv*.

full stop *n* (*Brit*) point *m*.

full-time [fōōl'tīm] *a* (*work*) à plein temps ♦ *n* (*SPORT*) fin *f* du match.

fully [fōōl'ē] *ad* entièrement, complètement; (*at least*): ~ **as big** au moins aussi grand.

fully-fledged [fōōl'ēflejd'] *a* (*Brit*) = **full-fledged.**

fulsome [fōōl'səm] *a* (*pej: praise*) excessif(ive); (: *manner*) exagéré(e).

fumble [fum'bəl] *vi* fouiller, tâtonner ♦ *vt* (*ball*) mal réceptionner, cafouiller.

fumble with *vt fus* tripoter.

fume [fyōōm] *vi* rager; ~**s** *npl* vapeurs *fpl*, émanations *fpl*, gaz *mpl*.

fumigate [fyōō'məgāt] *vt* désinfecter (par fumigation).

fun [fun] *n* amusement *m*, divertissement *m*; **to have** ~ s'amuser; **for** ~ pour rire; **it's not much** ~ ce n'est pas très drôle or amusant; **to make** ~ **of** se moquer de.

function [fungk'shən] *n* fonction *f*; (*reception, dinner*) cérémonie *f*, soirée officielle ♦ *vi*

fonctionner; **to** ~ **as** faire office de.

functional [fungk'shənəl] *a* fonctionnel(le).

function key *n* (*COMPUT*) touche *f* de fonction.

fund [fund] *n* caisse *f*, fonds *m*; (*source, store*) source *f*, mine *f*; ~**s** *npl* fonds *mpl*.

fundamental [fundəmen'təl] *a* fondamental(e); ~**s** *npl* principes *mpl* de base.

fundamentalist [fundəmen'təlist] *n* intégriste *m/f*.

fundamentally [fundəmen'təlē] *ad* fondamentalement.

fund-raising [fund'rāzing] *n* collecte *f* de fonds.

funeral [fyōō'nūrəl] *n* enterrement *m*, obsèques *fpl* (*more formal occasion*).

funeral director *n* entrepreneur *m* des pompes funèbres.

funeral home, (*Brit*) **funeral parlour** *n* dépôt *m* mortuaire.

funeral service *n* service *m* funèbre.

funereal [fyōōnē'rēəl] *a* lugubre, funèbre.

funfair [fun'fär] *n* (*Brit*) fête (foraine).

fungus, *pl* **fungi** [fung'gəs, -jī] *n* champignon *m*; (*mould*) moisissure *f*.

funicular [fyōōnik'yəlûr] *n* (*also:* ~ **railway**) funiculaire *m*.

funnel [fun'əl] *n* entonnoir *m*; (*of ship*) cheminée *f*.

funnily [fun'ilē] *ad* (*see funny*) drôlement; curieusement.

funny [fun'ē] *a* amusant(e), drôle; (*strange*) curieux(euse), bizarre.

funny bone *n* endroit sensible du coude.

fur [fûr] *n* fourrure *f*; (*Brit: in kettle etc*) (dépôt *m* de) tartre *m*.

fur coat *n* manteau *m* de fourrure.

furious [fyōōr'ēəs] *a* furieux(euse); (*effort*) acharné(e); **to be** ~ **with sb** être dans une fureur noire contre qn.

furiously [fyōōr'ēəslē] *ad* furieusement; avec acharnement.

furl [fûrl] *vt* rouler; (*NAUT*) ferler.

furlong [fûr'lông] *n* = *201.17 m* (*terme d'hippisme*).

furlough [fûr'lō] *n* permission *f*, congé *m*.

furnace [fûr'nis] *n* fourneau *m*.

furnish [fûr'nish] *vt* meubler; (*supply*) fournir; ~**ed apartment** meublé *m*.

furnishings [fûr'nishingz] *npl* mobilier *m*, articles *mpl* d'ameublement.

furniture [fûr'nichûr] *n* meubles *mpl*, mobilier *m*; **piece of** ~ meuble *m*.

furniture mover *n* déménageur *m*.

furniture polish *n* encaustique *f*.

furore [fyōōr'ôr] *n* (*protests*) protestations *fpl*.

furrier [fûr'ēûr] *n* fourreur *m*.

furrow [fûr'ō] *n* sillon *m*.

furry [fûr'ē] *a* (*animal*) à fourrure; (*toy*) en peluche.

further [fûr'thûr] *a* supplémentaire, autre; nouveau(nouvelle) ♦ *ad* plus loin; (*more*) davantage; (*moreover*) de plus ♦ *vt* faire avancer or progresser, promouvoir; **how much** ~ **is it?** quelle distance or combien reste-t-il à parcourir?; **until** ~ **notice** jusqu'à nouvel ordre or avis; ~ **to your letter of ...** (*Brit COMM*) suite à votre lettre du ....

further education *n* enseignement *m* postscolaire *(recyclage, formation professionnelle)*.

furthermore [fûr'thurmôr] *ad* de plus, en outre.

furthermost [fûr'thurmōst] *a* le(la) plus éloigné(e).

furthest [fûr'thist] *superlative of* **far**.

furtive [fûr'tiv] *a* furtif(ive).

furtively [fûr'tivlē] *ad* furtivement.

fury [fyoor'ē] *n* fureur *f*.

fuse [fyooz] *n* fusible *m*; *(Brit: for bomb etc)* amorce *f*, détonateur *m* ♦ *vt, vi (metal)* fondre; *(fig)* fusionner; *(Brit ELEC)*: **to ~ the lights** faire sauter les fusibles *or* les plombs; **a ~ has blown** un fusible a sauté.

fuse box *n* boîte *f* à fusibles.

fuselage [fyoo'səlâzh] *n* fuselage *m*.

fuse wire *n* fusible *m*.

fusillade [fyoos'əlād] *n* fusillade *f*; *(fig)* feu roulant.

fusion [fyoo'zhən] *n* fusion *f*.

fuss [fus] *n (anxiety, excitement)* chichis *mpl*, façons *fpl*; *(commotion)* tapage *m*; *(complaining, trouble)* histoire(s) *f(pl)* ♦ *vi* faire des histoires ♦ *vt (person)* embêter; **to make a ~** faire des façons (*or* des histoires).

fuss over *vt fus (person)* dorloter.

fussy [fus'ē] *a (person)* tatillon(ne), difficile; chichiteux(euse); *(dress, style)* tarabiscoté(e); **I'm not ~** *(col)* ça m'est égal.

futile [fyoo'təl] *a* futile.

futility [fyootil'ətē] *n* futilité *f*.

future [fyoo'chûr] *a* futur(e) ♦ *n* avenir *m*; *(LING)* futur *m*; **in (the) ~** à l'avenir; **in the near/immediate ~** dans un avenir proche/immédiat.

futures [fyoo'chûrz] *npl (COMM)* opérations *fpl* à terme.

futuristic [fyoochəris'tik] *a* futuriste.

fuze [fyooz] *(US) n (for bomb etc)* amorce *f*, détonateur *m* ♦ *vt, vi* = **fuse**.

fuzzy [fuz'ē] *a (PHOT)* flou(e); *(hair)* crépu(e).

fwd. *abbr* = **forward**.

fwy *abbr (US)* = **freeway**.

FY *abbr* = **fiscal year**.

FYI *abbr* = *for your information*.

G

G, g [jē] *n (letter)* G, g *m*; *(MUS)*: **G** sol *m*; **G for George** G comme Gaston.

G [jē] *n abbr (US CINEMA*: = *general (audience))* ≈ tous publics; *(Brit SCOL*: = *good)* b (= *bien*).

g [jē] *abbr (= gram, gravity)* g.

GA *abbr (US MAIL)* = *Georgia*.

gab [gab] *n (col)*: **to have the gift of the ~** avoir la langue bien pendue.

gabble [gab'əl] *vi* bredouiller; jacasser.

gaberdine [gab'ûrdēn] *n* gabardine *f*.

gable [gā'bəl] *n* pignon *m*.

Gabon [gābân'] *n* Gabon *m*.

gad about [gad əbout'] *vi (col)* se balader.

gadget [gaj'it] *n* gadget *m*.

Gaelic [gā'lik] *a, n* gaélique *(m)*.

gaffe [gaf] *n* gaffe *f*.

gag [gag] *n* bâillon *m*; *(joke)* gag *m* ♦ *vt* bâillonner.

gaga [gâ'gâ] *a*: **to go ~** devenir gaga *or* gâteux(euse).

gage [gāj] *n, vt (US)* = **gauge**.

gaiety [gā'ətē] *n* gaieté *f*.

gaily [gā'lē] *ad* gaiement.

gain [gān] *n* gain *m*, profit *m* ♦ *vt* gagner ♦ *vi (watch)* avancer; **to ~ in/by** gagner en/à; **to ~ 3lbs (in weight)** prendre 3 livres; **to ~ ground** gagner du terrain.

gain (up)on *vt fus* rattraper.

gainful [gān'fəl] *a* profitable, lucratif(ive).

gainsay [gānsā'] *vt irg (like* **say***)* contredire; nier.

gait [gāt] *n* démarche *f*.

gal. *abbr* = **gallon**.

gala [gā'lə] *n* gala *m*; **swimming ~** grand concours de natation.

Galapagos (Islands) [gəlâ'pəgōs (ī'ləndz)] *npl*: **the ~** les (îles *fpl*) Galapagos *fpl*.

galaxy [gal'əksē] *n* galaxie *f*.

gale [gāl] *n* coup *m* de vent; **~ force 10** vent *m* de force 10.

gall [gôl] *n (ANAT)* bile *f*; *(fig)* effronterie *f* ♦ *vt* ulcérer, irriter.

gall. *abbr* = **gallon**.

gallant [gal'ənt] *a* vaillant(e), brave; [gəlânt'] *(towards ladies)* empressé(e), galant(e).

gallantry [gal'əntrē] *n* bravoure *f*, vaillance *f*; empressement *m*, galanterie *f*.

gall bladder *n* vésicule *f* biliaire.

galleon [gal'ēən] *n* galion *m*.

gallery [gal'ûrē] *n* galerie *f*; *(for spectators)* tribune *f*; *(: in theater)* dernier balcon; *(also:* **art ~**) musée *m*; *(: private)* galerie.

galley [gal'ē] *n (ship's kitchen)* cambuse *f*; *(ship)* galère *f*; *(also:* **~ proof**) placard *m*, galée *f*.

Gallic [gal'ik] *a (of Gaul)* gaulois(e); *(French)* français(e).

galling [gô'ling] *a* irritant(e).

gallon [gal'ən] *n* gallon *m* (= *8 pints; US* = *3.785 l; Brit* = *4.543 l*).

gallop [gal'əp] *n* galop *m* ♦ *vi* galoper; **~ing inflation** inflation galopante.

gallows [gal'ōz] *n* potence *f*.

gallstone [gôl'stōn] *n* calcul *m* (biliaire).

galore [gəlôr'] *ad* en abondance, à gogo.

galvanize [gal'vəniz] *vt* galvaniser; *(fig)*: **to ~ sb into action** galvaniser qn.

Gambia [gam'bēə] *n* Gambie *f*.

gambit [gam'bit] *n (fig)*: **(opening) ~** manœuvre *f* stratégique.

gamble [gam'bəl] *n* pari *m*, risque calculé ♦ *vt, vi* jouer; **to ~ on the Stock Exchange** jouer en *or* à la Bourse; **to ~ on** *(fig)* miser sur.

gambler [gam'blûr] *n* joueur *m*.

gambling [gam'bling] *n* jeu *m*.

gambol [gam'bəl] *vi* gambader.

game [gām] *n* jeu *m*; *(event)* match *m*; *(HUNTING)* gibier *m* ♦ *a* brave; *(ready)*: **to be ~ (for sth/to do)** être prêt(e) (à qch/à faire), se sentir de taille (à faire); **a ~ of**

football/tennis une partie de football/tennis;
~s (*SCOL*) sport *m*; **big ~** gros gibier.
game bird *n* gibier *m* à plume.
gamekeeper [gām'kēpûr] *n* garde-chasse *m*.
gamely [gām'lē] *ad* vaillamment.
game reserve *n* réserve animalière.
gamesmanship [gāmz'mənship] *n* roublardise
f.
gammon [gam'ən] *n* (*bacon*) quartier *m* de
lard fumé; (*ham*) jambon fumé.
gamut [gam'ət] *n* gamme *f*.
gang [gang] *n* bande *f*, groupe *m* ♦ *vi*: **to ~ up**
on sb se liguer contre qn.
Ganges [gan'jēz] *n*: **the ~** le Gange.
gangling [gang'gling] *a* dégingandé(e).
gangplank [gang'plangk] *n* passerelle *f*.
gangrene [gang'grēn] *n* gangrène *f*.
gangster [gang'stûr] *n* gangster *m*, bandit *m*.
gangway [gang'wā] *n* passerelle *f*; (*Brit: of*
bus) couloir central.
gantry [gan'trē] *n* portique *m*; (*for rocket*)
tour *f* de lancement.
GAO *n abbr* (*US:* = *General Accounting*
Office) ≈ Cour *f* des comptes.
gaol [jāl] *n*, *vt* (*Brit*) = **jail**.
gap [gap] *n* trou *m*; (*in time*) intervalle *m*;
(*fig*) lacune *f*; vide *m*.
gape [gāp] *vi* être or rester bouche bée.
gaping [gā'ping] *a* (*hole*) béant(e).
garage [gərãzh'] *n* garage *m*.
garb [gârb] *n* tenue *f*, costume *m*.
garbage [gâr'bij] *n* ordures *fpl*, détritus *mpl*;
(*fig: col*) conneries *fpl*.
garbage can *n* (*US*) poubelle *f*, boîte *f* à
ordures.
garbage disposal unit *n* (*US*) broyeur *m*
d'ordures.
garbage dump *n* (*US: in town*) décharge publique, dépotoir *m*.
garbageman [gâr'bijman] *n* (*US*) éboueur *m*.
garbled [gâr'bəld] *a* déformé(e); faussé(e).
garden [gâr'dən] *n* jardin *m* ♦ *vi* jardiner; **~s**
npl (*public*) jardin public; (*private*) parc *m*.
garden center *n* garden-centre *m*, pépinière
f.
gardener [gârd'nûr] *n* jardinier *m*.
gardening [gâr'dəning] *n* jardinage *m*.
gargle [gâr'gəl] *vi* se gargariser ♦ *n* gargarisme *m*.
gargoyle [gâr'goil] *n* gargouille *f*.
garish [gär'ish] *a* criard(e), voyant(e).
garland [gâr'lənd] *n* guirlande *f*; couronne *f*.
garlic [gâr'lik] *n* ail *m*.
garment [gâr'mənt] *n* vêtement *m*.
garner [gâr'nûr] *vt* engranger, amasser.
garnish [gâr'nish] *vt* garnir.
garret [gar'it] *n* mansarde *f*.
garrison [gar'isən] *n* garnison *f* ♦ *vt* mettre en
garnison, stationner.
garrison cap *n* (*US*) calot *m*.
garrulous [gar'ələs] *a* volubile, loquace.
garter [gâr'tûr] *n* jarretière *f*; (*US: suspender*)
jarretelle *f*.
garter belt *n* (*US*) porte-jarretelles *m inv*.
gas [gas] *n* gaz *m*; (*used as anesthetic*): **to be**
given ~ se faire endormir; (*US: gasoline*)
essence *f* ♦ *vt* asphyxier; (*MIL*) gazer.
gas can *n* (*US*) bidon *m* à essence.
Gascony [gas'kənē] *n* Gascogne *f*.

gas cylinder *n* bouteille *f* de gaz.
gaseous [gas'ēəs] *a* gazeux(euse).
gash [gash] *n* entaille *f*; (*on face*) balafre *f* ♦
vt tailler; balafrer.
gasket [gas'kit] *n* (*AUT*) joint *m* de culasse.
gas mask *n* masque *m* à gaz.
gas meter *n* compteur *m* à gaz.
gas(oline) [gas(əlēn')] *n* (*US*) essence *f*.
gasp [gasp] *vi* haleter; (*fig*) avoir le souffle
coupé.
gasp out *vt* (*say*) dire dans un souffle or
d'une voix entrecoupée.
gas pedal *n* (*US*) accélérateur *m*.
gas-permeable [gaspûr'mēəbəl] *a* (*contact*
lenses) perméable à l'air.
gas pump *n* (*US*) pompe *f* à essence.
gas ring *n* brûleur *m*.
gas station *n* (*US*) station-service *f*.
gas stove *n* réchaud *m* à gaz; (*cooker*) cuisinière *f* à gaz.
gassy [gas'ē] *a* gazeux(euse).
gas tank *n* (*US AUT*) réservoir *m* d'essence.
gas tap *n* bouton *m* (de cuisinière à gaz); (*on*
pipe) robinet *m* à gaz.
gastric [gas'trik] *a* gastrique.
gastric ulcer *n* ulcère *m* de l'estomac.
gastroenteritis [gastrōēntərī'tis] *n* gastro-
entérite *f*.
gastronomy [gastrân'əmē] *n* gastronomie *f*.
gasworks [gas'wûrks] *n*, *npl* usine *f* à gaz.
gate [gāt] *n* (*of garden*) portail *m*; (*of farm, at*
level crossing) barrière *f*; (*of building, town,*
at airport) porte *f*; (*of lock*) vanne *f*.
gateau, *pl* **~x** [gatō', z] *n* (*Brit*) gros gâteau à
la crème.
gate-crash [gāt'krash] *vt* s'introduire sans
invitation dans.
gate-crasher [gat'krashûr] *n* intrus/e.
gateway [gāt'wā] *n* porte *f*.
gather [gath'ûr] *vt* (*flowers, fruit*) cueillir;
(*pick up*) ramasser; (*assemble*) rassembler,
réunir; recueillir; (*understand*) comprendre
♦ *vi* (*assemble*) se rassembler; (*dust*)
s'amasser; (*clouds*) s'amonceler; **to ~**
(from/that) conclure or déduire (de/que); **as**
far as I can ~ d'après ce que je comprends;
to ~ speed prendre de la vitesse.
gathering [gath'ûring] *n* rassemblement *m*.
GATT [gat] *n abbr* (= *General Agreement on*
Tariffs and Trade) GATT *m*.
gauche [gōsh] *a* gauche, maladroit(e).
gaudy [gô'dē] *a* voyant(e).
gauge [gāj] *n* (*standard measure*) calibre *m*;
(*RAIL*) écartement *m*; (*instrument*) jauge *f* ♦
vt jauger; (*fig: sb's capabilities, character*)
juger de; **to ~ the right moment** calculer le
moment propice; **gas ~**, (*Brit*) **petrol ~** jauge d'essence.
Gaul [gôl] *n* (*country*) Gaule *f*; (*person*)
Gaulois/e.
gaunt [gônt] *a* décharné(e); (*grim, desolate*)
désolé(e).
gauntlet [gônt'lit] *n* (*fig*): **to throw down the**
~ jeter le gant; **to run the ~ through an an-**
gry crowd se frayer un passage à travers
une foule hostile or entre deux haies de manifestants *etc* hostiles.
gauze [gôz] *n* gaze *f*.
gave [gāv] *pt of* **give**.

gavel [gav'əl] n marteau m.
gawky [gó'kē] a dégingandé(e), godiche.
gawp [gôp] vi: **to ~ at** regarder bouche bée.
gay [gā] a (homosexual) homosexuel(le); (slightly old-fashioned: cheerful) gai(e), réjoui(e); (color) gai, vif(vive).
gaze [gāz] n regard m fixe ♦ vi: **to ~ at** vt fixer du regard.
gazelle [gəzel'] n gazelle f.
gazette [gəzet'] n (newspaper) gazette f; (official publication) journal officiel.
gazetteer [gazitēr'] n dictionnaire m géographique.
GB abbr = **Great Britain**.
GCE n abbr (Brit) = General Certificate of Education.
GCSE n abbr (Brit) = General Certificate of Secondary Education.
Gdns. abbr = Gardens.
GDP n abbr = **gross domestic product**.
GDR n abbr (= German Democratic Republic) RDA f.
gear [gēr] n matériel m, équipement m; (TECH) engrenage m; (AUT) vitesse f ♦ vt (fig: adapt) adapter; **high** or (Brit) **top/low/bottom ~** quatrième (or cinquième)/deuxième/première vitesse; **in ~** en prise; **out of ~** au point mort; **our service is ~ed to meet the needs of the disabled** notre service répond de façon spécifique aux besoins des handicapés.
 gear up vi: **to ~ up (to do)** se préparer (à faire).
gear box n boîte f de vitesse.
gear shift, (Brit) **gear lever** n levier m de vitesse.
GED n abbr (US SCOL) = general educational development.
geese [gēs] npl of **goose**.
Geiger counter [gī'gûr koun'tûr] n compteur m Geiger.
gel [jel] n gelée f; (CHEMISTRY) colloïde m.
gelatin(e) [jel'atin] n gélatine f.
gelignite [jel'ignīt] n plastic m.
gem [jem] n pierre précieuse.
Gemini [jem'ənī] n les Gémeaux mpl; **to be ~** être des Gémeaux.
gen [jen] n (Brit col): **to give sb the ~ on sth** mettre qn au courant de qch.
Gen. abbr (MIL: = general) Gal.
gen. abbr (= general, generally) gén.
gender [jen'dûr] n genre m.
gene [jēn] n (BIOL) gène m.
genealogy [jēnēāl'əjē] n généalogie f.
general [jen'ûrəl] n général m ♦ a général(e); **in ~** en général; **the ~ public** le grand public; **~ audit** (COMM) vérification annuelle.
general anesthetic n anesthésie générale.
general delivery n (US) poste restante.
general election n élection(s) législative(s).
generalization [jenûrələzā'shən] n généralisation f.
generalize [jen'ûrəlīz] vi généraliser.
generally [jen'ûrəlē] ad généralement.
general manager n directeur général.
general practitioner (GP) n généraliste m/f; **who's your GP?** qui est votre médecin traitant?
general strike n grève générale.

generate [jen'ərāt] vt engendrer; (electricity) produire.
generation [jenərā'shən] n génération f; (of electricity etc) production f.
generator [jen'ərātûr] n générateur m.
generic [jənär'ik] a générique.
generosity [jenərâs'ətē] n générosité f.
generous [jen'ûrəs] a généreux(euse); (copious) copieux(euse).
genesis [jen'əsis] n genèse f.
genetic [jinet'ik] a génétique; **~ engineering** génie m génétique.
genetics [jənet'iks] n génétique f.
Geneva [jənē'və] n Genève; **Lake ~** le lac Léman.
genial [jē'nēəl] a cordial(e), chaleureux(euse); (climate) clément(e).
genitals [jen'itəlz] npl organes génitaux.
genitive [jen'ətiv] n génitif m.
genius [jēn'yəs] n génie m.
Genoa [jen'əwə] n Gênes.
genocide [jen'əsīd] n génocide m.
genteel [jentēl'] a de bon ton, distingué(e).
gentle [jen'təl] a doux(douce).
gentleman [jen'təlmən] n monsieur m; (wellbred man) gentleman m; **~'s agreement** gentleman's agreement m.
gentlemanly [jen'təlmənlē] a bien élevé(e).
gentleness [jen'təlnis] n douceur f.
gently [jen'tlē] ad doucement.
gentry [jen'trē] n petite noblesse.
genuine [jen'yōōin] a véritable, authentique; (person, emotion) sincère.
genuinely [jen'yōōinlē] ad sincèrement, vraiment.
geographer [jēâg'rəfûr] n géographe m/f.
geographic(al) [jēəgraf'ik(əl)] a géographique.
geography [jēâg'rəfē] n géographie f.
geological [jēəlâj'ikəl] a géologique.
geologist [jēâl'əjist] n géologue m/f.
geology [jēâl'əjē] n géologie f.
geometric(al) [jēəmet'rik(əl)] a géométrique.
geometry [jēâm'ətrē] n géométrie f.
geranium [jərā'nēəm] n géranium m.
geriatric [järēat'rik] a gériatrique.
germ [jûrm] n (MED) microbe m; (BIO, fig) germe m.
German [jûr'mən] a allemand(e) ♦ n Allemand/e; (LING) allemand m.
German measles n rubéole f.
German shepherd n (US: dog) berger allemand.
Germany [jûr'mənē] n Allemagne f.
germination [jûrmənā'shən] n germination f.
germ warfare n guerre f bactériologique.
gerrymandering [jär'ēmandûring] n tripotage m du découpage électoral.
gestation [jestā'shən] n gestation f.
gesticulate [jestik'yəlāt] vi gesticuler.
gesture [jes'chûr] n geste m; **as a ~ of friendship** en témoignage d'amitié.
get, pt, pp **got,** (US) pp **gotten** [get, gât, gât'ən] vt (obtain) avoir, obtenir; (receive) recevoir; (find) trouver, acheter; (catch) attraper; (fetch) aller chercher; (take, move) emmener; (understand) comprendre, saisir; (have): **to have got** avoir; (become): **to ~ rich/old** s'enrichir/vieillir; (col: annoy): **he really ~s me!** il me porte sur les nerfs! ♦ vi

(*go*): **to ~ to** (*place*) aller à; arriver à; parvenir à; (*modal auxiliary vb*): **you've got to do it** il faut que vous le fassiez; **he got across the bridge/under the fence** il a traversé le pont/est passé par-dessous la barrière; **to ~ sth for sb** obtenir qch pour qn, procurer qch à qn; (*fetch*) aller chercher qch (pour qn); **~ me Mr Jones, please** (*TEL*) appelez-moi Mr Jones (au téléphone), s'il vous plaît; **can I ~ you a drink?** puis-je vous offrir quelque chose à boire?; **to ~ ready/ washed/shaved** *etc* se préparer/laver/raser *etc*; **to ~ sth done** (*do*) faire qch; arriver à faire qch; (*have done*) faire faire qch; **to ~ sth/sb ready** préparer qch/qn; **to ~ one's hair cut** se faire couper les cheveux; **to ~ sb to do sth** faire faire qch à qn; **to ~ sth through/out of** faire passer qch par/sortir qch de; **let's ~ going** *or* **started!** allons-y!

get about *vi* se déplacer; (*news*) se répandre.

get across *vt*: **to ~ across (to)** (*message, meaning*) faire passer (à) ♦ *vi*: **to ~ across to** (*subj: speaker*) se faire comprendre (par).

get along *vi* (*agree*): **to ~ along (with)** s'entendre (avec); (*depart*) s'en aller; (*manage*) = **to get by.**

get around *vi*: **to ~ around to doing sth** se mettre (finalement) à faire qch ♦ *vt fus* contourner; (*fig: person*) entortiller.

get at *vt fus* (*attack*) s'en prendre à; (*reach*) attraper, atteindre; **what are you ~ting at?** à quoi voulez-vous en venir?

get away *vi* partir, s'en aller; (*escape*) s'échapper.

get away with *vt fus* en être quitte pour; se faire passer *or* pardonner.

get back *vi* (*return*) rentrer ♦ *vt* récupérer, recouvrer; **to ~ back to** (*start again*) retourner *or* revenir à; (*contact again*) recontacter.

get back at *vt fus* (*col*): **to ~ back at sb** rendre la monnaie de sa pièce à qn.

get by *vi* (*pass*) passer; (*manage*) se débrouiller; **I can ~ by in Dutch** je me débrouille en hollandais.

get down *vi*, *vt fus* descendre ♦ *vt* descendre; (*depress*) déprimer.

get down to *vt fus* (*work*) se mettre à (faire); **to ~ down to business** passer aux choses sérieuses.

get in *vi* entrer; (*train*) arriver; (*arrive home*) rentrer ♦ *vt* (*bring in: harvest*) rentrer; (*: coal*) faire rentrer; (*: supplies*) faire des provisions de.

get into *vt fus* entrer dans; (*vehicle*) monter dans; (*clothes*) mettre, enfiler; **to ~ into bed/a rage** se mettre au lit/en colère.

get off *vi* (*from train etc*) descendre; (*depart: person, car*) s'en aller; (*escape*) s'en tirer ♦ *vt* (*remove: clothes, stain*) enlever; (*send off*) expédier; (*have as leave: day, time*): **we got 2 days off** nous avons eu 2 jours de congé ♦ *vt fus* (*train, bus*) descendre de; **to ~ off to a good start** (*fig*) prendre un bon départ.

get on *vi* (*at exam etc*) se débrouiller; (*agree*): **to ~ on (with)** s'entendre (avec) ♦

vt fus monter dans; (*horse*) monter sur; **how are you ~ting on?** comment ça va?

get on to *vt fus* (*Brit: deal with: problem*) s'occuper de; (*: contact: person*) contacter.

get out *vi* sortir; (*of vehicle*) descendre; (*news etc*) s'ébruiter ♦ *vt* sortir.

get out of *vt fus* sortir de; (*duty etc*) échapper à, se soustraire à.

get over *vt fus* (*illness*) se remettre de ♦ *vt* (*communicate: idea etc*) communiquer; (*finish*): **let's ~ it over (with)** finissons-en.

get round *vi*, *vt fus* (*Brit*) = **get around.**

get through *vi* (*TEL*) avoir la communication ♦ *vt fus* (*finish: work, book*) finir, terminer.

get through to *vt fus* (*TEL*) atteindre.

get together *vi* se réunir ♦ *vt* rassembler.

get up *vi* (*rise*) se lever ♦ *vt fus* monter.

get up to *vt fus* (*reach*) arriver à; (*Brit: prank etc*) faire.

getaway [get'əwā] *n* fuite *f*.

getaway car *n* voiture prévue pour prendre la fuite.

get-together [get'təgeťhûr] *n* petite réunion, petite fête.

get-up [get'up] *n* (*col: outfit*) accoutrement *m*.

get-well card [getwel' kârd] *n* carte *f* de vœux de bon rétablissement.

geyser [gī'zûr] *n* (*GEO*) geyser *m*.

Ghana [gän'ə] *n* Ghana *m*.

Ghanaian [gənā'ēən] *a* ghanéen(ne) ♦ *n* Ghanéen/ne.

ghastly [gast'lē] *a* atroce, horrible; (*pale*) livide, blême.

gherkin [gûr'kin] *n* cornichon *m*.

ghetto [get'ō] *n* ghetto *m*.

ghetto blaster [get'ō blast'ûr] *n* (*col*) grosse radio-cassette.

ghost [gōst] *n* fantôme *m*, revenant *m* ♦ *vt* (*sb else's book*) écrire.

ghostly [gōst'lē] *a* fantomatique.

ghostwriter [gōst'rītûr] *n* nègre *m* (*fig*).

ghoul [gōōl] *n* (*ghost*) vampire *m*.

ghoulish [gōōl'ish] *a* (*tastes etc*) morbide.

GHQ *n abbr* (*MIL*: = *general headquarters*) GQG *m*.

GI *n abbr* (*US col*: = *government issue*) soldat de l'armée américaine, GI *m*.

giant [jī'ənt] *n* géant/e ♦ *a* géant(e), énorme; **~ (size) packet** paquet géant.

gibber [jib'ûr] *vi* émettre des sons inintelligibles.

gibberish [jib'ûrish] *n* charabia *m*.

gibe [jīb] *n* sarcasme *m* ♦ *vi*: **to ~ at** railler.

giblets [jib'lits] *npl* abats *mpl*.

Gibraltar [jibrôl'tûr] *n* Gibraltar *m*.

giddiness [gid'ēnis] *n* vertige *m*.

giddy [gid'ē] *a* (*dizzy*): **to be (or feel) ~** avoir le vertige; (*height*) vertigineux(euse); (*thoughtless*) sot(te), étourdi(e).

gift [gift] *n* cadeau *m*, présent *m*; (*donation*) don *m*; (*COMM: also*: **free ~**) cadeau(-réclame) *m*; (*talent*): **to have a ~ for sth** avoir des dons pour *or* le don de qch.

gift certificate *n* (*US*) bon *m* d'achat.

gifted [gif'tid] *a* doué(e).

gift token *n* (*Brit*) bon *m* d'achat.

gig [gig] *n* (*col: of musician*) gig *f*.

gigantic [jīgan'tik] *a* gigantesque.

giggle [gig'əl] *vi* pouffer, ricaner sottement ♦ *n* petit rire sot, ricanement *m*.

GIGO [gīg'ō] *abbr* (*COMPUT col:* = *garbage in, garbage out*) qualité d'entrée = qualité de sortie.

gild [gild] *vt* dorer.

gill [jil] *n* (*measure*) = 0.25 pints (*US* = 0.118 *l*; *Brit* = 0.148 *l*).

gills [gilz] *npl* (*of fish*) ouïes *fpl*, branchies *fpl*.

gilt [gilt] *n* dorure *f* ♦ *a* doré(e).

gilt-edged [gilt'ejd] *a* (*stocks, securities*) de premier ordre.

gimlet [gim'lit] *n* vrille *f*.

gimmick [gim'ik] *n* truc *m*; **sales** ~ offre promotionnelle.

gin [jin] *n* gin *m*.

ginger [jin'jûr] *n* gingembre *m*.

ginger up *vt* secouer; animer.

ginger ale, ginger beer *n* boisson gazeuse au gingembre.

gingerbread [jin'jûrbred] *n* pain *m* d'épices.

ginger group *n* (*Brit*) groupe *m* de pression.

ginger-haired [jin'jûrhärd] *a* roux(rousse).

gingerly [jin'jûrlē] *ad* avec précaution.

gingham [ging'əm] *n* vichy *m*.

gipsy [jip'sē] *n* = **gypsy**.

giraffe [jəraf'] *n* girafe *f*.

girder [gûr'dûr] *n* poutrelle *f*.

girdle [gûr'dəl] *n* (*corset*) gaine *f* ♦ *vt* ceindre.

girl [gûrl] *n* fille *f*, fillette *f*; (*young unmarried woman*) jeune fille; (*daughter*) fille; **an English** ~ une jeune Anglaise; **a little English** ~ une petite Anglaise.

girl Friday *n* aide *f* de bureau.

girlfriend [gûrl'frend] *n* (*of girl*) amie *f*; (*of boy*) petite amie.

girlish [gûr'lish] *a* de jeune fille.

Girl Scout *n* (*US*) guide *f*.

Giro [jī'rō] *n*: **the National ~** (*Brit*) ≈ les comptes chèques postaux.

giro [jī'rō] *n* (*Brit: bank* ~) virement *m* bancaire; (: *post office* ~) mandat *m*.

girth [gûrth] *n* circonférence *f*; (*of horse*) sangle *f*.

gist [jist] *n* essentiel *m*.

give [giv] *n* (*of fabric*) élasticité *f* ♦ *vb* (*pt* **gave**, *pp* **given** [gāv, giv'ən]) *vt* donner ♦ *vi* (*break*) céder; (*stretch: fabric*) se prêter; **to** ~ **sb sth**, ~ **sth to sb** donner qch à qn; **to** ~ **a cry/sigh** pousser un cri/un soupir; **how much did you** ~ **for it?** combien (l')avez-vous payé?; **12 o'clock,** ~ **or take a few minutes** midi, à quelques minutes près; **to** ~ **way** *vi* céder; (*Brit AUT*) donner la priorité.

give away *vt* donner; (*give free*) faire cadeau de; (*betray*) donner, trahir; (*disclose*) révéler; (*bride*) conduire à l'autel.

give back *vt* rendre.

give in *vi* céder ♦ *vt* donner.

give off *vt* dégager.

give out *vt* (*food etc*) distribuer; (*news*) annoncer ♦ *vi* (*be exhausted: supplies*) s'épuiser; (*fail*) lâcher.

give up *vi* renoncer ♦ *vt* renoncer à; **to** ~ **up smoking** arrêter de fumer; **to** ~ **o.s. up** se rendre.

give-and-take [giv'əntāk'] *n* concessions mutuelles.

giveaway [giv'əwā] *n* (*col*): **her expression was a** ~ son expression la trahissait; **the exam was a** ~! cet examen, c'était du gâteau! ♦ *cpd*: ~ **prices** prix sacrifiés.

given [giv'ən] *pp* of **give** ♦ *a* (*fixed: time, amount*) donné(e), déterminé(e) ♦ *cj*: ~ **the circumstances** ... étant donné les circonstances ..., vu les circonstances ...; ~ **that** ... étant donné que ....

glacial [glā'shəl] *a* (*GEO*) glaciaire; (*wind, weather*) glacial(e).

glacier [glā'shûr] *n* glacier *m*.

glad [glad] *a* content(e); **to be** ~ **about sth/ that** être heureux(euse) *or* bien content de qch/que; **I was** ~ **of his help** (*Brit*) j'étais bien content de (pouvoir compter sur) son aide *or* qu'il m'aide.

gladden [glad'ən] *vt* réjouir.

glade [glād] *n* clairière *f*.

gladioli [gladēō'lē] *npl* glaïeuls *mpl*.

gladly [glad'lē] *ad* volontiers.

glamorous [glam'ûrəs] *a* séduisant(e).

glamour [glam'ûr] *n* éclat *m*, prestige *m*.

glance [glans] *n* coup *m* d'œil ♦ *vi*: **to** ~ **at** jeter un coup d'œil à.

glance off *vt fus* (*bullet*) ricocher sur.

glancing [glan'sing] *a* (*blow*) oblique.

gland [gland] *n* glande *f*.

glandular [glan'jəlûr] *a*: ~ **fever** (*Brit*) mononucléose infectieuse.

glare [glär] *n* lumière éblouissante ♦ *vi* briller d'un éclat aveuglant; **to** ~ **at** lancer un *or* des regard(s) furieux à.

glaring [glär'ing] *a* (*mistake*) criant(e), qui saute aux yeux.

glass [glas] *n* verre *m*; (*also:* **looking** ~) miroir *m*.

glass-blowing [glas'blōing] *n* soufflage *m* (du verre).

glasses [glas'iz] *npl* lunettes *fpl*.

glass fiber *n* fibre *f* de verre.

glasshouse [glas'hous] *n* (*Brit*) serre *f*.

glassware [glas'wär] *n* verrerie *f*.

glassy [glas'ē] *a* (*eyes*) vitreux(euse).

glaze [glāz] *vt* (*door*) vitrer; (*pottery*) vernir; (*CULIN*) glacer ♦ *n* vernis *m*; (*CULIN*) glaçage *m*.

glazed [glāzd] *a* (*eye*) vitreux(euse); (*pottery*) verni(e); (*tiles*) vitrifié(e).

glazier [glā'zhûr] *n* vitrier *m*.

gleam [glēm] *n* lueur *f* ♦ *vi* luire, briller; **a** ~ **of hope** une lueur d'espoir.

gleaming [glē'ming] *a* luisant(e).

glean [glēn] *vt* (*information*) recueillir.

glee [glē] *n* joie *f*.

gleeful [glē'fəl] *a* joyeux(euse).

glen [glen] *n* vallée *f*.

glib [glib] *a* qui a du bagou; facile.

glide [glīd] *vi* glisser; (*AVIAT, bird*) planer ♦ *n* glissement *m*; vol plané.

glider [glī'dûr] *n* (*AVIAT*) planeur *m*.

gliding [glī'ding] *n* (*AVIAT*) vol *m* à voile.

glimmer [glim'ûr] *vi* luire ♦ *n* lueur *f*.

glimpse [glimps] *n* vision passagère, aperçu *m* ♦ *vt* entrevoir, apercevoir; **to catch a** ~ **of** entrevoir.

glint [glint] *n* éclair *m* ♦ *vi* étinceler.

glisten [glis'ən] *vi* briller, luire.

glitter [glit'ûr] *vi* scintiller, briller ♦ *n* scintillement *m*.

glitz [glits] n (col) clinquant m.
gloat [glōt] vi: **to ~ (over)** jubiler (à propos de).
global [glō'bəl] a (world-wide) mondial(e); (overall) global(e).
globe [glōb] n globe m.
globe-trotter [glōb'trâtûr] n globe-trotter m.
globule [glâb'yōōl] n (ANAT) globule m; (of water etc) gouttelette f.
gloom [glōōm] n obscurité f; (sadness) tristesse f, mélancolie f.
gloomy [glōō'mē] a sombre, triste, mélancolique; **to feel ~** avoir or se faire des idées noires.
glorification [glôrəfəkā'shən] n glorification f.
glorify [glôr'əfī] vt glorifier.
glorious [glôr'ēəs] a glorieux(euse); (beautiful) splendide.
glory [glôr'ē] n gloire f; splendeur f ♦ vi: **to ~ in** se glorifier de.
glory hole n (col) capharnaüm m.
Glos abbr (Brit) = Gloucestershire.
gloss [glôs] n (shine) brillant m, vernis m; (also: ~ **paint**) peinture brillante or laquée.
  gloss over vt fus glisser sur.
glossary [glâs'ûrē] n glossaire m, lexique m.
glossy [glâs'ē] a brillant(e), luisant(e) ♦ n (also: ~ **magazine**) revue f de luxe.
glove [gluv] n gant m.
glove compartment n (AUT) boîte f à gants, vide-poches m inv.
glow [glō] vi rougeoyer; (face) rayonner ♦ n rougeoiement m.
glower [glou'ûr] vi lancer des regards mauvais.
glowing [glō'ing] a (fire) rougeoyant(e); (complexion) éclatant(e); (report, description etc) dithyrambique.
glow-worm [glō'wûrm] n ver luisant.
glucose [glōō'kōs] n glucose m.
glue [glōō] n colle f ♦ vt coller.
glue-sniffing [glōō'snifing] n inhalation f de colle.
glum [glum] a maussade, morose.
glut [glut] n surabondance f ♦ vt rassasier; (market) encombrer.
glutinous [glōōt'ənəs] a visqueux(euse).
glutton [glut'ən] n glouton/ne; **a ~ for work** un bourreau de travail.
gluttonous [glut'ənəs] a glouton(ne).
gluttony [glut'ənē] n gloutonnerie f; (sin) gourmandise f.
glycerin(e) [glis'ûrin] n glycérine f.
gm abbr (= gram) g.
GMAT n abbr (US: = Graduate Management Admissions Test) examen d'admission dans le 2e cycle de l'enseignement supérieur.
GMT abbr (= Greenwich Mean Time) GMT.
gnarled [nârld] a noueux(euse).
gnash [nash] vt: **to ~ one's teeth** grincer des dents.
gnat [nat] n moucheron m.
gnaw [nô] vt ronger.
gnome [nōm] n gnome m, lutin m.
GNP n abbr = gross national product.
go [gō] vb (pt went, pp gone [went, gôn]) vi aller; (depart) partir, s'en aller; (work) marcher; (be sold): **to ~ for $10** se vendre 10 dollars; (fit, suit): **to ~ with** aller avec; (be-

come): **to ~ pale/moldy** pâlir/moisir; (break etc) céder ♦ n (pl: ~es): **to have a ~ (at)** essayer (de faire); **to be on the ~** être en mouvement; **whose ~ is it?** à qui est-ce de jouer?; **to ~ by car/on foot** aller en voiture/à pied; **he's ~ing to do it** il va faire, il est sur le point de faire; **to ~ for a walk** aller se promener; **to ~ dancing/shopping** aller danser/faire les courses; **to ~ looking for sb/sth** aller or partir à la recherche de qn/qch; **to ~ to sleep** s'endormir; **to ~ and see sb, to ~ to see sb** aller voir qn; **how is it ~ing?** comment ça marche?; **how did it ~?** comment est-ce que ça s'est passé?; **to ~ round the back/by the shop** passer par derrière/devant le magasin; **my voice has gone** il y a une extinction de voix; **the cake is all gone** il n'y a plus de gâteau; **I'll take whatever is ~ing** (Brit) je prendrai ce qu'il y a (or ce que vous avez); **... to ~** (US: food) ... à emporter.
  go about vt fus: **how do I ~ about this?** comment dois-je m'y prendre (pour faire ceci)? ♦ vi (Brit) **= go around**; **to ~ about one's business** s'occuper de ses affaires.
  go after vt fus (pursue) poursuivre, courir après; (job, record etc) essayer d'obtenir.
  go against vt fus (be unfavorable to) être défavorable à; (be contrary to) être contraire à.
  go ahead vi (make progress) avancer; (get going) y aller.
  go along vi aller, avancer ♦ vt fus longer, parcourir; **as you ~ along (with your work)** au fur et à mesure (de votre travail); **to ~ along with** (accompany) accompagner; (agree with: idea) être d'accord sur; (: person) suivre.
  go around vi (circulate: news, rumor) circuler; (revolve) tourner; (wander around) aller çà et là; (visit): **to ~ around to sb's** passer chez qn; aller chez qn; (make a detour): **to ~ around (by)** faire un détour (par); (suffice) suffire (pour tout le monde).
  go away vi partir, s'en aller.
  go back vi rentrer; revenir; (go again) retourner.
  go back on vt fus (promise) revenir sur.
  go by vi (years, time) passer, s'écouler ♦ vt fus s'en tenir à; (believe) en croire.
  go down vi descendre; (ship) couler; (sun) se coucher ♦ vt fus descendre; **that should ~ down well with him** (fig) ça devrait lui plaire.
  go for vt fus (fetch) aller chercher; (like) aimer; (attack) s'en prendre à; attaquer.
  go in vi entrer.
  go in for vt fus (competition) se présenter à; (like) aimer.
  go into vt fus entrer dans; (investigate) étudier, examiner; (embark on) se lancer dans.
  go off vi partir, s'en aller; (food) se gâter; (bomb) sauter; (lights etc) s'éteindre; (event) se dérouler ♦ vt fus ne plus aimer, ne plus avoir envie de; **the gun went off** le coup est parti; **to ~ off to sleep** s'endormir; **the party went off well** la fête s'est bien passée or était très réussie.

go on *vi* continuer; (*happen*) se passer; (*lights*) s'allumer ♦ *vt fus* (*be guided by: evidence etc*) se fonder sur; **to ~ on doing** continuer à faire; **what's ~ing on here?** qu'est-ce qui se passe ici?

go on at *vt fus* (*nag*) tomber sur le dos de.

go on with *vt fus* poursuivre, continuer.

go out *vi* sortir; (*fire, light*) s'éteindre; (*tide*) descendre; **to ~ out with sb** sortir avec qn.

go over *vi* (*ship*) chavirer ♦ *vt fus* (*check*) revoir, vérifier; **to ~ over sth in one's mind** repasser qch dans son esprit.

go round *vi* (*Brit*) = **go around**.

go through *vt fus* (*town etc*) traverser; (*search through*) fouiller; (*examine: list, book*) lire *or* regarder en détail, éplucher; (*perform: lesson*) réciter; (*: formalities*) remplir; (*: program*) exécuter.

go through with *vt fus* (*plan, crime*) aller jusqu'au bout de.

go under *vi* (*sink: also fig*) couler; (*: person*) succomber.

go up *vi* monter; (*price*) augmenter ♦ *vt fus* gravir; **to ~ up in flames** flamber, s'enflammer brusquement.

go without *vt fus* se passer de.

goad [gōd] *vt* aiguillonner.

go-ahead [gō'əhed] *a* dynamique, entreprenant(e) ♦ *n* feu vert.

goal [gōl] *n* but *m*.

goalkeeper [gōl'kēpûr] *n* gardien *m* de but.

goal post *n* poteau *m* de but.

goat [gōt] *n* chèvre *f*.

gobble [gâb'əl] *vt* (*also:* **~ down**, **~ up**) engloutir.

gobbledygook [gâb'əldēgōōk] *n* charabia *m*.

go-between [gō'bitwēn] *n* médiateur *m*.

Gobi Desert [gō'bē dez'ûrt] *n* désert *m* de Gobi.

goblet [gâb'lit] *n* goblet *m*.

goblin [gâb'lin] *n* lutin *m*.

go-cart [gō'kârt] *n* kart *m* ♦ *cpd:* **~ racing** *n* karting *m*.

god [gâd] *n* dieu *m*; **G~** Dieu.

godchild [gâd'chīld] *n* filleul/e.

goddamn [gâd'dam'] *n* (*US col!*): **this ~** ... ce foutu ..., ce putain de ....

goddaughter [gâd'dôtûr] *n* filleule *f*.

goddess [gâd'is] *n* déesse *f*.

godfather [gâd'fâthûr] *n* parrain *m*.

godforsaken [gâd'fûrsā'kən] *a* maudit(e).

godmother [gâd'muthûr] *n* marraine *f*.

godparents [gâd'pârənts] *npl*: **the ~** le parrain et la marraine.

godsend [gâd'send] *n* aubaine *f*.

godson [gâd'sun] *n* filleul *m*.

goes [gōz] *vb see* **go**.

gofer [gō'fûr] *n* (*US*) bonne *f* à tout faire, tâcheron *m*.

go-getter [gō'get'ûr] *n* arriviste *m/f*.

goggle [gâg'əl] *vi*: **to ~ at** regarder avec des yeux ronds.

goggles [gâg'əlz] *npl* lunettes *fpl* (protectrices) (*de motocycliste etc*).

going [gō'ing] *n* (*conditions*) état *m* du terrain ♦ *a*: **the ~ rate** le tarif (en vigueur); **a ~ concern** une affaire prospère; **it was slow ~** les progrès étaient lents, ça n'avançait pas

vite.

goings-on [gō'ingzân'] *npl* (*col*) manigances *fpl*.

go-kart [gō'kârt] *n* = **go-cart**.

gold [gōld] *n or m* ♦ *a* en or; (*reserves*) d'or.

golden [gōl'dən] *a* (*made of gold*) en or; (*gold in color*) doré(e).

golden age *n* âge *m* d'or.

golden rule *n* règle *f* d'or.

goldfish [gōld'fish] *n* poisson *m* rouge.

gold leaf *n or m* en feuille.

gold medal *n* (*SPORT*) médaille *f* d'or.

goldmine [gōld'mīn] *n* mine *f* d'or.

gold-plated [gōldplā'tid] *a* plaqué(e) or *inv*.

goldsmith [gōld'smith] *n* orfèvre *m*.

gold standard *n* étalon-or *m*.

golf [gâlf] *n* golf *m*.

golf ball *n* balle *f* de golf; (*on typewriter*) boule *f*.

golf club *n* club *m* de golf; (*stick*) club *m*, crosse *f* de golf.

golf course *n* terrain *m* de golf.

golfer [gâl'fûr] *n* joueur/euse de golf.

gondola [gân'dələ] *n* gondole *f*.

gondolier [gândəliûr'] *n* gondolier *m*.

gone [gôn] *pp of* **go** ♦ *a* parti(e).

gong [gông] *n* gong *m*.

good [gōōd] *a* bon(ne); (*kind*) gentil(le); (*child*) sage ♦ *n* bien *m*; **~!** bon!, très bien!; **to be ~ at** être bon en; **it's ~ for you** c'est bon pour vous; **it's a ~ thing you were there** heureusement que vous étiez là; **she is ~ with children/her hands** elle sait bien s'occuper des enfants/sait se servir de ses mains; **to feel ~** se sentir bien; **it's ~ to see you** ça me fait plaisir de vous voir, je suis content de vous voir; **he's up to no ~** il prépare quelque mauvais coup; **it's no ~ complaining** cela ne sert à rien de se plaindre; **for the common ~** dans l'intérêt commun; **for ~** (*for ever*) pour de bon, une fois pour toutes; **would you be ~ enough to** ...? auriez-vous la bonté *or* l'amabilité de ...?; **that's very ~ of you** c'est très gentil de votre part; **is this any ~?** (*will it do?*) est-ce que ceci fera l'affaire?, est-ce que cela peut vous rendre service?; (*what's it like?*) qu'est-ce que ça vaut?; **a ~ deal (of)** beaucoup (de); **a ~ many** beaucoup (de); **~ morning/afternoon!** bonjour!; **~ evening!** bonsoir!; **~ night!** bonsoir!; (*on going to bed*) bonne nuit!

goodbye [gōōdbī'] *excl* au revoir!; **to say ~** to dire au revoir à.

good faith *n* bonne foi.

good-for-nothing [gōōd'fərnuth'ing] *a* bon(ne) *or* propre à rien.

Good Friday *n* Vendredi saint.

good-humored [gōōd'hyōō'mûrd] *a* (*person*) jovial(e); (*remark, joke*) sans malice.

good-looking [gōōd'lōōk'ing] *a* bien *inv*.

good-natured [gōōd'nā'chûrd] *a* (*person*) qui a un bon naturel; (*discussion*) enjoué(e).

goodness [gōōd'nis] *n* (*of person*) bonté *f*; **for ~ sake!** je vous en prie!; **~ gracious!** mon Dieu!

goods [gōōdz] *npl* marchandise *f*, articles *mpl*; (*COMM etc*) marchandises; **~ and chattels** biens *mpl* et effets *mpl*.

goods train n (Brit) train m de marchandises.

goodwill [good'wil'] n bonne volonté; (COMM) réputation f (auprès de la clientèle).

goody-goody [good'ēgood'ē] n (pej) petit saint, sainte nitouche.

goof [goof] vi (US col) gaffer.

goose, pl **geese** [goos, gēs] n oie f.

gooseberry [goos'bärē] n groseille f à maquereau; **to play** ~ (Brit) tenir la chandelle.

gooseflesh [goos'flesh] n, **goosepimples** [goos'pimpəlz] npl chair f de poule.

goose step n (MIL) pas m de l'oie.

GOP n abbr (US POL: col: = Grand Old Party) parti républicain.

gore [gôr] vt encorner ♦ n sang m.

gorge [gôrj] n gorge f ♦ vt: **to** ~ **o.s. (on)** se gorger (de).

gorgeous [gôr'jəs] a splendide, superbe.

gorilla [gəril'ə] n gorille m.

gorse [gôrs] n ajoncs mpl.

gory [gôr'ē] a sanglant(e).

go-slow [gō'slō'] n (Brit) grève perlée.

gospel [gâs'pəl] n évangile m.

gossamer [gâs'əmûr] n (cobweb) fils mpl de la vierge; (light fabric) étoffe très légère.

gossip [gâs'əp] n bavardages mpl; (malicious) commérage m, cancans mpl; (person) commère f ♦ vi bavarder; cancaner, faire des commérages; **a piece of** ~ un ragot, un racontar.

gossip column n (PRESS) échos mpl.

got [gât] pt, pp of **get**.

Gothic [gâth'ik] a gothique.

gotten [gât'ən] (US) pp of **get**.

gouge [gouj] vt (also: ~ **out**: hole etc) évider; (: initials) tailler; **to** ~ **sb's eyes out** crever les yeux à qn.

gourd [gôrd] n calebasse f, gourde f.

gourmet [goormā'] n gourmet m, gastronome m/f.

gout [gout] n goutte f.

govern [guv'ûrn] vt (gen, LING) gouverner.

governess [guv'ûrnis] n gouvernante f.

governing [guv'ûrning] a (POL) au pouvoir, au gouvernement; ~ **body** conseil m d'administration.

government [guv'ûrnmənt] n gouvernement m; (Brit: ministers) ministère m ♦ cpd de l'Etat; **local** ~ administration locale.

governmental [guvûrnmen'təl] a gouvernemental(e).

government housing n (US) logements sociaux.

government stock n titres mpl d'État.

governor [guv'ûrnûr] n (of colony, state, bank) gouverneur m; (of school, hospital etc) administrateur/trice; (Brit: of prison) directeur/trice.

Govt abbr (= government) gvt.

gown [goun] n robe f; (of teacher; Brit: of judge) toge f.

GP n abbr (MED) = **general practitioner**.

GPO n abbr (US) = Government Printing Office.

gr. abbr (COMM) = **gross**.

grab [grab] vt saisir, empoigner; (property, power) se saisir de ♦ vi: **to** ~ **at** essayer de saisir.

grace [grās] n grâce f ♦ vt honorer; **5 days'** ~ répit m de 5 jours; **to say** ~ dire le bénédicité; (after meal) dire les grâces; **with a good/bad** ~ de bonne/mauvaise grâce; **his sense of humor is his saving** ~ il se rachète par son sens de l'humour.

graceful [grās'fəl] a gracieux(euse), élégant(e).

gracious [grā'shəs] a (kind) charmant(e), bienveillant(e); (elegant) plein(e) d'élégance, d'une grande élégance; (formal: pardon etc) miséricordieux(euse) ♦ excl: **(good)** ~! mon Dieu!

gradation [grādā'shən] n gradation f.

grade [grād] n (COMM) qualité f; calibre m; catégorie f; (in hierarchy) grade m, échelon m; (US: SCOL) note f; classe f; (: gradient) pente f ♦ vt classer; calibrer; graduer; **to make the** ~ (fig) réussir.

grade crossing n (US) passage m à niveau.

grade school n (US) école f primaire.

gradient [grā'dēənt] n inclinaison f, pente f; (GEOM) gradient m.

gradual [graj'ōōəl] a graduel(le), progressif(ive).

gradually [graj'ōōəlē] ad peu à peu, graduellement.

graduate n [graj'ōōit] diplômé/e d'université; (US) diplômé/e de fin d'études ♦ vi [graj'ōōāt] obtenir un diplôme d'université (or de fin d'études).

graduated pension [graj'ōōātid pen'shən] n retraite calculée en fonction des derniers salaires.

graduation [grajōōā'shən] n cérémonie f de remise des diplômes.

graffiti [grəfē'tē] npl graffiti mpl.

graft [graft] n (AGR, MED) greffe f; (bribery) corruption f ♦ vt greffer; **hard** ~ (Brit col) boulot acharné.

grain [grān] n grain m; (no pl: cereals) céréales fpl; (US) blé m; **it goes against the** ~ cela va à l'encontre de sa (or ma etc) nature.

gram [gram] n gramme m.

grammar [gram'ûr] n grammaire f.

grammatical [grəmat'ikəl] a grammatical(e).

gramme [gram] n = **gram**.

granary [grā'nûrē] n grenier m.

grand [grand] a splendide, imposant(e); (terrific) magnifique, formidable; (also humorous: gesture etc) noble ♦ n (col: thousand) mille livres fpl (or dollars mpl).

grandchildren [gran'chil'drən] npl petits-enfants mpl.

granddad [gran'dad] n grand-papa m.

granddaughter [gran'dôtûr] n petite-fille f.

grandeur [gran'jûr] n magnificence f, splendeur f; (of position etc) éminence f.

grandfather [gran'fâthûr] n grand-père m.

grandiose [gran'dēōs] a grandiose; (pej) pompeux(euse).

grand jury n (US) jury m d'accusation (formé de 12 à 23 jurés).

grandma [gran'mə] n grand-maman f.

grandmother [gran'muthûr] n grand-mère f.

grandpa [gran'pə] n = **granddad**.

grandparent [gran'pârənt] n grand-père/grand-mère.

grand piano n piano m à queue.

Grand Prix [grand prē'] *n* (*AUT*) grand prix automobile.

grandson [gran'sun] *n* petit-fils *m*.

grandstand [gran'stand] *n* (*SPORT*) tribune *f*.

grand total *n* total général.

granite [gran'it] *n* granit *m*.

granny [gran'ē] *n* grand-maman *f*.

grant [grant] *vt* accorder; (*a request*) accéder à; (*admit*) concéder ♦ *n* (*SCOL*) bourse *f*; (*ADMIN*) subside *m*, subvention *f*; **to take sth for ~ed** considérer qch comme acquis; **to ~ that** admettre que.

granulated [gran'yəlātid] *a*: **~ sugar** sucre *m* en poudre.

granule [gran'yool] *n* granule *m*.

grape [grāp] *n* raisin *m*; **a bunch of ~s** une grappe de raisin.

grapefruit [grāp'frōot] *n* pamplemousse *m*.

grapevine [grāp'vīn] *n* vigne *f*; **I heard it on the ~** (*fig*) je l'ai appris par le téléphone arabe.

graph [graf] *n* graphique *m*, courbe *f*.

graphic [graf'ik] *a* graphique; (*vivid*) vivant(e).

graphic designer *n* graphiste *m/f*.

graphics [graf'iks] *n* (*art*) arts *mpl* graphiques; (*process*) graphisme *m*; (*pl: drawings*) illustrations *fpl*.

graphite [graf'īt] *n* graphite *m*.

graph paper *n* papier millimétré.

grapple [grap'əl] *vi*: **to ~ with** être aux prises avec.

grappling iron [grap'ling ī'ûrn] *n* (*NAUT*) grappin *m*.

grasp [grasp] *vt* saisir, empoigner; (*understand*) saisir, comprendre ♦ *n* (*grip*) prise *f*; (*fig*) compréhension *f*, connaissance *f*; **to have sth within one's ~** avoir qch à sa portée; **to have a good ~ of sth** (*fig*) bien comprendre qch.

grasp at *vt fus* (*rope etc*) essayer de saisir; (*fig: opportunity*) sauter sur.

grasping [gras'ping] *a* avide.

grass [gras] *n* herbe *f*; (*Brit col: informer*) mouchard/e; (*: ex-terrorist*) balanceur/euse.

grasshopper [gras'hápûr] *n* sauterelle *f*.

grassland [gras'land] *n* prairie *f*.

grass roots *npl* (*fig*) base *f*.

grass snake *n* couleuvre *f*.

grassy [gras'ē] *a* herbeux(euse).

grate [grāt] *n* grille *f* de cheminée ♦ *vi* grincer ♦ *vt* (*CULIN*) râper.

grateful [grāt'fəl] *a* reconnaissant(e).

gratefully [grāt'fəlē] *ad* avec reconnaissance.

grater [grā'tûr] *n* râpe *f*.

gratification [gratəfəkā'shən] *n* satisfaction *f*.

gratify [grat'əfī] *vt* faire plaisir à; (*whim*) satisfaire.

gratifying [grat'əfīing] *a* agréable; satisfaisant(e).

grating [grā'ting] *n* (*iron bars*) grille *f* ♦ *a* (*noise*) grinçant(e).

gratitude [grat'ətōod] *n* gratitude *f*.

gratuitous [grətoo'itəs] *a* gratuit(e).

gratuity [grətoo'itē] *n* pourboire *m*.

grave [grāv] *n* tombe *f* ♦ *a* grave, sérieux(euse).

gravedigger [grāv'digûr] *n* fossoyeur *m*.

gravel [grav'əl] *n* gravier *m*.

gravely [grāv'lē] *ad* gravement, sérieusement; **~ ill** gravement malade.

gravestone [grāv'stōn] *n* pierre tombale.

graveyard [grāv'yârd] *n* cimetière *m*.

gravitate [grav'ətāt] *vi* graviter.

gravity [grav'itē] *n* (*PHYSICS*) gravité *f*; pesanteur *f*; (*seriousness*) gravité, sérieux *m*.

gravy [grā'vē] *n* jus *m* (de viande); sauce *f* (au jus de viande).

gravy boat *n* saucière *f*.

gravy train *n* (*col*): **to ride the ~** avoir une bonne planque.

gray [grā] *a* (*US*) gris(e); (*dismal*) sombre; **to go ~** (*commencer à*) grisonner.

gray-haired [grā'härd] *a* aux cheveux gris.

grayhound [grā'hound] *n* lévrier *m*.

graze [grāz] *vi* paître, brouter ♦ *vt* (*touch lightly*) frôler, effleurer; (*scrape*) écorcher ♦ *n* écorchure *f*.

grazing [grā'zing] *n* (*pasture*) pâturage *m*.

grease [grēs] *n* (*fat*) graisse *f*; (*lubricant*) lubrifiant *m* ♦ *vt* graisser; lubrifier; **to ~ the skids** (*US: fig*) huiler les rouages.

grease gun *n* graisseur *m*.

greasepaint [grēs'pānt] *n* produits *mpl* de maquillage.

greaseproof paper [grēs'prōof pā'pûr] *n* (*Brit*) papier sulfurisé.

greasy [grē'sē] *a* gras(se), graisseux(euse); (*hands, clothes*) graisseux; (*Brit: road, surface*) glissant(e).

great [grāt] *a* grand(e); (*heat, pain etc*) très fort(e), intense; (*col*) formidable; **they're ~ friends** ils sont très amis, ce sont de grands amis; **we had a ~ time** nous nous sommes bien amusés; **it was ~!** c'était fantastique *or* super!; **the ~ thing is that ...** ce qu'il y a de vraiment bien c'est que ...

Great Barrier Reef *n*: **the ~** la Grande Barrière.

Great Britain *n* Grande-Bretagne *f*.

great-grandchild, *pl* **-children** [grāt'gran'chīld, -chil'drən] *n* arrière-petit(e)-enfant.

great-grandfather [grāt'gran'fâthûr] *n* arrière-grand-père *m*.

great-grandmother [grāt'gran'muthûr] *n* arrière-grand-mère *f*.

Great Lakes *npl*: **the ~** les Grands Lacs.

greatly [grāt'lē] *ad* très, grandement; (*with verbs*) beaucoup.

greatness [grāt'nis] *n* grandeur *f*.

Grecian [grē'shən] *a* grec(grecque).

Greece [grēs] *n* Grèce *f*.

greed [grēd] *n* (*also*: **~iness**) avidité *f*; (*for food*) gourmandise *f*.

greedily [grē'dilē] *ad* avidement; avec gourmandise.

greedy [grē'dē] *a* avide; gourmand(e).

Greek [grēk] *a* grec(grecque) ♦ *n* Grec/Grecque; (*LING*) grec *m*; **ancient/modern ~** grec classique/moderne.

green [grēn] *a* vert(e); (*inexperienced*) (bien) jeune, naïf(ïve) ♦ *n* (*color, of golf course*) vert *m*; (*stretch of grass*) pelouse *f*; (*also*: **village ~**) ≈ place *f* du village; **~s** *npl* légumes verts; **to have a ~ thumb** *or* (*Brit*) **~ fingers** (*fig*) avoir le pouce vert.

greenback [grēn'bak] *n* (*US col*) billet *m* d'un dollar, dolluche *m* (col).

green bean *n* haricot vert.
green belt *n* (*round town*) ceinture verte.
green card *n* permis *m* de travail; (*Brit AUT*) carte verte.
greenery [grē'nûrē] *n* verdure *f.*
greenfly [grēn'flī] *n* (*Brit*) puceron *m.*
greengage [grēn'gāj] *n* reine-claude *f.*
greengrocer [grēn'grōsûr] *n* (*Brit*) marchand *m* de fruits et légumes.
greenhouse [grēn'hous] *n* serre *f.*
greenhouse effect *n* effet *m* de serre.
greenish [grē'nish] *a* verdâtre.
Greenland [grēn'lənd] *n* Groenland *m.*
Greenlander [grēn'ləndûr] *n* Groenlandais/e.
green pepper *n* poivron (vert).
green pound *n* (*ECON*) livre verte.
greet [grēt] *vt* accueillir.
greeting [grē'ting] *n* salutation *f;* **Christmas/ birthday** ~s souhaits *mpl* de Noël/de bon anniversaire.
greeting(s) card *n* carte *f* de vœux.
gregarious [grigär'ēəs] *a* grégaire; sociable.
grenade [grinād'] *n* (*also:* **hand** ~) grenade *f.*
grew [grōō] *pt of* **grow.**
grey [grā] *etc a* (*Brit*) = **gray** *etc.*
grid [grid] *n* grille *f;* (*ELEC*) réseau *m;* (*US AUT*) intersection *f* (*matérialisée par des marques au sol*).
griddle [grid'əl] *n* (*on stove*) plaque chauffante.
gridiron [grid'īûrn] *n* gril *m.*
grief [grēf] *n* chagrin *m,* douleur *f;* **to come to** ~ (*plan*) échouer; (*person*) avoir un malheur.
grievance [grē'vəns] *n* doléance *f,* grief *m;* (*cause for complaint*) grief.
grieve [grēv] *vi* avoir du chagrin; se désoler ♦ *vt* faire de la peine à, affliger; **to** ~ **at** se désoler de; pleurer.
grievous [grē'vəs] *a* grave; cruel(le); ~ **bodily harm** (*LAW*) coups *mpl* et blessures *fpl.*
grill [gril] *n* (*on stove*) gril *m* ♦ *vt* griller; (*question*) interroger longuement, cuisiner.
grille [gril] *n* grillage *m;* (*AUT*) calandre *f.*
grill(room) [gril'(rōōm)] *n* rôtisserie *f.*
grim [grim] *a* sinistre, lugubre.
grimace [grim'əs] *n* grimace *f* ♦ *vi* grimacer, faire une grimace.
grime [grīm] *n* crasse *f.*
grimy [grīm'ē] *a* crasseux(euse).
grin [grin] *n* large sourire *m* ♦ *vi* sourire; **to** ~ **(at)** faire un grand sourire (à).
grind [grīnd] *vb* (*pt, pp* **ground** [ground]) *vt* écraser; (*coffee, pepper etc*) moudre; (*US: meat*) hacher; (*make sharp*) aiguiser; (*polish: gem, lens*) polir ♦ *vi* (*car gears*) grincer ♦ *n* (*work*) corvée *f;* **to** ~ **one's teeth** grincer des dents; **to** ~ **to a halt** (*vehicle*) s'arrêter dans un grincement de freins; (*fig*) s'arrêter, s'immobiliser; **the daily** ~ (*col*) le train-train quotidien.
grinder [grīn'dûr] *n* (*machine: for coffee*) moulin *m* (à café); (: *for meat*) hachoir *m;* (: *for waste disposal etc*) broyeur *m.*
grindstone [grīnd'stōn] *n:* **to keep one's nose to the** ~ travailler sans relâche.
grip [grip] *n* (*control, grasp*) étreinte *f;* (*hold*) prise *f;* (*handle*) poignée *f;* (*carryall*) sac *m* de voyage ♦ *vt* saisir, empoigner; étreindre;

to come to ~s **with** se colleter avec, en venir aux prises avec; **to** ~ **the road** (*AUT*) adhérer à la route; **to lose one's** ~ lâcher prise; (*fig*) perdre les pédales, être dépassé(e).
gripe [grīp] *n* (*MED*) coliques *fpl;* (*col: complaint*) ronchonnement *m,* rouspétance *f* ♦ *vi* (*col*) râler.
gripping [grip'ing] *a* prenant(e), palpitant(e).
grisly [griz'lē] *a* sinistre, macabre.
grist [grist] *n* (*fig*): **it's (all)** ~ **to his mill** ça l'arrange, ça apporte de l'eau à son moulin.
gristle [gris'əl] *n* cartilage *m* (*de poulet etc*).
grit [grit] *n* gravillon *m;* (*courage*) cran *m* ♦ *vt* (*road*) sabler; **to** ~ **one's teeth** serrer les dents; **to have a piece of** ~ **in one's eye** (*Brit*) avoir une poussière *or* une saleté dans l'œil.
grits [grits] *npl* (*US*) gruau *m* de maïs.
grizzle [griz'əl] *vi* (*Brit*) pleurnicher.
grizzly [griz'lē] *n* (*also:* ~ **bear**) grizzli *m,* ours gris.
groan [grōn] *n* gémissement *m;* grognement *m* ♦ *vi* gémir; grogner.
grocer [grō'sûr] *n* épicier *m;* **at the** ~'s à l'épicerie, chez l'épicier.
groceries [grō'sûrēz] *npl* provisions *fpl.*
grocery [grō'sûrē] *n* (*also:* ~ **store**) épicerie *f.*
grog [grâg] *n* grog *m.*
groggy [grâg'ē] *a* groggy *inv.*
groin [groin] *n* aine *f.*
groom [grōōm] *n* palefrenier *m;* (*also:* **bride**~) marié *m* ♦ *vt* (*horse*) panser; (*fig*): **to** ~ **sb for** former qn pour.
groove [grōōv] *n* sillon *m,* rainure *f.*
grope [grōp] *vi* tâtonner; **to** ~ **for** *vt fus* chercher à tâtons.
grosgrain [grō'grān] *n* gros-grain *m.*
gross [grōs] *a* grossier(ière); (*COMM*) brut(e) ♦ *n* (*pl inv*) (*twelve dozen*) grosse *f* ♦ *vt* (*COMM*): **to** ~ **$500,000** gagner 500.000 dollars avant impôt.
gross domestic product (GDP) *n* produit brut intérieur (PIB).
grossly [grōs'lē] *ad* (*greatly*) très, grandement.
gross national product (GNP) *n* produit national brut (PNB).
grotesque [grōtesk'] *a* grotesque.
grotto [grât'ō] *n* grotte *f.*
grotty [grât'ē] *a* (*Brit col*) minable.
grouch [grouch] (*col*) *vi* rouspéter ♦ *n* (*person*) rouspéteur/euse.
ground [ground] *pt, pp of* **grind** ♦ *n* sol *m,* terre *f;* (*land*) terrain *m,* terres *fpl;* (*SPORT*) terrain; (*reason: gen pl*) raison *f;* (*US: also:* ~ **wire**) terre *f* ♦ *vt* (*plane*) empêcher de décoller, retenir au sol; (*US ELEC*) équiper d'une prise de terre, mettre à la terre ♦ *vi* (*ship*) s'échouer ♦ *a* (*coffee etc*) moulu(e); (*US: meat*) haché(e); ~s *npl* (*gardens etc*) parc *m,* domaine *m;* (*of coffee*) marc *m;* **on the** ~, **to the** ~ par terre; **below** ~ sous terre; **to gain/lose** ~ gagner/perdre du terrain; **common** ~ terrain d'entente; **he covered a lot of** ~ **in his lecture** sa conférence a traité un grand nombre de questions *or* la question en profondeur.
ground cloth *n* (*US*) tapis *m* de sol.

ground control n (AVIAT, SPACE) centre m de contrôle (au sol).

ground floor n (Brit) rez-de-chaussée m.

grounding [groun'ding] n (in education) connaissances fpl de base.

groundless [ground'lis] a sans fondement.

ground meat n (US) viande hachée, hachis m.

groundnut [ground'nut] n arachide f.

ground rent n (Brit) fermage m.

groundsheet [ground'shēt] n (Brit) = **ground cloth.**

groundskeeper [groundz'kēpûr] n (US: SPORT) gardien m de stade.

groundsman [groundz'mən], n (Brit) = **groundskeeper.**

ground staff n équipage m au sol.

groundswell [ground'swel] n lame f or vague f de fond.

ground-to-ground [ground'təground'] a: ~ **missile** missile m sol-sol.

groundwork [ground'wûrk] n préparation f.

group [grōōp] n groupe m ♦ vt (also: ~ **together**) grouper ♦ vi (also: ~ **together**) se grouper.

grouse [grous] n (pl inv) (bird) grouse f (sorte de coq de bruyère) ♦ vi (complain) rouspéter, râler.

grove [grōv] n bosquet m.

grovel [gruv'əl] vi (fig): **to ~ (before)** ramper (devant).

grow, pt **grew**, pp **grown** [grō, grōō, grōn] vi (plant) pousser, croître; (person) grandir; (increase) augmenter, se développer; (become): **to ~ rich/weak** s'enrichir/s'affaiblir ♦ vt cultiver, faire pousser.

grow apart vi (fig) se détacher (l'un de l'autre).

grow away from vt fus (fig) s'éloigner de.

grow on vt fus: **that painting is ~ing on me** je finirai par aimer ce tableau.

grow out of vt fus (clothes) devenir trop grand pour; (habit) perdre (avec le temps); **he'll ~ out of it** ça lui passera.

grow up vi grandir.

grower [grō'ûr] n producteur m; (AGR) cultivateur/trice.

growing [grō'ing] a (fear, amount) croissant(e), grandissant(e); ~ **pains** (MED) fièvre f de croissance; (fig) difficultés fpl de croissance.

growl [groul] vi grogner.

grown [grōn] pp of **grow** ♦ a adulte.

grown-up [grōn'up'] n adulte m/f, grande personne.

growth [grōth] n croissance f, développement m; (what has grown) pousse f; poussée f; (MED) grosseur f, tumeur f.

growth rate n taux m de croissance.

grub [grub] n larve f; (col: food) bouffe f.

grubby [grub'ē] a crasseux(euse).

grudge [gruj] n rancune f ♦ vt: **to ~ sb sth** donner qch à qn à contre-cœur; reprocher qch à qn; **to bear sb a ~ (for)** garder rancune or en vouloir à qn (de); **he ~s spending** il rechigne à dépenser.

grudgingly [gruj'inglē] ad à contre-cœur, de mauvaise grâce.

gruel(l)ing [grōō'əling] a exténuant(e).

gruesome [grōō'səm] a horrible.

gruff [gruf] a bourru(e).

grumble [grum'bəl] vi rouspéter, ronchonner.

grumpy [grum'pē] a grincheux(euse).

grunt [grunt] vi grogner ♦ n grognement m.

GSA n abbr (US) = General Services Administration.

G-string [jē'string] n (garment) cache-sexe m inv.

GSUSA n abbr = Girl Scouts of the United States of America.

GU abbr (US MAIL) = Guam.

guarantee [garəntē'] n garantie f ♦ vt garantir; **he can't ~ (that) he'll come** il n'est pas absolument certain de pouvoir venir.

guarantor [gar'əntôr] n garant/e.

guard [gârd] n garde f, surveillance f; (squad, BOXING, FENCING) garde f; (one man) garde m; (in prison) gardien/ne; (Brit RAIL) chef m de train; (safety device: on machine) dispositif m de sûreté; (also: **fire~**) garde-feu m inv ♦ vt garder, surveiller; (protect): **to ~ (against or from)** protéger (contre); **to be on one's ~** (fig) être sur ses gardes.

guard against vi: **to ~ against doing sth** se garder de faire qch.

guard dog n chien m de garde.

guarded [gâr'did] a (fig) prudent(e).

guardian [gâr'dēən] n gardien/ne; (of minor) tuteur/trice.

guardrail [gârd'rāl] n rail m de sécurité.

guard's van [gârdz' van] n (Brit RAIL) fourgon m.

Guatemala [gwâtəmâl'ə] n Guatémala m.

guerrilla [gəril'ə] n guérillero m.

guerrilla warfare n guérilla f.

guess [ges] vi deviner ♦ vt deviner; (US) croire, penser ♦ n supposition f, hypothèse f; **to take or have a ~** essayer de deviner; **to keep sb ~ing** laisser qn dans le doute or l'incertitude, tenir qn en haleine.

guesstimate [ges'təmit] n (col) estimation f.

guesswork [ges'wûrk] n hypothèse f; **I got the answer by ~** j'ai deviné la réponse.

guest [gest] n invité/e; (in hotel) client/e; **be my ~** faites comme chez vous.

guest book n livre m d'or.

guesthouse [gest'hous] n pension f.

guest room n chambre f d'amis.

guffaw [gufô'] n gros rire ♦ vi pouffer de rire.

guidance [gīd'əns] n conseils mpl; **under the ~ of** conseillé(e) or encadré(e) par, sous la conduite de; **vocational ~** orientation professionnelle; **marriage ~** conseils conjugaux.

guide [gīd] n (person, book etc) guide m; (Brit: also: **girl ~**) guide f ♦ vt guider; **to be ~d by sb/sth** se laisser guider par qn/qch.

guidebook [gīd'bŏŏk] n guide m.

guided missile [gī'did mis'əl] n missile téléguidé.

guide dog n chien m d'aveugle.

guided tour [gīd'id tŏŏr] n visite guidée.

guidelines [gīd'līnz] npl (fig) instructions générales, conseils mpl.

guild [gild] n corporation f; cercle m, association f.

guile [gīl] n astuce f.

guileless [gīl'lis] a candide.

guillotine [gil'ətēn] n guillotine f; (for paper) massicot m.

guilt [gilt] *n* culpabilité *f*.

guilty [gil'tē] *a* coupable; **to plead ~/not ~** plaider coupable/non coupable; **to feel ~ about doing sth** avoir mauvaise conscience à faire qch.

Guinea [gin'ē] *n*: **Republic of ~** (République *f* de) Guinée *f*.

guinea pig *n* cobaye *m*.

guise [gīz] *n* aspect *m*, apparence *f*.

guitar [gitâr'] *n* guitare *f*.

guitarist [gitâr'ist] *n* guitariste *m/f*.

gulch [gulch] *n* (*US*) ravin *m*.

gulf [gulf] *n* golfe *m*; (*abyss*) gouffre *m*; **the (Persian) G~** le golfe Persique.

Gulf States *npl*: **the ~** (*in Middle East*) les pays *mpl* du Golfe.

Gulf Stream *n*: **the ~** le Gulf Stream.

gull [gul] *n* mouette *f*.

gullet [gul'it] *n* gosier *m*.

gullibility [guləbil'ətē] *n* crédulité *f*.

gullible [gul'əbəl] *a* crédule.

gully [gul'ē] *n* ravin *m*; ravine *f*; couloir *m*.

gulp [gulp] *vi* avaler sa salive; (*from emotion*) avoir la gorge serrée, s'étrangler ♦ *vt* (*also*: **~ down**) avaler ♦ *n* (*of drink*) gorgée *f*; **at one ~** d'un seul coup.

gum [gum] *n* (*ANAT*) gencive *f*; (*glue*) colle *f*; (*sweet*) boule *f* de gomme; (*also*: **chewing- ~**) chewing-gum *m* ♦ *vt* coller.

gum up *vt*: **to ~ up the works** (*col*) bousiller tout.

gumboil [gum'boil] *n* abcès *m* dentaire.

gumboots [gum'bōōts] *npl* (*Brit*) bottes *fpl* en caoutchouc.

gun [gun] *n* (*small*) revolver *m*, pistolet *m*; (*rifle*) fusil *m*, carabine *f*; (*cannon*) canon *m* ♦ *vt* (*also*: **~ down**) abattre; **to stick to one's ~s** (*fig*) ne pas en démordre.

gunboat [gun'bōt] *n* canonnière *f*.

gun dog *n* chien *m* de chasse.

gunfire [gun'fûr] *n* fusillade *f*.

gunk [gungk] *n* (*col*) saleté *f*.

gunman [gun'mən] *n* bandit armé.

gunner [gun'ûr] *n* artilleur *m*.

gunpoint [gun'point] *n*: **at ~** sous la menace du pistolet (*or* fusil).

gunpowder [gun'poudûr] *n* poudre *f* à canon.

gunrunner [gun'runûr] *n* trafiquant *m* d'armes.

gunrunning [gun'runing] *n* trafic *m* d'armes.

gunshot [gun'shât] *n* coup *m* de feu; **within ~** à portée de fusil.

gunsmith [gun'smith] *n* armurier *m*.

gurgle [gûr'gəl] *n* gargouillis *m* ♦ *vi* gargouiller.

guru [gōō'rōō] *n* gourou *m*.

gush [gush] *n* jaillissement *m*, jet *m* ♦ *vi* jaillir; (*fig*) se répandre en effusions.

gusset [gus'it] *n* gousset *m*, soufflet *m*; (*in tights, pants*) entre-jambes *m*.

gust [gust] *n* (*of wind*) rafale *f*; (*of smoke*) bouffée *f*.

gusto [gus'tō] *n* enthousiasme *m*.

gut [gut] *n* intestin *m*, boyau *m*; (*MUS etc*) boyau ♦ *vt* (*poultry, fish*) vider; (*building*) ne laisser que les murs de; **~s** *npl* boyaux *mpl*; (*col*: *courage*) cran *m*; **to hate sb's ~s** ne pas pouvoir voir qn en peinture *or* sentir qn.

gut reaction *n* réaction instinctive.

gutter [gut'ûr] *n* (*of roof*) gouttière *f*; (*in street*) caniveau *m*; (*fig*) ruisseau *m*.

guttural [gut'ûrəl] *a* guttural(e).

guy [gī] *n* (*also*: **~rope**) corde *f*; (*col*: *man*) type *m*; (*figure*) effigie de Guy Fawkes.

Guyana [gēân'ə] *n* Guyane *f*.

guzzle [guz'əl] *vi* s'empiffrer ♦ *vt* avaler glou-tonnement.

gym [jim] *n* (*also*: **gymnasium**) gymnase *m*; (*also*: **gymnastics**) gym *f*.

gymkhana [jimkâ'nə] *n* gymkhana *m*.

gymnasium [jimnâ'zēəm] *n* gymnase *m*.

gymnast [jim'nast] *n* gymnaste *m/f*.

gymnastics [jimnas'tiks] *n*, *npl* gymnastique *f*.

gym shoes *npl* chaussures *fpl* de gym(nastique).

gym slip *n* (*Brit*) tunique *f* (d'écolière).

gynecologist, (*Brit*) **gynaecologist** [gīnəkâl'əjist] *n* gynécologue *m/f*.

gynecology, (*Brit*) **gynaecology** [gīnəkâl'əjē] *n* gynécologie *f*.

gypsy [jip'sē] *n* gitan/e, bohémien/ne ♦ *cpd*: **~ caravan** *n* roulotte *f*.

gyrate [jī'rāt] *vi* tournoyer.

gyroscope [jī'rəskōp] *n* gyroscope *m*.

H

H, h [āch] *n* (*letter*) H, h *m*; **H for How** H comme Henri.

habeas corpus [hā'bēəs kôr'pəs] *n* (*LAW*) habeas corpus *m*.

haberdashery [hab'ûrdashrē] *n* (*Brit*) mercerie *f*.

habit [hab'it] *n* habitude *f*; (*costume*) habit *m*, tenue *f*; **to get out of/into the ~ of doing sth** perdre/prendre l'habitude de faire qch.

habitable [hab'itəbəl] *a* habitable.

habitat [hab'itat] *n* habitat *m*.

habitation [habitā'shən] *n* habitation *f*.

habitual [həbich'ōōəl] *a* habituel(le); (*drinker, liar*) invétéré(e).

habitually [həbich'ōōəlē] *ad* habituellement, d'habitude.

hack [hak] *vt* hacher, tailler ♦ *n* (*cut*) entaille *f*; (*blow*) coup *m*; (*pej*: *writer*) nègre *m*; (*old horse*) canasson *m*.

hacker [hak'ûr] *n* (*COMPUT*) pirate *m* informatique.

hackles [hak'əlz] *npl*: **to make sb's ~ rise** (*fig*) mettre qn hors de soi.

hackney cab [hak'nē kab] *n* fiacre *m*.

hackneyed [hak'nēd] *a* usé(e), rebattu(e).

had [had] *pt, pp of* **have**.

haddock, *pl ~ or* [had'ək] **~s** *n* églefin *m*; **smoked ~** haddock *m*.

hadn't [had'ənt] = **had not**.

haematology [hēmətâl'əjē] *n* (*Brit*) hématologie *f*.

haemoglobin [hē'məglōbin] *n* (*Brit*) hémoglobine *f*.

haemophilia [hēməfil'ēə] *n* (*Brit*) hémophilie

f.

haemorrhage [hem'ûrij] *n* (*Brit*) hémorragie *f.*

haemorrhoids [hem'əroidz] *npl* (*Brit*) hémorroïdes *fpl.*

hag [hag] *n* (*ugly*) vieille sorcière; (*nasty*) chameau *m*, harpie *f*; (*witch*) sorcière.

haggard [hag'ûrd] *a* hagard(e), égaré(e).

haggis [hag'is] *n* haggis *m.*

haggle [hag'əl] *vi* marchander; **to ~ over** chicaner sur.

haggling [hag'ling] *n* marchandage *m.*

Hague [hāg] *n:* **The ~** La Haye.

hail [hāl] *n* grêle *f* ♦ *vt* (*call*) héler; (*greet*) acclamer ♦ *vi* grêler; (*originate*): **he ~s from Scotland** il est originaire d'Écosse.

hailstone [hāl'stōn] *n* grêlon *m.*

hailstorm [hāl'stôrm] *n* averse *f* de grêle.

hair [hār] *n* cheveux *mpl*; (*on body*) poils *mpl*, pilosité *f*; (*single hair: on head*) cheveu *m*; (: *on body*) poil *m*; **to do one's ~** se coiffer.

hairbrush [hār'brush] *n* brosse *f* à cheveux.

haircut [hār'kut] *n* coupe *f* (de cheveux).

hairdo [hār'dōō] *n* coiffure *f.*

hairdresser [hār'dresûr] *n* coiffeur/euse.

hair dryer *n* sèche-cheveux *m.*

hair gel *n* gel *m.*

hairgrip [hār'grip] *n* (*Brit*) pince *f* à cheveux.

hairline [hār'līn] *n* naissance *f* des cheveux.

hairline fracture *n* fêlure *f.*

hairnet [hār'net] *n* résille *f.*

hair oil *n* huile *f* capillaire.

hairpiece [hār'pēs] *n* postiche *m.*

hairpin [hār'pin] *n* épingle *f* à cheveux.

hairpin curve, (*Brit*) **hairpin bend** *n* virage *m* en épingle à cheveux.

hair-raising [hār'rāzing] *a* à (vous) faire dresser les cheveux sur la tête.

hair remover *n* dépilateur *m.*

hair spray *n* laque *f* (pour les cheveux).

hairstyle [hār'stīl] *n* coiffure *f.*

hairy [hār'ē] *a* poilu(e); chevelu(e); (*fig*) effrayant(e).

Haiti [hā'tē] *n* Haïti *m.*

hake [hāk] *n* colin *m*, merlu *m.*

halcyon [hal'sēən] *a* merveilleux(euse).

hale [hāl] *a:* **~ and hearty** robuste, en pleine santé.

half [haf] *n* (*pl* **halves** [havz]) moitié *f*; (*SPORT: of match*) mi-temps *f*; (: *of ground*) moitié (du terrain) ♦ *a* demi(e) ♦ *ad* (à) moitié, à demi; **~ an hour** une demi-heure; **~ a dozen** une demi-douzaine; **~ a pound** une demi-livre, ≈ 250 g; **two and a ~** deux et demi; **a week and a ~** une semaine et demie; **~ (of it)** la moitié; **~ (of)** la moitié de; **~ the amount of** la moitié de; **to cut sth in ~** couper qch en deux; **~ after three** trois heures et demie; **~ empty/closed** à moitié vide/fermé; **to go halves (with sb)** se mettre de moitié avec qn.

halfback [haf'bak] *n* (*SPORT*) demi *m.*

half-baked [haf'bākt'] *a* (*col: idea, scheme*) qui ne tient pas debout.

half-breed [haf'brēd] *n* = **halfcaste.**

half-brother [haf'bruth̦ûr] *n* demi-frère *m.*

half-caste [haf'kast] *n* métis/se.

half-hearted [haf'hâr'tid] *a* tiède, sans enthousiasme.

half-hour [haf'our'] *n* demi-heure *f.*

half-mast [haf'mast'] *n:* **at ~** (*flag*) en berne, à mi-mât.

half note *n* (*US*) blanche *f.*

halfpenny [hā'pənē] *n* demi-penny *m.*

half-price [haf'prīs'] *a* à moitié prix ♦ *ad* (*also:* **at ~**) à moitié prix.

half term *n* (*Brit SCOL*) congé *m* de demi-trimestre.

half-time [haf'tīm'] *n* mi-temps *f.*

halfway [haf'wā'] *ad* à mi-chemin; **to meet sb ~** (*fig*) parvenir à un compromis avec qn.

half-yearly [haf'yēr'lē] *ad* deux fois par an ♦ *a* semestriel(le).

halibut [hal'əbət] *n* (*pl inv*) flétan *m.*

halitosis [halitō'sis] *n* mauvaise haleine.

hall [hôl] *n* salle *f*; (*entrance way*) hall *m*, entrée *f*; (*corridor*) couloir *m*; (*mansion*) château *m*, manoir *m*; **~ of residence** *n* (*Brit*) pavillon *m or* résidence *f* universitaire.

hallmark [hôl'mârk] *n* poinçon *m*; (*fig*) marque *f.*

hallo [həlō'] *excl* (*Brit*) = **hello.**

Hallowe'en [haləwēn'] *n* veille *f* de la Toussaint.

hallucination [həlōōsənā'shən] *n* hallucination *f.*

hallway [hôl'wā] *n* vestibule *m*; couloir *m.*

halo [hā'lō] *n* (*of saint etc*) auréole *f*; (*of sun*) halo *m.*

halt [hôlt] *n* halte *f*, arrêt *m* ♦ *vt* faire arrêter ♦ *vi* faire halte, s'arrêter; **to call a ~ to sth** (*fig*) mettre fin à qch.

halter [hôl'tûr] *n* (*for horse*) licou *m.*

halterneck [hôl'tûrnek] *a* (*Brit: dress*) (avec) dos nu *inv.*

halve [hav] *vt* (*apple etc*) partager *or* diviser en deux; (*reduce by half*) réduire de moitié.

halves [havz] *npl of* **half.**

ham [ham] *n* jambon *m*; (*col: also:* **radio ~**) radio-amateur *m*; (: *also:* **~ actor**) cabotin/e.

Hamburg [ham'bûrg] *n* Hambourg.

hamburger [ham'bûrgûr] *n* hamburger *m.*

ham-handed [ham'handid] *a* maladroit(e).

hamlet [ham'lit] *n* hameau *m.*

hammer [ham'ûr] *n* marteau *m* ♦ *vt* (*fig*) éreinter, démolir ♦ *vi* (*at door*) frapper à coups redoublés; **to ~ a point home to sb** faire rentrer qch dans la tête de qn.

hammer out *vt* (*metal*) étendre au marteau; (*fig: solution*) élaborer.

hammock [ham'ək] *n* hamac *m.*

hamper [ham'pûr] *vt* gêner ♦ *n* panier *m* (d'osier).

hamster [ham'stûr] *n* hamster *m.*

hamstring [ham'string] *n* (*ANAT*) tendon *m* du jarret.

hand [hand] *n* main *f*; (*of clock*) aiguille *f*; (*handwriting*) écriture *f*; (*at cards*) jeu *m*; (*measurement: of horse*) paume *f*; (*worker*) ouvrier/ière ♦ *vt* passer, donner; **to give sb a ~** donner un coup de main à qn; **at ~** à portée de la main; **in ~** en main; (*work*) en cours; **we have the situation in ~** nous avons la situation bien en main; **to be on ~** (*person*) être disponible; (*emergency services*) se tenir prêt(e) (à intervenir); **to ~** (*information etc*) sous la main, à portée de la main; **to force sb's ~** forcer la main à qn; **to have a free ~** avoir carte blanche; **to**

have sth **in one's** ~ tenir qch à la main; **on the one** ~ ..., **on the other** ~ d'une part ..., d'autre part.

hand down vt passer; (*tradition, heirloom*) transmettre; (*US: sentence, verdict*) prononcer.

hand in vt remettre.

hand out vt distribuer.

hand over vt remettre; (*powers etc*) transmettre.

hand round vt (*Brit: information*) faire circuler; (: *chocolates etc*) faire passer.

handbag [hand'bag] n sac m à main.

handball [hand'bôl] n handball m.

hand basin n lavabo m.

handbook [hand'bŏŏk] n manuel m.

handbrake [hand'brāk] n frein m à main.

hand cream n crème f pour les mains.

handcuffs [hand'kufs] npl menottes fpl.

handful [hand'fŏŏl] n poignée f.

handicap [hand'ēkap] n handicap m ♦ vt handicaper; **mentally/physically ~ped** handicapé(e) mentalement/physiquement.

handicraft [hand'ēkraft] n travail m d'artisanat, technique artisanale.

handiwork [hand'ēwûrk] n ouvrage m; **this looks like his** ~ (*pej*) ça a. tout l'air d'être son œuvre.

handkerchief [hang'kûrchif] n mouchoir m.

handle [han'dəl] n (*of door etc*) poignée f; (*of cup etc*) anse f; (*of knife etc*) manche m; (*of saucepan*) queue f; (*for winding*) manivelle f ♦ vt toucher, manier; (*deal with*) s'occuper de; (*treat: people*) prendre; "~ **with care**" "fragile".

handlebar(s) [han'dəlbâr(z)] n(pl) guidon m.

handling charges [hand'ling chär'jəz] npl frais mpl de manutention; (*BANKING*) agios mpl.

hand luggage n bagages mpl à main.

handmade [hand'mād'] a fait(e) à la main.

handout [hand'out] n documentation f, prospectus m; (*press* ~) communiqué m de presse.

hand-picked [hand'pikt'] a (*produce*) cueilli(e) à la main; (*staff etc*) trié(e) sur le volet.

handrail [hand'rāl] n (*on staircase etc*) rampe f, main courante.

handshake [hand'shāk] n poignée f de main; (*COMPUT*) établissement m de la liaison.

handsome [han'səm] a beau(belle); (*gift*) généreux(euse); (*profit*) considérable.

hands-on [handz'ân] a: ~ **experience** expérience f sur le tas.

handstand [hand'stand] n: **to do a** ~ faire l'arbre droit.

hand-to-mouth [hand'təmouth'] a (*existence*) au jour le jour.

handwriting [hand'rīting] n écriture f.

handwritten [hand'ritən] a manuscrit(e), écrit(e) à la main.

handy [han'dē] a (*person*) adroit(e); (*close at hand*) sous la main; (*convenient*) pratique; **to come in** ~ être (or s'avérer) utile.

handyman [han'dēman] n bricoleur m; (*servant*) homme m à tout faire.

hang, pt, pp **hung** [hang, hung] vt accrocher; (*criminal: pt, pp* **hanged**) pendre ♦ vi pendre; (*hair, drapery*) tomber; **to get the** ~ **of (doing)** sth (*col*) attraper le coup pour faire qch.

hang about vi flâner, traîner.

hang back vi (*hesitate*): **to** ~ **back (from doing)** être réticent(e) (pour faire).

hang on vi (*wait*) attendre ♦ vt fus (*depend on*) dépendre de; **to** ~ **on to** (*keep hold of*) ne pas lâcher; (*keep*) garder.

hang out vt (*washing*) étendre (dehors) ♦ vi pendre; (*col: live*) habiter, percher.

hang together vi (*argument etc*) se tenir, être cohérent(e).

hang up vi (*TEL*) raccrocher ♦ vt accrocher, suspendre; **to** ~ **up on sb** (*TEL*) raccrocher au nez de qn.

hangar [hang'ûr] n hangar m.

hangdog [hang'dôg] a (*look, expression*) de chien battu.

hanger [hang'ûr] n cintre m, portemanteau m.

hanger-on [hang'ûrân'] n parasite m.·

hang-gliding [hang'glīding] n vol m libre or sur aile delta.

hanging [hang'ing] n (*execution*) pendaison f.

hangman [hang'mən] n bourreau m.

hangover [hang'ōvûr] n (*after drinking*) gueule f de bois.

hang-up [hang'up] n complexe m.

hank [hangk] n écheveau m.

hanker [hang'kûr] vi: **to** ~ **after** avoir envie de.

hankie, hanky [hang'kē] n abbr = **handkerchief.**

hanky-panky [hang'kēpang'kē] n (*pej*) tripotage m.

Hants abbr (*Brit*) = **Hampshire.**

haphazard [hap'haz'ûrd] a fait(e) au hasard, fait(e) au petit bonheur.

hapless [hap'lis] a malheureux(euse).

happen [hap'ən] vi arriver, se passer, se produire; **what's** ~**ing?** que se passe-t-il?; **she** ~**ed to be free** il s'est trouvé (or se trouvait) qu'elle était libre; **if anything** ~**ed to him** s'il lui arrivait quoi que ce soit; **as it** ~**s** justement.

happen (up)on vt fus tomber sur.

happening [hap'əning] n événement m.

happily [hap'ilē] ad heureusement.

happiness [hap'ēnis] n bonheur m.

happy [hap'ē] a heureux(euse); ~ **with** (*arrangements etc*) satisfait(e) de; **yes, I'd be** ~ **to** oui, avec plaisir or (bien) volontiers; ~ **birthday!** bon anniversaire!; ~ **Christmas/New Year!** joyeux Noël/bonne année!

happy-go-lucky [hap'ēgōluk'ē] a insouciant(e).

harangue [hərang'] vt haranguer.

harass [həras'] vt accabler, tourmenter.

harassed [hərast'] a tracassé(e).

harassment [həras'mənt] n tracasseries fpl.

harbor, (*Brit*) **harbour** [hâr'bûr] n port m ♦ vt héberger, abriter; (*hopes, suspicions*) entretenir; **to** ~ **a grudge against sb** en vouloir à qn.

harbo(u)r dues npl droits mpl de port.

harbo(u)r master n capitaine m du port.

hard [hârd] a dur(e) ♦ ad (*work*) dur; (*think, try*) sérieusement; **to look** ~ **at** regarder fixement; regarder de près; **to drink ~** boire sec; **~ luck!** pas de veine!; **no ~ feelings!** sans rancune!; **to be ~ of hearing** être dur(e) d'oreille; **to be ~ on sb** être dur(e) avec qn; **I find it ~ to believe that ...** je n'arrive pas à croire que ....

hard-and-fast [hârd'ənfast] *a* strict(e), absolu(e).

hardback [hârd'bak] *n* livre relié.

hardboard [hârd'bôrd] *n* Isorel *m* ®.

hard-boiled egg [hârd'boild' eg] *n* œuf dur.

hard cash *n* espèces *fpl.*

hard copy *n* (COMPUT) sortie *f* or copie *f* papier.

hard-core [hârd'kôr'] *a* (*pornography*) (dit(e)) dur(e); (*supporters*) inconditionnel(le).

hard court *n* (TENNIS) court *m* en dur.

hard disk *n* (COMPUT) disque dur.

harden [hâr'dən] *vt* durcir; (*steel*) tremper; (*fig*) endurcir ♦ *vi* (*substance*) durcir.

hardened [hâr'dənd] *a* (*criminal*) endurci(e); **to be ~ to sth** s'être endurci(e) à qch, être (devenu(e)) insensible à qch.

hardening [hâr'dəning] *n* durcissement *m.*

hard-headed [hârd'hed'id] *a* réaliste; décidé(e).

hard-hearted [hârd'hâr'tid] *a* dur(e), impitoyable.

hard labor *n* travaux forcés.

hardliner [hârdlī'nûr] *n* intransigeant/e, dur/e.

hardly [hârd'lē] *ad* (*scarcely*) à peine; (*harshly*) durement; **it's ~ the case** ce n'est guère le cas; **~ anywhere/ever** presque nulle part/jamais; **I can ~ believe it** j'ai du mal à le croire.

hardness [hârd'nis] *n* dureté *f.*

hard sell *n* vente agressive.

hardship [hârd'ship] *n* épreuves *fpl*; privations *fpl.*

hard shoulder *n* (AUT) accotement stabilisé.

hard up *a* (col) fauché(e).

hardware [hârd'wär] *n* quincaillerie *f*; (COMPUT) matériel *m.*

hardware dealer *n* (US) marchand *m* de couleurs.

hardware shop *n* quincaillerie *f.*

hard-wearing [hârd'wär'ing] *a* solide.

hard-working [hârd'wûr'king] *a* travailleur(euse), consciencieux(euse).

hardy [hâr'dē] *a* robuste; (*plant*) résistant(e) au gel.

hare [här] *n* lièvre *m.*

harebrained [här'brānd] *a* farfelu(e); écervelé(e).

harelip [här'lip] *n* (MED) bec-de-lièvre *m.*

harem [här'əm] *n* harem *m.*

hark back [hârk bak] *vi:* **to ~ back to** (en) revenir toujours à.

harm [hârm] *n* mal *m*; (*wrong*) tort *m* ♦ *vt* (*person*) faire du mal or du tort à; (*thing*) endommager; **to mean no ~** ne pas avoir de mauvaises intentions; **there's no ~ in trying** on peut toujours essayer; **out of ~'s way** à l'abri du danger, en lieu sûr.

harmful [hârm'fəl] *a* nuisible.

harmless [hârm'lis] *a* inoffensif(ive); sans méchanceté.

harmonic [hârmân'ik] *a* harmonique.

harmonica [hârmân'ikə] *n* harmonica *m.*

harmonics [hârmân'iks] *npl* harmoniques *mpl* or *fpl.*

harmonious [hârmō'nēəs] *a* harmonieux(euse).

harmonium [hârmō'nēəm] *n* harmonium *m.*

harmonize [hâr'mənīz] *vt* harmoniser ♦ *vi* s'harmoniser.

harmony [hâr'mənē] *n* harmonie *f.*

harness [hâr'nis] *n* harnais *m* ♦ *vt* (*horse*) harnacher; (*resources*) exploiter.

harp [hârp] *n* harpe *f* ♦ *vi:* **to ~ on about** parler tout le temps de.

harpist [hâr'pist] *n* harpiste *m/f.*

harpoon [hârpōōn'] *n* harpon *m.*

harpsichord [hârp'sikôrd] *n* clavecin *m.*

harrow [har'ō] *n* (AGR) herse *f.*

harrowing [har'ōing] *a* déchirant(e).

harry [har'ē] *vt* (MIL, fig) harceler.

harsh [hârsh] *a* (*hard*) dur(e), sévère; (*rough: surface*) rugueux(euse); (*: sound*) discordant(e); (*: taste*) âpre.

harshly [hârsh'lē] *ad* durement, sévèrement.

harshness [hârsh'nis] *n* dureté *f*, sévérité *f.*

harvest [hâr'vist] *n* (*of corn*) moisson *f*; (*of fruit*) récolte *f*; (*of grapes*) vendange *f* ♦ *vi, vt* moissonner; récolter; vendanger.

harvester [hâr'vistûr] *n* (*machine*) moissonneuse *f*; (*also:* **combine ~**) moissonneuse-batteuse(-lieuse) *f*; (*person*) moissonneur/euse.

has [haz] *vb* see **have**.

has-been [haz'bin] *n* (*col: person*): **he/she's a ~** il/elle a fait son temps *or* est fini(e).

hash [hash] *n* (CULIN) hachis *m*; (*fig: mess*) gâchis *m* ♦ *n abbr* (col) = **hashish**.

hashish [hash'ēsh] *n* haschisch *m.*

hasn't [haz'ənt] = **has not**.

hassle [has'əl] *n* (*col: fuss*) histoire(s) *f(pl)*.

haste [hāst] *n* hâte *f*, précipitation *f*; **in ~** à la hâte, précipitamment.

hasten [hā'sən] *vt* hâter, accélérer ♦ *vi* se hâter, s'empresser; **I ~ to add that ...** je m'empresse d'ajouter que ....

hastily [hās'tilē] *ad* à la hâte, précipitamment.

hasty [hās'tē] *a* hâtif(ive), précipité(e).

hat [hat] *n* chapeau *m.*

hatbox [hat'bâks] *n* carton *m* à chapeau.

hatch [hach] *n* (NAUT: also: **~way**) écoutille *f* ♦ *vi* éclore ♦ *vt* faire éclore; (*fig: scheme*) tramer, ourdir.

hatchback [hach'bak] *n* (AUT) modèle *m* avec hayon arrière.

hatchet [hach'it] *n* hachette *f.*

hate [hāt] *vt* haïr, détester ♦ *n* haine *f*; **to ~ to do** *or* **doing** détester faire; **I ~ to trouble you, but ...** désolé de vous déranger, mais ....

hateful [hāt'fəl] *a* odieux(euse), détestable.

hatred [hā'trid] *n* haine *f.*

hat trick *n* (Brit SPORT, also fig): **to get a ~** réussir trois coups (*or* gagner trois matchs *etc*) consécutifs.

haughty [hô'tē] *a* hautain(e), arrogant(e).

haul [hôl] *vt* traîner, tirer; (*by truck*) camionner; (NAUT) haler ♦ *n* (*of fish*) prise *f*; (*of stolen goods etc*) butin *m.*

haulage [hô'lij] *n* transport routier.

haulage contractor *n* (*company*) entreprise *f* de transport (routier); (*person*) transporteur routier.

hauler [hô'lûr], (*Brit*) **haulier** [hôl'ēûr] *n* transporteur (routier), camionneur *m*.

haunch [hônch] *n* hanche *f*.

haunt [hônt] *vt* (*subj: ghost, fear*) hanter; (*: person*) fréquenter ♦ *n* repaire *m*.

haunted [hôn'tid] *a* (*castle etc*) hanté(e); (*look*) égaré(e), hagard(e).

haunting [hôn'ting] *a* (*sight, music*) obsédant(e).

Havana [həvan'ə] *n* La Havane.

have, *pt, pp* **had** [hav, had] *vt* avoir; (*meal, shower*) prendre ♦ *auxiliary vb*: **to ~ eaten** avoir mangé; **to ~ arrived** être arrivé(e); **to ~ breakfast** prendre son petit déjeuner; **to ~ lunch** déjeuner; **to ~ dinner** dîner; **I'll ~ a coffee** je prendrai un café; **to ~ an operation** se faire opérer; **to ~ a party** donner une réception *or* une soirée; **to ~ sth done** faire faire qch; **he had a suit made** il s'est fait faire un costume; **let me ~ a try** laissez-moi essayer; **she has to do it** il faut qu'elle le fasse, elle doit le faire; **I had better leave** je ferais mieux de partir; **I won't ~ it** cela ne se passera pas ainsi; **he's been had** (*col*) il s'est fait avoir *or* rouler.

have in *vt*: **to ~ it in for sb** (*col*) avoir une dent contre qn.

have on *vt*: **~ you anything on tomorrow?** (*Brit*) est-ce que vous êtes pris demain?; **I don't ~ any money on me** je n'ai pas d'argent sur moi; **to ~ sb on** (*Brit col*) faire marcher qn.

have out *vt*: **to ~ it out with sb** s'expliquer (franchement) avec qn.

haven [hā'vən] *n* port *m*; (*fig*) havre *m*.

haversack [hav'ûrsak] *n* sac *m* à dos.

haves [havz] *npl* (*col*): **the ~ and have-nots** les riches et les pauvres.

havoc [hav'ək] *n* ravages *mpl*; **to play ~ with** (*fig*) désorganiser; détraquer.

Hawaii [həwī'yē] *n* (îles *fpl*) Hawaii *m*.

Hawaiian [həwī'ən] *a* hawaïen(ne) ♦ *n* Hawaïen/ne; (*LING*) hawaïen *m*.

hawk [hôk] *n* faucon *m* ♦ *vt* (*goods for sale*) colporter.

hawker [hô'kûr] *n* colporteur *m*.

hawthorn [hô'thôrn] *n* aubépine *f*.

hay [hā] *n* foin *m*.

hay fever *n* rhume *m* des foins.

haystack [hā'stak] *n* meule *f* de foin.

haywire [hā'wīûr] *a* (*col*): **to go ~** perdre la tête; mal tourner.

hazard [haz'ûrd] *n* (*chance*) hasard *m*, chance *f*; (*risk*) danger *m*, risque *m* ♦ *vt* risquer, hasarder; **to be a health/fire ~** présenter un risque d'incendie/pour la santé; **to ~ a guess** émettre *or* hasarder une hypothèse.

hazardous [haz'ûrdəs] *a* hasardeux(euse), risqué(e).

hazardous pay *n* (*US*) prime *f* de risque.

hazard warning lights *npl* (*Brit*: *AUT*) feux *mpl* de détresse.

haze [hāz] *n* brume *f*.

hazel [hā'zəl] *n* (*tree*) noisetier *m* ♦ *a* (*eyes*) noisette *inv*.

hazelnut [hā'zəlnut] *n* noisette *f*.

hazy [hā'zē] *a* brumeux(euse); (*idea*) vague; (*photograph*) flou(e).

H-bomb [āch'bâm] *n* bombe *f* H.

h & c *abbr* (*Brit*) = *hot and cold (water)*.

HE *abbr* = *high explosive*; (*REL, DIPLOMACY*) = *His (or Her) Excellency*.

he [hē] *pronoun* il; **it is ~ who** ... c'est lui qui ...; **here ~ is** le voici; **~-bear** *etc* ours *etc* mâle.

head [hed] *n* tête *f*; (*leader*) chef *m* ♦ *vt* (*list*) être en tête de; (*group*) être à la tête de; **~s** (*on coin*) (le côté) face; **~s or tails** pile ou face; **~ first** la tête la première; **~ over heels in love** follement *or* éperdument amoureux(euse); **to ~ the ball** faire une tête; **10 francs a** *or* **per ~** 10 F par personne; **to sit at the ~ of the table** présider la tablée; **to have a ~ for business** avoir des dispositions pour les affaires; **to have no ~ for heights** (*Brit*) être sujet(te) au vertige; **to come to a ~** (*fig: situation etc*) devenir critique.

head for *vt fus* se diriger vers.

head off *vt* (*threat, danger*) détourner.

headache [hed'āk] *n* mal *m* de tête; **to have a ~** avoir mal à la tête.

headcheese [hed'chēz] *n* (*US*) fromage *m* de tête.

head cold *n* rhume *m* de cerveau.

headdress [hed'dres] *n* coiffure *f*.

header [hed'ûr] *n* (*Brit col*: *SOCCER*) (coup *m* de) tête *f*; (*: fall*) chute *f* (*or* plongeon *m*) la tête la première.

headhunter [hed'huntûr] *n* chasseur *m* de têtes.

heading [hed'ing] *n* titre *m*; (*subject title*) rubrique *f*.

headlamp [hed'lamp] *n* (*Brit*) = **headlight**.

headland [hed'land] *n* promontoire *m*, cap *m*.

headlight [hed'līt] *n* phare *m*.

headline [hed'līn] *n* titre *m*; **to make the ~** être à la une des journaux.

headlong [hed'lông] *ad* (*fall*) la tête la première; (*rush*) tête baissée.

headmaster [hed'mas'tûr] *n* (*Brit*) directeur *m*, proviseur *m*.

headmistress [hed'mis'tris] *n* (*Brit*) directrice *f*.

head office *n* siège *m*, direction *f* (générale).

head-on [hed'ân'] *a* (*collision*) de plein fouet.

headphones [hed'fōnz] *npl* casque *m* (à écouteurs).

headquarters (HQ) [hed'kwôrtûrz] *npl* (*of business*) siège *m*, direction *f* (générale); (*MIL*) quartier général.

headrest [hed'rest] *n* appui-tête *m*.

headroom [hed'rōom] *n* (*in car*) hauteur *f* de plafond; (*under bridge*) hauteur limite; dégagement *m*.

headscarf [hed'skârf] *n* foulard *m*.

headset [hed'set] *n* = **headphones**.

headstone [hed'stōn] *n* (*on grave*) pierre tombale.

headstrong [hed'strông] *a* têtu(e), entêté(e).

head waiter *n* maître *m* d'hôtel.

headway [hed'wā] *n*: **to make ~** avancer, faire des progrès.

headwind [hed'wind] *n* vent *m* contraire.

heady [hed'ē] *a* capiteux(euse); enivrant(e).

heal [hēl] *vt, vi* guérir.

health [helth] *n* santé *f*; **Department of H~** (*US*) ≈ ministère *m* de la Santé.

health benefit *n* (*US*) (prestations *fpl* de

l')assurance-maladie f.
health centre n (Brit) centre m de santé.
health food(s) n(pl) aliment(s) naturel(s).
health food store n magasin m diététique.
health hazard n risque m pour la santé.
Health Service n: **the ~** (Brit) ≈ la Sécurite Sociale.
healthy [hel'thē] a (person) en bonne santé; (climate, food, attitude etc) sain(e).
heap [hēp] n tas m, monceau m ♦ vt entasser, amonceler; **~s (of)** (col: lots) des tas (de); **to ~ favors/praise/gifts** etc **on sb** combler qn de faveurs/d'éloges/de cadeaux etc.
hear, pt, pp **heard** [hēr, hûrd] vt entendre; (news) apprendre; (lecture) assister à, écouter ♦ vi entendre; **to ~ about** entendre parler de; (have news of) avoir des nouvelles de; **did you ~ about the move?** tu es au courant du déménagement?; **I've never heard of that book** je n'ai jamais entendu parler de ce livre.
hear out vt écouter jusqu'au bout.
hearing [hē'ring] n (sense) ouïe f; (of witnesses) audition f; (of a case) audience f; (of committee) séance f; **to give sb a ~** écouter ce que qn a à dire.
hearing aid n appareil m acoustique.
hearsay [hēr'sā] n on-dit mpl, rumeurs fpl; **by ~** ad par ouï-dire.
hearse [hûrs] n corbillard m.
heart [hârt] n cœur m; **~s** npl (CARDS) cœur; **at ~** au fond; **by ~** (learn, know) par cœur; **to have a weak ~** avoir le cœur malade, avoir des problèmes de cœur; **to lose ~** perdre courage, se décourager; **to take ~** prendre courage; **to set one's ~ on sth/on doing sth** vouloir absolument qch/faire qch; **the ~ of the matter** le fond du problème.
heart attack n crise f cardiaque.
heartbeat [hârt'bēt] n battement m de cœur.
heartbreak [hârt'brāk] n immense chagrin m.
heartbreaking [hârt'brāking] a navrant(e), déchirant(e).
heartbroken [hârt'brōkən] a: **to be ~** avoir beaucoup de chagrin.
heartburn [hârt'bûrn] n brûlures fpl d'estomac.
heartening [hâr'təning] a encourageant(e), réconfortant(e).
heart failure n (MED) arrêt m du cœur.
heartfelt [hârt'felt] a sincère.
hearth [hârth] n foyer m, cheminée f.
heartily [hâr'təlē] ad chaleureusement; (laugh) de bon cœur; (eat) de bon appétit; **to agree ~** être entièrement d'accord; **to be ~ sick of** (Brit) en avoir ras le bol de.
heartland [hârt'land] n centre m, cœur m; **France's ~s** la France profonde.
heartless [hârt'lis] a sans cœur, insensible; cruel(le).
heart-to-heart [hârt'təhârt'] a, ad à cœur ouvert.
heart transplant n greffe f du cœur.
heartwarming [hârt'wórming] a réconfortant(e).
hearty [hâr'tē] a chaleureux(euse); robuste; vigoureux(euse).
heat [hēt] n chaleur f; (fig) ardeur f; feu m;

(SPORT: also: **qualifying ~**) éliminatoire f; (ZOOL): **in** or (Brit) **on ~** en chaleur ♦ vt chauffer.
heat up vi (liquids) chauffer; (room) se réchauffer ♦ vt réchauffer.
heated [hē'tid] a chauffé(e); (fig) passionné(e); échauffé(e), excité(e).
heater [hē'tûr] n appareil m de chauffage; radiateur m.
heath [hēth] n (Brit) lande f.
heathen [hē'thən] a, n païen(ne).
heather [heth'ûr] n bruyère f.
heating [hē'ting] n chauffage m.
heat-resistant [hēt'rizistənt] a résistant(e) à la chaleur.
heatstroke [hēt'strōk] n coup m de chaleur.
heat wave n vague f de chaleur.
heave [hēv] vt soulever (avec effort) ♦ vi se soulever; (retch) avoir des haut-le-cœur ♦ n (push) poussée f; **to ~ a sigh** pousser un gros soupir.
heaven [hev'ən] n ciel m, paradis m; **~ forbid!** surtout pas!; **thank ~!** Dieu merci!; **for ~'s sake!** (pleading) je vous en prie!; (protesting) mince alors!
heavenly [hev'ənlē] a céleste, divin(e).
heavily [hev'ilē] ad lourdement; (drink, smoke) beaucoup; (sleep, sigh) profondément.
heavy [hev'ē] a lourd(e); (work, rain, user, eater) gros(se); (drinker, smoker) grand(e); **it's ~ going** ça ne va pas tout seul, c'est pénible.
heavy cream n (US) crème fraîche épaisse.
heavy-duty [hev'ēdōō'tē] a à usage intensif.
heavy goods vehicle (HGV) n (Brit) poids lourd m (P.L.).
heavy-handed [hev'ēhan'did] a (fig) maladroit(e), qui manque de tact.
heavyweight [hev'ēwāt] n (SPORT) poids lourd.
Hebrew [hē'brōō] a hébraïque ♦ n (LING) hébreu m.
heckle [hek'əl] vt interpeller (un orateur).
heckler [hek'lûr] n interrupteur m; élément m perturbateur.
hectic [hek'tik] a agité(e), trépidant(e); (busy) trépidant.
hector [hek'tûr] vt rudoyer, houspiller.
he'd [hēd] = **he would**, **he had**.
hedge [hej] n haie f ♦ vi se défiler; **to ~ one's bets** (fig) se couvrir; **as a ~ against inflation** pour se prémunir contre l'inflation.
hedge in vt entourer d'une haie.
hedgehog [hej'hág] n hérisson m.
hedgerow [hej'rō] n haie(s) f(pl).
hedonism [hēd'ənizəm] n hédonisme m.
heed [hēd] vt (also: **take ~ of**) tenir compte de, prendre garde à.
heedless [hēd'lis] a insouciant(e).
heel [hēl] n talon m ♦ vt (shoe) retalonner; **to bring to ~** (dog) faire venir à ses pieds; (fig: person) rappeler à l'ordre; **to take to one's ~s** prendre ses jambes à son cou.
hefty [hef'tē] a (person) costaud(e); (parcel) lourd(e); (piece, price) gros(se).
heifer [hef'ûr] n génisse f.
height [hīt] n (of person) taille f, grandeur f; (of object) hauteur f; (of plane, mountain)

altitude *f*; (*high ground*) hauteur, éminence *f*; (*fig: of glory*) sommet *m*; (*: of stupidity*) comble *m*; **what ~ are you?** combien mesurez-vous?, quelle est votre taille?; **of average ~** de taille moyenne; **to be afraid of ~s** être sujet(te) au vertige; **it's the ~ of fashion** c'est le dernier cri.

heighten [hīt'ən] *vt* hausser, surélever; (*fig*) augmenter.

heinous [hā'nəs] *a* odieux(euse), atroce.

heir [är] *n* héritier *m*.

heir apparent *n* héritier présomptif.

heiress [är'is] *n* héritière *f*.

heirloom [är'lōōm] *n* meuble *m* (*or* bijou *m or* tableau *m*) de famille.

heist [hīst] *n* (*US col: hold-up*) casse *m*.

held [held] *pt*, *pp of* **hold**.

helicopter [hel'əkâptûr] *n* hélicoptère *m*.

heliport [hel'əpôrt] *n* (*AVIAT*) héliport *m*.

helium [hē'lēəm] *n* hélium *m*.

hell [hel] *n* enfer *m*; **a ~ of a** ... (*col*) un(e) sacré(e) ...; **oh ~!** (*col*) merde!

he'll [hēl] = **he will, he shall**.

hellish [hel'ish] *a* infernal(e).

hello [helō'] *excl* bonjour!; salut! (*to sb one addresses as 'tu'*); (*surprise*) tiens!

hell's angel [helz ān'jəl] *n* blouson *m* noir.

helm [helm] *n* (*NAUT*) barre *f*.

helmet [hel'mit] *n* casque *m*.

helmsman [helmz'mən] *n* timonier *m*.

help [help] *n* aide *f*; (*cleaner*) femme *f* de ménage; (*assistant etc*) employé/e ♦ *vt* aider; **~!** au secours!; **~ yourself (to bread)** servez-vous (de pain); **are you being ~ed?** (*US*) est-ce qu'on s'occupe de vous?; **can I ~ you?** (*in store*) vous désirez?; **with the ~ of** (*person*) avec l'aide de; (*tool etc*) à l'aide de; **to be of ~ to sb** être utile à qn; *"~ wanted"* (*US PRESS*) "offres d'emploi"; **to ~ sb (to) do sth** aider qn à faire qch; **I can't ~ saying** je ne peux pas m'empêcher de dire; **he can't ~ it** il n'y peut rien.

helper [hel'pûr] *n* aide *m/f*, assistant/e.

helpful [help'fəl] *a* serviable, obligeant(e); (*useful*) utile.

helping [hel'ping] *n* portion *f*.

helpless [help'lis] *a* impuissant(e); (*baby*) sans défense.

helplessly [help'lislē] *ad* (*watch*) sans pouvoir rien faire.

Helsinki [hel'singkē] *n* Helsinki.

helter-skelter [hel'tûrskel'tûr] *n* (*Brit*: *at amusement park*) toboggan *m*.

hem [hem] *n* ourlet *m* ♦ *vt* ourler.

hem in *vt* cerner; **to feel ~med in** (*fig*) avoir l'impression d'étouffer, se sentir oppressé(e) *or* écrasé(e).

he-man [hē'man] *n* (*col*) macho *m*.

hematology [hēmətâl'əjē] *n* hématologie *f*.

hemisphere [hem'isfēr] *n* hémisphère *m*.

hemlock [hem'lâk] *n* cigüe *f*.

hemoglobin [hē'məglōbin] *n* hémoglobine *f*.

hemophilia [hēməfil'eə] *n* hémophilie *f*.

hemorrhage [hem'ûrij] *n* hémorragie *f*.

hemorrhoids [hem'əroidz] *npl* hémorroïdes *fpl*.

hemp [hemp] *n* chanvre *m*.

hen [hen] *n* poule *f*; (*female bird*) femelle *f*.

hence [hens] *ad* (*therefore*) d'où, de là; **2**

years ~ d'ici 2 ans.

henceforth [hens'fôrth] *ad* dorénavant.

henchman [hench'mən] *n* (*pej*) acolyte *m*, séide *m*.

henna [hen'ə] *n* henné *m*.

hen party *n* (*col*) réunion *f or* fête *f* entre femmes.

henpecked [hen'pekt] *a* dominé par sa femme.

hepatitis [hepətī'tis] *n* hépatite *f*.

her [hûr] *pronoun* (*direct*) la, l' + *vowel or h mute*; (*indirect*) lui; (*stressed, after prep*) elle; *see note at* **she** ♦ *a* son(sa), ses *pl*; **I see ~** je la vois; **give ~ a book** donne-lui un livre; **after ~** après elle.

herald [här'əld] *n* héraut *m* ♦ *vt* annoncer.

heraldic [hiral'dik] *a* héraldique.

heraldry [här'əldrē] *n* héraldique *f*; (*coat of arms*) blason *m*.

herb [ûrb] *n* herbe *f*; **~s** *npl* (*CULIN*) fines herbes.

herbaceous [hûrbā'shəs] *a* herbacé(e).

herbal [hûr'bəl] *a* à base de plantes; **~ tea** tisane *f*.

herbicide [hûr'bisīd] *n* herbicide *m*.

herd [hûrd] *n* troupeau *m*; (*of wild animals, swine*) troupeau, troupe *f* ♦ *vt* (*drive: animals, people*) mener, conduire; (*gather*) rassembler; **~ed together** parqués (comme du bétail).

here [hēr] *ad* ici ♦ *excl* tiens!, tenez!; **~!** présent!; **~ is, ~ are** voici; **~'s my sister** voici ma sœur; **~ he/she is** le/la voici; **~ she comes** la voici qui vient; **come ~!** viens ici!; **~ and there** ici et là.

hereabouts [hē'rəbouts] *ad* par ici, dans les parages.

hereafter [hēraf'tûr] *ad* après, plus tard; ci-après ♦ *n*: **the ~** l'au-delà *m*.

hereby [hērbī'] *ad* (*in letter*) par la présente.

hereditary [həred'itärē] *a* héréditaire.

heredity [həred'itē] *n* hérédité *f*.

heresy [här'isē] *n* hérésie *f*.

heretic [här'itik] *n* hérétique *m/f*.

heretical [həret'ikəl] *a* hérétique.

herewith [hērwith'] *ad* avec ceci, ci-joint.

heritage [här'itij] *n* héritage *m*, patrimoine *m*; **our national ~** notre patrimoine national.

hermetically [hûrmet'iklē] *ad* hermétiquement; **~ sealed** hermétiquement fermé *or* clos.

hermit [hûr'mit] *n* ermite *m*.

hernia [hûr'nēə] *n* hernie *f*.

hero, *pl* **~es** [hē'rō] *n* héros *m*.

heroic [hirō'ik] *a* héroïque.

heroin [här'ōin] *n* héroïne *f*.

heroin addict *n* héroïnomane *m/f*.

heroine [här'ōin] *n* héroïne *f* (*femme*).

heroism [här'ōizəm] *n* héroïsme *m*.

heron [här'ən] *n* héron *m*.

hero worship *n* culte *m* (du héros).

herring [här'ing] *n* hareng *m*.

hers [hûrz] *pronoun* le(la) sien(ne), les siens(siennes); **a friend of ~** un(e) ami(e) à elle, un(e) de ses ami(e)s; **this is ~** c'est à elle, c'est le sien.

herself [hûrself'] *pronoun* (*reflexive*) se; (*emphatic*) elle-même; (*after prep*) elle.

Herts *abbr* (*Brit*) = *Hertfordshire*.

he's [hēz] = **he is, he has.**

hesitant [hez'ətənt] *a* hésitant(e), indécis(e); **to be ~ about doing sth** hésiter à faire qch.

hesitate [hez'ətāt] *vi*: **to ~ (about/to do)** hésiter (sur/à faire).

hesitation [hezətā'shən] *n* hésitation *f*; **I have no ~ in saying (that)** ... je n'hésiterai pas à dire (que) ....

hessian [hesh'ən] *n* (toile *f* de) jute *m*.

heterogeneous [hetûrəjē'nēəs] *a* hétérogène.

heterosexual [hetûrəsek'shōōəl] *a, n* hétérosexuel(le).

het up [het up] *a* (*col*) agité(e), excité(e).

HEW *n abbr* (*US*: *formerly*: = *Department of Health, Education and Welfare*) ministère de la santé publique, de l'enseignement et du bien-être.

hew [hyōō] *vt* tailler (*à la hache*).

hex [heks] (*US*) *n* sort *m* ♦ *vt* jeter un sort sur.

hexagon [hek'səgân] *n* hexagone *m*.

hexagonal [heksag'ənəl] *a* hexagonal(e).

hey [hā] *excl* hé!

heyday [hā'dā] *n*: **the ~ of** l'âge *m* d'or de, les beaux jours de.

HF *n abbr* (= *high frequency*) HF *f*.

HGV *n abbr* (*Brit*) = **heavy goods vehicle.**

HI *abbr* (*US MAIL*) = *Hawaii.*

hi [hī] *excl* salut!

hiatus [hīā'təs] *n* trou *m*, lacune *f*; (*LING*) hiatus *m*.

hibernate [hī'bûrnāt] *vi* hiberner.

hibernation [hībûrnā'shən] *n* hibernation *f*.

hiccough, hiccup [hik'up] *vi* hoqueter ♦ *n* hoquet *m*; **to have (the) ~s** avoir le hoquet.

hick [hik] *n* (*US*) rustre *m*, péquenaud *m*.

hid [hid] *pt of* **hide.**

hidden [hid'ən] *pp of* **hide** ♦ *a*: **there are no ~ extras** absolument tout est compris dans le prix.

hide [hīd] *n* (*skin*) peau *f* ♦ *vb* (*pt* **hid,** *pp* **hidden** [hid, hid'ən]) *vt*: **to ~ sth (from sb)** cacher qch (à qn); (*feelings, truth*) dissimuler qch (à qn) ♦ *vi*: **to ~ (from sb)** se cacher de qn.

hide-and-seek [hīd'ənsēk'] *n* cache-cache *m*.

hideaway [hīd'əwā] *n* cachette *f*.

hideous [hid'ēəs] *a* hideux(euse); atroce.

hide-out [hīd'out] *n* cachette *f*.

hiding [hī'ding] *n* (*beating*) correction *f*, volée *f* de coups; **to be in ~** (*concealed*) se tenir caché(e).

hiding place *n* cachette *f*.

hierarchy [hī'ərârkē] *n* hiérarchie *f*.

hieroglyphic [hīûrəglif'ik] *a* hiéroglyphique; **~s** *npl* hiéroglyphes *mpl*.

hi-fi [hī'fī'] *a, n abbr* (= *high fidelity*) hi-fi (*f*) *inv.*

higgledy-piggledy [hig'əldēpig'əldē] *ad* pêlemêle, dans le plus grand désordre.

high [hī] *a* haut(e); (*speed, respect, number*) grand(e); (*price*) élevé(e); (*wind*) fort(e), violent(e); (*voice*) aigu(aiguë); (*col: person: on drugs*) défoncé(e), fait(e); (: *on drink*) soûl(e), bourré(e); (*Brit CULIN: meat, game*) faisandé(e); (: *spoilt*) avarié(e) ♦ *ad* haut, en haut ♦ *n*: **exports have reached a new ~** les exportations ont atteint un nouveau record; **20 m ~** haut(e) de 20 m; **to pay a ~ price for sth** payer cher pour qch.

highball [hī'bôl] *n* (*US*) whisky *m* à l'eau avec des glaçons.

highboy [hī'boi] *n* (*US*) grande commode.

highbrow [hī'brou] *a, n* intellectuel(le).

highchair [hī'chär] *n* chaise haute (*pour enfant*).

high-class [hī'klas'] *a* (*neighborhood, hotel*) chic *inv*, de grand standing; (*performance etc*) de haut niveau.

high court *n* (*LAW*) cour *f* suprême.

higher [hī'ûr] *a* (*form of life, study etc*) supérieur(e) ♦ *ad* plus haut.

higher education *n* études supérieures.

high finance *n* la haute finance.

high-flier [hī'flī'ûr] *n* étudiant/e (*or* employé/e) particulièrement doué(e) et ambitieux(euse).

high-flying [hī'flī'ing] *a* (*fig*) ambitieux(euse), de haut niveau.

high-handed [hī'han'did] *a* très autoritaire; très cavalier(ière).

high-heeled [hī'hēld] *a* à hauts talons.

highjack [hī'jak] *n, vt* = **hijack.**

high jump *n* (*SPORT*) saut *m* en hauteur.

highlands [hī'ləndz] *npl* région montagneuse.

high-level [hī'level] *a* (*talks etc*) à un haut niveau; **~ language** (*COMPUT*) langage évolué.

highlight [hī'līt] *n* (*fig: of event*) point culminant ♦ *vt* faire ressortir, souligner; **~s** *npl* (*hairstyle*) reflets *mpl*.

highlighter [hī'lītûr] *n* (*pen*) surligneur (lumineux).

highly [hī'lē] *ad* très, fort, hautement; **~ paid** très bien payé(e); **to speak ~ of** dire beaucoup de bien de.

highly-strung [hī'lēstrung'] *a* (*Brit*) = **highstrung.**

High Mass *n* grand-messe *f*.

highness [hī'nis] *n* hauteur *f*; **Her H~** son Altesse *f*.

high-pitched [hī'picht'] *a* aigu(ë).

high-powered [hī'pou'ûrd] *a* (*engine*) performant(e); (*fig: person*) dynamique; (: *job, businessman*) très important(e).

high-pressure [hī'presh'ûr] *a* à haute pression.

high-rise block [hī'rīz'blâk] *n* tour *f* (d'habitation).

high school *n* lycée *m*; (*US*) établissement *m* d'enseignement secondaire.

high season *n* haute saison.

high spirits *npl* pétulance *f*; **to be in ~** être plein(e) d'entrain.

high street *n* (*Brit*) grand-rue *f*.

high-strung [hī'strung'] *a* (*US*) nerveux(euse), toujours tendu(e).

highway [hī'wā] *n* grand'route *f*, route nationale; **it's ~ robbery!** c'est le coup de barre!

Highway Code *n* (*Brit*) code *m* de la route.

highwayman [hī'wāmən] *n* voleur *m* de grand chemin.

hijack [hī'jak] *vt* détourner (*par la force*) ♦ *n* (*also*: **~ing**) détournement *m* (d'avion).

hijacker [hī'jakûr] *n* auteur *m* d'un détournement d'avion, pirate *m* de l'air.

hike [hīk] *vi* aller à pied ♦ *n* excursion *f* à pied, randonnée *f*; (*col: in prices etc*) augmentation *f* ♦ *vt* (*col*) augmenter.

hiker [hī'kûr] *n* promeneur/euse, excursionniste *m/f*.

hiking [hī'king] *n* excursions *fpl* à pied,

randonnée f.

hilarious [hilär'ēəs] a (behavior, event) désopilant(e).

hilarity [hilar'itē] n hilarité f.

hill [hil] n colline f; (fairly high) montagne f; (on road) côte f.

hillbilly [hil'bilē] n (US) montagnard/e du sud des USA; (pej) péquenaud m.

hillock [hil'ək] n petite colline, butte f.

hillside [hil'sīd] n (flanc m de) coteau m.

hill start n (AUT) démarrage m en côte.

hilly [hil'ē] a vallonné(e); montagneux(euse); (road) à fortes côtes.

hilt [hilt] n (of sword) garde f; **to the ~** (fig: support) à fond.

him [him] pronoun (direct) le, l' + vowel or h mute; (stressed, indirect, after prep) lui; **I see ~** je le vois; **give ~ a book** donne-lui un livre; **after ~** après lui.

Himalayas [himəlā'əz] npl: **the ~** l'Himalaya m.

himself [himself'] pronoun (reflexive) se; (emphatic) lui-même; (after prep) lui.

hind [hīnd] a de derrière ♦ n biche f.

hinder [hin'dûr] vt gêner; (delay) retarder; (prevent): **to ~ sb from doing** empêcher qn de faire.

hindquarters [hīnd'kwôrtûrz] npl (ZOOL) arrière-train m.

hindrance [hin'drəns] n gêne f, obstacle m.

hindsight [hīnd'sīt] n bon sens m coup; **with the benefit of ~** avec du recul, rétrospectivement.

Hindu [hin'dōō] n Hindou/e.

hinge [hinj] n charnière f ♦ vi (fig): **to ~ on** dépendre de.

hint [hint] n allusion f; (advice) conseil m ♦ vt: **to ~ that** insinuer que ♦ vi: **to ~ at** faire une allusion à; **to drop a ~** faire une allusion or insinuation; **give me a ~** (clue) mettez-moi sur la voie, donnez-moi une indication.

hip [hip] n hanche f; (BOT) fruit m de l'églantier or du rosier.

hip flask n flacon m (pour la poche).

hippie, hippy [hip'ē] n hippie m/f.

hip pocket n poche-revolver f.

hippopotamus, pl ~**es** or **hippopotami** [hipəpât'əməs, -pât'əmī] n hippopotame m.

hippy [hip'ē] n = **hippie.**

hire [hīûr] vt (Brit: car, equipment) louer; (worker) embaucher, engager ♦ n location f; **for ~** à louer; (taxi) libre; **on ~** en location.

hire out vt louer.

hire(d) car n (Brit) voiture louée.

hire purchase (H.P.) n (Brit) achat m (or vente f) à tempérament or crédit; **to buy sth on ~** acheter qch en location-vente.

his [hiz] pronoun le(la) sien(ne), les siens(siennes) ♦ a son(sa), ses pl; **this is ~** c'est à lui, c'est le sien.

hiss [his] vi siffler ♦ n sifflement m.

histogram [his'təgram] n histogramme m.

historian [histôr'ēən] n historien/ne.

historic(al) [histôr'ik(əl)] a historique.

history [his'tûrē] n histoire f; **medical ~** (of patient) passé médical.

histrionics [histrēân'iks] n gestes mpl dramatiques, cinéma m (fig).

hit [hit] vt (pt, pp **hit**) frapper; (knock against) cogner; (reach: target) atteindre, toucher; (collide with: car) entrer en collision avec, heurter; (fig: affect) toucher; (find) tomber sur ♦ n coup m; (success) coup réussi; succès m; (song) chanson f à succès, tube m; **to ~ it off with sb** bien s'entendre avec qn; **to ~ the road** (col) se mettre en route.

hit back vi: **to ~ back at sb** prendre sa revanche sur qn.

hit out at vt fus envoyer un coup à; (fig) attaquer.

hit (up)on vt fus (answer) trouver (par hasard); (solution) tomber sur (par hasard).

hit-and-run driver [hit'ənrun' drī'vûr] n chauffard m.

hitch [hich] vt (fasten) accrocher, attacher; (also: ~ **up**) remonter d'une saccade ♦ n (knot) nœud m; (difficulty) anicroche f, contretemps m; **to ~ a lift** faire du stop; **technical ~** incident m technique.

hitch up vt (horse, cart) atteler; see also **hitch.**

hitchhike [hich'hīk] vi faire de l'auto-stop.

hitchhiker [hich'hīkûr] n auto-stoppeur/euse.

hi-tech [hī'tek'] a à la pointe de la technologie, technologiquement avancé(e) ♦ n high-tech m.

hitherto [hith'ûrtōō] ad jusqu'ici, jusqu'à présent.

hit man n tueur m.

hit-or-miss [hit'ərmis'] a fait(e) au petit bonheur; **it's ~ whether...** il est loin d'être certain que... + sub.

hit parade n hit parade m.

hive [hīv] n ruche f; **the shop was a ~ of activity** (fig) le magasin était une véritable ruche.

hive off vt (col) mettre à part, séparer.

hl abbr (= hectoliter) hl.

HM abbr (= His (or Her) Majesty) SM.

HMG abbr (Brit) = His (or Her) Majesty's Government.

HMO n abbr (US: = health maintenance organization) organisme médical assurant un forfait entretien de santé.

HMS abbr (Brit) = His (or Her) Majesty's Ship.

hoard [hôrd] n (of food) provisions fpl, réserves fpl; (of money) trésor m ♦ vt amasser.

hoarding [hôr'ding] n (Brit) panneau m d'affichage or publicitaire.

hoarfrost [hôr'frâst] n givre m.

hoarse [hôrs] a enroué(e).

hoax [hōks] n canular m.

hob [hâb] n plaque chauffante.

hobble [hâb'əl] vi boitiller.

hobby [hâb'ē] n passe-temps favori.

hobbyhorse [hâb'ēhôrs] n cheval m à bascule; (fig) dada m.

hobnob [hâb'nâb] vi: **to ~ with** frayer avec, fréquenter.

hobo [hō'bō] n (US) vagabond m.

hock [hâk] n (of animal, CULIN) jarret m; (Brit: wine) vin m du Rhin; (col): **to be in ~** (person) avoir des dettes; (object) être en gage or au clou.

hockey [hák'ē] *n* hockey *m*.

hocus-pocus [hō'kəspō'kəs] *n* (*trickery*) supercherie *f*; (*words: of magician*) formules *fpl* magiques; (: *jargon*) galimatias *m*.

hodgepodge [háj'páj] *n* mélange *m* hétéroclite.

hoe [hō] *n* houe *f*, binette *f* ♦ *vt* (*ground*) biner; (*plants etc*) sarcler.

hog [hóg] *n* sanglier *m* ♦ *vt* (*fig*) accaparer; **to go the whole ~** aller jusqu'au bout.

hoist [hoist] *n* palan *m* ♦ *vt* hisser.

hold [hōld] *vb* (*pt, pp* **held** [held]) *vt* tenir; (*contain*) contenir; (*keep back*) retenir; (*believe*) maintenir, considérer; (*possess*) avoir; détenir ♦ *vi* (*withstand pressure*) tenir (bon); (*be valid*) valoir ♦ *n* prise *f*; (*fig*) influence *f*; (*NAUT*) cale *f*; **to catch** *or* **get (a) ~ of** saisir; **to get ~ of** (*fig*) .trouver; **to get ~ of o.s.** se contrôler; **~ the line!** (*TEL*) ne quittez pas!; **to ~ one's own** (*fig*) (bien) se défendre; **to ~ office** (*POL*) avoir un portefeuille; **to ~ firm** *or* **fast** tenir bon; **he ~s the view that ...** il pense *or* estime que ..., d'après lui ...; **to ~ sb responsible for sth** tenir qn pour responsable de qch.

    hold back *vt* retenir; (*secret*) cacher; **to ~ sb back from doing sth** empêcher qn de faire qch.

    hold down *vt* (*person*) maintenir à terre; (*job*) occuper.

    hold forth *vi* pérorer.

    hold off *vt* tenir à distance ♦ *vi* (*rain*): **if the rain ~s off** s'il ne pleut pas, s'il ne se met pas à pleuvoir.

    hold on *vi* tenir bon; (*wait*) attendre; **~ on!** (*TEL*) ne quittez pas!

    hold on to *vt fus* se cramponner à; (*keep*) conserver, garder.

    hold out *vt* offrir ♦ *vi* (*resist*): **to ~ out (against)** résister (devant), tenir bon (devant).

    hold over *vt* (*meeting etc*) ajourner, reporter.

    hold up *vt* (*raise*) lever; (*support*) soutenir; (*delay*) retarder; (: *traffic*) ralentir; (*rob*) braquer.

holdall [hōld'ól] *n* (*Brit*) fourre-tout *m inv*.

holder [hōl'dûr] *n* (*of ticket, record*) détenteur/trice; (*of office, title, passport etc*) titulaire *m/f*.

holding [hōl'ding] *n* (*share*) intérêts *mpl*; (*farm*) ferme *f*.

holding company *n* holding *m*.

holdup [hōld'up] *n* (*robbery*) hold-up *m*; (*delay*) retard *m*; (*in traffic*) embouteillage *m*.

hole [hōl] *n* trou *m* ♦ *vt* trouer, faire un trou dans; **~ in the heart** (*MED*) communication *f* interventriculaire; **to pick ~s (in)** (*fig*) chercher des poux (dans).

    hole up *vi* se terrer.

holiday [hál'idā] *n* (*Brit: vacation*) vacances *fpl*; (*day off*) jour *m* de congé; (*public*) jour férié; **to be on ~** être en congé; **tomorrow is a ~** demain c'est fête, on a congé demain.

holiday camp *n* (*Brit: for children*) colonie *f* de vacances; (: *also:* **holiday centre**) camp *m* de vacances.

holidaymaker [hál'idāmākûr] *n* (*Brit*) vacancier/ière.

holiday pay *n* (*Brit*) paie *f* des vacances.

holiday resort *n* centre *m* de villégiature *or* de vacances.

holiday season *n* (*US*) fêtes *fpl* de fin d'année; (*Brit*) période *f* des vacances.

holiness [hō'lēnis] *n* sainteté *f*.

Holland [hál'ənd] *n* Hollande *f*.

hollow [hál'ō] *a* creux(euse); (*fig*) faux(fausse) ♦ *n* creux *m*; (*in land*) dépression *f* (de terrain), cuvette *f* ♦ *vt*: **to ~ out** creuser, évider.

holly [hál'ē] *n* houx *m*.

hollyhock [hál'ēhák] *n* rose trémière.

holocaust [hál'əkóst] *n* holocauste *m*.

holster [hōl'stûr] *n* étui *m* de revolver.

holy [hō'lē] *a* saint(e); (*bread, water*) bénit(e); (*ground*) sacré(e).

Holy Communion *n* la (sainte) communion.

Holy Ghost, Holy Spirit *n* Saint-Esprit *m*.

Holy Land *n*: **the ~** la Terre Sainte.

holy orders *npl* ordres (majeurs).

homage [hám'ij] *n* hommage *m*; **to pay ~ to** rendre hommage à.

home [hōm] *n* foyer *m*, maison *f*; (*country*) pays natal, patrie *f*; (*institution*) maison ♦ *a* de famille; (*ECON, POL*) national(e), intérieur(e); (*SPORT: team*) qui reçoit; (: *match, win*) sur leur (*or* notre) terrain ♦ *ad* chez soi, à la maison; au pays natal; (*right in: nail etc*) à fond; **at ~** chez soi, à la maison; **to go** (*or* **come**) **~** rentrer (chez soi), rentrer à la maison (*or* au pays); **make yourself at ~** faites comme chez vous; **near my ~** près de chez moi.

    home in on *vt fus* (*missiles*) se diriger automatiquement vers *or* sur.

home address *n* domicile permanent.

home-brew [hōm'brōō'] *n* vin *m* (*or* bière *f*) maison.

homecoming [hōm'kuming] *n* retour *m* (au bercail).

home computer *n* ordinateur *m* domestique.

home economics *n* économie *f* domestique.

home furnishings [hōm fûr'nishingz] *npl* (*drapes etc*) tissus *mpl* d'ameublement.

home-grown [hōm'grōn'] *a* (*not foreign*) du pays; (*from garden*) du jardin.

homeland [hōm'land] *n* patrie *f*.

homeless [hōm'lis] *a* sans foyer, sans abri; **the ~** *npl* les sans-abri *mpl*.

home loan *n* prêt *m* sur hypothèque.

homely [hōm'lē] *a* simple, sans prétention; accueillant(e).

home-made [hōm'mād'] *a* fait(e) à la maison.

Home Office *n* (*Brit*) ministère *m* de l'Intérieur.

homeopath [hō'mēəpath] *n* homéopath *m/f*.

homeopathy [hōmēăp'əthē] *n* homéopathe *f*.

homeowner [hōm'ōnûr] *n* propriétaire occupant.

home rule *n* autonomie *f*.

Home Secretary *n* (*Brit*) ministre *m* de l'Intérieur.

homesick [hōm'sik] *a*: **to be ~** avoir le mal du pays; (*missing one's family*) s'ennuyer de sa famille.

homestead [hōm'sted] *n* propriété *f*; (*farm*) ferme *f*.

home town *n* ville natale.

homeward [hōm'wûrd] *a (journey)* du retour.
homeward(s) [hōm'wûrd(z)] *ad* vers la maison.
homework [hōm'wûrk] *n* devoirs *mpl*.
homicidal [hâmisīd'əl] *a* homicide.
homicide [hám'isīd] *n (US)* homicide *m*.
homily [hám'ilē] *n* homélie *f*.
homing [hō'ming] *a (device, missile)* à tête chercheuse; ~ **pigeon** pigeon voyageur.
homoeopathy [hōmēǎp'əthē] *etc (Brit)* = **homeopathy** *etc*.
homogeneous [hōməjē'nēəs] *a* homogène.
homogenize [həmâj'əniz] *vt* homogénéiser.
homosexual [hōməsek'shōōəl] *a, n* homosexuel(le).
Hon. *abbr* (= *honorable, honorary*) dans un titre.
Honduras [hundōō'rəs] *n* Honduras *m*.
hone [hōn] *n* pierre *f* à aiguiser ♦ *vt* affûter, aiguiser.
honest [ân'ist] *a* honnête; *(sincere)* franc(franche); **to be quite ~ with you** ... à dire vrai ....
honestly [ân'istlē] *ad* honnêtement; franchement.
honesty [ân'istē] *n* honnêteté *f*.
honey [hun'ē] *n* miel *m*; *(US col: darling)* chéri/e.
honeycomb [hun'ēkōm] *n* rayon *m* de miel; *(pattern)* nid *m* d'abeilles, motif alvéolé ♦ *vt (fig)*: **to ~ with** cribler de.
honeymoon [hun'ēmōōn] *n* lune *f* de miel, voyage *m* de noces.
honeysuckle [hun'ēsukəl] *n* chèvrefeuille *m*.
Hong Kong [hâng' kông'] *n* Hong Kong.
honk [hângk] *n (AUT)* coup *m* de klaxon ♦ *vi* klaxonner.
Honolulu [hânəlōō'lōō] *n* Honolulu.
honor [ân'ûr] *(US) vt* honorer ♦ *n* honneur *m*; **in ~ of** en l'honneur de.
honorable [ân'ûrəbəl] *a* honorable.
honorary [ân'ərārē] *a* honoraire; *(duty, title)* honorifique.
honor-bound [an'ûrbound'] *a*: **to be ~ to do** se devoir de faire.
honors degree *n (SCOL)* licence *avec mention*.
honour [ân'ûr] *etc (Brit)* = **honor** *etc*.
Hons. *abbr (SCOL)* = **honors degree**.
hood [hōōd] *n* capuchon *m*; *(US AUT)* capot *m*; *(Brit AUT)* capote *f*; *(col)* truand *m*.
hoodlum [hōōd'ləm] *n* truand *m*.
hoodwink [hōōd'wingk] *vt* tromper.
hoof, *pl* ~**s** *or* **hooves** [hōōf, hōōvz] *n* sabot *m*.
hook [hōōk] *n* crochet *m*; *(on dress)* agrafe *f*; *(for fishing)* hameçon *m* ♦ *vt* accrocher; *(dress)* agrafer; ~ **and eye** agrafe; **by ~ or by crook** de gré ou de force, coûte que coûte; **to be ~ed (on)** *(col)* être accroché(e) (par); *(person)* être dingue (de).
hook up *vt (RADIO, TV etc)* faire un duplex entre.
hooker [hōōk'ûr] *n (col: pej)* putain *f*.
hooky [hōōk'ē] *n*: **to play ~** faire l'école buissonnière.
hooligan [hōō'ligən] *n* voyou *m*.
hoop [hōōp] *n* cerceau *m*; *(of barrel)* cercle *m*.
hoot [hōōt] *vi (siren)* mugir; *(owl)* hululer;

(Brit AUT) klaxonner ♦ *vt (jeer at)* huer ♦ *n* huée *f*; coup *m* de klaxon; mugissement *m*; hululement *m*; **to ~ with laughter** rire aux éclats.
hooter [hōō'tûr] *n (NAUT, factory)* sirène *f*; *(Brit AUT)* klaxon *m*.
hoover [hōō'vûr] ® *(Brit) n* aspirateur *m* ♦ *vt (room)* passer l'aspirateur dans; *(carpet)* passer l'aspirateur sur.
hooves [hōōvz] *npl of* **hoof**.
hop [hâp] *vi* sauter; *(on one foot)* sauter à cloche-pied ♦ *n* saut *m*.
hope [hōp] *vt, vi* espérer ♦ *n* espoir *m*; **I ~ so** je l'espère; **I ~ not** j'espère que non.
hopeful [hōp'fəl] *a (person)* plein(e) d'espoir; *(situation)* prometteur(euse), encourageant(e); **I'm ~ that she'll manage to come** j'ai bon espoir qu'elle pourra venir.
hopefully [hōp'fəlē] *ad* avec espoir, avec optimisme; ~, **they'll come back** espérons bien qu'ils reviendront.
hopeless [hōp'lis] *a* désespéré(e), sans espoir; *(useless)* nul(le).
hopelessly [hōp'lislē] *ad (live etc)* sans espoir; ~, **confused** *etc* complètement désorienté *etc*.
hopper [hâp'ûr] *n (chute)* trémie *f*.
hops [hâps] *npl* houblon *m*.
horde [hôrd] *n* horde *f*.
horizon [hərī'zən] *n* horizon *m*.
horizontal [hôrizân'təl] *a* horizontal(e).
hormone [hôr'mōn] *n* hormone *f*.
horn [hôrn] *n* corne *f*; *(MUS)* cor *m*; *(AUT)* klaxon *m*.
horned [hôrnd] *a (animal)* à cornes.
hornet [hôr'nit] *n* frelon *m*.
horny [hôr'nē] *a* corné(e); *(hands)* calleux(euse); *(col: aroused)* excité(e).
horoscope [hôr'əskōp] *n* horoscope *m*.
horrendous [hôren'dəs] *a* horrible, affreux(euse).
horrible [hôr'əbəl] *a* horrible, affreux(euse).
horrid [hôr'id] *a* méchant(e), désagréable.
horrific [hôrif'ik] *a* horrible.
horrify [hôr'əfī] *vt* horrifier.
horrifying [hôr'əfīing] *a* horrifiant(e).
horror [hôr'ûr] *n* horreur *f*.
horror film *n* film *m* d'épouvante.
horror-struck [hôr'ûrstruk], **horror-stricken** [hôr'ûrstrikən] *a* horrifié(e).
hors d'oeuvre [ôr dûrv'] *n* hors d'œuvre *m*.
horse [hôrs] *n* cheval *m*.
horseback [hôrs'bak]: **on ~** *a, ad* à cheval; **to go ~ riding** faire du cheval.
horsebox [hôrs'bâks] *n (Brit)* = **horse trailer**.
horse chestnut *n* marron *m* (d'Inde).
horse-drawn [hôrs'drôn] *a* tiré(e) par des chevaux.
horsefly [hôrs'flī] *n* taon *m*.
horseman [hôrs'mən] *n* cavalier *m*.
horsemanship [hôrs'mənship] *n* talents *mpl* de cavalier.
horseplay [hôrs'plā] *n* chahut *m* *(blagues etc)*.
horsepower (hp) [hôrs'pouûr] *n* puissance *f* (en chevaux); cheval-vapeur *m* (CV).
horse racing *n* courses *fpl* de chevaux.
horseradish [hôrs'radish] *n* raifort *m*.
horseshoe [hôrs'shōō] *n* fer *m* à cheval.
horse show *n* concours *m* hippique.

horse-trading [hôrs'trãding] *n* maquignonage *m*.

horse trailer *n* (*US*) van *m*.

horse trials *npl* = **horse show**.

horsewhip [hôrs'hwip] *vt* cravacher.

horsewoman [hôrs'woomən] *n* cavalière *f*.

horsey [hôr'sē] *a* féru(e) d'équitation *or* de cheval; (*appearance*) chevalin(e).

horticulture [hôr'təkulchûr] *n* horticulture *f*.

hose [hōz] *n* (*also:* **~pipe**) tuyau *m*; (*also:* **garden ~**) tuyau d'arrosage.
   hose down *vt* laver au jet.

hosiery [hō'zhûrē] *n* (*in store*) (rayon *m* des) bas *mpl*.

hospice [hâs'pis] *n* hospice *m*.

hospitable [hâspit'əbəl] *a* hospitalier(ière).

hospital [hâs'pitəl] *n* hôpital *m*; **in the ~**, (*Brit*) **in ~** à l'hôpital.

hospitality [hâspətal'itē] *n* hospitalité *f*.

hospitalize [hâs'pitəlīz] *vt* hospitaliser.

host [hōst] *n* hôte *m*; (*in hotel etc*) patron *m*; (*TV, RADIO*) présentateur/trice, animateur/trice; (*large number*): **a ~ of** une foule de; (*REL*) hostie *f* ♦ *vt* (*TV program*) présenter, animer.

hostage [hâs'tij] *n* otage *m*.

host country *n* pays *m* d'accueil, pays-hôte *m*.

hostel [hâs'təl] *n* foyer *m*; (*also:* **youth ~**) auberge *f* de jeunesse.

hostelling [hâs'təling] *n*: **to go (youth) ~** faire une virée *or* randonnée en séjournant dans des auberges de jeunesse.

hostess [hōs'tis] *n* hôtesse *f*; (*AVIAT*) hôtesse de l'air; (*in nightclub*) entraîneuse *f*.

hostile [hâs'təl] *a* hostile.

hostility [hâstil'ətē] *n* hostilité *f*.

hot [hât] *a* chaud(e); (*as opposed to only warm*) très chaud; (*spicy*) fort(e); (*fig*) acharné(e); brûlant(e); violent(e), passionné(e); **to be ~** (*person*) avoir chaud; (*thing*) être (très) chaud; (*weather*) faire chaud.
   hot up (*Brit col*) *vi* (*situation*) devenir tendu(e); (*party*) s'animer ♦ *vt* (*pace*) accélérer, forcer; (*engine*) gonfler.

hot-air balloon [hâtär' bəloon'] *n* montgolfière *f*, ballon *m*.

hotbed [hât'bed] *n* (*fig*) foyer *m*, pépinière *f*.

hotchpotch [hâch'pâch] *n* (*Brit*) = **hodge-podge**.

hot dog *n* hot-dog *m*.

hotel [hōtel'] *n* hôtel *m*.

hotelier [ōtelyā'] *n* hôtelier/ière.

hotel industry *n* industrie hôtelière.

hotel room *n* chambre *f* d'hôtel.

hotfoot [hât'foot] *ad* à toute vitesse.

hotheaded [hât'hedid] *a* impétueux(euse).

hothouse [hât'hous] *n* serre chaude.

hot line [hât līn] *n* (*POL*) téléphone *m* rouge, ligne directe.

hotly [hât'lē] *ad* passionnément, violemment.

hot pad *n* (*US*) dessous-de-plat *m inv*.

hotplate [hât'plāt] *n* (*on stove*) plaque chauffante.

hotpot [hât'pât] *n* (*Brit CULIN*) ragoût *m*.

hot seat *n* (*fig*) poste chaud.

hot spot *n* point chaud.

hot spring *n* source thermale.

hot-tempered [hât'tem'pûrd] *a* emporté(e).

hot-water bottle [hâtwôt'ûr bâtəl] *n* bouillotte *f*.

hound [hound] *vt* poursuivre avec acharnement ♦ *n* chien courant; **the ~s** la meute.

hour [ou'ûr] *n* heure *f*; **at 30 miles an ~** ≈ à 50 km à l'heure; **lunch ~** heure du déjeuner; **to pay sb by the ~** payer qn à l'heure.

hourly [ouûr'lē] *a* toutes les heures; (*rate*) horaire; **~ paid** *a* payé(e) à l'heure.

house *n* [hous] (*pl:* **~s** [hou'zəz]) maison *f*; (*POL*) chambre *f*; (*THEATER*) salle *f*; auditoire *m* ♦ *vt* [houz] (*person*) loger, héberger; **at** (*or* **to**) **my ~** chez moi; **the H~ (of Representatives)** (*US*) la Chambre des représentants; **the H~ (of Commons)** (*Brit*) la Chambre des communes; **on the ~** (*fig*) aux frais de la maison.

house arrest *n* assignation *f* à domicile.

houseboat [hous'bōt] *n* bateau (aménagé en habitation).

housebound [hous'bound] *a* confiné(e) chez soi.

housebreaking [hous'brāking] *n* cambriolage *m* (avec effraction).

house-broken [hous'brōkən] *a* (*US: animal*) propre.

housecoat [hous'kōt] *n* peignoir *m*.

household [hous'hōld] *n* ménage *m*; (*people*) famille *f*, maisonnée *f*; **~ name** nom connu de tout le monde.

householder [hous'hōldûr] *n* propriétaire *m/f*; (*head of house*) chef *m* de ménage *or* de famille.

house hunting *n*: **to go ~** se mettre en quête d'une maison (*or* d'un appartement).

housekeeper [hous'kēpûr] *n* gouvernante *f*.

housekeeping [hous'kēping] *n* (*work*) ménage *m*; (*also:* **~ money**) argent *m* du ménage; (*COMPUT*) gestion *f* (des disques).

houseman [hous'mən] *n* (*Brit MED*) ≈ interne *m*.

house-proud [hous'proud] *a* qui tient à avoir une maison impeccable.

house-to-house [houstəhous'] *a* (*enquiries etc*) chez tous les habitants (du quartier *etc*).

house-trained [hous'trānd] *a* (*Brit*) = **house-broken**.

house-warming [hous'wôrming] *n* (*also:* **~ party**) pendaison *f* de crémaillère.

housewife [hous'wīf] *n* ménagère *f*; femme *f* du foyer.

housework [hous'wûrk] *n* (travaux *mpl* du) ménage *m*.

housing [hou'zing] *n* logement *m* ♦ *cpd* (*problem, shortage*) de *or* du logement.

housing association *n* fondation *f* charitable fournissant des logements.

housing conditions *npl* conditions *fpl* de logement.

housing development, (*Brit*) **housing estate** *n* cité *f*; lotissement *m*.

hovel [huv'əl] *n* taudis *m*.

hover [huv'ûr] *vi* planer; **to ~ around sb** rôder *or* tourner autour de qn.

hovercraft [huv'ûrkraft] *n* aéroglisseur *m*.

hoverport [huv'ûrpôrt] *n* hoverport *m*.

how [hou] *ad* comment; **~ are you?** comment allez-vous?; **~ do you do?** bonjour; (*on*

being introduced) enchanté(e); ~ **far is it to
...?** combien y a-t-il jusqu'à ...?; ~ **long have
you been here?** depuis combien de temps
êtes-vous là?; ~ **lovely!** que *or* comme c'est
joli!; ~ **many/much?** combien?; ~ **many
people/much milk** combien de gens/lait; ~
old are you? quel âge avez-vous?; ~**'s life?**
(*col*) comment ça va?; ~ **about a drink?** si
on buvait quelque chose?; ~ **is it that ...?**
comment se fait-il que ... + *sub*?

however [houev'ûr] *cj* pourtant, cependant ♦
ad de quelque façon *or* manière que + *sub*;
(+ *adjective*) quelque *or* si ... que + *sub*; (*in
questions*) comment.

howitzer [hou'itsûr] *n* (*MIL*) obusier *m*.

howl [houl] *n* hurlement *m* ♦ *vi* hurler.

howler [hou'lûr] *n* gaffe *f*, bourde *f*.

HP *n abbr* (*Brit*) = **hire purchase**.

hp *abbr* (*AUT*) = **horsepower**.

HQ *n abbr* (= *headquarters*) QG *m*.

HR *n abbr* (*US*) = **House of Representatives**.

HRH *abbr* (= *His* (*or Her*) *Royal Highness*)
SAR.

hr(s) *abbr* (= *hour(s)*) h.

HS *abbr* (*US*) = **high school**.

HST *abbr* (*US*: = *Hawaiian Standard Time*)
heure de Hawaii.

hub [hub] *n* (*of wheel*) moyeu *m*; (*fig*) centre
m, foyer *m*.

hubbub [hub'ub] *n* brouhaha *m*.

hub cap *n* (*AUT*) enjoliveur *m*.

HUD *n abbr* (*US*: = *Department of Housing
and Urban Development*) ministère de
l'urbanisme et du logement.

huddle [hud'əl] *vi*: **to ~ together** se blottir les
uns contre les autres.

hue [hyōō] *n* teinte *f*, nuance *f*; ~ **and cry** *n*
tollé (général), clameur *f*.

huff [huf] *n*: **in a ~** fâché(e); **to get into a ~**
prendre la mouche.

hug [hug] *vt* serrer dans ses bras; (*shore,
curb*) serrer ♦ *n* étreinte *f*; **to give sb a ~**
serrer qn dans ses bras.

huge [hyōōj] *a* énorme, immense.

hulk [hulk] *n* (*ship*) vieux rafiot; (*car,
building*) carcasse *f*; (*person*) mastodonte *m*,
malabar *m*.

hulking [hul'king] *a* balourd(e).

hull [hul] *n* (*of ship, nuts*) coque *f*; (*of peas*)
cosse *f*.

hullabaloo [huləbəlōō'] *n* (*col: noise*) tapage
m, raffut *m*.

hullo [həlō'] *excl* = **hello**.

hum [hum] *vt* (*tune*) fredonner ♦ *vi* fredonner;
(*insect*) bourdonner; (*plane, tool*) vrombir ♦
n fredonnement *m*; bourdonnement *m*;
vrombissement *m*.

human [hyōō'mən] *a* humain(e) ♦ *n* (*also*: ~
being) être humain.

humane [hyōōmān'] *a* humain(e), humanitaire.

humanism [hyōō'mənizəm] *n* humanisme *m*.

humanitarian [hyōōmanitār'ēən] *a* humanitaire.

humanity [hyōōman'itē] *n* humanité *f*.

humanly [hyōō'mənlē] *ad* humainement.

humanoid [hyōō'mənoid] *a, n* humanoïde (*m/
f*).

humble [hum'bəl] *a* humble, modeste ♦ *vt* hu-

milier.

humbly [hum'blē] *ad* humblement, modeste-
ment.

humbug [hum'bug] *n* fumisterie *f*; (*Brit:
candy*) bonbon *m* à la menthe.

humdrum [hum'drum] *a* monotone, routi-
nier(ière).

humid [hyōō'mid] *a* humide.

humidifier [hyōōmid'əfiûr] *n* humidificateur *m*.

humidity [hyōōmid'ətē] *n* humidité *f*.

humiliate [hyōōmil'ēāt] *vt* humilier.

humiliation [hyōōmilēā'shən] *n* humiliation *f*.

humility [hyōōmil'ətē] *n* humilité *f*.

humor [hyōō'mûr] (*US*) *n* humour *m*; (*mood*)
humeur *f* ♦ *vt* (*person*) faire plaisir à; se prêter aux caprices de; **sense of ~** sens *m* de
l'humour; **to be in a good/bad ~** être de
bonne/mauvaise humeur.

humorist [hyōō'mûrist] *n* humoriste *m/f*.

humorless [hyōō'mûrlis] *a* dépourvu(e) d'humour.

humorous [hyōō'mûrəs] *a* humoristique;
(*person*) plein(e) d'humour.

humour [hyōō'mûr] *etc* (*Brit*) = **humor** *etc*.

hump [hump] *n* bosse *f*.

humpback [hump'bak] *n* bossu/e.

humus [hyōō'məs] *n* humus *m*.

hunch [hunch] *n* bosse *f*; (*premonition*) intuition *f*; **I have a ~ that** j'ai (comme une vague) idée que.

hunchback [hunch'bak] *n* bossu/e.

hunched [huncht] *a* arrondi(e), voûté(e).

hundred [hun'drid] *num* cent; **about a ~
people** une centaine de personnes; ~**s of
people** des centaines de gens; **I'm a ~ per
cent sure** j'en suis absolument certain.

hundredweight [hun'dridwāt] *n* (*US*) = 45.3
kg; 100 lb; (*Brit*) = 50.8 *kg; 112 lb*.

hung [hung] *pt, pp of* **hang**.

Hungarian [hunggãr'ēən] *a* hongrois(e) ♦ *n*
Hongrois/e; (*LING*) hongrois *m*.

Hungary [hung'gûrē] *n* Hongrie *f*.

hunger [hung'gûr] *n* faim *f* ♦ *vi*: **to ~ for**
avoir faim de, désirer ardemment.

hunger strike *n* grève *f* de la faim.

hungrily [hung'grilē] *ad* voracement; (*fig*) avidement.

hungry [hung'grē] *a* affamé(e); **to be ~** avoir
faim; ~ **for** (*fig*) avide de.

hung up *a* (*col*) complexé(e); bourré(e) de
complexes.

hunk [hungk] *n* gros morceau; (*col: man*)
beau mec.

hunt [hunt] *vt* (*seek*) chercher; (*SPORT*)
chasser ♦ *vi* chasser ♦ *n* chasse *f*.
hunt down *vt* pourchasser.

hunter [hun'tûr] *n* chasseur *m*; (*Brit: horse*)
cheval *m* de chasse.

hunting [hun'ting] *n* chasse *f*.

hurdle [hûr'dəl] *n* (*for fences*) claie *f*; (*SPORT*)
haie *f*; (*fig*) obstacle *m*.

hurl [hûrl] *vt* lancer (avec violence).

hurrah, hurray [hərã', hərā'] *n* hourra *m*.

hurricane [hûr'əkān] *n* ouragan *m*.

hurried [hûr'ēd] *a* pressé(e), précipité(e);
(*work*) fait(e) à la hâte.

hurriedly [hûr'ēdlē] *ad* précipitamment, à la
hâte.

hurry [hûr'ē] *n* hâte *f*, précipitation *f* ♦ *vi* se

presser, se dépêcher ♦ *vt* (*person*) faire presser, faire se dépêcher; (*work*) presser; **to be in a ~** être pressé(e); **to do sth in a ~** faire qch en vitesse; **to ~ in/out** entrer/ sortir précipitamment; **to ~ home** se dépêcher de rentrer.

hurry along *vi* marcher d'un pas pressé.
hurry away, hurry off *vi* partir précipitamment.
hurry up *vi* se dépêcher.
hurt [hûrt] *vb* (*pt, pp* **hurt**) *vt* (*cause pain to*) faire mal à; (*injure, fig*) blesser; (*damage: business, interests etc*) nuire à, faire du tort à ♦ *vi* faire mal ♦ *a* blessé(e); **I ~ my arm** je me suis fait mal au bras; **where does it ~?** où avez-vous mal?, où est-ce que ça vous fait mal?
hurtful [hûrt'fəl] *a* (*remark*) blessant(e).
hurtle [hûr'təl] *vt* lancer (de toutes ses forces) ♦ *vi*: **to ~ past** passer en trombe; **to ~ down** dégringoler.
husband [huz'bənd] *n* mari *m*.
hush [hush] *n* calme *m*, silence *m* ♦ *vt* faire taire; **~!** chut!
hush up *vt* (*fact*) étouffer.
hush-hush [hush'hush] *a* (*col*) ultra-secret(ète).
husk [husk] *n* (*of wheat*) balle *f*; (*of rice, maize*) enveloppe *f*; (*of peas*) cosse *f*.
husky [hus'kē] *a* rauque; (*burly*) costaud(e) ♦ *n* chien *m* esquimau *or* de traîneau.
hustings [hus'tingz] *npl* (*Brit* POL) plate-forme électorale.
hustle [hus'əl] *vt* pousser, bousculer ♦ *n* bousculade *f*; **~ and bustle** *n* tourbillon *m* (d'activité).
hut [hut] *n* hutte *f*; (*shed*) cabane *f*.
hutch [huch] *n* clapier *m*.
hyacinth [hī'əsinth] *n* jacinthe *f*.
hybrid [hī'brid] *a, n* hybride (*m*).
hydrant [hī'drənt] *n* prise *f* d'eau; (*also*: **fire ~**) bouche *f* d'incendie.
hydraulic [hīdrô'lik] *a* hydraulique.
hydraulics [hīdrô'liks] *n* hydraulique *f*.
hydrochloric [hīdrəklôr'ik] *a*: **~ acid** acide *m* chlorhydrique.
hydroelectric [hīdrōilek'trik] *a* hydro-électrique.
hydrofoil [hī'drəfoil] *n* hydrofoil *m*.
hydrogen [hī'drəjən] *n* hydrogène *m*.
hydrogen bomb *n* bombe *f* à hydrogène.
hydrophobia [hīdrəfō'bēə] *n* hydrophobie *f*.
hydroplane [hī'drəplān] *n* (*seaplane*) hydra-vion *m*; (*jetfoil*) hydroglisseur *m*.
hyena [hīē'nə] *n* hyène *f*.
hygiene [hī'jēn] *n* hygiène *f*.
hygienic [hījēen'ik] *a* hygiénique.
hymn [him] *n* hymne *m*; cantique *m*.
hype [hīp] *n* (*col*) matraquage *m* publicitaire *or* médiatique.
hyperactive [hīpûrak'tiv] *a* hyperactif(ive).
hypermarket [hī'pûrmârkit] *n* (*Brit*) hypermarché *m*.
hypertension [hīpûrten'chən] *n* (MED) hypertension *f*.
hyphen [hī'fən] *n* trait *m* d'union.
hypnosis [hipnō'sis] *n* hypnose *f*.
hypnotic [hipnät'ik] *a* hypnotique.
hypnotism [hip'nətizəm] *n* hypnotisme *m*.

hypnotist [hip'nətist] *n* hypnotiseur/euse.
hypnotize [hip'nətīz] *vt* hypnotiser.
hypoallergenic [hīpōalûrjcn'ik] *a* hypoallergi-que.
hypochondriac [hīpəkán'drēak] *n* hypo-condriaque *m/f*.
hypocrisy [hipák'rəsē] *n* hypocrisie *f*.
hypocrite [hip'əkrit] *n* hypocrite *m/f*.
hypocritical [hipəkrit'ikəl] *a* hypocrite.
hypodermic [hīpədûr'mik] *a* hypodermique ♦ *n* (*syringe*) seringue *f* hypodermique.
hypothermia [hīpōthûr'mēə] *n* hypothermie *f*.
hypothesis, *pl* **hypotheses** [hīpáth'əsis, -sēz] *n* hypothèse *f*.
hypothetic(al) [hīpəthet'ik(əl)] *a* hypothétique.
hysterectomy [histərek'təmē] *n* hystérectomie *f*.
hysteria [histē'rēə] *n* hystérie *f*.
hysterical [histär'ikəl] *a* hystérique; **to become ~** avoir une crise de nerfs.
hysterics [histär'iks] *npl* (violente) crise de nerfs; (*laughter*) crise de rire; **to have ~** avoir une crise de nerfs; attraper un fou rire.
Hz *abbr* (= *hertz*) Hz.

I

I, i [ī] *n* (*letter*) I, i *m*; **I for Item** I comme Irma.
I [ī] *pronoun* je; (*before vowel*) j'; (*stressed*) moi ♦ *abbr* (= *island, isle*) I; (*US*) = **inter-state (highway)**.
IA *abbr* (US MAIL) = *Iowa*.
IAEA *n abbr* = **International Atomic Energy Agency**.
IBA *n abbr* (*Brit*: = *Independent Broadcasting Authority*) ≈ CNCL *f* (= *Commission natio-nale de la communication audio-visuelle*).
Iberian [ibēr'ēən] *a* ibérien, ibérien(ne).
Iberian Peninsula *n*: **the ~** la péninsule Ibé-rique.
IBEW *n abbr* (US: = *International Brother-hood of Electrical Workers*) syndicat interna-tional des électriciens.
i/c *abbr* (*Brit*) = **in charge**.
ICC *n abbr* (= *International Chamber of Commerce*) CCI *f*; (*US*) = *Interstate Commerce Commission*.
ice [īs] *n* glace *f*; (*on road*) verglas *m* ♦ *vt* (*cake*) glacer; (*drink*) faire rafraîchir ♦ *vi* (*also*: **~ over**) geler; (*also*: **~ up**) se givrer; **to put sth on ~** (*fig*) mettre qch en attente.
Ice Age *n* ère *f* glaciaire.
ice ax, (*Brit*) **ice axe** *n* piolet *m*.
iceberg [īs'bûrg] *n* iceberg *m*; **the tip of the ~** (*also fig*) la partie émergée de l'iceberg.
icebox [īs'báks] *n* (US) réfrigérateur *m*; (*Brit*) compartiment *m* à glace; (*insulated box*) gla-cière *f*.
icebreaker [īs'brākûr] *n* brise-glace *m*.
ice bucket *n* seau *m* à glace.
ice-cold [īs'kōld] *a* glacé(e).

ice cream n glace f.

ice cube n glaçon m.

iced [īst] a (drink) frappé(e); (coffee, tea, also cake) glacé(e).

ice hockey n hockey m sur glace.

Iceland [īs'lənd] n Islande f.

Icelander [īs'lândûr] n Islandais/e.

Icelandic [īslan'dik] a islandais(e) ♦ n (LING) islandais m.

ice lolly [īs lâl'ē] n (Brit) Esquimau m ®.

ice pick n pic m à glace.

ice rink n patinoire f.

ice-skate [īs'skāt] n patin m à glace ♦ vi faire du patin à glace.

ice-skating [īs'skāting] n patinage m (sur glace).

icicle [ī'sikəl] n glaçon m (naturel).

icing [ī'sing] n (AVIAT etc) givrage m; (CULIN) glaçage m.

icing sugar n (Brit) sucre m glace.

ICJ n abbr = **International Court of Justice.**

icon [ī'kân] n icône f.

ICR n abbr (US) = Institute for Cancer Research.

ICU n abbr = **intensive care unit.**

icy [ī'sē] a glacé(e); (road) verglacé(e); (weather, temperature) glacial(e).

ID abbr (US MAIL) = Idaho.

I'd [īd] = I would, I had.

Ida. abbr (US) = Idaho.

ID card n carte f d'identité.

idea [īdē'ə] n idée f; **good ~!** bonne idée!; **to have an ~ that** ... avoir idée que ...; **I haven't the least ~** je n'ai pas la moindre idée.

ideal [īdē'əl] n idéal m ♦ a idéal(e).

idealist [īdē'əlist] n idéaliste m/f.

ideally [īdē'əlē] ad idéalement, dans l'idéal; ~ **the book should have** ... l'idéal serait que le livre ait ....

identical [īden'tikəl] a identique.

identification [īdentəfəkā'shən] n identification f; **means of ~** pièce f d'identité.

identify [īden'təfī] vt identifier ♦ vi: **to ~ with** s'identifier à.

Identikit [īden'təkit] n ® (Brit): ~ **(picture)** portrait-robot m.

identity [īden'titē] n identité f.

identity card n (Brit) carte f d'identité.

identity parade n (Brit) parade f d'identification.

ideological [īdēəlâj'ikəl] a idéologique.

ideology [īdēâl'əjē] n idéologie f.

idiocy [id'ēəsē] n idiotie f, stupidité f.

idiom [id'ēəm] n langue f, idiome m; (phrase) expression f idiomatique.

idiomatic [idēəmat'ik] a idiomatique.

idiosyncrasy [idēəsing'krəsē] n particularité f, caractéristique f.

idiot [id'ēət] n idiot/e, imbécile m/f.

idiotic [idēât'ik] a idiot(e), bête, stupide.

idle [ī'dəl] a sans occupation, désœuvré(e); (lazy) oisif(ive), paresseux(euse); (unemployed) au chômage; (machinery) au repos; (question, pleasures) vain(e), futile ♦ vi (engine) tourner au ralenti; **to lie ~** être arrêté, ne pas fonctionner.

　idle away vt: to ~ **away one's time** passer son temps à ne rien faire.

idleness [ī'dəlnis] n désœuvrement m; oisi-

veté f.

idler [īd'lûr] n désœuvré/e; oisif/ive.

idle time n (COMM) temps mort.

idol [ī'dəl] n idole f.

idolize [ī'dəlīz] vt idolâtrer, adorer.

idyllic [īdil'ik] a idyllique.

i.e. abbr (= id est: that is) c. à d., c'est-à-dire.

if [if] cj si ♦ n: **there are a lot of ~s and buts** il y a beaucoup de si mpl et de mais mpl; **I'd be pleased ~ you could do it** je serais très heureux si vous pouviez le faire; ~ **necessary** si nécessaire, le cas échéant; ~ **only he were here** si seulement il était là; ~ **only to show him my gratitude** ne serait-ce que pour lui témoigner ma gratitude.

igloo [ig'lōō] n igloo m.

ignite [ignīt'] vt mettre le feu à, enflammer ♦ vi s'enflammer.

ignition [ignish'ən] n (AUT) allumage m; **to switch on/off the ~** mettre/couper le contact.

ignition key n (AUT) clé f de contact.

ignoble [ignō'bəl] a ignoble, indigne.

ignominious [ignəmin'ēəs] a honteux(euse), ignominieux(euse).

ignoramus [ignərā'məs] n personne f ignare.

ignorance [ig'nûrəns] n ignorance f; **to keep sb in ~ of sth** tenir qn dans l'ignorance de qch.

ignorant [ig'nûrənt] a ignorant(e); **to be ~ of** (subject) ne rien connaître en; (events) ne pas être au courant de.

ignore [ignôr'] vt ne tenir aucun compte de, ne pas relever; (person) faire semblant de ne pas reconnaître, ignorer; (fact) méconnaître.

ikon [ī'kân] n = **icon.**

IL abbr (US MAIL) = Illinois.

ILA n abbr (US: = International Longshoremen's Association) syndicat international des dockers.

ILGWU n abbr (US: = International Ladies' Garment Workers Union) syndicat des employés de l'habillement féminin.

Ill. abbr (US) = Illinois.

ill [il] a (sick) malade; (bad) mauvais(e) ♦ n mal m ♦ ad: **to speak/think ~ of sb** dire/penser du mal de qn; **to take** or **be taken ~** tomber malade.

I'll [īl] = I will, I shall.

ill-advised [il'advīzd'] a (decision) peu judicieux(euse); (person) malavisé(e).

ill-at-ease [il'ətēz'] a mal à l'aise.

ill-considered [il'kənsid'ûrd] a (plan) inconsidéré(e), irréfléchi(e).

ill-disposed [il'dispōzd'] a: **to be ~ towards sb/sth** être mal disposé(e) envers qn/qch.

illegal [ilē'gəl] a illégal(e).

illegally [ilē'gəlē] ad illégalement.

illegible [ilej'əbəl] a illisible.

illegitimate [ilijit'əmit] a illégitime.

ill-fated [il'fā'tid] a malheureux(euse); (day) néfaste.

ill-favored, (Brit) ill-favoured [il'fā'vûrd] a déplaisant(e).

ill feeling n (Brit) ressentiment m, rancune f.

ill-gotten [il'gât'ən] a (gains etc) mal acquis(e).

illicit [ilis'it] a illicite.

ill-informed [il'infôrmd'] a (judgment) erro-

né(e); (person) mal renseigné(e).
illiterate [ilit'ûrit] a illettré(e); (letter) plein(e) de fautes.
ill-mannered [il'man'ûrd] a impoli(e), grossier(ière).
illness [il'nis] n maladie f.
illogical [ilâj'ikəl] a illogique.
ill-suited [il'sōō'tid] a (couple) mal assorti(e); **he is ~ to the job** il n'est pas vraiment fait pour ce travail.
ill-timed [il'tîmd] a inopportun(e).
ill-treat [il'trēt] vt maltraiter.
ill-treatment [il'trēt'mənt] n mauvais traitement.
illuminate [ilōō'mənāt] vt (room, street) éclairer; (building) illuminer; **~d sign** n enseigne lumineuse.
illuminating [ilōō'mənāting] a éclairant(e).
illumination [ilōōmənā'shən] n éclairage m; illumination f.
illusion [ilōō'zhən] n illusion f; **to be under the ~ that** avoir l'illusion que.
illusive [ilōō'siv], **illusory** [ilōō'sərē] a illusoire.
illustrate [il'əstrāt] vt illustrer.
illustration [iləstrā'shən] n illustration f.
illustrator [il'əstrātûr] n illustrateur/trice.
illustrious [ilus'trēəs] a illustre.
ill will n malveillance f.
ILO n abbr (= International Labour Organization) OIT f.
ILWU n abbr (US: = International Longshoremen's and Warehousemen's Union) syndicat international des dockers et des magaziniers.
I'm [īm] = I am.
image [im'ij] n image f; (public face) image de marque.
imagery [im'ijrē] n images fpl.
imaginable [imaj'ənəbəl] a imaginable.
imaginary [imaj'ənârē] a imaginaire.
imagination [imajənā'shən] n imagination f.
imaginative [imaj'ənətiv] a imaginatif(ive), plein(e) d'imagination.
imagine [imaj'in] vt s'imaginer; (suppose) imaginer, supposer.
imbalance [imbal'əns] n déséquilibre m.
imbecile [im'bəsil] n imbécile m/f.
imbue [imbyōō'] vt: **to ~ sth with** imprégner qch de.
IMF n abbr = International Monetary Fund.
imitate [im'ətāt] vt imiter.
imitation [imətā'shən] n imitation f.
imitator [im'ətātûr] n imitateur/trice.
immaculate [imak'yəlit] a impeccable; (REL) immaculé(e).
immaterial [imətē'rēəl] a sans importance, insignifiant(e).
immature [imətōōr'] a (fruit) qui n'est pas mûr(e); (person) qui manque de maturité.
immaturity [imətōō'ritē] n immaturité f.
immeasurable [imezh'ûrəbəl] a incommensurable.
immediacy [imē'dēəsē] n (of events etc) caractère or rapport immédiat; (of needs) urgence f.
immediate [imē'dēit] a immédiat(e).
immediately [imē'dēitlē] ad (at once) immédiatement; **~ next to** juste à côté de.
immense [imens'] a immense; énorme.
immensity [imen'sitē] n immensité f.

immerse [imûrs'] vt immerger, plonger; **to ~ sth in** plonger qch dans.
immersion heater [imûr'zhən hē'tûr] n chauffe-eau m électrique.
immigrant [im'əgrənt] n immigrant/e; (already established) immigré/e.
immigration [iməgrā'shən] n immigration f.
immigration authorities npl service m de l'immigration.
immigration laws npl lois fpl sur l'immigration.
imminent [im'ənənt] a imminent(e).
immobile [imō'bəl] a immobile.
immobilize [imō'bəlīz] vt immobiliser.
immoderate [imâd'ûrit] a immodéré(e), démesuré(e).
immodest [imâd'ist] a (indecent) indécent(e); (boasting) pas modeste, présomptueux(euse).
immoral [imôr'əl] a immoral(e).
immorality [imərəl'itē] n immoralité f.
immortal [imôr'təl] a, n immortel(le).
immortalize [imôr'təlīz] vt immortaliser.
immovable [imōō'vəbəl] a (object) fixe; immobilier(ière); (person) inflexible; (opinion) immuable.
immune [imyōōn'] a: **~ (to)** immunisé(e) (contre).
immunity [imyōō'nitē] n immunité f; **diplomatic ~** immunité diplomatique.
immunization [imyōōnəzā'shən] n immunisation f.
immunize [im'yənīz] vt immuniser.
imp [imp] n (small devil) lutin m; (child) petit diable.
impact [im'pakt] n choc m, impact m; (fig) impact.
impair [impär'] vt détériorer, diminuer.
impale [impāl'] vt empaler.
impart [impârt'] vt (make known) communiquer, transmettre; (bestow) confier, donner.
impartial [impâr'shəl] a impartial(e).
impartiality [impârshēal'itē] n impartialité f.
impassable [impas'əbəl] a infranchissable; (road) impraticable.
impasse [im'pas] n (fig) impasse f.
impassioned [impash'ənd] a passionné(e).
impassive [impas'iv] a impassible.
impatience [impā'shəns] n impatience f.
impatient [impā'shənt] a impatient(e); **to get** or **grow ~** s'impatienter.
impeach [impēch'] vt accuser, attaquer; (public official) mettre en accusation.
impeachment [impēch'mənt] n (LAW) (mise f en) accusation f.
impeccable [impek'əbəl] a impeccable, parfait(e).
impecunious [impəkyōō'nēəs] a sans ressources.
impede [impēd'] vt gêner.
impediment [imped'əmənt] n obstacle m; (also: **speech ~**) défaut m d'élocution.
impel [impel'] vt (force): **to ~ sb (to do sth)** forcer qn (à faire qch).
impending [impen'ding] a imminent(e).
impenetrable [impen'itrəbəl] a impénétrable.
imperative [impär'ətiv] a nécessaire; urgent(e), pressant(e); (tone) impérieux(euse) ♦ n (LING) impératif m.
imperceptible [impûrsep'təbəl] a impercep-

tible.

imperfect [impûr'fïkt] *a* imparfait(e); *(goods etc)* défectueux(euse) ♦ *n* (*LING*: *also*: ~ **tense**) imparfait *m*.

imperfection [impûrfek'shən] *n* imperfection *f*; défectuosité *f*.

imperial [impēr'ēəl] *a* impérial(e); (*Brit*: *measure*) légal(e).

imperialism [impēr'ēəlizəm] *n* impérialisme *m*.

imperil [impär'əl] *vt* méttre en péril.

imperious [impēr'ēəs] *a* impérieux(euse).

impersonal [impûr'sənəl] *a* impersonnel(le).

impersonate [impûr'sənāt] *vt* se faire passer pour; (*THEATER*) imiter.

impersonation [impûrsənā'shən] *n* (*LAW*) usurpation *f* d'identité; (*THEATER*) imitation *f*.

impersonator [impûr'sənātûr] *n* imposteur *m*; (*THEATER*) imitateur/trice.

impertinence [impûr'tənəns] *n* impertinence *f*, insolence *f*.

impertinent [impûr'tənənt] *a* impertinent(e), insolent(e).

imperturbable [impûrtûr'bəbəl] *a* imperturbable.

impervious [impûr'vēəs] *a* imperméable; (*fig*): ~ **to** insensible à; inaccessible à.

impetuous [impech'ōōəs] *a* impétueux(euse), fougueux(euse).

impetus [im'pitəs] *n* impulsion *f*; (*of runner*) élan *m*.

impinge [impinj'] : **to** ~ **on** *vt fus* (*person*) affecter, toucher; (*rights*) empiéter sur.

impish [imp'ish] *a* espiègle.

implacable [implak'əbəl] *a* implacable.

implant [implant'] *vt* (*MED*) implanter; (*fig*) inculquer.

implausible [implô'zəbəl] *a* peu plausible.

implement *n* [im'pləmənt] outil *m*, instrument *m*; (*for cooking*) ustensile *m* ♦ *vt* [im'pləmənt] exécuter, mettre à effet.

implicate [im'plikāt] *vt* impliquer, compromettre.

implication [implikā'shən] *n* implication *f*; **by** ~ indirectement.

implicit [implis'it] *a* implicite; (*complete*) absolu(e), sans réserve.

implicitly [implis'itlē] *ad* implicitement; absolument, sans réserve.

implore [implôr'] *vt* implorer, supplier.

imply [implī'] *vt* (*hint*) suggérer, laisser entendre; (*mean*) indiquer, supposer.

impolite [impəlīt'] *a* impoli(e).

imponderable [impän'dûrəbəl] *a* impondérable.

import *vt* [impôrt'] importer ♦ *n* [im'pôrt] (*COMM*) importation *f*; (*meaning*) portée *f*, signification *f* ♦ *cpd* (*duty, license etc*) d'importation.

importance [impôr'təns] *n* importance *f*; **to be of great/little** ~ avoir beaucoup/peu d'importance.

important [impôr'tənt] *a* important(e); **it is** ~ **that** il importe que, il est important que; **it's not** ~ c'est sans importance, ce n'est pas important.

importantly [impôr'təntlē] *ad* (*with an air of importance*) d'un air important;

(*essentially*): **but, more** ~ ... mais, (ce qui est) plus important encore ....

importation [impôrtā'shən] *n* importation *f*.

imported [impôr'tid] *a* importé(e), d'importation.

importer [impôr'tûr] *n* importateur/trice.

impose [impōz'] *vt* imposer ♦ *vi*: **to** ~ **on sb** abuser de la gentillesse de qn.

imposing [impō'zing] *a* imposant(e), impressionnant(e).

imposition [impəzish'ən] *n* (*of tax etc*) imposition *f*; **to be an** ~ **on** (*person*) abuser de la gentillesse *or* la bonté de.

impossibility [impâsəbil'itē] *n* impossibilité *f*.

impossible [impâs'əbəl] *a* impossible; **it is** ~ **for me to leave** il m'est impossible de partir.

impostor [impâs'tûr] *n* imposteur *m*.

impotence [im'pətəns] *n* impuissance *f*.

impotent [im'pətənt] *a* impuissant(e).

impound [impound'] *vt* confisquer, saisir.

impoverished [impâv'ûrisht] *a* pauvre, appauvri(e).

impracticable [imprak'tikəbəl] *a* impraticable.

impractical [imprak'tikəl] *a* pas pratique; (*person*) qui manque d'esprit pratique.

imprecise [imprisīs'] *a* imprécis(e).

impregnable [impreg'nəbəl] *a* (*fortress*) imprenable; (*fig*) inattaquable; irréfutable.

impregnate [impreg'nāt] *vt* imprégner; (*fertilize*) féconder.

impresario [imprəsâ'rēō] *n* impresario *m*.

impress [impres'] *vt* impressionner, faire impression sur; (*mark*) imprimer, marquer; **to** ~ **sth on sb** faire bien comprendre qch à qn.

impression [impresh'ən] *n* impression *f*; (*of stamp, seal*) empreinte *f*; **to make a good/bad** ~ **on sb** faire bonne/mauvaise impression sur qn; **to be under the** ~ **that** avoir l'impression que.

impressionable [impresh'ənəbəl] *a* impressionnable, sensible.

impressionist [impresh'ənist] *n* impressionniste *m/f*.

impressive [impres'iv] *a* impressionnant(e).

imprint [im'print] *n* empreinte *f*; (*PUBLISHING*) notice *f*; (: *label*) nom *m* (de collection *or* d'éditeur).

imprinted [imprin'tid] *a*: ~ **on** imprimé(e) sur; (*fig*) imprimé(e) *or* gravé(e) dans.

imprison [impriz'ən] *vt* emprisonner, mettre en prison.

imprisonment [impriz'ənmənt] *n* emprisonnement *m*.

improbable [impráb'əbəl] *a* improbable; (*excuse*) peu plausible.

impromptu [imprâmp'tōō] *a* impromptu(e) ♦ *ad* impromptu.

improper [imprâp'ûr] *a* (*wrong*) incorrect(e); (*unsuitable*) déplacé(e), de mauvais goût; indécent(e).

impropriety [imprəprī'ətē] *n* inconvenance *f*; (*of expression*) impropriété *f*.

improve [improōv'] *vt* améliorer ♦ *vi* s'améliorer; (*pupil etc*) faire des progrès.

improve (up)on *vt fus* (*offer*) enchérir sur.

improvement [improōv'mənt] *n* amélioration *f*; (*of pupil etc*) progrès *m*; **to make** ~**s to** apporter des améliorations à.

improvisation [imprəvəzā'shən] *n* improvisa-

tion *f*.
improvise [im'prəvīz] *vt*, *vi* improviser.
imprudence [imprōōd'əns] *n* imprudence *f*.
imprudent [imprōōd'ənt] *a* imprudent(e).
impudent [im'pyədənt] *a* impudent(e).
impugn [impyōōn'] *vt* contester, attaquer.
impulse [im'puls] *n* impulsion *f*; **on** ~ impulsivement, sur un coup de tête.
impulse buying [im'puls bī'ing] *n* achat *m* d'impulsion.
impulsive [impul'siv] *a* impulsif(ive).
impunity [impyōō'nitē] *n*: **with** ~ impunément.
impure [impyōōr'] *a* impur(e).
impurity [impyōōr'itē] *n* impureté *f*.
IN *abbr* (*US MAIL*) = *Indiana*.
in [in] *prep* dans; (*with time: during, within*): ~ **May/2 days** en mai/2 jours; (: *after*): ~ **2 weeks** dans 2 semaines; (*with substance*) en; (*with town*) à; (*with country*): **it's** ~ **France/Portugal** c'est en France/au Portugal ♦ *ad* dedans, à l'intérieur; (*fashionable*) à la mode; **is he** ~? est-il là?; ~ **the United States** aux États-Unis; ~ **1992** en 1992; ~ **spring/fall** au printemps/en automne; ~ **the morning** le matin; **dans la matinée**; ~ **the country** à la campagne; ~ **town** en ville; ~ **here/there** ici/là(-dedans); ~ **the sun** au soleil; ~ **the rain** sous la pluie; ~ **French** en français; ~ **writing** par écrit; ~ **pencil** au crayon; **to pay** ~ **dollars** payer en dollars; **a man** ~ **10** un homme sur 10; **once** ~ **a hundred years** une fois tous les cent ans; ~ **hundreds** par centaines; **the best pupil** ~ **the class** le meilleur élève de la classe; **to be** ~ **insurance/publishing** être dans l'assurance/l'édition; ~ **saying this** en disant ceci; **their party is** ~ leur parti est au pouvoir; **to ask sb** ~ inviter qn à entrer; **to run/limp** *etc* ~ entrer en courant/boitant *etc*; **the** ~**s and outs of** les tenants et aboutissants de.
in., **ins** *abbr* = **inch(es)**.
inability [inəbil'ətē] *n* incapacité *f*; ~ **to pay** incapacité de payer.
inaccessible [inakses'əbəl] *a* inaccessible.
inaccuracy [inak'yûrəsē] *n* inexactitude *f*; manque *m* de précision.
inaccurate [inak'yûrit] *a* inexact(e); (*person*) qui manque de précision.
inaction [inak'shən] *n* inaction *f*, inactivité *f*.
inactivity [inaktiv'itē] *n* inactivité *f*.
inadequacy [inad'əkwəsē] *n* insuffisance *f*.
inadequate [inad'əkwit] *a* insuffisant(e), inadéquat(e).
inadmissible [inədmis'əbəl] *a* (*behavior*) inadmissible; (*LAW: evidence*) irrecevable.
inadvertent [inədvûr'tənt] *a* (*mistake*) commis(e) par inadvertance.
inadvertently [inədvûr'təntlē] *ad* par mégarde.
inadvisable [inədvī'zəbəl] *a* à déconseiller; **it is** ~ **to** il est déconseillé de.
inane [inān'] *a* inepte, stupide.
inanimate [inan'əmit] *a* inanimé(e).
inapplicable [inap'likəbəl] *a* inapplicable.
inappropriate [inəprō'prēit] *a* inopportun(e), mal à propos; (*word, expression*) impropre.
inapt [inapt'] *a* inapte; peu approprié(e).

inaptitude [inap'tətōōd] *n* inaptitude *f*.
inarticulate [inârtik'yəlit] *a* (*person*) qui s'exprime mal; (*speech*) indistinct(e).
inasmuch as [inəzmuch' az] *ad* dans la mesure où; (*seeing that*) attendu que.
inattention [inəten'chən] *n* manque *m* d'attention.
inattentive [inəten'tiv] *a* inattentif(ive), distrait(e);r négligent(e).
inaudible [inô'dəbəl] *a* inaudible.
inaugural [inô'gyûrəl] *a* inaugural(e).
inaugurate [inô'gyərāt] *vt* inaugurer; (*president, official*) investir de ses fonctions.
inauguration [inôgyərā'shən] *n* inauguration *f*; investiture *f*.
inauspicious [inôspish'əs] *a* peu propice.
in-between [in'bitwēn'] *a* entre les deux.
inborn [in'bôrn] *a* (*feeling*) inné(e); (*defect*) congénital(e).
inbred [in'bred] *a* inné(e), naturel(le); (*family*) consanguin(e).
inbreeding [in'brēding] *n* croisement *m* d'animaux de même souche; unions consanguines.
Inc. *abbr* = **incorporated**.
Inca [ing'kə] *a* (*also*: ~**n**) inca *inv* ♦ *n* Inca *m/f*.
incalculable [inkal'kyələbəl] *a* incalculable.
incapability [inkāpəbil'ətē] *n* incapacité *f*.
incapable [inkā'pəbəl] *a*: ~ (**of**) incapable (de).
incapacitate [inkəpas'ətāt] *vt*: **to** ~ **sb from doing** rendre qn incapable de faire.
incapacitated [inkəpas'ətātid] *a* (*LAW*) frappé(e) d'incapacité.
incapacity [inkəpas'itē] *n* incapacité *f*.
incarcerate [inkâr'sûrit] *vt* incarcérer.
incarnate *a* [inkâr'nit] incarné(e) ♦ *vt* [inkâr'nāt] incarner.
incarnation [inkârnā'shən] *n* incarnation *f*.
incendiary [insen'dēârē] *a* incendiaire ♦ *n* (*bomb*) bombe *f* incendiaire.
incense *n* [in'sens] encens *m* ♦ *vt* [insens'] (*anger*) mettre en colère.
incense burner *n* encensoir *m*.
incentive [insen'tiv] *n* encouragement *m*, raison *f* de se donner de la peine.
incentive scheme *n* système *m* de primes d'encouragement.
inception [insep'shən] *n* commencement *m*, début *m*.
incessant [inses'ənt] *a* incessant(e).
incessantly [inses'əntlē] *ad* sans cesse, constamment.
incest [in'sest] *n* inceste *m*.
inch [inch] *n* pouce *m* (= 25 mm; 12 in a foot); **within an** ~ **of** à deux doigts de; **he wouldn't give an** ~ (*fig*) il n'a pas voulu céder d'un pouce *or* faire la plus petite concession.
inch forward *vi* avancer petit à petit.
incidence [in'sidəns] *n* (*of crime, disease*) fréquence *f*.
incident [in'sidənt] *n* incident *m*; (*in book*) péripétie *f*.
incidental [insiden'təl] *a* accessoire; (*unplanned*) accidentel(le); ~ **to** qui accompagne; ~ **expenses** faux frais *mpl*.
incidentally [insiden'təlē] *ad* (*by the way*) à propos.

incidental music *n* musique *f* de fond.

incinerate [insin'ərāt] *vt* incinérer.

incinerator [insin'ərātŭr] *n* incinérateur *m*.

incipient [insip'ēənt] *a* naissant(e).

incision [insizh'ən] *n* incision *f*.

incisive [insī'siv] *a* incisif(ive); mordant(e).

incisor [insī'zŭr] *n* incisive *f*.

incite [insīt'] *vt* inciter, pousser.

incl. *abbr* = **including, inclusive (of)**.

inclement [inklem'ənt] *a* inclément(e), rigoureux(euse).

inclination [inklənā'shən] *n* inclination *f*.

incline *n* [in'klīn] pente *f*, plan incliné ♦ *vb* [inklīn'] *vt* incliner ♦ *vi*: **to ~ to** avoir tendance à; **to be ~d to do** être enclin(e) à faire; *(have a tendency to do)* avoir tendance à faire; **to be well ~d towards sb** être bien disposé(e) à l'égard de qn.

include [inklood'] *vt* inclure, comprendre; **the tip is/is not ~d** le service est compris/n'est pas compris.

including [inklood'ing] *prep* y compris; **~ tip** service compris.

inclusion [inkloo'zhən] *n* inclusion *f*.

inclusive [inkloo'siv] *a* inclus(e), compris(e); **$50 ~ of all surcharges** 50 dollars tous frais compris.

inclusive terms *npl* *(Brit)* prix tout compris.

incognito [inkâgnē'tō] *ad* incognito.

incoherent [inkōhē'rənt] *a* incohérent(e).

income [in'kum] *n* revenu *m*; **gross/net ~** revenu brut/net; **~ and expenditure account** compte *m* de recettes et de dépenses.

income tax *n* impôt *m* sur le revenu.

income tax auditor, *(Brit)* **income tax inspector** *n* inspecteur *m* des contributions directes.

income tax return *n* déclaration *f* des revenus.

incoming [in'kuming] *a* *(passengers, mail)* à l'arrivée; *(government, tenant)* nouveau(nouvelle); **~ tide** marée montante.

incommunicado [inkəmyōōnəkâ'dō] *a*: **to hold sb ~** tenir qn au secret.

incomparable [inkâm'pûrəbəl] *a* incomparable.

incompatible [inkəmpat'əbəl] *a* incompatible.

incompetence [inkâm'pitəns] *n* incompétence *f*, incapacité *f*.

incompetent [inkâm'pitənt] *a* incompétent(e), incapable.

incomplete [inkəmplēt'] *a* incomplet(ète).

incomprehensible [inkâmprihen'səbəl] *a* incompréhensible.

inconceivable [inkənsē'vəbəl] *a* inconcevable.

inconclusive [inkənkloo'siv] *a* peu concluant(e); *(argument)* peu convaincant(e).

incongruous [inkâng'grōōəs] *a* peu approprié(e); *(remark, act)* incongru(e), déplacé(e).

inconsequential [inkânsəkwen'chəl] *a* sans importance.

inconsiderable [inkənsid'ûrəbəl] *a*: **not ~** non négligeable.

inconsiderate [inkənsid'ûrit] *a* *(action)* inconsidéré(e); *(person)* qui manque d'égards.

inconsistency [inkânsis'tənsē] *n* *(of actions etc)* inconséquence *f*; *(of work)* irrégularité

f; *(of statement etc)* incohérence *f*.

inconsistent [inkânsis'tənt] *a* inconséquent(e); irregulier(ière); peu cohérent(e); **~ with** en contradiction avec.

inconsolable [inkânsō'ləbəl] *a* inconsolable.

inconspicuous [inkənspik'yōōəs] *a* qui passe inaperçu(e); *(color, dress)* discret(ète); **to make o.s. ~** ne pas se faire remarquer.

inconstant [inkân'stənt] *a* inconstant(e); variable.

incontinence [inkân'tənəns] *n* incontinence *f*.

incontinent [inkân'tənənt] *a* incontinent(e).

incontrovertible [inkântrəvûr'təbəl] *a* irréfutable.

inconvenience [inkənvēn'yəns] *n* inconvénient *m*; *(trouble)* dérangement *m* ♦ *vt* déranger; **don't ~ yourself** ne vous dérangez pas.

inconvenient [inkənvēn'yənt] *a* malcommode; *(time, place)* mal choisi(e), qui ne convient pas; **that time is very ~ for me** c'est un moment qui ne me convient pas du tout.

incorporate [inkôr'pûrāt] *vt* incorporer; *(contain)* contenir ♦ *vi* fusionner; *(two firms)* se constituer en société.

incorporated [inkôr'pərātid] *a*: **~ company** *(US: abbr* **Inc.***)* ≈ société *f* anonyme (S.A.).

incorrect [inkərekt'] *a* incorrect(e); *(opinion, statement)* inexact(e).

incorrigible [inkôr'ijəbəl] *a* incorrigible.

incorruptible [inkərup'təbəl] *a* incorruptible.

increase *n* [in'krēs] augmentation *f* ♦ *vi*, *vt* [inkrēs'] augmenter; **an ~ of 5%** une augmentation de 5%; **to be on the ~** être en augmentation.

increasing [inkrēs'ing] *a* croissant(e).

increasingly [inkrēs'inglē] *ad* de plus en plus.

incredible [inkred'əbəl] *a* incroyable.

incredulous [inkrej'ələs] *a* incrédule.

increment [in'krəmənt] *n* augmentation *f*.

incriminate [inkrim'ənāt] *vt* incriminer, compromettre.

incriminating [inkrim'ənāting] *a* compromettant(e).

incrust [inkrust'] *vt* = **encrust**.

incubate [in'kyəbāt] *vt* *(egg)* couver, incuber ♦ *vi* *(eggs)* couver; *(disease)* couver.

incubation [inkyəbā'shən] *n* incubation *f*.

incubation period *n* période *f* d'incubation.

incubator [in'kyəbātûr] *n* incubateur *m*; *(for babies)* couveuse *f*.

inculcate [in'kulkāt] *vt*: **to ~ sth in sb** inculquer qch à qn.

incumbent [inkum'bənt] *a*: **it is ~ on him to ...** il lui incombe *or* appartient de ... ♦ *n* titulaire *m/f*.

incur [inkûr'] *vt* *(expenses)* encourir; *(anger, risk)* s'exposer à; *(debt)* contracter; *(loss)* subir.

incurable [inkyōōr'əbəl] *a* incurable.

incursion [inkûr'zhən] *n* incursion *f*.

Ind. *abbr* *(US)* = *Indiana*.

indebted [indet'id] *a*: **to be ~ to sb (for)** être redevable à qn (de).

indecency [indē'sənsē] *n* indécence *f*.

indecent [indē'sənt] *a* indécent(e), inconvenant(e).

indecent assault *n* *(Brit)* attentat *m* à la pudeur.

indecent exposure *n* outrage *m* public à la

pudeur.

indecipherable [indisï'fûrəbəl] *a* indéchiffrable.

indecision [indisizh'ən] *n* indécision *f*.

indecisive [indisï'siv] *a* indécis(e); (*discussion*) peu concluant(e).

indeed [indēd'] *ad* en effet, effectivement; (*furthermore*) d'ailleurs; **yes** ~! certainement!

indefatigable [indifat'əgəbəl] *a* infatigable.

indefensible [indifen'səbəl] *a* (*conduct*) indéfendable.

indefinable [indifï'nəbəl] *a* indéfinissable.

indefinite [indef'ənit] *a* indéfini(e); (*answer*) vague; (*period, number*) indéterminé(e).

indefinitely [indef'ənitlē] *ad* (*wait*) indéfiniment; (*speak*) vaguement, avec imprécision.

indelible [indel'əbəl] *a* indélébile.

indelicate [indel'əkit] *a* (*tactless*) indélicat(e), grossier(ière); (*not polite*) inconvenant(e), malséant(e).

indemnify [indem'nəfï] *vt* indemniser, dédommager.

indemnity [indem'nitē] *n* (*insurance*) assurance *f*, garantie *f*; (*compensation*) indemnité *f*.

indent [indent'] *vt* (*text*) commencer en retrait.

indentation [indentä'shən] *n* découpure *f*; (*TYP*) alinéa *m*; (*on metal*) bosse *f*.

independence [indipen'dəns] *n* indépendance *f*.

independent [indipen'dənt] *a* indépendant(e); **to become** ~ s'affranchir.

independently [indipen'dəntlē] *ad* de façon indépendante; ~ **of** indépendamment de.

indescribable [indiskrī'bəbəl] *a* indescriptible.

indeterminate [inditûr'mənit] *a* indéterminé(e).

index [in'dəks] *n* (*pl*: ~**es**: *in book*) index *m*; (: *in library etc*) catalogue *m*; (*pl*: **indices** [in'dīsēz]) (*ratio, sign*) indice *m*.

index card *n* fiche *f*.

indexed [in'dəkst] *a* (*US*) indexé(e) (sur le coût de la vie *etc*).

index finger *n* index *m*.

index-linked [in'dəkslingkt'] *a* (*Brit*) = **indexed**.

India [in'dēə] *n* Inde *f*.

Indian [in'dēən] *a* indien(ne) ♦ *n* Indien/ne.

Indian ink *n* encre *f* de Chine.

Indian Ocean *n*: **the** ~ l'océan Indien.

Indian summer *n* (*fig*) été indien, beaux jours en automne.

India paper *n* papier *m* bible.

indicate [in'dikāt] *vt* indiquer ♦ *vi* (*Brit AUT*): **to** ~ **left/right** mettre son clignotant à gauche/à droite.

indication [indikā'shən] *n* indication *f*, signe *m*.

indicative [indik'ətiv] *a* indicatif(ive) ♦ *n* (*LING*) indicatif *m*; **to be** ~ **of sth** être symptomatique de qch.

indicator [in'dikātûr] *n* (*sign*) indicateur *m*; (*Brit AUT*) clignotant *m*.

indices [in'disēz] *npl of* **index**.

indict [indīt'] *vt* accuser.

indictable [indīt'əbəl] *a* (*person*) passible de poursuites; ~ **offense** délit *m* tombant sous le coup de la loi.

indictment [indīt'mənt] *n* accusation *f*.

indifference [indif'ûrəns] *n* indifférence *f*.

indifferent [indif'ûrənt] *a* indifférent(e); (*poor*) médiocre, quelconque.

indigenous [indij'ənəs] *a* indigène.

indigestible [indijes'təbəl] *a* indigeste.

indigestion [indijes'chən] *n* indigestion *f*, mauvaise digestion.

indignant [indig'nənt] *a*: ~ (**at sth/with sb**) indigné(e) (de qch/contre qn).

indignation [indignā'shən] *n* indignation *f*.

indignity [indig'nitē] *n* indignité *f*, affront *m*.

indigo [in'dəgō] *a* indigo *inv* ♦ *n* indigo *m*.

indirect [indirekt'] *a* indirect(e).

indirectly [indirekt'lē] *ad* indirectement.

indiscreet [indiskrēt'] *a* indiscret(ète); (*rash*) imprudent(e).

indiscretion [indiskresh'ən] *n* (*see* **indiscreet**) indiscrétion *f*; imprudence *f*.

indiscriminate [indiskrim'ənit] *a* (*person*) qui manque de discernement; (*admiration*) aveugle; (*killings*) commis(e) au hasard.

indispensable [indispen'səbəl] *a* indispensable.

indisposed [indispōzd'] *a* (*unwell*) indisposé(e), souffrant(e).

indisposition [indispəzish'ən] *n* (*illness*) indisposition *f*, malaise *m*.

indisputable [indispyōō'təbəl] *a* incontestable, indiscutable.

indistinct [indistingkt'] *a* indistinct(e); (*memory, noise*) vague.

indistinguishable [indisting'gwishəbəl] *a* impossible à distinguer.

individual [indəvij'ōōəl] *n* individu *m* ♦ *a* individuel(le); (*characteristic*) particulier(ière), original(e).

individualist [indəvij'ōōəlist] *n* individualiste *m/f*.

individuality [indəvijōōal'itē] *n* individualité *f*.

individually [indəvij'ōōəlē] *ad* individuellement.

indivisible [indəviz'əbəl] *a* indivisible; (*MATH*) insécable.

Indo-China [in'dōchī'nə] *n* Indochine *f*.

indoctrinate [indâk'trənāt] *vt* endoctriner.

indoctrination [indâktrənā'shən] *n* endoctrinement *m*.

indolent [in'dələnt] *a* indolent(e), nonchalant(e).

Indonesia [indənē'zhə] *n* Indonésie *f*.

Indonesian [indənē'zhən] *a* indonésien(ne) ♦ *n* Indonésien/ne.

indoor [in'dôr] *a* d'intérieur; (*plant*) d'appartement; (*swimming pool*) couvert(e); (*sport, games*) pratiqué(e) en salle.

indoors [indôrz'] *ad* à l'intérieur; (*at home*) à la maison.

indubitable [indōō'bitəbəl] *a* indubitable, incontestable.

induce [indōōs'] *vt* persuader; (*bring about*) provoquer; **to** ~ **sb to do sth** inciter *or* pousser qn à faire qch.

inducement [indōōs'mənt] *n* incitation *f*; (*incentive*) but *m*; (*pej: bribe*) pot-de-vin *m*.

induct [indukt'] *vt* établir dans ses fonctions; (*fig*) initier.

induction [induk'shən] *n* (*MED: of birth*)

accouchement provoqué.
induction course n (*Brit*) stage m de mise au courant.
indulge [indulj'] vt (*whim*) céder à, satisfaire; (*child*) gâter ♦ vi: **to ~ in sth** s'offrir qch, se permettre qch; se livrer à qch.
indulgence [indul'jəns] n fantaisie f (que l'on s'offre); (*leniency*) indulgence f.
indulgent [indul'jənt] a indulgent(e).
industrial [indus'trēəl] a industriel(le); (*injury*) du travail; (*dispute*) ouvrier(ière).
industrial action n (*Brit*) action revendicative.
industrial estate n (*Brit*) zone industrielle.
industrialist [indus'trēəlist] n industriel m.
industrialize [indus'trēəlīz] vt industrialiser.
industrial park n (*US*) zone industrielle.
industrial relations npl relations fpl dans l'entreprise.
industrial tribunal n (*Brit*) ≈ conseil m de prud'hommes.
industrial unrest n (*Brit*) agitation sociale, conflits sociaux.
industrious [indus'trēəs] a travailleur(euse).
industry [in'dəstrē] n industrie f; (*diligence*) zèle m, application f.
inebriated [inēb'rēātid] a ivre.
inedible [ined'əbəl] a immangeable; (*plant etc*) non comestible.
ineffective [inifek'tiv], **ineffectual** [inefek'chooəl] a inefficace; incompétent(e).
inefficiency [inifish'ənsē] n inefficacité f.
inefficient [inifish'ənt] a inefficace.
inelegant [inel'əgənt] a peu élégant(e), inélégant(e).
ineligible [inel'ijəbəl] a (*candidate*) inéligible; **to be ~ for sth** ne pas avoir droit à qch.
inept [inept'] a inepte.
ineptitude [inep'tətōōd] n ineptie f.
inequality [inikwâl'itē] n inégalité f.
inequitable [inek'witəbəl] a inéquitable, inique.
ineradicable [inirad'ikəbəl] a indéracinable, tenace.
inert [inûrt'] a inerte.
inertia [inûr'shə] n inertie f.
inertia-reel seat belt [inûr'shərēl sēt' belt] n ceinture f de sécurité à enrouleur.
inescapable [inəskā'pəbəl] a inéluctable, inévitable.
inessential [inisen'chəl] a superflu(e).
inestimable [ines'təməbəl] a inestimable, incalculable.
inevitable [inev'itəbəl] a inévitable.
inevitably [inev'itəblē] ad inévitablement, fatalement.
inexact [in'igzakt'] a inexact(e).
inexcusable [inikskyōō'zəbəl] a inexcusable.
inexhaustible [inigzôs'təbəl] a inépuisable.
inexorable [inek'sûrəbəl] a inexorable.
inexpensive [inikspen'siv] a bon marché inv.
inexperience [inikspēr'ēəns] n inexpérience f, manque m d'expérience.
inexperienced [inikspēr'ēənst] a inexpérimenté(e); **to be ~ in sth** manquer d'expérience dans qch.
inexplicable [ineks'plikəbəl] a inexplicable.
inexpressible [inikspres'əbəl] a inexprimable; indicible.

inextricable [ineks'trikəbəl] a inextricable.
infallibility [infaləbil'ətē] n infaillibilité f.
infallible [infal'əbəl] a infaillible.
infamous [in'fəməs] a infâme, abominable.
infamy [in'fəmē] n infamie f.
infancy [in'fənsē] n petite enfance, bas âge; (*fig*) enfance, débuts mpl.
infant [in'fənt] n (*baby*) nourrisson m; (*young child*) petit(e) enfant.
infantile [in'fəntīl] a infantile.
infant mortality n mortalité f infantile.
infantry [in'fəntrē] n infanterie f.
infantryman [in'fəntrēmən] n fantassin m.
infant school n (*Brit*) classes fpl préparatoires (*entre 5 et 7 ans*).
infatuated [infach'ōōātid] a: **~ with** entiché(e) de; **to become ~ (with sb)** s'enticher (de qn).
infatuation [infachōōā'shən] n toquade f; engouement m.
infect [infekt'] vt infecter, contaminer; (*fig: pej*) corrompre; **~ed with** (*illness*) atteint(e) de; **to become ~ed** (*wound*) s'infecter.
infection [infek'shən] n infection f; contagion f.
infectious [infek'shəs] a infectieux(euse); (*also fig*) contagieux(euse).
infer [infûr'] vt: **to ~ (from)** conclure (de), déduire (de).
inference [in'fûrəns] n conclusion f, déduction f.
inferior [infē'rēûr] a inférieur(e); (*goods*) de qualité inférieure ♦ n inférieur/e; (*in rank*) subalterne m/f; **to feel ~** avoir un sentiment d'infériorité.
inferiority [infērēôr'itē] n infériorité f.
inferiority complex n complexe m d'infériorité.
infernal [infûr'nəl] a infernal(e).
infernally [infûr'nəlē] ad abominablement.
inferno [infûr'nō] n enfer m; brasier m.
infertile [infûr'təl] a stérile.
infertility [infûrtil'ətē] n infertilité f, stérilité f.
infested [infes'tid] a: **~ (with)** infesté(e) (de).
infidelity [infidel'itē] n infidélité f.
infighting [in'fiting] n querelles fpl internes.
infiltrate [infil'trāt] vt (*troops etc*) faire s'infiltrer; (*enemy line etc*) s'infiltrer dans ♦ vi s'infiltrer.
infinite [in'fənit] a infini(e); (*time, money*) illimité(e).
infinitely [in'fənitlē] ad infiniment.
infinitesimal [infinites'əməl] a infinitésimal(e).
infinitive [infin'ətiv] n infinitif m.
infinity [infin'ətē] n infinité f; (*also MATH*) infini m.
infirm [infûrm'] a infirme.
infirmary [infûr'mûrē] n hôpital m; (*in school, factory*) infirmerie f.
infirmity [infûr'mitē] n infirmité f.
inflamed [inflāmd'] a enflammé(e).
inflammable [inflam'əbəl] a inflammable.
inflammation [infləmā'shən] n inflammation f.
inflammatory [inflam'ətôrē] a (*speech*) incendiaire.
inflatable [inflā'təbəl] a gonflable.
inflate [inflāt'] vt (*tire, balloon*) gonfler; (*fig*) grossir; gonfler; faire monter.
inflated [inflā'tid] a (*style*) enflé(e); (*value*)

exagéré(e).

inflation [inflā'shən] *n* (*ECON*) inflation *f*.

inflationary [inflā'shənārē] *a* inflationniste.

inflection [inflek'shən] *n* inflexion *f*; (*ending*) désinence *f*.

inflexible [inflek'səbəl] *a* inflexible, rigide.

inflict [inflikt'] *vt*: **to ~ on** infliger à.

infliction [inflik'shən] *n* infliction *f*; affliction *f*.

in-flight [in'flīt] *a* (*refuelling*) en vol; (*service etc*) à bord.

inflow [in'flō] *n* afflux *m*.

influence [in'flŌŌəns] *n* influence *f* ♦ *vt* influencer; **under the ~ of** sous l'effet de; **under the ~ of drink** en état d'ébriété.

influential [inflŌŌen'chəl] *a* influent(e).

influenza [inflŌŌen'zə] *n* grippe *f*.

influx [in'fluks] *n* afflux *m*.

inform [infôrm'] *vt*: **to ~ sb (of)** informer *or* avertir qn (de) ♦ *vi*: **to ~ on sb** dénoncer qn, informer contre qn; **to ~ sb about** renseigner qn sur, mettre qn au courant de.

informal [infôr'məl] *a* (*person, manner*) simple, sans cérémonie; (*announcement, visit*) non officiel(le); **"dress ~"** ''tenue de ville''.

informality [infôrmal'itē] *n* simplicité *f*, absence *f* de cérémonie; caractère non officiel.

informal language *n* langage *m* de la conversation.

informally [infôr'məlē] *ad* sans cérémonie, en toute simplicité; non officiellement.

informant [infôr'mənt] *n* informateur/trice.

information [infûrmā'shən] *n* information(s) *f(pl)*; renseignements *mpl*; (*knowledge*) connaissances *fpl*; **to get ~ on** se renseigner sur; **a piece of ~** un renseignement; **for your ~** à titre d'information.

information bureau *n* bureau *m* de renseignements.

information desk *n* guichet *m* de renseignements.

information processing *n* traitement *m* de l'information.

information retrieval *n* recherche *f* (informatique) de renseignements.

information technology (IT) *n* informatique *f*.

informative [infôr'mətiv] *a* instructif(ive).

informed [infôrmd'] *a* (bien) informé(e); **an ~ guess** une hypothèse fondée sur la connaissance des faits.

informer [infôr'mûr] *n* dénonciateur/trice; (*also*: **police ~**) indicateur/trice.

infra dig [in'frə dig] *a abbr* (*col*: = *infra dignitatem*) au-dessous de ma (*or* sa *etc*) dignité.

infra-red [in'frəred'] *a* infrarouge.

infrastructure [in'frəstruk'chûr] *n* infrastructure *f*.

infrequent [infrē'kwint] *a* peu fréquent(e), rare.

infringe [infrinj'] *vt* enfreindre ♦ *vi*: **to ~ on** empiéter sur.

infringement [infrinj'mənt] *n*: **~ (of)** infraction *f* (à).

infuriate [infyŌŌr'ēāt] *vt* mettre en fureur.

infuriating [infyŌŌr'ēāting] *a* exaspérant(e).

infuse [infyŌŌz'] *vt*: **to ~ sb with sth** (*fig*) insuffler qch à qn.

infusion [infyŌŌ'zhən] *n* (*tea etc*) infusion *f*.

ingenious [injēn'yəs] *a* ingénieux(euse).

ingenuity [injənŌŌ'itē] *n* ingéniosité *f*.

ingenuous [injen'yŌŌəs] *a* franc(franche), ouvert(e).

ingot [ing'gət] *n* lingot *m*.

ingrained [ingrānd'] *a* enraciné(e).

ingratiate [ingrā'shēāt] *vt*: **to ~ o.s. with** s'insinuer dans les bonnes grâces de, se faire bien voir de.

ingratiating [ingrā'shēāting] *a* (*smile, speech*) insinuant(e); (*person*) patelin(e).

ingratitude [ingrat'ətŌŌd] *n* ingratitude *f*.

ingredient [ingrē'dēənt] *n* ingrédient *m*; élément *m*.

ingrowing [in'grōing], **ingrown** [in'grōn] *a*: **~ toenail** ongle incarné.

inhabit [inhab'it] *vt* habiter.

inhabitable [inhab'itəbəl] *a* habitable.

inhabitant [inhab'ətənt] *n* habitant/e.

inhale [inhāl'] *vt* inhaler; (*perfume*) respirer ♦ *vi* (*in smoking*) avaler la fumée.

inherent [inhär'ent] *a*: **~ (in *or* to)** inhérent(e) (à).

inherently [inhär'entlē] *ad* (*easy, difficult*) en soi; (*lazy*) fondamentalement.

inherit [inhär'it] *vt* hériter (de).

inheritance [inhär'itəns] *n* héritage *m*; **law of ~** droit *m* de la succession.

inheritance tax *n* droits *mpl* de succession.

inhibit [inhib'it] *vt* (*PSYCH*) inhiber; **to ~ sb from doing** empêcher *or* retenir qn de faire.

inhibited [inhib'itid] *a* (*person*) inhibé(e).

inhibiting [inhib'iting] *a* gênant(e).

inhibition [inibish'ən] *n* inhibition *f*.

inhospitable [inhàspit'əbəl] *a* inhospitalier(ière).

inhuman [inhyŌŌ'mən] *a* inhumain(e).

inhumane [inhyŌŌmān'] *a* inhumain(e).

inimitable [inim'itəbəl] *a* inimitable.

iniquity [inik'witē] *n* iniquité *f*.

initial [inish'əl] *a* initial(e) ♦ *n* initiale *f* ♦ *vt* parafer; **~s** *npl* initiales *fpl*; (*as signature*) parafe *m*.

initialize [inish'əlīz] *vt* (*COMPUT*) initialiser.

initially [inish'əlē] *ad* initialement, au début.

initiate [inish'ēāt] *vt* (*start*) entreprendre; amorcer; lancer; (*person*) initier; **to ~ sb into a secret** initier qn à un secret; **to ~ proceedings against sb** (*LAW*) intenter une action à qn, engager des poursuites contre qn.

initiation [inishēā'shən] *n* (*into secret etc*) initiation *f*.

initiative [inish'ēativ] *n* initiative *f*; **to take the ~** prendre l'initiative.

inject [injekt'] *vt* (*liquid, fig: money*) injecter; (*person*) faire une piqûre à.

injection [injek'shən] *n* injection *f*, piqûre *f*; **to have an ~** se faire faire une piqûre.

injudicious [injŌŌdish'əs] *a* peu judicieux(euse).

injunction [injungk'shən] *n* (*LAW*) injonction *f*, ordre *m*.

injure [in'jûr] *vt* blesser; (*wrong*) faire du tort à; (*damage: reputation etc*) compromettre; (*feelings*) heurter; **to ~ o.s.** se blesser.

injured [in'jûrd] *a* (*person, leg etc*) blessé(e); (*tone, feelings*) offensé(e); **~ party** (*LAW*) partie lésée.

injurious [injŏŏr'ēəs] *a*: ~ **(to)** préjudiciable (à).

injury [in'jûrē] *n* blessure *f*; (*wrong*) tort *m*; **to escape without** ~ s'en sortir sain et sauf.

injury time *n* (SPORT) arrêts *mpl* de jeu.

injustice [injus'tis] *n* injustice *f*; **you do me an** ~ vous êtes injuste envers moi.

ink [ingk] *n* encre *f*.

ink-jet printer [ingk'jet prin'tûr] *n* imprimante *f* à jet d'encre.

inkling [ingk'ling] *n* soupçon *m*, vague idée *f*.

inkpad [ingk'pad] *n* tampon *m* encreur.

inky [ing'kē] *a* taché(e) d'encre.

inlaid [in'lād] *a* incrusté(e); (*table etc*) marqueté(e).

inland [in'land] *a* intérieur(e) ♦ *ad* à l'intérieur, dans les terres; ~ **waterways** canaux *mpl* et rivières *fpl*.

Inland Revenue *n* (*Brit*) fisc *m*.

in-laws [in'lóz] *npl* beaux-parents *mpl*; belle famille.

inlet [in'let] *n* (GEO) crique *f*.

inlet pipe *n* (TECH) tuyau *m* d'arrivée.

inmate [in'māt] *n* (*in prison*) détenu/e; (*in asylum*) interné/e.

inmost [in'mōst] *a* le(la) plus profond(e).

inn [in] *n* auberge *f*.

innards [in'ûrdz] *npl* (*col*) entrailles *fpl*.

innate [ināt'] *a* inné(e).

inner [in'ûr] *a* intérieur(e).

inner city *n* (vieux quartiers du) centre urbain (*souffrant souvent de délabrement, d'embouteillages etc*).

innermost [in'ûrmōst] *a* le(la) plus profond(e).

inner tube *n* (*of tire*) chambre *f* à air.

innings [in'ingz] *n* (SPORT) tour *m* de batte.

innocence [in'əsəns] *n* innocence *f*.

innocent [in'əsənt] *a* innocent(e).

innocuous [inák'yŏŏəs] *a* inoffensif(ive).

innovation [inəvā'shən] *n* innovation *f*.

innuendo, ~**es** [inyŏŏen'dō] *n* insinuation *f*, allusion (malveillante).

Innuit [in'ŏŏwit] *a* esquimau(de), eskimo ♦ *n* Esquimau/de.

innumerable [inŏŏ'mûrəbəl] *a* innombrable.

inoculate [inák'yəlāt] *vt*: **to** ~ **sb with sth** inoculer qch à qn; **to** ~ **sb against sth** vacciner qn contre qch.

inoculation [inákyəlā'shən] *n* inoculation *f*.

inoffensive [inəfen'siv] *a* inoffensif(ive).

inopportune [inápûrtŏŏn'] *a* inopportun(e).

inordinate [inôr'dənit] *a* démesuré(e).

inordinately [inôr'dənitlē] *ad* démesurément.

inorganic [inôrgan'ik] *a* inorganique.

inpatient [in'pāshənt] *n* malade hospitalisé(e).

input [in'pŏŏt] *n* (ELEC) énergie *f*, puissance *f*; (*of machine*) consommation *f*; (*of computer*) information fournie ♦ *vt* (COMPUT) introduire, entrer.

inquest [in'kwest] *n* enquête (criminelle).

inquire [inkwîûr'] *vi* demander ♦ *vt* demander, s'informer de; **to** ~ **about** s'informer de, se renseigner sur; **to** ~ **when/where/whether** demander quand/où/si.

inquire after *vt fus* demander des nouvelles de.

inquire into *vt fus* faire une enquête sur.

inquiring [inkwîûr'ing] *a* (*mind*) curieux(euse), investigateur(trice).

inquiry [inkwîûr'ē] *n* demande *f* de renseignements; (LAW) enquête *f*, investigation *f*; **to hold an** ~ **into sth** enquêter sur qch.

inquiry desk *n* (*Brit*) guichet *m* de renseignements.

inquiry office *n* (*Brit*) bureau *m* de renseignements.

inquisition [inkwizish'ən] *n* enquête *f*, investigation *f*; (REL): **the l**~ l'Inquisition.

inquisitive [inkwiz'ətiv] *a* curieux(euse).

inroads [in'rōdz] *npl*: **to make** ~ **into** (*savings, supplies*) entamer.

insane [insān'] *a* fou(folle); (MED) aliéné(e).

insanitary [insan'itārē] *a* insalubre.

insanity [insan'itē] *n* folie *f*; (MED) aliénation (mentale).

insatiable [insā'shəbəl] *a* insatiable.

inscribe [inskrīb'] *vt* inscrire; (*book etc*): **to** ~ **(to sb)** dédicacer (à qn).

inscription [inskrip'shən] *n* inscription *f*; (*in book*) dédicace *f*.

inscrutable [inskrŏŏ'təbəl] *a* impénétrable.

inseam [in'sēm] *n* (US): ~ **measurement** hauteur *f* d'entre-jambe.

insect [in'sekt] *n* insecte *m*.

insect bite *n* piqûre *f* d'insecte.

insecticide [insek'tisīd] *n* insecticide *m*.

insect repellent *n* crème *f* anti-insectes.

insecure [insikyŏŏr'] *a* peu solide; peu sûr(e); (*person*) anxieux(euse).

insecurity [insikyŏŏr'itē] *n* insécurité *f*.

insensible [insen'səbəl] *a* insensible; (*unconscious*) sans connaissance.

insensitive [insen'sətiv] *a* insensible.

insensitivity [insensətiv'itē] *n* insensibilité *f*.

inseparable [insep'ûrəbəl] *a* inséparable.

insert *vt* [insûrt'] insérer ♦ *n* [in'sûrt] insertion *f*.

insertion [insûr'shən] *n* insertion *f*.

in-service [in'sûr'vis] *a* (*training*) continu(e); (*course*) d'initiation; de perfectionnement; de recyclage.

inshore [in'shôr] *a* côtier(ière) ♦ *ad* près de la côte; vers la côte.

inside [in'sīd'] *n* intérieur *m*; (*of road*: US, *Europe etc*) côté *m* droit (*de la route*); (: *Brit*) côté *m* gauche (*de la route*) ♦ *a* intérieur(e) ♦ *ad* à l'intérieur, dedans ♦ *prep* à l'intérieur de; (*of time*): ~ **10 minutes** en moins de 10 minutes; ~**s** *npl* (*col*) intestins *mpl*; ~ **out** *ad* à l'envers; **to turn sth** ~ **out** retourner qch; **to know sth** ~ **out** connaître qch à fond *or* comme sa poche; ~ **information** renseignements *mpl* à la source; ~ **story** histoire racontée par un témoin.

inside forward *n* (SPORT) intérieur *m*.

inside lane *n* (AUT: *in US, Europe*) voie *f* de droite; (: *in Britain*) voie *f* de gauche.

inside leg measurement *n* (*Brit*) hauteur *f* d'entre-jambe.

insider [insī'dûr] *n* initié/e.

insider dealing *n* (STOCK EXCHANGE) délit *m* d'initié(s).

insidious [insid'ēəs] *a* insidieux(euse).

insight [in'sīt] *n* perspicacité *f*; (*glimpse, idea*) aperçu *m*; **to gain (an)** ~ **into** parvenir à comprendre.

insignia [insig'nēə] *npl* insignes *mpl*.
insignificant [insignif'ikənt] *a* insignifiant(e).
insincere [insinsēr'] *a* hypocrite.
insincerity [insinsär'itē] *n* manque *m* de sincérité, hypocrisie *f*.
insinuate [insin'yōōāt] *vt* insinuer.
insinuation [insinyōōā'shən] *n* insinuation *f*.
insipid [insip'id] *a* insipide, fade.
insist [insist'] *vi* insister; **to ~ on doing** insister pour faire; **to ~ that** insister pour que; (*claim*) maintenir *or* soutenir que.
insistence [insis'təns] *n* insistance *f*.
insistent [insis'tənt] *a* insistant(e), pressant(e).
insole [in'sōl] *n* semelle intérieure; (*fixed part of shoe*) première *f*.
insolence [in'sələns] *n* insolence *f*.
insolent [in'sələnt] *a* insolent(e).
insoluble [insâl'yəbəl] *a* insoluble.
insolvency [insâl'vənsē] *n* insolvabilité *f*; faillite *f*.
insolvent [insâl'vənt] *a* insolvable; (*bankrupt*) en faillite.
insomnia [insâm'nēə] *n* insomnie *f*.
insomniac [insâm'nēak] *n* insomniaque *m/f*.
inspect [inspekt'] *vt* inspecter; (*Brit: ticket*) contrôler.
inspection [inspek'shən] *n* inspection *f*; contrôle *m*.
inspector [inspek'tûr] *n* inspecteur/trice; contrôleur/euse.
inspiration [inspərā'shən] *n* inspiration *f*.
inspire [inspīr'] *vt* inspirer.
inspired [inspīrd'] *a* (*writer, book etc*) inspiré(e); **in an ~ moment** dans un moment d'inspiration.
inspiring [inspīr'ing] *a* inspirant(e).
inst. *abbr* (*Brit COMM:* = *instant*): **of the 16th ~** du 16 courant.
instability [instəbil'ətē] *n* instabilité *f*.
install [instôl'] *vt* installer.
installation [instəlā'shən] *n* installation *f*.
installment, (*Brit*) **instalment** [instôl'mənt] *n* acompte *m*, versement partiel; (*of TV serial etc*) épisode *m*; **in ~s** (*pay*) à tempérament; (*receive*) en plusieurs fois.
installment plan *n* (*US*) achat *m* (*or* vente *f*) à tempérament *or* crédit.
instance [in'stəns] *n* exemple *m*; **for ~** par exemple; **in many ~s** dans bien des cas; **in that ~** dans ce cas; **in the first ~** tout d'abord, en premier lieu.
instant [in'stənt] *n* instant *m* ♦ *a* immédiat(e); urgent(e); (*coffee, food*) instantané(e), en poudre; **the 10th ~** le 10 courant.
instantaneous [instəntā'nēəs] *a* instantané(e).
instantly [in'stəntlē] *ad* immédiatement, tout de suite.
instant replay *n* (*US TV*) retour *m* sur une séquence.
instead [insted'] *ad* au lieu de cela; **~ of** au lieu de; **~ of sb** à la place de qn.
instep [in'step] *n* cou-de-pied *m*; (*of shoe*) cambrure *f*.
instigate [in'stəgāt] *vt* (*rebellion, strike, crime*) inciter à; (*new ideas etc*) susciter.
instigation [instəgā'shən] *n* instigation *f*; **at sb's ~** à l'instigation de qn.
instill, (*Brit*) **instil** [instil'] *vt*: **to ~ (into)**

inculquer (à); (*courage*) insuffler (à).
instinct [in'stingkt] *n* instinct *m*.
instinctive [instingk'tiv] *a* instinctif(ive).
instinctively [instingk'tivlē] *ad* instinctivement.
institute [in'stitōōt] *n* institut *m* ♦ *vt* instituer, établir; (*inquiry*) ouvrir; (*proceedings*) entamer.
institution [institōō'shən] *n* institution *f*; (*school*) établissement *m* (scolaire); (*for care*) établissement (psychiatrique *etc*).
institutional [institōō'shənəl] *a* institutionnel(le); **~ care** soins *mpl* fournis par un établissement médico-social.
instruct [instrukt'] *vt* instruire, former; **to ~ sb in sth** enseigner qch à qn; **to ~ sb to do** charger qn *or* ordonner à qn de faire.
instruction [instruk'shən] *n* instruction *f*; **~s** *npl* directives *fpl*; **~s for use** mode *m* d'emploi.
instruction book *n* manuel *m* d'instructions.
instructive [instruk'tiv] *a* instructif(ive).
instructor [instruk'tûr] *n* professeur *m*; (*for skiing, driving*) moniteur *m*.
instrument [in'strəmənt] *n* instrument *m*.
instrumental [instrəmen'təl] *a* (*MUS*) instrumental(e); **to be ~ in sth/in doing sth** contribuer à qch/à faire qch.
instrumentalist [instrəmen'təlist] *n* instrumentiste *m/f*.
instrument panel *n* tableau *m* de bord.
insubordinate [insəbôr'dənit] *a* insubordonné(e).
insubordination [insəbôrdənā'shən] *n* insubordination *f*.
insufferable [insuf'ûrəbəl] *a* insupportable.
insufficient [insəfish'ənt] *a* insuffisant(e).
insufficiently [insəfish'əntlē] *ad* insuffisamment.
insular [in'sələr] *a* insulaire; (*outlook*) étroit(e); (*person*) aux vues étroites.
insulate [in'səlāt] *vt* isoler; (*against sound*) insonoriser.
insulating tape [in'səlāting tāp] *n* ruban isolant.
insulation [insəlā'shən] *n* isolation *f*; insonorisation *f*.
insulin [in'səlin] *n* insuline *f*.
insult *n* [in'sult] insulte *f*, affront *m* ♦ *vt* [insult'] insulter, faire un affront à.
insulting [insul'ting] *a* insultant(e), injurieux(euse).
insuperable [insōō'pûrəbəl] *a* insurmontable.
insurance [inshûr'əns] *n* assurance *f*; **fire/life ~** assurance-incendie/-vie; **to take out ~ (against)** s'assurer (contre).
insurance agent *n* agent *m* d'assurances.
insurance broker *n* courtier *m* en assurances.
insurance policy *n* police *f* d'assurance.
insurance premium *n* prime *f* d'assurance.
insure [inshōōr'] *vt* assurer; **to ~ sb/sb's life** assurer qn/la vie de qn; **to be ~d for $5000** être assuré(e) pour 5000 dollars.
insured [inshōōrd'] *n*: **the ~** l'assuré/e.
insurer [inshōō'rûr] *n* assureur *m*.
insurgent [insûr'jənt] *a, n* insurgé(e).
insurmountable [insûrmoun'təbəl] *a* insurmontable.

insurrection [insərɛk'shən] *n* insurrection *f*.
intact [intakt'] *a* intact(e).
intake [in'tāk] *n* (*TECH*) admission *f*; adduction *f*; (*of food*) consommation *f*; (*Brit SCOL*): **an ~ of 200 a year** 200 admissions par an.
intangible [intan'jəbəl] *a* intangible; (*assets*) immatériel(le).
integral [in'təgrəl] *a* intégral(e); (*part*) intégrant(e).
integrate [in'təgrāt] *vt* intégrer ♦ *vi* s'intégrer.
integrated circuit [in'təgrātid sûr'kit] *n* (*COMPUT*) circuit intégré.
integration [intəgrā'shən] *n* intégration *f*; **racial ~** intégration raciale.
integrity [intɛg'ritē] *n* intégrité *f*.
intellect [in'təlɛkt] *n* intelligence *f*.
intellectual [intəlɛk'chooəl] *a*, *n* intellectuel(le).
intelligence [intɛl'ijəns] *n* intelligence *f*; (*MIL etc*) informations *fpl*, renseignements *mpl*.
intelligence quotient (IQ) *n* quotient intellectuel (QI).
Intelligence Service *n* services *mpl* de renseignements.
intelligence test *n* test *m* d'intelligence.
intelligent [intɛl'ijənt] *a* intelligent(e).
intelligently [intɛl'ijəntlē] *ad* intelligemment.
intelligible [intɛl'ijəbəl] *a* intelligible.
intemperate [intɛm'pûrit] *a* immodéré(e); (*drinking too much*) adonné(e) à la boisson.
intend [intɛnd'] *vt* (*gift etc*): **to ~ sth for** destiner qch à; **to ~ to do** avoir l'intention de faire.
intended [intɛn'did] *a* (*insult*) intentionnel(le); (*journey*) projeté(e); (*effect*) voulu(e).
intense [intɛns'] *a* intense; (*person*) véhément(e).
intensely [intɛns'lē] *ad* intensément; (*moving*) profondément.
intensify [intɛn'səfī] *vt* intensifier.
intensity [intɛn'sitē] *n* intensité *f*.
intensive [intɛn'siv] *a* intensif(ive).
intensive care *n*: **to be in ~** être en réanimation; **~ unit** *n* service *m* de réanimation.
intent [intɛnt'] *n* intention *f* ♦ *a* attentif(ive), absorbé(e); **to all ~s and purposes** en fait, pratiquement; **to be ~ on doing sth** être (bien) décidé à faire qch.
intention [intɛn'chən] *n* intention *f*.
intentional [intɛn'chənəl] *a* intentionnel(le), délibéré(e).
intently [intɛnt'lē] *ad* attentivement.
inter [intûr'] *vt* enterrer.
interact [intûrakt'] *vi* avoir une action réciproque.
interaction [intûrak'shən] *n* interaction *f*.
interactive [intûrak'tiv] *a* interactif(ive).
intercede [intûrsēd'] *vi*: **to ~ with sb/on behalf of sb** intercéder auprès de qn/en faveur de qn.
intercept [intûrsɛpt'] *vt* intercepter; (*person*) arrêter au passage.
interception [intûrsɛp'shən] *n* interception *f*.
interchange *n* [in'tûrchānj] (*exchange*) échange *m*; (*on freeway*) échangeur *m* ♦ *vt* [intûrchānj'] échanger; mettre à la place l'un(e) de l'autre.
interchangeable [intûrchān'jəbəl] *a* interchangeable.
intercity [in'tûrsitē] *a*: **~ (train)** train *m* rapide.
intercom [in'tûrkâm] *n* interphone *m*.
interconnect [intûrkənɛkt'] *vi* (*rooms*) communiquer.
intercontinental [intûrkântənən'təl] *a* intercontinental(e).
intercourse [in'tûrkôrs] *n* rapports *mpl*; **sexual ~** rapports sexuels.
interdependent [intûrdipɛn'dənt] *a* interdépendant(e).
interest [in'trist] *n* intérêt *m*; (*COMM*: *stake, share*) participation *f*, intérêts *mpl* ♦ *vt* intéresser; **compound/simple ~** intérêt composé/simple; **American ~s in the Middle East** les intérêts américains au Moyen-Orient; **his main ~ is** ... ce qui l'intéresse le plus est ....
interested [in'tristid] *a* intéressé(e); **to be ~ in** s'intéresser à.
interest-free [in'tristfrē] *a* sans intérêt.
interesting [in'tristing] *a* intéressant(e).
interest rate *n* taux *m* d'intérêt.
interface [in'tûrfās] *n* (*COMPUT*) interface *f*.
interfere [intûrfēr'] *vi*: **to ~ in** (*quarrel, other people's business*) se mêler à; **to ~ with** (*object*) tripoter, toucher à; (*plans*) contrecarrer; (*duty*) être en conflit avec; **don't ~** mêlez-vous de vos affaires.
interference [intûrfēr'əns] *n* (*gen*) intrusion *f*; (*PHYSICS*) interférence *f*; (*RADIO, TV*) parasites *mpl*.
interfering [intûrfēr'ing] *a* importun(e).
interim [in'tûrim] *a* provisoire; (*post*) intérimaire ♦ *n*: **in the ~** dans l'intérim.
interior [intē'rēûr] *n* intérieur *m* ♦ *a* intérieur(e).
interior decorator, interior designer *n* décorateur/trice d'intérieur.
interjection [intûrjɛk'shən] *n* interjection *f*.
interlock [intûrlâk'] *vi* s'enclencher ♦ *vt* enclencher.
interloper [intûrlō'pûr] *n* intrus/e.
interlude [in'tûrlōōd] *n* intervalle *m*; (*THEATER*) intermède *m*.
intermarry [intûrmar'ē] *vi* former des alliances entre familles (*or* tribus); former des unions consanguines.
intermediary [intûrmē'dēârē] *n* intermédiaire *m/f*.
intermediate [intûrmē'dēit] *a* intermédiaire; (*SCOL*: *course, level*) moyen(ne).
interminable [intûr'mənəbəl] *a* sans fin, interminable.
intermission [intûrmish'ən] *n* pause *f*; (*THEATER, CINEMA*) entracte *m*.
intermittent [intûrmit'ənt] *a* intermittent(e).
intermittently [intûrmit'əntlē] *ad* par intermittence, par intervalles.
intern *vt* [intûrn'] interner ♦ *n* [in'tûrn] (*US*) interne *m/f*.
internal [intûr'nəl] *a* interne; (*dispute, reform etc*) intérieur(e); **~ injuries** lésions *fpl* internes.
internally [intûr'nəlē] *ad* intérieurement; **"not to be taken ~"** "pour usage externe".
Internal Revenue (Service) (IRS) *n* (*US*) fisc *m*.

international [intûrnash'ənəl] *a* internatio-
nal(e) ♦ *n* (*Brit SPORT*) international *m*.
**International Atomic Energy Agency
(IAEA)** *n* Agence Internationale de l'Energie
Atomique (AIEA).
International Court of Justice (ICJ) *n*
Cour internationale de justice (CIJ).
international date line *n* ligne *f* de changement de date.
internationally [intûrnash'ənəlē] *ad* dans le
monde entier.
International Monetary Fund (IMF) *n*
Fonds *m* monétaire international (FMI).
internecine [intûrnē'sīn] *a* mutuellement des-
tructeur(trice).
internee [intûrnē'] *n* interné/e.
internment [intûrn'mənt] *n* internement *m*.
interplay [in'tûrplā] *n* effet *m* réciproque, jeu
m.
Interpol [in'tûrpōl] *n* Interpol *m*.
interpret [intûr'prit] *vt* interpréter ♦ *vi* servir
d'interprète.
interpretation [intûrpritā'shən] *n* interprétation *f*.
interpreter [intûr'pritûr] *n* interprète *m/f*.
interpreting [intûr'priting] *n* (*profession*)
interprétariat *m*.
interrelated [intərilā'tid] *a* en corrélation, en
rapport étroit.
interrogate [intär'əgāt] *vt* interroger; (*suspect
etc*) soumettre à un interrogatoire.
interrogation [intärəgā'shən] *n* interrogation
f; interrogatoire *m*.
interrogative [intərâg'ətiv] *a* interroga-
teur(trice) ♦ *n* (*LING*) interrogatif *m*.
interrogator [intär'əgātûr] *n* interrogateur/
trice.
interrupt [intərupt'] *vt* interrompre.
interruption [intərup'shən] *n* interruption *f*.
intersect [intûrsekt'] *vt* couper, croiser;
(*MATH*) intersecter ♦ *vi* se croiser, se couper; s'intersecter.
intersection [intûrsek'shən] *n* intersection *f*;
(*of roads*) croisement *m*.
intersperse [intûrspûrs'] *vt*: **to ~ with** parsemer de.
interstate (highway) [in'tûrstāt (hī'wā)] *n*
(*US*) route nationale.
intertwine [intûrtwīn'] *vt* entrelacer ♦ *vi* s'entrelacer.
interval [in'tûrvəl] *n* intervalle *m*; (*Brit:
THEATER*) entracte *m*; (: *SPORT*) mi-temps *f*;
bright ~s (*in weather*) éclaircies *fpl*; **at ~s**
par intervalles.
intervene [intûrvēn'] *vi* (*time*) s'écouler
(entre-temps); (*event*) survenir; (*person*)
intervenir.
intervention [intûrven'chən] *n* intervention *f*.
interview [in'tûrvyōō] *n* (*RADIO, TV etc*)
interview *f*; (*for job*) entrevue *f* ♦ *vt* interviewer; avoir une entrevue avec.
interviewer [in'tûrvyōōûr] *n* interviewer *m*.
intestate [intes'tāt] *a* intestat.
intestinal [intes'tənəl] *a* intestinal(e).
intestine [intes'tin] *n* intestin *m*; **large ~** gros
intestin; **small ~** intestin grêle.
intimacy [in'təməsē] *n* intimité *f*.
intimate *a* [in'təmit] intime; (*knowledge*) ap-
profondi(e) ♦ *vt* [in'təmāt] suggérer, laisser

entendre; (*announce*) faire savoir.
intimately [in'təmitlē] *ad* intimement.
intimation [intəmā'shən] *n* annonce *f*.
intimidate [intim'idāt] *vt* intimider.
intimidation [intimidā'shən] *n* intimidation *f*.
into [in'tōō] *prep* dans; **~ pieces/French** en
morceaux/français; **to change pounds ~
dollars** changer des livres en dollars.
intolerable [intâl'ûrəbəl] *a* intolérable.
intolerance [intâl'ûrəns] *n* intolérance *f*.
intolerant [intâl'ûrənt] *a*: **~ (of)** intolérant(e)
(de); (*MED*) intolérant (à).
intonation [intōnā'shən] *n* intonation *f*.
intoxicate [intâk'sikāt] *vt* enivrer.
intoxicated [intâk'sikātid] *a* ivre.
intoxication [intâksikā'shən] *n* ivresse *f*.
intractable [intrak'təbəl] *a* (*child, temper*)
indocile, insoumis(e); (*problem*) insoluble;
(*illness*) incurable.
intransigent [intran'sijənt] *a* intransigeant(e).
intransitive [intran'sətiv] *a* intransitif(ive).
intra-uterine device (IUD) [intrəyōō'tûrin di-
vīs'] *n* dispositif intra-utérin (DIU), stérilet
m.
intravenous [intrəvē'nəs] *a* intravei-
neux(euse).
in-tray [in'trā] *n* courrier *m* "arrivée".
intrepid [intrep'id] *a* intrépide.
intricacy [in'trəkəsē] *n* complexité *f*.
intricate [in'trəkit] *a* complexe, compliqué(e).
intrigue [intrēg'] *n* intrigue *f* ♦ *vt* intriguer ♦
vi intriguer, comploter.
intriguing [intrē'ging] *a* fascinant(e).
intrinsic [intrin'sik] *a* intrinsèque.
introduce [intrədōōs'] *vt* introduire; **to ~ sb
(to sb)** présenter qn (à qn); **to ~ sb to** (*pastime, technique*) initier qn à; **may I ~ ...?** je
vous présente ....
introduction [intrəduk'shən] *n* introduction *f*;
(*of person*) présentation *f*; **a letter of ~** une
lettre de recommendation.
introductory [intrəduk'tûrē] *a* préliminaire, in-
troductif(ive); **~ remarks** remarques *fpl* li-
minaires; **an ~ offer** une offre de lancement.
introspection [intrəspek'shən] *n* introspection
f.
introspective [intrəspek'tiv] *a* in-
trospectif(ive).
introvert [in'trəvûrt] *a*, *n* introverti(e).
intrude [intrōōd'] *vi* (*person*) être
importun(e); **to ~ on** *or* **into** (*conversation
etc*) s'immiscer dans; **am I intruding?** est-ce
que je vous dérange?
intruder [intrōō'dûr] *n* intrus/e.
intrusion [intrōō'zhən] *n* intrusion *f*.
intrusive [intrōō'siv] *a* importun(e), gênant(e).
intuition [intōōish'ən] *n* intuition *f*.
intuitive [intōō'ətiv] *a* intuitif(ive).
inundate [in'undāt] *vt*: **to ~ with** inonder de.
inure [inyōōr'] *vt*: **to ~ (to)** habituer (à).
invade [invād'] *vt* envahir.
invader [invā'dûr] *n* envahisseur *m*.
invalid *n* [in'vəlid] malade *m/f*; (*with disability*) invalide *m/f* ♦ *a* [inval'id] (*not valid*)
invalide, non valide.
invalidate [inval'idāt] *vt* invalider, annuler.
invalid chair *n* (*Brit*) fauteuil *m* d'infirme.
invaluable [inval'yōōəbəl] *a* inestimable, inappréciable.

invariable [invär'ēəbəl] *a* invariable; (*fig*) immanquable.

invariably [invär'ēəblē] *ad* invariablement; **she is ~ late** elle est toujours en retard.

invasion [invā'zhən] *n* invasion *f*.

invective [invek'tiv] *n* invective *f*.

inveigle [invē'gəl] *vt*: **to ~ sb into (doing) sth** amener qn à (faire) qch (par la ruse *or* la flatterie).

invent [invent'] *vt* inventer.

invention [inven'chən] *n* invention *f*.

inventive [inven'tiv] *a* inventif(ive).

inventiveness [inven'tivnis] *n* esprit inventif *or* d'invention.

inventor [inven'tûr] *n* inventeur/trice.

inventory [in'vəntôrē] *n* inventaire *m*.

inventory control *n* (*COMM*) contrôle *m* des stocks.

inverse [invûrs'] *a* inverse ♦ *n* inverse *m*, contraire *m*; **in ~ proportion (to)** inversement proportionel(le) (à).

inversely [invûrs'lē] *ad* inversement.

invert [invûrt'] *vt* intervertir; (*cup, object*) retourner.

invertebrate [invûr'təbrit] *n* invertébré *m*.

inverted commas [invûr'tid kâm'əz] *npl* (*Brit*) guillemets *mpl*.

invest [invest'] *vt* investir; (*endow*): **to ~ sb with sth** conférer qch à qn ♦ *vi* faire un investissement, investir; **to ~ in** placer de l'argent *or* investir dans; (*acquire*) s'offrir, faire l'acquisition de.

investigate [inves'təgāt] *vt* étudier, examiner; (*crime*) faire une enquête sur.

investigation [investəgāshən] *n* examen *m*; (*of crime*) enquête *f*, investigation *f*.

investigative [inves'təgātiv] *a*: **~ journalism** journalisme *m* d'enquête.

investigator [inves'təgātûr] *n* investigateur/trice; **private ~** détective privé.

investiture [inves'tichûr] *n* investiture *f*.

investment [invest'mənt] *n* investissement *m*, placement *m*.

investment income *n* revenu *m* de placement.

investment trust *n* société *f* d'investissements.

investor [inves'tûr] *n* épargnant/e; (*shareholder*) actionnaire *m/f*.

inveterate [invet'ûrit] *a* invétéré(e).

invidious [invid'ēəs] *a* injuste; (*task*) déplaisant(e).

invigilator [invij'əlātûr] *n* (*Brit*) surveillant *m* (d'examen).

invigorating [invig'ərāting] *a* vivifiant(e); stimulant(e).

invincible [invin'səbəl] *a* invincible.

inviolate [invī'əlit] *a* inviolé(e).

invisible [inviz'əbəl] *a* invisible.

invisible ink *n* encre *f* sympathique.

invisible mending *n* stoppage *m*.

invitation [invitā'shən] *n* invitation *f*; **by ~ only** sur invitation; **at sb's ~** à la demande de qn.

invite [invīt'] *vt* inviter; (*opinions etc*) demander; (*trouble*) chercher; **to ~ sb (to do)** inviter qn (à faire); **to ~ sb to dinner** inviter qn à dîner.

invite out *vt* inviter (à sortir).

invite over *vt* inviter (chez soi).

inviting [invī'ting] *a* engageant(e), attrayant(e); (*gesture*) encourageant(e).

invoice [in'vois] *n* facture *f* ♦ *vt* facturer; **to ~ sb for goods** facturer des marchandises à qn.

invoke [invōk'] *vt* invoquer.

involuntary [invâl'əntärē] *a* involontaire.

involve [invâlv'] *vt* (*entail*) impliquer; (*concern*) concerner; (*require*) nécessiter; **to ~ sb in** (*theft etc*) impliquer qn dans; (*activity, meeting*) faire participer qn à.

involved [invâlvd'] *a* complexe; **to feel ~** se sentir concerné(e); **to become ~** (*in love etc*) s'engager.

involvement [invâlv'mənt] *n* (*personal role*) participation *f*; (*of resources, funds*) mise *f* en jeu.

invulnerable [invul'nûrəbəl] *a* invulnérable.

inward [in'wûrd] *a* (*movement*) vers l'intérieur; (*thought, feeling*) profond(e), intime.

inwardly [in'wûrdlē] *ad* (*feel, think etc*) secrètement, en son for intérieur.

inward(s) [in'wûrd(z)] *ad* vers l'intérieur.

I/O *abbr* (*COMPUT*: = *input/output*) E/S.

IOC *n abbr* (= *International Olympic Committee*) CIO *m* (= *Comité international olympique*).

iodine [ī'ədīn] *n* iode *m*.

ion [ī'ən] *n* ion *m*.

Ionian Sea [īō'nēən sē] *n*: **the ~** la mer Ionienne.

iota [īō'tə] *n* (*fig*) brin *m*, grain *m*.

IOU *n abbr* (= *I owe you*) reconnaissance *f* de dette.

IOW *abbr* (*Brit*) = *Isle of Wight*.

IPA *n abbr* (= *International Phonetic Alphabet*) A.P.I. *m*.

IQ *n abbr* = **intelligence quotient**.

IRA *n abbr* (= *Irish Republican Army*) IRA *f*; (*US*) = *individual retirement account*.

Iran [iran'] *n* Iran *m*.

Iranian [irā'nēən] *a* iranien(ne) ♦ *n* Iranien/ne; (*LING*) iranien *m*.

Iraq [irak'] *n* Irak *m*.

Iraqi [irák'ē] *a* irakien(ne) ♦ *n* Irakien/ne; (*LING*) irakien *m*.

irascible [iras'əbəl] *a* irascible.

irate [irāt'] *a* courroucé(e).

Ireland [īûr'lənd] *n* Irlande *f*; **Republic of ~** République *f* d'Irlande.

iris, ~es [ī'ris] *n* iris *m*.

Irish [ī'rish] *a* irlandais(e) ♦ *n* (*LING*) irlandais *m*; **the ~** *npl* les Irlandais.

Irishman [ī'rishmən] *n* Irlandais *m*.

Irish Sea *n*: **the ~** la mer d'Irlande.

Irishwoman [ī'rishwŏōmən] *n* Irlandaise *f*.

irk [ûrk] *vt* ennuyer.

irksome [ûrk'səm] *a* ennuyeux(euse).

IRO *n abbr* (*US*) = *International Refugee Organization*.

iron [ī'ûrn] *n* fer *m*; (*for clothes*) fer *m* à repasser ♦ *a* de *or* en fer ♦ *vt* (*clothes*) repasser; **~s** *npl* (*chains*) fers *mpl*, chaînes *fpl*.

iron out *vt* (*crease*) faire disparaître au fer; (*fig*) aplanir; faire disparaître.

Iron Curtain *n*: **the ~** le rideau de fer.

iron foundry *n* fonderie *f* de fonte.

ironic(al) [īrân'ik(əl)] *a* ironique.

ironically [īrân'iklē] *ad* ironiquement.
ironing [ī'ûrning] *n* repassage *m*.
ironing board *n* planche *f* à repasser.
ironmonger [ī'ûrnmunggûr] *n* (*Brit*) quincailler *m*; **~'s (shop)** quincaillerie *f*.
iron ore [ī'ûrn ôr] *n* minerai *m* de fer.
ironworks [ī'ûrnwûrks] *n* usine *f* sidérurgique.
irony [ī'rɔnē] *n* ironie *f*.
irrational [irash'ənəl] *a* irrationnel(le); déraisonnable; qui manque de logique.
irreconcilable [irek'ɔnsīlɔbəl] *a* irréconciliable; (*opinion*): **~ with** inconciliable avec.
irredeemable [iridē'məbəl] *a* (*COMM*) non remboursable.
irrefutable [irifyōō'təbəl] *a* irréfutable.
irregular [ireg'yəlûr] *a* irrégulier(ière).
irregularity [iregyəlar'itē] *n* irrégularité *f*.
irrelevance [irel'əvəns] *n* manque *m* de rapport *or* d'à-propos.
irrelevant [irel'əvənt] *a* sans rapport, hors de propos.
irreligious [irilij'əs] *a* irréligieux(euse).
irreparable [irep'ûrəbəl] *a* irréparable.
irreplaceable [iriplā'səbəl] *a* irremplaçable.
irrepressible [iripres'əbəl] *a* irrépressible.
irreproachable [iriprō'chəbəl] *a* irréprochable.
irresistible [irizis'təbəl] *a* irrésistible.
irresolute [irez'əlōōt] *a* irrésolu(e), indécis(e).
irrespective [irispek'tiv] : **~ of** *prep* sans tenir compte de.
irresponsible [irispân'səbəl] *a* (*act*) irréfléchi(e); (*person*) qui n'a pas le sens des responsabilités.
irretrievable [iritrē'vəbəl] *a* irréparable, irrémédiable; (*object*) introuvable.
irreverent [irev'ûrənt] *a* irrévérencieux(euse).
irrevocable [irev'əkəbəl] *a* irrévocable.
irrigate [ir'igāt] *vt* irriguer.
irrigation [irigā'shən] *n* irrigation *f*.
irritable [ir'itəbəl] *a* irritable.
irritate [ir'ətāt] *vt* irriter.
irritation [iritā'shən] *n* irritation *f*.
IRS *n abbr* (*US*) = **Internal Revenue Service**.
is [iz] *vb see* **be**.
ISBN *n abbr* (= *International Standard Book Number*) ISBN *m*.
Islam [ish'lâm] *n* Islam *m*.
island [ī'lənd] *n* île *f*; (*also*: **traffic ~**) refuge *m* (pour piétons).
islander [ī'ləndûr] *n* habitant/e d'une île, insulaire *m/f*.
isle [īl] *n* île *f*.
isn't [iz'ənt] = **is not**.
isolate [ī'səlāt] *vt* isoler.
isolated [ī'səlātid] *a* isolé(e).
isolation [īsəlā'shən] *n* isolement *m*.
isolationism [īsəlā'shənizəm] *n* isolationnisme *m*.
isotope [ī'sətōp] *n* isotope *m*.
Israel [iz'rāəl] *n* Israël *m*.
Israeli [izrā'lē] *a* israélien(ne) ♦ *n* Israélien/ne.
issue [ish'ōō] *n* question *f*, problème *m*; (*outcome*) résultat *m*, issue *f*; (*of banknotes etc*) émission *f*; (*of newspaper etc*) numéro *m*; (*offspring*) descendance *f* ♦ *vt* (*rations, equipment*) distribuer; (*orders*) donner; (*book*) faire paraître, publier; (*banknotes, checks, stamps*) émettre, mettre en circulation ♦ *vi*: **to ~ from** provenir de; **at ~** en

jeu, en cause; **to avoid the ~** éluder le problème; **to take ~ with sb (over sth)** exprimer son désaccord avec qn (sur qch); **to make an ~ of sth** faire de qch un problème; **to confuse** *or* **obscure the ~** embrouiller la question.
Istanbul [istambōōl'] *n* Istamboul, Istanbul.
isthmus [is'məs] *n* isthme *m*.
IT *n abbr* = **information technology**.
it [it] *pronoun* (*subject*) il(elle); (*direct object*) le(la), l'; (*indirect object*) lui; (*impersonal*) il; ce, cela, ça; **of ~, from ~, about ~, out of ~** *etc* en; **in ~, to ~, at ~** *etc* y; **above ~, over ~** (au-dessus); **below ~, under ~** (en-)dessous; **in front of/behind ~** devant/derrière; **who is ~?** qui est-ce?; **~'s me** c'est moi; **what is ~?** qu'est-ce que c'est?; **where is ~?** où est-ce?, où est-ce que c'est?; **~'s Friday tomorrow** demain, c'est vendredi; **~'s raining** il pleut; **~'s 6 o'clock** il est 6 heures; **~'s 2 hours by train** c'est à 2 heures de train; **I've come from ~** j'en viens; **it's on ~** c'est dessus; **he's proud of ~** il en est fier; **he agreed to ~** il y a consenti.
Italian [ital'yən] *a* italien(ne) ♦ *n* Italien/ne; (*LING*) italien *m*.
italic [ital'ik] *a* italique; **~s** *npl* italique *m*.
Italy [it'əlē] *n* Italie *f*.
itch [ich] *n* démangeaison *f* ♦ *vi* (*person*) éprouver des démangeaisons; (*part of body*) démanger; **I'm ~ing to do** l'envie me démange de faire.
itching [ich'ing] *n* démangeaison *f*.
itchy [ich'ē] *a* qui démange; **my back is ~** j'ai le dos qui me démange.
it'd [it'əd] = **it would, it had**.
item [ī'təm] *n* (*gen*) article *m*; (*on agenda*) question *f*, point *m*; (*in program*) numéro *m*; (*also*: **news ~**) nouvelle *f*; **~s of clothing** articles vestimentaires.
itemize [ī'təmīz] *vt* détailler, spécifier.
itinerant [ītin'ûrənt] *a* itinérant(e); (*musician*) ambulant(e).
itinerary [ītin'ərärē] *n* itinéraire *m*.
it'll [it'əl] = **it will, it shall**.
its [its] *a* son(sa), ses *pl* ♦ *pronoun* le(la) sien(ne), les siens(siennes).
it's [its] = **it is, it has**.
itself [itself'] *pronoun* (*emphatic*) lui-même(elle-même); (*reflexive*) se.
ITV *n abbr* (*Brit*: = *Independent Television*) chaîne de télévision commerciale.
IUD *n abbr* = **intra-uterine device**.
I.V. *n* (*US MED*) goutte-à-goutte *m inv*, perfusion *f*; **to put sb on an ~** alimenter qn au goutte-à-goutte *or* par perfusion.
I've [īv] = **I have**.
ivory [ī'vûrē] *n* ivoire *m*.
Ivory Coast *n* Côte *f* d'Ivoire.
ivory tower *n* (*fig*) tour *f* d'ivoire.
ivy [ī'vē] *n* lierre *m*.
Ivy League *n* (*US*) *les grandes universités du nord-est des États Unis (Harvard, Yale, Princeton etc)*.

J

J, j [jā] *n* (*letter*) J, j *m*; **J for Jig** J comme Joseph.
JA *n abbr* = **judge advocate**.
J/A *abbr* = **joint account**.
jab [jab] *vt*: **to ~ sth into** enfoncer *or* planter qch dans ♦ *n* coup *m*; (*MED col*) piqûre *f*.
jabber [jab'ûr] *vt, vi* bredouiller, baragouiner.
jack [jak] *n* (*AUT*) cric *m*; (*Brit BOWLS*) cochonnet *m*; (*CARDS*) valet *m*.
  jack in *vt* (*col*) laisser tomber.
  jack up *vt* soulever (au cric).
jackal [jak'əl] *n* chacal *m*.
jackass [jak'as] *n* (*also fig*) âne *m*.
jackdaw [jak'dô] *n* choucas *m*.
jacket [jak'it] *n* veste *f*, veston *m*; (*of boiler etc*) enveloppe *f*; (*of book*) couverture *f*, jaquette *f*.
jack-in-the-box [jak'inthəbáks] *n* diable *m* à ressort.
jackknife [jak'nīf] *n* couteau *m* de poche ♦ *vi*: **the truck ~d** la remorque (du camion) s'est mise en travers.
jack-of-all-trades [jak'əvôltrādz'] *n* bricoleur *m*.
jack plug *n* (*Brit*) jack *m*.
jackpot [jak'pât] *n* gros lot.
jacuzzi [jəkōō'zē] *n* ® jacuzzi *m* ®.
jade [jād] *n* (*stone*) jade *m*.
jaded [jā'did] *a* éreinté(e), fatigué(e).
JAG *n abbr* = **Judge Advocate General**.
jagged [jag'id] *a* dentelé(e).
jaguar [jag'wâr] *n* jaguar *m*.
jail [jāl] *n* prison *f* ♦ *vt* emprisonner, mettre en prison.
jailbird [jāl'bûrd] *n* récidiviste *m/f*.
jailbreak [jāl'brāk] *n* évasion *f*.
jailer [jā'lûr] *n* geôlier/ière.
jalopy [jəláp'ē] *n* (*col*) vieux clou.
jam [jam] *n* confiture *f*; (*of shoppers etc*) cohue *f*; (*also*: **traffic ~**) embouteillage *m* ♦ *vt* (*passage etc*) encombrer, obstruer; (*mechanism, drawer etc*) bloquer, coincer; (*RADIO*) brouiller ♦ *vi* (*mechanism, sliding part*) se coincer, se bloquer; (*gun*) s'enrayer; **to get sb out of a ~** (*col*) sortir qn du pétrin; **to ~ sth into** entasser *or* comprimer qch dans; **enfoncer qch dans**; **the telephone lines are ~med** les lignes (téléphoniques) sont encombrées.
Jamaica [jəmā'kə] *n* Jamaïque *f*.
Jamaican [jəmā'kən] *a* jamaïquain(e) ♦ *n* Jamaïquain/e.
jamb [jam] *n* jambage *m*.
jam-packed [jam'pakt'] *a*: **~ (with)** bourré(e) (de).
jam session *n* jam session *f*.
Jan. *abbr* (= *January*) janv.
jangle [jang'gəl] *vi* cliqueter.
janitor [jan'itûr] *n* (*caretaker*) huissier *m*;

concierge *m*.
January [jan'yōōwärē] *n* janvier *m*; *for phrases see also* **July**.
Japan [jəpan'] *n* Japon *m*.
Japanese [japənēz'] *a* japonais(e) ♦ *n* (*pl inv*) Japonais/e; (*LING*) japonais *m*.
jar [jâr] *n* (*container*) pot *m*, bocal *m* ♦ *vi* (*sound*) produire un son grinçant *or* discordant; (*colors etc*) détonner, jurer ♦ *vt* (*shake*) ébranler, secouer.
jargon [jâr'gən] *n* jargon *m*.
jarring [jâr'ing] *a* (*sound, color*) discordant(e).
Jas. *abbr* = *James*.
jasmin(e) [jaz'min] *n* jasmin *m*.
jaundice [jôn'dis] *n* jaunisse *f*.
jaundiced [jôn'dist] *a* (*fig*) envieux(euse), désapprobateur(trice).
jaunt [jônt] *n* balade *f*.
jaunty [jôn'tē] *a* enjoué(e); désinvolte.
Java [jâv'ə] *n* Java *f*.
javelin [jav'lin] *n* javelot *m*.
jaw [jô] *n* mâchoire *f*.
jawbone [jô'bōn] *n* maxillaire *m*.
jay [jā] *n* geai *m*.
jaywalker [jā'wôkûr] *n* piéton indiscipliné.
jazz [jaz] *n* jazz *m*.
  jazz up *vt* animer, égayer.
jazz band *n* orchestre *m or* groupe *m* de jazz.
jazzy [jaz'ē] *a* bariolé(e), tapageur(euse).
JCC *n abbr* (*US*) = *Junior Chamber of Commerce*.
JCS *n abbr* (*US*) = *Joint Chiefs of Staff*.
JD *n abbr* (*US*: = *Doctor of Laws*) titre universitaire; (: = *Justice Department*) ministère de la Justice.
jealous [jel'əs] *a* jaloux(ouse).
jealously [jel'əslē] *ad* jalousement.
jealousy [jel'əsē] *n* jalousie *f*.
jeans [jēnz] *npl* (blue-)jean *m*.
jeep [jēp] *n* jeep *f*.
jeer [jēr] *vi*: **to ~ (at)** huer; se moquer cruellement (de), railler.
jeering [jē'ring] *a* railleur(euse), moqueur(euse) ♦ *n* huées *fpl*.
jeers [jērz] *npl* huées *fpl*; sarcasmes *mpl*.
jelly [jel'ē] *n* gelée *f*.
jellyfish [jel'ēfish] *n* méduse *f*.
jeopardize [jep'ûrdīz] *vt* mettre en danger *or* péril.
jeopardy [jep'ûrdē] *n*: **in ~** en danger *or* péril.
jerk [jûrk] *n* secousse *f*; saccade *f*; sursaut *m*, spasme *m*; (*col*) pauvre type *m*; (: *idiot*) andouille *f* ♦ *vt* donner une secousse à ♦ *vi* (*vehicles*) cahoter.
jerkin [jûr'kin] *n* blouson *m*.
jerky [jûr'kē] *a* saccadé(e); cahotant(e).
jerry-built [jär'ēbilt] *a* de mauvaise qualité.
jerry can [jär'ē kan] *n* bidon *m*.
jersey [jûr'zē] *n* tricot *m*; (*fabric*) jersey *m*.
Jerusalem [jərōō'sələm] *n* Jérusalem.
jest [jest] *n* plaisanterie *f*; **in ~** en plaisantant.
jester [jes'tûr] *n* (*HIST*) plaisantin *m*.
Jesus [jē'səs] *n* Jésus *m*; **~ Christ** Jésus-Christ.
jet [jet] *n* (*of gas, liquid*) jet *m*; (*AUT*) gicleur *m*; (*AVIAT*) avion *m* à réaction, jet *m*.
jet-black [jet'blak'] *a* (d'un noir) de jais.
jet engine *n* moteur *m* à réaction.
jet lag *n* décalage *m* horaire.
jetsam [jet'səm] *n* objets jetés à la mer (et re-

jetés sur la côte).
jettison |jɛt'əsən| *vt* jeter par-dessus bord.
jetty |jɛt'ē| *n* jetée *f*, digue *f*.
Jew |jōō| *n* Juif *m*.
jewel |jōō'əl| *n* bijou *m*, joyau *m*.
jeweler, (*Brit*) **jeweller** |jōō'əlûr| *n* bijoutier/
ière, joaillier *m*; **~'s** (**shop**) *n* bijouterie *f*,
joaillerie *f*.
jewelry, (*Brit*) **jewellery** |jōō'əlrē| *n* bijoux
mpl.
Jewess |jōō'is| *n* Juive *f*.
Jewish |jōō'ish| *a* juif(juive).
JFK *n abbr* (*US*) = *John Fitzgerald Kennedy*
International Airport.
jib |jib| *n* (*NAUT*) foc *m*; (*of crane*) flèche *f* ♦
vi (*horse*) regimber; **to ~ at doing sth** rechigner à faire qch.
jibe |jīb| *n* sarcasme *m*.
jiffy |jif'ē| *n* (*col*): **in a ~** en un clin d'œil.
jig |jig| *n* (*dance, tune*) gigue *m*.
jigsaw |jig'sô| *n* (*also*: **~ puzzle**) puzzle *m*;
(*tool*) scie sauteuse.
jilt |jilt| *vt* laisser tomber, plaquer.
jingle |jing'gəl| *n* (*advertising* **~**) couplet *m* pu-
blicitaire ♦ *vi* cliqueter, tinter.
jingoism |jing'gōizəm| *n* chauvinisme *m*.
jinx |jingks| *n* (*col*) (mauvais) sort.
jitters |jit'ûrz| *npl* (*col*): **to get the ~** avoir la
trouille *or* la frousse.
jittery |jit'ûrē| *a* (*col*) froussard(e).
jiujitsu |jōōjit'sōō| *n* jiu-jitsu *m*.
job |jäb| *n* travail *m*; (*employment*) emploi *m*,
poste *m*, place *f*; **a part-time/full-time ~** un
emploi à temps partiel/à plein temps; **he's**
only doing his ~ il fait son boulot; **it's a**
good ~ that ... c'est heureux *or* c'est une
chance que ...; **just the ~!** (c'est) juste *or*
exactement ce qu'il faut!
job action *n* (*US*) action revendicative.
jobber |jäb'ûr| *n* (*Brit STOCK EXCHANGE*) né-
gociant *m* en titres.
jobbing |jäb'ing| *a* (*Brit*: *workman*) à la
tâche, à la journée.
Jobcentre |jäb'sentûr| *n* (*Brit*) agence *f* pour
l'emploi.
job creation scheme *n* (*Brit*) plan *m* pour
la création d'emplois.
job description *n* description *f* du poste.
jobless |jäb'lis| *a* sans travail, au chômage.
job lot *n* lot *m* (d'articles divers).
job satisfaction *n* satisfaction professionnelle.
job security *n* sécurité *f* de l'emploi.
job specification *n* caractéristiques *fpl* du
poste.
jockey |jäk'ē| *n* jockey *m* ♦ *vi*: **to ~ for posi-**
tion manœuvrer pour être bien placé.
jocular |jäk'yəlûr| *a* jovial(e), enjoué(e); facé-
tieux(euse).
jog |jäg| *vt* secouer ♦ *vi* (*SPORT*) faire du
jogging; **to ~ along** cahoter; trotter; **to ~**
sb's memory rafraîchir la mémoire de qn.
jogger |jäg'ûr| *n* jogger *m/f*.
jogging |jäg'ing| *n* jogging *m*.
john |jän| *n* (*US col*) w.-c. *mpl*, petit coin.
join |join| *vt* unir, assembler; (*become*
member of) s'inscrire à; (*meet*) rejoindre,
retrouver; se joindre à ♦ *vi* (*roads, rivers*) se
rejoindre, se rencontrer ♦ *n* raccord *m*; **will**

you **~** us for dinner? vous dînerez bien avec
nous?; **I'll ~ you later** je vous rejoindrai plus
tard; **to ~ forces** (**with**) s'associer (à).
join in *vi* se mettre de la partie ♦ *vt* se mêler à.
join up *vi* s'engager.
joiner |joi'nûr| *n* menuisier *m*.
joinery |joi'nûrē| *n* menuiserie *f*.
joint |joint| *n* (*TECH*) jointure *f*; joint *m*;
(*ANAT*) articulation *f*, jointure; (*Brit CULIN*)
rôti *m*; (*col*: *place*) boîte *f* ♦ *a* commun(e);
(*committee*) mixte, paritaire; **~ respon-**
sibility coresponsabilité *f*.
joint account (J/A) *n* compte joint.
jointly |joint'lē| *ad* ensemble, en commun.
joint ownership *n* copropriété *f*.
joint-stock company |joint'stâk' kum'pənē| *n*
société *f* par actions.
joint venture *n* entreprise commune.
joist |joist| *n* solive *f*.
joke |jōk| *n* plaisanterie *f*; (*also*: **practical ~**)
farce *f* ♦ *vi* plaisanter; **to play a ~ on** jouer
un tour à, faire une farce à.
joker |jō'kûr| *n* plaisantin *m*, blagueur/euse;
(*CARDS*) joker *m*.
joking |jō'king| *n* plaisanterie *f*.
jollity |jäl'itē| *n* réjouissances *fpl*, gaieté *f*.
jolly |jäl'ē| *a* gai(e), enjoué(e) ♦ *ad* (*Brit col*)
rudement, drôlement; **~ good!** (*Brit*) formidable!
jolt |jōlt| *n* cahot *m*, secousse *f* ♦ *vt* cahoter,
secouer.
Jordan |jôr'dun| *n* (*country*) Jordanie *f*; (*ri-*
ver) Jourdain *m*.
Jordanian |jôrdā'nēən| *a* jordanien(ne) ♦ *n*
Jordanien/ne.
joss stick |jäs stik| *n* bâton *m* d'encens.
jostle |jäs'əl| *vt* bousculer, pousser ♦ *vi* jouer
des coudes.
jot |jät| *n*: **not one ~** pas un brin.
jot down *vt* inscrire rapidement, noter.
jotter |jät'ûr| *n* (*Brit*) cahier *m* (de brouillon);
bloc-notes *m*.
journal |jûr'nəl| *n* journal *m*.
journalese |jûrnəlēz'| *n* (*pej*) style *m* journa-
listique.
journalism |jûr'nəlizəm| *n* journalisme *m*.
journalist |jûr'nəlist| *n* journaliste *m/f*.
journey |jûr'nē| *n* voyage *m*; (*distance cov-*
ered) trajet *m*; **a 5-hour ~** un voyage de 5
heures ♦ *vi* voyager.
jovial |jō'vēəl| *a* jovial(e).
jowl |joul| *n* mâchoire *f* (*inférieure*); bajoue *f*.
joy |joi| *n* joie *f*.
joyful |joi'fəl|, **joyous** |joi'əs| *a* joyeux(euse).
joy ride *n* virée *f* (*gén avec une voiture vo-*
lée).
joystick |joi'stik| *n* (*AVIAT*) manche *m* à balai;
(*COMPUT*) manche à balai, manette *f* (de
jeu).
JP *n abbr* = **Justice of the Peace**.
Jr. *abbr* = **junior**.
JTPA *n abbr* (*US*: = *Job Training Partnership*
Act) programme gouvernemental de formation.
jubilant |jōō'bələnt| *a* triomphant(e); ré-
joui(e).
jubilation |jōōbələ'shən| *n* jubilation *f*.
jubilee |jōō'bəlē| *n* jubilé *m*; **silver ~** (jubilé

du) vingt-cinquième anniversaire.

judge [juj] *n* juge *m* ♦ *vt* juger; (*estimate: weight, size etc*) apprécier; (*consider*) estimer ♦ *vi*: **judging** *or* **to ~ by his expression** d'après son expression; **as far as I can ~** autant que je puisse en juger; **I ~d it necessary to inform him** j'ai jugé nécessaire de l'informer.

judge advocate (JA) *n* (*MIL*) magistrat *m* militaire.

Judge Advocate General (JAG) *n* (*MIL*) magistrat *m* militaire en chef.

judg(e)ment [juj'mənt] *n* jugement *m*; (*punishment*) châtiment *m*; **in my ~** à mon avis; **to pass ~ on** (*LAW*) prononcer un jugement (sur).

judicial [jōōdish'əl] *a* judiciaire; (*fair*) impartial(e).

judiciary [jōōdish'ēārē] *n* (pouvoir *m*) judiciaire *m*.

judicious [jōōdish'əs] *a* judicieux(euse).

judo [jōō'dō] *n* judo *m*.

jug [jug] *n* pot *m*, cruche *f*.

juggernaut [jug'ûrnôt] *n* (*Brit: huge truck*) mastodonte *m*.

juggle [jug'əl] *vi* jongler.

juggler [jug'lûr] *n* jongleur *m*.

Jugoslav [yōō'gōslâv] *a*, *n* = **Yugoslav**.

jugular [jug'yəlûr] *a*: **~ (vein)** veine *f* jugulaire.

juice [jōōs] *n* jus *m*; (*col: gas*): **we've run out of ~** c'est la panne sèche.

juicy [jōō'sē] *a* juteux(euse).

jukebox [jōōk'bâks] *n* juke-box *m*.

Jul. *abbr* (= *July*) juil.

July [julī'] *n* juillet *m*; **the first of ~** le premier juillet; **(on) the eleventh of ~** le onze juillet; **in the month of ~** au mois de juillet; **at the beginning/end of ~** au début/à la fin (du mois) de juillet, début/fin juillet; **in the middle of ~** au milieu (du mois) de juillet, à la mi-juillet; **during ~** pendant le mois de juillet; **in ~ of next year** en juillet de l'année prochaine; **each** *or* **every ~** tous les ans *or* chaque année en juillet; **~ was wet this year** il a beaucoup plu cette année en juillet.

jumble [jum'bəl] *n* fouillis *m* ♦ *vt* (*also:* **~ up**, **~ together**) mélanger, brouiller.

jumble sale *n* (*Brit*) vente *f* de charité.

jumbo [jum'bō] *a*: **~ jet** (avion) gros porteur (à réaction); **~ size** format maxi *or* extra-grand.

jump [jump] *vi* sauter, bondir; (*start*) sursauter; (*increase*) monter en flèche ♦ *vt* sauter, franchir ♦ *n* saut *m*, bond *m*; sursaut *m*; (*fence*) obstacle *m*.

jump about *vi* sautiller.

jump at *vt fus* (*fig*) sauter sur; **he ~ed at the offer** il s'est empressé d'accepter la proposition.

jump down *vi* sauter (pour descendre).

jump up *vi* se lever (d'un bond).

jumped-up [jumpt'up] *a* (*Brit pej*) parvenu(e).

jumper [jum'pûr] *n* (*US: pinafore dress*) robe-chasuble *f*; (*Brit: pullover*) pull-over *m*; (*SPORT*) sauteur/euse.

jumper cables, (*Brit*) **jump leads** *npl* câbles *mpl* de démarrage.

jump rope *n* (*US*) corde *f* à sauter.

jump suit *n* combinaison *f* (d'aviateur).

jumpy [jum'pē] *a* nerveux(euse), agité(e).

Jun. *abbr* = **June**.

Jun., Junr *abbr* = **junior**.

junction [jungk'shən] *n* (*of rails*) embranchement *m*; (*Brit: of roads*) carrefour *m*.

juncture [jungk'chûr] *n*: **at this ~** à ce moment-là, sur ces entrefaites.

June [jōōn] *n* juin *m*; *for phrases see also* **July**.

jungle [jung'gəl] *n* jungle *f*.

junior [jōōn'yûr] *a*, *n*: **he's ~ to me (by 2 years)**, **he's my ~ (by 2 years)** il est mon cadet (de 2 ans), il est plus jeune que moi (de 2 ans); **he's ~ to me** (*seniority*) il est en dessous de moi (dans la hiérarchie), j'ai plus d'ancienneté que lui.

junior executive *n* cadre moyen.

junior high school *n* (*US*) ≈ collège *m* d'enseignement secondaire.

junior partner *n* associé(-adjoint) *m*.

junior school *n* (*Brit*) école *f* primaire, cours moyen.

junior sizes *npl* (*COMM*) tailles *fpl* fillettes/garçonnets.

juniper [jōō'nəpûr] *n*: **~ berry** baie *f* de genièvre.

junk [jungk] *n* (*trash*) bric-à-brac *m inv*; (*ship*) jonque *f* ♦ *vt* (*col*) abandonner, mettre au rancart.

junk dealer *n* brocanteur/euse.

junket [jung'kit] *n* (*CULIN*) lait caillé; (*Brit col*): **to go on a ~**, **go ~ing** voyager aux frais de la princesse.

junk foods *npl* snacks *mpl* (vite prêts).

junkie [jung'kē] *n* (*col*) junkie *m*, drogué/e.

junk room *n* débarras *m*.

junk shop *n* (boutique *f* de) brocanteur *m*.

junkyard [jungk'yârd] *n* parc *m* à ferrailles; (*for cars*) cimetière *m* de voitures.

junta [hōōn'tə] *n* junte *f*.

Jupiter [jōō'pitûr] *n* (*planet*) Jupiter *f*.

jurisdiction [jōōrisdik'shən] *n* juridiction *f*; **it falls** *or* **comes within/outside our ~** cela est/n'est pas de notre compétence *or* ressort.

jurisprudence [jōōrisprōōd'əns] *n* jurisprudence *f*.

juror [jōō'rûr] *n* juré *m*.

jury [jōō'rē] *n* jury *m*.

jury box *n* banc *m* des jurés.

juryman [jōōr'ēmən] *n* = **juror**.

just [just] *a* juste ♦ *ad*: **he's ~ done it/left** il vient de le faire/partir; **~ as I expected** exactement *or* précisément comme je m'y attendais; **~ right/two o'clock** exactement *or* juste ce qu'il faut/deux heures; **we were ~ going** nous partions; **I was ~ about to phone** j'allais téléphoner; **~ as he was leaving** au moment *or* à l'instant précis où il partait; **~ before/enough/here** juste avant/assez/là; **it's ~ me/a mistake** ce n'est que moi/(rien) qu'une erreur; **~ missed/caught** manqué/attrapé de justesse; **~ listen to this!** écoutez un peu ça!; **~ ask someone the way** vous n'avez qu'à demander votre chemin à quelqu'un; **it's ~ as good** c'est (vraiment) aussi bon; **it's ~ as well that you ...** heureusement que vous ...; **not ~ now** pas tout de suite; ~ **a minute!**, ~ **one moment!** un instant (s'il vous plaît)!

justice [jus'tis] *n* justice *f*; **this photo doesn't do you** ~ cette photo ne vous avantage pas.

Justice of the Peace (JP) *n* juge *m* de paix.

justifiable [jus'tifiəbəl] *a* justifiable.

justifiably [jus'təfiəblē] *ad* légitimement, à juste titre.

justification [justəfəkā'shən] *n* justification *f*.

justify [jus'təfī] *vt* justifier; **to be justified in doing sth** être en droit de faire qch.

justly [just'lē] *ad* avec raison, justement.

justness [just'nis] *n* justesse *f*.

jut [jut] *vi* (*also*: ~ **out**) dépasser, faire saillie.

jute [jōōt] *n* jute *m*.

juvenile [jōō'vənəl] *a* juvénile; (*court, books*) pour enfants ♦ *n* adolescent/e.

juvenile delinquency *n* délinquance *f* juvénile.

juxtapose [jukstəpōz'] *vt* juxtaposer.

juxtaposition [jukstəpəzish'ən] *n* juxtaposition *f*.

K

K, k [kā] *n* (*letter*) K, k *m*; **K for King** K comme Kléber.

K [kā] *abbr* (= *kilobyte*) Ko ♦ *n abbr* (= *one thousand*) K.

kaftan [kaf'tən] *n* cafetan *m*.

Kalahari Desert [káləhâr'ē dez'ûrt] *n* désert *m* de Kalahari.

kale [kāl] *n* chou frisé.

kaleidoscope [kəlī'dəskōp] *n* kaléidoscope *m*.

Kampala [kâmpâl'ə] *n* Kampala.

Kampuchea [kampōōchē'ə] *n* Kampuchéa *m*.

kangaroo [kanggərōō'] *n* kangourou *m*.

Kans. *abbr* (*US*) = *Kansas*.

kaput [kəpōōt'] *a* (*col*) kapout, capout.

karate [kərâ'tē] *n* karaté *m*.

Kashmir [kash'mēr] *n* Cachemire *m*.

kd *abbr* (*US*: = *knocked down*) en pièces détachées.

kebab [kəbáb'] *n* kébab *m*.

keel [kēl] *n* quille *f*; **on an even** ~ (*fig*) à flot.

keel over *vi* (*NAUT*) chavirer, dessaler; (*person*) tomber dans les pommes.

keen [kēn] *a* (*interest, desire, competition*) vif(vive); (*eye, intelligence*) pénétrant(e); (*edge*) effilé(e); (*eager*) plein(e) d'enthousiasme; **to be** ~ **to do** *or* **on doing sth** désirer vivement faire qch, tenir beaucoup à faire qch; **to be** ~ **on sth/sb** aimer beaucoup qch/qn; **I'm not** ~ **on going** je ne suis pas chaud pour aller, je n'ai pas très envie d'y aller.

keenly [kēn'lē] *ad* (*enthusiastically*) avec enthousiasme; (*feel*) vivement, profondément; (*look*) intensément.

keenness [kēn'nis] *n* (*eagerness*) enthousiasme *m*; ~ **to do** vif désir de faire.

keep [kēp] *vb* (*pt, pp* **kept** [kept]) *vt* (*retain,*

preserve) garder; (*hold back*) retenir; (*a store, the books, a diary*) tenir; (*feed: one's family etc*) entretenir, assurer la subsistance de; (*a promise*) tenir; (*chickens, bees, pigs etc*) élever ♦ *vi* (*food*) se conserver; (*remain: in a certain state or place*) rester ♦ *n* (*of castle*) donjon *m*; (*food etc*): **enough for his** ~ assez pour (assurer) sa subsistance; **to** ~ **doing sth** continuer à faire qch; faire qch continuellement; **to** ~ **sb from doing/sth from happening** empêcher qn de faire *or* que qn (ne) fasse/que qch (n')arrive; **to** ~ **sb happy/a place tidy** faire que qn soit content/qu'un endroit reste propre; **to** ~ **sb waiting** faire attendre qn; **to** ~ **an appointment** ne pas manquer un rendez-vous; **to** ~ **a record of sth** prendre note de qch; **to** ~ **sth to o.s.** garder qch pour soi, tenir qch secret; **to** ~ **sth (back) from sb** cacher qch à qn; **to** ~ **time** (*clock*) être à l'heure, ne pas retarder.

keep away *vt*: **to** ~ **sth/sb away from sb** tenir qch/qn éloigné de qn ♦ *vi*: **to** ~ **away (from)** ne pas s'approcher (de).

keep back *vt* (*crowds, tears, money*) retenir ♦ *vi* rester en arrière.

keep down *vt* (*control: prices, spending*) empêcher d'augmenter, limiter; (*retain: food*) garder ♦ *vi* (*person*) rester assis(e); rester par terre.

keep in *vt* (*invalid, child*) garder à la maison; ♦ *vi* (*col*): **to** ~ **in with sb** rester en bons termes avec qn.

keep off *vi* ne pas s'approcher; "~ **off the grass**" "pelouse interdite".

keep on *vi* continuer; **to** ~ **on doing** continuer à faire.

keep out *vt* empêcher d'entrer ♦ *vi* rester en dehors; "~ **out**" "défense d'entrer".

keep up *vi* se maintenir; (*fig: in comprehension*) suivre ♦ *vt* continuer, maintenir; **to** ~ **up with** se maintenir au niveau de; **to** ~ **up with sb** (*in race etc*) aller aussi vite que qn, être du même niveau que qn.

keeper [kē'pûr] *n* gardien/ne.

keep-fit [kēp'fit'] *n* (*Brit*) gymnastique *f* de maintien.

keeping [kē'ping] *n* (*care*) garde *f*; **in** ~ **with** à l'avenant de; en accord avec.

keeps [kēps] *n*: **for** ~**s** (*col*) pour de bon, pour toujours.

keepsake [kēp'sāk] *n* souvenir *m*.

keg [keg] *n* barrique *f*, tonnelet *m*.

Ken. *abbr* (*US*) = *Kentucky*.

kennel [ken'əl] *n* niche *f*; ~**s** *npl* chenil *m*.

Kenya [ken'yə] *n* Kenya *m*.

Kenyan [ken'yən] *a* Kenyen(ne) ♦ *n* Kenyen/ne.

kept [kept] *pt, pp* of **keep.**

kerb [kûrb] *n* (*Brit*) bordure *f* du trottoir.

kernel [kûr'nəl] *n* amande *f*; (*fig*) noyau *m*.

kerosene [kär'əsēn] *n* kérosène *m*.

ketchup [kech'əp] *n* ketchup *m*.

kettle [ket'əl] *n* bouilloire *f*.

kettle drums *npl* timbales *fpl*.

key [kē] *n* (*gen, MUS*) clé *f*; (*of piano, typewriter*) touche *f*; (*on map*) légende *f* ♦ *cpd* (-)clé.

key in *vt* (*text*) introduire au clavier.

keyboard [kē'bôrd] *n* clavier *m* ♦ *vt* (*text*)

saisir.
keyed up [kēd up] *a*: **to be (all)** ~ être surexcité(e).

keyhole [kē'hōl] *n* trou *m* de la serrure.

keynote [kē'nōt] *n* (*MUS*) tonique *f*; (*fig*) note dominante.

keypad [kē'pad] *n* pavé *m* numérique.

key ring *n* porte-clés *m*.

keystroke [kē'strōk] *n* frappe *f*.

kg *abbr* (= *kilogram*) K.

KGB *n abbr* KGB *m*.

khaki [kak'ē] *a*, *n* kaki (*m*).

kibbutz [kibōōts'] *n* kibboutz *m*.

kick [kik] *vt* donner un coup de pied à ♦ *vi* (*horse*) ruer ♦ *n* coup *m* de pied; (*of rifle*) recul *m*; (*col*: *thrill*): **he does it for** ~**s** il le fait parce que ça l'excite, il le fait pour le plaisir.
kick around *vi* (*col*) traîner.
kick off *vi* (*SPORT*) donner le coup d'envoi.

kickoff [kik'ôf] *n* (*SPORT*) coup *m* d'envoi.

kick-start [kik'stârt] *n* - (*Brit*: *also*: ~**er**) lanceur *m* au pied.

kid [kid] *n* (*col*: *child*) gamin/e, gosse *m/f*; (*animal*, *leather*) chevreau *m* ♦ *vi* (*col*) plaisanter, blaguer.

kidnap [kid'nap] *vt* enlever, kidnapper.

kidnap(p)er [kid'napûr] *n* ravisseur/euse.

kidnap(p)ing [kid'naping] *n* enlèvement *m*.

kidney [kid'nē] *n* (*ANAT*) rein *m*; (*CULIN*) rognon *m*.

kidney bean *n* haricot *m* rouge.

kidney machine *n* (*MED*) rein artificiel.

Kilimanjaro [kiləmənjâr'ō] *n*: **Mount** ~ Kilimandjaro *m*.

kill [kil] *vt* tuer; (*fig*) faire échouer; détruire; supprimer ♦ *n* mise *f* à mort; **to** ~ **time** tuer le temps.
kill off *vt* exterminer; (*fig*) éliminer.

killer [kil'ûr] *n* tueur/euse; meurtrier/ière.

killing [kil'ing] *n* meurtre *m*; tuerie *f*, massacre *m*; (*col*): **to make a** ~ se remplir les poches, réussir un beau coup ♦ *a* (*col*) tordant(e).

killjoy [kil'joi] *n* rabat-joie *m inv*.

kiln [kiln] *n* four *m*.

kilo [kē'lō] *n abbr* (= *kilogram*) kilo *m*.

kilobyte [kil'əbīt] *n* kilo-octet *m*.

kilogram, (*Brit*) **kilogramme** [kil'əgram] *n* kilogramme *m*.

kilometer, (*Brit*) **kilometre** [kil'əmētûr] *n* kilomètre *m*.

kilowatt [kil'əwât] *n* kilowatt *m*.

kilt [kilt] *n* kilt *m*.

kilter [kil'tûr] *n*: **out of** ~ déréglé(e), détraqué(e).

kimono [kimō'nō] *n* kimono *m*.

kin [kin] *n see* **next**, **kith**.

kind [kīnd] *a* gentil(le), aimable ♦ *n* sorte *f*, espèce *f*; (*species*) genre *m*; **to be two of a** ~ se ressembler; **would you be** ~ **enough to ...?, would you be so** ~ **as to ...?** auriez-vous la gentillesse *or* l'obligeance de ...?; **it's very** ~ **of you (to do)** c'est très aimable à vous (de faire); **in** ~ (*COMM*) en nature; (*fig*): **to repay sb in** ~ rendre la pareille à qn.

kindergarten [kin'dûrgârtən] *n* jardin *m* d'enfants.

kind-hearted [kīnd'hâr'tid] *a* bon(bonne).

kindle [kin'dəl] *vt* allumer, enflammer.

kindling [kin'dling] *n* petit bois.

kindly [kīnd'lē] *a* bienveillant(e), plein(e) de gentillesse ♦ *ad* avec bonté; **will you** ~ ... auriez-vous la bonté *or* l'obligeance de ...; **he didn't take it** ~ il l'a mal pris.

kindness [kīnd'nis] *n* bonté *f*, gentillesse *f*.

kindred [kin'drid] *a* apparenté(e); ~ **spirit** âme *f* sœur.

kinetic [kinet'ik] *a* cinétique.

king [king] *n* roi *m*.

kingdom [king'dəm] *n* royaume *m*.

kingfisher [king'fishûr] *n* martin-pêcheur *m*.

kingpin [king'pin] *n* (*TECH*) pivot *m*; (*fig*) cheville ouvrière.

king-size(d) [king'sīz(d)] *a* (*cigarette*) (format) extra-long(ue).

kink [kingk] *n* (*of rope*) entortillement *m*; (*in hair*) ondulation *f*; (*col*: *fig*) aberration *f*.

kinky [king'kē] *a* (*fig*) excentrique; (*pej*) aux goûts spéciaux.

kinship [kin'ship] *n* parenté *f*.

kinsman [kinz'mən] *n* parent *m*.

kinswoman [kinz'wōōmən] *n* parente *f*.

kiosk [kēâsk'] *n* kiosque *m*; (*Brit*: *also*: **telephone** ~) cabine *f* (téléphonique); (: *also*: **newspaper** ~) kiosque à journaux.

kipper [kip'ûr] *n* hareng fumé et salé.

kiss [kis] *n* baiser *m* ♦ *vt* embrasser; **to** ~ **(each other)** s'embrasser; **to** ~ **sb goodbye** dire au revoir à qn en l'embrassant; ~ **of life** *n* (*Brit*) bouche à bouche *m*.

kit [kit] *n* équipement *m*, matériel *m*; (*set of tools etc*) trousse *f*; (*for assembly*) kit *m*; **tool** ~ nécessaire *m* à outils.
kit out *vt* (*Brit*) équiper.

kitbag [kit'bag] *n* sac *m* de voyage *or* de marin.

kitchen [kich'ən] *n* cuisine *f*.

kitchen garden *n* jardin *m* potager.

kitchen sink *n* évier *m*.

kitchen unit *n* (*Brit*) élément *m* de cuisine.

kitchenware [kich'ənwär] *n* vaisselle *f*; ustensiles *mpl* de cuisine.

kite [kīt] *n* (*toy*) cerf-volant *m*; (*ZOOL*) milan *m*.

kith [kith] *n*: ~ **and kin** parents et amis *mpl*.

kitten [kit'ən] *n* petit chat, chaton *m*.

kitty [kit'ē] *n* (*money*) cagnotte *f*.

KKK *n abbr* (*US*) = *Ku Klux Klan*.

Kleenex [klē'neks] *n* ® Kleenex *m* ®.

kleptomaniac [kleptəmā'nēak] *n* kleptomane *m/f*.

km *abbr* (= *kilometer*) km.

km/h *abbr* (= *kilometers per hour*) km/h.

knack [nak] *n*: **to have the** ~ **(of doing)** avoir le coup (pour faire); **there's a** ~ il y a un coup à prendre or une combine.

knapsack [nap'sak] *n* musette *f*.

knave [nāv] *n* (*CARDS*) valet *m*.

knead [nēd] *vt* pétrir.

knee [nē] *n* genou *m*.

kneecap [nē'kap] *n* rotule *f*.

knee-deep [nē'dēp] *a*: **the water was** ~ l'eau arrivait aux genoux.

kneel, *pt*, *pp* **knelt** [nēl, nelt] *vi* (*also*: ~ **down**) s'agenouiller.

kneepad [nē'pad] *n* genouillère *f*.

knell [nɛl] *n* glas *m*.
knelt [nɛlt] *pt, pp of* **kneel**.
knew [nōō] *pt of* **know**.
knickers [nik'ûrz] *npl* (*Brit*) culotte *f* (de femme).
knick-knack [nik'nak] *n* colifichet *m*.
knife [nīf] *n* (*pl* **knives**) couteau *m* ♦ *vt* poignarder, frapper d'un coup de couteau; ~, **fork and spoon** couvert *m*.
knight [nīt] *n* chevalier *m*; (*CHESS*) cavalier *m*.
knighthood [nīt'hōōd] *n* chevalerie *f*; (*title*): **to get a ~** être fait chevalier.
knit [nit] *vt* tricoter; (*fig*): **to ~ together** unir ♦ *vi* (*broken bones*) se ressouder.
knitted [nit'id] *a* en tricot.
knitting [nit'ing] *n* tricot *m*.
knitting machine *n* machine *f* à tricoter.
knitting needle *n* aiguille *f* à tricoter.
knitting pattern *n* modèle *m* (pour tricot).
knitwear [nit'wär] *n* tricots *mpl*, lainages *mpl*.
knives [nīvz] *npl of* **knife**.
knob [nâb] *n* bouton *m*; (*Brit*): **a ~ of butter** une noix de beurre.
knobby [nâb'ē], (*Brit*) **knobbly** [nâb'lē] *a* (*wood, surface*) noueux(euse); (*knees*) noueux.
knock [nâk] *vt* frapper; (*make: hole etc*): **to ~ a hole in** faire un trou dans, trouer; (*Brit: force: nail etc*): **to ~ a nail into** enfoncer un clou dans; (*fig: col*) dénigrer ♦ *vi* (*engine*) cogner; (*at door etc*): **to ~ at/on** frapper à/sur ♦ *n* coup *m*; **he ~ed at the door** il frappa à la porte.
knock down *vt* renverser; (*price*) réduire.
knock off *vi* (*col: finish*) s'arrêter (de travailler) ♦ *vt* (*vase, object*) faire tomber; (*fig: from price etc*): **to ~ off $10** faire une remise de 10 dollars; (*col: steal*) piquer.
knock out *vt* assommer; (*BOXING*) mettre k.-o.
knock over *vt* (*object*) faire tomber; (*pedestrian*) renverser.
knockdown [nâk'doun] *a* (*price*) sacrifié(e); (*furniture etc*) démontable.
knocker [nâk'ûr] *n* (*on door*) heurtoir *m*.
knock-for-knock [nâk'fûrnâk'] *a* (*Brit*): **~ agreement** convention entre compagnies d'assurances par laquelle chacune s'engage à dédommager son propre client.
knocking [nâk'ing] *n* coups *mpl*.
knock-kneed [nâk'nēd] *a* aux genoux cagneux.
knock-on effect [nâk'ân ifekt'] *n* répercussions *fpl* en chaîne.
knockout [nâk'out] *n* (*BOXING*) knock-out *m*, K.-O. *m*.
knot [nât] *n* (*gen*) nœud *m* ♦ *vt* nouer; **to tie a ~** faire un nœud.
knotty [nât'ē] *a* (*fig*) épineux(euse).
know [nō] *vt* (*pt* **knew**, *pp* **known** [nōō, nōn]) savoir; (*person, place*) connaître; **to ~ that** savoir que; **to ~ how to do** savoir faire; **to ~ about/of sth** être au courant de/connaître qch; **to get to ~ sth** (*fact*) apprendre qch; (*place*) apprendre à connaître qch; **I don't ~ him** je ne le connais pas; **to ~ right from wrong** savoir distinguer le bon du mauvais; **as far as I ~ ...** à ma connaissance ...,

autant que je sache ....
know-all [nō'ôl] *n* (*Brit*) = **know-it-all**.
know-how [nō'hou] *n* savoir-faire *m*, technique *f*, compétence *f*.
knowing [nō'ing] *a* (*look etc*) entendu(e).
knowingly [nō'inglē] *ad* sciemment; d'un air entendu.
know-it-all [nō'itôl] *n* (*US pej*) je-sais-tout *m/f*.
knowledge [nâl'ij] *n* connaissance *f*; (*learning*) connaissances, savoir *m*; **to have no ~ of** ignorer; **not to my ~** pas à ma connaissance; **without my ~** à mon insu; **to have a working ~ of French** se débrouiller en français; **it is common ~ that ...** chacun sait que ...; **it has come to my ~ that ...** j'ai appris que ....
knowledgeable [nâl'ijəbəl] *a* bien informé(e).
known [nōn] *pp of* **know** ♦ *a* (*thief, facts*) notoire; (*expert*) célèbre.
knuckle [nuk'əl] *n* articulation *f* (des phalanges), jointure *f*.
knuckle under *vi* (*col*) céder.
knuckle-duster [nuk'əldustûr] *n* coup-de-poing américain.
KO *abbr* (= *knock out*) *n* K.-O. *m* ♦ *vt* mettre K.-O.
koala [kōâl'ə] *n* (*also*: **~ bear**) koala *m*.
kook [kōōk] *n* (*US col*) loufoque *m/f*.
Koran [kôrân'] *n* Coran *m*.
Korea [kôrē'ə] *n* Corée *f*; **North/South ~** Corée du Nord/Sud.
Korean [kôrē'ən] *a* coréen(ne) ♦ *n* Coréen/ne.
kosher [kō'shûr] *a* kascher *inv*.
kowtow [kou'tou] *vi*: **to ~ to sb** s'aplatir devant qn.
Kremlin [krem'lin] *n*: **the ~** le Kremlin.
KS *abbr* (*US MAIL*) = *Kansas*.
Kuala Lumpur [kōōâ'lə lōōm'pōōr] *n* Kuala Lumpur.
kudos [kyōō'dōs] *n* gloire *f*, lauriers *mpl*.
Kuwait [kōōwāt'] *n* Koweït *f*, Kuweït *f*.
Kuwaiti [kōōāt'ē] *a* koweïtien(ne) ♦ *n* Koweïtien/ne.
kW *abbr* (= *kilowatt*) kW.
KY *abbr* (*US MAIL*) = *Kentucky*.

L

L, l [el] *n* (*letter*) L, l *m*; **L for Love** L comme Louis.
L *abbr* (= *lake, large*) L; (= *left*) g; (*Brit AUT*: = *learner*) signale un conducteur débutant.
l *abbr* (= *liter*) l.
La. *abbr* (*US*) = *Louisiana*.
LA *n abbr* (*US*) = *Los Angeles* ♦ *abbr* (*US MAIL*) = *Louisiana*.
Lab. *abbr* (*Canada*) = *Labrador*.
lab [lab] *n abbr* (= *laboratory*) labo *m*.
label [lā'bəl] *n* étiquette *f*; (*brand: of record*) marque *f* ♦ *vt* étiqueter; **to ~ sb a ...** quali-

fier qn de ....

labor |lā'bûr| *(US)* *n* *(task)* travail *m*; *(workmen)* main-d'œuvre *f*; *(MED)* travail, accouchement *m* ♦ *vi*: **to ~ (at)** travailler dur (à), peiner (sur); **in ~** *(MED)* en travail.

laboratory |lab'rətôrē| *n* laboratoire *m*.

labor camp *n* camp *m* de travaux forcés.

labor cost *n* coût *m* de la main-d'œuvre; coût de la façon.

Labor Day *n* fête *f* du travail.

labor dispute *n* conflit social.

labored |lā'bûrd| *a* lourd(e), laborieux(euse); *(breathing)* difficile, pénible; *(style)* lourd, embarrassé(e).

laborer |lā'bûrûr| *n* manœuvre *m*; *(on farm)* ouvrier *m* agricole.

labor force *n* main-d'œuvre *f*.

labor-intensive |lā'bûrintensiv| *a* intensif(ive) en main-d'œuvre.

laborious |ləbôr'ēəs| *a* laborieux(euse).

labor market *n* marché *m* du travail.

labor pains *npl* douleurs *fpl* de l'accouchement.

labor relations *npl* relations *fpl* dans l'entreprise.

labor-saving |lā'bûrsā'ving| *a* qui simplifie le travail.

labor union *n* *(US)* syndicat *m*.

labor unrest *n* agitation sociale.

Labour |lā'bûr| *n* *(Brit POL: also*: **the ~ Party)** le parti travailliste, les travaillistes *mpl*.

labour *etc* |lā'bûr| *(Brit)* = **labor** *etc*.

labyrinth |lab'ûrinth| *n* labyrinthe *m*, dédale *m*.

lace |lās| *n* dentelle *f*; *(of shoe etc)* lacet *m* ♦ *vt* *(shoe)* lacer; *(drink)* arroser, corser.

lacemaking |lās'māking| *n* fabrication *f* de dentelle.

laceration |lasərā'shən| *n* lacération *f*.

lace-up |lās'up| *a* *(shoes etc)* à lacets.

lack |lak| *n* manque *m* ♦ *vt* manquer de; **through** *or* **for ~ of** faute de, par manque de; **to be ~ing** manquer, faire défaut; **to be ~ing in** manquer de.

lackadaisical |lakədā'zikəl| *a* nonchalant(e), indolent(e).

lackey |lak'ē| *n* *(also fig)* laquais *m*.

lackluster, *(Brit)* lacklustre |lak'lustûr| *a* terne.

laconic |ləkân'ik| *a* laconique.

lacquer |lak'ûr| *n* laque *f*.

lacy |lā'sē| *a* comme de la dentelle, qui ressemble à de la dentelle.

lad |lad| *n* garçon *m*, gars *m*; *(Brit: in stable etc)* lad *m*.

ladder |lad'ûr| *n* échelle *f*; *(Brit: in tights)* maille filée ♦ *vt*, *vi* *(Brit: tights)* filer.

laden |lā'dən| *a*: **~ (with)** chargé(e) (de); **fully ~** *(truck, ship)* en pleine charge.

ladle |lā'dəl| *n* louche *f*.

lady |lā'dē| *n* dame *f*; **L~ Smith** lady Smith; **the ladies' (room)** les toilettes *fpl* des dames; **a ~ doctor** une doctoresse, une femme médecin.

ladybird |lā'dēbûrd| *n* *(Brit)* coccinelle *f*.

ladybug |lā'dēbug| *n* *(US)* coccinelle *f*.

lady finger *n* *(US)* boudoir *m*.

lady-in-waiting |lā'dēinwā'ting| *n* dame *f*

d'honneur.

ladykiller |lā'dēkilûr| *n* don Juan *m*.

ladylike |lā'dēlik| *a* distingué(e).

lag |lag| *n* = **time ~** ♦ *vi* *(also:* **~ behind)** rester en arrière, traîner ♦ *vt* *(pipes)* calorifuger.

lager |lâ'gûr| *n* bière blonde.

lagging |lag'ing| *n* enveloppe isolante, calorifuge *m*.

lagoon |ləgōōn'| *n* lagune *f*.

Lagos |lâg'ōs| *n* Lagos.

laid |lād| *pt*, *pp* of **lay**.

laid-back |lād'bak'| *a* *(col)* relaxe, décontracté(e).

lain |lān| *pp* of **lie**.

lair |lär| *n* tanière *f*, gîte *m*.

laissez-faire |les'āfär'| *n* libéralisme *m*.

laity |lā'itē| *n* laïques *mpl*.

lake |lāk| *n* lac *m*.

lamb |lam| *n* agneau *m*.

lamb chop *n* côtelette *f* d'agneau.

lambskin |lam'skin| *n* (peau *f* d')agneau *m*.

lambswool |lams'wōōl| *n* *(Brit)* laine *f* d'agneau.

lame |lām| *a* boiteux(euse); **~ duck** *(fig)* canard boiteux.

lamely |lām'lē| *ad* *(fig)* sans conviction.

lament |ləment'| *n* lamentation *f* ♦ *vt* pleurer, se lamenter sur.

lamentable |lam'əntəbəl| *a* déplorable, lamentable.

laminated |lam'ənātid| *a* laminé(e); *(windshield)* (en verre) feuilleté.

lamp |lamp| *n* lampe *f*.

lamplight |lamp'lït| *n*: **by ~** à la lumière de la (*or* d'une) lampe.

lampoon |lampōōn'| *n* pamphlet *m*.

lamppost |lamp'pōst| *n* réverbère *m*.

lampshade |lamp'shād| *n* abat-jour *m* *inv*.

lance |lans| *n* lance *f* ♦ *vt* *(MED)* inciser.

lance corporal *n* *(Brit)* ≈ (soldat *m* de) première classe *m*.

lancet |lan'sit| *n* *(MED)* bistouri *m*.

Lancs |langks| *abbr* *(Brit)* = Lancashire.

land |land| *n* *(as opposed to sea)* terre *f* *(ferme)*; *(country)* pays *m*; *(soil)* terre; terrain *m*; *(estate)* terre(s), domaine(s) *m(pl)* ♦ *vi* *(from ship)* débarquer; *(AVIAT)* atterrir; *(fig: fall)* (re)tomber ♦ *vt* *(passengers, goods)* débarquer; *(obtain)* décrocher; **to go/travel by ~** se déplacer par voie de terre; **to own ~** être propriétaire foncier; **to ~ on one's feet** *(also fig)* retomber sur ses pieds.

land up *vi* atterrir, (finir par) se retrouver.

landing |lan'ding| *n* *(from ship)* débarquement *m*; *(AVIAT)* atterrissage *m*; *(of staircase)* palier *m*.

landing card *n* carte *f* de débarquement.

landing craft *n* péniche *f* de débarquement.

landing gear *n* train *m* d'atterrissage.

landing strip *n* piste *f* d'atterrissage.

landlady |land'lādē| *n* propriétaire *f*, logeuse *f*.

landlocked |land'lâkt| *a* entouré(e) de terre(s), sans accès à la mer.

landlord |land'lôrd| *n* propriétaire *m*, logeur *m*; *(of pub etc)* patron *m*.

landlubber |land'lubûr| *n* terrien/ne.

landmark |land'mârk| *n* (point *m* de) repère

m; **to be a** ~ *(fig)* faire date *or* époque.

landowner [land'ōnûr] *n* propriétaire foncier *or* terrien.

landscape [land'skāp] *n* paysage *m.*

landscape architect, landscape gardener *n* paysagiste *m/f.*

landscape painting *n* (*ART*) paysage *m.*

landslide [land'slīd] *n* (*GEO*) glissement *m* (de terrain); *(fig: POL)* raz-de-marée (électoral).

lane [lān] *n* (*in country*) chemin *m;* (*in town*) ruelle *f;* (*AUT*) voie *f;* file *f;* (*in race*) couloir *m;* **shipping** ~ route *f* maritime *or* de navigation.

language [lang'gwij] *n* langue *f;* (*way one speaks*) langage *m;* **bad** ~ grossièretés *fpl,* langage grossier.

language laboratory *n* laboratoire *m* de langues.

languid [lang'gwid] *a* languissant(e); langoureux(euse).

languish [lang'gwish] *vi* languir.

lank [langk] *a* (*hair*) raide et terne.

lanky [lang'kē] *a* grand(e) et maigre, efflanqué(e).

lanolin(e) [lan'əlin] *n* lanoline *f.*

lantern [lan'tûrn] *n* lanterne *f.*

Laos [lā'ōs] *n* Laos *m.*

lap [lap] *n* (*of track*) tour *m* (de piste); (*of body*): **in** *or* **on one's** ~ sur les genoux ♦ *vt* (*also:* ~ **up**) laper ♦ *vi* (*waves*) clapoter.

   lap up *vt* *(fig)* boire comme du petit-lait, se gargariser de; *(: lies etc)* gober.

La Paz [lä pâs'] *n* La Paz.

lapdog [lap'dôg] *n* chien *m* d'appartement.

lapel [ləpel'] *n* revers *m.*

Lapland [lap'lənd] *n* Laponie *f.*

lapse [laps] *n* défaillance *f;* (*in behavior*) écart *m* (de conduite) ♦ *vi* (*LAW*) cesser d'être en vigueur; se périmer; **to** ~ **into bad habits** prendre de mauvaises habitudes; ~ **of time** laps *m* de temps, intervalle *m;* **a** ~ **of memory** un trou de mémoire.

laptop [lap'tâp] *n* (*also:* ~ **computer**) portatif *m.*

larceny [lâr'sənē] *n* vol *m.*

lard [lârd] *n* saindoux *m.*

larder [lâr'dûr] *n* garde-manger *m inv.*

large [lârj] *a* grand(e); (*person, animal*) gros(grosse); **to make** ~**r** agrandir; **a** ~ **number of people** beaucoup de gens; **by and** ~ en général; **on a** ~ **scale** sur une grande échelle; **at** ~ (*free*) en liberté; (*generally*) en général; pour la plupart.

largely [lârj'lē] *ad* en grande partie.

large-scale [lârj'skāl] *a* (*map, drawing etc*) à grande échelle; *(fig)* important(e).

lark [lârk] *n* (*bird*) alouette *f;* (*joke*) blague *f,* farce *f.*

   lark about *vi* faire l'idiot, rigoler.

larva, *pl* **larvae** [lâr'və, lâr'vā] *n* larve *f.*

laryngitis [larənjī'tis] *n* laryngite *f.*

larynx [lar'ingks] *n* larynx *m.*

lascivious [ləsiv'ēəs] *a* lascif(ive).

laser [lā'zûr] *n* laser *m.*

laser beam *n* rayon *m* laser.

laser printer *n* imprimante *f* laser.

lash [lash] *n* coup *m* de fouet; (*also:* **eye**~) cil *m* ♦ *vt* fouetter; (*tie*) attacher.

   lash down *vt* attacher; amarrer; arrimer ♦

vi (*rain*) tomber avec violence.

   lash out *vi:* **to** ~ **out** (**at** *or* **against sb/sth**) attaquer violemment (qn/qch); **to** ~ **out** (**on sth**) *(col: spend)* se fendre (de qch).

lass [las] *n* (jeune) fille *f.*

lasso [las'ō] *n* lasso *m* ♦ *vt* prendre au lasso.

last [last] *a* dernier(ière) ♦ *ad* en dernier ♦ *vi* durer; ~ **week** la semaine dernière; ~ **night** hier soir; la nuit dernière; **at** ~ enfin; **next to (the)** ~ avant-dernier(ière); **the** ~ **time** la dernière fois; **it** ~**s (for) 2 hours** ça dure 2 heures.

last-ditch [last'dich] *a* ultime, désespéré(e).

lasting [las'ting] *a* durable.

lastly [last'lē] *ad* en dernier lieu, pour finir.

last-minute [last'min'it] *a* de dernière minute.

latch [lach] *n* loquet *m.*

   latch on to *vt* (*cling to: person*) s'accrocher à; (*: idea*) trouver bon(ne).

latchkey [lach'kē] *n* clé *f* (de la porte d'entrée).

late [lāt] *a* (*not on time*) en retard; (*far on in day etc*) dernier(ière); tardif(ive); (*recent*) récent(e), dernier; (*former*) ancien(ne); (*dead*) défunt(e) ♦ *ad* tard; (*behind time, schedule*) en retard; **to be** ~ avoir du retard; **to be 10 minutes** ~ avoir 10 minutes de retard; **to work** ~ travailler tard; ~ **in life** sur le tard, à un âge avancé; **of** ~ dernièrement; **in** ~ **May** vers la fin (du mois) de mai, fin mai; **the** ~ **Mr X** feu M. X.

latecomer [lāt'kumûr] *n* retardataire *m/f.*

lately [lāt'lē] *ad* récemment.

lateness [lāt'nis] *n* (*of person*) retard *m;* (*of event*) heure tardive.

latent [lā'tənt] *a* latent(e); ~ **defect** vice caché.

later [lā'tûr] *a* (*date etc*) ultérieur(e); (*version etc*) plus récent(e) ♦ *ad* plus tard; ~ **on today** plus tard dans la journée.

lateral [lat'ûrəl] *a* latéral(e).

latest [lā'tist] *a* tout(e) dernier(ière); **the** ~ **news** les dernières nouvelles; **at the** ~ au plus tard.

latex [lā'teks] *n* latex *m.*

lath, *pl* ~**s** [lath, lathz] *n* latte *f.*

lathe [lāth] *n* tour *m.*

lather [lath'ûr] *n* mousse *f* (de savon) ♦ *vt* savonner ♦ *vi* mousser.

Latin [lat'in] *n* latin *m* ♦ *a* latin(e).

Latin America *n* Amérique latine.

Latin American *a* latino-américain(e), d'Amérique latine ♦ *n* Latino-Américain/e.

latitude [lat'ətōōd] *n* (*also fig*) latitude *f.*

latrine [lətrēn'] *n* latrines *fpl.*

latter [lat'ûr] *a* deuxième, dernier(ière) ♦ *n:* **the** ~ ce dernier, celui-ci.

latterly [lat'ûrlē] *ad* dernièrement, récemment.

lattice [lat'is] *n* treillis *m;* treillage *m.*

lattice window *n* fenêtre treillissée, fenêtre à croisillons.

Latvia [lat'vēə] *n* Lettonie *f.*

laudable [lôd'əbəl] *a* louable.

laudatory [lôd'ətôrē] *a* élogieux(euse).

laugh [laf] *n* rire *m* ♦ *vi* rire.

   laugh at *vt fus* se moquer de; (*joke*) rire de.

   laugh off *vt* écarter *or* rejeter par une plaisanterie *or* par une boutade.

laughable [laf'əbəl] *a* risible, ridicule.

laughing [laf'ing] *a* rieur(euse); **this is no ~ matter** il n'y a pas de quoi rire, ça n'a rien d'amusant.

laughing gas *n* gaz hilarant.

laughing stock *n*: **the ~ of** la risée de.

laughter [laf'tûr] *n* rire *m*; (*people laughing*) rires *mpl*.

launch [lônch] *n* lancement *m*; (*boat*) chaloupe *f*; (*also*: **motor ~**) vedette *f* ♦ *vt* (*ship, rocket, plan*) lancer.

   launch out *vi*: **to ~ out (into)** se lancer (dans).

launching [lôn'ching] *n* lancement *m*.

launch(ing) pad *n* rampe *f* de lancement.

launder [lôn'dûr] *vt* blanchir.

launderette [lôndəret'] *n* (*Brit*) laverie *f* (automatique).

laundromat [lôn'drəmat] *n* (*US*) laverie *f* (automatique).

laundry [lôn'drē] *n* blanchisserie *f*; (*clothes*) linge *m*; **to do the ~** faire la lessive.

laureate [lôr'ēit] *a see* **poet laureate**.

laurel [lôr'əl] *n* laurier *m*; **to rest on one's ~s** se reposer sur ses lauriers.

lava [lâv'ə] *n* lave *f*.

lavatory [lav'ətôrē] *n* toilettes *fpl*.

lavender [lav'əndûr] *n* lavande *f*.

lavish [lav'ish] *a* copieux(euse); somptueux(euse); (*giving freely*): **~ with** prodigue de ♦ *vt*: **to ~ sth on sb** prodiguer qch à qn.

lavishly [lav'ishlē] *ad* (*give, spend*) sans compter; (*furnished*) luxueusement.

law [lô] *n* loi *f*; (*science*) droit *m*; **against the ~** contraire à la loi; **to study ~** faire du droit; **~ and order** *n* l'ordre public.

law-abiding [lô'əbīding] *a* respectueux(euse) des lois.

lawbreaker [lô'brākûr] *n* personne *f* qui transgresse la loi.

law court *n* tribunal *m*, cour *f* de justice.

lawful [lô'fəl] *a* légal(e); permis(e).

lawfully [lô'fəlē] *ad* légalement.

lawless [lô'lis] *a* sans loi.

lawmaker [lô'mākûr] *n* législateur/trice.

lawn [lôn] *n* pelouse *f*.

lawnmower [lôn'mōûr] *n* tondeuse *f* à gazon.

lawn tennis *n* tennis *m*.

law school *n* faculté *f* de droit.

law student *n* étudiant/e en droit.

lawsuit [lô'sōōt] *n* procès *m*; **to bring a ~ against** engager des poursuites contre.

lawyer [lô'yûr] *n* (*consultant, with company*) juriste *m*; (*for sales, wills etc*) ≈ notaire *m*; (*partner, in court*) ≈ avocat *m*.

lax [laks] *a* relâché(e).

laxative [lak'sətiv] *n* laxatif *m*.

laxity [lak'sitē] *n* relâchement *m*.

lay [lā] *pt of* **lie** ♦ *a* laïque; profane ♦ *vt* (*pt, pp* **laid** [lād]) poser, mettre; (*eggs*) pondre; (*trap*) tendre; (*plans*) élaborer; **to ~ the table** (*Brit*) mettre la table; **to ~ the facts/ one's proposals before sb** présenter les faits/ses propositions à qn; **to get laid** (*col!*) baiser (!); se faire baiser (!).

lay aside, **lay by** *vt* mettre de côté.

lay down *vt* poser; **to ~ down the law**

(*fig*) faire la loi.

lay in *vt* accumuler, s'approvisionner en.

lay into *vi* (*col*: *attack*) tomber sur; (: *scold*) passer une engueulade à.

lay off *vt* (*workers*) licencier.

lay on *vt* (*water, gas*) mettre, installer; (*provide*: *meal etc*) fournir; (*paint*) étaler.

lay out *vt* (*design*) dessiner, concevoir; (*display*) disposer; (*spend*) dépenser.

lay up *vt* (*to store*) amasser; (*car*) remiser; (*ship*) désarmer; (*subj*: *illness*) forcer à s'aliter.

layabout [lā'əbáut] *n* (*Brit*) fainéant/e.

lay-by [lā'bī] *n* (*Brit*) aire *f* de stationnement (sur le bas-côté).

lay days *npl* (*NAUT*) estarie *f*.

layer [lā'ûr] *n* couche *f*.

layette [lāet'] *n* layette *f*.

layman [lā'mən] *n* laïque *m*; profane *m*.

layoff [lā'ôf] *n* licenciement *m*.

layout [lā'áut] *n* disposition *f*, plan *m*, agencement *m*; (*PRESS*) mise *f* en page.

layover [lā'ōvûr] *n* (*US*) escale *f*.

laze [lāz] *vi* paresser.

laziness [lā'zēnis] *n* paresse *f*.

lazy [lā'zē] *a* paresseux(euse).

LB *abbr* (*Canada*) = Labrador.

lb. *abbr* (= *libra*: *pound*) unité de poids.

LC *n abbr* (*US*) = Library of Congress.

lc *abbr* (*TYP*: = *lower case*) b.d.c.

L/C *abbr* = **letter of credit**.

LCD *n abbr* = **liquid crystal display**.

LDS *n abbr* (= *Latter-day Saints*) *Église de Jésus-Christ des Saints du dernier jour*.

lead [lēd] *n* (*front position*) tête *f*; (*distance, time ahead*) avance *f*; (*clue*) piste *f*; (*to battery*) raccord *m*; (*ELEC*) fil *m*; (*for dog*) laisse *f*; (*THEATER*) rôle principal; [led] (*metal*) plomb *m*; (*in pencil*) mine *f* ♦ *vb* (*pt, pp* **led** [led]) *vt* mener, conduire; (*induce*) amener; (*be leader of*) être à la tête de; (*SPORT*) être en tête de; (*orchestra*: *US*) diriger; (: *Brit*) être le premier violon de ♦ *vi* mener, être en tête; **to ~ to** mener à; (*result in*) conduire à; aboutir à; **to ~ sb astray** détourner qn du droit chemin; **to be in the ~** (*SPORT*: *in race*) mener, être en tête; (: *match*) mener (à la marque); **to take the ~** (*SPORT*) passer en tête, prendre la tête; mener; (*fig*) prendre l'initiative; **to ~ sb to believe that ...** amener qn à croire que ...; **to ~ sb to do sth** amener qn à faire qch.

lead away *vt* emmener.

lead back *vt* ramener.

lead off *vi* (*in game etc*) commencer.

lead on *vt* (*tease*) faire marcher; **to ~ sb on to** (*induce*) amener qn à.

lead up to *vt* conduire à.

leaded [led'id] *a* (*gas*) avec plomb; (*windows*) à petits carreaux.

leaden [led'ən] *a* de *or* en plomb.

leader [lē'dûr] *n* (*of team*) chef *m*; (*of party etc*) dirigeant/e, leader *m*; (*of orchestra*: *US*) chef *m* d'orchestre; (: *Brit*) premier violon; (*Brit*: *in newspaper*) éditorial *m*; **they are ~s in their field** (*fig*) ils sont à la pointe du progrès dans leur domaine.

leadership [lē'dûrship] *n* direction *f*; **under the ~ of ...** sous la direction de ...; **qualities**

of ~ qualités *fpl* de chef *or* de meneur.
lead-free [lēdfrē'] *a* sans plomb.
leading [lē'ding] *a* de premier plan; (*main*) principal(e); **a ~ question** une question tendancieuse; **~ role** rôle prépondérant *or* de premier plan.
leading lady *n* (THEATER) vedette (féminine).
leading light *n* (*person*) sommité *f*, personnalité *f* de premier plan.
leading man *n* (THEATER) vedette (masculine).
lead pencil *n* crayon noir *or* à papier.
lead poisoning *n* saturnisme *m*.
lead time *n* (COMM) délai *m* de livraison.
lead weight *n* plomb *m*.
leaf, *pl* **leaves** [lēf, lēvz] *n* feuille *f*; (*of table*) rallonge *f*; **to turn over a new ~** (*fig*) changer de conduite *or* d'existence; **to take a ~ out of sb's book** (*fig*) prendre exemple sur qn.
leaf through *vt* (*book*) feuilleter.
leaflet [lēf'lit] *n* prospectus *m*, brochure *f*; (POL, REL) tract *m*.
leafy [lē'fē] *a* feuillu(e).
league [lēg] *n* ligue *f*; (SOCCER) championnat *m*; (*measure*) lieue *f*; **to be in ~ with** avoir partie liée avec, être de mèche avec.
leak [lēk] *n* (*out, also fig*) fuite *f*; (*in*) infiltration *f* ♦ *vi* (*pipe, liquid etc*) fuir; (*shoes*) prendre l'eau ♦ *vt* (*liquid*) répandre; (*information*) divulguer.
leak out *vi* fuir; (*information*) être divulgué(e).
leakage [lē'kij] *n* (*also fig*) fuite *f*.
leaky [lē'kē] *a* (*pipe, bucket*) qui fuit, percé(e); (*roof*) qui coule; (*shoe*) qui prend l'eau; (*boat*) qui fait eau.
lean [lēn] *a* maigre ♦ *n* (*of meat*) maigre *m* ♦ *vb* (*pt, pp* **leaned** *or* **leant** [lent]) *vt*: **to ~ sth on** appuyer qch sur ♦ *vi* (*slope*) pencher; (*rest*): **to ~ against** s'appuyer contre; être appuyé(e) contre; **to ~ on** s'appuyer sur.
lean back *vi* se pencher en arrière.
lean forward *vi* se pencher en avant.
lean out *vi*: **to ~ out (of)** se pencher au dehors (de).
lean over *vi* se pencher.
leaning [lē'ning] *a* penché(e) ♦ *n*: **~ (towards)** penchant *m* (pour); **the ~ Tower of Pisa** la tour penchée de Pise.
leant [lent] *pt, pp of* **lean.**
lean-to [lēn'tōō] *n* appentis *m*.
leap [lēp] *n* bond *m*, saut *m* ♦ *vi* (*pt, pp* **leaped** *or* **leapt** [lept]) bondir, sauter; **to ~ at an offer** saisir une offre.
leap up *vi* (*person*) faire un bond; se lever d'un bond.
leapfrog [lēp'frág] *n* jeu *m* de saute-mouton.
leapt [lept] *pt, pp of* **leap.**
leap year *n* année *f* bissextile.
learn, *pt, pp* **learned** *or* **learnt** [lûrn, -t] *vt, vi* apprendre; **to ~ how to do sth** apprendre à faire qch; **we were sorry to ~ that ...** nous apprenons avec regret que ...; **to ~ about sth** (SCOL) étudier qch; (*hear*) apprendre qch.
learned [lûr'nid] *a* érudit(e), savant(e).
learner [lûr'nûr] *n* débutant/e; (*Brit: also:* ~

driver) (conducteur/trice) débutant(e).
learning [lûr'ning] *n* savoir *m*.
lease [lēs] *n* bail *m* ♦ *vt* louer à bail; **on ~** en location.
lease back *vt* (*Brit*) vendre en cession-bail.
leaseback [lēs'bak] *n* (*Brit*) cession-bail *f*.
leasehold [lēs'hōld] *n* (*contract*) bail *m* ♦ *a* loué(e) à bail.
leash [lēsh] *n* laisse *f*.
least [lēst] *a*: **the ~** + *noun* le(la) plus petit(e), le(la) moindre; (*smallest amount of*) le moins de; **the ~** + *adjective* le(la) moins; **the ~ money** le moins d'argent; **the ~ expensive** le moins cher; **at ~** au moins; **not in the ~** pas le moins du monde.
leather [leth'ûr] *n* cuir *m* ♦ *cpd* en *or* de cuir; **~ goods** maroquinerie *f*.
leave [lēv] *vb* (*pt, pp* **left** [left]) *vt* laisser; (*go away from*) quitter ♦ *vi* partir, s'en aller ♦ *n* (*time off*) congé *m*; (MIL, *also: consent*) permission *f*; **to be left** rester; **there's some milk left over** il reste du lait; **to ~ school** quitter l'école, terminer sa scolarité; **~ it to me!** laissez-moi faire!, je m'en occupe!; **on ~** en permission; **to take one's ~ of** prendre congé de; **~ of absence** un congé exceptionnel; (MIL) permission spéciale.
leave behind *vt* (*also fig*) laisser; (*opponent in race*) distancer; (*forget*) laisser, oublier.
leave off *vt* (*cover, lid, heating*) ne pas (re)mettre; (*light*) ne pas (r)allumer, laisser éteint(e).
leave on *vt* (*coat etc*) garder, ne pas enlever; (*lid*) laisser dessus; (*light, fire, stove*) laisser allumé(e).
leave out *vt* oublier, omettre.
leaves [lēvz] *npl of* **leaf.**
leavetaking [lēv'tāking] *n* adieux *mpl*.
Lebanese [lebənēz'] *a* libanais(e) ♦ *n* (*pl inv*) Libanais/e.
Lebanon [leb'ənən] *n* Liban *m*.
lecherous [lech'ûrəs] *a* lubrique.
lectern [lek'tûrn] *n* lutrin *m*, pupitre *m*.
lecture [lek'chûr] *n* conférence *f*; (SCOL) cours (magistral) ♦ *vi* donner des cours; enseigner ♦ *vt* (*reprove*) sermonner, réprimander; **to ~ on** faire un cours (*or* son cours) sur; **to give a ~ (on)** faire une conférence (sur); faire un cours (sur).
lecture hall *n* amphithéâtre *m*.
lecturer [lek'chûrûr] *n* (*speaker*) conférencier/ière; (*Brit: at university*) chargé/e de cours, ≈ maître assistant (*inv*).
LED *n abbr* (= *light-emitting diode*) LED *f*, diode électroluminescente.
led [led] *pt, pp of* **lead.**
ledge [lej] *n* (*of window, on wall*) rebord *m*; (*of mountain*) saillie *f*, corniche *f*.
ledger [lej'ûr] *n* registre *m*, grand livre.
lee [lē] *n* côté *m* sous le vent; **in the ~ of** à l'abri de.
leech [lēch] *n* sangsue *f*.
leek [lēk] *n* poireau *m*.
leer [lēr] *vi*: **to ~ at sb** regarder qn d'un air mauvais *or* concupiscent, lorgner qn.
leeward [lē'wûrd] *a, ad* sous le vent ♦ *n* côté *m* sous le vent; **to ~** sous le vent.
leeway [lē'wā] *n* (*fig*): **to make up ~** rattra-

per son retard; **to have some** ~ avoir une certaine liberté d'action.

left [left] *pt, pp of* **leave** ♦ *a* gauche ♦ *ad* à gauche ♦ *n* gauche *f*; **on the ~, to the ~** à gauche; **the L~** (*POL*) la gauche.

left-hand drive [left'hand' drīv] *n* conduite *f* à gauche.

left-handed [left'han'did] *a* gaucher(ère); (*scissors etc*) pour gauchers.

left-hand side [left'hand' sīd] *n* gauche *f*, côté *m* gauche.

leftist [lef'tist] *a* (*POL*) gauchiste, de gauche.

left-luggage (office) [leftlug'ij (ôf'is)] *n* (*Brit*) consigne *f*.

leftovers [left'ō'vûrz] *npl* restes *mpl*.

left wing *n* (*MIL, SPORT*) aile *f* gauche; (*POL*) gauche *f* ♦ *a*: **left-wing** (*POL*) de gauche.

left-winger [left'wing'ûr] *n* (*POL*) membre *m* de la gauche; (*SPORT*) ailier *m* gauche.

leg [leg] *n* jambe *f*; (*of animal*) patte *f*; (*of furniture*) pied *m*; (*CULIN: of chicken*) cuisse *f*; **lst/2nd ~** (*SPORT*) match *m* aller/retour; (*of journey*) 1ère/2ème étape; **~ of lamb** (*CULIN*) gigot *m* d'agneau; **to stretch one's ~s** se dégourdir les jambes.

legacy [leg'əsē] *n* (*also fig*) héritage *m*, legs *m*.

legal [lē'gəl] *a* légal(e); **to take ~ action** *or* **proceedings against sb** poursuivre qn en justice.

legal adviser *n* conseiller/ère juridique.

legal holiday *n* (*US*) jour férié.

legality [lēgal'itē] *n* légalité *f*.

legalize [lē'gəlīz] *vt* légaliser.

legally [lē'gəlē] *ad* légalement; **~ binding** juridiquement contraignant(e).

legal tender *n* monnaie légale.

legation [ligā'shən] *n* légation *f*.

legend [lej'ənd] *n* légende *f*.

legendary [lej'əndārē] *a* légendaire.

-legged [leg'id] *suffix*: **two~** à deux pattes (*or* jambes *or* pieds).

leggings [leg'ingz] *npl* jambières *fpl*, guêtres *fpl*.

legibility [lejəbil'ətē] *n* lisibilité *f*.

legible [lej'əbəl] *a* lisible.

legibly [lej'əblē] *ad* lisiblement.

legion [lē'jən] *n* légion *f*.

legionnaire [lējənär'] *n* légionnaire *m*; **~'s disease** maladie *f* du légionnaire.

legislate [lej'islāt] *vi* légiférer.

legislation [lejislā'shən] *n* législation *f*; **a piece of ~** un texte de loi.

legislative [lej'islātiv] *a* législatif(ive).

legislator [lej'islātûr] *n* législateur/trice.

legislature [lej'islāchûr] *n* corps législatif.

legitimacy [lijit'əməsē] *n* légitimité *f*.

legitimate [lijit'əmit] *a* légitime.

legitimize [lijit'əmīz] *vt* légitimer.

legroom [leg'rōōm] *n* place *f* pour les jambes.

leg warmers [leg' wôrm'ûrz] *npl* jambières *fpl*.

Leics *abbr* (*Brit*) = *Leicestershire.*

leisure [lē'zhûr] *n* (*time*) loisir *m*, temps *m*; (*free time*) temps libre, loisirs *mpl*; **at ~** (*tout*) à loisir; à tête reposée.

leisurely [lē'zhûrlē] *a* tranquille; fait(e) sans se presser.

leisure suit *n* survêtement *m* (mode).

lemon [lem'ən] *n* citron *m*.

lemonade [lemənād'] *n* limonade *f*.

lemon cheese, lemon curd *n* crème *f* de citron.

lemon juice *n* jus *m* de citron.

lemon juicer [lem'ən jōō'sûr] *n* presse-citron *m inv.*

lemon tea *n* thé *m* au citron.

lend, *pt, pp* **lent** [lend, lent] *vt*: **to ~ sth (to sb)** prêter qch (à qn); **to ~ a hand** donner un coup de main.

lender [len'dûr] *n* prêteur/euse.

lending library [len'ding li'brärē] *n* bibliothèque *f* de prêt.

length [lengkth] *n* longueur *f*; (*section: of road, pipe etc*) morceau *m*, bout *m*; **~ of time** durée *f*; **what ~ is it?** quelle longueur fait-il?; **it is 2 meters in ~** cela fait 2 mètres de long; **to fall full ~** tomber de tout son long; **at ~** (*at last*) enfin, à la fin; (*lengthily*) longuement; **to go to any ~(s) to do sth** faire n'importe quoi pour faire qch, ne reculer devant rien pour faire qch.

lengthen [lengk'thən] *vt* allonger, prolonger ♦ *vi* s'allonger.

lengthwise [lengkth'wīz] *ad* dans le sens de la longueur, en long.

lengthy [lengk'thē] *a* (très) long(longue).

leniency [lē'nēənsē] *n* indulgence *f*, clémence *f*.

lenient [lē'nēənt] *a* indulgent(e), clément(e).

leniently [lē'nēəntlē] *ad* avec indulgence *or* clémence.

lens [lenz] *n* lentille *f*; (*of spectacles*) verre *m*; (*of camera*) objectif *m*.

Lent [lent] *n* Carême *m*.

lent [lent] *pt, pp of* **lend**.

lentil [len'təl] *n* lentille *f*.

Leo [lē'ō] *n* le Lion; **to be ~** être du Lion.

leopard [lep'ûrd] *n* léopard *m*.

leotard [lē'ətärd] *n* maillot *m* (*de danseur etc*).

leper [lep'ûr] *n* lépreux/euse.

leper colony *n* léproserie *f*.

leprosy [lep'rəsē] *n* lèpre *f*.

lesbian [lez'bēən] *n* lesbienne *f* ♦ *a* lesbien(ne).

lesion [lē'zhən] *n* (*MED*) lésion *f*.

Lesotho [lisōō'tōō] *n* Lesotho *m*.

less [les] *a* moins de ♦ *pronoun, ad* moins; **~ than that/you** moins que cela/vous; **~ than half** moins de la moitié; **~ than 1/a kilo/3 meters** moins de un/d'un kilo /de 3 mètres; **~ and ~** de moins en moins; **the ~ he works** ... moins il travaille ....

lessee [lesē'] *n* locataire *m/f* (à bail), preneur/ euse du bail.

lessen [les'ən] *vi* diminuer, s'amoindrir, s'atténuer ♦ *vt* diminuer, réduire, atténuer.

lesser [les'ûr] *a* moindre; **to a ~ extent** *or* **degree** à un degré moindre.

lesson [les'ən] *n* leçon *f*; **a math ~** une leçon *or* un cours de maths; **to give ~s in** donner des cours de; **it taught him a ~** (*fig*) cela lui a servi de leçon.

lessor [les'ôr] *n* bailleur/eresse.

lest [lest] *cj* de peur de + *infinitive*, de peur que + *sub*.

let, *pt, pp* **let** [let] *vt* laisser; (*Brit: lease*) louer; **to ~ sb do sth** laisser qn faire qch; **to ~ sb know sth** faire savoir qch à qn, prévenir qn de qch; **he ~ me go** il m'a laissé partir; **~ the water boil and ...** faites bouillir l'eau et ...; **~'s go** allons-y; **~ him come** qu'il vienne; "**to ~**" (*Brit*) "à louer".

let down *vt* (*lower*) baisser; (*dress*) rallonger; (*hair*) défaire; (*Brit: tire*) dégonfler; (*disappoint*) décevoir.

let go *vi* lâcher prise ♦ *vt* lâcher.

let in *vt* laisser entrer; (*visitor etc*) faire entrer; **what have you ~ yourself in for?** à quoi t'es-tu engagé?

let off *vt* (*allow to leave*) laisser partir; (*not punish*) ne pas punir; (*subj: taxi driver, bus driver*) déposer; (*firework etc*) faire partir; (*smell etc*) dégager; **to ~ off steam** (*fig: col*) se défouler, décharger sa rate *or* bile.

let on *vi* (*col*): **to ~ on that ...** révéler que ..., dire que ....

let out *vt* laisser sortir; (*dress*) élargir; (*scream*) laisser échapper; (*rent out*) louer.

let up *vi* diminuer, s'arrêter.

letdown [let'dâun] *n* (*disappointment*) déception *f*.

lethal [lē'thəl] *a* mortel(le), fatal(e).

lethargic [ləthâr'jik] *a* léthargique.

lethargy [leth'ûrjē] *n* léthargie *f*.

letter [let'ûr] *n* lettre *f*; **~s** *npl* (*LITERATURE*) lettres; **small/capital ~** minuscule *f*/majuscule *f*; **~ of credit** lettre *f* de crédit.

letter bomb *n* lettre piégée.

letterbox [let'ûrbâks] *n* (*Brit*) boîte *f* aux *or* à lettres.

letterhead [let'ûrhed] *n* en-tête *m*.

lettering [let'ûring] *n* lettres *fpl*; caractères *mpl*.

letter opener *n* coupe-papier *m*.

letterpress [let'ûrpres] *n* (*method*) typographie *f*.

letter quality *n* qualité *f* "courrier".

letters patent *npl* brevet *m* d'invention.

lettuce [let'is] *n* laitue *f*, salade *f*.

letup [let'up] *n* répit *m*, détente *f*.

leukemia, (*Brit*) **leukaemia** [lookē'mēə] *n* leucémie *f*.

level [lev'əl] *a* plat(e), plan(e), uni(e); horizontal(e) ♦ *n* niveau *m*; (*flat place*) terrain plat; (*also*: **spirit ~**) niveau à bulle ♦ *vt* niveler, aplanir; (*gun*) pointer, braquer; (*accusation*): **to ~** (*against*) lancer *or* porter (contre) ♦ *vi* (*col*): **to ~ with sb** être franc(franche) avec qn; "**A**" **~s** *npl* (*Brit*) ≈ baccalauréat *m*; "**O**" **~s** *npl* (*Brit*) ≈ B.E.P.C; **a ~ spoonful** (*CULIN*) une cuillerée à raser; **to be ~ with** être au même niveau que; **to draw ~ with** (*team*) arriver à égalité de points avec, égaliser avec; arriver au même classement que; (*runner, car*) arriver à la hauteur de, rattraper; **on the ~** à l'horizontale; (*fig: honest*) régulier(ière).

level off, **level out** *vi* (*prices etc*) se stabiliser ♦ *vt* (*ground*) aplanir, niveler.

level crossing *n* (*Brit*) passage *m* à niveau.

levelheaded [lev'əlhed'id] *a* équilibré(e).

leveling, (*Brit*) **levelling** [lev'əling] *a* (*process, effect*) de nivellement.

lever [le'vûr] *n* levier *m* ♦ *vt*: **to ~ up/out**

soulever/extraire au moyen d'un levier.

leverage [lev'ûrij] *n*: **~ (on** *or* **with)** prise *f* (sur).

levity [lev'itē] *n* manque *m* de sérieux, légèreté *f*.

levy [lev'ē] *n* taxe *f*, impôt *m* ♦ *vt* prélever, imposer; percevoir.

lewd [lood] *a* obscène, lubrique.

LF *abbr* (= *low frequency*) BF.

LI *abbr* (*US*) = Long Island.

liabilities [līəbil'ətēz] *npl* (*COMM*) obligations *fpl*, engagements *mpl*; (*on balance sheet*) passif *m*.

liability [līəbil'ətē] *n* responsabilité *f*; (*handicap*) handicap *m*.

liability insurance *n* (*US*) assurance *f* au tiers.

liable [lī'əbəl] *a* (*subject*): **~ to** sujet(te) à; passible de; (*responsible*): **~ (for)** responsable (de); (*likely*): **~ to do** susceptible de faire; **to be ~ to a fine** être passible d'une amende.

liaise [lēāz'] *vi*: **to ~ with** rester en liaison avec.

liaison [lēā'zân] *n* liaison *f*.

liar [lī'ûr] *n* menteur/euse.

libel [lī'bəl] *n* écrit *m* diffamatoire; diffamation *f* ♦ *vt* diffamer.

libelous, (*Brit*) **libellous** [lī'bələs] *a* diffamatoire.

liberal [lib'ûrəl] *a* libéral(e); (*generous*): **~ with** prodigue de, généreux(euse) avec ♦ *n*: **L~** (*POL*) libéral/e.

liberality [libərəl'itē] *n* (*generosity*) générosité *f*, libéralité *f*.

liberalize [lib'ûrəlīz] *vt* libéraliser.

liberal-minded [lib'ûrəlmīn'did] *a* libéral(e), tolérant(e).

liberate [lib'ərāt] *vt* libérer.

liberation [libərā'shən] *n* libération *f*.

Liberia [lībē'rēə] *n* Libéria *m*, Liberia *m*.

Liberian [lībē'rēən] *a* libérien(ne) ♦ *n* Libérien/ne.

liberty [lib'ûrtē] *n* liberté *f*; **at ~ to do** libre de faire; **to take the ~ of** prendre la liberté de, se permettre de.

libido [libē'dō] *n* libido *f*.

Libra [lēb'rə] *n* la Balance; **to be ~** être de la Balance.

librarian [lībrär'ēən] *n* bibliothécaire *m/f*.

library [lī'brärē] *n* bibliothèque *f*.

library book *n* livre *m* de bibliothèque.

libretto [libret'ō] *n* livret *m*.

Libya [lib'ēə] *n* Libye *f*.

Libyan [lib'ēən] *a* libyen(ne), de Libye ♦ *n* Libyen/ne.

lice [līs] *npl* of **louse**.

licence [lī'səns] *n* (*Brit*) = **license**.

license [lī'səns] *n* (*US*) autorisation *f*, permis *m*; (*COMM*) licence *f*; (*RADIO, TV*) redevance *f*; (*also*: **driver's ~**, (*Brit*) **driving ~**) permis *m* (de conduire); (*excessive freedom*) licence; **import ~** licence d'importation; **produced under ~** fabriqué(e) sous licence ♦ *vt* donner une licence à; (*car*) acheter la vignette de; délivrer la vignette de.

licensed [lī'sənst] *a* (*for alcohol*) patenté(e) pour la vente des spiritueux, qui a une patente de débit de boissons.

license plate n (esp US AUT) plaque f miné- ralogique.

licentious [līsen'chəs] a licentieux(euse).

lichen [lī'kən] n lichen m.

lick [lik] vt lécher; (col: defeat) écraser, flanquer une piquette or raclée à ♦ n coup m de langue; **a ~ of paint** un petit coup de peinture.

licorice [lik'ûris] n (US) réglisse m.

lid [lid] n couvercle m; **to take the ~ off sth** (fig) exposer or étaler qch au grand jour.

lido [lē'dō] n piscine f en plein air; complexe m balnéaire.

lie [lī] n mensonge m ♦ vi mentir; (pt **lay**, pp **lain** [lā, lān]) (rest) être étendu(e) or allongé(e) or couché(e); (in grave) être enterré(e), reposer; (of object: be situated) se trouver, être; **to ~ low** (fig) se cacher, rester caché(e); **to tell ~s** mentir.

lie around vi (things) traîner; (person) traînasser, flemmarder.

lie back vi se renverser en arrière.

lie down vi se coucher, s'étendre.

lie up vi (hide) se cacher.

Liechtenstein [lēch'tenstīn] n Liechtenstein m.

lie detector n détecteur m de mensonges.

lieu [lōō]: **in ~ of** prep au lieu de, à la place de.

Lieut. abbr (= lieutenant) Lt.

lieutenant [lōōten'ənt] n lieutenant m.

lieutenant colonel n lieutenant-colonel m.

life, pl **lives** [līf, līvz] n vie f ♦ cpd de vie; de la vie; à vie; **true to ~** réaliste, fidèle à la réa- lité; **to paint from ~** peindre d'après nature; **to be sent to prison for ~** être condamné(e) (à la réclusion criminelle) à perpétuité; **country/city ~** la vie à la campagne/à la ville.

life annuity n pension f, rente viagère.

life belt n bouée f de sauvetage.

lifeblood [līf'blud] n (fig) élément moteur.

lifeboat [līf'bōt] n canot m or chaloupe f de sauvetage.

life buoy n bouée f de sauvetage.

life expectancy n espérance f de vie.

lifeguard [līf'gârd] n surveillant m de baigna- de.

life imprisonment n prison f à vie; (LAW) réclusion f à perpétuité.

life insurance n assurance-vie f.

life jacket n gilet m or ceinture f de sauveta- ge.

lifeless [līf'lis] a sans vie, inanimé(e); (dull) qui manque de vie or de vigueur.

lifelike [līf'līk] a qui semble vrai(e) or vi- vant(e); ressemblant(e).

lifeline [līf'līn] n corde f de sauvetage.

lifelong [līf'lông] a de toute une vie, de tou- jours.

life preserver [līf prēzûrv'ûr] n (US) gilet m or ceinture f de sauvetage.

life raft n radeau m de sauvetage.

lifesaver [līf'sāvûr] n surveillant m de baignade.

life sentence n condamnation f à vie or à perpétuité.

life-sized [līf'sīzd] a grandeur nature inv.

life span n (durée f de) vie f.

life style n style m de vie.

life support system n (MED) respirateur artificiel.

lifetime [līf'tīm] n: **in his ~** de son vivant; **the chance of a ~** la chance de ma (or sa etc) vie, une occasion unique.

lift [lift] vt soulever, lever; (steal) prendre, vo- ler ♦ vi (fog) se lever ♦ n (Brit: elevator) ascenseur m; **to give sb a ~** (Brit) emme- ner or prendre qn en voiture.

lift off vi (rocket, helicopter) décoller.

lift out vt sortir; (troops, evacuees etc) éva- cuer par avion or hélicoptère.

lift up vt soulever.

lift-off [lift'âf] n décollage m.

ligament [lig'əmənt] n ligament m.

light [līt] n lumière f; (daylight) lumière, jour m; (lamp) lampe f; (AUT: traffic ~, rear ~) feu m; (: headlamp) phare m; (for cigarette etc): **have you got a ~?** avez-vous du feu? ♦ vt (pt, pp **lighted** or **lit** [lit]) (candle, ciga- rette, fire) allumer; (room) éclairer ♦ a (room, color) clair(e); (not heavy, also fig) léger(ère) ♦ ad (travel) avec peu de baga- ges; **to turn the ~ on/off** allumer/éteindre; **to cast** or **shed** or **throw ~ on** éclaircir; **to come to ~** être dévoilé(e) or découvert(e); **in the ~ of** à la lumière de; étant donné; **to make ~ of sth** (fig) prendre qch à la légère, faire peu de cas de qch.

light up vi s'allumer; (face) s'éclairer ♦ vt (illuminate) éclairer, illuminer.

light bulb n ampoule f.

lighten [lī'tən] vi s'éclairer ♦ vt (give light to) éclairer; (make lighter) éclaircir; (make less heavy) alléger.

lighter [lī'tûr] n (also: **cigarette ~**) briquet m; (: in car) allume-cigare m inv; (boat) pé- niche f.

lighter fluid n gaz m à briquet.

light-fingered [līt'finggûrd] a cha- pardeur(euse).

light-headed [līt'hed'id] a étourdi(e), écerve- lé(e).

lighthearted [līt'hâr'tid] a gai(e), joyeux(euse), enjoué(e).

lighthouse [līt'hâus] n phare m.

lighting [lī'ting] n (on road) éclairage m; (in theater) éclairages.

lightly [līt'lē] ad légèrement; **to get off ~** s'en tirer à bon compte.

light meter n (PHOT) photomètre m, posemè- tre m.

lightness [līt'nis] n clarté f; (in weight) légè- reté f.

lightning [līt'ning] n éclair m, foudre f.

lightning conductor n (Brit) paratonnerre m.

lightning rod n (US) paratonnerre m.

lightning strike n (Brit) grève f surprise.

light pen n crayon m optique.

lightship [līt'ship] n bateau-phare m.

lightweight [līt'wāt] a (suit) léger(ère); (boxer) poids léger inv.

light-year [līt'yēr] n année-lumière f.

like [līk] vt aimer (bien) ♦ prep comme ♦ a semblable, pareil(le) ♦ n: **the ~** un(e) pa- reil(le) or semblable; le(la) pareil(le); (pej) (d')autres du même genre or acabit; **his ~s and dislikes** ses goûts mpl or préférences *fpl*; **I would** ~, **I'd** ~ je voudrais, j'aimerais; **would you** ~ **a coffee?** voulez-vous du café?; **to be/look** ~ **sb/sth** ressembler à qn/qch; **what's he** ~**?** comment est-il?; **what's the weather** ~**?** quel temps fait-il?; **that's just** ~ **him** c'est bien de lui, ça lui ressemble; **something** ~ **that** quelque chose comme ça; **I feel** ~ **a drink** je boirais bien quelque chose; **if you** ~ si vous voulez; **there's nothing** ~ ... il n'y a rien de tel que ....

likeable [lī'kəbəl] *a* sympathique, agréable.

likelihood [līk'lēhōōd] *n* probabilité *f*; **in all** ~ selon toute vraisemblance.

likely [līk'lē] *a* (*result, outcome*) probable; (*excuse*) plausible; **he's** ~ **to leave** il va sûrement partir, il risque fort de partir; **not** ~**!** (*col*) pas de danger!

like-minded [līk'mīn'did] *a* de même opinion.

liken [lī'kən] *vt*: **to** ~ **sth to** comparer qch à.

likeness [līk'nis] *n* ressemblance *f*.

likewise [līk'wīz] *ad* de même, pareillement.

liking [lī'king] *n* affection *f*, penchant *m*; goût *m*; **to take a** ~ **to sb** se prendre d'amitié pour qn; **to be to sb's** ~ être au goût de qn, plaire à qn.

lilac [lī'lək] *n* lilas *m* ♦ *a* lilas *inv*.

lilt [lilt] *n* rythme *m*, cadence *f*.

lilting [lil'ting] *a* aux cadences mélodieuses; chantant(e).

lily [lil'ē] *n* lis *m*; ~ **of the valley** muguet *m*.

Lima [lē'mə] *n* Lima.

limb [lim] *n* membre *m*; **to be out on a** ~ (*fig*) être isolé(e).

limber [lim'bûr] **to** ~ **up** *vi* se dégourdir, se mettre en train.

limbo [lim'bō] *n*: **to be in** ~ (*fig*) être tombé(e) dans l'oubli.

lime [līm] *n* (*tree*) tilleul *m*; (*fruit*) citron vert, lime *f*; (*GEO*) chaux *f*.

lime juice *n* jus *m* de citron vert.

limelight [līm'līt] *n*: **in the** ~ (*fig*) en vedette, au premier plan.

limerick [lim'ûrik] *n* petit poème humoristique.

limestone [līm'stōn] *n* pierre *f* à chaux; (*GEO*) calcaire *m*.

limit [lim'it] *n* limite *f* ♦ *vt* limiter; **weight/speed** ~ limite de poids/de vitesse.

limitation [limitā'shən] *n* limitation *f*, restriction *f*.

limited [lim'itid] *a* limité(e), restreint(e); ~ **edition** édition *f* à tirage limité.

limited (liability) company (Ltd) *n* (*Brit*) ≈ société *f* anonyme (SA).

limitless [lim'itlis] *a* illimité(e).

limousine [lim'əzēn] *n* limousine *f*.

limp [limp] *n*: **to have a** ~ boiter ♦ *vi* boiter ♦ *a* mou(molle).

limpet [lim'pit] *n* patelle *f*; **like a** ~ (*fig*) comme une ventouse.

limpid [lim'pid] *a* limpide.

linchpin [linch'pin] *n* esse *f*; (*fig*) pivot *m*.

Lincs [lingks] *abbr* (*Brit*) = *Lincolnshire*.

line [līn] *n* (*gen*) ligne *f*; (*rope*) corde *f*; (*wire*) fil *m*; (*of poem*) vers *m*; (*row, series*) rangée *f*; file *f*, queue *f*; (*COMM: series of goods*) article(s) *m(pl)*, ligne de produits ♦ *vt* (*clothes*): **to** ~ (**with**) doubler (de); (*box*): **to** ~ (**with**) garnir *or* tapisser (de); (*subj*:

trees, crowd) border; **to cut in** ~ (*US*) passer avant son tour; **in his** ~ **of business** dans sa partie, dans son rayon; **on the right** ~**s** sur la bonne voie; **a new** ~ **in cosmetics** une nouvelle ligne de produits de beauté; **hold the** ~ **please** (*Brit TEL*) ne quittez pas; **to be in** ~ **for sth** (*fig*) être en lice pour qch; **in** ~ **with** en accord avec, en conformité avec; **to bring sth into** ~ **with sth** aligner qch sur qch; **to draw the** ~ **at (doing) sth** (*fig*) se refuser à (faire) qch; ne pas tolérer (*or* admettre (qu'on fasse) qch; **to take the** ~ **that** ... être d'avis *or* de l'opinion que ....

line up *vi* s'aligner, se mettre en rang(s) ♦ *vt* aligner; (*set up, have ready*) prévoir; trouver; **to have sb/sth** ~**d up** avoir qn/qch en vue *or* de prévu(e).

linear [lin'ēûr] *a* linéaire.

lined [līnd] *a* (*paper*) réglé(e); (*face*) marqué(e), ridé(e); (*clothes*) doublé(e).

line feed *n* (*COMPUT*) interligne *m*.

linen [lin'ən] *n* linge *m* (de corps *or* de maison); (*cloth*) lin *m*.

line printer *n* imprimante *f* (ligne par ligne).

liner [lī'nûr] *n* paquebot *m* de ligne.

linesman [līnz'mən] *n* (*TENNIS*) juge *m* de ligne; (*SOCCER*) juge de touche.

lineup [līn'up] *n* file *f*; (*also*: **police** ~) parade *f* d'identification; (*SPORT*) (composition *f* de l')équipe *f*.

linger [ling'gûr] *vi* s'attarder; traîner; (*smell, tradition*) persister.

lingerie [lân'jərā] *n* lingerie *f*.

lingering [ling'gûring] *a* persistant(e); qui subsiste; (*death*) lent(e).

lingo, ~es [ling'gō] *n* (*pej*) jargon *m*.

linguist [ling'gwist] *n* linguiste *m/f*; personne douée pour les langues.

linguistic [linggwis'tik] *a* linguistique.

linguistics [linggwis'tiks] *n* linguistique *f*.

lining [lī'ning] *n* doublure *f*; (*TECH*) revêtement *m*; (: *of brakes*) garniture *f*.

link [lingk] *n* (*of a chain*) maillon *m*; (*connection*) lien *m*, rapport *m* ♦ *vt* relier, lier, unir; **rail** ~ liaison *f* ferroviaire.

link up *vt* relier ♦ *vi* se rejoindre; s'associer.

links [lingks] *npl* (terrain *m* de) golf *m*.

linkup [lingk'up] *n* lien *m*, rapport *m*; (*of roads*) jonction *f*, raccordement *m*; (*of spaceships*) arrimage *m*; (*RADIO, TV*) liaison *f*; (: *program*) duplex *m*.

linoleum [linō'lēəm] *n* linoléum *m*.

linseed oil [lin'sēd oil] *n* huile *f* de lin.

lint [lint] *n* tissu ouaté (*pour pansements*).

lintel [lin'təl] *n* linteau *m*.

lion [lī'ən] *n* lion *m*.

lion cub *n* lionceau *m*.

lioness [lī'ənis] *n* lionne *f*.

lip [lip] *n* lèvre *f*; (*of cup etc*) rebord *m*; (*insolence*) insolences *fpl*.

lip-read [lip'rēd] *vi* lire sur les lèvres.

lip salve [lip sav] *n* pommade *f* pour les lèvres, pommade rosat.

lip service *n*: **to pay** ~ **to sth** ne reconnaître le mérite de qch que pour la forme *or* qu'en paroles.

lipstick [lip'stik] *n* rouge *m* à lèvres.

liquefy [lik'wəfī] *vt* liquéfier ♦ *vi* se liquéfier.

liqueur [likûr'] *n* liqueur *f*.
liquid [lik'wid] *n* liquide *m* ♦ *a* liquide.
liquid assets *npl* liquidités *fpl*, disponibilités *fpl*.
liquidate [lik'widāt] *vt* liquider.
liquidation [likwidā'shən] *n* liquidation *f*; **to go into** ~ déposer son bilan.
liquidation value *n* (*US COMM*) valeur *f* de liquidation.
liquidator [lik'widātûr] *n* liquidateur *m*.
liquid crystal display (LCD) *n* affichage *m* à cristaux liquides.
liquidize [lik'widīz] *vt* (*CULIN*) passer au mixer.
liquidizer [lik'widīzûr] *n* (*Brit CULIN*) mixer *m*.
Liquid Paper *n* ® Tipp-Ex *m* ®.
liquor [lik'ûr] *n* spiritueux *m*, alcool *m*.
liquorice [lik'ûris] *n* (*Brit*) réglisse *m*.
liquor store *n* (*US*) débit *m* de vins et de spiritueux.
Lisbon [liz'bən] *n* Lisbonne.
lisp [lisp] *n* zézaiement *m*.
lissom [lis'əm] *a* souple, agile.
list [list] *n* liste *f*; (*of ship*) inclinaison *f* ♦ *vt* (*write down*) inscrire; faire la liste de; (*enumerate*) énumérer; (*COMPUT*) lister ♦ *vi* (*ship*) gîter, donner de la bande; **shopping** ~ liste des courses.
listed company [lis'tid kum'panē] *n* société cotée en bourse.
listen [lis'ən] *vi* écouter; **to** ~ **to** écouter.
listener [lis'ənûr] *n* auditeur/trice.
listing [lis'ting] *n* (*COMPUT*) listage *m*; (: *hard copy*) liste *f*, listing *m*.
listless [list'lis] *a* indolent(e), apath. ue.
listlessly [list'lislē] *ad* avec indolence *or* apathie.
list price *n* prix *m* de catalogue.
lit [lit] *pt*, *pp of* **light**.
litany [lit'ənē] *n* litanie *f*.
liter [lē'tûr] *n* (*US*) litre *m*.
literacy [lit'ûrəsē] *n* degré *m* d'alphabétisation, fait *m* de savoir lire et écrire.
literal [lit'ûrəl] *a* littéral(e).
literally [lit'ûrəlē] *ad* littéralement.
literary [lit'ərārē] *a* littéraire.
literate [lit'ûrit] *a* qui sait lire et écrire, instruit(e).
literature [lit'ûrəchûr] *n* littérature *f*; (*brochures etc*) copie *f* publicitaire, prospectus *mpl*.
lithe [līth] *a* agile, souple.
lithography [lithág'rəfē] *n* lithographie *f*.
Lithuania [lithōoā'nēə] *n* Lituanie *f*.
litigate [lit'əgāt] *vt* mettre en litige ♦ *vi* plaider.
litigation [litəgā'shən] *n* litige *m*; contentieux *m*.
litmus [lit'məs] *n*: ~ **paper** papier *m* de tournesol.
litre [lē'tûr] *n* (*Brit*) litre *m*.
litter [lit'ûr] *n* (*garbage*) détritus *mpl*, ordures *fpl*; (*young animals*) portée *f* ♦ *vt* éparpiller; laisser des détritus dans; ~**ed with** jonché(e) de, couvert(e) de.
litter bin *n* (*Brit*) boîte *f* à ordures, poubelle *f*.
litterbug [lit'ûrbug] *n* personne qui jette des détritus par terre.

little [lit'əl] *a* (*small*) petit(e); (*not much*): **it's** ~ c'est peu; ~ **milk** peu de lait ♦ *ad* peu; **a** ~ **un peu (de)**; **a** ~ **milk** un peu de lait; **for a** ~ **while** pendant un petit moment; **with** ~ **difficulty** sans trop de difficulté; **as** ~ **as possible** le moins possible; ~ **by** ~ petit à petit, peu à peu; **to make** ~ **of** faire peu de cas de.
liturgy [lit'ûrjē] *n* liturgie *f*.
live *vi* [liv] vivre; (*reside*) vivre, habiter ♦ *a* [līv] (*animal*) vivant(e), en vie; (*wire*) sous tension; (*broadcast*) (transmis(e)) en direct; (*issue*) d'actualité, brûlant(e); (*unexploded*) non explosé(e); **to** ~ **in Chicago** habiter (à) Chicago; **to** ~ **together** vivre ensemble, cohabiter; ~ **ammunition** munitions *fpl* de combat.
live down *vt* faire oublier (avec le temps).
live in *vi* être logé(e) et nourri(e); être interne.
live off *vt* (*land, fish etc*) vivre de; (*pej*: *parents etc*) vivre aux crochets de.
live on *vt fus* (*food*) vivre de ♦ *vi* survivre; **to** ~ **on $150 a week** vivre avec 150 dollars par semaine.
live out *vi* (*Brit*: *students*) être externe ♦ *vt*: **to** ~ **out one's days** *or* **life** passer sa vie.
live up *vt*: **to** ~ **it up** (*col*) faire la fête; mener la grande vie.
live up to *vt fus* se montrer à la hauteur de.
livelihood [līv'lēhōod] *n* moyens *mpl* d'existence.
liveliness [līv'lēnis] *n* vivacité *f*, entrain *m*.
lively [līv'lē] *a* vif(vive), plein(e) d'entrain.
liven up [lī'vən up] *vt* (*room etc*) égayer; (*discussion, evening*) animer.
liver [liv'ûr] *n* foie *m*.
liverish [liv'ûrish] *a* qui a mal au foie; (*fig*) grincheux(euse).
livery [liv'ûrē] *n* livrée *f*.
lives [līvz] *npl of* **life**.
livestock [līv'stâk] *n* cheptel *m*, bétail *m*.
livid [liv'id] *a* livide, blafard(e); (*furious*) furieux(euse), furibond(e).
living [liv'ing] *a* vivant(e), en vie ♦ *n*: **to earn** *or* **make a** ~ gagner sa vie; **cost of** ~ coût *m* de la vie; **within** ~ **memory** de mémoire d'homme.
living conditions *npl* conditions *fpl* de vie.
living expenses *npl* dépenses courantes.
living room *n* salle *f* de séjour.
living wage *n* salaire *m* permettant de vivre (décemment).
lizard [liz'ûrd] *n* lézard *m*.
llama [lâm'ə] *n* lama *m*.
LLB *n abbr* (= *Bachelor of Laws*) titre universitaire.
LLD *n abbr* (= *Doctor of Laws*) titre universitaire.
load [lōd] *n* (*weight*) poids *m*; (*thing carried*) chargement *m*, charge *f*; (*ELEC, TECH*) charge ♦ *vt* (*truck, ship*): **to** ~ **(with)** charger (de); (*gun, camera*): **to** ~ **(with)** charger (avec); (*COMPUT*) charger; **a** ~ **of**, ~**s of** (*fig*) un *or* des tas de, des masses de.
loaded [lō'did] *a* (*dice*) pipé(e); (*question*) insidieux(euse); (*col*: *rich*) bourré(e) de fric; (: *drunk*) bourré.

loading dock [lō'ding dâk] *n* (*US*) aire *f* de chargement.

loaf, *pl* **loaves** [lōf, lōvz] *n* pain *m*, miche *f* ♦ *vi* (*also*: ~ **about,** ~ **around**) fainéanter, traîner.

loafer [lō'fûr] *n* fainéant/e.

loam [lōm] *n* terreau *m*.

loan [lōn] *n* prêt *m* ♦ *vt* prêter; **on** ~ prêté(e), en prêt; **public** ~ emprunt public.

loan account *n* compte *m* de prêt.

loan capital *n* capital-obligations *m*.

loath [lōth] *a*: **to be** ~ **to do** répugner à faire.

loathe [lōth] *vt* détester, avoir en horreur.

loathing [lō'thing] *n* dégoût *m*, répugnance *f*.

loathsome [lōth'səm] *a* répugnant(e), détestable.

loaves [lōvz] *npl of* **loaf.**

lob [lâb] *vt* (*ball*) lober.

lobby [lâb'ē] *n* hall *m*, entrée *f*; (*POL*) groupe *m* de pression, lobby *m* ♦ *vt* faire pression sur.

lobbyist [lâb'ēist] *n* membre *m/f* d'un groupe de pression.

lobe [lōb] *n* lobe *m*.

lobster [lâb'stûr] *n* homard *m*.

lobster pot *n* casier *m* à homards.

local [lō'kəl] *a* local(e) ♦ *n* (*Brit*: *pub*) pub *m* or café *m* du coin; **the** ~**s** *npl* les gens *mpl* du pays or du coin.

local anesthetic *n* anesthésie locale.

local authority (*Brit*) *n* collectivité locale, municipalité *f*.

local call *n* (*TEL*) communication urbaine.

local government *n* administration locale or municipale.

locality [lōkal'itē] *n* région *f*, environs *mpl*; (*position*) lieu *m*.

localize [lō'kəlīz] *vt* localiser.

locally [lō'kəlē] *ad* localement; dans les environs or la région.

locate [lō'kāt] *vt* (*find*) trouver, repérer; (*situate*) situer.

location [lōkā'shən] *n* emplacement *m*; **on** ~ (*CINEMA*) en extérieur.

loch [lâkh] *n* lac *m*, loch *m*.

lock [lâk] *n* (*of door, box*) serrure *f*; (*of canal*) écluse *f*; (*of hair*) mèche *f*, boucle *f* ♦ *vt* (*with key*) fermer à clé; (*immobilize*) bloquer ♦ *vi* (*door etc*) fermer à clé; (*wheels*) se bloquer; ~ **stock and barrel** (*fig*) en bloc.

lock away *vt* (*valuables*) mettre sous clé; (*criminal*) mettre sous les verrous, enfermer.

lock out *vt* enfermer dehors; (*on purpose*) mettre à la porte; (: *workers*) lock-outer.

lock up *vi* tout fermer (à clé).

locker [lâk'ûr] *n* casier *m*.

locker room *n* (*US*) vestiaire *m*.

locket [lâk'it] *n* médaillon *m*.

lockjaw [lâk'jô] *n* tétanos *m*.

lockout [lâk'out] *n* (*INDUSTRY*) lock-out *m*, grève patronale.

locksmith [lâk'smith] *n* serrurier *m*.

lock-up [lâk'up] *n* (*prison*) prison *f*; (*cell*) cellule *f* provisoire.

locomotive [lōkəmō'tiv] *n* locomotive *f*.

locum tenens [lō'kəm tē'nənz] *n* (*MED*) suppléant/e (de médecin).

locust [lō'kəst] *n* locuste *f*, sauterelle *f*.

lodge [lâj] *n* pavillon *m* (de gardien); (*FREE-*

MASONRY) loge *f* ♦ *vi* (*person*): **to** ~ **with** être logé(e) chez, être en pension chez ♦ *vt* (*appeal etc*) présenter; déposer; **to** ~ **a complaint** porter plainte; **to** ~ **(itself) in/between** se loger dans/entre.

lodger [lâj'ûr] *n* locataire *m/f*; (*with room and meals*) pensionnaire *m/f*.

lodging [lâj'ing] *n* logement *m*; *see also* **board.**

lodgings [lâj'ingz] *n* chambre *f*, meublé *m*.

loft [lôft] *n* grenier *m*; (*US*) grenier aménagé (en appartement) (*gén dans ancien entrepôt ou fabrique*).

lofty [lôf'tē] *a* élevé(e); (*haughty*) hautain(e); (*sentiments, aims*) noble.

log [lôg] *n* (*of wood*) bûche *f*; (*book*) = **logbook** ♦ *n abbr* (= *logarithm*) log *m* ♦ *vt* enregistrer.

log in, log on *vi* (*COMPUT*) ouvrir une session, entrer dans le système.

log off, log out *vi* (*COMPUT*) clore une session, sortir du système.

logarithm [lôg'ərithəm] *n* logarithme *m*.

logbook [lôg'bŏŏk] *n* (*NAUT*) livre *m* or journal *m* de bord; (*AVIAT*) carnet *m* de vol; (*of truck-driver*) carnet de route; (*of events, movement of goods etc*) registre *m*; (*of car*) ≈ carte grise.

log cabin *n* cabane *f* en rondins.

log fire *n* feu *m* de bois.

loggerheads [lôg'ûrhedz] *npl*: **at** ~ **(with)** à couteaux tirés (avec).

logic [lâj'ik] *n* logique *f*.

logical [lâj'ikəl] *a* logique.

logically [lâj'iklē] *ad* logiquement.

logistics [lōjis'tiks] *n* logistique *f*.

logo [lō'gō] *n* logo *m*.

loin [loin] *n* (*CULIN*) filet *m*, longe *f*; ~**s** *npl* reins *mpl*.

loincloth [loin'klôth] *n* pagne *m*.

loiter [loi'tûr] *vi* s'attarder; **to** ~ **(about)** traîner, musarder; (*pej*) rôder.

loll [lâl] *vi* (*also*: ~ **about**) se prélasser, fainéanter.

lollipop [lâl'ēpâp] *n* sucette *f*.

London [lun'dən] *n* Londres.

Londoner [lun'dənûr] *n* Londonien/ne.

lone [lōn] *a* solitaire.

loneliness [lōn'lēnis] *n* solitude *f*, isolement *m*.

lonely [lōn'lē] *a* seul(e); (*childhood etc*) solitaire; (*place*) solitaire, isolé(e); **to feel** ~ se sentir seul.

loner [lō'nûr] *n* solitaire *m/f*.

lonesome [lōn'səm] *a* seul(e); solitaire.

long [lông] *a* long(longue) ♦ *ad* longtemps ♦ *n*: **the** ~ **and the short of it is that ...** (*fig*) le fin mot de l'histoire c'est que ... ♦ *vi*: **to** ~ **for sth/to do** avoir très envie de qch/de faire; attendre qch avec impatience/impatience de faire; **he had** ~ **understood that ...** il avait compris depuis longtemps que ...; **how** ~ **is this river/course?** quelle est la longueur de ce fleuve/la durée de ce cours?; **6 meters** ~ (long) de 6 mètres; **6 months** ~ qui dure 6 mois, de 6 mois; **all night** ~ toute la nuit; **he no** ~**er comes** il ne vient plus; ~ **before** longtemps avant; **before** ~ (+ *future*) avant peu, dans peu de temps; (+ *past*) peu de temps après; ~ **ago** il y a longtemps; **don't be** ~! fais vite!, dépêche-toi!; **I won't be** ~ je n'en ai pas pour longtemps; **at** ~ **last** enfin; **in the** ~ **run** à la longue; finalement; **so** or **as** ~ **as** pourvu que.

long-distance [lông'dis'təns] a (race) de fond; (call) interurbain(e).

long-haired [lông'härd] a (person) aux cheveux longs; (animal) aux longs poils.

longhand [lông'hand] n écriture normale or courante.

longing [lông'ing] n désir m, envie f, nostalgie f ♦ a plein(e) d'envie or de nostalgie.

longingly [lông'inglē] ad avec désir or nostalgie.

longitude [lân'jətōōd] n longitude f.

long johns [lông jânz] npl caleçons longs.

long jump n saut m en longueur.

long-lost [lông'lôst] a perdu(e) depuis longtemps.

long-playing [lông'plā'ing] a: ~ **record (LP)** (disque m) 33 tours m inv.

long-range [lông'rānj'] a à longue portée; (weather forecast) à long terme.

longshoreman [lông'shôrmən] n (US) docker m, débardeur m.

longsighted [lông'sītid] a presbyte; (fig) prévoyant(e).

long-standing [lông'standing] a de longue date.

long-suffering [lông'suf'ûring] a empreint(e) d'une patience résignée; extrêmement patient(e).

long-term [lông'tûrm'] a à long terme.

long wave n (RADIO) grandes ondes, ondes longues.

long-winded [lông'win'did] a intarissable, interminable.

loo [lōō] n (Brit col) w.-c. mpl, petit coin.

loofah [lōō'fə] n (Brit) sorte d'éponge végétale.

look [lōōk] vi regarder; (seem) sembler, paraître, avoir l'air; (building etc): to ~ **south/on to the sea** donner au sud/sur la mer ♦ n regard m; (appearance) air m, allure f, aspect m; ~**s** npl physique m, beauté f; **to** ~ **like** ressembler à; **it** ~**s like him** on dirait que c'est lui; **it** ~**s about 4 meters long** je dirais que ça fait 4 mètres de long, à vue de nez, ça fait 4 mètres de long; **it** ~**s all right to me** ça me paraît bien; **to have a** ~ **at sth** jeter un coup d'œil à qch; **to have a** ~ **for sth** chercher qch; **to** ~ **ahead** regarder devant soi; (fig) envisager l'avenir.

look after vt fus s'occuper de, prendre soin de; (baggage etc: watch over) garder, surveiller.

look around vi regarder autour de soi; (turn) regarder derrière soi, se retourner; **to** ~ **around for sth** chercher qch.

look at vt fus regarder.

look back vi: **to** ~ **back at sth/sb** se retourner pour regarder qch/qn; **to look back on** (event, period) évoquer, repenser à.

look down on vt fus (fig) regarder de haut, dédaigner.

look for vt fus chercher.

look forward to vt fus attendre avec impatience; **I'm not** ~**ing forward to** it cette

perspective ne me réjouit guère; ~**ing forward to hearing from you** (in letter) dans l'attente de vous lire.

look in vi: **to** ~ **in on sb** passer voir qn.

look into vt fus (matter, possibility) examiner, étudier.

look on vi regarder (en spectateur).

look out vi (beware): **to** ~ **out (for)** prendre garde (à), faire attention (à).

look out for vt fus être à la recherche de; guetter.

look over vt (essay) jeter un coup d'œil à; (town, building) visiter (rapidement); (person) jeter un coup d'œil à; examiner de la tête aux pieds.

look round vi (Brit) = **look around**.

look through vt fus (papers, book) examiner; (: briefly) parcourir; (telescope) regarder à travers.

look to vt fus veiller à; (rely on) compter sur.

look up vi lever les yeux; (improve) s'améliorer ♦ vt (word) chercher; (friend) passer voir.

look up to vt fus avoir du respect pour.

lookout [lōōk'âut] n poste m de guet; guetteur m; **to be on the** ~ **(for)** guetter.

look-up table [lōōk'up tā'bəl] n (COMPUT) table f à consulter.

LOOM n abbr (US: = Loyal Order of Moose) association charitable.

loom [lōōm] n métier m à tisser ♦ vi surgir; (fig) menacer, paraître imminent(e).

loony [lōō'nē] a, n (col) timbré(e), cinglé(e) (m/f).

loop [lōōp] n boucle f; (contraceptive) stérilet m.

loophole [lōōp'hōl] n porte f de sortie (fig); échappatoire f.

loose [lōōs] a (knot, screw) desserré(e); (stone) branlant(e); (clothes) vague, ample, lâche; (animal) en liberté, échappé(e); (life) dissolu(e); (morals, discipline) relâché(e); (thinking) peu rigoureux(euse), vague; (translation) approximatif(ive) ♦ vt (free: animal) lâcher; (: prisoner) relâcher, libérer; (slacken) détendre, relâcher; desserrer; défaire; donner du mou à; donner du ballant à; ~ **connection** (ELEC) mauvais contact; **to be at** ~ **ends** or (Brit) **at a** ~ **end** (fig) ne pas trop savoir quoi faire; **to tie up** ~ **ends** (fig) mettre au point or régler les derniers détails.

loose change n petite monnaie.

loose-fitting [lōōs'fit'ing] a (clothes) ample.

loose-leaf [lōōs'lēf] a: ~ **binder** or **folder** classeur m à feuilles or feuillets mobiles.

loosely [lōōs'lē] ad sans serrer; approximativement.

loosen [lōō'sən] vt desserrer, relâcher, défaire.

loosen up vi (before game) s'échauffer; (col: relax) se détendre, se laisser aller.

loot [lōōt] n butin m ♦ vt piller.

looter [lōō'tûr] n pillard m, casseur m.

looting [lōō'ting] n pillage m.

lop [lâp] : **to** ~ **off** vt couper, trancher.

lopsided [lâp'sīdid] a de travers, asymétrique.

lord [lôrd] n seigneur m; **L**~ **Smith** lord

Smith; **the L~** (REL) le Seigneur; **the (House of) L~s** (Brit) la Chambre des Lords.
lordly [lôrd'lē] a noble, majestueux(euse); (arrogant) hautain(e).
lore [lôr] n tradition(s) f(pl).
lorry [lôr'ē] n (Brit) camion m.
lorry driver n (Brit) camionneur m, routier m.
lose, pt, pp **lost** [lōōz, lôst] vt perdre; (opportunity) manquer, perdre; (pursuers) distancer, semer ♦ vi perdre; **to ~ (time)** (clock) retarder; **to ~ no time (in doing sth)** ne pas perdre de temps (à faire qch); **to get lost** vi (person) se perdre; **my watch has got lost** ma montre est perdue.
loser [lōō'zûr] n perdant/e; **to be a good/bad ~** être beau/mauvais joueur.
loss [lôs] n perte f; **to cut one's ~es** limiter les dégâts; **to make a ~** enregistrer une perte; **to sell sth at a ~** vendre qch à perte; **to be at a ~** être perplexe or embarrassé(e); **to be at a ~ to do** se trouver incapable de faire.
loss adjuster n (INSURANCE) responsable m/f de l'évaluation des dommages.
loss leader n (COMM) article sacrifié.
lost [lôst] pt, pp of **lose** ♦ a perdu(e); **~ in thought** perdu dans ses pensées; **~ and found property** n (US) objets trouvés; **~ and found** n (US) (bureau m des) objets trouvés.
lost property n (Brit) objets trouvés; **~ office** or **department** n (Brit) (bureau m des) objets trouvés.
lot [lât] n (at auctions) lot m; (destiny) sort m, destinée f; (US: plot of land) lot m (de terrain), lotissement m; **the ~** le tout; **tous** mpl, toutes fpl; **a ~** beaucoup; **a ~ of** beaucoup de; **~s** des tas de; **to draw ~s (for sth)** tirer (qch) au sort.
lotion [lō'shən] n lotion f.
lottery [lât'ûrē] n loterie f.
loud [loud] a bruyant(e), sonore, fort(e); (gaudy) voyant(e), tapageur(euse) ♦ ad (speak etc) fort; **out ~** tout haut.
loudly [loud'lē] ad fort, bruyamment.
loudspeaker [loud'spēkûr] n haut-parleur m.
lounge [lounj] n salon m; (of airport) salle f ♦ vi se prélasser, paresser.
lounge bar n (salle f de) bar m.
lounge suit n (Brit) complet m; (: on invitation) "tenue de ville".
louse, pl **lice** [lous, līs] n pou m.
louse up vt (col) gâcher.
lousy [lou'zē] a (fig) infect(e), moche.
lout [lout] n rustre m, butor m.
louver, (Brit) **louvre** [lōō'vûr] a (door, window) à claire-voie.
lovable [luv'əbəl] a très sympathique; adorable.
love [luv] n amour m ♦ vt aimer; aimer beaucoup; **to ~ to do** aimer beaucoup or adorer faire; **I'd ~ to come** cela me ferait très plaisir (de venir); **"15 ~"** (TENNIS) "15 à rien or zéro"; **to be/fall in ~ with** être/tomber amoureux(euse) de; **to make ~** faire l'amour; **~ at first sight** le coup de foudre; **to send one's ~ to sb** adresser ses amitiés à qn; **~ from Anne, ~, Anne** affectueusement, Anne.

love affair n liaison (amoureuse).
love letter n lettre f d'amour.
love life n vie sentimentale.
lovely [luv'lē] a (house, garden) ravissant(e); (friend, wife) charmant(e); (vacation, surprise) très agréable, merveilleux(euse); **we had a ~ time** c'était vraiment très bien, nous avons eu beaucoup de plaisir.
lover [luv'ûr] n amant m; (amateur): **a ~ of** un(e) ami(e) de, un(e) amoureux(euse) de.
lovesick [luv'sik] a qui se languit d'amour.
lovesong [luv'sông] n chanson f d'amour.
loving [luv'ing] a affectueux(euse), tendre, aimant(e).
low [lō] a bas(basse) ♦ ad bas ♦ n (METEOROLOGY) dépression f ♦ vi (cow) mugir; **to feel ~** se sentir déprimé(e); **he's very ~** (ill) il est bien bas or très affaibli; **to turn (down) ~** vt baisser; **to reach a new** or **an all-time ~** tomber au niveau le plus bas.
lowbrow [lō'brou] a sans prétentions intellectuelles.
low-calorie [lō'kal'ûrē] a hypocalorique.
low-cut [lō'kut'] a (dress) décolleté(e).
lowdown [lō'doun] n (col): **he gave me the ~ (on it)** il m'a mis au courant ♦ a (mean) méprisable.
lower [lō'ûr] a, ad comparative of **low** ♦ vt baisser; (resistance) diminuer; (US AUT: lights) mettre en code, baisser ♦ vi [lou'ûr] (person): **to ~ at sb** jeter un regard mauvais or noir à qn; (sky, clouds) être menaçant.
low-fat [lō'fat'] a maigre.
low-key [lō'kē'] a modéré(e); discret(ète).
lowland [lō'lənd] n plaine f.
low-level [lō'lɛvəl] a bas(basse); (flying) à basse altitude.
lowly [lō'lē] a humble, modeste.
low-lying [lō'lī'ing] a à faible altitude.
low-paid [lō'pād'] a mal payé(e), aux salaires bas.
loyal [loi'əl] a loyal(e), fidèle.
loyalist [loi'əlist] n loyaliste m/f.
loyalty [loi'əltē] n loyauté f, fidélité f.
lozenge [lâz'inj] n (MED) pastille f; (GEOM) losange m.
LP n abbr = **long-playing record**.
L-plates [el'plāts] npl (Brit) plaques fpl (obligatoires) d'apprenti conducteur.
LPN n abbr (US: = Licensed Practical Nurse) infirmier/ière diplômé(e).
LSAT n abbr (US) = Law School Admissions Test.
LSD n abbr (= lysergic acid diethylamide) LSD m.
LSE n abbr = London School of Economics.
LST abbr (US: = local standard time) heure locale.
LT abbr (ELEC: = low tension) BT.
Lt. abbr (= lieutenant) Lt.
Ltd abbr (Brit: COMM) = **limited**.
lubricant [lōōb'rikənt] n lubrifiant m.
lubricate [lōōb'rikāt] vt lubrifier, graisser.
lucid [lōō'sid] a lucide.
lucidity [lōōsid'itē] n lucidité f.
luck [luk] n chance f; **bad ~** malchance f, malheur m; **to be in ~** avoir de la chance; **to be out of ~** ne pas avoir de chance; **good**

~! bonne chance!

luckily [luk'ilē] *ad* heureusement, par bonheur.

lucky [luk'ē] *a* (*person*) qui a de la chance; (*coincidence*) heureux(euse); (*number etc*) qui porte bonheur.

lucrative [lōōk'rətiv] *a* lucratif(ive), rentable, qui rapporte.

ludicrous [lōō'dəkrəs] *a* ridicule, absurde.

luffa [luf'ə] *n* (*US*) sorte d'éponge végétale.

lug [lug] *vt* traîner, tirer.

luggage [lug'ij] *n* bagages *mpl*.

luggage car *n* (*US RAIL*) fourgon *m* (à bagages).

luggage lockers *npl* consigne *f sg* automatique.

luggage rack *n* (*in train*) porte-bagages *m inv*; (: *made of string*) filet *m* à bagages; (*on car*) galerie *f*.

lugubrious [lōōgōō'brēəs] *a* lugubre.

lukewarm [lōōk'wôrm'] *a* tiède.

lull [lul] *n* accalmie *f* ♦ *vt* (*child*) bercer; (*person, fear*) apaiser, calmer.

lullaby [lul'əbī] *n* berceuse *f*.

lumbago [lumbā'gō] *n* lumbago *m*.

lumber [lum'bûr] *n* bric-à-brac *m inv*; (*wood*) bois *m* de charpente ♦ *vt* (*Brit col*): **to ~ sb with sth/sb** coller *or* refiler qch/qn à qn ♦ *vi* (*also*: **~ about**, **~ along**) marcher pesamment.

lumberjack [lum'bûrjak] *n* bûcheron *m*.

lumberyard [lum'bûryárd] *n* entrepôt *m* de bois.

luminous [lōō'minəs] *a* lumineux(euse).

lump [lump] *n* morceau *m*; (*in sauce*) grumeau *m*; (*swelling*) grosseur *f* ♦ *vt* (*also*: **~ together**) réunir, mettre en tas.

lump sum *n* somme globale *or* forfaitaire.

lumpy [lum'pē] *a* (*sauce*) qui a des grumeaux.

lunacy [lōō'nəsē] *n* démence *f*, folie *f*.

lunar [lōō'nûr] *a* lunaire.

lunatic [lōō'nətik] *n* fou/folle, dément/e ♦ *a* fou(folle), dément(e); **the ~ fringe** les enragés *mpl*.

lunatic asylum *n* asile *m* d'aliénés.

lunch [lunch] *n* déjeuner *m* ♦ *vi* déjeuner; **it is his ~ hour** c'est l'heure où il déjeune; **to invite sb to** *or* **for ~** inviter qn à déjeuner.

luncheon [lun'chən] *n* déjeuner *m*.

luncheon meat *n* sorte de saucisson.

lunchtime [lunch'tīm] *n* l'heure *f* du déjeuner.

lung [lung] *n* poumon *m*.

lung cancer *n* cancer *m* du poumon.

lunge [lunj] *vi* (*also*: **~ forward**) faire un mouvement brusque en avant; **to ~ at sb** envoyer *or* assener un coup à qn.

lupin [lōō'pin] *n* lupin *m*.

lurch [lûrch] *vi* vaciller, tituber ♦ *n* écart *m* brusque, embardée *f*; **to leave sb in the ~** laisser qn se débrouiller *or* se dépêtrer tout(e) seul(e).

lure [lōōr] *n* appât *m*, leurre *m* ♦ *vt* attirer *or* persuader par la ruse.

lurid [lōō'rid] *a* affreux(euse), atroce.

lurk [lûrk] *vi* se tapir, se cacher.

luscious [lush'əs] *a* succulent(e), appétissant(e).

lush [lush] *a* luxuriant(e).

lust [lust] *n* luxure *f*; lubricité *f*; désir *m*;

(*fig*): **~ for** soif *f* de.

lust after *vt fus* convoiter, désirer.

luster [lus'tûr] *n* (*US*) lustre *m*, brillant *m*.

lustful [lust'fəl] *a* lascif(ive).

lustre [lus'tûr] *n* (*Brit*) = **luster**.

lusty [lus'tē] *a* vigoureux(euse), robuste.

lute [lōōt] *n* luth *m*.

Luxembourg [luk'səmbûrg] *n* Luxembourg *m*.

luxuriant [lōōgzhōō'rēənt] *a* luxuriant(e).

luxurious [lōōgzhōō'rēəs] *a* luxueux(euse).

luxury [luk'shûrē] *n* luxe *m* ♦ *cpd* de luxe.

LW *abbr* (*RADIO*: = *long wave*) GO.

lying [lī'ing] *n* mensonge(s) *m(pl)* ♦ *a* (*statement, story*) mensonger(ère), faux(fausse); (*person*) menteur(euse).

lynch [linch] *vt* lyncher.

lynx [lingks] *n* lynx *m inv*.

Lyons [lī'ənz] *n* Lyon *m*.

lyre [lī'ûr] *n* lyre *f*.

lyric [lir'ik] *a* lyrique; **~s** *npl* (*of song*) paroles *fpl*.

lyrical [lir'ikəl] *a* lyrique.

lyricism [lir'əsizəm] *n* lyrisme *m*.

M

M, m [em] *n* (*letter*) M, m *m*; **M for Mike** M comme Marcel.

M [em] *n abbr* (*Brit*: = *motorway*): **the M8** ≈ l'A8 ♦ *abbr* (= *medium*) M.

m [em] *abbr* (= *meter*) m; (= *million*) M; (= *mile*) mi.

MA *n abbr* (*SCOL*) = **Master of Arts**; (*US*) = *military academy*; (*US MAIL*) = Massachusetts.

mac [mak] *n* (*Brit*) imper(méable) *m*.

macabre [məkâ'brə] *a* macabre.

macaroni [makərō'nē] *n* macaronis *mpl*.

macaroon [makərōōn'] *n* macaron *m*.

mace [mās] *n* masse *f*; (*spice*) macis *m*.

machinations [makənā'shənz] *npl* machinations *fpl*, intrigues *fpl*.

machine [məshēn'] *n* machine *f* ♦ *vt* (*dress etc*) coudre à la machine; (*TECH*) usiner.

machine code *n* (*COMPUT*) code *m* machine.

machine gun *n* mitrailleuse *f*.

machine language *n* (*COMPUT*) langage *m* machine.

machine-readable [məshēn'rē'dəbəl] *a* (*COMPUT*) exploitable par une machine.

machinery [məshē'nûrē] *n* machinerie *f*, machines *fpl*; (*fig*) mécanisme(s) *m(pl)*.

machine shop *n* atelier *m* d'usinage.

machine tool *n* machine-outil *f*.

machine washable *a* (*garment*) lavable en machine.

machinist [məshē'nist] *n* machiniste *m/f*.

macho [mâch'ō] *a* macho *m inv*.

mackerel [mak'ûrəl] *n* (*pl inv*) maquereau *m*.

mackintosh [mak'intâsh] *n* (*Brit*) imperméable *m*.

macro... [mak'rō] *prefix* macro....

macroeconomics [makrōěkənâm'iks] *n* macro-économie *f*.

mad [mad] *a* fou(folle); (*foolish*) insensé(e); (*angry*) furieux(euse); **to go ~** devenir fou; **to be ~ (keen) about** *or* **on sth** (*col*) être follement passionné de qch, être fou de qch.

madam [mad'əm] *n* madame *f*; **yes ~** oui Madame; **M~ Chairman** Madame la Présidente.

madden [mad'ən] *vt* exaspérer.

maddening [mad'əning] *a* exaspérant(e).

made [mād] *pt, pp of* **make.**

Madeira [mədē'rə] *n* (*GEO*) Madère *f*; (*wine*) madère *m*.

made-to-measure [mād'təmezh'ûr] *a* (*Brit*) fait(e) sur mesure.

made-to-order [mād'tōȯr'dûr] *a* (*US*) fait(e) sur mesure.

madly [mad'lē] *ad* follement.

madman [mad'man] *n* fou *m*, aliéné *m*.

madness [mad'nis] *n* folie *f*.

Madrid [mədrid'] *n* Madrid.

Mafia [mâf'ēə] *n* maf(f)ia *f*.

magazine [magəzēn'] *n* (*PRESS*) magazine *m*, revue *f*; (*MIL*: *store*) dépôt *m*, arsenal *m*; (*of firearm*) magasin *m*.

maggot [mag'ət] *n* ver *m*, asticot *m*.

magic [maj'ik] *n* magie *f* ♦ *a* magique.

magical [maj'ikəl] *a* magique.

magician [məjish'ən] *n* magicien/ne.

magistrate [maj'istrāt] *n* magistrat *m*; juge *m*.

magnanimous [magnan'əməs] *a* magnanime.

magnate [mag'nāt] *n* magnat *m*.

magnesium [magnē'zēəm] *n* magnésium *m*.

magnet [mag'nit] *n* aimant *m*.

magnetic [magnet'ik] *a* magnétique.

magnetic disk *n* (*COMPUT*) disque *m* magnétique.

magnetic tape *n* bande *f* magnétique.

magnetism [mag'nitizəm] *n* magnétisme *m*.

magnification [magnəfəkā'shən] *n* grossissement *m*.

magnificence [magnif'isəns] *n* magnificence *f*.

magnificent [magnif'əsənt] *a* superbe, magnifique.

magnify [mag'nəfī] *vt* grossir; (*sound*) amplifier.

magnifying glass [mag'nəfīing glas] *n* loupe *f*.

magnitude [mag'nətōōd] *n* ampleur *f*.

magnolia [magnōl'yə] *n* magnolia *m*.

magpie [mag'pī] *n* pie *f*.

mahogany [məhâg'ənē] *n* acajou *m* ♦ *cpd* en (bois d')acajou.

maid [mād] *n* bonne *f*; **old ~** (*pej*) vieille fille.

maiden [mād'ən] *n* jeune fille *f* ♦ *a* (*aunt etc*) non mariée; (*speech, voyage*) inaugural(e).

maiden name *n* nom *m* de jeune fille.

mail [māl] *n* poste *f*; (*letters*) courrier *m* ♦ *vt* envoyer (par la poste); **by ~** par la poste.

mailbag [māl'bag] *n* sac postal; (*mailman's*) sacoche *f*.

mailbox [māl'bâks] *n* (*US: for letters etc*; *COMPUT*) boîte *f* aux lettres.

mailing [mā'ling] *n* publipostage *m*, mailing *m*.

mailing list [mā'ling list] *n* liste *f* d'adresses.

mailman [māl'man] *n* (*US*) facteur *m*.

mail order *n* vente *f* *or* achat *m* par correspondance ♦ *cpd*: **mail-order house** *or* (*Brit*) **firm** maison *f* de vente par correspondance.

mailshot [māl'shât] *n* (*Brit*) = **mailing.**

mail train *n* train postal.

mail truck *n* (*US AUT*) voiture *f* *or* fourgonnette *f* des postes.

mail van *n* (*Brit*: *AUT*) voiture *f* *or* fourgonnette *f* des postes; (: *RAIL*) wagonposte *m*.

maim [mām] *vt* mutiler.

main [mān] *a* principal(e) ♦ *n* (*pipe*) conduite principale, canalisation *f*; **the ~s** (*ELEC*) le secteur; **in the ~** dans l'ensemble.

main course *n* (*CULIN*) plat *m* de résistance.

mainframe [mān'frām] *n* (*also*: **~ computer**) (gros) ordinateur, unité centrale.

mainland [mān'lənd] *n* continent *m*.

mainline [mān'līn] *a* (*RAIL*) de grande ligne ♦ *vb* (*drugs slang*) *vt* se shooter à ♦ *vi* se shooter.

main line *n* (*RAIL*) grande ligne.

mainly [mān']ē] *ad* principalement, surtout.

main road *n* grand axe, route nationale.

mainstay [mān'stā] *n* (*fig*) pilier *m*.

mainstream [mān'strēm] *n* (*fig*) courant principal.

maintain [māntān'] *vt* entretenir; (*continue*) maintenir, préserver; (*affirm*) soutenir; **to ~ that** ... soutenir que ....

maintenance [mān'tənəns] *n* entretien *m*; (*LAW*: *alimony*) pension *f* alimentaire.

maintenance contract *n* contrat *m* d'entretien.

maintenance order *n* (*LAW*) obligation *f* alimentaire.

maisonette [māzənet'] *n* (*Brit*) appartement *m* en duplex.

maize [māz] *n* maïs *m*.

Maj. *abbr* (*MIL*) = **major.**

majestic [məjes'tik] *a* majestueux(euse).

majesty [maj'istē] *n* majesté *f*.

major [mā'jûr] *n* (*MIL*) commandant *m* ♦ *a* important(e), principal(e); (*MUS*) majeur(e) ♦ *vi* (*US SCOL*): **to ~ (in)** se spécialiser (en); **a ~ operation** (*MED*) une grosse opération.

Majorca [məyôr'kə] *n* Majorque *f*.

major general *n* (*MIL*) général *m* de division.

majority [məjôr'itē] *n* majorité *f* ♦ *cpd* (*verdict, holding*) majoritaire.

make [māk] *vt* (*pt, pp* **made** [mād]) faire; (*manufacture*) faire, fabriquer; (*cause to be*): **to ~ sb sad** *etc* rendre qn triste *etc*; (*force*): **to ~ sb do sth** obliger qn à faire qch, faire faire qch à qn; (*equal*): **2 and 2 ~ 4** 2 et 2 font 4 ♦ *n* fabrication *f*; (*brand*) marque *f*; **to ~ it** (*in time etc*) y arriver; (*succeed*) réussir; **what time do you ~ it?** quelle heure avez-vous?; **to ~ good** *vi* (*succeed*) faire son chemin, réussir ♦ *vt* (*deficit*) combler; (*losses*) compenser; **to ~ do with** se contenter de; se débrouiller avec.

make for *vt fus* (*place*) se diriger vers.

make off *vi* filer.

make out *vt* (*write out*) écrire; (*understand*) comprendre; (*see*) distinguer; (*claim, imply*) prétendre, vouloir faire croire; **to ~ out a case for sth** présenter des arguments solides en faveur de qch.

make over *vt* (*assign*): **to ~ over (to)** céder (à), transférer (au nom de).

make up *vt* (*invent*) inventer, imaginer; (*parcel*) faire ♦ *vi* se réconcilier; (*with cosmetics*). se maquiller, se farder; **to be made up of** se composer de.

make up for *vt fus* compenser; racheter.

make-believe [māk'bilēv] *n*: **a world of** ~ un monde de chimères *or* d'illusions; **it's just** ~ c'est de la fantaisie; c'est une illusion.

maker [mā'kúr] *n* fabricant *m*.

makeshift [māk'shift] *a* provisoire, improvisé(e).

make-up [māk'up] *n* maquillage *m*.

make-up bag *n* trousse *f* de maquillage.

make-up remover *n* démaquillant *m*.

making [mā'king] *n* (*fig*): **in the** ~ en formation *or* gestation; **he has the** ~**s of an actor** il a l'étoffe d'un acteur.

maladjusted [maləjus'tid] *a* inadapté(e).

malaise [malāz'] *n* malaise *m*.

malaria [məlär'ēə] *n* malaria *f*, paludisme *m*.

Malawi [mə'lâwē] *n* Malawi *m*.

Malay [məlā'] *a* malais(e) ♦ *n* (*person*) Malais/e; (*language*) malais *m*.

Malaya [malā'yə] *n* Malaisie *f*.

Malayan [məlā'yən] *a*, *n* = **Malay**.

Malaysia [məlā'zhə] *n* Malaisie *f*.

Malaysian [məlā'zhən] *a* malaisien(ne) ♦ *n* Malaisien/ne.

Maldives [mal'dīvz] *npl*: **the** ~ les Maldives *fpl*.

male [māl] *n* (*BIOL*, *ELEC*) mâle *m* ♦ *a* (*sex*, *attitude*) masculin(e); mâle; (*child etc*) du sexe masculin; ~ **and female students** étudiants et étudiantes.

male chauvinist *n* phallocrate *m*.

male nurse *n* infirmier *m*.

malevolence [məlev'ələns] *n* malveillance *f*.

malevolent [məlev'ələnt] *a* malveillant(e).

malfunction [malfungk'shən] *n* fonctionnement défectueux.

malice [mal'is] *n* méchanceté *f*, malveillance *f*.

malicious [məlish'əs] *a* méchant(e), malveillant(e); (*LAW*) avec intention criminelle.

malign [məlīn'] *vt* diffamer, calomnier.

malignant [məlig'nənt] *a* (*MED*) malin(igne).

malingerer [məling'gúrúr] *n* simulateur/trice.

mall [môl] *n* (*also*: **shopping** ~) centre commercial.

malleable [mal'ēəbəl] *a* malléable.

mallet [mal'it] *n* maillet *m*.

malnutrition [malnōōtrish'ən] *n* malnutrition *f*.

malpractice [malprak'tis] *n* faute professionnelle; négligence *f*.

malt [môlt] *n* malt *m* ♦ *cpd* (*whisky*) pur malt.

Malta [môl'tə] *n* Malte *f*.

Maltese [môltēz'] *a* maltais(e) ♦ *n* (*pl inv*) Maltais/e; (*LING*) maltais *m*.

maltreat [maltrēt'] *vt* maltraiter.

mammal [mam'əl] *n* mammifère *m*.

mammoth [mam'əth] *n* mammouth *m* ♦ *a* géant(e), monstre.

Man. *abbr* (*Canada*) = *Manitoba*.

man [man], *pl* **men** [man, men] *n* homme *m*; (*CHESS*) pièce *f*; (*CHECKERS*) pion *m* ♦ *vt* garnir d'hommes; servir, assurer le fonctionnement de; être de service à; **an old** ~ un vieillard; ~ **and wife** mari et femme.

manacles [man'əkəlz] *npl* menottes *fpl*.

manage [man'ij] *vi* se débrouiller; y arriver, réussir ♦ *vt* (*business*) gérer; (*team, operation*) diriger; (*device, things to do, carry etc*) arriver à se débrouiller avec, s'en tirer avec; **to** ~ **to do** se débrouiller pour faire; (*succeed*) réussir à faire.

manageable [man'ijəbəl] *a* maniable; (*task etc*) faisable.

management [man'ijmənt] *n* administration *f*, direction *f*; (*persons: of business, firm*) dirigeants *mpl*, cadres *mpl*; (: *of hotel, store, theater*) direction; **"under new** ~**"** "changement de gérant", "changement de propriétaire".

management accounting *n* comptabilité *f* de gestion.

management consultant *n* conseiller/ère de direction.

manager [man'ijûr] *n* (*of business*) directeur *m*; (*of institution etc*) administrateur *m*; (*of department, unit*) responsable *m/f*, chef *m*; (*of hotel etc*) gérant *m*; (*of artist*) impresario *m*; **sales** ~ responsable *or* chef des ventes.

manageress [man'ijûris] *n* directrice *f*; (*of hotel etc*) gérante *f*.

managerial [manijē'rēəl] *a* directorial(e); ~ **staff** cadres *mpl*.

managing director (MD) [man'ijing direk'tûr] *n* directeur général.

mandarin [man'dûrin] *n* (*also:* ~ **orange**) mandarine *f*; (*person*) mandarin *m*.

mandate [man'dāt] *n* mandat *m*.

mandatory [man'dətôrē] *a* obligatoire; (*powers etc*) mandataire.

mandolin(e) [man'dəlin] *n* mandoline *f*.

mane [mān] *n* crinière *f*.

maneuvrable [mənōō'vrəbəl] *a* facile à manoeuvrer.

maneuver [mənōō'vúr] (*US*) *vt, vi* manoeuvrer ♦ *n* manoeuvre *f*; **to** ~ **sb into doing sth** manipuler qn pour lui faire faire qch.

manfully [man'fəlē] *ad* vaillamment.

manganese [mang'gənēz] *n* manganèse *m*.

mangle [mang'gəl] *vt* déchiqueter; mutiler ♦ *n* essoreuse *f*; calandre *f*.

mango, ~**es** [mang'gō] *n* mangue *f*.

mangrove [mang'grōv] *n* palétuvier *m*.

mangy [mān'jē] *a* galeux(euse).

manhandle [man'handəl] *vt* (*mistreat*) maltraiter, malmener; (*move by hand*) manutentionner.

manhole [man'hōl] *n* trou *m* d'homme.

manhood [man'hŏŏd] *n* âge *m* d'homme; virilité *f*.

man-hour [man'ouûr] *n* heure-homme *f*, heure *f* de main-d'œuvre.

manhunt [man'hunt] *n* chasse *f* à l'homme.

mania [mā'nēə] *n* manie *f*.

maniac [mā'nēak] *n* maniaque *m/f*.

manic [man'ik] *a* maniaque.

manic-depressive [man'ikdipres'iv] *a*, *n* (*PSYCH*) maniaco-dépressif(ive).

manicure [man'əkyŏŏr] *n* manucure *f* ♦ *vt* (*person*) faire les mains à.

manicure set *n* trousse *f* à ongles.

manifest [man'əfest] *vt* manifester ♦ *a* manifeste, évident(e) ♦ *n* (*AVIAT, NAUT*) manifeste *m*.

manifestation [manəfestā'shən] *n* manifestation *f*.

manifesto [manəfes'tō] *n* manifeste *m* (*POL*).

manifold [man'əfōld] *a* multiple, varié(e) ♦ *n* (*AUT etc*): **exhaust** ~ collecteur *m* d'échappement.

Manila [mənil'ə] *n* Manille, Manila.

manila *a*: ~ **paper** papier *m* bulle.

manipulate [mənip'yəlāt] *vt* manipuler.

manipulation [mənipyəlā'shən] *n* manipulation *f*.

mankind [man'kīnd'] *n* humanité *f*, genre humain.

manliness [man'lēnis] *n* virilité *f*.

manly [man'lē] *a* viril(e); courageux(euse).

man-made [man'mād] *a* artificiel(le).

manna [man'ə] *n* manne *f*.

mannequin [man'əkin] *n* mannequin *m*.

manner [man'ûr] *n* manière *f*, façon *f*; (**good**) ~**s** (bonnes) manières; **bad** ~**s** mauvaises manières; **all** ~ **of** toutes sortes de.

mannerism [man'ərizəm] *n* particularité *f* de langage (*or* de comportement), tic *m*.

mannerly [man'ûrlē] *a* poli(e), courtois(e).

manoeuvre [mənōō'vûr] *etc* (*Brit*) = **maneuver**.

manor [man'ûr] *n* (*also*: ~ **house**) manoir *m*.

manpower [man'pouûr] *n* main-d'œuvre *f*.

Manpower Services Commission *n* (*Brit*) *agence nationale pour l'emploi*.

manservant, *pl* **menservants** [man'sûrvənt, men-] *n* domestique *m*.

mansion [man'chən] *n* château *m*, manoir *m*.

manslaughter [man'slôtûr] *n* homicide *m* involontaire.

mantelpiece [man'təlpēs] *n* cheminée *f*.

mantle [man'təl] *n* cape *f*; (*fig*) manteau *m*.

man-to-man [man'təman'] *a*, *ad* d'homme à homme.

manual [man'yōōəl] *a* manuel(le) ♦ *n* manuel *m*.

manual worker *n* travailleur manuel.

manufacture [manyəfak'chûr] *vt* fabriquer ♦ *n* fabrication *f*.

manufactured goods [manyəfak'chûrd gōōdz] *npl* produits manufacturés.

manufacturer [manyəfak'chûrûr] *n* fabricant *m*.

manufacturing industries [manyəfak'chûring in'dəstrēz] *npl* industries *fpl* de transformation.

manure [mənōōr'] *n* fumier *m*; (*artificial*) engrais *m*.

manuscript [man'yəskript] *n* manuscrit *m*.

many [men'ē] *a* beaucoup de, de nombreux(euses) ♦ *pronoun* beaucoup, un grand nombre; **how** ~**?** combien?; **a great** ~ un grand nombre (de); **too** ~ **difficulties** trop de difficultés; **twice as** ~ deux fois plus; ~ **a ...** bien des ..., plus d'un(e) ....

map [map] *n* carte *f* ♦ *vt* dresser la carte de.

map out *vt* tracer; (*fig: career, vacation*) organiser, préparer (à l'avance); (*: essay*) faire le plan de.

maple [mā'pəl] *n* érable *m*.

Mar. *abbr* = **March**.

mar [mâr] *vt* gâcher, gâter.

marathon [mar'əthán] *n* marathon *m* ♦ *a*: **a** ~ **session** une séance-marathon.

marathon runner *n* coureur/euse de marathon, marathonien/ne.

marauder [mərôd'ûr] *n* maraudeur/euse.

marble [mâr'bəl] *n* marbre *m*; (*toy*) bille *f*; ~**s** *n* (*game*) billes.

marble mason *n* (*US*) marbrier *m*.

March [mârch] *n* mars *m*; *for phrases see also* **July.**

march [mârch] *vi* marcher au pas; (*demonstrators*) défiler ♦ *n* marche *f*; (*demonstration*) rallye *m*; **to** ~ **out of/into** *etc* sortir de/entrer dans *etc* (*de manière décidée ou impulsive*).

marcher [mâr'chûr] *n* (*demonstrator*) manifestant/e, marcheur/euse.

marching [mâr'ching] *n*: **to give sb his** ~ **orders** (*fig*) renvoyer qn; envoyer promener qn.

march-past [mârch'past] *n* défilé *m*.

mare [mär] *n* jument *f*.

marg. [mârj] *n abbr* (*col*) = **margarine**.

margarine [mâr'jûrin] *n* margarine *f*.

margin [mâr'jin] *n* marge *f*.

marginal [mâr'jinəl] *a* marginal(e); ~ **seat** (*POL*) siège disputé.

marginally [mâr'jinəlē] *ad* très légèrement, sensiblement.

marigold [mar'əgōld] *n* souci *m*.

marijuana [marəwâ'nə] *n* marijuana *f*.

marina [mərē'nə] *n* marina *f*.

marinade [mar'ənād] *n* marinade *f* ♦ *vt* = **marinate**.

marinate [mar'ənāt] *vt* (faire) mariner.

marine [mərēn'] *a* marin(e) ♦ *n* fusilier marin; (*US*) marine *m*.

marine insurance *n* assurance *f* maritime.

marital [mar'itəl] *a* matrimonial(e); ~ **status** situation *f* de famille.

maritime [mar'itīm] *a* maritime.

maritime law *n* droit *m* maritime.

marjoram [mâr'jûrəm] *n* marjolaine *f*.

mark [mârk] *n* marque *f*; (*of skid etc*) trace *f*; (*Brit SCOL*) note *f*; (*SPORT*) cible *f*; (*currency*) mark *m*; (*Brit TECH*): **M~ 2/3** 2ème/3ème série *f or* version *f* ♦ *vt* (*also SPORT: player*) marquer; (*stain*) tacher; (*Brit SCOL*) noter; corriger; **punctuation** ~**s** signes *mpl* de ponctuation; **to** ~ **time** marquer le pas; **to be quick off the** ~ (**in doing**) (*fig*) ne pas perdre de temps (pour faire); **up to the** ~ (*in efficiency*) à la hauteur.

mark down *vt* (*prices, goods*) démarquer, réduire le prix de.

mark off *vt* (*tick off*) cocher, pointer.

mark out *vt* désigner.

mark up *vt* (*price*) majorer.

marked [mârkt] *a* marqué(e), net(te).

markedly [mâr'kidlē] *ad* visiblement, manifestement.

marker [mâr'kûr] *n* (*sign*) jalon *m*; (*bookmark*) signet *m*.

market [mâr'kit] *n* marché *m* ♦ *vt* (*COMM*) commercialiser; **to be on the** ~ être sur le marché; **on the open** ~ en vente libre; **to play the** ~ jouer à la *or* spéculer en Bourse.

marketable [mâr'kitəbəl] *a* commercialisable.

market analysis *n* analyse *f* de marché.

market day *n* jour *m* de marché.

market demand n besoins mpl du marché.

market forces npl tendances fpl du marché.

market garden n (Brit) jardin maraîcher.

marketing [mâr'kiting] n marketing m.

marketplace [mâr'kitplās] n place f du marché; (COMM) marché m.

market price n prix marchand.

market research n étude f de marché.

market value n valeur marchande; valeur du marché.

marking [mâr'king] n (on animal) marque f, tache f; (on road) signalisation f.

marksman [mârks'mən] n tireur m d'élite.

marksmanship [mârks'mənship] n adresse f au tir.

markup [mârk'up] n (COMM: margin) marge f (bénéficiaire); (: increase) majoration f.

marmalade [mâr'məlād] n confiture f d'oranges.

maroon [mərōōn'] vt (fig): **to be ~ed (in** or **at)** être bloqué(e) (à) ♦ a bordeaux inv.

marquee [mârkē'] n chapiteau m.

marquess, marquis [mâr'kwis] n marquis m.

Marrakech, Marrakesh [mâr'əkesh] n Marrakech.

marriage [mar'ij] n mariage m.

marriage bureau n agence matrimoniale.

marriage certificate n extrait m d'acte de mariage.

marriage counseling, (Brit) **marriage guidance** n conseils conjugaux.

married [mar'ēd] a marié(e); (life, love) conjugal(e).

marrow [mar'ō] n moelle f; (vegetable) courge f.

marrow squash n (US) courge f.

marry [mar'ē] vt épouser, se marier avec; (subj: father, priest etc) marier ♦ vi (also: **get married**) se marier.

Mars [mârz] n (planet) Mars f.

Marseilles [mârsā'] n Marseille.

marsh [mârsh] n marais m, marécage m.

marshal [mâr'shəl] n maréchal m; (US: fire, police) ≈ capitaine m ♦ vt rassembler.

marshalling yard [mâr'shəling yârd] n (Brit RAIL) gare f de triage.

marshmallow [mârsh'melō] n (BOT) guimauve f; (sweet) pâte f de) guimauve.

marshy [mâr'shē] a marécageux(euse).

marsupial [mârsōō'pēəl] a marsupial(e) ♦ n marsupial m.

martial [mâr'shəl] a martial(e).

martial law n loi martiale.

Martian [mâr'shən] n Martien/ne.

martin [mâr'tən] n (also: **house ~**) martinet m.

martyr [mâr'tûr] n martyr/e ♦ vt martyriser.

martyrdom [mâr'tûrdəm] n martyre m.

marvel [mâr'vəl] n merveille f ♦ vi: **to ~ (at)** s'émerveiller (de).

marvelous, (Brit) **marvellous** [mâr'vələs] a merveilleux(euse).

Marxism [mârk'sizəm] n marxisme m.

Marxist [mâr'ksist] a, n marxiste (m/f).

marzipan [mâr'zəpan] n pâte f d'amandes.

mascara [maskar'ə] n mascara m.

mascot [mas'kət] n mascotte f.

masculine [mas'kyəlin] a masculin(e) ♦ n masculin m.

masculinity [maskyəlin'itē] n masculinité f.

MASH [mash] n abbr (US MIL) = mobile army surgical hospital.

mash [mash] vt (CULIN) faire une purée de.

mashed [masht] a: **~ potatoes** purée f de pommes de terre.

mask [mask] n masque m ♦ vt masquer.

masochism [mas'əkizəm] n masochisme m.

masochist [mas'əkist] n masochiste m/f.

mason [mā'sən] n (also: **stone~**) maçon m; (also: **free~**) franc-maçon m.

masonic [məsân'ik] a maçonnique.

masonry [mā'sənrē] n maçonnerie f.

masquerade [maskərād'] n bal masqué; (fig) mascarade f ♦ vi: **to ~ as** se faire passer pour.

Mass. abbr (US) = Massachusetts.

mass [mas] n multitude f, masse f; (PHYSICS) masse; (REL) messe f ♦ vi se masser; **the ~es** les masses; **to go to ~** aller à la messe.

massacre [mas'əkûr] n massacre m ♦ vt massacrer.

massage [məsâzh'] n massage m ♦ vt masser.

masseur [masûr'] n masseur m.

masseuse [məsōōs'] n masseuse f.

massive [mas'iv] a énorme, massif(ive).

mass market n marché m grand public.

mass media [mas mē'dēə] npl mass-media mpl.

mass meeting n rassemblement m de masse.

mass-produce [mas'prədōōs'] vt fabriquer en série.

mass production n fabrication f en série.

mast [mast] n mât m; (RADIO, TV) pylône m.

master [mas'tûr] n maître m; (Brit: in high school) professeur m; (title for boys): **M~ X** Monsieur X ♦ vt maîtriser; (learn) apprendre à fond; (understand) posséder parfaitement or à fond; **~ of ceremonies (MC)** n maître des cérémonies; **M~ of Arts/Science (MA/ MSc)** n ≈ titulaire m/f d'une maîtrise (en lettres/science); **M~ of Arts/Science degree (MA/MSc)** n ≈ maîtrise f; **M~'s degree** n ≈ maîtrise.

master disk n (COMPUT) disque original.

masterful [mas'tûrfəl] a autoritaire, impérieux(euse).

master key n passe-partout m inv.

masterly [mas'tûrlē] a magistral(e).

mastermind [mas'tûrmīnd] n esprit supérieur ♦ vt diriger, être le cerveau de.

masterpiece [mas'tûrpēs] n chef-d'œuvre m.

master plan n stratégie f d'ensemble.

masterstroke [mas'tûrstrōk] n coup m de maître.

mastery [mas'tûrē] n maîtrise f; connaissance parfaite.

mastiff [mas'tif] n mastiff m.

masturbate [mas'tûrbāt] vi se masturber.

masturbation [mastûrbā'shən] n masturbation f.

mat [mat] n petit tapis; (also: **door~**) paillasson m ♦ a = **matt**.

match [mach] n allumette f; (game) match m, partie f; (fig) égal/e; mariage m; parti m ♦ vt assortir; (go well with) aller bien avec, s'assortir à; (equal) égaler, valoir ♦ vi être assorti(e); **to be a good ~** être bien

assorti(e).
match up *vt* assortir.
matchbox [mach'bâks] *n* boîte *f* d'allumettes.
matching [mach'ing] *a* assorti(e).
matchless [mach'lis] *a* sans égal.
mate [māt] *n* (*animal*) partenaire *m/f*, mâle/
femelle; (in *merchant navy*) second *m*;
(*Brit*: *colleague*) camarade *m/f* de travail; (:
col) copain/copine ♦ *vi* s'accoupler ♦ *vt*
accoupler.
material [mətē'rēəl] *n* (*substance*) matière *f*,
matériau *m*; (*cloth*) tissu *m*, étoffe *f* ♦ *a* ma-
tériel(le); (*important*) essentiel(le); **~s** *npl*
matériaux *mpl*; **reading** ~ de quoi lire, de la
lecture.
materialistic [mətērēəlis'tik] *a* matérialiste.
materialize [mətēr'ēəlīz] *vi* se matérialiser, se
réaliser.
materially [mətēr'ēəlē] *ad* matériellement;
essentiellement.
maternal [mətûr'nəl] *a* maternel(le).
maternity [mətûr'nitē] *n* maternité *f* ♦ *cpd* de
maternité, de grossesse.
maternity benefit *n* prestation *f* de maternité.
maternity hospital *n* maternité *f*.
math. [math] *n* *abbr* (*US*: = *mathematics*)
maths *fpl*.
mathematical [mathəmat'ikəl] *a* mathématique.
mathematician   [mathəmətish'ən]   *n*
mathématicien/ne.
mathematics [mathəmat'iks] *n* mathématiques
fpl.
maths [maths] *n abbr* (*Brit*: = *mathematics*)
maths *fpl*.
matinée [matənā'] *n* matinée *f*.
mating [mā'ting] *n* accouplement *m*.
mating call *n* appel *m* du mâle.
mating season *n* saison *f* des amours.
matriarchal [mātrēâr'kəl] *a* matriarcal(e).
matrices [māt'risēz] *npl of* **matrix**.
matriculation [mətrikyəlā'shən] *n* inscription *f*.
matrimonial [matrəmō'nēəl] *a* matrimo-
nial(e), conjugal(e).
matrimony [mat'rəmōnē] *n* mariage *m*.
matrix, *pl* **matrices** [mā'triks, māt'risēz] *n* matrice *f*.
matron [mā'trən] *n* (*in hospital*) infirmière-
chef *f*; (*in school*) infirmière.
matronly [mā'trənlē] *a* de matrone; impo-
sant(e).
matt [mat] *a* mat(e).
matted [mat'id] *a* emmêlé(e).
matter [mat'ûr] *n* question *f*; (*PHYSICS*) matière *f*, substance *f*; (*content*) contenu *m*,
fond *m*; (*MED*: *pus*) pus *m* ♦ *vi* importer; **it
doesn't** ~ cela n'a pas d'importance; (*I don't
mind*) cela ne fait rien; **what's the** ~?
qu'est-ce qu'il y a?, qu'est-ce qui ne va pas?;
no ~ **what** quoiqu'il arrive; **that's another**
~ c'est une autre affaire; **as a** ~ **of course**
tout naturellement; **as a** ~ **of fact** en fait;
it's a ~ **of habit** c'est une question d'habitude; **printed** ~ imprimés *mpl*; **reading** ~ de
quoi lire, de la lecture.
matter-of-fact [mat'ûrəvfakt'] *a* terre à terre,
neutre.

matting [mat'ing] *n* natte *f*.
mattress [mat'ris] *n* matelas *m*.
mature [mətōōr'] *a* mûr(e); (*cheese*) fait(e) ♦
vi mûrir; se faire.
maturity [mətōō'ritē] *n* maturité *f*.
maudlin [môd'lin] *a* larmoyant(e).
maul [môl] *vt* lacérer.
Mauritania [môritā'nēə] *n* Mauritanie *f*.
Mauritius [môrish'ēəs] *n* l'île *f* Maurice.
mausoleum [môsəlē'əm] *n* mausolée *m*.
mauve [mōv] *a* mauve.
maverick [mav'ûrik] *n* (*fig*) franc-tireur *m*,
non-conformiste *m/f*.
mawkish [môk'ish] *a* mièvre; fade.
max. *abbr* = **maximum**.
maxim [mak'sim] *n* maxime *f*.
maxima [mak'səm] *npl of* **maximum**.
maximize [mak'səmīz] *vt* (*profits etc, chances*)
maximiser.
maximum [mak'səmən] *a* maximum ♦ *n* (*pl*
maxima [mak'səmə]) maximum *m*.
May [mā] *n* mai *m*; *for phrases see also* **July**.
may [mā] *vi* (*conditional*: **might**) (*indicating
possibility*): **he** ~ **come** il se peut qu'il
vienne; (*be allowed to*): ~ **I smoke?** puis-je
fumer?; (*wishes*): ~ **God bless you!** (que)
Dieu vous bénisse!; ~ **I sit here?** vous
permettez que je m'assoie ici?; **he might be
there** il pourrait être y être, il se pourrait
qu'il y soit; **I might as well go** je ferais
aussi bien d'y aller, autant y aller; **you
might like to try** vous pourriez (peut-être)
essayer.
maybe [mā'bē] *ad* peut-être; ~ **he'll** ... peut-
être qu'il ...; ~ **not** peut-être pas.
May Day *n* le Premier mai.
mayday [mā'dā] *n* S.O.S. *m*.
mayhem [mā'hem] *n* grabuge *m*.
mayonnaise [māənāz'] *n* mayonnaise *f*.
mayor [mā'ûr] *n* maire *m*.
mayoress [mā'ûris] *n* maire *m*; épouse *f* du
maire.
maypole [mā'pōl] *n* mât enrubanné (*autour
duquel on danse*).
maze [māz] *n* labyrinthe *m*, dédale *m*.
MB *abbr* (*COMPUT*) = **megabyte**; (*Canada*) =
Manitoba.
MBA *n abbr* (= *Master of Business Administration*) *titre universitaire*.
MBBS, MBChB *n abbr* (*Brit*: = *Bachelor of
Medicine and Surgery*) *titre universitaire*.
MC *n abbr* = **master of ceremonies**.
MCAT *n abbr* (*US*) = *Medical College Admissions Test*.
MCP *n abbr* (*Brit col*: = *male chauvinist pig*)
phallocrate *m*.
MD *n abbr* (= *Doctor of Medicine*) *titre universitaire*; (*COMM*) = **managing director** ♦
abbr (*US MAIL*) = *Maryland*.
ME *abbr* (*US MAIL*) = *Maine* ♦ *n abbr* (*US
MED*) = *medical examiner*; (*MED*: = *myalgic
encephalomyelitis*).
me [mē] *pronoun* me, m' + *vowel*; (*stressed,
after prep*) moi; **it's** ~ c'est moi; **it's for** ~
c'est pour moi.
meadow [med'ō] *n* prairie *f*, pré *m*.
meager, (*Brit*) **meagre** [mē'gûr] *a* maigre.
meal [mēl] *n* repas *m*; (*flour*) farine *f*; **to go
out for a** ~ sortir manger.

meal ticket *n* (*US*) chèque-repas *m*, ticket-repas *m*.

mealtime [mēl'tīm] *n* heure *f* du repas.

mealy-mouthed [mē'lēmouťhd] *a* mielleux(euse).

mean [mēn] *a* (*with money*) avare, radin(e); (*unkind*) mesquin(e), méchant(e); (*US col: animal*) méchant, vicieux(euse); (: *person*) vache; (*average*) moyen(ne) ♦ *vt* (*pt, pp* **meant** [ment]) (*signify*) signifier, vouloir dire; (*intend*): **to ~ to do** avoir l'intention de faire ♦ *n* moyenne *f*; **to be meant for** être destiné(e) à; **do you ~ it?** vous êtes sérieux?; **what do you ~?** que voulez-vous dire?

meander [mēan'dûr] *vi* faire des méandres; (*fig*) flâner.

meaning [mē'ning] *n* signification *f*, sens *m*.

meaningful [mē'ningfəl] *a* significatif(ive); (*relationship*) valable.

meaningless [mē'ninglis] *a* dénué(e) de sens.

meanness [mēn'nis] *n* avarice *f*; mesquinerie *f*.

means [mēnz] *npl* moyens *mpl*; **by ~ of** par l'intermédiaire de; au moyen de; **by all ~** je vous en prie.

means test *n* (*ADMIN*) contrôle *m* des conditions de ressources.

meant [ment] *pt, pp of* **mean**.

meantime [mēn'tīm] *ad* (*also*: **in the ~**) pendant ce temps.

meanwhile [mēn'wīl] *ad* pendant ce temps.

measles [mē'zəlz] *n* rougeole *f*.

measly [mēz'lē] *a* (*col*) minable.

measurable [mezh'ûrəbəl] *a* mesurable.

measure [mezh'ûr] *vt, vi* mesurer ♦ *n* mesure *f*; (*ruler*) règle (graduée); **a liter ~** un litre; **some ~ of success** un certain succès; **to take ~s to do sth** prendre des mesures pour faire qch.

measure up *vi*: **to ~ up (to)** être à la hauteur (de).

measured [mezh'ûrd] *a* mesuré(e).

measurement [mezh'ûrmənt] *n*: **chest/hip ~** tour *m* de poitrine/hanches; **~s** *npl* mesures *fpl*; **to take sb's ~s** prendre les mesures de qn.

meat [mēt] *n* viande *f*; **cold ~s** (*Brit*) viandes froides; **crab ~** crabe *f*.

meatball [mēt'bôl] *n* boulette *f* de viande.

meat pie *n* pâté *m* en croûte.

meaty [mē'tē] *a* avec beaucoup de viande, plein(e) de viande; (*fig*) substantiel(le).

Mecca [mek'ə] *n* la Mecque; (*fig*): **a ~ (for)** la Mecque (de).

mechanic [məkan'ik] *n* mécanicien *m*.

mechanical [məkan'ikəl] *a* mécanique.

mechanical engineering *n* (*science*) mécanique *f*; (*industry*) construction *f* mécanique.

mechanical pencil *n* (*US*) porte-mine *m inv*.

mechanics [məkan'iks] *n* mécanique *f* ♦ *npl* mécanisme *m*.

mechanism [mek'ənizəm] *n* mécanisme *m*.

mechanization [mekənizā'shən] *n* mécanisation *f*.

MEd *n abbr* (= *Master of Education*) titre universitaire.

medal [med'əl] *n* médaille *f*.

medalist [med'əlist] *n* (*US SPORT*) médaillé/e.

medallion [mədal'yən] *n* médaillon *m*.

medallist [med'əlist] *n* (*Brit*) = **medalist**.

meddle [med'əl] *vi*: **to ~ in** se mêler de, s'occuper de; **to ~ with** toucher à.

meddlesome [med'əlsəm], **meddling** [med'ling] *a* indiscret(ète), qui se mêle de ce qui ne le (*or* la) regarde pas; touche-à-tout *inv*.

media [mē'dēə] *npl* media *mpl*.

mediaeval [mēdēē'vəl] *a* = **medieval**.

median [mē'dēən] *n* (*US*: *also*: **~ strip**) bande médiane.

media research *n* étude *f* de l'audience.

mediate [mē'dēāt] *vi* s'interposer; servir d'intermédiaire.

mediation [mēdēā'shən] *n* médiation *f*.

mediator [mē'dēātûr] *n* médiateur/trice.

medical [med'ikəl] *a* médical(e) ♦ *n* (*also*: **~ examination**) visite médicale; examen médical.

medical certificate *n* certificat médical.

medical examiner *n* (*US*) médecin *m* légiste.

medical student *n* étudiant/e en médecine.

Medicare [med'əkär] *n* (*US*) régime d'assurance maladie.

medicated [med'ikātid] *a* traitant(e), médicamenteux(euse).

medication [medikā'shən] *n* (*drugs etc*) médication *f*.

medicinal [mədis'ənəl] *a* médicinal(e).

medicine [med'isin] *n* médecine *f*; (*drug*) médicament *m*.

medicine chest *n* pharmacie *f* (*murale ou portative*).

medicine man *n* sorcier *m*.

medieval [mēdēē'vəl] *a* médiéval(e).

mediocre [mē'dēōkûr] *a* médiocre.

mediocrity [mēdēâk'ritē] *n* médiocrité *f*.

meditate [med'ətāt] *vi*: **to ~ (on)** méditer (sur).

meditation [meditā'shən] *n* méditation *f*.

Mediterranean [meditərā'nēən] *a* méditerranéen(ne); **the ~ (Sea)** la (mer) Méditerranée.

medium [mē'dēəm] *a* moyen(ne) ♦ *n* (*pl* **media**) (*means*) moyen *m*; (*pl* **mediums**) (*person*) médium *m*; **the happy ~** le juste milieu.

medium-sized [mē'dēəmsīzd] *a* de taille moyenne.

medium wave *n* (*RADIO*) ondes moyennes, petites ondes.

medley [med'lē] *n* mélange *m*.

meek [mēk] *a* doux(douce), humble.

meet, *pt, pp* **met** [mēt, met] *vt* rencontrer; (*by arrangement*) retrouver, rejoindre; (*for the first time*) faire la connaissance de; (*go and fetch*): **I'll ~ you at the station** j'irai te chercher à la gare; (*problem*) faire face à; (*requirements*) satisfaire à, répondre à; (*bill, expenses*) régler, honorer ♦ *vi* se rencontrer; se retrouver; (*in session*) se réunir; (*join: objects*) se joindre ♦ *n* (*US SPORT*) rencontre *f*, meeting *m*; (*Brit*: *HUNTING*) rendez-vous *m* de chasse; **pleased to ~ you!** enchanté!

meet up *vi*: **to ~ up with sb** rencontrer qn.

meet with *vt fus* rencontrer.

meeting [mē'ting] *n* rencontre *f*; (*session: of club etc*) réunion *f*; (*formal*) assemblée *f*; (SPORT: *rally*) rencontre, meeting *m*; (*interview*) entrevue *f*; **she's at a** ~ (COMM) elle est en conférence; **to call a** ~ convoquer une réunion.

meeting place *n* lieu *m* de (la) réunion; (*for appointment*) lieu de rendez-vous.

megabyte [meg'əbīt] *n* (COMPUT) méga-octet *m*.

megalomaniac [megəlōmā'nēak] *n* mégalomane *m/f*.

megaphone [meg'əfōn] *n* porte-voix *m inv*.

melancholy [mel'ənkâlē] *n* mélancolie *f* ♦ *a* mélancolique.

mellow [mel'ō] *a* velouté(e); doux(douce); (*color*) riche et profond(e); (*fruit*) mûr(e) ♦ *vi* (*person*) s'adoucir.

melodious [məlō'dēəs] *a* mélodieux(euse).

melodrama [mel'ədrâmə] *n* mélodrame *m*.

melodramatic [melədrəmat'ik] *a* mélodramatique.

melody [mel'ədē] *n* mélodie *f*.

melon [mel'ən] *n* melon *m*.

melt [melt] *vi* fondre; (*become soft*) s'amollir; (*fig*) s'attendrir ♦ *vt* faire fondre; (*person*) attendrir.

melt away *vi* fondre complètement.

melt down *vt* fondre.

meltdown [melt'doun] *n* fusion *f* (du cœur d'un réacteur nucléaire).

melting point [melt'ing point] *n* point *m* de fusion.

melting pot [melt'ing pât] *n* (*fig*) creuset *m*; **to be in the** ~ être encore en discussion.

member [mem'bûr] *n* membre *m*; (*of club, political party*) membre, adhérent/e ♦ *cpd*: ~ **country/state** *n* pays *m*/état *m* membre; **M~ of Congress (MC)** *n* (US) membre du Congrès; **M~ of the House of Representatives (MHR)** *n* (US) membre de la Chambre des représentants; **M~ of Parliament (MP)** *n* (*Brit*) député *m*; **M~ of the European Parliament (MEP)** *n* Eurodéputé *m*.

membership [mem'bûrship] *n* (*becoming a member*) adhésion *f*; admission *f*; (*being a member*) qualité *f* de membre, fait *m* d'être membre; (*the members*) membres *mpl*, adhérents *mpl*; (*number of members*) nombre *m* des membres *or* adhérents.

membership card *n* carte *f* de membre.

membrane [mem'brān] *n* membrane *f*.

memento [məmen'tō] *n* souvenir *m*.

memo [mem'ō] *n* note *f* (de service).

memoir [mem'wâr] *n* mémoire *m*, étude *f*; ~**s** *npl* mémoires.

memo pad *n* bloc-notes *m*.

memorable [mem'ûrəbəl] *a* mémorable.

memorandum, *pl* **memoranda** [meməran'dəm, -də] *n* note *f* (de service); (DIPLOMACY) mémorandum *m*.

memorial [məmô'rēəl] *n* mémorial *m* ♦ *a* commémoratif(ive).

memorize [mem'ərīz] *vt* apprendre *or* retenir par cœur.

memory [mem'ûrē] *n* mémoire *f*; (*recollection*) souvenir *m*; **to have a good/bad** ~ avoir une bonne/mauvaise mémoire; **loss of** ~ perte *f* de mémoire; **in** ~ **of** à la mé-

moire de.

men [men] *npl of* **man**.

menace [men'is] *n* menace *f*; (*col: nuisance*) peste *f*, plaie *f* ♦ *vt* menacer; **a public** ~ un danger public.

menacing [men'ising] *a* menaçant(e).

menagerie [mənaj'ûrē] *n* ménagerie *f*.

mend [mend] *vt* réparer; (*darn*) raccommoder, repriser ♦ *n* reprise *f*; **on the** ~ en voie de guérison.

mending [mend'ing] *n* raccommodages *mpl*.

menial [mē'nēəl] *a* de domestique, inférieur(e); subalterne.

meningitis [meninjī'tis] *n* méningite *f*.

menopause [men'əpóz] *n* ménopause *f*.

menservants [men'sûrvənts] *npl of* **manservant.**

menstruate [men'strōoāt] *vi* avoir ses règles.

menstruation [menstrōoā'shən] *n* menstruation *f*.

mental [men'təl] *a* mental(e); ~ **illness** maladie mentale.

mentality [mental'itē] *n* mentalité *f*.

mentally [men'təlē] *ad*: **to be** ~ **handicapped** être handicapé/e mental(e).

menthol [men'thôl] *n* menthol *m*.

mention [men'chən] *n* mention *f* ♦ *vt* mentionner, faire mention de; **don't** ~ **it!** je vous en prie, il n'y a pas de quoi!; **I need hardly** ~ **that ...** est-il besoin de rappeler que ...?; **not to** ~ **...**, **without** ~**ing ...** sans parler de ..., sans compter ....

mentor [men'tûr] *n* mentor *m*.

menu [men'yōō] *n* (*in restaurant*, COMPUT) menu *m*; (*printed*) carte *f*.

menu-driven [men'yōōdriv'ən] *a* (COMPUT) piloté(e) par menu.

meow [mēou'] *vi* miauler.

MEP *n abbr* = **Member of the European Parliament.**

mercantile [mûr'kəntil] *a* marchand(e); (*law*) commercial(e).

mercenary [mûr'sənerē] *a* mercantile ♦ *n* mercenaire *m*.

merchandise *n* [mûr'chəndīs] marchandises *fpl* ♦ *vt* [mûr'chəndīz] commercialiser.

merchandiser [mûr'chəndīzûr] *n* marchandiseur *m*.

merchant [mûr'chənt] *n* négociant *m*, marchand *m*; **timber/wine** ~ négociant en bois/vins, marchand de bois/vins.

merchant bank *n* (*Brit*) banque *f* d'affaires.

merchantman [mûr'chəntmən] *n* navire marchand.

merchant marine, (*Brit*) **merchant navy** *n* marine marchande.

merciful [mûr'sifəl] *a* miséricordieux(euse), clément(e).

mercifully [mûr'sifəlē] *ad* avec clémence; (*fortunately*) par bonheur, Dieu merci.

merciless [mûr'silis] *a* impitoyable, sans pitié.

mercurial [mûrkyōō'rēəl] *a* changeant(e); (*lively*) vif(vive).

mercury [mûrk'yûrē] *n* mercure *m*.

mercy [mûr'sē] *n* pitié *f*, merci *f*; (REL) miséricorde *f*; **to have** ~ **on sb** avoir pitié de qn; **at the** ~ **of** à la merci de.

mercy killing *n* euthanasie *f*.

mere [mēr] *a* simple.

merely |mēr'lē| *ad* simplement, purement.
merge |mûrj| *vt* unir; (*COMPUT*) fusionner, interclasser ♦ *vi* se fondre; (*COMM*) fusionner.
merger |mûr'jûr| *n* (*COMM*) fusion *f*.
meridian |mərid'ēən| *n* méridien *m*.
meringue |mərang'| *n* meringue *f*.
merit |mär'it| *n* mérite *m*, valeur *f* ♦ *vt* mériter.
meritocracy |märitâk'rəsē| *n* méritocratie *f*.
mermaid |mûr'mād| *n* sirène *f*.
merrily |mär'ilē| *ad* joyeusement, gaiement.
merriment |mär'imənt| *n* gaieté *f*.
merry |mär'ē| *a* gai(e); **M~ Christmas!** joyeux Noël!
merry-go-round |mär'ēgōround| *n* manège *m*.
mesh |mesh| *n* maille *f*; filet *m* ♦ *vi* (*gears*) s'engrener; **wire ~** grillage *m* (métallique), treillis *m* (métallique).
mesmerize |mez'mərīz| *vt* hypnotiser; fasciner.
mess |mes| *n* désordre *m*, fouillis *m*, pagaille *f*; (*MIL*) mess *m*, cantine *f*; **to be (in) a ~** être en désordre; **to be/get o.s. in a ~** (*fig*) être/se mettre dans le pétrin.
mess about *vi* (*Brit*) = **mess around**.
mess around *vi* (*col*) faire l'imbécile; (: *waste time*) traînasser.
mess around with *vt fus* (*col*) chambarder, tripoter.
mess up *vt* salir; chambarder; gâcher.
message |mes'ij| *n* message *m*; **to get the ~** (*fig*: *col*) saisir, piger.
message switching *n* (*COMPUT*) commutation *f* de messages.
messenger |mes'injûr| *n* messager *m*.
Messiah |misī'ə| *n* Messie *m*.
Messrs, Messrs. |mes'ûrz| *abbr* (*on letters*: = *messieurs*) MM.
messy |mes'ē| *a* sale; en désordre.
Met |met| *n abbr* (*US*) = *Metropolitan Opera*.
met |met| *pt, pp of* **meet** ♦ *a abbr* (*Brit*: = *meteorological*) météo *inv*.
metabolism |mətab'əlizəm| *n* métabolisme *m*.
metal |met'əl| *n* métal *m* ♦ *vt* empierrer.
metallic |mital'ik| *a* métallique.
metallurgy |met'əlûrjē| *n* métallurgie *f*.
metalwork |met'əlwûrk| *n* (*craft*) ferronnerie *f*.
metamorphosis, *pl* **-phoses** |metəmôr'fəsis, -ēz| *n* métamorphose *f*.
metaphor |met'əfôr| *n* métaphore *f*.
metaphysics |metəfiz'iks| *n* métaphysique *f*.
mete |mēt| : **to ~ out** *vt fus* infliger.
meteor |mē'tēôr| *n* météore *m*.
meteoric |mētēôr'ik| *a* (*fig*) fulgurant(e).
meteorite |mē'tēərīt| *n* météorite *m or f*.
meteorological |mētēûrəlâj'ikəl| *a* météorologique.
meteorology |mētēərâl'əjē| *n* météorologie *f*.
meter |mē'tûr| *n* (*instrument*) compteur *m*; (*also*: **parking ~**) parc(o)mètre *m*; (*US*: *measurement*) mètre *m*.
methane |meth'ān| *n* méthane *m*.
method |meth'əd| *n* méthode *f*; **~ of payment** mode *m* or modalité *f* de paiement.
methodical |məthâd'ikəl| *a* méthodique.
Methodist |meth'ədist| *a, n* méthodiste *(m/f)*.
methylated spirit(s) |meth'əlātid spir'its| *n*

(*Brit: also*: **meths**) alcool *m* à brûler.
meticulous |mətik'yələs| *a* méticuleux(euse).
metre |mē'tûr| *n* (*Brit: measurement*) mètre *m*.
metric |met'rik| *a* métrique; **to go ~** adopter le système métrique.
metrical |met'rikəl| *a* métrique.
metrication |metrikā'shən| *n* conversion *f* au système métrique.
metric system *n* système *m* métrique.
metric ton *n* tonne *f*.
metronome |met'rənōm| *n* métronome *m*.
metropolis |mitrâp'əlis| *n* métropole *f*.
metropolitan |metrəpâl'itən| *a* métropolitain(e).
Metropolitan Police *n* (*Brit*): **the ~** la police londonienne.
mettle |met'əl| *n* courage *m*.
mew |myōō| *vi* (*cat*) miauler.
mews |myōōz| *n* (*Brit*): **~ cottage** maisonnette aménagée dans une ancienne écurie ou remise.
Mexican |mek'səkən| *a* mexicain(e) ♦ *n* Mexicain/e.
Mexico |mek'səkō| *n* Mexique *m*.
Mexico City *n* Mexico.
mezzanine |mez'ənēn| *n* mezzanine *f*; (*of shops, offices*) entresol *m*.
MFA *n abbr* (*US*: = *Master of Fine Arts*) titre universitaire.
mfr *abbr* = **manufacture, manufacturer**.
mg *abbr* (= *milligram*) mg.
Mgr *abbr* (= *Monseigneur, Monsignor*) Mgr; (= *manager*) dir.
MHR *n abbr* (*US*) = **Member of the House of Representatives**.
MHz *abbr* (= *megahertz*) MHz.
MI *abbr* (*US MAIL*) = *Michigan*.
MI5 *n abbr* (*Brit*: = *Military Intelligence 5*) ≈ DST *f*.
MI6 *n abbr* (*Brit*: = *Military Intelligence 6*) ≈ DGSE *f*.
MIA *abbr* (= *missing in action*) disparu au combat.
mice |mīs| *npl of* **mouse**.
Mich. *abbr* (*US*) = *Michigan*.
microbe |mī'krōb| *n* microbe *m*.
microbiology |mīkrōbīál'əjē| *n* microbiologie *f*.
microchip |mī'krəchip| *n* (*ELEC*) puce *f*.
micro(computer) |mīkrō(kəmpyōō'tûr)| *n* micro(-ordinateur) *m*.
microcosm |mī'krəkázəm| *n* microcosme *m*.
microeconomics |mīkrōēkənám'iks| *n* microéconomie *f*.
microfiche |mī'krōfēsh| *n* microfiche *f*.
microfilm |mī'krəfilm| *n* microfilm *m* ♦ *vt* microfilmer.
micrometer |mīkrâm'itûr| *n* palmer *m*, micromètre *m*.
microphone |mī'krəfōn| *n* microphone *m*.
microprocessor |mīkrōprás'esûr| *n* microprocesseur *m*.
microscope |mī'krəskōp| *n* microscope *m*; **under the ~** au microscope.
microscopic |mī'krəskâp'ik| *a* microscopique.
microwave |mī'krōwāv| *n* (*also*: **~ oven**) four *m* à micro-ondes.
mid |mid| *a*: **~ May** la mi-mai; **~ afternoon**

le milieu de l'après-midi; **in ~ air** en plein ciel; **he's in his ~ thirties** il a dans les trente-cinq ans.

midday [mid'dā] n midi m.

middle [mid'əl] n milieu m; (waist) ceinture f, taille f ♦ a du milieu; **in the ~ of the night** au milieu de la nuit; **I'm in the ~ of reading it** je suis (justement) en train de le lire.

middle age n tranche d'âge aux limites floues, entre la quarantaine et le début du troisième âge.

middle-aged [mid'əlājd'] a (people) see middle age; d'un certain âge, ni vieux ni jeune; (pej: values, outlook) conventionnel(le), rassis(e).

Middle Ages npl: **the ~** le moyen âge.

middle class n: **the ~(es)** ≈ les classes moyennes ♦ a (also: **middle-class**) ≈ (petit(e)-)bourgeois(e).

Middle East n: **the ~** le Proche-Orient, le Moyen-Orient.

middleman [mid'əlman] n intermédiaire m.

middle management n cadres moyens.

middle name n second prénom.

middle-of-the-road [mid'əlʌvthərōd'] a (policy) modéré(e), du juste milieu; (music etc) plutôt classique, assez traditionnel(le).

middleweight [mid'əlwāt] n (BOXING) poids moyen.

middling [mid'ling] a moyen(ne).

Middx abbr (Brit) = Middlesex.

midge [mij] n moucheron m.

midget [mij'it] n nain/e ♦ a minuscule.

midnight [mid'nīt] n minuit m; **at ~** à minuit.

midriff [mid'rif] n estomac m, taille f.

midst [midst] n: **in the ~ of** au milieu de.

midsummer [mid'sum'ûr] n milieu m de l'été.

midway [mid'wā] a, ad: **~ (between)** à mi-chemin (entre).

midweek [mid'wēk] n milieu m de la semaine ♦ ad au milieu de la semaine, en pleine semaine.

midwife, midwives [mid'wīf, -vz] n sage-femme f.

midwifery [mid'wīfûrē] n obstétrique f.

midwinter [mid'win'tûr] n milieu m de l'hiver.

might [mīt] vb see **may** ♦ n puissance f, force f.

mighty [mī'tē] a puissant(e) ♦ ad (col) rudement.

migraine [mī'grān] n migraine f.

migrant [mī'grənt] n (bird, animal) migrateur m; (person) migrant/e; nomade m/f ♦ a migrateur(trice); migrant(e); nomade; (worker) saisonnier(ière).

migrate [mī'grāt] vi émigrer.

migration [mīgrā'shən] n migration f.

mike [mīk] n abbr (= microphone) micro m.

Milan [milan'] n Milan.

mild [mīld] a doux(douce); (reproach) léger(ère); (illness) bénin(igne) ♦ n bière légère.

mildew [mil'dōō] n mildiou m.

mildly [mīld'lē] ad doucement; légèrement; **to put it ~** (col) c'est le moins qu'on puisse dire.

mildness [mīld'nis] n douceur f.

mile [mīl] n mil(l)e m (= 1609 m); **to do 30 ~s per gallon** ≈ faire 9,4 litres aux cent.

mileage [mī'lij] n distance f en milles, ≈ kilométrage m.

mileage allowance n ≈ indemnité f kilométrique.

mileometer [mīlâm'itûr] n (Brit) = **milometer.**

milestone [mīl'stōn] n borne f; (fig) jalon m.

milieu [mēlyōō'] n milieu m.

militant [mil'ətənt] a, n militant(e).

militarism [mil'itərizəm] n militarisme m.

militaristic [militəris'tik] a militariste.

military [mil'itārē] a militaire ♦ n: **the ~** l'armée f, les militaires mpl.

militate [mil'ətāt] vi: **to ~ against** militer contre.

militia [milish'ə] n milice f.

milk [milk] n lait m ♦ vt (cow) traire; (fig) dépouiller, plumer.

milk chocolate n chocolat m au lait.

milk float n (Brit) = **milk truck.**

milking [mil'king] n traite f.

milkman [milk'man] n laitier m.

milk shake n milk-shake m.

milk tooth n dent f de lait.

milk truck n (US) voiture f or camionnette f du or de laitier.

milky [mil'kē] a lacté(e); (color) laiteux(euse).

Milky Way n Voie lactée.

mill [mil] n moulin m; (factory) usine f, fabrique f; (spinning ~) filature f; (flour ~) minoterie f ♦ vt moudre, broyer ♦ vi (also: **~ around**) grouiller.

millennium, pl ~s or millennia [milen'ēəm, -len'ēə] n millénaire m.

miller [mil'ûr] n meunier m.

millet [mil'it] n millet m.

milli... [mil'ə] prefix milli....

milligram(me) [mil'əgram] n milligramme m.

milliliter, (Brit) millilitre [mil'əlētûr] n millilitre m.

millimeter, (Brit) millimetre [mil'əmētûr] n millimètre m.

milliner [mil'inûr] n modiste f.

millinery [mil'ənārē] n modes fpl.

million [mil'yən] n million m.

millionaire [milyənär'] n millionnaire m.

millipede [mil'əpēd] n mille-pattes m inv.

millstone [mil'stōn] n meule f.

millwheel [mil'wēl] n roue f de moulin.

milometer [mīlō'mētûr] n (Brit) ≈ compteur m kilométrique.

mime [mīm] n mime m ♦ vt, vi mimer.

mimic [mim'ik] n imitateur/trice ♦ vt, vi imiter, contrefaire.

mimicry [mim'ikrē] n imitation f; (ZOOL) mimétisme m.

Min. abbr (Brit POL) = **ministry.**

min. abbr (= minute) mn.; (= minimum) min.

minaret [minəret'] n minaret m.

mince [mins] vt hacher ♦ vi (in walking) marcher à petits pas maniérés ♦ n (Brit CULIN) viande hachée, hachis m; **he does not ~ (his) words** il ne mâche pas ses mots.

mincemeat [mins'mēt] n hachis de fruits secs utilisés en pâtisserie.

mince pie n sorte de tarte aux fruits secs.

mincer [min'sûr] n hachoir m.

mincing [min'sing] *a* affecté(e).

mind [mīnd] *n* esprit *m* ♦ *vt* (*attend to, look after*) s'occuper de; (*be careful*) faire attention à; (*object to*): I don't ~ the noise je ne crains pas le bruit, le bruit ne me dérange pas; do you ~ if ...? est-ce que cela vous gêne si ...?; I don't ~ cela ne me dérange pas; ~ you, ... remarquez, ...; never ~ peu importe, ça ne fait rien; it is on my ~ cela me préoccupe; to change one's ~ changer d'avis; to be of two ~s about sth être indécis(e) *or* irrésolu(e) en ce qui concerne qch; to my ~ à mon avis, selon moi; to be out of one's ~ ne plus avoir toute sa raison; to keep sth in ~ ne pas oublier qch; to bear sth in ~ tenir compte de qch; to have sb/sth in ~ avoir qn/qch en tête; to have in ~ to do avoir l'intention de faire; it went right out of my ~ ça m'est complètement sorti de la tête; to bring *or* call sth to ~ se rappeler qch; to make up one's ~ se décider.

-minded [mīn'did] *a*: fair~ impartial(e); an industrially~ nation une nation orientée vers l'industrie.

minder [mīnd'ûr] *n* (*child* ~) gardienne *f*; (*bodyguard*) ange gardien (*fig*).

mindful [mīnd'fəl] *a*: ~ of attentif(ive) à, soucieux(euse) de.

mindless [mīnd'lis] *a* irréfléchi(e); (*violence, crime*) insensé(e).

mine [mīn] *pronoun* le(la) mien(ne), les miens(miennes); this book is ~ ce livre est à moi ♦ *n* mine *f* ♦ *vt* (*coal*) extraire; (*ship, beach*) miner.

mine detector *n* détecteur *m* de mines.

minefield [mīn'fēld] *n* champ *m* de mines.

miner [mīn'ûr] *n* mineur *m*.

mineral [min'ûrəl] *a* minéral(e) ♦ *n* minéral *m*; ~s *npl* (*Brit: soft drinks*) boissons gazeuses (sucrées).

mineralogy [minərâl'əjē] *n* minéralogie *f*.

mineral water *n* eau minérale.

minesweeper [mīn'swēpûr] *n* dragueur *m* de mines.

mingle [ming'gəl] *vt* mêler, mélanger ♦ *vi*: to ~ with se mêler à.

mingy [min'jē] *a* (*col*) radin(e).

miniature [min'ēəchûr] *a* (en) miniature ♦ *n* miniature *f*.

miniature golf *n* golf-miniature *m*.

minibus [min'ēbus] *n* minibus *m*.

minicab [min'ēkab] *n* (*Brit*) minitaxi *m*.

minicomputer [min'ēkəmpyōōtûr] *n* mini-ordinateur *m*.

minim [min'əm] *n* (*MUS*) blanche *f*.

minima [min'əmə] *npl of* **minimum**.

minimal [min'əməl] *a* minimale(e).

minimize [min'əmīz] *vt* minimiser.

minimum [min'əməm] *n* (*pl*: **minima** [min'əmə]) minimum *m* ♦ *a* minimum; to reduce to a ~ réduire au minimum.

minimum lending rate (MLR) *n* (*ECON*) taux *m* de crédit minimum.

mining [mī'ning] *n* exploitation minière ♦ *a* minier(ière); de mineurs.

minion [min'yən] *n* (*pej*) laquais *m*; favori/te.

miniskirt [min'ēskûrt] *n* mini-jupe *f*.

minister [min'istûr] *n* (*Brit POL*) ministre *m*;

(*REL*) pasteur *m* ♦ *vi*: to ~ to sb donner ses soins à qn; to ~ to sb's needs pourvoir aux besoins de qn.

ministerial [ministēr'ēəl] *a* (*Brit POL*) ministériel(le).

ministry [min'istrē] *n* (*Brit POL*) ministère *m*; (*REL*): to go into the ~ devenir pasteur.

mink [mingk] *n* vison *m*.

mink coat *n* manteau *m* de vison.

Minn. *abbr* (*US*) = Minnesota.

minnow [min'ō] *n* vairon *m*.

minor [mī'nûr] *a* petit(e), de peu d'importance; (*MUS*) mineur(e) ♦ *n* (*LAW*) mineur/e; (*US SCOL*) matière *f* secondaire.

Minorca [minôr'kə] *n* Minorque *f*.

minority [minôr'itē] *n* minorité *f*; to be in a ~ être en minorité.

minster [min'stûr] *n* église abbatiale.

minstrel [min'strəl] *n* trouvère *m*, ménestrel *m*.

mint [mint] *n* (*plant*) menthe *f*; (*candy*) bonbon *m* à la menthe ♦ *vt* (*coins*) battre; the (US) M~, (*Brit*) the (Royal) M~ ≈ l'hôtel *m* de la Monnaie; in ~ condition à l'état de neuf.

mint sauce *n* sauce *f* à la menthe.

minuet [minyōōet'] *n* menuet *m*.

minus [mī'nəs] *n* (*also*: ~ sign) signe *m* moins ♦ *prep* moins.

minute [n mīnōōt'] minuscule; (*detailed*) minutieux(euse) ♦ *n* [min'it] minute *f*; (*official record*) procès-verbal *m*, compte rendu; ~s *npl* procès-verbal; it is 5 ~s past 3 il est 3 heures 5; wait a ~! (attendez) un instant!; at the last ~ à la dernière minute; up to the ~ (*fashion*) dernier cri; (*news*) de dernière minute; (*machine, technology*) de pointe; in ~ detail par le menu.

minute book *n* registre *m* des procès-verbaux.

minute hand *n* aiguille *f* des minutes.

minutely [mīnōōt'lē] *ad* (*by a small amount*) de peu, de manière infime; (*in detail*) minutieusement, dans les moindres détails.

miracle [mir'əkəl] *n* miracle *m*.

miraculous [mirak'yələs] *a* miraculeux(euse).

mirage [mirâzh'] *n* mirage *m*.

mire [mī'ûr] *n* bourbe *f*, boue *f*.

mirror [mir'ûr] *n* miroir *m*, glace *f* ♦ *vt* refléter.

mirror image *n* image inversée.

mirth [mûrth] *n* gaieté *f*.

misadventure [misədven'chûr] *n* mésaventure *f*; death by ~ (*Brit*) décès accidentel.

misanthropist [misan'thrəpist] *n* misanthrope *m/f*.

misapply [misəplī'] *vt* mal employer.

misapprehension [misaprihen'chən] *n* malentendu *m*, méprise *f*.

misappropriate [misəprō'prēāt] *vt* détourner.

misappropriation [misəprōprēā'shən] *n* escroquerie *f*, détournement *m*.

misbehave [misbihāv'] *vi* se conduire mal.

misbehavior, (*Brit*) **misbehaviour** [misbihāv'yûr] *n* mauvaise conduite.

misc. *abbr* = **miscellaneous**.

miscalculate [miskal'kyəlāt] *vt* mal calculer.

miscalculation [miskalkyəlā'shən] *n* erreur *f* de calcul.

miscarriage [miskar'ij] *n* (*MED*) fausse couche; ~ **of justice** erreur *f* judiciaire.

miscarry [miskar'ē] *vi* (*MED*) faire une fausse couche; (*fail: plans*) échouer, mal tourner.

miscellaneous [misəlā'nēəs] *a* (*items, expenses*) divers(es); (*selection*) varié(e).

miscellany [mis'əlānē] *n* recueil *m*.

mischance [mischans'] *n* malchance *f*; **by (some)** ~ par malheur.

mischief [mis'chif] *n* (*naughtiness*) sottises *fpl*; (*harm*) mal *m*, dommage *m*; (*maliciousness*) méchanceté *f*.

mischievous [mis'chəvəs] *a* (*naughty*) coquin(e), espiègle; (*harmful*) méchant(e).

misconception [miskənsep'shən] *n* idée fausse.

misconduct [miskân'dukt] *n* inconduite *f*; **professional** ~ faute professionnelle.

misconstrue [miskənstrōō'] *vt* mal interpréter.

miscount [miskount'] *vt, vi* mal compter.

misdeed [misdēd'] *n* méfait *m*.

misdemeanor, (*Brit*) **misdemeanour** [misdimē'nûr] *n* écart *m* de conduite; infraction *f*.

misdirect [misdirekt'] *vt* (*person*) mal renseigner; (*letter*) mal adresser.

miser [mī'zûr] *n* avare *m/f*.

miserable [miz'ùrəbəl] *a* malheureux(euse); (*wretched*) misérable; **to feel** ~ avoir le cafard.

miserably [miz'ûrəblē] *ad* (*smile, answer*) tristement; (*live, pay*) misérablement; (*fail*) lamentablement.

miserly [mī'zûrlē] *a* avare.

misery [miz'ûrē] *n* (*unhappiness*) tristesse *f*; (*pain*) souffrances *fpl*; (*wretchedness*) misère *f*.

misfire [misfīr'] *vi* rater; (*car engine*) avoir des ratés.

misfit [mis'fit] *n* (*person*) inadapté/e.

misfortune [misfôr'chən] *n* malchance *f*, malheur *m*.

misgiving(s) [misgiv'ing(z)] *n(pl)* craintes *fpl*, soupçons *mpl*; **to have ~s about sth** avoir des doutes quant à qch.

misguided [misgī'did] *a* malavisé(e).

mishandle [mis·han'dəl] *vt* (*treat roughly*) malmener; (*mismanage*) mal s'y prendre pour faire *or* résoudre *etc*.

mishap [mis'hap] *n* mésaventure *f*.

mishear [mis·hiûr'] *vt, vi irg* mal entendre.

mishmash [mish'mash] *n* (*col*) fatras *m*, méli-mélo *m*.

misinform [misinfôrm'] *vt* mal renseigner.

misinterpret [misintûr'prit] *vt* mal interpréter.

misinterpretation [misintûrpritā'shən] *n* interprétation erronée, contresens *m*.

misjudge [misjuj'] *vt* méjuger, se méprendre sur le compte de.

mislay [mislā'] *vt irg* égarer.

mislead [mislēd'] *vt irg* induire en erreur.

misleading [mislē'ding] *a* trompeur(euse).

misled [misled'] *pt, pp of* **mislead**.

mismanage [misman'ij] *vt* mal gérer; mal s'y prendre pour faire *or* résoudre *etc*.

mismanagement [misman'ijmənt] *n* mauvaise gestion.

misnomer [misnō'mûr] *n* terme *or* qualificatif trompeur *or* peu approprié.

misogynist [misâj'ənist] *n* misogyne *m/f*.

misplace [misplās'] *vt* égarer; **to be ~d** (*trust etc*) être mal placé(e).

misprint [mis'print] *n* faute *f* d'impression.

mispronounce [misprənouns'] *vt* mal prononcer.

misquote [miskwōt'] *vt* citer erronément *or* inexactement.

misread [misrēd'] *vt irg* mal lire.

misrepresent [misreprizent'] *vt* présenter sous un faux jour.

Miss [mis] *n* Mademoiselle; **Dear ~ Smith** Chère Mademoiselle Smith.

miss [mis] *vt* (*fail to get*) manquer, rater; (*appointment, class*) manquer; (*escape, avoid*) échapper à, éviter; (*notice loss of: money etc*) s'apercevoir de l'absence de; (*regret the absence of*): **I ~ him/it** il/cela me manque ♦ *vi* manquer ♦ *n* (*shot*) coup manqué; **the bus just ~ed the wall** le bus a évité le mur de justesse; **you're ~ing the point** vous êtes à côté de la question.

miss out *vt* (*Brit*) oublier.

miss out on *vt fus* (*fun, party*) rater, manquer; (*chance, bargain*) laisser passer.

Miss. *abbr* (*US*) = **Mississippi**.

missal [mis'əl] *n* missel *m*.

misshapen [mis-shā'pən] *a* difforme.

missile [mis'əl] *n* (*AVIAT*) missile *m*; (*object thrown*) projectile *m*.

missile base *n* base *f* de missiles.

missile launcher *n* lance-missiles *m*.

missing [mis'ing] *a* manquant(e); (*after escape, disaster: person*) disparu(e); **to go ~** disparaître; **~ person** personne disparue, disparu/e.

mission [mish'ən] *n* mission *f*; **on a ~ to sb** en mission auprès de qn.

missionary [mish'ənārē] *n* missionnaire *m/f*.

missive [mis'iv] *n* missive *f*.

misspell [misspel'] *vt* (*irg: like* **spell**) mal orthographier.

misspent [misspent'] *a*: **his ~ youth** sa folle jeunesse.

mist [mist] *n* brume *f*, brouillard *m* ♦ *vi* (*also*: ~ **over**, ~ **up**) devenir brumeux(euse); (*Brit: windows*) s'embuer.

mistake [mistāk'] *n* erreur *f*, faute *f* ♦ *vt* (*irg: like* **take**) (*meaning*) mal comprendre; (*intentions*) se méprendre sur; **to ~ for** prendre pour; **by ~** par erreur, par inadvertance; **to make a ~** (*in writing*) faire une faute; (*in calculating etc*) faire une erreur; **to make a ~ about sb/sth** se tromper sur le compte de qn/sur qch.

mistaken [mistā'kən] *pp of* **mistake** ♦ *a* (*idea etc*) erroné(e); **to be ~** faire erreur, se tromper.

mistaken identity *n* erreur *f* d'identité.

mistakenly [mistā'kənlē] *ad* par erreur, par mégarde.

mister [mis'tûr] *n* (*col*) Monsieur *m*; *see* **Mr**.

mistletoe [mis'əltō] *n* gui *m*.

mistook [mistōōk'] *pt of* **mistake**.

mistranslation [mistranzlā'shən] *n* erreur *f* de traduction, contresens *m*.

mistreat [mistrēt'] *vt* maltraiter.

mistress [mis'tris] *n* maîtresse *f*; (*Brit: in elementary school*) institutrice *f*; *see* **Mrs**.

mistrust [mistrust'] vt se méfier de ♦ n: ~ (of) méfiance f (à l'égard de).

mistrustful [mistrust'fəl] a: ~ (of) méfiant(e) (à l'égard de).

misty [mis'tē] a brumeux(euse).

misty-eyed [mis'tēīd'] a les yeux embués de larmes; (fig) sentimental(e).

misunderstand [misundûrstand'] vt, vi irg mal comprendre.

misunderstanding [misundûrstan'ding] n méprise f, malentendu m.

misunderstood [misundûrsto͞od'] pt, pp of misunderstand.

misuse n ₁ [misyo͞os'] mauvais emploi; (of power) abus m ♦ vt [misyo͞oz'] mal employer; abuser de.

MIT n abbr (US) = Massachusetts Institute of Technology.

mite [mīt] n (small quantity) grain m, miette f.

miter [mī'tûr] n (US) mitre f; (CARPENTRY) onglet m.

mitigate [mit'əgāt] vt atténuer; **mitigating circumstances** circonstances atténuantes.

mitigation [mitəgā'shən] n atténuation f.

mitre [mī'tûr] n (Brit) = **miter**.

mitt(en) [mit'(ən)] n mitaine f; moufle f.

mix [miks] vt mélanger ♦ vi se mélanger ♦ n mélange m; dosage m; **to ~ sth with sth** mélanger qch à qch; **to ~ business with pleasure** unir l'utile à l'agréable; **cake ~** préparation f pour gâteau.

mix in vt incorporer, mélanger.

mix up vt mélanger; (confuse) confondre; **to be ~ed up in sth** être mêlé(e) à qch or impliqué(e) dans qch.

mixed [mikst] a (assorted) assortis(ies); (school etc) mixte.

mixed doubles npl (SPORT) double m mixte.

mixed economy n économie f mixte.

mixed grill n (Brit) assortiment m de grillades.

mixed-up [mikst'up] a (person) désorienté(e) (fig).

mixer [mik'sûr] n (for food) batteur m, mixeur m; (person): **he is a good ~** il est très sociable.

mixture [miks'chûr] n assortiment m, mélange m; (MED) préparation f.

mix-up [miks'up] n confusion f.

MK abbr (Brit TECH) = **mark**.

mk abbr = **mark** (currency).

mkt abbr = **market**.

MLitt n abbr (= Master of Literature, Master of Letters) titre universitaire.

MLR n abbr (Brit) = **minimum lending rate**.

mm abbr (= millimeter) mm.

MN abbr (Brit) = **Merchant Navy**; (US MAIL) = Minnesota.

MO n abbr (MED) = medical officer; (US col: = modus operandi) méthode f ♦ abbr (US MAIL) = Missouri.

mo abbr = **month**.

m.o. abbr = **money order**.

moan [mōn] n gémissement m ♦ vi gémir; (col: complain): **to ~ (about)** se plaindre (de).

moaning [mō'ning] n gémissements mpl.

moat [mōt] n fossé m, douves fpl.

mob [mâb] n foule f; (disorderly) cohue f; (pej): **the ~** la populace ♦ vt assaillir.

mobile [mō'bəl] a mobile ♦ n (ART) mobile m.

mobile home n caravane f.

mobility [mōbil'ətē] n mobilité f.

mobilize [mō'bəlīz] vt, vi mobiliser.

moccasin [mâk'əsin] n mocassin m.

mock [mâk] vt ridiculiser, se moquer de ♦ a faux(fausse).

mockery [mâk'ûrē] n moquerie f, raillerie f; **to make a ~ of** ridiculiser, tourner en dérision.

mocking [mâk'ing] a moqueur(euse).

mockingbird [mâk'ingbûrd] n moqueur m.

mock-up [mâk'up] n maquette f.

MOD n abbr (Brit) = **Ministry of Defence**.

mod cons [mâd kânz] npl abbr (Brit) = **modern conveniences**.

mode [mōd] n mode m; (of transport) moyen m.

model [mâd'əl] n modèle m; (person: for fashion) mannequin m; (: for artist) modèle ♦ vt modeler ♦ vi travailler comme mannequin ♦ a (railroad: toy) modèle réduit inv; (child, factory) modèle; **to ~ clothes** présenter des vêtements; **to ~ sb/sth on** modeler qn/qch sur.

model apartment n (US) appartement-témoin.

modeler [mâd'əlûr] n (US) modeleur m; (model maker) maquettiste m/f; fabricant m de modèles réduits.

modeling clay [mâd'ling klā] n pâte f à modeler.

modeller [mâd'əlûr] n (Brit) = **modeler**.

modem [mō'dem] n modem m.

moderate a, n [mâd'ûrit] a modéré(e) ♦ n (POL) modéré(e) ♦ vb [mâd'ərāt] vi se modérer, se calmer ♦ vt modérer.

moderately [mâd'ûritlē] ad (act) avec modération or mesure; (expensive, difficult) moyennement; (pleased, happy) raisonnablement, assez; **~ priced** à un prix raisonnable.

moderation [mâdərā'shən] n modération f, mesure f; **in ~** à dose raisonnable, pris(e) or pratiqué(e) modérément.

modern [mâd'ûrn] a moderne; **~ languages** langues vivantes.

modernization [mâdûrnəzā'shən] n modernisation f.

modernize [mâd'ûrnīz] vt moderniser.

modest [mâd'ist] a modeste.

modesty [mâd'istē] n modestie f.

modicum [mâd'əkəm] n: **a ~ of** un minimum de.

modification [mâdəfəkā'shən] n modification f; **to make ~s** faire or apporter des modifications.

modify [mâd'əfī] vt modifier.

modular [mâj'ələr] a (filing, unit) modulaire.

modulate [mâj'əlāt] vt moduler.

modulation [mâjəlā'shən] n modulation f.

module [mâj'o͞ol] n module m.

mogul [mō'gəl] n (fig) nabab m; (SKI) bosse f.

mohair [mō'här] n mohair m.

Mohammed [mōham'id] n Mahomet m.

moist [moist] a humide, moite.

moisten [mois'ən] vt humecter, mouiller légèrement.

moisture [mois'chûr] *n* humidité *f*; (*on glass*) buée *f*.

moisturize [mois'chəriz] *vt* (*skin*) hydrater.

moisturizer [mois'chərizûr] *n* produit hydratant.

molar [mō'lûr] *n* molaire *f*.

molasses [məlas'iz] *n* mélasse *f*.

mold [mōld] (*US*) *n* moule *m*; (*mildew*) moisissure *f* ♦ *vt* mouler, modeler; (*fig*) façonner.

molder [mōl'dûr] *vi* (*US*: *decay*) moisir.

molding [mōl'ding] *n* (*US ARCHIT*) moulure *f*.

moldy [mōl'dē] *a* (*US*) moisi(e).

mole [mōl] *n* (*animal*) taupe *f*; (*spot*) grain *m* de beauté.

molecule [mâl'əkyōōl] *n* molécule *f*.

molehill [mōl'hil] *n* taupinière *f*.

molest [məlest'] *vt* tracasser; molester.

mollusc [mâl'əsk] *n* mollusque *m*.

mollycoddle [mâl'ēkâdəl] *vt* chouchouter, couver.

molt [mōlt] *vi* (*US*) muer.

molten [mōl'tən] *a* fondu(e).

mom [mâm] *n* (*US*) maman *f*.

moment [mō'mənt] *n* moment *m*, instant *m*; (*importance*) importance *f*; **at the ~** en ce moment; **for the ~** pour l'instant; **in a ~** dans un instant; **"one ~ please"** (*TEL*) ''ne quittez pas''.

momentarily [mōməntâr'ilē] *ad* momentanément; (*US*: *soon*) bientôt.

momentary [mō'məntârē] *a* momentané(e), passager(ère).

momentous [mōmen'təs] *a* important(e), capital(e).

momentum [mōmen'təm] *n* élan *m*, vitesse acquise; **to gather ~** prendre de la vitesse.

mommy [mâm'ē] *n* (*US*) maman *f*.

Mon. *abbr* (= *Monday*) l.

Monaco [mân'əkō] *n* Monaco *f*.

monarch [mân'ûrk] *n* monarque *m*.

monarchist [mân'ûrkist] *n* monarchiste *m/f*.

monarchy [mân'ûrkē] *n* monarchie *f*.

monastery [mân'əstârē] *n* monastère *m*.

monastic [mənas'tik] *a* monastique.

Monday [mun'dā] *n* lundi *m*; *for phrases see also* **Tuesday**.

monetarist [mân'itârist] *n* monétariste *m/f*.

monetary [mân'itârē] *a* monétaire.

money [mun'ē] *n* argent *m*; **to make ~** (*person*) gagner de l'argent; (*business*) rapporter; **I've got no ~ left** je n'ai plus d'argent, je n'ai plus un sou.

moneyed [mun'ēd] *a* riche.

moneylender [mun'ēlendûr] *n* prêteur/euse.

moneymaking [mun'ēmāking] *a* lucratif(ive), qui rapporte (de l'argent).

money market *n* marché financier.

money order *n* mandat *m*.

money-spinner [mun'ēspinûr] *n* (*col*) mine *f* d'or (*fig*).

money supply *n* masse *f* monétaire.

Mongol [mâng'gəl] *n* Mongol/e; (*LING*) mongol *m*.

mongol [mâng'gəl] *a*, *n* (*MED*) mongolien(ne).

Mongolia [mânggō'lcə] *n* Mongolie *f*.

Mongolian [mânggō'lēən] *a* mongol(e) ♦ *n* Mongol/e; (*LING*) mongol *m*.

mongoose [mâng'gōōs] *n* mangouste *f*.

mongrel [mung'grəl] *n* (*dog*) bâtard *m*.

monitor [mân'itûr] *n* (*US SCOL*) surveillant *m* (d'examen); (*Brit SCOL*) chef *m* de classe; (*TV*, *COMPUT*) écran *m*, moniteur *m* ♦ *vt* contrôler; (*foreign station*) être à l'écoute de.

monk [mungk] *n* moine *m*.

monkey [mung'kē] *n* singe *m*.

monkey nut *n* (*Brit*) cacahuète *f*.

monkey wrench *n* clé *f* à molette.

mono [mân'ō] *a* mono *inv*.

mono... [mân'ō] *prefix* mono....

monochrome [mân'əkrōm] *a* monochrome.

monocle [mân'əkəl] *n* monocle *m*.

monogram [mân'əgram] *n* monogramme *m*.

monolith [mân'əlith] *n* monolithe *m*.

monologue [mân'əlóg] *n* monologue *m*.

mononucleosis [mânōnōōklēō'sis] *n* (*US*) mononucléose infectieuse.

monoplane [mân'əplān] *n* monoplan *m*.

monopolize [mənâp'əliz] *vt* monopoliser.

monopoly [mənâp'əlē] *n* monopole *m*; **Monopolies and Mergers Commission** (*Brit*) *Commission britannique d'enquête sur les monopoles*.

monorail [mân'ərāl] *n* monorail *m*.

monosodium glutamate (MSG) [mânəsō'dēəm glōō'təmāt] *n* glutamate *m* de sodium.

monosyllabic [mânəsilab'ik] *a* monosyllabique; (*person*) laconique.

monosyllable [mân'əsiləbəl] *n* monosyllabe *m*.

monotone [mân'ətōn] *n* ton *m* (*or* voix *f*) monocorde; **to speak in a ~** parler sur un ton monocorde.

monotonous [mənât'ənəs] *a* monotone.

monotony [mənât'ənē] *n* monotonie *f*.

monoxide [mənâk'sīd] *n*: **carbon ~** oxyde *m* de carbone.

monsoon [mânsōōn'] *n* mousson *f*.

monster [mân'stûr] *n* monstre *m*.

monstrosity [mânstrás'ətē] *n* monstruosité *f*, atrocité *f*.

monstrous [mân'strəs] *a* (*huge*) gigantesque; (*atrocious*) monstrueux(euse), atroce.

Mont. *abbr* (*US*) = *Montana*.

montage [mântâzh'] *n* montage *m*.

Mont Blanc [mânt blangk'] *n* Mont Blanc *m*.

month [munth] *n* mois *m*; **every ~** tous les mois; **$300 a ~** 300 dollars par mois.

monthly [munth'lē] *a* mensuel(le) ♦ *ad* mensuellement ♦ *n* (*magazine*) mensuel *m*, publication mensuelle; **twice ~** deux fois par mois.

Montreal [mântrēôl'] *n* Montréal.

monument [mân'yəmənt] *n* monument *m*.

monumental [mânyəmen'təl] *a* monumental(e).

moo [mōō] *vi* meugler, beugler.

mood [mōōd] *n* humeur *f*, disposition *f*; **to be in a good/bad ~** être de bonne/mauvaise humeur; **to be in the ~ for** être d'humeur à, avoir envie de.

moody [mōō'dē] *a* (*variable*) d'humeur changeante, lunatique; (*sullen*) morose, maussade.

moon [mōōn] *n* lune *f*.

moonbeam [mōōn'bēm] *n* rayon *m* de lune.

moon landing *n* alunissage *m*.

moonlight [mōōn'līt] *n* clair *m* de lune ♦ *vi*

travailler au noir.

moonlighting [mōōn'līting] *n* travail *m* au noir.

moonlit [mōōn'lit] *a* éclairé(e) par la lune; **a ~ night** une nuit de lune.

moonshot [mōōn'shât] *n* (SPACE) tir *m* lunaire.

moonstruck [mōōn'struk] *a* fou(folle), dérangé(e).

Moor [mōōr] *n* Maure/Mauresque.

moor [mōōr] *n* lande *f* ♦ *vt* (*ship*) amarrer ♦ *vi* mouiller.

moorings [mōōr'ingz] *npl* (*chains*) amarres *fpl*; (*place*) mouillage *m*.

Moorish [mōō'rish] *a* maure(mauresque).

moorland [mōōr'land] *n* lande *f*.

moose [mōōs] *n* (*pl inv*) élan *m*.

moot [mōōt] *vt* soulever ♦ *a*: ~ **point** point *m* discutable.

mop [mâp] *n* balai *m* à laver ♦ *vt* éponger, essuyer; ~ **of hair** tignasse *f*.

mop up *vt* éponger.

mope [mōp] *vi* avoir le cafard, se morfondre.

mope around *vi* broyer du noir, se morfondre.

moped [mō'ped] *n* cyclomoteur *m*.

moquette [mōket'] *n* moquette *f*.

moral [môr'əl] *a* moral(e) ♦ *n* morale *f*; ~**s** *npl* moralité *f*.

morale [məral'] *n* moral *m*.

morality [məral'itē] *n* moralité *f*.

moralize [môr'əlīz] *vi*: **to** ~ (**about**) moraliser (sur).

morally [môr'əlē] *ad* moralement.

morass [məras'] *n* marais *m*, marécage *m*.

moratorium [môrətôr'ēəm] *n* moratoire *m*.

morbid [môr'bid] *a* morbide.

more [môr] *a* plus de, davantage de ♦ *ad* plus; ~ **people** plus de gens; **I want** ~ j'en veux plus *or* davantage; **is there any** ~? est-ce qu'il en reste?; **many/much** ~ beaucoup plus; ~ **and** ~ de plus en plus; **once** ~ encore une fois, une fois de plus; **no** ~, **not any** ~ ne ... plus; **and what's** ~ ... et de plus ..., et qui plus est ...; ~ **dangerous than** plus dangereux que; ~ **or less** plus ou moins; ~ **than ever** plus que jamais.

moreover [môrō'vûr] *ad* de plus.

morgue [môrg] *n* morgue *f*.

MORI [mō'rē] *n abbr* (*Brit*: = *Market & Opinion Research Institute*) *institut de sondage*.

moribund [môr'əbund] *a* moribond(e).

morning [môr'ning] *n* matin *m*; (*as duration*) matinée *f*; **in the** ~ le matin; **7 o'clock in the** ~ 7 heures du matin; **this** ~ ce matin.

morning sickness *n* nausées matinales.

Moroccan [mərâk'ən] *a* marocain(e) ♦ *n* Marocain/e.

Morocco [mərâk'ō] *n* Maroc *m*.

moron [môr'ân] *n* idiot/e, minus *m/f*.

moronic [mərân'ik] *a* idiot(e), imbécile.

morose [mərōs'] *a* morose, maussade.

morphine [môr'fēn] *n* morphine *f*.

Morse [môrs] *n* (*also*: ~ **code**) morse *m*.

morsel [môr'səl] *n* bouchée *f*.

mortal [môr'təl] *a*, *n* mortel(le).

mortality [môrtal'itē] *n* mortalité *f*.

mortality rate *n* (taux *m* de) mortalité *f*.

mortar [môr'tûr] *n* mortier *m*.

mortgage [môr'gij] *n* hypothèque *f*; (*loan*) prêt *m* (*or* crédit *m*) hypothécaire ♦ *vt* hypothéquer; **to take out a** ~ prendre une hypothèque, faire un emprunt.

mortgage company *n* (*US*) société *f* de crédit immobilier.

mortgagee [môrgəjē'] *n* prêteur/euse (sur hypothèque).

mortgagor [môr'gəjûr] *n* emprunteur/euse (sur hypothèque).

mortician [môrtish'ən] *n* (*US*) entrepreneur *m* de pompes funèbres.

mortified [môr'təfīd] *a* mortifié(e).

mortise lock [môr'tis lâk] *n* serrure encastrée.

mortuary [môr'chōōärē] *n* dépôt *m* mortuaire; (*Brit*) morgue *f*.

mosaic [mōzā'ik] *n* mosaïque *f*.

Moscow [mâs'kou] *n* Moscou.

Moslem [mâz'ləm] *a*, *n* = **Muslim**.

mosque [mâsk] *n* mosquée *f*.

mosquito, ~es [məskē'tō] *n* moustique *m*.

mosquito net *n* moustiquaire *f*.

moss [môs] *n* mousse *f*.

mossy [môs'ē] *a* moussu(e).

most [mōst] *a* la plupart de; le plus de ♦ *pronoun* la plupart ♦ *ad* le plus; (*very*) très, extrêmement; **the** ~ (*also*: + *adjective*) le plus; ~ **fish** la plupart des poissons; ~ **of** la plus grande partie de; ~ **of them** la plupart d'entre eux; **at the** (**very**) ~ au plus; **to make the** ~ **of** profiter au maximum de.

mostly [mōst'lē] *ad* surtout, principalement.

MOT *n abbr* (*Brit*: = *Ministry of Transport*): **the** ~ (**test**) *visite technique (annuelle) obligatoire des véhicules à moteur*.

motel [mōtel'] *n* motel *m*.

moth [môth] *n* papillon *m* de nuit; mite *f*.

mothball [môth'bôl] *n* boule *f* de naphtaline.

moth-eaten [môth'ētən] *a* mité(e).

mother [muth'ûr] *n* mère *f* ♦ *vt* (*care for*) dorloter.

mother board *n* (*COMPUT*) carte-mère *f*.

motherhood [muth'ûrhŏod] *n* maternité *f*.

mother-in-law [muth'ûrinlô] *n* belle-mère *f*.

motherly [muth'ûrlē] *a* maternel(le).

mother-of-pearl [muth'ûrəvpûrl'] *n* nacre *f*.

mother's help *n* aide *f or* auxiliaire *f* familiale.

mother-to-be [muth'ûrtəbē'] *n* future maman.

mother tongue *n* langue maternelle.

mothproof [môth'prŏof] *a* traité(e) à l'antimite.

motif [mōtēf'] *n* motif *m*.

motion [mō'shən] *n* mouvement *m*; (*gesture*) geste *m*; (*at meeting*) motion *f*; (*Brit: also*: **bowel** ~) selles *fpl* ♦ *vt, vi*: **to** ~ (**to**) **sb to do** faire signe à qn de faire; **to be in** ~ (*vehicle*) être en marche; **to set in** ~ mettre en marche; **to go through the** ~**s of doing sth** (*fig*) faire qch machinalement *or* sans conviction.

motionless [mō'shənlis] *a* immobile, sans mouvement.

motion picture *n* film *m*.

motivate [mō'təvāt] *vt* motiver.

motivated [mō'təvātid] *a* motivé(e).

motivation [mōtəvā'shən] *n* motivation *f*.

motive [mō'tiv] *n* motif *m*, mobile *m* ♦ *a* moteur(trice); **from the best (of)** ~s avec les meilleures intentions (du monde).

motley [mât'lē] *a* hétéroclite; bigarré(e), bariolé(e).

motor [mō'tûr] *n* moteur *m*; (*Brit col: vehicle*) auto *f* ♦ *a* moteur(trice).

motorbike [mō'tûrbīk] *n* moto *f*.

motorboat [mō'tûrbōt] *n* bateau *m* à moteur.

motorcar [mō'tûrkâr] *n* (*Brit*) automobile *f*.

motorcoach [mō'tûrkōch] *n* (*Brit*) car *m*.

motorcycle [mō'tûrsī'kəl] *n* vélomoteur *m*.

motorcyclist [mō'tûrsīklist] *n* motocycliste *m*/*f*.

motor home *n* (*US*) camping-car *m*, autocaravane *f*.

motoring [mō'tûring] (*Brit*) *n* tourisme *m* automobile ♦ *a* (*accident*) de voiture, de la route; ~ **holiday** (*Brit*) vacances *fpl* en voiture; ~ **offence** (*Brit*) infraction *f* au code de la route.

motorist [mō'tûrist] *n* automobiliste *m*/*f*.

motorize [mō'tərīz] *vt* motoriser.

motor oil *n* huile *f* de graissage.

motor racing *n* (*Brit*) course *f* automobile.

motor scooter *n* scooter *m*.

motor vehicle *n* véhicule *m* automobile.

motorway [mō'tûrwā] *n* (*Brit*) autoroute *f*.

mottled [mât'əld] *a* tacheté(e), marbré(e).

motto, ~es [mât'ō] *n* devise *f*.

mould [mōld] *etc* (*Brit*) = **mold**.

moult [mōlt] *vi* (*Brit*) = **molt**.

mound [mound] *n* monticule *m*, tertre *m*.

mount [mount] *n* mont *m*, montagne *f*; (*horse*) monture *f*; (*for jewel etc*) monture ♦ *vt* monter; (*exhibition*) organiser, monter; (*picture*) monter sur carton; (*stamp*) coller dans un album ♦ *vi* (*also*: ~ **up**) s'élever, monter.

mountain [moun'tən] *n* montagne *f* ♦ *cpd* de (la) montagne; **to make a ~ out of a molehill** (*fig*) se faire une montagne d'un rien.

mountaineer [mountənēr'] *n* alpiniste *m*/*f*.

mountaineering [mountənē'ring] *n* alpinisme *m*; **to go ~** faire de l'alpinisme.

mountainous [moun'tənəs] *a* montagneux(euse).

mountain rescue team *n* colonne *f* de secours.

mountainside [moun'tənsīd] *n* flanc *m* or versant *m* de la montagne.

mounted [moun'tid] *a* monté(e).

Mount Everest [mount ev'ûrist] *n* le mont Everest.

mourn [môrn] *vt* pleurer ♦ *vi*: **to ~ (for)** se lamenter (sur).

mourner [môr'nûr] *n* parent/e *or* ami/e du défunt; personne *f* en deuil *or* venue rendre hommage au défunt.

mournful [môrn'fəl] *a* triste, lugubre.

mourning [môr'ning] *n* deuil *m* ♦ *cpd* (*dress*) de deuil; **in ~** en deuil.

mouse, *pl* **mice** [mous, mīs] *n* (*also COMPUT*) souris *f*.

mousetrap [mous'trap] *n* souricière *f*.

mousse [mōōs] *n* mousse *f*.

moustache [məstash'] *n* (*Brit*) = **mustache**.

mousy [mou'sē] *a* (*person*) effacé(e); (*hair*) d'un châtain terne.

mouth, ~s [mouth, -t͟hz] *n* bouche *f*; (*of dog,*

cat) gueule *f*; (*of river*) embouchure *f*; (*of bottle*) goulot *m*; (*opening*) orifice *m*.

mouthful [mouth'fōōl] *n* bouchée *f*.

mouth organ *n* harmonica *m*.

mouthpiece [mouth'pēs] *n* (*of musical instrument*) bec *m*, embouchure *f*; (*spokesman*) porte-parole *m inv*.

mouth-to-mouth [mouth'təmouth'] *a*: ~ **resuscitation** bouche à bouche *m*.

mouthwash [mouth'wôsh] *n* eau *f* dentifrice.

mouth-watering [mouth'wôtûring] *a* qui met l'eau à la bouche.

movable [mōō'vəbəl] *a* mobile.

move [mōōv] *n* (*movement*) mouvement *m*; (*in game*) coup *m*; (: *turn to play*) tour *m*; (*change of house*) déménagement *m* ♦ *vt* déplacer, bouger; (*emotionally*) émouvoir; (*POL: resolution etc*) proposer ♦ *vi* (*gen*) bouger, remuer; (*traffic*) circuler; (*also*: ~ **house**) déménager; **to ~ towards** se diriger vers; **to ~ sb to do sth** pousser *or* inciter qn à faire qch; **to get a ~ on** se dépêcher, se remuer.

move about *vi* (*Brit*) = **move around**.

move around *vi* (*fidget*) remuer; (*travel*) voyager, se déplacer.

move along *vi* se pousser.

move away *vi* s'en aller, s'éloigner.

move back *vi* revenir, retourner.

move forward *vi* avancer ♦ *vt* avancer; (*people*) faire avancer.

move in *vi* (*to a house*) emménager.

move off *vi* s'éloigner, s'en aller.

move on *vi* se remettre en route ♦ *vt* (*onlookers*) faire circuler.

move out *vi* (*of house*) déménager.

move over *vi* se pousser, se déplacer.

move up *vi* avancer; (*employee*) avoir de l'avancement.

movement [mōōv'mənt] *n* mouvement *m*; ~ **(of the bowels)** (*MED*) selles *fpl*.

mover [mōō'vûr] *n* auteur *m* d'une proposition; (*furniture* ~) déménageur *m*; (*firm*) entreprise *f* de déménagement.

movie [mōō'vē] *n* film *m*; **the ~s** le cinéma.

movie camera *n* caméra *f*.

moviegoer [mōō'vēgōūr] *n* cinéphile *m*/*f*.

movie projector *n* (*US*) projecteur *m* de cinéma.

movie theater *n* (*US*) cinéma *m*.

moving [mōō'ving] *a* en mouvement; (*touching*) émouvant(e) ♦ *n* (*US*) déménagement *m*.

moving van *n* (*US*) camion *m* de déménagement.

mow, *pt* **mowed,** *pp* **mowed** *or* **mown** [mō, -n] *vt* faucher; (*lawn*) tondre.

mow down *vt* faucher.

mower [mō'ûr] *n* (*also*: **lawn~**) tondeuse *f* à gazon.

Mozambique [mōzambēk'] *n* Mozambique *m*.

MP *n abbr* (= *Military Police*) PM; (*Brit*) = **Member of Parliament**; (*Canada*) = **Mounted Police**.

mpg *n abbr* = *miles per gallon* (*30 mpg = 9,4 l. aux 100 km*).

mph *abbr* = *miles per hour* (*60 mph = 96 km/h*).

MPhil *n abbr* (*US*: = *Master of Philosophy*)

titre universitaire.

Mr, Mr. [mis'tûr] *n*: ~ **X** Monsieur X, M. X.

Mrs, Mrs. [mis'iz] *n*: ~ **X** Madame X, Mme X.

MS *n abbr* (= *manuscript*) ms; (= *multiple sclerosis*) SEP *f*; (*US*: = *Master of Science*) *titre universitaire* ♦ *abbr* (*US MAIL*) = *Mississippi.*

Ms, Ms. [miz] *n* (= *Miss or Mrs*): ~ **X** Madame X, Mme X.

MSA *n abbr* (*US*: = *Master of Science in Agriculture*) *titre universitaire.*

MSc *n abbr* = **Master of Science.**

MSG *n abbr* = **monosodium glutamate.**

MST *abbr* (*US*: = *Mountain Standard Time*) *heure d'hiver des Montagnes Rocheuses.*

MSW *n abbr* (*US*: = *Master of Social Work*) *titre universitaire.*

MT *n abbr* (= *machine translation*) TM ♦ *abbr* (*US MAIL*) = Montana.

Mt *abbr* (*GEO*: = *mount*) Mt.

much [much] *a* beaucoup de ♦ *ad*, *n or pronoun* beaucoup; ~ **milk** beaucoup de lait; **how ~ is it?** combien est-ce que ça coûte?; **it's not** ~ ce n'est pas beaucoup; **too** ~ trop (de); **so** ~ tant (de); **I like it very/so** ~ j'aime beaucoup/tellement ça; **thank you very** ~ merci beaucoup; ~ **to my amazement** ... à mon grand étonnement ....

muck [muk] *n* (*mud*) boue *f*; (*dirt*) ordures *fpl.*

   muck about *or* **around** *vi* (*Brit*) = **mess around.**

   muck in *vi* (*Brit col*) donner un coup de main.

   muck out *vt* (*stable*) nettoyer.

   muck up *vt* (*col: ruin*) gâcher, esquinter; (: *dirty*) salir.

muckraking [muk'rāk'ing] *n* (*fig: col*) déterrement *m* d'ordures.

mucky [muk'ē] *a* (*dirty*) boueux(euse), sale.

mucus [myōo'kəs] *n* mucus *m.*

mud [mud] *n* boue *f.*

muddle [mud'əl] *n* pagaille *f*; désordre *m*, fouillis *m* ♦ *vt* (*also:* ~ **up**) brouiller, embrouiller; **to be in a** ~ (*person*) ne plus savoir ou l'on en est; **to get in a** ~ (*while explaining etc*) s'embrouiller.

   muddle along *vi* aller son chemin tant bien que mal.

   muddle through *vi* se débrouiller.

muddle-headed [mud'əlhedid] *a* (*person*) à l'esprit embrouillé *or* confus, dans le brouillard.

muddy [mud'ē] *a* boueux(euse).

mud flats *npl* plage *f* de vase.

mudguard [mud'gârd] *n* garde-boue *m inv.*

mudpack [mud'pak] *n* masque *m* de beauté.

mudslinging [mud'slinging] *n* médisance *f*, dénigrement *m.*

muff [muf] *n* manchon *m* ♦ *vt* (*col: shot, catch etc*) rater, louper; **to** ~ **it** rater *or* louper son coup.

muffin [muf'in] *n* petit pain rond et plat.

muffle [muf'əl] *vt* (*sound*) assourdir, étouffer; (*against cold*) emmitoufler.

muffled [muf'əld] *a* étouffé(e), voilé(e).

muffler [muf'lûr] *n* (*scarf*) cache-nez *m inv*; (*US AUT*) silencieux *m.*

mufti [muf'tē] *n*: **in** ~ en civil.

mug [mug] *n* (*cup*) tasse *f* (*sans soucoupe*); (: *for beer*) chope *f*; (*col: face*) bouille *f*; (: *fool*) poire *f* ♦ *vt* (*assault*) agresser.

   mug up *vt* (*Brit col: also:* ~ **up on**) bosser, bûcher.

mugger [mug'ûr] *n* agresseur *m.*

mugging [mug'ing] *n* agression *f.*

muggy [mug'ē] *a* lourd(e), moite.

mulatto, ~**es** [məlat'ō] *n* mulâtre/esse.

mulberry [mul'bärē] *n* (*fruit*) mûre *f*; (*tree*) mûrier *m.*

mule [myōōl] *n* mule *f.*

mull [mul]: **to** ~ **over** *vt* réfléchir à, ruminer.

mulled [muld] *a*: ~ **wine** vin chaud.

multi... [mul'tē] *prefix* multi....

multi-access [multēak'ses] *a* (*COMPUT*) à accès multiple.

multicolored, (*Brit*) **multicoloured** [mul'tikulûrd] *a* multicolore.

multifarious [multəfär'ēəs] *a* divers(es); varié(e).

multilateral [multilat'ûrəl] *a* (*POL*) multilatéral(e).

multilevel [multēlev'əl] *a* (*US: building*) à étages; (: *car park*) à étages or niveaux multiples.

multimillionaire [multēmilyənär'] *n* milliardaire *m/f.*

multinational [multənash'ənəl] *n* multinationale *f* ♦ *a* multinational(e).

multiple [mul'təpəl] *a* multiple ♦ *n* multiple *m*; (*Brit: also:* ~ **store**) magasin *m* à succursales (multiples).

multiple choice *a* à choix multiple.

multiple crash *n* carambolage *m.*

multiple sclerosis (MS) [mul'təpəl sklirō'sis] *n* sclérose *f* en plaques.

multiplication [multəpləkā'shən] *n* multiplication *f.*

multiplication table *n* table *f* de multiplication.

multiplicity [multəplis'ətē] *n* multiplicité *f.*

multiply [mul'təplī] *vt* multiplier ♦ *vi* se multiplier.

multiracial [multērā'shəl] *a* multiracial(e).

multistorey [multēstôr'ē] *a* (*Brit*) = **multilevel.**

multitude [mul'tətōōd] *n* multitude *f.*

mum [mum] (*Brit*) *n* maman *f* ♦ *a*: **to keep** ~ ne pas souffler mot; ~**'s the word!** motus et bouche cousue!

mumble [mum'bəl] *vt*, *vi* marmotter, marmonner.

mummify [mum'əfi] *vt* momifier.

mummy [mum'ē] *n* (*Brit: mother*) maman *f*; (*embalmed*) momie *f.*

mumps [mumps] *n* oreillons *mpl.*

munch [munch] *vt*, *vi* mâcher.

mundane [mundān'] *a* banal(e), terre à terre *inv.*

municipal [myōōnis'əpəl] *a* municipal(e).

municipality [myōōnisəpəl'itē] *n* municipalité *f.*

munitions [myōōnish'ənz] *npl* munitions *fpl.*

mural [myōōr'əl] *n* peinture murale.

murder [mûr'dûr] *n* meurtre *m*, assassinat *m* ♦ *vt* assassiner; **to commit** ~ commettre un meurtre.

murderer [mûr'dûrûr] *n* meurtrier *m*, assas-

sin *m*.
murderess |mûr'dŭris| *n* meurtrière *f*.
murderous |mûr'dûrəs| *a* meurtrier(ière).
murk |mûrk| *n* obscurité *f*.
murky |mûr'kē| *a* sombre, ténébreux(euse).
murmur |mûr'mûr| *n* murmure *m* ♦ *vt*, *vi*
murmurer; **heart** ~ (*MED*) souffle *m* au cœur.
MusB(ac) *n abbr* (= *Bachelor of Music*) titre universitaire.
muscle |mus'əl| *n* muscle *m*.
   muscle in *vi* s'imposer, s'immiscer.
muscular |mus'kyələr| *a* musculaire; (*person, arm*) musclé(e).
MusD(oc) *n abbr* (= *Doctor of Music*) titre universitaire.
muse |myo͞oz| *vi* méditer, songer ♦ *n* muse *f*.
museum |myo͞ozē'əm| *n* musée *m*.
mush |mush| *n* bouillie *f*; (*pej*) sentimentalité *f* à l'eau de rose.
mushroom |mush'ro͞om| *n* champignon *m* ♦ *vi* (*fig*) pousser comme un (*or* des) champignon(s).
mushy |mush'ē| *a* en bouillie; (*pej*) à l'eau de rose.
music |myo͞o'zik| *n* musique *f*.
musical |myo͞o'zikəl| *a* musical(e); (*person*) musicien(ne) ♦ *n* (*show*) comédie musicale.
musical instrument *n* instrument *m* de musique.
music box *n* boîte *f* à musique.
music hall *n* music-hall *m*.
musician |myo͞ozish'ən| *n* musicien/ne.
music stand *n* pupitre *m* à musique.
musk |musk| *n* musc *m*.
musket |mus'kit| *n* mòusquet *m*.
muskrat |musk'rat| *n* rat musqué.
musk rose *n* (*BOT*) rose *f* muscade.
Muslim |muz'lim| *a*, *n* musulman(e).
muslin |muz'lin| *n* mousseline *f*.
musquash |mus'kwâsh| *n* loutre *f*; (*fur*) rat *m* d'Amérique, ondatra *m*.
mussel |mus'əl| *n* moule *f*.
must |must| *auxiliary vb* (*obligation*): **I** ~ **do it** je dois le faire, il faut que je le fasse; (*probability*): **he** ~ **be there by now** il doit y être maintenant, il y est probablement maintenant; **I** ~ **have made a mistake** j'ai dû me tromper ♦ *n* nécessité *f*, impératif *m*; **it's a** ~ c'est indispensable.
mustache |məstash'| *n* (*US*) moustache(s) *f(pl)*.
mustard |mus'tûrd| *n* moutarde *f*.
mustard gas *n* ypérite *f*, gaz *m* moutarde.
muster |mus'tûr| *vt* rassembler; (*also:* ~ **up:** *strength, courage*) rassembler.
mustiness |mus'tēnis| *n* goût *m* de moisi; odeur *f* de moisi *or* de renfermé.
mustn't |mus'ənt| = **must not**.
musty |mus'tē| *a* qui sent le moisi *or* le renfermé.
mutant |myo͞o'tənt| *a* mutant(e) ♦ *n* mutant *m*.
mutate |myo͞o'tāt| *vi* subir une mutation.
mutation |myo͞otā'shən| *n* mutation *f*.
mute |myo͞ot| *a*, *n* muet(te).
muted |myo͞o'tid| *a* (*noise*) sourd(e), assourdi(e); (*criticism*) voilé(e); (*MUS*) en sourdine; (*: trumpet*) bouché(e).

mutilate |myo͞o'təlāt| *vt* mutiler.
mutilation |myo͞otəlā'shən| *n* mutilation *f*.
mutinous |myo͞o'tənəs| *a* (*troops*) mutiné(e); (*attitude*) rebelle.
mutiny |myo͞o'tənē| *n* mutinerie *f* ♦ *vi* se mutiner.
mutter |mut'ûr| *vt*, *vi* marmonner, marmotter.
mutton |mut'ən| *n* mouton *m*.
mutual |myo͞o'cho͞oəl| *a* mutuel(le), réciproque.
mutual fund *n* (*US*) fonds commun de placement, FCP *m*.
mutually |myo͞o'cho͞oəlē| *ad* mutuellement, réciproquement.
muzzle |muz'əl| *n* museau *m*; (*protective device*) muselière *f*; (*of gun*) gueule *f* ♦ *vt* museler.
MVP *n abbr* (*US SPORT*) = *most valuable player*.
MW *abbr* (= *medium wave*) PO.
my |mī| *a* mon(ma), mes *pl*.
myopic |miăp'ik| *a* myope.
myriad |mir'ēəd| *n* myriade *f*.
myself |mīself'| *pronoun* (*reflexive*) me; (*emphatic*) moi-même; (*after prep*) moi.
mysterious |mistēr'ēəs| *a* mystérieux(euse).
mystery |mis'tûrē| *n* mystère *m*.
mystery story *n* roman *m* à suspense.
mystic |mis'tik| *n* mystique *m/f* ♦ *a* (*mysterious*) ésotérique.
mystical |mis'tikəl| *a* mystique.
mystify |mis'təfī| *vt* mystifier; (*puzzle*) ébahir.
mystique |mistēk'| *n* mystique *f*.
myth |mith| *n* mythe *m*.
mythical |mith'ikəl| *a* mythique.
mythological |mithəlâj'ikəl| *a* mythologique.
mythology |mithâl'əjē| *n* mythologie *f*.

N

N, n |en| *n* (*letter*) N, n *m*; **N for Nan** N comme Nicolas.
N |en| *abbr* (= *north*) N.
NA *n abbr* (*US*: = *Narcotics Anonymous*) association d'aide aux drogués; (*US*) = *National Academy*.
n/a *abbr* (= *not applicable*) n.a.; (*COMM etc*) = *no account*.
NAACP *n abbr* (*US*) = *National Association for the Advancement of Colored People*.
nab |nab| *vt* (*col*) pincer, attraper.
NACU *n abbr* (*US*) = *National Association of Colleges and Universities*.
nadir |nā'dûr| *n* (*ASTRONOMY*) nadir *m*; (*fig*) fond *m*, point *m* extrême.
nag |nag| *vt* (*person*) être toujours après, reprendre sans arrêt ♦ *n* (*pej*: *horse*) canasson *m*; (*person*): **she's an awful** ~ elle est constamment après lui (*or* eux *etc*), elle est terriblement casse-pieds.
nagging |nag'ing| *a* (*doubt, pain*) persistant(e) ♦ *n* remarques continuelles.

nail [nāl] *n* (*human*) ongle *m*; (*metal*) clou *m* ♦ *vt* clouer; **to ~ sb down to a date/price** contraindre qn à accepter *or* donner une date/un prix; **to pay cash on the ~** (*Brit*) payer rubis sur l'ongle.

nailbrush [nāl'brush] *n* brosse *f* à ongles.

nailfile [nāl'fīl] *n* lime *f* à ongles.

nail polish *n* vernis *m* à ongles.

nail polish remover *n* dissolvant *m*.

nail scissors *npl* ciseaux *mpl* à ongles.

nail varnish *n* (*Brit*) = **nail polish**.

Nairobi [nīrō'bē] *n* Nairobi.

naïve [nīēv'] *a* naïf(ïve).

naïveté, naïvety [nīēvtā'] *n* naïveté *f*.

naked [nā'kid] *a* nu(e); **with the ~ eye** à l'œil nu.

nakedness [nā'kidnis] *n* nudité *f*.

NAM *n abbr* (*US*) = *National Association of Manufacturers*.

name [nām] *n* nom *m*; (*reputation*) réputation *f* ♦ *vt* nommer; citer; (*price, date*) fixer, donner; **by ~** par son nom; de nom; **in the ~ of** au nom de; **what's your ~?** quel est votre nom?; **my ~ is Peter** je m'appelle Peter; **to take sb's ~ and address** relever l'identité de qn *or* les nom et adresse de qn; **to make a ~ for o.s.** se faire un nom; **to get (o.s.) a bad ~** se faire une mauvaise réputation; **to call sb ~s** traiter qn de tous les noms.

name dropping *n* mention *f* (*pour se faire valoir*) *du nom de personnalités qu'on connaît (ou prétend connaître)*.

nameless [nām'lis] *a* sans nom; (*witness, contributor*) anonyme.

namely [nām'lē] *ad* à savoir.

nameplate [nām'plāt] *n* (*on door etc*) plaque *f*.

namesake [nām'sāk] *n* homonyme *m*.

nanny [nan'ē] *n* bonne *f* d'enfants.

nanny goat *n* chèvre *f*.

nap [nap] *n* (*sleep*) (petit) somme ♦ *vi*: **to be caught ~ping** être pris(e) à l'improviste *or* en défaut.

NAPA *n abbr* (*US*: = *National Association of Performing Artists*) *syndicat des gens du spectacle*.

napalm [nā'pâm] *n* napalm *m*.

nape [nāp] *n*: **~ of the neck** nuque *f*.

napkin [nap'kin] *n* serviette *f* (de table).

Naples [nā'pəlz] *n* Naples.

Napoleonic [nəpōlēän'ik] *a* napoléonien(ne).

nappy [nap'ē] *n* (*Brit*) couche *f* (*gen pl*).

narcissistic [nârsisis'tik] *a* narcissique.

narcissus, *pl* **narcissi** [nârsis'əs, -sī] *n* narcisse *m*.

narcotic [nârkât'ik] *n* (*MED*) narcotique *m*; **~s** *npl* (*drugs*) stupéfiants *mpl*.

narrate [nar'āt] *vt* raconter, narrer.

narration [narā'shən] *n* narration *f*.

narrative [nar'ətiv] *n* récit *m* ♦ *a* narratif(ive).

narrator [nar'ātûr] *n* narrateur/trice.

narrow [nar'ō] *a* étroit(e); (*fig*) restreint(e), limité(e) ♦ *vi* devenir plus étroit, se rétrécir; **to have a ~ escape** l'échapper belle; **to ~ sth down** to réduire qch à.

narrow gauge *a* (*RAIL*) à voie étroite.

narrowly [nar'ōlē] *ad*: **he ~ missed injury/the tree** il a failli se blesser/rentrer dans l'arbre; **he only ~ missed the target** il a manqué la cible de peu *or* de justesse.

narrow-minded [nar'ōmīn'did] *a* à l'esprit étroit, borné(e).

NAS *n abbr* (*US*) = *National Academy of Sciences*.

NASA [nas'ə] *n abbr* (*US*: = *National Aeronautics and Space Administration*) NASA *f*.

nasal [nā'zəl] *a* nasal(e).

Nassau [nas'ô] *n* (*in Bahamas*) Nassau.

nastily [nas'tilē] *ad* (*say, act*) méchamment.

nastiness [nas'tēnis] *n* (*of person, remark*) méchanceté *f*.

nasturtium [nəstûr'shəm] *n* capucine *f*.

nasty [nas'tē] *a* (*person*) méchant(e); très désagréable; (*smell*) dégoûtant(e); (*wound, situation*) mauvais(e), vilain(e); (*weather*) affreux(euse); **to turn ~** (*situation*) mal tourner; (*weather*) se gâter; (*person*) devenir méchant; **it's a ~ business** c'est une sale affaire.

nation [nā'shən] *n* nation *f*.

national [nash'ənəl] *a* national(e) ♦ *n* (*abroad*) ressortissant/e; (*when home*) national/e.

national anthem *n* hymne national.

national debt *n* dette publique.

national dress *n* costume national.

National Forest Service *n* (*US*) ≈ Office National des Forêts.

National Guard *n* (*US*) milice *f* (*de volontaires dans chaque Etat*).

National Health Service (NHS) *n* (*Brit*) service national de santé, ≈ Sécurité Sociale.

National Insurance *n* (*Brit*) ≈ Sécurité Sociale.

nationalism [nash'ənəlizəm] *n* nationalisme *m*.

nationalist [nash'nəlist] *a*, *n* nationaliste (*m/f*).

nationality [nashənal'ətē] *n* nationalité *f*.

nationalization [nashnələzā'shən] *n* nationalisation *f*.

nationalize [nash'nəlīz] *vt* nationaliser.

nationally [nash'nəlē] *ad* du point de vue national; dans le pays entier.

national park *n* parc national.

national press *n* presse nationale.

National Security Council *n* (*US*) conseil national de sécurité.

national service *n* (*MIL*) service *m* militaire.

National Weather Service *n* (*US*) ≈ météo *inv*.

nationwide [nā'shənwīd'] *a* s'étendant à l'ensemble du pays; (*problem*) à l'échelle du pays entier ♦ *ad* à travers *or* dans tout le pays.

native [nā'tiv] *n* habitant/e du pays, autochtone *m/f*; (*in colonies*) indigène *m/f* ♦ *a* du pays, indigène; (*country*) natal(e); (*language*) maternel(le); (*ability*) inné(e); **a ~ of Russia** une personne originaire de Russie; **a ~ speaker of French** une personne de langue maternelle française.

Nativity [nətiv'ətē] *n* (*REL*): **the ~** la Nativité.

NATO [nā'tō] *n abbr* (= *North Atlantic Treaty Organization*) OTAN *f*.

natter [nat'ûr] *vi* (*Brit*) bavarder.

natural [nach'ûrəl] *a* naturel(le); **to die of ~ causes** mourir d'une mort naturelle.

natural childbirth *n* accouchement *m* sans douleur.

natural gas *n* gaz naturel.

naturalist [nach'ûrəlist] *n* naturaliste *m/f*.

naturalization [nachûrələzā'shən] n naturalisation f; acclimatation f.

naturalize [nach'ûrəlīz] vt naturaliser; (plant) acclimater; **to become ~d** (person) se faire naturaliser.

naturally [nach'ûrəlē] ad naturellement.

naturalness [nach'ûrəlnis] n naturel m.

natural resources npl ressources naturelles.

natural wastage n (INDUSTRY) départs naturels et volontaires.

nature [nā'chûr] n nature f; **by ~** par tempérament, de nature; **documents of a confidential ~** documents à caractère confidentiel.

nature reserve n (Brit) réserve naturelle.

nature trail n sentier de découverte de la nature.

naturist [nā'chûrist] n naturiste m/f.

naught [nôt] n = **nought**.

naughtiness [nôt'ēnis] n (of child) désobéissance f; (of story etc) grivoiserie f.

naughty [nôt'ē] a (child) vilain(e), pas sage; (story, film) grivois(e).

nausea [nô'zēə] n nausée f.

nauseate [nô'zēāt] vt écœurer, donner la nausée à.

nauseating [nô'zēāting] a écœurant(e), dégoûtant(e).

nauseous [nô'shəs] a nauséabond(e), écœurant(e); (feeling sick): **to be ~** avoir des nausées.

nautical [nô'tikəl] a nautique.

nautical mile n mille marin (= 1853 m).

naval [nā'vəl] a naval(e).

naval officer n officier m de marine.

nave [nāv] n nef f.

navel [nā'vəl] n nombril m.

navigable [nav'əgəbəl] a navigable.

navigate [nav'əgāt] vt diriger, piloter ♦ vi naviguer; (AUT) indiquer la route à suivre.

navigation [navəgā'shən] n navigation f.

navigator [nav'əgātûr] n navigateur m.

navvy [nav'ē] n (Brit) terrassier m.

navy [nā'vē] n marine f; **Department of the N~** (US) ministère m de la Marine.

navy (blue) a bleu marine inv.

Nazareth [naz'ûrith] n Nazareth.

Nazi [nát'sē] a nazi(e) ♦ n Nazi/e.

NB abbr (= nota bene) NB; (Canada) = New Brunswick.

NBA n abbr (US) = National Basketball Association, National Boxing Association.

NBC n abbr (US: = National Broadcasting Company) chaîne de télévision.

NBS n abbr (US: = National Bureau of Standards) office de normalisation.

NC abbr (COMM etc) = no charge; (US MAIL) = North Carolina.

NCC n abbr (US) = National Council of Churches.

NCO n abbr = **non-commissioned officer**.

ND abbr (US MAIL) = North Dakota.

N. Dak. abbr (US) = North Dakota.

NE abbr (US MAIL) = Nebraska, New England.

NEA n abbr (US) = National Education Association.

neap [nēp] n (also: **~ tide**) mortes-eaux fpl.

Neapolitan [nēəpál'ətən] a napolitain(e) ♦ n Napolitain/e.

near [nēr] a proche ♦ ad près ♦ prep (also: **~ to**) près de ♦ vt approcher de; **~ here/there** près d'ici/non loin de là; **in the ~ future** dans un proche avenir; **the building is ~ing completion** le bâtiment est presque terminé; **to come ~** vi s'approcher.

nearby [nēr'bī'] a proche ♦ ad tout près, à proximité.

Near East n: **the ~** le Proche-Orient.

nearer [nē'rûr] a plus proche ♦ ad plus près.

nearly [nēr'lē] ad presque; **I ~ fell** j'ai failli tomber; **it's not ~ big enough** ce n'est vraiment pas assez grand, c'est loin d'être assez grand.

near miss n collision évitée de justesse; (when aiming) coup manqué de peu or de justesse.

nearness [nēr'nis] n proximité f.

nearside [nēr'sīd] (AUT) n (right-hand drive) côté m gauche; (left-hand drive) côté droit ♦ a de gauche; de droite.

nearsighted [nēr'sītid] a myope.

neat [nēt] a (person, work) soigné(e); (room etc) bien tenu(e) or rangé(e); (solution, plan) habile; (spirits) pur(e); **I drink it ~** je le bois sec or sans eau.

neatly [nēt'lē] ad avec soin or ordre; habilement.

neatness [nēt'nis] n (tidiness) netteté f; (skillfulness) habileté f.

Nebr. abbr (US) = Nebraska.

nebulous [neb'yələs] a nébuleux(euse).

necessarily [nesəsär'ilē] ad nécessairement; **not ~** pas nécessairement or forcément.

necessary [ncs'isärē] a nécessaire; **if ~** si besoin est, le cas échéant.

necessitate [nəses'ətāt] vt nécessiter.

necessity [nəses'itē] n nécessité f; chose nécessaire or essentielle; **in case of ~** en cas d'urgence.

neck [nek] n cou m; (of horse, garment) encolure f; (of bottle) goulot m ♦ vi (col) se peloter; **~ and ~** à égalité; **to stick one's ~ out** (col) se mouiller.

necklace [nek'lis] n collier m.

neckline [nek'līn] n encolure f.

necktie [nek'tī] n (esp US) cravate f.

nectar [nek'tûr] n nectar m.

nectarine [nektərēn'] n brugnon m, nectarine f.

née [nā] a: **~ Scott** née Scott.

need [nēd] n besoin m ♦ vt avoir besoin de; **to ~ to do** devoir faire; avoir besoin de faire; **you don't ~ to go** vous n'avez pas besoin or vous n'êtes pas obligé de partir; **a signature is ~ed** il faut une signature; **to be in ~ of** or **have ~ of** avoir besoin de; **$10 will meet my immediate ~s** 10 dollars suffiront pour mes besoins immédiats; **in case of ~** en cas de besoin, au besoin; **there's no ~ to do ...** il n'y a pas lieu de faire ..., il n'est pas nécessaire de faire ...; **there's no ~ for that** ce n'est pas la peine, cela n'est pas nécessaire.

needle [nē'dəl] n aiguille f; (on record player) saphir m ♦ vt (col) asticoter, tourmenter.

needless [nēd'lis] a inutile; **~ to say, ...** inutile de dire que ....

needlessly [nēd'lislē] ad inutilement.

needlework [nēd'əlwûrk] *n* (*activity*) travaux *mpl* d'aiguille; (*object*) ouvrage *m*.

needn't [nēd'ənt] = **need not**.

needy [nē'dē] *a* nécessiteux(euse).

negation [nigā'shən] *n* négation *f*.

negative [neg'ətiv] *n* (*PHOT, ELEC*) négatif *m*; (*LING*) terme *m* de négation ♦ *a* négatif(ive); **to answer in the** ~ répondre par la négative.

neglect [niglekt'] *vt* négliger ♦ *n* (*of person, duty, garden*) le fait de négliger; **(state of)** ~ abandon *m*; **to** ~ **to do sth** négliger *or* omettre de faire qch.

neglected [niglek'tid] *a* négligé(e), à l'abandon.

neglectful [niglekt'fəl] *a* (*gen*) négligent(e); **to be** ~ **of sb/sth** négliger qn/qch.

negligee [neg'ləzhā] *n* déshabillé *m*.

negligence [neg'lijəns] *n* négligence *f*.

negligent [neg'lijənt] *a* négligent(e).

negligently [neg'lijəntlē] *ad* par négligence; (*offhandedly*) négligemment.

negligible [neg'lijəbəl] *a* négligeable.

negotiable [nigō'shəbəl] *a* négociable; **not** ~ (*check*) non négociable.

negotiate [nigō'shēāt] *vi* négocier ♦ *vt* (*COMM*) négocier; (*obstacle*) franchir, négocier; (*curve in road*) négocier; **to** ~ **with sb for sth** négocier avec qn en vue d'obtenir qch.

negotiation [nigōshēā'shən] *n* négociation *f*, pourparlers *mpl*; **to enter into** ~s **with sb** engager des négociations avec qn.

negotiator [nigō'shēātûr] *n* négociateur/trice.

Negress [nēg'ris] *n* négresse *f*.

Negro [nēg'rō] *a* (*gen*) noir(e); (*music, arts*) nègre, noir ♦ *n* (*pl:* ~es) Noir/e.

neigh [nā] *vi* hennir.

neighbor [nā'bûr] *n* (*US*) voisin/e.

neighborhood [nā'bûrhood] *n* quartier *m*; voisinage *m*.

neighboring [nā'bûring] *a* voisin(e), avoisinant(e).

neighborly [nā'bûrlē] *a* obligeant(e); (*relations*) de bon voisinage.

neighbour [nā'bûr] *etc* (*Brit*) = **neighbor**.

neither [nē'thûr] *a, pronoun* aucun(e) (des deux), ni l'un(e) ni l'autre ♦ *cj:* **I didn't move and** ~ **did Claude** je n'ai pas bougé, (et) Claude non plus; ..., ~ **did I refuse** ..., (et *or* mais) je n'ai pas non plus refusé ♦ *ad:* ~ **good nor bad** ni bon ni mauvais.

neo... [nē'ō] *prefix* néo-.

neolithic [nēəlith'ik] *a* néolithique.

neologism [nēál'əjizəm] *n* néologisme *m*.

neon [nē'án] *n* néon *m*.

neon light *n* lampe *f* au néon.

neon sign *n* enseigne (lumineuse) au néon.

Nepal [nəpôl'] *n* Népal *m*.

nephew [nef'yōō] *n* neveu *m*.

nepotism [nep'ətizəm] *n* népotisme *m*.

nerve [nûrv] *n* nerf *m*; (*bravery*) sang-froid *m*, courage *m*; (*cheek*) aplomb *m*, toupet *m*; **he gets on my** ~s il m'énerve; **to have a fit of** ~s avoir le trac; **to lose one's** ~ (*self-confidence*) perdre son sang-froid.

nerve center *n* (*ANAT*) centre nerveux; (*fig*) centre névralgique.

nerve gas *n* gaz *m* neuroplégique.

nerve-racking [nûrv'raking] *a* angoissant(e).

nervous [nûr'vəs] *a* nerveux(euse); (*apprehensive*) inquiet(ète), plein(e) d'appréhension.

nervous breakdown *n* dépression nerveuse.

nervously [nûr'vəslē] *ad* nerveusement.

nervousness [nûr'vəsnis] *n* nervosité *f*; inquiétude *f*, appréhension *f*.

nest [nest] *n* nid *m* ♦ *vi* (se) nicher, faire son nid; ~ **of tables** table *f* gigogne.

nest egg *n* (*fig*) bas *m* de laine, magot *m*.

nestle [nes'əl] *vi* se blottir.

nestling [nest'ling] *n* oisillon *m*.

NET *abbr* (*US*) = *National Educational Television*.

net [net] *n* (*also fabric*) filet *m* ♦ *a* net(te) ♦ *vt* (*fish etc*) prendre au filet; (*money: subj: person*) toucher; (: *deal, sale*) rapporter; ~ **of tax** net d'impôt; **he earns $10,000** ~ **per year** il gagne 10 000 dollars net par an.

netball [net'bôl] *n* netball *m*.

net curtains *npl* (*Brit*) voilages *mpl*.

Netherlands [neth'ûrləndz] *npl:* **the** ~ les Pays-Bas *mpl*.

net profit *n* bénéfice net.

nett [net] *a* = **net**.

netting [net'ing] *n* (*for fence etc*) treillis *m*, grillage *m*; (*fabric*) voile *m*.

nettle [net'əl] *n* ortie *f*.

network [net'wûrk] *n* réseau *m* ♦ *vt* (*RADIO, TV*) diffuser sur l'ensemble du réseau; (*computers*) interconnecter.

neuralgia [nōōral'jə] *n* névralgie *f*.

neurosis, *pl* **neuroses** [nōōrō'sis, -sēz] *n* névrose *f*.

neurotic [nōōrât'ik] *a, n* névrosé(e).

neuter [nōō'tûr] *a, n* neutre (*m*) ♦ *vt* (*cat etc*) châtrer, couper.

neutral [nōō'trəl] *a* neutre ♦ *n* (*AUT*) point mort.

neutrality [nōōtral'itē] *n* neutralité *f*.

neutralize [nōō'trəlīz] *vt* neutraliser.

neutron bomb [nōō'trân bâm] *n* bombe *f* à neutrons.

Nev. *abbr* (*US*) = *Nevada*.

never [nev'ûr] *ad* (ne ...) jamais; ~ **again** plus jamais; ~ **in my life** jamais de ma vie; *see also* **mind**.

never-ending [nev'ûren'ding] *a* interminable.

nevertheless [nevûrthəles'] *ad* néanmoins, malgré tout.

new [nōō] *a* nouveau(nouvelle); (*brand new*) neuf(neuve); **as good as** ~ comme neuf.

newborn [nōō'bôrn] *a* nouveau-né(e).

newcomer [nōō'kumûr] *n* nouveau venu/ nouvelle venue.

newfangled [nōō'fang'gəld] *a* (*pej*) ultramoderne (et farfelu(e)).

newfound [nōō'found] *a* de fraîche date; (*friend*) nouveau(nouvelle).

Newfoundland [nōō'fəndland] *n* Terre-Neuve *f*.

New Guinea [nōō gin'ē] *n* Nouvelle-Guinée *f*.

newly [nōō'lē] *ad* nouvellement, récemment.

newlyweds [nōō'lēwedz] *npl* jeunes mariés *mpl*.

new moon *n* nouvelle lune.

newness [nōō'nis] *n* nouveauté *f*; (*of fabric, clothes etc*) état neuf.

New Orleans [nōō ôr'lēənz] *n* la Nouvelle-

Orléans.

news [nooz] *n* nouvelle(s) *f(pl)*; (*RADIO, TV*) informations *fpl*; **a piece of** ~ une nouvelle; **good/bad** ~ bonne/mauvaise nouvelle; **financial** ~ (*PRESS, RADIO, TV*) page financière.

news agency *n* agence *f* de presse.

newsagent [nooz'ājənt] *n* (*Brit*) = **newsdealer.**

news bulletin *n* (*RADIO, TV*) bulletin *m* d'informations.

newscaster [nooz'kastûr] *n* (*RADIO, TV*) présentateur/trice.

newsdealer [nooz'dēlûr] *n* (*US*) marchand *m* de journaux.

news flash *n* flash *m* d'information.

newsletter [nooz'letûr] *n* bulletin *m*.

newspaper [nooz'pāpûr] *n* journal *m*; **daily** ~ quotidien *m*; **weekly** ~ hebdomadaire *m*.

newsprint [nooz'print] *n* papier *m* (de) journal.

newsreader [nooz'rēdûr] *n* (*Brit*) = newscaster.

newsreel [nooz'rēl] *n* actualités (filmées).

newsroom [nooz'room] *n* (*PRESS*) salle *f* de rédaction; (*RADIO, TV*) studio *m*.

newsstand [nooz'stand] *n* kiosque *m* à journaux.

newt [noot] *n* triton *m*.

New Year *n* Nouvel An; **Happy** ~! Bonne Année!; **to wish sb a happy** ~ souhaiter la Bonne Année à qn.

New Year's Day *n* le jour de l'An.

New Year's Eve *n* la Saint-Sylvestre.

New York [noo yórk] *n* New York; (*also:* ~ **State**) New York *m*.

New Zealand [noo zē'lənd] *n* Nouvelle-Zélande *f* ♦ *a* néo-zélandais(e).

New Zealander [noo zē'ləndûr] *n* Néo-Zélandais/e.

next [nekst] *a* (*seat, room*) voisin(e), d'à côté; (*meeting, bus stop*) suivant(e); prochain(e) ♦ *ad* la fois suivante; la prochaine fois; (*afterwards*) ensuite; ~ **to** *prep* à côté de; ~ **to nothing** presque rien; ~ **time** *ad* la prochaine fois; **the** ~ **day** le lendemain, le jour suivant *or* d'après; ~ **week** la semaine prochaine; **the** ~ **week** la semaine suivante; ~ **year** l'année prochaine; **"turn to the** ~ **page"** "voir page suivante"; **who's** ~? c'est à qui?; **the week after** ~ dans deux semaines; **when do we meet** ~? quand nous revoyons-nous?

next door *ad* à côté.

next-of-kin [nekst'əvkin'] *n* parent *m* le plus proche.

NF *n abbr* (*Brit POL*: = *National Front*) ≈ FN ♦ *abbr* (*Canada*) = *Newfoundland.*

NFL *n abbr* (*US*) = *National Football League.*

Nfld. *abbr* (*Canada*) = *Newfoundland.*

NG *abbr* (*US*) = **National Guard.**

NGO *n abbr* (*US*: = *non-governmental organization*) ONG *f*.

NH *abbr* (*US MAIL*) = *New Hampshire.*

NHL *n abbr* (*US*) = *National Hockey League.*

NHS *n abbr* (*Brit*) = **National Health Service.**

NI *abbr* = *Northern Ireland*; (*Brit*) = **National Insurance.**

Niagara Falls [nīag'rə fólz] *npl* chutes *fpl* du

Niagara.

nib [nib] *n* (*of pen*) (bec *m* de) plume *f*.

nibble [nib'əl] *vt* grignoter.

Nicaragua [nikərág'wə] *n* Nicaragua *m*.

Nicaraguan [nikərág'wən] *a* nicaraguayen(ne) ♦ *n* Nicaraguayen/ne.

nice [nīs] *a* (*vacation, trip, taste*) agréable; (*apartment, picture*) joli(e); (*person*) gentil(le); (*distinction, point*) subtil(e).

nice-looking [nīs'look'ing] *a* joli(e).

nicely [nīs'lē] *ad* agréablement; joliment; gentiment; subtilement; **that will do** ~ ce sera parfait.

niceties [nī'sətēz] *npl* subtilités *fpl*.

niche [nich] *n* (*ARCHIT*) niche *f*.

nick [nik] *n* encoche *f* ♦ *vt* (*cut*): **to** ~ **o.s.** se couper; (*col: steal*) faucher, piquer; (: *Brit: arrest*) choper, pincer; **in the** ~ **of time** juste à temps.

nickel [nik'əl] *n* nickel *m*; (*US*) pièce *f* de 5 cents.

nickname [nik'nām] *n* surnom *m* ♦ *vt* surnommer.

Nicosia [nikōsē'ə] *n* Nicosie.

nicotine [nik'ətēn] *n* nicotine *f*.

niece [nēs] *n* nièce *f*.

nifty [nif'tē] *a* (*col: car, jacket*) qui a du chic *or* de la classe; (: *gadget, tool*) astucieux(euse).

Niger [nī'jûr] *n* (*country, river*) Niger *m*.

Nigeria [nījē'rēə] *n* Nigéria *m or f*.

Nigerian [nījē'rēən] *a* nigérien(ne) ♦ *n* Nigérien/ne.

niggardly [nig'ûrdlē] *a* (*person*) parcimonieux(euse), pingre; (*allowance, amount*) misérable.

nigger [nig'ûr] *n* (*col!: highly offensive*) nègre/négresse.

niggle [nig'əl] *vt* tracasser ♦ *vi* (*find fault*) trouver toujours à redire; (*fuss*) n'être jamais content(e).

niggling [nig'ling] *a* tatillon(ne); (*detail*) insignifiant(e); (*doubt, pain*) persistant(e).

night [nīt] *n* nuit *f*; (*evening*) soir *m*; **at** ~ la nuit; **by** ~ de nuit; **in the** ~, **during the** ~ pendant la nuit; **the** ~ **before last** avant-hier soir.

nightcap [nīt'kap] *n* boisson prise avant le coucher.

nightclub [nīt'klub] *n* boîte *f* de nuit.

nightdress [nīt'dres] *n* chemise *f* de nuit.

nightfall [nīt'fól] *n* tombée *f* de la nuit.

nightgown [nīt'goun] *n* chemise *f* de nuit.

nightie [nī'tē] *n* (*Brit*) chemise *f* de nuit.

nightingale [nī'təngāl] *n* rossignol *m*.

night life *n* vie *f* nocturne.

nightly [nīt'lē] *a* de chaque nuit *or* soir; (*by night*) nocturne ♦ *ad* chaque nuit *or* soir; nuitamment.

nightmare [nīt'mär] *n* cauchemar *m*.

night owl *n* (*fig*) couche-tard *m inv*, noctambule *m/f*.

night porter *n* gardien *m* de nuit, concierge *m* de service la nuit.

night safe *n* coffre *m* de nuit.

night school *n* cours *mpl* du soir.

nightshade [nīt'shād] *n*: **deadly** ~ (*BOT*) belladone *f*.

night shift *n* équipe *f* de nuit.

nightstick [nīt'stik] *n* (*US*) bâton *m* (d'agent de police).

night-time [nīt'tīm] *n* nuit *f.*

night watchman *n* veilleur *m* de nuit; poste *m* de nuit.

NIH *n abbr* (*US*) = *National Institutes of Health.*

nihilism [nē'əlizəm] *n* nihilisme *m.*

nil [nil] *n* rien *m*; zéro *m.*

Nile [nīl] *n*: **the ~** le Nil.

nimble [nim'bəl] *a* agile.

nine [nīn] *num* neuf.

nineteen [nīn'tēn'] *num* dix-neuf.

ninety [nīn'tē] *num* quatre-vingt-dix.

ninth [nīnth] *num* neuvième.

nip [nip] *vt* pincer ♦ *vi* (*Brit col*): **to ~ out/down/up** sortir/descendre/monter en vitesse ♦ *n* pincement *m*; (*drink*) petit verre; **to ~ into a store** faire un saut dans un magasin.

nipple [nip'əl] *n* (*ANAT*) mamelon *m*, bout *m* du sein.

nippy [nip'ē] *a* (*Brit*: *person*) alerte, leste; (: *car*) nerveux(euse).

nit [nit] *n* (*in hair*) lente *f.*

nit-pick [nit'pik] *vi* (*col*) être tatillon(ne).

nitrogen [nī'trəjən] *n* azote *m.*

nitroglycerin(e) [nītrəglis'ûrin] *n* nitroglycérine *f.*

nitty-gritty [nit'ēgrit'ē] *n* (*fam*): **to get down to the ~** en venir au fond du problème.

nitwit [nit'wit] *n* (*col*) nigaud/e.

NJ *abbr* (*US MAIL*) = *New Jersey.*

NLF *n abbr* (= *National Liberation Front*) FLN *m.*

NLQ *abbr* (= *near letter quality*) qualité *f* courrier.

NLRB *n abbr* (*US*: = *National Labor Relations Board*) *organisme de protection des travailleurs.*

NM *abbr* (*US MAIL*) = *New Mexico.*

N. Mex. *abbr* (*US*) = *New Mexico.*

no [nō] *a* pas de, aucun(e) + *sg* ♦ *ad*, *n* non (*m*); **I have ~ more wine** je n'ai plus de vin; **"~ entry"** "défense d'entrer"; **"~ dogs"** "les chiens ne sont pas admis"; **I won't take ~ for an answer** il n'est pas question de refuser.

no. *abbr* (= *number*) nº.

nobble [nâb'əl] *vt* (*Brit col*: *bribe*: *person*) soudoyer, acheter; (: *person: to speak to*) mettre le grappin sur; (*RACING*: *horse, dog*) droguer (*pour l'empêcher de gagner*).

Nobel prize [nō'bel prīz'] *n* prix *m* Nobel.

nobility [nōbil'ətē] *n* noblesse *f.*

noble [nō'bəl] *a* noble.

nobleman [nō'bəlmən] *n* noble *m.*

nobly [nō'blē] *ad* noblement.

nobody [nō'bâdē] *pronoun* personne (*with negative*).

no-claims bonus [nō'klāmz bō'nəs] *n* (*Brit*) bonus *m.*

no-claims discount [nō'klāmz dis'kount] *n* (*US*) bonus *m.*

nocturnal [nâktûr'nəl] *a* nocturne.

nod [nâd] *vi* faire un signe de (la) tête (*affirmatif ou amical*); (*sleep*) somnoler ♦ *vt*: **to ~ one's head** faire un signe de (la) tête; (*in agreement*) faire signe que oui ♦ *n* signe *m* de (la) tête; **they ~ded their agree-**

-ment ils ont acquiescé d'un signe de la tête.

nod off *vi* s'assoupir.

no fault agreement *n* (*US*) *convention entre compagnies d'assurance par laquelle chacune s'engage à dédommager son propre client.*

noise [noiz] *n* bruit *m.*

noiseless [noiz'lis] *a* silencieux(euse).

noisily [noi'zílē] *ad* bruyamment.

noisy [noi'zē] *a* bruyant(e).

nomad [nō'mad] *n* nomade *m/f.*

nomadic [nōmad'ik] *a* nomade.

no man's land *n* no man's land *m.*

nominal [nâm'ənəl] *a* (*rent, fee*) symbolique; (*value*) nominal(e).

nominate [nâm'ənāt] *vt* (*propose*) proposer; (*elect*) nommer.

nomination [nâmənā'shən] *n* nomination *f.*

nominee [nâmənē'] *n* candidat agréé; personne nommée.

non- [nân] *prefix* non-.

nonalcoholic [nânalkəhôl'ik] *a* non-alcoolisé(e).

nonbreakable [nânbrā'kəbəl] *a* incassable.

nonce word [nâns' wûrd] *n* mot créé pour l'occasion.

nonchalant [nânshəlânt'] *a* nonchalant(e).

noncommissioned [nânkəmish'ənd] *a*: **~ officer** sous-officier *m.*

noncommittal [nânkəmit'əl] *a* évasif(ive).

nonconformist [nânkənfôr'mist] *n* non-conformiste *m/f* ♦ *a* non-conformiste, dissident(e).

noncontributory [nânkəntrib'yətôrē] *a*: **~ pension plan** *or* (*Brit*) **scheme** *régime de retraite payée par l'employeur.*

noncooperation [nânkōâpərā'shən] *n* refus *m* de coopérer, non-coopération *f.*

nondescript [nân'diskript] *a* quelconque, indéfinissable.

none [nun] *pronoun* aucun/e; **~ of you** aucun d'entre vous, personne parmi vous; **I have ~** je n'en ai pas; **I have ~ left** je n'en ai plus; **~ at all** (*not one*) aucun(e); **how much milk?** — **~ at all** combien de lait? — pas du tout; **he's ~ the worse for it** il ne s'en porte pas plus mal.

nonentity [nânen'titē] *n* personne insignifiante.

nonessential [nânəsen'chəl] *a* accessoire, superflu(e) ♦ *n*: **~s** le superflu.

nonetheless [nun'ᵺəles'] *ad* néanmoins.

nonexecutive [nânigzek'yətiv] *a*: **~ director** administrateur/trice, conseiller/ère de direction.

nonexistent [nânigzis'tənt] *a* inexistant(e).

nonfiction [nânfik'shən] *n* littérature *f* non-romanesque.

nonflammable [nânflam'əbəl] *a* ininflammable.

nonintervention [nânintûrven'chən] *n* non-intervention *f.*

non obst. *abbr* (= *non obstante*: *notwithstanding*) nonobstant.

nonpayment [nânpā'mənt] *n* non-paiement *m.*

nonplussed [nânplust'] *a* perplexe.

nonprofit-making [nânprâf'itmāking] *a* à but non lucratif.

nonsense [nân'sens] *n* absurdités *fpl*, idioties *fpl*; **~!** ne dites pas d'idioties!; **it is ~ to say that ...** il est absurde de dire que ....

nonskid [nânskid'] *a* antidérapant(e).
nonsmoker [nânsmō'kûr] *n* non-fumeur *m*.
nonstick [nânstik'] *a* qui n'attache pas.
nonstop [nân'stâp'] *a* direct(e), sans arrêt (*or* escale) ♦ *ad* sans arrêt.
nontaxable [nântak'səbəl] *a*: ~ **income** revenu *m* non imposable.
nonvolatile [nânvál'ətəl] *a*: ~ **memory** (*COMPUT*) mémoire rémanente *or* non volatile.
nonvoting [nânvō'ting] *a*: ~ **shares** actions *fpl* sans droit de vote.
nonwhite [nânwīt'] *a* de couleur ♦ *n* personne *f* de couleur.
noodles [nōō'dəlz] *npl* nouilles *fpl*.
nook [nŏŏk] *n*: ~**s and crannies** recoins *mpl*.
noon [nōōn] *n* midi *m*.
no one [nō' wun] *pronoun* = **nobody**.
noose [nōōs] *n* nœud coulant; (*hangman's*) corde *f*.
nor [nôr] *cj* = **neither** ♦ *ad see* **neither**.
Norf *abbr* (*Brit*) = *Norfolk*.
norm [nôrm] *n* norme *f*.
normal [nôr'məl] *a* normal(e) ♦ *n*: **to return to** ~ redevenir normal(e).
normality [nôrmal'itē] *n* normalité *f*.
normally [nôr'məlē] *ad* normalement.
Normandy [nôr'məndē] *n* Normandie *f*.
north [nôrth] *n* nord *m* ♦ *a* du nord, nord *inv* ♦ *ad* au *or* vers le nord.
North Africa *n* Afrique *f* du Nord.
North African *a* nord-africain(e), d'Afrique du Nord ♦ *n* Nord-Africain/e.
North America *n* Amérique *f* du Nord.
North American *n* Nord-Américain/e ♦ *a* nord-américain(e), d'Amérique du Nord.
Northants [nôrthants'] *abbr* (*Brit*) = *Northamptonshire*.
northbound [nôrth'bound'] *a* (*traffic*) en direction du nord; (*lane*) nord *inv*.
Northd *abbr* (*Brit*) = *Northumberland*.
northeast [nôrthēst'] *n* nord-est *m*.
northerly [nôr'thûrlē] *a* (*wind, direction*) du nord.
northern [nôr'thûrn] *a* du nord, septentrional(e).
Northern Ireland *n* Irlande *f* du Nord.
North Pole *n*: **the** ~ le pôle Nord.
North Sea *n*: **the** ~ la mer du Nord.
North Sea oil *n* pétrole *m* de la mer du Nord.
northward(s) [nôrth'wûrd(z)] *ad* vers le nord.
northwest [nôrthwest'] *n* nord-ouest *m*.
Norway [nôr'wā] *n* Norvège *f*.
Norwegian [nôrwē'jən] *a* norvégien(ne) ♦ *n* Norvégien/ne; (*LING*) norvégien *m*.
nos. *abbr* (= *numbers*) n°.
nose [nōz] *n* nez *m*; (*fig*) flair *m* ♦ *vi* (*also*: ~ **one's way**) avancer précautionneusement; **to pay through the** ~ **(for sth)** (*col*) payer un prix excessif (pour qch).
nose around *vi* fouiner *or* fureter (partout).
nosebleed [nōz'blēd] *n* saignement *m* de nez.
nose dive *n* (descente *f* en) piqué *m*.
nose drops *npl* gouttes *fpl* pour le nez.
nosey [nō'zē] *a* curieux(euse).
nostalgia [nəstal'jə] *n* nostalgie *f*.
nostalgic [nəstal'jik] *a* nostalgique.

nostril [nâs'trəl] *n* narine *f*; (*of horse*) naseau *m*.
nosy [nō'zē] *a* = **nosey**.
not [nât] *ad* (ne ...) pas; **I hope** ~ j'espère que non; ~ **at all** pas du tout; (*after thanks*) de rien; **you must** ~ *or* **mustn't do this** tu ne dois pas faire ça; **he isn't** ... il n'est pas ....
notable [nō'təbəl] *a* notable.
notably [nō'təblē] *ad* en particulier.
notary [nō'tûrē] *n* (*also*: ~ **public**) notaire *m*.
notation [nōtā'shən] *n* notation *f*.
notch [nâch] *n* encoche *f* ♦ *vt* (*score*) marquer; (*victory*) remporter.
note [nōt] *n* note *f*; (*letter*) mot *m*; (*banknote*) billet *m* ♦ *vt* (*also*: ~ **down**) noter; (*notice*) constater; **just a quick** ~ **to let you know** ... juste un mot pour vous dire ...; **to take** ~**s** prendre des notes; **to compare** ~**s** (*fig*) échanger des (*or* leurs *etc*) impressions; **to take** ~ **of** prendre note de; **a person of** ~ une personne éminente.
notebook [nōt'bŏŏk] *n* carnet *m*; (*for shorthand etc*) bloc-notes *m*.
note-case [nōt'kās] *n* (*Brit*) porte-feuille *m*.
noted [nō'tid] *a* réputé(e).
notepad [nōt'pad] *n* bloc-notes *m*.
notepaper [nōt'pāpûr] *n* papier *m* à lettres.
noteworthy [nōt'wûrthē] *a* remarquable.
nothing [nuth'ing] *n* rien *m*; **he does** ~ il ne fait rien; ~ **new** rien de nouveau; **for** ~ (*free*) pour rien, gratuitement; ~ **at all** rien du tout.
notice [nō'tis] *n* avis *m*; (*of leaving*) congé *m*; (*Brit: review: of play etc*) critique *f*, compte-rendu *m* ♦ *vt* remarquer, s'apercevoir de; **without** ~ sans préavis; **advance** ~ préavis *m*; **to give sb** ~ **of sth** notifier qn de qch; **at short** ~ dans un délai très court; **until further** ~ jusqu'à nouvel ordre; **to give** ~, **hand in one's** ~ (*subj: employee*) donner sa démission, démissionner; **to take** ~ **of** prêter attention à; **to bring sth to sb's** ~ porter qch à la connaissance de qn; **it has come to my** ~ **that** ... on m'a signalé que ...; **to escape** *or* **avoid** ~ (essayer de) passer inaperçu *or* ne pas se faire remarquer.
noticeable [nō'tisəbəl] *a* visible.
notice board *n* (*Brit*) panneau *m* d'affichage.
notification [nōtəfəkā'shən] *n* notification *f*.
notify [nō'təfī] *vt*: ~ **to** ~ **sth to sb** notifier qch à qn; **to** ~ **sb of sth** avertir qn de qch.
notion [nō'shən] *n* idée *f*; (*concept*) notion *f*.
notions [nō'shənz] *npl* (*US*) mercerie *f*.
notoriety [nōtərī'ətē] *n* notoriété *f*.
notorious [nōtôr'ēəs] *a* notoire (*souvent en mal*).
notoriously [nōtôr'ēəslē] *a* notoirement.
Notts [nâts] *abbr* (*Brit*) = *Nottinghamshire*.
notwithstanding [nâtwithstan'ding] *ad* néanmoins ♦ *prep* en dépit de.
nougat [nōō'gət] *n* nougat *m*.
nought [nôt] *n* zéro *m*.
noun [noun] *n* nom *m*.
nourish [nûr'ish] *vt* nourrir.
nourishing [nûr'ishing] *a* nourrissant(e).
nourishment [nûr'ishmənt] *n* nourriture *f*.
Nov. *abbr* (= *November*) nov.
Nova Scotia [nō'və skō'shə] *n* Nouvelle-Écosse *f*.

novel [nàv'əl] *n* roman *m* ♦ *a* nouveau(nouvelle), original(e).

novelist [nàv'əlist] *n* romancier *m*.

novelty [nàv'əltē] *n* nouveauté *f*.

November [nōvem'bûr] *n* novembre *m*; *for phrases see also* **July.**

novice [nàv'is] *n* novice *m/f*.

NOW [nou] *n abbr* (*US*) = *National Organization for Women.*

now [nou] *ad* maintenant ♦ *cj*: ~ **(that)** maintenant (que); **right** ~ tout de suite; **by** ~ à l'heure qu'il est; **I saw her right** ~ je viens de la voir, je l'ai vue à l'instant; **I'll read it right** ~ je vais le lire à l'instant or dès maintenant; ~ **and then**, ~ **and again** de temps en temps; **from** ~ **on** dorénavant; **in 3 days from** ~ dans or d'ici trois jours; **between** ~ **and Monday** d'ici (à) lundi; **that's all for** ~ c'est tout pour l'instant.

nowadays [nou'ədāz] *ad* de nos jours.

nowhere [nō'wär] *ad* nulle part; ~ **else** nulle part ailleurs.

noxious [nàk'shəs] *a* toxique.

nozzle [nàz'əl] *n* (*of hose*) jet *m*, lance *f*.

NP *n abbr* = **notary public.**

NS *abbr* (*Canada*) = *Nova Scotia.*

NSC *n abbr* (*US*) = **National Security Council.**

NSF *n abbr* (*US*) = *National Science Foundation.*

NSW *abbr* (*Australia*) = *New South Wales.*

NT *n abbr* (= *New Testament*) NT *m* ♦ *abbr* (*Canada*) = *Northwest Territories.*

nth [enth] *a*: **for the** ~ **time** (*col*) pour la énième fois.

nuance [nōo'ânts] *n* nuance *f*.

nubile [nōo'bil] *a* nubile; (*attractive*) jeune et désirable.

nuclear [nōo'klēûr] *a* nucléaire.

nuclear disarmament *n* désarmement *m* nucléaire.

nucleus, *pl* **nuclei** [nōo'klēəs, nōo'klēī] *n* noyau *m*.

nude [nōod] *a* nu(e) ♦ *n* (*ART*) nu *m*; **in the** ~ (tout(e)) nu(e).

nudge [nuj] *vt* donner un (petit) coup de coude à.

nudist [nōo'dist] *n* nudiste *m/f*.

nudist colony *n* colonie *f* de nudistes.

nudity [nōo'ditē] *n* nudité *f*.

nugget [nug'it] *n* pépite *f*.

nuisance [nōo'səns] *n*: **it's a** ~ c'est (très) ennuyeux or gênant; **he's a** ~ il est assommant or casse-pieds; **what a** ~! quelle barbe!

nuke [nōok] *vt* (*attack*) lancer une attaque nucléaire contre; (*destroy*) détruire à l'arme nucléaire or atomique.

null [nul] *a*: ~ **and void** nul(le) et non avenu(e).

nullify [nul'əfī] *vt* invalider.

numb [num] *a* engourdi(e) ♦ *vt* engourdir; ~ **with cold** engourdi(e) par le froid, transi(e) (de froid); ~ **with fear** transi de peur, paralysé(e) par la peur.

number [num'bûr] *n* nombre *m*; (*numeral*) chiffre *m*; (*of house, car, telephone, newspaper*) numéro *m* ♦ *vt* numéroter; (*include*) compter; **a** ~ **of** un certain nombre de; **to be**

~**ed among** compter parmi; **the staff** ~**s 20** le nombre d'employés s'élève à or est de 20; **wrong** ~ (*TEL*) mauvais numéro.

numbered account [num'bûrd əkount'] *n* (*in bank*) compte numéroté.

number plate *n* (*Brit AUT*) plaque *f* minéralogique or d'immatriculation.

Number Ten *n* (*Brit*: = *10 Downing Street*) résidence du Premier ministre.

numbness [num'nis] *n* torpeur *f*; (*due to cold*) engourdissement *m*.

numeral [nōo'mûrəl] *n* chiffre *m*.

numerical [nōomär'ikəl] *a* numérique.

numerous [nōo'mûrəs] *a* nombreux(euse).

nun [nun] *n* religieuse *f*, sœur *f*.

nuptial [nup'shəl] *a* nuptial(e).

nurse [nûrs] *n* infirmière *f*; (*also*: ~**maid**) bonne *f* d'enfants ♦ *vt* (*patient, cold*) soigner; (*baby*: *US*) allaiter, nourrir; (: *Brit*) bercer (dans ses bras); (*hope*) nourrir *m*.

nursery [nûr'sûrē] *n* (*room*) nursery *f*; (*institution*) pouponnière *f*; (*for plants*) pépinière *f*.

nursery rhyme *n* comptine *f*, chansonnette *f* pour enfants.

nursery school *n* école maternelle.

nursery slope *n* (*Brit SKI*) piste *f* pour débutants.

nursing [nûrs'ing] *n* (*profession*) profession *f* d'infirmière ♦ *a* (*mother*) qui allaite.

nursing home *n* clinique *f*; maison *f* de convalescence.

nurture [nûr'chûr] *vt* élever.

nut [nut] *n* (*of metal*) écrou *m*; (*fruit*) noix *f*, noisette *f*, cacahuète *f* (*terme générique en anglais*) ♦ *a* (*chocolate etc*) aux noisettes.

nutcase [nut'kās] *n* (*Brit col*) dingue *m/f*.

nutcracker [nut'krakûr] *n* casse-noix *m inv*, casse-noisette(s) *m*.

nutmeg [nut'meg] *n* (*noix f*) muscade *f*.

nutrient [nōo'trēənt] *a* nutritif(ive) ♦ *n* substance nutritive.

nutrition [nōotrish'ən] *n* nutrition *f*, alimentation *f*.

nutritionist [nōotrish'ənist] *n* nutritionniste *m/f*.

nutritious [nōotrish'əs] *a* nutritif(ive), nourrissant(e).

nuts [nuts] *a* (*col*): **he's** ~ il est dingue ♦ *excl* zut!

nutshell [nut'shel] *n* coquille *f* de noix; **in a** ~ en un mot.

nuzzle [nuz'əl] *vi*: **to** ~ **up to** fourrer son nez contre.

NV *abbr* (*US MAIL*) = *Nevada.*

NWT *abbr* (*Canada*) = *Northwest Territories.*

NY *abbr* (*US MAIL*) = *New York.*

NYC *abbr* (*US MAIL*) = *New York City.*

nylon [nī'lân] *n* nylon *m* ♦ *a* de or en nylon; ~**s** *npl* bas *mpl* nylon.

nymph [nimf] *n* nymphe *f*.

nymphomaniac [nimfəmā'nēak] *a*, *n* nymphomane (*f*).

NYSE *n abbr* (*US*) = *New York Stock Exchange.*

NZ *abbr* = *New Zealand.*

O

O, o [ō] *n* (*letter*) O, o *m*; (*US SCOL:* = *outstanding*) tb (= *très bien*); **O for Oboe** O comme Oscar.

oaf [ōf] *n* balourd *m*.

oak [ōk] *n* chêne *m* ♦ *cpd* de *or* en (bois de) chêne.

OAP *n abbr* (*Brit*) = **old-age pensioner.**

oar [ōr] *n* aviron *m*, rame *f*; **to put** *or* **shove one's ~ in** (*fig: col*) mettre son grain de sel.

oarlock [ōr'låk] *n* (*US*) dame *f* de nage, tolet *m*.

oarsman [ōrz'mən], **oarswoman** [ōrz'woomən] *n* rameur/euse.

OAS *n abbr* (= *Organization of American States*) OEA *f* (= *Organisation des états américains*).

oasis, pl oases [ōā'sis, ōā'sēz]] *n* oasis *f*.

oath [ōth] *n* serment *m*; (*swear word*) juron *m*; **to take the ~** prêter serment; **under** *or* **on** (*Brit*) **~** sous serment; assermenté(e).

oatmeal [ōt'mēl] *n* flocons *mpl* d'avoine.

oats [ōts] *n* avoine *f*.

OAU *n abbr* (= *Organization of African Unity*) OUA *f* (= *Organisation de l'unité africaine*).

obdurate [åb'dyərit] *a* obstiné(e); impénitent(e); intraitable.

obedience [ōbē'dēəns] *n* obéissance *f*; **in ~ to** conformément à.

obedient [ōbē'dēənt] *a* obéissant(e); **to be ~ to sb/sth** obéir à qn/qch.

obelisk [åb'əlisk] *n* obélisque *m*.

obesity [ōbē'sitē] *n* obésité *f*.

obey [ōbā'] *vt* obéir à; (*instructions, regulations*) se conformer à ♦ *vi* obéir.

obituary [ōbich'ōōårē] *n* nécrologie *f*.

object *n* [åb'jikt] objet *m*; (*purpose*) but *m*, objet; (*LING*) complément *m* d'objet ♦ *vi*: [əbjekt'] **to ~ to** (*attitude*) désapprouver; (*proposal*) protester contre, élever une objection contre; **I ~!** je proteste!; **he ~ed that ...** il a fait valoir *or* a objecté que ...; **do you ~ to my smoking?** est-ce que cela vous gêne si je fume?; **what's the ~ of doing that?** quel est l'intérêt de faire cela?; **money is no ~** l'argent n'est pas un problème.

objection [əbjek'shən] *n* objection *f*; (*drawback*) inconvénient *m*; **if you have no ~ to** si vous n'y voyez pas d'inconvénient; **to make** *or* **raise an ~** élever une objection.

objectionable [əbjek'shənəbəl] *a* très désagréable; choquant(e).

objective [əbjek'tiv] *n* objectif *m* ♦ *a* objectif(ive).

objectivity [åbjektiv'ətē] *n* objectivité *f*.

object lesson *n* (*fig*) (bonne) illustration.

objector [əbjek'tûr] *n* opposant/e.

obligation [åbləgā'shən] *n* obligation *f*, devoir *m*; (*debt*) dette *f* de reconnaissance); **"without ~"** "sans engagement".

obligatory [əblig'ətôrē] *a* obligatoire.

oblige [əblīj'] *vt* (*force*): **to ~ sb to do** obliger *or* forcer qn à faire; (*do a favor*) rendre service à, obliger; **to be ~d to sb for sth** être obligé(e) à qn de qch; **anything to ~!** (*col*) (toujours prêt à rendre) service!

obliging [əblī'jing] *a* obligeant(e), serviable.

oblique [əblēk'] *a* oblique; (*allusion*) indirect(e) ♦ *n* (*Brit TYP*): **~ (stroke)** barre *f* oblique.

obliterate [əblit'ərāt] *vt* effacer.

oblivion [əbliv'ēən] *n* oubli *m*.

oblivious [əbliv'ēəs] *a*: **~ of** oublieux(euse) de.

oblong [åb'lông] *a* oblong(ue) ♦ *n* rectangle *m*.

obnoxious [əbnåk'shəs] *a* odieux(euse); (*smell*) nauséabond(e).

o.b.o. *abbr* (*US:* = *or best offer*: *in classified ads*) ≈ à discuter.

oboe [ō'bō] *n* hautbois *m*.

obscene [əbsēn'] *a* obscène.

obscenity [əbsen'itē] *n* obscénité *f*.

obscure [əbskyōōr'] *a* obscur(e) ♦ *vt* obscurcir; (*hide: sun*) cacher.

obscurity [əbskyōōr'itē] *n* obscurité *f*.

obsequious [əbsē'kwēəs] *a* obséquieux(euse).

observable [əbzûr'vəbəl] *a* observable; (*appreciable*) notable.

observance [əbzûr'vəns] *n* observance *f*, observation *f*; **religious ~s** observances religieuses.

observant [əbzûr'vənt] *a* observateur(trice).

observation [åbzûrvā'shən] *n* observation *f*; (*by police etc*) surveillance *f*.

observation post *n* (*MIL*) poste *m* d'observation.

observatory [əbzûr'vətôrē] *n* observatoire *m*.

observe [əbzûrv'] *vt* observer; (*remark*) faire observer *or* remarquer.

observer [əbzûr'vûr] *n* observateur/trice.

obsess [əbses'] *vt* obséder; **to be ~ed by** *or* **with sb/sth** être obsédé(e) par qn/qch.

obsession [əbsesh'ən] *n* obsession *f*.

obsessive [əbses'iv] *a* obsédant(e).

obsolescence [åbsəles'əns] *n* vieillissement *m*; obsolescence *f*; **built-in** *or* **planned ~** (*COMM*) désuétude calculée.

obsolescent [åbsəles'ənt] *a* obsolescent(e), en voie d'être périmé(e).

obsolete [åbsəlēt'] *a* dépassé(e), périmé(e).

obstacle [åb'stəkəl] *n* obstacle *m*.

obstacle race *n* course *f* d'obstacles.

obstetrics [åbstet'riks] *n* obstétrique *f*.

obstinacy [åb'stənəsē] *n* obstination *f*.

obstinate [åb'stənit] *a* obstiné(e); (*pain, cold*) persistant(e).

obstreperous [åbstrep'ûrəs] *a* turbulent(e).

obstruct [əbstrukt'] *vt* (*block*) boucher, obstruer; (*halt*) arrêter; (*hinder*) entraver.

obstruction [əbstruk'shən] *n* obstruction *f*; obstacle *m*.

obstructive [əbstruk'tiv] *a* obstructionniste.

obtain [əbtān'] *vt* obtenir ♦ *vi* avoir cours.

obtainable [əbtān'əbəl] *a* qu'on peut obtenir.

obtrusive [əbtrōō'siv] *a* (*person*) importun(e); (*smell*) pénétrant(e); (*building etc*) trop en évidence.

obtuse [əbtōōs'] *a* obtus(e).

obverse [åb'vûrs] *n* (*of medal, coin*) côté *m*

face; (fig) contrepartie f.
obviate [âb'vćãt] vt parer à, obvier à.
obvious [âb'vēəs] a évident(e), manifeste.
obviously [âb'vēəslē] ad manifestement; (of course): ~, **he** ... or **he** ~ ... il est bien évident qu'il ...; ~**!** bien sûr!; ~ **not!** évidemment pas!, bien sûr que non!
OCAS n abbr (= Organization of Central American States) ODEAC f (= Organisation des États d'Amérique Centrale).
occasion [əkā'zhən] n occasion f; (event) événement m ♦ vt occasionner, causer; **on that** ~ à cette occasion; **to rise to the** ~ se montrer à la hauteur de la situation.
occasional [əkā'zhənəl] a pris(e) (or fait(e) etc) de temps en temps; occasionnel(le).
occasionally [əkā'zhənəlē] ad de temps en temps; **very** ~ (assez) rarement.
occasional table n table décorative.
occult [əkult'] a occulte ♦ n: **the** ~ le surnaturel.
occupancy [âk'yəpənsē] n occupation f.
occupant [âk'yəpənt] n occupant m.
occupation [âkyəpā'shən] n occupation f; (job) métier m, profession f; **unfit for** ~ (house) impropre à l'habitation.
occupational [âkyəpā'shənəl] a (accident, disease) du travail; (hazard) du métier.
occupational pension n retraite professionnelle.
occupational therapy n ergothérapie f.
occupied [âk'yəpīd] a (busy, in use) occupé(e).
occupier [âk'yəpīûr] n occupant/e.
occupy [âk'yəpī] vt occuper; **to** ~ **o.s. with** or **by doing** s'occuper à faire; **to be occupied with sth** être occupé avec qch.
occur [əkûr'] vi se produire; (difficulty, opportunity) se présenter; (phenomenon, error) se rencontrer; **to** ~ **to sb** venir à l'esprit de qn.
occurrence [əkûr'əns] n présence f, existence f; cas m, fait m.
ocean [ō'shən] n océan m; ~**s of** (col) des masses de.
ocean bed n fond (sous-)marin.
ocean-going [ō'shəngōing] a de haute mer.
Oceania [ōshēan'ēə] n Océanie f.
ocean liner n paquebot m.
ocher, (Brit) **ochre** [ō'kûr] a ocre.
o'clock [əklâk'] ad: **it is 5** ~ il est 5 heures.
OCR n abbr = **optical character reader, optical character recognition**.
Oct. abbr (= October) oct.
octagonal [âktag'ənəl] a octogonal(e).
octane [âk'tān] n octane m; **high-**~ **gas** or (Brit) **petrol** essence f à indice d'octane élevé.
octave [âk'tiv] n octave f.
October [âktō'bûr] n octobre m; for phrases see also **July**.
octogenarian [âktəjənär'ēən] n octogénaire m/f.
octopus [âk'təpəs] n pieuvre f.
odd [âd] a (strange) bizarre, curieux(euse); (number) impair(e); (left over) qui reste, en plus; (not of a set) dépareillé(e); **60**~ 60 et quelques; **at** ~ **times** de temps en temps; **the** ~ **one out** l'exception f.

oddball [âd'bôl] n (col) excentrique m/f.
oddity [âd'itē] n bizarrerie f; (person) excentrique m/f.
odd-job man [âdjâb' man] n homme m à tout faire.
odd jobs npl petits travaux divers.
oddly [âd'lē] ad bizarrement, curieusement.
oddments [âd'mənts] npl (Brit COMM) fins fpl de série.
odds [âdz] npl (in betting) cote f; **the** ~ **are against his coming** il y a peu de chances qu'il vienne; **it makes no** ~ cela n'a pas d'importance; **to succeed against all the** ~ réussir contre toute attente; ~ **and ends** de petites choses; **at** ~ en désaccord.
ode [ōd] n ode f.
odious [ō'dēəs] a odieux(euse), détestable.
odometer [ōdâm'itûr] n (US) ≈ compteur m kilométrique.
odor [ō'dûr] n (US) odeur f.
odorless [ō'dûrlis] a inodore.
odour [ō'dûr] etc (Brit) = **odor** etc.
OECD n abbr (= Organization for Economic Cooperation and Development) OCDE f (= Organisation de coopération et de développement économique).
oesophagus [isâf'əgəs] n (Brit) œsophage m.
oestrogen [es'trəjən] n (Brit) œstrogène m.
of [uv] prep de; **a friend** ~ **ours** un de nos amis; **3** ~ **them went** 3 d'entre eux y sont allés; **the 5th** ~ **July** le 5 juillet; **a boy** ~ **10** un garçon de 10 ans; **made** ~ **wood** (fait) en bois; **a kilo** ~ **flour** un kilo de farine; **that was very kind** ~ **you** c'était très gentil de votre part; **a quarter** ~ **4** (US) 4 heures moins le quart.
off [ôf] a, ad (engine) coupé(e); (faucet) fermé(e); (Brit: food) mauvais(e), avancé(e); (: milk) tourné(e); (absent) absent(e); (cancelled) annulé(e); (removed): **the lid was** ~ le couvercle était retiré or n'était pas mis ♦ prep de; sur; **to be** ~ (to leave) partir, s'en aller; **I must be** ~ il faut que je file; **to be** ~ **sick** être absent pour cause de maladie; **a day** ~ un jour de congé; **to have an** ~ **day** n'être pas en forme; **he had his coat** ~ il avait enlevé son manteau; **the hook is** ~ le crochet s'est détaché; le crochet n'est pas mis; **10%** ~ (COMM) 10% de rabais; **5 km** ~ **(the road)** à 5 km (de la route); ~ **the coast** au large de la côte; **a house** ~ **the main road** une maison à l'écart de la grand-route; **it's a long way** ~ c'est loin (d'ici); **I'm** ~ **meat** je ne mange plus de viande; je n'aime plus la viande; **on the** ~ **chance** à tout hasard; **to be well/badly** ~ être bien/mal loti; (financially) être aisé/dans la gêne; ~ **and on, on and** ~ de temps à autre; **to be** ~ **in one's calculations** s'être trompé dans ses calculs; **that's a bit** ~ (fig: col) c'est un peu fort.
offal [ôf'əl] n (CULIN) abats mpl.
offbeat [ôf'bēt] a excentrique.
off-center [ôf'sen'tûr] a décentré(e), excentré(e).
off-colour [ôf'kul'ûr] a (Brit: ill) malade, mal fichu(e); **to feel** ~ être mal fichu.
offence [əfens'] n (Brit) = **offense**.
offend [əfend'] vt (person) offenser, blesser ♦

vi: **to ~ against** (*law, rule*) contrevenir à, enfreindre.

offender [ǝfen'dûr] *n* délinquant/e; (*against regulations*) contrevenant/e.

offense [ǝfens'] *n* (*US*) (*crime*) délit *m*, infraction *f*; **to give ~ to** blesser, offenser; **to take ~ at** se vexer de, s'offenser de; **to commit an ~** commettre une infraction.

offensive [ǝfen'siv] *a* offensant(e), choquant(e); (*smell etc*) très déplaisant(e); (*weapon*) offensif(ive) ♦ *n* (*MIL*) offensive *f*.

offer [ôf'ûr] *n* offre *f*, proposition *f* ♦ *vt* offrir, proposer; **to make an ~** faire une offre pour qch; **to ~ sth to sb, ~ sb sth** offrir qch à qn; **to ~ to do sth** proposer de faire qch; **"on ~"** (*Brit COMM*) "en promotion".

offering [ôf'ûring] *n* offrande *f*.

offhand [ôf'hand'] *a* désinvolte ♦ *ad* spontané- ment; **I can't tell you ~** je ne peux pas vous le dire comme ça.

office [ôf'is] *n* (*place*) bureau *m*; (*position*) charge *f*, fonction *f*; **doctor's ~** (*US*) cabinet (médical); **to take ~** entrer en fonctions; **through his good ~s** (*fig*) grâce à ses bons offices.

office automation *n* bureautique *f*.

office bearer *n* (*Brit*) = **office holder**.

office boy *n* garçon *m* de bureau.

office building, (*Brit*) **office block** *n* immeuble *m* de bureaux.

office holder *n* (*US*: *of club etc*) membre *m* du bureau.

office hours *npl* heures *fpl* de bureau; (*US MED*) heures de consultation.

office manager *n* responsable administratif(ive).

officer [ôf'isûr] *n* (*MIL etc*) officier *m*; (*of club*) membre *m* du bureau; (*of organization*) membre du bureau directeur; (*also:* **police ~**) agent *m* (de police).

office work *n* travail *m* de bureau.

office worker *n* employé/e de bureau.

official [ǝfish'ǝl] *a* (*authorized*) officiel(le) ♦ *n* officiel *m*; (*civil servant*) fonctionnaire *m/f*; employé/e.

officialdom [ǝfish'ǝldǝm] *n* bureaucratie *f*.

officially [ǝfish'ǝlē] *ad* officiellement.

officiate [ǝfish'ēat] *vi* (*REL*) officier; **to ~ as Mayor** exercer les fonctions de maire; **to ~ at a marriage** célébrer un mariage.

officious [ǝfish'ǝs] *a* trop empressé(e).

offing [ôf'ing] *n*: **in the ~** (*fig*) en perspective.

off-key [ôfkē'] *a* faux(fausse) ♦ *ad* faux.

off-licence [ôf'līsǝns] *n* (*Brit*: *store*) débit *m* de vins et de spiritueux.

off-limits [ôf'lim'its] *a* (*esp US*) dont l'accès est interdit.

off line *a* (*COMPUT*) (en mode) autonome; (*: switched off*) non connecté(e).

off-load [ôf'lōd'] *vt*: **to ~ sth (onto)** (*goods*) décharger qch (sur); (*job*) se décharger de qch (sur).

off-peak [ôf'pēk'] *a* aux heures creuses.

off-putting [ôf'poot'ing] *a* (*Brit*) rébarbatif(ive); rebutant(e), peu engageant(e).

off-ramp [ôf'ramp] *n* (*US AUT*) bretelle *f* d'accès.

off-season [ôf'sēzǝn] *a*, *ad* hors-saison (*inv*).

offset *vt irg* [ôfset'] (*counteract*) contreba-

lancer, compenser ♦ *n* [ôf'set] (*also: ~ printing*) offset *m*.

offshoot [ôf'shōōt] *n* (*fig*) ramification *f*, antenne *f*; (*: of discussion etc*) conséquence *f*.

offshore [ôf'shôr'] *a* (*breeze*) de terre; (*island*) proche du littoral; (*fishing*) côtier(ière); **~ oilfield** gisement *m* pétrolifère en mer.

offside [ôf'sīd'] *n* (*AUT*: *with right-hand drive*) côté droit; (*: with left-hand drive*) côté gauche ♦ *a* (*AUT*) de droite; de gauche; (*SPORT*) hors jeu.

offspring [ôf'spring] *n* progéniture *f*.

offstage [ôf'stāj'] *ad* dans les coulisses.

off-the-cuff [ôf'thǝkuf'] *ad* au pied levé; de chic.

off-the-job [ôf'thǝjáb'] *a*: **~ training** formation professionnelle extérieure.

off-the-rack [ôf'thǝrak'], (*Brit*) **off-the-peg** [ôf'thǝpeg'] *ad* en prêt-à-porter.

off-the-wall [ôf'thǝwôl'] *a* (*col*) bizarre, dingue.

off-white [ôf'wīt] *a* blanc cassé *inv*.

off-year election [ôf'yĕr ilek'shǝn] *n* (*US*) élection (législative) partielle.

often [ôf'ǝn] *ad* souvent; **how ~ do you go?** vous y allez tous les combien?; **how ~ have you gone there?** vous y êtes allé combien de fois?; **as ~ as not** la plupart du temps.

ogle [ō'gǝl] *vt* lorgner.

ogre [ō'gûr] *n* ogre *m*.

OH *abbr* (*US MAIL*) = *Ohio*.

oh [ō] *excl* ô!, oh!, ah!

OHMS *abbr* (*Brit*) = *On His (or Her) Majesty's Service*.

oil [oil] *n* huile *f*; (*petroleum*) pétrole *m*; (*for central heating*) mazout *m* ♦ *vt* (*machine*) graisser.

oilcan [oil'kan] *n* burette *f* de graissage; (*for storing*) bidon *m* à huile.

oil change *n* vidange *f*.

oilfield [oil'fēld] *n* gisement *m* de pétrole.

oil filter *n* (*AUT*) filtre *m* à huile.

oil-fired [oil'fīûrd] *a* au mazout.

oil gauge *n* jauge *f* de niveau d'huile.

oil industry *n* industrie pétrolière.

oil level *n* niveau *m* d'huile.

oil painting *n* peinture *f* à l'huile.

oil pan *n* (*US AUT*) carter *m*.

oil refinery *n* raffinerie *f* de pétrole.

oil rig *n* derrick *m*; (*at sea*) plate-forme pétrolière.

oilskins [oil'skinz] *npl* (*Brit*) ciré *m*.

oil slick *n* nappe *f* de mazout.

oil tanker *n* pétrolier *m*.

oil well *n* puits *m* de pétrole.

oily [oi'lē] *a* huileux(euse); (*food*) gras(se).

ointment [oint'mǝnt] *n* onguent *m*.

OJT *abbr* (*US*) = **on-the-job training**.

OK *abbr* (*US MAIL*) = *Oklahoma*.

O.K., okay [ōkā'] (*col*) *excl* d'accord! ♦ *vt* approuver, donner son accord à ♦ *n*: **to give sth one's ~** donner son accord à qch ♦ *a* en règle; en bon état; sain et sauf; acceptable; **is it ~?, are you ~?** ça va?; **are you ~ for money?** ça va or ira question argent?; **it's ~ with** or **by me** ça me va, c'est d'accord en ce qui me concerne.

Okla. *abbr* (*US*) = *Oklahoma*.

old |ōld] *a* vieux(vieille); (*person*) vieux, âgé(e); (*former*) ancien(ne), vieux; **how ~ are you?** quel âge avez-vous?; **he's 10 years ~** il a 10 ans, il est âgé de 10 ans; **~er brother/sister** frère/sœur aîné(e); **any ~ thing will do** n'importe quoi fera l'affaire.

old age *n* vieillesse *f*.

old-age pensioner (OAP) |ōld'āj pen'chənúr] *n* (*Brit*) retraité/e.

old-fashioned |ōld'fash'ənd] *a* démodé(e); (*person*) vieux jeu *inv*.

old folk's home *n* maison *f* de retraite.

old maid *n* vieille fille.

old-time |ōld'tīm'] *a* du temps jadis, d'autrefois.

old-timer |ōld'tī'mûr] *n* ancien *m*.

old wives' tale *n* conte *m* de bonne femme.

olive |âl'iv] *n* (*fruit*) olive *f*; (*tree*) olivier *m* ♦ *a* (*also*: **~-green**) (vert) olive *inv*.

olive oil *n* huile *f* d'olive.

Olympic |ōlim'pik] *a* olympique; **the ~ Games, the ~s** les Jeux *mpl* olympiques.

O&M *n abbr* = *organization and method*.

Oman |ō'mân] *n* Oman *m*.

OMB *n abbr* (*US*: = *Office of Management and Budget*) service conseillant le président en matière budgétaire.

omelet(te) |âm'lit] *n* omelette *f*; **ham/cheese ~** omelette au jambon/fromage.

omen |ō'mən] *n* présage *m*.

ominous |âm'ənəs] *a* menaçant(e), inquiétant(e); (*event*) de mauvais augure.

omission |ōmish'ən] *n* omission *f*.

omit |ōmit'] *vt* omettre; **to ~ to do sth** négliger de faire qch.

omnivorous |âmniv'ûrəs] *a* omnivore.

ON *abbr* (*Canada*) = *Ontario*.

on |ân] *prep* sur ♦ *ad* (*machine*) en marche; (*light, radio*) allumé(e); (*tap*) ouvert(e); **is the meeting still ~?** est-ce que la réunion a bien lieu?; la réunion dure-t-elle encore?; **when is this film ~?** quand passe or passe-t-on ce film?; **~ the train** dans le train; **~ the wall** sur le or au mur; **~ television** à la télévision; **~ the Continent** sur le continent; **a book ~ physics** un livre de physique; **~ learning this** en apprenant cela; **~ arrival** à l'arrivée; **~ the left** à gauche; **~ Friday** vendredi; **~ Fridays** le vendredi; **~ vacation**, (*Brit*) **~ holiday** en vacances; **I haven't any money ~ me** je n'ai pas d'argent sur moi; **this round's ~ me** c'est ma tournée; **to have one's coat ~** avoir (mis) son manteau; **to walk** *etc* **~** continuer à marcher *etc*; **from that day ~** depuis ce jour; **that's not ~!** (*not acceptable*) cela ne se fait pas!; (*not possible*) pas question!; **~ and off** de temps à autre.

once |wuns] *ad* une fois; (*formerly*) autrefois ♦ *cj* une fois que; **~ he had left/it was done** une fois qu'il fut parti/que ce fut terminé; **at ~** tout de suite, immédiatement; (*simultaneously*) à la fois; **all at ~** *ad* tout d'un coup; **~ a week** une fois par semaine; **~ more** encore une fois; **I knew him ~** je l'ai connu autrefois; **~ and for all** une fois pour toutes; **~ upon a time** il y avait une fois, il était une fois.

oncoming |ân'kuming] *a* (*traffic*) venant en sens inverse.

one |wun] *a, num* un(e) ♦ *pronoun* un(e); (*impersonal*) on; **this ~** celui-ci/celle-ci; **that ~** celui-là/celle-là; **the ~ book which ...** l'unique livre que ...; **~ by ~** un(e) par un(e); **~ never knows** on ne sait jamais; **~ another** l'un(e) l'autre; **it's ~** (*o'clock*) il est une heure; **which ~ do you want?** lequel voulez-vous?; **to be ~ up on sb** avoir l'avantage sur qn; **to be at ~ (with sb)** être d'accord (avec qn).

one-armed bandit |wun'ârmd ban'dit] *n* machine *f* à sous.

one-day excursion |wun'dā ikskûr'zhən] *n* (*US*) billet *m* d'aller-retour (valable pour la journée).

one-man |wun'man] *a* (*business*) dirigé(e) *etc* par un seul homme.

one-man band *n* homme-orchestre *m*.

one-off |wun'ôf] (*Brit col*) *n* exemplaire *m* unique ♦ *a* unique.

one-piece |wun'pēs] *a*: **~ bathing suit** maillot *m* une pièce.

onerous |ân'ûrəs] *a* (*task, duty*) pénible; (*responsibility*) lourd(e).

oneself |wunself'] *pronoun* se; (*after prep, also emphatic*) soi-même; **by ~** tout seul.

one-shot |wun'shât] *a* (*US col*) unique.

one-sided |wun'sīdid] *a* (*decision*) unilatéral(e); (*judgment, account*) partial(e); (*contest*) inégal(e).

one-time |wun'tīm] *a* d'autrefois.

one-to-one |wun'təwun'] *a* (*relationship*) univoque.

one-upmanship |wunup'mənship] *n*: **the art of ~** l'art de faire mieux que les autres.

one-way |wun'wā'] *a* (*street, traffic*) à sens unique.

one-way ticket *n* aller *m* (simple).

ongoing |ân'gōing] *a* en cours; suivi(e).

onion |un'yən] *n* oignon *m*.

on line *a* (*COMPUT*) en ligne; (: *switched on*) connecté(e).

onlooker |ân'lŏōkûr] *n* spectateur/trice.

only |ōn'lē] *ad* seulement ♦ *a* seul(e), unique ♦ *cj* seulement, mais; **an ~ child** un enfant unique; **not ~** non seulement; **I ~ took one** j'en ai seulement pris un, je n'en ai pris qu'un; **I saw her ~ yesterday** je l'ai vue hier encore; **I'd be ~ too pleased to help** je ne serais que trop content de vous aider; **I would come, ~ I'm very busy** je viendrais bien mais j'ai beaucoup à faire.

ono *abbr* (*Brit*: = *or nearest offer*: *in classified ads*) ≈ à discuter.

on-ramp |ân'ramp] *n* (*US AUT*) bretelle *f* d'accès.

onset |ân'set] *n* début *m*; (*of winter, old age*) approche *f*.

onshore |ân'shôr'] *a* (*wind*) du large.

onslaught |ân'slôt] *n* attaque *f*, assaut *m*.

Ont. *abbr* (*Canada*) = *Ontario*.

on-the-job |ânthəjâb'] *a*: **~ training** formation *f* en cours d'emploi.

onto |ân'tōō] *prep* = **on to**.

onus |ō'nəs] *n* responsabilité *f*; **the ~ is upon him to prove it** c'est à lui de le prouver.

onward(s) |ân'wûrd(z)] *ad* (*move*) en avant.

onyx [ân'iks] *n* onyx *m*.

ooze [ōōz] *vi* suinter.

opacity [ōpas'itē] *n* opacité *f*.

opal [ō'pəl] *n* opale *f*.

opaque [ōpāk'] *a* opaque.

OPEC [ō'pek] *n abbr* (= *Organization of Petroleum-Exporting Countries*) OPEP *f* (= *Organisation des pays exportateurs de pétrole*).

open [ō'pən] *a* ouvert(e); (*car*) découvert(e); (*road, view*) dégagé(e); (*meeting*) public(ique); (*admiration*) manifeste; (*question*) non résolu(e); (*enemy*) déclaré(e) ♦ *vt* ouvrir ♦ *vi* (*flower, eyes, door, debate*) s'ouvrir; (*store, bank, museum*) ouvrir; (*book etc: commence*) commencer, débuter; **in the ~** (*air*) en plein air; **the ~ sea** le large; **~ ground** (*among trees*) clairière *f*; (*waste ground*) terrain *m* vague; **to have an ~ mind (on sth)** avoir l'esprit ouvert (sur qch).

  open on to *vt fus* (*subj: room, door*) donner sur.

  open out *vt* ouvrir ♦ *vi* s'ouvrir.

  open up *vt* ouvrir; (*blocked road*) dégager ♦ *vi* s'ouvrir.

open-air [ō'pənär'] *a* en plein air.

open-and-shut [ō'pənənshut'] *a*: **~ case** cas *m* limpide.

open day *n* (*Brit*) journée *f* portes ouvertes.

open-ended [ō'pənen'did] *a* (*fig*) non limité(e).

opener [ō'pənûr] *n* (*also*: **can ~, tin ~**) ouvre-boîtes *m*.

open-faced sandwich [ō'pənfāst' sand'wich] *n* (*US*) canapé *m*.

open-heart surgery [ō'pənhârt sûr'jûrē] *n* chirurgie *f* à cœur ouvert.

open house *n*: **to keep ~** tenir table ouverte.

opening [ō'pəning] *n* ouverture *f*; (*opportunity*) occasion *f*; débouché *m*; (*job*) poste vacant.

opening night *n* (*THEATER*) première *f*.

openly [ō'pənlē] *ad* ouvertement.

open-minded [ō'pənmīn'did] *a* à l'esprit ouvert.

open-necked [ō'pənnekt'] *a* à col ouvert.

openness [ō'pənnis] *n* (*frankness*) franchise *f*.

open-plan [ō'pənplan'] *a* sans cloisons.

open sandwich *n* (*Brit*) canapé *m*.

open shop *n entreprise qui admet les travailleurs non syndiqués*.

Open University *n* (*Brit*) *cours universitaires par correspondance*.

opera [âp'rə] *n* opéra *m*.

opera glasses *npl* jumelles *fpl* de théâtre.

opera house *n* opéra *m*.

opera singer *n* chanteur/euse d'opéra.

operate [âp'ərāt] *vt* (*machine*) faire marcher, faire fonctionner; (*system*) pratiquer ♦ *vi* fonctionner; (*drug*) faire effet; **to ~ on sb (for)** (*MED*) opérer qn (de).

operatic [âpərat'ik] *a* d'opéra.

operating [âp'ərāting] *a* (*COMM: costs, profit*) d'exploitation; (*MED*): **~ table** table *f* d'opération; **~ room** (*US*) *or* **theatre** (*Brit*) salle *f* d'opération.

operating system *n* (*COMPUT*) système *m* d'exploitation.

operation [âpərā'shən] *n* opération *f*; (*of machine*) fonctionnement *m*; **to have an ~ (for)** se faire opérer (de); **to be in ~** (*machine*) être en service; (*system*) être en vigueur.

operational [âpərā'shənəl] *a* opérationnel(le); (*ready for use or action*) en état de marche; **when the service is fully ~** lorsque le service fonctionnera pleinement.

operative [âp'ûrətiv] *a* (*measure*) en vigueur ♦ *n* (*in factory*) ouvrier/ière; **the ~ word** le mot clef.

operator [âp'ərātûr] *n* (*of machine*) opérateur/trice; (*TEL*) téléphoniste *m/f*.

operetta [âpəret'ə] *n* opérette *f*.

ophthalmologist [âfthalmâl'əjist] *n* ophtalmologiste *m/f*, ophtalmologue *m/f*.

opinion [əpin'yən] *n* opinion *f*, avis *m*; **in my ~** à mon avis; **to seek a second ~** demander un deuxième avis.

opinionated [əpin'yənātid] *a* aux idées bien arrêtées.

opinion poll *n* sondage *m* d'opinion.

opium [ō'pēəm] *n* opium *m*.

opponent [əpō'nənt] *n* adversaire *m/f*.

opportune [âpûrtōōn'] *a* opportun(e).

opportunist [âpûrtōō'nist] *n* opportuniste *m/f*.

opportunity [âpûrtyōō'nitē] *n* occasion *f*; **to take the ~ to do** *or* **of doing** profiter de l'occasion pour faire.

oppose [əpōz'] *vt* s'opposer à; **~d to a** opposé(e) à; **as ~d to** par opposition à.

opposing [əpōz'ing] *a* (*side*) opposé(e).

opposite [âp'əzit] *a* opposé(e); (*house etc*) d'en face ♦ *ad* en face ♦ *prep* en face de ♦ *n* opposé *m*, contraire *m*; (*of word*) contraire; **"see ~ page"** ''voir ci-contre''.

opposite number *n* (*Brit*) homologue *m/f*.

opposite sex *n*: **the ~** l'autre sexe.

opposition [âpəzish'ən] *n* opposition *f*.

oppress [əpres'] *vt* opprimer.

oppression [əpresh'ən] *n* oppression *f*.

oppressive [əpres'iv] *a* oppressif(ive).

opprobrium [əprō'brēəm] *n* (*formal*) opprobre *m*.

opt [âpt] *vi*: **to ~ for** opter pour; **to ~ to do** choisir de faire; **to ~ out of** choisir de quitter.

optical [âp'tikəl] *a* optique; (*instrument*) d'optique.

optical character reader/recognition (OCR) *n* lecteur *m*/lecture *f* optique.

optical fiber *n* fibre *f* optique.

optician [âptish'ən] *n* opticien/ne.

optics [âp'tiks] *n* optique *f*.

optimism [âp'təmizəm] *n* optimisme *m*.

optimist [âp'təmist] *n* optimiste *m/f*.

optimistic [âptəmis'tik] *a* optimiste.

optimum [âp'təməm] *a* optimum.

option [âp'shən] *n* choix *m*, option *f*; (*SCOL*) matière *f* à option; (*COMM*) option; **~s** *npl* accessoires *mpl* en option, options; **to keep one's ~s open** (*fig*) ne pas s'engager; **I have no ~** je n'ai pas le choix.

optional [âp'shənəl] *a* facultatif(ive); (*COMM*) en option; **~ extras** (*Brit*) accessoires *mpl* en option, options *fpl*.

opulence [âp'yələns] *n* opulence *f*; abondance *f*.

opulent [âp'yələnt] *a* opulent(e); abondant(e).
OR *abbr* (*US MAIL*) = Oregon.
or [ôr] *cj* ou; (*with negative*): **he hasn't seen ~ heard anything** il n'a rien vu ni entendu; **~ else** sinon; ou bien, ou alors.
oracle [ôr'əkəl] *n* oracle *m*.
oral [ôr'əl] *a* oral(e) ♦ *n* oral *m*.
orange [ôr'inj] *n* (*fruit*) orange *f* ♦ *a* orange *inv*.
orangeade [ôrinjād'] *n* orangeade *f*.
orange juice *n* jus *m* d'orange.
oration [ôrā'shən] *n* discours solennel.
orator [ôr'ətûr] *n* orateur/trice.
oratorio [ôrətôr'ēō] *n* oratorio *m*.
orb [ôrb] *n* orbe *m*.
orbit [ôr'bit] *n* orbite *f* ♦ *vt* décrire une *or* des orbite(s) autour de; **to be in/go into ~ (around)** être/entrer en orbite (autour de).
orchard [ôr'chûrd] *n* verger *m*; **apple ~** verger de pommiers.
orchestra [ôr'kistrə] *n* orchestre *m*; (*US: THEATER*) (fauteuils *mpl* d')orchestre.
orchestral [ôrkes'trəl] *a* orchestral(e); (*concert*) symphonique.
orchestrate [ôr'kistrāt] *vt* (*MUS*, *fig*) orchestrer.
orchid [ôr'kid] *n* orchidée *f*.
ordain [ôrdān'] *vt* (*REL*) ordonner; (*decide*) décréter.
ordeal [ôrdēl'] *n* épreuve *f*.
order [ôr'dûr] *n* ordre *m*; (*COMM*) commande *f* ♦ *vt* ordonner; (*COMM*) commander; **in ~** en ordre; (*of document*) en règle; **out of ~** hors service; (*telephone*) en dérangement; **a machine in working ~** une machine en état de marche; **in ~ of size** par ordre de grandeur; **in ~ to do/that** pour faire/que + *sub*; **to ~ sb to do** ordonner à qn de faire; **to place an ~ for sth with sb** commander qch auprès de qn, passer commande de qch à qn; **to be on ~** être en commande; **made to ~** fait sur commande; **to be under ~s to do sth** avoir ordre de faire qch; **a point of ~** un point de procédure; **to the ~ of** (*BANKING*) à l'ordre de.
order book *n* carnet *m* de commandes.
order form *n* bon *m* de commande.
orderly [ôr'dûrlē] *n* (*MIL*) ordonnance *f* ♦ *a* (*room*) en ordre; (*mind*) méthodique; (*person*) qui a de l'ordre.
order number *n* numéro *m* de commande.
ordinal [ôr'dənəl] *a* (*number*) ordinal(e).
ordinary [ôr'dənärē] *a* ordinaire, normal(e); (*pej*) ordinaire, quelconque; **out of the ~** exceptionnel(le).
ordinary seaman *n* (*Brit*) matelot *m*.
ordinary shares *npl* (*Brit*) actions *fpl* ordinaires.
ordination [ôrdənā'shən] *n* ordination *f*.
ordnance [ôrd'nəns] *n* (*MIL*: *unit*) service *m* du matériel.
Ore. *abbr* (*US*) = Oregon.
ore [ôr] *n* minerai *m*.
Oreg. *abbr* (*US*) = Oregon.
organ [ôr'gən] *n* organe *m*; (*MUS*) orgue *m*, orgues *fpl*.
organic [ôrgan'ik] *a* organique; (*crops etc*) biologique, naturel(le).
organism [ôr'gənizəm] *n* organisme *m*.

organist [ôr'gənist] *n* organiste *m/f*.
organization [ôrgənəzā'shən] *n* organisation *f*.
organization chart *n* organigramme *m*.
organize [ôr'gənīz] *vt* organiser; **to get ~d** s'organiser.
organized labor *n* main-d'œuvre syndiquée.
organizer [ôr'gənīzûr] *n* organisateur/trice.
orgasm [ôr'gazəm] *n* orgasme *m*.
orgy [ôr'jē] *n* orgie *f*.
Orient [ôr'ēənt] *n*: **the ~** l'Orient *m*.
oriental [ôrēen'təl] *a* oriental(e) ♦ *n* Oriental/e.
orientate [ôr'ēentāt] *vt* orienter.
orifice [ôr'əfis] *n* orifice *m*.
origin [ôr'ijin] *n* origine *f*; **country of ~** pays *m* d'origine.
original [ərij'ənəl] *a* original(e); (*earliest*) originel(le) ♦ *n* original *m*.
originality [ərijənal'itē] *n* originalité *f*.
originally [ərij'ənəlē] *ad* (*at first*) à l'origine.
originate [ərij'ənāt] *vi*: **to ~ from** être originaire de; (*suggestion*) provenir de; **to ~ in** prendre naissance dans; avoir son origine dans.
originator [ərij'inātûr] *n* auteur *m*.
ornament [ôr'nəmənt] *n* ornement *m*; (*trinket*) bibelot *m*.
ornamental [ôrnəmen'təl] *a* décoratif(ive); (*garden*) d'agrément.
ornamentation [ôrnəməntā'shən] *n* ornementation *f*.
ornate [ôrnāt'] *a* très orné(e).
ornithologist [ôrnəthâl'əjist] *n* ornithologue *m/f*.
ornithology [ôrnəthâl'əjē] *n* ornithologie *f*.
orphan [ôr'fən] *n* orphelin/e ♦ *vt*: **to be ~ed** devenir orphelin.
orphanage [ôr'fənij] *n* orphelinat *m*.
orthodox [ôr'thədâks] *a* orthodoxe.
orthopedic, (*Brit*) **orthopaedic** [ôrthəpē'dik] *a* orthopédique.
O/S *abbr* = **out of stock**.
oscillate [âs'əlāt] *vi* osciller.
OSHA *n abbr* (*US*: = *Occupational Safety and Health Administration*) office de l'hygiène et de la sécurité au travail.
Oslo [âz'lō] *n* Oslo.
ostensible [âsten'səbəl] *a* prétendu(e); apparent(e).
ostensibly [âsten'səblē] *ad* en apparence.
ostentation [âstentā'shən] *n* ostentation *f*.
ostentatious [âstentā'shəs] *a* prétentieux(euse); ostentatoire.
osteopath [âs'tēəpath] *n* ostéopathe *m/f*.
ostracize [âs'trəsīz] *vt* frapper d'ostracisme.
ostrich [ôs'trich] *n* autruche *f*.
OT *n abbr* (= *Old Testament*) AT *m*.
OTB *n abbr* (*US*: = *off-track betting*) paris pris en dehors du champ de course.
O.T.E. *abbr* (*Brit*: = *on-target earnings*) primes sur objectifs inclus.
other [uth'ûr] *a* autre ♦ *pronoun*: **the ~ (one)** l'autre; **~s** (**~ people**) d'autres; **some ~ people have still to arrive** on attend encore quelques personnes; **the ~ day** l'autre jour; **~ than** autrement que; à part; **some actor or ~** (*Brit*) un certain acteur, je ne sais quel acteur; **somebody or ~** quelqu'un; **the car was none ~ than John's** la voiture n'était autre que celle de John.

otherwise [uth'ûrwīz] *ad*, *cj* autrement; **an ~ good piece of work** par ailleurs, un beau travail.

OTT *abbr* (*col*) = **over the top**; *see* **top**.

otter [ât'ûr] *n* loutre *f*.

ouch [ouch] *excl* aïe!

ought, *pt* **ought** [ôt] *auxiliary vb*: **I ~ to do it** je devrais le faire, il faudrait que je le fasse; **this ~ to have been corrected** cela aurait dû être corrigé; **he ~ to win** il devrait gagner; **you ~ to go and see it** vous devriez aller le voir.

ounce [ouns] *n* once *f* (= *28.35g; 16 in a pound*).

our [ou'ûr] *a* notre, nos *pl*.

ours [ou'ûrz] *pronoun* le(la) nôtre, les nôtres.

ourselves [ouûrselvz'] *pronoun pl* (*reflexive*, *after preposition*) nous; (*emphatic*) nous-mêmes; **we did it (all) by ~** nous avons fait ça tout seuls.

oust [oust] *vt* évincer.

out [out] *ad* dehors; (*published, not at home etc*) sorti(e); (*light, fire*) éteint(e); (*on strike*) en grève; **~ here** ici; **~ there** là-bas; **he's ~** (*absent*) il est sorti; (*unconscious*) il est sans connaissance; **to be ~ in one's calculations** (*Brit*) s'être trompé dans ses calculs; **to run/back etc ~** sortir en courant/en reculant *etc*; **to be ~ and around or** (*Brit*) **about again** être de nouveau sur pied; **before the week was ~** avant la fin de la semaine; **the journey ~** l'aller *m*; **the boat was 10 km ~** le bateau était à 10 km du rivage; **~ loud** *ad* à haute voix; **~ of** *prep* (*outside*) en dehors de; (*because of: anger etc*) par; (*from among*): **~ of 10** sur 10; (*without*): **~ of gas** sans essence, à court d'essence; **made ~ of wood** en *or* de bois; **~ of order** (*machine*) en panne; (*TEL: line*) en dérangement; **~ of stock** (*COMM: article*) épuisé(e); (: *store*) en rupture de stock.

outage [ou'tij] *n* (*esp US: power failure*) panne *f or* coupure *f* de courant.

out-and-out [out'əndout'] *a* véritable.

outback [out'bak] *n* campagne isolée; (*in Australia*) intérieur *m*.

outbid [outbid'] *vt* surenchérir.

outboard [out'bôrd] *n*: **~ (motor)** (moteur *m*) hors-bord *m*.

outbreak [out'brāk] *n* éruption *f*, explosion *f*; (*start*) déclenchement *m*.

outbuilding [out'bilding] *n* dépendance *f*.

outburst [out'bûrst] *n* explosion *f*, accès *m*.

outcast [out'kast] *n* exilé/e; (*socially*) paria *m*.

outclass [outklas'] *vt* surclasser.

outcome [out'kum] *n* issue *f*, résultat *m*.

outcrop [out'krâp] *n* affleurement *m*.

outcry [out'krī] *n* tollé (général).

outdated [outdā'tid] *a* démodé(e).

outdistance [outdis'təns] *vt* distancer.

outdo [outdōō'] *vt irg* surpasser; **to ~ o.s.** se surpasser.

outdoor [out'dôr] *a* de *or* en plein air.

outdoors [outdôrz'] *ad* dehors; au grand air.

outer [ou'tûr] *a* extérieur(e); **~ suburbs** grande banlieue.

outer space *n* espace *m* cosmique.

outfit [out'fit] *n* équipement *m*; (*clothes*) tenue *f*; (*col: COMM*) organisation *f*, boîte *f*.

outfitter [out'fitûr] *n*: "**~'s**" "confection pour hommes".

outgoing [out'gōing] *a* (*president, tenant*) sortant(e); (*character*) ouvert(e), extraverti(e).

outgoings [out'gōingz] *npl* (*Brit: expenses*) dépenses *fpl*.

outgrow [outgrō'] *vt irg* (*clothes*) devenir trop grand(e) pour.

outhouse [out'hous] *n* (*US*) cabinets extérieurs; (*Brit*) appentis *m*, remise *f*.

outing [ou'ting] *n* sortie *f*; excursion *f*.

outlandish [outlan'dish] *a* étrange.

outlast [outlast] *vt* survivre à.

outlaw [out'lô] *n* hors-la-loi *m inv* ♦ *vt* (*person*) mettre hors la loi; (*practice*) proscrire.

outlay [out'lā] *n* dépenses *fpl*; (*investment*) mise *f* de fonds.

outlet [out'let] *n* (*for liquid etc*) issue *f*, sortie *f*; (*for emotion*) exutoire *m*; (*for goods*) débouché *m*; (*also*: **retail ~**) point *m* de vente; (*US ELEC*) prise *f* de courant.

outline [out'lin] *n* (*shape*) contour *m*; (*summary*) esquisse *f*, grandes lignes.

outlive [outliv'] *vt* survivre à.

outlook [out'lōōk] *n* perspective *f*.

outlying [out'līing] *a* écarté(e).

outmaneuver, (*Brit*) **outmanoeuvre** [outmənōō'vûr] *vt* (*rival etc*) avoir au tournant.

outmoded [outmō'did] *a* démodé(e); dépassé(e).

outnumber [outnum'bûr] *vt* surpasser en nombre.

out-of-date [outəvdāt'] *a* (*passport, ticket*) périmé(e); (*theory, idea*) dépassé(e); (*custom*) désuet(ète); (*clothes*) démodé(e).

out-of-the-way [outəvthəwā'] *a* loin de tout; (*fig*) insolite.

outpatient [out'pāshənt] *n* malade *m/f* en consultation externe.

outpost [out'pōst] *n* avant-poste *m*.

output [out'pōot] *n* rendement *m*, production *f* ♦ *vt* (*COMPUT*) sortir.

outrage [out'rāj] *n* atrocité *f*, acte *m* de violence; scandale *m* ♦ *vt* outrager.

outrageous [outrā'jəs] *a* atroce; scandaleux(euse).

outrider [out'rīdûr] *n* (*on motorcycle*) motard *m*.

outright *ad* [outrīt'] complètement; catégoriquement; carrément; sur le coup ♦ *a* [out'rīt] complet(ète); catégorique.

outrun [outrun'] *vt irg* dépasser.

outset [out'set] *n* début *m*.

outshine [outshīn'] *vt irg* (*fig*) éclipser.

outside [out'sīd'] *n* extérieur *m* ♦ *a* extérieur(e); (*remote, unlikely*): **an ~ chance** une (très) faible chance ♦ *ad* (au) dehors, à l'extérieur ♦ *prep* hors de, à l'extérieur de; **at the ~** (*fig*) au plus *or* maximum; **~ left/right** *n* (*SOCCER*) ailier gauche/droit.

outside broadcast *n* (*RADIO, TV*) reportage *m*.

outside line *n* (*TEL*) ligne extérieure.

outsider [outsī'dûr] *n* (*in race etc*) outsider *m*; (*stranger*) étranger/ère.

outsize [out'sīz] *a* (*Brit*) énorme; (*clothes*)

grande taille *inv*.

outskirts [out'skûrts] *npl* faubourgs *mpl*.

outsmart [outsmárt'] *vt* se montrer plus malin(igne) *or* futé(e) que.

outspoken [out'spō'kən] *a* très franc(franche).

outspread [out'spred] *a* (*wings*) déployé(e).

outstanding [outstan'ding] *a* remarquable, exceptionnel(le); (*unfinished*) en suspens; en souffrance; non réglé(e); **your account is still ~** vous n'avez pas encore tout remboursé.

outstretched [outstrecht'] *a* (*hand*) tendu(e); (*body*) étendu(e).

outstrip [outstrip'] *vt* (*also fig*) dépasser.

out-tray [out'trā] *n* courrier *m* 'départ'.

outvote [outvōt'] *vt*: **to ~ sb (by)** mettre qn en minorité (par); **to ~ sth (by)** rejeter qch (par).

outward [out'wûrd] *a* (*sign, appearances*) extérieur(e); (*journey*) (d')aller.

outwardly [out'wûrdlē] *ad* extérieurement; en apparence.

outweigh [outwā'] *vt* l'emporter sur.

outwit [outwit'] *vt* se montrer plus malin que.

oval [ō'vəl] *a*, *n* ovale (*m*).

ovary [ō'vûrē] *n* ovaire *m*.

ovation [ōvā'shən] *n* ovation *f*.

oven [uv'ən] *n* four *m*.

ovenproof [uv'ənprōōf] *a* allant au four.

oven-ready [uv'ənred'ē] *a* prêt(e) à cuire.

ovenware [uv'ənwär] *n* plats *mpl* allant au four.

over [ō'vûr] *ad* (par-)dessus; (*excessively*) trop ♦ *a* (*or ad*) (*finished*) fini(e), terminé(e); (*too much*) en plus ♦ *prep* sur; pardessus; (*above*) au-dessus de; (*on the other side of*) de l'autre côté de; (*more than*) plus de; (*during*) pendant; **~ here** ici; **~ there** là-bas; **all ~** (*everywhere*) partout; (*finished*) fini(e); **~ and ~ (again)** à plusieurs reprises; **~ and above** en plus de; **to ask sb ~** inviter qn (à passer); **to go ~ to sb's** passer chez qn; **the world ~** dans le monde entier.

over... [ō'vûr] *prefix*: **~abundant** surabondant(e).

overact [ōvûrakt'] *vi* (*THEATER*) outrer son rôle.

overall *a*, *n* [ō'vûrôl] *a* (*length*) total(e); (*study*) d'ensemble ♦ *n* (*Brit*) blouse *f* ♦ *ad* [ōvûrôl'] dans l'ensemble, en général; **~s** *npl* bleus *mpl* (de travail).

overanxious [ōvûrangk'shəs] *a* trop anxieux(euse).

overawe [ōvûrô'] *vt* impressionner.

overbalance [ōvûrbal'əns] *vi* basculer.

overbearing [ōvûrbär'ing] *a* impérieux(euse), autoritaire.

overboard [ō'vûrbôrd] *ad* (*NAUT*) par-dessus bord; **to go ~ for sth** (*fig*) s'emballer (pour qch).

overbook [ō'vûrbōōk'] *vi* faire du surbooking.

overcapitalize [ōvûrkap'itəlīz] *vt* surcapitaliser.

overcast [ō'vûrkast] *a* couvert(e).

overcharge [ōvûrchárj'] *vt*: **to ~ sb for sth** faire payer qch trop cher à qn.

overcoat [ō'vûrkōt] *n* pardessus *m*.

overcome [ōvûrkum'] *vt irg* triompher de;

surmonter ♦ *a* (*emotionally*) bouleversé(e); **~ with grief** accablé(e) de douleur.

overconfident [ōvûrkán'fidənt] *a* trop sûr(e) de soi.

overcrowded [ōvûrkrou'did] *a* bondé(e).

overcrowding [ōvûrkrou'ding] *n* surpeuplement *m*; (*in bus*) encombrement *m*.

overdo [ōvûrdōō'] *vt irg* exagérer; (*overcook*) trop cuire; **to ~ it, to ~ things** (*work too hard*) en faire trop, se surmener.

overdose [ō'vûrdōs] *n* dose excessive.

overdraft [ō'vûrdraft] *n* découvert *m*.

overdrawn [ōvûrdrôn'] *a* (*account*) à découvert.

overdrive [ō'vûrdrīv] *n* (*AUT*) (vitesse) surmultipliée *f*.

overdue [ōvûrdōō'] *a* en retard; (*bill*) impayé(e); (*recognition*) tardif(ive); **that change was long ~** ce changement n'avait que trop tardé.

overestimate [ōvûres'təmāt] *vt* surestimer.

overexcited [ōvûriksī'tid] *a* surexcité(e).

overexertion [ōvûrigzûr'shən] *n* surmenage *m* (physique).

overexpose [ōvûrikspōz'] *vt* (*PHOT*) surexposer.

overflow *vi* [ōvûrflō'] déborder ♦ *n* [ō'vûrflō] trop-plein *m*; (*also:* **~ pipe**) tuyau *m* d'écoulement, trop-plein *m*.

overfly [ōvûrflī'] *vt irg* survoler.

overgenerous [ōvûrjen'ûrəs] *a* (*person*) prodigue; (*offer*) excessif(ive).

overgrown [ōvûrgrōn'] *a* (*garden*) envahi(e) par la végétation; **he's just an ~ schoolboy** (*fig*) c'est un écolier attardé.

overhang [ōvûrhang'] *vt irg* surplomber ♦ *vi* faire saillie.

overhaul *vt* [ōvûrhôl'] réviser ♦ *n* [ō'vûrhôl] révision *f*.

overhead *ad* [ō'vûrhed'] au-dessus ♦ [ō'vûrhed] *a* aérien(ne); (*lighting*) vertical(e) ♦ *n* (*US*) frais généraux.

overheads [ō'vûrhedz] *npl* (*Brit*) frais généraux.

overhear [ōvûrhiûr'] *vt irg* entendre (par hasard).

overheat [ōvûrhēt'] *vi* devenir surchauffé(e); (*engine*) chauffer.

overjoyed [ōvûrjoid'] *a* ravi(e), enchanté(e).

overkill [ō'vûrkil] *n* (*fig*): **it would be ~** ce serait de trop.

overland [ō'vûrland] *a*, *ad* par voie de terre.

overlap *vi* [ōvûrlap'] se chevaucher ♦ *n* [ō'vûrlap] chevauchement *m*.

overleaf [ō'vûrlēf] *ad* au verso.

overload [ō'vûrlōd] *vt* surcharger.

overlook [ō'vûrlōōk] *vt* (*have view of*) donner sur; (*miss*) oublier, négliger; (*forgive*) fermer les yeux sur.

overlord [ō'vûrlôrd] *n* chef *m* suprême.

overmanning [ōvûrman'ing] *n* sureffectif *m*, main-d'œuvre *f* pléthorique.

overnight *ad* [ōvûrnīt'] (*happen*) durant la nuit; (*fig*) soudain ♦ *a* [ō'vûrnīt] d'une (*or* de) nuit; soudain(e); **he stayed there ~** il y a passé la nuit; **if you travel ~ ...** si tu fais le voyage de nuit ...; **he'll be away ~** il ne rentrera pas ce soir.

overnight bag *n* sac *m* de voyage.

overpass [ō'vûrpas] *n* pont autoroutier; (*US*) passerelle *f*, pont *m*.

overpay [ōvûrpā'] *vt*: **to ~ sb by $50** donner à qn 50 dollars de trop.

overpower [ōvûrpou'ûr] *vt* vaincre; (*fig*) accabler.

overpowering [ōvûrpou'ûring] *a* irrésistible; (*heat, stench*) suffocant(e).

overproduction [ōvûrprəduk'shən] *n* surproduction *f*.

overrate [ōvərrāt'] *vt* surestimer.

overreact [ōvərēakt'] *vi* réagir de façon excessive.

override [ōvərīd'] *vt* (*irg*: *like* **ride**) (*order, objection*) passer outre à; (*decision*) annuler.

overriding [ōvərīd'ing] *a* prépondérant(e).

overrule [ōvərōōl'] *vt* (*decision*) annuler; (*claim*) rejeter.

overrun [ō'vərun] *vt irg* (*MIL*: *country etc*) occuper; (*time limit etc*) dépasser ♦ *vi irg* dépasser le temps imparti; **the town is ~ with tourists** la ville est envahie de touristes.

overseas *ad* [ō'vûrsēz'] outre-mer; (*abroad*) à l'étranger ♦ *a* [ō'vûrsēz] (*trade*) extérieur(e); (*visitor*) étranger(ère).

overseas cap *n* (*US*) calot *m*.

overseer [ō'vûrsēûr] *n* (*in factory*) contremaître *m*.

overshadow [ōvûrshad'ō] *vt* (*fig*) éclipser.

overshoot [ōvûrshōōt'] *vt irg* dépasser.

oversight [ō'vûrsīt] *n* omission *f*, oubli *m*; **due to an ~** par suite d'une inadvertance.

oversimplify [ōvûrsim'pləfī] *vt* simplifier à l'excès.

oversize [ō'vûrsīz] *a* (*US*) énorme; (*clothes*) grande taille *inv*.

oversleep [ōvûrslēp'] *vi irg* se réveiller (trop) tard.

overspend [ōvûrspend'] *vi irg* dépenser de trop; **we have overspent by $5,000** nous avons dépassé notre budget de 5000 dollars, nous avons dépensé 5000 dollars de trop.

overspill [ō'vûrspil] *n* excédent *m* de population.

overstaffed [ō'vûrstaft] *a*: **to be ~** avoir trop de personnel, être en surnombre.

overstate [ōvûrstāt'] *vt* exagérer.

overstatement [ōvûrstāt'mənt] *n* exagération *f*.

overstay [ōvûrstā'] *vt*: **to ~ one's welcome** abuser de l'hospitalité de son hôte.

overstep [ōvûrstep'] *vt*: **to ~ the mark** dépasser la mesure.

overstock [ōvûrstâk'] *vt* stocker en surabondance.

overstrike [ō'vûrstrīk] *n* (*on printer*) superposition *f*, double frappe *f* ♦ *vt irg* surimprimer.

overt [ōvûrt'] *a* non dissimulé(e).

overtake [ōvûrtāk'] *vt irg* dépasser; (*Brit AUT*) doubler.

overtaking [ōvûrtā'king] *n* (*Brit AUT*) dépassement *m*.

overtax [ōvûrtaks'] *vt* (*ECON*) surimposer; (*fig*: *strength, patience*) abuser de; **to ~ o.s.** se surmener.

overthrow [ōvûrthrō'] *vt irg* (*government*) renverser.

overtime [ō'vûrtīm] *n* heures *fpl* supplémentaires; (*US SPORT*) prolongation *f*; **to do** *or* **work ~** faire des heures supplémentaires.

overtime ban *n* refus *m* de faire des heures supplémentaires.

overtone [ō'vûrtōn] *n* (*also*: **~s**) note *f*, sous-entendus *mpl*.

overture [ō'vûrchûr] *n* (*MUS, fig*) ouverture *f*.

overturn [ōvûrtûrn'] *vt* renverser ♦ *vi* se retourner.

overweight [ōvûrwāt'] *a* (*person*) trop gros(se); (*baggage*) trop lourd(e).

overwhelm [ōvûrwelm'] *vt* accabler; submerger; écraser.

overwhelming [ōvûrwel'ming] *a* (*victory, defeat*) écrasant(e); (*desire*) irrésistible; **one's ~ impression is of heat** on a une impression dominante de chaleur.

overwhelmingly [ōvûrwel'minglē] *ad* (*vote*) en masse; (*win*) d'une manière écrasante.

overwork [ōvûrwûrk'] *n* surmenage *m* ♦ *vt* surmener ♦ *vi* se surmener.

overwrite [ōvərīt'] *vt* (*COMPUT*) écraser.

overwrought [ō'vərôt'] *a* excédé(e).

ovulation [âvyəlā'shən] *n* ovulation *f*.

owe [ō] *vt* devoir; **to ~ sb sth, to ~ sth to sb** devoir qch à qn.

owing to [ō'ing tōō] *prep* à cause de, en raison de.

owl [oul] *n* hibou *m*.

own [ōn] *vt* posséder ♦ *vi* (*Brit*): **to ~ to sth** reconnaître *or* avouer qch; **to ~ to having done sth** avouer avoir fait qch ♦ *a* propre; **a room of my ~** une chambre à moi, ma propre chambre; **can I have it for my (very) ~?** puis-je l'avoir pour moi (tout) seul?; **on one's ~** tout(e) seul(e); **to come into one's ~** trouver sa voie; trouver sa justification.

own up *vi* avouer.

own brand *n* (*COMM*) marque *f* de distributeur.

owner [ō'nûr] *n* propriétaire *m/f*.

owner-occupier [ō'nûr âk'yəpīûr] *n* (*Brit*) propriétaire occupant.

ownership [ō'nûrship] *n* possession *f*; **it's under new ~** (*store etc*) il y a eu un changement de propriétaire.

ox, *pl* **oxen** [âks, âk'sən] *n* bœuf *m*.

Oxfam [âks'fam] *n abbr* (*Brit*: = *Oxford Committee for Famine Relief*) association humanitaire.

oxide [âk'sīd] *n* oxyde *m*.

oxtail [âks'tāl] *n*: **~ soup** soupe *f* à la queue de bœuf.

oxyacetylene [âksēaset'əlin] *a* oxyacétylénique; **~ burner, ~ lamp** chalumeau *m* oxyacétylénique.

oxygen [âk'sijən] *n* oxygène *m*.

oxygen mask *n* masque *m* à oxygène.

oxygen tent *n* tente *f* à oxygène.

oyster [ois'tûr] *n* huître *f*.

oz. *abbr* = **ounce**.

ozone [ō'zōn] *n* ozone *m*.

P

P, p [pē] *n* (*letter*) P, p *m*; **P for Peter** P comme Pierre.

P [pē] *abbr.* = **president, prince.** ·

p [pē] *abbr* (= *page*) p; (*Brit*) = **penny, pence.**

PA *n abbr* = **personal assistant, public address system** ♦ *abbr* (*US* MAIL) = *Pennsylvania*.

pa [på] *n* (*col*) papa *m*.

p.a. *abbr* = *per annum*.

PAC *n abbr* (*US*) = *political action committee*.

pace [pās] *n* pas *m*; (*speed*) allure *f*; vitesse *f* ♦ *vi*: **to ~ up and down** faire les cent pas; **to keep ~ with** aller à la même vitesse que; (*events*) se tenir au courant de; **to set the ~** (*running*) donner l'allure; (*fig*) donner le ton; **to put sb through his ~s** (*fig*) mettre qn à l'épreuve.

pacemaker [pās'mākûr] *n* (MED) stimulateur *m* cardiaque.

pacific [pəsif'ik] *a* pacifique ♦ *n*: **the P~ (Ocean)** le Pacifique, l'océan *m* Pacifique.

pacification [pasəfəkā'shən] *n* pacification *f*.

pacifier [pas'əfiûr] *n* (*US*) tétine *f*.

pacifist [pas'əfist] *n* pacifiste *m/f*.

pacify [pas'əfi] *vt* pacifier; (*soothe*) calmer.

pack [pak] *n* paquet *m*; ballot *m*; (*of hounds*) meute *f*; (*of thieves, wolves etc*) bande *f*; (*of cards*) jeu *m* ♦ *vt* (*goods*) empaqueter, emballer; (*in suitcase etc*) emballer; (*box*) remplir; (*cram*) entasser; (*press down*) tasser; damer; (COMPUT) grouper, tasser ♦ *vi*: **to ~ (one's bags)** faire ses bagages; **to ~ into** (*room, stadium*) s'entasser dans; **to send sb ~ing** (*col*) envoyer promener qn.

pack in (*Brit col*) *vi* (*machine*) tomber en panne ♦ *vt* (*boyfriend*) plaquer.

pack off *vt* (*person*) envoyer (promener), expédier.

pack up *vt* (*belongings*) ranger; (*goods, presents*) empaqueter, emballer ♦ *vi* (*Brit col: machine*) tomber en panne; (: *person*) se tirer.

package [pak'ij] *n* paquet *m*; (*of goods*) emballage *m*, conditionnement *m*; (*also:* ~ **deal**) marché global; forfait *m*; (COMPUT) progiciel *m* ♦ *vt* empaqueter; (COMM: *goods*) conditionner.

package bomb *n* colis piégé.

package holiday *n* (*Brit*) vacances organisées.

package tour *n* voyage organisé.

packaging [pak'ijing] *n* conditionnement *m*.

packed [pakt] *a* (*crowded*) bondé(e); **~ lunch** (*Brit*) repas froid.

packer [pak'ûr] *n* (*person*) emballeur/euse; conditionneur/euse.

packet [pak'it] *n* paquet *m*.

packet switching *n* (COMPUT) commutation *f* de paquets.

pack ice [pak īs] *n* banquise *f*.

packing [pak'ing] *n* emballage *m*.

packing case *n* caisse *f* (d'emballage).

pact [pakt] *n* pacte *m*, traité *m*.

pad [pad] *n* bloc(-notes) *m*; (*for inking*) tampon encreur; (*col: apartment*) piaule *f* ♦ *vt* rembourrer ♦ *vi*: **to ~ in/around** *etc* entrer/aller et venir *etc* à pas feutrés.

padding [pad'ing] *n* rembourrage *m*; (*fig*) délayage *m*.

paddle [pad'əl] *n* (*oar*) pagaie *f*; (*US: for table tennis*) raquette *f* ♦ *vi* barboter, faire trempette ♦ *vt*: **to ~ a canoe** *etc* pagayer.

paddle steamer *n* bateau *m* à aubes.

paddling pool [pad'ling pōōl] *n* (*Brit*) petit bassin.

paddock [pad'ək] *n* enclos *m*; paddock *m*.

paddy [pad'ē] *n* (*also: US:* ~ **rice**) rizière *f*.

padlock [pad'låk] *n* cadenas *m* ♦ *vt* cadenasser.

paediatrics *etc* [pēdēat'riks] (*Brit*) = **pediatrics** *etc*.

pagan [pā'gən] *a*, *n* païen(ne).

page [pāj] *n* (*of book*) page *f*; (*also:* ~ **boy**) groom *m*, chasseur *m*; (*at wedding*) garçon *m* d'honneur ♦ *vt* (*in hotel etc*) (faire) appeler.

pageant [paj'ənt] *n* spectacle *m* historique; grande cérémonie.

pageantry [paj'əntrē] *n* apparat *m*, pompe *f*.

page break *n* fin *f* or saut *m* de page.

pager [pā'jûr] *n* système *m* de téléappel.

paginate [paj'ənāt] *vt* paginer.

pagination [pajənā'shən] *n* pagination *f*.

pagoda [pəgō'də] *n* pagode *f*.

paid [pād] *pt, pp of* **pay** ♦ *a* (*work, official*) rémunéré(e).

paid-up [pād'up] *a* (*member*) à jour de sa cotisation; (*shares*) libéré(e); **~ capital** capital versé.

pail [pāl] *n* seau *m*.

pain [pān] *n* douleur *f*; **to be in ~** souffrir, avoir mal; **to have a ~ in** avoir mal à *or* une douleur à *or* dans; **to take ~s to do** se donner du mal pour faire; **on ~ of death** sous peine de mort.

pained [pānd] *a* peiné(e), chagrin(e).

painful [pān'fəl] *a* douloureux(euse); (*difficult*) difficile, pénible.

painfully [pān'fəlē] *ad* (*fig: very*) terriblement.

painkiller [pān'kilûr] *n* calmant *m*.

painless [pān'lis] *a* indolore.

painstaking [pānz'tāking] *a* (*person*) soigneux(euse); (*work*) soigné(e).

paint [pānt] *n* peinture *f* ♦ *vt* peindre; (*fig*) dépeindre; **to ~ the door blue** peindre la porte en bleu; **to ~ in oils** faire de la peinture à l'huile.

paintbox [pānt'båks] *n* boîte *f* de couleurs.

paintbrush [pānt'brush] *n* pinceau *m*.

painter [pān'tûr] *n* peintre *m*.

painting [pān'ting] *n* peinture *f*; (*picture*) tableau *m*.

paint stripper *n* décapant *m*.

paintwork [pānt'wûrk] *n* (*Brit*) peintures *fpl*; (: *of car*) peinture *f*.

pair [pär] *n* (*of shoes, gloves etc*) paire *f*; (*couple*) couple *m*; (*twosome*) duo *m*; **~ of**

scissors (paire de) ciseaux *mpl*; ~ **of pants** pantalon *m*.

pair off *vi* se mettre par deux.

pajamas [pəjâm'əz] *npl* (*US*) pyjama *m*; **a pair of** ~ un pyjama.

Pakistan [pak'istan] *n* Pakistan *m*.

Pakistani [pak'əstan'ē] *a* pakistanais(e) ♦ *n* Pakistanais/e.

PAL [pal] *n abbr* (*TV*: *phase alternation line*) PAL *m*.

pal [pal] *n* (*col*) copain/copine.

palace [pal'is] *n* palais *m*.

palatable [pal'ətəbəl] *a* bon(bonne), agréable au goût.

palate [pal'it] *n* palais *m* (*ANAT*).

palatial [pəlā'shəl] *a* grandiose, magnifique.

palaver [pəlav'ûr] *n* palabres *fpl or mpl*; histoire(s) *f(pl)*.

pale [pāl] *a* pâle ♦ *vi* pâlir ♦ *n*: **to be beyond the** ~ être au ban de la société; **to grow** *or* **turn** ~ (*person*) pâlir; ~ **blue** *a* bleu pâle *inv*; **to** ~ **into insignificance (beside)** perdre beaucoup d'importance (par rapport à).

paleness [pāl'nis] *n* pâleur *f*.

Palestine [pal'istīn] *n* Palestine *f*.

Palestinian [palistin'ēən] *a* palestinien(ne) ♦ *n* Palestinien/ne.

palette [pal'it] *n* palette *f*.

paling [pā'ling] *n* (*stake*) palis *m*; (*fence*) palissade *f*.

palisade [palisād'] *n* palissade *f*.

pall [pól] *n* (*of smoke*) voile *m* ♦ *vi*: **to** ~ **(on)** devenir lassant (pour).

pallet [pal'it] *n* (*for goods*) palette *f*.

pallid [pal'id] *a* blême.

pallor [pal'ûr] *n* pâleur *f*.

pally [pal'ē] *a* (*col*) copain(copine).

palm [pâm] *n* (*ANAT*) paume *f*; (*also*: ~ **tree**) palmier *m*; (*leaf, symbol*) palme *f* ♦ *vt*: **to** ~ **sth off on sb** (*col*) refiler qch à qn.

palmist [pâm'ist] *n* chiromancien/ne.

Palm Sunday *n* le dimanche des Rameaux.

palpable [pal'pəbəl] *a* évident(e), manifeste.

palpitation [palpitā'shən] *n* palpitation *f*.

paltry [pól'trē] *a* dérisoire; piètre.

pamper [pam'pûr] *vt* gâter, dorloter.

pamphlet [pam'flit] *n* brochure *f*; (*political etc*) tract *m*.

pan [pan] *n* (*also*: **sauce**~) casserole *f*; (*also*: **frying** ~) poêle *f*; (*of lavatory*) cuvette *f* ♦ *vi* (*CINEMA*) faire un panoramique ♦ *vt* (*col*: *book, film*) éreinter; **to** ~ **for gold** laver du sable aurifère.

panacea [panəsē'ə] *n* panacée *f*.

Panama [pan'əmá] *n* Panama *m*.

Panama canal *n* canal *m* de Panama.

pancake [pan'kāk] *n* crêpe *f*.

Pancake Day *n* (*Brit*) mardi gras.

pancreas [pan'krēəs] *n* pancréas *m*.

panda [pan'də] *n* panda *m*.

pandemonium [pandəmō'nēəm] *n* tohu-bohu *m*.

pander [pan'dûr] *vi*: **to** ~ **to** flatter bassement; obéir servilement à.

pane [pān] *n* carreau *m* (de fenêtre).

panel [pan'əl] *n* (*of wood, cloth etc*) panneau *m*; (*RADIO, TV*) panel *m*, invités *mpl*; (*of experts*) table ronde, comité *m*.

panel game *n* jeu *m* (radiophonique/télévisé).

paneling, (*Brit*) **panelling** [pan'əling] *n* boiseries *fpl*.

panelist, (*Brit*) **panellist** [pan'əlist] *n* invité/e (*d'un panel*), membre d'un panel.

pang [pang] *n*: ~**s of remorse** pincements *mpl* de remords; ~**s of hunger/conscience** tiraillements *mpl* d'estomac/de la conscience.

panic [pan'ik] *n* panique *f*, affolement *m* ♦ *vi* s'affoler, paniquer.

panicky [pan'ikē] *a* (*person*) qui panique *or* s'affole facilement.

panic-stricken [pan'ikstrikən] *a* affolé(e).

pannier [pan'yûr] *n* (*on animal*) bât *m*; (*on bicycle*) sacoche *f*.

panorama [panəram'ə] *n* panorama *m*.

panoramic [panəram'ik] *a* panoramique.

pansy [pan'zē] *n* (*BOT*) pensée *f*; (*col*) tapette *f*, pédé *m*.

pant [pant] *vi* haleter.

panther [pan'thûr] *n* panthère *f*.

panties [pan'tēz] *npl* slip *m*, culotte *f*.

pantomime [pan'təmīm] *n* (*Brit*) spectacle *m* de Noël.

pantry [pan'trē] *n* garde-manger *m inv*; (*room*) office *f or m*.

pants [pants] *n* (*trousers*) pantalon *m*; (*Brit*: *woman's*) culotte *f*, slip *m*; (: *man's*) slip, caleçon *m*.

pants press *n* (*US*) presse-pantalon *m inv*.

pantsuit [pant'sōōt] *n* (*US*) tailleur-pantalon *m*.

pantyhose [pan'tēhōz] *n* (*US*) collant *m*.

papacy [pā'pəsē] *n* papauté *f*.

papal [pā'pəl] *a* papal(e), pontifical(e).

paper [pā'pûr] *n* papier *m*; (*also*: **wall**~) papier peint; (*also*: **news**~) journal *m*; (*study, article*) article *m*; (*exam*) épreuve écrite ♦ *a* en *or* de papier ♦ *vt* tapisser (de papier peint); **a piece of** ~ (*odd bit*) un bout de papier; (*sheet*) une feuille de papier; **to put sth down on** ~ mettre qch par écrit.

paper advance *n* (*on printer*) avance *f* (du) papier.

paperback [pā'pûrbak] *n* livre *m* de poche; livre broché *or* non relié ♦ *a*: ~ **edition** édition brochée.

paper bag *n* sac *m* en papier.

paperboy [pā'pûrboi] *n* (*selling*) vendeur *m* de journaux; (*delivering*) livreur *m* de journaux.

paper clip *n* trombone *m*.

paper handkerchief *n* (*Brit*) mouchoir *m* en papier.

paper mill *n* papeterie *f*.

paper money *n* papier-monnaie *m*.

paper profit *n* profit *m* théorique.

papers [pā'pûrz] *npl* (*also*: **identity** ~) papiers *mpl* (d'identité).

paperweight [pā'pûrwāt] *n* presse-papiers *m inv*.

paperwork [pā'pûrwûrk] *n* paperasserie *f*.

papier-mâché [pā'pûrməshā'] *n* papier mâché.

paprika [paprē'kə] *n* paprika *m*.

par [pâr] *n* pair *m*; (*GOLF*) normale *f* du parcours; **on a** ~ **with** à égalité avec, au même niveau que; **at** ~ au pair; **above/ below** ~ au-dessus/au-dessous du pair; **to feel below** *or* **under** *or* **not up to** ~ ne pas se sentir en forme.

parable [par'əbəl] *n* parabole *f* (*REL*).

parabola [pərab'ələ] *n* parabole *f* (*MATH*).
parachute [par'əshōot] *n* parachute *m* ♦ *vi* sauter en parachute.
parachute jump *n* saut *m* en parachute.
parachutist [par'əshōotist] *n* parachutiste *m/f*.
parade [pərād'] *n* défilé *m*; (*inspection*) revue *f*; (*street*) boulevard *m* ♦ *vt* (*fig*) faire étalage de ♦ *vi* défiler.
parade ground *n* terrain *m* de manœuvre.
paradise [par'ədīs] *n* paradis *m*.
paradox [par'ədâks] *n* paradoxe *m*.
paradoxical [parədâk'sikəl] *a* paradoxal(e).
paradoxically [parədâk'siklē] *ad* paradoxalement.
paraffin [par'əfin] *n* (*Brit*): ~ (**oil**) pétrole (lampant); **liquid** ~ huile *f* de paraffine.
paragon [par'əgân] *n* parangon *m*.
paragraph [par'əgraf] *n* paragraphe *m*; **to begin a new** ~ aller à la ligne.
Paraguay [par'əgwā] *n* Paraguay *m*.
Paraguayan [parəgwā'ən] *a* paraguayen(ne) ♦ *n* Paraguayen/ne.
parakeet [par'əkēt] *n* (*US*) perruche *f*.
parallel [par'əlel] *a*: ~ (**with** *or* **to**) parallèle (à); (*fig*) analogue (à) ♦ *n* (*line*) parallèle *f*; (*fig*, *GEO*) parallèle *m*.
paralysis, *pl* **paralyses** [pərəl'isis, -sēz] *n* paralysie *f*.
paralytic [parəlit'ik] *a* paralytique.
paralyze [par'əlīz] *vt* paralyser.
paramedic [parəmed'ik] *n* (*US*) ambulancier/ière; ~**s** *npl* (*US*) ≈ service *m* d'assistance médicale d'urgence (SAMU).
parameter [pəram'itûr] *n* paramètre *m*.
paramilitary [parəmil'itârē] *a* paramilitaire.
paramount [par'əmount] *a*: **of** ~ **importance** de la plus haute *or* grande importance.
paranoia [parənoi'ə] *n* paranoïa *f*.
paranoid [par'ənoid] *a* (*PSYCH*) paranoïaque; (*neurotic*) paranoïde.
paranormal [parənôr'məl] *a* paranormal(e).
paraphernalia [parəfûrnāl'yə] *n* attirail *m*, affaires *fpl*.
paraphrase [par'əfrāz] *vt* paraphraser.
paraplegic [parəplē'jik] *n* paraplégique *m/f*.
parapsychology [parəsīkâl'əjē] *n* parapsychologie *f*.
parasite [par'əsīt] *n* parasite *m*.
parasol [par'əsôl] *n* ombrelle *f*; (*at café etc*) parasol *m*.
paratrooper [par'ətrōopûr] *n* parachutiste *m* (*soldat*).
parcel [pâr'səl] *n* paquet *m*, colis *m* ♦ *vt* empaqueter.
parcel out *vt* répartir.
parcel bomb *n* (*Brit*) colis piégé.
parcel post *n* service *m* de colis postaux.
parch [pârch] *vt* dessécher.
parched [pârcht] *a* (*person*) assoiffé(e).
parchment [pârch'mənt] *n* parchemin *m*.
pardon [pâr'dən] *n* pardon *m*; grâce *f* ♦ *vt* pardonner à; (*LAW*) gracier; ~**!** pardon!; ~ **me!** excusez-moi!; **I beg your** ~! pardon!, je suis désolé!; ~ **me?**, (*Brit*) (**I beg your**) ~**?** pardon?
pare [pār] *vt* (*Brit*: *nails*) couper; (*fruit etc*) peler; (*fig*: *costs etc*) réduire.
parent [pär'ənt] *n* père *m* *or* mère *f*; ~**s** *npl* parents *mpl*.

parentage [pär'əntij] *n* naissance *f*; **of unknown** ~ de parents inconnus.
parental [pərɛn'təl] *a* parental(e), des parents.
parent company *n* société *f* mère.
parenthesis, *pl* **parentheses** [pərɛn'thəsis, -sēz] *n* parenthèse *f*; **in parentheses** entre parenthèses.
parenthood [pär'ənt·hōod] *n* paternité *f* *or* maternité *f*.
parenting [pär'ənting] *n* le métier de parent, le travail d'un parent.
Paris [par'is] *n* Paris.
parish [par'ish] *n* paroisse *f*; (*civil*) ≈ commune *f* ♦ *a* paroissial(e).
parish council *n* (*Brit*) ≈ conseil municipal.
parishioner [pərish'ənûr] *n* paroissien/ne.
Parisian [pərizh'ən] *a* parisien(ne) ♦ *n* Parisien/ne.
parity [par'itē] *n* parité *f*.
park [pârk] *n* parc *m*, jardin public ♦ *vt* garer ♦ *vi* se garer.
parka [pâr'kə] *n* parka *m*.
parking [pâr'king] *n* stationnement *m*; "**no** ~" "stationnement interdit".
parking lights *npl* feux *mpl* de stationnement.
parking lot *n* (*US*) parking *m*, parc *m* de stationnement.
parking meter *n* parcomètre *m*.
parking offence *n* (*Brit*) = **parking violation**.
parking place *n* place *f* de stationnement.
parking ticket *n* P.-V. *m*.
parking violation *n* (*US*) infraction *f* au stationnement.
parkway [pârk'wā] *n* (*US*) route *f* express (*en site vert ou aménagé*).
parlance [pâr'ləns] *n*: **in common/modern** ~ dans le langage courant/actuel.
parliament [pâr'ləmənt] *n* parlement *m*.
parliamentary [pârləmən'tûrē] *a* parlementaire.
parlor, (*Brit*) **parlour** [pâr'lûr] *n* salon *m*.
parlous [pâr'ləs] *a* (*formal*) précaire.
Parmesan [pâr'məzân] *n* (*also*: ~ **cheese**) Parmesan *m*.
parochial [pərō'kēəl] *a* paroissial(e); (*pej*) à l'esprit de clocher.
parody [par'ədē] *n* parodie *f*.
parole [pərōl'] *n*: **on** ~ en liberté conditionnelle.
paroxysm [par'əksizəm] *n* (*MED*, *of grief*) paroxysme *m*; (*of anger*) accès *m*.
parquet [pârkā'] *n*: ~ **floor(ing)** parquet *m*.
parrot [par'ət] *n* perroquet *m*.
parrot fashion *ad* comme un perroquet.
parry [par'ē] *vt* esquiver, parer à.
parsimonious [pârsəmō'nēəs] *a* parcimonieux(euse).
parsley [pârz'lē] *n* persil *m*.
parsnip [pârs'nip] *n* panais *m*.
parson [pâr'sən] *n* ecclésiastique *m*; (*Church of England*) pasteur *m*.
parsonage [pâr'sənij] *n* presbytère *m*.
part [pârt] *n* partie *f*; (*of machine*) pièce *f*; (*THEATER etc*) rôle *m*; (*MUS*) voix *f*; partie ♦ *a* partiel(le); (*US*: *in hair*) raie *f* ♦ *ad* = **partly** ♦ *vt* séparer ♦ *vi* (*people*) se séparer; (*roads*) se diviser; **to take** ~ **in** participer à,

prendre part à; **to take sb's** ~ prendre le parti de qn, prendre parti pour qn; **on his** ~ de sa part; **for my** ~ en ce qui me concerne; **for the most** ~ en grande partie; dans la plupart des cas; **for the better** ~ **of the day** pendant la plus grande partie de la journée; **to be** ~ **and parcel of** faire partie de; ~ **of speech** (*LING*) partie *f* du discours.
part with *vt fus* se séparer de; se défaire de.

partake [pârtāk'] *vi irg* (*formal*): **to** ~ **of sth** prendre part à qch, partager qch.

part exchange *n* (*Brit*): **in** ~ en reprise.

partial [pâr'shəl] *a* partiel(le); (*unjust*) partial(e); **to be** ~ **to** aimer, avoir un faible pour.

partially [pâr'shəlē] *ad* en partie, partiellement; partialement.

participant [pârtis'əpənt] *n:* ~ **(in)** participant/e (à).

participate [pârtis'əpāt] *vi:* **to** ~ **(in)** participer (à), prendre part (à).

participation [pârtisəpā'shən] *n* participation *f*.

participle [pâr'tisipəl] *n* participe *m*.

particle [pâr'tikəl] *n* particule *f*.

particleboard [pâr'tikəlbôrd] *n* (*US*) aggloméré *m*.

particular [pûrtik'yəlûr] *a* (*specific*) particulier(ière); (*special*) particulier, spécial(e); (*fussy*) difficile, exigeant(e); méticuleux(euse); ~**s** *npl* détails *mpl*; (*information*) renseignements *mpl*; **in** ~ surtout, en particulier.

particularly [pûrtik'yəlûrlē] *ad* particulièrement; (*in particular*) en particulier.

parting [pâr'ting] *n* séparation *f*; (*Brit: in hair*) raie *f* ♦ *a* d'adieu; **his** ~ **shot was ...** il lança en partant ....

partisan [pâr'tizən] *n* partisan/e ♦ *a* partisan(e); de parti.

partition [pârtish'ən] *n* (*POL*) partition *f*, division *f*; (*wall*) cloison *f*.

partly [pârt'lē] *ad* en partie, partiellement.

partner [pârt'nûr] *n* (*COMM*) associé/e; (*SPORT*) partenaire *m/f*; (*at dance*) cavalier/ière ♦ *vt* être l'associé *or* le partenaire *or* le cavalier de.

partnership [pârt'nûrship] *n* association *f*; **to go into** ~ **(with), form a** ~ **(with)** s'associer (avec).

part payment *n* acompte *m*.

partridge [pâr'trij] *n* perdrix *f*.

part-time [pârt'tīm'] *a, ad* à mi-temps, à temps partiel.

part-timer [pârttī'mûr] *n* (*also:* **part-time worker**) travailleur/euse à temps partiel.

party [pâr'tē] *n* (*POL*) parti *m*; (*team*) équipe *f*; groupe *m*; (*LAW*) partie *f*; (*celebration*) réception *f*; soirée *f*; réunion *f*, fête *f*; **dinner** ~ dîner *m*; **to give** *or* **throw a** ~ donner une réception; **we're having a** ~ **next Saturday** nous organisons une soirée *or* réunion entre amis samedi prochain; **it's for our son's birthday** ~ c'est pour la fête (*or* le goûter) d'anniversaire de notre garçon; **to be a** ~ **to a crime** être impliqué(e) dans un crime.

party line *n* (*POL*) ligne *f* politique; (*TEL*) ligne partagée.

par value *n* (*of share, bond*) valeur nominale.

pass [pas] *vt* (*time, object*) passer; (*place*) passer devant; (*car, friend*) croiser; (*exam*) être reçu(e) à, réussir; (*candidate*) admettre; (*overtake, surpass*) dépasser; (*approve*) approuver, accepter; (*law*) promulguer ♦ *vi* passer; (*SCOL*) être reçu(e) *or* admis(e), réussir ♦ *n* (*permit*) laissez-passer *m inv*; carte *f* d'accès *or* d'abonnement; (*in mountains*) col *m*; (*SPORT*) passe *f*; (*SCOL*): **to get a** ~ être reçu(e) (sans mention); **she could** ~ **for 25** on lui donnerait 25 ans; **to** ~ **sth through a ring** *etc* (faire) passer qch dans un anneau *etc*; **could you** ~ **the vegetables around?** pourriez-vous faire passer les légumes?; **to make a** ~ **at sb** (*col*) faire des avances à qn.
pass away *vi* mourir.
pass by *vi* passer ♦ *vt* négliger.
pass down *vt* (*customs, inheritance*) transmettre.
pass on *vi* (*die*) s'éteindre, décéder ♦ *vt* (*hand on*): **to** ~ **on (to)** transmettre (à); (: *illness*) passer (à); (: *price rises*) répercuter (sur).
pass out *vi* s'évanouir.
pass over *vt* (*ignore*) passer sous silence.
pass up *vt* (*opportunity*) laisser passer.

passable [pas'əbəl] *a* (*road*) praticable; (*work*) acceptable.

passage [pas'ij] *n* (*also:* ~**way**) couloir *m*; (*gen, in book*) passage *m*; (*by boat*) traversée *f*.

passbook [pas'bōōk] *n* livret *m*.

passenger [pas'injûr] *n* passager/ère.

passer-by [pasûrbi'] *n* passant/e.

passing [pas'ing] *a* (*fig*) passager(ère); **in** ~ en passant.

passing place *n* (*AUT*) aire *f* de croisement.

passion [pash'ən] *n* passion *f*; **to have a** ~ **for sth** avoir la passion de qch.

passionate [pash'ənit] *a* passionné(e).

passive [pas'iv] *a* (*also LING*) passif(ive).

passkey [pas'kē] *n* passe *m*.

Passover [pas'ōvûr] *n* Pâque juive.

passport [pas'pôrt] *n* passeport *m*.

passport control *n* contrôle *m* des passeports.

password [pas'wûrd] *n* mot *m* de passe.

past [past] *prep* (*further than*) au delà de, plus loin que; après; (*later than*) après ♦ *a* passé(e); (*president etc*) ancien(ne) ♦ *n* passé *m*; **quarter/half** ~ **four** quatre heures et quart/demie; **ten/twenty** ~ **four** quatre heures dix/vingt; **he's** ~ **forty** il a dépassé la quarantaine, il a plus de *or* passé quarante ans; **it's** ~ **midnight** il est plus de minuit, il est passé minuit; **for the** ~ **few/3 days** depuis quelques/3 jours; ces derniers/3 derniers jours; **to run** ~ passer en courant; **he ran** ~ **me** il m'a dépassé en courant; il a passé devant moi en courant; **in the** ~ (*gen*) dans le temps, autrefois; (*LING*) au passé; **I'm** ~ **caring** je ne m'en fais plus; **to be** ~ **one's prime** avoir passé l'âge.

pasta [pâs'tə] *n* pâtes *fpl*.

paste [pāst] *n* (*glue*) colle *f* (de pâte); (*jewelry*) strass *m*; (*CULIN*) pâté *m* (à tartiner); pâte *f* ♦ *vt* coller; **tomato** ~ concentré *m* de tomate, purée *f* de tomate.

pastel |pastel'| *a* pastel *inv.*

pasteurized |pas'chərīzd| *a* pasteurisé(e).

pastille |pastēl'| *n* pastille *f.*

pastime |pas'tīm| *n* passe-temps *m inv*, distraction *f.*

pastor |pas'tûr| *n* pasteur *m.*

pastoral |pas'tûrəl| *a* pastoral(e).

pastry |pās'trē| *n* pâte *f*; (*cake*) pâtisserie *f.*

pastry shop *n* (*US*) pâtisserie *f.*

pasture |pas'chûr| *n* pâturage *m.*

pasty *a* |pās'tē|' pâteux(euse); (*complexion*) terreux(euse) ♦ *n* |pas'tē| (*Brit*) petit pâté (en croûte).

pat |pat| *vt* donner une petite tape à ♦ *n*: **a ~ of butter** une noisette de beurre; **to give sb/ o.s. a ~ on the back** (*fig*) congratuler qn/se congratuler; **he has it down ~** il sait cela sur le bout des doigts.

patch |pach| *n* (*of material*) pièce *f*; (*spot*) tache *f*; (*of land*) parcelle *f* ♦ *vt* (*clothes*) rapiécer.

  patch up *vt* réparer.

patchwork |pach'wûrk| *n* patchwork *m.*

patchy |pach'ē| *a* inégal(e).

pate |pāt| *n*: **a bald ~** un crâne chauve *or* dégarni.

pâté |pâtā'| *n* pâté *m*, terrine *f.*

patent |pat'ənt| *n* brevet *m* (d'invention) ♦ *vt* faire breveter ♦ *a* patent(e), manifeste.

patent leather *n* cuir verni.

patently |pat'əntlē| *ad* manifestement.

patent medicine *n* spécialité *f* pharmaceutique.

patent office *n* bureau *m* des brevets.

paternal |pətûr'nəl| *a* paternel(le).

paternity |pətûr'nitē| *n* paternité *f.*

paternity suit *n* (*LAW*) action *f* en recherche de paternité.

path |path| *n* chemin *m*, sentier *m*; allée *f*; (*of planet*) course *f*; (*of missile*) trajectoire *f.*

pathetic |pəthet'ik| *a* (*pitiful*) pitoyable; (*very bad*) lamentable, minable; (*moving*) pathétique.

pathological |pathəlâj'ikəl| *a* pathologique.

pathologist |pəthál'əjist| *n* pathologiste *m/f.*

pathology |pəthál'əjē| *n* pathologie *f.*

pathos |pā'thâs| *n* pathétique *m.*

pathway |path'wā| *n* chemin *m*, sentier *m.*

patience |pā'shəns| *n* patience *f*; (*Brit CARDS*) réussite *f*; **to lose (one's) ~** perdre patience.

patient |pā'shənt| *n* patient/e; (*in hospital*) malade *m/f* ♦ *a* patient(e).

patiently |pā'shəntlē| *ad* patiemment.

patio |pat'ēō| *n* patio *m.*

patriot |pā'trēət| *n* patriote *m/f.*

patriotic |pātrēât'ik| *a* patriotique; (*person*) patriote.

patriotism |pā'trēətizəm| *n* patriotisme *m.*

patrol |pətrōl'| *n* patrouille *f* ♦ *vt* patrouiller dans; **to be on ~** être de patrouille.

patrol boat *n* patrouilleur *m.*

patrol car *n* voiture *f* de police.

patrolman |pətrōl'mən| *n* (*US*) agent *m* de police.

patron |pā'trən| *n* (*in shop*) client/e; (*of charity*) patron/ne; **~ of the arts** mécène *m.*

patronage |pā'trənij| *n* patronage *m*, appui *m.*

patronize |pā'trəniz| *vt* être (un) client *or* un habitué de; (*fig*) traiter avec condescen-

dance.

patronizing |pā'trənīzing| *a* condescendant(e).

patron saint *n* saint(e) patron/ne.

patter |pat'ûr| *n* crépitement *m*, tapotement *m*; (*sales talk*) boniment *m* ♦ *vi* crépiter, tapoter.

pattern |pat'ûrn| *n* modèle *m*; (*SEWING*) patron *m*; (*design*) motif *m*; (*sample*) échantillon *m*; **behavior ~** mode *m* de comportement.

patterned |pat'ûrnd| *a* à motifs.

paucity |pô'sitē| *n* pénurie *f*, carence *f.*

paunch |pônch| *n* gros ventre, bedaine *f.*

pauper |pô'pûr| *n* indigent/e; **~'s grave** *n* fosse commune.

pause |pôz| *n* pause *f*, arrêt *m*; (*MUS*) silence *m* ♦ *vi* faire une pause, s'arrêter; **to ~ for breath** reprendre son souffle; (*fig*) faire une pause.

pave |pāv| *vt* paver, daller; **to ~ the way for** ouvrir la voie à.

pavement |pāv'mənt| *n* (*US*) chaussée *f*; (*Brit*) trottoir *m.*

pavilion |pəvil'yən| *n* pavillon *m*; tente *f*; (*SPORT*) stand *m.*

paving |pā'ving| *n* pavage *m*, dallage *m.*

paving stone *n* pavé *m.*

paw |pô| *n* patte *f* ♦ *vt* donner un coup de patte à; (*subj: person: pej*) tripoter.

pawn |pôn| *n* gage *m*; (*CHESS, also fig*) pion *m* ♦ *vt* mettre en gage.

pawnbroker |pôn'brōkûr| *n* prêteur *m* sur gages.

pawnshop |pôn'shâp| *n* mont-de-piété *m.*

pay |pā| *n* salaire *m*; (*of manual worker*) paie *f* ♦ *vb* (*pt, pp* **paid** |pād|) *vt* payer; (*be profitable to: also fig*) rapporter à ♦ *vi* payer; (*be profitable*) être rentable; **how much did you ~ for it?** combien l'avez-vous payé?, vous l'avez payé combien?; **I paid $5 for that record** j'ai payé ce disque 5 dollars; **to ~ one's way** payer sa part; (*company*) couvrir ses frais; **to ~ dividends** (*fig*) porter ses fruits, s'avérer rentable; **it won't ~ you to do that** vous ne gagnerez rien à faire cela; **to ~ attention (to)** prêter attention (à).

pay back *vt* rembourser.

pay in *vt* verser.

pay off *vt* (*debts*) régler, acquitter; (*creditor, mortgage*) rembourser; (*workers*) licencier ♦ *vi* (*plan, patience*) se révéler payant(e); **to ~ sth off in installments** payer qch à tempérament.

pay out *vt* (*money*) payer, sortir de sa poche; (*rope*) laisser filer.

pay up *vt* (*debts*) régler; (*amount*) payer.

payable |pā'əbəl| *a* payable; **to make a check ~ to sb** établir un chèque à l'ordre de qn.

pay day *n* jour *m* de paie.

PAYE *n abbr* (*Brit*: = *pay as you earn*) système de retenue des impôts à la source.

payee |pāē'| *n* bénéficiaire *m/f.*

pay envelope *n* (*US*) (enveloppe *f* de) paie *f.*

paying |pā'ing| *a* payant(e); **~ guest** hôte payant.

payload |pā'lōd| *n* charge *f* utile.

payment |pā'mənt| *n* paiement *m*; (*of bill*) règlement *m*; (*of deposit, check*) versement *m*; **advance ~** (*part sum*) acompte *m*; (*total* *sum*) paiement anticipé; **deferred ~, ~ by installments** paiement par versements échelonnés; **monthly ~**, mensualité *f*; **in ~ for, in ~ of** en règlement de; **on ~ of $5** pour 5 dollars.

pay packet *n* (*Brit*) paie *f*.

pay phone *n* cabine *f* téléphonique, téléphone public.

payroll [pā'rōl] *n* registre *m* du personnel; **to be on a firm's ~** être employé par une entreprise.

pay slip *n* (*Brit*) bulletin *m* de paie, feuille *f* de paie.

pay station *n* (*US*) cabine *f* téléphonique.

PBS *n abbr* (*US*: = *Public Broadcasting Service*) *groupement d'aide à la réalisation d'émissions pour la TV publique.*

PBX *abbr* (= *private branch (telephone) exchange*) autocommutateur privé.

PC *n abbr* = **personal computer**; (*Brit*) = **police constable.**

pc *abbr* = **per cent, postcard.**

p/c *abbr* = **petty cash.**

PCB *n abbr* = **printed circuit board.**

PD *n abbr* (*US*) = **police department.**

pd *abbr* = **paid.**

PDT *abbr* (*US*: = *Pacific Daylight Time*) *heure d'été du Pacifique.*

PE *n abbr* (= *physical education*) EPS *f*.

pea [pē] *n* (petit) pois.

peace [pēs] *n* paix *f*; (*calm*) calme *m*, tranquillité *f*; **to be at ~ with sb/sth** être en paix avec qn/qch; **to keep the ~** (*subj: policeman*) assurer le maintien de l'ordre; (: *citizen*) ne pas troubler l'ordre.

peaceable [pē'səbəl] *a* paisible, pacifique.

Peace Corps *n* (*US*) ≈ coopération (civile).

peaceful [pēs'fəl] *a* paisible, calme.

peacekeeping [pēs'kēping] *n* maintien *m* de la paix.

peace offering *n* gage *m* de réconciliation; (*humorous*) gage de paix.

peach [pēch] *n* pêche *f*.

peacock [pē'kâk] *n* paon *m*.

peak [pēk] *n* (*mountain*) pic *m*, cime *f*; (*fig: highest level*) maximum *m*; (: *of career, fame*) apogée *m*.

peaked [pēkt] *a* (*US col*) fatigué(e).

peak-hour [pēk'ouûr] *a* (*traffic etc*) de pointe.

peak hours *npl* heures *fpl* d'affluence.

peak period *n* période *f* de pointe.

peaky [pē'kē] *a* (*Brit col*) = **peaked.**

peal [pēl] *n* (*of bells*) carillon *m*; **~s of laughter** éclats *mpl* de rire.

peanut [pē'nut] *n* arachide *f*, cacahuète *f*.

peanut butter *n* beurre *m* de cacahuète.

peanut oil *n* (*US*) huile *f* d'arachide.

pear [pär] *n* poire *f*.

pearl [pûrl] *n* perle *f*.

peasant [pez'ənt] *n* paysan/ne.

peat [pēt] *n* tourbe *f*.

pebble [peb'əl] *n* galet *m*, caillou *m*.

peck [pek] *vt* (*also: ~ at*) donner un coup de bec à; (*food*) picorer ♦ *n* coup *m* de bec; (*kiss*) bécot *m*.

pecking order [pek'ing ôrdûr] *n* ordre *m* hiérarchique.

peckish [pek'ish] *a* (*Brit col*): **I feel ~** je mangerais bien quelque chose, j'ai la dent.

peculiar [pikyōōl'yûr] *a* (*odd*) étrange, bizarre, curieux(euse); (*particular*) particulier(ière); **~ to** particulier à.

peculiarity [pikyōōlēar'itē] *n* bizarrerie *f*; particularité *f*.

pecuniary [pikyōō'nēārē] *a* pécuniaire.

pedal [ped'əl] *n* pédale *f* ♦ *vi* pédaler.

pedal bin *n* (*Brit*) poubelle *f* à pédale.

pedantic [pədan'tik] *a* pédant(e).

peddle [ped'əl] *vt* colporter; (*drugs*) faire le trafic de.

peddler [ped'lûr] *n* colporteur *m*; camelot *m*.

pedestal [ped'istəl] *n* piédestal *m*.

pedestrian [pədes'trēən] *n* piéton *m* ♦ *a* piétonnier(ière); (*fig*) prosaïque, terre à terre *inv*.

pedestrian crossing *n* passage clouté.

pedestrian precinct *n* (*Brit*) zone piétonne.

pediatrician [pēdēətrish'ən] *n* (*US*) pédiatre *m/f*.

pediatrics [pēdēat'riks] *n* (*US*) pédiatrie *f*.

pedigree [ped'əgrē] *n* ascendance *f*; (*of animal*) pedigree *m* ♦ *cpd* (*animal*) de race.

pedlar [ped'lûr] *n* = **peddler.**

pee [pē] *vi* (*col*) faire pipi, pisser.

peek [pēk] *vi* jeter un coup d'œil (furtif).

peel [pēl] *n* pelure *f*, épluchure *f*; (*of orange, lemon*) écorce *f* ♦ *vt* peler, éplucher ♦ *vi* (*paint etc*) s'écailler; (*wallpaper*) se décoller.

peel back *vt* décoller.

peeler [pē'lûr] *n* (*potato etc* ~) éplucheur *m*.

peelings [pē'lingz] *npl* pelures *fpl*, épluchures *fpl*.

peep [pēp] *n* (*Brit: look*) coup d'œil furtif; (*sound*) pépiement *m* ♦ *vi* (*Brit*) jeter un coup d'œil (furtif).

peep out *vi* (*Brit*) se montrer (furtivement).

peephole [pēp'hōl] *n* judas *m*.

peer [pēr] *vi*: **to ~ at** regarder attentivement, scruter ♦ *n* (*noble*) pair *m*; (*equal*) pair, égal/e.

peerage [pē'rij] *n* pairie *f*.

peerless [pēr'lis] *a* incomparable, sans égal.

peeved [pēvd] *a* irrité(e), ennuyé(e).

peevish [pē'vish] *a* grincheux(euse), maussade.

peg [peg] *n* cheville *f*; (*for coat etc*) patère *f*; (*Brit: also:* **clothes ~**) pince *f* à linge ♦ *vt* (*clothes*) accrocher; (*fig: prices, wages*) contrôler, stabiliser.

PEI *abbr* (*Canada*) = *Prince Edward Island.*

pejorative [pijór'ətiv] *a* péjoratif(ive).

Pekin [pē'kin] *n*, **Peking** [pēking'] *n* Pékin.

pekingese [pēkingēz'] *n* pékinois *m*.

pelican [pel'ikən] *n* pélican *m*.

pelican crossing *n* (*Brit AUT*) feu *m* à commande manuelle.

pellet [pel'it] *n* boulette *f*; (*of lead*) plomb *m*.

pell-mell [pel'mel'] *ad* pêle-mêle.

pelmet [pel'mit] *n* cantonnière *f*; lambrequin *m*.

pelt [pelt] *vt*: **to ~ sb (with)** bombarder qn (de) ♦ *vi* (*rain*) tomber à seaux ♦ *n* peau *f*.

pelvis [pel'vis] *n* bassin *m*.

pen [pen] *n* (*for writing*) stylo *m*; (*for sheep*) parc *m*; (*US col: prison*) taule *f*; **to put ~ to paper** prendre la plume.

penal [pē'nəl] *a* pénal(e).

penalize [pē'nəlīz] *vt* pénaliser; *(fig)* désavantager.

penal servitude [pē'nəl sûr'vətōōd] *n* travaux forcés.

penalty [pen'əltē] *n* pénalité *f;* sanction *f; (fine)* amende *f; (SPORT)* pénalisation *f; (SOCCER: also:* ~ **kick**) penalty *m.*

penalty clause *n* clause pénale.

penalty kick *n (SOCCER)* penalty *m.*

penance [pen'əns] *n* pénitence *f.*

pence [pens] *npl (Brit)* = **penny.**

penchant [pen'chənt] *n* penchant *m.*

pencil [pen'səl] *n* crayon *m* ♦ *vt:* **to** ~ **sth in** noter qch provisoirement.

pencil case *n* trousse *f* (d'écolier).

pencil sharpener *n* taille-crayon(s) *m inv.*

pendant [pen'dənt] *n* pendentif *m.*

pending [pen'ding] *prep* en attendant ♦ *a* en suspens.

pendulum [pen'jələm] *n* pendule *m; (of clock)* balancier *m.*

penetrate [pen'itrāt] *vt* pénétrer dans; pénétrer.

penetrating [pen'itrāting] *a* pénétrant(e).

penetration [penitrā'shən] *n* pénétration *f.*

pen friend *n* correspondant/e.

penguin [peng'gwin] *n* pingouin *m.*

penicillin [penisil'in] *n* pénicilline *f.*

peninsula [pənin'sələ] *n* péninsule *f.*

penis [pē'nis] *n* pénis *m,* verge *f.*

penitence [pen'itəns] *n* repentir *m.*

penitent [pen'itənt] *a* repentant(e).

penitentiary [peniten'chûrē] *n (US)* prison *f.*

penknife [pen'nīf] *n* canif *m.*

Penn., Penna. *abbr (US)* = *Pennsylvania.*

pen name [pen' nām] *n* nom *m* de plume, pseudonyme *m.*

pennant [pen'ənt] *n* flamme *f,* banderole *f.*

penniless [pen'ēlis] *a* sans le sou.

Pennines [pen'īnz] *npl* Pennines *fpl.*

penny, *pl* **pennies** *or* **pence** [pen'ē, pen'ēz, pens] *n (Brit)* penny *m (pl* pennies) *(new: 100 in a pound; old: 12 in a shilling; on tend à employer 'pennies' ou 'two-pence piece' etc pour les pièces, 'pence' pour la valeur); (US)* = **cent.**

pen pal *n* correspondant/e.

pension [pen'chən] *n* retraite *f; (MIL)* pension *f.*

 pension off *vt* mettre à la retraite.

pensionable [pen'chənəbəl] *a* qui a droit à une retraite.

pensioner [pen'chənûr] *n (Brit)* retraité/e.

pension fund *n* caisse *f* de retraite.

pensive [pen'siv] *a* pensif(ive).

pentagon [pen'təgən] *n* pentagone *m.*

Pentecost [pen'təkôst] *n* Pentecôte *f.*

penthouse [pent'hous] *n* appartement *m* (de luxe) en attique.

pent-up [pent'up'] *a (feelings)* refoulé(e).

penultimate [pinul'təmit] *a* pénultième, avant-dernier(ière).

penury [pen'yûrē] *n* misère *f.*

people [pē'pəl] *npl* gens *mpl;* personnes *fpl; (citizens)* peuple *m* ♦ *n (nation, race)* peuple *m* ♦ *vt* peupler; **several** ~ **came** plusieurs personnes sont venues; **I know** ~ **who** ... je connais des gens qui ...; **the room was full of** ~ la salle était pleine de monde *or* de

gens; ~ **say that** ... on dit *or* les gens disent que ...; **old** ~ les personnes âgées; **young** ~ les jeunes; **a man of the** ~ un homme du peuple.

pep [pep] *n (col)* entrain *m,* dynamisme *m.*

 pep up *vt (col)* remonter.

pepper [pep'ûr] *n* poivre *m; (vegetable)* poivron *m* ♦ *vt* poivrer.

pepper mill *n* moulin *m* à poivre.

peppermint [pep'ûrmint] *n (plant)* menthe poivrée; *(candy)* pastille *f* de menthe.

pepperpot [pep'ûrpât] *n (Brit)* poivrière *f.*

pepper shaker [pep'ûr shā'kûr] *n (US)* poivrière *f.*

pep talk *n (col)* (petit) discours d'encouragement.

per [pûr] *prep* par; ~ **hour** *(miles etc)* à l'heure; *(fee)* (de) l'heure; ~ **kilo** *etc* le kilo *etc;* ~ **day/person** par jour/personne; **as** ~ **your instructions** conformément à vos instructions.

per annum *ad* par an.

per capita *a, ad* par habitant, par personne.

perceive [pûrsēv'] *vt* percevoir; *(notice)* remarquer, s'apercevoir de.

percent [pûrsent'] *ad* pour cent; **a 20** ~ **discount** une réduction de 20 pour cent.

percentage [pûrsen'tij] *n* pourcentage *m;* **on a** ~ **basis** au pourcentage.

perceptible [pûrsep'təbəl] *a* perceptible.

perception [pûrsep'shən] *n* perception *f; (insight)* sensibilité *f.*

perceptive [pûrsep'tiv] *a (remark, person)* perspicace.

perch [pûrch] *n (fish)* perche *f; (for bird)* perchoir *m* ♦ *vi* (se) percher.

percolate [pûr'kəlāt] *vt, vi* passer.

percolator [pûr'kəlātûr] *n* percolateur *m;* cafetière *f* électrique.

percussion [pûrkush'ən] *n* percussion *f.*

peremptory [pəremp'tûrē] *a* péremptoire.

perennial [pəren'ēəl] *a* perpétuel(le); *(BOT)* vivace ♦ *n* plante *f* vivace.

perfect *a, n* [pûr'fikt] *a* parfait(e) ♦ *n (also:* ~ **tense**) parfait *m* ♦ *vt* [pərfekt'] parfaire; mettre au point; **he's a** ~ **stranger to me** il m'est totalement inconnu.

perfection [pûrfek'shən] *n* perfection *f.*

perfectionist [pûrfek'shənist] *n* perfectionniste *m/f.*

perfectly [pûr'fiktlē] *ad* parfaitement; **I'm** ~ **happy with the situation** cette situation me convient parfaitement; **you know** ~ **well** vous le savez très bien.

perforate [pûr'fûrāt] *vt* perforer, percer.

perforated ulcer *n (MED)* ulcère perforé.

perforation [pûrfərā'shən] *n* perforation *f; (line of holes)* pointillé *m.*

perform [pûrfôrm'] *vt (carry out)* exécuter, remplir; *(concert etc)* jouer, donner ♦ *vi* jouer.

performance [pûrfôr'məns] *n* représentation *f,* spectacle *m; (of an artist)* interprétation *f; (of player etc)* prestation *f; (of car, engine)* performance *f.*

performer [pûrfôr'mûr] *n* artiste *m/f.*

performing [pûrfôr'ming] *a (animal)* savant(e).

perfume [pûr'fyōōm] *n* parfum *m* ♦ *vt* parfumer.

perfunctory [pûrfungk'tûrē] *a* négligent(e), pour la forme.

perhaps [pûrhaps'] *ad* peut-être; ~ **he'll** ... peut-être qu'il ...; ~ **so/not** peut-être que oui/que non.

peril [pär'əl] *n* péril *m*.

perilous [pär'ələs] *a* périlleux(euse).

perilously [pär'ələslē] *ad*: **they came** ~ **close to being caught** ils ont été à deux doigts de se faire prendre.

perimeter [pərim'itûr] *n* périmètre *m*.

perimeter wall *n* mur *m* d'enceinte.

period [pēr'ēəd] *n* période *f*; (*HIST*) époque *f*; (*SCOL*) cours *m*; (*punctuation*) point *m*; (*MED*) règles *fpl* ♦ *a* (*costume, furniture*) d'époque; **for a** ~ **of three weeks** pour (une période de) trois semaines; **the vacation** ~ la période des vacances.

periodic [pērēâd'ik] *a* périodique.

periodical [pērēâd'ikəl] *a* périodique ♦ *n* périodique *m*.

periodically [pērēâd'iklē] *ad* périodiquement.

peripatetic [päripətet'ik] *a* (*salesman*) ambulant; (*teacher*) qui travaille dans plusieurs établissements.

peripheral [pərif'ûrəl] *a* périphérique ♦ *n* (*COMPUT*) périphérique *m*.

periphery [pərif'ûrē] *n* périphérie *f*.

periscope [pär'iskōp] *n* périscope *m*.

perish [pär'ish] *vi* périr, mourir; (*decay*) se détériorer.

perishable [pär'ishəbəl] *a* périssable.

perishables [pär'ishəbəlz] *npl* denrées *fpl* périssables.

peritonitis [pär'itənī'tis] *n* péritonite *f*.

perjure [pûr'jûr] *vt*: **to** ~ **o.s.** se parjurer.

perjury [pûr'jûrē] *n* (*LAW: in court*) faux témoignage; (*breach of oath*) parjure *m*.

perk [pûrk] *n* (*col*) avantage *m*, à-côté *m*.

perk up *vi* (*col: cheer up*) se ragaillardir.

perky [pûr'kē] *a* (*cheerful*) guilleret(te), gai(e).

perm [pûrm] *n* (*for hair*) permanente *f* ♦ *vt*: **to have one's hair** ~**ed** se faire faire une permanente.

permanence [pûr'mənəns] *n* permanence *f*.

permanent [pûr'mənənt] *a* permanent(e); (*job, position*) permanent, fixe; (*dye, ink*) indélébile; **I'm not** ~ **here** je ne suis pas ici à titre définitif; ~ **address** adresse habituelle.

permanently [pûr'mənəntlē] *ad* de façon permanente.

permeable [pûr'mēəbəl] *a* perméable.

permeate [pûr'mēāt] *vi* s'infiltrer ♦ *vt* s'infiltrer dans; pénétrer.

permissible [pûrmis'əbəl] *a* permis(e), acceptable.

permission [pûrmish'ən] *n* permission *f*, autorisation *f*; **to give sb** ~ **to do sth** donner à qn la permission de faire qch.

permissive [pûrmis'iv] *a* tolérant(e); **the** ~ **society** la société de tolérance.

permit *n* [pûr'mit] permis *m*; (*entrance pass*) autorisation *f*, laisser-passer *m*; (*for goods*) licence *f* ♦ *vt* [pərmit'] permettre; **to** ~ **sb to do** autoriser qn à faire, permettre à qn de faire; **weather** ~**ting** si le temps le permet.

permutation [pûrmyətā'shən] *n* permutation *f*.

pernicious [pûrnish'əs] *a* pernicieux(euse), nocif(ive).

pernickety [pûrnik'ətē] *a* (*Brit*) = **persnickety**.

perpendicular [pûrpəndik'yəlûr] *a*, *n* perpendiculaire (*f*).

perpetrate [pûr'pitrāt] *vt* perpétrer, commettre.

perpetual [pûrpech'ōōəl] *a* perpétuel(le).

perpetuate [pûrpech'ōōāt] *vt* perpétuer.

perpetuity [pûrpətōō'itē] *n*: **in** ~ à perpétuité.

perplex [pûrpleks'] *vt* rendre perplexe; (*complicate*) embrouiller.

perplexing [pûrplek'sing] *a* embarrassant(e).

perquisites [pûr'kwizits] *npl* (*also*: **perks**) avantages *mpl* annexes.

persecute [pûr'səkyōōt] *vt* persécuter.

persecution [pûrsəkyōō'shən] *n* persécution *f*.

perseverance [pûrsəvēr'əns] *n* persévérance *f*, ténacité *f*.

persevere [pûrsəvēr'] *vi* persévérer.

Persia [pûr'zhə] *n* Perse *f*.

Persian [pûr'zhən] *a* persan(e) ♦ *n* (*LING*) persan *m*; **the (~) Gulf** le golfe Persique.

persist [pûrsist'] *vi*: **to** ~ **(in doing)** persister (à faire), s'obstiner (à faire).

persistence [pûrsis'təns] *n* persistance *f*, obstination *f*; opiniâtreté *f*.

persistent [pûrsis'tənt] *a* persistant(e), tenace; (*lateness, rain*) persistant.

persnickety [pûrsnik'ətē] *a* (*US col*) pointilleux(euse), tatillon(ne); (*task*) minutieux(euse).

person [pûr'sən] *n* personne *f*; **in** ~ en personne; **on** *or* **about one's** ~ sur soi; ~ **to** ~ **call** (*TEL*) appel *m* avec préavis.

personable [pûr'sənəbəl] *a* de belle prestance, au physique attrayant.

personal [pûr'sənəl] *a* personnel(le); ~ **belongings**, ~ **effects** effets personnels; ~ **hygiene** hygiène *f* intime; **a** ~ **interview** un entretien.

personal allowance *n* (*TAX*) part *f* du revenu non imposable.

personal assistant (PA) *n* secrétaire personnel(le).

personal call *n* (*TEL*) communication *f* avec préavis.

personal column *n* annonces personnelles.

personal computer (PC) *n* ordinateur individuel, PC *m*.

personal details *npl* (*on form etc*) coordonnées *fpl*.

personality [pûrsənal'itē] *n* personnalité *f*.

personally [pûr'sənəlē] *ad* personnellement.

personal organizer *n* agenda *m* modulaire.

personal property *n* biens personnels.

personify [pûrsân'əfī] *vt* personnifier.

personnel [pûrsənel'] *n* personnel *m*.

personnel department *n* service *m* du personnel.

personnel manager *n* chef *m* du personnel.

perspective [pûrspek'tiv] *n* perspective *f*; **to get sth into** ~ ramener qch à sa juste mesure.

Perspex [pûr'speks] *n* ® (*Brit*) matière plastique transparente, employée surtout comme verre de sécurité.

perspicacity [pûrspəka'sitē] *n* perspicacité *f*.

perspiration [pûrspərā'shən] *n* transpiration *f*.

perspire [pûrspïûr'] *vi* transpirer.

persuade [pûrswād'] *vt*: **to ~ sb to do sth** persuader qn de faire qch, amener *or* décider qn à faire qch; **to ~ sb of sth/that** persuader qn de qch/que.

persuasion [pûrswā'zhən] *n* persuasion *f*; (*creed*) conviction *f*.

persuasive [pûrswā'siv] *a* persuasif(ive).

pert [pûrt] *a* coquin(e), mutin(e).

pertaining [pûrtān'ing]: **~ to** *prep* relatif(ive) à.

pertinent [pûr'tənənt] *a* pertinent(e).

perturb [pûrtûrb'] *vt* troubler, inquiéter.

perturbing [pûrtûrb'ing] *a* troublant(e).

Peru [pərōō'] *n* Pérou *m*.

perusal [pərōō'zəl] *n* lecture (attentive).

Peruvian [pərōō'vēən] *a* péruvien(ne) ♦ *n* Péruvien/ne.

pervade [pûrvād'] *vt* se répandre dans, envahir.

pervasive [pûrvā'siv] *a* (*smell*) pénétrant(e); (*influence*) insidieux(euse); (*gloom, ideas*) diffus(e).

perverse [pûrvûrs'] *a* pervers(e); (*stubborn*) entêté(e), contrariant(e).

perversion [pûrvûr'zhən] *n* perversion *f*.

perversity [pûrvûr'sitē] *n* perversité *f*.

pervert *n* [pûr'vûrt] perverti/e ♦ *vt* [pûrvûrt'] pervertir.

pessimism [pes'əmizəm] *n* pessimisme *m*.

pessimist [pes'əmist] *n* pessimiste *m/f*.

pessimistic [pesəmis'tik] *a* pessimiste.

pest [pest] *n* animal *m* (*or* insecte *m*) nuisible; (*fig*) fléau *m*.

pest control *n* lutte *f* contre les nuisibles.

pester [pes'tûr] *vt* importuner, harceler.

pesticide [pes'tisīd] *n* pesticide *m*.

pestilent [pes'tələnt], **pestilential** [pestəlen'shəl] *a* (*col: exasperating*) empoisonnant(e).

pestle [pes'əl] *n* pilon *m*.

pet [pet] *n* animal familier; (*favorite*) chouchou *m* ♦ *vt* choyer ♦ *vi* (*col*) se peloter; **~ lion** *etc* lion *etc* apprivoisé.

petal [pet'əl] *n* pétale *m*.

pet door *n* (*US*) chatière *f*.

peter [pē'tûr]: **to ~ out** *vi* s'épuiser; s'affaiblir.

petite [pətēt'] *a* menu(e).

petition [pətish'ən] *n* pétition *f* ♦ *vt* adresser une pétition à ♦ *vi*: **to ~ for divorce** demander le divorce.

pet name *n* (*Brit*) petit nom.

petrified [pet'rəfīd] *a* (*fig*) mort(e) de peur.

petrify [pet'rəfī] *vt* pétrifier.

petrochemical [petrōkem'ikəl] *a* pétrochimique.

petrodollars [petrōdâl'ûrz] *npl* pétrodollars *mpl*.

petrol [pet'rəl] *n* (*Brit*) essence *f*.

petrol can *n* (*Brit*) bidon *m* à essence.

petrol engine *n* (*Brit*) moteur *m* à essence.

petroleum [pətrō'lēəm] *n* pétrole *m*.

petroleum jelly *n* vaseline *f*.

petrol pump *n* (*Brit: in car, at garage*) pompe *f* à essence.

petrol station *n* (*Brit*) station-service *f*.

petrol tank *n* (*Brit*) réservoir *m* d'essence.

petticoat [pet'ēkōt] *n* jupon *m*.

pettifogging [pet'ēfâging] *a* chicanier(ière).

pettiness [pet'ēnis] *n* mesquinerie *f*.

petty [pet'ē] *a* (*mean*) mesquin(e); (*unimportant*) insignifiant(e), sans importance.

petty cash *n* caisse *f* des dépenses courantes, petite caisse.

petty officer *n* second-maître *m*.

petulant [pech'ələnt] *a* irritable.

pew [pyōō] *n* banc *m* (d'église).

pewter [pyōō'tûr] *n* étain *m*.

Pfc *abbr* (*US MIL*) = private first class.

PG *n* *abbr* (*CINEMA*: = *parental guidance*) avis des parents recommandé.

PGA *n* *abbr* = Professional Golfers Association.

PH *n* *abbr* (*US MIL*: = *Purple Heart*) décoration accordée aux blessés de guerre.

p&h *abbr* (*US*: = *postage and handling*) frais *mpl* de port.

PHA *n* *abbr* (*US*: = *Public Housing Administration*) organisme d'aide à la construction.

phallic [fal'ik] *a* phallique.

phantom [fan'təm] *n* fantôme *m*; (*vision*) fantasme *m*.

Pharaoh [fär'ō] *n* pharaon *m*.

pharmaceutical [fârməsōō'tikəl] *a* pharmaceutique ♦ *n*: **~s** produits *mpl* pharmaceutiques.

pharmacist [fâr'məsist] *n* pharmacien/ne.

pharmacy [fâr'məsē] *n* pharmacie *f*.

phase [fāz] *n* phase *f*, période *f* ♦ *vt*: **to ~ sth in/out** introduire/supprimer qch progressivement.

PhD *abbr* (= *Doctor of Philosophy*) *title* ≈ Docteur *m* en Droit *or* Lettres *etc* ♦ *n* ≈ doctorat *m*; titulaire *m* d'un doctorat.

pheasant [fez'ənt] *n* faisan *m*.

phenomenon, *pl* **phenomena** [finâm'ənán, -nə] *n* phénomène *m*.

phew [fyōō] *excl* ouf!

phial [fī'əl] *n* fiole *f*.

philanderer [filan'dûrûr] *n* don Juan *m*.

philanthropic [filənthrâp'ik] *a* philanthropique.

philanthropist [filan'thrəpist] *n* philanthrope *m/f*.

philatelist [filat'əlist] *n* philatéliste *m/f*.

philately [filat'əlē] *n* philatélie *f*.

Philippines [fil'ipēnz] *npl* (*also*: **Philippine Islands**): **the ~** les Philippines *fpl*.

philosopher [filâs'əfûr] *n* philosophe *m*.

philosophical [filâsâf'ikəl] *a* philosophique.

philosophy [filâs'əfē] *n* philosophie *f*.

phlegm [flem] *n* flegme *m*.

phlegmatic [flegmat'ik] *a* flegmatique.

phobia [fō'bēə] *n* phobie *f*.

phone [fōn] *n* téléphone *m* ♦ *vt* téléphoner à ♦ *vi* téléphoner; **to be on the ~** avoir le téléphone; (*be calling*) être au téléphone.
    phone back *vt, vi* rappeler.

phone book *n* annuaire *m*.

phone booth, (*Brit*) **phone box** *n* cabine *f* téléphonique.

phone call *n* coup *m* de fil *or* de téléphone.

phone-in [fōn'in] *n* (*Brit RADIO, TV*) programme *m* à ligne ouverte.

phonetics [fənet'iks] *n* phonétique *f*.

phoney [fō'nē] *a* faux(fausse), factice ♦ *n* (*person*) charlatan *m*; fumiste *m/f*.

phonograph [fō'nəgraf] *n* (*US*) électro-

phone *m*.
phony [fō'nē] *a, n* = **phoney**.
phosphate [fâs'fāt] *n* phosphate *m*.
phosphorus [fâs'fûrəs] *n* phosphore *m*.
photo [fō'tō] *n* photo *f*.
photo... [fō'tō] *prefix* photo....
photocopier [fō'təkâpēûr] *n* copieur *m*.
photocopy [fō'təkâpē] *n* photocopie *f* ♦ *vt* photocopier.
photoelectric [fōtōilek'trik] *a* photoélectrique;
~ **cell** cellule *f* photoélectrique.
photogenic [fōtəjen'ik] *a* photogénique.
photograph [fō'təgraf] *n* photographie *f* ♦ *vt*
photographier; **to take a ~ of sb** prendre qn
en photo.
photographer [fətâg'rəfûr] *n* photographe *m/f*.
photographic [fōtəgraf'ik] *a* photographique.
photography [fətâg'rəfē] *n* photographie *f*.
photostat [fō'təstat] *n* photocopie *f*, photostat
m.
photosynthesis [fōtəsin'thəsis] *n* photosyn-
thèse *f*.
phrase [frāz] *n* expression *f*; (*LING*) locution *f*
♦ *vt* exprimer; (*letter*) rédiger.
phrase book *n* recueil *m* d'expressions (pour
touristes).
physical [fiz'ikəl] *a* physique; ~ **examination**
examen médical; ~ **education** éducation physique; ~ **exercises** gymnastique *f*.
physically [fiz'iklē] *ad* physiquement.
physician [fizish'ən] *n* médecin *m*.
physicist [fiz'əsist] *n* physicien/ne.
physics [fiz'iks] *n* physique *f*.
physiological [fizēəlâj'ikəl] *a* physiologique.
physiology [fizēâl'əjē] *n* physiologie *f*.
physiotherapist [fizēōthär'əpist] *n* kinésithérapeute *m/f*.
physiotherapy [fizēōthär'əpē] *n* kinésithérapie
f.
physique [fizēk'] *n* (*appearance*) physique *m*;
(*health etc*) constitution *f*.
pianist [pēan'ist] *n* pianiste *m/f*.
piano [pēan'ō] *n* piano *m*.
piano accordion *n* (*Brit*) accordéon *m* à touches.
Picardy [pik'ûrdē] *n* Picardie *f*.
piccolo [pik'əlō] *n* piccolo *m*.
pick [pik] *n* (*tool: also:* ~**ax**) pic *m*, pioche *f* ♦
vt choisir; (*gather*) cueillir; (*scab, spot*)
gratter, écorcher; **take your ~** faites votre
choix; **the ~ of** le(la) meilleur(e) de; **to ~ a
bone** ronger un os; **to ~ one's nose** se mettre le doigt dans le nez; **to ~ one's teeth** se
curer les dents; **to ~ sb's brains** faire appel
aux lumières de qn; **to ~ pockets** pratiquer
le vol à la tire; **to ~ a fight with sb** chercher la bagarre avec qn.
pick off *vt* (*kill*) (viser soigneusement et)
abattre.
pick on *vt fus* (*person*) harceler.
pick out *vt* choisir; (*distinguish*) distinguer.
pick up *vi* (*improve*) remonter, s'améliorer
♦ *vt* ramasser; (*telephone*) décrocher;
(*collect*) passer prendre; (*AUT: give lift to*)
prendre; (*learn*) apprendre; (*RADIO, TV,
TEL*) capter; **to ~ up speed** prendre de la vitesse; **to ~ o.s. up** se relever; **to ~ up
where one left off** reprendre là où l'on s'est
arrêté.

pickax, (*Brit*) **pickaxe** [pik'aks] *n* pioche *f*.
picket [pik'it] *n* (*in strike*) gréviste *m/f* participant à un piquet de grève; piquet *m* de grève
♦ *vt* mettre un piquet de grève devant.
picket line *n* piquet *m* de grève.
pickings [pik'ingz] *npl*: **there are rich ~ to be
had in** ... il y a gros à gagner dans ....
pickle [pik'əl] *n* (*also:* ~**s:** *as condiment*)
pickles *mpl*; (*fig*): **in a ~** dans le pétrin ♦ *vt*
conserver dans du vinaigre *or* dans de la saumure.
pick-me-up [pik'mēup] *n* remontant *m*.
pickpocket [pik'pâkit] *n* pickpocket *m*.
pickup [pik'up] *n* (*also:* ~ **truck**) camionnette
f; (*Brit: on record player*) bras *m* pick-up.
picnic [pik'nik] *n* pique-nique *m* ♦ *vi* pique-
niquer.
picnicker [pik'nikûr] *n* pique-niqueur/euse.
pictorial [piktôr'ēəl] *a* illustré(e).
picture [pik'chûr] *n* (*also TV*) image *f*;
(*painting*) peinture *f*, tableau *m*; (*photograph*) photo(graphie) *f*; (*drawing*) dessin
m; (*film*) film *m* ♦ *vt* se représenter; (*describe*) dépeindre, représenter; **the ~s** (*Brit*)
le cinéma; **to take a ~ of sb/sth** prendre
qn/qch en photo; **the overall ~** le tableau
d'ensemble; **to put sb in the ~** mettre qn au
courant.
picture book *n* livre *m* d'images.
picturesque [pikchəresk'] *a* pittoresque.
picture window *n* baie vitrée, fenêtre *f* panoramique.
piddling [pid'ling] *a* (*col*) insignifiant(e).
pidgin [pij'in] *a*: ~ **English** pidgin *m*.
pie [pī] *n* tourte *f*; (*of meat*) pâté *m* en croûte.
piebald [pī'bôld] *a* pie *inv*.
piece [pēs] *n* morceau *m*; (*of land*) parcelle *f*;
(*item*): **a ~ of furniture/advice** un meuble/
conseil; (*CHECKERS etc*) pion *m* ♦ *vt*: **to ~
together** rassembler; **in ~s** (*broken*) en
morceaux, en miettes; (*not yet assembled*)
en pièces détachées; **to take to ~s** démonter; **in one ~** (*object*) intact(e); **to get
back all in one ~** (*person*) rentrer sain et
sauf; **a 10 cents ~** une pièce de 10 cents; ~
by ~ morceau par morceau; **a six-~ band**
un orchestre de six musiciens; **to say one's
~** réciter son morceau.
piecemeal [pēs'mēl] *ad* par bouts.
piece rate *n* taux *m or* tarif *m* à la pièce.
piecework [pēs'wûrk] *n* travail *m* aux pièces
or à la pièce.
pie chart *n* graphique *m* à secteurs, camembert *m*.
pie crust pastry *n* (*US*) pâte brisée.
Piedmont [pēd'mânt] *n* Piémont *m*.
pier [pēr] *n* jetée *f*; (*of bridge etc*) pile *f*.
pierce [pērs] *vt* percer, transpercer; **to have
one's ears ~d** se faire percer les oreilles.
piercing [pērs'ing] *a* (*cry*) perçant(e).
piety [pī'ətē] *n* piété *f*.
piffling [pif'ling] *a* insignifiant(e).
pig [pig] *n* cochon *m*, porc *m*.
pigeon [pij'ən] *n* pigeon *m*.
pigeonhole [pij'ənhōl] *n* casier *m*.
pigeon-toed [pij'əntōd] *a* marchant les pieds
en dedans.
piggy bank [pig'ē bangk] *n* tirelire *f*.
pigheaded [pig'hedid] *a* entêté(e), têtu(e).

piglet [pig'lit] *n* petit cochon, porcelet *m*.
pigment [pig'mənt] *n* pigment *m*.
pigmentation [pigməntā'shən] *n* pigmentation *f*.
pigmy [pig'mē] *n* = **pygmy**.
pigskin [pig'skin] *n* (peau *f* de) porc *m*.
pigsty [pig'stī] *n* porcherie *f*.
pigtail [pig'tāl] *n* natte *f*, tresse *f*.
pike [pīk] *n* (*spear*) pique *f*; (*fish*) brochet *m*.
pilchard [pil'chûrd] *n* pilchard *m* (*sorte de sardine*).
pile [pīl] *n* (*pillar, of books*) pile *f*; (*heap*) tas *m*; (*of carpet*) épaisseur *f* ♦ *vb* (*also*: ~ **up**) *vt* empiler, entasser ♦ *vi* s'entasser; **in a** ~ en tas.
  pile on *vt*: **to** ~ **it on** (*col*) exagérer.
piles [pīlz] *npl* hémorroïdes *fpl*.
pileup [pīl'up] *n* (*AUT*) télescopage *m*, collision *f* en série.
pilfer [pil'fûr] *vt* chaparder ♦ *vi* commettre des larcins.
pilfering [pil'fûring] *n* chapardage *m*.
pilgrim [pil'grim] *n* pèlerin *m*.
pilgrimage [pil'grəmij] *n* pèlerinage *m*.
pill [pil] *n* pilule *f*; **the** ~ la pilule; **to be on the** ~ prendre la pilule.
pillage [pil'ij] *vt* piller.
pillar [pil'ûr] *n* pilier *m*.
pillar box *n* (*Brit*) boîte *f* aux lettres.
pillion [pil'yən] *n* (*of motor cycle*) siège *m* arrière; **to ride** ~ être derrière; (*on horse*) être en croupe.
pillory [pil'ûrē] *n* pilori *m* ♦ *vt* mettre au pilori.
pillow [pil'ō] *n* oreiller *m*.
pillowcase [pil'ōkās], **pillowslip** [pil'ōslip] *n* taie *f* d'oreiller.
pilot [pī'lət] *n* pilote *m* ♦ *cpd* (*plan etc*) pilote, expérimental(e) ♦ *vt* piloter.
pilot boat *n* bateau-pilote *m*.
pilot light *n* veilleuse *f*.
pimento [pimen'tō] *n* piment *m*.
pimp [pimp] *n* souteneur *m*, maquereau *m*.
pimple [pim'pəl] *n* bouton *m*.
pimply [pim'plē] *a* boutonneux(euse).
pin [pin] *n* épingle *f*; (*TECH*) cheville *f*; (*US: also*: **clothes** ~) pince *f* à linge; (*Brit: drawing* ~) punaise *f*; (*in grenade*) goupille *f*; (*Brit ELEC: of plug*) broche *f* ♦ *vt* épingler; ~**s and needles** fourmis *fpl*; **to** ~ **sb against/to** clouer qn contre/à; **to** ~ **sth on sb** (*fig*) mettre qch sur le dos de qn.
  pin down *vt* (*fig*): **to** ~ **sb down** obliger qn à répondre; **there's something strange here but I can't quite** ~ **it down** il y a quelque chose d'étrange ici, mais je n'arrive pas exactement à savoir quoi.
pinafore [pin'əfôr] *n* tablier *m*.
pinafore dress *n* robe-chasuble *f*.
pinball [pin'bôl] *n* flipper *m*.
pincers [pin'sûrz] *npl* tenailles *fpl*.
pinch [pinch] *n* pincement *m*; (*of salt etc*) pincée *f* ♦ *vt* pincer; (*col: steal*) piquer, chiper ♦ *vi* (*shoe*) serrer; **at a** ~ à la rigueur; **to feel the** ~ (*fig*) se ressentir des restrictions (*or* de la récession *etc*).
pinched [pincht] *a* (*drawn*) tiré(e); ~ **with cold** transi(e) de froid; ~ **for** (*short of*): ~ **for money** à court d'argent; ~ **for space** à l'étroit.

pincushion [pin'kŏŏshən] *n* pelote *f* à épingles.
pine [pīn] *n* (*also*: ~ **tree**) pin *m* ♦ *vi*: **to** ~ **for** aspirer à, désirer ardemment.
  pine away *vi* dépérir.
pineapple [pīn'apəl] *n* ananas *m*.
pine nut, *n* pignon *m*.
ping [ping] *n* (*noise*) tintement *m*.
ping-pong [ping'pông] *n* ® ping-pong *m* ®.
pink [pingk] *a* rose ♦ *n* (*color*) rose *m*; (*BOT*) œillet *m*, mignardise *f*.
pinking shears [ping'king shirz], **pinking scissors** [ping'king siz'ûrz] *npl* ciseaux *mpl* à denteler.
pin money *n* argent *m* de poche.
pinnacle [pin'əkəl] *n* pinacle *m*.
pinpoint [pin'point] *vt* indiquer (avec précision).
pinstripe [pin'strīp] *n* rayure très fine.
pint [pīnt] *n* pinte *f* (*US = 0.47 l; Brit = 0.57 l*).
pinup [pin'up] *n* pin-up *f inv*.
pinwheel [pin'wēl] *n* (*US*) soleil *m* (*feu d'artifice*).
pioneer [pīənēr'] *n* explorateur/trice; (*early settler*) pionnier *m*; (*fig*) pionnier, précurseur *m* ♦ *vt* être un pionnier de.
pious [pī'əs] *a* pieux(euse).
pip [pip] *n* (*seed*) pépin *m*; (*Brit: time signal on radio*) top *m*.
pipe [pīp] *n* tuyau *m*, conduite *f*; (*for smoking*) pipe *f*; (*MUS*) pipeau *m* ♦ *vt* amener par tuyau; ~**s** *npl* (*also*: **bag**~**s**) cornemuse *f*.
  pipe down *vi* (*col*) se taire.
pipe cleaner *n* cure-pipe *m*.
piped music [pīpt myŏŏ'zik] *n* musique *f* de fond.
pipe dream *n* chimère *f*, utopie *f*.
pipeline [pīp'līn] *n* (*for gas*) gazoduc *m*, pipeline *m*; (*for oil*) oléoduc *m*, pipeline; **it is in the** ~ (*fig*) c'est en route, ça va se faire.
piper [pī'pûr] *n* joueur/euse de pipeau (*or* de cornemuse).
pipe tobacco *n* tabac *m* pour la pipe.
piping [pī'ping] *ad*: ~ **hot** très chaud(e).
piquant [pē'kənt] *a* piquant(e).
pique [pēk] *n* dépit *m*.
piracy [pī'rəsē] *n* piraterie *f*.
pirate [pī'rət] *n* pirate *m* ♦ *vt* (*record, video, book*) pirater.
pirate radio (station) *n* (station *f* de) radio *f* pirate.
pirouette [pirŏŏet'] *n* pirouette *f* ♦ *vi* faire une *or* des pirouette(s).
Pisces [pī'sēz] *n* les Poissons *mpl*; **to be** ~ être des Poissons.
piss [pis] *vi* (*col!*) pisser (*!*); ~ **off!** tire-toi! (*!*).
pissed [pist] *a* (*Brit col: drunk*) bourré(e).
pistol [pis'təl] *n* pistolet *m*.
piston [pis'tən] *n* piston *m*.
pit [pit] *n* trou *m*, fosse *f*; (*also*: **coal** ~) puits *m* de mine; (*also*: **orchestra** ~) fosse d'orchestre; (*US: of fruit*) noyau *m* ♦ *vt* (*US: fruit*) dénoyauter; **to** ~ **sb against sb** opposer qn à qn; **to** ~ **o.s. against** se mesurer à; ~**s** *npl* (*in motor racing*) aire *f* de service.
pitapat [pit'əpat] *ad*: **to go** ~ (*heart*) battre la chamade; (*rain*) tambouriner.
pitch [pich] *n* (*throw*) lancement *m*; (*MUS*) ton

m; (*of voice*) hauteur *f*; (*fig: degree*) degré *m*; (*also:* **sales ~**) baratin *m*, boniment *m*; (*Brit SPORT*) terrain *m*; (*NAUT*) tangage *m*; (*tar*) poix *f* ♦ *vt* (*throw*) lancer; (*tent*) dresser; (*set: price, message*) adapter, positionner ♦ *vi* (*NAUT*) tanguer; (*fall*): **to ~ into/off** tomber dans/de; **to be ~ed forward** être projeté(e) en avant; **at this ~** à ce rythme.

pitch-black [pich'blak'] *a* noir(e) comme poix.

pitched battle [picht bat'əl] *n* bataille rangée.

pitcher [pich'ûr] *n* cruche *f*.

pitchfork [pich'fôrk] *n* fourche *f*.

piteous [pit'ēəs] *a* pitoyable.

pitfall [pit'fôl] *n* trappe *f*, piège *m*.

pith [pith] *n* (*of plant*) moelle *f*; (*of orange*) intérieur *m* de l'écorce; (*fig*) essence *f*; vigueur *f*.

pithy [pith'ē] *a* piquant(e); vigoureux(euse).

pitiable [pit'ēəbəl] *a* pitoyable.

pitiful [pit'ifəl] *a* (*touching*) pitoyable; (*contemptible*) lamentable.

pitifully [pit'ifəlē] *ad* pitoyablement; lamentablement.

pitiless [pit'ilis] *a* impitoyable.

pittance [pit'əns] *n* salaire *m* de misère.

pitted [pit'id] *a*: **~ with** (*chickenpox*) grêlé(e) par; (*rust*) piqué(e) de.

pity [pit'ē] *n* pitié *f* ♦ *vt* plaindre; **what a ~!** quel dommage!; **it is a ~ that you can't come** c'est dommage que vous ne puissiez venir; **to have** *or* **take ~ on sb** avoir pitié de qn.

pitying [pit'ēing] *a* compatissant(e).

pivot [piv'ət] *n* pivot *m* ♦ *vi* pivoter.

pixel [pik'səl] *n* (*COMPUT*) pixel *m*.

pixie [pik'sē] *n* lutin *m*.

pizza [pēt'sə] *n* pizza *f*.

P&L *abbr* = **profit and loss**.

placard [plak'ârd] *n* affiche *f*.

placate [plā'kāt] *vt* apaiser, calmer.

placatory [plā'kətôrē] *a* d'apaisement, lénifiant(e).

place [plās] *n* endroit *m*, lieu *m*; (*proper position, rank, seat*) place *f*; (*house*) maison *f*, logement *m*; (*in street names*): **Laurel P~** ≈ rue des Lauriers; (*home*): **at/to his ~** chez lui ♦ *vt* (*position*) placer, mettre; (*identify*) situer; reconnaître; **to take ~** avoir lieu; (*occur*) se produire; **from ~ to ~** d'un endroit à l'autre; **all over the ~** partout; **out of ~** (*not suitable*) déplacé(e), inopportun(e); **I feel out of ~ here** je ne me sens pas à ma place ici; **in the first ~** d'abord, en premier; **to put sb in his ~** (*fig*) remettre qn à sa place; **he's going ~s** (*fig: col*) il fait son chemin; **it is not my ~ to do it** ce n'est pas à moi de le faire; **to ~ an order with sb (for)** (*COMM*) passer commande à qn (de); **to be ~d** (*in race, exam*) se placer; **how are you ~d next week?** comment ça se présente pour la semaine prochaine?

placebo [pləsē'bō] *n* placebo *m*.

place mat *n* set *m* de table; (*in linen etc*) napperon *m*.

placement [plās'mənt] *n* placement *m*; poste *m*.

place name *n* nom *m* de lieu.

placenta [pləsen'tə] *n* placenta *m*.

placid [plas'id] *a* placide.

placidity [pləsid'itē] *n* placidité *f*.

plagiarism [plā'jərizəm] *n* plagiat *m*.

plagiarist [plā'jûrist] *n* plagiaire *m/f*.

plagiarize [plā'jərīz] *vt* plagier.

plague [plāg] *n* fléau *m*; (*MED*) peste *f* ♦ *vt* (*fig*) tourmenter; **to ~ sb with questions** harceler qn de questions.

plaice [plās] *n* (*pl inv*) carrelet *m*.

plaid [plad] *n* tissu écossais.

plain [plān] *a* (*clear*) clair(e), évident(e); (*simple*) simple, ordinaire; (*frank*) franc(franche); (*not handsome*) quelconque, ordinaire; (*cigarette*) sans filtre; (*without seasoning etc*) nature *inv*; (*in one color*) uni(e) ♦ *ad* franchement, carrément ♦ *n* plaine *f*; **in ~ clothes** (*police*) en civil; **to make sth ~ to sb** faire clairement comprendre qch à qn.

plain chocolate *n* chocolat *m* à croquer.

plainly [plān'lē] *ad* clairement; (*frankly*) carrément, sans détours.

plainness [plān'nis] *n* simplicité *f*.

plaintiff [plān'tif] *n* plaignant/e.

plaintive [plān'tiv] *a* plaintif(ive).

plait [plat] *n* tresse *f*, natte *f* ♦ *vt* tresser, natter.

plan [plan] *n* plan *m*; (*scheme*) projet *m* ♦ *vt* (*think in advance*) projeter; (*prepare*) organiser ♦ *vi* faire des projets; **to ~ to do** projeter de faire; **how long do you ~ to stay?** combien de temps comptez-vous rester?

plane [plān] *n* (*AVIAT*) avion *m*; (*tree*) platane *m*; (*tool*) rabot *m*; (*ART, MATH etc*) plan *m* ♦ *a* plan(e), plat(e) ♦ *vt* (*with tool*) raboter.

planet [plan'it] *n* planète *f*.

planetarium [planitär'ēəm] *n* planétarium *m*.

plank [plangk] *n* planche *f*; (*POL*) point *m* d'un programme.

plankton [plangk'tən] *n* plancton *m*.

planner [plan'ûr] *n* planificateur/trice; (*chart*) planning *m*; **city** *or* (*Brit*) **town ~** urbaniste *m/f*.

planning [plan'ing] *n* planification *f*; **family ~** planning familial.

plant [plant] *n* plante *f*; (*machinery*) matériel *m*; (*factory*) usine *f* ♦ *vt* planter; (*bomb*) déposer, poser.

plantation [plantā'shən] *n* plantation *f*.

plant pot *n* (*Brit*) pot *m* de fleurs.

plaque [plak] *n* plaque *f*.

plasma [plaz'mə] *n* plasma *m*.

plaster [plas'tûr] *n* plâtre *m*; (*Brit: also:* **sticking ~**) pansement adhésif ♦ *vt* plâtrer; (*cover*): **to ~ with** couvrir de; **in ~** (*Brit: leg etc*) dans le plâtre; **~ of Paris** plâtre à mouler.

plaster cast *n* (*MED*) plâtre *m*; (*model, statue*) moule *m*.

plastered [plas'tûrd] *a* (*col*) soûl(e).

plasterer [plas'tərûr] *n* plâtrier *m*.

plastic [plas'tik] *n* plastique *m* ♦ *a* (*made of plastic*) en plastique; (*flexible*) plastique, malléable; (*art*) plastique.

plastic bag *n* sac *m* en plastique.

plastic surgery *n* chirurgie *f* esthétique.

plate [plāt] *n* (*dish*) assiette *f*; (*sheet of metal, on door, PHOT*) plaque *f*; (*TYP*) cliché *m*; (*in book*) gravure *f*; (*AUT: license ~*) plaque minéralogique; **gold/silver** ~ (*dishes*) vaisselle *f* d'or/d'argent.

plateau [plat'ō', -z] *n* plateau *m*.

plateful [plāt'fəl] *n* assiette *f*, assiettée *f*.

plate glass *n* verre *m* à vitre, vitre *f*.

platen [plat'ən] *n* (*on typewriter, printer*) rouleau *m*.

platform [plat'fôrm] *n* (*at meeting*) tribune *f*; (*Brit: of bus*) plate-forme *f*; (*stage*) estrade *f*; (*RAIL*) quai *m*; **the train leaves from** ~ **7** le train part de la voie 7.

platinum [plat'ənəm] *n* platine *m*.

platitude [plat'ətōōd] *n* platitude *f*, lieu commun.

platoon [plətōōn'] *n* peloton *m*.

platter [plat'ûr] *n* plat *m*.

plaudits [plô'dits] *npl* applaudissements *mpl*.

plausible [plô'zəbəl] *a* plausible; (*person*) convaincant(e).

play [plā] *n* jeu *m*; (*THEATER*) pièce *f* (de théâtre) ♦ *vt* (*game*) jouer à; (*team, opponent*) jouer contre; (*instrument*) jouer de; (*part, piece of music, note*) jouer ♦ *vi* jouer; **to bring** *or* **call into** ~ faire entrer en jeu; ~ **on words** jeu de mots; **to** ~ **a trick on sb** jouer un tour à qn; **they're** ~**ing at soldiers** ils jouent aux soldats; **to** ~ **for time** (*fig*) chercher à gagner du temps; **to** ~ **into sb's hands** (*fig*) faire le jeu de qn.

play around *vi* (*person*) s'amuser.

play along *vi* (*fig*): **to** ~ **along with** (*person*) entrer dans le jeu de.

play back *vt* repasser, réécouter.

play down *vt* minimiser.

play on *vt fus* (*sb's feelings, credulity*) jouer sur; **to** ~ **on sb's nerves** porter sur les nerfs de qn.

play up *vi* (*Brit: cause trouble*) faire des siennes.

playact [plā'akt] *vi* jouer la comédie.

playboy [plā'boi] *n* playboy *m*.

played-out [plād'out] *a* épuisé(e).

player [plā'ûr] *n* joueur/euse; (*THEATER*) acteur/trice; (*MUS*) musicien/ne.

playful [plā'fəl] *a* enjoué(e).

playgoer [plā'gōûr] *n* amateur/trice de théâtre, habitué/e des théâtres.

playground [plā'ground] *n* cour *f* de récréation.

playgroup [plā'grōōp] *n* garderie *f*.

playing card [plā'ing kârd] *n* carte *f* à jouer.

playing field *n* terrain *m* de sport.

playmate [plā'māt] *n* camarade *m/f*, copain/copine.

play-off [plā'ôf] *n* (*SPORT*) belle *f*.

playpen [plā'pen] *n* parc *m* (pour bébé).

playroom [plā'rōōm] *n* salle *f* de jeux.

plaything [plā'thing] *n* jouet *m*.

playtime [plā'tīm] *n* (*SCOL*) récréation *f*.

playwright [plā'rīt] *n* dramaturge *m*.

plc *abbr* (*Brit*) = **public limited company**.

plea [plē] *n* (*request*) appel *m*; (*excuse*) excuse *f*; (*LAW*) défense *f*.

plead [plēd] *vt* plaider; (*give as excuse*) invoquer ♦ *vi* (*LAW*) plaider; (*beg*): **to** ~ **with sb (for sth)** implorer qn (d'accorder qch); **to** ~ **for sth** implorer qch; **to** ~ **guilty/not guilty** plaider coupable/non coupable.

pleasant [plez'ənt] *a* agréable.

pleasantly [plez'əntlē] *ad* agréablement.

pleasantness [plez'əntnis] *n* (*of person*) amabilité *f*; (*of place*) agrément *m*.

pleasantry [plez'əntrē] *n* (*joke*) plaisanterie *f*; **pleasantries** *npl* (*polite remarks*) civilités *fpl*.

please [plēz] *vt* plaire à ♦ *vi* (*think fit*): **do as you** ~ faites comme il vous plaira; ~**!** s'il te (*or* vous) plaît; **my check,** ~ l'addition, s'il vous plaît; ~ **don't cry!** je t'en prie, ne pleure pas!; ~ **yourself!** (faites) comme vous voulez!

pleased [plēzd] *a*: ~ **(with)** content(e) (de); ~ **to meet you** enchanté (de faire votre connaissance); **we are** ~ **to inform you that** ... nous sommes heureux de vous annoncer que ....

pleasing [plē'zing] *a* plaisant(e), qui fait plaisir.

pleasurable [plezh'ûrəbəl] *a* très agréable.

pleasure [plezh'ûr] *n* plaisir *m*; "**it's a** ~" "je vous en prie"; **with** ~ avec plaisir; **is this trip for business or** ~? est-ce un voyage d'affaires ou d'agrément?

pleasure steamer *n* (*Brit*) vapeur *m* de plaisance.

pleat [plēt] *n* pli *m*.

plebiscite [pleb'isit] *n* plébiscite *m*.

plebs [plebs] *npl* (*pej*) bas peuple.

plectrum [plek'trəm] *n* plectre *m*.

pledge [plej] *n* gage *m*; (*promise*) promesse *f* ♦ *vt* engager; promettre; **to** ~ **support for sb** s'engager à soutenir qn; **to** ~ **$500 per year to a charity** s'engager à verser $500 par an à une œuvre de bienfaisance; **to** ~ **sb to secrecy** faire promettre à qn de garder le secret.

plenary [plē'nûrē] *a*: **in** ~ **session** en séance plénière.

plentiful [plen'tifəl] *a* abondant(e), copieux(euse).

plenty [plen'tē] *n* abondance *f*; ~ **of** beaucoup de; (*sufficient*) (bien) assez de; **we've got** ~ **of time** nous avons largement le temps.

pleurisy [plōōr'isē] *n* pleurésie *f*.

Plexiglas [plek'səglas] *n* ® (*US*) Plexiglas *m* ®.

pliable [plī'əbəl] *a* flexible; (*person*) malléable.

pliers [plī'ûrz] *npl* pinces *fpl*.

plight [plīt] *n* situation *f* critique.

plimsolls [plim'səlz] *npl* (*Brit*) (chaussures *fpl*) tennis *fpl*.

plinth [plinth] *n* socle *m*.

PLO *n abbr* (= *Palestine Liberation Organization*) OLP *f*.

plod [plâd] *vi* avancer péniblement; (*fig*) peiner.

plodder [plâd'ûr] *n* bûcheur/euse.

plodding [plâd'ing] *a* pesant(e).

plonk [plângk] (*col*) *n* (*Brit: wine*) pinard *m*, piquette *f*.

plot [plât] *n* complot *m*, conspiration *f*; (*of story, play*) intrigue *f*; (*of land*) lot *m* de terrain, lopin *m* ♦ *vt* (*mark out*) pointer; relever; (*conspire*) comploter ♦ *vi* comploter.

plotter [plât'ûr] *n* conspirateur/trice; (*COMPUT*) traceur *m*.

plough [plou] *etc* (*Brit*) = **plow** *etc*.

plow [plou] (*US*) *n* charrue *f* ♦ *vt* (*earth*) labourer.

plow back vt (*COMM*) réinvestir.
plow through vt fus (*snow etc*) avancer péniblement dans.
plowing [plou'ing] n labourage m.
plowman [plou'mən] n laboureur m.
ploy [ploi] n stratagème m.
pluck [pluk] vt (*fruit*) cueillir; (*musical instrument*) pincer; (*bird*) plumer ♦ n courage m, cran m; **to ~ one's eyebrows** s'épiler les sourcils; **to ~ up courage** prendre son courage à deux mains.
plucky [pluk'ē] a courageux(euse).
plug [plug] n bouchon m, bonde f; (*ELEC*) prise f de courant; (*AUT: also*: **spark ~**) bougie f ♦ vt (*hole*) boucher; (*col: advertise*) faire du battage pour, matraquer; **to give sb/sth a ~** (*col*) faire de la pub pour qn/qch.
plug in (*ELEC*) vt brancher ♦ vi se brancher.
plughole [plug'hōl] n (*Brit*) trou m (d'écoulement).
plum [plum] n (*fruit*) prune f ♦ a: **~ job** (*col*) travail m en or.
plumage [plōō'mij] n plumage m.
plumb [plum] a vertical(e) ♦ n plomb m ♦ ad (*exactly*) en plein ♦ vt sonder.
plumb in vt (*washing machine*) faire le raccordement de.
plumber [plum'ûr] n plombier m.
plumbing [plum'ing] n (*trade*) plomberie f; (*piping*) tuyauterie f.
plumbline [plum'līn] n fil m à plomb.
plume [plōōm] n plume f, plumet m.
plummet [plum'it] vi plonger, dégringoler.
plump [plump] a rondelet(te), dodu(e), bien en chair ♦ vt: **to ~ sth (down) on** laisser tomber qch lourdement sur.
plump up vt (*cushion*) battre (pour lui redonner forme).
plunder [plun'dûr] n pillage m ♦ vt piller.
plunge [plunj] n plongeon m ♦ vt plonger ♦ vi (*fall*) tomber, dégringoler; **to take the ~** se jeter à l'eau; **to ~ a room into darkness** plonger une pièce dans l'obscurité.
plunger [plun'jûr] n piston m; (*for blocked sink*) (débouchoir m à) ventouse f.
plunging [plun'jing] a (*neckline*) plongeant(e).
pluperfect [plōōpûr'fikt] n plus-que-parfait m.
plural [plōōr'əl] a pluriel(le) ♦ n pluriel m.
plus [plus] n (*also*: **~ sign**) signe m plus ♦ prep plus; **ten/twenty ~** plus de dix/vingt; **it's a ~** c'est un atout.
plus fours npl pantalon m (de) golf.
plush [plush] a somptueux(euse) ♦ n peluche f; **~ toy** (*US*) jouet m en peluche.
plutonium [plōōtō'nēəm] n plutonium m.
ply [plī] n (*of wool*) fil m; (*of wood*) feuille f, épaisseur f ♦ vt (*tool*) manier; (*a trade*) exercer ♦ vi (*ship*) faire la navette; **three ~ (wool)** n laine f trois fils; **to ~ sb with drink** donner continuellement à boire à qn.
plywood [plī'wŏŏd] n contre-plaqué m.
PM n abbr = **prime minister**.
p.m. ad abbr (= *post meridiem*) de l'après-midi.
pneumatic [nōōmat'ik] a pneumatique; **~ drill** marteau-piqueur m.
pneumonia [nyōōmōn'yə] n pneumonie f.
PO n abbr (= *Post Office*) PTT fpl; (*MIL*) =

petty officer.
po abbr (*Brit*) = **postal order.**
poach [pōch] vt (*cook*) pocher; (*steal*) pêcher (*or* chasser) sans permis ♦ vi braconner.
poached [pōcht] a (*egg*) poché(e).
poacher [pō'chûr] n braconnier m.
poaching [pō'ching] n braconnage m.
PO Box n abbr = **Post Office Box.**
pocket [pâk'it] n poche f ♦ vt empocher.
pocketbook [pâk'itbŏŏk] n (*wallet*) portefeuille m; (*notebook*) carnet m; (*US: purse*) sac m à main.
pocket knife n canif m.
pocket money n argent m de poche.
pockmarked [pâk'märkt] a (*face*) grêlé(e).
pod [pâd] n cosse f ♦ vt écosser.
podgy [pâj'ē] a rondelet(te).
podiatrist [pədī'ətrist] n (*US*) pédicure m/f.
podiatry [pədī'ətrē] n (*US*) pédicurie f.
podium [pō'dēəm] n podium m.
POE n abbr = *port of embarkation, port of entry*.
poem [pō'əm] n poème m.
poet [pō'it] n poète m.
poetic [pōet'ik] a poétique.
poet laureate [pō'it lô'rēit] n poète lauréat (*nommé et appointé par la Cour royale*).
poetry [pō'itrē] n poésie f.
poignant [poin'yənt] a poignant(e); (*sharp*) vif(vive).
point [point] n (*tip*) pointe f; (*in time*) moment m; (*in space*) endroit m; (*GEOM, SCOL, SPORT, on scale*) point m; (*subject, idea*) point, sujet m; (*also*: **decimal ~**): **2 ~ 3** (**2.3**) 2 virgule 3 (2,3); (*Brit ELEC: also*: **power ~**) prise f (de courant) ♦ vt (*show*) indiquer; (*wall, window*) jointoyer; (*gun etc*): **to ~ sth at** braquer *or* diriger qch sur ♦ vi montrer du doigt; **to ~ to** montrer du doigt; (*fig*) signaler; **~s** npl (*AUT*) vis platinées; (*RAIL*) aiguillage m; **good ~s** qualités fpl; **the train stops at Boston and all ~s south** le train dessert Boston et toutes les gares vers le sud; **to make a ~** faire une remarque; **to make a ~ of doing sth** ne pas manquer de faire qch; **to make one's ~** se faire comprendre; **to get the ~** comprendre, saisir; **to come to the ~** en venir au fait; **when it comes to the ~** le moment venu; **there's no ~ (in doing)** cela ne sert à rien (de faire); **to be on the ~ of doing sth** être sur le point de faire qch; **that's the whole ~!** précisément!; **to be beside the ~** être à côté de la question; **you've got a ~ there!** (c'est) juste!; **in ~ of fact** en fait, en réalité; **~ of departure** (*also fig*) point de départ; **~ of order** point de procédure; **~ of sale** (*COMM*) point de vente; **~ of view** point de vue.
point out vt faire remarquer, souligner.
point-blank [point'blangk'] ad (*also*: **at ~ range**) à bout portant ♦ a (*fig*) catégorique.
pointed [poin'tid] a (*shape*) pointu(e); (*remark*) plein(e) de sous-entendus.
pointedly [poin'tidlē] ad d'une manière significative.
pointer [poin'tûr] n (*stick*) baguette f; (*needle*) aiguille f; (*dog*) chien m d'arrêt; (*clue*) indication f; (*advice*) tuyau m.

pointless |point'lis| *a* inutile, vain(e).
poise |poiz| *n* (*balance*) équilibre *m*; (*of head, body*) port *m*; (*calmness*) calme *m* ♦ *vt* placer en équilibre; **to be ~d for** (*fig*) être prêt à.
poison |poi'zən| *n* poison *m* ♦ *vt* empoisonner.
poisoning |poi'zəning| *n* empoisonnement *m*.
poisonous |poi'zənəs| *a* (*snake*) venimeux(euse); (*substance etc*) vénéneux(euse); (*fumes*) toxique; (*fig*) pernicieux(euse).
poke |pōk| *vt* (*fire*) tisonner; (*jab with finger, stick etc*) piquer; pousser du doigt; (*put*): **to ~ sth into** fourrer *or* enfoncer qch dans ♦ *n* (*jab*) (petit) coup; (*to fire*) coup *m* de tisonnier; **to ~ one's head out of the window** passer la tête par la fenêtre; **to ~ fun at sb** se moquer de qn.
  poke around *vi* fureter.
poker |pō'kûr| *n* tisonnier *m*; (*CARDS*) poker *m*.
poker-faced |pō'kûrfāst'| *a* au visage impassible.
poky |pō'kē| *a* exigu(ë).
Poland |pō'lənd| *n* Pologne *f*.
polar |pō'lûr| *a* polaire.
polar bear *n* ours blanc.
polarize |pō'lərīz| *vt* polariser.
Pole |pōl| *n* Polonais/e.
pole |pōl| *n* (*of wood*) mât *m*, perche *f*; (*ELEC*) poteau *m*; (*GEO*) pôle *m*.
pole bean *n* (*US*) haricot *m* (à rames).
polecat |pōl'kat| *n* putois *m*; (*US: skunk*) mouffette *f*.
Pol. Econ. |pâl'ēkán| *n abbr* = *political economy*.
polemic |pəlem'ik| *n* polémique *f*.
polestar |pōl'stär| *n* étoile *f* polaire.
pole vault *n* saut *m* à la perche.
police |pəlēs'| *npl* police *f* ♦ *vt* maintenir l'ordre dans; **a large number of ~ were hurt** de nombreux policiers ont été blessés.
police captain *n* (*US*) ≈ commissaire *m*.
police car *n* voiture *f* de police.
police constable *n* (*Brit*) agent *m* de police.
police department *n* (*US*) services *mpl* de police.
police force *n* police *f*, forces *fpl* de l'ordre.
policeman |pəlēs'mən| *n* agent *m* de police, policier *m*; (*US: also*: **traffic ~**) contractuel/le.
police officer *n* agent *m* de police.
police record *n* casier *m* judiciaire.
police state *n* état policier.
police station *n* commissariat *m* de police.
policewoman |pəlēs'wŏŏmən| *n* femme-agent *f*.
policy |pâl'isē| *n* politique *f*; (*also*: **insurance ~**) police *f* (d'assurance); (*of newspaper, company*) politique générale; **to take out a ~** (*INSURANCE*) souscrire une police d'assurance.
policy holder *n* assuré/e.
polio |pō'lēō| *n* polio *f*.
Polish |pō'lish| *a* polonais(e) ♦ *n* (*LING*) polonais *m*.
polish |pâl'ish| *n* (*for shoes*) cirage *m*; (*for floor*) cire *f*, encaustique *f*; (*for nails*) vernis *m*; (*shine*) éclat *m*, poli *m*; (*fig: refinement*)

raffinement *m* ♦ *vt* (*put polish on*: *shoes, wood*) cirer; (*make shiny*) astiquer, faire briller; (*fig: improve*) perfectionner.
  polish off *vt* (*work*) expédier; (*food*) liquider.
polished |pâl'isht| *a* (*fig*) raffiné(e).
polite |pəlīt'| *a* poli(e); **it's not ~ to do that** ça ne se fait pas.
politely |pəlīt'lē| *ad* poliment.
politeness |pəlīt'nis| *n* politesse *f*.
politic |pâl'itik| *a* diplomatique.
political |pəlit'ikəl| *a* politique.
political asylum *n* asile *m* politique.
politically |pəlit'iklē| *ad* politiquement.
politician |pâlitish'ən| *n* homme/femme politique, politicien/ne.
politics |pâl'itiks| *npl* politique *f*.
polka |pōl'kə| *n* polka *f*.
polka dot *n* pois *m*.
poll |pōl| *n* scrutin *m*, vote *m*; (*also*: **opinion ~**) sondage *m* (d'opinion) ♦ *vt* obtenir; **to go to the ~s** (*voters*) aller aux urnes; (*government*) tenir des élections.
pollen |pâl'ən| *n* pollen *m*.
pollen count *n* taux *m* de pollen.
pollination |pâlənā'shən| *n* pollinisation *f*.
polling |pō'ling| *n* (*Brit POL*) élections *fpl*; (*TEL*) invitation *f* à émettre.
pollute |pəlōōt'| *vt* polluer.
pollution |pəlōō'shən| *n* pollution *f*.
polo |pō'lō| *n* polo *m*.
polo neck *n* col roulé ♦ *a* à col roulé.
poly |pâl'ē| *n abbr* (*Brit*) = **polytechnic**.
polyester |pâlēes'tûr| *n* polyester *m*.
polygamy |pəlig'əmē| *n* polygamie *f*.
Polynesia |pâlənē'zhə| *n* Polynésie *f*.
Polynesian |pâlənē'zhən| *a* polynésien(ne) ♦ *n* Polynésien/ne.
polyp |pâl'ip| *n* (*MED*) polype *m*.
polystyrene |pâlēstī'rēn| *n* polystyrène *m*.
polytechnic |pâlētek'nik| *n* (*college*) I.U.T. *m*, Institut *m* Universitaire de Technologie.
polythene |pâl'əthēn| *n* polyéthylène *m*.
polythene bag *n* sac *m* en plastique.
polyurethane |pâlēyōōr'əthān| *n* polyuréthane *m*.
pomegranate |pâm'əgranit| *n* grenade *f*.
pommel |pum'əl| *n* pommeau *m* ♦ *vt* = **pummel**.
pomp |pâmp| *n* pompe *f*, faste *f*, apparat *m*.
pompom |pâm'pâm|, **pompon** |pâm'pân| *n* pompon *m*.
pompous |pâm'pəs| *a* pompeux(euse).
pond |pând| *n* étang *m*; (*stagnant*) mare *f*.
ponder |pân'dûr| *vi* réfléchir ♦ *vt* considérer, peser.
ponderous |pân'dûrəs| *a* pesant(e), lourd(e).
pong |pông| (*Brit col*) *n* puanteur *f* ♦ *vi* schlinguer.
pontiff |pân'tif| *n* pontife *m*.
pontificate |pântif'ikāt| *vi* (*fig*): **to ~ (about)** pontifier (sur).
pontoon |pântōōn'| *n* ponton *m*; (*Brit CARDS*) vingt-et-un *m*.
pony |pō'nē| *n* poney *m*.
ponytail |pō'nētāl| *n* queue *f* de cheval.
pony trekking |pō'nē trek'ing| *n* (*Brit*) randonnée *f* équestre *or* à cheval.
poodle |pōō'dəl| *n* caniche *m*.

pooh-pooh [pōōpōō'] *vt* dédaigner.

pool [pōōl] *n* (*of rain*) flaque *f*; (*pond*) mare *f*; (*artificial*) bassin *m*; (*also:* **swimming** ~) piscine *f*; (*sth shared*) fonds commun; (*money at cards*) cagnotte *f*; (*billiards*) poule *f*; (*COMM: consortium*) pool *m*; (*US: monopoly trust*) trust *m* ♦ *vt* mettre en commun; **secretary** ~, (*Brit*) **typing** ~ pool *m* dactylographique; **to do the (football)** ~**s** (*Brit*) ≈ jouer au loto sportif.

pooped [pōōpt] *a* (*US col*) crevé(e).

poor [pōōr] *a* pauvre; (*mediocre*) médiocre, faible, mauvais(e) ♦ *npl:* **the** ~ les pauvres *mpl*.

poorly [pōōr'lē] *ad* pauvrement; médiocrement ♦ *a* souffrant(e), malade.

pop [pâp] *n* (*noise*) bruit sec; (*MUS*) musique *f* pop; (*col: drink*) soda *m*; (*US col: father*) papa *m* ♦ *vt* (*put*) fourrer, mettre (rapidement) ♦ *vi* éclater; (*cork*) sauter; **she** ~**ped her head out of the window** elle passa la tête par la fenêtre.

pop in *vi* entrer en passant.

pop out *vi* sortir.

pop up *vi* apparaître, surgir.

pop concert *n* concert *m* pop.

popcorn [pâp'kôrn] *n* pop-corn *m*.

pope [pōp] *n* pape *m*.

poplar [pâp'lûr] *n* peuplier *m*.

poplin [pâp'lin] *n* popeline *f*.

poppy [pâp'ē] *n* coquelicot *m*; pavot *m*.

poppycock [pâp'ēkâk] *n* (*col*) balivernes *fpl*.

Popsicle [pâp'sikəl] *n* ® (*US*) ≈ esquimau *m* ® (*glace*).

populace [pâp'yələs] *n* peuple *m*.

popular [pâp'yəlûr] *a* populaire; (*fashionable*) à la mode; **to be** ~ **(with)** (*person*) avoir du succès (auprès de); (*decision*) être bien accueilli(e) (par).

popularity [pâpyəlar'itē] *n* popularité *f*.

popularize [pâp'yələrīz] *vt* populariser; (*science*) vulgariser.

populate [pâp'yəlāt] *vt* peupler.

population [pâpyəlā'shən] *n* population *f*.

population explosion *n* explosion *f* démographique.

populous [pâp'yələs] *a* populeux(euse).

porcelain [pôr'səlin] *n* porcelaine *f*.

porch [pôrch] *n* porche *m*.

porcupine [pôr'kyəpīn] *n* porc-épic *m*.

pore [pôr] *n* pore *m* ♦ *vi:* **to** ~ **over** s'absorber dans, être plongé(e) dans.

pork [pôrk] *n* porc *m*.

pork chop *n* côte *f* de porc.

pornographic [pôrnəgraf'ik] *a* pornographique.

pornography [pôrnâ'grəfē] *n* pornographie *f*.

porous [pôr'əs] *a* poreux(euse).

porpoise [pôr'pəs] *n* marsouin *m*.

porridge [pôr'ij] *n* porridge *m*.

port [pôrt] *n* (*harbor*) port *m*; (*opening in ship*) sabord *m*; (*NAUT: left side*) bâbord *m*; (*wine*) porto *m*; (*COMPUT*) port *m*, accès *m* ♦ *cpd* portuaire, du port; **to** ~ (*NAUT*) à bâbord; ~ **of call** (port d')escale *f*.

portable [pôr'təbəl] *a* portatif(ive).

portal [pôr'təl] *n* portail *m*.

portcullis [pôrtkul'is] *n* herse *f*.

portend [pôrtend'] *vt* présager, annoncer.

portent [pôr'tent] *n* présage *m*.

porter [pôr'tûr] *n* (*for luggage*) porteur *m*; (*doorkeeper*) gardien/ne; portier *m*.

portfolio [pôrtfō'lēō] *n* portefeuille *m*; (*of artist*) portfolio *m*.

porthole [pôrt'hōl] *n* hublot *m*.

portico [pôr'tikō] *n* portique *m*.

portion [pôr'shən] *n* portion *f*, part *f*.

portly [pôrt'lē] *a* corpulent(e).

portrait [pôr'trit] *n* portrait *m*.

portray [pôrtrā'] *vt* faire le portrait de; (*in writing*) dépeindre, représenter.

portrayal [pôrtrā'əl] *n* portrait *m*, représentation *f*.

Portugal [pôr'chəgəl] *n* Portugal *m*.

Portuguese [pôrchəgēz'] *a* portugais(e) ♦ *n* (*pl inv*) Portugais/e; (*LING*) portugais *m*.

Portuguese man-of-war *n* (*jellyfish*) galère *f*.

pose [pōz] *n* pose *f*; (*pej*) affectation *f* ♦ *vi* poser; (*pretend*): **to** ~ **as** se poser en ♦ *vt* poser, créer; **to strike a** ~ poser (pour la galerie).

poser [pō'zûr] *n* question difficile *or* embarrassante; (*person*) = **poseur.**

poseur [pōzir'] *n* (*pej*) poseur/euse.

posh [pâsh] *a* (*col*) chic *inv*; **to talk** ~ parler d'une manière affectée.

position [pəzish'ən] *n* position *f*; (*job*) situation *f* ♦ *vt* mettre en place *or* en position; **to be in a** ~ **to do sth** être en mesure de faire qch.

positive [pâz'ətiv] *a* positif(ive); (*certain*) sûr(e), certain(e); (*definite*) formel(le), catégorique; (*clear*) indéniable, réel(le).

posse [pâs'ē] *n* (*US*) détachement *m*.

possess [pəzes'] *vt* posséder; **like one** ~**ed** comme un fou; **whatever can have** ~**ed you?** qu'est-ce qui vous a pris?

possession [pəzesh'ən] *n* possession *f*; **to take** ~ **of sth** prendre possession de qch.

possessive [pəzes'iv] *a* possessif(ive).

possessively [pəzes'ivlē] *ad* d'une façon possessive.

possessor [pəzes'ûr] *n* possesseur *m*.

possibility [pâsəbil'ətē] *n* possibilité *f*; éventualité *f*; **he's a** ~ **for the part** c'est un candidat possible pour le rôle.

possible [pâs'əbəl] *a* possible; (*solution*) envisageable, éventuel(le); **it is** ~ **to do it** il est possible de le faire; **as far as** ~ dans la mesure du possible, autant que possible; **if** ~ si possible; **as big as** ~ aussi gros que possible.

possibly [pâs'əblē] *ad* (*perhaps*) peut-être; **if you** ~ **can** si cela vous est possible; **I cannot** ~ **come** il ne m'est impossible de venir.

post [pōst] *n* (*Brit: mail*) poste *f*; (: *collection*) levée *f*; (: *letters, delivery*) courrier *m*; (*job, situation*) poste *m*; (*pole*) poteau *m*; (*trading* ~) comptoir (*commercial*) ♦ *vt* (*Brit: send by mail, MIL*) poster; (*Brit: appoint*): **to** ~ **to** affecter à; (*notice*) afficher; **by** ~ (*Brit*) par la poste; **by return of** ~ (*Brit*) par retour du courrier; **to keep sb** ~**ed** tenir qn au courant.

post... *prefix* post...; ~ **1990** *a* d'après 1990 ♦ *ad* après 1990.

postage [pōs'tij] *n* affranchissement *m*; ~ **paid** port payé; ~ **prepaid** (*US*) franco (de port).

postage meter n (US) machine f à affranchir.

postage stamp n timbre-poste m.

postal [pōs'təl] a postal(e).

postal order n (Brit) mandat(-poste) m.

postbag [pōst'bag] n (Brit) sac postal; (mailman's) sacoche f.

postbox [pōst'bâks] n (Brit) boîte f aux lettres.

postcard [pōst'kârd] n carte postale.

postcode [pōst'kōd] n (Brit) code postal.

postdate [pōst'dāt] vt (check) postdater.

poster [pōs'tûr] n affiche f.

posterior [pāstēr'ēûr] n (col) postérieur m, derrière m.

posterity [pâstär'itē] n postérité f.

poster paint n gouache f.

post exchange (PX) n (US MIL) magasin m de l'armée.

post-free [pōst'frē'] a (Brit) franco (de port).

postgraduate [pōstgraj'ōōit] n ≈ étudiant/e de troisième cycle.

posthumous [pâs'chəməs] a posthume.

posthumously [pâs'chəməslē] ad après la mort de l'auteur, à titre posthume.

postman [pōst'mən] n (Brit) facteur m.

postmark [pōst'mârk] n cachet m (de la poste).

postmaster [pōst'mastûr] n receveur m des postes.

Postmaster General n ≈ ministre m des Postes et Télécommunications.

postmistress [pōst'mistris] n receveuse f des postes.

post-mortem [pōstmôr'təm] n autopsie f.

postnatal [pōstnāt'əl] a post-natal(e).

post office n (building) poste f; (organization) postes fpl.

post office box (PO box) n boîte postale (B.P.).

post-paid [pōst'pād'] a port payé.

postpone [pōstpōn'] vt remettre (à plus tard), reculer.

postponement [pōstpōn'mənt] n ajournement m, renvoi m.

postscript [pōst'skript] n post-scriptum m.

postulate [pâs'chəlāt] vt postuler.

posture [pâs'chûr] n posture f, attitude f ♦ vi poser.

post-viral syndrome (PVS) [pōstvī'rəl sin'drōm] n syndrome m post-viral.

postwar [pōst'wôr'] a d'après-guerre.

posy [pō'zē] n petit bouquet.

pot [pât] n (for cooking) marmite f; casserole f; (for plants, jam) pot m; (piece of pottery) poterie f; (col: marijuana) herbe f ♦ vt (plant) mettre en pot; **to go to ~** aller à vau-l'eau; **~s of** (Brit col) beaucoup de, plein de.

potash [pât'ash] n potasse f.

potassium [pətas'ēəm] n potassium m.

potato, ~es [pətā'tō] n pomme f de terre.

potato chips, (Brit) **potato crisps** npl chips mpl.

potato flour n fécule f.

potato peeler [pətā'tō pē'lûr] n épluche-légumes m.

potbellied [pât'belēd] a (from overeating) be-

donnant(e); (from malnutrition) au ventre ballonné.

potency [pōt'ənsē] n puissance f, force f; (of drink) degré m d'alcool.

potent [pōt'ənt] a puissant(e); (drink) fort(e), très alcoolisé(e).

potentate [pât'əntāt] n potentat m.

potential [pəten'chəl] a potentiel(le) ♦ n potentiel m; **to have ~** être prometteur(euse); ouvrir des possibilités.

potentially [pəten'chəlē] ad potentiellement; **it's ~ dangerous** ça pourrait se révéler dangereux, il y a possibilité de danger.

pothole [pât'hōl] n (in road) nid m de poule; (Brit: underground) gouffre m, caverne f.

potholer [pât'hōlûr] n (Brit) spéléologue m/f.

potion [pō'shən] n potion f.

potluck [pât'luk] n: **to take ~** tenter sa chance.

potpourri [pōpərē'] n pot-pourri m.

pot roast n rôti m à la cocotte.

potshot [pât'shât] n: **to take ~s at** canarder.

potted [pât'id] a (food) en conserve; (plant) en pot; (fig: shortened) abrégé(e).

potter [pât'ûr] n potier m ♦ vi (Brit): **to ~ around, ~ about** bricoler; **~'s wheel** tour m de potier.

pottery [pât'ûrē] n poterie f; **a piece of ~** une poterie.

potty [pât'ē] n (child's) pot m.

potty training n apprentissage m de la propreté.

pouch [pouch] n (ZOOL) poche f; (for tobacco) blague f.

pouf(fe) [pōōf] n (stool) pouf m.

poultice [pōl'tis] n cataplasme m.

poultry [pōl'trē] n volaille f.

poultry farm n élevage m de volaille.

poultry farmer n aviculteur m.

pounce [pouns] vi: **to ~ (on)** bondir (sur), fondre (sur) ♦ n bond m, attaque f.

pound [pound] n livre f (weight = 453g, 16 ounces; money = 100 pence); (for dogs, cars) fourrière f ♦ vt (beat) bourrer de coups, marteler; (crush) piler, pulvériser; (with guns) pilonner ♦ vi (beat) battre violemment, taper; **half a ~ (of)** une demi-livre (de); **a five-~ note** un billet de cinq livres.

pounding [poun'ding] n: **to take a ~** (fig) prendre une râclée.

pound sterling n livre f sterling.

pour [pôr] vt verser ♦ vi couler à flots; (rain) pleuvoir à verse; **to come ~ing in** (water) entrer à flots; (letters) arriver par milliers; (cars, people) affluer.

pour away, pour off vt vider.

pour in vi (people) affluer, se précipiter.

pour out vi (people) sortir en masse ♦ vt vider; déverser; (serve: a drink) verser.

pouring [pôr'ing] a: **~ rain** pluie torrentielle.

pout [pout] n moue f ♦ vi faire la moue.

poverty [pâv'ûrtē] n pauvreté f, misère f.

poverty-stricken [pâv'ûrtēstrikən] a pauvre, déshérité(e).

POW n abbr = **prisoner of war**.

powder [pou'dûr] n poudre f ♦ vt poudrer; **to ~ one's nose** se poudrer; (euphemism) aller à la salle de bain; **~ed milk** lait m en poudre.

powder compact n poudrier m.
powdered sugar [pou'dúrd shōōg'ûr] n (US) sucre m semoule.
powder puff n houppette f.
powder room n toilettes fpl (pour dames).
powdery [pou'dúrē] a poudreux(euse).
power [pou'úr] n (strength) puissance f, force f; (ability, POL: of party, leader) pouvoir m; (MATH) puissance; (of speech, thought) faculté f; (ELEC) courant m ♦ vt faire marcher, actionner; **to do all in one's ~ to help sb** faire tout ce qui est en son pouvoir pour aider qn; **the world ~s** les grandes puissances; **to be in ~** être au pouvoir.
power cut n (Brit) coupure f de courant.
power-driven [pou'úrdrivən] a à moteur; (ELEC) électrique.
powered [pou'úrd] a: **~ by** actionné(e) par, fonctionnant à; **nuclear-~ submarine** sous-marin m (à propulsion) nucléaire.
power failure n panne f de courant.
powerful [pou'úrfəl] a puissant(e).
powerhouse [pou'úrhous] n (fig: person) fonceur m; **a ~ of ideas** une mine d'idées.
powerless [pou'úrlis] a impuissant(e).
power line n ligne f électrique.
power shovel n (US) pelle f mécanique.
power station n centrale f électrique.
power steering n direction assistée.
powwow [pou'wou] n conciliabule m.
pox [pâks] n see **chickenpox**.
pp abbr (= per procurationem: by proxy) p.p.
p&p abbr (Brit: = postage and packing) frais mpl de port.
PPS n abbr (= post postscriptum) PPS.
PQ abbr (Canada) = Province of Quebec.
PR n abbr = **proportional representation, public relations** ♦ abbr (US MAIL) = Puerto Rico.
Pr. abbr (= prince) Pce.
practicability [praktikəbil'ətē] n possibilité f de réalisation.
practicable [prak'tikəbəl] a (scheme) réalisable.
practical [prak'tikəl] a pratique.
practicality [praktikal'itē] n (of plan) aspect m pratique; (of person) sens m pratique; **practicalities** npl détails mpl pratiques.
practical joke n farce f.
practically [prak'tiklē] ad (almost) pratiquement.
practice [prak'tis] n pratique f; (of profession) exercice m; (at football etc) entraînement m; (business) cabinet m; clientèle f ♦ vt (US) (work at: piano, one's backhand etc) s'exercer à, travailler; (train for: skiing, running etc) s'entraîner à; (a sport, religion, method) pratiquer; (profession) exercer ♦ vi (US) s'exercer, travailler; (train) s'entraîner; **in ~** (in reality) en pratique; **out of ~** rouillé(e); **2 hours' piano ~** 2 heures de travail or d'exercices au piano; **target ~** exercices de tir; **it's common ~** c'est courant, ça se fait couramment; **to put sth into ~** mettre qch en pratique; **to ~ for a match** s'entraîner pour un match.
practiced [prak'tist] a (person) expérimenté(e); (: performance) impeccable; (: liar) invétéré(e); **with a ~ eye** d'un œil exercé.

practice test n (SCOL) examen blanc.
practicing [prak'tising] a (Christian etc) pratiquant(e); (lawyer) en exercice; (homosexual) déclaré.
practise [prak'tis] vt, vi (Brit) = **practice**.
practitioner [praktish'ənûr] n praticien/ne.
pragmatic [pragmat'ik] a pragmatique.
Prague [prâg] n Prague.
prairie [prär'ē] n savane f; (US): **the ~s** la Prairie.
praise [prāz] n éloge(s) m(pl), louange(s) f(pl) ♦ vt louer, faire l'éloge de.
praiseworthy [prāz'wûrthē] a digne de louanges.
pram [pram] n (Brit) landau m, voiture f d'enfant.
prance [prans] vi (horse) caracoler.
prank [prangk] n farce f.
prattle [prat'əl] vi jacasser.
prawn [prôn] n crevette f (rose).
pray [prā] vi prier.
prayer [prär] n prière f.
prayer book n livre m de prières.
pre... [prē] prefix pré...; **pre-1970** a d'avant 1970 ♦ ad avant 1970.
preach [prēch] vt, vi prêcher; **to ~ at sb** faire la morale à qn.
preacher [prē'chûr] n prédicateur m; (clergyman) pasteur m.
preamble [prē'ambəl] n préambule m.
prearranged [prēərānjd'] a organisé(e) or fixé(e) à l'avance.
precarious [prikär'ēəs] a précaire.
precaution [prikô'shən] n précaution f.
precautionary [prikô'shənārē] a (measure) de précaution.
precede [prisēd'] vt, vi précéder.
precedence [pres'idəns] n préséance f.
precedent [pres'idənt] n précédent m; **to establish** or **set a ~** créer un précédent.
preceding [prisē'ding] a qui précède (or précédait).
precept [prē'sept] n précepte m.
precinct [prē'singkt] n (round cathedral) pourtour m, enceinte f; (US: district) circonscription f, arrondissement m; **~s** npl (neighborhood) alentours mpl, environs mpl; **pedestrian ~** zone piétonne; **shopping ~** (Brit) centre commercial.
precious [presh'əs] a précieux(euse) ♦ ad (col): **~ little** or **few** fort peu.
precipice [pres'əpis] n précipice m.
precipitate [prisip'itit] (hasty) précipité(e) ♦ vt [prisip'itāt] précipiter.
precipitation [prisipitā'shən] n précipitation f.
precipitous [prisip'itəs] a (steep) abrupt(e), à pic.
précis, pl **précis** [prā'sē] n résumé m.
precise [prisīs'] a précis(e).
precisely [prisīs'lē] ad précisément.
precision [prisizh'ən] n précision f.
preclude [priklōōd'] vt exclure, empêcher; **to ~ sb from doing** empêcher qn de faire.
precocious [prikō'shəs] a précoce.
preconceived [prēkənsēvd'] a (idea) préconçu(e).
preconception [prēkənsep'shən] n idée préconçue.

precondition [prēkəndish'ən] *n* condition *f* nécessaire.

precursor [prikûr'sûr] *n* précurseur *m*.

predate [prēdāt'] *vt* (*precede*) antidater.

predator [pred'ətûr] *n* prédateur *m*, rapace *m*.

predatory [pred'ətôrē] *a* rapace.

predecessor [pred'isesûr] *n* prédécesseur *m*.

predestination [prēdestinā'shən] *n* prédestination *f*.

predetermine [prēditûr'min] *vt* déterminer à l'avance.

predicament [pridik'əmənt] *n* situation *f* difficile.

predicate [pred'əkit] *n* (*LING*) prédicat *m*.

predict [pridikt'] *vt* prédire.

predictable [pridikt'əbəl] *a* prévisible.

predictably [pridikt'əblē] *ad* (*behave, react*) de façon prévisible; ~ **she didn't arrive** comme on pouvait s'y attendre, elle n'est pas venue.

prediction [pridik'shən] *n* prédiction *f*.

predispose [prēdispōz'] *vt* prédisposer.

predominance [pridâm'ənəns] *n* prédominance *f*.

predominant [pridâm'ənənt] *a* prédominant(e).

predominantly [pridâm'ənəntlē] *ad* en majeure partie; surtout.

predominate [pridâm'ənāt] *vi* prédominer.

preeminent [prēem'ənənt] *a* prééminent(e).

preempt [prēempt'] *vt* acquérir par droit de préemption; (*fig*) anticiper sur; **to ~ the issue** conclure avant même d'ouvrir les débats.

preemptive [prēemp'tiv] *a*: ~ **strike** attaque (*or* action) préventive.

preen [prēn] *vt*: **to ~ itself** (*bird*) se lisser les plumes; **to ~ o.s.** s'admirer.

prefab [prē'fab] *n* bâtiment préfabriqué.

prefabricated [prēfab'rikātid] *a* préfabriqué(e).

preface [pref'is] *n* préface *f*.

prefect [prē'fekt] *n* (*Brit: in school*) élève chargé de certaines fonctions de discipline; (*in France*) préfet *m*.

prefer [prifûr'] *vt* préférer; (*LAW*): **to ~ charges** procéder à une inculpation; **to ~ coffee to tea** préférer le café au thé.

preferable [pref'ûrəbəl] *a* préférable.

preferably [prifûr'əblē] *ad* de préférence.

preference [pref'ûrəns] *n* préférence *f*; **in ~ to sth** plutôt que qch, de préférence à qch.

preference shares *npl* (*Brit*) = **preferred stock**.

preferential [prefəren'chəl] *a* préférentiel(le); ~ **treatment** traitement *m* de faveur.

preferred stock [prifûrd' stâk] *npl* (*US*) actions privilégiées.

prefix [prē'fiks] *n* préfixe *m*.

pregnancy [preg'nənsē] *n* grossesse *f*.

pregnant [preg'nənt] *a* enceinte *af*; **3 months ~** enceinte de 3 mois.

prehistoric [prēhistôr'ik] *a* préhistorique.

prehistory [prēhis'tûrē] *n* préhistoire *f*.

prejudge [prējuj'] *vt* préjuger de.

prejudice [prej'ədis] *n* préjugé *m*; (*harm*) tort *m*, préjudice *m* ♦ *vt* porter préjudice à; (*bias*): **to ~ sb in favor of/against** prévenir qn en faveur de/contre.

prejudiced [prej'ədist] *a* (*person*) plein(e) de préjugés; (*view*) préconçu(e), partial(e); **to be ~ against sb/sth** avoir un parti-pris contre qn/qch.

prelate [prel'it] *n* prélat *m*.

preliminaries [prilim'ənārēz] *npl* préliminaires *mpl*.

preliminary [prilim'ənārē] *a* préliminaire.

prelude [prā'lood] *n* prélude *m*.

premarital [prēmar'itəl] *a* avant le mariage.

premature [prēməchoor'] *a* prématuré(e); **to be ~ (in doing sth)** aller un peu (trop) vite (en faisant qch).

premeditated [primed'ətātid] *a* prémédité(e).

premeditation [primeditā'shən] *n* préméditation *f*.

premenstrual [prēmen'strōōəl] *a* prémenstruel(le).

premenstrual tension *n* irritabilité *f* avant les règles.

premier [primyēr'] *a* premier(ière), principal(e) ♦ *n* (*POL*) premier ministre.

première [primyēr'] *n* première *f*.

premise [prem'is] *n* prémisse *f*.

premises [prem'isiz] *npl* locaux *mpl*; **on the ~** sur les lieux; sur place; **business ~** locaux commerciaux.

premium [prē'mēəm] *n* prime *f*; **to be at a ~** (*fig: housing etc*) être très demandé(e), être rarissime; **to sell at a ~** (*shares*) vendre au-dessus du pair.

premium bond *n* (*Brit*) bon *m* à lots.

premium deal *n* (*COMM*) offre spéciale.

premium gas(oline) *n* (*US*) super *m*.

premonition [premənish'ən] *n* prémonition *f*.

prenatal [prēnāt'l] *a* (*US*) prénatal(e).

prenatal clinic *n* (*US*) service *m* de consultation prénatale.

preoccupation [prēâkyəpā'shən] *n* préoccupation *f*.

preoccupied [prēâk'yəpīd] *a* préoccupé(e).

prep [prep] *a abbr*: ~ **school** = **preparatory school**.

prepackaged [prēpak'ijd] *a* préempaqueté(e).

prepaid [prēpād'] *a* payé(e) d'avance.

preparation [prepərā'shən] *n* préparation *f*; ~**s** (*for trip, war*) préparatifs *mpl*; **in ~ for** en vue de.

preparatory [pripar'ətôrē] *a* préparatoire; ~ **to sth/to doing sth** en prévision de qch/avant de faire qch.

preparatory school *n* école primaire privée; (*US*) lycée privé.

prepare [pripār'] *vt* préparer ♦ *vi*: **to ~ for** se préparer à.

prepared [pripārd'] *a*: ~ **for** préparé(e) à; ~ **to** prêt(e) à.

preponderance [pripân'dûrəns] *n* prépondérance *f*.

preposition [prepəzish'ən] *n* préposition *f*.

prepossessing [prēpəzes'ing] *a* avenant(e), engageant(e).

preposterous [pripâs'tûrəs] *a* absurde.

prep school *n* = **preparatory school**.

prerecord [prērikôrd'] *vt*: ~**ed broadcast** émission *f* en différé; ~**ed cassette** cassette enregistrée.

prerequisite [prirek'wizit] *n* condition *f* préalable.

prerogative [prərăg'ətiv] *n* prérogative *f.*

presbyterian [prezbitĕr'ēən] *a, n* presbytérien(ne).

presbytery [prez'bitărē] *n* presbytère *m.*

preschool [prē'skool'] *a* préscolaire; (*child*) d'âge préscolaire.

prescribe [priskrīb'] *vt* prescrire.

prescription [priskrip'shən] *n* prescription *f*; (*MED*) ordonnance *f*; **to fill a ~** faire une ordonnance.

prescriptive [priskrip'tiv] *a* normatif(ive).

presence [prez'əns] *n* présence *f*; **~ of mind** présence d'esprit.

present [prez'ənt] *a* présent(e) ♦ *n* cadeau *m*; (*also*: **~ tense**) présent *m* ♦ *vt* [prizent'] présenter; (*give*): **to ~ sb with sth** offrir qch à qn; **to be ~ at** assister à; **those ~** les présents; **at ~** en ce moment; **to give sb a ~** offrir un cadeau à qn; **to ~ sb (to sb)** présenter qn (à qn).

presentable [prizen'təbəl] *a* présentable.

presentation [prezəntā'shən] *n* présentation *f*; (*gift*) cadeau *m*, présent *m*; (*ceremony*) remise *f* du cadeau; **on ~ of** (*voucher etc*) sur présentation de.

present-day [prez'əntdā'] *a* contemporain(e), actuel(le).

presenter [prizen'tûr] *n* (*RADIO, TV*) présentateur/trice.

presently [prez'əntlē] *ad* (*soon*) tout à l'heure, bientôt; (*at present*) en ce moment; (*US: now*) maintenant.

preservation [prezûrvā'shən] *n* préservation *f*, conservation *f.*

preservative [prizûr'vətiv] *n* agent *m* de conservation.

preserve [prizûrv'] *vt* (*keep safe*) préserver, protéger; (*maintain*) conserver, garder; (*food*) mettre en conserve ♦ *n* (*for game, fish*) réserve *f*; (*often pl: jam*) confiture *f*; (*: fruit*) fruits *mpl* en conserve.

preshrunk [prē'shrungk'] *a* irrétrécissable.

preside [prizīd'] *vi* présider.

presidency [prez'idənsē] *n* présidence *f.*

president [prez'idənt] *n* président/e; (*US: of company*) président-directeur général, PDG *m.*

presidential [prezidεn'chəl] *a* présidentiel(le).

press [pres] *n* (*tool, machine, newspapers*) presse *f*; (*for wine*) pressoir *m*; (*crowd*) cohue *f*, foule *f* ♦ *vt* (*push*) appuyer sur; (*squeeze*) presser, serrer; (*clothes: iron*) repasser; (*pursue*) talonner; (*insist*): **to ~ sth on sb** presser qn d'accepter qch; (*urge, entreat*): **to ~ sb to do** *or* **into doing sth** pousser qn à faire qch ♦ *vi* appuyer, peser; se presser; **we are ~ed for time** le temps nous manque; **to ~ for sth** faire pression pour obtenir qch; **to ~ sb for an answer** presser qn de répondre; **to ~ charges against sb** (*LAW*) engager des poursuites contre qn; **to go to ~** (*newspaper*) aller à l'impression; **to be in the ~** (*being printed*) être sous presse; (*in the newspapers*) être dans le journal.

press on *vi* continuer.

press agency *n* agence *f* de presse.

press clipping *n* coupure *f* de presse.

press conference *n* conférence *f* de presse.

press cutting *n* (*Brit*) = **press clipping.**

press-gang [pres'gang] *n* recruteurs *de la marine (jusqu'au 19ème siècle).*

pressing [pres'ing] *a* urgent(e), pressant(e) ♦ *n* repassage *m.*

press release *n* communiqué *m* de presse.

press stud *n* (*Brit*) bouton-pression *m.*

press-up [pres'up] *n* (*Brit*) traction *f.*

pressure [presh'ûr] *n* pression *f*; (*stress*) tension *f* ♦ *vt* = **to put ~ on; to put ~ on sb (to do sth)** faire pression sur qn (pour qu'il fasse qch).

pressure cooker *n* cocotte-minute *f.*

pressure gauge *n* manomètre *m.*

pressure group *n* groupe *m* de pression.

pressurize [presh'ərīz] *vt* pressuriser; (*Brit fig*): **to ~ sb (into doing sth)** faire pression sur qn (pour qu'il fasse qch).

pressurized [presh'ərīzd] *a* pressurisé(e).

prestige [prestēzh'] *n* prestige *m.*

prestigious [prestij'əs] *a* prestigieux(euse).

presumably [prizoo'məblē] *ad* vraisemblablement; **~ he did it** c'est sans doute lui (qui a fait cela).

presume [prizoom'] *vt* présumer, supposer; **to ~ to do** (*dare*) se permettre de faire.

presumption [prizump'shən] *n* supposition *f*, présomption *f*; (*boldness*) audace *f.*

presumptuous [prizump'chooəs] *a* présomptueux(euse).

presuppose [prēsəpōz'] *vt* présupposer.

pretax [prē'taks] *a* avant impôt(s).

pretence [pritens'] *n* (*Brit*) = **pretense.**

pretend [pritend'] *vt* (*feign*) feindre, simuler ♦ *vi* (*feign*) faire semblant; (*claim*): **to ~ to sth** prétendre à qch; **to ~ to do** faire semblant de faire.

pretense [pritens'] *n* (*US*) (*claim*) prétention *f*; (*pretext*) prétexte *m*; **she is devoid of all ~** elle n'est pas du tout prétentieuse; **to make a ~ of doing** faire semblant de faire; **on** *or* **under the ~ of doing sth** sous prétexte de faire qch.

pretension [priten'chən] *n* (*claim*) prétention *f*; **to have no ~s to sth/to being sth** n'avoir aucune prétention à qch/à être qch.

pretentious [priten'chəs] *a* prétentieux(euse).

preterite [pret'ûrit] *n* prétérit *m.*

pretext [prē'tekst] *n* prétexte *m*; **on** *or* **under the ~ of doing sth** sous prétexte de faire qch.

pretty [prit'ē] *a* joli(e) ♦ *ad* assez.

prevail [privāl'] *vi* (*win*) l'emporter, prévaloir; (*be usual*) avoir cours; (*persuade*): **to ~ (up)on sb to do** persuader qn de faire.

prevailing [privā'ling] *a* dominant(e).

prevalent [prev'ələnt] *a* répandu(e), courant(e); (*fashion*) en vogue.

prevarication [privarikā'shən] *n* (usage *m* de) faux-fuyants *mpl.*

prevent [privent'] *vt*: **to ~ (from doing)** empêcher (de faire).

preventable [privent'əbəl] *a* évitable.

preventative [privent'ətiv] *a* préventif(ive).

prevention [priven'chən] *n* prévention *f.*

preventive [priven'tiv] *a* préventif(ive).

preview [prē'vyoo] *n* (*of film*) avant-première *f*; (*fig*) aperçu *m.*

previous [prē'vēəs] *a* (*last*) précédent(e);

(*earlier*) antérieur(e); (*question, experience*) préalable; **I have a ~ engagement** je suis déjà pris(e); **~ to doing** avant de faire.

previously [prē'vēəslē] *ad* précédemment, auparavant.

prewar [prē'wôr'] *a* d'avant-guerre.

prey [prā] *n* proie *f* ♦ *vi*: **to ~ on** s'attaquer à; **it was ~ing on his mind** ça le rongeait *or* minait.

price [prīs] *n* prix *m*; (*BETTING: odds*) cote *f* ♦ *vt* (*goods*) fixer le prix de; tarifer; **what is the ~ of ...?** combien coûte ...?, quel est le prix de ...?; **to go up** *or* **rise in ~** augmenter; **to put a ~ on sth** chiffrer qch; **to be ~d out of the market** (*article*) être trop cher pour soutenir la concurrence; (*producer, nation*) ne pas pouvoir soutenir la concurrence; **he regained his freedom, but at a ~** il a retrouvé sa liberté, mais cela lui a coûté cher.

price control *n* contrôle *m* des prix.

price-cutting [prīs'kuting] *n* réductions *fpl* de prix.

priceless [prīs'lis] *a* sans prix, inestimable; (*col: amusing*) impayable.

price list *n* tarif *m*.

price range *n* gamme *f* de prix; **it's within my ~** c'est dans mes prix.

price tag *n* étiquette *f*.

price war *n* guerre *f* des prix.

pricey [prī'sē] *a* (*col*) chérot *inv*.

prick [prik] *n* piqûre *f*; (*col!*) bitte *f* (!); connard *m* (!) ♦ *vt* piquer; **to ~ up one's ears** dresser *or* tendre l'oreille.

prickle [prik'əl] *n* (*of plant*) épine *f*; (*sensation*) picotement *m*.

prickly [prik'lē] *a* piquant(e), épineux(euse); (*fig: person*) irritable.

prickly heat *n* fièvre *f* miliaire.

prickly pear *n* figue *f* de Barbarie.

pride [prīd] *n* (*feeling proud*) fierté *f*; (: *pej*) orgueil *m*; (*self-esteem*) amour-propre *m* ♦ *vt*: **to ~ o.s. on** se flatter de; s'enorgueillir de; **to take (a) ~ in** être (très) fier(ère) de; **to take a ~ in doing** mettre sa fierté à faire.

priest [prēst] *n* prêtre *m*.

priestess [prēs'tis] *n* prêtresse *f*.

priesthood [prēst'hood] *n* prêtrise *f*, sacerdoce *m*.

prig [prig] *n* poseur/euse, fat *m*.

prim [prim] *a* collet monté *inv*, guindé(e).

prima facie [prē'mə fā'sē] *a*: **to have a ~ case** (*LAW*) avoir une affaire qui paraît fondée.

primarily [prīmär'ilē] *ad* principalement, essentiellement.

primary [prī'märē] *a* primaire; (*first in importance*) premier(ière), primordial(e) ♦ *n* (*US: election*) (élection *f*) primaire.

primary color *n* couleur fondamentale.

primary products *npl* produits *mpl* de base.

primary school *n* (*Brit*) école primaire *f*.

primate *n* (*REL*) [prī'mit] primat *m*; (*ZOOL*) [prī'māt] primate *m*.

prime [prīm] *a* primordial(e), fondamental(e); (*excellent*) excellent(e) ♦ *vt* (*gun, pump*) amorcer; (*fig*) mettre au courant; **in the ~ of life** dans la fleur de l'âge.

prime minister *n* premier ministre *m*.

primer [prī'mûr] *n* (*book*) premier livre, manuel *m* élémentaire; (*paint*) apprêt *m*; (*of gun*) amorce *f*.

prime time *n* (*RADIO. TV*) heure(s) *f(pl)* de grande écoute.

primeval [prīmē'vəl] *a* primitif(ive).

primitive [prim'ətiv] *a* primitif(ive).

primrose [prim'rōz] *n* primevère *f*.

primus (stove) [prī'məs (stōv)] *n* ® (*Brit*) réchaud *m* de camping.

prince [prins] *n* prince *m*.

princess [prin'sis] *n* princesse *f*.

principal [prin'səpəl] *a* principal(e) ♦ *n* (*headmaster*) directeur *m*, principal *m*; (*in play*) rôle principal; (*money*) principal *m*.

principality [prinsəpal'itē] *n* principauté *f*.

principally [prin'səpəlē] *ad* principalement.

principle [prin'səpəl] *n* principe *m*; **in ~** en principe; **on ~** par principe.

print [print] *n* (*mark*) empreinte *f*; (*letters*) caractères *mpl*; (*fabric*) imprimé *m*; (*ART*) gravure *f*, estampe *f*; (*PHOT*) épreuve *f* ♦ *vt* imprimer; (*publish*) publier; (*write in capitals*) écrire en majuscules; **out of ~** épuisé(e).

print out *vt* (*COMPUT*) imprimer.

printed circuit board (PCB) *n* carte *f* à circuit imprimé.

printed matter *n* imprimés *mpl*.

printer [prin'tûr] *n* imprimeur *m*; (*machine*) imprimante *f*.

printhead [print'hed] *n* tête *f* d'impression.

printing [prin'ting] *n* impression *f*.

printing press *n* presse *f* typographique.

print-out [print'out] *n* listing *m*.

print shop *n* imprimerie *f*.

print wheel *n* marguerite *f*.

prior [prī'ûr] *a* antérieur(e), précédent(e) ♦ *n* (*REL*) prieur *m*; **~ to doing** avant de faire; **without ~ notice** sans préavis; **to have a ~ claim to sth** avoir priorité pour qch.

priority [prīôr'itē] *n* priorité *f*; **to have** *or* **take ~ over sth/sb** avoir la priorité sur qch/qn.

priory [prī'ərē] *n* prieuré *m*.

prise [prīz] *vt* (*Brit*): **to ~ open** forcer.

prism [priz'əm] *n* prisme *m*.

prison [priz'ən] *n* prison *f*.

prison camp *n* camp *m* de prisonniers.

prisoner [priz'ənûr] *n* prisonnier/ière; **the ~ at the bar** l'accusé/e; **to take sb ~** faire qn prisonnier; **~ of war** prisonnier de guerre.

prison warden *n* (*US*) directeur/trice de prison.

prissy [pris'ē] *a* bégueule.

pristine [pris'tēn] *a* virginal(e).

privacy [prī'vəsē] *n* intimité *f*, solitude *f*.

private [prī'vit] *a* (*not public*) privé(e); (*personal*) personnel(le); (*house, car, lesson*) particulier(ière) ♦ *n* (*US MIL*) soldat *m* de deuxième classe; "**~**" (*on envelope*) "personnelle"; **in ~** en privé; **in (his) ~ life** dans sa vie privée; **he is a very ~ person** il est très secret; **to be in ~ practice** être médecin (*or* dentiste *etc*) non conventionné; **~ hearing** (*LAW*) audience *f* à huis-clos.

private enterprise *n* entreprise privée.

private eye *n* détective privé.

private limited company *n* (*Brit*) société *f* à participation restreinte (*non cotée en*

Bourse).

privately [prī'vitlē] *ad* en privé; (*within one-self*) intérieurement.

private parts *npl* parties (génitales).

private property *n* propriété privée.

private school *n* école privée.

privation [prīvā'shən] *n* privation *f*.

privatize [prī'vətīz] *vt* privatiser.

privet [priv'it] *n* troène *m*.

privilege [priv'əlij] *n* privilège *m*.

privileged [priv'əlijd] *a* privilégié(e); **to be ~ to do sth** avoir le privilège de faire qch.

privy [priv'ē] *a*: **to be ~ to** être au courant de.

privy council *n* conseil privé.

prize [prīz] *n* prix *m* ♦ *a* (*example, idiot*) parfait(e); (*bull, novel*) primé(e) ♦ *vt* priser, faire grand cas de; (*US*): **to ~ open** forcer.

prize fight *n* combat professionnel.

prize giving *n* distribution *f* des prix.

prize money *n* argent *m* du prix.

prizewinner [prīz'winûr] *n* gagnant/e.

prizewinning [prīz'wining] *a* gagnant(e); (*novel, essay etc*) primé(e).

PRO *n abbr* = **public relations officer.**

pro [prō] *n* (*SPORT*) professionnel/le; **the ~s and cons** le pour et le contre.

pro- [prō] *prefix* (*in favor of*) pro-.

probability [prâbəbil'ətē] *n* probabilité *f*; **in all ~** très probablement.

probable [prâb'əbəl] *a* probable; **it is ~/ hardly ~ that ...** il est probable/peu probable que ....

probably [prâb'əblē] *ad* probablement.

probate [prō'bāt] *n* (*LAW*) validation *f*, homologation *f*.

probation [prəbā'shən] *n* (*in employment*) (période *f* d')essai *m*; (*LAW*) liberté surveillée; (*REL*) noviciat *m*, probation *f*; **on ~** (*employee*) à l'essai; (*LAW*) en liberté surveillée.

probationary [prəbā'shənârē] *a* (*period*) d'essai.

probe [prōb] *n* (*MED*, *SPACE*) sonde *f*; (*enquiry*) enquête *f*, investigation *f* ♦ *vt* sonder, explorer.

probity [prō'bitē] *n* probité *f*.

problem [prâb'ləm] *n* problème *m*; **to have ~s with the car** avoir des ennuis avec la voiture; **what's the ~?** qu'y a-t-il?, quel est le problème?; **I had no ~ in finding her** je n'ai pas eu de mal à la trouver; **no ~!** pas de problème!

problematic [prâbləmat'ik] *a* problématique.

procedure [prəsē'jûr] *n* (*ADMIN*, *LAW*) procédure *f*; (*method*) marche *f* à suivre, façon *f* de procéder.

proceed [prəsēd'] *vi* (*go forward*) avancer; (*go about it*) procéder; (*continue*): **to ~ (with)** continuer, poursuivre; **to ~ to aller à**; passer à; **to ~ to do se mettre à faire**; **I am not sure how to ~** je ne sais pas exactement comment m'y prendre; **to ~ against sb** (*LAW*) intenter des poursuites contre qn.

proceeding [prəsē'ding] *n* procédé *m*, façon *f* d'agir.

proceedings [prəsē'dingz] *npl* mesures *fpl*; (*LAW*) poursuites *fpl*; (*meeting*) réunion *f*, séance *f*; (*records*) compte rendu; actes *mpl*.

proceeds [prō'sēds] *npl* produit *m*, recette *f*.

process *n* [prâs'es] processus *m*; (*method*)

procédé *m* ♦ *vt* traiter ♦ *vi* [prases'] (*Brit formal: go in procession*) défiler; **in ~** en cours; **we are in the ~ of doing** nous sommes en train de faire.

process(ed) cheese [prâs'es(t) chēz] *n ≈* fromage fondu.

processing [prâs'esing] *n* traitement *m*.

procession [prəsesh'ən] *n* défilé *m*, cortège *m*; **funeral ~** cortège funèbre, convoi *m* mortuaire.

proclaim [prəklām'] *vt* déclarer, proclamer.

proclamation [prâkləmā'shən] *n* proclamation *f*.

proclivity [prōkliv'ətē] *n* inclination *f*.

procrastination [prōkrastənā'shən] *n* procrastination *f*.

procreation [prōkrēā'shən] *n* procréation *f*.

proctor [prâk'tûr] *n* (*US*) surveillant *m* d'examen.

procure [prəkyōor'] *vt* (*for o.s.*) se procurer; (*for sb*) procurer.

procurement [prəkyōor'mənt] *n* achat *m*, approvisionnement *m*.

prod [prâd] *vt* pousser ♦ *n* (*push, jab*) petit coup, poussée *f*.

prodigal [prâd'əgəl] *a* prodigue.

prodigious [prədij'əs] *a* prodigieux(euse).

prodigy [prâd'əjē] *n* prodige *m*.

produce *n* [prō'dōos] produits *mpl* ♦ *vt* [prədōos'] produire; (*to show*) présenter; (*cause*) provoquer, causer; (*THEATER*) monter, mettre en scène.

producer [prədōo'sûr] *n* (*THEATER*) metteur *m* en scène; (*AGR*, *CINEMA*) producteur *m*.

product [prâd'əkt] *n* produit *m*.

production [prəduk'shən] *n* production *f*; (*THEATER*) mise *f* en scène; **to put into ~** (*goods*) entreprendre la fabrication de.

production agreement *n* (*US*) accord *m* de productivité.

production control *n* contrôle *m* de production.

production line *n* chaîne *f* (de fabrication).

production manager *n* directeur/trice de la production.

productive [prəduk'tiv] *a* productif(ive).

productivity [prâdəktiv'ətē] *n* productivité *f*.

productivity agreement *n* (*Brit*) = **production agreement.**

productivity bonus *n* prime *f* de rendement.

Prof. [prâf] *abbr* (= *professor*) Prof.

profane [prəfān'] *a* sacrilège; (*lay*) profane.

profess [prəfes'] *vt* professer; **I do not ~ to be an expert** je ne prétends pas être spécialiste.

professed [prəfest'] *a* (*self-declared*) déclaré(e).

profession [prəfesh'ən] *n* profession *f*; **the ~s** les professions libérales.

professional [prəfesh'ənəl] *n* (*SPORT*) professionnel/le ♦ *a* professionnel(le); (*work*) de professionnel; **he's a ~ man** il exerce une profession libérale; **to seek ~ advice** consulter un spécialiste.

professionalism [prəfesh'ənəlizəm] *n* professionnalisme *m*.

professionally [prəfesh'ənəlē] *ad* professionnellement; (*SPORT: play*) en professionnel; **I only know him ~** je n'ai avec lui que des relations de travail.

professor [prəfes'ûr] n professeur m (titulaire d'une chaire); (US: teacher) professeur m.

professorship [prəfes'ûrship] n chaire f.

proffer [prâf'ûr] vt (hand) tendre; (remark) faire; (apologies) présenter.

proficiency [prəfish'ənsē] n compétence f, aptitude f.

proficient [prəfish'ənt] a compétent(e), capable.

profile [prō'fil] n profil m; **to keep a high/low ~** (fig) rester or être très en évidence/discret(ète).

profit [prâf'it] n (from trading) bénéfice m; (advantage) profit m ♦ vi: **to ~ (by** or **from)** profiter (de); **~ and loss statement** compte m de profits et pertes; **to make a ~** faire un or des bénéfice(s); **to sell sth at a ~** vendre qch à profit.

profitability [prâfitəbil'ətē] n rentabilité f.

profitable [prâf'itəbəl] a lucratif(ive), rentable; (fig: beneficial) avantageux(euse); (: meeting) fructueux(euse).

profit center n centre m de profit.

profiteering [prâfitēr'ing] n (pej) mercantilisme m.

profit-making [prâf'itmāking] a à but lucratif.

profit margin n marge f bénéficiaire.

profit sharing [prâf'it shä'ring] n intéressement m aux bénéfices.

profligate [prâf'ləgit] a (behavior, act) dissolu(e); (person) débauché(e); (extravagant): **~ (with)** prodigue (de).

pro forma [prō fôr'mə] a: **~ invoice** facture f pro-forma.

profound [prəfound'] a profond(e).

profuse [prəfyōōs'] a abondant(e).

profusely [prəfyōōs'lē] ad abondamment; (thank etc) avec effusion.

profusion [prəfyōō'zhən] n profusion f, abondance f.

progeny [prâj'ənē] n progéniture f; descendants mpl.

program (US) n [prō'grəm] programme m; (RADIO, TV) émission f ♦ vt [prō'gram] (also: Brit: COMPUT) programmer.

program(m)er [prō'gramûr] n programmeur/euse.

program(m)ing [prō'graming] n programmation f.

program(m)ing language n langage m de programmation.

programme [prō'gram] etc (Brit) = **program** etc.

progress [prâg'res] n progrès m ♦ vi [prəgres'] progresser, avancer; **in ~** en cours; **to make ~** progresser, faire des progrès, être en progrès; **as the match ~ed** au fur et à mesure que la partie avançait.

progression [prəgresh'ən] n progression f.

progressive [prəgres'iv] a progressif(ive); (person) progressiste.

progressively [prəgres'ivlē] ad progressivement.

progress report n (MED) bulletin m de santé; (ADMIN) rapport m d'activité; rapport sur l'état (d'avancement) des travaux.

prohibit [prōhib'it] vt interdire, défendre; **to ~ sb from doing sth** défendre or interdire à

qn de faire qch; **"smoking ~ed"** "défense de fumer".

prohibition [prōəbish'ən] n prohibition f.

prohibitive [prōhib'ətiv],a (price etc) prohibitif(ive).

project n [prâj'ekt] (plan) projet m, plan m; (venture) opération f, entreprise f; (gen SCOL: research) étude f, dossier m ♦ vb [prəjekt'] vt projeter ♦ vi (stick out) faire saillie, s'avancer.

projectile [prəjek'təl] n projectile m.

projection [prəjek'shən] n projection f; (overhang) saillie f.

projectionist [prəjek'shənist] n (CINEMA) projectionniste m/f.

projection room n (CINEMA) cabine f de projection.

projector [prəjek'tûr] n (CINEMA etc) projecteur m.

proletarian [prōlitär'ēən] a prolétarien(ne) ♦ n prolétaire m/f.

proletariat [prōlitär'ēət] n prolétariat m.

proliferate [prōlif'ərāt] vi proliférer.

proliferation [prōlifərā'shən] n prolifération f.

prolific [prōlif'ik] a prolifique.

prolog(ue) [prō'lôg] n prologue m.

prolong [prəlông'] vt prolonger.

prom [prâm] n abbr = **promenade**; (Brit) **promenade concert**; (US: ball) bal m d'étudiants.

promenade [prâmənād'] n (by sea) esplanade f, promenade f.

promenade concert n (Brit) concert m (de musique classique).

promenade deck n (NAUT) pont m promenade.

prominence [prâm'ənəns] n proéminence f; importance f.

prominent [prâm'ənənt] a (standing out) proéminent(e); (important) important(e); **he is ~ in the field of** ... il est très connu dans le domaine de ....

prominently [prâm'ənəntlē] ad (display, set) bien en évidence; **he figured ~ in the case** il a joué un rôle important dans l'affaire.

promiscuity [prâmiskyōō'itē] n (sexual) légèreté f de mœurs.

promiscuous [prəmis'kyōōəs] a (sexually) de mœurs légères.

promise [prâm'is] n promesse f ♦ vt, vi promettre; **to make sb a ~** faire une promesse à qn; **to ~ (sb) to do sth** promettre (à qn) de faire qch; **a young man of ~** un jeune homme plein d'avenir; **to ~ well** vi promettre.

promising [prâm'ising] a prometteur(euse).

promissory note [prâm'isôrē nōt] n billet m à ordre.

promontory [prâm'əntôrē] n promontoire m.

promote [prəmōt'] vt promouvoir; (venture, event) organiser, mettre sur pied; (new product) lancer; **the team was ~d to the second division** (Brit SOCCER) l'équipe est montée en 2e division.

promoter [prəmō'tûr] n (of event) organisateur/trice; (of cause etc) partisan/e, défenseur m.

promotion [prəmō'shən] n promotion f.

prompt [prâmpt] a rapide ♦ n (COMPUT)

message m (de guidage) ♦ vt inciter; (cause) entraîner, provoquer; (THEATER) souffler (son rôle or ses répliques) à; **they're very ~** (punctual) ils sont ponctuels; **at 8 o'clock ~** à 8 heures précises; **he was ~ to accept** il a tout de suite accepté; **to ~ sb to do** inciter or pousser qn à faire.

prompter [prâmp'tûr] n (THEATER) souffleur m.

promptly [prâmpt'lē] ad rapidement, sans délai; ponctuellement.

promptness [prâmpt'nis] n rapidité f; promptitude f; ponctualité f.

promulgate [prâm'əlgāt] vt promulguer.

prone [prōn] a (lying) couché(e) (face contre terre); (liable): **~ to** enclin(e) à; **to be ~ to illness** être facilement malade; **to be ~ to an illness** être sujet à une maladie; **she is ~ to burst into tears if** ... elle a tendance à tomber en larmes si ....

prong [prông] n pointe f; (of fork) dent f.

pronoun [prō'noun] n pronom m.

pronounce [prənouns'] vt prononcer ♦ vi: **to ~ (up)on** se prononcer sur; **they ~d him unfit to drive** ils l'ont déclaré inapte à la conduite.

pronounced [prənounst'] a (marked) prononcé(e).

pronouncement [prənouns'mənt] n déclaration f.

pronunciation [prənunsēā'shən] n prononciation f.

proof [proof] n preuve f; (test, of book, PHOT) épreuve f; (of alcohol) degré m ♦ a: **against** à l'épreuve de; **to be 35% ~** ≈ titrer 40 degrés.

proofreader [proof'rēdûr] n correcteur/trice (d'épreuves).

prop [prâp] n support m, étai m ♦ vt (also: **~ up**) étayer, soutenir; (lean): **to ~ sth against** appuyer qch contre or à.

Prop. abbr (COMM) = **proprietor.**

propaganda [prâpəgan'də] n propagande f.

propagation [prâpəgā'shən] n propagation f.

propel [prəpel'] vt propulser, faire avancer.

propeller [prəpel'ûr] n hélice f.

propelling pencil [prəpel'ing pen'səl] n (Brit) porte-mine m inv.

propensity [prəpen'sitē] n propension f.

proper [prâp'ûr] a (suited, right) approprié(e), bon(bonne); (seemly) correct(e), convenable; (authentic) vrai(e), véritable; (col: real) n + fini(e), vrai(e); **to go through the ~ channels** (ADMIN) passer par la voie officielle.

properly [prâp'ûrlē] ad correctement, convenablement; (really) bel et bien.

proper noun n nom m propre.

property [prâp'ûrtē] n (possessions) biens mpl; (house etc) propriété f; (land) terres fpl, domaine m; (CHEMISTRY etc: quality) propriété f; **it's their ~** cela leur appartient, c'est leur propriété.

property developer n (Brit) promoteur immobilier.

property owner n propriétaire m.

property tax n impôt foncier.

prophecy [prâf'isē] n prophétie f.

prophesy [prâf'isī] vt prédire ♦ vi prophétiser.

prophet [prâf'it] n prophète m.

prophetic [prəfet'ik] a prophétique.

prophylactic [prōfəlak'tik] n préservatif m.

proportion [prəpôr'shən] n proportion f; (share) part f; partie f ♦ vt proportionner; **to be in/out of ~ to** or **with sth** être à la mesure de/hors de proportion avec qch; **to see sth in ~** (fig) ramener qch à de justes proportions.

proportional [prəpôr'shənəl] a proportionnel(le).

proportional representation (PR) n (POL) représentation proportionnelle.

proportionate [prəpôr'shənit] a proportionnel(le).

proposal [prəpō'zəl] n proposition f, offre f; (plan) projet m; (of marriage) demande f en mariage.

propose [prəpōz'] vt proposer, suggérer; (have in mind): **to ~ sth/to do** or **doing sth** envisager qch/de faire qch ♦ vi faire sa demande en mariage; **to ~ to do** avoir l'intention de faire.

proposer [prəpō'zûr] n (of motion etc) auteur m.

proposition [prâpəzish'ən] n proposition f; **to make sb a ~** faire une proposition à qn.

propound [prəpound'] vt proposer, soumettre.

proprietary [prəprī'itārē] a de marque déposée; **~ article** article m or produit m de marque; **~ brand** marque déposée.

proprietor [prəprī'ətûr] n propriétaire m/f.

propriety [prəprī'ətē] n (seemliness) bienséance f, convenance f.

propulsion [prəpul'shən] n propulsion f.

pro rata [prō ra'tə] ad au prorata.

prosaic [prōzā'ik] a prosaïque.

Pros. Atty. abbr (US) = **prosecuting attorney.**

proscribe [prōskrīb'] vt proscrire.

prose [prōz] n prose f; (Brit SCOL: translation) thème m.

prosecute [prâs'əkyōōt] vt poursuivre.

prosecuting attorney (Pros. Atty.) n (US) procureur m.

prosecution [prâsəkyōo'shən] n poursuites fpl judiciaires; (accusing side) accusation f.

prosecutor [prâs'əkyōōtûr] n procureur m; (also: **public ~**) ministère public.

prospect [prâs'pekt] n perspective f; (hope) espoir m, chances fpl ♦ vt, vi prospecter; **we are faced with the ~ of leaving** nous risquons de devoir partir; **there is every ~ of an early victory** tout laisse prévoir une victoire rapide.

prospecting [prâs'pekting] n prospection f.

prospective [prəspek'tiv] a (possible) éventuel(le); (future) futur(e).

prospector [prâs'pektûr] n prospecteur m; **gold ~** chercheur m d'or.

prospects [prâs'pekts] npl (for work etc) possibilités fpl d'avenir, débouchés mpl.

prospectus [prəspek'təs] n prospectus m.

prosper [prâs'pûr] vi prospérer.

prosperity [prâspär'itē] n prospérité f.

prosperous [prâs'pûrəs] a prospère.

prostate [prâs'tāt] n (also: **~ gland**) prostate f.

prostitute [prâs'titōōt] n prostituée f; **male ~**

prostitué *m*.

prostitution [prâstitōō'shən] *n* prostitution *f*.

prostrate [prâs'trāt] *a* prosterné(e); *(fig)* prostré(e) ♦ *vt*: **to ~ o.s. (before sb)** se prosterner (devant qn).

protagonist [prōtag'ənist] *n* protagoniste *m*.

protect [prətekt'] *vt* protéger.

protection [prətek'shən] *n* protection *f*; **to be under sb's ~** être sous la protection de qn.

protectionism [prətek'shənizəm] *n* protectionnisme *m*.

protection racket *n* racket *m*.

protective [prətek'tiv] *a* protecteur(trice); **~ custody** (*LAW*) détention préventive.

protector [prətek'tûr] *n* protecteur/trice.

protégé [prō'təzhā] *n* protégé *m*.

protégée [prō'təzhā] *n* protégée *f*.

protein [prō'tēn] *n* protéine *f*.

pro tem [prō tem] *ad abbr* (= *pro tempore: for the time being*) provisoirement.

protest *n* [prō'test] protestation *f* ♦ *vb* [prōtest'] *vi*: **to ~ against/about** protester contre/à propos de ♦ *vt* protester de.

Protestant [prât'istənt] *a*, *n* protestant(e).

protester, protestor [prətes'tûr] *n* (*in demonstration*) manifestant/e.

protest march *n* manifestation *f*.

protocol [prō'təkól] *n* protocole *m*.

prototype [prō'tətip] *n* prototype *m*.

protracted [prōtrak'tid] *a* prolongé(e).

protractor [prōtrak'tûr] *n* (*GEOM*) rapporteur *m*.

protrude [prōtrōōd'] *vi* avancer, dépasser.

protuberance [prōtōō'bûrəns] *n* protubérance *f*.

proud [proud] *a* fier(ère); (*pej*) orgueilleux(euse); **to be ~ to do sth** être fier de faire qch; **to do sb ~** (*col*) faire honneur à qn; **to do o.s. ~** (*col*) ne se priver de rien.

proudly [proud'lē] *ad* fièrement.

prove [prōōv] *vt* prouver, démontrer ♦ *vi*: **to ~ correct** *etc* s'avérer juste *etc*; **to ~ o.s.** montrer ce dont on est capable; **to ~ o.s./ itself (to be) useful** *etc* se montrer *or* se révéler utile *etc*; **he was ~d right in the end** il s'est avéré qu'il avait raison.

proverb [prâv'ûrb] *n* proverbe *m*.

proverbial [prəvûr'bēəl] *a* proverbial(e).

provide [prəvīd'] *vt* fournir; **to ~ sb with sth** fournir qch à qn; **to be ~d with** (*person*) disposer de; (*thing*) être équipé(e) *or* muni(e) de.

provide for *vt fus* (*person*) subvenir aux besoins de; (*emergency*) prévoir.

provided [prəvī'did] *cj*: **~ (that)** à condition que + *sub*.

Providence [prâv'idəns] *n* la Providence.

providing [prəvī'ding] *cj* à condition que + *sub*.

province [prâv'ins] *n* province *f*.

provincial [prəvin'chəl] *a* provincial(e).

provision [prəvizh'ən] *n* (*supply*) provision *f*; (*supplying*) fourniture *f*; approvisionnement *m*; (*stipulation*) disposition *f*; **~s** *npl* (*food*) provisions *fpl*; **to make ~ for** (*one's future*) assurer; (*one's family*) assurer l'avenir de; **there's no ~ for this in the contract** le contrat ne prévoit pas cela.

provisional [prəvizh'ənəl] *a* provisoire ♦ *n*: **P~** (*Irish POL*) Provisional *m* (*membre de la tendance activiste de l'IRA*).

provisional licence *n* (*Brit AUT*) permis *m* provisoire.

provisionally [prəvizh'ənəlē] *ad* provisoirement.

proviso [prəvī'zō] *n* condition *f*; **with the ~ that** à la condition (expresse) que.

Provo [prō'vō] *n abbr* (*Irish POL*) = **Provisional**.

provocation [prâvəkā'shən] *n* provocation *f*.

provocative [prəvâk'ətiv] *a* provocateur(trice), provocant(e).

provoke [prəvōk'] *vt* provoquer; **to ~ sb to sth/to do** *or* **into doing sth** pousser qn à qch/à faire qch.

provoking [prəvōk'ing] *a* énervant(e), exaspérant(e).

provost [prâv'əst] *n* (*of university*) principal *m*; (*Scottish*) maire *m*.

prow [prou] *n* proue *f*.

prowess [prou'is] *n* prouesse *f*.

prowl [proul] *vi* (*also*: **~ around**) rôder ♦ *n*: **to be on the ~** rôder.

prowler [prou'lûr] *n* rôdeur/euse.

proximity [prâksim'itē] *n* proximité *f*.

proxy [prâk'sē] *n* procuration *f*; **by ~** par procuration.

prude [prōōd] *n* prude *f*.

prudence [prōō'dəns] *n* prudence *f*.

prudent [prōō'dənt] *a* prudent(e).

prudish [prōō'dish] *a* prude, pudibond(e).

prune [prōōn] *n* pruneau *m* ♦ *vt* élaguer.

pruning shears [prōōn'ing shirz] *npl* sécateur *m*.

pry [prī] *vi*: **to ~ into** fourrer son nez dans; **to ~ open** (*US*) forcer.

PS *n abbr* (= *postscript*) PS *m*.

psalm [sâm] *n* psaume *m*.

PSAT *n abbr* (*US*) = *Preliminary Scholastic Aptitude Test*.

pseudo- [sōō'dō] *prefix* pseudo-.

pseudonym [sōō'dənim] *n* pseudonyme *m*.

PST *abbr* (*US*: = *Pacific Standard Time*) heure d'hiver du Pacifique.

psyche [sī'kē] *n* psychisme *m*.

psychiatric [sīkēat'rik] *a* psychiatrique.

psychiatrist [siki'ətrist] *n* psychiatre *m/f*.

psychiatry [siki'ətrē] *n* psychiatrie *f*.

psychic [sī'kik] *a* (*also*: **~al**) (méta-) psychique; (*person*) doué(e) de télépathie *or* d'un sixième sens.

psychoanalyze, (*Brit*) **psychoanalyse** [sīkōan'əliz] *vt* psychanalyser.

psychoanalysis, *pl* **-lyses** [sīkōənal'isis, -sēz] *n* psychanalyse *f*.

psychoanalyst [sīkōan'əlist] *n* psychanalyste *m/f*.

psychological [sīkəlâj'ikəl] *a* psychologique.

psychologist [sīkâl'əjist] *n* psychologue *m/f*.

psychology [sīkâl'əjē] *n* psychologie *f*.

psychopath [sī'kəpath] *n* psychopathe *m/f*.

psychosis, *pl* **psychoses** [sīkō'sis, -sēz] *n* psychose *f*.

psychosomatic [sīkōsōmat'ik] *a* psychosomatique.

psychotherapy [sīkōthär'əpē] *n* psychothérapie *f*.

psychotic [sīkât'ik] *a*, *n* psychotique *(m/f)*.
PT *n abbr* (*Brit*: = *physical training*) EPS *f*.
pt *abbr* = **pint, point.**
PTA *n abbr* = *Parent-Teacher Association*.
PTO *abbr* (= *please turn over*) TSVP (= *tournez s'il vous plaît*).
PTV *n abbr* (*US*) = *pay television, public television*.
pub [pub] *n* (*Brit*) pub *m*.
puberty [pyoo'bûrtē] *n* puberté *f*.
pubic [pyoo'bik] *a* pubien(ne), du pubis.
public [pub'lik] *a* public(ique) ♦ *n* public *m*; **in ~** en public; **the general ~** le grand public; **to be ~ knowledge** être de notoriété publique; **to go ~** (*COMM*) être coté(e) en Bourse.
public address system (PA) *n* (système *m* de) sonorisation *f*, sono *f* (*col*).
publican [pub'likən] *n* patron *m* or gérant *m* de pub.
publication [publikā'shən] *n* publication *f*.
public company *n* société *f* anonyme (*cotée en Bourse*).
public convenience *n* (*Brit*) toilettes *fpl*.
public holiday *n* (*Brit*) jour férié.
public house *n* (*Brit*) pub *m*.
public housing unit *n* (*US*) habitation *f* à loyer modéré.
publicity [publis'ətē] *n* publicité *f*.
publicize [pub'ləsīz] *vt* faire connaître, rendre public.
public limited company (plc) *n* (*Brit*) ≈ société anonyme (SA) (*cotée en Bourse*).
publicly [pub'liklē] *ad* publiquement, en public.
public opinion *n* opinion publique.
public ownership *n*: **to be taken into ~** être nationalisé(e), devenir propriété de l'État.
public relations (PR) *n or npl* relations publiques (RP).
public relations officer (PRO) *n* responsable *m/f* des relations publiques.
public school *n* (*US*) école publique; (*Brit*) école privée.
public sector *n* secteur public.
public service vehicle (PSV) *n* (*Brit*) véhicule affecté au transport de personnes.
public-spirited [pub'likspir'itid] *a* qui fait preuve de civisme.
public transportation, (*Brit*) **public transport** *n* transports *mpl* en commun.
public utility *n* service public.
public works *npl* travaux publics.
publish [pub'lish] *vt* publier.
publisher [pub'lishûr] *n* éditeur *m*.
publishing [pub'lishing] *n* (*industry*) édition *f*; (*of a book*) publication *f*.
publishing company *n* maison *f* d'édition.
puce [pyoos] *a* puce.
puck [puk] *n* (*elf*) lutin *m*; (*ICE HOCKEY*) palet *m*.
pucker [puk'ûr] *vt* plisser.
pudding [pŏod'ing] *n* (*dessert*) dessert *m*, entremets *m*; **rice ~** ≈ riz *m* au lait.
puddle [pud'əl] *n* flaque *f* d'eau.
pudgy [puj'ē] *a* (*US*) rondelet(te).
puerile [pyoo'ûrəl] *a* puéril(e).
Puerto Rico [pwär'tō rē'kō] *n* Porto Rico *f*.
puff [puf] *n* bouffée *f* ♦ *vt*: **to ~ one's pipe** ti-

rer sur sa pipe; (*also*: **~ out**: *sails, cheeks*) gonfler ♦ *vi* sortir par bouffées; (*pant*) haleter; **to ~ out smoke** envoyer des bouffées de fumée.
puffed [puft] *a* (*col*: *out of breath*) tout(e) essoufflé(e).
puffin [puf'in] *n* macareux *m*.
puff paste, (*Brit*) **puff pastry** *n* pâte feuilletée.
puffy [puf'ē] *a* bouffi(e), boursouflé(e).
pugnacious [pugnā'shəs] *a* pugnace, batailleur(euse).
pull [pŏol] *n* (*tug*): **to give sth a ~** tirer sur qch; (*of moon, magnet, the sea etc*) attraction *f*; (*fig*) influence *f* ♦ *vt* tirer; (*strain: muscle, tendon*) se claquer ♦ *vi* tirer; **to ~ to pieces** mettre en morceaux; **to ~ one's punches** (*also fig*) ménager son adversaire; **to ~ one's weight** y mettre du sien; **to ~ o.s. together** se ressaisir; **to ~ sb's leg** (*fig*) faire marcher qn; **to ~ strings (for sb)** intervenir (en faveur de qn).
pull apart *vt* séparer; (*break*) mettre en pièces, démantibuler.
pull around *vt* (*handle roughly: object*) maltraiter; (: *person*) malmener.
pull down *vt* baisser, abaisser; (*house*) démolir; (*tree*) abattre.
pull in *vi* (*AUT*) se ranger; (*RAIL*) entrer en gare.
pull off *vt* enlever, ôter; (*deal etc*) conclure.
pull out *vi* démarrer, partir; (*withdraw*) se retirer; (*AUT: come out of line*) déboîter ♦ *vt* sortir; arracher; (*withdraw*) retirer.
pull over *vi* (*AUT*) se ranger.
pull through *vi* s'en sortir.
pull up *vi* (*stop*) s'arrêter ♦ *vt* remonter; (*uproot*) déraciner, arracher; (*stop*) arrêter.
pulley [pŏol'ē] *n* poulie *f*.
Pullman [pŏol'mən] *n* (*US*) wagon-lits *m*, voiture-lits *f*.
pull-out [pŏol'out] *n* (*of forces etc*) retrait *m* ♦ *cpd* (*magazine, pages*) détachable.
pullover [pŏol'ōvûr] *n* pull-over *m*, tricot *m*.
pulp [pulp] *n* (*of fruit*) pulpe *f*; (*for paper*) pâte *f* à papier; (*pej: also*: **~ magazines** *etc*) presse *f* à sensation or de bas étage; **to reduce sth to (a) ~** réduire qch en purée.
pulpit [pŏol'pit] *n* chaire *f*.
pulsate [pul'sāt] *vi* battre, palpiter; (*music*) vibrer.
pulse [puls] *n* (*of blood*) pouls *m*; (*of heart*) battement *m*; (*of music, engine*) vibrations *fpl*; **to feel** or **take sb's ~** prendre le pouls à qn.
pulses [pul'siz] *npl* (*CULIN*) légumineuses *fpl*.
pulverize [pul'vərīz] *vt* pulvériser.
puma [pyoo'mə] *n* puma *m*.
pumice [pum'is] *n* (*also*: **~ stone**) pierre *f* ponce.
pummel [pum'əl] *vt* rouer de coups.
pump [pump] *n* pompe *f*; (*shoe*) escarpin *m* ♦ *vt* pomper; (*fig: col*) faire parler; **to ~ sb for information** essayer de soutirer des renseignements à qn.
pump up *vt* gonfler.
pumpkin [pump'kin] *n* potiron *m*, citrouille *f*.
pun [pun] *n* jeu *m* de mots, calembour *m*.

punch [punch] n (blow) coup m de poing; (fig: force) vivacité f, mordant m; (tool) poinçon m; (drink) punch m ♦ vt (hit): **to ~ sb/sth** donner un coup de poing à qn/sur qch; (make a hole) poinçonner, perforer; **to ~ a hole (in)** faire un trou (dans).

punch in vi (US) pointer (en arrivant).

punch out vi (US) pointer (en partant).

punch-drunk [punch'drungk] a (Brit) sonné(e).

punch(ed) card [punch(t) kârd] n carte perforée.

punch line n (of joke) conclusion f.

punch-up [punch'up] n (Brit col) bagarre f.

punctual [pungk'chōōəl] a ponctuel(le).

punctuality [pungkchōōal'itē] n ponctualité f.

punctually [pungk'chōōəlē] ad ponctuellement; **it will start ~ at 6** cela commencera à 6 heures précises.

punctuate [pungk'chōōāt] vt ponctuer.

punctuation [pungkchōōā'shən] n ponctuation f.

punctuation mark n signe m de ponctuation.

puncture [pungk'chûr] n (Brit) crevaison f ♦ vt crever; **I have a ~** (AUT) j'ai (un pneu) crevé.

pundit [pun'dit] n individu m qui pontifie, pontife m.

pungent [pun'jənt] a piquant(e); (fig) mordant(e), caustique.

punish [pun'ish] vt punir; **to ~ sb for sth/for doing sth** punir qn de qch/d'avoir fait qch.

punishable [pun'ishəbəl] a punissable.

punishing [pun'ishing] a (fig: exhausting) épuisant(e) ♦ n punition f.

punishment [pun'ishmənt] n punition f, châtiment m; (fig: col): **to take a lot of ~** (boxer) encaisser; (car, person etc) être mis(e) à dure épreuve.

punk [pungk] n (person: also: **~ rocker**) punk m/f; (music: also: **~ rock**) le punk; (US col: hoodlum) voyou m.

punt [punt] n (boat) bachot m.

puny [pyoo'nē] a chétif(ive).

pup [pup] n chiot m.

pupil [pyoo'pəl] n élève m/f.

puppet [pup'it] n marionnette f, pantin m.

puppet government n gouvernement m fantoche.

puppy [pup'ē] n chiot m, petit chien.

purchase [pûr'chis] n achat m; (grip) prise f ♦ vt acheter; **to get a ~ on** trouver appui sur.

purchase order n ordre m d'achat.

purchase price n prix m d'achat.

purchaser [pûr'chisûr] n acheteur/euse.

purchasing power [pûr'chising pouùr] n pouvoir m d'achat.

pure [pyoor] a pur(e); **a ~ wool sweater** un pull en pure laine; **~ and simple** pur(e) et simple.

purebred [pyoor'bred'] a de race.

purée [pyoorā'] n purée f.

purely [pyoor'lē] ad purement.

purge [pûrj] n (MED) purge f; (POL) épuration f, purge ♦ vt purger; (fig) épurer, purger.

purification [pyoorəfəkā'shən] n purification f.

purify [pyoor'əfī] vt purifier, épurer.

purist [pyoor'ist] n puriste m/f.

puritan [pyoor'itən] n puritain/e.

puritanical [pyoorian'ikəl] a puritain(e).

purity [pyoor'itē] n pureté f.

purl [pûrl] n maille f à l'envers ♦ vt tricoter à l'envers.

purloin [pûrloin'] vt dérober.

purple [pûr'pəl] a violet(te); cramoisi(e).

purport [pərpôrt'] vi: **to ~ to be/do** prétendre être/faire.

purpose [pûr'pəs] n intention f, but m; **on ~** exprès; **for illustrative ~s** à titre d'illustration; **for teaching ~s** dans un but pédagogique; **for the ~s of this meeting** pour cette réunion; **to no ~** en pure perte.

purpose-built [pûr'pəsbilt'] a (Brit) fait(e) sur mesure.

purposeful [pûr'pəsfəl] a déterminé(e), résolu(e).

purposely [pûr'pəslē] ad exprès.

purr [pûr] n ronronnement m ♦ vi ronronner.

purse [pûrs] n (US) sac m (à main); (Brit) porte-monnaie m inv, bourse f ♦ vt serrer, pincer.

purser [pûr'sûr] n (NAUT) commissaire m du bord.

purse snatcher [pûrs' snach'ûr] n (US) voleur m à l'arraché.

pursue [pûrsoo'] vt poursuivre; (pleasures) rechercher; (inquiry, matter) approfondir.

pursuer [pûrsoo'ûr] n poursuivant/e.

pursuit [pûrsoot'] n poursuite f; (occupation) occupation f, activité f; **scientific ~s** recherches fpl scientifiques; **in (the) ~ of sth** à la recherche de qch.

purveyor [pûrvā'ûr] n fournisseur m.

pus [pus] n pus m.

push [poosh] n poussée f; (effort) gros effort; (drive) énergie f ♦ vt pousser; (button) appuyer sur; (thrust): **to ~ sth (into)** enfoncer qch (dans); (fig) mettre en avant, faire de la publicité pour ♦ vi pousser; appuyer; **to ~ a door open/shut** pousser une porte (pour l'ouvrir/pour la fermer); **"~"** (on door) "pousser"; (on bell) "appuyer"; **to ~ for** (better pay, conditions) réclamer; **to be ~ed for time/money** être à court de temps/d'argent; **she is ~ing fifty** (col) elle frise la cinquantaine; **at a ~** (Brit col) à la limite, à la rigueur.

push aside vt écarter.

push in vi s'introduire de force.

push off vi (col) filer, ficher le camp.

push on vi (continue) continuer.

push over vt renverser.

push through vt (measure) faire voter.

push up vt (total, prices) faire monter.

push button n bouton(-poussoir) m.

pushchair [poosh'châr] n (Brit) poussette f.

pusher [poosh'ûr] n (also: **drug ~**) revendeur/euse (de drogue), ravitailleur/euse (en drogue).

pushing [poosh'ing] a dynamique.

pushover [poosh'ōvûr] n (col): **it's a ~** c'est un jeu d'enfant.

push-up [poosh'up] n traction f.

pushy [poosh'ē] a (pej) arriviste.

pussycat [poos'ēkat] n minet m.

put [poot], pt, pp **put** vt mettre; (place) poser, placer; (say) dire, exprimer; (a question) poser; (estimate) estimer; **to ~ sb in a good/**

bad mood mettre qn de bonne/mauvaise humeur; **to ~ sb to bed** mettre qn au lit, coucher qn; **to ~ sb to a lot of trouble** déranger qn; **how shall I ~ it?** comment dirais-je?, comment dire?; **to ~ a lot of time into sth** passer beaucoup de temps à qch; **to ~ money on a horse** miser sur un cheval; **to stay ~** ne pas bouger.

put about *vi* (*NAUT*) virer de bord ♦ *vt* (*rumor*) faire courir.

put across *vt* (*ideas etc*) communiquer; faire comprendre.

put aside *vt* mettre de côté.

put away *vt* (*store*) ranger.

put back *vt* (*replace*) remettre, replacer; (*postpone*) remettre; (*delay, also: watch, clock*) retarder; **this will ~ us back 10 years** cela nous ramènera dix ans en arrière.

put down *vt* (*parcel etc*) poser, déposer; (*pay*) verser; (*in writing*) mettre par écrit, inscrire; (*suppress: revolt etc*) réprimer, faire cesser; (*attribute*) attribuer.

put forward *vt* (*ideas*) avancer, proposer; (*date, watch, clock*) avancer.

put in *vt* (*gas, electricity*) installer; (*application, complaint*) soumettre.

put in for *vt fus* (*job*) poser sa candidature pour; (*promotion*) solliciter.

put off *vt* (*light etc*) éteindre; (*postpone*) remettre à plus'tard, ajourner; (*discourage*) dissuader.

put on *vt* (*clothes, lipstick etc*) mettre; (*light etc*) allumer; (*play etc*) monter; (*extra bus, train etc*) mettre en service; (*food, meal*) servir; (*weight*) prendre; (*assume: accent, manner*) prendre; (: *airs*) se donner, prendre; (*brake*) mettre; (*col: tease*): **to ~ sb on** faire marcher qn; (*inform, indicate*): **to ~ sb on to sb/sth** indiquer qn/qch à qn.

put out *vt* mettre dehors; (*one's hand*) tendre; (*news, rumor*) faire courir, répandre; (*light etc*) éteindre; (*person: inconvenience*) déranger, gêner; (*Brit: dislocate*) se démettre ♦ *vi* (*NAUT*): **to ~ out to sea** prendre le large; **to ~ out from New York** quitter New York.

put through *vt* (*caller*) mettre en communication; (*call*) passer; **~ me through to Miss Blair** passez-moi Miss Blair.

put together *vt* mettre ensemble; (*assemble: furniture, toy etc*) monter, assembler; (*meal*) préparer.

put up *vt* (*raise*) lever, relever, remonter; (*pin up*) afficher; (*hang*) accrocher; (*build*) construire, ériger; (*a tent*) monter; (*increase*) augmenter; (*accommodate*) loger; (*incite*): **to ~ sb up to doing sth** pousser qn à faire qch; **to ~ sth up for sale** mettre qch en vente.

put upon *vt fus*: **to be ~ upon** (*imposed on*) se laisser faire.

put up with *vt fus* supporter.

putrid [pyōō'trid] *a* putride.

putt [put] *vt* poter (la balle) ♦ *n* coup roulé.

putter [put'ûr] *n* (*GOLF*) putter *m* ♦ *vi* (*US*): **to ~ around** bricoler.

putting green [put'ing grēn] *n* green *m*.

putty [put'ē] *n* mastic *m*.

put-up [pŏot'up] *a*: **~ job** affaire montée.

puzzle [puz'əl] *n* énigme *f*, mystère *m*;

(*jigsaw*) puzzle *m*; (*also:* **crossword ~**) problème *m* de mots croisés ♦ *vt* intriguer, rendre perplexe ♦ *vi* se creuser la tête; **to ~ over** chercher à comprendre; **to be ~d about sth** être perplexe au sujet de qch.

puzzling [puz'ling] *a* déconcertant(e), inexplicable.

PVC *n abbr* (= *polyvinyl chloride*) PVC *m*, polyvinyle *m*.

PVS *n abbr* = **post-viral syndrome**.

Pvt. *abbr* (*US MIL*) = **private**.

pw *abbr* (= *per week*) p.sem.

PX *n abbr* (*US MIL*) = **post exchange**.

pygmy [pig'mē] *n* pygmée *m/f*.

pyjamas [pəjâm'əz] *npl* (*Brit*) = **pajamas**.

pylon [pī'lân] *n* pylône *m*.

pyramid [pir'əmid] *n* pyramide *f*.

Pyrenean [pirənē'ən] *a* pyrénéen(ne), des Pyrénées.

Pyrenees [pir'ənēz] *npl*: **the ~** les Pyrénées *fpl*.

python [pī'thân] *n* python *m*.

Q

Q, q [kyōō] *n* (*letter*) Q, q *m*; **Q for Queen** Q comme Quintal.

Qatar [kətâr'] *n* Qatar *m*, Katar *m*.

QC *n abbr* (= *Queen's Counsel*) *titre donné à certains avocats.*

QED *abbr* (= *quod erat demonstrandum*) CQFD.

QM *n abbr* = **quartermaster**.

q.t. *n abbr* (*col: = quiet*): **on the ~** discrètement.

qty *abbr* (= *quantity*) qté.

quack [kwak] *n* (*of duck*) coin-coin *m inv*; (*pej: doctor*) charlatan *m* ♦ *vi* faire coin-coin.

quad [kwâd] *n abbr* = **quadruple, quadruplet, quadrangle**.

quadrangle [kwâd'ranggəl] *n* (*MATH*) quadrilatère *m*; (*courtyard: abbr:* **quad**) cour *f*.

quadruped [kwâd'rŏŏped] *n* quadrupède *m*.

quadruple [kwâdrŏŏ'pəl] *a*, *n* quadruple (*m*) ♦ *vt*, *vi* quadrupler.

quadruplet [kwâdru'plit] *n* quadruplé/e.

quagmire [kwag'mīur] *n* bourbier *m*.

quail [kwāl] *n* (*ZOOL*) caille *f* ♦ *vi*: **to ~ at** *or* **before** se décourager devant.

quaint [kwānt] *a* bizarre; (*old-fashioned*) désuet(ète); (*limitation*) vieillot, pittoresque.

quake [kwāk] *vi* trembler ♦ *n abbr* = **earthquake**.

Quaker [kwā'kûr] *n* quaker/esse.

qualification [kwâləfəkā'shən] *n* (*degree etc*) diplôme *m*; (*ability*) compétence *f*, qualification *f*; (*limitation*) réserve *f*, restriction *f*; **what are your ~s?** qu'avez-vous comme diplômes?; quelles sont vos qualifications?

qualified [kwâl'əfīd] *a* diplômé(e); (*able*) compétent(e), qualifié(e); (*limited*) conditionnel(le); **it was a ~ success** ce fut un succès mitigé; **~ for/to do** qui a les diplômes requis pour/pour faire; qualifié pour/pour faire.

qualify [kwâl'əfī] *vt* qualifier; (*limit: statement*) apporter des réserves à ♦ *vi:* **to ~ (as)** obtenir son diplôme (de); **to ~ (for)** remplir les conditions requises (pour); (*SPORT*) se qualifier (pour).

qualifying [kwâl'əfiing] *a:* **~ exam** examen *m* d'entrée; **~ round** éliminatoires *fpl*.

qualitative [kwâl'itātiv] *a* qualitatif(ive).

quality [kwâl'itē] *n* qualité *f* ♦ *cpd* de qualité; **of good/poor ~** de bonne/mauvaise qualité.

quality control *n* contrôle *m* de qualité.

qualm [kwâm] *n* doute *m*; scrupule *m*; **to have ~s about sth** avoir des doutes sur qch; éprouver des scrupules à propos de qch.

quandary [kwän'drē] *n:* **in a ~** devant un dilemme, dans l'embarras.

quantitative [kwän'titātiv] *a* quantitatif(ive).

quantity [kwän'titē] *n* quantité *f;* **in ~** en grande quantité.

quarantine [kwôr'əntēn] *n* quarantaine *f.*

quarrel [kwôr'əl] *n* querelle *f,* dispute *f* ♦ *vi* se disputer, se quereller; **to have a ~ with sb** se quereller avec qn; **I've no ~ with him** je n'ai rien contre lui; **I can't ~ with that** je ne vois rien à redire à cela.

quarrelsome [kwôr'əlsəm] *a* querelleur(euse).

quarry [kwôr'ē] *n* (*for stone*) carrière *f;* (*animal*) proie *f,* gibier *m* ♦ *vt* (*marble etc*) extraire.

quart [kwôrt] *n* ≈ litre *m.*

quarter [kwôr'tûr] *n* quart *m;* (*of year*) trimestre *m;* (*district*) quartier *m;* (*US, Canada: 25 cents*) (pièce *f* de) vingt-cinq cents *mpl* ♦ *vt* partager en quartiers *or* en quatre; (*MIL*) caserner, cantonner; **~s** *npl* logement *m;* (*MIL*) quartiers *mpl,* cantonnement *m;* **a ~ of an hour** un quart d'heure; **it's a ~ of 3,** (*Brit*) **it's a ~ to 3** il est 3 heures moins le quart; **it's a ~ after 3,** (*Brit*) **it's a ~ past 3** il est 3 heures et quart; **from all ~s** de tous côtés; **at close ~s** tout près.

quarter-deck [kwôr'tûrdek] *n* (*NAUT*) plage *f* arrière.

quarter final *n* quart *m* de finale.

quarterly [kwôr'tûrlē] *a* trimestriel(le) ♦ *ad* tous les trois mois ♦ *n* (*PRESS*) revue trimestrielle.

quartermaster [kwôr'tûrmastûr] *n* (*MIL*) intendant *m* militaire de troisième classe; (*NAUT*) maître *m* de manœuvre.

quarter note *n* (*US*) noire *f.*

quartet(te) [kwôrtet'] *n* quatuor *m;* (*jazz players*) quartette *m.*

quarto [kwôr'tō] *a, n* in-quarto (*m*) *inv.*

quartz [kwôrts] *n* quartz *m* ♦ *cpd* de *or* en quartz; (*watch, clock*) à quartz.

quash [kwâsh] *vt* (*verdict*) annuler, casser.

quasi- [kwā'zī] *prefix* quasi- + *noun;* quasi, presque + *adjective.*

quaver [kwā'vûr] *n* (*Brit MUS*) croche *f* ♦ *vi* trembler.

quay [kē] *n* (*also:* **~side**) quai *m.*

Que. *abbr* (*Canada*) = Quebec.

queasy [kwē'zē] *a* (*stomach*) délicat(e); **to feel ~** avoir mal au cœur.

Quebec [kwibek'] *n* Québec *m.*

queen [kwēn] *n* (*gen*) reine *f;* (*CARDS etc*) dame *f.*

queen mother *n* reine mère *f.*

queer [kwēr] *a* étrange, curieux(euse); (*suspicious*) louche; (*sick*): **I feel ~** je ne me sens pas bien ♦ *n* (*col*) homosexuel *m.*

quell [kwel] *vt* réprimer, étouffer.

quench [kwench] *vt* (*flames*) éteindre; **to ~ one's thirst** se désaltérer.

querulous [kwär'ələs] *a* (*person*) récriminateur(trice); (*voice*) plaintif(ive).

query [kwiûr'ē] *n* question *f;* (*doubt*) doute *m;* (*question mark*) point *m* d'interrogation ♦ *vt* (*disagree with, dispute*) mettre en doute, questionner.

quest [kwest] *n* recherche *f,* quête *f.*

question [kwes'chən] *n* question *f* ♦ *vt* (*person*) interroger; (*plan, idea*) mettre en question *or* en doute; **to ask sb a ~,** to put a **~ to sb** poser une question à qn; **to bring** *or* **call sth into ~** remettre qch en question; **the ~ is ...** la question est de savoir ...; **it's a ~ of doing** il s'agit de faire; **there's some ~ of doing** il est question de faire; **beyond ~** sans aucun doute; **out of the ~** hors de question.

questionable [kwes'chənəbəl] *a* discutable.

questioner [kwes'chənûr] *n* personne *f* qui pose une question (*or* qui a posé la question *etc*).

questioning [kwes'chəning] *a* interrogateur(trice) ♦ *n* interrogatoire *m.*

question mark *n* point *m* d'interrogation.

questionnaire [kweschənär'] *n* questionnaire *m.*

queue [kyōō] (*Brit*) *n* queue *f,* file *f* ♦ *vi* faire la queue; **to jump the ~** passer avant son tour.

quibble [kwib'əl] *vi* ergoter, chicaner.

quick [kwik] *a* rapide; (*reply*) prompt(e), rapide; (*mind*) vif(vive) ♦ *ad* vite, rapidement ♦ *n:* **cut to the ~** (*fig*) touché(e) au vif; **be ~!** dépêche-toi!; **to be ~ to act** agir tout de suite.

quicken [kwik'ən] *vt* accélérer, presser; (*rouse*) stimuler ♦ *vi* s'accélérer, devenir plus rapide.

quicklime [kwik'līm] *n* chaux vive.

quickly [kwik'lē] *ad* (*fast*) vite, rapidement; (*immediately*) tout de suite.

quickness [kwik'nis] *n* rapidité *f,* promptitude *f;* (*of mind*) vivacité *f.*

quicksand [kwik'sand] *n* sables mouvants.

quickstep [kwik'step] *n* fox-trot *m.*

quick-tempered [kwik'tempûrd] *a* emporté(e).

quick-witted [kwik'wit'id] *a* à l'esprit vif.

quid [kwid] *n* (*pl inv*) (*Brit col*) livre *f.*

quid pro quo [kwid' prō' kwō] *n* contrepartie *f.*

quiet [kwī'it] *a* tranquille, calme; (*not noisy: engine*) silencieux(euse); (*reserved*) réservé(e); (*not busy: day, business*) calme; (*ceremony, color*) discret(ète) ♦ *n* tranquillité *f,* calme *m* ♦ *vb* (*US: also:* **~ down**) *vi* se calmer, s'apaiser ♦ *vt* calmer, apaiser; **keep ~!** tais-toi!; **on the ~** en secret, discrètement; **I'll have a ~ word with him** je lui en parlerai discrètement.

quieten [kwī'itən] (*Brit: also:* **~ down**) *vi, vt*

= **quiet**.
quietly [kwī'itlē] *ad* tranquillement, calmement; discrètement.
quietness [kwī'itnis] *n* tranquillité *f*, calme *m*; silence *m*.
quill [kwil] *n* plume *f* (d'oie).
quilt [kwilt] *n* édredon *m*; (*continental* ~) couette *f*.
quilting [kwil'tiŋ] *n* ouatine *f*; molletonnage *m*.
quin [kwin] *n abbr* = **quintuplet**.
quince [kwins] *n* coing *m*; (*tree*) cognassier *m*.
quinine [kwī'nīn] *n* quinine *f*.
quintet(te) [kwintet'] *n* quintette *m*.
quintuplet [kwintu'plit] *n* quintuplé/e.
quip [kwip] *n* remarque piquante *or* spirituelle, pointe *f* ♦ *vt*: ... he ~ped ... lança-t-il.
quire [kwīur] *n* ≈ main *f* (*de papier*).
quirk [kwûrk] *n* bizarrerie *f*; **by some ~ of fate** par un caprice du hasard.
quit, *pt*, *pp* **quit** *or* **quitted** [kwit] *vt* quitter ♦ *vi* (*give up*) abandonner, renoncer; (*resign*) démissionner; **to ~ doing** arrêter de faire; ~ **stalling!** (*US col*) arrête de te dérober!; **notice to ~** (*Brit*) congé *m* (*signifié au locataire*).
quite [kwīt] *ad* (*rather*) assez, plutôt; (*entirely*) complètement, tout à fait; ~ **new** plutôt neuf; tout à fait neuf; **she's ~ pretty** elle est plutôt jolie; **I ~ understand** je comprends très bien; ~ **a few of them** un assez grand nombre d'entre eux; **that's not ~ right** ce n'est pas tout à fait juste; **not ~ as many as last time** pas tout à fait autant que la dernière fois; ~ **(so)!** exactement!
Quito [kē'tō] *n* Quito.
quits [kwits] *a*: ~ **(with)** quitte (envers); **let's call it ~** restons-en là.
quiver [kwiv'ûr] *vi* trembler, frémir ♦ *n* (*for arrows*) carquois *m*.
quiz [kwiz] *n* (*on TV*) jeu-concours *m* (télévisé); (*in magazine etc*) test *m* de connaissances ♦ *vt* interroger.
quizzical [kwiz'ikəl] *a* narquois(e).
quoits [kwoits] *npl* jeu *m* du palet.
quorum [kwôr'əm] *n* quorum *m*.
quota [kwō'tə] *n* quota *m*.
quotation [kwōtā'shən] *n* citation *f*; (*Brit*: *estimate*) devis *m*.
quotation marks *npl* guillemets *mpl*.
quote [kwōt] *n* citation *f*; (*estimate*) devis *m* ♦ *vt* (*sentence, author*) citer; (*price*) donner, soumettre; (*shares*) coter ♦ *vi*: **to ~ from** citer; **to ~ for a job** établir un devis pour des travaux; ~**s** *npl* (*col*) = **quotation marks**; **in ~s** entre guillemets; ~ ... **unquote** (*in dictation*) ouvrez les guillemets ... fermez les guillemets.
quotient [kwō'shənt] *n* quotient *m*.
qv *abbr* (= *quod vide: which see*) voir.
qwerty keyboard [kwûr'tē kē'bôrd] *n* (*Brit*) clavier *m* QWERTY.

R

R, r [âr] *n* (*letter*) R, r *m*; **R for Roger** R comme Raoul.
R [âr] *abbr* (= *right*) dr; (= *river*) riv., fl.; (= *Réaumur* (*scale*)) R; (*US CINEMA*: = restricted) *interdit aux moins de 17 ans*; (*US POL*) = **republican**; (*Brit*) = *Rex, Regina*.
RA *abbr* = **rear admiral**.
RAAF *n abbr* = *Royal Australian Air Force*.
Rabat [râbât'] *n* Rabat.
rabbi [rab'ī] *n* rabbin *m*.
rabbit [rab'it] *n* lapin *m*.
rabbit hole *n* terrier *m* (de lapin).
rabbit hutch *n* clapier *m*.
rabble [rab'əl] *n* (*pej*) populace *f*.
rabid [rab'id] *a* enragé(e).
rabies [rā'bēz] *n* rage *f*.
RAC *n abbr* (*Brit*: = *Royal Automobile Club*) ≈ ACF *m*.
raccoon [rakoon'] *n* raton *m* laveur.
race [rās] *n* race *f*; (*competition, rush*) course *f* ♦ *vt* (*person*) faire la course avec; (*horse*) faire courir; (*engine*) emballer ♦ *vi* courir; (*engine*) s'emballer; **the human ~** la race humaine; **to ~ in/out** *etc* entrer/sortir *etc* à toute vitesse.
race car *n* (*US*) voiture de course.
race car driver *n* (*US*) pilote de course.
racecourse [rās'kôrs] *n* champ *m* de courses.
racehorse [rās'hôrs] *n* cheval *m* de course.
race relations *npl* rapports *mpl* entre les races.
racetrack [rās'trak] *n* piste *f*.
racial [rā'shəl] *a* racial(e).
racialism [rā'shəlizəm] *n* racisme *m*.
racialist [rā'shəlist] *a*, *n* raciste (*m/f*).
racing [rā'siŋ] *n* courses *fpl*.
racing car *n* (*Brit*) = **race car**.
racing driver *n* (*Brit*) = **race car driver**.
racism [rā'sizəm] *n* racisme *m*.
racist [rā'sist] *a*, *n* (*pej*) raciste (*m/f*).
rack [rak] *n* (*also*: **luggage ~**) filet *m* à bagages; (*also*: **roof ~**) galerie *f* ♦ *vt* tourmenter; **magazine ~** porte-revues *m inv*; **shoe ~** étagère *f* à chaussures; **toast ~** porte-toast *m*; **to ~ one's brains** se creuser la cervelle; **to go to ~ and ruin** (*building*) tomber en ruine; (*business*) péricliter.
rack up *vt* accumuler.
rack-and-pinion [rak'əndpin'yən] *n* (*TECH*) crémaillère *f*.
racket [rak'it] *n* (*for tennis*) raquette *f*; (*noise*) tapage *m*, vacarme *m*; (*swindle*) escroquerie *f*; (*organized crime*) racket *m*.
racketeer [rakitēr'] *n* (*esp US*) racketteur *m*.
racoon [rakoon'] *n* = **raccoon**.
racquet [rak'it] *n* raquette *f*.
racy [rā'sē] *a* plein(e) de verve; osé(e).
radar [rā'dâr] *n* radar *m* ♦ *cpd* radar *inv*.
radar trap *n* contrôle *m* radar.

radial [rā'dēəl] *a* (*also:* ~-**ply**) à carcasse radiale.

radiance [rā'dēəns] *n* éclat *m*, rayonnement *m*.

radiant [rā'dēənt] *a* rayonnant(e); (*PHYSICS*) radiant(e).

radiate [rā'dēāt] *vt* (*heat*) émettre, dégager ♦ *vi* (*lines*) rayonner.

radiation [rādēā'shən] *n* rayonnement *m*; (*radioactive*) radiation *f*.

radiation sickness *n* mal *m* des rayons.

radiator [rā'dēātûr] *n* radiateur *m*.

radiator cap *n* bouchon *m* de radiateur.

radiator grill *n* calandre *f*.

radical [rad'ikəl] *a* radical(e).

radii [rā'dēī] *npl of* **radius**.

radio [rā'dēō] *n* radio *f* ♦ *vi:* **to** ~ **to sb** envoyer un message radio à qn ♦ *vt* (*information*) transmettre par radio; (*one's position*) signaler par radio; (*person*) appeler par radio; **on the** ~ à la radio.

radioactive [rādēōak'tiv] *a* radioactif(ive).

radioactivity [rādēōaktiv'ətē] *n* radioactivité *f*.

radio announcer *n* annonceur *m*.

radio-controlled [rā'dēōkəntrōld'] *a* radioguidé(e).

radiographer [rādēāg'rəfûr] *n* radiologue *m/f* (*technicien*).

radiography [rādēāg'rəfē] *n* radiographie *f*.

radiologist [rādēál'əjist] *n* radiologue *m/f* (*médecin*).

radiology [rādēál'əjē] *n* radiologie *f*.

radio station *n* station *f* de radio.

radio taxi *n* radio-taxi *m*.

radiotelephone [rādēōtel'əfōn] *n* radiotéléphone *m*.

radiotherapist [rādēōthär'əpist] *n* radiothérapeute *m/f*.

radiotherapy [rādēōthär'əpē] *n* radiothérapie *f*.

radish [rad'ish] *n* radis *m*.

radium [rā'dēəm] *n* radium *m*.

radius, *pl* **radii** [rā'dēəs, -ēī] *n* rayon *m*; (*ANAT*) radius *m*; **within a** ~ **of 50 miles** dans un rayon de 50 milles.

RAF *n abbr* (*Brit*) = **Royal Air Force.**

raffia [raf'ēə] *n* raphia *m*.

raffish [raf'ish] *a* dissolu(e); canaille.

raffle [raf'əl] *n* tombola *f* ♦ *vt* mettre comme lot dans une tombola.

raft [raft] *n* (*craft; also:* **life** ~) radeau *m*; (*logs*) train *m* de flottage.

rafter [raf'tûr] *n* chevron *m*.

rag [rag] *n* chiffon *m*; (*pej: newspaper*) feuille *f*, torchon *m*; (*for charity*) attractions organisées par les étudiants au profit d'œuvres de charité; ~**s** *npl* haillons *mpl*; **in** ~**s** (*person*) en haillons; (*clothes*) en lambeaux.

rag-and-bone man [ragənbōn' man] *n* (*Brit*) = **ragman.**

ragbag [rag'bag] *n* (*fig*) ramassis *m*.

rag doll *n* poupée *f* de chiffon.

rage [rāj] *n* (*fury*) rage *f*, fureur *f* ♦ *vi* (*person*) être fou(folle) de rage; (*storm*) faire rage, être déchaîné(e); **to fly into a** ~ se mettre en rage; **it's all the** ~ cela fait fureur.

ragged [rag'id] *a* (*edge*) inégal(e), qui accroche; (*cuff*) effiloché(e); (*appearance*) déguenillé(e).

raging [rā'jing] *a* (*sea, storm*) en furie; (*fever, pain*) violent(e); ~ **toothache** rage *f* de dents; **in a** ~ **temper** dans une rage folle.

ragman [rag'man] *n* chiffonnier *m*.

rag trade *n* (*col*): **the** ~ la confection.

raid [rād] *n* (*MIL*) raid *m*; (*criminal*) hold-up *m inv*; (*by police*) descente *f*, rafle *f* ♦ *vt* faire un raid sur *or* un hold-up dans *or* une descente dans.

raider [rā'dûr] *n* malfaiteur *m*.

rail [rāl] *n* (*on stair*) rampe *f*; (*on bridge, balcony*) balustrade *f*; (*of ship*) bastingage *m*; (*for train*) rail *m*; ~**s** *npl* rails *mpl*, voie ferrée; **by** ~ par chemin de fer, par le train.

railing(s) [rāl'ing(z)] *n(pl)* grille *f*.

railroad [rāl'rōd] *n* (*US*) chemin *m* de fer.

railroader [rāl'rōdûr] *n* (*US*) cheminot *m*.

railroad line *n* ligne *f* de chemin de fer.

railroad station *n* gare *f*.

railway [rāl'wā] *etc* (*Brit*) = **railroad** *etc.*

railway engine *n* (*Brit*) locomotive *f*.

railwayman [rāl'wāmən] *n* (*Brit*) = **railroader.**

rain [rān] *n* pluie *f* ♦ *vi* pleuvoir; **in the** ~ sous la pluie; **it's** ~**ing** il pleut; **it's** ~**ing cats and dogs** il pleut à torrents.

rainbow [rān'bō] *n* arc-en-ciel *m*.

raincoat [rān'kōt] *n* imperméable *m*.

raindrop [rān'dräp] *n* goutte *f* de pluie.

rainfall [rān'fôl] *n* chute *f* de pluie; (*measurement*) hauteur *f* des précipitations.

rainforest [rān'fôr'ist] *n* forêt tropicale.

rainproof [rān'prōōf] *a* imperméable.

rainstorm [rān'stôrm] *n* pluie torrentielle.

rainwater [rān'wôtûr] *n* eau *f* de pluie.

rainy [rā'nē] *a* pluvieux(euse).

raise [rāz] *n* augmentation *f* ♦ *vt* (*lift*) lever; hausser; (*end: siege, embargo*) lever; (*build*) ériger; (*increase*) augmenter; (*a protest, doubt*) provoquer, causer; (*a question*) soulever; (*cattle, family*) élever; (*crop*) faire pousser; (*army, funds*) rassembler; (*loan*) obtenir; **to** ~ **one's glass to sb/sth** porter un toast en l'honneur de qn/qch; **to** ~ **one's voice** élever la voix; **to** ~ **sb's hopes** donner de l'espoir à qn; **to** ~ **a laugh/a smile** faire rire/sourire.

raisin [rā'zin] *n* raisin sec.

Raj [räj] *n*: **the** ~ l'empire *m* (*aux Indes*).

rajah [rä'jə] *n* radja(h) *m*.

rake [rāk] *n* (*tool*) râteau *m*; (*person*) débauché *m* ♦ *vt* (*garden*) ratisser; (*fire*) tisonner; (*with machine gun*) balayer ♦ *vi:* **to** ~ **through** (*fig: search*) fouiller (dans).

rake-off [rāk'ôf] *n* (*col*) pourcentage *m*.

rakish [rā'kish] *a* dissolu(e); cavalier(ière).

rally [ral'ē] *n* (*POL etc*) meeting *m*, rassemblement *m*; (*AUT*) rallye *m*; (*TENNIS*) échange *m* ♦ *vt* rassembler, rallier ♦ *vi* se rallier; (*sick person*) aller mieux; (*Stock Exchange*) reprendre.

rally around *vi* venir en aide ♦ *vt fus* se rallier à; venir en aide à.

rallying point [ral'ēing point] *n* (*MIL*) point *m* de ralliement.

RAM [ram] *n abbr* (*COMPUT*) = **random access memory.**

ram [ram] *n* bélier *m* ♦ *vt* enfoncer; (*soil*) tasser; (*crash into*) emboutir; percuter; éperonner.

ramble [ram'bəl] *n* randonnée *f* ♦ *vi* (*pej: also:* ~ **on**) discourir, pérorer.

rambler [ram'blûr] *n* promeneur/euse, randonneur/euse; (*BOT*) rosier grimpant.

rambling [ram'bling] *a* (*speech*) décousu(e); (*house*) plein(e) de coins et de recoins; (*BOT*) grimpant(e).

rambunctious [rambungk'shəs] *a* (*US: person*) exubérante(e).

ramification [raməfəkā'shən] *n* ramification *f*.

ramp [ramp] *n* (*incline*) rampe *f*; dénivellation *f*; (*in garage*) pont *m*.

rampage [ram'pāj] *n*: **to be on the** ~ se déchaîner ♦ *vi*: **they went rampaging through the town** ils ont envahi les rues et ont tout saccagé sur leur passage.

rampant [ram'pənt] *a* (*disease etc*) qui sévit.

rampart [ram'pârt] *n* rempart *m*.

ramshackle [ram'shakəl] *a* (*house*) délabré(e); (*car etc*) déglingué(e).

ran [ran] *pt of* **run**.

ranch [ranch] *n* ranch *m*.

rancher [ran'chûr] *n* (*owner*) propriétaire *m* de ranch; (*ranch hand*) cowboy *m*.

rancid [ran'sid] *a* rance.

rancor, (*Brit*) **rancour** [rang'kûr] *n* rancune *f*, rancœur *f*.

random [ran'dəm] *a* fait(e) *or* établi(e) au hasard; (*COMPUT, MATH*) aléatoire ♦ *n*: **at** ~ au hasard.

random access memory (RAM) *n* (*COMPUT*) mémoire vive, RAM *f*.

randy [ran'dē] *a* (*Brit col*) excité(e); lubrique.

rang [rang] *pt of* **ring**.

range [rānj] *n* (*of mountains*) chaîne *f*; (*of missile, voice*) portée *f*; (*of products*) choix *m*, gamme *f*; (*also:* **shooting** ~) champ *m* de tir; (: *indoor*) stand *m* de tir; (*also:* **kitchen** ~) fourneau *m* (de cuisine) ♦ *vt* (*place*) mettre en rang, placer; (*roam*) parcourir ♦ *vi*: **to** ~ **over** couvrir; **to** ~ **from ... to** aller de ... à; **price** ~ éventail *m* des prix; **do you have anything else in this price** ~? avez-vous autre chose dans ces prix?; **within (firing)** ~ à portée (de tir); ~**d left/right** (*text*) justifié à gauche/à droite.

ranger [rān'jûr] *n* garde *m* forestier.

Rangoon [ranggōon'] *n* Rangoon.

rank [rangk] *n* rang *m*; (*MIL*) grade *m*; (*Brit: also:* **taxi** ~) station *f* de taxis ♦ *vi*: **to** ~ **among** compter *or* se classer parmi ♦ *vt*: **I** ~ **him sixth** je le place sixième ♦ *a* (*smell*) nauséabond(e); (*hypocrisy, injustice etc*) flagrant(e); **the** ~**s** (*MIL*) la troupe; **the** ~ **and file** (*fig*) la masse, la base; **to close** ~**s** (*MIL, fig*) serrer les rangs.

rankle [rang'kəl] *vi* (*insult*) rester sur le cœur.

ransack [ran'sak] *vt* fouiller (à fond); (*plunder*) piller.

ransom [ran'səm] *n* rançon *f*; **to hold sb to** ~ (*fig*) exercer un chantage sur qn.

rant [rant] *vi* fulminer.

ranting [ran'ting] *n* invectives *fpl*.

rap [rap] *n* petit coup sec; tape *f* ♦ *vt* frapper sur *or* à; taper sur.

rape [rāp] *n* viol *m*; (*BOT*) colza *m* ♦ *vt* violer.

rape(seed) oil [rāp'(sēd) oil] *n* huile *f* de colza.

rapid [rap'id] *a* rapide.

rapidity [rəpid'itē] *n* rapidité *f*.

rapidly [rap'idlē] *ad* rapidement.

rapids [rap'idz] *npl* (*GEO*) rapides *mpl*.

rapist [rā'pist] *n* auteur *m* d'un viol.

rapport [rapôr'] *n* entente *f*.

rapt [rapt] *a* (*attention*) extrême; **to be** ~ **in contemplation** être perdu(e) dans la contemplation.

rapture [rap'chûr] *n* extase *f*, ravissement *m*; **to go into** ~**s over** s'extasier sur.

rapturous [rap'chûrəs] *a* extasié(e); frénétique.

rare [rär] *a* rare; (*CULIN: steak*) saignant(e).

rarebit [rär'bit] *n see* **Welsh rarebit**.

rarefied [rär'əfīd] *a* (*air, atmosphere*) raréfié(e).

rarely [reûr'lē] *ad* rarement.

raring [rär'ing] *a*: **to be** ~ **to go** (*col*) être très impatient(e) de commencer.

rarity [rär'itē] *n* rareté *f*.

rascal [ras'kəl] *n* vaurien *m*.

rash [rash] *a* imprudent(e), irréfléchi(e) ♦ *n* (*MED*) rougeur *f*, éruption *f*; **to come out in a** ~ avoir une éruption.

rasher [rash'ûr] *n* fine tranche (de lard).

rasp [rasp] *n* (*tool*) lime *f* ♦ *vt* (*speak: also:* ~ **out**) dire d'une voix grinçante.

raspberry [raz'bärē] *n* framboise *f*.

raspberry bush *n* framboisier *m*.

rasping [ras'ping] *a*: ~ **noise** grincement *m*.

rat [rat] *n* rat *m*.

ratchet [rach'it] *n*: ~ **wheel** roue *f* à rochet.

rate [rāt] *n* (*ratio*) taux *m*, pourcentage *m*; (*speed*) vitesse *f*, rythme *m*; (*price*) tarif *m* ♦ *vt* classer; évaluer; **to** ~ **sb/sth as** considérer qn/qch comme; **to** ~ **sb/sth among** classer qn/qch parmi; **to** ~ **sb/sth highly** avoir une haute opinion de qn/qch; **at a** ~ **of 60 kph** à une vitesse de 60 km/h; ~ **of exchange** taux *or* cours *m* du change; ~ **of flow** débit *m*; ~ **of return** (taux de) rendement *m*; **pulse** ~ fréquence *f* des pulsations.

rates [rāts] *npl* (*Brit*) impôts locaux.

rather [rath'ûr] *ad* (*somewhat*) assez, plutôt; (*to some extent*) un peu; **it's** ~ **expensive** c'est assez cher; (*too much*) c'est un peu cher; **there's** ~ **a lot** (*Brit*) il y en a beaucoup; **I would** *or* **I'd** ~ **go** j'aimerais mieux *or* je préférerais partir; **I had** ~ **go** il vaudrait mieux que je parte; **I'd** ~ **not leave** j'aimerais mieux ne pas partir; **or** ~ (*more accurately*) ou plutôt.

ratification [ratəfəkā'shən] *n* ratification *f*.

ratify [rat'əfī] *vt* ratifier.

rating [rā'ting] *n* classement *m*; cote *f*; (*NAUT: category*) classe *f*; (: *sailor: Brit*) matelot *m*; ~**s** *npl* (*RADIO, TV*) indice(s) *m(pl)* d'écoute.

ratio [rā'shō] *n* proportion *f*; **in the** ~ **of 100 to 1** dans la proportion de 100 contre 1.

ration [rash'ən] *n* (*gen pl*) ration(s) *f(pl)* ♦ *vt* rationner.

rational [rash'ənəl] *a* raisonnable, sensé(e); (*solution, reasoning*) logique; (*MED*) lucide.

rationale [rashənal'] *n* raisonnement *m*; justification *f*.

rationalization [rashənələzā'shən] *n* rationalisation *f*.

rationalize [rash'ənəlīz] *vt* rationaliser;

(*conduct*) essayer d'expliquer *or* de motiver.
rationally [rash'ənəlē] *ad* raisonnablement; logiquement.
rationing [rash'əning] *n* rationnement *m*.
rat poison *n* mort-aux-rats *f inv*.
rat race *n* foire *f* d'empoigne.
rattan [ratan'] *n* rotin *m*.
rattle [rat'əl] *n* cliquetis *m*; (*louder*) bruit *m* de ferraille; (*object: of baby*) hochet *m*; (: *of sports fan*) crécelle *f* ♦ *vi* cliqueter; faire un bruit de ferraille *or* du bruit ♦ *vt* agiter (bruyamment); (*col: disconcert*) décontenancer; (: *annoy*) embêter.
rattlesnake [rat'əlsnāk] *n* serpent *m* à sonnettes.
ratty [rat'ē] *a* (*col: US: shabby*) miteux(euse); (: *Brit: annoyed*) en rogne.
raucous [rô'kəs] *a* rauque.
raucously [rô'kəslē] *ad* d'une voix rauque.
ravage [rav'ij] *vt* ravager.
ravages [rav'ijiz] *npl* ravages *mpl*.
rave [rāv] *vi* (*in anger*) s'emporter; (*with enthusiasm*) s'extasier; (*MED*) délirer ♦ *cpd*: ~ **review** (*col*) critique *f* dithyrambique.
raven [rā'vən] *n* grand corbeau.
ravenous [rav'ənəs] *a* affamé(e).
ravine [rəvēn'] *n* ravin *m*.
raving [rā'ving] *a*: ~ **lunatic** *n* fou furieux/folle furieuse.
ravings [rā'vingz] *npl* divagations *fpl*.
ravioli [ravēō'lē] *n* ravioli *mpl*.
ravish [rav'ish] *vt* ravir.
ravishing [rav'ishing] *a* enchanteur(eresse).
raw [rô] *a* (*uncooked*) cru(e); (*not processed*) brut(e); (*sore*) à vif, irrité(e); (*inexperienced*) inexpérimenté(e); ~ **deal** (*col: bad bargain*) sale coup *m*; (: *unfair treatment*): **to get a** ~ **deal** être traité(e) injustement.
Rawalpindi [râwəlpin'dē] *n* Rawalpindi.
raw material *n* matière première.
ray [rā] *n* rayon *m*; ~ **of hope** lueur *f* d'espoir.
rayon [rā'ân] *n* rayonne *f*.
raze [rāz] *vt* (*also*: ~ **to the ground**) raser.
razor [rā'zûr] *n* rasoir *m*.
razor blade *n* lame *f* de rasoir.
razzmatazz [raz'mətaz] *n* (*col*) tralala *m*, tapage *m*.
R&B *n abbr* = *rhythm and blues*.
RC *abbr* = **Roman Catholic**.
RCAF *n abbr* = *Royal Canadian Air Force*.
RCMP *n abbr* = *Royal Canadian Mounted Police*.
RCN *n abbr* = *Royal Canadian Navy*.
RD *abbr* (*US MAIL*) = *rural delivery*.
Rd *abbr* = **road**.
R&D *n abbr* (= *research and development*) R-D *f*.
R&R *n abbr* (*US MIL*) = *rest and recuperation*.
re [rā] *prep* concernant.
reach [rēch] *n* portée *f*, atteinte *f*; (*of river etc*) étendue *f* ♦ *vt* atteindre, arriver à ♦ *vi* s'étendre; (*stretch out hand*): **to** ~ **up/down/out** *etc* (**for sth**) lever/baisser/allonger *etc* le bras (pour prendre qch); **to** ~ **sb by phone** joindre qn par téléphone; **out of/within** ~ (*object*) hors de/à portée; **within easy** ~ (**of**) (*place*) à proximité (de), proche (de).
react [rēakt'] *vi* réagir.

reaction [rēak'shən] *n* réaction *f*.
reactionary [rēak'shənärē] *a, n* réactionnaire (*m/f*).
reactor [rēak'tûr] *n* réacteur *m*.
read, *pt, pp* **read** [rēd, red] *vi* lire ♦ *vt* lire; (*understand*) comprendre, interpréter; (*study*) étudier; (*subj: instrument etc*) indiquer, marquer; **to take sth as read** (*fig*) considérer qch comme accepté; **do you** ~ **me?** (*TEL*) est-ce que vous me recevez?
read out *vt* lire à haute voix.
read over *vt* relire.
read through *vt* (*quickly*) parcourir; (*thoroughly*) lire jusqu'au bout.
read up *vt*, **read up on** *vt fus* étudier.
readable [rē'dəbəl] *a* facile *or* agréable à lire.
reader [rē'dûr] *n* lecteur/trice; (*book*) livre *m* de lecture.
readership [rē'dûrship] *n* (*of paper etc*) (nombre *m* de) lecteurs *mpl*.
readily [red'əlē] *ad* volontiers, avec empressement; (*easily*) facilement.
readiness [red'ēnis] *n* empressement *m*; **in** ~ (*prepared*) prêt(e).
reading [rēd'ing] *n* lecture *f*; (*understanding*) interprétation *f*; (*on instrument*) indications *fpl*.
reading lamp *n* lampe *f* de bureau.
reading room *n* salle *f* de lecture.
readjust [rēəjust'] *vt* rajuster; (*instrument*) régler de nouveau ♦ *vi* (*person*): **to** ~ (**to**) se réadapter (à).
ready [red'ē] *a* prêt(e); (*willing*) prêt, disposé(e); (*quick*) prompt(e); (*available*) disponible ♦ *n*: **at the** ~ (*MIL*) prêt à faire feu; (*fig*) tout(e) prêt(e); ~ **for use** prêt à l'emploi; **to be** ~ **to do sth** être prêt à faire qch; **to get** ~ *vi* se préparer ♦ *vt* préparer.
ready cash *n* (argent *m*) liquide *m*.
ready-made [red'ēmād'] *a* tout(e) fait(e).
ready-mix [red'ēmiks] *n* (*for cakes etc*) préparation *f* en sachet.
ready-to-wear [red'ētəwär'] *a* (en) prêt-à-porter.
reagent [rēā'jənt] *n* réactif *m*.
real [rēl] *a* réel(le); (*genuine*) véritable; (*proper*) vrai(e) ♦ *ad* (*US col: very*) vraiment; **in** ~ **life** dans la réalité.
real estate *n* biens fonciers *or* immobiliers.
real estate agency *n* agence immobilière.
real estate agent *n* agent immobilier.
realism [rē'əlizəm] *n* réalisme *m*.
realist [rē'əlist] *n* réaliste *m/f*.
realistic [rēəlis'tik] *a* réaliste.
reality [rēal'itē] *n* réalité *f*; **in** ~ en réalité, en fait.
realization [rēələzā'shən] *n* prise *f* de conscience; réalisation *f*.
realize [rē'əlīz] *vt* (*understand*) se rendre compte de, prendre conscience de; (*a project, COMM: asset*) réaliser.
really [rē'əlē] *ad* vraiment.
realm [relm] *n* royaume *m*.
real-time [rēltīm'] *a* (*COMPUT*) en temps réel.
realtor [rē'əltûr] *n* (*US*) agent immobilier.
ream [rēm] *n* rame *f* (*de papier*); ~**s** (*fig: col*) des pages et des pages.
reap [rēp] *vt* moissonner; (*fig*) récolter.
reaper [rē'pûr] *n* (*machine*) moissonneuse *f*.

reappear [rēəpi'ûr] *vi* réapparaître, reparaître.
reappearance [rēəpēr'əns] *n* réapparition *f*.
reapply [rēəplī'] *vi*: **to ~ for** faire une nouvelle demande d'emploi concernant; reposer sa candidature à.
reappraisal [rēəprā'zəl] *n* réévaluation *f*.
rear [rēr] *a* de derrière, arrière *inv*; (AUT: *wheel etc*) arrière ♦ *n* arrière *m*, derrière *m* ♦ *vt* (*cattle, family*) élever ♦ *vi* (*also*: ~ **up**: *animal*) se cabrer.
rear admiral (RA) *n* vice-amiral *m*.
rear-engined [rēr'en'jənd] *a* (AUT) avec moteur à l'arrière.
rearguard [rēr'gärd] *n* arrière-garde *f*.
rearm [rēärm'] *vt, vi* réarmer.
rearmament [rēärm'əmənt] *n* réarmement *m*.
rearrange [rēərānj'] *vt* réarranger.
rear-view [rēr'vyōō'] : ~ **mirror** *n* (AUT) rétroviseur *m*.
reason [rē'zən] *n* raison *f* ♦ *vi*: **to ~ with sb** raisonner qn, faire entendre raison à qn; **the ~ for/why** la raison de/pour laquelle; **to have ~ to think** avoir lieu de penser; **it stands to ~ that** il va sans dire que; **she claims with good ~ that** ... elle affirme à juste titre que ...; **all the more ~ why** raison de plus pour + *infinitive or* pour que + *sub*.
reasonable [rē'zənəbəl] *a* raisonnable; (*not bad*) acceptable.
reasonably [rē'zənəblē] *ad* (*to behave*) raisonnablement; (*fairly*) assez; **one can ~ assume that** ... on est fondé à *or* il est permis de supposer que ....
reasoned [rē'zənd] *a* (*argument*) raisonné(e).
reasoning [rē'zəning] *n* raisonnement *m*.
reassemble [rēəsem'bəl] *vt* rassembler; (*machine*) remonter.
reassert [rēəsûrt'] *vt* réaffirmer.
reassurance [rēəshōōr'əns] *n* assurance *f*, garantie *f*; (*comfort*) réconfort *m*.
reassure [rēəshōōr'] *vt* rassurer; **to ~ sb of** donner à qn l'assurance répétée de.
reassuring [rēəshōōr'ing] *a* rassurant(e).
reawakening [rēəwā'kəning] *n* réveil *m*.
rebate [rē'bāt] *n* (*on product*) rabais *m*; (*on tax etc*) dégrèvement *m*; (*repayment*) remboursement *m*.
rebel *n* [reb'əl] rebelle *m/f* ♦ *vi* [ribel'] se rebeller, se révolter.
rebellion [ribel'yən] *n* rébellion *f*, révolte *f*.
rebellious [ribel'yəs] *a* rebelle.
rebirth [rēbûrth'] *n* renaissance *f*.
rebound *vi* [ribound'] (*ball*) rebondir ♦ *n* [rē'bound] rebond *m*.
rebuff [ribuf'] *n* rebuffade *f* ♦ *vt* repousser.
rebuild [rēbild'] *vt irg* reconstruire.
rebuke [ribyōōk'] *n* réprimande *f*, reproche *m* ♦ *vt* réprimander.
rebut [ribut'] *vt* réfuter.
rebuttal [ribut'əl] *n* réfutation *f*.
recalcitrant [rikal'sitrənt] *a* récalcitrant(e).
recall [rikôl'] *vt* rappeler; (*remember*) se rappeler, se souvenir de ♦ *n* rappel *m*; **beyond ~** *a* irrévocable.
recant [rikant'] *vi* se rétracter; (REL) abjurer.
recap [rē'kap] *n* récapitulation *f* ♦ *vt, vi* récapituler.
recapture [rēkap'chûr] *vt* reprendre; (*atmosphere*) recréer.

recd. *abbr* = *received*.
recede [risēd'] *vi* s'éloigner; reculer; redescendre.
receding [risē'ding] *a* (*forehead, chin*) fuyant(e); ~ **hairline** front dégarni.
receipt [risēt'] *n* (*document*) reçu *m*; (*for parcel etc*) accusé *m* de réception; (*act of receiving*) réception *f*; ~**s** *npl* (COMM) recettes *fpl*; **to acknowledge ~ of** accuser réception de; **we are in ~ of** ... nous avons reçu ....
receivable [risē'vəbəl] *a* (COMM) recevable; (: *owing*) à recevoir.
receive [risēv'] *vt* recevoir; (*guest*) recevoir, accueillir; **"~d with thanks"** (COMM) "pour acquit".
receiver [risē'vûr] *n* (TEL) récepteur *m*, combiné *m*; (RADIO) récepteur; (*of stolen goods*) receleur *m*; (COMM) administrateur *m* judiciaire.
recent [rē'sənt] *a* récent(e); **in ~ years** au cours de ces dernières années.
recently [rē'səntlē] *ad* récemment; **as ~ as** pas plus tard que; **until ~** jusqu'à il y a peu de temps encore.
receptacle [risep'təkəl] *n* récipient *m*.
reception [risep'shən] *n* réception *f*; (*welcome*) accueil *m*, réception.
reception center *n* centre *m* d'accueil.
reception desk *n* réception *f*.
receptionist [risep'shənist] *n* réceptionniste *m/f*.
receptive [risep'tiv] *a* réceptif(ive).
recess [rē'ses] *n* (*in room*) renfoncement *m*; (*for bed*) alcôve *f*; (*secret place*) recoin *m*; (POL etc: *vacation*) vacances *fpl*; (US LAW: *short break*) suspension *f* d'audience; (SCOL: *esp US*) récréation *f*.
recession [risesh'ən] *n* (ECON) récession *f*.
recharge [rēchärj'] *vt* (*battery*) recharger.
rechargeable [rēchär'jəbəl] *a* rechargeable.
recipe [res'əpē] *n* recette *f*.
recipient [risip'ēənt] *n* bénéficiaire *m/f*; (*of letter*) destinataire *m/f*.
reciprocal [risip'rəkəl] *a* réciproque.
reciprocate [risip'rəkāt] *vt* retourner, offrir en retour ♦ *vi* en faire autant.
recital [risīt'əl] *n* récital *m*.
recite [risīt'] *vt* (*poem*) réciter; (*complaints etc*) énumérer.
reckless [rek'lis] *a* (*driver etc*) imprudent(e); (*spender etc*) insouciant(e).
recklessly [rek'lislē] *ad* imprudemment; avec insouciance.
reckon [rek'ən] *vt* (*count*) calculer, compter; (*consider*) considérer, estimer; (*think*): **I ~ (that)** ... je pense (que) ..., j'estime (que) ... ♦ *vi*: **he is somebody to be ~ed with** il ne faut pas le sous-estimer; **to ~ without sb/ sth** ne pas tenir compte de qn/qch.
reckon on *vt fus* compter sur, s'attendre à.
reckoning [rek'əning] *n* compte *m*, calcul *m*; estimation *f*; **the day of ~** le jour du Jugement.
reclaim [riklām'] *vt* (*land*) amender; (: *from sea*) assécher; (: *from forest*) défricher; (*demand back*) réclamer (le remboursement *or* la restitution de).
reclamation [rekləmā'shən] *n* (*of land*) amendement *m*; assèchement *m*; défriche-

ment *m*.

recline |riklīn'| *vi* être allongé(e) *or* étendu(e).

reclining |riklīn'ing| *a* (*seat*) à dossier réglable.

recluse |rck'lōōs| *n* reclus/e, ermite *m*.

recognition |rckəgnish'ən| *n* reconnaissance *f*; **in** ~ **of** en reconnaissance de; **to gain** ~ être reconnu(e); **transformed beyond** ~ méconnaissable.

recognizable |rckəgnī'zəbəl| *a*: ~ **(by)** reconnaissable (à).

recognize |rek'əgnīz| *vt*: **to** ~ **(by/as)** reconnaître (à/comme étant).

recoil |rikoil'| *vi* (*person*): **to** ~ **(from)** reculer (devant) ♦ *n* (*of gun*) recul *m*.

recollect |rckəlckt'| *vt* se rappeler, se souvenir de.

recollection |rckəlck'shən| *n* souvenir *m*; **to the best of my** ~ autant que je m'en souvienne.

recommend |rckəmend'| *vt* recommander; **she has a lot to** ~ **her** elle a beaucoup de choses en sa faveur.

recommendation |rckəmcndā'shən| *n* recommandation *f*.

recommended retail price (RRP) *n* (*Brit*) prix conseillé.

recompense |rek'əmpcns| *vt* récompenser; (*compensate*) dédommager ♦ *n* récompense *f*; dédommagement *m*.

reconcilable |rek'ənsīləbəl| *a* (*ideas*) conciliable.

reconcile |rek'ənsīl| *vt* (*two people*) réconcilier; (*two facts*) concilier, accorder; **to** ~ **o.s. to** se résigner à.

reconciliation |rckənsilēā'shən| *n* réconciliation *f*; conciliation *f*.

recondite |rck'əndīt| *a* abstrus(e), obscur(e).

recondition |rēkəndi'shən| *vt* remettre à neuf, réviser entièrement.

reconnaissance |rikān'isəns| *n* (*MIL*) reconnaissance *f*.

reconnoiter, (*Brit*) **reconnoitre** |rēkənoi'tûr| (*MIL*) *vt* reconnaître ♦ *vi* faire une reconnaissance.

reconsider |rēkənsid'ûr| *vt* reconsidérer.

reconstitute |rēkán'stitōōt| *vt* reconstituer.

reconstruct |rēkənstrukt'| *vt* (*building*) reconstruire; (*crime*) reconstituer.

reconstruction |rēkənstruk'shən| *n* reconstruction *f*; reconstitution *f*.

record *n* |rek'ûrd| rapport *m*, récit *m*; (*of meeting etc*) procès-verbal *m*; (*register*) registre *m*; (*file*) dossier *m*; (*COMPUT*) article *m*; (*also*: **police** ~) casier *m* judiciaire; (*MUS: disc*) disque *m*; (*SPORT*) record *m* ♦ *vt* |rikôrd'| (*set down*) noter; (*relate*) rapporter; (*MUS: song etc*) enregistrer; **in** ~ **time** dans un temps record *inv*; **public** ~**s** archives *fpl*; **to keep a** ~ **of** noter; **to keep the** ~ **straight** (*fig*) mettre les choses au point; **he is on** ~ **as saying that** ... il a déclaré en public que ...; **Italy's excellent** ~ les excellents résultats obtenus par l'Italie; **off the** ~ *a* officieux(euse) ♦ *ad* officieusement.

record card *n* (*in file*) fiche *f*.

recorded delivery letter *n* (*Brit MAIL*) ≈ lettre recommandée.

recorder |rikôr'dûr| *n* (*MUS*) flûte *f* à bec.

record holder *n* (*SPORT*) détenteur/trice du record.

recording |rikôr'ding| *n* (*MUS*) enregistrement *m*.

recording studio *n* studio *m* d'enregistrement.

record library *n* discothèque *f*.

record player *n* électrophone *m*.

recount |rikount'| *vt* raconter.

re-count *n* |rē'kount| (*POL: of votes*) nouveau décompte (des suffrages) ♦ *vt* |rēkount'| recompter.

recoup |rikōōp'| *vt*: **to** ~ **one's losses** récupérer ce qu'on a perdu, se refaire.

recourse |rē'kôrs| *n* recours *m*; expédient *m*; **to have** ~ **to** recourir à, avoir recours à.

recover |rikuv'ûr| *vt* récupérer ♦ *vi* (*from illness*) se rétablir; (*from shock*) se remettre; (*country*) se redresser.

re-cover |rēkuv'ûr| *vt* (*chair etc*) recouvrir.

recovery |rikuv'ûrē| *n* récupération *f*; rétablissement *m*; redressement *m*.

re-create |rēkrēāt'| *vt* recréer.

recreation |rckrēā'shən| *n* récréation *f*, détente *f*.

recreation center *n* centre *m* de loisirs.

recreational |rckrēā'shənəl| *a* pour la détente, récréatif(ive).

recreational vehicle (RV) *n* (*US*) camping-car *m*.

recrimination |rikrimənā'shən| *n* récrimination *f*.

recruit |rikrōōt'| *n* recrue *f* ♦ *vt* recruter.

recruiting office |rikrōōt'ing ôf'is| *n* bureau *m* de recrutement.

recruitment |rikrōōt'mənt| *n* recrutement *m*.

rectangle |rek'tanggəl| *n* rectangle *m*.

rectangular |rektang'gyəlûr| *a* rectangulaire.

rectify |rek'təfī| *vt* (*error*) rectifier, corriger; (*omission*) réparer.

rector |rek'tûr| *n* (*REL*) pasteur *m*; (*in Scottish universities*) personnalité élue par les étudiants pour les représenter.

rectory |rek'tûrē| *n* presbytère *m*.

rectum |rek'təm| *n* (*ANAT*) rectum *m*.

recuperate |rikōō'pərāt| *vi* (*from illness*) se rétablir.

recur |rikûr'| *vi* se reproduire; (*idea, opportunity*) se retrouver; (*symptoms*) réapparaître.

recurrence |rikûr'əns| *n* répétition *f*; réapparition *f*.

recurrent |rikûr'ənt| *a* périodique, fréquent(e).

recurring |rikûr'ing| *a* (*MATH*) périodique.

recycle |rēsī'kəl| *vt* recycler.

red |red| *n* rouge *m*; (*POL: pej*) rouge *m/f* ♦ *a* rouge; **in the** ~ (*account*) à découvert; (*business*) en déficit.

red carpet treatment *n* réception *f* en grande pompe.

Red Cross *n* Croix-Rouge *f*.

redcurrant |red'kur'ənt| *n* groseille *f* (rouge).

redden |red'ən| *vt*, *vi* rougir.

reddish |red'ish| *a* rougeâtre; (*hair*) plutôt roux(rousse).

redecorate |rēdek'ərāt| *vt* refaire à neuf, repeindre et retapisser.

redecoration |rēdekərā'shən| *n* remise *f* à neuf.

redeem |ridēm'| *vt* (*debt*) rembourser; (*sth in pawn*) dégager; (*fig, also REL*) racheter.

redeemable [ridē'məbəl] *a* rachetable; remboursable, amortissable.

redeeming [ridē'ming] *a* (*feature*) qui sauve, qui rachète (le reste).

redeploy [rēdiploi'] *vt* (*MIL*) redéployer; (*staff, resources*) reconvertir.

redeployment [rēdiploi'mənt] *n* redéploiement *m*; reconversion *f*.

redevelop [rēdivel'əp] *vt* rénover.

redevelopment [rēdivel'əpmənt] *n* rénovation *f*.

red-haired [red'härd] *a* roux(rousse).

red-handed [red'han'did] *a*: **to be caught ~** être pris(e) en flagrant délit *or* la main dans le sac.

redhead [red'hed] *n* roux/rousse.

red herring *n* (*fig*) diversion *f*, fausse piste.

red-hot [red'hât'] *a* chauffé(e) au rouge, brûlant(e).

redirect [rēdərekt'] *vt* (*mail*) faire suivre.

redistribute [rēdistrib'yōōt] *vt* redistribuer.

red-letter day [red'let'ûr dā] *n* grand jour, jour mémorable.

red light *n*: **to go through a ~** (*AUT*) brûler un feu rouge.

red-light district *n* quartier réservé.

redness [red'nis] *n* rougeur *f*; (*of hair*) rousseur *f*.

redo [rēdōō'] *vt irg* refaire.

redolent [red'əlent] *a*: **~ of** qui sent; (*fig*) qui évoque.

redouble [rēdub'əl] *vt*: **to ~ one's efforts** redoubler d'efforts.

redraft [rēdraft'] *vt* remanier.

redress [ridres'] *n* réparation *f* ♦ *vt* redresser; **to ~ the balance** rétablir l'équilibre.

Red Sea *n*: **the ~** la mer Rouge.

redskin [red'skin] *n* Peau-Rouge *m/f*.

red tape *n* (*fig*) paperasserie (administrative).

reduce [ridōōs'] *vt* réduire; (*lower*) abaisser; **to ~ sth by/to** réduire qch de/à; **to ~ sb to tears** faire pleurer qn.

reduced [ridōōst'] *a* réduit(e); **"greatly ~ prices"** "gros rabais"; **at a ~ price** (*goods*) au rabais; (*ticket etc*) à prix réduit.

reduction [riduk'shən] *n* réduction *f*; (*of price*) baisse *f*; (*discount*) rabais *m*; réduction.

redundancy [ridun'dənsē] *n* (*Brit*) licenciement *m*, mise *f* au chômage; **compulsory ~** licenciement; **voluntary ~** départ *m* volontaire.

redundancy payment *n* (*Brit*) indemnité *f* de licenciement.

redundant [ridun'dənt] *a* (*Brit: worker*) licencié(e), mis(e) au chômage; (*detail, object*) superflu(e); **to be made ~** (*worker*) être licencié, être mis au chômage.

reed [rēd] *n* (*BOT*) roseau *m*; (*MUS: of clarinet etc*) anche *f*.

reedy [rē'dē] *a* (*voice, instrument*) ténu(e).

reef [rēf] *n* (*at sea*) récif *m*, écueil *m*.

reek [rēk] *vi*: **to ~ (of)** puer, empester.

reel [rēl] *n* bobine *f*; (*TECH*) dévidoir *m*; (*FISHING*) moulinet *m*; (*CINEMA*) bande *f* ♦ *vt* (*TECH*) bobiner; (*also:* **~ up**) enrouler ♦ *vi* (*sway*) chanceler; **my head is ~ing** j'ai la tête qui tourne.

reel off *vt* (*say*) énumérer, débiter.

re-election [rēilek'shən] *n* réélection *f*.

re-enter [rēen'tûr] *vt* (*also SPACE*) rentrer dans.

re-entry [rēen'trē] *n* (*also SPACE*) rentrée *f*.

re-export *vt* [rēekspôrt'] réexporter ♦ *n* [rēeks'pôrt] marchandise réexportée; (*act*) réexportation *f*.

ref [ref] *n abbr* (*col:* = *referee*) arbitre *m*.

ref. *abbr* (*COMM*: = *with reference to*) réf.

refectory [rifek'tûrē] *n* réfectoire *m*.

refer [rifûr'] *vt*: **to ~ sth to** (*dispute, decision*) soumettre qch à; **to ~ sb to** (*inquirer: for information*) adresser *or* envoyer qn à; (*reader: to text*) renvoyer qn à; **he ~red me to the manager** il m'a dit de m'adresser au directeur.

refer to *vt fus* (*allude to*) parler de, faire allusion à; (*apply to*) s'appliquer à; (*consult*) se reporter à; **~ring to your letter** (*COMM*) en réponse à votre lettre.

referee [refərē'] *n* arbitre *m*; (*TENNIS*) juge-arbitre *m*; (*Brit: for job application*) répondant/e ♦ *vt* arbitrer.

reference [ref'ûrəns] *n* référence *f*, renvoi *m*; (*mention*) allusion *f*, mention *f*; (*for job application: letter*) références; lettre *f* de recommandation; (*: person*) répondant/e; **with ~ to** en ce qui concerne; (*COMM: in letter*) me référant à; **"please quote this ~"** (*COMM*) "prière de rappeler cette référence".

reference book *n* ouvrage *m* de référence.

reference number *n* (*COMM*) numéro *m* de référence.

reference table *n* (*COMPUT*) table *f* à consulter.

referendum, *pl* **referenda** [refərən'dəm, -də] *n* référendum *m*.

refill *vt* [rēfil'] remplir à nouveau; (*pen, lighter etc*) recharger ♦ *n* [rē'fil] (*for pen etc*) recharge *f*.

refine [rifīn'] *vt* (*sugar, oil*) raffiner; (*taste*) affiner.

refined [rifīnd'] *a* (*person, taste*) raffiné(e).

refinement [rifīn'mənt] *n* (*of person*) raffinement *m*.

refinery [rifī'nûrē] *n* raffinerie *f*.

refit *n* [rē'fit] (*NAUT*) remise *f* en état ♦ *vt* [rēfit'] remettre en état.

reflate [rifāt'] *vt* (*economy*) relancer.

reflation [riflā'shən] *n* relance *f*.

reflationary [riflā'shənârē] *a* de relance.

reflect [riflekt'] *vt* (*light, image*) réfléchir, refléter; (*fig*) refléter ♦ *vi* (*think*) réfléchir, méditer.

reflect on *vt fus* (*discredit*) porter atteinte à, faire tort à.

reflection [riflek'shən] *n* réflexion *f*; (*image*) reflet *m*; (*criticism*):: **~ on** critique *f* de; atteinte *f* à; **on ~** réflexion faite.

reflector [riflek'tûr] *n* (*also AUT*) réflecteur *m*.

reflex [rē'fleks] *a, n* réflexe (*m*).

reflexive [riflek'siv] *a* (*LING*) réfléchi(e).

reforestation [rēfôrista'shən] *n* reboisement *m*.

reform [rifôrm'] *n* réforme *f* ♦ *vt* réformer.

reformat [rēfôr'mat] *vt* (*COMPUT*) reformater.

Reformation [refûrmā'shən] *n*: **the ~** la Réforme.

reformatory [rifôr'mətôrē] *n* centre *m* d'éducation surveillée.

reformed [rifôrmd'] *a* amendé(e), assagi(e).

reformer [rifôr'mûr] *n* réformateur/trice.

refrain [rifrān'] *vi:* **to ~ from doing** s'abstenir de faire ♦ *n* refrain *m*.

refresh [rifresh'] *vt* rafraîchir; *(subj: food, sleep etc)* redonner des forces à.

refresher course [rifresh'ûr kôrs] *n* cours *m* de recyclage.

refreshing [rifresh'ing] *a* rafraîchissant(e); *(sleep)* réparateur(trice); *(fact, idea etc)* qui réjouit par son originalité *or* sa rareté.

refreshment [rifresh'mənt] *n:* **for some ~** *(eating)* pour se restaurer *or* sustenter; **in need of ~** *(resting etc)* ayant besoin de refaire ses forces; **~(s)** rafraîchissement(s) *m(pl)*.

refreshment stand *n* buvette *f*.

refrigeration [rifrijərā'shən] *n* réfrigération *f*.

refrigerator [rifrij'ərātûr] *n* réfrigérateur *m*, frigidaire *m*.

refuel [rēfyōō'əl] *vt* ravitailler en carburant ♦ *vi* se ravitailler en carburant.

refuge [ref'yōōj] *n* refuge *m*; **to take ~ in** se réfugier dans.

refugee [refyōōjē'] *n* réfugié/e.

refugee camp *n* camp *m* de réfugiés.

refund *n* [rē'fund] remboursement *m* ♦ *vt* [rifund'] rembourser.

refurbish [rēfûr'bish] *vt* remettre à neuf.

refurnish [rēfûr'nish] *vt* remeubler.

refusal [rifyōō'zəl] *n* refus *m*; **to have first ~ on sth** avoir droit de préemption sur qch.

refuse *n* [ref'yōōs] ordures *fpl*, détritus *mpl* ♦ *vt*, *vi* [rifyōōz'] refuser; **to ~ to do sth** refuser de faire qch.

refuse collection *n* (*Brit*) ramassage *m* d'ordures.

refuse collector *n* (*Brit*) éboueur *m*.

refuse disposal *n* (*Brit*) élimination *f* des ordures.

refute [rifyōōt'] *vt* réfuter.

regain [rigān'] *vt* regagner; retrouver.

regal [rē'gəl] *a* royal(e).

regale [rigāl'] *vt:* **to ~ sb with sth** régaler qn de qch.

regalia [rigā'lēə] *n* insignes *mpl* de la royauté.

regard [rigârd'] *n* respect *m*, estime *f*, considération *f* ♦ *vt* considérer; **to give one's ~s to** faire ses amitiés à; **"with kindest ~s"** "bien amicalement"; **as ~s, with ~ to** en ce qui concerne.

regarding [rigâr'ding] *prep* en ce qui concerne.

regardless [rigârd'lis] *ad* quand même; **~ of** sans se soucier de.

regatta [rigāt'ə] *n* régate *f*.

regency [rē'jənsē] *n* régence *f*.

regenerate [rējen'ûrāt] *vt* régénérer ♦ *vi* se régénérer.

regent [rē'jənt] *n* régent/e.

régime [rāzhēm'] *n* régime *m*.

regiment *n* [rej'əmənt] régiment *m* ♦ *vt* [rej'əment] imposer une discipline trop stricte à.

regimental [rejəmen'təl] *a* d'un *or* du régiment.

regimentation [rejəməntā'shən] *n* réglementation excessive.

region [rē'jən] *n* région *f*; **in the ~ of** (*fig*) aux alentours de.

regional [rē'jənəl] *a* régional(e).

regional development *n* aménagement *m* du territoire.

register [rej'istûr] *n* registre *m*; (*also:* **electoral ~**) liste électorale ♦ *vt* enregistrer, inscrire; (*birth*) déclarer; (*vehicle*) immatriculer; (*luggage*) enregistrer; (*letter*) envoyer en recommandé; (*subj: instrument*) marquer ♦ *vi* se faire inscrire; (*at hotel*) signer le registre; (*make impression*) être (bien) compris(e); **to ~ for a course** s'inscrire à un cours; **to ~ a protest** protester.

registered [rej'istûrd] *a* (*design*) déposé(e); (*Brit: letter*) recommandé(e); (*student, voter*) inscrit(e).

registered company *n* société immatriculée.

registered nurse *n* (*US*) infirmier/ière diplômé(e) d'État.

registered office *n* (*Brit*) siège social.

registered trademark *n* marque déposée.

registrar [rej'istrâr] *n* officier *m* de l'état civil; secrétaire (général).

registration [rejistrā'shən] *n* (*act*) enregistrement *m*; inscription *f*; (*Brit AUT: also:* **~ number**) numéro *m* d'immatriculation.

registry [rej'istrē] *n* bureau *m* de l'enregistrement.

registry office [rej'istrē ôfis] *n* (*Brit*) bureau *m* de l'état civil; **to get married in a ~** ≈ se marier à la mairie.

regret [rigret'] *n* regret *m* ♦ *vt* regretter; **to ~ that** regretter que + *sub*; **we ~ to inform you that ...** nous sommes au regret de vous informer que ...

regretfully [rigret'fəlē] *ad* à *or* avec regret.

regrettable [rigret'əbəl] *a* regrettable, fâcheux(euse).

regrettably [rigret'əblē] *ad* (*drunk, late*) fâcheusement; **~, he ...** malheureusement, il ....

regroup [rēgrōōp'] *vt* regrouper ♦ *vi* se regrouper.

regt *abbr* = **regiment**.

regular [reg'yəlûr] *a* régulier(ière); (*usual*) habituel(le), normal(e); (*listener, reader*) fidèle; (*soldier*) de métier; (*COMM: size*) ordinaire ♦ *n* (*client etc*) habitué/e; **~ (gas)** (*US*) essence *f* ordinaire.

regularity [regyəlar'itē] *n* régularité *f*.

regularly [reg'yəlûrlē] *ad* régulièrement.

regulate [reg'yəlāt] *vt* régler.

regulation [regyəlā'shən] *n* (*rule*) règlement *m*; (*adjustment*) réglage *m* ♦ *cpd* réglementaire.

rehabilitation [rēhəbilətā'shən] *n* (*of offender*) réhabilitation *f*; (*of disabled*) rééducation *f*, réadaptation *f*.

rehash [rēhash'] *vt* (*col*) remanier.

rehearsal [rihûr'səl] *n* répétition *f*; **dress ~** (répétition) générale.

rehearse [rihûrs'] *vt* répéter.

rehouse [rēhouz'] *vt* reloger.

reign [rān] *n* règne *m* ♦ *vi* régner.

reigning [rā'ning] *a* (*monarch*) régnant(e); (*champion*) actuel(le).

reimburse [rēimbûrs'] *vt* rembourser.

rein [rān] *n* (*for horse*) rêne *f*; **to give sb free ~** (*fig*) donner carte blanche à qn.

reincarnation [rēinkârnā'shən] *n* réincarnation f.

reindeer [rān'dēr] n (pl inv) renne m.

reinforce [rēinfôrs'] vt renforcer.

reinforced concrete [rēinfôrst' kân'krēt] n béton armé.

reinforcement [rēinfôrs'mənt] n (action) renforcement m; **~s** npl (MIL) renfort(s) m(pl).

reinstate [rēinstāt'] vt rétablir, réintégrer.

reinstatement [rēinstāt'mənt] n réintégration f.

reissue [rēish'ōō] vt (book) rééditer; (film) ressortir.

reiterate [rēit'ərāt] vt réitérer, répéter.

reject n [rē'jekt] (COMM) article m de rebut ♦ vt [rijekt'] refuser; (COMM: goods) mettre au rebut; (idea) rejeter.

rejection [rijek'shən] n rejet m, refus m.

rejoice [rijois'] vi: **to ~ (at** or **over)** se réjouir (de).

rejoinder [rijoin'dûr] n (retort) réplique f.

rejuvenate [rijōō'vənāt] vt rajeunir.

rekindle [rēkin'dəl] vt rallumer; (fig) raviver.

relapse [rilaps'] n (MED) rechute f.

relate [rilāt'] vt (tell) raconter; (connect) établir un rapport entre ♦ vi: **to ~ to** (connect) se rapporter à; (interact) établir un rapport or une entente avec.

related [rilā'tid] a apparenté(e).

relating [rilā'ting] : **~ to** prep concernant.

relation [rilā'shən] n (person) parent/e; (link) rapport m, lien m; **diplomatic/international ~s** relations diplomatiques/internationales; **in ~ to** en ce qui concerne; par rapport à; **to bear no ~ to** être sans rapport avec.

relationship [rilā'shənship] n rapport m, lien m; (personal ties) relations fpl, rapports; (also: **family ~**) lien de parenté; (affair) liaison f; **they have a good ~** ils s'entendent bien.

relative [rel'ətiv] n parent/e ♦ a relatif(ive); (respective) respectif(ive); **all her ~s** toute sa famille.

relatively [rel'ətivlē] ad relativement.

relax [rilaks'] vi se relâcher; (person: unwind) se détendre; (calm down) se calmer ♦ vt relâcher; (mind, person) détendre.

relaxation [rēlaksā'shən] n relâchement m; détente f; (entertainment) distraction f.

relaxed [rilakst'] a relâché(e); détendu(e).

relaxing [rilaks'ing] a délassant(e).

relay n [rē'lā] (SPORT) course f de relais ♦ vt [rēlā'] (message) retransmettre, relayer.

release [rilēs'] n (from prison, obligation) libération f; (of gas etc) émission f; (of film etc) sortie f; (record) disque m; (device) déclencheur m ♦ vt (prisoner) libérer; (book, film) sortir; (report, news) rendre public, publier; (gas etc) émettre, dégager; (free: from wreckage etc) dégager; (TECH: catch, spring etc) déclencher; (let go) relâcher; lâcher; desserrer; **to ~ one's grip** or **hold** lâcher prise; **to ~ the clutch** (AUT) débrayer.

relegate [rel'əgāt] vt reléguer; (SPORT): **to be ~d** descendre dans une division inférieure.

relent [rilent'] vi se laisser fléchir.

relentless [rilent'lis] a implacable.

relevance [rel'əvəns] n pertinence f; **~ of sth to sth** rapport m entre qch et qch.

relevant [rel'əvənt] a approprié(e); (fact) significatif(ive); (information) utile, pertinent(e); **~ to** ayant rapport à, approprié à.

reliability [rilīəbil'ətē] n sérieux m; fiabilité f.

reliable [rilī'əbəl] a (person, firm) sérieux(euse), fiable; (method, machine) fiable.

reliably [rilī'əblē] ad: **to be ~ informed** savoir de source sûre.

reliance [rilī'əns] n: **~ (on)** (trust) confiance f (en); (dependence) besoin m (de), dépendance f (de).

reliant [rilī'ənt] a: **to be ~ on sth/sb** dépendre de qch/qn.

relic [rel'ik] n (REL) relique f; (of the past) vestige m.

relief [rilēf'] n (from pain, anxiety) soulagement m; (help, supplies) secours m(pl); (of guard) relève f; (ART, GEO) relief m; **by way of light ~** pour faire diversion.

relief map n carte f en relief.

relief road n (Brit) route f de délestage.

relieve [rilēv'] vt (pain, patient) soulager; (bring help) secourir; (take over from: gen) relayer; (: guard) relever; **to ~ sb of sth** débarrasser qn de qch; **to ~ sb of his command** (MIL) relever qn de ses fonctions; **to ~ o.s.** (euphemism) se soulager, faire ses besoins.

religion [rilij'ən] n religion f.

religious [rilij'əs] a religieux(euse); (book) de piété.

reline [rēlīn'] vt (brakes) refaire la garniture de.

relinquish [riling'kwish] vt abandonner; (plan, habit) renoncer à.

relish [rel'ish] n (CULIN) condiment m; (enjoyment) délectation f ♦ vt (food etc) savourer; **to ~ doing** se délecter à faire.

relive [rēliv'] vt revivre.

reload [rēlōd'] vt recharger.

relocate [rēlō'kāt] vt (business) transférer ♦ vi se transférer, s'installer or s'établir ailleurs; **to ~ in** (déménager et) s'installer or s'établir à, se transférer à.

reluctance [riluk'təns] n répugnance f.

reluctant [riluk'tənt] a peu disposé(e), qui hésite; **to be ~ to do sth** hésiter à faire qch.

reluctantly [riluk'təntlē] ad à contrecœur, sans enthousiasme.

rely [rilī'] : **to ~ on** vt fus compter sur; (be dependent) dépendre de.

remain [rimān'] vi rester; **to ~ silent** garder le silence.

remainder [rimān'dûr] n reste m; (COMM) fin f de série.

remaining [rimā'ning] a qui reste.

remains [rimānz'] npl restes mpl.

remand [rimand'] n: **on ~** en détention préventive ♦ vt: **to ~ in custody** écrouer; renvoyer en détention provisoire.

remark [rimârk'] n remarque f, observation f ♦ vt (faire) remarquer, dire; (notice) remarquer; **to ~ on sth** faire une or des remarque(s) sur qch.

remarkable [rimâr'kəbəl] a remarquable.

remarry [rēmar'ē] vi se remarier.

remedial [rimē'dēəl] a (tuition, classes) de rattrapage.

remedy [rem'idē] n: **~ (for)** remède m (contre

or à) ♦ *vt* remédier à.

remember [rimem'bûr] *vt* se rappeler, se souvenir de; **I ~ seeing it**, **I ~ having seen it** je me rappelle l'avoir vu *or* que je l'ai vu; **she ~ed to do it** elle a pensé à le faire; **~ me to your wife** rappelez-moi au bon souvenir de votre femme.

remembrance [rimem'brəns] *n* souvenir *m*; mémoire *f*.

remind [rimīnd'] *vt*: **to ~ sb of sth** rappeler qch à qn; **to ~ sb to do** faire penser à qn à faire, rappeler à qn qu'il doit faire; **that ~s me!** j'y pense!

reminder [rimīnd'ûr] *n* rappel *m*; (*note etc*) pense-bête *m*.

reminisce [remənis'] *vi*: **to ~ (about)** évoquer ses souvenirs (de).

reminiscences [remənis'ənsiz] *npl* réminiscences *fpl*, souvenirs *mpl*.

reminiscent [remənis'ənt] *a*: **~ of** qui rappelle, qui fait penser à.

remiss [rimis'] *a* négligent(e); **it was ~ of me** c'était une négligence de ma part.

remission [rimish'ən] *n* rémission *f*; (*of debt, sentence*) remise *f*; (*of fee*) exemption *f*.

remit [rimit'] *vt* (*send: money*) envoyer.

remittance [rimit'əns] *n* envoi *m*, paiement *m*.

remnant [rem'nənt] *n* reste *m*, restant *m*; **~s** *npl* (*COMM*) coupons *mpl*; fins *fpl* de série.

remonstrate [rimán'strāt] *vi*: **to ~ (with sb about sth)** se plaindre (à qn de qch).

remorse [rimôrs'] *n* remords *m*.

remorseful [rimôrs'fəl] *a* plein(e) de remords.

remorseless [rimôrs'lis] *a* (*fig*) impitoyable.

remote [rimōt'] *a* éloigné(e), lointain(e); (*person*) distant(e); **there is a ~ possibility that** ... il est tout juste possible que ....

remote control *n* télécommande *f*.

remote-controlled [rimōt'kəntrōld'] *a* téléguidé(e).

remotely [rimōt'lē] *ad* au loin; (*slightly*) très vaguement.

remoteness [rimōt'nis] *n* éloignement *m*.

remould [rē'mōld] *n* (*Brit: tire*) pneu rechapé.

removable [rimōō'vəbəl] *a* (*detachable*) amovible.

removal [rimōō'vəl] *n* (*taking away*) enlèvement *m*; suppression *f*; (*Brit: from house*) déménagement *m*; (*from office: dismissal*) renvoi *m*; (*MED*) ablation *f*.

removal man *n* (*Brit*) déménageur *m*.

removal van *n* (*Brit*) camion *m* de déménagement.

remove [rimōōv'] *vt* enlever, retirer; (*employee*) renvoyer; (*stain*) faire partir; (*doubt, abuse*) supprimer; **first cousin once ~d** cousin/e au deuxième degré.

remover [rimōō'vûr] *n* (*for paint*) décapant *m*; (*for varnish*) dissolvant *m*; **make-up ~** démaquillant *m*; **~s** *npl* (*Brit: company*) entreprise *f* de déménagement.

remunerate [rimyōō'nərāt] *vt* rémunérer.

remuneration [rimyōōnərā'shən] *n* rémunération *f*.

rename [rēnām'] *vt* rebaptiser.

rend, *pt*, *pp* **rent** [rend, rent] *vt* déchirer.

render [ren'dûr] *vt* rendre; (*CULIN: fat*) clarifier.

rendering [ren'dûring] *n* (*MUS etc*) interpréta-

tion *f*.

rendezvous [rân'dāvōō] *n* rendez-vous *m inv* ♦ *vi* opérer une jonction, se rejoindre; (*spaceship*) effectuer un rendez-vous (dans l'espace); **to ~ with sb** rejoindre qn.

renegade [ren'əgād] *n* rénégat/e.

renew [rinōō'] *vt* renouveler; (*negotiations*) reprendre; (*acquaintance*) renouer.

renewable [rinōō'əbəl] *a* renouvelable.

renewal [rinōō'əl] *n* renouvellement *m*; reprise *f*.

renounce [rinouns'] *vt* renoncer à; (*disown*) renier.

renovate [ren'əvāt] *vt* rénover; (*work of art*) restaurer.

renovation [renəvā'shən] *n* rénovation *f*; restauration *f*.

renown [rinoun'] *n* renommée *f*.

renowned [rinound'] *a* renommé(e).

rent [rent] *pt*, *pp of* **rend** ♦ *n* loyer *m* ♦ *vt* louer; (*car, TV*) louer, prendre en location; (*also: ~ out: car, TV*) louer, donner en location; **"for rent"** "à louer".

rental [ren'təl] *n* (*for television, car*) (prix *m* de) location *f*.

rental car *n* (*US*) voiture louée.

renunciation [rinunsēā'shən] *n* renonciation *f*; (*self-denial*) renoncement *m*.

reopen [rēō'pən] *vt* rouvrir.

reopening [rēō'pəning] *n* réouverture *f*.

reorder [rēôr'dûr] *vt* commander de nouveau; (*rearrange*) réorganiser.

reorganize [rēôr'gənīz] *vt* réorganiser.

rep [rep] *n abbr* (*COMM*) = **representative**; (*THEATER*) = **repertory**.

Rep. *abbr* (*US POL*) = **representative**, **republican**.

repair [ripär'] *n* réparation *f* ♦ *vt* réparer; **in good/bad ~** en bon/mauvais état; **under ~** en réparation.

repair kit *n* trousse *f* de réparations.

repair man *n* réparateur *m*.

repair shop *n* (*AUT etc*) atelier *m* de réparations.

repartee [repûrtē'] *n* repartie *f*.

repast [ripast'] *n* (*formal*) repas *m*.

repatriate [rēpā'trēāt] *vt* rapatrier.

repay [ripā'] *vt irg* (*money, creditor*) rembourser; (*sb's efforts*) récompenser.

repayment [ripā'mənt] *n* remboursement *m*; récompense *f*.

repeal [ripēl'] *n* (*of law*) abrogation *f*; (*of sentence*) annulation *f* ♦ *vt* abroger; annuler.

repeat [ripēt'] *n* (*RADIO, TV*) reprise *f* ♦ *vt* répéter; (*pattern*) reproduire; (*promise, attack, also COMM: order*) renouveler; (*SCOL: a class*) redoubler ♦ *vi* répéter.

repeatedly [ripēt'idlē] *ad* souvent, à plusieurs reprises.

repel [ripel'] *vt* repousser.

repellent [ripel'ənt] *a* repoussant(e) ♦ *n*: **insect ~** insectifuge *m*; **moth ~** produit *m* antimite(s).

repent [ripent'] *vi*: **to ~ (of)** se repentir (de).

repentance [ripen'təns] *n* repentir *m*.

repercussion [rēpûrkush'ən] *n* (*consequence*) répercussion *f*.

repertoire [rep'ûrtwâr] *n* répertoire *m*.

repertory [rep'ûrtôrē] *n* (*also: ~ theater*)

théâtre *m* de répertoire.
repertory company *n* troupe théâtrale permanente.
repetition [rɛpitish'ən] *n* répétition *f*.
repetitious [rɛpitish'əs] *a* (*speech*) plein(e) de redites.
repetitive [ripɛt'ətiv] *a* (*movement, work*) répétitif(ive); (*speech*) plein(e) de redites.
replace [riplās'] *vt* (*put back*) remettre, replacer; (*take the place of*) remplacer; (*TEL*): "~ **the receiver**" "raccrochez".
replacement [riplās'mənt] *n* replacement *m*; remplacement *m*; (*person*) remplaçant/e.
replacement part *n* pièce *f* de rechange.
replay [rēplā'] *n* (*of match*) match rejoué; (*of tape, film*) répétition *f*.
replenish [riplen'ish] *vt* (*glass*) remplir (de nouveau); (*stock etc*) réapprovisionner.
replete [riplēt'] *a* rempli(e); (*well-fed*): ~ (**with**) rassasié(e) (de).
replica [rep'ləkə] *n* réplique *f*, copie exacte.
reply [riplī'] *n* réponse *f* ♦ *vi* répondre; **in** ~ (**to**) en réponse (à).
report [ripôrt'] *n* rapport *m*; (*PRESS etc*) reportage *m*; (*Brit: also*: **school** ~) bulletin *m* (scolaire); (*of gun*) détonation *f* ♦ *vt* rapporter, faire un compte rendu de; (*PRESS etc*) faire un reportage sur; (*bring to notice: occurrence*) signaler; (: *person*) dénoncer ♦ *vi* (*make a report*): **to** ~ (**on**) faire un rapport (sur); (*for newspaper*) faire un reportage (sur); (*present o.s.*): **to** ~ (**to sb**) se présenter (chez qn); **it is** ~**ed that** on dit or annonce que; **it is** ~**ed from Berlin that** on nous apprend de Berlin que.
report card *n* (*US, Scottish*) bulletin *m* (scolaire).
reportedly [ripôr'tidlē] *ad*: **she is** ~ **living in Spain** elle habiterait en Espagne; **he** ~ **ordered them to** ... il leur aurait ordonné de ....
reporter [ripôr'tûr] *n* reporter *m*.
repose [ripōz'] *n*: **in** ~ en or au repos.
repossess [rēpəzes'] *vt* saisir.
reprehensible [reprihen'səbəl] *a* répréhensible.
represent [reprizent'] *vt* représenter; (*explain*): **to** ~ **to sb that** expliquer à qn que.
representation [reprizentā'shən] *n* représentation *f*; ~**s** *npl* (*protest*) démarche *f*.
representative [reprizen'tətiv] *n* représentant/e; (*COMM*) représentant/e (de commerce); (*US POL*) député *m* ♦ *a*: ~ (**of**) représentatif(ive) (de), caractéristique (de).
repress [ripres'] *vt* réprimer.
repression [ripresh'ən] *n* répression *f*.
repressive [ipres'iv] *a* répressif(ive).
reprieve [riprēv'] *n* (*LAW*) grâce *f*; (*fig*) sursis *m*, délai *m* ♦ *vt* gracier; accorder un sursis or un délai à.
reprimand [rep'rəmand] *n* réprimande *f* ♦ *vt* réprimander.
reprint *n* [rē'print] réimpression *f* ♦ *vt* [rēprint'] réimprimer.
reprisal [riprī'zəl] *n* représailles *fpl*; **to take** ~**s** user de représailles.
reproach [riprōch'] *n* reproche *m* ♦ *vt*: **to** ~ **sb with sth** reprocher qch à qn; **beyond** ~ irréprochable.

reproachful [riprōch'fəl] *a* de reproche.
reproduce [rēprədōōs'] *vt* reproduire ♦ *vi* se reproduire.
reproduction [rēprəduk'shən] *n* reproduction *f*.
reproductive [rēprəduk'tiv] *a* reproducteur(trice).
reproof [riprōōf'] *n* reproche *m*.
reprove [riprōōv'] *vt* (*action*) réprouver; (*person*): **to** ~ (**for**) blâmer (de).
reproving [riprōō'ving] *a* réprobateur(trice).
reptile [rep'tīl] *n* reptile *m*.
Repub. *abbr* (*US POL*) = **republican**.
republic [ripub'lik] *n* république *f*.
republican [ipub'likən] *a, n* républicain(e).
repudiate [ripyōō'dēāt] *vt* (*ally, behavior*) désavouer; (*accusation*) rejeter; (*wife*) répudier.
repugnant [ripug'nənt] *a* répugnant(e).
repulse [ripuls'] *vt* repousser.
repulsion [ripul'shən] *n* répulsion *f*.
repulsive [ripul'siv] *a* repoussant(e), répulsif(ive).
reputable [rep'yətəbəl] *a* de bonne réputation; (*occupation*) honorable.
reputation [repyətā'shən] *n* réputation *f*; **to have a** ~ **for** être réputé(e) pour; **he has a** ~ **for being awkward** il a la réputation de ne pas être commode.
repute [ripyōōt'] *n* (*bonne*) réputation.
reputed [ripyōō'tid] *a* réputé(e); **he is** ~ **to be rich/intelligent** *etc* on dit qu'il est riche/intelligent *etc*.
reputedly [ripyōō'tidlē] *ad* d'après ce qu'on dit.
request [rikwest'] *n* demande *f*; (*formal*) requête *f* ♦ *vt*: **to** ~ (**of or from sb**) demander (à qn); **at the** ~ **of** à la demande de.
request stop *n* (*Brit: for bus*) arrêt facultatif.
requiem [rek'wēəm] *n* requiem *m*.
require [rikwīûr'] *vt* (*need: subj: person*) avoir besoin de; (: *thing, situation*) nécessiter, demander; (*demand*) exiger, requérir; (*order*): **to** ~ **sb to do sth/sth of sb** exiger que qn fasse qch/qch de qn; **if** ~**d** s'il le faut; **what qualifications are** ~**d?** quelles sont les qualifications requises?; ~**d by law** requis par la loi.
required [rikwīûrd'] *a* requis(e), voulu(e).
requirement [rikwīûr'mənt] *n* exigence *f*; besoin *m*; condition *f* (requise).
requisite [rek'wizit] *n* chose *f* nécessaire ♦ *a* requis(e), nécessaire; **toilet** ~**s** accessoires *mpl* de toilette.
requisition [rekwizish'ən] *n*: ~ (**for**) demande *f* (de) ♦ *vt* (*MIL*) réquisitionner.
reroute [rērout'] *vt* (*train etc*) dérouter.
resale [rē'sāl] *n* revente *f*.
resale price maintenance [rē'sāl prīs mān'tənəns] *n vente au détail à prix imposé*.
rescind [risind'] *vt* annuler; (*law*) abrog◌ (*judgment*) rescinder.
rescue [res'kyōō] *n* sauvetage *m*; (*hel* cours *mpl* ♦ *vt* sauver; **to come to** ◌ venir au secours de qn.
rescue party *n* équipe *f* de sauvetag◌
rescuer [res'kyōōûr] *n* sauveteur *m*◌
research [risûrch'] *n* recherche(◌

faire des recherches sur ♦ *vi*: **to ~ (into sth)**
faire des recherches (sur qch); **a piece of ~**
un travail de recherche; **~ and development
(R & D)** recherche-développement (R-D).
researcher [risûr'chûr] *n* chercheur/euse.
research work *n* recherches *fpl*.
resell [rēsel'] *vt irg* revendre.
resemblance [rizem'bləns] *n* ressemblance *f*;
  to bear a strong ~ to ressembler beaucoup
  à.
resemble [rizem'bəl] *vt* ressembler à.
resent [rizent'] *vt* éprouver du ressentiment
  de, être contrarié(e) par.
resentful [rizent'fəl] *a* irrité(e), plein(e) de
  ressentiment.
resentment [rizent'mənt] *n* ressentiment *m*.
reservation [rezûrvā'shən] *n* (*booking*) réservation *f*; (*doubt*) réserve *f*; (*protected
  area*) réserve, (*Brit* AUT: *also*: **central ~**)
  bande médiane; **to make a ~ (in an hotel/a
  restaurant/on a plane)** réserver *or* retenir
  une chambre/une table/une place; **with ~s**
  (*doubts*) avec certaines réserves.
reservation desk *n* (*US: in hotel*) réception
  f.
reserve [rizûrv'] *n* réserve *f*; (SPORT)
  remplaçant/e ♦ *vt* (*seats etc*) réserver, retenir; **~s** *npl* (MIL) réservistes *mpl*; **in ~** en
  réserve.
reserve currency *n* monnaie *f* de réserve.
reserved [rizûrvd'] *a* réservé(e).
reserve price *n* (*Brit*) mise *f* à prix, prix *m*
  de départ.
reservist [rizûr'vist] *n* (MIL) réserviste *m*.
reservoir [rez'ûrvwâr] *n* réservoir *m*.
reset [rēset'] *vt irg* remettre; (*clock, watch*)
  mettre à l'heure; (COMPUT) remettre à zéro.
reshape [rēshāp'] *vt* (*policy*) réorganiser.
reshuffle [rēshuf'əl] *n*: **Cabinet ~** (POL) remaniement ministériel.
reside [rizīd'] *vi* résider.
residence [rez'idəns] *n* résidence *f*; **to take up
  ~** s'installer; **in ~** (*queen etc*) en résidence;
  (*doctor*) résidant(e).
resident [rez'idənt] *n* résident/e ♦ *a* rési-
  dant(e).
residential [reziden'chəl] *a* de résidence;
  (*area*) résidentiel(le).
residue [rez'idōō] *n* reste *m*; (CHEMISTRY,
  PHYSICS) résidu *m*.
resign [rizīn'] *vt* (*one's post*) se démettre de ♦
  vi: **to ~ (from)** démissionner (de); **to ~ o.s.
  to** (*endure*) se résigner à.
resignation [rezignā'shən] *n* démission *f*; résignation *f*; **to tender one's ~** donner sa démission.
resigned [rizīnd'] *a* résigné(e).
resilience [rizil'yəns] *n* (*of material*) élasticité
  f; (*of person*) ressort *m*.
resilient [rizil'yənt] *a* (*person*) qui réagit, qui a
  du ressort.
resin [rez'in] *n* résine *f*.
resist [rizist'] *vt* résister à.
resistance [rizis'təns] *n* résistance *f*.
resistant [rizis'tənt] *a*: **~ (to)** résistant(e) (à).
resolute [rez'əlōōt] *a* résolu(e).
resolution [rezəlōō'shən] *n* résolution *f*; **to
  make a ~** prendre une résolution.
resolve [rizâlv'] *n* résolution *f* ♦ *vt* (*decide*): **to**

~ to do résoudre *or* décider de faire; (*problem*) résoudre.
resolved [rizâlvd'] *a* résolu(e).
resonance [rez'ənəns] *n* résonance *f*.
resonant [rez'ənənt] *a* résonnant(e).
resort [rizôrt'] *n* (*town*) station *f* (de vacances); (*recourse*) recours *m* ♦ *vi*: **to ~ to**
  avoir recours à; **seaside/winter sports ~**
  station balnéaire/de sports d'hiver; **in the
  last ~** en dernier ressort.
resound [rizound'] *vi*: **to ~ (with)** retentir
  (de).
resounding [rizoun'ding] *a* retentissant(e).
resource [rē'sôrs] *n* ressource *f*; **~s** *npl*
  ressources; **natural ~s** ressources naturelles;
  to leave sb to his (*or* **her**) **own ~s** (*fig*) livrer qn à lui-même (*or* elle-même).
resourceful [risôrs'fəl] *a* plein(e) de ressource,
  débrouillard(e).
resourcefulness [risôrs'fəlnis] *n* ressource *f*.
respect [rispekt'] *n* respect *m*; (*point, detail*):
  in some ~s à certains égards ♦ *vt* respecter;
  ~s *npl* respects, hommages *mpl*; **to have** *or*
  show ~ for sb/sth respecter qn/qch; **out of
  ~ for** par respect pour; **with ~ to** en ce qui
  concerne; **in ~ of** sous le rapport de, quant
  à; **in this ~** sous ce rapport, à cet égard;
  with due ~ I ... malgré le respect que je
  vous dois, je ....
respectability [rispektəbil'ətē] *n* respectabilité
  f.
respectable [rispek'təbəl] *a* respectable;
  (*quite good: result etc*) honorable; (*player*)
  assez bon(bonne).
respectful [rispekt'fəl] *a* respectueux(euse).
respective [rispek'tiv] *a* respectif(ive).
respectively [rispek'tivlē] *ad* respectivement.
respiration [respərā'shən] *n* respiration *f*.
respirator [res'pərātûr] *n* respirateur *m*.
respiratory [res'pûrətôrē] *a* respiratoire.
respite [res'pit] *n* répit *m*.
resplendent [risplen'dənt] *a* resplendissant(e).
respond [rispând'] *vi* répondre; (*to treatment*)
  réagir.
respondent [rispân'dənt] *n* (LAW) défendeur/
  deresse.
response [rispâns'] *n* réponse *f*; (*to treatment*)
  réaction *f*; **in ~ to** en réponse à.
responsibility [rispânsəbil'ətē] *n* responsabilité
  f; **to take ~ for sth/sb** accepter la responsabilité de qch/d'être responsable de qn.
responsible [rispân'səbəl] *a* (*liable*): **~ (for)**
  responsable (de); (*person*) digne de
  confiance; (*job*) qui comporte des responsabilités; **to be ~ to sb (for sth)** être responsable devant qn (de qch).
responsibly [rispân'səblē] *ad* avec sérieux.
responsive [rispân'siv] *a* qui n'est pas ré-
  servé(e) *or* indifférent(e).
rest [rest] *n* repos *m*; (*stop*) arrêt *m*, pause *f*;
  (MUS) silence *m*; (*support*) support *m*, appui
  m; (*remainder*) reste *m*, restant *m* ♦ *vi* se
  reposer; (*be supported*): **to ~ on** appuyer *or*
  reposer sur; (*remain*) rester ♦ *vt* (*lean*): **to
  ~ sth on/against** appuyer qch sur/contre;
  the ~ of them les autres; **to set sb's mind
  at ~** tranquilliser qn; **it ~s with him to**
  c'est à lui de; **~ assured that ...** soyez assuré que ....

rest area *n* (*US AUT*) aire *f* de stationnement (sur le bas-côté).

restart [rēstârt'] *vt* (*engine*) remettre en marche; (*work*) reprendre.

restaurant [res'tûrənt] *n* restaurant *m*.

restaurant car *n* (*Brit*) wagon-restaurant *m*.

rest cure *n* cure *f* de repos.

restful [rest'fəl] *a* reposant(e).

rest home *n* maison *f* de repos.

restitution [restitōō'shən] *n* (*act*) restitution *f*; (*reparation*) réparation *f*.

restive [res'tiv] *a* agité(e), impatient(e); (*horse*) rétif(ive).

restless [rest'lis] *a* agité(e); **to get ~** s'impatienter.

restlessly [rest'lislē] *ad* avec agitation.

restock [rēståk'] *vt* réapprovisionner.

restoration [restərā'shən] *n* restauration *f*; restitution *f*.

restorative [ristôr'ətiv] reconstituant(e) ♦ *n* reconstituant *m*.

restore [ristôr'] *vt* (*building*) restaurer; (*sth stolen*) restituer; (*peace, health*) rétablir.

restorer [ristôr'ûr] *n* (*ART etc*) restaurateur/trice (d'œuvres d'art).

restrain [ristrān'] *vt* (*feeling*) contenir; (*person*): **to ~ (from doing)** retenir (de faire).

restrained [ristrānd'] *a* (*style*) sobre; (*manner*) mesuré(e).

restraint [ristrānt'] *n* (*restriction*) contrainte *f*; (*moderation*) retenue *f*; (*of style*) sobriété *f*; **wage ~** limitations salariales.

restrict [ristrikt'] *vt* restreindre, limiter.

restricted area *n* (*AUT*) zone *f* à vitesse limitée.

restriction [ristrik'shən] *n* restriction *f*, limitation *f*.

restrictive [ristrik'tiv] *a* restrictif(ive).

restrictive practices *npl* (*INDUSTRY*) pratiques *fpl* entravant la libre concurrence.

rest room *n* (*US*) toilettes *fpl*.

rest stop *n* (*US AUT*) aire *f* de stationnement (sur le bas-côté).

restructure [rēstruk'chûr] *vt* restructurer.

result [rizult'] *n* résultat *m* ♦ *vi*: **to ~ (from)** résulter (de); **to ~ in** aboutir à, se terminer par; **as a ~ it is too expensive** il en résulte que c'est trop cher; **as a ~ of** à la suite de.

resultant [rizul'tənt] *a* résultant(e).

resume [rēzoom'] *vt* (*work, journey*) reprendre; (*sum up*) résumer ♦ *vi* (*work etc*) reprendre.

résumé [rez'ōōmā'] *n* (*summary*) résumé *m*; (*US: curriculum vitae*) curriculum vitae *m inv*.

resumption [rizump'shən] *n* reprise *f*.

resurgence [risûr'jəns] *n* réapparition *f*.

resurrection [rezərek'shən] *n* résurrection *f*.

resuscitate [risus'ətāt] *vt* (*MED*) réanimer.

resuscitation [risusətā'shən] *n* réanimation *f*.

retail [rē'tāl] *n* (vente *f* au) détail *m* ♦ *cpd* de or au détail ♦ *vt* vendre au détail ♦ *vi*: **to ~ at 10 francs** se vendre au détail à 10 F.

retailer [rē'tālûr] *n* détaillant/e.

retail outlet *n* point *m* de vente.

retail price *n* prix *m* de détail.

retail price index *n* ≈ indice *m* des prix.

retain [ritān'] *vt* (*keep*) garder, conserver; (*employ*) engager.

retainer [ritā'nûr] *n* (*servant*) serviteur *m*; (*fee*) acompte *m*, provision *f*.

retaliate [rital'ēāt] *vi*: **to ~ (against)** se venger (de); **to ~ (on sb)** rendre la pareille (à qn).

retaliation [ritalēā'shən] *n* représailles *fpl*, vengeance *f*; **in ~ for** par représailles pour.

retaliatory [rital'ēətôrē] *a* de représailles.

retarded [ritâr'did] *a* retardé(e).

retch [rech] *vi* avoir des haut-le-cœur.

retentive [riten'tiv] *a*: **~ memory** excellente mémoire.

rethink [rēthingk'] *vt* repenser.

reticence [ret'isəns] *n* réticence *f*.

reticent [ret'isənt] *a* réticent(e).

retina [ret'ənə] *n* rétine *f*.

retinue [ret'ənōō] *n* suite *f*, cortège *m*.

retire [ritūr'] *vi* (*give up work*) prendre sa retraite; (*withdraw*) se retirer, partir; (*go to bed*) (aller) se coucher.

retired [ritūrd'] *a* (*person*) retraité(e).

retirement [ritūr'mənt] *n* retraite *f*.

retirement age *n* âge *m* de la retraite.

retiring [ritūr'ing] *a* (*person*) réservé(e); (*chairman etc*) sortant(e).

retort [ritôrt'] *n* (*reply*) riposte *f*; (*container*) cornue *f* ♦ *vi* riposter.

retrace [rētrās'] *vt* reconstituer; **to ~ one's steps** revenir sur ses pas.

retract [ritrakt'] *vt* (*statement, claws*) rétracter; (*undercarriage, aerial*) rentrer, escamoter ♦ *vi* se rétracter; rentrer.

retractable [ritrakt'əbəl] *a* escamotable.

retrain [rētrān'] *vt* recycler ♦ *vi* se recycler.

retraining [rētrā'ning] *n* recyclage *m*.

retread *vt* [rētred'] (*AUT: tire*) rechaper ♦ *n* [re'tred] pneu rechapé.

retreat [ritrēt'] *n* retraite *f* ♦ *vi* battre en retraite; (*flood*) reculer; **to beat a hasty ~** (*fig*) partir avec précipitation.

retrial [rētrī'] *n* nouveau procès.

retribution [retrəbyōō'shən] *n* châtiment *m*.

retrieval [ritrē'vəl] *n* récupération *f*; réparation *f*; recherche *f* et extraction *f*.

retrieve [ritrēv'] *vt* (*sth lost*) récupérer; (*situation, honor*) sauver; (*error, loss*) réparer; (*COMPUT*) rechercher.

retriever [ritrē'vûr] *n* chien *m* d'arrêt.

retroactive [retrōak'tiv] *a* rétroactif(ive).

retrograde [ret'rəgrad] *a* rétrograde.

retrospect [ret'rəspekt] *n*: **in ~** rétrospectivement, après coup.

retrospective [retrəspek'tiv] *a* (*law*) rétroactif(ive) ♦ *n* (*ART*) rétrospective *f*.

return [ritûrn'] *n* (*going or coming back*) retour *m*; (*of sth stolen etc*) restitution *f*; (*recompense*) récompense *f*; (*FINANCE: from land, shares*) rapport *m*; (*report*) relevé *m*, rapport ♦ *cpd* (*journey*) de retour; (*Brit: ticket*) aller et retour; (*match*) retour ♦ *vi* (*person etc: come back*) revenir; (: *go back*) retourner ♦ *vt* rendre; (*bring back*) rapporter; (*send back*) renvoyer; (*put back*) remettre; (*POL: candidate*) élire; **~s** *npl* (*COMM*) recettes *fpl*; bénéfices *mpl*; (: **~ed goods**) marchandises renvoyées; **many happy ~s (of the day)!** bon anniversaire!; **by ~ mail** par retour (du courrier); **in ~ (for)** en échange (de).

returnable [ritûr'nəbəl] *a* (*bottle etc*) consigné(e).

return key *n* (*COMPUT*) touche *f* de retour.

return on investment (ROI) *n* (*US*) rentabilité *f* de l'investissement.

reunion [rēyōōn'yən] *n* réunion *f*.

reunite [rēyōōnīt'] *vt* réunir.

rev [rev] *n abbr* (= *revolution*: *AUT*) tour *m* ♦ *vb* (*also*: ~ **up**) *vt* emballer ♦ *vi* s'emballer.

revaluation [rēval'yōōāshən] *n* réévaluation *f*.

revamp [rēvamp'] *vt* (*house*) retaper; (*firm*) réorganiser.

Rev(d). *abbr* = **reverend**.

reveal [rivēl'] *vt* (*make known*) révéler; (*display*) laisser voir.

revealing [rivē'ling] *a* révélateur(trice); (*dress*) au décolleté généreux *or* suggestif.

reveille [rev'əlē] *n* (*MIL*) réveil *m*.

revel [rev'əl] *vi*: **to** ~ **in** sth/in doing se délecter de qch/à faire.

revelation [revəlā'shən] *n* révélation *f*.

reveler, (*Brit*) **reveller** [rev'əlûr] *n* fêtard *m*.

revelry [rev'əlrē] *n* festivités *fpl*.

revenge [rivenj'] *n* vengeance *f*; (*in game etc*) revanche *f* ♦ *vt* venger; **to take** ~ se venger.

revengeful [rivenj'fəl] *a* vengeur(eresse); vindicatif(ive).

revenue [rev'ənōō] *n* revenu *m*.

reverberate [rivûr'bərāt] *vi* (*sound*) retentir, se répercuter; (*light*) se réverbérer.

reverberation [rivûrbərā'shən] *n* répercussion *f*; réverbération *f*.

revere [rivēr'] *vt* vénérer, révérer.

reverence [rev'ûrəns] *n* vénération *f*, révérence *f*.

reverend [rev'ûrənd] *a* vénérable; **the R~ John Smith** (*Anglican*) le révérend John Smith; (*Catholic*) l'abbé John Smith; (*Protestant*) le pasteur John Smith.

reverent [rev'ûrənt] *a* respectueux(euse).

reverie [rev'ûrē] *n* rêverie *f*.

reversal [rivûr'səl] *n* (*of opinion*) revirement *m*.

reverse [rivûrs'] *n* contraire *m*, opposé *m*; (*back*) dos *m*, envers *m*; (*AUT*: *also*: ~ **gear**) marche *f* arrière ♦ *a* (*order, direction*) opposé(e), inverse ♦ *vt* (*turn*) renverser, retourner; (*change*) renverser, changer complètement; (*LAW*: *judgment*) réformer ♦ *vi* (*Brit AUT*) faire marche arrière; **to go into** ~ faire marche arrière; **in** ~ **order** en ordre inverse.

reversed charge call *n* (*Brit TEL*) communication *f* en PCV.

reverse video *n* vidéo *m* inverse.

reversible [rivûr'səbəl] *a* (*garment*) réversible; (*procedure*) révocable.

reversing lights [rivûr'sing līts] *npl* (*Brit AUT*) feux *mpl* de marche arrière *or* de recul.

reversion [rivûr'zhən] *n* retour *m*.

revert [rivûrt'] *vi*: **to** ~ **to** revenir à, retourner à.

review [rivyōō'] *n* revue *f*; (*of book, film*) critique *f* ♦ *vt* passer en revue; faire la critique de; (*US SCOL*) réviser; **to come under** ~ être révisé(e).

reviewer [rivyōō'ûr] *n* critique *m*.

revile [rivīl'] *vt* injurier.

revise [rivīz'] *vt* (*manuscript*) revoir, corriger; (*opinion*) réviser, modifier; (*study: subject, notes*) réviser; ~**d edition** édition revue et corrigée.

revision [rivizh'ən] *n* révision *f*; (*revised version*) version corrigée.

revitalize [rēvī'təlīz] *vt* revitaliser.

revival [rivī'vəl] *n* reprise *f*; rétablissement *m*; (*of faith*) renouveau *m*.

revive [rivīv'] *vt* (*person*) ranimer; (*custom*) rétablir; (*hope, courage*) redonner; (*play, fashion*) reprendre ♦ *vi* (*person*) reprendre connaissance; (*hope*) renaître; (*activity*) reprendre.

revoke [rivōk'] *vt* révoquer; (*promise, decision*) revenir sur.

revolt [rivōlt'] *n* révolte *f* ♦ *vi* se révolter, se rebeller.

revolting [rivōl'ting] *a* dégoûtant(e).

revolution [revəlōō'shən] *n* révolution *f*; (*of wheel etc*) tour *m*, révolution.

revolutionary [revəlōō'shənärē] *a*, *n* révolutionnaire *(m/f)*.

revolutionize [revəlōō'shənīz] *vt* révolutionner.

revolve [rivälv'] *vi* tourner.

revolver [riväl'vûr] *n* revolver *m*.

revolving [riväl'ving] *a* (*chair*) pivotant(e); (*light*) tournant(e).

revolving credit [rivâl'ving kred'it] *n* crédit *m* à renouvellement automatique.

revolving door *n* (*porte f* à) tambour *m*.

revue [rivyōō'] *n* (*THEATER*) revue *f*.

revulsion [rivul'shən] *n* dégoût *m*, répugnance *f*.

reward [riwôrd'] *n* récompense *f* ♦ *vt*: **to** ~ **(for)** récompenser (de).

rewarding [riwôrd'ing] *a* (*fig*) qui (en) vaut la peine, gratifiant(e); **financially** ~ financièrement intéressant(e).

rewind [rēwīnd'] *vt irg* (*watch*) remonter; (*ribbon etc*) réembobiner.

rewire [rēwīûr'] *vt* (*house*) refaire l'installation électrique de.

reword [rēwûrd'] *vt* formuler *or* exprimer différemment.

rewrite [rērīt'] *vt irg* récrire.

Reykjavik [rā'kyəvik] *n* Reykjavik.

RFD *abbr* (*US MAIL*) = *rural free delivery*.

Rh *abbr* (= *rhesus*) Rh.

rhapsody [rap'sədē] *n* (*MUS*) rhapsodie *f*; (*fig*) éloge délirant.

Rh factor *n* (*MED*) facteur *m* rhésus.

rhetoric [ret'ûrik] *n* rhétorique *f*.

rhetorical [ritôr'ikəl] *a* rhétorique.

rheumatic [rōōmat'ik] *a* rhumatismal(e).

rheumatism [rōō'mətizəm] *n* rhumatisme *m*.

rheumatoid arthritis [rōō'mətoid ärthrī'tis] *n* polyarthrite *f* chronique.

Rhine [rīn] *n*: **the** ~ le Rhin.

rhinestone [rīn'stōn] *n* faux diamant.

rhinoceros [rīnâs'ûrəs] *n* rhinocéros *m*.

Rhodes [rōdz] *n* Rhodes *f*.

Rhodesia [rōdē'zhə] *n* Rhodésie *f*.

Rhodesian [rōdē'zhən] *a* rhodésien(ne) ♦ *n* Rhodésien/ne.

rhododendron [rōdəden'drən] *n* rhododendron *m*.

Rhone [rōn] *n*: **the** ~ le Rhône.

rhubarb [roo'bárb] *n* rhubarbe *f*.
rhyme [rīm] *n* rime *f*; (*verse*) vers *mpl* ♦ *vi*:
to ~ (with) rimer (avec); without ~ or
reason sans rime ni raison.
rhythm [riਰ'əm] *n* rythme *m*.
rhythmic(al) [riਰ'mik(əl)] *a* rythmique.
rhythmically [riਰ'miklē] *ad* avec rythme.
RI *abbr* (*US MAIL*) = Rhode Island.
rib [rib] *n* (*ANAT*) côte *f* ♦ *vt* (*mock*) taquiner.
ribald [rib'əld] *a* paillard(e).
ribbed [ribd] *a* (*knitting*) à côtes; (*shell*)
strié(e).
ribbon [rib'ən] *n* ruban *m*; in ~s (*torn*) en
lambeaux.
rice [rīs] *n* riz *m*.
ricefield [rīs'fēld] *n* rizière *f*.
rich [rich] *a* riche; (*gift, clothes*)
somptueux(euse); the ~ *npl* les riches *mpl*;
~es *npl* richesses *fpl*; to be ~ in sth être
riche en qch.
richly [rich'lē] *ad* richement; (*deserved,
earned*) largement, grandement.
richness [rich'nis] *n* richesse *f*.
rickets [rik'its] *n* rachitisme *m*.
rickety [rik'ətē] *a* branlant(e).
rickshaw [rik'shô] *n* pousse(-pousse) *m inv*.
ricochet [rikəshā'] *n* ricochet *m* ♦ *vi* ricocher.
rid, *pt, pp* **rid** [rid] *vt*: to ~ sb of débarrasser
qn de; to get ~ of se débarrasser de.
riddance [rid'əns] *n*: good ~! bon débarras!
ridden [rid'ən] *pp* of **ride**.
riddle [rid'əl] *n* (*puzzle*) énigme *f* ♦ *vt*: to be
~d with être criblé(e) de.
ride [rīd] *n* promenade *f*, tour *m*; (*distance
covered*) trajet *m* ♦ *vb* (*pt* **rode**, *pp* **ridden**
[rōd, rid'ən]) *vi* (*as sport*) monter (à cheval),
faire du cheval; (*go somewhere: on horse, bicycle*) aller (à cheval *or* bicyclette *etc*); to
give sb a ~ (*to work etc*) emmener *or* prendre qn en voiture; (*journey: on bicycle,
motor cycle, bus*) rouler ♦ *vt* (*a certain
horse*) monter; (*distance*) parcourir, faire;
we rode all day/all the way nous sommes
restés toute la journée en selle/avons fait tout
le chemin en selle *or* à cheval; to ~ a
horse/bicycle/camel monter à cheval/à
bicyclette/à dos de chameau; can you ~ a
bike? est-ce que tu sais monter à bicyclette?; to ~ at anchor (*NAUT*) être à l'ancre; horse/car ~ promenade *or* tour à
cheval/en voiture; to go for a ~ faire une
promenade (en voiture *or* à bicyclette *etc*);
to give sb a ~ (*to work etc*) emmener *or*
prendre qn en voiture; to take sb for a ~
(*fig*) faire marcher qn; rouler qn.
ride out *vt*: to ~ out the storm (*fig*)
surmonter les difficultés.
rider [rī'dûr] *n* cavalier/ière; (*in race*) jockey
m; (*on bicycle*) cycliste *m/f*; (*on motorcycle*)
motocycliste *m/f*; (*in document*) annexe *f*,
clause additionnelle.
ridge [rij] *n* (*of hill*) faîte *m*; (*of roof,
mountain*) arête *f*; (*on object*) strie *f*.
ridicule [rid'əkyōōl] *n* ridicule *m*; dérision *f* ♦
vt ridiculiser, tourner en dérision; to hold
sb/sth up to ~ tourner qn/qch en ridicule.
ridiculous [ridik'yələs] *a* ridicule.
riding [rī'ding] *n* équitation *f*.
riding school *n* manège *m*, école *f* d'équitation.

rife [rīf] *a* répandu(e); ~ with abondant(e) en.
riffraff [rif'raf] *n* racaille *f*.
rifle [rī'fəl] *n* fusil *m* (à canon rayé) ♦ *vt* vider,
dévaliser.
rifle through *vt fus* fouiller dans.
rifle range *n* champ *m* de tir; (*indoor*) stand
m de tir.
rift [rift] *n* fente *f*, fissure *f*; (*fig: disagreement*) désaccord *m*.
rig [rig] *n* (*also*: oil ~: *on land*) derrick *m*; (:
at sea) plate-forme pétrolière ♦ *vt* (*election
etc*) truquer.
rig up *vt* arranger, faire avec des moyens
de fortune.
rigging [rig'ing] *n* (*NAUT*) gréement *m*.
right [rīt] *a* (*true*) juste, exact(e); (*correctly
chosen: answer, road etc*) bon(bonne); (*suitable*) approprié(e), convenable; (*just*) juste,
équitable; (*morally good*) bien *inv*; (*not left*)
droit(e) ♦ *n* (*title, claim*) droit *m*; (*not left*)
droite *f* ♦ *ad* (*answer*) correctement; (*not on
the left*) à droite ♦ *vt* redresser ♦ *excl* bon!;
the ~ time (*precise*) l'heure exacte; (*not
wrong*) la bonne heure; to be ~ (*person*)
avoir raison; (*answer*) être juste *or*
correct(e); to get sth ~ ne pas se tromper
sur qch; let's get it ~ this time! essayons de
ne pas nous tromper cette fois-ci!; you did
the ~ thing vous avez bien fait; ~ now en
ce moment même; tout de suite; ~ before/
after juste avant/après; ~ off sans hesiter;
(*at once*) tout de suite; ~ against the wall
tout contre le mur; ~ ahead tout droit; droit
devant; ~ in the middle en plein milieu; ~
away immédiatement; to go ~ to the end
of sth aller jusqu'au bout de qch; by ~s en
toute justice; on the ~ à droite; ~ and
wrong le bien et le mal; to be in the ~
avoir raison; film ~s droits d'adaptation
cinématographique; ~ of way droit *m* de
passage; (*AUT*) priorité *f*.
right angle *n* angle droit.
righteous [rī'chəs] *a* droit(e), vertueux(euse);
(*anger*) justifié(e).
righteousness [rī'chəsnis] *n* droiture *f*, vertu
f.
rightful [rīt'fəl] *a* (*heir*) légitime.
rightfully [rīt'fəlē] *ad* à juste titre, légitimement.
right-handed [rīt'handid] *a* (*person*) droi-
tier(ière).
right-hand man [rīt'hand' man] *n* bras droit
(*fig*).
right-hand side [rīt'hand' sīd] *n* côté droit.
rightly [rīt'lē] *ad* bien, correctement; (*with
reason*) à juste titre; if I remember ~ (*Brit*)
si je me souviens bien.
right-minded [rīt'mīndid] *a* sensé(e), sain(e)
d'esprit.
rights issue *n* (*STOCK EXCHANGE*) émission
préférentielle *or* de droit de souscription.
right wing *n* (*MIL, SPORT*) aile droite; (*POL*)
droite *f* ♦ *a*: right-wing (*POL*) de droite.
right-winger [rīt'wing'ûr] *n* (*POL*) membre *m*
de la droite; (*SPORT*) ailier droit.
rigid [rij'id] *a* rigide; (*principle*) strict(e).
rigidity [rijid'itē] *n* rigidité *f*.
rigidly [rij'idlē] *ad* rigidement; (*behave*)

inflexiblement.

rigmarole |rig'mərōl| *n* galimatias *m*, comédie *f*.

rigor |rig'ûr| *n* (*US*) rigueur *f*.

rigor mortis |rig'ûr môr'tis| *n* rigidité *f* cadavérique.

rigorous |rig'ûrəs| *a* rigoureux(euse).

rigorously |rig'ûrəslē| *ad* rigoureusement.

rigour |rig'ûr| *n* (*Brit*) = **rigor**.

rig-out |rig'out| *n* (*Brit col*) tenue *f*.

rile |rīl| *vt* agacer.

rim |rim| *n* bord *m*; (*of spectacles*) monture *f*; (*of wheel*) jante *f*.

rimless |rim'lis| *a* (*spectacles*) à monture invisible.

rind |rīnd| *n* (*of bacon*) couenne *f*; (*of lemon etc*) écorce *f*.

ring |ring| *n* anneau *m*; (*on finger*) bague *f*; (*also:* **wedding** ~) alliance *f*; (*for napkin*) rond *m*; (*of people, objects*) cercle *m*; (*of spies*) réseau *m*; (*of smoke etc*) rond; (*arena*) piste *f*, arène *f*; (*for boxing*) ring *m*; (*sound of bell, US TEL:* tone) sonnerie *f*; (*telephone call*) coup *m* de téléphone ♦ *vb* (*pt* **rang**, *pp* **rung** |rang, rung|) *vi* (*person, bell*) sonner; (*also:* ~ **out**: *voice, words*) retentir; (*TEL*) téléphoner ♦ *vt* (*Brit TEL:* also: ~ **up**) téléphoner à; **to** ~ **the bell** sonner; **to give sb a** ~ (*TEL*) passer un coup de téléphone or de fil à qn; **that has the** ~ **of truth about it** cela sonne vrai; **the name doesn't** ~ **a bell (with me)** ce nom ne me dit rien.

ring back *vt, vi* (*Brit TEL*) rappeler.

ring off *vi* (*Brit TEL*) raccrocher.

ring binder *n* classeur *m* à anneaux.

ring finger *n* annulaire *m*.

ringing |ring'ing| *n* (*of bell*) tintement *m*; (*louder, also of telephone*) sonnerie *f*; (*in ears*) bourdonnement *m*.

ringing tone *n* (*TEL*) sonnerie *f*.

ringleader |ring'lēdûr| *n* (*of gang*) chef *m*, meneur *m*.

ringlets |ring'lits| *npl* anglaises *fpl*.

ring road *n* (*Brit*) route *f* de ceinture.

rink |ringk| *n* (*also:* **ice** ~) patinoire *f*; (*for roller-skating*) skating *m*.

rinse |rins| *n* rinçage *m* ♦ *vt* rincer.

Rio (de Janeiro) |rē'ō (dē zhənər'ō)| *n* Rio de Janeiro.

riot |rī'ət| *n* émeute *f*, bagarres *fpl* ♦ *vi* manifester avec violence; **a** ~ **of colors** une débauche *or* orgie de couleurs; **to run** ~ se déchaîner.

rioter |rī'ətûr| *n* émeutier/ière, manifestant/e.

riotous |rī'ətəs| *a* tapageur(euse); tordant(e).

riotously |rī'ətəslē| *ad:* ~ **funny** tordant(e).

riot police *n* forces *fpl* de police intervenant en cas d'émeute; **hundreds of** ~ des centaines de policiers casqués et armés.

RIP *abbr* (= *rest in peace*) RIP.

rip |rip| *n* déchirure *f* ♦ *vt* déchirer ♦ *vi* se déchirer.

rip up *vt* déchirer.

ripcord |rip'kôrd| *n* poignée *f* d'ouverture.

ripe |rīp| *a* (*fruit*) mûr(e); (*cheese*) fait(e).

ripen |rī'pən| *vt* mûrir ♦ *vi* mûrir; se faire.

ripeness |rīp'nis| *n* maturité *f*.

rip-off |rip'ôf| *n* (*col*): **it's a** ~! c'est du vol manifeste!

riposte |ripōst'| *n* riposte *f*.

ripple |rip'əl| *n* ride *f*, ondulation *f*; égrènement *m*, cascade *f* ♦ *vi* se rider, onduler ♦ *vt* rider, faire onduler.

rise |rīz| *n* (*slope*) côte *f*, pente *f*; (*hill*) élévation *f*; (*increase: in prices, temperature*) hausse *f*, augmentation; (: *in wages* : *Brit*) augmentation *f*; (*fig*) ascension *f* ♦ *vi* (*pt* **rose**, *pp* **risen** |rōs, riz'ən|) s'élever, monter; (*prices*) augmenter, monter; (*waters, river*) monter; (*sun, wind, person: from chair, bed*) se lever; (*also:* ~ **up:** *rebel*) se révolter; se rebeller; ~ **to power** montée *f* au pouvoir; **to give** ~ **to** donner lieu à; **to** ~ **to the occasion** se montrer à la hauteur.

rising |rī'zing| *a* (*increasing: number, prices*) en hausse; (*tide*) montant(e); (*sun, moon*) levant(e) ♦ *n* (*uprising*) soulèvement *m*, insurrection *f*.

rising damp *n* (*Brit*) humidité *f* (montant des fondations).

risk |risk| *n* risque *m*, danger *m*; (*deliberate*) risque ♦ *vt* risquer; **to take** *or* **run the** ~ **of doing** courir le risque de faire; **at** ~ en danger; **at one's own** ~ à ses risques et périls; **it's a fire/health** ~ cela présente un risque d'incendie/pour la santé; **I'll** ~ **it** je vais risquer le coup.

risk capital *n* capital-risques *m*.

risky |ris'kē| *a* risqué(e).

risqué |riskā'| *a* (*joke*) risqué(e).

rissole |ris'āl| *n* croquette *f*.

rite |rīt| *n* rite *m*; **the last** ~s les derniers sacrements.

ritual |rich'ōōəl| *a* rituel(le) ♦ *n* rituel *m*.

rival |rī'vəl| *n* rival/e; (*in business*) concurrent/e ♦ *a* rival(e); qui fait concurrence ♦ *vt* être en concurrence avec; **to** ~ **sb/sth in** rivaliser avec qn/qch de.

rivalry |rī'vəlrē| *n* rivalité *f*; concurrence *f*.

river |riv'ûr| *n* rivière *f*; (*major, also fig*) fleuve *m* ♦ *cpd* (*port, traffic*) fluvial(e); **up/down** ~ en amont/aval.

riverbank |riv'ûrbangk| *n* rive *f*, berge *f*.

riverbed |riv'ûrbed| *n* lit *m* (de rivière *or* de fleuve).

riverside |riv'ûrsīd| *n* bord *m* de la rivière *or* du fleuve.

rivet |riv'it| *n* rivet *m* ♦ *vt* riveter; (*fig*) river, fixer.

riveting |riv'iting| *a* (*fig*) fascinant(e).

Riviera |rivēûr'ə| *n:* **the (French)** ~ la Côte d'Azur; **the Italian** ~ la Riviera (italienne).

Riyadh |rēyâd'| *n* Riyad.

RN *n abbr* (*US*) = **registered nurse**; (*Brit*) = **Royal Navy**.

RNA *n abbr* (= *ribonucleic acid*) ARN *m*.

road |rōd| *n* route *f*; (*in town*) rue *f*; (*fig*) chemin, voie *f*; **main** ~ grande route; **major** ~ route principale *or* à priorité; **minor** ~ voie secondaire; **it takes four hours by** ~ il y a quatre heures de route.

roadblock |rōd'blâk| *n* barrage routier.

road haulage *n* transports routiers.

road hog *n* chauffard *m*.

road map *n* carte routière.

road safety *n* sécurité routière.

roadside |rōd'sīd| *n* bord *m* de la route, bas-côté *m* ♦ *cpd* (situé(e) *etc*) au bord de la rou-

te; **by the** ~ au bord.de la route.
road sign *n* panneau *m* de signalisation.
roadsweeper [rōd'swēpûr] *n* (*Brit: person*) balayeur/euse.
road transport *n* transports routiers.
road user *n* usager *m* de la route.
roadway [rōd'wā] *n* chaussée *f*.
roadworthy [rōd'wûrt̸hē] *a* en bon état de marche.
roam [rōm] *vi* errer, vagabonder ♦ *vt* parcourir, errer par.
roar [rôr] *n* rugissement *m*; (*of crowd*) hurlements *mpl*; (*of vehicle, thunder, storm*) grondement *m* ♦ *vi* rugir; hurler; gronder; **to** ~ **with laughter** éclater de rire.
roaring [rôr'ing] *a*: **a** ~ **fire** une belle flambée; **a** ~ **success** un succès fou; **to do a** ~ **trade** faire des affaires d'or.
roast [rōst] *n* rôti *m* ♦ *vt* (*meat*) (faire) rôtir.
roast beef *n* rôti *m* de bœuf, rosbif *m*.
rob [râb] *vt* (*person*) voler; (*bank*) dévaliser; **to** ~ **sb of sth** voler *or* dérober qch à qn; (*fig: deprive*) priver qn de qch.
robber [râb'ûr] *n* bandit *m*, voleur *m*.
robbery [râb'ûrē] *n* vol *m*.
robe [rōb] *n* (*for ceremony etc*) robe *f*; (*also:* **bath**~) peignoir *m* ♦ *vt* revêtir (d'une robe).
robin [râb'in] *n* rouge-gorge *m*.
robot [rō'bət] *n* robot *m*.
robotics [rōbât'iks] *n* robotique *m*.
robust [rōbust'] *a* robuste; (*material, appetite*) solide.
rock [râk] *n* (*substance*) roche *f*, roc *m*; (*boulder*) rocher *m*; roche; (*Brit: candy*) ≈ sucre *m* d'orge ♦ *vt* (*swing gently: cradle*) balancer; (*: child*) bercer; (*shake*) ébranler, secouer ♦ *vi* (se) balancer; être ébranlé(e) *or* secoué(e); **on the** ~**s** (*drink*) avec des glaçons; (*ship*) sur les écueils; (*marriage etc*) en train de craquer; **to** ~ **the boat** (*fig*) jouer les trouble-fête.
rock and roll *n* rock (and roll) *m*, rock'n'roll *m*.
rock-bottom [râk'bât'əm] *n* (*fig*) niveau le plus bas ♦ *a* (*fig: prices*) sacrifié(e); **to reach** *or* **touch** ~ (*price, person*) tomber au plus bas.
rock climber *n* varappeur/euse.
rock climbing *n* varappe *f*.
rocket [râk'it] *n* fusée *f*; (*MIL*) fusée, roquette *f* ♦ *vi* (*prices*) monter en flèche.
rocket launcher [râk'it lônch'ûr] *n* lance-roquettes *m inv*.
rock face *n* paroi rocheuse.
rock fall *n* chute *f* de pierres.
rock garden *n* (jardin *m* de) rocaille *f*.
rocking chair [râk'ing chär] *n* fauteuil *m* à bascule.
rocking horse [râk'ing hôrs] *n* cheval *m* à bascule.
rocky [râk'ē] *a* (*hill*) rocheux(euse); (*path*) rocailleux(euse); (*unsteady: table*) branlant(e).
Rocky Mountains *npl*: **the** ~ les (montagnes *fpl*) Rocheuses *fpl*.
rod [râd] *n* (*metallic*) tringle *f*; (*TECH*) tige *f*; (*wooden*) baguette *f*; (*also:* **fishing** ~) canne *f* à pêche.
rode [rōd] *pt of* **ride**.
rodent [rō'dənt] *n* rongeur *m*.

rodeo [rō'dēō] *n* rodéo *m*.
roe [rō] *n* (*species: also:* ~ **deer**) chevreuil *m*; (*of fish: also:* **hard** ~) œufs *mpl* de poisson; **soft** ~ laitance *f*.
roe deer *n* chevreuil *m*; chevreuil femelle.
rogue [rōg] *n* coquin/e.
roguish [rō'gish] *a* coquin(e).
ROI *n abbr* (*US*) = **return on investment**.
role [rōl] *n* rôle *m*.
roll [rōl] *n* rouleau *m*; (*of banknotes*) liasse *f*; (*also:* **bread** ~) petit pain; (*register*) liste *f*; (*sound: of drums etc*) roulement *m*; (*movement: of ship*) roulis *m* ♦ *vt* rouler; (*also:* ~ **up**: *string*) enrouler; (*also:* ~ **out**: *pastry*) étendre au rouleau ♦ *vi* rouler; (*wheel*) tourner; **cheese** ~ ≈ sandwich *m* au fromage (*dans une petit pain*).
roll about, roll around *vi* rouler çà et là; (*person*) se rouler par terre.
roll by *vi* (*time*) s'écouler, passer.
roll in *vi* (*mail, cash*) affluer.
roll over *vi* se retourner.
roll up *vi* (*col: arrive*) arriver, s'amener ♦ *vt* (*carpet, cloth, map*) rouler; (*sleeves*) retrousser; **to** ~ **o.s. up into a ball** se rouler en boule.
roll call *n* appel *m*.
roller [rō'lûr] *n* rouleau *m*; (*wheel*) roulette *f*.
roller coaster *n* montagnes *fpl* russes.
roller skates *npl* patins *mpl* à roulettes.
rollicking [râl'iking] *a* bruyant(e) et joyeux(euse); (*play*) bouffon(ne); **to have a** ~ **time** s'amuser follement.
rolling [rō'ling] *a* (*landscape*) onduleux(euse).
rolling mill *n* laminoir *m*.
rolling pin *n* rouleau *m* à pâtisserie.
rolling stock *n* (*RAIL*) matériel roulant.
ROM [râm] *n abbr* (*COMPUT:* = *read-only memory*) mémoire morte, ROM *f*.
romaine (lettuce) [rōmān' (let'is)] *n* (*US*) (laitue *f*) romaine *f*.
Roman [rō'mən] *a* romain(e) ♦ *n* Romain/e.
Roman Catholic *a*, *n* catholique (*m/f*).
romance [rōmans'] *n* histoire *f* (or film *m* or aventure *f*) romanesque; (*charm*) poésie *f*; (*love affair*) idylle *f*.
Romanesque [rōmənesk'] *a* roman(e).
Romania [rōmā'nēə] *n* Roumanie *f*.
Romanian [rəmā'nēən] *a* roumain(e) ♦ *n* Roumain/e; (*LING*) roumain *m*.
Roman numeral *n* chiffre romain.
romantic [rōman'tik] *a* romantique; (*play, attachment*) sentimental(e).
romanticism [rōman'tisizəm] *n* romantisme *m*.
Romany [rōm'ənē] *a* de bohémien ♦ *n* bohémien/ne; (*LING*) romani *m*.
Rome [rōm] *n* Rome.
romp [râmp] *n* jeux bruyants ♦ *vi* (*also:* ~ **about**) s'ébattre, jouer bruyamment; **to** ~ **home** (*horse*) arriver bon premier.
rompers [râm'pûrz] *npl* barboteuse *f*.
rondo [rân'dō] *n* (*MUS*) rondeau *m*.
roof [rōōf] *n* toit *m*; (*of tunnel, cave*) plafond *m* ♦ *vt* couvrir (d'un toit); **the** ~ **of the mouth** la voûte du palais.
roof garden *n* toit-terrasse *m*.
roofing [rōō'fing] *n* toiture *f*.
roof rack *n* (*AUT*) galerie *f*.
rook [rōōk] *n* (*bird*) freux *m*; (*CHESS*) tour *f* ♦

vt (*col: cheat*) rouler, escroquer.

room [room] *n* (*in house*) pièce *f*; (*also:* **bed~**) chambre *f* (à coucher); (*in school etc*) salle *f*; (*space*) place *f*; **~s** *npl* (*lodging*) meublé *m*; "**~s for rent**", (*Brit*) "**~s to let**" "chambres à louer"; **is there ~ for this?** est-ce qu'il y a de la place pour ceci?; **to make ~ for sb** faire de la place à qn; **there is ~ for improvement** on peut faire mieux.

rooming house [roo'ming hous] *n* (*US*) maison *f* de rapport.

roommate [room'māt] *n* camarade *m/f* de chambre.

room service *n* service *m* des chambres (*dans un hôtel*).

room temperature *n* température ambiante; "**serve at ~**" (*wine*) "servir chambré".

roomy [roo'mē] *a* spacieux(euse); (*garment*) ample.

roost [roost] *n* juchoir *m* ♦ *vi* se jucher.

rooster [roos'tûr] *n* coq *m*.

root [root] *n* (*BOT, MATH*) racine *f*; (*fig: of problem*) origine *f*, fond *m* ♦ *vi* (*plant*) s'enraciner; **to take ~** (*plant, idea*) prendre racine.

   root around, (*Brit*) **root about** *vi* (*fig*) fouiller.

   root for *vt fus* (*col*) applaudir.

   root out *vt* extirper.

rope [rōp] *n* corde *f*; (*NAUT*) cordage *m* ♦ *vt* (*box*) corder; (*climbers*) encorder; **to jump** *or* **skip ~** (*US*) sauter à la corde; **to ~ sb in** (*fig*) embringuer qn; **to know the ~s** (*fig*) être au courant, connaître les ficelles; **at the end of one's ~** à bout (de patience).

rope ladder *n* échelle *f* de corde.

rosary [rō'zûrē] *n* chapelet *m*.

rose [rōz] *pt of* **rise** ♦ *n* rose *f*; (*also:* **~bush**) rosier *m*; (*on watering can*) pomme *f* ♦ *a* rose.

rosé [rōzā'] *n* rosé *m*.

rosebed [rōz'bed] *n* massif *m* de rosiers.

rosebud [rōz'bud] *n* bouton *m* de rose.

rosebush [rōz'boosh] *n* rosier *m*.

rosemary [rōz'märē] *n* romarin *m*.

rosette [rōzet'] *n* rosette *f*; (*larger*) cocarde *f*.

roster [râs'tûr] *n*: **duty ~** tableau *m* de service.

rostrum [râs'trəm] *n* tribune *f* (*pour un orateur etc*).

rosy [rō'zē] *a* rose; **a ~ future** un bel avenir.

rot [rât] *n* (*decay*) pourriture *f*; (*fig: pej*) idioties *fpl*, balivernes *fpl* ♦ *vt*, *vi* pourrir; **to stop the ~** (*Brit fig*) rétablir la situation; **dry ~** pourriture sèche (*du bois*); **wet ~** pourriture (du bois).

rota [rō'tə] *n* liste *f*, tableau *m* de service; **on a ~ basis** par roulement.

rotary [rō'tûrē] *a* rotatif(ive).

rotate [rō'tāt] *vt* (*revolve*) faire tourner; (*change round: crops*) alterner; (*: jobs*) faire à tour de rôle ♦ *vi* (*revolve*) tourner.

rotating [rō'tāting] *a* (*movement*) tournant(e).

rotation [rōtā'shən] *n* rotation *f*; **in ~** à tour de rôle.

rote [rōt] *n*: **by ~** machinalement, par cœur.

rotor [rō'tûr] *n* rotor *m*.

rotten [rât'ən] *a* (*decayed*) pourri(e); (*dishonest*) corrompu(e); (*col: bad*) mauvais(e),

moche; **to feel ~** (*ill*) être mal fichu(e).

rotting [rât'ing] *a* pourrissant(e).

rotund [rōtund'] *a* rondelet(te); arrondi(e).

rouge [roozh] *n* rouge *m* (à joues).

rough [ruf] *a* (*cloth, skin*) rêche, rugueux(euse); (*terrain*) accidenté(e); (*path*) rocailleux(euse); (*voice*) rauque, rude; (*person, manner: coarse*) rude, fruste; (*: violent*) brutal(e); (*district, weather*) mauvais(e); (*plan*) ébauché(e); (*guess*) approximatif(ive) ♦ *n* (*GOLF*) rough *m*; **the sea is ~ today** la mer est agitée aujourd'hui; **to have a ~ time (of it)** en voir de dures; **~ estimate** approximation *f*; **to ~ it** vivre à la dure; **to play ~** jouer avec brutalité.

rough out *vt* (*draft*) ébaucher.

roughage [ruf'ij] *n* fibres *fpl* diététiques.

rough-and-ready [ruf'ənred'ē] *a* (*accommodation, method*) rudimentaire.

rough-and-tumble [ruf'əntum'bəl] *n* agitation *f*.

roughcast [ruf'kast] *n* crépi *m*.

rough copy, rough draft *n* brouillon *m*.

roughen [ruf'ən] *vt* (*a surface*) rendre rude *or* rugueux(euse).

roughly [ruf'lē] *ad* (*handle*) rudement, brutalement; (*make*) grossièrement; (*approximately*) à peu près, en gros; **~ speaking** en gros.

roughness [ruf'nis] *n* (*of cloth, skin*) rugosité *f*; (*of person*) rudesse *f*; brutalité *f*.

roughshod [ruf'shâd] *ad*: **to ride ~ over** ne tenir aucun compte de.

rough work *n* (*Brit: at school etc*) brouillon *m*.

roulette [roolet'] *n* roulette *f*.

Roumania [roomā'nēə] *etc* = **Romania** *etc*.

round [round] *a* rond(e) ♦ *n* rond *m*, cercle *m*; (*Brit: of toast*) tranche *f*; (*duty: of policeman, milkman etc*) tournée *f*; (*: of doctor*) visites *fpl*; (*game: of cards, in competition*) partie *f*; (*BOXING*) round *m*; (*of talks*) série *f* ♦ *vt* (*corner*) tourner; (*bend*) prendre; (*cape*) doubler ♦ *prep* autour de ♦ *ad*: **right ~** tout autour; **all the year ~** toute l'année; **in ~ figures** en chiffres ronds; **she arrived ~ (about) noon** (*Brit*) elle est arrivée vers midi; **to go the ~s** (*disease, story*) circuler; **the daily ~** (*fig*) la routine quotidienne; **~ of ammunition** cartouche *f*; **~ of applause** ban *m*, applaudissements *mpl*; **~ of drinks** tournée *f*; **~ of sandwiches** (*Brit*) sandwich *m*; *see also* **around**.

round off *vt* (*speech etc*) terminer.

round up *vt* rassembler; (*criminals*) effectuer une rafle de; (*prices*) arrondir (au chiffre supérieur).

roundabout [round'əbout] *n* (*Brit AUT*) rondpoint *m* (à sens giratoire); (*at fair*) manège *m* (de chevaux de bois) ♦ *a* (*route, means*) détourné(e).

rounded [roun'did] *a* arrondi(e); (*style*) harmonieux(euse).

rounders [roun'dûrz] *npl* (*game*) ≈ balle *f* au camp.

roundly [round'lē] *ad* (*fig*) tout net, carrément.

round-shouldered [round'shōldûrd] *a* au dos rond.

round trip *n* (voyage *m*) aller et retour *m*.

round trip ticket n (US) (billet m d')aller et retour m.

roundup [round'up] n rassemblement m; (of criminals) rafle f; **a ~ of the latest news** un rappel des derniers événements.

rouse [rouz] vt (wake up) réveiller; (stir up) susciter; provoquer; éveiller.

rousing [rou'zing] a (welcome) enthousiaste.

rout [rout] n (MIL) déroute f ♦ vt mettre en déroute.

route [rōōt] n itinéraire m; (of bus) parcours m; (of trade, shipping) route f; "all ~s" (AUT) "toutes directions"; **the best ~ to Chicago** le meilleur itinéraire pour aller à Chicago; **en ~ for** en route pour.

routine [rōōtēn'] a (work) ordinaire, courant(e); (procedure) d'usage ♦ n routine f; (THEATER) numéro m; **daily ~** occupations journalières.

roving [rō'ving] a (life) vagabond(e).

roving reporter n reporter volant.

row [rō] n (line) rangée f; (of people, seats, KNITTING) rang m; (behind one another: of cars, people) file f; (rou) (noise) vacarme m; (dispute) dispute f, querelle f; (scolding) réprimande f, savon m ♦ vi (in boat) ramer; (as sport) faire de l'aviron; (rou) se disputer, se quereller ♦ vt (boat) faire aller à la rame or à l'aviron; **in a ~** (fig) d'affilée; **to have a ~** se disputer, se quereller.

rowboat [rō'bōt] n (US) canot m (à rames).

rowdiness [rou'dēnis] n tapage m, chahut m; (fighting) bagarre f.

rowdy [rou'dē] a chahuteur(euse); bagarreur(euse) ♦ n voyou m.

rowdyism [rou'dēizəm] n tendances fpl à la violence; actes mpl de violence.

rowing [rō'ing] n canotage m; (as sport) aviron m.

rowing boat n (Brit) = **rowboat.**

rowlock [rō'lâk] n (Brit) dame f de nage, tolet m.

royal [roi'əl] a royal(e).

Royal Air Force (RAF) n (Brit) armée de l'air britannique.

royal blue a bleu roi inv.

royalist [roi'əlist] a, n royaliste (m/f).

Royal Navy (RN) n (Brit) marine de guerre britannique.

royalty [roi'əltē] n (royal persons) (membres mpl de la) famille royale; (payment: to author) droits mpl d'auteur; (: to inventor) royalties fpl.

RP n abbr (Brit: = received pronunciation) prononciation f standard.

rpm abbr (= revolutions per minute) t/mn (= tours/minute).

RR abbr (US) = **railroad.**

R&R n abbr (US MIL) = rest and recreation.

RSVP abbr (= répondez s'il vous plaît) RSVP.

Rt Hon. abbr (Brit: = Right Honourable) titre donné aux députés de la Chambre des communes.

Rt Rev. abbr (= Right Reverend) très révérend.

rub [rub] n (with cloth) coup m de chiffon or de torchon; (on person) friction f ♦ vt frotter; frictionner; **to ~ sb** or (Brit) **~ sb up the wrong way** prendre qn à rebrousse-poil.

rub down vt (body) frictionner; (horse) bouchonner.

rub in vt (ointment) faire pénétrer.

rub off vi partir; **to ~ off on** déteindre sur.

rub out vt effacer ♦ vi s'effacer.

rubber [rub'ûr] n caoutchouc m; (US col) préservatif m; (Brit: eraser) gomme f (à effacer).

rubber band n élastique m.

rubber plant n caoutchouc m (plante verte).

rubber stamp n tampon m.

rubber-stamp [rub'ûrstamp'] vt (fig) approuver sans discussion.

rubbery [rub'ûrē] a caoutchouteux(euse).

rubbing alcohol [rub'ing al'kəhôl] n (US) alcool m à 90°.

rubbish [rub'ish] n (fig: pej) choses fpl sans valeur; camelote f; (nonsense) bêtises fpl, idioties fpl; (Brit: from household) ordures fpl ♦ vt (Brit col) dénigrer, rabaisser; **what you've just said is ~** tu viens de dire une bêtise.

rubbish bin n (Brit) boîte f à ordures, poubelle f.

rubbish dump n (Brit: in town) décharge publique, dépotoir m.

rubbishy [rub'ishē] a (Brit col) qui ne vaut rien, moche.

rubble [rub'əl] n décombres mpl; (smaller) gravats mpl.

ruble [rōō'bəl] n rouble m.

ruby [rōō'bē] n rubis m.

RUC n abbr (Brit) = Royal Ulster Constabulary.

rucksack [ruk'sak] n sac m à dos.

rudder [rud'ûr] n gouvernail m.

ruddy [rud'ē] a (face) coloré(e).

rude [rōōd] a (impolite: person) impoli(e); (: word, manners) grossier(ière); (shocking) indécent(e), inconvenant(e); **to be ~ to sb** être grossier envers qn.

rudely [rōōd'lē] ad impoliment; grossièrement.

rudeness [rōōd'nis] n impolitesse f; grossièreté f.

rudiment [rōō'dəmənt] n rudiment m.

rudimentary [rōōdəmən'tûrē] a rudimentaire.

rueful [rōō'fəl] a triste.

ruff [ruf] n fraise f, collerette f.

ruffian [ruf'ēən] n brute f, voyou m.

ruffle [ruf'əl] vt (hair) ébouriffer; (clothes) chiffonner; (water) agiter; (fig: person) émouvoir, faire perdre son flegme à.

rug [rug] n petit tapis.

rugby [rug'bē] n (also: ~ football) rugby m.

rugged [rug'id] a (landscape) accidenté(e); (features, kindness, character) rude; (determination) farouche.

ruin [rōō'in] n ruine f ♦ vt ruiner; (spoil: clothes) abîmer; **~s** npl ruine(s); **in ~s** en ruine.

ruination [rōōinā'shən] n ruine f.

ruinous [rōō'inəs] a ruineux(euse).

rule [rōōl] n règle f; (regulation) règlement m; (government) autorité f, gouvernement m; (dominion etc): **under British ~** sous l'autorité britannique ♦ vt (country) gouverner; (person) dominer; (decide) décider ♦ vi commander; décider; (LAW): **to ~ against/ in favor of/on** statuer contre/en faveur de/

sur; **to ~ that** (*umpire, judge etc*) décider que; **it's against the ~s** c'est contraire au règlement; **the ~s of the road** le code de la route; **by ~ of thumb** à vue de nez; **as a ~** normalement, en règle générale.

rule out *vt* exclure; **murder cannot be ~d out** l'hypothèse d'un meurtre ne peut être exclue.

ruled [rōold] *a* (*paper*) réglé(e).

ruler [rōo'lûr] *n* (*sovereign*) souverain/e; (*leader*) chef *m* (d'État); (*for measuring*) règle *f*.

ruling [rōo'ling] *a* (*party*) au pouvoir; (*class*) dirigeant(e) ♦ *n* (*LAW*) décision *f*.

rum [rum] *n* rhum *m*.

Rumania [rōomā'nēə] *etc* = **Romania** *etc*.

rumble [rum'bəl] *n* grondement *m*; gargouillement *m* ♦ *vi* gronder; (*stomach, pipe*) gargouiller.

rumbustious [rumbus'chəs] *a* (*person*) exubérant(e).

rummage [rum'ij] *vi* fouiller.

rummage sale *n* vente *f* de charité.

rumor, (*Brit*) **rumour** [rōo'mûr] *n* rumeur *f*, bruit *m* (qui court) ♦ *vt*: **it is ~ed that** le bruit court que.

rump [rump] *n* (*of animal*) croupe *f*; (*also*: ~ **steak**) romsteck *m*.

rumple [rum'pəl] *vt* (*hair*) ébouriffer; (*clothes*) chiffonner, friper.

rumpus [rum'pəs] *n* (*col*) tapage *m*, chahut *m*; (*quarrel*) prise *f* de bec; **to kick up a ~** faire toute une histoire.

run [run] *n* (*race etc*) course *f*; (*trip*) tour *m or* promenade *f* (en voiture); (*journey*) parcours *m*, trajet *m*; (*series*) suite *f*, série *f*; (*THEATER*) série de représentations; (*SKI*) piste *f*; (*in tights, stockings*) maille filée, échelle *f* ♦ *vb* (*pt* **ran**, *pp* **run** [ran, run]) *vt* (*business*) diriger; (*competition, course*) organiser; (*hotel, house*) tenir; (*COMPUT: program*) exécuter; (*force through: rope, pipe*): **to ~ sth through** faire passer qch à travers; (*to pass: hand, finger*): **to ~ sth over** promener *or* passer qch sur; (*water, bath*) faire couler ♦ *vi* courir; (*pass: road etc*) passer; (*work: machine, factory*) marcher; (*bus, train*) circuler; (*continue: play*) se jouer, être à l'affiche; (*: contract*) être valide *or* en vigueur; (*slide: drawer etc*) glisser; (*flow: river, bath*) couler; (*colors, washing*) déteindre; (*in election*) être candidat, se présenter; **to go for a ~** aller courir *or* faire un peu de course à pied; (*in car*) faire un tour *or* une promenade (en voiture); **to break into a ~** se mettre à courir; **a ~ of luck** une série de coups de chance; **to have the ~ of sb's house** avoir la maison de qn à sa disposition; **there was a ~ on** (*meat, tickets*) les gens se sont rués sur; **in the long ~** à longue échéance; à la longue; en fin de compte; **in the short ~** à brève échéance, à court terme; **on the ~** en fuite; **to make a ~ for it** s'enfuir; **I'll ~ you to the station** je vais vous emmener *or* conduire à la gare; **to ~ a stoplight** (*US*) griller un feu rouge; **to ~ errands** faire des commissions; **the train ~s between New York and Boston** le train assure le service entre New York et Boston; **the bus ~s every 20 minutes** il y a un auto-

bus toutes les 20 minutes; **it's very cheap to ~** (*car, machine*) c'est très économique; **to ~ on gas** *or* (*Brit*) **petrol/on diesel/off batteries** marcher à l'essence/au diesel/sur piles; **to ~ for president** être candidat à la présidence; **their losses ran into millions** leurs pertes se sont élevées à plusieurs millions.

run about *vi* (*Brit*) = **run around**.

run across *vt fus* (*find*) trouver par hasard.

run around *vi* (*children*) courir çà et là.

run away *vi* s'enfuir.

run down *vi* (*clock*) s'arrêter (faute d'avoir été remonté) ♦ *vt* (*AUT*) renverser; (*Brit: reduce: production*) réduire progressivement; (*: factory/shop*) réduire progressivement la production/l'activité de; (*criticize*) critiquer, dénigrer; **to be ~ down** être fatigué(e) *or* à plat.

run in *vt* (*Brit: car*) roder.

run into *vt fus* (*meet: person*) rencontrer par hasard; (*: trouble*) se heurter à; (*collide with*) heurter; **to ~ into debt** contracter des dettes.

run off *vi* s'enfuir ♦ *vt* (*water*) laisser s'écouler.

run out *vi* (*person*) sortir en courant; (*liquid*) couler; (*lease*) expirer; (*money*) être épuisé(e).

run out of *vt fus* se trouver à court de; **I've ~ out of gas** *or* (*Brit*) **petrol** je suis en panne d'essence.

run over *vt* (*AUT*) écraser ♦ *vt fus* (*revise*) revoir, reprendre.

run through *vt fus* (*instructions*) reprendre, revoir.

run up *vt* (*debt*) laisser accumuler; **to ~ up against** (*difficulties*) se heurter à.

runaway [run'əwā] *a* (*horse*) emballé(e); (*truck*) fou(folle); (*inflation*) galopant(e).

rundown [run'doun] *n* (*Brit: of industry etc*) réduction progressive.

rung [rung] *pp of* **ring** ♦ *n* (*of ladder*) barreau *m*.

run-in [run'in] *n* (*col*) accrochage *m*, prise *f* de bec.

runner [run'ûr] *n* (*in race: person*) coureur/euse; (*: horse*) partant *m*; (*on sleigh*) patin *m*; (*for drawer etc*) coulisseau *m*; (*carpet: in hall etc*) chemin *m*.

runner bean *n* (*Brit*) haricot *m* (à rames).

runner-up [runûrup'] *n* second/e.

running [run'ing] *n* (*in race etc*) course *f*; (*of business*) direction *f*; (*of event*) organisation *f*; (*of machine etc*) marche *f*, fonctionnement *m* ♦ *a* (*water*) courant(e); (*commentary*) suivi(e); **6 days ~** 6 jours de suite; **to be in/out of the ~ for sth** être/ne pas être sur les rangs pour qch.

running costs *npl* (*of business*) frais *mpl* de gestion; (*of car*): **the ~ are high** elle revient cher.

running head *n* (*TYP etc*) titre courant.

running mate *n* (*US POL*) *candidat à la vice-présidence*.

runny [run'ē] *a* qui coule.

run-off [run'ôf] *n* (*in contest, election*) deuxième tour *m*; (*extra race etc*) épreuve *f* supplémentaire.

run-of-the-mill [runəvᵗẖəmil'] *a* ordinaire, banal(e).

runt [runt] *n* (*also pej*) avorton *m*.

run-through [run'thrōō] *n* répétition *f*, essai *m*.

run-up [run'up] *n* (*Brit*): ~ **to sth** période *f* précédant qch.

runway [run'wā] *n* (*AVIAT*) piste *f* (d'envol *or* d'atterrissage).

rupee [rōō'pē] *n* roupie *f*.

rupture [rup'chûr] *n* (*MED*) hernie *f* ♦ *vt*: **to ~ o.s.** se donner une hernie.

rural [rōōr'əl] *a* rural(e).

ruse [rōōz] *n* ruse *f*.

rush [rush] *n* course précipitée; (*of crowd*) ruée *f*, bousculade *f*; (*hurry*) hâte *f*, bousculade; (*current*) flot *m*; (*BOT*) jonc *m*; (*for chair*) paille *f* ♦ *vt* transporter *or* envoyer d'urgence; (*attack: town etc*) prendre d'assaut ♦ *vi* se précipiter; **don't ~ me!** laissez-moi le temps de souffler!; **to ~ sth off** (*do quickly*) faire qch à la hâte; (*send*) envoyer d'urgence; **is there any ~ for this?** est-ce urgent?; **we've had a ~ of orders** nous avons reçu une avalanche de commandes; **I'm in a ~ (to do)** je suis vraiment pressé (de faire); **gold ~** ruée vers l'or.

rush through *vt fus* (*work*) exécuter à la hâte ♦ *vt* (*COMM: order*) exécuter d'urgence.

rush hour *n* heures *fpl* de pointe *or* d'affluence.

rush job *n* travail urgent.

rush matting [rush mat'ing] *n* natte *f* de paille.

rusk [rusk] *n* biscotte *f*.

Russia [rush'ə] *n* Russie *f*.

Russian [rush'ən] *a* russe ♦ *n* Russe *m/f*; (*LING*) russe *m*.

rust [rust] *n* rouille *f* ♦ *vi* rouiller.

rustic [rus'tik] *a* rustique ♦ *n* (*pej*) rustaud/e.

rustle [rus'əl] *vi* bruire, produire un bruissement ♦ *vt* (*paper*) froisser; (*US: cattle*) voler.

rustproof [rust'prōōf] *a* inoxydable.

rustproofing [rust'prōōfing] *n* traitement *m* antirouille.

rusty [rus'tē] *a* rouillé(e).

rut [rut] *n* ornière *f*; (*ZOOL*) rut *m*; **to be in a ~** (*fig*) suivre l'ornière, s'encroûter.

rutabaga [rōōtəbā'gə] *n* (*US*) rutabaga *m*.

ruthless [rōōth'lis] *a* sans pitié, impitoyable.

ruthlessness [rōōth'lisnis] *n* dureté *f*, cruauté *f*.

RV *abbr* (= *revised version*) traduction anglaise de la Bible de 1885 ♦ *n abbr* (*US*) = **recreational vehicle**.

rye [rī] *n* seigle *m*.

rye bread *n* pain *m* de seigle.

S

S, s [es] *n* (*letter*) S, s *m*; (*US SCOL*: = *sat-*

isfactory) ≈ assez bien; **S for Sugar** S comme Suzanne.

S [es] *abbr* (= *south, small*) S; (= *saint*) St.

SA *n abbr* = **South Africa, South America**.

Sabbath [sab'əth] *n* (*Jewish*) sabbat *m*; (*Christian*) dimanche *m*.

sabbatical [səbat'ikəl] *a*: ~ **year** année *f* sabbatique.

sabotage [sab'ətâzh] *n* sabotage *m* ♦ *vt* saboter.

saccharin(e) [sak'ûrin] *n* saccharine *f*.

sachet [sashā'] *n* sachet *m*.

sack [sak] *n* (*bag*) sac *m* ♦ *vt* (*dismiss*) renvoyer, mettre à la porte; (*plunder*) piller, mettre à sac; **to get the ~** être renvoyé(e) *or* mis(e) à la porte.

sackful [sak'fəl] *n*: **a ~ of** un (plein) sac de.

sacking [sak'ing] *n* toile *f* à sac; (*dismissal*) renvoi *m*.

sacrament [sak'rəmənt] *n* sacrement *m*.

sacred [sā'krid] *a* sacré(e).

sacrifice [sak'rəfīs] *n* sacrifice *m* ♦ *vt* sacrifier; **to make ~s (for sb)** se sacrifier *or* faire des sacrifices (pour qn).

sacrilege [sak'rəlij] *n* sacrilège *m*.

sacrosanct [sak'rōsangkt] *a* sacro-saint(e).

sad [sad] *a* (*unhappy*) triste; (*deplorable*) triste, fâcheux(euse).

sadden [sad'ən] *vt* attrister, affliger.

saddle [sad'əl] *n* selle *f* ♦ *vt* (*horse*) seller; **to be ~d with sth** (*col*) avoir qch sur les bras.

saddlebag [sad'əlbag] *n* sacoche *f*.

sadism [sā'dizəm] *n* sadisme *m*.

sadist [sā'dist] *n* sadique *m/f*.

sadistic [sədis'tik] *a* sadique.

sadly [sad'lē] *ad* tristement; (*regrettably*) malheureusement.

sadness [sad'nis] *n* tristesse *f*.

sae *abbr* (*Brit*: = *stamped addressed envelope*) enveloppe affranchie pour la réponse.

safari [səfâ'rē] *n* safari *m*.

safari park *n* réserve *f*.

safe [sāf] *a* (*out of danger*) hors de danger, en sécurité; (*not dangerous*) sans danger; (*cautious*) prudent(e); (*sure: bet etc*) assuré(e) ♦ *n* coffre-fort *m*; ~ **from** à l'abri de; ~ **and sound** sain(e) et sauf(sauve); **(just) to be on the ~ side** pour plus de sûreté, par précaution; **to play ~** ne prendre aucun risque; **it is ~ to say that ...** on peut dire sans crainte que ...; ~ **journey!** bon voyage!

safe-breaker [sāf'brākûr] *n* (*Brit*) = **safe-cracker**.

safe-conduct [sāf'kán'dukt] *n* sauf-conduit *m*.

safe-cracker [sāf'krakûr] *n* perceur *m* de coffre-fort.

safe-deposit [sāf'dipâzit] *n* (*vault*) dépôt *m* de coffres-forts; (*box*) coffre-fort *m*.

safeguard [sāf'gárd] *n* sauvegarde *f*, protection *f* ♦ *vt* sauvegarder, protéger.

safekeeping [sāfkē'ping] *n* bonne garde.

safely [sāf'lē] *ad* sans danger, sans risque; (*without mishap*) sans accident; **I can ~ say** ... je peux dire à coup sûr ....

safety [sāf'tē] *n* sécurité *f*; ~ **first!** la sécurité d'abord!

safety belt *n* ceinture *f* de sécurité.

safety curtain *n* rideau *m* de fer.

safety net n filet m de sécurité.
safety pin n épingle f de sûreté or de nourrice.
safety valve n soupape f de sûreté.
saffron [saf'rən] n safran m.
sag [sag] vi s'affaisser, fléchir; pendre.
saga [sâ'gə] n saga f; (fig) épopée f.
sage [sāj] n (herb) sauge f; (man) sage m.
Sagittarius [sajitär'ēəs] n le Sagittaire; **to be ~** être du Sagittaire.
sago [sā'gō] n sagou m.
Sahara [səhär'ə] n: **the ~ (Desert)** le (désert du) Sahara m.
Sahel [sâhel] n Sahel m.
said [sed] pt, pp of **say**.
Saigon [sīgän'] n Saigon.
sail [sāl] n (on boat) voile f; (trip): **to go for a ~** faire un tour en bateau ♦ vt (boat) manœuvrer, piloter ♦ vi (travel: ship) avancer, naviguer; (: passenger) aller or se rendre (en bateau); (set off) partir, prendre la mer; (SPORT) faire de la voile; **they ~ed into Le Havre** ils sont entrés dans le port du Havre.
sail through vi, vt fus (fig) réussir haut la main.
sailboard [sāl'bôrd] n planche f à voile.
sailboat [sāl'bōt] n (US) bateau m à voiles, voilier m.
sailing [sā'ling] n (SPORT) voile f; **to go ~** faire de la voile.
sailing boat n (Brit) = **sailboat**.
sailing ship n grand voilier.
sailor [sā'lûr] n marin m, matelot m.
saint [sānt] n saint/e.
saintly [sānt'lē] a saint(e), plein(e) de bonté.
sake [sāk] n: **for the ~ of** (out of concern for) pour, dans l'intérêt de; (out of consideration for) par égard pour; (in order to achieve) pour plus de, par souci de; **arguing for arguing's ~** discuter pour (le plaisir de) discuter; **for the ~ of argument** à titre d'exemple; **for heaven's ~!** pour l'amour du ciel!
salad [sal'əd] n salade f; **tomato ~** salade de tomates.
salad bowl n saladier m.
salad cream n (Brit) (sorte f de) mayonnaise f.
salad dressing n vinaigrette f.
salad oil n huile f de table.
salami [səlâ'mē] n salami m.
salaried [sal'ûrēd] a (staff) salarié(e), qui touche un traitement.
salary [sal'ûrē] n salaire m, traitement m.
salary scale n échelle f des traitements.
sale [sāl] n vente f; (at reduced prices) soldes mpl; **"for ~"** "à vendre"; **on ~** en vente; **on ~ or return** vendu(e) avec faculté de retour; **liquidation ~** liquidation f (avant fermeture); **~ and lease back** n cession-bail f.
saleroom [sāl'rōōm] n (Brit) = **salesroom**.
sales assistant n (Brit) = **sales clerk**.
sales clerk n (US) vendeur/euse.
sales conference n réunion f de vente.
sales drive n campagne commerciale, animation f des ventes.
sales force n (ensemble m du) service des ventes.
salesman [sālz'mən] n vendeur m; (representative) représentant m de commerce.

sales manager n directeur commercial.
salesmanship [sālz'mənship] n art m de la vente.
salesroom [sālz'rōōm] n (US) salle f des ventes.
sales slip n ticket m de caisse.
sales tax n (US) taxe f à l'achat.
saleswoman [sālz'wōōmən] n vendeuse f.
salient [sā'lēənt] a saillant(e).
saline [sā'lēn] a salin(e).
saliva [səlī'və] n salive f.
sallow [sal'ō] a cireux(euse).
salmon [sam'ən] n (pl inv) saumon m.
salmon trout n truite saumonée.
saloon [səlōōn'] n (US) bar m; (Brit AUT) berline f; (ship's lounge) salon m.
Salop [sal'əp] n abbr (Brit) = **Shropshire**.
SALT [sôlt] n abbr = Strategic Arms Limitation Talks/Treaty) SALT m.
salt [sôlt] n sel m ♦ vt saler ♦ cpd de sel; (CULIN) salé(e); **an old ~** un vieux loup de mer.
salt away vt mettre de côté.
saltcellar [sôlt'selûr] n (Brit) salière f.
salt-free [sôlt'frē'] a sans sel.
salt shaker [sôlt shā'kûr] n (US) salière f.
saltwater [sôlt'wôtûr] a (fish etc) (d'eau) de mer.
salty [sôl'tē] a salé(e).
salubrious [səlōō'brēəs] a salubre.
salutary [sal'yətārē] a salutaire.
salute [səlōōt'] n salut m ♦ vt saluer.
salvage [sal'vij] n (saving) sauvetage m; (things saved) biens sauvés or récupérés ♦ vt sauver, récupérer.
salvage vessel n bateau m de sauvetage.
salvation [salvā'shən] n salut m.
Salvation Army n Armée f du Salut.
salver [sal'vûr] n plateau m de métal.
salvo [sal'vō] n salve f.
same [sām] a même ♦ pronoun: **the ~** le(la) même, les mêmes; **the ~ book** as le même livre que; **on the ~ day** le même jour; **at the ~ time** en même temps; **all or just the ~** tout de même, quand même; **they're one and the ~** (person/thing) c'est une seule et même personne/chose; **to do the ~** faire de même, en faire autant; **to do the ~ as sb** faire comme qn; **and the ~ to you!** et à vous de même!; (after insult) toi-même!; **~ here!** moi aussi!; **the ~ again!** (in bar etc) la même chose!
sample [sam'pəl] n échantillon m; (MED) prélèvement m ♦ vt (food, wine) goûter; **to take a ~** prélever un échantillon; **free ~** échantillon gratuit.
sanatorium, pl **sanatoria** [sanətôr'ēəm, -tôr'ēə] n (Brit) = **sanitarium**.
sanctify [sangk'təfī] vt sanctifier.
sanctimonious [sangktəmō'nēəs] a moralisateur(trice).
sanction [sangk'shən] n sanction f ♦ vt cautionner, sanctionner; **to impose economic ~s on** or **against** prendre des sanctions économiques contre.
sanctity [sangk'titē] n sainteté f, caractère sacré.
sanctuary [sangk'chōōârē] n (holy place) sanctuaire m; (refuge) asile m; (for wild

life) réserve *f*..

sand [sand] *n* sable *m* ♦ *vt* sabler; (*also:* ~ **down**: *wood etc*) poncer.

sandal [san'dəl] *n* sandale *f*.

sandbag [sand'bag] *n* sac *m* de sable.

sandblast [sand'blast] *vt* décaper à la sableuse.

sandbox [sand'bâks] *n* (*US: for children*) tas *m* de sable.

sand castle *n* château *m* de sable.

sand dune *n* dune *f* de sable.

sandpaper [sand'pāpúr] *n* papier *m* de verre.

sand pie *n* pâté *m* (de sable).

sandpit [sand'pit] *n* (*Brit*) = **sandbox**.

sands [sandz] *npl* plage *f* (de sable).

sandstone [sand'stōn] *n* grès *m*.

sandstorm [sand'stórm] *n* tempête *f* de sable.

sandwich [sand'wich] *n* sandwich *m* ♦ *vt* (*also:* ~ **in**) intercaler; ~**ed between** pris en sandwich entre; **cheese/ham** ~ sandwich au fromage/jambon.

sandwich board *n* panneau *m* publicitaire (porté par un homme-sandwich).

sandy [san'dē] *a* sablonneux(euse); couvert(e) de sable; (*color*) sable *inv*, blond roux *inv*.

sane [sān] *a* (*person*) sain(e) d'esprit; (*outlook*) sensé(e), sain(e).

sang [sang] *pt of* **sing**.

sanguine [sang'gwin] *a* optimiste.

sanitarium, *pl* **sanitaria** [sanitär'ēəm, -tär'ēə] *n* sanatorium *m*.

sanitary [san'itärē] *a* (*system, arrangements*) sanitaire; (*clean*) hygiénique.

sanitary napkin *n* serviette *f* hygiénique.

sanitation [sanitā'shən] *n* (*in house*) installations *fpl* sanitaires; (*in town*) système *m* sanitaire.

sanitation department *n* (*US*) service *m* de voirie.

sanity [san'itē] *n* santé mentale; (*common sense*) bon sens.

sank [sangk] *pt of* **sink**.

San Marino [san mərē'nō] *n* Saint-Marin *m*.

Santa Claus [san'tə klôz] *n* le Père Noël.

Santiago [santēâ'gō] *n* (*also:* ~ **de Chile**) Santiago (du Chili).

sap [sap] *n* (*of plants*) sève *f* ♦ *vt* (*strength*) saper, miner.

sapling [sap'ling] *n* jeune arbre *m*.

sapphire [saf'īúr] *n* saphir *m*.

sarcasm [sâr'kazəm] *n* sarcasme *m*, raillerie *f*.

sarcastic [sârkas'tik] *a* sarcastique.

sarcophagus, *pl* **sarcophagi** [sârkâf'əgəs, -gī] *n* sarcophage *m*.

sardine [sârdēn'] *n* sardine *f*.

Sardinia [sârdin'ēə] *n* Sardaigne *f*.

Sardinian [sârdin'ēən] *a* sarde ♦ *n* Sarde *m/f*; (*LING*) sarde *m*.

sardonic [sârdân'ik] *a* sardonique.

sari [sâ'rē] *n* sari *m*.

sartorial [sârtôr'ēəl] *a* vestimentaire.

SAS *n abbr* (*Brit MIL*: = *Special Air Service*) ≈ GIGN *m*.

SASE *n abbr* (*US*: = *self-addressed stamped envelope*) enveloppe affranchie pour la réponse..

sash [sash] *n* écharpe *f*.

sash window *n* fenêtre *f* à guillotine.

Sask. *abbr* (*Canada*) = *Saskatchewan*.

sassy [sas'ē] *a* (*US*) effronté(e), culotté(e).

SAT *n abbr* (*US*) = *Scholastic Aptitude Test*.

Sat. *abbr* (= *Saturday*) sa.

sat [sat] *pt, pp of* **sit**.

Satan [sā'tən] *n* Satan *m*.

satanic [sətan'ik] *a* satanique, démoniaque.

satchel [sach'əl] *n* cartable *m*.

sated [sā'tid] *a* repu(e); blasé(e).

satellite [sat'əlīt] *a, n* satellite *(m)*.

satellite dish *n* antenne *f* parabolique.

satiate [sā'shēāt] *vt* rassasier.

satin [sat'ən] *n* satin *m* ♦ *a* en *or* de satin, satiné(e); **with a ~ finish** satiné(e).

satire [sat'īúr] *n* satire *f*.

satirical [sətir'ikəl] *a* satirique.

satirist [sat'ûrist] *n* (*writer*) auteur *m* satirique; (*cartoonist*) caricaturiste *m/f*.

satirize [sat'ərīz] *vt* faire la satire de, satiriser.

satisfaction [satisfak'shən] *n* satisfaction *f*.

satisfactory [satisfak'tûrē] *a* satisfaisant(e).

satisfy [sat'isfī] *vt* satisfaire, contenter; (*convince*) convaincre, persuader; **to** ~ **the requirements** remplir les conditions; **to** ~ **sb (that)** convaincre qn (que); **to** ~ **o.s. of sth** vérifier qch, s'assurer de qch.

satisfying [sat'isfīing] *a* satisfaisant(e).

saturate [sach'ûrāt] *vt*: **to** ~ **(with)** saturer (de).

saturation [sachərā'shən] *n* saturation *f*.

Saturday [sat'ûrdā] *n* samedi *m*; *for phrases see also* **Tuesday**.

sauce [sôs] *n* sauce *f*.

saucepan [sôs'pan] *n* casserole *f*.

saucer [sô'sûr] *n* soucoupe *f*.

saucy [sôs'ē] *a* impertinent(e).

Saudi Arabia [sou'dē ərā'bēə] *n* Arabie *f* Saoudite *or* Séoudite.

Saudi (Arabian) [sou'dē (ərā'bēən)] *a* saoudien(ne) ♦ *n* Saoudien/ne.

sauna [sô'nə] *n* sauna *m*.

saunter [sôn'tûr] *vi*: **to** ~ **to** aller en flânant *or* se balader jusqu'à.

sausage [sô'sij] *n* saucisse *f*; (*salami etc*) saucisson *m*.

sausage roll *n* friand *m*.

sauté [sôtā'] *a* (*CULIN: potatoes*) sauté(e); (*: onions*) revenu(e) ♦ *vt* faire sauter; faire revenir.

savage [sav'ij] *a* (*cruel, fierce*) brutal(e), féroce; (*primitive*) primitif(ive), sauvage ♦ *n* sauvage *m/f* ♦ *vt* attaquer férocement.

savagery [sav'ijrē] *n* sauvagerie *f*, brutalité *f*, férocité *f*.

save [sāv] *vt* (*person, belongings*) sauver; (*money*) mettre de côté, économiser; (*time*) (faire) gagner; (*food*) garder; (*COMPUT*) sauvegarder; (*avoid: trouble*) éviter ♦ *vi* (*also:* ~ **up**) mettre de l'argent de côté ♦ *n* (*SPORT*) arrêt *m* (du ballon) ♦ *prep* sauf, à l'exception de; **it will** ~ **me an hour** ça me fera gagner une heure; **to** ~ **face** sauver la face; **God** ~ **the Queen!** vive la Reine!

saving [sā'ving] *n* économie *f* ♦ *a*: **the** ~ **grace of** ce qui rachète; ~**s** *npl* économies *fpl*; **to make** ~**s** faire des économies.

savings account *n* compte *m* d'épargne.

savings and loan association *n* (*US*) société *f* de crédit immobilier.

savings bank *n* caisse *f* d'épargne.

savior, (*Brit*) **saviour** [sāv'yûr] *n* sauveur *m*.

savor [sā'vûr] (*US*) *n* saveur *f*, goût *m* ◆ *vt* savourer.

savory [sā'vûrē] *a* savoureux(euse); (*dish: not sweet*) salé(e).

savour [sā'vûr] *etc* (*Brit*) = **savor** *etc*.

savvy [sav'ē] *n* (*col*) jugeote *f*.

saw [sô] *pt of* **see** ◆ *n* (*tool*) scie *f* ◆ *vt* (*pt* **sawed**, *pp* **sawed** *or* (*Brit*) **sawn** [sôn]) scier; **to ~ sth up** débiter qch à la scie.

sawdust [sô'dust] *n* sciure *f*.

sawed-off [sôd'ôf] *a* (*US*): **~ shotgun** carabine *f* à canon scié.

sawmill [sô'mil] *n* scierie *f*.

sawn-off [sôn'ôf] *a* (*Brit*) = **sawed-off**.

saxophone [sak'səfōn] *n* saxophone *m*.

say [sā] *n*: **to have one's ~** dire ce qu'on a à dire; **to have a ~** avoir voix au chapitre ◆ *vt* (*pt, pp* **said** [sed]) dire; **could you ~ that again?** pourriez-vous répéter ceci?; **to ~ yes/no** dire oui/non; **she said (that) I was to give you this** elle m'a chargé de vous remettre ceci; **my watch ~s 3 o'clock** ma montre indique 3 heures, il est 3 heures à ma montre; **shall we ~ Tuesday?** disons mardi?; **that doesn't ~ much for him** ce n'est pas vraiment à son honneur; **when all is said and done** en fin de compte, en définitive; **there is something** *or* **a lot to be said for it** cela a des avantages; **that is to ~** c'est-à-dire; **to ~ nothing of** sans compter; **~ that ... mettons** *or* **disons que ...**; **that goes without ~ing** cela va sans dire, cela va de soi.

saying [sā'ing] *n* dicton *m*, proverbe *m*.

SBA *n abbr* (*US*: = *Small Business Administration*) *organisme d'aide aux PME*.

SC *n abbr* (*US*) = **supreme court** ◆ *abbr* (*US MAIL*) = *South Carolina*.

s/c *abbr* = **self-contained**.

scab [skab] *n* croûte *f*; (*pej*) jaune *m*.

scabby [skab'ē] *a* croûteux(euse).

scaffold [skaf'əld] *n* échafaud *m*.

scaffolding [skaf'əlding] *n* échafaudage *m*.

scald [skôld] *n* brûlure *f* ◆ *vt* ébouillanter.

scalding [skôl'ding] *a* (*also*: **~ hot**) brûlant(e), bouillant(e).

scale [skāl] *n* (*of fish*) écaille *f*; (*MUS*) gamme *f*; (*of ruler, thermometer etc*) graduation *f*, échelle (graduée); (*of salaries, fees etc*) barème *m*; (*of map, also size, extent*) échelle ◆ *vt* (*mountain*) escalader; (*fish*) écailler; **pay ~ échelle des salaires; ~ of charges** tarif *m* (des consultations *or* prestations *etc*); **on a large ~** sur une grande échelle, en grand; **to draw sth to ~** dessiner qch à l'échelle; **small-~ model** modèle réduit.

scale down *vt* réduire.

scale drawing *n* dessin *m* à l'échelle.

scale model *n* modèle *m* à l'échelle.

scales [skālz] *npl* balance *f*; (*larger*) bascule *f*.

scallion [skal'yən] *n* oignon *m*; (*US: shallot*) échalote *f*; (*: leek*) poireau *m*.

scallop [skâl'əp] *n* coquille *f* Saint-Jacques.

scalp [skalp] *n* cuir chevelu ◆ *vt* scalper.

scalpel [skal'pəl] *n* scalpel *m*.

scalper [skal'pûr] *n* (*US col: of tickets*) revendeur *m* de billets.

scamp [skamp] *vt* bâcler.

scamper [skam'pûr] *vi*: **to ~ away, ~ off** détaler.

scampi [skam'pē] *npl* langoustines (frites), scampi *mpl*.

scan [skan] *vt* scruter, examiner; (*glance at quickly*) parcourir; (*poetry*) scander; (*TV, RADAR*) balayer ◆ *n* (*MED*) scanographie *f*.

scandal [skan'dəl] *n* scandale *m*; (*gossip*) ragots *mpl*.

scandalize [skan'dəlīz] *vt* scandaliser, indigner.

scandalous [skan'dələs] *a* scandaleux(euse).

Scandinavia [skandənā'vēə] *n* Scandinavie *f*.

Scandinavian [skandənā'vēən] *a* scandinave ◆ *n* Scandinave *m/f*.

scanner [skan'ûr] *n* (*RADAR, MED*) scanner *m*, scanographe *m*.

scant [skant] *a* insuffisant(e).

scantily [skan'tilē] *ad*: **~ clad** *or* **dressed** vêtu(e) du strict minimum.

scanty [skan'tē] *a* peu abondant(e), insuffisant(e), maigre.

scapegoat [skāp'gōt] *n* bouc *m* émissaire.

scar [skâr] *n* cicatrice *f* ◆ *vt* laisser une cicatrice *or* une marque à.

scarce [skârs] *a* rare, peu abondant(e).

scarcely [skârs'lē] *ad* à peine, presque pas; **~ anybody** pratiquement personne; **I can ~ believe it** j'ai du mal à le croire.

scarcity [skâr'sitē] *n* rareté *f*, manque *m*, pénurie *f*.

scarcity value *n* valeur *f* de rareté.

scare [skär] *n* peur *f*, panique *f* ◆ *vt* effrayer, faire peur à; **to ~ sb stiff** faire une peur bleue à qn; **bomb ~** alerte *f* à la bombe.

scare away, scare off *vt* faire fuir.

scarecrow [skär'krō] *n* épouvantail *m*.

scared [skärd] *a*: **to be ~** avoir peur.

scaremonger [skär'munggûr] *n* alarmiste *m/f*.

scarf, *pl* **scarves** [skârf, skârvz] *n* (*long*) écharpe *f*; (*square*) foulard *m*.

scarlet [skâr'lit] *a* écarlate.

scarlet fever *n* scarlatine *f*.

scarves [skârvz] *npl of* **scarf**.

scary [skär'ē] *a* (*col*) qui fiche la frousse.

scathing [skā'ᵺing] *a* cinglant(e), acerbe; **to be ~ about sth** être très critique vis-à-vis de qch.

scatter [skat'ûr] *vt* éparpiller, répandre; (*crowd*) disperser ◆ *vi* se disperser.

scatterbrained [skat'ûrbrānd] *a* écervelé(e), étourdi(e).

scattered [skat'ûrd] *a* épars(e), dispersé(e).

scatty [skat'ē] *a* (*Brit col*) loufoque.

scavenge [skav'inj] *vi* (*person*): **to ~ (for)** faire les poubelles (pour trouver); **to ~ for food** (*hyenas etc*) se nourrir de charognes.

scavenger [skav'injûr] *n* éboueur *m*.

scenario [sinär'ēō] *n* scénario *m*.

scene [sēn] *n* (*THEATER, fig etc*) scène *f*; (*of crime, accident*) lieu(x) *m(pl)*, endroit *m*; (*sight, view*) spectacle *m*, vue *f*; **behind the ~s** (*also fig*) dans les coulisses; **to make a ~** (*col: fuss*) faire une scène *or* toute une histoire; **to appear on the ~** (*also fig*) faire son apparition, arriver; **the political ~** la situation politique.

scenery [sē'nûrē] *n* (*THEATER*) décor(s) *m(pl)*; (*landscape*) paysage *m*.

scenic [sē'nik] *a* scénique; offrant de beaux paysages *or* panoramas.

scent [sent] *n* parfum *m*, odeur *f*; (*fig: track*) piste *f*; (*sense of smell*) odorat *m* ♦ *vt* parfumer; (*smell, also fig*) flairer; **to put** *or* **throw sb off the** ~ (*fig*) mettre *or* lancer qn sur une mauvaise piste.

scepter [sep'tûr] *n* (*US*) sceptre *m*.

sceptic [skep'tik] *etc* (*Brit*) = **skeptic** *etc*.

sceptre [sep'tûr] *n* (*Brit*) = **scepter**.

schedule [skej'ōōl, (*Brit*) shed'yōōl] *n* programme *m*, plan *m*; (*of trains*) horaire *m*; (*of prices etc*) barème *m*, tarif *m* ♦ *vt* prévoir; **as** ~**d** comme prévu; **on** ~ à l'heure (prévue); à la date prévue; **to be ahead of/behind** ~ avoir de l'avance/du retard; **we are working to a very tight** ~ notre programme de travail est très serré *or* intense; **everything went according to** ~ tout s'est passé comme prévu.

scheduled [skej'ōōld, (*Brit*) shed'yōōld] *a* (*date, time*) prévu(e), indiqué(e); (*visit, event*) programmé(e), prévu; (*train, bus, stop, flight*) régulier(ière).

schematic [skēmat'ik] *a* schématique.

scheme [skēm] *n* plan *m*, projet *m*; (*method*) procédé *m*; (*dishonest plan, plot*) complot *m*, combine *f*; (*arrangement*) arrangement *m*, classification *f* ♦ *vt, vi* comploter, manigancer; **color** ~ combinaison *f* de(s) couleurs.

scheming [skēm'ing] *a* rusé(e), intrigant(e) ♦ *n* manigances *fpl*, intrigues *fpl*.

schism [skiz'əm] *n* schisme *m*.

schizophrenia [skitsəfrē'nēə] *n* schizophrénie *f*.

schizophrenic [skitsəfren'ik] *a* schizophrène.

scholar [skâl'ûr] *n* érudit/e.

scholarly [skâl'ûrlē] *a* érudit(e), savant(e).

scholarship [skâl'ûrship] *n* érudition *f*; (*grant*) bourse *f* (d'études).

school [skōōl] *n* (*gen*) école *f*; (*in university*) faculté *f*; (*high school*) collège *m*, lycée *m*; (*of fish*) banc *m* ♦ *cpd* scolaire ♦ *vt* (*animal*) dresser.

school age *n* âge *m* scolaire.

school bag *n* cartable *m*.

schoolbook [skōōl'bŏŏk] *n* livre *m* scolaire *or* de classe.

schoolboy [skōōl'boi] *n* écolier *m*; collégien *m*, lycéen *m*.

schoolchild, *pl* **-children** [skōōl'chīld, -children] *n* écolier/ière, collégien/ne, lycéen/ne.

schooldays [skōōl'dāz] *npl* années *fpl* de scolarité.

schoolgirl [skōōl'gûrl] *n* écolière *f*; collégienne *f*, lycéenne *f*.

schooling [skōō'ling] *n* instruction *f*, études *fpl*.

school-leaving age [skōōl'lēving āj] *n* âge *m* de fin de scolarité.

schoolmaster [skōōl'mastûr] *n* (*elementary*) instituteur *m*; (*high*) professeur *m*.

schoolmistress [skōōl'mistris] *n* (*elementary*) institutrice *f*; (*high*) professeur *m*.

schoolroom [skōōl'rōōm] *n* (salle *f* de) classe *f*.

schoolteacher [skōōl'tēchûr] *n* (*elementary*) instituteur/trice; (*high*) professeur *m*.

schoolyard [skōōl'yârd] *n* cour *f* de récréation.

schooner [skōō'nûr] *n* (*ship*) schooner *m*, goélette *f*; (*glass*) grand verre (à xérès).

sciatica [sīat'ikə] *n* sciatique *f*.

science [sī'əns] *n* science *f*; **the** ~**s** les sciences; (*SCOL*) les matières *fpl* scientifiques.

science fiction *n* science-fiction *f*.

scientific [sīəntif'ik] *a* scientifique.

scientist [sī'əntist] *n* scientifique *m/f*; (*eminent*) savant *m*.

sci-fi [sī'fī'] *n abbr* (*col*: = *science fiction*) SF *f*.

scintillating [sin'təlāting] *a* scintillant(e), étincelant(e); (*wit etc*) brillant(e).

scissors [siz'ûrz] *npl* ciseaux *mpl*; **a pair of** ~ une paire de ciseaux.

sclerosis [sklirō'sis] *n* sclérose *f*.

scoff [skâf] *vi*: **to** ~ (**at**) (*mock*) se moquer (de).

scold [skōld] *vt* gronder, attraper, réprimander.

scolding [skōld'ing] *n* réprimande *f*.

scone [skōn] *n* sorte de petit pain rond au lait.

scoop [skōōp] *n* pelle *f* (à main); (*for ice cream*) boule *f* à glace; (*PRESS*) reportage exclusif *or* à sensation.

scoop out *vt* évider, creuser.

scoop up *vt* ramasser.

scooter [skōō'tûr] *n* (*motorcycle*) scooter *m*; (*toy*) trottinette *f*.

scope [skōp] *n* (*capacity: of plan, undertaking*) portée *f*, envergure *f*; (*: of person*) compétence *f*, capacités *fpl*; (*opportunity*) possibilités *fpl*; **within the** ~ **of** dans les limites de; **there is plenty of** ~ **for improvement** (*Brit*) cela pourrait être beaucoup mieux.

scorch [skôrch] *vt* (*clothes*) brûler (légèrement), roussir; (*earth, grass*) dessécher, brûler.

scorched earth policy *n* politique *f* de la terre brûlée.

scorcher [skôr'chûr] *n* (*col: hot day*) journée *f* torride.

scorching [skôrch'ing] *a* torride, brûlant(e).

score [skôr] *n* score *m*, décompte *m* des points; (*MUS*) partition *f*; (*twenty*) vingt ♦ *vt* (*goal, point*) marquer; (*success*) remporter; (*cut: leather, wood, card*) entailler, inciser ♦ *vi* marquer des points; (*SOCCER*) marquer un but; (*keep* ~) compter les points; **on that** ~ sur ce chapitre, à cet égard; **to have an old** ~ **to settle with sb** (*fig*) avoir un (vieux) compte à régler avec qn; ~**s of** (*fig*) des tas de; **to** ~ **well/6 out of 10** obtenir un bon résultat/6 sur 10.

score out *vt* rayer, barrer, biffer.

scoreboard [skôr'bôrd] *n* tableau *m*.

scorecard [skôr'kârd] *n* (*SPORT*) carton *m*, feuille *f* de marque.

scorer [skôr'ûr] *n* (*SOCCER*) auteur *m* du but; buteur *m*; (*keeping score*) marqueur *m*.

scorn [skôrn] *n* mépris *m*, dédain *m* ♦ *vt* mépriser, dédaigner.

scornful [skôrn'fəl] *a* méprisant(e), dédaigneux(euse).

Scorpio [skôr'pēō] *n* le Scorpion; **to be** ~ être du Scorpion.

scorpion [skôr'pēən] *n* scorpion *m*.

Scot [skȧt] *n* Écossais/e.

Scotch [skȧch] *n* whisky *m*, scotch *m*.

scotch [skȧch] *vt* faire échouer; enrayer; étouffer.

Scotch tape *n* ® (*US*) scotch *m* ®, ruban adhésif.

scot-free [skȧt'frē'] *a*: **to get off ~** s'en tirer sans être puni(e) (*or* sans payer); s'en sortir indemne.

Scotland [skȧt'lənd] *n* Écosse *f*.

Scots [skȧts] *a* écossais(e).

Scotsman [skȧts'mən] *n* Écossais *m*.

Scotswoman [skȧts'wōōmən] *n* Écossaise *f*.

Scottish [skȧt'ish] *a* écossais(e).

scoundrel [skoun'drəl] *n* vaurien *m*.

scour [skour] *vt* (*clean*) récurer; frotter; décaper; (*search*) battre, parcourir.

scourer [skour'ûr] *n* (*powder*) poudre *f* à récurer; (*Brit*) = **scouring pad**.

scourge [skûrj] *n* fléau *m*.

scouring pad [skour'ing pad] *n* tampon abrasif *or* à récurer.

scout [skout] *n* (*MIL*) éclaireur *m*; (*also*: **boy ~**) scout *m*.
  scout around *vi* chercher.

scowl [skoul] *vi* se renfrogner, avoir l'air maussade; **to ~ at** regarder de travers.

scrabble [skrab'əl] *vi* (*claw*): **to ~ (at)** gratter; **to ~ about** *or* **around for sth** chercher qch à tâtons ♦ *n*: **S~** ® Scrabble *m* ®.

scraggy [skrag'ē] *a* décharné(e), efflanqué(e), famélique.

scram [skram] *vi* (*col*) ficher le camp.

scramble [skram'bəl] *n* bousculade *f*, ruée *f* ♦ *vi* avancer tant bien que mal (à quatre pattes *or* en grimpant); **to ~ for** se bousculer *or* se disputer pour (avoir); **to go scrambling** (*SPORT*) faire du trial.

scrambled eggs [skram'bəld egz] *npl* œufs brouillés.

scrap [skrap] *n* bout *m*, morceau *m*; (*fight*) bagarre *f*; (*also*: **~ iron**) ferraille *f* ♦ *vt* jeter, mettre au rebut; (*fig*) abandonner, laisser tomber; **~s** *npl* (*waste*) déchets *mpl*; **to sell sth for ~** vendre qch à la casse *or* à la ferraille.

scrapbook [skrap'bōōk] *n* album *m*.

scrap dealer *n* marchand *m* de ferraille.

scrape [skrāp] *vt, vi* gratter, racler ♦ *n*: **to get into a ~** s'attirer des ennuis.
  scrape through *vi* (*in exam etc*) réussir de justesse.

scraper [skrā'pûr] *n* grattoir *m*, racloir *m*.

scrapheap [skrap'hēp] *n* tas *m* de ferraille; (*fig*): **on the ~** au rancart *or* rebut.

scrap metal *n* ferraille *f*.

scrap paper *n* papier *m* brouillon.

scrappy [skrap'ē] *a* fragmentaire, décousu(e).

scrap yard *n* (*Brit*) parc *m* à ferrailles; (: *for cars*) cimetière *m* de voitures.

scratch [skrach] *n* égratignure *f*, rayure *f*; éraflure *f*; (*from claw*) coup *m* de griffe ♦ *vt* (*record*) rayer; (*paint etc*) érafler; (*with claw, nail*) griffer ♦ *vi* (se) gratter; **to start from ~** partir de zéro; **to be up to ~** être à la hauteur.

scrawl [skrôl] *n* gribouillage *m* ♦ *vi* gribouiller.

scrawny [skrô'nē] *a* décharné(e).

scream [skrēm] *n* cri perçant, hurlement *m* ♦

vi crier, hurler; **to be a ~** (*col*) être impayable; **to ~ at sb to do sth** crier *or* hurler à qn de faire qch.

scree [skrē] *n* éboulis *m*.

screech [skrēch] *n* cri strident, hurlement *m*; (*of tires, brakes*) crissement *m*, grincement *m* ♦ *vi* hurler; crisser, grincer.

screen [skrēn] *n* écran *m*, paravent *m*; (*CINEMA, TV*) écran; (*fig*) écran, rideau *m* ♦ *vt* masquer, cacher; (*from the wind etc*) abriter, protéger; (*film*) projeter; (*candidates etc*) filtrer; (*for illness*): **to ~ sb for sth** faire subir un test de dépistage de qch à qn.

screen editing *n* (*COMPUT*) édition *f* or correction *f* sur écran.

screening [skrē'ning] *n* (*of film*) projection *f*; (*MED*) test *m* (*or* tests) de dépistage; (*for security*) filtrage *m*.

screen memory *n* (*COMPUT*) mémoire *f* écran.

screenplay [skrēn'plā] *n* scénario *m*.

screen test *n* bout *m* d'essai.

screw [skrōō] *n* vis *f*; (*propeller*) hélice *f* ♦ *vt* visser; (*col!: woman*) baiser (*!*); **to ~ sth to the wall** visser qch au mur; **to have one's head ~ed on** (*fig*) avoir la tête sur les épaules.
  screw up *vt* (*paper, material*) froisser; (*col: ruin*) bousiller; **to ~ up one's face** faire la grimace.

screwball [skrōō'bôl] *n* (*col*) cinglé/e, tordu/e.

screwdriver [skrōō'drīvûr] *n* tournevis *m*.

screwy [skrōō'ē] *a* (*col*) dingue, cinglé(e).

scribble [skrib'əl] *n* gribouillage *m* ♦ *vt* gribouiller, griffonner; **to ~ sth down** griffonner qch.

scribe [skrīb] *n* scribe *m*.

script [skript] *n* (*CINEMA etc*) scénario *m*, texte *m*; (*in exam*) copie *f*; (*writing*) (écriture *f*) script *m*.

scripted [skrip'tid] *a* (*RADIO, TV*) préparé(e) à l'avance.

Scripture [skrip'chûr] *n* Écriture Sainte.

scriptwriter [skript'rītûr] *n* scénariste *m/f*, dialoguiste *m/f*.

scroll [skrōl] *n* rouleau *m* ♦ *vt* (*COMPUT*) faire défiler (sur l'écran).

scrotum [skrō'təm] *n* scrotum *m*.

scrounge [skrounj] (*col*) *vt*: **to ~ sth (off** *or* **from sb)** se faire payer qch (par qn), emprunter qch (à qn) ♦ *vi*: **to ~ on sb** vivre aux crochets de qn.

scrounger [skrounj'ûr] *n* parasite *m*.

scrub [skrub] *n* (*clean*) nettoyage *m* (à la brosse); (*land*) broussailles *fpl* ♦ *vt* (*floor*) nettoyer à la brosse; (*pan*) récurer; (*washing*) frotter; (*reject*) annuler.

scrub brush *n* brosse dure.

scrubbing brush [skrub'ing brush] *n* (*Brit*) = **scrub brush**.

scruff [skruf] *n*: **by the ~ of the neck** par la peau du cou.

scruffy [skruf'ē] *a* débraillé(e).

scrum(mage) [skrum'(ij)] *n* (*RUGBY*) mêlée *f*.

scruple [skrōō'pəl] *n* scrupule *m*; **to have no ~s about doing sth** n'avoir aucun scrupule à faire qch.

scrupulous [skrōō'pyələs] *a* scrupuleux(euse).

scrupulously [skrōō'pyələslē] *ad* scrupuleusement; **to be ~ honest** être d'une honnêteté scrupuleuse.

scrutinize [skrōō'tənīz] *vt* scruter, examiner minutieusement.

scrutiny [skrōō'tənē] *n* examen minutieux; **under the ~ of sb** sous la surveillance de qn.

scuba [skōō'bə] *n* scaphandre *m* (autonome).

scuba diving *n* plongée sous-marine (autonome).

scuff [skuf] *vt* érafler.

scuffle [skuf'əl] *n* échauffourée *f*, rixe *f*.

scull [skul] *n* aviron *m*.

scullery [skul'ûrē] *n* arrière-cuisine *f*.

sculptor [skulp'tûr] *n* sculpteur *m*.

sculpture [skulp'chûr] *n* sculpture *f*.

scum [skum] *n* écume *f*, mousse *f*; *(pej: people)* rebut *m*, lie *f*.

scurrilous [skûr'ələs] *a* haineux(euse), virulent(e); calomnieux(euse).

scurry [skûr'ē] *vi* filer à toute allure; **to ~ off** détaler, se sauver.

scurvy [skûr'vē] *n* scorbut *m*.

scuttle [skut'əl] *n* (*NAUT*) écoutille *f*; *(also:* **coal ~**) seau *m* (à charbon) ♦ *vt (ship)* saborder ♦ *vi (scamper):* **to ~ away, ~ off** détaler.

scythe [sīth] *n* faux *f*.

SD *abbr (US MAIL)* = *South Dakota.*

S.Dak. *abbr (US)* = *South Dakota.*

SDI *n abbr (= Strategic Defense Initiative)* IDS *f*.

SDLP *n abbr (Brit POL)* = *Social Democratic and Labour Party.*

SDP *n abbr (Brit POL)* = *Social Democratic Party.*

sea [sē] *n* mer *f* ♦ *cpd* marin(e), de (la) mer, maritime; **on the ~** *(boat)* en mer; *(town)* au bord de la mer; **by** *or* **beside the ~** *(vacation)* au bord de la mer; *(village)* près de la mer; **by ~** par mer, en bateau; **out to ~** au large; **(out)** *at* ~ en mer; **heavy** *or* **rough ~(s)** grosse mer, mer agitée; **a ~ of faces** *(fig)* une multitude de visages.

sea bed *n* fond *m* de la mer.

sea bird *n* oiseau *m* de mer.

seaboard [sē'bôrd] *n* côte *f*.

sea breeze *n* brise *f* de mer.

seafarer [sē'fârûr] *n* marin *m*.

seafaring [sē'fâring] *a (life)* de marin; **~ people** les gens *mpl* de mer.

seafood [sē'fōōd] *n* fruits *mpl* de mer.

sea front *n* bord *m* de mer.

seagoing [sē'gōing] *a (ship)* de haute mer.

seagull [sē'gul] *n* mouette *f*.

seal [sēl] *n (animal)* phoque *m*; *(stamp)* sceau *m*, cachet *m*; *(impression)* cachet, estampille *f* ♦ *vt* sceller; *(envelope)* coller; *(: with seal)* cacheter; *(decide: sb's fate)* décider (de); *(: bargain)* conclure; **~ of approval** approbation *f*.

seal off *vt (close)* condamner; *(forbid entry to)* interdire l'accès de.

sea level *n* niveau *m* de la mer.

sealing wax [sē'ling waks] *n* cire *f* à cacheter.

sea lion *n* lion *m* de mer.

sealskin [sēl'skin] *n* peau *f* de phoque.

seam [sēm] *n* couture *f*; *(of coal)* veine *f*, filon *m*; **the hall was bursting at the ~s** la salle était pleine à craquer.

seaman [sē'mən] *n* marin *m*.

seamanship [sē'mənship] *n* qualités *fpl* de marin.

seamless [sēm'lis] *a* sans couture(s).

seamy [sē'mē] *a* louche, mal famé(e).

seance [sā'áns] *n* séance *f* de spiritisme.

seaplane [sē'plān] *n* hydravion *m*.

seaport [sē'pôrt] *n* port *m* de mer.

search [sûrch] *n (for person, thing)* recherche(s) *f(pl)*; *(of drawer, pockets)* fouille *f*; *(LAW: at sb's home)* perquisition *f* ♦ *vt* fouiller; *(examine)* examiner minutieusement; scruter ♦ *vi:* **to ~ for** chercher; **in ~ of** à la recherche de; **"~ and replace"** *(COMPUT)* "rechercher et remplacer".

search through *vt fus* fouiller.

searcher [sûr'chûr] *n* chercheur/euse.

searching [sûr'ching] *a (look, question)* pénétrant(e); *(examination)* minutieux(euse).

searchlight [sûrch'līt] *n* projecteur *m*.

search party *n* expédition *f* de secours.

search warrant *n* mandat *m* de perquisition.

searing [sē'ring] *a (heat)* brûlant(e); *(pain)* aigu(ë).

seashore [sē'shôr] *n* rivage *m*, plage *f*, bord *m* de (la) mer; **on the ~** sur le rivage.

seasick [sē'sik] *a:* **to be ~** avoir le mal de mer.

seaside [sē'sīd] *n* bord *m* de la mer.

seaside resort *n* station *f* balnéaire.

season [sē'zən] *n* saison *f* ♦ *vt* assaisonner, relever; **to be in/out of ~** être/ne pas être de saison; **the busy ~** *(for shops)* la période de pointe; *(for hotels etc)* la pleine saison; **the open ~** *(HUNTING)* saison *f* de la chasse.

seasonal [sē'zənəl] *a* saisonnier(ière).

seasoned [sē'zənd] *a (wood)* séché(e); *(fig: worker, actor, troops)* expérimenté(e); **a ~ campaigner** un vieux militant, un vétéran.

seasoning [sē'zəning] *n* assaisonnement *m*.

season ticket *n* carte *f* d'abonnement.

seat [sēt] *n* siège *m*; *(in bus, train: place)* place *f*; *(PARLIAMENT)* siège; *(buttocks)* postérieur *m*; *(of pants)* fond *m* ♦ *vt* faire asseoir, placer; *(have room for)* avoir des places assises pour, pouvoir accueillir; **are there any ~s left?** est-ce qu'il reste des places?; **to take one's ~** prendre place; **to be ~ed** être assis; **please be ~ed** veuillez vous asseoir.

seat belt *n* ceinture *f* de sécurité.

seating capacity [sē'ting kəpas'itē] *n* nombre *m* de places assises.

seating room [sē'ting rōōm] *n* places assises.

SEATO [sē'tō] *n abbr (= Southeast Asia Treaty Organization)* OTASE *f* (= *Organisation du traité de l'Asie du Sud-Est*).

sea water *n* eau *f* de mer.

seaweed [sē'wēd] *n* algues *fpl*.

seaworthy [sē'wûrthē] *a* en état de naviguer.

SEC *n abbr (US: = Securities and Exchange Commission)* ≈ COB *f* (= *Commission des opérations de Bourse*).

sec. *abbr* (= *second*) sec.

secateurs [sek'ətûrz] *npl (Brit)* sécateur *m*.

secede [sisēd'] *vi* faire sécession.

secluded [siklōō'did] *a* retiré(e), à l'écart.

seclusion [siklōō'zhən] *n* solitude *f*.

second [sek'ənd] *num* deuxième, second(e) ♦ *ad (in race etc)* en seconde position ♦ *n (unit* *of time*) seconde *f*; (*in series, position*) deuxième *m/f*, second/e; (*Brit scol*) ≈ licence *f* avec mention bien *or* assez bien; (*AUT: also:* ~ **gear**) seconde *f*; (*COMM: imperfect*) article *m* de second choix ♦ *vt* (*motion*) appuyer; [sikând'] (*employee*) détacher, mettre en détachement; **Charles the S~** Charles II; **just a ~**! une seconde!, un instant!; (*stopping sb*) pas si vite!; ~ **floor** (*US*) premier (étage) *m*; (*Brit*) deuxième (étage) *m*; **to ask for a ~ opinion** (*MED*) demander l'avis d'un autre médecin; **to have ~ thoughts (about doing sth)** changer d'avis (à propos de faire qch); **on ~ thought** *or* (*Brit*) **thoughts** à la réflexion.

secondary [sek'əndârē] *a* secondaire.

secondary picket *n* piquet *m* (de grève) secondaire.

secondary school *n* (*Brit*) collège *m*, lycée *m*.

second-best [sek'əndbest'] *n* deuxième choix *m*; **as a ~** faute de mieux.

second-class [sek'əndklas'] *a* de deuxième classe ♦ *ad*: **to send sth ~** envoyer qch à tarif réduit; **to travel ~** voyager en seconde; ~ **citizen** citoyen/ne de deuxième classe.

second cousin *n* cousin/e issu(e) de germains.

seconder [sek'əndûr] *n* personne *f* qui appuie une motion.

secondhand [sek'əndhand'] *a* d'occasion; ♦ *ad* (*buy*) d'occasion; **to hear sth ~** apprendre qch indirectement.

second hand *n* (*on clock*) trotteuse *f*.

second-in-command [sek'əndinkəmand'] *n* (*MIL*) commandant *m* en second; (*ADMIN*) adjoint/e, sous-chef *m*.

secondly [sek'əndlē] *ad* deuxièmement.

second-rate [sek'əndrrāt'] *a* de deuxième ordre, de qualité inférieure.

secrecy [sē'krisē] *n* secret *m*; **in ~** en secret, dans le secret.

secret [sē'krit] *a* secret(ète) ♦ *n* secret *m*; **in ~** *ad* en secret, secrètement, en cachette; **to keep sth ~ from sb** cacher qch à qn, ne pas révéler qch à qn; **keep it ~** n'en parle à personne; **to make no ~ of sth** ne pas cacher qch.

secret agent *n* agent secret.

secretarial [sekritār'ēəl] *a* de secrétaire, de secrétariat.

secretariat [sekritār'ēət] *n* secrétariat *m*.

secretary [sek'ritârē] *n* secrétaire *m/f*; (*COMM*) secrétaire général; **S~ of State** (*US POL*) ≈ ministre *m* des Affaires étrangères; (*Brit POL*): **S~ of State (for)** ministre *m* (de).

secrete [sikrēt'] *vt* (*ANAT, BIOL, MED*) sécréter; (*hide*) cacher.

secretion [sikrē'shən] *n* sécrétion *f*.

secretive [sē'kritiv] *a* réservé(e); (*pej*) cachottier(ière), dissimulé(e).

secretly [sē'kritlē] *ad* en secret, secrètement, en cachette.

sect [sekt] *n* secte *f*.

sectarian [sektār'ēən] *a* sectaire.

section [sek'shən] *n* coupe *f*, section *f*; (*department*) section; (*COMM*) rayon *m*; (*of document*) section, article *m*, paragraphe *m* ♦ *vt* sectionner; **the business** *etc* ~ (*PRESS*)

la page des affaires *etc*.

sectional [sek'shənl] *a* (*drawing*) en coupe.

sector [sek'tûr] *n* secteur *m*.

secular [sek'yəlûr] *a* profane; laïque; séculier(ière).

secure [sikyōōr'] *a* (*free from anxiety*) sans inquiétude, sécurisé(e); (*firmly fixed*) solide, bien attaché(e) (*or* fermé(e) *etc*); (*in safe place*) en lieu sûr, en sûreté ♦ *vt* (*fix*) fixer, attacher; (*get*) obtenir, se procurer; (*COMM: loan*) garantir; **to make sth ~** bien fixer *or* attacher qch; **to ~ sth for sb** obtenir qch pour qn, procurer qch à qn.

secured creditor [sikyōōrd' krēd'itûr] *n* créancier/ière privilégié(e).

security [sikyōōr'itē] *n* sécurité *f*, mesures *fpl* de sécurité; (*for loan*) caution *f*, garantie *f*; **securities** *npl* (*STOCK EXCHANGE*) valeurs *fpl*, titres *mpl*; **to increase** *or* **tighten ~** renforcer les mesures de sécurité; ~ **of tenure** stabilité *f* d'un emploi, titularisation *f*.

security forces *npl* forces *fpl* de sécurité.

security guard *n* garde chargé de la sécurité; (*transporting money*) convoyeur *m* de fonds.

security risk *n* menace *f* pour la sécurité de l'état (*or* d'une entreprise *etc*).

secy *abbr* (= *secretary*) secr.

sedan [sidan'] *n* (*US AUT*) berline *f*.

sedate [sidāt'] *a* calme; posé(e) ♦ *vt* donner des sédatifs à.

sedation [sidā'shən] *n* (*MED*) sédation *f*; **to be under ~** être sous calmants.

sedative [sed'ətiv] *n* calmant *m*, sédatif *m*.

sedentary [sed'əntârē] *a* sédentaire.

sediment [sed'əmənt] *n* sédiment *m*, dépôt *m*.

sedition [sidish'ən] *n* sédition *f*.

seduce [sidōōs'] *vt* séduire.

seduction [siduk'shən] *n* séduction *f*.

seductive [siduk'tiv] *a* séduisant(e), séducteur(trice).

see [sē] *vb* (*pt* **saw**, *pp* **seen** [sô, sēn]) *vt* (*gen*) voir; (*accompany*): **to ~ sb to the door** reconduire *or* raccompagner qn jusqu'à la porte ♦ *vi* voir ♦ *n* évêché *m*; **to ~ that** (*ensure*) veiller à ce que + *sub*, faire en sorte que + *sub*, s'assurer que; **there was nobody to be ~n** il n'y avait pas un chat; **let me ~** (*show me*) fais(-moi) voir; (*let me think*) voyons (un peu); **to go and ~ sb** aller voir qn; ~ **for yourself** voyez vous-même; **I don't know what she ~s in him** je ne sais pas ce qu'elle lui trouve; **as far as I can ~** pour autant que je puisse en juger; ~ **you!** au revoir!, à bientôt!; ~ **you soon/later/tomorrow!** à bientôt/plus tard/demain!

see about *vt fus* (*deal with*) s'occuper de.

see off *vt* accompagner (à la gare *or* à l'aéroport *etc*).

see through *vt* mener à bonne fin ♦ *vt fus* voir clair dans.

see to *vt fus* s'occuper de, se charger de.

seed [sēd] *n* graine *f*; (*fig*) germe *m*; (*TENNIS*) tête *f* de série; **to go to ~** monter en graine; (*fig*) se laisser aller.

seedless [sēd'lis] *a* sans pépins.

seedling [sēd'ling] *n* jeune plant *m*, semis *m*.

seedy [sē'dē] *a* (*shabby*) minable, miteux(euse).

seeing [sē'ing] *cj*: ~ **(that)** vu que, étant donné que.

seek, *pt, pp* **sought** [sēk, sôt] *vt* chercher, rechercher; **to ~ advice/help from sb** demander conseil/de l'aide à qn.
 seek out *vt* (*person*) chercher.

seem [sēm] *vi* sembler, paraître; **there ~s to be** ... il semble qu'il y a ..., on dirait qu'il y a ...; **it ~s (that)** ... il semble que ...; **what ~s to be the trouble?** qu'est-ce qui ne va pas?

seemingly [sē'minglē] *ad* apparemment.

seen [sēn] *pp of* **see**.

seep [sēp] *vi* suinter, filtrer.

seer [sēr] *n* prophète/prophétesse, voyant/e.

seersucker [sēr'sukûr] *n* cloqué *m*, étoffe cloquée.

seesaw [sē'sô] *n* (jeu *m* de) bascule *f*.

seethe [sēth] *vi* être en effervescence; **to ~ with anger** bouillir de colère.

see-through [sē'thrōō] *a* transparent(e).

segment [seg'mənt] *n* segment *m*.

segregate [seg'rəgāt] *vt* séparer, isoler.

segregation [segrəgā'shən] *n* ségrégation *f*.

Seine [sān] *n*: **the ~** la Seine.

seismic [sīz'mik] *a* sismique.

seize [sēz] *vt* (*grasp*) saisir, attraper; (*take possession of*) s'emparer de; (*LAW*) saisir.
 seize up *vi* (*TECH*) se gripper.
 seize (up)on *vt fus* saisir, sauter sur.

seizure [sē'zhûr] *n* (*MED*) crise *f*, attaque *f*; (*LAW*) saisie *f*.

seldom [sel'dəm] *ad* rarement.

select [silekt'] *a* choisi(e), d'élite; (*hotel, restaurant, club*) chic *inv*, sélect *inv* ♦ *vt* sélectionner, choisir; **a ~ few** quelques privilégiés.

selection [silek'shən] *n* sélection *f*, choix *m*.

selection committee *n* comité *m* de sélection.

selective [silek'tiv] *a* sélectif(ive); (*school*) à recrutement sélectif.

selector [silek'tûr] *n* (*person*) sélectionneur/euse; (*TECH*) sélecteur *m*.

self [self] *n* (*pl* **selves** [selvz]): **the ~** le moi *inv* ♦ *prefix* auto-.

self-addressed [self'ədrest'] *a*: **~ envelope** enveloppe *f* à mon (*or* votre *etc*) nom; **~ stamped envelope (SASE)** (*US*) enveloppe affranchie pour la réponse.

self-adhesive [self'adhē'siv] *a* autocollant(e).

self-assertive [self'əsûr'tiv] *a* autoritaire.

self-assurance [self'əshōōr'əns] *n* assurance *f*.

self-assured [self'əshōōrd'] *a* sûr(e) de soi, plein(e) d'assurance.

self-catering [self'kā'tûring] *a* (*Brit: apartment*) avec cuisine, où l'on peut faire sa cuisine; (: *holiday*) en appartement (*or* chalet *etc*) loué.

self-centered [self'sen'tûrd] *a* égocentrique.

self-cleaning [self'klē'ning] *a* autonettoyant(e).

self-colored [self'kul'ûrd] *a* uni(e).

self-confessed [self'kənfest'] *a* (*alcoholic etc*) déclaré(e), qui ne s'en cache pas.

self-confidence [self'kán'fidəns] *n* confiance *f* en soi.

self-conscious [self'kán'chəs] *a* timide, qui manque d'assurance.

self-contained [self'kəntānd'] *a* (*Brit:* *apartment*) avec entrée particulière, indépendant(e).

self-control [self'kəntrōl'] *n* maîtrise *f* de soi.

self-defeating [self'difē'ting] *a* qui a un effet contraire à l'effet recherché.

self-defense [self'difens'] *n* légitime défense *f*.

self-discipline [self'dis'əplin] *n* discipline personnelle.

self-employed [self'imploid'] *a* qui travaille à son compte.

self-esteem [self'əstēm'] *n* amour-propre *m*.

self-evident [self'ev'idənt] *a* évident(e), qui va de soi.

self-explanatory [self'iksplan'ətôrē] *a* qui se passe d'explication.

self-governing [self'guv'ûrning] *a* autonome.

self-help [self'help'] *n* initiative personnelle, efforts personnels.

self-importance [self'impôr'təns] *n* suffisance *f*.

self-indulgent [self'indul'jənt] *a* qui ne se refuse rien.

self-inflicted [self'inflik'tid] *a* volontaire.

self-interest [self'in'trist] *n* intérêt personnel.

selfish [sel'fish] *a* égoïste.

selfishness [sel'fishnis] *n* égoïsme *m*.

selfless [self'lis] *a* désintéressé(e).

selflessly [self'lislē] *ad* sans penser à soi.

self-made man [self'mād' man'] *n* self-made man *m*.

self-pity [self'pit'ē] *n* apitoiement *m* sur soi-même.

self-portrait [self'pôr'trit] *n* autoportrait *m*.

self-possessed [self'pəzest'] *a* assuré(e).

self-preservation [self'prezûrvā'shən] *n* instinct *m* de conservation.

self-raising [self'rā'zing] *a* (*Brit*) = **self-rising**.

self-reliant [self'rili'ənt] *a* indépendant(e).

self-respect [self'rispekt'] *n* respect *m* de soi, amour-propre *m*.

self-respecting [self'rispekt'ing] *a* qui se respecte.

self-righteous [self'rī'chəs] *a* satisfait(e) de soi, pharisaïque.

self-rising [self'rī'zing] *a* (*US*): **~ flour** farine *f* pour gâteaux (*avec levure incorporée*).

self-sacrifice [self'sak'rəfīs] *n* abnégation *f*.

self-same [self'sām] *a* même.

self-satisfied [self'sat'isfīd] *a* content(e) de soi, suffisant(e).

self-sealing [self'sēl'ing] *a* (*envelope*) autocollant(e).

self-service [self'sûr'vis] *a, n* libre-service (*m*), self-service (*m*).

self-styled [self'stīld] *a* soi-disant *inv*.

self-sufficient [self'səfish'ənt] *a* indépendant(e).

self-supporting [self'səpôrt'ing] *a* financièrement indépendant(e).

self-taught [self'tôt'] *a* autodidacte.

self-test [self'test'] *n* (*COMPUT*) test *m* automatique.

sell, *pt, pp* **sold** [sel, sōld] *vt* vendre ♦ *vi* se vendre; **to ~ at *or* for 10 F** se vendre 10 F; **to ~ sb an idea** (*fig*) faire accepter une idée à qn.
 sell off *vt* liquider.
 sell out *vi*: **to ~ out (to)** (*COMM*) vendre son fonds *or* son affaire (à) ♦ *vt* vendre tout son stock de; **the tickets are all sold out** il

ne reste plus de billets.

sell-by date [sel'bī dāt] *n* date *f* limite de vente.

seller [sel'ûr] *n* vendeur/euse, marchand/e; ~'s **market** marché *m* à la hausse.

selling price [sel'ing prīs] *n* prix *m* de vente.

sellotape [sel'ətāp] *n* ® (*Brit*) papier collant, scotch *m* ®.

sellout [sel'out] *n* trahison *f*, capitulation *f*; (*of tickets*): **it was a** ~ tous les billets ont été vendus.

selves [selvz] *npl of* **self**.

semantic [siman'tik] *a* sémantique.

semantics [siman'tiks] *n* sémantique *f*.

semaphore [sem'əfôr] *n* signaux *mpl* à bras; (*RAIL*) sémaphore *m*.

semblance [sem'bləns] *n* semblant *m*.

semen [sē'mən] *n* sperme *m*.

semester [simes'tûr] *n* semestre *m*.

semi... [sem'ē] *prefix* semi-, demi-; à demi, à moitié ♦ *n* (*Brit*): **semi = semidetached (house)**.

semiannual [sem'ēan'yōōəl] *a* (*US*) semes-triel(le).

semiannually [sem'ēan'yōōəlē] *ad* (*US*) deux fois par an.

semibreve [sem'ēbrēv] *n* (*Brit*) = **whole note**.

semicircle [sem'ēsûrkəl] *n* demi-cercle *m*.

semicircular [sem'ēsûr'kyəlûr] *a* en demi-cercle, semi-circulaire.

semicolon [sem'ēkōlən] *n* point-virgule *m*.

semiconductor [semēkənduk'tûr] *n* semi-conducteur *m*.

semiconscious [semēkän'chəs] *a* à demi conscient(e).

semidetached (house) [semēditacht' (hous')] *n* (*Brit*) maison jumelée *or* jumelle.

semifinal [semēfī'nəl] *n* demi-finale *f*.

seminar [sem'ənâr] *n* séminaire *m*.

seminary [sem'ənārē] *n* (*REL: for priests*) sé-minaire *m*.

semiprecious [semēpresh'əs] *a* semi-précieux(euse).

semiquaver [sem'ēkwāvûr] *n* (*Brit*) = **sixteenth note**.

semiskilled [semēskild'] *a*: ~ **worker** *n* ouvrier/ière spécialisé(e).

semitone [sem'ētōn] *n* (*MUS*) demi-ton *m*.

semi(trailer) [sem'ē(trā'lûr)] *n* (*US*) (camion *m*) semi-remorque *m*.

semolina [seməlē'nə] *n* semoule *f*.

Sen., sen. *abbr* = **senator, senior**.

senate [sen'it] *n* sénat *m*.

senator [sen'ətûr] *n* sénateur *m*.

send, *pt, pp* **sent** [send, sent] *vt* envoyer; **to** ~ **by mail** envoyer *or* expédier par la poste; **to** ~ **sb for sth** envoyer qn chercher qch; **to** ~ **word that ...** faire dire que ...; **she** ~s **(you) her love** elle vous adresse ses amitiés; **to** ~ **sb to sleep** endormir qn; **to** ~ **sb into fits of laughter** faire rire qn aux éclats; **to** ~ **sth flying** envoyer valser qch.

send (a)round *vt* (*letter, document etc*) faire circuler.

send away *vt* (*letter, goods*) envoyer, expé-dier.

send away for *vt fus* commander par correspondance, se faire envoyer.

send back *vt* renvoyer.

send for *vt fus* envoyer chercher; faire ve-nir; (*by mail*) se faire envoyer, commander par correspondance.

send in *vt* (*report, application, resignation*) remettre.

send off *vt* (*goods*) envoyer, expédier.

send on *vt* (*letter*) faire suivre; (*luggage etc: in advance*) (faire) expédier à l'avance.

send out *vt* (*invitation*) envoyer (par la poste); (*emit: light, heat, signals*) émettre.

send up *vt* (*person, price*) faire monter.

sender [send'ûr] *n* expéditeur/trice.

send-off [send'ôf] *n*: **a good** ~ des adieux chaleureux.

Senegal [sen'əgâl] *n* Sénégal *m*.

Senegalese [senəgəlēz'] *a* sénégalais(e) ♦ *n* (*pl inv*) Sénégalais/e.

senile [sē'nīl] *a* sénile.

senility [sinil'ətē] *n* sénilité *f*.

senior [sēn'yûr] *a* (*older*) aîné(e), plus âgé(e); (*of higher rank*) supérieur(e) ♦ *n* aîné/e; (*in service*) personne *f* qui a plus d'ancienneté; **P. Jones** ~ P. Jones père.

senior citizen *n* personne âgée.

senior high school *n* (*US*) ≈ lycée *m*.

seniority [sēnyôr'itē] *n* priorité *f* d'âge, ancienneté *f*; (*in rank*) supériorité *f* (hiérar-chique).

sensation [sensā'shən] *n* sensation *f*; **to create a** ~ faire sensation.

sensational [sensā'shənəl] *a* qui fait sensation; (*marvellous*) sensationnel(le).

sense [sens] *n* sens *m*; (*feeling*) sentiment *m*; (*meaning*) signification *f*; (*wisdom*) bon sens ♦ *vt* sentir, pressentir; ~s *npl* raison *f*; **it makes** ~ c'est logique; ~ **of humor** sens de l'humour; **there is no** ~ **in (doing) that** cela n'a pas de sens; **to come to one's** ~s (*re-gain consciousness*) reprendre conscience; (*become reasonable*) revenir à la raison; **to take leave of one's** ~s perdre la tête.

senseless [sens'lis] *a* insensé(e), stupide; (*unconscious*) sans connaissance.

sensibility [sensəbil'ətē] *n* sensibilité *f*; **sensi-bilities** *npl* susceptibilité *f*.

sensible [sen'səbəl] *a* sensé(e), raisonnable; (*shoes etc*) pratique.

sensitive [sen'sətiv] *a*: ~ **(to)** sensible (à); **he is very** ~ **about it** c'est un point très sensible (chez lui).

sensitivity [sensətiv'ətē] *n* sensibilité *f*.

sensual [sen'shōōəl] *a* sensuel(le).

sensuous [sen'shōōəs] *a* voluptueux(euse), sensuel(le).

sent [sent] *pt, pp of* **send**.

sentence [sen'təns] *n* (*LING*) phrase *f*; (*LAW: judgment*) condamnation *f*, sentence *f*; (: *punishment*) peine *f* ♦ *vt*: **to** ~ **sb to death/ to 5 years** condamner qn à mort/à 5 ans; **to pass** ~ **on sb** prononcer une peine contre qn.

sentiment [sen'təmənt] *n* sentiment *m*; (*opin-ion*) opinion *f*, avis *m*.

sentimental [sentəmen'təl] *a* sentimental(e).

sentimentality [sentəmental'itē] *n* sentimenta-lité *f*, sensiblerie *f*.

sentry [sen'trē] *n* sentinelle *f*, factionnaire *m*.

sentry duty *n*: **to be on** ~ être de faction.

Seoul [sōl] *n* Séoul.

separable [sep'ûrəbəl] *a* séparable.

separate *a* [sep'rit] séparé(e), indépendant(e), différent(e) ♦ *vb* [sep'erāt] *vt* séparer ♦ *vi* se séparer; **~ from** distinct(e) de; **under ~ cover** (*COMM*) sous pli séparé; **to ~ into** diviser en.

separately [sep'ritlĕ] *ad* séparément.

separates [sep'rits] *npl* (*clothes*) coordonnés *mpl*.

separation [separā'shən] *n* séparation *f*.

Sept. *abbr* (= *September*) sept.

September [septem'bûr] *n* septembre *m*; *for phrases see also* **July**.

septic [sep'tik] *a* septique; (*wound*) infecté(e); **to go ~** s'infecter.

septicemia, (*Brit*) **septicaemia** [septisē'mēə] *n* septicémie *f*.

septic tank *n* fosse *f* septique.

sequel [sē'kwəl] *n* conséquence *f*; séquelles *fpl*; (*of story*) suite *f*.

sequence [sē'kwins] *n* ordre *m*, suite *f*; **in ~** par ordre, dans l'ordre, les uns après les autres; **~ of tenses** concordance *f* des temps.

sequential [sikwen'chəl] *a*: **~ access** (*COMPUT*) accès séquentiel.

sequin [sē'kwin] *n* paillette *f*.

Serbo-Croat [sûr'bōkrōat] *n* (*LING*) serbocroate *m*.

serenade [särənad'] *n* sérénade *f* ♦ *vt* donner une sérénade à.

serene [sərēn'] *a* serein(e), calme, paisible.

serenity [səren'itē] *n* sérénité *f*, calme *m*.

sergeant [sâr'jənt] *n* sergent *m*; (*POLICE*) brigadier *m*.

sergeant major *n* sergent-major *m*.

serial [sēr'ēəl] *n* feuilleton *m* ♦ *a* (*COMPUT*: *interface, printer*) série *inv*; (: *access*) séquentiel(le).

serialize [sēr'ēəliz] *vt* publier (*or* adapter) en feuilleton.

serial number *n* numéro *m* de série.

series [sēr'ēz] *n* série *f*; (*PUBLISHING*) collection *f*.

serious [sēr'ēəs] *a* sérieux(euse); (*accident etc*) grave; **are you ~ (about it?)** parlez-vous sérieusement?

seriously [sē'rēəslē] *ad* sérieusement, gravement; **to take sth/sb ~** prendre qch/qn au sérieux.

seriousness [sē'rēəsnis] *n* sérieux *m*, gravité *f*.

sermon [sûr'mən] *n* sermon *m*.

serrated [sēr'ätid] *a* en dents de scie.

serum [sēr'əm] *n* sérum *m*.

servant [sûr'vənt] *n* domestique *m/f*; (*fig*) serviteur/servante.

serve [sûrv] *vt* (*employer etc*) servir, être au service de; (*purpose*) servir à; (*customer, food, meal*) servir; (*apprenticeship*) faire, accomplir; (*prison term*) faire; purger ♦ *vi* (*also TENNIS*) servir; (*be useful*): **to ~ as/for/to do** servir de/à/à faire ♦ *n* (*TENNIS*) service *m*; **are you being ~d?** (*Brit*) est-ce qu'on s'occupe de vous?; **to ~ on a committee/jury** faire partie d'un comité/jury; **it ~s him right** c'est bien fait pour lui; **it ~s my purpose** cela fait mon affaire.

serve up *vt* (*food*) servir.

service [sûr'vis] *n* (*gen*) service *m*; (*AUT: maintenance*) révision *f*; (*REL*) office *m* ♦ *vt* (*car, washing machine*) réviser; **the Armed S~s** *npl* les forces armées; **to be of ~ to sb, to do sb a ~** rendre service à qn; **to put one's car in for ~** donner sa voiture à réviser; **dinner ~** service de table.

serviceable [sûr'visəbəl] *a* pratique, commode.

service area *n* (*on motorway*) aire *f* de services.

service charge *n* (*Brit*) service *m*.

service industries *npl* les industries *fpl* de service, les services *mpl*.

serviceman [sûr'visman] *n* militaire *m*.

service station *n* station-service *f*.

serviette [sûrvēet'] *n* (*Brit*) serviette *f* (de table).

servile [sûr'vil] *a* servile.

serving cart [sûr'ving kârt] *n* (*US*) table roulante.

session [sesh'ən] *n* (*sitting*) séance *f*; (*SCOL*) année *f* scolaire (*or* universitaire); **to be in ~** siéger, être en session *or* en séance.

set [set] *n* série *f*, assortiment *m*; (*of tools etc*) jeu *m*; (*RADIO, TV*) poste *m*; (*TENNIS*) set *m*; (*group of people*) cercle *m*, milieu *m*; (*CINEMA*) plateau *m*; (*THEATER: stage*) scène *f*; (: *scenery*) décor *m*; (*MATH*) ensemble *m*; (*HAIRDRESSING*) mise *f* en plis ♦ *a* (*fixed*) fixe, déterminé(e); (*ready*) prêt(e) ♦ *vb* (*pt, pp* **set**) *vt* (*place*) mettre, poser, placer; (*table*) mettre; (*fix, establish*) fixer; (: *record*) établir; (*assign: task, homework*) donner; (*adjust*) régler; (*decide: rules etc*) fixer, choisir; (*TYP*) composer ♦ *vi* (*sun*) se coucher; (*jam, jelly, concrete*) prendre; **to be ~ on doing** être résolu(e) à faire; **to be all ~ to do** être (fin) prêt(e) pour faire; **to be (dead) ~ against** être (totalement) opposé(e); **he's ~ in his ways** il n'est pas très souple, il tient à ses habitudes; **to ~ to music** mettre en musique; **to ~ on fire** mettre le feu à; **to ~ free** libérer; **to ~ sth going** déclencher qch; **to ~ sail** partir, prendre la mer; **a ~ phrase** une expression toute faite, une locution; **a ~ of false teeth** un dentier; **a ~ of dining-room furniture** une salle à manger.

set about *vt fus* (*task*) entreprendre, se mettre à; **to ~ about doing sth** se mettre à faire qch.

set aside *vt* mettre de côté.

set back *vt* (*in time*): **to ~ back (by)** retarder (de); (*place*): **a house ~ back from the road** une maison située en retrait de la route.

set in *vi* (*infection, bad weather*) s'installer; (*complications*) survenir, surgir; **the rain has ~ in for the day** c'est parti pour qu'il pleuve toute la journée.

set off *vi* se mettre en route, partir ♦ *vt* (*bomb*) faire exploser; (*cause to start*) déclencher; (*show up well*) mettre en valeur, faire valoir.

set out *vi*: **to ~ out to do** entreprendre de faire; avoir pour but *or* intention de faire ♦ *vt* (*arrange*) disposer; (*state*) présenter, exposer; **to ~ out (from)** partir (de).

set up *vt* (*organization*) fonder, constituer; (*monument*) ériger; **to ~ up shop** (*fig*) s'établir, s'installer.

setback [set'bak] *n* (*hitch*) revers *m*, contretemps *m*; (*in health*) rechute *f*.

set menu n menu m.
set square n (Brit) équerre f.
settee [setē'] n canapé m.
setting [set'ing] n cadre m; (of jewel) monture f.
settle [set'əl] vt (argument, matter, account) régler; (problem) résoudre; (MED: calm) calmer; (colonize: land) coloniser ♦ vi (bird, dust etc) se poser; (sediment) se déposer; (also: ~ **down**) s'installer, se fixer; (: become calmer) se calmer; se ranger; **to ~ to sth** se mettre sérieusement à qch; **to ~ for sth** accepter qch, se contenter de qch; **to ~ on sth** opter pour qch; **that's ~d then** alors, c'est d'accord!; **to ~ one's stomach** calmer des maux d'estomac.
settle in vi s'installer.
settle up vi: **to ~ up with sb** régler (ce que l'on doit à) qn.
settlement [set'əlmənt] n (payment) règlement m; (agreement) accord m; (colony) colonie f; (village etc) établissement m; hameau m; **in ~ of our account** (COMM) en règlement de notre compte.
settler [set'lûr] n colon m.
setup [set'up] n (arrangement) manière f dont les choses sont organisées; (situation) situation f, allure f des choses.
seven [sev'ən] num sept.
seventeen [sev'əntēn'] num dix-sept.
seventh [sev'ənth] num septième; **to be in ~ heaven** être au septième ciel.
seventy [sev'əntē] num soixante-dix.
sever [sev'ûr] vt couper, trancher; (relations) rompre.
several [sev'ûrəl] a, pronoun plusieurs (m/fpl); **~ of us** plusieurs d'entre nous; **~ times** plusieurs fois.
severance [sev'ûrəns] n (of relations) rupture f.
severance pay n indemnité f de licenciement.
severe [sivēr'] a sévère, strict(e); (serious) grave, sérieux(euse); (hard) rigoureux(euse), dur(e); (plain) sévère, austère.
severely [sivēr'lē] ad sévèrement; (wounded, ill) gravement.
severity [sivär'itē] n sévérité f; gravité f; rigueur f.
sew, pt sewed, pp sewn [sō, sōd, sōn] vt, vi coudre.
sew up vt (re)coudre; **it is all sewn up** (fig) c'est dans le sac or dans la poche.
sewage [sōō'ij] n vidange(s) f(pl).
sewer [sōō'ûr] n égout m.
sewing [sō'ing] n couture f.
sewing machine n machine f à coudre.
sewn [sōn] pp of **sew**.
sex [seks] n sexe m; **to have ~ with** avoir des rapports (sexuels) avec.
sex act n acte sexuel.
sexism [sek'sizəm] n sexisme m.
sexist [sek'sist] a sexiste.
sextet [sekstet'] n sextuor m.
sexual [sek'shōōəl] a sexuel(le); **~ assault** attentat m à la pudeur; **~ intercourse** rapports sexuels.
sexy [sek'sē] a sexy inv.
Seychelles [sāshel'] npl: **the ~** les Seychelles fpl.

SF n abbr (= science fiction) SF f.
SG n abbr (US) = **Surgeon General.**
Sgt abbr (= sergeant) Sgt.
shabbiness [shab'ēnis] n aspect miteux; mesquinerie f.
shabby [shab'ē] a miteux(euse); (behavior) mesquin(e), méprisable.
shack [shak] n cabane f, hutte f.
shackles [shak'əlz] npl chaînes fpl, entraves fpl.
shade [shād] n ombre f; (for lamp) abat-jour m inv; (of color) nuance f, ton m; (US: window ~) store m; (small quantity): **a ~ of** un soupçon de ♦ vt abriter du soleil, ombrager; **~s** npl (sunglasses) lunettes fpl de soleil; **in the ~** à l'ombre; **a ~ smaller** un tout petit peu plus petit.
shadow [shad'ō] n ombre f ♦ vt (follow) filer; **without** or **beyond a ~ of doubt** sans l'ombre d'un doute.
shadow cabinet n (Brit POL) cabinet parallèle formé par le parti qui n'est pas au pouvoir.
shadowy [shad'ōē] a ombragé(e); (dim) vague, indistinct(e).
shady [shā'dē] a ombragé(e); (fig: dishonest) louche, véreux(euse).
shaft [shaft] n (of arrow, spear) hampe f; (AUT, TECH) arbre m; (of mine) puits m; (of elevator) cage f; (of light) rayon m, trait m; **ventilator ~** conduit m d'aération or de ventilation.
shaggy [shag'ē] a hirsute; en broussaille.
shake [shāk] vb (pt shook, pp shaken [shōōk, shā'kən]) vt secouer; (bottle, cocktail) agiter; (house, confidence) ébranler ♦ vi trembler ♦ n secousse f; **to ~ one's head** (in refusal etc) dire or faire non de la tête; (in dismay) secouer la tête; **to ~ hands with sb** serrer la main à qn.
shake off vt secouer; (fig) se débarrasser de.
shake up vt secouer.
shake-up [shāk'up] n grand remaniement.
shakily [shā'kilē] ad (reply) d'une voix tremblante; (walk) d'un pas mal assuré; (write) d'une main tremblante.
shaky [shā'kē] a (hand, voice) tremblant(e); (building) branlant(e), peu solide; (memory) chancelant(e); (knowledge) incertain(e).
shale [shāl] n schiste argileux.
shall [shal] auxiliary vb: **I ~ go** j'irai.
shallot [shəlât'] n échalote f.
shallow [shal'ō] a peu profond(e); (fig) superficiel(le), qui manque de profondeur.
sham [sham] n frime f; (jewelry, furniture) imitation f ♦ a feint(e), simulé(e) ♦ vt feindre, simuler.
shambles [sham'bəlz] n confusion f, pagaïe f, fouillis m; **the economy is (in) a complete ~** l'économie est dans la confusion la plus totale.
shame [shām] n honte f ♦ vt faire honte à; **it is a ~ (that/to do)** c'est dommage (que + sub/de faire); **what a ~!** quel dommage!; **to put sb/sth to ~** (fig) faire honte à qn/qch.
shamefaced [shām'fāst] a honteux(euse), penaud(e).
shameful [shām'fəl] a honteux(euse), scanda-

leux(euse).

shameless [shām'lis] *a* éhonté(e), effronté(e); (*immodest*) impudique.

shampoo [shampoo'] *n* shampooing *m* ♦ *vt* faire un shampooing à; ~ **and set** shampooing et mise *f* en plis.

shamrock [sham'răk] *n* trèfle *m* (*emblème national de l'Irlande*).

shandy [shan'dē] *n* bière panachée.

shan't [shant] = **shall not.**

shanty town [shan'tē toun] *n* bidonville *m*.

SHAPE [shāp] *n abbr* (= *Supreme Headquarters Allied Powers, Europe*) quartier général des forces alliées en Europe.

shape [shāp] *n* forme *f* ♦ *vt* façonner, modeler; (*clay, stone*) donner forme à; (*statement*) formuler; (*sb's ideas, character*) former; (*sb's life*) déterminer; (*course of events*) influer sur le cours de ♦ *vi* (*also*: ~ **up**: *events*) prendre tournure; (: *person*) faire des progrès, s'en sortir; **to take** ~ prendre forme *or* tournure; **in the** ~ **of a heart** en forme de cœur; **I can't bear gardening in any** ~ **or form** je déteste le jardinage sous quelque forme que ce soit; **to get o.s. into** ~ (re)trouver la forme.

-shaped [shāpt] *suffix:* **heart**~ en forme de cœur.

shapeless [shāp'lis] *a* informe, sans forme.

shapely [shāp'lē] *a* bien proportionné(e), beau(belle).

share [shär] *n* (*thing received, contribution*) part *f*; (COMM) action *f* ♦ *vt* partager; (*have in common*) avoir en commun; **to** ~ **out (among** *or* **between)** partager (entre); **to** ~ **in** (*joy, sorrow*) prendre part à; (*profits*) participer à, avoir part à; (*work*) partager.

share capital *n* capital social.

share certificate *n* certificat *m or* titre *m* d'action.

shareholder [shär'hōldûr] *n* actionnaire *m/f*.

share index *n* indice *m* de la Bourse.

shark [shârk] *n* requin *m*.

sharp [shârp] *a* (*razor, knife*) tranchant(e), bien aiguisé(e); (*point*) aigu(ë); (*nose, chin*) pointu(e); (*outline*) net(te); (*curve, bend*) brusque; (*cold, pain*) vif(vive); (MUS) dièse; (*voice*) coupant(e); (*person: quick-witted*) vif(vive), éveillé(e); (: *unscrupulous*) malhonnête ♦ *n* (MUS) dièse *m* ♦ *ad:* **at 2 o'clock** ~ à 2 heures pile *or* tapantes; **turn** ~ **left** tournez immédiatement à gauche; **to be** ~ **with sb** être brusque avec qn; **look** ~! dépêche-toi!

sharpen [shâr'pən] *vt* aiguiser; (*pencil*) tailler; (*fig*) aviver.

sharpener [shâr'pənûr] *n* (*also*: **pencil** ~) taille-crayon(s) *m inv*; (*also*: **knife** ~) aiguisoir *m*.

sharp-eyed [shârp'īd] *a* à qui rien n'échappe.

sharply [shârp'lē] *ad* (*abruptly*) brusquement; (*clearly*) nettement; (*harshly*) sèchement, vertement.

sharp-tempered [shârp'tempûrd] *a* prompt(e) à se mettre en colère.

sharp-witted [shârp'wit'id] *a* à l'esprit vif, malin(igne).

shatter [shat'ûr] *vt* fracasser, briser, faire voler en éclats; (*fig: upset*) bouleverser; (:

ruin) briser, ruiner ♦ *vi* voler en éclats, se briser, se fracasser.

shattered [shat'ûrd] *a* (*overwhelmed, grief-stricken*) bouleversé(e); (*col: exhausted*) éreinté(e).

shatterproof [shat'ûrproof] *a* incassable.

shave [shāv] *vt* raser ♦ *vi* se raser ♦ *n:* **to have a** ~ se raser.

shaven [shā'vən] *a* (*head*) rasé(e).

shaver [shā'vûr] *n* (*also:* **electric** ~) rasoir *m* électrique.

shaving [shā'ving] *n* (*action*) rasage *m*; ~**s** *npl* (*of wood etc*) copeaux *mpl*.

shaving brush *n* blaireau *m*.

shaving cream *n* crème *f* à raser.

shaving soap *n* savon *m* à barbe.

shawl [shôl] *n* châle *m*.

she [shē] *pronoun* elle; **there** ~ **is** la voilà; ~-**elephant** *etc* éléphant *etc* femelle; *NB: for ships, countries follow the gender of your translation.*

sheaf, *pl* **sheaves** [shēf, shēvz] *n* gerbe *f*.

shear [shē'ûr] *vt* (*pt* ~**ed**, *pp* ~**ed** *or* **shorn** [shôrn]) (*sheep*) tondre.

shear off *vt* tondre; (*branch*) élaguer.

shears [shē'ûrz] *npl* (*for hedge*) cisaille(s) *f(pl)*.

sheath [shēth] *n* gaine *f*, fourreau *m*, étui *m*; (*contraceptive*) préservatif *m*.

sheathe [shēth] *vt* gainer; (*sword*) rengainer.

sheath knife *n* couteau *m* à gaine.

sheaves [shēvz] *npl of* **sheaf.**

shed [shed] *n* remise *f*, resserre *f*; (INDUSTRY, RAIL) hangar *m* ♦ *vt* (*pt, pp* **shed**) (*leaves, fur etc*) perdre; (*tears*) verser, répandre; **to** ~ **light on** (*problem, mystery*) faire la lumière sur.

she'd [shēd] = **she had, she would.**

sheen [shēn] *n* lustre *m*.

sheep [shēp] *n* (*pl inv*) mouton *m*.

sheepdog [shēp'dôg] *n* chien *m* de berger.

sheep farmer *n* éleveur *m* de moutons.

sheepish [shē'pish] *a* penaud(e), timide.

sheepskin [shēp'skin] *n* peau *f* de mouton.

sheepskin jacket *n* canadienne *f*.

sheer [shē'ûr] *a* (*utter*) pur(e), pur et simple; (*steep*) à pic, abrupt(e); (*almost transparent*) extrêmement fin(e) ♦ *ad* à pic, abruptement; **by** ~ **chance** par pur hasard.

sheer curtains *npl* (US) voilages *mpl*.

sheet [shēt] *n* (*on bed*) drap *m*; (*of paper*) feuille *f*; (*of glass, metal*) feuille, plaque *f*.

sheet feed *n* (*on printer*) alimentation *f* en papier (feuille à feuille).

sheet lightning *n* éclair *m* en nappe(s).

sheet metal *n* tôle *f*.

sheet music *n* partition(s) *f(pl)*.

sheik(h) [shēk] *n* cheik *m*.

shelf, *pl* **shelves** [shelf, shelvz] *n* étagère *f*, rayon *m*; **set of shelves** rayonnage *m*.

shelf life *n* (COMM) durée *f* de conservation (avant la vente).

shell [shel] *n* (*on beach*) coquillage *m*; (*of egg, nut etc*) coquille *f*; (*explosive*) obus *m*; (*of building*) carcasse *f* ♦ *vt* (*crab, prawn etc*) décortiquer; (*peas*) écosser; (MIL) bombarder (d'obus).

shell out *vi* (*col*): **to** ~ **out (for)** casquer (pour).

she'll [shēl] = **she will, she shall**.

shellfish [shel'fish] *n* (*pl inv*) (*crab etc*) crustacé *m*; (*scallop etc*) coquillage *m*; (*pl: as food*) crustacés; coquillages.

shelter [shel'tûr] *n* abri *m*, refuge *m* ♦ *vt* abriter, protéger; (*give lodging to*) donner asile à ♦ *vi* s'abriter, se mettre à l'abri; **to take ~ (from)** s'abriter (de).

sheltered [shel'tûrd] *a* (*life*) retiré(e), à l'abri des soucis; (*spot*) abrité(e).

shelve [shelv] *vt* (*fig*) mettre en suspens *or* en sommeil.

shelves [shelvz] *npl of* **shelf**.

shelving [shel'ving] *n* (*shelves*) rayonnage(s) *m(pl)*.

shepherd [shep'ûrd] *n* berger *m* ♦ *vt* (*guide*) guider, escorter.

shepherdess [shep'ûrdis] *n* bergère *f*.

shepherd's pie *n* ≈ hachis *m* Parmentier.

sherbet [shûr'bit] *n* (*US: dessert*) sorbet *m*; (*Brit: powder*) poudre acidulée.

sheriff [shär'if] *n* shérif *m*.

sherry [shär'ē] *n* xérès *m*, sherry *m*.

she's [shēz] = **she is, she has**.

Shetland [shet'lənd] *n* (*also:* **the ~s, the ~ Isles** *or* **Islands**) les îles *fpl* Shetland.

shield [shēld] *n* bouclier *m* ♦ *vt:* **to ~ (from)** protéger (de *or* contre).

shift [shift] *n* (*change*) changement *m*; (*of workers*) équipe *f*, poste *m* ♦ *vt* déplacer, changer de place; (*remove*) enlever ♦ *vi* changer de place, bouger; **the wind has ~ed to the south** le vent a tourné au sud; **a ~ in demand** (COMM) un déplacement de la demande.

shift key *n* (*on typewriter*) touche *f* de majuscule.

shiftless [shift'lis] *a* fainéant(e).

shift work *n* travail *m* par roulement; **to do ~** travailler par roulement.

shifty [shif'tē] *a* sournois(e); (*eyes*) fuyant(e).

shilling [shil'ing] *n* (*Brit*) shilling *m* (= 12 old pence; 20 in a pound).

shilly-shally [shil'ēshalē] *vi* tergiverser, atermoyer.

shimmer [shim'ûr] *n* miroitement *m*, chatoiement *m* ♦ *vi* miroiter, chatoyer.

shin [shin] *n* tibia *m* ♦ *vi:* **to ~ up/down a tree** grimper dans un/descendre d'un arbre.

shindig [shin'dig] *n* (*col*) bamboula *f*.

shine [shīn] *n* éclat *m*, brillant *m* ♦ *vb* (*pt, pp* **shone** [shōn]) *vi* briller ♦ *vt* faire briller *or* reluire; (*flashlight*): **to ~ on** braquer sur.

shingle [shing'gəl] *n* (*on beach*) galets *mpl*; (*on roof*) bardeau *m*.

shingles [shing'gəlz] *n* (MED) zona *m*.

shining [shī'ning] *a* brillant(e).

shiny [shī'nē] *a* brillant(e).

ship [ship] *n* bateau *m*; (*large*) navire *m* ♦ *vt* transporter (par mer); (*send*) expédier (par mer); (*load*) charger, embarquer; **on board ~** à bord.

shipbuilder [ship'bildûr] *n* constructeur *m* de navires.

shipbuilding [ship'bilding] *n* construction navale.

ship canal *n* canal *m* maritime *or* de navigation.

ship chandler [ship chan'dlûr] *n* fournisseur

m maritime, shipchandler *m*.

shipment [ship'mənt] *n* cargaison *f*.

shipowner [ship'ōnûr] *n* armateur *m*.

shipper [ship'ûr] *n* affréteur *m*, expéditeur *m*.

shipping [ship'ing] *n* (*ships*) navires *mpl*; (*traffic*) navigation *f*.

shipping agent *n* agent *m* maritime.

shipping company *n* compagnie *f* de navigation.

shipping lane *n* couloir *m* de navigation.

shipping line *n* = **shipping company**.

shipshape [ship'shāp] *a* en ordre impeccable.

shipwreck [ship'rek] *n* épave *f*; (*event*) naufrage *m* ♦ *vt:* **to be ~ed** faire naufrage.

shipyard [ship'yârd] *n* chantier naval.

shirk [shûrk] *vt* esquiver, se dérober à.

shirt [shûrt] *n* chemise *f*; **in ~ sleeves** en bras de chemise.

shit [shit] *excl* (*col!*) merde (!).

shiver [shiv'ûr] *n* frisson *m* ♦ *vi* frissonner.

shoal [shōl] *n* (*Brit: of fish*) banc *m*.

shock [shâk] *n* (*impact*) choc *m*, heurt *m*; (ELEC) secousse *f*, décharge *f*; (*emotional*) choc; (MED) commotion *f*, choc ♦ *vt* (*scandalize*) choquer, scandaliser; (*upset*) bouleverser; **suffering from ~** (MED) commotionné(e); **it gave us a ~** ça nous a fait un choc; **it came as a ~ to hear that ...** nous avons appris avec stupeur que ....

shock absorber [shâk' absôrb'ûr] *n* amortisseur *m*.

shocking [shâk'ing] *a* choquant(e), scandaleux(euse); (*weather, handwriting*) épouvantable.

shockproof [shâk'prōōf] *a* anti-choc *inv*.

shock therapy, shock treatment *n* (MED) (traitement *m* par) électrochoc(s) *m(pl)*.

shod [shâd] *pt, pp of* **shoe; well-~** bien chaussé(e).

shoddy [shâd'ē] *a* de mauvaise qualité, mal fait(e).

shoe [shōō] *n* chaussure *f*, soulier *m*; (*also:* **horse~**) fer *m* à cheval; (*also:* **brake ~**) mâchoire *f* de frein ♦ *vt* (*pt, pp* **shod** [shâd]) (*horse*) ferrer.

shoe brush *n* brosse *f* à chaussures.

shoehorn [shōō'hôrn] *n* chausse-pied *m*.

shoelace [shōō'lās] *n* lacet *m* (de soulier).

shoemaker [shōō'mākûr] *n* cordonnier *m*, fabricant *m* de chaussures.

shoe polish *n* cirage *m*.

shoe shop *n* magasin *m* de chaussures.

shoestring [shōō'string] *n:* **on a ~** (*fig*) avec un budget dérisoire; avec des moyens très restreints.

shoetree [shōō'trē] *n* embauchoir *m*.

shone [shōn] *pt, pp of* **shine**.

shoo [shōō] *excl* (allez,) ouste! ♦ *vt* (*also:* **~ away, ~ off**) chasser.

shook [shōōk] *pt of* **shake**.

shoot [shōōt] *n* (*on branch, seedling*) pousse *f*; (*shooting party*) partie *f* de chasse ♦ *vb* (*pt, pp* **shot** [shât]) *vt* (*game: Brit*) chasser; tirer; abattre; (*person*) blesser (*or* tuer) d'un coup de fusil (*or* de revolver); (*execute*) fusiller; (CINEMA) tourner ♦ *vi* (*with gun, bow*): **to ~ (at)** tirer (sur); (SOCCER) shooter, tirer; **to ~ past sb** passer en flèche devant qn; **to ~ in/out** entrer/sortir comme

une flèche.
shoot down vt (plane) abattre.
shoot up vi (fig) monter en flèche.
shooting [shoo͞'ting] n (shots) coups mpl de
feu; (attack) fusillade f; (: murder) homicide m (à l'aide d'une arme à feu); (HUNT-
ING) chasse f; (CINEMA) tournage m.
shooting range n stand m de tir.
shooting star n étoile filante.
shop [shâp] n magasin m; (workshop) atelier
m ♦ vi (also: **go ~ping**) faire ses courses or
ses achats; **repair ~** atelier de réparations;
to talk ~ (fig) parler boutique.
  shop around vi faire le tour des magasins
  (pour comparer les prix); (fig) se renseigner
  avant de choisir or decider.
shop assistant n (Brit) vendeur/euse.
shop floor n (fig) ouvriers mpl.
shopkeeper [shâp'kēpûr] n marchand/e,
commerçant/e.
shoplift [shâp'lift] vi voler à l'étalage.
shoplifter [shâp'liftûr] n voleur/euse à l'étalage.
shoplifting [shâp'lifting] n vol m à l'étalage.
shopper [shâp'ûr] n personne f qui fait ses
courses, acheteur/euse.
shopping [shâp'ing] n (goods) achats mpl,
provisions fpl.
shopping bag n sac m (à provisions).
shopping cart n (US) caddie m.
shopping center n centre commercial.
shopping mall n centre commercial.
shop-soiled [shâp'soild] a (Brit) = **shopworn.**
shop steward n (INDUSTRY) délégué/e syndi-
cal(e).
shop window n vitrine f.
shopworn [shâp'wôrn] a (US) défraîchi(e),
qui a fait la vitrine.
shore [shôr] n (of sea, lake) rivage m, rive f ♦
vt: **to ~ (up)** étayer; **on ~** à terre.
shore leave n (NAUT) permission f à terre.
shorn [shôrn] pp of **shear;** **~ of** dépouillé(e)
de.
short [shôrt] a (not long) court(e); (soon
finished) court, bref(brève); (person, step)
petit(e); (curt) brusque, sec(sèche);
(insufficient) insuffisant(e) ♦ n (also: **~ film**)
court métrage; **to be ~ of sth** être à court
de or manquer de qch; **to be in ~ supply**
manquer, être difficile à trouver; **I'm 3 ~** il
m'en manque 3; **in ~** bref; en bref; **~ of
doing** à moins de faire; **everything ~ of** tout
sauf; **it is ~ for** c'est l'abréviation or le diminutif de; **a ~ time ago** il y a peu de temps;
in the ~ term à court terme; **to cut ~**
(speech, visit) abréger, écourter; (person)
couper la parole à; **to fall ~ of** ne pas être à
la hauteur de; **to stop ~** s'arrêter net; **to
stop ~ of** ne pas aller jusqu'à.
shortage [shôr'tij] n manque m, pénurie f.
shortbread [shôrt'bred] n ≈ sablé m.
shortchange [shôrt'chânj'] vt: **to ~ sb** ne pas
rendre assez à qn.
short circuit n court-circuit m.
short-circuit [shôrtsûr'kit] vt court-circuiter ♦
vi se mettre en court-circuit.
shortcoming [shôrt'kuming] n défaut m.
short(crust) pastry [shôrt('krust) pās'trē] n
(Brit) pâte brisée.

shortcut [shôrt'kut] n raccourci m.
shorten [shôr'tən] vt raccourcir; (text, visit)
abréger.
shortening [shôr'təning] n (CULIN) matière
grasse.
shortfall [shôrt'fôl] n déficit m.
shorthand [shôrt'hand] n sténo(graphie) f; **to
take sth down in ~** prendre qch en sténo.
shorthand notebook n bloc m sténo.
shorthand typist n (Brit) sténodactylo m/f.
short list n (for job) liste f des candidats sé-
lectionnés.
short-lived [shôrt'livd'] a de courte durée.
shortly [shôrt'lē] ad bientôt, sous peu.
shortness [shôrt'nis] n brièveté f.
shorts [shôrts] npl (also: **a pair of ~**) un
short.
shortsighted [shôrt'sī'tid] a myope; (fig) qui
manque de clairvoyance.
short-staffed [shôrt'staft'] a à court de
personnel.
short story n nouvelle f.
short-tempered [shôrt'tempûrd] a qui
s'emporte facilement.
short-term [shôrt'tûrm'] a (effect) à court
terme.
short time n: **to work ~, to be on ~**
(INDUSTRY) être en chômage partiel, travailler à horaire réduit.
short wave n (RADIO) ondes courtes.
shot [shât] pt, pp of **shoot** ♦ n coup m (de
feu); (shotgun pellets) plombs mpl; (person)
tireur m; (try) coup, essai m; (MED) piqûre
f; (PHOT) photo f; **to fire a ~ at sb/sth** tirer
sur qn/qch; **to have a ~ at (doing) sth**
essayer de faire qch; **like a ~** comme une
flèche; (very readily) sans hésiter; **to get ~
of sb/sth** (col) se débarrasser de qn/qch; **a
big ~** (col) un gros bonnet.
shotgun [shât'gun] n fusil m de chasse.
should [shood] auxiliary vb: **I ~ go now** je
devrais partir maintenant; **he ~ be there
now** il devrait être arrivé maintenant; **~ he
phone ...** si jamais il téléphone ....
shoulder [shōl'dûr] n épaule f; (Brit: of
road): **hard ~** accotement m ♦ vt (fig)
endosser, se charger de; **to look over one's
~** regarder derrière soi (en tournant la tête);
to rub ~s with sb (fig) côtoyer qn; **to give
sb the cold ~** (fig) battre froid à qn.
shoulder bag n sac m à bandoulière.
shoulder blade n omoplate f.
shoulder strap n bretelle f.
shouldn't [shood'ənt] = **should not.**
shout [shout] n cri m ♦ vt crier ♦ vi crier,
pousser des cris; **to give sb a ~** appeler qn.
  shout down vt huer.
shouting [shout'ing] n cris mpl.
shove [shuv] vt pousser; (col: put): **to ~ sth
in** fourrer or ficher qch dans ♦ n poussée f;
he ~d me out of the way il m'a écarté en
me poussant.
  shove off vi (NAUT) pousser au large; (fig:
  col) ficher le camp.
shovel [shuv'əl] n pelle f ♦ vt pelleter, enlever
(or enfourner) à la pelle.
show [shō] n (of emotion) manifestation f, démonstration f; (semblance) semblant m,
apparence f; (exhibition) exposition f, salon

m; (*THEATER*) spectacle *m*, représentation *f*; (*CINEMA*) séance *f* ♦ *vb* (*pt* ~**ed**, *pp* **shown** [shŏd, shōn]) *vt* montrer; (*courage etc*) faire preuve de, manifester; (*exhibit*) exposer ♦ *vi* se voir, être visible; **to ~ sb to his seat/to the door** accompagner qn jusqu'à sa place/la porte; **to ~ a profit/loss** (*COMM*) indiquer un bénéfice/une perte; **it just goes to ~ that ...** ça prouve bien que ...; **to ask for a ~ of hands** demander que l'on vote à main levée; **to be on ~** être exposé(e); **it's just for ~** c'est juste pour l'effet; **who's running the ~ here?** (*col*) qui est-ce qui commande ici?
show in *vt* faire entrer.
show off *vi* (*pej*) crâner ♦ *vt* (*display*) faire valoir; (*pej*) faire étalage de.
show out *vt* reconduire à la porte.
show up *vi* (*stand out*) ressortir; (*col: turn up*) se montrer ♦ *vt* démontrer; (*unmask*) démasquer, dénoncer.
show business *n* le monde du spectacle.
showcase [shō'kās] *n* vitrine *f*.
showdown [shō'doun] *n* épreuve *f* de force.
shower [shou'ûr] *n* (*also:* ~ **bath**) douche *f*; (*rain*) averse *f*; (*of stones etc*) pluie *f*, grêle *f*; (*US: party*) réunion organisée pour la remise de cadeaux ♦ *vi* prendre une douche, se doucher ♦ *vt*: **to ~ sb with** (*gifts etc*) combler qn de; (*abuse etc*) accabler qn de; (*missiles*) bombarder qn de; **to have** *or* **take a ~** prendre une douche, se doucher.
shower cap *n* bonnet *m* de douche.
showerproof [shou'ûrprōōf] *a* imperméable.
showery [shou'ûrē] *a* (*weather*) pluvieux(euse).
showground [shō'ground] *n* (*Brit*) champ *m* de foire.
showing [shō'ing] *n* (*of film*) projection *f*.
show jumping [shō' jum'ping] *n* concours *m* hippique.
showman [shō'mən] *n* (*at fair, circus*) forain *m*; (*fig*) comédien *m*.
showmanship [shō'mənship] *n* art *m* de la mise en scène.
shown [shōn] *pp of* **show**.
show-off [shō'ôf] *n* (*col: person*) crâneur/euse, m'as-tu-vu/e.
showpiece [shō'pēs] *n* (*of exhibition etc*) joyau *m*, clou *m*; **that hospital is a ~** cet hôpital est un modèle du genre.
showroom [shō'rōōm] *n* magasin *m or* salle *f* d'exposition.
showy [shō'ē] *a* tapageur(euse).
shrank [shrangk] *pt of* **shrink**.
shrapnel [shrap'nəl] *n* éclats *mpl* d'obus.
shred [shred] *n* (*gen pl*) lambeau *m*, petit morceau; (*fig: of truth, evidence*) parcelle *f* ♦ *vt* mettre en lambeaux, déchirer; (*documents*) détruire; (*CULIN*) râper; couper en lanières.
shredder [shred'ûr] *n* (*for vegetables*) râpeur *m*; (*for documents, papers*) déchiqueteuse *f*.
shrewd [shrōōd] *a* astucieux(euse), perspicace.
shrewdness [shrōōd'nis] *n* perspicacité *f*.
shriek [shrēk] *n* cri perçant *or* aigu, hurlement *m* ♦ *vt*, *vi* hurler, crier.
shrift [shrift] *n*: **to give sb short ~** expédier qn sans ménagements.

shrill [shril] *a* perçant(e), aigu(ë), strident(e).
shrimp [shrimp] *n* crevette grise.
shrine [shrīn] *n* châsse *f*; (*place*) lieu *m* de pèlerinage.
shrink [shringk], *pt* **shrank**, *pp* **shrunk** [shringk, shrangk, shrungk] *vi* rétrécir; (*fig*) se réduire; se contracter ♦ *vt* (*wool*) (faire) rétrécir ♦ *n* (*col: pej*) psychanalyste *m/f*; **to ~ from (doing) sth** reculer devant (la pensée de faire) qch.
shrinkage [shringk'ij] *n* (*of clothes*) rétrécissement *m*.
shrink-wrap [shringk'rap] *vt* emballer sous film plastique.
shrivel [shriv'əl] (*also:* ~ **up**) *vt* ratatiner, flétrir ♦ *vi* se ratatiner, se flétrir.
shroud [shroud] *n* linceul *m* ♦ *vt*: ~**ed in mystery** enveloppé(e) de mystère.
Shrove Tuesday [shrōv tōōz'dā] *n* (le) Mardi gras.
shrub [shrub] *n* arbuste *m*.
shrubbery [shrub'ûrē] *n* massif *m* d'arbustes.
shrug [shrug] *n* haussement *m* d'épaules ♦ *vt*, *vi*: **to ~ (one's shoulders)** hausser les épaules.
shrug off *vt* faire fi de; (*cold, illness*) se débarrasser de.
shrunk [shrungk] *pp of* **shrink**.
shrunken [shrungk'ən] *a* ratatiné(e).
shudder [shud'ûr] *n* frisson *m*, frémissement *m* ♦ *vi* frissonner, frémir.
shuffle [shuf'əl] *vt* (*cards*) battre; **to ~ (one's feet)** traîner les pieds.
shun [shun] *vt* éviter, fuir.
shunt [shunt] *vt* (*RAIL: direct*) aiguiller; (: *divert*) détourner ♦ *vi*: **to ~ (to and fro)** faire la navette.
shunting [shun'ting] *n* (*RAIL*) triage *m*.
shush [shush] *excl* chut!
shut, *pt*, *pp* **shut** [shut] *vt* fermer ♦ *vi* (se) fermer.
shut down *vt* fermer définitivement; (*machine*) arrêter ♦ *vi* fermer définitivement.
shut off *vt* couper, arrêter.
shut out *vt* (*person, cold*) empêcher d'entrer; (*noise*) éviter d'entendre; (*block: view*) boucher; (: *memory of sth*) chasser de son esprit.
shut up *vi* (*col: keep quiet*) se taire ♦ *vt* (*close*) fermer; (*silence*) faire taire.
shutdown [shut'doun] *n* fermeture *f*.
shutter [shut'ûr] *n* volet *m*; (*PHOT*) obturateur *m*.
shuttle [shut'əl] *n* navette *f*; (*also:* ~ **service**) (service *m* de) navette *f* ♦ *vi* (*vehicle, person*) faire la navette ♦ *vt* (*passengers*) transporter par un système de navette.
shuttlecock [shut'əlkâk] *n* volant *m* (*de badminton*).
shy [shī] *a* timide; **to fight ~ of** se dérober devant; **to be ~ of doing sth** hésiter à faire qch, ne pas oser faire qch ♦ *vi*: **to ~ away from doing sth** (*fig*) craindre de faire qch.
shyness [shī'nis] *n* timidité *f*.
Siam [sīam'] *n* Siam *m*.
Siamese [sīəmēz'] *a*: ~ **cat** chat siamois; ~ **twins** (frères *mpl*) siamois, (sœurs *fpl*) siamoises.
Siberia [sībē'rēə] *n* Sibérie *f*.

siblings [sib'lingz] *npl* (*formal*) enfants *mpl* d'un même couple.

Sicilian [sisil'yən] *a* sicilien(ne) ♦ *n* Sicilien/ne.

Sicily [sis'ilē] *n* Sicile *f*.

sick [sik] *a* (*ill*) malade; (*vomiting*): **to be** ~ vomir; (*humor*) noir(e), macabre; **to feel** ~ **to one's stomach** avoir envie de vomir, avoir mal au cœur; **to fall** ~ tomber malade; **to be (off)** ~ être absent(e) pour cause de maladie; **a** ~ **person** un(e) malade; **to be** ~ **of** (*fig*) en avoir assez de.

sick bay *n* infirmerie *f*.

sick benefit *n* (*US*) (prestations *fpl* de l')assurance-maladie *f*.

sicken [sik'ən] *vt* écœurer.

sickening [sik'əning] *a* (*fig*) écœurant(e), révoltant(e), répugnant(e).

sickle [sik'əl] *n* faucille *f*.

sick leave *n* congé *m* de maladie.

sickly [sik'lē] *a* maladif(ive), souffreteux(euse); (*causing nausea*) écœurant(e).

sickness [sik'nis] *n* maladie *f*; (*vomiting*) vomissement(s) *m(pl)*.

sickness benefit *n* (Brit) = **sick benefit**.

sick pay *n* indemnité *f* de maladie.

sickroom [sik'rōōm] *n* infirmerie *f*.

side [sīd] *n* côté *m*; (*of animal*) flanc *m*; (*of lake, road*) bord *m*; (*of mountain*) versant *m*; (*fig: aspect*) côté, aspect *m*; (*team: SPORT*) équipe *f* ♦ *cpd* (*door, entrance*) latéral(e) ♦ *vi*: **to** ~ **with sb** prendre le parti de qn, se ranger du côté de qn; **by the** ~ **of** au bord de; ~ **by** ~ côte à côte; **the right/ wrong** ~ le bon/mauvais côté, l'endroit/ l'envers *m*; **they are on our** ~ ils sont avec nous; **from all** ~**s** de tous côtés; **to take** ~**s (with)** prendre parti (pour); **a** ~ **of beef** ≈ un quartier de bœuf.

sideboard [sīd'bôrd] *n* buffet *m*.

sideburns [sīd'bûrnz] *npl* (*whiskers*) pattes *fpl*.

sidecar [sīd'kâr] *n* side-car *m*.

side dish *n* (plat *m* d')accompagnement *m*.

side drum *n* (*MUS*) tambour plat, caisse claire.

side effect *n* (*MED*) effet *m* secondaire.

sidekick [sīd'kik] *n* (col) sous-fifre *m*.

sidelight [sīd'līt] *n* (*AUT*) veilleuse *f*.

sideline [sīd'līn] *n* (*SPORT*) (ligne *f* de) touche *f*; (*fig*) activité *f* secondaire.

sidelong [sīd'lông] *a*: **to give sb a** ~ **glance** regarder qn du coin de l'œil.

side plate *n* petite assiette.

side road *n* petite route, route transversale.

sidesaddle [sīd'sadəl] *ad* en amazone.

sideshow [sīd'shō] *n* attraction *f*.

sidestep [sīd'step] *vt* (*question*) éluder; (*problem*) éviter ♦ *vi* (*BOXING etc*) esquiver.

side street *n* rue transversale.

sidetrack [sīd'trak] *vt* (*fig*) faire dévier de son sujet.

sidewalk [sīd'wôk] *n* (*US*) trottoir *m*.

sideways [sīd'wāz] *ad* de côté.

siding [sī'ding] *n* (*RAIL*) voie *f* de garage.

sidle [sī'dəl] *vi*: **to** ~ **up (to)** s'approcher furtivement (de).

siege [sēj] *n* siège *m*; **to lay** ~ **to** assiéger.

siege economy *n* économie *f* de (temps de) siège.

Sierra Leone [sēăr'ə lēōn'] *n* Sierra Leone *f*.

sieve [siv] *n* tamis *m*, passoire *f* ♦ *vt* tamiser, passer (au tamis).

sift [sift] *vt* passer au tamis *or* au crible; (*fig*) passer au crible ♦ *vi* (*fig*): **to** ~ **through** passer en revue.

sigh [sī] *n* soupir *m* ♦ *vi* soupirer, pousser un soupir.

sight [sīt] *n* (*faculty*) vue *f*; (*spectacle*) spectacle *m*; (*on gun*) mire *f* ♦ *vt* apercevoir; **in** ~ visible; (*fig*) en vue; **out of** ~ hors de vue; **on** ~ (*COMM*) à vue; **at first** ~ à première vue, au premier abord; **I know her by** ~ je la connais de vue; **to catch** ~ **of sb/sth** apercevoir qn/qch; **to lose** ~ **of sb/ sth** perdre qn/qch de vue; **to set one's** ~**s on sth** jeter son dévolu sur qch.

sighted [sī'tid] *a* qui voit; **partially** ~ qui a un certain degré de vision.

sightseeing [sīt'sēing] *n* tourisme *m*; **to go** ~ faire du tourisme.

sightseer [sīt'sēr] *n* touriste *m/f*.

sign [sīn] *n* (*gen*) signe *m*; (*with hand etc*) signe, geste *m*; (*notice*) panneau *m*, écriteau *m*; (*also*: **road** ~) panneau de signalisation ♦ *vt* signer; **as a** ~ **of** en signe de; **it's a good/bad** ~ c'est bon/mauvais signe; **plus/ minus** ~ signe plus/moins; **there's no** ~ **of a change of mind** rien ne laisse présager un revirement; **he was showing** ~**s of improvement** il commençait visiblement à faire des progrès; **to** ~ **one's name** signer.

sign away *vt* (*rights etc*) renoncer officiellement à.

sign in *vi* signer le registre (en arrivant).

sign off *vi* (*RADIO, TV*) terminer l'émission.

sign on *vi* (*as unemployed*) s'inscrire au chômage; (*enrol*): **to** ~ **on for a course** s'inscrire pour un cours ♦ *vt* (*MIL*) engager; (*employee*) embaucher.

sign out *vi* signer le registre (en partant).

sign over *vt*: **to** ~ **sth over to sb** céder qch par écrit à qn.

sign up (*MIL*) *vt* engager ♦ *vi* s'engager.

signal [sig'nəl] *n* signal *m* ♦ *vi* (*AUT*) mettre son clignotant ♦ *vt* (*person*) faire signe à; (*message*) communiquer par signaux; **to** ~ **a left/right turn** (*AUT*) indiquer *or* signaler que l'on tourne à gauche/droite; **to** ~ **to sb (to do sth)** faire signe à qn (de faire qch).

signal box *n* (Brit *RAIL*) poste *m* d'aiguillage.

signalman [sig'nəlmən] *n* (*RAIL*) aiguilleur *m*.

signatory [sig'nətôrē] *n* signataire *m/f*.

signature [sig'nəchûr] *n* signature *f*.

signature tune *n* indicatif musical.

signet ring [sig'nit ring] *n* chevalière *f*.

significance [signif'əkəns] *n* signification *f*; importance *f*; **that is of no** ~ ceci n'a pas d'importance.

significant [signif'ikənt] *a* significatif(ive); (*important*) important(e), considérable.

significantly [signif'ikəntlē] *ad* (*improve, increase*) sensiblement; (*smile*) d'un air entendu, éloquemment; ~, ... fait significatif, ...

signify [sig'nəfī] *vt* signifier.

sign language *n* langage *m* par signes.

signpost [sīn'pōst] *n* poteau indicateur.

silage [sī'lij] *n* (*fodder*) fourrage vert; (*meth-*

od) ensilage *m*.

silence [sī'ləns] *n* silence *m* ♦ *vt* faire taire, réduire au silence.

silencer [sī'lənsûr] *n* (*on gun, Brit AUT*) silencieux *m*.

silent [sī'lənt] *a* silencieux(euse); (*film*) muet(te); **to keep** *or* **remain** ~ garder le silence, ne rien dire.

silently [sī'ləntlē] *ad* silencieusement.

silent partner *n* (*US COMM*) bailleur *m* de fonds, commanditaire *m*.

silhouette [silōōet'] *n* silhouette *f* ♦ *vt*: ~**d against** se profilant sur, se découpant contre.

silicon [sil'ikən] *n* silicium *m*.

silicon chip [sil'ikən chip'] *n* puce *f* électronique.

silicone [sil'əkōn] *n* silicone *f*.

silk [silk] *n* soie *f* ♦ *cpd* de *or* en soie.

silky [sil'kē] *a* soyeux(euse).

sill [sil] *n* (*also*: **window~**) rebord *m* (de la fenêtre); (*of door*) seuil *m*; (*AUT*) bas *m* de marche.

silly [sil'ē] *a* stupide, sot(te), bête; **to do something** ~ faire une bêtise.

silo [sī'lō] *n* silo *m*.

silt [silt] *n* vase *f*; limon *m*.

silver [sil'vûr] *n* argent *m*; (*money*) monnaie *f* (en pièces d'argent); (*also*: ~**ware**) argenterie *f* ♦ *cpd* d'argent, en argent.

silver foil *n* papier *m* d'argent *or* d'étain.

silver-plated [sil'vûrplā'tid] *a* plaqué(e) argent.

silversmith [sil'vûrsmith] *n* orfèvre *m/f*.

silverware [sil'vûrwär] *n* argenterie *f*.

silver wedding (anniversary) *n* noces *fpl* d'argent.

silvery [sil'vûrē] *a* argenté(e).

similar [sim'əlûr] *a*: ~ **(to)** semblable (à).

similarity [siməlar'itē] *n* ressemblance *f*, similarité *f*.

similarly [sim'əlûrlē] *ad* de la même façon, de même.

simile [sim'əlē] *n* comparaison *f*.

simmer [sim'ûr] *vi* cuire à feu doux, mijoter.

simmer down *vi* (*fig: col*) se calmer.

simper [sim'pûr] *vi* minauder.

simpering [sim'pûring] *a* stupide.

simple [sim'pəl] *a* simple; **the** ~ **truth** la vérité pure et simple.

simple interest *n* (*MATH. COMM*) intérêts *mpl* simples.

simple-minded [sim'pəlmīn'did] *a* simplet(te), simple d'esprit.

simpleton [sim'pəltən] *n* nigaud/e, niais/e.

simplicity [simplis'ətē] *n* simplicité *f*.

simplification [simpləfəkā'shən] *n* simplification *f*.

simplify [sim'pləfī] *vt* simplifier.

simply [sim'plē] *ad* simplement; (*without fuss*) avec simplicité.

simulate [sim'yəlāt] *vt* simuler, feindre.

simulation [simyəlā'shən] *n* simulation *f*.

simultaneous [sīməltā'nēəs] *a* simultané(e).

simultaneously [sīməltā'nēəslē] *ad* simultanément.

sin [sin] *n* péché *m* ♦ *vi* pécher.

Sinai [sī'nī] *n* Sinaï *m*.

since [sins] *ad*, *prep* depuis ♦ *cj* (*time*) depuis que; (*because*) puisque, étant donné que,

comme; ~ **then** depuis ce moment-là; ~ **Monday** depuis lundi; **(ever)** ~ **I arrived** depuis mon arrivée, depuis que je suis arrivé.

sincere [sinsēr'] *a* sincère.

sincerely [sinsēr'lē] *ad* sincèrement; ~ **yours**, (*Brit*) **yours** ~ (*at end of letter*) veuillez agréer, Monsieur (*or* Madame), l'expression de mes sentiments distingués *or* les meilleurs.

sincerity [sinsär'itē] *n* sincérité *f*.

sine [sīn] *n* (*MATH*) sinus *m*.

sinew [sin'yōō] *n* tendon *m*; ~**s** *npl* muscles *mpl*.

sinful [sin'fəl] *a* coupable.

sing, *pt* **sang**, *pp* **sung** [sing, sang, sung] *vt*, *vi* chanter.

Singapore [sing'gəpôr] *n* Singapour *m*.

singe [sinj] *vt* brûler légèrement; (*clothes*) roussir.

singer [sing'ûr] *n* chanteur/euse.

Singhalese [singəlēz'] *a* = **Sinhalese**.

singing [sing'ing] *n* (*of person, bird*) chant *m*; façon *f* de chanter; (*of kettle, bullet, in ears*) sifflement *m*.

single [sing'gəl] *a* seul(e), unique; (*unmarried*) célibataire; (*not double*) simple ♦ *n* (*Brit: also*: ~ **ticket**) aller *m* (simple); (*record*) 45 tours *m*; **not a** ~ **one was left** il n'en est pas resté un(e) seul(e); **every** ~ **day** chaque jour sans exception.

single out *vt* choisir; distinguer.

single bed *n* lit à une place.

single-breasted [sing'gəlbres'tid] *a* droit(e).

single file *n*: **in** ~ en file indienne.

single-handed [sing'gəlhan'did] *ad* tout(e) seul(e), sans (aucune) aide.

single-minded [sing'gəlmīn'did] *a* résolu(e), tenace.

single parent *n* parent unique (*or* célibataire).

single room *n* chambre *f* à un lit *or* pour une personne.

singles [sing'gəlz] *npl* (*TENNIS*) simple *m*; (*US: single people*) célibataires *m/fpl*.

singly [sing'glē] *ad* séparément.

singsong [sing'sông] *a* (*tone*) chantant(e).

singular [sing'gyəlûr] *a* singulier(ière); (*odd*) singulier, étrange; (*LING*) (au) singulier, du singulier ♦ *n* (*LING*) singulier *m*; **in the feminine** ~ au féminin singulier.

singularly [sing'gyəlûrlē] *ad* singulièrement, étrangement.

Sinhalese [sinhəlēz'] *a* cingalais(e).

sinister [sin'istûr] *a* sinistre.

sink [singk] *n* évier *m* ♦ *vb* (*pt* **sank**, *pp* **sunk** [sangk, sungk]) *vt* (*ship*) couler, faire sombrer; (*foundations*) creuser; (*piles etc*): **to** ~ **sth into** enfoncer qch dans ♦ *vi* couler, sombrer; (*ground etc*) s'affaisser; **he sank into a chair/the mud** il s'est enfoncé dans un fauteuil/la boue; **a** ~**ing feeling** un serrement de cœur.

sink in *vi* s'enfoncer, pénétrer; (*explanation*): **it took a long time to** ~ **in** il a fallu longtemps pour que ça rentre.

sinking fund [sing'king fund] *n* fonds *mpl* d'amortissement.

sink unit *n* bloc-évier *m*.

sinner [sin'ûr] *n* pécheur/eresse.

Sino- [sī'nō] *prefix* sino-.
sinuous [sin'yŌŌəs] *a* sinueux(euse).
sinus [sī'nəs] *n* (ANAT) sinus *m inv*.
sip [sip] *n* petite gorgée ♦ *vt* boire à petites gorgées.
siphon [sī'fən] *n* siphon *m* ♦ *vt* (*also:* ~ **off**) siphonner; (: *fig: funds*) transférer; (: *illegally*) détourner.
sir [sûr] *n* monsieur *m*; **S~ John Smith** sir John Smith; **yes** ~ oui Monsieur; **Dear S~** (*in letter*) Monsieur.
siren [sī'rən] *n* sirène *f*.
sirloin [sûr'loin] *n* aloyau *m*.
sirloin steak [sûr'loin stāk'] *n* bifteck *m* dans l'aloyau.
sirocco [sərák'ō] *n* sirocco *m*.
sisal [sī'səl] *n* sisal *m*.
sissy [sis'ē] *n* (*col: coward*) poule mouillée.
sister [sis'tûr] *n* sœur *f*; (*nun*) religieuse *f*, (bonne) sœur; (*Brit: nurse*) infirmière *f* en chef ♦ *cpd*: ~ **organization** organisation *f* sœur; ~ **ship** sister(-)ship *m*.
sister-in-law [sis'tûrinlô] *n* belle-sœur *f*.
sit, *pt, pp* **sat** [sit, sat] *vi* s'asseoir; (*assembly*) être en séance, siéger; (*for painter*) poser; (*dress etc*) tomber ♦ *vt* (*exam*) passer, se présenter à; **to** ~ **on a committee** faire partie d'un comité; **to** ~ **tight** ne pas bouger.
sit about *vi* (*Brit*) = **sit around**.
sit around *vi* être assis(e) *or* rester à ne rien faire.
sit back *vi* (*in seat*) bien s'installer, se carrer.
sit down *vi* s'asseoir; **to be ~ting down** être assis(e).
sit in *vi*: **to** ~ **in on a discussion** assister à une discussion.
sit up *vi* s'asseoir; (*not go to bed*) rester debout, ne pas se coucher.
sitcom [sit'kâm] *n abbr* (TV: = *situation comedy*) série *f* comique.
sit-down [sit'doun] *a*: **a** ~ **strike** une grève sur le tas; **a** ~ **meal** un repas assis.
site [sīt] *n* emplacement *m*, site *m*; (*also:* **building** ~) chantier *m* ♦ *vt* placer.
sit-in [sit'in] *n* (*demonstration*) sit-in *m inv*, occupation *f* de locaux.
siting [sī'ting] *n* (*location*) emplacement *m*.
sitter [sit'ûr] *n* (*also:* **baby**~) baby-sitter *m/f*.
sitting [sit'ing] *n* (*of assembly etc*) séance *f*; (*in canteen*) service *m*.
sitting member *n* (POL) parlementaire *m/f* en exercice.
sitting room *n* salon *m*.
situate [sich'ŌŌāt] *vt* situer.
situated [sich'ŌŌātid] *a* situé(e).
situation [sichŌŌā'shən] *n* situation *f*.
situation comedy *n* (THEATER) comédie *f* de situation.
six [siks] *num* six.
sixteen [siks'tēn'] *num* seize.
sixteenth note [siks'tēnth' nōt] *n* (US) double croche *f*.
sixth [siksth] *a* sixième; **the upper/lower** ~ (*Brit* SCOL) la terminale/la première.
sixty [siks'tē] *num* soixante.
size [sīz] *n* dimensions *fpl*; (*of person*) taille *f*; (*of estate, area*) étendue *f*; (*of problem*) ampleur *f*; (*of company*) importance *f*; (*of clothing*) taille; (*of shoes*) pointure *f*; (*glue*) colle *f*; **I take** ~ **14** (*of dress etc*) ≈ je prends du 42 *or* la taille 42; **the small/large** ~ (*of soap powder etc*) le petit/grand modèle; **it's the** ~ **of** ... c'est de la taille (*or* grosseur) de ..., c'est grand (*or* gros) comme ...; **cut to** ~ découpé(e) aux dimensions voulues.
size up *vt* juger, jauger.
sizeable [sī'zəbəl] *a* assez grand(e) *or* gros(se); assez important(e).
sizzle [siz'əl] *vi* grésiller.
SK *abbr* (*Canada*) = *Saskatchewan*.
skate [skāt] *n* patin *m*; (*fish: pl inv*) raie *f* ♦ *vi* patiner.
skate over, skate around *vt* (*problem, issue*) éluder.
skateboard [skāt'bôrd] *n* skateboard *m*, planche *f* à roulettes.
skater [skā'tûr] *n* patineur/euse.
skating [skā'ting] *n* patinage *m*.
skating rink *n* patinoire *f*.
skeleton [skel'itən] *n* squelette *m*; (*outline*) schéma *m*.
skeleton key *n* passe-partout *m*.
skeleton staff *n* effectifs réduits.
skeptic [skep'tik] *n* (US) sceptique *m/f*.
skeptical [skep'tikəl] *a* sceptique.
skepticism [skep'tisizəm] *n* scepticisme *m*.
sketch [skech] *n* (*drawing*) croquis *m*, esquisse *f*; (THEATER) sketch *m*, saynète *f* ♦ *vt* esquisser, faire un croquis *or* une esquisse de.
sketch book *n* carnet *m* à dessin.
sketch pad *n* bloc *m* à dessin.
sketchy [skech'ē] *a* incomplet(ète), fragmentaire.
skew [skyŌŌ] *n* (*Brit*): **on the** ~ de travers, en biais.
skewer [skyŌŌ'ûr] *n* brochette *f*.
ski [skē] *n* ski *m* ♦ *vi* skier, faire du ski.
ski boot *n* chaussure *f* de ski.
skid [skid] *n* dérapage *m* ♦ *vi* déraper; **to go into a** ~ déraper.
skid mark *n* trace *f* de dérapage.
skier [skē'ûr] *n* skieur/euse.
skiing [skē'ing] *n* ski *m*; **to go** ~ (aller) faire du ski.
ski instructor *n* moniteur/trice de ski.
ski jump *n* (*ramp*) tremplin *m*; (*event*) saut *m* à skis.
skilful [skil'fəl] *etc* = **skillful** *etc*.
ski lift *n* remonte-pente *m inv*.
skill [skil] *n* (*ability*) habileté *f*, adresse *f*, talent *m*; (*art, craft*) technique(s) *f(pl)*, compétences *fpl*.
skilled [skild] *a* habile, adroit(e); (*worker*) qualifié(e).
skillet [skil'it] *n* poêlon *m*.
skillful [skil'fəl] *a* (US) habile, adroit(e).
skillfully [skil'fəlē] *ad* habilement, adroitement.
skim [skim] *vt* (*milk*) écrémer; (*soup*) écumer; (*glide over*) raser, effleurer ♦ *vi*: **to** ~ **through** (*fig*) parcourir.
skimmed milk [skimd milk] *n* lait écrémé.
skimp [skimp] *vt* (*work*) bâcler, faire à la va-vite; (*cloth etc*) lésiner sur.
skimpy [skim'pē] *a* étriqué(e); maigre.
skin [skin] *n* peau *f* ♦ *vt* (*fruit etc*) éplucher; (*animal*) écorcher; **wet** *or* **soaked to the** ~

trempé(e) jusqu'aux os.

skin-deep [skin'dēp'] *a* superficiel(le).

skin diver *n* plongeur/euse sous-marin(e).

skin diving *n* plongée sous-marine.

skinflint [skin'flint] *n* grippe-sou *m*.

skin graft *n* greffe *f* de peau.

skinny [skin'ē] *a* maigre, maigrichon(ne).

skin test *n* cuti(-réaction) *f*.

skintight [skin'tīt] *a* (*dress etc*) collant(e), ajusté(e).

skip [skip] *n* petit bond *or* saut; (*Brit: container*) benne *f* ♦ *vi* gambader, sautiller; (*with rope*) sauter à la corde ♦ *vt* (*pass over*) sauter; **to ~ school** (*esp US*) faire l'école buissonnière.

ski pants *npl* pantalon *m* de ski.

ski pole *n* bâton *m* de ski.

skipper [skip'ûr] *n* (*NAUT, SPORT*) capitaine *m* ♦ *vt* (*boat*) commander; (*team*) être le chef de.

skipping rope [skip'ing rōp] *n* (*Brit*) corde *f* à sauter.

ski resort *n* station *f* de sports d'hiver.

skirmish [skûr'mish] *n* escarmouche *f*, accrochage *m*.

skirt [skûrt] *n* jupe *f* ♦ *vt* longer, contourner.

skirting board [skûr'ting bōrd] *n* (*Brit*) plinthe *f*.

ski run *n* piste *f* de ski.

ski suit *n* combinaison *f* de ski.

skit [skit] *n* sketch *m* satirique.

ski tow *n* = **ski lift**.

skittle [skit'əl] *n* quille *f*; **~s** (*game*) (jeu *m* de) quilles *fpl*.

skive [skīv] *vi* (*Brit col*) tirer au flanc.

skulk [skulk] *vi* rôder furtivement.

skull [skul] *n* crâne *m*.

skullcap [skul'kap] *n* calotte *f*.

skunk [skungk] *n* mouffette *f*; (*fur*) sconse *m*.

sky [skī] *n* ciel *m*; **to praise sb to the skies** porter qn aux nues.

sky-blue [skī'blōō'] *a* bleu ciel *inv*.

sky-high [skī'hī'] *ad* très haut ♦ *a*: **prices are ~** les prix sont exorbitants.

skylark [skī'lârk] *n* (*bird*) alouette *f* (des champs).

skylight [skī'līt] *n* lucarne *f*.

skyline [skī'līn] *n* (*horizon*) (ligne *f* d')horizon *m*; (*of city*) ligne des toits.

skyscraper [skī'skrāpûr] *n* gratte-ciel *m inv*.

slab [slab] *n* plaque *f*; dalle *f*; (*of wood*) bloc *m*; (*of meat, cheese*) tranche épaisse.

slack [slak] *a* (*loose*) lâche, desserré(e); (*slow*) stagnant(e); (*careless*) négligent(e), peu sérieux(euse) *or* consciencieux(euse); (*COMM: market*) peu actif(ive); (: *demand*) faible; (*period*) creux(euse) ♦ *n* (*in rope etc*) mou *m*; **business is ~** les affaires vont mal.

slacken [slak'ən] (*also*: **~ off**) *vi* ralentir, diminuer ♦ *vt* relâcher.

slacks [slaks] *npl* pantalon *m*.

slag [slag] *n* scories *fpl*.

slag heap *n* crassier *m*.

slain [slān] *pp of* **slay**.

slake [slāk] *vt* (*one's thirst*) étancher.

slalom [slâ'ləm] *n* slalom *m*.

slam [slam] *vt* (*door*) (faire) claquer; (*throw*) jeter violemment, flanquer; (*criticize*) éreinter, démolir ♦ *vi* claquer.

slander [slan'dûr] *n* calomnie *f*; (*LAW*) diffamation *f* ♦ *vt* calomnier; diffamer.

slanderous [slan'dûrəs] *a* calomnieux(euse); diffamatoire.

slang [slang] *n* argot *m*.

slant [slant] *n* inclinaison *f*; (*fig*) angle *m*, point *m* de vue.

slanted [slan'tid] *a* tendancieux(euse).

slanting [slan'ting] *a* en pente, incliné(e); couché(e).

slap [slap] *n* claque *f*, gifle *f*; (*on the back*) tape *f* ♦ *vt* donner une claque *or* une gifle (*or* une tape) à ♦ *ad* (*directly*) tout droit, en plein.

slapdash [slap'dash] *a* (*work*) fait(e) sans soin *or* à la va-vite; (*person*) insouciant(e), négligent(e).

slapstick [slap'stik] *n* (*comedy*) grosse farce, style *m* tarte à la crème.

slash [slash] *vt* entailler, taillader; (*fig: prices*) casser.

slat [slat] *n* (*of wood*) latte *f*, lame *f*.

slate [slāt] *n* ardoise *f* ♦ *vt* (*fig: criticize*) éreinter, démolir.

slaughter [slô'tûr] *n* carnage *m*, massacre *m*; (*of animals*) abattage *m* ♦ *vt* (*animal*) abattre; (*people*) massacrer.

slaughterhouse [slô'tûrhous] *n* abattoir *m*.

Slav [slâv] *a* slave.

slave [slāv] *n* esclave *m/f* ♦ *vi* (*also*: **~ away**) trimer, travailler comme un forçat; **to ~ (away) at sth/at doing sth** se tuer à qch/à faire qch.

slave labor *n* travail *m* d'esclave; **it's just ~** (*fig*) c'est de l'esclavage.

slaver [slā'vûr] *vi* (*dribble*) baver.

slavery [slā'vûrē] *n* esclavage *m*.

Slavic [slâv'ik] *a* slave.

slavish [slā'vish] *a* servile.

Slavonic [sləvân'ik] *a* slave.

slay [slā], *pt* **slew** [slōō], *pp* **slain** [slā, slōō, slān] *vt* (*literary*) tuer.

SLD *n abbr* (*Brit POL*) = **Social and Liberal Democratic Party**.

sleazy [slē'zē] *a* miteux(euse), minable.

sled [sled] *n* (*US*) luge *f*.

sledge [slej] *n* (*Brit*) = **sled**.

sledgehammer [slej'hamûr] *n* marteau *m* de forgeron.

sleek [slēk] *a* (*hair, fur*) brillant(e), luisant(e); (*car, boat*) aux lignes pures *or* élégantes.

sleep [slēp] *n* sommeil *m* ♦ *vi* (*pt, pp* **slept** [slept]) dormir; (*spend night*) dormir, coucher ♦ *vt*: **we can ~ 4** on peut coucher *or* loger 4 personnes; **to go to ~** s'endormir; **to have a good night's ~** passer une bonne nuit; **to put to ~** (*patient*) endormir; (*animal: euphemism: kill*) piquer; **to ~ lightly** avoir le sommeil léger; **to ~ with sb** (*euphemism*) coucher avec qn.

sleep in *vi* (*lie late*) faire la grasse matinée; (*oversleep*) se réveiller trop tard.

sleeper [slē'pûr] *n* (*person*) dormeur/euse; (*US: for baby*) grenouillère *f*; (*Brit RAIL: on track*) traverse *f*; (: *train*) train *m* de voitures-lits; (: *carriage*) wagon-lits *m*, voiture-lits *f*; (: *berth*) couchette *f*.

sleepily [slēp'ilē] *ad* d'un air endormi.

sleeping [slē'ping] *a* qui dort, endormi(e).
sleeping bag [slē'ping bag] *n* sac *m* de couchage.
sleeping car *n* wagon-lits *m*, voiture-lits *f*.
sleeping partner *n* (*Brit* COMM) = **silent partner**.
sleeping pill *n* somnifère *m*.
sleepless [slēp'lis] *a*: **a ~ night** une nuit blanche.
sleeplessness [slēp'lisnis] *n* insomnie *f*.
sleepwalker [slēp'wôkûr] *n* somnambule *m/f*.
sleepy [slē'pē] *a* qui a envie de dormir; (*fig*) endormi(e); **to be** *or* **feel ~** avoir sommeil, avoir envie de dormir.
sleet [slēt] *n* neige fondue.
sleeve [slēv] *n* manche *f*; (*of record*) pochette *f*.
sleeveless [slēv'lis] *a* (*garment*) sans manches.
sleigh [slā] *n* traîneau *m*.
sleight [slīt] *n*: **~ of hand** tour *m* de passe-passe.
slender [slen'dûr] *a* svelte, mince; (*fig*) faible, ténu(e).
slept [slept] *pt, pp of* **sleep**.
sleuth [slōōth] *n* (*col*) détective (privé).
slew [slōō] *vi* (*Brit*) = **slue** ♦ *pt of* **slay**.
slice [slīs] *n* tranche *f*; (*round*) rondelle *f* ♦ *vt* couper en tranches (*or* en rondelles); **~d bread** pain *m* en tranches.
slick [slik] *a* brillant(e) en apparence; mielleux(euse) ♦ *n* (*also*: **oil ~**) nappe *f* de pétrole, marée noire.
slid [slid] *pt, pp of* **slide**.
slide [slīd] *n* (*in playground*) toboggan *m*; (*PHOT*) diapositive *f*; (*Brit*: *also*: **hair ~**) barrette *f*; (*microscope ~*) (lame *f*) porte-objet *m*; (*in prices*) chute *f*, baisse *f* ♦ *vb* (*pt, pp* **slid** [slid]) *vt* (*faire*) glisser ♦ *vi* glisser; **to let things ~** (*fig*) laisser les choses aller à la dérive.
slide projector *n* (*PHOT*) projecteur *m* de diapositives.
slide rule *n* règle *f* à calcul.
sliding [slī'ding] *a* (*door*) coulissant(e); **~ roof** (*AUT*) toit ouvrant.
sliding scale *n* échelle *f* mobile.
slight [slīt] *a* (*slim*) mince, menu(e); (*frail*) frêle; (*trivial*) faible, insignifiant(e); (*small*) petit(e), léger(ère) (*before n*) ♦ *n* offense *f*, affront *m* ♦ *vt* (*offend*) blesser, offenser; **the ~est** le (*or* la) moindre; **not in the ~est** pas le moins du monde, pas du tout.
slightly [slīt'lē] *ad* légèrement, un peu; **~ built** fluet(te).
slim [slim] *a* mince ♦ *vi* maigrir, suivre un régime amaigrissant.
slime [slīm] *n* vase *f*; substance visqueuse.
slimming [slim'ing] *n* amaigrissement *m* ♦ *a* (*diet, pills*) amaigrissant(e), pour maigrir.
slimy [slī'mē] *a* visqueux(euse), gluant(e); (*covered with mud*) vaseux(euse).
sling [sling] *n* (*MED*) écharpe *f* ♦ *vt* (*pt, pp* **slung** [slung]) lancer, jeter; **to have one's arm in a ~** avoir le bras en écharpe.
slingshot [sling'shät] *n* (*US*) lance-pierres *m inv*, fronde *f*.
slink, *pt, pp* **slunk** [slingk, slungk] *vi*: **to ~ away** *or* **off** s'en aller furtivement.

slip [slip] *n* faux pas; (*mistake*) erreur *f*, bévue *f*; (*underskirt*) combinaison *f*; (*of paper*) petite feuille, fiche *f* ♦ *vt* (*slide*) glisser ♦ *vi* (*slide*) glisser; (*move smoothly*): **to ~ into/out of** se glisser *or* se faufiler dans/hors de; (*decline*) baisser; **to let a chance ~ by** laisser passer une occasion; **to ~ sth on/off** enfiler/enlever qch; **it ~ped from her hand** cela lui a glissé des mains; **to give sb the ~** fausser compagnie à qn; **a ~ of the tongue** un lapsus.
slip away *vi* s'esquiver.
slip in *vt* glisser.
slip out *vi* sortir.
slip-on [slip'än] *a* facile à enfiler; **~ shoes** mocassins *mpl*.
slipped disc [slipt disk] *n* déplacement *m* de vertèbres.
slipper [slip'ûr] *n* pantoufle *f*.
slippery [slip'ûrē] *a* glissant(e); (*fig: person*) insaisissable.
slip road *n* (*Brit*: *to freeway*) bretelle *f* d'accès.
slipshod [slip'shäd] *a* négligé(e), peu soigné(e).
slip-up [slip'up] *n* bévue *f*.
slipway [slip'wā] *n* cale *f* (de construction *or* de lancement).
slit [slit] *n* fente *f*; (*cut*) incision *f*; (*tear*) déchirure *f* ♦ *vt* (*pt, pp* **slit**) fendre; couper; inciser; déchirer; **to ~ sb's throat** trancher la gorge à qn.
slither [slith'ûr] *vi* glisser, déraper.
sliver [sliv'ûr] *n* (*of glass, wood*) éclat *m*; (*of cheese, sausage*) petit morceau.
slob [släb] *n* (*col*) rustaud/e.
slog [släg] *n* (*Brit*) gros effort; tâche fastidieuse ♦ *vi* travailler très dur.
slogan [slō'gən] *n* slogan *m*.
slop [släp] *vi* (*also*: **~ over**) se renverser; déborder ♦ *vt* répandre; renverser.
slope [slōp] *n* pente *f*; (*side of mountain*) versant *m*; (*slant*) inclinaison *f* ♦ *vi*: **to ~ down** être *or* descendre en pente; **to ~ up** monter.
sloping [slō'ping] *a* en pente, incliné(e); (*handwriting*) penché(e).
sloppy [släp'ē] *a* (*work*) peu soigné(e), bâclé(e); (*appearance*) négligé(e), débraillé(e); (*film etc*) sentimental(e).
slosh [släsh] *vi* (*col*): **to ~ around** (*children*) patauger; (*liquid*) clapoter.
sloshed [släsht] *a* (*col: drunk*) bourré(e).
slot [slät] *n* fente *f*; (*fig*: *in timetable, RADIO, TV*) créneau *m*, plage *f* ♦ *vt*: **to ~ into** encastrer *or* insérer dans ♦ *vi*: **to ~ into** s'encastrer *or* s'insérer dans.
sloth [slôth] *n* (*vice*) paresse *f*; (*ZOOL*) paresseux *m*.
slot machine *n* (*for gambling*) appareil *m or* machine *f* à sous; (*Brit*: *vending machine*) distributeur *m* (automatique), machine à sous.
slouch [slouch] *vi* avoir le dos rond, être voûté(e).
slouch about, slouch around *vi* traîner à ne rien faire.
slovenly [sluv'ənlē] *a* sale, débraillé(e), négligé(e).

slow [slō] *a* lent(e); (*watch*): **to be ~** retarder ♦ *ad* lentement ♦ *vt, vi* (*also:* **~ down, ~ up**) ralentir; **at a ~ speed** à petite vitesse; **to be ~ to act/decide** être lent à agir/décider; **my watch is 20 minutes ~** ma montre retarde de 20 minutes; **business is ~** les affaires marchent au ralenti; **to go ~** (*driver*) rouler lentement; (*in industrial dispute*) faire la grève perlée.

slow-acting [slō'ak'ting] *a* qui agit lentement, à action lente.

slowdown [slō'doun] *n* grève perlée.

slowly [slō'lē] *ad* lentement.

slow motion *n*: **in ~** au ralenti.

slowness [slō'nis] *n* lenteur *f*.

slowpoke [slō'pōk] *n* (*US*) tortue *f*.

sludge [sluj] *n* boue *f*.

slue [slōō] *vi* (*US*) (*also:* **~ around**) virer, pivoter.

slug [slug] *n* limace *f*; (*bullet*) balle *f*.

sluggish [slug'ish] *a* mou(molle), lent(e); (*business, sales*) stagnant(e).

sluice [slōōs] *n* écluse *f*; (*also:* **~ gate**) vanne *f* ♦ *vt*: **to ~ down** *or* **out** laver à grande eau.

slum [slum] *n* taudis *m*.

slumber [slum'bûr] *n* sommeil *m*.

slump [slump] *n* baisse soudaine, effondrement *m*; crise *f* ♦ *vi* s'effondrer, s'affaisser.

slung [slung] *pt, pp of* **sling**.

slunk [slungk] *pt, pp of* **slink**.

slur [slûr] *n* bredouillement *m*; (*smear*): **~ (on)** atteinte *f* (à); insinuation *f* (contre) ♦ *vt* mal articuler; **to be a ~ on** porter atteinte à.

slurred [slûrd] *a* (*pronunciation*) inarticulé(e), indistinct(e).

slush [slush] *n* neige fondue.

slush fund *n* caisse noire, fonds secrets.

slushy [slush'ē] *a* (*snow*) fondu(e); (*street*) couvert(e) de neige fondue; (*Brit fig*) à l'eau de rose.

slut [slut] *n* souillon *f*.

sly [slī] *a* rusé(e); sournois(e); **on the ~** en cachette.

smack [smak] *n* (*slap*) tape *f*; (*on face*) gifle *f* ♦ *vt* donner une tape à; gifler; (*child*) donner la fessée à ♦ *vi*: **to ~ of** avoir des relents de, sentir ♦ *ad* (*col*): **it fell ~ in the middle** c'est tombé en plein milieu *or* en plein dedans; **to ~ one's lips** se lécher les babines.

smacker [smak'ûr] *n* (*col: kiss*) bisou *m or* bise *f* sonore; (*: US: dollar bill*) dollar *m*; (*: Brit: pound note*) livre *f*.

small [smôl] *a* petit(e); (*letter*) minuscule ♦ *n*: **the ~ of the back** le creux des reins; **to get** *or* **grow ~er** diminuer; **to make ~er** (*amount, income*) diminuer; (*object, garment*) rapetisser; **a ~ storekeeper** un petit commerçant.

small ads *npl* (*Brit*) petites annonces.

small change *n* petite *or* menue monnaie.

smallholding [smôl'hōlding] *n* (*Brit*) petite ferme.

small hours *npl*: **in the ~** au petit matin.

smallish [smô'lish] *a* plutôt *or* assez petit(e).

small-minded [smôl'mīn'did] *a* mesquin(e).

smallpox [smôl'päks] *n* variole *f*.

small print *n* (*in contract etc*) clause(s) imprimée(s) en petits caractères.

small-scale [smôl'skāl] *a* (*map, model*) à échelle réduite, à petite échelle; (*business, farming*) peu important(e), modeste.

small talk *n* menus propos.

small-time [smôl'tim'] *a* (*farmer etc*) petit(e); **a ~ thief** un voleur à la petite semaine.

smart [smârt] *a* élégant(e), chic *inv*; (*clever*) intelligent(e); (*pej*) futé(e); (*quick*) vif(vive), prompt(e) ♦ *vi* faire mal, brûler; **the ~ set** le beau monde; **to look ~** être élégant(e); **my eyes are ~ing** j'ai les yeux irrités *or* qui me piquent.

smart-ass [smârt'as] *n* (*US col*) je-sais-tout *m/f*.

smarten up [smâr'tən up] *vi* devenir plus élégant(e), se faire beau(belle) ♦ *vt* rendre plus élégant(e).

smash [smash] *n* (*also:* **~-up**) collision *f*, accident *m*; (*sound*) fracas *m* ♦ *vt* casser, briser, fracasser; (*opponent*) écraser; (*hopes*) ruiner, détruire; (*SPORT: record*) pulvériser ♦ *vi* se briser, se fracasser; s'écraser.

smash up *vt* (*car*) bousiller; (*room*) tout casser dans.

smash hit *n* (grand) succès.

smattering [smat'ûring] *n*: **a ~ of** quelques notions de.

smear [smē'ûr] *n* tache *f*, salissure *f*; trace *f*; (*MED*) frottis *m*; (*insult*) calomnie *f* ♦ *vt* enduire; (*fig*) porter atteinte à; **his hands were ~ed with oil/ink** il avait les mains maculées de cambouis/d'encre.

smear campaign *n* campagne *f* de dénigrement.

smell [smel] *n* odeur *f*; (*sense*) odorat *m* ♦ *vb* (*pt, pp* **~ed** *or* **smelt** [smeld, smelt]) *vt* sentir ♦ *vi* (*food etc*): **to ~ (of)** sentir; (*pej*) sentir mauvais; **it ~s good** ça sent bon.

smelly [smel'ē] *a* qui sent mauvais, malodorant(e).

smelt [smelt] *pt, pp of* **smell** ♦ *vt* (*ore*) fondre.

smile [smīl] *n* sourire *m* ♦ *vi* sourire.

smiling [smī'ling] *a* souriant(e).

smirk [smûrk] *n* petit sourire suffisant *or* affecté.

smith [smith] *n* maréchal-ferrant *m*; forgeron *m*.

smithy [smith'ē] *n* forge *f*.

smitten [smit'ən] *a*: **~ with** pris(e) de; frappé(e) de.

smock [smäk] *n* blouse *f*, sarrau *m*.

smog [smäg] *n* brouillard mêlé de fumée.

smoke [smōk] *n* fumée *f* ♦ *vt, vi* fumer; **to have a ~** fumer une cigarette; **do you ~?** est-ce que vous fumez?; **to go up in ~** (*house etc*) brûler; (*fig*) partir en fumée.

smoked [smōkt] *a* (*bacon, glass*) fumé(e).

smokeless fuel [smōk'lis fyōō'əl] *n* combustible non polluant.

smoker [smō'kûr] *n* (*person*) fumeur/euse; (*RAIL*) wagon *m* fumeurs.

smoke screen *n* rideau *m or* écran *m* de fumée; (*fig*) paravent *m*.

smoking [smō'king] *n*: **"no ~"** (*sign*) "défense de fumer"; **he's given up ~** il a arrêté de fumer.

smoking car *n* wagon *m* fumeurs.

smoking room *n* fumoir *m*.

smoky [smō'kē] *a* enfumé(e).

smolder [smōl'dûr] *vi* (*US*) couver.
smooth [smōōᵺ] *a* lisse; (*sauce*)
onctueux(euse); (*flavor, whiskey*) moel-
leux(euse); (*cigarette*) doux(douce); (*movement*) régulier(ière), sans à-coups *or* heurts;
(*landing, take-off*) en douceur; (*flight*) sans
secousses; (*person*) doucereux(euse), miel-
leux(euse) ♦ *vt* lisser, défroisser; (*also:* ~
out: *creases, difficulties*) faire disparaître.
   smooth over *vt*: **to** ~ **things over** (*fig*)
arranger les choses.
smoothly [smōōᵺ'lē] *ad* (*easily*) facilement,
sans difficulté(s); **everything went** ~ tout
s'est bien passé.
smother [smuᵺ'ûr] *vt* étouffer.
smoulder [smōl'dûr] *vi* (*Brit*) = **smolder**.
smudge [smuj] *n* tache *f*, bavure *f* ♦ *vt* salir,
maculer.
smug [smug] *a* suffisant(e), content(e) de soi.
smuggle [smug'əl] *vt* passer en contrebande *or*
en fraude; **to** ~ **in/out** (*goods etc*) faire
entrer/sortir clandestinement *or* en fraude.
smuggler [smug'lûr] *n* contrebandier/ière.
smuggling [smug'ling] *n* contrebande *f*.
smut [smut] *n* (*grain of soot*) grain *m* de suie;
(*mark*) tache *f* de suie; (*in conversation etc*)
obscénités *fpl*.
smutty [smut'ē] *a* (*fig*) grossier(ière), obscène.
snack [snak] *n* casse-croûte *m inv*; **to have a**
~ prendre un en-cas, manger quelque chose
(de léger).
snack bar *n* snack(-bar) *m*.
snag [snag] *n* inconvénient *m*, difficulté *f*.
snail [snāl] *n* escargot *m*.
snake [snāk] *n* serpent *m*.
snap [snap] *n* (*sound*) claquement *m*, bruit
sec; (*photograph*) photo *f*, instantané *m*;
(*game*) sorte de jeu de bataille ♦ *a* subit(e);
fait(e) sans réfléchir ♦ *vt* faire claquer;
(*break*) casser net ♦ *vi* se casser net *or* avec
un bruit sec; (*fig: person*) craquer; **to** ~ **at**
sb (*subj: person*) parler d'un ton brusque à
qn; (*: dog*) essayer de mordre qn; **to** ~
open/shut s'ouvrir/se refermer brusquement;
to ~ **one's fingers at** (*fig*) se moquer de; **a**
cold ~ (*of weather*) un refroidissement soudain de la température.
   snap off *vt* (*break*) casser net.
   snap up *vt* sauter sur, saisir.
snap fastener *n* bouton-pression *m*.
snappy [snap'ē] *a* prompt(e); (*slogan*) qui a
du punch; **make it** ~! (*col: hurry up*)
grouille-toi!, magne-toi!
snapshot [snap'shät] *n* photo *f*, instantané *m*.
snare [snär] *n* piège *m* ♦ *vt* attraper, prendre
au piège.
snarl [snärl] *n* grondement *m or* grognement *m*
féroce ♦ *vi* gronder ♦ *vt*: **to get** ~**ed up**
(*wool, plans*) s'emmêler; (*traffic*) se bloquer.
snatch [snach] *n* (*fig*) vol *m*; (*small amount*):
~**es of** des fragments *mpl or* bribes *fpl* de ♦
vt saisir (*d'un geste vif*); (*steal*) voler.
   snatch up *vt* saisir, s'emparer de.
sneak [snēk] *vi*: **to** ~ **in/out** entrer/sortir
furtivement *or* à la dérobée ♦ *vt*: **to** ~ **a look**
at sth regarder furtivement qch.
sneakers [snē'kûrz] *npl* chaussures *fpl* de
tennis *or* basket.
sneaking [snē'king] *a*: **to have a** ~ **feeling** *or*

suspicion that ... avoir la vague impression
que ....
sneaky [snē'kē] *a* sournois(e).
sneer [snēr] *n* ricanement *m* ♦ *vi* ricaner, sourire d'un air sarcastique; **to** ~ **at sb/sth** se
moquer de qn/qch avec mépris.
sneeze [snēz] *n* éternuement *m* ♦ *vi* éternuer.
snicker [snik'ûr] *n* ricanement *m*; rire moquer
♦ *vi* ricaner; pouffer de rire.
snide [snīd] *a* sarcastique, narquois(e).
sniff [snif] *n* reniflement *m* ♦ *vi* renifler ♦ *vt* renifler, flairer; (*glue, drug*) sniffer, respirer.
   sniff at *vt fus*: **it's not to be** ~**ed at** il ne
faut pas cracher dessus, ce n'est pas à dédaigner.
snigger [snig'ûr] *n, vi* = **snicker**.
snip [snip] *n* petit bout; (*bargain*) (bonne)
occasion *or* affaire *f* ♦ *vt* couper.
sniper [snī'pûr] *n* (*marksman*) tireur
embusqué.
snippet [snip'it] *n* bribes *fpl*.
snivel(l)ing [sniv'əling] *a* larmoyant(e),
pleurnicheur(euse).
snob [snäb] *n* snob *m/f*.
snobbery [snäb'ûrē] *n* snobisme *m*.
snobbish [snäb'ish] *a* snob *inv*.
snooker [snōōk'ûr] *n* sorte de jeu de billard.
snoop [snōōp] *vi*: **to** ~ **on sb** espionner qn; **to**
~ **around somewhere** fourrer son nez
quelque part.
snooper [snōō'pûr] *n* fureteur/euse.
snooty [snōō'tē] *a* snob *inv*, prétentieux(euse).
snooze [snōōz] *n* petit somme ♦ *vi* faire un petit somme.
snore [snôr] *vi* ronfler ♦ *n* ronflement *m*.
snoring [snôr'ing] *n* ronflement(s) *m(pl)*.
snorkel [snôr'kəl] *n* (*of swimmer*) tuba *m*.
snort [snôrt] *n* grognement *m* ♦ *vi* grogner;
(*horse*) renâcler ♦ *vt* (*col: drugs*) sniffer.
snotty [snät'ē] *a* morveux(euse).
snout [snout] *n* museau *m*.
snow [snō] *n* neige *f* ♦ *vi* neiger ♦ *vt*: **to be**
~**ed under with work** être débordé(e) de
travail.
snowball [snō'bôl] *n* boule *f* de neige.
snowbound [snō'bound] *a* enneigé(e), blo-
qué(e) par la neige.
snowcapped [snō'kapt] *a* (*peak, mountain*)
couvert(e) de neige.
snowdrift [snō'drift] *n* congère *f*.
snowdrop [snō'dräp] *n* perce-neige *m*.
snowfall [snō'fôl] *n* chute *f* de neige.
snowflake [snō'flāk] *n* flocon *m* de neige.
snowman [snō'man] *n* bonhomme *m* de neige.
snowmobile [snō'mōbēl] *n* motoneige *f*.
snowplow, (*Brit*) **snowplough** [snō'plou] *n*
chasse-neige *m inv*.
snowshoe [snō'shōō] *n* raquette *f* (*pour la
neige*).
snowstorm [snō'stôrm] *n* tempête *f* de neige.
snowy [snō'ē] *a* neigeux(euse); (*covered with
snow*) enneigé(e).
SNP *n abbr* (*Brit POL*) = Scottish National
Party.
snub [snub] *vt* repousser, snober ♦ *n* rebuffade
f.
snub-nosed [snub'nōzd] *a* au nez retroussé.
snuff [snuf] *n* tabac *m* à priser ♦ *vt* (*also:* ~
out: *candle*) moucher.

snug [snug] *a* douillet(te), confortable; **it's a ~ fit** c'est bien ajusté(e).

snuggle [snug'əl] *vi*: **to ~ down in bed/up to sb** se pelotonner dans son lit/contre qn.

SO *abbr* (*BANKING*) = **standing order.**

so [sō] *ad* (*degree*) si, tellement; (*manner: thus*) ainsi, de cette façon ♦ *cj* donc, par conséquent; **~ as to do** afin de *or* pour faire; **~ that** (*purpose*) afin de + *infinitive*, pour que *or* afin que + *sub*; (*result*) si bien que, de (telle) sorte que; **~ that's the reason!** c'est donc (pour) ça!; **~ do I, ~ am I** *etc* moi *etc* aussi; **~ it is!, ~ it does!** c'est vrai!; **if ~** si oui; **I hope ~** je l'espère; **10 or ~** 10 à peu près *or* environ; **quite ~!** exactement!, c'est bien ça!; **even ~** quand même, tout de même; **~ far** jusqu'ici, jusqu'à maintenant; (*in past*) jusque-là; **~ long!** à bientôt!, au revoir!; **~ many** tant de; **~ much** *ad* tant ♦ *a* tant de; **~ to speak** pour ainsi dire; **~ (what)?** (*col*) (bon) et alors?, et après?

soak [sōk] *vt* faire *or* laisser tremper ♦ *vi* tremper; **to be ~ed through** être trempé jusqu'aux os.

soak in *vi* pénétrer, être absorbé(e).

soak up *vt* absorber.

soaking [sō'king] *a* (*also*: **~ wet**) trempé(e).

so and so *n* un tel/une telle.

soap [sōp] *n* savon *m*.

soapflakes [sōp'flāks] *npl* paillettes *fpl* de savon.

soap opera *n* feuilleton télévisé (*quotidienneté réaliste ou embellie*).

soap powder *n* lessive *f*, détergent *m*.

soapsuds [sōp'sudz] *npl* mousse *f* de savon.

soapy [sō'pē] *a* savonneux(euse).

soar [sôr] *vi* monter (en flèche), s'élancer; **~ing prices** prix qui grimpent.

sob [sâb] *n* sanglot *m* ♦ *vi* sangloter.

s.o.b. *n abbr* (*US col!*: = *son of a bitch*) salaud *m* (!).

sober [sō'bûr] *a* qui n'est pas (*or* plus) ivre; (*sedate*) sérieux(euse), sensé(e); (*moderate*) mesuré(e); (*color, style*) sobre, discret(ète).

sober up *vt* dégriser ♦ *vi* se dégriser.

sobriety [səbrī'ətē] *n* (*not being drunk*) sobriété *f*; (*seriousness, sedateness*) sérieux *m*.

Soc. *abbr* (= *society*) Soc.

so-called [sō'kôld'] *a* soi-disant *inv*.

soccer [sâk'ûr] *n* football *m*.

soccer player *n* footballeur *m*.

sociable [sō'shəbəl] *a* sociable.

social [sō'shəl] *a* social(e) ♦ *n* (petite) fête.

social climber *n* arriviste *m/f*.

social club *n* amicale *f*, foyer *m*.

Social Democrat *n* social-démocrate *m/f*.

socialism [sō'shəlizəm] *n* socialisme *m*.

socialist [sō'shəlist] *a*, *n* socialiste (*m/f*).

socialite [sō'shəlīt] *n* personnalité mondaine.

socialize [sō'shəlīz] *vi* voir *or* rencontrer des gens, se faire des amis; **to ~ with** fréquenter; lier connaissance *or* parler avec.

socially [sō'shəlē] *ad* socialement, en société.

social science *n* sciences humaines.

social security *n* aide sociale; **Department of S~ S~** (*Brit*) *ministère de la Sécurité Sociale.*

social welfare *n* sécurité sociale.

social work *n* assistance sociale.

social worker *n* assistant/e social(e).

society [səsī'ətē] *n* société *f*; (*club*) société, association *f*; (*also*: **high ~**) (haute) société, grand monde ♦ *cpd* (*party*) mondain(e).

socioeconomic [sōshēōēkənâm'ik] *a* socio-économique.

sociological [sōsēəláj'ikəl] *a* sociologique.

sociologist [sōsēâl'əjist] *n* sociologue *m/f*.

sociology [sōsēâl'əjē] *n* sociologie *f*.

sock [sâk] *n* chaussette *f* ♦ *vt* (*col: hit*) flanquer un coup à; **to pull one's ~s up** (*fig*) se secouer (les puces).

socket [sâk'it] *n* cavité *f*; (*ELEC: also:* **wall ~**) prise *f* de courant; (: *for light bulb*) douille *f*.

sod [sâd] *n* (*of earth*) motte *f*; (*Brit col!*) con *m* (!); salaud *m* (!).

soda [sō'də] *n* (*CHEMISTRY*) soude *f*; (*also:* **~ water**) eau *f* de Seltz; (*US: also:* **~ pop**) soda *m*.

sodden [sâd'ən] *a* trempé(e); détrempé(e).

sodium [sō'dēəm] *n* sodium *m*.

sodium chloride *n* chlorure *m* de sodium.

sofa [sō'fə] *n* sofa *m*, canapé *m*.

Sofia [sō'fēə] *n* Sofia.

soft [sôft] *a* (*not rough*) doux(douce); (*not hard*) doux; mou(molle); (*not loud*) doux, léger(ère); (*kind*) doux, gentil(le); (*weak*) indulgent(e); (*stupid*) stupide, débile.

soft-boiled [sôft'boild'] *a* (*egg*) à la coque.

soft drink *n* boisson non alcoolisée.

soft drugs *npl* drogues douces.

soften [sôf'ən] *vt* (r)amollir; adoucir; atténuer ♦ *vi* se ramollir; s'adoucir; s'atténuer.

softener [sôf'ənûr] *n* (*water ~*) adoucisseur *m*; (*fabric ~*) produit assouplissant.

softhearted [sôft'hâr'tid] *a* au cœur tendre.

softly [sôft'lē] *ad* doucement; légèrement; gentiment.

softness [sôft'nis] *n* douceur *f*.

soft sell *n* promotion *f* de vente discrète.

soft toy *n* jouet *m* en peluche.

software [sôft'wär] *n* logiciel *m*, software *m*.

software package *n* progiciel *m*.

soggy [sâg'ē] *a* trempé(e); détrempé(e).

soil [soil] *n* (*earth*) sol *m*, terre *f* ♦ *vt* salir; (*fig*) souiller.

soiled [soild] *a* sale; (*COMM*) défraîchi(e).

sojourn [sō'jûrn] *n* (*formal*) séjour *m*.

solace [sâl'is] *n* consolation *f*, réconfort *m*.

solar [sō'lûr] *a* solaire.

solarium, *pl* **solaria** [sōlär'ēəm, -lär'ēə] *n* solarium *m*.

solar plexus [sō'lûr plek'səs] *n* (*ANAT*) plexus *m* solaire.

sold [sōld] *pt*, *pp* of **sell.**

solder [sâd'ûr] *vt* souder (*au fil à souder*) ♦ *n* soudure *f*.

soldier [sōl'jûr] *n* soldat *m*, militaire *m*; **toy ~** petit soldat.

sold out *a* (*COMM*) épuisé(e).

sole [sōl] *n* (*of foot*) plante *f*; (*of shoe*) semelle *f*; (*fish: pl inv*) sole *f* ♦ *a* seul(e), unique; **the ~ reason** la seule et unique raison.

solely [sōl'lē] *ad* seulement, uniquement; **I will hold you ~ responsible** je vous en tiendrai pour seul responsable.

solemn [sâl'əm] *a* solennel(le); sérieux(euse), grave.

sole trader *n* (*COMM*) chef *m* d'entreprise individuelle.

solicit [sɔlis'it] *vt* (*request*) solliciter ♦ *vi* (*prostitute*) racoler.

solicitor [sɔlis'itûr] *n* (*Brit: for wills etc*) ≈ notaire *m*; (: *in court*) ≈ avocat *m*.

solid [sâl'id] *a* (*not hollow*) plein(e), compact(e), massif(ive); (*strong, sound, reliable, not liquid*) solide; (*meal*) consistant(e), substantiel(le); (*vote*) unanime ♦ *n* solide *m*; **to be on** ~ **ground** être sur la terre ferme; (*fig*) être en terrain sûr; **we waited 2** ~ **hours** nous avons attendu deux heures entières.

solidarity [sâlidar'itē] *n* solidarité *f*.

solidify [sɔlid'əfī] *vi* se solidifier ♦ *vt* solidifier.

solidity [sɔlid'itē] *n* solidité *f*.

solid-state [sâl'idstāt'] *a* (*ELEC*) à circuits intégrés.

soliloquy [sɔlil'əkwē] *n* monologue *m*.

solitaire [sâl'itär] *n* (*US: card game*) réussite *f*; (*gem, Brit: game*) solitaire *m*.

solitary [sâl'itärē] *a* solitaire.

solitary confinement *n* (*LAW*) isolement *m* (cellulaire).

solitude [sâl'ətōōd] *n* solitude *f*.

solo [sō'lō] *n* solo *m*.

soloist [sō'lōist] *n* soliste *m/f*.

Solomon Islands [sâl'əmən ī'ləndz] *npl:* **the** ~ **les** (îles *fpl*) Salomon *fpl*.

solstice [sâl'stis] *n* solstice *m*.

soluble [sâl'yəbəl] *a* soluble.

solution [sɔlōō'shən] *n* solution *f*.

solve [sâlv] *vt* résoudre.

solvency [sâl'vənsē] *n* (*COMM*) solvabilité *f*.

solvent [sâl'vənt] *a* (*COMM*) solvable ♦ *n* (*CHEMISTRY*) (dis)solvant *m*.

solvent abuse *n* usage *m* de solvants hallucinogènes.

Som. *abbr* (*Brit*) = *Somerset*.

Somali [sōmâ'lē] *a* somali(e), somalien(ne) ♦ *n* Somali/e, Somalien/ne.

Somalia [sōmâl'ēə] *n* (République *f* de) Somalie *f*.

somber, (*Brit*) **sombre** [sâm'bûr] *a* sombre, morne.

some [sum] *a* (*a few*) quelques; (*certain*) certains(certaines); (*a certain number or amount) see phrases below*; (*unspecified*) un(e) ... (quelconque) ♦ *pronoun* quelques uns(unes); un peu ♦ *ad:* ~ **10 people** quelque 10 personnes, 10 personnes environ; ~ **children came** des enfants sont venus; ~ **people say that** ... certains disent que ...; **have** ~ **tea/ice-cream/water** prends du thé/ de la glace/de l'eau; **there's** ~ **milk in the fridge** il y a du lait *or* un peu de lait dans le frigo; ~ (**of it**) **was left** il en est resté un peu; **could I have** ~ **of that cheese?** pourriez-vous me donner un peu de ce fromage?; **I've got** ~ (*i.e. books etc*) j'en ai (quelques uns); (*i.e. milk, money etc*) j'en ai (un peu); **would you like** ~? est-ce que vous en voulez?, en voulez-vous?; **after** ~ **time** après un certain temps; **at** ~ **length** assez longuement; **in** ~ **form or other** sous une forme ou une autre, sous une forme quelconque.

somebody [sum'bâdē] *pronoun* quelqu'un; ~

or other quelqu'un, je ne sais qui.

someday [sum'dā] *ad* un de ces jours, un jour ou l'autre.

somehow [sum'hou] *ad* d'une façon ou d'une autre; (*for some reason*) pour une raison ou une autre.

someone [sum'wun] *pronoun* = **somebody.**

someplace [sum'plās] *ad* (*US*) = **somewhere.**

somersault [sum'ûrsôlt] *n* culbute *f*, saut périlleux ♦ *vi* faire la culbute *or* un saut périlleux; (*car*) faire un tonneau.

something [sum'thing] *pronoun* quelque chose *m;* ~ **interesting** quelque chose d'intéressant; ~ **to do** quelque chose à faire; **he's** ~ **like me** il est un peu comme moi; **it's** ~ **of a problem** il y a là un problème.

sometime [sum'tīm] *ad* (*in future*) un de ces jours, un jour ou l'autre; (*in past*): ~ **last month** au cours du mois dernier.

sometimes [sum'tīmz] *ad* quelquefois, parfois.

somewhat [sum'wut] *ad* quelque peu, un peu.

somewhere [sum'wär] *ad* quelque part; ~ **else** ailleurs, autre part.

son [sun] *n* fils *m*.

sonar [sō'nâr] *n* sonar *m*.

sonata [sənât'ə] *n* sonate *f*.

song [sông] *n* chanson *f*.

songbook [sông'bōōk] *n* chansonnier *m*.

songwriter [sông'rī'tûr] *n* auteur-compositeur *m*.

sonic [sân'ik] *a* (*boom*) supersonique.

son-in-law [sun'inlô] *n* gendre *m*, beau-fils *m*.

sonnet [sân'it] *n* sonnet *m*.

sonny [sun'ē] *n* (*col*) fiston *m*.

soon [sōōn] *ad* bientôt; (*early*) tôt; ~ **afterwards** peu après; **quite** ~ sous peu; **how** ~ **can you do it?** combien de temps vous faut-il pour le faire, au plus pressé?; **how** ~ **can you come back?** quand *or* dans combien de temps pouvez-vous revenir, au plus tôt; **see you** ~! à bientôt!; *see also* **as.**

sooner [sōō'nûr] *ad* (*time*) plus tôt; (*preference*): **I would** ~ **do** j'aimerais autant *or* je préférerais faire; ~ **or later** tôt ou tard; **no** ~ **said than done** sitôt dit, sitôt fait; **the** ~ **the better** le plus tôt sera le mieux; **no** ~ **had we left than** ... à peine étions-nous partis que ....

soot [sōōt] *n* suie *f*.

soothe [sōōth] *vt* calmer, apaiser.

soothing [sōō'thing] *a* (*ointment etc*) lénitif(ive), lénifiant(e); (*tone, words etc*) apaisant(e); (*drink, bath*) relaxant(e).

SOP *n abbr* = *standard operating procedure*.

sop [sâp] *n:* **that's only a** ~ c'est pour nous (*or les etc*) amadouer.

sophisticated [səfis'tikātid] *a* raffiné(e), sophistiqué(e); (*system etc*) très perfectionné(e), sophistiqué.

sophistication [səfis'tikā'shən] *n* raffinement *m;* (niveau *m* de) perfectionnement *m*.

sophomore [sâf'əmôr] *n* (*US*) étudiant/e de seconde année.

soporific [sâpərif'ik] *a* soporifique ♦ *n* somnifère *m*.

sopping [sâp'ing] *a* (*also:* ~ **wet**) tout(e) trempé(e).

soprano [səpran'ō] *n* (*voice*) soprano *m;* (*singer*) soprano *m/f*.

sorbet |sórbā'| *n* sorbet *m*.

sorcerer |sór'sərûr| *n* sorcier *m*.

sordid |sór'did| *a* sordide.

sore |sór| *a* (*painful*) douloureux(euse), sensible; (*offended*) contrarié(e), vexé(e) ♦ *n* plaie *f*; **to have a ~ throat** avoir mal à la gorge; **it's a ~ point** (*fig*) c'est un point délicat.

sorely |sór'lē| *ad* (*tempted*) fortement.

sorrel |sór'əl| *n* oseille *f*.

sorrow |sår'ō| *n* peine *f*, chagrin *m*.

sorrowful |sår'ōfəl| *a* triste.

sorry |sår'ē| *a* désolé(e); (*condition, excuse, tale*) triste, déplorable; (*sight*) désolant(e); **~!** pardon!, excusez-moi!; **to feel ~ for sb** plaindre qn; **I'm ~ to hear that ...** je suis désolé(e) or navré(e) d'apprendre que ...; **to be ~ about sth** regretter qch.

sort |sórt| *n* genre *m*, espèce *f*, sorte *f*; (*make: of coffee, car etc*) marque *f* ♦ *vt* (*also:* **~ out:** *papers*) trier; classer; ranger; (: *letters etc*) trier; (: *problems*) résoudre, régler; (*COMPUT*) trier; **what ~ do you want?** quelle sorte or quel genre voulez-vous?; **what ~ of car?** quelle marque de voiture?; **I'll do nothing of the ~!** je ne ferai rien de tel!; **it's ~ of awkward** (*col*) c'est plutôt gênant.

sortie |sór'tē| *n* sortie *f*.

sorting office |sór'ting ò'fis| *n* (*MAIL*) bureau *m* de tri.

SOS |es'ō'es'| *n abbr* (= *save our souls*) SOS *m*.

so-so |sō'sō'| *ad* comme ci comme ça.

soufflé |sōōflā'| *n* soufflé *m*.

sought |sót| *pt, pp* of **seek**.

sought-after |sót'af'tûr| *a* recherché(e).

soul |sōl| *n* âme *f*; **the poor ~ had nowhere to sleep** le pauvre n'avait nulle part où dormir; **I didn't see a ~** je n'ai vu (absolument) personne.

soul-destroying |sōl'distroiing| *a* démoralisant(e).

soulful |sōl'fəl| *a* plein(e) de sentiment.

soulless |sōl'lis| *a* sans cœur, inhumain(e).

soul mate *n* âme *f* sœur.

soul-searching |sōl'sûrching| *n*: **after much ~, I decided ...** j'ai longuement réfléchi avant de décider ...

sound |sound| *a* (*healthy*) en bonne santé, sain(e); (*safe, not damaged*) solide, en bon état; (*reliable, not superficial*) sérieux(euse), solide; (*sensible*) sensé(e); ♦ *ad*: **~ asleep** dormant d'un profond sommeil ♦ *n* (*noise*) son *m*; bruit *m*; (*GEO*) détroit *m*, bras *m* de mer ♦ *vt* (*alarm*) sonner; (*also:* **~ out:** *opinions*) sonder ♦ *vi* sonner, retentir; (*fig: seem*) sembler (être); **to be of ~ mind** être sain(e) d'esprit; **I don't like the ~ of it** ça ne me dit rien qui vaille; **to ~ one's horn** (*AUT*) klaxonner, actionner son avertisseur; **to ~ like** ressembler à; **it ~s as if ...** il semblerait que ..., j'ai l'impression que ....

sound off *vi* (*col*): **to ~ off (about)** la ramener (sur).

sound barrier *n* mur *m* du son.

sound effects *npl* bruitage *m*.

sound engineer *n* ingénieur *m* du son.

sounding |soun'ding| *n* (*NAUT etc*) sondage *m*.

sounding board *n* (*MUS*) table *f* d'harmonie;

(*fig*): **to use sb as a ~ for one's ideas** essayer ses idées sur qn.

soundly |sound'lē| *ad* (*sleep*) profondément; (*beat*) complètement, à plate couture.

soundproof |sound'prōōf| *vt* insonoriser ♦ *a* insonorisé(e).

sound track *n* (*of film*) bande *f* sonore.

sound wave *n* (*PHYSICS*) onde *f* sonore.

soup |sōōp| *n* soupe *f*, potage *m*; **in the ~** (*fig*) dans le pétrin.

soup course *n* potage *m*.

soup kitchen *n* soupe *f* populaire.

soup plate *n* assiette creuse or à soupe.

soupspoon |sōōp'spōōn| *n* cuiller *f* à soupe.

sour |sou'ûr| *a* aigre, acide; (*milk*) tourné(e), aigre; (*fig*) acerbe, aigre; revêche; **to go** or **turn ~** (*milk, wine*) tourner; (*fig: relationship, plans*) mal tourner; **it's ~ grapes** c'est du dépit.

source |sórs| *n* source *f*; **I have it from a reliable ~ that** je sais de source sûre que.

south |south| *n* sud *m* ♦ *a* sud *inv*, du sud ♦ *ad* au sud, vers le sud; (*to the*) **~ of** au sud de; **to travel ~** aller en direction du sud; **the S~ of France** le Sud de la France, le Midi.

South Africa *n* Afrique *f* du Sud.

South African *a* sud-africain(e) ♦ *n* Sud-Africain/e.

South America *n* Amérique *f* du Sud.

South American *a* sud-américain(e) ♦ *n* Sud-Américain/e.

southbound |south'bound'| *a* en direction du sud; (*carriageway*) sud *inv*.

southeast |southēst'| *n* sud-est *m*.

Southeast Asia *n* le Sud-Est asiatique.

southerly |suth'ûrlē| *a* du sud; au sud.

southern |suth'ûrn| *a* (du) sud; méridional(e); **with a ~ aspect** orienté(e) or exposé(e) au sud; **the ~ hemisphere** l'hémisphère sud or austral.

South Pole *n* Pôle *m* Sud.

South Sea Islands *npl*: **the ~** l'Océanie *f*.

South Seas *npl*: **the ~** les mers *fpl* du Sud.

southward(s) |south'wûrd(z)| *ad* vers le sud.

southwest |southwest'| *n* sud-ouest *m*.

souvenir |sōōvənēr'| *n* souvenir *m* (*objet*).

sovereign |såv'rin| *a*, *n* souverain(e).

sovereignty |såv'rəntē| *n* souveraineté *f*.

soviet |sō'vēit| *a* soviétique.

Soviet Union *n*: **the ~** l'Union *f* soviétique.

sow *n* |sou| truie *f* ♦ *vt* |sō| (*pt* **~ed**, *pp* **sown** |sōn|) semer.

soy |soi| *n* soja *m*.

soya |soi'ə| *n* (*Brit*) = **soy**.

soybean |soi'bēn| *n* graine *f* de soja.

soy sauce *n* sauce *f* au soja.

spa |spå| *n* (*town*) station thermale; (*US: also:* **health ~**) établissement *m* de cure de rajeunissement.

space |spås| *n* (*gen*) espace *m*; (*room*) place *f*; espace; (*length of time*) laps *m* de temps ♦ *cpd* spatial(e) ♦ *vt* (*also:* **~ out**) espacer; **to clear a ~ for sth** faire de la place pour qch; **in a confined ~** dans un espace réduit or restreint; **in a short ~ of time** dans peu de temps; **(with)in the ~ of an hour** en l'espace d'une heure.

space bar *n* (*on typewriter*) barre *f* d'espacement.

spacecraft [spās'kraft] *n* engin spatial.
spaceman [spās'man] *n* astronaute *m*, cosmonaute *m*.
spaceship [spās'ship] *n* engin *or* vaisseau spatial.
space shuttle *n* navette spatiale.
spacesuit [spās'sōōt] *n* combinaison spatiale.
spacewoman [spās'wōōmən] *n* astronaute *f*, cosmonaute *f*.
spacing [spā'sing] *n* espacement *m*; **single/ double** ~ (*TYP etc*) interligne *m* simple/ double.
spacious [spā'shəs] *a* spacieux(euse), grand(e).
spade [spād] *n* (*tool*) bêche *f*, pelle *f*; (*child's*) pelle; **~s** *npl* (*CARDS*) pique *m*.
spadework [spād'wûrk] *n* (*fig*) gros *m* du travail.
spaghetti [spəget'ē] *n* spaghetti *mpl*.
Spain [spān] *n* Espagne *f*.
span [span] *pt of* **spin** ♦ *n* (*of bird, plane*) envergure *f*; (*of arch*) portée *f*; (*in time*) espace *m* de temps, durée *f* ♦ *vt* enjamber, franchir; (*fig*) couvrir, embrasser.
Spaniard [span'yûrd] *n* Espagnol/e.
spaniel [span'yəl] *n* épagneul *m*.
Spanish [span'ish] *a* espagnol(e), d'Espagne ♦ *n* (*LING*) espagnol *m*; **the** ~ *npl* les Espagnols; ~ **omelette** omelette *f* à l'espagnole.
spank [spangk] *vt* donner une fessée à.
spanner [span'ûr] *n* (*Brit*) clé *f* (de mécanicien).
spar [spâr] *n* espar *m* ♦ *vi* (*BOXING*) s'entraîner.
spare [spär] *a* de réserve, de rechange; (*surplus*) de *or* en trop, de reste ♦ *n* (*part*) pièce *f* de rechange, pièce détachée ♦ *vt* (*do without*) se passer de; (*afford to give*) donner, accorder, passer; (*refrain from hurting*) épargner; (*refrain from using*) ménager; **to** ~ (*surplus*) en surplus, de trop; **to** ~ **no expense** ne pas reculer devant la dépense; **can you** ~ **the time?** est-ce que vous avez le temps?; **there is no time to** ~ il n'y a pas de temps à perdre; **I've a few minutes to** ~ je dispose de quelques minutes.
spare part *n* pièce *f* de rechange, pièce détachée.
spare room *n* chambre *f* d'ami.
spare time *n* moments *mpl* de loisir.
spare tire, (*Brit*) **spare tyre** *n* (*AUT*) pneu *m* de rechange.
spare wheel *n* (*AUT*) roue *f* de secours.
sparing [spär'ing] *a*: **to be** ~ **with** ménager.
sparingly [spär'inglē] *ad* avec modération.
spark [spârk] *n* étincelle *f*; (*fig*) étincelle, lueur *f*.
spark plug [spârk' plug] *n* bougie *f*.
sparkle [spâr'kəl] *n* scintillement *m*, étincellement *m*, éclat *m* ♦ *vi* étinceler, scintiller; (*bubble*) pétiller.
sparkling [spâr'kling] *a* étincelant(e), scintillant(e); (*wine*) mousseux(euse), pétillant(e).
sparrow [spar'ō] *n* moineau *m*.
sparse [spârs] *a* clairsemé(e).
spartan [spâr'tən] *a* (*fig*) spartiate.
spasm [spaz'əm] *n* (*MED*) spasme *m*; (*fig*) accès *m*.

spasmodic [spazmâd'ik] *a* (*fig*) intermittent(e).
spastic [spas'tik] *n* handicapé/e moteur.
spat [spat] *pt, pp of* **spit** ♦ *n* (*US*) prise *f* de bec.
spate [spāt] *n* (*fig*): ~ **of** avalanche *f or* torrent *m* de; **in** ~ (*river*) en crue.
spatial [spā'shəl] *a* spatial(e).
spatter [spat'ûr] *n* éclaboussure(s) *f(pl)* ♦ *vt* éclabousser ♦ *vi* gicler.
spatula [spach'ələ] *n* spatule *f*.
spawn [spón] *vt* pondre; (*pej*) engendrer ♦ *vi* frayer ♦ *n* frai *m*.
SPCA *n abbr* (*US*: = *Society for the Prevention of Cruelty to Animals*) ≈ SPA *f*.
SPCC *n abbr* (*US*) = *Society for the Prevention of Cruelty to Children*.
speak, *pt* **spoke**, *pp* **spoken** [spēk, spōk, spō'kən] *vt* (*language*) parler; (*truth*) dire ♦ *vi* parler; (*make a speech*) prendre la parole; **to** ~ **to sb/of** *or* **about sth** parler à qn/de qch; ~**ing!** (*on telephone*) c'est moi-même!; **to** ~ **one's mind** dire ce que l'on pense; **it** ~**s for itself** c'est évident; ~ **up!** parle plus fort!; **he has no money to** ~ **of** il n'a pas d'argent.
speak for *vt fus*: **to** ~ **for sb** parler pour qn; **that picture is already spoken for** (*in shop*) ce tableau est déjà réservé.
speaker [spē'kûr] *n* (*in public*) orateur *m*; (*also*: **loud~**) haut-parleur *m*; (*POL*): **the S**~ le président de la Chambre des représentants (*US*) *or* des communes (*Brit*); **are you a Welsh ~?** parlez-vous gallois?
speaking [spē'king] *a* parlant(e); **French-~ people** les francophones; **to be on** ~ **terms** se parler.
spear [spi'ûr] *n* lance *f* ♦ *vt* transpercer.
spearhead [spēr'hed] *n* fer *m* de lance; (*MIL*) colonne *f* d'attaque ♦ *vt* (*attack etc*) mener.
spearmint [spēr'mint] *n* (*BOT etc*) menthe verte.
special [spesh'əl] *a* spécial(e) ♦ *n* (*train*) train spécial; **take** ~ **care** soyez particulièrement prudents; **nothing** ~ rien de spécial; "**on special**" (*US COMM*) en promotion; **today's** ~ (*at restaurant*) le plat du jour.
special agent *n* agent secret.
special correspondent *n* envoyé spécial.
special delivery *n* (*MAIL*): **by** ~ en exprès.
specialist [spesh'əlist] *n* spécialiste *m/f*; **heart** ~ cardiologue *m/f*.
speciality [speshēal'ətē] *n* (*Brit*) = **specialty**.
specialize [spesh'əlīz] *vi*: **to** ~ (**in**) se spécialiser (dans).
specially [spesh'əlē] *ad* spécialement, particulièrement.
special offer *n* (*COMM*) réclame *f*.
specialty [spesh'əltē] *n* (*US*) spécialité *f*.
species [spē'shēz] *n* (*pl inv*) espèce *f*.
specific [spisif'ik] *a* (*not vague*) précis(e), explicite; (*particular*) particulier(ière); (*BOT, CHEMISTRY etc*) spécifique; **to be** ~ **to** être particulier à, être le *or* un caractère (*or* les caractères spéciaux) de.
specifically [spisif'iklē] *ad* explicitement, précisément; (*intend, ask, design*) expressément, spécialement; (*exclusively*) exclusivement, spécifiquement.

specification [spesəfəkā'shən] *n* spécification *f*; stipulation *f*; ~s *npl* (*of car, building etc*) spécification.

specify [spes'əfī] *vt* spécifier, préciser; **unless otherwise specified** sauf indication contraire.

specimen [spes'əmən] *n* spécimen *m*, échantillon *m*; (*MED*) prélèvement *m*.

specimen copy *n* spécimen *m*.

specimen signature *n* spécimen *m* de signature.

speck [spek] *n* petite tache, petit point; (*particle*) grain *m*; **to have a ~ in one's eye** (*US*) avoir une poussière *or* une saleté dans l'œil.

speckled [spek'əld] *a* tacheté(e), moucheté(e).

specs [speks] *npl* (*col*) lunettes *fpl*.

spectacle [spek'təkəl] *n* spectacle *m*.

spectacles [spek'təkəlz] *npl* (*Brit*) lunettes *fpl*.

spectacular [spektak'yəlûr] *a* spectaculaire ♦ *n* (*CINEMA etc*) superproduction *f*.

spectator [spek'tātûr] *n* spectateur/trice.

specter, (*Brit*) **spectre** [spek'tûr] *n* spectre *m*, fantôme *m*.

spectrum, *pl* **spectra** [spek'trəm, -rə] *n* spectre *m*; (*fig*) gamme *f*.

speculate [spek'yəlāt] *vi* spéculer; (*try to guess*): **to ~ about** s'interroger sur.

speculation [spekyəlā'shən] *n* spéculation *f*; conjectures *fpl*.

speculative [spek'yəlātiv] *a* spéculatif(ive).

speculator [spek'yəlātûr] *n* spéculateur/trice.

speech [spēch] *n* (*faculty*) parole *f*; (*talk*) discours *m*, allocution *f*; (*manner of speaking*) façon *f* de parler, langage *m*; (*language*) langage *m*; (*enunciation*) élocution *f*.

speech day *n* (*Brit SCOL*) distribution *f* des prix.

speech impediment *n* défaut *m* d'élocution.

speechless [spēch'lis] *a* muet(te).

speech therapy *n* orthophonie *f*.

speed [spēd] *n* vitesse *f*; (*promptness*) rapidité *f* ♦ *vi* (*pt, pp* **sped** [sped]): **to ~ along/by** *etc* aller/passer *etc* à toute vitesse; (*AUT*: *exceed ~ limit*) faire un excès de vitesse; **at full** *or* **top ~** à toute vitesse *or* allure; **at a ~ of 70 km/h** à une vitesse de 70 km/h; **shorthand/typing ~s** nombre *m* de mots à la minute en sténographie/dactylographie; **five-~ transmission** boîte cinq vitesses.

speed up, *pt, pp* **~ed up** *vi* aller plus vite, accélérer ♦ *vt* accélérer.

speedboat [spēd'bōt] *n* vedette *f*, hors-bord *m inv*.

speedily [spē'dilē] *ad* rapidement, promptement.

speeding [spē'ding] *n* (*AUT*) excès *m* de vitesse.

speed limit *n* limitation *f* de vitesse, vitesse maximale permise.

speedometer [spēdâm'itûr] *n* compteur *m* (de vitesse).

speed trap *n* (*AUT*) piège *m* de police pour contrôle de vitesse.

speedway [spēd'wā] *n* (*SPORT*) piste *f* de vitesse pour motos; (: *also*: **~ racing**) épreuve(s) *f(pl)* de vitesse de motos.

speedy [spē'dē] *a* rapide, prompt(e).

speleologist [spēlēál'əjist] *n* spéléologue *m/f*.

spell [spel] *n* (*also*: **magic ~**) sortilège *m*,

charme *m*; (*period of time*) (courte) période *f* ♦ *vt* (*pt, pp* **~ed** *or* **spelt** [speld, spelt]) (*in writing*) écrire, orthographier; (*aloud*) épeler; (*fig*) signifier; **to cast a ~ on sb** jeter un sort à qn; **he can't ~** il fait des fautes d'orthographe; **how do you ~ your name?** comment écrivez-vous votre nom?; **can you ~ it for me?** pouvez-vous me l'épeler?

spellbound [spel'bound] *a* envoûté(e), subjugué(e).

spelling [spel'ing] *n* orthographe *f*.

spelt [spelt] *pt, pp of* **spell**.

spelunker [spēlung'kûr] *n* (*US*) spéléologue *mf*.

spend, *pt, pp* **spent** [spend, spent] *vt* (*money*) dépenser; (*time, life*) passer; (*devote*): **to ~ time/money/effort on sth** consacrer du temps/de l'argent/de l'énergie à qch.

spending [spen'ding] *n* dépenses *fpl*; **government ~** les dépenses publiques.

spending money *n* argent *m* de poche.

spending power *n* pouvoir *m* d'achat.

spendthrift [spend'thrift] *n* dépensier/ière.

spent [spent] *pt, pp of* **spend** ♦ *a* (*patience*) épuisé(e), à bout; (*cartridge, bullets*) vide.

sperm [spûrm] *n* spermatozoïde *m*; (*semen*) sperme *m*.

sperm whale *n* cachalot *m*.

spew [spyōō] *vt* vomir.

sphere [sfēr] *n* sphère *f*; (*fig*) sphère, domaine *m*.

spherical [sfär'ikəl] *a* sphérique.

sphinx [sfingks] *n* sphinx *m*.

spice [spīs] *n* épice *f* ♦ *vt* épicer.

spick-and-span [spik'ənspan'] *a* impeccable.

spicy [spī'sē] *a* épicé(e), relevé(e); (*fig*) piquant(e).

spider [spī'dûr] *n* araignée *f*; **~'s web** toile *f* d'araignée.

spiel [spēl] *n* laïus *m inv*.

spike [spīk] *n* pointe *f*; (*ELEC*) pointe de tension; **~s** *npl* (*SPORT*) chaussures *fpl* à pointes.

spike heel *n* (*US*) talon *m* aiguille.

spiky [spī'kē] *a* (*bush, branch*) épineux(euse); (*animal*) plein(e) de piquants.

spill, *pt, pp* **~ed** *or* **spilt** [spil, -d, -t] *vt* renverser; répandre ♦ *vi* se répandre; **to ~ the beans** (*col*) vendre la mèche; (: *confess*) lâcher le morceau.

spill out *vi* sortir à flots, se répandre.

spill over *vi* déborder.

spin [spin] *n* (*revolution of wheel*) tour *m*; (*AVIAT*) (chute *f* en) vrille *f*; (*trip in car*) petit tour, balade *f* ♦ *vb* (*pt* **spun, span**, *pp* **spun** [spun, span]) *vt* (*wool etc*) filer; (*wheel*) faire tourner; (*Brit: clothes*) essorer ♦ *vi* tourner, tournoyer; **to ~ a yarn** débiter une longue histoire.

spin out *vt* faire durer.

spinach [spin'ich] *n* épinard *m*; (*as food*) épinards.

spinal [spī'nəl] *a* vertébral(e), spinal(e).

spinal column *n* colonne vertébrale.

spinal cord *n* moelle épinière.

spindly [spind'lē] *a* grêle, filiforme.

spin-dry [spindrī'] *vt* essorer.

spin-dryer [spindrī'ûr] *n* (*Brit*) essoreuse *f*.

spine [spīn] *n* colonne vertébrale; (*thorn*)

épine f, piquant m.
spine-chilling [spīn'chiling] a terrifiant(e).
spineless [spīn'lis]   a   invertébré(e);   (fig)
mou(molle), sans caractère.
spinner [spin'ûr] n (of thread) fileur/euse.
spinning [spin'ing] n (of thread) filage m; (by
machine) filature f.
spinning top n toupie f.
spinning wheel n rouet m.
spin-off [spin'ôf] n sous-produit m; avantage
inattendu.
spinster [spin'stûr] n célibataire f; vieille fille.
spiral [spī'rəl] n spirale f ♦ a en spirale ♦ vi
(fig: prices etc) monter en flèche; **the inflationary ~** la spirale inflationniste.
spiral staircase n escalier m en colimaçon.
spire [spī'ûr] n flèche f, aiguille f.
spirit [spir'it] n (soul) esprit m, âme f; (ghost)
esprit, revenant m; (mood) esprit, état m
d'esprit; (courage) courage m, énergie f; **~s**
npl (drink) spiritueux mpl, alcool m; **in good
~s** de bonne humeur; **in low ~s** démorali-
sé(e); **community ~** solidarité f; **public ~**
civisme m.
spirit duplicator n duplicateur m à alcool.
spirited [spir'itid] a vif(vive), fougueux(euse),
plein(e) d'allant.
spirit level n niveau m à bulle.
spiritual [spir'ichōoəl] a spirituel(le); reli-
gieux(euse) ♦ n (also: **Negro ~**) spiritual m.
spiritualism [spir'ichōoəlizəm] n spiritisme m.
spit [spit] n (for roasting) broche f; (spittle)
crachat m; (saliva) salive f ♦ vi (pt, pp **spat**
[spat]) cracher; (sound) crépiter.
spite [spīt] n rancune f, dépit m ♦ vt contrarier, vexer; **in ~ of** en dépit de, malgré.
spiteful [spīt'fəl]   a   malveillant(e),
rancunier(ière).
spitroast [spit'rōst] vt faire rôtir à la broche.
spitting [spit'ing] n: **"~ prohibited"** "défense
de cracher''   ♦ a: **to be the ~ image of sb**
être le portrait tout craché de qn.
spittle [spit'əl] n salive f; bave f; crachat m.
splash [splash] n éclaboussement m; (of color)
tache f ♦ excl (sound) plouf! ♦ vt éclabousser
♦ vi (also: **~ about**) barboter, patauger.
splashdown [splash'doun] n amerrissage m.
splay [splā] a: **~footed** marchant les pieds en
dehors.
spleen [splēn] n (ANAT) rate f.
splendid [splen'did] a splendide, superbe, magnifique.
splendor,   (Brit)   **splendour**   [splen'dûr]   n
splendeur f, magnificence f.
splice [splīs] vt épisser.
splint [splint] n attelle f, éclisse f.
splinter [splin'tûr] n (wood) écharde f; (metal)
éclat m ♦ vi se fragmenter.
splinter group n groupe dissident.
split [split] n fente f, déchirure f; (fig: POL)
scission f ♦ vb (pt, pp **split**) vt fendre, déchirer; (party) diviser; (work, profits) partager,
répartir ♦ vi (break) se fendre, se briser; (divide) se diviser; **let's ~ the difference** coupons la poire en deux; **to do the ~s** faire le
grand écart.
  split up vi (couple) se séparer, rompre;
(meeting) se disperser.
split-level [split'lev'əl] a (house) à deux or plu-

sieurs niveaux.
split peas npl pois cassés.
split personality n double personnalité f.
split second n fraction f de seconde.
splitting [split'ing] a: **a ~ headache** un mal de
tête atroce.
splutter [splut'ûr] vi = **sputter.**
spoil, pt, pp **~ed** or **spoilt** [spoil, -d, -t] vt
(damage) abîmer; (mar) gâcher; (child) gâ-
ter; (ballot paper) rendre nul ♦ vi: **to be
~ing for a fight** chercher la bagarre.
spoiler [spoi'lûr] n spoiler m.
spoils [spoilz] npl butin m.
spoilsport [spoil'spôrt] n trouble-fête m/f inv,
rabat-joie m inv.
spoilt [spoilt] pt, pp **of spoil.**
spoke [spōk] pt of **speak** ♦ n rayon m.
spoken [spō'kən] pp of **speak.**
spokesman [spōks'mən] n porte-parole m inv.
sponge [spunj] n éponge f; (CULIN: also: **~
cake**) ≈ biscuit m de Savoie ♦ vt éponger ♦
vi: **to ~ off sb** vivre aux crochets de qn.
sponge bag n (Brit) trousse f de toilette.
sponge cake n ≈ biscuit m de Savoie.
sponger [spun'jûr] n (pej) parasite m.
spongy [spun'jē] a spongieux(euse).
sponsor [spän'sûr] n sponsor m, personne f
(ou organisme m) qui assure le parrainage;
(of new member) parrain m/marraine f ♦ vt
(program, competition etc) parrainer, patronner, sponsoriser; (POL: bill) présenter;
(new member) parrainer; **I ~ed him at 25¢
a mile** (in fund-raising race) je me suis engagé à lui donner 25 cents par mile.
sponsorship [spän'sûrship] n patronage m,
parrainage m.
spontaneity [späntənē'itē] n spontanéité f.
spontaneous [späntā'nēəs] a spontané(e).
spooky [spōō'kē] a qui donne la chair de
poule.
spool [spōōl] n bobine f.
spoon [spōōn] n cuiller f.
spoon-feed [spōōn'fēd] vt nourrir à la cuiller;
(fig) mâcher le travail à.
spoonful [spōōn'fōōl] n cuillerée f.
sporadic [spôrad'ik] a sporadique.
sport [spôrt] n sport m; (amusement) divertissement m; (person) chic type/chic fille
♦ vt arborer; **indoor/outdoor ~s** sports en
salle/de plein air; **to say sth in ~** dire qch
pour rire.
sporting [spôr'ting] a sportif(ive); **to give sb
a ~ chance** donner sa chance à qn.
sports car [spôrts kâr] n voiture f de sport.
sport(s) coat n (US) veste f de sport.
sports field n terrain m de sport.
sports jacket n (Brit) = **sport(s) coat.**
sportsman [spôrts'mən] n sportif m.
sportsmanship [spôrts'mənship]   n   esprit
sportif, sportivité f.
sports page n page f des sports.
sportswear [spôrts'weûr] n vêtements mpl de
sport.
sportswoman [spôrts'wōōmən] n sportive f.
sporty [spôr'tē] a sportif(ive).
spot [spät] n tache f; (dot: on pattern) pois m;
(pimple) bouton m; (place) endroit m, coin
m; (also: **~ advertisement**) message m publicitaire; (small amount): **a ~ of** un peu de

♦ vt (notice) apercevoir, repérer; **on the ~** sur place, sur les lieux; (immediately) sur le champ; **to pay cash on the ~** (US) payer rubis sur l'ongle; **to put sb on the ~** (fig) mettre qn dans l'embarras; **to come out in ~s** se couvrir de boutons, avoir une éruption de boutons.

spot check n contrôle intermittent.

spotless [spât'lis] a immaculé(e).

spotlight [spât'līt] n projecteur m; (AUT) phare m auxiliaire.

spot price n prix m sur place.

spotted [spât'id] a tacheté(e), moucheté(e); à pois; **~ with** tacheté(e) de.

spotty [spât'ē] a (face) boutonneux(euse).

spouse [spous] n époux/épouse.

spout [spout] n (of jug) bec m; (of liquid) jet m ♦ vi jaillir.

sprain [sprān] n entorse f, foulure f ♦ vt: **to ~ one's ankle** se fouler or se tordre la cheville.

sprang [sprang] pt of **spring**.

sprawl [sprôl] vi s'étaler ♦ n: **urban ~** expansion urbaine; **to send sb ~ing** envoyer qn rouler par terre.

spray [sprā] n jet m (en fines gouttelettes); (container) vaporisateur m, bombe f; (of flowers) petit bouquet ♦ vt vaporiser, pulvériser; (crops) traiter ♦ cpd (deodorant etc) en bombe or atomiseur.

spread [spred] n (distribution) répartition f; (CULIN) pâte f à tartiner; (PRESS, TYP: two pages) double page f ♦ vb (pt, pp **spread**) vt (paste, contents) étendre, étaler; (rumor, disease) répandre, propager; (repayments) échelonner, étaler; (wealth) répartir ♦ vi s'étendre; se répandre; se propager; **middle-age ~** embonpoint m (pris avec l'âge).

spread-eagled [spred'ēgəld] a: **to be** or **lie ~** être étendu(e) bras et jambes écartés.

spreadsheet [spred'shēt] n (COMPUT) tableur m.

spree [sprē] n: **to go on a ~** faire la fête.

sprig [sprig] n rameau m.

sprightly [sprīt'lē] a alerte.

spring [spring] n (leap) bond m, saut m; (coiled metal) ressort m; (bounciness) élasticité f; (season) printemps m; (of water) source f ♦ vb (pt **sprang**, pp **sprung** [sprang, sprung]) vi bondir, sauter ♦ vt: **to ~ a leak** (pipe etc) se mettre à fuir; **he sprang the news on me** il m'a annoncé la nouvelle de but en blanc; **in ~, in the ~** au printemps; **to ~ from** provenir de; **to ~ into action** passer à l'action; **to walk with a ~ in one's step** marcher d'un pas souple.

spring up vi (problem) se présenter, surgir.

springboard [spring'bôrd] n tremplin m.

spring-clean [spring'klēn'] n (also: **~ing**) grand nettoyage de printemps.

spring onion n (Brit) ciboule f, cive f.

springtime [spring'tīm] n printemps m.

springy [spring'ē] a élastique, souple.

sprinkle [spring'kəl] vt (pour) répandre; verser; **to ~ water** etc **on, ~ with water** etc asperger d'eau etc; **to ~ sugar** etc **on, ~ with sugar** etc saupoudrer de sucre etc; **~d with** (fig) parsemé(e) de.

sprinkler [spring'klûr] n (for lawn etc) arro-

seur m; (to put out fire) diffuseur m d'extincteur automatique d'incendie.

sprinkling [spring'kling] n (of water) quelques gouttes fpl; (of salt) pincée f; (of sugar) légère couche.

sprint [sprint] n sprint m ♦ vi sprinter.

sprinter [sprin'tûr] n sprinteur/euse.

sprite [sprīt] n lutin m.

sprocket [sprâk'it] n (on printer etc) picot m.

sprout [sprout] vi germer, pousser.

sprouts [sprouts] npl (also: **Brussels ~**) choux mpl de Bruxelles.

spruce [sprōos] n épicéa m ♦ a net(te), pimpant(e).

spruce up vt (smarten up: room etc) apprêter; **to ~ o.s. up** se faire beau(belle).

sprung [sprung] pp of **spring**.

spry [sprī] a alerte, vif(vive).

SPUC n abbr = Society for the Protection of Unborn Children.

spud [spud] n (col: potato) patate f.

spun [spun] pt, pp of **spin**.

spur [spûr] n éperon m; (fig) aiguillon m ♦ vt (also: **~ on**) éperonner; aiguillonner; **on the ~ of the moment** sous l'impulsion du moment.

spurious [spyōōr'ēəs] a faux(fausse).

spurn [spûrn] vt repousser avec mépris.

spurt [spûrt] n jet m; (of energy) sursaut m ♦ vi jaillir, gicler; **to put in** or **on a ~** (runner) piquer un sprint; (fig: in work etc) donner un coup de collier.

sputter [sput'ûr] vi bafouiller; postillonner.

spy [spī] n espion/ne ♦ vi: **to ~ on** espionner, épier ♦ vt (see) apercevoir ♦ cpd (film, story) d'espionnage.

spying [spī'ing] n espionnage m.

Sq. abbr (in address) = **square**.

sq. abbr (MATH etc) = **square**.

squabble [skwâb'əl] n querelle f, chamaillerie f ♦ vi se chamailler.

squad [skwâd] n (MIL, POLICE) escouade f, groupe m; (SOCCER) contingent m.

squad car n (POLICE) voiture f de police.

squadron [skwâd'rən] n (MIL) escadron m; (AVIAT, NAUT) escadrille f.

squalid [skwâl'id] a sordide, ignoble.

squall [skwôl] n rafale f, bourrasque f.

squalor [skwâl'ûr] n conditions fpl sordides.

squander [skwân'dûr] vt gaspiller, dilapider.

square [skwär] n carré m; (in town) place f; (US: block) îlot m, pâté m de maisons; (instrument) équerre f ♦ a carré(e); (honest) honnête, régulier(ière); (col: ideas, tastes) vieux jeu inv, qui retarde ♦ vt (arrange) régler; arranger; (MATH) élever au carré; (reconcile) concilier ♦ vi (agree) cadrer, s'accorder; **all ~** quitte; à égalité; **a ~ meal** un repas convenable; **2 meters ~** (de) 2 mètres sur 2; **1 ~ meter** 1 mètre carré; **we're back to ~ one** (fig) on se retrouve à la case départ.

square bracket n (TYP) crochet m.

squarely [skwär'lē] ad carrément; (honestly, fairly) honnêtement, équitablement.

square root n racine carrée.

squash [skwâsh] n (SPORT) squash m; (vegetable) courge f; (Brit: drink): **lemon/orange ~** citronnade/orangeade f ♦ vt écraser.

squat [skwât] *a* petit(e) et épais(se), ramassé(e) ♦ *vi* s'accroupir; (*on property*) squatter, squattériser.
squatter [skwât'ûr] *n* squatter *m*.
squawk [skwôk] *vi* pousser un *or* des glousse-ment(s).
squeak [skwēk] *n* (*of hinge, wheel etc*) grince-ment *m*; (*of shoes*) craquement *m*; (*of mouse etc*) petit cri aigu ♦ *vi* grincer, crier.
squeal [skwēl] *vi* pousser un *or* des cri(s) aigu(s) *or* perçant(s).
squeamish [skwē'mish] *a* facilement dégoû-té(e); facilement scandalisé(e).
squeeze [skwēz] *n* pression *f*; (*also*: **credit** ~) encadrement *m* du crédit, restrictions *fpl* de crédit ♦ *vt* presser; (*hand, arm*) serrer ♦ *vi*: **to ~ past/under sth** se glisser avec (beau-coup de) difficulté devant/sous qch; **a ~ of lemon** quelques gouttes de citron.
squeeze out *vt* exprimer; (*fig*) soutirer.
squelch [skwelch] *vi* faire un bruit de succion; patauger.
squib [skwib] *n* pétard *m*.
squid [skwid] *n* calmar *m*.
squiggle [skwig'əl] *n* gribouillis *m*.
squint [skwint] *vi* loucher ♦ *n*: **he has a ~** il louche, il souffre de strabisme; **to ~ at sth** regarder qch du coin de l'œil; (*quickly*) jeter un coup d'œil à qch.
squirm [skwûrm] *vi* se tortiller.
squirrel [skwûr'əl] *n* écureuil *m*.
squirt [skwûrt] *n* jet *m* ♦ *vi* jaillir, gicler.
Sr *abbr* = **senior, sister** (*REL*).
Sri Lanka [srē lângk'ə] *n* Sri Lanka *m or f*.
SRO *abbr* (*US*) = *standing room only*.
SS *abbr* (= *steamship*) S/S.
SSA *n abbr* (*US*: = *Social Security Adminis-tration*) organisme de sécurité sociale.
SST *n abbr* (*US*) = *supersonic transport*.
St *abbr* (= *saint*) St; (= *street*) R.
stab [stab] *n* (*with knife etc*) coup *m* (de cou-teau *etc*); (*col: try*): **to have a ~ at (doing) sth** s'essayer à (faire) qch ♦ *vt* poignarder; **to ~ sb to death** tuer qn à coups de couteau.
stabbing [stab'ing] *n*: **there's been a ~** quelqu'un a été attaqué à coups de couteau ♦ *a* (*pain, ache*) lancinant(e).
stability [stəbil'ətē] *n* stabilité *f*.
stabilization [stābiləzā'shən] *n* stabilisation *f*.
stabilize [stā'bəlīz] *vt* stabiliser ♦ *vi* se stabili-ser.
stabilizer [stā'bəlīzûr] *n* stabilisateur *m*.
stable [stā'bəl] *n* écurie *f* ♦ *a* stable; **riding ~s** centre *m* d'équitation.
stableboy [stā'bəlboi] *n* garçon *m* d'écurie.
staccato [stəkä'tō] *ad* staccato ♦ *a* (*MUS*) pi-qué(e); (*noise, voice*) saccadé(e).
stack [stak] *n* tas *m*, pile *f* ♦ *vt* empiler, entasser.
stadium [stā'dēəm] *n* stade *m*.
staff [staf] *n* (*work force*) personnel *m*; (*Brit SCOL: also*: **teaching** ~) professeurs *mpl*, enseignants *mpl*, personnel enseignant; (*servants*) domestiques *mpl*; (*MIL*) état-major *m*; (*stick*) perche *f*, bâton *m* ♦ *vt* pourvoir en personnel.
Staffs *abbr* (*Brit*) = *Staffordshire*.
stag [stag] *n* cerf *m*; (*Brit STOCK EXCHANGE*) loup *m*.

stage [stāj] *n* scène *f*; (*profession*): **the ~** le théâtre; (*point*) étape *f*, stade *m*; (*platform*) estrade *f* ♦ *vt* (*play*) monter, mettre en scène; (*demonstration*) organiser; (*fig: re-covery etc*) effectuer; **in ~s** par étapes, par degrés; **to go through a difficult ~** traverser une période difficile; **in the early ~s** au dé-but; **in the final ~s** à la fin.
stagecoach [stāj'kōch] *n* diligence *f*.
stage door *n* entrée *f* des artistes.
stage fright *n* trac *m*.
stagehand [stāj'hand] *n* machiniste *m*.
stage-manage [stāj'man'ij] *vt* (*fig*) orchestrer.
stage manager *n* régisseur *m*.
stagger [stag'ûr] *vi* chanceler, tituber ♦ *vt* (*person*) stupéfier; bouleverser; (*hours, vaca-tion*) étaler, échelonner.
staggering [stag'ûring] *a* (*amazing*) stupé-fiant(e), renversant(e).
stagnant [stag'nənt] *a* stagnant(e).
stagnate [stag'nāt] *vi* stagner, croupir.
stagnation [stagnā'shən] *n* stagnation *f*.
stag party *n* enterrement *m* de vie de garçon.
staid [stād] *a* posé(e), rassis(e).
stain [stān] *n* tache *f*; (*coloring*) colorant *m* ♦ *vt* tacher; (*wood*) teindre.
stained glass window [stānd' glas win'dō] *n* vitrail *m*.
stainless [stān'lis] *a* (*steel*) inoxydable.
stain remover *n* détachant *m*.
stair [stär] *n* (*step*) marche *f*; ~**s** *npl* escalier *m*; **on the ~s** dans l'escalier.
staircase [stär'kās], **stairway** [stär'wā] *n* esca-lier *m*.
stairwell [stär'wel] *n* cage *f* d'escalier.
stake [stāk] *n* pieu *m*, poteau *m*; (*BETTING*) enjeu *m* ♦ *vt* risquer, jouer; (*also*: ~ **out**: *area*) marquer, délimiter; **to be at ~** être en jeu; **to have a ~ in sth** avoir des intérêts (en jeu) dans qch; **to ~ a claim (to sth)** re-vendiquer (qch).
stalactite [stəlak'tīt] *n* stalactite *f*.
stalagmite [stəlag'mīt] *n* stalagmite *f*.
stale [stāl] *a* (*bread*) rassis(e); (*beer*) éventé(e); (*smell*) de renfermé.
stalemate [stāl'māt] *n* pat *m*; (*fig*) impasse *f*.
stalk [stôk] *n* tige *f* ♦ *vt* traquer ♦ *vi*: **to ~ in/ out** *etc* entrer/sortir *etc* avec raideur.
stall [stôl] *n* (*in stable*) stalle *f*; (*Brit: in street, market etc*) éventaire *m*, étal *m* ♦ *vt* (*AUT*) caler ♦ *vi* (*AUT*) caler; (*fig*) essayer de gagner du temps; ~**s** *npl* (*Brit: in cine-ma, theater*) orchestre *m*; **a newspaper/ flower ~** un kiosque à journaux/de fleuriste.
stallholder [stôl'hōldûr] *n* (*Brit*) marchand/e en plein air.
stallion [stal'yən] *n* étalon *m* (*cheval*).
stalwart [stôl'wûrt] *n* partisan *m* fidèle.
stamen [stā'mən] *n* étamine *f*.
stamina [stam'inə] *n* vigueur *f*, endurance *f*.
stammer [stam'ûr] *n* bégaiement *m* ♦ *vi* bé-gayer.
stamp [stamp] *n* timbre *m*; (*mark, also fig*) empreinte *f*; (*on document*) cachet *m* ♦ *vi* (*also*: ~ **one's foot**) taper du pied ♦ *vt* tamponner, estamper; (*letter*) timbrer; ~**ed addressed envelope (sae)** (*Brit*) enveloppe affranchie pour la réponse.
stamp out *vt* (*fire*) piétiner; (*crime*) éradi-

quer; (*opposition*) éliminer.
stamp album *n* album *m* de timbres(-poste).
stamp collecting *n* philatélie *f*.
stampede [stampĕd'] *n* ruée *f*; (*of cattle*) débandade *f*.
stamp machine *n* distributeur *m* de timbres-poste.
stance [stans] *n* position *f*.
stand [stand] *n* (*position*) position *f*; (*MIL*) résistance *f*; (*structure*) guéridon *m*; support *m*; (*COMM*) étalage *m*, stand *m*; (*SPORT*) tribune *f*; (*also*: **music ~**) pupitre *m* ♦ *vb* (*pt*, *pp* **stood** [stŏŏd]) *vi* être *or* se tenir (debout); (*rise*) se lever, se mettre debout; (*be placed*) se trouver ♦ *vt* (*place*) mettre, poser; (*tolerate, withstand*) supporter; **to make a ~** prendre position; **to take a ~ on an issue** prendre position sur un problème; **to ~ for parliament** (*Brit*) se présenter aux élections (*comme candidat à la députation*); **to ~ guard** *or* **watch** (*MIL*) monter la garde; **it ~s to reason** c'est logique; cela va de soi; **as things ~** dans l'état actuel des choses; **to ~ sb a drink/meal** payer à boire/à manger à qn; **I can't ~ him** je ne peux pas le voir.
stand aside *vi* s'écarter.
stand by *vi* (*be ready*) se tenir prêt(e) ♦ *vt fus* (*opinion*) s'en tenir à.
stand down *vi* (*withdraw*) se retirer; (*LAW*) renoncer à ses droits.
stand for *vt fus* (*signify*) représenter, signifier; (*tolerate*) supporter, tolérer.
stand in for *vt fus* remplacer.
stand out *vi* (*be prominent*) ressortir.
stand up *vi* (*rise*) se lever, se mettre debout.
stand up for *vt fus* défendre.
stand up to *vt fus* tenir tête à, résister à.
stand-alone [stand'əlōn'] *a* (*COMPUT*) autonome.
standard [stan'dûrd] *n* (*reference*) norme *f*; (*level*) niveau *m*; (*flag*) étendard *m* ♦ *a* (*size etc*) ordinaire, normal(e); (*model, feature*) standard *inv*; (*practice*) courant(e); (*text*) de base **~s** *npl* (*morals*) morale *f*, principes *mpl*; **to be** *or* **come up to ~** être du niveau voulu *or* à la hauteur; **to apply a double ~** avoir *or* appliquer deux poids deux mesures; **~ of living** niveau de vie.
standardization [standûrdəzā'shən] *n* standardisation *f*.
standardize [stan'dûrdīz] *vt* standardiser.
standard lamp *n* (*Brit*) lampadaire *m*.
standard time *n* heure légale.
standby [stand'bī] *n* remplaçant/e ♦ *a* (*provisions*) de réserve; (*generator*) de secours; (*ticket, passenger*) sans garantie; **to be on ~** se tenir prêt(e) (à intervenir); (*doctor*) être de garde.
stand-in [stand'in] *n* remplaçant/e; (*CINEMA*) doublure *f*.
standing [stan'ding] *a* debout *inv*; (*permanent: rule*) immuable; (*army*) de métier; (*grievance*) constant(e), de longue date ♦ *n* réputation *f*, rang *m*, standing *m*; (*duration*): **of 6 months'** ~ qui dure depuis 6 mois; **of many years'** ~ qui dure *or* existe depuis longtemps; **he was given a ~ ovation** on s'est levé pour l'acclamer; **it's a ~ joke** c'est

un vieux sujet de plaisanterie; **a man of some ~** un homme estimé; **"no ~"** (*US AUT*) "stationnement interdit".
standing committee *n* commission permanente.
standing order *n* (*Brit*: *at bank*) virement permanent; **~s** *npl* (*MIL*) règlement *m*.
standing room *n* places *fpl* debout.
standoffish [standôf'ish] *a* distant(e), froid(e).
standpat [stand'pat] *a* (*US*) inflexible, rigide.
standpipe [stand'pīp] *n* colonne *f* d'alimentation.
standpoint [stand'point] *n* point *m* de vue.
standstill [stand'stil] *n*: **at a ~** à l'arrêt; (*fig*) au point mort; **to come to a ~** s'immobiliser, s'arrêter.
stank [stangk] *pt of* **stink**.
stanza [stan'zə] *n* strophe *f*; couplet *m*.
staple [stā'pəl] *n* (*for papers*) agrafe *f*; (*chief product*) produit *m* de base ♦ *a* (*food, crop, industry etc*) de base, principal(e) ♦ *vt* agrafer.
stapler [stā'plûr] *n* agrafeuse *f*.
star [stâr] *n* étoile *f*; (*celebrity*) vedette *f* ♦ *vi*: **to ~ (in)** être la vedette (de) ♦ *vt* (*CINEMA*) avoir pour vedette; **4-~ hotel** hôtel *m* 4 étoiles; **4-~ petrol** (*Brit*) super *m*.
star attraction *n* grande attraction.
starboard [stâr'bûrd] *n* tribord *m*; **to ~** à tribord.
starch [stârch] *n* amidon *m*.
starched [stârcht] *a* (*collar*) amidonné(e), empesé(e).
starchy [stâr'chē] *a* riche en féculents; (*person*) guindé(e).
stardom [stâr'dəm] *n* célébrité *f*.
stare [stär] *n* regard *m* fixe ♦ *vi*: **to ~ at** regarder fixement.
starfish [stâr'fish] *n* étoile *f* de mer.
stark [stârk] *a* (*bleak*) désolé(e), morne; (*simplicity, color*) austère; (*reality, poverty*) nu(e) ♦ *ad*: **~ naked** complètement nu(e).
starlet [stâr'lit] *n* (*CINEMA*) starlette *f*.
starlight [stâr'līt] *n*: **by ~** à la lumière des étoiles.
starling [stâr'ling] *n* étourneau *m*.
starlit [stâr'lit] *a* étoilé(e); illuminé(e) par les étoiles.
starry [stâr'ē] *a* étoilé(e).
starry-eyed [stâr'ēīd] *a* (*innocent*) ingénu(e).
star-studded [stâr'studid] *a*: **a ~ cast** une distribution prestigieuse.
start [stârt] *n* commencement *m*, début *m*; (*of race*) départ *m*; (*sudden movement*) sursaut *m*; (*advantage*) avance *f* ♦ *vt* commencer; (*found: business, newspaper*) lancer, créer ♦ *vi* partir, se mettre en route; (*jump*) sursauter; **to ~ doing sth** se mettre à faire qch; **at the ~** au début; **for a ~** d'abord, pour commencer; **to make an early ~** partir *or* commencer de bonne heure; **to ~ (off) with** ... (*firstly*) d'abord ...; (*at the beginning*) au commencement ...
start off *vi* commencer; (*leave*) partir.
start over *vi* (*US*) recommencer.
start up *vi* commencer; (*car*) démarrer ♦ *vt* déclencher; (*car*) mettre en marche.
starter [stâr'tûr] *n* (*AUT*) démarreur *m*; (*SPORT: official*) starter *m*; (: *runner, horse*)

partant *m*; (*Brit CULIN*) entrée *f*; **for ~s** d'abord, pour commencer.

starting point [stár'ting point] *n* point *m* de départ.

starting price [stár'ting prīs] *n* prix initial.

startle [stár'təl] *vt* faire sursauter; donner un choc à.

startling [stárt'ling] *a* surprenant(e), saisissant(e).

starvation [stárvā'shən] *n* faim *f*, famine *f*; **to die of ~** mourir de faim *or* d'inanition.

starve [stárv] *vi* mourir de faim; être affamé(e) ♦ *vt* affamer; **I'm starving** je meurs de faim.

state [stāt] *n* état *m*; (*pomp*): **in ~** en grande pompe ♦ *vt* (*declare*) déclarer, affirmer; (*specify*) indiquer, spécifier; **to be in a ~** être dans tous ses états; **~ of emergency** état d'urgence; **~ of mind** état d'esprit; **the ~ of the art** l'état actuel de la technologie (*or* des connaissances).

state control *n* contrôle *m* de l'État.

stated [stā'tid] *a* fixé(e), prescrit(e).

State Department *n* (*US*) Département *m* d'État, ≈ ministère *m* des Affaires étrangères.

state highway *n* (*US AUT*) route nationale.

stateless [stāt'lis] *a* apatride.

stately [stāt'lē] *a* majestueux(euse), imposant(e).

statement [stāt'mənt] *n* déclaration *f*; (*LAW*) déposition *f*; (*ECON*) relevé *m*; **official ~** communiqué officiel; **~ of account, bank ~** relevé de compte.

state-owned [stāt'ōnd'] *a* étatisé(e).

States [stāts] *npl*: **the ~** les États-Unis *mpl*.

state secret *n* secret *m* d'État.

statesman [stāts'mən] *n* homme *m* d'État.

statesmanship [stāts'mənship] *n* qualités *fpl* d'homme d'état.

static [stat'ik] *n* (*RADIO*) parasites *mpl*; (*also*: **~ electricity**) électricité *f* statique ♦ *a* statique.

station [stā'shən] *n* gare *f*; (*MIL*, *POLICE*) poste *m* (militaire *or* de police *etc*); (*rank*) condition *f*, rang *m* ♦ *vt* placer, poster; **action ~s** postes de combat; **to be ~ed in** (*MIL*) être en garnison à.

stationary [stā'shənärē] *a* à l'arrêt, immobile.

stationer [stā'shənûr] *n* papetier/ière; **~'s (shop)** papeterie *f*.

stationery [stā'shənärē] *n* papier *m* à lettres, petit matériel de bureau.

station master *n* (*RAIL*) chef *m* de gare.

station wagon *n* (*US*) break *m*.

statistic [stətis'tik] *n* statistique *f*.

statistical [stətis'tikəl] *a* statistique.

statistics [stətis'tiks] *n* (*science*) statistique *f*.

statue [stach'ōō] *n* statue *f*.

statuesque [stachōōesk'] *a* sculptural(e).

statuette [stachōōet'] *n* statuette *f*.

stature [stach'ûr] *n* stature *f*; (*fig*) envergure *f*.

status [stā'təs] *n* position *f*, situation *f*; (*prestige*) prestige *m*; (*ADMIN*, *official position*) statut *m*.

status quo [stā'təs kwō] *n*: **the ~** le statu quo.

status symbol *n* marque *f* de standing, signe

extérieur de richesse.

statute [stach'ōōt] *n* loi *f*; **~s** *npl* (*of club etc*) statuts *mpl*.

statute book *n* ≈ code *m*, textes *mpl* de loi.

statutory [stach'ōōtôrē] *a* statutaire, prévu(e) par un article de loi; **~ meeting** assemblée constitutive *or* statutaire.

staunch [stônch] *a* sûr(e), loyal(e) ♦ *vt* étancher.

stave [stāv] *n* (*MUS*) portée *f* ♦ *vt*: **to ~ off** (*attack*) parer; (*threat*) conjurer.

stay [stā] *n* (*period of time*) séjour *m*; (*LAW*): **~ of execution** sursis *m* à statuer ♦ *vi* rester; (*reside*) loger; (*spend some time*) séjourner; **to ~ put** ne pas bouger; **to ~ with friends** loger chez des amis; **to ~ the night** passer la nuit.

stay behind *vi* rester en arrière.

stay in *vi* (*at home*) rester à la maison.

stay on *vi* rester.

stay out *vi* (*of house*) ne pas rentrer; (*strikers*) rester en grève.

stay up *vi* (*at night*) ne pas se coucher.

staying power [stā'ing pou'ûr] *n* endurance *f*.

STD *n abbr* (*Brit*: = *subscriber trunk dialling*) l'automatique *m*; (= *sexually transmitted disease*) MST *f*.

stead [sted] *n*: **in sb's ~** à la place de qn.

steadfast [sted'fast] *a* ferme, résolu(e).

steadily [sted'ilē] *ad* régulièrement; fermement; d'une voix *etc* ferme.

steady [sted'ē] *a* stable, solide, ferme; (*regular*) constant(e), régulier(ière); (*person*) calme, pondéré(e) ♦ *vt* assurer, stabiliser; (*voice*) assurer; **to ~ oneself** reprendre son aplomb.

steak [stāk] *n* (*meat*) bifteck *m*, steak *m*; (*fish*) tranche *f*.

steakhouse [stāk'hous] *n* ≈ grill-room *m*.

steal, *pt* **stole,** *pp* **stolen** [stēl, stōl, stō'lən] *vt*, *vi* voler.

steal away, steal off *vi* s'esquiver.

stealth [stelth] *n*: **by ~** furtivement.

stealthy [stel'thē] *a* furtif(ive).

steam [stēm] *n* vapeur *f* ♦ *vt* passer à la vapeur; (*CULIN*) cuire à la vapeur ♦ *vi* fumer; (*ship*): **to ~ along** filer; **under one's own ~** (*fig*) par ses propres moyens; **to run out of ~** (*fig: person*) caler; être à bout; **to let off ~** (*fig: col*) se défouler.

steam up *vi* (*window*) se couvrir de buée; **to get ~ed up about sth** (*fig: col*) s'exciter à propos de qch.

steam engine *n* locomotive *f* à vapeur.

steamer [stē'mûr] *n* (bateau *m* à) vapeur *m*; (*CULIN*) ≈ couscoussier *m*.

steam iron *n* fer *m* à repasser à vapeur.

steamroller [stēm'rōlûr] *n* rouleau compresseur.

steamy [stē'mē] *a* embué(e), humide.

steed [stēd] *n* (*literary*) coursier *m*.

steel [stēl] *n* acier *m* ♦ *cpd* d'acier.

steel band *n* steel band *m*.

steel industry *n* sidérurgie *f*.

steel mill *n* aciérie *f*, usine *f* sidérurgique.

steelworks [stēl'wûrks] *n* aciérie *f*.

steely [stē'lē] *a* (*determination*) inflexible; (*eyes, gaze*) d'acier.

steep [stēp] *a* raide, escarpé(e); (*price*) très

élevé(e), excessif(ive) ♦ *vt* (faire) tremper.

steeple [stē'pəl] *n* clocher *m*.

steeplechase [stē'pəlchās] *n* steeple(-chase) *m*.

steeplejack [stē'pəljak] *n* réparateur *m* de clochers et de hautes cheminées.

steeply [stēp'lē] *ad* en pente raide.

steer [stēr] *n* bœuf *m* ♦ *vt* diriger, gouverner; (*lead*) guider ♦ *vi* tenir le gouvernail; **to ~ clear of sb/sth** (*fig*) éviter qn/qch.

steering [stēr'ing] *n* (*AUT*) conduite *f*.

steering column *n* (*AUT*) colonne *f* de direction.

steering committee *n* comité *m* d'organisation.

steering wheel *n* volant *m*.

stellar [stel'ûr] *a* stellaire.

stem [stem] *n* (*of plant*) tige *f*; (*of leaf, fruit*) queue *f*; (*of glass*) pied *m* ♦ *vt* contenir, endiguer, juguler.

stem from *vt fus* provenir de, découler de.

stench [stench] *n* puanteur *f*.

stencil [sten'səl] *n* stencil *m*; pochoir *m* ♦ *vt* polycopier.

stenographer [stənâg'rəfûr] *n* (*US*) sténographe *m/f*.

stenography [stənâg'rəfē] *n* (*US*) sténo(graphie) *f*.

step [step] *n* pas *m*; (*stair*) marche *f*; (*action*) mesure *f*, disposition *f* ♦ *vi*: **to ~ forward** faire un pas en avant, avancer; **~ by ~** pas à pas; (*fig*) petit à petit; **to be in ~ (with)** (*fig*) aller dans le sens (de); **to be out of ~ (with)** (*fig*) être déphasé(e) (par rapport à).

step down *vi* (*fig*) se retirer, se désister.

step in *vi* (*fig*) intervenir.

step off *vt fus* descendre de.

step over *vt fus* enjamber.

step up *vt* augmenter; intensifier.

stepbrother [step'bruᵗẖûr] *n* demi-frère *m*.

stepchild [step'chīld] *n* beau-fils/belle-fille.

stepdaughter [step'dôtûr] *n* belle-fille *f*.

stepfather [step'fâᵗẖûr] *n* beau-père *m*.

stepladder [step'ladûr] *n* escabeau *m*.

stepmother [step'muᵗẖûr] *n* belle-mère *f*.

stepping stone [step'ing stōn] *n* pierre *f* de gué; (*fig*) tremplin *m*.

stepsister [step'sistûr] *n* demi-sœur *f*.

stepson [step'sun] *n* beau-fils *m*.

stereo [stär'ēō] *n* (*system*) stéréo *f*; (*record player*) chaîne *f* stéréo ♦ *a* (*also*: **~phonic**) stéréophonique; **in ~** en stéréo.

stereotype [stär'ēətīp] *n* stéréotype *m* ♦ *vt* stéréotyper.

sterile [stär'əl] *a* stérile.

sterility [stəril'ətē] *n* stérilité *f*.

sterilization [stärələzā'shən] *n* stérilisation *f*.

sterilize [stär'əlīz] *vt* stériliser.

sterling [stûr'ling] *a* sterling *inv*; (*silver*) de bon aloi, fin(e); (*fig*) à toute épreuve, excellent(e) ♦ *n* (*currency*) livre *f* sterling *inv*; **a pound ~** une livre sterling.

sterling area *n* zone *f* sterling *inv*.

stern [stûrn] *a* sévère ♦ *n* (*NAUT*) arrière *m*, poupe *f*.

sternum [stûr'nəm] *n* sternum *m*.

steroid [stär'oid] *n* stéroïde *m*.

stethoscope [steth'əskōp] *n* stéthoscope *m*.

stew [stōō] *n* ragoût *m* ♦ *vt*, *vi* cuire à la casserole; **~ed tea** thé trop infusé; **~ed fruit** fruits cuits *or* en compote.

steward [stōō'ûrd] *n* (*AVIAT, NAUT, RAIL*) steward *m*; (*in club etc*) intendant *m*; (*also*: **shop ~**) délégué syndical.

stewardess [stōō'ûrdis] *n* hôtesse *f*.

stew meat, (*Brit*) **stewing steak** [stōō'ing stāk] *n* bœuf *m* à braiser.

stewpan [stōō'pan] *n* fait-tout *m inv*, faitout *m*.

St. Ex. *abbr* = **stock exchange**.

stg *abbr* = **sterling**.

stick [stik] *n* bâton *m*; (*of chalk etc*) morceau *m* ♦ *vb* (*pt, pp* **stuck** [stuk]) *vt* (*glue*) coller; (*thrust*): **to ~ sth into** piquer *or* planter *or* enfoncer qch dans; (*col: put*) mettre, fourrer; (*: tolerate*) supporter ♦ *vi* (*adhere*) coller; (*remain*) rester; (*get jammed: door, elevator*) se bloquer; **to ~ to** (*one's word, promise*) s'en tenir à; (*principles*) rester fidèle à.

stick around *vi* (*col*) rester (dans les parages).

stick out *vi* dépasser, sortir ♦ *vt*: **to ~ it out** (*col*) tenir le coup.

stick up *vi* dépasser, sortir.

stick up for *vt fus* défendre.

sticker [stik'ûr] *n* auto-collant *m*.

sticking plaster [stik'ing plas'tûr] *n* sparadrap *m*, pansement adhésif.

stickleback [stik'əlbak] *n* épinoche *f*.

stickler [stik'lûr] *n*: **to be a ~ for** être pointilleux(euse) sur.

stick-up [stik'up] *n* (*col*) braquage *m*, hold-up *m*.

sticky [stik'ē] *a* poisseux(euse); (*label*) adhésif(ive).

stiff [stif] *a* (*gen*) raide, rigide; (*door, brush*) dur(e); (*difficult*) difficile, ardu(e); (*cold*) froid(e), distant(e); (*strong, high*) fort(e), élevé(e); **to be** *or* **feel ~** (*person*) avoir des courbatures; **to have a ~ back** avoir mal au dos; **~ neck** torticolis *m*.

stiffen [stif'ən] *vt* raidir, renforcer ♦ *vi* se raidir; se durcir.

stiffness [stif'nis] *n* raideur *f*.

stifle [stī'fəl] *vt* étouffer, réprimer.

stifling [stīf'ling] *a* (*heat*) suffocant(e).

stigma, *pl* (*BOT, MED, REL*) **~ta,** (*fig*) **~s** [stigmə, stigmâ'tə] *n* stigmate *m*.

stile [stīl] *n* échalier *m*.

stiletto [stilet'ō] *n* (*Brit: also*: **~ heel**) talon *m* aiguille.

still [stil] *a* (*motionless*) immobile; (*calm*) calme, tranquille; (*Brit: orange drink etc*) non gazeux(euse) ♦ *ad* (*up to this time*) encore, toujours; (*even*) encore; (*nonetheless*) quand même, tout de même ♦ *n* (*CINEMA*) photo *f*; **to stand ~** rester immobile, ne pas bouger; **keep ~!** ne bouge pas!; **he ~ hasn't arrived** il n'est pas encore arrivé, il n'est toujours pas arrivé.

stillborn [stil'bôrn] *a* mort-né(e).

still life *n* nature morte.

stilt [stilt] *n* échasse *f*; (*pile*) pilotis *m*.

stilted [stil'tid] *a* guindé(e), emprunté(e).

stimulant [stim'yələnt] *n* stimulant *m*.

stimulate [stim'yəlāt] *vt* stimuler.

stimulating [stim'yəlāting] *a* stimulant(e).

stimulation [stimyəlā'shən] *n* stimulation *f*.

stimulus, *pl* **stimuli** [stim'yələs, stim'yəlī] *n* stimulant *m*; (*BIOL, PSYCH*) stimulus *m*.

sting [sting] *n* piqûre *f*; (*organ*) dard *m*; (*col: confidence trick*) arnaque *m* ♦ *vt* (*pt, pp* **stung** [stung]) piquer ♦ *vi* piquer; **my eyes are ~ing** j'ai les yeux qui piquent.

stingy [stin'jē] *a* avare, pingre, chiche.

stink [stingk] *n* puanteur *f* ♦ *vi* (*pt* **stank,** *pp* **stunk** [stangk, stungk]) puer, empester.

stinker [stingk'ûr] *n* (*col: problem, exam*) vacherie *f*; (: *person*) dégueulasse *m/f*.

stinking [sting'king] *a* (*fig: col*) infect(e); **~ rich** bourré(e) de pognon.

stint [stint] *n* part *f* de travail ♦ *vi*: **to ~ on** lésiner sur, être chiche de.

stipend [stī'pend] *n* (*of vicar etc*) traitement *m*.

stipendiary [stīpen'dēārē] *a*: **~ magistrate** juge *m* de tribunal d'instance.

stipulate [stip'yəlāt] *vt* stipuler.

stipulation [stipyəlā'shən] *n* stipulation *f*, condition *f*.

stir [stûr] *n* agitation *f*, sensation *f* ♦ *vt* remuer ♦ *vi* remuer, bouger; **to give sth a ~** remuer qch; **to cause a ~** faire sensation.

stir up *vt* exciter.

stirring [stûr'ing] *a* excitant(e); émouvant(e).

stirrup [stûr'əp] *n* étrier *m*.

stitch [stich] *n* (*SEWING*) point *m*; (*KNITTING*) maille *f*; (*MED*) point de suture; (*pain*) point de côté ♦ *vt* coudre, piquer; suturer.

stoat [stōt] *n* hermine *f* (*avec son pelage d'été*).

stock [stäk] *n* réserve *f*, provision *f*; (*COMM*) stock *m*; (*AGR*) cheptel *m*, bétail *m*; (*CULIN*) bouillon *m*; (*FINANCE*) valeurs *fpl*, titres *mpl*; (*RAIL: also*: **rolling ~**) matériel roulant; (*descent, origin*) souche *f* ♦ *a* (*fig: reply etc*) courant(e); classique ♦ *vt* (*have in stock*) avoir, vendre; **well-~ed** bien approvisionné(e) or fourni(e); **in ~** en stock, en magasin; **out of ~** épuisé(e); **to take ~** (*fig*) faire le point; **~s and shares** valeurs (mobilières), titres; **government ~** fonds *mpl* publics.

stock up *vi*: **to ~ up (with)** s'approvisionner (en).

stockade [stäkād'] *n* palissade *f*.

stockbroker [stäk'brōkûr] *n* agent *m* de change.

stock control *n* (*COMM*) gestion *f* des stocks.

stock cube *n* (*Brit CULIN*) bouillon-cube *m*.

stock exchange *n* Bourse *f* (des valeurs).

stockholder [stäk'hōldûr] *n* actionnaire *m/f*.

Stockholm [stäk'hōm] *n* Stockholm.

stocking [stäk'ing] *n* bas *m*.

stock-in-trade [stäk'intrād'] *n* (*fig*): **it's his ~** c'est sa spécialité.

stockist [stäk'ist] *n* (*Brit*) stockiste *m*.

stock market *n* Bourse *f*, marché financier.

stock phrase *n* cliché *m*.

stockpile [stäk'pīl] *n* stock *m*, réserve *f* ♦ *vt* stocker, accumuler.

stockroom [stäk'rōōm] *n* réserve *f*, magasin *m*.

stocktaking [stäk'tāking] *n* (*Brit COMM*) inventaire *m*.

stocky [stäk'ē] *a* trapu(e), râblé(e).

stodgy [stäj'ē] *a* bourratif(ive), lourd(e).

stoic [stō'ik] *n* stoïque *m/f*.

stoical [stō'ikəl] *a* stoïque.

stoke [stōk] *vt* garnir, entretenir; chauffer.

stoker [stō'kûr] *n* (*RAIL, NAUT etc*) chauffeur *m*.

stole [stōl] *pt of* **steal** ♦ *n* étole *f*.

stolen [stō'lən] *pp of* **steal**.

stolid [stäl'id] *a* impassible, flegmatique.

stomach [stum'ək] *n* estomac *m*; (*abdomen*) ventre *m* ♦ *vt* supporter, digérer; **to have no ~ for heights** être sujet(te) au vertige.

stomachache [stum'əkāk] *n* mal *m* à l'estomac *or* au ventre.

stomach pump *n* pompe stomacale.

stomach ulcer *n* ulcère *m* à l'estomac.

stomp [stämp] *vi*: **to ~ in/out** entrer/sortir d'un pas bruyant.

stone [stōn] *n* pierre *f*; (*pebble*) caillou *m*, galet *m*; (*in fruit*) noyau *m*; (*MED*) calcul *m*; (*Brit: weight*) = 6.348 kg; 14 pounds ♦ *cpd* de *or* en pierre ♦ *vt* dénoyauter; **within a ~'s throw of the station** à deux pas de la gare.

Stone Age *n*: **the ~** l'âge *m* de pierre.

stone-cold [stōn'kōld'] *a* complètement froid(e).

stoned [stōnd] *a* (*col: drunk*) bourré(e); (: *on drugs*) défoncé(e).

stone-deaf [stōn'def'] *a* sourd(e) comme un pot.

stonemason [stōn'māsən] *n* tailleur *m* de pierre(s).

stonework [stōn'wûrk] *n* maçonnerie *f*.

stony [stō'nē] *a* pierreux(euse), rocailleux(euse).

stood [stōōd] *pt, pp of* **stand**.

stool [stōōl] *n* tabouret *m*.

stoop [stōōp] *vi* (*also*: **have a ~**) être voûté(e); (*bend*) se baisser, se courber; (*fig*): **to ~ to sth/doing sth** s'abaisser jusqu'à qch/ jusqu'à faire qch.

stop [stäp] *n* arrêt *m*; (*short stay*) halte *f*; (*in punctuation*) point *m* ♦ *vt* arrêter; (*break off*) interrompre; (*also*: **put a ~ to**) mettre fin à; (*prevent*) empêcher ♦ *vi* s'arrêter; (*rain, noise etc*) cesser, s'arrêter; **to ~ doing sth** cesser *or* arrêter de faire qch; **to ~ sb (from) doing sth** empêcher qn de faire qch; **to ~ dead** *vi* s'arrêter net; **~ it!** arrête!

stop by *vi* s'arrêter (au passage).

stop off *vi* faire une courte halte.

stop up *vt* (*hole*) boucher.

stopcock [stäp'käk] *n* robinet *m* d'arrêt.

stopgap [stäp'gap] *n* (*person*) bouche-trou *m*; (*also*: **~ measure**) mesure *f* intérimaire.

stoplights [stäp'līts] *npl* (*AUT*) signaux *mpl* de stop, feux *mpl* arrière.

stopover [stäp'ōvûr] *n* halte *f*; (*AVIAT*) escale *f*.

stoppage [stäp'ij] *n* arrêt *m*; (*of pay*) retenue *f*; (*strike*) arrêt de travail.

stopper [stäp'ûr] *n* bouchon *m*.

stop press *n* (*Brit*) nouvelles *fpl* de dernière heure.

stopwatch [stäp'wäch] *n* chronomètre *m*.

storage [stōr'ij] *n* emmagasinage *m*; (*of nuclear waste etc*) stockage *m*; (*in house*) rangement *m*; (*COMPUT*) mise *f* en mémoire *or* réserve.

storage heater *n* (*Brit*) radiateur *m* électrique par accumulation.

storage room *n* (*US*) débarras *m*.

store [stôr] *n* provision *f*, réserve *f*; (*depot*) entrepôt *m*; magasin *m*; (*Brit*: *large shop*) grand magasin ♦ *vt* emmagasiner; (*nuclear waste etc*) stocker; (*in filing system*) classer, ranger; (*COMPUT*) mettre en mémoire; ~**s** *npl* provisions; **who knows what is in ~ for us?** qui sait ce que l'avenir nous réserve *or* ce qui nous attend?; **to set great/little ~ by sth** faire grand cas/peu de cas de qch.

store up *vt* mettre en réserve, emmagasiner.

storehouse [stôr'hous] *n* entrepôt *m*.

storekeeper [stôr'kēpûr] *n* commerçant/e.

storeroom [stôr'rōōm] *n* réserve *f*, magasin *m*.

storey [stôr'ē] *n* (*Brit*) étage *m*.

stork [stôrk] *n* cigogne *f*.

storm [stôrm] *n* tempête *f*; (*also*: **electric ~**) orage *m* ♦ *vi* (*fig*) fulminer ♦ *vt* prendre d'assaut.

storm cloud *n* nuage *m* d'orage.

storm door *n* double-porte (extérieure).

stormy [stôr'mē] *a* orageux(euse).

story [stôr'ē] *n* histoire *f*; récit *m*; (*PRESS*: *article*) article *m*; (: *subject*) affaire *f*; (*US*: *floor*) étage *m*.

storybook [stôr'ēbōōk] *n* livre *m* d'histoires *or* de contes.

storyteller [stôr'ētelûr] *n* conteur/euse.

stout [stout] *a* solide; (*brave*) intrépide; (*fat*) gros(se), corpulent(e) ♦ *n* bière brune.

stove [stōv] *n* (*for cooking*) fourneau *m*; (: *small*) réchaud *m*; (*for heating*) poêle *m*; **gas/electric ~** (*cooker*) cuisinière *f* à gaz/électrique.

stow [stō] *vt* ranger; cacher.

stowaway [stō'əwā] *n* passager/ère clandestin(e).

straddle [strad'əl] *vt* enjamber, être à cheval sur.

strafe [stráf] *vt* mitrailler.

straggle [strag'əl] *vi* être (*or* marcher) en désordre; ~**d along the coast** disséminé(e) tout au long de la côte.

straggler [strag'lûr] *n* traînard/e.

straggling [strag'ling], **straggly** [strag'lē] *a* (*hair*) en désordre.

straight [strāt] *a* droit(e); (*frank*) honnête, franc(franche); (*plain, uncomplicated*) simple; (*THEATER*: *part, play*) sérieux(euse); (*col*: *not bent*) normal(e); réglo *inv* ♦ *ad* (*tout*) droit; (*drink*) sec, sans eau ♦ *n*: **the ~** (*SPORT*) la ligne droite; **to put** *or* **get ~** mettre en ordre, mettre de l'ordre dans; **let's get this ~** mettons les choses au point; **10 ~ wins** 10 victoires d'affilée; **to go ~ home** rentrer directement à la maison; **~ away, ~ off** (*at once*) tout de suite.

straighten [strā'tən] *vt* (*also*: **~ out**) redresser; **to ~ things out** arranger les choses.

straight-faced [strāt'fāst] *a* impassible ♦ *ad* en gardant son sérieux.

straightforward [strātfôr'wûrd] *a* simple; (*frank*) honnête, direct(e).

strain [strān] *n* (*TECH*) tension *f*; pression *f*; (*physical*) effort *m*; (*mental*) tension (nerveuse); (*MED*) entorse *f*; (*streak, trace*) tendance *f*; élément *m*; (*breed*) variété *f*; (*of virus*) souche *f*; ~**s** *npl* (*of music*) accents *mpl*, accords *mpl* ♦ *vt* tendre fortement; mettre à l'épreuve; (*filter*) passer, filtrer ♦ *vi* peiner, fournir un gros effort; **he's been under a lot of ~** il a traversé des moments très difficiles, il est très éprouvé nerveusement.

strained [strānd] *a* (*laugh etc*) forcé(e), contraint(e); (*relations*) tendu(e).

strainer [strā'nûr] *n* passoire *f*.

strait [strāt] *n* (*GEO*) détroit *m*; **to be in dire ~s** (*fig*) être dans une situation désespérée.

straitjacket [strāt'jakit] *n* camisole *f* de force.

strait-laced [strāt'lāst] *a* collet monté *inv*.

strand [strand] *n* (*of thread*) fil *m*, brin *m* ♦ *vt* (*boat*) échouer.

stranded [stran'did] *a* en rade, en plan.

strange [strānj] *a* (*not known*) inconnu(e); (*odd*) étrange, bizarre.

strangely [strānj'lē] *ad* étrangement, bizarrement.

stranger [strān'jûr] *n* (*unknown*) inconnu/e; (*from somewhere else*) étranger/ère; **I'm a ~ here** je ne suis pas d'ici.

strangle [strang'gəl] *vt* étrangler.

stranglehold [strang'gəlhōld] *n* (*fig*) emprise totale, mainmise *f*.

strangulation [stranggyəlā'shən] *n* strangulation *f*.

strap [strap] *n* lanière *f*, courroie *f*, sangle *f*; (*of slip, dress*) bretelle *f* ♦ *vt* attacher (avec une courroie *etc*).

straphanging [strap'hanging] *n* (fait *m* de) voyager debout (dans le métro *etc*).

strapless [strap'lis] *a* (*bra, dress*) sans bretelles.

strapping [strap'ing] *a* bien découplé(e), costaud(e).

Strasbourg [stras'bûrg] *n* Strasbourg.

strata [strā'tə] *npl of* **stratum**.

stratagem [strat'əjəm] *n* stratagème *m*.

strategic [strətē'jik] *a* stratégique.

strategist [strat'ijist] *n* stratège *m*.

strategy [strat'ijē] *n* stratégie *f*.

stratosphere [strat'əsfēr] *n* stratosphère *f*.

stratum, *pl* **strata** [strā'təm, strā'tə] *n* strate *f*, couche *f*.

straw [strô] *n* paille *f*; **that's the last ~!** ça c'est le comble!

strawberry [strô'bārē] *n* fraise *f*; (*plant*) fraisier *m*.

stray [strā] *a* (*animal*) perdu(e), errant(e) ♦ *vi* s'égarer; ~ **bullet** balle perdue.

streak [strēk] *n* raie *f*, bande *f*, filet *m*; (*fig*: *of madness etc*): **a ~ of** une *or* des tendance(s) à ♦ *vt* zébrer, strier ♦ *vi*: **to ~ past** passer à toute allure; **to have ~s in one's hair** s'être fait faire des mèches; **a winning/losing ~** une bonne/mauvaise série *or* période.

streaky [strē'kē] *a* zébré(e), strié(e).

streaky bacon *n* (*Brit*) ≈ lard *m* (maigre).

stream [strēm] *n* (*brook*) ruisseau *m*; (*current*) courant *m*, flot *m*; (*of people*) défilé ininterrompu, flot ♦ *vt* (*SCOL*) répartir par niveau ♦ *vi* ruisseler; **to ~ in/out** entrer/sortir

à flots; **against the** ~ à contre courant.
streamer [strē'mûr] *n* serpentin *m*, banderole *f*.
streamline [strēm'līn] *vt* donner un profil aéro-dynamique à; (*fig*) rationaliser.
streamlined [strēm'līnd] *a* (*AVIAT*) fuselé(e), profilé(e); (*AUT*) aérodynamique; (*fig*) rationalisé(e).
street [strēt] *n* rue *f*; **the back** ~s les quartiers pauvres; **to walk the** ~s (*homeless*) être à la rue *or* sans abri; (*as prostitute*) faire le trottoir.
streetcar [strēt'kâr] *n* (*US*) tramway *m*.
streetlight [strēt'līt] *n* réverbère *m*.
street lighting *n* éclairage public.
street map, street plan *n* plan *m* des rues.
street market *n* marché *m* à ciel ouvert.
streetsweeper [strēt'swēp'ûr] *n* (*US: person*) balayeur/euse.
streetwise [strēt'wīz] *a* (*col*) futé(e), réaliste.
strength [strengkth] *n* force *f*; (*of girder, knot etc*) solidité *f*; (*of chemical solution*) titre *m*; (*of wine*) degré *m* d'alcool; **on the** ~ **of** en vertu de; **at full** ~ au grand complet; **below** ~ à effectifs réduits.
strengthen [strengk'thən] *vt* renforcer; (*muscle*) fortifier.
strenuous [stren'yōōəs] *a* vigoureux(euse), énergique; (*tiring*) ardu(e), fatigant(e).
stress [stres] *n* (*force, pressure*) pression *f*; (*mental strain*) tension (nerveuse); (*accent*) accent *m*; (*emphasis*) insistance *f* ♦ *vt* insister sur, souligner; **to lay great** ~ **on sth** insister beaucoup sur qch; **to be under** ~ être stressé(e).
stressful [stres'fəl] *a* (*job*) stressant(e).
stretch [strech] *n* (*of sand etc*) étendue *f*; (*of time*) période *f* ♦ *vi* s'étirer; (*extend*): **to** ~ **to** *or* **as far as** s'étendre jusqu'à; (*be enough: money, food*): **to** ~ **to** aller pour ♦ *vt* tendre, étirer; (*spread*) étendre; (*fig*) pousser (au maximum); **at a** ~ sans discontinuer, sans interruption; **to** ~ **a muscle** se distendre un muscle; **to** ~ **one's legs** se dégourdir les jambes.
  stretch out *vi* s'étendre ♦ *vt* (*arm etc*) allonger, tendre; (*to spread*) étendre; **to** ~ **out for sth** allonger la main pour prendre qch.
stretcher [strech'ûr] *n* brancard *m*, civière *f*.
stretcher-bearer [strech'ûrbârûr] *n* brancardier *m*.
stretch marks *npl* (*on skin*) vergetures *fpl*.
strewn [strōōn] *a*: ~ **with** jonché(e) de.
stricken [strik'ən] *a* très éprouvé(e); dévasté(e); ~ **with** frappé(e) *or* atteint(e) de.
strict [strikt] *a* strict(e); **in** ~ **confidence** tout à fait confidentiellement.
strictly [strikt'lē] *ad* strictement; ~ **confidential** strictement confidentiel(le); ~ **speaking** à strictement parler.
strictness [strikt'nis] *n* sévérité *f*.
stride [strīd] *n* grand pas, enjambée *f* ♦ *vi* (*pt* **strode**, *pp* **stridden** [strōd, strid'ən]) marcher à grands pas; **to take in one's** ~ (*fig: changes etc*) accepter sans sourciller.
strident [strīd'ənt] *a* strident(e).
strife [strīf] *n* conflit *m*, dissensions *fpl*.
strike [strīk] *n* grève *f*; (*of oil etc*) découverte

f; (*attack*) raid *m* ♦ *vb* (*pt, pp* **struck** [struk])
vt frapper; (*oil etc*) trouver, découvrir; (*make: agreement, deal*) conclure ♦ *vi* faire grève; (*attack*) attaquer; (*clock*) sonner; **to go on** *or* **come out on** ~ se mettre en grève, faire grève; **to** ~ **a match** frotter une allumette; **to** ~ **a balance** (*fig*) trouver un juste milieu.
strike back *vi* (*MIL, fig*) contre-attaquer.
strike down *vt* (*fig*) terrasser.
strike off *vt* (*from list*) rayer; (: *doctor etc*) radier.
strike out *vt* rayer.
strike up *vt* (*MUS*) se mettre à jouer; **to** ~ **up a friendship with** se lier d'amitié avec.
strikebreaker [strīk'brākûr] *n* briseur *m* de grève.
striker [strī'kûr] *n* gréviste *m/f*; (*SPORT*) buteur *m*.
striking [strī'king] *a* frappant(e), saisissant(e).
string [string] *n* ficelle *f*, fil *m*; (*row: of beads*) rang *m*; (: *of onions, excuses*) chapelet *m*; (: *of people, cars*) file *f*; (*MUS*) corde *f*; (*COMPUT*) chaîne *f* ♦ *vt* (*pt, pp* **strung** [strung]): **to** ~ **out** échelonner; **to** ~ **together** enchaîner; **to** ~ **sb along** faire marcher qn; **the** ~s (*MUS*) les instruments *mpl* à cordes; **to get a job by pulling** ~s obtenir un emploi en faisant jouer le piston; **with no** ~s **attached** (*fig*) sans conditions.
string bean *n* haricot vert.
string(ed) instrument [string(d)' in'strəmənt] *n* (*MUS*) instrument *m* à cordes.
stringent [strin'jənt] *a* rigoureux(euse); (*need*) impérieux(euse).
string quartet *n* quatuor *m* à cordes.
strip [strip] *n* bande *f* ♦ *vt* déshabiller; (*fig*) dégarnir, dépouiller; (*also:* ~ **down:** *machine*) démonter ♦ *vi* se déshabiller.
stripe [strīp] *n* raie *f*, rayure *f*.
striped [strīpt] *a* rayé(e), à rayures.
strip light *n* (*Brit*) (tube *m* au) néon *m*.
stripper [strip'ûr] *n* strip-teaseuse *f*.
striptease [strip'tēz] *n* strip-tease *m*.
strive [strīv], *pt* **strove**, *pp* **striven** [strīv, strōv, striv'ən] *vi*: **to** ~ **to do** s'efforcer de faire.
strode [strōd] *pt of* **stride**.
stroke [strōk] *n* coup *m*; (*MED*) attaque *f*; (*caress*) caresse *f*; (*SWIMMING: style*) (sorte *f* de) nage *f*; (*of piston*) course *f* ♦ *vt* caresser; **at a** ~ d'un (seul) coup; **on the** ~ **of 5** à 5 heures sonnantes; **a** ~ **of luck** un coup de chance; **a 2-**~ **engine** un moteur à 2 temps.
stroll [strōl] *n* petite promenade ♦ *vi* flâner, se promener nonchalamment; **to go for a** ~ aller se promener *or* faire un tour.
stroller [strō'lûr] *n* (*US*) poussette *f*.
strong [strông] *a* (*gen*) fort(e); (*healthy*) vigoureux(euse); (*object, material*) solide; (*distaste, desire*) vif(vive); (*drugs, chemicals*) puissant(e) ♦ *ad*: **to be going** ~ (*company*) marcher bien; (*person*) être toujours solide; **they are 50** ~ ils sont au nombre de 50.
strong-arm [strông'ârm] *a* (*tactics, methods*) musclé(e).
strongbox [strông'bâks] *n* coffre-fort *m*.
strong drink *n* boisson alcoolisée.
stronghold [strông'hōld] *n* bastion *m*.

strong language *n* grossièretés *fpl*.

strongly [strông'lē] *ad* fortement, avec force; vigoureusement; solidement; **I feel ~ about it** c'est une question qui me tient particulièrement à cœur; (*negatively*) j'y suis profondément opposé(e).

strongman [strông'man] *n* hercule *m*, colosse *m*; (*fig*) homme *m* à poigne.

strongroom [strông'rōōm] *n* chambre forte.

strove [strōv] *pt of* **strive**.

struck [struk] *pt*, *pp of* **strike**.

structural [struk'chŭrəl] *a* structural(e); (*CONSTR*) de construction; affectant les parties portantes.

structurally [struk'chŭrəlē] *ad* du point de vue de la construction.

structure [struk'chŭr] *n* structure *f*; (*building*) construction *f*.

struggle [strug'əl] *n* lutte *f* ♦ *vi* lutter, se battre; **to have a ~ to do sth** avoir beaucoup de mal à faire qch.

strum [strum] *vt* (*guitar*) gratter de.

strung [strung] *pt*, *pp of* **string**.

strut [strut] *n* étai *m*, support *m* ♦ *vi* se pavaner.

strychnine [strik'nīn] *n* strychnine *f*.

stub [stub] *n* bout *m*; (*of ticket etc*) talon *m*, souche *f* ♦ *vt*: **to ~ one's toe (on sth)** se heurter le doigt de pied (contre qch).
   stub out *vt* écraser.

stubble [stub'əl] *n* chaume *m*; (*on chin*) barbe *f* de plusieurs jours.

stubborn [stub'ûrn] *a* têtu(e), obstiné(e), opiniâtre.

stubby [stub'ē] *a* trapu(e); gros(se) et court(e).

stucco [stuk'ō] *n* stuc *m*.

stuck [stuk] *pt*, *pp of* **stick** ♦ *a* (*jammed*) bloqué(e), coincé(e); **to get ~** se bloquer *or* coincer.

stuck-up [stuk'up'] *a* prétentieux(euse).

stud [stud] *n* clou *m* (à grosse tête); (*collar ~*) bouton *m* de col; (*of horses*) écurie *f*, haras *m*; (*also:* **~ horse**) étalon *m* ♦ *vt* (*fig*): **~ded with** parsemé(e) *or* criblé(e) de.

student [stōō'dənt] *n* étudiant/e; (*US: at school*) élève *m/f* ♦ *cpd* estudiantin(e); universitaire; d'étudiant; **law/medical ~** étudiant en droit/médecine.

student driver *n* (*US*) (conducteur/trice) débutant(e).

student teacher *n* professeur *m* stagiaire.

studied [stud'ēd] *a* étudié(e), calculé(e).

studio [stōō'dēō] *n* studio *m*, atelier *m*.

studio apartment *n* studio *m*.

studious [stōō'dēəs] *a* studieux(euse), appliqué(e); (*studied*) étudié(e).

studiously [stōō'dēəslē] *ad* (*carefully*) soigneusement.

study [stud'ē] *n* étude *f*; (*room*) bureau *m* ♦ *vt* étudier ♦ *vi* étudier, faire ses études; **to make a ~ of sth** étudier qch, faire une étude de qch; **to ~ for an exam** préparer un examen.

stuff [stuf] *n* (*gen*) chose(s) *f(pl)*, truc *m*; (*belongings*) affaires *fpl*, trucs; (*substance*) substance *f* ♦ *vt* rembourrer; (*CULIN*) farcir; (*animal: for exhibition*) empailler; **my nose is ~ed up** j'ai le nez bouché; **get ~ed!** (*col!*)

va te faire foutre! (!); **~ed toy** jouet *m* en peluche.

stuffing [stuf'ing] *n* bourre *f*, rembourrage *m*; (*CULIN*) farce *f*.

stuffy [stuf'ē] *a* (*room*) mal ventilé(e) *or* aéré(e); (*ideas*) vieux jeu *inv*.

stumble [stum'bəl] *vi* trébucher.
   stumble across *vt fus* (*fig*) tomber sur.

stumbling block [stum'bling blâk] *n* pierre *f* d'achoppement.

stump [stump] *n* souche *f*; (*of limb*) moignon *m* ♦ *vt*: **to be ~ed** sécher, ne pas savoir que répondre.

stun [stun] *vt* (*subj: blow*) étourdir; (: *news*) abasourdir, stupéfier.

stung [stung] *pt*, *pp of* **sting**.

stunk [stungk] *pp of* **stink**.

stunning [stun'ing] *a* étourdissant(e); (*fabulous*) stupéfiant(e), sensationnel(le).

stunt [stunt] *n* tour *m* de force; truc *m* publicitaire; (*AVIAT*) acrobatie *f* ♦ *vt* retarder, arrêter.

stunted [stun'tid] *a* rabougri(e).

stuntman [stunt'mən] *n* cascadeur *m*.

stupefaction [stōōpəfak'shən] *n* stupéfaction *f*, stupeur *f*.

stupefy [stōō'pəfī] *vt* étourdir; abrutir; (*fig*) stupéfier.

stupendous [stōōpen'dəs] *a* prodigieux(euse), fantastique.

stupid [stōō'pid] *a* stupide, bête.

stupidity [stōōpid'itē] *n* stupidité *f*, bêtise *f*.

stupidly [stōō'pidlē] *ad* stupidement, bêtement.

stupor [stōō'pûr] *n* stupeur *f*.

sturdy [stûr'dē] *a* robuste, vigoureux(euse), solide.

sturgeon [stûr'jən] *n* esturgeon *m*.

stutter [stut'ûr] *n* bégaiement *m* ♦ *vi* bégayer.

sty [stī] *n* (*of pigs*) porcherie *f*.

stye [stī] *n* (*MED*) orgelet *m*.

style [stīl] *n* style *m*; (*of dress etc*) genre *m*; (*distinction*) allure *f*, cachet *m*, style; **in the latest ~** à la dernière mode; **hair ~** coiffure *f*.

stylish [stī'lish] *a* élégant(e), chic *inv*.

stylist [stī'list] *n* (*hair ~*) coiffeur/euse; (*literary ~*) styliste *m/f*.

stylized [stī'līzd] *a* stylisé(e).

stylus, *pl* **styli** *or* **styluses** [stī'ləs, -lī] *n* (*of record player*) pointe *f* de lecture.

suave [swâv] *a* doucereux(euse), onctueux(euse).

sub [sub] *n abbr* = **submarine**, **subscription**.

sub... [sub] *prefix* sub..., sous-.

subcommittee [sub'kəmitē] *n* sous-comité *m*.

subconscious [subkân'chəs] *a* subconscient(e) ♦ *n* subconscient *m*.

subcontinent [subkân'tənənt] *n*: **the (Indian) ~** le sous-continent indien.

subcontract *n* [subkân'trakt] contrat *m* de sous-traitance ♦ *vt* [subkəntrakt'] sous-traiter.

subcontractor [subkân'traktûr] *n* sous-traitant *m*.

subdivide [subdivīd'] *vt* subdiviser.

subdivision [sub'divizhən] *n* subdivision *f*.

subdue [səbdōō'] *vt* subjuguer, soumettre.

subdued [səbdōōd'] *a* contenu(e), atténué(e); (*light*) tamisé(e); (*person*) qui a perdu de son entrain.

subject *n* [sub'jikt] sujet *m*; (*SCOL*) matière *f*
♦ *vt* [səbjekt']: **to ~ to** soumettre à; exposer
à; **to be ~ to** (*law*) être soumis(e) à; (*disease*) être sujet(te) à; **~ to confirmation in
writing** sous réserve de confirmation écrite;
to change the ~ changer de conversation.

subjection [səbjek'shən] *n* soumission *f*, sujétion *f*.

subjective [səbjek'tiv] *a* subjectif(ive).

subject matter *n* sujet *m*; contenu *m*.

sub judice [sub jōō'disē] *a* (*LAW*) devant les
tribunaux.

subjugate [sub'jəgāt] *vt* subjuguer.

subjunctive [səbjungk'tiv] *a* subjonctif(ive) ♦
n subjonctif *m*.

sublease [sublēs'] (*US*) *vt* vendre en cession-
bail ♦ *n* cession-bail *f*.

sublet [sublet'] *vt* sous-louer.

sublime [səblīm'] *a* sublime.

subliminal [sublim'ənəl] *a* subliminal(e).

submachine gun [subməshēn' gun] *n* fusil-
mitrailleur *m*.

submarine [sub'mərēn] *n* sous-marin *m*.

submerge [səbmûrj'] *vt* submerger; immerger
♦ *vi* plonger.

submersion [səbmûr'zhən] *n* submersion *f*;
immersion *f*.

submission [səbmish'ən] *n* soumission *f*; (*to
committee etc*) présentation *f*.

submissive [səbmis'iv] *a* soumis(e).

submit [səbmit'] *vt* soumettre ♦ *vi* se soumettre.

subnormal [subnôr'məl] *a* au-dessous de la
normale; (*person*) arriéré(e).

subordinate [səbôr'dənit] *a*, *n* subordonné(e).

subpoena [səpē'nə] (*LAW*) *n* citation *f*, assignation *f* ♦ *vt* citer *or* assigner (à comparaître).

subroutine [subrōōtēn'] *n* (*COMPUT*) sous-
programme *m*.

subscribe [səbskrīb'] *vi* cotiser; **to ~ to** (*opinion, fund*) souscrire à; (*newspaper*)
s'abonner à; être abonné(e) à.

subscriber [səbskrīb'ûr] *n* (*to periodical, telephone*) abonné/e.

subscript [sub'skript] *n* (*TYP*) indice inférieur.

subscription [səbskrip'shən] *n* (*to fund*) souscription *f*; (*to magazine etc*) abonnement *m*;
(*membership dues*) cotisation *f*; **to take out
a ~ to** s'abonner à.

subsequent [sub'səkwənt] *a* ultérieur(e), sui-
vant(e); **~ to** *prep* à la suite de.

subsequently [sub'səkwəntlē] *ad* par la suite.

subservient [səbsûr'vēənt] *a* obséquieux(euse).

subside [səbsīd'] *vi* s'affaisser; (*flood*)
baisser; (*wind*) tomber.

subsidence [səbsīd'əns] *n* affaissement *m*.

subsidiary [səbsid'ēàrē] *a* subsidiaire;
accessoire; (*Brit SCOL: subject*) complémentaire ♦ *n* filiale *f*.

subsidize [sub'sidīz] *vt* subventionner.

subsidy [sub'sidē] *n* subvention *f*.

subsist [səbsist'] *vi*: **to ~ on sth** (arriver à)
vivre avec *or* subsister avec qch.

subsistence [səbsis'təns] *n* existence *f*,
subsistance *f*.

subsistence allowance *n* indemnité *f* de séjour.

subsistence level *n* niveau *m* de vie mini-

mum.

substance [sub'stəns] *n* substance *f*; (*fig*)
essentiel *m*; **a man of ~** un homme jouissant
d'une certaine fortune; **to lack ~** être plutôt
mince (*fig*).

substandard [substan'dûrd] *a* (*goods*) de qualité inférieure, qui laisse à désirer; (*housing*)
inférieur(e) aux normes requises.

substantial [səbstan'chəl] *a* substantiel(le);
(*fig*) important(e).

substantially [səbstan'chəlē] *ad* considérablement; en grande partie.

substantiate [səbstan'chēāt] *vt* étayer, fournir
des preuves à l'appui de.

substitute [sub'stitōōt] *n* (*person*)
remplaçant/e; (*thing*) succédané *m* ♦ *vt*: **to
~ sth/sb for** substituer qch/qn à, remplacer
par qch/qn.

substitute teacher *n* (*US*) suppléant/e.

substitution [substitōō'shən] *n* substitution *f*.

subterfuge [sub'tûrfyōōj] *n* subterfuge *m*.

subterranean [subtərā'nēən] *a* souterrain(e).

subtitle [sub'tītəl] *n* (*CINEMA*) sous-titre *m*.

subtle [sut'əl] *a* subtil(e).

subtlety [sut'əltē] *n* subtilité *f*.

subtly [sut'lē] *ad* subtilement.

subtotal [subtō'təl] *n* total partiel.

subtract [səbtrakt'] *vt* soustraire, retrancher.

subtraction [səbtrak'shən] *n* soustraction *f*.

subtropical [subtrâp'ikəl] *a* subtropical(e).

suburb [sub'ûrb] *n* faubourg *m*; **the ~s** la
banlieue.

suburban [səbûr'bən] *a* de banlieue, su-
burbain(e).

suburbia [səbûr'bēə] *n* la banlieue.

subvention [səbven'chən] *n* (*subsidy*)
subvention *f*.

subversion [səbvûr'zhən] *n* subversion *f*.

subversive [səbvûr'siv] *a* subversif(ive).

subway [sub'wā] *n* (*US*) métro *m*; (*Brit*)
passage souterrain.

subway station *n* (*US*) station *f* de métro.

sub-zero [sub'zē'rō] *a* au-dessous de zéro.

succeed [səksēd'] *vi* réussir ♦ *vt* succéder à;
to ~ in doing réussir à faire.

succeeding [səksē'ding] *a* suivant(e), qui suit
(*or* suivent *or* suivront *etc*).

success [səkses'] *n* succès *m*; réussite *f*.

successful [səkses'fəl] *a* qui a du succès;
(*candidate*) choisi(e), agréé(e); (*business*)
prospère, qui réussit; (*attempt*) couronné(e)
de succès; **to be ~ (in doing)** réussir (à
faire).

successfully [səkses'fəlē] *ad* avec succès.

succession [səksesh'ən] *n* succession *f*; **in ~**
successivement; **3 years in ~** 3 ans de suite.

successive [səkses'iv] *a* successif(ive); **on 3 ~
days** 3 jours de suite *or* consécutifs.

successor [səkses'ûr] *n* successeur *m*.

succinct [səksingkt'] *a* succinct(e),
bref(brève).

succulent [suk'yələnt] *a* succulent(e) ♦ *n*
(*BOT*): **~s** plantes grasses.

succumb [səkum'] *vi* succomber.

such [such] *a* tel(telle); (*of that kind*): **~ a
book** un livre de ce genre *or* pareil, un tel livre; **~ books** des livres de ce genre *or* pa-
reils, de tels livres; (*so much*): **~ courage**
un tel courage ♦ *ad* si; **~ a long trip** un si

long voyage; ~ **good books** de si bons livres; ~ **a long trip that** un voyage si *or* tellement long que; ~ **a lot of** tellement *or* tant de; **making** ~ **a noise that** faisant un tel bruit que *or* tellement de bruit que; ~ **a long time ago** il y a si *or* tellement longtemps; ~ **as** (*like*) tel(telle) que, comme; **a noise** ~ **as to** un bruit de nature à; ~ **books as I have** les quelques livres que j'ai; **as** ~ *ad* en tant que tel(telle), à proprement parler.

such-and-such [such'ənsuch] *a* tel(telle) ou tel(telle).

suchlike [such'līk] *pronoun* (*col*): **and** ~ et le reste.

suck [suk] *vt* sucer; (*breast, bottle*) téter; (*subj: pump, machine*) aspirer.

sucker [suk'ûr] *n* (BOT, ZOOL, TECH) ventouse *f*; (*col*) naïf/ive, poire *f*.

suckle [suk'əl] *vt* allaiter.

suction [suk'shən] *n* succion *f*.

suction pump *n* pompe aspirante.

Sudan [sōōdan'] *n* Soudan *m*.

Sudanese [sōōdənēz'] *a* soudanais(e) ♦ *n* Soudanais/e.

sudden [sud'ən] *a* soudain(e), subit(e); **all of a** ~ soudain, tout à coup.

suddenly [sud'ənlē] *ad* brusquement, tout à coup, soudain.

suds [sudz] *npl* eau savonneuse.

sue [sōō] *vt* poursuivre en justice, intenter un procès à ♦ *vi*: **to** ~ **(for)** intenter un procès (pour); **to** ~ **for divorce** engager une procédure de divorce; **to** ~ **sb for damages** poursuivre qn en dommages-intérêts.

suede [swād] *n* daim *m*, cuir suédé ♦ *cpd* de daim.

suet [sōō'it] *n* graisse *f* de rognon *or* de bœuf.

Suez Canal [sōōez' kənal'] *n* canal *m* de Suez.

Suff. *abbr* (*Brit*) = *Suffolk*.

suffer [suf'ûr] *vt* souffrir, subir; (*bear*) tolérer, supporter, subir ♦ *vi* souffrir; **to** ~ **from** (*illness*) souffrir de, avoir; **to** ~ **from the effects of alcohol/a fall** se ressentir des effets de l'alcool/des conséquences d'une chute.

sufferance [suf'ûrəns] *n*: **he was only there on** ~ sa présence était seulement tolérée.

sufferer [suf'ûrûr] *n* malade *m/f*; victime *m/f*.

suffering [suf'ûring] *n* souffrance(s) *f(pl)*.

suffice [səfīs'] *vi* suffire.

sufficient [səfish'ənt] *a* suffisant(e); ~ **money** suffisamment d'argent.

sufficiently [səfish'əntlē] *ad* suffisamment, assez.

suffix [suf'iks] *n* suffixe *m*.

suffocate [suf'əkāt] *vi* suffoquer; étouffer.

suffocation [sufəkā'shən] *n* suffocation *f*; (MED) asphyxie *f*.

suffrage [suf'rij] *n* suffrage *m*; droit *m* de suffrage *or* de vote.

suffuse [səfyōoz'] *vt* baigner, imprégner; **the room was ~d with light** la pièce baignait dans la lumière *or* était imprégnée de lumière.

sugar [shōog'ûr] *n* sucre *m* ♦ *vt* sucrer.

sugar beet *n* betterave sucrière.

sugar bowl *n* sucrier *m*.

sugar cane *n* canne *f* à sucre.

sugar-coated [shōog'ûrkō'tid] *a* dragéifié(e).

sugar lump *n* morceau *m* de sucre.

sugar refinery *n* raffinerie *f* de sucre.

sugary [shōog'ûrē] *a* sucré(e).

suggest [səgjest'] *vt* suggérer, proposer; (*indicate*) laisser supposer, suggérer; **what do you** ~ **I do?** que vous me suggérez de faire?

suggestion [səgjes'chən] *n* suggestion *f*.

suggestive [səgjes'tiv] *a* suggestif(ive).

suicidal [sōōisīd'əl] *a* suicidaire.

suicide [sōō'isīd] *n* suicide *m*; **to commit** ~ se suicider.

suicide attempt, suicide bid *n* tentative *f* de suicide.

suit [sōōt] *n* (*man's*) costume *m*, complet *m*; (*woman's*) tailleur *m*, ensemble *m*; (CARDS) couleur *f*; (*law*~) procès *m* ♦ *vt* aller à; convenir à; (*adapt*): **to** ~ **sth to** adapter *or* approprier qch à; **to be ~ed to sth** (*suitable for*) être adapté(e) *or* approprié(e) à qch; **well ~ed** (*couple*) faits l'un pour l'autre, très bien assortis; **to bring a** ~ **against sb** intenter un procès contre qn; **to follow** ~ (*fig*) faire de même.

suitable [sōō'təbəl] *a* qui convient; approprié(e), adéquat(e); **would tomorrow be** ~? est-ce que demain vous conviendrait?; **we found somebody** ~ nous avons trouvé la personne qui'il nous faut.

suitably [sōō'təblē] *ad* comme il se doit (*or* se devait *etc*), convenablement.

suitcase [sōōt'kās] *n* valise *f*.

suite [swēt] *n* (*of rooms, also* MUS) suite *f*; (*furniture*): **bedroom/dining room** ~ (ensemble *m* de) chambre *f* à coucher/salle *f* à manger; **a three-piece** ~ un salon (canapé et deux fauteuils).

suitor [sōō'tûr] *n* soupirant *m*, prétendant *m*.

sulfate [sul'fāt] *n* (US) sulfate *m*; **copper** ~ sulfate de cuivre.

sulfur [sul'fûr] *n* (US) soufre *m*.

sulfuric [sulfyōōr'ik] *a*: ~ **acid** acide *m* sulfurique.

sulk [sulk] *vi* bouder.

sulky [sul'kē] *a* boudeur(euse), maussade.

sullen [sul'ən] *a* renfrogné(e), maussade; morne.

sulphate [sul'fāt] *n* (Brit) = **sulfate**.

sulphur [sul'fûr] *etc* (Brit) = **sulfur** *etc*.

sultan [sul'tən] *n* sultan *m*.

sultana [sultan'ə] *n* (*fruit*) raisin (sec) de Smyrne.

sultry [sul'trē] *a* étouffant(e).

sum [sum] *n* somme *f*; (SCOL *etc*) calcul *m*.

sum up *vt* résumer; (*evaluate rapidly*) récapituler ♦ *vi* résumer.

Sumatra [sōōmát'rə] *n* Sumatra.

summarize [sum'ərīz] *vt* résumer.

summary [sum'ûrē] *n* résumé *m* ♦ *a* (*justice*) sommaire.

summer [sum'ûr] *n* été *m* ♦ *cpd* d'été, estival(e); **in (the)** ~ en été, pendant l'été.

summer camp *n* (US) colonie *f* de vacances.

summerhouse [sum'ûrhous] *n* (*in garden*) pavillon *m*.

summertime [sum'ûrtīm] *n* (*season*) été *m*.

summer time *n* (*by clock*) heure *f* d'été.

summery [sum'ûrē] *a* estival(e); d'été.

summing-up [sum'ingup'] *n* résumé *m*, récapitulation *f.*

summit [sum'it] *n* sommet *m;* (*also:* ~ **conference**) (conférence *f* au) sommet *m.*

summon [sum'ən] *vt* appeler, convoquer; **to ~ a witness** citer *or* assigner un témoin.

summon up *vt* rassembler, faire appel à.

summons [sum'ənz] *n* citation *f,* assignation *f* ♦ *vt* citer, assigner; **to serve a ~ on sb** remettre une assignation à qn.

sump [sump] *n* (*Brit AUT*) carter *m.*

sumptuous [sump'chōōəs] *a* somptueux(euse).

Sun. *abbr* (= *Sunday*) dim.

sun [sun] *n* soleil *m;* **in the ~** au soleil; **to catch the ~** prendre le soleil; **everything under the ~** absolument tout.

sunbathe [sun'bāth] *vi* prendre un bain de soleil.

sunbeam [sun'bēm] *n* rayon *m* de soleil.

sunbed [sun'bed] *n* (*Brit*) lit pliant; (: *with sun lamp*) lit à ultra-violets.

sunburn [sun'bûrn] *n* coup *m* de soleil.

sunburnt [sun'bûrnt], **sunburned** [sun'bûrnd] *a* bronzé(e), hâlé(e); (*painfully*) brûlé(e) par le soleil.

sundae [sun'dē] *n* sundae *m,* coupe glacée.

Sunday [sun'dā] *n* dimanche *m; for phrases see also* **Tuesday.**

Sunday school *n* ≈ catéchisme *m.*

sundial [sun'dīl] *n* cadran *m* solaire.

sundown [sun'doun] *n* coucher *m* du soleil.

sundries [sun'drēz] *npl* articles divers.

sundry [sun'drē] *a* divers(e), différent(e); **all and ~** tout le monde, n'importe qui.

sunflower [sun'flouûr] *n* tournesol *m.*

sung [sung] *pp of* **sing.**

sunglasses [sun'glasiz] *npl* lunettes *fpl* de soleil.

sunk [sungk] *pp of* **sink.**

sunken [sung'kən] *a* (*rock, ship*) submergé(e); (*eyes, cheeks*) creux(euse); (*bath*) encastré(e).

sunlamp [sun'lamp] *n* lampe *f* à rayons ultra-violets.

sunlight [sun'līt] *n* (lumière *f* du) soleil *m.*

sunlit [sun'lit] *a* ensoleillé(e).

sunny [sun'ē] *a* ensoleillé(e); (*fig*) épanoui(e), radieux(euse); **it is ~** il fait (du) soleil, il y a du soleil.

sunrise [sun'rīz] *n* lever *m* du soleil.

sun roof *n* (*AUT*) toit ouvrant.

sunset [sun'set] *n* coucher *m* du soleil.

sunshade [sun'shād] *n* (*lady's*) ombrelle *f;* (*over table*) parasol *m.*

sunshine [sun'shīn] *n* (lumière *f* du) soleil *m.*

sunspot [sun'spät] *n* tache *f* solaire.

sunstroke [sun'strōk] *n* insolation *f,* coup *m* de soleil.

suntan [sun'tan] *n* bronzage *m.*

suntan lotion *n* lotion *f or* lait *m* solaire.

suntanned [sun'tand] *a* bronzé(e).

suntan oil *n* huile *f* solaire.

super [sōō'pûr] *a* (*col*) formidable.

superannuation [sōōpûranyōōā'shən] *n* cotisations *fpl* pour la pension.

superb [sōōpûrb'] *a* superbe, magnifique.

supercilious [sōōpûrsil'ēəs] *a* hautain(e), dédaigneux(euse).

superficial [sōōpûrfish'əl] *a* superficiel(le).

superficially [sōōpûrfish'əlē] *ad* superficielle-

ment.

superfluous [sōōpûr'flōōəs] *a* superflu(e).

superhuman [sōōpûrhyōō'mən] *a* surhumain(e).

superimpose [sōōpûrimpōz'] *vt* superposer.

superintend [sōōpûrintend'] *vt* surveiller.

superintendent [sōōpûrinten'dənt] *n* directeur/trice; (*Brit POLICE*) ≈ commissaire *m.*

superior [səpēr'ēûr] *a* supérieur(e); (*COMM: goods, quality*) de qualité supérieure; (*smug*) condescendant(e), méprisant(e) ♦ *n* supérieur/e; **Mother S~** (*REL*) Mère supérieure.

superiority [səpērēôr'itē] *n* supériorité *f.*

superlative [səpûr'lətiv] *a* sans pareil(le), suprême ♦ *n* (*LING*) superlatif *m.*

superman [sōō'pûrman] *n* surhomme *m.*

supermarket [sōō'pûrmârkit] *n* supermarché *m.*

supernatural [sōōpûrnach'ûrəl] *a* surnaturel(le).

superpower [sōō'pûrpou'ûr] *n* (*POL*) superpuissance *f.*

supersede [sōōpûrsēd'] *vt* remplacer, supplanter.

supersonic [sōōpûrsân'ik] *a* supersonique.

superstition [sōōpûrstish'ən] *n* superstition *f.*

superstitious [sōōpûrstish'əs] *a* superstitieux(euse).

superstore [sōō'pûrstôr] *n* (*Brit*) hypermarché *m,* grand surface.

supertanker [sōō'pûrtangkûr] *n* pétrolier géant, superpétrolier *m.*

supertax [sōō'pûrtaks] *n* tranche supérieure de l'impôt.

supervise [sōō'pûrvīz] *vt* (*children etc*) surveiller; (*organization, work*) diriger.

supervision [sōōpûrvizh'ən] *n* surveillance *f;* direction *f;* **under medical ~** sous contrôle du médecin.

supervisor [sōō'pûrvīzûr] *n* surveillant/e; (*in shop*) chef *m* de rayon; (*SCOL*) directeur/trice de thèse.

supervisory [sōōpûrvī'zûrē] *a* de surveillance.

supine [sōō'pīn] *a* couché(e) *or* étendu(e) sur le dos.

supper [sup'ûr] *n* dîner *m;* (*late*) souper *m;* **to have ~** dîner; souper.

supplant [səplant'] *vt* supplanter.

supple [sup'əl] *a* souple.

supplement *n* [sup'ləmənt] supplément *m* ♦ *vt* [sup'ləment] ajouter à, compléter.

supplementary [supləmen'tûrē] *a* supplémentaire.

supplementary benefit *n* (*Brit*) allocation *f* supplémentaire d'aide sociale.

supplier [səplī'ûr] *n* fournisseur *m.*

supply [səplī'] *vt* (*goods*): **to ~ sth** (**to sb**) fournir qch (à qn); (*people, organization*): **to ~ sb** (**with sth**) approvisionner *or* ravitailler qn (en qch); fournir qn (en qch), fournir qch à qn; (*system, machine*): **to ~ sth** (**with sth**) alimenter qch (en qch); (*a need*) répondre à ♦ *n* provision *f,* réserve *f;* (*supplying*) approvisionnement *m;* (*TECH*) alimentation; **supplies** *npl* (*food*) vivres *mpl;* (*MIL*) subsistances *fpl;* **office supplies** fournitures *fpl* de bureau; **to be in short ~** être rare, manquer; **the electricity/water/gas** ~ l'alimentation en électricité/eau/gaz; ~ **and demand** l'offre *f* et la demande; **it comes supplied with an adaptor** il (*or* elle) est pourvu(e) d'un adaptateur.

supply teacher *n* (*Brit*) suppléant/e.

support [səpôrt'] *n* (*moral, financial etc*) soutien *m*, appui *m*; (*TECH*) support *m*, soutien ♦ *vt* soutenir, supporter; (*financially*) subvenir aux besoins de; (*uphold*) être pour, être partisan de, appuyer; (*SPORT: team*) être pour; **to ~ o.s.** (*financially*) gagner sa vie.

supporter [səpôr'tûr] *n* (*POL etc*) partisan/e; (*SPORT*) supporter *m*.

supporting [səpôr'ting] *a* (*THEATER etc: role*) secondaire; (*: actor*) qui a un rôle secondaire.

suppose [səpōz'] *vt, vi* supposer; imaginer; **to be ~d to do/be** être censé(e) faire/être; **I don't ~ she'll come** je suppose qu'elle ne viendra pas, cela m'étonnerait qu'elle vienne.

supposedly [səpō'zidlē] *ad* soi-disant.

supposing [səpō'zing] *cj* si, à supposer que + *sub*.

supposition [supəzish'ən] *n* supposition *f*, hypothèse *f*.

suppository [səpâz'itôrē] *n* suppositoire *m*.

suppress [səpres'] *vt* (*revolt, feeling*) réprimer; (*publication*) supprimer; (*scandal*) étouffer.

suppression [səpresh'ən] *n* suppression *f*, répression *f*.

suppressor [səpres'ûr] *n* (*ELEC etc*) dispositif *m* antiparasite.

supremacy [səprem'əsē] *n* suprématie *f*.

supreme [səprēm'] *a* suprême.

Supreme Court *n* (*US*) Cour *f* suprême.

Supt. *abbr* (*POLICE*) = **superintendent**.

surcharge [sûr'chârj] *n* surcharge *f*; (*extra tax*) surtaxe *f*.

sure [shōōr] *a* (*gen*) sûr(e); (*definite, convinced*) sûr, certain(e) ♦ *ad* (*col: esp US*): **that ~ is pretty, that's ~ pretty** c'est drôlement joli(e); **~!** (*of course*) bien sûr!; **~ enough** effectivement; **I'm not ~ how/ why/when** je ne sais pas très bien comment/ pourquoi/quand; **to be ~ of o.s.** être sûr de soi; **to make ~ of** s'assurer de; vérifier.

sure-footed [shōōr'fŏŏt'id] *a* au pied sûr.

surely [shōōr'lē] *ad* sûrement; certainement; **~ you don't mean that!** vous ne parlez pas sérieusement!

surety [shōōr'ətē] *n* caution *f*; **to go** *or* **stand ~ for sb** se porter caution pour qn.

surf [sûrf] *n* ressac *m*.

surface [sûr'fis] *n* surface *f* ♦ *vt* (*road*) poser le revêtement de ♦ *vi* remonter à la surface; faire surface; **on the ~** (*fig*) au premier abord.

surface area *n* superficie *f*, aire *f*.

surface mail *n* courrier *m* par voie de terre (*or* maritime).

surfboard [sûrf'bôrd] *n* planche *f* de surf.

surfeit [sûr'fit] *n*: **a ~ of** un excès de; une indigestion de.

surfer [sûrf'ûr] *n* surfiste *m/f*.

surfing [sûrf'ing] *n* surf *m*.

surge [sûrj] *n* vague *f*, montée *f*; (*ELEC*) pointe *f* de courant ♦ *vi* déferler; **to ~ for-**

ward se précipiter (en avant).

surgeon [sûr'jən] *n* chirurgien *m*.

Surgeon General *n* (*US*) chef *m* du service fédéral de la santé publique.

surgery [sûr'jûrē] *n* chirurgie *f*; (*Brit: room*) cabinet *m* (de consultation); (*: session*) consultation *f*; (*: of MP etc*) permanence *f* (*où le député etc reçoit les électeurs etc*); **to undergo ~** être opéré(e).

surgery hours *npl* (*Brit*) heures *fpl* de consultation.

surgical [sûr'jikəl] *a* chirurgical(e).

surgical spirit *n* (*Brit*) alcool *m* à 90°.

surly [sûr'lē] *a* revêche, maussade.

surmise [sûrmīz'] *vt* présumer, conjecturer.

surmount [sûrmount'] *vt* surmonter.

surname [sûr'nām] *n* nom *m* de famille.

surpass [sûrpas'] *vt* surpasser, dépasser.

surplus [sûr'pləs] *n* surplus *m*, excédent *m* ♦ *a* en surplus, de trop; **it is ~ to our requirements** cela dépasse nos besoins; **~ stock** surplus *m*.

surprise [sûrprīz'] *n* (*gen*) surprise *f*; (*astonishment*) étonnement *m* ♦ *vt* surprendre; étonner; **to take by ~** (*person*) prendre au dépourvu; (*MIL: town, fort*) prendre par surprise.

surprising [sûrprī'zing] *a* surprenant(e), étonnant(e).

surprisingly [sûrprī'zinglē] *ad* (*easy, helpful*) étonnamment, étrangement; (*somewhat*) ~, **he agreed** curieusement, il a accepté.

surrealism [sərē'əlizəm] *n* surréalisme *m*.

surrealist [sərē'əlist] *a, n* surréaliste (*m/f*).

surrender [sərən'dûr] *n* reddition *f*, capitulation *f* ♦ *vi* se rendre, capituler ♦ *vt* (*claim, right*) renoncer à.

surrender value *n* valeur *f* de rachat.

surreptitious [sûrəptish'əs] *a* subreptice, furtif(ive).

surrogate [sûr'əgit] *n* (*substitute*) substitut *m* ♦ *a* de substitution, de remplacement; **a food** ~ un succédané alimentaire; **~ coffee** (*Brit*) ersatz *m or* succédané *m* de café.

surrogate mother *n* mère porteuse *or* de substitution.

surround [səround'] *vt* entourer; (*MIL etc*) encercler.

surrounding [səroun'ding] *a* environnant(e).

surroundings [səroun'dingz] *npl* environs *mpl*, alentours *mpl*.

surtax [sûr'taks] *n* surtaxe *f*.

surveillance [sûrvā'ləns] *n* surveillance *f*.

survey *n* [sûr'vā] enquête *f*, étude *f*; (*Brit: in house buying etc*) inspection *f*, (rapport *m* d')expertise *f*; (*of land*) levé *m*; (*comprehensive view: of situation etc*) vue *f* d'ensemble ♦ *vt* [sûrvā'] passer en revue; enquêter sur; inspecter; (*building*) expertiser; (*land*) faire le levé de.

surveying [sûrvā'ing] *n* arpentage *m*.

surveyor [sûrvā'ûr] *n* (*of building*) expert *m*; (*of land*) (arpenteur *m*) géomètre *m*.

survival [sûrvī'vəl] *n* survie *f*; (*relic*) vestige *m* ♦ *cpd* (*course, kit*) de survie.

survive [sûrvīv'] *vi* survivre; (*custom etc*) subsister ♦ *vt* survivre à, réchapper de; (*person*) survivre à.

survivor [sûrvī'vûr] *n* survivant/e.

susceptible [səsep'təbəl] *a*: ~ **(to)** sensible (à); (*disease*) prédisposé(e) (à).

suspect *a, n* [sus'pekt] suspect(e) ♦ *vt* [səspekt'] soupçonner, suspecter.

suspend [səspend'] *vt* suspendre.

suspended sentence [səspen'did sen'təns] *n* condamnation *f* avec sursis.

suspender belt [səspen'dûr belt] *n* (*Brit*) porte-jarretelles *m inv.*

suspenders [səspen'dûrz] *npl* (*US*) bretelles *fpl.*

suspense [səspens'] *n* attente *f*; (*in film etc*) suspense *m.*

suspense account *n* compte *m* d'attente.

suspension [səspen'chən] *n* (*gen, AUT*) suspension *f*; (*of driver's license*) retrait *m* provisoire.

suspension bridge *n* pont suspendu.

suspicion [səspish'ən] *n* soupçon(s) *m(pl)*; **to be under** ~ être considéré(e) comme suspect(e), être suspecté(e); **arrested on** ~ **of murder** arrêté sur présomption de meurtre.

suspicious [səspish'əs] *a* (*suspecting*) soupçonneux(euse), méfiant(e); (*causing suspicion*) suspect(e); **to be** ~ **of** *or* **about sb/sth** avoir des doutes à propos de qn/sur qch, trouver qn/qch suspect(e).

suss out [sus out] *vt* (*Brit col: discover*) supputer; (: *understand*) piger.

sustain [səstān'] *vt* supporter; soutenir; corroborer; (*suffer*) subir; recevoir.

sustained [səstānd'] *a* (*effort*) soutenu(e), prolongé(e).

sustenance [sus'tənəns] *n* nourriture *f*; moyens *mpl* de subsistance.

suture [sōō'chûr] *n* suture *f.*

SW *abbr* (= *short wave*) OC.

swab [swâb] *n* (*MED*) tampon *m*; prélèvement *m* ♦ *vt* (*NAUT: also:* ~ **down**) nettoyer.

swagger [swag'ûr] *vi* plastronner, parader.

swallow [swâl'ō] *n* (*bird*) hirondelle *f*; (*of food etc*) gorgée *f* ♦ *vt* avaler; (*fig*) gober.
   swallow up *vt* engloutir.

swam [swam] *pt of* **swim.**

swamp [swâmp] *n* marais *m*, marécage *m* ♦ *vt* submerger.

swampy [swâmp'ē] *a* marécageux(euse).

swan [swân] *n* cygne *m.*

swank [swangk] *vi* (*col*) faire de l'épate.

swan song *n* (*fig*) chant *m* du cygne.

swap [swâp] *n* échange *m*, troc *m* ♦ *vt*: **to** ~ **(for)** échanger (contre), troquer (contre).

swarm [swôrm] *n* essaim *m* ♦ *vi* essaimer; fourmiller, grouiller.

swarthy [swôr'thē] *a* basané(e), bistré(e).

swashbuckling [swâsh'bukling] *a* (*film*) de cape et d'épée.

swastika [swâs'tikə] *n* croix gammée.

swathe [swâth] *vt*: **to** ~ **in** (*bandages, blankets*) emboîner de.

swatter [swât'ûr] *n* (*also:* **fly** ~) tapette *f.*

sway [swā] *vi* se balancer, osciller; tanguer ♦ *vt* (*influence*) influencer ♦ *n* (*rule, power*): ~ **(over)** emprise *f* (sur); **to hold** ~ **over sb** avoir de l'emprise sur qn.

Swaziland [swâ'zēland] *n* Swaziland *m.*

swear, *pt* **swore,** *pp* **sworn** [swe'ûr, swôr, swôrn] *vi* jurer; **to** ~ **to sth** jurer de qch; **to** ~ **an oath** prêter serment.
   swear in *vt* assermenter.

swearword [swär'wûrd] *n* gros mot, juron *m.*

sweat [swet] *n* sueur *f*, transpiration *f* ♦ *vi* suer; **in a** ~ en sueur.

sweatband [swet'band] *n* (*SPORT*) bandeau *m.*

sweater [swet'ûr] *n* tricot *m*, pull *m.*

sweatshirt [swet'shûrt] *n* sweat-shirt *m.*

sweatshop [swet'shâp] *n* atelier *m* où les ouvriers sont exploités.

sweat suit *n* survêtement *m.*

sweaty [swet'ē] *a* en sueur, moite *or* mouillé(e) de sueur.

Swede [swēd] *n* Suédois/e.

swede [swēd] *n* (*Brit*) rutabaga *m.*

Sweden [swēd'ən] *n* Suède *f.*

Swedish [swē'dish] *a* suédois(e) ♦ *n* (*LING*) suédois *m.*

sweep [swēp] *n* coup *m* de balai; (*curve*) grande courbe; (*range*) champ *m*; (*also:* **chimney** ~) ramoneur *m* ♦ *vb* (*pt, pp* **swept** [swept]) *vt* balayer; (*fashion, craze*) se répandre dans ♦ *vi* avancer majestueusement *or* rapidement; s'élancer; s'étendre.
   sweep away *vt* balayer; entraîner; emporter.
   sweep past *vi* passer majestueusement *or* rapidement.
   sweep up *vt, vi* balayer.

sweeping [swē'ping] *a* (*gesture*) large; circulaire; (*changes, reforms*) radical(e); **a** ~ **statement** une généralisation hâtive.

sweepstake [swēp'stāk] *n* sweepstake *m.*

sweet [swēt] *n* (*Brit*) dessert *m*; (*candy*) bonbon *m* ♦ *a* doux(douce); (*not savory*) sucré(e); (*fresh*) frais(fraîche), pur(e); (*kind*) gentil(le); (*cute*) mignon(ne) ♦ *ad*: **to smell** ~ sentir bon; **to taste** ~ avoir un goût sucré; ~ **and sour** *a* aigre-doux(douce).

sweetbread [swēt'bred] *n* ris *m* de veau.

sweetcorn [swēt'kôrn] *n* maïs doux.

sweeten [swēt'ən] *vt* sucrer; (*fig*) adoucir.

sweetener [swēt'ənûr] *n* (*CULIN*) édulcorant *m.*

sweetheart [swēt'hârt] *n* amoureux/euse.

sweetly [swēt'lē] *ad* (*smile*) gentiment; (*sing, play*) mélodieusement.

sweetness [swēt'nis] *n* douceur *f*; (*of taste*) goût sucré.

sweet pea *n* pois *m* de senteur.

sweet potato *n* patate douce.

sweetshop [swēt'shâp] *n* (*Brit*) confiserie *f.*

sweet tooth *n*: **to have a** ~ aimer les sucreries.

swell [swel] *n* (*of sea*) houle *f* ♦ *a* (*col: excellent*) chouette ♦ *vb* (*pt* ~**ed,** *pp* **swollen** *or* ~**ed** [swō'lən]) *vt* augmenter; grossir ♦ *vi* grossir, augmenter; (*sound*) s'enfler; (*MED*) enfler.

swelling [swel'ing] *n* (*MED*) enflure *f*; grosseur *f.*

sweltering [swel'tûring] *a* étouffant(e), oppressant(e).

swept [swept] *pt, pp of* **sweep.**

swerve [swûrv] *vi* faire une embardée *or* un écart; dévier.

swift [swift] *n* (*bird*) martinet *m* ♦ *a* rapide, prompt(e).

swiftly [swift'lē] *ad* rapidement, vite.

swiftness [swift'nis] *n* rapidité *f*.
swig [swig] *n* (*col: drink*) lampée *f*.
swill [swil] *n* pâtée *f* ♦ *vt* (*also*: ~ **out**, ~ **down**) laver à grande eau.
swim [swim] *n*: **to go for a** ~ aller nager *or* se baigner ♦ *vb* (*pt* **swam**, *pp* **swum** [swam, swum]) *vi* nager; (*SPORT*) faire de la natation; (*fig: head, room*) tourner ♦ *vt* traverser (à la nage); (*distance*) faire (à la nage); **to** ~ **a length** nager une longueur; **to go** ~**ming** aller nager.
swimmer [swim'ûr] *n* nageur/euse.
swimming [swim'ing] *n* nage *f*, natation *f*.
swimming baths *npl* (*Brit*) piscine *f*.
swimming cap *n* bonnet *m* de bain.
swimming costume *n* (*Brit*) maillot *m* (de bain).
swimming pool *n* piscine *f*.
swimming trunks *npl* maillot *m* de bain.
swimsuit [swim'sōōt] *n* maillot *m* (de bain).
swindle [swin'dəl] *n* escroquerie *f* ♦ *vt* escroquer.
swindler [swind'lûr] *n* escroc *m*.
swine [swīn] *n* (*pl inv*) pourceau *m*, porc *m*; (*col!*) salaud *m* (!).
swing [swing] *n* balançoire *f*; (*movement*) balancement *m*, oscillations *fpl*; (*MUS*) swing *m*; rythme *m* ♦ *vb* (*pt, pp* **swung** [swung]) *vt* balancer, faire osciller; (*also*: ~ **around**) tourner, faire virer ♦ *vi* se balancer, osciller; (*also*: ~ **around**) virer, tourner; **a** ~ **to the left** (*POL*) un revirement en faveur de la gauche; **to be in full** ~ battre son plein; **to get into the** ~ **of things** se mettre dans le bain; **the road** ~**s south** la route prend la direction sud.
swing bridge *n* pont tournant.
swing door *n* (*Brit*) porte battante.
swingeing [swin'jing] *a* (*Brit*) écrasant(e); considérable.
swinging [swing'ing] *a* rythmé(e); entraînant(e); (*col*) dans le vent.
swinging door *n* (*US*) porte battante.
swipe [swīp] *n* grand coup; gifle *f* ♦ *vt* (*hit*) frapper à toute volée; gifler; (*col: steal*) piquer.
swirl [swûrl] *n* tourbillon *m* ♦ *vi* tourbillonner, tournoyer.
swish [swish] *vi* (*whip*) siffler; (*skirt, long grass*) bruire.
Swiss [swis] *a* suisse ♦ *n* (*pl inv*) Suisse/esse.
Swiss French *a* suisse romand(e).
Swiss German *a* suisse-allemand(e).
Swiss roll *n* gâteau roulé.
switch [swich] *n* (*for light, radio etc*) bouton *m*; (*change*) changement *m*, revirement *m* ♦ *vt* (*change*) changer; (*exchange*) intervertir; (*invert*): **to** ~ (**around** *or* **over**) changer de place.
  switch off *vt* éteindre; (*engine*) arrêter.
  switch on *vt* allumer; (*engine, machine*) mettre en marche.
switchback [swich'bak] *n* (*Brit*) montagnes *fpl* russes.
switchblade [swich'blād] *n* (*also*: ~ **knife**) couteau *m* à cran d'arrêt.
switchboard [swich'bôrd] *n* (*TEL*) standard *m*.
switchboard operator *n* (*TEL*) standardiste

m/f.
switchtower [swich'touûr] *n* (*US*) poste *m* d'aiguillage.
switchyard [swich'yârd] *n* (*US*) voies *fpl* de garage *or* de triage.
Switzerland [swit'sûrlənd] *n* Suisse *f*.
swivel [swiv'əl] *vi* (*also*: ~ **around**) pivoter, tourner.
swollen [swō'lən] *pp* of **swell** ♦ *a* (*ankle etc*) enflé(e).
swoon [swōōn] *vi* se pâmer.
swoop [swōōp] *n* (*by police etc*) rafle *f*, descente *f*; (*of bird etc*) descente *f* en piqué ♦ *vi* (*also*: ~ **down**) descendre en piqué, piquer.
swop [swâp] *n, vt* = **swap**.
sword [sôrd] *n* épée *f*; **to be at** ~**s' points with sb** (*US*) être à couteaux tirés avec qn.
swordfish [sôrd'fish] *n* espadon *m*.
swore [swôr] *pt* of **swear**.
sworn [swôrn] *pp* of **swear**.
swot [swât] *vt, vi* bûcher, potasser.
swum [swum] *pp* of **swim**.
swung [swung] *pt, pp* of **swing**.
sycamore [sik'əmôr] *n* sycomore *m*.
sycophant [sik'əfənt] *n* flagorneur/euse.
sycophantic [sikəfan'tik] *a* flagorneur(euse).
Sydney [sid'nē] *n* Sydney.
syllable [sil'əbəl] *n* syllabe *f*.
syllabus [sil'əbəs] *n* programme *m*; **on the** ~ au programme.
symbol [sim'bəl] *n* symbole *m*.
symbolic(al) [simbâl'ik(əl)] *a* symbolique.
symbolism [sim'bəlizəm] *n* symbolisme *m*.
symbolize [sim'bəlīz] *vt* symboliser.
symmetrical [simet'rikəl] *a* symétrique.
symmetry [sim'itrē] *n* symétrie *f*.
sympathetic [simpəthet'ik] *a* (*showing pity*) compatissant(e); (*understanding*) bienveillant(e), compréhensif(ive); ~ **towards** bien disposé(e) envers.
sympathetically [simpəthet'iklē] *ad* avec compassion (*or* bienveillance).
sympathize [sim'pəthīz] *vi*: **to** ~ **with sb** (*in grief*) être de tout cœur avec qn, compatir à la douleur de qn; (*in predicament*) partager les sentiments de qn; **to** ~ **with** (*sb's feelings*) comprendre.
sympathizer [sim'pəthīzûr] *n* (*POL*) sympathisant/e.
sympathy [sim'pəthē] *n* compassion *f*; **in** ~ **with** en accord avec; (*strike*) en *or* par solidarité avec; **with our deepest** ~ en vous priant d'accepter nos sincères condoléances.
symphonic [simfân'ik] *a* symphonique.
symphony [sim'fənē] *n* symphonie *f*.
symphony orchestra *n* orchestre *m* symphonique.
symposium [simpō'zēəm] *n* symposium *m*.
symptom [simp'təm] *n* symptôme *m*; indice *m*.
symptomatic [simptəmat'ik] *a* symptomatique.
synagogue [sin'əgâg] *n* synagogue *f*.
synchromesh [sing'krəmesh] *n* (*AUT*) synchronisation *f*.
synchronize [sing'krənīz] *vt* synchroniser ♦ *vi*: **to** ~ **with** se produire en même temps que.
syncopated [sing'kəpātid] *a* syncopé(e).
syndicate [sin'dəkit] *n* syndicat *m*, coopérative

f; (*PRESS*) agence *f* de presse.

syndrome [sin'drōm] *n* syndrome *m*.

synonym [sin'ənim] *n* synonyme *m*.

synonymous [sinán'əməs] *a*: ~ **(with)** synonyme (de).

synopsis, *pl* **synopses** [sinâp'sis, -sēz] *n* résumé *m*, synopsis *m* or *f*.

syntax [sin'taks] *n* syntaxe *f*.

synthesis, *pl* **syntheses** [sin'thəsis, -sēz] *n* synthèse *f*.

synthesizer [sin'thisīzûr] *n* (*MUS*) synthétiseur *m*.

synthetic [sinthet'ik] *a* synthétique ♦ *n* matière *f* synthétique; ~**s** *npl* textiles artificiels.

syphilis [sif'əlis] *n* syphilis *f*.

syphon [sī'fən] *n*, *vb* = **siphon**.

Syria [sēr'ēə] *n* Syrie *f*.

Syrian [sēr'ēən] *a* syrien(ne) ♦ *n* Syrien/ne.

syringe [sərinj'] *n* seringue *f*.

syrup [sir'əp] *n* sirop *m*; (*Brit*: *also*: **golden** ~) mélasse raffinée.

syrupy [sir'əpē] *a* sirupeux(euse).

system [sis'təm] *n* système *m*; (*order*) méthode *f*; (*ANAT*) organisme *m*.

systematic [sistəmat'ik] *a* systématique; méthodique.

system disk *n* (*COMPUT*) disque *m* système.

systems analyst [sis'təmz an'əlist] *n* analyste-programmeur *m/f*.

T

T, t [tē] *n* (*letter*) T, t *m*; **T for Tommy** T comme Thérèse.

ta [tä] *excl* (*Brit col*) merci!

tab [tab] *n abbr* = **tabulator** ♦ *n* (*loop on coat etc*) attache *f*; (*label*) étiquette *f*; **to keep** ~**s on** (*fig*) surveiller.

tabby [tab'ē] *n* (*also*: ~ **cat**) chat/te tigré(e).

tabernacle [tab'ûrnakəl] *n* tabernacle *m*.

table [tā'bəl] *n* table *f*; **to lay** *or* **set the** ~ mettre le couvert *or* la table; **to clear the** ~ débarrasser la table; ~ **of contents** table des matières.

tablecloth [tā'bəlklòth] *n* nappe *f*.

table d'hôte [tab'əl dōt'] *a* (*meal*) à prix fixe.

table lamp *n* lampe décorative.

tableland [tā'bəlland] *n* plateau *m*.

tablemat [tā'bəlmat] *n* (*Brit*: *for plate*) napperon *m*, set *m*; (: *for hot dish*) dessous-de-plat *m inv*.

table salt *n* sel fin *or* de table.

tablespoon [tā'bəlspōōn] *n* cuiller *f* de service; (*also*: ~**ful**: *as measurement*) cuillerée *f* à soupe.

tablet [tab'lit] *n* (*MED*) comprimé *m*; (: *for sucking*) pastille *f*; (*for writing*) bloc *m*; (*of stone*) plaque *f*.

table tennis *n* ping-pong *m*, tennis *m* de table.

table wine *n* vin *m* de table.

tabloid [tab'loid] *n* (*newspaper*) tabloïde *m*;

the ~**s** les journaux *mpl* populaires.

taboo [tabōō'] *a*, *n* tabou (*m*).

tabulate [tab'yəlāt] *vt* (*data*, *figures*) mettre sous forme de table(s).

tabulator [tab'yəlātûr] *n* tabulateur *m*.

tachograph [tak'əgraf] *n* tachygraphe *m*.

tachometer [təkâm'ətûr] *n* tachymètre *m*.

tacit [tas'it] *a* tacite.

taciturn [tas'itûrn] *a* taciturne.

tack [tak] *n* (*nail*) petit clou; (*stitch*) point *m* de bâti; (*NAUT*) bord *m*, bordée *f* ♦ *vt* clouer; bâtir ♦ *vi* tirer un *or* des bord(s); **to change** ~ virer de bord; **on the wrong** ~ (*fig*) sur la mauvaise voie; **to** ~ **sth on to (the end of) sth** (*of letter*, *book*) rajouter qch à la fin de qch.

tackle [tak'əl] *n* matériel *m*, équipement *m*; (*for lifting*) appareil *m* de levage; (*FOOTBALL*, *SOCCER*, *RUGBY*) plàquage *m* ♦ *vt* (*difficulty*) s'attaquer à; (*SOCCER*, *RUGBY*) plaquer.

tacky [tak'ē] *a* collant(e); pas sec(sèche); (*col*: *shabby*) moche.

tact [takt] *n* tact *m*.

tactful [takt'fəl] *a* plein(e) de tact.

tactfully [takt'fəlē] *ad* avec tact.

tactical [tak'tikəl] *a* tactique; ~ **error** erreur *f* de tactique.

tactics [tak'tiks] *n*, *npl* tactique *f*.

tactless [takt'lis] *a* qui manque de tact.

tactlessly [takt'lislē] *ad* sans tact.

tadpole [tad'pōl] *n* têtard *m*.

taffy [taf'ē] *n* (*US*) (bonbon *m* au) caramel *m*.

tag [tag] *n* étiquette *f*; **price/name** ~ étiquette (portant le prix/le nom).

tag along *vi* suivre.

Tahiti [təhē'tē] *n* Tahiti *m*.

tail [tāl] *n* queue *f*; (*of shirt*) pan *m* ♦ *vt* (*follow*) suivre, filer; **to turn** ~ se sauver à toutes jambes; *see also* **head**.

tail away, **tail off** *vi* (*in size*, *quality etc*) baisser peu à peu.

tailback [tāl'bak] *n* (*Brit*) bouchon *m*.

tail coat *n* habit *m*.

tail end *n* bout *m*, fin *f*.

tailgate [tāl'gāt] *n* (*AUT*) hayon *m* arrière.

taillight [tāl'līt] *n* (*AUT*) feu *m* arrière.

tailor [tā'lûr] *n* tailleur *m* (*artisan*) ♦ *vt*: **to** ~ **sth (to)** adapter qch exactement (à); ~**'s (shop)** (boutique *f* de) tailleur *m*.

tailoring [tā'lûring] *n* (*cut*) coupe *f*.

tailor-made [tā'lûrmād] *a* fait(e) sur mesure; (*fig*) conçu(e) spécialement.

tailwind [tāl'wind] *n* vent *m* arrière *inv*.

taint [tānt] *vt* (*meat*, *food*) gâter; (*fig*: *reputation*) salir.

tainted [tānt'id] *a* (*food*) gâté(e); (*water*, *air*) infecté(e); (*fig*) souillé(e).

Taiwan [tī'wân'] *n* Taiwan (*no article*).

take [tāk] *vb* (*pt* **took**, *pp* **taken** [tōōk, tā'kən]) *vt* prendre; (*gain*: *prize*) remporter; (*require*: *effort*, *courage*) demander; (*tolerate*) accepter, supporter; (*hold*: *passengers etc*) contenir; (*accompany*) emmener, accompagner; (*bring*, *carry*) apporter, emporter; (*exam*) passer, se présenter à; (*conduct*: *meeting*) présider ♦ *vi* (*dye*, *fire etc*) prendre ♦ *n* (*CINEMA*) prise *f* de vues; **to** ~ **sth from** (*drawer etc*) prendre qch dans; (*person*)

prendre qch à; **I ~ it that** je suppose que; **I took him for a doctor** je l'ai pris pour un docteur; **to ~ sb's hand** prendre qn par la main; **to ~ for a walk** (*child, dog*) emmener promener; **to be taken ill** tomber malade; **to ~ it upon o.s. to do sth** prendre sur soi de faire qch; **~ the first (street) on the left** prenez la première à gauche; **it won't ~ long** ça ne prendra pas longtemps; **I was quite taken with her/it** elle/cela m'a beaucoup plu.
take after *vt fus* ressembler à.
take apart *vt* démonter.
take away *vt* emporter; (*remove*) enlever; (*subtract*) soustraire ♦ *vi*: **to ~ away from** diminuer.
take back *vt* (*return*) rendre, rapporter; (*one's words*) retirer.
take down *vt* (*building*) démolir; (*dismantle: scaffolding*) démonter; (*letter etc*) prendre, écrire.
take in *vt* (*deceive*) tromper, rouler; (*understand*) comprendre, saisir; (*include*) couvrir, inclure; (*lodger*) prendre; (*orphan, stray dog*) recueillir; (*dress, waistband*) reprendre.
take off *vi* (AVIAT) décoller; (*leave*) décamper ♦ *vt* (*remove*) enlever; (*imitate*) imiter, pasticher.
take on *vt* (*work*) accepter, se charger de; (*employee*) prendre, embaucher; (*opponent*) accepter de se battre contre.
take out *vt* sortir; (*remove*) enlever; (*license*) prendre, se procurer; **to ~ sth out of** enlever qch de; prendre qch dans; **don't ~ it out on me!** ne t'en prends pas à moi!
take over *vt* (*business*) reprendre ♦ *vi*: **to ~ over from sb** prendre la relève de qn.
take to *vt fus* (*person*) se prendre d'amitié pour; (*activity*) prendre goût à; **to ~ to doing sth** prendre l'habitude de faire qch.
take up *vt* (*one's story, a dress*) reprendre; (*occupy: time, space*) prendre, occuper; (*engage in: hobby etc*) se mettre à; (*accept: offer, challenge*) accepter; (*absorb: liquids*) absorber ♦ *vi*: **to ~ up with sb** se lier d'amitié avec qn.
takeaway [tā'kəwā] *a* (*Brit*) = **takeout.**
take-home pay [tāk'hōm pā] *n* salaire net.
taken [tā'kən] *pp of* **take.**
takeoff [tāk'ôf] *n* (AVIAT) décollage *m*.
takeout [tāk'out] *a* (*US: food*) à emporter.
takeover [tāk'ōvûr] *n* (COMM) rachat *m*.
takeover bid *n* offre publique d'achat, OPA *f*.
takings [tā'kingz] *npl* (COMM) recette *f*.
talc [talk] *n* (*also:* **~um powder**) talc *m*.
tale [tāl] *n* (*story*) conte *m*, histoire *f*; (*account*) récit *m*; (*pej*) histoire; **to tell ~s** (*fig*) rapporter.
talent [tal'ənt] *n* talent *m*, don *m*.
talented [tal'əntid] *a* doué(e), plein(e) de talent.
talent scout *n* découvreur *m* de vedettes (*or* joueurs *etc*).
talk [tôk] *n* propos *mpl*; (*gossip*) racontars *mpl* (*pej*); (*conversation*) discussion *f*; (*interview*) entretien *m*; (*a speech*) causerie *f*, exposé *m* ♦ *vi* (*chatter*) bavarder; **~s** *npl* (POL *etc*) entretiens *mpl*; conférence *f*; **to give a ~ about** parler

de; (*converse*) s'entretenir *or* parler de; **~ing of films, have you seen ...?** à propos de films, avez-vous vu ...?; **to ~ sb out of/into doing** persuader qn de ne pas faire/de faire; **to ~ shop** parler métier *or* affaires.
talk over *vt* discuter (de).
talkative [tô'kətiv] *a* bavard(e).
talker [tô'kûr] *n* causeur/euse; (*pej*) bavard/e.
talking point [tô'king point] *n* sujet *m* de conversation.
talking-to [tô'kingtōō] *n*: **to give sb a good ~** passer un savon à qn.
talk show *n* (TV, RADIO) causerie (télévisée *or* radiodiffusée).
tall [tôl] *a* (*person*) grand(e); (*building, tree*) haut(e); **to be 6 feet ~** ≈ mesurer 1 mètre 80; **how ~ are you?** combien mesurez-vous?
tallboy [tôl'boi] *n* (*Brit*) grande commode.
tallness [tôl'nis] *n* grande taille; hauteur *f*.
tall story *n* histoire *f* invraisemblable.
tally [tal'ē] *n* compte *m* ♦ *vi*: **to ~ (with)** correspondre (à); **to keep a ~ of sth** tenir le compte de qch.
talon [tal'ən] *n* griffe *f*; (*of eagle*) serre *f*.
tambourine [tam'bərēn] *n* tambourin *m*.
tame [tām] *a* apprivoisé(e); (*fig: story, style*) insipide.
tamper [tam'pûr] *vi*: **to ~ with** toucher à (*en cachette ou sans permission*).
tampon [tam'pân] *n* tampon *m* hygiénique *or* périodique.
tan [tan] *n* (*also:* **sun~**) bronzage *m* ♦ *vt, vi* bronzer, brunir ♦ *a* (*color*) brun roux *inv*; **to get a ~** bronzer.
tandem [tan'dəm] *n* tandem *m*.
tang [tang] *n* odeur (*or* saveur) piquante.
tangent [tan'jənt] *n* (MATH) tangente *f*; **to go off at a ~** (*fig*) changer complètement de direction.
tangerine [tanjərēn'] *n* mandarine *f*.
tangible [tan'jəbəl] *a* tangible; **~ assets** biens réels.
Tangier [tanjiûr'] *n* Tanger *m*.
tangle [tang'gəl] *n* enchevêtrement *m* ♦ *vt* enchevêtrer; **to get in(to) a ~** s'emmêler.
tango [tang'gō] *n* tango *m*.
tank [tangk] *n* réservoir *m*; (*for processing*) cuve *f*; (*for fish*) aquarium *m*; (MIL) char *m* d'assaut, tank *m*.
tankard [tangk'ûrd] *n* chope *f*.
tanker [tangk'ûr] *n* (*ship*) pétrolier *m*, tanker *m*; (*truck*) camion-citerne *m*; (RAIL) wagon-citerne *m*.
tanned [tand] *a* bronzé(e).
tannin [tan'in] *n* tanin *m*.
tanning [tan'ing] *n* (*of leather*) tannage *m*.
tantalizing [tan'təlīzing] *a* (*smell*) extrêmement appétissant(e); (*offer*) terriblement tentant(e).
tantamount [tan'təmount] *a*: **~ to** qui équivaut à.
tantrum [tan'trəm] *n* accès *m* de colère; **to throw a ~** piquer une colère.
Tanzania [tanzənē'ə] *n* Tanzanie *f*.
Tanzanian [tanzənē'ən] *a* tanzanien(ne) ♦ *n* Tanzanien/ne.
tap [tap] *n* (*on sink etc*) robinet *m*; (*gentle blow*) petite tape ♦ *vt* frapper *or* taper légèrement; (*resources*) exploiter, utiliser; (*tele-*

phone) mettre sur écoute; **on** ~ (*beer*) en tonneau; (*fig: resources*) disponible.

tap-dancing [tap'dansing] *n* claquettes *fpl*.

tape [tāp] *n* ruban *m*; (*also:* **magnetic** ~) bande *f* (magnétique) ♦ *vt* (*record*) enregistrer (au magnétophone *or* sur bande); **on** ~ (*song etc*) enregistré(e).

tape deck *n* platine *f* d'enregistrement.

tape measure *n* mètre *m* à ruban.

taper [tā'pûr] *n* cierge *m* ♦ *vi* s'effiler.

tape-record [tāp'rikôrd] *vt* enregistrer (au magnétophone *or* sur bande).

tape recorder *n* magnétophone *m*.

tape recording *n* enregistrement *m* (au magnétophone).

tapered [tā'pûrd], **tapering** [tā'pûring] *a* fuselé(e), effilé(e).

tapestry [tap'istrē] *n* tapisserie *f*.

tapeworm [tāp'wûrm'] *n* ver *m* solitaire, ténia *m*.

tapioca [tapēō'kə] *n* tapioca *m*.

tappet [tap'it] *n* (*AUT*) poussoir *m* (de soupape).

tar [târ] *n* goudron *m*; **low-/middle-~ cigarettes** cigarettes *fpl* à faible/moyenne teneur en goudron.

tarantula [təran'chələ] *n* tarentule *f*.

tardy [târ'dē] *a* tardif(ive).

target [târ'git] *n* cible *f*; (*fig: objective*) objectif *m*; **to be on** ~ (*project*) progresser comme prévu.

target practice *n* exercices *mpl* de tir (à la cible).

tariff [tar'if] *n* (*COMM*) tarif *m*; (*taxes*) tarif douanier.

tariff barrier *n* barrière douanière.

tarmac [târ'mak] *n* (*AVIAT*) aire *f* d'envol; (*Brit: on road*) macadam *m*.

tarnish [târ'nish] *vt* ternir.

tarpaulin [târpô'lin] *n* bâche goudronnée.

tarragon [tar'əgən] *n* estragon *m*.

tart [târt] *n* (*CULIN*) tarte *f*; (*Brit col: pej: woman*) poule *f* ♦ *a* (*flavor*) âpre, aigrelet(te).
tart up *vt* (*col*): **to** ~ **o.s. up** se faire beau(belle); (: *pej*) s'attifer.

tartan [târ'tən] *n* tartan *m* ♦ *a* écossais(e).

tartar [târ'tûr] *n* (*on teeth*) tartre *m*.

tartar sauce *n* sauce *f* tartare.

task [task] *n* tâche *f*; **to take to** ~ prendre à partie.

task force *n* (*MIL, POLICE*) détachement spécial.

taskmaster [task'mastûr] *n*: **he's a hard** ~ il est très exigeant dans le travail.

Tasmania [tazmā'nēə] *n* Tasmanie *f*.

tassel [tas'əl] *n* gland *m*; pompon *m*.

taste [tāst] *n* goût *m*; (*fig: glimpse, idea*) idée *f*, aperçu *m* ♦ *vt* goûter ♦ *vi*: **to** ~ **of** (*fish etc*) avoir le *or* un goût de; **it** ~**s like fish** ça a un *or* le goût de poisson, on dirait du poisson; **what does it** ~ **like?** quel goût ça a?; **you can** ~ **the garlic (in it)** on sent bien l'ail; **can I have a** ~ **of this wine?** puis-je goûter un peu de ce vin?; **to have a** ~ **of sth** goûter (à) qch; **to have a** ~ **for sth** aimer qch, avoir un penchant pour qch; **to be in good/bad** *or* **poor** ~ être de bon/mauvais goût.

taste bud *n* papille *f*.

tasteful [tāst'fəl] *a* de bon goût.

tastefully [tāst'fəlē] *ad* avec goût.

tasteless [tāst'lis] *a* (*food*) qui n'a aucun goût; (*remark*) de mauvais goût.

tasty [tās'tē] *a* savoureux(euse), délicieux(euse).

tattered [tat'ûrd] *a see* **tatters**.

tatters [tat'ûrz] *npl*: **in** ~ (*also:* **tattered**) en lambeaux.

tattoo [tatōō'] *n* tatouage *m*; (*spectacle*) parade *f* militaire ♦ *vt* tatouer.

tatty [tat'ē] *a* (*Brit col*) défraîchi(e), en piteux état.

taught [tôt] *pt, pp of* **teach**.

taunt [tônt] *n* raillerie *f* ♦ *vt* railler.

Taurus [tôr'əs] *n* le Taureau; **to be** ~ être du Taureau.

taut [tôt] *a* tendu(e).

tavern [tav'ûrn] *n* taverne *f*.

tawdry [tô'drē] *a* (d'un mauvais goût) criard.

tawny [tô'nē] *a* fauve (*couleur*).

tax [taks] *n* (*on goods etc*) taxe *f*; (*on income*) impôts *mpl*, contributions *fpl* ♦ *vt* taxer; imposer; (*fig: strain: patience etc*) mettre à l'épreuve; **before/after** ~ avant/après l'impôt; **free of** ~ exonéré(e) d'impôt.

taxable [tak'səbəl] *a* (*income*) imposable.

tax allowance *n* part *f* du revenu non imposable, abattement *m* à la base.

taxation [taksā'shən] *n* taxation *f*; impôts *mpl*, contributions *fpl*; **system of** ~ système fiscal.

tax avoidance *n* évasion fiscale.

tax collector *n* percepteur *m*.

tax disc *n* (*Brit AUT*) vignette *f* (automobile).

tax evasion *n* fraude fiscale.

tax exemption *n* exonération fiscale, exemption *f* d'impôts.

tax exile *n* personne qui s'expatrie pour fuir une fiscalité excessive.

tax-free [taks'frē'] *a* exempt(e) d'impôts.

tax haven *n* paradis fiscal.

taxi [tak'sē] *n* taxi *m* ♦ *vi* (*AVIAT*) rouler (lentement) au sol.

taxidermist [tak'sidûrmist] *n* empailleur/euse (*d'animaux*).

taxi driver *n* chauffeur *m* de taxi.

taximeter [tak'simētûr] *n* taximètre *m*.

tax inspector *n* (*Brit*) percepteur *m*.

taxi stand, (*Brit*) **taxi rank** *n* station *f* de taxis.

tax payer *n* contribuable *m/f*.

tax rebate *n* ristourne *f* d'impôt.

tax relief *n* dégrèvement *or* allègement fiscal, réduction *f* d'impôt.

tax return *n* déclaration *f* d'impôts *or* de revenus.

tax year *n* année fiscale.

TB *n abbr* = **tuberculosis.**

TD *n abbr* (*US*) = **Treasury Department;** (: *FOOTBALL*) = **touchdown.**

tea [tē] *n* thé *m*; (*Brit: snack: for children*) goûter *m*; **high** ~ (*Brit*) collation combinant goûter et dîner.

tea bag *n* sachet *m* de thé.

tea break *n* (*Brit*) pause-thé *f*.

teach, *pt, pp* **taught** [tēch, tôt] *vt*: **to** ~ **sb sth,** ~ **sth to sb** apprendre qch à qn; (*in*

school etc) enseigner qch à qn ♦ *vi* enseigner; **it taught him a lesson** (*fig*) ça lui a
servi de leçon.
teacher [tē'chûr] *n* (*in high school*) professeur
m; (*in elementary school*) instituteur/trice;
French ~ professeur de français.
teacher training college *n* (*for elementary
schools*) ≈ école normale d'instituteurs; (*for
high schools*) collège *m* de formation pédagogique (*pour l'enseignement secondaire*).
teaching [tē'ching] *n* enseignement *m*.
teaching aids *npl* supports *mpl* pédago-
giques.
teaching hospital *n* C.H.U. *m*, centre *m*
hospitalo-universitaire.
tea cosy *n* couvre-théière *m*.
teacup [tē'kup] *n* tasse *f* à thé.
teak [tēk] *n* teck *m* ♦ *a* en *or* de teck.
tea leaves *npl* feuilles *fpl* de thé.
team [tēm] *n* équipe *f*; (*of animals*) attelage
m.
team up *vi*: **to** ~ **up (with)** faire équipe
(avec).
team games *npl* jeux *mpl* d'équipe.
teamwork [tēm'wûrk] *n* travail *m* d'équipe.
tea party *n* thé *m* (*réception*).
teapot [tē'pât] *n* théière *f*.
tear *n* [tär] déchirure *f*; [tēr] larme *f* ♦ *vb* [tär]
(*pt* **tore**, *pp* **torn** [tôr, tôrn]) *vt* déchirer ♦ *vi*
se déchirer; **in** ~**s** en larmes; **to burst into**
~**s** fondre en larmes; **to** ~ **to pieces** *or* **to
bits** *or* **to shreds** mettre en pièces; (*fig*) démolir.
tear along *vi* (*rush*) aller à toute vitesse.
tear apart *vt* (*also fig*) déchirer.
tear away *vt*: **to** ~ **o.s. away (from sth)**
(*fig*) s'arracher (de qch).
tear out *vt* (*sheet of paper, check*) arracher.
tear up *vt* (*sheet of paper etc*) déchirer,
mettre en morceaux *or* pièces.
tearaway [tär'əwā] *n* (*Brit: col*) casse-cou *m*
inv.
teardrop [tēr'drâp] *n* larme *f*.
tearful [tēr'fəl] *a* larmoyant(e).
tear gas *n* gaz *m* lacrymogène.
tearoom [tē'rōōm] *n* salon *m* de thé.
tease [tēz] *n* taquin/e ♦ *vt* taquiner; (*unkindly*)
tourmenter; (*hair*) crêper.
tea set *n* service *m* à thé.
teashop [tē'shâp] *n* (*Brit*) pâtisserie-salon de
thé *f*.
teaspoon [tē'spōōn] *n* petite cuiller; (*also:*
~**ful:** *as measurement*) ≈ cuillerée *f* à café.
tea strainer *n* passoire *f* (à thé).
teat [tēt] *n* tétine *f*.
teatime [tē'tīm] *n* l'heure *f* du thé.
tea towel *n* (*Brit*) torchon *m* (à vaisselle).
tea urn *n* fontaine *f* à thé.
tech [tek] *n abbr* (*col*) = **technology, technical
college**.
technical [tek'nikəl] *a* technique.
technical college *n* C.E.T. *m*, collège *m*
d'enseignement technique.
technicality [teknikal'itē] *n* technicité *f*; (*detail*) détail *m* technique; **on a legal** ~ à
cause de (*or* grâce à) l'application à la lettre
d'une subtilité juridique; pour vice de forme.
technically [tek'niklē] *ad* techniquement.

technician [teknish'ən] *n* technicien/ne.
technique [teknēk'] *n* technique *f*.
technocrat [tek'nəkrat] *n* technocrate *m/f*.
technological [teknəlâj'ikəl] *a* technologique.
technologist [teknâl'əjist] *n* technologue *m/f*.
technology [teknâl'əjē] *n* technologie *f*.
teddy (bear) [ted'ē bär] *n* ours *m* (en peluche).
tedious [tē'dēəs] *a* fastidieux(euse).
tedium [tē'dēəm] *n* ennui *m*.
tee [tē] *n* (*GOLF*) tee *m*.
teem [tēm] *vi*: **to** ~ **(with)** grouiller (de).
teenage [tēn'āj] *a* (*fashions etc*) pour jeunes,
pour adolescents.
teenager [tēn'ājûr] *n* jeune *m/f*, adolescent/e.
teens [tēnz] *npl*: **to be in one's** ~ être ado-
lescent(e).
tee shirt *n* = **T-shirt.**
teeter [tē'tûr] *vi* chanceler, vaciller.
teeth [tēth] *npl of* **tooth.**
teethe [tēth] *vi* percer ses dents.
teething ring [tē'thing ring] *n* anneau *m* (*pour
bébé qui perce ses dents*).
teething troubles [tē'thing trub'əlz] *npl* (*fig*)
difficultés initiales.
teetotal [tētōt'əl] *a* (*person*) qui ne boit jamais
d'alcool.
teetotaler, (*Brit*) **teetotaller** [tētōt'əlûr] *n*
personne *f* qui ne boit jamais d'alcool.
TEFL [tef'əl] *n abbr* = *Teaching of English as a
Foreign Language.*
Teheran [teərân'] *n* Téhéran.
tel. *abbr* (= *telephone*) tél.
Tel Aviv [tel'əvēv'] *n* Tel Aviv.
telecast [tel'əkast] *vt* télédiffuser, téléviser.
telecommunications [teləkəmyōōnikā'shənz]
n télécommunications *fpl.*
telegram [tel'əgram] *n* télégramme *m*.
telegraph [tel'əgraf] *n* télégraphe *m*.
telegraphic [teləgraf'ik] *a* télégraphique.
telegraph pole *n* poteau *m* télégraphique.
telegraph wire *n* fil *m* télégraphique.
telepathic [teləpath'ik] *a* télépathique.
telepathy [təlep'əthē] *n* télépathie *f*.
telephone [tel'əfōn] *n* téléphone *m* ♦ *vt*
(*person*) téléphoner à; (*message*) téléphoner;
to have a ~ (*subscriber*) être abonné(e) au
téléphone; **to be on the** ~ (*be speaking*) être
au téléphone.
telephone booth, (*Brit*) **telephone box** *n*
cabine *f* téléphonique.
telephone call *n* appel *m* téléphonique,
communication *f* téléphonique.
telephone directory *n* annuaire *m* (du téléphone).
telephone exchange *n* central *m* (téléphonique).
telephone kiosk *n* (*Brit*) cabine *f* téléphonique.
telephone number *n* numéro *m* de téléphone.
telephone operator téléphoniste *m/f*,
standardiste *m/f*.
telephone tapping [tel'əfōn ta'ping] *n* mise *f*
sur écoute.
telephonist [tel'əfōnist] *n* (*Brit*) téléphoniste
m/f.
telephoto [teləfō'tō] *a*: ~ **lens** téléobjectif *m*.
teleprinter [tel'əprintûr] *n* téléscripteur *m*.

telescope [tel'əskōp] *n* télescope *m* ♦ *vi* se télescoper ♦ *vt* télescoper.
telescopic [teliskåp'ik] *a* télescopique; (*umbrella*) à manche télescopique.
teletext [tel'ətekst] *n* télétexte *m*.
telethon [tel'əthân] *n* téléthon *m*.
televiewer [tel'əvyōōūr] *n* téléspectateur/trice.
televise [tel'əvīz] *vt* téléviser.
television [tel'əvizhən] *n* télévision *f*.
television licence *n* (*Brit*) redevance *f* (de l'audio-visuel).
television program *n* émission *f* de télévision.
television set *n* poste *m* de télévision, téléviseur *m*.
telex [tel'eks] *n* télex *m* ♦ *vt* (*message*) envoyer par télex; (*person*) envoyer un télex à ♦ *vi* envoyer un télex.
tell, *pt*, *pp* **told** [tel, tōld] *vt* dire; (*relate: story*) raconter; (*distinguish*): **to ~ sth from** distinguer qch de ♦ *vi* (*talk*): **to ~ (of)** parler (de); (*have effect*) se faire sentir, se voir; **to ~ sb to do** dire à qn de faire; **to ~ sb about sth** (*place, object etc*) parler de qch à qn; (*what happened etc*) raconter qch à qn; **to ~ the time** (*know how to*) savoir lire l'heure; **can you ~ me the time?** pourriez-vous me dire l'heure?; **(I) ~ you what ...** écoute, ...; **I can't ~ them apart** je n'arrive pas à les distinguer.
tell off *vt* réprimander, gronder.
tell on *vt fus* (*inform against*) dénoncer, rapporter contre.
teller [tel'ûr] *n* (*in bank*) caissier/ière.
telling [tel'ing] *a* (*remark, detail*) révélateur(trice).
telltale [tel'tāl] *a* (*sign*) éloquent(e), révélateur(trice).
telly [tel'ē] *n abbr* (*Brit col: = television*) télé *f*.
temerity [təmär'itē] *n* témérité *f*.
temp [temp] *abbr* (*Brit col: = temporary*) *n* intérimaire *m/f* ♦ *vi* travailler comme intérimaire.
temper [tem'pûr] *n* (*nature*) caractère *m*; (*mood*) humeur *f*; (*fit of anger*) colère *f* ♦ *vt* (*moderate*) tempérer, adoucir; **to be in a ~** être en colère; **to lose one's ~** se mettre en colère; **to keep one's ~** rester calme.
temperament [tem'pûrəmənt] *n* (*nature*) tempérament *m*.
temperamental [tempûrəmen'təl] *a* capricieux(euse).
temperance [tem'pûrəns] *n* modération *f*; (*in drinking*) tempérance *f*.
temperate [tem'pûrit] *a* modéré(e); (*climate*) tempéré(e).
temperature [tem'pûrəchûr] *n* température *f*; **to have** *or* **run a ~** avoir de la fièvre.
temperature chart *n* (*MED*) feuille *f* de température.
tempered [tem'pûrd] *a* (*steel*) trempé(e).
tempest [tem'pist] *n* tempête *f*.
tempestuous [tempes'chōōəs] *a* (*fig*) orageux(euse); (*: person*) passionné(e).
tempi [tem'pē] *npl of* **tempo**.
template [tem'plit] *n* patron *m*.
temple [tem'pəl] *n* (*building*) temple *m*; (*ANAT*) tempe *f*.

templet [tem'plit] *n* = **template**.
tempo, **~s** *or* **tempi** [tem'pō, tem'pē] *n* tempo *m*; (*fig: of life etc*) rythme *m*.
temporal [tem'pûrəl] *a* temporel(le).
temporarily [tempərär'ilē] *ad* temporairement; provisoirement.
temporary [tem'pərärē] *a* temporaire, provisoire; (*job, worker*) temporaire; **~ license** (*US AUT*) permis *m* provisoire; **~ secretary** (secrétaire *f*) intérimaire *f*; **a ~ teacher** un professeur remplaçant *or* suppléant.
temporize [tem'pəriz] *vi* atermoyer; transiger.
tempt [tempt] *vt* tenter; **to ~ sb into doing** induire qn à faire; **to be ~ed to do sth** être tenté(e) de faire qch.
temptation [temptā'shən] *n* tentation *f*.
tempting [temp'ting] *a* tentant(e).
ten [ten] *num* dix ♦ *n*: **~s of thousands** des dizaines *fpl* de milliers.
tenable [ten'əbəl] *a* défendable.
tenacious [tənā'shəs] *a* tenace.
tenacity [tənas'itē] *n* ténacité *f*.
tenancy [ten'ənsē] *n* location *f*; état *m* de locataire.
tenant [ten'ənt] *n* locataire *m/f*.
tend [tend] *vt* s'occuper de; (*sick etc*) soigner ♦ *vi*: **to ~ to do** avoir tendance à faire; (*color*): **to ~ to** tirer sur.
tendency [ten'dənsē] *n* tendance *f*.
tender [ten'dûr] *a* tendre; (*delicate*) délicat(e); (*sore*) sensible; (*affectionate*) tendre, doux(douce) ♦ *n* (*COMM: offer*) soumission *f*; (*money*): **legal ~** cours légal ♦ *vt* offrir; **to ~ one's resignation** donner *or* remettre sa démission; **to put in a ~ (for)** faire une soumission (pour).
tenderize [ten'dəriz] *vt* (*CULIN*) attendrir.
tenderly [ten'dûrlē] *ad* tendrement.
tenderness [ten'dûrnis] *n* tendresse *f*; (*of meat*) tendreté *f*.
tendon [ten'dən] *n* tendon *m*.
tenement [ten'əmənt] *n* immeuble *m* (de rapport).
Tenerife [tenərēf'] *n* Ténérife *f*.
tenet [ten'it] *n* principe *m*.
Tenn. *abbr* (*US*) = *Tennessee*.
tenner [ten'ûr] *n* (*col: US*) billet *m* de dix dollars; (*: Brit*) billet *m* de dix livres.
tennis [ten'is] *n* tennis *m* ♦ *cpd* (*club, match, racket, player*) de tennis.
tennis ball *n* balle *f* de tennis.
tennis court *n* (court *m* de) tennis *m*.
tennis elbow *n* (*MED*) synovite *f* du coude.
tennis shoes *npl* (chaussures *fpl* de) tennis *mpl*.
tenor [ten'ûr] *n* (*MUS*) ténor *m*; (*of speech etc*) sens général.
tenpin bowling [ten'pin bō'ling] *n* (*Brit*) = **tenpins**.
tenpins [ten'pinz] *n* (*US*) bowling *m* (à 10 quilles).
tense [tens] *a* tendu(e); (*person*) tendu, crispé(e) ♦ *n* (*LING*) temps *m* ♦ *vt* (*tighten: muscles*) tendre.
tenseness [tens'nis] *n* tension *f*.
tension [ten'chən] *n* tension *f*.
tent [tent] *n* tente *f*.
tentacle [ten'təkəl] *n* tentacule *m*.
tentative [ten'tətiv] *a* timide, hésitant(e);

(*conclusion*) provisoire.

tenterhooks [tɛn'tûrhŏŏks] *npl*: **on ~** sur des charbons ardents.

tenth [tenth] *num* dixième.

tent peg *n* piquet *m* de tente.

tent pole *n* montant *m* de tente.

tenuous [ten'yŏŏəs] *a* ténu(e).

tenure [ten'yûr] *n* (*of property*) bail *m*; (*of job*) période *f* de jouissance; statut *m* de titulaire.

tepid [tep'id] *a* tiède.

term [tûrm] *n* (*limit*) terme *m*; (*word*) terme, mot *m*; (*SCOL*) trimestre *m*; (*LAW*) session *f* ♦ *vt* appeler; **~s** *npl* (*conditions*) conditions *fpl*; (*COMM*) tarif *m*; **~ of imprisonment** peine *f* de prison; **his ~ of office** la période où il était en fonction; **in the short/long ~** à court/long terme; **"easy ~s"** (*COMM*) "facilités de paiement"; **to come to ~s with** (*problem*) faire face à; **to be on good ~s with** bien s'entendre avec, être en bons termes avec.

terminal [tûr'mənəl] *a* terminal(e); (*disease*) dans sa phase terminale ♦ *n* (*ELEC*) borne *f*; (*for oil, ore etc, also COMPUT*) terminal *m*; (*also*: **air ~**) aérogare *f*; (*Brit: also*: **coach ~**) gare routière.

terminate [tûr'mənāt] *vt* mettre fin à ♦ *vi*: **to ~ in** finir en *or* par.

termination [tûrmənā'shən] *n* fin *f*; cessation *f*; (*of contract*) résiliation *f*; **~ of pregnancy** (*MED*) interruption *f* de grossesse.

termini [tûr'mənē] *npl of* **terminus**.

terminology [tûrmənál'əjē] *n* terminologie *f*.

terminus, *pl* **termini** [tûr'mənəs, tûr'mənē] *n* terminus *m inv*.

termite [tûr'mīt] *n* termite *m*.

Ter(r). *abbr* = **terrace**.

terrace [tär'əs] *n* terrasse *f*; (*Brit: row of houses*) rangée *f* de maisons (*attenantes les unes aux autres*); **the ~s** (*Brit SPORT*) les gradins *mpl*.

terraced [tär'əst] *a* (*garden*) en terrasses; (*in a row: house, cottage etc*) attenant(e) aux maisons voisines.

terracotta [tärəkát'ə] *n* terre cuite.

terrain [tərān'] *n* terrain *m* (*sol*).

terrible [tär'əbəl] *a* terrible, atroce; (*weather, work*) affreux(euse), épouvantable.

terribly [tär'əblē] *ad* terriblement; (*very badly*) affreusement mal.

terrier [tär'ēûr] *n* terrier *m* (*chien*).

terrific [tərif'ik] *a* fantastique, incroyable, terrible; (*wonderful*) formidable, sensationnel(le).

terrify [tär'əfī] *vt* terrifier.

territorial [täritôr'ēəl] *a* territorial(e).

territorial waters *npl* eaux territoriales.

territory [tär'itôrē] *n* territoire *m*.

terror [tär'ûr] *n* terreur *f*.

terrorism [tär'ərizəm] *n* terrorisme *m*.

terrorist [tär'ûrist] *n* terroriste *m/f*.

terrorize [tär'ərīz] *vt* terroriser.

terse [tûrs] *a* (*style*) concis(e); (*reply*) laconique.

tertiary [tûr'shēärē] *a* tertiaire.

Terylene [tär'əlēn] *n* ® (*Brit*) tergal *m* ®.

TESL [tes'əl] *n abbr* = *Teaching of English as a Second Language*.

test [test] *n* (*trial, check*) essai *m*; (: *of goods in factory*) contrôle *m*; (*of courage etc*) épreuve *f*; (*MED*) examens *mpl*; (*CHEM*) analyses *fpl*; (*exam: of intelligence etc*) test *m* (d'aptitude); (: *in school*) interrogation *f* de contrôle; (*also*: **driving ~**) (examen du) permis *m* de conduire ♦ *vt* essayer; contrôler; mettre à l'épreuve; examiner; analyser; tester; faire subir une interrogation (de contrôle) à; **to put sth to the ~** mettre qch à l'épreuve.

testament [tes'təmənt] *n* testament *m*; **the Old/New T~** l'Ancien/le Nouveau Testament.

test ban *n* (*also*: **nuclear ~**) interdiction *f* des essais nucléaires.

test case *n* (*LAW, fig*) affaire-test *f*.

test flight *n* vol *m* d'essai.

testicle [tes'tikəl] *n* testicule *m*.

testify [tes'təfī] *vi* (*LAW*) témoigner, déposer; **to ~ to sth** (*LAW*) attester qch; (*gen*) témoigner de qch.

testimonial [testimō'nēəl] *n* (*gift*) témoignage *m* d'estime; (*Brit: reference*) recommandation *f*.

testimony [tes'təmōnē] *n* (*LAW*) témoignage *m*, déposition *f*.

testing [tes'ting] *a* (*situation, period*) difficile.

testing ground *n* banc *m* d'essai.

test match *n* (*CRICKET, RUGBY*) match international.

test paper *n* (*SCOL*) interrogation écrite.

test pilot *n* pilote *m* d'essai.

test tube *n* éprouvette *f*.

test-tube baby [test'tŏŏb bā'bē] *n* bébé-éprouvette *m*.

testy [tes'tē] *a* irritable.

tetanus [tet'ənəs] *n* tétanos *m*.

tetchy [tech'ē] *a* hargneux(euse).

tether [teth'ûr] *vt* attacher ♦ *n*: **at the end of one's ~** (*Brit*) à bout (de patience).

Tex. *abbr* (*US*) = *Texas*.

text [tekst] *n* texte *m*.

textbook [tekst'bŏŏk] *n* manuel *m*.

textile [teks'təl] *n* textile *m*.

texture [teks'chûr] *n* texture *f*; (*of skin, paper etc*) grain *m*.

TGIF *abbr* (*col*) = *thank God it's Friday*.

Thai [tī] *a* thaïlandais(e) ♦ *n* Thaïlandais/e; (*LING*) thaï *m*.

Thailand [tī'lənd] *n* Thaïlande *f*.

thalidomide [thəlid'əmīd] *n* ® thalidomide *f* ®.

Thames [temz] *n*: **the ~** la Tamise.

than [than, then] *cj* que; (*with numerals*): **more ~ 10/once** plus de 10/d'une fois; **I have more/less ~ you** j'en ai plus/moins que toi; **she has more apples ~ pears** elle a plus de pommes que de poires; **it is better to phone ~ to write** il vaut mieux téléphoner (plutôt) qu'écrire; **no sooner did he leave ~ the phone rang** il venait de partir quand le téléphone a sonné.

thank [thangk] *vt* remercier, dire merci à; **~ you (very much)** merci (beaucoup); **~ heavens, ~ God** Dieu merci.

thankful [thangk'fəl] *a*: **~ (for)** reconnaissant(e) (de); **~ for/that** (*relieved*) soulagé(e) de/que.

thankfully [thangk'fəlē] *ad* avec reconnaissance; avec soulagement; ~ **there were few victims** il y eut fort heureusement peu de victimes.

thankless [thangk'lis] *a* ingrat(e).

thanks [thangks] *npl* remerciements *mpl* ♦ *excl* merci!; ~ **to** *prep* grâce à.

Thanksgiving (Day) [thangksgiv'ing (dā)] *n* jour *m* d'action de grâce.

that [tǔat, tǔət] *cj* que ♦ *a* (*pl* **those**) ce(cet + *vowel or h mute*), *f* cette; (*not "this"*): ~ **book** ce livre-là ♦ *pronoun* (*pl* **those**) ce; (*not "this one"*) cela, ça; (*the one*) celui(celle); (*relative: subject*) qui; (*: object*) que, *prep* + lequel(laquelle); (*with time*): **on the day** ~ **he came** le jour où il est venu ♦ *ad*: ~ **high** aussi haut; si haut; **it's about** ~ **high** c'est à peu près de cette hauteur; ~ **one** celui-là(celle-là); ~ **one over there** celui-là (*or* celle-là) là-bas; **what's** ~? qu'est-ce que c'est?; **who's** ~? qui est-ce?; **is** ~ **you?** c'est toi?; ~'**s what he said** c'est *or* voilà ce qu'il a dit; ~ **is** ... c'est-à-dire ..., à savoir ...; **all** ~ tout cela, tout ça; **I can't work** ~ **much** je ne peux pas travailler autant que cela; **at** *or* **with** ~, **she** ... là-dessus, elle ...; **do it like** ~ fais-le comme ça; **not** ~ **I know of** pas à ma connaissance.

thatched [thacht] *a* (*roof*) de chaume; ~ **cottage** chaumière *f*.

thaw [thô] *n* dégel *m* ♦ *vi* (*ice*) fondre; (*food*) dégeler ♦ *vt* (*food*) (faire) dégeler; **it's** ~**ing** (*weather*) il dégèle.

the [tǔə, tǔē] *definite article* le, *f* la, (l' + vowel or h mute), *pl* les (NB: *à* + *le*(*s*) = au(x); *de* + *le* = du; *de* + *les* = des); (*in titles*): **Richard** ~ **Second** Richard Deux ♦ *ad*: ~ **more he works** ~ **more he earns** plus il travaille, plus il gagne d'argent; ~ **sooner** ~ **better** le plus tôt sera le mieux; ~ **rich and** ~ **poor** les riches et les pauvres.

theater, (*Brit*) **theatre** [thē'ətûr] *n* théâtre *m*.

theatergoer [thē'ətûrgōūr] *n* habitué/e du théâtre.

theatrical [thēat'rikəl] *a* théâtral(e); ~ **company** troupe *f* de théâtre.

theft [theft] *n* vol *m* (*larcin*).

their [tǔär] *a* leur, *pl* leurs.

theirs [tǔärz] *pronoun* le(la) leur, les leurs; **it is** ~ c'est à eux; **a friend of** ~ un de leurs amis.

them [tǔem, tǔəm] *pronoun* (*direct*) les; (*indirect*) leur; (*stressed, after prep*) eux(elles); **I see** ~ je les vois; **give** ~ **the book** donne-leur le livre; **give me a few of** ~ donnez m'en quelques uns (*or* quelques unes).

theme [thēm] *n* thème *m*.

theme song *n* chanson principale.

themselves [tǔəmselvz'] *pl pronoun* (*reflexive*) se; (*emphatic*) eux-mêmes(elles-mêmes); **between** ~ entre eux(elles).

then [tǔen] *ad* (*at that time*) alors, à ce moment-là; (*next*) puis, ensuite; (*and also*) et puis ♦ *cj* (*therefore*) alors, dans ce cas ♦ *a*: **the** ~ **president** le président d'alors *or* de l'époque; **by** ~ (*past*) à ce moment-là; (*future*) d'ici là; **from** ~ **on** dès lors; **before** ~ avant; **until** ~ jusqu'à ce moment-là, jusque-là; **and** ~ **what?** et puis après?; **what do you want me to do** ~? (*afterwards*) que

veux-tu que je fasse ensuite?; (*in that case*) bon alors, qu'est-ce que je fais?

theologian [thēəlō'jən] *n* théologien/ne.

theological [thēəlâj'ikəl] *a* théologique.

theology [thēāl'əjē] *n* théologie *f*.

theorem [thēr'əm] *n* théorème *m*.

theoretical [thēəret'ikəl] *a* théorique.

theorize [thē'ərīz] *vi* élaborer une théorie; (*pej*) faire des théories.

theory [thiûr'ē] *n* théorie *f*.

therapeutic(al) [thärəpyōōtik(əl)] *a* thérapeutique.

therapist [thär'əpist] *n* thérapeute *m/f*.

therapy [thär'əpē] *n* thérapie *f*.

there [tǔär] *ad* là, là-bas; ~, ~! allons, allons!; **it's** ~ c'est là; **he went** ~ il y est allé; ~ **is**, ~ **are** il y a; ~ **he is** le voilà; ~ **has been** il y a eu; **on/in** ~ là-dessus/-dedans; **back** ~ là-bas; **down** ~ là-bas en bas; **over** ~ là-bas; **through** ~ par là; **to go** ~ **and back** faire l'aller et retour.

thereabouts [tǔär'əbouts] *ad* (*place*) par là, près de là; (*amount*) environ, à peu près.

thereafter [tǔäraf'tûr] *ad* par la suite.

thereby [tǔärbī'] *ad* ainsi.

therefore [tǔär'fôr] *ad* donc, par conséquent.

there's [tǔärz] = **there is, there has.**

thereupon [tǔärəpän'] *ad* (*at that point*) sur ce; (*formal: on that subject*) à ce sujet.

thermal [thûr'məl] *a* thermique; ~ **paper/printer** papier *m*/imprimante *f* thermique.

thermodynamics [thûrmōdīnam'iks] *n* thermodynamique *f*.

thermometer [thûrmäm'itûr] *n* thermomètre *m*.

thermonuclear [thûrmōnōō'klēûr] *a* thermonucléaire.

Thermos [thûr'məs] *n* ® thermos *m or f inv* ®.

thermostat [thûr'məstat] *n* thermostat *m*.

thesaurus [thisôr'əs] *n* dictionnaire *m* synonymique.

these [tǔēz] *pl pronoun* ceux-ci(celles-ci) ♦ *pl a* ces; (*not "those"*): ~ **books** ces livres-ci.

thesis, *pl* **theses** [thē'sis, -sēz] *n* thèse *f*.

they [tǔā] *pl pronoun* ils(elles); (*stressed*) eux(elles); ~ **say that** ... (*it is said that*) on dit que ....

they'd [tǔād] = **they had, they would.**

they'll [tǔāl] = **they shall, they will.**

they're [tǔär] = **they are.**

they've [tǔāv] = **they have.**

thick [thik] *a* épais(se); (*crowd*) dense; (*stupid*) bête, borné(e) ♦ *n*: **in the** ~ **of** au beau milieu de, en plein cœur de; **it's 20 cm** ~ ça a 20 cm d'épaisseur.

thicken [thik'ən] *vi* s'épaissir ♦ *vt* (*sauce etc*) épaissir.

thicket [thik'it] *n* fourré *m*, hallier *m*.

thickly [thik'lē] *ad* (*spread*) en couche épaisse; (*cut*) en tranches épaisses; ~ **populated** à forte densité de population.

thickness [thik'nis] *n* épaisseur *f*.

thickset [thik'set'] *a* trapu(e), costaud(e).

thickskinned [thik'skind] *a* (*fig*) peu sensible.

thief, *pl* **thieves** [thēf, thēvz] *n* voleur/euse.

thieving [thē'ving] *n* vol *m* (*larcin*).

thigh [thī] *n* cuisse *f*.

thighbone [thī'bōn] *n* fémur *m*.

thimble [thim'bəl] *n* dé *m* (à coudre).

thin [thin] *a* mince; (*person*) maigre; (*soup*) peu épais(se); (*hair, crowd*) clairsemé(e); (*fog*) léger(ère) ◆ *vt* (*hair*) éclaircir; (*also:* ~ **down**: *sauce, paint*) délayer ◆ *vi* (*fog*) s'éclaircir; (*also:* ~ **out**: *crowd*) se disperser; **his hair is** ~**ning** il se dégarnit.

thing [thing] *n* chose *f*; (*object*) objet *m*; (*contraption*) truc *m*; ~**s** *npl* (*belongings*) affaires *fpl*; **first** ~ (**in the morning**) à la première heure, tout de suite (le matin); **last** ~ (**at night**), **he** ... juste avant de se coucher, il ...; **the** ~ **is** ... c'est que ...; **for one** ~ d'abord; **the best** ~ **would be to** le mieux serait de; **how are** ~**s?** comment ça va?; **she's got a** ~ **about** ... elle déteste ...; **poor** ~**!** le (*or* la) pauvre!

think, *pt, pp* **thought** [thingk, thôt] *vi* penser, réfléchir ◆ *vt* penser, croire; (*imagine*) s'imaginer; **to** ~ **of** penser à; **what do you** ~ **of it?** qu'en pensez-vous?; **what did you** ~ **of them?** qu'avez-vous pensé d'eux?; **to** ~ **about sth/sb** penser à qch/qn; **I'll** ~ **about it** je vais y réfléchir; **to** ~ **of doing** avoir l'idée de faire; **I** ~ **so/not** je crois *or* pense que oui/non; **to** ~ **well of** avoir une haute opinion de; ~ **again!** attention, réfléchis bien!; **to** ~ **aloud** penser tout haut.

think out *vt* (*plan*) bien réfléchir à; (*solution*) trouver.

think over *vt* bien réfléchir à; **I'd like to** ~ **things over** (*offer, suggestion*) j'aimerais bien y réfléchir un peu.

think through *vt* étudier dans tous les détails.

think up *vt* inventer, trouver.

thinking [thingk'ing] *n*: **to my (way of)** ~ selon moi.

think tank *n* groupe *m* de réflexion.

thinly [thin'lē] *ad* (*cut*) en tranches fines; (*spread*) en couche mince.

thinness [thin'is] *n* minceur *f*; maigreur *f*.

third [thûrd] *num* troisième ◆ *n* troisième *m/f*; (*fraction*) tiers *m*; **a** ~ **of** le tiers de.

third-degree burns [thûrd'digrē bûrnz] *npl* brûlures *fpl* au troisième degré.

thirdly [thûrd'lē] *ad* troisièmement.

third party insurance *n* (*Brit*) assurance *f* au tiers.

third-rate [thûrd'rāt'] *a* de qualité médiocre.

Third World *n*: **the** ~ le Tiers-Monde.

thirst [thûrst] *n* soif *f*.

thirsty [thûrs'tē] *a* qui a soif, assoiffé(e); **to be** ~ avoir soif.

thirteen [thûr'tēn'] *num* treize.

thirtieth [thûr'tēith] *num* trentième.

thirty [thûr'tē] *num* trente.

this [this] *a* (*pl* **these**) ce(cet + *vowel or h mute*), *f* cette; (*not* "*that*"): ~ **book** ce livre-ci ◆ *pronoun* (*pl* **these**) ce; ceci; (*not* "*that one*") celui-ci(celle-ci) ◆ *ad*: ~ **high** aussi haut; si haut; **it's about** ~ **high** c'est à peu près de cette hauteur; **who is** ~**?** qui est-ce?; **what is** ~**?** qu'est-ce que c'est?; ~ **is Mr Brown** (*in photo*) voici M. Brown; (*in introduction*) je vous présente M. Brown; (*on telephone*) (c'est) M. Brown à l'appareil; ~ **is what he said** voici ce qu'il a dit; ~ **time** cette fois-ci; ~ **time last year** l'année dernière à la même époque; ~ **way** (*in this direction*) par ici; (*in this fashion*) de cette façon, ainsi; **they were talking of** ~ **and that** ils parlaient de choses et d'autres.

thistle [this'əl] *n* chardon *m*.

thong [thông] *n* lanière *f*.

thorn [thôrn] *n* épine *f*.

thorny [thôr'nē] *a* épineux(euse).

thorough [thûr'ō] *a* (*search*) minutieux(euse); (*knowledge, research*) approfondi(e); (*work*) consciencieux(euse); (*cleaning*) à fond.

thoroughbred [thûr'ōbred] *n* (*horse*) pur-sang *m inv*.

thoroughfare [thûr'ōfär] *n* rue *f*.

thoroughly [thûr'ōlē] *ad* minutieusement; en profondeur; à fond; **he** ~ **agreed** il était tout à fait d'accord.

thoroughness [thûr'ōnis] *n* soin (méticuleux).

those [thōz] *pl pronoun* ceux-là(celles-là) ◆ *pl a* ces; (*not* "*these*"): ~ **books** ces livres-là.

though [thō] *cj* bien que + *sub*, quoique + *sub* ◆ *ad* pourtant; **even** ~ quand bien même + *conditional*; **it's not easy,** ~ pourtant, ce n'est pas facile.

thought [thôt] *pt, pp of* **think** ◆ *n* pensée *f*; (*opinion*) avis *m*; (*intention*) intention *f*; **after much** ~ après mûre réflexion; **I've just had a** ~ je viens de penser à quelque chose; **to give sb some** ~ réfléchir à qch.

thoughtful [thôt'fəl] *a* pensif(ive); (*considerate*) prévenant(e).

thoughtfully [thôt'fəlē] *ad* pensivement; avec prévenance.

thoughtless [thôt'lis] *a* étourdi(e); qui manque de considération.

thoughtlessly [thôt'lislē] *ad* inconsidérément.

thousand [thou'zənd] *num* mille; **one** ~ mille; ~**s of** des milliers de.

thousandth [thou'zəndth] *num* millième.

thrash [thrash] *vt* rouer de coups; donner une correction à; (*defeat*) battre à plate(s) couture(s).

thrash about *vi* se débattre.

thrash out *vt* débattre de.

thrashing [thrash'ing] *n*: **to give sb a** ~ = **to thrash sb**.

thread [thred] *n* fil *m*; (*of screw*) pas *m*, filetage *m* ◆ *vt* (*needle*) enfiler; **to** ~ **one's way between** se faufiler entre.

threadbare [thred'bär] *a* râpé(e), élimé(e).

threat [thret] *n* menace *f*; **to be under** ~ **of** être menacé(e) de.

threaten [thret'ən] *vi* (*storm*) menacer ◆ *vt*: **to** ~ **sb with sth/to do** menacer qn de qch/de faire.

threatening [thret'əning] *a* menaçant(e).

three [thrē] *num* trois.

three-dimensional [thrē'dimen'chənəl] *a* à trois dimensions; (*film*) en relief.

threefold [thrē'fōld] *ad*: **to increase** ~ tripler.

three-piece [thrē'pēs] : ~ **suit** *n* complet *m* (avec gilet); ~ **suite** *n* salon *m* comprenant un canapé et deux fauteuils assortis.

three-ply [thrē'plī] *a* (*wood*) à trois épaisseurs; (*wool*) trois fils *inv*.

three-quarters [thrē'kwôr'tûrz] *npl* trois-quarts *mpl*; ~ **full** aux trois-quarts plein.

thresh [thresh] *vt* (*AGR*) battre.

threshing machine [thresh'ing məshēn'] *n*

batteuse *f*.

threshold [thresh'ōld] *n* seuil *m*; **to be on the ~ of** (*fig*) être au seuil de.

threshold agreement *n* (*ECON*) accord *m* d'indexation des salaires.

threw [thrōō] *pt of* **throw**.

thrift [thrift] *n* économie *f*.

thrifty [thrif'tē] *a* économe.

thrill [thril] *n* frisson *m*, émotion *f* ♦ *vi* tressaillir, frissonner ♦ *vt* (*audience*) électriser; **to be ~ed** (*with gift etc*) être ravi(e).

thriller [thril'ûr] *n* film *m* (*or* roman *m or* pièce *f*) à suspense.

thrilling [thril'ing] *a* (*book, play etc*) saisissant(e); (*news, discovery*) excitant(e).

thrive, *pt* **thrived, throve**, *pp* **thrived, thriven** [thrīv, thrōv, thriv'ən] *vi* pousser *or* se développer bien; (*business*) prospérer; **he ~s on it** cela lui réussit.

thriving [thrīv'ing] *a* vigoureux(euse); (*industry etc*) prospère.

throat [thrōt] *n* gorge *f*; **to have a sore ~** avoir mal à la gorge.

throb [thrâb] *n* (*of heart*) pulsation *f*; (*of engine*) vibration *f*; (*of pain*) élancement *m* ♦ *vi* (*heart*) palpiter; (*engine*) vibrer; (*pain*) lanciner; (*wound*) causer des élancements; **my head is ~bing** j'ai des élancements dans la tête.

throes [thrōz] *npl*: **in the ~ of** au beau milieu de; en proie à; **in the ~ of death** à l'agonie.

thrombosis [thrâmbō'sis] *n* thrombose *f*.

throne [thrōn] *n* trône *m*.

throng [thrông] *n* foule *f* ♦ *vt* se presser dans.

throttle [thrât'əl] *n* (*AUT*) accélérateur *m* ♦ *vt* étrangler.

through [thrōō] *prep* à travers; (*time*) pendant, durant; (*by means of*) par l'intermédiaire de; (*owing to*) à cause de ♦ *a* (*ticket, train, passage*) direct(e) ♦ *ad* à travers; **(from) Monday ~ Friday** (*US*) de lundi à vendredi; **to let sb ~** laisser passer qn; **to put sb ~ to sb** (*TEL*) passer qn à qn; **to be ~** (*TEL*) avoir la communication; (*have finished*) avoir fini; **"no ~ traffic"** (*US*) "passage interdit"; **"no ~ road"** "impasse".

throughout [thrōōout'] *prep* (*place*) partout dans; (*time*) durant tout(e) le(la) ♦ *ad* partout.

throughput [thrōō'pŏŏt] *n* (*of goods, materials*) quantité de matières premières utilisée; (*COMPUT*) débit *m*.

throve [thrōv] *pt of* **thrive**.

throw [thrō] *n* jet *m*; (*SPORT*) lancer *m* ♦ *vt* (*pt* **threw**, *pp* **thrown** [thrōō, thrōn]) lancer, jeter; (*SPORT*) lancer; (*rider*) désarçonner; (*fig*) décontenancer; (*pottery*) tourner; **to ~ a party** donner une réception.

throw about *vt* (*Brit*) = **throw around**.

throw around *vt* (*litter etc*) éparpiller.

throw away *vt* jeter.

throw off *vt* se débarrasser de.

throw out *vt* jeter dehors; (*reject*) rejeter.

throw together *vt* (*clothes, meal etc*) assembler à la hâte; (*essay*) bâcler.

throw up *vi* vomir.

throwaway [thrō'əwā] *a* à jeter.

throwback [thrō'bak] *n*: **it's a ~ to** ça nous

etc ramène à.

throw-in [thrō'in] *n* (*SPORT*) remise *f* en jeu.

thru [thrōō] *prep, a, ad* (*US*) = **through**.

thrush [thrush] *n* (*ZOOL*) grive *f*; (*MED: esp in children*) muguet *m*; (: *Brit: in women*) muguet vaginal.

thrust [thrust] *n* (*TECH*) poussée *f* ♦ *vt* (*pt, pp* **thrust**) pousser brusquement; (*push in*) enfoncer.

thrusting [thrust'ing] *a* dynamique; qui se met trop en avant.

thud [thud] *n* bruit sourd.

thug [thug] *n* voyou *m*.

thumb [thum] *n* (*ANAT*) pouce *m* ♦ *vt* (*book*) feuilleter; **to ~ a lift** faire de l'auto-stop, arrêter une voiture; **to give sb/sth the ~s up** (*approve*) donner le feu vert à qn/qch.

thumb index *n* répertoire *m* (à onglets).

thumbnail [thum'nāl] *n* ongle *m* du pouce.

thumbnail sketch *n* croquis *m*.

thumbtack [thum'tak] *n* (*US*) punaise *f* (*clou*).

thump [thump] *n* grand coup *m*; (*sound*) bruit sourd ♦ *vt* cogner sur ♦ *vi* cogner, frapper.

thunder [thun'dûr] *n* tonnerre *m* ♦ *vi* tonner; (*train etc*): **to ~ past** passer dans un grondement *or* un bruit de tonnerre.

thunderbolt [thun'dûrbōlt] *n* foudre *f*.

thunderclap [thun'dûrklap] *n* coup *m* de tonnerre.

thunderous [thun'dûrəs] *a* étourdissant(e).

thunderstorm [thun'dûrstôrm] *n* orage *m*.

thunderstruck [thun'dûrstruk] *a* (*fig*) abasourdi(e).

thundery [thun'dûrē] *a* orageux(euse).

Thur(s). *abbr* (= *Thursday*) jeu.

Thursday [thûrz'dā] *n* jeudi *m*; *for phrases see also* **Tuesday**.

thus [thus] *ad* ainsi.

thwart [thwôrt] *vt* contrecarrer.

thyme [tīm] *n* thym *m*.

thyroid [thī'roid] *n* thyroïde *f*.

tiara [tēar'ə] *n* (*woman's*) diadème *m*.

Tibet [tibet'] *n* Tibet *m*.

Tibetan [tibet'ən] *a* tibétain(e) ♦ *n* Tibétain/e; (*LING*) tibétain *m*.

tibia [tib'ēə] *n* tibia *m*.

tic [tik] *n* tic (nerveux).

tick [tik] *n* (*sound: of clock*) tic-tac *m*; (*mark*) coche *f*; (*ZOOL*) tique *f* ♦ *vi* faire tic-tac ♦ *vt* cocher; **to put a ~ against sth** cocher qch.

tick off *vt* cocher; (*person*) réprimander, attraper.

tick over *vi* (*Brit: engine*) tourner au ralenti; (: *fig*) aller *or* marcher doucettement.

ticker tape [tik'ûr tāp] *n* bande *f* de téléscripteur; (*US: in celebrations*) ≈ serpentin *m*.

ticket [tik'it] *n* billet *m*; (*for bus, subway*) ticket *m*; (*in store: on goods*) étiquette *f*; (: *from cash register*) reçu *m*, ticket; (*US POL*) liste électorale (*soutenue par un parti*); **to get a (parking) ~** (*AUT*) attraper une contravention (pour stationnement illégal).

ticket agency *n* (*THEATER*) agence *f* de spectacles.

ticket collector *n* contrôleur/euse.

ticket holder *n* personne munie d'un billet.

ticket inspector *n* (*Brit*) contrôleur/euse.

ticket office *n* guichet *m*, bureau *m* de vente

des billets.

tickle [tik'əl] *n* chatouillement *m* ♦ *vt* chatouiller; *(fig)* plaire à; faire rire.

ticklish [tik'lish] *a (person)* chatouilleux(euse); *(which tickles: blanket)* qui chatouille; *(: cough)* qui irrite.

tidal [tīd'əl] *a* à marée.

tidal wave *n* raz-de-marée *m inv.*

tidbit [tid'bit] *n (US: food)* friandise *f*; *(: before meal)* amuse-gueule *m inv*; *(: news)* potin *m.*

tiddlywinks [tid'lēwingks] *n* jeu *m* de puce.

tide [tīd] *n* marée *f*; *(fig: of events)* cours *m* ♦ *vt*: **to ~ sb over** dépanner qn; **high/low ~** marée haute/basse.

tidily [tī'dilē] *ad* avec soin, soigneusement.

tidiness [tī'dēnis] *n* bon ordre; goût *m* de l'ordre.

tidy [tī'dē] *a (room)* bien rangé(e); *(dress, work)* net(nette), soigné(e); *(person)* ordonné(e), qui a de l'ordre; *(: in character)* soigneux(euse); *(mind)* méthodique ♦ *vt (also: ~ up)* ranger; **to ~ o.s. up** s'arranger.

tie [tī] *n (string etc)* cordon *m*; *(US RAIL)* traverse *f*; *(Brit: also:* **neck~**) cravate *f*; *(fig: link)* lien *m*; *(SPORT: draw)* égalité *f* de points; match nul; *(: match)* rencontre *f* ♦ *vt (parcel)* attacher; *(ribbon)* nouer ♦ *vi (SPORT)* faire match nul; finir à égalité de points; **"black/white ~"** "smoking/habit de rigueur"; **family ~s** liens de famille; **to ~ sth in a bow** faire un nœud à *or* avec qch; **to ~ a knot in sth** faire un nœud à qch.

tie down *vt* attacher; *(fig)*: **to ~ sb down to** contraindre qn à accepter.

tie in *vi*: **to ~ in (with)** *(correspond)* correspondre (à).

tie on *vt (Brit: label etc)* attacher (avec une ficelle).

tie up *vt (parcel)* ficeler; *(dog, boat)* attacher; *(arrangements)* conclure; **to be ~d up** *(busy)* être pris *or* occupé.

tie-break(er) [tī'brāk(ûr)] *n (TENNIS)* tie-break *m*; *(in quiz)* question *f* subsidiaire.

tie-on [tī'ân] *a (Brit: label)* qui s'attache.

tiepin [tī'pin] *n (Brit)* épingle *f* de cravate.

tier [tēr] *n* gradin *m*; *(of cake)* étage *m.*

Tierra del Fuego [tēär'ə del fwā'gō] *n* Terre *f* de Feu.

tie tack *n (US)* épingle *f* de cravate.

tiff [tif] *n* petite querelle.

tiger [tī'gûr] *n* tigre *m.*

tight [tīt] *a (rope)* tendu(e), raide; *(clothes)* étroit(e), très juste; *(budget, schedule, curve)* serré(e); *(control)* strict(e), sévère; *(col: drunk)* ivre, rond(e) ♦ *ad (squeeze)* très fort; *(shut)* à bloc, hermétiquement; **to be packed ~** *(suitcase)* être bourré(e); *(people)* être serré(e); **everybody hold ~!** accrochez-vous bien!

tighten [tīt'ən] *vt (rope)* tendre; *(screw)* resserrer; *(control)* renforcer ♦ *vi* se tendre; se resserrer.

tightfisted [tīt'fis'tid] *a* avare.

tightly [tīt'lē] *ad (grasp)* bien, très fort.

tightrope [tīt'rōp] *n* corde *f* raide.

tightrope walker *n* funambule *m/f.*

tights [tīts] *npl (Brit)* collant *m.*

tigress [tī'gris] *n* tigresse *f.*

tilde [til'də] *n* tilde *m.*

tile [tīl] *n (on roof)* tuile *f*; *(on wall or floor)* carreau *m* ♦ *vt (floor, bathroom etc)* carreler.

tiled [tīld] *a* en tuiles; carrelé(e).

till [til] *n* caisse (enregistreuse) ♦ *vt (land)* cultiver ♦ *prep, cj* = **until.**

tiller [til'ûr] *n (NAUT)* barre *f* (du gouvernail).

tilt [tilt] *vt* pencher, incliner ♦ *vi* pencher, être incliné(e) ♦ *n (slope)* inclinaison *f*; **to wear one's hat at a ~** porter son chapeau incliné sur le côté; **(at) full ~** à toute vitesse.

timber [tim'bûr] *n (material)* bois *m* de construction; *(trees)* arbres *mpl.*

time [tīm] *n* temps *m*; *(epoch: often pl)* époque *f*, temps; *(by clock)* heure *f*; *(moment)* moment *m*; *(occasion, also MATH)* fois *f*; *(MUS)* mesure *f* ♦ *vt (race)* chronométrer; *(program)* minuter; *(remark etc)* choisir le moment de; **a long ~** un long moment, longtemps; **for the ~ being** pour le moment; **from ~ to ~** de temps en temps; **~ after ~, ~ and again** bien des fois; **in ~** *(soon enough)* à temps; *(after some time)* avec le temps, à la longue; *(MUS)* en mesure; **in a week's ~** dans une semaine; **in no ~** en un rien de temps; **on ~** à l'heure; **to be 30 minutes behind/ahead of ~** avoir 30 minutes de retard/d'avance; **by the ~ he arrived** quand il est arrivé, le temps qu'il arrive *(sub)*; **5 ~s 5** 5 fois 5; **what ~ is it?** quelle heure est-il?; **to have a good ~** bien s'amuser; **we** *(or they etc)* **had a hard ~** ça a été difficile *or* pénible; **~'s up!** c'est l'heure!; **I've no ~ for it** *(fig)* cela m'agace; **he'll do it in his own (good) ~** *(without being hurried)* il le fera quand il en aura le temps; **he'll do it on** *or* **in his own ~** *(out of working hours)* il le fera à ses heures perdues; **to be behind the ~s** retarder (sur son temps).

time-and-motion study [tīm'ənmōshən stu'dē] *n* étude *f* des cadences.

time bomb *n* bombe *f* à retardement.

time clock *n* horloge pointeuse.

time-consuming [tīm'kənsōōming] *a* qui prend beaucoup de temps.

time difference *n* décalage *m* horaire.

time-honored [tīm'ânûrd] *a* consacré(e).

timekeeper [tīm'kēpûr] *n (SPORT)* chronomètre *m.*

time lag *n (Brit)* décalage *m*; *(: in travel)* décalage horaire.

timeless [tīm'lis] *a* éternel(le).

time limit *n* limite *f* de temps, délai *m.*

timely [tīm'lē] *a* opportun(e).

time off *n* temps *m* libre.

timeout [tīm'out'] *n (US)* temps mort.

timer [tī'mûr] *n (in kitchen)* compte-minutes *m inv*; *(TECH)* minuteur *m.*

timesaving [tīm'sāving] *a* qui fait gagner du temps.

time scale *n* délais *mpl.*

time sharing [tīm' shā'ring] *n (COMPUT)* temps partagé.

time sheet *n* feuille *f* de présence.

time signal *n* signal *m* horaire.

time switch *n (Brit)* minuteur *m*; *(: for*

lighting) minuterie *f*.

timetable [tīm'tābǝl] *n* (*RAIL*) (indicateur *m*) horaire *m*; (*SCOL*) emploi *m* du temps; (*program of events etc*) programme *m*.

time zone *n* fuseau *m* horaire.

timid [tim'id] *a* timide; (*easily scared*) peureux(euse).

timidity [timid'itē] *n* timidité *f*.

timing [tī'ming] *n* minutage *m*; chronométrage *m*; **the ~ of his resignation** le moment choisi pour sa démission.

timing device *n* (*on bomb*) mécanisme *m* de retardement.

timpani [tim'pǝnē] *npl* timbales *fpl*.

tin [tin] *n* étain *m*; (*also:* ~ **plate**) fer-blanc *m*; (*Brit: can*) boîte *f* (de conserve); (*: for baking*) moule *m* (à gâteau); **a ~ of paint** un pot de peinture.

tin foil *n* papier *m* d'étain.

tinge [tinj] *n* nuance *f* ♦ *vt*: ~d **with** teinté(e) de.

tingle [ting'gǝl] *n* picotement *m*; frisson *m* ♦ *vi* picoter.

tinker [tingk'ûr] *n* rétameur ambulant; (*gipsy*) romanichel *m*.

   tinker with *vt fus* bricoler, rafistoler.

tinkle [ting'kǝl] *vi* tinter ♦ *n* (*col*): **to give sb a ~** passer un coup de fil à qn.

tin mine *n* mine *f* d'étain.

tinned [tind] *a* (*Brit: food*) en boîte, en conserve.

tinny [tin'ē] *a* métallique.

tin opener [tin' ōpǝnúr] *n* (*Brit*) ouvre-boîte(s) *m*.

tinsel [tin'sǝl] *n* guirlandes *fpl* de Noël (*argentées*).

tint [tint] *n* teinte *f*; (*for hair*) shampooing colorant ♦ *vt* (*hair*) faire un shampooing colorant à.

tinted [tin'tid] *a* (*hair*) teint(e); (*glass*) teinté(e).

T-intersection [tē'intǝrsek'shǝn] *n* (*US*) croisement *m* en T.

tiny [tī'nē] *a* minuscule.

tip [tip] *n* (*end*) bout *m*; (*protective: on umbrella etc*) embout *m*; (*gratuity*) pourboire *m*; (*Brit: for garbage*) décharge *f*; (*advice*) tuyau *m* ♦ *vt* (*waiter*) donner un pourboire à; (*tilt*) incliner; (*overturn: also:* ~ **over**) renverser; (*empty: also:* ~ **out**) déverser; (*predict: winner etc*) pronostiquer.

tip off *vt* prévenir, avertir.

tip-off [tip'ôf] *n* (*hint*) tuyau *m*.

tipped [tipt] *a* (*Brit: cigarette*) (à bout) filtre *inv*; **steel-~** à bout métallique, à embout de métal.

Tipp-Ex [tip'eks] *n* ® (*Brit*) Tipp-Ex *m* ®.

tipple [tip'ǝl] (*Brit*) *vi* picoler ♦ *n*: **to have a ~** boire un petit coup.

tippy-toe [tip'ētō] *n* (*US*): **on ~** sur la pointe des pieds.

tipsy [tip'sē] *a* un peu ivre, éméché(e).

tiptoe [tip'tō] *n* (*Brit*) = **tippy-toe**.

tiptop [tip'tâp] *a*: **in ~ condition** en excellent état.

tire [tīûr'] *n* pneu *m* ♦ *vt* fatiguer ♦ *vi* se fatiguer.

   tire out *vt* épuiser.

tired [tīûrd'] *a* fatigué(e); **to be/feel/look ~**

être/se sentir/avoir l'air fatigué; **to be ~ of** en avoir assez de, être las(lasse) de.

tiredness [tīûrd'nis] *n* fatigue *f*.

tireless [tīûr'lis] *a* infatigable, inlassable.

tire pressure *n* (*US*) pression *f* de gonflage.

tiresome [tīûr'sǝm] *a* ennuyeux(euse).

tiring [tīûr'ing] *a* fatigant(e).

tissue [tish'ōō] *n* tissu *m*; (*paper handkerchief*) mouchoir *m* en papier, kleenex *m* ®.

tissue paper *n* papier *m* de soie.

tit [tit] *n* (*bird*) mésange *f*; (*col: breast*) nichon *m*; **to give ~ for tat** rendre coup pour coup.

titanium [tītā'nēǝm] *n* titane *m*.

titbit [tit'bit] *n* (*Brit*) = **tidbit**.

titillate [tit'ǝlāt] *vt* titiller, exciter.

titivate [tit'ǝvāt] *vt* pomponner.

title [tīt'ǝl] *n* titre *m*; (*LAW: right*): ~ **(to)** droit *m* (à).

title deed *n* (*LAW*) titre (constitutif) de propriété.

title page *n* page *f* de titre.

title role *n* rôle principal.

titter [tit'ûr] *vi* rire (bêtement).

tittle-tattle [tit'ǝltatǝl] *n* bavardages *mpl*.

titular [tich'ǝlûr] *a* (*in name only*) nominal(e).

tizzy [tiz'ē] *n*: **to be in a ~** être dans tous ses états.

T-junction [tējung'kshǝn] *n* (*Brit*) = **T-intersection**.

TM *n abbr* = **trademark, transcendental meditation**.

TN *abbr* (*US MAIL*) = *Tennessee*.

TNT *n abbr* (= *trinitrotoluene*) TNT *m*.

to [tōō, tōō] *prep* à; (*towards*) vers; envers ♦ *with vb* (*simple infinitive*): ~ **go/eat** aller/manger; (*following another vb*): **to want/try ~ do** vouloir faire/essayer de faire; (*purpose, result*) pour, afin de; **to give sth ~ sb** donner qch à qn; **give it ~ me** donne-le-moi; **the key ~ the front door** la clé de la porte d'entrée; **it belongs ~ him** cela lui appartient, c'est à lui; **the main thing is ~ ...** l'important est de ...; **to go ~ France/ Portugal** aller en France/au Portugal; **the road ~ Philadelphia** la route de Philadelphie; **I went ~ Claude's** je suis allé chez Claude; **to go ~ town/school** aller en ville/à l'école; **8 apples ~ the kilo** 8 pommes le kilo; **it's 25 ~ 3** il est 3 heures moins 25; **pull/push the door ~** tirez/poussez la porte; **to go ~ and fro** aller et venir; **he did it ~ help you** il l'a fait pour t'aider; **I don't want ~** je ne veux pas; **I have things ~ do** j'ai des choses à faire; **ready ~ go** prêt à partir.

toad [tōd] *n* crapaud *m*.

toadstool [tōd'stōōl] *n* champignon (vénéneux).

toady [tō'dē] *vi* flatter bassement.

toast [tōst] *n* (*CULIN*) pain grillé, toast *m*; (*drink, speech*) toast ♦ *vt* (*CULIN*) faire griller; (*drink to*) porter un toast à; **a piece** *or* **slice of ~** un toast.

toaster [tōs'tûr] *n* grille-pain *m inv*.

toastmaster [tōst'mastûr] *n* animateur *m* pour réceptions.

toast rack *n* porte-toast *m inv*.

tobacco [tǝbak'ō] *n* tabac *m*; **pipe ~** tabac à pipe.

tobacconist |təbak'ənist| *n* marchand/e de tabac; ~'s **(shop)** (bureau *m* de) tabac *m*.

Tobago |tōbā'gō| *n see* **Trinidad and Tobago.**

toboggan |təbág'ən| *n* toboggan *m*; (*child's*) luge *f*.

today |tədā'| *ad, n (also fig)* aujourd'hui *(m)*; **what day is it** ~? quel jour sommes-nous aujourd'hui?; **what date is it** ~? quelle est la date aujourd'hui?; ~ **is the 4th of March** aujourd'hui nous sommes le 4 mars; **a week ago** ~ il y a huit jours aujourd'hui.

toddler |tåd'lûr| *n* enfant *m/f* qui commence à marcher, bambin *m*.

toddy |tåd'ē| *n* grog *m*.

to-do |tədoo'| *n (fuss)* histoire *f*, affaire *f*.

toe |tō| *n* doigt *m* de pied, orteil *m*; *(of shoe)* bout *m* ♦ *vt:* **to** ~ **the line** *(fig)* obéir, se conformer; **big** ~ gros orteil; **little** ~ petit orteil.

toehold |tō'hōld| *n* prise *f*.

toenail |tō'nāl| *n* ongle *m* de l'orteil.

toffee |tôf'ē| *n* caramel *m*.

tofu |tō'foo| *n* tofou *m*.

toga |tō'gə| *n* toge *f*.

together |tōōgeth'ûr| *ad* ensemble; *(at same time)* en même temps; ~ **with** *prep* avec.

togetherness |tōōgeth'ûrnis| *n* camaraderie *f*; intimité *f*.

toggle switch |tåg'əl swich| *n (COMPUT)* interrupteur *m* à bascule.

Togo |tō'gō| *n* Togo *m*.

togs |tågz| *npl (col: clothes)* fringues *fpl*.

toil |toil| *n* dur travail, labeur *m* ♦ *vi* travailler dur; peiner.

toilet |toi'lit| *n (Brit: lavatory)* toilettes *fpl*, cabinets *mpl* ♦ *cpd (bag, soap etc)* de toilette; **to go to the** ~ aller aux toilettes.

toilet bag *n (Brit)* nécessaire *m* de toilette.

toilet bowl *n* cuvette *f* des W.-C.

toilet paper *n* papier *m* hygiénique.

toiletries |toi'litrēz| *npl* articles *mpl* de toilette.

toilet roll *n* rouleau *m* de papier hygiénique.

toilet water *n* eau *f* de toilette.

token |tō'kən| *n (sign)* marque *f*, témoignage *m*; *(voucher)* bon *m*, coupon *m* ♦ *cpd (fee, strike)* symbolique; **by the same** ~ *(fig)* de même.

Tokyo |tō'kēyō| *n* Tokyo.

told |tōld| *pt, pp of* **tell.**

tolerable |tål'ûrəbəl| *a (bearable)* tolérable; *(fairly good)* passable.

tolerably |tål'ûrəblē| *ad:* ~ **good** tolérable.

tolerance |tål'ûrəns| *n (also TECH)* tolérance *f*.

tolerant |tål'ûrənt| *a:* ~ **(of)** tolérant(e) (à l'égard de).

tolerate |tål'ərāt| *vt* supporter; *(MED, TECH)* tolérer.

toleration |tålərā'shən| *n* tolérance *f*.

toll |tōl| *n (tax, charge)* péage *m* ♦ *vi (bell)* sonner; **the accident** ~ **on the roads** le nombre des victimes de la route.

tollbridge |tōl'brij| *n* pont *m* à péage.

toll-free |tōl'frē'| *a (US TEL):* ~ **number)** numéro vert.

tomato, ~**es** |təmā'tō| *n* tomate *f*.

tomb |tōōm| *n* tombe *f*.

tomboy |tåm'boi| *n* garçon manqué.

tombstone |tōōm'stōn| *n* pierre tombale.

tomcat |tåm'kat| *n* matou *m*.

tomorrow |təmôr'ō| *ad, n (also fig)* demain *(m)*; **the day after** ~ après-demain; **a week** ~ demain en huit; ~ **morning** demain matin.

ton |tun| *n* tonne *f (US: also:* **short** ~ = *907 kg; Brit:* = *1016 kg; metric* = *1000 kg); (NAUT: also:* **register** ~) tonneau *m* (= *2.83 cu.m).*

tonal |tō'nəl| *a* tonal(e).

tone |tōn| *n* ton *m*; *(of radio, Brit TEL)* tonalité *f* ♦ *vi* s'harmoniser.

tone down *vt (color, criticism)* adoucir; *(sound)* baisser.

tone up *vt (muscles)* tonifier.

tone-deaf |tōn'def| *a* qui n'a pas d'oreille.

toner |tō'nûr| *n (for photocopier)* encre *f*.

Tonga |tång'gə| *n* îles *fpl* Tonga.

tongs |tôngz| *npl* pinces *fpl; (for coal)* pincettes *fpl; (for hair)* fer *m* à friser.

tongue |tung| *n* langue *f*; ~ **in cheek** *ad* ironiquement.

tongue-tied |tung'tīd| *a (fig)* muet(te).

tongue twister |tung' twistûr| *n* phrase *f* très difficile à prononcer.

tonic |tån'ik| *n (MED)* tonique *m*; *(MUS)* tonique *f; (also:* ~ **water)** tonic *m*.

tonight |tənīt'| *ad, n* cette nuit; *(this evening)* ce soir; **(I'll) see you** ~! à ce soir!

tonnage |tun'ij| *n (NAUT)* tonnage *m*.

tonsil |tån'səl| *n* amygdale *f*; **to have one's** ~**s out** se faire opérer des amygdales.

tonsillitis |tånsəli'tis| *n* amygdalite *f*; **to have** ~ avoir une angine or une amygdalite.

too |tōō| *ad (excessively)* trop; *(also)* aussi; **it's** ~ **sweet** c'est trop sucré; **I went** ~ moi aussi, j'y suis allé; ~ **much** *ad* trop ♦ *a* trop de; ~ **many** a trop de; ~ **bad!** tant pis!

took |tōōk| *pt of* **take.**

tool |tōōl| *n* outil *m*; *(fig)* instrument *m* ♦ *vt* travailler, ouvrager.

tool box *n* boîte *f* à outils.

tool kit *n* trousse *f* à outils.

toot |tōōt| *n* coup *m* de sifflet *(or* de klaxon) ♦ *vi* siffler; *(with car-horn)* klaxonner.

tooth, *pl* **teeth** |tōōth, tēth| *n (ANAT, TECH)* dent *f*; **to have a** ~ **pulled** *or (Brit)* **out** se faire arracher une dent; **to brush one's teeth** se laver les dents; **by the skin of one's teeth** *(fig)* de justesse.

toothache |tōōth'āk| *n* mal *m* de dents; **to have** ~ avoir mal aux dents.

toothbrush |tōōth'brush| *n* brosse *f* à dents.

toothpaste |tōōth'pāst| *n* (pâte *f*) dentifrice *m*.

toothpick |tōōth'pik| *n* cure-dent *m*.

tooth powder *n* poudre *f* dentifrice.

top |tåp| *n (of mountain, head)* sommet *m*; *(of page, ladder)* haut *m*; *(of list, line)* commencement *m*; *(of box, cupboard, table)* dessus *m; (lid: of box, jar)* couvercle *m*; *(: of bottle)* bouchon *m; (US AUT)* capote *f; (toy)* toupie *f; (DRESS: blouse etc)* haut *m; (of pajamas)* veste *f* ♦ *a* du haut; *(in rank)* premier(ière); *(best)* meilleur(e) ♦ *vt (exceed)* dépasser; *(be first in)* être en tête de; **at the** ~ **of the stairs/page/street** en haut de l'escalier/de la page/de la rue; **on** ~ **of** sur; *(in addition to)* en plus de; **at the** ~ **of the list** en tête de liste; **at the** ~ **of one's voice**

à tue-tête; **at ~ speed** à toute vitesse; **over the ~** (*col: behavior etc*) qui dépasse les limites.
   top off, (*Brit*) **top up** *vt* remplir.

topaz [tŏ'paz] *n* topaze *f*.

topcoat [tåp'kŏt] *n* pardessus *m*.

topflight [tåp'flīt'] *a* excellent(e).

top floor *n* dernier étage.

top hat *n* haut-de-forme *m*.

top-heavy [tåp'hevē] *a* (*object*) trop lourd(e) du haut.

topic [tåp'ik] *n* sujet *m*, thème *m*.

topical [tåp'ikəl] *a* d'actualité.

topless [tåp'lis] *a* (*bather etc*) aux seins nus; **~ swimsuit** monokini *m*.

top-level [tåp'lev'əl] *a* (*talks*) à l'échelon le plus élevé.

topmost [tåp'mŏst] *a* le(la) plus haut(e).

topography [təpåg'rəfē] *n* topographie *f*.

topping [tåp'ing] *n* (*CULIN*) couche *f* de crème, fromage etc qui recouvre un plat.

topple [tåp'əl] *vt* renverser, faire tomber ♦ *vi* basculer; tomber.

top-ranking [tåp'rang'king] *a* très haut placé(e).

top-secret [tåp'sē'krit] *a* ultra-secret(ète).

topsy-turvy [tåp'sētûr'vē] *a*, *ad* sens dessus-dessous.

top-up [tåp'up] *n* (*Brit*): **would you like a ~?** je vous en remets or rajoute?

torch [tôrch] *n* torche *f*; (*Brit: electric*) lampe *f* de poche.

tore [tôr] *pt of* **tear**.

torment *n* [tôr'ment] tourment *m* ♦ *vt* [tôrment'] tourmenter; (*fig: annoy*) agacer.

torn [tôrn] *pp of* **tear** ♦ *a*: **~ between** (*fig*) tiraillé(e) entre.

tornado, **~es** [tôrnā'dŏ] *n* tornade *f*.

torpedo, **~es** [tôrpē'dŏ] *n* torpille *f*.

torpedo boat *n* torpilleur *m*.

torpor [tôr'pûr] *n* torpeur *f*.

torque [tôrk] *n* couple *m* de torsion.

torrent [tôr'ənt] *n* torrent *m*.

torrential [tôren'chəl] *a* torrentiel(le).

torrid [tôr'id] *a* torride; (*fig*) ardent(e).

torso [tôr'sŏ] *n* torse *m*.

tortoise [tôr'təs] *n* tortue *f*.

tortoiseshell [tor'təs-shel] *a* en écaille.

tortuous [tôr'chōōəs] *a* tortueux(euse).

torture [tôr'chûr] *n* torture *f* ♦ *vt* torturer.

torturer [tôr'chûrûr] *n* tortionnaire *m*.

Tory [tôr'ē] *a* (*Brit POL*) tory (*pl* tories), conservateur(trice) ♦ *n* tory *m/f*, conservateur/trice.

toss [tôs] *vt* lancer, jeter; (*head*) rejeter en arrière ♦ *n* (*movement: of head etc*) mouvement soudain; (*of coin*) tirage *m* à pile ou face; **to ~ a coin** jouer à pile ou face; **to ~ and turn** (*in bed*) se tourner et se retourner; **to win/lose the ~** gagner/perdre à pile ou face; (*SPORT*) gagner/perdre le tirage au sort.

tot [tåt] *n* (*Brit: drink*) petit verre; (*child*) bambin *m*.

total [tŏt'əl] *a* total(e) ♦ *n* total *m* ♦ *vt* (*add up*) faire le total de, totaliser; (*amount to*) s'élever à; **in ~** au total.

totalitarian [tŏtalitär'ēən] *a* totalitaire.

totality [tŏtal'itē] *n* totalité *f*.

totally [tŏ'təlē] *ad* totalement.

tote bag [tŏt' bag] *n* fourre-tout *m inv*.

totem pole [tŏ'təm pōl] *n* mât *m* totémique.

totter [tât'ûr] *vi* chanceler; (*object, government*) être chancelant(e).

touch [tuch] *n* contact *m*, toucher *m*; (*sense, also skill: of pianist etc*) toucher; (*fig: note, also SOCCER*) touche *f* ♦ *vt* (*gen*) toucher; (*tamper with*) toucher à; **the personal ~** la petite note personnelle; **to put the finishing ~es to sth** mettre la dernière main à qch; **a ~ of** (*fig*) un petit peu de; une touche de; **in ~ with** en contact or rapport avec; **to get in ~ with** prendre contact avec; **I'll be in ~** je resterai en contact; **to lose ~** (*friends*) se perdre de vue; **to be out of ~ with events** ne pas être au courant de ce qui se passe.

touch on *vt fus* (*topic*) effleurer, toucher.

touch up *vt* (*paint*) retoucher.

touch-and-go [tuch'əngŏ'] *a* incertain(e); **it was ~ whether we did it** nous avons failli ne pas le faire.

touchdown [tuch'doun] *n* atterrissage *m*; (*on sea*) amerrissage *m*; (*US FOOTBALL*) touché-en-but *m*.

touched [tucht] *a* touché(e); (*col*) cinglé(e).

touching [tuch'ing] *a* touchant(e), attendrissant(e).

touchline [tuch'līn] *n* (*SPORT*) (ligne *f* de) touche *f*.

touch-type [tuch'tīp] *vi* taper au toucher.

touchy [tuch'ē] *a* (*person*) susceptible.

tough [tuf] *a* dur(e); (*resistant*) résistant(e), solide; (*meat*) dur, coriace; (*journey*) pénible; (*task, problem, situation*) difficile; (*rough*) dur ♦ *n* (*gangster etc*) dur *m*; **~ luck!** pas de chance!; tant pis!

toughen [tuf'ən] *vt* rendre plus dur(e) (or plus résistant(e) or plus solide).

toughness [tuf'nis] *n* dureté *f*; résistance *f*; solidité *f*.

toupee [tōōpā'] *n* postiche *m*.

tour [tōōr] *n* voyage *m*; (*also:* **package ~**) voyage organisé; (*of town, museum*) tour *m*, visite *f*; (*by artist*) tournée *f* ♦ *vt* visiter; **to go on a ~ of** (*museum, region*) visiter; **to go on ~** partir en tournée.

touring [tōō'ring] *n* voyages *mpl* touristiques, tourisme *m*.

tourism [tōōr'izəm] *n* tourisme *m*.

tourist [tōōr'ist] *n* touriste *m/f* ♦ *ad* (*travel*) en classe touriste ♦ *cpd* touristique; **the ~ trade** le tourisme.

tourist office *n* syndicat *m* d'initiative.

tournament [tōōr'nəmənt] *n* tournoi *m*.

tourniquet [tûr'nikit] *n* (*MED*) garrot *m*.

tour operator [tōōr' åp'ərātûr] *n* (*Brit*) organisateur *m* de voyages, tour-opérateur *m*.

tousled [tou'zəld] *a* (*hair*) ébouriffé(e).

tout [tout] *vi*: **to ~ for** essayer de raccrocher, racoler ♦ *n* (*Brit: ticket ~*) revendeur *m* de billets.

tow [tŏ] *n*: **to give sb a ~** (*AUT*) remorquer qn ♦ *vt* remorquer; **"in ~"**, (*Brit*) **"on ~"** (*AUT*) "véhicule en remorque".

toward(s) [tôrd(z)] *prep* vers; (*of attitude*) envers, à l'égard de; (*of purpose*) pour; **~ noon/the end of the year** vers midi/la fin de l'année; **to feel friendly ~ sb** être bien disposé envers qn.

towel [tou'əl] *n* serviette *f* (de toilette); **to throw in the ~** (*fig*) jeter l'éponge.

towelling [tou'əling] *n* (*fabric*) tissu-éponge *m*.

towel rack, (*Brit*) **towel rail** *n* porte-serviettes *m inv*.

tower [tou'ûr] *n* tour *f* ♦ *vi* (*building, mountain*) se dresser (majestueusement); **to ~ above** *or* **over sb/sth** dominer qn/qch.

tower block *n* (*Brit*) tour *f* (d'habitation).

towering [tou'ûring] *a* très haut(e), imposant(e).

towline [tō'līn] *n* (câble *m* de) remorque *f*.

town [toun] *n* ville *f*; **to go to ~** aller en ville; (*fig*) y mettre le paquet; **in the ~** dans la ville, en ville; **to be out of ~** (*person*) être en déplacement.

town center *n* centre *m* de la ville, centre-ville *m*.

town clerk *n* ≈ secrétaire *m/f* de mairie.

town council *n* conseil municipal.

town hall *n* ≈ mairie *f*.

town house *n* maison *f* en ville; (*US: in a complex*) maison mitoyenne.

town planner *n* (*Brit*) urbaniste *m/f*.

town planning *n* (*Brit*) urbanisme *m*.

townspeople [tounz'pēpəl] *npl* citadins *mpl*.

towpath [tō'path] *n* (chemin *m* de) halage *m*.

towrope [tō'rōp] *n* (câble *m* de) remorque *f*.

tow truck *n* (*US*) dépanneuse *f*.

toxic [tâk'sik] *a* toxique.

toxin [tâk'sin] *n* toxine *f*.

toy [toi] *n* jouet *m*.

  toy with *vt fus* jouer avec; (*idea*) caresser.

toyshop [toi'shâp] *n* magasin *m* de jouets.

trace [trās] *n* trace *f* ♦ *vt* (*draw*) tracer, dessiner; (*follow*) suivre la trace de; (*locate*) retrouver; **without ~** (*disappear*) sans laisser de traces; **there was no ~ of it** il n'y en avait pas trace.

trace element *n* oligo-élément *m*.

trachea [trā'kēə] *n* (*ANAT*) trachée *f*.

tracing paper [trā'sing pā'pûr] *n* papier-calque *m*.

track [trak] *n* (*mark*) trace *f*; (*path: gen*) chemin *m*, piste *f*; (*: of bullet etc*) trajectoire *f*; (*: of suspect, animal*) piste; (*RAIL*) voie ferrée, rails *mpl*; (*on tape*, COMPUT, SPORT) piste; (*on record*) plage *f* ♦ *vt* suivre la trace or la piste de; **to keep ~ of** suivre; **to be on the right ~** (*fig*) être sur la bonne voie.

  track down *vt* (*prey*) trouver et capturer; (*sth lost*) finir par retrouver.

tracked [trakt] *a* (AUT) à chenille.

track events *npl* (SPORT) épreuves *fpl* sur piste.

tracking station [trak'ing stā'shən] *n* (SPACE) centre *m* d'observation de satellites.

track record *n*: **to have a good ~** (*fig*) avoir fait ses preuves.

tracksuit [trak'sōōt] *n* survêtement *m*.

tract [trakt] *n* (GEO) étendue *f*, zone *f*; (*pamphlet*) tract *m*; **respiratory ~** (ANAT) système *m* respiratoire.

traction [trak'shən] *n* traction *f*.

tractor [trak'tûr] *n* tracteur *m*.

tractor feed *n* (*on printer*) entraînement *m* par ergots.

trade [trād] *n* commerce *m*; (*skill, job*) métier *m* ♦ *vi* faire du commerce; **to ~ with/in** faire du commerce avec/le commerce de; **foreign ~** commerce extérieur; **Department of T~ and Industry (DTI)** (*Brit*) ministère *m* du Commerce et de l'Industrie.

  trade in *vt* (*old car etc*) faire reprendre.

trade barrier *n* barrière commerciale.

trade deficit *n* déficit extérieur.

trade discount *n* remise *f* au détaillant.

trade fair *n* foire(-exposition) commerciale.

trade-in [trād'in] *n* reprise *f*.

trade-in price *n* prix *m* à la reprise.

trademark [trād'mârk] *n* marque *f* de fabrique.

trade mission *n* mission commerciale.

trade name *n* marque déposée.

trader [trā'dûr] *n* commerçant/e, négociant/e.

trade secret *n* secret *m* de fabrication.

tradesman [trādz'mən] *n* (*storekeeper*) commerçant.

trade union *n* syndicat *m*.

trade unionist [trād yōōn'yənist] *n* syndicaliste *m/f*.

trade wind *n* alizé *m*.

trading [trā'ding] *n* affaires *fpl*, commerce *m*.

trading estate *n* (*Brit*) zone industrielle.

trading stamp *n* timbre-prime *m*.

tradition [trədish'ən] *n* tradition *f*; **~s** *npl* coutumes *fpl*, traditions.

traditional [trədish'ənəl] *a* traditionnel(le).

traffic [traf'ik] *n* trafic *m*; (*cars*) circulation *f* ♦ *vi*: **to ~ in** (*pej: liquor, drugs*) faire le trafic de.

traffic circle *n* (*US*) rond-point *m*.

traffic island *n* refuge *m* (pour piétons).

traffic jam *n* embouteillage *m*.

trafficker [traf'ikûr] *n* trafiquant/e.

traffic lights *npl* feux *mpl* (de signalisation).

traffic offence *n* (*Brit*) = **traffic violation**.

traffic sign *n* panneau *m* de signalisation.

traffic violation *n* (*US*) infraction *f* au code de la route.

traffic warden *n* contractuel/le.

tragedy [traj'idē] *n* tragédie *f*.

tragic [traj'ik] *a* tragique.

trail [trāl] *n* (*tracks*) trace *f*, piste *f*; (*path*) chemin *m*, piste; (*of smoke etc*) traînée *f* ♦ *vt* traîner, tirer; (*follow*) suivre ♦ *vi* traîner; **to be on sb's ~** être sur la piste de qn.

  trail away, **trail off** *vi* (*sound, voice*) s'évanouir; (*interest*) disparaître.

  trail behind *vi* traîner, être à la traîne.

trailer [trā'lûr] *n* (AUT) remorque *f*; (*US*) caravane *f*; (CINEMA) bande-annonce *f*.

trailer park *n* (*US*) camping *m* pour caravanes.

trailer truck *n* (*US*) (camion *m*) semi-remorque *m*.

train [trān] *n* train *m*; (*in subway*) rame *f*; (*of dress*) traîne *f*; (*Brit: series*): **~ of events** série *f* d'événements ♦ *vt* (*apprentice, doctor etc*) former; (*sportsman*) entraîner; (*dog*) dresser; (*memory*) exercer; (*point: gun etc*): **to ~ sth on** braquer qch sur ♦ *vi* recevoir sa formation; s'entraîner; **one's ~ of thought** le fil de sa pensée; **to go by ~** voyager par le train *or* en train; **to ~ sb to do sth** apprendre à qn à faire qch; (*employee*) former qn à faire qch.

train attendant *n* (*US*) employé/e des wagons-lits.

trained [trānd] *a* qualifié(e), qui a reçu une formation; dressé(e).

trainee [trānē'] *n* stagiaire *m/f*; (*in trade*) apprenti/e.

trainer [trā'nûr] *n* (*SPORT*) entraîneur/euse; (*of dogs etc*) dresseur/euse; ~**s** *npl* (*shoes*) chaussures *fpl* de sport.

training [trā'ning] *n* formation *f*; entraînement *m*; dressage *m*; **in** ~ (*SPORT*) à l'entraînement; (*fit*) en forme.

training college *n* école professionnelle; (*for teachers*) ≈ école normale.

training course *n* cours *m* de formation professionnelle.

training shoes *npl* chaussures *fpl* de sport.

train station *n* gare *f*.

traipse [trāps] *vi* (se) traîner, déambuler.

trait [trāt] *n* trait *m* (de caractère).

traitor [trā'tûr] *n* traître *m*.

trajectory [trəjek'tûrē] *n* trajectoire *f*.

tram [tram] *n* (*Brit: also:* ~**car**) tram(way) *m*.

tramline [tram'līn] *n* ligne *f* de tram(way).

tramp [tramp] *n* (*person*) vagabond/e, clochard/e; (*col: pej: woman*): **to be a** ~ être coureuse ♦ *vi* marcher d'un pas lourd ♦ *vt* (*walk through: town, streets*) parcourir à pied.

trample [tram'pəl] *vt*: **to** ~ (**underfoot**) piétiner; (*fig*) bafouer.

trampoline [trampəlēn'] *n* trampolino *m*.

trance [trans] *n* transe *f*; (*MED*) catalepsie *f*; **to go into a** ~ entrer en transe.

tranquil [trang'kwil] *a* tranquille.

tranquil(l)ity [trangkwil'itē] *n* tranquillité *f*.

tranquil(l)izer [trang'kwəlīzûr] *n* (*MED*) tranquillisant *m*.

transact [transakt'] *vt* (*business*) traiter.

transaction [transak'shən] *n* transaction *f*; ~**s** *npl* (*minutes*) actes *mpl*; **cash** ~ transaction au comptant.

transatlantic [transətlan'tik] *a* transatlantique.

transcend [transend'] *vt* transcender; (*excel over*) surpasser.

transcendental [transenden'təl] *a*: ~ **meditation** méditation transcendantale.

transcribe [transkrīb'] *vt* transcrire.

transcript [tran'skript] *n* transcription *f* (*texte*).

transcription [transkrip'shən] *n* transcription *f*.

transcriptionist [transkrip'shənist] *n* (*US*) audiotypiste *m/f*.

transept [tran'sept] *n* transept *m*.

transfer *n* [trans'fûr] (*gen, also SPORT*) transfert *m*; (*POL: of power*) passation *f*; (*of money*) virement *m*; (*picture, design*) décalcomanie *f* ♦ *vt* [transfûr'] transférer; passer; virer; décalquer; **by bank** ~ par virement bancaire.

transferable [transfûr'əbəl] *a* transmissible, transférable; **"not** ~**"** "personnel".

transfix [transfiks'] *vt* transpercer; (*fig*): ~**ed with fear** paralysé(e) par la peur.

transform [transfôrm'] *vt* transformer.

transformation [transfûrmā'shən] *n*

transformation *f*.

transformer [transfôr'mûr] *n* (*ELEC*) transformateur *m*.

transfusion [transfyōō'zhən] *n* transfusion *f*.

transgress [transgres'] *vt* transgresser.

transient [tran'shənt] *a* transitoire, éphémère.

transistor [tranzis'tûr] *n* (*ELEC*; *also*: ~ **radio**) transistor *m*.

transit [tran'sit] *n*: **in** ~ en transit.

transit camp *n* camp *m* de transit.

transition [tranzish'ən] *n* transition *f*.

transitional [tranzish'ənəl] *a* transitoire.

transitive [tran'sətiv] *a* (*LING*) transitif(ive).

transit lounge *n* salle *f* de transit.

transitory [tran'sitôrē] *a* transitoire.

translate [tranz'lāt] *vt*: **to** ~ (**from/into**) traduire (du/en).

translation [tranzlā'shən] *n* traduction *f*; (*SCOL: as opposed to prose*) version *f*.

translator [translā'tûr] *n* traducteur/trice.

translucent [translōō'sənt] *a* translucide.

transmission [transmish'ən] *n* transmission *f*.

transmit [transmit'] *vt* transmettre; (*RADIO, TV*) émettre.

transmitter [transmit'ûr] *n* émetteur *m*.

transom [tran'səm] *n* (*US*) vasistas *m*.

transparency [transpär'ənsē] *n* (*PHOT*) diapositive *f*.

transparent [transpär'ənt] *a* transparent(e).

transpire [transpiûr'] *vi* (*become known*): **it finally** ~**d that** ... on a finalement appris que ...; (*happen*) arriver.

transplant *vt* [tranzplant'] transplanter; (*seedlings*) repiquer ♦ *n* [tranz'plant] (*MED*) transplantation *f*; **to have a heart** ~ subir une greffe du cœur.

transport *n* [trans'pôrt] transport *m* ♦ *vt* [transpôrt'] transporter; **Department of T**~ (*Brit*) ministère *m* des Transports.

transportation [transpûrtā'shən] *n* (*moyen de*) transport *m*; (*of prisoners*) transportation *f*; **public** ~ transports en commun; **Department of T**~ (*US*) ministère *m* des Transports.

transport café *n* (*Brit*) ≈ relais *m* routier.

transpose [tranzpōz'] *vt* transposer.

transship [transship'] *vt* transborder.

transverse [transvûrs'] *a* transversal(e).

transvestite [transves'tīt] *n* travesti/e.

trap [trap] *n* (*snare, trick*) piège *m*; (*carriage*) cabriolet *m* ♦ *vt* prendre au piège; (*immobilize*) bloquer; (*jam*) coincer; **to set** *or* **lay a** ~ (**for sb**) tendre un piège (à qn); **to shut one's** ~ (*col*) la fermer.

trap door *n* trappe *f*.

trapeze [trapēz'] *n* trapèze *m*.

trapper [trap'ûr] *n* trappeur *m*.

trappings [trap'ingz] *npl* ornements *mpl*; attributs *mpl*.

trash [trash] *n* (*pej: goods*) camelote *f*; (: *nonsense*) sottises *fpl*; (*garbage*) ordures *fpl*; *vt* (*US col*): **to** ~ **sb** dénigrer qn.

trash can *n* (*US*) boîte *f* à ordures.

trauma [trou'mə] *n* traumatisme *m*.

traumatic [trômat'ik] *a* traumatisant(e).

travel [trav'əl] *n* voyage(s) *m(pl)* ♦ *vi* voyager; (*move*) aller, se déplacer ♦ *vt* (*distance*) parcourir; **this wine doesn't** ~ **well** ce vin voyage mal.

travel agency n agence f de voyages.
travel agent n agent m de voyages.
travel brochure n brochure f touristique.
traveler, (Brit) **traveller** [trav'əlúr] n voyageur/euse; (COMM) représentant m de commerce.
traveler's check, (Brit) **traveller's cheque** n chèque m de voyage.
traveling [trav'əling] (US) n voyage(s) m(pl) ♦ a (circus, exhibition) ambulant(e) ♦ cpd (bag, clock) de voyage; (expenses) de déplacement.
traveling salesman n voyageur m de commerce.
travelling etc [trav'əling] (Brit) = **traveling** etc.
travelog(ue) [trav'əlôg] n (book, talk) récit m de voyage; (film) documentaire m de voyage.
travel sickness n mal m de la route (or de mer or de l'air).
traverse [trav'úrs] vt traverser.
travesty [trav'istē] n parodie f.
trawler [trô'lúr] n chalutier m.
tray [trā] n (for carrying) plateau m; (on desk) corbeille f.
treacherous [trech'úrəs] a traître(sse); **road conditions are** ~ l'état des routes est dangereux.
treachery [trech'úrē] n traîtrise f.
treacle [trē'kəl] n (Brit) mélasse f.
tread [tred] n pas m; (sound) bruit m de pas; (of tire) chape f, bande f de roulement ♦ vi (pt **trod,** pp **trodden** [trâd, trâd'ən]) marcher.
tread on vt fus marcher sur.
treadle [tred'əl] n pédale f (de machine).
treas. abbr = **treasurer.**
treason [trē'zən] n trahison f.
treasure [trezh'úr] n trésor m ♦ vt (value) tenir beaucoup à; (store) conserver précieusement.
treasure hunt n chasse f au trésor.
treasurer [trezh'úrúr] n trésorier/ière; (US) économe m/f.
treasury [trezh'úrē] n trésorerie f; (US) économat m; **the T~ Department,** (Brit) **the T~** ≈ le ministère des Finances.
treasury bill n bon m du Trésor.
treat [trēt] n petit cadeau, petite surprise ♦ vt traiter; **it was a** ~ ça m'a (or nous a etc) vraiment fait plaisir; **to** ~ **sb to sth** offrir qch à qn; **to** ~ **sth as a joke** prendre qch à la plaisanterie.
treatise [trē'tis] n traité m (ouvrage).
treatment [trēt'mənt] n traitement m; **to have** ~ **for sth** (MED) suivre un traitement pour qch.
treaty [trē'tē] n traité m.
treble [treb'əl] a triple ♦ n (MUS) soprano m ♦ vt, vi tripler.
treble clef n clé f de sol.
tree [trē] n arbre m.
tree-lined [trē'līnd] a bordé(e) d'arbres.
treetop [trē'tâp] n cime f d'un arbre.
tree trunk n tronc m d'arbre.
trek [trek] n voyage m; randonnée f; (tiring walk) tirée f ♦ vi (as vacation) faire de la randonnée.
trellis [trel'is] n treillis m, treillage m.
tremble [trem'bəl] vi trembler.

trembling [trem'bling] n tremblement m ♦ a tremblant(e).
tremendous [trimen'dəs] a énorme, formidable; (excellent) fantastique, formidable.
tremendously [trimen'dəslē] ad énormément, extrêmement + adjective; formidablement.
tremor [trem'úr] n tremblement m; (also: earth ~) secousse f sismique.
trench [trench] n tranchée f.
trench coat n trench-coat m.
trench warfare n guerre f de tranchées.
trend [trend] n (tendency) tendance f; (of events) cours m; (fashion) mode f; ~ **towards/away from doing** tendance à faire/à ne pas faire; **to set the** ~ donner le ton; **to set a** ~ lancer une mode.
trendy [tren'dē] a (idea) dans le vent; (clothes) dernier cri inv.
trepidation [trepidā'shən] n vive agitation.
trespass [tres'pas] vi: **to** ~ **on** s'introduire sans permission dans; (fig) empiéter sur; **"no ~ing"** "propriété privée", "défense d'entrer".
trespasser [tres'pasúr] n intrus/e; **"~s will be prosecuted"** "interdiction d'entrer sous peine de poursuites".
tress [tres] n boucle f de cheveux.
trestle [tres'əl] n tréteau m.
trestle table n table f à tréteaux.
trial [trīl] n (LAW) procès m, jugement m; (test: of machine etc) essai m; (hardship) épreuve f; (worry) souci m; **~s** npl (SPORT) épreuves éliminatoires; **horse ~s** concours m hippique; ~ **by jury** jugement par jury; **to be sent for** ~ être traduit(e) en justice; **to be on** ~ passer en jugement; **by** ~ **and error** par tâtonnements.
trial balance n (COMM) balance f de vérification.
trial basis n: **on a** ~ pour une période d'essai.
trial run n essai m.
triangle [trī'anggəl] n (MATH, MUS) triangle m; (US) équerre f.
triangular [trīang'gyəlúr] a triangulaire.
tribal [trī'bəl] a tribal(e).
tribe [trīb] n tribu f.
tribesman [trībz'mən] n membre m de la tribu.
tribulation [tribyəlā'shən] n tribulation f, malheur m.
tribunal [trībyōō'nəl] n tribunal m.
tributary [trib'yətárē] n (river) affluent m.
tribute [trib'yōōt] n tribut m, hommage m; **to pay** ~ **to** rendre hommage à.
trice [trīs] n: **in a** ~ en un clin d'œil.
trick [trik] n ruse f; (clever act) astuce f; (prank) tour m; (CARDS) levée f ♦ vt attraper, rouler; **to play a** ~ **on sb** jouer un tour à qn; **to** ~ **sb into doing sth** persuader qn par la ruse de faire qch; **to** ~ **sb out of sth** obtenir qch de qn par la ruse; **it's a** ~ **of the light** c'est une illusion d'optique causée par la lumière; **that should do the** ~ (col) ça devrait faire l'affaire.
trickery [trik'úrē] n ruse f.
trickle [trik'əl] n (of water etc) filet m ♦ vi couler en un filet or goutte à goutte; **to** ~ **in/out** (people) entrer/sortir par petits

groupes.
trick question n question-piège f.
trickster [trik'stûr] n arnaqueur/euse, filou m.
tricky [trik'ē] a difficile, délicat(e).
tricycle [trī'sikəl] n tricycle m.
trifle [trī'fəl] n bagatelle f; (CULIN) ≈ diplomate m ♦ ad: **a ~ long** un peu long ♦ vi: **to ~ with** traiter à la légère.
trifling [trīf'ling] a insignifiant(e).
trigger [trig'ûr] n (of gun) gâchette f.
  trigger off vt déclencher.
trigonometry [trigənâm'ətrē] n trigonométrie f.
trilby [tril'bē] n (Brit: also: ~ **hat**) chapeau mou, feutre m.
trill [tril] n (of bird, MUS) trille m.
trillion [tril'yən] n (US) billion m.
trilogy [tril'əjē] n trilogie f.
trim [trim] a net(te); (house, garden) bien tenu(e); (figure) svelte ♦ n (haircut etc) légère coupe; (embellishment) finitions fpl; (on car) garnitures fpl ♦ vt couper légèrement; (decorate): **to ~ (with)** décorer (de); (NAUT: a sail) gréer; **to keep in (good) ~** maintenir en (bon) état.
trimmings [trim'ingz] npl décorations fpl; (extras: gen CULIN) garniture f.
Trinidad and Tobago [trin'idad and tōbā'gō] n Trinité et Tobago f.
Trinity [trin'itē] n: **the ~** la Trinité.
trinket [tring'kit] n bibelot m; (piece of jewelry) colifichet m.
trio [trē'ō] n trio m.
trip [trip] n voyage m; (excursion) excursion f; (stumble) faux pas ♦ vi faire un faux pas, trébucher; (go lightly) marcher d'un pas léger; **on a ~** en voyage.
  trip up vi trébucher ♦ vt faire un croc-en-jambe à.
tripartite [trīpâr'tīt] a triparti(e).
tripe [trīp] n (CULIN) tripes fpl; (pej: rubbish) idioties fpl.
triple [trip'əl] a triple ♦ ad: **~ the distance/the speed** trois fois la distance/la vitesse.
triplets [trip'lits] npl triplés/ées.
triplicate [trip'ləkit] n: **in ~** en trois exemplaires.
tripod [trī'pâd] n trépied m.
Tripoli [trip'əlē] n Tripoli.
tripwire [trip'wiûr] n fil m de déclenchement.
trite [trīt] a banal(e).
triumph [trī'əmf] n triomphe m ♦ vi: **to ~ (over)** triompher (de).
triumphal [trīum'fəl] a triomphal(e).
triumphant [trīum'fənt] a triomphant(e).
trivia [triv'ēə] npl futilités fpl.
trivial [triv'ēəl] a insignifiant(e); (commonplace) banal(e).
triviality [trivēal'ətē] n caractère insignifiant; banalité f.
trivialize [triv'ēəlīz] vt rendre banal(e).
trod [trâd] pt of **tread**.
trodden [trâd'ən] pp of **tread**.
trolley [trâl'ē] n (Brit) chariot m.
trolley bus n trolleybus m.
trollop [trâl'əp] n prostituée f.
trombone [trâmbōn'] n trombone m.
troop [trōōp] n bande f, groupe m ♦ vi: **to ~ in/out** entrer/sortir en groupe.

troop carrier n (plane) avion m de transport de troupes; (NAUT: also: **troopship**) transport m (navire).
trooper [trōō'pûr] n (MIL) soldat m de cavalerie; (US: policeman) ≈ gendarme m.
troops [trōōps] npl (MIL) troupes fpl; (: men) hommes mpl, soldats mpl.
troopship [trōōp'ship] n transport m (navire).
trophy [trō'fē] n trophée m.
tropic [trâp'ik] n tropique m; **in the ~s** sous les tropiques; **T~ of Cancer/Capricorn** tropique du Cancer/Capricorne.
tropical [trâp'ikəl] a tropical(e).
trot [trât] n trot m ♦ vi trotter; **on the ~** (Brit: fig) d'affilée.
  trot out vt (excuse, reason) débiter; (names, facts) réciter les uns après les autres.
trouble [trub'əl] n difficulté(s) f(pl), problème(s) m(pl); (worry) ennuis mpl, soucis mpl; (bother, effort) peine f; (POL) conflit(s) m(pl), troubles mpl; (MED): **stomach etc ~** troubles gastriques etc ♦ vt déranger, gêner; (worry) inquiéter ♦ vi: **to ~ to do** prendre la peine de faire; **~s** npl (POL etc) troubles mpl; **to be in ~** avoir des ennuis; (ship, climber etc) être en difficulté; **to have ~ doing sth** avoir du mal à faire qch; **to go to the ~ of doing** se donner le mal de faire; **it's no ~!** je vous en prie!; **please don't ~ yourself** je vous en prie, ne vous dérangez pas!; **the ~ is ...** le problème, c'est que ...; **what's the ~?** qu'est-ce qui ne va pas?
troubled [trub'əld] a (person) inquiet(ète); (epoch, life) agité(e).
trouble-free [trub'əlfrē] a sans problèmes or ennuis.
troublemaker [trub'əlmākûr] n élément perturbateur, fauteur m de troubles.
troubleshooter [trub'əlshōōtûr] n (in conflict) conciliateur m.
troublesome [trub'əlsəm] a ennuyeux(euse), gênant(e).
trouble spot n point chaud (fig).
trough [trôf] n (also: **drinking ~**) abreuvoir m; (also: **feeding ~**) auge f; (channel) chenal m; **~ of low pressure** (METEOROLOGY) dépression f.
trounce [trouns] vt (defeat) battre à plates coutures.
troupe [trōōp] n troupe f.
trouser press n (Brit) presse-pantalon m inv.
trousers [trou'zûrz] npl pantalon m; **short ~** (Brit) culottes courtes.
trouser suit n (Brit) tailleur-pantalon m.
trousseau, pl **~x** or **~s** [trōō'sō, z] n trousseau m.
trout [trout] n (pl inv) truite f.
trowel [trou'əl] n truelle f.
truant [trōō'ənt] n: **to be** or (Brit) **play ~** faire l'école buissonnière.
truce [trōōs] n trêve f.
truck [truk] n camion m; (RAIL) wagon m à plate-forme; (for luggage) chariot m (à bagages).
truck driver n camionneur m.
trucker [truk'ûr] n (esp US) camionneur m.
truck farm n (US) jardin maraîcher.
trucking [truk'ing] n (esp US) transport rou-

tier.

trucking company n (US) entreprise f de transport (routier).

truck stop n (US) relais m routier.

truculent [truk'yələnt] a agressif(ive).

trudge [truj] vi marcher lourdement, se traîner.

true [trōō] a vrai(e); (accurate) exact(e); (genuine) vrai, véritable; (faithful) fidèle; (wall) d'aplomb; (beam) droit(e); (wheel) dans l'axe; **to come** ~ se réaliser; ~ **to life** réaliste.

truffle [truf'əl] n truffe f.

truly [trōō'lē] ad vraiment, réellement; (truthfully) sans mentir; (faithfully) fidèlement; **yours** ~ (in letter) je vous prie d'agréer, Monsieur (or Madame etc), l'expression de mes sentiments respectueux.

trump [trump] n atout m; **to turn up** ~**s** (fig) faire des miracles.

trump card n atout m; (fig) carte maîtresse f.

trumped-up [trumpt'up'] a inventé(e) (de toutes pièces).

trumpet [trum'pit] n trompette f.

truncated [trung'kātid] a tronqué(e).

truncheon [trun'chən] n bâton m (d'agent de police); matraque f.

trundle [trun'dəl] vt, vi: **to** ~ **along** rouler bruyamment.

trunk [trungk] n (of tree, person) tronc m; (of elephant) trompe f; (case) malle f; (US AUT) coffre m.

trunk road n (Brit) ≈ (route) nationale.

trunks [trungks] npl (also: **swimming** ~) maillot m or slip m de bain.

truss [trus] n (MED) bandage m herniaire ♦ vt: **to** ~ **(up)** (CULIN) brider.

trust [trust] n confiance f; (LAW) fidéicommis m; (COMM) trust m ♦ vt (rely on) avoir confiance en; (entrust): **to** ~ **sth to sb** confier qch à qn; (hope): **to** ~ **(that)** espérer (que); **to take sth on** ~ accepter qch sans garanties (or sans preuves); **in** ~ (LAW) par fidéicommis.

trust company n société f fiduciaire.

trusted [trus'tid] a en qui l'on a confiance.

trustee [trustē'] n (LAW) fidéicommissaire m/f; (of school etc) administrateur/trice.

trustful [trust'fəl] a confiant(e).

trust fund n fonds m en fidéicommis.

trusting [trus'ting] a confiant(e).

trustworthy [trust'wûrt̸hē] a digne de confiance.

trusty [trus'tē] a fidèle.

truth, ~**s** [trōōth, trōōt̸hz] n vérité f.

truthful [trōōth'fəl] a (person) qui dit la vérité; (description) exact(e), vrai(e).

truthfully [trōōth'fəlē] ad sincèrement, sans mentir.

truthfulness [trōōth'fəlnis] n véracité f.

try [trī] n essai m, tentative f; (RUGBY) essai ♦ vt (LAW) juger; (test: sth new) essayer, tester; (strain) éprouver ♦ vi essayer; **to** ~ **to do** essayer de faire; (seek) chercher à faire; **to** ~ **one's (very) best** or **one's (very) hardest** faire de son mieux; **to give sth a** ~ essayer qch.

try on vt (clothes) essayer; **to** ~ **it on** (fig)

tenter le coup, bluffer.

try out vt essayer, mettre à l'essai.

trying [trī'ing] a pénible.

tsar [zär] n tsar m.

T-shirt [tē'shûrt] n tee-shirt m.

T-square [tē'skwär] n équerre f en T.

TT abbr (US MAIL) = Trust Territory ♦ a abbr (Brit col) = **teetotal.**

tub [tub] n cuve f; baquet m; (bath) baignoire f.

tuba [tōō'bə] n tuba m.

tubby [tub'ē] a rondelet(te).

tube [tōōb] n tube m; (for tire) chambre f à air; (col: television): **the** ~ la télé; (Brit: subway) métro m; **down the** ~**s** (col) fichu(e), foutu(e) (!).

tubeless [tōōb'lis] a (tire) sans chambre à air.

tuber [tōō'bûr] n (BOT) tubercule m.

tuberculosis [tōōbûrkyəlō'sis] n tuberculose f.

tube station n [tōōb' stā'shən] n (Brit) station f de métro.

tubing [tōō'bing] n tubes mpl; **a piece of** ~ un tube.

tubular [tōō'byəlûr] a tubulaire.

TUC n abbr (Brit: = Trades Union Congress) confédération f des syndicats britanniques.

tuck [tuk] n (SEWING) pli m, rempli m ♦ vt (put) mettre.

tuck away vt cacher, ranger.

tuck in vt rentrer; (child) border ♦ vi (eat) manger de bon appétit; attaquer le repas.

tuck up vt (child) border.

Tue(s). abbr (= Tuesday) ma.

Tuesday [tōōz'dā] n mardi m; **(the date) today is** ~ **23rd March** nous sommes aujourd'hui le mardi 23 mars; **on** ~ mardi; **on** ~**s** le mardi; **every** ~ tous les mardis, chaque mardi; **every other** ~ un mardi sur deux; **last/next** ~ mardi dernier/prochain; ~ **next** mardi qui vient; **the following** ~ le mardi suivant; **a week on** ~, ~ **week** mardi en huit; **the** ~ **before last** l'autre mardi; **the** ~ **after next** mardi en huit; ~ **morning/lunchtime/afternoon/evening** mardi matin/midi/après-midi/soir; ~ **night** mardi soir; (overnight) la nuit de mardi (à mercredi); ~**'s newspaper** le journal de mardi.

tuft [tuft] n touffe f.

tug [tug] n (ship) remorqueur m ♦ vt tirer (sur).

tug-of-war [tug'əvwôr'] n lutte f à la corde.

tuition [tōōish'ən] n (US: fees) frais mpl de scolarité; (Brit: lessons) leçons fpl.

tulip [tōō'lip] n tulipe f.

tumble [tum'bəl] n (fall) chute f, culbute f ♦ vi tomber, dégringoler; (somersault) faire une or des culbute(s) ♦ vt renverser, faire tomber; **to** ~ **to sth** (col) réaliser qch.

tumbledown [tum'bəldoun] a délabré(e).

tumble dryer n (Brit) séchoir m (à linge) à air chaud.

tumbler [tum'blûr] n verre (droit), gobelet m.

tummy [tum'ē] n (col) ventre m.

tumor, (Brit) **tumour** [tōō'mûr] n tumeur f.

tumult [tōō'məlt] n tumulte m.

tumultuous [tōōmul'chōōəs] a tumultueux(euse).

tuna [tōō'nə] n (pl inv) (also: ~ **fish**) thon m.

tune [tōōn] n (melody) air m ♦ vt (MUS)

accorder; (*RADIO*, *TV*, *AUT*) régler, mettre au point; **to be in/out of** ~ (*instrument*) être accordé/désaccordé; (*singer*) chanter juste/faux; **to be in/out of** ~ **with** (*fig*) être en accord/désaccord avec; **she was robbed to the** ~ **of $10,000** (*fig*) on lui a volé la jolie somme de 10 000 dollars.
  tune in *vi* (*RADIO*, *TV*): **to** ~ **in** (**to**) se mettre à l'écoute (de).
  tune up *vi* (*musician*) accorder son instrument.
tuneful [tōōn'fəl] *a* mélodieux(euse).
tuner [tōō'nûr] *n* (*radio set*) radio-préamplificateur *m*; **piano** ~ accordeur *m* de pianos.
tuner amplifier *n* radio-ampli *m*.
tungsten [tung'stən] *n* tungstène *m*.
tunic [tōō'nik] *n* tunique *f*.
tuning [tōō'ning] *n* réglage *m*.
tuning fork *n* diapason *m*.
Tunis [tōō'nis] *n* Tunis.
Tunisia [tōōnē'zhə] *n* Tunisie *f*.
Tunisian [tōōnē'zhən] *a* tunisien(ne) ♦ *n* Tunisien/ne.
tunnel [tun'əl] *n* tunnel *m*; (*in mine*) galerie *f* ♦ *vi* creuser un tunnel (or une galerie).
tunny [tun'ē] *n* thon *m*.
turban [tûr'bən] *n* turban *m*.
turbid [tûr'bid] *a* boueux(euse).
turbine [tûr'bīn] *n* turbine *f*.
turbojet [tûr'bōjet] *n* turboréacteur *m*.
turboprop [tûr'bōpräp] *n* (*engine*) turbopropulseur *m*.
turbot [tûr'bət] *n* (*pl inv*) turbot *m*.
turbulence [tûr'byələns] *n* (*AVIAT*) turbulence *f*.
turbulent [tûr'byələnt] *a* turbulent(e); (*sea*) agité(e).
tureen [tərēn'] *n* soupière *f*.
turf [tûrf] *n* gazon *m*; (*clod*) motte *f* (de gazon) ♦ *vt* gazonner; **the T~** le turf, les courses *fpl*.
  turf out *vt* (*col*) jeter; jeter dehors.
turgid [tûr'jid] *a* (*speech*) pompeux(euse).
Turin [tōō'rin] *n* Turin.
Turk [tûrk] *n* Turc/Turque.
Turkey [tûr'kē] *n* Turquie *f*.
turkey [tûr'kē] *n* dindon *m*, dinde *f*.
Turkish [tûr'kish] *a* turc(turque) ♦ *n* (*LING*) turc *m*.
Turkish bath *n* bain turc.
Turkish delight *n* loukoum *m*.
turmeric [tûr'mûrik] *n* curcuma *m*.
turmoil [tûr'moil] *n* trouble *m*, bouleversement *m*.
turn [tûrn] *n* tour *m*; (*in road*) tournant *m*; (*tendency: of mind, events*) tournure *f*; (*performance*) numéro *m*; (*MED*) crise *f*, attaque *f* ♦ *vt* tourner; (*collar, steak*) retourner; (*milk*) faire tourner; (*change*): **to** ~ **sth into** changer qch en; (*shape: wood, metal*) tourner ♦ *vi* tourner; (*person: look back*) se (re)tourner; (*reverse direction*) faire demi-tour; (*change*) changer; (*become*) devenir; **to** ~ **into** se changer en, se transformer en; **a good** ~ un service; **a bad** ~ un mauvais tour; **it gave me quite a** ~ ça m'a fait un coup; **"no left ~"** (*AUT*) "défense de tourner à gauche"; **the first** ~ **on**

the right (*US*) la première (rue or route) à droite; **it's your** ~ c'est (à) votre tour; **in** ~ à son tour; **to take** ~**s** se relayer; **to take** ~**s at** faire à tour de rôle; **at the** ~ **of the year/century** à la fin de l'année/du siècle; **to take a** ~ **for the worse** (*situation, events*) empirer; **his health** or **he has taken a** ~ **for the worse** son état s'est aggravé.
  turn around *vi* faire demi-tour; (*rotate*) tourner.
  turn away *vi* se détourner, tourner la tête ♦ *vt* (*reject: person*) renvoyer; (*: business*) refuser.
  turn back *vi* revenir, faire demi-tour.
  turn down *vt* (*refuse*) rejeter, refuser; (*reduce*) baisser; (*fold*) rabattre.
  turn in *vi* (*col: go to bed*) aller se coucher ♦ *vt* (*fold*) rentrer.
  turn off *vi* (*from road*) tourner ♦ *vt* (*light, radio etc*) éteindre; (*engine*) arrêter.
  turn on *vt* (*light, radio etc*) allumer; (*engine*) mettre en marche.
  turn out *vt* (*light, gas*) éteindre; (*produce: goods, novel, good pupils*) produire ♦ *vi* (*appear, attend: troops, doctor etc*) être présent(e); **to** ~ **out to be** ... s'avérer ..., se révéler ...
  turn over *vi* (*person*) se retourner ♦ *vt* (*object*) retourner; (*page*) tourner.
  turn round *vi* (*Brit*) = **turn around**.
  turn up *vi* (*person*) arriver, se pointer; (*lost object*) être retrouvé(e) ♦ *vt* (*collar*) remonter; (*increase: sound, volume etc*) mettre plus fort.
turnabout [tûr'nəbout], **turnaround** [tûr'nəround] *n* volte-face *f inv*.
turncoat [tûrn'kōt] *n* rénégat/e.
turned-up [tûrnd'up] *a* (*nose*) retroussé(e).
turning [tûr'ning] *n* (*in road*) tournant *m*; **the first** ~ **on the right** (*Brit*) la première (rue or route) à droite.
turning circle *n* (*Brit*) = **turning radius**.
turning point *n* (*fig*) tournant *m*, moment décisif.
turning radius *n* (*US*) rayon *m* de braquage.
turnip [tûr'nip] *n* navet *m*.
turnout [tûrn'out] *n* (nombre *m* de personnes dans l')assistance *f*.
turnover [tûrn'ōvûr] *n* (*COMM: amount of money*) chiffre *m* d'affaires; (*: of goods*) roulement *m*; (*CULIN*) sorte de chausson; **there is a rapid** ~ **in staff** le personnel change souvent.
turnpike [tûrn'pīk] *n* (*US*) autoroute *f* à péage.
turn signal *n* (*US AUT*) clignotant *m*.
turnstile [tûrn'stīl] *n* tourniquet *m* (*d'entrée*).
turntable [tûrn'tābəl] *n* (*on record player*) platine *f*.
turn-up [tûrn'up] *n* (*Brit: on pants*) revers *m*.
turpentine [tûr'pəntīn] *n* (*also:* **turps**) (essence *f* de) térébenthine *f*.
turquoise [tûr'koiz] *n* (*stone*) turquoise *f* ♦ *a* turquoise *inv*.
turret [tûr'it] *n* tourelle *f*.
turtle [tûr'təl] *n* tortue marine.
turtleneck (sweater) [tûr'təlnek (swet'ûr)] *n* pullover *m* à col montant.
Tuscany [tus'kənē] *n* Toscane *f*.

tusk [tusk] *n* défense *f (d'éléphant)*.
tussle [tus'əl] *n* bagarre *f*, mêlée *f*.
tutor [tōō'tûr] *n (private teacher)* précepteur/trice; *(Brit SCOL)* directeur/trice d'études.
tutorial [tōōtôr'ēəl] *n (SCOL)* (séance *f* de) travaux *mpl* pratiques.
tuxedo [tuksē'dō] *n* smoking *m*.
TV [tēvē] *n abbr (= television)* télé *f*, TV *f*.
TV dinner *n* plateau-repas *m*.
TVP *n abbr (= texturized vegetable protein)* protéine végétale texturisée.
twaddle [twâd'əl] *n* balivernes *fpl*.
twang [twang] *n (of instrument)* son vibrant; *(of voice)* ton nasillard ♦ *vi* vibrer ♦ *vt (guitar)* pincer les cordes de.
tweak [twēk] *vt (nose)* tordre; *(ear, hair)* tirer.
tweed [twēd] *n* tweed *m*.
tweezers [twē'zûrz] *npl* pince *f* à épiler.
twelfth [twelfth] *num* douzième.
Twelfth Night *n* la fête des Rois.
twelve [twelv] *num* douze; **at** ~ **(o'clock)** à midi; *(midnight)* à minuit.
twentieth [twen'tēith] *num* vingtième.
twenty [twen'tē] *num* vingt.
twerp [twûrp] *n (col)* imbécile *m/f*.
twice [twīs] *ad* deux fois; ~ **as much** deux fois plus; ~ **a week** deux fois par semaine; **she is** ~ **your age** elle a deux fois ton âge.
twiddle [twid'əl] *vt, vi*: **to** ~ **(with) sth** tripoter qch; **to** ~ **one's thumbs** *(fig)* se tourner les pouces.
twig [twig] *n* brindille *f* ♦ *vt, vi (col)* piger.
twilight [twī'līt] *n* crépuscule *m*; *(morning)* aube *f*; **in the** ~ dans la pénombre.
twill [twil] *n* sergé *m*.
twin [twin] *a, n* jumeau(elle) ♦ *vt* jumeler.
twin beds *npl* lits *mpl* jumeaux.
twin-carburetor [twinkâr'bərātûr] *a* à double carburateur.
twine [twīn] *n* ficelle *f* ♦ *vi (plant)* s'enrouler.
twin-engined [twin'enjənd] *a* bimoteur; ~ **aircraft** bimoteur *m*.
twinge [twinj] *n (of pain)* élancement *m*; *(of conscience)* remords *m*.
twinkle [twing'kəl] *n* scintillement *m*; pétillement *m* ♦ *vi* scintiller; *(eyes)* pétiller.
twin town *n* ville jumelée.
twirl [twûrl] *n* tournoiement *m* ♦ *vt* faire tournoyer ♦ *vi* tournoyer.
twist [twist] *n* torsion *f*, tour *m*; *(in wire, cord)* tortillon *m*; *(bend: in road)* tournant *m*; *(in story)* coup *m* de théâtre ♦ *vt* tordre; *(weave)* entortiller; *(roll around)* enrouler; *(fig)* déformer ♦ *vi* s'entortiller; s'enrouler; *(road)* serpenter; **to** ~ **one's ankle/wrist** *(MED)* se tordre la cheville/le poignet.
twisted [twis'tid] *a (wire, rope)* entortillé(e); *(ankle, wrist)* tordu(e), foulé(e); *(fig: logic, mind)* tordu.
twit [twit] *n (col)* crétin/e.
twitch [twich] *n* saccade *f*; *(nervous)* tic *m* ♦ *vi* se convulser; avoir un tic.
two [tōō] *num* deux; ~ **by** ~, **in** ~**s** par deux; **to put** ~ **and** ~ **together** *(fig)* faire le rapport.
two-door [tōō'dôr] *a (AUT)* à deux portes.
two-faced [tōō'fāst] *a (pej: person)* faux(fausse).

twofold [tōō'fōld] *ad*: **to increase** ~ doubler ♦ *a (increase)* de cent pour cent; *(reply)* en deux parties.
two-piece [tōō'pēs] *n (also:* ~ **suit)** (costume *m)* deux-pièces *m inv*; *(also:* ~ **swimsuit)** (maillot *m* de bain) deux-pièces.
two-seater [tōō'sē'tûr] *n (plane)* (avion *m)* biplace *m*; *(car)* voiture *f* à deux places.
twosome [tōō'səm] *n (people)* couple *m*.
two-stroke [tōō'strōk'] *n (also:* ~ **engine)** moteur *m* à deux temps ♦ *a* à deux temps.
two-tone [tōō'tōn'] *a (in color)* à deux tons.
two-way [tōō'wā'] *a (traffic)* dans les deux sens; ~ **radio** émetteur-récepteur *m*.
TX *abbr (US MAIL)* = *Texas*.
tycoon [tīkōōn'] *n*: **(business)** ~ gros homme d'affaires.
type [tīp] *n (category)* genre *m*, espèce *f*; *(model)* modèle *m*; *(example)* type *m*; *(TYP)* type, caractère *m* ♦ *vt (letter etc)* taper (à la machine); **what** ~ **do you want?** quel genre voulez-vous?; **in bold/italic** ~ en caractères gras/en italiques.
typecast [tīp'kast] *a* condamné(e) à toujours jouer le même rôle.
typeface [tīp'fās] *n* police *f* (de caractères).
typescript [tīp'skript] *n* texte dactylographié.
typeset [tīp'set] *vt* composer *(en imprimerie)*.
typesetter [tīp'setûr] *n* compositeur *m*.
typewriter [tīp'rītûr] *n* machine *f* à écrire.
typewritten [tīp'ritən] *a* dactylographié(e).
typhoid [tī'foid] *n* typhoïde *f*.
typhoon [tīfōōn'] *n* typhon *m*.
typhus [tī'fəs] *n* typhus *m*.
typical [tip'ikəl] *a* typique, caractéristique.
typify [tip'əfī] *vt* être caractéristique de.
typing [tī'ping] *n* dactylo(graphie) *f*.
typing error *n* faute *f* de frappe.
typing pool *n* pool *m* de dactylos.
typist [tī'pist] *n* dactylo *m/f*.
typo [tī'pō] *n abbr (col:* = *typographical error)* coquille *f*.
typography [tīpàg'rəfē] *n* typographie *f*.
tyranny [tēr'ənē] *n* tyrannie *f*.
tyrant [tī'rənt] *n* tyran *m*.
tyre [tīûr'] *n (Brit)* pneu *m*.
tyre pressure *n (Brit)* pression *f* (de gonflage).
Tyrol [tirōl'] *n* Tyrol *m*.
Tyrolean [tīrō'lēən], **Tyrolese** [tirəlēz'] *a* tyrolien(ne) ♦ *n* Tyrolien/ne.
Tyrrhenian Sea [tīrē'nēən sē'] *n*: **the** ~ la mer Tyrrhénienne.
tzar [zâr] *n* = **tsar**.

U

U, u [yōō] *n (letter)* U, u *m*; **U for Uncle** U comme Ursule.
U [yōō] *n abbr (Brit CINEMA*: = *universal)* ≈ tous publics.
UAW *n abbr (US*: = *United Automobile*

Workers) *syndicat des ouvriers de l'automobile.*

U-bend [yōō'bɛnd] *n* (*Brit* AUT) coude *m*, virage *m* en épingle à cheveux; (*in pipe*) coude.

ubiquitous [yōōbik'witəs] *a* doué(e) d'ubiquité, omniprésent(e).

UDA *n abbr* (*Brit*) = *Ulster Defence Association.*

udder [ud'ûr] *n* pis *m*, mamelle *f*.

UDI *n abbr* (*Brit* POL) = *unilateral declaration of independence.*

UDR *n abbr* (*Brit*) = *Ulster Defence Regiment.*

UEFA [yōōā'fa] *n abbr* (= *Union of European Football Associations*) UEFA *f*.

UFO [yōōefō'] *n abbr* (= *unidentified flying object*) ovni *m* (= *objet volant non identifié*).

Uganda [yōōgan'də] *n* Ouganda *m*.

Ugandan [yōōgan'dən] *a* ougandais(e) ♦ *n* Ougandais/e.

ugh [u] *excl* pouah!

ugliness [ug'lēnis] *n* laideur *f*.

ugly [ug'lē] *a* laid(e), vilain(e); (*fig*) répugnant(e).

UHF *abbr* (= *ultra-high frequency*) UHF.

UHT *a abbr* (= *ultra-heat treated*): ~ **milk** *n* lait UHT *or* longue conservation.

UK *n abbr* = **United Kingdom**.

ulcer [ul'sûr] *n* ulcère *m*; **mouth** ~ aphte *f*.

Ulster [ul'stûr] *n* Ulster *m*.

ulterior [ultēr'ēûr] *a* ultérieur(e); ~ **motive** arrière-pensée *f*.

ultimate [ul'təmit] *a* ultime, final(e); (*authority*) suprême ♦ *n*: **the** ~ **in luxury** le summum du luxe.

ultimately [ul'təmitlē] *ad* (*in the end*) en fin de compte; (*at last*) finalement; (*eventually*) par la suite.

ultimatum, *pl* ~**s** *or* **ultimata** [ultimā'təm, -tə] *n* ultimatum *m*.

ultralight [ultrəlīt] *n* (*US*) ULM *m* (= *ultra léger motorisé*).

ultrasonic [ultrəsân'ik] *a* ultrasonique.

ultrasound [ul'trəsound] *n* (MED) ultrason *m*.

ultraviolet [ultrəvī'əlit] *a* ultraviolet(te).

umbilical [umbil'ikəl] *a*: ~ **cord** cordon ombilical.

umbrage [um'brij] *n*: **to take** ~ prendre ombrage, se froisser.

umbrella [umbrel'ə] *n* parapluie *m*; (*fig*): **under the** ~ **of** sous les auspices de; chapeauté(e) par.

umpire [um'pīûr] *n* arbitre *m*; (TENNIS) juge *m* de chaise ♦ *vt* arbitrer.

umpteen [ump'tēn'] *a* je ne sais combien de; **for the** ~**th time** pour la nième fois.

UMW *n abbr* (= *United Mineworkers of America*) *syndicat des mineurs.*

UN *n abbr* = **United Nations**.

unabashed [unəbasht'] *a* nullement intimidé(e).

unabated [unəbā'tid] *a* non diminué(e).

unable [unā'bəl] *a*: **to be** ~ **to** ne (pas) pouvoir, être dans l'impossibilité de; (*not capable*) être incapable de.

unabridged [unəbrijd'] *a* complet(ète), intégral(e).

unacceptable [unaksep'təbəl] *a* (*behavior*)

inadmissible; (*price, proposal*) inacceptable.

unaccompanied [unəkum'pənēd] *a* (*child, lady*) non accompagné(e); (*singing, song*) sans accompagnement.

unaccountably [unəkount'əblē] *ad* inexplicablement.

unaccounted [unəkoun'tid] *a*: **two passengers are** ~ **for** on est sans nouvelles de deux passagers.

unaccustomed [unəkus'təmd] *a* inaccoutumé(e), inhabituel(le); **to be** ~ **to sth** ne pas avoir l'habitude de qch.

unacquainted [unəkwān'tid] *a*: **to be** ~ **with** ne pas connaître.

unadulterated [unədul'tərātid] *a* pur(e), naturel(le).

unaffected [unəfɛk'tid] *a* (*person, behavior*) naturel(le); (*emotionally*): **to be** ~ **by** ne pas être touché(e) par.

unafraid [unəfrād'] *a*: **to be** ~ ne pas avoir peur.

unaided [unā'did] *a* sans aide, tout(e) seul(e).

unanimity [yōōnənim'itē] *n* unanimité *f*.

unanimous [yōōnan'əməs] *a* unanime.

unanimously [yōōnan'əməslē] *ad* à l'unanimité.

unanswered [unan'sûrd] *a* (*question, letter*) sans réponse.

unappetizing [unap'itīzing] *a* peu appétissant(e).

unappreciative [unəprē'shēətiv] *a* indifférent(e).

unarmed [unârmd'] *a* (*person*) non armé(e); (*combat*) sans armes.

unashamed [unəshāmd'] *a* sans honte; impudent(e).

unassisted [unəsis'tid] *a* non assisté(e) ♦ *ad* sans aide, tout(e) seul(e).

unassuming [unəsōō'ming] *a* modeste, sans prétentions.

unattached [unətacht'] *a* libre, sans attaches.

unattended [unətɛn'did] *a* (*car, child, luggage*) sans surveillance.

unattractive [unətrak'tiv] *a* peu attrayant(e).

unauthorized [unôth'ərīzd] *a* non autorisé(e), sans autorisation.

unavailable [unəvā'ləbəl] *a* (*article, room, book*) (qui n'est) pas disponible; (*person*) (qui n'est) pas libre.

unavoidable [unəvoi'dəbəl] *a* inévitable.

unavoidably [unəvoi'dəblē] *ad* inévitablement.

unaware [unəwär'] *a*: **to be** ~ **of** ignorer, ne pas savoir, être inconscient(e) de.

unawares [unəwärz'] *ad* à l'improviste, au dépourvu.

unbalanced [unbal'ənst] *a* déséquilibré(e).

unbearable [unbär'əbəl] *a* insupportable.

unbeatable [unbē'təbəl] *a* imbattable.

unbeaten [unbēt'ən] *a* invaincu(e); (*record*) non battu(e).

unbecoming [unbikum'ing] *a* (*unseemly: language, behavior*) malséant(e), inconvenant(e); (*unflattering: garment*) peu seyant(e).

unbeknown(st) [unbinōn(st)'] *ad*: ~ **to** à l'insu de.

unbelief [unbilēf'] *n* incrédulité *f*.

unbelievable [unbilē'vəbəl] *a* incroyable.

unbelievingly [unbilē'vinglē] *ad* avec incrédulité.

unbend |unbend'| *vb (irg) vi* se détendre ♦ *vt (wire)* redresser, détordre.

unbending |unben'ding| *a (fig)* inflexible.

unbias(s)ed |unbī'əst| *a* impartial(e).

unblemished |unblem'isht| *a* impeccable.

unblock |unblāk'| *vt (pipe)* déboucher; *(road)* dégager.

unborn |unbôrn'| *a* à naître.

unbounded |unboun'did| *a* sans bornes, illimité(e).

unbreakable |unbrā'kəbəl| *a* incassable.

unbridled |unbrī'dəld| *a* débridé(e), déchaîné(e).

unbroken |unbrō'kən| *a* intact(e); *(line)* continu(e); *(record)* non battu(e).

unbuckle |unbuk'əl| *vt* déboucler.

unburden |unbûr'dən| *vt*: **to ~ o.s.** s'épancher, se livrer.

unbutton |unbut'ən| *vt* déboutonner.

uncalled-for |unkôld'fôr| *a* déplacé(e), injustifié(e).

uncanny |unkan'ē| *a* étrange, troublant(e).

unceasing |unsē'sing| *a* incessant(e), continu(e).

unceremonious |unsärəmō'nēəs| *a (abrupt, rude)* brusque.

uncertain |unsûr'tən| *a* incertain(e); **we were ~ whether ...** nous ne savions pas vraiment si ...; **in no ~ terms** sans équivoque possible.

uncertainty |unsûr'təntē| *n* incertitude *f*, doutes *mpl*.

unchallenged |unchal'injd| *a (gen)* incontesté(e); *(information)* non contesté(e); **to go ~** ne pas être contesté.

unchanged |unchānjd'| *a* inchangé(e).

uncharitable |unchar'itəbəl| *a* peu charitable.

uncharted |unchär'tid| *a* inexploré(e).

unchecked |unchekt'| *a* non réprimé(e).

uncivilized |unsiv'ilīzd| *a* non civilisé(e); *(fig)* barbare.

uncle |ung'kəl| *n* oncle *m*.

unclear |unkliûr'| *a* (qui n'est) pas clair(e) *or* évident(e); **I'm still ~ about what I'm supposed to do** je ne sais pas encore exactement ce que je dois faire.

uncoil |unkoil'| *vt* dérouler ♦ *vi* se dérouler.

uncomfortable |unkumf'təbəl| *a* inconfortable; *(uneasy)* mal à l'aise, gêné(e); *(situation)* désagréable.

uncomfortably |unkumf'təblē| *ad* inconfortablement; d'un ton *etc* gêné *or* embarrassé; désagréablement.

uncommitted |unkəmit'id| *a (attitude, country)* non engagé(e).

uncommon |unkâm'ən| *a* rare, singulier(ière), peu commun(e).

uncommunicative |unkəmyōō'nikətiv| *a* réservé(e).

uncomplicated |unkâm'plikātid| *a* simple, peu compliqué(e).

uncompromising |unkâm'prəmīzing| *a* intransigeant(e), inflexible.

unconcerned |unkənsûrnd'| *a (unworried)*: **to be ~ (about)** ne pas s'inquiéter (de).

unconditional |unkəndish'ənəl| *a* sans conditions.

uncongenial |unkənjēn'yəl| *a* peu agréable.

unconnected |unkənek'tid| *a (unrelated)*: **~ (with)** sans rapport (avec).

unconscious |unkân'chəs| *a* sans connaissance, évanoui(e); *(unaware)* inconscient(e) ♦ *n*: **the ~** l'inconscient *m*; **to knock sb ~** assommer qn.

unconsciously |unkân'chəslē| *ad* inconsciemment.

unconstitutional |unkânstitōō'shənəl| *a* anticonstitutionnel(le).

uncontested |unkəntes'tid| *a (champion)* incontesté(e); *(POL: seat)* non disputé(e).

uncontrollable |unkəntrō'ləbəl| *a (child, dog)* indiscipliné(e); *(emotion)* irrépressible.

uncontrolled |unkəntrōld'| *a (laughter, price rises)* incontrôlé(e).

unconventional |unkənven'chənəl| *a* non conventionnel(le).

unconvinced |unkənvinst'| *a*: **to be ~** ne pas être convaincu(e).

unconvincing |unkənvin'sing| *a* peu convaincant(e).

uncork |unkôrk'| *vt* déboucher.

uncorroborated |unkərâb'ərātid| *a* non confirmé(e).

uncouth |unkōōth'| *a* grossier(ière), fruste.

uncover |unkuv'ûr| *vt* découvrir.

uncovered |unkuv'ûrd| *a (US: check)* sans provision.

unctuous |ungk'chōōəs| *a* onctueux(euse), mielleux(euse).

undamaged |undam'ijd| *a (goods)* intact(e), en bon état; *(fig: reputation)* intact.

undaunted |undôn'tid| *a* non intimidé(e), inébranlable.

undecided |undisī'did| *a* indécis(e), irrésolu(e).

undelivered |undiliv'ûrd| *a* non remis(e), non livré(e).

undeniable |undinī'əbəl| *a* indéniable, incontestable.

under |un'dûr| *prep* sous; *(less than)* (de) moins de; au-dessous de; *(according to)* selon, en vertu de ♦ *ad* au-dessous; **from ~ sth** de dessous *or* de sous qch; **~ there** là-dessous; **in ~ 2 hours** en moins de 2 heures; **~ anesthetic** sous anesthésie; **~ discussion** en discussion; **~ the circumstances** étant donné les circonstances; **~ repair** en (cours de) réparation.

under... *prefix* sous-.

underage |ŭndûrāj'| *a* qui n'a pas l'âge réglementaire.

underarm |un'dûrârm| *ad* par en-dessous ♦ *a (throw)* par en-dessous; *(deodorant)* pour les aisselles.

undercapitalized |undûrkap'itəlīzd| *a* sous-capitalisé(e).

undercarriage |un'dûrkârij| *n (Brit AVIAT)* train *m* d'atterrissage.

undercharge |undûrchârj'| *vt* ne pas faire payer assez à.

underclothes |un'dûrklōz| *npl* sous-vêtements *mpl*; *(women's only)* dessous *mpl*.

undercoat |un'dûrkōt| *n (paint)* couche *f* de fond ♦ *vt (US AUT)* traiter contre la rouille.

undercover |undûrkuv'ûr| *a* secret(ète), clandestin(e).

undercurrent |un'dûrkûrənt| *n* courant sous-jacent.

undercut [undûrkut'] *vt irg* vendre moins cher que.

underdeveloped [un'dûrdivel'əpt] *a* sous-développé(e).

underdog [un'dûrdôg] *n* opprimé *m*.

underdone [un'dûrdun'] *a* (*food*) pas assez cuit(e).

underemployment [undûremploi'mənt] *n* sous-emploi *m*.

underestimate [undûres'təmāt] *vt* sous-estimer, mésestimer.

underexposed [undûrikspōzd'] *a* (*PHOT*) sous-exposé(e).

underfed [undûrfed'] *a* sous-alimenté(e).

underfoot [undûrfōōt'] *ad* sous les pieds.

undergo [undûrgō'] *vt irg* subir; (*treatment*) suivre; **the car is ~ing repairs** la voiture est en réparation.

undergraduate [undûrgraj'ōōit] *n* étudiant/e (qui prépare la licence) ♦ *cpd*: **~ courses** cours *mpl* préparant à la licence.

underground [un'dûrground] *a* souterrain(e); (*fig*) clandestin(e) ♦ *n* (*Brit*) métro *m*; (*POL*) clandestinité *f*.

undergrowth [un'dûrgrōth] *n* broussailles *fpl*, sous-bois *m*.

underhand(ed) [un'dûrhand(id)] *a* (*fig*) sournois(e), en dessous.

underinsured [undûrinshōōrd'] *a* sous-assuré(e).

underlie [undûrlī'] *vt irg* être à la base de; **the underlying cause** la cause sous-jacente.

underline [undûrlīn'] *vt* souligner.

underling [un'dûrling] *n* (*pej*) sous-fifre *m*, subalterne *m*.

undermanning [un'dûrman'ing] *n* pénurie *f* de main-d'œuvre.

undermentioned [un'dûrmenchənd] *a* mentionné(e) ci-dessous.

undermine [undûrmīn'] *vt* saper, miner.

underneath [undûrnēth'] *ad* (en) dessous ♦ *prep* sous, au-dessous de.

undernourished [undûrnûr'isht] *a* sous-alimenté(e).

underpaid [undûrpād'] *a* sous-payé(e).

underpants [un'dûrpants] *npl* caleçon *m*, slip *m*.

underpass [un'dûrpas] *n* passage souterrain; (*Brit: on freeway*) passage inférieur.

underpin [undûrpin'] *vt* (*argument, case*) étayer.

underplay [undûrplā'] *vt* minimiser.

underpopulated [un'dûrpâp'yəlātid] *a* sous-peuplé(e).

underprice [undûrprīs'] *vt* vendre à un prix trop bas.

underprivileged [undûrpriv'əlijd] *a* défavorisé(e), déshérité(e).

underrate [undərāt'] *vt* sous-estimer, mésestimer.

underscore [undûrskôr'] *vt* souligner.

underseal [un'dûrsēl] *vt* (*Brit*) traiter contre la rouille.

undersecretary [un'dûrsek'ritärē] *n* sous-secrétaire *m*.

undersell [undûrsel'] *vt* (*competitors*) vendre moins cher que.

undershirt [un'dûrshûrt] *n* (*US*) tricot *m* de corps.

undershorts [un'dûrshôrts] *npl* (*US*) caleçon *m*, slip *m*.

underside [un'dûrsīd] *n* dessous *m*.

undersigned [un'dûrsīnd] *a, n* soussigné(e) (*m/f*).

underskirt [un'dûrskûrt] *n* jupon *m*.

understaffed [undûrstaft'] *a* qui manque de personnel.

understand [undûrstand'] *vb* (*irg: like* **stand**) *vt, vi* comprendre; **I ~ that** ... je me suis laissé dire que ...; je crois comprendre que ...; **to make o.s. understood** se faire comprendre.

understandable [undûrstan'dəbəl] *a* compréhensible.

understanding [undûrstan'ding] *a* compréhensif(ive) ♦ *n* compréhension *f*; (*agreement*) accord *m*; **to come to an ~ with sb** s'entendre avec qn; **on the ~ that** ... à condition que ....

understate [undûrstāt'] *vt* minimiser.

understatement [undûrstāt'mənt] *n*: **that's an ~** c'est (bien) peu dire, le terme est faible.

understood [undûrstōōd'] *pt, pp of* **understand** ♦ *a* entendu(e); (*implied*) sous-entendu(e).

understudy [un'dûrstudē] *n* doublure *f*.

undertake [undûrtāk'] *vt irg* (*job, task*) entreprendre; (*duty*) se charger de; **to ~ to do sth** s'engager à faire qch.

undertaker [un'dûrtākûr] *n* entrepreneur *m* des pompes funèbres, croque-mort *m*.

undertaking [un'dûrtāking] *n* entreprise *f*; (*promise*) promesse *f*.

undertone [un'dûrtōn] *n* (*low voice*): **in an ~** à mi-voix; (*of criticism etc*) nuance cachée.

undervalue [undûrval'yōō] *vt* sous-estimer.

underwater [un'dûrwôt'ûr] *ad* sous l'eau ♦ *a* sous-marin(e).

underwear [un'dûrwär] *n* sous-vêtements *mpl*; (*women's only*) dessous *mpl*.

underweight [un'dûrwāt] *a* d'un poids insuffisant; (*person*) (trop) maigre.

underworld [un'dûrwûrld] *n* (*of crime*) milieu *m*, pègre *f*.

underwrite [un'dərīt] *vt* (*FINANCE*) garantir; (*INSURANCE*) souscrire.

underwriter [un'dərītûr] *n* (*INSURANCE*) souscripteur *m*.

undeserving [undizûr'ving] *a*: **to be ~ of** ne pas mériter.

undesirable [undizīûr'əbəl] *a* peu souhaitable; indésirable.

undeveloped [undivel'əpt] *a* (*land, resources*) non exploité(e).

undies [un'dēz] *npl* (*col*) dessous *mpl*, lingerie *f*.

undiluted [undilōō'tid] *a* pur(e), non dilué(e).

undiplomatic [undipləmat'ik] *a* peu diplomatique, maladroit(e).

undischarged [undischârjd'] *a*: **~ bankrupt** failli/e non réhabilité(e).

undisciplined [undis'əplind] *a* indiscipliné(e).

undisguised [undisgīzd'] *a* (*dislike, amusement etc*) franc(franche).

undisputed [undispyōō'tid] *a* incontesté(e).

undistinguished [undisting'gwisht] *a* médiocre, quelconque.

undisturbed [undistûrbd'] *a* (*sleep*) tranquille,

paisible; **to leave** ~ ne pas déranger.

undivided [undiv'i'did] *a*: **can I have your** ~ **attention?** puis-je avoir toute votre attention?

undo [undoo̅'] *vt irg* défaire.

undoing [undoo̅'ing] *n* ruine *f*, perte *f*.

undone [undun'] *pp of* **undo**; **to come** ~ se défaire.

undoubted [undou'tid] *a* indubitable, certain(e).

undoubtedly [undou'tidlē] *ad* sans aucun doute.

undress [undres'] *vi* se déshabiller ♦ *vt* déshabiller.

undrinkable [undringk'əbəl] *a* (*unpalatable*) imbuvable; (*poisonous*) non potable.

undue [undoo̅'] *a* indu(e), excessif(ive).

undulating [un'jəlāting] *a* ondoyant(e), onduleux(euse).

unduly [undoo̅'lē] *ad* trop, excessivement.

undying [undī'ing] *a* éternel(le).

unearned [unûrnd'] *a* (*praise, respect*) immérité(e); ~ **income** rentes *fpl*.

unearth [unûrth'] *vt* déterrer; (*fig*) dénicher.

unearthly [unûrth'lē] *a* surnaturel(le); (*hour*) indu(e), impossible.

uneasy [unē'zē] *a* mal à l'aise, gêné(e); (*worried*) inquiet(ète); **to feel** ~ **about doing sth** se sentir mal à l'aise à l'idée de faire qch.

uneconomic(al) [unēkənâm'ik(əl)] *a* peu économique; peu rentable.

uneducated [unej'oo̅kātid] *a* sans éducation.

unemployed [unemploid'] *a* sans travail, au chômage ♦ *n*: **the** ~ les chômeurs *mpl*.

unemployment [unemploi'mənt] *n* chômage *m*.

unemployment compensation, (*Brit*) **unemployment benefit** *n* allocation *f* de chômage.

unending [unen'ding] *a* interminable.

unenviable [unen'vēəbəl] *a* peu enviable.

unequal [unēk'wəl] *a* inégal(e).

unequaled, (*Brit*) **unequalled** [unēk'wəld] *a* inégalé(e).

unequivocal [unikwiv'əkəl] *a* (*answer*) sans équivoque; (*person*) catégorique.

unerring [unûr'ing] *a* infaillible, sûr(e).

UNESCO [yoo̅nes'kō] *n abbr* (= *United Nations Educational, Scientific and Cultural Organization*) UNESCO *f*.

unethical [uneth'ikəl] *a* (*methods*) immoral(e); (*doctor's behavior*) qui ne respecte pas l'éthique.

uneven [unē'vən] *a* inégal(e); irrégulier(ière).

uneventful [univent'fəl] *a* tranquille, sans histoires.

unexceptional [uniksep'shənəl] *a* banal(e), quelconque.

unexciting [uniksī'ting] *a* pas passionnant(e).

unexpected [unikspek'tid] *a* inattendu(e), imprévu(e).

unexpectedly [unikspek'tidlē] *ad* contre toute attente; (*arrive*) à l'improviste.

unexplained [unikspländ'] *a* inexpliqué(e).

unexploded [uniksplō'did] *a* non explosé(e) or éclaté(e).

unfailing [unfā'ling] *a* inépuisable; infaillible.

unfair [unfär'] *a*: ~ **(to)** injuste (envers); **it's** ~ **that** ... il n'est pas juste que ....

unfair dismissal *n* licenciement abusif.

unfairly [unfär'lē] *ad* injustement.

unfaithful [unfāth'fəl] *a* infidèle.

unfamiliar [unfəmil'yûr] *a* étrange, inconnu(e); **to be** ~ **with sth** mal connaître qch.

unfashionable [unfash'ənəbəl] *a* (*clothes*) démodé(e); (*district*) déshérité(e), pas à la mode.

unfasten [unfas'ən] *vt* défaire; détacher.

unfathomable [unfath'əməbəl] *a* insondable.

unfavorable [unfā'vûrəbəl] *a* (*US*) défavorable.

unfavorably [unfā'vûrəblē] *ad*: **to look** ~ **upon** ne pas être favorable à.

unfavourable [unfā'vûrəbəl] *etc* (*Brit*) = **unfavorable** *etc*.

unfeeling [unfē'ling] *a* insensible, dur(e).

unfinished [unfin'isht] *a* inachevé(e).

unfit [unfit'] *a* (*physically*) pas en forme; (*incompetent*): ~ **(for)** impropre (à); (*work, service*) inapte (à).

unflagging [unflag'ing] *a* infatigable, inlassable.

unflappable [unflap'əbəl] *a* imperturbable.

unflattering [unflat'ûring] *a* (*dress, hairstyle*) qui n'avantage pas; (*remark*) peu flatteur(euse).

unflinching [unflin'ching] *a* stoïque.

unfold [unfōld'] *vt* déplier; (*fig*) révéler, exposer ♦ *vi* se dérouler.

unforeseeable [unfôrsē'əbəl] *a* imprévisible.

unforeseen [unfôrsēn'] *a* imprévu(e).

unforgettable [unfûrget'əbəl] *a* inoubliable.

unforgivable [unfûrgiv'əbəl] *a* impardonnable.

unformatted [unfôr'matid] *a* (*disk, text*) non formaté(e).

unfortunate [unfôr'chənit] *a* malheureux(euse); (*event, remark*) malencontreux(euse).

unfortunately [unfôr'chənitlē] *ad* malheureusement.

unfounded [unfoun'did] *a* sans fondement.

unfriendly [unfrend'lē] *a* froid(e), inamical(e).

unfulfilled [unfoo̅lfild'] *a* (*ambition, prophecy*) non réalisé(e); (*desire*) insatisfait(e); (*promise*) non tenu(e); (*terms of contract*) non rempli(e); (*person*) qui n'a pas su se réaliser.

unfurl [unfûrl'] *vt* déployer.

unfurnished [unfûr'nisht] *a* non meublé(e).

ungainly [ungān'lē] *a* gauche, dégingandé(e).

ungodly [ungâd'lē] *a* impie; **at an** ~ **hour** à une heure indue.

ungrateful [ungrāt'fəl] *a* qui manque de reconnaissance, ingrat(e).

unguarded [ungâr'did] *a*: ~ **moment** moment *m* d'inattention.

unhappily [unhap'ilē] *ad* tristement; (*unfortunately*) malheureusement.

unhappiness [unhap'ēnis] *n* tristesse *f*, peine *f*.

unhappy [unhap'ē] *a* triste, malheureux(euse); (*unfortunate: remark etc*) malheureux(euse); (*not pleased*): ~ **with** mécontent(e) de, peu satisfait(e) de.

unharmed [unhârmd'] *a* indemne, sain(e) et sauf(sauve).

unhealthy [unhel'thē] *a* (*gen*) malsain(e); (*person*) maladif(ive).

unheard-of [unhûrd'əv] *a* inouï(e), sans précédent.

unhelpful [unhelp'fəl] *a* (*person*) peu serviable; (*advice*) peu utile.

unhesitating [unhez'itāting] *a* (*loyalty*) spontané(e); (*reply, offer*) immédiat(e).

unhook [unhŏŏk'] *vt* décrocher; dégrafer.

unhurt [unhûrt'] *a* indemne, sain(e) et sauf(sauve).

unhygienic [unhījēen'ik] *a* antihygiénique.

UNICEF [yŏŏ'nisef] *n abbr* (= *United Nations International Children's Emergency Fund*) UNICEF *m*, FISE *m*.

unicolor, (*Brit*) **unicolour** [yŏŏnəkul'ûr] *a* uni(e).

unicorn [yŏŏ'nəkôrn] *n* licorne *f*.

unidentified [unīden'təfīd] *a* non identifié(e).

uniform [yŏŏ'nəfôrm] *n* uniforme *m* ♦ *a* uniforme.

uniformity [yŏŏnəfôr'mitē] *n* uniformité *f*.

unify [yŏŏ'nəfī] *vt* unifier.

unilateral [yŏŏnəlat'ûrəl] *a* unilatéral(e).

unimaginable [unimaj'ənəbəl] *a* inimaginable, inconcevable.

unimaginative [unimaj'ənətiv] *a* sans imagination.

unimpaired [unimpärd'] *a* intact(e).

unimportant [unimpôr'tənt] *a* sans importance.

unimpressed [unimprest'] *a* pas impressionné(e).

uninhabited [uninhab'itid] *a* inhabité(e).

uninhibited [uninhib'itid] *a* sans inhibitions; sans retenue.

uninjured [unin'jûrd] *a* indemne.

unintelligent [unintel'ijənt] *a* inintelligent(e).

unintentional [uninten'chənəl] *a* involontaire.

unintentionally [uninten'chənəlē] *ad* sans le vouloir.

uninvited [uninvī'tid] *a* (*guest*) qui n'a pas été invité(e).

uninviting [uninvī'ting] *a* (*place*) peu attirant(e); (*food*) peu appétissant(e).

union [yŏŏn'yən] *n* union *f*; (*also:* **trade** ~) syndicat *m* ♦ *cpd* du syndicat, syndical(e).

unionize [yŏŏn'yənīz] *vt* syndiquer.

Union Jack *n* drapeau du *Royaume-Uni.*

Union of Soviet Socialist Republics (USSR) *n* Union *f* des républiques socialistes soviétiques (URSS).

union shop *n* entreprise où tous les travailleurs doivent être syndiqués.

unique [yŏŏnēk'] *a* unique.

unisex [yŏŏ'niseks] *a* unisexe.

unison [yŏŏ'nisən] *n*: **in** ~ à l'unisson, en chœur.

unit [yŏŏ'nit] *n* unité *f*; (*section: of furniture etc*) élément *m*, bloc *m*; (*team, squad*) groupe *m*, service *m*; **production** ~ atelier *m* de fabrication; **sink** ~ bloc-évier *m*.

unit cost *n* coût *m* unitaire.

unite [yŏŏnīt'] *vt* unir ♦ *vi* s'unir.

united [yŏŏnī'tid] *a* uni(e); unifié(e); (*efforts*) conjugué(e).

United Arab Emirates *npl* Émirats Arabes Unis.

United Kingdom (UK) *n* Royaume-Uni *m*

(R.U.).

United Nations (Organization) (UN, UNO) *n* (Organisation *f* des) Nations unies (ONU).

United States (of America) (US, USA) *n* États-Unis *mpl*.

unit price *n* prix *m* unitaire.

unit trust *n* (*Brit COMM*) fonds commun de placement, FCP *m*.

unity [yŏŏ'nitē] *n* unité *f*.

Univ. *abbr* = **university.**

universal [yŏŏnəvûr'səl] *a* universel(le).

universe [yŏŏ'nəvûrs] *n* univers *m*.

university [yŏŏnəvûr'sitē] *n* université *f* ♦ *cpd* (*student, professor*) d'université; (*education, year, degree*) universitaire.

unjust [unjust'] *a* injuste.

unjustifiable [unjus'tifīəbəl] *a* injustifiable.

unjustified [unjus'təfīd] *a* injustifié(e); (*text*) non justifié(e).

unkempt [unkempt'] *a* mal tenu(e), débraillé(e); mal peigné(e).

unkind [unkīnd'] *a* peu gentil(le), méchant(e).

unkindly [unkīnd'lē] *ad* (*treat, speak*) avec méchanceté.

unknown [unnōn'] *a* inconnu(e); ~ **to me** sans que je le sache; ~ **quantity** (*MATH, fig*) inconnue *f*.

unladen [unlā'dən] *a* (*ship, weight*) à vide.

unlawful [unlô'fəl] *a* illégal(e).

unleaded [unled'id] *a* sans plomb.

unleash [unlēsh'] *vt* détacher; (*fig*) déchaîner, déclencher.

unleavened [unlev'ənd] *a* sans levain.

unless [unles'] *cj*: ~ **he leaves** à moins qu'il (ne) parte; ~ **we leave** à moins de partir, à moins que nous (ne) partions; ~ **otherwise stated** sauf indication contraire; ~ **I am mistaken** si je ne me trompe.

unlicensed [unlī'sənst] *a* (*Brit*) non patenté(e) pour la vente des spiritueux.

unlike [unlīk'] *a* dissemblable, différent(e) ♦ *prep* à la différence de, contrairement à.

unlikelihood [unlīk'lēhŏŏd] *a* improbabilité *f*.

unlikely [unlīk'lē] *a* (*result, event*) improbable; (*explanation*) invraisemblable.

unlimited [unlim'itid] *a* illimité(e).

unlisted [unlis'tid] *a* (*US TEL*) sur la liste rouge; (*STOCK EXCHANGE*) non coté(e) en bourse.

unlit [unlit'] *a* (*room*) non éclairé(e).

unload [unlōd'] *vt* décharger.

unlock [unlâk'] *vt* ouvrir.

unlucky [unluk'ē] *a* malchanceux(euse); (*object, number*) qui porte malheur; **to be** ~ (*person*) ne pas avoir de chance.

unmanageable [unman'ijəbəl] *a* (*unwieldy: tool, vehicle*) peu maniable; (: *situation*) inextricable.

unmanned [unmand'] *a* sans équipage.

unmannerly [unman'ûrlē] *a* mal élevé(e), impoli(e).

unmarked [unmârkt'] *a* (*unstained*) sans marque; ~ **police car** voiture de police banalisée.

unmarried [unmar'ēd] *a* célibataire.

unmask [unmask'] *vt* démasquer.

unmatched [unmacht'] *a* sans égal(e).

unmentionable [unmen'chənəbəl] *a* (*topic*)

dont on ne parle pas; (*word*) qui ne se dit pas.

unmerciful [unmûr'sifəl] *a* sans pitié.

unmistakable [unmistā'kəbəl] *a* indubitable; qu'on ne peut pas ne pas reconnaître.

unmitigated [unmit'əgātid] *a* non mitigé(e), absolu(e), pur(e).

unnamed [unnāmd'] *a* (*nameless*) sans nom; (*anonymous*) anonyme.

unnatural [unnach'ûrəl] *a* non naturel(le); contre nature.

unnecessary [unnes'isärē] *a* inutile, superflu(e).

unnerve [unnûrv'] *vt* faire perdre son sang-froid à.

unnoticed [unnō'tist] *a* inaperçu(e).

UNO [ōō'nō] *n abbr* = **United Nations Organization**.

unobservant [unəbzûr'vənt] *a* pas observateur(trice).

unobtainable [unəbtā'nəbəl] *a* (*TEL*) impossible à obtenir.

unobtrusive [unəbtrōō'siv] *a* discret(ète).

unoccupied [unäk'yəpīd] *a* (*seat, table, also MIL*) libre; (*house*) inoccupé(e).

unofficial [unəfish'əl] *a* non officiel(le); (*strike*) ≈ non sanctionné(e) par la centrale.

unopposed [unəpōzd'] *a* sans opposition.

unorthodox [unôr'thədäks] *a* peu orthodoxe.

unpack [unpak'] *vi* défaire sa valise, déballer ses affaires.

unpaid [unpād'] *a* (*bill*) impayé(e); (*vacation*) non-payé(e), sans salaire; (*work*) non rétribué(e); (*worker*) bénévole.

unpalatable [unpal'ətəbəl] *a* (*truth*) désagréable (à entendre).

unparalleled [unpar'əleld] *a* incomparable, sans égal.

unpatriotic [unpātrēăt'ik] *a* (*person*) manquant de patriotisme; (*speech, attitude*) antipatriotique.

unplanned [unpland'] *a* (*visit*) imprévu(e); (*baby*) non prévu(e).

unpleasant [unplez'ənt] *a* déplaisant(e), désagréable.

unplug [unplug'] *vt* débrancher.

unpolluted [unpəlōō'tid] *a* non pollué(e).

unpopular [unpäp'yəlûr] *a* impopulaire; **to make o.s. ~ (with)** se rendre impopulaire (auprès de).

unprecedented [unpres'identid] *a* sans précédent.

unpredictable [unpridik'təbəl] *a* imprévisible.

unprejudiced [unprej'ədist] *a* (*not biased*) impartial(e); (*having no prejudices*) qui n'a pas de préjugés.

unprepared [unpripärd'] *a* (*person*) qui n'est pas suffisamment préparé(e); (*speech*) improvisé(e).

unprepossessing [unprēpəzes'ing] *a* peu avenant(e).

unpretentious [unpriten'chəs] *a* sans prétention(s).

unprincipled [unprin'səpəld] *a* sans principes.

unproductive [unprəduk'tiv] *a* improductif(ive); (*discussion*) stérile.

unprofessional [unprəfesh'ənəl] *a* (*conduct*) contraire à la déontologie.

unprofitable [unpräf'itəbəl] *a* non rentable.

unprovoked [unprəvōkt'] *a* (*attack*) sans provocation.

unpunished [unpun'isht] *a* impuni(e).

unqualified [unkwâl'əfīd] *a* (*teacher*) non diplômé(e), sans titres; (*success*) sans réserve, total(e).

unquestionably [unkwes'chənəblē] *ad* incontestablement.

unquestioning [unkwes'chəning] *a* (*obedience, acceptance*) inconditionnel(le).

unravel [unrav'əl] *vt* démêler.

unreal [unrēl'] *a* irréel(le).

unrealistic [unrēəlis'tik] *a* (*idea*) irréaliste; (*estimate*) peu réaliste.

unreasonable [unrē'zənəbəl] *a* qui n'est pas raisonnable; **to make ~ demands on sb** exiger trop de qn.

unrecognizable [unrek'əgnīzəbəl] *a* pas reconnaissable.

unrecognized [unrek'əgnīzd] *a* (*talent, genius*) méconnu(e).

unrecorded [unrikôr'did] *a* non enregistré(e).

unrefined [unrifīnd'] *a* (*sugar, petroleum*) non raffiné(e).

unrehearsed [unrihûrst'] *a* (*THEATER etc*) qui n'a pas été répété(e); (*spontaneous*) spontané(e).

unrelated [unrilā'tid] *a* sans rapport; sans lien de parenté.

unrelenting [unrilen'ting] *a* implacable; acharné(e).

unreliable [unrilī'əbəl] *a* sur qui (*or* quoi) on ne peut pas compter, peu fiable.

unrelieved [unrilēvd'] *a* (*monotony*) constant(e), uniforme.

unremitting [unrimit'ing] *a* inlassable, infatigable, acharné(e).

unrepeatable [unripē'təbəl] *a* (*offer*) unique, exceptionnel(le).

unrepentant [unripen'tənt] *a* impénitent(e).

unrepresentative [unreprizen'tətiv] *a*: **~ (of)** peu représentatif(ive) (de).

unreserved [unrizûrvd'] *a* (*seat*) non réservé(e); (*approval, admiration*) sans réserve.

unresponsive [unrispän'siv] *a* insensible.

unrest [unrest'] *n* agitation *f*, troubles *mpl*.

unrestricted [unristrik'tid] *a* illimité(e); **to have ~ access to** avoir librement accès *or* accès en tout temps à.

unrewarded [unriwôr'did] *a* pas récompensé(e).

unripe [unrīp'] *a* pas mûr(e).

unrivaled, (*Brit*) **unrivalled** [unrī'vəld] *a* sans égal, incomparable.

unroll [unrōl'] *vt* dérouler.

unruffled [unruf'əld] *a* (*person*) imperturbable; (*hair*) qui n'est pas ébouriffé(e).

unruly [unrōō'lē] *a* indiscipliné(e).

unsafe [unsāf'] *a* (*machine, wiring*) dangereux(euse); (*method*) hasardeux(euse); **~ to drink/eat** non potable/comestible.

unsaid [unsed'] *a*: **to leave sth ~** passer qch sous silence.

unsalable, (*Brit*) **unsaleable** [unsā'ləbəl] *a* invendable.

unsatisfactory [unsatisfak'tûrē] *a* qui laisse à désirer.

unsavory, (*Brit*) **unsavoury** [unsā'vûrē] *a* (*fig*) peu recommandable, répugnant(e).

unscathed [unskāᵗʰd'] a indemne.

unscientific [unsīəntif'ik] a non scientifique.

unscrew [unskrōō'] vt dévisser.

unscrupulous [unskrōō'pyələs] a sans scrupules.

unsecured [unsikyōōrd'] a: ~ **creditor** créancier/ière sans garantie.

unseemly [unsēm'lē] a inconvenant(e).

unseen [unsēn'] a (person) invisible; (danger) imprévu(e).

unselfish [unsel'fish] a désintéressé(e).

unsettled [unset'əld] a (restless) perturbé(e); (unpredictable) instable; incertain(e); (not finalized) non résolu(e).

unsettling [unset'ling] a qui a un effet perturbateur.

unshak(e)able [unshā'kəbəl] a inébranlable.

unshaven [unshā'vən] a non or mal rasé(e).

unsightly [unsīt'lē] a disgracieux(euse), laid(e).

unskilled [unskild'] a: ~ **worker** manœuvre m.

unsociable [unsō'shəbəl] a (person) peu sociable; (behavior) qui manque de sociabilité.

unsocial [unsō'shəl] a (hours) en dehors de l'horaire normal.

unsold [unsōld'] a invendu(e), non vendu(e).

unsolicited [unsolis'itid] a non sollicité(e).

unsophisticated [unsəfis'tikātid] a simple, naturel(le).

unsound [unsound'] a (health) chancelant(e); (floor, foundations) peu solide; (policy, advice) peu judicieux(euse).

unspeakable [unspē'kəbəl] a indicible; (awful) innommable.

unspoken [unspō'kən] a (word) qui n'est pas prononcé(e); (agreement, approval) tacite.

unsteady [unsted'ē] a mal assuré(e), chancelant(e), instable.

unstinting [unstin'ting] a (support) total(e), sans réserve; (generosity) sans limites.

unstuck [unstuk'] a: **to come** ~ se décoller; (fig) faire fiasco.

unsubstantiated [unsəbstan'chēātid] a (rumor) qui n'est pas confirmé(e); (accusation) sans preuve.

unsuccessful [unsəkses'fəl] a (attempt) infructueux(euse); (writer, proposal) qui n'a pas de succès; (marriage) malheureux(euse), qui ne réussit pas; **to be** ~ (in attempting sth) ne pas réussir; ne pas avoir de succès; (application) ne pas être retenu(e).

unsuccessfully [unsəkses'fəlē] ad en vain.

unsuitable [unsōō'təbəl] a qui ne convient pas, peu approprié(e); inopportun(e).

unsuited [unsōō'tid] a: **to be** ~ **for** or **to** être inapte or impropre à.

unsupported [unsəpôr'tid] a (claim) non soutenu(e); (theory) qui n'est pas corroboré(e).

unsure [unshōōr'] a pas sûr(e); **to be** ~ **of o.s.** ne pas être sûr de soi, manquer de confiance en soi.

unsuspecting [unsəspek'ting] a qui ne se méfie pas.

unsweetened [unswēt'ənd] a non sucré(e).

unswerving [unswûr'ving] a inébranlable.

unsympathetic [unsimpəthet'ik] a hostile; (unpleasant) antipathique; ~ **to** indiffé-

rent(e) à.

untangle [untang'gəl] vt démêler, débrouiller.

untapped [untapt'] a (resources) inexploité(e).

untaxed [untakst'] a (goods) non taxé(e); (income) non imposé(e).

unthinkable [unthingk'əbəl] a impensable, inconcevable.

untidy [untī'dē] a (room) en désordre; (appearance) désordonné(e), débraillé(e); (person) sans ordre, désordonné; débraillé; (work) peu soigné(e).

untie [untī'] vt (knot, parcel) défaire; (prisoner, dog) détacher.

until [until'] prep jusqu'à; (after negative) avant ♦ cj jusqu'à ce que + sub, en attendant que + sub; (in past, after negative) avant que + sub; ~ **now** jusqu'à présent, jusqu'ici; ~ **then** jusque-là; **from morning** ~ **night** du matin au soir or jusqu'au soir.

untimely [untīm'lē] a inopportun(e); (death) prématuré(e).

untold [untōld'] a incalculable; indescriptible.

untouched [untucht'] a (not used etc) tel(le) quel(le), intact(e); (safe: person) indemne; (unaffected) ~ **by** indifférent(e) à.

untoward [untôrd'] a fâcheux(euse), malencontreux(euse).

untrammeled, (Brit) **untrammelled** [untram'əld] a sans entraves.

untranslatable [untranz'lātəbəl] a intraduisible.

untrue [untrōō'] a (statement) faux(fausse).

untrustworthy [untrust'wûrᵗʰē] a (person) pas digne de confiance, peu sûr(e).

unusable [unyōō'zəbəl] a inutilisable.

unused [unyōōzd'] a (new) neuf(neuve); [unyōōst']: **to be** ~ **to sth/to doing sth** ne pas avoir l'habitude de qch/de faire qch.

unusual [unyōō'zhōōəl] a insolite, exceptionnel(le), rare.

unusually [unyōō'zhōōəlē] ad exceptionnellement, particulièrement.

unveil [unvāl'] vt dévoiler.

unwanted [unwôn'tid] a non désiré(e).

unwarranted [unwôr'əntid] a injustifié(e).

unwary [unwär'ē] a imprudent(e).

unwavering [unwā'vûring] a inébranlable.

unwelcome [unwel'kəm] a importun(e); **to feel** ~ se sentir de trop.

unwell [unwel'] a indisposé(e), souffrant(e); **to feel** ~ ne pas se sentir bien.

unwieldy [unwēl'dē] a difficile à manier.

unwilling [unwil'ing] a: **to be** ~ **to do** ne pas vouloir faire.

unwillingly [unwil'inglē] ad à contrecœur, contre son gré.

unwind [unwīnd'] vb (irg) vt dérouler ♦ vi (relax) se détendre.

unwise [unwīz'] a imprudent(e), peu judicieux(euse).

unwitting [unwit'ing] a involontaire.

unworkable [unwûr'kəbəl] a (plan etc) inexploitable.

unworthy [unwûr'ᵗʰē] a indigne.

unwrap [unrap'] vt défaire; ouvrir.

unwritten [unrit'ən] a (agreement) tacite.

unzip [unzip'] vt ouvrir (la fermeture éclair de).

up [up] *prep*: **to go/be** ~ **sth** monter/être sur qch ♦ *ad* en haut; **en l'air** ♦ *vi* (*col*): **she ~ped and left** elle a fichu le camp sans plus attendre ♦ *vt* (*col*: *price etc*) augmenter; ~ **there** là-haut; ~ **above** au-dessus; ~ **to** jusqu'à; **"this side ~"** ''haut''; **to be** ~ (*out of bed*) être levé(e), être debout *inv*; **to be** ~ **(by)** (*of price, value*) avoir augmenté (de); **when the year was** ~ (*finished*) à la fin de l'année; **time's** ~ c'est l'heure; **it is** ~ **to you** c'est à vous de décider, ça ne tient qu'à vous; **what is he** ~ **to?** qu'est-ce qu'il peut bien faire?; **he is not** ~ **to it** il n'en est pas capable; **what's** ~? (*col*) qu'est-ce qui ne va pas?; **what's** ~ **with him?** (*col*) qu'est-ce qui lui arrive?; **~s and downs** *npl* (*fig*) hauts et bas *mpl*.

up-and-coming [upənkum'ing] *a* plein(e) d'avenir *or* de promesses.

upbeat [up'bēt] *n* (*MUS*) levé *m*; (*in economy, prosperity*) amélioration *f* ♦ *a* (*optimistic*) optimiste.

upbraid [upbrād'] *vt* morigéner.

upbringing [up'bringing] *n* éducation *f*.

update [updāt'] *vt* mettre à jour.

upend [upend'] *vt* mettre debout.

upgrade [upgrād'] *vt* (*person*) promouvoir; (*job*) revaloriser; (*property, equipment*) moderniser.

upheaval [uphē'vəl] *n* bouleversement *m*; branle-bas *m*; crise *f*.

uphill *a* [up'hil'] qui monte; (*fig: task*) difficile, pénible ♦ *ad* [uphil'] (*face, look*) en amont, vers l'amont; (*go, move*) vers le haut, en haut; **to go** ~ monter.

uphold [uphōld'] *vt irg* maintenir; soutenir.

upholstery [uphōl'stûrē] *n* rembourrage *m*; (*of car*) garniture *f*.

UPI *abbr* = *United Press International*.

upkeep [up'kēp] *n* entretien *m*.

up-market [up'mâr'kit] *a* (*product*) haut de gamme *inv*.

upon [əpân'] *prep* sur.

upper [up'ûr] *a* supérieur(e); du dessus ♦ *n* (*of shoe*) empeigne *f*.

upper class *n*: **the** ~ ≈ la haute bourgeoisie ♦ *a*: **upper-class** (*district*) élégant(e), huppé(e); (*accent, attitude*) caractéristique des classes supérieures.

upper hand *n*: **to have the** ~ avoir le dessus.

uppermost [up'ûrmōst] *a* le(la) plus haut(e); en dessus; **it was** ~ **in my mind** j'y pensais avant tout autre chose.

Upper Volta [up'ûr võl'tə] *n* Haute Volta.

upright [up'rīt] *a* droit(e); vertical(e); (*fig*) droit, honnête ♦ *n* montant *m*.

uprising [up'rīzing] *n* soulèvement *m*, insurrection *f*.

uproar [up'rôr] *n* tumulte *m*, vacarme *m*.

uproot [uprōōt'] *vt* déraciner.

upset *n* [up'set] dérangement *m* ♦ *vt* [upset'] (*irg: like* **set**) (*glass etc*) renverser; (*plan*) déranger; (*person: offend*) contrarier; (: *grieve*) faire de la peine à; bouleverser ♦ *a* [upset'] contrarié(e); peiné(e); (*stomach*) détraqué(e), dérangé(e); **to get** ~ (*sad*) devenir triste; (*offended*) se vexer; **to have a stomach** ~ (*Brit*) avoir une indigestion.

upset price *n* (*US, Scottish*) mise *f* à prix, prix *m* de départ.

upsetting [upset'ing] *a* (*offending*) vexant(e); (*annoying*) ennuyeux(euse).

upshot [up'shât] *n* résultat *m*; **the** ~ **of it all was that** ... il a résulté de tout cela que ....

upside down [up'sid doun'] *ad* à l'envers.

upstairs [up'stärz] *ad* en haut ♦ *a* (*room*) du dessus, d'en haut ♦ *n*: **there's no** ~ il n'y a pas d'étage.

upstart [up'stârt] *n* parvenu/e.

upstream [up'strēm] *ad* en amont.

upsurge [up'sûrj] *n* (*of enthusiasm etc*) vague *f*.

uptake [up'tāk] *n*: **he is quick/slow on the** ~ il comprend vite/est lent à comprendre.

uptight [up'tīt'] *a* (*col*) très tendu(e), crispé(e).

up-to-date [up'tədāt'] *a* moderne; très récent(e).

upturn [up'tûrn] *n* (*in economy*) reprise *f*.

upturned [uptûrnd'] *a* (*nose*) retroussé(e).

upward [up'wûrd] *a* ascendant(e); vers le haut.

upward(s) [up'wûrd(z)] *ad* vers le haut; **and** ~ et plus, et au-dessus.

URA *n abbr* (*US*) = *Urban Renewal Administration*.

Ural Mountains [yōōr'əl moun'tənz] *npl*: **the** ~ (*also*: **the Urals**) les monts *mpl* Oural, l'Oural *m*.

uranium [yōōrā'nēəm] *n* uranium *m*.

Uranus [yōōr'ānəs] *n* Uranus *f*.

urban [ûr'bən] *a* urbain(e).

urbane [ûrbān'] *a* urbain(e), courtois(e).

urbanization [ûrbənəzā'shən] *n* urbanisation *f*.

urchin [ûr'chin] *n* gosse *m*, garnement *m*; **sea** ~ oursin *m*.

urge [ûrj] *n* besoin (impératif), envie (pressante) ♦ *vt* (*caution etc*) recommander avec insistance; (*person*): **to** ~ **sb to do** presser qn de faire, recommander avec insistance à qn de faire.

urge on *vt* pousser, presser.

urgency [ûr'jənsē] *n* urgence *f*; (*of tone*) insistance *f*.

urgent [ûr'jənt] *a* urgent(e); (*plea, tone*) pressant(e).

urgently [ûr'jəntlē] *ad* d'urgence, de toute urgence; (*need*) sans délai.

urinal [yōōr'ənəl] *n* (*Brit*) urinoir *m*.

urinate [yōōr'ənāt] *vi* uriner.

urine [yōōr'in] *n* urine *f*.

urn [ûrn] *n* urne *f*; (*also*: **tea** ~) fontaine *f* à thé.

Uruguay [yōō'rəgwā] *n* Uruguay *m*.

Uruguayan [yōōrəgwā'ən] *a* uruguayen(ne) ♦ *n* Uruguayen/ne.

US *n abbr* = **United States**.

us [us] *pronoun* nous.

USA *n abbr* = **United States of America**; (*MIL*) = *United States Army*.

usable [yōō'zəbəl] *a* utilisable.

USAF *n abbr* = *United States Air Force*.

usage [yōō'sij] *n* usage *m*.

USCG *n abbr* = *United States Coast Guard*.

USDA *n abbr* = *United States Department of Agriculture*.

USDI *n abbr* = *United States Department of*

the Interior.

use *n* [yōōs] emploi *m*, utilisation *f*; usage *m* ♦
vt [yōōz] se servir de, utiliser, employer; **she**
~**d to do it** elle le faisait (autrefois), elle
avait coutume de le faire; **in** ~ en usage;
out of ~ hors d'usage; **to be of** ~ servir,
être utile; **to make** ~ **of sth** utiliser qch;
ready for ~ prêt à l'emploi; **to be of** ~ être
utile; **it's no** ~ ça ne sert à rien; **to have**
the ~ **of** avoir l'usage de; **what's this** ~**d**
for? à quoi est-ce que ça sert?; [yōōst']: **to be**
~**d to** avoir l'habitude de, être habitué(e) à;
to get ~**d to** s'habituer à.
use up [yōōz up] *vt* finir, épuiser; *(food)*
consommer.
used [yōōzd] *a (car)* d'occasion; *(match)*
vieux(vieille).
useful [yōōs'fəl] *a* utile; **to come in** ~ être utile.
usefulness [yōōs'fəlnis] *n* utilité *f*.
useless [yōōs'lis] *a* inutile.
user [yōō'zûr] *n* utilisateur/trice, usager *m*.
user-friendly [yōō'zûrfrend'lē] *a* convivial(e),
facile d'emploi.
USES *n abbr* = *United States Employment*
Service.
usher [ush'ûr] *n* placeur *m* ♦ *vt*: **to** ~ **sb in**
faire entrer qn.
usherette [ushəret'] *n (in cinema)* ouvreuse *f*.
USIA *n abbr* = *United States Information*
Agency.
USM *n abbr* = *United States Mail*, *United*
States Mint.
USN *n abbr* = *United States Navy.*
USPHS *n abbr* = *United States Public Health*
Service.
USPS *n abbr* = *United States Postal Service.*
USS *abbr* = *United States Ship.*
USSR *n abbr* = **Union of Soviet Socialist Re-**
publics.
usu. *abbr* = **usually.**
usual [yōō'zhōōəl] *a* habituel(le); **as** ~ comme
d'habitude.
usually [yōō'zhōōəlē] *ad* d'habitude, d'ordinaire.
usurer [yōō'zhûrûr] *n* usurier/ière.
usurp [yōōsûrp'] *vt* usurper.
UT *abbr (US MAIL)* = *Utah.*
utensil [yōōten'səl] *n* ustensile *m*; **kitchen** ~**s**
batterie *f* de cuisine.
uterus [yōō'tûrəs] *n* utérus *m*.
utilitarian [yōōtilitâr'ēən] *a* utilitaire.
utility [yōōtil'itē] *n* utilité *f*; *(also:* **public** ~*)*
service public.
utility room *n* buanderie *f*.
utilization [yōōtəlizā'shən] *n* utilisation *f*.
utilize [yōō'təliz] *vt* utiliser; exploiter.
utmost [ut'mōst] *a* extrême, le(la) plus
grand(e) ♦ *n*: **to do one's** ~ faire tout son
possible; **of the** ~ **importance** d'une
importance capitale, de la plus haute
importance.
utter [ut'ûr] *a* total(e), complet(ète) ♦ *vt* prononcer, proférer; émettre.
utterance [ut'ûrəns] *n* paroles *fpl*.
utterly [ut'ûrlē] *ad* complètement, totalement.
U-turn [yōō'tûrn] *n* demi-tour *m*; *(fig)* volte-
face *f inv*.

V

V, v [vē] *n (letter)* V, v *m*; **V for Victor** V
comme Victor.
v [vak] *abbr* (= *verse*, = *vide: see*) v.; (=
versus) c.; (= *volt*) V.
VA *abbr (US MAIL)* = *Virginia.*
vac [vak] *n abbr (Brit col)* = **vacation.**
vacancy [vā'kənsē] *n (room)* chambre *f* disponible; *(Brit: job)* poste vacant; **"no va-**
cancies" "complet".
vacant [vā'kənt] *a (post)* vacant(e); *(seat etc)*
libre, disponible; *(expression)* distrait(e).
vacant lot *n* terrain inoccupé; *(for sale)*
terrain à vendre.
vacate [vā'kāt] *vt* quitter.
vacation [vākā'shən] *n (esp US)* vacances *fpl*;
to take a ~ prendre des vacances; **on** ~ en
vacances.
vacation course *n* cours *mpl* de vacances.
vacationer [vākā'shənûr] *n (US)* vacancier/ère.
vacation pay *n (US)* paie *f* des vacances.
vacation season *n (US)* période *f* des vacances.
vaccinate [vak'sənāt] *vt* vacciner.
vaccination [vak'sənā'shən] *n* vaccination *f*.
vaccine [vaksēn'] *n* vaccin *m*.
vacuum [vak'yōōm] *n* vide *m*; *(also:* ~
cleaner) aspirateur *m* ♦ *vt* passer l'aspirateur.
vacuum bottle *n (US)* bouteille *f* thermos ®.
vacuum flask *n (Brit)* = **vacuum bottle.**
vacuum-packed [vak'yōōmpakt'] *a* emballé(e)
sous vide.
vagabond [vag'əbând] *n* vagabond/e; *(tramp)*
chemineau *m*, clochard/e.
vagary [vā'gûrē] *n* caprice *m*.
vagina [vəji'nə] *n* vagin *m*.
vagrancy [vā'grənsē] *n* vagabondage *m*.
vagrant [vā'grənt] *n* vagabond/e, mendiant/e.
vague [vāg] *a* vague, imprécis(e); *(blurred:*
photo, memory) flou(e); **I haven't the** ~**st**
idea je n'en ai pas la moindre idée.
vaguely [vāg'lē] *ad* vaguement.
vain [vān] *a (useless)* vain(e); *(conceited)* va-
niteux(euse); **in** ~ en vain.
valance [val'əns] *n (of bed)* tour *m* de lit.
valedictory [validik'tûrē] *a* d'adieu.
valentine [val'əntīn] *n (also:* ~ **card)** carte *f*
de la Saint-Valentin.
valet [valā'] *n* valet *m* de chambre.
valet parking *n* parcage *m* par les soins du
personnel (de l'hôtel *etc*).
valet service *n (for clothes)* pressing *m*; *(for*
car) nettoyage complet.
valiant [val'yənt] *a* vaillant(e), coura-
geux(euse).
valid [val'id] *a* valide, valable; *(excuse)* valable.
validate [val'idāt] *vt (contract, document)* valider; *(argument, claim)* prouver la justesse

de, confirmer.
validity [vəlid'itē] *n* validité *f*.
valise [vəlēs'] *n* sac *m* de voyage.
valley [val'ē] *n* vallée *f*.
valor, *(Brit)* **valour** [val'ûr] *n* courage *m*.
valuable [val'yōōəbəl] *a* (*jewel*) de grande valeur; (*time*) précieux(euse); ~s *npl* objets *mpl* de valeur.
valuation [valyōōā'shən] *n* évaluation *f*, expertise *f*.
value [val'yōō] *n* valeur *f* ♦ *vt* (*fix price*) évaluer, expertiser; (*cherish*) tenir à; **you get good ~ (for money) in that store** vous en avez pour votre argent dans ce magasin; **to lose (in)** ~ (*currency*) baisser; (*property*) se déprécier; **to gain (in)** ~ (*currency*) monter; (*property*) prendre de la valeur; **to be of great ~ to sb** (*fig*) être très utile à qn.
value added tax (VAT) *n* taxe *f* à la valeur ajoutée (TVA).
valued [val'yōōd] *a* (*appreciated*) estimé(e).
valuer [val'yōōûr] *n* expert *m* (en estimations).
valve [valv] *n* (*in machine*) soupape *f*; (*on tire*) valve *f*; (*in radio*) lampe *f*.
vampire [vam'pīûr] *n* vampire *m*.
van [van] *n* (*AUT*) camionnette *f*; (*Brit RAIL*) fourgon *m*.
vandal [van'dəl] *n* vandale *m/f*.
vandalism [van'dəlizəm] *n* vandalisme *m*.
vandalize [van'dəlīz] *vt* saccager.
vanguard [van'gârd] *n* avant-garde *m*.
vanilla [vənil'ə] *n* vanille *f* ♦ *cpd* (*ice cream*) à la vanille.
vanish [van'ish] *vi* disparaître.
vanity [van'itē] *n* vanité *f*.
vanity case *n* sac *m* de toilette.
vantage [van'tij] *n*: ~ **point** bonne position.
vaporize [vā'pərīz] *vt* vaporiser ♦ *vi* se vaporiser.
vapor [vā'pûr] *n* (*US*) vapeur *f*; (*on window*) buée *f*.
vapor trail *n* (*AVIAT*) traînée *f* de condensation.
vapour [vā'pûr] *etc* (*Brit*) = **vapor** *etc*.
variable [vär'ēəbəl] *a* variable; (*mood*) changeant(e) ♦ *n* variable *f*.
variance [vär'ēəns] *n*: **to be at ~ (with)** être en désaccord (avec); (*facts*) être en contradiction (avec).
variant [vär'ēənt] *n* variante *f*.
variation [värēā'shən] *n* variation *f*; (*in opinion*) changement *m*.
varicose [var'əkōs] *a*: ~ **veins** varices *fpl*.
varied [vär'ēd] *a* varié(e), divers(e).
variety [vərī'ətē] *n* variété *f*; (*quantity*): **a wide ~ of ...** une quantité *or* un grand nombre de ... (différent(e)s *or* divers(es)); **for a ~ of reasons** pour diverses raisons.
variety show *n* (spectacle *m* de) variétés *fpl*.
various [vär'ēəs] *a* divers(e), différent(e); (*several*) divers, plusieurs; **at ~ times** (*different*) en diverses occasions; (*several*) à plusieurs reprises.
varnish [vär'nish] *n* vernis *m*; (*for nails*) vernis (à ongles) ♦ *vt* vernir; **to ~ one's nails** se vernir les ongles.
vary [vär'ē] *vt, vi* varier, changer; **to ~ with** *or* **according to** varier selon.
varying [vär'ēing] *a* variable.

vase [vās] *n* vase *m*.
vasectomy [vasek'təmē] *n* vasectomie *f*.
vaseline [vas'əlēn] *n* ® vaseline *f*.
vast [vast] *a* vaste, immense; (*amount, success*) énorme.
vastly [vast'lē] *ad* infiniment, extrêmement.
vastness [vast'nis] *n* immensité *f*.
VAT [vat] *n abbr* = **value added tax**.
vat [vat] *n* cuve *f*.
Vatican [vat'ikən] *n*: **the ~** le Vatican.
vault [vôlt] *n* (*of roof*) voûte *f*; (*tomb*) caveau *m*; (*in bank*) salle *f* des coffres; chambre forte; (*jump*) saut *m* ♦ *vt* (*also*: ~ **over**) sauter (d'un bond).
vaunted [vôn'tid] *a*: **much-~** tant célébré(e).
VC *n abbr* = **vice-chairman**.
VCR *n abbr* = **video cassette recorder**.
VD *n abbr* = **venereal disease**.
VDU *n abbr* = **visual display unit**.
veal [vēl] *n* veau *m*.
veer [vēr] *vi* tourner; virer.
vegan [vē'gən] *n* végétalien/ne.
vegetable [vej'təbəl] *n* légume *m* ♦ *a* végétal(e).
vegetable garden *n* (jardin *m*) potager *m*.
vegetarian [vejitär'ēən] *a, n* végétarien(ne).
vegetate [vej'itāt] *vi* végéter.
vegetation [vejitā'shən] *n* végétation *f*.
vehemence [vē'əməns] *n* véhémence *f*, violence *f*.
vehement [vē'əmənt] *a* violent(e), impétueux(euse); (*impassioned*) ardent(e).
vehicle [vē'ikəl] *n* véhicule *m*.
vehicular [vēhik'yəlûr] *a*: **"no ~ traffic"** "interdit à tout véhicule".
veil [vāl] *n* voile *m* ♦ *vt* voiler; **under a ~ of secrecy** (*fig*) dans le plus grand secret.
veiled [vāld] *a* voilé(e).
vein [vān] *n* veine *f*; (*on leaf*) nervure *f*; (*fig: mood*) esprit *m*.
vellum [vel'əm] *n* (*writing paper*) vélin *m*.
velocity [vəlâs'itē] *n* vitesse *f*, vélocité *f*.
velvet [vel'vit] *n* velours *m*.
vending machine [ven'ding məshēn'] *n* distributeur *m* automatique.
vendor [ven'dûr] *n* vendeur/euse; **street ~** marchand ambulant.
veneer [vənēr'] *n* placage *m* de bois; (*fig*) vernis *m*.
venerable [ven'ûrəbəl] *a* vénérable.
venereal [vənēr'ēəl] *a*: ~ **disease (VD)** maladie vénérienne.
Venetian [vənē'shən] *a*: ~ **blind** store vénitien.
Venezuela [venizwā'lə] *n* Venezuela *m*.
Venezuelan [venizwā'lən] *a* vénézuélien(ne) ♦ *n* Vénézuélien/ne.
vengeance [ven'jəns] *n* vengeance *f*; **with a ~** (*fig*) vraiment, pour de bon.
vengeful [venj'fəl] *a* vengeur(geresse).
Venice [ven'is] *n* Venise.
venison [ven'isən] *n* venaison *f*.
venom [ven'əm] *n* venin *m*.
venomous [ven'əməs] *a* venimeux(euse).
vent [vent] *n* conduit *m* d'aération; (*in dress, jacket*) fente *f* ♦ *vt* (*fig: one's feelings*) donner libre cours à.
ventilate [ven'təlāt] *vt* (*room*) ventiler, aérer.
ventilation [ventəlā'shən] *n* ventilation *f*, aéra-

tion *f*.
ventilation shaft *n* conduit *m* de ventilation *or* d'aération.
ventilator [ven'tǝlātûr] *n* ventilateur *m*.
ventriloquist [ventril'ǝkwist] *n* ventriloque *m/ f*.
venture [ven'chûr] *n* entreprise *f* ♦ *vt* risquer, hasarder ♦ *vi* s'aventurer, se risquer; **a business ~** une entreprise commerciale; **to ~ to do sth** se risquer à faire qch.
venture capital *n* capital-risques *m*.
venue [ven'yōō] *n* (*of conference etc*) lieu *m* de la réunion (*or* manifestation *etc*); (*of game*) lieu de la rencontre.
Venus [vē'nǝs] *n* (*planet*) Vénus *f*.
veracity [vǝras'itē] *n* véracité *f*.
veranda(h) [vǝrandǝ] *n* véranda *f*.
verb [vûrb] *n* verbe *m*.
verbal [vûr'bǝl] *a* verbal(e); (*translation*) littéral(e).
verbally [vûr'bǝlē] *ad* verbalement.
verbatim [vûrbā'tim] *a, ad* mot pour mot.
verbose [vûrbōs'] *a* verbeux(euse).
verdict [vûr'dikt] *n* verdict *m*; **~ of guilty/not guilty** verdict de culpabilité/de non-culpabilité.
verge [vûrj] *n* bord *m*; **on the ~ of doing** sur le point de faire.
  verge on *vt fus* approcher de.
verger [vûr'jûr] *n* (*REL*) bedeau *m*.
verification [värǝfǝkā'shǝn] *n* vérification *f*.
verify [vär'ǝfī] *vt* vérifier.
veritable [vär'itǝbǝl] *a* véritable.
vermin [vûr'min] *npl* animaux *mpl* nuisibles; (*insects*) vermine *f*.
vermouth [vûrmōōth'] *n* vermouth *m*.
vernacular [vûrnak'yǝlûr] *n* langue *f* vernaculaire, dialecte *m*.
versatile [vûr'sǝtǝl] *a* polyvalent(e).
verse [vûrs] *n* vers *mpl*; (*stanza*) strophe *f*; (*in bible*) verset *m*; **in ~** en vers.
versed [vûrst] *a*: (**well-)~ in** versé(e) dans.
version [vûr'zhǝn] *n* version *f*.
versus [vûr'sǝs] *prep* contre.
vertebra, *pl* **~e** [vûr'tǝbrǝ, -brē] *n* vertèbre *f*.
vertebrate [vûr'tǝbrāt] *n* vertébré *m*.
vertical [vûr'tikǝl] *a* vertical(e) ♦ *n* verticale *f*.
vertically [vûr'tiklē] *ad* verticalement.
vertigo [vûr'tǝgō] *n* vertige *m*; **to suffer from ~** avoir des vertiges.
verve [vûrv] *n* brio *m*; enthousiasme *m*.
very [vär'ē] *ad* très ♦ *a*: **the ~ book which** le livre même que; **the ~ thought (of it)** ... rien que d'y penser ...; **at the ~ end** tout à la fin; **the ~ last** le tout dernier; **at the ~ least** au moins; **~ well** très bien; **~ little** très peu; **~ much** beaucoup.
vespers [ves'pûrz] *npl* vêpres *fpl*.
vessel [ves'ǝl] *n* (*ANAT, NAUT*) vaisseau *m*; (*container*) récipient *m*.
vest [vest] *n* (*US*) gilet *m*; (*Brit*) tricot *m* de corps ♦ *vt*: **to ~ sb with sth, to ~ sth in sb** investir qn de qch.
vested interest [ves'tid in'trist] *n*: **to have a ~ in doing** avoir tout intérêt à faire; **~s** *npl* (*COMM*) droits acquis.
vestibule [ves'tǝbyōōl] *n* vestibule *m*.
vestige [ves'tij] *n* vestige *m*.
vestry [ves'trē] *n* sacristie *f*.

Vesuvius [vǝsōō'vēǝs] *n* Vésuve *m*.
vet [vet] *n abbr* (= *veterinary surgeon*) vétérinaire *m/f* ♦ *vt* examiner minutieusement; (*text*) revoir; (*candidate*) se renseigner soigneusement sur, soumettre à une enquête approfondie.
veteran [vet'ûrǝn] *n* vétéran *m*; (*also*: **war ~**) ancien combattant ♦ *a*: **she's a ~ campaigner for** ... cela fait très longtemps qu'elle lutte pour ....
veteran car *n* voiture *f* d'époque.
veterinarian [vetûrǝnär'ēǝn] *n* (*US*) vétérinaire *m/f*.
veterinary [vet'ûrǝnärē] *a* vétérinaire.
veterinary surgeon *n* (*Brit*) = **veterinarian**.
veto [vē'tō] *n* (*pl* **~es**) veto *m* ♦ *vt* opposer son veto à; **to put a ~ on** mettre (*or* opposer) son veto à.
vex [veks] *vt* fâcher, contrarier.
vexed [vekst] *a* (*question*) controversé(e).
VFD *n abbr* (*US*) = *voluntary fire department*.
VHF *abbr* (= *very high frequency*) VHF.
VI *abbr* (*US MAIL*) = *Virgin Islands*.
via [vī'ǝ] *prep* par, via.
viability [vīǝbil'ǝtē] *n* viabilité *f*.
viable [vī'ǝbǝl] *a* viable.
viaduct [vī'ǝdukt] *n* viaduc *m*.
vibrant [vī'brǝnt] *a* (*sound, color*) vibrant(e).
vibrate [vī'brāt] *vi*: **to ~ (with)** vibrer (de); (*resound*) retentir (de).
vibration [vībrā'shǝn] *n* vibration *f*.
vicar [vik'ûr] *n* pasteur *m* (*de l'Église anglicane*).
vicarage [vik'ûrij] *n* presbytère *m*.
vicarious [vīkär'ēǝs] *a* (*pleasure, experience*) indirect(e).
vice [vīs] *n* (*evil*) vice *m*; (*TECH*) étau *m*.
vice- *prefix* vice-.
vice-chairman [vīs'chär'mǝn] *n* vice-président/e.
vice-chancellor [vīs'chan'sǝlûr] *n* (*Brit*) ≈ président·e d'université.
vice-president [vīs'prez'idǝnt] *n* vice-président/e.
vice-principal [vīs'prin'sǝpǝl] *n* (*SCOL*) censeur *m*.
vice squad *n* ≈ brigade mondaine.
vice versa [vīs'vûr'sǝ] *ad* vice versa.
vicinity [visin'ǝtē] *n* environs *mpl*, alentours *mpl*.
vicious [vish'ǝs] *a* (*remark*) cruel(le), méchant(e); (*blow*) brutal(e); **a ~ circle** un cercle vicieux.
viciousness [vish'ǝsnis] *n* méchanceté *f*, cruauté *f*; brutalité *f*.
vicissitudes [visis'ǝtōōdz] *npl* vicissitudes *fpl*.
victim [vik'tim] *n* victime *f*; **to be the ~ of** être victime de.
victimization [viktimǝzā'shǝn] *n* brimades *fpl*; représailles *fpl*.
victimize [vik'tǝmīz] *vt* brimer; exercer des représailles sur.
victor [vik'tûr] *n* vainqueur *m*.
Victorian [viktôr'ēǝn] *a* victorien(ne).
victorious [viktôr'ēǝs] *a* victorieux(euse).
victory [vik'tûrē] *n* victoire *f*; **to win a ~ over sb** remporter une victoire sur qn.
video [vid'ēō] *n* (**~ film**) vidéo *f*; (*also*: **~ cassette**) vidéocassette *f*; (*also*: **~ cassette**

recorder) magnétoscope *m* ♦ *cpd* vidéo *inv*.
video cassette *n* vidéocassette *f*.
video cassette recorder (VCR) *n* magnétoscope *m*.
video recording *n* enregistrement *m* (en) vidéo.
video tape *n* bande *f* vidéo *inv*; (*cassette*) vidéocassette *f*.
video tape recorder (VTR) magnétoscope *m* (à bande).
videotex |vid'cōtcks| *n* télétexte *m*.
vie |vī| *vi*: **to ~ with** lutter avec, rivaliser avec.
Vienna |vēen'ə| *n* Vienne.
Vietnam, Viet Nam |vĕctnâm'| *n* Viet-Nam *or* Vietnam *m*.
Vietnamese |vĕctnâméz'| *a* vietnamien(ne) ♦ *n* (*pl inv*) Vietnamien/ne; (*LING*) vietnamien *m*.
view |vyōō| *n* vue *f*; (*opinion*) avis *m*, vue ♦ *vt* (*situation*) considérer; (*house*) visiter; **on ~** (*in museum etc*) exposé(e); **in full ~ of sb** sous les yeux de qn; **to be within ~ (of sth)** être à portée de vue (de qch); **an overall ~ of the situation** une vue d'ensemble de la situation; **in my ~** à mon avis; **in ~ of the fact that** étant donné que; **with a ~ to doing sth** dans l'intention de faire qch.
viewdata |vyōō'dātə| *n* (*Brit*) télétexte *m* (*version téléphonique*).
viewer |vyōō'ûr| *n* (*viewfinder*) viseur *m*; (*small projector*) visionneuse *f*; (*TV*) téléspectateur/trice.
viewfinder |vyōō'fîndûr| *n* viseur *m*.
viewpoint |vyōō'point| *n* point *m* de vue.
vigil |vij'əl| *n* veille *f*; **to keep ~** veiller.
vigilance |vij'ələns| *n* vigilance *f*.
vigilance committee *n* comité *m* d'autodéfense.
vigilant |vij'ələnt| *a* vigilant(e).
vigor |vig'ûr| *n* (*US*) vigueur *f*.
vigorous |vig'ûrəs| *a* vigoureux(euse).
vigour |vig'ûr| *n* (*Brit*) = **vigor**.
vile |vīl| *a* (*action*) vil(e); (*smell*) abominable; (*temper*) massacrant(e).
vilify |vil'əfī| *vt* calomnier, vilipender.
villa |vil'ə| *n* villa *f*.
village |vil'ij| *n* village *m*.
villager |vil'ijûr| *n* villageois/e.
villain |vil'in| *n* (*scoundrel*) scélérat *m*; (*criminal*) bandit *m*; (*in novel etc*) traître *m*.
VIN *n* *abbr* (*US*) = *vehicle identification number*.
vindicate |vin'dikāt| *vt* défendre avec succès; justifier.
vindication |vindikā'shən| *n*: **in ~ of** pour justifier.
vindictive |vindik'tiv| *a* vindicatif(ive), rancunier(ière).
vine |vīn| *n* vigne *f*; (*climbing plant*) plante grimpante.
vinegar |vin'əgûr| *n* vinaigre *m*.
vine grower *n* viticulteur *m*.
vine-growing |vīn'grōing| *a* viticole ♦ *n* viticulture *f*.
vineyard |vin'yûrd| *n* vignoble *m*.
vintage |vin'tij| *n* (*year*) année *f*, millésime *m*; **the 1970 ~** le millésime 1970.
vintage car *n* voiture ancienne.

vintage wine *n* vin *m* de grand cru.
vinyl |vī'nil| *n* vinyle *m*.
viola |vēō'lə| *n* alto *m*.
violate |vī'əlāt| *vt* violer.
violation |vīəlā'shən| *n* violation *f*; **in ~ of** (*rule, law*) en infraction à, en violation de.
violence |vī'ələns| *n* violence *f*; (*POL etc*) incidents violents.
violent |vī'ələnt| *a* violent(e); **a ~ dislike of sb/sth** une aversion profonde pour qn/qch.
violently |vī'ələntlē| *ad* violemment; (*ill, angry*) terriblement.
violet |vī'əlit| *a* (*color*) violet(te) ♦ *n* (*plant*) violette *f*.
violin |vīəlin'| *n* violon *m*.
violinist |vīəlin'ist| *n* violoniste *m/f*.
VIP *n* *abbr* (= *very important person*) VIP *m*.
viper |vī'pûr| *n* vipère *f*.
virgin |vûr'jin| *n* vierge *f* ♦ *a* vierge; **she is a ~** elle est vierge; **the Blessed V~** la Sainte Vierge.
virginity |vûrjin'ətē| *n* virginité *f*.
Virgo |vûr'gō| *n* la Vierge; **to be ~** être de la Vierge.
virile |vir'əl| *a* viril(e).
virility |vəril'ətē| *n* virilité *f*.
virtual |vûr'chōōəl| *a* (*COMPUT, PHYSICS*) virtuel(le); (*in effect*): **it's a ~ impossibility** c'est pratiquement impossible; **the ~ leader** le chef dans la pratique.
virtually |vûr'chōōəlē| *ad* (*almost*) pratiquement; **it is ~ impossible** c'est quasiment impossible.
virtue |vûr'chōō| *n* vertu *f*; (*advantage*) mérite *m*, avantage *m*; **by ~ of** par le fait de.
virtuoso |vûrchōō'sō| *n* virtuose *m/f*.
virtuous |vûr'chōōəs| *a* vertueux(euse).
virulent |vir'yələnt| *a* virulent(e).
virus |vī'rəs| *n* (*also COMPUT*) virus *m*.
visa |vē'zə| *n* visa *m*.
vis-à-vis |vēzâvē'| *prep* vis-à-vis de.
viscount |vī'kount| *n* vicomte *m*.
viscous |vis'kəs| *a* visqueux(euse), gluant(e).
vise |vīs| *n* (*US TECH*) étau *m*.
visibility |vizəbil'ətē| *n* visibilité *f*.
visible |viz'əbəl| *a* visible; **~ exports/imports** exportations/importations *fpl* visibles.
visibly |viz'əblē| *ad* visiblement.
vision |vizh'ən| *n* (*sight*) vue *f*, vision *f*; (*foresight, in dream*) vision.
visionary |vizh'ənärē| *n* visionnaire *m/f*.
visit |viz'it| *n* visite *f*; (*stay*) séjour *m* ♦ *vt* (*person*) rendre visite à; (*place*) visiter; **on a private/official ~** en visite privée/officielle.
visiting |viz'iting| *a* (*speaker, team*) invité(e), de l'extérieur.
visiting card *n* carte *f* de visite.
visiting hours *npl* heures *fpl* de visite.
visiting professor *n* ≈ professeur associé.
visitor |viz'itûr| *n* visiteur/euse; (*in hotel*) client/e.
visitors' book *n* livre *m* d'or; (*in hotel*) registre *m*.
visor |vī'zûr| *n* visière *f*.
VISTA |vis'tə| *n* *abbr* (= *Volunteers in Service to America*) programme d'assistance bénévole aux régions pauvres.
vista |vis'tə| *n* vue *f*, perspective *f*.
visual |vizh'ōōəl| *a* visuel(le).

visual aid n support visuel (pour l'enseignement).

visual display unit (VDU) n console f de visualisation, visuel m.

visualize [vizh'ōōəlīz] vt se représenter; (foresee) prévoir.

visually [vizh'ōōəlē] ad visuellement; ~ **handicapped** handicapé(e) visuel(le).

vital [vīt'əl] a vital(e); **of** ~ **importance (to sb/sth)** d'une importance capitale (pour qn/ qch).

vitality [vītal'itē] n vitalité f.

vitally [vī'təlē] ad extrêmement.

vital statistics npl (of population) statistiques fpl démographiques; (col: woman's) mensurations fpl.

vitamin [vī'təmin] n vitamine f.

vitiate [vish'ēāt] vt vicier.

vitreous [vit'rēəs] a (china) vitreux(euse); (enamel) vitrifié(e).

vitriolic [vitrēal'ik] a (fig) venimeux(euse).

viva [vē'və] n (also: ~ **voce**) (examen) oral.

vivacious [vivā'shəs] a animé(e), qui a de la vivacité.

vivacity [vivas'itē] n vivacité f.

vivid [viv'id] a (account) frappant(e); (light, imagination) vif(vive).

vividly [viv'idlē] ad (describe) d'une manière vivante; (remember) de façon précise.

vivisection [vivisek'shən] n vivisection f.

vixen [vik'sən] n renarde f; (pej: woman) mégère f.

viz abbr (= videlicet: namely) à savoir, c. à d.

VLF abbr = very low frequency.

V-neck [vē'nek] n décolleté m en V.

VOA n abbr = Voice of America) voix f de l'Amérique (émissions de radio à destination de l'étranger).

vocabulary [vōkab'yəlārē] n vocabulaire n.

vocal [vō'kəl] a vocal(e); (articulate) qui n'hésite pas à s'exprimer, qui sait faire entendre ses opinions; ~**s** npl voix fpl.

vocal cords npl cordes vocales.

vocalist [vō'kəlist] n chanteur/euse.

vocation [vōkā'shən] n vocation f.

vocational [vōkā'shənəl] a professionnel(le); ~ **guidance/training** orientation/formation professionnelle; ~ **guidance counselor** (US) conseiller/ère d'orientation (professionnelle).

vociferous [vōsif'ûrəs] a bruyant(e).

vodka [vâd'kə] n vodka f.

vogue [vōg] n mode f; (popularity) vogue f; **to be in** ~ être en vogue or à la mode.

voice [vois] n voix f; (opinion) avis m ♦ vt (opinion) exprimer, formuler; **in a loud/soft** ~ à voix haute/basse; **to give** ~ **to** exprimer.

void [void] n vide m ♦ a (invalid) nul(le); (empty): ~ **of** vide de, dépourvu(e) de.

voile [voil] n voile m (tissu).

vol. abbr (= volume) vol.

volatile [vâl'ətəl] a volatil(e); (fig) versatile.

volcanic [vâlkan'ik] a volcanique.

volcano, ~**es** [vâlkā'nō] n volcan m.

volition [vōlish'ən] n: **of one's own** ~ de son propre gré.

volley [vâl'ē] n (of gunfire) salve f; (of stones etc) pluie f, volée f; (TENNIS etc) volée f.

volleyball [vâl'ēbôl] n volley(-ball) m.

volt [vōlt] n volt m.

voltage [vōl'tij] n tension f, voltage m; **high/ low** ~ haute/basse tension.

voluble [vâl'yəbəl] a volubile.

volume [vâl'yōōm] n volume m; (of tank) capacité f; ~ **one/two** (of book) tome un/deux; **his expression spoke** ~**s** son expression en disait long.

volume control n (RADIO, TV) bouton m de réglage du volume.

volume discount n (COMM) remise f sur la quantité.

voluminous [vəlōō'minəs] a volumineux(euse).

voluntarily [vâləntär'ilē] ad volontairement; bénévolement.

voluntary [vâl'əntärē] a volontaire; (unpaid) bénévole.

voluntary liquidation n (COMM) dépôt m de bilan.

voluntary redundancy n (Brit) départ m volontaire (en cas de licenciements).

volunteer [vâləntēr'] n volontaire m/f ♦ vi (MIL) s'engager comme volontaire; **to** ~ **to do** se proposer pour faire.

voluptuous [vəlup'chōōəs] a voluptueux(euse).

vomit [vâm'it] n vomissure f ♦ vt, vi vomir.

vote [vōt] n vote m, suffrage m; (cast) voix f, vote; (franchise) droit m de vote ♦ vt (bill) voter; (chairman) élire ♦ vi voter; **to put sth to the** ~, **to take a** ~ **on sth** mettre qch aux voix, procéder à un vote sur qch; ~ **for or in favor of/against** vote pour/contre; **to** ~ **to do sth** voter en faveur de faire qch; ~ **of censure** motion f de censure; ~ **of thanks** discours m de remerciement.

voter [vō'tûr] n électeur/trice.

voting [vō'ting] n scrutin m.

voting right n droit m de vote.

vouch [vouch]: **to** ~ **for** vt fus se porter garant de.

voucher [vou'chûr] n (for meal, gasoline) bon m; (receipt) reçu m; **travel** ~ bon m de transport.

vow [vou] n vœu m, serment m ♦ vi jurer; **to take or make a** ~ **to do sth** faire le vœu de faire qch.

vowel [vou'əl] n voyelle f.

voyage [voi'ij] n voyage m par mer, traversée f.

VP n abbr = **vice-president**.

vs abbr (= versus) c.

VSO n abbr (Brit: = Voluntary Service Overseas) ≈ coopération civile.

VT abbr (US MAIL) = Vermont.

VTR n abbr = **video tape recorder**.

vulgar [vul'gûr] a vulgaire.

vulgarity [vulgar'itē] n vulgarité f.

vulnerability [vulnûrəbil'ətē] n vulnérabilité f.

vulnerable [vul'nûrəbəl] a vulnérable.

vulture [vul'chûr] n vautour m.

W

W, w [dub'əlyōō] *n* (*letter*) W, w *m*; **W for William** W comme William.

W [dub'əlyōō] *abbr* (= *west*) O; (*ELEC*: = *watt*) W.

WA *abbr* (*US MAIL*) = *Washington*.

wad [wâd] *n* (*of absorbent cotton, paper*) tampon *m*; (*of banknotes etc*) liasse *f*.

wadding [wâd'ing] *n* rembourrage *m*.

waddle [wâd'əl] *vi* se dandiner.

wade [wād] *vi*: **to ~ through** marcher dans, patauger dans ♦ *vt* passer à gué.

wading pool [wād'ing pōōl] *n* (*US*) petit bassin.

wafer [wā'fûr] *n* (*CULIN*) gaufrette *f*; (*REL*) pain *m* d'hostie; (*COMPUT*) tranche *f* (de silicium).

wafer-thin [wā'fûrthin'] *a* ultra-mince, mince comme du papier à cigarette.

waffle [wâf'əl] *n* (*CULIN*) gaufre *f*; (*col*) rabâchage *m*; remplissage *m* ♦ *vi* parler pour ne rien dire; faire du remplissage.

waffle iron *n* gaufrier *m*.

waft [waft] *vt* porter ♦ *vi* flotter.

wag [wag] *vt* agiter, remuer ♦ *vi* remuer; **the dog ~ged its tail** le chien a remué la queue.

wage [wāj] *n* (*also*: **~s**) salaire *m*, paye *f* ♦ *vt*: **to ~ war** faire la guerre; **a day's ~s** un jour de salaire.

wage claim *n* demande *f* d'augmentation de salaire.

wage differential *n* éventail *m* des salaires.

wage earner *n* salarié/e; (*breadwinner*) soutien *m* de famille.

wage freeze *n* blocage *m* des salaires.

wage packet *n* (*Brit*) (enveloppe *f* de) paye *f*.

wager [wā'jûr] *n* pari *m* ♦ *vt* parier.

waggle [wag'əl] *vt, vi* remuer.

wagon, (*Brit*) **waggon** [wag'ən] *n* (*horse-drawn*) chariot *m*; (*Brit RAIL*) wagon *m* (de marchandises).

wail [wāl] *n* gémissement *m*; (*of siren*) hurlement *m* ♦ *vi* gémir; hurler.

waist [wāst] *n* taille *f*, ceinture *f*.

waistcoat [wāst'kōt] *n* (*Brit*) gilet *m*.

waistline [wāst'līn] *n* (tour *m* de) taille *f*.

wait [wāt] *n* attente *f* ♦ *vi* attendre; **to ~ for sb/sth** attendre qn/qch; **to keep sb ~ing** faire attendre qn; **~ a minute!** un instant!; "**repairs while you ~**" "réparations minute"; **I can't ~ to ...** (*fig*) je meurs d'envie de ...; **to lie in ~ for** guetter.

wait behind *vi* rester (à attendre).

wait on *vt fus* servir.

wait up *vi* attendre, ne pas se coucher; **don't ~ up for me** ne m'attendez pas pour aller vous coucher.

waiter [wā'tûr] *n* garçon *m* (de café), serveur *m*.

waiting list [wāt'ing list] *n* liste *f* d'attente.

waiting room *n* salle *f* d'attente.

waitress [wā'tris] *n* serveuse *f*.

waive [wāv] *vt* renoncer à, abandonner.

waiver [wā'vûr] *n* dispense *f*.

wake [wāk] *vb* (*pt* **woke, ~d**, *pp* **woken, ~d** [wōk, wō'kən]) *vt* (*also*: **~ up**) réveiller ♦ *vi* (*also*: **~ up**) se réveiller ♦ *n* (*for dead person*) veillée *f* mortuaire; (*NAUT*) sillage *m*; **to ~ up to sth** (*fig*) se rendre compte de qch; **in the ~ of** (*fig*) à la suite de; **to follow in sb's ~** (*fig*) marcher sur les traces de qn.

waken [wā'kən] *vt, vi* = **wake**.

Wales [wālz] *n* pays *m* de Galles.

walk [wôk] *n* promenade *f*; (*short*) petit tour; (*gait*) démarche *f*; (*pace*): **at a quick ~** d'un pas rapide; (*path*) chemin *m*; (*in park etc*) allée *f* ♦ *vi* marcher; (*for pleasure, exercise*) se promener ♦ *vt* (*distance*) faire à pied; (*dog*) promener; **10 minutes' ~ from** à 10 minutes de marche de; **to go for a ~** se promener; faire un tour; **I'll ~ you home** je vais vous raccompagner chez vous; **from all ~s of life** de toutes conditions sociales.

walk out *vi* (*go out*) sortir; (*as protest*) partir (en signe de protestation); (*strike*) se mettre en grève; **to ~ out on sb** quitter qn.

walker [wôk'ûr] *n* (*person*) marcheur/euse.

walkie-talkie [wô'kētô'kē] *n* talkie-walkie *m*.

walking [wô'king] *n* marche *f* à pied; **it's within ~ distance** on peut y aller à pied.

walking shoes *npl* chaussures *fpl* de marche.

walking stick *n* canne *f*.

walk-on [wôk'ân] *a* (*THEATER*: *part*) de figurant/e.

walkout [wôk'out] *n* (*of workers*) grève-surprise *f*.

walkover [wôk'ōvûr] *n* (*col*) victoire *f or* examen *m etc* facile.

walkway [wôk'wā] *n* promenade *f*, cheminement piéton.

wall [wôl] *n* mur *m*; (*of tunnel, cave*) paroi *f*; **to go to the ~** (*fig*: *firm etc*) faire faillite.

wall in *vt* (*garden etc*) entourer d'un mur.

wall cupboard *n* placard mural.

walled [wôld] *a* (*city*) fortifié(e).

wallet [wâl'it] *n* portefeuille *m*.

wallflower [wôl'flouûr] *n* giroflée *f*; **to be a ~** (*fig*) faire tapisserie.

wall hanging *n* tenture (murale), tapisserie *f*.

wallop [wâl'əp] *vt* (*col*) taper sur, cogner.

wallow [wâl'ō] *vi* se vautrer; **to ~ in one's grief** se complaire à sa douleur.

wallpaper [wôl'pāpûr] *n* papier peint.

wall-to-wall [wôl'təwôl'] *a*: **~ carpeting** moquette *f*.

wally [wâ'lē] *n* (*Brit col*) imbécile *m/f*.

walnut [wôl'nut] *n* noix *f*; (*tree*) noyer *m*.

walrus, *pl* **~** *or* **~es** [wôl'rəs] *n* morse *m*.

waltz [wôlts] *n* valse *f* ♦ *vi* valser.

wan [wán] *a* pâle; triste.

wand [wând] *n* (*also*: **magic ~**) baguette *f* (magique).

wander [wán'dûr] *vi* (*person*) errer, aller sans but; (*thoughts*) vagabonder; (*river*) serpenter ♦ *vt* errer dans.

wanderer [wán'dûrûr] *n* vagabond/e.

wandering [wán'dûring] *a* (*tribe*) nomade;

(*minstrel, actor*) ambulant(e).

wane [wān] *vi* (*moon*) décroître; (*reputation*) décliner.

wangle [wang'gəl] (*col*) *vt* se débrouiller pour avoir; carotter ♦ *n* combine *f*, magouille *f*.

want [wônt] *vt* vouloir; (*need*) avoir besoin de; (*lack*) manquer de ♦ *n* (*poverty*) pauvreté *f*, besoin *m*; **~s** *npl* (*needs*) besoins *mpl*; **for ~ of** par manque de, faute de; **to ~ to do** vouloir faire; **to ~ sb to do** vouloir que qn fasse; **you're ~ed on the phone** on vous demande au téléphone; **"cook ~ed"** "on demande un cuisinier".

want ads *npl* (*US*) petites annonces.

wanting [wôn'ting] *a*: **to be ~ (in)** manquer (de); **to be found ~** ne pas être à la hauteur.

wanton [wân'tən] *a* capricieux(euse); dévergondé(e).

war [wôr] *n* guerre *f*; **to go to ~** se mettre en guerre.

warble [wôr'bəl] *n* (*of bird*) gazouillis *m* ♦ *vi* gazouiller.

war cry *n* cri *m* de guerre.

ward [wôrd] *n* (*in hospital*) salle *f*; (*LAW: child*) pupille *m/f*.

ward off *vt* parer, éviter.

warden [wôr'dən] *n* (*US: of prison*) directeur/trice; (*of park, game reserve*) gardien/ne; (*Brit: of institution*) directeur/trice; (*also:* **traffic ~**) contractuel/le.

warder [wôr'dûr] *n* (*Brit*) gardien *m* de prison.

wardrobe [wôrd'rōb] *n* (*closet*) armoire *f*; (*clothes*) garde-robe *f*; (*THEATER*) costumes *mpl*.

warehouse [wär'hous] *n* entrepôt *m*.

wares [wärz] *npl* marchandises *fpl*.

warfare [wôr'fär] *n* guerre *f*.

war game *n* jeu *m* de stratégie militaire.

warhead [wôr'hed] *n* (*MIL*) ogive *f*.

warily [wär'ilē] *ad* avec prudence, avec précaution.

warlike [wôr'līk] *a* guerrier(ière).

warm [wôrm] *a* chaud(e); (*person, greeting, welcome, applause*) chaleureux(euse); (*supporter*) ardent(e), enthousiaste; **it's ~** il fait chaud; **I'm ~** j'ai chaud; **to keep sth ~** tenir qch au chaud; **with my ~est thanks/ congratulations** avec mes remerciements/ mes félicitations les plus sincères.

warm up *vi* (*person, room*) se réchauffer; (*water*) chauffer; (*athlete, discussion*) s'échauffer ♦ *vt* réchauffer; chauffer; (*engine*) faire chauffer.

warm-blooded [wôrm'blud'id] *a* (*ZOOL*) à sang chaud.

war memorial *n* monument *m* aux morts.

warm-hearted [wôrm'hâr'tid] *a* affectueux(euse).

warmly [wôrm'lē] *ad* chaudement; chaleureusement.

warmonger [wôr'munggûr] *n* belliciste *m/f*.

warmongering [wôr'munggûring] *n* propagande *f* belliciste, bellicisme *m*.

warmth [wôrmth] *n* chaleur *f*.

warm-up [wôrm'up] *n* (*SPORT*) période *f* d'échauffement.

warn [wôrn] *vt* avertir, prévenir; **to ~ sb not to do sth** *or* **against doing sth** prévenir qn de ne pas faire qch.

warning [wôr'ning] *n* avertissement *m*; (*notice*) avis *m*; **without (any) ~** (*suddenly*) inopinément; (*without notifying*) sans prévenir; **gale ~** (*METEOROLOGY*) avis de grand vent.

warning light *n* avertisseur lumineux.

warning triangle *n* (*AUT*) triangle *m* de présignalisation.

warp [wôrp] *n* (*TEXTILES*) chaîne *f* ♦ *vi* (*wood*) travailler, se voiler *or* gauchir ♦ *vt* voiler; (*fig*) pervertir.

warped [wôrpt] *a* (*wood*) gauchi(e); (*fig*) perverti(e).

warrant [wôr'ənt] *n* (*guarantee*) garantie *f*; (*LAW: to arrest*) mandat *m* d'arrêt; (*: to search*) mandat de perquisition ♦ *vt* (*justify, merit*) justifier.

warrant officer *n* (*MIL*) adjudant *m*; (*NAUT*) premier-maître *m*.

warranty [wôr'əntē] *n* garantie *f*; **under ~** (*COMM*) sous garantie.

warren [wôr'ən] *n* (*of rabbits*) terriers *mpl*, garenne *f*.

warring [wô'ring] *a* (*nations*) en guerre; (*interests etc*) contradictoire, opposé(e).

warrior [wôr'ēûr] *n* guerrier/ière.

Warsaw [wôr'sô] *n* Varsovie.

warship [wôr'ship] *n* navire *m* de guerre.

wart [wôrt] *n* verrue *f*.

wartime [wôr'tīm] *n*: **in ~** en temps de guerre.

wary [wär'ē] *a* prudent(e); **to be ~ about** *or* **of doing sth** hésiter beaucoup à faire qch.

was [wuz] *pt of* **be**.

wash [wâsh] *vt* laver; (*sweep, carry: sea etc*) emporter, entraîner; (*: ashore*) rejeter ♦ *vi* se laver ♦ *n* (*paint*) badigeon *m*; (*washing program*) lavage *m*; (*of ship*) sillage *m*; **to give sth a ~** laver qch; **to have a ~** se laver, faire sa toilette; **he was ~ed overboard** il a été emporté par une vague.

wash away *vt* (*stain*) enlever au lavage; (*subj: river etc*) emporter.

wash down *vt* laver; laver à grande eau.

wash off *vi* partir au lavage.

wash up *vi* faire la vaisselle; (*US: have a wash*) se débarbouiller.

Wash. *abbr* (*US*) = *Washington*.

washable [wâsh'əbəl] *a* lavable.

washbag [wâsh'bag] *n* trousse *f* de toilette.

washbasin [wâsh'bāsin] *n* lavabo *m*.

washcloth [wâsh'klôth] *n* (*US*) gant *m* de toilette.

washer [wâsh'ûr] *n* (*TECH*) rondelle *f*, joint *m*.

washing [wâsh'ing] *n* (*Brit: linen etc*) lessive *f*.

washing line *n* (*Brit*) corde *f* à linge.

washing machine *n* machine *f* à laver.

washing powder *n* (*Brit*) lessive *f* (en poudre).

Washington [wâsh'ingtən] *n* (*city, state*) Washington *m*.

washing-up [wâsh'ingup'] *n* (*Brit*) vaisselle *f*.

washing-up liquid *n* (*Brit*) produit *m* pour la vaisselle.

wash-out [wâsh'out] *n* (*col*) désastre *m*.

washroom [wâsh'rōŏm] *n* toilettes *fpl*.
wasn't [wuz'ənt] = **was not**.
Wasp, WASP [wâsp] *n abbr* (*US col*: = *White Anglo-Saxon Protestant*) surnom, souvent péjoratif, donné à l'américain de souche anglosaxonne, aisé et de tendance conservatrice.
wasp [wâsp] *n* guêpe *f*.
waspish [wâs'pish] *a* irritable.
wastage [wās'tij] *n* gaspillage *m*; (*in manufacturing, transport etc*) déchet *m*.
waste [wāst] *n* gaspillage *m*; (*of time*) perte *f*; (*garbage*) déchets *mpl*; (*also*: **household** ∼) ordures *fpl* ♦ *a* (*material*) de rebut; (*energy, heat*) perdu(e); (*food*) inutilisé(e); (*land, ground: in city*) à l'abandon; (: *in country*) inculte, en friche ♦ *vt* gaspiller; (*time, opportunity*) perdre; ∼**s** *npl* étendue *f* désertique; **it's a** ∼ **of money** c'est de l'argent jeté en l'air; **to go to** ∼ être gaspillé(e); **to lay** ∼ (*destroy*) dévaster.
waste away *vi* dépérir.
wastebin [wāst'bin] *n* (*Brit*) corbeille *f* à papier; (*in kitchen*) boîte *f* à ordures.
wasteful [wāst'fəl] *a* gaspilleur(euse); (*process*) peu économique.
waste ground *n* (*Brit*) terrain *m* vague.
wasteland [wāst'land] *n* terres *fpl* à l'abandon; (*in town*) terrain(s) *m(pl)* vague(s).
wastepaper basket [wāst'pāpûr bas'kit] *n* corbeille *f* à papier.
waste products *n* (*INDUSTRY*) déchets *mpl* (de fabrication).
watch [wâch] *n* montre *f*; (*act of watching*) surveillance *f*; guet *m*; (*guard*: *MIL*) sentinelle *f*; (: *NAUT*) homme *m* de quart; (*NAUT: spell of duty*) quart *m* ♦ *vt* (*look at*) observer; (: *match, program*) regarder; (*spy on, guard*) surveiller; (*be careful of*) faire attention à ♦ *vi* regarder; (*keep guard*) monter la garde; **to keep a close** ∼ **on sb/sth** surveiller qn/qch de près; ∼ **what you're doing** fais attention à ce que tu fais.
watch out *vi* faire attention.
watchband [wâch'band] *n* (*US*) bracelet *m* de montre.
watchdog [wâch'dôg] *n* chien *m* de garde; (*fig*) gardien/ne.
watchful [wâch'fəl] *a* attentif(ive), vigilant(e).
watchmaker [wâch'mākûr] *n* horloger/ère.
watchman [wâch'mən] *n* gardien *m*; (*also*: **night** ∼) veilleur *m* de nuit.
watch stem *n* (*US*) remontoir *m*.
watch strap *n* bracelet *m* de montre.
watchword [wâch'wûrd] *n* mot *m* de passe.
water [wô'tûr] *n* eau *f* ♦ *vt* (*plant*) arroser ♦ *vi* (*eyes*) larmoyer; **a drink of** ∼ un verre d'eau; **in British** ∼**s** dans les eaux territoriales Britanniques; **to pass** ∼ uriner; **to make sb's mouth** ∼ mettre l'eau à la bouche de qn.
water down *vt* (*milk*) couper d'eau; (*fig: story*) édulcorer.
water closet *n* (*Brit*) w.-c. *mpl*, waters *mpl*.
watercolor, (*Brit*) **watercolour** [wô'tûrkulûr] *n* aquarelle *f*; ∼**s** *npl* couleurs *fpl* pour aquarelle.
water-cooled [wô'tûrkōōld] *a* à refroidissement par eau.

watercress [wô'tûrkres] *n* cresson *m* (de fontaine).
waterfall [wô'tûrfôl] *n* chute *f* d'eau.
waterfront [wô'tûrfrunt] *n* (*seafront*) front *m* de mer; (*at docks*) quais *mpl*.
water heater *n* chauffe-eau *m*.
water hole *n* mare *f*.
watering can [wô'tûring kan] *n* arrosoir *m*.
water level *n* niveau *m* de l'eau; (*of flood*) niveau des eaux.
water lily *n* nénuphar *m*.
waterline [wô'tûrlīn] *n* (*NAUT*) ligne *f* de flottaison.
waterlogged [wô'tûrlôgd] *a* détrempé(e); imbibé(e) d'eau.
water main *n* canalisation *f* d'eau.
watermark [wô'tûrmârk] *n* (*on paper*) filigrane *m*.
watermelon [wô'tûrmelən] *n* pastèque *f*.
water polo *n* water-polo *m*.
waterproof [wô'tûrprōōf] *a* imperméable.
water-repellent [wô'təripel'ənt] *a* hydrofuge.
watershed [wô'tûrshed] *n* (*GEO*) ligne *f* de partage des eaux; (*fig*) moment *m* critique, point décisif.
water-skiing [wô'tûrskēing] *n* ski *m* nautique.
water softener *n* adoucisseur *m* d'eau.
water tank *n* réservoir *m* d'eau.
watertight [wô'tûrtīt] *a* étanche.
water vapor *n* vapeur *f* d'eau.
waterway [wô'tûrwā] *n* cours *m* d'eau navigable.
waterworks [wô'tûrwûrks] *npl* station *f* hydraulique.
watery [wô'tûrē] *a* (*color*) délavé(e); (*coffee*) trop faible.
WATS *abbr* (*US*: = *Wide Area Telecommunications Service*) service téléphonique longue distance à tarif forfaitaire.
watt [wât] *n* watt *m*.
wattage [wât'ij] *n* puissance *f* or consommation *f* en watts.
wattle [wât'əl] *n* clayonnage *m*.
wave [wāv] *n* vague *f*; (*of hand*) geste *m*, signe *m*; (*RADIO*) onde *f*; (*in hair*) ondulation *f*; (*fig: of enthusiasm, strikes etc*) vague *f* ♦ *vi* faire signe de la main; (*flag*) flotter au vent ♦ *vt* (*handkerchief*) agiter; (*stick*) brandir; (*hair*) onduler; **to** ∼ **goodbye to sb** dire au revoir de la main à qn; **short/medium** ∼ (*RADIO*) ondes courtes/moyennes; **long** ∼ (*RADIO*) grandes ondes; **the new** ∼ (*CINEMA, MUS*) la nouvelle vague.
wave aside, **wave away** *vt* (*person*): **to** ∼ **sb aside** faire signe à qn de s'écarter; (*fig: suggestion, objection*) rejeter, repousser; (: *doubts*) chasser.
waveband [wāv'band] *n* bande *f* de fréquences.
wavelength [wāv'lengkth] *n* longueur *f* d'ondes.
waver [wā'vûr] *vi* vaciller; (*voice*) trembler; (*person*) hésiter.
wavy [wā'vē] *a* ondulé(e); onduleux(euse).
wax [waks] *n* cire *f*; (*for skis*) fart *m* ♦ *vt* cirer; (*car*) lustrer ♦ *vi* (*moon*) croître.
waxen [wak'sən] *a* cireux(euse).
wax paper *n* papier sulfurisé.
waxworks [waks'wûrks] *npl* personnages *mpl*

de cire; musée *m* de cire.

way [wā] *n* chemin *m*, voie *f*; (*path, access*) passage *m*; (*distance*) distance *f*; (*direction*) chemin, direction *f*; (*manner*) façon *f*, manière *f*; (*habit*) habitude *f*, façon; (*condition*) état *m*; **which ~?** — **this ~** par où *or* de quel côté? — par ici; **to crawl one's ~ to ...** ramper jusqu'à ...; **to lie one's ~ out of it** s'en sortir par un mensonge; **to lose one's ~** perdre son chemin; **on the ~** (to) en route (pour); **to be on one's ~** être en route; **be in the ~** bloquer le passage; (*fig*) gêner; **to keep out of sb's ~** éviter qn; **it's a long ~ away** c'est loin d'ici; **the village is rather out of the ~** le village est plutôt à l'écart *or* isolé; **to go out of one's ~ to do** (*fig*) se donner beaucoup de mal pour faire; **to be under ~** (*work, project*) être en cours; **to make ~ (for sb/sth)** faire place (à qn/qch), s'écarter pour laisser passer (qn/qch); **to get one's own ~** arriver à ses fins; **put it the right ~ up** (*Brit*) mettez-le dans le bon sens; **to be the wrong ~ around** être à l'envers, ne pas être dans le bon sens; **he's in a bad ~** il va mal; **in a ~** d'un côté; **in some ~s** à certains égards; d'un côté; **in the ~ of** en fait de, comme; **by ~ of** (*through*) en passant par, via; (*as a sort of*) en guise de; **~ in** entrée *f*; **~ out** sortie *f*; **the ~ back** le chemin du retour; **this ~ and that** par-ci par-là; **"give ~"** (*Brit AUT*) "cédez la priorité"; **no ~!** (*col*) pas question!

waybill [wā'bil] *n* (*COMM*) récépissé *m*.

waylay [wālā'] *vt irg* attaquer; (*fig*): **I got waylaid** quelqu'un m'a accroché.

wayside [wā'sid] *n* bord *m* de la route; **to fall by the ~** (*fig*) abandonner; (*morally*) quitter le droit chemin.

way station *n* (*US: RAIL*) petite gare; (: *fig*) étape *f*.

wayward [wā'wûrd] *a* capricieux(euse), entêté(e).

WC *n abbr* (*Brit*: = *water closet*) w.-c. *mpl*, waters *mpl*.

WCC *n abbr* (= *World Council of Churches*) COE *m* (= *Conseil œcuménique des Églises*).

we [wē] *pl pronoun* nous.

weak [wēk] *a* faible; (*health*) fragile; (*beam etc*) peu solide; (*tea, coffee*) léger(ère); **to grow ~(er)** s'affaiblir, faiblir.

weaken [wē'kən] *vi* faiblir ♦ *vt* affaiblir.

weak-kneed [wēk'nēd] *a* (*fig*) lâche, faible.

weakling [wēk'ling] *n* gringalet *m*; faible *m/f*.

weakly [wēk'lē] *a* chétif(ive) ♦ *ad* faiblement.

weakness [wēk'nis] *n* faiblesse *f*; (*fault*) point *m* faible.

wealth [wclth] *n* (*money, resources*) richesse(s) *f(pl)*; (*of details*) profusion *f*.

wealth tax *n* impôt *m* sur la fortune.

wealthy [wcl'thē] *a* riche.

wean [wēn] *vt* sevrer.

weapon [wep'ən] *n* arme *f*.

wear [wär] *n* (*use*) usage *m*; (*deterioration through use*) usure *f*; (*clothing*): **sports/baby~** vêtements *mpl* de sport/pour bébés; **evening ~** tenue *f* de soirée ♦ *vb* (*pt* **wore**, *pp* **worn** [wôr, wôrn]) *vt* (*clothes*) porter; (*beard etc*) avoir; (*damage: through use*) user ♦ *vi* (*last*) faire de l'usage; (*rub etc*

through) s'user; **~ and tear** usure *f*; **to ~ a hole in sth** faire (à la longue) un trou dans qch.

wear away *vt* user, ronger ♦ *vi* s'user, être rongé(e).

wear down *vt* user; (*strength*) épuiser.

wear off *vi* disparaître.

wear on *vi* se poursuivre; passer.

wear out *vt* user; (*person, strength*) épuiser.

wearable [wär'əbəl] *a* mettable.

wearily [wē'rilē] *ad* avec lassitude.

weariness [wē'rēnis] *n* épuisement *m*, lassitude *f*.

wearisome [wē'rēsəm] *a* (*tiring*) fatigant(e); (*boring*) ennuyeux(euse).

wear resistant *a* (*US*) solide.

weary [wēr'ē] *a* (*tired*) épuisé(e); (*dispirited*) las(lasse); abattu(e) ♦ *vt* lasser ♦ *vi*: **to ~ of** se lasser de.

weasel [wē'zəl] *n* (*ZOOL*) belette *f*.

weather [weth'ûr] *n* temps *m* ♦ *vt* (*wood*) faire mûrir; (*tempest, crisis*) essuyer, être pris(e) dans; survivre à, tenir le coup durant; **what's the ~ like?** quel temps fait-il?; **under the ~** (*fig: ill*) mal fichu(e).

weather-beaten [weth'ûrbētən] *a* (*person*) hâlé(e); (*building*) dégradé(e) par les intempéries.

weather cock *n* girouette *f*.

weather forecast *n* prévisions *fpl* météorologiques, météo *f*.

weatherman [weth'ûrman] *n* météorologue *m*.

weatherproof [weth'ûrprōōf] *a* (*garment*) imperméable; (*building*) étanche.

weather report *n* bulletin *m* météo, météo *f*.

weather strip(ping) [weth'ûr strip('ing)] *n* bourrelet *m*.

weather vane *n* = **weather cock**.

weave [wēv] *vt* **wove**, *pp* **woven** [wēv, wōv, wō'vən] *vt* (*cloth*) tisser; (*basket*) tresser ♦ *vi* (*fig: pt, pp ~d: move in and out*) se faufiler.

weaver [wē'vûr] *n* tisserand/e.

weaving [wē'ving] *n* tissage *m*.

web [web] *n* (*of spider*) toile *f*; (*on foot*) palmure *f*; (*fabric, also fig*) tissu *m*.

webbed [webd] *a* (*foot*) palmé(e).

webbing [web'ing] *n* (*on chair*) sangles *fpl*.

wed [wed] *vt* (*pt, pp* **wedded**) épouser ♦ *n*: **the newly-~s** les jeunes mariés.

Wed. *abbr* (= *Wednesday*) me.

we'd [wēd] = **we had, we would**.

wedded [wed'id] *pt, pp of* **wed**.

wedding [wed'ing] *n* mariage *m*.

wedding anniversary *n* anniversaire *m* de mariage; **silver/golden ~** noces *fpl* d'argent/d'or.

wedding day *n* jour *m* du mariage.

wedding dress *n* robe *f* de mariage.

wedding present *n* cadeau *m* de mariage.

wedding ring *n* alliance *f*.

wedge [wej] *n* (*of wood etc*) coin *m*; (*under door etc*) cale *f*; (*of cake*) part *f* ♦ *vt* (*fix*) caler; (*push*) enfoncer, coincer.

wedge-heeled shoes [wej'hēld shōōz'] *npl* chaussures *fpl* à semelles compensées.

wedlock [wed'lâk] *n* (*union f du*) mariage *m*.

Wednesday [wenz'dā] *n* mercredi *m*; *for*

phrases see also **Tuesday**.

wee [wē] *a* (*Scottish*) petit(e); tout(e) petit(e).

weed [wēd] *n* mauvaise herbe ♦ *vt* désherber.

weedkiller [wēd'kilûr] *n* désherbant *m*.

weedy [wē'dē] *a* (*man*) gringalet.

week [wēk] *n* semaine *f*; **once/twice a ~** une fois/deux fois par semaine; **in two ~s' time** dans quinze jours; **Tuesday ~, a ~ from Tuesday** mardi en huit.

weekday [wēk'dā] *n* jour *m* de semaine; (*COMM*) jour ouvrable; **on ~s** en semaine.

weekend [wēk'end] *n* week-end *m*.

weekend case *n* sac *m* de voyage.

weekly [wēk'lē] *ad* une fois par semaine, chaque semaine ♦ *a*, *n* hebdomadaire *(m)*.

weep, *pt*, *pp* **wept** [wēp, wept] *vi* (*person*) pleurer; (*MED*: *wound etc*) suinter.

weeping willow [wē'ping wil'ō] *n* saule pleureur.

weft [weft] *n* (*TEXTILES*) trame *f*.

weigh [wā] *vt*, *vi* peser; **to ~ anchor** lever l'ancre; **to ~ the pros and cons** peser le pour et le contre.

  weigh down *vt* (*branch*) faire plier; (*fig*: *with worry*) accabler.

  weigh out *vt* (*goods*) peser.

  weigh up *vt* examiner.

weighing machine [wā'ing məshēn'] *n* balance *f*, bascule *f*.

weight [wāt] *n* poids *m* ♦ *vt* alourdir; (*fig*: *factor*) pondérer; **sold by ~** vendu au poids; **to put on/lose ~** grossir/maigrir; **~s and measures** poids et mesures.

weighting [wā'ting] *n*: **~ allowance** indemnité *f* de résidence.

weightlessness [wāt'lisnis] *n* apesanteur *f*.

weight lifter [wāt' liftûr] *n* haltérophile *m*.

weighty [wā'tē] *a* lourd(e).

weir [wēr] *n* barrage *m*.

weird [wērd] *a* bizarre; (*eerie*) surnaturel(le).

welcome [wel'kəm] *a* bienvenu(e) ♦ *n* accueil *m* ♦ *vt* accueillir; (*also*: **bid ~**) souhaiter la bienvenue à; (*be glad of*) se réjouir de; **to be ~** être le(la) bienvenu(e); **to make sb ~** faire bon accueil à qn; **you're ~ to try** vous pouvez essayer si vous voulez; **you're ~!** (*after thanks*) de rien, il n'y a pas de quoi.

welcoming [wel'kəming] *a* accueillant(e); (*speech*) d'accueil.

weld [weld] *n* soudure *f* ♦ *vt* souder.

welder [weld'ûr] *n* (*person*) soudeur *m*.

welding [weld'ing] *n* soudure *f* (autogène).

welfare [wel'fär] *n* bien-être *m*; **to be on ~** (*US*) recevoir l'aide sociale.

welfare state *n* État-providence *m*.

welfare work *n* travail social.

well [wel] *n* puits *m* ♦ *ad* bien ♦ *a*: **to be ~** aller bien ♦ *excl* eh bien!; bon!; enfin!; **~ done!** bravo!; **I don't feel ~** je ne me sens pas bien; **get ~ soon!** remets-toi vite!; **to do ~ in sth** bien réussir en *or* dans qch; **to think ~ of sb** penser du bien de qn; **as ~** (*in addition*) aussi, également; **you might as ~ tell me** tu ferais aussi bien de me le dire; **~ as** aussi bien que *or* de; en plus de; **~, as I was saying ...** donc, comme je disais ....

  well up *vi* (*tears*, *emotions*) monter.

we'll [wēl] = **we will**, **we shall**.

well-behaved [welbihāvd'] *a* sage,

obéissant(e).

well-being [wel'bē'ing] *n* bien-être *m*.

well-bred [wel'bred'] *a* bien élevé(e).

well-built [wel'bilt'] *a* (*house*) bien construit(e); (*person*) bien bâti(e).

well-chosen [wel'chō'zən] *a* (*remarks, words*) bien choisi(e), pertinent(e).

well-developed [wel'divel'əpt] *a* (*girl*) bien fait(e).

well-disposed [wel'dispōzd'] *a*: **~ to(wards)** bien disposé(e) envers.

well-dressed [wel'drest'] *a* bien habillé(e), bien vêtu(e).

well-earned [wel'ûrnd'] *a* (*rest*) bien mérité(e).

well-groomed [wel'grōōmd] *a* très soigné(e) de sa personne.

well-heeled [wel'hēld'] *a* (*col: wealthy*) fortuné(e), riche.

well-informed [wel'infôrmd'] *a* (*having knowledge of sth*) bien renseigné(e); (*having general knowledge*) cultivé(e).

Wellington [wel'ingtən] *n* Wellington.

wellingtons [wel'ingtənz] *npl* (*also*: **wellington boots**) bottes *fpl* de caoutchouc.

well-kept [wel'kept'] *a* (*house, grounds*) bien tenu(e), bien entretenu(e); (*secret*) bien gardé(e); (*hair, hands*) soigné(e).

well-known [wel'nōn'] *a* (*person*) bien connu(e).

well-mannered [wel'man'ûrd] *a* bien élevé(e).

well-meaning [wel'mē'ning] *a* bien intentionné(e).

well-nigh [wel'nī'] *ad*: **~ impossible** pratiquement impossible.

well-off [wel'ôf'] *a* aisé(e), assez riche.

well-read [wel'red'] *a* cultivé(e).

well-spoken [wel'spō'kən] *a* (*person*) qui parle bien; (*words*) bien choisi(e).

well-stocked [wel'stäkt'] *a* bien approvisionné(e).

well-timed [wel'tīmd'] *a* opportun(e).

well-to-do [wel'tədōō'] *a* aisé(e), assez riche.

well-wisher [wel'wishûr] *n* ami/e, admirateur/trice; **scores of ~s had gathered** de nombreux amis et admirateurs s'étaient rassemblés; **letters from ~s** des lettres d'encouragement.

Welsh [welsh] *a* gallois(e) ♦ *n* (*LING*) gallois *m*; **the ~** *npl* les Gallois.

Welshman, Welshwoman [welsh'mən, -wōōmən] *n* Gallois/e.

Welsh rarebit [welsh rär'bit] *n* croûte *f* au fromage.

welter [wel'tûr] *n* fatras *m*.

went [went] *pt of* **go**.

wept [wept] *pt, pp of* **weep**.

were [wûr] *pt of* **be**.

we're [wēr] = **we are**.

weren't [wûr'ənt] = **were not**.

werewolf, *pl* **-wolves** [wär'wōōlf, -wōōlvz] *n* loup-garou *m*.

west [west] *n* ouest *m* ♦ *a* ouest *inv*, de *or* à l'ouest ♦ *ad* à *or* vers l'ouest; **the W~** l'Occident *m*, l'Ouest.

westbound [west'bound] *a* (*traffic*) en direction de l'ouest; (*lane*) ouest *inv*.

West Country *n*: **the ~** le sud-ouest de l'Angleterre.

westerly [wes'tûrlē] *a* (*situation*) à l'ouest; (*wind*) d'ouest.

western [wes'tûrn] *a* occidental(e), de *or* à l'ouest ♦ *n* (*CINEMA*) western *m*.

westernized [wes'tûrnîzd] *a* occidentalisé(e).

West German *a* ouest-allemand(e) ♦ *n* Allemand/e de l'Ouest.

West Germany *n* Allemagne *f* de l'Ouest.

West Indian *a* antillais(e) ♦ *n* Antillais/e.

West Indies [west in'dēz] *npl*: **the** ~ les Antilles *fpl*.

westward(s) [west'wûrd(z)] *ad* vers l'ouest.

wet [wet] *a* mouillé(e); (*damp*) humide; (*soaked*) trempé(e); (*rainy*) pluvieux(euse) ♦ *vt*: **to** ~ **one's pants** *or* **o.s.** mouiller sa culotte, faire pipi dans sa culotte; **to get** ~ se mouiller; "~ **paint**" "attention peinture fraîche".

wet blanket *n* (*fig*) rabat-joie *m inv*.

wetness [wet'nis] *n* humidité *f*.

wet suit *n* combinaison *f* de plongée.

we've [wēv] = **we have.**

whack [wak] *vt* donner un grand coup à.

whale [wāl] *n* (*ZOOL*) baleine *f*.

whaler [wā'lûr] *n* (*ship*) baleinier *m*.

wharf, *pl* **wharves** [wôrf, wôrvz] *n* quai *m*.

what [wut] *excl* quoi!, comment! ♦ *a* quel(le) ♦ *pronoun* (*interrogative*) que, *prep* + quoi; (*relative, indirect: object*) ce que; (: *subject*) ce qui; ~ **are you doing?** que fais-tu?, qu'est-ce que tu fais?; ~ **has happened?** que s'est-il passé?, qu'est-ce qui s'est passé?; ~**'s in there?** qu'y a-t-il là-dedans?, qu'est-ce qu'il y a là-dedans?; **for** ~ **reason?** pour quelle raison?; **I saw** ~ **you did/is on the table** j'ai vu ce que vous avez fait/ce qui est sur la table; **I don't know** ~ **to do** je ne sais pas que *or* quoi faire; ~ **a mess!** quel désordre!; ~ **is his address?** quelle est son adresse?; ~ **will it cost?** combien est-ce que ça coûtera?; ~ **is it called?** comment est-ce que ça s'appelle?; **I want is a cup of tea** ce que je veux, c'est une tasse de thé; ~ **about doing ...?** et si on faisait ...?; ~ **about me?** et moi?

whatever [wutev'ûr] *a*: ~ **book** quel que soit le livre que (*or* qui) + *sub*; n'importe quel livre ♦ *pronoun*: **do** ~ **is necessary** faites (tout) ce qui est nécessaire; ~ **happens** quoi qu'il arrive; **no reason** ~ *or* **whatsoever** pas la moindre raison; **nothing** ~ *or* **whatsoever** rien du tout.

wheat [wēt] *n* blé *m*, froment *m*.

wheat germ *n* germe *m* de blé.

wheatmeal [wēt'mēl] *n* farine bise.

wheedle [wēd'əl] *vt*: **to** ~ **sb into doing sth** cajoler *or* enjôler qn pour qu'il fasse qch; **to** ~ **sth out of sb** obtenir qch de qn par des cajoleries.

wheel [wēl] *n* roue *f*; (*AUT: also*: **steering** ~) volant *m*; (*NAUT*) gouvernail *m* ♦ *vt* pousser, rouler ♦ *vi* (*also*: ~ **around**) tourner.

wheelbarrow [wēl'barō] *n* brouette *f*.

wheelbase [wēl'bās] *n* empattement *m*.

wheelchair [wēl'chär] *n* fauteuil roulant.

wheel clamp *n* (*Brit AUT*) sabot *m* (de Denver).

wheeler-dealer [wē'lûrdē'lûr] *n* (*pej*) combinard/e, affairiste *m/f*.

wheeling [wē'ling] *n*: ~ **and dealing** (*pej*) manigances *fpl*, magouilles *fpl*.

wheeze [wēz] *n* respiration bruyante (*d'asthmatique*) ♦ *vi* respirer bruyamment.

when [wen] *ad* quand ♦ *cj* quand, lorsque; (*whereas*) alors que; **on the day** ~ **I met him** le jour où je l'ai rencontré.

whenever [wenev'ûr] *ad* quand donc ♦ *cj* quand; (*every time that*) chaque fois que; **I go** ~ **I can** j'y vais quand *or* chaque fois que je le peux.

where [wär] *ad, cj* où; **this is** ~ **c'est là que; ~ are you from?** d'où venez vous?

whereabouts [wär'əbouts] *ad* où donc ♦ *n*: **sb's** ~ l'endroit où se trouve qn.

whereas [wäraz'] *cj* alors que.

whereby [wärbī'] *ad* (*formal*) par lequel (*or* laquelle *etc*).

whereupon [wärəpân'] *ad* sur quoi, et sur ce.

wherever [wärev'ûr] *ad* où donc ♦ *cj* où que + *sub*; **sit** ~ **you like** asseyez-vous (là) où vous voulez.

wherewithal [wär'withôl] *n*: **the** ~ **(to do sth)** les moyens *mpl* (de faire qch).

whet [wet] *vt* aiguiser.

whether [weth'ûr] *cj* si; **I don't know** ~ **to accept** *or* **not** je ne sais pas si je dois accepter ou non; **it's doubtful** ~ **il est peu probable que; ~ you go or not** que vous y alliez ou non.

whey [wā] *n* petit-lait *m*.

which [wich] *a* (*interrogative*) quel(le), *pl* quels(quelles); ~ **one of you?** le-quel(laquelle) d'entre vous?; **tell me** ~ **one you want** dis-moi lequel tu veux *or* celui que tu veux ♦ *pronoun* (*interrogative*) le-quel(laquelle), *pl* lesquels(lesquelles); (*indirect*) celui(celle) qui (*or* que); (*relative: subject*) qui; (: *object*) que, *prep* + le-quel(laquelle) (NB: à + *lequel* = auquel; *de* + *lequel* = duquel); ~ **do you want?** lequel *or* laquelle *etc* veux-tu?; **I don't mind** ~ peu importe lequel; **the apple** ~ **you ate/**~ **is on the table** la pomme que vous avez mangée/qui est sur la table; **the chair on** ~ la chaise sur laquelle; **the book of** ~ le livre dont *or* duquel; **he said he knew,** ~ **is true/I feared** il a dit qu'il le savait, ce qui est vrai/ce que je craignais; **after** ~ après quoi; **in** ~ **case** auquel cas; **by** ~ **time ...** heure (*or* moment) à laquelle(auquel) ..., et à ce moment-là ....

whichever [wichev'ûr] *a*: **take** ~ **book you prefer** prenez le livre que vous préférez, peu importe lequel; ~ **book you take** quel que soit le livre que vous preniez; ~ **way you** de quelque façon que vous + *sub*.

whiff [wif] *n* bouffée *f*; **to catch a** ~ **of sth** sentir l'odeur de qch.

while [wīl] *n* moment *m* ♦ *cj* pendant que; (*as long as*) tant que; (*as, whereas*) alors que; (*though*) quoique + *sub*; **for a** ~ pendant quelque temps; **in a** ~ dans un moment; **all the** ~ pendant tout ce temps-là; **we'll make it worth your** ~ nous vous récompenserons de votre peine.

while away *vt* (*time*) (faire) passer.

whilst [wīlst] *cj* = **while.**

whim [wim] *n* caprice *m*.

whimper [wim'pûr]. *n* geignement *m* ♦ *vi*

geindre.

whimsical [wim'zikəl] a (person) capricieux(euse); (look) étrange.

whine [wīn] n gémissement m ♦ vi gémir, geindre; pleurnicher.

whip [wip] n fouet m; (for riding) cravache f; (POL: person) chef m de file (assurant la discipline dans son groupe parlementaire) ♦ vt fouetter; (snatch) enlever (or sortir) brusquement.

whip up vt (cream) fouetter; (col: meal) préparer en vitesse; (stir up: support) stimuler; (: feeling) attiser, aviver.

whiplash [wip'lash] n (MED: also: ~ injury) coup m du lapin.

whipped cream [wipt krēm] n crème fouettée.

whipping boy [wip'ing boi] n (fig) bouc m émissaire.

whip-round [wip'round] n (Brit) collecte f.

whirl [wûrl] n tourbillon m ♦ vt faire tourbillonner; faire tournoyer ♦ vi tourbillonner.

whirlpool [wûrl'pōōl] n tourbillon m.

whirlwind [wûrl'wind] n tornade f.

whirr [wär] vi bruire; ronronner; vrombir.

whisk [wisk] n (CULIN) fouet m ♦ vt fouetter, battre; **to ~ sb away** or **off** emmener qn rapidement.

whiskers [wis'kûrz] npl (of animal) moustaches fpl; (of man) favoris mpl.

whiskey (US, Ireland), **whisky** (Brit) [wis'kē] n whisky m.

whisper [wis'pûr] n chuchotement m; (fig: of leaves) bruissement m; (rumor) rumeur f ♦ vt, vi chuchoter; **to ~ sth to sb** chuchoter qch à (l'oreille de) qn.

whispering [wis'pûring] n chuchotement(s) m(pl).

whist [wist] n (Brit) whist m.

whistle [wis'əl] n (sound) sifflement m; (object) sifflet m ♦ vi siffler ♦ vt siffler, siffloter.

whistle-stop [wis'əlstâp] a: **to make a ~ tour of** (POL) faire la tournée électorale des petits patelins de.

Whit [wit] n la Pentecôte.

white [wit] a blanc(blanche); (with fear) blême ♦ n blanc m; (person) blanc/blanche; **to turn** or **go ~** (person) pâlir, blêmir; (hair) blanchir; **the ~s** (washing) le linge blanc; **tennis ~s** tenue f de tennis.

whitebait [wīt'bāt] n blanchaille f.

white coffee n (Brit) café m au lait, (café) crème m.

white-collar worker [wīt'kâl'ûr wûr'kûr] n employé/e de bureau.

white elephant n (fig) objet dispendieux et superflu.

white goods npl (appliances) (gros) électroménager m; (linen etc) linge m de maison.

white-hot [wīt'hât'] a (metal) incandescent(e).

white lie n pieux mensonge.

whiteness [wīt'nis] n blancheur f.

white noise n son m blanc.

whiteout [wīt'out] n jour blanc.

white paper n (POL) livre blanc.

whitewash [wīt'wâsh] n (paint) lait m de

chaux ♦ vt blanchir à la chaux; (fig) blanchir.

whiting [wī'ting] n (pl inv) (fish) merlan m.

Whit Monday n le lundi de Pentecôte.

Whitsun [wit'sən] n la Pentecôte.

whittle [wit'əl] vt: **to ~ away**, **~ down** (costs) réduire, rogner.

whizz [wiz] vi aller (or passer) à toute vitesse.

whizz kid n (col) petit prodige.

WHO n abbr (= World Health Organization) OMS f (= Organisation mondiale de la Santé).

who [hōō] pronoun qui.

whodunit [hōōdun'it] n (col) roman policier.

whoever [hōōev'ûr] pronoun: **~ finds it** celui(celle) qui le trouve (, qui que ce soit), quiconque le trouve; **ask ~ you like** demandez à qui vous voulez; **~ he marries** qui que ce soit or quelle que soit la personne qu'il épouse; **~ told you that?** qui a bien pu vous dire ça?, qui donc vous a dit ça?

whole [hōl] a (complete) entier(ière), tout(e); (not broken) intact(e), complet(ète) ♦ n (total) totalité f; (sth not broken) tout m; **the ~ lot (of it)** tout; **the ~ lot (of them)** tous (sans exception); **the ~ of the time** tout le temps; **the ~ of the town** la ville tout entière; **~ villages were destroyed** des villages entiers ont été détruits; **on the ~**, **as a ~** dans l'ensemble.

wholefoods [hōl'fōōdz] npl aliments naturels.

wholehearted [hōl'hâr'tid] a sans réserve(s), sincère.

wholemeal [hōl'mēl] a (Brit) = **wholewheat**.

whole milk n (US) lait entier.

whole note n (US) ronde f.

wholesale [hōl'sāl] n (vente f en) gros m ♦ a de gros; (destruction) systématique.

wholesaler [hōl'sālûr] n grossiste m/f.

wholesome [hōl'səm] a sain(e); (advice) salutaire.

wholewheat [hōl'wēt] a (US: flour, bread) complet(ète).

wholly [hō'lē] ad entièrement, tout à fait.

whom [hōōm] pronoun que, prep + qui (check syntax of French verb used); (interrogative) qui; **those to ~ I spoke** ceux à qui j'ai parlé.

whooping cough [wōō'ping kôf] n coqueluche f.

whoosh [wōōsh] n, vi: **the skiers ~ed past**, **the skiers came by with a ~** les skieurs passèrent dans un glissement rapide.

whopper [wâp'ûr] n (col: lie) gros bobard; (: large thing) monstre m, phénomène m.

whopping [wâp'ing] a (col: big) énorme.

whore [hôr] n (col: pej) putain f.

whose [hōōz] a: **~ book is this?** à qui est ce livre?; **~ pencil have you taken?** à qui est le crayon que vous avez pris?, c'est le crayon de qui que vous avez pris?; **the man ~ son you rescued** l'homme dont or de qui vous avez sauvé le fils; **the girl ~ sister you were speaking to** la fille à la sœur de qui or laquelle vous parliez ♦ pronoun: **~ is this?** à qui est ceci?; **I know ~ it is** je sais à qui c'est.

Who's Who [hōōz' hōō'] n ≈ Bottin Mondain.

why [wī] ad pourquoi ♦ excl eh bien!, tiens!; **the reason ~** la raison pour laquelle; **~ is**

he late? pourquoi est-il en retard?

whyever [wī'evûr] *ad* pourquoi donc, mais pourquoi.

WI *abbr* (*GEO*) = **West Indies**; (*US MAIL*) = Wisconsin.

wick [wik] *n* mèche *f* (*de bougie*).

wicked [wik'id] *a* foncièrement mauvais(e), inique; (*mischievous*: *grin*, *look*) espiègle, malicieux(euse); (*terrible*: *prices*, *weather*) épouvantable.

wicker [wik'ûr] *n* osier *m*; (*also*: ~**work**) vannerie *f*.

wicket [wik'it] *n* (*CRICKET*) guichet *m*; espace compris entre les deux guichets.

wide [wīd] *a* large; (*region*, *knowledge*) vaste, très étendu(e); (*choice*) grand(e) ♦ *ad*: **to open** ~ ouvrir tout grand; **to shoot** ~ tirer à côté; **it is 3 meters** ~ cela fait 3 mètres de large.

wide-angle lens [wīd'ang'gəl lenz] *n* objectif *m* grand-angulaire.

wide-awake [wīd'əwāk'] *a* bien éveillé(e).

wide-eyed [wīd'īd] *a* aux yeux écarquillés; (*fig*) naïf(ïve), crédule.

widely [wīd'lē] *ad* (*different*) radicalement; (*spaced*) sur une grande étendue; (*believed*) généralement; **to be** ~ **read** (*author*) être beaucoup lu(e); (*reader*) avoir beaucoup lu, être cultivé(e).

widen [wī'dən] *vt* élargir.

wideness [wīd'nis] *n* largeur *f*.

wide open *a* grand(e) ouvert(e).

wide-ranging [wīd'rān'jing] *a* (*survey*, *report*) vaste; (*interests*) divers(e).

widespread [wīdspred'] *a* (*belief etc*) très répandu(e).

widow [wid'ō] *n* veuve *f*.

widowed [wid'ōd] *a* (qui est devenu(e)) veuf(veuve).

widower [wid'ôûr] *n* veuf *m*.

width [width] *n* largeur *f*; **it's 7 meters in** ~ cela fait 7 mètres de large.

widthwise [width'wīz] *ad* en largeur.

wield [wēld] *vt* (*sword*) manier; (*power*) exercer.

wife, *pl* **wives** [wīf, wīvz] *n* femme (mariée), épouse *f*.

wig [wig] *n* perruque *f*.

wiggle [wig'əl] *vt* agiter, remuer ♦ *vi* (*loose screw etc*) branler; (*worm*) se tortiller.

wiggly [wig'lē] *a* (*line*) ondulé(e).

wild [wīld] *a* sauvage; (*sea*) déchaîné(e); (*idea*, *life*) fou(folle); extravagant(e); (*col*: *angry*) hors de soi, furieux(euse); (: *enthusiastic*): **to be** ~ **about** être fou(folle) *or* dingue de ♦ *n*: **the** ~ la nature; ~**s** *npl* régions *fpl* sauvages.

wild card *n* (*COMPUT*) caractère *m* de remplacement.

wildcat [wīld'kat] *n* chat *m* sauvage.

wildcat strike *n* grève *f* sauvage.

wilderness [wil'dûrnis] *n* désert *m*, région *f* sauvage.

wildfire [wīld'fiûr] *n*: **to spread like** ~ se répandre comme une traînée de poudre.

wild game reserve *n* (*US*) réserve *f*.

wild-goose chase [wīld'goōs' chās] *n* (*fig*) fausse piste.

wildlife [wīld'līf] *n* faune *f* (et flore *f*) sau-

vage(s).

wildly [wīld'lē] *ad* (*applaud*) frénétiquement; (*hit*, *guess*) au hasard; (*happy*) follement.

wiles [wīlz] *npl* ruses *fpl*, artifices *mpl*.

wilful [wil'fəl] *a* (*Brit*) = **willful**.

will [wil] *auxiliary vb*: **he** ~ **come** il viendra; **you won't lose it,** ~ **you?** vous ne le perdrez pas, n'est-ce pas?; **that** ~ **be the mailman** c'est probablement *or* ça doit être le facteur; ~ **you sit down** voulez-vous vous asseoir; **the car won't start** la voiture ne veut pas démarrer ♦ *vt* (*pt*, *pp* ~**ed**) exhorter par la pensée; **he** ~**ed himself to go on** par un suprême effort de volonté, il continua ♦ *n* volonté *f*; (*LAW*) testament *m*; **to do sth of one's own free** ~ faire qch de son propre gré; **against one's** ~ à contre-cœur.

willful [wil'fəl] *a* (*US*) (*person*) obstiné(e); (*action*) délibéré(e); (*crime*) prémédité(e).

willing [wil'ing] *a* de bonne volonté, serviable ♦ *n*: **to show** ~ faire preuve de bonne volonté; **he's** ~ **to do it** il est disposé à le faire, il veut bien le faire.

willingly [wil'inglē] *ad* volontiers.

willingness [wil'ingnis] *n* bonne volonté.

will-o'-the wisp [wil'ōŧhə wisp'] *n* (*also fig*) feu follet *m*.

willow [wil'ō] *n* saule *m*.

will power *n* volonté *f*.

willy-nilly [wil'ēnil'ē] *ad* bon gré mal gré.

wilt [wilt] *vi* dépérir.

Wilts [wilts] *abbr* (*Brit*) = **Wiltshire**.

wily [wī'lē] *a* rusé(e).

wimp [wimp] *n* (*col*) mauviette *f*.

win [win] *n* (*in sports etc*) victoire *f* ♦ *vb* (*pt*, *pp* **won** [wun]) *vt* (*battle*, *money*) gagner; (*prize*, *contract*) remporter; (*popularity*) acquérir ♦ *vi* gagner.

win over, (*Brit*) **win round** *vt* gagner, se concilier.

wince [wins] *n* tressaillement *m* ♦ *vi* tressaillir.

winch [winch] *n* treuil *m*.

Winchester disk [win'chestûr ⁄ disk] *n* (*COMPUT*) disque *m* Winchester.

wind *n* [wind] (*also MED*) vent *m* ♦ *vb* [wīnd] (*pt*, *pp* **wound** [wound]) *vt* enrouler; (*wrap*) envelopper; (*clock*, *toy*) remonter; (*take breath away*: [wind]) couper le souffle à ♦ *vi* (*road*, *river*) serpenter; **the** ~(**s**) (*MUS*) les instruments *mpl* à vent; **into** *or* **against the** ~ contre le vent; **to get** ~ **of sth** (*fig*) avoir vent de qch; **to break** ~ avoir des gaz.

wind down [wīnd doun] *vt* (*car window*) baisser; (*fig*: *production*, *business*) réduire progressivement.

wind up [wīnd up] *vt* (*clock*) remonter; (*debate*) terminer, clôturer.

windbreak [wind'brāk] *n* brise-vent *m inv*.

windbreaker [wind'brākûr] *n* (*US*) anorak *m*.

windfall [wind'fôl] *n* coup *m* de chance.

winding [wīn'ding] *a* (*road*) sinueux(euse); (*staircase*) tournant(e).

wind instrument [wind in'strəmənt] *n* (*MUS*) instrument *m* à vent.

windmill [wind'mil] *n* moulin *m* à vent.

window [win'dō] *n* fenêtre *f*; (*in car*, *train*, *also*: ~**pane**) vitre *f*; (*in store etc*) vitrine *f*.

window box *n* jardinière *f*.

window cleaner *n* (*person*) laveur/euse de vitres.

window dressing *n* arrangement *m* de la vitrine.

window envelope *n* enveloppe *f* à fenêtre.

window frame *n* châssis *m* de fenêtre.

window ledge *n* rebord *m* de la fenêtre.

window pane *n* vitre *f*, carreau *m*.

window-shopping [win'dōshâping] *n*: **to go ~** faire du lèche-vitrines.

windowsill [win'dōsil] *n* (*inside*) appui *m* de la fenêtre; (*outside*) rebord *m* de la fenêtre.

windpipe [wind'pīp] *n* gosier *m*.

windscreen [wind'skrēn] *n* (*Brit*) = **windshield.**

windshield [wind'shēld] *n* (*US*) pare-brise *m inv.*

windshield washer *n* lave-glace *m inv.*

windshield wiper *n* essuie-glace *m inv.*

windsurfing [wind'sûrfing] *n* planche *f* à voile.

windswept [wind'swept] *a* balayé(e) par le vent.

wind tunnel *n* soufflerie *f*.

windy [win'dē] *a* venté(e), venteux(euse); **it's ~** il y a du vent.

wine [wīn] *n* vin *m* ♦ *vt*: **to ~ and dine sb** offrir un dîner bien arrosé à qn.

wine cellar *n* cave *f* à vins.

wineglass [wīn'glas] *n* verre *m* à vin.

wine list *n* carte *f* des vins.

wine merchant *n* marchand/e de vins.

wine tasting *n* dégustation *f* (de vins).

wine waiter *n* sommelier *m*.

wing [wing] *n* aile *f*; (*in air force*) groupe *m* d'escadrilles; (*SPORT*) ailier *m*; **~s** *npl* (*THEATER*) coulisses *fpl*.

winger [wing'ûr] *n* (*Brit SPORT*) ailier *m*.

wing mirror *n* (*Brit*) rétroviseur latéral.

wing nut *n* papillon *m*, écrou *m* à ailettes.

wingspan [wing'span] *n*, **wingspread** [wing'spred] *n* envergure *f*.

wink [wingk] *n* clin *m* d'œil ♦ *vi* faire un clin d'œil; (*blink*) cligner des yeux.

winkle [win'kəl] *n* bigorneau *m*.

winner [win'ûr] *n* gagnant/e.

winning [win'ing] *a* (*team*) gagnant(e); (*goal*) décisif(ive); (*charming*) charmeur(euse).

winning post *n* poteau *m* d'arrivée.

winnings [win'ingz] *npl* gains *mpl*.

winsome [win'səm] *a* avenant(e), engageant(e).

winter [win'tûr] *n* hiver *m* ♦ *vi* hiverner.

winter sports *npl* sports *mpl* d'hiver.

wintry [win'trē] *a* hivernal(e).

wipe [wīp] *n* coup *m* de torchon (*or* de chiffon *or* d'éponge) ♦ *vt* essuyer; **to give sth a ~** donner un coup de torchon à qch; **to ~ one's nose** se moucher.

wipe off *vt* essuyer.

wipe out *vt* (*debt*) régler; (*memory*) oublier; (*destroy*) anéantir.

wipe up *vt* essuyer.

wire [wī'ûr] *n* fil *m* (de fer); (*ELEC*) fil électrique; (*TEL*) télégramme *m* ♦ *vt* (*fence*) grillager; (*house*) faire l'installation électrique de; (*also*: **~ up**) brancher.

wire brush *n* brosse *f* métallique.

wire cutters *npl* cisaille *f*.

wire netting *n* treillis *m* métallique,

grillage *m*.

wiretapping [wī'ûrtaping] *n* écoute *f* téléphonique.

wiring [wīûr'ing] *n* (*ELEC*) installation *f* électrique.

wiry [wīûr'ē] *a* noueux(euse), nerveux(euse).

Wis., Wisc. *abbr* (*US*) = Wisconsin.

wisdom [wiz'dəm] *n* sagesse *f*; (*of action*) prudence *f*.

wisdom tooth *n* dent *f* de sagesse.

wise [wīz] *a* sage, prudent(e), judicieux(euse); **I'm none the ~r** je ne suis pas plus avancé(e) pour autant.

wise up *vi* (*col*): **to ~ up to** commencer à se rendre compte de.

wisecrack [wīz'krak] *n* sarcasme *m*.

wish [wish] *n* (*desire*) désir *m*; (*specific desire*) souhait *m*, vœu *m* ♦ *vt* souhaiter, désirer, vouloir; **best ~es** (*on birthday etc*) meilleurs vœux; **with best ~es** (*in letter*) bien amicalement; **give her my best ~es** faites-lui mes amitiés; **to ~ sb goodbye** dire au revoir à qn; **he ~ed me well** il me souhaitait de réussir; **to ~ to do/sb to do** désirer *or* vouloir faire/que qn fasse; **to ~ for** souhaiter; **to ~ sth on sb** souhaiter qch à qn.

wishful [wish'fəl] *a*: **it's ~ thinking** c'est prendre ses désirs pour des réalités.

wishy-washy [wish'ēwâshē] *a* (*col: person*) qui manque de caractère, falot(e); (: *ideas, thinking*) faiblard(e).

wisp [wisp] *n* fine mèche (*de cheveux*); (*of smoke*) mince volute *f*; **a ~ of straw** un fétu de paille.

wistful [wist'fəl] *a* mélancolique.

wit [wit] *n* (*gen pl: intelligence*) intelligence *f*, esprit *m*; (*presence of mind*) présence *f* d'esprit; (*wittiness*) esprit; (*person*) homme/femme d'esprit; **to be at one's ~s' end** (*fig*) ne plus savoir que faire; **to have one's ~s about one** avoir toute sa présence d'esprit, ne pas perdre la tête; **to ~ *ad*** à savoir.

witch [wich] *n* sorcière *f*.

witchcraft [wich'kraft] *n* sorcellerie *f*.

witch doctor *n* sorcier *m*.

witch-hunt [wich'hunt] *n* chasse *f* aux sorcières.

with [with, with] *prep* avec; **red ~ anger** rouge de colère; **to shake ~ fear** trembler de peur; **the man ~ the gray hat** l'homme au chapeau gris; **to stay overnight ~ friends** passer la nuit chez des amis; **to be ~ it** (*fig*) être dans le vent; **I am ~ you** (*I understand*) je vous suis.

withdraw [withdrô'] *vb* (*irg*) *vt* retirer ♦ *vi* se retirer; (*go back on promise*) se rétracter; **to ~ into o.s.** se replier sur soi-même.

withdrawal [withdrô'əl] *n* retrait *m*; (*MED*) état *m* de manque.

withdrawal symptoms *npl*: **to have ~** être en état de manque, présenter les symptômes *mpl* de sevrage.

withdrawn [withdrôn'] *pp of* **withdraw** ♦ *a* (*person*) renfermé(e).

wither [with'ûr] *vi* se faner.

withered [with'ûrd] *a* fané(e), flétri(e); (*limb*) atrophié(e).

withhold [withhōld'] *vt irg* (*money*) retenir;

(decision) remettre; (permission): **to ~ (from)** refuser (à); (information): **to ~ (from)** cacher (à).

within [wi‹hin'] prep à l'intérieur de ♦ ad à l'intérieur; **~ sight of** en vue de; **~ a mile of** à moins d'un mille de; **~ the week** avant la fin de la semaine; **~ an hour from now** d'ici une heure; **to be ~ the law** être légal(e) or dans les limites de la légalité.

without [wi‹hout'] prep sans; **~ anybody knowing** sans que personne le sache; **to go** or **do ~ sth** se passer de qch.

withstand [withstand'] vt irg résister à.

witness [wit'nis] n (person) témoin m; (evidence) témoignage m ♦ vt (event) être témoin de; (document) attester l'authenticité de; **to bear ~ to sth** témoigner de qch; **~ for the prosecution/defense** témoin à charge/à décharge; **to ~ to sth/having seen sth** témoigner de qch/d'avoir vu qch.

witness stand, (Brit) **witness box** n barre f des témoins.

witticism [wit'əsizəm] n mot m d'esprit.

witty [wit'ē] a spirituel(le), plein(e) d'esprit.

wives [wīvz] npl of **wife**.

wizard [wiz'ûrd] n magicien m.

wizened [wiz'ənd] a ratatiné(e).

wk abbr = **week**.

Wm. abbr = **William**.

WO n abbr = **warrant officer**.

wobble [wâb'əl] vi trembler; (chair) branler.

wobbly [wâb'lē] a tremblant(e); branlant(e).

woe [wō] n malheur m.

woke [wōk] pt of **wake**.

woken [wō'kən] pp of **wake**.

wolf, pl **wolves** [wŏŏlf, wŏŏlvz] n loup m.

woman, pl **women** [wŏŏm'ən, wim'ən] n femme f ♦ cpd: **~ doctor** femme f médecin; **~ friend** amie f; **~ teacher** professeur m femme; **young ~** jeune femme; **women's page** (PRESS) page f des lectrices.

womanize [wŏŏm'əniz] vi jouer les séducteurs.

womanly [wŏŏm'ənlē] a féminin(e).

womb [wŏŏm] n (ANAT) utérus m.

women [wim'ən] npl of **woman**.

Women's (Liberation) Movement n (also: **women's lib**) mouvement m de libération de la femme, MLF m.

won [wun] pt, pp of **win**.

wonder [wun'dûr] n merveille f, miracle m; (feeling) émerveillement m ♦ vi: **to ~ whether** se demander si; **to ~ at** s'étonner de; s'émerveiller de; **to ~ about** songer à; **it's no ~ that** il n'est pas étonnant que + sub.

wonderful [wun'dûrfəl] a merveilleux(euse).

wonderfully [wun'dûrfəlē] ad (+ adjective) merveilleusement; (+ vb) à merveille.

wonky [wâng'kē] a (Brit col) qui ne va or ne marche pas très bien.

won't [wōnt] = **will not**.

woo [wŏŏ] vt (woman) faire la cour à.

wood [wŏŏd] n (timber, forest) bois m ♦ cpd de bois, en bois.

wood alcohol n (US) alcool m à brûler.

wood carving n sculpture f en or sur bois.

wooded [wŏŏd'id] a boisé(e).

wooden [wŏŏd'ən] a en bois; (fig) raide; inex-

pressif(ive).

woodland [wŏŏd'land] n forêt f, région boisée.

woodpecker [wŏŏd'pekûr] n pic m (oiseau).

wood pigeon n ramier m.

woodwind [wŏŏd'wind] n (MUS) bois m; **the ~** (MUS) les bois.

woodwork [wŏŏd'wûrk] n menuiserie f.

woodworm [wŏŏd'wûrm] n ver m du bois.

woof [wŏŏf] n (of dog) aboiement m ♦ vi aboyer; **~, ~!** oua, oua!

wool [wŏŏl] n laine f; **to pull the ~ over sb's eyes** (fig) en faire accroire à qn.

woolen, (Brit) **woollen** [wŏŏl'ən] a de laine; (industry) lainier(ière) ♦ n: **~s** lainages mpl.

wooly, (Brit) **woolly** [wŏŏl'ē] a laineux(euse); (fig: ideas) confus(e).

word [wûrd] n mot m; (spoken) mot, parole f; (promise) parole; (news) nouvelles fpl ♦ vt rédiger, formuler; **~ for ~** (repeat) mot pour mot; (translate) mot à mot; **what's the ~ for "pen" in French?** comment dit-on "pen" en français?; **to put sth into ~s** exprimer qch; **in other ~s** en d'autres termes; **to have a ~ with sb** toucher un mot à qn; **to have ~s with sb** (quarrel) avoir des mots avec qn; **to break/keep one's ~** manquer à/tenir sa parole; **I'll take your ~ for it** je vous crois sur parole; **to send ~ of** prévenir de; **to leave ~ (with sb/for sb) that** ... laisser un mot (à qn/pour qn) disant que ....

wording [wûr'ding] n termes mpl, langage m; libellé m.

word-perfect [wûrd'pûrfikt] a: **he was ~ (in his speech** etc), **his speech** etc **was ~** il savait son discours etc sur le bout du doigt.

word processing n traitement m de texte.

word processor n machine f de traitement de texte.

wordwrap [wûrd'rap] n (COMPUT) retour m (automatique) à la ligne.

wordy [wûr'dē] a verbeux(euse).

wore [wôr] pt of **wear**.

work [wûrk] n travail m; (ART, LITERATURE) œuvre f ♦ vi travailler; (mechanism) marcher, fonctionner; (plan etc) marcher; (medicine) agir ♦ vt (clay, wood etc) travailler; (mine etc) exploiter; (machine) faire marcher or fonctionner ♦ cpd (day, tools etc, conditions) de travail; **to go to ~** aller travailler; **to set to ~, to start ~** se mettre à l'œuvre; **to be at ~ (on sth)** travailler (sur qch); **to be out of ~** être au chômage; **"~ wanted"** (US) "demandes fpl d'emploi"; **to ~ hard** travailler dur; **to ~ loose** se défaire, se desserrer.

work on vt fus travailler à; (principle) se baser sur.

work out vi (plans etc) marcher; (SPORT) s'entraîner ♦ vt (problem) résoudre; (plan) élaborer; **it ~s out at $100** ça fait 100 dollars.

workable [wûr'kəbəl] a (solution) réalisable.

workaholic [wûrkəhâl'ik] n bourreau m de travail.

workbench [wûrk'bench] n établi m.

workbook [wûrk'bŏŏk] n cahier m d'exercices.

work council n comité m d'entreprise.

worked up [wûrkt up] *a*: **to get** ~ se mettre dans tous ses états.

worker [wûr'kûr] *n* travailleur/euse, ouvrier/ière; **office** ~ employé/e de bureau.

work force *n* main-d'œuvre *f*.

work-in [wûrk'in] *n* (*Brit*) occupation *f* d'usine *etc* (*sans arrêt de la production*).

working [wûr'king] *a* (*Brit: day, tools etc, conditions*) de travail; (*wife*) qui travaille; (*partner, population*) actif(ive); **in** ~ **order** en état de marche; **a** ~ **knowledge of English** une connaissance toute pratique de l'anglais.

working capital *n* (*COMM*) fonds *mpl* de roulement.

working class *n* classe ouvrière ♦ *a*: **working-class** ouvrier(ière), de la classe ouvrière.

working man *n* travailleur *m*.

working model *n* modèle opérationnel.

working-week *n* (*Brit*) semaine *f* de travail.

work-in-progress [wûrkinprâg'res] *n* (*COMM*) en-cours *m inv*; (*: value*) valeur *f* des en-cours.

workload [wûrk'lōd] *n* charge *f* de travail.

workman [wûrk'mən] *n* ouvrier *m*.

workmanship [wûrk'mənship] *n* métier *m*, habileté *f*; facture *f*.

workmate [wûrk'māt] *n* collègue *m/f*.

workout [wûrk'out] *n* (*SPORT*) séance *f* d'entraînement.

work party *n* groupe *m* de travail.

work permit *n* permis *m* de travail.

works [wûrks] *n* (*Brit: factory*) usine *f* ♦ *npl* (*of clock, machine*) mécanisme *m*; **road** ~ travaux *mpl* (d'entretien des routes).

work sheet *n* (*COMPUT*) feuille *f* de programmation.

workshop [wûrk'shâp] *n* atelier *m*.

work station *n* poste *m* de travail.

work study *n* étude *f* du travail.

work-to-rule [wûrk'tərōōl'] *n* (*Brit*) grève *f* du zèle.

work week *n* (*US*) semaine *f* de travail.

world [wûrld] *n* monde *m* ♦ *cpd* (*champion*) du monde; (*power, war*) mondial(e); **all over the** ~ dans le monde entier, partout dans le monde; **to think the** ~ **of sb** (*fig*) ne jurer que par qn; **what in the** ~ **is he doing?** qu'est-ce qu'il peut bien être en train de faire?; **to do sb a** ~ **of good** faire le plus grand bien à qn; **W**~ **War One/Two** la Première/Deuxième guerre mondiale; **out of this** ~ *a* extraordinaire.

World Cup *n*: **the** ~ (*SOCCER*) la Coupe du monde.

world-famous [wûrldfā'məs] *a* de renommée mondiale.

worldly [wûrld'lē] *a* de ce monde.

worldwide [wûrld'wīd'] *a* universel(le) ♦ *ad* dans le monde entier.

worm [wûrm] *n* ver *m*.

worn [wôrn] *pp* of **wear** ♦ *a* usé(e).

worn-out [wôrn'out'] *a* (*object*) complètement usé(e); (*person*) épuisé(e).

worried [wûr'ēd] *a* inquiet(ète); **to be** ~ **about sth** être inquiet au sujet de qch.

worrier [wûr'ēûr] *n* inquiet/ète.

worrisome [wûr'ēsəm] *a* inquiétant(e).

worry [wûr'ē] *n* souci *m* ♦ *vt* inquiéter ♦ *vi* s'inquiéter, se faire du souci; **to** ~ **about** or **over sth/sb** se faire du souci pour or à propos de qch/qn.

worrying [wûr'ēing] *a* inquiétant(e).

worse [wûrs] *a* pire, plus mauvais(e) ♦ *ad* plus mal ♦ *n* pire *m*; **to get** ~ (*condition, situation*) empirer, se dégrader; **a change for the** ~ une détérioration; **he is none the** ~ **for it** il ne s'en porte pas plus mal; **so much the** ~ **for you!** tant pis pour vous!

worsen [wûr'sən] *vt*, *vi* empirer.

worse off *a* moins à l'aise financièrement; (*fig*): **you'll be** ~ **this way** ça ira moins bien de cette façon; **he is now** ~ **than before** il se retrouve dans une situation pire qu'auparavant.

worship [wûr'ship] *n* culte *m* ♦ *vt* (*God*) rendre un culte à; (*person*) adorer; **Your W**~ (*Brit: to mayor*) Monsieur le Maire; (*: to judge*) Monsieur le Juge.

worship(p)er [wûr'shipûr] *n* adorateur/trice; (*in church*) fidèle *m/f*.

worst [wûrst] *a* le(la) pire, le(la) plus mauvais(e) ♦ *ad* le plus mal ♦ *n* pire *m*; **at** ~ au pis aller; **if** ~ **comes to** ~, (*Brit*) **if the** ~ **comes to the** ~ si le pire doit arriver.

worsted [wōōs'tid] *n*: **(wool)** ~ laine peignée.

worth [wûrth] *n* valeur *f* ♦ *a*: **to be** ~ valoir; **how much is it** ~? ça vaut combien?; **it's** ~ **it** cela en vaut la peine; **$2** ~ **of apples** (pour) 2 dollars de pommes.

worthless [wûrth'lis] *a* qui ne vaut rien.

worthwhile [wûrth'wīl'] *a* (*activity*) qui en vaut la peine; (*cause*) louable; **a** ~ **book** un livre qui vaut la peine d'être lu.

worthy [wûr'thē] *a* (*person*) digne; (*motive*) louable; ~ **of** digne de.

would [wōōd] *auxiliary vb*: **she** ~ **come** elle viendrait; **he** ~ **have come** il serait venu; ~ **you like a cookie?** voulez-vous or voudriez-vous un biscuit?; ~ **you close the door, please?** voulez-vous fermer la porte, s'il vous plaît; **he** ~ **go there on Mondays** il y allait le lundi; **you WOULD say that,** ~**n't you!** bien évidemment tu dis ça!; c'est bien de toi de dire ça!; **she** ~**n't leave** elle a refusé de partir.

would-be [wōōd'bē'] *a* (*pej*) soi-disant.

wound *vb* [wound] *pt*, *pp* of **wind** ♦ *n*, *vt* [wōōnd] *n* blessure *f* ♦ *vt* blesser; ~**ed in the leg** blessé à la jambe.

wove [wōv] *pt* of **weave**.

woven [wō'vən] *pp* of **weave**.

WP *n abbr* = **word processing, word processor**.

WPC *n abbr* (*Brit*) = *woman police constable*.

wpm *abbr* (= *words per minute*) mots/minute.

wrangle [rang'gəl] *n* dispute *f* ♦ *vi* se disputer.

wrap [rap] *n* (*stole*) écharpe *f*; (*cape*) pèlerine *f* ♦ *vt* (*also:* ~ **up**) envelopper; **under** ~**s** (*fig: plan, scheme*) secret(ète).

wrapper [rap'ûr] *n* (*on chocolate etc*) papier *m*.

wrapping paper [rap'ing pā'pûr] *n* papier *m* d'emballage; (*for gift*) papier cadeau.

wrath [rath] *n* courroux *m*.

wreak [rēk] *vt* (*destruction*) entraîner; **to** ~

havoc faire des ravages; **to ~ vengeance on** se venger de, exercer sa vengeance sur.

wreath, **~s** [rēth, rēthz] *n* couronne *f*.

wreck [rek] *n* (*sea disaster*) naufrage *m*; (*ship*) épave *f*; (*pej: person*) loque (humaine) ♦ *vt* démolir; (*ship*) provoquer le naufrage de; (*fig*) briser, ruiner.

wreckage [rek'ij] *n* débris *mpl*; (*of building*) décombres *mpl*; (*of ship*) naufrage *m*.

wrecker [rek'ûr] *n* (*US*) dépanneuse *f*.

wren [ren] *n* (*ZOOL*) roitelet *m*.

wrench [rench] *n* (*TECH*) clé *f* (à écrous); (*tug*) violent mouvement de torsion; (*fig*) arrachement *m* ♦ *vt* tirer violemment sur, tordre; **to ~ sth from** arracher qch (violemment) à *or* de.

wrest [rest] *vt*: **to ~ sth from sb** arracher *or* ravir qch à qn.

wrestle [res'əl] *vi*: **to ~ (with sb)** lutter (avec qn); **to ~ with** (*fig*) se débattre avec, lutter contre.

wrestler [res'lûr] *n* lutteur/euse.

wrestling [res'ling] *n* lutte *f*.

wrestling match *n* rencontre *f* de lutte (*or* de catch).

wretch [rech] *n* pauvre malheureux/euse; **little ~!** (*often humorous*) petit(e) misérable!

wretched [rech'id] *a* misérable; (*col*) maudit(e).

wriggle [rig'əl] *n* tortillement *m* ♦ *vi* se tortiller.

wring, *pt*, *pp* **wrung** [ring, rung] *vt* tordre; (*wet clothes*) essorer; (*fig*): **to ~ sth out of** arracher qch à.

wringer [ring'ûr] *n* essoreuse *f*.

wringing [ring'ing] *a* (*also: ~ wet*) tout mouillé(e), trempé(e).

wrinkle [ring'kəl] *n* (*on skin*) ride *f*; (*on paper etc*) pli *m* ♦ *vt* rider, plisser ♦ *vi* se plisser.

wrinkled [ring'kəld], **wrinkly** [ring'klē] *a* (*fabric, paper*) froissé(e), plissé(e); (*surface*) plissé; (*skin*) ridé(e), plissé.

wrist [rist] *n* poignet *m*.

wristwatch [rist'wâch] *n* montre-bracelet *f*.

writ [rit] *n* acte *m* judiciaire; **to issue a ~ against sb, serve a ~ on sb** assigner qn en justice.

write, *pt* **wrote,** *pp* **written** [rīt, rōt, rit'ən] *vt*, *vi* écrire; **to ~ sb a letter** écrire une lettre à qn.

write away *vi*: **to ~ away for** (*information*) (écrire pour) demander; (*goods*) (écrire pour) commander.

write down *vt* noter; (*put in writing*) mettre par écrit.

write off *vt* (*debt*) passer aux profits et pertes; (*depreciate*) amortir; (*smash up: car etc*) démolir complètement.

write out *vt* écrire; (*copy*) recopier.

write up *vt* rédiger.

write-off [rīt'ôf] *n* perte totale; **the car is a ~** (*Brit*) la voiture est bonne pour la casse.

write-protect [rīt'prətekt'] *vt* (*COMPUT*) protéger contre l'écriture.

writer [rī'tûr] *n* auteur *m*, écrivain *m*.

write-up [rīt'up] *n* (*review*) critique *f*.

writhe [rīth] *vi* se tordre.

writing [rī'ting] *n* écriture *f*; (*of author*) œuvres *fpl*; **in ~** par écrit; **in my own ~** écrit(e) de ma main.

writing case *n* nécessaire *m* de correspondance.

writing desk *n* secrétaire *m*.

writing paper *n* papier *m* à lettres.

written [rit'ən] *pp of* **write.**

wrong [rông] *a* faux(fausse); (*incorrectly chosen: number, road etc*) mauvais(e); (*not suitable*) qui ne convient pas; (*wicked*) mal; (*unfair*) injuste ♦ *ad* faux ♦ *n* tort *m* ♦ *vt* faire du tort à, léser; **to be ~** (*answer*) être faux(fausse); (*in doing/saying*) avoir tort (de dire/faire); **you are ~ to do it** tu as tort de le faire; **it's ~ to steal, stealing is ~** c'est mal de voler; **you are ~ about that, you've got it ~** tu te trompes; **to be in the ~** avoir tort; **what's ~?** qu'est-ce qui ne va pas?; **there's nothing ~** tout va bien; **what's ~ with the car?** qu'est-ce qu'elle a, la voiture?; **to go ~** (*person*) se tromper; (*plan*) mal tourner; (*machine*) se détraquer.

wrongful [rông'fəl] *a* injustifié(e); **~ dismissal** (*INDUSTRY*) licenciement abusif.

wrongly [rông'lē] *ad* à tort; (*answer, do, count*) mal, incorrectement; (*treat*) injustement.

wrong number *n* (*TEL*): **you have the ~** vous vous êtes trompé de numéro.

wrong side *n* (*of cloth*) envers *m*.

wrote [rōt] *pt of* **write.**

wrought [rôt] *a*: **~ iron** fer forgé.

wrung [rung] *pt*, *pp of* **wring.**

wry [rī] *a* désabusé(e).

wt. *abbr* (= *weight*) pds.

WV *abbr* (*US MAIL*) = *West Virginia.*

W.Va. *abbr* (*US*) = *West Virginia.*

WY *abbr* (*US MAIL*) = *Wyoming.*

Wyo. *abbr* (*US*) = *Wyoming.*

WYSIWYG [wiz'ēwig] *abbr* (*COMPUT*: = *what you see is what you get*) ce que vous voyez est ce que vous aurez.

X

X, x [eks] *n* (*letter*) X, x *m*; **X for Xmas** X comme Xavier.

Xerox [zē'râks] ® *n* (*also: ~ machine*) photocopieuse *f*; (*photocopy*) photocopie *f* ♦ *vt* photocopier.

XL *abbr* (= *extra large*) XL.

Xmas [eks'mis] *n abbr* = **Christmas.**

X-rated [eks'rātid] *a* (*US: film*) interdit(e) aux moins de 18 ans.

X-ray [eks'rā] *n* rayon *m* X; (*photograph*) radio(graphie) *f* ♦ *vt* radiographier.

xylophone [zī'ləfōn] *n* xylophone *m*.

Y

Y, y [wī] *n* (*letter*) Y, y *m*; **Y for Yoke** Y comme Yvonne.

yacht [yât] *n* voilier *m*; (*motor, luxury* ~) yacht *m*.

yachting [yât'ing] *n* yachting *m*, navigation *f* de plaisance.

yachtsman [yâts'mən] *n* yacht(s)man *m*.

yam [yam] *n* igname *f*.

Yank [yangk], **Yankee** [yang'kē] *n* (*pej*) Amerloque *m/f*, Ricain/e.

yank [yangk] *vt* tirer d'un coup sec.

yap [yap] *vi* (*dog*) japper.

yard [yârd] *n* (*of house etc*) cour *f*; (*US: garden*) jardin *m*; (*measure*) yard *m* (= *914 mm; 3 feet*); **builder's** ~ chantier *m*.

yardstick [yârd'stik] *n* (*fig*) mesure *f*, critère *m*.

yarn [yârn] *n* fil *m*; (*tale*) longue histoire.

yawn [yôn] *n* bâillement *m* ♦ *vi* bâiller.

yawning [yôn'ing] *a* (*gap*) béant(e).

yd *abbr* = **yard**.

yeah [ye] *ad* (*col*) ouais.

year [yēr] *n* an *m*, année *f*; (*Brit SCOL etc*) année; **every** ~ tous les ans, chaque année; **this** ~ cette année; **a** *or* **per** ~ par an; ~ **in**, ~ **out** année après année; **to be 8** ~**s old** avoir 8 ans; **an eight-**~**-old child** un enfant de huit ans.

yearbook [yēr'bŏŏk] *n* annuaire *m*.

yearly [yēr'lē] *a* annuel(le) ♦ *ad* annuellement; **twice** ~ deux fois par an.

yearn [yûrn] *vi*: **to** ~ **for sth/to do** aspirer à qch/à faire, languir après qch.

yearning [yûr'ning] *n* désir ardent, envie *f*.

yeast [yēst] *n* levure *f*.

yell [yel] *n* hurlement *m*, cri *m* ♦ *vi* hurler.

yellow [yel'ō] *a, n* jaune (*m*); (**at**) ~ (*US AUT*) à l'orange.

yellow fever *n* fièvre *f* jaune.

yellowish [yel'ōish] *a* qui tire sur le jaune, jaunâtre (*péj*).

Yellow Sea *n*: **the** ~ la mer Jaune.

yelp [yelp] *n* jappement *m*; glapissement *m* ♦ *vi* japper; glapir.

Yemen [yem'ən] *n* Yémen *m*.

yen [yen] *n* (*currency*) yen *m*; (*craving*): ~ **for/to do** grand(e) envie *f* *or* désir *m* de/de faire.

yeoman [yō'mən] *n*: **Y**~ **of the Guard** hallebardier *m* de la garde royale.

yes [yes] *ad* oui; (*answering negative question*) si ♦ *n* oui *m*; **to say** ~ (**to**) dire oui (à).

yes man *n* béni-oui-oui *m inv*.

yesterday [yes'tûrdā] *ad, n* hier (*m*); ~ **morning/evening** hier matin/soir; **the day before** ~ avant-hier; **all day** ~ toute la journée d'hier.

yet [yet] *ad* encore; déjà ♦ *cj* pourtant, néanmoins; **it is not finished** ~ ce n'est pas encore fini *or* toujours pas fini; **the best** ~ le meilleur jusqu'ici *or* jusque-là; **as** ~ jusqu'ici, encore; **a few days** ~ encore quelques jours; ~ **again** une fois de plus.

yew [yōō] *n* if *m*.

YHA *n abbr* (*Brit*) = *Youth Hostels Association*.

Yiddish [yid'ish] *n* yiddish *m*.

yield [yēld] *n* production *f*, rendement *m*; (*FINANCE*) rapport *m* ♦ *vt* produire, rendre, rapporter; (*surrender*) céder ♦ *vi* céder; (*US AUT*) céder la priorité; **a** ~ **of 5%** un rendement de 5%.

YMCA *n abbr* (= *Young Men's Christian Association*) ≈ union chrétienne de jeunes gens (UCJG).

yodel [yōd'əl] *vi* faire des tyroliennes, jodler.

yoga [yō'gə] *n* yoga *m*.

yog(h)ourt, yog(h)urt [yō'gûrt] *n* yaourt *m*.

yoke [yōk] *n* joug *m* ♦ *vt* (*also:* ~ **together**: *oxen*) accoupler.

yolk [yōk] *n* jaune *m* (d'œuf).

yonder [yân'dûr] *ad* là(-bas).

Yorks [] *abbr* (*Brit*) = Yorkshire.

you [yōō] *pronoun* tu; (*polite form*) vous; (*pl*) vous; (*complement*) te, t' + *vowel*; vous; (*stressed*) toi; vous; (*impersonal: one*) on; **if I was** *or* **were** ~ si j'étais vous, à votre place; **fresh air does** ~ **good** l'air frais (vous) fait du bien; ~ **never know** on ne sait jamais.

you'd [yōōd] = **you had, you would**.

you'll [yōōl] = **you will, you shall**.

young [yung] *a* jeune ♦ *npl* (*of animal*) petits *mpl*; (*people*): **the** ~ les jeunes, la jeunesse; **a** ~ **man** un jeune homme; **a** ~ **lady** (*unmarried*) une jeune fille, une demoiselle; (*married*) une jeune femme *or* dame; **my** ~**er brother** mon frère cadet; **the** ~**er generation** la jeune génération.

youngish [yung'ish] *a* assez jeune.

youngster [yung'stûr] *n* jeune *m/f*; (*child*) enfant *m/f*.

your [yōōr] *a* ton(ta), tes *pl*; (*polite form, pl*) votre, vos *pl*.

you're [yōōr] = **you are**.

yours [yōōrz] *pronoun* le(la) tien(ne), les tiens(tiennes); (*polite form, pl*) le(la) vôtre, les vôtres; **is it** ~? c'est à toi (*or* à vous)?; **a friend of** ~ un(e) de tes (*or* de vos) amis.

yourself [yōōrself'] *pronoun* (*reflexive*) te; (: *polite form*) vous; (*after prep*) toi; vous; (*emphatic*) toi-même; vous-même; **you** ~ **told me** c'est vous qui me l'avez dit, vous me l'avez dit vous-même.

yourselves [yōōrselvz'] *pl pronoun* vous; (*emphatic*) vous-mêmes.

youth [yōōth] *n* jeunesse *f*; (*young man*) (*pl* ~**s** [yōōthz]) jeune homme *m*; **in my** ~ dans ma jeunesse, quand j'étais jeune.

youth club *n* centre *m* de jeunes.

youthful [yōōth'fəl] *a* jeune; (*enthusiasm etc*) juvénile; (*misdemeanor*) de jeunesse.

youthfulness [yōōth'fəlnis] *n* jeunesse *f*.

youth hostel *n* auberge *f* de jeunesse.

youth movement *n* mouvement *m* de jeunes.

you've [yōōv] = **you have**.

yowl [youl] *n* hurlement *m*; miaulement *m* ♦